Pub Guide
2013

AA Lifestyle Guides

16th edition September 2012.
© AA Media Limited 2012.
AA Media Limited retains the copyright in the current edition © 2012 and in all subsequent editions, reprints and amendments to editions. The information contained in this directory is sourced entirely from the AA's information resources. All rights reserved. No part of this publication may be reproduced, stored in a retrieval system, or transmitted in any form or by any means - electronic, photocopying, recording or otherwise - unless the written permission of the publishers has been obtained beforehand. This book may not be sold, resold, hired out or otherwise disposed of by way of trade in any form of binding or cover other than that in which it is published, without the prior consent of all relevant Publishers.

Assessments of AA inspected establishments are based on the experience of the Hotel and Restaurant Inspectors on the occasion(s) of their visit(s) and therefore descriptions given in this guide necessarily contain an element of subjective opinion which may not reflect or dictate a reader's own opinion on another occasion. See pages 6–7 for a clear explanation of how, based on our Inspectors' inspection experiences, establishments are graded. If the meal or meals experienced by an Inspector or Inspectors during an inspection fall between award levels the restaurant concerned may be awarded the lower of any award levels considered applicable.

AA Media Limited strives to ensure accuracy of the information in this guide at the time of printing. Nevertheless, the Publisher cannot be held responsible for any errors or omissions, or for changes in the details given in this guide, or for the consequences of any reliance on the information provided by the same. This does not affect your statutory rights. Due to the constantly evolving nature of the subject matter the information is subject to change. AA Media Limited will gratefully receive any advice from our readers of any necessary updated information.

Please contact:
Advertising Sales Department: advertisingsales@theAA.com
Editorial Department: lifestyleguides@theAA.com
AA Hotel Scheme Enquiries: 01256 844455

Web site addresses are included in some entries and specified by the respective establishment. Such web sites are not under the control of AA Media Limited and as such AA Media Limited has no control over them and will not accept any responsibility or liability in respect of any and all matters whatsoever relating to such web sites including access, content, material and functionality. By including the addresses of third party web sites the AA does not intend to solicit business or offer any security to any person in any country, directly or indirectly.

Typeset/Repro: Servis Filmsetting Ltd, Stockport.
Printed and bound by Graficas Estella, Spain.

Directory compiled by the AA Lifestyle Guides Department and managed in the Librios Information Management System and generated from the AA establishment database system.

Pub descriptions have been contributed by the following team of writers: Phil Bryant, David Foster, David Halford, David Hancock, Mark Taylor and Jenny White.

Published by AA Publishing, a trading name of AA Media Limited, whose registered office is Fanum House, Basing View, Basingstoke RG21 4EA. Registered number 06112600.
A CIP catalogue for this book is available from the British Library.
ISBN: 978-0-7495-7362-1
A04887

Maps prepared by the Mapping Services Department of AA Publishing.

Maps © AA Media Limited 2012.

Contains Ordnance Survey data © Crown copyright and database right 2012. Licence number 100021153.

Information on National Parks in England provided by the Countryside Agency (Natural England).

Information on National Parks in Scotland provided by Scottish Natural Heritage.

Information on National Parks in Wales provided by The Countryside Council for Wales.

Contents

1 LOCATION

Guide order Pubs are listed alphabetically by name (ignoring The) under their village or town. Towns and villages are listed alphabetically within their county (a county map appears at the back of the guide). The guide has entries for England, Channel Islands, Isle of Man, Scotland and Wales in that order. Some village pubs prefer to be initially located under the nearest town, in which case the village name is included in the address and directions.

Pick of the Pubs Over 800 of the best pubs in Britain have been selected by the editor and inspectors and these are highlighted. They have longer, more detailed descriptions. Over 240 of these have a full page entry and two photographs.

2 MAP REFERENCE

The map reference number denotes the map page number in the atlas section at the back of the book and (except for London maps) the National Grid reference. The London map references help locate their position on the Central and Greater London maps.

3 ESTABLISHMENT NAME AND SYMBOLS

See Key to symbols in the panel on page 5.

4 ADDRESS AND POSTCODE DETAILS

This gives the street name and the postcode, and if necessary the name of the village is included (see 1 above). This may be up to five miles from the named location.

☎ **Telephone number, e-mail and websites:** Wherever possible we have included an e-mail address.

5 DIRECTIONS

Directions are given only when they have been supplied by the proprietor.

6 DESCRIPTION

Description of the pub and food.

7 OPEN

Indicates the hours and dates when the establishment is open and closed.

8 BAR MEALS

Indicates the times and days when proprietors tell us bar food can be ordered, and the average price of a main

---

1 3 4 14 5 2

EWEN   Map 4 SU09

The Wild Duck ★★★★ INN

GL7 6BY ☎ 01285 770310
e-mail: duckreservations@aol.com
web: www.thewildduckinn.co.uk
dir: *From Cirencester take A429 towards Malmesbury. At Kemble left to Ewen. Inn in village centre*

6   Children and canine companions are welcome at this inn, built from honeyed Cotswold stone in 1563; the source of the Thames and the Cotswold Water Park are near by. Family-owned for more than 20 years, the pub has oil portraits, log fires, oak beams and a resident ghost. Deep red walls give the Post Horn bar a warm feel, as does the extensive choice of real ales. The rambling restaurant has a lunch menu of wholesome pub favourites, while dinner may extend to wild duck antipasto, followed by luxury fish bouillabaisse. Booking for meals may be required.

7   **Open** all day all wk Closed: 25 Dec (eve) **Bar Meals** L **8** served Mon-Fri 12-2, Sat-Sun all day D served all wk 6.30-10 Av main course £15 **Restaurant** L served Mon-Fri 12-2, Sat-Sun all day D served all wk 6.30-10 Av 3 course à la carte fr £30 ⊕ FREE HOUSE ◗ The Wild Duck Duckpond Bitter, Butcombe Bitter, Wye Valley Dorothy Goodbody's Country Ale, Greene King Abbot Ale, Morland Old Speckled Hen, Bath Gem Ö Ashton Press, Westons Stowford Press, Aspall. ♀ 32 **Facilities** ❖ Children welcome Children's menu Children's portions Garden Parking Wi-fi ▬ **Rooms** 12

10 12 9 11

---

course as supplied by the proprietor. Please be aware that last orders could vary by up to 30 minutes.

9 RESTAURANT

Indicates the times and days when proprietors tell us food can be ordered from the restaurant. The average cost of a 3-course à la carte meal and a 3- or 4-course fixed-price menu are shown as supplied by the proprietor. Last orders may be approximately 30 minutes before the times stated.

10 BREWERY AND COMPANY

⊕ indicates the name of the Brewery to which the pub is tied, or the Company that owns it. A free house is where the pub is independently owned and run.

◧ indicates the principal beers sold by the pub. The pub's top cask or hand-pulled beers are listed. Many pubs have a much greater selection, with several guest beers each week.

11 FACILITIES

Indicates if a pub has a children's menu, children's portions, a garden, children's play area, is dog-friendly (NEW for 2013), holds a beer festival, offers parking, accepts coach parties. For further information please phone the pub.

12 ROOMS

Only accommodation that has been AA inspected and rated is indicated, with the number of en suite bedrooms listed. Many pubs have rooms, but we only indicate those that are AA rated.

13 NOTES

As so many establishments take one or more of the major credit cards we only indicate if a pub does not take cards.

14 AA STARS/DESIGNATORS

AA Stars (and designators as appropriate) are shown at the beginning of an entry. The AA, in partnership with the national tourist bodies (VisitBritain, VisitScotland and VisitWales) has introduced new Quality Standards for inspected accommodation. See pages 6-7 for details of AA ratings.

AA Classifications & Awards

Many of the pubs in this Guide offer accommodation. Where a Star rating appears next to an entry's name in the Guide, the establishment has been inspected by the AA under common Quality Standards agreed between the AA, VisitBritain, VisitScotland and VisitWales. These ratings are for the accommodation, and ensure that it meets the highest standards of cleanliness, with an emphasis on professionalism, proper booking procedures and prompt and efficient services. Some of the pubs in this Guide offer accommodation but do not belong to a rating scheme. In this case the accommodation is not included in their entry.

AA recognised establishments pay an annual fee that varies according to the classification and the number of bedrooms. The establishments receive an unannounced inspection from a qualified AA inspector who recommends the appropriate classification. Return visits confirm that standards are maintained; the classification is not transferable if an establishment changes hands.

The annual *AA Hotel Guide* and *AA Bed & Breakfast Guide* give further details of recognised establishments and the classification schemes. Details of AA recognised hotels, guest accommodation, restaurants and pubs are also available at **theAA.com,** along with a useful Route Planner.

AA Hotel Classification

Hotels are classified on a 5-point scale, with one star ★ being the simplest, and five stars offering a luxurious service at the top of the range. The AA's top hotels in Britain and Ireland are identified by red stars. (★)

In addition to the main **Hotel** (HL) classification which applies to some pubs in this Guide, there are other categories of hotel which may be applicable to pubs, as follows:

Town House Hotel (TH) - A small, individual city or town centre property, which provides a high degree of personal service and privacy.

Country House Hotel (CHH) - Quietly located in a rural area.

Small Hotel (SHL) - Has fewer than 20 bedrooms and is owner managed.

Metro Hotel (MET) - A hotel in an urban location that does not offer an evening meal.

Budget Hotel (BUD) - These are usually purpose-built modern properties offering inexpensive accommodation. Often located near motorways and in town or city centres. **They are not awarded stars.**

AA Guest Accommodation

Guest accommodation is also classified on a scale of one to five stars, with one ★ being the most simple, and five being more luxurious. Gold stars (★) indicate the very best B&Bs, Guest Houses, Farmhouses, Inns and Guest Accommodation in the 3, 4 and 5 star ratings. A series of designators appropriate to the type of accommodation offered is also used, as follows:

Inn (INN) – Accommodation provided in a fully licensed establishment. The bar will be open to non-residents and provide food in the evenings.

Bed & Breakfast (B&B) – Accommodation provided in a private house, run by the owner and with no more than six paying guests.

Guest House (GH) – Accommodation provided for more than six paying guests and run on a more commercial basis than a B&B. Usually more services, for example dinner, provided by staff as well as the owner.

Farmhouse (FH) – B&B or guest house rooms provided on a working farm or smallholding.

Restaurant with Rooms (RR) – Destination restaurant offering overnight accommodation. The restaurant is the main business and is open to non-residents. A high standard of food should be offered, at least five nights a week. A maximum of 12 bedrooms. Most Restaurants with Rooms have been awarded AA Rosettes for their food.

Guest Accommodation (GA) – Any establishment which meets the entry requirements for the Scheme can choose this designator.

U A small number of pubs have this symbol because their Star classification was not confirmed at the time of going to press.

A Refers to hotels rated by another organisation, eg VisitBritain.

Rosette Awards

Out of the thousands of restaurants in the British Isles, the AA identifies, with its Rosette Awards, around 2,000 as the best. What to expect from restaurants with AA Rosette Awards is outlined here; for a more detailed explanation of Rosette criteria please see **theAA.com**

◉ Excellent local restaurants serving food prepared with care, understanding and skill and using good quality ingredients.

◉◉ The best local restaurants, which consistently aim for and achieve higher standards and where a greater precision is apparent in the cooking. Obvious attention is paid to the selection of quality ingredients.

◉◉◉ Outstanding restaurants that demand recognition well beyond their local area.

◉◉◉◉ Amongst the very best restaurants in the British Isles, where the cooking demands national recognition.

◉◉◉◉◉ The finest restaurants in the British Isles, where the cooking stands comparison with the best in the world.

The AA Pub of the Year for England, Scotland and Wales have been selected with the help of our AA inspectors; we have chosen three very worthy winners for this prestigious annual award.

The winners stand out for being great all-round pubs or inns, combining a good pub atmosphere, a warm welcome from friendly, efficient hosts and staff, excellent food and well-kept beers.

ENGLAND

THE BLACK SWAN ★★★★ INN
RAVENSTONEDALE, CUMBRIA Page 128

The Black Swan nestles below Wild Boar Fell beside the frothy headwaters of the appropriately named River Eden. The enterprising owners of this family-run residential inn, which has gained four AA Gold Stars Award for the quality of the individually styled bedrooms and Breakfast and Dinner awards for the food, have placed themselves right at the heart of the community, with an on-site village store; being part of the 'Pub is the Hub' campaign; and specialising in locally produced foods and goodies. Relax in the inn's tranquil riverside garden after you've walked the Howgill Fells, explored the Lakes or toured the Yorkshire Dales, all of which are on the doorstep. The ever-changing selection of northern beers includes the likes of Dent, Hesket Newmarket and Tirril breweries. The menu might include a starter of layered terrine of smoked trout, mackerel and salmon, wrapped in smoked salmon, a robust precursor to steak, venison and ale cobbler. Vegetarians may relish the vegetable Wellington stuffed with celeriac, broccoli and spinach in a creamy cheese sauce. Menus tend to be seasonal with daily-changing specials; there's also a good choice of snacks and light bites.

SCOTLAND

WEST BREWERY
GLASGOW Page 628

This buzzy brewery pub/restaurant occupies the old Winding House of the former Templeton Carpet Factory, one of Glasgow's most unique Victorian buildings, modelled on the Doge's Palace in Venice. West is the only brewery in the UK to produce all of its beers according to the German Purity Law, which means they are free from artificial additives, colourings and preservatives. Look down into the brewhouse from the beer hall and watch the brewers making the lagers and wheat beers, including St Mungo, Dunkel, Munich and Hefeweizen, with equipment imported from Germany. Brewery tours are conducted on selected days of the week. The all-day menu offers German dishes like Wiener schnitzel, spätzle (Bavarian noodles with caramelised onions and melted cheese) and Nuremberg sausages served with sauerkraut. Grills, burgers and British pub grub also feature. For dessert is the adults-only Hefeweizen ice cream, made by hand and infused with their award-winning wheat beer. Brunch is available at weekends. Look out for the Oktoberfest beer festival.

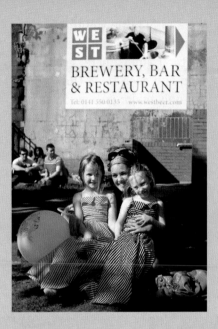

WALES

THE INN AT PENALLT ★★★★ INN ◎
PENALLT, MONMOUTHSHIRE Page 666

Built as a farmhouse in the 17th century, Bush Farm started serving cider, ale and perry in the early 1800s before becoming the Bush Inn in the 1890s. Spruced up and renamed by Jackie and Andrew Murphy a few years ago, this traditional village pub in the beautiful Wye Valley maintains its time-honoured reputation for serving quality local ales and ciders from breweries within 30 miles, alongside AA-Rosette standard food made from sustainable produce. Tuck into seared scallops, pea purée, roasted garlic and smoked Welsh bacon; home-made faggots and creamed mashed potato with onion gravy and crushed peas; or goat's cheese and spinach ravioli. Finish with lemon-scented treacle tart with ginger ice cream; or white chocolate and rosemary

pannacotta. Dogs are warmly welcomed in the bar and large garden, while dog-friendly accommodation is also available. The inn makes and ideal base for walking Offa's Dyke Path and the Three Castles Walk.

Welcome to the Guide

We aim to bring you the country's best pubs, selected for their atmosphere, great food and good beer. Ours is the only major pub guide to feature colour photographs, and to highlight the 'Pick of the Pubs', revealing Britain's finest hostelries. Updated every year, this edition includes lots of old favourites, as well as plenty of new destinations for eating and drinking, and great places to stay across Britain.

Who's in the Guide?

We make our selection by seeking out pubs that are worth making a detour - 'destination' pubs - with publicans exhibiting real enthusiasm for their trade and offering a good selection of well-kept drinks and good food. We also choose neighbourhood pubs supported by locals and attractive to passing motorists or walkers. Our selected pubs make no payment for their inclusion in our guide. They are included entirely at our discretion.

Tempting Food

We are looking for menus that show a commitment to home cooking, making good use of local produce wherever possible, and offering an appetising range of freshly-prepared dishes. Pubs presenting well-executed traditional dishes like ploughman's or pies, or those offering innovative bar or restaurant food, are all in the running. In keeping with recent trends in pub food, we are keen to include those where particular emphasis is placed on imaginative modern dishes and those specialising in fresh fish. Occasionally we include pubs that serve no food, or just snacks, but are very special in other ways.

That Special Place

We look for pubs that offer something special: pubs where the time-honoured values of a convivial environment for conversation while supping or eating have not been forgotten. They may be

attractive, interesting, unusual or in a good location. Some may be very much a local pub or they may draw customers from further afield, while others may be included because they are in an exceptional place. Interesting towns and villages, eccentric or historic buildings, and rare settings can all be found within this guide.

Pick of the Pubs and Full Page Entries

Some of the pubs included in the guide are particularly special, and we have highlighted these as Pick of the Pubs. For 2013 over 800 pubs have been selected by the personal knowledge of our editorial team, our AA inspectors, and suggestions from our readers.

These pubs have a more detailed description. From these, over 240 have chosen to enhance their entry in the 2013 Guide by purchasing two photographs as part of a full-page entry.

Smoking Regulations

A law banning smoking in public places came into force in July 2007. This covers all establishments in this guide. Some pubs provide a private area in, for example an outbuilding, for smokers. If the freedom to smoke is important to you, we recommend that you check with the pub when you book.

Tell us what you think

We welcome your feedback about the pubs included and about the guide itself. We are also delighted to receive suggestions about good pubs you have visited and loved. A Reader Report form appears at the back of the book, so please write in or e-mail us at lifestyleguides@theAA.com to help us improve future editions. The pubs also feature on the AA website, **theAA.com**, along with our inspected restaurants, hotels and bed & breakfast accommodation.

Pub Grub
– the new specials

By FIONA GRIFFITHS

There was a time when pubs up and down the country would serve the same predictable menu, but flick through the pages of this guide and you'll find pubs specialising in all manner of different foods – from sausages to Indian, Thai cuisine to pizzas.

Fiona Griffiths has been meeting some of the people leading the pub grub revolution...

Inside and out, The Star Inn in Ringwood, Hampshire, looks like any other traditional old pub.

But look a little closer and you'll see chopsticks on the tables, blackboards listing specials with a distinctly Oriental slant, and customers tucking into steaming plates of noodles and Thai curries.

The Star Inn has been specialising in Thai food for well over a decade, and without any other Thai restaurants in the town, it's been a highly successful move for landlord Ian Pepperell.

"There are Chinese take-aways in Ringwood but we're the only sit-down Thai restaurant in the town, so if people want Thai they come here," says Pepperell.

Lunches are particularly big business:

although the pub offers a few alternatives at lunchtime like sandwiches, salads and cod and chips, 75 per cent of diners typically choose from the Thai menu.

"It's works very well," says landlord Ian Pepperell.

"For lunchtime it's ideal because people are often tight for time and with Thai food all the preparation is done in advance and it's just a case of stir-frying it to order."

In the evenings the menu is exclusively Thai, and Pepperell encourages his two Thai chefs to put more authentic dishes on the specials board, particularly seafood-based options like steamed sea bass, king prawns and scallops, soft-shelled crab and salt and pepper squid.

"The chefs tend to Westernise the

Above: Malaysian noodles at The Star Inn in Ringwood

dishes a bit and I'm trying to get them away from that and to express what Thai food really is," says Pepperell.

Take-aways can be ordered at the bar – not on the phone – with the idea that people can have a pint while they wait for their meal to be ready.

"We started doing them about five years ago and it works well. People were asking for doggy bags to take away what they couldn't manage, so we had boxes for that anyway and thought why not utilise that and do a take-away service as well?" explains Pepperell.

Pepperell has found that Sunday trade doesn't work in a Thai pub, so he only opens for drinks on Sundays.

And recruiting Thai chefs can be a problem too.

"That's probably the hardest thing – finding good chefs who are already permitted to reside in the UK, so it's not necessary for us to fund them through immigration," says Pepperell.

But he believes these difficulties far outweigh the benefits of running a pub that's a little bit different from all the rest.

"There are so many pubs offering the same thing: egg and chips, scampi and chips – you pretty much know what you're going to get in most pubs.

"To have a 470-year-old pub offering a full Thai menu is quite a strange mixture, but it's nice to be doing something different."

So, what other types of cuisine can you expect to find in pubs these days?

The Mexican Pub

When Gareth Finney took over The Albion Tavern in Faversham, Kent, eight years ago, there was no question over what kind of food he would serve.

Finney had previously been the group chef for a chain of Mexican pubs, and Faversham didn't have a Mexican restaurant, so The Albion quickly became The Albion Taverna, serving the likes of fajitas, quesadillas and burritos.

"I thought The Albion was the perfect spot for that type of food with my experience in Mexican cooking and the fact that Faversham didn't have a Mexican restaurant.

"So I turned it into a Mexican pub and pretty much doubled the trade straight away," says Finney.

From day one the most popular dish has been chicken fajitas, which are served on a sizzling skillet with a selection of accompaniments on a spinning board in the middle of the table.

"It's like an enormous lazy Susan – I think people like it because it's a bit different," says Finney.

"We do serve some English dishes as well, because although most people who come here want Mexican, grandma might not."

Finney tries to use as much local produce as possible, while his beers are from the Shepherd Neame brewery just opposite the pub.

He also serves a couple of Mexican beers – Corona and Sol – as "people expect to get those with Mexican food".

Finney says: "I think every town should have a pub like this specialising in a type of food that's a bit different.

"We're the only place in town serving fajitas, burritos and enchiladas, so if anyone wants Mexican in Faversham they come to us."

The Pizza Pub

The sleepy village of Corfe Castle in Dorset isn't the sort of place you'd naturally expect to find some of the best pizzas in the country, but head to The Bankes Arms and that's exactly what you'll get.

Since Jacci Pestana took over the pub in April 2011 and installed an electric pizza oven in the kitchen, freshly made pizzas have become a huge draw, especially for tourists staying in the area's many campsites.

"I bought the pizza oven three years ago from a friend who ran an Italian restaurant and I thought why not put it in the pub?" explains Pestana.

"I was lucky enough to find a master

Above: Oyster & Otter, Feniscowles

Below: The Albion Taverna, Faversham

"We do serve some English dishes as well, because although most people who come here want Mexican, grandma might not."

pizza chef, and since we put pizzas on the menu they've outsold everything by five to one.

"It has a lot to do with the number of campsites in the area, as lots of tourists buy pizza to take away."

The dough and tomato sauce are made freshly every day, with the most popular pizzas on the menu including the Siciliana with anchovies, capers, sun-dried tomatoes and mozzarella, and the Diavola with salami, chorizo, peppers, onion, chilli and mozzarella.

In 2013 Pestana plans to build a wood-fired oven from Purbeck stone in the garden, which will take over from the electric one and give the pizzas an even more authentic taste.

Alongside pizzas The Bankes Arms offers a mostly Mediterranean menu, although there are a few traditional pub dishes available too, such as a home-made burger and fish pie.

Pestana says, "When you're running a pub these days there's so much competition that you have to become known for something. We haven't been

here long but now everyone knows about our authentic pizzas and our seafood paella."

The Gourmet Burger Pub

People come in their droves for the award-winning burgers served up in various guises ('the classic', 'the Italian', 'the New Yorker') at The Wheatsheaf at Oaksey in Wiltshire.

Chef-patron Tony Robson-Burrell sells 250-300 burgers a week – so many, in fact, that he's had to stop making his own baps and instead buy them from a local baker to cope with demand.

But business hasn't always been this good: before Robson-Burrell launched his gourmet burger menu in late 2011, the number of people coming to eat at the pub had dwindled to a worrying level.

"I think the climate has changed a lot in this country – the fine-dining food I was doing was really good but it wasn't attracting the right footfall, because people thought it was too expensive.

"I was seeing my turnover decreasing

and I thought I needed to do something about this," explains Robson-Burrell.

Having won a national award for his burger recipe (using 30-day hung rump steak) from the English Beef and Lamb Executive in 2007, Robson-Burrell decided gourmet burgers could be the answer.

"I've always thought in the back of my head 'I'm missing a trick here', so I launched the gourmet burger menu and since then customers have increased by 40 per cent.

"Now 80 per cent of my customers go for the burgers. All round it's been a great move for me."

Best-sellers include the 'smokin' (smokey barbecue sauce, melted cheese, salad and mayonnaise), and the double cheese (melted pecorino and Isle of Mull cheddar, beef tomato and mayonnaise).

And popular with Japanese workers at the nearby Honda plant in Swindon and Mitsubishi's office in Cirencester is the burger made from highly-prized Wagyu beef (£20).

Left: Gourmet burger at The Wheatsheaf at Oaksey

Below: Lobster dish by the Seafood Pub Company

"That's attracted a lot of Japanese people to the pub," says Robson-Burrell.

"We even had a Japanese family in recently who drove for two hours from London just because they'd heard about our Wagyu burger."

The Seafood Pub

If you love fish and you live in the North West then you're very lucky, because the Seafood Pub Company, set up by father and daughter Chris and Joycelyn Neve in early 2011, is growing fast.

The first two pubs run by the Neves – Oyster & Otter in Feniscowles near Blackburn and The Assheton Arms in Downham – are to be joined by another eight seafood-orientated pubs in the

next few years if Joycelyn's dream goes to plan.

The Neves launched the Seafood Pub Company after spotting a gap in the market for super-fresh fish and seafood served in a casual pub environment.

All fish is supplied by Chris's small wholesale business, which means freshness is guaranteed and costs are kept low, with those savings passed on to the customer.

Joycelyn says, "Any fish that's just landed that's brilliant quality my dad will send over to me and we'll put it straight on the specials board.

"Our customers know they're going to get something really good when they come to one of our pubs – and

often something they can't get hold of themselves."

The menu varies between the two sites but popular dishes include the Malaysian seafood curry, seasonal fish pie, fish and chips, and monkfish bourguignon.

"When we first opened the Oyster & Otter, we thought we needed to play it safe with the menu because it was a new concept, but we couldn't have been more wrong," says Joycelyn.

"There isn't anything that doesn't sell. The first time we put a raw plate on – oysters, tuna sashimi and scallop ceviche – we sold out within two hours."

So next time you fancy a pizza, a spot of Thai, or perhaps a plate of sushi or sashimi, don't dismiss your local pub.

Beer festivals, or their equivalent, are as old as the hills. The brewing of hops goes back to the beginning of human civilisation, and the combination of common crop and a fermenting process that results in alcoholic liquid has long been a cause of celebration. Beer festivals officially began in Germany with the first Munich Oktoberfest in 1810. Wherever in the world beer is brewed, today and for the last few millennia, admirers, enthusiasts, aficionados – call them what you will – have gathered together to sample and praise its unique properties. It happens throughout Europe, in Australia and New Zealand, and in America and Canada, and annual events are held in pubs all over Britain.

Beer festivals are often occasions for the whole family, when entertainment is laid on for children as well as adults. Summer is naturally a popular season for festivals, when the action can be taken outdoors. Other festivals are held in October, traditionally harvest time, but they can be at any time of the year. Beer festivals are sometimes large and well advertised gatherings that attract a wide following for sometimes several days of unselfconscious consumption of unusual or award-winning ales; or they might be local but none the less enthusiastic get-togethers of neighbourhood or pub micro-breweries.

We list here the pubs that appear in this guide, who have told us they hold annual beer festivals.
For up-to-date information, please check directly with the pub.
We would love to hear from our readers about their favourite beer festivals. E-mail us at lifestyleguides@theAA.com

ENGLAND

BEDFORDSHIRE

The Globe Inn
LINSLADE   01525 373338

The Bell
ODELL   01234 720254
Summer

BERKSHIRE

The White Horse of Hermitage
HERMITAGE   01635 200325
Jun

Bird In Hand Country Inn
KNOWL HILL   01628 826622
Jun & Nov

The Flowing Spring
READING   0118 969 9878
Midsummer over a wknd.
At least 12 real ales, live music and barbecue. Dates vary

The Bell
WALTHAM ST LAWRENCE
          0118 934 1788
Annual - 30 real ales, 10 Ciders

The Broad Street Tavern
WOKINGHAM   0118 977 3706
4 times a year

BRISTOL

The Albion
BRISTOL   0117 973 3522
Annual beer and cider

BUCKINGHAMSHIRE

Hit or Miss Inn
AMERSHAM   01494 713109
Middle wknd Jul

The King's Head
AYLESBURY   01296 718812

The Black Horse Inn
CHESHAM   01494 784656

The Swan
CHESHAM   01494 783075
Aug BH

The Unicorn
CUBLINGTON   01296 681261
May & Aug BHs

The Falcon Inn
DENHAM   01895 832125
See website

The Palmer Arms
DORNEY   01628 666612
End Jul selection of local ales and local ciders

The White Horse
HEDGERLEY   01753 643225
Three times a year, Etr, end of May BH & Aug BH

The Whip Inn
LACEY GREEN   01844 344060
May & Sep

The Full Moon
LITTLE KINGSHILL   01494 862397

The Derehams Inn
LOUDWATER   01494 530965

Carrington Arms
MOULSOE   01908 218050
Summer

The White Hart
PRESTON BISSETT   01280 847969
Spring BH

CAMBRIDGESHIRE

Cambridge Blue
CAMBRIDGE   01223 471680
Feb, Jun, Oct

The Black Horse
DRY DRAYTON   01954 782600
St George's Day wknd

The Crown Inn
ELTON   01832 280232

The Cock Pub and Restaurant
HEMINGFORD GREY   01480 463609
Aug BH wknd

The Red Lion Inn
HINXTON   01799 530601
Aug BH wknd

Red Lion
HISTON   01223 564437
Etr & 1st wk Sep

The Horseshoe Inn
OFFORD D'ARCY   01480 810293
Midsummer

Charters Bar & East Restaurant
PETERBOROUGH   01733 315700
Etr Thu-Etr Mon

The Lazy Otter
STRETHAM   01353 649780

CHESHIRE

The Bhurtpore Inn
ASTON   01270 780917
Jul - 130 beers

Old Harkers Arms
CHESTER   01244 344525
Early Feb & Oct

The Jolly Cricketers
SEER GREEN   01494 676308
Etr wknd & Aug BH

The Chequers Inn
WHEELER END   01494 883070
Whitsun BH

The Cholmondeley Arms
CHOLMONDELEY   01829 720300

Swan Inn
KETTLESHULME   01663 732943
1st wknd Sep

The Dog Inn
KNUTSFORD   01625 861421
1st wknd Aug

The Bulls Head
MOBBERLEY   01565 873345
Jun

The Ship Hotel
PARKGATE   0151 336 3931

The Yew Tree Inn
SPURSTOW   01829 260274
Good Fri-Etr Mon

The Bunbury Arms
STOAK   01244 301665
Held in marquee, camping available

The Hanging Gate Inn
SUTTON LANE ENDS   01260 252238
May or Aug BH

CORNWALL & ISLES OF SCILLY

The Blisland Inn
BLISLAND   01208 850739
May

Manor House Inn
CALLINGTON   01579 362354
1st wknd Sep

The Smugglers' Den Inn
CUBERT   01637 830209
May Day BH wknd

Godolphin Arms
MARAZION   01736 710202

The Plume of Feathers
MITCHELL   01872 510387
May

The Bush Inn
MORWENSTOW   01288 331242

PICK OF THE FESTIVALS

OLD HALL INN

CHINLEY, Derbyshire, 01633 750529
www.old-hall-inn.co.uk

September Beer and Cider Festival – 3rd weekend September

The September beer and cider festival held by the Old Hall Inn features live music on Friday and Saturday evenings, and over 100 beers and ciders. A barbecue is on offer all day, every day.

Old Mill House Inn
POLPERRO   01503 272362
1st wknd Oct

Driftwood Spars
ST AGNES   01872 552428
Mid-Mar Mini beer festival
& May Day BH wknd

The Watermill
ST IVES   01736 757912
Jun & Nov

The Cornish Arms
ST MERRYN   01841 532700
Beer & Mussel festival

The New Inn
TRESCO   01720 422844
Mid-May & early Sep

CUMBRIA

Brook House Inn
BOOT   01946 7 23288
Boot Beer Festival 1st or 2nd wknd
Jun involving village pubs

Hare & Hounds Country Inn
BOWLAND BRIDGE   015395 68333
May Day BH

Blacksmiths Arms
BROUGHTON-IN-FURNESS
                  01229 716824
1st wknd Oct

The Masons Arms
CARTMEL   015395 68486
Jun - Lake District Brewers

The Britannia Inn
ELTERWATER   015394 37210
2wks mid-Nov

Kirkstile Inn
LOWESWATER   01900 85219

Wheatsheaf Inn
LOW LORTON   01900 85199
Late Mar

The Cross Keys
MILNTHORPE   015395 62115
Annual

Newfield Inn
SEATHWAITE   01229 716208
Oct

The Strickland Arms
SIZERGH   015395 61010

Farmers Arms Hotel
ULVERSTON   01229 584469

Wasdale Head Inn
WASDALE HEAD   019467 26229
1st Sun Oct

DERBYSHIRE

The Old Poets Corner
ASHOVER   01246 590888
Mar & Oct, Thu-Sun 40 beers
and ciders with live music

Rowley's
BASLOW   01246 583880
Thornbridge Brewery annual beer
and food evening

Red Lion Inn
BIRCHOVER   01629 650363
Mid-Jul

The Barley Mow
BONSALL   01629 825685
3-4 annually on BHs

The Peaks Inn
CASTLETON   01433 620247
Jul

Ye Olde Nags Head
CASTLETON   01433 620248
Summer

Old Hall Inn
CHINLEY   01633 750529
4th wknd Feb; September Beer and
Cider Festival 3rd wknd Sept

The Alexandra Hotel
DERBY   01332 293993
Late Jun with barbecue

The Brunswick Inn
DERBY   01332 290677
1st wknd Oct

Miners Arms
EYAM   01433 630853
3 per year

Bentley Brook Inn
FENNY BENTLEY   01335 350278

The Mill Wheel
HARTSHORNE   01283 550335

The Royal Hotel
HAYFIELD   01663 742721
1st wknd Oct

The Old Crown Inn
SHARDLOW   01332 792392
Apr & Oct

DEVON

The Quarrymans Rest
BAMPTON   01398 331480
May BH

The Fountain Head
BRANSCOMBE   01297 680359
Mid-Jun

The Masons Arms
BRANSCOMBE   01297 680300
Jul 30 ales & ciders, live music,
barbecue

Dartbridge Inn
BUCKFASTLEIGH   01364 642214
Annual

The Skylark Inn
CLEARBROOK   01822 853258
Aug BH

Red Lion Hotel
CLOVELLY   01237 431237
Late May BH

The Anchor Inn
COCKWOOD   01626 890203
Halloween, Spring

The Duke of York
IDDESLEIGH   01837 810253
Last wknd Jul

The Old Inn
KILMINGTON   01297 32096
Late May BH Sat & late Aug BH Sat

The Elizabethan Inn
LUTON (NEAR CHUDLEIGH)
          01626 775425
Jun

The Royal Oak Inn
MEAVY   01822 852944
Cider festival, Aug BH. Cider & Bean
fest, mid-Nov. Real Ale 3rd wknd Jun

The Wild Goose Inn
NEWTON ABBOT   01626 872241
Early May BH wknd

The Blacksmiths Arms
PLYMTREE   01884 277474
Biannual Jul

The Lamb Inn
SANDFORD   01363 773676

Dukes
SIDMOUTH   01395 513320
1st wk Aug

The Tower Inn
SLAPTON   01548 580216
Various dates, check with pub

Steam Packet Inn
TOTNES   01803 863880
Mid-May (4 days)

The Maltsters Arms
TUCKENHAY   01803 732350
Annual

DORSET

Stapleton Arms
BUCKHORN WESTON 01963 370396

The Chetnole Inn
CHETNOLE   01935 872337

The Bankes Arms
CORFE CASTLE   01929 480206
Aug - Beer & Music Festival

The Greyhound Inn
CORFE CASTLE   01929 480205
Aug BH wknd

The Acorn Inn
EVERSHOT   01935 83228
Cider & beer festival

The Drovers Inn
GUSSAGE ALL SAINTS 01258 840084
Etr

The Hambro Arms
MILTON ABBAS   01258 880233
Jul

The Three Elms
NORTH WOOTTON   01935 812881

The Cricketers
SHROTON or IWERNE COURTNEY
          01258 860421

The Bankes Arms Hotel
STUDLAND   01929 450225
Mid-Aug 4 days with live music &
200 beers & ciders

The Castle Inn
WEST LULWORTH   01929 400311

The Ship Inn
WEST STOUR   01747 838640
Jun or Jul

The Square and Compass
WORTH MATRAVERS 01929 439229
Beer and Pumpkin Festival
1st Sat Oct

DURHAM, CO

The Morritt Arms Hotel
BARNARD CASTLE   01833 627232

The George & Dragon Inn
BOLDRON   01833 638215
Early May

Duke of York Inn
FIR TREE   01388 767429

The Black Bull Inn
FROSTERLEY   01388 527784

Vane Arms
LONGNEWTON   01642 580401
Black Sheep wknd Oct, Mini Beer
Festival Jul

Ship Inn
MIDDLESTONE   01388 810904
May & Nov

**The Stables Pub
and Restaurant**
STANLEY   01207 288750
3rd wknd in Sep

ESSEX

The Bell Inn
CASTLE HEDINGHAM 01787 460350
3 per year

The Swan Inn
CHAPPEL   01787 222353
Spring & Aug BHs

The Sun Inn
FEERING   01376 570442
May & Oct

The Square & Compasses
FULLER STREET   01245 361477
Jun

The Chequers Inn
GOLDHANGER   01621 788203
Mar & Sep

The Ducane
GREAT BRAXTED   01621 891697

Rainbow & Dove
HASTINGWOOD   01279 415419

The White Hart Inn
MARGARETTING TYE 01277 840478
Jul & Nov

The Thatchers Arms
MOUNT BURES   01787 227460
May & Oct

The Duck Pub & Dining
NEWNEY GREEN   01245 421894
Aug BH

The Hoop
STOCK   01277 841137
Jun over 100 real ales & ciders,
barbecue

Hurdlemakers Arms
WOODHAM MORTIMER
          01245 225169
Last wknd Jun, 25+ real ales
& ciders

GLOUCESTERSHIRE

The Gardeners Arms
ALDERTON   01242 620257
Spring BH & Boxing Day (5 days
each)

Boat Inn
ASHLEWORTH   01452 700272

Catherine Wheel
BIBURY   01285 740250
Aug BH

Craven Arms Inn
BROCKHAMPTON   01242 820410
Annual

The Gloucester Old Spot
CHELTENHAM   01242 680321
May Day BH Annual cider festival

The Royal Oak Inn
CHELTENHAM   01242 522344
Whitsun BH Beer festival, Aug BH
Cider festival

The Yew Tree
CLIFFORD'S MESNE 01531 820719
Annually in Oct

The Tunnel House Inn
COATES   01285 770280
Jul

The Old Spot Inn
DURSLEY   01453 542870
3 times a year

The Trout Inn
LECHLADE ON THAMES
01367 252313
Jun

Bathurst Arms
NORTH CERNEY   01285 831281
Jan, Apr, Jul & Oct

The George Inn
STONEHOUSE   01453 822302
Aug BH

The Priory Inn
TETBURY   01666 502251
May Day BH - Real ale & cider

GREATER MANCHESTER

Marble Arch
MANCHESTER   0161 832 5914

The Nursery Inn
STOCKPORT   0161 432 2044
3 times a year with 8 guests on
handpump

The Lord Raglan
WALMERSLEY   0161 764 6680
Summer & Autumn

HAMPSHIRE

The Furze Bush Inn
BALL HILL   01635 253228
24-26 Dec

The Drift Inn
BEAULIEU   023 8029 2342

The Three Tuns Country Inn
BRANSGORE   01425 672232
Sep

The Red Lion
CHALTON   023 9259 2246
Late Jul-early Aug

The White Hart Inn
CHARTER ALLEY   01256 850048

The Flower Pots Inn
CHERITON   01962 771318

Turfcutters Arms
EAST BOLDRE   01590 612331

The Sussex Brewery
EMSWORTH   01243 371533
Annual Jun/Jul

The Shoe Inn
EXTON   01489 877526

The Augustus John
FORDINGBRIDGE   01425 652098
May BH

Hawkley Inn
HAWKLEY   01730 827205
End May-early Jun

The Kings Head
HURSLEY   01962 775208
2 per year - Aug BH & Dec

New Forest Inn
LYNDHURST   023 8028 4690
2nd wknd Jul

Half Moon & Spread Eagle
MICHELDEVER   01962 774339

The Red Lion
MORTIMER WEST END
                      0118 970 0169
Sep

The Fox
NORTH WALTHAM   01256 397288
Late Apr

The Crown
OLD BASING   01256 321424
Annually

The White Horse Inn
PETERSFIELD   01420 588387
Jun

The Fleur de Lys
PILLEY   01590 672158
Jul

The Alice Lisle
ROCKFORD   01425 474700

The Dukes Head
ROMSEY   01794 514450
May & Sep

The Selborne Arms
SELBORNE   01420 511247
1st wknd Oct

The Tichborne Arms
TICHBORNE   01962 733760
3rd wknd Aug

The Bell Inn
WINCHESTER   01962 865284
Summer

The Westgate Inn
WINCHESTER   01962 820222

HEREFORDSHIRE

England's Gate Inn
BODENHAM   01568 797286
Jul

Live and Let Live
BRINGSTY COMMON   01886 821462
Etr wknd

The New Harp Inn
HOARWITHY   01432 840900
BHs

The Grape Vaults
LEOMINSTER   01568 611404
2nd Sat in Dec - same day as the
Victorian Street Market

The Wellington
WELLINGTON   01432 830367
Jun

The Crown Inn
WOOLHOPE   01432 860468
May Day BH

HERTFORDSHIRE

The Valiant Trooper
ALDBURY   01442 851203

The Waggoners
AYOT GREEN   01707 324241

The Fox & Hounds
BARLEY   01763 849400
Every BH wknd

The Old Mill
BERKHAMSTED   01442 879590

**The Land of Liberty,
Peace and Plenty**
HERONSGATE   01923 282226
Winter ales, Etr, Aug BH, Xmas

The Radcliffe Arms
HITCHIN   01462 456111
2-3 annually

The Cow Roast Inn
TRING   01442 822287

The Fox
WILLIAN   01462 480233
Guinness & Oyster Festival Mar

KENT

The Red Lion
CANTERBURY   01227 721339
Aug BH wknd

The Bowl Inn
CHARING   01233 712256
Mid-Jul

The White Horse
CHILHAM   01227 730355
Summer

Albion Taverna
FAVERSHAM   01795 591411
Early Sep, annual Hop Festival

Rose & Crown
HALSTEAD   01959 533120
Spring, Summer & Autumn

The Red Lion
HERNHILL   01227 751207

The Peacock
IDEN GREEN   01580 211233

The Bull
ROLVENDEN   01580 241212

The Rose and Crown
SELLING   01227 752214

The Chequers Inn
SMARDEN   01233 770217

The Coastguard
ST MARGARET'S BAY   01304 853176
Historic Food Festival Sep

LANCASHIRE

Owd Nell's Tavern
BILSBORROW   01995 640010
Oyster Festival 1st wk Sep;
Oktoberfest last wk Oct; Cider
Festival last wk Jul

The Sun Hotel and Bar
LANCASTER   01524 66006
Summer festival

The White Cross
LANCASTER   01524 33999
Late Apr - Beer & Pie Festival

The Eagle & Child
PARBOLD   01257 462297
1st May BH

The Royal Arms
TOCKHOLES   01254 705373
Sep

LEICESTERSHIRE

The Royal Oak
LONG WHATTON   01509 843694
30 real ales plus 10 ciders

The Swan in the Rushes
LOUGHBOROUGH   01509 217014
Twice a year late May & mid-Nov

Cow and Plough
OADBY   0116 2720852
Quarterly

LINCOLNSHIRE

The Tally Ho Inn
ASWARBY   01529 455170
Aug BH - Real ales, hog roast, live
music & family fun

The Wishing Well Inn
BOURNE   01778 422970
Aug BH

The Goat
FROGNALL   01778 347629
Annually in Jun

The Victoria
LINCOLN   01522 541000
Halloween & Winter

The Willoughby Arms
LITTLE BYTHAM   01780 410276
Aug BH

Kings Head Inn
THEDDLETHORPE ALL SAINTS
                      01507 339798

LONDON

The Peasant
EC1   020 7336 7726
Apr & Nov

Ye Olde Mitre
EC1   020 7405 4751
May, Aug & Dec

The Charles Lamb
N1   020 7837 5040
Late May BH

The Drapers Arms
N1   020 7619 0348
Aug

The Engineer
NW1   020 7483 1890
Seasonal

The Prince Albert
NW1   020 7485 0270
3-day Real Ale Festival held 2-3
times a year

The Queens
NW1   020 7586 0408
During British Food Fortnight

The Holly Bush
NW3   020 7435 2892

The Junction Tavern
NW5   020 7485 9400
2-3 per year & mini festivals

The Lord Palmerston
NW5   020 7485 1578
Feb

William IV Bar & Restaurant
NW10   020 8969 5944

The Sands End Pub
SW6   020 7731 7823
Jun/Jul

The White Horse
SW6   020 7736 2115
4 per year. American, Great British,
Old Ale, Belgian

The Alma Tavern
SW18   020 8870 2537
Annual Young's Mini Festival

The Prince Bonaparte
W2   020 7313 9491
3rd week in Mar

The Albion
W14   020 7603 2826
Etr wknd

The Havelock Tavern
W14   020 7603 5374

The George
WC2   020 7353 9638
Mar - Real ale & Cider fest

GREATER LONDON

The Sun
CARSHALTON   020 8773 4549
Jun & Nov

The Five Bells
CHELSFIELD   01689 821044
Etr & Oct

NORFOLK

Chequers Inn
BINHAM   01328 830297

The Jolly Sailors
BRANCASTER STAITHE
   01485 210314
Norfolk Ale & Music Festival mid to
late Jun

**The Brisley Bell Inn
& Restaurant**
BRISLEY   01362 668686

The Crown
BURSTON   01379 741257
2-3 per year

PICK OF THE FESTIVALS

VICTORIA HOTEL
BEESTON, Nottinghamshire, 0115 9254049
www.victoriabeeston.co.uk

Easter Beer Festival

The Victoria Hotel's beer festival has up to 30 ales available at any
one time and speciality continental bottled beers. Bands play live
music on the Saturday and Sunday and festival food is served
throughout the day in the marquee.

The Red Lion Food and Rooms
CROMER   01263 514964
Annually in Autumn

The Butchers Arms
EAST RUSTON   01692 650237
Annually

Earle Arms
HEYDON   01263 587376
St George's Day

The Ancient Mariner Inn
HUNSTANTON   01485 536390
Last wknd Jun

The Hunny Bell
HUNWORTH   01263 712300
Aug BH

**The Stuart House Hotel,
Bar & Restaurant**
KING'S LYNN   01553 772169

Angel Inn
LARLING   01953 717963
Early Aug

The Mad Moose Arms
NORWICH   01603 627687
May & Oct

The Parson Woodforde
WESTON LONGVILLE   01603 881675

Fishermans Return
WINTERTON-ON-SEA   01493 393305
Aug BH

NORTHAMPTONSHIRE

The Great Western Arms
AYNHO   01869 338288
1st wknd Oct

Royal Oak @ Eydon
EYDON   01327 263167

The Falcon Inn
FOTHERINGHAY   01832 226254

The White Swan
HARRINGWORTH   01572 747543
Welland Valley Beer Festival

The George
KILSBY   01788 822229
St George's Day wknd

The Althorp Coaching Inn
NORTHAMPTON   01604 770651

The Chequered Skipper
OUNDLE   01832 273494
Twice yearly

The King's Head
WADENHOE   01832 720024
Aug

NORTHUMBERLAND

The Feathers Inn
HEDLEY ON THE HILL   01661 843607
Etr

**Battlesteads Hotel &
Restaurant**
HEXHAM   01434 230209
Summer

Miners Arms Inn
HEXHAM   01434 603909

The Bamburgh Castle Inn
SEAHOUSES   01665 720283
Annual

NOTTINGHAMSHIRE

Victoria Hotel
BEESTON   0115 9254049
4 per year - end Jan; Easter Beer
Festival; last 2wks Jul; Oct

The Dovecote Inn
LAXTON   01777 871586
Last wknd Aug

The Prince Rupert
NEWARK-ON-TRENT   01636 918121
Every BH

Ye Olde Trip to Jerusalem
NOTTINGHAM   0115 947 3171
2-3 per year

OXFORDSHIRE

The Elephant & Castle
BLOXHAM   0845 873 7358
Early May (part of Bloxfest Music
Festival)

The Red Lion
BRIGHTWELL-CUM-SOTWELL
   01491 837373
Beer & Live Music - 2 days in
Summer (local beer & musicians)

The Highway Inn
BURFORD   01993 823661

Horse & Groom
CAULCOTT   01869 343257
Jul

The George
DORCHESTER   01865 340404

The Woodman Inn
FERNHAM   01367 820643
Annually

The Butchers Arms
FRINGFORD   01869 277363
Jun

The White Hart
FYFIELD   01865 390585
Check with pub

The Falkland Arms
GREAT TEW   01608 683653

The Plough Inn
KELMSCOTT   01367 253543

The Magdalen Arms
OXFORD   01865 243159
Annually

The Unicorn
ROTHERFIELD PEPPARD
   01491 628674

The George & Dragon
SHUTFORD   01295 780320
Annually in Jun

The Old Red Lion
TETSWORTH   01844 281274
Mini Etr Festival

The Thatch
THAME   01844 214340
National Cask Ale Week

Plough Inn
WEST HANNEY   01235 868674
May BH - Oxon Ales; Aug BH -
Champ Beers of Britain

The Three Horseshoes
WITNEY   01993 703086
Annually Aug BH

RUTLAND

Old White Hart
LYDDINGTON   01572 821703
Summer

**The Jackson Stops
Country Inn**
STRETTON   01780 410237

SHROPSHIRE

The New Inn
BASCHURCH   01939 260335
Annually - check with pub

The Three Tuns Inn
BISHOP'S CASTLE   01588 638797
2nd wknd Jul involving all pubs
in town

The White Horse Inn
CLUN   01588 640305
1st wknd Oct

The Sun Inn
CRAVEN ARMS   01584 861239
Early Oct

The Ragleth Inn
LITTLE STRETTON   01694 722711
1st wknd Jul

The George & Dragon
MUCH WENLOCK   01952 727312
Much Wenlock Festival Sep

Odfellows Wine Bar
SHIFNAL   01952 461517
Annual May

Fighting Cocks
STOTTESDON   01746 718270

SOMERSET

The Globe Inn
APPLEY   01823 672327
1st wknd Sep

The Star Inn
BATH   01225 425072
2 annual Cornish beer festivals

Candlelight Inn
BISHOPSWOOD   01460 234476

The Queens Arms
CORTON DENHAM   01963 220317

The George Inn
CROSCOMBE   01749 342306
Spring BH wknd

The Inn at Freshford
FRESHFORD   01225 722250
Aug

The Lord Poulett Arms
HINTON ST GEORGE   01460 73149

The Halfway House
PITNEY   01458 252513
Mar

The Bottom Ship
PORLOCK   01643 863288
1st wknd Jul

Duke of York
SHEPTON BEAUCHAMP
   01460 240314
Sep

The Crown and Victoria Inn
TINTINHULL   01935 823341

The Blue Ball
TRISCOMBE   01984 618242
Triscombefest 1st Sat in Sep

Crossways Inn
WEST HUNTSPILL   01278 783756
Aug BH

The Rest and Be Thankful Inn
WHEDDON CROSS   01643 841222
Check with pub

STAFFORDSHIRE

Burton Bridge Inn
BURTON UPON TRENT
01283 536596
Twice yearly

The George
ECCLESHALL 01785 850300
Etr wknd

The Holly Bush Inn
STAFFORD 01889 508234
Jun & Sep

Oddfellows in the Boat
SUMMERHILL 01543 361692

The Hand & Trumpet
WRINEHILL 01270 820048
Last wk in Jan

SUFFOLK

The Queens Head
BRANDESTON 01728 685307
Jun

The Old Cannon Brewery
BURY ST EDMUNDS 01284 768769
Aug BH wknd

The Ship at Dunwich
DUNWICH 01728 648219
24 & Mar, Sep

Elveden Inn
ELVEDEN 01842 890876
Mid-Jun with live bands

The Station Hotel
FRAMLINGHAM 01728 723455
Mid-Jul

The Kings Head
(The Low House)
LAXFIELD 01986 798395
May & Sep

The Lindsey Rose
LINDSEY TYE 01449 741424
1st wknd Aug

Anchor Inn
NAYLAND 01206 262313
Father's Day, Octoberfest

Sibton White Horse Inn
SIBTON 01728 660337

The Rose & Crown
STANTON 01359 250236

The Anchor
WALBERSWICK 01502 722112
Mid-Aug

SURREY

The Jolly Farmers Deli Pub & Restaurant
BUCKLAND 01737 221355
Annually

The Swan Inn
CHIDDINGFOLD 01428 684688
Sep

The Bat & Ball Freehouse
FARNHAM 01252 792108
2nd wknd Jun

The Bell
FETCHAM 01372 372624
Cask Ale Festival in Autumn

The Keystone
GUILDFORD 01483 575089
Cider Festival Jul

The Surrey Oaks
NEWDIGATE 01306 631200
Late May BH & Aug BH

The Duke of Cambridge
TILFORD 01252 792236
Cherryfest - Music & Beer;
Oktoberfest - Real Ale &
Traditional food

The Half Moon
WINDLESHAM 01276 473329

SUSSEX, EAST

The Blackboys Inn
BLACKBOYS 01825 890283
Annually

The Greys
BRIGHTON 01273 680734
Aug BH

The Merrie Harriers
COWBEECH 01323 833108
Aug BH Beer & Music

The Tiger Inn
EAST DEAN 01323 423209

The Hatch Inn
HARTFIELD 01342 822363
Jun 'Ashdown Forest' beer festival

The Queen's Head
ICKLESHAM 01424 814552
1st wknd Oct

SUSSEX, WEST

The Fountain Inn
ASHURST 01403 710219
Oct

Duke of Cumberland Arms
HENLEY 01428 652280
Dukefest - midsummer biannually

The Dog and Duck
KINGSFOLD 01306 627295
Once a year - call for dates. Raises money for St George's, Tooting

The Lamb Inn
LAMBS GREEN 01293 871336
Aug

The Gribble Inn
OVING 01243 786893
Summer & Winter

The Grove Inn
PETWORTH 01798 343659
Summer

The Royal Oak
WINEHAM 01444 881252

WARWICKSHIRE

The Holly Bush
ALCESTER 01789 762482
Jun & Oct

The Castle Inn
EDGEHILL 01295 670255

The Red Lion, Hunningham
HUNNINGHAM 01926 623715
The Red Lion Film & Beer Festival
Aug BH wknd

The Duck on the Pond
LONG ITCHINGTON 01926 815876
1st May BH

White Bear Hotel
SHIPSTON ON STOUR
01608 661558
Etr

The Rose & Crown
WARWICK 01926 411117
May

WEST MIDLANDS

The Old Joint Stock
BIRMINGHAM 0121 200 1892
Twice a year

WIGHT, ISLE OF

Horse & Groom
NINGWOOD 01983 760672
Sep

Buddle Inn
NITON 01983 730243
Jun & Sep

The Chequers
ROOKLEY 01983 840314

WILTSHIRE

The Blue Boar
ALDBOURNE 01672 540237
Twice a year in Apr & Oct

The Crown Inn
ALDBOURNE 01672 540214
3rd wknd May & Aug

The Quarrymans Arms
BOX 01225 743569
Mini ale weeks

The Queens Head Inn
BROAD CHALKE 01722 780344
Summer

The Fox
BROUGHTON GIFFORD
01225 782949
During summer months

The Shears Inn
COLLINGBOURNE DUCIS
01264 850304
Early Jun

The Red Lion Inn
CRICKLADE 01793 750776
1st wknd Jun

The Raven Inn
DEVIZES 01380 828271
Wadworth Shire Horses Holiday;
early Aug

Red Lion
EAST CHISENBURY 01980 671124
May BH

The Bath Arms at Longleat
HORNINGSHAM 01985 844308
Mid-Jun

Red Lion Inn
LACOCK 01249 730456

The Smoking Dog
MALMESBURY 01666 825823
Spring BH

The Malet Arms
NEWTON TONEY 01980 629279
Jul

Old Mill
SALISBURY 01722 327517
May & Oct

The Lamb on the Strand
SEMINGTON 01380 870263

The Somerset Arms
SEMINGTON 01380 870067
May BH, Aug

The Cross Keys Inn
UPPER CHUTE 01264 730295
Summer

Prince Leopold Inn
UPTON LOVELL 01985 850460

The George Inn
WARMINSTER 01985 840396
Aug

WORCESTERSHIRE

The Beckford
BECKFORD 01386 881532
Oct

The Mug House Inn & Angry Chef Restaurant
BEWDLEY 01299 402543
May Day BH wknd

The Fleece Inn
BRETFORTON 01386 831173
Mid-late Oct

Crown & Trumpet
BROADWAY 01386 853202
Xmas & New Year

The Talbot
KNIGHTWICK 01886 821235
2nd wknd Oct

Nags Head
MALVERN 01684 574373
St George's Day annually

YORKSHIRE, EAST RIDING OF

The Old Star Inn
KILHAM 01262 420619
Last wknd Sep 25+ real ales

YORKSHIRE, NORTH

The Craven Arms
APPLETREEWICK 01756 720270
Oct, 25+ beers

Ye Old Sun Inn
COLTON 01904 744261
Summer

The New Inn
CROPTON 01751 417330
Nov

The Green Dragon Inn
HARDRAW 01969 667392
May, Jul & Oct

The Forresters Arms Inn
KILBURN 01347 868386
St George's Day

The Shoulder of Mutton Inn
KIRBY HILL 01748 822772

The White Bear
MASHAM 01765 689319
1st wknd after midsummer

The George at Wath
RIPON 01765 641324
BHs

YORKSHIRE, SOUTH

The Fountain Inn Hotel
PENISTONE 01226 763125
May & Aug

Kelham Island Tavern
SHEFFIELD 0114 272 2482
Midsummer - nearest wknd 24 Jun

YORKSHIRE, WEST

The Three Pigeons
HALIFAX 01422 347001
May

Farmers Arms
HOLMFIRTH 01484 683713
Autumn

North Bar
LEEDS 0113 242 4540
Spring - Belgium/Holland, Summer - USA, Autumn/Winter - German

The Windmill Inn
LINTON 01937 582209
Jul

The Alma Inn & Fresco Italian Restaurant
SOWERBY BRIDGE 01422 823334
Oktoberfest late Sep

CHANNEL ISLANDS JERSEY

Old Court House Inn
ST AUBIN 01534 746433

ISLE OF MAN

The Creek Inn
PEEL 01624 842216
Mar

Falcon's Nest Hotel
PORT ERIN 01624 834077
Early May

SCOTLAND

ARGYLL & BUTE

George Hotel
INVERARAY 01499 302111
May BH & Aug BH

DUMFRIES & GALLOWAY

House O'Hill Hotel
BARGRENNAN 01671 840243
Mar & Sep

DUNDEE

The Royal Arch Bar
BROUGHTY FERRY 01382 779741
1st wknd Oct in aid of local charities

Speedwell Bar
DUNDEE 01382 667783
1st wknd Oct Rotary Charity Oktoberfest

EDINBURGH

The Bow Bar
EDINBURGH 0131 226 7667
Twice a year end Jan & end Jul for 10 days each

The Guildford Arms
EDINBURGH 0131 556 4312

Halfway House
EDINBURGH 0131 225 7101
Throughout year

The Bridge Inn
RATHO 0131 333 1320
Check with pub

GLASGOW

Bon Accord
GLASGOW 0141 248 4427
4 per year, each selling 90 different beers and ciders

West Brewery
GLASGOW 0141 550 0135
Oktoberfest

HIGHLANDS

The Anderson
FORTROSE 01381 620236
Burns Weekend Real Ale Festival in Jan, monthly mini-festivals

Clachaig Inn
GLENCOE 01855 811252
Hogmanay, FebFest & OctoberFest

The Torridon Inn
TORRIDON 01445 791242
Sep

NORTH LANAKSHIRE

Castlecary House Hotel
CUMBERNAULD 01324 840233
TBA. Once or twice a year, over a wknd

PERTH & KINROSS

Meikleour Hotel
MEIKLEOUR 01250 883206
Last Sun in May

RENFREWSHIRE

Fox & Hounds
HOUSTON 01505 612448
May & Aug

SCOTTISH BORDERS

Liddesdale
NEWCASTLETON 01387 375255
1st wknd Jul

PICK OF THE FESTIVALS

BLACK LION INN
BABELL, Flintshire, 01352 720239
www.theblacklionuk.com

Real Ale Trail – April

The Real Ale Trail features live music and five cask ales.

STIRLING

The Lade Inn
CALLANDER 01877 330152
Late Aug-early Sep

WEST LOTHIAN

The Four Marys
LINLITHGOW 01506 842171
Last wknd in May & Oct with 20 ales

WALES

BRIDGEND

Prince of Wales Inn
KENFIG 01656 740356

CONWY

Pen-y-Bryn
COLWYN BAY 01492 533360
Beer & Bangers wk, Pie & Ale wk

FLINTSHIRE

Black Lion Inn
BABELL 01352 720239
Real Ale Trail Apr

Glasfryn
MOLD 01352 750500
Oct Great British Pie and Champion Beers of Britain wk; Mar Welsh Food and Drink wk

GWYNEDD

Snowdonia Parc Brewpub & Campsite
WAUNFAWR 01286 650409
Usually mid May to coincide with Welsh Highland Railway Raleail Festival

MONMOUTHSHIRE

Clytha Arms
ABERGAVENNY 01873 840206
Whitsun BH, Aug BH

Goose and Cuckoo Inn
RHYD-Y-MEIRCH 01873 880277
Twice a year, end of May & end of Aug

Fountain Inn
TINTERN PARVA 01291 689303
Etr & Sep

The Lion Inn
TRELLECH 01600 860322
Jun & Nov

NEWPORT

The Bell at Caerleon
CAERLEON 01633 420613

POWYS

The Bell
GLANGRWYNEY 01873 811115
Etr & Aug BHs

The Coach & Horses
LLANGYNIDR 01874 730245
Annually in Jul

The Harp
OLD RADNOR 01544 350655
Jun

Star Inn
TALYBONT-ON-USK 01874 676635
Mid-Jun & mid-Oct

RHONDDA CYNON TAFF

Bunch of Grapes
PONTYPRIDD 01443 402934
Every 2 months, 20+ ales

SWANSEA

Kings Head
LLANGENNITH 01792 386212
Last wknd of Nov

VALE OF GLAMORGAN

The Cross Inn
COWBRIDGE 01446 772995
Mini Beer/Cider fest - late Apr & Sep

The Plough & Harrow
MONKNASH 01656 890209
Jun/Jul

Pub Insurance

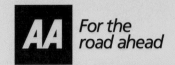

We could **save you £££'s** on your insurance.

Our fantastic Pub Insurance Package includes the following:

- ✔ Buildings and Contents, including frozen foods, wines & spirits
- ✔ Generous seasonal increases in stock cover
- ✔ Public Liability & Employers Liability
- ✔ Loss of Licence
- ✔ Business Interruption covered
- ✔ Money with personal accident & assault benefits
- ✔ Plus much more all tailored to your business

EXCLUSIVE RATES AVAILABLE

WHY CHOOSE US?

- Highly Competitive Rates
- Quick Quotes and Instant Cover
- Over 40 years experience in commercial insurance
- Pay in Instalments
- Live Entertainment Covered

- Winner of numerous industry awards
- Friendly, experienced team waiting to take your calls
- Can include Cover for Children's Outside Play Areas

Call us on
0800 107 1475

England

View over Ladybower Reservoir in the Peak District National Park, Derbyshire

BEDFORDSHIRE

BEDFORD
Map 12 TL04

The Embankment

6 The Embankment MK40 3PD ☎ 01234 261332
e-mail: embankment@peachpubs.com
dir: *From M1 junct 13, A421 to Bedford. Left onto A6 to town centre. Into left lane on river bridge. Into right lane signed Embankment. Follow around St Paul's Square into High St, into left lane. Left onto The Embankment*

At the heart of Bedford's beautifully landscaped Embankment, this imposing mock-Tudor pub sits behind an outdoor terrace overlooking the River Great Ouse. Dating from 1891, the building has been renovated to create a relaxed, hospitable atmosphere that reflects its late-Victorian heyday. Food choices range from deli boards to full meals, such as potato gnocchi with a spring onion, broad bean and gorgonzola sauce, followed by free-range chicken breast with a spring onion potato croquette and French-style peas, and Valrhona white chocolate mousse with home-made honeycomb for dessert.

Open all day all wk 7am-mdnt (Sat 7.30am-mdnt Sun 7.30am-11pm) Closed: 25 Dec **Bar Meals** Av main course £14 food served all day **Restaurant** Av 3 course à la carte fr £22 food served all day ⊕ PEACH PUBS ◀ Wells Eagle IPA & Bombardier, Young's ♂ Aspall. ♚ 13 **Facilities** ✿ Children welcome Children's portions Garden Parking Wi-fi ▦ (notice required)

The Park Pub & Kitchen **NEW**

PICK OF THE PUBS

98 Kimbolton Rd MK40 2PA ☎ 01234 273929
e-mail: info@theparkbedford.co.uk
dir: *M1 junct 14, A509 follow Newport Pagnell signs, then A422, A428 onto A6 right into Tavistock St (A600). Left on Broadway, 1st left into Kimbolton Rd. The Park in 0.5m*

Built in the 1900s, this fine-looking pub is a stone's throw from Bedford Park, just a little way out of town. If you expect the smartly decorated exterior to promise similar treatment inside, you won't be disappointed, because the interior, with its fireplaces, flagstone floors and beamed ceilings looks and feels very good. Beyond the wrap-around bar are a spacious restaurant, relaxing conservatory and airy garden room leading to an outdoor area, where heaters permit comfortable drinking and dining in less than heatwave conditions. In the bar is Eagle IPA from the town's Wells and Young's brewery, whose other flagship brew, Bombardier, is also on duty. Menus reflect local sourcing, with daily fish specials made from top-quality, market-fresh fish, and main dishes such as aubergine and spinach moussaka; chicken, leek and mushroom pie; honey and mustard pork sausages; and pot-roasted duck breast with sweet potato rösti.

Open all day all wk **Bar Meals** L served Mon-Sat 12-3, Sun 12-5 D served Mon-Sat 6-10, Sun 12-5 **Restaurant** L served Mon-Sat 12-3, Sun 12-5 D served Mon-Sat 6-10, Sun 12-5 ⊕ CHARLES WELLS ◀ Bombardier, Eagle IPA. ♚ 33 **Facilities** Children welcome Children's portions Garden Parking Wi-fi ▦ (notice required)

The Three Tuns

57 Main Rd, Biddenham MK40 4BD ☎ 01234 354847
e-mail: enquiries@threetunsbiddenham.com
dir: *On A428 from Bedford towards Northampton 1st left signed Biddenham. Into village, pub on left*

In a pretty village, this stone-built, thatched, Greene King pub has a large garden with a patio and decking, and a separate children's play area. Owner Chris Smith worked for French celebrity chef Jean-Christophe Novelli for a number of years and now produces dishes such as grilled tiger prawns in chilli and lime oil; pork and apple sausages with buttered mash, beer-battered onion rings and red wine jus; and Thai vegetable curry. In the garden is a long-disused, possibly haunted, morgue, the oldest building hereabouts. Booking for meals may be required.

Open all day all wk **Bar Meals** L served all wk 12-2.30 D served Mon-Sat 6-9.30 Av main course £12.50 **Restaurant** L served Mon-Sat 12-2.30, Sun 12-4 D served Mon-Sat 6-9.30 Av 3 course à la carte fr £20 ⊕ GREENE KING ◀ IPA, Guinness, Guest ale ♂ Aspall. ♚ 16 **Facilities** Children welcome Children's portions Play area Family room Garden Parking Wi-fi ▦

BOLNHURST
Map 12 TL05

The Plough at Bolnhurst ⊛

PICK OF THE PUBS

Kimbolton Rd MK44 2EX ☎ 01234 376274
e-mail: theplough@bolnhurst.com
dir: *On B660 N of Bedford*

This whitewashed Tudor country inn has tiny windows, thick walls, low beams and great open fires coupled with fresh, country-style décor. The impressive choice of real ales and inspired wine list are matched by a delicious menu prepared by Raymond Blanc-trained Martin Lee and his team of skilled chefs. The menu is driven by the freshest local and regional produce and specialist foods gathered from all corners. The result is an ever-changing choice of unique dishes, which have gained The Plough an AA Rosette. Start with nibbles such as lamb tikka or roast chorizo, then move on to diver-caught seared scallops with slow-cooked fennel and cardamom and fennel sauce, followed by breast of wood pigeon with beetroot purée, parsnip gratin, juniper and parsnip crisps. Rhubarb crème brûlée makes a tempting dessert but do leave room for the cheeseboard, with its astonishing choice of British, Italian and French varieties. Booking for meals may be required.

Open Tue-Sun 12-3 6.30-11 (Sun 12-3) Closed: 1 Jan, 2wks Jan, Mon & Sun eve **Bar Meals** L served Tue-Sun 12-2 D served Tue-Sat 6.30-9.30 Av main course £16.95 **Restaurant** L served Tue-Sun 12-2 D served Tue-Sat 6.30-9.30 Fixed menu price fr £12 Av 3 course à la carte fr £35 ⊕ FREE HOUSE ◀ Adnams Southwold Bitter, Potton Village Bike, Fuller's London Pride, Hopping Mad Brainstorm, Church End Goat's Milk ♂ Aspall Harry Sparrow. ♚ 13 **Facilities** Children welcome Children's portions Garden Parking Wi-fi ▦

BROOM
Map 12 TL14

The Cock

23 High St SG18 9NA ☎ 01767 314411
dir: *Off B658 SW of Biggleswade. 1m from A1*

Unspoilt to this day with its intimate quarry-tiled rooms with latched doors and panelled walls, this 17th-century establishment is known as 'The Pub with no Bar'. Real ales are served straight from casks racked by the cellar steps. A straightforward pub-grub menu includes burgers, jackets, sandwiches, omelettes and ploughman's. More substantial offerings are scampi and chicken nuggets. There are also veggie options (stilton and vegetable crumble; curry and rice) and specials (sirloin steak; half a roast chicken). A skittle room is available for hire.

Open 12-4 6-11 Closed: Sun eve **Bar Meals** L served all wk 12-2.15 D served Mon-Sat 7-9 Av main course £7.95 **Restaurant** L served all wk 12-2.15 D served Mon-Sat 7-9 ⊕ GREENE KING ◀ Abbot Ale, IPA, Ruddles County. **Facilities** ✿ Children welcome Children's menu Children's portions Play area Family room Garden Parking ▦ (notice required)

EATON BRAY
Map 11 SP92

The White Horse

Market Square LU6 2DG ☎ 01525 220231
e-mail: tom-dunnell@hotmail.co.uk
dir: *A5 N of Dunstable onto A505, left in 1m, follow signs*

Independently owned and managed by Tom Dunnell since December 2011, this 300-year-old village inn retains its reputation for a warm and cosy atmosphere, great home-cooked food and well-kept real ales. Oak beams and horse brasses add to the traditional charms of the interior. Chef Frank Lloyd has worked here for several years and continues to put together eclectic menus ranging from Japanese-style prawns with sweet chilli dip to homely beef in ale pie. Traditional desserts include steamed syrup pudding. Booking for meals may be required.

Open all wk 11.30-3 6.30-11 (Fri-Sun 11.30-11.30) **Bar Meals** L served all wk 12-2.15 D served all wk 7-9.30 **Restaurant** L served all wk 12-2.15 D served all wk 7-9.30 ⊕ PUNCH TAVERNS ◀ Greene King IPA, Shepherd Neame Spitfire ♂ Aspall. ♚ 10 **Facilities** Children welcome Children's menu Children's portions Play area Family room Garden Parking Wi-fi

HARROLD
Map 11 SP95

The Muntjac

PICK OF THE PUBS

71 High St MK43 7BJ ☎ 01234 721500
e-mail: muntjacharrold@hotmail.com
dir: *Telephone for directions*

Fine wines and ales and fine Indian cuisine is not how an inn normally sets out its stall, but this 17th-century former coaching inn is quite happy to be a little

Save on hotels. Book at **theAA.com/hotel**

BEDFORDSHIRE 29 **ENGLAND**

unorthodox. Independently run Harrold's Indian Cuisine restaurant offers dishes cooked to order to eat in or take away, its extensive menu featuring all the popular fish, meat, poultry and vegetarian dishes, as well as the less often encountered tandoori chicken mossallam, duck Darjeeling, and tawa specialities cooked using a traditional iron plate. A few English dishes are also available. The bar serves Ringwood Best, Abbot Ale, and regularly-changing guest ales from local breweries. Sports fans will appreciate the large-screen TVs. Members of the pub-sponsored local football team can often be found in the bar on Sunday lunchtimes after their match.

Open all wk Mon-Thu 5.30-11 (Fri 12.30-12 Sat 12-12 Sun 12.30-10.30) **Restaurant** D served Mon-Sat 5.30-11, Sun 5.30-10 ⊕ FREE HOUSE ◀ Ringwood Best Bitter, Greene King Abbot Ale, Guest ales Ö Symonds Founders Reserve. **Facilities** Children welcome Children's portions Garden Parking ⊨ (notice required) **Notes** ✆

IRELAND
Map 12 TL14

The Black Horse

SG17 5QL ☎ 01462 811398
e-mail: countrytaverns@aol.com
dir: *From S: M1 junct 12, A5120 to Flitwick. Onto A507 by Redbourne School. Follow signs for A1, Shefford (cross A6). Left onto A600 towards Bedford*

Built in the late 17th century, The Black Horse's traditional features combine with a bright, airy, chic interior where a mix of light and dark beams, inglenook fire and low ceilings invites you to tarry a little longer. The flower-rich garden and courtyard dining are popular in warmer weather. Grab a pint of Adnams, or choose from the excellent wine list, and settle down to appreciate the tempting range of dishes – a starter of poached Loch Duhart salmon, perhaps, followed by cashew and chickpea curry, and a dessert of orange and almond polenta cake. Individual dietary requirements are catered for. Booking for meals may be required.

Open all wk 12-3 6-12 (Sun 12-6) **Closed:** 25-26 Dec, 1 Jan **Bar Meals** L served Mon-Sat 12-2.30, Sun 12-5 D served Mon-Sat 6.30-10 Av main course £12.95 **Restaurant** L served Mon-Sat 12-2.30, Sun 12-5 D served Mon-Sat 6.30-10 Av 3 course à la carte fr £24.85 ⊕ FREE HOUSE ◀ Fuller's London Pride, St Austell Tribute, Adnams Ö Westons Stowford Press. ♥ 20 **Facilities** Children welcome Children's portions Garden Parking ⊨ (notice required)

KEYSOE
Map 12 TL06

The Chequers

Pertenhall Rd, Brook End MK44 2HR ☎ 01234 708678
e-mail: chequers.keysoe@tesco.net
dir: *On B660, 7m N of Bedford. 3m S of Kimbolton*

This peaceful 15th-century country pub has been in the same safe hands for over 25 years. No games machines, pool tables or jukeboxes disturb the simple pleasures of well-kept ales and great home-made food. The menu offers pub stalwarts like ploughman's; home-made

steak-and-ale pie; pan-fried trout; glazed lamb cutlets and a variety of grilled steaks; and a blackboard displays further choice plus the vegetarian options. For a lighter option try the home-made chicken liver pâté or soup, fried brie with cranberries, or plain or toasted sandwiches.

Open Wed-Sun 11.30-2.30 6.30-11 (Mon 11.30-2.30) **Closed:** Mon eve & Tue **Bar Meals** L served Wed-Mon 12-2 D served Wed-Sun 6.30-9 ⊕ FREE HOUSE ◀ Hook Norton Hooky Bitter, Fuller's London Pride Ö Westons Stowford Press. **Facilities** Children welcome Children's menu Children's portions Play area Family room Garden Parking ⊨ **Notes** ✆

LINSLADE
Map 11 SP92

The Globe Inn

Globe Ln, Old Linslade LU7 2TA ☎ 01525 373338
e-mail: 6458@greeneking.co.uk
dir: *N of Leighton Buzzard*

A very homely old pub, creaking with the character of the small Georgian farmhouse and stables it once was; beams, log fires, partial weatherboarding and a wrinkly roof line. Fronting the Grand Union Canal at the end of a no-through lane, it's a marvellous place to linger watching boating activity, supping on Greene King beers and choosing from a Pandora's Box of meals, varying from traditional meaty favourites like grilled pork chop to chicken fajitas, vegetarian lentil shepherd's pie, and smoked salmon and king prawn salad. There's a well-appointed restaurant, and children are made welcome with a play area in the tree-shaded garden.

Open all day all wk 11-11 (Sun 11-10.30) **Bar Meals** L served all wk 12-10 D served all wk 12-10 food served all day **Restaurant** L served all wk 12-10 D served all wk 12-10 food served all day ⊕ GREENE KING ◀ Abbot Ale & IPA, Morland Old Speckled Hen Ö Aspall. ♥ 16 **Facilities** ✿ Children welcome Children's menu Children's portions Play area Garden Beer festival Parking ⊨

NORTHILL
Map 12 TL14

The Crown

2 Ickwell Rd SG18 9AA ☎ 01767 627337
e-mail: victoria@doughtysbrasserie.com
dir: *Next to church & village green*

A delightful 16th-century pub with a new look and feel inside since refurbishment in 2010. Greene King ales are well kept, and Doughty's Brasserie is undoubtedly a major attraction. Lunch menus kick off with a range of organic baguettes and doorstep sandwiches, and continue with light bites such as Stornaway black pudding and poached egg salad. Main dishes excite the taste buds with the likes of roasted garlic and thyme chicken. The garden has plenty of tables for alfresco eating, and a children's play area. Booking for meals may be required.

Open all day all wk **Bar Meals** L served Mon-Fri 11-3, Sat-Sun 12-4 D served all wk 6.30-10 **Restaurant** L served Mon-Fri 12-2.30, Sat-Sun 12-10.30 ⊕ GREENE KING ◀ IPA & Abbot Ale, Morland Old Speckled Hen,

Hardys & Hansons Olde Trip, Guest ales Ö Aspall. ♥ 9 **Facilities** Children welcome Children's menu Children's portions Play area Garden Parking Wi-fi ⊨

ODELL
Map 11 SP95

The Bell

Horsefair Ln MK43 7AU ☎ 01234 720254
dir: *Telephone for directions*

Stone walls, open fireplaces and exposed beams provide the character for this 16th-century thatched village pub, with a spacious garden leading down to the River Ouse adding even more. But it doesn't stop there, not when you factor in the quality home-cooked food, such as ricotta and tomato tortellini; beef enchiladas; breaded fillet of haddock with home-made tartare sauce; and Irish beef stew. Sandwiches, baguettes and omelettes are also served at lunchtime. There is a summer beer festival. Booking for meals may be required.

Open all wk Mon-Thu 11.30-3 5-11.30 (Fri-Sun all day) **Bar Meals** L served Mon-Sat 11.30-2.30, Sun 12-4.30 D served all wk 6-9 ⊕ GREENE KING ◀ IPA, Abbot Ale, Seasonal ales Ö Westons Stowford Press. ♥ 8 **Facilities** ✿ Children welcome Children's menu Children's portions Garden Beer festival Parking ⊨

OLD WARDEN
Map 12 TL14

Hare and Hounds

PICK OF THE PUBS

SG18 9HQ ☎ 01767 627225
dir: *From Bedford turn right off A603 (or left from A600) to Old Warden. Also accessed from Biggleswade rdbt on A1*

This attractive 200-year-old building is situated in the charming Bedfordshire village of Old Warden and is part of the Shuttleworth Estate, home to the famous collection of classic cars and vintage aeroplanes. The interiors of the bar and the three chic dining rooms feature timbered walls, warm red and cream colours, fresh flowers and contemporary furnishings. Wines include some from the local Warden Abbey vineyard, whilst cracking beers come courtesy of Charles Wells, and cider from Aspall. Food is taken very seriously here; the menu lists a well-balanced choice of rustic traditional dishes and more modern offerings, with every effort made to use local produce. Typical starters include chicken liver parfait with red onion marmalade and toast. For a main course, try the beer-battered Billingsgate haddock with hand-cut chips, mushy peas and tartare sauce; or pie of the day. There's a monthly-changing set menu as well.

Open Tue-Sat 12-3 6-11 (Sun 12-10.30) **Closed:** 25 & 26 Dec, 1 Jan, Mon (ex BH) **Bar Meals** L served all wk 12-2 D served all wk 6.30-9 **Restaurant** L served Mon-Sat 12-2, Sun 12-3.30 D served Mon-Sat 6.30-9 ⊕ CHARLES WELLS ◀ Eagle IPA, Young's Ö Aspall. ♥ 13 **Facilities** ✿ Children welcome Children's portions Family room Garden Parking

SALFORD — Map 11 SP93

The Swan

PICK OF THE PUBS

2 Warendon Rd MK17 8BD ☎ 01908 281008
e-mail: swan@peachpubs.com
dir: *M1 junct 13, follow signs to Salford*

In this attractive village setting you'll find the tile-hung, Edwardian-era Swan. Painted in rich reds, the lively bar makes you feel instantly at home, as does the eating area, where the big French doors can be thrown open to the garden. Peer through the feature window into the kitchen to watch the chefs preparing dishes from top, locally supplied ingredients, including free-range meat and eggs, sustainable fish, and seasonal vegetables. Deli boards are available throughout the day – choose from the five on the menu or make up your own board from the selection. Lunch or dinner main courses include superfood salad, vegetable tagine, and coq au vin. A sensibly priced wine list offers plenty by the glass. The carefully restored barn with a large central dining table can be used as a memorable setting for a private dinner. There's a busy social calendar of events.

Open all day all wk 11am-mdnt (Sun 12-10.30) Closed: 25 Dec Bar Meals L served all wk 12-6 D served Mon-Sat 6-9.45, Sun 6-9.30 Av main course £12.20 food served all day Restaurant L served all wk 12-3 D served Mon-Sat 6-9.45, Sun 6-9.30 Av 3 course à la carte fr £18.50 ⊕ PEACH PUBS ◀ Fuller's London Pride ♂ Addlestones, Aspall. ♟ 12 Facilities ♣ Children welcome Children's portions Garden Parking Wi-fi ▬

SOULDROP — Map 11 SP96

The Bedford Arms

High St MK44 1EY ☎ 01234 781384
e-mail: thebedfordarms@tiscali.co.uk
dir: *From Rushden take A6 towards Bedford. In 6m right into Stocking Lane to Souldrop. Pub 50mtrs on right*

Thought to be over 300 years old, this pub has all the traditional attributes – low beams, horse brasses, tankards and skittles. Then there are the four well-kept real ales available in the bar with its cosy open fire in winter. Plus there is a pretty good selection of pub dishes served in the cottage-style dining room, with its country prints and shelves of china – chicken (or vegetable) tikka masala; sausage, mash and onion gravy; chicken and ham pie; home-made cottage pie; battered cod; and leek and stilton bread-and-butter pudding. It's a great place to start or end a walk.

Open 12-3 6-11 (Fri-Sun 12-11) Closed: Mon (ex BHs) Bar Meals L served Tue-Sat 12-2, Sun 12-4 D served Tue-Sat 12-2, Sun 12-4 Restaurant L served Tue-Sat 12-2, Sun 12-4 D served Tue-Sat 6.30-9 Av 3 course à la carte fr £22 ⊕ FREE HOUSE ◀ Phipps NBC Red Star, Greene King IPA, Black Sheep, Guest ale ♂ Westons Stowford Press. ♟ 9 Facilities Children welcome Children's menu Children's portions Garden Parking

SOUTHILL — Map 12 TL14

The White Horse

High St SG18 9LD ☎ 01462 813364
e-mail: whitehorsesouthill@live.co.uk
dir: *Telephone for directions*

A country pub with traditional values, happily accommodating the needs of children in the large patio gardens, and those who like to sit outside on cool days enjoying a well-kept pint (the patio has heaters). Offering traditional English food, fish, vegetarian and children's dishes, grilled steaks are a big draw in the restaurant but other main courses from the extensive menu include rack of barbecue spare ribs; home-made game or fisherman's pie; plus choices from the chef's specials board. Salads, ploughman's, sandwiches, baguettes and wraps are also available. Booking for meals may be required.

Open all wk 11.30-3 6-11 (Sat 11.30-11 Sun 12-10.30) Closed: 26 Dec Bar Meals L served Mon-Fri 12-2, Sat-Sun all day D served Mon-Fri 6-9.30, Sat-Sun all day Restaurant L served Mon-Fri 12-2, Sat-Sun all day D served Mon-Fri 6-9.30, Sat-Sun all day ⊕ ENTERPRISE INNS ◀ Greene King IPA, Banks & Taylor Golden Fox, Sharp's Doom Bar, John Smith's. ♟ 8 Facilities Children welcome Children's menu Play area Garden Parking Wi-fi ▬ (notice required)

STANBRIDGE — Map 11 SP92

The Five Bells

PICK OF THE PUBS

Station Rd LU7 9JF ☎ 01525 210224
e-mail: fivebells@fullers.co.uk
dir: *Off A505 E of Leighton Buzzard*

A stylish and relaxing setting for a drink or a meal is offered by this white-painted 400-year-old village inn, which has been delightfully renovated and revived. The bar features lots of bare wood as well as comfortable armchairs and polished, rug-strewn floors. The modern décor extends to the bright, airy 75-cover dining room with its oak beams and walls adorned with paintings. There's also a spacious garden with patio and lawns. The inn uses local suppliers where possible to offer farm-assured chicken and beef, as well as sustainable seafood. The menu typically includes sharing boards and dishes such as Woburn Abbey venison burger; chicken and ham pudding; slow-cooked pressed Suffolk pork belly; and roast guinea fowl breast. These dishes are complemented by light lunches and traditional blackboard daily specials. Leave room for chocolate and hazelnut torte or a British cheeseboard.

Open all day all wk 11-11 (Sun 12-10.30) Bar Meals L served Mon-Sat 12-10, Sun 12-9 D served Mon-Sat 12-10, Sun 12-9 food served all day Restaurant food served all day ⊕ FULLER'S ◀ London Pride & Chiswick Bitter, George Gale & Co Seafarers ♂ Aspall. ♟ 8 Facilities ♣ Children welcome Children's menu Children's portions Garden Parking ▬

SUTTON — Map 12 TL24

John O'Gaunt Inn

30 High St SG19 2NE ☎ 01767 260377
dir: *Off B1040 between Biggleswade & Potton*

Situated in one of Bedfordshire's most picturesque villages, the John O'Gaunt is a pretty village inn at the centre of the community and many rural walks. Ales are supplied in rotation from various breweries. Piped music is notable by its absence, though you may be encouraged to join in the regular folk music sessions; 30 different clubs and societies are hosted here. Good traditional fare is on offer, such as gammon steak, lamb shank, fisherman's pie, and mixed vegetable lasagne, plus various balti dishes. The pub has a large beer garden, and welcoming winter fires.

Open all wk 9-4 6.30-11.30 Bar Meals L served all wk 11-3 D served all wk 6.30-9.30 Restaurant L served all wk 11-3 D served all wk 6.30-9.30 ⊕ FREE HOUSE ◀ Rotating - Woodforde's Wherry, Fuller's London Pride, Potton Porter, Sharp's Doom Bar, Timothy Taylor Landlord, Black Sheep ♂ Westons Old Rosie. ♟ 8 Facilities ♣ Children welcome Garden Parking Wi-fi ▬ Notes ⊛

TILSWORTH — Map 11 SP92

The Anchor Inn

1 Dunstable Rd LU7 9PU ☎ 01525 211404
dir: *Exit A5 at Tilsworth. In 1m pub on right at 3rd bend*

The only pub in a Saxon village, The Anchor dates from 1878. The restaurant is a recent addition to the side of the pub, and the whole building has been refurbished. The licensees pride themselves on their fresh food and well-kept beers and guest ales. An acre of garden includes patio seating for alfresco dining, an adventure playground and a barbecue. There's been a recent change of hands, but a current menu lists the likes of sausage and mash; shin of beef stew; pan-fried veal liver and bacon; and pie of the week. Also available are a selection of Thai curries, sandwiches, baguettes and jacket potatoes. Booking for meals may be required.

Open all day all wk 12-11.30 Bar Meals L served all wk 12-5 D served all wk 5-10 food served all day Restaurant L served all wk 12-5 D served all wk 5-10 food served all day ⊕ GREENE KING ◀ IPA & Abbot Ale, Guest ales. Facilities Children welcome Children's menu Children's portions Play area Garden Parking Wi-fi ▬ (notice required)

WOBURN — Map 11 SP93

The Birch at Woburn

20 Newport Rd MK17 9HX ☎ 01525 290295
e-mail: ctaverns@aol.com
dir: *Telephone for directions*

Close to Woburn Abbey and the Safari Park, this smart family-run establishment is located opposite Woburn Championship Golf Course and a short hop from junction 13 of the M1. The pub has built its reputation on friendly service and freshly cooked food; the kitchen team is passionate about sourcing ingredients from local farms and estates. The menu offers a range of English and continental dishes, and there is a griddle area where customers can select their steaks and fish, which are then cooked to your liking by the chefs. Booking for meals may be required.

Open 12-3 6-12 Closed: 25-26 Dec, 1 Jan, Sun eve **Bar Meals** L served all wk 12-2.30 D served Mon-Sat 6-10 Av main course £13.95 **Restaurant** L served all wk 12-2.30 D served Mon-Sat 6-10 Av 3 course à la carte fr £27.85 ⊕ FREE HOUSE ◀ Fuller's London Pride, Adnams. ▾ 12 **Facilities** Children welcome Children's portions Parking ▬ (notice required)

The Black Horse

1 Bedford St MK17 9QB ☎ 01525 290210
e-mail: blackhorse@peachpubs.com
dir: In town centre on A4012

Right in the middle of the pretty village of Woburn, this 18th-century inn cuts an elegant figure. Behind the Georgian frontage, the original coaching-inn feel of the cosy bar has been retained and complemented with a chic, relaxed dining area where seasonal, locally sourced food drives the all-day menus. As well as sandwiches and deli boards to share, main courses might include free-range coq au vin with creamy mash; Jimmy Butler slow-braised collar of pork, chorizo and butter bean cassoulet; winter vegetable tagine with almond and orange couscous; or Welsh sea bass fillets with sautéed new potatoes and pesto sauce.

Open all day all wk 11-11 (Sat 11am-11.30pm) Closed: 25 Dec **Bar Meals** L served all wk 12-6 D served all wk 6-9.45 food served all day **Restaurant** L served all wk 12-3 D served all wk 6-9.45 ⊕ PEACH PUBS ◀ Greene King IPA & Abbot Ale, Hardys & Hansons Olde Trip, Guest ale ♂ Aspall. ▾ 10 **Facilities** Children's portions Garden Wi-fi ▬

The Tavistock Bar & Lounge

The Inn at Woburn, George St MK17 9PX
☎ 01525 290441
e-mail: inn@woburn.co.uk
dir: M1 junct 13, left to Woburn, in Woburn turn left at T-junct

The Inn at Woburn has been a welcome sight for travellers for nearly 300 years. Originally a coaching inn, it was a popular spot for Royal Mail coaches travelling from London to the North. The inn's Tavistock Bar offers an informal setting to enjoy real ales and a wide range of wines – including 28 by the glass. In addition, an all-day bar menu of light snacks and meals might feature croque-monsieur, steak baguette or venison burger.

Open all day all wk **Bar Meals** L served all wk 12-10 D served all wk 12-10 food served all day **Restaurant** L served all wk 12-2 D served all wk 6.30-9.30 ⊕ FREE HOUSE ◀ Wells Bombardier, Eagle IPA. ▾ 28 **Facilities** Children welcome Children's menu Children's portions Parking Wi-fi ▬ (notice required)

ALDERMASTON   Map 5 SU56

Hinds Head

Wasing Ln RG7 4LX ☎ 0118 971 2194
e-mail: hindshead@fullers.co.uk
dir: M4 junct 12, A4 towards Newbury, left on A340 towards Basingstoke, 2m to village

This 17th-century inn with its distinctive clock and bell tower still incorporates the village lock-up, which was last used in 1865. The former brewhouse behind the pub has been refurbished to create an additional dining area. The menu features home-made British choices with international influences. Dishes range from a meze board to share; country pie of the week; rice noodle salad with prawns; leek and cheese crumble; honey-glazed roast salmon; and lunchtime jackets and sandwiches.

Open all wk Mon-Thu 11-11 (Fri-Sat 11am-mdnt Sun 11-10.30) **Bar Meals** L served Mon-Sat 12-3, Sun 12-6 D served Mon-Sat 6-9 **Restaurant** L served Mon-Sat 12-3, Sun 12-6 D served Mon-Sat 6-9 ⊕ FULLER'S ◀ London Pride & ESB, Guest ales ♂ Aspall. ▾ 12 **Facilities** ✿ Children welcome Children's menu Children's portions Family room Garden Parking Wi-fi

ALDWORTH   Map 5 SU57

The Bell Inn

PICK OF THE PUBS

RG8 9SE ☎ 01635 578272
dir: Just off B4009 (Newbury to Streatley road)

One might be surprised to discover that an establishment without a restaurant can hold its own in a world of smart dining pubs and modish gastro-pubs. Well, be surprised. The Bell not only survives, it positively prospers and, to be fair, it does serve some food, if only hot, crusty, generously filled rolls. And since it is one of the few truly unspoiled country pubs left, and serves cracking pints of Arkell's, West Berkshire and guest real ales, plus ciders, this limitation has been no disadvantage. The Bell is old, very old, beginning life in 1340 as a five-bay cruck-built manor hall. It has reputedly been in the same family for 200 years: ask Mr Macaulay, the landlord - he's been here for more than 30 of them, and he has no plans to change it from the time warp it is. A 300-year-old, one-handed clock still stands in the taproom 'keeping imperfect time', and the rack for the spit-irons and clockwork roasting jack are still over the fireplace. Taller customers may bump their heads at the glass-panelled bar hatch.

Open Tue-Sat 11-3 6-11 (Sun 12-3 7-10.30) Closed: 25 Dec, Mon (open BH Mon L only) **Bar Meals** L served Tue-Sat 11-2.30, Sun 12-2.30 D served Tue-Sat 6-9.30, Sun 7-9 ⊕ FREE HOUSE ◀ Arkell's Kingsdown Special Ale & 3B, West Berkshire Old Tyler & Maggs' Magnificent Mild, Guest ales ♂ Upton's Farmhouse, Tutts Clump, Lilley's Pear & Apple. **Facilities** ✿ Children welcome Garden Parking **Notes** ☺

ASCOT   Map 6 SU96

The Thatched Tavern

Cheapside Rd SL5 7QG ☎ 01344 620874
e-mail: enquiries@thethatchedtavern.co.uk
dir: Follow Ascot Racecourse signs. Through Ascot 1st left (Cheapside). 1.5m, pub on left

En route to Windsor Castle, Queen Victoria's carriage was allegedly sometimes spotted outside this 400-year-old, flagstone-floored, low-ceilinged pub, while what the history books call 'her faithful servant' John Brown knocked a few back inside. The sheltered garden makes a fine spot to enjoy a Fuller's real ale, a glass of wine and, for lunch, beef stew suet pudding; or London Pride-battered fish and chips. For dinner, try pan-fried chicken supreme; cider-marinated pressed pork belly and celeriac purée; or spaghetti, tenderstem broccoli, asparagus and cherry tomatoes. Baguettes and sandwiches are available too. Booking for meals may be required.

Open all wk Mon-Thu 12-3 5.30-11 (Fri-Sun all day) **Bar Meals** L served Mon-Sat 12-2.30 **Restaurant** L served Mon-Sat 12-2.30, Sun 12-3 D served Mon-Sat 7-9.45, Sun 7-9 ⊕ FREE HOUSE ◀ Fuller's London Pride, Guinness ♂ Westons Stowford Press. ▾ 11 **Facilities** Children welcome Children's portions Garden Parking Wi-fi

ASHMORE GREEN   Map 5 SU56

The Sun in the Wood

Stoney Ln RG18 9HF ☎ 01635 42377
e-mail: info@suninthewood.co.uk
dir: From A34 at Robin Hood Rdbt left to Shaw, at mini rdbt right then 7th left into Stoney Ln 1.5m, pub on left

Top licensees Philip and Lauren Davison are proudly anticipating their 17th year at this award-winning Wadworth country pub and restaurant, which is surrounded by beautiful mature woodland. A new look to the interior early in 2012 introduced colourful wallpaper to the lounge bar and restaurant, and beams and tables were stripped back to their natural hue. The menu proffers reliable starters such as Scottish smoked salmon and prawn mayonnaise salad; a typical main course from the carte is turkey, ham and leek pie; and home-made puddings cater for most allergy sufferers. Booking for meals may be required.

Open 12-2.30 6-11 (Sat 12-11 Sun 12-5) Closed: Mon **Bar Meals** L served Tue-Fri 12-2, Sat 12-2.30, Sun 12-4 D served Tue-Fri 6-9.30, Sat 5.30-9.30 Av main course £11 **Restaurant** L served Tue-Fri 12-2, Sat 12-2.30, Sun 12-4 D served Tue-Fri 6-9.30, Sat 5.30-9.30 Fixed menu price fr £20 Av 3 course à la carte fr £20 ⊕ WADWORTH ◀ 6X, Henry's Original IPA ♂ Westons Stowford Press. ▾ 15 **Facilities** Children welcome Children's menu Children's portions Play area Garden Parking Wi-fi ▬

BOXFORD — Map 5 SU47

The Bell at Boxford

Lambourn Rd RG20 8DD ☎ 01488 608721
e-mail: paul@bellatboxford.com
dir: *M4 junct 14 onto A338 towards Wantage. Turn right onto B4000 to x-rds, signed Boxford; From junct 13 onto A34 to Hungerford, right at rdbt onto B4000. At xrds turn right to Boxford, signed*

This mock-Tudor country pub is at the heart of the glorious Lambourn Valley, noted for its pretty villages and sweeping Downland scenery. The main bar is located in the earliest part of the building, dating from the 17th century. There is also a patio, which is popular throughout the year with its array of flowers and outdoor heating, hog roasts, barbecues and parties. Menus might include rib-eye steak served with field mushroom and tomato on a bed of chips; tiger prawn linguine; or pan-fried lemon sole with lemon and caper sauce.

Open all day all wk **Bar Meals** L served Mon-Sat 12-2 (pizza Mon-Sat 2.30-7), Sun 12-9 D served Mon-Sat 7-9.30, Sun 7-9 (pizza Sun 6.30-11) **Restaurant** L served Mon-Sat 12-2.30, Sun 12-7 D served Mon-Sat 7-9.30, Sun 7-9 ⊕ FREE HOUSE ◀ Wadworth The Bishop's Tipple, 6X & Henry's Original IPA, Guinness Ö Lilley's Apples & Pears, Bee Sting Pear. ♀ 60 **Facilities** ✿ Children welcome Children's portions Garden Parking Wi-fi ▄▄ (notice required)

BRAY — Map 6 SU97

The Crown Inn ◉

High St SL6 2AH ☎ 01628 621936
dir: *M4 junct 8/9, exit to Maidenhead Central. At next rdbt, take exit to Bray & Windsor (A308). 0.5m, left at the Bray sign (B3028). In village, pub on left*

Since celebrity chef Heston Blumenthal acquired this 16th-century village pub in 2010, subtle but necessary improvements have been made to the décor and furnishings to bring it up-to-date, while leaving untouched the historic low beams and grand open fireplaces. The modern British food with one AA Rosette includes lunchtime sandwiches and main courses such as roast Loch Duart salmon with crushed Jersey Royals; baked suet, steak-and-ale pie; and macaroni, baby leeks and chanterelle mushrooms. Guests may also dine outside in the courtyard with its overhanging grape vines. Heston's world-famous Fat Duck restaurant is next door. Booking for meals may be required.

Open all wk 12-3 6-11 Closed: 26-27 Dec **Bar Meals** L served Mon-Fri 12-2.30, Sat-Sun 12-3 D served all wk 6.30-10 **Restaurant** L served Mon-Fri 12-2.30, Sat-Sun 12-3 D served all wk 6.30-10 ⊕ SCOTTISH & NEWCASTLE ◀ Courage Best & Directors, Shepherd Neame Spitfire. ♀ 13 **Facilities** Children welcome Children's menu Children's portions Garden Parking ▄▄

The Hinds Head ◉◉

PICK OF THE PUBS

See Pick of the Pubs on opposite page

BURCHETT'S GREEN — Map 5 SU88

The Crown NEW

Burchett's Green Rd SL6 6QZ ☎ 01628 826184
e-mail: thecrown@thecrownburchettsgreen.co.uk
dir: *From Maidenhead take A4 towards Reading. At mini rdbt right signed Burchett's Green. Pub in village centre*

New landlords took over this traditional brick-built village local in 2011 and have maintained its reputation for imaginative pub food cooked from local seasonal ingredients, including home-grown salads, herbs and vegetables. From the spanking new kitchen chefs deliver seared scallops with black pudding; cod wrapped in Parma ham with pea risotto and sauce vierge; venison with honey-roast roots, mash and redcurrant jelly; white chocolate pannacotta; and cracking Sunday roasts. The atmosphere is pubby and informal – bag a table by the blazing fire in the homely bar. Booking for meals may be required.

Open 12-3 6-11 (Sun 12-9) Closed: Mon L **Bar Meals** L served Tue-Sun 12-3 D served Mon-Sat 6-9 Av main course £14 **Restaurant** L served Tue-Sat 12-2.30, Sun 12-3.30 D served Mon-Sat 6.30-9 Fixed menu price fr £13 ⊕ GREENE KING ◀ Morland Original, Old Speckled Hen Ö Aspall. ♀ 10 **Facilities** ✿ Children welcome Children's menu Children's portions Garden Parking Wi-fi ▄▄ (notice required)

CHIEVELEY — Map 5 SU47

The Crab at Chieveley ★ ★ ★ ★ GA ◉◉

North Heath, Wantage Rd RG20 8UE ☎ 01635 247550
e-mail: info@crabatchieveley.com
dir: *M4 junct 13. 1.5m W of Chieveley on B4494*

This lovely old thatched dining pub has an award-winning seafood restaurant, which makes it the perfect place to break a tedious M4 journey or chill out at on a summer evening. Specialising in fish dishes and with fresh deliveries daily, the continuously-changing menu in the maritime-themed restaurant offers mouth-watering starters such as Carlingford Loch oysters, followed by catch of the day, venison loin, bouillabaisse or Cornish lobster thermidor. The interesting dessert menu has treacle and pistachio tart with apricot purée and pistachio anglaise. Beers are from West Berkshire Brewery and 13 boutique bedrooms complete the package. Dogs are welcome.

Open all day all wk 11-11 **Bar Meals** L served all wk 12-2.30 D served all wk 6-10 **Restaurant** L served all wk 12-2.30 D served all wk 6-10 ⊕ FREE HOUSE ◀ West Berkshire. ♀ 20 **Facilities** ✿ Children welcome Children's menu Children's portions Garden Parking Wi-fi **Rooms** 13

COLNBROOK — Map 6 TQ07

The Ostrich NEW

High St SL3 0JZ ☎ 01753 682628
e-mail: enquiries@theostrichcolnbrook.co.uk
dir: *M25 junct 14 towards Poyle. Right at 1st rdbt, over next 2 rdbts. Left at sharp right bend into High St. Left at mini rdbt, pub on left*

Close to Heathrow and just minutes from the motorway stands, surprisingly, one of England's oldest pubs. Dating from 1106 and once a coaching inn on the old London-Bath road, the vast and rambling Ostrich oozes history, with its heavily timbered façade, cobbled courtyard and an interior filled with wonky oak beams, massive fireplaces and crooked stairs. Cross Oak Inns have revamped it in contemporary style, so expect glass doors, a steel bar, chunky furnishings and vibrant colours. Equally modern, the menu takes in chicken terrine with rustic bread, pork belly with cider jus, and milk chocolate fondant.

Open all wk 12-3 5-11 (Sun all day) **Bar Meals** L served all wk 12-3 D served all wk 6-9.30 Av main course £12 **Restaurant** L served all wk 12-3 D served all wk 6-9.30 Av 3 course à la carte fr £25 ⊕ FREE HOUSE/CROSS OAK INNS ◀ Sharp's Doom Bar, Windsor & Eton Windsor Knot & Knight of the Garter, Fuller's London Pride, Hook Norton Hooky Bitter Ö Aspall. ♀ 10 **Facilities** Children welcome Children's menu Children's portions Garden Parking Wi-fi ▄▄ (notice required)

COOKHAM DEAN — Map 5 SU88

The Chequers Brasserie

PICK OF THE PUBS

See Pick of the Pubs on page 34

PICK OF THE PUBS

The Hinds Head ⚜⚜

BRAY   Map 6 SU97

High St SL6 2AB ☎ 01628 626151
e-mail: info@hindsheadbray.com
web: www.hindsheadbray.com
dir: *M4 junct 8/9 take Maidenhead Central exit. Next rdbt take Bray/Windsor exit. 0.5m, B3028 to Bray*

Heston Blumenthal's younger sibling to his eponymous Fat Duck restaurant has, not surprisingly, become a gastronomic destination, yet the striking 15th-century building remains very much a village local. Its origins are a little obscure, with some saying it was used as a royal hunting lodge and others as a guest house for the local Abbot of Cirencester. What is known is that Queen Elizabeth II dined with European royalty at the pub in 1963. Expect an informal atmosphere in the traditional bar, with its beams, sturdy oak panelling, log fires, leather chairs, and pints of Rebellion available at the bar. On the ground floor is the main restaurant, while upstairs are two further dining areas, the Vicars Room, and the larger Royal Room. Having worked alongside the team in the Tudor kitchens at Hampton Court Palace, Heston rediscovered the origins of British cuisine, and has reintroduced some classic recipes that echo the pub's Tudor roots. Top-notch ingredients are used in gutsy dishes that are cooked simply and delivered in an unfussy

manner by head chef Kevin Love. Take bar snacks or starters like tea-smoked salmon with soda bread or hash of snails, with main courses taking in veal chop with cabbage and onion and sauce 'Reform', chicken thigh with liver butter, bacon, onion, mushrooms and red wine sauce; Cornish day-boat brill with artichokes, clams and cider butter sauce; and rib-eye steak with bone marrow sauce and triple-cooked chips. Room should be left for a memorable pudding, perhaps rhubarb and custard quaking pudding; hazelnut and chocolate with blood orange sorbet; or a plate of British cheese with oatcakes and pear chutney. Well selected, widely sourced wines complete the picture. Booking for meals may be required.

Open all wk 11.30-11 (Sun 12-7) Closed: 25 Dec **Bar Meals** L served Mon-Sat 12-2.30, Sun 12-4 D served Mon-Sat 6.30-9.30 **Restaurant** L served Mon-Sat 12-2.30, Sun 12-4 D served Mon-Sat 6.30-9.30 ⊕ FREE HOUSE ◀ Rebellion IPA & Seasonal ales, Cotswold, Windsor & Eton Seasonal ale Ö Lilley's Star Gazer. ☐ 15 **Facilities** Children welcome Children's menu Children's portions Parking

PICK OF THE PUBS

The Chequers Brasserie

COOKHAM DEAN Map 5 SU88

Dean Ln SL6 9BQ ☎ 01628 481232
e-mail: info@chequersbrasserie.co.uk
web: www.chequersbrasserie.co.uk
dir: *From A4094 in Cookham High St
towards Marlow, over rail line. Pub 1m
on right*

Kenneth Grahame, who wrote *The Wind
in the Willows*, spent his childhood in
these parts. This historic pub is tucked
away between Marlow and Maidenhead,
in one of the prettiest villages in the
Thames Valley. Striking Victorian and
Edwardian villas around the green set
the tone, whilst the surrounding wooded
hills and dales have earned Cookham
Dean a reputation as a centre for
wonderful walks. The brasserie is what
this operation is all about, established
now for over 15 years. But wooden
beams, an open fire and comfortable
seating welcome drinkers to the small
bar, with Rebellion's fine ales and top
real ciders among the refreshments on
offer. Dining takes place in the main
older part of the building, or in the
conservatory; a private dining room can
be reserved for parties. The menus of
expertly prepared dishes are based on
fresh, quality ingredients enhanced by
careful use of cosmopolitan flavours.
Who can resist an appetiser of sweet
baby red peppers stuffed with feta
cheese? They could precede a starter of
Shetland Isles scallops with pea purée,
black pudding and crisp pancetta. You

could continue with a fillet of smoked
haddock with hollandaise sauce; or a
corn-fed chicken breast wrapped in
Parma ham. The specials list pushes
the bar even higher; here you may find
lobster bisque, fresh clams and Avrugar
caviar; vegetarians delight in smoked
goat's cheese beignets with charred
baby artichokes and mixed bean
cassoulet. There's no end to the
temptation with an excellent choice of
dessert wines to accompany the likes of
Morello cherry cheesecake or chocolate
fondant. Accompanying children can be
served smaller portions from the menu;
dogs are welcome in the garden only.

Open all wk Mon-Thu 12-3 5.30-11
(Fri-Sat 12-11.30 Sun 12-6) **Bar Meals**
L served Mon-Sat 12-2.30, Sun 12-5 D

served Mon-Thu 6.30-9.30, Fri-Sat 6.30-
10 **Restaurant** L served Mon-Sat 12-
2.30, Sun 12-5 D served Mon-Thu 6.30-
9.30, Fri-Sat 6.30-10 ⌂ FREE HOUSE
◖ Rebellion IPA & Smuggler, Morland
Old Speckled Hen, Guinness, Guest ales
Ŏ Thatchers Cox's & Katy, Cotswold,
Westons Stowford Press. ♟ 14 **Facilities**
Children welcome Children's portions
Garden Parking Wi-fi 🚌 🐾

Save on hotels. Book at **theAA.com/hotel**

BERKSHIRE 35 **ENGLAND**

CRAZIES HILL — Map 5 SU78

The Horns

PICK OF THE PUBS

RG10 8LY ☎ 0118 940 6222
dir: Off A321 NE of Wargrave

In tranquil surroundings near Wargrave, The Horns is a beautifully restored 16th-century pub with oak beams, terracotta walls and stripped wooden floors. There are three interconnecting rooms full of old pine tables, warmed by open fires; the main dining room is in an elegantly converted barn, which was added 200 years ago. The peaceful atmosphere makes it a great place to enjoy a pint of Brakspear's Bitter or Oxford Gold, or you can eat and drink outside in the secluded garden when the weather is fine. The evening menu might offer starters of filo prawns, devilled whitebait and garlic mushrooms on toast, while main courses encompass pub classics such as coq au vin; sausage and mash; beef and ale pie; mushroom and pepper Stroganoff; and rib-eye steak. There's a good choice of puddings, too: treacle tart, chocolate fondant, apple crumble, sticky toffee pudding, and Baileys and coffee cheesecake.

Open 12-3 6-11 (Mon 12-3 Sun 12-6) Closed: Sun eve, Mon eve **Bar Meals** L served Mon-Sat 12-2.30, Sun 12-4 D served Tue-Sat 6.30-9.30 **Restaurant** L served Mon-Sat 12-2.30, Sun 12-4 D served Tue-Sat 6.30-9.30 ⊕ BRAKSPEAR ◼ Bitter, Oxford Gold, Marston's Pedigree. ♟ 8 **Facilities** ❧ Children welcome Children's menu Children's portions Play area Family room Garden Parking 🚐

EAST GARSTON — Map 5 SU37

The Queen's Arms Country Inn ★★★★ INN

PICK OF THE PUBS

See Pick of the Pubs on page 36

FRILSHAM — Map 5 SU57

The Pot Kiln ◉◉

PICK OF THE PUBS

RG18 0XX ☎ 01635 201366
e-mail: admin@potkiln.org
web: www.potkiln.org
dir: From Yattendon follow Pot Kiln signs, cross over motorway. Continue for 0.25m pub on right

The 18th-century Pot Kiln country pub may take some finding but the rewards of fine food and good beer make the journey worth it. It could be the commitment to real ale, with three on tap at any one time, from the award-winning West Berkshire Brewery (which originated at the pub, since relocated), but like-as-not it's the exceptional food which draws crowds to this former kiln-workers' old beerhouse secluded along back lanes in beautiful unspoilt countryside. Chef-patron Mike Robinson is renowned for shooting much of the game he then crafts into extraordinary dishes such as pie of fallow deer. Signature dishes include pan-fried breast of wood pigeon; confit of pork belly; and fillet of salmon with chorizo, mussel and clam chowder. Local pike and trout and crayfish from the River Kennet may also feature. The small public bar serves excellent bar food including the pub's famous venison burgers and venison steak sandwiches. Booking for meals may be required.

Open Mon & Wed-Fri 12-3 6-11 (Sat-Sun 12-11) Closed: 25 Dec, Tue **Bar Meals** L served Wed-Mon 12-2.30 D served Wed-Mon 6.30-8.30 Av main course £8.50 **Restaurant** L served Wed-Mon 12-2 D served Wed-Mon 7-9 Fixed menu price fr £14.95 Av 3 course à la carte fr £30 ⊕ FREE HOUSE ◼ Brick Kiln, West Berkshire Mr Chubb's Lunchtime Bitter & Maggs' Magnificent Mild ♎ Thatchers, Cotswold. **Facilities** ❧ Children welcome Children's menu Children's portions Play area Garden Parking Wi-fi

HERMITAGE — Map 5 SU57

The White Horse of Hermitage

Newbury Rd RG18 9TB ☎ 01635 200325
e-mail: whoh@btconnect.com
dir: 5m from Newbury on B4009. From M4 junct 13 follow signs for Newbury Showground, right into Priors Court Rd, left at mini rdbt, pub approx 50yds on right

A family friendly pub dating back at least 160 years, The White Horse has achieved a solid reputation for its pub

food, using the freshest and finest local produce to create a daily menu that typically includes burgers, pies, steaks and dishes such as smoked haddock fishcakes followed by lemon and paprika chicken. The interior bar and restaurant is contemporary in décor, and outside you choose between the Mediterranean-style patio or the large garden, which is equipped with swings, a bouncy castle and animal enclosures.

Open all day summer (Mon 5-11 Tue-Fri 12-3 5-11 Sat 12-11 Sun 12-10 winter) Closed: Mon L (ex BH) **Bar Meals** L served Tue-Sat 12-3 D served Mon-Thu 5-9, Fri-Sat 5-9.30, Sun 12-6 **Restaurant** L served Tue-Sat 12-3 D served Mon-Thu 5-9, Fri-Sat 5-9.30, Sun 12-6 ⊕ GREENE KING ◼ Abbot Ale & IPA, Guinness, Guest ales ♎ Westons Stowford Press. ♟ 9 **Facilities** ❧ Children welcome Children's menu Children's portions Play area Garden Beer festival Parking Wi-fi 🚐 (notice required)

HUNGERFORD — Map 5 SU36

The Crown & Garter ★★★★ INN

PICK OF THE PUBS

Inkpen Common RG17 9QR ☎ 01488 668325
e-mail: gill.hern@btopenworld.com
dir: From A4 to Kintbury & Inkpen. At village store left into Inkpen Rd, follow signs for Inkpen Common 2m

James II is said to have dropped in to this 17th-century inn en route to visit one of his mistresses; whether he needed Dutch courage, history doesn't relate. In 1676, the bodies of murderers George Broomham and Dorothy Newman were executed on nearby Combe Gibbet and their bodies were laid out in the barn. Today the historic charm of this family-run free house is best seen in the bar, where there's a huge inglenook fireplace and criss-crossing beams, and where Fuller's, Sharp's and West Berkshire beers are on tap. In addition to the bar you may eat in the candlelit, wood-panelled restaurant, on the patio, or even under an oak tree in the garden. A sample meal might consist of Brixham-landed potted shrimps with brown toast; pot roast of English lamb shank; and apple strudel with toffee ice cream. The spacious en suite bedrooms are built round a pretty garden. Booking for meals may be required.

Open 12-3 5.30-11 (Sun 12-5 7-10.30) Closed: Mon L & Tue L **Bar Meals** L served Wed-Sat 12-2, Sun 12-2.30 D served Mon-Sat 6.30-9.30 Av main course £11.95 **Restaurant** L served Wed-Sat 12-2, Sun 12-2.30 D served Mon-Sat 6.30-9.30 Av 3 course à la carte fr £25 ⊕ FREE HOUSE ◼ Crown & Garter Gibbet Ale, West Berkshire Good Old Boy, Fuller's London Pride, Sharp's Doom Bar, Guinness ♎ Westons Stowford Press. ♟ 9 **Facilities** Garden Parking Wi-fi **Rooms** 9

PICK OF THE PUBS

The Queen's Arms Country Inn ★★★★INN

EAST GARSTON   Map 5 SU37

RG17 7ET ☎ 01488 648757
e-mail: info@queensarmshotel.co.uk
web: www.queensarmshotel.co.uk
dir: *M4 junct 14, 4m onto A338 to Great Shefford, then East Garston*

The oldest part of this inn started life as a farmer's cottage in the 18th century, becoming licensed later – probably around 1856, the year of Queen Victoria's Silver Jubilee. Several years ago it joined the small and select group of Miller's Collection inns. It's pleasantly located in the small village of East Garston in the Lambourn Valley, home to over 2,000 racehorses and more than 50 racing yards. Hardly surprising, then, that the pub acts as quasi-headquarters for British racing, with owners, trainers and jockeys among its clientele. They may tell you they come for the local cask ales, pulled at the bar decorated with horse-racing memorabilia. Or perhaps their preference is for an excellent glass of wine – the carte lists the personal selections of an award-winning Master Sommelier. The kitchen's exceptional food is obviously a huge attraction, but the clincher is probably The Queen's mobile phone booster, which gives the pub the best reception in the valley. No matter who enters, the welcome is warm and the setting is stylishly traditional.

So with a glass of Henry's IPA in hand, and a listening ear tuned for an indiscreet tip, take your time over your choice from the menu. The innovative English country dishes are prepared from fresh ingredients, all sourced as locally as possible, with game high on the list of the head chef's favourite ingredients. A sample three-course treat could start with pan-roasted pigeon breast with bacon, black pudding, lentils and juices. Follow this with stuffed slow-roasted pork shoulder, served with pease pudding, apple sauce and crackling. Jam roly-poly with custard is one of the classic desserts with which to finish. If the wine carte is likely to be irresistible, book ahead for one of the eight elegant en suite rooms.

Open all day all wk 11-11 **Bar Meals** L served Mon-Sat 12-2.30, Sun 12-3.30 D served Mon-Sat 6.30-9.30, Sun 7-9 **Restaurant** L served Mon-Sat 12-2.30, Sun 12-3.30 D served Mon-Sat 6.30-9.30, Sun 7-9 ⊕ FREE HOUSE ◀ Wadworth Henry's Original IPA, Guinness, Guest ales ♂ Westons Stowford Press. **Facilities** Children welcome Children's portions ♣ Garden Parking Wi-fi ▄ **Rooms** 8

HUNGERFORD *continued*

The Pheasant Inn ★★★★ INN

Ermin St, Shefford Woodlands RG17 7AA
☎ **01488 648284**
e-mail: enquiries@thepheasant-inn.co.uk
dir: *From M4 junct 14 take A338 towards Wantage. Left onto B4000 towards Lambourn*

This old drovers' retreat in the Lambourn Valley used to be called The Paraffin House because it was licensed to sell fuel alongside ale. Now a notable food pub with 11 contemporary-styled bedrooms, the pub remains unchanged with beams, wood-panelling and a stone floor. The Berkshire Downs are at the heart of horse-racing country, a fact more than hinted at in the bar/restaurant, which serves ham hock and cider fritters with fried quail eggs, or fish pie with buttered peas and white wine sauce. Wash it down with Pheasant Plucker cider.

Open all day all wk Closed: 25 Dec, 31 Dec eve **Bar Meals** L served all wk 12-2.30 D served all wk 7-9 **Restaurant** L served all wk 12-2.30 D served all wk 7-9 ⊕ FREE HOUSE ◀ Wadworth, Sharp's ♂ Pheasant Plucker. ♀12 **Facilities** ♣ Children welcome Children's portions Garden Parking Wi-fi ▭ **Rooms** 11

The Swan Inn ★★★★ INN

PICK OF THE PUBS

Craven Rd, Lower Green, Inkpen RG17 9DX
☎ **01488 668326**
e-mail: enquiries@theswaninn-organics.co.uk
web: www.theswaninn-organics.co.uk
dir: *S on Hungerford High St, past rail bridge, left to Hungerford Common, right signed Inkpen*

This award-winning 17th-century village free house, which stands in fine walking country just below Combe Gibbet and Walbury Hill in the North Wessex Downs, is presided over by organic beef farmers Mary and Bernard Harris. The beamed interior has old photographic prints and open winter fires. Almost everything on the menu is prepared using their own fresh produce; meats are 100% organic and butchered on the premises; all beef is supplied by their organic farm in Inkpen. Fresh pasta and bread are cooked daily on the premises. Even the wine is organic. The menu offers traditional English favourites and classic Italian dishes, such as chicken liver pâté; home-cured bresaola; spaghetti napoletana; meat loaf; braised ox tail; mixed seafood risotto; and ricotta and spinach cannelloni. There is an organic farm shop and butchery attached to the pub (Soil Association

registered), and ten en suite bedrooms available. An attractive terraced garden sets the scene for alfresco summer dining. Booking for meals may be required.

Open all wk 12-2.30 7-10 (Sat 12-11 Sun 12-4) Closed: 25-26 Dec **Bar Meals** L served all wk 12-2 D served Tue-Sat 7-9.30 Av main course £9.50 **Restaurant** L served Wed-Sun 12-2.30 D served Wed-Sat 7-9.30 Av 3 course à la carte fr £19.50 ⊕ FREE HOUSE ◀ Butts Traditional, Jester & Blackguard Porter, Guest ales. **Facilities** Children welcome Children's menu Children's portions Play area Garden Parking Wi-fi ▭ (notice required) **Rooms** 10

HURLEY	Map 5 SU88

The Olde Bell Inn ★★★★★ INN ֎֎

High St SL6 5LX ☎ **01628 825881**
e-mail: oldebellreception@coachinginn.co.uk
dir: *M4 junct 8/9 follow signs for Henley. At rdbt take A4130 to Hurley, turn right to Hurley, 800yds on right*

Heritage seeps from the very framework of this smart village inn, parts of which date to 1135 when it was a guest house for pilgrims to a nearby priory. Its charming old bar has seen a republican plot (appropriately, Rebellion beers are sold here) and wartime visits by Churchill and Eisenhower. Today's visitors are drawn by the superb accommodation and accomplished gastro-pub menu, which may feature a starter of marinated octopus as prelude to braised ox cheek with roast butternut squash. The terrace and wildflower meadow-style beer garden are delightful. Booking for meals may be required.

Open all day all wk 10am-11pm **Bar Meals** L served Mon-Sat 12.30-2.30, Sun 12-3.30 D served Mon-Sat 6-10, Sun 6.30-9 **Restaurant** L served Mon-Sat 12.30-2.30, Sun 12-3.30 D served Mon-Sat 6-10, Sun 6.30-9 ⊕ FREE HOUSE ◀ Rebellion. ♀10 **Facilities** ♣ Children welcome Children's portions Play area Garden Parking Wi-fi ▭ **Rooms** 48

HURST	Map 5 SU77

The Green Man

Hinton Rd RG10 0BP ☎ **0118 934 2599**
e-mail: phil@thegreenman.uk.com
web: www.thegreenman.uk.com
dir: *Off A321, adjacent to Hurst Cricket Club*

Built from timbers of decommissioned ships from Portsmouth, the pub gained its first licence in 1602, and Brakspear purchased a 1,000 year lease on the building in 1646. The old black beams, low in places, are still to

be seen and you'll find open fires, hand-drawn beer and good food. The seasonal main menu offers the likes of spicy Cajun chicken breast, Mexican beef chilli, game pie, and pan-fried sea bass fillet. There are weekend specials, such as oven-baked lemon sole or grilled Gressingham duck breast. The garden, open to fields and woodland, includes a children's play area. Booking for meals may be required.

Open all wk 11-3 5.30-11 (Sat-Sun all day) **Bar Meals** L served all wk 12-2.30 D served all wk 6-9.30 **Restaurant** L served all wk 12-2.30 D served all wk 6-9.30 ⊕ BRAKSPEAR ◀ Bitter & Seasonal ales, Wychwood Hobgoblin. ♀8 **Facilities** Children welcome Children's menu Children's portions Play area Garden Parking Wi-fi

KINTBURY	Map 5 SU36

The Dundas Arms

PICK OF THE PUBS

53 Station Rd RG17 9UT ☎ **01488 658263**
e-mail: info@dundasarms.co.uk
web: www.dundasarms.co.uk
dir: *M4 junct 13, A34 to Newbury, A4 towards Hungerford, left to Kintbury. Pub 1m*

On the banks of both the Kennet & Avon Canal and the River Kennet itself, this late-18th-century free house has been in the same family for more than 40 years, with proprietor David Dalzell-Piper working and cooking here throughout that time. The bar offers beers from Adnams, West Berkshire and Ramsbury breweries, and a blackboard selection of food. When David received a real ale award in 2009, he said: "We do great food, but good beer has been the mainstay throughout good times and bad". You can watch narrowboats on the canal from the auberge-style restaurant, where a starter like home-potted brown shrimps on toast might be followed by grilled Longhorn sirloin steak, or roast breast of Creedy Carver duck with cider and apple sauce. By all means, take your drinks and food outside to the patio or canalside jetty. Booking for meals may be required.

Open all wk 11-2.30 6-11 Closed: 25-26 & 31 Dec, Sun eve **Bar Meals** L served Mon-Sat 12-2 D served Tue-Sat 7-9 Av main course £13.50 **Restaurant** L served Mon-Sat 12-2 D served Tue-Sat 7-9 Av 3 course à la carte fr £26 ⊕ FREE HOUSE ◀ Adnams Southwold Bitter, West Berkshire Good Old Boy, Ramsbury Gold, Flack Manor ♂ Westons Stowford Press. ♀ **Facilities** Children welcome Children's menu Family room Parking

---

Bird In Hand Country Inn

PICK OF THE PUBS

Bath Rd RG10 9UP ☎ 01628 826622 & 822781
e-mail: info@birdinhand.co.uk
dir: *On A4, 5m W of Maidenhead, 7m E of Reading*

Proprietor Caroline Shone is a third-generation member of her family to run this part-14th-century inn, where some three centuries ago George III probably slipped in for a swift one while his horse was being re-shod at the forge next door. Had he still been waiting, his choice today of local real ales in the wood-panelled Oak Lounge bar would have been considerably wider. Or he could have selected one or two of the 20 wines by the glass from the 50-bin wine list, including some from nearby Stanlake Park vineyard. In the attractive restaurant, which overlooks a courtyard and fountain, the menu (also available in the bar) offers salads, vegetarian meze, jacket potatoes, omelettes and pizzas, with typical main meals of roast beef with Yorkshire pudding; poached smoked haddock; pork Stroganoff; or green vegetable risotto. There are beer festivals in June and November.

Open all day all wk **Bar Meals** Av main course £12.95 food served all day **Restaurant** L served all wk 12-2.30 D served all wk 6.30-10 Fixed menu price fr £12.95 Av 3 course à la carte fr £25 ⊕ FREE HOUSE ◀ Binghams Twyford Tipple, 5 Guest ales ♂ Thatchers. ♀ 20 **Facilities** ❖ Children welcome Children's menu Children's portions Garden Beer festival Parking Wi-fi 🚌

The Stag

PICK OF THE PUBS

Shop Ln RG20 8QG ☎ 01488 638436
dir: *6m from Newbury on B4494*

The white-painted Stag lies just off the village green in a sleepy downland village, close to the Ridgeway long-distance path and Snelsmore Common, home to nightjar, woodlark and grazing Exmoor ponies. During the winter months the wood-burning stove is always ready. The bar and restaurant walls are painted in warm red, or left as bare brick, while old black-and-white photographs tell of village life many years ago. Surrounding farms and growers supply all produce, including venison, pheasant and fresh river trout. Aberdeen Angus beef from cattle raised next door may also feature as a special, and those lucky enough to find it there agree that its taste and texture are sublime. Other possibilities are venison and redcurrant sausages with butternut squash mash; pork loin with creamy mushroom sauce; or traditional beer-battered fish and chips with mushy peas. There are around 20 red and white wines, among them varieties from Australia, California and France. Booking for meals may be required.

Open all day 12-3 6-11 Closed: Sun eve & Mon L **Bar Meals** L served Tue-Sat 12-2, Sun 12-3.30 D served

Tue-Sat 6-9 Av main course £10 **Restaurant** L served Tue-Sat 12-2, Sun 12-3.30 D served Tue-Sat 6-9 ⊕ FREE HOUSE ◀ Morland Original, West Berkshire Good Old Boy, Guest ales ♂ Aspall. **Facilities** ❖ Children welcome Children's menu Children's portions Garden Parking Wi-fi 🚌 (notice required)

The George on the Green

Holyport SL6 2JL ☎ 01628 628317
e-mail: natalie@thegeorgeonthegreen.com
dir: *M4 junct 8/9, at rdbt 2nd exit onto A308(M). At rdbt 3rd exit onto A308. At rdbt take 2nd exit signed Holyport. Pub in village centre*

Facing the vast, eponymous green, this low-beamed 16th-century pub may possibly have played host to Charles II and Nell Gwynne when the actress lived locally. Today's locals can look forward to great beers from Rebellion Brewery in nearby Marlow Bottom coupled with a selective, well thought-out menu; maybe baked crab gratin to start, then smoked chicken, leek and butternut squash risotto, or slow-roasted half shoulder of lamb with sweet potato boulangère. From outside tables, views stretch across the green to the tree-shaded village duck pond.

Open 12-3 5-11 (Sat 12-11 Sun 12-6) Closed: Mon ⊕ ENTERPRISE INNS ◀ Rebellion Mutiny & IPA, Fuller's London Pride. **Facilities** Children welcome Children's portions Garden Parking

---

The Red House

RG20 8LY ☎ 01635 582017
e-mail: info@theredhousepub.com
dir: *5m from Hungerford, 3m from Newbury, 400yds off A4*

This thatched village local is set in beautiful countryside and provides a welcoming and relaxed atmosphere. There is a bar with local ales and cosy log fire, a charming restaurant, and a patio and garden for the summer. Run by experienced French chef-patron Laurent Lebeau, his essentially British menu might include free-range chicken and leek pudding with French beans; cauliflower gratin with chips and peas; and roasted corn-fed guinea fowl supreme with roasted apple and black pudding in a mustard gravy. As for the wines, Laurent chooses well.

Open all day all wk **Bar Meals** L served all wk 12-10 D served all wk 12-10 Av main course £12.50 food served all day **Restaurant** L served all wk 12-10 D served all wk 12-10 Fixed menu price fr £13.95 Av 3 course à la carte fr £28 food served all day ⊕ FREE HOUSE ◀ West Berkshire Good Old Boy & Mr Chubb's Lunchtime Bitter, Guest ales ♂ Westons Stowford Press. **Facilities** ❖ Children welcome Children's menu Children's portions Garden Parking Wi-fi 🚌 (notice required)

The White Hart

SL6 2ND ☎ 01628 621460
e-mail: admin@thewhitehartholyport.co.uk
dir: *2m S from Maidenhead. M4 junct 8/9, follow Holyport signs then Moneyrow Green. Pub by petrol station*

This traditional coaching inn dates back to the 19th century and its close proximity to the M4 makes it a popular spot for those heading to nearby Maidenhead and Windsor. The wood-panelled lounge bar is furnished with leather chesterfields, and quality home-made food and real ales can be enjoyed in a cosy atmosphere with an open fire. Typical mains are North African-style chicken curry; home-made bolognese; and mushroom and spinach pasta. There are large gardens to enjoy in summer with a children's playground and petanque pitch.

Open all day all wk 12-11.30 (Fri-Sat 12-12 Sun 12-11) **Bar Meals** L served Tue-Sat 12-2.30, Sun 12.30-4 D served Tue-Sat 6-9 Av main course £8.50 ⊕ GREENE KING ◀ IPA, Morland Old Speckled Hen, Guinness, Guest ales ♂ Westons Stowford Press, Koppaberg, Aspall. ♀ **Facilities** ❖ Children welcome Children's menu Children's portions Play area Garden Parking Wi-fi 🚌 (notice required)

The Yew Tree Inn ⊛

PICK OF THE PUBS

Hollington Cross, Andover Rd, Highclere RG20 9SE ☎ 01635 253360
e-mail: info@theyewtree.net
dir: *M4 junct 13, A34 S, 4th junct on left signed Highclere/Wash Common, turn right towards Andover A343, inn on right*

This fine 17th-century free house occupies a pleasant setting close to Highclere Castle. Full of charm and character, the pub blends original features like old beams, tiled floors, and logs smouldering in the inglenook fireplaces with the contemporary refinements of crisp linen and sparkling glassware. Several interconnecting rooms provide a choice of dining areas, and unusual real ales, ciders and 15 wines by the glass are served in the bar. The kitchen offers traditional British food and time-honoured classics from the French culinary canon. The Anglo-French cooking takes a brasserie approach, with the menu split into sections like hors d'oeuvres, fish and seafood, pies and puddings, and roasts and grills, and delivers accomplished, well-presented dishes that are driven by quality ingredients. A memorable meal might kick off with potted duck with Agen prunes and Madeira jelly, before moving on to roast venison 'Pierre Koffmann' with chocolate sauce. The dessert menu could include blackberry and apple crumble or sherry trifle.

Open all day all wk 10am-11pm **Bar Meals** L served Mon-Sat 12-2.30, Sun 12-3 D served Mon-Sat 6-9.30, Sun 6-9 **Restaurant** L served Mon-Sat 12-2.30, Sun 12-3 D served Mon-Sat 6-9.30, Sun 6-9 ⊕ FREE HOUSE ◀ Butts Barbus barbus, Wychwood Hobgoblin, Timothy

---

Save on hotels. Book at theAA.com/hotel

BERKSHIRE 39 ENGLAND

Taylor, Black Sheep, Local guest ales ○ Westons Old Rosie, Tutts Clump. ♥ 15 **Facilities** ✿ Children welcome Children's portions Garden Parking Wi-fi

PALEY STREET   Map 5 SU87

The Royal Oak Paley Street ◉◉◉

PICK OF THE PUBS

Littlefield Green SL6 3JN ☎ 01628 620541
e-mail: info@theroyaloakpaleystreet.com
dir: *From Maidenhead take A330 towards Ascot for 2m, turn right onto B3024 signed Twyford, 2nd pub on left*

In summer, fields of wheat appear to surround this 17th-century, oak-beamed gastro-pub, popularly known as Parky's Pub. This is because Sir Michael Parkinson, the former TV chat-show host, eats here most days of the week. And why does he do that? Because his son Nick owns it. The head chef is Dominic Chapman, who includes three AA Rosettes among his collection of prestigious awards for exemplary dishes such as seared South Devon mackerel with beetroot, horseradish cream and watercress; Iberico ham de Bellota; Norfolk brown hare and trotter pie; and warm salad of wood pigeon, Cumbrian ham, radicchio, pine-nuts, sultanas and quail eggs. Desserts can be expressed more simply: Yorkshire rhubarb trifle; bread-and-butter pudding; and soufflé of raspberries, for instance. From a list of over 330 wines, some 25 are by the glass, while on handpump in the bar are London Pride and Seafarers. Booking for meals may be required.

Open all wk 12-3 6-11 (Sun 12-4) **Restaurant** L served Mon-Sat 12-3, Sun 12-4 D served Mon-Thu 6.30-9.30, Fri-Sat 6.30-10 Fixed menu price fr £25 Av 3 course à la carte fr £35 ⊞ FULLER'S ◀ London Pride, George Gale & Co Seafarers. ♥ 25 **Facilities** Children welcome Garden Parking

READING   Map 5 SU77

The Flowing Spring

Henley Rd, Playhatch RG4 9RB ☎ 0118 969 9878
e-mail: info@theflowingspringpub.co.uk
web: www.theflowingspringpub.co.uk
dir: *3m N of Reading on A4155 towards Henley*

A midsummer beer festival promising a dozen ales, live music and barbecue is one of a myriad of exciting events that take place throughout the year at this rural Fuller's establishment. Unusually the pub is on the first floor, which slopes steeply from one end of the bar to the other;

the verandah overlooks Thames Valley countryside. Its quirky character notwithstanding, the pub has been recognised for its well-kept ales and cellar, and the menu of no-nonsense pub favourites is backed by a comprehensive range of vegetarian, gluten-free and dairy-free options. The huge garden is bounded by streams.

Open all day Closed: Mon **Bar Meals** L served Tue-Sat 12-2.30, Sun 12-3 D served Tue-Sat 6-9 Av main course £9.95 **Restaurant** L served Tue-Sat 12-2.30, Sun 12-3 D served Tue-Sat 6-9 ⊞ FULLER'S ◀ London Pride, Chiswick Bitter & ESB, Guest ale ○ Aspall. ♥ 10 **Facilities** ✿ Children welcome Children's portions Play area Garden Beer festival Parking Wi-fi 🚌 (notice required)

See advert below

READING *continued*

The Shoulder of Mutton

Playhatch RG4 9QU ☎ 0118 947 3908

e-mail: shoulderofmutton@hotmail.co.uk

dir: From Reading follow signs to Caversham, then onto A4155 to Henley-on-Thames. At rdbt left to Binfield Heath, pub on left

An inviting combination of rustic, cosy village inn and contemporary dining in the airy conservatory restaurant draws a dedicated crowd keen to share chef-proprietor Alan Oxlade's passion for the finest foodstuffs. The pub, true to its name, specialises in mutton dishes, and is proud to be a member of HRH The Prince of Wales' Mutton Renaissance Club. The signature dish is Welsh organic mountain mutton, slow roasted for seven hours. All the dishes have inventive names: 'Tender Moment' is mutton fillet topped with a herb crust; 'Sirocco Breeze', chicken supreme stuffed with goat's cheese, sundried tomatoes and pine kernels wrapped in Parma ham. The walled garden is a popular retreat. Booking for meals may be required.

Open 12-3 6-11 (Mon 12-3 7-11 Sat 12-3 6.30-11 Sun 12-3) Closed: 26-30 Dec, 1 Jan, Sun eve Bar Meals L served all wk 12-2 D served Mon 7-9, Tue-Sat 6.30-9 Av main course £12.50 Restaurant L served all wk 12-2 D served Mon 7-9, Tue-Sat 6.30-9 Av 3 course à la carte fr £25 ⊕ GREENE KING ◀ IPA, Loddon Hullabaloo ♂ Aspall. Facilities Children welcome Children's portions Garden Parking ▭ (notice required)

RUSCOMBE   Map 5 SU77

Buratta's at the Royal Oak

Ruscombe Ln RG10 9JN ☎ 0118 934 5190

e-mail: enquiries@burattas.co.uk

dir: From A4 (Wargrave rdbt) take A321 to Twyford (signed Twyford/Wokingham). Straight on at 1st lights, right at 2nd lights onto A3032. Right onto A3024 (Ruscombe Rd which becomes Ruscombe Ln). Pub on left on brow of hill

Built in the 1840s, The Royal Oak was originally a one-bar pub, but it has been extended over the years and the old cottage next door is now the kitchen. With Binghams Brewery and Fuller's London Pride as resident ales, the relaxed restaurant offers a wide range of meals, from hearty bar snacks and sandwiches to regularly changing à la carte choices, such as confit of duck with bacon and flageolet beans. The large garden, complete with resident ducks, is dog friendly. The pub even has its own antiques shop and nearly everything in the pub is for sale. Booking for meals may be required.

Open Tue-Sat 12-3 6-11 (Sun-Mon 12-3) Closed: Sun eve & Mon eve Bar Meals L served all wk 12-2.30 D served Tue-Sat 7-9.30 Av main course £9 Restaurant L served all wk 12-2.30 D served Tue-Sat 7-9.30 Av 3 course à la carte fr £25 ⊕ ENTERPRISE INNS ◀ Fuller's London Pride, Binghams, Guest ales. ₹ 12 Facilities ♣ Children welcome Children's menu Children's portions Garden Parking ▭ (notice required)

SINDLESHAM   Map 5 SU76

The Walter Arms

Bearwood Rd RG41 5BP ☎ 0118 977 4903

e-mail: mail@thewalterarms.com

dir: From Wokingham take A329 towards Reading. In 1.5m left onto B3030. 5m left into Bearwood Rd. Pub 200yds on left

A typically solid Victorian building built about 1850 by John Walter III, grandson of the man who founded *The Times* newspaper. The idea was that it should be a working men's club for the workers on the Bearwood Estate, where Walter lived. Now a popular dining pub, the seasonal menus offer traditional English dishes, such as pan-roasted rump of lamb, and beer-battered sustainable haddock; as well as pasta, stone-baked pizzas and oriental- and Arabian-style 'smörgåsbord'. The beer garden is a good spot for a pint of London Pride or Courage Best. Booking for meals may be required.

Open all day all wk Bar Meals L served Mon-Fri 12-3, Sat 12-10, Sun 12-9 D served Mon-Fri 6-10, Sat-Sun all day Restaurant L served Mon-Fri 12-3, Sat 12-10, Sun 12-9 D served Mon-Fri 6-10, Sat-Sun all day Av 3 course à la carte fr £20 ⊕ FREE HOUSE ◀ Fuller's London Pride, Courage Best ♂ Westons Stowford Press. Facilities Children welcome Children's menu Children's portions Garden Parking

SONNING   Map 5 SU77

The Bull Inn

High St RG4 6UP ☎ 0118 969 3901

e-mail: bullinn@fullers.co.uk

dir: From Reading take A4 towards Maidenhead. Left onto B4446 to Sonning

Two minutes' walk from the River Thames in the pretty village of Sonning, this olde-worlde inn can trace its roots back 500 years or more; it can also boast a mention in Jerome K. Jerome's classic *Three Men in a Boat*. With Fuller's ales on tap and log fires in the grate, The Bull charms locals and visitors alike. It's a great place to eat too, with specials changing daily – perhaps 'fabulous fish stew' served with fresh crab dumplings and crispy bread; or cinnamon and apple spiced pork belly with mulled wine cabbage and roasted almonds.

Open all day all wk 11-11 Bar Meals L served all wk 10-9.30 D served all wk 6.30-9.30 food served all day Restaurant L served all wk 10-9.30 D served all wk 6.30-9.30 food served all day ⊕ FULLER'S ◀ London Pride, Chiswick Bitter, Discovery & Organic Honey Dew, George Gale & Co HSB, Guest ale. ₹ 24 Facilities ♣ Children welcome Children's portions Garden Parking Wi-fi ▭

STANFORD DINGLEY   Map 5 SU57

The Old Boot Inn

RG7 6LT ☎ 0118 974 4292

e-mail: johnintheboot@hotmail.co.uk

dir: M4 junct 12, A4/A340 to Pangbourne. 1st left to Bradfield. Through Bradfield, follow Stanford Dingley signs

John Haley's 18th-century free house in the Pang Valley serves locally brewed beers from the Brakspear and West Berkshire breweries. Study his carte for good old pub grub like home-made steak and kidney pudding; escalope of veal; and Barnsley chop with roasted garlic, red wine jus and dauphinoise potatoes. Or, from the specials, fillet of venison with creamed cabbage, bacon and port jus; and whole lemon sole with herb butter, both dishes with seasonal vegetables and new potatoes. To follow, see if he's offering chocolate brownie with pistachio ice cream.

Open all wk 11-3 6-11 (Sat-Sun all day) Bar Meals L served all wk 12-2 D served all wk 7-9 Restaurant L served all wk 12-2 D served all wk 7-9 ⊕ FREE HOUSE ◀ Brakspear Bitter, Bass, West Berkshire Dr Hexters, O'Hanlon's Thomas Hardy's Ale & Royal Oak, Archers ♂ Westons Stowford Press. ₹ 10 Facilities ♣ Children welcome Children's menu Children's portions Play area Garden Parking Wi-fi ▭ (notice required)

SWALLOWFIELD   Map 5 SU76

The George & Dragon

PICK OF THE PUBS

Church Rd RG7 1TJ ☎ 0118 988 4432

e-mail: dining@georgeanddragonswallowfield.co.uk

dir: M4, junct 11, A33 towards Basingstoke. Left at Barge Ln to B3349 into The Street, right into Church Rd

Formerly a farm, this award-winning country pub and restaurant looks very much the part with its low, stripped beams, log fires, rug-strewn floors and warm earthy tones. It has been under the same ownership for the last 17 years, and regular customers know what to expect from the internationally inspired seasonal menus, sourced extensively from local suppliers. Starters that may be available are herbed spinach and button mushroom pancake with mornay sauce; and soy- and chilli-braised octopus with pineapple, orange and tomato salsa. Typical main courses include local venison loin steak with haggis mash and redcurrant jus; baked meatballs in a rich Barolo wine tomato sauce, with zesty gremolata and pasta; and monkfish on sweet potato bubble-and-squeak. The garden overlooks beautiful countryside and makes a great place to head for after walking the long-distance Blackwater Valley Path, which follows the river from its source in Rowhill Nature Reserve to Swallowfield. Booking for meals may be required.

Open all day all wk Bar Meals L served Mon-Sat 12-2.30, Sun 12-3 D served Mon-Sat 7-9.30, Sun 7-9 Restaurant L served Mon-Sat 12-2.30, Sun 12-3 D served Mon-Sat 7-9.30, Sun 7-9 ⊕ FREE HOUSE ◀ Fuller's London Pride, Ringwood Best Bitter, Sharp's Doom Bar ♂ Thatchers Gold. Facilities Children welcome Children's menu Children's portions Garden Parking

PICK OF THE PUBS

The Royal Oak Hotel

YATTENDON   Map 5 SU57

The Square RG18 0UG
☎ **01635 201325**
e-mail: info@royaloakyattendon.com
web: www.royaloakyattendon.co.uk
dir: *M4 junct 12, A4 to Newbury, right at 2nd rdbt to Pangbourne then 1st left. From junct 13, A34 N 1st left, right at T-junct. Left then 2nd right to Yattendon*

In the heart of this historic village, deep in shooting country, The Royal Oak was where Oliver Cromwell and his Roundheads dined and planned their strategy for what became the second Battle of Newbury in 1664. Their adversary, King Charles I, sought refuge here after the fighting was over. Part of a row of 16th-century cottages, the old building wears its history well, with log fires in the bar, oak beams, quarry-tiled and wood floors in the adjoining lounge and dining rooms, and an assortment of pine and mahogany tables on which to be served delicious home-cooked food. From the regularly changing menu, order a sandwich, perhaps filled with fish fingers and tartare sauce, or begin a more serious relationship with French onion soup and cheddar toast, or devilled kidneys on toast. Then, for a main course, why not choose smoked haddock kedgeree, soft poached egg and curry leaves; braised beef, horseradish dumplings and Jerusalem artichoke gratin; or one of the daily specials from the blackboard, such as roast wood pigeon stuffed with black

pudding? Finally, round off with apple and cinnamon pie and custard, or chocolate and orange torte with clotted cream. Give four days' notice and your private dinner party (minimum of eight) can enjoy a whole roast suckling pig with rosemary and cider sauce in one of the private rooms. French windows lead to a walled rear garden with smart garden furniture and a vine-laden trellis, plus a boules piste, making a perfect spot for a summer drink or meal. Owner Rob McGill offers tip-top real ales from the West Berkshire Brewery in the village, including Good Old Boy and Mr Chubb's Lunchtime Bitter.

Open all day all wk **Bar Meals** L served Mon-Fri 12-2.30, Sat-Sun 12-3 D served Mon-Thu 6.30-9.30, Fri-Sat 6.30-10, Sun 6.30-9 Av main course £15

Restaurant L served Mon-Fri 12-2.30, Sat-Sun 12-3 D served Mon-Thu 6.30-9.30, Fri-Sat 6.30-10, Sun 6.30-9 Fixed menu price fr £12.95 Av 3 course à la carte fr £25 ⊕ FREE HOUSE ◀ West Berkshire Good Old Boy & Mr Chubb's Lunchtime Bitter, Guest ale ♂ Westons Stowford Press. ♟ 10 **Facilities** Children welcome Children's menu Children's portions ♣ Garden Parking Wi-fi

WALTHAM ST LAWRENCE · Map 5 SU87

The Bell

The Street RG10 0JJ ☎ 0118 934 1788
e-mail: info@thebellwalthamstlawrence.co.uk
dir: *On B3024 E of Twyford. From A4 turn at Hare Hatch*

This 14th-century free house is renowned for its ciders and an ever-changing range of real ales selected from small independent breweries. The building was given to the community in 1608 and profits from the rent still help village charities. Iain and Scott Ganson took over in 2004, and have built a local reputation for good food. Everything possible is made on the premises, including all charcuterie and preparation of game. Start with yellow split pea soup with Bell beer bread or Welsh rarebit, then continue with pan-fried trout with Puy lentils, rainbow chard and horseradish dressing; or confit of pork belly with fondant potato, haricot beans, spinach and salsa verde. Don't miss the annual beer festival in June.

Open all wk 12-3 5-11 (Sat 12-11 Sun 12-10.30) **Bar Meals** L served Mon-Fri 12-2, Sat-Sun 12-3 D served all wk 7-9.30 ◀ FREE HOUSE ◀ Binghams Twyford Tipple, 5 Guest ales ♂ Pheasant Plucker, Westons Old Rosie. ♥ 19 **Facilities** ✿ Children welcome Children's menu Children's portions Play area Garden Beer festival Parking

WHITE WALTHAM · Map 5 SU87

The Beehive

Waltham Rd SL6 3SH ☎ 01628 822877
e-mail: beehivepub@aol.com
dir: *M4 junct8/9, A404, follow White Waltham signs*

This is a cracking country local in an idyllic village setting. The glass conservatory has been replaced by a brick-built pitched roof extension; its tri-folding doors give wide and easy access to the front patio which overlooks the cricket pitch. Renowned for its relaxing atmosphere and choice of real ales, which includes a local Loddon brew, The Beehive is also a great place to eat. In addition to its lunchtime bar meals menu, fresh seasonal dishes may feature Grimsby cod; calves' liver; and slow-roasted pork belly with bubble-and-squeak. Booking for meals may be required.

Open all wk 11-3 5-11 (Sat 11am-mdnt Sun 12-10.30) Closed: 26 Dec **Bar Meals** L served Mon-Fri 12-2.30, Sat 12-9.30, Sun 12-8.30 D served Mon-Fri 5-9.30, Sat 12-9.30, Sun 12-8.30 **Restaurant** L served Mon-Fri 12-2.30, Sat 12-9.30, Sun 12-8.30 D served Mon-Fri 5-9.30, Sat 12-9.30, Sun 12-8.30 ⊕ ENTERPRISE INNS ◀ Fuller's London Pride, Greene King Abbot Ale, Rebellion, Brakspear, Loddon guest ale. ♥ 14 **Facilities** ✿ Children welcome Children's menu Children's portions Garden Parking ▄▄▄

WINKFIELD · Map 6 SU97

Rose & Crown

Woodside, Windsor Forest SL4 2DP ☎ 01344 882051
dir: *M3 junct 3, from Ascot Racecourse on A332 take 2nd exit from Heatherwood Hosp rdbt, 2nd left*

A 200-year-old traditional pub complete with old beams and low ceilings. Hidden down a country lane, it has a peaceful garden overlooking open fields. A typical menu includes tapas; charcuterie platters; breaded whitebait with saffron mayonnaise; or gambas pil pil – sizzling tiger prawns with garlic chilli oil. To follow maybe egg Catalan; lamb shank and mashed potato; or home-cured Bagshot Park honey-roasted ham, hand-cut chips and a fried duck egg. Booking for meals may be required.

Open all day all wk ⊕ GREENE KING ◀ IPA, Morland Original, Guest ale. **Facilities** Children welcome Children's menu Children's portions Play area Garden Parking Wi-fi

WINTERBOURNE · Map 5 SU47

The Winterbourne Arms

RG20 8BB ☎ 01635 248200
e-mail: mail@winterbournearms.com
dir: *M4 junct 13 into Chieveley Services, follow Donnington signs to Winterbourne sign. Turn right into Arlington Ln, right at T-junct, left into Winterbourne*

Steeped in 300 years of history, warmth and charm, yet only five minutes from the M4, this privately owned, pretty village pub offers a high standard from both its big and gutsy food and the range of drinks. Real ales may include Whistle Wetter, while ten wines served by the glass and 20 more by the bottle make for a comprehensive list. Traditional British menus include flaked ham hock in a butter bean and parsley sauce and short crust pie of the week, which can be served in candlelight and by the winter fires or out in the large gardens in summer.

Open all wk 12-3 6-11 (Sun 12-10.30) **Bar Meals** L served all wk 12-2.30 D served all wk 6-10 **Restaurant** L served all wk 12-2.30 D served all wk 6-10 ⊕ FREE HOUSE ◀ Winterbourne Whistle Wetter, Ramsbury Gold, Guinness. ♥ 10 **Facilities** Children welcome Children's portions Garden Parking ▄▄▄ (notice required)

WOKINGHAM · Map 5 SU86

The Broad Street Tavern

29 Broad St RG40 1AU ☎ 0118 977 3706
e-mail: broadstreettavern@wadworth.co.uk
dir: *In town centre, adjacent to Pizza Express*

Four beer festivals are hosted every year in this town-centre watering hole. Housed in a handsome detached period building fronted by elegant railings, the adults-only Wadworth-owned 'Tav' offers leather armchairs and sofas in the bar, and an extensive decked garden area with a summer bar and barbecue. Snacks range from organic baguettes to tapas dishes of crispy battered onion rings; grilled haloumi with tomato and rosemary bruschetta; and stuffed cream cheese jalapeños. More filling classics include pie of the day; honey-roast gammon with two free-range eggs; and gourmet burgers.

Open all day all wk Closed: 25 Dec **Bar Meals** L served all wk 12-2.30 D served all wk 6-9.30 ⊕ WADWORTH ◀ 6X, Henry's Original IPA, Bishop's Tipple ♂ Westons Old Rosie. ♥ 17 **Facilities** ✿ Garden Beer festival Wi-fi ▄▄▄ (notice required)

YATTENDON · Map 5 SU57

The Royal Oak Hotel

PICK OF THE PUBS

See Pick of the Pubs on page 41

BRISTOL

BRISTOL · Map 4 ST57

The Albion

Boyces Av, Clifton BS8 4AA ☎ 0117 973 3522
e-mail: info@thealbionclifton.co.uk
dir: *From A4 take B3129 towards city centre. Right into Clifton Down Rd. 3rd left into Boyces Av*

This handsome Grade II listed coaching inn dates from the 17th century and was refurbished a few years ago by owner and designer Owain George. A top gastro-pub, it has become one of Bristol's premier dining destinations, as well as a popular pub to enjoy local ales and ciders. In the enclosed courtyard you can order jugs of Pimm's in summer or sip mulled cider under heaters in the winter. The modern British cooking, created by head chef Clarke Oldfield, uses local produce in dishes such as rabbit croquette with braised baby turnips and clotted cream mash; and West Country beef and Guinness pie with braised red cabbage.

Open all day 12-12 (Sat 11am-mdnt Sun 11-11) Closed: 25-26 Dec, Mon L **Bar Meals** L served Tue-Fri 12-3, Sat 11-3, Sun 11-3.30 D served Tue-Sat 7-10 **Restaurant** L served Tue-Fri 12-3, Sat 11-3, Sun 11-3.30 D served Tue-Sat 7-10 ⊕ ENTERPRISE INNS ◀ Otter Bitter, Sharp's Doom Bar, Bath Gem ♂ Thatchers Cheddar Valley, Westons Stowford Press. ♥ 12 **Facilities** ✿ Children welcome Children's menu Children's portions Garden Beer festival Wi-fi ▄▄▄

Cornubia

142 Temple St BS1 6EN ☎ 0117 925 4415
e-mail: philjackithecornubia@hotmail.co.uk
dir: *Opposite Bristol Fire Station*

Hidden among tall office buildings in the centre of Bristol, this welcoming Georgian pub was originally built as two houses. The pub's name is the Latinised version for Cornwall. Local workers love it, not just because of its convenience, but also for its choice of changing real ales, including its own Cornubia, two draught ciders and a serious collection of malts and bottled beers. Weekday lunchtime bar snacks include baguettes, Phil's specials of the day, and the pub's famous pork pies. There is a raised decking area at the front and live entertainment every week.

Open all day Mon-Sat 12-11 Closed: 25-26 Dec, 1 Jan, Sun **Bar Meals** L served Mon-Sat 12-2.30 ⊕ FREE HOUSE ◀ Cornubia, Guest ales Ó Thatchers Cheddar Valley & Gold, Guest ciders. **Facilities** ❖ Parking Wi-fi 🚐 (notice required)

The Hare on the Hill

41 Thomas St North, Kingsdown BS2 8LX
☎ **0117 908 1982**
e-mail: harehill@bathales.co.uk
dir: *Telephone for directions*

If you can find it in the maze of streets that is Kingsdown, this is a gem – a small, street-corner local from the good old days, remaining close to the heart of the community. If all you want is a pint of one of Bath Ales' award-winning brews, malt whisky or a European-style beer, come here. All food (except fresh fish) is sourced from within a 40-mile radius. Typical dishes are steak-and-ale pie; home-made faggots, mash and onion gravy; plus a roast on Sundays. There are Monday night quizzes and major sports fixtures are shown on TV.

Open all wk 12-2.30 5-11.30 (Fri-Sat 12-12 Sun 12-11.30) **Bar Meals** food served all day **Restaurant** food served all day ⊕ BATH ALES ◀ Gem, SPA, Barnsey Ó Bath Ciders Bounders. **Facilities** Children welcome Wi-fi

Highbury Vaults

164 St Michaels Hill, Cotham BS2 8DE
☎ **0117 973 3203**
e-mail: highburyvaults@youngs.co.uk
dir: *Take A38 to Cotham from inner ring dual carriageway*

Once a turnpike station, this 1840s pub has retained much of its Victorian atmosphere. In days when hangings took place on nearby St Michael's Hill, many victims partook of their last meal in the vaults. Today, it's a business crowd by day and students at night, feasting on chilli (veggie and meat), burgers, nachos, and jacket potatoes. No fussy foods, no music or fruit machines here, but a popular heated garden terrace. Look carefully and you'll spot a little train running the length of the pub.

Open all day all wk 12-12 (Sun 12-11) **Bar Meals** L served Mon-Fri 12-2, Sat 12-2.30, Sun 12-4 D served Mon-Fri 5.30-8.30 Av main course £7 ⊕ YOUNG'S ◀ Special & Bitter, Bath Gem, St Austell Tribute, Brains SA, Guest ales Ó Addlestones, Thatchers Gold. **Facilities** Children welcome Garden 🚐 (notice required) **Notes** ☺

The Kensington Arms

PICK OF THE PUBS

35-37 Stanley Rd BS6 6NP ☎ **0117 944 6444**
e-mail: info@thekensingtonarms.co.uk
dir: *From Redland Rail Station into South Rd, then Kensington Rd. 4th right into Stanley Rd*

In the heart of Bristol's leafy Redland district, this Victorian corner pub is popular with locals as well as the many university students living nearby. Inside is a smart bar and a dining room packed with mismatched antique furniture and Victorian prints, with views into the open kitchen. The modern British food utilises the very best local produce and the menu changes daily. In the bar, try mussels with cider and cream, or a Kensington burger. Typical restaurant dishes are truffled duck egg and brioche; whole lemon sole with sorrel butter sauce; and lemon posset and shortbread for dessert.

Open all day all wk Closed: 26 Dec **Bar Meals** L served Mon-Fri 12-3 D served Mon-Sat 6-10 Av main course £13.95 **Restaurant** L served Mon-Fri 12-3, Sat 10-3, Sun 12-4 D served Mon-Sat 6-10 Av 3 course à la carte fr £24 ⊕ GREENE KING ◀ IPA & Abbot Ale, Morland Ó Westons Stowford Press, Thatchers Gold. ♟ 14 **Facilities** ❖ Children welcome Children's portions Garden Wi-fi 🚐 (notice required)

Robin Hood's Retreat

197 Gloucester Rd BS7 8BG ☎ **0117 924 8639**
web: www.robinhoodsretreat.co.uk
dir: *At main rdbt at Broad Mead take Gloucester Rd exit, St Pauls. Road leads into Gloucester Rd (A38)*

In the heart of Bristol, this Victorian red-brick pub is popular with real ale lovers, who usually have several to choose from. The interior has been superbly appointed, with original features retained and with the addition of richly coloured wood panelling and furniture. There's plenty of attention to detail in the food too, which is all prepared on the premises. Favourites are slow-cooked British dishes such as braised brisket of salt beef with toffee carrots and dripping roast potatoes, and several seafood options. Booking for meals may be required.

Open all wk Sun-Wed 10.30am-11pm (Thu-Sat 10.30am-mdnt) Closed: 25 Dec **Bar Meals** L served Mon-Sat 10.30-9.30, Sun 12-5 D served Mon-Sat 6-9.30, Sun 6-9 **Restaurant** L served Mon-Sat 10.30-9.30, Sun 12-5 D served Mon-Sat 10.30-9.30, Sun 6-9 ⊕ ENTERPRISE INNS ◀ Sharp's Doom Bar, St Austell Tribute, Badger Tanglefoot, Butcombe Ó Westons Stowford Press. ♟ 15 **Facilities** Children welcome Children's portions Garden

AMERSHAM   Map 6 SU99

Hit or Miss Inn

Penn Street Village HP7 0PX ☎ **01494 713109**
e-mail: hit@ourpubs.co.uk
dir: *M25 junct 18, A404 (Amersham to High Wycombe road) to Amersham. Past crematorium on right, 2nd left into Whielden Ln (signed Winchmore Hill). 1.25m, pub on right*

Overlooking the cricket ground from which its name is taken, this is an 18th-century cottage-style dining pub. It has a beautiful country garden with lawn, patio and picnic tables for warmer days, while inside you'll find fires, old-world beams, Badger ales and a warm welcome from owners Michael and Mary Macken. Options on the menu range from tempting sandwiches and baked potatoes to dishes like chicken, chorizo and prosciutto roulade; turkey schnitzel; and seafood linguine. There are daily specials, Sunday roasts and a children's menu, too. There is a village beer festival in mid-July.

Open all day all wk 11-11 (Sun 12-10.30) **Bar Meals** L served Mon-Sat 12-2.30, Sun 12-8 D served Mon-Sat 6.30-9.30, Sun 12-8 Av main course £12 **Restaurant** L served Mon-Sat 12-2.30, Sun 12-8 D served Mon-Sat 6.30-9.30, Sun 12-8 Av 3 course à la carte fr £23 ⊕ HALL & WOODHOUSE ◀ Badger Dorset Best, Tanglefoot, K&B Sussex, Hopping Hare Ó Westons Stowford Press. ♟ 10 **Facilities** ❖ Children welcome Children's menu Children's portions Garden Beer festival Parking Wi-fi 🚐 (notice required)

AYLESBURY   Map 11 SP81

The King's Head

Market Square HP20 2RW ☎ **01296 718812**
e-mail: info@farmersbar.co.uk
dir: *Access on foot only. From Market Square access cobbled passageway. Pub entrance under archway on right*

A well-preserved coaching inn dating from 1455, with many fascinating architectural features. Today, The King's Head is the award-winning brewery tap for the Chiltern Brewery, one of the oldest micro-breweries in the country. Come at lunchtime for a beer-bread sandwich and a pint, perhaps in the cobbled courtyard; or dine inside on broccoli and stilton mornay, or hearty ham, egg and chips. Rothschild's supplies the wines from its former family seat at nearby National Trust-owned Waddesdon Manor. Beer festivals are held here; contact the pub for details.

Open all day all wk 11-11 (Sun 12-10.30) Closed: 25 Dec **Bar Meals** L served Mon-Fri 12-2, Sat-Sun 12-3 Av main course £8.50 ⊕ FREE HOUSE/CHILTERN BREWERY ◀ Beechwood Bitter, Ale, 300s Old Ale Ó Westons Stowford Press & Wyld Wood Organic. ♟ 11 **Facilities** Children welcome Children's menu Children's portions Family room Garden Beer festival 🚐 (notice required)

PICK OF THE PUBS

The Crooked Billet ❀

BLETCHLEY   Map 11 SP83

**2 Westbrook End, Newton Longville
MK17 0DF ☎ 01908 373936**
e-mail: john@thebillet.co.uk
web: www.thebillet.co.uk
dir: *M1 junct 13, follow signs to
Buckingham. 6m, signed at Bottledump
rdbt to Newton Longville*

Timbers from a vessel surplus to
requirements around the time of Sir
Francis Drake were recycled to create the
core of this magnificently thatched
village pub, and it remained for
centuries a farming community local in a
rural village setting. Time and tide wait
for no one, however, and the countryside
became part of greater Milton Keynes,
Newton just remaining detached from
the new town; the fascinating Bletchley
Park World War II code-breaking centre is
just down the road. Fortunately, the soul
of the rural alehouse remains; crackling
winter log fires (the house bacon is
smoked in the inglenook) cast flickering
shadows across oak beams whilst a
glimpse of village green life is recalled
by the huge lawned gardens. Top
sommelier John Gilchrist and wife/chef
Emma took on the run-down Billet a
decade ago and realised their dream of
running a high-end destination dining
pub together. Local foodies flock to the
two intimate wine-themed dining rooms
for Emma's menus, which are based on
the finest, freshest ingredients from a
multitude of small, local specialist food
producers and suppliers. The emphasis
is on taste, combined with modern

presentation; a cosmopolitan mix of
contemporary and classical with definite
English and French influences. Set lunch
and dinner menus change daily, whilst
the carte selection reads like a
gastronome's wish list; all meals are
matched on the menus to particular
wines, astonishingly well over 200 are
listed, all available by the glass. An
opening gambit could be truffle and
thyme marinated pan-fried pigeon
breast, pinot noir reduced Puy lentils,
bacon and tarragon parsnip purée;
paving the way for guinea fowl breast
with spinach and roasted garlic stuffing,
creamed pearl barley and chimney
smoked bacon with leek gratin, roasted
salsify and a port reduction; or pan-fried
cod fillet and crispy squid linguine nero
with lemon marinated fennel salad,
chive and chervil cream. The sweets and

cheeseboard are equally fulfilling, whilst
evening luxury taster menus, including
vegetarian, are available. Booking for
meals may be required.

Open 12-2.30 5-11 (Sun 12-4 7-10.30)
Closed: 27-28 Dec, Mon L ⊕ GREENE
KING ◀ Ruddles County, Morland Old
Speckled Hen, Badger Tanglefoot,
Wychwood Hobgoblin. **Facilities** Children
welcome Children's portions Garden
Parking

Save on hotels. Book at **theAA.com/hotel**

BUCKINGHAMSHIRE 45 ENGLAND

PICK OF THE PUBS

The Royal Oak

Frieth Rd SL7 2JF ☎ 01628 488611
e-mail: info@royaloakmarlow.co.uk
web: www.royaloakmarlow.co.uk
dir: *A4155 from Marlow. 300yds right signed Bovingdon Green. 0.75m, pub on left*

Just up the hill from town on the edge of Marlow Common, this little old whitewashed pub stands in sprawling, flower-filled gardens. It's one of five in the well-regarded Salisbury Pubs mini-empire in and around the Chilterns, all of which have entries in this guide.* Inside, it's spacious yet cosy, with dark floorboards, rich fabrics, a rosy red dining room and a wood-burning stove. All this sets the tone for early evening regulars gathered round a challenging crossword with a pint of Rebellion from Marlow, or Tutts Clump draught cider from West Berkshire. The imaginative modern British menu, put together with good food ethics in mind, is designed to appeal to all, beginning with 'small plates', or starters such as Dorset crab with cucumber, apple and Bloody Mary dressing, and crispy shredded five-spice duck leg, sesame beansprouts, tamarind and hoi sin dressing. Main courses cover ground from pan-fried lamb cutlet, seared kidney and liver, fondant potato, crushed peas and mint oil; and root vegetable with coconut and coriander curry with lime raita and cardamom pilaff rice; to British coastal

shellfish linguine with tomato marinara and lemon brioche crumbs. Perhaps to follow, Black Forest marshmallow arctic roll with hot chocolate shot, or warm pecan pie with Chantilly cream. An exclusively European wine list includes 22 by the glass and a wide choice of pudding wines, including one from Worcestershire. Free Wi-fi is available if you're planning a working lunch or dinner. Outside are a sunny summer terrace, pétanque piste and, if you're lucky, red kites wheeling around in the sky. Booking for meals may be required.

*Alford Arms, Hemel Hempstead, Hertfordshire; and in Buckinghamshire, The Swan Inn, Denham; The Old Queens Head, Penn; and The Black Horse, Fulmer.

Open all day all wk 11-11 (Sun 12-10.30) Closed: 25-26 Dec **Bar Meals** L served Mon-Fri 12-2.30, Sat

12-3, Sun 12-4 D served Sun-Thu 6.30-9.30, Fri-Sat 6.30-10 Av main course £14.75 **Restaurant** L served Mon-Fri 12-2.30, Sat 12-3, Sun 12-4 D served Sun-Thu 6.30-9.30, Fri-Sat 6.30-10 Av 3 course à la carte fr £27.25 ⊕ SALISBURY PUBS LTD ◖ Rebellion IPA & Smuggler Ō Thatchers, Tutts Clump. ♀ 22 **Facilities** Children welcome Children's portions ✿ Garden Parking Wi-fi

BEACONSFIELD Map 6 SU99

The Royal Standard of England

PICK OF THE PUBS

Brindle Ln, Forty Green HP9 1XT ☎ 01494 673382
e-mail: theoldestpub@btinternet.com
dir: A40 to Beaconsfield, right at church rdbt onto B474
towards Penn, left onto Forty Green Rd, 1m

Set in the beautiful Chilterns village of Forty Green, this
inn can trace its roots to Saxon times. It's apt then that
tales from its history abound, many recounted on the
back of the menu. Ramblers can use the large car park
before setting out on circular walks around this historic
alehouse, reputedly the oldest in England. Along with a
good selection of real ales and ciders, hearty food is the
order of the day, served amid the striking stained-glass
windows, beams and flagstone floors, and around the
large inglenook fireplace that warms the old walls in
winter. Seasonal wild game is a regular feature on the
specials board, supported by an extensive bill of fare.
Start, perhaps, with onion soup with gruyère cheese and
croûtons; continue with sausages and mash; or Welsh
lamb's liver and bacon with mashed potatoes and onion
gravy; and finish with traditional delights such as spotted
dick. Wash it down with ales from the pub's own new
brewery.

Open all day all wk 11-11 **Bar Meals** Av main course
£12.50 food served all day **Restaurant** food served all day
⊕ FREE HOUSE ◀ Chiltern Ale, Brakspear Bitter,
Rebellion IPA, Theakston Old Peculier, Guest ales
Ö Cotswold, The Orchard Pig, Westons Perry. ♀ 11
Facilities Children welcome Children's portions Family
room Garden Parking Wi-fi ▭

BLEDLOW Map 5 SP70

The Lions of Bledlow

Church End HP27 9PE ☎ 01844 343345
web: www.lionsofbledlow.co.uk
dir: M40 junct 6, B4009 to Princes Risborough, through
Chinnor into Bledlow

This lovely old free house dates back to the 1500s and is
often used as a filming location for programmes such as
Midsomer Murders. Low beams and careworn flooring give
the pub a timeless feeling, underlined by the steam trains
chugging past on the heritage railway beyond the village
green. Ramblers dropping down from the wooded Chiltern
scarp can fill up on generously filled baguettes and rustic
home-made meals like beef lasagne with garlic bread;

and hot smoked mackerel fillets with salad and boiled
potatoes, boosted by daily-changing specials.

Open all wk 11.30-3 6-11 (Sun 12-4 7-10.30 BHs &
summer wknds all day) **Bar Meals** L served all wk
12-2.30 D served Mon-Sat 6.30-9.30, Sun 7-9 Av main
course £7-£13 **Restaurant** L served all wk 12-2.30
D served Mon-Sat 6.30-9.30, Sun 7-9 ⊕ FREE HOUSE
◀ Wadworth 6X, Guest ales Ö Westons Stowford Press.
♀ 12 **Facilities** Children welcome Children's menu
Children's portions Family room Garden Parking ▭

BLETCHLEY Map 11 SP83

The Crooked Billet ◉

PICK OF THE PUBS

See Pick of the Pubs on page 44

BOVINGDON GREEN Map 5 SU88

The Royal Oak

PICK OF THE PUBS

See Pick of the Pubs on page 45

BRILL Map 11 SP61

The Pheasant Inn

Windmill St HP18 9TG ☎ 01844 239370
e-mail: info@thepheasant.co.uk
dir: In village centre, by windmill

Occupying a fine hilltop position on the edge of Brill
Common, with impressive views over the Vale of Aylesbury
and the Chilterns, this 17th-century beamed inn stands
next to Brill Windmill, one of the oldest postmills in the
country. A simple menu offers hearty modern pub dishes,
including starters of spiced potted beef with horseradish
cream, and main courses like venison with game chips
and cranberry jus; and pot-roasted lamb shank with root
vegetables and mash. Salads, filled baps and
ploughman's lunches are served at lunchtime – best
enjoyed in the garden in summer. Booking for meals may
be required.

Open all day all wk 12-11 (Fri-Sat 12-12 Sun 12-10.30)
Bar Meals L served Mon-Sat 12-2, Sun 12-6 D served all
wk 6.30-9 Av main course £13 **Restaurant** L served all wk
12-2 D served all wk 6.30-9 Av 3 course à la carte fr £22
⊕ FREE HOUSE ◀ St Austell Tribute, 2 Guest ales
Ö Thatchers. **Facilities** Children welcome Children's
portions Garden Parking Wi-fi ▭ (notice required)

BUCKINGHAM Map 11 SP63

The Old Thatched Inn

Main St, Adstock MK18 2JN ☎ 01296 712584
e-mail: manager@theoldthatchedinn.co.uk
web: www.theoldthatchedinn.co.uk
dir: Telephone for directions

Dating back to 1702, this lovely old thatched inn still
boasts traditional beams and inglenook fireplace. The
spacious interior consists of a formal conservatory and a
bar with comfy furniture and a welcoming, relaxed
atmosphere. Using the freshest, seasonal ingredients
from local and regional suppliers, the evening menu
takes in devilled kidneys with caramelised onions; pork
belly with black pudding and confit apple purée; and
banana Eton Mess. Typical lunchtime dishes include
smoked haddock linguine, and home-made beefburger
with pickles and hand-cut chips.

Open all day all wk Closed: 26 Dec **Bar Meals** L served
Mon-Fri 12-2.30, Sat 12-3, Sun 12-9 D served Mon-Sat
6-9.30, Sun 12-9 Av main course £13.95 **Restaurant**
Fixed menu price fr £13.95 Av 3 course à la carte fr £25
⊕ FREE HOUSE ◀ Hook Norton Hooky Bitter, Morland Old
Speckled Hen, Fuller's London Pride, Timothy Taylor
Ö Aspall. ♀ 14 **Facilities** Children welcome Children's
menu Children's portions Parking Wi-fi

See advert on opposite page

CHALFONT ST GILES Map 6 SU99

The Ivy House

PICK OF THE PUBS

See Pick of the Pubs on page 48

PICK OF THE PUBS

The Ivy House

CHALFONT ST GILES Map 6 SU99

London Rd HP8 4RS ☎ **01494 872184**
e-mail: ivyhouse@fullers.co.uk
web: www.fullers.co.uk
dir: *On A413 2m S of Amersham & 1.5m
N of Chalfont St Giles*

The Ivy House is a beautiful 250-year-old brick and flint coaching inn with amazing views of the Chiltern Vale, and set close to poet John Milton's cottage in Chalfont St Giles. In a great location for country walks as well as several nearby golf courses (including Harewood Downs), the pub is well known for its friendly welcome, great food and extensive wine list. Old beams, open fires, comfy armchairs and brasses all give the place a welcoming, cosy atmosphere. There's even the odd ghost story to be told about sightings of a shadowy stable lad dressed in 17th-century costume. Whisky-lovers will appreciate the range of over 30 malts, including some of the landlord's favourite rarities. Fuller's London Pride and a guest ale are among the beers, while Symonds provides the cider. Meals are served in the bar, the former coach house and the restaurant, and in fine weather you can dine alfresco in the garden, enjoying the fantastic views over the Chiltern Hills. The fresh rustic menus change every season, and also feature daily specials, with the

emphasis on quality local produce and fresh fish. Vegetarian meals are always available and special diets are catered for. Booking for meals may be required.

Open all day all wk **Bar Meals** L served Mon-Fri 12-2.45, Sat-Sun all day D served Mon-Fri 6-9.15, Sat-Sun all day Av main course £12 **Restaurant** L served Mon-Fri 12-2.45, Sat-Sun all day D served Mon-Fri 6-9.15, Sat-Sun all day Fixed menu price fr £13.50 Av 3 course à la carte fr £22 ⊕ FULLER'S ◖ London Pride, Guest ale ♂ Symonds. ♟ 10 **Facilities** Children welcome Children's menu Children's portions ❖ Garden Parking Wi-fi 🚌 (notice required)

PICK OF THE PUBS

The Greyhound Inn

CHALFONT ST PETER   Map 6 TQ09

SL9 9RA ☎ 01753 883404
e-mail: reception@thegreyhoundinn.net
web: www.thegreyhoundinn.net
dir: *M40 junct 1/M25 junct 16, follow signs for Gerrards Cross, then Chalfont St Peter*

On the London Road and set beside the River Misbourne, this historic coaching inn has been at the heart of Chalfont St Peter since the 14th century. Over the years, it has welcomed many a weary traveller, including Winston Churchill, Oliver Cromwell and local landowner Judge Jeffreys, who held his famous assizes here in the 1680s before sending his victims to the gallows by the nearby river. Much of the pub's original character has been retained, including the massive beams supporting the weight of the inn, plus the huge brick chimneys. These days, visitors and villagers can establish a presence in the imposing panelled, flagstoned bar or chic restaurant, and chinwag with the locals over a pint of London Pride or one of the ten wines available by the glass. A continental-style menu of light dishes and sandwiches includes sirloin steak sandwich with fried onions, or chicken liver parfait with red onion marmalade on toasted brioche. For those with larger appetites, look forward to choosing from the extensive modern British menu,

where a starter of pea and goat's cheese tart with rocket salad and red pepper coulis, or a sharing platter of fish or meat whets the appetite for steak and ale pie with bubble-and-squeak; squid ink linguine with clams, crayfish, shallot and roasted cherry tomato sauce; or grilled corn-fed chicken breast with chorizo potatoes and thyme sauce. Make sure you leave some room for one of the tempting desserts: apple tart with vanilla ice cream and Calvados raisins, perhaps, or chocolate fondant with candied orange and clotted cream. Local cheeses, biscuits and quince jelly round things off nicely. Booking for meals may be required.

Open all day all wk Mon-Wed 6.30am-10.30pm (Thu 6.30am-11.30pm Fri-Sat

6.30am-1am Sun 8.30am-10.30pm) **Bar Meals** L served Mon-Sat 12-2.30, Sun 12-6 D served Mon-Sat 6-9.30 Av main course £9 **Restaurant** L served Mon-Sat 12-2.30, Sun 12-6 D served Mon-Sat 6-9.30 Av 3 course à la carte fr £25 ⊕ ENTERPRISE INNS ◀ Fuller's London Pride, Sharp's Doom Bar, Adnams. ⬤ 10 **Facilities** Children welcome Children's menu Children's portions ❀ Garden Parking Wi-fi

The Greyhound Inn

PICK OF THE PUBS

See Pick of the Pubs on page 49

The Old Swan

58 High St LU7 0RQ ☎ 01296 668226
e-mail: oldswancheddington@btconnect.com
dir: *From Tring towards Marsworth take B489, 0.5m. Left towards Cooks Wharf onto Cheddington, pub on left*

Formed out of three cottages in the 15th century, this delightful thatched pub is known not only for its real ales and traditional charm but also for its food. Using fresh, locally sourced ingredients and game, fish and seafood supplies from sustainable sources, the menus offer modern British dishes. Lunchtime food ranges from hot paninis and ciabatta sandwiches to smaller and larger plates like potato cakes with salmon and mascarpone. Imaginative evening meals could be chickpea terrine or chicken saltimbocca. Children are made very welcome and there's a good play area in the attractive garden.

Open all day all wk **Bar Meals** L served Mon-Thu 12-3, Fri-Sat 12-5, Sun 12-4 D served Mon-Thu 6-9, Fri-Sat 6-9.30 **Restaurant** L served Mon-Thu 12-3, Fri-Sat 12-5, Sun 12-4 D served Mon-Thu 6-9, Fri-Sat 6-9.30 ⊕ PUNCH TAVERNS ◀ St Austell Tribute, Shepherd Neame Spitfire, Adnams Broadside & Explorer, Guest ales ○ Westons Stowford Press. ♦ 20 **Facilities** ❖ Children welcome Children's portions Play area Garden Parking Wi-fi ▄▄▄

The Red Lion

PICK OF THE PUBS

See Pick of the Pubs on opposite page

The Black Horse Inn

Chesham Vale HP5 3NS ☎ 01494 784656
e-mail: enquiries@black-horse-inn.co.uk
dir: *A41 from Berkhamsted, A416 through Ashley Green, 0.75m before Chesham right to Vale Rd, at bottom of Mashleigh Hill, 1m, inn on left*

Under new ownership since August 2011, this 500-year-old pub is set in some beautiful valley countryside and is ideal for enjoying a cosy, traditional environment without electronic games or music. During the winter there are roaring log fires to take the chill off those who may spot one of the resident ghosts. An ever-changing menu includes an extensive range of snacks, while the main menu features hearty lamb

casserole; baked fillet of sea bass with prawns in garlic butter; home-made pies; and steaks. In summer, eat in the large garden.

Open 12-3 6-11 (Sun 12-6) Closed: Sun eve **Bar Meals** L served Mon-Sat 12-2, Sun 12-3 D served Mon-Sat 6-9 **Restaurant** L served Mon-Sat 12-2, Sun 12-3 D served Mon-Sat 6-9 ⊕ PUNCH TAVERNS ◀ Tring Side Pocket For a Toad, Fuller's London Pride, 2 Guest ales ○ Westons Stowford Press. **Facilities** ❖ Children welcome Garden Beer festival Parking Wi-fi ▄▄▄ (notice required)

The Swan

Ley Hill HP5 1UT ☎ 01494 783075
e-mail: swanleyhill@btconnect.com
dir: *1.5m E of Chesham by golf course*

A beautiful 16th-century pub set in the delightful village of Ley Hill, this was once where condemned prisoners would drink a 'last and final ale' on the way to the nearby gallows. During World War II, Glen Miller and Clark Gable cycled here for a pint from their base. These days, it is a free house offering a warm welcome, real ales and good food, plus a large inglenook fireplace and original beams. Potted shrimps; chicken and chorizo tagliatelle; and pan-fried calves' liver and bacon are typical choices. Look out for the Bank Holiday beer festival in August. Booking for meals may be required.

Open all wk 12-3 5.30-11 (Sun 12-10.30) **Bar Meals** L served all wk 12-2.30 D served Tue-Sat 6.30-9.30 **Restaurant** L served all wk 12-2.30 D served Tue-Sat 6.30-9.30 ⊕ FREE HOUSE ◀ Adnams Southwold Bitter, St Austell Tribute, Timothy Taylor Landlord, Tring Side Pocket for a Toad, Guest ales. **Facilities** Children welcome Children's menu Garden Beer festival Parking ▄▄▄

The Full Moon

PICK OF THE PUBS

Hawridge Common HP5 2UH ☎ 01494 758959
e-mail: info@thefullmoonpub.com
dir: *At Tring on A41 follow signs for Wiggington & Cholesbury. On Cholesbury Common pub by windmill*

Known as The Half Moon when it was first built as a coaching inn in the 17th century, this alehouse graduated to The Full Moon in 1812. Something of an ideal country pub, it is situated on the edge of Cholesbury Common in the Chilterns; views to the windmill behind can be enjoyed from the large garden with heated paved patio, pergola and giant parasols. Inside are beams, flagstones, winter fires and cask ales which include Timothy Taylor Landlord and two weekly-changing guests. Comprehensive menus cover a range of possibilities, from wraps and sandwiches to toad-in-the-hole and jacket potatoes; from confit of duck leg on potato rösti to (vegetarian) shepherdess pie. Finish with a lemon and lime tart with vanilla ice cream. In 1907, the landlord

was fined for permitting drunkenness on the premises; these days the clientele is much better behaved. Booking for meals may be required.

Open all day all wk 12-11 (Sun 12-10.30) Closed: 25 Dec **Bar Meals** L served Mon-Fri 12-2, Sat 12-9, Sun 12-8 D served Mon-Fri 6.30-9, Sat 12-9, Sun 12-8 Av main course £9.95 **Restaurant** L served Mon-Fri 12-2, Sat 12-9, Sun 12-8 D served Mon-Fri 6.30-9, Sat 12-9, Sun 12-8 Fixed menu price fr £19.95 Av 3 course à la carte fr £19.95 ⊕ ADMIRAL TAVERNS ◀ Fuller's London Pride, Timothy Taylor Landlord, Sharp's Doom Bar, Brakspear, Adnams, Guest ales. ♦ 9 **Facilities** ❖ Children welcome Children's menu Children's portions Garden Parking Wi-fi ▄▄▄ (notice required)

The Unicorn ◉◉

High St LU7 0LQ ☎ 01296 681261
e-mail: theunicornpub@btconnect.com
dir: *2m N of A418 (between Aylesbury & Leighton Buzzard). In village centre*

The Unicorn is a 17th-century village free house overflowing with character from the low-beamed bar, real fires and good beers to the mismatched furniture, wooden floors and welcoming atmosphere. Relax in the secluded garden with a pint of Doom Bar or Spitfire. In the restaurant, the seasonal menus of hearty pub staples made from local ingredients have gained two AA Rosettes. Perhaps begin with duck liver and brandy pâté, followed by slow-roasted pork belly, or beetroot and fennel risotto. Finish with passionfruit cheesecake. There are May and August Bank Holiday beer festivals, regular quiz nights and live music events. Booking for meals may be required.

Open all day all wk 10.30am-11pm (Fri-Sat 10.30am-mdnt) **Bar Meals** Av main course £12 food served all day **Restaurant** L served Mon-Sat 12-2, Sun 12-3 D served Mon-Sat 6.30-9, Sun 6.30-8.30 Fixed menu price fr £15.50 Av 3 course à la carte fr £19.50 ⊕ FREE HOUSE ◀ Sharp's Doom Bar, Shepherd Neame Spitfire ○ Westons Stowford Press, Thatchers. **Facilities** Children welcome Children's menu Children's portions Play area Garden Beer festival Parking Wi-fi ▄▄▄ (notice required)

PICK OF THE PUBS

The Red Lion

CHENIES   Map 6 TQ09

WD3 6ED ☎ **01923 282722**

e-mail: theredlionchenies@hotmail.co.uk
web: www.theredlionchenies.co.uk
dir: *Between Rickmansworth &
Amersham on A404, follow signs for
Chenies & Latimer*

Set in the Chess Valley, in a picture-
book village, complete with a pretty
green and an ancient parish church,
and just up the lane from Chenies
Manor. The unassuming, white-painted
Red Lion's owners Mike and Heather
Norris have over 20 years' experience
behind them, and they firmly believe the
17th-century inn's popularity stems
from being a pub that serves good food,
not a restaurant that serves beer.
Expect a plain, simply furnished main
bar, a charming, snug dining area
housed in the original cottage to the
rear with a tiled floor, old inglenook and
rustic furniture, a restaurant, and Mike
talking passionately about his real ales.
Lion's Pride, brewed by Rebellion in
Marlow, is available here and here
alone; other local beers come from Vale
Brewery in Haddenham. Heather cooks
everything, including fresh daily pastas;
bangers with bubble-and-squeak; big
chunks of oven-baked leg of lamb
(much like Greek kleftiko); roast pork
belly on leek and potato mash; game
pie; fishcakes with horseradish and
beetroot dip; Orkneys rump steak;

curries; poached haddock with peppered
red wine sauce; and sausage, apple and
cheddar pie. Speaking of pies, brace
yourself for the famous lamb version,
which a visiting American serviceman
once declared beat a rival pub's pies
hands down. Ever since, its entry on the
menu has acquired an additional
adjective every time it is rewritten.
Today, therefore, it reads (take a deep
breath) 'The awesome, internationally
acclaimed, world-renowned,
aesthetically and palatably pleasing,
not knowingly genetically modified,
hand-crafted, well-balanced, famous,
original Chenies lamb pie'. Outside, on
the pub's sunny side, is a small seating
area. Booking for meals may be
required.

Open all wk Mon-Sat 11-2.30 5.30-11
(Sun 12-3 6.30-10.30) Closed: 25 Dec
🍺 FREE HOUSE 🍺 Wadworth 6X,
Rebellion Lion's Pride, Vale Best Bitter,
Guest ales ⌚ Thatchers Gold.
Facilities Garden Parking

PICK OF THE PUBS

The Swan Inn

DENHAM   Map 6 TQ08

Village Rd UB9 5BH ☎ 01895 832085
e-mail: info@swaninndenham.co.uk
web: www.swaninndenham.co.uk
dir: *A40 onto A412. 200yds follow*
'Denham village' sign. Through village,
over bridge, last pub on left

In the picturesque village of Denham you're surprisingly close to London and motorways, yet you just wouldn't know it. Georgian, double-fronted and covered in wisteria, this traditional country inn's large log fire and collection of rather interesting pictures picked up at auction give it a really homely feel. Outside, a secluded terrace and large gardens are ideal for families with children. It's one of five in the well-regarded Salisbury Pubs mini-empire in and around the Chilterns, all of which have entries in this guide.* Locals help to maintain a thriving bar trade, drawn in by well-kept Marlow Rebellion IPA and guests, perhaps Caledonian's Flying Scotsman. Fresh seasonal produce underpins a menu and daily-changing specials that feature more than a few old favourites. For a starter, look to the 'small plates' section of the menu, possibly featuring Little Marlow rabbit, prune, pistachio and bacon terrine, local plum, apple and elderberry chutney and toasted treacle bread. Then, among the main courses you'll find plenty of variety, from pan-fried devilled lamb's liver with roast beetroot, new potatoes,

chive sour cream and thyme jus; and Grimsby smoked haddock fishcake with wilted spinach and grain mustard and cream sauce; to parsnip, sweet potato, red onion and kidney bean pasty with purple sprouting broccoli and truffled cream sauce. Among the puddings are warm spiced carrot, apple and raisin muffin with cinnamon ice cream; and rhubarb knickerbocker glory with ginger tuile. An exclusively European wine list includes 22 by the glass and a wide choice of pudding wines, including an Austrian and one from Puglia. A private dining room is also available for family occasions or business meetings. Booking for meals may be required.

*Alford Arms, Hemel Hempstead, Hertfordshire: and in Buckinghamshire, The Royal Oak, Bovingdon Green; The Old Queens Head, Penn; and The Black Horse, Fulmer.

Open all day all wk 11-11 (Sun 12-10.30) Closed: 25-26 Dec **Bar Meals** L served Mon-Fri 12-2.30, Sat 12-3, Sun 12-4 D served Sun-Thu 6.30-9.30, Fri-Sat 6.30-10 Av main course £14.50 **Restaurant** L served Mon-Fri 12-2.30, Sat 12-3, Sun 12-4 D served Sun-Thu 6.30-9.30, Fri-Sat 6.30-10 Av 3 course à la carte fr £27 ⊕ SALISBURY PUBS LTD ◀ Rebellion IPA, Caledonian Flying Scotsman ♂ Thatchers. ♟ 22 **Facilities** Children welcome Children's portions ✿ Garden Parking Wi-fi

CUDDINGTON   Map 5 SP71

The Crown
PICK OF THE PUBS

Spurt St HP18 0BB ☎ **01844 292222**
e-mail: david@anniebaileys.com
dir: *Off A418 between Aylesbury & Thame*

Cuddington is a picturesque village, which is why it has often featured in the TV series *Midsomer Murders*. Some scenes were filmed at this thatched and whitewashed listed pub, with its atmospheric interior that includes a locals' bar and several low-beamed dining areas filled with prints and evening candlelight. Fuller's London Pride, Adnams and guest ales are on tap, and there's also an extensive wine list. Seafood dishes are a major attraction, and might include seafood pie; smoked haddock with grilled Welsh rarebit, tomato salad and chips; sea bass with crab risotto; and scallops with pancetta, salad leaves and truffle vinaigrette. Among other modern, internationally influenced options are rib-eye steak with grilled tomato, mushrooms and chips; slow-roast pork belly with Savoy cabbage, smoked bacon, mash and vanilla jus; and aubergine parmigiana with green salad. Sandwiches, salads and 'small plates' are also available. A compact patio area provides outside seating.

Open all wk 12-3 6-11 (Sun all day) **Bar Meals** L served all wk 12-2.15 D served Mon-Sat 6.30-9.15 **Restaurant** L served all wk 12-2.15 D served Mon-Sat 6.30-9.15 ⊕ FULLER'S ◀ London Pride & ESB, Adnams, Guest ales. ▾ 12 **Facilities** Children welcome Children's portions Garden Parking Wi-fi ▰

DENHAM   Map 6 TQ08

The Falcon Inn ★★★★ INN

Village Rd UB9 5BE ☎ **01895 832125**
e-mail: mail@falcondenham.com
web: www.falcondenham.com
dir: *M40 junct 1, follow A40/Gerrards Cross signs. Approx 200yds turn right onto Old Mill Rd. Pass church on right, enter village. Pub opposite village green*

A perfect place to refuel when exploring the nearby Colne Valley Country Park, this lovely old coaching inn is located opposite the green in the charming conversation village of Denham. Expect well-kept real ales and brasserie-style food in the cosy restaurant: smoked haddock and spring

onion fishcake, or baked camembert with redcurrant jelly to start, and main courses such as chicken wrapped in Parma ham; steak and Merlot pie; or Thai green curry. Four beamed bedrooms with original features are also available.

Open all day all wk **Bar Meals** L served all wk 12-2.30 D served all wk 5-9.30 Av main course £8 **Restaurant** L served all wk 12-2.30 D served all wk 5-9.30 Fixed menu price fr £13 Av 3 course à la carte fr £17 ⊕ ENTERPRISE INNS ◀ Timothy Taylor Landlord, Wells Bombardier, Brakspear, Guest ales Õ Westons Stowford Press. **Facilities** ✿ Children welcome Children's portions Garden Beer festival Wi-fi ▰ **Rooms** 4

The Swan Inn
PICK OF THE PUBS

See Pick of the Pubs on opposite page

DORNEY   Map 6 SU97

The Palmer Arms

Village Rd SL4 6QW ☎ **01628 666612**
e-mail: chrys@thepalmerarms.com
dir: *From A4 take B3026, over M4 to Dorney*

Engaging chickens take dust baths in the sun trap garden of this family-friendly community pub in pretty Dorney, just a short stroll from the Thames Path and Boveney Lock. Its 15th-century origins are disguised behind contemporary décor and furnishings, with winter open fires adding atmosphere, whilst a thoroughly modern menu adds spice: crispy chilli beef salad may precede a main of pan-fried duck breast with creamy mash, pak choi, cherry and port sauce, or slow-roasted belly pork with dauphinoise potatoes, spinach, apple purée and red wine jus. A summer beer festival features local beers and ciders.

Open all day all wk 11am-11.30pm (Sun 12-10.30) **Bar Meals** food served all day **Restaurant** food served all day ⊕ GREENE KING ◀ Abbot Ale & IPA, Guinness Õ Aspall. ▾ 18 **Facilities** ✿ Children welcome Children's menu Children's portions Play area Garden Beer festival Parking ▰

EASINGTON   Map 5 SP61

Mole and Chicken
PICK OF THE PUBS

HP18 9EY ☎ **01844 208387**
e-mail: enquiries@themoleandchicken.co.uk
dir: *M40 juncts 8 or 8a, A418 to Thame. At rdbt left onto B4011 signed Long Crendon & Bicester. In Long Crendon right into Carters Lane signed Dorton & Chilton. At T-junct left into Chilton Rd signed Chilton. Approx 0.75m to pub*

Set high on the border between Oxfordshire and Buckinghamshire, there are magnificent views across

rolling countryside from the terraced garden of this attractive pub. It was built in 1831 as part of the workers' estate, later becoming the village store and pub that sold only beer and cider until 1918. Inside it's all exposed beams and unusual flagged floors, two roaring log fires, and a motley collection of oak and pine tables and chairs. Although self-styled as a restaurant with rooms, the atmosphere is friendly and relaxed despite the emphasis on food, and local Old Hooky and Vale Best ales are served on tap. Modern pub food draws an appreciative crowd, the seasonal menu typically offering chilli-fried Cornish squid with garlic, lemon and olive oil, or cream of celeriac soup; followed by pot-roasted corn-fed chicken leg, root vegetables, shallots and sauté potatoes, or glazed Old Spot pork belly, champ, sprouting broccoli and red cabbage. To finish there's turmeric pannacotta, lime Chantilly and ginger shortbread, or a plate of British cheeses. Booking for meals may be required.

Open all wk 12-3 6-11 **Restaurant** L served Mon-Sat 12-2.30, Sun all day D served Mon-Sat 6-9, Sun all day Fixed menu price fr £12.95 Av 3 course à la carte fr £25 ⊕ FREE HOUSE ◀ Hook Norton Old Hooky, Vale Best Bitter. **Facilities** Children welcome Children's menu Children's portions Garden Parking Wi-fi

FARNHAM COMMON   Map 6 SU98

The Foresters

The Broadway SL2 3QQ ☎ **01753 643340**
e-mail: info@theforesterspub.com
dir: *Telephone for directions*

At first sight looking older than its 1930's origins, this handsome building has a funky interior where old meets new - crystal chandeliers and log fires, real ales and cocktails, chesterfields and velvet thrones. Front and rear gardens contribute to the overall smart appearance. Typical dishes include warm applewood-smoked salmon with gnocchi, butter emulsion and baby beetroot; roasted breast of guinea fowl with red cabbage, celeriac remoulade and spiced cranberries; Foresters beefburger with bacon, smoked cheese, onion jam and shoestring fries; and Bloody Mary pasta.

Open all day all wk **Bar Meals** L served all wk 12-3 D served all wk 6.30-10 **Restaurant** L served all wk 12-3 D served all wk 6.30-10 ⊕ PUNCH TAVERNS ◀ Fuller's London Pride, Young's, Guest ales Õ Aspall. ▾ **Facilities** Children welcome Children's menu Children's portions Garden Parking Wi-fi ▰ (notice required)

FARNHAM ROYAL   Map 6 SU98

The Emperor

Blackpond Ln SL2 3EG ☎ 01753 643006
e-mail: bookings@theemperorpub.co.uk
dir: *Telephone for directions*

Off the beaten track, this old village inn is a pub for all seasons thanks to its log fire in winter and alfresco tables in the summer. A wealth of polished wood floors and original beams runs through the bar, conservatory and refurbished barn. British food based on fresh seasonal fare drives the menu, which might include rolled pork loin with mash, pear purée and spinach; and smoked haddock fishcake with wasabi and lime mayonnaise dip. Tuesday is steak night, when exotic choices might include springbok.

Open all day all wk **Bar Meals** L served Mon-Thu 12-3, Fri-Sat 12-10, Sun 12-6 D served Mon-Thu 6-10, Fri-Sat 12-10, Sun 12-6 ⊕ ORIGINAL PUB CO LTD ◼ Fuller's London Pride, Rebellion, 3 Guest ales. ▮ 8 **Facilities** ❖ Children welcome Children's menu Children's portions Garden Parking Wi-fi ▭ (notice required)

FORD   Map 5 SP70

The Dinton Hermit ★★★ INN

PICK OF THE PUBS

Water Ln HP17 8XH ☎ 01296 747473
e-mail: relax@dintonhermit.co.uk
dir: *Off A418 between Aylesbury & Thame*

A character called John Biggs inspired the name of this 16th-century, stone-built inn (now in new hands) in the Vale of Aylesbury. Local legend suggests that Biggs had been King Charles I's executioner in 1649, so he thought it prudent to go to ground and live as a recluse. At the bar you'll find real ales from Vale Brewery and monthly guests, as well as a wide selection of wines. Both the restaurant and the bar menus offer locally sourced regular favourites and seasonal specials. To convey the style, take a typical evening meal of seared breast of wood pigeon on Puy lentils, crispy leeks and pan juices as a starter; a main course of baked fillet of hake with crushed new potatoes, samphire and mussel broth; and, for dessert, glazed lemon tart with mascarpone ice cream. Contemporary accommodation includes six newly refurbished Barn Rooms. The garden is quite splendid.

Open all day all wk 10am-11pm (Sun 12-10.30) **Bar Meals** L served Mon-Fri 12-2, Sat-Sun 12-3 D served all wk 6.30-8.45 **Restaurant** L served Mon-Fri 12-2, Sat-Sun 12-3 D served all wk 6.30-8.45 ⊕ FREE HOUSE ◼ Vale Best Bitter, Guest ales Ö Westons Stowford Press. **Facilities** ❖ Children welcome Children's menu Children's portions Garden Parking Wi-fi **Rooms** 13

FRIETH   Map 5 SU79

The Prince Albert

RG9 6PY ☎ 01494 881683
dir: *4m N of Marlow. Follow Frieth road from Marlow. Straight across at x-rds on Fingest road. Pub 200yds on left*

Dating back to the 1700s, this traditional country pub set in the Chilterns prides itself on old-world values. There are no televisions, jukeboxes or games - just good conversation, great beers and a welcoming atmosphere. With copper pots and pans and jugs hanging in the bar, warming open fires enhance the mood in winter and there is a garden with seating to admire the views. Expect traditional pub food with jacket potatoes, fishcakes and country pâté with toast among the small bites, while the main courses typically include local cured ham; Torre Meadow steak burger; gammon steak with egg (or pineapple) and chips; and Berkshire sausages.

Open all day all wk 11-11 (Sun 12-10.30) **Bar Meals** L served Mon-Sat 12.15-2.30, Sun 12.30-3 D served Fri-Sat 7.30-9.30 ⊕ BRAKSPEAR ◼ Bitter, Seasonal ales. ▮ 9 **Facilities** ❖ Children welcome Children's portions Garden Parking

FULMER   Map 6 SU98

The Black Horse

PICK OF THE PUBS

See Pick of the Pubs on opposite page

GREAT HAMPDEN   Map 5 SP80

The Hampden Arms

HP16 9RQ ☎ 01494 488255
dir: *From M40 junct 4 take A4010, turn right before Princes Risborough. Great Hampden signed*

The large garden of this mock-Tudor free house on the wooded Hampden Estate sits beside the common, where you might watch a game of cricket during the season. Chef-proprietor Constantine Lucas includes some Greek signature dishes such as kleftiko and Greek salad alongside more traditional choices such as breaded chicken escalope; steak, ale and mushroom pie; and mixed pepper and aubergine risotto. Guest ales support regular brews from Adnams and Vale Brewery.

Open all wk 12-3 6-12 ⊕ FREE HOUSE ◼ Adnams Southwold Bitter, Vale, Fuller's London Pride, Guest ales Ö Addlestones. **Facilities** Children welcome Children's portions Family room Garden Parking

GREAT MISSENDEN   Map 6 SP80

The Nags Head ★★★★ INN ◉

PICK OF THE PUBS

See Pick of the Pubs on page 57
See advert on page 56

The Polecat Inn

PICK OF THE PUBS

170 Wycombe Rd, Prestwood HP16 0HJ ☎ 01494 862253
e-mail: polecatinn@btinternet.com
dir: *On A4128 between Great Missenden & High Wycombe*

The Polecat dates back to the 17th century, and its beautiful three-acre garden, set amidst rolling Chilterns countryside, is part of its great attraction. John Gamble bought the closed and dilapidated pub over 20 years ago, renovating and extending it to create an attractive free house, while retaining many original features. The small low-beamed rooms radiating from the central bar give many options when it comes to choosing where to eat or drink. Dishes are prepared from local ingredients, including herbs from the garden. Lunchtime snacks (sandwiches, warm baguettes, jackets and ploughman's) are backed by a main menu ranging from melon and passionfruit with a wild strawberry coulis as a starter to main courses such as magret of duck in a orange and Cognac sauce, or bean and vegetable hotpot with a smoked cheese and potato gratin; and for pudding, chocolate and biscuit terrine. Daily blackboard specials add to the choice – mushroom and gorgonzola bruschetta with chopped walnuts may be on offer.

Open 11-2.30 6-11 (Sun 12-3) Closed: 25-26 Dec, 1 Jan, Sun eve **Bar Meals** L served all wk 12-2 D served Mon-Sat 6.30-9 Av main course £12 ⊕ FREE HOUSE ◼ Marston's Pedigree, Morland Old Speckled Hen, Brakspear Bitter, Ringwood Best Bitter Ö Thatchers Gold. ▮ 16 **Facilities** Children welcome Children's portions Play area Family room Garden Parking ▭ (notice required)

PICK OF THE PUBS

The Black Horse

FULMER   Map 6 SU98

Windmill Ln SL3 6HD ☎ **01753 663183**
e-mail: info@blackhorsefulmer.co.uk
web: www.blackhorsefulmer.co.uk
dir: *A40 E of Gerrards Cross. Follow Fulmer/Wexham signs. Pub in 1.5m*

A short hop from central London, The Black Horse is tucked away in a pretty conservation village between Gerrards Cross and Slough. It's one of five in the well-regarded Salisbury Pubs mini-empire in and around the Chilterns, all of which have entries in this guide.* Originally 17th-century cottages housing local craftsmen building the Church of St James next door, the main building is essentially a warren of small rooms filled with antique furniture, pictures from local salerooms and rich Zoffany fabrics. Its proximity to Pinewood Studios means that you just might see a famous face at the bar with a pint of Old Speckled Hen or London Glory. The menu, described as earthy British Colonial, is driven by local produce, even to the extent that the chefs themselves go out foraging. For a light lunch, a good starting point is a 'small plate', perhaps steamed Cornish mussels with lemongrass, chilli and coriander, or crispy Stockings Farm pork belly fritters, cauliflower purée and crackling. Among the mains expect slow-cooked steak-and-kidney suet pudding with buttered curly kale; honey-glazed Barbary duck breast with braised lentils, roast salsify and wilted spinach; and wild mushroom and rocket bread-and-butter pudding with purple sprouting broccoli and roast shallots. Puddings are essentially traditional: warm treacle sponge with vanilla custard, and warm lemon meringue crêpes with lemon syrup and stem ginger ice cream. The garden is large enough to 'lose' children while you enjoy one of the 22 wines by the glass on the peaceful terrace. Happy, chatty staff have been well chosen and clearly enjoy working here. Booking for meals may be required.

*Alford Arms, Hemel Hempstead, Hertfordshire: and in Buckinghamshire, The Swan Inn, Denham; The Royal Oak, Bovingdon Green; and The Old Queens Head, Penn.

Open all day all wk 11-11 (Sun 12-10.30) Closed: 25-26 Dec **Bar Meals** L

served Mon-Fri 12-2.30, Sat 12-3, Sun 12-4 D served Sun-Thu 6.30-9.30, Fri-Sat 6.30-10 Av main course £14.50 **Restaurant** L served Mon-Fri 12-2.30, Sat 12-3, Sun 12-4 D served Sun-Thu 6.30-9.30, Fri-Sat 6.30-10 Av 3 course à la carte fr £27 ⊕ SALISBURY PUBS LTD ◀ Greene King IPA & London Glory, Morland Old Speckled Hen ⓒ Aspall. ☙ 22 **Facilities** Children welcome Children's portions ☙ Garden Parking Wi-fi

The Nags Head
Country Inn & Restaurant

The AA 4 star Nags Head Inn has now been awarded a Rosette for its culinary excellence and has received many accolades in the last few years.

It has tastefully been refurbished to a high standard retaining its original 15th century country inn features including, low oak beams and a large inglenook fireplace.

Situated in the valley of the River Misbourne within the glorious Chilterns, it's ideally located within walking distance of the picturesque village of Great Missenden, near all major road and rail routes.

The Nags Head Inn has been viewed in past TV series including recent travel programmes and is featured in children's author, Roald Dahl's "Fantastic Mr Fox" animated film based in Great Missenden.

It boasts a beautiful restaurant and refurnished bedrooms all with private ensuite facilities.

The menu has a British and French fusion theme using local produce where possible.

Local game and their home smoked produce is a must along with a great Sunday roast and home made desserts.

A great wine list of more than 150 with local ales and beers should satisfy most budgets and tastes. Enjoy!

London Road, Great Missenden, Buckinghamshire HP16 0DG
Tel: 01494 862200 • Fax: 01494 862685
Website: www.nagsheadbucks.com • Email: goodfood@nagsheadbucks.com

PICK OF THE PUBS

The Nags Head ★★★★INN ✿

GREAT MISSENDEN Map 6 SP80

London Rd HP16 0DG ☎ 01494 862200
e-mail: goodfood@nagsheadbucks.com
web: www.nagsheadbucks.com
dir: *N of Amersham on A413, left at Chiltern hospital into London Rd signed Great Missenden*

It has been five years since the Michaels family restored this 15th-century inn tucked away in the sleepy valley of the River Misbourne in the picturesque Chiltern Hills. As they did with such success at the Bricklayers Arms in Flaunden, Hertfordshire (see entry), the family has helped this former coaching inn to gain a formidable reputation for food and hospitality. Originally three small cottages, features include low oak beams and an inglenook fireplace, which have been carefully retained as a backdrop for the stylish new bar. The late Roald Dahl used to be a regular here and the dining room is decorated with limited edition prints by the children's author, who drew inspiration from the pub for his famous book *Fantastic Mr Fox*. Food is taken seriously here, and executive head chef Claude Paillet sources the finest ingredients from local suppliers wherever possible, for a menu that fuses English with French. Lunch and dinner menus may offer starters like crab with home-smoked salmon, chive cream and blinis,

or goat's cheese artichoke crumble with confit root vegetables and apple dressing. Main courses range from fillet of local pork with black pudding, Bramley apple crumble and a sage and cider jus, to steak, kidney and ale pie with chive mash and salad. Leave room for a tempting pudding; typical choices include bourbon vanilla crème brûlée or crêpe filled with citrus fruits and Cointreau-flavoured mascarpone. In summer, relax over a drink or a meal whilst gazing out over the Chiltern Hills from the pub's lovely informal garden. Alternatively, stay overnight in one of the five beautifully refurbished and contemporary bedrooms. Booking for meals may be required.

Open all day all wk Closed: 25 Dec **Bar Meals** L served Mon-Sat 12-2.30, Sun 12-3.30 D served all wk 6.30-9.30 **Restaurant** L served Mon-Sat 12-2.30, Sun 12-3.30 D served all wk 6.30-9.30 🛢 FREE HOUSE ◨ Fuller's London Pride, Rebellion, Tring, Vale Ŏ Aspall. ♟ 19 **Facilities** Children welcome Children's portions ❤ Garden Parking Wi-fi **Rooms** 5

Grove Lock

LU7 0QU ☎ 01525 380940
dir: *From A4146 (S of Leighton Buzzard) take B4146 signed Ivinghoe & Tring. Pub 0.5m on left*

This pub is situated next to Lock 28 on the Grand Union Canal, and is less than a mile from the scene of the 1963 Great Train Robbery. Its lofty open-plan bar has leather sofas, assorted tables and chairs and canal-themed artworks. The restaurant, once the lock-keeper's cottage, serves breaded chicken Caesar salad; butternut squash risotto; sausages and mash; and smoked belly of pork. Plenty of outdoor seating means you can watch the barges, while enjoying a pint of Fuller's. Catch a summer barbecue and hog roast. Booking for meals may be required.

Open all day all wk **Bar Meals** L served Mon-Sat 12-9 D served Sun 12-7 Av main course £9.95 food served all day **Restaurant** L served Mon-Sat 12-9 D served Sun 12-7 Av 3 course à la carte fr £20 food served all day ⊕ FULLER'S ◀ London Pride, Chiswick Bitter, Discovery, ESB. ₹ 14 **Facilities** Children welcome Children's menu Children's portions Garden Parking Wi-fi

The Stag & Huntsman Inn ⓤ

RG9 6RP ☎ 01491 571227
dir: *5m from Henley-on-Thames on A4155 towards Marlow, left at Mill End towards Hambleden*

Close to the glorious beech-clad Chilterns, this 400-year-old brick and flint village pub has featured in countless films and television series. After being completely refurbished, the pub reopened in spring 2012. Ever-changing guest ales are served in the public bar, larger lounge bar and cosy snug. Food is available in the bars as well as the dining room, from an extensive menu of home-made pub favourites prepared with local seasonal produce. Opt for the likes of pan-fried fillet of salmon; rib-eye steak; or oven-roasted peppers filled with spiced couscous. Hambleden Estate game features strongly when in season, and there is a pizza and barbecue menu to enjoy in the garden during the summer months.

Open all wk Mon-Sat all day (Sun 11-10.30) **Bar Meals** L served all wk 12-2.30 D served Mon-Sat 6.30-9 ⊕ FREE HOUSE ◀ Rebellion, Sharp's, Loddon, Guest ales ♂ Thatchers & Gold. **Facilities** ❄ Children welcome Garden Parking ⬛ **Rooms** 9

The White Horse

SL2 3UY ☎ 01753 643225
dir: *Telephone for directions*

An ale drinker's paradise if ever there was one, parts of which date back 500 years. With three beer festivals a year (Easter, Spring Holiday and August Bank Holiday) and barely a pause between them, this pub can almost claim to run a single year-long celebration, with over 1,000 real ales consumed annually. Real cider and Belgian bottled beers augment the already mammoth range. A large well-kept garden at the rear hosts summer barbecues; otherwise the menu of home-cooked pub favourites ranges from a salad bar with quiches, sandwiches and ploughman's, through to curries, chilli, pasta dishes, pies and steaks (lunchtime only).

Open all wk 11-2.30 5-11 (Sat 11-11 Sun 11-10.30) **Bar Meals** L served Mon-Fri 12-2, Sat-Sun 12-2.30 ⊕ FREE HOUSE ◀ 8 Rotating ales ♂ 3 Guest ciders. ₹ 10 **Facilities** Children welcome Children's portions Family room Garden Beer festival Parking ⬛

The Sausage Tree

Saffron Rd HP13 6AB ☎ 01494 452204
e-mail: sausagetreepub@hotmail.co.uk
dir: *M40 junct 4, take A404 signed Town Centre & Amersham. At rdbt 2nd exit signed Beaconsfield, Amersham, A404. At rdbt 2nd exit signed Beaconsfield. Left into Stuart Rd, left into Easton Terrace, left into Saffron Rd*

The Chilterns may not be famous for exotic meats but this pub on the outskirts of High Wycombe has made a name for itself with its vast range of sausages, including ostrich, kangaroo and springbok. Try to decide just which types of sausage will be your repast: Armenian lamb; lemon chicken and tarragon; and smoked beer and beef are just three examples. Maybe plump instead for one of the 100 speciality beers on offer with a steak cooked at your table on fearsomely hot volcanic rock platters.

Open 12-3 5-11 Closed: Sun **Bar Meals** L served Mon-Sat 12-3 D served Mon-Sat 5.30-10 **Restaurant** L served Mon-Sat 12-3 D served Mon-Sat 5.30-11 ⊕ ENTERPRISE INNS ◀ Guest ales. ₹ **Facilities** Garden Wi-fi

The Whip Inn

Pink Rd HP27 0PG ☎ 01844 344060
dir: *1m of A4010 (Princes Risborough to High Wycombe road). Adjacent to windmill*

A picturesque old smock windmill catches the breeze on the ridge top where this 150-year-old pub also stands, high above the Vale of Aylesbury; five counties are visible on clear days. Ramblers on the Chiltern Way join locals in appreciating some of 700 real ales offered each year, as well as real Millwhites cider. A robust menu of home-made classic favourites and seasonally based specials seals the deal at this rustic, music- and fruit-machine free country inn. The Whip holds a beer festival twice a year in May and September. Booking for meals may be required.

Open all day all wk **Bar Meals** L served all wk 12-2.30 D served all wk 6.30-9 **Restaurant** L served all wk 12-2.30 D served all wk 6.30-9 ⊕ FREE HOUSE ◀ Over 700 guest ales a year ♂ Thatchers, Millwhites. ₹ 22 **Facilities** Children welcome Children's menu Children's portions Garden Beer festival Parking

Grouse & Ale **NEW**

High St HP14 3JG ☎ 01494 882299
e-mail: info@grouseandale.co.uk
dir: *On B482 in village*

Built as a manor house in 1679 and a pub since 1909, when it was called the Clayton Arms, this striking building became the Grouse & Ale in 2006 following major refurbishment. On a back road, equidistant between junctions 4 and 5 of the M40, it makes a peaceful pitstop, the draw being the cosy bar and dining area, where you can relax and peruse the papers with a pint. Modern pub food ranges from a lunchtime steak and red onion ciabatta to pub favourites like sausages with mash and onion gravy, and daily specials, perhaps pork belly with mustard sauce. There's a secluded suntrap courtyard for summer alfresco meals.

Open all day all wk Closed: 1 Jan **Bar Meals** L served Mon-Sat 12-2.30, Sun 12-4 D served Mon-Sat 6-9.30 Av main course £11 **Restaurant** L served Mon-Sat 12-2.30, Sun 12-4 D served Mon-Sat 6-9.30 Av 3 course à la carte fr £23 ⊕ HEINEKEN ◀ Adnams Broadside, Caledonian Deuchars IPA, Courage. ₹ 27 **Facilities** ❄ Children welcome Children's menu Children's portions Garden Parking Wi-fi

PICK OF THE PUBS

The Hand & Flowers ❀❀❀

MARLOW   Map 5 SU88

126 West St SL7 2BP ☎ **01628 482277**
e-mail: reservations@thehandandflowers.co.uk
web: www.thehandandflowers.co.uk
dir: *M4 junct 9, A404 to Marlow, A4155 towards Henley-on-Thames. Pub on right*

Tom and Beth Kerridge bought the lease of this whitewashed 18th-century pub in 2005 and it quickly became a destination for food-lovers as much as locals in search of a pint of Abbot Ale and a pork pie. An unassuming pub on the outskirts of this upmarket town, The Hand & Flowers remains a class act and a gastronomic hotspot. Despite gaining three AA Rosettes in the first year, the pub remains a relaxed and unpretentious place, with flagstone floors, old beams and timbers, roaring winter log fires, walls lined with striking modern art, leather banquettes and cloth-less, smartly-set tables. A small bar area serves decent real ale, and a cracking set lunch that features dishes like tomato soup with basil pesto; crispy lamb breast with pomme boulangère; profiteroles with dark chocolate sauce. The friendly, knowledgeable service also helps to set the tone of the place. Tom's cooking is intelligently straightforward and elegant, with simplicity, flavour and skill top of his agenda. The style is broadly modern British, underpinned by classical French techniques, and the

seasonally-changing menu is built around top-notch produce. Considerable skill and confidence can be seen in dishes such as starters of salt cod Scotch egg with chorizo and red pepper sauce; parsley soup with smoked eel, bacon and parmesan tortellini, and main dishes of line-caught cod with pastrami, herb crust and etuvé of leek; loin of Cotswold venison with ox tongue, Bérigoule mushroom, English lettuce and prickly ash; and Essex lamb 'bun' with sweetbreads and salsa verde. Be wowed by desserts such as tonka bean pannacotta with poached rhubarb, or passionfruit soufflé with kaffir lime ice cream and warm toffee. The Thames is close for revitalising river walks. Booking for meals may be required.

Open 12-2.30 6.30-9.30 (Sun 12-3.30) Closed: 24-26 Dec, 1 Jan Dinner, Sun eve ⊕ GREENE KING 🍺 Abbot Ale & IPA, Morland Original. **Facilities** Children welcome Children's portions Garden Parking

LITTLE KINGSHILL
Map 6 SU89

The Full Moon NEW

Hare Ln HP16 0EE ☎ 01494 862397
e-mail: email@thefullmoon.info
dir: *SW of Great Missenden, accessed from either A413 or A4128*

Wonderful walks through the Chiltern Hills radiate from the front door of this traditional brick-built village pub, which makes it a popular post-ramble refuelling stop, especially as both dogs and children are warmly welcomed inside. The pub is noted for it's tip-top Fuller's London Pride and the weekly-changing guest ales, and the pub throngs during the late June beer festival. Walking appetites will be satisfied with one of the sharing platters, a rib-eye steak sandwich or hearty mains courses like lamb shank in red wine and rosemary sauce, and beer-battered haddock and chips. Booking for meals may be required.

Open all day all wk **Bar Meals** L served all wk 12-3 D served all wk 6-10 Av main course £11 **Restaurant** L served all wk 12-3 D served all wk 6-10 Fixed menu price fr £5 Av 3 course à la carte fr £22 ⊕ PUNCH TAVERNS ◼ Fuller's London Pride, Young's, Adnams, Guest ale. ☂ 21 **Facilities** ✿ Children welcome Children's menu Children's portions Play area Garden Beer festival Parking 🚐 (notice required)

LONG CRENDON
Map 5 SP60

The Angel Inn ◉

PICK OF THE PUBS

47 Bicester Rd HP18 9EE ☎ 01844 208268
e-mail: info@angelrestaurant.co.uk
dir: *M40 junct 7, A418 to Thame, B4011 to Long Crendon. Inn on B4011*

Set in a picturesque village on the Bucks and Oxfordshire borders, this smartly refurbished old coaching inn dates from the 15th century. Much of its character has been retained with original fireplaces and wattle-and-daub walls alongside modern features including an airy conservatory, and tasteful natural materials and fabrics throughout. The inn's main focus is food but you'll also find real ales like Oxford Blue on offer as well as cocktails, champagne, wine by the glass and an impressive selection of whiskies. At lunch, choose between tempting sandwiches and the more substantial fare on offer. Similar choices abound at dinner, offering the likes of Cornish crab and salmon fishcake; and chargrilled fillet of beef on bubble-and-squeak with oxtail jus. An impressive array of fish dishes might include lightly curried cod on new potato and spinach sag aloo. In warmer weather, head for the heated alfresco terrace.

Open all day Closed: Sun eve **Bar Meals** L served all wk 12-2.30 D served Mon-Sat 7-9.30 Av main course £5.50 **Restaurant** L served all wk 12-2.30 D served Mon-Sat 7-9.30 Fixed menu price fr £14.95 Av 3 course à la carte fr £30 ⊕ FREE HOUSE ◼ Morrells Oxford Blue, Vale Wychert, Brakspear. ☂ 18 **Facilities** Children welcome Children's portions Garden Parking Wi-fi

LOUDWATER
Map 6 SU99

The Derehams Inn

5 Derehams Ln HP10 9RH ☎ 01494 530965
e-mail: derehams@hotmail.co.uk
dir: *From A40 (London Rd) from High Wycombe towards Beaconsfield turn left onto Derehams Ln*

All low beams and brasses, panelling and pewter, The Derehams, which originated as 18th-century farm cottages, shouts timeless English village pub loud and clear. A bevy of beer-wickets dispense a great range of local ales. Maggie's kitchen rustles up anything from light bites and sandwiches to home-made burgers, chicken curry, veggie chilli, wholetail scampi, cottage pie and solid Sunday roasts. They also host an annual summer beer festival here with local real ales, live music and a hog roast.

Open all wk Mon-Thu 11.30-3.30 5.30-11 (Fri-Sun all day) **Bar Meals** L served Mon-Sat 12-2.30, Sun 2-5 ⊕ FREE HOUSE ◼ Fuller's London Pride, Loddon, Brakspear, Guest ales. **Facilities** Children welcome Children's menu Children's portions Garden Beer festival Parking Wi-fi 🚐

MARLOW
Map 5 SU88

The Hand & Flowers ◉◉◉

PICK OF THE PUBS

See Pick of the Pubs on page 59

The Kings Head

Church Rd, Little Marlow SL7 3RZ ☎ 01628 484407
e-mail: clive.harvison@sky.com
dir: *M40 junct 4 take A4040 S, then A4155 towards Bourne End. Pub 0.5m on right*

A good range of real ales, including a couple from the Rebellion brewery in Marlow, awaits visitors to this charming 16th-century pub a few minutes' walk from the Thames Path. The open-plan interior features original beams and log fires, or there's the large garden. As well as sandwiches, baguettes, paninis and jacket potatoes, the food includes home-cooked steaks, chicken curry and rice, lasagna verdi and vegetarian risotto. Friday is fish day, typically North Atlantic haddock. Tell staff you've parked the car, go for a walk and return for a meal. Booking for meals may be required.

Open all day all wk Closed: 26 Dec **Bar Meals** L served Mon-Sat 12-2.15, Sun 12-7 D served all wk 6.30-9.30 Av main course £10.25 **Restaurant** L served Mon-Sat 12-2.15, Sun 12-7 D served all wk 6.30-9.30 ⊕ ENTERPRISE INNS ◼ Fuller's London Pride, Timothy Taylor Landlord, Adnams Broadside, Rebellion IPA & Smuggler Ö Aspall. ☂ 13 **Facilities** Children welcome Children's menu Children's portions Garden Parking 🚐 (notice required)

MEDMENHAM
Map 5 SU88

The Dog and Badger NEW

Henley Rd SL7 2HE ☎ 01491 571362
e-mail: info@thedogandbadger.com
dir: *On A4155, midway between Marlow & Henley-on-Thames*

Surrounded by peaceful Chiltern countryside, this traditional inn between Marlow and Henley was built around 1390 as a meeting house in the grounds of Medmenham Abbey. Since then, visitors have included the noted Satanist James Dashwood and Nell Gwynn, who is said to have met certain admirers at the pub. Modern-day visitors can be assured of a friendly welcome, good real ales and a menu of home-cooked dishes such as slow-roast belly of pork with caramelised apple, creamy mash and cider jus, or duck and black bean stirfry.

Open 12-3 6-11 Closed: Sun eve **Bar Meals** L served Mon-Thu 12-2, Fri-Sat 12-2.30, Sun 12-3 (Sun 12-4 summer) D served Mon-Thu 6-9, Fri-Sat 6-10 Av main course £14 **Restaurant** L served Mon-Thu 12-2, Fri-Sat 12-2.30, Sun 12-3 (Sun 12-4 summer) D served Mon-Thu 6-9, Fri-Sat 6-10 Fixed menu price fr £5 ⊕ ENTERPRISE INNS ◼ Rebellion IPA, Fuller's London Pride. ☂ 9 **Facilities** ✿ Children welcome Children's portions Garden Parking Wi-fi 🚐 (notice required)

MENTMORE
Map 11 SP91

The Stag Inn

PICK OF THE PUBS

The Green LU7 0QF ☎ 01296 668423
e-mail: info@thestagmentmore.com
dir: *Telephone for directions*

High-quality service is the keynote at the imposing Stag Inn, which offers a distinctive flair in the treatment of modern British dishes. The pub stands in a picture-postcard village overlooking the huge Elizabethan-style stately home of Mentmore Towers, which was built in 1855 for Baron Amschel de Rothschild. The surrounding farmland supplies head chef Chris West with fresh seasonal produce for his popular menus. Typical of the starters are baked free-range duck egg with potato and herb hash; and the inn's own maple-smoked duck breast with celeriac coleslaw. Loin and confit leg of rabbit with fondant potato and white onion purée appeals as a main course. Familiar sweets, such as sticky toffee pudding, appear among lesser known ones; if in doubt, go for the assiette of five miniature desserts. The full menu is available in the bar and restaurant, as well as in the pub's lovely summer garden, although the kitchen is closed on Mondays.

Open 12-2.30 5-11 (Mon 5-9 Sat 12-11 Sun 12-10.30) Closed: Mon L (ex BHs) **Bar Meals** L served Tue-Fri 12-2.30, Sat all day, Sun 12-4.30 D served Tue-Fri 6-9.30, Sat all day Av main course £15 **Restaurant** L served Tue-Fri 12-2.30, Sat all day, Sun 12-4.30 D served Tue-Fri 6-9.30, Sat all day ⊕ CHARLES WELLS ◼ Bombardier, Young's Bitter. **Facilities** Garden Parking 🚐

PICK OF THE PUBS

The Old Queens Head

PENN Map 6 SU99

Hammersley Ln HP10 8EY
☎ 01494 813371
e-mail: info@oldqueensheadpenn.co.uk
web: www.oldqueensheadpenn.co.uk
dir: *B474 into School Rd, 500yds, left into Hammersley Ln*

Between the delightful villages of Penn and Tylers Green, this old pub has bags of character and atmosphere. It's one of five in the well-regarded Salisbury Pubs mini-empire in and around the Chilterns, all of which have entries in this guide.* The timber-built dining room dates from 1666 (word of the Great Fire of London clearly hadn't reached here) and although it has seen several additions since then, the cosy corners, undulating floors and real fires are reminders of its history. The owners have spent many hours at local auctions finding lovely old furniture and pictures in keeping with the age of the pub, whose warm heritage colours look good against the dark floorboards, flagstones and rugs. A sunny terrace overlooks the village church, and there's a large garden in which to eat and drink. The kitchen team has created a modern British menu with starters of twice-baked peppered goat's cheese soufflé with melba toast and apple and fig chutney; and pickled quail's egg with béarnaise sauce. Main course options are similarly appetising: slow-cooked spiced Buckinghamshire venison hotpot with sautéed curly kale, Savoy cabbage and bacon; pan-roast Scottish salmon fillet with creamy leek, new potato and pea fricassée, and chorizo oil; and roast squash, red onion, fennel and pearl barley crumble with Wookey Hole cheddar and walnut crust. For pudding, consider rhubarb and star anise meringue pie with raspberry sorbet bonbon, or caramelised banana bread-and-butter pudding with clotted cream. A well-considered wine list includes 22 by the glass and a separate pudding wine selection. Settle by the fire with a pint of Ruddles County or a mug of hot chocolate and marshmallows. Booking for meals may be required.

*Alford Arms, Hemel Hempstead, Hertfordshire: and in Buckinghamshire, The Swan Inn, Denham; The Royal Oak, Bovingdon Green; and The Black Horse, Fulmer

Open all day all wk 11-11 (Sun 12-10.30) Closed: 25-26 Dec **Bar Meals** L served Mon-Fri 12-2.30, Sat 12-3, Sun 12-4 D served Sun-Thu 6.30-9.30, Fri-Sat 6.30-10 Av main course £14.50 **Restaurant** L served Mon-Fri 12-2.30, Sat 12-3, Sun 12-4 D served Sun-Thu 6.30-9.30, Fri-Sat 6.30-10 Av 3 course à la carte fr £27 SALISBURY PUBS LTD Greene King Ruddles County & IPA, Guinness Aspall. 22 **Facilities** Children welcome Children's portions Garden Parking Wi-fi

MILTON KEYNES
Map 11 SP83

The Swan Inn

Broughton Rd, Milton Keynes Village MK10 9AH
☎ **01908 665240**
e-mail: info@theswan-mkvillage.co.uk
dir: *M1 junct 14 towards Milton Keynes. Pub off V11 or H7*

In the heart of the original Milton Keynes village, the beautiful 13th-century Swan Inn offers everything you could wish for from an ancient thatched pub. Sympathetically renovated, the interior is an eclectic mix of traditional charm and contemporary chic. It has flagstone floors, an open fire in the inglenook in winter keeps things cosy, and an orchard garden for those warmer days. The open-plan kitchen creates simple yet creative dishes such as ham hock terrine with spiced pear chutney, piccalilli dressing and toasted ciabatta, followed by slow-roasted pork belly with truffle mash and creamed wild mushroom, with banoffee crème brûlée and coconut shortbread for pudding. Booking for meals may be required.

Open all day all wk **Bar Meals** L served all wk 12-3 D served all wk 6-9.30 Av main course £12 **Restaurant** L served all wk 12-3 D served all wk 6-9.30 Av 3 course à la carte fr £22.50 ⊕ FRONT LINE INNS ◀ Wells Bombardier, Young's, Guest ales ♂ Symonds. ♚ 34 **Facilities** ♣ Children welcome Children's portions Garden Parking Wi-fi ➡ (notice required)

MOULSOE
Map 11 SP94

The Carrington Arms

Cranfield Rd MK16 0HB ☎ **01908 218050**
e-mail: enquiries@thecarringtonarms.co.uk
dir: *M1 junct 14, A509 to Newport Pagnell 100yds, turn right signed Moulsoe & Cranfield. Pub on right*

Dating from 1860, this Grade II listed building is set in the picturesque village of Moulsoe. The Dodman family took over the pub in 2008 and have created a 'Best of British' restaurant offering seasonal menus. Customers can choose their own cuts of meat, fish and seafood from a special counter. Typical choices might be venison with chestnut mash, curly kale and blackberry sauce; spicy bean and tomato casserole with garlic and rosemary ciabatta; or Bourbon-marinated steak. There's a summer beer and cider festival featuring local breweries and a barbecue. Booking for meals may be required.

Open all day all wk 12-11 **Bar Meals** food served all day **Restaurant** food served all day ⊕ FREE HOUSE ◀ Fuller's London Pride, Guest ales ♂ Aspall. ♚ 10 **Facilities** Children welcome Children's menu Garden Beer festival Parking Wi-fi ➡

OVING
Map 11 SP72

The Black Boy

Church Ln HP22 4HN ☎ **01296 641258**
dir: *4.6m N of Aylesbury*

Oliver Cromwell and his soldiers camped in The Black Boy's huge garden after sacking nearby Bolebec Castle during the Civil War. Today, the 16th-century pub is a rural oasis, with spectacular views over the Vale of Aylesbury to Stowe School and beyond. At lunch wash down a seafood platter to share, beer-battered fish with chunky chips and tartare sauce, or lamb and apricot casserole, with a pint of local Vale Best Bitter. Evening extras may include sea bass with lemon and herb sauce, and pan-fried duck with wild mushroom and red wine sauce. Good value set and Sunday lunch menus.

Open all wk 12-3 6-11 (Sat all day Sun 12-5) **Bar Meals** L served Mon-Sat 12-2, Sun 12-3 D served Mon-Thu 6.30-9, Fri-Sat 6-9.30 **Restaurant** L served Mon-Sat 12-2, Sun 12-3 D served Mon-Thu 6.30-9, Fri-Sat 6-9.30 ⊕ FREE HOUSE ◀ Vale Best Bitter, Sharp's Doom Bar, Guest ales ♂ Westons Old Rosie, Thatchers Gold. ♚ 10 **Facilities** ♣ Children welcome Children's menu Children's portions Garden Parking Wi-fi ➡

PENN
Map 6 SU99

The Old Queens Head
PICK OF THE PUBS

See Pick of the Pubs on page 61

PRESTON BISSETT
Map 11 SP62

The White Hart

Pound Ln MK18 4LX ☎ **01280 847969**
dir: *2.5m from A421*

A pretty 18th-century, thatched and timbered village pub with three unpretentious low-beamed rooms, log fires and a simple matchboarded bar front. Outside is a secluded garden and patio. Regular real ales include Hooky Bitter, The Rev. James and Doom Bar, while a small but considered seasonal menu offers steak-and-ale pie; slow-cooked belly of pork; pan-fried sea bass; roast vegetable lasagne; and Sunday roasts. Home-made bread-and-butter pudding, and apple and mixed nut crumble are characteristic desserts. A beer festival is held on Spring Bank Holiday. Booking for meals may be required.

Open 12-2.30 6-11 (Sat-Sun 12-11) Closed: Mon **Bar Meals** L served Tue-Sun 12-2.30 D served Tue-Sun 6-11 **Restaurant** L served Tue-Sun 12-2.30 D served Tue-Sun 6-10 ⊕ FREE HOUSE ◀ Hook Norton Hooky Bitter & Old Hooky, Timothy Taylor Landlord, Brains The Rev. James, St Austell Tribute, Sharp's Doom Bar. **Facilities** ♣ Children welcome Children's menu Children's portions Garden Beer festival Parking ➡

RADNAGE
Map 5 SU79

The Three Horseshoes Inn

Horseshoe Rd, Bennett End HP14 4EB ☎ **01494 483273**
e-mail: threehorseshoe@btconnect.com
dir: *From M40 junct 5, A40 towards High Wycombe, after unrestricted mileage sign turn left signed Radnage (Mudds Bank). 1.8m, 1st left into Bennett End Rd, inn on right*

When award-winning chef-patron Simon Crawshaw bought this beautiful old building in 2005, he knew it would be something special. Down a leafy lane, it is truly traditional – worn flagstones, blackened beams and original inglenook fireplace. On his modern English and European menus he typically offers terrine of foie gras with fig chutney and toasted brioche; seared sea bream with pak choi and crispy potatoes; and vanilla Décor crème brûlée. Enjoy Marlow's Rebellion ale in the bar or in the lovely garden. Booking for meals may be required.

Open 12-3 6-11 (Mon 6-11 Sat all day Sun 12-6) Closed: Sun eve, Mon L **Bar Meals** L served Tue-Sat 12-2.30, Sun 12-3 D served Mon-Sat 6-9 **Restaurant** L served Tue-Sat 12-2.30, Sun 12-3 D served Mon-Sat 6-9 ⊕ FREE HOUSE ◀ Rebellion. ♚ 12 **Facilities** Children welcome Children's portions Garden Parking Wi-fi ➡

SEER GREEN
Map 6 SU99

The Jolly Cricketers ⊚

24 Chalfont Rd HP9 2YG ☎ **01494 676308**
dir: *M40 junct 2, A355 signed Beaconsfield A40, Amersham. At Pyebush rdbt 1st exit, A40 signed Beaconsfield, Amersham, A355. At rdbt, A355 signed Amersham. Right into Longbottom Ln signed Seer Green. Left into Bottom Ln, right into Orchard Rd, left into Church Rd, right into Chalfont Rd*

In the heart of the picture-postcard village of Seer Green, Chris Lillitou and Amanda Baker's 19th-century, wisteria-clad free house appeals to all-comers: locals chatting over pints of Marlow's Rebellion IPA, quiz addicts on Sunday nights, live jazz fans, beer festival-goers, dog-walkers. Their signature dish is ale- and cider-braised ham with crispy poached egg, pineapple chutney and triple-cooked chips, served on locally crafted wooden boards. There's plenty more on the AA-Rosette menu, such as pan-fried stone bass with winter minestrone, cockles, clams and Tuscan olive oil, followed by a dessert of warm chocolate fondant with banana brittle and lemon curd ice cream. Booking for meals may be required.

Open Tue-Thu 12-11.30 (Mon 5-11.30 Fri-Sat 12-12 Sun 12-10.30) Closed: 2wks Jan, Mon until 5 **Bar Meals** L served Tue-Sat 12-2.30 D served Tue-Sat 6.30-9 Av main course £17 **Restaurant** L served Tue-Fri 12-2.30, Sat-Sun 12-3.30 D served Tue-Sat 6.30-9 Av 3 course à la carte fr £28 ⊕ FREE HOUSE ◀ Rebellion IPA, Fuller's London Pride, Chiltern Beechwood Bitter, Vale VPA ♂ Millwhites, Artisan bottle selection. ♚ 16 **Facilities** ♣ Children welcome Children's menu Children's portions Garden Beer festival Parking Wi-fi

PICK OF THE PUBS

The Frog

SKIRMETT   Map 5 SU79

RG9 6TG ☎ 01491 638996
e-mail: info@thefrogatskirmett.co.uk
web: www.thefrogatskirmett.co.uk
dir: *Exit A4155 at Mill End, pub in 3m*

The Hamble Brook flows behind this 18th-century coaching inn, while buzzards and red kites float on thermals above the wooded hills at the heart of the Chilterns Area of Outstanding Natural Beauty. In summer the garden is a relaxing place to be, perhaps resting after a ramble to the famous windmill on nearby Turville Hill. Winter warmth is guaranteed in the charming public bar where oak beams, bare floorboards and leather seating combine with colourful textiles to create a welcoming atmosphere. Where better to settle with a pint of Rebellion or Sharp's? The wine list, a combination of Old World and New, is definitely worth a look, and the range of Scottish and Irish whiskies is also attractive. Perhaps the time to indulge is during one of the pub's themed evenings with special dinner menus or live music – the diary is full of them from New Year's Eve onwards. Head chef and co-owner Jim Crowe has developed excellent relationships with his suppliers, resulting in superb fresh local produce to satisfy the most discerning of palates. Jim's cooking style is adventurous yet classic, with modern

takes on British and European dishes. So on the entrée list, alongside a prawn cocktail with Marie Rose dressing, you'll find a fried soft-shell crab with chilli, spring onion and mango salad. For main courses, you can go with the pie of the day served with mash and mushy peas, or try the roast guinea fowl breast stuffed with oxtail and served with garlic risotto, Grand Marnier sauce and confit leg. Vegetarians may come across linguine with wild mushrooms, shallots and artichoke hearts in a saffron cream sauce. Take your choice between two dining rooms, both appealing yet quite different from each other, with contemporary interior design that manages to highlight the historical nature of this lovely building.

Open 11.30-3 6-11 Closed: 25 Dec, Sun eve (Oct-Apr) **Bar Meals** L served all wk 12-2.30 D served all wk 6-9.30 **Restaurant** L served all wk 12-2.30 D served all wk 6-9.30 ⊕ FREE HOUSE
◨ Leaping Frog, Rebellion IPA, Sharp's Doom Bar, Wadworth Henry's Original IPA ♂ Thatchers. ♀ 15
Facilities Children welcome Children's menu Children's portions Family room
🐾 Garden Parking 🚌

PICK OF THE PUBS

The Bull & Butcher

TURVILLE Map 5 SU79

RG9 6QU ☎ 01491 638283
e-mail: info@thebullandbutcher.com
web: www.thebullandbutcher.com
dir: *M40 junct 5, follow Ibstone signs.
Right at T-junct. Pub 0.25m on left*

Built in 1550, this quintessentially
English pub received its first licence in
1617 after workmen building the nearby
church refused to continue without
refreshments. Originally known as the
'Bullen Butcher' – a reference to Henry
VIII and his second wife Anne Boleyn –
the name was later adapted to its
modern form. Even on your first visit,
you'll probably recognise The Bull &
Butcher, for Turville village and its
tenth-century church has played a
starring role in numerous film and
television productions, including *The
Vicar of Dibley* and *Midsomer Murders*.
Once inside, you'll soon feel at home in
the relaxed atmosphere of the Windmill
Lounge or the Well Bar, where a 50-foot
well discovered in 1999 now features as
a table. Original beams and large open
fires add to the pub's charm; there's
also a large garden and patio area, as
well as a function room that's perfect
for family or corporate occasions. So,
after an exhilarating walk amid the
glorious Chilterns scenery, drop down
from the Cobstone Windmill on Turville
Hill, immortalised in the film *Chitty
Chitty Bang Bang*, and unwind with a

pint and a plate of home-cooked food.
Pub favourites include Oxford pork
sausages with creamy mash and sticky
onion gravy; and beef and Guinness pie
with salt-roasted new potatoes and
seasonal greens. More adventurous
tastes might kick off with whole baked
camembert, rosemary and garlic, before
moving on to confit belly pork with Puy
lentil broth, apple and pea purée; or
Brixham fish of the day with thyme-
roasted new potatoes, fine beans and
caper butter sauce. Typical puds include
apple and winter berry crumble with
crème anglaise; and classic lemon tart
with raspberry sorbet. Booking for meals
may be required.

Open all day all wk Summer 12-11 (Sat
noon-1am) Winter 12-3 5.30-11 **Bar**

Meals L served Mon-Sat 12-2.30, Sun
12-3 D served Mon-Sat 6-9.30
Restaurant L served Mon-Sat 12-2.30,
Sun 12-3 D served Mon-Sat 6-9.30
⊕ BRAKSPEAR ◀ Bitter & Oxford Gold,
Guest ales Ö Symonds. ♇ 36
Facilities Children welcome Children's
menu ☘ Garden Parking Wi-fi
🚌 (notice required)

SKIRMETT   Map 5 SU79

The Frog

PICK OF THE PUBS

See Pick of the Pubs on page 63

TURVILLE   Map 5 SU79

The Bull & Butcher

PICK OF THE PUBS

See Pick of the Pubs on opposite page

WEST WYCOMBE   Map 5 SU89

The George and Dragon Hotel

PICK OF THE PUBS

High St HP14 3AB ☎ 01494 535340
e-mail: georgeanddragon@live.co.uk
dir: *On A40*

Visitors to the area will enjoy exploring West Wycombe Caves, and the stately houses at Cliveden and Hughenden. After a day's hard touring, a visit to this traditional coaching inn with 14th-century origins in a National Trust village will be nicely relaxing. It wasn't always the case – it was once a hideout for highwaymen stalking travellers between London and Oxford; indeed, one unfortunate guest robbed and murdered here is rumoured still to haunt its corridors. The hotel is reached through a cobbled archway and comprises a delightful jumble of whitewashed, timber-framed buildings. Reliable real ales include St Austell Tribute and Skinner's Smugglers. Also reliable is the varied menu, which offers freshly-prepared dishes cooked to order such as beef and ale pie; beer-battered haddock; a button mushroom, brie and cranberry filo parcel; and succulent rib-eye steaks.

Open all wk 12-12 (Fri-Sat noon-1am Sun 12-11.30) **Bar Meals** L served Mon-Sat 12-2.30, Sun 12-3 D served Mon-Thu 6-9, Fri-Sat 6-9.30 **Restaurant** L served Mon-Sat 12-2.30, Sun 12-3 D served Mon-Thu 6-9, Fri-Sat 6-9.30 ⊕ ENTERPRISE INNS ◀ St Austell Tribute, Skinner's Smugglers Ale. ♈ 9 **Facilities** ❧ Children welcome Play area Family room Garden Parking Wi-fi ▥

WHEELER END   Map 5 SU89

The Chequers Inn

Bullocks Farm Ln HP14 3NH ☎ 01494 883070
e-mail: chequersinn2@btconnect.com
dir: *4m N of Marlow*

This picturesque 17th-century inn, with its low-beamed ceilings, roaring winter fires and two attractive beer gardens, is ideally located for walkers on the edge of Wheeler End Common (families and dogs are welcome). Lunchtime dishes include pub favourites such as ham, egg and chips or bangers and mash with gravy. Typical evening choices are melting goat's cheese salad with sun blushed tomato and beetroot dressing followed by pan-fried fillet of sea bream with chilli and lime butter,

sautéed new potatoes and carrot julienne. There's a beer festival at Whitsun.

Open 12-3 6-11 (Sun 12-6 winter) Closed: Sun eve, Mon L **Bar Meals** L served Tue-Sat 12-2, Sun 12-3.30 D served Tue-Thu & Sat 6-9, Fri 6-9.30 **Restaurant** L served Tue-Sat 12-2, Sun 12-3.30 D served Tue-Thu & Sat 6-9, Fri 6-9.30 ⊕ FULLER'S ◀ London Pride & ESB, Guest ale ⚬ Aspall. ♈ 12 **Facilities** ❧ Children welcome Children's menu Children's portions Garden Beer festival Parking Wi-fi ▥ (notice required)

WOOBURN COMMON   Map 6 SU98

Chequers Inn ★★★ HL ◉

PICK OF THE PUBS

Kiln Ln HP10 0JQ ☎ 01628 529575
e-mail: info@chequers-inn.com
dir: *M40 junct 2, A40 through Beaconsfield towards High Wycombe. Left into Broad Ln, signed Taplow/Burnham/Wooburn Common. 2m to pub*

Tucked away in Buckinghamshire's neck of the picturesque Thames Valley, this 17th-century inn is an absolute charmer; so you may wish to book one of the 17 beautifully appointed bedrooms. The inn has been owned and run by the same family for over 35 years, ensuring a friendly, relaxed and welcoming atmosphere. Oak posts and beams, flagstone floors and a wonderful open fireplace blackened by a million blazing logs characterise the pub's interior. The lounge has leather sofas and low tables. The extensive bar menu has a tempting list of small plates, as well as pub staples like chilli con carne and fishcakes. Dishes served in the attractively decorated restaurant include honey-roast root vegetable pithivier with chestnut cappuccino and herb salad; tea-smoked duck with sweetcorn custard, baby chard and pomegranate dressing; and salmon and dill ravioli with leek compôte and a sweet pepper coulis. Outside, a small enclosed patio offers alfresco dining. Booking for meals may be required.

Open all day all wk 12-12 **Bar Meals** L served Mon-Fri 12-2.30, Sat 12-10, Sun 12-9.30 D served Mon-Thu 6-9.30, Fri 6-10, Sat 12-10, Sun 12-9.30 Av main course £9.95-£10.95 **Restaurant** L served all wk 12-2.30 D served all wk 7-9.30 Fixed menu price fr £17.95 Av 3 course à la carte fr £28.85 ⊕ FREE HOUSE ◀ Rebellion Smuggler, Morland Old Speckled Hen ⚬ Westons Stowford Press. ♈ 14 **Facilities** Children welcome Children's menu Children's portions Garden Parking Wi-fi **Rooms** 17

CAMBRIDGESHIRE

BABRAHAM   Map 12 TL55

The George Inn at Babraham

PICK OF THE PUBS

High St CB2 4AG ☎ 01223 833800
e-mail: info@thegeorgebabraham.co.uk
dir: *In High St, just off A11/A505 & A1307*

Just four miles from Cambridge, this 18th-century coaching inn occupies an enviable position in the picturesque village of Babraham at the county's rural heart. Exposed beams and brickwork characterise most areas, lending a friendly and relaxed air to the place. A mix of leather sofas and solid oak furniture add to the appeal, and the dining room has been refurbished. Devastated by fire in 2004, the pub has been restored to its former glory and the new kitchen and three restaurant areas have helped to build its reputation as a destination dining venue serving well-kept Greene King beers and enjoyable home-cooked food. A typical menu might offer sticky pork belly slice, beef lasagne, or home-made salmon and crab fishcakes. An attractive rear patio with heaters and parasols leads to a garden, and special culinary and music events are hosted throughout the year.

Open all day all wk 12-11 (Sun 12-5) **Bar Meals** L served all wk 12-2 D served Mon-Sat 5.30-9 Av main course £8.95 **Restaurant** L served Mon-Fri 12-2, Sat-Sun 12-3 D served Mon-Sat 5.30-9 Av 3 course à la carte fr £16.95 ⊕ GREENE KING ◀ IPA, Morland Old Speckled Hen, Guest ale ⚬ Aspall. ♈ 8 **Facilities** Children welcome Children's menu Children's portions Garden Parking Wi-fi ▥

BARRINGTON   Map 12 TL34

The Royal Oak

31 West Green CB22 7RZ ☎ 01223 870791
e-mail: info@royaloakbarrington.co.uk
dir: *From Barton off M11, S of Cambridge*

One of the oldest thatched and timbered pubs in England, this rambling 16th-century building overlooks a 30-acre village green. Much has changed in last couple of years – new management, new chefs, new menu and a new, contemporary finish to the interior. The value-for-money menu lists the classic dishes for which the pub has long been known, such as pie of the day, and a tempting carte with pan-roasted duck breast; and herb-crusted North Atlantic baked cod. Roast beef, lamb and pork on Sundays could be accompanied by a Potton Brewery or Adnams pint. Booking for meals may be required.

Open all wk 12-3 6-11 (Sun 12-11) **Bar Meals** L served all wk 12-3 D served all wk 6-9.30 Av main course £15 **Restaurant** L served all wk 12-3 D served Mon-Sat 6-9.30, Sun 7-9 Av 3 course à la carte fr £25 ⊕ FREE HOUSE ◀ Potton Shannon IPA, Young's Bitter, Morland Original, Adnams. ♈ 8 **Facilities** ❧ Children welcome Children's menu Children's portions Garden Parking Wi-fi ▥ (notice required)

The Crown Inn

PICK OF THE PUBS

Bridge Rd PE28 3AY ☎ 01487 824428
e-mail: info@thecrowninnrestaurant.co.uk
dir: *A141 from Huntingdon towards Warboys. Left to Broughton*

In the mid-19th century, this picturesque village inn incorporated a saddler's shop, thatched stables and piggeries. The livestock has long gone, and today it focuses on being a popular village pub and restaurant at the heart of a thriving local community. The bar offers real ales from local breweries, and you'll also find Aspall cider. The restaurant combines a traditional pub look with contemporary design and it's here you'll be able to eat modern European dishes cooked using the best sustainable fish caught by day boats, the highest quality meats, and excellent seasonal vegetables. Menus change regularly, so when you visit you may find one offering starters of seafood terrine or seared pigeon breast. Typical main courses are roast cod on a bed of sautéed celeriac, or confit duck leg with rissolé potatoes. Round off with cappuccino and hazelnut praline gâteau.

Open all wk Mon-Sat 11.30-3 6.30-11 (Sun 11.30-8) **Bar Meals** L served Mon-Sat 12-2.15, Sun 12-3.30 D served Mon-Sat 6.30-9.15 **Restaurant** L served Mon-Sat 12-2.15, Sun 12-3.30 D served Mon-Sat 6.30-9.15 ⊕ FREE HOUSE ◀ Nethergate Sweeney Todd, Timothy Taylor Landlord, Adnams Southwold Bitter, Guest ales Ò Aspall. ♟ 10 **Facilities** ❄ Children welcome Children's menu Children's portions Play area Garden Parking

The Anchor

PICK OF THE PUBS

Silver St CB3 9EL ☎ 01223 353554
e-mail: 7614@greeneking.co.uk
dir: *Telephone for directions*

Situated at the end of the medieval lane that borders Queens' College in the heart of the University city, this attractive waterside pub appeals to students and visitors alike. Hard by the bridge over the River Cam, in fine weather the riverside patio is an ideal spot for enjoying one of a range of good ales, including guest beers, while watching the activities on the water. The more adventurous can hire a punt for a leisurely trip to Grantchester (of Rupert Brooke and Jeffrey Archer fame), and on return sample a choice of hearty meals from a range that includes lasagne, home-made pie, and roast beef.

Open all wk Mon-Thu & Sun 11-11 (Fri-Sat 11am-mdnt) **Bar Meals** L served all wk 11-10 food served all day ⊕ GREENE KING ◀ IPA, Abbot Ale & St Edmunds, Morland Old Speckled Hen, Guest ales Ò Aspall. ♟ 12 **Facilities** Children welcome Children's menu

Cambridge Blue

PICK OF THE PUBS

85 Gwydir St CB1 2LG ☎ 01223 471680
dir: *In city centre. Access by car to Gwydir St from Mill Rd only (no access by car from Norfolk St). Gwydir St parking available*

A friendly 1860s backstreet pub, built to serve the terrace that housed railway workers, with an unexpected large sun trap garden and an amazing range of beers, from 200 bottled beers from around the world to a mind-boggling choice of 14 real ales from micro-breweries on handpump in the taproom – try a pint of Oakham Inferno or Woodforde's Wherry. Inside are two real fires, lots of memorabilia and a lively, buzzy vibe. Good-value pub grub made on the premises comes in the form of steak-and-kidney pie; fish pie; sausages and mash; a daily curry; and a range of filled ciabatta sandwiches and jacket potatoes (plus there are always vegetarian options). Don't miss the February, June and October beer festivals.

Open all day all wk Mon-Sat 12-11 (Sun 12-10.30) **Bar Meals** L served Mon-Sat 12-10, Sun 12-9 food served all day ⊕ FREE HOUSE ◀ Woodforde's Wherry, Oakham Inferno, Guest ales Ò Pickled Pig, Thatchers. ♟ 8 **Facilities** ❄ Children welcome Children's portions Family room Garden Beer festival Wi-fi

Free Press

Prospect Row CB1 1DU ☎ 01223 368337
e-mail: craig.bickley@ntlworld.com
dir: *Telephone for directions*

A pub for over 120 years, the Free Press gets its name from when part of it was a printing press which circulated a free Cambridge newspaper. Now a haunt for students, academics, locals and visitors, this atmospheric and picturesque backstreet pub near the city centre has open fires and a beautiful walled garden – but no music, mobile phones or gaming machines. Punters are attracted by first-rate real ales and great home-made food such as toasted ciabattas; seafood platter; lamb's liver and bacon with bubble-and-squeak and gravy.

Open all wk 12-2.30 6-11 (Fri-Sat 12-11 Sun 12-3 7-10.30) Closed: 25-26 Dec, 1 Jan **Bar Meals** L served Mon-Fri 12-2, Sat-Sun 12-2.30 D served Mon-Fri 6-9, Sun 7-9 ⊕ GREENE KING ◀ IPA & Abbot Ale, Hardys & Hansons Dark Mild, Guest ales Ò Westons Stowford Press, Aspall. ♟ 10 **Facilities** ❄ Children welcome Children's portions Garden ▭

The Old Spring

1 Ferry Path CB4 1HB ☎ 01223 357228
e-mail: theoldspring@hotmail.co.uk
dir: *Just off Chesterton Rd, (A1303) in city centre, near Midsummer Common*

You'll find this bustling neighbourhood pub in the leafy suburb of De Freville, just a short stroll from the River Cam and its many boatyards, which makes its splendid decked patio popular as a post-workout refreshment spot

for rowers. The bright and airy interior offers rug-covered wood floors, comfy sofas and large family tables. Sip a pint of Abbot Ale, one of several real ales on tap, or one of 20 wines by the glass while choosing from the array of freshly prepared food, perhaps pan-fried gnocchi with pesto; a home-made lamb burger, coleslaw and straw fries; or warm goat's cheese and roasted sweet potato salad.

Open all day all wk 11.30-11 (Sun 12-10.30) **Bar Meals** L served Mon-Fri 12-2.30, Sat-Sun 12-4 D served Mon-Sun 6-9.30 Av main course £9-£14 ⊕ GREENE KING ◀ IPA & Abbot Ale, Hardys & Hansons Olde Trip, Morland Old Speckled Hen, Guest ales Ò Aspall. ♟ 20 **Facilities** Children welcome Children's menu Children's portions Garden Parking Wi-fi

The Punter

3 Pound Hill CB3 0AE ☎ 01223 363322
e-mail: thepunter@hotmail.co.uk
dir: *Telephone for directions*

This beautifully renovated coaching house, with its eclectic mix of pine furniture and relaxed ambience, is just two minutes' walk from the city centre. Popular with visitors, locals and students alike, drinkers can sit alongside diners and enjoy well-priced rustic food. Serving bar snacks, a three-course set menu and a daily-changing seasonal menu, dishes might include braised pig cheeks with Jerusalem artichoke purée and hazelnuts; guinea fowl, truffled pomme purée with spinach and pickled mushroom; and apple tarte Tatin with ginger mascarpone. In the delightful courtyard garden pots of home-grown produce are sold. Booking for meals may be required.

Open all day all wk Closed: 25 Dec **Bar Meals** L served Mon-Fri 12-10, Sat-Sun all day Av main course £13.50 food served all day **Restaurant** L served Mon-Fri 12-3, Sat-Sun all day D served Mon-Fri 6-10, Sat-Sun all day Fixed menu price fr £25 Av 3 course à la carte fr £26.40 ⊕ PUNCH TAVERNS ◀ Adnams Explorer, Broadside Ò Aspall. **Facilities** ❄ Children welcome Children's portions Garden Wi-fi

The Black Horse **NEW**

35 Park St CB23 8DA ☎ 01954 782600
e-mail: blackhorse.info@btinternet.com
dir: *A14 junct 30, follow signs for Dry Drayton. In village turn right to pub. Signed*

Just five miles from Cambridge, The Black Horse has been at the heart of this quiet village for more than 300 years. Gary and Denise Glover took the keys of this lovely free house in 2011 and chef Marcello Silveira has already built a reputation for notable food. Much as local ales are showcased in the bar, local suppliers dominate the menu in the restaurant. A starter of pan-seared pigeon breast, black pudding and game jus might be followed by Aldeburgh stone bass with green lentils, spinach and mussel sauce. The pub holds an annual beer festival over

Save on hotels. Book at theAA.com/hotel

CAMBRIDGESHIRE 67 ENGLAND

St George's Day weekend. Booking for meals may be required.

Open all day 12-3 6-11 (Sun 12-4) Closed: Mon **Bar Meals** L served Tue-Sun 12-2 Av main course £9 **Restaurant** L served Tue-Sun 12-2.30 D served Tue-Sat 6-9.30 Fixed menu price fr £12 Av 3 course à la carte fr £35 ⊕ FREE HOUSE ◖ Black Horse, Milton Pegasus, Glebe Farm Gladiator, Guest ale ⊘ Aspall. **Facilities** ✿ Children welcome Children's portions Garden Beer festival Parking Wi-fi

---

DUXFORD   Map 12 TL44

The John Barleycorn
PICK OF THE PUBS

3 Moorfield Rd CB2 4PP ☎ 01223 832699
e-mail: info@johnbarleycorn.co.uk
dir: Exit A505 into Duxford

If you need somewhere to relax after a day's racing at Newmarket, head for The John Barleycorn. During World War II, it was a favourite watering hole for the brave young airmen of Douglas Bader's Duxford Wing. Step through the door of the thatched and whitewashed 17th-century former coach house into the low-beamed and softly lit bar. There's a rustic mix of country furniture, a large brick fireplace and an old tiled floor, with cushioned painted pews and hop-adorned beams. It's a cosy, comfortable and relaxing place in which to enjoy a hearty home-cooked meal, washed down with a refreshing pint of Greene King IPA or Ruddles County. You can nibble on a bowl of olives and roasted almonds while making your menu selections: seared scallops wrapped in Parma ham, perhaps, followed by confit duck leg. Summer alfresco eating can be enjoyed on the flower-festooned rear patio. Booking for meals may be required.

Open all day all wk **Bar Meals** L served all wk D served all wk Av main course £10.95 food served all day **Restaurant** Av 3 course à la carte fr £25 food served all day ⊕ FREE HOUSE/REDCOMB PUBS LTD ◖ Greene King IPA, Abbot Ale, Ruddles Best & Ruddles County, Morland Old Speckled Hen. ☗ 12 **Facilities** Children welcome Children's menu Children's portions Play area Garden Parking Wi-fi ⛍ (notice required)

ELSWORTH   Map 12 TL36

The George & Dragon
41 Boxworth Rd CB3 8JQ ☎ 01954 267236
dir: SE of A14 between Cambridge & Huntingdon

Set in a pretty village just outside Cambridge, this pub offers a friendly, relaxed environment, great beers and a wide range of satisfying food for locals and visitors alike. Aberdeen Angus steaks and fish fresh from Lowestoft are a draw here on the seasonal menu. Look out for wedges of breaded brie; hot potted crab with chilli; chicken and wild mushroom Stroganoff; and home-made fish pie. Friday night is steak night, Wednesday night is fish and chip supper, and there are special menus for occasions such as Valentine's Day, St George's Day and Mother's Day.

Open all wk 11-2.30 6-11 (all day Sun Mar-Dec) **Bar Meals** L served Mon-Sat 12-2, Sun 12-8.30 D served Mon-Sat 6-9.30, Sun 12-8.30 **Restaurant** L served Mon-Sat 12-2, Sun 12-8.30 D served Mon-Sat 6-9.30, Sun 12-8.30 ⊕ FREE HOUSE ◖ Greene King IPA, Morland Old Speckled Hen, Guest ales ⊘ Aspall. ☗ 13 **Facilities** Children welcome Children's menu Children's portions Garden Parking ⛍

ELTON   Map 12 TL09

The Black Horse
PICK OF THE PUBS

14 Overend PE8 6RU ☎ 01832 280240 & 280875
e-mail: theblackhorseelton@gmail.com
dir: Off A605 (Peterborough to Northampton road)

Antique furnishings and open log fires crank up the old-world charm in this 17th-century inn, while the delightful one-acre rear garden overlooks Elton's famous church and rolling open countryside. The real ales include Everards Tiger, seasonal brews, and Barnwell Bitter, which is brewed locally. The superb selection of food ranges from bar snacks to a full à la carte. Among the 'snacks' are sandwiches, filled baguettes, jacket potatoes, a home-made pie of the day, and seasonal salads. Or you might start with baked scallops with endives in a daube sauce; or cauliflower soup with croûtons. Typical main courses include grilled chicken breast with tarragon sauce and mash; lamb neck fillet with chunky vegetables and dried fruit crumble; and grilled Dingley Dell pork chop with spicy home-made sausage, aubergine and apples.

Open all day Mon-Thu 12-10 (Fri-Sat 12-11 Sun 12-9) ⊕ FREE HOUSE ◖ Everards Tiger, Digfield Barnwell Bitter, Oakham JHB. **Facilities** Children welcome Children's menu Play area Family room Garden Parking

---

The Crown Inn ★★★★★ INN
PICK OF THE PUBS

See Pick of the Pubs on page 68

ELY   Map 12 TL58

The Anchor Inn ★★★★ RR ◉
PICK OF THE PUBS

Sutton Gault CB6 2BD ☎ 01353 778537
e-mail: anchorinn@popmail.bta.com
dir: From A14, B1050 to Earith, take B1381 to Sutton. Sutton Gault on left

The Anchor is ideally situated for exploring East Anglia, with the cathedral city of Ely and Cambridge both within easy reach. In 1630 the Earl of Bedford engaged the Dutch engineer Cornelius Vermuyden to drain the surrounding lawless and disease-ridden fens for agricultural use; The Anchor was constructed on the bank of the New Bedford River to accommodate Vermuyden's workforce. Today, scrubbed pine tables on gently

undulating tiled floors, antique prints and winter log fires lend character to the cosy, intimate atmosphere of this family-run free house. Summer meals can be enjoyed on the terrace overlooking the river. Modern British cuisine is the strength here, with an emphasis on seasonal and traditional ingredients. Smoked salmon cheesecake with tomato and roast pepper essence makes a great starter, which could be followed by beef stew and dumplings with braised red cabbage. Desserts may include Key lime pie with gin and tonic sorbet. Accommodation is available. Booking for meals may be required.

Open Mon-Fri 12-2.30 7-10.30 (Sat 12-3 6.30-11 Sun 12-4 6.30-10) Closed: 25-26 Dec eve **Restaurant** L served Mon-Sat 12-2, Sun 12-2.30 D served Mon-Fri 7-9, Sat 6.30-9.30, Sun 6.30-8.30 Av 3 course à la carte fr £25 ⊕ FREE HOUSE ◖ Humpty Dumpty Little Sharpie, City of Cambridge Hobson's Choice. ☗ 12 **Facilities** Children welcome Children's portions Garden Parking Wi-fi ⛍ (notice required) **Rooms** 4

FEN DITTON   Map 12 TL46

Ancient Shepherds
PICK OF THE PUBS

High St CB5 8ST ☎ 01223 293280
e-mail: ancientshepherds@hotmail.co.uk
dir: From A14 take B1047 signed Cambridge/Airport

Easily recognised by its whitewashed walls and hanging baskets in summer, this heavily beamed pub was named after the ancient order of Shepherds who once met here; it was built originally as three cottages in 1540. Tucked away in a peaceful riverside village three miles from Cambridge it is a popular dining destination sway from the bustle of the city. The two bars, a lounge and a dining room all boast inglenook fireplaces and the pub is delightfully free of music, darts and pool. The menus range from filled baguettes, home-made soup, ploughman's, and ham, egg and chips for lunch, to specials such as smoked haddock and spring onion fishcakes, and home-made beef and Guinness pie. In the restaurant follow a plate of Bottisham smoked salmon, with braised lamb shank with minted red wine and rosemary gravy, and sticky toffee pudding for dessert. Booking for meals may be required.

Open 12-2.30 6-11 Closed: 25-26 Dec, 1 Jan, Sun eve, Mon eve **Bar Meals** L served all wk 12-2 Av main course £9.95 **Restaurant** L served all wk 12-2 D served Tue-Sat 6.30-9 Av 3 course à la carte fr £25 ⊕ PUNCH TAVERNS ◖ Adnams Southwold Bitter, Greene King IPA, Fuller's London Pride ⊘ Aspall. ☗ 8 **Facilities** Children welcome Children's portions Garden Parking

PICK OF THE PUBS

The Crown Inn ★★★★★ INN

ELTON   Map 12 TL09

8 Duck St PE8 6RQ ☎ 01832 280232
e-mail: inncrown@googlemail.com
web: www.thecrowninn.org
dir: *A1(M) junct 17, W on A605 signed Oundle/Northampton. In 3.5m right to Elton, 0.9m left signed Nassington. Inn 0.3m on right*

Tucked away behind a towering chestnut tree in the heart of the unspoilt village of Elton, this 17th-century thatched stone inn simply oozes with character and charm. Click open the door latch to reveal oak beams and natural stone aplenty, with soothing pastel shades and a crackling winter fire in the inglenook. Golden Crown Bitter – locally brewed by the Tydd Steam brewery – takes pole position amongst the real ales at the bar, supported by Old Rosie and Glebe Farm ciders. Chef-patron Marcus Lamb places great emphasis on the food, with the finest local ingredients forming the basis for the freshly prepared dishes from his kitchen. Bar lunches feature sandwiches, baguettes and omelettes, as well as pub favourites such as home-cooked glazed ham with fried duck egg and hand-cut chips. In the evening, pheasant and chestnut terrine served with chutney and crusty bread might herald roast Aylesbury duck with dauphinoise potatoes, braised red cabbage and port wine sauce; or wild mushroom and parmesan tart with dressed leaves and mushroom cream sauce. Warm fig and frangipane tart with mascarpone cream is a typical dessert. With five individually furnished en suite bedrooms, this is an ideal base for exploring the surrounding area. Local attractions include Elton Hall and the River Nene, thought to have inspired Kenneth Graham's classic *The Wind in the Willows*. Oundle, Stamford and Peterborough are also within easy reach, whilst children will enjoy the Nene Valley Railway Museum and Sacrewell Farm and Country Centre. Annual treats include a May Day hog roast and a summer beer festival. Booking for meals may be required.

Open all wk 12-11 (Mon 5-11 (BH 12-11)) Closed: 1-7 Jan (Restaurant) **Bar Meals** L

served Tue-Sun 12-2 D served Mon-Sat 6.30-8.45 Av main course £13 **Restaurant** L served Tue-Sun 12-2 D served Tue-Sat 6.30-8.45 Av 3 course à la carte fr £25 ⊕ FREE HOUSE ◖ Tydd Steam Golden Crown Bitter, Greene King IPA, Black Sheep, Digfield, Oakham, Adnams ♂ Westons Old Rosie, Glebe Farm. ♥ 8 **Facilities** Children welcome Children's menu Children's portions ☺ Beer festival Parking Wi-fi 🚌 (notice required) **Rooms** 5

FENSTANTON   Map 12 TL36

King William IV

High St PE28 9JF ☎ 01480 462467
e-mail: kingwilliamfenstanton@btconnect.com
dir: Off A14 junct 27 between Cambridge & Huntingdon

This rambling 17th-century village pub features oak beams, old brickwork and a wonderful central fireplace. Lunchtime offerings include a range of hot and cold sandwiches but also light bites such as roast confit duck leg with an oriental salad, or parmesan, leek and thyme tart with red onion jam. Diners looking for something more substantial can choose from classic grilled dishes such as spatchcock chicken, or enjoy Moroccan spiced stuffed chicken leg or pan-roasted mackerel. There is live music on Wednesday evenings and twice monthly at Sunday lunchtimes.

Open all wk Mon-Thu 12-3 5-11 (Fri-Sun all day) **Bar Meals** L served all wk 12-2.30 D served Mon-Wed 6-9, Thu-Sat 5.30-9.30 **Restaurant** L served all wk 12-2.30 D served Mon-Wed 6-9, Thu-Sat 5.30-9.30 ⊕ GREENE KING ◀ IPA, Guest ales Ö Aspall. ♟ 13 **Facilities** ❖ Children welcome Children's portions Garden Parking Wi-fi ▭ (notice required)

FORDHAM   Map 12 TL67

White Pheasant

PICK OF THE PUBS

CB7 5LQ ☎ 01638 720414
e-mail: chef@whitepheasant.com
dir: From Newmarket A142 to Ely, approx 5m to Fordham. Pub on left in village

This 18th-century building stands in a fenland village between Ely and Newmarket. In recent years its considerable appeal has been subtly enhanced by improvements that preserve its period charm. You can enjoy locally brewed ale, a glass of wine, home-made lemonade or strawberryade while perusing the menus. Food is taken seriously here, with quality, presentation and flavour taking top priority, using produce sourced as locally as possible. Starters could be free-range chicken terrine with cranberry and chervil; crispy whitebait with garlic salt, lemon and tartare sauce. Following on with pan-fried Suffolk-reared beef fillet, wild mushrooms and red wine with thick-cut chips; roasted Gressingham duck breast, braised red cabbage with rapeseed oil mash; and buffalo mozzarella, plum tomato and parmesan gratin tart. Honey and lavender pannacotta with white chocolate, honeycomb and strawberries is among the desserts. Booking for meals may be required.

Open 12-3 6-11 (Sun 12-4) Closed: 26-29 Dec, 1 Jan, Sun eve ⊕ FREE HOUSE ◀ Brandon Rusty Bucket, Nethergate Ö Aspall. **Facilities** ❖ Children welcome Children's portions Garden Parking

FOWLMERE   Map 12 TL44

The Chequers

High St SG8 7SR ☎ 01763 208369
e-mail: info@thechequersfowlmere.co.uk
web: www.thechequersfowlmere.co.uk
dir: From M11, A505, 2nd right to Fowlmere. 8m S of Cambridge, 4m E of Royston

The pub's sign – blue and red chequers – honours the British and American squadrons based nearby during World War II, though the pub dates from the 16th century and Samuel Pepys was a visitor in 1660. These days The Chequers is known for its imaginative dishes made from local produce, which are served in the galleried restaurant, conservatory, bar or attractive garden. Their wide-ranging menu might include a starter of Louisiana crab cakes with celeriac remoulade, and mains of pan-fried pork loin escalopes served on potato rösti with stir-fried cabbage and pancetta, or featherblade of beef braised in a Portobello mushroom, red wine and thyme sauce.

Open all wk 12-3 6-11 (Sun 12-4 7-10) Closed: 25 Dec, 26 Dec eve & 1 Jan eve **Bar Meals** L served Mon-Sat 12-2, Sun 12-2.30 D served Mon-Sat 6.30-9.30, Sun 7-9 **Restaurant** L served Mon-Sat 12-2, Sun 12-2.30 D served Mon-Sat 6.30-9.30, Sun 7-9 ⊕ FREE HOUSE ◀ Sharp's Doom Bar, Adnams Ö Aspall. ♟ 19 **Facilities** Children welcome Garden Parking Wi-fi

GRANTCHESTER   Map 12 TL45

The Rupert Brooke ◉

2 Broadway CB3 9NQ ☎ 01223 840295
e-mail: info@therupertbrooke.com
dir: M11 junct 12, follow Grantchester signs

Named after the World War I poet who lived nearby, this inn sits only five minutes from the centre of Cambridge in an idyllic location overlooking the famous Grantchester meadows, which inspired the Pink Floyd song of the same name. Inside, you'll find timber beams and winter log fires, with relaxing sofas and tub chairs, plus a good selection of real ales. Watch the chefs at work in the theatre-style kitchen, creating their AA Rosette-awarded dishes made with local, seasonal produce – moules marinière; pan-fried beef medallions with roast polenta, braised red cabbage and red wine jus; and white and milk chocolate pannacotta, for example.

Open all day all wk Closed: 25 Dec **Bar Meals** L served Mon-Fri 12-3, Sat 12-4, Sun 12-8 D served Mon-Thu 6-9, Fri-Sat 6-9.30, Sun 12-8 **Restaurant** L served Mon-Fri

12-3, Sat 12-4, Sun 12-8 D served Mon-Thu 6-9, Fri-Sat 6-9.30, Sun 12-8 ⊕ ENTERPRISE INNS ◀ Woodforde's Wherry, Sharp's Doom Bar, Flowers IPA Ö Westons Stowford Press. ♟ 10 **Facilities** ❖ Children welcome Children's menu Children's portions Garden Parking Wi-fi ▭ (notice required)

GREAT CHISHILL   Map 12 TL43

The Pheasant

24 Heydon Rd SG8 8SR ☎ 01763 838535
dir: Off B1039 between Royston & Saffron Walden

Stunning views and roaring log fires characterise this traditional, beamed village free house, where Nethergate and Woodforde's are a couple of the real ale choices. There are no gaming machines or piped music to disturb the friendly, sociable bar, and children under 14 are not allowed in. In summer, bird song holds sway in the idyllic pub garden. Freshly made sandwiches come complete with chips and salad garnish, or there is a deal to include home-made soup as well. Home-made dishes like four-rib rack of lamb; calves' liver and bacon; and wild mushroom and tarragon linguine cater for larger appetites.

Open all wk 12-3 6-11 (Sat-Sun all day) **Bar Meals** L served all wk 12-2 D served all wk 6-9.30 Av main course £12 **Restaurant** L served all wk 12-2 D served all wk 6-9.30 Av 3 course à la carte fr £25 ⊕ FREE HOUSE ◀ Fuller's London Pride, Woodforde's Wherry, Nethergate Ö Westons Stowford Press. ♟ 8 **Facilities** ❖ Garden Parking Wi-fi ▭ (notice required)

HEMINGFORD GREY   Map 12 TL27

The Cock Pub and Restaurant

PICK OF THE PUBS

See Pick of the Pubs on page 70

HILDERSHAM   Map 12 TL54

The Pear Tree Inn

High St CB21 6BU ☎ 01223 891680
e-mail: peartreeinn@btconnect.com
dir: 5m E of Cambridge, take A1307 to Haverhill, turn left to Hildersham

This has been a village pub for more than 200 years but became a free house in 2011 and now offers several real ales. Standing opposite the village green and close to a Roman road, the present building took over the Pear Tree name in the 19th century, and there's a picture of the former thatched pub in the bar. Home-cooked food could include wholetail Whitby scampi; sweet potato and chickpea curry; pie of the day; sirloin or rump steak; and lamb's liver in onion gravy. Try Belgian chocolate pudding for dessert. There are excellent walks from the pub.

Open 6.30-11 (Fri 6-11 Sun 12-2.30 7-10.30) Closed: Mon & Tue **Bar Meals** L served Sun 12-2.30 D served Wed-Sat 6.30-9.30, Sun 7-9 ⊕ FREE HOUSE ◀ Adnams Southwold Bitter, Broadside Ö Aspall. **Facilities** ❖ Children welcome Children's menu Children's portions Garden Parking

PICK OF THE PUBS

The Cock Pub and Restaurant

HEMINGFORD GREY Map 12 TL27

47 High St PE28 9BJ ☎ 01480 463609
e-mail: cock@cambscuisine.com
web: www.thecockhemingford.co.uk
dir: *Between A14 juncts 25 & 26 follow village signs*

Weary, hungry and stuck in traffic on the A14 near Huntingdon, then shun the services and follow signs for Hemingford Grey to find The Cock, a pretty 17th-century pub dozing on the main street in this idyllic village of thatched, timbered and brick cottages. It's a world away from the A14 throng, although just a mile away, and you can relax with peaceful views across the willow-bordered Great Ouse river. Other than the peaceful location, the detour is well worth taking as the food on offer is excellent – the set lunch menu is a steal. The stylishly revamped interior comprises a contemporary bar for drinks only, and a restaurant with bare boards, dark or white-painted beams, wood-burning stoves, and church candles on an eclectic mix of old dining tables. Cooking is modern British, with the occasional foray further afield, and fresh local produce is used in preparing the short, imaginative carte, while daily deliveries of fresh fish dictate the chalkboard menu choice, perhaps seared scallops with celeriac purée and

chorizo; and grey mullet with braised Puy lentils, Savoy cabbage and salsa verde. A typical meal might kick off with coarse pork and herb terrine with honeyed figs and pork crackling. Follow with steamed game suet pudding with bacon and gravy; beef Wellington with dauphinois, roasted root vegetables and port sauce; or sausages (made by the owner) and mash; then round off with chocolate and orange mousse with pistachio biscuit, or a plate of unusual cheeses. The wine list specialises in the Languedoc and the choice of real ales favours local micro-breweries, perhaps Great Oakley Wagtail, Oldershaw Best Bitter and Brewster's Hophead. There is a beer festival every August Bank Holiday weekend.

Open all wk 11.30-3 6-11 **Bar Meals** Av main course £14 **Restaurant** L served all wk 12-2.30 D served all wk 6.15-9.30 Fixed menu price fr £12 Av 3 course à la carte fr £26 🛢 FREE HOUSE 🍺 Brewster's Hophead, Great Oakley Wagtail, Oldershaw Best Bitter Ö Cromwell. 🍷 18 **Facilities** Children welcome Children's portions Garden Beer festival Parking 🚌 (notice required)

Save on hotels. Book at **theAA.com/hotel**

CAMBRIDGESHIRE 71 **ENGLAND**

HILTON — Map 12 TL26

The Prince of Wales ★★★ INN

Potton Rd PE28 9NG ☎ 01480 830257
e-mail: bookings@thehiltonpow.co.uk
dir: *On B1040 between A14 & A428 S of St Ives*

The Prince of Wales is a traditional, 1830s two-bar village inn with four comfortable bedrooms. To drink, choose from Adnams, Timothy Taylor Landlord or a guest ale. Food options range from bar snacks to full meals, among which are grills, fish, curries brought in from a local Indian restaurant, and daily specials, such as lamb hotpot. Home-made puddings include crème brûlée and sherry trifle. The village's 400-year-old grass maze was where locals used to escape the devil.

Open 12-2.30 6-11 Closed: Mon L **Bar Meals** L served Tue-Sun 12-2 D served all wk 7-9 Av main course £7.50 **Restaurant** L served Tue-Sun 12-2 D served all wk 7-9 ⊕ FREE HOUSE ◀ Timothy Taylor Landlord, Adnams, Guest ales ♂ Aspall. ♀ 9 **Facilities** ♥ Children welcome Children's menu Children's portions Garden Parking Wi-fi ⇔ **Rooms** 4

HINXTON — Map 12 TL44

The Red Lion Inn ★★★★ INN ⑯

PICK OF THE PUBS

32 High St CB10 1QY ☎ 01799 530601
e-mail: info@redlionhinxton.co.uk
dir: *N'bound only: M11 junct 9, towards A11, left onto A1301. Turn left to Hinxton. Or M11 junct 10, take A505 towards A11/Newmarket. At rdbt take 3rd exit onto A1301, right to Hinxton*

In a pretty conservation village, this 16th-century, pink-washed free house and restaurant is privately owned and run. Some customers like to eat informally on settles in the bar, where the ceilings are low, and green chesterfield sofas sit on the wooden floors; others prefer the loftier ceilings and pegged oak rafters of the restaurant, or the lovely award-winning walled garden. Locally sourced, modern British menus apply throughout, offering chargrilled rib-eye steak; Thai-style salmon fishcake; home-made chicken and leek pie; tournedos Rossini (a French steak dish); spicy red pepper risotto; and baguettes and sandwiches. The four real ales are also locally sourced: Adnams Bitter, Greene King IPA and Woodforde's Wherry are permanent fixtures, with other East Anglian micro-breweries supplying another on a rotational basis. A beer festival is held over the August Bank Holiday weekend. Guest rooms are set apart in a private garden area.

Open all day all wk **Bar Meals** L served Mon-Thu 12-2, Fri-Sun 12-2.30 D served Mon-Thu 6.30-9, Fri-Sat 6.30-9.30, Sun 7-9 Av main course £13 **Restaurant** L served Mon-Thu 12-2, Fri-Sun 12-2.30 D served Mon-Thu 6.30-9, Fri-Sat 6.30-9.30, Sun 7-9 Av 3 course à la carte fr £25 ⊕ FREE HOUSE ◀ Greene King IPA, Woodforde's Wherry, Brandon Rusty Bucket, Adnams, Guest ales ♂ Aspall. ♀ 20 **Facilities** ♥ Children welcome Children's portions Garden Beer festival Parking Wi-fi ⇔ (notice required) **Rooms** 8

HISTON — Map 12 TL46

Red Lion

27 High St CB24 9JD ☎ 01223 564437
dir: *M11 junct 14, A14 towards. Exit at junct 32 onto B1049 for Histon*

A pub since 1836, this popular village local on Cambridge's northern fringe has been run by Mark Donachy for almost two decades. A dyed-in-the-wool pub man, Mark's real ales include Oakham Bishops Farewell, as well as Pickled Pig Porker's Snout cider. There are also over 30 different Belgian bottled beers. The bar has now been extended in order to offer food in the evenings, as well as lunchtimes. Expect cheerful service, winter log fires and a good-sized neat garden. Time a visit for the Easter or early September beer festivals.

Open all day all wk 10.30am-11pm (Fri 10.30am-mdnt Sun 12-11) **Bar Meals** L served Mon-Sat 12-2.30, Sun 12.30-5 D served Tue-Thu & Sat 6.30-10 Av main course £8.50 ⊕ FREE HOUSE ◀ Batemans XB, Tring Blonde, Oakham Bishops Farewell, Theakston Lightfoot ♂ Pickled Pig Porker's Snout, Westons Perry. **Facilities** Children welcome Children's portions Garden Beer festival Parking Wi-fi ⇔ (notice required) **Notes** ⊜

HOLYWELL — Map 12 TL37

The Old Ferryboat Inn ★★★ INN

Back Ln PE27 4TG ☎ 01480 463227
e-mail: 8638@greeneking.co.uk
dir: *From Cambridge on A14 right onto A1096, then right onto A1123, right to Holywell*

Renowned as England's oldest inn, built some time in the 11th century, but with a hostelry history that goes back to the sixth. In a tranquil setting beside the Great Ouse River, The Old Ferryboat has immaculately maintained thatch, white stone walls, a cosy interior and bags of charm and character. It's a pleasant place — despite the resident ghost of a lovelorn teenager — in which to enjoy grilled pork chop and apple fritter; British beef and Ruddles ale pie; chicken tikka masala; or a surf 'n' turf burger. There are seven en suite bedrooms available.

Open all wk 11-11 (Sun 12-10.30) **Bar Meals** L served Mon-Sat 12-10, Sun 12-9 D served Mon-Sat 12-10, Sun 12-9 **Restaurant** L served Mon-Sat 12-10, Sun 12-9 D served Mon-Sat 12-10, Sun 12-9 ⊕ OLD ENGLISH INNS & HOTELS ◀ Greene King IPA & XX Mild, Morland Old Speckled Hen, Guest ales. ♀ 18 **Facilities** ♥ Children welcome Garden Parking ⇔ **Rooms** 7

HORNINGSEA — Map 12 TL46

The Crown & Punchbowl

CB5 9JG ☎ 01223 860643
e-mail: info@thecrownandpunchbowl.co.uk
dir: *Telephone for directions*

An 18th-century, tiled and whitewashed coaching inn, The Crown & Punchbowl stands in a little one-street village. Soft colours and wooden floors create a friendly atmosphere, while in the low-beamed restaurant innovative influences are at play with starters such as smoked salmon roulade with pickled mooli, radish, turnips and lime jelly; and devilled Cromer crab with parmesan crumble. Typical mains are roast loin of Suffolk lamb with spinach purée, walnuts and red wine jus; pan-fried halibut with rösti potatoes and confit of lamb shoulder; and wild mushroom cannelloni, winter vegetable salad and truffle cream. Booking for meals may be required.

Open 12-3 6.30-9.30 Closed: Sun eve & BH eve **Restaurant** L served all wk 12-3 D served Mon-Sat 6.30-9.30 ⊕ FREE HOUSE ◀ Thwaites Original ♂ Aspall. **Facilities** Children welcome Children's portions Garden Parking Wi-fi

KEYSTON — Map 11 TL07

Pheasant Inn ⑯⑯

PICK OF THE PUBS

Village Loop Rd PE28 0RE ☎ 01832 710241
e-mail: info@thepheasant-keyston.co.uk
dir: *0.5m off A14, clearly signed, 10m W of Huntingdon, 14m E of Kettering*

Following a five-year gap, John and Julia Hoskins have bought back this 16th-century, thatched village pub, which their family first acquired in 1964. The large bar, which serves Adnams and Nene Valley, is a traditional and unspoilt mixture of oak beams, stripped boards, large open fires and simple wooden furniture. The airy Garden Room opens to a sunny patio and herb garden beyond. Chef-patron is Simon Cadge, who relies greatly on local producers and suppliers, leaving only smoked fish from Uig Lodge on the Isle of Lewis, and fine British cheeses from Neal's Yard Dairy in London to travel any great distance. A typical meal features ribollita, a rustic Tuscan soup; fillet of salmon, crushed potatoes and crab and cockle velouté; or pork and leek sausages with mash, white onion and mustard sauce; and poached pear with hot chocolate sauce. John, a Master of Wine, compiles the wine list. Booking for meals may be required.

Open 12-3 6-11 Closed: Mon & Sun eve **Bar Meals** L served Tue-Sat 12-2 D served Tue-Sat 6.30-9.30 Av main course £9.95 **Restaurant** L served Tue-Sat 12-2, Sun 12-3.30 D served Tue-Sat 6.30-9.30 Fixed menu price fr £14.95 ⊕ FREE HOUSE ◀ Adnams Broadside, Nene Valley NVB ♂ Aspall. ♀ 16 **Facilities** ♥ Children welcome Children's menu Children's portions Garden Parking Wi-fi ⇔ (notice required)

KIMBOLTON Map 12 TL16

The New Sun Inn

20-22 High St PE28 0HA ☎ 01480 860052
e-mail: newsunninn@btinternet.com
dir: *From A1 N take B645 for 7m. From A1 S take B661 for 7m. From A14 take B660 for 5m*

Its pink-washed, profusely flower-basketed frontage makes this 17th-century inn easy to spot from a distance. Serving Wells Bombardier, Eagle IPA and a weekly guest, it also offers bar, conservatory and formal restaurant dining, from hot and cold tapas, to comprehensive lunch and evening menus featuring favourites like steak-and-kidney pudding. Other weekly changing possibilities are hake in pancetta with baby squid and chorizo; chargrilled chicken cassoulet; and goat's cheese, red onion and pine nut tart. Malteser cheesecake is a dessert. Themed events include lunch with the landlord and landlady.

Open all wk Mon-Thu 11.30-2.30 6-11 (Fri-Sun & mid Jun to mid Sep all day) **Bar Meals** L served Mon-Sat 12-2.15, Sun 12-2.30 D served Tue-Sat 7-9.30 **Restaurant** L served Mon-Sat 12-2.15, Sun 12-2.30 D served Tue-Sat 7-9.30 ⊕ CHARLES WELLS ◀ Bombardier & Eagle IPA, Guest ales Ö Aspall. ♀ 17 **Facilities** ✿ Children welcome Children's portions Garden ▭ (notice required)

LITTLE WILBRAHAM Map 12 TL55

Hole in the Wall @

PICK OF THE PUBS

2 High St CB21 5JY ☎ 01223 812282
dir: *Telephone for directions*

In 2010, Masterchef finalist Alex Rushmer was in the garden of this heavily timbered, 16th-century village pub and restaurant between Cambridge and Newmarket wondering where he could find and buy a pub of his own. Shortly afterwards, the Hole in the Wall came on to the market, so Alex bought it. The name recalls how farm workers used to collect their jugs of beer through a hole in the wall so as not to upset the gentry in the bar. Today, whatever their social standing, Alex's customers can drink Elgood's Cambridge Bitter, Milton's Sparta, and Woodforde's Nelson's Revenge and Wherry in the hop-adorned bar. His first-class modern British cooking is prepared from fresh local produce and includes pork belly and beans with confit duck leg; and whole roast lemon sole with courgettes at lunch and, in the evening, halibut, smoked haddock and bacon chowder; and chicken and chanterelle mushroom risotto. Booking for meals may be required.

Open 11.30-3 6.30-11 Closed: 2wks Jan, 25 Dec, Mon, Tue L, Sun eve **Bar Meals** L served Wed-Sun 12-2 D served Tue-Sat 7-9 **Restaurant** L served Wed-Sun 12-2 D served Tue-Sat 7-9 Av 3 course à la carte fr £30 ⊕ FREE HOUSE ◀ Woodforde's Wherry & Nelson's Revenge, Elgood's Cambridge Bitter, Milton Sparta. ♀ 10 **Facilities** Children welcome Children's portions Garden Parking Wi-fi

MADINGLEY Map 12 TL36

The Three Horseshoes

PICK OF THE PUBS

High St CB3 8AB ☎ 01954 210221
e-mail: 3hs@btconnect.com
dir: *M11 junct 13, 1.5m from A14*

With its large garden overlooking meadowland and the local cricket pitch, this quintessential thatched village inn enjoys a picturesque location. Inside is a small, bustling bar serving a great selection of beers and 22 wines by the glass, and a pretty conservatory restaurant. Chef-patron Richard Stokes has eaten his way around the world, and his success can be gauged by the long queues for tables; prior booking is advisable. Richard's own style is a modern take on Italian cuisine, characterised by seasonal and imaginative dishes with intense flavours. After trying the Puglian olives marinated with lemon, garlic and rosemary, you could choose seared, peppered beef fillet with grated beetroot, rocket and horseradish; or king prawn, cockle and clam risotto with tomato, fennel, Cognac and parsley. Then perhaps penne with cavolo nero purée, fresh red chilli and parmesan; or roast haunch of venison with wild mushrooms, potato purée, Savoy cabbage and pan juices. Desserts might include the popcorn pannacotta with cola granité and caramelised popcorn.

Open all wk 11.30-3 6-11 (Sun 11.30-3 6-9.30) **Bar Meals** L served Mon-Fri 12-2, Sat-Sun 12-2.30 D served all wk 6.30-9.30 Av main course £14 **Restaurant** L served all wk 12-2.30 D served Mon-Sat 6.30-9.30 Av 3 course à la carte fr £35 ⊕ FREE HOUSE ◀ Adnams Southwold Bitter, Hook Norton Old Hooky, Smiles Best Bitter, City of Cambridge Hobson's Choice, Guest ales Ö Westons Stowford Press. ♀ 22 **Facilities** Children welcome Children's portions Garden Parking

NEWTON Map 12 TL44

The Queen's Head

PICK OF THE PUBS

Fowlmere Rd CB22 7PG ☎ 01223 870436
dir: *6m S of Cambridge on B1368, 1.5m off A10 at Harston, 4m from A505*

For 50 years now the Short family have owned and operated their tiny and very traditional village pub. Unchanging and unmarred by gimmickry, the simple, stone-tiled bars, replete with log fires, pine settles and old school benches, draw an eclectic clientele, from Cambridge dons to local farm workers. They all come for tip-top Adnams ale direct from the drum, the friendly, honest atmosphere and straightforward pub dishes. Food is simple – at lunch, soup served in mugs, excellent sandwiches and Aga-baked potatoes. In the evening, just soup, toast and beef dripping, and cold platters (roast beef, smoked ham, smoked salmon or a variety of cheeses) are on the menu. Village tradition is kept alive with time-honoured pub games – try your hand at dominoes, table skittles, shove ha'penny and nine men's Morris. There is a green opposite for summer sipping.

Open all wk 11.30-2.30 6-11 (Sun 12-2.30 7-10.30) Closed: 25-26 Dec **Bar Meals** L served all wk 12-2.15 D served all wk 7-9.30 Av main course £3.90-£6.50 ⊕ FREE HOUSE ◀ Adnams Southwold Bitter, Broadside, Fisherman, Regatta Ö Crones. ♀ 9 **Facilities** ✿ Children welcome Children's portions Family room Parking **Notes** @

OFFORD D'ARCY Map 12 TL26

The Horseshoe Inn

90 High St PE19 5RH ☎ 01480 810293
e-mail: info@theoffordshoe.co.uk
dir: *Between Huntingdon & St Neots. 1.5m from Buckden on A1*

Built by a yeoman farmer in 1626, this spruced up pub-restaurant stands close to the River Ouse in a sleepy village just off the A1. Famished travellers keen to escape the faceless services will find two comfortable bars serving good local real ales – try a pint of Oakham JHB – and an imaginative changing menu. Chef-patron Richard Kennedy offers dishes such as scallops with black pudding and celeriac purée; pork belly with creamed leeks, mustard mash and cider jus; steaks with all the trimmings; and lunchtime pub classics like steak-and-ale pie. A midsummer beer festival is held on the green. Booking for meals may be required.

Open all day 12-11 Closed: 2-4 Jan, Jan-Mar Mon **Bar Meals** L served Mon-Sat 12-2.30 D served Mon-Sat 6-9.30 Av main course £16.50 **Restaurant** L served all wk 12-2.30 D served Mon-Sat 6-9.30 Fixed menu price fr £15 Av 3 course à la carte fr £19.95 ⊕ FREE HOUSE ◀ Adnams Southwold Bitter, Sharp's Doom Bar, Potton Shannon IPA, Oakham JHB. ♀ 17 **Facilities** ✿ Children welcome Children's portions Play area Garden Beer festival Parking Wi-fi ▭ (notice required)

PETERBOROUGH Map 12 TL19

The Brewery Tap

80 Westgate PE1 2AA ☎ 01733 358500
e-mail: brewerytap.manager@oakagroup.com
dir: *Opposite bus station*

Located in the old labour exchange on Westgate, this striking American-style pub is home to the multi-award winning Oakham Brewery and it is one of the largest brewpubs in Europe. Visitors can see the day-to-day running of the brewery through a glass wall spanning half the length of the bar. As if the appeal of the 12 real ales and the vast range of bottled beers were not enough, Thai chefs beaver away producing delicious snacks, soups, salads, stirfries and curries. Look out for live music nights.

Open all day all wk 12-11 (Fri-Sat 12-12) Closed: 25-26 Dec, 1 Jan **Bar Meals** L served Sun-Thu 12-2.30, Fri-Sat 12-10.30 D served Sun-Thu 6-9.30, Fri-Sat 12-10.30 **Restaurant** L served Sun-Thu 12-2.30, Fri-Sat 12-10.30 D served Sun-Thu 6-9.30, Fri-Sat 12-10.30 ⊕ FREE HOUSE ◀ Oakham Inferno, Citra, JHB & Bishops Farewell, Elgood's Black Dog, 7 Guest ales Ö Westons 1st Quality. **Facilities** ✿ Children welcome Children's portions Wi-fi ▭

Charters Bar & East Restaurant

Upper Deck, Town Bridge PE1 1FP
☎ 01733 315700 & 315702 (bkgs)
e-mail: charters.manager@oakagroup.com
dir: *A1/A47 towards Wisbech, 2m for city centre & town bridge (River Nene). Barge moored at Town Bridge (west side)*

The largest floating real ale emporium in Britain can be found moored in the heart of Peterborough. The 176-ft converted barge promises 'brews, blues and fine views'. It motored from Holland across the North Sea in 1991, and is now a haven for real-ale and cider-lovers. Twelve hand pumps dispense a continually changing repertoire of cask ales, while entertainment, dancing, live blues music and an Easter beer festival are regular features. The East part of the name applies to the oriental restaurant on the upper deck which offers a comprehensive selection of pan-Asian dishes. Booking for meals may be required.

Open all day all wk 12-11 (Fri-Sat noon-2am) Closed: 25-26 Dec, 1 Jan **Bar Meals** L served all wk 12-2.30 **Restaurant** L served Mon-Sat 12-2.30, Sun 12-3.30 D served Sun-Thu 5.30-10.30, Fri-Sat 5.30-11 ⊕ FREE HOUSE ◀ Oakham JHB, Bishops Farewell, Citra, Inferno & Scarlet Macaw, Guest ales Ŏ Westons Old Rosie & Traditional. ⬤ 10 **Facilities** ❖ Children welcome Garden Beer festival Parking Wi-fi ▭ (notice required)

REACH   Map 12 TL56

Dyke's End

CB25 0JD ☎ 01638 743816
dir: *Telephone for directions*

Located in the centre of the village, overlooking the green, this pub was saved from closure by villagers in the 1990s. They ran it as a co-operative until 2003, when it was bought by Frank Feehan, who further refurbished and extended it. Frank's additions included the Devil's Dyke micro-brewery, which continues to be run by new owners Catherine and George Gibson, who took over in 2012. The pub has a strong local following for its food and beers. The menu is seasonal with daily-changing specials, although pub favourites like beer-battered haddock and steak frites are always popular.

Open 12-2.30 6-11 (Sat-Sun 12-11) Closed: Mon L **Bar Meals** L served Tue-Sun 12-2 D served all wk 7-9 Av main course £15 ⊕ FREE HOUSE ◀ Devil's Dyke, Thwaites Wainwright, Adnams Southwold Bitter Ŏ Aspall, Westons Old Rosie. ⬤ 8 **Facilities** ❖ Children welcome Children's portions Play area Family room Garden Parking Wi-fi

STAPLEFORD   Map 12 TL45

The Rose at Stapleford

81 London Rd CB22 5DE ☎ 01223 843349
e-mail: paulnbeer@aol.com
dir: *Telephone for directions*

Paul and Karen Beer have made a success of The George & Dragon at Elsworth (see entry) and they're also weaving their magic at The Rose, a traditional village pub close to Cambridge and Duxford Imperial War Museum. Expect a stylish interior, replete with low beams and inglenook fireplaces, and extensive menus that draw on local Suffolk produce, particularly meat, with fish from Lowestoft. As well as a good selection of seafood appetisers, typical main dishes include home-made vegetable curry; warm Cajun chicken salad; wild mushroom Stroganoff; and beef lasagne.

Open 12-2.30 5.30-11 (Sun winter 12-5 summer 12-8.30) Closed: Sun eve (winter only) **Bar Meals** L served all wk 12-2 D served Mon-Sat 5.30-9.30 **Restaurant** L served all wk 12-2 D served Mon-Sat 5.30-9.30 ⊕ ENTERPRISE INNS ◀ Adnams Southwold Bitter, St Austell Tribute, Guest ale Ŏ Aspall. ⬤ 13 **Facilities** Children welcome Children's menu Children's portions Garden Parking ▭

STILTON   Map 12 TL18

The Bell Inn Hotel ★★★ HL ⊛

PICK OF THE PUBS

Great North Rd PE7 3RA ☎ 01733 241066
e-mail: reception@thebellstilton.co.uk
dir: *From A1(M) junct 16 follow signs for Stilton. Hotel on main road in village centre*

Famous as the birthplace of stilton cheese, the pub has just started making it again. They call it Bell Blue, because EU food protection law says that the real thing must come from only Derbyshire, Leicestershire and Nottinghamshire. A Bell Inn has stood here since 1500, although this one is mid-17th century; even so, it is reputedly the oldest coaching inn on the old Great North Road, with an impressive façade and a fine original interior. It once welcomed (or maybe not!) highwayman Dick Turpin, as well as Lord Byron and Clark Gable, who was stationed nearby in 1943. Modern British dishes in the Galleried Restaurant include fillet of English beef Rossini; roast cod fillet; and stilton, rocket and aubergine quiche. In the Bar/Bistro try Guinness-braised shank of lamb, or seared fillet of sea bass. Note the magnificent inn sign, a replica of the original. All the bedrooms are en suite. Booking for meals may be required.

Open all wk 12-2.30 6-11 (Sat 12-3 6-12 Sun 12-11) Closed: 25 Dec **Bar Meals** L served Mon-Sat 12-2.30, Sun all day D served all wk 6-9.30 Av main course £13.95 **Restaurant** L served Sun 12-2 D served Mon-Sat 7-9.30 Fixed menu price fr £29.50 ⊕ FREE HOUSE ◀ Greene King IPA, Oakham Bishops Farewell, Morland Old Speckled Hen, Digfield Fool's Nook. ⬤ 8 **Facilities** Children welcome Children's menu Children's portions Garden Parking Wi-fi ▭ (notice required) **Rooms** 22

STRETHAM   Map 12 TL57

The Lazy Otter

Cambridge Rd CB6 3LU ☎ 01353 649780
e-mail: thelazyotter@btconnect.com
dir: *Telephone for directions*

When fire destroyed the original pub here in 1844, locals blamed a match salesman the landlord had upset. By a marina on the River Great Ouse, its replacement has a riverside restaurant and a large garden. Snacks include New York bagels and gourmet burgers, and main meals take in pan-fried duck breast; chicken Stroganoff; seafood linguine; and mixed bean cobbler. Look for guest ales from the Milton and Wolf breweries, and Old Rosie cloudy scrumpy from Westons. Check with the pub for beer festival details. Booking for meals may be required.

Open all day all wk 7am-11pm (Sun 8.30am-10.30pm) **Bar Meals** Av main course £8.25 food served all day **Restaurant** Av 3 course à la carte fr £23 food served all day ⊕ FREE HOUSE ◀ Greene King IPA, Guest ales Ŏ Westons Stowford Press & Old Rosie. ⬤ 10 **Facilities** ❖ Children welcome Children's menu Children's portions Play area Garden Beer festival Parking Wi-fi ▭

The Red Lion NEW

47 High St CB6 3LD ☎ 01353 648132
e-mail: redlion@charnwoodpubco.co.uk
dir: *Exit A10 between Cambridge & Ely into Stretham. Left into High St, pub on right*

Ten miles north of Cambridge, this former coaching inn is in the village of Stretham. In the busy locals' bar, enjoy a pint of Adnams beer or Pickled Pig cider with bar meals such as spicy meatball melt or a bucket of potato wedges topped with barbecue chicken wings. Alternatively, head to the conservatory-style restaurant for traditional favourites such as home-cooked ham, eggs and chips; minted lamb stew; hand-made burger; or one of the steaks from the grill. Booking for meals may be required.

Open all day all wk **Bar Meals** L served all wk 12-2.30 D served all wk 6-9 Av main course £8 **Restaurant** L served all wk 12-2.30 D served all wk 6-9 ◀ Greene King IPA, Wychwood Hobgoblin, Adnams, Marston's Ŏ Pickled Pig. ⬤ 8 **Facilities** Children welcome Children's menu Children's portions Garden Parking Wi-fi ▭ (notice required)

UFFORD   Map 12 TF00

The White Hart ★★★★ INN

Main St PE9 3BH ☎ 01780 740250
e-mail: info@whitehartufford.co.uk
dir: From Stamford take B1443 signed Barnack. Through Barnack and follow signs to Ufford

Salvaged cast-iron railway signs and old agricultural tools embellish the bar of this 17th-century country inn, serving Aspall Suffolk Cyder and four real ales, three from the on-site Ufford Ales micro-brewery. An extensive wine list reflects the help of Master of Wine, John Atkinson. Locally sourced produce including game ends up on the seasonal menus, perhaps alongside traditional Lincolnshire sausages, mash and onion gravy; Thai-style seafood casserole; and wild mushroom, spinach and smoked Lincolnshire Poacher cheese risotto. Four individually styled bedrooms are in the main building, two in the converted cart shed. Booking for meals may be required.

Open all day all wk **Bar Meals** L served Mon-Sat 12-2.30, Sun 12-5 D served Mon-Sat 6-9.30 Av main course £14 **Restaurant** L served Mon-Sat 12-2.30, Sun 12-5 D served Mon-Sat 6-9.30 Fixed menu price fr £25 Av 3 course à la carte fr £30 ⊕ FREE HOUSE ◀ Ufford White Hart & Rupert's War Dog, Adnams ♻ Aspall. ♟ 10 **Facilities** ❀ Children welcome Children's menu Children's portions Play area Garden Parking Wi-fi 🚌 (notice required) **Rooms** 6

CHESHIRE

ALDFORD   Map 15 SJ45

The Grosvenor Arms

PICK OF THE PUBS

Chester Rd CH3 6HJ ☎ 01244 620228
e-mail: grosvenor.arms@brunningandprice.co.uk
dir: On B5130, S of Chester

This 'delight of higgledy-piggledy rooflines and soft, warm Cheshire brick' dates from 1864. The architect was John Douglas, who designed around 500 buildings, many of them in Cheshire. Its spacious, open-plan interior includes an airy conservatory and a panelled, book-filled library. Outside, a terrace leads into a small but pleasing garden, and on out to the village green. On the bistro-style menu are snacks such as warm goat's cheese and Provençal vegetables on ciabatta; starters may feature smoked trout and pickled cucumber salad with herb crème fraîche; look for a main course of David Joinson's award-winning traditional pork sausages and mash; and don't forget that the puddings can be served with custard. This is a Brunning & Price pub, so expect lots of different real ales from small breweries around the country. No wonder the locals are fond of it.

Open all day all wk **Bar Meals** Av main course £12.50 food served all day ⊕ FREE HOUSE/BRUNNING & PRICE ◀ Original Bitter, Weetwood Eastgate Ale, Phoenix, Guest ales ♻ Westons Stowford Press, Aspall. ♟ 20 **Facilities** Children welcome Children's portions Garden Parking

ASTON   Map 15 SJ64

The Bhurtpore Inn

PICK OF THE PUBS

See Pick of the Pubs on opposite page

BOLLINGTON   Map 16 SJ97

The Church House Inn

Church St SK10 5PY ☎ 01625 574014
e-mail: info@thechurchhouseinn-bollington.co.uk
dir: From A34 take A538 towards Macclesfield. Through Prestbury, then follow Bollington signs

After a gap of eight years, Julie and Steve Robinson are back at this stone-built free house dating from Bollington's days as a cotton-milling village. Its exposed beams and log fires look just the part for a traditional village local, whose varied menu includes home-made soup, home-made sausages and pies, and other time-honoured British favourites. Vegetarian options feature on the daily specials board, which will go down well with a pint of Adnams, and there's a good-value senior citizens' menu.

Open all wk 12-3 5.30-11 (Sun 12-10.30) **Bar Meals** L served Mon-Sat 12-2, Sun 12-8.30 D served Mon-Thu 6-9, Sat-Sun 6-9.30, Sun 12-8.30 ⊕ FREE HOUSE ◀ Timothy Taylor Golden Best, Adnams, Duchess IPA. **Facilities** Children welcome Children's menu Children's portions Parking Wi-fi 🚌

BROXTON   Map 15 SJ45

Egerton Arms

Whitchurch Rd CH3 9JW ☎ 01829 782241
e-mail: egertonarms@woodwardandfalconer.com
dir: On A41 between Whitchurch & Chester

A little gem in the heart of the rolling Cheshire plains, where the aim is to cosset customers with a combination of lovely ales, a wide selection of wines, food that hits the spot, and excellent service from the enthusiastic and friendly staff. With a pint of Piffle in hand, choosing a dish to tickle your taste buds is not a problem – the menu covers all preferences, from toad-in-the-hole to warm duck salad or vegetable burrito. The spacious gardens are another bonus, and occasional special events represent excellent value.

Open all day all wk Closed: 25 Dec **Bar Meals** L served all wk 12-5.30 D served Mon-Sat 5.30-9.30, Sun 5.30-9 food served all day **Restaurant** L served all wk 12-5.30 D served Mon-Sat 5.30-9.30, Sun 5.30-9 food served all day ⊕ WOODWARD & FALCONER PUBS LTD ◀ Woodward & Falconer Piffle, Weetwood Eastgate Ale, Theakston. ♟ 18 **Facilities** Children welcome Children's menu Children's portions Play area Garden Parking 🚌

BUNBURY   Map 15 SJ55

The Dysart Arms

PICK OF THE PUBS

Bowes Gate Rd CW6 9PH ☎ 01829 260183
e-mail: dysart.arms@brunningandprice.co.uk
dir: Between A49 & A51, by Shropshire Union Canal

A classic English village pub with open fires, lots of old oak, full-height bookcases and a pretty garden with views to two castles and the neighbouring parish church. Built as a farmhouse in the mid-18th century and licensed since the late 1800s, it once functioned simultaneously as a farm, an abattoir and a pub; the abattoir building was demolished by a German bomber on its way home from 'rearranging' the Liverpool docks. The hostelry is named after local landowners, the Earls of Dysart, whose coat of arms is above the door. An ever-changing line-up of ales is served in the central bar, around which are several airy rooms perfect for drinking and eating. Snacks include a home-made fish finger butty; starters may list venison carpaccio with candied red cabbage; and main courses range from breast of pheasant with bacon and chestnut hash cake, to a pine nut-encrusted hake fillet.

Open all day all wk 11.30-11 (Sun 12-10.30) **Bar Meals** L served all wk D served all wk food served all day **Restaurant** L served all wk D served all wk food served all day ⊕ FREE HOUSE/BRUNNING & PRICE ◀ Original Bitter, Weetwood Best Cask, Timothy Taylor Landlord ♻ Aspall. ♟ 18 **Facilities** Children welcome Children's portions Garden Parking

BURLEYDAM   Map 15 SJ64

The Combermere Arms

SY13 4AT ☎ 01948 871223
e-mail: combermere.arms@brunningandprice.co.uk
dir: From Whitchurch take A525 towards Nantwich, at Newcastle/Audlem/Woore sign, turn right at junct. Pub 100yds on right

Popular with local shoots, walkers and town folk alike, this classic 17th-century country inn is full of character and warmth. Three roaring fires complement the wealth of oak, nooks and crannies, pictures and old furniture. Food options range from sandwiches to a hearty meal of garlic wild mushrooms on toasted brioche, followed by chicken, ham and leek pie with buttered mash and white wine cream sauce, with raspberry Bakewell tart for dessert. There is a great choice of real ales and ciders, an informative wine list and impressive cheese list.

Open all day all wk 11.30-11 **Bar Meals** food served all day **Restaurant** food served all day ⊕ FREE HOUSE/BRUNNING & PRICE ◀ Original Bitter, Woodlands Oak Beauty, Weetwood Cheshire Cat, St Austell Tribute, Morland Old Speckled Hen ♻ Weston Stowford Press, Thatchers Old Rascal, Aspall. ♟ 20 **Facilities** Children welcome Children's portions Garden Parking

PICK OF THE PUBS

The Bhurtpore Inn

ASTON   Map 15 SJ64

Wrenbury Rd CW5 8DQ
☎ **01270 780917**
e-mail: simonbhurtpore@yahoo.co.uk
web: www.bhurtpore.co.uk
dir: *Just off A530 between Nantwich &
Whitchurch. Follow Wrenbury signs at
x-rds in village*

A pub since at least 1778, when it was
called the Queen's Head. It subsequently
became the Red Lion, but it was Lord
Combermere's success at the Siege of
Bhurtpore in India in 1826 that inspired
the name that has stuck. Simon and
Nicky George came across it in 1991,
boarded-up and stripped-out. Simon is
a direct descendant of Joyce George,
who leased the pub from the
Combermere Estate in 1849, so was
motivated by his family history to take
on the hard work of restoring the
interior; the pub reopened in early 1992.
Since then, 'award winning' hardly does
justice to the accolades heaped upon
this hostelry. In the bar, 11 ever-
changing real ales are always available,
mostly from local micro-breweries, as
are real ciders, continental draught
lagers and around 150 of the world's
bottled beers. An annual beer festival,
reputedly Cheshire's largest, is in its
17th year, with around 130 real ales.
The pub has also been shortlisted five
times for the 'National Whisky Pub of
the Year' award, and there is a long soft
drinks menu. Recognition extends to the

kitchen too, where unfussy dishes of
classic pub fare are prepared. Among
the hearty British ingredients you'll find
seasonal game, such as venison haunch
on cabbage with smoked bacon and
cream; and rabbit loin with a pork and
black pudding stuffing. Curries and
balti dishes are always on the
blackboard; these usually comprise at
least six options, based on meat, as well
as vegetables and Quorn. Vintage
vehicles bring their owners here on the
first Thursday of the month, and folk
musicians play on the third Tuesday.

Open all wk 12-2.30 6.30-11.30 (Fri-Sat
12-12 Sun 12-11) Closed: 25-26 Dec, 1
Jan **Bar Meals** L served Mon-Fri 12-2 D
served Mon-Fri 6.30-9.30, Sat 12-9.30,
Sun 12-9 **Restaurant** L served Mon-Fri

12-2 D served Mon-Fri 6.30-9.30, Sat
12-9.30, Sun 12-9 ⊕ FREE HOUSE
◀ Salopian Golden Thread, Abbeydale
Absolution, Weetwood Oast-House Gold,
Copper Dragon Golden Pippin, Hobson's
Mild ♂ Thatchers Cheddar Valley,
Moonshine, Westons Old Rosie. ♟ 12
Facilities Children welcome Children's
menu Children's portions ♣ Garden
Beer festival Parking ▅ (notice
required)

BURWARDSLEY
Map 15 SJ55

The Pheasant Inn ★★★★★ INN

PICK OF THE PUBS

See Pick of the Pubs on opposite page

CHESTER
Map 15 SJ46

Albion Inn

PICK OF THE PUBS

Park St CH1 1RN ☎ 01244 340345
e-mail: christina.mercer@tesco.net
dir: *In city centre adjacent to Citywalls & Newgate*

A few decades back many a good local was ruined when the brewery turned it into a theme pub. This theme pub, however, wasn't a brewery's idea, yet it's still a fine local. A living memorial to the First World War, Michael Mercer has run it for some 40 years, his inspiration the nearby drill hall where many a lad signed up before a few reflective jars in here. In fact, the home fires still burn on winter nights in the splendid Victorian cast-iron fireplaces in the original Vault, Snug and Lounge, adorned with sepia photographs, 1914 wallpaper, enamelled advertisements, and vintage artefacts. Locally and regionally sourced 'trench rations' include boiled gammon and pease pudding; fish pie with mashed potato and parmesan cheese; and Staffordshire oatcakes with various fillings. Several cask ales are on tap. Please note that children are not allowed.

Open all wk 12-3 & Tue-Fri 5-11 Sat 6-11 Sun 7-10.30 Mon 5.30-11 Closed: 25-26 Dec, 1-2 Jan **Bar Meals** L served Mon-Fri 12-2, Sat 12-2.30 D served Mon-Fri 5-8, Sat 6-8.30 Av main course £9.90 **Restaurant** L served all wk 12-2 D served Mon-Fri 5-8, Sat 6-8.30 ⊕ PUNCH TAVERNS ◼ Black Sheep, Adnams, Guest ales ♂ Westons Wyld Wood Organic. **Facilities** ❖ Wi-fi **Notes** ☺

The Brewery Tap NEW

52-54 Lower Bridge St CH1 1RU ☎ 01244 340999
e-mail: drink@the-tap.co.uk
web: www.the-tap.co.uk
dir: *From B5268 in Chester into Lower Bridge St towards river*

This building started a new life as The Brewery Tap in 2008 as the first acquisition for the Spitting Feathers Brewery in Waverton. It is situated in part of Gamul House, named after Sir Francis Gamul, a wealthy merchant and mayor of Chester who built the edifice in 1620. This is reputedly where Charles I stayed when his troops were defeated at Rowton Moor, shortly before the king's final and fatal flight to Wales. Relax and enjoy the pub's myriad period details, and choose from a menu of robust pub favourites such as devilled kidneys on toast; English veal burger with fat chips; and caramelised rice pudding.

Open all day all wk Closed: 25-26 Dec **Bar Meals** L served all wk 12-9.30 D served all wk 12-9.30 Av main course £8.95 food served all day ⊕ FREE HOUSE/SPITTING FEATHERS ◼ Thirstquencher, Old Wavertonian Stout ♂ Gwynt y Ddraig Black Dragon. ♚ 14 **Facilities** Children welcome Wi-fi

See advert below

PICK OF THE PUBS

The Pheasant Inn ★★★★★ INN

BURWARDSLEY   Map 15 SJ55

CH3 9PF ☎ 01829 770434
e-mail: info@thepheasantinn.co.uk
web: www.thepheasantinn.co.uk
dir: *A41 (Chester to Whitchurch), 4m,*
left to Burwardsley. Follow 'Cheshire
Workshops' signs

In a peaceful corner of Cheshire lie the Peckforton Hills, a sandstone ridge liberally covered by thick woodlands. High on their west-facing slopes is this some 300-year-old former farmhouse and barn, where only five families have been licensees since it first became an alehouse. It stands high enough for there to be panoramic views taking in the Cheshire Plain, the Welsh hills and even the distant tower of Liverpool Cathedral, yet Chester, whose cathedral is also visible, is only 15 minutes' drive away. Among those who know it well are the walkers on the Sandstone Trail long-distance footpath from Frodsham on the Mersey to Whitchurch in Shropshire. On a summer's day the obvious place to be is outside in the flower-filled courtyard or on the terrace, but if the winter weather dictates otherwise, there are big open fires waiting. Four real ales, usually drawn from the Weetwood Brewery near Tarporley, are always on tap in the wooden-floored, heftily-beamed bar, and well chosen wines too. The kitchen (with an AA Dinner Award) makes extensive use of produce from local estates, with the menu in the restaurant offering a wide choice of modern British and European dishes. A duck cromesquis (like a fritter) with plum and rhubarb compôte might be followed by fresh North Sea haddock in beer batter, with hand-cut chips and mushy peas; or perhaps a 28-day-aged Bowland rib-eye steak on a skillet with roast tomato, mushroom, bell peppers and chips. Vegetarians may opt for spinach, leek and wild mushroom cannelloni, while the children's selection includes corn-fed chicken strips, penne pasta and home-made chargrilled steak burger. Warm sticky toffee pudding and lemon posset are among the desserts. If planning to stay overnight, there is comfortable en suite accommodation in both the main building and the ivy-clad stable wing.

Open all day all wk **Bar Meals** L served all wk (no food Mon 3-6) D served all wk (no food Mon 3-6) food served all day

Restaurant L served all wk (no food Mon 3-6) D served all wk (no food Mon 3-6) food served all day ⊕ FREE HOUSE ◀ Weetwood Old Dog Premium Bitter, Eastgate Ale & Best Cask Bitter, Guest ale ♂ Kingstone Press.
Facilities Children welcome Children's menu Children's portions ♥ Garden Parking Wi-fi 🚌 (notice required)
Rooms 12

CHESTER *continued*

Old Harkers Arms

1 Russell St CH3 5AL ☎ **01244 344525**
e-mail: harkers.arms@brunningandprice.co.uk
dir: *Close to railway station, on canal side*

Striking tall windows, lofty ceilings, wooden floors and a bar constructed from salvaged doors make this former Victorian chandler's warehouse beside the Shropshire Union Canal one of Chester's more unusual pubs. A buzzy city watering hole, the bar offers over 100 malt whiskies and Weetwood Cheshire Cat and Titanic Stout among the hand pumps. The daily-changing menu runs from light dishes such as pitta bread filled with lamb, haloumi and tzatziki through to main courses such as beef, red wine and baby onion suet pudding. The pub holds events such as 'Pie & Ale Week'. Booking for meals may be required.

Open all day all wk 11.30-11 (Sun 12-10.30) Closed: 25 Dec **Bar Meals** L served all wk 12-9.30 D served all wk 12-9.30 Av main course £11.95 **Restaurant** L served all wk 12-9.30 D served all wk 12-9.30 Av 3 course à la carte fr £21.95 ⊕ FREE HOUSE/BRUNNING & PRICE ◀ Original Bitter, Weetwood Cheshire Cat, Flowers Original, Titanic Stout, Crouch Vale Brewers Gold, Spitting Feathers ♂ Westons Wyld Wood Organic & Old Rosie, Aspall, Thatchers. ♀ 15 **Facilities** ♣ Beer festival

| CHOLMONDELEY | Map 15 SJ55 |

The Cholmondeley Arms

PICK OF THE PUBS

See Pick of the Pubs on page 80

| CHRISTLETON | Map 15 SJ46 |

Ring O'Bells **NEW**

Village Rd CH3 7AS ☎ **01244 335422**
e-mail: ringobells@mbt.cc
web: www.ringobellschester.co.uk
dir: *Village 3m from Chester between A51 towards Nantwich & A41 towards Whitchurch*

Wine tastings, 'Meet the Brewer' nights and a monthly produce market in the car park are just some of the events that draw drinkers and diners to this spruced-up village pub close to Chester. In summer, be spoilt by the choice of alfresco dining areas, perhaps choosing the decked suntrap terrace for savouring a pint of Liverpool Organic with a roast beef, horseradish and rocket sandwich, or one of the freshly-baked pizzas. The kitchen makes good use of local produce and the menu combines

pub classics (battered cod with hand-cut chips) with Mediterranean-influenced dishes like haddock and leek risotto. Booking for meals may be required.

Open all day all wk **Bar Meals** L served Mon-Fri 12-3, Sat-Sun 12-5 D served Mon-Thu 5-9, Fri-Sat 5-9.30, Sun 5-8 Av main course £10.95 **Restaurant** L served Mon-Fri 12-3, Sat-Sun 12-5 D served Mon-Thu 5-9, Fri-Sat 5-9.30, Sun 5-8 Av 3 course à la carte fr £21.95 ⊕ TRUST INNS ◀ Spitting Feathers, Weetwood, Liverpool Organic. ♀ **Facilities** ♣ Children welcome Children's menu Children's portions Play area Garden Parking Wi-fi 🚐 (notice required)

See advert on opposite page

| CONGLETON | Map 16 SJ86 |

Egerton Arms Country Inn ★★★★ INN

Astbury Village CW12 4RQ ☎ **01260 273946**
e-mail: egertonastbury@totalise.co.uk
dir: *1.5m SW of Congleton off A34, by St Mary's Church*

A buzzing village local with a good name for dependable real ales and freshly prepared fodder. It's a family-run establishment, with Grace and Allen at the helm. Set at the edge of one of Cheshire's picture-perfect villages, near the ancient church and flowery green, the Egerton Arms enjoys views from the peaceful beer garden onto the nearby Bosley Cloud Hill. Take a stroll along the paths there or stroll along the Macclesfield Canal towpath. The restaurant is newly refurbished, and offers a nice selection including pan-fried lamb's liver and onions; bacon chops with cranberry topping; and a variety of baguettes and sandwiches. Stay awhile in the comfortable accommodation and you may meet the ghost, a local lady murdered next door in 1922!

Open all day all wk **Bar Meals** L served Mon-Sat 11.30-2, Sun 12-8 D served Mon-Sat 6-9, Sun 12-8 Av main course £10.50 **Restaurant** L served Mon-Sat 12-1.45, Sun 12-8 D served Mon-Sat 6.30-8.45, Sun 12-8 Fixed menu price fr £15.50 Av 3 course à la carte fr £22 ⊕ FREDERIC ROBINSON ◀ Unicorn, Dizzy Blonde, Double Hop, Seasonal ales. ♀ 12 **Facilities** ♣ Children welcome Children's menu Children's portions Play area Garden Parking Wi-fi **Rooms** 6

The Plough At Eaton ★★★★ INN

Macclesfield Rd, Eaton CW12 2NH ☎ **01260 280207**
e-mail: theploughinn@hotmail.co.uk
web: www.theploughinnateaton.co.uk
dir: *On A536 (Congleton to Macclesfield road)*

Set well back from the main road in the hamlet of Eaton, this 400-year-old Cheshire-brick inn is a far cry from its genesis as a farmers' local in a farmhouse. It's now a popular destination gastro-pub with a very accomplished menu, available throughout the very traditional interior or in the restaurant housed in a remarkable cruck barn moved here from Wales. From bar snacks such as grilled fresh sardines, the choice of dishes balloons to include pink roasted duck breast, with additional changing specials. Handy for visiting Gawsworth Hall and Macclesfield's museums, the comfortable, en suite rooms are in a separate annexe. Beers are largely from local Cheshire craft breweries.

Open all day all wk 11am-mdnt **Bar Meals** L served Mon-Thu 12-2.30, Fri-Sat 12-9.30, Sun 12-8 D served Mon-Thu 6-9.30, Fri-Sat 12-9.30, Sun 12-8 **Restaurant** L served Mon-Thu 12-2.30, Fri-Sat 12-9.30, Sun 12-8 D served Mon-Sat 6-9.30, Fri-Sat 12-9.30, Sun 12-8 ⊕ FREE HOUSE ◀ Hydes, Storm, Flowers, Guest ales. ♀ 10 **Facilities** Children welcome Children's menu Garden Parking 🚐 **Rooms** 17

| COTEBROOK | Map 15 SJ56 |

Fox & Barrel **NEW**

Foxbank CW6 9DZ ☎ **01829 760529**
e-mail: info@foxandbarrel.co.uk
web: www.foxandbarrel.co.uk
dir: *On A49, 2.8m N of Tarporley*

The rather cute explanation for the pub's name is that a fox being chased by the local hunt ran into the cellar, where the landlord gave it sanctuary. And who's to say otherwise? Restored and refreshed features include a huge open log fire, old beams and half-panelled walls;

Save on hotels. Book at **theAA.com/hotel**

CHESHIRE 79 **ENGLAND**

the snug bar is the perfect spot for a pint of Weetwood. Classic pub food includes Cumberland sausage and mash with onion gravy; fish pie; and spicy vegetable and chickpea hotpot. Outside is a secluded landscaped garden surrounded by unspoilt Cheshire countryside.

Fox & Barrel

Open all day all wk Closed: 25-26 Dec pm, 31 Dec am, 1 Jan pm **Bar Meals** Av main course £13.95 food served all day ⊕ FREE HOUSE ◀ Weetwood Eastgate Ale, Caledonian Deuchars IPA. ☂ 20 **Facilities** ✿ Children welcome Children's portions Garden Parking Wi-fi

---

FARNDON   Map 15 SJ45

The Farndon ★★★★ INN

High St CH3 6PU ☎ 01829 270570
e-mail: enquiries@thefarndon.co.uk
dir: *From Wrexham take A534 towards Nantwich. Follow signs for Farndon on left*

Close to the River Dee, this family-run 16th-century coaching inn is at the heart of Farndon and the warmth of the welcome is matched by the log fire, lots of candles and an ambience of stylish renovation. Several local real ales are on tap, and menus are tweaked every week. The brasserie-style dishes, built around local produce, might include a starter of wild mushroom tartlet with caramelised onions, followed by a main course of pan-fried lamb's liver with tomato and smoked bacon jus. There are four boutique guest bedrooms and a suite.

Open all wk 5-11 (Sat 12-11 Sun 12-10.30) **Bar Meals** L served Sat-Sun 12-9.30 D served Mon-Fri 6-9, Sat-Sun 12-9.30 Av main course £10.50 **Restaurant** D served Mon-Thu 6-9, Fri 6-9.30, Sat 12-9.30, Sun 12-8 Fixed menu price fr £15 Av 3 course à la carte fr £20 ⊕ FREE HOUSE ◀ Timothy Taylor Landlord, Weetwood Cheshire Cat & Eastgate Ale, Spitting Feathers Thirstquencher, Sandstone. **Facilities** Children welcome Children's menu Children's portions Garden Parking Wi-fi 🚌 (notice required) **Rooms** 5

GAWSWORTH   Map 16 SJ86

Harrington Arms

Church Ln SK11 9RJ ☎ 01260 223325
dir: *From Macclesfield take A536 towards Congleton. Turn left for Gawsworth*

Part farmhouse, part pub, the little-changed interior comprises a main bar serving Robinsons real ales and quirky rooms with open fires and rustic furnishings. Memorable for its impression of timelessness, it dates from 1664 and has been licensed since 1710. On offer is good pub food made extensively from the wealth of local produce, some from the pub's own fields, including home-made cottage pie; rib-eye, sirloin and gammon steaks; scampi and chips; vegetarian sausage and mash; and daily specials. Early October sees the annual conker championship here.

Open all wk 12-3 5-11.30 (Sun 12-4 7-11) Closed: 25 Dec **Bar Meals** L served Mon-Sat 12-2.30, Sun 12-3.30 D served Mon-Sat 5-8.30 Av main course £7.75 ⊕ FREDERIC ROBINSON ◀ Unicorn, 1892, Build a Rocket Boys!, Dizzy Blonde & Seasonal ale, Guinness ○ Westons Stowford Press. ☂ 8 **Facilities** Children welcome Children's portions Garden Parking 🚌 (notice required)

Ring O' Bells

Village Rd, Christleton, Chester CH3 7AS
Website: www.ringobellschester.co.uk
Email: ringobells@mbt.cc • Tel: 01244 335422

This charming pub situated in the picturesque village of Christleton just outside of Chester was voted Best Pub in Chester at the Chester Food and Drink Awards 2011-12 as well as receiving a highly commended top 3 place in the Cheshire Life Dining Pub of the Year 2011. *The Ring O' Bells* possesses a warm and friendly atmosphere where old meets new and contemporary meets traditional. The pub provides high-class quality food using locally sourced produce as well as having a large selection of wines from around the world and a range of well-kept locally brewed cask ales. *The Ring O' Bells* is also well known for it's hand stretched stone baked pizzas (2 for 1 every Wednesday) and its great customer service.

The exterior of the pub boasts many features such as an al fresco dining terrace, a decked "sun trap", as well as a family lawn with picnic tables & a children's' play area to keep every guest happy. Whether you're after a quick drink after work, a casual family Sunday lunch or an intimate meal on a Friday evening the *The Ring O' Bells* has something to offer everyone.

PICK OF THE PUBS

The Cholmondeley Arms

CHOLMONDELEY Map 15 SJ55

SY14 8HN ☎ 01829 720300
e-mail: info@cholmondeleyarms.co.uk
web: www.cholmondeleyarms.co.uk
dir: *On A49, between Whitchurch & Tarporley*

Set in rolling Cheshire countryside virtually opposite Cholmondeley Castle on the A49, and still part of the Vicount's estate, is this red-brick former schoolhouse (closed 1982). Quirky and eclectic, it's surely one of England's more unique pubs, the décor and artefacts, including family heirlooms, educational memorabilia, bell tower without and blackboards within add tremendously to the atmosphere of the cavernous interior. No longer a draughty institute, new owners Tim and Mary Bird have spruced the old school up and you'll find a warm and inviting interior, with fat church candles on old school desks, fresh flowers, glowing log fires and a relaxing atmosphere. After exploring the local countryside, visiting nearby Cholmondeley Castle, country seat of Lord and Lady Cholmondeley or the fabulous ruins at Beeston, stapled to Cheshire's hilly sandstone spine, it's the perfect place to unwind, sup a pint of Shropshire Gold or Cholmondeley Best (only micro-brewery beers from a 30-mile radius can be found on the five handpumps), or delve into the mind-

boggling list of over 80 different gins behind the bar. Allow time to taste some of the best produce from Cheshire's burgeoning larder, including seasonal game from the estate. Nibble and natter over a pork pie with piccalilli, or pint of prawns, then start with a seafood sharing plate, devilled lambs' kidneys on toast, or chicken, mushroom and tarragon terrine. 'Old School Favourites' take in a classic burger with chips and fennel coleslaw; lamb faggots with bubble-and-squeak; spicy goat stew with roasted pumpkin and crusty bread; and duck leg and lentil hotpot with prunes and winter vegetables; leaving room for warm Bakewell tart with raspberry ripple ice cream – school meals were never like this!

Open all day all wk **Bar Meals** L served all wk 12-9.30 D served all wk 12-9.30 Av main course £12 food served all day **Restaurant** food served all day ⊞ FREE HOUSE ◀ Cholmondeley Best Bitter, Salopian Shropshire Gold, 3 Guest ales. ♟ 16 **Facilities** Children welcome Children's portions ❀ Garden Beer festival Parking Wi-fi 🚌 (notice required)

Save on hotels. Book at **theAA.com/hotel**

CHESHIRE 81 ENGLAND

HANDLEY   Map 15 SJ45

The Calveley Arms

Whitchurch Rd CH3 9DT ☎ 01829 770619
e-mail: calveleyarms@btconnect.com
dir: *5m S of Chester, signed from A41. Follow signs for Handley & Aldersey Green Golf Course*

The spruced-up old coaching inn, first licensed in 1636, stands opposite the church with views of the distant Welsh hills. Chock full of old timbers, jugs, pots, pictures, prints and ornaments, the rambling bars provide an atmospheric setting in which to sample some cracking beers and decent pub food. Typically, tuck into lunchtime filled baguettes (hot beef), steak-and-kidney pie, sirloin steak with pepper sauce, speciality salads, and a good selection of pasta dishes. There are spacious gardens to enjoy in summer.

Open all wk 12-3 6-11 (Sun 12-3 7-11) **Bar Meals** L served all wk 12-3 D served Mon-Sat 6-9, Sun 7-9 ⊕ ENTERPRISE INNS ◀ Castle Eden Ale, Marston's Pedigree, Theakston Black Bull Bitter, Wells Bombardier, Greene King IPA. **Facilities** Children welcome Children's portions Play area Garden Parking 🚌

HAUGHTON MOSS   Map 15 SJ55

The Nags Head

Long Ln CW6 9RN ☎ 01829 260265
e-mail: roryk1@ournagshead.co.uk
dir: *Exit A49 S of Tarporley at Beeston/Haughton sign into Long Ln. 1.75m to pub*

An inn for all seasons, this 17th-century black-and-white timbered village pub has glorious summer gardens, suntrap patios and a bowling green. In winter, retreat inside the former smithy to find cosy, low-ceilinged rooms with old beams, exposed brickwork and open log fires. Owners Rory and Debbie and chef Karl Prince are committed to providing a broad range of home-cooked food; perhaps oven-roasted black pudding with warm tomato chutney and bacon lardons, followed by fillet of beef Stroganoff on a bed of rice, or vegetable frittata.

Open all day all wk 11am-mdnt **Bar Meals** L served all wk 12-10 D served all wk 12-10 Av main course £10 food served all day **Restaurant** L served all wk 12-10 D served all wk 12-10 Fixed menu price fr £8 Av 3 course à la carte fr £20 food served all day ⊕ FREE HOUSE ◀ Flowers IPA, Sharp's Doom Bar, Weetwood, Guest ales ♂ Kingstone Press. ☙12 **Facilities** Children welcome Children's menu Children's portions Play area Garden Parking Wi-fi 🚌 (notice required)

KETTLESHULME   Map 16 SJ97

Swan Inn

SK23 7QU ☎ 01663 732943
e-mail: the.swan.kettleshulme@googlemail.co.uk
dir: *On B5470 between Whaley Bridge (2m) and Macclesfield (5m)*

The Swan is a glorious, tiny 15th-century village inn huddled in the shadow of the craggy Windgather Rocks in the Cheshire Peak District. A consortium of locals bought the place over six years ago to save it from closure. Now safe and thriving in private hands again, the eclectic and international menu has interesting dishes such as 'stifado', a Greek rabbit stew slow-cooked with red wine, cinnamon, shallots and currants; and chicken jambonette, a chicken leg stuffed with duck and sausage meat, wrapped in proscuitto ham and smoky bacon. Local craft beers keep ramblers and locals very contented, especially at the pub's beer festival on the first weekend in September. Booking for meals may be required.

Open all wk Mon 5-11 Tue 12-3 5-11 Wed-Sun all day Closed: 25-26 Dec, 1 Jan, Mon L **Bar Meals** L served Tue 12-2, Wed 12-9, Thu-Fri 12-7, Sat 12-9, Sun 12-4 D served Tue 6.30-8.30, Wed 12-9, Thu-Fri 12-7, Sat 12-9 ⊕ FREE HOUSE ◀ Marston's, Marble, Thornbridge, Phoenix. **Facilities** ✿ Children welcome Children's portions Garden Beer festival

KNUTSFORD   Map 15 SJ77

The Dog Inn ★★★★ INN

PICK OF THE PUBS

See Pick of the Pubs on page 82

LACH DENNIS   Map 15 SJ77

The Duke of Portland

Penny's Ln CW9 7SY ☎ 01606 46264
e-mail: info@dukeofportland.com
dir: *M6 junct 19, A556 towards Northwich. Left onto B5082 to Lach Dennis*

This award-winning family-run pub has made a name for itself with its use of local and regional produce from across the Cheshire and Lancashire area. The kitchen's highly regarded suppliers are listed on the menus, which might include Goosnargh chicken in a basket; slow-roasted shoulder of Lune Valley lamb; cured ham hock with colcannon potatoes; or beef, Guinness and mushroom pie. Finish with rum baba or Bramley apple and rhubarb crumble. A sunny, landscaped garden complements the attractive building. Booking for meals may be required.

Open all day all wk **Bar Meals** L served all wk 12-3 D served all wk 5.30-9.30 Av main course £12 **Restaurant** L served all wk 12-3 D served all wk 5.30-9.30 Fixed menu price fr £10.95 Av 3 course à la carte fr £30 ⊕ MARSTON'S ◀ Banks's Original, Brakspear Oxford Gold, Jennings Cocker Hoop & Cumberland Ale ♂ Thatchers Gold. **Facilities** Children welcome Children's menu Children's portions Garden Parking Wi-fi 🚌

LITTLE NESTON   Map 15 SJ27

The Harp Inn

19 Quay Side CH64 0TB ☎ 0151 336 6980
e-mail: jonesalbert@sky.com
dir: *From Neston town centre, at 2nd mini rdbt, turn right onto Marshlands Rd. At bottom turn left, 200yds ahead*

Popular with walkers, cyclists and bird-watchers, this isolated pub enjoys beautiful scenery and sunsets, with views over the River Dee and across to Wales. The building was formerly miners' cottages before becoming a pub around 150 years ago; on the walls mining artefacts and pictures testify to its history. Although renovated over the years, it remains a simple two-roomed pub, with quarry-tiled floors and low beams. A good range of real ales is kept – six available all the time, and simple plates of food. There is a boules pitch in the beer garden.

Open all day all wk 12-12 **Bar Meals** L served Mon-Fri 12-2 ⊕ ADMIRAL TAVERNS ◀ Joseph Holt, Timothy Taylor Landlord, Wadworth 6X, Guest ales. **Facilities** Children welcome Children's menu Children's portions Family room Garden Parking 🚌 **Notes** ⊕

LOWER WHITLEY   Map 15 SJ67

Chetwode Arms NEW

Street Ln WA4 4EN ☎ 01925 730203
e-mail: info@chetwode-arms.co.uk
web: www.chetwode-arms.co.uk
dir: *M56 junct 10, 2m S on A49*

In the heart of Cheshire's farming countryside, it is easy to miss this tucked away 400-year-old brick-built coaching inn, despite its close proximity to the M56. Enjoy well-kept real ales in the intimate bar, which is listed due to its double-hinged door dating back to the days when coffins were taken on their last journey to the church – 'one for the road'. The food can be enjoyed in one of the many cosy dining rooms or passageways, with most meat and fish dishes being served on volcanic stone grills. Booking for meals may be required.

Open all wk 12.30-2.30 5-11 (Sun 12-7) **Bar Meals** L served Tue 12-2.30, Sun 12-7 D served Mon-Thu 5-9, Fri-Sat 5-9.30, Sun 12-7 Av main course £7.50 **Restaurant** L served Tue 12-2.30, Sun 12-7 D served Mon-Thu 5-9, Fri-Sat 5-9.30, Sun 12-7 Fixed menu price fr £10 Av 3 course à la carte fr £30 ⊕ PUNCH TAVERNS ◀ Adnams Broadside, Greene King Ruddles County, 2 Guest ales ♂ Westons Old Rosie. **Facilities** ✿ Children welcome Children's portions Family room Garden Parking Wi-fi 🚌 (notice required)

PICK OF THE PUBS

The Dog Inn ★★★★ INN

KNUTSFORD Map 15 SJ77

Well Bank Ln, Over Peover WA16 8UP
☎ **01625 861421**
e-mail: thedoginnpeover@btconnect.com
web: www.doginn-overpeover.co.uk
dir: *S from Knutsford take A50. Turn into Stocks Ln at The Whipping Stocks pub. 2m*

Before you go in, enjoy the pub sign here because there cannot possibly be another in Britain featuring a boxer dog with a turquoise ice-pack on its head! Serving ale for about two centuries, this timbered inn has in its time been a row of cottages, a grocer's, a shoemaker's and a farm. Colourful flowerbeds, tubs and hanging baskets create quite a display in summer, while year-round appeal derives from the cask-conditioned ales from Hydes in Manchester, Weetwood in Tarporley and Moorhouse's in Burnley, and large array of malt whiskies. There's classic English food too, prepared from produce sourced largely within Cheshire and which might appear on the menu as crudités to share, and barbecued spare ribs of pork as starters, with main courses of 14-oz king cod and mushy peas; crispy roast half-duck with port and mushroom sauce; and, for vegetarians, Congleton oatcakes with leeks, stilton and mushrooms. Ever-popular desserts include chocolate fudge cake and bread-and-butter pudding. For

something lighter, choose from the excellent range of sandwiches and hot baguettes. There are six attractive guest rooms if you want to stay over and explore this part of the world, or maybe attend the annual beer festival, which begins on the first Friday in August and staggers through to the Sunday, and for which more than 30 real ales and ciders are marshalled for visitors' pleasure. On that same Sunday the pub is also the venue for the Over Peover Gooseberry Show, when you can find out what possesses grown men and women to try and grow Cheshire's biggest gooseberry. Given the pub's name, it should come as no surprise to learn that dogs are welcome everywhere, except of course the restaurant.

Open all wk 11.30-3 4.30-11 (Sat-Sun all day) **Bar Meals** L served Mon-Fri 12-2.30, Sat-Sun all day D served Mon-Fri 6-9, Sat-Sun all day **Restaurant** L served all wk 12-2.30 D served all wk 6-9 ⊕ FREE HOUSE ◖ Weetwood Best Bitter, Copper Dragon, Hydes, Moorhouse's. ♟ 10 **Facilities** Children welcome Children's menu Children's portions Garden ❀ Beer festival Parking Wi-fi 🚌 **Rooms** 6

MARTON
Map 16 SJ86

The Davenport Arms
PICK OF THE PUBS

Congleton Rd SK11 9HF ☎ 01260 224269
e-mail: info@thedavenportarms.co.uk
dir: *3m from Congleton on A34*

A farmhouse in the 18th century, this charming old pub occupies a lovely spot opposite Marton church – said to be the oldest half-timbered church still in use in Europe – and close to the Marton Oak, which at 1,200 years is possibly the oldest surviving tree in England. An independent free house, the traditional bar is furnished with cushioned settles and leather armchairs around a log fire; an old fresh-water well covered by plate glass adds appeal of its own to the restaurant. Food is all freshly made on the premises using local ingredients. Seasonal specials change daily and there's always a good fresh fish selection – fillet of Cajun salmon with sweet potato rösti and chive crème fraîche might appear alongside sticky pork ribs with garlic mayo and home-made chips, or honeyed duck breast, fondant potato with blackberry sauce. The large garden contains a thatched summerhouse and a play area for children. Booking for meals may be required.

Open 12-3 6-12 (Fri-Sun 12-12) Closed: Mon L (ex BH) **Bar Meals** L served Tue-Sat 12-2.30, Sun 12-3 D served Mon-Fri 6-9, Sun 6-8.30 Av main course £10 **Restaurant** L served Tue-Fri 12-2.30, Sat 12-9, Sun 12-8 D served Tue-Fri 6-9, Sat 12-9, Sun 12-8 Av 3 course à la carte fr £20 ⊕ FREE HOUSE ◀ Copper Dragon, Storm, Weetwood, Theakston, Beartown, Courage Directors. ♀ 9 **Facilities** Children welcome Children's menu Play area Garden Parking Wi-fi ▩ (notice required)

MOBBERLEY
Map 15 SJ77

The Bulls Head NEW

Mill Ln WA16 7HX ☎ 01565 873345
e-mail: info@thebullsheadpub.com
web: www.thebullsheadpub.com
dir: *From Knutsford take A537, A5085 to Mobberley*

The sister pub to the Cholmondeley Arms (see entry) pushed open its doors in May 2010 following major refurbishment. This little gem, tucked away in sleepy Mobberley, now thrives as a community local and as destination for cracking real ales from Cheshire micro-breweries and wholesome home-cooked food.

Traditional rooms have been gently smartened up and provide a comfortable and convivial setting for savouring delicious Sunday roasts, ale-battered haddock, a classic burger with hand-cut chips and fennel coleslaw, and sticky whisky toffee pudding. There's a super summer garden and don't miss the June beer festival.

Open all day all wk **Bar Meals** Av main course £12 food served all day **Restaurant** food served all day ⊕ FREE HOUSE ◀ Bulls Head Bitter, Mobberley Wobbly Ale, 1812 Overture Ale, Blonde Bull. ♀ 16 **Facilities** ✿ Children welcome Children's portions Garden Beer festival Parking Wi-fi ▩ (notice required)

MOULDSWORTH
Map 15 SJ57

The Goshawk
PICK OF THE PUBS

Station Rd CH3 8AJ ☎ 01928 740900
e-mail: goshawk@woodwardandfalconer.com
dir: *A51 from Chester onto A54. Left onto B5393 towards Frodsham. Into Mouldsworth, pub on left*

This sturdy old railway inn has a hint of Edwardian grandeur whilst benefitting from contemporary comforts; print-clad walls and dado rails, comfy sofas and open fires. Its village setting makes the most of the area's delights, including the many miles of footpaths, cycle trails and mysterious meres of nearby Delamere Forest, one of the largest in northwest England, whilst historic Chester is just one stop away on the train. The terrace and large grassy beer garden offer views across the heart of Cheshire, and the local motor museum is an interesting diversion. Cheshire ales from Weetwood draw an appreciative crowd of locals, whilst the wide-ranging menu is matched by an extensive wine list. Starters tempt with manchego cheese with roast figs, or confit duck stack; mains browse a wide choice: sesame-rolled tuna steak with oriental noodles; mozzarella-topped chicken breast stuffed with chorizo; and the Goshawk steak burger. There's a good range of vegetarian dishes and a choice of 21-day aged steaks.

Open all day all wk 12-11 (Sun 12-10.30) Closed: 25 Dec & 1 Jan **Bar Meals** food served all day **Restaurant** food served all day ⊕ WOODWARD & FALCONER PUBS ◀ Piffle, Weetwood Eastgate Ale & Best Bitter, Guest ales. ♀ 14 **Facilities** Children welcome Children's menu Children's portions Play area Family room Garden Parking ▩

NANTWICH
Map 15 SJ65

The Thatch Inn

Wrexham Rd, Faddiley CW5 8JE ☎ 01270 524223
dir: *Follow signs for Wrexham from Nantwich, inn 4m from Nantwich on A534*

The pretty black-and-white Thatch Inn is believed to be the oldest (and one of the prettiest) pubs in south Cheshire. It has a three-quarter acre garden, while inside there are plentiful oak beams, and open fires in winter. Starters might be salmon, haddock and spring onion fishcakes with home-made tartare sauce, or black pudding and streaky bacon with a creamy wholegrain mustard sauce. For mains, maybe home-made steak, mushroom and ale pie, or chargrilled pork loin on creamy mash with an apple fritter, braised red cabbage and cider and apple jus. Children have their own menu.

Open Mon-Tue 6-11, Wed-Thu 12-3 5.30-11, Fri-Sat 12-11, Sun 12-10.30 Closed: Mon L & Tue L **Bar Meals** L served Wed-Thu 12-3, Fri-Sat 12-9, Sun 12-8.30 D served Mon-Thu 6-9, Fri-Sat 12-9, Sun 12-8.30 ⊕ ENTERPRISE INNS ◀ Weetwood Eastgate Ale, Salopian Shropshire Gold. ♀ 24 **Facilities** Children welcome Children's menu Play area Family room Garden Parking ▩

NETHER ALDERLEY
Map 16 SJ87

The Wizard Inn NEW

Macclesfield Rd SK10 4UB ☎ 01625 584000
e-mail: wizardrestaurant@googlemail.com
dir: *On B5087 between Alderley Edge & Macclesfield. Next to National Trust car park*

In National Trust woodlands below the red sandstone escarpment of Alderley Edge, The Wizard has all the country-pub hallmarks – stone floors, beams, scrubbed wood tables... Only the finest locally and responsibly sourced ingredients go into modern classics and specials, such as chargrilled rump steak with garlic prawns and triple-cooked beef-dripping chips; roast salmon with wild mushrooms, green kale and walnut pesto; and chicken curry with basmati and tomato and red onion salsa. The wine list is admirably brief; Pouilly Fumé is 'Fresh, light and bone dry', for example.

Open all wk 12-3 5.30-11 (Sat 12-11 Sun 12-10) Closed: 25 Dec **Bar Meals** L served Mon-Fri 12-2, Sat 12-9.30, Sun 12-8 D served Mon-Fri 6.30-9.30, Sat 12-9.30, Sun 12-8 Av main course £13 **Restaurant** L served Mon-Fri 12-2, Sat 12-9.30, Sun 12-8 D served Mon-Fri 6.30-9.30, Sat 12-9.30, Sun 12-8 Av 3 course à la carte fr £25 ⊕ FREE HOUSE ◀ Storm Ale Force, Thwaites Wainwright. ♀ 14 **Facilities** ✿ Children welcome Children's portions Garden Parking Wi-fi

NORTHWICH
Map 15 SJ67

The Red Lion ★★★ INN

277 Chester Rd, Hartford CW8 1QL ☎ 01606 74597
e-mail: cathy.iglesias@tesco.net
dir: *From A556 take Hartford exit. Red Lion at 1st junct on left next to church*

This engaging inn was the village fire station until a century or so ago, and many artefacts remain from that. Hunker down with a pint of Black Sheep, tuck in to hearty pub grub like home-made lamb hotpot, or take on the locals at darts or dominoes. This is a thriving community local where visitors to the nearby Delamere Forest or Oulton Park motor-racing circuit can also bed down in the en suite accommodation here. Out the back there is an enclosed beer garden with smoking shelter.

Open all day all wk **Bar Meals** L served Mon-Sat 12-2 D served Mon-Sat 6-8 Av main course £5.50 **Restaurant** L served Mon-Sat 12-2 D served Mon-Sat 6-8 ⊕ PUNCH TAVERNS ◀ Marston's Pedigree, Black Sheep. ☗ **Facilities** ☙ Children welcome Family room Garden Parking Wi-fi **Rooms** 3

PARKGATE
Map 15 SJ27

The Boat House

1 The Parade CH64 6RN ☎ 0151 336 4187
dir: *On B5135, 3m from Heswall*

With magnificent views across the Dee Estuary to Wales, this striking black-and-white timbered pub is a haven for both bird-watchers and food-lovers. Thirsty twitchers head straight for the bar and a pint of Piffle – the pub's own brew. If food is the priority, look to the airy dining room with views across salt marshes, or take a seat in the cosy modernised bars. Freshly supplied fish and seafood are the major attraction here, with plenty of lovingly prepared dishes. Look out for the flooding, about four times a year, when high tide reaches the walls of the pub.

Open all day all wk 11-11 (Sun 11-10.30) Closed: 25 Dec, 1 Jan **Bar Meals** L served Mon-Sat 12-9.30, Sun 12-9 D served Mon-Sat 12-9.30, Sun 12-9 **Restaurant** L served all wk 12-5 D served Mon-Sat 5-9.30, Sun 5-9 ⊕ FREE HOUSE ◀ John Smith's, Morland Old Speckled Hen, Woodward & Falconer Piffle, Weetwood Eastgate Ale. ☗ 17 **Facilities** Children welcome Children's portions Garden Parking Wi-fi ▭ (notice required)

The Ship Hotel

The Parade CH64 6SA ☎ 0151 336 3931
e-mail: info@the-shiphotel.co.uk
dir: *A540 (Chester towards Neston) left then immediately right onto B5136 (Liverpool Rd). In Neston town centre, left onto B5135. Follow to The Parade in Parkgate, hotel 50yds on right*

Although silting put paid to Parkgate's days as a thriving port, visitors to this free house with rooms can still enjoy fine views across the tranquil, wildlife-rich Dee Estuary to the coast and mountains of North Wales. The Ship's origins can be traced to the 18th century, but the hotel was rebuilt and enlarged in the 19th century. Enjoy home-made food by the roaring fire or on the heated patio. The options on the daily menus are traditional in style – fish finger sandwich; rump burger; and sweet potato and vegetable crumble, with the specials board adding further choice. There's a beer festival in April.

Open all day all wk **Bar Meals** L served all wk 12-2.30 D served all wk 6-8.30 **Restaurant** L served all wk 12-2.30 D served all wk 6-8.30 ⊕ FREE HOUSE ◀ Brimstage Trapper's Hat, Peerless Storr, Woodlands Oak Beauty, Weetwood Oast-House Gold. **Facilities** Children welcome Children's menu Children's portions Beer festival Parking Wi-fi ▭ (notice required)

PLUMLEY
Map 15 SJ77

The Golden Pheasant Hotel

Plumley Moor Rd WA16 9RX ☎ 01565 722261 & 722125
dir: *M6 junct 19, A556 signed Chester. 2m, left at Plumley/Peover signs. Through Plumley, pub 1m opp rail station*

This 200-year-old traditional wayside inn has a wealth of beams, low ceilings and a magnificent carved oak bar servery. Set in beautiful Cheshire countryside, it is convenient for Chester and Manchester, with trains from the station opposite hourly. Expect a great choice of real ales, an extensive wine list and home-cooked, locally sourced food. Typical choices are black pudding with soft poached egg and creamy pepper sauce, followed by pan-fried fillet of sea bass with goat's cheese crushed potatoes, yellow pepper coulis and beetroot glaze. Expect roaring log fires, comfy sitting areas, alfresco dining, a children's play area and a locals' bar with a darts board.

Open all day all wk 11-11 (Sun 12-10.30) **Bar Meals** Av main course £10.95 food served all day **Restaurant** Fixed menu price fr £17.95 Av 3 course à la carte fr £21.95 food served all day ⊕ J W LEES ◀ Bitter, John Willies Premium Bitter & Dragon's Fire, Great Budworth Best Bitter, Guinness. ☗ 14 **Facilities** Children welcome Children's menu Children's portions Play area Garden Parking Wi-fi ▭

The Smoker

WA16 0TY ☎ 01565 722338
e-mail: thesmokerinn@aol.com
dir: *From M6 junct 19 take A556 W. Pub 1.75m on left*

In the Cheshire countryside, this 400-year-old thatched coaching inn was named after a white racehorse bred by the Prince Regent. The pub's striking wood-panelled interior of three connecting rooms welcomes drinkers as well as diners, all enjoying the warm welcome of log fires, comfortable sofas, beams and copper kettles. To drink, choose from Robinsons Dizzy Blonde, Old Stockport and Long Kiss Goodnight, among other ales. The menu has an appealing array of starters such as crispy duck pancake, while main courses include sweet chilli chicken. Desserts tempt with tarte au citron, Eton Mess and baked Alaska. Booking for meals may be required.

Open all wk 10-3 6-11 (Sun 10am-10.30pm) **Bar Meals** L served Mon-Sat 10-2.30, Sun 10-9 D served Mon-Sat 6-9.30, Sun 10-9 Av main course £11.95 **Restaurant** L served Mon-Sat 10-2.30, Sun 10-9 D served Mon-Sat 6-9.30, Sun 10-9 Fixed menu price fr £14.95 Av 3 course à la carte fr £20 ⊕ FREDERIC ROBINSON ◀ Unicorn, Old Stockport, Dizzy Blonde, Hannibal's Nectar, Long Kiss Goodnight ♻ Westons Stowford Press. ☗ 10 **Facilities** Children welcome Children's menu Children's portions Play area Garden Parking

PRESTBURY
Map 16 SJ87

The Legh Arms

The Village SK10 4DG ☎ 01625 829130
e-mail: legharms@hotmail.co.uk
dir: *On A538 (New Road)*

A characterful gabled and part-timbered old inn at the heart of trendy Prestbury, where premiership footballers trip over each other on the pavements. They're lucky to have The Legh Arms on their doorstep, dispensing fine ales from Robinsons Brewery near by and serving good food all day every day. At lunchtime you can opt for simpler fare such as macaroni cheese; pie of the day; or a half roasted chicken served with salad and fries. For a celeb-spotting special dinner, look to the specials for great local estate meat and game. Booking for meals may be required.

Open all day all wk **Bar Meals** food served all day **Restaurant** L served Mon-Fri 12-2, Sat-Sun 12-10 D served Sat 12-10, Sun 12-9.30 ⊕ FREDERIC ROBINSON ◀ Hatters, Unicorn. ☗ **Facilities** Children welcome Children's portions Garden Parking Wi-fi

Save on hotels. Book at **theAA.com/hotel**

CHESHIRE 85 ENGLAND

PICK OF THE PUBS

The Swettenham Arms

SWETTENHAM Map 15 SJ86

Swettenham Ln CW12 2LF
☎ 01477 571284

e-mail: info@swettenhamarms.co.uk
web: www.swettenhamarms.co.uk
dir: *M6 junct 18 to Holmes Chapel, then A535 towards Jodrell Bank. 3m right (Forty Acre Lane) to Swettenham*

If you rely on your Sat Nav you may well end up in the middle of the local ford, but this pub's well worth the search once you find it. Formerly a nunnery, it's been in the capable hands of the Cunninghams for many years, although there's still the occasional ghostly sighting of a nun. With a polished copper bar, three welcoming open fireplaces and shiny brasses it is obvious that a traditional approach still reigns, and it certainly proves a sure-fire hit with both drinkers and diners. Thomas Ludecke and his brigade are now in their third year in the kitchen and the menu is as modern as the pub is traditional. The short menus indicate the reliance on the freshest, locally-sourced, seasonal ingredients. Home grown vegetables, bee hives and the pub's own hens were introduced last year. The seasonally-changing menus offer plenty of choice, from satisfying pub classics such as steak, mushroom and ale suet pudding to restaurant-style English rump of lamb with Puy lentils and root vegetable ragout, tomato and tarragon jus. For dessert, the hot mango and coconut soufflé with mango sauce is worth the wait of 15 minutes; the ice creams are home-made too. The good selection of

English farmhouse cheeses and a coffee make a great finish to a delightful meal. At lunchtime, light bites and sandwiches feature too, and there's a choice of roasts on a Sunday. In summer, a stroll round the stunning lavender and sunflower meadow to the rear of the pub should not be missed, or at any time of year you can wander in the adjoining 33-acre Quinta Arboretum (5,000 trees) where there are plenty of easy-walking and wheelchair-friendly routes. Booking for meals may be required.

Open all day all wk 11.30-close **Food** L served Mon-Fri 12-2.30, Sat-Sun 12-6 D served Mon-Sat 6-9.30, Sun 6-8.30 Early bird menu Mon-Fri from 5 Av main course £10, fixed price menu fr £9, Av 3 course à la carte £26.50 ⊕ FREE HOUSE

◗ Timothy Taylor Landlord, Sharp's Doom Bar, Bollington Best, Courage Directors, Moorhouse's Pride of Pendle, Slater's Top Totty, Hydes, Black Sheep, Beartown ♂ Addlestones. ♟ 12 **Facilities** Children welcome Children's menu ♣ Garden Parking Wi-fi 🚌

SPURSTOW
Map 15 SJ55

The Yew Tree Inn NEW

Long Ln CW6 9RD ☎ 01829 260274
e-mail: info@theyewtreebunbury.com
dir: *400mtrs from A49 on Long Ln*

Built by the Earl of Crewe, this is a sympathetically refurbished 19th-century village pub. Inside, the original beams and open fires are a reminder of the pub's history, while a new terrace is a more modern addition and perfect for summer dining. Beer is taken seriously here, with up to eight real ales available and the Easter beer festival is not to be missed. A seasonal menu is driven by local produce and might include faggots, buttered mash and onion gravy or home-made fish pie. Booking for meals may be required.

Open all day all wk **Bar Meals** L served Mon-Fri 12-2.30, Sat 12-10, Sun brunch 11-1, Sun 12-8 D served Mon-Thu 6-9.30, Fri 6-10, Sat 12-10, Sun 12-8 Av main course £11 **Restaurant** L served Mon-Fri 12-2.30, Sat 12-10, Sun brunch 11-1, Sun 12-8 D served Mon-Thu 6-9.30, Fri 6-10, Sat 12-10, Sun 12-8 Av 3 course à la carte fr £25 ⊕ FREE HOUSE ◀ Stonehouse Station Bitter, 7 Guest ales Ŏ Westons. ♟ 14 **Facilities** ❖ Children welcome Children's menu Children's portions Garden Beer festival Parking Wi-fi ▭ (notice required)

STOAK
Map 15 SJ47

The Bunbury Arms

Little Stanney Ln CH2 4HW ☎ 01244 301665
e-mail: bunburyarmschester@gmail.com
dir: *From M53/M56 junct 11/15 take A5117. 1st left into Little Stanney Ln*

This traditional alehouse is located in a small wooded hamlet. Inside, the snug is exactly that – with open fire, TV, board games and darts, not forgetting an award-winning selection of real ales and extensive wine list. The Bunbury developed a fine reputation under the ownership of Alan Frain, who had run the pub since the '70s and who sadly passed away in 2011. Now in the experienced hands of his wife Janet, the pub continues to pride itself on its hospitality and good food. Chicken and seafood paella; Lebanese-style meatballs; and beef bordelaise all appear on the evening menu. The pub's handy for the Cheshire Oaks retail outlet, Chester Zoo and Blue Planet Aquarium.

Open all day all wk **Bar Meals** L served all wk 12-6 D served Mon-Thu 6-9, Fri-Sat 6-9.30 food served all day **Restaurant** L served Mon-Sat 12-6, Sun 12-8 D served Mon-Thu 6-9, Fri-Sat 6-9.30, Sun 12-8 food served all day ⊕ FREE HOUSE ◀ Robinsons Unicorn, JW Lees Coronation Street, Joseph Holt, Cains. ♟ 26 **Facilities** ❖ Children welcome Children's menu Children's portions Garden Beer festival Parking Wi-fi ▭ (notice required)

SUTTON LANE ENDS
Map 16 SJ97

The Hanging Gate Inn

Meg Ln, Higher Sutton SK11 0NG ☎ 01260 252238
dir: *From S of Macclesfield take A523 (signed Leek). At lights left into Byron's Ln signed Sutton, Langley & Wincle. Bear left into Jarman, left onto Ridge Hill, becomes Meg Lane. 2nd right to pub on left*

Clinging to the hillside high above Rossendale, The Hanging Gate boasts breathtaking views across Cheshire into Wales. An old drovers' inn dating from 1661, the pub marks the spot where poachers on the Royal Macclesfield Forest were hanged. Quaff a pint of local ale in one of the three unspoilt rooms or tuck into regional produce, perhaps pheasant with smoked bacon, red wine sauce, and bubble-and-squeak. On a fine day bag a seat in the garden or time a visit with the May or August Bank Holiday beer festivals.

Open all wk 12-3 6-11 (Sat-Sun 12-11) **Bar Meals** L served Mon-Fri 12-2, Sat-Sun 12-2.30 D served all wk 6-9 Av main course £12 **Restaurant** L served Mon-Fri 12-2, Sat-Sun 12-2.30 D served all wk 6-9 Fixed menu price fr £19.95 Av 3 course à la carte fr £35 ⊕ HYDES BREWERY ◀ Original, Manchester Finest, Craft Ales. ♟ 10 **Facilities** ❖ Children welcome Children's menu Children's portions Family room Garden Beer festival Parking Wi-fi ▭ (notice required)

Sutton Hall

PICK OF THE PUBS

Bullocks Ln SK11 0HE ☎ 01260 253211
e-mail: sutton.hall@brunningandprice.co.uk
dir: *A523 from Macclesfield. At lights left into Byron's Ln (signed Sutton, Langley & Wincle) to village. Pub on left*

The family seat of the Earls of Lucan, this striking half-timbered and gritstone manor house is surrounded by its own estate. Dating from the 16th century, but considerably added to since, it conceals a wealth of nooks and crannies, a snug, a library and seven different dining areas, with terraces and gardens outside. The Macclesfield Canal runs nearby, while in the other direction are the steeply wooded hills and crags of Macclesfield Forest. As part of the Brunning & Price chain

of dining pubs, it offers the company's own Original Bitter alongside Lord Lucan, a local brew whose whereabouts are no mystery; the wine list is well compiled and there are over 100 whiskies. A typical starter is potted smoked mackerel, crayfish and apple and fennel salad. Sample mains include honey-roast duck breast; pan-fried sea bass with chorizo, caper and tomato dressing; and Moroccan spiced pepper with couscous, aubergine and okra salad. Booking for meals may be required.

Open all day all wk 11.30-11 (Sun 12-10.30) **Bar Meals** L served Mon-Sat 12-10, Sun 12-9.30 D served Mon-Sat 12-10, Sun 12-9.30 food served all day **Restaurant** L served Mon-Sat 12-10, Sun 12-9.30 D served Mon-Sat 12-10, Sun 12-9.30 food served all day ⊕ FREE HOUSE/ BRUNNING & PRICE ◀ Brunning & Price Original Bitter, Flowers Original, Wincle Lord Lucan Ŏ Aspall, Westons Wyld Wood Organic. ♟ 21 **Facilities** ❖ Children welcome Children's portions Play area Garden Parking

SWETTENHAM
Map 15 SJ86

The Swettenham Arms

PICK OF THE PUBS

See Pick of the Pubs on page 85

TARPORLEY
Map 15 SJ56

Alvanley Arms Inn ★★★★ INN

Forest Rd, Cotebrook CW6 9DS ☎ 01829 760200
e-mail: info@alvanleyarms.co.uk
dir: *On A49, 1.5m N of Tarporley*

The landlords of this charming 16th-century former coaching inn also own the Cotebrook Shire Horse Centre next door, so expect a horse-themed décor – rosettes, harnesses and horseshoes – in the traditional oak-beamed bar. Hand-pulled ales complement a range of freshly prepared dishes, based on ingredients from local family businesses. Dishes range from chicken liver pâté with apple and date chutney, and Thai salmon fishcakes with sweet chilli sauce to roast leg of pork with mash and apple sauce. Renovations uncovered original beams in the individually designed bedrooms. Booking for meals may be required.

Open all wk 12-3 5.30-11.30 (Sat-Sun 12-11) **Bar Meals** L served Mon-Fri 12-2, Sat-Sun 12-9 D served Mon-Fri 6-9, Sat-Sun 12-9 **Restaurant** L served Mon-Fri 12-2, Sat-Sun 12-9 D served Mon-Fri 6-9, Sat-Sun 12-9 Fixed menu price fr £10.95 ⊕ FREDERIC ROBINSON ◀ Unicorn, Guest ales. ♟ 12 **Facilities** Children welcome Children's menu Children's portions Garden Parking Wi-fi ▭ (notice required) **Rooms** 7

PICK OF THE PUBS

The Bear's Paw ★★★★★ INN ❀

WARMINGHAM   Map 15 SJ76

School Ln CW11 3QN ☎ 01270 526317
e-mail: info@thebearspaw.co.uk
web: www.thebearspaw.co.uk
dir: *M6 junct 18, A54, A533 towards Sandbach. Follow signs for village*

With its prominent central gable and some nods towards typical Cheshire black-and-white half-timbering, this stylish 19th-century gastro inn has clearly had a lot of money spent on it. Acres — well it seems like acres — of reclaimed antique oak flooring, leather sofas surrounding two huge open fireplaces, bookshelves offering plenty of choice for a good read, and more than 200 pictures and archive photos lining the oak-panelled walls. The bar, in which stands a carved wooden bear with a salmon in its mouth, offers a half dozen cask ales from local micro-breweries, including the somewhat appropriate Beartown in Congleton, Weetwood in Tarporley, and Tatton in Knutsford, as well as some real ciders. Whether you're sitting out front looking across to the churchyard or in the clubby interior, there's plenty of comfortable dining space in which to sample wholesome, locally sourced food from wide-ranging daily menus that expertly blend the classic with the modern. Take, for example, starters like baked field mushrooms with Blacksticks Blue cheese, rocket, pine nuts and balsamic vinegar, and main dishes such as chargrilled Bowland lamb steak, chive-crushed new potatoes, Jerusalem artichoke purée and watercress; fresh North Sea haddock in beer batter with mushy peas, home-made

tartare sauce and hand-cut chips; and half a Goosnargh duck, stir-fried vegetables in a crisp filo basket, rice and hoi sin sauce. Great for sharing are the imaginative deli boards, which come laden with local cheeses, charcuterie or pickled and smoked fish, and don't miss the Sunday roast lunches. For something lighter, think in terms of a filled jacket potato, or a sandwich, baguette or wrap. The Bear's Paw is owned and operated by family-owned Nelson Hotels, whose distinctive boutique-style en suite bedrooms, with their exquisite décor and furnishings are a real treat to stay in.

Open all day all wk **Bar Meals** L served Mon-Thu 12-9.30, Fri-Sat 12-10, Sun 12-8 D served Mon-Thu 12-9.30, Fri-Sat 12-10, Sun 12-8 **Restaurant** L served Mon-Thu 12-9.30, Fri-Sat 12-10, Sun

12-8 D served Mon-Thu 12-9.30, Fri-Sat 12-10, Sun 12-8 ⊕ FREE HOUSE ◀ Weetwood Best Bitter & Cheshire Cat, Moorhouse's Black Cat, Spitting Feathers, Beartown, Tatton ⏾ Westons Stowford Press, Kingstone Press. ♟ 10 **Facilities** Children welcome Children's menu Children's portions ❣ Garden Parking Wi-fi ▭ (notice required) **Rooms** 17

TARPORLEY *continued*

The Swan, Tarporley

50 High St CW6 0AG ☎ 01829 733838
e-mail: info@theswantarporley.co.uk
web: www.theswantarporley.co.uk
dir: *From junct of A49 & A51 into Tarporley. Pub on right in village centre*

An old coaching inn on the Shrewsbury to Chester road, this hostelry is one of the most historic inns in the area. It's been home to the Tarporley Hunt Club, known as the Green Collars, since it was formed in 1762, and is full of nook-and-cranny-imbued character. Regulars favour the open-fired Pantry Bar, but the Hayes and Pickering Rooms are also welcoming, the latter for locally sourced plates of home-made Scotch egg; and the village butcher's half-pound bacon chop. The afternoon tea-for-two tempts with a half bottle of champagne and smoked salmon and cream cheese sandwiches.

Open all day all wk **Bar Meals** L served Mon-Sat 7am-9pm, Sun 8-8 D served Mon-Sat 7am-9pm, Sun 8-8 Av main course £12 food served all day **Restaurant** L served Mon-Sat 7am-9pm, Sun 8-8 D served Mon-Sat 7am-9pm, Sun 8-8 food served all day ⊕ FREE HOUSE ◀ Weetwood Best Bitter & Eastgate Ale, Black Sheep ○ Westons Wyld Wood Organic Classic & Stowford Press. ⓨ 10 **Facilities** Children welcome Children's menu Children's portions Family room Garden Parking Wi-fi

---

TUSHINGHAM CUM GRINDLEY   Map 15 SJ54

Blue Bell Inn

PICK OF THE PUBS

SY13 4QS ☎ 01948 662172
dir: *A41, 4m N of Whitchurch, signed Bell O' the Hill*

In what must be a unique tale from the annals of pub-haunting, this inn reputedly has a ghost duck, whose spirit is sealed in a bottle buried in the bottom step of the cellar. Believe that or not, the Blue Bell remains a charming pub. A lovely black-and-white building that oozes character with its abundance of beams, open fires and horse brasses, its oldest part dates to approximately 1550, and the main building was completed in 1667. It has all the features you'd expect of a timber-framed building of this date, including one of the largest working chimneys in Cheshire and a priest hole. Curios that have been discovered from within the wall structure are on show in the pub. A menu of hearty, home-cooked pub food includes curries, steak and chips, and chilli with garlic bread. Drink options include well-kept ales, real cider and a selection of wines. Booking for meals may be required.

Open 12-3 6-11.30 Closed: Mon (ex BH) **Bar Meals** L served Tue-Sun 12-2 D served Tue-Sat 6-9 **Restaurant** L served Tue-Sun 12-2 D served Tue-Sat 6-9 ⊕ FREE HOUSE ◀ Salopian Shropshire Gold, Oakham JHB, Guest ales ○ Thatchers Cheddar Valley, Westons Old Rosie. **Facilities** ❤ Children welcome Children's portions Family room Garden Parking ▭

WARMINGHAM   Map 15 SJ76

The Bear's Paw ★★★★★ INN ◉

PICK OF THE PUBS

See Pick of the Pubs on page 87

WINCLE   Map 16 SJ96

The Ship Inn

Barlow Hill SK11 0QE ☎ 01260 227217
e-mail: shipinnwincle@btconnect.com
dir: *From Buxton towards Congleton on A54 left into Barlow Hill at x-roads, follow signs for Wincle (0.75m) & Swythamley & brown signs to pub (Spoon & Fork)*

Dating back to the 17th-century, The Ship Inn is located in the small, vibrant village of Wincle in the heart of the Peak District National Park. With several circular trails nearby, walkers and their dogs are welcome in the flag-stoned taproom, as well as the beer garden with its splendid views. In the more formal dining area, enjoy a pint of JW Lees Coronation Street ale and choose from the extensive and regularly changing menu, which focuses on local produce. Typical dishes might include slow-roasted wild duck in a red wine, orange and lemon sauce, or ham hock and chicken terrine.

Open 12-3 evening times vary Closed: Mon (ex BHs) **Bar Meals** L served Tue-Sat 12-2.30, Sun 12-3 D served Tue-Sat 7-9 Av main course £11.95 **Restaurant** L served Tue-Sat 12-2.30, Sun 12-3 D served Tue-Sat 7-9 Av 3 course à la carte fr £23.95 ⊕ J W LEES ◀ Bitter, Coronation Street. ⓨ 13 **Facilities** ❤ Children welcome Children's portions Family room Garden Parking

---

WRENBURY   Map 15 SJ54

The Dusty Miller

CW5 8HG ☎ 01270 780537
dir: *Telephone for directions*

This beautifully converted 18th-century corn mill is beside the Llangollen Canal in the rural village of Wrenbury. The pub's large arched windows offer views of passing boats, while a black-and-white lift bridge, designed by Thomas Telford, completes the picture-postcard setting. With a good choice of real ales, the menu, which mainly relies on ingredients from the region, offers pan-fried king scallops with pea purée; braised shallot and fig tarte Tatin; roasted chicken supreme; pan-fried salmon with new potatoes; and 28-day matured rib-eye steak.

Open 12-12 Closed: Mon in winter **Bar Meals** L served Mon-Fri 12-3, Sat 12-9.30, Sun 12-8 D served Mon-Fri 6-9 **Restaurant** L served Mon-Fri 12-3, Sat 12-9.30, Sun 12-8 D served Mon-Fri 6-9 ⊕ FREE HOUSE ◀ Robinsons Unicorn, Old Tom & Dizzy Blonde, Guest ales ○ Westons Stowford Press & Traditional. ⓨ 12 **Facilities** ❤ Children welcome Children's menu Children's portions Garden Parking ▭

CORNWALL & ISLES OF SCILLY

BLISLAND   Map 2 SX17

The Blisland Inn

PL30 4JF ☎ 01208 850739
dir: *5m from Bodmin towards Launceston. 2.5m off A30 signed Blisland. On village green*

Beside one of Cornwall's few remaining village greens, this old stone inn hosts a beer festival each May when milds are promoted, augmenting the Cornish bitters, local ciders and countless guest beers that have gained the pub national recognition. Inside there's no jukebox or fruit machines, but beams, toby jugs, local photos, a huge collection of barometers and a slate floor produce a timeless atmosphere. Reliable pub grub includes home-made chicken and ham pie and bowls of thick soup, ideal for warming up after walking on nearby Bodmin Moor. Booking for meals may be required.

Open all day all wk **Bar Meals** L served all wk 12-2 D served all wk 6.30-9 ⊕ FREE HOUSE ◀ Sharp's, Skinner's, Guest ales ○ Cornish Orchards, Winkleigh, Haye Farm. **Facilities** Children welcome Children's portions Family room Garden Beer festival ▭

BOLVENTOR   Map 2 SX17

Jamaica Inn

PL15 7TS ☎ 01566 86250
e-mail: enquiry@jamaicainn.co.uk
dir: *Follow A30 from Exeter. 10m after Launceston take Bolventor road, follow signs*

The setting for Daphne du Maurier's famous novel of the same name, this 18th-century inn stands high on Bodmin Moor. Its Smugglers Museum houses fascinating artefacts, while the Daphne du Maurier room honours the great writer. The place is big on atmosphere, with a cobbled courtyard, beamed ceilings and roaring fires, plus a children's play area and beautiful gardens. Breakfasts, mid-morning snacks and lunches provide an inviting choice, while the evening menu offers steaks, fish, chicken and vegetarian options.

Open all day all wk 9am-11pm ⊕ FREE HOUSE ◀ Jamaica Inn Ale, Sharp's Doom Bar, St Austell Tribute. **Facilities** Children welcome Play area Garden Parking

BOSCASTLE   Map 2 SX09

Cobweb Inn

The Bridge PL35 0HE ☎ 01840 250278
e-mail: cobweb.inn@virgin.net
dir: *In village centre*

Built in the 1600s, this immense, five-storey stone edifice used to be a bonded warehouse where customs agents guarded taxable imported goods. Rumour has it that despite this, one could drink illicitly in the beamed, flag-floored back room, today the bottle- and jug-festooned bar, where Cornwall-brewed real ales and farm ciders can be ordered without subterfuge. Eat here or in the charming white-painted restaurant, where seafood, steaks, pasties and a great deal more feature on the extensive menu and daily specials boards. Each Saturday sees a live music event. Booking for meals may be required.

Open all day all wk **Bar Meals** L served all wk 11-2.30 D served all wk 6-9.30 Av main course £7.50 **Restaurant** D served all wk 6.15-9 ⊕ FREE HOUSE ◀ Sharp's Doom Bar, St Austell Tribute, Tintagel Harbour Special, Guest ales Ŏ Healey's Cornish Rattler, Westons Stowford Press. **Facilities** Children welcome Children's menu Children's portions Family room Garden Parking Wi-fi 🚌 (notice required)

The Wellington Hotel ★★ HL ◉

PICK OF THE PUBS

The Harbour PL35 0AQ ☎ 01840 250202
e-mail: info@wellingtonhotelboscastle.com
dir: *A30/A395 at Davidstow follow Boscastle signs. B3266 to village. Right into New Rd*

Known affectionately as 'The Welly' by both locals and loyal guests, this listed 16th-century coaching inn with its castellated tower was renamed in 1852 in honour of the Duke of Wellington. It nestles on one of England's

most stunning coastlines at the end of a glorious wooded valley where the rivers Jordan and Valency meet. It was fully restored after devastating floods a few years ago, but retains much of its original charm, including beamed ceilings and real log fires. The traditional Long Bar, complete with minstrels' gallery and log fires, proffers a good selection of Cornish ales and ciders, malt whiskies and bar snacks, together with pub favourites and a specials board – trio of pork sausages with mash and peas; mozzarella, tomato and basil tart; or shellfish linguine. Perhaps try the lemon posset for dessert. Children can choose from a separate menu. There is also a fine dining restaurant. Accommodation is available. Booking for meals may be required.

Open all day all wk 11-11 (Sun 12-10) **Bar Meals** L served Mon-Fri 12-3, Sat-Sun 12-9 D served Mon-Fri 6-9, Sat-Sun 12-9 Av main course £10.75 **Restaurant** D served all wk 6.30-9 Av 3 course à la carte fr £22.50 ⊕ FREE HOUSE ◀ St Austell Tribute, Skinner's Spriggan Ale, Tintagel Harbour Special Ŏ Healey's Cornish Rattler & Pear Rattler, Thatchers. ☿ 13 **Facilities** Children welcome Children's menu Children's portions Garden Parking Wi-fi 🚌 (notice required) **Rooms** 14

CADGWITH   Map 2 SW71

Cadgwith Cove Inn

TR12 7JX ☎ 01326 290513
e-mail: david@cadgwithcoveinn.com
dir: *A3083 from Helston towards Lizard. Left to Cadgwith*

Once frequented by smugglers, this 300-year-old pub will be familiar to anyone who watched the BBC TV series *The Fisherman's Apprentice*. It sits in an unspoilt fishing hamlet of thatched cottages on the rugged Lizard coastline. In summer, ramblers mingle with tourists and locals on the sunny front patio, which affords views across the old pilchard cellar to the peaceful cove. The atmospheric, simply furnished bars are adorned with relics that record a rich seafaring history, and it's easy to imagine that the ghosts of smugglers still gather within these cosy walls. As we went to press we learnt the pub had changed hands.

Open all wk Mon-Thu 12-3 6-11 winter (Fri noon-1am Sat 12-11 Sun 12-10) Mon-Sat 12-11 summer ⊕ PUNCH TAVERNS ◀ Sharp's, Skinner's, Guest ales. **Facilities** Children welcome Children's menu Children's portions Family room Garden Parking

CALLINGTON   Map 3 SX36

Manor House Inn

Rilla Mill PL17 7NT ☎ 01579 362354
e-mail: dcproctor@btinternet.com
dir: *5m from Callington, just off B3257*

Standing by the River Lynher on the edge of Bodmin Moor, this former granary once supplied the neighbouring mill. Today it offers Cornish real ales and ciders, a selection of paninis and wraps; home-made steak-and-ale pie; fish and chips; chilli con carne; and chargrilled burgers. Or, cook your self-selected pieces of meat, fish, cheese or

vegetables on the Black Rock Grill, adding mushrooms, chips and salad to the result. A whole roast chicken serving four is offered on Sundays. There's a beer festival on the first weekend in September.

Open Mon 5-11 Tue-Fri 11-3 5-11 (Sat-Sun all day) Closed: Mon L **Bar Meals** L served Tue-Sun 11.30-2 D served Tue-Sun 6-9 Av main course £9 **Restaurant** L served Tue-Sun 11.30-2 D served Tue-Sun 6-9 Av 3 course à la carte fr £22 ⊕ FREE HOUSE ◀ Sharp's Own, Special & Doom Bar, St Austell Tribute Ŏ Thatchers Gold, Westons, Healey's Cornish Rattler. **Facilities** Children welcome Children's menu Children's portions Garden Beer festival Parking 🚌 (notice required)

CONSTANTINE   Map 2 SW72

Trengilly Wartha Inn

PICK OF THE PUBS

See Pick of the Pubs on page 90

CRAFTHOLE   Map 3 SX35

The Finnygook Inn

PL11 3BQ ☎ 01503 230338
e-mail: eat@finnygook.co.uk
dir: *10m W of Tamar Bridge take A374 S. 3m turn right for Crafthole & follow pub signs. From Torpoint take A374, 5m to Antony. Left in Antony, 1m to T-junct. 3m to Crafthole*

They say the ghost of smuggler Silas Finny walks abroad on the cliffs and byways hereabouts; so, too, do ramblers and visitors seeking to share the inspirational beers and food available at this pub. The Finnygook is a refurbished old coaching inn located in a hamlet above Portwrinkle's cove-nibbled coast. Peninsula-brewed beers from the likes of St Austell and Penpont breweries set the scene for tempting fodder featuring seafood dishes, backed by a host of reliable pub favourites (gammon steak, Cumberland sausage) taken by the log fire, in the library room or on the terrace with distant views up the Tamar estuary.

Open all day Closed: Mon in Nov-Mar **Bar Meals** L served all wk 12-9 (Nov-Mar Tue-Sun 12.30-2.30) D served all wk 12-9 (Nov-Mar Tue-Sun 6-9) Av main course £11.95 **Restaurant** L served all wk 12-9 (Nov-Mar Tue-Sun 12.30-2.30) D served all wk 12-9 (Nov-Mar Tue-Sun 6-9) Fixed menu price fr £9.95 Av 3 course à la carte fr £18.95 ⊕ FREE HOUSE ◀ Sharp's Doom Bar, St Austell Tribute & Proper Job, Penpont Cornish Arvor, Dartmoor. ☿ 10 **Facilities** 🐾 Children welcome Children's menu Children's portions Garden Parking Wi-fi

PICK OF THE PUBS

Trengilly Wartha Inn

CONSTANTINE Map 2 SW72

Nancenoy TR11 5RP ☎ 01326 340332
e-mail: reception@trengilly.co.uk
web: www.trengilly.co.uk
dir: *Follow signs to Constantine, left towards Gweek until 1st sign for inn, left & left again at next sign, continue to inn*

In the half dozen or so years since William and Lisa Lea arrived at Trengilly Wartha, they have established it as one of Cornwall's leading inns. The Cornish name of this friendly free house means a settlement above the trees – although it actually lies at the foot of a densely wooded valley. Originally built as a small farmstead in the late 18th century, the building was sold for just £300 in 1946. Over the next decade, the Ballamy family renovated and extended the building with help from German prisoners of war, who installed the double staircase. A full liquor licence was granted as recently as 1960, and today the black-beamed bar with its cricketing memorabilia offers Skinner's Cornish Knocker amongst other local ales and ciders. There's also an extensive wine list with 15 varieties offered by the glass, and over 40 malt whiskies. Meanwhile, the menu includes locally sourced Cornish produce wherever possible. Expect classic lunchtime fare, including a range of traditional ploughman's with home-made granary bread, pickles and chutneys; and hot dishes like Tywardreath sausages, mustard mash and gravy. Fish and

seafood feature strongly in the restaurant, with starters like Falmouth River mussels, or smoked whiting with herb butter. Main course fish dishes might include wild sea bass, or fillet of brill with sundried tomato and baby spinach. Meat-eaters and vegetarians will also find plenty of choice – pork fillet with prune, apple and brandy sauce; and leek, broccoli and mushroom pancakes are typical choices, whilst home-made sweets with seasonal organic fruit are offered on the chalkboard. A pretty beer garden and vine-shaded pergola complete the picture, surrounded by the three meadows that formed part of the original smallholding. Booking for meals may be required.

Open all wk 11-3 6-12 **Bar Meals** L served all wk 12-2.15 D served all wk

6.30-9.30 **Restaurant** L served all wk 12-2.15 D served all wk 6.30-9.30 ⊕ **FREE HOUSE** ◀ Skinner's Cornish Knocker & Betty Stogs, Sharp's Doom Bar & Eden Ale, Guest ales ☼ Henley's Cornish Rattler, Thatchers Gold. 🍷 15 **Facilities** Children welcome Children's menu Children's portions Play area Family room 🐾 Garden Parking Wi-fi 🚌

CUBERT   Map 2 SW75

The Smugglers' Den Inn

Trebellan TR8 5PY ☎ 01637 830209
e-mail: info@thesmugglersden.co.uk
web: www.thesmugglersden.co.uk
dir: *From Newquay take A3075 to Cubert x-rds, then right, then left signed Trebellan, 0.5m*

Look to the blackboard for fish specials in this thatched 16th-century pub situated less than 15 minutes from Newquay; the table d'hôte menu includes catch of the day too. Popular with locals and visitors alike, the pub comprises a long bar, family room, children's play area, courtyards and huge beer garden. Local suppliers are listed at the bottom of the no-nonsense modern menu, where a salt and chilli squid could be followed by a slow-roasted shoulder of Cornish lamb. A real ale, cider and pie festival is held over the May Day Bank Holiday weekend. Booking for meals may be required.

Open all wk 11.30-3 6-11 (Sat 11-3 6-12 Sun & summer open all day) Closed: 25 Dec 12-3 **Bar Meals** L served all wk 12-2.30 (winter 12-2) D served all wk 6-9.30 (winter Sun-Thu 6-9, Fri-Sat 6-9.30) **Restaurant** L served all wk 12-2.30 (winter 12-2) D served all wk 6-9.30 (winter Sun-Thu 6-9, Fri-Sat 6-9.30) ⊕ FREE HOUSE ◀ Skinner's Smugglers Ale, Sharp's Doom Bar, St Austell Tribute, Guest ales ○ Healey's Cornish Rattler, Thatchers Gold. ♟ 10 **Facilities** ✿ Children welcome Children's menu Play area Family room Garden Beer festival Parking Wi-fi ▭

See advert below

DUNMERE   Map 2 SX06

The Borough Arms

PL31 2RD ☎ 01208 73118
e-mail: borougharms@hotmail.co.uk
dir: *From A30 take A389 to Wadebridge, pub approx 1m from Bodmin*

Although it was built in the 1850s to refresh rail workers transporting china clay from the moors down to the port at Padstow, The Borough seems much older. These days walkers, cyclists, horseriders and summertime tourists drop in as they follow the now-disused railway line which has become the 17-mile Camel Trail. Ales include Dartmoor and Tribute, while food options range from pub favourites (scampi, burgers, filled jacket potatoes, pie of the day) to dishes such as gammon steak, and leek and stilton pancakes, plus a carvery. Children's portions are marked on the menu.

Open all day all wk **Bar Meals** L served all wk 12-9 D served all wk 12-9 Av main course £7.95 food served all day **Restaurant** L served all wk 12-9 D served all wk 12-9 Fixed menu price fr £8.95 Av 3 course à la carte fr £15 food served all day ⊕ ST AUSTELL BREWERY ◀ Tribute, Dartmoor, Bass. **Facilities** ✿ Children welcome Children's menu Children's portions Play area Family room Garden Parking ▭

PICK OF THE PUBS

The Halzephron Inn

GUNWALLOE Map 2 SW62

TR12 7QB ☎ 01326 240406
e-mail: halzephroninn@tiscali.co.uk
web: www.halzephron-inn.co.uk
dir: *3m S of Helston on A3083, right to Gunwalloe, through village. Inn on left*

The 500-year-old inn commands an enviable position perched high above Gunwalloe Fishing Cove, with stunning views across Mount's Bay to Penzance, it's rugged stone exterior feeling the full force of 2,000 miles of Atlantic weather on wild winter days. The name of this ancient inn derives from Als Yfferin, old Cornish for 'Cliffs of Hell', an appropriate description that conjures up images of smugglers and wreckers along this hazardous stretch of coastline. But you can expect a genuine warm welcome from Angela Thomas, the former opera singer who has been at the helm of this Cornish treasure for nearly 20 years. The two spick-and-span interconnecting bars are simply, yet tastefully kitted out, featuring attractive checked fabrics, scatter cushions on padded wall benches, warming log fires, fishing memorabilia, and original watercolours of Cornish scenes. Daily-changing menus utilise the best Cornish produce available, including fresh seafood and herbs from a neighbouring farm. Everything is home-made, with the likes of fish chowder with tarragon

and cream; chicken liver paté with apple and sultana chutney; and baked St Anthony goat's cheese with olive and tomato salsa among the starters. For main courses there's winter vegetable and pearl barley stew; confit duck leg on garlic crushed potatoes with purple sprouting broccoli and rosemary jus; whole roasted sea bass with sautéed potatoes and chilli oil; and beer-battered fish and chips. Among the list of desserts you might find cherry and almond flan, treacle tart and baked American cheesecake. Arrive early on sunny days to bag a front bench and savour a pint of Skinner's Betty Stogs looking out across Mount's Bay to St Michael's Mount. Booking for meals may be required.

Open all wk 11-3 6-11 Closed: 25 Dec **Bar Meals** L served all wk 12-2 D served all wk 7-9 **Restaurant** L served all wk 12-2 D served all wk 7-9 ⊞ FREE HOUSE ◀ Sharp's Own, Doom Bar & Special, St Austell Tribute, Skinner's Betty Stogs, Lizard Kernow Gold Ö Healey's Cornish Rattler, Skinner's Press Gang. ♟ 9 **Facilities** Children welcome Children's menu Children's portions Play area Family room ☘ Garden Parking Wi-fi

FEOCK   Map 2 SW83

The Punchbowl & Ladle

Penelewey TR3 6QY ☎ 01872 862237
e-mail: punchbowlandladle@googlemail.com
dir: *From Truro take A39 Truro towards Falmouth, after Shell garage at Playing Place rdbt follow for King Harry Ferry signs. 0.5m, pub on right*

Local rumour has it that the bar fireplace at this attractive, thatched pub close to the King Harry Ferry was used to burn contraband when customs officers used the building. Head for the suntrap walled garden or patio with a glass of St Austell Proper Job beer or Cornish Rattler cider. Alternatively, settle down on the comfortable sofas in the low-beamed bar and await your choice from the locally sourced menu, which features great comfort dishes such as home-cooked honey-roast ham, egg and chips, or sausages and mash.

Open all day all wk 10.30am-11pm (Fri-Sat 10.30am-mdnt Sun 12-11) **Bar Meals** L served Mon-Sat 12-2.30, Sun 12-3 D served all wk 6-9 ⊕ ST AUSTELL BREWERY ◼ Tribute, Tinners Ale, Proper Job Ö Healey's Cornish Rattler. ♇ 8 **Facilities** ✿ Children welcome Children's portions Garden Parking Wi-fi ▭

FOWEY   Map 2 SX15

The Ship Inn

Trafalgar Square PL23 1AZ ☎ 01726 832230
e-mail: shipinnfowey@hotmail.com
dir: *From A30 take B3269 & A390*

One of Fowey's oldest buildings, The Ship was built in 1570 by John Rashleigh, who sailed to the Americas with Walter Raleigh. Given Fowey's riverside position, assume a good choice of fish, including peppered smoked mackerel, breaded scampi, and Ship Inn fish pie. Other options include chilli con carne or local butcher's sausages and mash. St Austell ales, real fires and a long tradition of genial hospitality add the final touches.

Open all day all wk 11am-mdnt (Fri-Sat 11am-1am) **Bar Meals** food served all day **Restaurant** food served all day ⊕ ST AUSTELL BREWERY ◼ Tribute & Proper Job, Dartmoor IPA Ö Healey's Cornish Rattler & Pear Rattler. **Facilities** ✿ Children welcome Children's menu Children's portions Family room ▭

GOLDSITHNEY   Map 2 SW53

The Trevelyan Arms

Fore St TR20 9JU ☎ 01736 710453
e-mail: trevelyanarms@live.co.uk
dir: *5m from Penzance. A394 signed to Goldsithney*

The former manor house for Lord Trevelyan, this 17th-century property stands at the centre of the picturesque village just a mile from the sea. It has also been a coaching inn and a bank/post office in its time, but these days is very much the traditional family-run Cornish pub. Food is fresh and locally sourced, offering good value for money. Typical dishes are T-bone steaks,

home-made pies and curries, pasta dishes and local fish. There are also vegetarian options and a separate children's menu.

Open all wk 4-12 (Sat-Sun 12-12) **Bar Meals** L served Sun D served all wk 6-9 **Restaurant** L served Sun D served all wk 6-9 ⊕ PUNCH TAVERNS ◼ Morland Old Speckled Hen, St Austell Tribute, Guinness Ö Thatchers Green Goblin, Westons Stowford Press. ♇ 10 **Facilities** ✿ Children welcome Children's menu Children's portions Garden Wi-fi

GUNNISLAKE   Map 3 SX47

The Rising Sun Inn

Calstock Rd PL18 9BX ☎ 01822 832201
dir: *From Tavistock take A390 to Gunnislake. Left after lights into Calstock Rd. Inn approx 500mtrs on right*

Overlooking the stunning Tamar Valley, this traditional two-roomed picture-postcard pub is a popular stop for walkers, wildlife enthusiasts and cyclists; great walks start and finish from the pub. In warmer weather, enjoy a pint of real ale in the award-winning gardens or order from the simple menu of locally sourced, home-cooked food, perhaps chicken liver pâté, or soup of the day to start, and a warm duck salad or vegetable lasagne to follow.

Open all wk 12-3 5-11 **Bar Meals** L served all wk 12-3 D served all wk 5-9 ⊕ FREE HOUSE ◼ Skinner's Betty Stogs, St Austell Tribute, Tintagel Gull Rock, Otter, Dartmoor Ö Westons Stowford Press. ♇ 25 **Facilities** ✿ Children welcome Children's menu Children's portions Garden Parking

GUNWALLOE   Map 2 SW62

The Halzephron Inn
PICK OF THE PUBS

See Pick of the Pubs on opposite page

HELFORD PASSAGE   Map 2 SW72

The Ferryboat Inn **NEW**

TR11 5LB ☎ 01326 250625
e-mail: manager@ferryboatinnhelford.com
dir: *In village centre, 1st turn after Trebah Gardens*

This award-winning waterside pub dates back 300 years and offers fabulous views over the Helford estuary. Whether it's a plate of oysters and a glass of fizz on the sunny, south-facing terrace or cottage pie by the warmth of the granite fireplace inside, this is a venue for all weathers. Everything is made on the premises and the Ferryboat burger is especially popular. The pub is owned by Wright Brothers, custodians of the Duchy of Cornwall's oyster farm, so the quality of the shellfish and seafood speaks for itself. Booking for meals may be required.

Open all day Closed: Mon (low season) **Bar Meals** Av main course £14 **Restaurant** L served all wk 12-2.30 D served all wk 6-8.30 ⊕ FREE HOUSE ◼ St

Austell Tribute, Dartmoor Ö Healey's Cornish Rattler. **Facilities** Children welcome Children's menu Children's portions Parking Wi-fi ▭ (notice required)

HELSTON   Map 2 SW62

The Queens Arms ★★★ INN

Breage TR13 9PD ☎ 01326 573485
e-mail: chris-brazier@btconnect.com
dir: *Village off A394 (Penzance to Helston). Pub adjacent to church*

It's not so apparent from outside, but this is a 15th-century pub where the workmen building St Breaca's Church lived. Its age is more obvious indoors, particularly in the beamed, open-fired bar, where real ales include Penzance Brewing's Potion No 9. Simple home-cooked food makes good use of local produce, including pub-allotment-grown vegetables. Bar and restaurant menus offer breaded wholetail scampi, chips and peas; Thai green chicken curry and rice; and roasted vegetables with fruited couscous. Added attractions are a DIY barbecue, children's play area and two en suite double rooms.

Open all wk Mon-Thu 11.30-3 5-11.30 (Fri-Sun 11.30-11.30) **Bar Meals** L served all wk 12-2 D served Mon-Sat 6.30-9 (ex Tue Oct-Mar) **Restaurant** L served all wk 12-2 D served Mon-Sat 6.30-9 (ex Tue Oct-Mar) ⊕ PUNCH TAVERNS ◼ Sharp's Doom Bar, Penzance Potion No 9 Ö Addlestones. **Facilities** Children welcome Children's menu Children's portions Play area Garden Parking Wi-fi **Rooms** 2

KINGSAND   Map 3 SX45

The Halfway House Inn

Fore St PL10 1NA ☎ 01752 822279
e-mail: info@halfwayinn.biz
dir: *From Torpoint Ferry or Tamar Bridge follow signs to Mount Edgcumbe*

So named because the pub stands at the point that once marked the spot of the Devon and Cornwall border, this friendly inn has been serving locals and visitors since 1850. Hidden amongst the narrow lanes and colourful houses of a quaint fishing village, the stone-walled bar offers plenty of original fireplaces and beams, all of which makes for a relaxing place to enjoy a pint of Betty Stogs. Alternatively, you can tuck into locally caught mackerel, sea bass and crab in the cosy restaurant.

Open all wk **Bar Meals** L served all wk 11-2 D served all wk 6-9 **Restaurant** L served all wk 11-2 D served all wk 6-9 ⊕ FREE HOUSE ◼ Sharp's Doom Bar & Own, Skinner's, Betty Stogs, Guinness Ö Westons Stowford Press & Old Rosie. ♇ 12 **Facilities** ✿ Children welcome Children's menu Children's portions Wi-fi

LAMORNA
Map 2 SW42

Lamorna Wink

TR19 6XH ☎ 01736 731566
dir: 4m on B3315 towards Land's End, then 0.5m to turn on left

This oddly named pub was one of the original Kiddleywinks, a product of the 1830 Beer Act that enabled any householder to buy a liquor licence. Popular with walkers and not far from the Merry Maidens standing stones, the Wink provides a selection of local beers including Skinner's Betty Stogs. A simple menu includes sandwiches, jacket potatoes and fresh local crab. The management have been at the Wink for over 30 years and pride themselves on providing diners with as much local produce as possible.

Open all wk Mon-Sat 11-2.30 (Sun 12-2.30) **Bar Meals** L served Mon-Sat 11-2, Sun 12-2 ⊕ FREE HOUSE ◀ Sharp's Doom Bar, Skinner's Betty Stogs. **Facilities** Children welcome Family room Garden Parking ☞ **Notes** ☺

LANLIVERY
Map 2 SX05

The Crown Inn ★★★ INN

PICK OF THE PUBS

See Pick of the Pubs on opposite page

LOOE
Map 2 SX25

The Ship Inn ★★★ INN

Fore St PL13 1AD ☎ 01503 263124
dir: In town centre

This lively St Austell Brewery-owned pub stands on a corner in the heart of this charming old fishing town, a minute's walk from the working harbour. Locals and tourists join together in the appreciation of a pint of Tribute, and select their favourites from the menu – a burger or hot baguette for some, while others go for steak-and-ale pie or hunter's chicken. A quiz is held on Mondays throughout the year, live bands play regularly, and well-equipped bedrooms are available for those wanting to tarry awhile.

Open all day all wk **Bar Meals** food served all day ⊕ ST AUSTELL BREWERY ◀ Tribute, Tinners, HSD ♨ Healey's Cornish Rattler. ♇ **Facilities** Children welcome Children's menu Children's portions Family room **Rooms** 8

LUDGVAN
Map 2 SW53

White Hart

Churchtown TR20 8EY ☎ 01736 740574
e-mail: info@whitehartludgvan.co.uk
dir: From A30 take B3309 at Crowlas

Standing opposite the church, the White Hart is one of the oldest pubs in Cornwall and retains the peaceful atmosphere of a bygone era. There are splendid views across St Michael's Mount, and a great selection of real

ales is sold from the back of the bar. The food is as popular as ever, with choices such as duck stirfry with egg noodles; roasted salmon fillet with mustard butter crust; and grilled goat's cheese with portabella mushroom and red pepper salad. Booking for meals may be required.

Open all wk 12-3 6-late **Bar Meals** L served all wk 12-2.30 D served all wk 6-9.30 **Restaurant** L served all wk 12-2.30 D served all wk 6-9.30 ⊕ PUNCH TAVERNS ◀ Sharp's Doom Bar, Skinner's Betty Stogs, Hamish Traditional Cornish Ale ♨ Thatchers. ♇ 8 **Facilities** Children welcome Children's portions Garden Parking ☞

MALPAS
Map 2 SW84

The Heron Inn

Trenhaile Ter TR1 1SL ☎ 01872 272773
e-mail: theheron@hotmail.co.uk
dir: From Trafalgar rdbt in Truro exit towards BBC Radio Cornwall, & pub sign. Follow Malpas Rd for 2m into village. Pub on left

To overlook not one, not two, but three rivers is what helps to make The Heron such an attractive destination, for it's here that the Tresilian and Truro combine to become the Fal. Local produce features in pan-fried chicken breast with a chilli, lime and garlic butter; honey-roast pork sausages; and chickpea and vegetable curry. There is a terrace area with wonderful views and is the perfect place to enjoy a pint of ale from St Austell Brewery. Although walkable in 40 minutes from Truro, mooring the yacht at Malpas Marina is more stylish. Booking for meals may be required.

Open all wk 11.30-3 6-11 (Fri-Sat all day Sun 11.30-5; summer all day every day) Closed: 25 Dec **Restaurant** L served Mon-Thu 12-2, Fri-Sun 12-2.30 D served Mon-Sat 6.30-9 ⊕ ST AUSTELL BREWERY ◀ Tribute, Proper Job ♨ Healey's Cornish Rattler. ♇ 11 **Facilities** Children welcome Children's menu Children's portions Garden Parking Wi-fi ☞

MANACCAN
Map 2 SW72

The New Inn

TR12 6HA ☎ 01326 231323
e-mail: penny@stmartin.wanadoo.co.uk
dir: 7m from Helston

This thatched village pub, deep in Daphne du Maurier country near the Helford River, dates back to Cromwellian times, although obviously Cromwell forbade his men to drink here. Attractions include the homely bars and large, natural garden full of flowers. At lunchtime you might opt for a roast beef and horseradish sandwich, in the evening perhaps fillets of monkfish sautéed in a creamy Pernod sauce or steak and stilton pie. There are separate menus dedicated to crab dishes and steaks.

Open all wk 12-3 6-11 (Sat-Sun all day in summer) **Bar Meals** L served all wk 12-2.30 D served all wk 6-9 **Restaurant** L served all wk D served all wk ⊕ PUNCH TAVERNS ◀ Sharp's Doom Bar ♨ Westons Stowford

Press. ♇ 10 **Facilities** ♣ Children welcome Children's menu Play area Garden Parking ☞

MARAZION
Map 2 SW53

Godolphin Arms

PICK OF THE PUBS

TR17 0EN ☎ 01736 710202
e-mail: enquiries@godolphinarms.co.uk
dir: From A30 just outside Penzance follow Marazion signs. Pub 1st large building on right in Marazion, opposite St Michael's Mount

The Godolphin Arms stands atop the sea wall at the end of the causeway to St Michael's Mount. There are superb views across the bay from the traditional bar and beer terrace, as well as from the restaurant. With direct access to a large sandy beach where at low tide the causeway is revealed, the sea is so close that it splashes at the windows in winter as you watch the fishing boats returning with their catch. Seafood from the Newlyn fish market is listed on the daily specials board; crab in particular is a speciality. Other options include traditional pub favourites like bangers and mash, or sample a Cornish cream tea in the afternoon. Cornish steaks and chicken from the chargrill come with potatoes and fresh vegetables, and the Sunday carvery offers a choice of roasts as well as a vegetarian option. The Goldolphin also holds a beer festival.

Open all day all wk 8am-mdnt **Bar Meals** L served all wk 12-9 D served all wk 12-9 food served all day **Restaurant** food served all day ⊕ FREE HOUSE ◀ St Austell Tribute, Sharp's Doom Bar, Skinner's Betty Stogs ♨ Healey's Cornish Rattler, Cornish Orchard. **Facilities** Children welcome Garden Beer festival Parking ☞

MEVAGISSEY
Map 2 SX04

The Ship Inn

Fore St PL26 6UQ ☎ 01726 843324
dir: 7m S of St Austell

This 400-year-old inn stands just a few yards from Mevagissey's picturesque fishing harbour, so the choice of fish and seafood dishes comes as no surprise on a menu of home-cooked dishes: moules marinière, beer-battered cod, and oven-baked fillet of haddock topped with prawns and Cornish Tiskey cheese. The popular bar has low-beamed ceilings, flagstone floors and a strong nautical feel. The inn hosts local musicians in the winter months.

Open all day all wk 11am-mdnt **Bar Meals** L served all wk 12-3 D served all wk 6-9 ⊕ ST AUSTELL BREWERY ◀ St Austell ♨ Healey's Cornish Rattler. ♇ 8 **Facilities** ♣ Children welcome Children's menu ☞

PICK OF THE PUBS

The Crown Inn ★★★ INN

LANLIVERY　　Map 2 SX05

PL30 5BT ☎ 01208 872707
e-mail: thecrown@wagtailinns.com
web: www.wagtailinns.com
dir: *Signed from A390. Follow brown sign approx 1.5m W of Lostwithiel*

This moorland village above a tributary of the Fowey River is home to one of Cornwall's oldest pubs. It's a former long house, with characteristic thick stone walls, low beams, granite and slate floors, open fires and an unusual bread oven. Much of the present building dates from the 12th century, when it housed the stonemasons constructing the charming church of St Brevita nearby. Passing right by is the Saints Way, a 30-mile drovers' route from Padstow to Fowey once used by Irish cattle drovers 'fat-walking' their cattle overland to avoid the dangerous sea passage round Land's End. At Fowey they and their animals would then sail for France. The pub has been extensively but sympathetically restored over the years, at one point the work uncovering a huge, deep well, now covered by glass, under the porch. With the sea only a few miles away, expect a menu offering plenty of fresh fish and seafood, as well as other local produce. A typical meal might begin with grilled sardines, fennel relish and toasted ciabatta, or celeriac with poached apple and walnut salad. Popular main courses are Cornish ale-battered fish with chips, crushed

peas and home-made tartare sauce; pan-fried lamb's liver, smoked bacon, bubble-and-squeak and red wine sauce; and saffron and winter vegetable chowder and toasted baguette. At lunchtime, enjoy a fresh Fowey crab sandwich or a local butcher's proper Cornish pasty. Doom Bar real ale comes from Sharp's in Rock and Betty Stogs (a character in Cornish folklore) from Skinner's of Truro, while a reasonably priced wine list offers seven wines by the glass. The pretty garden is a lovely spot to enjoy a summer evening, perhaps with a glass of Pimm's. The impressively appointed bedrooms are very much in keeping with the 21st century, and dogs (with owners obviously) are welcome to stay. Booking or meals may be required.

Open all day all wk **Bar Meals** food served all day **Restaurant** food served all day ⊕ FREE HOUSE ◀ Sharp's Doom Bar, Skinner's Betty Stogs, Guest ales ♂ Westons 1st Quality.
Facilities Children welcome Children's menu Children's portions ❖ Garden Parking Wi-fi 🚐 (notice required)
Rooms 9

The Plume of Feathers ★★★★ INN

PICK OF THE PUBS

TR8 5AX ☎ 01872 510387
e-mail: theplume@hospitalitycornwall.com
dir: *Exit A30 to Mitchell/Newquay*

In the peaceful village of Mitchell, this successful destination pub restaurant dates from the 16th century and has welcomed various historical figures in its time – Sir Walter Raleigh lived nearby and John Wesley preached Methodism from the pillared entrance. Today, with its roaring log fires, beamed ceilings and cosy ambience, it offers a choice of real ales, holds a beer festival every May, and the imaginative kitchen has an excellent reputation for its food. Dishes are based on a fusion of modern European and classical British, with an emphasis on fresh fish and the best Cornish ingredients; bread is baked fresh daily and some fruit and veg is grown on site. Expect starters such as seared breast of local pigeon, followed by mains of fish pie, or Fowey River mussels. Choose from a selection of desserts including white chocolate brûlée. Seven stylish bedrooms and a conservatory complete the picture.

Open all day all wk 9am-11pm/mdnt (25 Dec 11-4) **Bar Meals** food served all day **Restaurant** food served all day ⊕ FREE HOUSE ◀ Sharp's Doom Bar, John Smith's Extra Smooth, Skinner's. **Facilities** Children welcome Play area Garden Beer festival Parking **Rooms** 7

The Miners Arms

TR5 0QF ☎ 01872 552375
e-mail: minersarms@live.co.uk
dir: *From A30 at Chiverton Cross rdbt take A3075 signed Newquay. At Pendown Cross left onto B3284 signed Perranporth. Left, left again to Mithian*

The curiously light interior of this historic 16th-century pub adds yet another layer of mystery to the legends of its past. Over the centuries it has served as a courthouse, a venue for inquests, a smugglers' lair and even a house of ill repute. Relax beneath the low-beamed ceilings while admiring the wall paintings of Elizabeth I, and choose from the menu of dishes freshly cooked to order from local produce: hake topped with pesto; steak of the day; vegetable tagine; and the Miners fish pie is a must. Booking for meals may be required.

Open all day all wk 12-11.30 **Bar Meals** L served all wk 12-2.30 D served all wk 6-9 **Restaurant** L served all wk 12-2.30 D served all wk 6-9 ⊕ PUNCH TAVERNS ◀ Sharp's Doom Bar, Guest ales Ö Westons Stowford Press. **Facilities** Children welcome Children's menu Children's portions Garden Parking **

The Bush Inn

PICK OF THE PUBS

EX23 9SR ☎ 01288 331242
e-mail: coryfarmltd@aol.com
dir: *Exit A39, 3m N of Kilkhampton, 2nd right into Shop. 1.5m to Crosstown, pub on left*

The Bush is a 13th-century pub set in an isolated cliff-top hamlet, close to a dramatic stretch of the north Cornish coast, a natural haunt for smugglers and wreckers a couple of centuries ago. The historic interior features flagstone floors, old stone fireplaces and a 'leper's squint', a tiny window through which food scraps were passed for the needy. Cornish ales are on tap, and menus featuring produce fresh from Cornwall's larder are served all day, every day. The pub's kitchen garden is productive, and beef comes from the inn's own farm. Game from local shoots is used in robust winter warmers such as venison stew, while summer days are ideal for a bowl of mussels. Among the fish dishes may be found beer-battered pollock, while desserts include apple and cherry crumble. The large garden overlooking the beautiful Tidna Valley and Atlantic Ocean has sturdy wooden play equipment for children. Look out for the beer festival.

Open all day all wk 11am-12.30am **Bar Meals** L served all wk D served all wk food served all day **Restaurant** L served all wk D served all wk food served all day ⊕ FREE HOUSE ◀ St Austell HSD & Tribute, Sharp's Doom Bar, Skinner's Betty Stogs Ö Thatchers, Cornish Orchards. ₹ 9 **Facilities** Children welcome Children's menu Children's portions Play area Garden Beer festival Parking **

The Pandora Inn

PICK OF THE PUBS

Restronguet Creek TR11 5ST ☎ 01326 372678
e-mail: info@pandorainn.com
dir: *From Truro/Falmouth follow A39, left at Carclew, follow signs to pub*

The name stems from the good ship *Pandora*, sent to Tahiti in 1790 to capture the *Bounty* mutineers. Badly damaged by fire in March 2011, The Pandora reopened a year later after a careful restoration that has painstakingly retained much of the inn's original 13th-century features. Its breathtakingly beautiful situation, right on the banks of the Restronguet Creek, affords panoramic views across the water. You can reach this thatched inn on foot, by bicycle or boat, as well as by car. In the bar, the flagstone floors and low beams suggest little has changed since it first opened and local ales such as Trelawny and Proper Job can be enjoyed along with 15 wines by the glass. Chef Tom Milby tries to use as many local farms, growers and fishermen as possible: Falmouth Bay scallops with black pudding might be followed by local sirloin steak or fish pie.

Open all day all wk 10.30am-11pm **Bar Meals** L served all wk 10.30-9.30 D served all wk 10.30-9.30 Av main course £13 food served all day **Restaurant** food served all day ⊕ ST AUSTELL BREWERY ◀ HSD, Tribute, Proper Job & Trelawny, Bass. ₹ 15 **Facilities** ❀ Children welcome Children's menu Children's portions Garden Parking Wi-fi **

The Lewinnick Lodge Bar & Restaurant

Pentire Headland TR7 1NX ☎ 01637 878117
e-mail: thelodge@hospitalitycornwall.com
dir: *From Newquay take Pentire Rd 0.5m, pub on right*

On the rugged Pentire Headland, this late 18th-century former cottage must have one of the best coastal views in the county. With a great reputation for modern British food, particularly fresh fish, The Lewinnick offers starters of pork and duck liver terrine; and twice-baked Cornish Yarg soufflé, followed perhaps by sautéed potato gnocchi; slow-braised Cornish lamb shank; or Falmouth Bay moules marinière. Signature dishes are the tasting plate of seafood and the fishcakes. Relax on the patio or deck with a pint of Betty Stogs or Doom Bar.

Open all day all wk **Bar Meals** L served all wk 12-5 D served all wk 5-10 food served all day **Restaurant** L served all wk 12-5 D served all wk 5-10 food served all day ⊕ FREE HOUSE ◀ Sharp's Doom Bar, Skinner's Betty Stogs Ö Cornish Orchards. **Facilities** Children welcome Children's menu Garden Parking Wi-fi **

The Royal Inn ★★★★ INN

66 Eastcliffe Rd PL24 2AJ ☎ 01726 815601
e-mail: info@royal-inn.co.uk
dir: *A3082 Par, follow brown tourist signs for 'Newquay Branch line' or railway station. Pub opp rail station*

Travellers and employees of the Great Western Railway once frequented this 19th-century inn, which was named after a visit by King Edward VII to a local copper mine. The pub is now on the Atlantic Coast line of the 'Rail Ale Trail', and the building is much extended, with an open-plan bar serving a variety of real ales. Leading off are the dining areas which comprise a cosy beamed room and conservatory. The long bar menu offers everything from pizzas and burgers to sandwiches, salads and omelettes, and grills and jackets. The restaurant menu includes three cheese tortellini, loin of cod, and chicken tikka masala. Fifteen comfortable rooms are available.

Open all day all wk 11.30-11 (Sun 12-10.30) **Bar Meals** L served all wk 12-2 D served all wk 6.30-9 **Restaurant** L served all wk 12-2 D served all wk 6.30-9 ⊕ FREE HOUSE ◀ Sharp's Doom Bar & Special, Wells Bombardier, Shepherd Neame Spitfire, Cotleigh Barn Owl Ö Healey's Cornish Rattler, Thatchers Gold. ₹ 13 **Facilities** Children welcome Children's menu Children's portions Garden Parking Wi-fi ** **Rooms** 15

PENZANCE   Map 2 SW43

The Coldstreamer Inn ★★★ INN ◉
NEW

Gulval TR18 3BB ☎ 01736 362072
e-mail: info@coldstreamer-penzance.co.uk
dir: *From Penzance take B3311 towards St Ives. In Gulval right into School Ln. Pub in village centre*

Young Tom Penhaul (ex-Abbey Restaurant) is cooking up a storm at this unassuming inn tucked away in a sleepy village close to Penzance and the heliport. In keeping with the contemporary dining room – smart décor, pine tables, wooden floors – menus are modern and evolve with the seasons, with quality, fresh local produce key to Tom's innovative dishes. Tuck into game terrine with plum chutney; hake with home-made tagliatelle, crab, dill and shellfish cream; and cinnamon rice pudding. Excellent light lunches, a cracking bar with local ales and traditional bar games, and contemporary bedrooms complete the picture.

Open all day all wk **Bar Meals** L served all wk 12-3 D served all wk 6-9.30 (summer), 6-9 (winter) Av main course £10.50-£13 **Restaurant** L served all wk 12-3 D served all wk 6-9.30 (summer), 6-9 (winter) Fixed menu price fr £14 ⊕ PUNCH TAVERNS ◀ Skinner's Betty Stogs, Otter Bitter. ☗ 12 **Facilities** ☙ Children welcome Children's menu Children's portions Garden Wi-fi ▬ (notice required) **Rooms** 3

Dolphin Tavern ★★★ INN

Quay St TR18 4BD ☎ 01736 364106
e-mail: dolphin@tiscali.co.uk
dir: *From rail station follow road along harbour. Tavern on corner opposite Scilonian Ferry Terminal*

Sir Walter Raleigh is said to have smoked the first pipe of tobacco in England at this lovely 16th-century pub, the central part of which was once used as a courtroom by Judge Jeffreys. These days, the Dolphin serves great home-made food accompanied by a full range of St Austell beers, plus accommodation. Fresh, locally caught fish features on the daily specials board, and the menu offers a tempting selection of meat, vegetarian and children's dishes. A typical menu might feature steak-and-ale pie or Newlyn crab salad.

Open all day all wk Closed: 25 Dec **Bar Meals** food served all day **Restaurant** food served all day ⊕ ST AUSTELL BREWERY ◀ HSD, Tinners Ale, Tribute ♻ Healey's Cornish Rattler. ☗ 10 **Facilities** Children welcome Children's menu Children's portions Play area Family room Garden Wi-fi ▬ **Rooms** 2

The Turks Head Inn

Chapel St TR18 4AF ☎ 01736 363093
e-mail: turks@fsmail.net
dir: *Telephone for directions*

Dating from around 1233, this is the oldest pub in Penzance and was the first in the country to be given the Turks Head name. Sadly, a Spanish raiding party destroyed much of the original building in the 16th century, but an old smugglers' tunnel leading directly to the harbour still exists. The food offering includes picnic lunches, filled jacket potatoes, and a range of sandwiches and paninis served with chips and a dressed salad. A sunny flower-filled garden lies at the rear. Booking for meals may be required.

Open all day all wk **Bar Meals** L served all wk 12-2.30 D served all wk 6-9.30 **Restaurant** L served all wk 12-2.30 D served all wk 6-9.30 ⊕ PUNCH TAVERNS ◀ Skinner's Betty Stogs, Wadworth 6X, Sharp's Doom Bar, Guest ale ♻ Westons Old Rosie, Thatchers. ☗ 22 **Facilities** ☙ Children welcome Children's menu Children's portions Family room Garden ▬ (notice required)

PERRANUTHNOE   Map 2 SW52

The Victoria Inn ★★★ INN ◉
PICK OF THE PUBS

TR20 9NP ☎ 01736 710309
e-mail: enquiries@victoriainn-penzance.co.uk
dir: *Off A394 (Penzance to Helston road), signed Perranuthnoe*

With imaginative pub food and easy access to a safe sandy beach and the coastal footpath, this striking, pink-washed village inn is a favoured summer destination for rest and refreshment. Arrive early for a seat in the Mediterranean-style patio garden. Dating from the 12th century it is reputedly Cornwall's oldest inn. The typically Cornish stone-walled bar, adorned with various seafaring and fishing memorabilia, is popular with famished coast path walkers and families strolling up from the beach. Food is taken seriously here, with chef-patron Stewart Eddy cooking the best fish, seafood and quality seasonal ingredients with care and simplicity. The result is earthy, flavoursome dishes that pack a punch. At dinner, perhaps follow slow-roasted Primrose Herd pork belly with a selection of cheeses from artisan producers. Add traditional lunch dishes, Sharp's Doom Bar and St Austell Tribute on tap, and two individually decorated en suite bedrooms, and you have a cracking Cornish coastal gem. Booking for meals may be required.

Open 12-3 6.30-11 (Jun-Sep all day) Closed: 25-26 Dec, 1 Jan, 1wk Jan, Sun eve & Mon (off season) **Bar Meals** L served Mon-Sat 12-2, Sun 12-3 D served all wk 6.30-9 Av main course £14.95 **Restaurant** L served Mon-Sat 12-2, Sun 12-2.30 D served all wk 6.30-9 Av 3 course à la carte fr £21.20 ⊕ FREE HOUSE ◀ Sharp's Doom Bar, St Austell Tribute, Skinner's Betty Stogs, Cornish Chough Serpentine ♻ Healey's Cornish Orchards. **Facilities** Children welcome Children's menu Children's portions Garden Parking Wi-fi **Rooms** 2

PHILLEIGH   Map 2 SW83

Roseland Inn

TR2 5NB ☎ 01872 580254
dir: *From Truro take A39 towards Falmouth. Turn left onto B3289 towards St Mawes. Turn left at sharp right bend for Philleigh*

Phil and Debbie Heslip take pride in the quality of their home-prepared modern British cooking at this highly appealing, traditional rural 16th-century inn. The character of the interior owes much to the low-beamed ceilings, brassware, paintings and prints. Phil brews his ornithologically themed Cornish Shag, Chough to Bits and High-as-a-Kite beers on site. So, in winter cosy up to the fire for a drink or a meal prepared using the best of local Cornish produce, or in warmer weather head outside to the picnic tables. Just to the west is the famous King Harry Ferry over the River Fal.

Open all wk 11-3 6-11.30 **Bar Meals** L served all wk 12-2.30 D served all wk 6-9 **Restaurant** L served all wk 12-2.30 D served all wk 6-9 ⊕ PUNCH TAVERNS ◀ Skinner's Betty Stogs, Roseland Cornish Shag, High-as-a-Kite & Chough to Bits ♻ Westons Stowford Press. **Facilities** Children welcome Children's menu Children's portions Garden Parking Wi-fi ▬

POLKERRIS   Map 2 SX05

The Rashleigh Inn

PL24 2TL ☎ 01726 813991
e-mail: jonspode@aol.com
web: www.rashleighinnpolkerris.co.uk
dir: *Off A3082 outside Fowey*

Once a coastguard station, this 300-year-old pub at the end of a no-through road to Polkerris beach faces west, so watching the sun set over St Austell Bay is a delight. In the bar there's a good selection of real ales from Cornwall and elsewhere, real cider, local organic soft drinks and a water bowl and Bonio biscuits for visiting dogs. Good, locally sourced food is typically slow-roasted Cornish belly pork; pan-fried fillet of wild sea bass; roasted darnes of gurnard; mushroom ravioli; and tapas, served on a slate platter. Booking for meals may be required.

Open all day all wk **Bar Meals** L served all wk 12-3, snacks 3-5 D served all wk 6-9 **Restaurant** L served all wk 12-3, snacks 3-5 D served all wk 6-9 ⊕ FREE HOUSE ◀ Timothy Taylor Landlord, Skinner's Betty Stogs, St Austell HSD, Otter Bitter, Black Sheep Best Bitter ♻ Westons Stowford Press, Addlestones. ☗ **Facilities** ☙ Children welcome Children's menu Children's portions Garden Parking Wi-fi

Old Mill House Inn

Mill Hill PL13 2RP ☎ **01503 272362**
e-mail: enquiries@oldmillhouseinn.co.uk
dir: *Telephone for directions*

In the heart of historic Polperro, this old inn was once the house and storage area of a grain mill built in the early 17th century. It has survived serious flood damage in the past – photographs recording the disaster can be seen on the walls. Here you can sample well-kept local ales and cider beside a log fire in the bar, or sit out over lunch in the riverside garden during fine weather. Local ingredients are the foundation of dishes on the restaurant menu and firm favourites are steak-and-ale pie; and beer-battered locally caught cod. A beer festival is held on the first weekend in October.

Open all day all wk 10am-12.30am (Sun 10am-11.30pm) **Bar Meals** L served all wk 10-2.30 D served all wk 5.30-9 Av main course £8 **Restaurant** D served all wk 5.30-9 ⊕ FREE HOUSE ◀ Skinner's Mill House Ale, Sharp's Doom Bar ♂ Westons Stowford Press & Old Rosie. ♀ **Facilities** ❧ Children welcome Children's menu Children's portions Garden Beer festival Wi-fi

Port Gaverne Hotel

PICK OF THE PUBS

PL29 3SQ ☎ **01208 880244**
e-mail: graham@port-gaverne-hotel.co.uk
dir: *Signed from B3314, S of Delabole via B3267 on E of Port Isaac*

The secluded cove just down from this delightful 17th-century inn is where women once loaded sea-bound ketches with slate from the great quarry at Delabole. But after the railway arrived in 1893, sea trade declined and tranquillity returned to the port. The bar has slate floors (naturally!), low wooden beams and the customary log fire. Locally supplied produce includes plenty of fresh fish, destined to appear, for example, as crab salad, Port Isaac Bay lobster thermidor, and whole grilled Dover sole. Other possibilities include honey-roasted breast of duck with brandy, cream and green peppercorn sauce; and ploughman's with Cornish Yarg and chutney. Walkers from the Heritage Coast Path are always pausing for a pint of Sharp's or St Austell in the small beer garden.

Open all day all wk **Bar Meals** L served all wk 12-2.30 D served all wk 6-9 **Restaurant** D served all wk 7-9 ⊕ FREE HOUSE ◀ Sharp's Doom Bar & Cornish Coaster, St Austell Tribute. ♀ 9 **Facilities** Children welcome Children's menu Children's portions Garden Parking Wi-fi 🚌

The Ship Inn

TR13 9JS ☎ **01326 564204**
e-mail: cjoakden@yahoo.co.uk
dir: *From Helston follow signs to Porthleven, 2.5m. On entering village continue to harbour. Take W road by side of harbour to inn*

Dating from the 17th century, this smugglers' inn is actually built into the cliffs, and is approached by a flight of stone steps. During the winter, two log fires warm the interior, while the flames of a third flicker in the separate Smithy children's room. Expect a good selection of locally caught fish and seafood, such as crab and prawn mornay, or the smoked fish platter, all smoked in Cornwall. The pub has declared itself a 'chip-free zone'.

Open all day all wk 11.30-11.30 (Sun 12-10.30) **Bar Meals** L served all wk 12-2 D served all wk 6.30-9 ⊕ FREE HOUSE ◀ Courage Best, Sharp's Doom Bar, Guest ales ♂ Cornish Orchards. ♀ 8 **Facilities** ❧ Children welcome Children's menu Family room Garden

Basset Arms

Tregea Ter TR16 4NG ☎ **01209 842077**
e-mail: bassettarms@btconnect.com
dir: *From Redruth take B3300 to Portreath. Pub on left near seafront*

Tin-mining and shipwreck paraphernalia adorn the low-beamed interior of this early 19th-century Cornish stone cottage, built as a pub to serve harbour workers. At one time it served as a mortuary for ill-fated seafarers, so there are plenty of ghost stories! The menu makes the most of local seafood, such as mussels with fries, and home-made fish pie, but also provides a wide selection of alternatives, including half a chicken in barbecue sauce; 12oz gammon steak; curry of the day; and salads including crab, when available. Wash down your meal with a pint of Skinner's real ale.

Open all day all wk 11-11 (Fri-Sat 11am-mdnt Sun 11-10.30) **Bar Meals** L served all wk 12-2 D served all wk 6-9 **Restaurant** L served all wk 12-2 D served all wk 6-9 ⊕ FREE HOUSE ◀ Sharp's Doom Bar, Skinner's ♂ Healey's Cornish Rattler. **Facilities** Children welcome Children's menu Children's portions Play area Garden Parking 🚌

The Kings Head

TR2 5NX ☎ **01872 501263**
e-mail: contact@kings-head-roseland.co.uk
dir: *3m from Tregony Bridge on A3078*

This traditional country pub set deep in the Roseland countryside has a warm and welcoming atmosphere. Roaring winter fires, beamed ceilings and mulled wine contrasts with summer days relaxing on the terrace with a jug of Pimm's, a pint of Betty Stogs or Stowford Press cider. Whatever the time of year, the chef responds with seasonal dishes using the best of local produce, ranging from duo of Cornish sausages and prime Cornish steaks to Mediterranean chicken and fish pie. Look out for the signature dish, too – slow-roasted Terras Ruan duckling with pepper sauce. Booking for meals may be required.

Open 12-2.30 6-11 Closed: Sun eve, Mon (Oct-Etr) **Restaurant** L served all wk 12.30-2 D served all wk 6.30-9 ⊕ FREE HOUSE ◀ Skinner's Kings Ruan, Betty Stogs ♂ Westons Stowford Press. ♀ 9 **Facilities** Children welcome Garden Parking

Driftwood Spars ★★★★ GA

PICK OF THE PUBS

See Pick of the Pubs on opposite page

The Old Inn & Restaurant

Churchtown, Bodmin Moor PL30 4PP ☎ **01208 850711**
e-mail: theoldinn@macace.net
dir: *A30 to Bodmin. 16m, right just after Temple, follow signs to St Breward. B3266 (Bodmin to Camelford road) turn to St Breward, follow brown signs*

On the edge of Bodmin Moor, this is not just Cornwall's highest inn (720ft above sea level), it's one of the oldest too, having been built in the 11th century for monks to live in. It's believed to have been a pub since the 15th century, although records only go back to 1806. You can see ancient granite fireplaces and sloping ceilings in the bars, where Sharp's Doom Bar and Orchard cider are in the line-up. It is owned and run by local man Darren Wills, the latest licensee in its 1,000-year history. Mixed grills, over 25 daily changing specials, a pie of the day, locally caught fish, and all-day Sunday carvery are served in the bars, spacious restaurant or large garden. Cream teas are also a speciality. Booking for meals may be required.

Open all day all wk **Bar Meals** L served Sun-Fri 11-2, Sat 11-9 D served Sun-Fri 6-9, Sat 11-9 Av main course £9.95 **Restaurant** L served Mon-Fri 11-2, Sat-Sun 12-9 D served Mon-Fri 6-9, Sat-Sun 12-9 ⊕ FREE HOUSE ◀ Sharp's Doom Bar & Special, Guest ales ♂ Sharp's Orchard. ♀ 15 **Facilities** ❧ Children welcome Children's menu Children's portions Family room Garden Parking Wi-fi 🚌

PICK OF THE PUBS

Driftwood Spars ★★★★GA

ST AGNES　　　Map 3 SW75

Trevaunance Cove TR5 0RT
☎ **01872 552428**
e-mail: info@driftwoodspars.co.uk
web: www.driftwoodspars.co.uk
dir: *A30 onto B3285, through St Agnes, down steep hill, left at Peterville Inn, follow Trevaunance Cove sign*

Adjacent to the South West Coastal Path in the stunning Trevaunance Cove, this family-run pub occupies a 300-year-old tin miners' store, chandlery and sail loft, complete with its own smugglers' tunnel; it takes its name from spars salvaged from nearby shipwrecks. Around here the ancient Celtic landscape of dramatic cliffs, crashing surf, small fields and moorland abounds with legend and intrigue; in spring, watch for the Giant Bolster who rears his head in search of the lovely maid St Agnes. Altogether this award-winning establishment comprises 15 bedrooms (some with stunning sea views); a dining room with sea view; two beer gardens; three bars sparkling with real fires, old brass and lanterns; a micro-brewery; and a shop. Among the seven hand-pulled real ales are some of the 11 quality beers brewed on site, including the award-winning Alfie's Revenge, alongside guests, a 35-bin wine list, 35 malts and an impressive selection of 'alcoholic curiosities'. On the menu, seafood figures strongly in dishes such as beer-battered 'catch of the day' with crushed peas, fries and home-made tartare sauce, or trawlerman's fish pie with buttered greens. Other dishes range from pub

classics such as pan-fried whitebait followed by a 'gourmet' beefburger with organic leaf salad, to international favourites including fresh egg tagliatelle with fricassée of forest mushrooms; Thai green chicken curry with steamed basmati rice; and beef bourguignon with creamy mash and seasonal greens. The Sunday roast comes highly recommended. Tempting desserts might include saffron bread-and-butter pudding with vanilla bean ice cream or warm traditional treacle tart with Cornish clotted cream. There is a mini beer festival mid-March and on May Day Bank Holiday weekend. Booking for meals may be required.

Open all day all wk 11-11 (Fri-Sat 11am-1am 25 Dec 11am-2pm) **Bar Meals** L served all wk 12-2.30 D served all wk 6.30-9.30 (winter 6.30-8.30) Av main course £9.95 **Restaurant** L served

Sun 12-2.30 D served all wk 7-9 (winter Fri-Sat 7-8.30) Av 3 course à la carte fr £25 ⊕ FREE HOUSE ◄ Driftwood Spars Red Mission, Blue Hills Bitter, Lou's Brew & Alfie's Revenge, St Austell Tribute, Sharp's Doom Bar ⌀ Healey's Cornish Rattler, Thatchers. ♟ 9 **Facilities** Children welcome Children's menu Children's portions ❀ Garden Beer festival Parking Wi-fi ⛟ (notice required) **Rooms** 15

ST EWE
Map 2 SW94

The Crown Inn

PL26 6EY ☎ 01726 843322
e-mail: phigham@fsnet.co.uk
dir: *From St Austell take B3273. At Tregiskey x-rds turn right. St Ewe signed on right*

Taken over by a new landlord in October 2011, this pretty 16th-century village inn is only a mile away from the famous 'Lost Gardens of Heligan'. Rest and refuel by the fire in the traditional bar or relax in the peaceful flower-festooned garden in summer. Quaff a pint of St Austell ale and tuck into a hearty lunchtime bar snack or look to the board for evening specials like pan-fried kidneys with pepper sauce; hake with mussels; crushed potatoes and fish cream; or seared lamb rump with sweet potato mash and minted gravy.

Open all wk 12-2.30 5.30-close (summer all day) **Bar Meals** L served all wk 12-2 D served Mon-Sat 6-9.30 Av main course £9-£12 **Restaurant** L served all wk 12-2 D served Mon-Sat 6-9.30 ⊞ ST AUSTELL BREWERY ◀ Tribute, Tinners Ale & Proper Job, Guest ale ♻ Healey's Cornish Rattler. **Facilities** ♣ Children welcome Children's menu Children's portions Play area Family room Garden Parking Wi-fi ▭

ST IVES
Map 2 SW54

The Queens ★★★★ INN ⊛ NEW

2 High St TR26 1RR ☎ 01736 796468
e-mail: info@queenshotelstives.com
dir: *5min walk from St Ives Station*

Minutes from the harbourside and beaches stands St Ives' new gastro-pub with rooms, an impressive late-Georgian granite building where informed locals and tourists have found spruced-up bedrooms (some have sea views) and top-notch pub food. Scrubbed tables, wooden floors, squashy sofas, daily papers and log fires set the informal scene for sampling tip-top St Austell ales and some delicious food. Expect big flavours, local produce and home-baked bread, with game terrine with cranberry chutney; sea bass with onion and herb dressing; and roast partridge featuring on the daily chalkboard menu.

Open all day all wk **Bar Meals** L served Tue-Sat 12-2.30, Sun 12-4 D served Tue-Sat 6.30-9.30 Av main course £10 **Restaurant** Fixed menu price fr £10 ⊞ ST AUSTELL BREWERY ◀ Tribute, HSD ♻ Healey's Cornish Rattler. ♟ 16 **Facilities** ♣ Children welcome Children's portions Wi-fi ▭ (notice required) **Rooms** 8

The Sloop Inn ★★★ INN

The Wharf TR26 1LP ☎ 01736 796584
e-mail: sloopinn@btinternet.com
dir: *On St Ives harbour by middle slipway*

A trip to St Ives wouldn't be complete without visiting this 700-year-old pub perched right on the harbourside. Slate floors, beamed ceilings and nautical artefacts dress

some of the several bars and dining areas, whilst the cobbled forecourt is an unbeatable spot for people- and harbour-watching, preferably with a pint of local Doom Bar. The menu majors on local seafood, from line-caught St Ives Bay mackerel and fries to home-made Newlyn cod, smoked haddock and smoked bacon fishcakes. Most of the comfortably appointed bedrooms overlook the pretty bay. Booking for meals may be required.

Open all day all wk **Bar Meals** L served all wk 12-3 D served all wk 5-10 Av main course £8 **Restaurant** D served Mon-Sat 6-10 Av 3 course à la carte fr £23 ⊞ ENTERPRISE INNS ◀ Sharp's Doom Bar ♻ Thatchers Gold. **Facilities** Children welcome Wi-fi ▭ (notice required) **Rooms** 18

The Watermill

Lelant Downs, Hayle TR27 6LQ ☎ 01736 757912
e-mail: watermill@btconnect.com
dir: *Exit A30 at junct for St Ives/A3074, turn left at 2nd mini rdbt*

Set in extensive gardens on the old St Ives coach road, with glorious valley views towards Trencrom Hill, The Watermill is a cosy, family-friendly pub and restaurant created in the 18th-century Lelant Mill. The old mill machinery is still in place and the iron waterwheel continues to turn, gravity fed by the mill stream. Downstairs is the old beamed bar and wood-burning stove, while upstairs in the open-beamed mill loft is the atmospheric restaurant where steaks and fish (sea bass, sardines and mackerel perhaps) are specialities. There are beer festivals in June and November with live music all weekend. Booking for meals may be required.

Open all day all wk 12-11 **Bar Meals** L served all wk 12-2.30 D served all wk 6-9 **Restaurant** D served all wk 6-9 ⊞ FREE HOUSE ◀ Sharp's Doom Bar, Skinner's Betty Stogs, Guest ales ♻ Healey's Cornish Rattler. **Facilities** ♣ Children welcome Children's menu Play area Garden Beer festival Parking ▭

ST JUST (NEAR LAND'S END)
Map 2 SW33

Star Inn
PICK OF THE PUBS

TR19 7LL ☎ 01736 788767
dir: *Telephone for directions*

Plenty of tin-mining and fishing stories are told at this traditional Cornish pub, located in the town of St Just, near Land's End. It dates back a few centuries, and was reputedly built to house workmen constructing the 15th-century church. John Wesley is believed to have been among the Star's more illustrious guests over the years, but these days the pub is most likely to be recognised for having featured in several television and film productions due to its immense charm and character. A choice of local beers is served, but there is no food. Monday night is folk night, and there's live music on Thursdays and Saturdays, too, in a whole range of styles.

Open all day all wk 11am-12.30am ⊞ ST AUSTELL BREWERY ◀ HSD, Tinners Ale, Tribute, Dartmoor, Proper Job ♻ Healey's Cornish Rattler. **Facilities** ♣ Children welcome Family room Garden **Notes** ⊛

The Wellington ★★ INN

Market Square TR19 7HD ☎ 01736 787319
e-mail: wellingtonhotel@msn.com
dir: *Take A30 to Penzance, then A3071 W of Penzance to St Just*

Standing in the market square of the historic mining town of St Just, this attractive family-run inn makes an ideal base for visiting Land's End and St Ives, as well as exploring the spectacular beaches and countryside – walking, climbing and bird-watching. Low ceilings, solid stonework and a secluded walled garden help evoke the atmosphere of Cornwall as it once was. St Austell beers and Cornish Rattler cider are served in the bar, while the menu offers a selection of grills, pasta dishes, sandwiches, daily specials, traditional pub dishes, and the popular Welly burger – either beef or vegetarian. Accommodation is available.

Open all day all wk **Bar Meals** L served all wk 12-2 D served all wk 6-9 (winter 6-8.30) Av main course £8.50 **Restaurant** D served all wk 6-9 (summer) ⊞ ST AUSTELL BREWERY ◀ Dartmoor, Tribute, HSD ♻ Healey's Cornish Rattler. **Facilities** Children welcome Children's menu Children's portions Play area Garden Wi-fi ▭ (notice required) **Rooms** 11

ST KEW
Map 2 SX07

St Kew Inn NEW

Churchtown PL30 3HB ☎ 01208 841259
e-mail: stkewinn@btconnect.com
dir: *From Wadebridge N on A39. Left to St Kew*

A classic stone-built village pub with 15th-century origins, in summer the exterior makes a chocolate-box picture of flower tubs and creepers. Inside, traditional features include a huge open fire. St Austell beers and Rattler cider are the prime refreshments, while menus proffer carefully sourced and prepared British dishes with cosmopolitan touches. Choose between four eating areas – five if you include the garden – when ordering your lunchtime snack of Welsh rarebit on ciabatta with a fried egg. Alternatively try the pork, Tribute and thyme sausages with mustard mash, followed by steamed chocolate pudding with clotted cream.

Open all wk 11-3 5.30-11 (summer all day) **Bar Meals** L served all wk 12-2, summer all day D served all wk 6-9, summer all day Av main course £12.95 **Restaurant** L served all wk 12-2, summer all day D served all wk 6-9, summer all day Av 3 course à la carte fr £25 ⊞ ST AUSTELL BREWERY ◀ Tribute, HSD, Proper Job ♻ Healey's Cornish Rattler. **Facilities** ♣ Children welcome Children's menu Children's portions Family room Garden Parking Wi-fi

PICK OF THE PUBS

The Victory Inn

ST MAWES   Map 2 SW83

Victory Hill TR2 5DQ ☎ 01326 270324
e-mail: contact@victory-inn.co.uk
web: www.victory-inn.co.uk
dir: *A3078 to St Mawes. Pub adjacent to harbour*

Located near the harbour, this friendly fishermen's local is named after Nelson's flagship but adopts a modern approach to its daily lunch and dinner menus. You may eat downstairs in the traditional bar, or in the modern and stylish first-floor Seaview Restaurant (white walls, white linen and wicker chairs), with a terrace that looks across the town's rooftops to the harbour and the River Fal. High on the list of ingredients is fresh seafood – all from Cornish waters, of course – the choice changing virtually daily to include crab risotto, fisherman's pie, and beer-battered cod and hand-cut chips, with chicken breast cordon bleu, lamb shank provençale, and curry or casserole of the day among the other favourites. Children are provided with paper, crayons and their own menu; dogs are

given treats too. Wines are all carefully chosen and excellent in quality, as are the real ales from Cornwall's own Roseland, Sharp's and Skinner's breweries. There is outside seating with views over the harbour. Booking for meals is definitely advisable in the summer months. Ever-popular St Mawes boasts lovely safe beaches, and if you choose to venture further afield the dramatic Cornish coastal scenery is close at hand.

Open all day all wk 11am-mdnt **Bar Meals** L served all wk 12-3 D served all wk 6-9.30 **Restaurant** L served all wk 12-3 D served all wk 6-9.15 ⊕ PUNCH TAVERNS ◧ Wadworth 6X, Roseland Cornish Shag, Skinner's Betty Stogs, Bass, Sharp's. **Facilities** Children welcome Children's menu Children's portions ⚹ Garden Wi-fi 🚌

PICK OF THE PUBS

The Falcon Inn ★★★★ INN

ST MAWGAN Map 2 SW86

TR8 4EP ☎ 01637 860225
e-mail: thefalconinnstmawgan@gmail.com
web: www.thefalconinnstmawgan.co.uk
dir: *From A30 (8m W of Bodmin) follow signs to Newquay Airport. Turn right 200mtrs before airport terminal into St Mawgan, pub at bottom of hill*

This attractive stone building in the Vale of Lanherne traces its ancestry back as far as 1758, and is thought to have been kept as the New Inn during the late 18th century. By 1813 the pub was known as the Gardeners' Arms, and in about 1880 the name was changed again to The Falcon Inn, an allusion to the nearby estate's coat of arms. Throughout much of the 20th century the inn was run by members of the Fry family; they relinquished control in 1966, and the present innkeepers are David Carbis and Sarah Lawrence. The interior of the wisteria-covered Falcon is cosy and relaxed, with flagstone floors and log fires in winter; there's a large attractive garden, magnificent magnolia tree and cobbled courtyard for alfresco summer dining. Beers from St Austell Brewery are augmented by Rattler cider, and a dozen wines are served by the glass. Lunchtime brings snacks like home-made fishcakes or grilled local goat's cheese, plus an appetising range of hot open toasted sandwiches. There's

also a good selection of home-made hot dishes, including fresh battered Newlyn fish and chips; Falcon burger with blue cheese and red onion marmalade; and three cheese lasagne. An à la carte evening menu is served in the more formal restaurant; main courses always include fresh fish options, and vegetarians are well catered for. Comfortable, individually furnished en suite bedrooms are also available. Nearby, traces of a sixth-century Celtic monastery can be found in what became the Arundel family manor house – today a convent housing nuns and friars.

Open all wk 11-3 6-11 (Jul-Aug all day) Closed: 25 Dec (open 12-2) **Bar Meals** L served all wk 12-2 D served all wk 6-9

Av main course £9.75 **Restaurant** L served all wk 12-2 D served all wk 6-9 ⊕ ST AUSTELL BREWERY ◀ HSD, Tribute & Dartmoor, Guest ales ♂ Healey's Cornish Rattler. ♟ 12 **Facilities** Children welcome Children's menu ♣ Garden Parking Wi-fi 🚌 (notice required) **Rooms** 2

ST MAWES	Map 2 SW83

The Victory Inn
PICK OF THE PUBS

See Pick of the Pubs on page 101

ST MAWGAN	Map 2 SW86

The Falcon Inn ★★★★ INN
PICK OF THE PUBS

See Pick of the Pubs on opposite page

ST MERRYN	Map 2 SW87

The Cornish Arms
PICK OF THE PUBS

Churchtown PL28 8ND ☎ 01841 532700
e-mail: reservations@rickstein.com
dir: *From Padstow follow signs for St Merryn then Churchtown*

When Rick and Jill Stein took over this ancient village pub, situated across the road from the parish church and overlooking a peaceful valley, the locals feared their treasured boozer would become a fancy gastro-pub. Luckily, the Steins loved their local pub just as it was, replete with slate floors, beams and roaring log fires. They have kept the food offering equally traditional, the chalkboard listing simple pub classics prepared from fresh produce: ham, egg and chips; mussels with bread and butter; and ploughman's. Wash it down with a decent pint of St Austell Tribute ale, or a glass of Chalky's Bite, named after their much-missed rough-haired Jack Russell. Check with the pub for details of themed nights and beer festivals.

Open all day all wk 11-11 **Bar Meals** L served all wk 12-2.30 D served all wk 6-8.30 Av main course £10 **Restaurant** L served all wk 12-2.30 D served all wk 6-8.30 Av 3 course à la carte fr £19 ⊕ ST AUSTELL BREWERY ◀ Tribute, Proper Job, Trelawny, Chalky's Bite ♂ Healey's Cornish Rattler. ♟ 15 **Facilities** ♣ Children welcome Children's menu Children's portions Garden Beer festival Parking Wi-fi 🚌

SALTASH	Map 3 SX45

The Crooked Inn ★★★★ INN

Stoketon Cottage, Trematon PL12 4RZ
☎ 01752 848177
e-mail: info@crooked-inn.co.uk
dir: *Telephone for directions*

Overlooking the lush Lyher Valley and run by the same family for more than 25 years, this delightful inn once housed staff from Stoketon Manor, whose ruins lie on the other side of the courtyard. It is set in ten acres of lawns and woodland, yet only 15 minutes from Plymouth. There is an extensive menu including evening specials with plenty of fresh fish and vegetarian dishes. The children's playground has friendly animals, swings, slides, a

trampoline and a treehouse. Spacious bedrooms are individually designed and decorated.

Open all day all wk 11-11 (Sun 12-10.30) Closed: 25 Dec **Bar Meals** L served all wk 11-2.30 D served all wk 6-9.30 ⊕ FREE HOUSE ◀ St Austell HSD, Dartmoor Jail Ale, Guest ales ♂ Thatchers Gold. **Facilities** ♣ Children welcome Children's menu Play area Garden Parking Wi-fi 🚌 **Rooms** 18

SENNEN	Map 2 SW32

The Old Success Inn

Sennen Cove TR19 7DG ☎ 01736 871232
e-mail: oldsuccess@staustellbrewery.co.uk
dir: *Telephone for directions*

Once the haunt of smugglers and now a focal point for the Sennen Lifeboat crew, this 17th-century inn enjoys a glorious location overlooking Cape Cornwall. Its name comes from the days when fishermen gathered here to count their catch and share out their 'successes'. Fresh local seafood is to the fore, and favourites include Tribute-battered catch of the day and Cornish fish pie. Non-fishy choices include Cajun-style chicken, goat's cheese tart, Cornish pasty with chips, and casserole of the day. Booking for meals may be required.

Open all wk Mon-Sat 10am-11pm (Sun 11-10.30) **Bar Meals** L served all wk 12-3 D served all wk 6-9 **Restaurant** L served all wk 12-3 D served all wk 6-9 ⊕ ST AUSTELL BREWERY ◀ Tribute, HSD, Proper Job, Trelawny ♂ Healey's Cornish Rattler. ♟ 18 **Facilities** ♣ Children welcome Children's menu Children's portions Garden Parking Wi-fi 🚌 (notice required)

TORPOINT	Map 3 SX45

Edgcumbe Arms
PICK OF THE PUBS

Cremyll PL10 1HX ☎ 01752 822294
dir: *Telephone for directions*

The inn dates from the 15th century and is located right on the Tamar estuary, next to Mount Edgcumbe Country Park, and close to the foot ferry from Plymouth. Views from the bow window seats and waterside terrace are glorious, taking in Drakes Island, the Royal William Yard and the marina. Real ales from St Austell like Proper Job, plus Cornish Rattler cider, and quality home-cooked food are served in a series of rooms (the same menu is offered throughout), which are full of character with American oak panelling and flagstone floors. Dishes are a mixture of international and traditional British: Cornish sardines on toast or Chinese duck pancakes to start, followed by Thai sweet chilli chicken or honey-roast ham. Lighter bites and a carvery are available daily. The inn has a first-floor function room with sea views, and a courtyard garden.

Open all day all wk 11-11 Closed: Nov, Jan-Feb Mon-Tue eve **Bar Meals** food served all day **Restaurant** food served all day ⊕ ST AUSTELL BREWERY ◀ Tribute, Proper Job, Trelawny ♂ Healey's Cornish Rattler. ♟ 10 **Facilities** ♣ Children welcome Children's menu Children's portions Garden Parking Wi-fi 🚌 (notice required)

TREBARWITH	Map 2 SX08

The Mill House Inn
PICK OF THE PUBS

See Pick of the Pubs on page 104

The Port William

Trebarwith Strand PL34 0HB ☎ 01840 770230
e-mail: theportwilliam@staustellbrewery.co.uk
dir: *From A39 onto B3314 signed Tintagel. Right onto B3263, follow Trebarwith Strand signs, then brown Port William signs*

Occupying one of the best locations in Cornwall, this former harbourmaster's house lies directly on the coastal path, 50 yards from the sea, which means the views are amazing. There is an entrance to a smugglers' tunnel at the rear of the ladies' toilet! Focus on the daily-changing specials board for such dishes as artichoke and roast pepper salad, warm smoked trout platter, and spinach and ricotta tortelloni.

Open all wk 10am-11pm (Sun 10am-10.30pm) **Bar Meals** L served all wk 12-3, 3-6 D served all wk 6-9 ⊕ ST AUSTELL BREWERY ◀ Tribute & Trelawny, Guest ales ♂ Healey's Cornish Rattler. ♟ 8 **Facilities** ♣ Children welcome Children's menu Children's portions Family room Garden Parking Wi-fi

TREBURLEY	Map 3 SX37

The Springer Spaniel
PICK OF THE PUBS

See Pick of the Pubs on page 105

TREGADILLETT	Map 3 SX28

Eliot Arms

PL15 7EU ☎ 01566 772051
dir: *From Launceston take A30 towards Bodmin. Then follow brown signs to Tregadillett*

The extraordinary décor in this charming creeper-clad coaching inn, dating back to 1625, includes Masonic regalia, horse brasses and grandfather clocks. It was believed to have been a Masonic lodge for Napoleonic prisoners, and even has its own friendly ghost! Customers can enjoy real fires in winter and lovely hanging baskets in summer. Food, based on locally sourced meat and fresh fish and shellfish caught off the Cornish coast, is served in the bar or bright and airy restaurant. Expect home-made soups, pie and curry of the day; steak and chips; chargrills; and home-made vegetarian dishes. Booking for meals may be required.

Open all day all wk 11.30-11 (Fri-Sat 11.30am-mdnt Sun 12-10.30) **Bar Meals** L served all wk 12-2 D served all wk 6-9 **Restaurant** L served all wk 12-2 D served all wk 6-9 ⊕ FREE HOUSE ◀ Sharp's Doom Bar, Courage Best Bitter, St Austell Tribute. ♟ 9 **Facilities** ♣ Children welcome Family room Parking 🚌

PICK OF THE PUBS

The Mill House Inn

TREBARWITH Map 2 SX08

PL34 0HD ☎ 01840 770200

e-mail: management@themillhouseinn.co.uk
web: www.themillhouseinn.co.uk
dir: *From Tintagel take B3263 S, right after Trewarmett to Trebarwith Strand. Pub 0.5m on right*

This charming 18th-century corn mill dates from 1760, and was still working in the late 1930s, when it became first a private house, then a guest house and finally, in 1960, a pub and hotel. Set in seven acres of woodland on the north Cornish coast, it's half a mile from the surfing beach at Trebarwith Strand, one of the finest in Cornwall, while also nearby is Tintagel Castle, birthplace of the legendary King Arthur. The log fires in this beautifully atmospheric stone building are quite capable of warming the residents' lounge and informally furnished, slate-floored bar, where wooden tables and chapel chairs help create a relaxed, family-friendly feel. Locally brewed real ales are furnished by Sharp's and Tintagel breweries, and the ciders are Cornish Orchards and Cornish Rattler. The cosmopolitan wine list features an especially good choice of half bottles and should appeal to everyone. Lunches, evening drinks and barbecues are particularly enjoyable out on the attractive split-level terraces, while dinner in the Millstream Restaurant is intended to be an intimate and romantic experience. Regularly changing dishes use the best fresh fish, meat, vegetables and other ingredients that Cornwall can supply so,

starting with the bar menu, there's sweet chilli beef strips with stir-fried vegetables and noodles; and Porthilly mussels in garlic and white wine cream sauce. From the carte, a typical dinner might involve crispy duck with shredded cucumber, spring onions, steamed pancakes and hoi sin sauce; then lemon and sea salt-roasted halibut fillet, pancetta and bean fricassée, and rocket; and to follow, lavender crème brûlée. Regular live events feature local musicians and comedians, while calendar fixtures such as Halloween, Guy Fawkes' Night and New Year are not to be missed. Staff will organise water sports, including surfing and deep-water soloing on the rugged sea cliffs.

Open all day all wk 11-11 (Fri-Sat 11am-mdnt Sun 12-10.30) **Bar Meals** L served Mon-Sat 12-2.30, Sun 12-3

D served all wk 6.30-8.30 Av main course £9.95 **Restaurant** D served all wk 7-9 Av 3 course à la carte fr £25 ⊕ FREE HOUSE ◧ Sharp's Doom Bar, Tintagel Harbour Special & Cornwall's Pride Ŏ Cornish Orchards, Healey's Cornish Rattler. **Facilities** Children welcome Children's menu Children's portions Play area Family room Garden Parking Wi-fi ▭ (notice required)

PICK OF THE PUBS

The Springer Spaniel

TREBURLEY   Map 3 SX37

PL15 9NS ☎ 01579 370424

e-mail: enquiries@thespringerspaniel.org.uk
web: www.thespringerspaniel.org.uk
dir: *On A388 halfway between Launceston & Callington*

An inn for the last two centuries, Roger and Lavinia Halliday's traditional hostelry offers Cornish and guest ales, delicious food, fine wines and friendly service. The inviting bar is furnished with high-backed wooden settles, farmhouse-style chairs and a wood-burning stove which, no doubt, the dogs will seek out while their owners chat, read the daily paper or cast a curious eye over the many books in the snug. The restaurant is full of plants and flowers, and flickering candles in the evenings add to the romantic atmosphere. In summer the landscaped, sheltered garden is a great place to relax and enjoy the sun with a pint of Doom Bar or Betty Stogs, or one of the half dozen wines by the glass. The fact that food is such a big draw here is partly down to where it comes from: fresh fish and seafood from Cornish waters; meat, game and dairy produce from local farmers and country estates; grass-fed pedigree South Devon cattle and Lleyn sheep from the owners' 100-hectare, Soil Association-approved farm; and vegetables and fragrant herbs from the region. Then there are the seasonally-inspired menus, cooked by chefs Francis Denford, veteran of many a top Cornish and London restaurant, and Martin Putt. Bar lunches range from the ever-popular ploughman's and hot filled focaccias, to old faithfuls like cottage pie. A three-course meal might begin with gravad lax or mushrooms sautéed with bacon and cream, flamed in brandy and topped with melted cheddar cheese, before a main course of salmon en papillote; lamb and vegetable casserole; or a special of pan-fried venison loin with parsnip mash and red wine jus. Treacle and almond, and cranberry Bakewell tarts are among the desserts. Children should enjoy organically-reared beef sausages, and wild mushroom and cashew nut Stroganoff on the 'Little Jack Russell' menu.

Open all wk 12-2.30 6-10.30 **Bar Meals** L served all wk 12-1.45 D served all wk 6.15-8.45 Av main course £12.95 **Restaurant** L served all wk 12-1.45 D served all wk 6.15-8.45 ⊞ FREE HOUSE ◀ Sharp's Doom Bar, Skinner's Betty Stogs, Guest ale ♂ Thatchers. **Facilities** Children welcome Children's menu Children's portions Family room ❖ Garden Parking

TRESCO (ISLES OF SCILLY)   Map 2 SV81

The New Inn ★★★★ INN ◉
PICK OF THE PUBS

New Grimsby TR24 0QQ ☎ 01720 422844
e-mail: newinn@tresco.co.uk
dir: *By New Grimsby Quay*

Nowadays, as the only pub on the island, this has to be, as landlord Robin Lawson says, the 'Best Pub on Tresco'. Everywhere you look is maritime history, much of it, such as the signboard, mahogany bar and wall-planking, salvaged from wrecks. An AA Rosette recognises the quality of food - served from the same menu wherever you dine - in the quiet restaurant, the livelier Driftwood Bar, the Pavillion, or outside. Accompany a lunchtime beefburger with a pint of Scillonian real ale or Cornish Rattler cider. For dinner, seek out Scilly crab salad; seared salmon fillet with couscous salad; or butternut squash, Cornish goat's cheese and sage risotto; finish with sticky toffee sponge or dark chocolate fondant. Traditional roasts are served on Sundays. There are beer festivals in mid-May and early September. Some of the stylish rooms available have ocean views. Booking for meals may be required.

Open all wk all day (Apr-Oct) phone for winter opening **Bar Meals** L served all wk 12-2.15 D served all wk 6.30-9 **Restaurant** D served all wk 6.30-9 ⊕ FREE HOUSE/ TRESCO ESTATE ◀ Skinner's Betty Stogs, Tresco Tipple, Ales of Scilly Scuppered & Firebrand, St Austell Proper Job Ò Healey's Cornish Rattler & Pear Rattler. ♈ 13 **Facilities** Children welcome Children's menu Children's portions Garden Beer festival Wi-fi **Rooms** 16

TRURO   Map 2 SW84

Old Ale House

7 Quay St TR1 2HD ☎ 01872 271122
e-mail: jamie@oahtruro.com
dir: *In town centre*

This traditional city centre pub right next to the main bus station in Truro offers a large selection of Skinner's real ales and guest beers, as well as live music and various quiz and games nights. The extensive menus include 'huge hands of hot bread' (quarter or half a bloomer covered in a topping of your choice and baked), sandwiches and the pub's famous skillets – perhaps the five-spice chicken, the Cantonese prawns or the sizzling beef.

Open all wk 11-11 (Fri-Sat 11am-mdnt Sun 12-10.30) Closed: 25-26 Dec, 1 Jan **Bar Meals** L served all wk 12-3 Av main course £6.50 **Restaurant** L served all wk 12-3 ⊕ ENTERPRISE INNS ◀ Skinner's Kiddlywink, Shepherd Neame Spitfire, Greene King Abbot Ale, Fuller's London Pride, Courage, Guest ales. ♈ 9 **Facilities** Children welcome Children's portions ▭ (notice required)

The Wig & Pen Inn

Frances St TR1 3DP ☎ 01872 273028
e-mail: wigandpentruro@hotmail.com
dir: *In city centre near Law Courts. 10 mins from rail station*

Tim and Georgina Robinson took over the reins of this Truro city-centre pub in 2011, bringing with them their respective skills in the kitchen and top quality front-of-house experience. There's a menu full of interesting, modern dishes, freshly prepared on the premises. Kick off with a shareable chips and dips, or beer-battered squid rings with chilli mayo, then Cornish crab hash cakes with red pepper salsa; or trio of smoked meats with beetroot chutney, followed by roast skate wing with pork belly and lentil stew; Mediterranean fish stew; or rare venison with celeriac dauphinoise, red cabbage and jus. Those with a sweet tooth will be tempted by the Baileys and Malteser cheesecake. Regular themed evenings take place, and plans for further refurbishment are scheduled in 2012.

Open all day all wk Closed: 25-26 Dec, 1 Jan **Bar Meals** L served all wk 12-2.30 D served all wk 6-9.30 Av main course £10 ⊕ ST AUSTELL BREWERY ◀ Tribute, HSD, Trelawny Ò Healey's Cornish Rattler & Pear Rattler. ♈ 12 **Facilities** ☙ Children welcome Children's portions Garden ▭

VERYAN   Map 2 SW93

The New Inn

TR2 5QA ☎ 01872 501362
e-mail: newinnveryan@gmail.com
dir: *From St Austell take A390 towards Truro, in 2m left to Tregony. Through Tregony, follow signs to Veryan*

In the centre of a pretty village on the Roseland Peninsula, this unspoiled, part-thatched pub comprises a pair of 16th-century cottages. It has a single bar, open fires, a beamed ceiling and a warm, welcoming atmosphere. The emphasis is on good ales and home cooking. Sunday lunch is a speciality; other choices during the week might include hand-breaded Cornish brie with redcurrant jelly, followed by home-made steak and St Austell ale pie; home-made lasagne with garlic bread; or hand-carved Cornish ham with egg and fries. Booking for meals may be required.

Open all day all wk 12-3 5.30-11 (Sun 7-11) **Bar Meals** L served all wk 12-2 D served Mon-Sat 6.30-9, Sun 7-9 **Restaurant** L served all wk 12-2 D served Mon-Sat 6.30-9, Sun 7-9 ⊕ ST AUSTELL BREWERY ◀ Tribute, Proper Job, Dartmoor Ò Healey's Cornish Rattler. ♈ **Facilities** ☙ Children welcome Children's menu Children's portions Garden Wi-fi ▭

WADEBRIDGE   Map 2 SW97

The Quarryman Inn

Edmonton PL27 7JA ☎ 01208 816444
e-mail: thequarryman@live.co.uk
web: www.thequarryman.co.uk
dir: *Off A39 opposite Royal Cornwall Showground*

Close to the famous Camel Trail, this friendly 18th-century free house has evolved from a courtyard of cottages once home to slate workers from the nearby quarry. Several bow windows, one of which features a stained-glass quarryman panel, add character to this unusual inn. The pub's signature dishes are chargrilled steaks served on sizzling platters and fresh local seafood; puddings are on the blackboard. Meals and drinks can be enjoyed outside in the slate courtyard in summer, or by a roaring fire in colder months. Booking for meals may be required.

Open all day all wk 12-11 Closed: 25 Dec **Bar Meals** L served all wk 12-2.30 D served all wk 6-9 Av main course £10.90 ⊕ FREE HOUSE ◀ Timothy Taylor Landlord, Sharp's, Skinner's, Guest ales Ò Westons Stowford Press. **Facilities** Children welcome Children's menu Children's portions Garden Parking Wi-fi ▭ (notice required)

Swan

9 Molesworth St PL27 7DD ☎ 01208 812526
e-mail: reservations@smallandfriendly.co.uk
dir: *In centre of Wadebridge on corner of Molesworth St & The Platt*

Bursting with life and at the heart of the local community, this white-painted town-centre corner hotel is an ideal base for exploring north Cornwall and the nearby Camel Trail. Popular with families, the main bar provides a comfortable place to relax and enjoy a drink or a meal. Typical pub food in the Cygnet restaurant includes locally smoked salmon; Cornish ham, egg and chips; local crab cakes; and beer-battered fish and chips with peas. There's also a good selection from the grill. Booking for meals may be required.

Open all day all wk **Bar Meals** L served all wk 12-9 Av main course £8.95 food served all day **Restaurant** D served all wk 6.30-9 ⊞ ST AUSTELL BREWERY ◀ Tribute, Proper Job, Guinness Ö Healey's Cornish Rattler. ♚ 13 **Facilities** ✿ Children welcome Children's menu Children's portions Family room Garden Wi-fi ▦ (notice required)

WIDEMOUTH BAY — Map 2 SS20

Bay View Inn

Marine Dr EX23 0AW ☎ 01288 361273
e-mail: thebayviewinn@aol.com
dir: *On Marine Drive adjacent to beach in Widemouth Bay*

Dating back around 100 years, this welcoming, family-run pub was a guest house for many years before becoming an inn in the 1960s. True to its name, the pub has fabulous views of the rolling Atlantic from its restaurant and the large raised decking area outside. The menu makes excellent use of local produce, as in the signature dish of fish pie; and sea bass fillets with Florentine potatoes and tiger prawn and saffron sauce. Other choices include home-made pies, casseroles and burgers.

Open all day all wk **Bar Meals** L served Mon-Fri 12-2.30, Sat-Sun 12-9 D served Mon-Fri 5.30-9, Sat-Sun 12-9 Av main course £10-£15 **Restaurant** L served Mon-Fri 12-2.30, Sat-Sun 12-9 D served Mon-Fri 5.30-9, Sat-Sun 12-9 ⊞ FREE HOUSE ◀ Skinner's Betty Stogs & Spriggan Ale, Sharp's Doom Bar Ö Thatchers. ♚ 14 **Facilities** ✿ Children welcome Children's menu Children's portions Play area Garden Parking Wi-fi ▦ (notice required)

ZENNOR — Map 2 SW43

The Gurnard's Head ★★★ INN ◉

PICK OF THE PUBS

Treen TR26 3DE ☎ 01736 796928
e-mail: enquiries@gurnardshead.co.uk
dir: *5m from Penzance. 5m from St Ives on B3306*

In a fabulous location, remote amidst a latticework of stone-walled pastures atop the high cliff of Gurnard's Head, this pub has fabulous views across the Penwith peninsula. The rugged setting is more than matched by

the robust meals created under the tutelage of head chef Bruce Rennie. Choose a table in the multi-roomed interior, all colourwash, scrubbed tables, rugs and local art, and contemplate a fare that kicks in with striking starters like quail, squid ink risotto and parsley, followed by main of gurnard, smoked haddock, mashed potatoes and leeks. Other mains are equally arresting; sample pork loin with Puy lentils, broccoli and salsa verde. Cornish beers wet the whistle of diners and walkers, whilst there's also an extraordinary wine list, with 16 by the glass. Accommodation is available if you would like to stay over and explore the area. Booking for meals may be required.

Open all day all wk 11-11 Closed: 25 Dec **Bar Meals** L served Mon-Sat 12.30-2.30, Sun 12-2.30 D served all wk 6.30-9.30 **Restaurant** L served Mon-Sat 12.30-2.30, Sun 12-2.30 D served all wk 6.30-9.30 ⊞ FREE HOUSE ◀ St Austell Tribute, Skinner's Betty Stogs & Splendid Tackle Ö Westons Stowford Press, Wickwar Screech. ♚ 16 **Facilities** ✿ Children welcome Children's menu Children's portions Garden Parking **Rooms** 7

The Tinners Arms

PICK OF THE PUBS

TR26 3BY ☎ 01736 796927
e-mail: tinners@tinnersarms.com
dir: *Take B3306 from St Ives towards St Just. Zennor approx 5m*

Built around 700 years ago to accommodate masons working on the beautiful church next door, D H Lawrence reputedly stayed here during World War I, when he was writing *Women in Love*. The only pub in the village, this 13th-century granite-built free house is close to the South West Coastal Path, so muddy booted walkers taking a well-earned rest are usually found among its clientele. It has changed little over the years: its stone floors and low ceilings are warmed by open fires in winter, when cushioned settles and mixed chairs around solid wood tables greet locals and visitors alike; outside is a large terrace with sea views. The dinner menu, based on ingredients from local suppliers, might offer pigeon breast with mushrooms and tarragon sauce; Terras Farm duck breast with braised peas and new potatoes; chocolate fudge cake with clotted cream; or 'Moomaid' ice cream made on the local farm.

Open all wk **Bar Meals** L served all wk 12-2.30 D served all wk 6.30-9 (ex Sun & Mon eve winter) ⊞ FREE HOUSE ◀ Zennor Mermaid, St Austell Tinners Ale, Sharp's Own Ö Burrow Hill. ♚ 10 **Facilities** Children welcome Children's menu Children's portions Garden Parking

CUMBRIA

AMBLESIDE — Map 18 NY30

Drunken Duck Inn ★★★★★ INN ◉◉

PICK OF THE PUBS

See Pick of the Pubs on page 108

Wateredge Inn ★★★★ INN

Waterhead Bay LA22 0EP ☎ 015394 32332
e-mail: stay@wateredgeinn.co.uk
dir: *M6 junct 36, A591 to Ambleside, 5m from Windermere station*

With large gardens and plenty of seating running down to the shores of Lake Windermere, the Wateredge Inn has been run by the same family for over 28 years. The inn was converted from two 17th-century fishermen's cottages, and now offers a stylish bar/restaurant and pretty, spacious en suite bedrooms. The extensive menus range from chicken, leek and bacon pie to honey, lime and chilli-glazed chicken, and warm Lancashire cheese and chive tart. Try the chocolate espresso fudge cake with Chantilly cream to finish.

Open all day all wk 10.30am-11pm Closed: 23-26 Dec **Bar Meals** L served Mon-Fri 12-2.30, Sat-Sun 12-4 D served all wk 5.30-9 food served all day ⊞ FREE HOUSE ◀ Theakston, Barngates Tag Lag & Cat Nap, Watermill Collie Wobbles Ö Symonds. ♚ 15 **Facilities** ✿ Children welcome Children's menu Children's portions Garden Parking Wi-fi **Rooms** 22

APPLEBY-IN-WESTMORLAND — Map 18 NY62

The Royal Oak Appleby

Bongate CA16 6UN ☎ 017683 51463
e-mail: jan@royaloakappleby.co.uk
dir: *M6 junct 38, B6260 to Appleby-in-Westmorland. Through square, over bridge, right onto B6542, Pub in 0.25m. Or from A66 take B6542 through Appleby, pub on left*

Parts of this award-winning former coaching inn date back to 1100, with 17th-century additions. The building has been sympathetically and painstakingly refurbished to provide a classic dog-friendly tap-room with blackened beams, an oak-panelled lounge with open fire, and a comfortable restaurant. The modern British menu uses the best of local ingredients and features dishes rack of lamb with a garlic, rosemary and redcurrant gravy; stuffed chicken breast with Cumberland sausage and wrapped in bacon; and spinach and ricotta cannelloni. Enjoy your visit with a pint of Hawkshead.

Open all day all wk 8am-mdnt **Bar Meals** L served Mon-Fri 8-3, Sat-Sun all day D served Mon-Fri 5-9, Sat-Sun all day **Restaurant** L served Mon-Fri 8-3, Sat-Sun all day D served Mon-Fri 5-9, Sat-Sun all day ⊞ FREE HOUSE ◀ Hawkshead, Black Sheep, Timothy Taylor, Copper Dragon. ♚ 9 **Facilities** ✿ Children welcome Children's menu Children's portions Garden Parking Wi-fi ▦

PICK OF THE PUBS

Drunken Duck Inn ★★★★★INN ❀❀

AMBLESIDE　　　　Map 18 NY30

Barngates LA22 0NG ☎ 015394 36347
e-mail: info@drunkenduckinn.co.uk
web: www.drunkenduckinn.co.uk
dir: *From Kendal on A591 to Ambleside,
then follow Hawkshead sign. In 2.5m
inn sign on right, 1m up hill*

There are fabulous views towards Lake
Windermere from this 17th-century inn,
which stands at a lonely crossroads
close to Tarn Hows in glorious Lakeland
countryside between Ambleside and
Hawkshead. In the same ownership
since the mid-1970s, the 'Duck'
continues to offer good service, with
excellent food and drink in a friendly,
relaxed atmosphere. The amusing title
dates back to Victorian times, when the
landlady found her ducks motionless in
the road. Thinking that they were dead,
she began to pluck them for the pot,
unaware that they were merely legless
from drinking beer that had leaked into
their feed. Legend has it that after the
ducks recovered on their way to the
oven, the good lady knitted them
waistcoats to wear until their feathers
grew back. No such risk today – the
adjoining Barngates Brewery takes good
care of its award-winning real ales,
which are served in the oak-floored bar
with its open fire, leather club chairs
and beautiful slate bar top. Excellent,
locally sourced food is served in three
informal restaurant areas. Lunchtime
brings a range of soups and
sandwiches, as well as hot dishes like
pumpkin and sage risotto; fisherman's
pie; and braised beef shin with garlic
mash and red wine jus. At dinner, begin
with seared scallops with tomato, crab
and coriander broth, followed by lamb
rump with braised sweet red cabbage.
Leave room for prune and Armagnac
soufflé with vanilla ice cream. Each of
the 17 bedrooms comes complete with
antique furniture, prints and designer
fabrics. After an invigorating walk
there's nothing better than relaxing on
the front verandah with a pint of
Barngates Cracker Ale, whilst soaking
up the view to Lake Windermere. Booking
for meals may be required.

Open all day all wk Closed: 25 Dec
🍺 FREE HOUSE 🛢 Barngates Cracker
Ale, Chesters Strong & Ugly, Tag Lag,
Cat Nap, Mothbag & Westmorland Gold,
Guest ale. **Facilities** Children welcome
Children's portions Garden Parking Wi-fi
Rooms 17

Save on hotels. Book at **theAA.com/hotel**

CUMBRIA 109 ENGLAND

PICK OF THE PUBS

The Pheasant ★★★HL 🌹

BASSENTHWAITE Map 18 NY23

CA13 9YE ☎ 017687 76234
e-mail: info@the-pheasant.co.uk
web: www.the-pheasant.co.uk
dir: *A66 to Cockermouth, 8m N of Keswick on left*

First a farmhouse, then a coaching inn, this 500-year-old Lake District favourite is surrounded by lovely gardens and today combines the role of traditional Cumbrian hostelry with that of an internationally renowned modern hotel. Even so, you still sense the history the moment you walk through the door – the legendary foxhunter John Peel, who's "view halloo would awaken the dead", according to the song, was a regular. In the warmly inviting bar, with polished parquet flooring, panelled walls and oak settles, hang two of Cumbrian artist and former customer Edward H Thompson's paintings. Here, order a pint of Cumberland Ale from Jennings, the Cockermouth brewery that resumed production within weeks of catastrophic flood damage in 2009, or cast your eyes over the extensive selection of malt whiskies. The high standard of food, recognised by an AA Rosette, is well known for miles around; meals are served in the attractive beamed restaurant, bistro, bar and lounges overlooking the gardens. Light lunches served in the lounge and bar include open sandwiches, ploughman's, home-made pork pie, and chicken Caesar salad. A three-course dinner in

the restaurant could feature crab and cucumber cannelloni with soy marshmallow and chilled cucumber velouté; fillet of smoked haddock with creamed leeks; slowly cooked loin of wild Cumbrian venison with creamy pearl barley, jellied balsamic, beetroot and peanut butter; or poached breast of wood pigeon with apricot chutney, watercress, cumin jus and natural yogurt. Treat the family to afternoon tea with home-made scones and rum butter. A private dining room is available for small parties, and there are individually decorated en suite bedrooms with beautiful fabrics, antique pieces and impressive bathrooms. Booking for meals may be required.

Open all wk Mon-Thu 11-2.30 5.30-10.30 (Fri-Sat 11-2.30 5.30-11

Sun 12-2.30 6-10.30) Closed: 25 Dec
Bar Meals L 12-2 D 6-9 Av main course £14 **Restaurant** L Sun 12.30-1.30 D 7-8.30 Fixed price menu £35
⊕ FREE HOUSE ◾ Coniston Bluebird, Jennings Cumberland Ale, Hawkshead Red ♂ Thatchers Gold. ♉ 12
Facilities Children welcome Children's menu Children's portions ❧ Garden Parking Wi-fi **Rooms** 15

APPLEBY-IN-WESTMORLAND *continued*

Tufton Arms Hotel

PICK OF THE PUBS

Market Square CA16 6XA ☎ 017683 51593
e-mail: info@tuftonarmshotel.co.uk
dir: *In town centre*

A 16th-century coaching inn, rebuilt in Victorian times with tall ceilings, and now Grade II listed. The elegant interior displays co-owner Teresa Milsom's design skills with its attractive wallpapers, engravings and prints, heavy drapes and period furniture, all harmonising contentedly with contemporary fabrics, soft tones and modern lighting. At the heart of the hotel, overlooking a cobbled mews courtyard, is the Conservatory Restaurant, where David Milsom and his kitchen team's award-winning cuisine is complemented by a serious wine list. Naturally lit during the day, this room takes on an attractive glow in the evening when the curtains are closed and the dimmer switches have been turned down. Typical meals made from top-quality fresh local ingredients are potted Morecambe Bay shrimps, followed by Lakeland lamb rump; or perhaps Appleby cheddar and leek cake, followed by roast vegetable tagine and spicy couscous. On handpump in the bar are Cumberland Corby and the Tufton Arms house beer.

Open all day all wk 7.30am-11pm Closed: 25-26 Dec **Bar Meals** L served all wk 12-2 D served all wk 6-9 **Restaurant** L served all wk 12-2 D served all wk 6-9 ⊕ FREE HOUSE ◀ Tufton Arms Ale, Cumberland Corby Ale. ₹ 15 **Facilities** ♣ Children welcome Children's portions Parking Wi-fi ⚌

ARMATHWAITE   Map 18 NY54

The Dukes Head Inn

Front St CA4 9PB ☎ 016974 72226
e-mail: peterrose_51@hotmail.co.uk
dir: *9m from Penrith, 10m from Carlisle between junct 41 & 42 of M6*

First licensed when the Carlisle to Settle railway was being built, this homely, whitewashed inn stands in the heart of a tiny village in the beautiful Eden Valley. Follow a fabulous walk or cycle ride along the banks of the River Eden with a pint of Black Sheep and a hearty meal in the civilised lounge bar, with its stone walls, open fires and sturdy oak settles and tables. There's a full à la carte menu on offer, along with lunchtime specials, and curry and steak nights. Visitors can also arrive here on the Carlisle to Settle Railway and alight at the pub's own unique railway station. Recent change of hands.

Open all wk 11am-mdnt (Fri-Sat 11am-1am) **Bar Meals** L served all wk 12-9 D served all wk 6.30-9 food served all day **Restaurant** L served Mon-Sat 12-2, Sun 12-9 D served all wk 6.30-9 Fixed menu price fr £6.95 Av 3 course à la carte fr £18 ⊕ PUNCH TAVERNS ◀ Jennings Cumberland Ale, Black Sheep Bitter, Moorhouse's Black Cat, Lancaster Blonde, Guest ales. ₹ 9 **Facilities** ♣ Children welcome Children's menu Children's portions Garden Parking Wi-fi ⚌ (notice required)

BAMPTON   Map 18 NY51

Mardale Inn

PICK OF THE PUBS

CA10 2RQ ☎ 01931 713244
e-mail: info@mardaleinn.co.uk
dir: *Telephone for directions*

Found on the rural eastern edge of the Lake District, in perfect walking, biking and fishing country, the Mardale Inn forms part of a terrace of 18th-century cottages in a small farming village. The spruced-up interior is a refreshing mix of flagstone floors, exposed stone and brick, old beams, open fireplaces and rustic furniture and more modern colours and design. Expect to find a great selection of guest ales to enjoy while perusing the menu. At lunch refuel on decent sandwiches and classic pub meals prepared from locally sourced produce. At dinner, typically tuck into Morecambe Bay potted shrimps, or caramelised onion tart, followed by lamb cutlets with minted pea mash and braised beetroot, or sea bass with fennel and dill sauce, and bread-and-butter pudding for dessert. Dogs are welcome in all public areas, and fans of cult movie, *Withnail and I*, will find plenty of the film's locations in the area.

Open all wk 8.30am-mdnt **Bar Meals** L served all wk 12-6 D served all wk 6-9 food served all day ⊕ FREE HOUSE ◀ 5 Guest ales ♂ Westons. **Facilities** ♣ Children welcome Children's menu Children's portions Parking Wi-fi ⚌

BARBON   Map 18 SD68

The Barbon Inn

LA6 2LJ ☎ 015242 76233
e-mail: info@barbon-inn.co.uk
dir: *3.5m N of Kirkby Lonsdale on A683*

Sitting happily in the Lune Valley, between the River Lune and the looming fells rising to Whernside, this whitewashed small village inn oozes the character only centuries of heritage can generate. The cosy Coach Lamp bar is particularly welcoming, with its vast fireplace and old furnishings, and it serves 20 wines by the glass. The Oak Room restaurant is equally enticing; secure one of the polished old settles and contemplate the very best that Cumbria, Yorkshire and Lancashire can provide, from grand beers brewed in Dent and Kirkby Lonsdale to pan-fried breast of pheasant, grouse and pigeon with dauphinoise potatoes, pancetta and juniper sauce. Booking for meals may be required.

Open all wk 12-2 6-11 (Sun 12-2 6-10.30) Closed: 25 Dec **Bar Meals** L served all wk 12-2 D served all wk 6-9 Av main course £8.95 **Restaurant** L served all wk 12-2 D served all wk 6-9 Fixed menu price fr £17.50 Av 3 course à la carte fr £20 ⊕ FREE HOUSE ◀ York, Dent, Tirril, Kirkby Lonsdale ♂ Addlestones. ₹ 20 **Facilities** Children welcome Children's menu Children's portions Garden Parking Wi-fi ⚌ (notice required)

BASSENTHWAITE   Map 18 NY23

The Pheasant ★★★ HL ◉

PICK OF THE PUBS

See Pick of the Pubs on page 109

BEETHAM   Map 18 SD47

The Wheatsheaf at Beetham

PICK OF THE PUBS

LA7 7AL ☎ 015395 62123
e-mail: info@wheatsheafbeetham.com
dir: *On A6 5m N of junct 35*

Run with passion and enthusiasm by the Skelton family, this atmospheric 16th-century former coaching inn stands in the heart of Beetham close to the River Bela. Inside, expect to find wood panelling, low lighting, period pictures and floral displays with the small bar counter screened from the lounge featuring lots of polished wood. Jennings Cumberland Ale heads up the choice of three real ales, while several wines by the glass span classic European with New World offerings. As far as possible, seasonal menus use the freshest and finest local produce. Lunchtime light meals include hot and cold sandwiches, and simple dishes such as potted shrimps and tomato, rocket and parmesan tart with basil dressing. At dinner, start with chicken liver and garlic pâté with apple marmalade, moving on to minted lamb Henry, or halibut with garlic prawns, lemon and white wine risotto and scallop cream. Finish with rich chocolate pot or sticky toffee pudding with caramel sauce.

Open all day all wk 12-11 Closed: 25 Dec ⊕ FREE HOUSE ◀ Jennings Cumberland Ale, Thwaites Wainwright, Tirril Queen Jean ♂ Kingstone Press. **Facilities** Garden Parking

BOOT   Map 18 NY10

Brook House Inn ★★★★ INN

PICK OF THE PUBS

CA19 1TG ☎ 019467 23288
e-mail: stay@brookhouseinn.co.uk
dir: *M6 junct 36, A590 follow Barrow signs. A5092, then A595. Past Broughton-in-Furness then right at lights to Ulpha. Cross river, next left signed Eskdale, & on to Boot. (NB not all routes to Boot are suitable in bad weather conditions)*

Few locations can rival this: Lakeland fells rise behind the inn to England's highest peak, whilst golden sunsets illuminate tranquil Eskdale. Footpaths string to nearby Stanley Ghyll's wooded gorge with its falls and red squirrels, and the charming La'al Ratty narrow gauge railway steams to and from the coast. It's a magnet for ramblers and cyclists, so a small drying room for wet adventurers is greatly appreciated. Up to seven real ales are kept, including Yates Best Bitter and Langdale from Cumbrian Legendary Ales, and an amazing selection of 170 malt whiskies. Award-winning home-made food prepared from Cumbria's finest (ducks and saddleback pigs reside beside the inn) is available in the restaurant, bar and snug all day. Temper the local drizzle with a rewarding starter of Brook House pâté with Cumberland sausage and crostini; then indulge in beef-and-beer pie or pan-fried chicken with a tangy blue cheese sauce, followed by blackcurrant pie and custard. Much too much for one day, so stay in the light, airy bedrooms before exploring the mountain roads across to Wordsworth's favourite Duddon Valley. This great community pub also takes a full role in the famous Boot Beer Festival each June. Booking for meals may be required.

Open all day all wk Closed: 25 Dec **Bar Meals** food served all day **Restaurant** L served by arrangement D served 6-8.30 ⊕ FREE HOUSE ◀ Hawkshead Bitter, Jennings Cumberland Ale, Cumbrian Legendary Langdale, Yates Best Bitter, Guest ales ♂ Westons Old Rosie. ♟ 10 **Facilities** Children welcome Children's menu Family room Garden Beer festival Parking Wi-fi 🚌 **Rooms** 8

BORROWDALE　　　　**Map 18 NY21**

The Langstrath Country Inn

CA12 5XG ☎ 017687 77239
e-mail: info@thelangstrath.com
dir: B5289 past Grange, through Rosthwaite, left to Stonethwaite. Inn on left after 1m

Nestling in the stunning Langstrath Valley, this lovely family-run 16th-century inn is an ideal base for those attempting England's highest peak, Scafell Pike; the inn also sits on the coast-to-coast and Cumbrian Way walks. Refurbishments over the years include the addition of a restaurant positioned to maximise the spectacular views. Here hungry ramblers enjoy high quality Lakeland dishes based on local ingredients. A typical choice could include smoked trout and avocado salad; and breast of Lowther free-range corn-fed chicken. Local cask-conditioned ales include some from the Keswick Brewery.

Open 12-10.30 Closed: Jan, Mon **Bar Meals** L served Tue-Sun 12-2.30 D served Tue-Sun 6-9 **Restaurant** L served Tue-Sun 12-2.30 D served Tue-Sun 6-9 ⊕ FREE HOUSE ◀ Jennings Bitter & Cocker Hoop, Hawkshead Bitter, Black Sheep, Keswick Thirst Rescue ♂ Thatchers Gold. ♟ 9 **Facilities** Children welcome Children's menu Children's portions Garden Parking Wi-fi 🚌 (notice required)

BOWLAND BRIDGE　　　　**Map 18 SD48**

Hare & Hounds Country Inn
PICK OF THE PUBS

LA11 6NN ☎ 015395 68333
e-mail: info@hareandhoundsbowlandbridge.co.uk
dir: M6 onto A591, left after 3m onto A590, right after 3m onto A5074, after 4m sharp left & next left after 1m

In the pretty little hamlet of Bowland Bridge, not far from Bowness, this 17th-century coaching inn has gorgeous views all round, especially of Cartmel Fell. A traditional country-pub atmosphere is fostered by the flagstone floors, exposed oak beams, ancient pews warmed by open fires, and cosy niches. Very much at the heart of the

community, the pub hosts the Post Office on Tuesday and Thursday afternoons. Excellent links with local food producers result in exclusively reared pork and lamb featuring on the menu and Hare of the Dog beer – brewed for the pub by Tirril Brewery – is a permanent fixture at the bar. Visit at lunchtime and take your pick from sandwiches and salads or hearty meals such as pork, sweet chilli and black pudding terrine with home-made chutney, followed by beer-battered haddock with hand-cut chips, home-made mushy peas and home-made tartare sauce. Finish with home-made seasonal fruit crumble. Booking for meals may be required.

Open all day all wk 12-11 **Bar Meals** L served Mon-Fri 12-2, Sat 12-9, Sun 12-8.30 D served Mon-Fri 6-9, Sat 12-9, Sun 12-8.30 Av main course £11 **Restaurant** Fixed menu price fr £12.95 ⊕ FREE HOUSE ◀ Tirril, Coniston, Ulverston, Hawkshead, Kirkby Lonsdale ♂ Cowmire Hall. ♟ 10 **Facilities** ♣ Children welcome Children's menu Children's portions Garden Beer festival Parking Wi-fi 🚌

BRAITHWAITE　　　　**Map 18 NY22**

Coledale Inn

CA12 5TN ☎ 017687 78272
e-mail: info@coledale-inn.co.uk
dir: M6 junct 50, A66 towards Cockermouth for 18m. Turn to Braithwaite then towards Whinlatter Pass. Follow sign on left, over bridge to Inn

Dating from about 1824, the Coledale Inn began life as a woollen mill. Today, the interior is attractively decked out with Victorian prints, furnishings and antiques, whilst footpaths leading off from the large gardens make it ideal for exploring the nearby fells. Two homely bars serve a selection of local ales while traditional lunch and dinner menus are served in the dining room. Typical choices include poached salmon in a white wine and dill sauce; chilli con carne; and aubergine and tomato bake.

Open all day all wk **Bar Meals** L served all wk 12-2 D served all wk 6-9 ⊕ FREE HOUSE ◀ Cumberland Corby Ale, Hesket Newmarket, Yates, Keswick, Tirril. **Facilities** ♣ Children welcome Children's menu Children's portions Play area Garden Parking Wi-fi 🚌

The Royal Oak ★★★ INN

CA12 5SY ☎ 017687 78533
e-mail: tpfranks@hotmail.com
dir: Exit M6 junct 40, A66 to Keswick, 20m. Bypass Keswick & Portinscale juncts, take next left, pub in village centre

Surrounded by high fells and beautiful scenery, The Royal Oak is set in the centre of the village and is the perfect base for walkers. The interior is all oak beams and log fires, and the menu offers hearty pub food, such as slow-roasted pork belly on apple mash; home-made fish pie; and slow-roasted lamb rump with mint gravy, all served alongside local ales, such as Sneck Lifter or Cumberland Ale. Visitors can extend the experience by staying over in the comfortable en suite bedrooms.

Open all day all wk **Bar Meals** L served all wk 12-2 D served all wk 6-9 Av main course £10 **Restaurant** L served all wk 12-2 D served all wk 6-9 ⊕ MARSTON'S ◀ Jennings Lakeland Stunner, Cumberland Ale, Cocker Hoop, Sneck Lifter. ♟ 8 **Facilities** Children welcome Children's menu Children's portions Garden Parking Wi-fi 🚌 **Rooms** 10

BRAMPTON　　　　**Map 21 NY56**

Blacksmiths Arms ★★★★ INN

Talkin Village CA8 1LE ☎ 016977 3452
e-mail: blacksmithsarmstalkin@yahoo.co.uk
web: www.blacksmithstalkin.co.uk
dir: From M6 take A69 E, after 7m straight over rdbt, follow signs to Talkin Tarn then Talkin Village

This attractive free house with en suite accommodation stands in some of northern Cumbria's most scenic countryside. The original 1700 smithy dates remains part of the inn. A traditional weekly menu of good home cooking lists fisherman's pie, beef lasagne, loin of lamb and mushroom Stroganoff, while appearing among the specials might be supreme of pheasant with creamy mushroom and bacon sauce; goujons of plaice with Thai-battered prawns; breaded scampi with sweet chilli dip; and chickpea, sweet potato and spinach curry. The beer garden is a good size. Booking for meals may be required.

Open all wk 12-3 6-12 **Bar Meals** L served all wk 12-2 D served all wk 6-9 Av main course £9 **Restaurant** L served all wk 12-2 D served all wk 6-9 Av 3 course à la carte fr £22 ⊕ FREE HOUSE ◀ Geltsdale Cold Fell, Yates, Brampton, Black Sheep. ♟ 16 **Facilities** Children welcome Children's menu Children's portions Garden Parking Wi-fi **Rooms** 8

BROUGHTON-IN-FURNESS　　　　**Map 18 SD28**

Blacksmiths Arms
PICK OF THE PUBS

See Pick of the Pubs on page 112

PICK OF THE PUBS

Blacksmiths Arms

BROUGHTON-IN-FURNESS   Map 18 SD28

Broughton Mills LA20 6AX
☎ **01229 716824**
e-mail: blacksmithsarms@aol.com
web: www.theblacksmithsarms.com
dir: *A593 from Broughton-in-Furness
towards Coniston, in 1.5m left signed
Broughton Mills, pub 1m on left*

Originally a farmhouse called
Broadstones, this whitewashed Lakeland
pub dating from 1577 would have cut its
teeth serving ale in the kitchen to local
workers and travellers. By 1748 its role
had been formalised, with records now
listing it not just as an inn, but also as a
blacksmith's. It stands in the secluded
Lickle Valley, with miles of glorious walks
radiating from the front door. The internal
structure remains largely unchanged, with
oak-panelled corridors, slate floors from
local quarries, oak-beamed ceilings and
four log fires, one in the original kitchen
range; should the electricity fail, gaslights
in the dining room and bar are lit. Michael
and Sophie Lane own and run it, he
dividing his time between the kitchen and
the bar, she running front of house. The
bar is reserved for drinking only, with
Jennings Cumberland Ale from
Cockermouth always available, alongside
regular visitors from Barngates,
Hawkshead and Dent micro-breweries
and, in summer, a farmhouse cider. The
Lanes use only suppliers who guarantee
quality produce, thus you will often find
locally sourced Herdwick lamb, beef,
pheasant and venison on the menu. Apart
from sandwiches and baguettes at

lunchtime, there are light meals such as
braised salt beef with pickles and home-
made chips; and honey-roast ham with
poached egg and tomato and spinach
salad. In the evening the menu typically
features slow-braised shoulder of minted
lamb Henry; chargrilled steaks; chicken,
ham hock and leek pie; roasted breast of
guinea fowl; beer-battered hake fillet; and
goat's cheese and courgette tart. Among
the desserts is lemon meringue pie with
mixed fruit compôte. Sandwiches and
light meals are available at lunchtime,
and the under-12s have their own menu.
The sheltered, flower-filled front patio
garden is great for warm-weather dining.
Catch the beer festival during the first
weekend in October. Booking for meals
may be required.

Open all wk Mon 5-11 Tue-Fri 12-2.30
5-11 (Sat-Sun 12-11) Closed: 25 Dec,

Mon L **Bar Meals** L served Tue-Sun 12-2
D served all wk 6-9 Av main course
£12.50 **Restaurant** L served Tue-Sun
12-2 D served all wk 6-9 Av 3 course à
la carte fr £23 🛢 FREE HOUSE
🍺 Jennings Cumberland Ale, Dent
Aviator, Barngates Tag Lag,
Moorhouse's Pride of Pendle,
Hawkshead Bitter. **Facilities** Children
welcome Children's menu Garden Beer
festival Parking

BUTTERMERE Map 18 NY11

Bridge Hotel

CA13 9UZ ☎ **017687 70252**
e-mail: enquiries@bridge-hotel.com
dir: *M6 junct 40, A66 to Keswick. Continue on A66 to avoid Keswick centre, exit at Braithwaite. Over Newlands Pass, follow Buttermere signs. (if weather bad follow Whinlatter Pass via Lorton). Hotel in village*

Surrounded by the Buttermere Fells in an outstandingly beautiful area, this 18th-century former coaching inn is set between Buttermere and Crummock Water with lovely walks right from the front door. Good food and real ales are served in the character bars, and a four-course dinner in the dining room might include cushion of Fellside lamb on dauphinoise potatoes with root vegetables and rosemary and redcurrant jus, or roast breast of Gressingham duck on apple and potato rösti. Booking for meals may be required.

Open all day all wk 10.30am-11.30pm **Bar Meals** L served all wk 12-9.30 D served all wk 12-9.30 food served all day **Restaurant** D served all wk 6-8.30 ⊕ FREE HOUSE ◖ Jennings Cumberland Ale, Smooth Bitter & Corby Blonde, Guinness. **Facilities** Children welcome Children's menu Children's portions Garden Parking Wi-fi ⊞

CALDBECK Map 18 NY34

Oddfellows Arms

CA7 8EA ☎ **016974 78227**
dir: *Telephone for directions*

A popular spot for both walkers and coast-to-coast cyclists on the Cumbrian Way, this 17th-century former coaching inn is in the scenic conservation village of Caldbeck. A tied house, it serves real ales from Jennings in Cockermouth, and lunchtime snacks include filled jacket potatoes and sandwiches. Typical choices on the main menu include local Gilcrux trout, roast duck with gooseberry sauce, and teriyaki pork, as well as vegetarian dishes and blackboard specials. Admire the views of the northern fells from the peaceful beer garden. Booking for meals may be required.

Open all day all wk **Bar Meals** L served all wk 12-2 D served all wk 6.15-8.30 Av main course £8.95 **Restaurant** L served all wk 12-1.30 D served all wk 6.15-8.30 Av 3 course à la carte fr £18 ⊕ MARSTON'S ◖ Jennings Bitter, Cumberland Ale. **Facilities** Children welcome Children's menu Children's portions Garden Parking ⊞ (notice required)

CARTMEL Map 18 SD37

The Cavendish Arms

PICK OF THE PUBS

LA11 6QA ☎ **015395 36240**
e-mail: info@thecavendisharms.co.uk
dir: *M6 junct 36, A590 signed Barrow-in-Furness. Cartmel signed. In village take 1st right*

Situated within the village walls, this 450-year-old coaching inn is Cartmel's longest-surviving hostelry. Many traces of its history remain, from the mounting block outside the main door to the bar itself, which used to be the stables. Oak beams, uneven floors and an open fire create a traditional, cosy atmosphere, and outside a stream flows past a tree-lined garden. The food, from the lunchtime sandwiches to the cheeses served at the end of dinner, owes much to its local origins (and, of course, to the skilled kitchen team). Perhaps begin your meal with seafood chowder or smoked cheese wrapped in ham. Then move on to roast lamb with a mint and redcurrant gravy; steak-and-ale pie; or goat's cheese lasagne. Desserts include hazelnut meringue and fruit crumble served with custard. The owners have teamed up with a local company that offers carriage tours of the village. This popular area is ideal for walking, horse riding, and visiting Lake Windermere.

Open all day all wk 9am-11pm **Bar Meals** L served all wk 12-9 D served all wk 12-9 **Restaurant** L served all wk 12-9 D served all wk 12-9 ⊕ SCOTTISH & NEWCASTLE ◖ Caledonian Deuchars IPA, Jennings Cumberland Ale, Cumberland Corby Ale, Theakston, Guest ales. ♥ 8 **Facilities** ❤ Children welcome Children's menu Children's portions Garden Parking ⊞

The Masons Arms **NEW**

Strawberry Bank LA11 6NW ☎ **015395 68486**
e-mail: info@masonsarms.info
dir: *M6 junct 36, A590 toward Barrow. Right onto A5074 signed Bowness/Windermere. 5m, left at Bowland Bridge. Through village, pub on right*

Overlooking the Winster Valley and beyond, this quaint, award-winning inn presents an atmospheric bar with low, beamed ceilings, old fireplaces and quirky furniture. Real ale-drinkers will have their work cut out choosing from the huge selection of Lake District brews; in fact, many return for further sampling during the June beer festival. Waiting staff manoeuvre through the busy bar, dining rooms and heated, covered terraces with popular dishes such as Lakeland damson and pork sausage; local game; roasted belly pork; Cartmel lamb shank; and smoked haddock fishcakes. Booking for meals may be required.

Open all day all wk **Bar Meals** L served Mon-Fri 12-2.30, Sat-Sun 12-9 D served Mon-Fri 6-9, Sat-Sun 12-9 Av main course £13.95 **Restaurant** L served Sat-Sun 12-9 D served Mon-Fri 6-9, Sat-Sun 12-9 ⊕ FREE HOUSE/ INDIVIDUAL INNS LTD ◖ Thwaites Wainwright, Cumbrian Legendary Esthwaite Bitter, Hawkshead Ö Cowmire Hall, Kopparberg. ♥ 12 **Facilities** Children welcome Children's menu Children's portions Garden Beer festival Parking Wi-fi

CLIFTON Map 18 NY52

George and Dragon

PICK OF THE PUBS

CA10 2ER ☎ **01768 865381**
e-mail: enquiries@georgeanddragonclifton.co.uk
dir: *M6 junct 40, A66 towards Appleby-in-Westmorland, A6 S to Clifton*

The historic Lowther Estate fringes the eastern Lake District near Ullswater; the ruined castle-mansion is set at the heart of pasture, woodland and fells alongside the rushing River Lowther and pretty villages of Askham and Clifton. The latter saw the last battle to take place on British soil, when in 1745 the retreating army of Bonnie Prince Charlie was defeated here; behind the inn is the Rebel Oak, marking the burial place of some of the victims. It's more peaceful today; in 2008 the pub was bought by the Charles Lowther and meticulously renovated in sympathy with the Georgian building, creating a traditional inn with contemporary comforts. There's an extremely comfortable menu, too, overseen by respected chef Paul McKinnon and majoring on the bountiful produce of the estate. Beef is from pedigree shorthorns; pork from home-reared rare breed stock; vegetables from the estate kitchen gardens; game and most fish from local waters. Settle in with a pint of Hawkshead Bitter and secure a starter of pan-fried wood pigeon, smoked black pudding mash and a soft boiled egg, leading up to monkfish, saffron potatoes and cucumber. The menu changes monthly, as do the daily specials. There is a secluded stone-walled courtyard and garden for the summer. Booking for meals may be required.

Open all day all wk Closed: 26 Dec **Bar Meals** L served all wk 12-2.30 D served all wk 6-9 Av main course £12-£15 **Restaurant** L served all wk 12-2.30 D served all wk 6-9 ⊕ FREE HOUSE ◖ Lancaster Blonde, Hawkshead Bitter Ö Westons Stowford Press. ♥ **Facilities** ❤ Children welcome Children's menu Children's portions Garden Parking Wi-fi

COCKERMOUTH — Map 18 NY13

The Trout Hotel ★★★★ HL

Crown St CA13 0EJ ☎ **01900 823591**
e-mail: enquiries@trouthotel.co.uk
dir: In town centre

Overlooking the River Derwent, The Trout is a popular black-and-white Grade II listed town-centre inn. At the bar several Jennings ales are backed by guests from Corby Brewery, and wine drinkers have their work cut out choosing between 24 wines served by the glass. Throughout the menu The Trout's small army of local suppliers are referenced, so diners know the ingredients are locally sourced and fresh. A typical choice could be Thornby Moor goat's cheese mousse to start, followed by pan-fried Gilcrux trout fillets with saffron potatoes. Booking for meals may be required.

Open all day all wk **Bar Meals** Av main course £8.95 food served all day **Restaurant** D served all wk 7-9.30 Av 3 course à la carte fr £22 ⊕ FREE HOUSE ◀ Jennings Cumberland Ale, Cooper Hoop, Corby Blonde ⭘ Thatchers. ☗ 24 **Facilities** Children welcome Children's menu Garden Parking 🚌 **Rooms** 49

CONISTON — Map 18 SD39

The Black Bull Inn & Hotel

PICK OF THE PUBS

1 Yewdale Rd LA21 8DU ☎ **015394 41335 & 41668**
e-mail: i.s.bradley@btinternet.com
dir: M6 junct 36, A590. 23m from Kendal via Windermere & Ambleside

The Black Bull, a 16th-century coaching inn with open fires, uneven floors and oak beams, is a cosy refuge in the heart of the Lake District. Set at the foot of the Old Man of Coniston and adjacent to Coniston Water, it has been under the same ownership for 36 years. As a further enticement to venture inside, all the beers, stout and lager served here are produced at the pub's own on-site Coniston micro-brewery. In its time, the inn has welcomed some famous faces. These include Coleridge and Turner, as well as Donald Campbell when attempting his water speed records, and Anthony Hopkins who starred in the film of Campbell's last 60 days. Hungry ramblers calling in at lunchtime will find an unfussy range of snacks and daily specials, whilst the restaurant menu changes seasonally and might feature Cumberland lamb hotpot with red cabbage, or home-made beef chilli with rice. Booking for meals may be required.

Open all day all wk **Bar Meals** L served all wk 12-9 D served all wk 12-9 Av main course £10 food served all day **Restaurant** L served all wk 12-2 D served all wk 6-9 Av 3 course à la carte fr £20 ⊕ FREE HOUSE ◀ Coniston Bluebird Bitter, Bluebird Premium XB, Old Man Ale, Winter Warmer Blacksmiths Ale, Special Oatmeal Stout. ☗ 10 **Facilities** ✿ Children welcome Children's menu Children's portions Family room Garden Parking Wi-fi 🚌 (notice required)

The Sun, Coniston

PICK OF THE PUBS

LA21 8HQ ☎ **015394 41248**
e-mail: info@thesunconiston.com
dir: M6 junct 36, A590, A591 to Ambleside, A593 to Coniston. Pub signed in village

In an enviable Lakeland location, set above Coniston village, yet below the famous Old Man mountain, this 16th-century inn and hotel makes the most of its stunning location, with both the conservatory dining room and large garden enjoying wonderful fell views. The refurbished old pub oozes traditional charm, boasting beams and timbers, stone walls and floors, a blazing fire in the Victorian range, and several real ales on tap, including Cumbrian-brewed Coniston Bluebird and Hawkshead Bitter. The Coniston Bluebird is particularly apt, as Donald Campbell stayed at The Sun during his later and last record attempts. From an eclectic menu, which makes sound use of quality local ingredients, start with devilled whitebait with paprika, horseradish and garlic mayonnaise, or guinea fowl and pistachio terrine with red onion marmalade, then follow with lamb shank with minted stout gravy; braised beef with red wine and caper sauce; or sea bass with garlic sautéed potatoes. Finish with sticky toffee pudding or a plate of Cumbrian cheeses.

Open all day all wk 11am-mdnt **Bar Meals** L served all wk 12-2.30 D served all wk 5.30-8.30 ⊕ FREE HOUSE ◀ Coniston Bluebird Bitter, Hawkshead Bitter, Copper Dragon, 4 Guest ales. **Facilities** ✿ Children welcome Children's menu Children's portions Play area Family room Garden Parking Wi-fi 🚌 (notice required)

CROOK — Map 18 SD49

The Sun Inn

LA8 8LA ☎ **01539 821351**
dir: Off B5284

An oak-beamed, open fire-warmed country pub that has evolved over time from a row of early 18th-century cottages. Hand-pumps in the bar dispense Coniston Bluebird and Hawkshead, and seasonal menus feature a fine range of starters and light snacks, as well as locally sourced dishes such as Cajun chicken with garlic mayonnaise dip; grilled lamb's liver and bacon; and spinach and ricotta cannelloni. The restaurant carte and specials boards have their share of interesting dishes too, with medallions of pork; grilled salmon fillet; and mushroom Stroganoff. Booking for meals may be required.

Open all wk Mon-Fri 12-2.30 6-11 (Sat 12-11 Sun 12-10.30) **Bar Meals** L served Mon-Fri 12-2.30, Sat 12-9, Sun 12-8 D served Mon-Fri 6-9, Sat 12-9, Sun 12-8 Av main course £9 **Restaurant** L served Mon-Fri 12-2.30, Sat 12-9, Sun 12-8 D served Mon-Fri 6-9, Sat 12-9, Sun 12-8 Av 3 course à la carte fr £22 ⊕ SCOTTISH & NEWCASTLE ◀ Coniston Bluebird Bitter, Thwaites Wainwright, Hawkshead, Theakston. **Facilities** Children welcome Children's menu Children's portions Garden Parking 🚌 (notice required)

CROSTHWAITE — Map 18 SD49

The Punch Bowl Inn ★★★★★ INN ⊛⊛

PICK OF THE PUBS

See Pick of the Pubs on opposite page

ELTERWATER — Map 18 NY30

The Britannia Inn

PICK OF THE PUBS

LA22 9HP ☎ **015394 37210**
e-mail: info@britinn.co.uk
dir: In village centre

This whitewashed free house in a Langdale Valley village is over 400 years old, with slate walls several feet thick. A short drive away are some of the Lake District's top destinations – Ambleside, Wordsworth's Grasmere, Lake Windermere, Hawkshead and Coniston, while walks and mountain-bike trails head off in all directions from the front door. The bar area is essentially a series of small, cosy rooms with low-beamed oak ceilings and winter coal fires, and very popular they are, especially in summer, when the bar staff are pulling pints of Dent Aviator, Hawkshead, Coniston Bluebird, Jennings and guest beers nineteen to the dozen. An even wider selection of real ales is available during the two-week beer festival in mid November. The inn offers a wide choice of fresh, home-cooked food, with an evening meal typically featuring beer-battered haloumi; home-made steak, ale and mushroom pie; and Cumbrian cheese and biscuits. Booking for meals may be required.

Open all day all wk 10am-11pm **Bar Meals** L served all wk 12-9.30 D served all wk 12-9.30 Av main course £13 food served all day **Restaurant** D served all wk 6.30-9.30 ⊕ FREE HOUSE ◀ Jennings Bitter, Coniston Bluebird Bitter & Britannia Inn Special Edition, Dent Aviator, Hawkshead Bitter, Guest ales. **Facilities** ✿ Children welcome Children's menu Children's portions Garden Beer festival Parking Wi-fi 🚌 (notice required)

Save on hotels. Book at **theAA.com/hotel**

CUMBRIA 115 ENGLAND

PICK OF THE PUBS

The Punch Bowl Inn ★★★★★ INN

CROSTHWAITE   Map 18 SD49

LA8 8HR ☎ 015395 68237
e-mail: info@the-punchbowl.co.uk
web: www.the-punchbowl.co.uk
dir: *M6 junct 36, A590 towards Barrow,*
A5074, follow Crosthwaite signs. Pub by
church

Very much a destination dining inn, The
Punch Bowl stands alongside the village
church in the delightfully unspoilt Lyth
Valley. The slates on the bar floor were
found beneath the old dining room and
complement the Brathay slate bar top and
antique furniture, while in the restaurant
are polished oak floorboards, comfortable
leather chairs and an eye-catching stone
fireplace. Two rooms off the bar add extra
space to eat or relax with a pint and a daily
paper in front of an open fire. The kitchen
team concentrates on providing meals
featuring the best of local, seasonal
produce and has two AA Rosettes to show
for its expertise. Sourcing extensively from
the area's estates, farms and coastal
villages, the lunch and dinner menus in
both the bar and the restaurant might
begin with potato and roast garlic soup,
chorizo and parsley; or black pudding,
bubble-and-squeak, crispy hen's egg and
apple caramel. For a main course, possibly
pan-roasted breast of pheasant with
fondant potato, Jerusalem artichokes,
truffle and curly kale; fillet of sea bass with
potato rösti, cauliflower romanesco and
shrimp cream; or glazed gnocchi with wild
mushrooms, rosemary, lemon butter and
rocket. And for dessert, why not nutmeg

crème brûlée with white chocolate,
pistachio and cranberry biscotti, or a
selection of Neal's Yard English cheeses
and port jelly? While still on the food,
typical specials are slow-roasted breast of
lamb with pumpkin purée, samphire, deep-
fried clams and salsa verde; and oxtail and
pheasant roly-poly with braised red
cabbage, baby carrots, purple sprouting
broccoli and peppercorn sauce. The owners
are great supporters of Cumbrian micro-
breweries, witness Tag Lag and
Westmorland Gold from Barngates, and
Bluebird from the Coniston brewery. Luxury,
individually furnished guest rooms are
available. Booking for meals may be
required.

Open all day all wk **Bar Meals** L served
all wk 12-9 D served all wk 12-9 Av
main course £14.95 **Restaurant** L
served all wk 12-9 D served all wk 12-9
Fixed menu price fr £12.95 Av 3 course
à la carte fr £25 ⊞ FREE HOUSE
◀ Barngates Westmorland Gold & Tag
Lag, Coniston Bluebird Bitter
◑ Thatchers Gold. ♟ 14
Facilities Children welcome Children's
menu Children's portions ✿ Garden
Parking Wi-fi **Rooms** 9

ESKDALE GREEN — Map 18 NY10

Bower House Inn

PICK OF THE PUBS

CA19 1TD ☎ **019467 23244**
e-mail: info@bowerhouseinn.co.uk
dir: *4m off A595, 0.5m W of Eskdale Green*

Hidden away in the fabulously unspoilt Eskdale Valley, this traditional Lake District hotel has been serving locals and walkers since the 17th century. Less than four miles from the main Cumbria coast road, it is ideally placed for visitors heading to the western lakes. Inside, oak beams, ticking clocks and crackling log fires create a comfortable setting to enjoy a pint of Bower House bitter in the bar, which opens out on to an attractive enclosed garden. The restaurant is a charming room with candlelit tables, exposed stone, log fires and equestrian pictures. Here, typical starters may include hand-pressed Cumberland terrine with tomato chutney, which might be followed by pan-fried duck breast with burnt orange sauce, fondant potato and vegetables or local Cumberland sausages with mash, peas and onion gravy. Dog-lovers may want to time a visit to coincide with the UK's largest annual meeting of Staffordshires in May.

Open all day all wk **Bar Meals** L served Mon-Fri 12-2, Sat-Sun 12-9 D served Mon-Fri 6-9, Sat-Sun 12-9 Av main course £13 **Restaurant** D served all wk 6-9 ⊕ FREE HOUSE ◀ Bower House Ale, Theakston Best Bitter, Hesket Newmarket Scafell Blonde. **Facilities** Children welcome Children's menu Children's portions Play area Garden Parking Wi-fi 🚌 (notice required)

FAUGH — Map 18 NY55

The String of Horses Inn

CA8 9EG ☎ **01228 670297**
e-mail: info@stringofhorses.com
dir: *M6 junct 43, A69 towards Hexham. In 5-6m right at 1st lights at Corby Hill/Warwick Bridge. 1m, through Heads Nook, in 1m bear sharp right. Left into Faugh. Pub on left down hill*

Well tucked away in a sleepy village, this traditional Lakeland inn has all the charm you'd expect from a 17th-century building. There are oak beams, wood panelling, old settles and log fires in the restaurant, where imaginative pub food is on offer, and in the bar, where you'll find real ales from Brampton Brewery and Theakston. Grilled curried salmon with side salad; chicken enchiladas in rich tomato sauce; half shoulder of lamb in mint and redcurrant gravy; and tagliatelle al arrabbiata admirably represent what's on a typical menu.

Open Tue-Sun 6-11 Closed: Mon **Bar Meals** D served Tue-Sun 6-8.45 Av main course £11.50 **Restaurant** D served Tue-Sun 6-8.45 Av 3 course à la carte fr £17.50 ⊕ FREE HOUSE ◀ Brampton Best, Theakston Best Bitter, John Smith's, Guinness. ☮ 8 **Facilities** Children welcome Children's menu Parking Wi-fi 🚌

GRASMERE — Map 18 NY30

The Travellers Rest Inn

Keswick Rd LA22 9RR ☎ **015394 35604**
e-mail: stay@lakedistrictinns.co.uk
web: www.lakedistrictinns.co.uk
dir: *From M6 take A591 to Grasmere, pub 0.5m N of Grasmere*

Located on the edge of picturesque Grasmere and handy for touring and exploring the ever-beautiful Lake District, The Travellers Rest has been a pub for more than 500 years. Inside, a roaring log fire complements the welcoming atmosphere of the beamed and inglenook bar area. Along with ales like Sneck Lifter, an extensive menu of traditional home-cooked fare is offered, ranging from Westmorland terrine and eggs Benedict, to wild mushroom gratin and rump of Lakeland lamb.

Open all day all wk 12-11 **Bar Meals** L served all wk 12-9.30 D served all wk 12-9.30 food served all day **Restaurant** L served all wk 12-9.30 D served all wk 12-9.30 food served all day ⊕ FREE HOUSE ◀ Jennings Bitter, Cocker Hoop, Cumberland Ale & Sneck Lifter, Guest ales. ☮ 10 **Facilities** 🐾 Children welcome Children's menu Children's portions Family room Garden Parking Wi-fi 🚌

GREAT LANGDALE — Map 18 NY20

The New Dungeon Ghyll Hotel ★★★ HL

LA22 9JX ☎ **015394 37213**
e-mail: enquiries@dungeon-ghyll.com
dir: *From Ambleside follow A593 towards Coniston for 3m, at Skelwith Bridge right onto B5343 towards 'The Langdales'*

In a spectacular location at the foot of the Langdale Pikes and Pavey Ark, this traditional stone building was once a farmhouse before being transformed into a hotel in 1832.

Full of character and charm, the rustic bar is popular with walkers returning from the fells. Local specialities are served in the bar and smart dining room. In the bar tuck into Cumberland sausages with mash and gravy, or beefburger with chutney and chips. A meal in the dining room may take in game spring rolls, venison with thyme and port sauce, and sticky toffee pudding. Booking for meals may be required.

Open all day all wk **Bar Meals** L served all wk 12-9 food served all day **Restaurant** D served all wk 6-8.30 ⊕ FREE HOUSE ◀ Thwaites Original, Langdale Tup, Wainwright ♻ Kingstone Press. ☮ 8 **Facilities** Children welcome Children's menu Children's portions Garden Parking Wi-fi 🚌 **Rooms** 22

GREAT SALKELD — Map 18 NY53

The Highland Drove Inn and Kyloes Restaurant

PICK OF THE PUBS

See Pick of the Pubs on opposite page

HAWKSHEAD — Map 18 SD39

Kings Arms ★★★ INN

The Square LA22 0NZ ☎ **015394 36372**
e-mail: info@kingsarmshawkshead.co.uk
dir: *M6 junct 36, A590 to Newby Bridge, right at 1st junct past rdbt, over bridge, 8m to Hawkshead*

Overlooking the picturesque square at the heart of this virtually unchanged Elizabethan Lakeland village, made famous by Beatrix Potter who lived nearby, this 16th-century inn throngs in summer. In colder weather, bag a table by the fire in the traditional carpeted bar, quaff a pint of Hawkshead Bitter and tuck into lunchtime light bites such as minute steak and sautéed red onion jacket; alternatively try main courses like steak and Hawkshead ale pie, or the chef's own home-made gourmet lamb and mint burger. Look out for the carved figure of a king in the bar. Cosy, thoughtfully equipped bedrooms are available. Booking for meals may be required.

Open all day all wk 11am-mdnt **Bar Meals** L served all wk 12-2.30 D served all wk 6-9.30 **Restaurant** L served all wk 12-2.30 D served all wk 6-9.30 ⊕ FREE HOUSE ◀ Hawkshead Gold & Bitter, Coniston Bluebird, Cumbrian Legendary, Guest ales. **Facilities** 🐾 Children welcome Children's menu Children's portions Garden Wi-fi 🚌 (notice required) **Rooms** 8

Save on hotels. Book at **theAA.com/hotel**

CUMBRIA 117 ENGLAND

PICK OF THE PUBS

The Highland Drove and Kyloes Restaurant

GREAT SALKELD　　　　Map 18 NY53

CA11 9NA ☎ 01768 898349
e-mail: highlanddrove@kyloes.co.uk
web: www.kyloes.co.uk
dir: *M6 junct 40, A66 E'bound, A686 to Alston. 4m, left onto B6412 for Great Salkeld & Lazonby*

Nestling on an old drove road by a village church deep in the lovely Eden Valley, Donald and Christine Newton's 300-year-old country inn is named after the original Highland cattle that were bred in the Western Isles and then driven over the short channels of water to the mainland. Looking more like an old farmhouse, the pub is a great all-rounder with a well-deserved reputation for high-quality food and conviviality. Despite the excellence of the food, The Highland Drove is still an award-winning pub where locals come to enjoy the wide range of cask-conditioned real ales and a good selection of wines. Inside, there's an attractive brick and timber bar, old tables and settles in the main bar area, and a lounge with log fire, dark wood furniture and tartan fabrics. The upstairs restaurant has a unique hunting lodge feel, with a verandah and lovely country views. Menus list traditional local dishes, alongside daily specials reflecting the availability of local game and fish, and meat from herds reared and matured in Cumbria. Typical meals might be black pudding and apple fritter on sweet potato and parsnip purée with whole grain mustard sauce; twice-baked goat's cheese soufflé with a roasted tomato and garlic sauce; fillet of beef on a turnip fondant with pomme purée, leek and haggis cannelloni served with a rich Madeira sauce; curried aubergine and mushrooms with a potato and pea samosa, braised onion rice and spiced cauliflower. Leave room for steamed chocolate sponge pudding with chocolate and mint sauce or home-made lemon tart and raspberry coulis.

Open all wk 12-2 6-late Closed: Mon L, 25 Dec ⊞ FREE HOUSE ◖ Theakston Black Bull Bitter, Best & Traditional Mild, John Smith's Cask & Smooth, Guest ale. **Facilities** Children welcome Children's menu Children's portions Garden Parking Wi-fi 🚐

HAWKSHEAD *continued*

The Queen's Head Inn & Restaurant ★★★★ INN

PICK OF THE PUBS

Main St LA22 0NS ☎ 015394 36271
e-mail: info@queensheadhawkshead.co.uk
dir: *M6 junct 36, A590 to Newby Bridge, 1st right, 8m to Hawkshead*

Surrounded by fells and forests and a stone's throw from Esthwaite Water, The Queen's Head is the perfect base for exploring the southern Lakes. Hawkshead has impressive literary links – William Wordsworth attended the local grammar school, and Beatrix Potter lived just up the road. You'll find the 16th-century inn on the village's main street. Behind the pub's flower-bedecked exterior, there are low oak-beamed ceilings, wood-panelled walls, slate floors and welcoming fires. Real ales and an extensive wine list promise excellent refreshment, while a full menu and an ever-changing specials board brim with quality local produce. At lunchtime sandwiches served with French fries and salad refuel the ramblers. In the evening you may start with mussels or potted brown shrimps; follow with lamb rack or turbot fillet. Vegetarians may plump for a dish of aloo gobi, or goat's cheese and butternut squash tortellini. Home-made desserts and local cheeses are written on the blackboard. Change of hands. Booking for meals may be required.

Open all day all wk 11am-11.45pm (Sun 12-11.45) **Bar Meals** L served Mon-Fri 12-2.30, Sat 12-4.30, Sun 12-5 D served all wk 6.15-9.30 **Restaurant** L served Mon-Sat 12-2.30, Sun 12-5 D served all wk 6.15-9.30 ⊕ FREDERIC ROBINSON ◀ Double Hop, Hartleys Cumbria Way, Guest ale. ♀ 11 **Facilities** ♣ Children welcome Children's menu Family room Garden Wi-fi ▭ (notice required) **Rooms** 13

The Sun Inn ★★★★ INN

Main St LA22 0NT ☎ 015394 36236
e-mail: rooms@suninn.co.uk
dir: *N on M6 junct 36, A591 to Ambleside, B5286 to Hawkshead. S on M6 junct 40, A66 to Keswick, A591 to Ambleside, B5286 to Hawkshead*

Taken over by Alex Godfrey in July 2011, this listed 17th-century coaching inn is at the heart of the charming village where Wordsworth went to school. Inside are two resident ghosts – a giggling girl and a drunken landlord – and outside is a paved terrace with seating. The wood-panelled bar has low, oak-beamed ceilings, and hill walkers and others will enjoy the log fires, real ales and locally sourced food. Choices range from steak and vegetable Westmorland pie; vegetable bake; and Lancashire hotpot to venison burger and fillet of plaice. There are modern bedrooms, including a four-poster room.

Open all day all wk 10am-mdnt **Bar Meals** L served all wk 12-2.30 D served all wk 6-9 ⊕ FREE HOUSE ◀ Cumbrian Legendary Loweswater Gold, Jennings, Guest ale. **Facilities** ♣ Children welcome Children's menu Children's portions Garden Wi-fi ▭ **Rooms** 8

KESWICK Map 18 NY22

Farmers Arms

Portinscale CA12 5RN ☎ 017687 72322
e-mail: thefarmers.arms@hotmail.com
dir: *M6 junct 40, A66, bypass Keswick. After B5289 junct turn left to Portinscale*

Set in the pretty village of Portinscale, about a mile from Keswick, this 18th-century pub has traditional décor with an open fire. Ben and Sharon warmly welcome their locals and touring visitors, serving good quality, well-kept ales, and traditional home-cooked food. Typical of the menu are cod goujons with a sweet chilli mayonnaise; Cumberland sausage with gravy; and lamb and mint suet pudding. Favourites from the dessert menu such as ginger pudding round things off nicely. Look out for live music and quiz nights. The beer garden to the rear has views of the mountain range.

Open all day all wk **Bar Meals** L served all wk 12-2 D served all wk 6-9 Av main course £9 **Restaurant** L served all wk 12-2 D served all wk 6-9 ⊕ MARSTON'S ◀ Jennings Bitter, Cumberland Ale, Cocker Hoop & Sneck Lifter, Guest ale. ♀ **Facilities** ♣ Children welcome Children's menu Children's portions Family room Garden Parking Wi-fi ▭

The George ★★★ INN

3 St John's St CA12 5AZ ☎ 017687 72076
e-mail: rooms@thegeorgekeswick.co.uk
dir: *M6 junct 40 onto A66, take left filter road signed Keswick, pass pub on left. At x-rds turn left onto Station St, 150yds on left*

Keswick's oldest coaching inn is a handsome 17th-century building in the heart of this popular Lakeland town. Restored to its former glory, retaining its traditional black panelling, Elizabethan beams, ancient settles and log fires, it makes a comfortable base from which to explore the fells and lakes. Expect to find local Jennings ales on tap and classic pub food prepared from local ingredients. Typical dishes include trio of Cumbrian pork, seafood pasta, venison casserole, cow (steak) pie, apple crumble cheesecake, and sticky toffee pudding. There are 12 comfortable bedrooms available. Booking for meals may be required.

Open all day all wk **Bar Meals** L served Mon-Thu 12-2.30, Fri-Sun 12-5 D served all wk 5.30-9 **Restaurant** L served Mon-Thu 12-2.30, Fri-Sun 12-5 D served all wk 5.30-9 ⊕ JENNINGS ◀ Cumberland Ale, Sneck Lifter & Cocker Hoop, Guest ales. ♀ 10 **Facilities** Children welcome Children's menu Garden Parking ▭ **Rooms** 12

The Horse & Farrier Inn

PICK OF THE PUBS

See Pick of the Pubs on opposite page

Save on hotels. Book at **theAA.com/hotel**

CUMBRIA 119 ENGLAND

PICK OF THE PUBS

The Horse & Farrier Inn

KESWICK   Map 18 NY22

Threlkeld Village CA12 4SQ
☎ **017687 79688**
e-mail: info@horseandfarrier.com
web: www.horseandfarrier.com
dir: *M6 junct 40, A66 signed Keswick, 12m, right signed Threlkeld. Pub in village centre*

For over 300 years this solid Lakeland inn has seen poets, playwrights and lead miners wending their way along the Glenderamackin Valley. This ancient route between Keswick and Penrith in the northern outpost of the Lake District National Park is tucked beneath the challenging mountains of Blencathra, Skiddaw and Helvellyn. Little wonder that it's a hot spot for serious walkers, who take their rest in the beer garden here – a case of up hill and down ale, perhaps. Within the thick, whitewashed stone walls of this long, low old building you'll find slate-flagged floors, beamed ceilings and crackling log fires, with hunting prints decorating the traditional bars and a memorable panelled snug. The inn has an excellent reputation for good food, from hearty Lakeland breakfasts to home-cooked lunches and dinners served in either the bar or the charming period restaurant. The chefs make full use of local and seasonal produce. The lunchtime bar menu has all the old favourites, from home-made curry of the day to steak-and-kidney pie

in rich ale gravy. In the restaurant, starters embrace a seared trio of fresh Morecambe Bay scallops served on a roulade of black pudding; or a broader medley of seafood in a puff pastry case finished with fresh dill. Look for the local produce in the main courses. There are pan-fried sirloin or fillet steaks cooked to your liking; slow-roasted belly pork served on a cushion of grain mustard mash; and a pan-griddled duo of Cumberland sausages made with beef, pork, and the pub's own blend of herbs and spices. If your visit coincides with teatime, you could ask for a round of cheese or Cumbrian ham sandwiches, with scone, jam and cream; or the home-made soup of the day with a hot Cumbrian rarebit.

Open all day all wk 7.30am-mdnt
⊕ JENNINGS ◀ Jennings Bitter, Cocker Hoop, Sneck Lifter & Cumberland Ale, Guest ale. **Facilities** Children welcome Children's menu Children's portions Family room Garden Parking Wi-fi

PICK OF THE PUBS

The Inn at Keswick ★★★★ INN

KESWICK Map 18 NY22

Main St CA12 5HZ ☎ 017687 74584
e-mail: relax@theinnkeswick.co.uk
web: www.theinnkeswick.co.uk
dir: *M6 junct 40, A66 to Keswick town
centre to war memorial x-rds. Left into
Station St. Inn 100yds*

Located on the corner of Keswick's vibrant market square, this large yet friendly 18th-century coaching inn combines contemporary comfort with charming reminders of its place in local history. It is understandably popular with walkers – it's within a few strides of England's three highest peaks; dogs are permitted in the bar and some of the bedrooms, an important consideration for many. Lancaster Bomber is one of the award-winning Thwaites ales on tap, and Kingstone Press cider is popular too. The wine selection is small but perfectly formed, with some bottles coming in below the £20 mark. The kitchen's careful sourcing of ingredients from ethical suppliers ensures sustainability as well as freshness, and local artisans such as Thornby Moor Dairy are supported and named on the menu. The slight price premium for these policies is all but unnoticeable, as the menu represents excellent value for money. From noon until teatime, hot sandwiches such as tuna savoury with

cheddar are available, alongside cold sandwiches, light dishes such as tiger prawn tempura, and home comforts such as beefsteak and ale pie topped with puff pastry. Deli boards showing off a selection of local cheeses or meats are great for sharing. In the evening the chargrill is fired up, producing a delicious range of beef, gammon and chicken main courses. Alternatively, go for the hotpot of Fellside lamb topped with sliced potatoes – the inn's best-selling dish. For those with a nagging sweet tooth, a plate of warm treacle tart with clotted cream should hit the spot. If you book to stay in one of the 19 en suite rooms, a wholesome Cumbrian breakfast will set you up for the ramble you have planned.

Open all day all wk **Bar Meals** L served Mon-Sat 11-9, Sun 12-9 D served Mon-Sat 11-9, Sun 12-9 food served all day **Restaurant** food served all day ⬛ THWAITES INNS OF CHARACTER ◀ Wainwright, Original, Lancaster Bomber. ↻ Kingstone Press **Facilities** Children welcome Children's menu Children's portions 🐾 🚌 **Rooms** 19

Save on hotels. Book at **theAA.com/hotel**

CUMBRIA 121 ENGLAND

PICK OF THE PUBS

The Kings Head

KESWICK　　　　　　　　**Map 18 NY22**

Thirlspot CA12 4TN ☎ 017687 72393
e-mail: stay@lakedistrictinns.co.uk
web: www.lakedistrictinns.co.uk
dir: *From M6 take A66 to Keswick then A591, pub 4m S of Keswick*

Hotel management stints in France, Switzerland, Barbados, Florida, New York and London were the perfect background for Derek and Lynne Sweeney before, with Derek's brother Graham, acquiring this 17th-century coaching inn. Above it towers Helvellyn, the third highest peak in England, the view of which, according to a tongue-in-cheek website comment, a guest liked so much that he didn't identify his bedroom in case he found it booked next time! With Thirlmere a couple of fields away, this long (there are 15 first-floor windows at the front alone), whitewashed building and its delightful beer garden also offer spectacular views of the surrounding fells, while indoors the traditional bar features old beams and an inglenook fireplace. In addition to several regulars from the Jennings Brewery in nearby Cockermouth, there are guest real ales and a fine selection of wines and malt whiskies. In the refurbished bar, paninis, sandwiches and jacket potatoes head the lunchtime options, which also feature grilled asparagus and poached egg; tomato and mozzarella salad; oven-baked sea bream; and fennel- and lemon-glazed Lakeland lamb shank. It's in the St Johns

Restaurant, which looks out to the glacial valley of St Johns in the Vale, that dinner might begin with pan-fried chicken livers with wild mushrooms, bacon and garlic croûte; to be followed by home-made steak-and-kidney pudding; or Jennings beer-battered haddock with chips and mushy peas; and end with Pavlova meringue with seasonal berries, fruit coulis and cream; or a locally made ice cream with shortbread biscuits. Home-made polenta gnocchi is a vegetarian option. From Monday to Saturday chargrilled steaks, ham, pork and salmon extend the daily range. Booking is advisable for Sunday roasts – usually beef, lamb and chicken. An in-house Lakeland Produce Store offers a wide range of local food, drinks and gifts. Booking for meals may be required.

Open all day all wk 12-11 **Bar Meals** L served all wk 12-9.30 food served all day **Restaurant** D served all wk 7-8.30 ⊕ FREE HOUSE ◀ Jennings Bitter, Cumberland Ale, Sneck Lifter & Cocker Hoop, Guest ales. ♟ 9 **Facilities** Children welcome Children's menu Family room ✿ Garden Parking Wi-fi 🚌

KESWICK *continued*

The Inn at Keswick ★★★★ INN

PICK OF THE PUBS

See Pick of the Pubs on page 120
See advert on page 118

The Kings Head

PICK OF THE PUBS

See Pick of the Pubs on page 121

Pheasant Inn

Crosthwaite Rd CA12 5PP ☎ 017687 72219
dir: *On A66 Keswick rdbt towards town centre, 60yds on right*

An open-fired, traditional Lakeland inn, owned by Jennings Brewery, so expect their regular range on tap, and a monthly guest. For the seasonal menus, the kitchen produces home-cooked, locally sourced food, including starters of whitebait with smoked paprika sauce; and "gooey" baked camembert with ciabatta dipping sticks and chilli, red onion and tomato relish. Follow with an old favourite like red Thai chicken and mango curry, or a chef's speciality, such as prime Cumbrian rump steak; pan-fried swordfish marinated in basil and lemon; or oven-roasted chicken supreme on fettuccine pasta.

Open all day all wk Closed: 25 Dec **Bar Meals** L served all wk 12-4 (12-2 low season) D served all wk 6-9 Av main course £10-£14 **Restaurant** L served all wk 12-2 D served all wk 6-9 ⊕ JENNINGS ◀ Bitter, Cumberland Ale, Cocker Hoop, Sneck Lifter, Guest ale. ☗ 8 **Facilities** ✤ Children welcome Children's menu Garden Parking

The Swinside Inn

Newlands Valley CA12 5UE ☎ 017687 78253
e-mail: booking@swinsideinn.com
dir: *1m from A66, signed for Newlands/Swinside*

Situated at the entrance to the quiet Newlands Valley, in the heart of the Lake District, the Swinside Inn is a listed building dating back to about 1642. From the pub there are superb views of Causey Pike and Cat Bells among other landmarks. The pub has a lounge bar and landscaped beer garden, plus a cosy themed bar, The Refuge Bar, with a pool table, TV and games. You'll also find traditional open fires and oak-beamed ceilings. The extensive bar menu may offer lamb Henry, Cumberland sausage, Swinside chicken, and fresh grilled Borrowdale trout. There was a change of hands in 2011.

Open all day all wk **Bar Meals** L served all wk 12-2 D served all wk 6-9 ⊕ SCOTTISH & NEWCASTLE ◀ Jennings Cumberland Ale, John Smith's Extra Smooth, Caledonian Deuchars IPA, Guest ales. **Facilities** ✤ Children welcome Children's menu Children's portions Family room Garden Parking Wi-fi ◚

KIRKBY LONSDALE Map 18 SD67

The Pheasant Inn

PICK OF THE PUBS

Casterton LA6 2RX ☎ 01524 271230
e-mail: info@pheasantinn.co.uk
web: www.pheasantinn.co.uk
dir: *M6 junct 36, A65 for 7m, left onto A683 at Devils Bridge, 1m to Casterton centre*

A sleepy hamlet close to Kirkby Lonsdale on the edge of the beautiful Lune Valley is the setting for this whitewashed 18th-century coaching inn. It is also perfectly situated for exploring the Dales, the Trough of Bowland and the Cumbrian Lakes. The Dixon family and staff ensure a warm welcome and traditional food is served daily in both the oak-panelled restaurant and the bar, where beams and open fireplaces add to the relaxing atmosphere. Local ales, malt whiskies and a broad choice of wines can be sampled while perusing the menu of quality produce sourced from the valley farms. Dishes may include smoked mackerel mousse to start, followed by traditional beef-and-ale pie with shortcrust pastry; slow-roasted shoulder of lamb; whole sea bass baked in olive oil and sea salt; and pork fillet in pepper cream sauce. In fine weather you can sit outside and enjoy the lovely views of the fells. Booking for meals may be required.

Open 12-3 6-11 Closed: 2wks mid-Jan, Mon **Bar Meals** L served Tue-Sun 12-2 D served all wk 6-9 **Restaurant** L served Tue-Sun 12-2 D served all wk 6-9 ⊕ FREE HOUSE ◀ Theakston Best Bitter & Cool Cask, Black Sheep Best Bitter, Dent Aviator, Timothy Taylor Landlord. ☗ 8 **Facilities** Children welcome Children's portions Garden Parking ◚ (notice required)

The Sun Inn ★★★★★ INN ◉

PICK OF THE PUBS

Market St LA6 2AU ☎ 01524 271965
e-mail: email@sun-inn.info
dir: *From M6 junct 36 take A65 for Kirkby Lonsdale. In 5m left signed Kirkby Lonsdale. At next T-junct turn left. Right at bottom of hill*

You'll find this welcoming 17th-century free house just a few minutes' walk from the famous Ruskin's View. There are natural stone walls, oak floors, log fires and furniture hand-made by the landlady's father, a cabinet maker. Some of the chairs were previously used on the RMS *Mauretania*. The selection of cask ales is backed by an extensive wine choice with helpful tasting notes. 'Meats,

fishes, loaves and dishes' is the carte for starter-size meals for grazing or nibbling; served between midday and 10pm. You'll find the likes of sausages with mustard dips, haddock goujons with herb mayonnaise, and an award-winning pork and damson pie. The restaurant menu changes seasonally. Starters may embrace ham hock and chicken terrine, while hearty main courses such as wild mushroom and chestnut ravioli or slow-roasted Lune Valley lamb shoulder keep the customers satisfied. Eleven bedrooms blend modern comforts with character and charm, making The Sun an ideal base from which to explore the Lake District and Yorkshire Dales.

Open all wk Mon 3-11, Tue-Sun 10am-11pm **Bar Meals** L served Tue-Sun 12-10 D served Mon 4-10, Tue-Sun 12-10 Av main course £9.95 food served all day **Restaurant** L served Tue-Sun 12-2.30 D served all wk 7-9 Fixed menu price fr £25.95 Av 3 course à la carte fr £27.90 ⊕ FREE HOUSE ◀ Kirkby Lonsdale Radical, Thwaites Wainwright, Hawkshead Bitter. ☗ 9 **Facilities** ✤ Children welcome Children's menu Children's portions Wi-fi **Rooms** 11

The Whoop Hall ★★ HL

Skipton Rd LA6 2HP ☎ 015242 71284
e-mail: info@whoophall.co.uk
dir: *From M6 junct 36 take A65. Pub 1m SE of Kirkby Lonsdale*

This 16th-century converted coaching inn was once the kennels for local foxhounds. In an imaginatively converted barn you can relax and enjoy Yorkshire ales and a good range of dishes based on local produce. Oven-baked fillet of sea bass with tagliatelle verde and tiger prawns, and stir-fried honey-roast duck with vegetables and water chestnuts are among the popular favourites. The bar offers traditional hand-pulled ales and roaring log fires, while outside is a terrace and children's area.

Open all wk **Bar Meals** L served all wk 12-9 ⊕ FREE HOUSE ◀ Jennings Cumberland Cream & Cumberland Ale, Black Sheep ☼ Thatchers Gold. ☗ 14 **Facilities** ✤ Children welcome Play area Family room Garden Parking ◚ **Rooms** 24

LITTLE LANGDALE Map 18 NY30

Three Shires Inn ★★★★ INN

PICK OF THE PUBS

See Pick of the Pubs on opposite page

LOWESWATER Map 18 NY12

Kirkstile Inn ★★★★ INN

PICK OF THE PUBS

See Pick of the Pubs on page 124

Save on hotels. Book at **theAA.com/hotel**

CUMBRIA 123 ENGLAND

PICK OF THE PUBS

Three Shires Inn ★★★★INN

LITTLE LANGDALE Map 18 NY30

LA22 9NZ ☎ 015394 37215
e-mail: enquiry@threeshiresinn.co.uk
web: www.threeshiresinn.co.uk
dir: *Exit A593, 2.3m from Ambleside at 2nd junct signed 'The Langdales'. 1st left 0.5m. Inn in 1m*

This newly refurbished, traditional Cumbrian slate and stone inn enjoys a stunning location in the beautiful Little Langdale Valley. Personally run by the Stephenson family since 1983, its name refers to its situation near the meeting point of three county shires – Westmorland, Cumberland and Lancashire. A perfect pitstop for lunch on walks through the Langdale valleys and for travellers negotiating the Hardknott and Wrynose passes, it has a blazing fire in the traditional beamed bar during the winter months, while the landscaped garden with its magnificent fell views is the place to savour a pint of local real ale in summer. Everyone – including families with children and dogs – is welcomed in the bar. The award-winning food is freshly prepared using local Lakeland ingredients. At lunch you can enjoy filled baguettes (brie with cranberry sauce; warm Cumberland sausage with home-made chutney) or hearty favourites such as Aberdeen Angus steak burger with fried onions in a roll, served with salad or chips; or beef-and-ale pie with a flaky pastry crust. The evening menu kicks off with the likes of deep-fried black pudding fritter with herb and apple mash, rich pan gravy and onion marmalade, or slices of smoked venison loin with balsamic syrup and mixed leaf salad, perhaps followed by Lakeland beef pie with Charlotte potatoes, or half a local duckling oven roasted with an orange, thyme and honey glaze, finished with rich pan gravy. Comforting desserts include dark chocolate tart with heather honey ice cream; and home-made clotted cream rice pudding with raspberry jam. Booking for meals may be required.

Open all wk 11-3 6-10.30 Dec-Jan, 11-10.30 Feb-Nov (Fri-Sat 11-11) Closed: 25 Dec **Bar Meals** L served all wk 12-2 (ex 24-25 Dec) D served all wk 6-8.45 (ex mid-wk Dec-Jan) Av main course £14.95 **Restaurant** D served all wk 6-8.45 (ex mid-wk Dec-Jan) Av 3 course à la carte fr £25 ⊕ FREE HOUSE ◀ Cumbrian Legendary Melbreak Bitter, Jennings Bitter & Cumberland Ale, Coniston Old Man Ale, Hawkshead Bitter, Ennerdale Blonde.
Facilities Children welcome Children's menu 🐾 Garden Parking Wi-fi **Rooms** 10

PICK OF THE PUBS

Kirkstile Inn ★★★★INN

LOWESWATER   Map 18 NY12

CA13 0RU ☎ 01900 85219
e-mail: info@kirkstile.com
web: www.kirkstile.com
dir: *From A66 Keswick take Whinlatter Pass at Braithwaite. Take B5292, at T-junct left onto B5289. 3m to Loweswater. From Cockermouth B5289 to Lorton, past Low Lorton, 3m to Loweswater. At red phone box left, 200yds*

Stretching as far as the eye can see, the woods, fells and lakes are as much a draw today as they must have been in the inn's infancy some 400 years ago. The beck below meanders under a stone bridge, oak trees fringing its banks with the mighty Melbreak towering impressively above. Tucked away next to an old church, this classic Cumbrian inn stands just half a mile from the Loweswater and Crummock lakes and makes an ideal base for walking, climbing, boating and fishing. The whole place has an authentic, traditional and well-looked-after feel – whitewashed walls, low beams, solid polished tables, cushioned settles, a well-stoked fire and the odd horse harness remind you of times gone by. You can call in for afternoon tea, but better still would be to taste one of the Cumbrian Legendary Ales – Loweswater Gold, Grasmoor Dark Ale, Esthwaite Bitter - brewed by landlord Roger Humphreys in Esthwaite Water near Hawkshead. The dining room dates back to 1549 and is the oldest part of the inn, facing south down the Buttermere Valley.

Traditional pub food is freshly prepared using local produce and the lunchtime menu brims with wholesome dishes that will satisfy the hearty appetites of famished hikers and climbers. They can tuck into beef and chutney sandwiches; steak-and-kidney pie with shortcrust pastry and hand-cut chips; Lakeland lamb tatie pot; beer-battered hake with mushy peas, chips and tartare sauce; and a platter of local cheeses with chutney. Evening additions and daily specials may take in rabbit, duck and pheasant terrine with pear chutney; slow-roasted lamb shoulder with red wine and rosemary sauce; and home-made game suet pudding with shallot and Madeira sauce. Leave room for hot sticky toffee pudding with toffee sauce and local vanilla ice cream. Don't miss the spring beer festival.

Open all day all wk Closed: 25 Dec **Bar Meals** L served all wk 12-2, light menu 2-4.30 D served all wk 6-9 Av main course £9 **Restaurant** D served all wk 6-9 Av 3 course à la carte fr £17 🛢 FREE HOUSE ◀ Cumbrian Legendary Loweswater Gold, Esthwaite Bitter, Grasmoor Dark Ale, Langdale ♻ Westons Stowford Press. ♟ 9 **Facilities** Children welcome Children's menu Children's portions Family room Garden Beer festival Parking **Rooms** 10

PICK OF THE PUBS

The Plough Inn ★★★★★ INN ●

LUPTON   Map 18 SD58

Cow Brow LA6 1PJ ☎ 015395 67700
e-mail: info@theploughatlupton.co.uk
web: www.theploughatlupton.co.uk
dir: *M6 junct 36, A65 towards Kirkby*
Lonsdale. Pub on right in Lupton

In 2009 the owners of the renowned
Punch Bowl at Crosthwaite (see entry)
took on this failing country pub and set
about transforming it into a sublime
dining establishment. The place was
stripped, gutted, a few walls were
ripped out, floors came up and the roof
came down, and finally the pub was
reborn as a beautiful open space with
wood burning stoves, stunning oak
beams and antique furniture. Located in
the hills between Kendal and Kirkby
Lonsdale, the immense limestone
whaleback of Farleton Fell rises behind
the inn, whilst the sunset view across
towards Morecambe Bay and the lower
Furness Fells can be stunning. Beers,
including Kirkby Lonsdale Monumental
and Jennings Cumberland Ale, are
available to deserving ramblers who've
tackled the fell, but this is primarily a
top-notch food destination, overseen by
smartly uniformed staff. Fires blaze,
country prints decorate and quirky
stuffed creatures take the eye
momentarily from a menu that delivers
with a punch, from simple small plate
light bites (salt and pepper squid or
beetroot and orange salad with goat's

cheese) to full meals such as ham hock
terrine with piccalilli followed by
Cumberland sausages, mashed potato
and onion gravy, with warm chocolate
brownie, ginger ice cream and
crystallised ginger for dessert. Besides
the traditional British options there are
internationally inspired dishes such as
mussels in black bean sauce or
tagliatelle with wild mushroom. Wash it
down with a wine chosen from the
magnificent list kept in rustic 'wine
caves' viewable to the rear. If you visit
in the afternoon a further option is
afternoon tea, featuring the full
complement of scones, cakes and
sandwiches.

Open all day all wk **Bar Meals** L served
all wk 12-9 D served all wk 12-9 Av

main course £12.95 food served all day
Restaurant L served all wk 12-9
D served all wk 12-9 Av 3 course à la
carte fr £18.50 food served all day
⊕ FREE HOUSE ◼ Kirkby Lonsdale
Monumental, Jennings Cumberland Ale
ర్ Thatchers Gold, Westons Wyld Wood
Organic. ♟ 14 **Facilities** Children
welcome Children's menu Children's
portions ❖ Garden Parking Wi-fi
Rooms 5

LOW LORTON — Map 18 NY12

The Wheatsheaf Inn

CA13 9UW ☎ 01900 85199 & 85268
e-mail: j.williams53@sky.com
dir: From Cockermouth take B5292 to Lorton. Right onto B5289 to Low Lorton

The Wheatsheaf is a friendly and welcoming village local hidden away in the Vale of Lorton. Close to the Whinlatter Forest and its walking and mountain biking trails, the pub is popular for its local ales and traditional food. Seek it out for its stunning setting and savour the panoramic views of the Lakeland fells with a pint of Jennings Bitter in the tranquil garden. The menu ranges from pub classics like liver casserole and beef to fresh fish nights (Thursday and Friday). Look out for the March beer festival.

Open Tue-Sun Closed: Mon & Tue eve in Jan & Feb **Bar Meals** L served Fri 12-2, Sat 12-3, Sun 12-8.30 D served Mon-Sat 6-8.30, Sun 12-8.30 **Restaurant** L served all wk D served Mon-Sat 6-8.30, Sun 12-8.30 ⊕ MARSTON'S ◧ Pedigree, Jennings Bitter & Cumberland Ale, Brakspear Oxford Gold. **Facilities** Children welcome Children's menu Children's portions Family room Garden Beer festival Parking ▭

LUPTON — Map 18 SD58

The Plough Inn ★★★★★ INN ⊚

PICK OF THE PUBS

See Pick of the Pubs on page 125

MILNTHORPE — Map 18 SD48

The Cross Keys

1 Park Rd LA7 7AB ☎ 015395 62115
e-mail: stay@thecrosskeyshotel.co.uk
dir: M6 junct 35, to junct 35A then A6 N to Milnthorpe; or M6 junct 36, A65 towards Kendal. At Crooklands left onto B6385 to Milnthorpe. Pub at x-rds in village centre

Levens Hall, Leighton Moss Nature Reserve and Morecambe Bay are all within reach of this imposing former coaching inn. Set in the heart of Milnthorpe village, it makes a good pitstop for cask-conditioned ales and hearty pub food. Menus offer sandwiches, salads and pub favourites like roast topside of beef in a giant Yorkshire pudding; fresh fish and chips; beef madras curry; and burgers. Puddings are a speciality — look out for the local favourite, sticky toffee.

Open all day all wk **Bar Meals** L served Mon-Fri 12-2, Sat-Sun all day D served Mon-Fri 5.30-8.30, Sat-Sun all day Av main course £7-£10 **Restaurant** L served Mon-Fri 12-2, Sat-Sun all day D served Mon-Fri 5-8.30, Sat-Sun all day Fixed menu price fr £7 Av 3 course à la carte fr £20 ⊕ FREDERIC ROBINSON ◧ Dizzy Blonde, Hartleys XB, Veltins, Guest ale ♥ Westons Stowford Press. **Facilities** Children welcome Children's menu Children's portions Garden Beer festival Parking Wi-fi ▭ (notice required)

NEAR SAWREY — Map 18 SD39

Tower Bank Arms

PICK OF THE PUBS

See Pick of the Pubs on opposite page

OUTGATE — Map 18 SD39

Outgate Inn

LA22 0NQ ☎ 015394 36413
e-mail: info@outgateinn.co.uk
dir: Exit M6 junct 36, by-passing Kendal, A591 towards Ambleside. At Clappersgate take B5285 to Hawkshead then Outgate 3m

Once a mineral water manufacturer and now part of Robinsons and Hartleys Brewery, this 17th-century Lakeland inn is full of traditional features including oak beams and a real fire in winter. The secluded beer garden at the rear is a tranquil place to enjoy the summer warmth. Food options include salads and light bites such as a beefburger or ham, egg and chips; and hearty options such as braised blade of beef carved onto horseradish mash with port jus; or grilled chicken wrapped in bacon with bubble-and-squeak and red wine and thyme sauce. Home-made Baileys and chocolate cheesecake is a typical dessert. Booking for meals may be required.

Open all day all wk **Bar Meals** L served all wk 12-4 D served all wk 12-9 food served all day **Restaurant** L served all wk 12-4 D served all wk 12-9 food served all day ⊕ FREDERIC ROBINSON ◧ Dizzy Blonde, Hartleys XB. **Facilities** ✿ Children welcome Children's menu Children's portions Garden Parking Wi-fi ▭ (notice required)

PENRITH — Map 18 NY53

Cross Keys Inn

Carleton Village CA11 8TP ☎ 01768 865588
e-mail: crosskeys@kyloes.co.uk
dir: From A66 in Penrith take A686 to Carleton Village, inn on right

At the edge of Penrith, this much-refurbished old drovers' and coaching inn offers sweeping views to the nearby North Pennines from the upstairs restaurant where timeless, traditional pub meals are the order of the day; beer-battered haddock with hand-cut chips or home-made steak-and-ale pie for example. Kyloes Grill here is particularly well thought of, with only Cumbrian meats used. Beers crafted in nearby Broughton Hall by Tirril Brewery draw an appreciative local clientele, warming their toes by the ferocious log-burner or laying a few tiles on the domino tables.

Open all wk Mon-Fri 12-2.30 5-12 (Sat-Sun all day) **Bar Meals** L served Mon-Sat 12-2.30 **Restaurant** L served all wk 12-2.30 D served Sun-Thu 6-9, Fri-Sat 5.30-9 ⊕ FREE HOUSE ◧ Theakston Black Bull Bitter, Tirril 1823, Guest ale. ♥ 10 **Facilities** ✿ Children welcome Children's menu Children's portions Garden Parking Wi-fi ▭ (notice required)

RAVENSTONEDALE — Map 18 NY70

The Black Swan ★★★★ INN

PICK OF THE PUBS

See Pick of the Pubs on page 128

The Fat Lamb Country Inn ★★ HL

PICK OF THE PUBS

See Pick of the Pubs on page 129

SEATHWAITE — Map 18 SD29

Newfield Inn

LA20 6ED ☎ 01229 716208
dir: From Broughton-in-Furness take A595 signed Whitehaven & Workington. Right into Smithy Ln signed Ulpha. Through Ulpha to Seathwaite

Paul Batten's 16th-century cottage-style pub can be found tucked away in the peaceful Duddon Valley. Wordsworth's favourite valley is also popular with walkers and climbers, and the slate-floored bar regularly throngs with parched outdoor types quaffing pints of Cumberland Ale and Esthwaite Bitter. Served all day, food is hearty and traditional and uses local farm meats; the choice ranges from fresh rolls, salads and lunchtime snacks like ham, egg and chips, to steak pie, sirloin steak and chips, and home-made bread-and-butter pudding. Escape to the garden in summer and savour cracking fell views, or come for the beer festival in October.

Open all day all wk **Bar Meals** Av main course £10 food served all day **Restaurant** food served all day ⊕ FREE HOUSE ◧ Cumberland Corby Ale, Jennings Cumberland Ale, Cumbrian Legendary Esthwaite Bitter. ♥ 8 **Facilities** ✿ Children welcome Children's portions Play area Garden Beer festival Parking ▭

Save on hotels. Book at **theAA.com/hotel**

CUMBRIA 127 ENGLAND

PICK OF THE PUBS

Tower Bank Arms

NEAR SAWREY   Map 18 SD39

LA22 0LF ☎ 015394 36334
e-mail: enquiries@towerbankarms.com
web: www.towerbankarms.com
dir: *On B5285 SW of Windermere.1.5m
from Hawkshead. 2m from Windermere
via ferry*

When author Beatrix Potter died in 1943
she left her old home, called Hill Top, to
the National Trust. Standing on the
quieter, west side of Lake Windermere,
its neighbour is this 17th-century
Lakeland pub, which the Trust also
owns, although it is run independently.
Once known as The Blue Pig and later
The Albion, it has been the Tower Bank
Arms for over a century and Potter
illustrated it perfectly in her *Tale of
Jemima Puddleduck*, although history
appears not to record whether she ever
slipped in for a swift half during a break
from sketching! The literary connection
brings out the Peter Rabbit fan club in
force, particularly in summer, so the
delightfully unspoilt rustic charm of this
little treasure may be easier to
appreciate out of season. In the low-
beamed, slate-floored main bar, where
there's an open log fire, fresh flowers
and ticking grandfather clock, and local
brews on handpump from Cumbrian
Legendary, Hawkshead and Barngates
breweries. The full lunch and dinner
menus are available throughout all areas
for both lunch and dinner. Hearty
country food makes good use of local
produce, whether snack, such as a
freshly cut Lakeland ham sandwich, or
main dish, such as Cumbrian beef and
ale stew with herby dumplings;
Woodall's Cumberland sausage, mash
and rich onion gravy; baked fillet of
salmon with a herb crust; or puff pastry
vegetable Wellington with Eden
Chieftain cheese. Daily specials could
feature locally reared rib-eye steak, and
'surf and turf'. Desserts include the
firmly traditional, sticky toffee pudding
with custard; bread-and-butter pudding
with vanilla ice cream; and local
cheeses on a slate. From the garden you
can see the village of Near Sawrey and a
panorama of farms, fells and fields.
Booking for meals may be required.

Open all wk (all day Etr-Oct) **Meals** L
served all wk 12-2 D served Mon-Sat
6-9, Sun & BH 6-8 (Mon-Thu in winter)
Av main course £12.50 Av 3 course à la
carte fr £20.45 ⊕ FREE HOUSE
◖ Barngates Tag Lag & Cat Nap,
Hawkshead Bitter & Brodie's Prime
⚲ Westons Wyld Wood Organic Vintage.
Facilities Children welcome Children's
portions ❦ Garden Parking Wi-fi
🚌 (notice required)

PICK OF THE PUBS

The Black Swan ★★★★ INN

AA PUB OF THE YEAR FOR ENGLAND 2012-2013

RAVENSTONEDALE Map 18 NY70

CA17 4NG ☎ 015396 23204
e-mail: enquiries@blackswanhotel.com
web: www.blackswanhotel.com
dir: *M6 junct 38, A685 E towards Brough*

The Black Swan nestles below Wild Boar Fell beside the frothy headwaters of the appropriately named River Eden. The enterprising owners of this family-run residential inn, which has gained a four AA Gold Stars Award for the quality of the individually styled bedrooms and Breakfast and Dinner awards for the food, have placed themselves right at the heart of the community, with the on-site village store being opened by HRH Prince Charles in 2008; being part of the 'Pub is the Hub' campaign; and specialising in locally produced foods and goodies. Relax in the tranquil riverside garden, home to red squirrels which will let you share their space after you've walked the Howgill Fells, explored the Lakes or toured the Yorkshire Dales, all of which are on the doorstep. The ever-changing selection of northern beers includes the likes of Dent, Hesket Newmarket and Tirril breweries. This local pride ethos is also strongly evident in the choice of dishes, with all meat traceable locally and detailed for lucky guests to contemplate. The menu might include a starter of layered terrine of smoked trout, mackerel and salmon,

wrapped in smoked salmon with horseradish and artisan bread, a robust precursor to steak, venison and ale cobbler with a choice of potato accompaniment. Vegetarians may relish the vegetable Wellington stuffed with celeriac, broccoli and spinach in a creamy cheese sauce accompanied by braised red cabbage, chestnuts and new potatoes. Making the most of the local country's largesse, menus tend to be seasonal with daily-changing specials; there's also a good choice of snacks and light bites. Booking for meals may be required.

Open all day all wk 8am-11.30pm **Bar Meals** L served all wk 12-2 D served all

wk 6-9 **Restaurant** L served all wk 12-2 D served all wk 6-9 ⊕ FREE HOUSE
◀ Black Sheep Ale & Best Bitter, Dent, Tirril, Hawkshead, Hesket Newmarket, Cumberland, Guinness, Guest ales
Ö Thatchers Gold. ♟ **Facilities** Children welcome Children's menu Children's portions Garden Parking Wi-fi ⛟
Rooms 14

Save on hotels. Book at **theAA.com/hotel**

CUMBRIA 129 **ENGLAND**

PICK OF THE PUBS

The Fat Lamb Country Inn ★★ HL

RAVENSTONEDALE   Map 18 NY70

Crossbank CA17 4LL ☎ 015396 23242
e-mail: enquiries@fatlamb.co.uk
web: www.fatlamb.co.uk
dir: *On A683 between Sedbergh & Kirkby Stephen*

High above the green meadows of Ravenstonedale in the furthest corner of old Westmorland, this 350-year-old stone coaching inn blends modern amenities with old fashioned hospitality. From The Fat Lamb's gardens, your gaze will fall on some of England's most precious, under-visited and remote countryside and it's no surprise that ramblers and country lovers compete to stay in the comfy AA-rated en suite bedrooms at this free house. A short, post-prandial constitutional could take you through the inn's own nature reserve – seven acres of open water and wetlands, surrounded by flower rich meadows. Over 80 species of bird have been recorded, sharing their glorious surroundings with badgers, foxes, otters, roe deer and bats. An open fire in the traditional Yorkshire range warms the bar in winter; this is the oldest part of the building and was converted from the former kitchen and living area. Here, visitors and locals mingle and natter without the intrusion of electronic entertainments. Snacks and meals are served both here and in the traditional and relaxed restaurant, which is decorated with old prints and plates.

Bar snacks take the form of sandwiches and warm baguettes, local sausage platters, Yorkshire gammon and eggs or the pie of the day. The five-course set menu may offer sautéed scampi tails in Pernod and cucumber cream sauce, followed by a home-made tomato and basil soup and then slow-cooked beef in mushroom and brandy sauce. If you go à la carte, warm salad of seared pigeon breast with Bury black pudding makes an excellent start, which could be followed by roast leg of Fell-bred lamb with champ and a rosemary and redcurrant sauce. Alternatively, check out the day's specials board. Whatever you choose, it will have been prepared on site using the best available local ingredients. Booking for meals may be required.

Open all day all wk **Bar Meals** L served all wk 12-2 D served all wk 6-9 Av main course £10 **Restaurant** L served all wk 12-2 D served all wk 6-9 Fixed menu price fr £25 ⊕ FREE HOUSE ◼ Black Sheep Best Bitter ♺ Westons Stowford Press. **Facilities** Children welcome Children's menu Children's portions Play area ❀ Garden Parking Wi-fi 🚌 (notice required) **Rooms** 12

SIZERGH   Map 18 SD48

The Strickland Arms

PICK OF THE PUBS

LA8 8DZ ☎ 015395 61010

e-mail: thestricklandarms@yahoo.co.uk

dir: *From Kendal A591 S. At Brettargh Holt junct branch left, at rdbt 3rd exit onto A590 (dual carriageway) signed Barrow. Follow brown signs for Sizergh Castle. Into right lane, turn right across dual carriageway. Pub on left*

Beside the lane leading to the National Trust's Sizergh Castle and just a stride from paths alongside the lively River Kent, this slightly severe-looking building (also NT-owned) slumbers amidst low hills above the Lyth Valley at the southern fringe of the Lake District National Park. Visitors to the valley's renowned damson blossom extravaganza in April can enjoy produce gleaned from this bounteous harvest, maybe including a damson beer from one of the local micro-breweries whose ales stock the bar here; an annual beer festival scoops many more Lake District breweries into the fold. The essentially open-plan interior is contemporary-Edwardian, with high ceilings, flagstoned floors, grand fires and Farrow & Ball finish to the walls, creating an instantly welcoming atmosphere. Re-opened after years of closure a couple of seasons ago, the great beers and fine food made an immediate impact, and the inn is a popular destination dining pub. Home-made chicken liver and brandy pâté with Hawkshead damson chutney, salad and crusty bread is a good foundation for a main of sweet cured pork loin steak with black pudding and free-range eggs; all local produce when possible. Recent change of hands.

Open all wk Mon-Thu 12-3 5.30-11 (Fri-Sun all day) Closed: 25 Dec **Bar Meals** L served Mon-Fri 12-2, Sat 12-2.30, Sun 12-8.30 D served Mon-Sat 6-9, Sun 12-8.30 **Restaurant** L served Mon-Fri 12-2, Sat 12-2.30, Sun 12-8.30 D served Mon-Sat 6-9, Sun 12-8.30 ⊕ FREE HOUSE ◀ Thwaites Langdale Tup & Lancaster Bomber, Coniston Bluebird Bitter, Cumbrian Legendary Loweswater Gold, Kirkby Lonsdale Monumental. ₹ 9 **Facilities** ✿ Children welcome Children's menu Children's portions Garden Beer festival Parking Wi-fi ⇌

TEMPLE SOWERBY   Map 18 NY62

The Kings Arms ★★★★ INN

CA10 1SB ☎ 017683 62944

e-mail: enquiries@kingsarmstemplesowerby.co.uk

dir: *M6 junct 40, E on A66 to Temple Sowerby. Inn in town centre*

This 400-year-old coaching inn, just a few miles from Penrith, was where William Wordsworth and Samuel Coleridge set off for their exploration of the Lake District. The owners fully refurbished the property to create a traditional inn with rooms. The kitchen serves a mix of old pub-grub favourites, including prawn cocktail, Whitby Bay scampi, and chicken Kiev; and modern classics such as black pudding filo tartlet, chorizo spiced mushrooms, pan-seared tuna steak, and chicken al forno. Booking for meals may be required.

Open all wk 10-3 6-11 **Bar Meals** L served all wk 12-2 D served all wk 6-9 Av main course £10 **Restaurant** L served all wk 12-2 D served all wk 6-9 ⊕ FREE HOUSE ◀ Black Sheep, Guest ales ♂ Westons Stowford Press. **Facilities** ✿ Children welcome Children's menu Children's portions Garden Parking Wi-fi ⇌ (notice required) **Rooms** 8

TIRRIL   Map 18 NY52

Queen's Head Inn

PICK OF THE PUBS

CA10 2JF ☎ 01768 863219

e-mail: margarethodge567@btinternet.com

dir: *A66 towards Penrith then A6 S towards Shap. In Eamont Bridge turn right just after Crown Hotel. Tirril in 1m on B5320*

Situated on the edge of the Lake District National Park, this traditional English country inn dates from 1719 and is chock-full of beams, flagstones and memorabilia as you would expect from an old inn. While enjoying a pint of Unicorn, Cumbria Way or Dizzy Blonde in the bar, look for the Wordsworth Indenture, signed by the great poet himself, his brother, Christopher, and local wheelwright John Bewsher, to whom the Wordsworths sold the pub in 1836. You can eat in the bar or restaurant, and a meal might include bacon and black pudding salad; oven-baked chicken stuffed with Blengdale Blue and spinach; and chocolate and orange tart. In August every year the Cumbrian beer and sausage festival is held here. The village shop is located at the back of the inn.

Open all day all wk Sun-Thu 12-11 (Fri-Sat 12-12) **Bar Meals** L served all wk 12-2.30 D served all wk 5.30-8.30 **Restaurant** L served all wk 12-2.30 D served all wk 5.30-8.30 ⊕ FREDERIC ROBINSON ◀ Unicorn & Dizzy Blonde, Hartleys Cumbria Way & XB, Guest ales ♂ Westons Stowford Press. ₹ 10 **Facilities** ✿ Children welcome Children's portions Beer festival Parking ⇌

TORVER   Map 18 SD29

Church House Inn

LA21 8AZ ☎ 01539 441282

e-mail: churchhouseinn@hotmail.co.uk

dir: *Take A539 from Coniston towards Broughton-in-Furness. Inn on left in Torver before junct with A5084 towards Ulverston*

Footpaths wind to the bank of Coniston Water whilst the ridges of the Coniston Horseshoe mountains rise steeply from sloping pastures opposite. Sitting plum in the middle, the 15th-century Church House Inn revels in this idyllic location, offering a great range of Lakeland beers and satisfying meals sourced from local farms and estates; Cumberland tattie hotpot based on slow-braised Herdwick lamb hits the spot, enjoyed in the olde-worlde rambling interior or sheltered beer garden. Booking for meals may be required.

Open all day all wk 10.30am-mdnt **Bar Meals** L served all wk 12-3 D served all wk 6-9 **Restaurant** L served all wk 12-3 D served all wk 6-9 ⊕ ENTERPRISE INNS ◀ Hawkshead Bitter & Lakeland Gold, Barngates Tag

Lag, Cumbrian Legendary Loweswater Gold. **Facilities** ✿ Children welcome Children's portions Family room Garden Parking Wi-fi ⇌

TROUTBECK   Map 18 NY40

Queen's Head ★★★★ INN

PICK OF THE PUBS

See Pick of the Pubs on opposite page
See advert on page 132

ULVERSTON   Map 18 SD27

Farmers Arms Hotel

Market Place LA12 7BA ☎ 01229 584469

dir: *In town centre*

Landlord Roger Chattaway takes pride in serving quality ales and food at his lively 16th-century inn at the heart of this historic market town. Expect a warm welcome in the comfortable and relaxing beamed front bar, where you'll find local Hawkshead Bitter on tap and an open fire in winter. Sunday lunches are famous locally, and there's a varied specials menu, deli boards to share, pizzas; pub classics like brisket of beef on red onion mash with a rich gravy, chargrilled steaks; and seafood delights like mussels cooked in white wine, chilli, ginger and cream; and hot steak sandwiches at lunchtime. Booking for meals may be required.

Open all day all wk **Bar Meals** L served all wk 9-3 D served all wk 6-9 Av main course £10 **Restaurant** Av 3 course à la carte fr £20 ⊕ FREE HOUSE ◀ Hawkshead Bitter, John Smith's, Courage Directors, Yates ♂ Symonds. ₹ 12 **Facilities** Children welcome Children's menu Children's portions Garden Beer festival Wi-fi ⇌ (notice required)

The Stan Laurel Inn

31 The Ellers LA12 0AB ☎ 01229 582814

e-mail: thestanlaurel@aol.com

dir: *M6 junct 36, A590 to Ulverston. Straight on at Booths rdbt, left at 2nd rdbt in The Ellers, pub on left after Ford garage*

In 1890, when the old market town of Ulverston's most famous son – the comic actor Stan Laurel – was born, this town-centre pub was still a farmhouse with two cottages surrounded by fields and orchards. Owners Trudi and Paul Dewar serve a selection of locally brewed real ales and a full menu of traditional pub food plus a specials board. Take your pick from starters such as seafood pancake, spicy chicken strips, or battered brie wedges. Among tasty mains are a chilli tortilla stack, and barbecued baby back ribs from the grill. Booking for meals may be required.

Open Mon 7pm-11.30pm Tue-Thu 12-2.30 6-11.30 Fri-Sat 12-2.30 6-12 Sun 12-11.30 Closed: Mon L **Bar Meals** L served Tue-Sat 12-2, Sun 12-8 D served Tue-Sat 6-9, Sun 12-8 **Restaurant** L served Tue-Sat 12-2, Sun 12-8 D served Tue-Sat 6-9, Sun 12-8 ⊕ FREE HOUSE ◀ Thwaites Original, Ulverston, Barngates, Salamander. **Facilities** Children welcome Children's menu Children's portions Parking Wi-fi

Save on hotels. Book at **theAA.com/hotel**

CUMBRIA 131 **ENGLAND**

PICK OF THE PUBS

Queen's Head ★★★★ INN

TROUTBECK   Map 18 NY40

Townhead LA23 1PW ☎ 015394 32174
e-mail:
reservations@queensheadtroutbeck.co.uk
web: www.queensheadtroutbeck.co.uk
dir: *M6 junct 36, A590, A591 towards*
Windermere, right at mini-rdbt onto
A592 signed Penrith/Ullswater. Pub 2m
on left

Nooks and crannies, a log fire throughout
the year, and low beams stuffed with old
pennies by farmers on their way home
from market all help to make this smart
17th-century coaching inn hard to beat
in the traditional English inn stakes. It
stands in the lovely undulating valley of
Troutbeck which, bordered by impressive
fells criss-crossed by footpaths, is a real
magnet for ramblers. But you don't have
to wear walking boots to enjoy the food
or drink, or the comfortable
accommodation in bedrooms with
delightfully uneven walls and four-poster
beds in the original building, and in the
beautifully transformed old barn. And,
while on the subject of four-posters,
there's one in the bar; in fact, it is the
bar, although it once saw service in
Appleby Castle. Look below bar counter
level at the striking carved panelling
while ordering a pint of Hartleys XB or
Robinsons Old Tom. The chef and his
team's reputation for accomplished
cooking is widely recognised for their
menus of interestingly prepared
international dishes, with typical first

courses of home-made black pudding
with rösti potato, poached egg, English
mustard sauce and pancetta; and
Garstang Blue cheese mousse with
crispy apple Tatin and beetroot salad.
Main courses of note – and there are
many – include beer-braised brisket
cottage pie; locally sourced steamed
lamb and cockle pudding; fish mixed
grill with crab fondue; and wild
mushroom and buttered spinach home-
made macaroni. The cast list continues
with desserts of steamed lemon sponge
with honey and whisky syrup; sticky
toffee pudding; and a selection of local
cheeses. Well-behaved dogs on leads are
allowed on the slated area in the bar,
and in two of the guest rooms in the
annexe. Toys and games are available
for young children in the bar and

restaurant area. Booking for meals may
be required.

Open all day all wk **Bar Meals** food
served all day **Restaurant** food served
all day ⊕ FREDERIC ROBINSON ◀ Dizzy
Blonde, Old Tom & Double Hop, Hartleys
Cumbria Way & XB. ☙ 8
Facilities Children welcome Children's
menu Children's portions Parking Wi-fi
🚌 **Rooms** 15

WASDALE HEAD Map 18 NY10

Wasdale Head Inn ★★★ INN

CA20 1EX ☎ 019467 26229
e-mail: reception@wasdale.com
dir: *From A595 follow Wasdale signs. Inn at head of valley*

Dramatically situated at the foot of England's highest mountain, adjacent to England's smallest church and not far from the deepest lake, this historical inn is reputedly the birthplace of British climbing – photographs decorating the oak-panelled walls reflect the passion for this activity. Expect local ales and hearty food such as goulash soup followed by shepherd's pie with a golden cheesy topping or Thai green vegetable curry. A beer festival on the first Sunday in October is a great reason to hang up the climbing boots for a day and maybe stay over in one of the comfortable bedrooms. Booking for meals may be required.

Open all day all wk **Bar Meals** L served all wk 12-9 D served all wk 12-9 Av main course £10.50 food served all day **Restaurant** D served all wk 7-8 ⊕ FREE HOUSE ◀ Cumbrian Legendary Loweswater Gold & Esthwaite Bitter, Great Gable Yewbarrow & Iron Awe, Jennings. **Facilities** ❀ Children welcome Children's menu Children's portions Garden Beer festival Parking **Rooms** 12

WINDERMERE Map 18 SD49

The Angel Inn

Helm Rd LA23 3BU ☎ 015394 44080
e-mail: rooms@the-angelinn.com
dir: *From Rayrigg Rd (parallel to lake) into Crag Brow, then right into Helm Rd*

Just five minutes' walk from Lake Windermere, in the centre of Bowness-on-Windermere, this family-owned and run gastro-pub offers plenty of city-chic style. Unusual local ales vie with international beers at the bar, and good food based on local produce is available throughout the day from a choice of menus: sandwiches and light lunches; starters, nibbles and salads; cheese plates or main courses – try wild boar and apple sausage or Cumbrian Fellbred steak – desserts and a children's menu. In summer customers can enjoy the gardens and grounds; the terrace offers fantastic views.

Open all day all wk 9am-11pm Closed: 25 Dec **Bar Meals** L served all wk 9.30-4 D served all wk 5-9 **Restaurant** L served all wk 9.30-4 D served all wk 5-9 ⊕ FREE HOUSE ◀ Coniston Bluebird Bitter, Hawkshead Bitter, Tirril Old Faithful, Stringers West Coast Blond, Jennings Cumberland Ale. ♀ 12 **Facilities** Children welcome Children's menu Children's portions Garden Parking Wi-fi

Eagle & Child Inn

Kendal Rd, Staveley LA8 9LP ☎ 01539 821320
e-mail: info@eaglechildinn.co.uk
dir: *M6 junct 36, A590 towards Kendal then A591 towards Windermere. Staveley approx 2m*

The rivers Kent and Gowan meet at the gardens of this friendly inn, and it's surrounded by miles of excellent walking, cycling and fishing country. Several pubs in Britain share the same name, which refers to a legend of a baby found in an eagle's nest. With a good range of beers to chose from, dishes include Hawkshead ale, beef, mushroom and onion pie; vegetarian shepherd's pie; local Cumberland sausage; 'Eagle & Child' hotpot; and a changing selection of 'Chef's Fishy Specials'. Finish with some delicious bread-and-butter pudding with honey and Drambuie.

Open all day all wk **Bar Meals** L served Mon-Fri 12-2.30, Sat-Sun 12-3 D served all wk 6-9 Av main course £9.95 ⊕ FREE HOUSE ◀ Hawkshead Bitter, Yates Best Bitter, Tirril, Coniston, Dent ð Westons, Cowmire Hall Ancient Orchard, Cumbrian. ♀ 10 **Facilities** Children welcome Children's menu Children's portions Garden Parking Wi-fi 🚐

Save on hotels. Book at **theAA.com/hotel**

CUMBRIA 133 ENGLAND

PICK OF THE PUBS

The Yanwath Gate Inn

YANWATH   Map 18 NY52

CA10 2LF ☎ 01768 862386
e-mail: enquiries@yanwathgate.com
web: www.yanwathgate.com
dir: *Telephone for directions*

Evolving over centuries from a toll gate, or 'yat', on the long road from Kendal to Scotland, today's incarnation is a classy mix of traditional pub and fine restaurant; timeless ambience (the pub is around 330 years old) and top-notch dishes, where 'free range' and 'organic' are words constantly at the forefront of Matt Edwards' mantra. Lunch and evening menus will vary, and content depends on seasonal or specialist availability, but could encompass starters of spicy Tuscan bean soup, or pigeon and fig terrine with pickled walnut and watercress. For main course, perhaps try confit duck leg with warm potato, chorizo and black pudding salad; the stuffed belly of Lakeland lamb with Crofton cheese mash and Madeira and thyme jus; or the Moroccan vegetable tagine with spicy lemon harrissa dressing and coriander couscous. Leave room for sticky date pudding with toffee sauce and vanilla ice cream, or an impressive selection of local cheeses served with home-made chutney. To accompany, there's authentic Trappist beer, an excellent list

of wines (12 by the glass), or take a leaf out of locals' and Matt's book and indulge in a beer from one of the reliable craft breweries within a few miles of the inn, perhaps a pint from the range of Hesket Newmarket, Tirril and Barngates ales. The location is stunning — on one horizon rise the lofty North Pennines; to another the hills and moors bounding nearby Ullswater draw the eye. In between is the Eden Valley, source of much of the food prepared at this well-respected dining inn. So, famished M6 travellers should note the location of this fine gastro-pub — it's only two miles from junction 40 at Penrith. Booking for meals may be required.

Open all day all wk **Bar Meals** L served all wk 12-2.30 D served all wk 6-9 Av main course £16 **Restaurant** L served all wk 12-2.30 D served all wk 6-9 Av 3 course à la carte fr £26 ⊞ FREE HOUSE ◀ Hesket Newmarket, Tirril, Barngates Ŏ Westons Old Rosie. ♈ 12 **Facilities** Children welcome Children's menu Garden Parking Wi-fi 🚌 (notice required)

The Brown Horse Inn **NEW**

LA22 9BG ☎ 015394 43443
e-mail: steve@thebrownhorseinn.co.uk
dir: *On A5074 between Bowness-on-Windermere & A590 (Kendal to Barrow-in-Furness road)*

The beautiful Winster Valley is a perfect location for this inn full of original features. Despite all the time-worn charm, the décor has a subtly modern edge. It's an inn of many talents: much of the food (even the pork) is home grown and ales are brewed on site. Food ranges from grilled steaks to confit belly pork with crisply fried onions, black pudding and apple purée, followed by tournedos of salmon with spiced lentils and foie gras.

Open all day all wk **Bar Meals** L served all wk 12-2 D served all wk 6-9 Av main course £12 **Restaurant** L served all wk 12-2 D served all wk 6-9 Av 3 course à la carte fr £22 ⊕ FREE HOUSE ◀ Winster Valley Best Bitter, Old School, Hurdler, Chaser. ♀ 12 **Facilities** Children welcome Children's menu Children's portions Garden Parking Wi-fi ▦ (notice required)

The Old Ginn House

Great Clifton CA14 1TS ☎ 01900 64616
e-mail: enquiries@oldginnhouse.co.uk
dir: *Just off A66, 3m from Workington & 4m from Cockermouth*

When this was a farm, ginning was the process by which horses were used to turn a grindstone that crushed grain. It took place in the rounded area known today as the Ginn Room and which is now the main bar, serving Jennings and Coniston beers. The dining areas, all butter yellow, bright check curtains and terracotta tiles, rather bring the Mediterranean to mind, although the extensive menu and specials are both cosmopolitan and traditional.

Open all day all wk Closed: 24-26 Dec, 1 Jan **Bar Meals** L served all wk 12-2 D served all wk 6-9.30 **Restaurant** L served all wk 12-2 D served all wk 6-9.30 ⊕ FREE HOUSE ◀ Jennings Bitter, John Smith's, Coniston Bluebird Bitter. **Facilities** Children welcome Children's menu Children's portions Garden Parking ▦

The Yanwath Gate Inn
PICK OF THE PUBS

See Pick of the Pubs on page 133

The Old Poets Corner

Butts Rd S45 0EW ☎ 01246 590888
e-mail: enquiries@oldpoets.co.uk
dir: *From Matlock take A632 signed Chesterfield. Right onto B6036 to Ashover*

Ale and cider aficionados flock to this traditional village local, and no wonder. It dispenses eight ciders, and ten cask ales include five from the Ashover Brewery behind the pub. The March and October beer festivals see these numbers multiply. There's live music here twice a week, quizzes, special events and Sunday night curries. Hearty home-cooked pub dishes range from meat and potato pie to devilled lamb's kidneys. Squeeze in a sweet served with your choice of cream, ice cream or custard before walking it off in the scenic Derbyshire countryside. Booking for meals may be required.

Open all day all wk **Bar Meals** L served Mon-Fri 12-2, Sat-Sun 12-3 D served Mon-Thu 6.30-9, Fri-Sat 6-9.30, Sun 7-9 Av main course £7.25 **Restaurant** L served Mon-Fri 12-2, Sat-Sun 12-3 D served Mon-Thu 6.30-9, Fri-Sat 6-9.30, Sun 7-9 Fixed menu price fr £9.50 ⊕ FREE HOUSE ◀ Ashover, Thornbridge, Oakham Ò Broadoak Perry & Moonshine, Westons Old Rosie. **Facilities** ✿ Children welcome Family room Beer festival Parking ▦ (notice required)

The Bull's Head
PICK OF THE PUBS

Church St, Ashford-in-the-Water DE45 1QB ☎ 01629 812931
dir: *Off A6, 2m N of Bakewell, 5m from Chatsworth Estate*

Debbie Shaw's family has run this popular 17th-century coaching inn for more than half a century. With an abundance of oak beams, open fires, carved settles, and jazz playing quietly in the background, a relaxed time is guaranteed here and Debbie and husband/chef Carl have picked up a number of impressive accolades in the 12 years they have been at the helm. With a clear preference for using local produce including pork reared by the owners themselves, Carl develops appealing menus that always feature steak and Old Stockport ale pie, and may well include pork and tomato sausages on minted mash with red wine gravy, or roast chicken breast in white wine, celery and lovage sauce. Rhubarb mousse with Cognac ice cream is one of the tempting desserts. A snack or sandwich in the attractive beer garden, followed by a game of boules is well worth considering in summer.

Open all wk 12-3 6-11 (Sun 12-3.30 7-10.30) **Bar Meals** L served Mon-Sat 12-2, Sun 12-2.30 D served Mon-Sat (ex Thu in winter) 6.30-9, Sun 7-9 ⊕ FREDERIC ROBINSON ◀ Old Stockport, Unicorn, Seasonal ales. **Facilities** Children welcome Children's portions Play area Family room Garden Parking

The Monsal Head Hotel ★★ HL ⊚
PICK OF THE PUBS

See Pick of the Pubs on opposite page

Yorkshire Bridge Inn
PICK OF THE PUBS

See Pick of the Pubs on page 136

Ragley Boat Stop

Deepdale Ln, Off Sinfin Ln DE73 1HH ☎ 01332 703919
e-mail: pippa@king-henrys-taverns.co.uk
dir: *Telephone for directions*

This spacious free house has a lovely garden sloping down to the Trent and Mersey Canal. There are plenty of sofas to relax in, a good choice of eating areas, and a huge balcony overlooking the gardens and canal – an ideal spot for a quiet drink whilst watching the world go by. The menu of freshly prepared dishes has choices to suit every appetite. Beef in all its forms is a major attraction; alternatively international flavours abound in dishes such as spicy Cajun chicken and ribs, lasagne, and curries.

Open all day all wk 11.30-11 **Bar Meals** food served all day **Restaurant** food served all day ⊕ FREE HOUSE/KING HENRY'S TAVERNS ◀ Greene King IPA, Marston's Pedigree, Guinness. ♀ 16 **Facilities** Children welcome Children's menu Children's portions Garden Parking ▦

Rowley's ⊚⊚
PICK OF THE PUBS

See Pick of the Pubs on page 137

Save on hotels. Book at **theAA.com/hotel**

DERBYSHIRE 135 ENGLAND

PICK OF THE PUBS

The Monsal Head Hotel ★★HL ❀

BAKEWELL   Map 16 SK26

Monsal Head DE45 1NL
☎ **01629 640250**
e-mail: enquiries@monsalhead.com
web: www.monsalhead.com
dir: *A6 from Bakewell towards Buxton. 1.5m to Ashford. Follow Monsal Head signs, B6465 for 1m*

A ten-minute drive from Chatsworth House will deliver you to Monsal Head and its famous railway viaduct, with the River Wye meandering beneath. The hotel's real ale pub, the Stables bar, reflects its earlier role as the home of railway horses collecting passengers from Monsal Dale station. It has a rustic ambience with an original flagstone floor, seating in horse stalls and a log fire – the perfect place to enjoy wines by the bottle or glass, or a range of cask ales from Derbyshire micro-breweries. The Longstone restaurant is spacious and airy with large windows to appreciate the views, again with an open fire in the colder weather. Although the menu has influences from around the world, such as pressed confit of duck, with a five-spice dressing, pickled cucumber, spring onion salsa and cucumber jelly, it demonstrates an extensive use of local produce, as in home-made local wild boar Scotch egg, home-made piccalilli and rocket salad. For a main course try braised beef with home-smoked garlic mash, Chantenay carrots, pancetta crisps with red wine and wild mushroom jus; or maybe slow-cooked shoulder of lamb with warm pea and mint pannacotta, fondant potato and a rich lamb jus. There are always fish and vegetarian options available and special diets can be easily catered for. Desserts include a fantastic sticky toffee pudding with butterscotch sauce and vanilla ice cream; a malt cheesecake with white chocolate 'snow' and chocolate crème anglaise; and a three counties cheeseboard with traditional Yorkshire pepper cake. The bedrooms, although very traditional, do have Freeview digital TV, beverage-making facilities and complimentary toiletries. Breakfasts and morning coffee are available everyday, and the same menu is offered from noon in the bar, restaurant, or weather permitting, in the large outdoor seating area.

Open all day all wk 8am-mdnt **Bar Meals** L served Mon-Sat 12-9.30, Sun 12-9 D served Mon-Sat 12-9.30, Sun

12-9 Av main course £12 food served all day **Restaurant** L served Mon-Sat 12-9.30, Sun 12-9 D served Mon-Sat 12-9.30, Sun 12-9 Av 3 course à la carte fr £20 food served all day ⊕ FREE HOUSE ◼ Peakstones Rock Black Hole, Bradfield, Abbeydale, Buxton, Wincle. ▮ 17 **Facilities** Children welcome Children's menu Children's portions 🐾 Garden Parking 🚐 (notice required) **Rooms** 7

PICK OF THE PUBS

Yorkshire Bridge Inn

BAMFORD Map 16 SK28

Ashopton Rd S33 0AZ ☎ 01433 651361
e-mail: info@yorkshire-bridge.co.uk
web: www.yorkshire-bridge.co.uk
dir: *From Sheffield A57 towards Glossop,
left onto A6013, pub 1m on right*

In the heart of wonderful Peak District
walking country, this inn dates from
1826; it's named after an old packhorse
bridge over the River Derwent. The
village of Derwent was one of two
villages (the other being Ashopton)
which were sacrificed to the waters of
the Ladybower Reservoir, the largest of
the Derwent dams and famed for the
Dambuster training runs. Today it is but
a short stroll to the Ladybower from this
lovely old free house. Views from the
beamed and chintz-curtained bars take
in the peak of Whin Hill, a beautiful
setting in which to enjoy a pint of Easy
Rider and good-quality pub food made
with fresh local produce. 'Soup and a
sandwich' is a popular lunchtime
combination for the day's intake of
ramblers, with fillings from tuna
mayonnaise to Derbyshire beef. Starters
include a classic prawn cocktail, or crab
fishcakes. Hot main courses range from
home-made steak-and-kidney pie to
pot-roasted lamb; favourites such as
beef lasagne are served with garlic

bread, while chilli con carne comes with
either rice or chips and a side of cheesy
nachos. If you're hanging up your boots
for the day, look to the grill for a T-bone
or rib-eye steak cooked to your liking.
Hungry children polish off plates of pork
sausages with mash, or a battered fillet
of fresh fish with chips and baked
beans or salad. A seasonal crumble and
custard makes a great dessert, or you
may simply round off with a hot
chocolate topped with whipped cream.
Nearby attractions include Chatsworth,
Haddon Hall, Dovedale, Buxton and
Bakewell.

Open all day all wk **Bar Meals** L served
Mon-Sat 12-2, Sun 12-8.30 D served
Mon-Thu 6-9, Fri-Sat 6-9.30, Sun 12-
8.30 ⊕ FREE HOUSE ◖ Peak Bakewell
Best Bitter & Chatsworth Gold, Kelham
Island Easy Rider ♉ Thatchers. ☗ 11
Facilities Children welcome Children's
menu Children's portions Garden
Parking Wi-fi 🚌

Save on hotels. Book at **theAA.com/hotel**

DERBYSHIRE 137 ENGLAND

PICK OF THE PUBS

Rowley's 🌹🌹

BASLOW Map 16 SK27

Church Ln DE45 1RY ☎ 01246 583880
e-mail: info@rowleysrestaurant.co.uk
web: www.rowleysrestaurant.co.uk
dir: *A619/A623 signed Chatsworth.
Baslow on edge of Chatsworth Estate*

The team behind Fischer's Restaurant in nearby Baslow Hall have transformed the former Prince of Wales pub into a thoroughly modern bar and restaurant. Set in a peaceful village overlooking the church and open for coffee from 10am, Rowley's offers an informal mix of stone-flagged bar area, where you can sup a pint of local ale by the log-burning stove, alongside the chic, more contemporary feel of its three dining areas upstairs. Very much a dining destination (the food has been awarded two AA Rosettes), the kitchen is headed by Craig Skinner under the watchful eye of Rupert Rowley, award-winning head chef of Fischer's. Menus feature an appealing mix of modern and traditional British dishes, with an emphasis on quality local produce. At lunch, simply presented dishes may take in ham hock terrine with piccalilli, followed by slow-roasted Derbyshire pork belly with celeriac mash, curly kale and wholegrain mustard sauce. In the evening the kitchen shifts up a gear, offering the likes of pan-fried black

pudding sausage with champ potatoes, crispy air-dried ham and a soft poached hen's egg, ahead of a main course of corn-fed chicken breast stuffed with chorizo, wrapped in pancetta and served with soft polenta and piperade. Attractive meat-free options include butternut squash risotto with parmesan shavings, and baked Puy lentil moussaka with griddled oregano flatbread and Yorkshire Fine Fettle cheese. For dessert, maybe buttermilk pannacotta with winter berry compôte and toasted granola, or warm Yorkshire parkin with spiced custard and banana ice cream. Children's choices are home made by the chefs too. Booking for meals may be required.

Open all day Closed: 26 Dec, Sun eve
Bar Meals L served Mon-Sat 12-2.30,
Sun 12-3 D served Mon-Fri 5.30-9
Restaurant L served Mon-Sat 12-2.30,
Sun 12-3 D served Mon-Fri 5.30-9, Sat
6-9.30 ⊞ FREE HOUSE 🍺 Peak, Local
ale. ♟ 10 **Facilities** Children welcome
Children's menu Children's portions
Beer festival Parking Wi-fi

BEELEY
Map 16 SK26

The Devonshire Arms at Beeley ★★★★ INN ◉◉

PICK OF THE PUBS

Devonshire Square DE4 2NR ☎ 01629 733259
e-mail: res@devonshirehotels.co.uk
dir: *B6012 towards Matlock, pass Chatsworth House. After 1.5m turn left, 2nd entrance to Beeley*

This handsome 18th-century village inn is surrounded by classic Peak District scenery and stands on the Chatsworth Estate. It became a thriving coaching inn; Charles Dickens was a frequent visitor; and it is rumoured that King Edward VII often met his mistress Alice Keppel here. The comfortably civilised and neatly furnished interior comprises three attractive beamed rooms, with flagstone floors, roaring log fires, antique settles and farmhouse tables; the rustic taproom is perfect for walkers with muddy boots. In contrast, the brasserie dining room is modern, bright and colourful, with stripey chairs and bold artwork. Come for beers brewed at Chatsworth's brewery and some sublime modern British food (two AA Rosettes) cooked by chef-patron Alan Hill. Using estate-reared and -grown produce, dishes include classics like beer-battered haddock and chips; beef cobbler; tempura skate wing with lobster sauce; and Chatsworth venison spit-roasted over the fire. There are wonderful walks from the front door.

Open all day all wk **Bar Meals** L served all wk 12-3 D served all wk 6-9.30 Av main course £18 **Restaurant** L served all wk 12-3 D served all wk 6-9.30 Fixed menu price fr £14.95 Av 3 course à la carte fr £30 ⊕ FREE HOUSE/DEVONSHIRE HOTELS & RESTAURANTS ◀ Peak Chatsworth Gold, Buxton Blonde, Thornbridge Jaipur. ♈ 10 **Facilities** Children welcome Children's menu Children's portions Garden Parking Wi-fi **Rooms** 8

BIRCHOVER
Map 16 SK26

The Druid Inn

PICK OF THE PUBS

Main St DE4 2BL ☎ 01629 650302
e-mail: thedruidinn@hotmail.co.uk
dir: *From A6 between Matlock & Bakewell take B5056 signed Ashbourne. Approx 2m left to Birchover*

Although the pub has been here since 1607, this family-run food pub has been under new management since December 2011 and new head chef Wayne Rodgers has quickly gained a reputation for his high-quality cooking. Utilising plenty of Peak District produce, the menu combines traditional with contemporary dishes, all of which can be enjoyed in one of the four dining areas. Lunch (and maybe a pint of Druid Bitter) in the bar and snug; a more formal meal in the upper or lower restaurant; or outside on the terrace, from where you can survey the surrounding countryside. The constantly evolving menu ranges from light bites and sandwiches to two- and three-course meals. A starter such as jellied

pig's head with piccalilli and sourdough bread could precede Chatsworth Estate fallow deer stew with Yorkshire stump and juniper dumplings. End with Yorkshire blue cheese, pannacotta and Pontefract cake ice cream. Booking for meals may be required.

Open 11.30-11.30 (Tue 11.30-3 Sat 11.30am-mdnt Sun 11.30-4) Closed: 25 Dec, Mon-Tue Oct-Apr (open during Xmas) **Bar Meals** L served Mon-Sat 12-2.30, Sun 12-3 D served Mon-Thu 6-9, Fri-Sat 6-9.30 Av main course £12 **Restaurant** L served Mon-Sat 12-2.30, Sun 12-3 D served Mon-Thu 6-9, Fri-Sat 6-9.30 ⊕ FREE HOUSE ◀ Druid Bitter, Guest ale. ♈ 11 **Facilities** ✿ Children welcome Children's menu Children's portions Garden Parking ﹇ (notice required)

Red Lion Inn

PICK OF THE PUBS

Main St DE4 2BN ☎ 01629 650363
e-mail: red.lion@live.co.uk
dir: *5.5m from Matlock, off A6 onto B5056*

Built in 1680, The Red Lion started life as a farmhouse and gained its first licence in 1722. Its old well, now glass-covered, still remains in the taproom. Follow a walk to nearby Rowter Rocks, a gritstone summit affording stunning valley and woodland views, cosy up in the oak-beamed bar with its exposed stone walls, scrubbed oak tables, worn quarry-tiled floor, and welcoming atmosphere. Quaff a pint of locally brewed Nine Ladies or one of the other real ales on tap that change weekly, and refuel with a plate of home-cooked food prepared from predominantly local ingredients. Start with a Sardinian speciality from owner Matteo Frau's homeland, perhaps a selection of cured meats, cheese and olives, then follow with pork loin medallions with lemon, caper and sage butter, or field mushroom tart Tatin with Birchover blue cheese. Don't miss the Sardinian nights in winter and mid-July beer festival.

Open 12-2.30 6-11.30 (Sat & BH Mon 12-12 Sun 12-11) Closed: Mon in winter **Bar Meals** L served Tue-Sat 12-2, Sun 12-7 (winter) D served Tue-Sat 6-9 **Restaurant** L served Tue-Sat 12-2, Sun 12-7 (winter) D served Tue-Sat 6-9 ⊕ FREE HOUSE ◀ Peak Swift Nick, Nine Ladies, Peakstones Rock, Buxton, Thornbridge, Ichinusa (Sardinian) Ŏ Westons Perry & Old Rosie. **Facilities** Children welcome Children's portions Garden Beer festival Parking ﹇

BIRCH VALE
Map 16 SK08

The Waltzing Weasel Inn

PICK OF THE PUBS

New Mills Rd SK22 1BT ☎ 01663 743402
e-mail: info@waltzingweasel.co.uk
dir: *Village at junct of A6015 & A624, halfway between Glossop & Chapel-en-le-Frith*

Dramatic views of Kinder Scout set this 400-year-old quintessential English inn apart from the crowd. Situated beside the Sett Valley trail, it is an ideal spot for walkers. Although refurbished, the bar is still warmed by a real fire

and furnished with country antiques, while the restaurant enjoys more of those wonderful views from its mullioned windows. No games machines or piped music sully the atmosphere, so sit back with a pint of Sneck Lifter and choose from a menu of robust and reasonably priced dishes. In addition to soups, filled jackets, sandwiches and light bites, the lunch menu embraces starters such as button mushroom and blue cheese bake; or corned beef hash with soft poached egg. Main courses include proper steak-and-ale pie in a puff pastry case; and chargrilled gammon steak with hand-cut chunky chips.

Open all day all wk **Bar Meals** L served Mon-Fri 12-2, Sat-Sun all day D served Mon-Thu 6-9, Fri 6-9.30, Sat-Sun all day **Restaurant** L served Mon-Fri 12-2, Sat-Sun all day D served Mon-Thu 6-9, Fri 6-9.30, Sat-Sun all day ⊕ FREE HOUSE ◀ Jennings Sneck Lifter, Greene King IPA, Morland Old Speckled Hen, Worthington's, Guest ales. ♈ 10 **Facilities** Children welcome Children's menu Children's portions Garden Parking Wi-fi ﹇

BONSALL
Map 16 SK25

The Barley Mow NEW

The Dale DE4 2AY ☎ 01629 825685
e-mail: david.j.wragg@gmail.com
dir: *S from Matlock on A6 to Cromford. Right onto A5012 (Cromwell Hill). Right into Water Ln (A5012). Right in Clatterway towards Bonsall. Left at memorial into The Dale. Pub 400mtrs on right*

There are several reasons to visit this intimate, former lead miner's cottage: Bonsall is apparently Europe's UFO capital; the pub hosts the World Championship Hen Races; and landlords Colette and David display an unshakeable commitment to Peak District and other regional real ales, as their bank holiday beer festivals help to confirm. The simple menu is all about home-cooked pub grub, such as ham, egg and chips; scampi and chips; extra-mature rump steak; chicken curry; sausages and mash; beef chilli; and gammon steak.

Open 6-11 (Sat-Sun 12-11) Closed: Mon **Bar Meals** L served Sat-Sun 12-3 D served all wk 6-9 Av main course £8.95 ⊕ FREE HOUSE ◀ Thornbridge, Whim, Abbeydale, Blue Monkey Ŏ Hecks, Westons Perry. ♈ 10 **Facilities** ✿ Children welcome Children's menu Children's portions Beer festival Parking Wi-fi ﹇

BRASSINGTON
Map 16 SK25

Ye Olde Gate Inn

PICK OF THE PUBS

Well St DE4 4HJ ☎ 01629 540448
e-mail: info@oldgateinnbrassington.co.uk
dir: *2m from Carsington Water off A5023 between Wirksworth & Ashbourne*

Sitting beside an old London to Manchester turnpike in the heart of Brassington, a hill village on the southern edge of the Peak District, this venerable inn dates back to 1616. Aged beams (allegedly salvaged from the wrecked

Armada fleet), a black cast-iron log burner, an antique clock, charmingly worn quarry-tiled floors and a delightful mishmash of polished furniture give the inn plenty of character – as does the reputed ghost. Hand-pumped Jennings Cumberland takes pride of place behind the bar, alongside other Marston's beers and guest ales. The menu offers firm lunchtime favourites, such as home-made curry; or a range of filled baguettes. In the evening you may find a fillet of pork in pepper sauce served with rice; poached salmon fillet with a prawn and white wine sauce; or duck breast served with an orange and Cointreau sauce. Desserts range from a traditional apple crumble to a black cherry and white chocolate torte.

Open Tue eve-Sun Closed: Mon (ex BH), Tue L **Bar Meals** L served Wed-Sat 12-1.45, Sun 12.30-2.30 D served Tue-Sat 6.30-8.45 ⊕ MARSTON'S ◄ Pedigree, Jennings Cumberland Ale, Guest ales. **Facilities** Children welcome Children's portions Family room Garden Parking

CASTLETON　　　　　Map 16 SK18

The Peaks Inn

How Ln S33 8WJ ☎ 01433 620247
e-mail: info@peaksinn.com
dir: *On A6187 in centre of village*

There has been a change of hands at this refurbished stone-built pub standing below the ruins of Peveril Castle. An ideal place to recover after a country walk, the bar is warm and welcoming, with leather armchairs and open log fires plus a great range of real ales. The menu showcases plenty of local ingredients in dishes such as braised featherblade of beef with horseradish mash and Buxton Blue cheese and red onion tart. There is a heated garden and the pub hosts a beer festival in July.

Open all day all wk **Bar Meals** L served Mon-Fri 12-3, Sat 12-8.30, Sun 12-4 D served Mon-Fri 5.30-8.30, Sat 12-8.30 Av main course £8 **Restaurant** D served Mon-Fri 5.30-8.30 ⊕ PUNCH TAVERNS ◄ Kelham Island Easy Rider, Morland Old Speckled Hen, Guest ale ⓣ Westons Old Rosie & Traditional. ♥ 9 **Facilities** ♣ Children welcome Children's menu Children's portions Garden Beer festival Parking Wi-fi ▭

Ye Olde Nags Head

Cross St S33 8WH ☎ 01433 620248
e-mail: info@yeoldenagshead.co.uk
dir: *A625 from Sheffield, W through Hope Valley, through Hathersage & Hope. Pub on main road*

Situated in the heart of the Derbyshire Peak District National Park, close to Chatsworth House and Haddon Hall, this traditional 17th-century coaching inn continues to welcome thirsty travellers. Miles of wonderful walks and country lanes favoured by cyclists bring visitors seeking a warm welcome and refreshment in the cosy bars warmed by open fires. A recent refurbishment successfully mixes the contemporary with the traditional, a theme also reflected in the menu: expect the likes of bangers and mash pick 'n' mix and giant Yorkies –

Yorkshire puddings filled with the likes of game casserole.

Open all day all wk **Bar Meals** Av main course £9 food served all day **Restaurant** Fixed menu price fr £9.95 Av 3 course à la carte fr £19.95 food served all day ⊕ FREE HOUSE ◄ Timothy Taylor Landlord, Buxton Kinder Sunset, Kelham Island Riders on the Storm, Black Sheep, Guinness. **Facilities** ♣ Children welcome Children's menu Children's portions Beer festival Parking ▭

CHELMORTON　　　　Map 16 SK16

The Church Inn

SK17 9SL ☎ 01298 85319
e-mail: justinsatur@tiscali.co.uk
dir: *From A515 or A6 take A5270 between Bakewell & Buxton. Chelmorton signed*

Originally the Blacksmith's Arms, there has been a pub here since 1742. In the warm and welcoming bar, the modern décor combines well with original features. A menu of freshly prepared pub favourites might include Barnsley lamb chop with a rich minty gravy; rabbit pie topped with suet crust pastry; or mushroom Stroganoff with rice, salad and garlic bread, all washed down with a foaming pint of Marston's. Pennine Way walkers take note of this traditional stone inn between Buxton and Bakewell, as the long-distance trail passes the front door.

Open all wk 12-3 6-12 (Fri-Sun 12-12) **Bar Meals** L served Mon-Thu 12-2.30, Fri-Sun 12-9 D served all wk 6-9 Av main course £9.95 **Restaurant** L served Mon-Thu 12-2.30, Fri-Sun 12-9 D served all wk 6-9 ⊕ FREE HOUSE ◄ Marston's Burton Bitter & Pedigree, Adnams Southwold Bitter, Local ales. **Facilities** Children welcome Children's menu Children's portions Garden Wi-fi ▭

CHESTERFIELD　　　Map 16 SK37

Red Lion Pub & Bistro
PICK OF THE PUBS

Darley Rd, Stone Edge S45 0LW ☎ 01246 566142
e-mail: dine@redlionpubandbistro.co.uk
dir: *Telephone for directions*

On the edge of the Peak District National Park, the Red Lion dates back to 1788. Although it has seen many changes, it has retained much of its character. The original wooden beams and stone walls are now complemented by discreet lighting and comfy leather armchairs which add a thoroughly contemporary edge. Striking black-and-white photographs decorate the walls, whilst local jazz bands liven up the bar on Thursday evenings. Meals are served in the bar and bistro, or beneath umbrellas in the large garden. Seasonal produce drives the menu and the chefs make everything, from sauces to the hand-cut chips. Typical choices might start with pan-seared king scallops with black pudding and pea purée, followed by roast pepper and brie tart with red onion, tomato and herb salad, or Manor Farm lamb shank with creamed potato, caramelised onions and braised red

cabbage. Leave space for desserts like caramelised apple tart with Chantilly cream and mango coulis.

Open all day all wk **Bar Meals** L served Sun-Thu 12-9, Fri-Sat 12-9.30 D served Sun-Thu 12-9, Fri-Sat 12-9.30 food served all day **Restaurant** L served Sun-Thu 12-9, Fri-Sat 12-9.30 D served Sun-Thu 12-9, Fri-Sat 12-9.30 food served all day ⊕ FREE HOUSE ◄ Guest ales. ♥ **Facilities** Children welcome Children's menu Children's portions Garden Parking Wi-fi ▭

CHINLEY　　　　　Map 16 SK08

Old Hall Inn
PICK OF THE PUBS

See Pick of the Pubs on page 140

DERBY　　　　　　Map 11 SK33

The Alexandra Hotel

203 Siddals Rd DE1 2QE ☎ 01332 293993
e-mail: alexandrahotel@castlerockbrewery.co.uk
dir: *150yds from rail station*

This small hotel was built in 1871 and is named after the Danish princess who married the Prince of Wales, later Edward VII. It was also known as the Midland coffee house after the Midland Railway company, one of Derby's major employers. It is noted for its real ales from seven handpumps, and an annual beer festival confirms its serious approach to the amber liquid; real ciders, and bottled and draught continental beers complete the line-up at the bar. Simple food offerings include pies and filled rolls.

Open all day all wk 12-11 (Fri 12-12 Sat 11am-mdnt) **Bar Meals** food served all day ⊕ CASTLE ROCK ◄ Elsie Mo, Harvest Pale ⓣ Westons Old Rosie & Stowford Press. **Facilities** ♣ Children welcome Children's portions Garden Beer festival Parking Wi-fi

The Brunswick Inn

1 Railway Ter DE1 2RU ☎ 01332 290677
e-mail: thebrunswickinn@btconnect.com
dir: *From rail station turn right. Pub 100yds*

'A True Ale House and Brewery' it says on the sign outside this Grade II listed pub, which the Midland Railway built in the 1840s. It has no fewer than 16 handpumps, six for Brunswick ales brewed on the premises, the rest for guest beers. Real ciders are brought up from the cellar. Bar lunches are typically ploughman's, steak-and-ale pie, and chilli and cheese (either cheddar or stilton), which is billed on the menu as 'cha-cha-cha'. There's a beer festival during the first weekend in October.

Open all day all wk **Bar Meals** L served Mon-Wed 11.30-2.30, Fri-Sat 11.30-5, Sun 12-4 ⊕ BRUSWICK ◄ Brunswick, Guest ales ⓣ Westons Old Rosie, Westons 1st Quality. **Facilities** ♣ Children welcome Children's portions Family room Garden Beer festival ▭ **Notes** ▭

PICK OF THE PUBS

Old Hall Inn

CHINLEY　　　　Map 16 SK08

Whitehough SK23 6EJ
☎ **01663 750529**
e-mail: info@old-hall-inn.co.uk
web: www.old-hall-inn.co.uk
dir: *B5470 W from Chapel-en-le-Frith.
Right into Whitehough Head Ln. 0.8m to
inn*

Prime Peak District walking country lies all around this family-run, 16th-century pub attached to Whitehough Hall, an Elizabethan former manor house. Within easy reach are the iconic landscape features of Kinder Scout, Mam Tor and Stanage Edge, all very popular with climbers and fell-walkers, who head here and refreshment following their exertions. The good news is that there's a drinks list as long as your arm because the inn is a strong supporter of local breweries, and the popular bar delivers beers from Kelham Island, Red Willow, Thornbridge and many more, with Sheppy's from Somerset among the real ciders and perries. These are backed by all manner of bottled beers, particularly Belgian wheat, fruit and Trappist varieties, a remarkable choice of malts and gins, around 80 wines and various teas and herbal infusions. The food is greatly sought after too and the pub opens into the Minstrels' Gallery restaurant in the old manor house, where a short seasonal menu and daily specials offer freshly made 'small plates' of Derbyshire pressed lamb terrine in prosciutto with cumin and mint dressing; and haddock pieces in local ale batter with home-made tartare sauce. Larger

options are steaks, cooked six ways from blue to well done; pan-fried chicken supreme with sautéed chorizo; home-made Gloucester Old Spot pork sausages; roasted salmon fillet with lemon and dill cream sauce; and chicken and spinach curry. Desserts, some accompanied by Hilly Billy ice cream from nearby Blaze Farm, are all home-made, as are all the chutneys, pickles and sauces. Sandwiches are served at lunchtimes. This is very much a community pub and there's usually something going on, possibly one of the two annual beer and cider festivals (third weekend in September, fourth weekend in February). Booking for meals may be required.

Open all day all wk **Bar Meals** L served Mon-Sat 12-2, Sun 12-7.30 D served Mon-Thu 5-9, Fri-Sat 5-9.30, Sun 12-7.30 Av main course £10

Restaurant L served Mon-Sat 12-2, Sun 12-7.30 D served Mon-Thu 5-9, Fri-Sat 5-9.30, Sun 12-7.30 Av 3 course à la carte fr £18 ⊕ FREE HOUSE
◀ Marston's, Thornbridge, Phoenix, Abbeydale, Storm, Kelham Island, Red Willow ☼ Thatchers, Sheppy's, Westons.
♀ 12 **Facilities** Children welcome Children's menu Children's portions Garden Beer festival Parking Wi-fi 🚌

DOE LEA   Map 16 SK46

Hardwick Inn

Hardwick Park S44 5QJ ☎ 01246 850245
e-mail: batty@hardwickinn.co.uk
web: www.hardwickinn.co.uk
dir: M1 junct 29 take A6175. 0.5m left (signed Stainsby/
Hardwick Hall). After Stainsby, 2m, left at staggered
junct. Follow brown tourist signs

Dating from the 15th century and built of locally quarried
sandstone, this striking building was once the lodge for
Hardwick Hall (NT) and stands at the south gate of
Hardwick Park. Owned by the Batty family for three
generations, the pub has a rambling interior and features
period details such as mullioned windows, oak beams
and stone fireplaces. Traditional food takes in a popular
daily carvery roast, a salad bar, hearty home-made pies,
pot roasts and casseroles, as well as selections of fish
and vegetarian dishes. A handy pitstop for M1 travellers.
Booking for meals may be required.

Open all day all wk **Bar Meals** food served all day
Restaurant L served Tue-Sat 12-2, Sun 12-1 & 4-5.30 D
served Tue-Sat 6.30-8.30 ⊕ FREE HOUSE ◀ Theakston
Old Peculier & XB, Wells Bombardier, Bess of Hardwick,
Black Sheep ♻ Addlestones. ♟ 10 **Facilities** Children
welcome Children's menu Children's portions Play area
Family room Garden Parking ⛟

See advert below

EYAM   Map 16 SK27

Miners Arms

Water Ln S32 5RG ☎ 01433 630853
dir: Off B6521, 5m N of Bakewell

This welcoming 17th-century inn and restaurant was
built just before the plague hit Eyam; the village tailor
brought damp cloth from London and hung it to dry in
front of the fire so releasing the infected fleas. The pub
gets its name from the local lead mines of Roman times.
Now owned by Greene King, there's always the option to
pop in for a pint of their IPA or Ruddles Best bitter, or
enjoy a meal. A beer festival is held three times a year.

Open all wk Mon 12-3 5.30-12 Tue-Sun 12-12 **Bar
Meals** L served Mon-Sat 12-2, Sun 12-3 D served Mon
6-8, Tue-Fri 6-9, Sat 7-9 **Restaurant** L served Mon-Sat
12-2, Sun 12-3 D served Mon 6-8, Tue-Fri 6-9, Sat 7-9
⊕ GREENE KING ◀ IPA, Ruddles Best, Guest ales.
Facilities ✿ Children welcome Children's menu
Children's portions Garden Beer festival Parking ⛟

Bentley Brook Inn ★★★ INN

PICK OF THE PUBS

DE6 1LF ☎ **01335 350278**
e-mail: all@bentleybrookinn.co.uk
dir: *Telephone for directions*

This substantial farmhouse was created in 1805 from the shell of a medieval building that served the local manor. It became a restaurant in 1954, a full drinks licence was granted in the early 1970s, and in 2006/7 it was completely restored and refurbished. The substantial gabled, timbered frontage surveys the three acres of gardens and grounds. Beer fans will revel in the annual beer festival, held in late May or early June. Settle by the central open log fire in the bar and play dominoes, cards or chess, or peruse the menu. In the restaurant, which overlooks the terrace and garden, locally sourced, seasonal menus might offer starters of home-made chicken pâté with toasted foccacia or melon 'lasagne', a combination of melon and seasonal berries. Mains could include roasted fillet of salmon; home-made steak-and-ale pie with suet pastry crust; or rack of pork ribs. Eleven bedrooms make this inn the ideal base for exploring the peaceful Derbyshire Dales. Booking for meals may be required.

Open all day all wk 11-11 **Bar Meals** L served all wk 12-9 D served all wk 12-9 **Restaurant** L served all wk 12-9 D served all wk 12-9 ⊕ FREE HOUSE ◀ Leatherbritches Dr Johnson, Shepherd Neame Goldings, Marston's Pedigree, Sharp's Doom Bar. ♥ 10 **Facilities** ✿ Children welcome Play area Garden Beer festival Parking Wi-fi ⤶ **Rooms** 11

The Coach and Horses Inn

DE6 1LB ☎ **01335 350246**
e-mail: coachandhorses2@btconnect.com
dir: *On A515 (Ashbourne to Buxton road), 2.5m from Ashbourne*

A cosy refuge in any weather, this family-run, 17th-century coaching inn stands on the edge of the Peak District National Park. Besides the beautiful location, its charms include stripped wood furniture and low beams, real log-burning fires plus a welcoming and friendly atmosphere. Expect a great selection of real ales and good home cooking that is hearty and uses the best of local produce. Expect local specials and dishes like chicken breast wrapped in bacon with a stilton sauce; Tissington pork and leek sausages with red onion gravy and mash; or vegetable and three-cheese tart served with

ratatouille. Hot and cold sandwiches and baguettes provide lighter options.

Open all day all wk 11-11 (Sun 12-10.30) **Bar Meals** food served all day **Restaurant** food served all day ⊕ FREE HOUSE ◀ Marston's Pedigree, Oakham JHB, Peak Swift Nick, Whim Hartington Bitter, Derby. **Facilities** Children welcome Children's menu Family room Garden Parking ⤶ (notice required)

The Bulls Head Inn ★★★★ INN

S32 5QR ☎ **01433 630873**
e-mail: wilbnd@aol.com
dir: *Just off A623, N of Stoney Middleton*

In an upland village surrounded by a lattice-work of dry-stone walls, this 19th-century former coaching inn is the epitome of the English country pub. Well, with open fires, oak beams, flagstone floors, great views and good food and beer, it has to be. The bar serves Black Sheep and Peak Ales, lunchtime snacks and sandwiches, while main meals include Cumberland sausages and Yorkshire pudding; beef Wellington with red wine gravy; sea bream fillets with lemon butter; Mediterranean vegetable hotpot; and even ostrich steak with brandied game gravy. Bedrooms are well-equipped.

Open 12-3 6.30-11 (Sun all day) Closed: Mon (ex BH) **Bar Meals** L served Tue-Sun 12-2 D served Tue-Sun 6.30-9 Av main course £10 **Restaurant** L served Tue-Sun 12-2 D served Tue-Sun 6.30-9 Av 3 course à la carte fr £20 ⊕ FREE HOUSE ◀ Black Sheep, Peak, Adnams, Tetley. **Facilities** ✿ Children welcome Children's menu Children's portions Parking ⤶ **Rooms** 3

The Chequers Inn ★★★★ INN ◉

PICK OF THE PUBS

Froggatt Edge S32 3ZJ ☎ **01433 630231**
e-mail: info@chequers-froggatt.com
dir: *On A625, 0.5m N of Calver*

The Chequers is an excellent base for exploring the Peak District, with Chatsworth House in close proximity. Originally four stone-built 18th-century cottages, this traditional country inn nestles below beautiful Froggatt Edge. A haven for walkers, its westward panorama is reached by a steep, wild woodland footpath from the elevated secret garden. The comfortable interior of wooden floors, antiques and blazing log fires is perfect for a relaxing pint of Bakewell Best Bitter or one of the guest ales. The food on the innovative modern European menu is prepared from locally sourced produce, such as sausages from Paul Bowyer Butchers in Hathersage and ice cream from Bradwell's. Starters, desserts and specials are listed on the blackboards. Mains take in chicken and chorizo risotto with parmesan crisp and chorizo oil; and spinach and goat's cheese tagliatelle. There are six en suite bedrooms available.

Open all day all wk Closed: 25 Dec **Bar Meals** L served Mon-Fri 12-2.30, Sat 12-9.30, Sun 12-9 D served Mon-Fri

6-9.30, Sat 12-9.30, Sun 12-9 Av main course £13-£17 ⊕ FREE HOUSE ◀ Kelham Island Easy Rider, Peak Bakewell Best Bitter, Wells Bombardier, Bradfield Farmers Blonde, Guest ales. ♥ 10 **Facilities** Children welcome Children's menu Children's portions Garden Parking Wi-fi **Rooms** 6

The Queen Anne Inn ★★★ INN

SK17 8RF ☎ **01298 871246**
e-mail: angelaryan100@aol.com
dir: *A623 onto B6049, turn off at Anchor pub towards Bradwell, 2nd right to Great Hucklow*

The sheltered south-facing garden of this traditional country free house has stunning open views. The inn dates from 1621; a licence has been held for over 300 years, and the names of all the landlords are known. Inside you'll find an open fire in the stone fireplace, good food made using locally sourced produce, and an ever-changing range of cask ales. The inn has an AA Dinner Award in recognition of the quality of the food on offer; popular choices include sea bass fillet with parmesan crust; steak-and-kidney pudding; and steamed mussels with freshly baked bread. There is a child-friendly south-facing garden and two guest bedrooms available.

Open 12-2.30 5-11 (Fri-Sun 12-11) Closed: Mon **Bar Meals** L served Tue-Sun 12-2 D served Tue-Thu 6-8.30, Fri-Sat 6-9, Sun 6-8 **Restaurant** L served Tue-Sun 12-2 D served Tue-Thu 6-8.30, Fri-Sat 6-9, Sun 6-8 ⊕ FREE HOUSE ◀ Tetley's Cask, Local guest ales ○ Westons Stowford Press. ♥ 9 **Facilities** ✿ Children welcome Children's menu Children's portions Family room Garden Parking ⤶ **Rooms** 2

The Maynard ★★★ HL ◉◉

PICK OF THE PUBS

Main Rd S32 2HE ☎ **01433 630321**
e-mail: enquiries@themaynard.co.uk
dir: *From M1 junct 30 take A619 into Chesterfield, then onto Baslow. A623 to Calver, right into Grindleford*

Formerly a coaching inn, this imposing stone hotel stands below the steep, wooded crags of Froggatt Edge overlooking the village and the Derwent Valley beyond, and is situated in the heart of the Peak National Park. The capacious beer garden offers stunning panoramas across moorland and river valley. Continuing the Peakland theme, beer from Chatsworth's own estate brewery may be sampled in the Longhaw Bar, where a good-value lunch menu might include twice-baked smoked salmon soufflé, or fish and garden pea pie. For some of the best cuisine in the Midlands, however, head for the Maynard Restaurant where chef Ben Hickinson creates menus which have gained two AA Rosettes; rabbit and smoked bacon ravioli with thyme and mustard cream might be followed by venison with baked potato cake and carrot and tarragon purée, or baked sea trout with chive and caviar cream sauce. For pudding, try the warm chocolate tart with red berry sorbet.

Open all day all wk 11-9 **Bar Meals** L served all wk 12-2 D served all wk 7-9 **Restaurant** L served all wk 12-2 D served all wk 7-9 ⊕ FREE HOUSE ◀ Abbeydale Moonshine, Peak Bakewell Best Bitter. **Facilities** Children welcome Children's menu Garden Parking Wi-fi 🚌 **Rooms** 10

HARDSTOFT   Map 16 SK46

The Shoulder at
Hardstoft ★★★★ INN ⊛⊛ NEW

Deep Ln S45 8AF ☎ **01246 850276**
e-mail: info@thefamousshoulder.co.uk
dir: *From B6039 follow signs for Hardwick Hall. 1st right into car park*

Just ten minutes from the M1, this refurbished 300-year-old pub is an ideal base for exploring the Peak District and Sherwood Forest. Peak Ales Bakewell Best is one of the local beers available in the bar, with its open log fires. The kitchen sources all ingredients within 15 miles of the pub where possible, with the exception of fish, which is from sustainable sources. In the two AA Rosette restaurant, a typical menu might include hand-dived scallops with glazed pig's cheek followed by Chatsworth lamb with sage gnocchi. Accommodation is available.

Open all day all wk **Bar Meals** food served all day **Restaurant** Fixed menu price fr £15 food served all day ⊕ FREE HOUSE ◀ Peak Bakewell Best Bitter, Thornbridge Jaipur, Greene King Abbot Ale. 🍷 10 **Facilities** 🐾 Children welcome Children's portions Parking Wi-fi 🚌 (notice required) **Rooms** 4

HARTSHORNE   Map 10 SK32

The Mill Wheel ★★★★ INN ⊛

Ticknall Rd DE11 7AS ☎ **01283 550335**
e-mail: info@themillwheel.co.uk
dir: *M42 junct 2 follow signs for A511 to Woodville, left onto A514 towards Derby to Hartshorne*

This building's long life has included stints as a corn mill, saw mill and an iron furnace. Its huge mill wheel has survived for some 250 years. Since being restored and converted into a pub, the wheel has been slowly turning once again, and is very much the focus of attention in the bar and restaurant. Mill Wheel Bitter is available along with the AA-Rosette cuisine. The à la carte menu changes monthly and offers dishes such as pan-fried delice of salmon, aromatic rice, wilted spinach with damson and ginger coulis. If you want to stay over, there are modern bedrooms available.

Open all wk (Sat-Sun all day) **Bar Meals** L served Mon-Sat 12-2.30, Sun 12-7 D served Mon-Thu 6-9.15, Fri-Sat 6-9.30, Sun 12-7 Av main course £8.95 **Restaurant** L served Mon-Sat 12-2.30, Sun 12-7 D served Mon-Thu 6-9.15, Fri-Sat 6-9.30, Sun 12-7 Av 3 course à la carte fr £24.20 ⊕ FREE HOUSE ◀ Mill Wheel Bitter, Greene King Abbot Ale, Hop Back Summer Lightning,

Marston's Pedigree, Bass. **Facilities** Children welcome Children's portions Garden Beer festival Parking Wi-fi 🚌 **Rooms** 4

HASSOP   Map 16 SK27

Eyre Arms

DE45 1NS ☎ **01629 640390**
e-mail: nick@eyrearms.com
dir: *On B6001 N of Bakewell*

Ivy-clad and resolutely traditional, this charming free house started life as a farmstead and 17th-century coaching inn and has been proudly run by the same family for 18 years. Views of rolling Peak District countryside from the secluded garden can only be improved with a pint of Bakewell Best in hand, brewed on the nearby Chatsworth Estate. Oak settles, low ceilings and cheery log fires create a cosy atmosphere, ideal surroundings for enjoying dishes such as Grand Marnier duckling; local rainbow trout baked with butter and almonds; or braised pheasant cooked in a Madeira, mushroom and bacon sauce.

Open all wk 11-3 6.30-11 Closed: 25 Dec **Bar Meals** L served all wk 12-2 D served all wk 6.30-9 Av main course £10.95 ⊕ FREE HOUSE ◀ Peak Bakewell Best Bitter, Swift Nick & Chatsworth Gold, Black Sheep ⚬ Westons Stowford Press. 🍷 9 **Facilities** Children welcome Children's menu Children's portions Garden Parking

HATHERSAGE   Map 16 SK28

Millstone Inn ★★★★ INN

Sheffield Rd S32 1DA ☎ **01433 650258**
e-mail: enquiries@millstoneinn.co.uk
dir: *Telephone for directions*

Striking views over the picturesque Hope Valley are afforded from this former coaching inn, set amid the beauty of the Peak District yet convenient for the city of Sheffield. The atmospheric bar serves six traditional cask ales all year round and the menu offers a good choice of dishes prepared from local produce, including a popular Sunday carvery of freshly roasted joints. Accommodation is available.

Open all day all wk 11.30-11 **Bar Meals** L served all wk 12-9 D served all wk 12-9 **Restaurant** L served all wk 12-9 D served all wk 12-9 ⊕ FREE HOUSE ◀ Timothy Taylor Landlord, Black Sheep, Guest ales. 🍷 16 **Facilities** 🐾 Children welcome Garden Parking 🚌 **Rooms** 8

The Plough Inn ★★★★ INN ⊛

PICK OF THE PUBS

See Pick of the Pubs on page 144

The Scotsmans Pack Country
Inn ★★★★ INN

School Ln S32 1BZ ☎ **01433 650253**
e-mail: scotsmans.pack@btinternet.com
web: www.scotsmanspack.com
dir: *Hathersage is on A625 8m from Sheffield. Pub near church and Little John's Grave*

Set in the beautiful Hope Valley on one of the old packhorse trails used by Scottish 'packmen', this traditional inn is a short walk from Hathersage church and Little John's Grave. The pub offers hearty dishes such as lamb's liver and bacon or rabbit casserole, best washed down with a pint of Jennings Cumberland. Weather permitting, head outside onto the sunny patio, next to the trout stream. A perfect base for walking and touring the Peak District, it has five individually designed en suite bedrooms for those who wish to stay. Booking for meals may be required.

Open all day all wk 11-3 6-12 (Fri-Sun all day) **Bar Meals** L served Mon-Fri 12-2, Sat-Sun 12-9 D served Mon-Fri 6-9, Sat-Sun 12-9 ⊕ MARSTON'S ◀ Pedigree, Jennings Cumberland Ale, Mansfield Original Bitter. 🍷 10 **Facilities** Children welcome Children's menu Children's portions Family room Garden Parking Wi-fi 🚌 **Rooms** 5

HAYFIELD   Map 16 SK08

The Royal Hotel

Market St SK22 2EP ☎ **01663 742721**
e-mail: enquiries@theroyalhayfield.co.uk
dir: *Off A624*

Dating from 1755, this is a fine-looking former vicarage in an attractive High Peak village. The oak-panelled bar offers Hydes and guest ales, and traditional snacks and light dishes; the Dining Room offers a good choice from the carte. Or you could try the family lounge, popular with the local cricket team whose ground is next door. From the patio, the windswept plateau of Kinder Scout looks impressive. A beer festival is held during the first weekend in October.

Open all day all wk 9am-mdnt **Bar Meals** L served Mon-Fri 12-2.30, Sat 12-9, Sun 12-6 D served Mon-Fri 6-9, Sat 12-9, Sun 12-6 **Restaurant** L served Mon-Fri 12-2.30, Sat 12-9, Sun 12-6 D served Mon-Fri 6-9, Sat 12-9, Sun 12-6 ⊕ FREE HOUSE ◀ Hydes, Guest ales ⚬ Westons Stowford Press. 🍷 **Facilities** Children welcome Children's menu Children's portions Family room Garden Beer festival Parking Wi-fi 🚌 (notice required)

PICK OF THE PUBS

The Plough Inn ★★★★ INN ❀

HATHERSAGE Map 16 SK28

Leadmill Bridge S32 1BA
☎ **01433 650319 & 650180**
e-mail: sales@theploughinn-hathersage.co.uk
web: www.theploughinn-hathersage.co.uk
dir: *M1 junct 29, take A617W, A619, A623, then B6001 N to Hathersage*

The lively waters of Highlow Brook were once harnessed here to drive waterwheels which turned stones, first to grind corn and later crushers to release lead ore from rock mined in the hills of the surrounding Peak District. Trains of packhorses would have moved the ore; perhaps the overseers had home-brewed beer here three centuries ago, starting a tradition which has culminated in today's notable roadside inn near the banks of the glorious River Derwent; the inn's nine-acre riverside estate stretches to the old bridge carrying the Derwent Valley Heritage Way across the rapids here. Smart red tartan carpets complement open fires, wooden beams and copper details on the bar, where Adnams, Black Sheep and Timothy Taylor ales are hand pulled. An extensive British menu featuring carefully sourced local produced has achieved the award of one AA Rosette for Bob Emery and his enthusiastic team. The homely bar and restaurant, cobbled courtyard or glorious beer garden are all great locations to settle in and anticipate some well-prepared

dishes. Typically, begin with home-smoked venison with blackberry vinaigrette; or scallops with maple-glazed pork belly and five-spice roast quince. Move on to seared lambs' liver with champ, French beans and red wine jus; or roast salmon with crushed potato, wilted rocket and a tomato beurre blanc. Sandwiches, salads and lighter meals like lasagne and salad; and butternut squash, goat's cheese and sage risotto are served during the day. Guests can stroll through the landscaped grounds before retiring to the beautifully appointed accommodation in the inn or converted barns across the secluded courtyard. Booking for meals may be required.

Open all day all wk 11-11 (Sun 12-10.30) Closed: 25 Dec **Bar Meals** Av main course £15 food served all day **Restaurant** Fixed menu price fr £24 Av 3 course à la carte fr £30 food served all day ⊕ FREE HOUSE ◼ Adnams, Black Sheep, Timothy Taylor, Bass Extra Smooth. ⬤ 15 **Facilities** Children welcome Children's menu Children's portions ❖ Garden Parking Wi-fi **Rooms** 5

HOGNASTON Map 16 SK25

The Red Lion Inn

Main St DE6 1PR ☎ 01335 370396
e-mail: enquiries@redlionhognaston.org.uk
web: www.redlionhognaston.org.uk
dir: *From Ashbourne take B5035 towards Wirksworth. Approx 5m follow Carsington Water signs. Turn right to Hognaston*

A traditional 17th-century pub with an open fire, old-style furnishings and abundant antiques, overlooking Carsington Water on the edge of the Peak District. The menu features dishes made from top-quality Derbyshire produce, including those old favourites steak-and-ale pie, and fish and chips, as well as beef Stroganoff and basmati rice; Gressingham duck breast with black cherry sauce; fresh haddock and leeks in creamy white sauce; and vegetarian Wellington. With the weather on your side, enjoy a Derbyshire-brewed beer in the garden and try your hand at boules.

Open all wk 12-3 6-11 **Bar Meals** L served all wk 12-2.30 D served all wk 6.30-9 **Restaurant** L served all wk 12-2.30 D served all wk 6.30-9 FREE HOUSE Marston's Pedigree, Greene King Ruddles County, Derby, Black Sheep, Guinness Westons Old Rosie. 9 **Facilities** Children welcome Children's portions Garden Parking Wi-fi

HOPE Map 16 SK18

Cheshire Cheese Inn

Edale Rd S33 6ZF ☎ 01433 620381
e-mail: laura@thecheshirecheeseinn.co.uk
dir: *On A6187 between Sheffield & Castleton, turn N at Hope Church onto Edale Rd*

Originally a farm, this 17th-century inn used to provide salt-carriers crossing the Pennines to Yorkshire with overnight lodgings, for which they paid in cheese. In the unspoilt atmosphere of today's pub payment is made the conventional way, but cheese with tomato, onion or pickle makes a good sandwich with a locally brewed real ale. Other home-made food includes main meals such as gammon steak with fried egg and chips; steak-and-kidney pudding; beer-battered Grimsby haddock; and large Yorkshire pud with local sausages. Dogs are welcome in the inn and beer garden. Booking for meals may be required.

Open Tue-Sun 12-3 6-late (Sat-Sun all day) Closed: Mon (out of season) **Bar Meals** L served Tue-Fri 12-2, Sat 12-3, Sun 12-4 D served Tue-Sat 6-9 Av main course £10-£15 ENTERPRISE INNS Peak Swift Nick, Bradfield Farmers Blonde, Kelham Island Easy Rider Addlestones. **Facilities** Children welcome Children's portions Family room Garden Parking Wi-fi (notice required)

INGLEBY Map 11 SK32

The John Thompson Inn & Brewery

DE73 7HW ☎ 01332 862469
e-mail: nick@johnthompsoninn.com
dir: *From A38 between Derby and Burton upon Trent take A5132 towards Barrow upon Trent. At mini rdbt right onto B5008 (signed Repton). At rdbt 1st exit into Brook End. Right onto Milton Rd. Left, left again to Ingleby*

This 15th-century farmhouse became a pub in 1968, taking its name from licensee and owner John Thompson. Now run by son Nick, this traditional brewpub is set in idyllic countryside beside the banks of the River Trent with views of the neighbouring National Forest. This relaxed inn has a wealth of original features and is a friendly place to enjoy a pint of home-brewed JTS XXX and tuck into sarnies, jacket potatoes or order from the carvery menu. Other options include salads; gammon, egg and chips; and Mediterranean vegetable risotto.

Open Tue-Fri 11-2.30 6-11 (Sat-Sun 11-11 Mon 6-11) Closed: Mon L **Bar Meals** L served Tue-Sun 12-2 Av main course £7.45 **Restaurant** L served Tue-Sun 12-2 FREE HOUSE John Thompson JTS XXX, St Nick's, Gold, Rich Porter. 9 **Facilities** Children welcome Children's portions Family room Garden Parking Wi-fi

KIRK IRETON Map 16 SK25

Barley Mow Inn

DE6 3JP ☎ 01335 370306
dir: *Telephone for directions*

Built on the edge of the Peak District National Park by the Storer family of yeomen farmers in the 16th century, the building became an inn during the early 1700s. The imposing free house has remained largely unchanged over the years, and has been run by Mary Short since 1976. Six nine-gallon barrels of beer stand behind the bar, with cheese and pickle or salami rolls and bar snacks on offer at lunchtime. Tea and coffee is always available. Close to Carsington Water, there are good walking opportunities on nearby marked paths.

Open all wk 12-2 7-11 (Sun 12-2 7-10.30) Closed: 25 Dec, 1 Jan FREE HOUSE Whim Hartington Bitter, Guest ales Thatchers. **Facilities** Children welcome Garden Parking **Notes**

LITTLE HAYFIELD Map 16 SK08

Lantern Pike

45 Glossop Rd SK22 2NG ☎ 01663 747590
e-mail: tomandstella@lanternpikeinn.co.uk
dir: *On A624, between Glossop and Chapel-en-le-Frith*

Dating from 1783 when it was built as a farmhouse, this creeper-clad building in the Peak District was converted into a pub in 1844. Over a century later it was renamed the Lantern Pike, after an ancient beacon on the hill behind the inn. Hungry ramblers and riders indulge in seasonal dishes created by chef Chris Caldwell, such as black pudding tartlet, peppered mackerel, and stuffed peppers. Relax in the patio-garden with its grand vista of Lantern Pike hill, or indulge in a bit of 'Corrie' nostalgia – it was here that Tony Warren created the series; the original Rover's Return swing doors adorn the bar. Booking for meals may be required.

Open Mon 5-12, Tue-Fri 12-3 5-12 (Sat-Sun all day) Closed: 25 Dec, Mon L **Bar Meals** L served Tue-Fri 12-2.30, Sat-Sun 12-8.30 D served Mon 5-8, Tue-Fri 5-8.30, Sat-Sun 12-8.30 Av main course £10 **Restaurant** L served Tue-Fri 12-2.30, Sat-Sun 12-8.30 D served Mon 5-8, Tue-Fri 5-8.30, Sat-Sun 12-8.30 Av 3 course à la carte fr £17 ENTERPRISE INNS Timothy Taylor Landlord, Whim Hartington Bitter, Castle Rock Harvest Pale. **Facilities** Children welcome Children's menu Children's portions Garden Parking Wi-fi (notice required)

LITTON Map 16 SK17

Red Lion Inn

SK17 8QU ☎ 01298 871458
e-mail: theredlionlitton@yahoo.co.uk
dir: *Just off A623 (Chesterfield to Stockport road), 1m E of Tideswell*

The Red Lion is a beautiful, traditional pub on the village green, very much at the heart of the local community. It became a pub in 1787 when it was converted from three farm cottages. With its wood fires, selection of well-kept real ales and friendly atmosphere, it's a favourite with walkers and holiday-makers too. The menu offers hearty pub food at reasonable prices, such as Thai fishcakes with sweet chilli dip to start; Derbyshire lamb hotpot; steak-and-kidney pie; or South African Bobotie to follow; and apple and berry crumble with custard to finish. A gluten-free menu is available. Only children over six years of age are welcome.

Open all day all wk **Bar Meals** L served Mon-Wed 12-8, Thu-Sun 12-8.30 D served Mon-Wed 12-8, Thu-Sun 12-8.30 food served all day **Restaurant** food served all day ENTERPRISE INNS Abbeydale Absolution, 2 Guest ales. 10 **Facilities** Children's portions

MATLOCK — Map 16 SK35

The Red Lion ★★★ INN

65 Matlock Green DE4 3BT ☎ 01629 584888

dir: *From Chesterfield, A632 into Matlock, on right just before junct with A615*

This friendly, family-run free house makes a good base for exploring local attractions like Chatsworth House, Carsington Water and Dovedale. Spectacular walks in the local countryside help to work up an appetite for bar lunches, or great tasting home-cooked dishes in the homely restaurant. On Sunday there's a popular carvery with freshly cooked gammon, beef, pork, lamb and turkey. In the winter months, open fires burn in the lounge and games room, and there's a boules area in the attractive beer garden for warmer days. Some of the ales from the bar were brewed on the Chatsworth Estate. There are six comfortable bedrooms.

Open all day all wk **Bar Meals** L served Tue-Fri 12-2 **Restaurant** L served Sun 12-2.45 D served Tue-Sat 7-9 ⊕ FREE HOUSE ◀ Marston's Pedigree, Morland Old Speckled Hen, Peak, Guest ales. **Facilities** Garden Parking Wi-fi ➡ **Rooms** 6

MELBOURNE — Map 11 SK32

The Melbourne Arms ★★★ INN

92 Ashby Rd DE73 8ES ☎ 01332 864949 & 863990

e-mail: info@melbournearms.co.uk

dir: *M1 junct 23A, A453 signed East Midlands (airport) to Isley Walton, right signed Melbourne, pass Donington Park to Melbourne*

On the outskirts of the Georgian market town of Melbourne and close to East Midlands Airport, this Grade II listed, 18th-century inn has housed a popular Indian restaurant for 15 years now. There are two bars, a coffee lounge and a traditionally decorated restaurant where an extensive menu of authentic Indian dishes is offered. Popular with families, you can stay over in one of the modern, thoughtfully equipped bedrooms, many of which have views of the countryside. Booking for meals may be required.

Open all day all wk Closed: 26 Dec **Bar Meals** L served all wk 12-3 D served all wk 3-6 Av main course £11 **Restaurant** L served all wk 12-3.30 D served all wk 3.30-11.30 Fixed menu price fr £15 Av 3 course à la carte fr £16 food served all day ⊕ FREE HOUSE/DARSHANTI UK LTD ◀ Marston's Pedigree. **Facilities** Children welcome Children's menu Children's portions Play area Garden Parking Wi-fi ➡ (notice required) **Rooms** 10

MIDDLE HANDLEY — Map 16 SK47

Devonshire Arms NEW

Lightwood Ln S21 5RN ☎ 01246 434800

dir: *B6052 from Eckington towards Chesterfield. 1.5m*

This stone-built pub dates back 150 years but a tasteful refurbishment five years ago restored it to its original splendour. The stylish interior mixes contemporary touches with original features including a grandfather clock and open fireplace. In the separate dining room with its view of the partially open kitchen, the focus is on modern British dishes created from top-top local produce – perhaps black pudding potato cake with soft poached egg and mustard mayonnaise, followed by herb-crusted rack of lamb. Wash it down with a pint of local Chatsworth Gold ale.

Open all day Closed: Mon ex BHs **Bar Meals** L served Tue-Thu 12-9, Fri-Sat 12-10, Sun 12-6 D served Tue-Thu 12-9, Fri-Sat 12-10, Sun 12-6 food served all day **Restaurant** L served Tue-Thu 12-9, Fri-Sat 12-10, Sun 12-6 D served Tue-Thu 12-9, Fri-Sat 12-10, Sun 12-6 Fixed menu price fr £13.95 food served all day ⊕ FREE HOUSE ◀ Bradfield Farmers Blonde, Kelham Island Pride of Sheffield, Peak Chatsworth Gold. **Facilities** ❤ Children welcome Children's menu Children's portions Parking Wi-fi

MILLTOWN — Map 16 SK36

The Nettle Inn

S45 0ES ☎ 01246 590462

e-mail: marcus.sloan@thenettleinn.co.uk

dir: *Telephone for directions*

A 16th-century hostelry on the edge of the Peak District, this inn has all the traditional charm you could wish for, from flower-filled hanging baskets to log fires and a stone-flagged taproom floor. Expect well-kept ales such as Bakewell Best, and impressive home-made food using the best of seasonal produce. Typical bar options are Armstrong's chicken and leek pie or chargrilled pork chop and plenty of sandwiches, while on the restaurant menu dishes such as wild salmon roulade or roast broccoli and rosemary filo parcel may tempt.

Open all wk 12-2.30 5.30-11 (Sun 12-10) **Bar Meals** Av main course £9.75 **Restaurant** Av 3 course à la carte fr £27 ⊕ FREE HOUSE ◀ Peak Swift Nick, Bakewell Best Bitter, DPA. ₹ 9 **Facilities** Children welcome Children's menu Children's portions Garden Parking Wi-fi ➡

NEW MILLS — Map 16 SK08

Pack Horse Inn

Mellor Rd SK22 4QQ ☎ 01663 742365

e-mail: info@packhorseinn.co.uk

dir: *From A6 at Newtown take A6015 to New Mills. At lights left into Union Rd (B6101) signed Marple. At mini rdbt right into Market St, becomes Spring Bank Rd. Approx 1m left into Mellor Rd. 0.5m to pub*

Overlooking the valley of the River Sett, with views towards Kinder Scout, the Pack Horse is situated in the heart of the Peak District. This former farmhouse is an ideal base to explore the surrounding countryside or a pleasant pitstop between Sheffield and Manchester. The pub uses as much local produce as possible and the enticing menu might include Peak-reared lamb cutlets, mushrooms, tomatoes and peas, or local butchers' sausages with onion gravy and mash. Booking for meals may be required.

Open all wk 12-3 5-11 (Fri-Sat 12-12 Sun 12-10.30) **Bar Meals** L served Mon-Thu 12-2, Fri-Sun all day D served Mon-Thu 5-9.30, Fri-Sat until 9.30pm, Sun until 8pm **Restaurant** L served Mon-Thu 12-2, Fri-Sun all day D served Mon-Thu 5-9.30, Fri-Sat until 9.30pm, Sun until 8pm ⊕ FREE HOUSE ◀ Phoenix Arizona, 2 Guest ales. ₹ 14 **Facilities** Children welcome Children's menu Children's portions Garden Parking Wi-fi

PILSLEY — Map 16 SK27

The Devonshire Arms at Pilsley ★★★ INN

High St DE45 1UL ☎ 01246 583258

e-mail: res@devonshirehotels.co.uk

dir: *From A619, in Baslow, at rdbt take 1st exit onto B6012. Follow signs to Chatsworth, 2nd right to Pilsley*

Here is a fabulous old stone pub nestling in an estate village amidst the rolling parkland surrounding Chatsworth House, the 'Palace of The Peaks'. It's also an ideal base for visiting Matlock Bath and Castleton. There are open fires, Peak Ales from the estate's brewery and meats, game and greens from the adjacent estate shop, all sourced from these productive acres at the heart of the Peak District. A mixed grill, corned beef hash or minted lamb hotpot is a filling repast after a day's exploration of the area. Stop over at the luxurious accommodation designed by the Duchess of Devonshire.

Open all day all wk **Bar Meals** L served all wk 12-2.30 D served all wk 5-9 ⊕ FREE HOUSE ◀ Thornbridge Jaipur, Peak Chatsworth Gold, Guest ales. ₹ 12 **Facilities** Children welcome Children's menu Children's portions Parking Wi-fi **Rooms** 7

ROWSLEY — Map 16 SK26

The Grouse & Claret ★★★★ INN

Station Rd DE4 2EB ☎ 01629 733233

dir: *On A6 between Matlock & Bakewell*

A venue popular with local anglers, this 18th-century pub takes its name from a fishing fly. Situated at the gateway to the Peak District National Park, it is handy for visits to the stately homes of Haddon Hall and Chatsworth House. After quenching the thirst with a pint of Marston's, the colourful menu promises a selection of well-priced and tasty pub meals: garlic mushrooms; pâté in a pot; pork rump in plum sauce; and Creole chicken are typical. Parents look on enviously as their offspring consume toffee apple wedges from the children's menu.

Open all day all wk **Bar Meals** L served Mon-Sat 12-9, Sun 12-8 D served Mon-Sat 12-9, Sun 12-8 Av main course £7.95 food served all day **Restaurant** L served Mon-Sat 12-9, Sun 12-8 D served Mon-Sat 12-9, Sun 12-8 food served all day ⊕ MARSTON'S ◀ Pedigree, Bank's Bitter, Jennings Cumberland Ale. ₹ 16 **Facilities** Children welcome Children's portions Play area Garden Parking Wi-fi ➡ **Rooms** 8

SHARDLOW   Map 11 SK43

The Old Crown Inn

Cavendish Bridge DE72 2HL ☎ 01332 792392
e-mail: jamesvize@hotmail.co.uk
dir: *M1 junct 24 take A6 towards Derby. Left before river,
bridge into Shardlow*

Up to nine real ales are served at this family-friendly pub
on the south side of the River Trent, where there's a beer
festival twice a year. Built as a coaching inn during the
17th century, it retains its warm and atmospheric
interior. Several hundred water jugs hang from the
ceilings, while the walls display an abundance of brewery
and railway memorabilia. Traditional food is lovingly
prepared by the landlady; main meals focus on pub
classics such as home-made steak-and-kidney pie; ham,
eggs and chips; lasagne; curry; steaks; and daily
specials. Monday night is quiz night, and there's folk
music every Tuesday.

Open all day all wk 11am-11.30pm (Fri-Sat
11am-12.30am Sun 11-11) **Bar Meals** L served Tue-Fri
12-2, Sat 12-8, Sun 12-3 D served Tue-Fri 5-8, Sat 12-8
Restaurant L served Tue-Fri 12-2, Sat 12-8, Sun 12-3
D served Tue-Fri 5-8, Sat 12-8 ∰ MARSTON'S ◀ Pedigree
& Old Empire, Jennings Cocker Hoop, Guest ales.
Facilities Children welcome Children's menu Children's
portions Play area Garden Beer festival Parking
▭ (notice required)

STANTON IN PEAK   Map 16 SK26

The Flying Childers Inn

Main Rd DE4 2LW ☎ 01629 636333
dir: *From A6 (between Matlock & Bakewell) follow
Youlgrave signs. Onto B5056 to Ashbourne. Follow
Stanton in Peak signs*

Set in the heart of the Peak District and surrounded by
beautiful walking country, The Flying Childers was named
after a champion racehorse owned by the 4th Duke of
Devonshire. This stone-built village pub is now a cosy
bolt-hole offering open fires, real ales, a well-considered
wine list and reasonably priced lunchtime food such as
liver and vegetable casserole, filled cobs (including
pheasant) and toasties. Canine visitors are treated just
as well as their owners with doggy bar snacks. Head
outside to the lovely beer garden in summer.

Open all wk 12-2 7-11 (Mon-Tue 7pm-11pm Sat-Sun
12-3 7-11) **Bar Meals** L served Wed-Sun 12-2 Av main
course £3.80 ∰ FREE HOUSE ◀ Wells Bombardier, Guest
ales. **Facilities** ✿ Children welcome Garden Parking
Notes ▭

TIDESWELL   Map 16 SK17

The George Hotel

Commercial Rd SK17 8NU ☎ 01298 871382
e-mail: simon@tght.co.uk
dir: *A619 to Baslow, A623 towards Chapel-en-le-Frith,
0.25m*

Built in 1730, this delightful stone-built coaching inn
stands in the shadow of St John the Baptist's church,
known locally as the Cathedral of the Peak. It is
conveniently placed for exploring the National Park and
visiting Buxton, Chatsworth and Eyam. Since taking over
the licence in 2010, Simon Easter has introduced a
distinctive range of 'volcanic grills' served whilst still
cooking on smooth slabs of hot volcanic rock. Other food
options include sandwiches, filled jacket potatoes,
stone-baked pizzas and pub favourites. There's a special
children's selection, and traditional Sunday roasts.

Open all day all wk ∰ GREENE KING ◀ IPA & Abbot Ale,
Morland Old Speckled Hen. **Facilities** Children welcome
Children's menu Children's portions Parking Wi-fi

Three Stags' Heads

Wardlow Mires SK17 8RW ☎ 01298 872268
dir: *At junct of A623 (Baslow to Stockport road) & B6465*

A remarkable survivor, this unspoilt and rustic
17th-century moorland longhouse stands in renowned
walking country and features a stone-flagged bar and
huge range fire. The bar counter, a 1940s addition, sells
Abbeydale beers, including the heady Black Lurcher and
Brimstone bitter, and several real ciders. Hearty food
includes pea and ham soup, chicken casserole, roast
partridge and bread-and-butter pudding. Note the
restricted opening hours, which allow owners Geoff and
Pat Fuller time to make pottery, which you can buy. Sorry,
it's not a pub for children.

Open all day Sat-Sun 12-12 (Fri 6-12) Closed: Mon-Thu
(ex BH) **Bar Meals** L served Sat-Sun 12-3.30 D served
Fri-Sun 6-9.30 Av main course £8.50 **Restaurant** L served
Sat-Sun 12-2.30 D served Fri-Sun 6-9.30 ∰ FREE HOUSE
◀ Abbeydale Matins, Absolution, Black Lurcher,
Brimstone ♻ Dunkertons Black Fox, Hecks Kingston
Black, Gawtkin Yarlington Mill. **Facilities** Parking **Notes**
▭

DEVON

ASHBURTON   Map 3 SX77

The Rising Sun

Woodland TQ13 7JT ☎ 01364 652544
e-mail: admin@therisingsunwoodland.co.uk
dir: *From A38 E of Ashburton take lane signed Woodland/
Denbury. Pub on left, approx 1.5m*

A former drovers' pub set in beautiful countryside, The
Rising Sun is run by Paul and Louise Cheakley. Paul, who
is also the chef, is totally committed to local produce,
including daily delivered crab, lobster, cod and other
freshly caught fish from Brixham. There's a bar menu, a
carte and a specials board, on one or more of which
mixed fish grill, chicken korma, Greek salad, West Country
cheeses, and home-made puddings are likely to appear.
Children can choose from their own menu.

Open all wk 12-3 6-11 (Sun 12-3 6.30-11) Closed: 25-26
Dec **Bar Meals** L served Mon-Sat 12-2.15, Sun 12-2.30
D served Mon-Sat 6-9.15, Sun 6.30-9.15 **Restaurant** L
served Mon-Sat 12-2.15, Sun 12-2.30 D served Mon-Sat
6-9.15, Sun 6.30-9.15 ∰ FREE HOUSE ◀ Dartmoor Jail
Ale, Guest ales ♻ Thatchers. ▾ 16 **Facilities** ✿ Children
welcome Children's menu Children's portions Play area
Family room Garden Parking Wi-fi ▭

AVONWICK   Map 3 SX75

The Turtley Corn Mill

PICK OF THE PUBS

TQ10 9ES ☎ 01364 646100
e-mail: eat@turtleycornmill.com
dir: *From A38 at South Brent/Avonwick junction, take
B3372, then follow signs for Avonwick, 0.5m*

This sprawling old free house began life as a corn mill,
then spent many years as a chicken hatchery before
being converted to a pub in the 1970s and renovated a
few years ago. The six-acre site is bordered by a river and
includes a lake complete with ducks and its own small
island, whilst the interior is light and fresh with old
furniture and oak and slate floors. You'll find plenty of
newspapers and books to browse through while enjoying
a whisky or supping a pint of Tribute or Tamar ale. The
daily-changing modern British menus for breakfast/
brunch, lunch and dinner are extensively based on local
produce from around the pub's idyllic South Hams
location. Typical main-course choices include pheasant
casserole; root vegetable gratin; smoked haddock and
Jerusalem artichoke bake; and a catch of the day. Warm
chocolate fondant is a typical dessert. Booking for meals
may be required.

Open all day all wk Closed: 25 Dec **Bar Meals** L served all
wk 12-10 D served all wk 12-10 food served all day
Restaurant L served all wk 12-10 D served all wk 12-10
food served all day ∰ FREE HOUSE ◀ Holsworthy Tamar
Sauce, Dartmoor Jail Ale, St Austell Tribute, Sharp's Doom
Bar, Guest ales ♻ Thatchers. ▾ 8 **Facilities** ✿ Children
welcome Children's portions Garden Parking Wi-fi

AXMOUTH
Map 4 SY29

The Harbour Inn
PICK OF THE PUBS

Church St EX12 4AF ☎ 01297 20371
dir: Main street opposite church, 1m from Seaton

A pebble's throw from the Axe Estuary in the picturesque village of Axmouth, this cosy, oak-beamed harbourside inn is a popular place for walkers and birdwatchers to refuel. Local ingredients are sourced for the food here and the bar and bistro menu offers comforting classics like local butcher's ham sandwiches; half a pint of king prawns; and smoked haddock and Somerset cheddar fishcakes. From a daily updated blackboard menu, you might want to consider oven-roasted salmon fillet with roasted fennel, caper and lemon butter sauce; breaded plaice fillets with peas and triple-fried chips; or steak and Poachers Ale pie. Leave room for apple and blackberry oat crunch crumble with vanilla custard; or banana Eton Mess with butterscotch sauce, meringue and honeycomb ice cream. The Harbour makes a great stop if you are walking the South West Coastal Path between Lyme Regis and Seaton.

Open all wk 11-11 (Fri-Sat 11am-mdnt Sun 11-10.30)
Bar Meals L served all wk 12-9.30 food served all day
Restaurant L served all wk 12-9.30 food served all day
⊕ HALL & WOODHOUSE ◀ Badger First Gold, Tanglefoot, K&B Sussex ♂ Badger Applewood, Westons Stowford Press. **Facilities** ♣ Children welcome Children's menu Children's portions Play area Garden Parking

The Ship Inn

EX12 4AF ☎ 01297 21838
dir: 1m S of A3052 between Lyme & Sidmouth. Signed to Seaton at Boshill Cross

Built soon after the original Ship burnt down on Christmas Day 1879, this creeper-clad family-run inn is able to trace its landlords back to 1769. Well-kept real ales and draught cider complement an extensive menu, including daily blackboard specials featuring local fish and game cooked with home-grown herbs. Typical choices include sausages and mash with red onion gravy; mushroom Stroganoff; and whole baked trout with new potatoes. The pub has a skittles alley, and there are long views over the Axe estuary from the beer garden. Booking for meals may be required.

Open all wk 12-3 5.30-11 **Bar Meals** L served all wk 12-2.30 D served all wk 6-9 **Restaurant** L served all wk 12-2.30 D served all wk 6-9 ⊕ FREE HOUSE ◀ Otter Bitter, Guinness ♂ Westons Stowford Press, Sheppy's. **Facilities** ♣ Children welcome Children's menu Children's portions Garden Parking Wi-fi ▥

BAMPTON
Map 3 SS92

The Quarrymans Rest ★★★★ INN ◉

Briton St EX16 9LN ☎ 01398 331480
e-mail: info@thequarrymansrest.co.uk
dir: M5 junct 27 towards Tiverton on A361, at rdbt right signed Bampton. At next rdbt take 2nd exit signed Bampton, on right

The local Ordnance Survey map marks the disused quarries whose workers once drank here. There's a small seating area out front, a patio and grassed area to the rear, and an inviting bar with tables the regular real ales are Otter, Doom Bar and Exmoor. In the quieter dining room, try the one AA-Rosette dishes: beer-battered Cornish haddock; rump of Exmoor lamb; or goat's cheese, sunblush tomato and mushroom tagliatelle. A beer festival is held during the May bank holiday, following which a night in one of the well-equipped guest rooms might be wise. Booking for meals may be required.

Open all day all wk Mon 12-11 Tue-Thu 11.45-11 Fri 11.45-11.45 Sat 11am-11.45pm Sun 12-7 (summer all wk 12-10.30) **Bar Meals** L served all wk 12-2 D served all wk 6-9.30 Av main course £14 **Restaurant** L served all wk 12-2 D served all wk 6-9.30 Av 3 course à la carte fr £26 ⊕ FREE HOUSE ◀ Sharp's Doom Bar, Otter, Exmoor, Guest ale ♂ Thatchers Gold & Pear. ☗ 16 **Facilities** ♣ Children welcome Children's portions Garden Beer festival Parking Wi-fi ▥ **Rooms** 3

BEER
Map 4 SY28

Anchor Inn ★★★★ INN

Fore St EX12 3ET ☎ 01297 20386
e-mail: 6403@greeneking.co.uk
dir: A3052 towards Lyme Regis. At Hangmans Stone take B3174 into Beer. Pub on seafront

A traditional inn overlooking the bay in the picture-perfect Devon village of Beer, this pretty colour-washed pub is perfectly situated for walking the Jurassic coastline. Fish caught by local boats features strongly on the menu, and the tempting starters might include a crabmeat pot with mixed leaves and granary bread, followed by home-made steak and Guinness pie; whole sea bass on king prawn and vegetable stirfry; or wild mushroom and spinach risotto. Six comfortable guest rooms are also available.

Open all day all wk 8am-11pm **Bar Meals** L served Mon-Fri 11-2.30, Sat-Sun 11-4 D served Sun-Thu 6-9, Fri-Sat 6-9.30 **Restaurant** L served Mon-Fri 12-2.30, Sat-Sun 12-3 D served Sun-Thu 6-9, Fri-Sat 6-9.30 ⊕ GREENE KING ◀ IPA & Abbot Ale, Otter Ale ♂ Aspall. ☗ 14 **Facilities** ♣ Children welcome Children's menu Garden Wi-fi ▥ (notice required) **Rooms** 6

BEESANDS
Map 3 SX84

The Cricket Inn ★★★★ INN ◉
PICK OF THE PUBS

TQ7 2EN ☎ 01548 580215
e-mail: enquiries@thecricketinn.com
dir: From Kingsbridge take A379 towards Dartmouth. At Stokenham mini rdbt turn right to Beesands

In the small South Hams fishing village of Beesands, The Cricket Inn first opened its doors in 1867 and is only metres from the sloping beach and clear waters of Start Bay. Fishing was the main source of employment here until the early 1970s but there are still three trawler captains living in the village, plus fishermen who bring their catch straight to The Cricket. The dog-friendly bar is the place to enjoy Otter Ale or Heron Valley cider but the extended restaurant with its sea views and one AA Rosette is the place to sample crab, lobster and scallops caught in the bay outside. Locally grown vegetables and meat from the local butcher means a menu that is dictated by what's best on the day. Hand-picked Start Bay crab sandwiches or fish pie make for a light lunch option. Two of the choices at dinner could be diver-caught Beesands scallops with shiitake mushrooms, cauliflower purée and crispy Parma ham, followed by whole lemon sole with lemon and chive butter. Bright and airy accommodation is available.

Open all wk 11-3 6-11 (May-Sep all day) **Bar Meals** L served all wk 12-2.30 D served all wk 6-8.30 **Restaurant** L served all wk 12-2.30 D served all wk 6-8.30 ⊕ HEAVITREE ◀ Otter Ale & Bitter, St Austell Tribute ♂ Aspall, Heron Valley. ☗ 10 **Facilities** ♣ Children welcome Children's menu Children's portions Parking Wi-fi **Rooms** 8

BICKLEIGH
Map 3 SS90

Fisherman's Cot

EX16 8RW ☎ 01884 855237
e-mail: fishermanscot.bickleigh@marstons.co.uk
dir: Telephone for directions

Well-appointed thatched inn by Bickleigh Bridge over the River Exe with food all day and beautiful gardens, just a short drive from Tiverton and Exmoor. The Waterside Bar is the place for doorstep sandwiches, pies, snacks and afternoon tea, while the restaurant incorporates a carvery (on Sunday) and carte menus. Expect dishes such as farmhouse pâté; deep-fried baby squid; Thai red fish curry; slow-cooked pork shank; steak and Exeter Ale pie; and forest fruit crumble. Children's menu available.

Open all day all wk 11-11 (Sun 12-10.30) **Bar Meals** food served all day **Restaurant** food served all day ⊕ MARSTON'S ◀ Wychwood Hobgoblin, Ringwood. ☗ 8 **Facilities** ♣ Children welcome Children's menu Children's portions Garden Parking ▥ (notice required)

Save on hotels. Book at **theAA.com/hotel**

DEVON 149 ENGLAND

BIGBURY-ON-SEA   Map 3 SX64

Pilchard Inn

Burgh Island TQ7 4BG ☎ 01548 810514
e-mail: reception@burghisland.com
web: www.burghisland.com
dir: *From A38 turn off to Modbury then follow signs to Bigbury & Burgh Island*

Open all day all wk **Bar Meals** L served all wk 12-3
Av main course £5 **Restaurant** D served Fri 7-9 (curry buffet) Fixed menu price fr £18.75 ⊕ FREE HOUSE
◀ Pilchard Ale, The South Hams Eddystone & Devon Pride
Ò Thatchers Gold, Herron Valley. **Facilities** ❀ Children welcome Garden

See advert below

You can't simply park the car or even lean the bike against a wall here because this 14th-century smugglers' inn is on Burgh Island, cut off by the sea twice a day. Depending on the tide, you walk here or ride the 'sea tractor'. Expect beams, flagstones and log fires, picnic tables by the water's edge and lovely coastal views. Friday night curry apart (booking advisable), food is served only at lunchtime, typically locally landed shellfish; pan-fried John Dory and prawn risotto; and crisp duckling breast with confit leg and scrumpy reduction. Booking for meals may be required.

BLACKAWTON   Map 3 SX85

The Normandy Arms

PICK OF THE PUBS

Chapel St TQ9 7BN ☎ 01803 712884
e-mail: info@normandyarms.co.uk
dir: *From Dartmouth take A3122 towards Halwell. Turn right at Forces Tavern to Blackawton*

This revamped 16th-century inn was named in honour of the Normandy landings, for which training exercises took place on the nearby beaches in World War II. Located off the beaten track down narrow winding country lanes leading to the sleepy village of Blackawton, the pub is packed with character in the form of the beamed and slate-floored bar and the relaxing dining room, both with warming log-burning stoves. Expect imaginative seasonal menus that draw on top-notch South Hams produce, perhaps including sautéed Devon scallops with a lentil and bacon salad and tomato vinaigrette among the starters. Main dishes may take in saddle of Dartmoor venison, sweet potato fondants, curly kale and wild mushroom sauce, or fillet of line-caught Dartmouth cod and creamy vegetable curry with mussels and scallops, while puddings could feature apple and almond samosa with rum and raisin ice cream. The two-course set menus are a steal at £12.50. Booking for meals may be required.

Open 10.30-3 5-11 Closed: 2 Jan-1 Feb, Sun eve & Mon
Bar Meals L served Tue-Sun 12-2.30 D served Tue-Sat 6-9.30 **Restaurant** L served Tue-Sun 12-2.30 D served Tue-Sat 6-9.30 Fixed menu price fr £12.50 Av 3 course à la carte fr £27 ⊕ FREE HOUSE ◀ Dartmoor Legend, St Austell Trelawny, Cotleigh Ò The Orchard Pig, Thatchers Cheddar Valley. ☗ 12 **Facilities** ❀ Children welcome Children's menu Children's portions Garden Parking Wi-fi

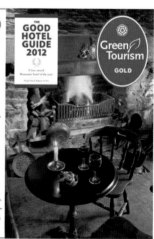

BRAMPFORD SPEKE — Map 3 SX99

The Lazy Toad Inn

EX5 5DP ☎ 01392 841591
e-mail: thelazytoadinn@btinternet.com
dir: From Exeter take A377 towards Crediton 1.5m, right signed Brampford Speke

There's much to commend this 19th-century, Grade II listed country inn just a short drive from Exeter. It stands in a picturesque thatched village in peaceful countryside, close to the Devonshire Heartland Way, Exe Valley Way and glorious riverside walks. Clive and Mo Walker's smallholding behind the pub supplies the soft fruit, herbs, vegetables, lamb and eggs to the kitchen, while meat and fish are cured in the pub smokery. Bag a table by the fire in one of the renovated beamed rooms, or outside in the courtyard or walled beer garden, and tuck into offerings from the daily-changing menu: grilled lamb's liver with chorizo, pine nuts and sage mash; or purple sprouting broccoli with parsley linguine, pine nuts and chilli oil.

Open 11.30-2.30 6-11 (Sun 12-3) Closed: 3wks Jan, Sun eve & Mon Bar Meals L served Tue-Sun 12-2 D served Tue-Sat 6.30-9 ⊕ FREE HOUSE ◀ Otter Ale, Toads Tipple ♻ Sandford Orchards Devon Red & Devon Mist. ♟ 12 Facilities Children welcome Children's menu Children's portions Family room Garden Parking

BRANSCOMBE — Map 4 SY18

The Fountain Head

EX12 3BG ☎ 01297 680359
dir: From Seaton on A3052 towards Sidmouth left at Branscombe Cross to pub

A true 500-year-old rural survivor tucked away in a peaceful Devon village a short walk from the coastal path. The old forge and cider house is often rammed with walkers and locals, drawn by the traditional charm of worn flagstones, crackling log fires, rustic furnishings, village-brewed beers (Branscombe Vale), and the chatty atmosphere – no intrusive music or electronic games here. Hearty pub food includes game pie; vegetable moussaka; lasagne; pheasant, pistachio and smoked bacon terrine; and fresh local hand-picked crab. There's a spit-roast and barbecue every Sunday evening between July and September. Don't miss the midsummer beer festival.

Open all wk 11-3 6-11 (Sun 12-3 6-10.30) Bar Meals L served all wk 12-2 D served all wk 6.30-9 Restaurant L served all wk 12-2 D served all wk 6.30-9 ⊕ FREE HOUSE ◀ Branscombe Vale Branoc, Jolly Geff, Summa That ♻ Thatchers Cheddar Valley. Facilities Children welcome Children's menu Children's portions Family room Garden Beer festival Parking ▭

The Masons Arms

PICK OF THE PUBS

See Pick of the Pubs on opposite page

BRAUNTON — Map 3 SS43

The Williams Arms

Wrafton EX33 2DE ☎ 01271 812360
e-mail: info@williamsarms.co.uk
dir: On A361 between Barnstaple & Braunton

This postcard-pretty thatched pub beside the popular Tarka Trail dates back to the 16th century and has been owned by the Squire family since the mid-70s. Its prime location sees weary walkers, cyclists and local diners pile in for the pub's famous daily carvery, which always features locally reared meat and seasonal vegetables. Alternatively, you can try Devon scallops in white wine and cream sauce; steak and real ale pie or lighter options like prawn salad or roast turkey panini, perfect washed down with a pint of Sharp's Doom Bar.

Open all day all wk 8.45am-11pm Bar Meals food served all day Restaurant L served Mon-Sat 12-2, Sun 12-3 D served all wk 6-9 ⊕ FREE HOUSE ◀ Worthington's Creamflow, Sharp's Doom Bar, Guinness ♻ Thatchers. Facilities Children welcome Children's menu Children's portions Play area Garden Parking ▭ (notice required)

BRENDON — Map 3 SS74

Rockford Inn

EX35 6PT ☎ 01598 741214
e-mail: enquiries@therockfordinn.com
dir: A39 through Minehead follow signs to Lynmouth. Turn left off A39 to Brendon approx 5m before Lynmouth

Standing alongside the East Lyn River in the tucked-away Brendon Valley, this traditional 17th-century free house stands in the heart of Exmoor and is handy for several walking routes. Thatchers ciders complement local cask ales such as Barn Owl and Devon Darter, and there's a choice of good home-made pub meals. Chicken and leek pie, River Exe moules marinière and slow-braised beef are typical menu choices; the specials board changes daily. Eat in the garden in warm weather, or head inside to the open fire when the weather changes. Booking for meals may be required.

Open all day Closed: Mon L Bar Meals L served Tue-Sun 12-3 D served Tue-Sun 6-8.30 Av main course £12 ⊕ FREE HOUSE ◀ Cotleigh Barn Owl & 25, St Austell Tribute, Clearwater Proper Ansome, Devon Darter & Real Smiler, Exmoor ♻ Thatchers, Addlestones. Facilities ☙ Children welcome Children's menu Children's portions Garden Parking Wi-fi

BRIDFORD — Map 3 SX88

The Bridford Inn NEW

EX6 7HT ☎ 01647 252250
e-mail: info@bridfordinn.co.uk
web: www.bridfordinn.co.uk
dir: Telephone for directions

Converted from three 17th-century cottages, this village inn and shop lies above the beautiful Teign Valley in Dartmoor National Park. Its elevated position provides glorious views over the surrounding area. Oak beams supporting the ceiling are timbers left over from construction of the replica Pilgrim Fathers' ship, *The Mayflower*. The unusual bar top was salvaged from an Exeter chemist's. Menus offer grilled rib-eye and sirloin steaks; sausage, mash and onion gravy; pie of the day; scampi, chips and peas; and vegetable lasagne. The bar serves Jail Ale from Dartmoor Brewery. Look out for the pub's cider festival.

Open 12-2.30 5-11 Closed: Tue L Bar Meals L served Mon & Wed-Sun 12-2 D served all wk 7-9.30 Av main course £10 Restaurant Av 3 course à la carte fr £17 ⊕ FREE HOUSE ◀ Dartmoor Jail Ale, St Austell Tribute, Sharp's Doom Bar, O'Hanlon's Port Stout & Yellow Hammer ♻ Sandford Orchards. Facilities ☙ Children welcome Children's portions Garden Parking Wi-fi ▭ (notice required)

Save on hotels. Book at **theAA.com/hotel**

DEVON 151 **ENGLAND**

PICK OF THE PUBS

The Masons Arms

BRANSCOMBE Map 4 SY18

EX12 3DJ ☎ 01297 680300
e-mail: masonsarms@staustellbrewery.co.uk
web: www.masonsarms.co.uk
dir: *Exit A3052 towards Branscombe,
down hill, Masons Arms at bottom of hill*

This creeper-clad inn dates from 1360,
when it was a cider house squeezed into
the middle of a row of cottages. Back
then it was a smugglers' haunt and its
interior has barely changed since those
days: slate floors, stone walls, ships'
beams, an old jail railing and a huge
open fireplace used for spit roasts on
Sundays all add to the time-warp
charm. Located in the picturesque
village of Branscombe, the inn is just a
ten-minute stroll from the beach; its
peaceful gardens have sea views across
a picturesque valley. Five real ales are
always available, including several that
are locally brewed, plus ciders such as
Thatchers Gold or Addlestones. Food is a
serious business here; where possible
all ingredients are grown, reared or
caught locally, especially lobster and
crab. Starters include moules marinière
from the River Axe and a hugely popular
chicken liver parfait. Main courses vary
from day to day but seafood stew is a
perennial fixture, and also popular is
grilled sea bass with a West Country
mussel and chervil cream velouté. Other
choices could include starters of Elston

Farm smoked venison, warm
Cumberland sauce and blue cheese
croûtons; and West Country scallops
with a roasted butternut squash purée;
followed by rack of lamb with aubergine
caviar and a light lamb jus. Indulgent
desserts such as Devon clotted cream
crème brûlée; apple and thyme tarte
Tatin; or chocolate and hazelnut parfait
with crème anglaise round things off
nicely. There are always simpler dishes
such as fish and chips, plus excellent
vegetarian options – maybe Cornish
Yarg soufflé followed by grilled
Mediterranean vegetable soft herb
risotto with a deep fried poached egg.
A three-day beer festival is held in the
middle of July. Booking for meals may
be required.

Open all day all wk **Bar Meals** L served
all wk 12-2.15 D served all wk 6-9
Restaurant D served all wk 7-9
⊞ ST AUSTELL BREWERY ◀ Tribute &
Dartmoor, Branscombe Vale Summa
That ♂ Addlestones, Thatchers Gold,
Healey's Pear Rattler. ♟ 14
Facilities Children welcome Children's
menu Children's portions ✿ Garden
Beer festival Parking Wi-fi

BROADHEMPSTON — Map 3 SX86

The Monks Retreat Inn

The Square TQ9 6BN ☎ 01803 812203
dir: Exit A381 (Newton Abbot to Totnes road) at Ipplepen, follow for Broadhempston signs for 3.5m

Apparently a friendly ghost of a monk inhabits this 1456 inn, formerly called Church House Inn. Certainly it's the sort of place you'd want to linger in: the building (listed as of outstanding architectural interest) is full of fascinating features, including a panelled oak screen typical of ancient Devon houses. Sit by one of the cosy log fires and enjoy a pint of Bath Gem or Jail Ale or some good food at this popular locals' pub. Booking for meals may be required.

Open 12-2 6-11 (Sun 12-2 7-11) Closed: Mon **Bar Meals** L served Tue-Sun 12-1.45 D served Tue-Sat 6.30-9, Sun 7-9 **Restaurant** L served Tue-Sun 12-1.45 D served Tue-Sat 6.30-9, Sun 7-9 ⊕ ENTERPRISE INNS ◖ Bath Gem, Dartmoor Jail Ale ♂ Thatchers Gold. **Facilities** Children welcome

BUCKFASTLEIGH — Map 3 SX76

Dartbridge Inn

Totnes Rd TQ11 0JR ☎ 01364 642214
e-mail: 6442@greeneking.co.uk
dir: From Exeter A38, take 1st Buckfastleigh turn, then left to Totnes. Inn on left

Wooden floors, leather chairs, sofas and real fires define the ambience in the spacious bar of the Dartbridge, where various guest ales vie for your trade; a dozen wines are served by the glass too. Outside, there are views through trees to the River Dart, and a prettily furnished terrace with parasols where you can dine alfresco. The menus comprise salads, gourmet burgers, lunchtime sandwiches, Black Angus steaks, and pub favourites made with good-quality produce, such as beef and Ruddles ale pie; chicken fajitas; Suffolk pork sausages with Devon cheddar mash; and lentil shepherd's pie. A children's menu and specials are also available.

Open all day all wk **Bar Meals** food served all day **Restaurant** food served all day ⊕ OLD ENGLISH INNS ◖ Greene King IPA & Abbot Ale, Morland Old Speckled Hen, Guest ales. ♀ 12 **Facilities** Children welcome Children's menu Children's portions Garden Beer festival Parking Wi-fi ╤ (notice required)

BUCKLAND MONACHORUM — Map 3 SX46

Drake Manor Inn Ⓤ

The Village PL20 7NA ☎ 01822 853892
e-mail: drakemanor@drakemanorinn.co.uk
dir: Off A386 near Yelverton

In the 12th century, when nearby St Andrew's church was being built, the masons needed a house to live in. Today's licensee of that now very old house is Mandy Robinson, who prides herself on running a 'proper pub', where her locally sourced menu includes bar snacks, vegetarian options, steaks and fresh fillet of smoked haddock on pea risotto, as well as pub favourites, such as home-made steak-and-kidney pie and chicken supreme. The sunny cottage garden is appealing.

Open all wk 11.30-2.30 6.30-11 (Fri 11.30-2.30 6.30-11.30 Sat 11.30-11.30 Sun 12-11) **Bar Meals** L served all wk 12-2 D served Mon-Sat 7-10, Sun 7-9.30 Av main course £9.95 **Restaurant** L served all wk 12-2 D served Mon-Sat 7-10, Sun 7-9.30 ⊕ PUNCH TAVERNS ◖ John Smith's, Sharp's Doom Bar, Otter Bitter ♂ Thatchers Gold. ♀ 9 **Facilities** ♣ Children welcome Children's portions Family room Garden Parking **Rooms** 4

BUTTERLEIGH — Map 3 SS90

The Butterleigh Inn

EX15 1PN ☎ 01884 855433
e-mail: thebutterleighinn1@btconnect.com
dir: 3m from M5 junct 28 turn right by Manor Hotel in Cullompton. Follow Butterleigh signs

Set in a delightful village opposite the 13th-century St Matthew's church and in the heart of the rolling Devon countryside, the 400-year-old Butterleigh is a traditional free house. There is a mass of local memorabilia throughout this friendly local, where customers can choose from a selection of changing real ales including Dartmoor Jail Ale, ciders including Devon Scrumpy from Sandford Orchards, and around 15 malt whiskies. Expect home-made dishes such as turkey and pork pie; curry of the day; lamb chops; broccoli, leek and stilton bake; and steaks from the grill. On fine days, the garden with its huge flowering cherry tree is very popular.

Open 12-2.30 6-11 (Fri-Sat 12-2.30 6-12 Sun 12-3) Closed: Sun eve, Mon L **Bar Meals** L served Tue-Sat 12-2 D served Tue-Sat 7-9 Av main course £9.50 **Restaurant** L served Tue-Sat 12-2 D served Tue-Sat 7-9 Av 3 course à la carte fr £18 ⊕ FREE HOUSE ◖ Cotleigh Tawny Ale, Otter Ale & Amber, Dartmoor IPA & Jail Ale, Guest ale ♂ Sandford Orchards Devon Scrumpy, Sheppy's. **Facilities** ♣ Children welcome Children's menu Children's portions Garden Parking Wi-fi

CHAGFORD — Map 3 SX78

Sandy Park Inn

PICK OF THE PUBS

TQ13 8JW ☎ 01647 433267
e-mail: info@sandyparkinn.co.uk
dir: From A30 exit at Whiddon Down, turn left towards Moretonhampstead. Inn 5m from Whiddon Down

In a beautiful setting near the River Teign on the edge of Dartmoor, this lovely thatched pub has a timeless quality about it. The beamed bar attracts locals and travellers alike, while dogs are frequently to be found slumped in front of the fire. Homely horse brasses and sporting prints adorn the walls of the bar where you can choose from an eclectic wine list and a good range of traditional local ales like Otter and Dartmoor Legend. Whether you eat in the bar, snug or candlelit dining room, menus of home-made dishes change with the seasons, blending pub classics with modern fusion and vegetarian options; a range of gourmet stone-baked pizzas is especially popular and include Hawaiian or Four Seasons. Sandwiches and salads are perfect for summer lunchtimes, when they can be served in the garden with its views towards the Castle Drogo estate and deer park.

Open all day 12-11 Closed: Sun eve & Mon Jan-Feb ex half term **Bar Meals** L served all wk 12-2.30 D served all wk 6-9 **Restaurant** L served all wk 12-2.30 D served all wk 6-9 ⊕ FREE HOUSE ◖ Otter Ale, Dartmoor Legend, Guest ale ♂ Thatchers. ♀ 9 **Facilities** ♣ Children welcome Children's portions Family room Garden Parking Wi-fi ╤

CHARDSTOCK — Map 4 ST30

The George Inn

EX13 7BX ☎ 01460 220241
e-mail: contactus@george-inn.com
dir: A358 from Taunton through Chard towards Axminster, left at Tytherleigh. Signed from A358

New owners have acquired this traditional, thatched 15th-century village inn on the edge of the Blackdown Hills. Lots of original features include superb linenfold oak panelling, and graffiti dated 1649. Several locals whose drinking histories here stretch back at least 40 years can usually be found in the bar's 'Compost Corner' with their pints of Otter Bitter or Sharp's Doom Bar. Sandwiches and more substantial meals are served at lunchtime, while in the evening you might fancy a 10oz Somerset rib-eye steak; pan-fried skate wing; or wild mushroom pappardelle.

Open Tue-Sat 12-3 6-11 (Mon 6-11 Sun 12-3) Closed: Sun eve, Mon L **Bar Meals** L served Tue-Sat 12-2, Sun 12-2.30 D served Mon-Sat 6.30-9.30 **Restaurant** D served Mon-Sat 6.30-9.30 ⊕ FREE HOUSE ◖ Otter Bitter, Sharp's Doom Bar, Guest ales ♂ Westons Stowford Press, Thatchers Gold. **Facilities** ♣ Children welcome Children's menu Children's portions Garden Parking ╤ (notice required)

Save on hotels. Book at **theAA.com/hotel**

DEVON 153 ENGLAND

PICK OF THE PUBS

The Five Bells Inn

CLYST HYDON Map 3 ST00

EX15 2NT ☎ 01884 277288
e-mail: info@fivebellsclysthydon.co.uk
web: www.fivebellsclysthydon.co.uk
dir: *B3181 towards Cullompton, right at Hele Cross towards Clyst Hydon. 2m turn right, then sharp right at left bend at village sign*

Once a farmhouse, this pretty 16th-century country pub takes its name from the five bells hanging in the village church tower: the pub was located next to the church in the centre of the village but apparently fell out with the church and moved to its present location in the late 19th century. The Five Bells is increasingly popular thanks to its family-friendly owners and a focus on well-kept local ales and ciders, good food and cheerful hospitality. The interior boasts two wood fires, numerous prints and watercolours, and brass and copper artefacts. Kick off a meal with one of the tempting starters – perhaps kiln-roasted salmon with whisky horseradish and potato salad; tiger prawns with whisky, lime and chilli glaze; or figs wrapped in prosciutto ham baked with goat's cheese; before tucking into mains of slowly cooked chicken breast with sherry, chorizo and onion sauce; half a roast duck with honey, rosemary and white wine sauce

or pork Valentine steak with mushroom, garlic and brandy sauce. Leave room for one of the delicious desserts: apricot bread-and-butter pudding, perhaps, or lemon and ginger steam pudding with custard. There is also a set lunch menu which changes daily and children get to choose from their own menu. The well-maintained garden is colourful all year round and a delight in summer, with 20 tables enjoying lovely views of the rolling east Devon countryside, and a children's play area.

Open Tue-Sat 11.30-3 6.30-11 (Sun 12-3, 6.30-10.30) Closed: Mon L **Bar Meals** L served Tue-Sat 11.30-2, Sun 12-2 D served all wk 6.30-9 Av main

course £11 ⊕ FREE HOUSE ◾ Cotleigh Tawny Owl, Otter Bitter, O'Hanlon's Ö Westons Stowford Press, Thatchers Gold, Berry Farm Cider. ⦿ 10
Facilities Children welcome Children's menu Children's portions Play area Family room Garden Parking Wi-fi 🚌 (notice required)

The Merry Harriers

PICK OF THE PUBS

Forches Corner EX15 3TR ☎ 01823 421270
e-mail: peter.gatling@btinternet.com
*dir: M5 junct 26 towards Wellington A38, turn onto Ford
Street (marked by brown tourist sign). At top of hill turn
left, 1.5m on right*

Set in beautiful countryside high on the Blackdown Hills,
this free house stands on the once notorious Forches
Corner, which was the scene of ambushes during the
17th-century Monmouth Rebellion. Highwaymen were
reputedly hanged outside the pub – which might explain
why it's said to be haunted. Originally a Devon longhouse
dating from 1492, the black-and-white building features
beamed ceilings, a cosy inglenook and attractive dining
areas, whilst the large mature garden is popular during
the summer months. Peter and Angela Gatling have
worked tirelessly to build the local drinks trade and
expand the food operation. More than 90 per cent of
kitchen ingredients come from the surrounding hills or
further afield in the West Country. A bar lunch might
feature fresh Fowey mussels served in a Bollhayes cider
cream, or for lighter appetites there are filled baguettes.
In the evening you could try oven-roasted whole Devon
rainbow trout or pan-roasted suprême of West Country
chicken served with seasonal vegetables. Booking for
meals may be required.

Open 12-3 6.30-11 Closed: Sun eve & Mon **Bar Meals** L
served Tue-Sat 12-2, Sun 12-2.15 D served Tue-Sat
6.30-9 Av main course £10 **Restaurant** L served Tue-Sat
12-2, Sun 12-2.15 D served Tue-Sat 6.30-9 Av 3 course à
la carte fr £16 ⊕ FREE HOUSE ◀ Otter Head & Amber,
Cotleigh Harrier, Exmoor Gold, St Austell Tinners
Ö Thatchers Gold, Bollhayes. ♀ 14 **Facilities** ❖ Children
welcome Children's menu Children's portions Play area
Family room Garden Parking Wi-fi ⛟ (notice required)

The Skylark Inn

PL20 6JD ☎ 01822 853258
e-mail: skylvic@btinternet.com
*dir: 5m N of Plymouth on A386 towards Tavistock. Take
2nd right signed Clearbrook*

Originally used by miners in the 18th century, The Skylark
is set in the Dartmoor National Park just ten minutes
from Plymouth and the area is ideal for cyclists and
walkers. Children are welcome and there is a special play
area available. The beamed bar with its large fireplace
and wood-burning stove characterises this attractive
village inn, where local ales and good wholesome food
are served. Dishes include classics like steak-and-ale
pie, beef lasagne, mushroom Stroganoff, and cod and
chips. Booking for meals may be required.

Open all wk 11.30-3 6-11.30 (Sat-Sun all day) **Bar
Meals** L served all wk 12-2 D served all wk 6.30-9
Av main course £9.50 **Restaurant** L served all wk 12-2
D served all wk 6.30-9 ⊕ UNIQUE PUB CO LTD ◀ Otter

Ale, St Austell Tribute, Dartmoor. **Facilities** ❖ Children
welcome Children's menu Children's portions Play area
Family room Garden Beer festival Parking ⛟ (notice
required)

Red Lion Hotel ★★ HL

PICK OF THE PUBS

The Quay EX39 5TF ☎ 01237 431237
e-mail: redlion@clovelly.co.uk
*dir: From Bideford rdbt, follow A39 to Bude for 10m. At
Clovelly Cross rdbt turn right, follow past Clovelly Visitor
Centre entrance, bear to left. Hotel at bottom of hill*

This charming whitewashed hostelry sits right on the
quay in Clovelly, the famously unspoilt 'village like a
waterfall' which descends down broad steps to a
14th-century harbour. Guests staying in the whimsically
decorated bedrooms can fall asleep to the sound of
waves lapping the shingle. Originally a beerhouse for
fishermen and other locals, the Red Lion has plenty of
character and offers Cornish ales such as Sharp's Doom
Bar in its snug bar, where you can rub shoulders with the
locals. Alternatively, you could settle in the Harbour Bar,
and sample the home-cooked food, the modern seasonal
menu specialising in fresh seafood, which is landed daily
right outside the door. Choose pan-fried John Dory or
poached brill with creamy mushroom sauce, or opt for
Clovelly Estate venison and game dishes, or pork fillet
with smoked bacon, apple purée and red wine jus. There
is an annual beer festival late May Bank Holiday. Booking
for meals may be required.

Open all day all wk **Bar Meals** L served all wk 12-2.30
D served all wk 6-8.30 Av main course £8.95-£18.50
Restaurant D served all wk 7-9 Av 3 course à la carte fr
£29.50 ⊕ FREE HOUSE ◀ Sharp's Doom Bar, Clovelly
Cobbler, Guinness Ö Thatchers, Winkleigh Sam's
Poundhouse. ♀ **Facilities** Children welcome Children's
menu Children's portions Family room Beer festival
Parking Wi-fi ⛟ **Rooms** 17

The Five Bells Inn

PICK OF THE PUBS

See Pick of the Pubs on page 153

The Anchor Inn

EX6 8RA ☎ 01626 890203
dir: Off A379 between Dawlish & Starcross

Reputedly over 450 years old, this former inn overlooks a
small landlocked harbour on the River Exe and changed
hands in 2011. Expect tales of smugglers and even a
friendly ghost with his dog. In summer customers spill
out onto the verandah and harbour wall, while real fires,
nautical bric-a-brac and low beams make the interior
cosy in winter. For fish-lovers, the comprehensive menu

will challenge the indecisive – there are 28 different ways
to eat mussels, fresh oyster and scallop dishes aplenty,
and fish platters. Meat-eaters and vegetarians are not
forgotten, and food allergies and dietary requirements are
catered for. Beer festival twice a year. Booking for meals
may be required.

Open all day all wk 11-11 (Sun 12-10.30 25 Dec 12-2)
Bar Meals Av main course £8.95 food served all day
Restaurant Av 3 course à la carte fr £30 food served all
day ⊕ HEAVITREE ◀ Otter Ale & Bitter, St Austell Tribute,
3 Guest ales. ♀ 10 **Facilities** ❖ Children welcome
Children's menu Garden Beer festival Parking ⛟ (notice
required)

The New Inn ★★★★ INN

PICK OF THE PUBS

EX17 5BZ ☎ 01363 84242
e-mail: enquiries@thenewinncoleford.co.uk
*dir: From Exeter take A377, 1.5m after Crediton left for
Coleford, 1.5m to inn*

The attractive 13th-century building with thatched roof
makes a perfect home for this friendly inn. The ancient
slate-floored bar with its old chests and polished brass
blends effortlessly with fresh white walls, original oak
beams and simple wooden furniture in the dining room.
Set beside the River Cole, the garden is perfect for
alfresco summer dining, when you can ponder on the
pub's history: it was used by travelling Cistercian monks
long before Charles I reviewed his troops from a nearby
house during the English Civil War. Menus change
regularly, and special events such as 'fish fest week' or
'sea shanty night' are interspersed throughout the year.
Home-made bar food includes a range of soups,
omelettes and platters, while a larger meal might include
chicken, ham and mushroom pie, or whole grilled sea
bass served with an orange and lemon butter sauce. The
pub's Amazon Blue parrot, called Captain, has been a
famous fixture here for nearly 30 years, greeting bar
regulars and guests booking into the six well-appointed
bedrooms.

Open all wk 12-3 6-11 (Sun 6-10.30 winter) Closed:
25-26 Dec **Bar Meals** L served all wk 12-2 D served all wk
6.30-9.30 Av main course £9.50 **Restaurant** L served all
wk 12-2 D served all wk 6.30-9.30 Av 3 course à la carte
fr £22 ⊕ FREE HOUSE ◀ Sharp's Doom Bar, Otter Ale,
Exmoor Ale, Shepherd Neame Spitfire, Brains The Rev.
James Ö Thatchers, Winkleigh Sam's. ♀ 20
Facilities Children welcome Children's menu Children's
portions Garden Parking **Rooms** 6

Save on hotels. Book at **theAA.com/hotel**

DEVON 155 ENGLAND

The Wheelwright Inn

Swan Hill Rd EX24 6QQ ☎ 01297 552585
e-mail: gary@wheelwright-inn.co.uk
web: www.wheelwright-inn.co.uk
dir: *Telephone for directions*

This pretty thatched inn has earned a reputation for outstanding food and service since the current landlords took over. The exterior of the 17th-century building belies the contemporary interior, but the low beams, wooden floors and log fire endorse its reassuringly authentic country feel. Well-kept Hall & Woodhouse beers are dispensed in the dog-friendly bar. The varied modern menu includes specials, some of which – such as kidneys turbigo, or River Teign mussels – can be ordered in starter or main course sizes. 'A taste of all our home-made puddings' will be irresistible to the sweet of tooth.

Open all day all wk Closed: 26 Dec **Bar Meals** food served all day **Restaurant** food served all day ⊕ HALL & WOODHOUSE ◀ Badger First Gold, Hopping Hare & K&B Sussex, Guinness ☼ Westons Stowford Press. ♟
Facilities ☙ Children welcome Children's menu Children's portions Family room Parking ▣

See advert below

The Tuckers Arms

PICK OF THE PUBS

EX13 7EG ☎ 01404 881342
e-mail: tuckersarms@tuckersarms.com
dir: *Exit A35 between Honiton & Axminster, follow Dalwood signs*

An 800-year-old, family-run Devon longhouse in a pretty setting between two ridges of the Blackdown Hills, a tranquil landscape of high plateaux, valleys and springs, dotted with farms and villages. Some sources suggest that the pub was built as living accommodation for the labourers constructing St Peter's church across the way, although at least one other source credits the Duke of Beaulieu for building it as a hunting lodge. The interior is everything you would expect of a traditional, thatched inn – inglenook fireplaces, low beams and flagstone floors. As the pub is only 15 minutes from the coast at Lyme Regis, fish and seafood have only a short distance to travel, so its freshness is assured. At lunchtime, choose beer-battered catch of the day with hand-cut chips and pea purée, or maybe prime beefburger topped with cheese. The evening menu offers Thai crab linguine; slow-roast pork belly; and West Country ham, eggs and chips.

Open all wk 11.30-3 6.30-11 ⊕ FREE HOUSE ◀ Otter Bitter, Branscombe Vale Branoc, Guest ales.
Facilities Children welcome Children's menu Children's portions Garden Parking Wi-fi

---

The Wheelwright Inn

We have a genuine enthusiasm for food and want this to shine through everything we do. From the first cooked meal of the day to the last fresh coffee of the evening, consistent quality is paramount. Our close-knit team of chefs fervently believe that offering the best food revolves entirely around the very freshest, locally sourced ingredients, simply prepared and elegantly presented. Nothing pretentious or unnecessarily complicated, just very good, honest food.

With a wealth of local Hall & Woodhouse beers, there's nothing to beat a properly pulled pint of beer at the Wheelwright Inn. We also hold a wine library of over 100 bins and 8 champagnes. You are welcome to peruse the wines on offer and learn more about each one.

Our menu is seasonally based, so you won't find fresh strawberries on the specials board in February, but you will find the very best in local produce that's low on food miles and high on quality. We cater for kids too, with a child's menu that's every bit as carefully thought out and planned as the adult's. The result of all this dedication is an audience of diners who are prepared to travel miles to eat with us, making us not just a pub and restaurant, but also a focal point for the local community.

Our dedication to quality has earned us 'Best Food Pub 2009' by Hall & Woodhouse and 'Best Dining Pub South West 2009' in the Great British Pub Awards. We offer everything from deli boards of cured meats, seafood and cheeses to daily specials such as venison casserole or grilled sea bass, always using fresh, locally sourced ingredients. Our growing reputation for excellent food is attracting a loyal clientele of locals and discerning diners from further a field.

Swan Hill Road, Colyford, Devon EX24 6QQ • Tel: 01297 552585 • Website: www.wheelwright-inn.co.uk • Email: gary@wheelwright-inn.co.uk

DARTMOUTH
Map 3 SX85

Royal Castle Hotel ★★★ HL

PICK OF THE PUBS

11 The Quay TQ6 9PS ☎ 01803 833033
e-mail: nic@royalcastle.co.uk
dir: *In town centre, overlooking inner harbour*

Commanding the best site overlooking the small harbour and the Dart estuary beyond, this handsome old coaching inn is a most welcoming and comfortable place to stay. Originally four Tudor houses built on either side of a narrow lane, which now forms the lofty and attractive hallway, it boasts period fireplaces, spiral staircases, oil paintings, and a magnificent bell board, while priest holes are other intriguing features, along with fine antique pieces including four-poster beds. Of the two bars, the Harbour Bar is distinctly pubby and lively throughout the day. The Grill Room restaurant on the first floor looks out over the river. A supporter of Taste of the West's 'buy local' campaign, the hotel offers an extensive seasonal menu that includes Dartmoor venison, South Hams beef and Dartmouth crab. Lunchtime sandwiches and ploughman's are served in the bar, supported by a good selection of hot dishes, perhaps lamb shank with rosemary jus, and game pie with wild mushroom sauce.

Open all day all wk 8am-11.30pm **Bar Meals** L served all wk 11.30-10 D served all wk 11.30-10 food served all day **Restaurant** L served all wk 12-2 D served all wk 6-10 ⊕ FREE HOUSE ◀ Dartmoor Jail Ale, Otter Amber, Sharp's Doom Bar Ö Thatchers Gold, Orchard's. ☂ 29 **Facilities** ☘ Children welcome Children's menu Children's portions Family room Parking Wi-fi ⬛ (notice required) **Rooms** 25

DENBURY
Map 3 SX86

The Union Inn

Denbury Green TQ12 6DQ ☎ 01803 812595
e-mail: enquiries@theunioninndenbury.co.uk
dir: *2m from Newton Abbot, signed Denbury*

Overlooking the village green, The Union Inn is at least 400 years old and counting. Inside are the original stone walls that once rang to the hammers of the blacksmiths and cartwrights who worked here many moons ago. The bar area has comfy leather sofas while the décor throughout is a mix of traditional and contemporary. Choose from the tapas and bar snack menu, the restaurant menu or the daily specials. Mouth-watering starters could include quail stuffed with pancetta or barbecued chicken wings. Follow with vegetable filo roulade; slow-cooked belly of Devon pork; seafood linguine; or the Union Inn burger.

Open all wk 12-3 6-11.30 (Thu-Sun 12-11) **Bar Meals** L served all wk 12-2.30 D served all wk 6.30-9.30 **Restaurant** L served all wk 12-2.30 D served all wk 6.30-9.30 ⊕ ENTERPRISE INNS ◀ Otter Bitter, Hunter's Denbury Dreamer, Guest ales Ö Westons. ☂ 10 **Facilities** ☘ Children welcome Children's menu Children's portions Garden Parking Wi-fi ⬛

DITTISHAM
Map 3 SX85

The Ferry Boat

PICK OF THE PUBS

Manor St TQ6 0EX ☎ 01803 722368
e-mail: simonfbi@hotmail.co.uk
dir: *Telephone for directions*

The only pub situated on the River Dart, The Ferry Boat inn dates back 300 years and the pontoon outside the entrance means that you can still arrive here by boat. Tables at the front of this waterside pub enjoy views across the river to Greenway House and Gardens, the National Trust property that used to be Agatha Christie's home. The pub has plenty of marine connections, being just a few miles upriver from the Royal Naval College in Dartmouth. The pontoon guarantees popularity with the boating fraternity, but the pub is also a favourite with walkers and families. With its year-round selection of four or five real ales, and open log fires crackling in the grates in winter, this really is a pub for all seasons. Menus of home-cooked food vary seasonally, based on fresh fish and seafood, and local meats and cheeses. Typical dishes might include home-made smoked haddock chowder, seafood linguine with tiger prawns and mussels or fresh crab salad. A beach barbecue in summer is often accompanied by live music from local musicians. Booking for meals may be required.

Open all day all wk Closed: 25 Dec **Bar Meals** L served all wk 12-2.30 (summer hols all day) D served all wk 7-9 (summer hols all day) ⊕ PUNCH TAVERNS ◀ Otter Ale, Dorset Jurassic, Sharp's Doom Bar, Guest ales Ö Addlestones, Westons Old Rosie & Stowford Press. ☂ 10 **Facilities** ☘ Children welcome Children's menu Children's portions Family room ⬛

DODDISCOMBSLEIGH
Map 3 SX88

The Nobody Inn ★★★★ INN

PICK OF THE PUBS

See Pick of the Pubs on opposite page

DOLTON
Map 3 SS51

Rams Head Inn

South St EX19 8QS ☎ 01805 804255
e-mail: ramsheadinn@btopenworld.com
dir: *8m from Torrington on A3124*

This 15th-century free house has retained much of its original character with huge old fireplaces, bread ovens and pot stands. The inn's central location places it on many inland tourist routes, whilst the Tarka Trail and Rosemoor Gardens are both nearby. Expect a selection of cask ales on tap, accompanied by popular and traditional meals on the restaurant menu, served at lunchtime and in the evening.

Open 10-3 6-11 (Fri-Sat 12-12 Sun 12-4 6-11) Closed: Mon winter **Bar Meals** L served all wk 12-2.30 D served Mon-Sat 6.30-9 Av main course £8 food served all day **Restaurant** L served all wk 12-2.30 D served Mon-Sat

6.30-9 Fixed menu price fr £11 food served all day ⊕ FREE HOUSE ◀ Country Life Golden Pig, Sharp's Own Ö Winkleigh. ☂ 14 **Facilities** Children welcome Garden Parking Wi-fi ⬛

DREWSTEIGNTON
Map 3 SX79

The Drewe Arms

PICK OF THE PUBS

The Square EX6 6QN ☎ 01647 281224
e-mail: mail@thedrewearms.co.uk
dir: *W of Exeter on A30 for 12m. Left at Woodleigh junct follow signs for 3m to Drewsteignton*

In a sleepy village square, this traditional thatched pub lies just within Dartmoor National Park. Built in 1646, it used to be the Druid Arms, but in the 1920s the Drewe family, who had commissioned Sir Edwin Lutyens to design nearby Castle Drogo, persuaded the brewery to change the pub's name. The Drewes' contribution? They paid for a pub sign showing the family coat of arms. Real ales are served from the cask in the taproom and served through a hatchway into the bar. Dine in The Dartmoor or Card Rooms, or in Aunt Mabel's Kitchen, named after Mabel Mudge, landlady for 75 years from 1919 to 1994. Enjoy grilled steaks; pizzas; fillet of cod; steak-and-kidney pudding; fresh mussels cooked several ways; and Teign Valley venison pie, as well as sandwiches and ploughman's lunches. In summer relax in the attractive gardens or enjoy a game of boules.

Open all day all wk 11am-mdnt (winter 11-3 6-12) **Bar Meals** L served all wk 12-10 (winter 12-2.30) D served all wk 12-10 (winter 6-9.30) food served all day **Restaurant** L served all wk 12-10 (winter 12-2.30) D served all wk 12-10 (winter 6-9.30) food served all day ⊕ FREE HOUSE ◀ Otter Ale, Local guest ales Ö Winkleigh. ☂ 10 **Facilities** ☘ Children welcome Children's menu Children's portions Garden Parking Wi-fi ⬛

EAST ALLINGTON
Map 3 SX74

Fortescue Arms

TQ9 7RA ☎ 01548 521215
e-mail: info@fortescue-arms.co.uk
dir: *Telephone for directions*

This charming old country inn is the only pub in the village and was taken over by Jacqui Clifford and Ged Smith in May 2011. The flagstone-floored bar offers Dartmoor Legend, Sharp's Doom Bar and guest real ales. In the restaurant, expect the likes of pan-seared local hand-dived scallops, followed by slow-braised shoulder of lamb with pan-fried lamb chop, creamy mint mash and redcurrant sauce. For dessert, maybe coffee crème brûlée with cinnamon doughnuts. Booking for meals may be required.

Open 12-2.30 6-11 Closed: Mon L **Bar Meals** L served Tue-Sun 12-2.30 D served all wk 6.30-9.15 **Restaurant** L served Tue-Sun 12-2.30 D served all wk 6.30-9.15 ⊕ FREE HOUSE ◀ Dartmoor Legend, RCH Pitchfork, Sharp's Doom Bar, Guinness, Guest ales Ö Ashton Press. **Facilities** ☘ Children welcome Children's menu Children's portions Family room Garden Parking Wi-fi

PICK OF THE PUBS

The Nobody Inn ★★★★INN

DODDISCOMBSLEIGH   Map 3 SX88

EX6 7PS ☎ 01647 252394
e-mail: info@nobodyinn.co.uk
web: www.nobodyinn.co.uk
dir: *3m SW of Exeter Racecourse (A38)*

Difficult to find, but this famous Devon inn is worth the tricky drive through narrow lanes off the A38 at Haldon Racecourse. Set in rolling countryside between the Haldon Hills and the Teign Valley, the inn's history can be traced back to 1591, although it was another two centuries before it became a hostelry. For many years it served as the village's unofficial church house and meeting place, becoming a de facto inn along the way. It was officially licensed as the New Inn in 1838, and acquired its unusual name after an unfortunate incident following the innkeeper's death in 1952. His corpse was accidentally left in the mortuary while the funeral took place around an empty coffin with 'no body'. The present owners – only the fifth since 1838 – have refurbished the pub, but have wisely bypassed the bar, which retains its traditional ambience. Here, the low ceilings, blackened beams, inglenook fireplace and antique furniture all contribute to the timeless atmosphere, and you can sample some 260 wines and 230 whiskies in addition to an ever-changing range of real ales. Fresh fish is delivered daily from Brixham and decent bar meals are

served daily from a regularly changing menu. A typical dinner might begin with chicken liver pâté or home-smoked salmon served with horseradish cream; continuing with sea bass with tempura battered king prawns and wasabi mayonnaise; lamb shank with a rich mint gravy; and Dartmoor beef fillet wrapped in Parma ham and served with chips and a peppercorn sauce. Finish with sticky ginger pudding with toffee sauce or a board of West Country cheeses. A small bar shop sells cheeses, wine and whisky. Five attractive bedrooms are available. Booking for meals may be required.

Open all day all wk 11-11 (Sun 12-10.30) **Bar Meals** L served Mon-Sat 12-2, Sun 12-3 D served Mon-Thu

6.30-9, Fri-Sat 6.30-9.30, Sun 7-9 **Restaurant** D served Tue-Thu 6.30-9, Fri-Sat 6.30-9.30 ⊕ FREE HOUSE ◗ Branscombe Vale Nobody's Bitter, Guest ales ♂ Brimblecombe's, Healey's Cornish Rattler, Thatchers Gold. ♟ 28 **Facilities** Children welcome Children's portions Garden Parking Wi-fi **Rooms** 5

EXETER
Map 3 SX99

The Hour Glass

21 Melbourne St EX2 4AU ☎ 01392 258722
e-mail: ajpthehourglass@yahoo.co.uk
dir: *From M5 junct 30, A370 signed Exeter. At Countess Weir rdbt 3rd exit onto Topsham Rd (B3182) signed City Centre. In approx 2m left into Melbourne St*

This distinctively shaped backstreet pub has built up a reputation for its friendly service and inventive food, not to mention its impressive range of local real ales. Expect beams, wood floors, an open fire and resident cats in the bar, where handpulled pints of Otter Bitter or Exeter Ferryman; can be enjoyed with curried eggs and watercress; or lamb, quince and Rioja stew with anchovy dumplings. Booking for meals may be required.

Open 12-3 5-close (Sat-Sun all day Mon 5-close) Closed: 25-26 Dec, Mon L **Bar Meals** L served Tue-Fri 12.30-2.30, Sat-Sun 12.30-3 D served Mon-Sat 7-9.30, Sun 6-9 Av main course £13 **Restaurant** L served Tue-Fri 12.30-2.30, Sat-Sun 12.30-3 D served Mon-Sat 7-9.30, Sun 6-9 Av 3 course à la carte fr £23 ⊕ ENTERPRISE INNS ◀ Otter Bitter, Exeter Ferryman, Bath SPA ♂ Burrow Hill. ♚ 24 **Facilities** Wi-fi

Red Lion Inn

Broadclyst EX5 3EL ☎ 01392 461271
dir: *On B3181 (Exeter to Cullompton)*

You'll find the Red Lion in a 16th-century listed building set at the heart of a delightful village in the National Trust's Killerton Estate. The interior has a wealth of beams and warming open fires, where pints of Stormstay and Yellow Hammer are cheerfully served and supped. The menu offers light bites such as a smoked salmon prawn wrap or turn to the main dishes among which Exmoor Ale rabbit stew may be found. Treat yourself to a home-made pud afterwards.

Open all wk 11-3.30 5.30-11.30 (Sat 11am-11.30pm Sun 12-11) **Bar Meals** L served Mon-Fri 12-2.30, Sat-Sun 12-9 D served Mon-Fri 6-9, Sat-Sun 12-9 Av main course £7 **Restaurant** L served Mon-Fri 12-2.30, Sat-Sun 12-9 D served Mon-Fri 6-9, Sat-Sun 12-9 Av 3 course à la carte fr £25 ⊕ FREE HOUSE ◀ Fuller's London Pride, O'Hanlon's Yellow Hammer & Stormstay, Otter Ale ♂ Thatchers. ♚ 8 **Facilities** Children welcome Children's menu Children's portions Garden Parking 🚍 (notice required)

EXTON
Map 3 SX98

The Puffing Billy

PICK OF THE PUBS

Station Rd EX3 0PR ☎ 01392 877888
e-mail: enquiries@thepuffingbilly.co.uk
dir: *A376 signed Exmouth, through Ebford. Follow signs for Puffing Billy, turn right into Exton*

Acquired some three years ago by an expanding Devon-based hotel and restaurant group, the 16th-century Puffing Billy overlooks the Exe estuary near its confluence with the River Clyst. Local Otter and O'Hanlon's ales are dispensed at the smartly designed bar. Head chef Sean McBride arrived in 2011 to take charge of the kitchen, where he is building on the contemporary restaurant's reputation for modern British seasonal food, augmented by cosmopolitan flavours. Beef and venison are sourced from Dartmoor, while much of the fresh fish is caught in the Exe estuary and off the Devon coast. So an excellent start to your meal here would be the local seafood bouillabaisse with garlic purée and herb croûtons. Follow with roasted rabbit with chorizo pudding. And how better to finish than with an apple crumble and clotted cream? Doze off as you watch the river traffic go by from the secluded garden. Booking for meals may be required.

Open all wk 12-3 6-11 (Apr-Sep all day) Closed: 25 Dec **Bar Meals** L served Mon-Sat 12-2 Av main course £11.50 **Restaurant** L served Mon-Sat 12-2, Sun 12-3 D served Mon-Sat 6.30-9.30, Sun 6-9 Fixed menu price fr £14.95 Av 3 course à la carte fr £22 ⊕ FREE HOUSE ◀ Otter Bitter, Bays Topsail, O'Hanlon's Yellow Hammer. ♚ 15 **Facilities** Children welcome Children's menu Children's portions Garden Parking Wi-fi

GEORGEHAM
Map 3 SS43

The Rock Inn

Rock Hill EX33 1JW ☎ 01271 890322
e-mail: therockgeorgeham@gmail.com
dir: *From A361 at Braunton follow Croyde Bay signs. Through Croyde, 1m to Georgeham. Pass shop & church. Inn on right*

A great watering hole for walkers and cyclists, this old inn is also handy for the famous surfing beaches at Woolacombe. Its friendly atmosphere, comprising a mix of happy banter from the locals and gentle jazz played at lunchtime, adds to the enjoyment of a pint selected from the five ales on offer. Choose between the traditional bar, the slightly more contemporary lower bar, or a bright conservatory decorated with local art. The tasty menu is hard to resist, extending from a light lunch of Dave Wong's salt and pepper chilli squid, to dinner dishes such as the Rock's fish pie.

Open all day all wk **Bar Meals** L served all wk 12-2.30 D served all wk 6-9.30 **Restaurant** L served all wk 12-2.30 D served all wk 6-9.30 ⊕ PUNCH TAVERNS ◀ Timothy Taylor Landlord, Exmoor Gold, Fuller's London Pride, St Austell Tribute, Sharp's Doom Bar ♂ Thatchers Gold. ♚ 12 **Facilities** Children welcome Children's menu Children's portions Garden Parking Wi-fi 🚍

HARBERTON
Map 3 SX75

The Church House Inn

TQ9 7SF ☎ 01803 863707
e-mail: info@churchhouseharberton.co.uk
dir: *From Totnes take A381 S. Turn right for Harberton, pub by church in village centre*

Nestling in the beautiful South Devon countryside, this 13th-century free house is tucked away but easily accessible from Totnes. With high oak beams and a cosy atmosphere, The Church House was built around 1100 to accommodate monks constructing the church next door. Among its historic features is a fine medieval oak screen separating the long bar with its wood burners from the comfortable family room. Popular favourites on the menu include home-made chicken liver pâté; grilled scallop and tiger prawn kebab; poached salmon; and gammon steak with pineapple or egg. Booking for meals may be required.

Open all wk all day (Mon-Tue 12-3 6-11) **Bar Meals** L served all wk 12-2 D served all wk 6.30-9 Av main course £10.50 **Restaurant** L served all wk 12-2 D served all wk 6.30-9 ⊕ FREE HOUSE ◀ Dartmoor Jail Ale, Skinner's Betty Stogs ♂ Addlestones, Sandford Devon Mist, Westons. ♚ 12 **Facilities** ♣ Children welcome Children's menu Children's portions Parking Wi-fi 🚍 (notice required)

HAYTOR VALE
Map 3 SX77

The Rock Inn ★★★★ INN ◉

PICK OF THE PUBS

See Pick of the Pubs on opposite page

HOLSWORTHY
Map 3 SS30

The Bickford Arms

Brandis Corner EX22 7XY ☎ 01409 221318
e-mail: info@bickfordarms.com
dir: *On A3072, 4m from Holsworthy towards Hatherleigh*

This pub stood on the Holsworthy to Hatherleigh road for 300 years before it was gutted by fire in 2003. Although totally rebuilt, it retains much period charm, with beams, a welcoming bar and two fireplaces. The bar serves international beers, local real ales and ciders. Choose from the same menu in the bar and restaurant – perhaps free-range Devon duck breast with redcurrant and red wine sauce, or home-made steak-and-ale pie. All food is prepared with locally sourced ingredients. On Sunday summer evenings, the beer garden hosts popular barbecues.

Open all wk 11-11 **Bar Meals** L served all wk 12-2.30 D served all wk 6-9 ⊕ FREE HOUSE ◀ Skinner's Betty Stogs, Sharp's Doom Bar, Dartmoor Legend, St Austell Tribute ♂ Healey's Cornish Rattler. **Facilities** ♣ Children welcome Children's menu Children's portions Garden Parking Wi-fi

Save on hotels. Book at **theAA.com/hotel**

DEVON 159 ENGLAND

PICK OF THE PUBS

The Rock Inn ★★★★ INN ❀

HAYTOR VALE   Map 3 SX77

TQ13 9XP ☎ **01364 661305**
e-mail: inn@rock-inn.co.uk
web: www.rock-inn.co.uk
dir: *A38 from Exeter, at Drum Bridges
rdbt take A382 for Bovey Tracey, 1st exit
at 2nd rdbt (B3387), 3m left to Haytor
Vale*

Sheltering below the Haytor Rocks, this beamed and flagstoned 18th-century inn is an oasis of calm and comfort on wild and windy Dartmoor. The old coaching inn occupies a stunning location just inside Dartmoor National Park, with wonderful surrounding walks. The nine upgraded and comfortable en suite bedrooms, all named after Grand National winners, make this family-run inn a peaceful base for exploring Dartmoor and south Devon's superb coastline. The old stables recall the pub's strategic position on the road between Widecombe-in-the-Moor and Newton Abbot. The characterful, traditional interior has sturdy old furnishings, plenty of antique tables, settles, prints and paintings, a grandfather clock, and various pieces of china over the two fireplaces, where logs crackle constantly on winter days and make a welcome respite from Dartmoor's wilderness. Both the classic main bar and the attractive adjoining rooms are popular settings in which to appreciate some solid modern British cooking, using top-notch local produce in attractively presented dishes.

After a day walking on the moor, healthy appetites can be satisfied with seared scallops served with celeriac and vanilla purée and crispy Parma ham; and rump of Devon lamb on a bed of wilted spinach with a rosemary fondant potato and parsnip purée. Leave room for a caramelised lemon tart with ginger ice cream, or vanilla pannacotta served with shortbread and plum compôte. Simpler, more traditional lunch dishes include beef stew, seafood platter and chicken Caesar salad — best enjoyed alfresco in the sheltered courtyard or in the peaceful garden across the lane. West Country cheese is a particular feature, alongside wine from the Sharpham Vineyard in Totnes and local ales, including Dartmoor Jail Ale or IPA. Booking for meals may be required.

Open all day all wk 11-11 (Sun 12-10.30) Closed: 25-26 Dec **Bar Meals** L served all wk 12-2 Av main course £10.95 **Restaurant** D served all wk 7-9 Fixed menu price fr £19 Av 3 course à la carte fr £28 ⊕ FREE HOUSE ◀ Dartmoor Jail Ale, IPA ♂ Luscombe. ♟ 12 **Facilities** Children welcome Children's menu Children's portions Family room Garden Parking Wi-fi **Rooms** 9

HONITON   Map 4 ST10

The Holt ⊛

PICK OF THE PUBS

178 High St EX14 1LA ☎ 01404 47707
e-mail: enquiries@theholt-honiton.com
dir: *Telephone for directions*

Brothers Joe and Angus McCaig's family has been in the brewing business for three generations and their pub in the heart of Honiton reaps the benefits. It serves the full range of the family's Otter ales in the downstairs bar, busy with timeworn pub tables and chairs and a spread of sofas. The open-plan kitchen provides plenty of buzz; in the candlelit upstairs dining area tables look down on the bar below, so you can still feel totally involved. The pub also has its own smokery, where locally sourced poultry, meats, game, fish, shellfish and cheese are prepared. The frequently-changing menu is supplemented by daily specials and tapas; such inventive cooking has gained The Holt an AA Rosette. A starter of maple-smoked duck breast with garlic toast, spiced figs and pickled apple might precede applewood smoked haddock and leek chowder with air-dried ham, For pudding, maybe spiced orange bavarois with a honey and nut crunch. Booking for meals may be required.

Open 11-3 5.30-12 Closed: 25-26 Dec, Sun & Mon **Bar Meals** L served Tue-Sat 12-2 D served Tue-Sat 6.30-9 **Restaurant** L served Tue-Sat 12-2 D served Tue-Sat 6.30-9.30 ⊕ FREE HOUSE ◀ Otter Bitter, Ale, Bright, Amber, Head. ☂ 9 **Facilities** Children welcome Children's portions Wi-fi 🚍

IDDESLEIGH   Map 3 SS50

The Duke of York

PICK OF THE PUBS

EX19 8BG ☎ 01837 810253
e-mail: john@dukeofyorkdevon.co.uk
dir: *Telephone for directions*

Set deep in rural mid-Devon in a small hamlet, this timeless thatched inn was originally three cottages housing craftsmen who were rebuilding the parish church; local records accurately date this work to 1387. All the features of a classic country pub remain – heavy old beams, scrubbed tables, farmhouse chairs and a huge inglenook fireplace with crackling log fires. There's no truck for piped music and electronic games here and new owner John Pittam plans to keep it that way. Popular with all, it offers Cotleigh Tawny and guest ale on tap and hearty home cooking, with everything freshly prepared using local produce, such as meat reared on nearby farms. Typically, tuck into crab mayonnaise; pork belly with mustard and thyme sauce; and aga-roasted lamb shank with rosemary, garlic and red wine sauce. Featured in Michael Morpurgo's book *War Horse*.

Open all day all wk 11-11 **Bar Meals** L served all wk 11-10 D served all wk 11-10 food served all day ⊕ FREE HOUSE ◀ Adnams Broadside, Cotleigh Tawny Owl, Guest ales Ⓑ Winkleigh. ☂ 10 **Facilities** ❈ Children welcome Children's menu Children's portions Garden Beer festival Wi-fi 🚍

ILFRACOMBE   Map 3 SS54

The George & Dragon

5 Fore St EX34 9ED ☎ 01271 863851
e-mail: linda.quinn5@btinternet.com
dir: *Telephone for directions*

The oldest pub in town, The George & Dragon dates from 1360 and is reputedly haunted. The food is of the simple, no-nonsense variety – typical examples include home-cooked boozy beef, chicken curry, mixed grills, and home-cooked crab from the harbour when available. there are no fruit machines or pool table, but if you are lucky there will be a little home-produced background music, along with a good choice of real ales and ciders.

Open all day all wk 10am-mdnt (Sun 12-12) **Bar Meals** L served all wk 12-3 D served all wk 6.30-9 **Restaurant** L served all wk 12-3 D served all wk 6.30-9 ⊕ PUNCH TAVERNS ◀ Shepherd Neame Spitfire, Skinner's Betty Stogs, Exmoor Ale. **Facilities** ❈ Children welcome Children's menu Children's portions 🚍 **Notes** ⊛

KILMINGTON   Map 4 SY29

The Old Inn **NEW**

EX13 7RB ☎ 01297 32096
e-mail: pub@oldinnkilmington.co.uk
web: www.oldinnkilmington.co.uk
dir: *From Axminster on A35 towards Honiton. Pub on left in 1m*

Duncan and Leigh Colvin's thatched Devon longhouse dates from 1650, when it was a staging house for changing post horses, and stands beside the A35 just west of Axminster. Weary travellers will find a cosy, beamed interior with a relaxed atmosphere, crackling log fires, and a fine range of local ales on tap. Order a pint of Otter to accompany a traditional pub meal, perhaps a Devon beef ploughman's lunch; ham, egg and chips; fish pie; or a daily chalkboard special like sea bass on sweet potato and fennel risotto. The south-facing garden is the venue for the Spring and August Bank Holiday beer festivals.

Open all wk 11-3 6-11 Closed: 25-26 Dec **Bar Meals** L served all wk 12-2 D served all wk 6-9 Av main course £11 **Restaurant** L served all wk 12-2 D served all wk 6-9 Av 3 course à la carte fr £18 ⊕ FREE HOUSE ◀ Otter Bitter, Branscombe Vale Branoc & Drayman's Best Ⓑ Ashton Still. ☂ 10 **Facilities** ❈ Children welcome Children's menu Children's portions Garden Beer festival Parking 🚍 (notice required)

KINGSBRIDGE   Map 3 SX74

The Crabshell Inn

Embankment Rd TQ7 1JZ ☎ 01548 852345
e-mail: info@thecrabshellinn.com
dir: *A38 towards Plymouth, follow signs for Kingsbridge*

A traditional sailors' watering hole on the Kingsbridge estuary – you can moor up to three hours either side of high tide. If arriving by road, the car park has capacity for 25 vehicles. As you would expect, the views from the outside tables – with a glass of Proper Job in hand – and from the first-floor restaurant are unbeatable. The concise menu and specials board use locally sourced produce and might include Sharpham brie sandwiches; fish pie topped with creamed potato and cheese; or a marinated butterfly chicken breast from the chargrill.

Open all day all wk **Bar Meals** L served all wk 12-3, all day Jul-Aug D served all wk 6-9, all day Jul-Aug Av main course £8.25 **Restaurant** L served all wk 12-3, all day Jul-Aug D served all wk 6-9, all day Jul-Aug Fixed menu price fr £8.25 ⊕ FREE HOUSE ◀ Sharp's Doom Bar & Cornish Coaster, Otter Ale, St Austell Proper Job Ⓑ Addlestones, Westons Stowford Press. ☂ **Facilities** ❈ Children welcome Children's menu Children's portions Play area Family room Garden Parking 🚍

KINGSKERSWELL   Map 3 SX86

Barn Owl Inn

Aller Mills TQ12 5AN ☎ 01803 872130
e-mail: barnowl.allermills@hall-woodhouse.co.uk
dir: *Telephone for directions*

Flagged floors, a black-leaded range and oak beams are amongst the many charming original features at this 16th-century former farmhouse. The renovated building, which is handy for Dartmoor and the English Riviera towns, also boasts a high-vaulted converted barn with a minstrels' gallery. Lunchtime snacks include toasties, wraps and baguettes, while the main menu features plenty of traditional pub favourites all washed down with a pint of Tanglefoot or Badger First Gold. Recent change of hands.

Open all day all wk 11-11 (Sun 12-10.30) **Bar Meals** L served all wk 12-9 D served all wk 12-9 food served all day **Restaurant** L served all wk 12-9 D served all wk 12-9 food served all day ⊕ WOODHOUSE INNS ◀ Badger First Gold, Tanglefoot. ☗ 16 **Facilities** ❀ Children welcome Children's menu Children's portions Garden Parking ▬

Bickley Mill Inn
PICK OF THE PUBS

TQ12 5LN ☎ **01803 873201**
e-mail: info@bickleymill.co.uk
dir: From Newton Abbot on A380 towards Torquay. Right at Barn Owl Inn, follow brown tourist signs

A short drive from Torquay and Newton Abbot, this former 13th-century flour mill occupies an enviably secluded location in the wooded Stoneycombe Valley. Now a family-owned free house, the spacious property blends old and new in a fresh contemporary style. It comprises an attractive bar with roaring log fires and comfy sofas, and a restaurant separated into three areas – The Fireside, The Mill Room and The Panel Room. While perusing the appealing menu enjoy a pint of Otter or Teignworthy ale. Dishes are freshly prepared using quality produce from the local area. Fish from Brixham is a feature of the daily specials, along with regulars slow-braised lamb shank, minted pea purée, champ and rosemary jus; supreme of chicken, wild mushroom, leek and Madeira sauce; and pan-fried sea bass fillets with creamy mashed potato, crayfish and cucumber butter. There is outside decking and a tranquil garden. Booking for meals may be required.

Open all wk Mon-Sat 11.30-3 6.30-11 (Sun 11.30-3 6-10.30) Closed: 1 Jan **Bar Meals** L served Mon-Sat 12-2, Sun 12-2.30 D served Mon-Sat 6.30-9.15, Sun 6-8.30 **Restaurant** L served Mon-Sat 12-2, Sun 12-2.30 D served all wk 6.30-9.15 ⊕ FREE HOUSE ◀ Otter Ale, Teignworthy, Bays. ☗ 9 **Facilities** ❀ Children welcome Children's menu Children's portions Garden Parking Wi-fi ▬

KINGS NYMPTON   Map 3 SS61

The Grove Inn
PICK OF THE PUBS

EX37 9ST ☎ **01769 580406**
e-mail: enquiry@thegroveinn.co.uk
dir: 2.5m from A377 (Exeter to Barnstaple road). 1.5m from B3226 (South Molton road)

The Grove is the epitome of what an English pub should be: thatched roof, beamed ceilings, stone walls, rustic furnishings, flagstone floor and blazing winter log fires. Look for the hundreds of bookmarks on the bar beams. The picturesque inn shares listed status with the generous array of thatched cottages in this secluded village. Moreover, The Grove has been at the vanguard of the localisation movement, working closely with north Devon farmers for nearly a decade to source truly fresh,

seasonal produce from just down the lane. The rare-breed sausages hail from Highland Hogs, the beef from Mays Farm, whilst the ice cream is from Parsonage Farm. Add wild rabbit stew or perhaps chickpea, spinach and cauliflower curry, and there's something for most palates. Lucky locals and visitors can indulge in memorable Devon farmhouse ciders or West Country beers such as Devon Darter. Booking for meals may be required.

Open 12-3 6-11 (BH 12-3) Closed: Sun D & Mon L ex BH **Bar Meals** L served Tue-Sat 12-2 **Restaurant** L served Tue-Sat 12-2, Sun 12-2.30 D served Mon summer 7-9, Tue-Sat 6.45-9 ⊕ FREE HOUSE ◀ Exmoor Ale, Sharp's Own, Clearwater Devon Dympsy & Devon Darter, Skinner's Betty Stogs ♂ Winkleigh & Sam's Dry. ☗ 26 **Facilities** ❀ Children welcome Children's menu Children's portions Garden ▬ (notice required)

KINGSTON   Map 3 SX64

The Dolphin Inn

TQ7 4QE ☎ **01548 810314**
e-mail: info@dolphininn.eclipse.co.uk
dir: From A379 (Plymouth to Kingsbridge road) take B3233 for Bigbury-on-Sea. Take the turning for Kingston and follow brown inn signs

A 16th-century inn originally built as cottages for stonemasons working on the adjacent village church, and subsequently occupied by fishermen's families. Off the beaten track just a mile from the beaches of the South Hams and the beautiful Erme estuary, it's a popular watering hole for walkers, golfers and water-sports enthusiasts. Refreshments include Haye Farm cider, and home-made food ranges from traditional steak-and-kidney pie, or liver and onions, to fish and seafood specials involving lobster, crab, sea bass and lemon sole.

Open 12-3 6-11 (Sun 12-3 7-10.30) Closed: Sun eve winter **Bar Meals** L served Mon-Fri 12-2, Sat-Sun 12-2.30 D served all wk 6-9, closed Sun eve winter Av main course £10.95 **Restaurant** L served Mon-Fri 12-2, Sat-Sun 12-2.30 D served all wk 6-9, closed Sun & Mon eve winter ⊕ PUNCH TAVERNS ◀ Teignworthy Spring Tide, Courage Best, Sharp's Doom Bar, Otter ♂ Haye Farm. **Facilities** ❀ Children welcome Children's menu Children's portions Play area Family room Garden Parking Wi-fi

LIFTON   Map 3 SX38

The Arundell Arms ★★★ HL ⊛⊛
PICK OF THE PUBS

PL16 0AA ☎ **01566 784666**
e-mail: reservations@arundellarms.com
dir: 1m off A30 dual carriageway, 3m E of Launceston

Visitors to this 300-year-old inn can enjoy a mix of first-rate accommodation and exceptional menus, while also enjoying the countless activities that have made The Arundell Arms a destination of choice for lovers both of countryside and country sports. Walkers and horse-riders can enjoy some of Devon's most unspoilt countryside, whilst the inn's own 20 miles of beats on the Tamar and tributaries attract fly-fishers. Local farms and estates host various shoots, as well as raising livestock that features across the menus of the three dining areas, and has earned the inn's restaurant two AA Rosettes. The Arundell Arms' pub, the Lifton Courthouse, was formerly the village police station and magistrates court – note the bars over two of the windows. Indoor sports such as alley skittles and table football are a popular feature enjoyed by locals and visitors alike, as are the real ales on offer such as St Austell Tribute. The Courthouse menu offers good robust bar food, including rump steak with home-made onion rings, and beer-battered haddock and chips.

Open all wk 12-3 6-11 **Bar Meals** L served all wk 12-2 D served all wk 6-9.30 Av main course £8.95 **Restaurant** Fixed menu price fr £18.50 Av 3 course à la carte fr £19.50 ⊕ FREE HOUSE ◀ St Austell Tribute, Dartmoor Jail Ale, Guest ales ♂ Thatchers, Healey's Cornish Rattler. ☗ 9 **Facilities** ❀ Children welcome Children's menu Children's portions Garden Parking Wi-fi **Rooms** 21

LUSTLEIGH   Map 3 SX78

The Cleave Pub

TQ13 9TJ ☎ **01647 277223**
e-mail: ben@thecleavelustleigh.com
dir: From Newton Abbot take A382, follow Bovey Tracey signs, then Moretonhampstead signs. Left to Lustleigh

Dating from the 16th century, this thatched, family-run pub is the only one in the village and is adjacent to the cricket pitch. It has a traditional snug bar, with beams, granite flooring and log fire; to the rear, formerly the old railway station waiting room, is now a light and airy dining area leading to a lovely cottage garden. The pub/ bistro has gained a reputation for an interesting and varied menu. Dishes include mushroom ravioli; seared kangaroo steak; and fresh fish and seafood, depending on the catch. The Cleave hosts regular films, quizzes, Wii nights, concerts and live music.

Open all day all wk 11-11 **Bar Meals** L served all wk all day D served all wk all day food served all day **Restaurant** L served all wk all day D served all wk all day food served all day ⊕ HEAVITREE ◀ Otter Ale, Bitter ♂ Aspall. **Facilities** ❀ Children welcome Children's menu Children's portions Garden Parking Wi-fi ▬ (notice required)

LUTON (NEAR CHUDLEIGH) — Map 3 SX97

The Elizabethan Inn

Fore St TQ13 0BL ☎ **01626 775425**
e-mail: elizabethaninn@btconnect.com
web: www.elizabethaninn.co.uk
dir: *Between Chudleigh & Teignmouth*

Good honest Devon food and drink attract diners and drinkers alike to this welcoming 16th-century free house, known locally as the Lizzie. There's a choice selection of Devon ales, as well as Thatchers Gold and local Reddaway's cider to drink beside a log fire in winter or in the pretty beer garden or on warmer days. The pub prides itself on using the best of local ingredients. The bar menu includes salad bowls and tradtional dishes, while the main menu might offer seared lamb's liver, Viennese-style Stroganoff, pan-fried sea bass fillet, and a vegetarian linguine. A take-away menu is available. A beer festival is held in June. Booking for meals may be required.

Open all wk 12-3 6-11.30 (Sun all day) Closed: 25-26 Dec, 1 Jan **Bar Meals** L served Mon-Sat 12-2, Sun 12-9 D served all wk 6-9.30, Sun 12-9 Av main course £12.50 **Restaurant** L served Mon-Sat 12-2, Sun 12-9 D served all wk 6-9.30, Sun 12-9 Fixed menu price fr £16.50 Av 3 course à la carte fr £28 ⊕ FREE HOUSE ◀ Fuller's London Pride, Teignworthy Reel Ale, Otter Ale, Dartmoor IPA, St Austell Tribute ⌀ Thatchers Gold, Reddaway's Farm. ♀ 11 **Facilities** ✿ Children welcome Children's menu Children's portions Garden Beer festival Parking Wi-fi

LYDFORD — Map 3 SX58

Dartmoor Inn ◉◉

PICK OF THE PUBS

EX20 4AY ☎ **01822 820221**
e-mail: info@dartmoorinn.co.uk
dir: *On A386 S of Okehampton*

Owners Karen and Philip Burgess have made their mark at this distinctive free house, which Charles Kingsley almost certainly described in his novel *Westward Ho!* The stylish, restrained décor extends through the cosy dining rooms and small bar, where real ales and high-class pub classics are on offer. Food is based on seasonal ingredients, sourced locally, and turned into top-notch dishes. In the New England-style restaurant you might start with corned beef terrine with mustard dressing, followed by pan-fried lamb's kidneys, bacon, black pudding and red wine sauce. After your meal, you can even browse for beautiful accessories and homeware in the inn's own boutique.

Open all day 11-3 6-11 Closed: Sun eve, Mon L (ex BHs) **Bar Meals** L served Tue-Sun 12-2.30 D served all wk 6.30-9.15 **Restaurant** L served Tue-Sun 12-2.30 D served all wk 6.30-9.15 ⊕ FREE HOUSE ◀ Otter Ale, St Austell Tribute. **Facilities** ✿ Children welcome Garden Parking

LYMPSTONE — Map 3 SX98

The Globe Inn

The Strand EX8 5EY ☎ **01395 263166**
dir: *Telephone for directions*

The arrival of a new chef has enhanced the good local reputation for food and drink at this friendly beamed village pub in the estuary village of Lympstone. Well-kept Bass, Otter and London Pride are the ales on offer in the bar, while the menu offers traditional dishes such as lambs' liver, bacon and onion; home-made fish pie and seafood platters to share. On Sundays, landlady Sheila's traditional roasts are especially popular. Occasional music nights and Tuesday is quiz night. There's no food on Mondays.

Open all day all wk 11-11 **Bar Meals** L served Tue-Sat 11.45-2.15, Sun 12-2 D served Tue-Sat 5.45-9.15 **Restaurant** L served Tue-Sat 11.45-2.15, Sun 12-2 D served Tue-Sat 5.45-9.15 ⊕ HEAVITREE ◀ Fuller's London Pride, Otter, Bass ⌀ Aspall, Addlestones. ♀ 10 **Facilities** ✿ Children welcome

LYNMOUTH — Map 3 SS74

Rising Sun Hotel ★★ HL ◉

PICK OF THE PUBS

Harbourside EX35 6EG ☎ **01598 753223**
e-mail: reception@risingsunlynmouth.co.uk
dir: *From M5 junct 25 follow Minehead signs. A39 to Lynmouth*

Overlooking Lynmouth's tiny harbour and bay is this 14th-century thatched smugglers' inn. In turn, overlooking them all, are Countisbury Cliffs, the highest in England. The building's long history is evident from the uneven oak floors, crooked ceilings and thick walls. Literary associations are plentiful: R D Blackmore wrote some of his wild Exmoor romance, *Lorna Doone*, here; the poet Shelley is believed to have honeymooned in the garden cottage, and Coleridge stayed too. Immediately behind rises Exmoor Forest and National Park, home to red deer, wild ponies and birds of prey. With moor and sea so close, game and seafood are in plentiful supply; appearing in dishes such as braised pheasant with pancetta and quince and Braunton greens; and roast shellfish – crab, mussels, clams and scallops in garlic, ginger and coriander. At night the oak-panelled, candlelit dining room is an example of romantic British inn-keeping at its best. Booking for meals may be required.

Open all day all wk 11am-mdnt Closed: 25 Dec **Bar Meals** L served all wk 12-2.30 D served all wk 6-9 **Restaurant** D served all wk 7-9 ⊕ FREE HOUSE ◀ Exmoor Gold, Fox, Antler, Ale ⌀ Thatchers Gold, Addlestones. **Facilities** ✿ 🚐 Rooms 14

MARLDON — Map 3 SX86

The Church House Inn

Village Rd TQ3 1SL ☎ **01803 558279**
dir: *Take Torquay ring road, follow signs to Marldon & Totnes, follow brown signs to pub*

Built as a hostel for the stonemasons of the adjoining village church, this ancient country inn dates from 1362. It was rebuilt in 1740 and many features from that period still remain, including beautiful Georgian windows; some of the original glass is intact despite overlooking the cricket pitch. These days it has an uncluttered, contemporary feel with additional seating in the garden. As well as sandwiches, the lunch menu includes Dartmouth smoked fish platter; aubergine and lentil moussaka; and cauliflower roulade. Typical evening offerings are slow-roasted shoulder of lamb and wild turbot.

Open all wk 11.30-2.30 5-11 (Fri-Sat 11.30-2.30 5-11.30 Sun 12-3 5.30-10.30) **Bar Meals** L served all wk 12-2 D served all wk 6.30-9.30 Av main course £14 **Restaurant** L served all wk 12-2 D served all wk 6.30-9.30 Av 3 course à la carte fr £25 ⊕ FREE HOUSE ◀ Morland Old Speckled Hen, Greene King IPA, Fuller's London Pride, Bass. ♀ 12 **Facilities** ✿ Children welcome Children's portions Garden Parking

MEAVY — Map 3 SX56

The Royal Oak Inn

PL20 6PJ ☎ **01822 852944**
e-mail: info@royaloakinn.org.uk
dir: *B3212 from Yelverton to Princetown. Right at Dousland to Meavy, past school. Pub opposite village green*

This traditional 15th-century inn is situated by a village green within Dartmoor National Park. Flagstone floors, oak beams and a welcoming open fire set the scene at this free house popular with cyclists and walkers. Local cask ales, ciders and fine wines accompany the carefully sourced ingredients in a menu ranging from lunchtime light bites to steak-and-ale pie; home-cooked ham, egg and chips; or local bangers and mash. Look out for cider and beer festivals during the year.

Open all wk Mon-Fri 11-3 6-11 (Sat-Sun & Apr-Oct all day) **Bar Meals** L served Mon-Fri 12-2.30, Sat-Sun 12-3 D served all wk 6-9 **Restaurant** L served Mon-Fri 12-2.30, Sat-Sun 12-3 D served all wk 6-9 ⊕ FREE HOUSE ◀ Dartmoor Jail Ale & IPA, St Austell Tribute, Sharp's Doom Bar, Guest ales ⌀ Westons Old Rosie, Sandford Orchards Devon Red. ♀ 12 **Facilities** Children welcome Children's menu Children's portions Garden Beer festival 🚐

MODBURY — Map 3 SX65

California Country Inn

PICK OF THE PUBS

See Pick of the Pubs on opposite page

PICK OF THE PUBS

California Country Inn

MODBURY Map 3 SX65

California Cross PL21 0SG
☎ **01548 821449**

e-mail: enquiries@californiacountryinn.co.uk
web: www.californiacountryinn.co.uk
dir: *On B3196 (NE of Modbury)*

This centuries-old inn stands in some of the most tranquil countryside in southern England, just a few miles from Dartmoor to the north and the cliffs and estuaries of the coast to the south. In fact, this Area of Outstanding Natural Beauty encompasses the hills and vales which can be seen from the pub's landscaped and lawned gardens. Dating from the 14th century, its unusual name is thought to derive from local adventurers in the mid-19th century who heeded the call to 'go west' and waited at the nearby crossroads for the stage to take them on the first part of their journey to America's west coast. They must have suffered wistful thoughts of home when recalling their local pub, with its wizened old beams, exposed dressed-stone walls and a fabulous, huge stone fireplace. Old rural prints and photographs, copper kettles, jugs, brasses and many other artefacts add to the rustic charm of the whitewashed pub's atmospheric interior. A family-run free house, the beers on tap are likely to include Sharp's and Fuller's, the wine list has award-winning Devon wines from nearby Sharpham Vineyard, and the good-value house wines come from — you guessed — California. Having won

accolades as a dining pub, head chef Tim Whiston's food is thoughtfully created and impressively flavoursome. Most ingredients are sourced from the bounty of the local countryside and waters, with meats from a supplier in nearby Loddiswell and fish from the renowned 'Catch of the Day' in Kingsbridge. Meals can be taken from the bar menu, but why not indulge in the à la carte menu from the inn's dining room? Appetising starters include five-spiced duck salad, and seafood pancake. The main course selection may include local guinea fowl (leg confit and pan-fried breast) with creamed wild mushrooms, or pan-fried sea bass fillets. Specials and desserts can be found on the ever-changing blackboards. Booking for meals may be required.

Open all day all wk **Bar Meals** L served Mon-Sat 12-2, Sun 12-2.30 D served Mon-Sat 6-9, Sun 6-8.30 Av main course £15 **Restaurant** L served Sun 12-2 D served Wed-Sun 6-9 Fixed menu price fr £10.95 ⊕ FREE HOUSE ◼ Otter Bitter, Fuller's London Pride, Sharp's Doom Bar. ♉ 3 draught ciders
Facilities Children welcome Children's menu Children's portions Family room
❀ Garden Parking Wi-fi 🚌

NEWTON ABBOT — Map 3 SX87

The Wild Goose Inn

Combeinteignhead TQ12 4RA ☎ 01626 872241
dir: *From A380 at Newton Abbot rdbt take B3195 (Shaldon road), signed Milber, 2.5m into village, right at sign*

Originally licensed as the Country House Inn in 1840, this inn was renamed in the 1960s when nearby geese began intimidating the pub's customers. Set in the heart of Combeinteignhead at the head of a long valley, it's a charming free house that boasts a sunny garden. A good range of real ales and ciders accompanies home-made pub food prepared from local ingredients such as rope-grown Torbay mussels. You can also order from the daily fresh fish and specials board plus there are lighter options – a bowl of soup; pâté of the day; or a bara gallega (a continental baked roll). There is a village store and deli within the pub selling local produce, plus a beer festival every May Day weekend. Booking for meals may be required.

Open all wk 11-3 5.30-11 (Sun 12-3 7-11) **Bar Meals** L served all wk 12-2 D served Mon-Sat 7-9.30, Sun 7-9 Av main course £10 **Restaurant** L served all wk 12-2 D served Mon-Sat 7-9.30, Sun 7-9 ⊕ FREE HOUSE ◀ Otter Ale, Skinner's Best Bitter, Teignworthy, Branscombe Vale, Exe Valley, Cotleigh, Sharp's Ŏ Skinner's Press Gang, Wiscombe Suicider, Milltop Gold. ♥ 10 **Facilities** Children welcome Children's menu Children's portions Family room Garden Beer festival Parking

NEWTON ST CYRES — Map 3 SX89

The Beer Engine

EX5 5AX ☎ 01392 851282
e-mail: info@thebeerengine.co.uk
web: www.thebeerengine.co.uk
dir: *From Exeter take A377 towards Crediton. Signed from A377 towards Sweetham. Pub opp rail station over the bridge*

Originally opened as a railway hotel in 1852, this pretty whitewashed free house sits opposite the Tarka line on the banks of the River Creedy, much favoured by dogs and their walkers. The Beer Engine is also home to one of Devon's leading micro-breweries, producing ales delighting in names such as Rail Ale and Sleeper Heavy. Freshly baked bread uses the wort (beer yeast) from the brewery; dishes may include cod in Beer Engine batter or Sleeper ale steak pie; and vegetarians will rejoice in the

range of soups and bakes. Booking for meals may be required.

Open all day all wk Tue-Sat 11-11 (Sun 12-10.30 Mon 11-10.30) **Bar Meals** L served all wk 12-2.15 D served Tue-Sat 6.30-9.15, Sun-Mon 6.30-8.15 **Restaurant** L served all wk 12-2.15 D served Tue-Sat 6.30-9.15, Sun-Mon 6.30-8.15 ⊕ FREE HOUSE ◀ The Beer Engine Piston Bitter, Rail Ale, Sleeper Heavy, Silver Bullet Ŏ Westons Stowford Press, Dragons Tears. **Facilities** ❖ Children welcome Children's portions Garden Parking Wi-fi ▭

NORTH BOVEY — Map 3 SX78

The Ring of Bells Inn

PICK OF THE PUBS

TQ13 8RB ☎ 01647 440375
e-mail: mail@ringofbells.net
dir: *1.5m from Moretonhampstead off B3212. 7m S of Whiddon Down junct on A30*

This thatched Dartmoor pub dates back to the 13th-century and was originally built to house the stonemasons building the parish church. Overlooking the green in the pretty village of North Bovey, The Ring of Bells draws Dartmoor visitors and walkers in for good food and local Otter Ale. The kitchen uses fresh, locally sourced produce and menus reflect the changing seasons; suppliers are proudly listed. Served in cosy low-beamed bars, with heavy oak doors, rustic furnishings, crackling winter log fires and evening candlelight, the short daily menu may list fig and foie gras terrine with spiced fruit chutney or carpaccio of beef fillet for starters, followed by hearty main dishes such as roast rump of Dartmoor lamb with braised Puy lentils, or baked fillet of Cornish cod with a light River Teign mussel and fennel velouté. Round off with warm chocolate and banana pudding with banana ice cream. Booking for meals may be required.

Open all day all wk Closed: 25 Dec drinks only **Bar Meals** L served all wk 12-2.30 D served all wk 6-9 Av main course £13 **Restaurant** L served all wk 12-2.30 D served all wk 6-9 Av 3 course à la carte fr £28 ⊕ FREE HOUSE ◀ Otter Ale, St Austell Tribute, Sharp's Doom Bar, Teignworthy Reel Ale Ŏ Thatchers, Sheppy's. ♥ 15 **Facilities** Children welcome Children's portions Family room Garden Wi-fi ▭ (notice required)

NOSS MAYO — Map 3 SX54

The Ship Inn

PICK OF THE PUBS

PL8 1EW ☎ 01752 872387
e-mail: ship@nossmayo.com
dir: *5m S of Yealmpton on River Yealm estuary*

This award-winning waterside free house is a popular haunt for sailing enthusiasts and occupies a lovely spot on Noss Mayo's tidal waterfront on the south bank of the stunning Yealm estuary. The deceptively spacious building, refurbished using reclaimed local stone and

English oak, remains cosy thanks to its wooden floors, old bookcases, log fires and local pictures. Regional ales such as Dartmoor IPA are complemented by an ever-changing menu of home-made dishes majoring on local produce. Order home-baked Devon ham, free-range egg and chips, or haddock fillet fried in real ale batter with chips and mushy peas from the bar menu; or dive into the main menu for dishes such as rump of lamb with dauphinoise potatoes, or sea bass fillets on crushed new potatoes with olives and salsa verde. Round off with apple and plum crumble with custard. Walkers, too, throng the bar, and dogs are allowed downstairs.

Open all day all wk **Bar Meals** L served Mon-Sat 12-9.30, Sun 12-9 D served Mon-Sat 12-9.30, Sun 12-9 Av main course £13.95 food served all day **Restaurant** L served Mon-Sat 12-9.30, Sun 12-9 D served Mon-Sat 12-9.30, Sun 12-9 Av 3 course à la carte fr £25 food served all day ⊕ FREE HOUSE ◀ Dartmoor Jail Ale & IPA, St Austell Tribute & Proper Job, Otter, Palmers. ♥ 13 **Facilities** ❖ Children welcome Children's portions Garden Parking

OTTERY ST MARY — Map 3 SY19

The Talaton Inn

Talaton EX5 2RQ ☎ 01404 822214
dir: *Take A30 to Fairmile, then follow signs to Talaton*

This well-maintained, timber-framed 16th-century inn is run by a brother and sister partnership. There is a good selection of real ales (Otter Ale, Otter Bright) and malts, and a fine collection of bar games. The regularly-changing evening blackboard menu might include brie wedges with cranberry dip; surf and turf; tuna steak au poivre; or gammon and egg. At Sunday lunchtimes (booking advisable), as well as the popular roast, there is also a pie and vegetarian choice. There is a patio for summer dining and themed food nights.

Open 12-3 7-11 Closed: Mon (winter) **Bar Meals** L served Tue-Sun 12-2 D served Tue-Sun 7-9 Av main course £5-£8.25 **Restaurant** L served Tue-Sun 12-2 D served Tue-Sun 7-9 Fixed menu price fr £11 ⊕ FREE HOUSE ◀ Otter Ale & Bright, Guest ale Ŏ Westons Stowford Press. **Facilities** Children welcome Children's menu Children's portions Parking ▭ (notice required)

PARRACOMBE — Map 3 SS64

The Fox & Goose

PICK OF THE PUBS

See Pick of the Pubs on opposite page

Save on hotels. Book at **theAA.com/hotel**

DEVON 165 ENGLAND

PICK OF THE PUBS

The Fox & Goose

PARRACOMBE   Map 3 SS64

EX31 4PE ☎ 01598 763239

e-mail: info@foxandgooseinnexmoor.co.uk

web: www.foxandgooseinnexmoor.co.uk

dir: *1m from A39 between Blackmoor Gate & Lynton. Follow Parracombe signs*

This imposing Victorian building was once just a couple of tiny thatched cottages serving the local farming community. Transformation into a hotel took place when a narrow-gauge railway arrived in 1898 to link Parracombe with the outside world, represented by Lynton and Barnstaple. The line closed in the 1930s, although a short section was reopened a few years ago. Decorating the pub's interior are farm memorabilia, a scarf-wearing stag's head and photographs of villagers who now drink in more celestial surroundings; here beer-drinkers have a choice of local Cotleigh and Exmoor, Otter from South Devon and cider from Winkleigh, just north of Dartmoor. Good home-made food comes from constantly changing blackboard menus that are likely to feature seasonal game from surrounding farms and estates, as well as fish and shellfish caught off the north Devon coast. Examples include bouillabaisse; pan-fried skate wing with brown shrimp and capers; brill fillets

poached in red wine; and roast cod wrapped in bacon with Puy lentils. Among the meat choices are trio of venison sausages with creamy mash and gravy; fillet steak with sautéed mushrooms and cherry vine tomatoes; and confit of duck with juniper and port sauce. For vegetarians there are mushroom Stroganoff with cream, mustard and Cognac; and pearl barley risotto with roasted squash and sage. To follow, there's a good board of South West cheeses; brioche bread-and-butter pudding; and lemon posset with vanilla sablé biscuits. Pizzas are also available – either to eat in or take away. Children and dogs are welcome and, if they want, they can let off steam in the paved courtyard garden overlooking the river.

Open 12-2.30 6-11 (Sun 12-2.30 7-10.30; summer all day) Closed 25 Dec **Bar meals** all wk 12-2 Mon-Sat 6-9, Sun 7-9 Av main course £13.95 **Restaurant** all wk 12-2 Mon-Sat 6-9, Sun 7-9 Av 3 course à la carte fr £25 ⊕ FREE HOUSE ◀ Cotleigh Barn Owl, Exmoor Fox, Otter Ale, Sharp's Doom Bar, Guinness ♂ Winkleigh. ♚ 10 **Facilities** ☙ Children welcome Children's menu Children's portions Garden Parking Wi-fi

PETER TAVY — Map 3 SX57

Peter Tavy Inn

PL19 9NN ☎ **01822 810348**

e-mail: chris@wording.freeserve.co.uk

dir: *From Tavistock take A386 towards Okehampton. In 2m right to Peter Tavy*

Although this building on the western flanks of Dartmoor dates from the 15th century, it is likely that it became a pub by the early 17th century. It is thought the inn was originally built as a type of farmhouse called a Devon longhouse. It is now as much a draw for its range of local real ales and ciders as it is for its food, much of it sourced locally. Their pies are the most popular main dishes, while there are always vegetarian and vegan options. Wash down belly of pork or teriyaki chicken with pints of Dartmoor Jail Ale or Sam's Poundhouse dry cider.

Open all wk 12-3 6-11 (Sun 12-3 6-10.30); all day Etr-Autumn Closed: 25 Dec **Bar Meals** L served all wk 12-2 D served all wk 6.30-9 Av main course £10.95 **Restaurant** L served all wk 12-2 D served all wk 6.30-9 Av 3 course à la carte fr £21.85 ⊕ FREE HOUSE ◀ Dartmoor Jail Ale, Otter Bright, Branscombe Vale Drayman's Best Bitter ♂ Winkleigh Sam's Poundhouse & Crisp. ♥ 9 **Facilities** ❖ Children welcome Children's menu Children's portions Garden Parking Wi-fi

PLYMOUTH — Map 3 SX45

The Fishermans Arms

31 Lambhay St, The Barbican **PL1 2NN**
☎ **01752 661457**

e-mail: info@thefishermansarms.com

dir: *At top of Lambhay Hill turn right, pass large car park, 2nd right into Lambhay St*

One wall of this city-centre pub in the historic Barbican area is the only surviving part of Plymouth Castle, which was demolished in the 15th century. Devoid of modern-day intrusions, it's a bustling local with log fires, regular quiz nights, tip-top St Austell ales, and award-winning food. Dishes range from moules frites to steak, mushroom and ale pie. There is even a 3ft wide tunnel underneath the bar of Plymouth's second oldest pub, which runs to the shoreline — smugglers perhaps?

Open all wk Mon 6-11 Tue-Thu 12-3 6-11 (Fri-Sun all day from 12) **Bar Meals** L served Tue-Sat 12-2, Sun 12-3 D served Tue-Sat 6.30-9.30 **Restaurant** L served Tue-Sat 12-2, Sun 12-3 D served Tue-Sat 6.30-9.30 ⊕ ST AUSTELL BREWERY ◀ Tribute, Tinners Ale, HSD ♂ Healey's Cornish Rattler. ♥ 12 **Facilities** Children welcome Children's portions ▭ (notice required)

PLYMTREE — Map 3 ST00

The Blacksmiths Arms

EX15 2JU ☎ **01884 277474**

e-mail: blacksmithsplymtree@yahoo.com

dir: *From A373 (Cullompton to Honiton road) follow Plymtree signs. Pub in village centre*

Situated in an idyllic Devon village, this traditional yet stylish free house with exposed beams, large oak mirrors, log fire and comfortable seating has the atmosphere of a proper West Country pub. With a reputation for serving quality, freshly prepared food using local ingredients, it is known for generous portions with punchy flavours. Pick from pan-fried duck, gourmet burger, beef bourguignon and vegetable tart. Well-kept local ales include Otter Amber, and there is a fine selection of world wines. A large beer garden with boules piste, children's play area and alfresco dining area complete the picture. A beer festival is held in July every even-numbered year.

Open Tue-Fri 6-11 (Sat 12-11 Sun 12-10 (Sun 12-4 Oct-Mar)) Closed: Mon **Bar Meals** L served Sat-Sun 12-2 D served Tue-Sun 6-9 **Restaurant** L served Sat-Sun 12-2 D served Tue-Sun 6-9 ⊕ FREE HOUSE ◀ O'Hanlon's Yellow Hammer, Otter Amber, Exmoor Fox, St Austell Proper Job ♂ Westons Stowford Press, Healey's Cornish Rattler. ♥ 8 **Facilities** ❖ Children welcome Children's menu Children's portions Play area Family room Garden Beer festival Parking Wi-fi ▭ (notice required)

PORTGATE — Map 3 SX48

The Harris Arms

PICK OF THE PUBS

See Pick of the Pubs on opposite page

POSTBRIDGE — Map 3 SX67

Warren House Inn

PL20 6TA ☎ **01822 880208**

dir: *On B3212 between Moretonhampstead & Princetown*

Isolated high on Dartmoor, the Warren House (named after the prolific rabbit activity all around) has no mains services; it uses generators for electricity and gravity-fed water from a spring. It was built to service the local tin mines, and furnishes the same warm hospitality today — the fire in the hearth is said to have been burning continuously since 1845. Four real ales and scrumpy cider are served, along with a menu of good home-cooked food: hearty soups, a selection of pies, beef and lamb raised on the moor, and vegetables supplied by local farms.

Open all day all wk 11-11 (winter Mon-Tue 11-5) **Bar Meals** L served all wk 12-9, Mon-Tue in winter 12-4.30 D served all wk 12-9, Mon-Tue in winter 12-4.30 food served all day **Restaurant** L served all wk 12-9, Mon-Tue in winter 12-4.30 D served all wk 12-9, Mon-Tue in winter 12-4.30 food served all day ⊕ FREE HOUSE ◀ Otter Ale, Sharp's Doom Bar, Guest ales ♂ Countryman Cider, Thatchers Gold. **Facilities** ❖ Children welcome Children's menu Family room Garden Parking ▭

RATTERY — Map 3 SX76

Church House Inn

TQ10 9LD ☎ **01364 642220**

e-mail: ray.hardy@btconnect.com

web: www.thechurchhouseinn.co.uk

dir: *1m from A38 Exeter to Plymouth Rd & 0.75m from A385 Totnes to South Brent Rd*

Tracing its history as far back as 1028, this venerable inn burgeons with brasses, bare beams, large fireplaces and other historic features. Some customers encounter the wandering spirit of a monk; fortunately he seems to be friendly. In the character dining room, dishes include deep-fried camembert with a cranberry sauce followed by venison sausages with spicy mash, peas and gravy. Fresh fish (local trout grilled in butter; monkfish with a brandy cream and mushroom sauce) features strongly. For dessert, maybe choose pecan pie. There is a large lawn beer garden and patio where you can enjoy a pint of Dartmoor ale in warmer months. Booking for meals may be required.

Open all wk 11-2.30 6-11 (Sun 12-3 6-10.30) **Bar Meals** L served Mon-Sat 11.30-2, Sun 12-2 D served all wk 6.30-9 **Restaurant** L served Mon-Sat 11.30-2, Sun 12-2 D served all wk 6.30-9 ⊕ FREE HOUSE ◀ Dartmoor Jail Ale & Legend, George Gale & Co Seafarers, Exmoor Ale ♂ Thatchers Gold & Katy. ♥ 10 **Facilities** ❖ Children welcome Children's menu Children's portions Garden Parking ▭ (notice required)

ROCKBEARE — Map 3 SY09

Jack in the Green Inn ◉◉

PICK OF THE PUBS

See Pick of the Pubs on page 168

Save on hotels. Book at **theAA.com/hotel**

DEVON 167 ENGLAND

PICK OF THE PUBS

The Harris Arms

PORTGATE Map 3 SX48

EX20 4PZ ☎ 01566 783331
e-mail: info@theharrisarms.co.uk
web: www.theharrisarms.co.uk
dir: *From A30 at Broadwoodwidger/
Roadford Lake follow signs to Lifton
then Portgate*

Not far off the A30 just before Devon
turns into Cornwall, this 16th-century
inn has a string of awards going back
the best part of a decade. It's an
accessible spot for honest food with
substance and style and certainly lives
up to its promotional strapline: 'Eat real
food and drink real wine', the last part
picking up on owners Rowena and Andy
Whiteman's spells running vineyards in
France and New Zealand. You can
therefore be confident of an extensive
list of wines that you probably won't find
in supermarkets. In the bar the real ales
are from Devon – Bays Best, Otter Ale
and Holsworthy Tamar Sauce; so too is
Sam's Poundhouse real cider. The menu
is very much locally sourced, from Port
Isaac fresh fish to West Country
artisanal cheeses. Sample starters from
the carte include slow-cooked pork
cheeks with sweet potato and
mushroom hash, and sage and cider
sauce; and olives with feta cheese and
bread, while main dishes continue the
emphasis on good ingredients with
crispy confit of duck, haricot bean and
chorizo ragout with gratin potato and
red wine sauce; and roast lamb rump

with rosemary and garlic sauce. Fish,
game, vegetarian and other dishes are
chalked up daily and pub classics, such
as beer-battered fish and chips, get a
look in too. Enjoy a plate of tapas or
open griddled steak sandwich on
ciabatta outside on the decked patio
and admire the view of Brent Tor and its
village church in the distance. You may
even catch a glimpse of 'The Beast of
Portgate', otherwise known as Reg, the
pub's large strawberry blonde cat, and
Jerry the cockerel and his harem of
hens. Booking for meals may be
required.

Open Tue-Sat 12-3 6.30-11 (Sun 12-3)
Closed: Sun eve & Mon **Bar Meals** L
served Tue-Sun 12-2 D served Tue-Sat
6.30-9 Av main course £12.95

Restaurant L served Tue-Sun 12-2
D served Tue-Sat 6.30-9 2-course menu
£9.95 (Tue-Sat 6-7.30) Booking
essential Av 3 course à la carte fr £23
⊕ FREE HOUSE ◀ Otter Ale, Bays Best,
Holsworthy Tamar Sauce ♂ Winkleigh
Sam's Poundhouse. ♟ 20
Facilities Children welcome Children's
menu Children's portions ♣ Garden
Parking

PICK OF THE PUBS

Jack in the Green Inn ❀❀

ROCKBEARE   Map 3 SY09

London Rd EX5 2EE ☎ 01404 822240
e-mail: info@jackinthegreen.uk.com
web: www.jackinthegreen.uk.com
dir: *M5 junct 29, A30 towards Honiton,*
left signed Rockbeare

Collecting accolades at a rate of knots,
this white-painted, roadside pub has been
run for two decades by rugby aficionado
Paul Parnell. This is a man who works
tirelessly at maintaining the Jack's well-
deserved reputation for upmarket modern
pub food, but he dislikes the term gastro-
pub as he doesn't want people, especially
families, to think that it's purely a dining
venue and drive on by. What he offers is
good West Country brews on tap and, in
the restaurant, a simple philosophy of
serving the best Devon produce (with two
AA Rosettes to prove it) in stylish
surroundings — neat open-plan bar with
wood-burning stoves and leather
armchairs, and a warren of cosy dining
rooms adorned with fresh flowers and
prints. Local artisan producers underpin
chef Matthew Mason's innovative menus,
be it the local shoots which supply the
game, or the growers of salad leaves and
seasonal vegetables who live within six
miles of the pub. Pressed to label the food
style, Paul and Matthew would say modern
British, exemplified by dishes like Brixham
fish stew with smoked paprika rarebit;
breast of Creedy Carver free-range duck
with parsnip purée; and supreme of
chicken with buttered cabbage, bacon and
portabello mushroom sauce. Among the
more traditional pub grub selection are

slow-braised Kenniford Farm belly pork
with Puy lentils; real ale-battered fish (or
grilled if you'd prefer) with chips and
mushy peas; and the newly introduced
Thai green cod and prawn curry. The
'Totally Devon' menu is good value at £25
for three courses, or why not push the boat
out and go for the six-course tasting
menu? Look to the chalkboard for daily
specials like hand-dived scallops from
Lyme Bay. Dine in the spacious rear
courtyard in summer, and listen to live
jazz on the second Friday of the summer
months.

Open all wk 11-3 5.30-11 (Sun 12-11)
Closed: 25 Dec-5 Jan **Bar Meals** L
served Mon-Sat 12-2, Sun 12-9 D
served Mon-Sat 6-9.30, Sun 12-9 Av
main course £15 **Restaurant** L served
Mon-Sat 12-2, Sun12-9 D served Mon-

Sat 6-9.30, Sun 12-9 Fixed menu price
fr £25 Av 3 course à la carte fr £35
⊞ FREE HOUSE ◀ Otter Ale & Amber,
Sharp's Doom Bar, Butcombe Bitter
Ŏ Dragon Tears, Luscombe, St Georges.
♟ 12 **Facilities** Children welcome
Children's menu Children's portions
Family room Garden Parking Wi-fi
🚍 (notice required)

Save on hotels. Book at theAA.com/hotel

DEVON 169 ENGLAND

PICK OF THE PUBS

Blue Ball Inn ★★★★ INN

SIDMOUTH   Map 3 SY18

Stevens Cross, Sidford EX10 9QL
☎ **01395 514062**
e-mail: rogernewton@blueballinn.net
web: www.blueballinnsidford.co.uk
dir: *M5 junct 30, A3052, through Sidford towards Lyme Regis, inn on left*

Postcard-pretty under its pristine thatched roof, the 14th-century cob-and-flint Blue Ball has been run by generations of the Newton family since 1912 and was painstakingly rebuilt after a disastrous fire in 2006. Roger and Linda Newton sourced old furniture, pictures and memorabilia to recapture the unique atmosphere of the original inn. The spruced-up inn is a hugely attractive and lovingly maintained building, festooned with colourful hanging baskets in summer, when the patio and landscaped gardens come into their own. Arrive early in winter to bag a seat by one of the three log fires within the rambling carpeted bars, which specialise in hand-pumped cask-conditioned ales – try a pint of local Otter Bitter. The food bar and large dining area offer extensive menus of family favourites interspersed with dishes for the more sophisticated palate. So a starter like home-made fishcakes with rocket salad and tomato relish, for example, could be followed by steak-and-kidney pudding with mash and red wine gravy; or beer-battered local fish and chips. Don't forget to check out the specials too, or you may miss the crab and avocado tian with a lemon and cream dressing; or Lyme Bay line-caught sea bass on saffron mash with wilted spinach, roasted vine cherry tomatoes and a caper and parsley vinaigrette. There are nine contemporary en suite bedrooms, including one on the ground floor suitable for guests with disabilities, as well as a function room with full conference facilities. Within easy reach of the M5, A303 and Exeter, and just minutes from stunning walks along the coast, the Blue Ball's AA-rated accommodation provides an ideal base for exploring the county, or for a night's stay en route to the southwest. Booking for meals may be required.

Open all day all wk Closed: 25 Dec eve
Bar Meals L served all wk 12-2.30
D served all wk 6-9 **Restaurant** L served
all wk 12-2.30 D served all wk 6-9
⊕ PUNCH TAVERNS ◼ Otter Bitter, St
Austell Tribute, Sharp's Doom Bar, Bass,
Guest ale. ♂ Westons Stowford Press,
Taunton Original ♥ 13 **Facilities**
Children welcome Children's menu
Children's portions Play area Family
room Garden Parking Wi-fi 🚐 **Rooms** 9

SALCOMBE — Map 3 SX73

The Victoria Inn

PICK OF THE PUBS

Fore St TQ8 8BU ☎ **01548 842604**
e-mail: info@victoriainn-salcombe.co.uk
dir: *In town centre, overlooking estuary*

Tim and Liz Hore run this friendly and inviting pub in the centre of town, keeping the log fire roaring in winter, and in milder weather welcoming mums, dads, children and pets to the huge family garden with its shady terrace and enclosed children's play area. The bar presents St Austell ales, in addition to a diverse selection of wines and spirits; if you have something to celebrate, champagne is served by the glass as well as the bottle. The first-floor restaurant gives stunning views of the pretty harbour and fishing boats bringing in the catch of the day. So expect to find an open sandwich of Salcombe white crabmeat; starters such as smoked haddock kedgeree or pan-fried West Country scallops; and a heart-warming selection of main dishes: sautéed pork fillet; chef's own steak-and-kidney pudding; and the inn's own 'scrummy' fish pie.

Open all day all wk 11.30-11 Closed: 25 Dec **Bar Meals** L served all wk 12-2.30 D served all wk 6-9 ⊕ ST AUSTELL BREWERY ◀ Tribute, Dartmoor, Proper Job ♻ Healey's Cornish Rattler. ♟ 20 **Facilities** ❅ Children welcome Children's portions Play area Garden Wi-fi

SANDFORD — Map 3 SS80

The Lamb Inn NEW

The Square EX17 4LW ☎ **01363 773676**
e-mail: thelambinn@gmail.com
dir: *A377 from Exeter to Crediton. 1st right signed Sandford & Tiverton. Left, left again, up hill. 1.5m left into village square*

Mark Hildyard has worked hard at making The Lamb a cracking all-round pub, one that offers top-notch pub food and operates as a thriving community local. Set in a sleepy Devon village, the pub's upstairs room is used as an art gallery, cinema, theatre, venue for open-mic nights and a meeting room for village groups. Downstairs, expect to find three log fires, candles on scrubbed tables, a cosy atmosphere and an imaginative chalkboard menu. Using the best Devon produce, dishes may include duck liver and port pâté with red onion marmalade; venison with fig tart, roasted celeriac and venison jus; and chocolate fondant. Everyone is welcome, including dogs and walkers in muddy boots.

Open all day all wk 11am-11.30pm **Bar Meals** Av main course £11.90 food served all day **Restaurant** L served all wk 12.30-2.15 D served all wk 6.30-9.15 Av 3 course à la carte fr £19 ⊕ FREE HOUSE ◀ Otter Bitter, O'Hanlon's Yellow Hammer, Dartmoor Jail Ale & Legend, Skinner's ♻ Sandford Orchards. ♟ 9 **Facilities** ❅ Children welcome Children's portions Garden Beer festival Wi-fi 🚌 (notice required)

SHEBBEAR — Map 3 SS40

The Devil's Stone Inn

EX21 5RU ☎ **01409 281210**
e-mail: churst1234@btinternet.com
dir: *From Okehampton right opposite White Hart, follow A386 towards Hatherleigh. At rdbt outside Hatherleigh take Holsworthy road to Highampton. Just after Highampton right, follow signs to Shebbear*

A farmhouse before it became a coaching inn some 400 years ago, this inn is reputedly one of England's top dozen most haunted pubs. That does not deter the country sports lovers who use it as a base for their activities; it is especially a haven for fly-fishermen, with beats, some of which the pub owns, on the middle and upper Torridge. The beamed and flagstone-floored interior has several open fires. Locally sourced and home-cooked food, a selection of real ales and ciders, a games room, separate dining room and large garden complete the picture. Booking for meals may be required.

Open all wk 12-3 6-11 (Fri-Sun all day fr 12) **Bar Meals** L served all wk 12-2.30 D served all wk 6-9.30 **Restaurant** L served all wk 12-2.30 D served all wk 6-9.30 ⊕ FREE HOUSE ◀ Sharp's Doom Bar, St Austell Tribute, Black Prince & HSD ♻ Healey's Cornish Rattler, Thatchers Gold. **Facilities** Children welcome Children's menu Children's portions Play area Garden Parking 🚌

SIDBURY — Map 3 SY19

The Hare & Hounds

Putts Corner EX10 0QQ ☎ **01404 41760**
e-mail: contact@hareandhounds-devon.co.uk
web: www.hareandhounds-devon.co.uk
dir: *From Honiton take A375 signed Sidmouth. In approx 0.75m pub at Seaton Rd x-rds*

Behind the whitewashed walls of this traditional Devon free house you'll find a comfortable interior with wooden beams and winter log fires. There's also a large garden with fantastic views down the valley to the sea at Sidmouth. Besides the daily carvery, the extensive menu features classic pub dishes and snacks. Main course options include beef in Guinness with roast potatoes, as well as fish dishes and vegetarian options. The permanent cask ales are brewed less than ten miles away by the Otter Brewery.

Open all day all wk 10am-11pm (Sun 11-10.30) **Bar Meals** L served Mon-Sat 12-9 D served Mon-Sat 12-9 **Restaurant** L served all wk 12-9 D served all wk 12-9 ⊕ FREE HOUSE ◀ Otter Bitter & Ale, Guest ales ♻ Wiscombe Suicider. **Facilities** ❅ Children welcome Children's menu Children's portions Play area Garden Parking Wi-fi

SIDMOUTH — Map 3 SY18

Blue Ball Inn ★★★★ INN

PICK OF THE PUBS

See Pick of the Pubs on page 169

Dukes ★★★★ INN

PICK OF THE PUBS

See Pick of the Pubs on page 172
See advert on opposite page

SLAPTON — Map 3 SX84

The Tower Inn

PICK OF THE PUBS

See Pick of the Pubs on page 173

Save on hotels. Book at **theAA.com/hotel**

DEVON 171 **ENGLAND**

Dukes

The Esplanade, Sidmouth, Devon EX10 8AR
Freephone: 08000 48 17 31 • Tel: 01395 513320 • Fax: 01395 519318
Website: www.dukessidmouth.co.uk
Email: dukes@sidmouthinn.co.uk

Dukes is a central part of the social fabric of Sidmouth and a meeting place for all ages. Situated at the heart of Sidmouth's town centre and a stone's through away from the beach, Dukes is a family-friendly Inn offering fantastic food, drink and accommodation.

Serving some of Devon's best including Luscombe organic fruit juices, Branscombe Vale ales and Sandford Orchard Ciders. Award winning Christopher Piper wines provide an exciting list with all wines available by the bottle or glass. A range of beverages include freshly ground Italian coffee, a choice of teas and our renowned hot chocolate – not forgetting freshly baked scones and cakes!

Sun yourself in our patio garden on a warm summer's day or relax on our comfortable leather sofas on a chilly winters evening.

Seasonal menus and daily specials provide something for all tastes. Our lunch and dinner menus include a range of dishes showcasing local suppliers and feature fresh Lyme Bay fish and Devon reared meat and game. Light snacks and our own traditional style pub favourites are also always available. All of this can be enjoyed in our sea facing conservatory and upper bar areas or on our large patio – great for alfresco dining.

PICK OF THE PUBS

Dukes ★★★★INN

SIDMOUTH   Map 3 SY18

The Esplanade EX10 8AR
☎ **01395 513320**
e-mail: dukes@innsidmouth.co.uk
web: www.dukessidmouth.co.uk
dir: *Exit A3052 to Sidmouth, left onto Esplanade*

Situated in the town centre, a stone's throw from the sea on the Regency esplanade, here is a contemporary, informal and family-friendly inn with a stylish and lively interior, a continental feel in the bar and public areas, and comfortable en suite bedrooms, most of which come with a range of home comforts, including Wi-fi, and views out over Lyme Bay. In fine weather, the patio garden, which also overlooks the sea, is a very pleasant place in which to bask in the sun with a freshly ground mid-morning coffee, a pot of tea or hot chocolate, and some freshly baked scones and cakes. Of course, it might be chilly, so that's when to relax inside on one of the comfortable leather sofas. Real ales come from local Branscombe Vale, O'Hanlon's, Otter and Yeovil breweries, and cider from Sandford Orchard, while award-winning Christopher Piper wines are all by the bottle or glass. Things get a little more formal in the restaurant and conservatory, where the menu and daily specials choices range from traditional English favourites to the more modern, but always featuring fresh fish from

Brixham and prime meats and game from West Country farms. Lunchtime usually brings deli platters, chargrilled chicken supreme and king prawn tempura, while in the evening expect braised shank of lamb; slow-roasted belly of pork; sautéed skate wing; and twice-baked Cornish Yarg cheese soufflé. For a snack there are sandwiches and pizzas, or Devon clotted cream tea. Light snacks and traditional pub favourites are also always available. Dukes has received an AA Dinner Award. A beer festival takes place during the first week of August. Booking for meals may be required.

Open all day all wk **Bar Meals** L served Sun-Thu 12-9, Fri-Sat 12-9.30 D served Sun-Thu 12-9, Fri-Sat 12-9.30 Av main

course £12 **Restaurant** L served Sun-Thu 12-9, Fri-Sat 12-9.30 D served Sun-Thu 12-9, Fri-Sat 12-9.30 ⊕ FREE HOUSE ◀ Branscombe Vale Branoc & Summa That, O'Hanlon's Firefly, Otter Ale, Yeovil ♂ Westons Stowford Press, Thatchers Burrow Hill, Sandford Orchard. ♟ 20 **Facilities** Children welcome Children's menu Children's portions ♣ Garden Beer festival Parking Wi-fi ﹈ (notice required) **Rooms** 13

PICK OF THE PUBS

The Tower Inn

SLAPTON   Map 3 SX84

Church Rd TQ7 2PN ☎ 01548 580216
e-mail: towerinn@slapton.org
web: www.thetowerinn.com
dir: *Exit A379 S of Dartmouth, left at*
Slapton Sands

Tucked up a narrow driveway behind cottages and the church in this unspoilt Devon village, the ancient ivy-clad tower (which gives this charming 14th-century inn its name) looms hauntingly above the pub. It is all that remains of the old College of Chantry Priests – the pub was built to accommodate the artisans who constructed the monastic college. Six hundred years on and this truly atmospheric village pub continues to welcome guests and the appeal, other than its peaceful location, is the excellent range of real ales on tap and the eclectic choice of modern pub grub prepared from locally sourced ingredients, which include smoked fish from Dartmouth, quality Devon-reared beef, and fresh fish and crab landed at Brixham. Expect hearty lunchtime sandwiches (try the delicious fresh crab and lemon mayonnaise), alongside the ploughman's platter laden with pork pie, cheddar cheese, home-made relish and crusty bread; and Thai fishcakes with dressed mixed leaves and sweet chilli sauce. A typical evening meal may take in carpaccio of Exmoor venison with rocket, olive tapenade and parmesan; followed by pork belly with curly kale and sage jus; or pan-fried wild sea bass with

braised fennel, crab dumplings and a crab bisque. Round off with apple and blueberry crumble with vanilla ice cream and wash down with a pint of Otter or St Austell Proper Job. Stone walls, open fires, low beams, scrubbed oak tables and flagstone floors characterise the welcoming interior, the atmosphere enhanced at night with candlelit tables. There's a splendid landscaped rear garden with church and tower views – perfect for summer alfresco meals. Visitors exploring Slapton Ley Nature Reserve and Slapton Sands should venture inland to seek out this ancient inn. Check for the dates of the pub's beer festivals.

Open 12-2.30 (12-3 summer) 6-11
Closed: 1st 2wks Jan, Sun eve during Winter **Bar Meals** L served all wk

12-2.30 D served all wk 6.30-9.30 Av main course £13.95 **Restaurant** L served all wk 12-2.30 D served all wk 6.30-9.30 Av 3 course à la carte fr £25 ⊕ FREE HOUSE ◖ Butcombe Bitter, Otter Bitter, St Austell Proper Job, Sharp's Doom Bar ♂ Addlestones, Sharp's Orchard. **Facilities** Children welcome Children's menu Children's portions 🐾 Garden Beer festival Parking Wi-fi 🚐

SOURTON — Map 3 SX59

The Highwayman Inn

EX20 4HN ☎ **01837 861243**
e-mail: info@thehighwaymaninn.net
web: www.thehighwaymaninn.net
dir: *On A386 (Okehampton to Tavistock road). From Exeter, exit A30 towards Tavistock. Pub 4m from Okehampton, 12m from Tavistock*

The Highwayman is a fascinating and unique place, full of legend, strange architecture, eccentric furniture and obscure bric-à-brac, with roots going back to 1282. John 'Buster' Jones began creating his vision in 1959 — features include part of a galleon, wood hauled from Dartmoor's bogs, and Gothic church arches; the entrance is through the old Okehampton to Launceston coach. The pub is now run by his daughter Sally. Popular with holidaymakers and international tourists, The Highwayman refreshes one and all with drinks that include real farmhouse cider and interesting bottled beers from local breweries; great pasties and pies are always available, and for residents only a more extensive menu featuring lobster thermidor and duck a l'orange is offered.

Open 11.30-2 6-10.30 (Sun 12-2 7-10.30) **Closed:** 25-28 Dec **Bar Meals** L served all wk 12-1.45 D served all wk 6-9 Av main course £5 ⊕ FREE HOUSE ◀ Marston's Pedigree, Wychwood Hobgoblin, Sharp's Doom Bar, Shepherd Neame Spitfire ♂ Grays. **Facilities** ✿ Family room Garden Parking Wi-fi **Notes** ⊛

SOUTH POOL — Map 3 SX74

The Millbrook Inn

PICK OF THE PUBS

See Pick of the Pubs on opposite page

SOWTON — Map 3 SX99

The Black Horse Inn

Old Honiton Rd EX5 2AN ☎ **01392 366649**
e-mail: blackhorse@wadworth.co.uk
dir: *On old A30 from Exeter towards Honiton, 0.5m from M5 junct 29; 1m from Exeter International Airport. Inn between Sowton & Clyst Honiton*

This Wadworth-owned village pub has greatly benefited from its refurbishment and contemporary new dining room. The relaxed atmosphere is the perfect setting to enjoy a menu that uses plenty of produce from local suppliers. At lunch, jacket potatoes, paninis and ploughman's offer a lighter option, but there's also steak and kidney suet pudding; fish pie and a trio of sausages and mash for those with a bigger appetite. Try the local ale while sitting on the terrace on warmer days.

Open all day all wk 11-11 (Fri-Sat 11am-mdnt) **Bar Meals** L served all wk 11.45-2.30 D served all wk 6-9.30 Av main course £9.95 **Restaurant** L served all wk 11.45-2.30 D served all wk 6-9.30 ⊕ WADWORTH ◀ Henry's Original IPA & 6X, Guest ales ♂ Thatchers. ♀ 11 **Facilities** ✿ Children welcome Children's menu Garden Parking Wi-fi **▭**

SPREYTON — Map 3 SX69

The Tom Cobley Tavern

PICK OF THE PUBS

EX17 5AL ☎ **01647 231314**
dir: *From A30 at Whiddon Down take A3124 N. Take 1st right after services then 1st right over bridge.*

It was from this peaceful, whitewashed pub, one day in 1802, that a certain Thomas Cobley and his companions set forth for Widecombe Fair, an event immortalised in song, and his cottage still stands in the village. This pub draws the crowds in summer due to its name and associations with the fair. It stands in a sleepy Dartmoor village and remains a traditional village local; the unspoilt main bar has a roaring log fire, cushioned settles, and a mind-boggling range of 20 tip-top real ales straight from the cask, for which it has won many awards. The pub also offers a great range of real ciders. Typically, order a pint of Cotleigh Tawny Ale or Sharp's Doom Bar to accompany some hearty pub food, which ranges from simple bar snacks to decent pies, salads, duck and fish dishes, as well as a good vegetarian selection. Finish off with one of the great ice creams or sorbets. Summer alfresco drinking can be enjoyed on the pretty flower-decked gravel terrace or in the rear garden with its far-reaching views. Booking for meals may be required.

Open 12-3 6-11 (Sun 12-4 7-11 Mon 6.30-11 Fri-Sat 12-3 6-1am) **Closed:** Mon L **Bar Meals** L served Tue-Sun 12-2 D served all wk 7-9 **Restaurant** L served Tue-Sun 12-2 D served all wk 7-9 ⊕ FREE HOUSE ◀ Cotleigh Tawny Ale, Teignworthy Gundog, Sharp's Doom Bar, St Austell Tribute & Proper Job, Dartmoor Jail Ale & Legend, Guest ales ♂ Winkleigh, Westons Stowford Press, Healey's Cornish Rattler & Pear Rattler, Sandford Orchards Devon

Scrumpy, Gwynt y Ddraig, Lilley's. **Facilities** ✿ Children welcome Children's menu Children's portions Garden Parking **▭** (notice required)

STAVERTON — Map 3 SX76

Sea Trout Inn

TQ9 6PA ☎ **01803 762274**
e-mail: info@theseatroutinn.co.uk
dir: *From A38 take A384 towards Totnes. Follow Staverton & Sea Trout Inn sign*

Apart from the occasional puff of a steam train drifting across the pretty Dart Valley from the South Devon Railway, this character village inn is the epitome of tranquility. Dating back 600 years, the Sea Trout ticks all the boxes for the authentic country pub, from the delightful locals' bar to the stylish restaurant, where trying to choose from the modern British menu can be agonising; slow-roast pork belly with chorizo bubble-and-squeak, or perhaps Massaman seafood curry, with well-kept Palmers ales the icing on the cake. Booking for meals may be required.

Open all day all wk **Bar Meals** L served Mon-Fri 12-2, Sat 12-2.30, Sun 12-3 D served Mon-Thu 6-9, Fri-Sat 6-9.30, Sun 6.30-9 Av main course £13 **Restaurant** L served Mon-Fri 12-2, Sat 12-2.30, Sun 12-3 D served Mon-Thu 6-9, Fri-Sat 6-9.30, Sun 6.30-9 Av 3 course à la carte fr £24 ⊕ PALMERS ◀ 200, Copper Ale, Best Bitter ♂ Thatchers. **Facilities** ✿ Children welcome Children's menu Children's portions Garden Parking Wi-fi **▭**

STOKE FLEMING — Map 3 SX84

The Green Dragon Inn

Church Rd TQ6 0PX ☎ **01803 770238**
e-mail: pcrowther@btconnect.com
dir: *Off A379 (Dartmouth to Kingsbridge coast road) opposite church*

Although there has been a building on this site since the 12th century, the first recorded landlord took charge in 1607. Two miles from Dartmouth, opposite the church in the village of Stoke Fleming, this South Hams pub has many seafaring connections and the current landlord has turned the interior into a haven of boating memorabilia, including charts and sailing pictures. Local beers such as Otter slake the thirst of walkers, whilst the great-value menu can satisfy the largest of appetites with venison burger, fish pie or braised oxtail.

Open all wk 11.30-3 5.30-11 (Sun 12-3.30 6.30-10.30) **Closed:** 25-26 Dec **Bar Meals** L served all wk 12-2 D served all wk 6.30-8.30 ⊕ HEAVITREE ◀ St Austell Tribute, Otter, Guest ale ♂ Aspall, Addlestones. ♀ 10 **Facilities** ✿ Children welcome Children's menu Children's portions Play area Garden Parking

PICK OF THE PUBS

The Millbrook Inn

SOUTH POOL — Map 3 SX74

TQ7 2RW ☎ 01548 531581
e-mail: info@millbrookinnsouthpool.co.uk
web: www.millbrookinnsouthpool.co.uk
dir: *Take A379 from Kingsbridge to Frogmore then E for 2m to South Pool*

Set at the head of South Pool creek on the Salcombe estuary, this quaint 16th-century village pub attracts boat owners from Salcombe and Kingsbridge, in summer when the tide is high. The draw is award-winning chef Jean Phillipe Bidart's famous paellas and barbecues in the pretty front courtyard and, if you arrive early, you can bag a sun-drenched table on the tiny rear terrace overlooking a babbling brook and fields. White-painted under its natural stone roof, The Millbrook has two cosy beamed bars with open fires and traditional pub décor. There is also a charming little dining room where booking is essential. Ian Dent and Diana Hunt are welcoming hosts, and the pub throngs with locals quaffing Red Rock and Driftwood ales. Diners are eager to sample JP's imaginative pub food, which draws on local, seasonal ingredients, notably oysters from Bigbury Bay, Start Bay crab, fish caught off the South Hams coast, local estate game, and allotment-grown vegetables. At lunch tuck into a steaming bowl of Exe mussels in a curried broth; smoked

haddock cassoulet; a hearty bouillabaisse; pig's trotter patties; broad bean, asparagus and pea risotto; or a home-made terrine with chutney and dressed salad. Alternatively, order a plate of rustic West Country and French cheeses. For supper there might be duck foie gras with a walnut and pear salad for starters; followed by sea bream linguine with mussels, chilli, ginger, spring onion and parsley; or pan-fried pheasant and partridge with juniper jus. For pudding, expect to find the likes of tarte Tatin, chocolate fondant and a pannacotta on the menu. On Sundays, the speciality is rib of beef with slow-braised ox cheek, followed by live music. Visit the Veg Shed and take home some of the surplus allotment vegetables.

Open all day all wk 12-11 (Sun 12-10.30) **Bar Meals** L served all wk 12-2 D served all wk 7-9 Av main course £14 **Restaurant** L served Mon-Sat 12-2, Sun 12-3 D served all wk 7-9 Av 3 course à la carte fr £28 ⊕ FREE HOUSE ◀ Red Rock, Driftwood, Millbrook ♂ Thatchers Heritage, Westons Old Rosie. ⊠ 10 **Facilities** Children welcome Children's portions ❖ Garden Wi-fi

PICK OF THE PUBS

The Golden Lion Inn

TIPTON ST JOHN Map 3 SY09

EX10 0AA ☎ 01404 812881
e-mail: info@goldenliontipton.co.uk
web: www.goldenliontipton.co.uk
dir: *Telephone or visit website for directions*

Michelle and Francois Teissier are currently celebrating their ninth year at the helm of this welcoming Devon village pub. So many things contribute to its traditional feel – the low wooden beams and stone walls, the winter log fire, the art-deco prints and Tiffany lamps, not to mention the paintings by Devonian and Cornish artists. And there's the bar, of course, where locally brewed Otter ales are the order of the day. Chef-patron Franky (as everyone calls him) trained in classical French cooking at a prestigious establishment in the Loire Valley, a grounding that accounts today for his rustic French, Mediterranean and British menus. Their delights may include moules frites; slow roasted lamb shank; escargots; crevettes in garlic butter; spinach and mushroom filled crêpes; chicken Xerez in light creamy sherry sauce. Given that the genteel seaside town of Sidmouth is just down the road, the seafood specials depend totally on that day's catch – cod, hake and sea bass are all candidates. For vegetarians there's likely to be creamy garlic mushrooms or deep-fried brie. Tempting white and granary bread sandwiches are filled

with fresh Lyme Bay crab, mature cheddar or home-cooked ham. The Sunday lunch menu offers roast West Country beef with Yorkshire pudding; roast lamb with mint sauce; and winter vegetable crêpe. As Franky sums up: 'When Michelle and I took over in 2003, our aim was to create a friendly, inviting village pub offering great value, high-quality food made from the freshest ingredients; with our combination of rustic French dishes and traditional British food with a Mediterranean twist, there's something for everyone!' Outside there is a grassy beer garden and terracotta-walled terrace area with tumbling grapevines. On summer evenings you can listen to jazz. Booking for meals may be required.

Open all wk 12-2.30 6-11 (Sun 12-2.30 7-10.30) **Bar Meals** L served all wk 12-2 D served Mon-Sat 6.30-8.30, Sun 7-8.30 Av main course £10-£15 **Restaurant** L served all wk 12-2 ⊕ HEAVITREE ◀ Bass, Otter Ale & Bitter. ♟ 12 **Facilities** Children welcome Children's menu Children's portions Garden Parking 🚐 (notice required)

THURLESTONE   Map 3 SX64

The Village Inn

TQ7 3NN ☎ 01548 563525
dir: *Take A379 from Plymouth towards Kingsbridge, at Bantham rdbt straight over onto B3197, then right into a lane signed Thurlestone, 2.5m*

Built in the 16th century using timbers salvaged from a wrecked Spanish Armada ship, this popular village pub is under the same ownership as the nearby Thurlestone Hotel. Expect traditional country pub décor, good service from the Grose family, well-kept ales and decent food. Seafood is a speciality, with Salcombe crabmeat, River Exe mussels and other local fish and shellfish to choose from on the seasonal menus. Alternative dishes may include beef Stroganoff, and pork and leek sausages with mash and onion gravy. Just minutes from the beach and coastal path.

Open all wk 11.30-3 6-11.30 (Sat-Sun & summer all day) **Bar Meals** L served Mon-Fri 12-2.30, Sat-Sun 12-9 D served Mon-Fri 6-9, Sat-Sun 12-9 Av main course £9.95 ⊕ FREE HOUSE ◀ Palmers Best Bitter, Sharp's Doom Bar, Guest ale ♂ Heron Valley. **Facilities** ✿ Children welcome Children's menu Parking Wi-fi 🚍 (notice required)

TIPTON ST JOHN   Map 3 SY09

The Golden Lion Inn
PICK OF THE PUBS

See Pick of the Pubs on opposite page

TOPSHAM   Map 3 SX98

Bridge Inn
PICK OF THE PUBS

Bridge Hill EX3 0QQ ☎ 01392 873862
e-mail: su3264@eclipse.co.uk
dir: *M5 junct 30 follow Sidmouth signs, in approx 400yds right at rdbt onto A376 towards Exmouth. In 1.8m cross mini rdbt. Right at next mini rdbt to Topsham. 1.2m, cross River Clyst. Inn on right*

This 'museum with beer' is substantially 16th century, although its constituent parts vary considerably in age. Most of the fabric is local stone, while the old brewhouse at the rear is traditional Devon cob. Four generations of the same family have run it since great-grandfather William Gibbings arrived in 1897, and it remains eccentrically and gloriously old fashioned – mobile phones are definitely out. Usually around ten real ales from local and further-flung breweries are served straight from their casks, the actual line-up varying by the week. There are no lagers and only a few wines, two from a local organic vineyard. Traditional, freshly prepared lunchtime bar food includes granary ploughman's (smoked chicken, stilton or cheddar), pork pies, veggie or meat pasties, and sandwiches, all made with local ingredients. Queen

Elizabeth II visited in 1998; it is believed this is the only time she has officially stepped inside an English pub.

Open all wk 12-2 6-10.30 (Sun 12-2 7-10.30) **Bar Meals** L served all wk 12-2 ⊕ FREE HOUSE ◀ Branscombe Vale Branoc, Adnams Broadside, Exe Valley, O'Hanlon's, Teignworthy, Jollyboat Plunder. **Facilities** ✿ Children welcome Garden Parking Wi-fi **Notes** ⊛

TORCROSS   Map 3 SX84

Start Bay Inn

TQ7 2TQ ☎ 01548 580553
e-mail: clair@startbayinn.co.uk
dir: *Between Dartmouth & Kingsbridge on A379*

Located on the beach and with a freshwater reserve on its other side, the patio of this 14th-century inn overlooks the sea. The fishermen working from Start Bay deliver their catch direct to the kitchen; so does a local crabber, who leaves his catch at the back door to be cooked and picked by the pub. The former landlord (father of landladies Clair and Gail) continues to dive for scallops. Be in no doubt therefore about the freshness of the seafood on the specials board. Look also for Dartmouth Smokehouse products, locally sourced steaks, burgers from the village butcher, and Salcombe Dairy ice creams. Ploughman's, sandwiches and jackets are also available.

Open all day all wk 11.30-11.30 **Bar Meals** L served all wk 11.30-2.15 D served all wk 6-9.30 winter, 6-10 summer Av main course £10 ⊕ HEAVITREE ◀ Bass, Otter Ale & Bitter, St Austell Tribute ♂ Heron Valley. ♀ 8 **Facilities** Children welcome Children's menu Children's portions Family room Garden Parking

TORQUAY   Map 3 SX96

The Cary Arms
PICK OF THE PUBS

Beach Rd, Babbacombe TQ1 3LX ☎ 01803 327110
e-mail: enquiries@caryarms.co.uk
dir: *From Exeter A380 towards Torquay. Left onto B3192. On entering Teignmouth, at bottom of hill at lights, right signed Torquay/A379. Cross River Teign. At mini rdbt follow Babbacombe/Seafront signs. Pass Babbacombe Model Village & Bygones, through lights, left into Babbacombe Downs Rd, left into Beach Rd*

This 'boutique inn' is so much more than just a pub on the beach; it tempts with an excellent menu. Unwind in the stone-walled bar, perhaps with a pint of Doom Bar in hand, contemplating the views across the bay. If it's a glorious summer's day, you will unquestionably wish to eat on one of the terraces that lead down to the water's edge; this is when the barbecue and wood-fired oven come into their own. Catch of the day will be a must for fish-lovers – perhaps dressed South Devon crab salad or roasted hake on crushed new potatoes with curly kale and a wild mushroom sauce. Other choices – such as pork terrine with an apple and sage stuffing, toasted brioche

and fig and cranberry compôte, followed by roast duck breast with sautéed potatoes and wild mushrooms finished in a shallot and bacon sauce – are equally hard to resist. Jazz, gastro, quiz and steak nights punctuate the year. Booking for meals may be required.

Open all day all wk 12-11 **Bar Meals** L served all wk 12-3 D served all wk 6.30-9 Av main course £11-£18 ⊕ FREE HOUSE ◀ Otter Ale, Bays Topsail, Sharp's Doom Bar ♂ Sheppy's, Sandford Devon Mist. ♀ 14 **Facilities** ✿ Children welcome Children's menu Children's portions Family room Garden Wi-fi

TOTNES   Map 3 SX86

The Durant Arms ★★★★ INN
PICK OF THE PUBS

See Pick of the Pubs on page 178

Royal Seven Stars Hotel

The Plains TQ9 5DD ☎ 01803 862125
e-mail: enquiry@royalsevenstars.co.uk
dir: *From A382 signed Totnes, left at 'Dartington' rdbt. Through lights towards town centre, through next rdbt, pass Morrisons car park on left. 200yds on right*

A Grade II listed property in the heart of Totnes, with three characterful bars and a grand ballroom. A champagne bar is a recent addition to the TQ9 brasserie; here bubbly is served by the glass or bottle from 5pm onwards, along with cocktails and wines. Excellent local brews and ciders are always on tap. Quality food at affordable prices is another strength – expect to find Brixham crab and local mussels among the starters, and main courses such as chicken breast with lemon, thyme and garlic. Booking for meals may be required.

Open all day all wk **Bar Meals** L served all wk 11-9.30 D served all wk 11-9.30 Av main course £9.95 food served all day **Restaurant** L served Sun 12-2.30 D served all wk 6.30-9.30 Fixed menu price fr £16.95 Av 3 course à la carte fr £25.00 ⊕ FREE HOUSE ◀ Sharp's Doom Bar, Bays Gold, Courage Best, Dartmoor Legend & Jail Ale ♂ Thatchers, Orchard's, Ashridge. ♀ 26 **Facilities** ✿ Children welcome Children's menu Children's portions Family room Parking Wi-fi

PICK OF THE PUBS

The Durant Arms ★★★★INN

TOTNES   Map 3 SX86

Ashprington TQ9 7UP ☎ 01803 732240
e-mail: info@durantarms.co.uk
web: www.durantarms.co.uk
dir: *A38, A381, A385 to Totnes. Take A381 towards Kingsbridge, 1m, left for Ashprington*

Off the tourist trail in a popular part of Devon and situated in the heart of a sleepy, picturesque village, the 18th-century Durant Arms stands in the shadow of a beautiful 16th-century church and has stunning views of the River Dart. Located just outside the Elizabethan town of Totnes, in the heart of the South Hams, the building was originally the counting house for the neighbouring 500-acre Sharpham Estate. Formerly known as The Ashprington Inn, a flagged entrance leads into the small main bar, which is fitted out in a traditional style, with work by local artists on display alongside the horse brasses, ferns and cheerful red velvet curtains – the perfect place to enjoy local Sharpham Vineyard wines or local real ales and ciders. Patrick and Linda Lawrance took over in 2011 and have maintained the high standards at this delightful inn. Bedrooms are well appointed and attractively decorated and the food is cooked to order, using locally sourced ingredients wherever possible. Typical dishes from the daily-changing blackboard menu include pub favourites such as home-cooked ham, eggs and chips; steak-and-kidney pie with shortcrust pastry; and beef lasagne. A more formal meal in the dining rooms might begin with creamy garlic mushrooms, chicken liver pâté; or scallops with black pudding and mustard sauce. Follow on, perhaps, with duck breast with plum sauce; scallops and tiger prawns with a white wine and cream sauce; or pork loin with stilton and mushroom sauce. Leave space for desserts such as blackberry and apple pie, plum and apple crumble or chocolate fondant. The little courtyard to the rear provides a cosy spot to linger over a summer meal.

Open all wk Sat-Sun all day **Bar Meals** L served all wk 12-2 D served all wk 7-9.15 **Restaurant** L served all wk 12-2 D served all wk 7-9.15 🍺 FREE HOUSE ◀ St Austell Tribute, Dartmoor ♻ Thatchers. ♟ 22 **Facilities** Children welcome Children's menu Children's portions Family room Garden Parking Wi-fi 🚌 **Rooms** 7

Save on hotels. Book at **theAA.com/hotel**

DEVON 179 **ENGLAND**

TOTNES *continued*

Rumour

30 High St TQ9 5RY ☎ 01803 864682
dir: *Follow signs for Totnes castle/town centre. On main street up hill above arch on left. 5 min walk from rail station*

This 17th-century building has a chequered history including stints as a milk bar, restaurant and wine bar. Named after Fleetwood Mac's landmark 1977 album, it is now comprehensively refurbished, with innovative heating and plumbing systems which reduce its environmental footprint. Hospitable staff add to its charm. Food offerings include an extensive hand-made pizza menu alongside more formal à la carte options; maybe grilled goat's cheese with roasted beetroot and truffle honey dressing, followed by pork sausages braised in red wine, shallots and mushrooms and served with mash. Booking for meals may be required.

Open all wk Mon-Sat 10am-11pm (Sun 6-11) **Bar Meals** L served Mon-Sat 12-3 D served Mon-Sat 6-10, Sun 6-9 **Restaurant** L served Mon-Sat 12-3 D served Mon-Sat 6-10, Sun 6-9 ⊕ FREE HOUSE ◀ Erdinger, Dartmoor Jail Ale, Hunter's, Quercus ♂ Thatchers. ⬤ 12 **Facilities** Children welcome Children's portions

Steam Packet Inn ★★★★ INN

St Peter's Quay TQ9 5EW ☎ 01803 863880
e-mail: steampacket@buccaneer.co.uk
web: www.steampacketinn.co.uk
dir: *Exit A38 towards Plymouth, 18m. A384 to Totnes 6m. Left at mini rdbt, pass Morrisons on left, over mini rdbt, 400yds on left*

Named after the passenger, cargo and mail steamers that once plied the Dart, this riverside pub, with four en suite rooms, makes full use of its riverside position. Great views, particularly from the conservatory restaurant, and plenty of seating on the heated, extensive waterside patio contribute to its popularity. Choices at lunch and dinner might include fresh fillets of Torbay plaice with brown shrimp butter; slow-cooked belly pork; or steak and kidney suet pudding. You're welcome to moor your boat alongside the inn. Look our for the beer festival in mid-May, occasional live music and summer barbecues.

Open all day all wk **Bar Meals** L served Mon-Fri 12-2.30, Sat-Sun 12-3 D served Mon-Sat 6-9.30, Sun 6-9 Av main course £10.95 **Restaurant** L served Mon-Fri 12-2.30, Sat-Sun 12-3 D served Mon-Sat 6-9.30, Sun 6-9 ⊕ FREE HOUSE/BUCCANEER ◀ Sharp's Doom Bar, Dartmoor Jail Ale, Guest ale ♂ Westons Stowford Press, Ashridge. ⬤ 11 **Facilities** ❤ Children welcome Children's menu Garden Beer festival Parking Wi-fi 🚐 (notice required) **Rooms** 4

The White Hart

PICK OF THE PUBS

Dartington Hall TQ9 6EL ☎ 01803 847111
e-mail: bookings@dartingtonhall.com
dir: *A38 onto A384 towards Totnes. Turn at Dartington church into Dartington Hall Estate*

Part of the splendid 14th-century Dartington Hall Estate and deer park, The White Hart is surrounded by landscaped gardens. Ancient tapestries hang above the original kitchen fire in the main restaurant, which is floored with flagstones and oak, lit by Gothic chandeliers, and furnished with limed oak settles. Local Devon real ales are available in the bar, again with a fire, and there's a patio for the warmer weather. The daily-changing bar and restaurant menu uses fresh, seasonal ingredients from south Devon and the estate itself – single-suckled beef, grass-reared lamb, additive-free and free-range chickens and eggs, and fish. Typical dishes might be pan-fried free-range Crediton chicken livers with pancetta, pine nuts, mixed leaves and Madeira dressing, followed by rump steak with anchovy and chilli butter, slow-roast tomatoes, roasted shallots and French fries. The pub also has its own cinema and hosts a variety of music and literary events. Booking for meals may be required.

Open all day all wk Mon-Sat 10am-11pm (Sun 10am-10.30pm) **Bar Meals** L served Mon-Fri 12-2.30, Sat-Sun 12-9 D served Mon-Fri 6-9, Sat-Sun 12-9 Av main course £11.95 **Restaurant** L served Mon-Fri 12-2.30, Sat-Sun 12-9 D served Mon-Fri 6-9, Sat-Sun 12-9 ⊕ FREE HOUSE ◀ St Austell Tribute, Local guest ales ♂ Thatchers. ⬤ 10 **Facilities** Children welcome Children's menu Children's portions Garden Parking Wi-fi 🚐 (notice required)

TRUSHAM	Map 3 SX88

Cridford Inn

PICK OF THE PUBS

See Pick of the Pubs on page 180

TUCKENHAY	Map 3 SX85

The Maltsters Arms

TQ9 7EQ ☎ 01803 732350
e-mail: maltsters@tuckenhay.com
dir: *A381 from Totnes towards Kingsbridge. 1m, at hill top turn left, follow signs to Tuckenhay, 3m*

A late 18th-century stone inn which refreshed busy locals working in commodities such as lime, paper, cider, roadstone and malt before these industries petered out in the 1940s. Overlooking the picturesque Bow Creek, it's a lovely spot for a sparkling pint of local cider and a plate of delectable food. Bar snacks include Bigbury Bay oysters, while the main menu embraces River Teign mussels; Yonder Park Farm bangers with black peppered mash; and a West Country cheese selection. Summertime special events and barbecues are followed by a beer festival in September. Booking for meals may be required.

Open all day all wk Mon-Thu & Sun 9am-11pm (Fri-Sat 9am-mdnt) **Bar Meals** L served all wk 12-3 D served all wk 7-9.30 Av main course £9.95 **Restaurant** L served all wk 12-3 D served all wk 7-9.30 Av 3 course à la carte fr £25 ⊕ FREE HOUSE ◀ Dartmoor IPA, Otter Ale, Sambrook's Wandle ♂ Thatchers Gold. ⬤ 10 **Facilities** ❤ Children welcome Children's menu Children's portions Family room Garden Beer festival Parking Wi-fi

TYTHERLEIGH	Map 4 ST30

The Tytherleigh Arms

EX13 7BE ☎ 01460 220214
e-mail: tytherleigharms@gmail.com
dir: *Equidistant from Chard & Axminster on A358*

A change of hands in December 2011 has seen a smart refurbishment at this 16th-century coaching inn on the borders of Devon, Dorset and Somerset. There are still plenty of original features, including beamed ceilings and huge fires, which makes for a lovely setting if you are popping in for a pint of Branoc ale, or making a beeline for the daily-changing menu. Local produce drives the menu, whether it's rabbit with flageolet beans and mustard sauce, or Lyme Bay skate wing with caper butter and new potatoes. Booking for meals may be required.

Open 11-4 6-12 (Sat-Sun all day) Closed: Sun eve winter **Bar Meals** L served Mon-Fri 12-2.30, Sat 12-3, Sun 12-4 D served Mon-Fri 6-9.30, Sat 6-10, Sun 6-9 Av main course £10 **Restaurant** L served Mon-Fri 12-2.30, Sat 12-3, Sun 12-4 D served Mon-Fri 6-9.30, Sat 6-10, Sun 6-9 Av 3 course à la carte fr £27 ⊕ FREE HOUSE ◀ Otter Ale & Bitter, Branscombe Vale Branoc ♂ Thatchers Gold, Westons Wyld Wood Organic. ⬤ 10 **Facilities** ❤ Children welcome Children's portions Garden Parking Wi-fi 🚐 (notice required)

WIDECOMBE IN THE MOOR	Map 3 SX77

The Old Inn

TQ13 7TA ☎ 01364 621207
e-mail: oldinn.widecombe@hall-woodhouse.co.uk
dir: *From Bovey Tracey take B3387 to Widecombe in the Moor*

This 14th-century pub in the heart of a quintessential village is the start and finishing point for several excellent Dartmoor walks. A pub for all seasons, enjoy the five log fires when the weather turns cold or sit outside in the beer garden with its water features. Cask ales include seasonal guests, with plenty of wines by the glass. Lunchtime brings jacket potatoes and baguettes with a range of fillings, while those with heartier appetites can tuck into gourmet burgers; Somerset chicken and ham hock pie or vegetable curry.

Open all wk all day (ex 26 Dec & 1 Jan close 4pm) Closed: 25 Dec - open for bookings only **Bar Meals** food served all day **Restaurant** food served all day ⊕ HALL & WOODHOUSE ◀ Badger, Guest ales ♂ Badger Applewood, Westons Stowford Press. ⬤ 23 **Facilities** ❤ Children welcome Children's menu Children's portions Garden Parking Wi-fi 🚐

PICK OF THE PUBS

Cridford Inn

TRUSHAM   Map 3 SX88

TQ13 0NR ☎ 01626 853694
e-mail:
reservations@vanillapod-cridfordinn.com
web: www.vanillapod-cridfordinn.com
dir: *From A38 exit at junct for Teign Valley, right, follow Trusham signs for 4m*

Heritage enthusiasts will be in seventh heaven here, where researchers have pieced together a remarkable history dating back over a thousand years, putting a ninth-century longhouse on the site before a modern rebuild took place in the 13th century. A mosaic floor in the Vanilla Pod restaurant and what is probably the oldest surviving window frame in a secular building add immense warmth and character, as do the rough stone walls, old fireplaces and the general atmosphere of this architectural treasure, which has medieval masons' marks still visible above the bar. The only chill in the air may be from the ghost of a nun (the place also served as a nunnery), whilst the shadow of a cavalier is also occasionally spotted abroad. This picturesque thatched inn crouches like an owl below towering trees near a brook in the Teign Valley just a brace of miles from Dartmoor National Park; a pretty terrace is an ideal summertime spot to mull over the alfresco lunchtime dishes with a pint of local Teignworthy bitter. Quite apart from the fine destination dining of the chic Vanilla Pod restaurant, the bar menu boasts

dishes prepared from the finest Devonshire ingredients and changes regularly to reflect seasonal largesse — chargrilled 8oz Occombe Farm sirloin steak with cognac and wild mushroom cream sauce; and pan-fried Gressingham duck breast with Seville orange, rosemary and cranberry jus. In the Vanilla Pod, start with avocado, Teignmouth crab and tiger prawn cocktail, followed by estate game such as pan-fried haunch of Teign Valley venison with braised red cabbage and red wine and thyme jus; or pan-fried local sea bass with fennel chips and tomato relish. Specials and vegetarian choices are on the blackboard near the bar. Booking for meals may be required.

Open all wk 11-3 6.15-11 (Sat 11-11 Sun 12-10.30) **Bar Meals** L served Mon-Fri 12-2.30 (Sat all day, Sun Oct-Feb

12-3, Sun Mar-Sep all day) D served all wk 7-9.30 Av main course £10 **Restaurant** L served Sun 12-2 D served Tue-Sat 7-9.30 Fixed menu price fr £26.50 Av 3 course à la carte fr £28.50 ⊕ FREE HOUSE ◀ Sharp's Doom Bar, Otter Ale, Teignworthy, Bays ♂ Thatchers. ♟ 10 **Facilities** Children welcome Children's menu Children's portions Family room Garden Parking 🚌

Save on hotels. Book at **theAA.com/hotel**

DEVON 181 **ENGLAND**

PICK OF THE PUBS

The Digger's Rest

WOODBURY SALTERTON   Map 3 SY08

EX5 1PQ ☎ 01395 232375
e-mail: bar@diggersrest.co.uk
web: www.diggersrest.co.uk
dir: *2.5m from A3052. Signed from
Westpoint Showground*

This picturesque free house is just a few minutes' drive from the Exeter junction of the M5. Standing in the delightful east Devon village of Woodbury Salterton, the 500-year-old building with its thatched roof, thick stone and cob walls, heavy beams and log fire was originally a cider house. Today the choice on the bar is much wider but cider is still well represented with Westons scrumpy and Stowford Press. Real ales feature Otter Bitter from Devon with guest appearances from other West Country brewers such as Exmoor, St Austell and Sharp's. Wine fans will appreciate the wine list which has been created by the independent Wine Merchant, Tanners of Shrewsbury. The food menus are created to make the best of seasonal produce. Sourcing locally plays a big role in freshness and quality control, and English and West Country organic produce is used wherever possible. The kitchen is also committed to supporting farmers who practise good husbandry. Menus feature fish landed at Brixham and Looe, West Country beef hung for 21 days and pork from a farm just up the road. As well as the main menu there is a blackboard which features special dishes the chef has created from prime cuts or rarer seasonal ingredients he has sought out. Many of the dishes can be served as smaller portions for children and there is also a children's menu. Whether you want to check your emails (free Wi-fi), have a drink, snack or a full meal, you will find a warm welcome at The Digger's Rest. It's also worth checking the website for details of food clubs, quizzes and events.

Open all wk 11-3 5.30-11 (Sun 12-3.30 5.30-10.30) **Bar Meals** L served all wk 12-2.15 D served Mon-Sat 6.30-9.15, Sun 6.30-9 ⊕ FREE HOUSE ◀ Otter Bitter, St Austell, Sharp's, Exmoor guest ales Ö Westons Stowford Press. **Facilities** Children welcome Children's menu Children's portions Garden Parking Wi-fi 🚌

WIDECOMBE IN THE MOOR *continued*

The Rugglestone Inn

PICK OF THE PUBS

TQ13 7TF ☎ 01364 621327
e-mail: enquiries@rugglestoneinn.co.uk
dir: *From village centre take road by church towards Venton. Inn down hill on left*

Originally a cottage, this unaltered Grade II listed building was converted to an inn around 1832. In the picturesque village of Widecombe in the Moor, the pub is surrounded by tranquil moorland and streams; the Rugglestone itself rises behind the pub, whilst Widecombe's famous church acts as a beacon for ramblers and riders seeking out the inn's rural location. Cosy little rooms, wood-burners and beers such as Teignworthy's Rugglestone Moor and farmhouse ciders such as Ashridge, tapped straight from barrels stillaged behind the snug bar, draw an appreciative crowd of regulars and visitors. The filling fare is a decent mix of classic pub staples and savoury dishes aimed at taking away the winter nip or fulfilling a summer evening's promise in the streamside garden. Hot pork baps with apple sauce; steak and stilton pie; and oven-baked trout with lemon and garlic are all part of the Dartmoor experience.

Open all wk Sat-Sun all day & BH **Bar Meals** L served all wk 12-2 D served all wk 6.30-9 Av main course £10 **Restaurant** L served all wk 12-2 D served all wk 6.30-9 ⊕ FREE HOUSE ◀ O'Hanlon's Yellow Hammer, Otter Bitter, Teignworthy Rugglestone Moor, Dartmoor Legend ♂ Ashton Press, Lower Widdon Farm, Ashridge, North Hall Manor. ♟ 10 **Facilities** ❖ Children welcome Children's menu Children's portions Garden Parking 🚐 (notice required)

WINKLEIGH — Map 3 SS60

The Kings Arms

Fore St EX19 8HQ ☎ 01837 83384
e-mail: kingsarmswinkleigh@googlemail.com
dir: *Village signed from B3220 (Crediton to Torrington road)*

This ancient thatched country inn is situated in the centre of a village that has been voted best place in the UK to raise a family. Scrubbed pine tables and traditional wooden settles set the scene, and wood-burning stoves warm the beamed bar and dining rooms in winter. The freshly made, locally sourced food ranges from sandwiches and omelettes, to dishes like chicken and spinach lasagne; cottage pie; salmon fishcakes; and lamb's liver and bacon. Puddings include marmalade bread-and-butter pudding. The village's own Winkleigh cider is available and Devon cream teas are served every day.

Open all day all wk 11-11 (Sun 12-10.30) **Bar Meals** L served Mon-Sat 11-9.30, Sun 12-9 D served Mon-Sat 11-9.30, Sun 12-9 food served all day **Restaurant** L served Mon-Sat 11-9.30, Sun 12-9 D served Mon-Sat 11-9.30, Sun 12-9 food served all day ⊕ ENTERPRISE

INNS ◀ Butcombe Bitter, Sharp's Doom Bar, Otter Bitter ♂ Winkleigh. **Facilities** ❖ Children welcome Children's portions Garden

WOODBURY SALTERTON — Map 3 SY08

The Digger's Rest

PICK OF THE PUBS

See Pick of the Pubs on page 181

YEALMPTON — Map 3 SX55

Rose & Crown

PICK OF THE PUBS

Market St PL8 2EB ☎ 01752 880223
e-mail: info@theroseandcrown.co.uk
dir: *Telephone for directions*

Directly opposite the famous 'Old Mother Hubbard' cottage, this stylish bar/restaurant in the South Hams reflects a perfect balance between contemporary and traditional, from its classic brown and cream décor to the comfy leather sofas and open fire. When owner Simon Warner took over the Rose & Crown a few years ago, he aimed to preserve the 'village local' atmosphere in the bar while serving restaurant-standard food at affordable prices. A good selection of real ales is backed by wines that are few in number but high on quality. The menu proffers traditional classics with an extra touch of class, allowing the kitchen's focus on quality, freshness and local supply to be maintained. A typical three-course choice could start with duck spring roll with pineapple salsa; continue with pork tenderloin, tagliatelle, creamy garlic sauce and wild mushroom salsa; and finish with red wine poached pears with plum sorbet. Booking for meals may be required.

Open all wk 12-2.30 6-11 (Sun all day) **Bar Meals** L served all wk 12-2.30 D served all wk 6.30-9.30 **Restaurant** L served all wk 12-2.30 D served all wk 6.30-9.30 ⊕ ENTERPRISE INNS ◀ Sharp's Doom Bar, Fuller's London Pride, Courage Best, Greene King IPA, St Austell Tribute, Otter ♂ Thatchers Gold, Symonds. **Facilities** ❖ Children welcome Children's menu Children's portions Garden Parking Wi-fi 🚐 (notice required)

DORSET

ASKERSWELL — Map 4 SY59

The Spyway Inn ★★★★ INN

DT2 9EP ☎ 01308 485250
e-mail: spywayinn@sky.com
dir: *From A35 follow Askerswell sign, then follow Spyway Inn sign*

Handy for Dorchester and Bridport, this old beamed country inn offers magnificent views of the glorious Dorset countryside. Close to West Bay and an ideal base to explore the Jurassic Coast World Heritage Site at nearby West Bay, the pub boasts a landscaped, sloping beer garden with a pond and stream. It all makes for a lovely setting to enjoy a glass of Otter Ale and sample locally sourced, home-cooked fare like minted lamb chops with mash and vegetables or home-made fish pie. Accommodation is also available.

Open all wk 12-3 6-close **Bar Meals** L served all wk 12-3 D served all wk 6.30-9 **Restaurant** L served all wk 12-3 D served all wk 6.30-9 ⊕ FREE HOUSE ◀ Otter Ale, Bitter. ♟ **Facilities** Children welcome Children's menu Children's portions Play area Garden Parking Wi-fi 🚐 **Rooms** 3

BLANDFORD FORUM — Map 4 ST80

The Anvil Inn ★★★★ INN

Salisbury Rd, Pimperne DT11 8UQ ☎ 01258 453431
e-mail: theanvil.inn@btconnect.com
dir: *Telephone for directions*

In early 2012 Shaun Galvin and Karen O'Keefe took over this thatched, 16th-century inn, whose two bars offer a range of real ales, including Palmers Copper, and light meals. The charming beamed restaurant with log fire offers a full menu using Dorset produce, such as fresh fish landed on the nearby coast. Try the haddock and spring onion fishcakes; the Mediterranean vegetable lasagne; or maybe the home-made steak-and-ale pie (with shortcrust pastry, of course). The garden's lovely, especially by the pond. There are 12 en suite bedrooms.

Open all day all wk **Bar Meals** L served all wk 12-9.30 D served all wk 12-9.30 Av main course £9.95 food served all day **Restaurant** L served all wk 12-9.30 D served all wk 12-9.30 Av 3 course à la carte fr £19.95 food served all day ⊕ FREE HOUSE ◀ Fuller's London Pride, Palmers Copper Ale, Butcombe Bitter, Guinness ♂ Addlestones, Ashton Press. ♟ 9 **Facilities** ❖ Children welcome Children's menu Children's portions Garden Parking Wi-fi **Rooms** 12

Save on hotels. Book at **theAA.com/hotel**

DORSET 183 **ENGLAND**

Crown Hotel

West St DT11 7AJ ☎ 01258 456626
e-mail: crownhotel.blandford@hall-woodhouse.co.uk
dir: *M27 junct 1 W onto A31 to A350 junct, right to Blandford Forum. 100mtrs from town bridge*

Enjoying views across the water meadows of the River Stour and the Dorset market town of Blandford Forum, this 18th-century coaching inn replaces the original inn destroyed by fire in 1731. A more modern refurbishment has lost none of the historic character of this charming inn. An extensive bar menu includes sandwiches and light bites. In the restaurant, expect duck and herb pâté with fig relish to start. Mains might include a Stargazy pie of crayfish, prawns, scallops, monkfish and smoked haddock, or lemon and garlic roast chicken. There is a classic formal garden to enjoy in summer.

Open all wk 10am-11.30pm (Sun 12-10.30) ⊕ HALL & WOODHOUSE ◼ Badger Tanglefoot, First Gold.
Facilities Children welcome Children's menu Children's portions Garden Parking Wi-fi

BOURTON — Map 4 ST73

The White Lion Inn

High St SP8 5AT ☎ 01747 840866
e-mail: office@whitelionbourton.co.uk
dir: *Off A303, opposite B3092 to Gillingham*

Dating from 1723, The White Lion is a beautiful, stone-built, creeper-clad Dorset inn. The bar is cosy, with beams, flagstones and an open fire, and serves a range of real beers and ciders. Imaginative menus draw on the wealth of quality local produce, and dishes range from twice-baked cheddar soufflé or duck rillette to Moroccan tagine or roast venison.

Open all wk Mon-Thu 12-3 5-11 (Fri-Sat Sun all day) ⊕ FREE HOUSE/ADMIRAL TAVERNS ◼ Otter Amber, Sharp's Doom Bar, St Austell Tribute Ò Thatchers.
Facilities Children welcome Children's menu Children's portions Garden Parking Wi-fi

BRIDPORT — Map 4 SY49

The George Hotel

4 South St DT6 3NQ ☎ 01308 423187
dir: *In town centre, 1.5m from West Bay*

This handsome Georgian town house, with a Victorian-style bar and a mellow atmosphere, bustles all day. The George offers a traditional English breakfast, decent morning coffee and a good menu featuring fresh local plaice; natural smoked haddock; avocado and bacon salad; and the famous rabbit and bacon pie. Everything is home cooked using local produce and can be enjoyed with a selection of Palmers real ales. Recent change of hands.

Open all wk 11am-11.30pm (Wed 10am-11.30pm Fri-Sat 10am-mdnt Sun 12-10.30) **Bar Meals** L served all wk 12-2.30 D served Tue-Sat 6-9.30 ⊕ PALMERS ◼ Best Bitter, Copper Ale, Tally Ho!, 200. **Facilities** ✿ Children welcome Children's portions Family room ⬚ **Notes** ⊛

The Shave Cross Inn ★ ★ ★ ★ ★ INN

PICK OF THE PUBS

Shave Cross, Marshwood Vale DT6 6HW ☎ 01308 868358
e-mail: roy.warburton@virgin.net
dir: *From Bridport take B3162. In 2m left signed 'Broadoak/Shave Cross', then Marshwood*

Dorset thatch roofs this charming 14th-century cob-and-flint inn, which it delightfully situated off-the-beaten tracks down narrow lanes in the beautiful Marshwood Vale, deep in Thomas Hardy country. It was once a resting place for pilgrims and other monastic visitors on their way to Whitchurch Canonicorum to visit the shrine to St Candida and St Cross. While they were at the inn they had their tonsures trimmed, hence the pub's name. Step inside cosy bar to find head-cracking beams, stone floors, a huge inglenook fireplace, rustic furnishings, and local Branscombe Branoc ale on tap, as well as real farm ciders. The food here is both unusual and inspirational, with a strong Caribbean influence together with dishes originating as far afield as Fiji. A 'Genesis' starter may be spinach, coconut and crab soup, followed by a main course of Jamaican jerk pork tenderloin with pineapple compôte and fried plantin, or Creole whole sea bass. Leave room for chocolate truffle torte then retire to one of the individually designed luxury bedrooms. Booking for meals may be required.

Open 11-3 6-11.30 Closed: Mon (ex BH) **Bar Meals** L served Tue-Sun 12-2.30 D served Tue-Sun 6-7 Av main course £10 **Restaurant** L served Tue-Sun 12-2.30 D served Tue-Sun 6-9 (closed Sun eve winter) Av 3 course à la carte fr £32.50 ⊕ FREE HOUSE ◼ Branscombe Vale Branoc, Dorset, Local guest ales Ò Westons Old Rosie, Thatchers. ☙ 8 **Facilities** ✿ Children welcome Children's menu Children's portions Play area Garden Parking Wi-fi ⬚ **Rooms** 7

The West Bay

Station Rd, West Bay DT6 4EW ☎ 01308 422157
e-mail: enquiries@thewestbayhotel.co.uk
dir: *From A35 (Bridport by-pass) take B3157 (2nd exit) towards West Bay. After mini rdbt 1st left (Station Road). Pub on left*

Built in 1739, this traditional bar/restaurant lies at the foot of East Cliff, part of the impressive World Heritage Jurassic Coast, and in the picturesque harbour of West Bay. The pub specialises in fish and seafood with the latest catch shown as blackboard specials. Perhaps choose Thai crab cakes with sweet chilli prawn butter; then bouillabaisse with a hot baguette. For meat-eaters there's a good choice of steaks or maybe pot-roasted pork belly and cider jus. Palmers Brewery in Bridport furnishes the real ales, or you can ring the changes with a pint of Thatchers Gold cider. Booking for meals may be required.

Open all wk Mon-Thu 12-3 6-11 (Fri-Sun all day) **Bar Meals** L served all wk 12-2.30 D served all wk 6-9 **Restaurant** L served all wk 12-2.30 D served all wk 6-9 ⊕ PALMERS ◼ Best Bitter, Copper Ale, 200 & Tally Ho!, Guinness Ò Thatchers Gold. **Facilities** Children welcome Children's portions Garden Parking

BUCKHORN WESTON — Map 4 ST72

Stapleton Arms

PICK OF THE PUBS

Church Hill SP8 5HS ☎ 01963 370396
e-mail: relax@thestapletonarms.com
dir: *3.5m from Wincanton in village centre*

Tucked away in a pretty village on the Somerset, Wiltshire and Dorset border, the Stapleton Arms is a stylish and unstuffy country pub. There's an elegant dining room, secluded garden and a spacious bar offering real ales such as Butcombe and Moor Revival. In addition, the specialist cider and apple juice list includes draught ciders like Thatchers Cheddar Valley and Gold. The freshest seasonal ingredients from local producers lie behind an innovative modern menu. Starters like mackerel with a celeriac and pear remoulade herald main course offerings that might include tandoori pousin with spicy Indian slaw and raita. Banana and peanut crumble with peanut butter ice cream is a typical dessert. As well as regular beer tastings, festivals and events, there are some great walks in the area, and picnics and maps can be provided by the helpful staff. Booking for meals may be required.

Open all wk 11-3 6-11 (Sun 12-10.30) **Bar Meals** L served all wk 12-3 D served all wk 6-10 Av main course £12 **Restaurant** L served all wk 12-3 D served all wk 6-10 Av 3 course à la carte fr £21 ⊕ FREE HOUSE ◼ Moor Revival, Butcombe Ò Thatchers Cheddar Valley & Gold, The Orchard Pig. ☙ 30 **Facilities** ✿ Children welcome Children's menu Children's portions Play area Garden Beer festival Parking Wi-fi ⬚ (notice required)

BUCKLAND NEWTON — Map 4 ST60

Gaggle of Geese

PICK OF THE PUBS

DT2 7BS ☎ 01300 345249
e-mail: goose@thegaggle.co.uk
dir: *On B3143, N of Dorchester*

An extraordinary village inn with a heart of gold, the Gaggle harks back to times past when many villages could claim such a retreat. Now as rare as hen's teeth (there's a twice-yearly poultry auction here, so who knows…); step from the lane into the large front parlour, complete with sofas, wingbacks in front of the welcoming fire, bookshelves, matchboarding and scrubbed tables. A glance at the bar reveals well-lubricated handpumps dispensing beers from St Austell, Sharp's and Ringwood breweries, farmhouse ciders and a perry from the local Bridge Farm. The treats continue with a skittles alley, whilst the grounds host a cricket pitch, croquet lawn and orchard. Just like the Tardis, the inside expands to reveal a sizeable, well-appointed restaurant, where top-notch meals include many sourced from the home farm of landlord Mark Hammick. Be tempted by a starter of Pecker's pan-fried pigeon breast with poached egg, lardons and pan juices, but do leave room for pan-fried loin and fillet of Cheselbourne venison with miniature

continued

BUCKLAND NEWTON *continued*

venison cottage pie, braised red cabbage and fondant potato; or crispy skinned sea bass with Thai green butternut squash broth; completing with mulled wine poached pear with Blue Vinney ice cream. Booking for meals may be required.

Open all wk 10-3 6-11.30 (Sat-Sun all day in summer) **Bar Meals** L served Mon-Sat 12-2, Sun 12-3 D served Mon-Sat 7-9, Sun 6.30-8.30 **Restaurant** L served Mon-Sat 12-2, Sun 12-3 D served Mon-Sat 7-9, Sun 6.30-8.30 ⊕ FREE HOUSE ◄ St Austell Proper Job & Tribute, Sharp's Doom Bar, Ringwood, Guest ales ♂ Thatchers Gold, Lulworth Skipper, Bridge Farm Perry. ⬥ 10 **Facilities** ✿ Children welcome Children's portions Play area Garden Parking Wi-fi ▭

CATTISTOCK Map 4 SY59

Fox & Hounds Inn

Duck St DT2 0JH ☎ 01300 320444
e-mail: lizflight@yahoo.co.uk
dir: *On A37, between Dorchester & Yeovil, follow signs to Cattistock*

Expect a bar full of locals, children, dogs and even chickens under foot at this attractive award-winning pub. Situated in a picturesque village, the 17th-century inn has a welcoming and traditional atmosphere engendered by ancient beams, open fires in winter and huge inglenooks, one with an original bread oven. Palmers ales are on tap, along with Taunton cider, while home-made meals embrace Lyme Bay scallop and smoked bacon salad; vine tomato, fennel and basil pie; and lamb shank with redcurrant and rosemary sauce. Booking for meals may be required.

Open 12-2.30 6-11 Closed: Mon L **Bar Meals** L served Tue-Sun 12-2 D served Tue-Sat 7-11 Av main course £9.95 **Restaurant** L served Tue-Sun 12-2 D served Tue-Sat 7-11 ⊕ PALMERS ◄ Best Bitter, Copper Ale, 200, Dorset Gold ♂ Taunton Traditional, Thatchers Gold. **Facilities** ✿ Children welcome Children's portions Play area Garden Parking Wi-fi ▭ (notice required)

CHEDINGTON Map 4 ST40

Winyard's Gap Inn

Chedington Ln DT8 3HY ☎ 01935 891244
e-mail: enquiries@winyardsgap.com
dir: *5m S of Crewkerne on A356*

A family-owned free house with an extensive beer garden blessed with impressive views. Winyard's Gap itself is a cutting owned by the National Trust, just beyond which the road twists down into Somerset. Settle in the beamed bar with a pint of Dorset Piddle (it's a local river) and choose pan-fried pork fillet with thyme rösti; seared salmon on olive and chorizo potato cake; or perhaps brie with roasted winter vegetable, leek and parmesan crumble. A senior-citizens' menu offers two courses for £7.50 Monday to Friday lunchtimes, except Bank Holidays. Booking for meals may be required.

Open all wk 11.30-3 6-11 (Sat-Sun 11.30-11) Closed: 25 Dec **Bar Meals** L served Mon-Sat 12-2 D served all wk 6-9 Av main course £12 **Restaurant** L served all wk 12-2 D served all wk 6-9 Av 3 course à la carte fr £25 ⊕ FREE HOUSE ◄ Sharp's Doom Bar, Dorset Piddle, Exmoor Ale, Otter Ale ♂ Thatchers Gold, Westons Old Rosie & 1st Quality. ⬥ 8 **Facilities** Children welcome Children's menu Children's portions Garden Parking Wi-fi ▭ (notice required)

CHETNOLE Map 4 ST60

The Chetnole Inn NEW

DT9 6NU ☎ 01935 872337
e-mail: enquiries@thechetnoleinn.co.uk
dir: *A37 from Dorchester towards Yeovil. Left at Chetnole sign*

Close to Sherborne and just a 30-minute drive from the coast, this tucked-away country pub opposite the village church dates back to the early 16th century. There are three main areas in the pub plus an attractive beer garden where two giant rabbits reside. The food here has won awards for its quality and use of local produce – a starter of Capricorn goat's cheese with walnut salad might make way for slow-roast belly of Bridport pork and sage crushed new potatoes. Finish with pear and apple crumble with cream. Booking for meals may be required.

Open 12-3 6.30-close Closed: Sun eve & Mon (Sep-Apr) **Bar Meals** L served Tue-Sun 12-2 D served Tue-Sat 6.30-9 Av main course £14.20 **Restaurant** L served Tue-Sun 12-2 D served Tue-Sat 6.30-9 Fixed menu price fr £12.50 Av 3 course à la carte fr £25 ⊕ FREE HOUSE ◄ Sharp's Doom Bar, Otter Ale, Butcombe ♂ Ashton Press, Thatchers. ⬥ 12 **Facilities** ✿ Children welcome Children's menu Children's portions Garden Beer festival Parking Wi-fi ▭ (notice required)

CHIDEOCK Map 4 SY49

The Anchor Inn

Seatown DT6 6JU ☎ 01297 489215
dir: *On A35 turn S in Chideock opp church & follow single track rd for 0.75m to beach*

Originally a smugglers' haunt, The Anchor has an incredible setting in a little cove surrounded by National Trust land, beneath Golden Cap. The large sun terrace and cliffside beer garden overlooking the beach make it a premier destination for throngs of holidaymakers in the summer, while on winter weekdays it is blissfully quiet. The wide-ranging menu starts with snacks and light lunches - three types of ploughman's and a range of sandwiches might take your fancy. For something more substantial choose a freshly caught fish dish accompanied with one of the real ales or ciders.

Open all wk 11.30-10.30 **Bar Meals** L served all wk 12-9 D served all wk 12-9 ⊕ PALMERS ◄ 200, Best Bitter, Copper Ale ♂ Thatchers Traditional & Pear. **Facilities** ✿ Children welcome Children's menu Children's portions Family room Garden Parking

CHRISTCHURCH Map 5 SZ19

The Ship In Distress

66 Stanpit BH23 3NA ☎ 01202 485123
e-mail: shipindistress@rocketmail.com
web: www.ship-in-distress.co.uk
dir: *Telephone for directions*

The seafood menu at this 300-year-old smugglers' pub reflects the closeness of Mudeford Quay and the English Channel. Nautical memorabilia is everywhere, so either bag a seat by the woodburner with a pint of Ringwood Best Bitter or Fortyniner and traditional fish and chips or cottage pie; alternatively, head into the restaurant for salmon and scallion fishcake; fruits de mer; locally caught lobster; or whole Dorset crab. The full carte, including steaks, is on the blackboard. In summer enjoy the Shellfish Bar on the suntrap terrace.

Open all day all wk 11am-mdnt (Sun 11-11) **Bar Meals** L served Mon-Fri 12-2, Sat-Sun 12-2.30 D served Sun-Thu 6.30-9, Fri-Sat 6.30-9.30 Av main course £5.95 **Restaurant** L served Mon-Fri 12-2, Sat-Sun 12-2.30 D served Sun-Thu 6.30-9, Fri-Sat 6.30-9.30 Fixed menu price fr £9.95 Av 3 course à la carte fr £25 ⊕ PUNCH TAVERNS ◄ Ringwood Best Bitter & Fortyniner, Adnams Broadside, Guest ales ♂ Westons Stowford Press. **Facilities** ✿ Children welcome Children's menu Children's portions Garden Parking Wi-fi ▭

Save on hotels. Book at **theAA.com/hotel**

DORSET 185 **ENGLAND**

PICK OF THE PUBS

The Cock & Bottle

EAST MORDEN   Map 4 SY99

BH20 7DL ☎ **01929 459238**
e-mail: cockandbottle@btconnect.com
web: www.cockandbottlemorden.co.uk
dir: *From A35 W of Poole right onto B3075, pub 0.5m on left*

Parts of this old Dorset longhouse were built about 400 years ago; the pub was originally cob-walled and, though it was sheathed in brick some time around 1800, it retained its thatched roof until the mid-60s. Today, the unspoilt interiors with their low-beamed ceilings and a wealth of nooks and crannies are redolent of a bygone age. The lively locals' bar is simply furnished and comfortably rustic, with a large wooden settle on which to while away a winter's evening with a game of dominoes beside the cosy log fire. The fine range of real ales from the nearby Hall & Woodhouse brewery is also available in the lounge bar, and a modern restaurant at the back completes the picture. Fresh game and fish feature strongly on the ever-changing menu, which ranges from light lunches, bar meals and Sunday roasts to pub favourites like steak-and-kidney pudding or lamb shank. À la carte choices might include a starter of local dressed crab, or deep-fried brie wedges

with a Cumberland sauce. Moving on, rabbit pie with root vegetable and mushroom sauce; and grilled wild sea bass with crushed new potatoes, rocket and horseradish crème fraîche are typical main course options. Home-made desserts like orange and spiced rum crème brûlée; or dark and white chocolate terrine with a fruit coulis make a fitting finale to the meal. Lovely pastoral views over the surrounding farmland include the pub's paddock, which occasionally hosts vintage car and motorcycle meetings during the summer. Well-behaved dogs are welcome. Booking for meals may be required.

Open all wk 11.30-2.30 6-11 (Sun 12-3 7-10.30) **Bar Meals** L served all wk 12-2 D served Mon-Sat 6-9, Sun 7-9 **Restaurant** L served all wk 12-2 D served Mon-Sat 6-9, Sun 7-9 ⊕ HALL & WOODHOUSE ◖ Badger Dorset Best & Tanglefoot, Guest ale.
Facilities Children welcome Children's menu Children's portions Play area 🐾 Garden Parking 🚌

CHURCH KNOWLE — Map 4 SY98

The New Inn

BH20 5NQ ☎ 01929 480357
e-mail: maurice@newinn-churchknowle.co.uk
web: www.thenewinn-churchknowle.co.uk
dir: *From Wareham take A351 towards Swanage. At Corfe Castle turn right for Church Knowle. Pub in village centre*

Landlord Maurice Estop, whose family have run this part-thatched, stone-built, 16th-century village inn for 25 years, is only the fourth licensee in the last 150 years. Still in place are the old inglenook fireplaces and a brick alcove that used to be the kitchen oven from its days as a farmhouse. Real ales include Jurassic and changing guests, and there are draught ciders too, while fresh home-cooked food includes catch of the day, roasts, traditional pies, sandwiches and home-made desserts. The new Purbeck Lounge is tailor-made for family dining. Booking for meals may be required.

Open 10-3 6-11 (10-3 5-11 summer) Closed: Mon eve Jan & Feb **Bar Meals** L served all wk 12-2.15 D served all wk 6-9.15 (5-9.15 summer) Av main course £8.95-£16 **Restaurant** L served all wk 12-2.15 D served all wk 6-9.15 (5-9.15 summer) ⊕ PUNCH TAVERNS ◀ Dorset Jurassic, St Austell Tribute, Guest ales ♂ Westons Old Rosie, Stowford Press & Traditional. ♀ 10
Facilities Children welcome Children's menu Children's portions Family room Garden Parking 🚌 (notice required)

CORFE CASTLE — Map 4 SY98

The Bankes Arms ★★★ INN NEW

23 East St BH20 5ED ☎ 01929 480206
e-mail: bankescorfe@aol.com
dir: *From Wareham A351 to Corfe Castle. In village centre*

In the beautiful village of Corfe Castle, this lovely pub is located on the Isle of Purbeck with its famous Jurassic Coast World Heritage Site. With ten guest bedrooms, the inn is an ideal base to explore the many coastal walks and Dorset countryside. The team takes pride in sourcing fresh regional produce, cooked simply with a Mediterranean twist. Start with Lulworth Bay crab, move on to one of the hand-fired pizzas with a variety of toppings, or the gourmet beefburger, and finish with Belgain waffles. Mouthwatering cream teas are on offer too.

Open all day all wk **Bar Meals** L served all wk 12-9.30 D served all wk 12-9.30 Av main course £10 food served all day **Restaurant** L served all wk 12-9.30 D served all wk 12-9.30 Av 3 course à la carte fr £20 food served all day ⊕ ENTERPRISE INNS ◀ Sharp's Doom Bar, Ringwood ♂ Westons Stowford Press, Symonds. **Facilities** ❄ Children welcome Children's menu Children's portions Play area Family room Garden Beer festival Parking Wi-fi 🚌 (notice required) **Rooms** 10

The Greyhound Inn

The Square BH20 5EZ ☎ 01929 480205
e-mail: eat@greyhoundcorfe.co.uk
dir: *W from Bournemouth, take A35 to Dorchester, after 5m left onto A351, 10m to Corfe Castle*

This classic pub set beneath the ruins of Corfe Castle warmly welcomes all-comers, children and pets. Its large sun-drenched garden with views of Swanage Steam Railway is a highly-prized spot for the sampling of a summer pint of Hop Back. Food is served all day, so it's popular with nearby campsites, but fresh seasonal produce is nonetheless the kitchen's priority, appearing

in dishes such as hearty Dorset game pie, and Dorset baby back ribs in sticky barbecue sauce. Six food festivals are hosted throughout the year, as well as a beer festival on the August Bank Holiday weekend. Booking for meals may be required.

Open all day all wk 11am-1am **Bar Meals** Av main course £12-£15 food served all day **Restaurant** Av 3 course à la carte fr £25 food served all day ⊕ ENTERPRISE INNS ◀ Sharp's Doom Bar, Hop Back Summer Lightning, Guest ale ♂ Westons Stowford Press & Wyld Wood Organic Vintage, Thatchers, Purbeck Joe's. ♀ 9 **Facilities** ❄ Children welcome Children's menu Children's portions Play area Family room Garden Beer festival Wi-fi 🚌 (notice required)

EAST MORDEN — Map 4 SY99

The Cock & Bottle

PICK OF THE PUBS

See Pick of the Pubs on page 185

EVERSHOT — Map 4 ST50

The Acorn Inn ★★★★ INN ⊛

PICK OF THE PUBS

See Pick of the Pubs on opposite page
See advert below

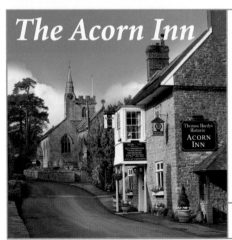

Save on hotels. Book at **theAA.com/hotel**

DORSET 187 ENGLAND

PICK OF THE PUBS

The Acorn Inn ★★★★INN 🏵

EVERSHOT   Map 4 ST50

DT2 0JW ☎ **01935 83228**
e-mail: stay@acorn-inn.co.uk
web: www.acorn-inn.co.uk
dir: *From A37 between Yeovil &
Dorchester, follow Evershot & Holywell
signs, 0.5m to inn*

Attractively set at the heart of a quaint,
historic village and surrounded by unspoilt
rolling countryside, this traditional 16th-
century village inn was the model for
Thomas Hardy's Sow and Acorn in *Tess of
the d'Urbervilles*. The infamous Judge
Jeffreys used one of the rooms in the inn
as a court. The Acorn is an excellent base
from which to explore Hardy Country and
the beautiful Dorset coastline, and many
of the comfortable bedrooms boast four-
poster beds. Oak-panelled bars with
flagstone floors and blazing log fires in
carved Hamstone fireplaces and elegantly
decorated dining areas adorned with
paintings offer a relaxed and civilised
ambience for savouring some imaginative
food. Using seasonal produce from local
farms and estates and fish from Bridport,
the modern British repertoire takes in
smoked venison with celeriac remoulade,
mixed leaves and truffle oil dressing; pork
belly with mixed bean and chorizo
cassoulet, braised fennel and pan juices;
venison hotpot with caramelised onions
and braised red cabbage; and chicken,
mushroom and tarragon pie with spring
onion mash and winter vegetables. Lighter
lunchtime options include smoked salmon

and crayfish open sandwich; cider-
steamed River Exe mussels with rosemary
and apple sauce; potted shrimps with
toast, radish and cucumber salad and
lemon dressing; and traditional bar
snacks like ploughman's, and baked ham,
egg and triple-cooked chips. Those with a
sweet tooth should leave room for warm
chocolate brownie with raspberry ripple
ice cream, or the apple crumble with
warm clove custard. To drink, there's Otter
and Doom Bar on tap and a list of 11
wines by the glass and 100 malt whiskies.
There are some wonderful walks from the
front door so don't forget to pack your
boots. Booking for meals may be required.

Open all day all wk 11am-11.30pm **Bar
Meals** L served all wk 12-2 D served all
wk 7-9 Av main course £8.95

Restaurant L served all wk 12-2
D served all wk 7-9 Av 3 course à la
carte fr £25 ⊕ FREE HOUSE ◀ Sharp's
Doom Bar, Otter ♂ Thatchers Gold &
Traditional. �$ 11 **Facilities** Children
welcome Children's portions Family
room 🐾 Garden Beer festival Parking
Wi-fi 🚐 (notice required) **Rooms** 10

FARNHAM
Map 4 ST91

The Museum Inn
PICK OF THE PUBS

DT11 8DE ☎ 01725 516261
e-mail: enquiries@museuminn.co.uk
dir: *From Salisbury take A354 to Blandford Forum, 12m. Farnham signed on right. Pub in village centre*

This award-winning country pub lies in Cranborne Chase, where kings used to hunt, and where in the 19th century General Augustus Pitt Rivers pioneered modern archaeological fieldwork. He built the inn for visitors to a small museum, now gone, where he displayed his finds. The sympathetically refurbished interior features the original inglenook fireplace, flagstone floors, a fashionable mismatch of furniture and a book-filled sitting room for relaxing with a pint of Flack Catcher or 6D Best. The name over the front door is that of new landlord James Harrison, although long-standing head chef Ricky Ford provides continuity, sourcing extensively from local estates and farms. His traditional Dorset lamb three ways (roasted saddle, sweetbreads and shepherd's pie) with neeps and tatties; and Brixham beer-battered cod, chips and crushed peas are highlights of the menu. A good many of the excellent wines are served by the glass. Booking for meals may be required.

Open all day all wk **Bar Meals** L served Mon-Fri 12-2, Sat 12-2.30, Sun 12-3 D served all wk 7-9.30 Av main course £8.50 **Restaurant** L served Sun 12-3 D served Fri-Sat 7-9.30 Fixed menu price fr £14.75 Av 3 course à la carte fr £26.95 ⊕ FREE HOUSE ◀ Sixpenny 6D Best, Flack Manor Flack Catcher Ŏ The Orchard Pig. ♀ 12 **Facilities** ❖ Children welcome Children's menu Children's portions Garden Parking Wi-fi ▅ (notice required)

GILLINGHAM
Map 4 ST82

The Kings Arms Inn

East Stour Common SP8 5NB ☎ 01747 838325
e-mail: nrosscampbell@aol.com
dir: *4m W of Shaftesbury on A30*

This is a 200-year-old, family-run village free house where Victorian fireplaces sit comfortably alongside modern wooden furniture and subtly coloured fabrics. Scottish touches – paintings by artist Mavis Makie, quotes by Robert Burns, the presence of haggis, skirlie and cranachan on the menus, and a wide choice of single malts – reflect the origin of the landlord and landlady. An extensive choice of dishes includes fillet of beef Wellington; steak and real ale suet pudding; pan-fried fillet of salmon; and Thai green vegetable curry. Doom Bar, Tribute and Greene King IPA are on tap. Booking for meals may be required.

Open all wk 12-3 5.30-11.30 (Sat-Sun 12-12) **Bar Meals** L served Mon-Sat 12-2.30, Sun 12-9.15 D served Mon-Sat 5.30-9.15, Sun 12-9.15 **Restaurant** L served Mon-Sat 12-2.30, Sun 12-9.15 D served Mon-Sat 5.30-9.15, Sun 12-9.15 ⊕ FREE HOUSE ◀ Sharp's Doom Bar, Greene King IPA, St Austell Tribute. ♀ **Facilities** ❖ Children welcome Children's menu Children's portions Family room Garden Parking Wi-fi ▅

GUSSAGE ALL SAINTS
Map 4 SU01

The Drovers Inn

BH21 5ET ☎ 01258 840084
e-mail: info@thedroversinn.biz
dir: *A31 Ashley Heath rdbt, right onto B3081 follow signs*

A rural 16th-century pub with a fine terrace and wonderful views from the garden, so it's something of a surprise to know it was rescued from closure in 2000. Its refurbished interior retains plenty of traditional appeal with flagstone floors and oak furniture. Landlord Jason is proud of the welcome he provides – ensuring, for example, that drinkers are never moved from tables to accommodate diners. Ales from Ringwood include seasonal guests, and the menu features carefully chosen rare-breed meats, vegetables from New Covent Garden via a local supplier, and fresh seafood from Poole. There is a beer festival around Easter time.

Open all wk 12-3 6-12 (Sat-Sun & BH all day) Closed: 26 Dec **Bar Meals** L served all wk 12-2 D served all wk 6-9 **Restaurant** L served all wk 12-2 D served all wk 6-9 ⊕ RINGWOOD BREWERY ◀ Best Bitter, Old Thumper, Fortyniner & Seasonal ales, Guest ales Ŏ Thatchers Gold & Traditional. ♀ 10 **Facilities** ❖ Children welcome Children's menu Children's portions Garden Beer festival Parking Wi-fi ▅

KING'S STAG
Map 4 ST71

The Greenman

DT10 2AY ☎ 01258 817338
dir: *E of Sherborne on A3030*

Legend has it that King's Stag in the Blackmore Vale owes its name to Henry III's favourite white hart, hunted down and killed by a local nobleman. Built around 1775 and full of oak beams, the pub has five separate dining areas where you can order anything from a snack to a banquet. The Sunday carvery offers a choice of five meats and eight vegetables – booking is essential. Children will enjoy the play area while parents can relax and enjoy a drink.

Open all wk 11-3 5.30-11 **Bar Meals** L served all wk 12-2 D served all wk 6-9 **Restaurant** L served all wk 12-2 D served all wk 6-9 ⊕ ENTERPRISE INNS ◀ 2 Guest ales. ♀ 9 **Facilities** ❖ Children welcome Play area Family room Garden Parking ▅

LODERS
Map 4 SY49

Loders Arms

DT6 3SA ☎ 01308 422431
dir: *Off A3066, 2m NE of Bridport*

This 17th-century, creeper-covered local, tucked away in a pretty village near the Dorset coast has recently undergone a change of hands. Child- and dog-friendly, it has a patio and garden with views over Boarsbarrow Hill. Alternatively, bag a seat in the long cosy bar with warming winter fires or in the homely dining room.

Open all wk **Bar Meals** L served all wk 12-2 D served all wk 6.30-9 Av main course £10 **Restaurant** L served all wk 12-2 D served all wk 6.30-9 Av 3 course à la carte fr £21 ⊕ PALMERS ◀ Copper Ale, Best Bitter, 200 Ŏ Thatchers Gold. **Facilities** ❖ Children welcome Children's menu Children's portions Garden Parking Wi-fi

LOWER ANSTY
Map 4 ST70

The Fox Inn ★★★★ INN

DT2 7PN ☎ 01258 880328
e-mail: fox@anstyfoxinn.co.uk
web: www.anstyfoxinn.co.uk
dir: *A35 from Dorchester towards Poole for 4m, exit signed Piddlehinton/Athelhampton House, left to Cheselbourne, then right. Pub in village opposite post office*

Built more than 250 years ago, The Fox Inn was once the home of Charles Hall, who went on to co-found the Hall & Woodhouse Brewery. The pub has undergone an extensive refurbishment and the main restaurant is now augmented by a light and airy garden eatery. The menu proffers chicken liver pâté with rum and raisins; honey and mustard glazed belly pork with sage, apple and smoked bacon, mashed potato and cider reduction. Badger beers are, naturally enough, served in the bar, and comfortable accommodation is available.

Open all day all wk **Bar Meals** L served all wk 12-2.30 D served all wk 6.30-9 Av main course £8.50 **Restaurant** L served all wk 12-2.30 D served all wk 6.30-9 Av 3 course à la carte fr £20 ⊕ HALL & WOODHOUSE ◀ Badger Tanglefoot, Dorset Best, Seasonal ale. ♀ 12 **Facilities** Children welcome Children's menu Children's portions Garden Parking Wi-fi ▅ (notice required) **Rooms** 11

Save on hotels. Book at **theAA.com/hotel**

DORSET 189 **ENGLAND**

LYME REGIS Map 4 SY39

The Mariners ★★★★ INN ◉

Silver St DT7 3HS ☎ 01297 442753
e-mail: enquiries@hotellymeregis.co.uk
dir: *A35 onto B3165 (Lyme Rd). Mariners is pink building opposite road to The Cobb (Pound Rd)*

This 17th-century coaching inn is handy for the renowned Jurassic Coast. The pub is steeped in Lyme's fossil history, having once been home to the Philpot sisters, famed as collectors in the early 19th century. Beatrix Potter is said to have stayed here too, reputedly writing *The Tale of Little Pig Robinson* – The Mariners is pictured in the book. The building combines traditional character with modern style. Simple menus feature the best of local seafood and other quality ingredients in dishes such as braised Dorset beef, and warm apple and plum crumble. Accommodation is available. Booking for meals may be required.

Open all day all wk **Bar Meals** L served all wk 12-2 D served all wk 6.30-9 Av main course £9.95 **Restaurant** L served all wk 12-2 D served all wk 6.30-9 Fixed menu price fr £12 Av 3 course à la carte fr £20 ⊕ FREE HOUSE ◀ Otter Bright, Mighty Hop Mighty Red IPA & Mainers Ale ♂ Thatchers Gold. **Facilities** Children welcome Children's menu Children's portions Garden Parking Wi-fi ▭ **Rooms** 14

Pilot Boat Inn

Bridge St DT7 3QA ☎ 01297 443157
dir: *Telephone for directions*

Old smuggling and sea rescue tales are associated with this busy town-centre pub, close to the seafront. Along with Palmers ales, there is a good range of food on regularly changing menus. Traditional recipes using local ingredients include steak-and-kidney pie and Dorset chicken in a cider and apple sauce. Sandwiches, salads and cold platters are also offered, plus local crab, real scampi and chips, and other fresh fish from Lyme Bay as available. There are always good vegetarian options, such as three bean casserole, and butternut squash and goat's cheese lasagne.

Open all day all wk Closed: 25 Dec **Bar Meals** food served all day **Restaurant** food served all day ⊕ PALMERS ◀ Best Bitter, 200, Bridport Bitter. ♛ 9 **Facilities** ❖ Children welcome Children's menu Children's portions Garden ▭

MILTON ABBAS Map 4 ST80

The Hambro Arms

DT11 0BP ☎ 01258 880233
e-mail: info@hambroarms.co.uk
dir: *A354 (Dorchester to Blandford road), turn off in Milborne St Andrew for Milton Abbas*

At one end of what is believed to have been the first planned village in England stands this long, whitewashed pub. The rest of the village street is lined by 36 identical thatched cottages built by Lord Milton in 1780. The pub, owned by a village partnership, serves Piddle Ales, Ringwood and Sharp's, and largely locally sourced dishes such as lamb chops in red wine and rosemary sauce; fennel-crusted fillet of salmon; and spinach and mushroom parcels with Dorset Blue Vinney sauce. A beer festival takes place in July.

Open all wk 11.30-3 6-11 (Sat-Sun 11.30-11.30) **Bar Meals** L served Mon-Fri 12-2.30, Sat-Sun 12-3 D served Mon-Thu 6-9, Fri-Sat 6-9.30 Av main course £9.50 **Restaurant** L served Mon-Fri 12-2.30, Sat-Sun 12-3 D served Mon-Thu 6-9, Fri-Sat 6-9.30 Av 3 course à la carte fr £22 ⊕ FREE HOUSE ◀ Sharp's Doom Bar, Ringwood, Piddle ♂ Westons Stowford Press. ♛ 8 **Facilities** Children welcome Children's menu Garden Beer festival Parking Wi-fi ▭

The Coppleridge Inn

Motcombe, Shaftesbury, Dorset SP7 9HW Tel: 01747 851980 Fax: 01747 851858
www.coppleridge.com

The Coppleridge inn is a family run traditional country inn set in 15 acres of Dorset countryside. Our 10 ground floor en suite bedrooms have all been superbly refurbished over the past 12 months. Our friendly bar and candlelit restaurant serving freshly cooked locally sourced meals creates the perfect location for exploring the beautiful and historic sights of Wessex.

MOTCOMBE — Map 4 ST82

The Coppleridge Inn ★★★ INN

SP7 9HW ☎ 01747 851980

e-mail: thecoppleridgeinn@btinternet.com
web: www.coppleridge.com
dir: Take A350 towards Warminster for 1.5m, turn left at brown tourist sign. Follow signs to inn

An 18th-century farmhouse, whose flagstone floors and log fires survive in today's pub, which is surrounded by meadows, woodland and gardens, with a secure children's playground. Run by Chris and Di Goodinge for more than 20 years, the bar offers a wide range of real ales, as well as constantly changing old favourites like beer-battered haddock and chips; casserole of the day; and home-made pancake stuffed with creamy spinach and stilton. Beef Wellington with port jus and fondant potato is a daily special. Ten spacious bedrooms are situated around a converted courtyard.

Open all wk 11-3 5-11 (Sat 11am-mdnt Sun 12-11) **Bar Meals** L served all wk 12-2.30 D served all wk 6-9 Av main course £10.50 **Restaurant** L served all wk 12-2.30 D served all wk 6-9 ⊕ FREE HOUSE ◀ Butcombe Bitter, Wadworth 6X, Fuller's London Pride, Sharp's Doom Bar, Ringwood Best Bitter Ö Ashton Press. ☶ 10 **Facilities** ✿ Children welcome Children's menu Children's portions Play area Family room Garden Parking Wi-fi ▭ (notice required) **Rooms** 10

See advert on page 189

NETTLECOMBE — Map 4 SY59

Marquis of Lorne

DT6 3SY ☎ 01308 485236

e-mail: info@themarquisoflorne.co.uk
dir: From A3066 (Bridport-Beaminster road) approx 1.5m N of Bridport follow Loders & Mangerton Mill signs. At junct left past Mangerton Mill, through West Milton. 1m to T-junct, straight over. Pub up hill, approx 300yds on left

The Marquis of Lorne, built as a farmhouse in the 16th century and converted into a pub in 1871, is now run by Steve and Tracey Brady. They have renewed the focus on local produce throughout the menus. Mustard and brown sugar-baked Dorset ham is presented with eggs, fries and home-made piccalilli, while oriental influences can be found in dishes such as warm salad of shredded duck with spring onion and cucumber in a hoi sin dressing. There are various special dinner evenings to look out for. The beautiful gardens are family friendly, too. Enjoy Palmers ales on tap.

Open all wk 12-2.30 6-11 **Bar Meals** L served all wk 12-2 D served all wk 6-9 Av main course £12.50 **Restaurant** L served all wk 12-2 D served all wk 6-9 Av 3 course à la carte fr £25 ⊕ PALMERS ◀ Copper Ale, Best Bitter, 200. **Facilities** Children welcome Children's menu Children's portions Play area Garden Parking Wi-fi ▭ (notice required)

NORTH WOOTTON — Map 4 ST61

The Three Elms

DT9 5JW ☎ 01935 812881

dir: From Sherborne take A352 towards Dorchester then A3030. Pub 1m on right

Now in new hands, and incorporating a shop and post office, this family-friendly pub near the beautiful Blackmore Vale has become the heart of the community. The bar is well stocked with local and weekly changing guest real ales and ciders, and freshly cooked pub classics served at candlelit tables include chicken Stroganoff and rice; scampi and chips; and bacon and mushroom tagliatelle carbonara. Among the 'two for £10' deals are Alweston Farm rabbit; faggots, mash and peas; and shepherd's pie. The large beer garden hosts summer barbecues and beer festivals.

Open all day all wk 11-11 (Sun 12-10.30) Closed: 26 Dec **Bar Meals** L served Mon-Sat 12-2.30, Sun 12-3 D served Mon-Sat 6-9.30, Sun 6-9 Av main course £10 **Restaurant** L served Mon-Sat 12-2.30, Sun 12-3 D served Mon-Sat 6-9.30, Sun 6-9 ⊕ FREE HOUSE ◀ Butcombe Bitter, Otter Bitter, St Austell Tribute Ö Thatchers & Gold, Ashton Still. **Facilities** ✿ Children welcome Children's menu Children's portions Play area Garden Beer festival Parking Wi-fi ▭

OSMINGTON MILLS — Map 4 SY78

The Smugglers Inn

DT3 6HF ☎ 01305 833125

e-mail: smugglersinn.weymouth@hall-woodhouse.co.uk
dir: 7m E of Weymouth towards Wareham, pub signed

Set on the cliffs at Osmington Mills with the South Coast Footpath running through the garden, the inn has beautiful views across Weymouth Bay. In the late 18th century (the inn dates back to the 13th century) it was the base of infamous smuggler Pierre La Tour who fell in love with the publican's daughter, Arabella Carless, who was shot dead while helping him to escape during a raid. Things are quieter now and you can enjoy a pint of Tanglefoot or one of the guest ales like Pickled Partridge. On the menu typical dishes are smoked haddock Benedict; venison sausages and mash; and steak and Tanglefoot pie.

Open all wk 11-11 (Sun 12-10.30) **Bar Meals** L served all wk 12-9.30 D served all wk 12-9.30 food served all day **Restaurant** L served all wk 12-9.30 D served all wk 12-9.30 food served all day ⊕ HALL & WOODHOUSE ◀ Badger Tanglefoot, Guest ale. ☶ 12 **Facilities** ✿ Children welcome Children's menu Children's portions Play area Garden Parking ▭

PIDDLEHINTON — Map 4 SY79

The Thimble Inn

DT2 7TD ☎ 01300 348270

e-mail: thethimbleinn@gmail.com
dir: A35 W'bound, right onto B3143, Piddlehinton in 4m

This friendly village local with open fires, traditional pub games and good food cooked to order was taken over new landlord Stuart Payne and landlady Heather Solonya in early 2012. The pub stands in a pretty valley on the banks of the River Piddle, and the riverside patio is popular in summer. Along with Palmers beers on tap, signature dishes from the menu range from Palmers beer-battered haddock to confit duck with braised sweet red cabbage, creamed potato and red wine jus. Booking for meals may be required.

Open 11.30-2.30 6-11 Closed: Mon **Bar Meals** L served all wk 11.30-2 D served all wk 6.30-9 **Restaurant** L served all wk 11.30-2 D served all wk 6.30-9 ⊕ PALMERS ◀ Copper Ale, Best Bitter, 200 Ö Thatchers Gold. **Facilities** ✿ Children welcome Children's menu Children's portions Garden Parking ▭

PIDDLETRENTHIDE — Map 4 SY79

The Piddle Inn

DT2 7QF ☎ 01300 348468

e-mail: piddleinn@aol.com
dir: 7m N of Dorchester on B3143, in village centre

Ramblers and visitors exploring the Dorset Area of Outstanding Natural Beauty just north of historic Dorchester can enjoy good food and local ales at The Piddle Inn. This idyllic, partly creeper-clad village inn is secluded in the valley of the eponymous chalk stream that courses behind the pub. Relax with gravity-dispensed beers from Dorset Piddle Brewery and indulge in meals created from the best local produce. Recent change of hands. Booking for meals may be required.

Open all wk 12-11.30 **Bar Meals** L served Mon-Sat 12-2, Sun 12-3 D served all wk 6-9.30 Av main course £11 **Restaurant** L served Mon-Sat 12-2, Sun 12-3 D served all wk 6-9.30 ⊕ FREE HOUSE ◀ St Austell Tribute, Sharp's Doom Bar, Greene King, Dorset Piddle Ö Thatchers Gold, Westons Stowford Press. **Facilities** ❄ Children welcome Children's menu Children's portions Garden Parking Wi-fi

The Poachers Inn

DT2 7QX ☎ 01300 348358
e-mail: info@thepoachersinn.co.uk
dir: *6m N from Dorchester on B3143. At church end of village*

Located in the pretty little village of Piddletrenthide in the heart of Thomas Hardy country, this 17th-century riverside pub is perfectly situated for exploring west Dorset and the Jurassic Coast. Classic pub meals (Dorset ham, egg and chips) vie with contemporary alternatives (marinated duck breast with soy and plum sauce) in the stylish bar and restaurant, or relax in the pool-side beer garden with a glass of Butcombe Bitter.

Open all day all wk 8am-mdnt **Bar Meals** L served all wk 12-2.30 D served all wk 6-9.30 Av main course £9.95 **Restaurant** L served all wk 12-2.30 D served all wk 6-9.30 ⊕ FREE HOUSE ◀ Sharp's Doom Bar, St Austell Tribute, Butcombe Bitter Ö Thatchers Gold. ☗ 9 **Facilities** ❄ Children welcome Children's menu Children's portions Garden Parking Wi-fi (notice required)

PLUSH   Map 4 ST70

The Brace of Pheasants ★★★★ INN

DT2 7RQ ☎ 01300 348357
e-mail: info@braceofpheasants.co.uk
dir: *A35 onto B3143, 5m to Piddletrenthide, then right to Mappowder & Plush*

With its welcoming open fire, oak beams and fresh flowers, this pretty 16th-century thatched village inn is an ideal place to start or end a walk. Tucked away in a fold of the hills in the heart of Hardy's beloved county, it offers a good selection of real ales and ciders and 18 wines by the glass. Food options might include local pigeon with roast beetroot and red watercress salad; pan-fried trio of lamb cutlets with honey and rosemary sauce and polenta roast potatoes; and treacle tart with double cream. The inn offers eight en suite bedrooms, four above the pub and four in the old skittle alley.

Open all wk 12-3 7-11 Closed: 25 Dec **Bar Meals** L served Tue-Sun 12-2.30 D served Tue-Sun 7-9 Av main course £13 **Restaurant** L served Tue-Sun 12-2.30 D served Tue-Sun 7-9 ⊕ FREE HOUSE ◀ Sharp's Doom Bar, Flack Manor Flack's Double Drop, Palmers, Dorset Piddle Ö Sharp's Orchard, Westons Traditional. ☗ 18

Facilities ❄ Children welcome Children's portions Garden Parking Wi-fi (notice required) **Rooms** 8

POOLE   Map 4 SZ09

The Guildhall Tavern

15 Market St BH15 1NB ☎ 01202 671717
e-mail: sewerynsevfred@aol.com
dir: *2 mins from Quay*

Two minutes from Poole's historic quay and located in the heart of the old town, this former cider house has been impressively refurbished without losing any of its traditional charm. Beautifully fresh seafood reflects the owners' Gallic roots, so you could start with snails in garlic butter, followed by pan-fried duck breast with Grand Marnier and orange gravy. Other main course options might include whole sea bass flambéed with Pernod or double-baked cheese soufflé. Leave room for hazelnut meringue filled with cream and raspberries. French themed evenings are held monthly.

Open Tue-Sat Closed: 1st 2wks Nov, Mon, Sun **Bar Meals** L served Tue-Sat 11.30-3 **Restaurant** L served Tue-Sat 11.30-3 D served Tue-Sat 6-10 ⊕ PUNCH TAVERNS ◀ Ringwood Best Bitter. **Facilities** Children welcome Children's menu Children's portions Parking ▦

The Rising Sun ◉◉

PICK OF THE PUBS

3 Dear Hay Ln BH15 1NZ ☎ 01202 771246
e-mail: paul@risingsunpoole.co.uk
dir: *7m from Wimborne B3073, A349 take A350 signed Poole/Channel Ferries*

This 18th-century pub just off the High Street in Poole is now a spruced-up and stylish, light and modern gastro-pub. A warm and relaxing atmosphere is guaranteed, whether you are popping for a pint of Flack's Double Drop in the elegant lounge bar, or heading for the charming restaurant to explore Greg Etheridge's innovative menus with two AA Rosettes. Both lunch and dinner menus successfully combine traditional pub classics with more adventurous dishes and make sound use of fresh local ingredients. Lunch offers inventive sandwiches and ciabattas, starters like warm salad of artichoke hearts, and main courses such as rope-grown Shetland mussels, and various grills. Evening extras may include chargrilled Honeybrook Farm chicken breast and roasted drumstick; slow-roast belly of pork with sautéed langoustines; and roasted fillet of cod and black olive crushed new potatoes. Seasonal specials are chalked on the blackboards daily. Booking for meals may be required.

Open all day Closed: 25 Dec, Sun **Bar Meals** L served Mon-Sat 12-2.30 D served Mon-Sat 6-9.30 Av main course £12.50 **Restaurant** L served Mon-Sat 12-2.30 D served Mon-Sat 6-9.30 Fixed menu price fr £15 Av 3 course à la carte fr £27.50 ⊕ ENTERPRISE INNS ◀ Flack Manor Flack's Double Drop, Guest ale Ö Westons Stowford Press. ☗ 12 **Facilities** Children welcome Children's portions Garden Wi-fi

---

POWERSTOCK   Map 4 SY59

Three Horseshoes Inn ★★★★ INN ◉

PICK OF THE PUBS

DT6 3TF ☎ 01308 485328
e-mail: threehorseshoespowerstock@live.co.uk
dir: *3m from Bridport off A3066 (Beaminster road)*

'The Shoes', as it is known locally, is a pretty Victorian inn belonging to Bridport's Palmers Brewery, in idyllic west Dorset countryside. The patio, terraced garden and guest rooms look out over the village, which lies at the foot of Eggardon hill fort, from which you can see Start Point in South Devon on a clear day. The one AA-Rosette cooking is inspired by traditional British pub food and produce from the surrounding area. Its reputation owes much to the kitchen's devotion to baking its own bread from organic flour, and making its own ingredients from scratch. The focus on local produce includes meat, game and poultry from Framptons of Bridport. Typical starters on the daily-changing menu of oyster fritters or Dorset snails could be followed by home-made veal burger; roe deer sausages; or one of the specials: West Bay scallops; smoked fishcake; or steak and kidney suet pudding.

Open 12-3 6.30-11.30 (Sun 12-3 6.30-10.30) Closed: Mon L **Bar Meals** L served Tue-Sat 12-2.30, Sun 12-3 D served all wk 6.30-9.30 Av main course £12 **Restaurant** L served Tue-Sat 12-2.30, Sun 12-3 D served all wk 6.30-9.30 Av 3 course à la carte fr £25 ⊕ PALMERS ◀ Best Bitter, Copper Ale, Tally Ho! Ö Thatchers Gold & Traditional. **Facilities** ❄ Children welcome Children's menu Children's portions Garden Parking Wi-fi **Rooms** 3

PUNCKNOWLE   Map 4 SY58

The Crown Inn

Church St DT2 9BN ☎ 01308 897711
e-mail: crownpuncknowle@btinternet.com
dir: *From A35, into Bridevally, through Litton Cheney. From B3157, inland at Swyre*

There's a traditional atmosphere within the rambling, low-beamed bars at this picturesque 16th-century thatched inn, which was once the haunt of smugglers on their way from nearby Chesil Beach to visit prosperous customers in Bath. Food ranges from light snacks and sandwiches to home-made dishes like lamb chops with mint sauce, and tuna steak with basil and tomato sauce. Accompany your meal with a glass of real ale or one of the wines by the glass.

Open 12-3 6-11 Closed: Sun eve in winter **Bar Meals** L served all wk 12-2 D served Mon-Sat 6-9 **Restaurant** L served all wk 12-2 D served Mon-Sat 6-9 ⊕ PALMERS ◀ Best Bitter, 200, Copper Ale, Seasonal ales Ö Thatchers Gold. ☗ 8 **Facilities** ❄ Children welcome Children's menu Children's portions Family room Garden Parking

---

The Anchor Inn

West St DT11 9LB ☎ 01258 857269
e-mail: anchor@shapwick.com
dir: *From Wimborne or Blandford Forum take B3082. Pub signed*

In 2006 this welcoming pub was saved from redevelopment; a group of 18 villagers clubbed together to purchase the freehold, then bought back the lease in 2011. Now the village owns The Anchor lock, stock and barrel. The current landlords are a retired BA captain and his ex-cabin-crew wife. You'll find Dorset Brewing Company ales and Cider by Rosie, an award-winning Dorset craft brew. Food is freshly prepared – a stone-baked ciabatta stuffed with tomato, basil and mozzarella makes a tasty light lunch, leaving space for a dessert of lemon tart with clotted cream.

Open 12-3 6-11 Closed: Sun eve **Bar Meals** L served all wk 12-2.30 D served Mon-Sat 6-9.30 Av main course £11.66 **Restaurant** L served all wk 12-2.30 D served Mon-Sat 6-9.30 Av 3 course à la carte fr £23.57 ⊕ FREE HOUSE ◀ Ringwood Best Bitter, Dorset Jurassic, Sharp's Doom Bar, Guest ales ♂ Thatchers, The Orchard Pig, Cider by Rosie. ▼ 23 **Facilities** ❤ Children welcome Children's portions Garden Parking ▄▄ (notice required)

The Kings Arms ★★★★★ INN

PICK OF THE PUBS

See Pick of the Pubs on opposite page
See advert below

The Cricketers

PICK OF THE PUBS

DT11 8QD ☎ 01258 860421
e-mail: info@thecricketersshroton.co.uk
web: www.heartstoneinns.co.uk
dir: *7m S of Shaftesbury on A350, turn right after Iwerne Minster. 5m N of Blandford Forum on A360, past Stourpaine, in 2m left into Shroton. Pub in village centre*

Maps show the village as Iwerne Courtney or Shroton, the latter being the name locals use and the one to ask for if lost in this beautiful Dorset countryside. Built early in the 20th century on the site of an earlier pub, The Cricketers is a real community local; it's also popular with walkers, lured from the Wessex Way as it passes conveniently through the secluded garden. In the light, open-plan interior Butcombe, Doom Bar and Tribute occupy the beer pumps, while wine-drinkers will find many available by the glass. In winter there's a welcoming log fire. The menu changes seasonally, with home-cooked, locally sourced ingredients delivering liver and bacon with minted mash; beer-battered cod and chips; chef's curry of the day; and root vegetable potato bake with optional cheese. There's also an ever-changing specials board, occasional summer barbecues and an annual beer festival.

Open all wk 12-3 6-11 (Sun 11-10.30) **Bar Meals** L served all wk 12-2.30 D served Mon-Sat 6.30-9.30 **Restaurant** L served all wk 12-2.30 D served Mon-Sat 6.30-9.30 ⊕ FREE HOUSE ◀ St Austell Tribute, Sharp's Doom Bar, Butcombe ♂ Westons Stowford Press. ▼ **Facilities** Children welcome Children's menu Children's portions Garden Beer festival Parking ▄▄ (notice required)

Saxon Arms

DT2 9WG ☎ 01305 260020
e-mail: rodsaxonlamont1@yahoo.co.uk
dir: *3m NW of Dorchester on A37. Pub between church & village hall*

Popular with villagers as much as visiting fishermen, cycling clubs and ramblers, this handsome, thatched flint-stone free house is ideally situated for riverside walks. Flagstone floors, a wood-burning stove and solid oak beams create a comfortable setting for a traditional English inn that offers a friendly welcome, a range of well-kept real ales and simple, carefully cooked food. Menu choices include Blue Vinney and real ale chutney baguettes; ham, egg and chips; Dorset sausage and mash; and chicken curry. Booking for meals may be required.

Open all wk 11-3 5.30-late (Sat-Sun 11am-late) **Bar Meals** L served Mon-Sat 11-2.15, Sun 12-9 D served Mon-Sat 6-9.15, Sun 12-9 Av main course £9.95 **Restaurant** L served Mon-Sat 11-2.15, Sun 12-9 D served Mon-Sat 6-9.15, Sun 12-9 ⊕ FREE HOUSE ◀ Fuller's London Pride, Palmers Best Bitter, Greene King Abbot Ale & Ruddles, Otter, Ringwood, Timothy Taylor, Butcombe, Guest ales ♂ Westons Stowford Press, Guest ciders. ▼ 15 **Facilities** ❤ Children welcome Children's menu Children's portions Garden Parking Wi-fi ▄▄ (notice required)

PICK OF THE PUBS

The Kings Arms ★★★★★INN

SHERBORNE　　　Map 4 ST61

North Rd, Charlton Horethorne DT9 4NL
☎ **01963 220281**
e-mail: admin@thekingsarms.co.uk
web: www.thekingsarms.co.uk
dir: *On A3145, N of Sherborne. Pub in village centre*

Behind its imposing façade, this elegant Edwardian building has been transformed by owners Tony and Sarah Lethbridge into a chic country pub and modern restaurant with boutique-style accommodation. The bar, where soft furnishings and pretty fabrics complement natural slate and oak flooring, is a coffee, lunch, afternoon tea and dinner rendezvous for the citizens of Sherborne and Wincanton. They, and many others, come too for the West Country real ales, including Kings Arms Tipple, and for Lawrence's cider from nearby Corton Denham. A wide walkway leads past a theatre-style kitchen and display of local artwork to the Georgian-mirrored dining room, from where doors lead to an extensive dining terrace overlooking a croquet lawn and the countryside. Fresh meats, fish, vegetables, cheeses and breads are provided by local suppliers, although the classically trained chefs make almost everything else, including pasta and ice cream. The cooking style is both traditional and modern British, with additional influences from around the world, thus the day's lunch menu might lead to something light like a ham and cheese toastie, or a Josper-oven cooked chicken fillet burger with tomato chutney and hand-cut chips. Main courses, either at lunch or in the evening, might include confit duck leg with fondant potato, baby spinach, chantenay carrots and quince; salmon fishcakes with creamy leeks and hand-cut chips; and butternut squash and feta risotto with a side salad. There's a dessert for everyone, from pannetone bread-and-butter pudding with fudge ice cream, to citrus posset with a stem ginger thin. Overnight guests have a choice of individually designed and furnished bedrooms – classic in style in the original building, contemporary in the new – but with a marble bathroom in both cases. Booking for meals may be required.

Open all day all wk **Bar Meals** L served all wk 12-2.30 D served Mon-Thu 7-9.30, Fri-Sat 7-10, Sun 7-9 **Restaurant** L served all wk 12-2.30 D served Mon-Thu 7-9.30, Fri-Sat 7-10, Sun 7-9 ⊕ FREE HOUSE ◀ Kings Arms Tipple, Sharp's Doom Bar, Butcombe ♂ Lawrence's. ♟ 13 **Facilities** Children welcome Children's menu Children's portions ❤ Garden Parking Wi-fi 🚌 (notice required) **Rooms** 10

STUDLAND Map 5 SZ08

The Bankes Arms Hotel

Watery Ln BH19 3AU ☎ **01929 450225**
dir: B3369 from Poole, across on Sandbanks chain ferry, or A35 from Poole, A351 then B3351

Standing above the wide sweep of Studland Bay, this part 15th-century creeper-clad inn was once a smugglers' dive. Nowadays the pub hosts an annual four-day festival in mid-August, featuring live music and some 200 beers and ciders that include award-winning ales from its own Isle of Purbeck brewery. Fresh fish and seafood salads are a speciality, but slow-braised lamb shank with rosemary mash; chilli con carne; and a daily curry are other examples from the menu.

Open all day all wk 11-11 (Sun 11-10.30) Closed: 25 Dec **Bar Meals** L served all wk 12-3 (summer & BH 12-9) D served all wk 6-9 (summer & BH 12-9) ⊕ FREE HOUSE ◀ Isle of Purbeck Fossil Fuel, Studland Bay Wrecked, Solar Power, Thermal Cheer, Harry's Harvest Ö Westons Old Rosie, Thatchers Cheddar Valley, Broadoak. **Facilities** Children welcome Children's menu Garden Beer festival ▄▄▄

SYDLING ST NICHOLAS Map 4 SY69

The Greyhound Inn ★★★★ INN ◉

PICK OF THE PUBS

See Pick of the Pubs on opposite page

TARRANT MONKTON Map 4 ST90

The Langton Arms ★★★★ INN

PICK OF THE PUBS

DT11 8RX ☎ **01258 830225**
e-mail: info@thelangtonarms.co.uk
dir: A31 from Ringwood, or A357 from Shaftesbury, or A35 from Bournemouth

This pretty 17th-century thatched inn sits close to the village church, surrounded by countryside immortalised in Thomas Hardy's novels. The award-winning pub has two bars, the Farmers and the Carpenters, both relaxing places for drinking from an ever-changing supply of outstanding real ales. The carte menu and traditional pub dishes are served in the bars, as well as in the Stables restaurant and conservatory. Expect choice West Country traditional fare made from local produce and vegetables grown in the vegetable patch: Langton Arms Dorset game pie; ballotine of Dorset chicken; and pan-seared Tarrant Valley venison liver; followed by chocolate cake, vanilla crème brûlée or a selection of local cheeses. There's also a choice of light bites and sharing platters, and a children's menu. All the comfortable and well-equipped bedrooms are on the ground floor, situated around an attractive courtyard.

Open all day all wk **Bar Meals** L served Mon-Fri 12-2.30, Sat-Sun all day D served Mon-Thu 6-9.30, Fri 6-10, Sat-Sun all day Av main course £12.50 **Restaurant** L served Mon-Fri 12-2.30, Sat-Sun all day D served

Mon-Thu 6-9.30, Fri 6-10, Sat-Sun all day Av 3 course à la carte fr £27 ⊕ FREE HOUSE ◀ Local guest ales. **Facilities** Children welcome Children's menu Children's portions Play area Family room Garden Parking Wi-fi ▄▄▄ **Rooms** 6

TRENT Map 4 ST51

Rose & Crown Trent

PICK OF THE PUBS

DT9 4SL ☎ **01935 850776**
e-mail: dine@roseandcrowntrent.co.uk
dir: Just off A30 between Sherborne & Yeovil

This ivy-clad, thatched inn in a conservation village dates from the 14th century, when workers erecting the spire of the church lived here. Today's structure owes more to its days as a farmhouse in the 18th century, but a few centuries aren't important when you can still enjoy the beams, flagstone floors and legend of Buff Biggins, an infamous former landlord. The lounge has a large, log-surrounded open fire and comfortable leather sofa; the main bar looks out over the fields, and from the restaurant you can survey the valley. Alternatively, the weather might be good enough to make the garden your destination. Quality local produce lies behind essentially traditional British food such as game casserole and colcannon mash; local trout on tomato, mussel, clam and brown shrimp fondue; and minted pea risotto with charred vegetables. Wadworth keeps the bar supplied with 6X and their other best-sellers. Booking for meals may be required.

Open 12-3 6-11 (Sat-Sun 12-11) Closed: Mon **Bar Meals** L served Tue-Sun 12-3 D served Tue-Sat 6-9 Av main course £10.95 **Restaurant** L served Tue-Sun 12-3 D served Tue-Sat 6-9 Fixed menu price fr £9.95 ⊕ WADWORTH ◀ 6X, Henry's Original IPA, Horizon & Bishop's Tipple, Guest ale Ö Westons Stowford Press, Thatchers Gold. ♥ 8 **Facilities** ❅ Children welcome Children's portions Family room Garden Parking ▄▄▄ (notice required)

WEST BEXINGTON Map 4 SY58

The Manor Hotel

DT2 9DF ☎ **01308 897660**
e-mail: relax@manorhoteldorset.com
dir: On B3157, 5m E of Bridport

Overlooking the Jurassic Coast's most famous feature, Chesil Beach, parts of this 16th-century manor house are thought to date from the 11th century. It offers an inviting mix of flagstones, Jacobean oak panelling, roaring fires and a cosy cellar bar serving Otter ales and locally sourced dishes.

Open all day all wk 11.30-10.30 Closed: 1st 2wks Jan **Bar Meals** L served all wk 12-2 D served Mon-Sat 6.30-9, Sun 6-8 ⊕ FREE HOUSE ◀ Otter Ale, Bitter. **Facilities** ❅ Children welcome Children's menu Garden Parking Wi-fi ▄▄▄ (notice required)

WEST LULWORTH Map 4 SY88

The Castle Inn

Main Rd BH20 5RN ☎ **01929 400311**
e-mail: office@lulworthinn.com
dir: Follow village signs from A352 (Dorchester to Wareham road). Inn on right on B3070 through West Lulworth. Car park opposite

In the heart of the Purbecks near Lulworth Cove, this award-winning 16th-century pub offers 13 real ciders, six regularly changing real ales and 15 single malt whiskies (complete with a booklet of tasting notes). The dog-friendly Castle is a traditional thatched inn with a wide-ranging menu of home-made dishes and daily specials. A selection includes chicken Stroganoff, chilli pasta bake, tuna steak, Dorset sausages and Mexican chip butty. Outside, you'll find large landscaped gardens packed with plants, and in summer there's a giant outdoor chess set. The pub holds a beer festival every year.

Open all wk 12-2.30 7-11 Closed: 25 Dec **Bar Meals** L served all wk 12-2 D served all wk 7-10 Av main course £9.90 ⊕ FREE HOUSE ◀ Sharp's, Isle of Purbeck, Dorset Piddle, Palmers, Plain, Flack Manor Ö Westons Old Rosie, 1st Quality & Country Perry, Hecks Kingston Black & Blakeney Red. ♥ 8 **Facilities** ❅ Children welcome Children's menu Children's portions Garden Beer festival Parking Wi-fi

Lulworth Cove Inn

Main Rd BH20 5RQ ☎ **01929 400333**
e-mail: lulworthcoveinn@hall-woodhouse.co.uk
dir: From A352 (Dorchester to Wareham road) follow Lulworth Cove signs. Inn at end of B3070, opposite car park

Lulworth Cove's famous horseshoe bay is just steps away from the front door of this inn, which changed hands in 2011. It was once a distribution point for the royal mail arriving by stage coach, plus many smugglers stories can be heard. Ramblers can sate their appetites from the extensive menu, which features light bites, filled baguettes and jacket potatoes, as well as main course dishes like glazed chicken supreme; chilli roast salmon; Moroccan vegetables with couscous; and pork and apple sausages.

Open all day all wk **Bar Meals** L served all wk 12-9 D served all wk 12-9 **Restaurant** L served all wk 12-9 D served all wk 12-9 ⊕ HALL & WOODHOUSE ◀ Badger Ö Westons Stowford Press. ♥ 10 **Facilities** ❅ Children welcome Children's menu Children's portions Garden Wi-fi ▄▄▄

Save on hotels. Book at **theAA.com/hotel**

DORSET 195 ENGLAND

PICK OF THE PUBS

The Greyhound Inn ★★★★INN ◉

SYDLING ST NICHOLAS   Map 4 SY69

DT2 9PD ☎ **01300 341303**
e-mail: info@dorsetgreyhound.co.uk
web: www.dorsetgreyhound.co.uk
dir: *From A37 (Yeovil to Dorchester road) exit at staggered x-rds signed Sydling St Nicholas & Cerne Abbas*

Tucked away among pastel-hued flint and stone houses in a valley formed by Sydling Water, this 17th-century pub is deep in Hardy Country. Hardy knew the village well, and it inspired him to write his short story, *The Grave at the Handcross*. Furthermore, the wedding scene in John Schlesinger's 1967 film *Far from the Madding Crowd* was shot at the parish church. Relax in the open-plan bar with a pint of Butcombe from across the border in Somerset, or a guest ale, usually something different every two weeks, unless the locals petition for its retention. The draught cider is Cornish Orchards, Peroni the draught lager, while wine-list staples include Chilean Merlot, French Pinot Noir, Chablis, Sancerre and, when available, some interesting bottles from Washington state, USA. There are four areas to eat in: the bar, with its open fire; the conservatory with oak, fruitwood and scrubbed wood tables and a deep chesterfield; the restaurant, with a glass-covered well from which coachmen used to pull up buckets of water for the horses during stagecoach stops; and finally, the suntrap front terrace. The food is fresh and menus

change every day. Fish, the pub's strength, is ordered the night before from the quaysides in Weymouth and Bridport, and there's usually venison, wild boar and other game in season. As one of The Greyhound's partners is a vegetarian, the veggie alternatives are more imaginative than in some places. Other dishes include open fish pie with sorrel mash and parmesan gratin; Ashdale rib-eye steak with field mushroom, watercress salad, hand-cut chips and béarnaise sauce; and slow-roasted pork belly with smoked ham hock rissole, parsnip purée and spiced apple sauce. What comes across strongly here is customer care. It should be a given, but not everywhere gets it as right as The Greyhound. Accommodation is available. Booking for meals may be required.

Open 11-3 6-11 Closed: Sun eve **Bar Meals** L served Mon-Sat 12-2, Sun 12-2.30 D served Mon-Sat 6-9 **Restaurant** L served Mon-Sat 12-2, Sun 12-2.30 D served Mon-Sat 6-9 ⊞ FREE HOUSE ◀ St Austell Tinners Ale, Butcombe, Guest ales ♂ Cornish Orchards. ♀ 12 **Facilities** Children welcome Children's menu Children's portions Play area ❀ Garden Parking Wi-fi **Rooms** 6

WEST STOUR — Map 4 ST72

The Ship Inn

SP8 5RP ☎ **01747 838640**
e-mail: mail@shipinn-dorset.com
dir: *On A30, 4m W of Shaftesbury (4m from Henstridge)*

Walkers can explore the footpaths, which pass through the picturesque Dorset countryside surrounding this coaching inn built in 1750. The main bar has a traditional flagstone floor, low ceiling and log fire, while the lounge bar has stripped oak floorboards and chunky farmhouse furniture. Both offer a selection of beers and ciders, with weekly-changing guest ales. Menus include daily-changing specials such as oven-roasted salmon supreme with a cream of spinach and leek sauce. Home-made desserts may include dark chocolate and brandy torte. Outside, a suntrap patio and large child-friendly garden host a festival every June or July showcasing up to 20 real ales and ciders. Booking for meals may be required.

Open all wk 12-3 6-11.30 **Bar Meals** L served all wk 12-2.30 D served all wk 6-9 Av main course £10.95 **Restaurant** L served all wk 12-2.30 D served all wk 6-9 Fixed menu price fr £10 Av 3 course à la carte fr £21.95 ⊕ FREE HOUSE ◀ Palmers IPA, Sharp's Doom Bar, Ringwood Fortyniner ♻ Thatchers Cheddar Valley & Heritage Westons Stowford Press. ♇ 9 **Facilities** ♣ Children welcome Children's menu Children's portions Garden Beer festival Parking Wi-fi

WEYMOUTH — Map 4 SY67

The Old Ship Inn

7 The Ridgeway DT3 5QQ ☎ **01305 812522**
e-mail: info@theoldshipupwey.co.uk
dir: *3m from Weymouth town centre, at bottom of The Ridgeway*

Thomas Hardy refers to this 400-year-old pub, now in new hands, in two of his novels. Copper pans, old clocks and a beamed open fire create a true period atmosphere, while the garden looks across Weymouth. A good selection of real ales includes Jurassic, Otter and Ringwood, with Addlestones cloudy cider as an alternative. A frequently changing menu of good home-cooked pub food offers trio of pork and leek sausages with bubble-and-squeak mash; twice-cooked blade of beef with horseradish mash; and cask ale-battered fish with hand-cut chips.

Open all wk **Bar Meals** L served Mon-Sat 12-2.30, Sun 12-6 D served Mon-Sat 6-9 Av main course £8.95 **Restaurant** Fixed menu price fr £8.55 Av 3 course à la carte fr £20 ⊕ PUNCH TAVERNS ◀ Sharp's Doom Bar, Ringwood Best Bitter, Dorset Jurassic, Otter, Guest ales ♻ Addlestones. **Facilities** ♣ Children welcome Children's menu Children's portions Garden Parking Wi-fi ▦

WIMBORNE ST GILES — Map 5 SU01

The Bull Inn

Coach Rd BH21 5NF ☎ **01725 517300**
e-mail: bullwsg@btconnect.com
dir: *From Salisbury take A354 towards Blandford Forum. Left onto B3081. Follow signs to Wimborne St Giles*

Situated in the heart of the Shaftesbury Estate on the edge of Cranborne Chase, there are three shoots within a five-minute drive of this award-winning pub, plus chalkwater stream fishing in the village. Much of the local produce ends up on the acclaimed menu – pigeon breast with smoked black pudding and apple salad might be followed by pork belly with bubble-and-squeak and rocket – all washed down with local Badger ales. Booking for meals may be required.

Open all wk 12-3 6-11 ⊕ HALL & WOODHOUSE ◀ Badger Tanglefoot, K&B Sussex, Hopping Hare ♻ The Orchard Pig. **Facilities** Children welcome Children's portions Garden Parking Wi-fi

WINTERBORNE ZELSTON — Map 4 SY89

Botany Bay Inne

DT11 9ET ☎ **01929 459227**
dir: *A31 between Bere Regis & Wimborne Minster*

The pub was built by the Hall & Woodhouse brewery (they're still the owners) in the 1920s to replace one in the village the local squire found offensive. Initially called the General Allenby, its name was changed in the 1980s in belated recognition of prisoners from Dorchester jail awaiting transportation to Australia. No such threat hangs over today's visitors here for locally sourced pub snacks and main dishes such as breaded wholetail scampi; steak and stilton pie; slow-roasted lamb shank; butterflied chicken breast; and sweet potato and red pepper cannelloni. Booking for meals may be required.

Open all wk 10-3 6-11.30 **Bar Meals** L served all wk (bkfst) 10-12, (lunch) 12-2.15 D served all wk 6.30-9.30 **Restaurant** L served all wk (bkst) 10-12, (lunch) 12-2.15 D served all wk 6.30-9.30 ⊕ HALL & WOODHOUSE ◀ Badger First Gold & Tanglefoot, Guest ales. ♇ 10 **Facilities** ♣ Children welcome Children's menu Children's portions Garden Parking ▦ (notice required)

WORTH MATRAVERS — Map 4 SY97

The Square and Compass

BH19 3LF ☎ **01929 439229**
dir: *Between Corfe Castle & Swanage. From B3069 follow signs for Worth Matravers*

Little has changed at this stone-built pub for the past century, during which time it has been run by the same family. This tucked-away inn boasts a simple interior with no bar, just a serving hatch and an abundance of flagstone floors, oak panels and a museum of local artefacts and fossils from the nearby Jurassic Coast. Award-winning West Country beers and ciders come straight from the barrel and food is limited to just pasties and pies. On the first Saturday in October there's a beer and pumpkin festival.

Open all wk 12-3 6-11 (12-11 in summer) ⊕ FREE HOUSE ◀ Palmers Copper Ale & Dorset Gold, RCH Pitchfork, Hop Back Summer Lightning ♻ Hecks Farmhouse, Seasonal home-produced. **Facilities** ♣ Children welcome Garden Beer festival ▦ **Notes** ⊛

DURHAM, CO

AYCLIFFE — Map 19 NZ22

The County ★★★★ RR

13 The Green, Aycliffe Village DL5 6LX ☎ **01325 312273**
e-mail: info@thecountyaycliffevillage.com
web: www.thecountyaycliffevillage.com
dir: *A1 (M) junct 59, off A167 into Aycliffe Village*

Back in 2000, this is where Tony Blair chose to bring the then French President, Jacques Chirac. It's an award-winning restaurant with a terrace overlooking the pretty village green, serving a good range of real ales backed by Green Goblin cider. On the doorstep are top-quality suppliers of fish, meat, game and other ingredients that go into the pub's seasonal menus and daily specials. History does not record M Chirac's choices, but today you can start with breaded Yellison Dairy goat's cheese salad; continue with Hartlepool naturally smoked haddock on grain mustard mash; and finish with baked ginger parkin with spiced treacle.

Open all wk 12-3 6-11 (Sun all day) Closed: 25 Dec, 1 Jan **Bar Meals** L served Mon-Sat 12-2, Sun 12-9 D served all wk 6-9 Av main course £13 **Restaurant** L served Mon-Sat 12-2, Sun 12-9 D served all wk 6-9 Av 3 course à la carte fr £28 ⊕ FREE HOUSE ◀ Jennings Bitter & Cocker Hoop, Black Sheep, Yorkshire Dales, Hawkshead ♻ Thatchers Green Goblin. ♇ 10 **Facilities** Children welcome Children's portions Parking **Rooms** 7

Save on hotels. Book at theAA.com/hotel

DURHAM, CO 197 ENGLAND

BARNARD CASTLE   Map 19 NZ01

The Morritt Arms Hotel ★★★★ HL ⊚

PICK OF THE PUBS

Greta Bridge DL12 9SE ☎ 01833 627232
e-mail: relax@themorritt.co.uk
dir: *At Scotch Corner take A66 towards Penrith, after 9m turn at Greta Bridge. Hotel over bridge on left*

This fine building dates from the late 17th century, when it served Carlisle- and London-bound coach travellers. Traditionally a fine-dining venue, the restaurant has been brought bang up to date with vibrant colours, a touch of black leather, comfortable armchairs, silk blinds over window seats and works by local artists. This association with art began in 1946, when local portraitist Jack Gilroy painted the mural of Dickensian characters you'll find in the bar. Here, the one AA-Rosette menu opens with a seafood platter, before featuring Mediterranean vegetable risotto; Neasham pork and leek sausages; and beer-battered cod. In the restaurant, venison loin with beetroot risotto; butter-fried plaice fillets; and wild mushroom and vegetable Wellington may well appear. Major Morritt beer, named after the hotel's former owner and namesake, was introduced at the pub's first cask ale festival in 2010. En suite bedrooms help to make this a popular function and wedding choice.

Open all day all wk 7am-11pm (Sun 7-10.30) ⊕ FREE HOUSE ◀ Morritt Arms Major Morritt, Timothy Taylor Landlord, Thwaites. **Facilities** Children welcome Children's menu Children's portions Play area Family room Garden Beer festival Parking Wi-fi **Rooms** 27

BOLDRON   Map 19 NZ01

The George & Dragon Inn NEW

DL12 9RF ☎ 01833 638215 & 07738 290298
e-mail: georgeanddragon_boldron@yahoo.com
dir: *Boldron signed from A66*

Famished A66 travellers should take note of this free house in sleepy Boldron, a picture-book village located just a mile from historic Barnard Castle and the main road. Ales from local micro-breweries and daily-changing menus await, the latter featuring an award-winning cheeseboard and salmon smoked on the premises. Start with a warming mug of soup with rustic oatcakes, follow with lamb's liver with bubble-and-squeak and thyme and mustard jus, or twice-baked local cheese soufflé, leaving room for a home-made pudding. The early May beer festival champions local brews and fine cheeses. Wonderful surrounding walks.

Open 11-2.30 5-11 Closed: Tue **Bar Meals** L served Mon & Wed-Sun 11-2.30 D served Mon & Wed-Sun 5-9 Av main course £12 **Restaurant** L served Mon & Wed-Sun 11-2.30 D served Mon & Wed-Sun 5-9 Av 3 course à la carte fr £22 ⊕ FREE HOUSE ◀ The Consett Ale Works Steel Town, Allendale Golden Plover & Wagtail. **Facilities** ✿ Children welcome Children's portions Garden Beer festival Parking Wi-fi 🚌

CHESTER-LE-STREET   Map 19 NZ25

The Moorings Hotel

Hett Hill DH2 3JU ☎ 0191 370 1597
e-mail: info@themooringsdurham.co.uk
dir: *A1(M) junct 63 to Chester-le-Street. Take B6313. Hotel on left*

Retaining a local feel and offering a cracking range of local beers (Rudgate, Consett and The Stables Beamish brews), the pub is part of an exclusive hotel complex and is popular with visitors to the famous Beamish Museum, and local ramblers and horse-riders. Signature dishes feature local steaks and North-East whitefish and shellfish, alongside the likes of Malayan chicken curry, Northumbrian ale pudding and home-made lasagne. Children are well catered for with a good choice of junior dishes. With a large patio and three acres of land, it's a peaceful spot to take time out at. Booking for meals may be required.

Open all day all wk **Bar Meals** L served all wk 11.30-9.30 D served all wk 11.30-9.30 Av main course £11 food served all day **Restaurant** L served Sun 11.30-4 D served Thu-Sat 6.30-9.30 Av 3 course à la carte fr £22 ⊕ FREE HOUSE ◀ Rudgate Battle Axe, Mordue Workie Ticket, The Stables Beamish Burn Brown Ale, The Consett Ale Works White Hot, Timothy Taylor Landlord. ♟ 10 **Facilities** Children welcome Children's menu Children's portions Garden Parking Wi-fi

COTHERSTONE   Map 19 NZ01

The Fox and Hounds

DL12 9PF ☎ 01833 650241
e-mail: ianswinburn999@btinternet.com
dir: *4m W of Barnard Castle. From A66 onto B6277, signed*

At the heart of beautiful Teesdale and just a stone's throw from the river's wooded gorge, The Fox and Hounds is huddled above one of the village greens in pretty Cotherstone. Beams, open fires and thickly cushioned wall seats tempt you to linger at this 360-year-old coaching inn, admiring the local photographs and country pictures while you sip a pint of Black Sheep. From the menu, tuck in to dishes made from the best of fresh, local ingredients: creamy garlic mushrooms; grilled Barnsley lamb chop marinated in mint and garlic; and vegetable stew with Cotherstone cheese gratin crust.

Open all wk 12-2.30 6.30-11 (Sun 12-2.30 6.30-10.30) Closed: 25-26 Dec **Bar Meals** L served all wk 12-2 D served all wk 6.30-9 **Restaurant** L served all wk 12-2 D served all wk 6.30-9 ⊕ FREE HOUSE ◀ Black Sheep Best Bitter & Ale, The Village Brewer Bull Premium Bitter, York Yorkshire Terrier, Daleside Ŏ Aspall. **Facilities** Children welcome Children's menu Children's portions Garden Parking Wi-fi

DURHAM   Map 19 NZ24

Victoria Inn

86 Hallgarth St DH1 3AS ☎ 0191 386 5269
dir: *In city centre*

This unique listed inn has scarcely changed since it was built in 1899 – not a jukebox, pool table or television to be found. Just five minutes' walk from the cathedral, it has been carefully nurtured by the Webster family for over three decades. Small rooms warmed by coal fires and a congenial atmosphere include the tiny snug, where a portrait of Queen Victoria still hangs above the upright piano. You'll find a few simple snacks to tickle the taste buds, but it's the cracking well-kept local ales, single malts, and over 40 Irish whiskies that are the main attraction.

Open all wk 11.45-3 6-11 ⊕ FREE HOUSE ◀ Wylam Gold Tankard, Durham Magus, Big Lamp Bitter, Hill Island. **Facilities** ✿ Children welcome Family room Parking Wi-fi 🚌

FIR TREE   Map 19 NZ13

Duke of York Inn

DL15 8DG ☎ 01388 767429
e-mail: gavinbowater@yahoo.com
dir: *On A68, 12m W of Durham. From Durham take A690 W. Left onto A68 to Fir Tree*

On the tourist route (A68) to Scotland, the Duke of York is a former drovers' and coaching inn dating from 1749, and was taken over by new landlord Gavin Bowater at the end of 2011. It has been refurbished inside and out to a high standard, keeping the traditional country feel with contemporary touches. Beers include Black Sheep Best Bitter and Camerons Smooth. Look out for the beer festival – call the pubs for the dates. Booking for meals may be required.

Open all day all wk **Bar Meals** L served all wk 12-9 D served all wk 12-9 Av main course £7-£17 food served all day **Restaurant** L served all wk 12-9 D served all wk 12-9 Fixed menu price fr £10 Av 3 course à la carte fr £20 food served all day ⊕ CAMERONS BREWERY ◀ Smooth, Black Sheep Best Bitter, John Smith's, Guinness. **Facilities** ✿ Children welcome Children's menu Children's portions Garden Beer festival Parking Wi-fi 🚌

FROSTERLEY
Map 19 NZ03

The Black Bull Inn NEW

DL13 2SL ☎ 01388 527784
dir: *From A68 onto A689 towards Stanhope. Left into Frosterley. Inn adjacent to railway station*

Next to Weardale steam railway station, this family-run, independent country pub has cosy, music-free rooms, a stone-flagged bar and open fires in Victorian ranges. Campanologists come here because, unique among pubs, it has its own peal of church bells. The bar and ad hoc beer festivals demonstrate unwavering backing for local micro-breweries, while the kitchen is equally supportive of the regional suppliers behind the food. Lunch might be toad-in-the-hole with black pudding mash, while dinner could feature potted North Shields crab; Morley Farm 28-day aged rib-eye steak; or pan-fried crispy salmon. Booking for meals may be required.

Open all day Closed: 1 Jan for 5wks, Sun eve, Mon, Tue **Bar Meals** L served Wed-Sun 12.30-2.30 D served Wed-Sat 7-9 Av main course £9.95-£18.95 **Restaurant** L served Wed-Sun 12.30-2.30 D served Wed-Sat 7-9 ⊕ FREE HOUSE ◀ Durham, Allendale, Wylam, Consett, York, Jarrow Ŏ Wilkins Farmhouse, Westons. **Facilities** Children welcome Children's portions Garden Beer festival Parking Wi-fi ▄ (notice required)

HURWORTH-ON-TEES
Map 19 NZ30

The Bay Horse NEW

45 The Green DL2 2AA ☎ 01325 720663
e-mail: mail@thebayhorsehurworth.com
dir: *From A66 at Darlington Football Club rdbt follow Hurworth sign*

Marcus Bennett and Jonathan Hall's dining pub is old, very old. Dating from the 1400s, extensive refurbishment in 2008 brought out its real character, enhanced by furnishings carefully sourced from antique fairs. With such highly regarded chefs as Messrs Bennett and Hall in charge of the tasting ladles, expect outstanding classic English dishes such as roasted partridge; loin of venison; pan-fried stone bass; and slow-cooked corn-fed chicken. Full descriptions of dishes are impossible here, but be assured that they make for a truly mouth-watering read. In the bar, Harviestoun and Jennings.

Open all day all wk Closed: 25-26 Dec **Bar Meals** L served Mon-Sat 12-2.30, Sun 12-4 D served all wk 6-close Av main course £16 **Restaurant** L served Mon-Sat 12-2.30, Sun 12-4 D served all wk 6-close Fixed menu price fr £12 Av 3 course à la carte fr £28 ⊕ FREE HOUSE ◀ Harviestoun Bitter & Twisted, Jennings Cumberland Ale. ▾ 12 **Facilities** Children welcome Children's menu Garden Parking Wi-fi

HUTTON MAGNA
Map 19 NZ11

The Oak Tree Inn ◉◉

PICK OF THE PUBS

DL11 7HH ☎ 01833 627371
dir: *From A1 at Scotch Corner take A66 W. 6.5m, right for Hutton Magna*

At this whitewashed, part 18th-century free house run by Alastair and Claire Ross, expect great food, a superb selection of drinks and a warm welcome. Alastair previously spent 14 years in London working at The Savoy, Leith's and, more recently, a private members' club on The Strand. The AA two-Rosette cuisine in the simply furnished dining room is based around the finest local ingredients, and dishes change daily depending on produce available. The refined cooking style combines classic techniques and occasional modern flavours: you could start with salt cod and saffron risotto with sweet peppers, or warm salad of confit pheasant and partridge with chorizo. After that, maybe seared duck breast with cabbage, bacon, parsnip purée and apple, or fillet of sea bass with garlic and parsley potato, purple broccoli and brown shrimps. As well as fine real ales, there's a menu of bottled beers from around the globe, and a list of over 20 malt whiskies. Booking for meals may be required.

Open 6-11 (Sun 5.30-10.30) Closed: Xmas & New Year, Mon **Bar Meals** Av main course £20 **Restaurant** D served Tue-Sun 6-9 Av 3 course à la carte fr £30 ⊕ FREE HOUSE ◀ Wells Bombardier, Timothy Taylor Landlord, Black Sheep Best Bitter. ▾ 10 **Facilities** Parking

LONGNEWTON
Map 19 NZ31

Vane Arms NEW

Darlington Rd TS21 1DB ☎ 01642 580401
e-mail: thevanearms@hotmail.com
dir: *W end of village, just off A66 midway between Stockton-on-Tees & Darlington*

Proving what the right approach can do, this 18th-century pub had been abandoned until villagers Jill and Paul Jackson bought it; now, it's loved again. No jukebox, pool or gaming machine, the TV is on only for special events, and background music plays quietly in the lounge. Sensibly priced pub grub includes home-made shortcrust steak and Black Sheep ale pie; pan-fried fish medley; and oven-roasted stuffed pepper. French cuisine night is Wednesday, while four real ales change frequently and there are beer festivals in July and October. A large garden looks towards the Cleveland Hills and the North Yorkshire Moors. Booking for meals may be required.

Open all wk Tue-Thu 12-2 5-11 (Mon 5-11 Fri-Sat 12-2 5-12 Sun 12-11) **Restaurant** L served Tue-Sat 12-2, Sun 12-4 D served Tue-Sat 5-8.30 Av 3 course à la carte fr £12.95 ⊕ FREE HOUSE ◀ Black Sheep Best Bitter, Guest ales Ŏ Hereford Dry. **Facilities** Children welcome Children's portions Garden Beer festival Parking Wi-fi ▄ (notice required)

MIDDLESTONE
Map 19 NZ23

Ship Inn

Low Rd DL14 8AB ☎ 01388 810904
e-mail: tony.theshipinn@googlemail.com
dir: *On B6287 (Kirk Merrington to Coundon road)*

A bustling local that knows how to generate community loyalty, not least through an ever-changing real ale portfolio and its May and November beer festivals. The lounge is all nautical memorabilia and walls festooned with old beer pump clips. At 550 feet above sea level the rooftop patio offers excellent views over the Tees Valley and Cleveland Hills. Home-cooked food is served in the bar, using locally reared beef, pork and lamb, with dishes such as corned beef pie and award-winning pork and leek sausages. Look out for regular themed evenings.

Open all wk 4-11 (Fri-Sun 12-11) **Bar Meals** L served Fri-Sun 12-2 D served Mon-Sat 6-9 Av main course £5.50 ⊕ FREE HOUSE ◀ 6 Guest ales Ŏ Westons. ▾ 9 **Facilities** ✿ Children welcome Children's menu Children's portions Play area Family room Beer festival Parking Wi-fi ▄

MIDDLETON-IN-TEESDALE
Map 18 NY92

The Teesdale Hotel ★★ HL

Market Place DL12 0QG ☎ 01833 640264
e-mail: enquiries@teesdalehotel.com
dir: *A1 to Scotch Corner, A66 to Barnard Castle, follow signs for Middleton-in-Teesdale*

This tastefully modernised, family-run former coaching inn sits in the quaint stone-built village of Middleton, amidst some of Britain's loveliest scenery. It has a striking 18th-century stone exterior and archway, and the interior is warm and friendly, with an open fire in the bar and well-kept real ales hand-pumped from the ancient cellar. Home-made food sourced from local produce results in hearty dishes such as partridge breast with black pudding followed by venison sausage with pickled cabbage and mustard mash.

Open all day all wk **Bar Meals** L served all wk 12.30-2.30 D served all wk 7-9 Av main course £10 **Restaurant** D served all wk 7-9 Av 3 course à la carte fr £17.30 ⊕ FREE HOUSE ◀ Jennings Smooth Bitter, Black Sheep Best Bitter, Bitburger, Guinness Ŏ Aspall. **Facilities** ✿ Children welcome Children's menu Children's portions Parking Wi-fi ▄ Rooms 14

Save on hotels. Book at **theAA.com/hotel**

DURHAM, CO 199 ENGLAND

PICK OF THE PUBS

Rose & Crown ★★HL ◉◉

ROMALDKIRK Map 19 NY92

DL12 9EB ☎ **01833 650213**
e-mail: hotel@rose-and-crown.co.uk
web: www.rose-and-crown.co.uk
dir: *6m NW from Barnard Castle on B6277*

In the middle of three village greens, this 18th-century, stone-built coaching inn overlooks the old stocks and water pump, while next door is the Saxon church known as 'The Cathedral of the Dale'. The name of the village is thought to have been derived from the obscure Saxon saint, St Rumwold. Step inside the pub to be greeted by fresh flowers, varnished oak panelling, old beams, and gleaming copper and brass artefacts, then enter the quirky little bar and you'll encounter oak settles, a vast dog grate, old prints, carriage lamps and rural curios; retire to a wing-backed chair in the secluded lounge and be lulled by the ticking of a grandfather clock, with maybe a glass of Allendale, Theakston or Black Sheep. Wines by the glass are listed on blackboards. Another option is a meal in the more formal panelled restaurant lit by candles in waxy old bottles, decorated with illustrations of fat, pompous waiters and holder of two AA Rosettes for over 20 years. Teesdale's farms and sporting estates, and east coast fishing ports produce some excellent food, on which the chefs rely to create the restaurant's daily-changing menu. This could start with rillettes of rabbit, fig and apple chutney; or baked local Cotherstone cheese soufflé with chive cream. Also on the menu might be mains of grilled fillet of brill with lightly spiced tomato, pepper and potato broth; steak, kidney and mushroom shortcrust pie; and wild mushroom and spinach risotto. Bar snacks include scrambled eggs with smoked salmon and crème fraîche; and sautéed lamb's liver with bacon and polenta. Stay in a comfortable bedroom in the inn or a contemporary suite adjoining the courtyard for a wine and food weekend. Booking for meals may be required.

Open all day all wk 11-11 Closed: 23-27 Dec **Bar Meals** L served all wk 12-1.30 D served all wk 6.30-9.30 Av main course £14 **Restaurant** L served Sun 12-1.30 D served all wk 7.30-8.45 Fixed menu price fr £18.95 ⊕ FREE HOUSE ◀ Theakston Best Bitter, Black Sheep Best Bitter, Allendale. ⬥ 14 **Facilities** Children welcome Children's menu Children's portions Parking Wi-fi **Rooms** 12

NEWTON AYCLIFFE — Map 19 NZ22

Blacksmiths Arms

Preston le Skerne, (off Ricknall Lane) DL5 6JH
☎ 01325 314873
dir: *Turn off A167 next to Gretna pub, into Ricknall Ln.
Blacksmiths Arms 0.5m*

Enjoying an excellent reputation locally as a good dining pub, this former smithy dates from the 1700s, and is still relatively isolated in its farmland setting. The menu offers starters of Capetian king prawns, roasted Tewkesbury cheese mushroom, or sautéed black pudding and smoked bacon. Requiring their own page on the menu are fish dishes such as green-lipped mussels, slow-roasted pesto salmon, and grilled swordfish with prawn sauce. There's also a good selection of vegetarian dishes and a gluten-free menu. There is an ever-changing selection of real ales served in the bar.

Open 11.30-2.30 6-11 Closed: 1 Jan, Mon **Bar Meals** L served Tue-Sun 11.30-2 D served Tue-Sun 6-9 Av main course £10 **Restaurant** L served Tue-Sun 11.30-2 D served Tue-Sun 6-9 Av 3 course à la carte fr £19 ⊕ FREE HOUSE ◀ Guest ales. ♟ 10 **Facilities** Children welcome Children's menu Play area Garden Parking 🚐 (notice required)

ROMALDKIRK — Map 19 NY92

Rose & Crown ★★ HL ◉◉

PICK OF THE PUBS

See Pick of the Pubs on page 199

SEAHAM — Map 19 NZ44

The Seaton Lane Inn ★★★★ INN

Seaton Ln SR7 0LP ☎ 0191 581 2036
e-mail: info@seatonlaneinn.com
dir: *S of Sunderland on A19 take B1404 towards
Houghton-le-Spring. In Seaton turn left for pub*

With a traditional bar area as well as a stylish restaurant and lounge, this boutique-type inn offers three real ales to keep the regulars happy, served from the central bar. The menu proffers many pub favourites – hot sandwiches such as the traditional BLT are served with chunky chips; pasta dishes, tortilla wraps and warm salads are all here as well as a good selection of main courses. A sample evening menu features Seaton Lane Inn seafood medley, paupiettes of plaice stuffed with Greenland prawns, fillet steaks, oven-baked best end of lamb, and vegetable curry. Bedrooms are modern, spacious and smartly furnished.

Open all day all wk **Bar Meals** L served all wk 7am-9.30pm D served all wk 7am-9.30pm Av main course £10 food served all day **Restaurant** L served all wk 7am-9.30pm D served all wk 7am-9.30pm Fixed menu price fr £12.95 Av 3 course à la carte fr £20 food served all day ⊕ FREE HOUSE ◀ Timothy Taylor Landlord, Wells Bombardier, Theakston Best Bitter. **Facilities** ✿ Children welcome Children's menu Children's portions Garden Parking Wi-fi 🚐 **Rooms** 18

STANLEY — Map 19 NZ15

The Stables Pub and Restaurant ★★★★ CHH

Beamish Hall Hotel, Beamish DH9 0YB
☎ 01207 288750 & 233733
e-mail: info@beamish-hall.co.uk
dir: *A693 to Stanley. Follow signs for Beamish Hall
Country House Hotel & Beamish Museum. Left at museum
entrance. Hotel on left 0.2m after golf club. Pub within
hotel grounds*

The Stables' stone-floored, beamed bar is the perfect spot to sample the pub's own real ales, brewed on site at their micro-brewery. The beer festival in the third week in September will get you even more closely acquainted. The pub has been creatively moulded from the estate workshops at a stunning country mansion and has excellent accommodation. Regional producers supply the best local ingredients from which are crafted exemplary meals. Snack on smoked ham and curried risotto, or sink into slow-roast belly pork with black pudding, creamed leeks, red wine sauce and English mustard cream.

Open all day all wk Mon-Thu 11-11 (Fri-Sat 11am-mdnt Sun 11-10.30) **Bar Meals** L served Mon-Thu 12-9, Fri-Sat 12-9.30, Sun 12-8 D served Mon-Thu 12-9, Fri-Sat 12-9.30, Sun 12-8 Av main course £8 food served all day **Restaurant** Av 3 course à la carte fr £20 food served all day ⊕ FREE HOUSE ◀ The Stables Beamish Hall Bitter, Beamish Burn Brown Ale, Old Miner Tommy, Silver Buckles ♂ Gwynt y Ddraig Haymaker & Farmhouse Pyder. ♟ **Facilities** Children welcome Children's menu Children's portions Play area Garden Beer festival Parking Wi-fi 🚐 **Rooms** 42

WINSTON — Map 19 NZ11

The Bridgewater Arms NEW

DL2 3RN ☎ 01325 730302
e-mail: paul.p.grundy@btinternet.com
dir: *Exit A67 between Barnard Castle & Darlington, onto
B6274 into Winston*

Between Barnard Castle and Darlington in Teesdale, this pub moved from its former site overlooking the bridge and river into a school house, now Grade II listed, after its closure in 1959. Original photographs of classmates and pantomime casts decorate the walls, and former pupils are among the pub's customers. Seating in the restaurant is augmented by the bar area, where daily-changing lunchtime and early evening specials can include seafood pancake thermidor; game casserole with red cabbage; and lamb tagine with pilau rice. Afterwards, the historic Winston Bridge and beautiful views to the church are a short stroll away.

Open 12-2.30 6-11 Closed: 25-26 Dec, Sun & Mon **Bar Meals** L served Tue-Sat 12-2 D served Tue-Sat 6-9 Av main course £12 **Restaurant** L served Tue-Sat 12-2 D served Tue-Sat 6-9 Av 3 course à la carte fr £27 ⊕ GREENE KING ◀ IPA, Timothy Taylor Landlord ♂ Aspall. ♟ 15 **Facilities** Children welcome Children's portions Garden Parking Wi-fi

ESSEX

ARKESDEN — Map 12 TL43

Axe & Compasses

PICK OF THE PUBS

See Pick of the Pubs on opposite page

AYTHORPE RODING — Map 6 TL51

Axe & Compasses

Dunmow Rd CM6 1PP ☎ 01279 876648
e-mail: axeandcompasses@msn.com
dir: *From A120 take junct for Dunmow*

A weather-boarded, 17th-century pub where the owners like to create a 'nostalgic pub experience'. In the bar, ales from small regional brewers such as Nethergate are backed by Westons ciders. David Hunt, a skilled self-taught chef, uses the best of seasonal produce and loves to offer dishes such as pan-fried pigeon breast, bacon salad and parsnip crisp or Mersea oysters to start; then calves' liver, crispy bacon, sage mash and caper butter; and ginger parkin, toffee sauce and home-made brandy ice cream to finish. Booking for meals may be required.

Open all day all wk 11am-11.30pm (Sun 12-11) ⊕ FREE HOUSE ◀ Brentwood Best, Nethergate Old Growler, Crouch Vale Brewers Gold, Woodforde's Wherry, Saffron ♂ Westons Old Rosie, Herefordshire Country Perry. **Facilities** Children welcome Children's portions Garden Parking Wi-fi

Save on hotels. Book at **theAA.com/hotel**

ESSEX 201 **ENGLAND**

PICK OF THE PUBS

Axe & Compasses

ARKESDEN Map 12 TL43

High St CB11 4EX ☎ 01799 550272
web: www.axeandcompasses.co.uk
dir: *From Buntingford take B1038*
towards Newport, left for Arkesden

The Axe & Compasses is the centrepiece of this sleepy, picture-postcard village, whose narrow main street runs alongside gentle Wicken Water, spanned by a succession of footbridges that give access to white, cream and pink-washed cottages. The thatched central part of the pub dates from 1650; the right-hand extension was added during the early 19th century and is now the public bar. It's run by Themis and Diane Christou from Cyprus, who between them have knocked up a good few awards for the marvellous things they do here. Easy chairs and settees, antique furniture, clocks and horse brasses fill their comfortable lounge and, in winter, there's an open fire. The pumps of Greene King hold sway in the bar, and it's with a pint of Abbot Ale that you can have a sandwich or light meal, such as monkfish served on a roasted red pepper sauce. In the softly lit restaurant area, which seats 50 on various levels, and where agricultural implements adorn the old beams, the slightly Greek-influenced menus offer a good selection of starters, including flat field mushrooms baked with garlic, thyme, lemon juice and olive oil; and

avocado, bacon and blue cheese crostini. There's a good choice of main courses too, examples being moussaka; supreme of chicken Kiev with mushroom duxelles in puff pastry and wholegrain mustard cream; tender rump of lamb with mint and red wine gravy; grilled halibut steak with creamed leeks; and fried spinach and potato cakes with tomato and basil sauce. Rounding off the menu are desserts from the trolley, such as trifle of the day, and summer pudding. The wine list is easy to navigate, with house reds and whites coming in at modest prices. On fine days many drinkers and diners head for the patio. Booking for meals may be required.

Open all wk 12-2.30 6-11 (Sun 12-3 7-10.30) **Bar Meals** L served all wk 12-2 D served all wk 6.45-9.30 **Restaurant** L served all wk 12-2 D served all wk 6.45-9.30 🛢 GREENE KING ◀ IPA & Abbot Ale, Morland Old Speckled Hen. ♟ 14 **Facilities** Children welcome Children's portions Garden Parking 🚌

PICK OF THE PUBS

The Bell Inn

CASTLE HEDINGHAM   Map 13 TL73

Saint James St CO9 3EJ
☎ **01787 460350**
e-mail: hedinghambell@zoho.com
web: www.hedinghambell.co.uk
dir: *On A1124 N of Halstead, right to Castle Hedingham*

Run by the same family since 1967, The Bell is a rambling former coaching inn whose Georgian façade conceals an interior dating back to the 15th century; heavy beams and wattle-and-daub walls hark back to these medieval foundations. There are four separate rooms inside, two with real log fires, connected by a warren of corridors. Victorian Prime Minister Benjamin Disraeli honed his early debating skills in the barrel-ceilinged assembly room on the first floor, and the unspoiled interior makes it easy to imagine this slice of history taking place. These days The Bell remains very much a traditional village pub offering unpretentious locally sourced food and well-kept real ale from Adnams and Mighty Oak. Settle at eye-catching period furniture by log fires or a shady spot on the patio and consider a wide-ranging menu of English favourites; all the meats come from welfare-accredited farms in Essex and Suffolk and go into the selection of pies available here; chicken and bacon or steak and ale, for example. As an extraordinary counterpoint, The Bell's

Turkish chef creates dishes inspired by his home country, including barbecued Mediterranean fish on Monday evenings and Turkish pizzas from the wood-fired oven on Wednesdays. Other choices could include starters of smoked mackerel pâté with granary toast, creamed horseradish and mixed baby leaves, or nachos with melted cheese, jalapeños, chilli salsa and sour cream, followed perhaps by steak-and-ale pie, bangers and mash, or salmon and broccoli fishcakes. Add a decent selection of ciders (including Delvin End and Pheasant Plucker), three annual beer festivals and live music on Fridays and the experience is complete.

Open all wk 11.45-3 6-11 (Fri-Sat 12-12 Sun 12-11) Closed: 25 Dec eve

Bar Meals L served Mon-Fri 12-2, Sat-Sun 12-2.30 D served Sun-Mon 7-9, Tue-Sat 7-9.30 Av main course £9 ⊕ GRAY & SONS ◀ Mighty Oak Maldon Gold & IPA, Adnams Southwold Bitter, Guest ale ☼ Aspall, Delvin End, Pheasant Plucker. **Facilities** Children welcome Children's menu Children's portions Play area Family room ☘ Garden Beer festival Parking Wi-fi ▦ (notice required)

Save on hotels. Book at **theAA.com/hotel**

ESSEX 203 **ENGLAND**

BLACKMORE
Map 6 TL60

The Leather Bottle

PICK OF THE PUBS

The Green CM4 0RL ☎ 01277 823538 & 821891
e-mail: leatherbottle@tiscali.co.uk
dir: *M25 junct 8 onto A1023, left onto A128, 5m. Left onto Blackmore Rd, 2m. Left towards Blackmore, 2m. Right then 1st left*

According to local legend, Henry VIII used to stable his horses here when he came to visit his mistress. There has been a pub on this site for over 400 years but the original pub building burned down in 1954 and was rebuilt two years later. The stone-floored bar is a cosy, welcoming place to savour real ales and ciders, while the restaurant is smart, with modern furnishings. Food is prepared with top-quality ingredients mainly from local suppliers. Options include a reasonably priced lunchtime menu, which might offer ham hock hash followed by liver and bacon with bubble-and-squeak. Typical dishes at other times are smoked haddock with asparagus and butter sauce, or chicken legs stuffed with black pudding. Friday night is fish and chip night, with a pint or glass of wine included in the price. The airy conservatory opens onto the spacious garden with covered patio. Booking for meals may be required.

Open all day all wk **Bar Meals** L served all wk 12-2 D served Mon-Sat 7-9, Sun 12-4 **Restaurant** L served Mon-Sat 12-2, Sun 12-4 D served Tue-Sat 7-9, Sun 12-4 ⊕ FREE HOUSE ◀ Adnams Southwold Bitter & Broadside, Sharp's Doom Bar, Woodforde's Wherry, Cottage Cactus Jack Ò Aspall, Westons Old Rosie. **Facilities** Children's portions Garden Parking

BRIGHTLINGSEA
Map 7 TM01

The Rosebud

66-67 Hurst Green CO7 0EH ☎ 01206 304571
e-mail: mark@rosebudpub.co.uk
dir: *From Colchester take A120 towards Harwich. Right to Brightlingsea. Follow High St (away from war memorial). 0.5m to Hurst Green*

Apparently, only the locals know about this quaint little pink-washed pub propping up a row of fishermen's cottages, named after a wrecked ship. Opened in 1849 for the oyster fishermen, the pub now has an on-site micro-brewery - the first bitter produced was called Nip in the Bud. Expect fresh fish and seafood, such as seafood kedgeree; cod loin wrapped in smoked salmon; and herb-crusted tuna; plus game pie; slow-braised beef; and roasted cherry tomato and brie quiche. Look for the tail in a bottle behind the bar – some say it belonged to a cat on the doomed *Rosebud*. Booking for meals may be required.

Open all wk Mon-Thu 4.30-11 (Fri-Sat 12-11 Sun 12-7 spring/summer all day) ⊕ FREE HOUSE ◀ Guest ales. **Facilities** Children welcome Children's portions Garden

BURNHAM-ON-CROUCH
Map 7 TQ99

Ye Olde White Harte Hotel

The Quay CM0 8AS ☎ 01621 782106
e-mail: whitehartehotel@gmail.com
dir: *Along high street, right before clocktower, right into car park*

Situated on the waterfront overlooking the River Crouch, the hotel dates from the 17th century and retains many original features, including beams and fireplaces. It also has its own private jetty. Enjoy fresh local produce and fish in The Waterside Restaurant, or eat in the bar or on the terrace. The dining room offers a wide range of starters, as well as main course options that include vegetarian dishes and a daily roast. The bar menu might feature lasagne and salad; or locally caught skate with new potatoes and vegetables.

Open all day all wk **Bar Meals** L served all wk 12-2.15 D served all wk 6.30-9 Av main course £9 **Restaurant** L served all wk 12-2.15 D served all wk 7-9 Av 3 course à la carte fr £25 ⊕ FREE HOUSE ◀ Adnams Southwold Bitter, Crouch Vale Brewers Gold. **Facilities** ✿ Children welcome Children's portions Parking 🚌

CASTLE HEDINGHAM
Map 13 TL73

The Bell Inn

PICK OF THE PUBS

See Pick of the Pubs on opposite page

CHAPPEL
Map 13 TL82

The Swan Inn

CO6 2DD ☎ 01787 222353
e-mail: swan@cipubs.com
dir: *Pub visible just off A1124 (Colchester to Halstead road), from Colchester 1st left after viaduct*

Under the constant gaze of a magnificent railway viaduct and surrounded by beautiful countryside, this 14th-century, low-beamed free house has a well-founded reputation for food, especially fresh fish. Other typical dishes include toad-in-the-hole; lamb's liver and bacon; and Mediterranean vegetable lasagne. The River Colne runs through the gardens where, as in the sheltered courtyard, you can enjoy a meal. The bar serves plenty of wines by the glass and well-kept Adnams real ales; Essex and Suffolk brews appear at Spring and August Bank Holiday beer festivals.

Open all wk 11-3 6-11 (Sat 11-11 Sun 12-10.30) **Bar Meals** L served Mon-Sat 12-2.30, Sun 12-8 D served Mon-Sat 6-9.30, Sun 12-8 ⊕ FREE HOUSE ◀ Adnams Southwold Bitter & Broadside, Guest Ale Ò Aspall. ♚ 15 **Facilities** Children welcome Children's menu Children's portions Play area Garden Beer festival Parking Wi-fi 🚌

CHELMSFORD
Map 6 TL70

The Alma

37 Arbour Ln CM1 7RG ☎ 01245 256783
e-mail: alma@cipubs.com
dir: *Telephone for directions*

Named after the bloodiest battle of the Crimean War, The Alma was built in the late 19th century as an alehouse for soldiers recovering in the neighbouring hospital. There was a change of hands in early 2012. The menu has a stylish mix of traditional and modern dishes - perhaps pan-fried sea bass fillet with fennel and crayfish risotto and pesto dressing; chicken breast with tarragon and white wine sauce; or stilton-stuffed fillet of beef with a rich red wine and mushroom sauce. There is a front patio and more secluded rear garden for alfresco dining.

Open all day all wk 11-11 (Fri-Sat 11-mdnt Sun 12-10.30) ⊕ FREE HOUSE ◀ Adnams Ò Aspall. **Facilities** Children welcome Children's menu Children's portions Garden Parking Wi-fi

CHRISHALL
Map 12 TL43

The Red Cow **NEW**

11 High St SG8 8RN ☎ 01763 838792
e-mail: thepub@theredcow.com
dir: *M11 junct 10, A505 towards Royston. 2m, pass pet creamtorium, 1st left signed Chrishall. 3.5m, pub in village centre*

Anyone with a jaundiced view of Essex, courtesy of a popular TV series, should visit this thatched village pub, restaurant and shop to see how delightfully rural it can be. In the bar the real ales and cider are all East Anglian; on the menu are soups, sandwiches, jacket potatoes and other pub favourites, such as fish and chips, and sausage and mash. The seasonally changing restaurant carte typically offers braised shin of beef and Guinness pie; rib-eye steak; roasted chicken breast; and chestnut, red onion and goat's cheese tart. Booking for meals may be required.

Open 12-3 6-12 (Sat 12-12 Sun 12-11) Closed: Mon **Bar Meals** L served Tue-Sun 12-3 D served Tue-Thu 6-9, Fri-Sat 6-9.30 Av main course £8 **Restaurant** L served Tue-Sun 12-3 D served Tue-Thu 6-9, Fri-Sat 6-9.30 Fixed menu price fr £14.50 Av 3 course à la carte fr £28 ⊕ FREE HOUSE ◀ Adnams Southwold Bitter, Woodforde's Wherry & Nelson's Revenge Ò Aspall Harry Sparrow. **Facilities** ✿ Children welcome Children's menu Children's portions Play area Garden Parking Wi-fi 🚌 (notice required)

CLAVERING
Map 12 TL43

The Cricketers

PICK OF THE PUBS

See Pick of the Pubs on page 204

PICK OF THE PUBS

The Cricketers

CLAVERING   Map 12 TL43

CB11 4QT ☎ 01799 550442
e-mail: info@thecricketers.co.uk
web: www.thecricketers.co.uk
dir: *M11 junct 10, A505 E, A1301, B1383. At Newport take B1038*

Rural Essex is pretty. Take Clavering, for example, and you'll see what a large part of the county is like – lovely villages with thatched cottages, winding lanes, extensive woodland and rich arable farmland. The Cricketers (the pitch is just down the road) has served the local community for the best part of 500 years; all the signs are here – the beams, a forest of wooden pillars, old fireplaces with winter log fires, while outside a wisteria surrounds the door and tables dot a rose-fringed garden. Tastefully appointed, this relaxing dining pub offers customers seasonally changing menus and daily chalkboard specials, with dishes expertly prepared by head chef Justin Greig and his team. Meats are properly hung, the fish is always fresh, and local, organic produce is used wherever possible. Jamie Oliver, son of landlords Trevor and Sally (now over 30 years here), supplies the pub with seasonal vegetables, herbs and salads from his certified organic garden that is nearby. Begin with an English classics plank, which is a hand-made

pork pie with crackling, quail Scotch egg, Suffolk Gold cheese, green tomato chutney and piccalilli. A main course salad or pasta dish might follow, or you could try sautéed lambs' kidneys and bacon with bubble-and-squeak and red wine jus; a fish or seafood daily special; or roasted squash and spinach lasagne. There's always a Sunday roast, and children are particularly welcome as their own small menu testifies. The extensive wine list changes regularly and features some excellent house wines; there's also a popular Connoisseurs' Selection. Beers are mostly East Anglian and the cider is from Aspall.

Open all day all wk Closed: 25-26 Dec **Bar Meals** L served all wk 12-2 D served all wk 6.30-9.30 **Restaurant** L served all wk 12-2 D served all wk 6.30-9.30 ⊕ FREE HOUSE ◀ Adnams Broadside & Southwold Bitter, Tetley's Bitter, Greene King IPA, Woodforde's Wherry & Norfolk Nog ⚖ Aspall. ♚ 17 **Facilities** Children welcome Children's menu Children's portions Family room Garden Parking Wi-fi 🚌

COLCHESTER — Map 13 TL92

The Rose & Crown Hotel ★★★ HL

East St CO1 2TZ ☎ 01206 866677
e-mail: info@rose-and-crown.com
dir: *From M25 junct 28 take A12 N. Follow Colchester signs*

Just a few minutes' stroll from Colchester Castle, this beautiful timber-framed building dates from the 14th century and is believed to be the oldest hotel in the oldest town in England. The Tudor bar with its central roaring fire is a great place to relax with a drink. Food is served in the Oak Room or the Tudor Room brasserie, an informal alternative serving classic bar food. Typically, start with ham hock terrine or a sharing platter of shellfish, then follow with pork belly with butterbean, pancetta and chorizo cassoulet. Leave room for warm pear and almond tart. Accommodation is available.

Open all wk **Bar Meals** L served all wk 12–2.30 D served all wk 6.30–9.30 ⊕ FREE HOUSE ◀ Rose & Crown Bitter, Tetley's Bitter, Adnams Broadside. **Facilities** Children welcome Family room Parking Wi-fi ▦ **Rooms** 39

DEDHAM — Map 13 TM03

Marlborough Head Inn ★★★ INN

Mill Ln CO7 6DH ☎ 01206 323250
e-mail: jen.pearmain@tiscali.co.uk
dir: *E of A12, N of Colchester*

Tucked away in glorious Constable Country, this 16th-century building was once a clearing-house for local wool merchants. In 1660, after a slump in trade, it became an inn. Today it is as perfect for a pint, sofa and newspaper as it is for a good home-cooked family meal. Traditional favourites such as steak, Guinness and mushroom pie; and lamb shank with red wine and rosemary appear on the menu, plus fish is given centre stage on Fridays. There is a terrace and walled garden to enjoy in the warmer weather. Three en suite bedrooms are available.

Open all day all wk 11.30–11 ⊕ PUNCH TAVERNS ◀ Adnams Southwold Bitter, Greene King IPA, Woodforde's Wherry ♂ Aspall. **Facilities** Children welcome Children's menu Children's portions Family room Garden Parking **Rooms** 3

The Sun Inn ★★★★ INN ◉

PICK OF THE PUBS

High St CO7 6DF ☎ 01206 323351
e-mail: office@thesuninndedham.com
dir: *From A12 follow signs to Dedham for 1.5m, pub on High Street*

Piers Baker's lovely old inn has two informal bars, an open dining room, a snug oak-panelled lounge, three open fires, exposed timbers and beams and what he calls "meandering" floors. Outside is a suntrap terrace and walled garden, so take your pick of where to enjoy a quiet pint of Crouch Vale Brewers Gold, Adnams Broadside, a

guest ale, or one of over 20 wines by the glass. Locally sourced seasonal ingredients drive the daily-changing menu of traditional Mediterranean-style dishes, many clearly Italian-influenced. Over shared antipasti choose leg of saltmarsh lamb with aubergines, pinenuts, sultanas, tomatoes and basil; salmon fillet with chilli, mint, slow-cooked fennel and spinach; or Arborio rice with courgettes (and their flowers), Chardonnay and parmesan. The bar menu offers soup, sandwiches, ploughman's and more. If you can't tear yourself away, stay in an en suite guest room with a large comfy bed and character furniture.

Open all day all wk 11–11 Closed: 25–27 Dec **Bar Meals** L served Mon–Thu 12–2.30, Fri–Sun 12–3 D served Sun–Thu 6.30–9.30, Fri–Sat 6.30–10 Av main course £6.50 **Restaurant** L served Mon–Thu 12–2.30, Fri–Sun 12–3 D served Sun–Thu 6.30–9.30, Fri–Sat 6.30–10 Fixed menu price fr £12 Av 3 course à la carte fr £20 ⊕ FREE HOUSE ◀ Crouch Vale Brewers Gold, Adnams Broadside, 2 Guest ales ♂ Aspall. ▼ 25 **Facilities** ❤ Children welcome Children's menu Children's portions Garden Parking Wi-fi **Rooms** 7

FEERING — Map 7 TL82

The Sun Inn

Feering Hill CO5 9NH ☎ 01376 570442
e-mail: sunninnfeering@live.co.uk
dir: *On A12 between Colchester & Witham. Village 1m*

A pretty pub dating from 1525 with heavily carved beams to prove it. The bar has two inglenook fireplaces, no TV or games machines and sells Shepherd Neame's real ales, while outside are a large garden and courtyard. Home-cooked burgers; hot chilli with basmati rice; and wholetail scampi, chips and peas are backed by daily specials and, from May to September, a wood-burning pizza oven. Three roasts, together with other options, are offered on Sundays. Over 40 real ales and ciders are showcased at May and October beer festivals.

Open all wk Sat–Sun all day **Bar Meals** L served Mon–Sat 12–2.30, Sun 12–8 D served Mon–Sat 6–9.30, Sun 12–8 **Restaurant** L served Mon–Sat 12–2.30, Sun 12–8 D served Mon–Sat 6–9.30, Sun 12–8 ⊕ SHEPHERD NEAME ◀ Master Brew, Spitfire & Bishops Finger, Guest ales ♂ Thatchers Heritage. ▼ 12 **Facilities** ❤ Children welcome Children's menu Children's portions Garden Beer festival Parking ▦ (notice required)

FELSTED — Map 6 TL62

The Swan at Felsted

PICK OF THE PUBS

Station Rd CM6 3DG ☎ 01371 820245
e-mail: info@theswanatfelsted.co.uk
dir: *M11 junct 8, A120 signed Felsted. Pub in village centre*

Venture through the door of this red-brick and timbered building and a stylish gastro-pub awaits. Rebuilt after a disastrous fire in the early 1900s, the building was formerly the village bank, then a run-down boozer. In

2002 it was rescued and refurbished by Jono and Jane Clark. With polished wood floors, leather sofas and colourful modern art, it successfully balances traditional pub attributes with a quality dining experience. Locals come for cracking Greene King ales and over a dozen world wines served by the glass; if sharing a bottle, allow time to peruse the 80-plus choices on the list. Seasonally changing food menus champion locally sourced produce, offering an imaginative selection of modern European dishes that remain in touch with their pub roots. Starters include goat's cheese and apple mousse, and rabbit terrine. Main courses cater to all tastes: roasted duck breast; gnocchi served with pesto and purple sprouting broccoli; or beer-battered haddock and chips. There is a courtyard garden to enjoy in the warmer months. Booking for meals may be required.

Open all wk 11.30–3 5–11 (Sun 11.30–6) **Bar Meals** L served Mon–Sat 12–2.30, Sun 12–4 D served Mon–Thu 6–9.30, Fri–Sat 5.30–9.45 **Restaurant** L served Mon–Sat 12–2.30, Sun 12–4 D served Mon–Thu 6–9.30, Fri–Sat 5.30–9.45 ⊕ GREENE KING ◀ IPA, Guinness, Guest ale ♂ Aspall. ▼ 14 **Facilities** ❤ Children welcome Children's menu Children's portions Garden Parking

FINGRINGHOE — Map 7 TM02

The Whalebone

Chapel Rd CO5 7BG ☎ 01206 729307
e-mail: vicki@thewhaleboneinn.co.uk
dir: *Telephone for directions*

This Grade II listed 18th-century free house enjoys breathtaking views from its position at the top of the Roman River Valley. The unusual name comes from bones, once fastened above the door of the pub, which came from a locally beached whale. The converted barn has wooden floors, exposed beams and unique artwork, all combining to create a feeling of warmth and character. Hearty British cuisine is prepared on the premises from local ingredients, along with four cask ales and a couple of ciders. Lunchtime choices range from sandwiches and ploughman's to mains of scampi, gammon and burger, all served with thick-cut chips. Booking for meals may be required.

Open all wk 12–3 5.30–11 (Sat 12–11 Sun 12–10.30) **Bar Meals** L served Mon–Sat 12–2.30, Sun 12–6.45 D served Mon–Thu 6.30–9, Fri–Sat 6.30–9.30, Sun 12–6.45 Av main course £11.25 **Restaurant** L served Mon–Sat 12–2.30, Sun 12–6.45 D served Mon–Thu 6.30–9, Fri–Sat 6.30–9.30, Sun 12–6.45 Av 3 course à la carte fr £23 ⊕ FREE HOUSE ◀ 4 Guest ales ♂ Aspall. ▼ 13 **Facilities** Children welcome Children's menu Children's portions Play area Family room Garden Parking ▦ (notice required)

FULLER STREET
Map 6 TL71

The Square and Compasses

CM3 2BB ☎ 01245 361477
e-mail: info@thesquareandcompasses.co.uk
web: www.thesquareandcompasses.co.uk
dir: *From A131 (Chelmsford to Braintree) take Great Leighs exit, enter village, turn right into Boreham Rd. Turn left signed Fuller St & Terling. Pub on left on entering hamlet*

Just ten minutes from Chelmsford, this beautifully restored 17th-century village free house is known locally as The Stokehole. Originally two farm cottages, the building still retains its original beams and inglenook fireplaces, with antique furnishings. Food is simple and straightforward, served alongside a good selection of ciders and ales. As well as pub classics, the daily-changing specials might include creamed parsnip and apple soup; roast breast of local pheasant wrapped in smoked streaky bacon; and apple pie with vanilla ice cream. There is a picket fenced garden and Mediterranean-style decking area. A beer festival is held in June. Booking for meals may be required.

Open all wk 11.30-3 5.30-11 (Sat-Sun 12-11) **Bar Meals** L served Mon-Fri 12-2, Sat 12-2.30, Sun 12-6 D served Mon-Sat 6.30-9.30 **Restaurant** L served Mon-Fri 12-2, Sat 12-2.30, Sun 12-6 D served Mon-Sat 6.30-9.30 ⊕ FREE HOUSE ◀ Square and Compasses Stokers IPA & Essex, Dark Star Ö Westons. ♀ 14 **Facilities** ✿ Children welcome Children's portions Garden Beer festival Parking

GOLDHANGER
Map 7 TL90

The Chequers Inn

Church St CM9 8AS ☎ 01621 788203
e-mail: chequersgoldhang@aol.com
dir: *From B1026, 500mtrs to village centre*

Built in 1410, The Chequers can be found in the picturesque village of Goldhanger on the River Blackwater. The pub name comes from a chequerboard used by the tax collector in the pub many, many years ago. At around 30 feet above sea level, it reputedly has the 'lowest' bar in Britain, where you can enjoy a pint of Nelson's Revenge. Pride is taken in the preparation and presentation of food. Lite bites may include moules marinière or local asparagus wrapped in smoked salmon. Main courses on the carte are reasonably priced: home-baked steak and stout pie; bacon, sage and onion pudding; and chicken and seafood paella. There are beer

festivals in March and September. Booking for meals may be required.

Open all day all wk **Bar Meals** L served all wk 12-3 D served Mon-Sat 6.30-9 **Restaurant** L served all wk 12-3 D served Mon-Sat 6.30-9 ⊕ PUNCH TAVERNS ◀ Young's Bitter, Woodforde's Nelson's Revenge, Crouch Vale Brewers Gold, St Austell Tribute Ö Westons Old Rosie & Perry. ♀ 13 **Facilities** Children welcome Children's menu Children's portions Garden Beer festival Parking ▭

GOSFIELD
Map 13 TL72

The Green Man

The Street CO9 1TP ☎ 01787 273608
e-mail: info@thegreenmangosfield.co.uk
dir: *Take A131 N from Braintree then A1017 to village*

Close to the picturesque Gosfield Lake, this pink-washed medley of buildings houses a welcoming village dining pub. At lunchtime, enjoy a pint of Greene King IPA with a choice of crusty filled baguettes, or dishes such as breaded scampi and chips. Using the best of local produce, the dinner menu is based around classic British and international fare and offers the likes of asparagus spears topped with Serrano ham; swordfish steak with a soy, lime and chilli dressing; and toffee pecan meringue cheesecake. A different half-price classic pub meal is on offer every day. Call for dates of the live music and themed nights.

Open all day all wk **Bar Meals** L served Mon-Sat 12-2.30, Sun 12-4 D served Mon-Sat 6-9 **Restaurant** L served Mon-Sat 12-2.30, Sun 12-4 D served Mon-Sat 6-9 ⊕ GREENE KING ◀ IPA & Abbot Ale, Guest ales Ö Aspall, Kopparberg. ♀ 16 **Facilities** Children welcome Children's menu Children's portions Garden Parking Wi-fi ▭ (notice required)

GREAT BRAXTED
Map 7 TL81

The Ducane
PICK OF THE PUBS

See Pick of the Pubs on opposite page

GREAT TOTHAM
Map 7 TL81

The Bull at Great
Totham ★★★★ RR ◉◉ **NEW**

2 Maldon Rd CM9 8NH ☎ 01621 893385
e-mail: reservations@thebullatgreattotham.co.uk
dir: *Exit A12 at Witham junct to Great Totham*

Overlooking the village cricket green is this 16th-century coaching inn housing a gastro-pub and restaurant, while in a cottage in the grounds are highly appointed en suite bedrooms. The bar offers fine wines by the glass, Fuller's, Adnams and guest real ales, and snacks like crispy fried chicken with roasted garlic aïoli; and sticky rack of baby back ribs. Named after the ancient specimen tree in the lavender-filled garden is the fine-dining Willow Room,

holding two AA Rosettes. Here you might start with beetroot-cured organic salmon, horseradish cream, piccalilli and pumpernickel, then follow with steamed beef and kidney pudding with parsnip purée, or caramelised shallot tarte Tatin with red wine syrup, goat's cheese and mixed herb salad. Spiced plum fool with shortbread is a typical dessert. Musical and themed dining evenings and other events take place throughout the year. Booking for meals may be required.

Open all day all wk **Bar Meals** L served Mon-Fri 12-2.30 (light bites till 5.30), Sat 12-10, Sun 12-6.45 D served Mon-Thu 5.30-9, Fri 5.30-10, Sat 12-10 Av main course £15 food served all day **Restaurant** L served Wed-Sat 12-2.30, Sun 12-5 D served Wed-Sat 7-9 Fixed menu price fr £14.90 ⊕ FREE HOUSE ◀ Fuller's London Pride, Adnams, Guest ale. ♀ 50 **Facilities** Children welcome Children's menu Children's portions Garden Parking ▭ (notice required) **Rooms** 4

GREAT YELDHAM
Map 13 TL73

The White Hart ★★★★ RR ◉◉
PICK OF THE PUBS

Poole St CO9 4HJ ☎ 01787 237250
e-mail: mjwmason@yahoo.co.uk
dir: *On A1017 between Haverhill & Halstead*

Highwaymen were once locked up in a small prison beneath the stairs of this impressive 500-year-old timber-framed inn. Situated on the border of Essex and Suffolk, The White Hart enjoys a setting within 4.5 acres of gardens, close to Heddingham Castle, the Colne Valley and Newmarket. With its blend of traditional and contemporary, it's a popular wedding venue on the one hand, and a great place to sample Brandon Rusty Bucket on the other. The hard work put in by the establishment's owner, Matthew Mason, has resulted in many awards, including two AA Rosettes for the food. The express bar menu lists favourites such as Cumberland sausage ring with cheddar mash and onion gravy, while the à la carte choice includes ballotine of Yeldham wood pigeon among its starters, and Auberies Estate roast loin of venison as a main course. For dessert there's baked Alaska or warm pear frangipane. Eleven en suite and fully equipped rooms complete the picture.

Open all day all wk ⊕ FREE HOUSE ◀ Adnams Southwold Bitter, Black Sheep, Brandon Rusty Bucket, Sharp's Doom Bar Ö Aspall. **Facilities** Children welcome Children's menu Children's portions Play area Garden Parking Wi-fi **Rooms** 11

Save on hotels. Book at **theAA.com/hotel**

ESSEX 207 ENGLAND

PICK OF THE PUBS

The Ducane

GREAT BRAXTED Map 7 TL81

The Village CM8 3EJ ☎ 01621 891697
e-mail: eat@theducane.co.uk
web: www.theducane.co.uk
dir: *Great Braxted signed between Witham & Kelvedon on A12*

Refurbished with style and flair by award-winning chef Jonathan Brown and partner Louise Partis, this modern-looking pub dates from 1935 and forms part of a village that was displaced by Lord Du Cane in the 19th century. Expect a fresh, modern interior, a warm welcome and a great selection of ales from Mighty Oak, Mersea Island, Farmers and Wibblers. Jonathan's innovative menus champion local produce and local suppliers, including Braxted beef and lamb, Colchester oysters and seasonal goodies (plums, quinces, pears and figs) from the gardens and allotments of local residents. A superb-value set menu might open with cream of sweet potato, chestnut and chickpea soup with croûtons and locally baked bread; or pressing of duck confit, ham hock with cranberry and port compôte; followed by slow-braised locally reared beef with red wine and thyme, topped with a herb crust and served with new potatoes; or twice-baked cheddar cheese soufflé. For dessert, maybe bread-and-butter pudding with orange, cinnamon and mixed spices, maple syrup drizzle and vanilla ice cream; or rich dark chocolate ganache cake, whipped cream and

chocolate sauce. Dishes from the carte keep with the modern British theme: you could kick off with potted shrimps with leek, white crab and spring onion and herb butter with tossed salad and toast followed by slow-braised pork belly with bubble-and-squeak, apple compôte, sage gravy and spring greens; then finish with sticky toffee pudding with vanilla ice cream. For children there is an excellent separate menu of home-cooked favourites such as ham, egg and chips; fish and chips; or pasta with tomato sauce and cheese. The pub hosts regular steak and curry nights and a beer festival. Booking for meals may be required.

Open Tue-Fri 12-3 6-11.30 (Sat 12-3 6-12 Sun 12-4) Closed: Sun eve & Mon
Bar Meals L served Tue-Sun 12-2.30

D served Tue-Sat 7-9.30 Av main course £13.50 **Restaurant** L served Tue-Sun 12-2.30 D served Tue-Sat 7-9.30 Fixed menu price fr £13.50 Av 3 course à la carte fr £25 ⊕ FREE HOUSE ◀ Mighty Oak Maldon Gold, Farmers, Wibblers, Mersea Island ♂ Aspall. ♥ 10
Facilities Children welcome Children's menu Children's portions Garden Beer festival Parking Wi-fi 🚌 (notice required)

PICK OF THE PUBS

Bell Inn & Hill House

HORNDON ON THE HILL   Map 6 TQ68

High Rd SS17 8LD ☎ 01375 642463
e-mail: info@bell-inn.co.uk
web: www.bell-inn.co.uk
dir: *M25 junct 30/31 signed Thurrock*

Visitors to the Bell these days get a much friendlier welcome than travellers passing through the area in the 16th century. This former coaching inn had a chequered history, which included one local landowner being burnt at the stake for heresy on ground at the rear of the pub – a grisly event marked with a blue plaque on the front of the building. Since then, owners of the pub have stuck around much longer and it has been in the same family since 1938. Its history as a coaching inn can still be seen today: from the first-floor gallery that runs above the courtyard luggage would have been transferred to and from the top of the London stagecoaches. In the bars, regular brews like Sharp's Doom Bar and Crouch Vale Brewers Gold are backed by a selection of guest ales that changes every few days. Many bottles from the extensive wine list are served by the glass. The lunchtime bar menu offers open sandwiches and a popular selection of light meals but booking is essential in the bustling restaurant, where the daily-changing modern British menu is driven by the best seasonal produce. A typical meal might begin with pressed butternut squash

and Pernod terrine, ricotta, pine nuts, rosemary and lentil dressing; followed by roasted local partridge with Jerusalem artichoke, black pudding and caramelised apple. Decadent desserts include poached rhubarb and vanilla parfait with toasted marshmallow and orange. One quirky talking point in the pub are the hot cross buns hanging from the original king post that supports the inn's ancient roof timbers. Every year the oldest willing villager hangs another, an unusual tradition that dates back 100 years to when the pub happened to change hands on a Good Friday. Booking for meals may be required.

Open all wk Mon-Fri 11-3 5.30-11 (Sat 11-3 6-11 Sun 12-4 7-10.30) Closed:

25-26 Dec **Bar Meals** L served all wk 12-1.45 D served Sun-Fri 7-9.45, Sat 6-9.45 Av main course £9.95 **Restaurant** L served Mon-Sat 12-1.45, Sun 12-2.30 D served all wk 7-9.45 Av 3 course à la carte fr £23.95 ⊕ FREE HOUSE ◀ Greene King IPA, Crouch Vale Brewers Gold, Sharp's Doom Bar, Bass, Guest ales. ☘ 16 **Facilities** Children welcome Children's portions ✿ Garden Parking Wi-fi

HASTINGWOOD   Map 6 TL40

Rainbow & Dove

Hastingwood Rd CM17 9JX ☎ **01279 415419**
e-mail: rainbowanddove@hotmail.co.uk
dir: *Just off M11 junct 7*

A farmhouse, staging post, village shop and post office
before it became a pub, this beamed local may or may
not be able to trace its origins back to the Domesday
Book, but what is for sure is that English Heritage have
rated it as a Grade II historical building. Four real ales
include two guests, and menus revolve around fresh
produce. Fish from Billingsgate Market is bought,
delivered and cooked all on the same day, so you may find
skate, sea bass and bream on the blackboard. Other
dishes for which the pub is famous are hot salt-beef
sandwiches; English rump steak with grilled tomato and
mushrooms; and nut roast with goat's cheese and apricot
stuffing.

Open Mon-Sat 11.30-3.30 6-11 (Sun 12-4) Closed: Sun
eve **Bar Meals** L served Mon-Sat 12-2.30, Sun 12-3.30
D served Mon-Sat 7-9.30 **Restaurant** L served Mon-Sat
12-2.30, Sun 12-3.30 D served Mon-Sat 7-9.30 ⊕ FREE
HOUSE ◀ Rainbow & Dove, Adnams Broadside, Sharp's
Doom Bar, Guest ales ♨ Thatchers Gold. ♥ 10
Facilities Children welcome Children's menu Children's
portions Garden Beer festival Parking 🚐 (notice
required)

HATFIELD BROAD OAK   Map 6 TL51

The Duke's Head NEW

High St CM22 7HH ☎ **01279 718598**
e-mail: info@thedukeshead.co.uk
dir: *M11 junct 8, A120 towards Great Dunmow. Right
into B183 to Hatfield Broad Oak. Pub on left at 1st bend
in village*

At the heart of the beautiful Essex village of Hatfield
Broad Oak, this welcoming child- and dog-friendly pub
dates back to 1828. A real fire in the bar is crying out to
be enjoyed with a pint of London Pride or one of the
carefully selected wines on offer. The seasonal British
menu offers familiar favourites and reworked classics,
including locally sourced game and Colchester oysters.
Sausage and mash or omelette Arnold Bennett (named
after the novelist) might appear alongside slow-cooked
pork belly or home-made chicken Kiev. Sunday lunch is
served well into the evening – until 9pm. Booking for
meals may be required.

Open all wk 12-3 6-11.30 (Fri-Sun all day) Closed: 25-26
Dec **Bar Meals** L served Mon-Fri 12-2.30, Sat 12-3, Sun
12-9 D served Mon-Thu 6.30-9.30, Fri-Sat 6.30-10, Sun
12-9 Av main course £12.75 **Restaurant** L served Mon-Fri
12-2.30, Sat 12-3, Sun 12-9 D served Mon-Thu
6.30-9.30, Fri-Sat 6.30-10, Sun 12-9 Av 3 course à la
carte fr £25 ⊕ ENTERPRISE INNS ◀ Greene King IPA, St
Austell Tribute, Fuller's London Pride ♨ Aspall. ♥ 10
Facilities ❧ Children welcome Children's menu
Children's portions Play area Garden Parking Wi-fi

HORNDON ON THE HILL   Map 6 TQ68

Bell Inn & Hill House

PICK OF THE PUBS

See Pick of the Pubs on opposite page

INGATESTONE   Map 6 TQ69

The Red Lion

Main Rd, Margaretting CM4 0EQ ☎ **01277 352184**
dir: *From Chelmsford take A12 towards Brentwood.
Margaretting in 4m*

The phrase 'quintessential English pub' is something of a
cliché, but how else to describe the 17th-century Red
Lion? The bar is decorated in burgundy and aubergine,
the restaurant in coffee and cream. From an extensive
menu choose salmon and dill fishcakes with lemon and
ginger jam, or garlic mushrooms for starters, then follow
with minted lamb shank on mustard mash, or rib-eye
steak with all the trimmings. Wash down with a pint of
Greene King IPA. New landlords.

Open all wk 12-11 (Sun 12-6) **Bar Meals** L served all wk
12-3 D served all wk 6-9.30 Av main course £8.95
Restaurant L served all wk 12-3 D served all wk 6-9.30
⊕ GREENE KING ◀ IPA, Guest ales ♨ Westons Stowford
Press. ♥ 14 **Facilities** Children welcome Children's menu
Children's portions Play area Garden Parking Wi-fi
🚐 (notice required)

LANGHAM   Map 13 TM03

The Shepherd and Dog

Moor Rd CO4 5NR ☎ **01206 272711**
dir: *A12 from Colchester towards Ipswich, take 1st left
signed Langham*

Set in the attractive village of Langham deep in
Constable Country on the Suffolk/Essex border, this 1928
free house has all the classic styling of an English
country pub. Widely renowned for its food, it serves an
extensive variety of meat, fish and poultry dishes, plus a
vegetarian selection and a children's menu. A typical
meal could take in deep-fried brie with cranberry sauce
followed by home-made chicken curry, beer-battered cod,
or maybe rump steak and peppercorn sauce.

Open all wk **Bar Meals** L served Mon-Fri 12-3, Sat-Sun
12-9.30 D served Mon-Fri 6-9.30, Sat-Sun 12-9.30
Av main course £3.50-£6.50 **Restaurant** L served Mon-Fri
12-3, Sat-Sun 12-9.30 D served Mon-Fri 6-9.30, Sat-Sun
12-9.30 Fixed menu price fr £7.95 Av 3 course à la carte
fr £13.95 ⊕ FREE HOUSE ◀ Greene King IPA & Abbot Ale,
Guest ales. **Facilities** Children welcome Children's menu
Children's portions Garden Parking 🚐

LITTLE BRAXTED   Map 7 TL81

The Green Man

Green Man Ln CM8 3LB ☎ **01621 891659**
e-mail: info@thegreenmanlittlebraxted.co.uk
dir: *From A12 junct 22 take unclassified road (Little
Braxted Ln) through Little Braxted. Straight ahead into
Kelvedon Rd. Right into Green Man Ln*

Keep going past the parish church to locate this unspoilt
brick-and-tiled pub tucked away on the edge of the long,
straggling little hamlet. Dating from the early 1700s, it
has a traditional interior with collections of horse brasses
and old woodworking tools, and there's a tree-shaded
garden to the rear – ideal for summer drinking. The
attraction, other than its peaceful rural location, is the
excellent range of real ales and the home-cooked food,
perhaps beef in Guinness with horseradish gravy, Thai
chicken curry, and bread-and-butter pudding.

Open all wk Mon-Sat 11.30-3 5-11 (Sun 12-7) **Bar
Meals** L served Mon-Sat 12-2.30, Sun 12-6 D served
Mon-Sat 6-9 Av main course £8.95 **Restaurant** L served
Mon-Sat 12-2.30, Sun 12-6 D served Mon-Sat 6-9
⊕ GREENE KING ◀ IPA, Abbot Ale & Abbot Reserve,
Nethergate, Hydes, Guest ales. ♥ 9 **Facilities** ❧ Children
welcome Children's menu Children's portions Garden
Parking Wi-fi

LITTLE BURSTEAD   Map 6 TQ69

The Dukes Head NEW

Laindon Common Rd CM12 9TA ☎ **01277 651333**
e-mail: enquiry@dukesheadlittleburstead.co.uk
dir: *From Basildon take A176 (Noah Hill Rd) N toward
Billericay. Left into Laindon Common Rd to Little
Burstead. Pub on left*

Smart refurbished interiors and a friendly team
characterise the atmosphere in this large hostelry
between Brentwood and Basildon. Chunky wood tables,
leather-upholstered stools and relaxing armchairs
surround the open fire in the bar area, where the ales vie
for selection with an excellent range of wines served by
the glass. Modern British food ranges from pizzas and
pastas to the chef's daily specials. A full diary of events
includes a steak night every week, fabulous fish on
Fridays, and a surprise menu on the last Thursday of the
month. Booking for meals may be required.

Open all day all wk **Bar Meals** L served Mon-Thu 12-10,
Fri-Sat 12-10.30, Sun 12-9 D served Mon-Thu 12-10,
Fri-Sat 12-10.30, Sun 12-9 Av main course £12.95 food
served all day **Restaurant** L served Mon-Thu 12-10,
Fri-Sat 12-10.30, Sun 12-9 D served Mon-Thu 12-10,
Fri-Sat 12-10.30, Sun 12-9 Fixed menu price fr £12.50
Av 3 course à la carte fr £20.95 food served all day
⊕ MITCHELLS & BUTLERS ◀ Fuller's London Pride,
Sharp's Doom Bar, Adnams. ♥ 21 **Facilities** ❧ Children
welcome Children's menu Children's portions Garden
Parking 🚐 (notice required)

Lion & Lamb | The White House

Restaurant and Bar now offering Accommodation in conjunction with
The White House Luxury Country House

A traditional country restaurant and bar complete with oak beams and a large secluded garden overlooking farmland. Side the B1256 (the old A120) 5 mins from M11–J8 and Stansted Airport is the Lion & Lamb, a traditional country pub combined with a restaurant serving very modern food all day long – kangaroo, grilled dover sole, pork belly and roasted loin with a pumpkin puree, parsnips and a tarragon jus and wild mushroom risotto are just some of the temptations that could be offered. With its oak beams and cosy fireplace, the Lion & Lamb dates back to the 16th century and is very inviting. Bar snacks are available and diners are welcome to eat in the bar, dining area or conservatory. Children are welcome, making the Lion & Lamb a popular choice for family groups.

This carefully refurbished family home displays many original 16th-century features alongside modern comforts. The Grade II listed building is close to Stansted Airport and is enclosed by extensive gardens. Accommodation is stylish with large beds and ensuite and there is a luxurious Victorian bathroom.

Served around one table in the farmhouse-style kitchen, the full cooked breakfast is a wholesome start to the day. For other meals a range of interesting dishes, using quality local ingredients, is available in the Lion and Lamb pub a mile up the road, which is owned by the same proprietors who offer free transport to and fro.

Stortford Road (B1256), Little Canfield, Dunmow, Near Takeley CM6 1SR
Tel: 01279 870257   Fax: 01279 870423
Email: info@lionandlamb.co.uk or enquiries@whitehousestansted.co.uk
www.lionandlamb.co.uk or www.whitehousestansted.co.uk

Johansen
Conde
Nast

Save on hotels. Book at **theAA.com/hotel**

ESSEX 211 ENGLAND

The Queens Head Inn

High St CB11 4TD ☎ 01799 522251
e-mail: thequeenshead@fsmail.net
dir: *M11 junct 9A take B184 towards Saffron Walden.
Right onto B1383, S towards Wendens Ambo*

A beautiful family-run former coaching inn with open
fires, exposed beams and one of only two remaining
full-length settles in England. Very much at the centre of
the local community, the pub runs darts and football
teams and pétanque competitions; a large beer garden
with bouncy castle confirms its family-friendly
credentials. The kitchen aims to produce good
home-made pub grub at realistic prices, with a menu of
popular favourites from pizzas to pies, ciabattas to
curries. Booking for meals may be required.

Open Tue-Thu 12-3 5.30-11 (Fri 12-3 5.30-12 Sat 12-12
Sun 12-10.30) Closed: Mon ⊕ GREENE KING ◀ IPA,
Morland Old Speckled Hen, Guest ale ♻ Westons Stowford
Press, Aspall. **Facilities** Children welcome Children's
menu Children's portions Play area Garden Parking Wi-fi

The Lion & Lamb

CM6 1SR ☎ 01279 870257
e-mail: info@lionandlamb.co.uk
web: www.lionandlamb.co.uk
dir: *M11 junct 8, B1256 towards Takeley & Little Canfield*

Ideal for business or leisure, this traditional country pub
and restaurant was built as a coaching inn on what used
to be the main East Coast road. Now bypassed, travellers
on the way to Stansted Airport seek it out for a last
English pint before their trip, relaxing in the large and
well-furnished garden. Inside are oak beams, winter log
fires, an extensive food selection, real ales and up to
11 wines served by the glass. From the restaurant menu
a starter of smoked trout fillet could be followed by
roasted breast of Telmara duck with an apple and cream
sauce.

Open all day all wk 11-11 **Bar Meals** food served all day
Restaurant food served all day ⊕ GREENE KING ◀ IPA &
St Edmunds, Ridley's Old Bob, Guest ales. ♀ 11
Facilities Children welcome Children's menu Children's
portions Play area Garden Parking Wi-fi

See advert on opposite page

Flitch of Bacon

The Street CM6 3HT ☎ 01371 820323
dir: *B1256 to Braintree for 10m, turn off at Little
Dunmow, 0.5m pub on right*

A charming 15th-century country inn, looking out over the
fields, whose name refers to the ancient gift of half a
salted pig, or 'flitch', to couples who have been married
for a year and a day, and 'who have not had a cross
word'. There are always two guest ales in addition to
Greene King IPA. Children are welcome.

Open Mon eve-Sun Closed: Mon L ⊕ FREE HOUSE
◀ Greene King IPA, Guest ales. **Facilities** Children
welcome Children's portions Family room Garden Wi-fi
Notes ⊛

The Mistley Thorn ⊛⊛

PICK OF THE PUBS

See Pick of the Pubs on page 212

The White Hart Inn

Swan Ln CM4 9JX ☎ 01277 840478
e-mail: liz@thewhitehart.uk.com
dir: *From A12 junct 15, B1002 to Margaretting. At x-rds
in Margaretting left into Maldon Rd. Under rail bridge,
left. Right into Swan Ln, follow Margaretting Tye signs.
Follow to pub on right*

Parts of this award-winning pub, sitting proudly on a
green known locally as Tigers Island, are 250 years old.
Landlady Liz and her team revel in offering a great choice
of the best regional and local beers and ciders;
much-anticipated July and November beer festivals
testify to the popularity of this approach. The pub's
interior, all matchboarding, old pictures, brewery
memorabilia, dark posts, pillars, beams and fireplaces,
oozes character, while the solidly traditional menu and
specials board shout quality. Start with an Italian meat
platter, and move on to lamb's liver and bacon casserole;
grilled extra mature rib-eye steak; or roasted sea bass
fillets served on couscous.

Open all wk 11.30-3 6-12 (Sat-Sun 12-12) Closed:
25 Dec **Bar Meals** L served Mon-Fri 12-2, Sat 12-2.30,
Sun all day D served Tue-Thu 6.30-9, Fri-Sat 6-9.30
Av main course £8.50 ⊕ FREE HOUSE ◀ Adnams
Southwold Bitter & Broadside, Mighty Oak IPA & Oscar
Wilde Mild, Red Fox Hunter's Gold ♻ Aspall, Black Rat,
Rekorderlig. ♀ 10 **Facilities** ✿ Children welcome
Children's menu Family room Garden Beer festival
Parking Wi-fi (notice required)

The Thatchers Arms **NEW**

Hall Rd CO8 5AT ☎ 01787 227460
e-mail: hello@thatchersarms.co.uk
dir: *From A12 onto A1124 towards Halstead. Right
immediately after Chappel Viaduct. 2m, pub on right*

Built for thirsty 19th-century railway navvies, this
award-winning pub surveys the beautiful Stour Valley.
Today's thirsts are quenched by Crouch Vale, Adnams
and other cask ales, including a mild, and biannual beer
festivals. The traditional British pub menu and daily
specials use locally sourced produce, including
sustainable fish, such as bream, ling, jack mackerel and
witch (Torbay) sole. During the week, £6 light meals
include bangers and mash, devilled kidneys and maybe
balti curry. Sunday roast could be haunch of venison or
leg of Bures hogget. Booking for meals may be required.

Open 12-3 6-11 (Sat-Sun all day) Closed: Mon **Bar
Meals** L served Tue-Sat 12-2.30, Sun 12-8 D served
Tue-Sat 6-9, Sun 12-8 Av main course £9 **Restaurant** L
served Tue-Sat 12-2.30, Sun 12-8 D served Tue-Sat 6-9,
Sun 12-8 Fixed menu price fr £18 Av 3 course à la carte fr
£20 ⊕ FREE HOUSE ◀ Adnams Southwold Bitter, Crouch
Vale Brewers Gold, Guest ales. ♀ 10 **Facilities** ✿ Children
welcome Children's portions Garden Beer festival Parking
Wi-fi (notice required)

PICK OF THE PUBS

The Mistley Thorn ❀❀

MANNINGTREE Map 13 TM13

High St, Mistley CO11 1HE
☎ **01206 392821**
e-mail: info@mistleythorn.co.uk
web: www.mistleythorn.com
dir: *From Ipswich A12 junct 31 onto B1070, follow signs to East Bergholt, Manningtree & Mistley. From Colchester A120 towards Harwich. Left at Horsley Cross. Mistley in 3m*

This former coaching inn was built overlooking the estuary of the River Stour in 1723, which was shortly before the Paymaster General, Richard Rigby, commissioned renowned architect Robert Adam to design a number of buildings, including the Swan Basin opposite, for what was intended to become a fashionable saltwater spa, but which never quite took off. Inside, all the public spaces are light and airy with high ceilings. Co-owner and executive chef Sherri Singleton, who hails from California, also runs the Mistley Kitchen cookery school next door, which suggests she knows what's she's doing. Indeed she does, the two AA Rosettes here adding to the many accolades she has received for her cooking in establishments elsewhere. Outside the Thorn a hanging sign says 'Oysters', a hefty hint of what's in store, those from Mersea Island being available year-round and Colchester natives when in season. With seafood a speciality, menus change daily to reflect

availability: for example, house-cured organic salmon, celeriac remoulade, blini, Avruga caviar and mustard dill sauce to start, might be followed by grilled local silver mullet with chickpeas, roast tomato, spinach and tapenade. And for dessert, chocolat St Émilion with crème fraîche and dark chocolate sauce. All-day Sunday lunch features roast Red Poll beef and other dishes, such as local Sutton Hoo chicken, seafood and interesting vegetarian meals. Real ales come from the Adnams and Mersea Island breweries. From the inn there are views down the estuary, which the Essex Way part-follows between Mistley and the port of Harwich.

Open all wk 12-2.30 6.30-9 (Sat-Sun all day) **Bar Meals** L served Mon-Fri

12-2.30, Sat-Sun all day D served Mon-Fri 6.30-9, Sat 6.30-9.30 Av main course £12.95 **Restaurant** L served Mon-Fri 12-2.30, Sat-Sun all day D served Mon-Fri 6.30-9, Sat 6.30-9.30 Fixed menu price fr £10.95 Av 3 course à la carte fr £22.50 ⊞ FREE HOUSE ◀ Adnams Southwold Bitter, Mersea Island. ♟ 17 **Facilities** Children welcome Children's menu Children's portions 🐾 Parking Wi-fi

MOUNTNESSING   Map 6 TQ69

The George & Dragon NEW

294 Roman Rd CM15 0TZ ☎ 01277 352461
e-mail: enquiry@thegeorgeanddragonbrentwood.co.uk
dir: *In village centre*

Spruced-up in true contemporary gastro-pub style, the interior of this 18th-century former coaching inn successfully blends bold artwork, colourful leather chairs and chunky modern tables with preserved original wooden floors, exposed beams and brick fireplaces. In this relaxed and convivial setting tuck into Mediterranean-inspired British dishes from an extensive menu that should please all tastes and palates. There are sharing platters, salads and pasta dishes, a selection of stone-baked pizzas and main courses like calves' liver with champ and red wine jus; and sea bass with sweet potato and aubergine tagine. Booking for meals may be required.

Open all day all wk **Bar Meals** L served all wk 12-10 D served all wk 12-10 Av main course £12 food served all day **Restaurant** L served all wk 12-2.30 D served all wk 6.30-10 Fixed menu price fr £12.50 Av 3 course à la carte fr £30 ⊕ MITCHELLS & BUTLERS ◼ Fuller's London Pride, Adnams Broadside ♂ Aspall Harry Sparrow. ☗ 21 **Facilities** Children welcome Children's portions Garden Parking ▭ (notice required)

NEWNEY GREEN   Map 6 TL60

The Duck Pub & Dining

CM1 3SF ☎ 01245 421894
e-mail: theduckinn1@btconnect.com
dir: *From Chelmsford take A1060 (Sawbridgeworth). Straight on at mini rdbt, 4th left into Vicarage Rd (signed Roxwell & Willingate), left into Hoe St, becomes Gravelly Ln, left to pub*

This 17th-century inn formed from two agricultural cottages is in the tiny hamlet of Newney Green. Fully restored by the current owners in 2010, the friendly country inn offers up to six real ales and menus that reflect the region's produce. Choose from the extensive menu in the beamed dining room, from classics like Wick's Manor sausages and mash, or haddock and chips, to pork belly with braised red cabbage, and venison cottage pie. There is a garden with children's play area and an August Bank Holiday beer festival.

Open all day Closed: Mon **Bar Meals** L served Tue-Sun 12-9.30 D served Tue-Sun 12-9.30 food served all day **Restaurant** L served Tue-Sun 12-9.30 D served Tue-Sun 12-9.30 food served all day ⊕ FREE HOUSE ◼ Woodforde's Wherry, Adnams Broadside, Sharp's Doom Bar. ☗ 14 **Facilities** Children welcome Children's menu Children's portions Play area Family room Garden Beer festival Parking Wi-fi ▭

NORTH FAMBRIDGE   Map 7 TQ89

The Ferry Boat Inn

Ferry Ln CM3 6LR ☎ 01621 740208
dir: *From Chelmsford take A130 S, then A132 to South Woodham Ferrers, then B1012. Turn right to village*

Popular with yachtsmen, walkers and visitors to the nearby wildlife reserve (Essex Wildlife Trust's 600-acre sanctuary), this 500-year-old weather-boarded free house is tucked away in a lovely village beside the River Crouch and marina. It started out as three fishermen's cottages and is believed to have been an inn for at least 200 years. Low beams and winter fires add character to the bars where tip-top Greene King ales are on tap. Menu choices include traditional pub fare such as baguettes, jacket potatoes and omelettes, plus favourites like steak-and-kidney pie or half a roast duck, chips and salad. Booking for meals may be required.

Open all wk 11.30-3 6.30-11 (Sun 12-4 6.30-10.30 & all day in summer) ⊕ FREE HOUSE ◼ Greene King IPA & Abbot Ale, Morland. **Facilities** Children welcome Children's menu Children's portions Family room Garden Parking

PATTISWICK   Map 13 TL82

The Compasses at Pattiswick

PICK OF THE PUBS

Compasses Rd CM77 8BG ☎ 01376 561322
e-mail: info@thecompassesatpattiswick.co.uk
dir: *A120 from Braintree towards Colchester. After Bradwell 1st left to Pattiswick*

Years ago, two farm workers' cottages were amalgamated to form this friendly pub, still surrounded by the meadows and pocket woodlands of the Holifield Estate. The pub's owners source some of the raw materials for their menu direct from the estate. Support for local producers is at the centre of the pub's ethos, with minimising food miles a guiding principle. Hearty rural recipes and uncomplicated cooking allow the dishes to do the talking. The main menu is supplemented by a daily specials board, allowing the chefs to take full advantage of seasonal produce. The dinner menu might feature toad-in-the-hole; Mediterranean vegetable linguine; and roast mutton shepherd's pie. The wine list is very comprehensive and features some exclusive Bordeaux and Burgundies. A roaring log fire makes a welcoming sight in winter after a local walk, while in summer the large garden is inviting. Families are very well catered for here, with a play area and toy box to keep little diners entertained. Booking for meals may be required.

Open all wk 11-3 5.30-11 (Sat 11-3 5.30-12 Sun 12-4 5.30-9) ⊕ FREE HOUSE ◼ Woodforde's Wherry, Adnams Broadside, St Austell Tribute ♂ Aspall. **Facilities** Children welcome Children's menu Children's portions Play area Garden Parking Wi-fi

PELDON   Map 7 TL91

The Peldon Rose

Colchester Rd CO5 7QJ ☎ 01206 735248
e-mail: enquiries@thepeldonrose.co.uk
dir: *On B1025 Mersea Rd, just before causeway*

With well-kept real ales, a well-sourced wine list, and a well-deserved reputation for good food, this 500-year-old former smugglers' and coaching inn has character in spades. It boasts log fires in the bar in winter, original beams and leaded windows. A conservatory, perfect for summer dining, leads to the garden. The menu changes regularly with the seasons and availability, but a sample offers starters like Chinese five-spiced rabbit, or smoked duck breast with walnut pesto and watercress; mains like chickpea, spinach and aubergine curry; slow-braised lamb shank with pearl barley and root vegetable stew; and traditional beer-battered fish and chips; and afters like spiced apple cake and caramelised orange tart. Booking for meals may be required.

Open all day all wk Closed: 25 Dec **Bar Meals** L served all wk 12-2.30 D served all wk 6.30-9 Av main course £10.95 **Restaurant** L served all wk 12-2.30 D served all wk 6.30-9 Fixed menu price fr £10.95 Av 3 course à la carte fr £16.95 ⊕ FREE HOUSE ◼ Morland Old Speckled Hen, Greene King IPA, Adnams ♂ Aspall. ☗ 15 **Facilities** Children welcome Children's menu Children's portions Garden Parking ▭

STANSTED AIRPORT

See Little Canfield

STOCK   Map 6 TQ69

The Hoop ◉

21 High St CM4 9BD ☎ 01277 841137
e-mail: thehoopstock@yahoo.co.uk
web: www.thehoop.co.uk
dir: *On B1007 between Chelmsford & Billericay*

Every inch the traditional country pub, this 15th-century free house on Stock's village green offers a warm welcome, authentic pub interiors and a pleasing absence of music and fruit machines. There's an emphasis on food here, with menus offering gutsy dishes such as crispy pig's head with apple and celery followed by the chef's beef, mushroom and real ale pie, with baked Alaska for dessert. The annual beer festival (early June) has been going from strength to strength for over

continued

STOCK *continued*

30 years; you'll have over 100 real ales to choose from, not to mention fruit beers, perries and more. Booking for meals may be required.

Open all day all wk 11-11 (Sun 12-10.30) **Bar Meals** L served Mon-Fri 12-2.30, Sat 12-9.30, Sun 12-5 D served Mon-Thu 6-9, Fri 6-9.30, Sat 12-9.30 Av main course £10 **Restaurant** L served Tue-Fri 12-2, Sun 12-3 D served Tue-Sat 6-9 Av 3 course à la carte fr £28 ⊕ FREE HOUSE ◖ Adnams Southwold Bitter, Crouch Vale Brewers Gold, Young's, Guest ales Ὸ Westons. ♀ 12 **Facilities** ✿ Children welcome Children's portions Garden Beer festival Wi-fi

WOODHAM MORTIMER — Map 7 TL80

Hurdlemakers Arms

Post Office Rd CM9 6ST ☎ 01245 225169
e-mail: info@hurdlemakersarms.co.uk
dir: *From Chelmsford A414 to Maldon/Danbury. 4.5m, through Danbury into Woodham Mortimer. Over 1st rdbt, 1st left, pub on left. Behind golf driving range*

A pub since 1837, this 400-year-old listed building in the sleepy village of Woodham Mortimer used to be two cottages. The beamed interior still retains its open log fire and many original features, and ale-lovers will be delighted by the wide range of real ales including Crouch Vale and Wibblers. Home-made specials might include salmon en croûte; roasted duck breast à l'orange; and liver and bacon. There are weekend summer barbecues in the large garden, and a beer festival takes place on the last weekend of June.

Open all day all wk 12-11 (Sun 12-9) **Bar Meals** L served Mon-Fri 12-3, Sat 12-9.30, Sun 12-8 D served Mon-Fri 6-9.30, Sat 12-9.30, Sun 12-8 **Restaurant** L served Mon-Fri 12-3, Sat 12-9.30, Sun 12-8 D served Mon-Fri 6-9.30, Sat 12-9.30, Sun 12-8 ⊕ GRAY & SONS ◖ Greene King Abbot Ale, Mighty Oak, Crouch Vale, Farmers, Wibblers, Guest ales Ὸ Westons Old Rosie & Wyld Wood Organic. ♀ 8 **Facilities** Children welcome Children's menu Children's portions Play area Garden Beer festival Parking Wi-fi 🚌

GLOUCESTERSHIRE

ALDERTON — Map 10 SP03

The Gardeners Arms

Beckford Rd GL20 8NL ☎ 01242 620257
e-mail: gardeners1@btconnect.com
dir: *Telephone for directions*

This charming family-run 16th-century thatched free house has always been a pub. The quiet Cotswolds village of Alderton was created when plague hit nearby Great Washbourne, so villagers moved up the road to a place that wasn't 'cursed'. Today you can play boules in the large beer garden, and traditional bar games in the stone-walled bar. Seasonal local produce underpins the menu, while weekly-changing specials include fresh fish dishes. The pub hosts two five-day beer festivals, one in May and the other at Christmas. Booking for meals may be required.

Open all wk 10-2 5.30-10 (Sun all day, Fri 10-mdnt) ⊕ FREE HOUSE ◖ Sharp's Doom Bar, Butcombe Bitter, Courage Best Bitter, Local guest ales Ὸ Westons Stowford Press. **Facilities** Children welcome Children's menu Children's portions Garden Beer festival Parking Wi-fi

ALMONDSBURY — Map 4 ST68

The Bowl

16 Church Rd BS32 4DT ☎ 01454 612757
e-mail: bowlinn@sabrain.com
dir: *M5 junct 16 towards Thornbury. 3rd left onto Over Ln, 1st right onto Sundays Hill, next right onto Church Rd*

The Bowl nestles on the south-eastern edge of the Severn Vale, hence its name. Part of this pretty, whitewashed building dates from 1147, when monks were building the village church, so it was getting on when it became an inn in 1550. It has an atmospheric interior with exposed stonework and a wood burner for winter warmth. The freshly prepared food includes ham, egg and chips; steak-and-ale pie; beef bourguignon; and goat's cheese and Mediterranean vegetable tart; as well as meats from the grill. To drink, there's Thatchers Gold cider and St Austell Tribute ale.

Open all day all wk **Bar Meals** L served Mon-Thu 12-2.30, Fri-Sat 12-9.30, Sun 12-7.30 D served Mon-Thu 6-9.30 Av main course £8.95 ⊕ BRAINS ◖ Bitter & The Rev. James, St Austell Tribute, Butcombe Ὸ Thatchers Gold. **Facilities** Children welcome Children's menu Children's portions Parking Wi-fi

ARLINGHAM — Map 4 SO71

The Old Passage Inn ★★★★ RR ⊛⊛

PICK OF THE PUBS

Passage Rd GL2 7JR ☎ 01452 740547
e-mail: oldpassage@btconnect.com
dir: *A38 onto B4071 through Arlingham. Through village to river*

Occupying a stunning position on the banks of the River Severn, this seafood restaurant-with-rooms once provided refreshment to ferry passengers across the tidal river but now attracts people from afar for its quality food and air of tranquility. You will still find real ales like Wickwar and Westons Organic cider on tap, but the food and wine is what draws people down to this riverside retreat. Eating in the open and airy dining room, or on the popular riverside terrace in summer is a delight. Dishes may include fish soup with saffron mayonnaise; roast brill with cockles and clams; and hake with tarragon and lemon butter sauce. Carnivores will not be disappointed with roast pork belly with Savoy cabbage and black pudding. Saltwater tanks virtually guarantee that Pembrokeshire or Cornish lobsters will be on the menu – try one grilled with parsley and garlic butter. There are three modern en suite bedrooms here. Booking for meals may be required.

Open 10-3 7-close Closed: 25 Dec, Jan-Feb Tue & Wed eve, Sun eve & Mon **Bar Meals** L served Tue-Sat 12-2, Sun 12-3 D served Tue-Sat 7-9 **Restaurant** L served Tue-Sat 12-2, Sun 12-3 D served Tue-Sat 7-9 Fixed menu price fr £15 Av 3 course à la carte fr £32 ⊕ FREE HOUSE ◖ Wickwar Ὸ Westons Wyld Wood Organic. ♀ 12 **Facilities** Children welcome Children's portions Garden Parking Wi-fi **Rooms** 3

ASHLEWORTH — Map 10 SO82

Boat Inn

The Quay GL19 4HZ ☎ 01452 700272
e-mail: boatinn@hotmail.co.uk
dir: *From Gloucester take A417 towards Ledbury. At Hartpury follow signs for Ashleworth Quay*

This picturesque pub on the banks of the Severn was taken over by a new owner in 2011 after being in the same family for over 400 years. Renowned for its beer festivals and real ales, serving them straight from the barrel, the beers are sourced from smaller, local and regional brewers and are changed frequently. They could include Bristol Beer Factory, Arbor Ales, Gloucester Brewery and Three Tuns Brewery. The pub also has a great selection of ciders supplied by Westons, Oliver's and Hartland Farmhouse from Gloucestershire and Herefordshire. Traditionally filled rolls, perhaps with home-made tomato chutney, form the hub of the simple but delicious food offering, available only at lunchtimes.

Open 11.30-2.30 6.30-11.30 (Fri-Sun 11.30am-mdnt) Closed: Mon & Wed L **Bar Meals** L served Tue, Thu-Sun 12-2 ⊕ FREE HOUSE ◖ Bristol Beer Factory, Arbor, Gloucester, Three Tuns Ὸ Westons, Oliver's, Hartland Farmhouse. **Facilities** Children welcome Garden Beer festival Parking 🚌 **Notes** ⊛

PICK OF THE PUBS

The Village Pub ✿

BARNSLEY   Map 5 SP00

GL7 5EF ☎ 01285 740421
e-mail: reservations@thevillagepub.
co.uk
web: www.thevillagepub.co.uk
dir: *On B4425 4m NE of Cirencester*

The clever marketing that lies behind the name ensures that every time someone says, "Let's go to the village pub", they give it a free plug. Beautifully refurbished by the team behind neighbouring Barnsley House country hotel, it manages to be both the local and a chic pub-restaurant, without becoming just another Cotswold tourist honeypot. Polished flagstones, oak floorboards, exposed timbers and open fireplaces are all there in spades, and the civilised atmosphere continues in each of the five rambling dining rooms, all sporting an eclectic mix of furniture, rug-strewn floors, oil paintings, cosy settles and warm terracotta walls. Modern British pub food draws a discerning dining crowd, with daily menus featuring quality local ingredients, some organic, like the vegetables from the Barnsley House gardens. If you want just a snack (it is the village pub, remember), there's mini chorizo and honey mustard sausages; quail Scotch eggs; spicy chicken wings; and meze with grilled focaccia. Among the restaurant starters are home-made corned beef with piccalilli; creamed

tomatoes on toast; and Upton Smokery sea trout with beetroot, horseradish and spring onions. A good choice of main dishes includes pigeon breast with Jerusalem artichoke, watercress, bacon and a red wine dressing; pan-fried scallops with roast pumpkin purée and sage butter; Badminton venison with roast apple, red cabbage and Anna potatoes; Village Pub pie with creamed potatoes and buttered greens; and wild mushroom tagliatelle with pesto. And then for dessert, maybe sticky toffee pudding with vanilla ice cream, or orange steamed pudding and custard. Half portions are available for 'younger clientele'. Newly refurbished en suite bedrooms are available.

Open all wk 11-11 (Sun 11-10) **Bar Meals** L served Mon-Fri 12-2.30, Sat-Sun 12-3 D served Mon-Thu 6-9.30, Fri-Sat 6-10, Sun 6-9 Av main course £14.95 **Restaurant** Av 3 course à la carte fr £28 🛢 FREE HOUSE ◧ Hook Norton Hooky Bitter, Butcombe, Guest ales Ö Ashton Press. 🍷 10
Facilities Children welcome Children's portions ✿ Garden Parking Wi-fi

ASHLEWORTH *continued*

The Queens Arms

PICK OF THE PUBS

The Village GL19 4HT ☎ 01452 700395
web: www.queensarmsashleworth.co.uk
dir: *From Gloucester N on A417 for 5m. At Hartpury, opp Royal Exchange turn right at Broad St to Ashleworth. Pub 100yds past village green*

Set in a rural village between rolling hills and the River Severn, this is an engaging 16th-century inn. Tony and Gill Burreddu have made alterations over the years but they have left the original beams and iron fireplaces well alone, simply complementing them with comfortable armchairs, antiques and a gallery of local artists' work. With a loyal customer base, the pub has built a reputation for imaginative food made with local produce. The ever-changing menus have featured hog loin steaks marinated in honey and barbecue sauce; mushroom, parsnip and nut terrine; and Bobotie, the South African dish of spicy minced beef topped with a savoury egg custard. From the peaceful garden behind 200-year-old clipped yews, enjoy views of the surrounding hills, in one hand a pint of Timothy Taylor Landlord or a dry white wine; in the other a ping pong ball for amusing Talulah, the pub cat. Booking for meals may be required.

Open 12-3 7-11 Closed: 25-26 Dec & 1 Jan, Sun eve & Mon (ex BH wknds) **Bar Meals** L served Tue-Sun 12-2 D served Tue-Sat 7-9 Av main course £12.95 **Restaurant** L served Tue-Sun 12-2 D served Tue-Sat 7-9 Av 3 course à la carte fr £22.50 ⊕ FREE HOUSE ◀ Timothy Taylor Landlord, Donnington BB, Brains The Rev. James, Shepherd Neame Spitfire, Sharp's Doom Bar Ở Westons Stowford Press. ⬤ 14 **Facilities** Children welcome Garden Parking

BARNSLEY   Map 5 SP00

The Village Pub ◉

PICK OF THE PUBS

See Pick of the Pubs on page 215

BERKELEY   Map 4 ST69

The Malt House ★★★ INN

Marybrook St GL13 9BA ☎ 01453 511177
e-mail: the-malthouse@btconnect.com
web: www.themalthouse.uk.com
dir: *M5 junct 13/14, A38 towards Bristol. Pub on main road towards Sharpness*

Within walking distance of Berkeley Castle and its deer park, this family-run free house with accommodation is also handy for the Edward Jenner Museum, dedicated to the life of the founding father of immunology. Inside the heavily beamed pub you can choose between popular real ales and ciders while selecting home-cooked choices from the menu: the chef's specialities are always popular, and may include sizzling chilli beef; or pork loin with port and plums. Traditional desserts include treacle sponge and jam roly-poly. A skittle alley and function room can be booked.

Open all wk Mon-Thu 4.30-11 (Fri 4.30-12 Sat 12-12 Sun 12-3) **Bar Meals** L served Sat-Sun 12-2 D served Mon-Sat 6.30-8.30 Av main course £9.50 **Restaurant** L served Sat-Sun 12-2 D served Mon-Sat 6.30-8.30 ⊕ FREE HOUSE ◀ Sharp's Doom Bar, Theakston Best Bitter Ở Westons Stowford Press, Thatchers Gold. **Facilities** Children welcome Children's menu Garden Parking Wi-fi ▭ (notice required) **Rooms** 10

BIBURY   Map 5 SP10

Catherine Wheel ★★★★ INN

Arlington GL7 5ND ☎ 01285 740250
e-mail: info@catherinewheel-bibury.co.uk
dir: *On B4425, W of Bibury*

This former blacksmith's has changed hands many times since J Hathaway opened it as an inn in 1856 but a warm welcome, good ales and quality food remain its hallmarks. The beautiful Cotswold-stone building, stable courtyard and orchard date back to the 15th century and plenty of historical features remain. The short but

appetising menu might include seared scallops with crispy duck confit, squash purée and red wine syrup; pot-roasted chicken with truffle mash, smoked bacon, shallots and peas; and king prawn and mussel spaghetti. There is a beer festival held every August Bank Holiday. Booking for meals may be required.

Open all day all wk 9am-11pm **Bar Meals** L served Mon-Fri 12-9.30, Sun 12-9 D served 6-9.30 food served all day **Restaurant** L served Mon-Fri 12-9.30, Sun 12-9 D served 6-9.30 food served all day ⊕ FREE HOUSE/WHITE JAYS LTD ◀ Sharp's Doom Bar, Hook Norton Ở Westons Stowford Press. **Facilities** ♥ Children welcome Children's menu Children's portions Garden Beer festival Parking Wi-fi ▭ **Rooms** 4

BIRDLIP   Map 10 SO91

The Golden Heart

Nettleton Bottom GL4 8LA ☎ 01242 870261
e-mail: info@thegoldenheart.co.uk
dir: *On A417 (Gloucester to Cirencester road). 8m from Cheltenham. Pub at base of dip in Nettleton Bottom*

Enjoy glorious views over the valley from the terraced gardens of this centuries-old Cotswold-stone inn. It probably started life as a drovers' resting place, and retains plenty of original features. The main bar is divided into four cosy areas with log fires and traditional built-in settles. Excellent local ales and ciders are backed by a good selection of wines, while the extensive menus demonstrate commitment to local produce, particularly prize-winning meat from the region's livestock markets and shows. Perhaps try chicken curry, steak sandwich or an omelette with a choice of fillings. Vegetarian, vegan and gluten-free options are available.

Open all wk 11-3 5.30-11 (Fri-Sun & summer holidays open all day) Closed: 25 Dec **Bar Meals** L served Mon-Sat 12-3, Sun all day D served Mon-Sat 6-10, Sun all day **Restaurant** L served Mon-Sat 12-3, Sun all day D served Mon-Sat 12-3, Sun all day ⊕ FREE HOUSE ◀ Otter Bitter, Wickwar Cotswold Way, Wye Valley, Festival Gold Ở Westons, Henney's, Thatchers. ⬤ 10 **Facilities** ♥ Children welcome Family room Garden Parking Wi-fi ▭

BLAISDON   Map 10 SO71

The Red Hart Inn

GL17 0AH ☎ 01452 830477
dir: *Take A40 (NW of Gloucester) towards Ross-on-Wye. At lights left onto A4136 signed Monmouth. Left into Blaisdon Lane to Blaisdon*

A pub with appeal for customers of all ages: say hello to Esmerelda the pig and Spot the dog at this low-ceilinged, beamed village hostelry. In the flagstoned bar with its cosy fire, real ales are taken seriously – four are usually on offer, and real ciders too. Two restaurant areas see the serving of comprehensive menus. Start with whitebait, or crispy potato skins with bacon and cheese; follow with one of the specials – steak, ale and mushroom pie; or penne with chargrilled chicken and pine nuts. If the weather is clement, enjoy the beer garden with barbecue and play area.

Save on hotels. Book at theAA.com/hotel

GLOUCESTERSHIRE 217 **ENGLAND**

Open all wk 12-3 6-11.30 (Sun 12.30-4 7-11) **Bar Meals** L served 12-2.15 D served 6.30-9.30 Av main course £10.95 **Restaurant** L served 12-2.15 D served 6.30-9.30 Av 3 course à la carte fr £25 ⊕ FREE HOUSE ◀ 4 Guest ales ♻ Westons Stowford Press, Traditional & 1st Quality. **Facilities** Children welcome Children's menu Children's portions Play area Garden Parking Wi-fi 🚐

BLEDINGTON   Map 10 SP22

The Kings Head Inn ★★★★ INN ֎

PICK OF THE PUBS

The Green OX7 6XQ ☎ **01608 658365**
e-mail: info@kingsheadinn.net
dir: *On B4450 4m from Stow-on-the-Wold*

Stone-built and dating back to the 15th century, this perfect country retreat facing the village green is the quintessential Cotswold inn. Much of the original structure has survived, leaving sturdy beams, low ceilings, flagstone floors, exposed stone walls, and inglenook fireplace. Archie and Nicola Orr-Ewing have worked hard to earn an excellent reputation built on well-kept real ales, an extensive wine list and wonderful local produce in the kitchen. In the bar, Hook Norton Hooky Bitter is a mainstay, alongside guest ales from local micro-breweries, organic cider, local lagers, over 25 malt whiskies, and eight wines served by the glass. The menu is concise but some of the starters can be served as main courses, so choice is more than ample: asparagus with poached egg and wholegrain mustard might be followed by confit duck leg with crushed potatoes, spring greens, broad beans and pancetta. Sticky ginger cake is one of the popular desserts. Accommodation is available.

Open all wk 11.30-3 6-11 (May-Sep Sat-Sun 11.30-11) Closed: 25-26 Dec **Bar Meals** L served Mon-Fri 12-2, Sat-Sun 12-2.30 D served Sun-Thu 7-9, Fri-Sat 6.30-9.30 **Restaurant** L served Mon-Fri 12-2, Sat-Sun 12-2.30 D served Sun-Thu 7-9, Fri-Sat 6.30-9.30 ⊕ FREE HOUSE ◀ Hook Norton Hooky Bitter, Sharp's Doom Bar, Vale VPA, Wye Valley, Brakspear ♻ Westons Stowford Press. ₹ 8 **Facilities** Children welcome Children's menu Children's portions Garden Parking Wi-fi **Rooms** 12

BOURTON-ON-THE-HILL   Map 10 SP13

Horse and Groom

PICK OF THE PUBS

GL56 9AQ ☎ **01386 700413**
e-mail: greenstocks@horseandgroom.info
dir: *2m W of Moreton-in-Marsh on A44*

The Horse and Groom is a handsome Cotswold-stone, Grade II listed Georgian building that combines a contemporary feel with original period features. Owned and run by the Greenstock brothers, it's both a serious dining pub and a friendly place for a drink. The beer selection mixes local brews and guest ales, and over 20 wines are served by the glass. The blackboard menu changes daily, providing plenty of appeal for even the most regular of diners. With committed local suppliers

backed up by the pub's own vegetable patch, the kitchen has plenty of good produce to work with. A typical menu might feature slow-cooked Moroccan spiced lamb shank with chickpeas, or griddled Longhorn rib-eye steak; and puds such as apple and blueberry flapjack crumble. In summer, head for the mature garden with its panoramic hilltop views. Booking for meals may be required.

Open 11-3 6-11 Closed: 25 Dec, Sun eve **Bar Meals** L served all wk 12-2 D served Mon-Sat 7-9 Av main course £13 **Restaurant** L served all wk 12-2 D served Mon-Sat 7-9 ⊕ FREE HOUSE ◀ Wye Valley Bitter, Purity Pure UBU, Goffs Jouster, Cotswold Wheat Beer, North Cotswold ♻ Hogan's. ₹ 21 **Facilities** Children welcome Children's portions Garden Parking Wi-fi

---

BROCKHAMPTON   Map 10 SP02

Craven Arms Inn

GL54 5XQ ☎ **01242 820410**
e-mail: cravenarms@live.co.uk
dir: *From Cheltenham take A40 towards Gloucester. In Andoversford, at lights, left onto A436 signed Bourton & Stow. Left, follow signs for Brockhampton*

Hidden away at the end of a village driveway a few miles from Cheltenham, this beautiful 16th-century Cotswold inn is full of warmth and character. Landlords Bob and Barbara Price have worked hard to build their trade through well-kept real ales and menus built on high-quality seasonal ingredients. You can cook your own meat or fish at the table on hot grill stones; or choose specials such as whole baked camembert to start, followed by pan-fried duck breast with potato purée and green peppercorn sauce. A beer festival is held in the summer.

Open 12-3 6-11 Closed: Sun eve & Mon **Bar Meals** L served Tue-Sun 12-2.30 D served Tue-Thu 6.30-9, Fri-Sat 6.30-9.30 **Restaurant** L served Tue-Sat 12-2.30, Sun 12.30-3 D served Tue-Thu 6.30-9, Fri-Sat 6.30-9.30 ⊕ FREE HOUSE ◀ Otter, Butcombe ♻ Westons Stowford Press, Ashton Press. ₹ 9 **Facilities** 🐾 Children welcome Children's portions Garden Beer festival Parking Wi-fi 🚐

CHEDWORTH   Map 5 SP01

Hare & Hounds ★★★★ INN ֎

PICK OF THE PUBS

Foss Cross GL54 4NN ☎ **01285 720288**
e-mail: stay@hareandhoundsinn.com
dir: *On A429 (Fosse Way), 6m from Cirencester*

A memorable mix of old-world character and contemporary cuisine (gaining chef-patron Geraldo Ragosa one AA Rosette for the past decade); creepers cling to the sharply-pitched roofline of the 14th-century inn, the old inn sign swings beneath a shady oak, and a string of open fires welcomes ramblers from the countless local walks, visitors to the nearby Roman villa complex or fans of the turf breaking away from Cheltenham's racecourse just a few miles distant. The interior is an eclectic marriage of original features and modern chic;

the ideal foundation for relaxing with a glass of locally brewed Arkell's bitter to accompany the accomplished menu which is strong on seafood dishes with a nod to world cuisine. Grilled fillet of halibut on a bed of mild spiced celeriac, or spiced tofu and grilled haloumi cheese on an oriental vegetable stirfry could be on the regularly updated menu here. In summer eat alfresco in the suntrap garden or stay over in one of the smart and comfortable rooms. Booking for meals may be required.

Open all wk Mon-Sat 11.30-2.30 6-close (Sun 11.30-2.30 7-close) **Bar Meals** L served all wk 12-2.30 D served Mon-Sat 6.30-9.30, Sun 7-9 **Restaurant** L served all wk 12-2.30 D served Mon-Sat 6.30-9.30, Sun 7-9 ⊕ ARKELL'S ◀ 2B, 3B, Moonlight ♻ Westons Stowford Press. ₹ 8 **Facilities** 🐾 Children welcome Children's menu Children's portions Family room Garden Parking Wi-fi 🚐 **Rooms** 10

Seven Tuns

PICK OF THE PUBS

See Pick of the Pubs on page 218

CHELTENHAM   Map 10 SO92

The Gloucester Old Spot

Tewkesbury Rd, Piff's Elm GL51 9SY ☎ **01242 680321**
e-mail: eat@thegloucesteroldspot.co.uk
dir: *On A4019 on outskirts of Cheltenham towards Tewkesbury*

Quarry tile floors, roaring log fires and farmhouse furnishings – The Old Spot ticks all the boxes when it comes to a traditional farming pub. Real ales such as Wye Valley take centre stage at the bar, as do local ciders and perries; there are annual beer and cider festivals, too. The baronial dining room takes its inspiration from the local manor, and game and rare-breed pork make an appearance on a menu that offers crispy ox tongue with black pudding and fried egg; and slow-braised venison and juniper casserole.

Open all day all wk Closed: 25-26 Dec **Bar Meals** L served all wk 12-2 D served Mon-Sat 6-9 Av main course £12.50 **Restaurant** L served Mon-Sat 12-2, Sun all day D served Mon-Sat 6-9 Fixed menu price fr £12.50 Av 3 course à la carte fr £22.50 ⊕ ENTERPRISE INNS ◀ Timothy Taylor Landlord, Purity Mad Goose, Wye Valley HPA ♻ Thatchers, Westons Stowford Press, Black Rat, Gwynt y Ddraig. **Facilities** 🐾 Children welcome Children's menu Children's portions Garden Beer festival Parking Wi-fi 🚐 (notice required)

PICK OF THE PUBS

Seven Tuns

CHEDWORTH Map 5 SP01

Queen St GL54 4AE ☎ 01285 720242
e-mail: theseventuns@clara.co.uk
dir: *Exit A429 at junct to Chedworth.*
Approx halfway between Northleach &
Cirencester, follow signs to pub

Up in Chedworth Woods to the north of
this memorable Cotswold-stone inn is a
large Romano-British villa, during its
heyday in the fourth century home to
some of the richest people in the
country. For many today, this idyllic
country pub is arguably more of a
second home. It has stood here above
the Coln Valley, supposedly the longest
in England, since 1610 and is said to
take its name from its seven chimney
pots, rather than beer casks as you
might expect. Across the road from the
pub, there is a raised terrace with a
stream and a little waterfall, and a path
heads up past pretty cottages to St
Andrew's, the village church. Inside the
pub are the beams, bare floorboards
and stone walls implicitly promised by
the creeper-camouflaged exterior. At
lunchtime order a pint of Young's Bitter,
or one of the nine wines by the glass,
and enjoy something light such as a
ploughman's, or a mixed meat platter.
For something more substantial, try
herb-crusted seasonal fish pie with
mixed salad; home-cured ham with
eggs and home-made chips; or trio of

local sausages with creamy mash and
onion gravy. Typical of an evening meal
in the log-fire-warmed restaurant might
be pan-seared scallops with roasted
tomato salsa; traditional toad-in-the-
hole with rich onion gravy; and
Mediterranean vegetable and tomato
tagliatelle with home-made focaccia. In
the beer garden is a revolving South
African barbecue, a renovated skittle
alley and a newly added boules court.
The pub is renowned for live music
evenings and other events, such as its
Guy Fawkes Night, considered by some
to be the best pub display in the
Cotswolds.

Open all wk 12-3 6-11 (Sat 12-12 Sun
12-10.30; May-Sep all wk all day) **Bar**

Meals L served Mon-Fri 12-2.30, Sat-
Sun 12-3 D served Mon-Sat 6.30-9.30,
Sun 6.30-9 **Restaurant** L served Mon-Fri
12-2.30, Sat-Sun 12-3 D served Mon-
Sat 6.30-9.30, Sun 6.30-9 🛢 YOUNG'S
🍺 Bitter, St Austell Tribute 🍎 Westons
Stowford Press. 🍷 9 **Facilities** Children
welcome Children's menu Children's
portions Family room 🐾 Garden Parking
Wi-fi 🚌

Save on hotels. Book at theAA.com/hotel

GLOUCESTERSHIRE 219 **ENGLAND**

CHELTENHAM *continued*

The Royal Oak Inn

The Burgage, Prestbury GL52 3DL ☎ 01242 522344
e-mail: eat@royal-oak-prestbury.co.uk
dir: *From town centre follow signs for Winchcombe/
Prestbury & Racecourse. In Prestbury follow brown signs
for inn from Tatchley Ln*

On the outskirts of Cheltenham, The Royal Oak is the
closest pub to the town's famous racecourse. Built in the
16th century, the pub was once owned by England cricket
legend Tom Graveney and continues its sporting links to
this day. Hosts Simon and Kate have been here for over a
decade, and pride themselves on their hospitality. Enjoy
well-kept local cask ales, real ciders and delicious food in
the snug, the comfortable dining room or the heated patio
overlooking a pretty beer garden. The menu includes
braised rolled beef in juniper and red wine sauce;
pheasant breast with chestnut, bacon and Savoy
cabbage; or a choice of steaks and market fish. There is a
beer festival at Whitsun and a cider one on August Bank
Holiday. Booking for meals may be required.

Open all day all wk Closed: 25 Dec **Bar Meals** L served
Mon-Sat 12-2, Sun 12-9 Av main course £13.50
Restaurant L served Mon-Sat 12-2, Sun 12-9 D served
Mon-Sat 6.30-9, Sun 12-9 Av 3 course à la carte fr
£24.50 ⊕ ENTERPRISE INNS ◀ Timothy Taylor Landlord,
Purity Mad Goose, Butcombe Bitter Ö Thatchers, Westons
Stowford Press, Black Rat Perry. **Facilities** Children
welcome Children's menu Children's portions Garden
Beer festival Parking Wi-fi

CHIPPING CAMPDEN	Map 10 SP13

The Bakers Arms

Broad Campden GL55 6UR ☎ 01386 840515
e-mail: sally@bakersarmscampden.co.uk
dir: *1m from Chipping Campden*

Tucked away in the chocolate-box village of Broad
Campden, this traditional Cotswold country pub dates
back to the early 1700s. Enjoy one of the real ales in the
welcoming bar, which has exposed stone walls, beams
and a large inglenook fireplace. With your pint of
Donnington BB, order from a menu that includes
ploughman's, warm baguettes and filled giant Yorkshire
puddings, or main courses such as pork steaks cooked in
cider, cream and mushroom sauce, or smoked haddock
bake. There are also patio gardens and a children's play
area.

Open all wk 11.30-2.30 5.30-11 (Fri-Sat 11.30-11 Sun
12-10.30) Closed: 25-26 Dec & 31 Dec eve **Bar Meals** L
served Mon-Fri 12-2, Sat 12-2.30, Sun 12-6 D served
Mon-Sat 6-9 **Restaurant** L served Mon-Fri 12-2, Sat
12-2.30, Sun 12-6 D served Mon-Sat 6-9 ⊕ FREE HOUSE
◀ Stanway Stanney Bitter, Donnington BB, Wickwar
Ö Thatchers Heritage. **Facilities** Children welcome
Children's menu Children's portions Play area Garden
Parking ⊞ (notice required)

Eight Bells

PICK OF THE PUBS

Church St GL55 6JG ☎ 01386 840371
e-mail: neilhargreaves@bellinn.fsnet.co.uk
web: www.eightbellsinn.co.uk
dir: *In town centre*

Originally built in the 14th century to house the
stonemasons who constructed nearby St James' church,
this lovely inn was rebuilt in the 17th century and was
used to store the peel of eight bells that were hung in the
church tower. The cobbled entranceway leads into two
atmospheric beamed bars with open fireplaces and, in
the floor of one, a surviving priest's hole; outside is an
enclosed courtyard and terraced garden overlooking the
almshouses and church. Enjoy the Hook Norton and Purity
real ales and freshly prepared, locally sourced, seasonal
dishes, such as spicy meatballs and spaghetti; chicken
liver parfait; supreme of chicken wrapped in Parma ham;
roasted butternut squash and tomato risotto; and
toad-in-the-hole. Home-made puddings tempt with
chocolate crème brûlée; apple and cinnamon sponge
pudding served with custard; and lemon posset with a
red berry coulis and shortbread. Specials, a prix-fixe
menu and a children's menu are also available.

Open all day all wk 12-11 (Sun 12-10.30) Closed: 25 Dec
Bar Meals L served Mon-Thu 12-2, Fri-Sun 12-2.30
D served Mon-Thu 6.30-9, Fri-Sat 6.30-9.30, Sun
6.30-8.45 **Restaurant** L served Mon-Thu 12-2, Fri-Sun
12-2.30 D served Mon-Thu 6.30-9, Fri-Sat 6.30-9.30, Sun
6.30-8.45 ⊕ FREE HOUSE ◀ Hook Norton Hooky Bitter,
Purity Pure UBU & Gold, Goffs Jouster, Wye Valley HPA
Ö Westons Old Rosie, Perry & Stowford Press. ₹ 8
Facilities Children welcome Children's menu Children's
portions Garden Wi-fi ⊞

The Kings ★★★★ RR ⑧⑧

PICK OF THE PUBS

The Square GL55 6AW ☎ 01386 840256
e-mail: info@kingscampden.co.uk
dir: *Telephone for directions*

A lovely old townhouse facing the square of one of
England's prettiest towns. Sympathetically restored, yet
packed with character, the oldest parts include the
16th-century stone mullioned windows on the first floor.
The bar offers at least two real ales, including local Hook
Norton, as well as daily papers and traditional pub
games, but no noisy gaming machines. Bar snacks
include a good range of sandwiches and baguettes, while
main meals are served in the informal bar brasserie or
more formal two AA-Rosette restaurant overlooking the
square. The packed menu offers some imaginative
delights: tian of Salcombe crab with cherry tomatoes and
herb crème fraîche; braised shank of Lighthorne lamb
with dauphinoise potatoes, roast root vegetables and
rosemary sauce; and risotto of the day. The large grassed
garden and dining terrace is good to find in a town-centre
pub. Individually decorated bedrooms offer period
features with plenty of modern comforts. Booking for
meals may be required.

Open all day all wk 7am-11pm (Sat-Sun 8am-11pm)
⊕ FREE HOUSE ◀ Hook Norton Hooky Bitter Ö Thatchers
Gold. **Facilities** Children welcome Children's menu
Children's portions Garden Parking Wi-fi **Rooms** 19

Noel Arms Hotel ★★★ HL

PICK OF THE PUBS

See Pick of the Pubs on page 220

Seagrave Arms ★★★★ INN ⑧

PICK OF THE PUBS

See Pick of the Pubs on page 221

PICK OF THE PUBS

Noel Arms Hotel ★★★HL

CHIPPING CAMPDEN Map 10 SP13

High St GL55 6AT ☎ 01386 840317
e-mail: reception@noelarmshotel.com
web: www.noelarmshotel.com
dir: *On High St, opposite Town Hall*

If you are of a mind to visit Stratford and watch one of the bard's plays, and if a night or two in a luxury hotel suits your style, then look no further than the Noel Arms. Perhaps gardens are your passion – there are several in the area, including Hidcote Manor Gardens, Kiftsgate Court Gardens and Mill Dene Garden. Whatever your excuse, the Noel Arms is one of the oldest hotels in the Cotswolds. Here traditional appeal has been successfully preserved and interwoven seamlessly with contemporary comforts. Charles II reputedly stayed in this golden Cotswold-stone 16th-century coaching inn. It was through the carriage arch that packhorse trains used to carry bales of wool, the source of Chipping Campden's prosperity, to Bristol and Southampton. Absorb these details of the hotel's history while sipping a pint of Hook Norton in front of the log fire in Dover's Bar; read the papers over a coffee and pastry in the coffee shop; and enjoy brasserie-style food in the restaurant, prepared with local ingredients – some unique to the surrounding area. Start with a pressed terrine of smoked ham hock or a Caesar

salad. A half-pound beefburger embracing gently spiced beef, smoked Wensleydale cheese and bacon is served with triple-cooked chips and onion confit. Lighter main courses can be found in fish from the market; or pot-roasted Madgett's Farm chicken breast with thyme potato gratin. To conclude, a strawberry Eton Mess is among the classic puddings. An alternative to these modern English dishes is brought by Indunil, the hotel's award-winning chef. He creates his trademark curries daily, and loyal enthusiasts arrive for his celebrated Curry Club on the last Thursday evening of every month. Replete, you can retire to bed in a four-poster made in 1657.

Open all day all wk **Bar Meals** L served all wk 12-3 D served all wk 6-9.30 **Restaurant** L served all wk 12-3 D served all wk 6-9.30 ⊕ FREE HOUSE ◄ Hook Norton Hooky Bitter, Wye Valley Butty Bach, Purity Gold & Pure UBU, Guinness Ö Westons Stowford Press. ♟ **Facilities** Children welcome Children's menu Children's portions ✿ Garden Parking Wi-fi ➠ **Rooms** 28

Save on hotels. Book at **theAA.com/hotel**

GLOUCESTERSHIRE 221 **ENGLAND**

PICK OF THE PUBS

Seagrave Arms ★★★★ INN ✿

CHIPPING CAMPDEN   Map 10 SP13

Friday St, Weston Subedge GL55 6QH
☎ **01386 840192**
e-mail: info@seagravearms.co.uk
web: www.seagravearms.co.uk
dir: *From Moreton-in-Marsh take A44*
towards Evesham. 7m, right onto B4081
to Chipping Campden. Left at junct with
High St. 0.5m, straight on at x-rds to
Weston Subedge. Left at T-junct

A Grade II listed Georgian Cotswold house
that has been sympathetically restored to
retain many of its original features, the
Seagrave Arms offers open log fires in
winter and a sheltered courtyard for
alfresco dining in the summer. Set in a
delectable honey-stoned village between
the verdant Vale of Evesham and the
golden scarp of the Cotswolds, it's
perfectly located for exploring the
surrounding area; Stately Broadway Tower
is on the horizon, the delights of Hidcote
Manor and Garden are just a short
distance away, and the remarkable,
eccentric collections at Snowshill are
similarly handy. Touring visitors are
equally captivated by the inn's luxurious
accommodation. At the bar, outstanding
beers from Purity and Cotswold breweries
slake the thirst of locals and ramblers
diverting from the nearby Cotswold Way
footpath. With the bountiful foodstuffs of
the Cotswolds to choose from, the
proprietors revel in selecting the best local
produce to satisfy their restaurant's hard-
won one-AA Rosette status. You could
start with slow-cooked pork belly with
carrots, cumin purée and apple salad,
followed perhaps by venison bourguignon
with smoked bacon, mushrooms and baby
onions. Local fish and seafood make
regular appearances – perhaps grilled
Cornish herring with white bean stew and
shellfish sauce, or seared Cornish scallops
with black pudding and cauliflower purée.
For vegetarians there might be butternut
squash and sage risotto with crème
fraîche and parmesan shavings, followed
by gnocchi with roast tomato and basil
sauce, rocket and parmesan. Desserts
offer a playful take on classics such as
apple and cinnamon crumble with cream
and apple fizz, or banana cake with salt
caramel, rum and raisin ice cream and
peanut crumble. Alternatively you could
finish with a selection of cheeses from
nearby villages. Wash it down with a
sprightly Gloucestershire wine from Three
Choirs Vineyard. Booking for meals may be
required.

Open all day Closed: Mon **Bar Meals** Av
main course £14 food served all day
Restaurant L served Tue-Sun 12-3 D
served Tue-Sun 6-9.15 Fixed menu price
fr £15 Av 3 course à la carte fr £26
⊞ FREE HOUSE ◄ Hook Norton,
Cotswold, Purity ♂ Westons Stowford
Press. ♟ 13 **Facilities** Children welcome
Children's portions ❤ Garden Parking
Wi-fi **Rooms** 6

CHIPPING CAMPDEN *continued*

The Volunteer Inn

Lower High St GL55 6DY ☎ 01386 840688
e-mail: info@thevolunteerinn.net
web: www.thevolunteerinn.net
dir: *From Shipston on Stour take B4035 to Chipping Campden*

The Cotswold Way passes the front door of this 300-year-old inn set in the heart of Chipping Campden. In the mid-19th century this was where the able-bodies used to sign up for the militia, hence its name. Walkers and visitors to this charming small town will find log fires, Hook Norton ales and traditional pub dishes in the bar, and a pan-Asian menu in the Maharaja Restaurant – tandoori lamb chops and coriander chicken, for example. There's a peaceful beer garden for summer drinking. Booking for meals may be required.

Open all wk Mon-Thu 3-12 (Fri-Sun 11am-late) **Bar Meals** Av main course £9 **Restaurant** D served all wk 5-10.30 ⊕ FREE HOUSE ◀ Wychwood Hobgoblin, Volunteer Ale, Hook Norton. **Facilities** Children welcome Children's portions Play area Family room Garden 🚐

CIRENCESTER   **Map 5 SP00**

The Crown of Crucis ★★★ HL

PICK OF THE PUBS

Ampney Crucis GL7 5RS ☎ 01285 851806
e-mail: reception@thecrownofcrucis.co.uk
dir: *On A417 to Lechlade, 2m E of Cirencester*

This 16th-century former coaching inn stands beside Ampney Brook in the heart of the Cotswolds, and the quiet stream meandering past the lawns creates a perfect picture of quintessential rural England. Overlooking the village cricket green, the building retains its historical charm while feeling comfortably up-to-date. The name 'Crucis' refers to the Latin cross in the nearby churchyard. With its traditional beams, log fires and

warm, friendly atmosphere, the busy bar offers a large selection of draught and real ales, including their own Crown Bitter, and a choice of wines by the glass. Bar food is served all day and ranges from sandwiches, salads and pastas, to dishes from the grill and stove: Old Spot pork chop with caramelised apple and thyme mash in cider jus; sizzling fajitas with a choice of fillings; Thai chicken curry and steamed rice; steak and mushroom pie with peas and chips. The restaurant offers a fine dining menu. Booking for meals may be required.

Open all day all wk 8am-11pm Closed: 25 Dec **Bar Meals** L served all wk 12-5 D served all wk 5-10 food served all day **Restaurant** D served all wk 7-9 ⊕ FREE HOUSE ◀ Crown Bitter, Sharp's Doom Bar & Seasonal ales, Wickwar ♂ Westons Stowford Press. ♟ 17 **Facilities** 🐾 Children welcome Children's menu Garden Parking 🚐 (notice required) **Rooms** 25

The Fleece at Cirencester ★★★★★ INN **NEW**

41 Market Place GL7 2NZ ☎ 01285 658507
e-mail: relax@fleecehotel.co.uk
web: www.thefleececirencester.co.uk
dir: *In centre of Cirencester*

In the heart of Cirencester's market place, this 16th-century building is reputed to be where Charles II disguised himself as a manservant when in hiding. The bar, restaurant and lounge were completely refurbished early in 2012 but The Fleece's charms have been retained. Settle by one of the log fires with a pint of award-winning Thwaites ales, and select from the menu that mixes traditional with modern brasserie style. The head chef is French, which explains why the 'plats du jour' include mouth-watering cassoulet de Toulouse; moules frites; and confit de canard with Puy lentils, to name but three.

Open all day all wk **Bar Meals** L served all wk 12-6 D served Mon-Sat 6-9.30, Sun 6-8.30 Av main course £10 food served all day **Restaurant** L served all wk 12-6 D served Mon-Sat 6-9.30, Sun 6-8.30 Av 3 course à la

carte fr £20 food served all day ⊕ THWAITES ◀ Wainwright, Guest ales ♂ Kingstone Press. ♟ 9 **Facilities** Children welcome Children's menu Children's portions Garden Parking Wi-fi 🚐 (notice required) **Rooms** 28

See advert on opposite page

CLEARWELL   **Map 4 SO50**

The Wyndham Arms ★★★ HL ⊛

The Cross GL16 8JT ☎ 01594 833666
e-mail: dine@thewyndhamhotel.co.uk
dir: *M4 junct 21 onto M48 for Chepstow. Exit at junct 2 signed A48/Chepstow. At rdbt take A48 towards Gloucester. Take B4228 to Coleford & The Forest of Dean. 10m, through St Briavels, in 2m Clearwell signed on left*

With cosy open fires and oak floors, The Wyndham Arms is the perfect place to enjoy a pint of Humpty's Fuddle brewed by Kingstone Brewery at nearby Tintern. The exciting menu of British dishes, served in the stone-walled Old Spot restaurant, might include the likes of local pheasant filled with game mousse, and twists on old favourites like the Wyndham-reared pork burger on a toasted muffin with smoked tomato relish. Situated between the beautiful Wye Valley and the Royal Forest of Dean, The Wyndham Arms offers the closest accommodation to Clearwell Castle, a popular wedding venue.

Open all day all wk Closed: early Jan **Bar Meals** L served Mon-Sat 12-2, Sun 12-2.30 D served all wk 6.30-9 Av main course £12 **Restaurant** L served Mon-Sat 12-2, Sun 12-2.30 D served all wk 6.30-9 Av 3 course à la carte fr £20 ⊕ FREE HOUSE ◀ Kingstone Humpty's Fuddle IPA ♂ Severn. ♟ 10 **Facilities** 🐾 Children welcome Children's menu Children's portions Parking Wi-fi **Rooms** 18

CLEEVE HILL   **Map 10 SO92**

The Rising Sun ★★★ INN

GL52 3PX ☎ 01242 676281
e-mail: 9210@greeneking.co.uk
dir: *On B4632, 4m N of Cheltenham*

On a clear day you can see south Wales from this Victorian hotel on Cleeve Hill, which also boasts views across Cheltenham and the Malverns. Whether you are staying overnight or just popping in to relax, settle in the nicely modernised bar or, in summer, out in the garden, which is well furnished with trestle tables and benches. Food ranges from sandwiches and wraps to traditional English favourites served both at lunch and dinner, including a choice of Black Angus steaks, gourmet burgers and classics like chicken and mushroom pie.

Open all day all wk **Bar Meals** food served all day **Restaurant** food served all day ⊕ GREENE KING ◀ IPA, Abbot Ale ♂ Aspall. ♟ 15 **Facilities** Children welcome Children's menu Children's portions Family room Garden Parking Wi-fi 🚐 (notice required) **Rooms** 24

CLIFFORD'S MESNE — Map 10 SO72

The Yew Tree

PICK OF THE PUBS

See Pick of the Pubs on page 224

COATES — Map 4 SO90

The Tunnel House Inn

PICK OF THE PUBS

See Pick of the Pubs on page 225

COLESBOURNE — Map 10 SP01

The Colesbourne Inn

PICK OF THE PUBS

GL53 9NP ☎ 01242 870376
e-mail: colesbourneinn@wadworth.co.uk
dir: *Midway between Cirencester & Cheltenham on A435*

North of Cirencester in a picturesque Cotswold Valley, this handsome, stone-built inn is just a short meadow walk from the source of the Thames. It sits in two acres of grounds, which include a fine terrace and garden where you can sit with a pint of Wadworth 6X and savour the glorious country views. Dating back to 1827, the inn has been sympathetically restored and oozes historic charm and character in its bar and dining area, where you'll find original beams and roaring log fires aplenty. The seasonal menus combine traditional pub classics, including fish and chips with beer-batter and mushy peas, and honey- and mustard-glazed Cotswold ham with free-range egg and chips, with modern ideas, perhaps confit duck leg with orange, pomegranate and ginger jus; a natural smoked haddock and spring onion fishcake with creamed vegetables and fries; or roasted pumpkin curry with basmati rice and a naan bread.

Open all day all wk **Bar Meals** L served all wk 12-2.30 D served Mon-Sat 6-9.30, Sun 6-9 **Restaurant** L served all wk 12-2.30 D served Mon-Sat 6-9.30, Sun 6-9 ⊞ WADWORTH ◀ 6X, Henry's Original IPA, Horizon Ö Westons Stowford Press. ♟ 20 **Facilities** Children welcome Children's portions Garden Parking Wi-fi ⛟ (notice required)

COLN ST ALDWYNS — Map 5 SP10

The New Inn At Coln ★★★★★ INN ◉◉

PICK OF THE PUBS

GL7 5AN ☎ 01285 750651
e-mail: info@thenewinnatcoln.co.uk
dir: *Between Bibury (B4425) & Fairford (A417), 8m E of Cirencester*

Take a sleepy Cotswold village, a handsome Elizabethan coaching inn with a picture-postcard frontage of flower baskets and ivy, and a stone-walled, beamed interior with open fires. Result: The New Inn. In the Courtyard Bar the beer pumps dispense local Old Hooky and the house Old King Coln, while in the intimate, red-walled dining room the wine list is suitably global. Modern British cooking depends on fresh, high-quality ingredients, thus, in the bar try a deli-board of Bibury smoked trout, smoked salmon, prawns and rollmops; a ham salad and English mustard sandwich; or ale-battered fish, chips and mushy peas. At dinner, perhaps chicken liver parfait, red onion marmalade and toasted brioche; followed by mixed seafood linguine and creamy saffron mascarpone sauce; then rhubarb and apple crumble with vanilla ice cream. Eat on the terrace, if you wish. Individually designed bedrooms look out over the village, water meadows or terrace.

Open all day all wk 11-11 **Bar Meals** L served all wk 12.30-3 D served all wk 7-9 **Restaurant** L served all wk 12.30-3 D served all wk 7-9 ⊞ FREE HOUSE ◀ Hook Norton Old Hooky, Old King Coln. **Facilities** ♣ Children welcome Children's menu Children's portions Play area Garden Parking Wi-fi ⛟ **Rooms** 14

COWLEY — Map 10 SO91

The Green Dragon Inn ★★★★ INN

PICK OF THE PUBS

See Pick of the Pubs on page 226

CRANHAM — Map 10 SO81

The Black Horse Inn

GL4 8HP ☎ 01452 812217
dir: *A46 towards Stroud, follow signs for Cranham*

Near the Cotswold Way and the Benedictine Prinknash Abbey, in a small village surrounded by woodland and commons, this inn is popular with walkers, the cricket team and visiting Morris dancers. Mostly home-cooked traditional pub food includes cottage pie; roast pork, beef or turkey; kleftiko (half-shoulder of slow-cooked lamb in red wine, lemon and herbs); haggis and bacon; and roast vegetable, cranberry and goat's cheese nut roast. Among the real ales are Butcombe, Sharp's and Otter, and there are good ciders too in the cosy, open-fire-warmed bar.

Open 12-2 6.30-11 (Sun 12-2 8.30-11) Closed: 25 Dec, Mon (ex BH L) **Bar Meals** L served Tue-Sun 12-2 D served Tue-Sat 6.30-9 Av main course £10 ⊞ FREE HOUSE ◀ Sharp's Doom Bar, Otter, Butcombe, Guest ales Ö Thatchers Gold, Westons Stowford Press & Country Perry. ♟ 9 **Facilities** ♣ Children welcome Children's portions Garden Parking

PICK OF THE PUBS

The Yew Tree

CLIFFORD'S MESNE   Map 10 SO72

GL18 1JS ☎ **01531 820719**
e-mail: unwind@yewtreeinn.com
web: www.yewtreeinn.com
dir: *From Newent High Street follow
signs to Clifford's Mesne. Pub at far end
of village on road to Glasshouse*

Finding this welcoming pub may prove
tricky. It's up a little lane on the slopes
of the National Trust's May Hill,
Gloucestershire's highest point, from
where you can see the Welsh mountains,
the Malvern Hills and the River Severn.
The hill is capped by a clump of pine
trees planted in 1887 to commemorate
Queen Victoria's Golden Jubilee.
Formerly a cider press, the pub has a
quarry-tiled floor and winter log fires,
and offers a good choice of local real
ales from breweries like Wye Valley and
Cotswold Spring, and ciders from Lyne
Down and Swallowfield; these and many
more feature in the annual October beer
festival here. As for the food, the
emphasis is on tasty home cooking
using seasonal local produce, with
daily-changing menus and specials.
You can make your selection while
snacking on nibbles like olives, tapas
and pork crackling sticks with warm
apple sauce. Starters could include
carrot and coriander soup, and potted
stilton with toast. For a main course,
think about chargrilled Gloucester Old
Spot loin steaks with chilli and ginger
butter, hand-cut chips and roast

tomatoes; grilled sea bass fillet with
chervil beurre blanc and black olive
mash; or spicy Mexican black bean and
squash galette. Home-made desserts
recognise traditional favourites — ginger
pudding with chocolate fudge sauce;
lemon meringue pie; and bread pudding
and custard, to name just three. The
Yew Tree has its own wine shop, which
contains a diverse selection of
provincial wines, all available in the bar
(for a small mark up), plus a dozen
wines available by the glass or pichet.
While in the area visit the nearby
National Birds of Prey Centre, noted for
its flying displays. Booking for meals
may be required.

Open 12-2.30 6-11 (Sun 12-5) Closed:
Mon, Tue L, Sun eve **Bar Meals** L served

Wed-Sat 12-2 D served Tue-Sat 6-9 Av
main course £14 ⊕ FREE HOUSE ◀ Wye
Valley HPA, Cotswold Spring Stunner,
Sharp's Own, Gloucester Mariner, Local
ales ♂ Westons Stowford Press, Lyne
Down, Severn Cider & Perry,
Swallowfield Cider & Perry. ♟ 12
Facilities Children welcome Children's
menu Children's portions Play area 🐾
Garden Beer festival Parking Wi-fi

PICK OF THE PUBS

The Tunnel House Inn

COATES   Map 4 SO90

Tarlton Rd GL7 6PW ☎ 01285 770280
e-mail: info@tunnelhouse.com
web: www.tunnelhouse.com
dir: *A433 from Cirencester towards*
Tetbury, 2m, right towards Coates,
follow brown inn signs

Down an unmade track, this rural inn
was built for the navvies who spent five
years constructing the two-mile long
Sapperton Tunnel on the now-disused
Thames and Severn Canal. The inn
overlooks the entrance to the tunnel
which hasn't been navigated by a barge
since 1911. Three winter log fires warm
the curio-filled bar, where oddities
include an upside-down table
suspended from the ceiling. Food, all
home cooked, is served every day from
noon onwards and you may eat in the
bar or restaurant, starting perhaps with
pheasant, lardons and plum mixed leaf
salad with redcurrant and balsamic
reduction; or potted salt beef served
with toasted brioche, pickled onions and
gherkins. A typical spring menu might
offer main courses of goat's cheese-
and thyme-stuffed chicken breast,
wrapped in smoked bacon, with creamy
red pesto linguine; baked smoked
haddock stuffed with spinach and pine
nuts on a bed of lemon and thyme
risotto; and wild mushroom, leek and
blue cheese puff pastry pie with sweet
potato wedges and parsnip crisps.
Apple and red berry crumble with crème

anglaise may appear on the desserts
list, while Cotswold ice creams almost
certainly will. At lunchtime eat more
simply with a hot panini stuffed with
Cajun chicken and mozzarella; a mature
cheddar or stilton ploughman's; or
Wiltshire honey-roast ham with two
eggs, coleslaw and mixed leaves. The
garden is tailor-made for relaxing with a
pint of one of the mostly local real ales
– typically from Uley, Wye Valley and
Hook Norton breweries – or a Somerset
or Herefordshire real cider, while
enjoying the views over the fields. A beer
festival in July, a children's play area
and delightful walks in the surrounding
countryside – the Thames rises about a
mile away – add to the pub's popularity.

Open all day all wk noon-late **Bar
Meals** L served 12-9.30 D served
12-9.30 food served all day **Restaurant**
food served all day ⊕ FREE HOUSE
◖ Uley Old Spot & Bitter, Wye Valley
Bitter, Stroud Budding Pale Ale, Hook
Norton, Butcombe Ŏ Healey's Cornish
Rattler, Black Rat, Westons Wyld Wood
Organic. ♟ 9 **Facilities** Children
welcome Children's menu Children's
portions Play area Family room Garden
Beer festival Parking Wi-fi 🚌

PICK OF THE PUBS

The Green Dragon Inn ★★★★INN

COWLEY   Map 10 SO91

Cockleford GL53 9NW
☎ 01242 870271
e-mail: green-dragon@buccaneer.co.uk
web: www.green-dragon-inn.co.uk
dir: *Telephone for directions*

Although recorded as an inn in 1675, it was 1710 before Robert Jones, a churchwarden, became the first landlord, splitting his time between pew and pump for the next 31 years. Behind the rose-and creeper-covered Cotswold-stone façade is the stone-flagged Mouse Bar, where each piece of English oak furniture features a carved mouse, the trademark of Robert Thompson, the Mouseman of Kilburn. He died in 1955, but North Yorkshire craftsmen continue the tradition. There's even one of the little beggars running along the edge of the bar in front of the Butcombe, Hook Norton and Directors beer pumps. Lunch could be a light meal of chilli con carne with basmati rice; or maybe fillet of haddock in lemon batter with fries and mushy peas; or yet again, simply a sandwich (except on Sundays), perhaps filled with Mediterranean vegetable, rocket and goat's cheese; or Cajun chicken and balsamic focaccia. Evening starters include Thai-marinated king prawns with pineapple and watermelon salsa; and duck leg confit with celeriac crisps and parsnip purée. To follow could come grilled sea bass fillet served with chorizo, new potatoes and wilted spinach; slow-cooked belly pork in honey with black pudding, mash, glazed Bramley apples and cider mustard sauce; or sweet potato and parsnip lasagne accompanied by cranberries and mild pesto sauce. In summer the secluded patio garden overlooking a lake is an obvious spot to head for. With comfortable, AA-listed and individually furnished bedrooms, all en suite, or the St George's Suite, which has its own sitting room overlooking Cowley lakes, The Green Dragon is an ideal base for exploring the Cotswolds. One could start by heading for the local Miserden Gardens and Chedworth Roman Villa. Booking for meals may be required.

Open all day all wk Closed: 25 Dec eve & 1 Jan eve **Bar Meals** L served Mon-Fri

12-2.30, Sat 12-3, Sun 12-3.30 D served all wk 6-10 Av main course £15 **Restaurant** L served Mon-Fri 12-2.30, Sat 12-3, Sun 12-3.30 D served all wk 6-10 ⊞ FREE HOUSE/ BUCCANEER ◄ Courage Directors, Hook Norton, Butcombe, Guest ale Ŏ Westons Stowford Press. **Facilities** Children welcome Children's menu Garden Parking Wi-fi 🚌 **Rooms** 9

Save on hotels. Book at **theAA.com/hotel**

GLOUCESTERSHIRE 227 **ENGLAND**

DURSLEY Map 4 ST79

The Old Spot Inn

PICK OF THE PUBS

Hill Rd GL11 4JQ ☎ 01453 542870
e-mail: steveoldspot@hotmail.co.uk
dir: *From Tetbury on A4135 (or Uley on B4066) into Dursley, round Town Hall. Straight on at lights towards bus station, pub behind bus station. From Cam to lights in Dursley immediately prior to pedestrianised street. Right towards bus station*

This classic 18th-century free house is a former real ale pub of the year, so it's worth visiting to sample the regularly changing, tip-top real ales on handpump and to savour the cheerful buzzing atmosphere, as The Old Spot is a cracking community local. It sits smack on the Cotswold Way and was once three terraced farm cottages known as 'pig row.' It's apt, then that it should take its name from the Gloucestershire Old Spot pig. As well as organising three real ale festivals a year, landlord Steve Herbert organises a host of events, including brewery visits, cricket matches and celebrity chef nights. Devoid of modern-day intrusions, the rustic and traditional low-beamed bars are havens of peace, with just the comforting sound of crackling log fires and the hubbub of chatting locals filling the rambling little rooms. Food is wholesome and home-made, ranging from ploughman's lunches and doorstep sandwiches to a pork and apple burger; haddock and chive fishcakes; or chicken fajitas. Puddings include treacle tart and white chocolate cheesecake. There's also a pretty garden for summer alfresco sipping. Booking for meals may be required.

Open all day all wk 11-11 (Sun 12-11) **Bar Meals** L served all wk 12-3 D served Mon only 6-9 **Restaurant** L served all wk 12-3 D served Mon only 6-9 ⊕ FREE HOUSE ◀ Old Ric, Session, Guest ales ♻ Westons 1st Quality. 🍷 8 **Facilities** Children welcome Children's portions Family room Garden Beer festival Parking Wi-fi 🚌

EBRINGTON Map 10 SP14

The Ebrington Arms ★★★★ INN ◉◉

PICK OF THE PUBS

See Pick of the Pubs on page 228

EWEN Map 4 SU09

The Wild Duck ★★★★ INN

GL7 6BY ☎ 01285 770310
e-mail: duckreservations@aol.com
web: www.thewildduckinn.co.uk
dir: *From Cirencester take A429 towards Malmesbury. At Kemble left to Ewen. Inn in village centre*

Children and canine companions are welcome at this inn, built from honeyed Cotswold stone in 1563; the source of the Thames and the Cotswold Water Park are near by. Family-owned for more than 20 years, the pub has oil portraits, log fires, oak beams and a resident ghost. Deep red walls give the Post Horn bar a warm feel, as does the extensive choice of real ales. The rambling restaurant has a lunch menu of wholesome pub favourites, while dinner may extend to wild duck antipasto, followed by luxury fish bouillabaisse. Booking for meals may be required.

Open all day all wk Closed: 25 Dec (eve) **Bar Meals** L served Mon-Fri 12-2, Sat-Sun all day D served all wk 6.30-10 Av main course £15 **Restaurant** L served Mon-Fri 12-2, Sat-Sun all day D served all wk 6.30-10 Av 3 course à la carte fr £30 ⊕ FREE HOUSE ◀ The Wild Duck Duckpond Bitter, Butcombe Bitter, Wye Valley Dorothy Goodbody's Country Ale, Greene King Abbot Ale, Morland Old Speckled Hen, Bath Gem ♻ Ashton Press, Westons Stowford Press, Aspall. 🍷 32 **Facilities** ♣ Children welcome Children's menu Children's portions Garden Parking Wi-fi 🚌 **Rooms** 12

FORD Map 10 SP02

The Plough Inn ★★★★ INN

PICK OF THE PUBS

GL54 5RU ☎ 01386 584215
e-mail: info@theploughinnatford.co.uk
dir: *4m from Stow-on-the-Wold on B4077 towards Tewkesbury*

All manner of horse racing folk are to be found in the bar at this 16th-century inn, which is just across the street from the famous Jackdaws Castle racing stables and a short drive from Cheltenham racecourse. The interior décor celebrates the pub's love of all things racing; so committed is landlord Craig Brown that he rode as a novice at Aintree

on Grand National day in 2009. If you want to stay over after a day at the races, there are bedrooms situated in a restored stable block, adjacent to the large beer garden. This is a traditional English pub, with flagstone floors and log fires, sturdy pine furnishings, and remnants of the stocks that once held convicted sheep-stealers. Excellent Donnington Ales served in the bar are made from water drawn from a spring next to the brewery and hops that travel only from neighbouring Worcestershire. Meals are cooked to order from the best of local produce and typically include Asian duck salad with spring onions, sesame and soy sauce; home-made creamy fish pie topped with cheesy mashed potato; or pan-fried strips of beef with mushrooms in a black peppercorn sauce with saffron rice.

Open all wk Closed: 25 Dec **Bar Meals** L served Mon-Fri 10-2, Sat-Sun all day D served Mon-Fri 6-9, Sat-Sun all day **Restaurant** L served Mon-Fri 10-2, Sat-Sun all day D served Mon-Fri 6-9, Sat-Sun all day ⊕ DONNINGTON ◀ BB, SBA, XXX ♻ Westons Stowford Press. **Facilities** Children welcome Play area Garden Parking 🚌 **Rooms** 3

FOSSEBRIDGE Map 5 SP01

The Inn at Fossebridge ★★★★ INN

PICK OF THE PUBS

See Pick of the Pubs on page 229

FRAMPTON MANSELL Map 4 SO90

The Crown Inn ★★★★ INN

PICK OF THE PUBS

GL6 8JG ☎ 01285 760601
e-mail: enquiries@thecrowninn-cotswolds.co.uk
dir: *A419 halfway between Cirencester & Stroud*

Once a simple cider house, this classic award-winning Cotswold-stone inn is full of old-world charm, with honey-coloured stone walls, beams and open fireplaces where log fires are lit in winter. A handsome 17th-century inn right in the heart of the village, it is surrounded by the peace and quiet of the Golden Valley. There is also plenty of seating in the large garden for the warmer months. Gloucestershire beers, such as Stroud Organic and Laurie Lee's Bitter, are usually showcased alongside others from the region, and a good choice of wines by the glass is served in the restaurant and three inviting bars. Fresh local food with lots of seasonal specials may include black olive tapenade, or mini mackerel cake with grilled chicory to start, followed by fish, chips and garden peas; Gloucester Old Spot sausages; or steak salad. Comfortable annexe rooms are well appointed and ideal for both business and leisure guests. Booking for meals may be required.

Open all day all wk 12-11 **Bar Meals** L served Mon-Sat 12-2.30, Sun 12-8.30 D served Mon-Sat 6-9.30, Sun 12-8.30 **Restaurant** L served Mon-Sat 12-2.30, Sun 12-8.30 D served Mon-Sat 6-9.30, Sun 12-8.30 ⊕ FREE HOUSE ◀ Butcombe Bitter, Uley Laurie Lee's Bitter, Stroud Organic, Guest ales ♻ Ashton Press, Westons Stowford Press. 🍷 16 **Facilities** ♣ Children welcome Children's portions Garden Parking Wi-fi 🚌 **Rooms** 12

PICK OF THE PUBS

The Ebrington Arms ★★★★INN ❀❀

EBRINGTON Map 10 SP14

GL55 6NH ☎ 01386 593223
e-mail: jim@theebringtonarms.co.uk
web: www.theebringtonarms.co.uk
dir: *From Chipping Campden on B4035
towards Shipston on Stour. Left to
Ebrington signed after 0.5m*

Every inch the real McCoy of a village pub, this award-winning hidden gem is in the Cotswolds — the hills look lovely from the walled beer garden. Built in 1640, its abundance of character owes much to the heavy beams and original flagstones in both the bar and Old Bakehouse dining room, and the large inglenook fireplaces, which recall the building's days as the village bakery. Very much the hub of community life, it's where lucky locals (and visitors too, of course) are spoilt for choice with several real ales, some from nearby breweries like Stroud and Uley, while cider-drinkers can enjoy Thatchers, and even Cotswold-brewed lagers. Wine-wise, owners Jim and Claire Alexander researched the market thoroughly before plumping for local merchant Savage Wines, of whose proprietor wine critic Oz Clarke has said: "I don't think Mark Savage could buy a dull wine if he tried". As for the food, chef James Nixon, having grown up in the area, knows how to get his hands on the best freshly harvested, organic produce, as most of it is grown or reared in fields around the pub. That his culinary talents are

recognised with two AA Rosettes should therefore come as no surprise. One of his typical evening meals could feature tuna carpaccio with radish, parmesan shavings and lemon olive oil; noisettes of Cotswold lamb topped with wild mushroom gratin, celeriac dauphinoise, roasted squash and thyme jus; and passionfruit and orange glaze. A vegetarian's first two courses on the other hand might be bruschetta of marinated wild mushrooms with feta, spinach and basil mousse; and roasted root vegetable cassoulet with rocket salad. Music, games and quiz nights, and occasional themed food evenings are held. If you would like to stay, there are attractive en suite bedrooms. Booking for meals may be required.

Open all day all wk noon-close ⊞ FREE HOUSE ◀ Wye Valley Butty Bach, Uley Bitter, Stroud Organic, Hobsons Bitter ○ Thatchers Pear & Gold.
Facilities Children welcome Children's portions Garden Parking Wi-fi **Rooms** 3

PICK OF THE PUBS

The Inn at Fossebridge ★★★★ INN

FOSSEBRIDGE   Map 5 SP01

Stow Rd GL54 3JS ☎ 01285 720721
e-mail: info@fossebridgeinn.co.uk
web: www.fossebridgeinn.co.uk
dir: *M4 junct 15, A419 towards*
Cirencester, A429 towards Stow. Pub
approx 6m on left in a dip

A 17th-century award-winning, family-run
free house with accommodation, set in four
acres of riverside gardens with a lake.
Records show that there has been a building
here on the ancient Fosseway since at least
1634; in 1749 it became a coaching inn, the
Lord Chedworth's Arms, his lordship being
the wealthy local landowner after whom the
characterful old bar is named. Stone
archways divide the restaurant from the two
bar areas, each featuring exposed beams,
stone walls, flagstone flooring and an open
fire. Whichever you choose, there are six real
ales to weigh up, including Tribute, Bath
Gem, Cotswold, Hill Climb and Proper Job;
Westons and Thatchers supply the draught
ciders. Lunch options include grilled
mackerel fillet with stuffed red pepper,
rocket salad and kalamata olive tapenade;
and chargrilled sirloin minute steak with
mushrooms, tomato, hand-cut chips and
garlic butter. Alternatively, a warm bacon
and egg sandwich made with farmhouse
white or granary bread is a good bet.
Offering both lunch and dinner options, the
seasonal menu may feature potted Cornish
crab as a starter, followed by a main course
of Dorchester rib of beef for two with bone
marrow, horseradish galette, honey-roast
parsnips and roasting juices; or
Trawlerman's Catch, which translates as

fillet of red mullet, mini fish pie, thick-cut
chips and hollandaise. There are Fossebridge
Classics too, such as sausages of the day
with creamy mash and red onion gravy, and
the specials, perhaps turkey and leek puff
pastry pie. A vegetarian option might be
baked spinach with wild mushroom and
ricotta cannelloni. Among the home-made
puddings are salted caramel tart and
lavender crème brûlée. The nine bedrooms
– named after local towns and villages –
have been refurbished to a high standard
with excellent shower and bathroom
facilities. Booking for meals may be
required.

Open all day all wk 12-12 (Sun
12-11.30) **Bar Meals** L served Mon-Fri
12-2.30, Sat 12-3, Sun 12-3.30 D
served Thu-Sat 6-9.30 Apr-Sep, 6-9
Oct-Mar **Restaurant** L served Mon-Fri
12-2.30, Sat 12-3, Sun 12-3.30
D served all wk 6-9.30/10 Apr-Sep, all
wk 6-9 Oct-Mar ⊕ FREE HOUSE ◖ St
Austell Tribute & Proper Job, Prescott
Hill Climb, Bath Gem, Otter, Cotswold
Ŏ Westons Stowford Press, Thatchers
Gold. **Facilities** Children welcome
Children's menu Children's portions
Play area ❤ Garden Parking Wi-fi
🚌 (notice required) **Rooms** 9

GLOUCESTER — Map 10 SO81

Queens Head

Tewkesbury Rd, Longford GL2 9EJ ☎ 01452 301882
e-mail: queenshead@aol.com
dir: *On A38 (Tewkesbury to Gloucester road) in Longford*

Under the same ownership since 1995, this 250-year-old pub/restaurant is just out of town, but it cannot be missed in summer when it is festooned with hanging baskets. Inside, a lovely old flagstone-floored locals' bar proffers a great range of real ales and ciders, while two dining areas tempt with menus of modern British food: pan-fried chicken livers in a mushroom velouté could be followed by breast of guinea fowl pan-fried with candied fresh black grapes and pancetta. No children under 12 years. Booking for meals may be required.

Open all wk 11-3 5.30-11 **Bar Meals** L served all wk 12-2 D served all wk 6.30-9.30 **Restaurant** D served all wk 6.30-9.30 ⊕ FREE HOUSE ◀ Wye Valley Butty Bach, Brains The Rev. James, Gloucester Mariner, Skinner's Betty Stogs ♂ Ashton Press, Westons Stowford Press. ☂ **Facilities** Parking Wi-fi

GREAT BARRINGTON — Map 10 SP21

The Fox

PICK OF THE PUBS

OX18 4TB ☎ 01451 844385
e-mail: info@foxinnbarrington.com
dir: *3m W on A40 from Burford, turn N signed The Barringtons, pub approx 0.5m on right*

Set in the picturesque Windrush Valley, this busy 17th-century former coaching house is at the heart of this pretty village. Popular with walkers, cyclists and with those attending Cheltenham racecourse, this quintessential Cotswold inn is built of mellow local stone and characterised by low ceilings, beams and log fires. The inn offers a range of well-kept Donnington beers and a concise wine list. Enjoy a meal in the main bar or the riverside dining room. Quality produce from local suppliers dominates a menu that might offer dishes like filo parcels of Windrush goat's cheese, leek and mushrooms; Tagmoor Farm strip steak Stroganoff; local Bibury trout with salad; or whole roasted Cotswold pigeon with cranberry and orange stuffing. The pub has a delightful patio and large beer garden overlooking the River Windrush — on warm days it's a perfect summer watering hole and base for lovely local walks and cycle routes.

Open all day all wk 11am-close **Bar Meals** L served Mon-Fri 12-2.30, Sat-Sun all day D served Mon-Fri 6.30-9.30, Sat-Sun all day **Restaurant** L served Mon-Fri 12-2.30, Sat-Sun all day D served Mon-Fri 6.30-9.30, Sat-Sun all day ⊕ DONNINGTON ◀ BB, SBA ♂ Westons Stowford Press & Perry, Addlestones. **Facilities** ✿ Children welcome Children's portions Garden Parking Wi-fi ▥

GUITING POWER — Map 10 SP02

The Hollow Bottom

GL54 5UX ☎ 01451 850392
e-mail: hello@hollowbottom.com
dir: *Telephone for directions*

Often frequented by Cheltenham race-goers, this 18th-century Cotswold free house is decorated with all manner of horse-racing memorabilia – from badges and silks to framed newspaper cuttings. Its nooks and crannies are warmed by a blazing log fire and lend themselves to planning a punt with an intimate drink or meal; there's also a separate dining room, plus outside tables for fine weather. In addition to real ales and ciders, the bar proffers a grand selection of malt whiskies, wines and champagne. If you're after a snack, baked potatoes and freshly made baguettes have a choice of fillings. Other dishes of typical pub fare extend from home-made pie or roast of the day to wholetail scampi.

Open all day all wk 9am-12.30am **Bar Meals** L served Mon-Fri 12-2, Sat-Sun 12-4 D served all wk 6-9 **Restaurant** L served Mon-Fri 12-2, Sat-Sun 12-4 D served all wk 6-9 ⊕ FREE HOUSE ◀ Hollow Bottom Best Bitter, Donnington SBA, Guest ale ♂ Thatchers Gold & Cheddar Valley. ☂ 9 **Facilities** Children welcome Children's menu Children's portions Play area Garden Parking Wi-fi ▥

HINTON — Map 4 ST77

The Bull Inn

PICK OF THE PUBS

See Pick of the Pubs on opposite page

LECHLADE ON THAMES — Map 5 SU29

The Trout Inn

St Johns Bridge GL7 3HA ☎ 01367 252313
e-mail: chefpjw@aol.com
dir: *A40 onto A361 then A417. From M4 junct 15, A419, then A361 & A417 to Lechlade*

When workmen constructed a new bridge over the Thames in 1220, they built an almshouse to live in. It became an inn in 1472, and its flagstone floors and beams now overflow into the old boathouse. The extensive menu features meat, fish and vegetarian options, as well as pizzas, filled jacket potatoes and burgers. This family-friendly pub offers smaller portions for children, who also have their own separate menu. The large garden often hosts live jazz, and there's a beer festival in June.

Open all wk 10-3 6-11 (summer all wk 10am-11pm) Closed: 25 Dec **Bar Meals** L served all wk 12-2 D served all wk 7-10 **Restaurant** L served all wk 12-2 D served all wk 7-10 ⊕ ENTERPRISE INNS ◀ Courage Best, Sharp's Doom Bar & Cornish Coaster, Guest ales. ☂ 15 **Facilities** ✿ Children welcome Children's menu Children's portions Play area Family room Garden Beer festival Parking ▥

LEIGHTERTON — Map 4 ST89

The Royal Oak NEW

1 The Street GL8 8UN ☎ 01666 890250
e-mail: info@royaloakleighterton.co.uk
dir: *M4 junct 18, A46 towards Stroud. After Dunkirk left, continue on A46. Right signed Leighterton*

Paul and Antonia Whitbread have breathed new life into The Royal Oak. Set in a picture-postcard Cotswold village, close to Westonbirt Arboretum, the pub thrives as a popular dining venue, the bright, contemporary bar and dining room successfully blending exposed beams, open fires and antiques with modern furnishings. Food is classic British and everything is made on the premises from local seasonal ingredients. Typically, tuck into scallop thermidor; pork belly stuffed with prunes with apricot brandy broth and cinnamon mash; and rhubarb and custard tart.

Open all wk 11-3 5.30-11 (Sat 11-11 Sun 12-10.30) **Bar Meals** L served Mon-Fri 12-2, Sat 12-2.30, Sun 12-3 D served Mon-Fri 6-9, Sat 6-9.30 Av main course £16 **Restaurant** L served Mon-Fri 12-2, Sat 12-2.30, Sun 12-3 D served Mon-Fri 6-9, Sat 6-9.30 Fixed menu price fr £13.95 Av 3 course à la carte fr £27.50 ⊕ FREE HOUSE ◀ Wadworth Boundary & Henry's Original IPA, Otter Ale, Bath Barnsey, Wye Valley ♂ Westons Stowford Press, Sherston. ☂ 10 **Facilities** ✿ Children welcome Children's menu Children's portions Garden Parking ▥ (notice required)

LITTLETON-ON-SEVERN — Map 4 ST58

White Hart

BS35 1NR ☎ 01454 412275
e-mail: whitehart@youngs.co.uk
web: www.whitehartbristol.com
dir: *M48 junct 1 towards Chepstow left on rdbt, follow for 3m, 1st left to Littleton-on-Severn*

Secluded in a hamlet close to the Severn Estuary, views from the shrubby, suntrap beer garden of this lovely 17th-century inn encompass the distant wooded ridge of the Forest of Dean. Defiantly olde worlde with all the timeless trimmings, the enchanting beamed interior draws in beer-lovers to sample beers from Bath Ales and locally made cider Little Delight Saber, whilst diners can expect a wide choice from an inspiring menu featuring their famous 8oz hanger steak; potted Gloucester ham;

continued

Save on hotels. Book at **theAA.com/hotel**

GLOUCESTERSHIRE 231 ENGLAND

PICK OF THE PUBS

The Bull Inn

HINTON Map 4 ST77

SN14 8HG ☎ 0117 937 2332
e-mail: reservations@thebullathinton.co.uk
web: www.thebullathinton.co.uk
dir: *From M4 junct 18, A46 to Bath 1m, turn right 1m, down hill. Pub on right*

Formerly a farmhouse and a dairy dating back to the 17th century, the stone-built Bull became an inn just over 100 years ago and stands in sleepy Hinton on the southern edge of the Cotswolds, just five minutes' drive from the M4. Run with charm and personality by David and Elizabeth White, the Wadworth-owned pub oozes original character, with inglenook fireplaces, flagstone floors, old pews and big oak tables, which are candlelit in the evenings, in the beamed bar and dining room. Food is freshly prepared by head chef Wieslaw, who sources top-notch ingredients from local producers and suppliers, and who specialises in cooking game dishes, especially partridge and pheasant. Fruit and vegetables are grown in the garden and Gloucester Old Spot, Durok and Welsh Black pigs are reared out back, which also provide entertainment for children. Short, seasonal menus may take in classics like beef and ale pie with herb mash; the Bull burger with relish and

hand-cut chips; a rib-eye steak with pepper sauce and all the trimmings. Look to the chalkboard for Wieslaw's imaginative daily specials, which may include devilled lambs' kidneys on toasted bread, followed by rabbit casserole; pasta with sea bass, clams, prawns and mussels in a spicy sauce; and venison steak served with cider fondant potato and juniper jus. For pudding, try the apple and mixed berry crumble with lashings of custard, or chocolate brownie and clotted cream. The suntrap south-facing terrace and garden is the perfect spot for summer alfresco pints of 6X. A small conference room is available for all-day business meetings. Booking for meals may be required.

Open 12-3 6-12 (Sat-Sun & BH open all day) Closed: Mon L (ex BH) **Food** Mon 6-9, Tue-Fri 12-2 6-9, Sat 12-9.30, Sun 12-8.30 BHs 12-8 ⊕ WADWORTH ◀ 6X, Henry's Original IPA, Bishop's Tipple & Summersault, Guest ale ♂ Thatchers Gold, Westons Stowford Press. ♀ 11 **Facilities** Children welcome Children's menu Play area ✿ Garden Parking Wi-fi 🚌 (notice required)

LITTLETON-ON-SEVERN *continued*

and goat's cheese and mushroom Wellington; with a local fruit crumble to finish.

Open all day all wk 12-11 (Fri-Sun 12-12) **Bar Meals** L served Mon-Sat 12-2.30, Sun 12-8 D served Mon-Sat 6-9, Sun 12-8 **Restaurant** L served Mon-Sat 12-2.30, Sun 12-8 D served Mon-Sat 6-9, Sun 12-8 ⊕ YOUNG'S ◀ Bitter & Special, Bath Gem, Guest ales Ŏ Thatchers Heritage & Gold, Addlestones. ♀ 18 **Facilities** ♣ Children welcome Children's menu Children's portions Family room Garden Parking ▅▅

LITTLE WASHBOURNE — Map 10 SO93

The Hobnails Inn

GL20 8NQ ☎ **01242 620237**
e-mail: enquiries@thehobnailsinn.co.uk
dir: *M5 junct 9, A46 towards Evesham then B4077 to Stow-on-the-Wold. Inn 1.5m on left*

Dating from the 13th century, this charming Cotswold building is one of the oldest inns in the county. Its idyllic rural setting and lovely large garden attract summer visitors, while log fires warm the interior in winter. The philosophy here is to serve wholesome meals using seasonal produce, so settle into one of the leather sofas with a pint and a menu. Perhaps a 'big bap' — a 7-inch fresh bap filled with liver and onions, for example — will suffice. Alternatively the lunchtime carvery is backed by a great selection of classic English dishes.

Open all wk 12-3 5.30-11 (Sun all day) **Bar Meals** L served all wk 12-3 D served all wk 5.30-9 **Restaurant** L served all wk 12-3 D served all wk 5.30-9 ⊕ ENTERPRISE INNS ◀ Fuller's London Pride Ŏ Westons Stowford Press. **Facilities** ♣ Children welcome Children's menu Children's portions Garden Parking Wi-fi ▅▅

LONGHOPE — Map 10 SO61

The Glasshouse Inn

May Hill GL17 0NN ☎ **01452 830529**
e-mail: glasshouseinn@gmail.com
dir: *Village off A40 between Gloucester & Ross-on-Wye*

Dating back to 1450, The Glasshouse gets its name from Dutch glassmakers who settled locally in the 16th century. A gimmick-free traditional pub, it is located in a fabulous rural setting with a country garden and an elegant interior. The inn serves a range of real ales including Butcombe and home-cooked dishes include gammon and eggs; beef curry; steak sandwich; mushroom Stroganoff; and several fish and chip options.

Open 11.30-3 7-11 (Sun 12-3) Closed: Sun eve **Bar Meals** L served all wk 12-2 (booking required for parties of 6 or more) D served Mon-Sat 7-9 (booking required for parties of 6 or more) Av main course £10-£25 ⊕ FREE HOUSE ◀ Sharp's Doom Bar, Butcombe Ŏ Westons Stowford Press. ♀ 12 **Facilities** Garden Parking

LOWER ODDINGTON — Map 10 SP22

The Fox

PICK OF THE PUBS

GL56 0UR ☎ **01451 870555 & 870666**
e-mail: info@foxinn.net
dir: *A436 from Stow-on-the-Wold then right to Lower Oddington*

Set in a quintessential Cotswold village and dating back to the 17th century, this stone-built, creeper-clad free house enjoys a reputation for well-kept beers, good food and wine at reasonable prices. The interior boasts polished flagstone floors, beams and log fires, with fresh flowers and antique furniture creating a period feel in the bar. The regularly changing menus and the daily specials take full advantage of seasonal local produce and freshly caught Cornish fish. Typical starters include pan-fried Cornish sardines with wild garlic butter; and seared Scottish scallops with chorizo and mixed leaves. Move on to braised shank of Cotswold lamb with spiced couscous and tomato sauce, or an individually baked shin of beef and oxtail pie. Finish with sticky toffee pudding, butterscotch sauce and ice cream. In summer, there's a heated terrace for alfresco dining, as well as a pretty, traditional cottage garden. Booking for meals may be required.

Open all wk 12-2.30 6-11 or 12 (Sun 12-3.30 7-10.30) Closed: 25 Dec **Bar Meals** L served Mon-Sat 12-2, Sun 12-2.30 D served Mon-Sat 6.30-10, Sun 7-9 **Restaurant** L served Mon-Sat 12-2, Sun 12-2.30 D served Mon-Sat 6.30-10, Sun 7-9 ⊕ FREE HOUSE ◀ Hook Norton Hooky Bitter, Greene King Abbot Ale & Ruddles County, Wickwar's BOB, Purity Pure UBU Ŏ Westons Stowford Press. ♀ 15 **Facilities** Children welcome Children's portions Garden Parking Wi-fi

MARSHFIELD — Map 4 ST77

The Catherine Wheel

39 High St SN14 8LR ☎ **01225 892220**
e-mail: roo@thecatherinewheel.co.uk
dir: *Between Bath, Bristol & Chippenham on A420. 5m from M4 junct 18*

An impressive, mainly 17th-century inn on the edge of the Cotswolds, The Catherine Wheel has the expected exposed brickwork and large open fireplaces offset by simple, stylish décor. Menus are also simple and well presented, with favourites at lunchtime including jacket potatoes and ploughman's. In the evening look forward to moules marinière, followed perhaps by slow-cooked Moroccan lamb stew with Mediterranean couscous, or traditional fish and chips. A small but sunny patio is a lovely spot for a summertime pint brewed by nearby Cotswold and Bath-based breweries.

Open all day all wk **Bar Meals** L served Mon-Fri 12-2, Sat-Sun 12-3 D served Mon-Thu 6.30-9, Fri-Sat 6.30-9.30, Sun 6-8.30 **Restaurant** L served Mon-Fri 12-2, Sat-Sun 12-3 D served Mon-Thu 6.30-9, Fri-Sat 6.30-9.30, Sun 6-8.30 ⊕ FREE HOUSE ◀ Butcombe Bitter, Sharp's Doom Bar, Local guest ale Ŏ Ashton Press.

Facilities ♣ Children welcome Children's portions Garden Parking Wi-fi ▅▅ (notice required)

The Lord Nelson Inn

1 & 2 High St SN14 8LP ☎ **01225 891820**
e-mail: thelordnelsoninn.@btinternet.com
dir: *M4 junct 18 onto A46 towards Bath. Left at Cold Ashton rdbt towards Marshfield-Chippenham*

In a conservation village on the edge of the Cotswolds and surrounded by wonderful walks, this 16th-century former coaching inn draws a loyal local crowd for good home-made food and quality cask ales. A spacious bar that provides a chance to mix with the locals, a candlelit restaurant, log fires in winter and a patio for summer use complete its attractions. With the food emphasis on simplicity and quality, the varied menus take in light bar lunches (ham, egg and chips), hearty evening dishes like pheasant with red wine and redcurrant gravy, and a very popular Sunday carvery. Booking for meals may be required.

Open all wk 12-2.30 5-11 (Fri-Sun 12-11) **Bar Meals** L served Mon-Sat 12-2, Sun 12-3 D served Mon-Sat 6.30-9, Sun 6-8.30 Av main course £10 **Restaurant** L served Mon-Sat 12-2, Sun 12-3 D served Mon-Sat 6.30-9, Sun 6-8.30 ⊕ ENTERPRISE INNS ◀ Greene King IPA, Bath Gem, Sharp's Doom Bar Ŏ Thatchers Gold. ♀ 9 **Facilities** Children welcome Children's menu Children's portions Play area Garden Wi-fi ▅▅ (notice required)

MEYSEY HAMPTON — Map 5 SP10

The Masons Arms

28 High St GL7 5JT ☎ **01285 850164**
dir: *6m E of Cirencester off A417, beside village green*

This is a quintessential 17th-century stone-built Cotswold inn, which sits nestled alongside the green in the heart of the village. The hub of the community and welcoming to visitors, it offers something for everyone, from a warming log fire in the large inglenook to the range of well-kept Arkell's ales and Westons cider served in the convivial beamed bar. Good value home-made food could include local smoked trout salad or Gloucestershire pork loin with chips. Worth noting if visiting the Cotswold Water Park near by. Booking for meals may be required.

Open all wk 12-2 5.30-11 (Sat 12-11 Sun 12-10) **Bar Meals** L served all wk 12-2 D served all wk 6-9 Av main course £11 **Restaurant** L served all wk 12-2 D served all wk 6-9 Av 3 course à la carte fr £22 ⊕ ARKELL'S ◀ 3B, 2B, Kingsdown, Moonlight Ŏ Westons Stowford Press. **Facilities** ♣ Children welcome Children's portions Garden Wi-fi ▅▅ (notice required)

MINCHINHAMPTON — Map 4 SO80

The Weighbridge Inn

PICK OF THE PUBS

See Pick of the Pubs on opposite page

Save on hotels. Book at **theAA.com/hotel**

GLOUCESTERSHIRE 233 ENGLAND

PICK OF THE PUBS

The Weighbridge Inn

MINCHINHAMPTON   Map 4 SO80

GL6 9AL ☎ **01453 832520**
e-mail: enquiries@2in1pub.co.uk
web: www.2in1pub.co.uk
dir: *On B4014 between Nailsworth & Avening*

Parts of this beautifully positioned free house date back to the 17th century, when it stood adjacent to the original packhorse trail between Bristol and London. The trail is now a footpath and bridleway and the road in front (now the B4014) became a turnpike in the 1820s. The innkeeper at the time ran both the pub and the weighbridge for the local woollen mills — serving jugs of ale in between making sure tolls were paid. Associated memorabilia and other rural artefacts from the time are displayed around the inn, which has been carefully renovated to retain original features. From the patios and sheltered landscaped garden the Cotswolds are in full view. Up in the restaurant, which used to be the hayloft, for example, the old roof timbers reach almost to the floor. The drinking areas are, as you would expect, tailor-made for a decent pint — Wadworth 6X, maybe — but if beer is not to your taste, a heady Wicked Witch cider. The inn prides itself on the quality of its food, all cooked from scratch to appear on the regular menu as simple starter dishes of smoked salmon and scrambled eggs on truffle oil crostini and horseradish cream, for example. The hearty main courses include cauliflower cheese, cottage pie, bangers and mash from a local award-winning butcher, or the popular Weighbridge burger. The Weighbridge is also the home of '2 in 1 pies', half containing one of seven fillings of your choice, the rest with home-made cauliflower cheese — also available to take away and bake at home. Typical desserts include treacle and hazelnut sponge with toffee sauce and local vanilla ice cream, or cappuccino pannacotta. Lighter meals are available as salads, omelettes, jacket potatoes and filled baguettes.

Open all day all wk 12-11 (Sun 12-10.30) Closed: 25 Dec ⊕ FREE HOUSE ◀ Wadworth 6X, Uley Old Spot, Palmers Best Bitter ᶯ Westons Bounds, Thatchers Gold, Wicked Witch.
Facilities Children welcome Children's menu Children's portions Family room Garden Parking Wi-fi

The Red Lion Inn ★★★ INN

GL56 0RT ☎ **01608 674397**
e-mail: info@theredlionlittlecompton.co.uk
dir: *Between Chipping Norton & Moreton-in-Marsh on A44*

A pretty Cotswold-stone building quietly located on the edge of the village, this is one of 15 pubs owned by Donnington Brewery – a family concern that has been brewing since 1865. Set in a large mature garden, the building has exposed stone walls and beams, inglenook fireplaces and real fires; there is comfortable, stylishly presented accommodation, too. Public bar games include darts, dominoes, a jukebox and pool table. The restaurant offers a seasonal menu and sensibly priced daily-changing specials. Booking for meals may be required.

Open all wk 12-3 6-12 **Bar Meals** L served all wk 12-2 D served Mon-Sat 6-9, Sun 7-9 **Restaurant** L served all wk 12-2 D served Mon-Sat 6-9, Sun 7-9 ⊕ DONNINGTON ◀ BB, SBA. � 10 **Facilities** ✿ Children welcome Children's portions Garden Parking Wi-fi **Rooms** 2

The Britannia

PICK OF THE PUBS

Cossack Square GL6 0DG ☎ **01453 832501**
e-mail: pheasantpluckers2003@yahoo.co.uk
dir: *From A46 S'bound right at town centre rdbt. 1st left. Pub directly ahead*

This stone-built, 17th-century former manor house occupies a delightful position on the south side of Nailsworth's Cossack Square. The interior is bright and uncluttered with low ceilings, cosy fires and a blue slate floor. Outside you'll find a pretty garden with plenty of tables, chairs and parasols for sunny days. Whether inside or out, a pint of well-kept ale is sure to go down well. The brasserie-style menu offers an interesting blend of modern British and continental food, with ingredients bought from local suppliers and from Smithfield Market. You can go lightly with just a starter from a list that includes warm chorizo and rocket salad, and moules marinière; or plunge into hearty mains such as chargrilled rump steak, free-range lemon chicken or confit pork belly. Other options include stone-baked pizzas made with ingredients imported from Italy, and impressive meat-free options such as mushroom linguine. Great wines, too.

Open all wk 11-11 (Fri-Sat 11am-mdnt Sun 11-10.30) Closed: 25 Dec **Bar Meals** L served Mon-Fri 11-2.45, Sat-Sun 11-10 D served Mon-Fri 5.30-10, Sat-Sun 11-10 **Restaurant** L served Mon-Fri 11-2.45, Sat-Sun 11-10 D served Mon-Fri 5.30-10, Sat-Sun 11-10 ⊕ FREE HOUSE ◀ Sharp's Doom Bar, Buckham, Otter, Guest ales ⚇ Thatcher's Gold, Westons Stowford Press. ☜ 10 **Facilities** ✿ Children welcome Garden Parking 🚌

Tipputs Inn

PICK OF THE PUBS

Bath Rd GL6 0QE ☎ **01453 832466**
e-mail: pheasantpluckers2003@yahoo.co.uk
dir: *A46, 0.5m S of Nailsworth*

Mellow Cotswold stone and stripped floorboards blend nicely with modern, clean-lined furniture in this impeccably decorated 17th-century pub-restaurant. A giant candelabra adds a touch of grandeur. Located in the heart of the Cotswolds, the Tipputs Inn is owned by Nick Beardsley and Christophe Coquoin. They started out as chefs together more than 12 years ago, but admit to spending less time in the kitchen these days now that they have to create menus for this and their other Gloucestershire food pubs, plus they select and import some ingredients and wines direct from France. There are dishes for every eventuality, starting with tapas-style appetisers and extending through starters such as pan-fried haloumi or spicy prawn cocktail to pub classics (fish and chips; home-made burger and chips) and classy options to South Indian cuisine. Classic desserts include Eton Mess and vanilla crème brûlée.

Open all wk 10-30am-11pm ⊕ FREE HOUSE ◀ Otter Ale, Stroud ⚇ Westons Stowford Press. **Facilities** Children welcome Children's menu Garden Parking

The Feathered Nest Inn ★★★★★ INN ⑧⑧

PICK OF THE PUBS

See Pick of the Pubs on page 236
See advert on opposite page

The Ostrich Inn

PICK OF THE PUBS

See Pick of the Pubs on page 237

Bathurst Arms

PICK OF THE PUBS

GL7 7BZ ☎ **01285 831281**
e-mail: james@bathurstarms.com
dir: *5m N of Cirencester on A435*

The 17th-century Bathurst Arms offers the intimacy of a traditional inn combined with high standards of food and drink. The rambling creeper-covered building stands on the Earl of Bathurst's estate, in the picturesque village of North Cerney, right on the edge of the River Churn. The flagstoned bar exudes character with its beams and log fires, and on warmer days guests can enjoy the pretty riverside garden. Decent pub food prepared from locally sourced ingredients has starters such as sweet potato, lemongrass and coconut soup; and a tian of crab and crayfish with mango and apple salad. Main course options may include roast duck breast with Puy lentil casserole, or salmon fillet with a herb crust served with lemon crushed potatoes and a spinach and chive butter sauce. For those with a sweet tooth, cardamom cheesecake with vanilla poached apricots and berries will be irresistible. Beer festivals are held in January, April, July and October.

Open all day all wk **Bar Meals** L served all wk 12-2 D served all wk 6-9 Av main course £11 **Restaurant** L served all wk 12-2 D served all wk 6-9 Fixed menu price fr £10 Av 3 course à la carte fr £23 ⊕ FREE HOUSE ◀ Box Steam Golden Bolt, Wickwar Cotswold Way ⚇ Westons Stowford Press, Cotswold. ☜ 25 **Facilities** Children welcome Children's menu Children's portions Garden Beer festival Parking Wi-fi 🚌 (notice required)

The Wheatsheaf Inn **NEW**

West End GL54 3EZ ☎ **01451 860244**
e-mail: reservations@cotswoldswheatsheaf.com
dir: *Just off A40 between Oxford & Cheltenham*

The setting of this old stone coaching inn is everything anyone could wish for, with an outlook on to the broad main street of a historic Cotswold wool town, flagstone floors, beams, log fires and a vibrant, smartened-up feel throughout. It's the perfect weekend retreat – come for wonderful walks, or chill out in the bar with the papers, and enjoy some seriously good food. Monthly menus evolve with the season and may take in linguine with tomato, clams and chilli; confit duck with pickled red cabbage; and hot chocolate mousse with raspberry sorbet. One to watch! Booking for meals may be required.

Open all day all wk **Bar Meals** L served all wk 12-3 D served all wk 6-10 Av main course £12-£15 **Restaurant** L served all wk 12-3 D served all wk 6-10 Fixed menu price fr £12.75 Av 3 course à la carte fr £25 ⊕ FREE HOUSE ◀ Fuller's London Pride ⚇ Dunkertons. ☜ 10 **Facilities** ✿ Children welcome Children's menu Children's portions Play area Garden Parking Wi-fi 🚌 (notice required)

Save on hotels. Book at **theAA.com/hotel**

GLOUCESTERSHIRE 235 ENGLAND

PICK OF THE PUBS

The Feathered Nest Inn ★★★★★ INN

NETHER WESTCOTE Map 10 SP22

OX7 6SD ☎ 01993 833030
e-mail: info@thefeatherednestinn.co.uk
web: www.thefeatherednestinn.co.uk
dir: *A424 between Burford &
Stow-on-the-Wold, follow signs*

Set in the picturesque village of Nether Westcote on the border of Gloucestershire and Oxfordshire, The Feathered Nest has marvellous views over the Evenlode Valley. Originally an old malthouse, the pub has been updated and thoughtfully furnished whilst retaining the original character, especially in the cosy log-fired bar, where Hook Norton Hooky Bitter is one of the real ales on offer. Awarded two AA Rosettes, a daily blackboard menu offers relaxed eating in the bar, and the garden terrace when the weather allows. Many of the herbs and vegetables are grown in the kitchen garden, with local produce a backbone of the menu. Lunch brings a set-price 'market menu' offering the likes of crispy pork belly with black pudding, celeriac and apple ahead of roast breast of chicken with spiced red cabbage, shiitake mushrooms and spinach, with bread-and-butter pudding for dessert. The à la carte menu is available at lunch or dinner, offering a modern take on classic combinations such as duck liver with potato fondant and orange balm dressing, followed by local wild venison with bacon cabbage, pickled russet

apple and chocolate and juniper sauce. For simpler tastes there's a selection from the charcoal grill; maybe Cotswold 28-day aged sirloin steak with skinny chips, peppercorn sauce and mixed leaf salad. Be sure to leave room for desserts such as chocolate fondant with beetroot and orange, or coffee soufflé with walnuts and pickled pear sorbet. Individually decorated bedrooms furnished with antiques and comfortable beds are available; the pub makes an excellent base from which to explore the quaint and charming villages nearby and the beautiful rural surroundings. Look out for enjoyable events running throughout the year, including a pie and pint tasting evening; live jazz; and a quiz night. Booking for meals may be required.

Open all day Closed: 25 Dec, Mon **Bar Meals** L served Tue-Sun 12-2.30 D served Tue-Sun 6.30-9.30 **Restaurant** L served Tue-Sun 12-2.30 D served Tue-Sun 6.30-9.30 ⊕ FREE HOUSE ◀ Hook Norton Hooky Bitter, Wychwood Hobgoblin, Marston's Pedigree ♂ Thatchers Gold. ♀ 19
Facilities Children welcome Children's menu Children's portions Family room ☘ Garden Parking Wi-fi **Rooms** 4

PICK OF THE PUBS

The Ostrich Inn

NEWLAND　　　　　　　**Map 4 SO50**

GL16 8NP ☎ 01594 833260

e-mail: kathryn@theostrichinn.com
web: theostrichinn.com
dir: *Follow Monmouth signs from Chepstow (A466), Newland signed from Redbrook*

A 13th-century inn situated on the western edge of the Forest of Dean and adjoining the Wye Valley, both Areas of Outstanding Natural Beauty. Set in the middle of the pretty village of Newland opposite the church, The Ostrich is thought to have taken its name from the family emblem of the Probyns, local landowners in previous centuries. To this day it retains many of its ancient features, including a priest hole. With its warm welcome embracing all-comers and their dogs, The Ostrich is a thriving social centre for the village. Without doubt, it's a proper country pub – one of a diminishing number throughout the county, some would say. With wooden beams and an open log fire burning in the large lounge bar throughout the winter, customers relax immediately in the friendly atmosphere with a pint of their chosen brew. And what a choice! Eight cask-conditioned real ales such as Butty Bach and Pigs Ear are served at any one time; real ciders, too, are strongly represented. Diners settle down in the small and intimate restaurant, in

the larger lounge bar, or out in gardens. A treat awaits – the select Ostrich menu is full of good things. Bar meals punch way above their weight in dishes such as Newland smokies – fresh smoked haddock in cream, egg and horseradish topped with dauphinoise potatoes and mozzarella. The monthly-changing menu in the restaurant continues the sophisticated approach in accomplished dishes. Why not start with goose rillettes with gooseberry and elderflower chutney on sourdough toast? This could be followed by sea bass fillet and prawns with lemon cream sauce, samphire and butter crushed new potatoes. Don't forget to check the specials board, and desserts are written up too.

Open all wk 12-3 (Mon-Fri 6.30-11.30 Sat 6-11.30 Sun 6.30-10.30) **Bar Meals** L served all wk 12-2.30 D served Sun-Fri 6.30-9.30, Sat 6-9.30 **Restaurant** L served all wk 12-2.30 D served Sun-Fri 6.30-9.30, Sat 6-9.30 ⊞ FREE HOUSE ◖ Wye Valley Butty Bach, Uley Pigs Ear, Hook Norton Old Hooky, Adnams, Guest ales ♨ Westons Stowford Press & Old Rosie, Ty Gwyn, Severn Cider.
Facilities Children welcome ✿ Garden

OLDBURY-ON-SEVERN — Map 4 ST69

The Anchor Inn

Church Rd BS35 1QA ☎ 01454 413331
e-mail: info@anchorinnoldbury.co.uk
dir: *From N A38 towards Bristol, 1.5m then right, village signed. From S A38 through Thornbury*

Located on the original river bank in the village of Oldbury-on-Severn, parts of this Cotswold-stone pub date from 1540. The village has a long history dating back to the Iron Age, whilst the pub itself was formerly a mill. There is a large garden to enjoy, flower-filled in summer, and a boules area. A typical menu features dishes such as roast Severnvale topside of beef and Yorkshire pudding; smoked haddock and salmon fish pie; and roast duck breast in a plum and port sauce. Sticky toffee pudding and blackcurrant sundae are among the desserts. Booking for meals may be required.

Open all wk 11.30-2.30 6-11 (Sat 11.30am-mdnt Sun 12-10.30) **Bar Meals** L served Mon-Fri 12-2, Sat 12-2.30, Sun 12-3 D served Sat-Sun 6-9 Av main course £9.95 **Restaurant** L served Mon-Fri 12-2, Sat 12-2.30, Sun 12-3 D served Sat-Sun 6-9 Fixed menu price fr £9.45 Av 3 course à la carte fr £19.95 ⊕ FREE HOUSE ◀ Bass, Butcombe Bitter, Otter Bitter, Guest ales ♂ Ashton Press, Sheppy's, Ashton Still. ♀ 16 **Facilities** Children welcome Children's menu Family room Garden Parking

PAINSWICK — Map 4 SO80

The Falcon Inn

New St GL6 6UN ☎ 01452 814222
e-mail: info@falconpainswick.co.uk
dir: *On A46 in centre of Painswick, opposite St Mary's church*

Built in 1554, this refurbished small hotel, restaurant and pub spent over 200 years as a courthouse. Landlord David Nott offers a good choice of local real ales, including Stroud Budding, and tasty meals any time of day, from hearty, home-cooked breakfasts to evening meals, typically fresh figs and mozzarella salad with honey vinaigrette; pork tenderloin and Stowford cider cream sauce, black pudding, mashed potato and apple to follow; and lemon syllabub for dessert. A blackboard offers daily specials, steaks and pies. Events include an August cider festival.

Open all day all wk 10am-11pm **Bar Meals** L served all wk 12-3 D served all wk 7-9.30 Av main course £9.95 **Restaurant** D served all wk 6-9.30 Av 3 course à la carte fr £24 ⊕ ENTERPRISE INNS ◀ Otter Ale, Butcombe Blond & Bitter, Sharp's Doom Bar, Stroud Budding ♂ Weston Stowford Press. ♀ 10 **Facilities** ☺ Children welcome Children's menu Children's portions Garden Parking Wi-fi ⇌ (notice required)

PAXFORD — Map 10 SP13

The Churchill Arms ★★★★ INN ⚹⚹

PICK OF THE PUBS

See Pick of the Pubs on opposite page

POULTON — Map 5 SP00

The Falcon Inn

London Rd GL7 5HN ☎ 01285 851597 & 850878
e-mail: bookings@falconinnpoulton.co.uk
dir: *From Cirencester 4m E on A417 towards Fairford*

Husband and wife Gianni Gray and Natalie Birch bought this 300-year-old village pub in July 2010 and have put real ale and good food at the top of the agenda. Contemporary furnishings blend with original features and log fires to create an informal pub for locals who want to sup a pint of Hooky or one of the rotating guests beers. Diners will be tempted by parsnip and apple soup with parsnip chips; Braised Butt's Farm lamb shank with creamy mash and rosemary-roasted root vegetables; and lemon tart with thyme ice cream and raspberry coulis. Booking for meals may be required.

Open Tue-Sat 12-3 5-11 (Sun 12-4) Closed: 25 Dec, Mon **Bar Meals** L served Tue-Sat 12-2.30, Sun 12-3 D served Tue-Sat 6-9 Av main course £12.50 **Restaurant** L served Tue-Sat 12-2.30, Sun 12-3 D served Tue-Sat 6-9 Fixed menu price fr £12.50 Av 3 course à la carte fr £21.50 ⊕ FREE HOUSE ◀ Hook Norton Hooky Bitter, Guest ale ♂ Westons Stowford Press. ♀ 11 **Facilities** Children welcome Children's menu Children's portions Garden Parking Wi-fi

SAPPERTON — Map 4 SO90

The Bell at Sapperton

PICK OF THE PUBS

See Pick of the Pubs on page 240

SHEEPSCOMBE — Map 4 SO81

The Butchers Arms

PICK OF THE PUBS

GL6 7RH ☎ 01452 812113
e-mail: mark@butchers-arms.co.uk
web: www.butchers-arms.co.uk
dir: *1.5m S of A46 (Cheltenham to Stroud road), N of Painswick*

Tucked into the western scarp of the Cotswolds, pretty Sheepscombe radiates all of the mellow, sedate, bucolic charm you'd expect from such a haven. The village pub, dating from 1620 and a favourite haunt of *Cider with Rosie* author Laurie Lee, lives up to such expectations and then some. Views from the gardens are idyllic whilst within is all you'd hope for: log fires, clean-cut rustic furnishings, village chatter backed up by local beers from Severn Vale Brewery. Walkers, riders and locals all beat a path to the door beneath the pub's famous carved sign showing a butcher supping a pint of ale with a pig tied to his leg. The fulfilling fodder here includes locally sourced meats; the chicken, broccoli and ham pie is a cracker, as is the pork, apple and cider sausage dish, whilst the specials board slants towards fish and vegetarian choices. Nibblers can graze on great sandwiches like brie, apple and caramelised balsamic onions. Booking for meals may be required.

Open all wk 11.30-2.30 6.30-11 (Sat 11.30-11.30 Sun 12-10.30) **Bar Meals** L served Mon-Fri 12-2.30, Sat-Sun all day D served Mon-Sat 6.30-9.30, Sun 6.30-9 (ex Sun Jan & Feb) **Restaurant** L served Mon-Fri 12-2.30, Sat-Sun all day D served Mon-Sat 6.30-9.30, Sun 6.30-9 (ex Sun Jan & Feb) ⊕ FREE HOUSE ◀ Otter Bitter, Butcombe Bitter, St Austell Proper Job, Wye Valley Dorothy Goodbody's Country Ale, Severn Vale ♂ Westons Stowford Press & Traditional. **Facilities** Children welcome Children's menu Children's portions Garden Parking

PICK OF THE PUBS

The Churchill Arms ★★★★ INN ❀❀

PAXFORD　　　　　　Map 10 SP13

GL55 6XH ☎ 01386 594000
e-mail: info@thechurchillarms.com
web: www.thechurchillarms.com
dir: *2m E of Chipping Campden, 4m N of Moreton-in-Marsh*

Nestled among honey-stone cottages in the chocolate-box village of Paxford, The Churchill Arms offers glorious views over the local chapel towards the rolling countryside. Close to the historical wool town of Chipping Campden, this unpretentious 17th-century pub is the quintessential Cotswold inn. The pub draws an eclectic mix of customers, including drinkers, well-informed foodies and muddy walkers – the starting point of the Cotswold Way is a short stroll away. The setting for savouring the imaginative food and tip-top ales is suitably cosy with a rustic interior – expect flagstones, a beamed ceiling and large inglenook fireplace with wood-burning stove. The kitchen makes sound use of quality local supplies, and prepares innovative modern British dishes that evolve with the seasons, with clever twists on pub classics. Gratin of smoked salmon and new potatoes with chive and tomato butter sauce might be followed by grilled Cornish sea bass with crab beignets, creamed spinach and carrots; roast confit duck leg, creamed Savoy cabbage, creamed potato, wild mushrooms and red wine jus; or open ravioli of butternut squash and ricotta cheese. For traditionalists, there is roast gammon, pineapple compôte, hand-cut chips and parsley sauce. Desserts are a strength here and might include home-made honeycomb with vanilla ice cream and chocolate sauce, or mango and passion fruit pannacotta, mango sorbet and fresh pineapple. Hook Norton, Purity and Wye Valley ales are on tap, among others, and an impressive list of wines ensures there's a tipple to suit every taste and pocket. There is free Wi-Fi throughout and four comfortable en suite rooms complete the picture at a pub that is a perfect base for exploring the Cotswolds. Booking for meals may be required.

Open all wk 11-3 6-11 Closed: 25 Dec
Bar Meals L served all wk 12-2 D served all wk 7-9 Av main course £14
Restaurant L served all wk 12-2 D served all wk 7-9 ⊞ ENTERPRISE INNS ◀ Hook Norton Hooky Bitter, Wye Valley Butty Bach, Fuller's London Pride, Purity Mad Goose ♂ Westons Stowford Press.
Facilities Children welcome Children's menu Children's portions Garden Wi-fi 🚌 (notice required) **Rooms** 4

PICK OF THE PUBS

The Bell at Sapperton

SAPPERTON   Map 4 SO90

GL7 6LE ☎ **01285 760298**

e-mail: thebell@sapperton66.freeserve.co.uk
web: www.foodatthebell.co.uk
dir: *From A419 between Cirencester &*
Stroud follow Sapperton signs

This stylish, contemporary free house
continues to evolve, as it has since
proprietors Paul Davidson and Pat
LeJeune took over in 1999. Following a
complete renovation, they established
The Bell as a thriving enterprise that
still impresses local walkers, drinkers
and diners. The 300-year-old pub is
built of mellow Cotswold stone and set
in an idyllic village close to Cirencester
Park. Exposed stone walls, polished
flagstones and bare boards set the
scene, enhanced by individual tables
and chairs and winter log fires. On
warmer days, there's a secluded rear
courtyard and a landscaped front
garden for alfresco dining. Civilised in
every way, The Bell attracts discerning
folk from miles around for its innovative
pub food, served throughout four cosy
dining areas, each with their own
individual character. Now with a new
kitchen brigade, Paul and Pat are
raising their standards once again, with
a more contemporary style of dining
tailored to busy modern lifestyles and
smaller pockets. Menus change with the
seasons, but all are founded on fresh

produce from known suppliers and local
farms. Walkers calling in for a snack
might tuck into a ploughman's, or a
roast chicken sandwich with chips and
salad, washed down by a pint of local
Uley Old Spot ale. Meanwhile, serious
diners can choose from starters like
rabbit and ham hock terrine with
parsnip and date chutney; or a grilled
Crotin goat's cheese with local golden
beetroot salad and pickled walnuts.
Main course options include wild
mushroom and spinach linguine with
parmesan cream; and slow-braised
oxtail with roasted Evesham carrots and
horseradish mash. Booking for meals
may be required.

Open 11-3 6.30-11 (Sun 12-10.30)
Closed: 25 Dec **Bar Meals** L served all
wk 12-2.15 D served all wk 7-9.30 Av
main course £15 **Restaurant** Av 3
course à la carte fr £33 🛢 FREE HOUSE
◀ Uley Old Spot, Otter Bitter, St Austell
Tribute, Bath ♻ Westons Stowford
Press. ♟ 20 **Facilities** Children's
portions ❧ Garden Parking

Save on hotels. Book at **theAA.com/hotel**

GLOUCESTERSHIRE 241 ENGLAND

SOMERFORD KEYNES   Map 4 SU09

The Bakers Arms

GL7 6DN ☎ 01285 861298
e-mail: enquiries@thebakersarmssomerford.co.uk
dir: *Exit A419 signed Cotswold Water Park. Cross B4696,
1m, follow signs for Keynes Park & Somerford Keynes*

This beautiful chocolate-box Cotswold pub is a stone's
throw from the Thames Path and Cotswold Way, making it
a convenient watering hole for walkers. Dating from the
17th century, the building was formerly the village
bakery, and has low-beamed ceilings and inglenook
fireplaces. The mature gardens are ideal for alfresco
dining, while discreet children's play areas and heated
terraces add to its broad appeal. The home-cooked food
on offer runs along the lines of sandwiches, specials and
pub favourites – Gloucestershire pork pie, pâté of the day
on toast, honey-baked ham, breaded scampi, chicken
chasseur, and trio of sausages.

Open all day all wk 11-11 (Sun 12-10.30) **Bar Meals** L
served 12-9 D served 12-9 Av main course £12 food
served all day **Restaurant** L served 12-9 D served 12-9
food served all day ⊕ ENTERPRISE INNS ◀ Courage Best,
Butcombe Bitter, Stroud Budding Ò Thatchers Gold.
Facilities ❤ Children welcome Children's menu
Children's portions Play area Garden Parking ◼

SOUTH CERNEY   Map 5 SU09

The Old Boathouse ◉

**Cotswold Water Park Four Pillars Hotel, Spine Road
East GL7 5FP ☎ 01285 864111**
e-mail: oldboathouse@four-pillars.co.uk
dir: *M4 junct 15/A419 to Cirencester, turn onto B4696 &
follow signs for Cotswold Water Park Information Centre*

At the heart of the watery wonderland of the Cotswold
Water Park, this ultra-modern gastro-pub is a relaxing
spot at which to unwind after a day's hard touring of
honeyed villages or birdwatching amidst these flooded
gravel pits. A robust British menu includes potted Cornish
crab, roast rump of lamb, and seared cod supreme, or
simply nibble on a deli board and enjoy the views from
the terrace. A daily-changing specials board combines to
earn this unusual destination bar an AA Rosette.

Open all day all wk 11-11 (Sun 11-10.30) **Bar Meals** L
served 12-6 D served 6-9.30 food served all day
Restaurant L served 12-6 D served 6-9.30 food served all
day ⊕ FREE HOUSE ◀ Timothy Taylor Landord, Black
Sheep Ò Westons Stowford Press. ☙ 15
Facilities Children welcome Children's menu Children's
portions Play area Garden Parking ◼

STONEHOUSE   Map 4 SO80

The George Inn

Peter St, Frocester GL10 3TQ ☎ 01453 822302
e-mail: paul@georgeinn.co.uk
dir: *M5 junct 13, onto A419 at 1st rdbt 3rd exit signed
Eastington, left at next rdbt signed Frocester. Approx 2m
on right in village*

Look in vain for a fruit machine or jukebox in this
family-run, former coaching inn which has a history going
back to 1716; instead, enjoy what makes a pub good – a
sensible choice of real ales and locally sourced,
home-made food, which here means bacon-wrapped
chicken breast, faggots, filled omelettes, and fish pie. The
lovely courtyard garden is overlooked by the original
coaching stables, while the Cotswold Way and a network
of leafy paths help guide visitors to the August Bank
Holiday village beer festival. There's a Sunday carvery,
and a function room that seats up to 60.

Open all day all wk 7.30am-mdnt **Bar Meals** L served all
wk 12-9.30 D served all wk 12-9.30 Av main course £8.95
food served all day **Restaurant** L served all wk 12-9.30
D served all wk 12-9.30 food served all day
⊕ ENTERPRISE INNS ◀ Sharp's Doom Bar, Timothy
Taylor, 3 Guest ales Ò Westons Old Rosie & Stowford
Press, Thatchers Gold. ☙ 10 **Facilities** ❤ Children
welcome Children's menu Children's portions Play area
Family room Garden Beer festival Parking Wi-fi ◼

STOW-ON-THE-WOLD   Map 10 SP12

The Eagle and Child

GL54 1HY ☎ 01451 830670
e-mail: stay@theroyalisthotel.com
dir: *From Moreton-in-Marsh rail station take A429 to
Stow-on-the-Wold. At 2nd lights left into Sheep St, A436.
Establishment 100yds on left*

Reputedly the oldest inn in England, dating back to 947
AD and once a hospice to shelter lepers, The Eagle and
Child is part of the Royalist Hotel. The social hub of the
hotel and village, serving local ales on handpump, it also
delivers pub food that manages to be both rustic and
accomplished. Informality and flexibility go hand-in-hand
with flagstone floors, oak beams and rustic tables; the
light-flooded conservatory offering a striking contrast to
the low-ceilinged dining room. Expect a range of seasonal
pub classics, from braised lamb shank to fish and chips,
and more innovative plates like beetroot and smoked
cheese soufflé with roast shallot purée.

Open all wk 11-11 (Sun 11-10.30) ⊕ FREE HOUSE
◀ Hook Norton Hooky Bitter, Goffs Jouster, Donnington
Ò Westons Stowford Press. **Facilities** Children welcome
Garden Parking

The Unicorn

Sheep St GL54 1HQ ☎ 01451 830257
e-mail: reception@birchhotels.co.uk
dir: *Telephone for directions*

Set in the heart of Stow-on-the-Wold, this attractive
17th-century property is built from honey-coloured
limestone and bedecked with abundantly flowering
window boxes. The interior is stylishly presented with
Jacobean pieces, antique artefacts and open log fires.
Food is served in the oak-beamed bar, the stylish
contemporary restaurant or in the secluded garden if the
weather is fine. Typical dishes include grilled goat's
cheese with beetroot and balsamic dressing; tender
strips of pork in tangy sherry and mustard sauce with
mushrooms and chives; and sticky toffee pudding with
vanilla ice cream.

Open all day all wk **Bar Meals** Av main course £11.95
Restaurant L served all wk 12-2 D served all wk 7-9 Av 3
course à la carte fr £24 ⊕ FREE HOUSE ◀ Wye Valley
Dorothy Goodbody's Country Ale, Hook Norton Ò Westons.
Facilities Children welcome Children's menu Children's
portions Garden Parking Wi-fi ◼

White Hart Inn

The Square GL54 1AF ☎ 01451 830674
e-mail: info@theoldbutchers.com
dir: *From A429 into market square. Inn on left*

Some of the mellow stone buildings in this lovely
Cotswold town date to the 12th century, including parts
of the White Hart. Under the management of Louise and
Peter Robinson since 2010, it has been refurbished
throughout. Two cosy bars benefit from open fires, and an
atmospheric dining room serves lunchtime snacks such
as a Lincolnshire poacher and piccalilli sandwich. For
dinner, you could start with Cornish scallops with chorizo;
follow with local pheasant cooked with cloves and
cinnamon; and round off with chocolate marquis. There's
a spacious car park.

Open all day all wk Closed: 1wk May & 1wk Oct **Bar
Meals** L served all wk 12-2.30 D served Mon-Sat 6.30-9
Av main course £13 **Restaurant** L served all wk 12-2.30
D served Mon-Sat 6.30-9 Av 3 course à la carte fr £24
⊕ ARKELL'S ◀ 3B, 2B, Kingsdown Ò Westons Stowford
Press. ☙ 11 **Facilities** Children welcome Children's menu
Children's portions Garden Parking Wi-fi

STROUD — Map 4 SO80

Bear of Rodborough Hotel ★★★ HL

PICK OF THE PUBS

Rodborough Common GL5 5DE ☎ 01453 878522
e-mail: info@bearofrodborough.info
dir: *From M5 junct 13 follow signs for Stonehouse then Rodborough*

Surrounded by 300 acres of National Trust land, this 17th-century former alehouse takes its name from the bear-baiting that used to take place near by. The pub is worth seeking out for all sorts of reasons; the open log fires, stone walls and solid wooden floors to be sure, but don't overlook the interesting inscription over the front doors. Head to the bar for a pint of Wickwar before seeking a seat on the York stone terrace or in the gardens with walled croquet lawn. The bar menu has many delights, such as Welsh rarebit with local apples, and fond favourites: beer-battered haddock; Gloucester Old Spot sausages; and game pie with buttered cabbage and hand-cut chips. Look to the Library restaurant for a more formal affair, where you can try shellfish ravioli, slow-braised blade of beef, and raspberry crème brûlée, all the while enjoying the panoramic views of the Cotswold countryside. Accommodation is available.

Open all day all wk 10.30am-11pm **Bar Meals** L served all wk 12-2.30 D served all wk 6.30-10 **Restaurant** D served all wk 7-10 ⊕ FREE HOUSE ◀ Butcombe, Stroud, Wickwar ♂ Ashton Press. ♥ 10 **Facilities** ✿ Children welcome Children's menu Children's portions Play area Garden Parking Wi-fi ▦ (notice required) **Rooms** 46

The Ram Inn

South Woodchester GL5 5EL ☎ 01453 873329
e-mail: raminnwoodchester@hotmail.co.uk
dir: *A46 from Stroud to Nailsworth, right after 2m into South Woodchester, follow brown tourist signs*

In winter the warmth from its huge fireplace might prove more appealing than standing on the terrace of this 17th-century Cotswold-stone inn, admiring the splendid views. Originally a farm, it became an alehouse in 1811 and is still full of historic little gems. Food is all home cooked and, typically, breaded fillet of plaice might appear on the menu, with Italian sausage and bean hotpot featuring as a daily special, along with several vegetarian items. Bath SPA, Butcombe Bitter, Stroud Budding and Uley Old Spot will appeal to real ale drinkers.

Open all day all wk **Bar Meals** L served Mon-Fri 12-2, Sat all day, Sun 12-3 D served all wk 6-9 Av main course £8.95 **Restaurant** L served Mon-Fri 12-2, Sat all day, Sun 12-3 D served all wk 6-9 Fixed menu price fr £9.95 ⊕ FREE HOUSE ◀ Uley Old Spot, Stroud Budding, Butcombe Bitter, Bath SPA, Guest ales ♂ Westons Stowford Press. **Facilities** ✿ Children welcome Children's menu Children's portions Family room Garden Parking Wi-fi ▦ (notice required)

Rose & Crown Inn

PICK OF THE PUBS

The Cross, Nympsfield GL10 3TU ☎ 01453 860240
dir: *M5 junct 13 off B4066, SW of Stroud*

An imposing, 400-year-old coaching inn of honey-coloured local stone that could well be the highest pub in the Cotswolds, a fact that hardly matters since the views over the Severn are stunning anyway. Occupying a central position in the village, the closeness of the Cotswold Way makes it a popular stop for hikers and bikers. Inside, the inn's character is preserved with natural stone, wood panelling, a lovely open fire and some local real ales, like Stroud Organic and Wickwar Cotswold Way. In the galleried restaurant, the owners offer fresh, home-made food cooked to order — steak-and-ale pie, T-bone steak, Gressingham duck, lamb rump and vegetarian options. In the large garden, children will enjoy the playground area, which has a swing, slides and a climbing bridge.

Open all day all wk 11.30-11 (Sun 12-9) **Bar Meals** L served Mon-Sat 12-2.30, Sun 12-6 D served Mon-Sat 6-9 **Restaurant** L served Mon-Sat 12-2.30, Sun 12-6 D served Mon-Sat 6-9 ⊕ FREE HOUSE ◀ Stroud Organic, Sharp's Doom Bar, Wickwar Cotswold Way ♂ Westons Stowford Press, Aspall. **Facilities** ✿ Children welcome Children's menu Children's portions Play area Garden Parking ▦

The Woolpack Inn

Slad Rd, Slad GL6 7QA ☎ 01452 813429
e-mail: info@thewoolpackinn-slad.com
dir: *2m from Stroud, 8m from Gloucester*

Laurie Lee of *Cider With Rosie* fame used to be a regular at this friendly local in the beautiful Slad Valley close to the Cotswold Way. Although ale fans make a detour here to sample the Uley Pigs Ear, the food is of equal importance. A starter of crayfish and baby prawn salad with Bloody Mary dressing might be followed by Stroud and Gloucester Old Spot sausages with mash and spring greens. A popular place for walkers, muddy boots are not frowned upon, and children and dogs are welcome. Booking for meals may be required.

Open all day all wk **Bar Meals** L served Mon-Sat 12-2, Sun 12-3.30 D served Tue-Sat 6.30-9 Av main course £10 **Restaurant** L served Mon-Sat 12-2, Sun 12-3.30 D served Tue-Sat 6.30-9 Av 3 course à la carte fr £25 ⊕ FREE HOUSE ◀ Uley Pigs Ear, Old Spot & Bitter, Stroud Budding, Butcombe Bitter ♂ Westons Old Rosie & Stowford Press. **Facilities** ✿ Children welcome Children's portions Garden Parking Wi-fi

TETBURY — Map 4 ST89

Gumstool Inn

PICK OF THE PUBS

See Pick of the Pubs on opposite page

The Priory Inn ★★★ SHL

PICK OF THE PUBS

London Rd GL8 8JJ ☎ 01666 502251
e-mail: info@theprioryinn.co.uk
dir: *M4 junct 17, A429 towards Cirencester. Left onto B4014 to Tetbury. Over mini rdbt onto Long St, pub 100yds after corner on right*

Parts of this thriving gastro-pub and hotel date from the 16th century, when it was a stable block and grooms' cottages for the neighbouring priory. In the heart of charming Tetbury, the inn has an excellent selection of real ales, including Uley Bitter; real cider from Thatchers is also on tap; and a local bubbly from Bow in the Cloud vineyard near Malmesbury is sold by the glass. A '30-mile food zone' demonstrates the pub's commitment to serving food and drink from farms and suppliers within a 30-mile radius. Children are particularly welcome, with a specialised menu and junior cocktails, plus the opportunity to decorate a personalised wood-fired pizza. There are pizzas for the adults too, with toppings from pepperoni and chorizo to balsamic roasted caramelised pear with double Gloucester. Evening meal options might include slow-braised shoulder of lamb served on creamed leeks. Try apple and sultana crumble with custard for dessert. There is live music every Sunday evening, and local ale and cider days twice a year. Booking for meals may be required.

Open all day all wk 7am-11pm (Fri 7am-mdnt Sat 8am-mdnt Sun 8am-11pm) **Bar Meals** L served Mon-Thu 12-3, Fri-Sun & BH all day (bkfst served all wk 7-10.30) D served Mon-Thu 5-10, Fri-Sun & BH all day **Restaurant** L served Mon-Thu 12-3, Fri-Sun & BH all day (bkfst served all wk 7-10.30) D served Mon-Thu 5-10, Fri-Sun & BH all day Av 3 course à la carte fr £25 ⊕ FREE HOUSE ◀ Uley Bitter, 2 Guest ales ♂ Thatchers Gold, Cotswold, Guest Cider. ♥ 13 **Facilities** Children welcome Children's menu Children's portions Play area Family room Garden Beer festival Parking **Rooms** 14

Snooty Fox Hotel ★★★ SHL

Market Place GL8 8DD ☎ 01666 502436
e-mail: res@snooty-fox.co.uk
dir: *In town centre opposite covered market hall*

Slap bang in the centre of Tetbury, this 16th-century coaching inn retains many of its original features. Sit in a leather armchair in front of the log fire with a pint of Butcombe Bitter and order from the extensive bar menu — a pint of prawns with lemon and garlic mayonnaise or smoked chicken Caesar salad maybe. Alternatively, head for the restaurant and enjoy the likes of rabbit terrine with pear chutney; beef Wellington; or roast partridge with whisky sauce, haggis, neeps and tatties. Booking for meals may be required.

Open all day all wk ⊕ FREE HOUSE ◀ Wadworth 6X, Butcombe Bitter ♂ Ashton Press. **Facilities** Children welcome Children's portions Wi-fi **Rooms** 12

Save on hotels. Book at **theAA.com/hotel**

GLOUCESTERSHIRE 243 ENGLAND

PICK OF THE PUBS

Gumstool Inn

TETBURY   Map 4 ST89

Calcot Manor GL8 8YJ
☎ **01666 890391**
e-mail: reception@calcotmanor.co.uk
web: www.calcotmanor.co.uk
dir: *3m W of Tetbury at A4135 & A46 junct*

Set in 220 acres of beautiful Cotswold countryside, this stylish country inn is part of Calcot Manor Hotel, a stone farmhouse originally built by Cistercian monks in the 14th century. As a free house, the buzzy and comfortable Gumstool Inn has a real country-pub atmosphere and stocks a good selection of West Country ales such as Butcombe Gold, and local ciders including Ashton Press. An excellent choice of 26 wines are offered by the glass or bottle. The food here is of top-notch gastro-pub quality and there is a pronounced use of local suppliers. After nibbles of quail Scotch eggs and shell-on prawns with garlic and herb mayonnaise, move on to starters of twice-baked Arbroath smokie and Montgomery cheddar cheese soufflé; or warm Cornish crab and leek tart with rocket and frisée salad. A section of the menu proffers light main courses such as an English charcuterie platter with piccalilli and gherkins; and grilled haloumi cheese, polenta and wood-roasted Mediterranean vegetables. Among the main courses may be found Cornish fish pie; venison

steak au poivre with rösti potatoes; or steak-and-kidney pudding made from Calcot's own organic beef. A daily-changing specials board might offer the likes of mackerel on garlic toast with a tomato and rocket salad; deep-fried Cajun-spiced calamari salad with chilli jam and lime; or whole griddled lemon sole with nut brown butter and lemon. Desserts might include rich chocolate and cherry cake with crème fraîche, or Tetbury tart with blackcurrant sorbet. In the summer, grab a table on the pretty, flower-filled sun terrace, while winter evenings are warmed with cosy log fires. Booking for meals may be required.

Open all day all wk **Bar Meals** L served all wk 12-2.30 D served Mon-Sat 5.30-9.30, Sun 5.30-9 Av main course

£15 **Restaurant** L served Mon-Sat 12-2.30, Sun 12-4 D served Mon-Sat 5.30-9.30, Sun 5.30-9 Av 3 course à la carte fr £22.50 ⊕ FREE HOUSE ◄ Butcombe Bitter, Blond, Gold Ö Ashton Press. ♚ 26 **Facilities** Children welcome Children's menu Children's portions Play area Family room Garden Parking Wi-fi ⛟ (notice required)

PICK OF THE PUBS

The Farriers Arms

TODENHAM Map 10 SP23

Main St GL56 9PF ☎ **01608 650901**
e-mail: info@farriersarms.com
web: www.farriersarms.com
dir: *From Moreton-in-Marsh take A429
N. Right to Todenham*

This Cotswolds hostelry has a history going back to 1650, when monks rebuilding the church lived here. It became an ironworks in the 1700s and a third storey was added, then a smithy, before becoming a pub in 1830. After World War II the landlord was a certain Leonard Flanakin, and a pub sign with his name on is in the pub courtyard. Several books on local ghosts refer to the Farriers' priest-like figure with a pair of Jack Russell terriers. The property ticks all the country-pub boxes with its polished flagstone floors, exposed stone walls, wooden beams, and large inglenook fireplace with wood-burner – clearly the perfect surroundings for a pint of Wye Valley Butty Bach or one of the Warwickshire Beer Company's brews. If the weather's good, take your drink into the landscaped walled garden and suntrap patio at the rear to enjoy the views of the church spire and the countryside. The refurbished restaurant offers a daily-changing menu packed with local produce, and starters of king prawns in tempura batter with sweet chilli dip; and goat's cheese and red onion tart with pesto dressing. Typical main courses are sirloin steak with mushrooms and tomatoes; roast duck breast with braised cabbage, parsnip crisps and port and redcurrant sauce; and roast vegetable and goat's cheese cannelloni with parmesan cream. Good planning should leave room for a home-made dessert along traditional lines – banoffee pie or white and dark chocolate tart, for example. The bar menu lists baguettes and salad, ploughman's, tapas and a few dishes of a more substantial nature, including pie of the day; hand-carved ham, eggs and chips; and wholetail breaded scampi. On Sundays, in addition to the blackboard suggestions, there's a choice between roast beef and pork.

Open all wk 12-3 6-11 (Sun & winter 12-3 6.30-11) **Bar Meals** L served

Mon-Sat 12-2, Sun 12-2.30 D served Mon-Sat 6-9, Sun 6.30-9 **Restaurant** L served Mon-Sat 12-2, Sun 12-2.30 D served Mon-Sat 6-9, Sun 6.30-9 ⊕ FREE HOUSE ◀ Hook Norton Hooky Bitter, Wye Valley Butty Bach, Goffs, Warwickshire ♂ Westons Stowford Press. ☙ 10 **Facilities** Children welcome Children's menu Children's portions ✿ Garden Parking Wi-fi 🚌

TETBURY continued

The Trouble House

PICK OF THE PUBS

Cirencester Rd GL8 8SG ☎ 01666 502206
e-mail: contact@troublehousetetbury.co.uk
dir: *On A433 between Tetbury & Cirencester*

This historic inn stands beside the A433 between Tetbury and Cirencester and continues to thrive as a destination dining pub under Shane and Liam Parr (ex-Calcot Manor). Uniquely named after a series of unfortunate events at the pub, namely agricultural riots, two suicides and a disastrous fire, the pub has a rustic-chic interior, with scrubbed tables, wooden floors, pastel-painted walls and three warming log fires. Liam's modern British cooking draws restaurant tourists across the Cotswolds for a table – so do book. In addition to the printed menu there's a favourites board offering the likes of Salcombe crab gratin, or steak with duck fat chips and béarnaise sauce. Other options could include white onion soup with onion bhaji, followed by local lamb loin and shoulder with celeriac purée, kale and root vegetables. Finish with warm lardy cake with brown sugar ice cream. Booking for meals may be required.

Open 11.30-3 6.30-11 Closed: 25 Dec, 1st 2wks Jan, Sun eve, Mon (ex BHs **L**) **Bar Meals** L served Tue-Sun 12-2 D served Tue-Sat 7-9.30 Av main course £14 **Restaurant** L served Tue-Sun 12-2 D served Tue-Sat 7-9.30 Av 3 course à la carte fr £30 ⊕ WADWORTH ◀ 6X, Henry's Original IPA ♻ Westons Stowford Press. ♟ 12 **Facilities** ❖ Children welcome Children's portions Garden Parking

TODENHAM   Map 10 SP23

The Farriers Arms

PICK OF THE PUBS

See Pick of the Pubs on opposite page

TORMARTON   Map 4 ST77

Best Western Compass Inn

GL9 1JB ☎ 01454 218242
e-mail: info@compass-inn.co.uk
dir: *M4 junct 18, A46 N towards Stroud. After 200mtrs 1st right towards Tormarton. Inn in 300mtrs*

A charming 18th-century creeper-clad inn, set in six acres of grounds in the heart of the Gloucestershire countryside, right on the Cotswold Way. Light bites and more filling meals can be taken in the bar where real ales and cider are served. In the restaurant, dishes might include home-made chicken Kiev; grilled lamb in mint marinade; spinach and ricotta tortellini; and breaded wholetail scampi.

Open all day all wk 7am-11pm (Sat-Sun 8am-11pm) Closed: 25-26 Dec ⊕ FREE HOUSE ◀ Fuller's London Pride, Bass, Butcombe ♻ Ashton Press. **Facilities** Children welcome Children's menu Children's portions Garden Parking Wi-fi

UPPER ODDINGTON   Map 10 SP22

The Horse and Groom Inn

PICK OF THE PUBS

GL56 0XH ☎ 01451 830584
e-mail: info@horseandgroom.uk.com
dir: *1.5m S of Stow-on-the-Wold, just off A436*

Polished flagstones, beams and an inglenook log fire – what more could you ask for in a 16th-century inn in a conservation village in the Evenlode Valley? Well, you could add the grapevines outside and the pleasure of eating and drinking on the terrace or in the gardens bordered by dry-stone walls. Then there's the bar, offering an ever-changing choice of real ales – too many to mention, sadly – from regional breweries, cider and lagers from the Cotswold Brewing Co, and over 20 wines by the glass. The kitchen's commitment to neighbourhood sourcing of ingredients is impressive: bread, for instance, is made daily from locally milled flour, meats are from a Chipping Norton butcher's, and venison is from the Adlestrop Estate a mile away. Bear this localism in mind as you peruse menus typically featuring roast breast of bacon-wrapped chicken filled with chorizo; home-cooked honey-roast ham; smoked haddock kedgeree; and pan-fried polenta with butternut squash and mushrooms.

Open all wk 12-3 5.30-11 (Sun 12-3 6.30-10.30) **Bar Meals** L served all wk 12-2 D served Mon-Sat 6.30-9, Sun 7-9 **Restaurant** L served all wk 12-2 D served Mon-Sat 6.30-9, Sun 7-9 ⊕ FREE HOUSE ◀ Wye Valley Bitter & HPA, Wickwar BOB, Goffs Tournament, Box Steam Chuffin Ale ♻ Cotswold. ♟ 25 **Facilities** ❖ Children welcome Children's menu Children's portions Garden Parking Wi-fi

WINCHCOMBE   Map 10 SP02

The White Hart Inn and Restaurant

High St GL54 5LJ ☎ 01242 602359
e-mail: winchcombe@wineandsausage.co.uk
dir: *In centre of Winchcombe on B4632*

Popular with walkers, this 16th-century inn offers the perfect place to unwind in the cosy bar or intimate restaurant. The White Hart is in the heart of Winchcombe just outside Cheltenham, a small historic town set in the Cotswold countryside. There is a wine shop as well as the bar and restaurant. Specialising in an amazing choice of wines, there are also plenty of real ales, and simple and unpretentious British food sourced from local suppliers. Main dishes include Cotswold venison stew, roasted root vegetable tart and steamed sea bream.

Open all day all wk 10am-11pm (Fri-Sat 10am-mdnt Sun 10am-10.30pm) **Bar Meals** L served all wk 12-3, bar snacks all day food served all day **Restaurant** L served all wk 12-3 D served Sun-Thu 6-9.30, Fri-Sat 6-10 ⊕ FREE HOUSE ◀ Wadworth 6X, Morland Old Speckled Hen, Butcombe, Otter, Guest ales ♻ Westons Stowford Press, Addlestones. ♟ 8 **Facilities** ❖ Children welcome Children's menu Children's portions Garden Parking Wi-fi

WOODCHESTER   Map 4 SO80

The Old Fleece

PICK OF THE PUBS

Bath Rd, Rooksmoor GL5 5NB ☎ 01453 872582
e-mail: pheasantpluckers2003@yahoo.co.uk
dir: *2m S of Stroud on A46*

Set amid beautiful countryside with miles of footpaths to explore, this delightful coaching inn was built in the 18th century from Cotswold stone and has a traditional stone roof. From The Old Fleece, you can walk to Rodborough, Minchinhampton and Selsley commons, or go one step further and connect eventually with the scenic Cotswold Way long-distance trail. The beautifully refurbished interior includes wooden floors, wood panelling and exposed stone, and the bar serves well-kept Tom Long and Buckham Bitter. Predominantly French chefs offer a comprehensive menu of British and continental dishes, ranging from classics such as Old Spot sausage and mash with onion gravy, to the likes of confit duck leg with hoi sin noodles; whole sea bream with braised fennel; or pork loin steak with apple and Calvados purée.

Open all day all wk 11-11 (Sun 11-10.30) ⊕ PHEASANT PLUCKERS LTD ◀ Buckham Bitter, Stroud Tom Long, Guest ales ♻ Ashton Still. **Facilities** Children welcome Parking

GREATER MANCHESTER

ALTRINCHAM   Map 15 SJ78

The Victoria

PICK OF THE PUBS

See Pick of the Pubs on page 246

BIRTLE   Map 15 SD81

Pack Horse Inn

Elbut Ln BL9 7TU ☎ 0161 764 3620
e-mail: pack@jwlees.co.uk
dir: *From Bury towards Rochdale take B6222 (Bury & Rochdale Old Rd). Left at Fairfield General Hospital*

Just beyond this converted farmhouse, the lane gives way to marked moorland paths and tracks into the spectacular wooded chasm of the Cheesden Gorge. Ramblers and horse-riders rest awhile at this comfy, family-friendly pub, which offers classic pub meals and some interesting specials: Lancashire hotpot, roast of the day, Thai tuna sizzler, Vietnamese chicken soup, gammon steak, and Bury black pudding and chorizo salad. Good vegetarian dishes are available too, such as five bean chilli, veggie burger, Mexican nachos, vegetable curry, and cheese and onion pie. Head out to the patio on warmer days for fine views over farmland high above Bury.

Open all day all wk 11.30-11.30 (Sun 12-10.30) **Bar Meals** food served all day **Restaurant** food served all day ⊕ J W LEES ◀ Bitter, The Governor. ♟ 20 **Facilities** Children welcome Children's menu Children's portions Garden Parking 🚐

PICK OF THE PUBS

The Victoria

ALTRINCHAM Map 15 SJ78

Stamford St WA14 1EX
☎ **0161 613 1855**
e-mail: the.victoria@yahoo.co.uk
web: www.thevictoria-altrincham.co.uk
dir: *From rail station cross main road, right. 2nd left into Stamford St*

This compact, one-roomed street-corner pub in trendy Altrincham was a breath of fresh air for drinkers and discerning diners when it burst onto the scene in 2006. An old, dilapidated town-centre drinking den had been transformed into an airy destination of choice; a stylish wood-panelled drawing-room area set for dining twinned with a chic, slate-floored area fronting the bar, where bar stools offer refuge for those intent simply on a restful pint of Waggle Dance or Old Speckled Hen, just a step or two away from Altrincham's shops and galleries, and handy too for the nearby Metrolink tram and rail interchange. Playfully dubbed a 'Gin Palace and Dining Room' by owners Rachel Wetherill and Kevin Choudhary, their aim – to offer a tranquil, adult's retreat where home-cooked imaginative British food with a strong traditional influence takes the lead – has paid dividends. The menu changes every six to eight .weeks to reflect seasonal availability. Typical starters might include oxtail soup, English crab cakes, or slowly braised beef and prune hash. These

could be followed by home-made lamb and apricot pudding with hand-cut chips, or escalope of naturally raised veal on chunky sautéed potatoes with watercress and a lemon, caper and parsley butter sauce. For dessert, maybe tangy lemon tart with whipped cream; sticky toffee pudding with custard; or apple crumble and ice cream. On Sundays traditional roasts are available. The wine list features a choice of more than 30 carefully chosen wines. Hand-pulled cask ales are always available, and for drivers there is a temperance bar featuring locally produced favourites such as sarsaparilla and dandelion and burdock. Other rare treats include honey mead, English potato vodka, black beer and raisin wine.

Open all day all wk 12-11 (Sun 12-6) Closed: 26 Dec & 1 Jan **Bar Meals** L served Mon-Sat 12-3 D served Mon-Sat 5.30-9.30 Av main course £15.95 **Restaurant** L served Mon-Sat 12-3, Sun 12-4 D served Mon-Sat 5.30-9.30 Fixed menu price fr £13.95 Av 3 course à la carte fr £26.50 ⊕ FREE HOUSE ◾ Morland Old Speckled Hen, Wells Waggle Dance ♂ Westons Wyld Wood Organic. ♉ 10 **Facilities** Children welcome Children's portions

DENSHAW   Map 16 SD91

The Rams Head Inn

OL3 5UN ☎ 01457 874802

e-mail: info@ramsheaddenshaw.co.uk

dir: *M62 junct 22, A672 towards Oldham, 2m to inn*

Two miles from the M62 and 1,212 feet above sea level, this 450-year-old country inn has fabulous moorland views. Log fires and collections of memorabilia are features of the interior, which includes The Pantry, an in-house farm shop, deli, bakery and coffee shop selling everything from cheeses to chocolates. Game and seafood figure strongly on the menu, with dishes ranging from fish pie to wood pigeon with roast shallots, watercress, bread sauce and game crisps. Finish with the inn's 'famed' sticky toffee pudding. There's a garden area to the rear of the inn with bench seating and panoramic views.

Open Tue-Fri 12-2.30 6-10 (Sat 12-10.30 Sun 12-8.30) Closed: 25 Dec, Mon (ex BH) **Bar Meals** L served Tue-Fri 12-2.30, Sat-Sun 12-5.30 D served Tue-Sat 6-10, Sun 6-8.30 Av main course £13.95 **Restaurant** L served Tue-Fri 12-2.30, Sat-Sun 12-5.30 D served Tue-Sat 6-10, Sun 5.30-8.30 Fixed menu price fr £16.95 Av 3 course à la carte fr £26.95 ⊕ FREE HOUSE ◀ Timothy Taylor Landlord, Black Sheep Best Bitter ᴼ Thatchers Gold. ▾ 16 **Facilities** Children welcome Children's portions Garden Parking Wi-fi

DIDSBURY   Map 16 SJ89

The Metropolitan
PICK OF THE PUBS

2 Lapwing Ln M20 2WS ☎ 0161 438 2332

e-mail: info@the-metropolitan.co.uk

dir: *M60 junct 5, A5103, right onto Barlow Moor Rd, left onto Burton Rd. Pub at x-rds. Right onto Lapwing Ln for car park*

A former Victorian railway hotel, the 'Met' is well situated in the leafy suburb of West Didsbury. Originally a hotel for passengers riding the old Midland Railway into Manchester, the pub still punches above its weight architecturally - look in particular at the decorative floor tiling, the ornate windows and the delicate plasterwork. During the latter part of the 20th century the building became very run down, but it was given a sympathetic renovation in 1997, reopening as a gastro-pub. Its huge, airy interior is filled with antique tables and chairs, and deep sofas, which suit the mainly young, cosmopolitan clientele. Food ranges from starters and light bites (warm confit duck leg with watercress, small sandwiches) to main courses such as rack of lamb with black olive crust and ratatouille, or fillet of sea trout with peas and asparagus. Spacious outside terraces buzz with drinkers and diners in the summer.

Open all day all wk 11.30am-mdnt (Sun 12-11) Closed: 25 Dec ◀ Timothy Taylor Landlord, Caledonian Deuchars IPA, Guinness ᴼ Westons, Rekorderlig. **Facilities** Children welcome Children's portions Garden Parking Wi-fi

LITTLEBOROUGH   Map 16 SD91

The White House

Blackstone Edge, Halifax Rd OL15 0LG ☎ 01706 378456

dir: *On A58, 8m from Rochdale, 9m from Halifax*

1,300 feet above sea level on the Pennine Way, this 17th-century coaching house has panoramic views of the moors and Hollingworth Lake far below. Not surprising, then, that it attracts walkers and cyclists who rest up and sup on Black Sheep and Exmoor Gold. It's been known as The White House for over 100 years and has been in the same hands for just over 28 of them. A simple menu of pub grub ranges from sandwiches and starters like grilled haloumi cheese, to grills, curries, chilli, and traditional dishes such as battered scampi or Cumberland sausage with fried egg.

Open all wk Mon-Sat 12-3 6-10 (Sun 12-10.30) Closed: 25 Dec **Bar Meals** L served Mon-Sat 12-2, Sun 12-9 D served Mon-Sat 6.30-9.30, Sun 12-9 **Restaurant** L served Mon-Sat 12-2, Sun 12-9 D served Mon-Sat 6.30-9.30, Sun 12-9 ⊕ FREE HOUSE ◀ Timothy Taylor Landlord, Theakston Best Bitter, Exmoor Gold, Black Sheep, Phoenix, Moorhouse's. ▾ **Facilities** Children welcome Children's menu Parking 🚌

MANCHESTER   Map 16 SJ89

Dukes 92

14 Castle St, Castlefield M3 4LZ ☎ 0161 839 8642

e-mail: info@dukes92.com

dir: *In Castlefield town centre, off Deansgate*

A beautifully restored 19th-century stable building with a vast patio beside the 92nd lock of the Duke of Bridgewater Canal, which opened in 1762. The interior is full of surprises, with minimalist décor downstairs and an upper gallery displaying local artistic talent. At the bar you'll find Moorhouse's ales and Sweden's premium bottled cider. A grill restaurant is supplemented by a lunchtime bar menu and pizza range; choices from the renowned cheese and pâté counter, displaying over 40 British and European savoury products, are served with freshly baked granary bread.

Open all day all wk Closed: 25-26 Dec, 1 Jan **Bar Meals** L served all wk 12-3 **Restaurant** L served all wk 12-5 D served all wk 5-11 ⊕ FREE HOUSE ◀ Moorhouse's ᴼ Kopparberg. ▾ 15 **Facilities** Children welcome Children's menu Children's portions Garden Parking 🚌

Marble Arch

73 Rochdale Rd M4 4HY ☎ 0161 832 5914

dir: *In city centre (Northern Quarter)*

Built in 1888 by celebrated architect Alfred Darbyshire for Manchester brewery B&J McKenna, the Marble Arch is now part of the award-winning organic Marble Brewery. A listed building famous for its sloping floor, glazed brick walls and barrel-vaulted ceiling, it is a fine example of Manchester's Victorian heritage. Now an established favourite with beer aficionados and offering six regular ales and eight seasonal house beers, the pub offers a well-considered menu, from traditional bar meals of fish and chips to rabbit cassoulet. It also hosts its own beer festivals.

Open all day all wk Closed: 25 Dec **Bar Meals** L served Mon-Sat 12-8.45, Sun 12-7.45 D served Mon-Sat 12-8.45, Sun 12-7.45 Av main course £9.50 **Restaurant** L served Mon-Sat 12-8.45, Sun 12-7.45 D served Mon-Sat 12-8.45, Sun 12-7.45 Av 3 course à la carte fr £25 ⊕ FREE HOUSE ◀ Marble Manchester Bitter, Lagonda IPA, Ginger Marble ᴼ Moonshine. ▾ 10 **Facilities** Children welcome Garden Beer festival

MARPLE BRIDGE   Map 16 SJ98

Hare & Hounds

19 Mill Brow SK6 5LW ☎ 0161 427 4042

e-mail: gmarsh@bwanorth.co.uk

dir: *From Marple Bridge travelling towards Mellor, turn left up Hollins Ln. Follow road to T junct with Ley Ln. Turn right, pub is 0.25m on left.*

Dating from 1805, the Hare & Hounds is a hidden gem in the beautiful hamlet of Mill Brow, a genuine village community in a great rural setting. It is a comfortable country pub with great atmosphere, roaring fires in winter and a get-away from loud music and big TV screens. You can enjoy a pint of real ale or cider here, and peruse the menu. Freshly prepared food is offered using local ingredients where possible. Expect dishes like starters of smoked haddock and prawn gratin in cheddar and parmesan sauce, followed by Goyt Valley wild venison steak with cabbage, port-glazed shallots, wild mushrooms and a chocolate and chilli sauce; or sweet potato, chickpea and spinach curry. For dessert, enjoy peach, raspberry and ginger crumble or egg custard. Booking for meals may be required.

Open all wk 5-12 (Fri 12-3 5-12 Sat-Sun 12-12) **Bar Meals** L served Fri-Sat 12-2, Sun 1-7 D served Mon-Sat 6-9.30 Av main course £11-£18 **Restaurant** L served Fri-Sat 12-2, Sun 1-7 D served Mon-Sat 6-9.30 Av 3 course à la carte fr £21 ⊕ FREDERIC ROBINSON ◀ Unicorn, Hatters, Dizzy Blonde, Seasonal Ales ᴼ Westons Stowford Press. **Facilities** Children welcome Children's portions Garden Parking Wi-fi

MELLOR   Map 16 SJ98

The Moorfield Arms ★★★★ INN

Shiloh Rd SK6 5NE ☎ 0161 427 1580
e-mail: info@moorfieldarms.com
dir: *From Marple station down Brabyns Brow to lights.
Right into Town St. 3m, left into Shiloh Rd. 0.5m, pub
on left*

This old pub dates from 1640 and retains plenty of
old-world charm and atmosphere. With stunning views of
Kinder Scout and Lantern Pike, The Moorfield Arms makes
an ideal Peak District base and is popular with fell
walkers. The extensive menu includes fish specials and
slow-roasted lamb in mint gravy and finished with fresh
rosemary from the pub's own herb garden. When the sun
makes an appearance, head for the garden terrace.
Situated in a barn conversion, the en suite rooms are
comfortable and stylish.

Open Tue-Sat 12-2.30 6-12 (Sun 12-9) Closed: Mon **Bar
Meals** L served Tue-Sat 12-2, Sun 12-9 D served Tue-Sun
6-9 **Restaurant** L served Tue-Sun 12-2 D served Tue-Sun
6-9 ⊕ FREE HOUSE ◀ Wychwood Hobgoblin, Marston's
EPA. ♀ 12 **Facilities** Children welcome Children's menu
Garden Parking ▭ **Rooms** 4

OLDHAM   Map 16 SD90

The Roebuck Inn

Strinesdale OL4 3RB ☎ 0161 624 7819
e-mail: sehowarth1@hotmail.com
dir: *From Oldham Mumps Bridge take Huddersfield Rd
(A62), right at 2nd lights onto Ripponden Rd (A672), after
1m right at lights onto Turfpit Ln, follow for 1m*

A thousand feet up in Strinedale on the edge of
Saddleworth Moor, this traditionally styled inn provides a
menu with plenty of choice. Starters include Bury black
pudding with hot mustard sauce, and smoked salmon
and prawns, then comes a long list of main courses,
including fillet of beef Stroganoff; fajitas with sour cream
and guacamole; roast half-duck with orange stuffing;
and deep-fried haddock in batter. Vegetarians could well
find an option like spinach and ricotta tortellini with
roasted peppers. Beers come from the Black Sheep
Brewery in Masham. Booking for meals may be required.

Open all wk 12-3 5-11 (Fri-Sun 12-11) **Bar Meals** L
served all wk 12-2.15 D served all wk 5-9.15
Restaurant L served all wk 12-2.15 D served all wk
5-9.15 ⊕ FREE HOUSE ◀ Black Sheep. ♀ 9 **Facilities** ❄
Children welcome Children's menu Children's portions
Play area Garden Parking Wi-fi ▭

The White Hart Inn ◉

51 Stockport Rd, Lydgate OL4 4JJ ☎ 01457 872566
e-mail: bookings@thewhitehart.co.uk
dir: *From Manchester A62 to Oldham. Right onto bypass,
A669 through Lees. In 500yds past Grotton, at brow of hill
turn right onto A6050*

The Grade II listed coaching inn high on the hillside
overlooking Oldham and Manchester is owned by Charles
Brierley, who converted the ground floor into a smart bar
and brasserie. There's been a pub on this site since 1788,
when its vast cellars were used for brewing beer using
water from the well. A barn added to house the local
foxhounds later served as a police station, school and
weaver's cottage. The White Hart has retained its period
charm of beams, exposed stonework and open fireplaces,
blending these with contemporary décor. Head chef Mike
Shaw makes good use of local ingredients, creating
cosmopolitan menus. The brasserie menu could feature
snails with garlic and herb butter, followed by pan-fried
cod fillet with salmon gnocchi and buttered leeks. Book
the restaurant for cauliflower cappuccino with truffle
potato and scallops; and smoked corn-fed chicken with
creamed cabbage, morel mushrooms and garlic sauce.
The inn also an intimate library dining area, and
award-winning gardens. Booking for meals may be
required.

Open all day all wk Closed: 26 Dec **Bar Meals** L served
Mon-Sat 12-2.30, Sun 1-8 D served all wk 6-9.30 Av main
course £15.50 **Restaurant** L served Sun 1-3.30 D served
Mon & Wed-Sat 6-9.30 Fixed menu price fr £19.95 Av 3
course à la carte fr £25 ⊕ FREE HOUSE ◀ Timothy Taylor
Landlord & Golden Best, JW Lees Bitter, Copper Dragon
Ŏ Westons Stowford Press. ♀ 12 **Facilities** Children
welcome Children's menu Garden Parking Wi-fi

STOCKPORT   Map 16 SJ89

The Arden Arms

23 Millgate SK1 2LX ☎ 0161 480 2185
e-mail: steve@ardenarms.com
dir: *M60 junct 27 to town centre. Across mini rdbt, at
lights turn left. Pub on right of next rdbt behind Asda*

The classic unspoilt layout and original tiled floors of this
Grade II listed late-Georgian coaching inn rank high
among the country's timeless gems. The building was
last modernised in 1908, giving drinkers the opportunity
to order from the traditional curved bar before settling
down by the coal fire in the tiny snug. These days, this
historic inn offers great real ales plus guests, and good
food. On offer are interesting hot and cold sandwiches
and home-made soup, and a selection of hot dishes like
oven-roasted Cheshire pork steak, fish curry, or Scottish
smoked salmon, cream cheese and rocket in an open
toasted ciabatta sandwich. Look out for the
daily-changing specials board. There's always a
traditional Sunday roast, as well as jazz nights and
charity quizzes.

Open all wk 12-12 Closed: 25-26 Dec, 1 Jan **Bar Meals** L
served Mon-Fri 12-2.30, Sat-Sun 12-4 Av main course

£8.95 ⊕ FREDERIC ROBINSON ◀ Unicorn, Hatters, Double
Hop, Dizzy Blonde, Seasonal ales Ŏ Westons Stowford
Press. ♀ 8 **Facilities** ❄ Children welcome Garden Wi-fi

The Nursery Inn

Green Ln, Heaton Norris SK4 2NA ☎ 0161 432 2044
e-mail: nurseryinn@hydesbrewery.com
dir: *Green Ln off Heaton Moor Rd. Pass rugby club on
Green Ln, at end on right. Narrow cobbled road, pub
100yds on right*

Finding a pub with its own bowling green is challenging,
but possible at this classic, unspoilt Grade II listed 1930s
hostelry, down a cobbled lane in a pleasant Manchester
suburb, which has one at the rear. In the rambling
interior you can drink beers from Hydes and enjoy some
good value, home-cooked lunchtime snacks, sandwiches,
toasties, salads and pub-grub mains like home-made pie
or roast of the day. Eight guest real ales on handpump
are served at the three annual beer festivals.

Open all day all wk **Bar Meals** L served Tue-Fri 12-2.30,
Sat-Sun 12-4 **Restaurant** L served Tue-Sun 12-2.30
⊕ HYDES BREWERY ◀ Original, Jekyll's Gold & Seasonal
ales, Guest ales. **Facilities** ❄ Children welcome
Children's portions Garden Beer festival Parking Wi-fi
▭

WALMERSLEY   Map 15 SD81

The Lord Raglan

Nangreaves BL9 6SP ☎ 0161 764 6680
dir: *M66 junct 1, A56 to Walmersley. Left into Palatine
Drive, left into Ribble Drive, left into Walmersley Old Rd
to Nangreaves*

The Lord Raglan is set beside a cobbled lane high on the
moors above Bury at the head of a former weaving
hamlet, where lanes and tracks dissipate into deep,
secluded gorges rich in industrial heritage. Beers brewed
at the on-site Leyden Brewery may be taken in the garden,
where the throaty cough of steam engines on the East
Lancashire Railway echoes off the River Irwell's steep
valley sides below the towering Peel Monument. Reliable,
traditional pub grub takes the edge off walkers'
appetites, whilst a frequently changing specials menu
draws diners to the characterful dining room of this
rambling, stone-built pub. Try the home-made
steak-and-ale pie, the Cumberland sausage and egg, or
the nice bit of London mixed grill.

Open all wk 12-2.30 6-11 (Fri 12-2.30 5-11 Sat-Sun all
day) **Bar Meals** L served Mon-Fri 12-2, Sat 12-9, Sun
12-8 D served Mon-Thu 6-9, Fri 5-9, Sat 12-9, Sun 12-8
Restaurant L served Mon-Fri 12-2, Sat 12-9, Sun 12-8
D served Mon-Thu 6-9, Fri 5-9, Sat 12-9, Sun 12-8
⊕ FREE HOUSE ◀ Leyden Nanny Flyer, Crowning Glory,
Light Brigade, Black Pudding. ♀ 10 **Facilities** ❄ Children
welcome Children's menu Children's portions Garden
Beer festival Parking ▭

Save on hotels. Book at **theAA.com/hotel**

HAMPSHIRE 249 ENGLAND

HAMPSHIRE

ALTON   Map 5 SU73

The Anchor Inn ★★★★★ RR ◉◉

PICK OF THE PUBS

See Pick of the Pubs on page 250

AMPFIELD   Map 5 SU42

White Horse at Ampfield

Winchester Rd SO51 9BQ ☎ 01794 368356
e-mail: whitehorseinn@hotmail.co.uk
web: www.whitehorseampfield.co.uk
dir: *From Winchester take A3040, then A3090 towards
Romsey. Ampfield in 7m. Or M3 junct 13, A335 (signed
Chandler's Ford). At lights right onto B3043, follow
Chandler's Ford Industrial Estate then Hursley signs. Left
onto A3090 to Ampfield*

With roots as a pilgrims' inn in the 16th century, the
timber-framed White Horse is the only pub in the village
in which The Rev W. Awdry, *Thomas the Tank Engine*'s
creator, lived as a boy. The building is home to three
large inglenooks, the one in the public bar having an iron
fireback decorated with the crest of Charles I and hooks
on which to hang bacon sides on for smoking. Typical
dishes are pan-fried monkfish with chorizo and bean
cassoulet; mixed game hotpot; and aubergine and lentil
moussaka with 'Greek-style' sweet potato. Booking for
meals may be required.

Open all day all wk 11-11 (Sun 12-9) **Bar Meals** L served
Mon-Fri 12-2.30, Sat 12-9, Sun 12-5 D served Mon-Fri
6-9, Sat 12-9 Av main course £12 **Restaurant** L served
Mon-Fri 12-2.30, Sat 12-9, Sun 12-5 D served Mon-Fri
6-9, Sat 12-9 Av 3 course à la carte fr £25 ⊕ GREENE
KING ◀ Morland Old Speckled Hen, Wadworth 6X,
Ringwood Best Bitter. ♚ 14 **Facilities** Children welcome
Children's menu Children's portions Play area Garden
Parking Wi-fi 🚐 (notice required)

ANDOVER   Map 5 SU34

Wyke Down Country Pub & Restaurant

Wyke Down, Picket Piece SP11 6LX ☎ 01264 352048
e-mail: info@wykedown.co.uk
dir: *3m from Andover town centre/A303. Follow signs for
Wyke Down Caravan Park*

A diversified farm on the outskirts of Andover, this
establishment combines a pub/restaurant with a golf
driving range, but still raises its own beef cattle. The pub
started in a barn over 25 years ago and the restaurant
was built some years later. A typical meal might be chef's
own chicken liver pâté with onion marmalade and warm
toast followed by steamed pudding filled with steak,
bacon, onion and London Pride. Other choices include
plenty from the grill and international favourites such as
curry and Cajun chicken. Booking for meals may be
required.

Open all wk 12-3 6-11 Closed: 25 Dec-2 Jan **Bar Meals** L
served all wk 12-2 D served all wk 6-9 **Restaurant** L
served all wk 12-2 D served all wk 6-9 ⊕ FREE HOUSE
◀ Fuller's London Pride, Guinness. **Facilities** Children
welcome Children's menu Children's portions Play area
Garden Parking 🚐 (notice required)

BALL HILL   Map 5 SU46

The Furze Bush Inn

**Hatt Common, East Woodhay RG20 0NQ
☎ 01635 253228**
e-mail: info@furzebushinn.co.uk
dir: *From Newbury onto Andover Road (A343), signed*

Following a day at the Newbury Races, walking the
Berkshire Downs, or visiting Highclere Castle, the location
for the TV series *Downton Abbey*, seek refreshment and a
meal at this popular rural free house. The bar menu
features a good range of pub favourites, with more
adventurous dishes like braised lamb with port, rosemary
and garlic, or pasta with scallops, mussels, crayfish,
salmon and prawns in a creamy white wine sauce
available in the restaurant. There's a large front garden,
a rear patio with huge TV and parasol plus a children's
play area – perfect for summer drinking. Booking for
meals may be required.

Open all day all wk **Bar Meals** L served Sun-Thu 12-8.30,
Fri-Sat 12-9.30 D served Sun-Thu 12-8.30, Fri-Sat
12-9.30 Av main course £10 food served all day
Restaurant L served Sun-Thu 12-8.30, Fri-Sat 12-9.30
D served all wk 12-8.30 Fixed menu price fr £16 Av 3
course à la carte fr £24 food served all day ⊕ FREE
HOUSE ◀ Fuller's London Pride, Greene King Abbot Ale.
Facilities Children welcome Children's menu Play area
Garden Beer festival Parking Wi-fi 🚐

BAUGHURST   Map 5 SU56

The Wellington Arms ◉◉

PICK OF THE PUBS

See Pick of the Pubs on page 251

BEAULIEU   Map 5 SU30

The Drift Inn

Beaulieu Rd SO42 7YQ ☎ 023 8029 2342
e-mail: bookatable@driftinn.co.uk
dir: *From Lyndhurst take B3056 (Beaulieu Rd) signed
Beaulieu. Cross railway line, inn on left*

Part of the New Forest Hotels group, the inn is surrounded
by the glorious New Forest, its name being the
centuries-old round-up of its 3,000-plus free-wandering
ponies. Beers from Ringwood on the western side of the
forest and a guest ale are served in the bar, while in the
restaurant a competitively priced menu lists Thai-style
green vegetable curry; New Forest steak; and haddock
and chips. Outside are two children's play areas and
large gardens, although no one minds if you come inside
wearing walking boots and with your dog in tow.

Open all wk **Bar Meals** L served all wk 12-9 D served all
wk 12-9 food served all day **Restaurant** L served all wk
12-9 D served all wk 12-9 food served all day ⊕ FREE
HOUSE ◀ Ringwood Best Bitter, Old Thumper &
Boondoggle, Guest ales Ō Thatchers. ♀ **Facilities** ✿
Children welcome Children's menu Children's portions
Play area Garden Beer festival Parking Wi-fi

BEAUWORTH   Map 5 SU52

The Milburys

SO24 0PB ☎ 01962 771248
dir: *A272 towards Petersfield, after 6m turn right for
Beauworth*

Dating from the 17th century and taking its name from
the Bronze Age barrow nearby, this rustic hill-top pub is
noted for its massive, 250-year-old treadmill that used to
draw water from the 300-ft well in the bar. In summer,
sweeping views across Hampshire can be savoured from
the lofty garden. Inside you will find a great selection of
real ales which you can enjoy by the warming winter fires.
Traditional pub food, such as steak-and-ale pie and
battered cod, is served all week in the bar and restaurant.
There's a skittle alley, and rallies and club meetings are
held here.

Open all wk **Bar Meals** L served all wk 12-2 D served all
wk 6-9 Av main course £9.95 **Restaurant** L served all wk
12-2 D served all wk 6-9 ⊕ FREE HOUSE ◀ Milburys
Best, Goddards Ale of Wight, Hop Back Summer Lightning
& Crop Circle Ō Westons Stowford Press. **Facilities** ✿
Children welcome Children's menu Children's portions
Play area Family room Garden Parking 🚐

PICK OF THE PUBS

The Anchor Inn ★★★★★ RR ❀❀

Lower Froyle GU34 4NA
☎ **01420 23261**
e-mail: info@anchorinnatlowerfroyle.co.uk
web: www.anchorinnatlowerfroyle.co.uk
dir: *From A31 follow Bentley signs*

Part of the Miller's Collection of period inns, this old, tile-hung rural inn, has the quintessentially English feel that qualified it for membership. The low ceilings, wooden floors, exposed beams and open fires all give clues to the age of the 16th-century farmhouse that forms the nucleus of the building. In fact, even during the last 60 years very little can have changed in the intimate snug and saloon bar, generously dressed with antiques and old prints, apart from gentle refurbishment. The beers are local, with Alton's Pride from the town's Triple fff brewery and King John from Andwell, near Basingstoke. The acclaimed restaurant (with two AA Rosettes), where candlesticks and polished wooden tables combine with painted wall panelling, is run by Kevin Chandler, a passionate believer in the 'nose-to-tail' philosophy that ensures no part of an animal is wasted. His regularly changing menus offer simply cooked, seasonal food and use local suppliers wherever possible. Begin dinner with pork rillette, onion purée and pickled vegetable salad; or haricot beans on toast, with chorizo, rocket and parmesan. For a main, opt for braised salt beef, tongue and smoked bacon in vegetable and parsley broth; halibut fillet with crab risotto, purple sprouting broccoli and crab glaze; or pasta rotolo of butternut squash and goat's cheese, spinach, red onion and sage. Working closely with Kevin and his team is wine expert Vincent Gasnier, a Master Sommelier and former UK Sommelier of the Year, who has chosen the small but innovative selection of interesting and good-value wines. Country pursuits are taken seriously here and fly-fishing, and pheasant, partridge and clay-pigeon shooting days can be arranged. In keeping with the area's literary links (Rupert Brooke and Jane Austen both lived locally) the five beautifully designed guest rooms are named after famous war poets. Booking for meals may be required.

Open all day all wk **Bar Meals** L served all wk 12-2.30 D served all wk 6.30-9.30 **Restaurant** L served Mon-Sat 12-2.30, Sun 12-4 D served Mon-Fri 6.30-9.30, Sat 6.30-10, Sun 7-9 🍺 FREE HOUSE/MILLER'S COLLECTION ◀ Triple fff Alton's Pride, Andwell King John Ŏ Westons Stowford Press. ♔ 9 **Facilities** Children welcome Children's menu Children's portions Garden Parking Wi-fi 🚌 **Rooms** 5

PICK OF THE PUBS

The Wellington Arms ⚜⚜

BAUGHURST   Map 5 SU56

Baughurst Rd RG26 5LP
☎ **0118 982 0110**
e-mail: hello@thewellingtonarms.com
web: www.thewellingtonarms.com
dir: *From A4, E of Newbury, through Aldermaston. At 2nd rdbt 2nd exit signed Baughurst, left at T-junct, pub 1m*

Lost down a maze of lanes in peaceful countryside between Basingstoke and Newbury, the 'Welly', a former hunting lodge for the Duke of Wellington, draws discerning diners from miles around due to the combined efforts of Jason King and Simon Page, who have worked wonders with the place since taking over some eight years ago. Jason's award-winning, daily chalkboard menus offer plenty of interest and imagination and much of the produce is organic, local or home-grown. Salad leaves, herbs and vegetables are grown in the pub's polytunnel and raised vegetable beds, eggs come from their rare breed and rescue hens, and there are also seven Jacob sheep, five Tamworth pigs and three beehives. This might translate to a starter of a 'tiny' pie of Gregory's pheasants, ceps and thyme with red wine sauce; or twice-baked Marksbury cheddar soufflé on braised leeks, followed by potpie of Baughurst House roe deer slow-cooked in red wine and topped with a flaky pastry lid; or chargrilled home-reared Tamworth pork T-bone with a raw salad of red cabbage, green apple and ginger. Vegetarians will like the baked potato gnocchi pan-fried with garlic, caramelised butternut squash, sage, walnuts and parmesan. A flourless dark chocolate cake with espresso ice cream makes the perfect finish. Although the small dining room has been extended, booking is still advisable, or maybe just arrive early to secure a table. The well-tended garden is an extension for diners in the summer too, and if the weather is on the chilly side, just ask for a cosy mohair rug to keep you warm. Accommodation available. Booking for meals may be required.

Open 12-3.30 6-11 Closed: Sun eve **Restaurant** L served all wk 12-1.30 D served Mon-Sat 6-9.30 ⊕ FREE HOUSE 🛢 Wadworth 6X, West Berkshire Good Old Boy ⚉ Tutts Clump. 🍷 11 **Facilities** Children welcome Children's portions 🐾 Garden Parking Wi-fi

PICK OF THE PUBS

The Sun Inn

BENTWORTH   Map 5 SU64

Sun Hill GU34 5JT ☎ 01420 562338
e-mail: info@thesuninnbentworth.co.uk
web: www.thesuninnbentworth.co.uk
dir: *From A339 between Alton &*
Basingstoke follow Bentworth signs

Just as you think you're about to leave
the village behind, this pretty, foliage-
covered, rural free house comes into
view. Dating from the 17th century,
when it was built as a pair of traditional
cottages, little can have changed inside
in recent years, which is how landlady
Mary Holmes intends things to stay. The
floors in the three interlinked rooms are
laid with brick and board; the furniture
is a mix of scrubbed pine tables,
benches and settles; the old ceiling
beams are hung with horse brasses;
and assorted prints and plates decorate
the walls. Log fires may be burning,
while tasteful cosmetic touches –
magazines, fresh flowers, flickering
candlelight – enhance the period feel
still further. Apart from The Sun's
overall charm, people come here for its
good selection of real ales, including
from Andwell, Sharp's, Fuller's,
Ringwood and Stonehenge breweries, as
well as Aspall cider. They come too for
the extensive range of hearty home-
cooked dishes, which run from
ploughman's, home-made soup and
sandwiches, to tiger prawns and
scallops in garlic butter; chicken breast

in stilton and walnut sauce; steak,
mushroom and ale pie; and Yorkshire
pudding with vegetable sausages.
Game in season includes pheasant, and
venison cooked in Guinness with pickled
walnuts. The uncomplicated desserts
are typically warm chocolate brownie,
banoffee pie, and treacle tart. There's a
lot to see and do in the area: in
Selborne, there's the house where
naturalist Gilbert White lived and where
the Oates (of Scott's ill-fated 1911-12
Antarctic expedition fame) Collection is
now found, and Jane Austen's House at
Chawton is an easy drive too. A ride on
the Watercress Line from Alton about 15
minutes away takes you on a 10-mile
steam train journey through glorious
Hampshire countryside to Alresford and
back.

Open all wk 12-3 6-11 (Sun 12-10.30)
Bar Meals L served all wk 12-2 D served
all wk 7-9.30 ⊕ FREE HOUSE ◀ Andwell
Resolute, Ringwood Fortyniner, Sharp's
Doom Bar, Stonehenge Pigswill, Fuller's
London Pride, Black Sheep ♂ Aspall.
♟ 12 **Facilities** Children welcome
Children's menu Children's portions
Family room ✿ Garden Parking

Save on hotels. Book at **theAA.com/hotel**

HAMPSHIRE 253 **ENGLAND**

BENTLEY   Map 5 SU74

The Bull Inn

GU10 5JH ☎ 01420 22156
e-mail: enquiries@thebullinnbentley.co.uk
dir: *2m from Farnham on A31 towards Winchester*

Exposed beams, real fires and plenty of alfresco seating make this 15th-century coaching inn well worth a visit. There's also a great selection of food. Lunch brings light meals including jacket potatoes and omelettes with interesting fillings. More substantial offerings encompass sharing baskets of scampi and potato wedges, and sausages and mash with red onion marmalade and red wine jus. There's a decent selection of wines, including Châteauneuf du Pape, while beers include Fuller's London Pride and St Austell Tribute.

Open all day all wk 11-11 (Sun 12-10.30) **Bar Meals** L served Mon-Sat 12-2.30, Sun 12-4.30 D served Mon-Sat 6-9.30 Av main course £9 **Restaurant** L served Mon-Sat 12-2.30, Sun 12-4.30 D served Mon-Sat 6-9.30 Fixed menu price fr £9.95 Av 3 course à la carte fr £15 ⊕ ENTERPRISE INNS ◀ Fuller's London Pride, St Austell Tribute, Ringwood Best Bitter ♂ Aspall. **Facilities** Children welcome Children's menu Children's portions Garden Parking Wi-fi 🚐 (notice required)

BENTWORTH   Map 5 SU64

The Sun Inn

PICK OF THE PUBS

See Pick of the Pubs on opposite page

BOLDRE   Map 5 SZ39

The Hobler Inn

Southampton Rd, Battramsley SO41 8PT
☎ 01590 623944
e-mail: hedi@alcatraz.co.uk
dir: *2m from Brockenhurst, towards Lymington on main road*

On the main road between Brockenhurst and Lymington, The Hobler has a large grassed area and trestle tables ideal for families visiting the New Forest. The Hobler Inn is more London wine bar than local with stylish leather furniture, but still serves a well-kept pint of Ringwood. Hot lunchtime snacks like Welsh rarebit or Boston baked beans on toast are good value. Mains include a variation on the classic shepherd's pie but with added Nepalese spices.

Open all day all wk ◀ Ringwood Best Bitter, Timothy Taylor. **Facilities** Children welcome Garden Parking Wi-fi

The Red Lion

PICK OF THE PUBS

See Pick of the Pubs on page 254
See advert below

BRANSGORE   Map 5 SZ19

The Three Tuns Country Inn ⊛⊛

PICK OF THE PUBS

See Pick of the Pubs on page 255

BUCKLERS HARD   Map 5 SU40

The Master Builders House Hotel ★★★ HL ⊛

PICK OF THE PUBS

SO42 7XB ☎ 01590 616253
e-mail: enquiries@themasterbuilders.co.uk
dir: *From M27 junct 2 follow signs to Beaulieu. Left onto B3056. Left to Bucklers Hard. Hotel 2m on left*

During the great age of sail, this 18th-century building was home to master shipbuilder Henry Adams, who oversaw construction of the navy's fleet. Situated on the banks of the River Beaulieu, in the famous shipbuilding village of Bucklers Hard, visitors can enjoy the New Forest National Park, Lord Montagu's Beaulieu Palace and the National Motor Museum, which are all on the doorstep. Beams, open fires and maritime memorabilia set the scene in the Yachtsmans Bar, where food includes game sausage roll, bucket of Atlantic prawns, or Godminster board served with a choice of real ales or wines. The refurbished Riverside Restaurant has a contemporary feel and tranquil river views. In summer, guests can dine on the terrace under the stars. The modern menu combines excellent local ingredients and innovative ideas to produce dishes such as roast fillet and belly of pork with black pudding; linguine with crab, mussels and prawns; and lemon sole with sprouting broccoli and new potatoes. Booking for meals may be required.

Open all day all wk 11-11 (Sun 11-10.30) ⊕ FREE HOUSE/HILLBROOKE HOTELS ◀ Ringwood Best Bitter, Boondoggle ♂ Westons Stowford Press. **Facilities** Children welcome Children's menu Garden Parking Wi-fi **Rooms** 25

PICK OF THE PUBS

The Red Lion

BOLDRE Map 5 SZ39

Rope Hill SO41 8NE ☎ 01590 673177
web: www.theredlionboldre.co.uk
dir: *M27 junct 1, A337 through Lyndhurst & Brockenhurst towards Lymington, follow Boldre signs*

Set at a crossroads in the centre of an ancient village, this is a New Forest pub for all seasons. Consistent with its 15th-century origins, the rambling interior contains cosy, beamed rooms, log fires and authentic rural memorabilia; the rooms are alive with the glow of candlelight on antique copper and brass. Expect a genuinely warm welcome and simple, traditional values, with Ringwood ales on offer at the bar. The kitchen places a keen emphasis on traditional meals made using the very best of the forest's produce. Chef's specials follow seasonal availability of local shellfish, whole fresh fish, venison and other game. Typical starters include local goat's cheese on a crouton with home-made onion marmalade; and tempura-battered fried black pudding with an apple, celery and caramelised walnut salad. There's an impressive selection of fish and vegetarian dishes, such as home-made risotto of New Forest mushrooms and seasonal vegetables with salad or breaded crab and spring onion fishcakes with salad and chunky chips. Meat lovers could plump for the pub's celebrated Hampshire pork duo:

slow-roasted belly with a black pudding, apricot and herb stuffing on home-made horseradish mash with sliced pan-fried pork fillet on cabbage and bacon. For simpler appetites there are home-made burgers and a variety of grilled steaks with all the trimmings. Other 'traditional favourites' include sliced ham, home-cooked with ale and orange, with free-range eggs, chunky chips and peas; and traditional Ringwood ale hand-battered haddock with chunky chips and peas. In the summer, you can enjoy full table service outside on the new herb patio. Booking for meals may be required.

Open all wk 11-3 5.30-11 (Sun 12-8) (Sat 11-11 summer) **Bar Meals** L served Mon-Sat 12-2.30, Sun 12-8, summer

Sat 12-9.30 D served Mon-Sat 6-9.30 Sun 12-8, summer Sat 12-9.30 **Restaurant** L served Mon-Sat 12-2.30, Sun 12-8, summer Sat 12-9.30 D served Mon-Sat 6-9.30 Sun 12-8, summer Sat 12-9.30 🛢 FREE HOUSE 🍺 Ringwood Best Bitter & Fortyniner, Brakspear Oxford Gold, Guinness, Guest ales ⚲ Thatchers Gold. ♟ 15 **Facilities** Children welcome Children's portions 🐾 Garden Parking 🚐 (notice required)

Save on hotels. Book at theAA.com/hotel

HAMPSHIRE 255 ENGLAND

PICK OF THE PUBS

The Three Tuns Country Inn ❀❀

BRANSGORE
Map 5 SZ19

Ringwood Rd BH23 8JH
☎ **01425 672232**
e-mail: threetunsinn@btconnect.com
web: www.threetunsinn.com
dir: *1.5m from A35 Walkford junct. 3m from Christchurch & 1m from Hinton Admiral railway station*

One of the few remaining thatched pubs in the New Forest National Park, this picture-perfect, 17th-century survivor is also immediately recognisable for another reason – by the riot of flowers outside. There are five distinct public areas: a comfortable, music-, TV- and games-free lounge bar (with a winter log fire); an oak-beamed snug, similarly warmed, and with biscuits and water for the dog; a large terrace with a water feature; a huge south-facing garden, with over 2,500 square metres of lawn (and not a bouncy castle in sight, although on sunny days out comes the barbecue), surrounded by fields, trees and grazing ponies; and finally, the 60-seat restaurant. Here, fresh produce and seasonings from around the world are transformed into award-winning dishes and seasonal specials, recognised for their quality by two AA Rosettes. The menus offer something for everyone: if there's time for just a pint of Ringwood Best and a light bar snack, then maybe pick moules marinière; six Dorset snails in garlic tarragon butter; bangers and mash; venison pasty; deep-fried cod

and chips; or a sandwich. Or, for those with more time to spend, the specials menu offers pan-fried Mudeford sea bass with a fricassée of squid, olives, tomatoes and artichoke; Irish stew with suet dumplings and pearl barley; rabbit pie with penny bun mushrooms; and truffle risotto with crispy egg. For pudding, try the baked cheesecake with preserved fruits, or a plate of British and French artisan and farmhouse cheeses with home-made pickles. A listed barn provides space for functions. Booking for meals may be required.

Open all day all wk 11-11 (Sun 12-10.30) **Bar Meals** L served Mon-Fri 12-2.15, Sat-Sun 12-9.15 D served Mon-Fri 6.30-9.15, Sat-Sun 12-9.15 Av main course £14.95 **Restaurant**

L served Mon-Fri 12-2.15, Sat-Sun 12-9.15 D served Mon-Fri 6.30-9.15, Sat-Sun 12-9.15 ⊕ ENTERPRISE INNS ◀ St Austell Tribute, Ringwood Best Bitter & Fortyniner, Exmoor Gold, Otter Bitter, Timothy Taylor ♻ Thatchers Gold & Katy, New Forest Traditional ♀ 9 **Facilities** Children welcome Children's menu Children's portions ❖ Garden Beer festival Parking Wi-fi 🚌 (notice required)

BURGHCLERE — Map 5 SU46

Marco Pierre White The Carnarvon Arms

PICK OF THE PUBS

Winchester Rd RG20 9LE ☎ 01635 278222
e-mail: info@thecarnarvonarmshotel.com
dir: *M4 junct 13, A34 S to Winchester. Exit A34 at Tothill Services, follow Highclere Castle signs. Pub on right*

Built in the 1800s as a coaching inn providing a stop off for travellers to nearby Highclere Castle, home to the present Lord and Lady Carnarvon, this Grade II listed coaching inn is steeped in history. It was the 5th Earl of Carnarvon who famously opened Tutankhamun's tomb in 1922, dying the following year and triggering suggestions of a Mummy's Curse. Following a recent restoration by Marco Pierre White and his team, The Carnarvon Arms is now a modern country inn, decorated with an eclectic mix of artefacts and art, and with a fine dining ethos set in a relaxed country-pub environment. The kitchen team prepare dishes created by Marco, including potted duck with green peppercorns; fillet of smoked haddock with poached eggs; chicken and leek pie; and roast rump of lamb. There are also lunch, evening and Sunday set menus. Finish with Eton Mess, sherry trifle or bread-and-butter pudding.

Open all day all wk 8am-11.30pm (Fri-Sat 8am-12.30am) **Bar Meals** L served all wk 12-3 D served all wk 6-9.30 **Restaurant** L served all wk 12-3 D served all wk 6-9.30 ⊕ FREE HOUSE ◀ JW Lees The Governor, Guest ales ♻ Westons The Governor. ¶ 15 **Facilities** ❖ Children welcome Children's menu Children's portions Garden Parking Wi-fi ▭

BURLEY — Map 5 SU20

The Burley Inn

BH24 4AB ☎ 01425 403448
e-mail: info@theburleyinn.co.uk
dir: *4m SE of of Ringwood*

Once a GP's surgery, this fine Edwardian building makes a smart and atmospheric inn. Surrounded by an Area of Outstanding Natural Beauty, it sits on what was once a major smuggling route. Food is served all day, with a menu offering morning coffee, cream teas, freshly cut sandwiches, hot snacks, freshly baked pies, grills and vegetarian dishes. Take a glass of Ringwood Best Bitter or locally produced fruit wine out to the patio and decking area and watch the ponies, donkeys and cattle wandering freely through the village.

Open all day all wk **Bar Meals** L served all wk 12-10 D served all wk 12-10 food served all day **Restaurant** L served all wk 12-10 D served all wk 12-10 food served all day ⊕ FREE HOUSE ◀ Ringwood Best Bitter & Fortyniner, Guest ales ♻ Thatchers. ¶ 10 **Facilities** ❖ Children's menu Garden Parking Wi-fi ▭

CADNAM — Map 5 SU31

Sir John Barleycorn

Old Romsey Rd SO40 2NP ☎ 023 8081 2236
e-mail: sjb@alcatraz.co.uk
dir: *From Southampton M27 junct 1 into Cadnam*

This friendly thatched establishment is reputedly the oldest inn in the New Forest, formed from three 12th-century cottages, one of which was once home to the charcoal burner who discovered the body of King William Rufus. Its name comes from a folksong celebrating the transformation of barley to beer. The menu has something for everyone with quick snacks and sandwiches, a children's menu and traditional dishes like stuffed oven-baked chicken, slow-cooked lamb shank, and beer-battered cod and chips with minted mushy peas. Booking for meals may be required.

Open all day all wk 11-11 **Bar Meals** food served all day **Restaurant** food served all day ◀ Morland Old Speckled Hen, Ringwood ♻ Westons Stowford Press & Old Rosie. ¶ 10 **Facilities** Children welcome Children's menu Garden Parking ▭

CHALTON — Map 5 SU71

The Red Lion

PICK OF THE PUBS

PO8 0BG ☎ 023 9259 2246
e-mail: redlionchalton@fullers.co.uk
dir: *Just off A3 between Horndean & Petersfield. Follow signs for Chalton*

Ask someone who's never been to Britain to describe the typical English pub and the chances are it would be this one, all half-timbering, whitewash and thatch. Records show that it began life in 1147 as a residential workshop for the builders of St Michael's church opposite; by the time another three centuries had gone by, church and civic dignitaries were lodging there, then in 1503 it was granted its first licence to sell alcohol to travellers on the old London to Portsmouth road. Well known for its excellent food, the kitchen sources locally for the daily-changing main and pub snack menus. The garden offers stunning views of the South Downs and a beer festival takes place during the last weekend of July.

Open all day all wk 11.30-11 (Sun 12-10.30) **Bar Meals** food served all day **Restaurant** food served all day ⊕ FULLER'S ◀ London Pride & ESB, Geoge Gale & Co Seafarers & HSB, Guest ales ♻ Kopparberg, Aspall. ¶ 20 **Facilities** ❖ Children welcome Children's portions Family room Garden Beer festival Parking ▭

CHARTER ALLEY — Map 5 SU55

The White Hart Inn

White Hart Ln RG26 5QA ☎ 01256 850048
e-mail: enquiries@whitehartcharteralley.com
dir: *From M3 junct 6 take A339 towards Newbury. Turn right to Ramsdell. Right at church, then 1st left into White Hart Ln*

On the outskirts of the village overlooking open farmland and woods, this pub draws everyone from cyclists and walkers to real ale and whisky enthusiasts. Dating from 1818, it originally refreshed local woodsmen and coach drivers visiting the farrier next door. Today's ales on offer include Stonehenge Great Bustard and Moor Revival. The menu changes daily, and all food is locally sourced and home-cooked. Expect a range of game and meat dishes, such as slow-roasted crown of wood pigeon; pot-roasted pheasant; venison Wellington; game pie; and slow-cooked pork belly. Contact the inn for its beer festival dates. Booking for meals may be required.

Open all wk 12-2.30 7-11 (Sun 12-10.30) Closed: 25-26 Dec, 1 Jan **Bar Meals** L served all wk 12-2 D served Tue-Sat 7-9 Av main course £13.50 **Restaurant** L served Tue-Sun 12-2 D served Tue-Sat 7-9 ⊕ FREE HOUSE ◀ Palmers Best Bitter, Triple fff Alton Pride's, Stonehenge Great Bustard, Bowman Swift One, Moor Revival. **Facilities** ❖ Children welcome Children's menu Children's portions Family room Garden Beer festival Parking Wi-fi ▭ (notice required)

CHAWTON — Map 5 SU73

The Greyfriar

Winchester Rd GU34 1SB ☎ 01420 83841
e-mail: hello@thegreyfriar.co.uk
web: www.thegreyfriar.co.uk
dir: *Just off A31 near Alton. Access to Chawton via A31/A32 junct. Follow Jane Austen's House signs, The Greyfriar is opposite*

Fran and Trevor Jones arrived at this 16th-century pub, once a terrace of cottages, opposite Jane Austen's House Museum in 2010. With its friendly atmosphere and delightful village setting, the pub is Fuller's-owned and offers London Pride and Seafarers along with great food. A sample menu includes Brixham crab cakes with lime salsa or slow-roasted field mushroom with goat's cheese and red onion marmalade to start, followed by lasagne; rib-eye of beef with peppercorn sauce; spinach and ricotta tortellini or The Greyfriar home-made prime minced beefburger. Sandwiches, jackets and salads also available.

Open all day all wk 12-11 (Sun 12-10.30) **Bar Meals** L served Mon-Sat 12-2.30, Sun 12-7 D served Mon-Sat 6-9.30 Av main course £10 **Restaurant** L served Mon-Sat 12-2.30, Sun 12-7 D served Mon-Sat 6-9.30 Av 3 course à la carte fr £25 ⊞ FULLER'S ◀ London Pride, Geoge Gale & Co Seafarers, Seasonal ales ○ Aspall. **Facilities** ⚘ Children welcome Children's portions Play area Garden Parking Wi-fi ▭ (notice required)

CHERITON   Map 5 SU52

The Flower Pots Inn
PICK OF THE PUBS

S024 0QQ ☎ 01962 771318
dir: A272 towards Petersfield, left onto B3046, pub 0.75m on right

Known almost universally as The Pots, this popular village pub used to be a farmhouse and home to the head gardener of nearby Avington Park. These days, there are two bars: one rustic and pine-furnished, with a glass-covered well, the other with a sofa; both have open fires when it's cold. Local beer drinkers know the pub well for its award-winning Flower Pots Bitter and Goodens Gold, brewed across the car park in the pub's own micro-brewery. Simple home-made food includes toasted sandwiches, jacket potatoes and different hotpots - chilli con carne, lamb and apricot, beef bourguignon - served with garlic bread, basmati rice or a jacket potato. Ploughman's feature various cheeses, ham or beef, and baps come filled with cheddar cheese; pork steak with onions and apple sauce; or bacon and mushroom. A large, safe garden, with a covered patio, allows children to let off steam (under 14s are not allowed in the bar).

Open all wk 12-2.30 6-11 (Sun 12-3 7-10.30) ⊞ FREE HOUSE ◀ Flower Pots Bitter, Goodens Gold ○ Westons Old Rosie. **Facilities** Children welcome Children's portions Garden Beer festival Parking **Notes** ⊘

CRAWLEY   Map 5 SU43

The Fox and Hounds

S021 2PR ☎ 01962 776006
e-mail: foxandhoundscrawley@hotmail.co.uk
dir: A34 onto A272 then 1st right into Crawley

Rebuilt in impressive mock-Tudor style in 1910, this popular inn serves a well-to-do village close enough to affluent Winchester to attract its citizens too. Dining tables grouped round a central bar soon fill up for well prepared chicken with stilton and mushroom sauce; cod with basil and parmesan crust; home-made pies; and mushroom Stroganoff. To drink, there are 36 wines by the glass and the beers come from Ringwood, Wadworth and Wychwood. Just down the road is a proper village duckpond. Recent change of hands. Booking for meals may be required.

Open all wk 11-3 6-11 **Bar Meals** L served all wk 12-2 D served all wk 6.30-9 **Restaurant** L served all wk 12-2 D served all wk 6.30-9 ⊞ ENTERPRISE INNS ◀ Wadworth

6X, Ringwood Best Bitter & Fortyniner, Wychwood Hobgoblin, Guest ales ○ Westons Stowford Press. ♚ 36 **Facilities** ⚘ Children welcome Children's menu Children's portions Play area Garden Parking ▭

CROOKHAM VILLAGE   Map 5 SU75

The Exchequer

Crondall Rd GU51 5SU ☎ 01252 615336
e-mail: info@theexchequer.co.uk
dir: M3 junct 5, A287 towards Farnham for 5m. Left to Crookham Village

In the beautiful setting of Crookham Village, this whitewashed free house, previously known as the George and Lobster, is just a stone's throw from the A287. The Exchequer serves ales straight from the cask, popular Sunday roasts, and curries, salads and sharing platters. The pub's ethos of keeping things simple and local where possible is shown in dishes such as salmon en croûte with a lemon and mustard seed sauce; crispy honey-roast duck with an orange and Cointreau sauce; penne carbonara served with garlic bread and green salad; and Ringwood steak-and-ale pie. Leave room for almondy Toblerone tart or Belgian dark chocolate mousse.

Open 12-3 6-11 (Sat-Sun 12-11) Closed: Mon (ex BH) **Bar Meals** L served Tue-Fri 12-2, Sat 12-2.30, Sun 12-8 D served Tue-Fri 6-9, Sat 6-9.30, Sun 12-8 Av main course £8.50 **Restaurant** L served Tue-Fri 12-2, Sat 12-2.30, Sun 12-8 D served Tue-Fri 6-9, Sat 6-9.30, Sun 12-8 Av 3 course à la carte fr £23.50 ⊞ FREE HOUSE ◀ Sharp's Doom Bar, Brakspear, Cumberland ○ Thatchers. ♚ 10 **Facilities** Children welcome Children's menu Children's portions Garden Parking Wi-fi

DOWNTON   Map 5 SZ29

The Royal Oak

Christchurch Rd S041 0LA ☎ 01590 642297
e-mail: royal.oak.downton@gmail.com
dir: On A337 between Lymington & Christchurch

Fronted by a white-painted picket fence, this well renovated pub on the edge of the New Forest is a mile from the beach at Lymington, from where you can look across the Solent to the Isle of Wight and its famed Needles. With Ringwood's Best Bitter, the stronger Fortyniner or a weekly guest ale, the food changes daily on the chalkboard - traditional ploughman's or sandwich; local crab, lobster or fresh fish; steak or game in season; sausages from a butcher's in Sway; or a Sunday roast. Booking for meals may be required.

Open all day all wk 11am-11.30pm **Bar Meals** L served Mon-Fri 12-2.30, Sat-Sun all day D served Mon-Fri 6-9.30, Sat-Sun all day Av main course £9.95 **Restaurant** L served Mon-Fri 12-2.30, Sat-Sun all day D served Mon-Fri 6-9.30, Sat-Sun all day Fixed menu price fr £9.95 Av 3 course à la carte fr £12.95 ⊞ ENTERPRISE INNS ◀ Ringwood Best Bitter & Fortyniner, Guest ales ○ Thatchers Gold. ♚ 9 **Facilities** ⚘ Children welcome Children's menu Children's portions Garden Parking Wi-fi ▭

DROXFORD   Map 5 SU61

The Bakers Arms ◉
PICK OF THE PUBS

High St S032 3PA ☎ 01489 877533
e-mail: enquiries@thebakersarmsdroxford.com
dir: 10m E of Winchester on A32 between Fareham & Alton. 7m SW of Petersfield. 10m inland from Portsmouth

With an enviable position in the pretty Meon Valley in a lovely corner of rural Hampshire, this unpretentious, white-painted pub and restaurant is a perfect place to refuel. It has been opened up inside but still oozes country charm and character, the staff are friendly, and the locals clearly love the place. Over the big log fire a blackboard menu lists the simple, well cooked and locally sourced food, while in the bar customers make short work of its barrels of Wallops Wood from the village's own Bowman Brewery. They can snack, too, on home-made Cornish pasties, pickled eggs and onions, and hot filled baguettes. But the kitchen cooks to AA Rosette standard, so make the most of your visit if you're just passing through (much of the produce is grown or shot by the owner): roasted pigeon breast salad with pancetta and walnut dressing; fillet of gurnard with saffron and lemon risotto; and chocolate and fudge brownie with butterscotch ice cream will make you wish every village had a pub like this. Booking for meals may be required.

Open 11.45-3 6-11 (Sun 12-3) Closed: Sun eve & Mon **Bar Meals** L served Tue-Sun 12-2 D served Tue-Sat 7-9 Av main course £14 **Restaurant** L served Tue-Sun 12-2 D served Tue-Sat 7-9 Fixed menu price fr £13 Av 3 course à la carte fr £27 ⊞ FREE HOUSE ◀ Bowman Swift One, Wallops Wood ○ Westons Stowford Press. ♚ **Facilities** ⚘ Children welcome Children's portions Garden Parking Wi-fi

DUMMER   Map 5 SU54

The Queen Inn

Down St RG25 2AD ☎ 01256 397367
e-mail: richardmoore49@btinternet.com
dir: M3 junct 7, follow Dummer signs

You can dine by candlelight in the restaurant at this low-beamed, 16th-century inn with a huge open log fire. The main menu offers a wide choice: steaks and burgers; fillet of beef medallions; teriyaki salmon; curry of the day; and warm bacon, mushroom and asparagus salad. Or at lunchtime there are savouries like Welsh rarebit and flame-grilled chicken ciabatta. Children are encouraged to have small adult portions, but have their own menu if all entreaties fail. There's a good real ale line-up, including Courage Best, London Pride and guests. Booking for meals may be required.

Open all wk 11-3 6-11 (Sun 12-3 7-10.30) **Bar Meals** L served all wk 12-2.30 D served all wk 6.30-9.30 **Restaurant** L served all wk 12-2.30 D served all wk 6.30-9.30 ⊞ ENTERPRISE INNS ◀ Courage Best, Fuller's London Pride, Morland Old Speckled Hen, Guest ales. **Facilities** Children welcome Children's menu Children's portions Garden Parking Wi-fi ▭

DUMMER *continued*

The Sun Inn

A30 Winchester Rd RG25 2DJ ☎ 01256 397234
e-mail: thesuninndummer@hotmail.co.uk
dir: M3 junct 7, take A30 (Winchester Rd) towards Basingstoke. Left onto A30 towards Winchester. Inn on right

Following an extensive refurbishment inside and out, The Sun Inn's reputation as a gastro-pub and bar is growing fast. Its clean, modern look recalls little of its pre-makeover days, but it still feels warm and welcoming and is definitely worth leaving the M3 for. Pub classics include roast Hampshire chicken Caesar salad; local hand-made sausages; and pan-fried liver and bacon. As we went to press, we learnt of a change of hands here. Booking for meals may be required.

Open all wk 12-11 **Bar Meals** L served all wk 12-3 D served Mon-Sat 6-9 **Restaurant** L served all wk 12-3 D served Mon-Sat 6-9 ⊕ FREE HOUSE ◖ Triple fff Alton's Pride, Marston's Pedigree. ☻ 9 **Facilities** ❧ Children welcome Children's menu Children's portions Play area Garden Parking Wi-fi ▭

DUNBRIDGE	Map 5 SU32

The Mill Arms

Barley Hill SO51 0LF ☎ 01794 340401
e-mail: millarms@btconnect.com
dir: From Romsey take A3057 signed Stockbridge & Winchester. Left onto B3084 through Awbridge to Dunbridge. Pub on left before rail crossing

This attractive 18th-century inn is situated in the heart of the Test Valley and close to the River Test, one of the finest chalk streams in the world. Not surprisingly, the pub is popular with fishermen the world over. A traditional country inn with wood and stone floors, oak beams and open fires, the menus combine old favourites and contemporary dishes. An excellent grill menu showcases local produce including buffalo and rare-breed pork, and wood-fired pizzas are available to eat in or takeaway. Booking for meals may be required.

Open 12-2.30 6-11 (Sat 12-11 Sun winter 12-5 Sun summer 12-10) Closed: 25 Dec, Sun eve winter & Mon **Bar Meals** L served Mon-Fri 12-2.30, Sat 12-9.30, Sun 12-4 D served Mon-Thu 6-9, Fri-Sat 6-9.30 Av main course £10.50 **Restaurant** L served Mon-Fri 12-2.30, Sat 12-9.30, Sun 12-4 D served Mon-Thu 6-9, Fri-Sat 6-9.30 Av 3 course à la carte fr £20 ⊕ ENTERPRISE INNS ◖ Flack Manor Flack's Double Drop, Sharp's Doom Bar, Ringwood ♺ Addlestones. ☻ 10 **Facilities** ❧ Children welcome Children's menu Children's portions Garden Beer festival Parking Wi-fi ▭ (notice required)

EAST BOLDRE	Map 5 SU30

Turfcutters Arms

Main Rd SO42 7WL ☎ 01590 612331
e-mail: enquiries.turfcutters@gmail.com
dir: From Beaulieu take B3055 towards Brockenhurst. Left at Hatchet Pond onto B3054 towards Lymington, turn left, follow signs for East Boldre. Pub approx 0.5m

Cyclists, ramblers, dog-walkers and locals congregate here all year round. In winter the open fires warm the cockles, while the lovely garden comes into its own in summer. Good beer including Ringwood and draught ciders such as Thatchers Gold complement a menu of unpretentious pub grub including jacket potatoes, ploughman's and filled baguettes. Among the favourites are home-made chilli; barbecue ribs; and Wiltshire home-baked ham, egg and chips. Children have their own menu, and canine treats are handed out at the bar. Booking for meals may be required.

Open all day all wk **Bar Meals** L served all wk 12-3 D served all wk 6-9 Av main course £8-£10 **Restaurant** L served all wk 12-3 D served all wk 6-9 Fixed menu price fr £10.95 Av 3 course à la carte fr £25 ⊕ ENTERPRISE INNS ◖ Ringwood Best Bitter, Fortyniner, Boondoggle ♺ Thatchers Gold. **Facilities** ❧ Children welcome Children's menu Children's portions Play area Garden Beer festival Parking Wi-fi ▭ (notice required)

EAST END	Map 5 SZ39

The East End Arms

PICK OF THE PUBS

Main Rd SO41 5SY ☎ 01590 626223
e-mail: manager@eastendarms.co.uk
dir: From Lymington towards Beaulieu (past Isle of Wight ferry), 3m to East End

Close to Beaulieu and historic Bucklers Hard, this New Forest inn, owned by John Illsley, the bass player of Dire Straits, combines the authenticity of a proper local with a good reputation as a gastro-pub. Ringwood ales are drawn straight from the wood in the Foresters Bar, where stone floors and open fires create a homely, traditional feel. The atmospheric lounge bar, with its sofas and winter fires, is a comfortable setting for a meal from the daily-changing brasserie-style menu. Locally sourced fish/seafood make a strong showing in dishes such as baked red mullet, organic wild rice, braised leeks and herb velouté. Other dishes might be chargrilled venison steak with a garlic and herb butter; or braised pork belly, fondant potato, kale, parsnip and vanilla purée and pink peppercorn sauce. The pub is well worth the drive down country lanes, or a short diversion from the nearby Solent Way long distance footpath. Booking for meals may be required.

Open all wk 11.30-3 6-11 (Fri-Sun 11.30-11) **Bar Meals** L served Mon-Sat 12-2.30 Av main course £12 **Restaurant** L served all wk 12-2.30 D served Mon-Sat 7-9.30 ⊕ FREE HOUSE ◖ Ringwood Best Bitter & Fortyniner, Andwell's, Jennings, Cottage ♺ Thatchers & Katy. **Facilities** ❧ Children welcome Children's menu Children's portions Garden Parking

EAST MEON	Map 5 SU62

Ye Olde George Inn

Church St GU32 1NH ☎ 01730 823481
e-mail: yeoldegeorge@live.co.uk
dir: S of A272 (Winchester/Petersfield). 1.5m from Petersfield turn left opposite church

With a magnificent Norman church (where tapestry designs similar to Bayeux can be found) and the River Meon running close by, the setting for this delightful 15th-century coaching inn is hard to beat. If you want heavy beams, inglenook fireplaces and wooden floors, look no further – they're all here, creating an ideal atmosphere for a choice of real ales, freshly prepared bar snacks and monthly changing menus. Tuck into crayfish, saffron and pea risotto; twice-cooked belly of pork with jasmine rice and Asian salad; or Hampshire rabbit served with chips and apple coleslaw, all made using local seasonal produce.

Open all wk 11-3 6-11 (Sun 11-10) Closed: 25 Dec **Bar Meals** L served Mon-Sat 12-2.30, Sun 12-3 D served Mon-Sat 6.30-9.30, Sun 6.30-9 Av main course £12 **Restaurant** L served Mon-Sat 12-2.30, Sun 12-3 D served Mon-Sat 6.30-9.30, Sun 6.30-9 Fixed menu price fr £16.95 Av 3 course à la carte fr £25 ⊕ HALL & WOODHOUSE ◖ Badger Dorset Best, K&B Sussex, Tanglefoot ♺ Westons Stowford Press. ☻ 9 **Facilities** ❧ Children welcome Children's menu Children's portions Garden Parking Wi-fi ▭

EASTON	Map 5 SU53

The Chestnut Horse

PICK OF THE PUBS

SO21 1EG ☎ 01962 779257
e-mail: info@thechestnuthorse.com
dir: M3 junct 9, A33 towards Basingstoke, then B3047. 2nd right, 1st left

Hidden away in the idyllic village of Easton in the Itchen Valley, this gem of a 16th-century pub has an abundance of traditional English character and atmosphere; old tankards hang from the low-beamed ceilings in the two bar areas, and a large open fire is the central focus through the winter months. Award-winning English beers, such as Pickled Partridge and Chestnut Horse Special can be enjoyed in the bar or the garden. A good-value set price menu is offered Monday to Saturday lunchtime (12-2pm) or Monday to Friday early evening (6-7.30pm). This might include onion bhaji with minted yogurt to start, salmon fishcake with a chive hollandaise to follow, and profiteroles to finish. Typical à la carte choices are Hampshire venison casserole with sage and onion cobbler; roasted butternut loaf with sweet crispy kale; and coq au vin. Take your walking boots with you and you can walk off any excesses on one of the enjoyable countryside walks that start at the front door. Booking for meals may be required.

Open all wk 12-3.30 5.30-11 (Fri-Sat 12-11.30 Sun 12-10.30) **Bar Meals** L served Mon-Sat 12-2.30, Sun 12-8 D served Mon-Sat 6-9.30 Av main course £12

Restaurant L served Mon-Sat 12-2, Sun 12-8 D served Mon-Sat 6-9.30 Fixed menu price fr £12 Av 3 course à la carte fr £24 ⊕ HALL & WOODHOUSE ◀ Badger First Gold & Pickled Partridge, Chestnut Horse Special ◔ Westons Stowford Press. ☙ **Facilities** ☙ Children welcome Children's portions Garden Parking Wi-fi 🚌

EAST STRATTON   Map 5 SU54

Northbrook Arms

SO21 3DU ☎ 01962 774150

dir: *Follow brown pub sign from A33, 4m S of junct with A303*

Just a stone's throw from the green in the picturesque estate village of East Stratton, the Northbrook Arms has been in Lord Northbrook's family for many generations. Wendy, Nick and Sophie aim to deliver good beer, fun and food in equal measures, and their modern British menu incorporates ideas from around the globe. Expect lunchtime sandwiches and a special set menu; daily changing fish dishes; and main course choices such as Hampshire sausages with mashed potatoes and onion gravy. Otter and Bowman ales are served along with wines from around the world.

Open 12-3 6-11 (all day Sun in summer) Closed: Sun pm (winter) & Mon **Bar Meals** L served Tue-Sun 12-2 D served Tue-Sat 6.30-9 ⊕ FREE HOUSE ◀ Otter, Bowman Swift One, Flower Pots Cheriton Pots. ☙ 10 **Facilities** Children welcome Children's portions Garden Parking Wi-fi 🚌

EAST TYTHERLEY   Map 5 SU22

The Star Inn Tytherley

PICK OF THE PUBS

SO51 0LW ☎ 01794 340225

e-mail: info@starinn.co.uk

dir: *5m N of Romsey off A3057, left for Dunbridge on B3084. Left for Awbridge & Kents Oak. Through Lockerley then 1m*

The 16th-century Star Inn stands overlooking the village cricket green in the smallest village in the Test Valley. You'll find Andwell Brewery beers and other guest ales behind the bar, plus an extensive international wine list. Dine where you like, in the bar, at dark-wood tables in the main dining room, or outside on the patio in summer, where you can also play king-sized chess. Lunchtime brings a variety of platters (fish, Barkham Blue, or Winchester farmhouse cheese), sandwiches (perhaps smoked salmon, crème fraîche and dill; or Cumberland sausage with caramelised onion), and a good value two-course menu (stir-fried tiger prawns with chorizo and gremolata; and roast chicken supreme). The evening menu might offer crab soufflé with watercress and saffron cream; and braised belly pork with sage polenta and celeriac purée. There's a good choice at Sunday lunch, too, including traditional roasts. Booking for meals may be required.

Open 11-2.30 6-10 Closed: Sun eve & Mon (ex BH) ⊕ FREE HOUSE ◀ Flack Manor, Andwell, Guest ales

---

◔ Thatchers Gold. **Facilities** Children welcome Garden Parking

---

EMSWORTH   Map 5 SU70

The Sussex Brewery

36 Main Rd PO10 8AU ☎ 01243 371533

e-mail: info@sussexbrewery.com

dir: *On A259 (coast road), between Havant & Chichester*

Traditional values rule in this 17th-century pub with sawdust covered floors, real ales and open fires. It is set in the picturesque village of Emsworth, renowned for its annual food festival in September. The menu includes a large variety of sausages, from Cumberland and Lincolnshire to Cajun and Mexican (there's a good choice for vegetarians too). Other dishes include crispy whitebait with a lemon and dill mayonnaise; and an open lamb burger with freshly cut chips, tsatziki and a tomato and onion salad. Booking for meals may be required.

Open all day all wk 7am-mdnt **Bar Meals** L served all wk 12-2.30 D served all wk 6.30-9.30 Av main course £10 **Restaurant** L served all wk 12-2.30 D served all wk 6.30-9.30 Fixed menu price fr £10 Av 3 course à la carte fr £20 ⊕ YOUNG'S ◀ Special, Wells Waggle Dance & Bombardier, St Austell Tribute ◔ Westons Stowford Press. ☙ 12 **Facilities** ☙ Children welcome Children's menu Children's portions Garden Beer festival Parking Wi-fi 🚌 (notice required)

EVERSLEY   Map 5 SU76

The Golden Pot

PICK OF THE PUBS

Reading Rd RG27 0NB ☎ 0118 973 2104

e-mail: jcalder@golden-pot.co.uk

web: www.golden-pot.co.uk

dir: *Between Reading & Camberley on B3272 approx 0.25m from Eversley cricket ground*

Set in the heart of the village but within easy reach of the M3 and M4, this well-established free house dates back to the 1700s. The pub offers a fine selection of real ales from such brewers as Windsor & Eton, Bowman and Ascot; nine wines are sold by the glass. A double-sided warming fire connects the bar and restaurant, while outside the Snug and Vineyard, surrounded by colourful tubs and hanging baskets, are just the ticket for summer relaxation. Monday evenings see live music performed for appreciative audiences, while they tuck into home-cooked food augmented by a unique rösti menu. The innovative menu offers traditional or modern choices. Specials of the

---

day might include home-made venison burger; roasted fillet of veal with wilted spinach, truffle whipped potatoes and sauce béarnaise; or pan-fried fillet of sea bass with seared scallop, crab and spring onion risotto. Booking for meals may be required.

Open 11.30-3 5.30-10.30 Closed: 25-26 & 31 Dec, 1 Jan, Sun eve **Bar Meals** L served all wk 12-2 D served Mon-Sat 6-9 **Restaurant** L served all wk 12-2 D served Mon-Sat 6-9 ⊕ FREE HOUSE ◀ Andwell, Bowman, Ascot, Rebellion, Windsor & Eton. ☙ 9 **Facilities** ☙ Children welcome Children's menu Children's portions Garden Parking Wi-fi

---

EXTON   Map 5 SU62

The Shoe Inn

Shoe Ln SO32 3NT ☎ 01489 877526

e-mail: theshoeexton@googlemail.com

dir: *Exton on A32 between Fareham & Alton*

On warmer days, you can enjoy views of Old Winchester Hill from the garden of this popular pub in the heart of the Meon Valley. Food is key – local ingredients include those from its ever-expanding herb and organic vegetable garden. A typical selection of dishes could include local Southdown lamb's liver, bacon, onion gravy and mashed potato; slow-cooked Oxford Sandy belly pork with Savoy cabbage and cider jus. The bar offers well-kept Wadworth ales and over a dozen wines served by the glass. There is a beer festival each year.

Open all wk 11-3 6-11 (Sat-Sun all day) Closed: 25 Dec **Bar Meals** L served all wk 12-2.15 **Restaurant** L served all wk 12-2.15 D served all wk 6-9 ⊕ WADWORTH ◀ 6X, Henry's Original IPA, Bishop's Tipple ◔ Westons Stowford Press. ☙ 13 **Facilities** ☙ Children welcome Children's menu Children's portions Garden Beer festival Parking

---

FORDINGBRIDGE   Map 5 SU11

The Augustus John

116 Station Rd SP6 1DG ☎ 01425 652098

e-mail: enquiries@augustusjohnfordingbridge.co.uk

dir: *12m S of Salisbury on A338 towards Ringwood*

After 14 years as a member of staff, Lorraine Smallwood took over this former station pub in 2009. The Welsh post-impressionist painter Augustus John used to be a regular here, although today it's the Ringwood real ales and food that continues to attract locals and visitors. A typical menu might include lamb braised with mint; pan-fried pork fillet flamed with brandy and apricots; the chef's casserole of the day; or grilled salmon fillet with lemon and saffron sauce. Time a visit for the May Bank Holiday beer festival.

Open all wk 11.30-3 6.30-11.30 (Sun 12-3 7-11.30) **Bar Meals** L served all wk 12-2.30, closed Mon L during winter D served Mon-Sat 6.30-9, Sun 7-9 (booking advised Fri-Sun) **Restaurant** L served all wk 12-2.30, closed Mon L during winter D served Mon-Sat 6.30-9, Sun 7-9 (booking advised Fri-Sun) ⊕ MARSTON'S ◀ Ringwood Best Bitter, Fortyniner ◔ Thatchers Gold. **Facilities** ☙ Children welcome Children's menu Children's portions Garden Beer festival Parking Wi-fi 🚌

FRITHAM
Map 5 SU21

The Royal Oak

SO43 7HJ ☎ 023 8081 2606
e-mail: royaloak-fritham@btopenworld.co.uk
dir: M27 junct 1, B3078 signed Fordingbridge. 2m, then left at x-rds signed Ocknell & Fritham. Then follow signs to Fritham

Off the beaten track in the New Forest, this award-winning thatched pub dates back to the 15th century. With no fruit machine or jukebox, the pub is part of a working farm and it has remained unchanged for more than a 100 years. The three small bars focus on serving a range of local real ales and draught ciders. Simple, locally sourced food includes home-made quiches, home-smoked duck breast and pork pies made from the pub's own pigs. The pub has a large garden looking across open forest and farmland.

Open all wk (all day wknds & Jul-Sep) Bar Meals L served Mon-Fri 12-2.30, Sat-Sun 12-3 Av main course £7.50 ⊕ FREE HOUSE ◀ Ringwood Best Bitter & Fortyniner, Hop Back Summer Lightning, Palmers Dorset Gold, Bowman Swift One ♂ Aspall, Thatchers. ♟ 12 Facilities ✿ Children welcome Garden Parking ▭ (notice required) Notes ⊛

HAMBLE-LE-RICE
Map 5 SU40

The Bugle ⊛
PICK OF THE PUBS

High St SO31 4HA ☎ 023 8045 3000
e-mail: manager@buglehamble.co.uk
dir: M27 junct 8, follow signs to Hamble. In village centre turn right at mini rdbt into one-way cobbled street, pub at end

Matthew Boyle, owner of The White Star Tavern in Southampton (see entry) rescued this famous waterside pub from proposed demolition in 2005 and lovingly refurbished it using traditional methods and materials. Old features include exposed beams and brickwork, natural flagstone floors and the wonderful oak bar, while among the new is a large heated terrace with lovely views over the River Hamble - perfect for outdoor dining. A pint of locally-brewed ale makes an ideal partner for one of the deli boards (great for sharing), a roast beef, horseradish crème fraîche and rocket sandwich, or a pub classic like fish pie with buttered greens. From the dining room menu, go for ham hock terrine with home-made piccalilli to start, then order the whole Torbay sole with garlic sauté potatoes and bisque vièrge, and round off with a seasonal fruit crumble with thick custard. For private dining, there is the Captain's Table upstairs.

Open all day all wk ⊕ FREE HOUSE ◀ Rotating local ales, Courage Best Bitter. Facilities Children welcome Children's portions Wi-fi

HANNINGTON
Map 5 SU55

The Vine at Hannington
PICK OF THE PUBS

RG26 5TX ☎ 01635 298525
e-mail: info@thevineathannington.co.uk
dir: Hannington signed from A339 between Basingstoke & Newbury

Given the nature of North Hampshire's rolling chalk downland, you can expect rambling and cycling devotees to patronise this gabled Victorian inn. It used to be the Wellington Arms because it stands on what was once the Iron Duke's estate, but was renamed in 1960 after the Vine & Craven Hunt, whose kennels are nearby. A wood-burning stove heats the spacious, traditionally furnished bar areas and conservatory, where rural artefacts pop up here and there. The Ringwood Brewery represents Hampshire at the bar, the other real ales coming from Black Sheep, Hogs Back and Sharp's. Seasonal menus and daily specials feature marinated lamb and vegetable kebab, saffron rice and tomato and chilli sauce; medallions of beef with red wine, tarragon and mushroom sauce; and spinach and ricotta cannelloni. Many of the herbs, salads and vegetables used in the kitchen are grown in the large garden, where there's also a children's play area.

Open 12-3 6-11 (Sat-Sun all day) Closed: 25 Dec, Mon in winter Bar Meals L served Tue-Fri 12-2, Sat-Sun 12-2.30 D served all wk 6-9 Restaurant L served Tue-Fri 12-2, Sat 12-2.30, Sun 12-8 (Sun 12-4 in winter) D served all wk 6-9 ⊕ PUNCH TAVERNS ◀ Sharp's Doom Bar, Ringwood Best Bitter, Hogs Back TEA, Black Sheep ♂ Aspall. ♟ 11 Facilities ✿ Children welcome Children's menu Children's portions Play area Family room Garden Parking Wi-fi ▭ (notice required)

HAVANT
Map 5 SU70

The Royal Oak

19 Langstone High St, Langstone PO9 1RY
☎ 023 9248 3125
e-mail: 7955@greeneking.co.uk
dir: Telephone for directions

Smack on the water's edge and originally a row of cottages used in conjunction with the adjacent old mill, this historic 16th-century pub enjoys stunning views across Langstone Harbour. An individual rustic charm characterises the unspoilt interior, with flagstone floors, exposed beams and winter fires contrasting with the waterfront benches (arrive early!) and secluded rear garden for alfresco summer drinking. Extensive menus list traditional pub dishes, the choice ranging from rump steak ciabatta and battered haddock and chips to beef and red wine casserole and dark chocolate and walnut brownie. Wash down with a pint of Abbot Ale.

Open all day all wk 11-11 Bar Meals L served all wk 12-5 D served all wk 5-9 Restaurant L served all wk 12-5 D served all wk 5-9 ⊕ GREENE KING ◀ IPA, Ruddles County, Ruddles Best & Abbot Ale, Morland Old Speckled

Hen ♂ Aspall. ♟ 16 Facilities Children welcome Children's menu Children's portions Family room Garden Wi-fi

HAWKLEY
Map 5 SU72

The Hawkley Inn ★★★ INN

Pococks Ln GU33 6NE ☎ 01730 827205
e-mail: info@hawkleyinn.co.uk
dir: From A3 (Liss rdbt) towards Liss on B3006. Right at Spread Eagle, in 2.5m left into Pococks Ln

The inn sign saying 'Free Hoose' owes something to the moose head hanging over one of the fires; indeed, as landlord Simon Hawkins says, his country pub is quirky. With ten beer engines and a late-spring beer festival, the Hawkley is well known by real ale enthusiasts and cider lovers. Menus change daily, so you may be lucky to find chickpea and vegetable tagine; home-made steak-and-ale pie; or pan-fried sea bass. At lunchtime Simon makes sure that filled baguettes and ciabattas are available (except Sunday). Contemporary accommodation is available.

Open all wk Mon-Fri 12-3 5.30-11 (Sat-Sun all day) Bar Meals L served Mon-Sat 12-2, Sun 12-4 D served Mon-Sat 7-9 Restaurant L served Mon-Sat 12-2, Sun 12-4 D served Mon-Sat 7-9 ⊕ FREE HOUSE/WEYBOURNE INNS ◀ 7 Constantly changing ales, Guest ales ♂ Mr Whitehead's, Westons Bounds. Facilities ✿ Children welcome Children's portions Garden Beer festival Wi-fi Rooms 5

HERRIARD
Map 5 SU64

The Fur & Feathers

Herriard Rd RG25 2PN ☎ 01256 384170
e-mail: bookings@franskitchen.co.uk
dir: From Basingstoke take A339 towards Alton. After Herriard follow pub signs. Turn left to pub

Purpose-built 120 years ago to refresh local farm workers, The Fur & Feathers has to this day obligations in the upkeep of the church roof. Its high-ceilinged Victorian proportions translate into light and airy accommodation for drinkers and diners, and comfort too, with log-burning fireplaces at each end of the bar. Here a trio of ales are rotated, and menus of modern British cooking are perused. Typical dishes are corn-fed chicken breast with a creamy bacon and Alresford watercress sauce; and local venison ragout with home-made pappardelle. A large garden hosts entertainment, and chickens laying eggs for the pub's use. Booking for meals may be required.

Open Tue-Thu 12-3 6-11 (Fri-Sat 12-11 Sun 12-6) Closed: 25 Dec & 1 wk end of Dec, Sun eve & Mon Bar Meals Av main course £13.95 Restaurant L served Tue-Sat 12-2.30, Sun 12-3 D served Tue-Sat 7-9.30 Av 3 course à la carte fr £19.95 ⊕ FREE HOUSE ◀ Local ales, rotating Flack Manor Flack's Double Drop, Hogs Back TEA, Sharp's Doom Bar ♂ Mr Whitehead's. Facilities Children welcome Children's menu Children's portions Garden Parking Wi-fi ▭ (notice required)

HOLYBOURNE — Map 5 SU74

The White Hart Hotel

139 London Rd GU34 4EY ☎ 01420 87654
dir: *From M3 junct 5 follow Alton signs (A339). In Alton take A31 towards Farnham. Follow Holybourne signs*

The village of Holybourne is steeped in history: an old Roman fort lies under the cricket field, and the village also stands on the Pilgrims' Way. Rebuilt in the 1920s on the site of the original inn, The White Hart has been recently refurbished to create a comfortable, welcoming setting for a well-kept pint of Greene King IPA or a hearty meal. The pub changed hands in September 2011.

Open all day all wk **Bar Meals** L served all wk 12-3 D served all wk 6.30-9.30 Av main course £6 **Restaurant** L served all wk 12-3 D served all wk 6.30-9.30 ⊕ GREENE KING ◀ IPA, Courage Best Bitter, 3 Guest ales. ☂ 10 **Facilities** Children welcome Children's menu Children's portions Play area Garden Parking Wi-fi 🚐

HOOK — Map 5 SU75

Crooked Billet

London Rd RG27 9EH ☎ 01256 762118
e-mail: richardbarwise@aol.com
web: www.thecrookedbillethook.co.uk
dir: *From M3 take Hook ring road. At 3rd rdbt turn right onto A30 towards London, pub on left 0.5m by river*

A hostelry has stood on this site since the 1600s, though the present pub only dates back to 1935. The family-friendly Crooked Billet has a lovely river garden and children's play area. There is food to suit all appetites, including a children's menu. Expect sirloin steak, tomato and mushrooms; honey-glazed ham, local eggs and chips; or home-made chilli with rice or tortilla chips and melted cheese. There's also a range of ploughman's and open sandwiches, all to be washed down with beers from Andwell Brewery. The pub is home to the Hook Eagle Morris Men. Booking for meals may be required.

Open all wk Mon-Fri 11.30-3 6-12 (Sat-Sun 11.30am-mdnt) **Bar Meals** L served Mon-Sat 12-2.30, Sun 12-8 D served Mon-Fri 6.30-9.30, Sat 6.30-10 ⊕ FREE HOUSE ◀ Courage Best Bitter, Sharp's Doom Bar, Andwell, Guest ales ♂ Thatchers Green Goblin. **Facilities** ❧ Children welcome Children's menu Children's portions Play area Garden Parking 🚐

The Hogget Country Pub & Eating House

London Rd, Hook Common RG27 9JJ ☎ 01256 763009
e-mail: home@hogget.co.uk
dir: *M3 junct 5, A30, 0.5m, between Hook & Basingstoke*

Close to the M3 motorway, The Hogget's reputation as a relaxed and contemporary venue continues to evolve, with quality the watchword in all aspects of the operation. Guest ales support regular beers from Ringwood and Wychwood, whilst the wines are all priced equally; this unusual approach allows customers to choose a wine by appeal rather than cost. Carefully prepared English favourites predominate on the menu, but you may also find the likes of baked chermoula chicken – infused with North African spices, served with chilli and cucumber salad and coriander couscous. Booking for meals may be required.

Open all wk 12-3 5.30-11 (Sat 12-11 Sun 12-10.30) Closed: 25-26 Dec **Bar Meals** L served all wk 12-2.30 D served all wk 5.30-9 Av main course £12 **Restaurant** L served all wk 12-2.30 D served all wk 5.30-9 Av 3 course à la carte fr £22 ⊕ MARSTON'S ◀ Ringwood Best Bitter, Wychwood Hobgoblin, Guest ales ♂ Thatchers Gold. ☂ 12 **Facilities** Children welcome Children's menu Children's portions Garden Parking Wi-fi

HURSLEY — Map 5 SU42

The Dolphin Inn

SO21 2JY ☎ 01962 775209
dir: *Telephone for directions*

Like most of the village, this old coaching inn with magnificent chimneys once belonged to the Hursley Estate, now owned by IBM. It was built between 1540 and 1560, reputedly using timbers from a Tudor warship called HMS *Dolphin* (today's less glamorous 'ship' is a shore establishment in Gosport). On tap in the beamed bars are Ringwood Best, Hop Back Summer Lightning, George Gale & Co HSB and Green Goblin oak-aged cider. In addition to sandwiches, baguettes and jacket potatoes, favourites include Hursley-made faggots; lamb's liver and bacon; scampi and chips; and macaroni cheese. Booking for meals may be required.

Open all day all wk Mon-Sat 11-11 (Sun 12-10.30) **Bar Meals** L served Mon-Sat 12-2.30, Sun 12-8.30 D served Mon-Thu 6-9, Fri-Sat 6.30-9.30, Sun 12-8.30 ⊕ ENTERPRISE INNS ◀ Hop Back Summer Lightning, George Gale & Co HSB, Ringwood Best Bitter ♂ Thatchers & Green Goblin. ☂ 12 **Facilities** ❧ Children welcome Children's menu Children's portions Play area Family room Garden Parking 🚐 (notice required)

The Kings Head

Main Rd SO21 2JW ☎ 01962 775208
e-mail: info@kingsheadhursley.co.uk
dir: *On A3090 between Winchester & Romsey*

Built as a coaching inn in 1810, The Kings Head was bought, a couple of years ago, by five local farming families who extensively refurbished it with décor and furniture to reflect its Georgian origins. The menu follows suit, offering a winning mix of modernity and tradition. Try whitebait or confit chicken and leek terrine to start, followed by roast cod with crushed peas, potatoes, clams, parsley and lemon, or steak with hand-cut chips, grilled tomato and watercress. Beer festivals are held on August Bank Holiday and in December.

Open all day all wk **Bar Meals** L served Mon-Sat 12-2, Sun 12-3 D served all wk 6-9 Av main course £7 **Restaurant** L served Mon-Sat 12-2, Sun 12-3 D served all wk 6-9 Fixed menu price fr £13 ⊕ FREE HOUSE ◀ Sharp's Doom Bar, Ringwood, 5 Local ales ♂ Thatchers Gold. ☂ 10 **Facilities** ❧ Children welcome Children's menu Children's portions Garden Beer festival Parking Wi-fi 🚐 (notice required)

IBSLEY — Map 5 SU10

Old Beams Inn

Salisbury Rd BH24 3PP ☎ 01425 473387
e-mail: oldbeams@alcatraz.co.uk
dir: *On A338 between Ringwood & Salisbury*

Old Beams is a beautiful 13th-century thatched and timber-framed village inn located at the heart of the New Forest, with views of lovely countryside and the famous native ponies. It has a beer garden with a decked area and patio, and a cosy old-world interior. Pub food favourites, based on local and New Forest produce, dominate the menu, and on Friday night (fish night) there's a large selection.

Open all wk 11am-11.30pm ⊕ ALCATRAZ ◀ Morland Old Speckled Hen. **Facilities** Children welcome Children's menu Garden Parking Wi-fi

LEE-ON-THE-SOLENT Map 5 SU50

The Bun Penny

36 Manor Way PO13 9JH ☎ 023 9255 0214
e-mail: bar@bunpenny.co.uk
web: www.bunpenny.co.uk
dir: *From Fareham take B3385 to Lee-on-the-Solent. Pub 300yds before High St*

A short walk from the waterfront, this former farmhouse occupies a prominent position on the road into Lee-on-the-Solent. Every inch a classic country free house, it has a large patio at the front and an extensive back garden that's ideal for summer relaxation, while real fires and cosy corners are welcome in winter. Otter beer is sold direct from the cask, backed by hand-pulls including ales from the local Oakleaf Brewery. A typical meal might be paprika-crusted calamari with garlic mayonnaise and sweet chilli dip followed by fillet of pork Wellington, roasted root vegetables with a light scrumpy sauce. Change of hands.

Open all day all wk 11-11 (Fri-Sat 11am-mdnt Sun 12-10.30) **Bar Meals** L served Mon-Sat 12-2.30, Sun 12-9 D served Mon-Sat 6-9, Sun 12-9 Av main course £10.95 **Restaurant** L served Mon-Sat 12-2.30, Sun 12-9 D served Mon-Sat 6-9, Sun 12-9 ⊕ FREE HOUSE ◀ Otter Bitter, Oakleaf Hole Hearted, Guest ales Ō Westons. ♀ 13 **Facilities** Children welcome Children's menu Children's portions Garden Parking Wi-fi ▥ (notice required)

LINWOOD Map 5 SU10

The High Corner Inn

PICK OF THE PUBS

BH24 3QY ☎ 01425 473973
e-mail: highcorner@wadworth.co.uk
dir: *From A338 (Ringwood to Salisbury road) follow brown tourist signs into forest. Pass Red Shoot Inn, after 1m turn down gravel track at Green High Corner Inn*

Lost down a quarter-mile gravel track a mile from the village of Linwood, this much extended and modernised, early 18th-century inn is set in seven beautiful acres of woodland deep in the heart of the New Forest. The cluster of rambling buildings began life as a farm in the early 1700s. A quiet hideaway in winter, mobbed in summer, it is a popular retreat for families with its numerous bar-free rooms, flower-filled terrace, large garden, an outdoor adventure playground and miles of wildlife-rich forest and heathland walks and cycle trails. The beamed bars, replete with roaring winter log fires and the full

range of Wadworth ales on tap, and the lovely forest garden are very agreeable settings for sampling an extensive range of home-cooked meals and bar snacks; daily specials are shown on chalkboards and a carvery is available on Sunday. Rest and refuel during or following a forest ramble with a refreshing pint of 6X and a bowl of home-made soup, or a ploughman's lunch, or tuck into something more substantial from the traditional pub menu.

Open all wk Mon-Fri 12-3 6-11 (Sat 11-11 Sun 11-10.30 all day summer & school holidays) ⊕ WADWORTH ◀ 6X, Horizon, Henry's Original IPA, Seasonal Ales Ō Westons, Thatchers Gold. **Facilities** ♣ Children welcome Children's menu Play area Garden Parking

LISS Map 5 SU72

The Jolly Drover

London Rd, Hillbrow GU33 7QL ☎ 01730 893137
e-mail: thejollydrover@googlemail.com
dir: *From station in Liss at mini rdbt right into Hill Brow Rd (B3006) signed Rogate, Rake, Hill Brow. At junct with B2071 pub opposite. Cross dual carriageway*

This pub was built in 1844 by Mr Knowles - a drover - to offer cheer and sustenance to other drovers on the old London road. For 17 years it has been run by Anne and Barry Coe, who welcome all-comers with a large log fire, secluded garden, a covered and heated patio, a choice of real ales such as London Pride, and home-cooked food. The same menu is served in the bar and restaurant. Snacks include loaded nachos and potato skins, or choose from the English favourites such as locally-reared pheasant breast with redcurrant sauce; beef lasagne; or roast of the day. A gluten-free menu is available.

Open 10.30-3 5.30-11 (Sun 12-4) Closed: 25-26 Dec, 1 Jan, Sun eve **Bar Meals** L served Mon-Sat 10.30-2.15, Sun 12-3 D served Mon-Sat 6.30-9.30 Av main course £11 **Restaurant** L served Mon-Sat 10.30-2.15, Sun 12-3 D served Mon-Sat 6.30-9.30 Fixed menu price fr £12 ⊕ ENTERPRISE INNS/WHITBREAD ◀ Fuller's London Pride, Sharp's Doom Bar, Black Sheep Best Bitter. ♀ 14 **Facilities** Children welcome Children's portions Garden Parking Wi-fi ▥ (notice required)

LITTLETON Map 5 SU43

The Running Horse ★★★★ INN ◉◉

PICK OF THE PUBS

88 Main Rd SO22 6QS ☎ 01962 880218
e-mail: runninghorseinn@btconnect.com
dir: *3m from Winchester, 1m from Three Maids Hill, signed from Stockbridge Rd*

Just three miles from Winchester, this attractive food-led pub is especially popular with those who, despite the city's many good eating establishments, prefer the quieter surroundings of a village. The bar's limestone counter, stripped wooden floor, leather tub chairs and original fireplace draw those who enjoy locally brewed beers such as Itchen Valley's Godfathers and Longdog from Basingstoke. The focus on good eating helped The

Running Horse to gain two AA Rosettes for its contemporary cuisine, examples of which include whole roasted partridge with sautéed black pudding, girolle mushrooms, beetroot and red wine jus; duo of British lamb with pea and mint pannacotta; and oven-roasted sea bream with lemon confit and home-made spaghetti, sun-blushed tomatoes and piperade. The rear garden and front patio are large and peaceful – perfect for both dining and drinking. Beautifully appointed overnight accommodation is in a courtyard behind the main building.

Open all day all wk **Bar Meals** L served all wk 12-2 D served all wk 6-9.30 Av main course £11 **Restaurant** L served all wk 12-2 D served all wk 6-9.30 Av 3 course à la carte fr £26 ⊕ FREE HOUSE ◀ Morland Old Speckled Hen, Itchen Valley Godfathers, Longdog Ō Aspall. ♀ 14 **Facilities** Children welcome Children's menu Children's portions Garden Parking Wi-fi **Rooms** 9

LONGPARISH Map 5 SU44

The Plough Inn

PICK OF THE PUBS

SP11 6PB ☎ 01264 720358
e-mail: eat@theploughinn.info
dir: *M3 junct 8, A303 towards Andover. In approx 6m take B3048 towards Longparish*

This charming old 18th-century inn stands close to the centre of Longparish, just a few minutes' drive from Andover. The nearby River Test is one of southern England's finest chalk streams and the Test Way footpath runs through the inn's car park. This delightful location makes The Plough a popular stop for walkers, as well as for the fishermen and cyclists who are also drawn to this lovely valley. Expect Hampshire ales from the Itchen Valley Brewery, and a food offering that encompasses fish specials and pub classics as well as the à la carte menu. Typical dishes include duo of duck on rösti potato with sautéed Savoy cabbage and five spice jus; award-winning local sausages with mash and onion gravy; grilled goat's cheese and pimento polenta with balsamic glazed rocket; and locally smoked trout on toasted brioche with creamed leeks and dill dressing. Booking for meals may be required.

Open Mon-Sat 12-2.30 6-9.30 (Sun 12-8 summer 12-4 winter) Closed: Sun eve in winter ⊕ ENTERPRISE INNS ◀ Flack Manor Flack's Double Drop, Itchen Valley, Black Sheep Ō Thatchers. **Facilities** Children welcome Children's portions Garden Parking Wi-fi

Save on hotels. Book at **theAA.com/hotel**

HAMPSHIRE 263 **ENGLAND**

LOWER SWANWICK   Map 5 SU40

Old Ship

261 Bridge Rd SO31 7FN ☎ **01489 575646**
e-mail: simonoldship@gmail.com
dir: *Telephone for directions*

A 17th-century inn of great character on the banks of the River Hamble, the Old Ship has been an overall winner of Fareham in Bloom. It's popular with sailing types and families with dogs – the waterside patio is a great draw in summer. Inside are open fires in winter, dark wood panelling and beams, and a bar serving well-kept Fuller's beers. The spacious candlelit restaurant has a high-vaulted ceiling and nautical paraphernalia. Here home-cooked dishes include all the family favourites, from ploughman's and jackets to lasagne or Cajun chicken. Booking for meals may be required.

Open all day all wk **Bar Meals** L served Mon-Fri 12-2.15, Sat-Sun 12-9 D served Mon-Fri 6.30-9.30, Sat-Sun 12-9 Av main course £9.95 **Restaurant** L served Mon-Fri 12-2.15, Sat-Sun 12-9 D served Mon-Fri 6.30-9.30, Sat-Sun 12-9 ⊕ MERLIN INNS/FULLER'S ◀ Fuller's London Pride, George Gale & Co HSB, Guest ale. ♀ 8 **Facilities** ❖ Children welcome Children's menu Children's portions Family room Garden Parking 🚌

LOWER WIELD   Map 5 SU64

The Yew Tree

PICK OF THE PUBS

SO24 9RX ☎ **01256 389224**
dir: *Take A339 from Basingstoke towards Alton. Turn right for Lower Wield*

Set in wonderful countryside, opposite a picturesque cricket pitch, the popular landlord's simple mission statement promises 'Good honest food; great local beers; fine wines (lots of choice); and, most importantly, good fun for one and all'. This free house first served ale in 1845, when the eponymous, 650-year-old yew tree was just getting into its stride. Triple fff Moondance is the house beer, with 20 guest ale brewers on rotation, including Bowman Ales and Hogs Back. Most of the seasonal food is sourced from Hampshire or neighbouring counties, while keeping the regular favourites 'to avoid uproar'. Sample dishes include guinea fowl with balsamic roasted potatoes and shallots; and beef, smoked bacon, mushroom and thyme casserole, followed by Yew Tree fruity white chocolate pot or rhubarb, apple and berry crumble. The wines are mainly New World, but with some classic Burgundies and plenty available by the glass. There is an annual cricket match and sports day in summer, and 'silly' quiz nights in winter.

Open Tue-Sat 12-3 6-11 (Sun all day) Closed: 1st 2wks Jan, Mon **Bar Meals** L served Tue-Sun 12-2 D served Tue-Sat 6.30-9, Sun 6.30-8.30 Av main course £11.50 **Restaurant** L served Tue-Sun 12-2 D served Tue-Sat 6.30-9, Sun 6.30-8.30 ⊕ FREE HOUSE ◀ Flower Pots Cheriton Pots, Bowman Swift One, Triple fff Moondance, Hogs Back TEA, Hop Back GFB, Andwell Gold Muddler. ♀ 14 **Facilities** ❖ Children welcome Children's menu Children's portions Garden Parking

LYMINGTON   Map 5 SZ39

Mayflower Inn

Kings Saltern Rd SO41 3QD ☎ **01590 672160**
e-mail: manager@themayflowerlymington.co.uk
dir: *A337 towards New Milton, left at rdbt by White Hart, left to Rookes Ln, right at mini rdbt, pub 0.75m*

A favourite with yachtsmen and dog walkers, this solidly built mock-Tudor inn overlooks the Lymington River, with glorious views to the Isle of Wight. There's a magnificent garden with splendid sun terraces where you can enjoy a pint of Goddards Fuggle-Dee-Dum, a purpose-built play area for children and an on-going summer barbecue in fine weather. Menu prices are reasonable, with dishes that range from light bites like lemon and pepper monkfish goujons or a sharing platter, to main courses of black bean chicken stirfry, or sea bass fillet with prawn and saffron risotto.

Open all day all wk ⊕ ENTERPRISE INNS/COASTAL INNS & TAVERNS LTD ◀ Ringwood Best Bitter, Fuller's London Pride, Wadworth 6X, Goddards Fuggle-Dee-Dum Ō Thatchers. **Facilities** Children welcome Children's menu Children's portions Play area Garden Parking Wi-fi

The Walhampton Arms **NEW**

Walhampton Hill SO41 5RE ☎ **01590 673113**
e-mail: enquiries@walhamptonarms.co.uk
web: www.walhamptonarmslymington.co.uk
dir: *From Lymington take B3054 towards Beaulieu. Pub in 2m*

Originally an early 19th-century farm building, including a model dairy which supplied the Walhampton Estate. Today the pub is well known locally for its carvery, with steaks and surf 'n' turf representing excellent value; other popular dishes may include pork ribs; braised lamb shank; and beef lasagne. Desserts are all well tried and tested: choose between sticky toffee pudding, chocolate puddle pudding, and ice cream sundaes. Children too will find all their favourites on their own menus. Real ales come from Ringwood, with guest appearances from other local micro-breweries throughout the year.

Open all wk 10-3 6-11 (Mon & Sat 10am-11pm Sun 12-10.30) **Bar Meals** L served Mon & Sun 12-8, Tue-Fri 12-2.30, Sat 12-9.30 D served Mon & Sun 12-8, Tue-Fri 6-9, Sat 12-9.30 **Restaurant** L served Mon & Sun 12-8, Tue-Fri 12-2.30, Sat 12-9.30 D served Mon & Sun 12-8, Tue-Fri 6-9, Sat 12-9.30 ⊕ FREE HOUSE ◀ Ringwood Best Bitter, Guest ales. ♀ 12 **Facilities** Children welcome Children's menu Children's portions Parking Wi-fi 🚌 (notice required)

LYNDHURST   Map 5 SU30

New Forest Inn

Emery Down SO43 7DY ☎ **023 8028 4690**
e-mail: info@thenewforestinn.co.uk
dir: *M27 junct 1 follow signs for A35/Lyndhurst. In Lyndhurst follow signs for Christchurch, turn right at Swan Inn towards Emery Down*

In the heart of the New Forest with ponies passing (and occasionally entering) the front door, this traditional inn prides itself on its friendliness, great local atmosphere, and relaxed attitude to dogs. At least two guest cask ales are on offer throughout the year, in addition to the regular Ringwood Fortyniner and Flack Manor Flack's Double Drop. Food-wise, expect favourites such as duck liver and orange parfait with chutney and toast; braised game casserole with crusty bread; and honey-roasted ham with eggs and chips. There is a beer festival on the second weekend in July.

Open all day all wk **Bar Meals** Av main course £9.95 food served all day **Restaurant** food served all day ⊕ ENTERPRISE INNS ◀ Ringwood Fortyniner, Flack Manor Flack's Double Drop, Guest ales Ō Westons Stowford Press. **Facilities** ❖ Children welcome Children's menu Children's portions Garden Beer festival Parking Wi-fi 🚌 (notice required)

The Oak Inn

Pinkney Ln, Bank SO43 7FE ☎ **023 8028 2350**
e-mail: oakinn@fullers.co.uk
dir: *From Lyndhurst signed A35 to Christchurch, follow A35 1m, turn left at Bank sign*

New Forest ponies, pigs and deer graze outside this small but perfectly formed former cider house. Behind its bay windows lie a traditional wood-burner, antique pine furniture and bric-à-brac galore. Well-kept Fuller's ales change regularly, and you can relish your pint with a plate of simple and honest food sourced, if possible, in the county. If wine is preferred, many of those on the excellent list can be served by the glass. The kitchen's style is classically rustic with innovative modern twists: Oakwood Lop ham, for example, is roasted in maple syrup and served with free-range eggs from Fluffetts Farm. Booking for meals may be required.

Open all wk Mon-Fri 11.30-3.30 6-11 (Sat 11.30-11 Sun 12-10.30) **Bar Meals** L served Mon-Fri 12-2.30, Sat 12-9.30, Sun 12-9 D served Mon-Fri 6-9.30, Sat 12-9.30, Sun 12-9 **Restaurant** L served Mon-Fri 12-2.30, Sat 12-9.30, Sun 12-9 D served Mon-Fri 6-9.30, Sat 12-9.30, Sun 12-9 ⊕ FULLER'S ◀ London Pride, George Gale & Co HSB & Seafarers Ō Aspall. ♀ 12 **Facilities** ❖ Children welcome Children's menu Children's portions Garden Parking Wi-fi

MAPLEDURWELL   Map 5 SU65

The Gamekeepers

PICK OF THE PUBS

See Pick of the Pubs on page 264

PICK OF THE PUBS

The Gamekeepers

MAPLEDURWELL   Map 5 SU65

Tunworth Rd RG25 2LU
☎ **01256 322038 & 07786 998994**
e-mail: info@thegamekeepers.co.uk
web: www.thegamekeepers.co.uk
dir: *M3 junct 6, A30 towards Hook. Right
across dual carriageway after The Hatch
pub. Pub signed*

Joseph Phillips was a shoemaker when
he and his wife, Elizabeth, started living
here, but the appeal of making boots
obviously lost its shine because the
1861 census shows that Joseph had
changed tack. He became an innkeeper
and his house had become the Queen's
Head. When you go into the dining room,
look for two bricks, one each side of the
fireplace, marked with the couple's
initials and the date 1854, which was
probably when the building was granted
a licence. Acquiring its current name in
1973, it still displays much of its 19th-
century origin through its low beams,
flagstone floors and even an indoor well;
outside, a large garden overlooks the
gentle north Hampshire countryside.
Relax on a leather sofa with a pint of
real ale, and choose your meal from the
daily-changing menu and fish and
game specials, starting maybe with
moules marinière, or locally picked wild
mushrooms in a devilled cream sauce.
A main course to look out for is the
slow-cooked game hotpot, most likely
containing pheasant, partridge,
mallard, venison and pigeon, baked in

Tanglefoot real ale. Among the
alternatives: pan-fried Mapledurwell
lamb cutlets with mini shepherd's pie;
oven-baked fish pie; and chargrilled
pork, beer and watercress sausages
with chive mash. Apple crumble, sticky
toffee pudding, crème brûlée, chocolate
brownies and a Hampshire cheeseboard
are some of the desserts. Children are
welcome and can order smaller portions
of what mum and dad have, or maybe a
home-made burger if they prefer. The
carefully chosen wine list, although not
extensive, still covers both the New and
Old Worlds. Booking for meals may be
required.

Open all wk Mon-Fri 11-3 5.30-12 (Sat
11am-mdnt Sun 11-11) **Bar Meals** L
served Mon-Fri 11-2.30, Sat-Sun 11-9.30

D served Mon-Fri 5.30-9, Sat-Sun 11-9.30
Av main course £10-£12 **Restaurant** L
served Mon-Fri 11-2.30, Sat-Sun 11-9.30
D served Mon-Fri 5.30-9, Sat-Sun 11-9.30
Av 3 course à la carte fr £30 ⊕ FREE
HOUSE ◀ Badger First Gold, Tanglefoot,
Fursty Ferret, Hopping Hare, Firkin Fox,
Pickled Partridge ♂ Westons Stowford
Press. ♀ 10 **Facilities** Children welcome
Children's portions ✿ Garden Parking
Wi-fi ▭ (notice required)

Save on hotels. Book at theAA.com/hotel

HAMPSHIRE 265 ENGLAND

MICHELDEVER — Map 5 SU53

The Dove Inn ★★★★ INN ⚜

Andover Rd, Micheldever Station SO21 3AU
☎ **01962 774288**
e-mail: info@the-dove-inn.co.uk
dir: M3 junct 8 merge onto A303, take exit signed Micheldever Station, follow station signs onto Andover Rd, on left

Before the railway reached Andover 11 miles away, early-Victorian travellers arrived at Micheldever (then called Andover Road) Station and took the stagecoach from the neighbouring Western Road Hotel, now The Dove. A changing roster of three real ales is the norm in the several bars and eating areas, where menus feature home-made, locally sourced Thai-battered fish with hand-cut chips, noodle salad and coriander and caper dip; chargrilled rump steak; beefburger in toasted ciabatta; and creamy mushroom and garlic pasta. Overnight stays in the comfortable bedrooms include a good breakfast.

Open all wk 11-3 5.30-11 (Sat-Sun all day) **Bar Meals** L served Mon-Fri 12-2, Sat-Sun 12-2.30 D served Mon-Thu 6.30-9, Fri-Sat 6-9.30, Sun 6-8 **Restaurant** L served Mon-Fri 12-2, Sat-Sun 12-2.30 D served Mon-Thu 6.30-9, Fri-Sat 6-9.30, Sun 6-8 ⊕ FREE HOUSE ◀ Guest ales.
Facilities ❀ Children welcome Children's menu Children's portions Garden Parking Wi-fi 🚐 (notice required) **Rooms** 5

Half Moon & Spread Eagle

Winchester Rd SO21 3DG ☎ **01962 774339**
e-mail: liquidbrighton@hotmail.com
dir: From Winchester take A33 towards Basingstoke. In 5m turn left after small car garage. Pub 0.5m on right

Once known as the Dever Arms, this much improved former drovers' inn overlooks the cricket green in the heart of a pretty thatched and timbered Hampshire village. Under new management, the pub comprises three smartly furnished interconnecting rooms and it has a genuine local feel. An extensive menu takes in starters of pork and apple rillette, main courses of pan-seared chicken breast with red wine sauce, bacon, mushrooms and onions. Gourmet sandwiches and bar meals are also on offer and takeaway fish and chips is available every day. A beer festival is held in May.

Open all day all wk **Bar Meals** Av main course £8.50 food served all day **Restaurant** Fixed menu price fr £12 food served all day ⊕ GREENE KING ◀ Abbot Ale & London Glory, Hardys & Hansons Dark Mild, Butcombe, Guest ales Ŏ Aspall, Thatchers. ♟ 16 **Facilities** ❀ Children welcome Children's menu Children's portions Play area Garden Beer festival Parking Wi-fi 🚐 (notice required)

MORTIMER WEST END — Map 5 SU66

The Red Lion

Church Rd RG7 2HU ☎ **0118 970 0169**
e-mail: red-lionwestend@hotmail.co.uk
dir: Telephone for directions

Dating back to 1650, this traditional pub has a profusion of original oak beams and an inglenook fireplace. A range of real ales is served, plus stylish, unfussy cooking. Where possible produce is locally sourced, including free-range chicken and eggs, and English beef hung for 21 days. A bar menu offers traditional favourites while restaurant fare might start with jellied pork meat with home-made pickles and toast; followed by confit duck legs with fondant potato, orange purée and glazed chicory; then treacle tart and clotted cream. Look out for authentic Czech dishes.

Open all day all wk ⊕ HALL & WOODHOUSE ◀ Badger Tanglefoot, First Gold & K&B Sussex, Guinness Ŏ Westons Stowford Press. **Facilities** Children welcome Children's menu Children's portions Play area Family room Garden Beer festival Parking Wi-fi

NEW ALRESFORD — Map 5 SU53

The Bell Inn

12 West St SO24 9AT ☎ **01962 732429**
e-mail: info@bellalresford.com
dir: In village centre

This family-run free house in a restored 17th-century former coaching inn is right in the centre of this picturesque Georgian town. Sit at the bar with a local Upham Ale, a cider from Mr Whitehead's of Selborne, or one of the many wines available by the glass. Dine in the candlelit restaurant or bar on fresh, locally sourced monkfish tail, curried shrimps and coriander potatoes; fillet of Hampshire wild venison, chocolate sauce, fondant potato and root vegetable purée; or wild mushroom Stroganoff and braised rice. A £10, two-course deal runs on weekdays.

Open all day Closed: Sun eve **Bar Meals** L served all wk 12-3 D served Mon-Sat 6-9 Av main course £13 **Restaurant** L served Mon-Sat 12-3, Sun 12-4 D served Mon-Sat 6-9 Fixed menu price fr £10 ⊕ FREE HOUSE ◀ Sharp's Doom Bar, Itchen Valley Winchester Ale, Andwell Resolute, Upham Ale, Otter Ŏ Mr Whitehead's Heart of Hampshire. ♟ 18 **Facilities** ❀ Children welcome Children's menu Children's portions Garden Parking Wi-fi 🚐 (notice required)

NORTHINGTON — Map 5 SU53

The Woolpack Inn

PICK OF THE PUBS

Totford SO24 9TJ ☎ **0845 293 8066**
e-mail: info@thewoolpackinn.co.uk
dir: From Basingstoke take A339 towards Alton. Under motorway, turn right (across dual carriageway) onto B3036 signed Candovers & Alresford. Pub between Brown Candover & Northington

This Grade II listed drovers' inn stands in a tiny hamlet in the peaceful Candover Valley. Sympathetically smartened up, creating a sense of calm modernity while still retaining the classic feel of a country pub, The Woolpack is once again welcoming walkers and their dogs, families, cyclists and local foodies who cannot resist the cracking pub food. Ales include one named after The Woolpack, while an up-market wine list will please the cognoscenti. Eat in the traditional bar, where rugs on tiled or wood floors, a roaring log fire, rustic pine tables and the day's papers create a relaxing atmosphere; alternatives are the smart dining room or a heated terrace. The bar menu proffers grilled Old Spot ham with duck egg and hand-cut chips; or a toasted bap filled with roast pork and apricot stuffing. Typical dining room main courses are roasted partridge; or, not just for vegetarians, open ravioli with wild mushrooms, tarragon and white truffle sauce. As we went to press, we learnt of a change of hands.

Open all day all wk Closed: 25 Dec eve **Bar Meals** L served all wk 12-3 D served Mon-Sat 6-close, Sun 6-8.30 **Restaurant** L served all wk 12-3 D served Mon-Sat 6-close ⊕ FREE HOUSE ◀ The Woolpack Ale, Palmers Copper Ale, Otter Bitter, Flower Pots Ŏ Thatchers Gold. ♟ 12 **Facilities** ❀ Children welcome Children's menu Children's portions Play area Garden Parking Wi-fi 🚐

NORTH WALTHAM — Map 5 SU54

The Fox

PICK OF THE PUBS

See Pick of the Pubs on page 266

PICK OF THE PUBS

The Fox

NORTH WALTHAM   Map 5 SU54

RG25 2BE ☎ 01256 397288
e-mail: info@thefox.org
web: www.thefox.org
dir: *M3 junct 7, A30 towards Winchester. North Waltham signed on right. Take 2nd signed road*

A feature of the bar in this peaceful village pub down a country lane is its collection of miniatures – over 1,100 so far, and counting. It's an easy place to get to: if you're London-bound on the A303, leave just before it joins the M3, or if you're heading west on the motorway, turn off at junction 7. Built as three farm cottages in 1624, The Fox welcomes families, as you might guess from the children's adventure play area in the extensive beer garden. The garden fair blazes with colour in summer when the pretty flower borders and hanging baskets are in bloom. In the bar, landlord Rob MacKenzie serves well-looked after real ales from Ringwood, Brakspear, West Berkshire and a guest brewery, and an impressive malt whisky selection among which you'll find the relatively scarce Auchentoshan, Glenkinchie and Tomintoul. Rob's wife Izzy is responsible for the monthly menus and daily specials boards in the tartan-carpeted restaurant, which include coquilles St Jacques, and deep-fried camembert with redcurrant jelly. Among typical main courses you may encounter Scottish salmon en croûte with

new potatoes and mixed salad; pan-fried breast and confit leg of pheasant in apricot and wine sauce with dauphinoise potatoes and steamed green beans; steak-and-kidney pudding with mash and vegetables; and roasted nut loaf in pastry with broccoli and cranberry sauce. Check the blackboard for the day's specials. Home-made desserts are tempting too – there's banoffee cheesecake, passionfruit crème brûlée, and clafoutis, a tasty baked chocolate pudding with a hot fondant centre and butterscotch sauce. The Fox's events calendar features a late-April oyster festival, with a beer tent. Booking for meals may be required.

Open all day all wk 11-11 Closed: 25 Dec **Bar Meals** L served all wk 12-2.30 D served all wk 6-9.30 Av main course

£7.60 **Restaurant** L served all wk 12-2.30 D served all wk 6-9.30 Av 3 course à la carte fr £21.25 ⊕ FREE HOUSE ◀ Ringwood Best Bitter, West Berkshire Good Old Boy, Brakspear, Guest ale ♂ Aspall, Thatchers Gold, Westons Old Rosie. ♟ 14
Facilities Children welcome Children's menu Children's portions Play area 🐾 Garden Beer festival Parking 🚐 (notice required)

Save on hotels. Book at **theAA.com/hotel**

HAMPSHIRE 267 ENGLAND

OLD BASING   Map 5 SU65

The Crown NEW

The Street RG24 7BW ☎ 01256 321424
e-mail: sales@thecrownoldbasing.com
web: www.thecrownoldbasing.com
dir: *M3 junct 6 towards Basingstoke. At rdbt right onto A30. 1st left into Redbridge Ln, to T-junct. Right into The Street, pub on right*

A short drive from Basingstoke will bring you to the picturesque village of Old Basing, where The Crown reopened under new management in 2011. Reliable and popular national ales are backed by a good wine list, and food can take the form of bar snacks or dishes from the well-chosen menu. A typical choice could see a starter of rope-grown Fowey estuary mussels followed by a main course of slow-braised belly of Royal Berkshire pork. An exemplary range of cheeses competes with the likes of spiced pear and apple crumble with vanilla custard to finish. Look out for the annual beer festival. Booking for meals may be required.

Open all wk 11.30-2.30 5-11 (Fri-Sat 11.30-11.30 Sun 11.30-10) Closed: 1 Jan **Bar Meals** L served Mon-Thu 12-2, Fri-Sun 12-2.30 D served Mon-Thu 6-9, Fri-Sat 6-9.30 Av main course £12.95 **Restaurant** L served Mon-Thu 12-2, Fri-Sun 12-2.30 D served Mon-Thu 6-9, Fri-Sat 6-9.30 Fixed menu price fr £18 Av 3 course à la carte fr £22.95 ⊕ ENTERPRISE INNS ◀ Sharp's Doom Bar, Fuller's London Pride, Ringwood Old Thumper Ö Aspall. ᵀ 9 **Facilities** ❅ Children welcome Children's menu Children's portions Garden Beer festival Parking Wi-fi 🚌 (notice required)

OVINGTON   Map 5 SU53

The Bush

PICK OF THE PUBS

See Pick of the Pubs on page 268

PETERSFIELD   Map 5 SU72

The Trooper Inn

PICK OF THE PUBS

Alton Rd, Froxfield GU32 1BD ☎ 01730 827293
e-mail: info@trooperinn.com
dir: *From A3 follow A272 Winchester signs towards Petersfield (NB do not take A272). 1st exit at mini rdbt for Steep. 3m, pub on right*

This 17th-century free house stands in the heart of the countryside at one of Hampshire's highest points. Said to have been a recruiting centre at the outset of the Great War, the inn now boasts winter log fires, a spacious bar and a charming restaurant with a vaulted ceiling and wooden settles. Expect seasonal country cooking with fresh fish and game, much of it from local suppliers and producers. Pan-fried pork medallions, sweet potato cake, Savoy cabbage and Calvados sauce; Mr Morgan's home-made Cumberland sausages, mash, blue cheese sauce and onion rings; and spiced Moroccan seafood tagine with lemon and herb couscous are typical main course choices. The resident vegetarian chef creates dishes like parsnip, potato and wild rice cake. The inn backs onto Ashford Hangers National Nature Reserve, and is also well positioned for the South Downs National Park, Jane Austen's Chawton and Gilbert White's Selborne. Booking for meals may be required.

Open 12-3 6-11 Closed: 25-26 Dec & 1 Jan, Sun eve & Mon L **Bar Meals** L served Tue-Sat 12-2, Sun 12-2.30 D served Mon-Thu 6.30-9, Sat 7-9.30 **Restaurant** L served Tue-Sat 12-2, Sun 12-2.30 D served Mon-Fri 6.30-9, Sat 7-9.30 ⊕ FREE HOUSE ◀ Ringwood Best Bitter, Ballards, Local guest ales. ᵀ **Facilities** ❅ Children welcome Children's menu Children's portions Garden Parking Wi-fi 🚌 (notice required)

The White Horse Inn

Priors Dean GU32 1DA ☎ 01420 588387
e-mail: details@pubwithnoname.co.uk
dir: *A3/A272 to Winchester/Petersfield. In Petersfield left to Steep, 5m then right at small x-rds to East Tisted, take 2nd drive on right*

Also known as the 'Pub With No Name' as it has no sign, this splendid 17th-century farmhouse was originally used as a forge for passing coaches. The blacksmith sold beer to the travellers while their horses were attended to. Today there is an excellent range of beers including No Name Strong, and for something a little different there's rhubarb, damson and elderflower wines too. Menus offer the likes of Hampshire smoked platter; fishcakes; home-made pie of the day; selection of O'Hagans sausages with bubble-and-squeak. The pub holds a beer festival every June. Booking for meals may be required.

Open all wk 12-3 6-12 (Thu-Sun all day) ⊕ FULLER'S ◀ London Pride, George Gale & Co Seafarers, No Name Best & No Name Strong, Ringwood Fortyniner, Sharp's Doom Bar. **Facilities** Children welcome Children's menu Children's portions Family room Garden Beer festival Parking

PILLEY   Map 5 SZ39

The Fleur de Lys

Pilley St SO41 5QG ☎ 01590 672158
e-mail: nickchef1@hotmail.co.uk
dir: *From Lymington A337 to Brockenhurst. Cross Ampress Park rdbt, right to Boldre. At end of Boldre Ln turn right. Pub 0.5m*

Originally built as two foresters' cottages, ale has been sold here since the close of the 11th century. So The Fleur de Lys isn't just the oldest pub in the New Forest – it also claims to be the second oldest in England. Today it remains a traditional thatched inn with open fires, two wood-burning stoves and a large landscaped garden with wooden tables and chairs. The menu includes light bites like croque monsieur, as well as pizzas, burgers and vegetarian alternatives. A beer festival is held in July.

Open all day all wk 11-11 **Bar Meals** L served Mon-Fri 12-3, Sat-Sun all day D served Mon-Fri 6-9, Sat-Sun all day Av main course £8 **Restaurant** L served Mon-Fri 12-3, Sat-Sun all day D served Mon-Fri 6-9, Sat-Sun all day Av 3 course à la carte fr £22 ⊕ ENTERPRISE INNS ◀ Ringwood Best Bitter, Guest ales Ö Westons Stowford Press. **Facilities** ❅ Children welcome Children's menu Children's portions Family room Garden Beer festival Parking Wi-fi 🚌

PICK OF THE PUBS

The Bush

OVINGTON   Map 5 SU53

SO24 0RE ☎ 01962 732764
e-mail: thebushinn@wadworth.co.uk
web: www.thebushinn.co.uk
dir: *A31 from Winchester towards Alton & Farnham, approx 6m, left to Ovington. 0.5m to pub*

Located just off the A31 on a peaceful lane, this unspoilt 17th-century rose-covered cottage enjoys an enviable setting, close to the River Itchen chalk trout stream. Gentle riverside strolls are very popular, as are the rustic bars and bench-filled garden, both of which are often crammed with people, especially on fine summer weekends. Don't expect to find a jukebox or fruit machine; the intimate, softly lit and atmospheric rooms boast an assortment of sturdy tables, chairs and high-backed settles and a wealth of old artefacts, prints and stuffed fish. On cold winter nights the place to sit with a pint of traditional ale is in front of the roaring log fire. The regularly-changing menu is based on the freshest food the owners, Nick and Cathy Young, can source, including local farm cheeses, meats from Wiltshire, Hampshire and Scotland, and fish from the Dorset and Cornish coasts. Choices range from sandwiches, ploughman's lunches and other bar snacks, through to satisfying meals such as chicken liver pâté with grape chutney, or local smoked trout mousse; followed by Chinese-style braised belly

pork with spring onions, pak choi and apple purée; and a daily seasonal special like Italian sausages on cannellini bean and potato mash. Finish with sticky toffee pudding with caramel sauce, or Valrhona dark chocolate and raspberry crème brûlée. You will certainly find a wine to suit your palate, including from among the 19 served by the glass. Real ales keep their end up too, with Wadworth 6X and guest ales. Traditional afternoon tea is available on Fridays and every weekend throughout the year.

Open all wk Mon-Fri 11-3 6-11 Sat 11-11 Sun 12-10.30 (summer hols Mon-Sat 11-11 Sun 12-10.30) **Bar Meals** L served Mon-Fri 12-2.30, Sat 12-9.30, Sun 12-8.30, summer hols Mon-Sat

12-9, Sun 12-8.30 D served Mon-Fri 7-9, Sat 12-9.30, Sun 12-8.30, summer hols Mon-Sat 12-9, Sun 12-8.30 Av main course £11.50 **Restaurant** Fixed menu price fr £15 Av 3 course à la carte fr £17.50 ⊕ WADWORTH ◀ 6X, Henry's Original IPA, Farmers Glory, Old Timer & Horizon, Guest ales. ♟ 19
Facilities Children welcome Children's menu Children's portions Family room ♣ Garden Parking Wi-fi

Save on hotels. Book at theAA.com/hotel

HAMPSHIRE 269 ENGLAND

Purefoy Arms

Preston Candover, Hampshire RG25 2EJ
Tel: 01256 389777
Website: www.thepurefoyarms.co.uk
Email: info@thepurefoyarms.co.uk

Reopened after refurbishment a couple of years ago, this has two pairs of smallish linked rooms. On the left, the airy front bar has chunky tables, including ones so tall as to need bar stools, and a corner counter serving a fine changing choice of wines, as well as Andwell and Black Sheep Best on hand pump; this opens into a jute-floored back area with four dining tables and characterful mixed seats including old settles. The right-hand front room has red leather sofas and armchairs by a log fire, and goes back into a bare-boards area with three or four sturdy pale pine tables. An understated contemporary décor in grey and puce goes nicely with the informal friendliness of the service; there may be unobtrusive piped pop music. The sizeable sloping garden has well spaced picnic-sets, a Wendy house and perhaps a big hammock slung between two of its trees; there are teak tables on a terrace sheltered by the pub. This is an attractive village, with nearby snowdrop walks in February.

Good food changing daily includes lunchtime sandwiches, quality tapas and other inventive dishes such as a crayfish and blood orange salad, ballotine of quail and foie gras with Madeira jelly, burgers made with well hung rare breed steak, butternut squash risotto with sage and aged parmesan, and specials like slow-roasted shoulder of rare-breed pork with white beans and pata negra (cured Spanish ham), and whole plaice with Cornish crab gratin.

PRESTON CANDOVER — Map 5 SU64

Purefoy Arms NEW

Alresford Rd RG25 2EJ ☎ **01256 389777**
e-mail: info@thepurefoyarms.co.uk
web: www.thepurefoyarms.co.uk
dir: *On B3046, S of Basingstoke*

Expect the unexpected at this lovingly restored 19th-century brick village pub in the heart of the pretty Candover Valley. With a Spanish chef/owner the daily handwritten menus have a distinct Mediterranean flavour. Nibble on Serrano ham with caperberries, then try the asparagus and parmesan risotto, followed by confit duck leg with white beans and patanegra, or the Catalan hotpot. Find room for chocolate and apricot tart or a plate of artisan English and French cheeses. Fine wines and a cosy, convivial setting of wooden floors, open fires, exposed brick walls, warm textiles and chesterfield sofas complete the pleasing picture. Booking for meals may be required.

Open 12-3 6-11 (Sun 12-4) Closed: 26 Dec & 1 Jan, Sun eve & Mon **Bar Meals** L served Tue-Sat 12-3, Sun 12-4 D served Tue-Sat 6-10 Av main course £15 **Restaurant** L served Tue-Sat 12-3, Sun 12-4 D served Tue-Sat 6-10 Av 3 course à la carte fr £27 ⊕ FREE HOUSE ◀ Flack Manor Flack's Double Drop, Itchen Valley Ŏ Westons Bounds. ♀17 **Facilities** ✿ Children welcome Children's menu Children's portions Garden Parking Wi-fi 🚐 (notice required)

See advert on page 269

RINGWOOD — Map 5 SU10

The Star Inn NEW

12 Market Place BH24 1AW ☎ **01425 473105**
e-mail: thestarringwood@yahoo.co.uk
dir: *From A31 follow market place signs*

Ian Pepperell, the landlord of this 470-year-old pub on the square in this New Forest market town, has played a character in BBC Radio 4's *The Archers* for over 15 years. Away from his radio career he pulls pints of Ringwood Best for locals and helps serve the authentic Thai and oriental food that dominates the menu. Typical dishes include salt and pepper squid, deep-fried sea bass with chilli sauce, chicken in black bean sauce, and aromatic crispy duck. At lunch, you can also tuck into rib-eye steak and chips and tuna mayonnaise sandwiches. Booking for meals may be required.

Open all day all wk Closed: 1 Jan **Bar Meals** L served all wk 12-2.30 D served all wk 6-9.30 **Restaurant** L served all wk 12-2.30 D served all wk 6-9.30 ⊕ ENTERPRISE INNS ◀ Ringwood Best Bitter, Hop Back Summer Lightning, Fuller's London Pride, Black Sheep, Brains Ŏ Black Rat, Thatchers Green Goblin. ♀11 **Facilities** ✿ Garden Wi-fi 🚐 (notice required)

ROCKBOURNE — Map 5 SU11

The Rose & Thistle

PICK OF THE PUBS

SP6 3NL ☎ **01725 518236**
e-mail: enquiries@roseandthistle.co.uk
dir: *Follow Rockbourne signs from either A354 (Salisbury to Blandford Forum road) or A338 at Fordingbridge*

Standing at the top of a fine main street lined with picture-postcard period houses, this pub was originally two 17th-century thatched cottages. Long, low and whitewashed, the pub is quintessentially English with its stunning rose arch, hanging baskets round the door, and a quaint dovecote in the glorious front garden. Country-style fabrics, impressive floral arrangements and magazines to peruse are tasteful touches in the charming beamed bars, which boast two huge fireplaces for blazing winter warmth – perfect after a breezy downland walk. Expect a relaxing atmosphere, Palmers Copper Ale on tap and a selection of quality dishes from well-balanced menus. Lunchtime bar snacks take in Welsh rarebit with grilled bacon and tomato, and favourite puddings such as seasonal fruit crumble. If the occasion calls for more formal dining, you could start with Fjordling smoked fish platter; and follow with slow-cooked pork belly with a shallot and apple purée and herb crusted black pudding. Booking for meals may be required.

Open all wk 11-3 6-11 (Sat 11-11 Sun 12-8) **Bar Meals** L served all wk 12-2.30 D served Mon-Sat 7-9.30 Av main course £14.50 **Restaurant** L served all wk 12-2.30 D served Mon-Sat 7-9.30 ⊕ FREE HOUSE ◀ Fuller's London Pride, Palmers Copper Ale, Timothy Taylor Landlord Ŏ Westons, Black Rat. ♀12 **Facilities** Children welcome Children's portions Garden Parking Wi-fi 🚐 (notice required)

ROCKFORD — Map 5 SU10

The Alice Lisle

Rockford Green BH24 3NA ☎ **01425 474700**
e-mail: alicelisle@fullers.co.uk
dir: *From Ringwood A338 towards Fordingbridge after 1m turn right into Ivy Lane at end turn left cross cattle grid. Inn on left*

A picturesque, red-brick pub with a beautiful garden overlooking Blashford Lakes to the rear and Rockford Green to the front. Lady Alice Lisle, who lived down the road, was beheaded in 1685 for harbouring fugitives, following the failure of the Monmouth Rebellion. With the majority of produce sourced from New Forest Marque suppliers, choose from a menu including crab, fennel and chilli linguine; River Test trout fillet; gammon steak, chips and free-range eggs; and tomato and basil gnocchi. A Fuller's house, it hosts beer festivals in the summer. Booking for meals may be required.

Open all day all wk 10.30am-11pm **Bar Meals** L served Mon-Fri 12-2.30, Sat 12-3, Sun 12-6 D served Mon-Fri 6-9, Sat 5-9 **Restaurant** L served Mon-Fri 12-2.30, Sat 12-3, Sun 12-6 D served Mon-Fri 6-9, Sat 5-9 ⊕ FULLER'S ◀ London Pride, George Gale & Co Seafarers & HSB Ŏ New Forest Traditional. ♀10 **Facilities** ✿ Children welcome Children's menu Children's portions Play area Garden Beer festival Parking Wi-fi 🚐 (notice required)

ROMSEY — Map 5 SU32

The Cromwell Arms

23 Mainstone SO51 8HG ☎ **01794 519515**
e-mail: dining@thecromwellarms.com
dir: *From Romsey take A27 signed Ringwood, Bournemouth, Salisbury. Cross River Test, pub on right*

With Broadlands, former home of Lord Mountbatten and current home of Lord and Lady Brabourne, as its neighbour, The Cromwell Arms derives its name from Romsey's links with the English Civil War. It offers fresh, home-cooked food and attentive service with some unique twists on traditional gastro-pub favourites. Typical locally sourced dishes are home-made game terrine with spiced apple chutney; and twice-baked cheese and mushroom soufflé with new potatoes and mixed leaves. Its Hampshire-skewed offering of real ales includes Double Drop from the town's Flack Manor brewery, and a diverse selection of wines.

Open all day all wk **Bar Meals** L served Mon-Sat 12-9.30, Sun 12-8.30 D served Mon-Sat 12-9.30, Sun 12-8.30 Av main course £15.95 food served all day **Restaurant** L served Mon-Sat 12-9.30, Sun 12-8.30 D served Mon-Sat 12-9.30, Sun 12-8.30 Av 3 course à la carte fr £23.50 food served all day ⊕ FREE HOUSE ◀ Flack Manor Flack's Double Drop, Andwell Ruddy Darter, Ringwood Best Bitter Ŏ Thatchers Gold. ♀17 **Facilities** Children welcome Children's menu Children's portions Garden Parking Wi-fi 🚐 (notice required)

Save on hotels. Book at theAA.com/hotel

HAMPSHIRE 271 ENGLAND

The Dukes Head

PICK OF THE PUBS

Greatbridge Rd SO51 0HB ☎ 01794 514450
dir: Telephone for directions

Coins dated 1621 found during renovations some years ago support the belief that an inn has stood where the roads to Romsey, Salisbury and Stockbridge cross the River Test for many centuries. In summer its cream-painted façade and large front garden are rich with flowers, at the rear is a terrace, while its rambling interior incorporates a beamed bar with a big log fire, a cosy snug and four other comfortable rooms. The real ale roll-call is good, with Fuller's London Pride, Hop Back Summer Lightning, two from Ringwood and four weekly changing guests. Food suggestions for lunch or dinner include steak-and-ale pie with shortcrust pastry; rustic chilli with wild rice; deep-fried haddock in beer-batter; and duo of pork. Fresh fish and shellfish, including sometimes seared scallops, appear on the specials board. There are beer festivals in May and September. Booking for meals may be required.

Open all day all wk Closed: 25 Dec **Bar Meals** L served all wk 12-2.30 D served all wk 6-9.30 **Restaurant** L served all wk 12-2.30 D served all wk 6-9.30 ⊕ ENTERPRISE INNS ◀ Fuller's London Pride, Ringwood Best Bitter & Fortyniner, Hop Back Summer Lightning, Guinness, 4 Guest ales. ♥ 10 **Facilities** Children welcome Children's menu Children's portions Garden Beer festival Parking Wi-fi

The Three Tuns ◉

58 Middlebridge St SO51 8HL ☎ 01794 512639
e-mail: manager@the3tuns.co.uk
dir: Romsey bypass, 0.5m from main entrance of Broadlands Estate

Holding many awards for food, including an AA Rosette, and hospitality, this 300-year-old pub belongs to the owners of Winchester's highly regarded Chesil Rectory restaurant. Newly added smart wood panelling, vintage chandeliers and botanical prints have each made their own contribution to the characteristic visual appeal of oak beams and open fireplaces. A new simple British menu features many local ingredients for seasonal classics, daily specials, sharing platters and Sunday roasts. For a quiet fireside pint, there's Ringwood or a guest. The River Test flows under the stone bridge just along the street.

Open all wk 12-3 5-11 (Fri-Sun 12-11) summer all day (Sun 11-10.30) Closed: 25 Dec **Bar Meals** L served Mon-Thu 12-2.30, Fri-Sun 12-3 D served Mon-Thu 6-9, Fri-Sat 6-9.30 Av main course £10 **Restaurant** L served Mon-Thu 12-2.30, Fri-Sun 12-3 D served Mon-Thu 6-9, Fri-Sat 6-9.30 Av 3 course à la carte fr £20 ⊕ ENTERPRISE INNS ◀ Ringwood Best Bitter, Sharp's Doom Bar, 2 Guest ales Ŏ Westons Stowford Press. ♥ 12 **Facilities** Children welcome Children's portions Garden Parking

ROTHERWICK   Map 5 SU75

The Coach and Horses NEW

The Street RG27 9BG ☎ 01256 768976
e-mail: ian027@btinternet.com
dir: Follow brown signs from A32 Hook-Reading road

Close to the church in Rotherwick — a picturesque Hampshire village that has appeared in TV's *Midsomer Murders* — parts of this traditional inn can be traced back to the 17th century. Three of the four rooms benefit from log fires in winter, whilst the south-facing garden is a draw in the summer as a place for a relaxed pint of ale, an afternoon tea or a sensibly priced meal: home-made pub classics include smoked haddock and cheese fishcakes; and beef and ale pie. Look out for visiting Morris dancers throughout the summer.

Open 12-3 5.30-11 (Sat 12-11 Sun 12-6) Closed: Sun eve & Mon **Bar Meals** L served Tue-Sat 12-3, Sun 12-4 D served Tue-Sat 6-9 ⊕ HALL & WOODHOUSE ◀ Badger First Gold, Pickled Partridge, Firkin Fox, Fursty Ferret Ŏ Westons Stowford Press. **Facilities** ❖ Children welcome Children's menu Children's portions Garden Parking Wi-fi ▭ (notice required)

ST MARY BOURNE   Map 5 SU45

The Bourne Valley Inn

SP11 6BT ☎ 01264 738361
e-mail: enquiries@bournevalleyinn.com
dir: Telephone for directions

This popular, traditional inn is an oasis of tranquillity surrounded by fields on the outskirts of St Mary Bourne. Built around the end of the 19th century, it was known as The Railway Inn, due to its proximity to the now vanished railway line and station. Smartly furnished throughout, it has a large character bar with plenty of guest ales and a more intimate dining area, as well as a riverside garden abounding with wildlife where children can let off steam in the special play area. At lunch you could enjoy a 'country pub classic' such as lasagne, salad and chips; beer-batter cod; eggs and gammon; and mushroom and pepper Stroganoff.

Open all day all wk **Bar Meals** L served all wk 12-2.30 D served all wk 6-9 Av main course £9 **Restaurant** L served all wk 12-2.30 D served all wk 6-9 Fixed menu price fr £9 Av 3 course à la carte fr £16 ⊕ FREE HOUSE ◀ Guest ales. ♥ 12 **Facilities** ❖ Children welcome Children's menu Children's portions Play area Garden Parking Wi-fi ▭ (notice required)

SELBORNE   Map 5 SU73

The Selborne Arms

High St GU34 3JR ☎ 01420 511247
e-mail: info@selbornearms.co.uk
dir: From A3 follow B3006, pub on left in village centre

The massive chimney appearing to block the way in to this simply furnished village pub is known as a baffle entry. Once inside, you'll find homely bars with hop-strewn beams, a huge fireplace, up to seven (in summer) real ales from micro-breweries, and Mr Whitehead's cider. Keen supporters of Hampshire Fare (a community interest company), the kitchen prepares steamed oxtail and kidney pudding; Blackmoor pigeon faggot on bubble-and-squeak; and whole grilled plaice. A beer festival is held over the first weekend in October. The village, overlooked by glorious beech 'hangers', is where naturalist Gilbert White lived.

Open all wk 11-3 6-11 (Sat-11-11 Sun 12-11) **Bar Meals** L served all wk 12-2 D served Mon-Sat 7-9, Sun 7-8.30 **Restaurant** L served all wk 12-2 D served Mon-Sat 7-9, Sun 7-8.30 ⊕ FREE HOUSE ◀ Courage Best Bitter, Ringwood Fortyniner, Suthwyk Old Dick, Local guest ales Ŏ Mr Whitehead's. ♥ 10 **Facilities** Children welcome Children's menu Children's portions Play area Garden Beer festival Parking ▭ (notice required)

SILCHESTER   Map 5 SU66

Calleva Arms

Little London Rd, The Common RG7 2PH ☎ 0118 970 0305
dir: A340 from Basingstoke, signed Silchester. M4 junct 11, 20 mins signed Mortimer then Silchester

Overlooking the common, this pub is the perfect starting (or finishing) point for visitors to Calleva Atrebatum, a Roman town whose surviving walls are some of the best preserved in Britain. Two bar areas, with a log burner in the middle, lead to a pleasant conservatory and large enclosed garden. A comprehensive menu lists grilled steaks with fries; prawn and whitebait salad; vegetarian Glamorgan sausages served with Yorkshire pudding; chicken Kiev; and daily specials, with roasts every Sunday. Guest beers change frequently.

Open all wk 11-3 5.30-11 (Sat 11am-11.30pm Sun 12-11) **Bar Meals** L served all wk 12-2 D served all wk 6.30-9 **Restaurant** L served all wk 12-2 D served all wk 6.30-9 ⊕ FULLER'S ◀ London Pride, George Gale & Co HSB & Butser, Guinness Ŏ Aspall. ♥ 10 **Facilities** ❖ Children welcome Children's portions Garden Parking Wi-fi ▭ (notice required)

SOUTHAMPTON · Map 5 SU41

The White Star Tavern, Dining & Rooms ★★★★★ INN ◉◉

28 Oxford St SO14 3DJ ☎ 023 8082 1990
e-mail: reservations@whitestartavern.co.uk
dir: M3 junct 13, take A33 to Southampton, towards Ocean Village & Marina

Named after the famous White Star Line shipping company that used to set sail from Southampton, this stylish gastro-pub with rooms is set in cosmopolitan Oxford Street. With two AA Rosettes, the restaurant provides modern British cooking typified by smoked salmon fishcake, buttered spinach, watercress beurre blanc; free-range Hampshire pork belly, champ cake and cider gravy; New Forest strawberries with vanilla ice cream, black pepper and balsamic. Watch the world go by from the pavement tables, or stay a little longer in one of 13 smart and comfortable bedrooms.

Open all day all wk 7am-11pm (Fri 7am-mdnt Sat 8.30am-mdnt Sun 8.30am-10.30pm) Closed: 25 Dec **Bar Meals** L served Mon-Thu 7am-11am (bkfst) 12-2.30, Fri-Sat 7am-11am (bkfst) 12-3, Sun 7.30am-11am (bkfst) 12-8 D served Mon-Thu & Sat 6-9.30, Fri 6-10, Sun 6-8 **Restaurant** L served Mon-Thu 12-2.30, Fri-Sat 12-3, Sun 12-8 D served Mon-Thu 6-9.30, Fri-Sat 6-10 ⊕ ENTERPRISE INNS ◖ Fuller's London Pride, Bowman Swift One, Ringwood. ☗ 11 **Facilities** Children welcome Children's menu Children's portions Wi-fi **Rooms** 13

SPARSHOLT · Map 5 SU43

The Plough Inn

PICK OF THE PUBS

See Pick of the Pubs on opposite page

STEEP · Map 5 SU72

Harrow Inn

PICK OF THE PUBS

GU32 2DA ☎ 01730 262685
dir: A3 to A272, left through Sheet, take road opposite church (School Ln) then over A3 by-pass bridge

This 16th-century tile-hung gem is situated in a lovely rural location and has changed little over the years. The McCutcheon family has run it since 1929; sisters Claire and Nisa, both born and brought up here, are now the third generation with their names over the door. Tucked away off the road, it comprises two tiny bars - the 'public' is Tudor, with beams, tiled floor, inglenook fireplace, scrubbed tables, wooden benches, tree-trunk stools and a 'library'; the saloon (or Smoking Room, as it is still called) is Victorian. Beers are dispensed from barrels, there is no till and the toilets are across the road. Food is in keeping: ham and pea soup; hot Scotch eggs (some days); cheddar ploughman's; and various quiches. The large garden has

plenty of tables surrounded by country-cottage flowers and fruit trees. Quiz nights raise huge sums for charity, for which Claire's partner Tony grows and sells flowers outside. Ask about the Harrow Cook Book, a collection of customers' recipes on sale for charity.

Open 12-2.30 6-11 (Sat 11-3 6-11 Sun 12-3 7-10.30) Closed: Sun eve in winter **Bar Meals** L served all wk 12-2 D served all wk 7-9 Av main course £10.50 ⊕ FREE HOUSE ◖ Ringwood Best Bitter, Palmers Best Biiter, Hop Back GFB, Otter Ale, Bowman ♂ Thatchers Heritage. **Facilities** ✿ Garden Parking **Notes** ◉

STOCKBRIDGE · Map 5 SU33

The Greyhound Inn ◉◉

PICK OF THE PUBS

31 High St SO20 6EY ☎ 01264 810833
e-mail: enquiries@thegreyhound.info
dir: In village centre

Midway between Winchester and Salisbury, in the heart of fly-fishing country, this classy 15th-century village inn backs on to the River Test. Dine alfresco on the patio in the beautiful riverside garden; the inn is the only pub in the area to have fishing rights on this stretch of the magnificent chalk stream. The history-steeped bar and more contemporary lounge sport polished wood floors, old beams and timbers, subtle spot-lighting, open log fires, and deep comfy sofas. You could pop in for a pint of Ringwood Best or Upham Ale, but most people are drawn by the first-class modern British cooking, with occasional influences from France and Italy. Simplicity is key to the kitchen's approach, delivering cracking modern dishes with care, finesse and thoughtful composition. Try the lemon-scented fish crumble from the bar menu, or roast Hampshire partridge from the restaurant menu. Booking for meals may be required.

Open all day Closed: 24-26 & 31 Dec, 1 Jan, Sun eve **Bar Meals** L served Mon-Thu 12-2, Fri-Sat 12-2.30 Av main course £16 **Restaurant** L served Mon-Thu 12-2, Fri-Sun 12-2.30 D served Mon-Thu 7-9, Fri-Sat 7-9.30 Av 3 course à la carte fr £35 ⊕ FREE HOUSE ◖ Ringwood Best Bitter, Upham Ale ♂ Westons Stowford Press. ☗ 8 **Facilities** Children welcome Children's portions Garden Parking Wi-fi

Mayfly

Testcombe SO20 6AZ ☎ 01264 860283
dir: Between A303 & A30, on A3057

Standing right on the banks of the swiftly flowing River Test, the Mayfly is an iconic drinking spot. Inside the beamed old farmhouse with its traditional bar and bright conservatory you'll find a choice of draught ciders and up to six real ales. All-day bar food might include smoked haddock and spring onion fishcakes; stuffed roasted peppers with herb couscous; or pork chops with caramelised apple glaze. Arrive early on warm summer days to grab a bench on the large riverside terrace.

Open all day all wk 10am-11pm **Bar Meals** L served all wk 11.30-9 D served all wk 11.30-9 Av main course £11 food served all day **Restaurant** food served all day ⊕ FREE HOUSE ◖ Adnams Southwold Bitter, Wadworth 6X, Goddards Fuggle-Dee-Dum, Hop Back Summer Lightning, Palmers Dorset Gold, Flack Manor Flack's Double Drop ♂ Aspall, Thatchers Green Goblin & Gold. ☗ 20 **Facilities** ✿ Children welcome Children's portions Garden Parking 🚌

The Peat Spade Inn ◉

PICK OF THE PUBS

See Pick of the Pubs on page 274

The Three Cups Inn ★★★ INN

PICK OF THE PUBS

High St SO20 6HB ☎ 01264 810527
e-mail: manager@the3cups.co.uk
dir: M3 junct 8, A303 towards Andover. Left onto A3057 to Stockbridge

The pub's name apparently comes from an Old English phrase for a meeting of three rivers, although there's only one river here. That river happens to be the Test, generally regarded as the birthplace of modern fly fishing. One of these channels flows through the delightful rear garden of this 15th-century, timber-framed building, where brown trout may be spotted from the patio. The low-beamed bar to the right of the front door can be warmed by the centrally placed log fire; Itchen Valley and Flower Pots - Hampshire real ales - and a guest, are served here. You can eat in the bar, but the main, candlelit dining area is at the other end of the building. Modern European and traditional selections blend fresh regional ingredients to create starters such as smoked salmon and crème fraîche terrine with citrus dressing; and main courses of rabbit leg braised in sherry, saffron, Savoy cabbage and wild mushroom tortellini. Accommodation suites provide Egyptian cotton sheets and real ground coffee.

Open all day all wk 10am-10.30pm ⊕ FREE HOUSE ◖ Itchen Valley Fagins, Young's Bitter, Flower Pots, Guest ales ♂ Westons Stowford Press. **Facilities** Children welcome Children's portions Garden Parking **Rooms** 8

Save on hotels. Book at **theAA.com/hotel**

HAMPSHIRE 273 ENGLAND

PICK OF THE PUBS

The Plough Inn

SPARSHOLT   Map 5 SU43

Woodman Ln SO21 2NW
☎ 01962 776353
dir: *B3049 from Winchester towards Salisbury, left to Sparsholt, 1m*

Built as a coach house to serve Sparsholt Manor opposite, this popular village pub just a few miles from Winchester has been a popular local alehouse for more than 150 years. Inside, the main bar and dining areas blend harmoniously together, with farmhouse-style pine tables, wooden and upholstered seats, and miscellaneous agricultural implements, stone jars, wooden wine box end-panels and dried hops. Wadworth of Devizes supplies all the real ales, and there's a good wine selection. Lunchtime regulars know that 'doorstep' is a most apt description for the great crab and mayonnaise, beef and horseradish and other sandwiches, plus good soups and chicken liver parfait. The dining tables to the left of the entrance look over open fields to wooded downland, and it's at this end of the pub you'll find a daily-changing blackboard offering dishes such as salmon and crab fishcakes with saffron sauce; lamb's liver and bacon with mash and onion gravy; beef, ale and mushroom pie; and whole baked camembert with garlic and rosemary.

The menu board at the right-hand end of the bar offers the more substantial venison steak with celeriac mash and roasted beetroot; roast pork belly with bubble-and-squeak, five spice and sultana gravy; chicken breast filled with goat's cheese mousse; and fillet of sea bass with olive mash. Puddings include sticky toffee pudding and crème brûlée. The Plough is very popular, so it's best to book for any meal. The delightful flower- and shrub-filled garden has plenty of room for children to run around and play in. There's a jazz night on the first Sunday in August and carol singing with Father Christmas on 23rd December. Booking for meals may be required.

Open all wk 11-3 6-11 (Sun 12-3 6-10.30) Closed: 25 Dec **Bar Meals** L served all wk 12-2 D served Sun-Thu 6-9, Fri-Sat 6-9.30 **Restaurant** L served all wk 12-2 D served Sun-Thu 6-9, Fri-Sat 6-9.30 ⊕ WADWORTH ◀ Henry's Original IPA, 6X, Old Timer, JCB. ♟ 15 **Facilities** Children welcome Children's menu Children's portions Play area Family room Garden Parking

PICK OF THE PUBS

The Peat Spade Inn ❀

STOCKBRIDGE Map 5 SU33

Longstock SO20 6DR ☎ 01264 810612
e-mail: info@peatspadeinn.co.uk
web: www.peatspadeinn.co.uk
dir: *Telephone for directions*

The Peat Spade sits on the banks of the River Test in a corner of Hampshire countryside famed for being the fly-fishing capital of the world. Unusual paned windows overlook the peaceful village lane and idyllic heavily thatched cottages at this striking, red-brick and gabled Victorian pub. Located between Winchester and Salisbury, The Peat Spade is a reminder of a bygone England and its country sport traditions. You will find a relaxed atmosphere in the cosy fishing- and shooting-themed bar and dining room; a simple daily-changing menu lists classic English food combined with flavoursome European ingredients. Using locally-sourced produce as the base, including allotment fruit and vegetables, and game from the Leckford Estate, the choice may take in cured Trealy Farm venison carpaccio with mozzarella, roasted pepper, wild rocket and parmesan shavings. Fish-based main courses are particularly well represented: they may proffer beer-battered haddock with triple-cooked chips and minted pea purée; Cornish cod fillet with chorizo and haricot bean stew; or whole lemon sole with saffron potatoes, brown shrimp butter and wilted spinach. Sunday lunches embrace the three classic meat roasts, preceded by the likes of smoked salmon gravad lax with traditional garnish and watercress, and followed by desserts such as lemon tart with raspberry sauce. To drink there are local cask ales, and a small but innovative wine list which includes a choice of two champagnes served by the glass. Why not take a bottle and retire to the super summer terrace, where thoughts might turn to the one that got away? Booking for meals may be required.

Open all day all wk 11-11 (Sun 11-10.30) Closed: 25 Dec **Bar Meals** L served all wk 12-2.30 D served all wk 6.30-9.30 **Restaurant** L served all wk 12-2.30 D served all wk 6.30-9.30 ⊕ FREE HOUSE/MILLER'S COLLECTION ◀ Ringwood Best Bitter & Fortyniner, Guest ales. ♖ 11 **Facilities** Children welcome Children's menu Children's portions ✿ Garden Parking Wi-fi 🚌 (notice required)

Save on hotels. Book at **theAA.com/hotel**

HAMPSHIRE 275 **ENGLAND**

SWANMORE
Map 5 SU51

The Rising Sun

Hill Pound SO32 2PS ☎ 01489 896663
dir: From M27 junct 10 take A32. Through Wickham towards Alton. Turn left onto Bishop's Wood Rd, right at x-rds into Mislington Rd to Swanmore

In the beautiful Meon Valley, this 17th-century coaching inn has winter fires, low beams, uneven floors and lots of nooks and crannies. In summer, enjoy a pint of Ringwood Best and Sharp's Doom Bar in the secluded rear garden. Home-cooked food makes good use of locally sourced ingredients in simple snacks such as a ham and tomato sandwich through to hearty mains along the lines of home-made faggots with mash, peas and gravy, or home-made beef lasagne and chips.

Open all wk Mon-Sat 11.30-3 5.30-11 (Sun 12-4 5.30-10.30) **Bar Meals** L served Mon-Sat 12-2, Sun 12-2.30 D served Mon-Sat 6-9, Sun 6-8.30 **Restaurant** L served Mon-Sat 12-2, Sun 12-2.30 D served Mon-Sat 6-9, Sun 6-8.30 ⊕ FREE HOUSE ◀ Sharp's Doom Bar, Ringwood Best Bitter, Fuller's London Pride, Timothy Taylor Landlord ♂ Westons Stowford Press. ♟ 13 **Facilities** Children welcome Children's menu Children's portions Garden Parking 🚌 (notice required)

TANGLEY
Map 5 SU35

The Fox Inn

SP11 0RU ☎ 01264 730276
e-mail: info@foxinntangley.co.uk
dir: A343, 4m from Andover

Standing on a small crossroads, miles it seems from anywhere, this 300-year-old brick and flint cottage has been a pub since 1830. Its thoughtfully restored interior is made up of several different matchboard walled rooms, including a sofa-furnished bar, a restaurant and the Racing Room where a plasma TV is turned on for sporting events. Authentic Thai food includes soups, salads, stirfries and curries, although traditional English dishes and children's menus are also available. There's a front terrace with giant umbrella and heater, and another terrace at the back. Booking for meals may be required.

Open all day all wk 12-11 (Sun 12-10.30) Closed: 25 Dec, 1 Jan **Bar Meals** L served Mon-Sat 12-2.30, Sun 12-2.45 D served Mon-Sat 6-9.45, Sun 6-8 **Restaurant** L served Mon-Sat 12-2.30, Sun 12-2.45 D served Mon-Sat 6-9.45, Sun 6-8 ⊕ FREE HOUSE ◀ Fuller's London Pride, Ramsbury. ♟ 12 **Facilities** ♣ Children welcome Children's menu Children's portions Garden Parking Wi-fi

TICHBORNE
Map 5 SU53

The Tichborne Arms

PICK OF THE PUBS

SO24 0NA ☎ 01962 733760
e-mail: tichbornearms@xln.co.uk
dir: Off A31 towards Alresford, after 200yds right at Tichborne sign

Of the three pubs built on this site, the first in 1423 was destroyed by fire, as was its successor; the present free house, a thatched, red-brick building, dates from 1939. The River Itchen, having risen nearby, flows through the quiet hamlet, which hit the headlines in the late-1860s when a butcher's boy from Australia was convicted for falsely claiming to be the dead heir to Lady Tichborne. An eclectic mix of artefacts inside includes stuffed animals, antiques and a chiming grandfather clock. Owner Patrick Roper cooks to order from short daily menus, typically featuring pork loin escalopes with apples and pears in blue cheese sauce; fillet of salmon with lemon and lime hollandaise; and wild mushroom risotto with parmesan. Snacks include sandwiches, ploughman's and filled jacket potatoes. Beers are supplied by Hop Back, Palmers, Bowman and Sharp's. A beer festival is held on the third weekend in August.

Open all wk 11.45-3 6-11.30 (Sat open all day) **Bar Meals** L served all wk 12-2 D served all wk 6-9 **Restaurant** L served all wk 12-2 D served all wk 6-9 ⊕ FREE HOUSE ◀ Sharp's, Downton, Hop Back, Palmers, Bowman ♂ Mr Whitehead's Cirrus Minor & Strawberry. ♟ 10 **Facilities** ♣ Children welcome Children's portions Garden Beer festival Parking Wi-fi 🚌

UPPER FROYLE
Map 5 SU74

The Hen & Chicken Inn

GU34 4JH ☎ 01420 22115
e-mail: info@henandchicken.co.uk
dir: 2m from Alton, on A31 next to petrol station

Sitting beside the A31 between Alton and Farnham, this 18th-century former coaching inn was once a favoured resting stop for bishops travelling between Winchester and Canterbury. A traditional atmosphere pervades the open-plan bar and dining areas; you'll find a large inglenook fireplace complete with empty post boxes above, plus plenty of wood panelling and beams. Quaff a pint of Hall & Woodhouse and refuel with duck liver and orange pâté; pork and leek sausages with mashed potatoes; and mixed wild berry and vanilla cheesecake. Booking for meals may be required.

Open all wk 10-3 5.30-12 (Fri 10-3 5-12 Sat-Sun all day) **Bar Meals** L served all wk 10-2.30 D served all wk 6-9 **Restaurant** L served all wk 10-2.30 D served all wk 6-9 ⊕ HALL & WOODHOUSE ◀ Badger Tanglefoot, K&B Sussex ♂ Westons Stowford Press. ♟ **Facilities** Children welcome Children's menu Children's portions Play area Garden Parking Wi-fi 🚌

WARNFORD
Map 5 SU62

The George & Falcon ★★★★ INN

Warnford Rd SO32 3LB ☎ 01730 829623
e-mail: reservations@georgeandfalcon.com
dir: M27 junct 10, A32 signed Alton. Approx 10.5m to Warnford

Colonel Butler reputedly refreshed his men at this 18th-century inn before meeting Charles II on Winchester Hill. Today the proximity of the South Downs Way means this watering hole is ideally sited for walkers planning a stop; muddy boots and dogs are always welcome, and six en suite rooms make it perfect for an overnight stay. Ringwood ales are on tap, while the menu ranges from home-made pies to pan-fried sea bass stuffed with herbs and served with sautéed new potatoes, spinach and a creamy mushroom sauce. The beautiful garden leads down to the River Meon. Booking for meals may be required.

Open all day all wk 11-11 (Oct-Mar 11-3 6-11) **Bar Meals** L served all wk 11-3 D served all wk 6-9 Av main course £10 **Restaurant** L served all wk 12-3 D served all wk 6-9 Fixed menu price fr £10 Av 3 course à la carte fr £22 ⊕ MARSTON'S ◀ Ringwood Best Bitter, Fortyniner ♂ Thatchers Gold. ♟ 9 **Facilities** ♣ Children welcome Children's menu Children's portions Family room Garden Parking Wi-fi 🚌 (notice required) **Rooms** 6

WARSASH
Map 5 SU40

The Jolly Farmer Country Inn

29 Fleet End Rd SO31 9JH ☎ 01489 572500
e-mail: mail@thejollyfarmeruk.com
dir: Exit M27 junct 9 towards A27 Fareham, right onto Warsash Rd. Follow for 2m, left onto Fleet End Rd

The multi-coloured classic cars lined up outside make it hard to miss this friendly country inn. Farming equipment decorates the rustic-style bars, whilst the patio, beer garden and children's play area are popular on warmer days. The comprehensive menu ranges from locally caught seafood dishes, sandwiches, salads, grills and pub favourites to home-made dishes like vegetable stirfry; steak-and-ale pie; chicken with roasted red pepper and tomato ragout; and beef goulash. There's also a daily chalkboard menu of specials and desserts, and a children's menu.

Open all day all wk 11-11 **Bar Meals** L served Mon-Fri 12-2.30, Sat-Sun all day D served Mon-Fri 6-10, Sat-Sun all day Av main course £8.95 **Restaurant** L served all wk 12-2.30 D served all wk 6-10 Fixed menu price fr £12.50 Av 3 course à la carte fr £20 ◀ Fuller's London Pride, George Gale & Co HSB, Flowers IPA. ♟ 14 **Facilities** ♣ Children welcome Children's menu Children's portions Play area Family room Garden Parking Wi-fi 🚌 (notice required)

WELL
Map 5 SU74

The Chequers Inn

RG29 1TL ☎ 01256 862605
e-mail: info@thechequersatwell.co.uk
dir: *From Odiham High St turn right into Long Ln, follow for 3m, left at T-junct, pub 0.25m on top of hill*

Tucked away deep in the heart of the Hampshire countryside, in the village of Well near Odiham, this 15th-century pub is full of charm and old-world character, with a rustic, low-beamed bar, log fires, scrubbed tables and vine-covered front terrace. The menu offers good hearty food such as country terrine with home-made chutney and melba toast; belly of pork with black pudding, dauphinoise potatoes, broccoli and red wine jus; and sticky toffee pudding. There is also a selection of pub classics such as ham, egg and chips, or home-made steak, mushroom and ale pie. Booking for meals may be required.

Open all wk 12-3 6-11 (Sat 12-11 Sun 12-10.30) **Bar Meals** L served Mon-Fri 12-2, Sat 12-3, Sun 12-6 D served Mon-Thu 6.30-9, Fri-Sat 6.30-9.30 **Restaurant** L served Mon-Fri 12-2, Sat 12-3, Sun 12-6 D served Mon-Thu 6.30-9, Fri-Sat 6.30-9.30 ⊕ HALL & WOODHOUSE ◀ Badger First Gold & Tanglefoot, Guinness, Seasonal ales Ö Westons Stowford Press. ▾ 8 **Facilities** Children welcome Family room Garden Parking 🚐

WEST MEON
Map 5 SU62

The Thomas Lord ◉◉

PICK OF THE PUBS

High St GU32 1LN ☎ 01730 829244
dir: *M3 junct 9, A272 towards Petersfield, right at x-roads onto A32, 1st left*

Named after the founder of Lord's Cricket Ground, who retired to West Meon in 1830 and is buried in the churchyard, the pub has remained very much a rustic country inn rather than another identikit gastro-pub. The bar is decorated with cricketing memorabilia and is the setting for award-winning Bowman ales, backed by a sophisticated range of wines sourced from an upmarket vintner. The pub's own garden supplies the kitchen with herbs, salads and vegetables, as do local farms and small-scale producers. The pub even uses eggs from its own hens and quails. The result is a tempting menu of seasonal delights such as pan-seared pigeon breast and peppered swede tart; Hyden Farm duck breast with gratin potatoes and parsnip purée; and iced caramel, meringue and walnut parfait with caramel sauce and chocolate marquise. Quiz nights take place every Wednesday, when smart phones are severely frowned-upon; occasional wine-tasting dinners and live music complete the picture. Booking for meals may be required.

Open Tue-Fri 12-3 5-11 (Sat-Sun 12-11) Closed: Mon **Bar Meals** L served Tue-Fri 12-3, Sat-Sun 12-4 D served Tue-Sun 7-10 **Restaurant** L served Tue-Fri 12-3, Sat-Sun 12-4 D served Tue-Sun 7-10 ⊕ ENTERPRISE INNS ◀ Bowman Wallops Wood, Swift One Ö Westons Stowford

Press. ▾ 20 **Facilities** Children welcome Children's menu Children's portions Garden Parking Wi-fi 🚐

WEST TYTHERLEY
Map 5 SU22

The Black Horse **NEW**

The Village SP5 1NF ☎ 01794 340308
e-mail: info@theblackhorsepublichouse.co.uk
dir: *In village centre*

Smack on the Clarendon Way, the popular walking/cycling trail between Winchester and Salisbury, this traditional 17th-century former coaching inn is the perfect spot to rest and refuel. It's a proper village community pub, replete with skittle alley, regular quiz nights and locals supping pints of Bowman or Stonehenge ales by the blazing fire in the oak-beamed main bar. Food ranges from lunchtime filled ciabatta sandwiches to ham, egg and chips, buffalo burger (using meat from the local water buffalo herd), and the good-value Sunday lunch menu. Booking for meals may be required.

Open 12-3 6-11 (Sun 12-8) Closed: 2 days after New Year BH, Mon L & Tue L **Bar Meals** L served Wed-Sun D served Tue-Sun Av main course £10 **Restaurant** L served Wed-Sun D served Tue-Sun ⊕ FREE HOUSE ◀ Hop Back, Stonehenge, Bowman, Flower Pots Ö Westons 1st Quality. ▾ 8 **Facilities** ❀ Children welcome Children's menu Children's portions Play area Garden Parking Wi-fi 🚐 (notice required)

WHITCHURCH
Map 5 SU44

Watership Down Inn

Freefolk Priors RG28 7NJ ☎ 01256 892254
e-mail: watershipdowninn@live.co.uk
dir: *On B3400 between Basingstoke & Andover*

Enjoy an exhilarating walk on Watership Down before relaxing with a pint of well-kept local ale at this homely 19th-century inn named after Richard Adams' classic tale of rabbit life. The pub offers a menu that includes scampi, chips and peas; steak-and-ale pie; Caribbean chicken; plus baguettes, sandwiches and jacket potatoes. All dishes are available in smaller portions for children, and as takeaways.

Open all day all wk ⊕ PUNCH TAVERNS ◀ Ringwood Best Bitter, Young's Special, Sharp's Doom Bar, Wells Bombardier, Cumberland. **Facilities** Children welcome Children's portions Play area Garden Parking Wi-fi

WICKHAM
Map 5 SU51

Greens Restaurant & Bar

The Square PO17 5JQ ☎ 01329 833197
dir: *2m from M27, on corner of historic Wickham Square. 3m from Fareham*

Set on a corner of Wickham's picturesque square, Frank and Carol Duckworth have been welcoming customers to award-winning Greens for getting on for 30 years. Drinkers will find local ales and high standards of customer service that ensure a warm and welcoming

reception. Enjoy mulled wine and warming log fires in winter and head for the garden in warmer weather for Pimm's and a barbecue. The modern British menu includes starters like home-smoked duck with a warm confit leg salad served on an orange dressing, whilst main course options might include roasted loin of venison with purple sprouting broccoli, or pan-fried sea bass fillet with creamed potatoes and butternut squash puree. Booking for meals may be required.

Open 10-3 6-11 (Sun & BH 12-5 May-Sep all day) Closed: 19-20 May, Sun eve & Mon **Bar Meals** L served Tue-Sat 12-2.30, Sun 12-5 D served Tue-Sat 6-9.30 **Restaurant** L served Tue-Sat 12-2.30, Sun 12-5 D served Tue-Sat 6-9.30 Fixed menu price fr £11.95 Av 3 course à la carte fr £30 ⊕ FREE HOUSE ◀ Bowman Wallops Wood & Swift One, Shepherd Neame Spitfire. ▾ 12 **Facilities** Children welcome Children's portions Garden

WINCHESTER
Map 5 SU42

The Bell Inn

83 St Cross Rd SO23 9RE ☎ 01962 865284
dir: *M3 junct 11, B3355 towards city centre. Approx 1m pub on right*

Close to the 12th-century Hospital of St Cross & Almshouse of Noble Poverty, this community local is now run by David and Kerry Hicks. Greene King ales and good value food are served in the main bar, pine-furnished lounge and walled garden. Daily specials include pan-fried sirloin steak; oven-roasted chicken supreme stuffed with mozzarella and chorizo; pan-seared salmon fillet; and wild mushroom risotto. There's a children's selection too. A walk through the River Itchen water meadows leads to Winchester College and the city centre. Check the summer beer festival dates. Booking for meals may be required.

Open all day all wk 11-11 (Fri-Sat 12-12 Sun 12-10.30) **Bar Meals** L served Mon-Sat 12-2.30, Sun 12-4 D served Mon-Sat 6-9 Av main course £10 **Restaurant** Av 3 course à la carte fr £19 ⊕ GREENE KING ◀ Ruddles Best, Belhaven Grand Slam, Morland Old Speckled Hen Ö Westons Stowford Press. ▾ 10 **Facilities** ❀ Children welcome Children's menu Children's portions Play area Garden Beer festival Parking Wi-fi 🚐 (notice required)

Save on hotels. Book at **theAA.com/hotel**

HAMPSHIRE 277 ENGLAND

The Golden Lion

99 Alresford Road, Winchester, Hampshire, SO23 0JZ

Tel: 01962 865512
Web: www.thegoldenlionwinchester.co.uk
E-mail: derekandbrid@thegoldenlionwinchester.co.uk

We warmly invite you to *The Golden Lion Pub*, Winchester, for our cosy vintage style interiors, excellent home cooked food and great Irish welcome! We are located just on the eastern edge of the city, within very easy reach of the M3, the A272 and the A34, just a 10 minute walk into the beautiful heart of the city with all of its historic attractions and wealth of independent shops. We have a large car park as well as patio areas and beer gardens to the front and back, including a special enclosed area for doggies to have a run. We are a TV and gaming machine free zone so that you can relax in our friendly atmosphere and enjoy our great background music, and we also welcome children who are eating with their parents/guardians.

We are very proud to have received many awards for the services that we offer, including 'The Casque Mark' and 'The Beer Master Award' for our real ales, the certification of 'Excellent' for our food hygiene and we have won many First Prizes for our floral displays and hanging baskets. We were also very honoured to have been awarded the Wadworth Brewery 'Best Pub of the Year' award. We were delighted to recieve the Quality Assured Award in Hampshire Hospitality Awards 2011/2012.

We have regular live music sessions such as Bluegrass music on the last Tuesday and Irish music on the second Thursday evening of each month.

We are really pleased to receive regular visitors who return again and again for the traditional home-cooked food and the constantly changing daily specials menus – so much so that we would recommend booking a table to avoid disappointment! We can also offer to arrange all your party booking requirements, whether you are planning a formal sit-down meal, a more casual finger buffet or a barbecue in the summer under our recently installed canopied 'Garden Room'.

We very much look forward to welcoming you very soon!

WINCHESTER *continued*

The Golden Lion

99 Alresford Rd SO23 0JZ ☎ 01962 865512
e-mail: derekandbrid@thegoldenlionwinchester.co.uk
web: www.thegoldenlionwinchester.co.uk
dir: *From Union St in Winchester town centre follow 'All other routes' sign. At rdbt 1st exit onto High St. At rdbt 1st exit onto Bridge St (B3404) signed Alton/Alresford, (becomes Alresford Rd)*

Winners of Winchester in Bloom awards for multiple years, bedecked with flower baskets, Brid and Derek Phelan's 1932-built, delightfully cottage-style pub is on Winchester's eastern fringe. As well as Irish charm, expect main and specials menus offering plenty of straightforward hearty pub meals. Lasagne, home-baked ham, battered hake fillet, steak-and-ale pie, and chargrilled lamb cutlets all feature. Soft cushions are provided in the 'treasure chest' by the back door for those sitting in the large beer garden. Booking for meals may be required.

Open all wk Mon-Sat 11.30-3 5.30-11 (Sun 12-10.30) **Bar Meals** L served all wk 12-2.30 D served all wk 6-9 Av main course £8.95-£15.95 **Restaurant** L served all wk 12-2.30 D served all wk 6-9 ⊕ WADWORTH ◀ 6X, Henry's Original IPA, Seasonal ales Ŏ Westons Stowford Press. ♀ **Facilities** ❦ Children welcome Children's menu Children's portions Garden Parking Wi-fi ▬ (notice required)

See advert on page 277

The Old Vine ★★★★ INN

8 Great Minster St SO23 9HA ☎ 01962 854616
e-mail: reservations@oldvinewinchester.com
dir: *M3 junct 11 towards St Cross, turn right at Green Man Pub, left onto Symonds St, left onto Little Minster St*

Opposite Winchester's fine cathedral, this handsome 18th-century pub takes its name from the elderly vine rambling over the street frontage. The rolling selection of real ales in the oak-beamed bar always features at least one local brew – perhaps Ringwood Best. Freshly prepared, locally sourced British and European food is served in the restaurant, where typical dishes are home-made Hampshire steak, ale and mushroom pie; or pan-fried guinea fowl supreme. Five beautifully presented bedrooms feature Georgian, Arts and Crafts, Victorian and art deco furniture.

Open all day all wk Closed: 25 Dec **Bar Meals** L served Mon-Thu 12-2.30, Fri-Sun 12-6 D served Mon-Sat 6.30-9.30, Sun 6.30-9 Av main course £11.90 **Restaurant** L served Mon-Thu 12-2.30, Fri-Sun 12-3 D served Mon-Sat 6.30-9.30, Sun 6.30-9 Av 3 course à la carte fr £24.50 ⊕ ENTERPRISE INNS ◀ Ringwood Best Bitter, Guest ales. ♀ 11 **Facilities** ❦ Garden **Rooms** 5

The Westgate Inn ★★★ INN

2 Romsey Rd SO23 8TP ☎ 01962 820222
e-mail: wghguy@yahoo.co.uk
dir: *On corner of Romsey Rd & Upper High St, opposite Great Hall & Medieval West Gate*

Standing boldly on a street corner, the curving, Palladian-style façade of this 1860s inn overlooks the city's medieval Westgate. A well-known interest in real ales and ciders is backed up by an annual beer festival. Full English breakfasts and mid-morning brunches are followed by made-to-order lunchtime sandwiches, soups and uncomplicated three-egg omelettes with various fillings; bangers and mash; Spanish-style shepherd's pie with chorizo and patatas bravas; and 21-day aged Hampshire steaks, which landlords Guy and Helen Carpenter reckon are the best in the world. Attractive and good-sized accommodation is available.

Open all day all wk 12-11.30 **Bar Meals** L served all wk 7-2.30 D served all wk 6-9.30 Av main course £8 **Restaurant** L served all wk 12-2.30 D served all wk 6-9.30 Av 3 course à la carte fr £16 ⊕ MARSTON'S ◀ Burton Bitter, Jennings Cumberland Ale, Banks's Original, Guest ales Ŏ Thatchers Gold, Green Goblin. **Facilities** Beer festival Wi-fi **Rooms** 8

The Wykeham Arms

75 Kingsgate St SO23 9PE ☎ 01962 853834
e-mail: wykehamarms@fullers.co.uk
dir: *Near Winchester College & Winchester Cathedral*

A fine 270-year-old brick building located in the oldest part of the city between the cathedral close and Winchester's famous college. Full of character and always buzzing with activity it draws an eclectic mix of customers, from businessmen and barristers, clergy and college dons to tourists and local drinkers and diners. The rambling series of character bars and eating areas are furnished with old pine tables and old-fashioned college desks, and boast four welcoming winter log fires and an impressive collection of hats, fascinating pictures and military memorabilia adorn every available wall space. Follow a town or water meadow stroll with a satisfying choice from modern, seasonal menus, perhaps moules marinière, parsley and fennel; poached sea trout, semi dried grapes, oyster and parsley tagliatelle; or slow roasted lamb cassoulet with confit tomatoes and bacon, with a dessert of set lavender cream, honeycomb and caramel ice cream to finish things off. Light meals might be honey and clove glazed ham sandwich; or a warm smoked back bacon, soft brie and cranberry baguette. Wash down with a cracking pint of London Pride, or one of 20 excellent wines by the glass. Booking for meals may be required.

Open all day all wk **Bar Meals** L served all wk 12-3 D served all wk 6-9.30 Av main course £12 **Restaurant** L served all wk 12-3 D served all wk 6-9.30 Fixed menu price fr £15 Av 3 course à la carte fr £25 ⊕ FULLER'S ◀ London Pride & Bengal Lancer, Geoge Gale & Co HSB & Seafarers, Flower Pots Goodens Gold, Guest ales Ŏ Westons 1st Quality. ♀ 20 **Facilities** ❦ Garden Parking Wi-fi

Save on hotels. Book at **theAA.com/hotel**

HEREFORDSHIRE 279 ENGLAND

HEREFORDSHIRE

ASTON CREWS
Map 10 SO62

The Penny Farthing Inn
PICK OF THE PUBS

HR9 7LW ☎ 01989 750366
e-mail: pennyfarthing1980@hotmail.co.uk
dir: *5m E of Ross-on-Wye*

This whitewashed 17th-century blacksmith's shop and coaching inn is located high above the Wye Valley. Inside are lots of nooks and crannies with oak beams, antiques, saddlery and warming log fires. The menu capitalises on the wealth of local vegetable and fruit growers' produce, and top quality meat. Begin with sauté king prawns in coriander batter with sweet chilli dip, or creamy garlic mushrooms, then follow with slow-roast belly pork with red wine gravy; pan-fried guinea fowl supreme with thyme and bacon gravy; or one of the daily chalkboard specials, perhaps medallions of monkfish with king prawns in a saffron sauce. For those who want to pack their walking boots, footpaths radiate from the front door.

Open all wk Tue-Fri 12-3 6-11 (Mon 6-11 Sat 12-11 Sun 12-10.30) **Bar Meals** L served Tue-Sat 12-2.30, Sun 12-3 D served Tue-Sat 6-9 **Restaurant** L served Tue-Sat 12-2.30, Sun 12-3 D served Tue-Sat 6-9 ⊕ PUBFOLIO ◀ Wychwood Hobgoblin, Wadworth 6X, Black Sheep Ŏ Westons Stowford Press. **Facilities** ❤ Children welcome Children's menu Children's portions Play area Garden Parking Wi-fi ▥

AYMESTREY
Map 9 SO46

The Riverside Inn
PICK OF THE PUBS

See Pick of the Pubs on page 280

BODENHAM
Map 10 SO55

England's Gate Inn ★★★★ INN

HR1 3HU ☎ 01568 797286
e-mail: englandsgate@btconnect.com
dir: *Hereford A49, turn onto A417 at Bosey Dinmore hill, 2.5m on right*

A pretty black-and-white coaching inn dating from around 1540, with atmospheric beamed bars and blazing log fires in winter. A picturesque beer garden attracts a good summer following, and so does the food. The menu features such dishes as slow-roasted shank of Ledbury lamb with parsnip and cardamom purée in red wine jus; baked fillet of cod topped with a garlic and herb crumble; or wholemeal pancakes filled with spinach and cream cheese served with ratatouille. The annual beer and sausage festival, featuring locally produced beer and cider, is a well-known local event with live bands playing in the garden. Booking for meals may be required.

Open all day all wk ⊕ FREE HOUSE ◀ Wye Valley Bitter & Butty Bach, Wood's Shropshire Lad, Guest ales. **Facilities** Children welcome Children's menu Children's portions Garden Beer festival Parking Wi-fi **Rooms** 7

BRINGSTY COMMON
Map 10 SO75

Live and Let Live
PICK OF THE PUBS

WR6 5UW ☎ 01886 821462
e-mail: theliveandletlive@tiscali.co.uk
dir: *From A44 (Bromyard to Worcester road) turn at sign with cat onto track leading to the common. At 1st fork bear right. Pub 200yds on right*

Secluded on Bringsty Common amidst bracken and old orchards, this lovely thatched cider house dates from the 16th century, making it one of the oldest buildings in the area. It was closed for 11 years while planning permission was sought and an extensive renovation undertaken by owner Sue Dovery. It reopened with its sand-blasted timber framing exposed for all to appreciate. Local Oliver's cider is joined by beers from various south Marches micro-breweries. Bar meals and the intimate Thatch Restaurant major on seasonal food from the home area. Typical starters include pan-fried baby octopus on mixed leaves with a spicy dressing; and deep-fried seasoned whitebait with wholemeal bread. Main course options are chicken breast stuffed with sun-dried tomatoes, topped with melted mozzarella and served with duchess potatoes, fresh vegetables and a home-made cheese sauce; or meat from the grill. A four-day beer and cider festival runs over the Easter weekend, when live music adds to the entertainment.

Open Tue-Thu 12-2.30 5.30-11 (Fri-Sun & summer all day) Closed: Mon (ex BHs) **Bar Meals** L served Tue-Sun 12-2 D served Tue-Sun 6-9 Av main course £8.95 **Restaurant** D served Tue-Sun 6-9 Fixed menu price fr £9.95 ⊕ FREE HOUSE ◀ Malvern Hills, Ludlow, Wye Valley, Hobsons Ŏ Oliver's, Robinsons. **Facilities** Children welcome Children's portions Garden Beer festival Parking ▥ (notice required)

CAREY
Map 10 SO53

Cottage of Content

HR2 6NG ☎ 01432 840242
dir: *From x-rds on A49 between Hereford & Ross-on-Wye, follow Hoarwithy signs. In Hoarwithy branch right, follow Carey signs*

Just a short drive from Hereford and Ross-on-Wye and situated within beautiful, unspoilt countryside, this 15th-century inn started life as three labourers' cottages. A popular spot for walkers and ramblers, the pub offers local Wye Valley ales and local ciders, plus a simple menu that appeals to all, with children well catered for. Popular meal options include twice-baked smoked brie and chestnut soufflé, followed by monkfish with pesto crust on smoked mussel and saffron risotto, or local beef and ale crumble, finishing with chocolate cheesecake and Amaretto cream. Booking for meals may be required.

Open 12-2 6.30-11 (times vary summer & winter) Closed: 1wk Feb, 1wk Oct, Sun eve, Mon, Tue L (winter only) **Bar Meals** L served Tue-Sat 12-2 **Restaurant** L served Tue-Sun 12-2 D served Tue-Sat 6.30-9 ⊕ FREE HOUSE ◀ Wye Valley Butty Bach, Hobsons Best Bitter

Ŏ Ross-on-Wye, Carey Organic, Westons Stowford Press. **Facilities** Children welcome Children's menu Children's portions Garden Parking Wi-fi ▥ (notice required)

CRASWALL
Map 9 SO23

The Bulls Head

HR2 0PN ☎ 01981 510616
e-mail: info@thebullsheadcraswall.co.uk
dir: *From A465 turn at Pandy. Village in 11m*

Six miles south of Hay-on-Wye, this old drovers' inn is set in a remote spot at the foot of the Black Mountains and is popular with walkers and riders, who tie their horses at the rail outside. Real ales and farmhouse ciders are served through the hole in the wall servery in the bar with its flagstone floors and log fires. Typical dishes include a starter of pan-fried black pudding, braised apple and cider sauce; followed by daube of Hereford beef or pan-fried squid with linguine, cherry tomatoes and chilli.

Open Fri-Sun 12-3 7-late Closed: please telephone in Jan & Feb; Mon-Thu **Bar Meals** L served Fri-Sun 12-2.30 D served Fri-Sat 7-8.30 Av main course £15 **Restaurant** L served Fri-Sun 12-2.30 D served Fri-Sat 7-8.30 Av 3 course à la carte fr £28 ⊕ FREE HOUSE ◀ Wye Valley Butty Bach, Bitter Ŏ Gwatkin's Farmhouse, Westons Old Rosie, Dunkertons Premium Organic & Black Fox. **Facilities** Children welcome Garden Wi-fi

DORSTONE
Map 9 SO34

The Pandy Inn
PICK OF THE PUBS

See Pick of the Pubs on page 281

HAMPTON BISHOP
Map 10 SO53

The Bunch of Carrots

HR1 4JR ☎ 01432 870237
e-mail: bunchofcarrots@buccaneer.co.uk
dir: *From Hereford take A4103, A438, then B4224*

Named after a rock formation in the River Wye that runs beside this family-friendly free house, the pub's interior boasts real fires, old beams and flagstone floors. Outside there's a garden and children's play area, making this an ideal place in which to sample a pint of Wye Valley Bitter. The extensive menu of pub favourites offers baguettes and hand-cut sandwiches as well as hot dishes like fish pie and peas; or slow-roast belly pork and crackling. There's also a daily specials board, carvery and children's menu. Booking for meals may be required.

Open all day all wk **Bar Meals** L served Mon-Fri 12-2, Sat 12-9.30, Sun 12-9 D served Mon-Fri 5.30-9.30, Sat 12-9.30, Sun 12-9 Av main course £10.50 **Restaurant** L served Mon-Fri 12-2, Sat 12-9.30, Sun 12-9 D served Mon-Fri 5.30-9.30, Sat 12-9.30, Sun 12-9 Av 3 course à la carte fr £21 ⊕ FREE HOUSE ◀ Wye Valley Bitter, Sharp's Doom Bar, Courage Best Bitter Ŏ Westons Stowford Press. ♀ 10 **Facilities** Children welcome Children's menu Play area Garden Parking Wi-fi ▥

PICK OF THE PUBS

The Riverside Inn

AYMESTREY   Map 9 SO46

HR6 9ST ☎ **01568 708440**
e-mail: theriverside@btconnect.com
web: www.theriversideinn.org
dir: *On A4110, 18m N of Hereford*

On a still and foggy November night you may still hear the Roman infantry marching along Watling Street as it crosses the River Lugg beside this ancient free house. Built in 1580, the pub is halfway along the Mortimer Trail from Ludlow to Kington, and numerous circular walks, with plenty of wildlife to spot, start from the front door. Anglers are also drawn to stay at the inn, which offers its residents private fishing for brown trout and grayling. The wood-panelled interior with its low beams and log fires engenders a relaxed atmosphere that reflects the pub's long history. Real ales and ciders, drawing on the Marches' tradition of brewing and cider-making, include Wye Valley Bitter and Three Tuns XXX as well as Brook Farm cider from nearby Wigmore. Owner Richard Gresko aims to offer seriously good food that's 'truly seasonal and truly local'. He encourages visitors to take a stroll round the pub's extensive vegetable, herb and fruit gardens; strung above the secluded riverside beer garden, these are some of the nicest that you'll find anywhere. Diners are promised classic British dishes with a modern twist, produced from the finest ingredients by an award-winning team of chefs. As you'd expect,

the menus change constantly throughout the year, but a typical dinner might begin with pan-fried River Lugg trout with sweet garlic palette and a mint, parsley and caper dressing. Main course options could feature a rare-breed Herefordshire stew of best shin and oxtail with wild mushroom and garden kale, parsnip purée and parsnip crisps; or roasted winter root vegetables in a creamy spinach, mustard and local Monkland cheese sauce, with celeriac purée and frisée salad. Leave space for one of the tempting desserts such as garden rhubarb and apple hazelnut crumble with home-made elderflower ice cream. Booking for meals may be required.

Open Tue-Sat 11-3 6-11 (Sun 12-3)
Closed: 26 Dec & 1 Jan, Sun eve, Mon L,

Mon eve in winter **Bar Meals** Tue-Sat 11-3 6-11, Sun 12-3 D served Tue-Sat 6-11 Av main course £9 **Restaurant** Av 3 course à la carte fr £25.25 ⊞ FREE HOUSE ◖ Wye Valley Bitter & Butty Bach, Hobsons Best Bitter, Three Tuns XXX ⏻ Brook Farm Medium Dry, Westons Stowford Press, Robinsons.
Facilities Children welcome Children's portions ❀ Garden Parking Wi-fi 🚌 (notice required)

Save on hotels. Book at **theAA.com/hotel**

HEREFORDSHIRE 281 | ENGLAND

PICK OF THE PUBS

The Pandy Inn

DORSTONE   Map 9 SO34

HR3 6AN ☎ **01981 550273**
e-mail: info@pandyinn.co.uk
web: www.pandyinn.co.uk
dir: *Exit B4348 W of Hereford. Inn in village centre*

The Pandy is reputed to be one of the oldest inns in the county, so a fascinating history is to be expected. It certainly doesn't disappoint. Richard de Brito, one of the four Norman knights who murdered Thomas à Becket in Canterbury Cathedral in 1170, built a chapel at Dorstone as an act of atonement after 15 years in the Holy Land. He is also said to have built The Pandy to house the workers. Much later, Oliver Cromwell is known to have taken refuge here during the Civil War. You'll find The Pandy just a few miles from the book capital of Hay-on-Wye, and it's an ideal stop when touring the Brecon Beacons or the picturesque Golden Valley. The ancient hostelry is delightfully situated opposite the village green; the large garden, which offers plenty of tables and a children's playground, has views of Dorstone Hill. The interior retains some original flagstone floors and beams. In the dog-friendly bar you'll find Golden Valley Brewers Choice on handpump, or a pint of Stowford Press cider if you prefer. Bar

food takes the form of a range of baguettes served with chips, and pizzas can be ordered in two sizes. Alternatively The Pandy fish pie is cooked to the chef's recipe with salmon, smoked haddock, tiger prawns and dill; breaded Whitby Bay scampi is another seafood option. In the restaurant, the short but delicious range of dishes may start with tender slices of duck breast hot-smoked in the kitchen; and continue with a main course of braised lamb shank cooked to a traditional Welsh recipe. Desserts, also home-made, may include truffle torte made with Belgian chocolate, and some will find the range of coffee liqueurs hard to resist.

Open Tue-Fri 12-3 6-11 (Sat 12-11 Sun 12-3 6.30-10.30) Closed: Mon **Bar Meals** L served Tue-Sun 12-2 **Restaurant** L served Tue-Sun 12-2 D served Tue-Sun 6.30–9 ⊕ FREE HOUSE ◀ Wye Valley Butty Bach, Golden Valley Brewers Choice ♻ Westons Stowford Press. **Facilities** Children welcome Children's menu Children's portions Play area Garden Parking Wi-fi 🚌

HOARWITHY
Map 10 SO52

The New Harp Inn

HR2 6QH ☎ **01432 840900**

e-mail: adrianchef@btinternet.com

dir: *From Ross-on-Wye take A49 towards Hereford. Turn right for Hoarwithy*

Situated on the River Wye, this pub is popular with locals, fishermen, campers and visitors to the countryside. A real country pub, its slogan reads: 'Kids, dogs and muddy boots all welcome'. Begin with a great choice of local real ale, an unusual foreign bottled beer or a home-produced cider. The menu includes starters such as port and juniper marinated wild pigeon breast, and home-smoked Wye salmon, then moves on to mains like roasted vegetable and stilton pie; a selection of steaks; and belly pork roasted with Stowford cider sauce. There's also a board for specials, and outside are extensive gardens and a real babbling brook. Look out for beer festivals on Bank Holidays.

Open all wk 12-3 6-11 (Fri-Sun all day) **Bar Meals** L served Mon-Fri 12-3, Sat-Sun all day D served Mon-Fri 6-9, Sat-Sun all day Av main course £8.95 **Restaurant** L served Mon-Fri 12-3, Sat-Sun all day D served Mon-Fri 6-9, Sat-Sun all day Fixed menu price fr £16 Av 3 course à la carte fr £22 ⊕ FREE HOUSE ◀ Wye Valley Butty Bach, Malvern Hills Black Pear, Wickwar BOB, Hobsons Ö Westons Stowford Press, New Harp Reserve, Carey Organic, Ross-on-Wye. **Facilities** ♣ Children welcome Children's menu Children's portions Play area Garden Beer festival Parking Wi-fi 🚌

KILPECK
Map 9 SO43

The Kilpeck Inn

HR2 9DN ☎ **01981 570464**

e-mail: booking@kilpeckinn.com

web: www.kilpeckinn.com

dir: *From Hereford take A465 S. In 6m at Belmont rdbt left towards Kilpeck. Follow church & inn signs*

Seven years ago this 250-year-old pub escaped conversion into a private house and, to the village's delight, later reopened. The bar stocks Butcombe, Golden Valley and Wye Valley real ales, draught cider from Westons in Much Marcle and bottled Gwatkins cider from a local farm. Chargrilled steaks; grilled lamb's liver and bacon; battered hake and chips; and cream risotto with asparagus number among the typical locally sourced dishes. Commendably green, the pub uses a wood-pellet burner for underfloor heating; rainwater to flush the loos;

and solar panels for hot water. Booking for meals may be required.

Open all wk 12-2.30 5.30-11 (Sun & BH 11-11) **Bar Meals** L served all wk 12-2 D served all wk 6-9 **Restaurant** L served all wk 12-2 D served all wk 7-9 ◀ Butcombe Bitter, Wye Valley Butty Bach, Golden Valley .410 Ö Westons Stowford Press. ₹ 9 **Facilities** Children welcome Children's portions Garden Parking Wi-fi 🚌 (notice required)

KIMBOLTON
Map 10 SO56

Stockton Cross Inn

HR6 0HD ☎ **01568 612509**

e-mail: mb@ecolots.co.uk

web: www.stocktoncrossinn.co.uk

dir: *On A4112, 0.5m off A49, between Leominster & Ludlow*

You'll find this black-and-white former drovers' inn beside a lonely crossroads where witches were allegedly hanged. Picture-book pretty, the building is regularly photographed by tourists and has featured on calendars and chocolate boxes. Landlord Mike Bentley keeps a good range of ales, including local Wye Valley Butty Bach, and regular guest ales. Local organic produce is used in preparing the traditional pub food on offer. From lunchtime sandwiches and ploughman's, the menu takes in devilled whitebait; pork belly with black pudding mash and red wine sauce; and spotted dick and custard.

Open 12-3 7-11 Closed: Sun eve & Mon **Bar Meals** L served Tue-Sun 12-2 D served Tue-Sat 7-9 **Restaurant** L served Tue-Sun 12-2 D served Tue-Sat 7-9 ⊕ FREE HOUSE ◀ Wye Valley Butty Bach & HPA, Flowers Best Bitter, Guest ales Ö Robinsons Flagon, Westons Stowford Press. ₹ 8 **Facilities** Children welcome Children's menu Children's portions Garden Parking Wi-fi

KINGTON
Map 9 SO25

The Stagg Inn and Restaurant ◉◉
PICK OF THE PUBS

Titley HR5 3RL ☎ **01544 230221**

e-mail: reservations@thestagg.co.uk

dir: *Between Kington & Presteigne on B4355*

It seems likely that an inn has been here since medieval times. In sheep-droving days it was called The Balance, because it was where wool was weighed; in 1833, local diarist and reformer Eliza Greenley renamed it The Stag's Head, after her family crest. The extra 'g' crept in later. Farmhouse tables and log fires create a relaxed atmosphere in the rambling dining rooms and homely bar, where locals drink Ludlow Gold, Hobsons Best and draught and bottled Marches ciders, maybe with a bar snack of home-made faggots. A modern approach to cooking leads Roux-trained local boy Steve Reynolds to produce Hereford snails with chestnuts, bacon and mushroom; roast partridge with game chips and red cabbage; fillet of Herefordshire beef with horseradish cream and carrot purée; and halibut fillet with lemon beurre blanc and Parmentier potatoes. Desserts include

some 15 unpasteurised cheeses. Booking for meals may be required.

Open Tue-Sat 12-3 6.30-10.30 (Sun 12-3) Closed: 25-27 Dec, 2wks Nov, 2wks Jan & Feb, Sun eve & Mon **Bar Meals** L served Tue-Sat 12-2 D served Tue-Thu 6.30-9 Av main course £11.50 **Restaurant** L served Tue-Sun 12-2 D served Tue-Sat 6.30-9 Av 3 course à la carte fr £30 ⊕ FREE HOUSE ◀ Ludlow Gold, Hobsons Best Bitter Ö Dunkertons, Westons, Ralph's, Robinsons. ₹ 12 **Facilities** Children's menu Children's portions Garden Parking Wi-fi

LEDBURY
Map 10 SO73

The Farmers Arms

Horse Rd, Wellington Heath HR8 1LS ☎ **01531 632010**

dir: *Through Ledbury, pass rail station, right into Wellington Heath, 1st right for pub*

Standing at the bottom of a country lane, this charming country inn has an elevated position over the village green. Under new management in 2012, four cask-conditioned ales, as well as ciders, lagers and wines are available in the bar. The comprehensive menu makes good use of local produce, such as Ledbury faggots; chicken and chorizo cassoulet; escalope of Severn and Wye salmon; and Maynard Farm caramelised ham. Heated, covered seating on the beer terrace is tailor-made for outdoor eating; there's a children's play area too.

Open all wk ⊕ BERMILL LTD ◀ Fuller's London Pride, Sharp's Doom Bar, Wye Valley, Guest ales. **Facilities** Children welcome Children's menu Play area Garden Parking

Prince of Wales

Church Ln HR8 1DL ☎ **01531 632250**

e-mail: pebblewalk@gmail.com

dir: *M50 junct 2, A417 to Ledbury. Pub in town centre behind Market House (black & white building) on cobbled street (parking nearby)*

In an enchanting spot hidden between Ledbury's memorable half-timbered market house and the ancient church, a cobbled alley lined by eye-catching medieval houses hosts this cracking little pub. All low beams with bags of character, folk nights add to the craic at this half-timbered gem, where home-made pies or pork and beef sausages from an award-winning local butcher are firm favourites on the traditional pub menu. The local theme continues, with Westons Bounds scrumpy from neighbouring Much Marcle and beers from Wye Valley Brewery just down the road complementing a huge range of guest ales.

Open all day all wk **Bar Meals** L served all wk 12-2.30 D served all wk 6-8.30 ⊕ FREE HOUSE ◀ Hobsons Best Bitter, Wye Valley Butty Bach & HPA, Otter Bitter, Guest ales Ö Westons Bounds. **Facilities** Children welcome Children's menu Garden 🚌 (notice required)

Save on hotels. Book at **theAA.com/hotel**

HEREFORDSHIRE 283 **ENGLAND**

The Talbot

14 New St HR8 2DX ☎ 01531 632963
e-mail: talbot.ledbury@wadworth.co.uk
dir: *Follow Ledbury signs, turn into Bye St, 2nd left into Woodley Rd, over bridge to junct, left into New St. Pub on right*

The historic Talbot is a stunning half-timbered coaching inn that dates back to 1550 and overflows with history – it was the scene of fighting between the Cavaliers and Roundheads in 1745. The classic Oak Room features impressive panelling and Jacobean carvings. After a stroll in the nearby Malvern Hills or Leadon Valley, retire to the bar, warm up by the log fire, sip a Herefordshire-brewed Wye Valley Butty Bach or, unusually, local Westons Perry and tuck into steak-and-ale pie, Spanish garlic chicken, or a delicious Sunday roast, followed by chocolate brownie with treacle toffee ice cream. There's a super courtyard garden for summer sipping.

Open all day all wk **Bar Meals** L served all wk 12-3 D served all wk 5.30-9 **Restaurant** L served all wk 12-3 D served all wk 5.30-9 ⊕ WADWORTH ◀ 6X, Henry's Original IPA & Wadworth guest ales, Wye Valley Butty Bach ♂ Westons Stowford Press, Wyld Wood Organic & Perry. ♀ 15 **Facilities** Children's portions Garden Wi-fi

The Trumpet Inn

Trumpet HR8 2RA ☎ 01531 670277
e-mail: trumpet@wadworth.co.uk
dir: *4m from Ledbury, at junct of A438 & A417*

This former coaching inn and post house takes its name from the days when mail coaches blew their horns on approaching the crossroads. A traditional black and white building, it dates back to the late 14th century. The cosy bars feature a wealth of exposed beams, with open fireplaces and a separate dining area. There is camembert or fisherman's platters to share, and main courses like Mr Waller's trio of sausages with mash and onion gravy; Angus beefburgers; or risotto or pie of the day. Booking for meals may be required.

Open all day all wk ⊕ WADWORTH ◀ 6X, Henry's Original IPA ♂ Westons Stowford Press. **Facilities** Children welcome Garden Parking Wi-fi

LEOMINSTER Map 10 SO45

The Grape Vaults

Broad St HR4 8BS ☎ 01568 611404
e-mail: jusaxon@tiscali.co.uk
dir: *Telephone for directions*

This unspoilt pub is so authentic that even its fixed seating is Grade II listed. Its many charms include a small, homely bar complete with real fire. A good selection of real ale is a popular feature, and includes micro-brewery offerings. The unfussy food encompasses favourites like cottage pie, lasagne, chicken curry and various fresh fish and vegetarian choices. There are also plenty of jackets, baguettes, omelettes and other lighter meals available. No piped music, gaming machines or alcopops! There is live music every Sunday and in December a beer festival takes place on the same day as the Victorian street market.

Open all day all wk 11-11 **Bar Meals** L served all wk 12-2 D served Mon-Sat 5.30-9 ⊕ PUNCH TAVERNS ◀ Ludlow Best, Mayfields, Wood's, Malvern Hills, Guest ales ♂ Westons Stowford Press. **Facilities** ♣ Children welcome Children's portions Beer festival Wi-fi **Notes** ☺

LITTLE COWARNE Map 10 SO65

The Three Horseshoes Inn

HR7 4RQ ☎ 01885 400276
e-mail: info@threehorseshoes.co.uk
dir: *Off A456 (Hereford/Bromyard). At Stokes Cross follow Little Cowarne/Pencombe signs*

They no longer shoe horses at the blacksmith's next door, but this old ale house's long drinking pedigree - 200 years and counting - looks secure. Norman and Janet Whittall have seen over 20 years here and have redecorated throughout; their son Philip, the head chef, creates dishes sourced mainly from fresh, local ingredients; some are grown in the inn's garden. There's a good range of bar snacks but the restaurant menu could feature pork and pheasant pâté with pickled damsons; pan-fried Herefordshire venison with sloe gin sauce; or pheasant breast stuffed with spiced pear with elderberry sauce.

Open 11-3 6.30-11 (Sun 12-4 7-10.30) Closed: 25-26 Dec, 1 Jan, Tue, Sun eve in winter ⊕ FREE HOUSE ◀ Morland Old Speckled Hen, Wye Valley Bitter, Greene King Ruddles Best ♂ Westons Stowford Press, Oliver's. **Facilities** Children's menu Children's portions Family room Garden Parking

MADLEY Map 9 SO43

The Comet Inn

Stoney St HR2 9NJ ☎ 01981 250600
e-mail: thecometinn-madley@hotmail.co.uk
dir: *6m from Hereford on B4352*

Set at a crossroads deep in rural Herefordshire, the space-age parabolic dishes of the Madley Earth Station and the distant smudge of the Black Mountains provide contrasting skylines visible from the large grounds of this convivial local. Within, it retains much of the character of the old cottages from which it was converted over 100 years ago. Vicky Willison, the enthusiastic and welcoming owner, serves a select range of Herefordshire- and Worcestershire-brewed beers to accompany simple and hearty home-cooked pub food in the conservatory off the main bar, with smaller portions for smaller appetites if required. There is a large garden with children's play area.

Open all wk 12-3 6-11 (Fri-Sun all day) **Bar Meals** food served all day **Restaurant** food served all day ⊕ FREE HOUSE ◀ Wye Valley, St George's, Hereford ♂ Westons Stowford Press. **Facilities** Children welcome Children's menu Children's portions Play area Garden Parking Wi-fi 🚌 (notice required)

MUCH MARCLE Map 10 SO63

The Slip Tavern

Watery Ln HR8 2NG ☎ 01531 660246
e-mail: sliptavern@googlemail.com
dir: *Follow signs off A449 at Much Marcle junct*

Curiously named after a 1575 landslip which buried the local church, this country pub is delightfully surrounded by cider apple orchards. An attractive conservatory overlooks the award-winning garden, where summer dining is popular, and there's also a cosy bar with roaring fires in winter. Being situated next to Westons Cider Mill, cider is a favourite in the bar along with real ales from the cask. Popular dishes of Cajun-spiced catfish and West Indian chicken curry are influenced by Trinidadian owner Denyse. There are regular jazz and folk evenings. Booking for meals may be required.

Open all wk Tue-Fri 11.30-3 4-11 (Sat all day Sun 12-4 7-11) Closed: Mon (ex BH) **Bar Meals** L served Tue-Sun 12-3 D served Tue-Sat 6-9 Av main course £9.95 **Restaurant** L served Tue-Sun 12-3 D served Tue-Sat 6-9 Av 3 course à la carte fr £19.95 ⊕ FREE HOUSE ◀ Butcombe, Otter, Guest ales ♂ Westons, Stowford Press, Wyld Wood Organic Vintage, Wyld Wood Organic Pear. ♀ 9 **Facilities** ♣ Children welcome Children's portions Play area Garden Parking 🚌 (notice required)

ORLETON Map 9 SO46

The Boot Inn

SY8 4HN ☎ 01568 780228
e-mail: thebootinn@villagegreeninns.com
web: www.thebootinnorleton.co.uk
dir: *Follow A49 S from Ludlow (approx 7m) to B4362 (Woofferton), 1.5m off B4362 turn left. Inn in village centre*

A black and white, half-timbered, 16th-century village inn characterised by a large inglenook fireplace, oak beams, mullioned windows, and exposed wattle-and-daub. Herefordshire real ales and Robinsons cider accompany dishes such as slow-cooked belly pork; line-caught sea bass; and wild mushroom and spinach linguine. In the back room is a painting from which the figure of one-time regular Joe Vale was obliterated after arguing with the landlord. Occasionally, old Joe's ghost returns...

Open all wk 12-3 5.30-11 (Fri 12-3 5.30-12 Sat-Sun all day) **Bar Meals** L served Mon-Sat 12-2, Sun 12-3.30 D served all wk 6.30-9 **Restaurant** L served all wk 12-3

continued

ORLETON *continued*

D served all wk 6-9 ⊕ VILLAGE GREEN INNS ◀ Hobsons Best Bitter, Wye Valley, Purple Moose, Three Tuns, Otter, Ludlow, Local ales ◔ Robinsons, Westons Stowford Press. **Facilities** ♣ Children welcome Children's menu Play area Garden Parking 🚐

PEMBRIDGE Map 9 SO35

New Inn

Market Square HR6 9DZ ☎ 01544 388427
dir: *From M5 junct 7 take A44 W through Leominster towards Llandrindod Wells*

Formerly a courthouse and jail, and close to the last battle of the War of the Roses, this 14th-century black and white timbered free house has been under the same ownership for 27 years. Worn flagstone floors and winter fires characterise the cosy bar, and in summer customers spill out into the pub's outdoor seating area in the Old Market Square. Home-cooked English fare might include seafood stew with crusty bread; beef steak-and-ale pie; or leek, mushroom and Shropshire Blue cheese croustade with salad. Booking for meals may be required.

Open all wk 11-2.30 6-11 (summer 11-3 6-11) Closed: 1st wk Feb **Bar Meals** L served all wk 12-2 D served all wk 6.30-9 **Restaurant** L served all wk 12-2 D served all

wk 6.30-9 ⊕ FREE HOUSE ◀ Hobsons Town Crier, Sharp's Doom Bar, Hook Norton, Three Tuns, Ludlow ◔ Westons Stowford Press & Wyld Wood Organic, Dunkertons. ₹ 10 **Facilities** Children welcome Children's portions Family room Garden Parking

SHOBDON Map 9 SO46

The Bateman Arms ★★★★ INN

HR6 9LX ☎ 01568 708374
e-mail: diana@batemanarms.co.uk
dir: *On B4362 off A4110 NW of Leominster*

Inside this striking 18th-century coaching inn you can sit beneath ancient oak beams on 300-year-old wooden settles. The games room is decorated with military paraphernalia, and the large beer garden is a pleasant spot in which to relax with one of the guest ales. The menu caters for all tastes, from a simple sandwich to cooked dishes like lamb shank with mashed potatoes and roasted vegetables. There's a separate Sunday lunch menu and a regularly changing specials board, whilst comfortable en suite guest rooms complete the picture.

Open all day all wk **Bar Meals** L served all wk 12-2
D served Tue-Sat 7-9 **Restaurant** L served all wk 12-2
D served Tue-Sat 7-9 ⊕ FREE HOUSE ◀ John Smith's, Wychwood Hobgoblin, Guinness, Guest ales ◔ Westons

Stowford Press, Robinsons Flagon. **Facilities** Children welcome Children's menu Children's portions Garden Parking Wi-fi 🚐 **Rooms** 6

STAPLOW Map 10 SO64

The Oak Inn ★★★★ INN

PICK OF THE PUBS

See Pick of the Pubs on opposite page

SYMONDS YAT (EAST) Map 10 SO51

The Saracens Head Inn ★★★★ INN

PICK OF THE PUBS

See Pick of the Pubs on page 286
See advert below

The Saracens Head Inn

For centuries the *Saracens Head Inn* has occupied its spectacular position on the east bank of the River Wye, where the river flows into a steep wooded gorge. The Inn's own ferry across the river still operates by hand, just as it has for the past 200 years.

There's a relaxed atmosphere throughout the Inn, from the flagstoned bar to the cosy lounge and dining room. The riverside terraces are a great place to watch the world go by.

The Inn has a reputation for high quality food, using fresh local ingredients where possible, with a regularly changing menu and daily specials – not to mention a tempting choice of 6 real ales (featuring local breweries), and freshly-ground coffee.

Symonds Yat East is situated in an Area Of Outstanding Natural Beauty on the edge of the Forest of Dean, so a stay in one of the ten guest bedrooms is a must for exploring the unspoilt local countryside.

The Wye Valley Walk passes the Inn, as does the Peregrine cycle trail. Walking, cycling, mountain biking, river cruises, canoeing, kayaking, climbing and fishing are all available nearby.

Symonds Yat East, Ross-on-Wye, Herefordshire HR9 6JL
Tel: 01600 890435
Website: www.saracensheadinn.co.uk • Email: contact@saracensheadinn.co.uk

PICK OF THE PUBS

The Oak Inn ★★★★INN

STAPLOW   Map 10 SO64

HR8 1NP ☎ **01531 640954**
e-mail: oakinn@wyenet.co.uk
web: www.oakinnstaplow.co.uk
dir: *M50 junct 2, A417 to Ledbury. At rdbt take 2nd exit onto A449, then A438 (High St). Then take B4214 to Staplow*

Since acquiring it five years ago, Hylton Haylett and Julie Woollard have sympathetically refurbished this lovely old 17th-century black-and-white free house in the heart of rural Herefordshire. Just two miles north of the market town of Ledbury and close to the Malvern Hills, it's the only pub to abutt the Hereford to Gloucester Canal which closed in 1881. Three cosy bar areas have log-burning stoves, flagstone floors and old wooden beams adorned with hops. The Oak is a friendly drinkers' pub, welcoming locals and visitors alike with a choice of two local real ales and two guests. As befits what was once an old cider house, fermented apple juice is also a major strength here: Westons and Robinsons are both near by. The informally rustic restaurant area has an open-plan kitchen serving lunch and dinner every day. Dishes are traditional, prepared with care, and use locally sourced ingredients. If a sandwich will suffice, the Severn and Wye smoked salmon is a must; alternatively the grilled ciabatta melts are mouthwatering good. A proper lunch could start with twice-baked Hereford Hop cheese soufflé with a

tomato and caper sauce; and continue with home-baked free-range ham and eggs, served with hand-cut chips. Go à la carte in the evenings with a special such as a Barnsley chop of Teme Valley hogget lamb served with pearl barley risotto, spring vegetables and rosemary jus. The puddings board, always changing to accommodate seasonally available ingredients, may include apple and damson crumble; or treacle tart with clotted cream. Hylton and Julie describe their pub as 'definitely dog-friendly', and where better for your four-legged friend than The Oak, where public paths start at the door and lead out into the orchards? A choice of four spacious and stylish en suite rooms includes one with a terrace overlooking the fruit trees. Booking for meals may be required.

Open all day all wk **Bar Meals** L served all wk 12-2.30 D served all wk 6.30-9.30 **Restaurant** L served Mon-Sat 12-2.30, Sun 12-3 D served Mon-Sat 6.30-9.30, Sun 6.30-9 🌐 FREE HOUSE 🍺 Wye Valley Bitter, Bathams Best Bitter, Guest ales ♻ Westons Stowford Press, Robinsons. **Facilities** Children welcome Children's portions 🐾 Garden Parking Wi-fi **Rooms** 4

PICK OF THE PUBS

The Saracens Head Inn ★★★★INN

SYMONDS YAT (EAST)   Map 10 SO51

HR9 6JL ☎ **01600 890435**
e-mail: contact@saracensheadinn.co.uk
web: www.saracensheadinn.co.uk
dir: *Exit A40, signed Symonds Yat East, 2m to inn*

Dating from the 16th century, this former cider mill occupies a stunning position on the east bank of the River Wye, where the river flows into a steep wooded gorge on the edge of the Royal Forest of Dean. This is the yat, the local name for a gate or pass; it was named after Robert Symonds who was a Sheriff of Herefordshire in the 17th century. The inn's own ferry across the river still operates by hand, just as it has for the past 200 years. There's a relaxed atmosphere throughout the inn, from the flagstoned bar to the cosy lounge and stylish dining room, and you can also eat on one of the two sunny riverside terraces. Regularly changing menus and daily specials boards offer both the traditional: steak, kidney and Butty Bach ale pie with mash and greens, for example; and the modern: the sharing plate with a whole oven-baked camembert, served with local acacia honey, apple compôte and crusty bread. A typical three-course meal might start with smoked Wye and Severn Valley salmon and crab roulade with mixed leaves and orange dressing, followed by braised shank of Welsh lamb with winter vegetables and rosemary jus. Complete your meal with one of the desserts on the blackboard or you might opt for a slate of three local cheeses – Hereford Hop, Per Las and Golden Cenarth – served with grapes, crackers, and quince and rose petal jelly. The inn is situated in an Area of Outstanding Natural Beauty, so a stay in one of the ten en suite bedrooms is a must for exploring the unspoiled local countryside. Walking, cycling, mountain biking, canoeing, kayaking, climbing, abseiling and potholing are all available nearby, whilst fishing is free to residents.

Open all day all wk Closed: 25 Dec **Bar Meals** L served all wk 12-2.30 D served all wk 6.30-9 Av main course £11.95 **Restaurant** L served all wk 12-2.30

D served all wk 6.30-9 Av 3 course à la carte fr £26 ⊕ FREE HOUSE
◀ Theakston Old Peculier, Wye Valley HPA & Butty Bach, Otley 01, Mayfields Copper Fox, Kingstone Gold Fine Ale
ŏ Westons Wyld Wood Organic & Stowford Press, Lyne Down Roaring Meg.
♛ 10 **Facilities** Children welcome Children's menu Children's portions Garden Parking Wi-fi **Rooms** 10

PICK OF THE PUBS

The Mill Race

WALFORD   Map 10 SO52

HR9 5QS ☎ 01989 562891
e-mail: enquiries@millrace.info
web: www.millrace.info
dir: B4234 from Ross-on-Wye to
Walford. Pub 3m on right

There's another Walford in the north of
the county, so make sure the Sat Nav
has the correct postcode if you're
planning to head for this one. It lies on
the banks of the River Wye, just
upstream from the picturesque gorge at
Symonds Yat and the wooded hills of the
Forest of Dean. Standing majestically on
the other bank is Goodrich Castle, where
'Roaring Meg', the only surviving Civil
War mortar, which the Parliamentarians
used to breach its walls, is on display.
The pub's interior is suitably cosy and
welcoming, with a beamed and
flagstone-floored bar and rustically
furnished dining areas. Warm up in
winter by one of the log fires, or in
summer relax on the terrace, perhaps
with a pint of Wye Valley Bitter or Butty
Bach, and watch the buzzards drifting
overhead. At nearby Bishopwood is the
pub's own 1,000-acre farm estate,
which together with a dedicated supply
chain of ultra-reliable local producers,
allows landlord Luke Freeman and his
team to dedicate their days to producing
the award-winning food that is now
highly regarded within the burgeoning
Herefordshire Slow Food movement.
Lunch and evening menus will vary; a
typical midday meal might begin with
Severn and Wye Valley smoked haddock

cassoulet, with chargrilled Herefordshire
steak, roasted tomato, buttered field
mushrooms and chips to follow. Or, in
the evening, consider a starter of pan-
fried squid, parsley salad, grilled black
pudding and English mustard cream,
followed by buttered salmon with leek
sauce and cocotte potatoes. Wednesday
nights are fish nights, while every
Tuesday and Thursday the outdoor pizza
oven is fired up to produce, not the
expected margheritas and quattro
stagiones, but English-named versions,
such as Featherstone Flyer (pheasant
and chestnuts) and Hopcraft Hot One
(sweet chilli and jalapeño peppers).
You'll find wines from Herefordshire on
the globe-spanning list.

Open all wk 11-3 5-11 (Sat-Sun all day)
Bar Meals L served Mon-Fri 12-2, Sat
12-2.30, Sun all day D served Mon-Sat

6-9.30, Sun all day Av main course £10
Restaurant L served Mon-Fri 12-2, Sat
12-2.30, Sun all day D served Mon-Sat
6-9.30, Sun all day Fixed menu price fr
£12 Av 3 course à la carte fr £20
⊕ FREE HOUSE ◀ Wye Valley Bitter &
Butty Bach, Butcombe, Guinness
Ŏ Westons Stowford Press, Lyne Down
Roaring Meg. ♥ 25 **Facilities** Children
welcome Children's menu Children's
portions Garden Parking Wi-fi 🚌

TILLINGTON
Map 9 SO44

The Bell

HR4 8LE ☎ **01432 760395**
e-mail: glenn@thebellinntillington.co.uk
dir: *NE Hereford, on road to Weobley via Burghill*

Run by the Williams family for 25 years, this traditional village pub appeals as much to local beer drinkers as it does to those wanting good food. Indeed, it offers something for everybody, with extensive gardens, patio, grassed play area, dining room and two bars, one with an open fire and a drop-down screen for national sporting events. Prepared on site using local ingredients are light meals (at lunchtime) and a full menu offering seafood chowder; Szechuan chicken; marinated Herefordshire sirloin steak; and butternut squash bake. Home-made cider is served.

Open all wk 12-3 6-11 (Fri-Sun all day) **Bar Meals** L served Mon-Sat 12-2.30, Sun 12-3 D served Mon-Sat 6-9.30 **Restaurant** L served Mon-Sat 12-2.30, Sun 12-3 D served Mon-Sat 6-9.30 ◖ Sharp's Doom Bar, Hereford Best Bitter, Local ales. **Facilities** Children welcome Children's menu Play area Garden Parking Wi-fi

WALFORD
Map 10 SO52

The Mill Race

PICK OF THE PUBS

See Pick of the Pubs on page 287

WALTERSTONE
Map 9 SO32

Carpenters Arms

HR2 0DX ☎ **01873 890353**
dir: *Off A465 between Hereford & Abergavenny at Pandy*

There's plenty of character in this 300-year-old free house located on the edge of the Black Mountains where the owner, Mrs Watkins, was born. Here you'll find beams, antique settles and a leaded range with open fires that burn all winter; a perfect cosy setting for enjoying a pint of Ramblers Ruin. Popular food options include beef and Guinness pie, beef lasagne and thick lamb cutlets. Ask about the vegetarian selection, and large choice of home-made desserts. There are a few tables outside which can be a suntrap in summer.

Open all day all wk 12-11 Closed: 25 Dec **Bar Meals** food served all day ⊕ FREE HOUSE ◖ Wadworth 6X, Breconshire Golden Valley & Ramblers Ruin Ö Westons. **Facilities** Children welcome Children's portions Play area Family room Garden Parking ☷ Notes ⊛

WELLINGTON
Map 10 SO44

The Wellington

HR4 8AT ☎ **01432 830367**
e-mail: jpgsurman@gmail.com
dir: *Off A49 into village centre. Pub 0.25m on left*

John Gallagher has taken over at The Wellington, where he aims to combine fine dining and a casual atmosphere with lots of family appeal. The garden is sunny and secure, an ideal venue for the beer festival held here in early June. If the weather is inclement, the pub's restaurant and conservatory are also at the disposal of family groups. Here, a typical meal choice could comprise chargrilled squid with chilli jam; a fillet of salmon with crushed new potatoes; and a dark chocolate fondant with vanilla ice cream.

Open 12-3 6-11 Closed: 25-26 Dec, Mon L **Bar Meals** L served Tue-Sun 12-2 D served Mon-Sat 6.30-9 Av main course £5.50-£9.50 **Restaurant** L served Tue-Sun 12-2 D served Mon-Sat 7-9 Av 3 course à la carte fr £21 ⊕ FREE HOUSE ◖ Wye Valley Butty Bach & HPA, Hobsons, Guest ales Ö Westons. ⏹ 9 **Facilities** ✿ Children welcome Children's portions Garden Beer festival Parking Wi-fi ☷ (notice required)

WEOBLEY
Map 9 SO45

Ye Olde Salutation Inn

PICK OF THE PUBS

Market Pitch HR4 8SJ ☎ **01544 318443**
e-mail: info@salutation-inn.com
dir: *A44, then A4112, 8m from Leominster*

Proprietor Stuart Elder took over this 17th-century black and white timber-framed pub in April 2011 – 12 years after he worked here as a chef for the previous owners. The inn, sympathetically converted from an old alehouse and adjoining cottage, is the perfect base for exploring the Welsh Marches and enjoying a host of leisure activities, including fishing, horse riding, golf, walking, and clay shooting. The book capital of Hay-on-Wye and the cathedral city of Hereford are close by, as are the Wye Valley and Black Mountains. The inn's restaurant offers a range of tempting dishes created with the use of locally sourced ingredients. Chef's specials and old favourites are also served in the traditional lounge bar with its welcoming atmosphere and cosy inglenook fireplace. Start, perhaps, with smoked haddock, spring onion and ricotta tartlet; or pan-fried kidneys in tomato and mustard sauce. Continue with baked cod fillet on roast Mediterranean vegetables; stuffed aubergine rolls with chickpeas, pine nuts and vegetables in Moroccan spices, or steak-and-ale pie. Light bites, salads, rolls, sandwiches and omelettes are also available.

Open all day all wk 12-11 (Sun 12-10.30) **Bar Meals** L served all wk 12-3 D served all wk 6-9.30 Av main course £13 **Restaurant** L served all wk 12-3 D served all wk 6-9.30 Fixed menu price fr £13 Av 3 course à la carte fr £25 ⊕ FREE HOUSE ◖ Wye Valley Butty Bach, Wood's, Hobsons Ö Westons Stowford Press, Robinsons.

Facilities Children welcome Children's portions Garden Parking Wi-fi ☷ (notice required)

WOOLHOPE
Map 10 SO63

The Butchers Arms ⊛⊛

PICK OF THE PUBS

HR1 4RF ☎ **01432 860281**
e-mail: food@butchersarmswoolhope.co.uk
dir: *From Hereford take B4224 towards Ross-on-Wye. Follow signs for Woolhope on left in Fownhope.*

Dating from the 16th century, this picturesque, half-timbered black and white inn was once a butcher's shop that also brewed beer and baked the village's bread. Set by a stream in an Area of Outstanding Natural Beauty at the foot of the sublime Marcle Ridge, it's in the heart of cider country – so expect several local ciders at the bar as well as a decent selection of local cask ales. There's also a well-considered wine list to match the accessible menu created by the renowned chef-patron Stephen Bull. Awarded two AA Rosettes for quality, typical dishes include haggis fritters with beetroot relish, followed by fillet of Cornish gilt head bream with brown shrimps, new potatoes and tomato and herb butter sauce. Bull's famous puddings include chargrilled pineapple with lime and chilli syrup and vanilla ice cream; and a chocolate brownie with chocolate and orange tart and coffee cream.

Open 12-2.30 6.30-11 Closed: Sun eve, Mon (ex BHs) **Bar Meals** L served Tue-Sat 12-2, Sun 12-2.15 D served Tue-Sat 7-9 Av main course £13.50 **Restaurant** L served Tue-Sat 12-2, Sun 12-2.15 D served Tue-Sat 7-9 Av 3 course à la carte fr £22 ⊕ FREE HOUSE ◖ Local ales Ö Westons Stowford Press, Oliver's, Dragon Orchard, Gwatkin. ⏹ 10 **Facilities** ✿ Children welcome Children's portions Garden Parking Wi-fi

The Crown Inn

HR1 4QP ☎ **01432 860468**
e-mail: menu@crowninnwoolhope.co.uk
dir: *B4224 to Mordiford, left after Moon Inn. Pub in village centre*

A traditional village free house with large gardens, The Crown Inn is popular with walkers and well supported by locals and visitors alike. Excellent food and drink are a priority here, with good ales as well as 23 local ciders and perries. Daily specials include trout fishcakes with garlic mayonnaise; cider-braised ham with free-range eggs and chunky chips; pheasant Kiev with sweet potato mash and stir-fried cabbage. There is an outside summertime bar in the garden on Saturday nights and a May Day Bank Holiday beer and cider festival.

Open all wk 12-2.30 6.30-11 (Sat-Sun all day) **Bar Meals** L served all wk 12-2 D served all wk 6.30-9 Av main course £9 **Restaurant** L served all wk 12-2 D served all wk 6.30-9 Av 3 course à la carte fr £15 ⊕ FREE HOUSE ◖ Wye Valley HPA, Hobsons Best Bitter, Guest ales Ö Westons Stowford Press, Country Perry & Bounds, Local ciders. ⏹ 8 **Facilities** Children welcome Children's menu Children's portions Garden Beer festival Parking Wi-fi ☷ (notice required)

Save on hotels. Book at **theAA.com/hotel**

HERTFORDSHIRE 289 **ENGLAND**

HERTFORDSHIRE

ALDBURY
Map 6 SP91

The Greyhound Inn

19 Stocks Rd HP23 5RT ☎ **01442 851228**
e-mail: greyhound@aldbury.wanadoo.co.uk
dir: *Telephone for directions*

The village's ancient stocks and duck pond are popular with film-makers who frequently use Aldbury as a film location, allowing the pub's customers the chance to witness every clap of the clapperboard. In the oak-beamed restaurant, the comprehensive menu includes salads and platters, as well as king prawn spaghetti with smoky bacon, sundried tomatoes and a lemon and garlic oil; chargrilled butterflied chicken breast; and butternut squash, red onion, sage and pine nut risotto. Among the desserts are salted butternut toffee terrine; and caramel fondue with fresh fruit and marshmallows. The bar snacks are a local legend, especially when accompanied by Badger Best or Tanglefoot ale.

Open all day all wk 11.30-11 (Sun 12-10.30) Closed: 25 Dec **Bar Meals** L served all wk 12-2.30 D served all wk 6.30-9.30 Av main course £12 **Restaurant** L served all wk 12-2.30 D served all wk 6.30-9.30 Av 3 course à la carte fr £25 ⊕ HALL & WOODHOUSE ◀ Badger Dorset Best, Tanglefoot, K&B Sussex. ♛ 13 **Facilities** Children welcome Family room Garden Parking Wi-fi ▭

The Valiant Trooper

Trooper Rd HP23 5RW ☎ **01442 851203**
e-mail: valianttrooper@gmx.co.uk
dir: *A41 at Tring junct, follow rail station signs 0.5m, at village green turn right, 200yds on left*

For centuries lucky locals have been enjoying this old pub in the quintessential Chilterns village of Aldbury beneath the beech woods of Ashridge Park. The Duke of Wellington allegedly discussed strategy with his troops here; when the famous warrior died it was named in his honour. Now in the safe hands of Wendy Greenall, the bar proffers six real ales and the promise of a beer festival; telephone for details. Choice is there too on the menu, which ranges through pub favourites such as jackets and ploughman's, to smoked haddock fishcakes; or Brick Oak Farm sausages and mash.

Open all day all wk 12-11 (Sun 12-10.30) **Bar Meals** L served Mon-Fri 12-3, Sat 12-9, Sun 12-4 D served Mon-Fri 6-9, Sat 12-9 **Restaurant** L served Mon-Fri 12-3, Sat 12-9, Sun 12-4 D served Mon-Fri 6-9, Sat 12-9 ⊕ FREE HOUSE ◀ Fuller's London Pride, Brakspear Bitter. **Facilities** ♣ Children welcome Children's menu Children's portions Play area Family room Garden Beer festival Parking Wi-fi ▭

ARDELEY
Map 12 TL32

Jolly Waggoner

SG2 7AH ☎ **01438 861350**
dir: *From Stevenage take B1037, through Walkern, in 2m right to Ardeley*

Church Farm took on the stewardship of this 500-year-old village pub in 2011, so all of the meat and over 100 different vegetables, fruits and herbs served in the pub are grown at Church Farm across the road. Heritage varieties and rare breeds allow the pub to offer the very best local ingredients. Start with pressed bacon terrine with piccalilli; or Aylesbury duck liver pâté. Main courses include vegetable biryani, dry-cured gammon, pan-fried partridge breast, stuffed baked pancakes, and beer-battered haddock fillet. There are weekly live music and quiz nights, as well as curry night and pudding club. Booking for meals may be required.

Open all day all wk 12-11.30 (Fri-Sat noon-12.30am) **Bar Meals** L served Mon-Fri 12-2, Sat 12-9, Sun 12-7 D served Mon-Fri 6.30-9, Sat 12-9, Sun 12-7 Av main course £13 **Restaurant** L served Mon-Fri 12-2, Sat 12-9, Sun 12-7 D served Mon-Fri 6.30-9, Sat 12-9, Sun 12-7 Av 3 course à la carte fr £20 ⊕ FREE HOUSE ◀ Thwaites Highwayman, Fuller's London Pride, Adnams Broadside, Crouch Vale Brewers Gold, Dark Star, McMullen, Buntingford, Guest ales. ♛ 10 **Facilities** ♣ Children welcome Children's menu Children's portions Garden Parking Wi-fi ▭

ASHWELL
Map 12 TL23

Three Tuns

6 High St SG7 5NL ☎ **01462 742107**
e-mail: info@threetunshotel.co.uk
dir: *Telephone for directions*

The building, dating from 1806, replaced an earlier one first recorded as a public house in 1701. Original features survive in the two refurbished bars – a lounge bar with restaurant and a large public bar. The extensive menu offers devilled whitebait; moules marinière; scampi and chips; grilled sea bass with rosemary and lemon on steamed greens; pan-fried pork fillet with Calvados sauce; whole roast partridge with wild blackberry, apple and red wine jus; and fillet steak Diane. There is a large garden with mature borders and children's play area, and a patio. Booking for meals may be required.

Open all day all wk 11am-11.30pm (Fri-Sat 11am-12.30am) ⊕ GREENE KING ◀ IPA & Abbot Ale, Guest ale ♂ Aspall. **Facilities** Children welcome Children's menu Children's portions Play area Family room Garden Parking Wi-fi

AYOT GREEN
Map 6 TL21

The Waggoners ⊛

Brickwall Close AL6 9AA ☎ **01707 324241**
e-mail: laurent@thewaggoners.co.uk
dir: *Ayot Green on unclassified road off B197, S of Welwyn*

Overlooking a splendid village green, this 17th-century coaching inn was originally built to house the workers at nearby Brocket Hall. Now a busy food-driven pub run by experienced French owners, it retains much of its original charm in the cosy beamed bar where English ales are on offer alongside some 50 wines by the glass. In the comfortable restaurant, the French-inspired menus might include roast leg of lamb stuffed with rosemary and mushrooms, or orange and pomegranate cake. In summer, bag a table in the suntrap garden and sheltered terrace. Booking for meals may be required.

Open all day all wk **Bar Meals** L served all wk 12-2.45 D served all wk 6.30-9.30 Av main course £8.50 **Restaurant** L served all wk 12-2.45 D served all wk 6.30-9.30 Fixed menu price fr £15.95 Av 3 course à la carte fr £25 ⊕ PUNCH TAVERNS ◀ Fuller's London Pride, St Austell Tribute, Adnams Broadside, Greene King Abbot Ale. ♛ 50 **Facilities** ♣ Children welcome Children's portions Garden Beer festival Parking Wi-fi ▭ (notice required)

BARLEY
Map 12 TL43

The Fox & Hounds

High St SG8 8HU ☎ **01763 849400**
e-mail: foxandhoundsbarley@hotmail.co.uk
dir: *A505 onto B1368 at Flint Cross, pub 4m*

This 16th-century former hunting lodge is set in a beautiful and historic village in north Hertfordshire. Expect a wealth of exposed beams, fireplaces, wood-burners, original flooring and more nooks and crannies than you can shake a stick at. The pub has made a name for itself by serving top-quality real ales from micro-breweries and offering home-cooked food in the dedicated restaurant. A typical menu might include home-made beef lasagne and chicken curry. Child- and dog-friendly, you could also time your visit for one of the Bank Holiday beer festivals.

Open all day all wk 12-11 (Fri- Sat 12-12) **Bar Meals** L served all wk 12-2 D served all wk 6-9 Av main course £7.50 **Restaurant** L served all wk 12-2 D served all wk 6-9 Fixed menu price fr £7.50 Av 3 course à la carte fr £18 ⊕ FREE HOUSE ◀ Adnams Southwold Bitter, Flowers IPA, Woodforde's Wherry, Falstaff Phoenix, Greene King Abbot Ale ♂ Lyne Down Roaring Meg. ♛ 12 **Facilities** ♣ Children welcome Children's menu Children's portions Play area Garden Beer festival Parking Wi-fi ▭

BERKHAMSTED   Map 6 SP90

The Old Mill

London Rd HP4 2NB ☎ 01442 879590
e-mail: oldmill@peachpubs.com
dir: *At east end of London Rd in Berkhamsted centre*

This restored pub retains many of its original Georgian and Victorian features. Occupying a plum spot on the Grand Union Canal, it's a great place to enjoy real ales and deli boards while relaxing on big leather sofas in the low-beamed bar. Alternatively, head for the comfortable dining room for menus showcasing the best seasonal ingredients: shredded duck salad could be followed by Cornish lamb steak with roasted garlic, creamy mash, pea purée and jus, and then lemon curd cheesecake. The canal-side garden is a perfect place for relaxed alfresco dining or a quiet pint. Look out for the beer festival.

Open all day all wk 10am-mdnt Closed: 25 Dec **Bar Meals** Av main course £14 food served all day **Restaurant** Av 3 course à la carte fr £22 food served all day ⊕ PEACH PUBS ◼ Greene King IPA, Morland Old Speckled Hen, Tring Side Pocket for a Toad Ὄ Aspall. ☏ 13 **Facilities** ✿ Children welcome Children's portions Garden Beer festival Parking Wi-fi ▰ (notice required)

BUNTINGFORD   Map 12 TL32

The Sword Inn Hand ★★★★ INN

Westmill SG9 9LQ ☎ 01763 271356
e-mail: welcome@theswordinnhand.co.uk
dir: *Off A10 1.5m S of Buntingford*

Since the 14th century this old inn has been welcoming travellers needing a halfway break between London and Cambridge. Inside are the original oak beams, flagstone floors and open fireplace; outside is a large garden and pretty patio. Fresh produce is delivered daily for a good selection of bar snacks, specials and, taken from a typical evening menu, seared sea bass fillet with fresh asparagus; local sausages, creamy mash and red onion gravy; and caramelised onion, sweet pepper and goat's cheese tart. Accommodation is provided in four luxury ground floor bedrooms.

Open all wk 12-3 5-11 (Sun Sep-Apr 12-7 May-Aug 12-10) **Bar Meals** L served Mon-Sat 12-2.30, Sun 12-4 D served Mon-Sat 6.30-9.30 **Restaurant** L served Mon-Sat 12-2.30, Sun 12-4 D served Mon-Sat 6.30-9.30 ⊕ FREE HOUSE ◼ Greene King IPA, Young's Bitter, Timothy Taylor Landlord, Sharp's Doom Bar, Guest ales Ὄ Aspall. **Facilities** Children welcome Children's menu Children's portions Play area Garden Parking Wi-fi ▰ **Rooms** 4

COTTERED   Map 12 TL32

The Bull at Cottered

SG9 9QP ☎ 01763 281243
e-mail: cordell39@btinternet.com
dir: *On A507 in Cottered between Buntingford & Baldock*

A charming, traditional village local with low beams, antique furniture, cosy fires and pub games. The setting is picturesque, with a well-tended garden offering an additional place to eat and drink. Everything that can be, is home-made, the brasserie-style cooking typified by starters of wild mushroom risotto; and Serrano ham with warm goat's cheese; and main courses such as rack of lamb in herb breadcrumbs and port sauce; sirloin of Scotch beef with mushrooms and pepper sauce; and fillet of salmon with cheese, cream and leek sauce. Booking for meals may be required.

Open all wk 11.30-3 6.30-11 (Sun 12-10.30) **Bar Meals** L served Mon-Sat 12-2, Sun 12-4 D served Mon-Sat 6.30-9.30, Sun 6-9 Av main course £10 **Restaurant** L served Mon-Sat 12-2, Sun 12-4 D served Mon-Sat 6.30-9.30, Sun 6-9 Fixed menu price £21 Av 3 course à la carte fr £27.50 ⊕ GREENE KING ◼ IPA & Abbot Ale, Morland Old Speckled Hen. **Facilities** Children welcome Children's portions Garden Parking ▰

DATCHWORTH   Map 6 TL21

The Tilbury ◉

Walton Rd SG3 6TB ☎ 01438 815550
e-mail: info@thetilbury.co.uk
dir: *A1(M) junct 7, A602 signed Ware & Hertford. At Bragbury End right into Bragbury Ln to Datchworth*

A well selected wine list, real ales and a list of over 30 bottled beers are a nice introduction to this once-tired old village boozer, now turned into a notable dining pub by TV chef Paul Bloxham. Bare brick walls, wooden floors and interesting art suit the mood for the simply cooked, seasonally inspired modern British food. The fixed-price market menu represents special value, offering the likes of mini bouillabaisse with rouille and sourdough crisp, followed by chargrilled mutton koftas with couscous, pickled red cabbage and tzatziki. Desserts may include chocolate pot with shortbread. Booking for meals may be required.

Open 12-3 6-late Closed: Sun eve **Bar Meals** L served all wk 12-2 Av main course £14 **Restaurant** D served Mon-Sat 6-9.30 Fixed menu price fr £13.95 Av 3 course à la carte fr £28 ⊕ BRAKSPEAR ◼ Bitter, Oxford Gold Ὄ Westons Wyld Wood Organic. ☏ 30 **Facilities** Children welcome Children's menu Children's portions Garden Parking Wi-fi

EPPING GREEN   Map 6 TL20

The Beehive

SG13 8NB ☎ 01707 875959
e-mail: squirrell15@googlemail.com
dir: *South of Hertford*

This family-run free house has held its liquor license for over 200 years and featured in the *Catweazel* TV series in the 1970s. These days it retains plenty of traditional charms including exposed beams, a real fire in winter and decked and grassed areas for sunnier days. The kitchen specialises in fresh fish from Billingsgate Market – maybe poached fish pie or sea bass fillets with basil pesto. Alternatives include steak, mushroom and ale pudding, and Thai green chicken curry. At the bar you'll find two permanent ales and a changing guest. Booking for meals may be required.

Open all wk Mon-Sat 11.30-3 5.30-11 (Sun 11-11) **Bar Meals** L served Mon-Sat 12-2.30, Sun 12-4 D served Mon-Sat 6-9.30, Sun 6-8.30 **Restaurant** L served Mon-Sat 12-2.30, Sun 12-4 D served Mon-Sat 6-9.30, Sun 6-8.30 ⊕ FREE HOUSE ◼ Greene King IPA, Morland Old Speckled Hen, Guest ale. ☏ 8 **Facilities** Children welcome Children's portions Garden Parking Wi-fi ▰ (notice required)

FLAUNDEN   Map 6 TL00

The Bricklayers Arms ◉

PICK OF THE PUBS

See Pick of the Pubs on page 292
See advert on opposite page

HEMEL HEMPSTEAD   Map 6 TL00

Alford Arms

PICK OF THE PUBS

See Pick of the Pubs on page 293

HERONSGATE   Map 6 TQ09

The Land of Liberty, Peace and Plenty

Long Ln WD3 5BS ☎ 01923 282226
e-mail: beer@landoflibertypub.com
dir: *M25 junct 17, follow Heronsgate signs. 0.5m, pub on right*

Named after a Chartist settlement established in Heronsgate in 1847, this pub is believed to have the second longest name in the British Isles. A traditional pub with a large garden and covered decked area, the cosy single bar has a buzz of conversation from locals. The focus here are the real ales and real ciders, all of which can be enjoyed with bar snacks of pork pies, pasties and pots of nuts. Regular events and beer festivals are held during the year.

Open all wk 12-11 (Fri 12-12 Sat 11am-mdnt) **Bar Meals** food served all day ⊕ FREE HOUSE ◼ 6 Guest ales Ὄ Millwhites, Westons. **Facilities** ✿ Garden Beer festival Parking Wi-fi ▰ (notice required)

Bricklayers Arms

The Award Winning Bricklayers Arms now with an AA Rosette for its "culinary excellence" is tucked away in the tiny Hertfordshire Village of Flaunden which you can find at the end of the winding lanes which snake between the quaint villages of Chipperfield and Latimer. A picturesque pub in a beautiful location on the edge of the Chilterns.

The Michaels family recently refurbished this ivy clad 18th Century listed building. You are sure to receive a warm welcome and enjoy the atmosphere with the pub's low wooden beams and real log fire.

In the summer you can enjoy a meal on the terrace and garden surrounded by acres of fields and lush green countryside.

Over the past years, the Bricklayers Arms has certainly gained an excellent reputation for its English traditional and French fusion menu created buy its Michelin trained chef, Claude Pallait.

You can enjoy the same menu throughout the restaurant and pub seven days a week with dishes ranging at lunch time from their famous Steak and Kidney Ale Pie to matured Red Ruby Devonshire (locally grazed in Sarratt) fillet Steaks and local game. Organic and local produce is used whenever possible.

The Evening menu offers several starters including, Egg Meurettes with a shallot, bacon and red wine jus or their home smoked selection of fishes and meats to main courses of Best End of Little Missenden Lamb served with a pea flan: locally farmed rare-breed Pork with a Bramley apple compote & cider jus. There are always a number of fish dishes with daily specials on the menu.

There's an excellent range of ales and a selection of more than 140 wines, ports and Armagnacs.

"AA Herts Pick of the Pubs"

Hogpits Bottom, Flaunden HP3 0PH • Tel: 01442 833322
Website: www.bricklayersarms.com • **Email:** goodfood@bricklayersarms.com

PICK OF THE PUBS

The Bricklayers Arms ❀

FLAUNDEN   Map 6 TL00

Hogpits Bottom HP3 0PH
☎ 01442 833322
e-mail: goodfood@bricklayersarms.com
web: www.bricklayersarms.com
dir: *M25 junct 18, A404 (Amersham road). Right at Chenies for Flaunden*

The creeper-clad Bricklayers Arms is a low, cottagey tiled pub formed from a pair of 18th-century cottages. It was in 1832 that Benskin's brewery converted the first of the cottages into an alehouse; the other joined it in the 1960s. Lost down leafy Hertfordshire lanes in a peaceful and inviting location, the pub has featured in many fictional films and TV programmes, and is a favourite with locals, walkers, horse-riders and, well, just about everyone. In summer, the flower-festooned garden is the perfect place to savour an alfresco pint or meal. An ivy-covered façade gives way to an immaculate interior, complete with low beams, exposed brickwork, candlelight and open fires. The award-winning restaurant is housed in a converted outbuilding and barn. Here you'll find a happy marriage of traditional English and French cooking. The Gallic influence comes from experienced head chef, Claude Pallait, and his team who use fresh organic produce from local suppliers to create seasonal lunch and dinner menus, plus daily specials. For starters try egg meurette (with a shallot,

bacon and red wine jus), or duck liver parfait with a toasted nut and crouton crumble. To follow, maybe local rare-breed pork with a Bramley apple compôte and cider jus, or roast breast of guinea fowl with pheasant sausage and a liver mousse feuilleté. But don't stop there, as the pub is also held in high esteem for its pudding menu, on which you're likely to find lemon tart with pannacotta and raspberry ice cream; and orange and mandarin sponge cheesecake with lemon sorbet. Choose one of the 120 wines from all corners of the world and, in the summer, enjoy it with your lunch in the terraced garden. Booking for meals may be required.

Open all day all wk 12-11.30 (25 Dec 12-3) **Bar Meals** L served Mon-Sat

12-2.30, Sun 12-3.30 D served Mon-Sat 6.30-9.30, Sun 6.30-8.30 Av main course £16 **Restaurant** L served Mon-Sat 12-2.30, Sun 12-3.30 D served Mon-Sat 6.30-9.30, Sun 6.30-8.30 Fixed menu price fr £15 Av 3 course à la carte fr £25 ⊕ FREE HOUSE ◛ Fuller's London Pride, Tring Jack O'Legs, Sharp's Doom Bar, Rebellion ♺ Aspall. ♟ 16 **Facilities** Children welcome Children's portions Garden Parking Wi-fi

PICK OF THE PUBS

Alford Arms

HEMEL HEMPSTEAD   Map 6 TL00

Frithsden HP1 3DD ☎ 01442 864480
e-mail: info@alfordarmsfrithsden.co.uk
web: www.alfordarmsfrithsden.co.uk
dir: *From Hemel Hempstead on A4146, 2nd left at Water End. 1m, left at T-junct, right in 0.75m. Pub 100yds on right*

With historic Ashridge Park on the doorstep and surrounded by National Trust woodland, this pretty Victorian pub is almost all there is in the untouched hamlet of Frithsden. It's one of five in the well-regarded Salisbury Pubs mini-empire in and around the Chilterns, all of which have entries in this guide.* Cross the threshold and you'll immediately pick up on the warm and lively atmosphere, derived from the buzz of conversation, some soft jazz in the background, and from the rich colours and eclectic mix of old furniture and antique pictures in the dining room and bar from Tring's well-known salerooms. Also from Tring is real ale called Side Pocket, which shares bar space with Rebellion IPA and Sharp's Doom Bar. The seasonal menus and daily specials are a balance of modern British with more traditional dishes, all prepared from fresh local produce whenever possible. There's a great choice of light dishes or 'small plates', from the pan-roasted Halsey Estate pigeon breast with cauliflower rösti and beetroot and juniper purée, to Cornish crab croquettes with chorizo cream. Equally imaginative main meals include roast hake fillet with clam, mussel and ham hock chowder, and smoked chilli onion rings; chargrilled 21-day-aged British rib-eye steak with fat chips, watercress and harissa butter; and creamy leeks, wild mushrooms, gruyère scone, parsnip purée and curly kale. Seville orange curd and jelly trifle with pecan biscuit is one way to finish, or there's also the plate of British cheeses. Like all pubs in the Salisbury group, they do great Sunday roasts. Booking for meals may be required.

*The Black Horse, Fulmer; The Swan Inn, Denham; The Royal Oak, Bovingdon Green; and The Old Queens Head, Penn.

Open all day all wk 11-11 (Sun 12-10.30) Closed: 25-26 Dec **Bar**

Meals L served Mon-Fri 12-2.30, Sat 12-3, Sun 12-4 D served Sun-Thu 6.30-9.30, Fri-Sat 6.30-10 Av main course £14.50 **Restaurant** L served Mon-Fri 12-2.30, Sat 12-3, Sun 12-4 D served Sun-Thu 6.30-9.30, Fri-Sat 6.30-10 Av 3 course à la carte fr £27 ⊕ SALISBURY PUBS LTD ◄ Rebellion IPA, Sharp's Doom Bar, Tring Side Pocket for a Toad Ŏ Thatchers. ⬤ 22 **Facilities** Children welcome Children's portions ❀ Garden Parking Wi-fi

HEXTON
Map 12 TL13

The Raven

SG5 3JB ☎ **01582 881209**
e-mail: theraven@emeryinns.com
dir: *5m W of Hitchin. 5m N of Luton, just outside Barton-le-Clay*

This neat 1920s pub is named after Ravensburgh Castle in the neighbouring hills. Comfortable bars witness the serving of four weekly-changing guest ales, perhaps Sharp's Doom Bar or Timothy Taylor Landlord, while outside a large garden with heated terrace and a play area ensure family friendliness. Extensive menus embrace ranges of wraps, baguettes, jackets and baps if a snack is required. For a full meal expect the likes of crab and chilli fishcakes with sweet chilli sauce to start, followed by lamb chops with red wine and rosemary sauce or fisherman's pie, leaving room for treacle sponge pudding.

Open all wk 11-3 6-11 (Fri-Sun all day) **Bar Meals** Av main course £12 **Restaurant** Av 3 course à la carte fr £21 ⊕ FREE HOUSE ◀ Greene King IPA, Morland Old Speckled Hen, Fuller's London Pride, Timothy Taylor Landlord, Sharp's Doom Bar. ♀ 24 **Facilities** Children welcome Children's menu Children's portions Play area Garden Parking Wi-fi ⛟ (notice required)

HITCHIN
Map 12 TL12

The Dragon Inn

London Rd, St Ippolyts SG4 7NL ☎ **01462 440989**
e-mail: hitchindragoninn@gmail.com
dir: *1.5m S of Hitchin on B656*

There has been a pub on the site for 300 years although the current building dates from 1900. It sits in pleasant countryside and open farmland on the outskirts of Hitchin, with easy access to the M1 and Luton Airport. The menu centres on pan-Asian cuisine, offering plenty of favourites such as tempura prawns, sesame prawn on toast and sweet and crispy seaweed to start, followed perhaps by sizzling chicken with ginger and spring onion, or squid in Szechuan sauce. Finish with fruit fritters in syrup.

Open all wk 12-2.30 6-11.30 (Fri-Sat 12-2.30 6-12 Sun 12-3 6-11.30) **Bar Meals** L served Mon-Sat 12-2.30, Sun 12-3 D served Mon-Thu & Sun 6-11.30, Fri-Sat 6-12 **Restaurant** L served Mon-Sat 12-2.30, Sun 12-3 D served Mon-Thu & Sun 6-11.30, Fri-Sat 6-12 Fixed menu price fr £15 ⊕ FREE HOUSE ◀ Adnams, Guest ale. **Facilities** Children welcome Children's menu Children's portions Family room Parking ⛟

The Radcliffe Arms

31 Walsworth Rd SG4 9ST ☎ **01462 456111**
e-mail: enquiries@radcliffearms.co.uk
dir: *From Hitchin rail station turn left into Walsworth Rd (B656)*

Named after a Lancastrian family who moved to Hitchin in the 16th century, the red-brick Radcliffe Arms dates from 1855 and is located in the town's 'Victorian Triangle'. Restored to its former glory a couple of years ago, this popular free house offers a range of weekly-changing local real ales, ten different gins and a comprehensive wine list. The à la carte menu might include butter bean and garlic soup with tiger prawn and lemon oil to begin; twice-cooked blade of beef accompanied by herbed mash, red cabbage and crispy root vegetables to continue; and sticky carrot cake in a toffee sauce to finish. Look out for the beer festivals, which happen two or three times a year. Booking for meals may be required.

Open all day all wk 8am-mdnt Closed: 26 Dec & 1 Jan **Bar Meals** Av main course £16 **Restaurant** L served all wk 12-2.30 D served all wk 6-9.30 Av 3 course à la carte fr £28 ⊕ FREE HOUSE ◀ Buntingford Twitchell, Polar Star, Grain Oak Ö Aspall Perronelle's Blush. ♀ 30 **Facilities** ✿ Children welcome Children's menu Children's portions Garden Beer festival Parking Wi-fi ⛟ (notice required)

HUNSDON
Map 6 TL41

The Fox and Hounds

PICK OF THE PUBS

See Pick of the Pubs on opposite page

LITTLE HADHAM
Map 6 TL42

The Nags Head

The Ford SG11 2AX ☎ **01279 771555**
e-mail: paul.arkell@virgin.net
dir: *M11 junct 8 take A120 towards Puckeridge & A10. Left at lights in Little Hadham. Pub 1m on right*

This warm and relaxed country pub was built in 1595 and still retains its traditional atmosphere, with an old bakery oven and a good range of real ales at the bar. Fish dishes such as poached skate with black butter and capers feature strongly on the full à la carte menu, which also includes a choice of steaks and vegetarian meals. At lunchtime, sandwiches and jacket potatoes offer a lighter alternative to hot main courses. Sit out the front on a good day and enjoy the countryside. Booking for meals may be required.

Open all wk 11.30-2.30 6-11 (Sun 12-10.30) **Bar Meals** L served Mon-Sat 12-2, Sun all day D served Mon-Sat 6-9, Sun all day Av main course £8-£17 **Restaurant** L served Mon-Sat 12-2, Sun all day D served Mon-Sat 6-9, Sun all day ⊕ GREENE KING ◀ Abbot Ale, Ruddles County & IPA, Morland Old Speckled Hen, Marston's Pedigree. ♀ 12 **Facilities** Children welcome Children's menu Children's portions Garden ⛟

NORTHAW
Map 6 TL20

The Sun at Northaw

1 Judges Hill EN6 4NL ☎ **01707 655507**
e-mail: reservations@thesunatnorthaw.co.uk
dir: *From M25 junct 24, A111 to Potters Bar. Right onto A1000, becomes High Street (B156). Follow to Northaw, pub on left*

On a picturesque village green, this Grade II listed inn has gained a reputation for its real ale, with up to seven available at any time. There is also an excellent wine list to complement cooking from chef and owner Oliver Smith, whose menus are driven by local, seasonal produce. An appetiser of beer-battered cod cheeks with tartare sauce might precede a starter of ham hock terrine with chutney and toast, followed by a main course of beef and kidney pie with a suet crust, swede and turnips. Finish with lemon tart with raspberry sorbet. Booking for meals may be required.

Open 12-5 6-11 Closed: Sun eve & Mon **Bar Meals** L served Tue-Sun 12-4 D served Tue-Sat 6-10 Av main course £15 **Restaurant** L served Tue-Sun 12-4 D served Tue-Sat 6-10 Fixed menu price fr £12.50 Av 3 course à la carte fr £25 ⊕ FREE HOUSE ◀ Adnams, Buntingford, Saffron Ö Millwhites, Aspall. ♀ 12 **Facilities** ✿ Children welcome Children's menu Children's portions Garden Parking Wi-fi

PERRY GREEN
Map 6 TL41

The Hoops Inn

SG10 6EF ☎ **01279 843568**
e-mail: reservations@hoops-inn.co.uk
dir: *From Ware on B1004 towards Bishop's Stortford right onto unclassified road to Perry Green*

Once home to Henry Moore, Perry Green is dotted with his famous sculptures. This comfortable dining inn is part of the estate and it boasts a chic country décor, contemporary furnishings and Moore-inspired artefacts. The food here draws a crowd thanks to mains of poached sea trout with spring vegetables; or Cornish lamb with spring greens. Excellent Sunday roasts can be walked off by visiting the Moore Foundation's estate just across the village green. There is a large front terrace and back garden to enjoy in the warmer weather. Booking for meals may be required.

Open all day 11.30-11 Closed: Jan-Mar, Mon **Bar Meals** Av main course £12-£15 food served all day **Restaurant** L served Tue-Sun 12-2.30 D served Tue-Sun 6-9.30 ⊕ FREE HOUSE ◀ Adnams Southwold Bitter, Guinness Ö Aspall, Thatchers. **Facilities** Children welcome Children's portions Garden Parking ⛟ (notice required)

PICK OF THE PUBS

The Fox and Hounds

HUNSDON   Map 6 TL41

2 High St SG12 8NH ☎ 01279 843999
e-mail: info@foxandhounds-hunsdon.co.uk
web: www.foxandhounds-hunsdon.co.uk
dir: *From A414 between Ware & Harlow take B180 in Stanstead Abbotts N to Hunsdon*

Owned and run by chef James Rix and wife Bianca, this renowned gastro-pub may be set in a sleepy Hertfordshire village, but it attracts food lovers from afar. There's an easy-going atmosphere thanks to a cosy winter fire warming the old bar, liberally supplied with Victorian-style furnishings. There is no pressure to do anything other than enjoy a glass of Adnams beer as the local drinkers do, but resistance is futile when you see James's imaginative, Mediterranean-inspired menu, which changes daily and evolves with the seasons. There's no doubting that the food side of the pub is the main draw here, and lunch and dinner can be taken in the bar or elegant, chandeliered dining room. James successfully combines traditional pub favourites (with a twist) with French and rustic Italian influences, and his simply described dishes champion local produce. Expect interesting combinations of ingredients, bold flavours and difficulty in choosing what to eat. Kick off with Normandy black pudding, chestnuts and fried duck egg; pigeon breast with sautéed wild mushrooms, pancetta and baby onions; or fish soup with rouille and croutons; then savour roast cod with olive oil mash and cod, mussel and prawn

sauce; or whole roast partridge with roast potatoes and braised Savoy cabbage; or splash out on a 30-day aged belted Galloway Chateaubriand for two, served with fat chips and béarnaise. Finish with a calorific dessert such as hot chocolate pudding with espresso ice cream, or poached pear and almond tart with crème fraîche, accompanied by a delicious 2007 Montbazillac dessert wine. Be sure to book for the excellent set Sunday lunches, the highlight being the roast rib of beef with all the trimmings. The tree-shaded garden, together with the heated, covered terrace is popular with both drinkers and alfresco diners. Booking for meals may be required.

Open 12-4 6-11 Closed: 26 Dec, Sun eve, Mon & BHs eve (Tue after BHs) **Bar Meals** L served Tue-Sun 12-3 D served

Tue-Sat 6.30-9.30 Av main course £14 **Restaurant** L served Sun 12-3.30 D served Fri-Sat 6.30-9.30 Fixed menu price fr £12.50 Av 3 course à la carte fr £26.50 ⊕ FREE HOUSE ◀ Adnams Southwold Bitter & Broadside, Guinness, Local ales ♂ Aspall. ♀ 9 **Facilities** Children welcome Children's menu Children's portions Play area ❖ Garden Parking Wi-fi

POTTEN END — Map 6 TL00

Martins Pond NEW

The Green HP4 2QQ ☎ 01442 864318
web: www.martinspond.com
dir: *A41 onto A416 signed Chesham, follow signs to Berkhamsted town centre. At lights straight over into Lower Kings Rd. Pass station, into Station Rd. Left at pub on opposite side of village green*

The unusual name refers to the village green where this welcoming pub is located. A section of Grim's Dyke, an ancient bank-and-ditch earthwork, is clearly visible nearby. By comparison the pub – dating from 1924 – is relatively new, but there's been a public house here since the 17th century. These days it's a good destination for home-cooked food such as crispy duck and filo parcels with spiced plums and red chard, followed by venison and smoked bacon meatballs with buttered Savoy cabbage and a red wine and cranberry gravy.

Open all day all wk Closed: 26 Dec **Bar Meals** L served Mon-Sat 12-2.30, Sun 12-7.30 D served Mon-Sat 6-9, Sun 12-7.30 **Restaurant** L served Mon-Sat 12-2, Sun 12-7.30 D served Mon-Sat 6-9, Sun 12-7.30 ⊕ FREE HOUSE ◄ Fuller's London Pride, Tetley's. ¶ 13 **Facilities** ✿ Children welcome Children's portions Garden Parking Wi-fi

See advert on opposite page

POTTERS CROUCH — Map 6 TL10

The Holly Bush

AL2 3NN ☎ 01727 851792
e-mail: info@thehollybushpub.co.uk
dir: *Ragged Hall Ln off A405 or Bedmond Ln off A4147*

Recently refurbished after passing into the hands of the previous landlords' daughter and son-in-law, The Holly Bush is a picturesque country pub with a large enclosed garden. There is a delightfully welcoming atmosphere and traditional and modern pub fare is offered. At lunch there's ploughman's, jacket potatoes, salads, various platters, and toasted sandwiches; while on the evening menu there might be fish pie, cod and pancetta pancakes, roasted chicken supreme, beef Bourguignon, and lamb kofta with Greek salad, grilled pittas and tzatziki. The pub is close to St Albans with its Roman ruins and good local walks.

Open all wk 12-2.30 6-11 (Sun 12-3) **Bar Meals** L served Mon-Sat 12-2, Sun 12-2.30 D served Wed-Sat 6-9 ⊕ FULLER'S ◄ London Pride, Chiswick Bitter, ESB, Seasonal ales. **Facilities** Garden Parking 🚌

RICKMANSWORTH — Map 6 TQ09

The Rose and Crown

Harefield Rd WD3 1PP ☎ 01923 897680
e-mail: roseandcrown@morethanjustapub.co.uk
dir: *M25 junct 17/18, follow Northwood signs. Past Tesco, pub 1.5m on right*

This 16th-century former farmhouse first became licensed in the mid-1700s. Around the wisteria-clad building, you'll find a large garden looking out across the lovely Colne Valley; the local stables, Field Ways, is popular with the film industry and Russell Crowe has enjoyed a pint here. The bar still retains its historic charm with low-beamed ceilings and real fires, while the kitchen prepares local produce such as meat from Daltons of Ickenham and Flexmore Farm. Lunchtime sandwiches and sharing platters are backed by favourite pies such as game or fish, while the dinner range broadens to include chargrilled steaks.

Open all day all wk 11am-11.30pm ⊕ MORE THAN JUST A PUB CO LTD ◄ Fuller's London Pride, Caledonian Deuchars IPA, Timothy Taylor Landlord. **Facilities** Children welcome Children's menu Children's portions Play area Garden Parking Wi-fi

SARRATT — Map 6 TQ09

The Cock Inn

Church Ln WD3 6HH ☎ 01923 282908
e-mail: enquiries@cockinn.net
dir: *M25 junct 18, A404 signed Chorleywood, Amersham. Right follow signs to Sarratt. Pass church on left, pub on right*

Dating from the 17th century, this traditional village pub stands opposite Sarratt's Norman church in the heart of the Chess Valley, a favoured walking area. Originally called the Cock Horse, it has head-cracking low beams, an inglenook fireplace and Hall & Woodhouse ales at the bar, while the ancient timbered barn houses the restaurant. Expect classic and imaginative pub dishes such as home-made chicken liver pâté followed by pan-fried sea bass fillets on crushed new potatoes with a spinach and coconut sauce. Light bites and sandwiches are served in the bar. Booking for meals may be required.

Open all day all wk **Bar Meals** L served Mon-Sat 12-2.30, Sun 12-6 D served Mon-Sat 6-9 Av main course £10.95 **Restaurant** L served Mon-Sat 12-2.30, Sun 12-6 D served Mon-Sat 6-9 Fixed menu price fr £12.95 Av 3 course à la carte fr £23 ⊕ HALL & WOODHOUSE ◄ Badger Tanglefoot, K&B Sussex Õ Westons Stowford Press. **Facilities** ✿ Children welcome Children's menu Children's portions Play area Garden Parking 🚌 (notice required)

SHENLEY — Map 6 TL10

The White Horse, Shenley

37 London Rd WD7 9ER ☎ 01923 853054
e-mail: enquiry@whitehorseradlett.co.uk
dir: *M25 junct 22, B556 then B5378 to Shenley*

The White Horse belies its 170-year-old foundation as a village pub, offering contemporary comforts and dining at the fringe of this green-belt village, with country walks to the Hertfordshire Way from the door. Bright, light and cheerful inside, with some quirky décor, it's an ideal place to sup a Sharp's Doom Bar bitter over a Sunday roast or crack a bottle from the extensive wine list and indulge in soft shell crab with crispy calamari, soy, ginger and chilli dip followed by pork fillet wrapped in sage and prosciutto with pistachio and blue cheese sauce, with white chocolate brûlée for dessert. Booking for meals may be required.

Open all day all wk 11-11 **Bar Meals** L served all wk 12-10 D served all wk 12-10 Av main course £13.95 food served all day **Restaurant** L served all wk 12-10 D served all wk 12-10 Fixed menu price fr £12.95 Av 3 course à la carte fr £22 food served all day ⊕ FREE HOUSE/ MITCHELLS & BUTLERS PLC ◄ Sharp's Doom Bar, Young's Õ Aspall. ¶ 12 **Facilities** ✿ Children welcome Children's menu Children's portions Garden Parking 🚌 (notice required)

STAPLEFORD — Map 6 TL31

Papillon Woodhall Arms ★★★ INN

17 High Rd SG14 3NW ☎ 01992 535123
e-mail: info@papillon-woodhallarms.com
dir: *On A119, between A602 & Hertford*

This is a pink-washed twin-gabled building behind a neat white picket fence, just a five-minute drive from the centre of Hertford. The bar serves well-kept ales in a welcoming atmosphere, plus a huge selection of snacks and pub favourites, including chicken curry, spaghetti bolognese and fresh mussels. The restaurant menu has roast saddle of lamb, veal escalopes, butternut squash pastry parcels, grilled halibut steak, and sautéed scallops. Desserts include individual pear and almond crumble, and a selection of sorbets. Accommodation is available in ten en suite bedrooms. Booking for meals may be required.

Open all wk 12-2 6.30-10.30 (Sun 12-2.30 6.30-10.30) **Bar Meals** L served all wk 12-2 D served Sun-Fri 6.30-10 **Restaurant** L served all wk 12-2 D served all wk 6.30-10 ⊕ FREE HOUSE ◀ Greene King IPA, Young's Special, St Austell Tribute, Black Sheep ☼ Aspall. ☂ 10 **Facilities** Children welcome Children's menu Children's portions Family room Garden Parking Wi-fi ▅ (notice required) **Rooms** 10

TRING | Map 6 SP91

The Cow Roast Inn

Cow Roast, London Rd HP23 5RF ☎ 01442 822287
e-mail: cowroastinn@btconnect.com
dir: Between Berkhamstead & Tring on A4251

Expect the unexpected at this former 16th-century coaching inn between Berkhamstead and Tring, where you will find a full-blown modern Thai restaurant amidst a traditional setting of oak beams, open fires and flagstone floors. Originally called the Cow Rest, it was frequented by local farmers en route to the London markets, while archaeological studies have found there was an important Roman settlement on the site. As well as authentic Thai dishes you can order classic bar meals, the choice ranging from steak and kidney suet pudding and battered cod and chips to lamb shank with mint gravy.

Open all day all wk **Bar Meals** L served all wk food served all day **Restaurant** L served Mon-Sat 12-3, Sun 12-5 D served Mon-Sat 5-9 ◀ Greene King Abbot Ale, Tring Side Pocket for a Toad, Guest ales ☼ Westons. **Facilities** ✿ Children welcome Children's menu Children's portions Garden Beer festival Parking Wi-fi ▅ (notice required)

WELWYN | Map 6 TL21

The White Hart ★★★ HL ◉

2 Prospect Place AL6 9EN ☎ 01438 715353
e-mail: bookings@thewhitehearthotel.net
dir: Just off A1(M) junct 6. On corner of Prospect Place (just past fire station), at the top of Welwyn High St

Just minutes away from the A1 but tucked away in an idyllic village, this 17th-century coaching inn with 13 luxury en suite guest rooms was once close to Dick Turpin's hunting ground. The olde-worlde beams and inglenook fireplace remain, but today they blend easily with contemporary wood floors, leather chairs and bold artwork. With one AA Rosette, the menus mix contemporary European style with the best of local produce, so expect the likes of game, bacon and pistachio terrine; steamed Norfolk mussels in white wine, garlic and parsley cream; beer-braised blade of beef with horseradish potato gratin; and seasonal specials. Booking for meals may be required.

Open all day all wk 7am-mdnt (Sun 9am-10.30pm) **Bar Meals** L served Mon-Sat 12-2.30 D served Mon-Sat

6.30-9.30 **Restaurant** L served all wk 12-2.30 D served Mon-Sat 6.30-9.30, Sun 6-8.30 Fixed menu price fr £10.95 Av 3 course à la carte fr £25 ⊕ CHARLES WELLS ◀ Bombardier & Eagle IPA, Young's London Gold ☼ Westons Stowford Press. ☂ 14 **Facilities** Children welcome Children's menu Children's portions Parking Wi-fi ▅ (notice required) **Rooms** 13

WELWYN GARDEN CITY | Map 6 TL21

The Brocket Arms

Ayot St Lawrence AL6 9BT ☎ 01438 820250 & 07984 282800
e-mail: bookings@brocketarms.com
dir: A1(M) junct 4 follow signs to Wheathampstead, then Shaw's Corner. Pub past Shaw's Corner on right

Parts of The Brocket Arms date back to 1378 when it was built as a monks' hostel; it became a tavern in the 1630s. The pub is encircled by a picturesque village that was once home to George Bernard Shaw. Huge oak beams and hefty hearths greet you along with a great range of real ales and wines. Food options range from Spanish frittata in the bar, to full meals such as wild mushroom risotto infused with truffle oil, followed by fish of the day with saffron, chorizo, mussel, clam and new potato broth. Finish with classic crème brûlée. Booking for meals may be required.

Open all day all wk 12-11 (Sun 12-10.30) **Bar Meals** L served all wk 12-2.30 D served Mon-Sat 5-9 Av main course £9 **Restaurant** L served all wk 12-2.30 D served Mon-Sat 7-9 ⊕ FREE HOUSE ◀ Nethergate Brocket Bitter, Greene King IPA & Abbot Ale, Sharp's Doom Bar, Adnams Broadside, Black Sheep, Guest ales ☼ Aspall. ☂ 18 **Facilities** ✿ Children welcome Children's menu Children's portions Play area Garden Parking Wi-fi ▅

WILLIAN | Map 12 TL23

The Fox ◉

PICK OF THE PUBS

SG6 2AE ☎ 01462 480233
e-mail: restaurant@foxatwillian.co.uk
dir: A1(M) junct 9 towards Letchworth, 1st left to Willian, 0.5m on left

The imposing Georgian building sits opposite the village pond and right next to the church, ideal aspects for the pub's two beer gardens. The Fox is a popular award-winning destination, attracting locals, walkers and cyclists to its range of ales and menus of modern British cooking. A clean, crisp look defines the interior, while the glazed restaurant atrium and enclosed courtyard are both pleasant places to settle down with a menu. It's overseen by Cliff Nye, known for his Norfolk coast pubs. No surprise, then, to find East Anglian brews from Woodforde's and Adnams at the bar; a fifth handpump dispenses guest ales from the pub's own Brancaster Brewery. Snacks include Jerusalem artichoke soup with truffle oil; or a more hearty beef and pork burger with cheese, sweet chilli relish and chips. For a proper meal look to the chef's specials for the likes of

rabbit and tarragon ballotine, followed by pan-seared chicken breast with Parisienne potatoes. Booking for meals may be required.

Open all day all wk 12-11 (Fri-Sat 12-12 Sun 12-10.30) **Bar Meals** L served Mon-Fri 12-2, Sat 12-6, Sun 12-3 D served Mon-Thu 6.30-9 Av main course £14.20 **Restaurant** L served Mon-Sat 12-2, Sun 12-3 D served Mon-Thu 6.45-9, Fri-Sat 6.30-9.15 Av 3 course à la carte fr £25.65 ⊕ FREE HOUSE ◀ Adnams Southwold Bitter, Woodforde's Wherry, Fuller's London Pride, Brancaster guest ales ☼ Aspall. ☂ 14 **Facilities** ✿ Children welcome Children's portions Garden Beer festival Parking Wi-fi

KENT

BEARSTED
Map 7 TQ85

The Oak on the Green

Bearsted Green ME14 4EJ ☎ 01622 737976
e-mail: headoffice@villagegreenrestaurants.com
dir: *In village centre next to green*

As its name suggests, this refurbished 17th-century pub overlooks Bearsted's pretty green and the front terrace, canopied under huge blue umbrellas, makes the most of its pleasant location. Once the village courthouse and prison, it is now a thriving gastro-pub. An eclectic modern menu offers an extensive choice, including Scottish steak (dry-aged up to 55 days) and pies (steak, port and stilton), alongside classic dishes like home-made sausages and mash, and imaginative specials, perhaps seared squid with garlic, chilli and coriander; and roast pork belly with rosemary and garlic gravy. Booking for meals may be required.

Open all day all wk Closed: 25 Dec **Bar Meals** L served Mon-Sat 12-5 D served Mon-Sat 12-10.30, Sun 12-9.45 food served all day **Restaurant** L served Mon-Sat 12-5 D served Mon-Sat 12-10.30, Sun 12-9.45 food served all day ⊕ FREE HOUSE ◀ Fuller's London Pride & ESB, Ringwood Old Thumper, 1648 Bee-Head Ŏ Biddenden. **Facilities** ❖ Children welcome Children's menu Children's portions Garden Parking 🚌

BENENDEN
Map 7 TQ83

The Bull at Benenden

PICK OF THE PUBS

The Street TN17 4DE ☎ 01580 240054
e-mail: enquiries@thebullatbenenden.co.uk
dir: *From A229 onto B2086 to Benenden. Or from Tenterden take A28 S towards Hastings. Right onto B2086*

In a classic Wealden village setting overlooking the village green and attractive cottages, The Bull dates from 1601 and has striking and unusual chinoiserie windows. The sympathetically refurbished interior boasts wooden floors, fat candles on scrubbed tables and an eclectic array of comfortable antique furniture. From the kitchen, expect top-notch pub food prepared from locally sourced ingredients, with main menu dishes including steak-and-kidney pudding, fresh cod in beer-batter, and wild rabbit stew. Daily specials include pan-fried Rye Bay scallops and vegetable balti, and don't miss the famous Sunday roasts – booking essential. The main bar, centring on an inglenook with integral seats, is where landlord Mark dispenses terrific local real ales – try a pint of Rother Valley Level Best - Biddenden cider and a decent perry selection. In summer, head outside to the secret garden or watch an innings or two from tables overlooking the cricket green.

Open all day all wk noon-2am **Bar Meals** L served Mon-Sat 12-2.30, Sun 12-4 D served Mon-Sat 6-9.20 **Restaurant** D served Fri-Sun 6-9.20 ⊕ FREE HOUSE ◀ Dark Star Hophead, Rother Valley Level Best, Larkins, Harvey's, Guest ales Ŏ Biddenden. **Facilities** ❖ Children

welcome Children's menu Children's portions Garden Parking 🚌 (notice required)

BIDDENDEN
Map 7 TQ83

The Three Chimneys

PICK OF THE PUBS

Biddenden Rd TN27 8LW ☎ 01580 291472
dir: *From A262 midway between Biddenden & Sissinghurst, follow Frittenden signs. (Pub seen from main road). Pub immediately on left in hamlet of Three Chimneys*

Worth remembering if visiting nearby Sissinghurst Castle, this 15th-century timbered treasure has every natural advantage of being a classic country pub, its original, small-roomed layout and old-fashioned furnishings remain delightfully intact. There are old settles, low beams, wood-panelled walls, worn brick floors, crackling log fires, soft evening candlelight, and an absence of music and electronic games. Modern-day demand for dining space has seen the addition of the rear Garden Room and a tasteful conservatory, and drinkers and diners spill out onto the secluded heated side patio and vast shrub-filled garden, which are perfect for summer eating. Food is seasonally bang up to date and listed on daily-changing chalkboards. Tuck into a hearty ploughman's lunch or salmon and smoked haddock fishcakes with tartare sauce, or something more substantial, perhaps roast duck with bubble-and-squeak and port jus, or pan-fried rib-eye steak with garlic butter. If you have room for afters, try the delicious sticky toffee pudding. Adnams ales and the heady Biddenden cider are tapped direct from cask. Booking for meals may be required.

Open all wk 11.30-3 5.30-11 (Sat-Sun 11.30-4 5.30-11) Closed: 25 Dec **Bar Meals** L served all wk 12-2.30 D served all wk 6.30-9.30 **Restaurant** L served all wk 12-2.30 D served all wk 6.30-9.30 ⊕ FREE HOUSE ◀ Harvey's Sussex Old Ale, Adnams Ŏ Biddenden. ▼ 10 **Facilities** ❖ Children welcome Children's portions Garden Parking

BOSSINGHAM
Map 7 TR14

The Hop Pocket

The Street CT4 6DY ☎ 01227 709866
dir: *Telephone for directions*

Birds of prey and an animal corner for children are among the more unusual attractions at this family pub in the heart of Kent. Canterbury is only five miles away and the county's delightfully scenic coast and countryside are within easy reach. As this is a free house there is a good range of ales to accompany dishes like fish pie, supreme of chicken, spicy salmon, Cajun beef, chilli nachos and fish platter. There is also an extensive range of sandwiches and omelettes.

Open all wk 11-3 6-12 (Sat & Sun all day) ⊕ FREE HOUSE ◀ Fuller's London Pride, Wadworth 6X, Adnams, Purity. **Facilities** Children welcome Children's portions Play area Garden Parking Wi-fi

BRABOURNE
Map 7 TR14

The Five Bells Inn

The Street TN25 5LP ☎ 01303 813334
e-mail: visitus@fivebellsinnbrabourne.com
dir: *5m E of Ashford*

Alison and John Rogers took over this 16th-century free house pub in 2010. A wood-fired oven is central to the menu, with many of the 'small plate' starters also available as main courses. Typical choices include pie or chargrilled breast of chicken with home-made barbecue sauce and topped with Kentish cheese and streaky bacon. The pub is surrounded by rolling hills and orchards, and is the perfect pitstop for walkers and cyclists who can enjoy a glass of local beer, cider and wine.

Open all day all wk ⊕ FREE HOUSE ◀ Goacher's, Hopdaemon, Brabourne Stout, Guest ales Ŏ Curious Brew, Biddenden. **Facilities** Children welcome Garden Parking Wi-fi

BROOKLAND
Map 7 TQ92

The Royal Oak

PICK OF THE PUBS

High St TN29 9QR ☎ 01797 344215
e-mail: info@royaloakbrookland.co.uk
dir: *A259, 5m E of Rye. In village by church*

The Royal Oak was built as a house in 1570 and connected to the church of St Augustine, one of only four churches in England with a separate bell tower. Since 1736 the Grade II listed marshland pub has been providing shelter and sustenance to locals and visitors to Romney Marsh. Its uncluttered, smart interior is a pleasing combination of original features and modern furnishings. The menus cater for everything from speedy lunchtime snacks to leisurely three-course dining. Regularly changing dishes draw on local, seasonal produce. Options could include pan-seared breasts of local wood pigeon; roasted stuffed red peppers; slow-cooked shank of Romney Marsh lamb; and chargrilled beefburger. The Sunday lunch menu offers traditional roasts of beef or lamb served with Yorkshire pudding, roast potatoes, seasonal vegetables and gravy. Every Wednesday evening is an inglenook spit-roast (booking essential). A well-kept and tranquil garden borders the churchyard.

Open 12-3 6-11 Closed: Sun eve & Mon **Bar Meals** L served Tue-Fri 12-2, Sat-Sun 12-2.30 D served Tue-Fri 6.30-9, Sat 6.30-9.30 **Restaurant** L served Tue-Fri 12-2, Sat-Sun 12-2.30 D served Tue-Fri 6.30-9, Sat 6.30-9.30 ⊕ ENTERPRISE INNS ◀ Harvey's Sussex Best Bitter, Adnams Southwold Bitter, Woodforde's Wherry, Guest ale Ŏ Westons Stowford Press. ▼ 20 **Facilities** ❖ Children's portions Garden Parking Wi-fi 🚌 (notice required)

2013 PUB GUIDE

Save on hotels. Book at theAA.com/hotel

KENT 299 ENGLAND

Woolpack Inn

PICK OF THE PUBS

Beacon Ln TN29 9TJ ☎ 01797 344321
dir: 1.5m past Brookland towards Rye on A259

Partly built of old timbers salvaged from local shipwrecks and isolated down a lane deep in Kentish marshland, this 15th-century cottage oozes character and charm. Built when smuggling was rife on Romney Marsh, it's rumoured that at one time the Woolpack had a secret tunnel used by smugglers to escape the Excise men. The old spinning wheel mounted on the bar ceiling was used to divide up their contraband; but, nowadays, the pub is ideally situated for those who wish to explore this unique and beautiful area of Kent. Open beams and a vast inglenook fireplace (you can sit in it!) add to the atmosphere. The chef makes extensive use of fresh produce including local game, and fish from the local fishermen. Lunchtime brings ploughman's, sandwiches and filled jacket potatoes. On the main menu, expect pub favourites like chicken Kiev, lamb shank and battered cod. Finish with the likes of bitter chocolate and orange sponge. There are barbecues in the two beer gardens on summer evenings.

Open all wk 11-3 6-11 (Sat 11-11 Sun 12-10.30 (open all day BH & school hols)) ◀ Shepherd Neame Spitfire, Master Brew. **Facilities** Children welcome Children's menu Children's portions Play area Family room Garden Parking

BURHAM
Map 6 TQ76

The Golden Eagle

80 Church St ME1 3SD ☎ 01634 668975
e-mail: kathy@thegoldeneagle.org
dir: S from M2 junct 3 or N from M20 junct 6 on A229, follow signs to Burham

Commanding striking views across the Medway Valley, this traditional Kentish village pub, which dates from 1850, has been famous locally for 30 years for its authentic Malaysian food. Expect to find an extensive menu, enhanced by chef specialities on the chalkboard, and featuring king prawn sambal; wortip crispy chicken; sweet and sour crispy pork; pad Thai chicken; and traditional puddings like apple crumble.

Open all wk Closed: 25-26 Dec ⊕ FREE HOUSE ◀ Wadworth 6X ♂ Westons Stowford Press. **Facilities** Parking

CANTERBURY
Map 7 TR15

The Chapter Arms

New Town St, Chartham Hatch CT4 7LT
☎ 01227 738340
e-mail: info@chapterarms.com
dir: 3m from Canterbury. Off A28 in Chartham Hatch or A2 at Upper Harbledown

This charming and picturesque free house sits on the North Downs Way in over an acre of gardens overlooking apple orchards and oast houses. It was once three cottages owned by Canterbury Cathedral's Dean and Chapter – hence the name. A comely choice of ales is offered in the bar, and food is freshly prepared to order by the talented kitchen team. Menus include lunch dishes such as traditional Aberdeen Angus beef suet pudding; home-baked honey-roast ham, eggs and hand-cut chunky chips; and Kentish lamb rump with spring onion mash, buttered leeks and mint velouté. There is also a good choice of local fish options. Look out for the Spoofers' Bar, where you can enjoy a game of spoof.

Open all wk 11-3 6-11 (Fri-Sun all day Jun-Sep) **Bar Meals** L served all wk 12-2.30 D served Mon-Sat 6.30-9 Av main course £10 **Restaurant** L served Mon-Sat 12-2.30, Sun 12-3 D served Mon-Sat 6.30-9 Av 3 course à la carte fr £23 ⊕ FREE HOUSE ◀ Shepherd Neame Master Brew, Wells Bombardier, Greene King IPA, Adnams, Harvey's, Young's, Guest ales ♂ Thatchers. ₸ 10 **Facilities** ✿ Children welcome Children's menu Children's portions Play area Garden Parking Wi-fi ▩

The Dove Inn ◉

PICK OF THE PUBS

Plum Pudding Ln, Dargate ME13 9HB ☎ 01227 751360
e-mail: doveatdargate@hotmail.com
dir: 6m from Canterbury; 4m from Whitstable. Telephone for detailed directions

Tucked down the delightfully named Plum Pudding Lane in a sleepy hamlet surrounded by orchards and farmland, the unpretentious honeysuckle- and rose-clad Dove draws discerning diners from far and wide for its top-notch food. The interior is simple and relaxed with stripped wooden floors and scrubbed tables. Outside is a gorgeous cottage garden where, appropriately, a dovecote and doves present an agreeably scenic backdrop for an alfresco meal or quiet pint. The Dove's menu is sensibly short and draws on quality local ingredients, which are soundly handled, offering a balanced choice of contemporary rustic dishes. After breads and olives for nibbles, start with pan-fried scallops with black pudding and parsnip purée, or foie gras and chicken liver parfait with shallot marmalade. For a main course, try the hake fillet with sautéed spinach and brown shrimps, or the aged rib-eye steak with triple-cooked chips and red wine jus, leaving room for apple and ginger crumble. Booking for meals may be required.

Open 12-3 6-12 (Fri 12-12 Sun 12-9 (Apr-Oct) 12-4 (Nov-Mar)) Closed: Mon **Bar Meals** L served Tue-Sat 12-2.30 D served Wed-Sat 6.30-9 Av main course £13.50 **Restaurant** L served Tue-Sun 12-2.30 D served Wed-Sat 7-9 Av 3 course à la carte fr £25 ⊕ SHEPHERD NEAME ◀ Master Brew, Spitfire, Seasonal ales. **Facilities** ✿ Children welcome Children's portions Garden Parking Wi-fi ▩ (notice required)

The Granville ◉

PICK OF THE PUBS

Street End, Lower Hardres CT4 7AL ☎ 01227 700402
e-mail: info@thegranvillecanterbury.com
dir: On B2068, 2m from Canterbury towards Hythe

Not far from Canterbury, this light and airy destination dining pub has a striking feature central fireplace/flue which draws the eye, at least temporarily, away from the series of roll-over art exhibitions and installations (lino cuts, photographs, sculptures) which add to its unique and contemporary character. With ample parking, a patio and large beer garden where summer barbecues take place, this Shepherd Neame pub is good for families and dogs, whilst locals indulge in a more traditional public bar. Don't, however, expect typical pub grub from the short, lively menu; the confident approach to utilising the best that Kent and the enfolding seas can provide has gained an AA Rosette for Gabrielle Harris and her team. You could start with chicken liver parfait with toast and pickles, followed perhaps by coq au vin or roast salmon fillet with pea sauce and crispy pancetta. To finish, maybe cherry Bakewell tart with whipped cream and Kirsch syrup. Booking for meals may be required.

Open 12-3 5.30-11 Closed: 26 Dec, Mon **Bar Meals** L served Tue-Sat 12-2 D served Tue-Sat 7-9 Av main course £15.95 **Restaurant** L served Tue-Sun 12-2 D served Tue-Sat 7-9 Fixed menu price fr £12.95 Av 3 course à la carte fr £27 ⊕ SHEPHERD NEAME ◀ Master Brew, Seasonal ale. **Facilities** ✿ Children welcome Children's portions Garden Parking Wi-fi

The Red Lion

PICK OF THE PUBS

High St, Stodmarsh CT3 4BA ☎ 01227 721339
e-mail: redlionstodmarsh@btconnect.com
dir: From Canterbury take A257 towards Sandwich, left into Stodmarsh Rd to Stodmarsh

Set in a tiny hamlet, The Red Lion has changed little since it was rebuilt after a fire in 1720. Surrounded by reed beds, which are home to marsh harriers, bearded tits and bitterns, the pub's interior, warmed by two large log fires, is adorned with traditional hop garlands, curios, antiques and a collection of international menus. From the kitchen expect a cosmopolitan and seasonally-changing menu blended with local produce. Salads come from allotments and gardens, meats from local farms, and wild mushrooms from surrounding woodland. Classic plates with a modern twist include deep-fried rabbit, fries and aïoli, or slow-cooked pork belly with butterbeans, chorizo and tomato. Outside is an extensive garden where an antique forge doubles as a barbecue during the summer months; here you'll find an abundance of flowers and hop bines, with ducks, chickens and rabbits wandering about. Over the August Bank Holiday weekend the pub holds a beer festival. Booking for meals may be required.

Open 11.30-3 5.30-11 (Sun 12-5) Closed: Sun eve & Mon **Bar Meals** L served Tue-Sat 12-2.15, Sun 12-2.30 D served Tue-Sat 6.30-9.15 Av main course £5-£8 **Restaurant** L served Tue-Sat 12-2.15, Sun 12-2.30 D served Tue-Sat 6.30-9.15 Av 3 course à la carte fr £23 ⊕ FREE HOUSE ◀ Greene King IPA & Ruddles County, Morland Old Speckled Hen, Hopdaemon Golden Braid ♂ Thatchers. **Facilities** Children welcome Children's menu Children's portions Play area Family room Garden Beer festival Parking Wi-fi ▩

CHARING — Map 7 TQ94

The Bowl Inn

Egg Hill Rd TN27 0HG ☎ 01233 712256
e-mail: info@bowl-inn.co.uk
dir: *M20 junct 8/9, A20 to Charing, then A252 towards Canterbury. Left at top of Charing Hill down Bowl Rd, 1.25m*

Standing high on top of the North Downs in an Area of Outstanding Natural Beauty, this popular pub was originally built as a farmhouse in 1512. For the past two decades, it has been run by the Paine family, who have retained the old-world charm courtesy of warming winter fires in the large inglenook fireplace. The well-priced menu includes bar snacks of spinach and feta cheese goujons, plus a main menu featuring cheese and ham ploughman's, sausage sandwiches and steak baps. An annual beer festival takes place in mid-July.

Open all wk Mon-Sat 12-12 Sun 12-11 (Mon-Thu 4-11 Fri-Sun 12-12 winter) **Bar Meals** L served all wk 12-9.30 summer only D served all wk 12-9.30 summer only food served all day ⊕ FREE HOUSE ◀ Fuller's London Pride, Adnams Southwold Bitter, Harvey's Sussex Best Bitter, Whitstable East India Pale Ale, Young's Bitter. **Facilities** Children welcome Garden Beer festival Parking Wi-fi 🚐

The Oak

5 High St TN27 0HU ☎ 01233 712612
e-mail: info@theoakcharing.co.uk
dir: *M20 junct 9, A20 towards Maidstone. 5m to Charing. Right into High St*

This gabled old inn in one of Kent's prettiest villages makes the most of its location, sourcing beers from Nelson, across the North Downs in Chatham, and harvesting produce from the bountiful surrounding acres of the 'Garden of England'. High-quality ingredients are sourced for the robust modern English menus. Fish from Hythe and Rye, pork and lamb from downland farms, and vegetables from local growers feature in dishes such as pan-seared fillet of smoked haddock on sautéed leeks with crème fraîche mash. Booking for meals may be required.

Open all wk 11-11 (Sun 12-10.30) ⊕ FREE HOUSE ◀ Shepherd Neame Master Brew, Nelson ☼ Thatchers Gold. **Facilities** Children welcome Children's menu Children's portions Garden Parking Wi-fi

CHIDDINGSTONE — Map 6 TQ54

Castle Inn
PICK OF THE PUBS

See Pick of the Pubs on opposite page

CHILHAM — Map 7 TR05

The White Horse
PICK OF THE PUBS

The Square CT4 8BY ☎ 01227 730355
e-mail: info@thewhitehorsechilham.co.uk
dir: *Take A28 from Canterbury then A252, in 1m turn left*

Set next to St Mary's church and opposite the 15th-century village square where the annual May Fair is held, this is one of the most photographed pubs in Britain. The square is a delightfully haphazard mix of gabled, half-timbered houses, shops, and inns dating from the late Middle Ages, with the North Downs Way passing through. Changing hands in 2011, this flint and stone inn offers a traditional atmosphere and modern cooking from menus based on fresh local produce, mainly organic. A meal might include brie and redcurrant parcel; chilli con carne; all-day breakfast salad; and home-made steak-and-ale pie. The bar menu offers sandwiches and ploughman's. Chocolate mousse, lemon posset and banoffee pie are among the desserts. There is a wide selection of real ales from local Kentish and more well-known breweries. Look out for live music nights. Booking for meals may be required.

Open all day all wk noon-close Closed: 25 Dec ⊕ ENTERPRISE INNS ◀ Shepherd Neame Master Brew, Guest ale. **Facilities** Children welcome Children's menu Children's portions Garden Beer festival

CHILLENDEN — Map 7 TR25

The Griffins Head
PICK OF THE PUBS

See Pick of the Pubs on page 302

CRANBROOK — Map 7 TQ73

The George Hotel

Stone St TN17 3HE ☎ 01580 713348
e-mail: georgehotel@shepherd-neame.co.uk
dir: *From A21 follow signs to Goudhurst. At large rdbt take 3rd exit to Cranbrook (A229). Hotel on left*

One of Cranbrook's landmark buildings, the 14th-century George Hotel traditionally served visiting buyers of locally made Cranbrook cloth. Magistrates held court here for over 300 years, and today the sophisticated interior mixes period features with contemporary décor, making the hotel a comfortable base for exploring Kent and Sussex. Two separate menus have been created; the brasserie offers a take on classic English cuisine - baked salmon fillet with spiced lentils and a sweet potato and pumpkin tarte Tatin, while in the restaurant diners can sample modern English dishes - honey-roasted duck breast and stuffed provençale courgettes with an orange and green peppercorn sauce perhaps.

Open all day all wk **Bar Meals** L served Sun-Fri 12-3, Sat all day D served Mon-Sat 6-9.30, Sun 6-9 Av main course £11.50 **Restaurant** L served Sun-Fri 12-3, Sat all day D served Mon-Sat 6-9.30, Sun 6-9 Fixed menu price fr £20 Av 3 course à la carte fr £28 ⊕ SHEPHERD NEAME ◀ Master Brew, Spitfire ☼ Thatchers. ♥ 16 **Facilities** ✿ Children welcome Children's menu Children's portions Garden Parking 🚐 (notice required)

DARTFORD — Map 6 TQ57

The Rising Sun Inn ★★★ INN

Fawkham Green, Fawkham, Longfield DA3 8NL ☎ 01474 872291
web: www.risingsun-fawkham.co.uk
dir: *0.5m from Brands Hatch Racing Circuit & 5m from Dartford*

Standing on the green in a picturesque village not far from Brands Hatch, The Rising Sun has been a pub since 1702. Inside you will find a bar full of character, complete with inglenook log fire, and Inglenooks restaurant where home-made traditional house specials and a large fish menu, using the best local produce, are served. There is also a front patio and garden for alfresco dining in warmer weather, plus comfortable en suite bedrooms if you would like to stay over.

Open all day all wk **Bar Meals** food served all day **Restaurant** L served all wk 12-3 D served all wk 6.30-9.30 ⊕ FREE HOUSE ◀ Courage Best & Directors, Fuller's London Pride, Timothy Taylor Landlord, Harvey's. ♥ 9 **Facilities** Children's portions Garden Parking Wi-fi **Rooms** 5

Save on hotels. Book at **theAA.com/hotel**

KENT 301 ENGLAND

PICK OF THE PUBS

Castle Inn

CHIDDINGSTONE   Map 6 TQ54

TN8 7AH ☎ 01892 870247
e-mail: info@castleinn-kent.co.uk
web: www.castleinn-kent.co.uk
dir: *1.5m S of B2027 between Tonbridge & Edenbridge*

If the Castle Inn strikes you as familiar there's probably a good reason: the pub is situated in the National Trust village of Chiddingstone, which has featured in many films and TV period dramas. The tile-hung inn dates from 1420 and boasts leaded casement windows and projecting upper gables. The pub sits at the end of a unique, unspoilt row of Tudor timbered houses opposite the parish church. The charming interior has remained delightfully unchanged over the years; the traditional bar has a quarry-tiled floor, and there are beams and old brick fireplaces, as well as rustic wall benches in the public bar. When the sun shines, head for the vine-hung courtyard or the peaceful, flower-filled garden. Chef-patron John McManus took over in 2010 and has significantly improved the food offering – which is hardly a surprise when you consider his impressive CV that includes time spent at top London restaurants Le Gavroche (where he was sous chef under Albert Roux) and The Connaught, where he worked with Michel Bourdin. Not that the food is excessively fancy; it matches the pubby setting perfectly. At lunchtime small appetites are satisfied by sandwiches (maybe Cumberland sausage with HP

Sauce and slow-cooked onions, or smoked salmon with lemon and chive cream cheese). For those seeking something more substantial by day or evening there are starters of potted smoked haddock with lime tartare sauce and parmesan salad, or potato and herb gnocchi with crispy salsify and fennel, followed by mains such as free-range chicken breast with bubble-and-squeak, wilted spinach and tarragon velouté; or shepherd's pie with pickled red cabbage and cheddar mash. Puddings such as treacle tart with almond and Chantilly cream or apple and rhubarb crumble with English custard keep with the traditional vibe. Larkins ales, nine wines by the glass and set Sunday lunches complete the picture.

Open all day all wk 11-11 (Sun 12-10.30) **Bar Meals** L served Mon-Fri

12-2, Sat-Sun 12-4 D served Mon-Sat 7-9.30 **Restaurant** L served Mon-Fri 12-2, Sat-Sun 12-4 D served Mon-Sat 7-9.30 ⊕ FREE HOUSE ◖ Larkins Traditional, Porter & Platinum Blonde, Harvey's Sussex ♨ Westons Stowford Press. ⬤ 9 **Facilities** Children welcome Children's menu Children's portions ✤ Garden Wi-fi ⌨ (notice required)

PICK OF THE PUBS

The Griffins Head

CHILLENDEN   Map 7 TR25

CT3 1PS ☎ 01304 840325
web: www.griffinsheadchillenden.co.uk
dir: *A2 from Canterbury towards Dover,*
then B2046. Village on right

Dating from 1286, when Edward I was on the English throne, this fine black-and-white, half-timbered Wealden hall house is an architectural gem. It was once part of the estate of John de Chillenden and for centuries was a farm and brewhouse, until in 1766 it was granted a full licence to serve travellers on what then was the main road from Canterbury to Deal, although it's hard to believe today. The building you see is Tudor, constructed around the original wattle-and-daub walls, some of which can be seen in one of the three mercifully unspoilt flagstone-floored rooms. Here you can sit at old scrubbed pine tables and on recycled church pews and take in the exposed brick walls and beams above your head. Owned by Shepherd Neame, it has been managed for more than 26 years by Jerry and Karen Copestake, who have won awards as testament to how well they do things here. The constantly changing seasonal menu is typically English and specialises in game from local estates and locally caught fish, especially haddock, cod, sea bass and sea bream. Typical dishes might include red-wine-marinated shoulder of lamb; warm salads with steak and roasted vegetables; chicken and ham pie; beef bourguignon; and traditional pub favourites like lambs' or calves' liver and bacon. Desserts include apple crumble, and home-made ice creams flavoured with passionfruit, ginger, raspberry or strawberry. The pretty garden, full of rambling roses and clematis, is especially popular during summer weekend barbecues. On the first Sunday of every month vintage and classic car enthusiasts turn up in their Armstrong Siddeleys, Austin 7s, MG TCs and other venerable vehicles. Local cricketers like to meet here too. Children are not allowed indoors. Booking for meals may be required.

Open all day Closed: Sun pm **Bar Meals** L served all wk 12-2 D served Mon-Sat 7-9.30 **Restaurant** L served all wk 12-2 D served Mon-Sat 7-9.30 ⊕ SHEPHERD NEAME ◗ Shepherd Neame. ☙ 10 **Facilities** Garden Parking

DOVER   Map 7 TR34

The White Cliffs Hotel ★★★ HL ◉

High St, St Margaret's at Cliffe CT15 6AT
☎ **01304 852400 & 852229**
e-mail: mail@thewhitecliffs.com
dir: *3m NE of Dover in centre of village*

A contemporary atmosphere and a refreshingly independent way of thinking characterise this traditional Kentish weather-boarded establishment. The hotel, with 15 bedrooms, has a stylish, contemporary feel without compromising the charm of this delightful historic building, with its winter log fires and bar leading out onto the rose-filled summer garden. Gavin Oakley brings imagination and flair to menus at The Bay Restaurant, which has earned him an AA Rosette, where main course offerings might include roasted corn-fed chicken breast with sweetcorn, rainbow chard and Madeira jus; and poached Hebridean loch salmon with chorizo, cannellini beans and mussels.

Open all wk ⊕ FREE HOUSE ◖ Adnams, Gadds' ♂ Westons Wyld Wood Organic, Aspall. **Facilities** Children welcome Children's menu Children's portions Garden Parking Wi-fi **Rooms** 15

FAVERSHAM   Map 7 TR06

Albion Taverna **NEW**

29 Front Brents ME13 7DH ☎ 01795 591411
e-mail: albiontaverna@yahoo.co.uk

Located near the Faversham swing bridge, the Albion Taverna looks directly onto the attractive waterfront area. Billed as a Mexican and English cook house, it has a colourful menu of spicy dishes such as shredded duck tacos followed by smoked chipotle meatballs with a tomato and chorizo sauce, Mexican rice, green salad and tzatziki dip. Other treats include mussels cooked country style, Spanish style or Mexican style; nachos with a variety of toppings; and quesadillas with a choice of fillings. For dessert, try churros with dark chocolate fondue.

Open all wk 12-3 6-11.30 (Sat-Sun 12-11.30) **Bar Meals** Av main course £10-£12 **Restaurant** L served Mon-Fri 12-3, Sat-Sun 12-10 D served Mon-Fri 6-10, Sat-Sun 12-10 ⊕ SHEPHERD NEAME ◖ Master Brew ♂ Thatchers Gold. **Facilities** Children welcome Children's menu Children's portions Play area Garden Beer festival Parking Wi-fi ▭ (notice required)

Shipwright's Arms

PICK OF THE PUBS

Hollowshore ME13 7TU ☎ 01795 590088
dir: *A2 through Ospringe then right at rdbt. Right at T-junct then left opposite Davington School, follow signs*

Although there has been a building on this site since the 13th century, the creekside Shipwright's Arms was first licensed in 1738 and has been a well-known spot for sailors and fishermen ever since. Once a popular haunt for pirates and smugglers, this homely brick and weatherboarded pub stands in a remote location on the Swale marshes. Best reached on foot or by boat, the effort in getting here is well rewarded as this charming, unspoilt tavern oozes historic character. Step back in time in the relaxed and comfortable bars, which boast nooks and crannies, original timbers, built-in settles, well-worn sofas, wood-burning stoves, and a wealth of maritime artefacts. Locally-brewed Goacher's and Whitstable ales are tapped straight from the cask, and make for a perfect match for the simple, traditional bar food: hot smoked mackerel; mushroom Stroganoff; macaroni cheese; sausage, mash and peas; and fresh fish caught by the local trawler.

Open 11-3 6-10 (Sat-Sun 11-4 6-11 in winter; Sat 11-11 Sun 12-10.30 in summer) Closed: Mon (Oct-Mar) **Bar Meals** L served Mon-Sat 11-2.30, Sun 12-2.30 D served Tue-Sat 7-9 (no food Tue-Thu eve in winter) **Restaurant** L served Tue-Sat 11-2.30, Sun 12-2.30 D served Tue-Sat 7-9 (no food Tue-Thu eve in winter) ⊕ FREE HOUSE ◖ Goacher's, Hopdaemon, Whitstable, Local ales. ♟12 **Facilities** Children welcome Children's menu Children's portions Family room Garden Parking ▭

FORDCOMBE   Map 6 TQ54

Chafford Arms

TN3 0SA ☎ 01892 740267
e-mail: chaffordarms@btconnect.com
web: www.chaffordarms.com
dir: *On B2188 (off A264) between Tunbridge Wells, East Grinstead & Penshurst*

This visually striking country inn, with multiple gables and tall chimneys has hints of Arts and Crafts about it. Set in The Weald high above the Medway Valley, close to Penshurst Place and handy for Hever Castle, fine walking on the Weald Way is rewarded by the prospect of beers from local micro-breweries and a menu of comforting, home-made pub meals like fisherman's pie or Italian

meatball linguine. Hunker down beside roaring log fires or rest awhile in the rose-scented garden, with great views of pretty countryside.

Open all day all wk 11am-mdnt **Bar Meals** L served Mon-Sat 12-9, Sun 12-7 D served Mon-Sat 12-9, Sun 12-7 food served all day **Restaurant** L served Mon-Sat 12-9, Sun 12-7 D served Mon-Sat 12-9, Sun 12-7 food served all day ⊕ ENTERPRISE INNS ◖ Larkins Best Bitter, Harvey's Sussex Best Bitter. ♟9 **Facilities** ✿ Children welcome Children's menu Garden Parking ▭

GOODNESTONE   Map 7 TR25

The Fitzwalter Arms

The Street CT3 1PJ ☎ 01304 840303
e-mail: fitzwalterarms@gmail.com
dir: *Signed from B2046 & A2*

A pub since 1702, the 'Fitz' is hostelry to the Fitzwalter Estate. Quintessentially English, it is a place of conviviality and conversation. Jane Austen was a frequent visitor to nearby Goodnestone Park after her brother, Edward, married into the family. Look out for daily home-made pies such as steak and kidney, ham and chicken and cottage pie, and a range of roasts on Sundays. Change of hands. Booking for meals may be required.

Open Tue-Thu 12-3 6-11 (Mon 6-11 Fri-Sat noon-1am Sun 12-11) Closed: Mon L **Bar Meals** L served Tue-Sun 12-3 D served all wk 6-9 Av main course £9 **Restaurant** L served Tue-Sat 12-3, Sun 12-7 D served all wk 6-9 Fixed menu price fr £9.50 ⊕ SHEPHERD NEAME ◖ Master Brew, Spitfire, Early Bird. **Facilities** Children welcome Children's portions Garden Wi-fi ▭ (notice required)

GOUDHURST   Map 6 TQ73

Green Cross Inn

TN17 1HA ☎ 01580 211200
dir: *A21 from Tonbridge towards Hastings turn left onto A262 towards Ashford. 2m, Goudhurst on right*

In an unspoiled corner of Kent, close to Finchcocks Manor, and originally built to serve the Paddock Wood–Goudhurst railway line, which closed in 1968, this thriving dining pub specialises in fresh seafood. Arrive early to bag a table in the dining room, prettily decorated with fresh flowers, and tuck into Cornish cock crab, sea bass with spring onions, ginger, soy sauce and white wine, or seafood paella, or go for the fillet steak pan fried with peppercorns, brandy and cream, followed by pannacotta with raspberry coulis; all freshly prepared by the chef-owner who is Italian and classically trained. Booking for meals may be required.

Open all wk 12-3 6-11 Closed: Sun eve **Bar Meals** L served all wk 12-2.30 D served Mon-Sat 7-9.45 Av main course £12 **Restaurant** L served all wk 12-2.30 D served Mon-Sat 7-9.45 Av 3 course à la carte fr £25 ⊕ FREE HOUSE ◖ Harvey's Sussex Best Bitter, Guinness ♂ Biddenden. **Facilities** Children welcome Children's portions Garden Parking ▭ (notice required)

GOUDHURST continued

The Star & Eagle ★★★★ INN

PICK OF THE PUBS

High St TN17 1AL ☎ 01580 211512
e-mail: starandeagle@btconnect.com
dir: *Just off A21 towards Hastings. Take A262 into Goudhurst. Pub at top of hill next to church*

At 400 feet above sea level the 14th-century Star & Eagle has outstanding views of the orchards and hop fields that helped earn Kent the accolade 'The Garden of England'. The vaulted stonework suggests that this rambling, big-beamed building may once have been a monastery, and the tunnel from the cellars probably surfaces underneath the neighbouring parish church. The ten bedrooms and the public rooms boast original features and much character. Adnams and Harvey's are the mainstays in the bar, and there's plenty of choice in wines served by the glass. While supping, unwind and enjoy choosing between the fine traditional and continental dishes prepared under the guidance of Spanish chef-proprietor Enrique Martinez. Typical dishes are large grilled Portuguese sardines; and roast pork belly with caramelised apples, dauphinoise potatoes, braised red cabbage and sultanas, and a cream and red wine sauce. Finish with apple, blackberry and hazelnut crumble and custard.

Open all day all wk 11-11 (Sun 12-3 6.30-10.30) **Bar Meals** L served all wk 12-2.30 D served all wk 7-9.30 **Restaurant** L served all wk 12-2.30 D served all wk 7-9.30 ⊕ FREE HOUSE ◀ Adnams Southwold Bitter, Harvey's. ☞ 14 **Facilities** Children welcome Children's menu Children's portions Family room Garden Parking Wi-fi ☞ **Rooms** 10

GRAVESEND — Map 6 TQ67

The Cock Inn

Henley St, Luddesdowne DA13 0XB ☎ 01474 814208
e-mail: andrew.r.turner@btinternet.com
dir: *Telephone for directions*

Dating from 1713, this award-winning whitewashed free house in the beautiful Luddesdowne Valley has two traditional beamed bars with wood-burning stoves and open fires. Always available are seven well-kept real ales, Köstritzer and other German beers, and not a fruit machine, jukebox or television in sight. All food is ordered at the bar: expect filled submarine rolls, basket meals and home-made cod and chips; steak, mushroom and Irish stout pie; and spinach and ricotta ravioli. As an adults-only pub, no-one under 18 is allowed.

Open all day all wk 12-11 (Sun 12-10.30) **Bar Meals** L served all wk 12-3 D served all wk 6-8 ⊕ FREE HOUSE ◀ Adnams Southwold Bitter, Broadside & Lighthouse, Shepherd Neame Master Brew, Goacher's Real Mild Ale, Woodforde's Wherry. **Facilities** ☜ Garden Parking

HALSTEAD — Map 6 TQ46

Rose & Crown

Otford Ln TN14 7EA ☎ 01959 533120
e-mail: info@roseandcrownhalstead.co.uk
dir: *M25 junct 4, follow A21, London (SE), Bromley, Orpington signs. At Hewitts Rdbt 1st exit onto A224 signed Dunton Green. At rdbt 3rd exit into Shoreham Ln. In Halstead left into Station Rd, left into Otford Ln*

This flint-and-brick free house knows how to win friends and influence people, thanks to its impressive six-pump array of real ales, including Larkins Traditional, Whitstable East India Pale and even a mild. The food in this lively local appeals too, of course, with all-day home-made baps and sandwiches, jacket potatoes, salads and dishes such as lamb shank; chicken and rib combo; scampi and chips; and macaroni cheese. Regular events include spring, summer and autumn beer festivals, barbecues, hog roasts and live jazz. The refurbished Stables serves cream teas and cakes.

Open all day all wk **Bar Meals** L served all wk 12-11 D served all wk 12-11 food served all day **Restaurant** L served all wk 12-11 D served all wk 12-11 food served all day ⊕ FREE HOUSE ◀ Larkins Traditional, Whitstable East India Pale Ale, Guest ales Ò Westons. ☞ **Facilities** Children welcome Children's menu Children's portions Play area Garden Beer festival Parking Wi-fi ☞

HARRIETSHAM — Map 7 TQ85

The Pepper Box Inn

ME17 1LP ☎ 01622 842558
e-mail: enquiries@thepepperboxinn.co.uk
dir: *From A20 in Harrietsham take Fairbourne Heath turn. 2m to x-rds, straight over, 200yds, pub on left*

High up on the Greensand Ridge this delightful 15th-century country pub enjoys far-reaching views over the Weald of Kent from its terrace. Run by the same family since 1958, it takes its name from an early type of pistol, a replica of which hangs behind the bar. Using the best of local seasonal produce, food ranges from bar snacks of ham, egg and chips or chicken curry through to tiger prawns pan fried in garlic, chilli and ginger butter, followed by slow-roasted belly pork with cider, apples, thyme and mashed potatoes. Booking for meals may be required.

Open all wk 11-3 6-11 ⊕ SHEPHERD NEAME ◀ Master Brew, Spitfire, Late Red. **Facilities** Garden Parking

HAWKHURST — Map 7 TQ73

The Black Pig at Hawkhurst

Moor Hill TN18 4PF ☎ 01580 752306
e-mail: enquiries@theblackpigathawkhurst.co.uk
dir: *On A229, S of Hawkhurst*

A year on and Mark and Lucy Barron-Reid's second pub, a stylishly refurbished community pub on Moor Hill, continues to thrive and gain praise for its locally sourced food. Like their first pub, the Bull at Benenden (see entry) a few miles east, the ethos is to specialise in food and drink from Kent and Sussex, so expect to find Copper Top ale from the Old Dairy Brewery in Rolvenden, and simple, home-cooked food – mixed seafood risotto, local rabbit burger, shoulder of lamb with mustard mash, garlic and rosemary jus, and a fish and seafood sharing platter. Booking for meals may be required.

Open all day all wk 11am-mdnt **Bar Meals** L served Mon-Sat 12-2.30, Sun 12-4 D served all wk 6.30-9.30 ⊕ FREE HOUSE ◀ Dark Star Hophead, Larkins Traditional, Old Dairy Copper Top, Harvey's Ò Biddenden. **Facilities** ☜ Children welcome Children's menu Children's portions Garden ☞

The Great House

PICK OF THE PUBS

Gills Green TN18 5EJ ☎ 01580 753119
e-mail: enquiries@thegreathouse.net
dir: *Just off A229 between Cranbrook & Hawkhurst*

This wonderfully atmospheric 16th-century free house with its network of exposed beams, roaring log fires and stone floors is set in the heart of the Kentish Weald. The three dining areas are complemented by the magnificent Orangery that opens on to a Mediterranean-style terrace and a garden with a lychgate. The French chef creates traditional English and regional French brasserie-style cuisine. The food is fresh, seasonal and, in the case of the meat, organic too. Start with a deli board to share, Thai crab cakes or Maldon oysters. The sophisticated main course choices include lamb rump with fondant potato, braised red cabbage, fine beans and redcurrant juice; spicy root vegetable tagine with orange and almond couscous and harissa dressing; and king prawn linguine with sweet chilli, tomato, garlic, ginger and coriander. Desserts range from chocolate brownie to Drambuie crème brûlée. Seventy world wines include some from nearby Tenterden.

Open all day all wk 11.30-11 **Bar Meals** L served Mon-Fri 12-3, Sat-Sun 12-9.45 D served Mon-Fri 6-9.45, Sat-Sun 12-9.45 Av main course £12 **Restaurant** L served Mon-Fri 12-3, Sat-Sun 12-9.45 D served Mon-Fri 6-9.45, Sat-Sun 12-9.45 Av 3 course à la carte fr £24 ⊕ FREE HOUSE ◀ Harvey's, Guinness Ò Biddenden, Aspall. ☞ 20 **Facilities** Children welcome Children's portions Garden Parking Wi-fi

HERNHILL   Map 7 TR06

The Red Lion NEW

Crockham Ln ME9 9JR ☎ 01227 751207
e-mail: enquiries@theredlion.org
dir: M2 junct 7, A299 signed Whitstable, Herne Bay & Ramsgate. Follow Fostall sign, up slip road. Right, signed Fostall & Hernhill. In Hernhill pub on left

Overlooking the church and green in a picturesque village near the bustling town of Faversham, this traditional inn dates back to the 14th century and contains many original features in the beamed, flagstoned bar and upstairs restaurant. The food is just as traditional and the menu offers old favourites such as steak-and-kidney pudding or beer-battered cod and chips alongside more contemporary dishes as Thai chicken with rice. The enclosed beer garden includes a large play area for children. Look out for the summer beer festival. Booking for meals may be required.

Open all wk 11.30-3 6-11 (Fri-Sat 12-11 Sun 12-10.30) **Bar Meals** L served Mon-Sat 12-3, Sun 12-8 D served Mon-Sat 6-9, Sun 12-8 Av main course £8-£9 **Restaurant** L served Mon-Sat 12-3, Sun 12-8 D served Mon-Sat 6-9, Sun 12-8 Av 3 course à la carte fr £15.50 ⊕ FREE HOUSE ◀ Sharp's Doom Bar, Fuller's London Pride, Adnams Broadside. ♇ 12 **Facilities** ♣ Children welcome Children's menu Children's portions Play area Family room Garden Beer festival Parking Wi-fi ☁

HEVER   Map 6 TQ44

The Wheatsheaf

Hever Rd, Bough Beech TN8 7NU ☎ 01732 700254
dir: M25 & A21 take exit for Hever Castle & follow signs. 1m past Castle on right

Originally built as a hunting lodge for Henry V, this splendid creeper-clad inn has some stunning original features, including a crown post revealed during renovation in 1997. Timbered ceilings and massive Tudor fireplaces set off various curios, such as the mounted jaw of a man-eating shark, and a collection of musical instruments. Food served all day encompasses light lunches from Monday to Saturday; the daily board menu may include houmous with olives and pitta bread, followed by lightly spiced pork casserole. Real ales include Harvey's Sussex Best and interesting ciders like Kentish Biddenden served by handpump.

Open all day all wk 11am-11.30pm ⊕ FREE HOUSE ◀ Harvey's Sussex Best Bitter, Westerham Grasshopper ⊘ Biddenden, Westons Stowford Press. **Facilities** Children welcome Children's menu Garden Parking

HODSOLL STREET   Map 6 TQ66

The Green Man

TN15 7LE ☎ 01732 823575
e-mail: the.greenman@btinternet.com
dir: On North Downs between Brands Hatch & Gravesend off A227

This 300-year-old, family-run pub is loved for its decent food and real ales. It stands in the picturesque village of Hodsoll Street on the North Downs, surrounded by beautiful Kent countryside, with a large garden for warmer weather. Food is prepared to order using fresh local produce, and includes a wide variety of fish such as stuffed trout with Thai prawns or salmon fillet with hollandaise sauce, as well as a range of steaks and grills, plus dishes like lamb shank with red wine jus, cherry tomato and stilton risotto; and roast duck with plum sauce and onion marmalade.

Open all wk 11-2.30 6-11 (Fri-Sun all day) **Bar Meals** L served Mon-Fri 12-2, Sat 12-3, Sun all day D served Mon-Sat 6.30-9.30, Sun all day **Restaurant** L served Mon-Fri 12-2, Sat 12-3, Sun all day D served Mon-Sat 6.30-9.30, Sun all day ⊕ HAYWOOD PUB COMPANY LTD ◀ Timothy Taylor Landlord, Morland Old Speckled Hen, Harvey's, Guest ale. **Facilities** Children welcome Children's menu Children's portions Play area Garden Parking ☁

ICKHAM   Map 7 TR25

The Duke William ★★★ INN

The Street CT3 1QP ☎ 01227 721308 & 721244
e-mail: goodfood@dukewilliam.biz
dir: A257 Canterbury to Sandwich. In Littlebourne turn left opposite The Anchor, into Nargate St. 0.5m turn right into Drill Ln, then right into The Street

This family-friendly, whitewashed free house with a log fire and four guest rooms is in the heart of Ickham village. Traditional, locally sourced and home-cooked food is the keynote here; the Sunday lunches are particularly popular. Menu choices might include fresh fish, venison or slow-roast pork, all served with local vegetables. Chicken liver pâté and rabbit casserole could appear on the daily specials menu. The lovely garden features a covered patio, as well as a children's play area with a swing and slide. Booking for meals may be required.

Open all day all wk **Bar Meals** L served all wk 12-3 D served all wk 6.30-10 Av main course £9.95 **Restaurant** L served all wk 12-2.30 D served all wk 6.30-10 Fixed menu price fr £9.95 Av 3 course à la carte fr £20 ⊕ FREE HOUSE ◀ Shepherd Neame Master Brew, Harvey's, Adnams ⊘ Westons Stowford Press. ♇ 9 **Facilities** ♣ Children welcome Children's menu Children's portions Play area Garden Wi-fi ☁ (notice required) **Rooms** 4

IDEN GREEN   Map 6 TQ73

The Peacock

Goudhurst Rd TN17 2PB ☎ 01580 211233
dir: A21 from Tunbridge Wells to Hastings, onto A262, pub 1.5m past Goudhurst

A Grade II listed building dating from the 14th century with exposed brickwork, low beams, an inglenook fireplace, and ancient oak doors. Seasonal ales can be found amongst the Shepherd Neame handles in the convivial bar. Popular with families, The Peacock offers a wide range of traditional pub food made using produce from local farmers; children may be served smaller portions from the main carte or choose from their own menu, and in summer they can use the large enclosed garden with fruit trees and picnic tables on one side of the building.

Open all day all wk 12-11 (Sun 12-6) **Bar Meals** L served Mon-Fri 12-2.30, Sat all day, Sun 12-3 D served Mon-Fri 6-8.45, Sat all day Av main course £9 **Restaurant** L served Mon-Fri 12-2.30, Sat all day, Sun 12-3 D served Mon-Fri 6-8.45, Sat all day ⊕ SHEPHERD NEAME ◀ Master Brew, Spitfire, Seasonal ales. **Facilities** ♣ Children welcome Children's menu Children's portions Family room Garden Beer festival Parking Wi-fi ☁ (notice required)

IGHTHAM   Map 6 TQ55

The Harrow Inn

PICK OF THE PUBS

Common Rd TN15 9EB ☎ 01732 885912
dir: 1.5m from Borough Green on A25 to Sevenoaks, signed Ightham Common, turn left into Common Rd. Inn 0.25m on left

Tucked away down country lanes, yet easily accessible from both the M20 and M26, this creeper-hung, stone-built free house dates back to at least the 17th century. The two-room bar area has a great brick fireplace, open to both sides and piled high with logs, while the restaurant's vine-clad conservatory opens on to a terrace that's ideal for a pint of Loddon Hoppit or Gravesend Shrimpers and warm weather dining. Menus vary with the seasons, and seafood is a particular speciality: fish lovers can enjoy dishes such as crab and ginger spring roll; swordfish with Cajun spice and salsa; or pan-fried fillets of sea bass with lobster cream and spinach. Other main courses may include baked sausage with gammon, fennel, red onions and garlic; and tagliatelle with wild mushroom, fresh herb, lemongrass and chilli ragout. The car park is fairly small, although there's adequate street parking. Booking for meals may be required.

Open 12-3 6-11 Closed: 1wk between Xmas & New Year, Sun eve & Mon ⊕ FREE HOUSE ◀ Loddon Hoppit, Gravesend Shrimpers. **Facilities** Children welcome Children's portions Family room Garden Parking

IVY HATCH — Map 6 TQ55

The Plough at Ivy Hatch

PICK OF THE PUBS

See Pick of the Pubs on opposite page

LAMBERHURST — Map 6 TQ63

The Vineyard NEW

Lamberhurst Down TN3 8EU ☎ 01892 890222
e-mail: enquiries@thevineyard.com
dir: *From A21 follow brown Vineyard signs onto B2169 towards Lamberhurst. Left, continue to follow Vineyard signs. Straight on at x-rds, pub on right*

Next to the historic Lamberhurst vineyards, this 17th-century country inn re-opened at the start of 2012 after a major refurbishment. The new rustic look incorporates chunky wood furniture with murals telling the story of the region's winemaking history. Local produce dominates the menu, which might feature pea and mint soup followed by new season rack of lamb or fish pie. Enjoy a pint of Harvey's ale or one of the 20 wines available by the glass in the bar or in the large garden if the weather dictates.

Open all day all wk 11.30-11 **Bar Meals** L served Mon-Fri 12-6, Sat-Sun 12-9.30 D served Mon-Fri 6-9.45, Sat-Sun 12-9.30 Av main course £14.95 food served all day **Restaurant** L served Mon-Fri 12-3, Sat-Sun 12-9.45 D served Mon-Fri 6-9.45, Sat-Sun 12-9.45 Av 3 course à la carte fr £24 ⊕ FREE HOUSE ◀ Sharp's Doom Bar, Harvey's, Old Dairy Ŏ Aspall. ♇ 20 **Facilities** ♣ Children welcome Children's portions Garden Parking

LEIGH — Map 6 TQ54

The Greyhound Charcott

Charcott TN11 8LG ☎ 01892 870275
e-mail: ghatcharcott@aol.com
dir: *From Tonbridge take B245 N towards Hildenborough. Left onto Leigh road, right onto Stocks Green road. Through Leigh, right then left at T-junct, right into Charcott (Camp Hill)*

This cosy pub has been welcoming locals and visitors for around 120 years and you can expect a traditional atmosphere in which music, pool table and fruit machine have no place. Winter brings log fires, while in summer you can relax in the garden with a pint of locally brewed Westerham British Bulldog. From a changing menu begin with leek and mussel crumble before tucking into monkfish and crayfish risotto, or braised local pheasant served with roasted root vegetables and a thyme and red wine sauce. Snacks include ploughman's, sandwiches and classics like cod and chips.

Open all wk 12-3 5.30-11 (Sat-Sun all day) **Bar Meals** L served Mon-Sat 12-2, Sun 12-3 D served Mon-Sat 6.30-9.30 **Restaurant** L served Mon-Sat 12-2, Sun 12-3 D served Mon-Sat 6.30-9.30 ⊕ ENTERPRISE INNS ◀ Woodforde's Wherry, Westerham British Bulldog BB, Harvey's Ŏ Westons Stowford Press. ♇ 12

Facilities Children welcome Children's portions Garden Parking Wi-fi 🚌 (notice required)

LINTON — Map 7 TQ75

The Bull Inn

Linton Hill ME17 4AW ☎ 01622 743612
e-mail: food@thebullatlinton.co.uk
dir: *S of Maidstone on A229 (Hastings road)*

Built in 1674, this part-timbered former coaching inn stands high on the Greensand Ridge, with wonderful views and sunsets over the Weald from the garden and large decked area. Inside there is a large inglenook fireplace and lots of beams, and a bar serving Shepherd Neame and a wide-ranging menu that includes hearty sandwiches and pub classics – perfect sustenance for walkers tackling the Greensand Way. Along with a popular Sunday carvery, the bistro offers Goan-style tiger prawn curry, wild boar steak with plum sauce, and sticky toffee pudding.

Open all day all wk 11am-11.30pm (Sun 12-10.30) **Bar Meals** L served all wk 12-9 D served all wk 12-9 food served all day **Restaurant** L served all wk 12-9 D served all wk 12-9 food served all day ◀ Shepherd Neame Master Brew, Kent's Best, Late Red Ŏ Thatchers Gold. **Facilities** ♣ Children welcome Children's menu Children's portions Garden Parking Wi-fi 🚌

MAIDSTONE — Map 7 TQ75

The Black Horse Inn ★★★★ INN

Pilgrim's Way, Thurnham ME14 3LD ☎ 01622 737185
e-mail: info@wellieboot.net
dir: *M20 junct 7, A249, right into Detling. Opposite Cock Horse Pub turn onto Pilgrim's Way*

Converted from a forge in the mid-18th century, this popular free house is smack beside the Pilgrim's Way and tucked just below the North Downs ridge. You'll find plenty of old-world Kentish charm in the beamed bar with its open fires - perfect for quaffing pints of Harvey's Sussex Best Bitter and local Biddenden cider. The candlelit restaurant serves a good range of imaginative British and continental cuisine, including smoked duck and celeriac remoulade. There are 27 stylish annexe bedrooms to the rear of the inn. Enjoy your drink or dine outside in the lovely garden with its fish and duck pond.

Open all day all wk **Bar Meals** L served all wk 12-6 D served all wk 6-10 Av main course £10 food served all day **Restaurant** L served all wk 12-6 D served all wk 6-10 Fixed menu price fr £12 Av 3 course à la carte fr £25 food served all day ⊕ FREE HOUSE ◀ Greene King IPA, Wychwood Hobgoblin, Westerham Grasshopper, Harvey's Sussex Best Bitter, Black Sheep Ŏ Biddenden. ♇ 21 **Facilities** ♣ Children welcome Children's menu Children's portions Garden Parking 🚌 (notice required) **Rooms** 27

MARKBEECH — Map 6 TQ44

The Kentish Horse

Cow Ln TN8 5NT ☎ 01342 850493
dir: *3m from Edenbridge & 7m from Tunbridge Wells. 1m S of Hever Castle*

Surrounded by Kent countryside, this pub is popular with ramblers, cyclists and families, as well as having a strong local following. Situated in four acres with views over Ashdown Forest, there is an extensive garden and children's play area. The menu is cooked simply from fresh ingredients, and can be served anywhere in the pub or garden. Real ales always available are Harvey's and locally-brewed Larkins.

Open all day all wk **Bar Meals** L served Mon-Sat 12-2.30, Sun 12-3.30 D served Mon-Sat 7-9.30 ⊕ FREE HOUSE ◀ Harvey's, Larkins. **Facilities** Children welcome Play area Garden Parking 🚌

NEWNHAM — Map 7 TQ95

The George Inn

44 The Street ME9 0LL ☎ 01795 890237
e-mail: hotchefpaul@msn.com
dir: *4m from Faversham*

Landlords Paul and Lisa Burton's attractive country inn was first licensed in 1718, after decades as a farm. It almost has its own bus - well, the timetable for the 344 from Sittingbourne shows it as a stop. Beams, wooden floors, inglenook and candlelit tables instil it with great character. Locally sourced food includes lunchtime home-made soups and ploughman's; at dinner, pan-fried sea bass; slow-roasted belly pork in cider; and juicy sirloin steaks. The pub calendar is full of events. James Pimm, inventor of the eponymous fruit cup, came from Newnham. Booking for meals may be required.

Open all wk 11.30-3 6.30-11 (Sun 11.30-6.30) Closed: 26 Dec **Bar Meals** L served Mon-Sat 12-2.30, Sun 12-4.30 D served Mon-Sat 7-9.30 **Restaurant** L served Mon-Sat 12-2.30, Sun 12-4.30 D served Mon-Sat 7-9.30 ⊕ SHEPHERD NEAME ◀ Master Brew, Kent's Best, Seasonal ale Ŏ Thatchers Gold. ♇ 8 **Facilities** Children welcome Children's menu Children's portions Garden Parking Wi-fi 🚌 (notice required)

Save on hotels. Book at **theAA.com/hotel**

KENT 307 **ENGLAND**

PICK OF THE PUBS

The Plough at Ivy Hatch

IVY HATCH Map 6 TQ55

High Cross Rd TN15 0NL
☎ **01732 810100**
e-mail: info@theploughivyhatch.co.uk
web: www.theploughivyhatch.co.uk
dir: *Exit A25 between Borough Green &
Sevenoaks, follow Ightham Mote signs*

This tile-hung 17th-century free house
stands in the picturesque village of Ivy
Hatch, just a short walk from the National
Trust's Ightham Mote, Britain's best
preserved medieval house. Owners Miles
and Anna have renovated the bar area,
conservatory and dining room to restore
the pub to the centre of its small
community. The Plough offers everything
from drinks for weary walkers to full meals
for hungry families – and the smart oak
flooring and seating area around the
fireplace make this the perfect spot for a
lingering lunch or supper. Beers are from
the Tunbridge Wells Brewery and the wine
list covers New and Old World. The modern
British menu with its European highlights
aims to please all tastes and budgets.
Menus are updated daily, driven by locally
produced seasonal ingredients including
south coast seafood and seasonal game
from local shoots, and the food is freshly
cooked with no frozen or bought-in dishes.
The comfort food bar menu offers venison
liver and bacon with mash; local sausages
with black pudding; and brunch – bacon,
sausage, poached egg and trimmings.
Starters from the main menu might
include spiced parsnip soup, field
mushroom and spinach on toast with
garlic butter and a poached egg, or
Cornish smoked paprika squid. Moving on
to the main course, expect dishes like
pan-fried grey mullet fillet; confit leg and
pan-fried breast of pheasant with bubble-
and-squeak or filo pastry basket with wild
mushrooms, butternut squash, spinach
and roquefort. Desserts include baked
apple with amaretti crumble and hazelnut
praline ice cream, or brioche and
chocolate chip bread-and-butter pudding.
There is also a great sweet and savoury
pancake menu. With lots of good walks in
the area, there is no need to worry about
squelching back to the pub in muddy
boots, as the terrace and garden are ideal
for alfresco dining. The Plough is now
open for brunch, Monday to Friday
mornings from 9am.

Open all wk 9-3 6-11 (Sat 12-11 Sun
10-6) Closed: 1 Jan **Bar Meals/
Restaurant** L served Mon-Sat 12-2.45,
Sun 12-6 D served Mon-Sat 6-9.30
⊞ FREE HOUSE ◖ Tunbridge Wells
Royal, Porter & Dipper, Kent Pale
Ŏ Westons Stowford Press. ♥ 10
Facilities Children welcome Children's
menu Children's portions Garden
Parking Wi-fi 🚌 (notice required)

PICK OF THE PUBS

The Bottle House Inn

PENSHURST Map 6 TQ54

Coldharbour Rd TN11 8ET
☎ **01892 870306**
e-mail: info@thebottlehouseinnpenshurst.co.uk
web: www.thebottlehouseinnpenshurst.co.uk
dir: *A264 W from Tunbridge Wells onto B2188 N. After Fordcombe left towards Edenbridge & Hever. Pub 500yds after staggered x-rds*

Down a country lane is the historic, weatherboarded Bottle House, and a handsome sight it is. Built as a farmhouse in 1492, it wasn't until 1806 that it was granted a licence to sell ales and ciders, later diversifying to function as a shop, farrier's and cobbler's too. Major refurbishment in 1938 unearthed hundreds of old bottles, the reason, of course, for its unusual name. Later improvements, all tastefully executed, include ancient oak beams sandblasted back to their natural colour, brickwork exposed and walls painted in pleasingly neutral shades. At the copper-topped bar counter choose between Harveys of Lewes and Chiddingstone-brewed Larkins hand-pumped beers, or a wine from one of the 11 served by the glass, then settle at a bench seat on the patio or in the garden. The menus change regularly to capitalise on the availability of seasonal produce, while the specials board is never the same from one day to the next. Light bites might include baked whole camembert with Rusbridge artisan bread and house chutney; and chilli con carne and rice topped with sour cream and cheese. Starters are equally appealing – chicken liver and cranberry pâté with toasted brioche; or

pan-fried scallops with pea purée, black pudding and red pepper coulis, for instance. Among the dozen or so main course options to choose from are chicken breast wrapped in bacon, stuffed with mozzarella and basil, and served with dauphinoise potato, fine beans and spicy tomato sauce; Bottle House burger with smoked cheddar and house chutney; and oven-roasted skate wing with lime and coriander butter. Among the home-made desserts, you're likely to find mango and passionfruit cheesecake with fruit coulis; and cappuccino crème brûlée with crushed amaretti brittle. On Sundays, in addition to the carte, three different roast meats are served.

Open all day all wk 11-11 (Sun 11-10.30) Closed: 25 Dec **Bar Meals** L served Mon-Sat 12-10, Sun & BH 12-9

D served Mon-Sat 12-10, Sun & BH 12-9 Av main course £13 food served all day **Restaurant** L served Mon-Sat 12-10, Sun & BH 12-9 D served Mon-Sat 12-10, Sun & BH 12-9 Fixed menu price fr £22.50 Av 3 course à la carte fr £22.50 food served all day ⊕ FREE HOUSE ◀ Harvey's Sussex Best Bitter, Larkins. ▼ 11 **Facilities** Children welcome Children's menu Children's portions ❦ Garden Parking ▭ (notice required)

Save on hotels. Book at **theAA.com/hotel**

KENT 309 ENGLAND

PENSHURST
Map 6 TQ54

The Bottle House Inn
PICK OF THE PUBS

See Pick of the Pubs on opposite page

The Leicester Arms

High St TN11 8BT ☎ **01892 870551**
dir: From Tunbridge Wells take A26 towards Tonbridge. Left onto B21765 towards Penshurst

A large and picturesque country inn at the centre of an attractive village, The Leicester Arms stands in its own pretty gardens looking out over the River Medway. It was once part of the Penshurst Place Estate. The wood-panelled dining room is worth a visit for the views over the Weald and river alone. Dishes range from traditional pub food in the bar to the likes of pressed pork belly with crackling, chicken curry, or Moroccan vegetable tagine from the carte menu.

Open all wk 11am-mdnt ⊕ FREE HOUSE/ENTERPRISE INNS ◀ Harvey's Sussex Best Bitter, Shepherd Neame Master Brew, Sharp's Doom Bar ♂ Westons Stowford Press. **Facilities** Children welcome Children's menu Garden Parking

The Spotted Dog
PICK OF THE PUBS

Smarts Hill TN11 8EE ☎ **01892 870253**
e-mail: chezzy47@gmail.com
dir: Off B2188 between Penshurst & Fordcombe

This weatherboarded inn started life as a row of old cottages, and which now form a welcoming pub with open fires, a forest of low beams and oak-board floors. There's also a terrace with fantastic views in the summer. The Spotted Dog is nestled in the folds of the Weald close to two magnificent stately homes, Penshurst Place and

Hever Castle. Kentish ales from Larkins are just another excellent reason to stop here, along with the bang up-to-date menu, making the most of the produce grown in this richly endowed countryside. Sample a starter of baked figs stuffed with camembert and drizzled with honey, precursor to game casserole; grilled sea bass fillets served with sautéed potatoes; or fishcakes of the day – traditional English with a twist, enhanced by a daily-changing specials board.

Open all day all wk **Bar Meals** L served Mon-Fri 12-2.30, Sat 12-9.30 D served Mon-Fri 6-9, Sat 12-9.30 Av main course £10 **Restaurant** L served Mon-Fri 12-2.30, Sat 12-9.30, Sun 12-5.30 D served Mon-Fri 6-9, Sat 12-9.30 Fixed menu price fr £9.95 Av 3 course à la carte fr £22 ⊕ FREE HOUSE ◀ Sharp's Doom Bar, Larkins Traditional, Harvey's, Guest ale ♂ Chiddingstone. ♟ 10 **Facilities** ❧ Children welcome Children's menu Children's portions Garden Parking Wi-fi 🚌

PLUCKLEY
Map 7 TQ94

The Dering Arms
PICK OF THE PUBS

Station Rd TN27 0RR ☎ **01233 840371**
e-mail: jim@deringarms.com
dir: M20 junct 8, A20 to Ashford. Right onto B2077 at Charing to Pluckley

Follow signs to Pluckley Station to locate this imposing-looking pub. Built as a hunting lodge in 1840 for the Dering family, this handsome building boasts curving Dutch gables, rounded triple lancet 'Dering' windows, and a rather spooky grandeur. The interior is all high ceilings, flagstone and board floors, open log fires, oak panelling, and there's a family room with a baby grand piano (there to be played). The extensive daily menus reflect the chef's love of fresh fish and seafood, as in starters of Provençale fish soup, sardines grilled with rosemary butter, and garlic king prawns. In addition to Jim's seafood special for two people – a platter

overflowing with traditional fruits de mer, there's confit duck with bubble-and-squeak, and rib-eye steak with black pepper, brandy and cream. There is a classic car meet on the second Sunday of the month.

Open Mon-Fri 11.30-3.30 6-11 (Sat 9am-11pm Sun 9-5) Closed: 26-29 Dec, Sun eve **Bar Meals** L served Mon-Fri 12-2.30, Sat all day, Sun 9-5 D served Mon-Sat 6.30-9 Av main course £12.50 **Restaurant** L served Mon-Fri 12-2.30, Sat all day, Sun 9-5 D served Mon-Sat 6.30-9 Av 3 course à la carte fr £30 ⊕ FREE HOUSE ◀ Goacher's Best Dark Ale, Gold Star Ale, Old Ale ♂ Biddenden. ♟ 8 **Facilities** ❧ Children welcome Children's portions Family room Garden Parking

ROLVENDEN
Map 7 TQ83

The Bull

1 Regent St TN17 4PB ☎ **01580 241212**
e-mail: thebullinnkent@yahoo.com
dir: Just off A28, approx 3m from Tenterden

Close to the walled garden that inspired Frances Hodgson Burnett's classic tale *The Secret Garden* and handy, too, for steam trains of the Kent and East Sussex Railway, this handsome, tile hung village inn dates, in part, back to the 13th century. There's a welcome focus on local beers and produce, with a heart-warming, pubby menu enhanced by modern dishes like scallops with a Martini and cream sauce, followed by sea bream and flash-fried calamari with lemon and dill sauce and crushed new potatoes. There's a great beer garden overlooking the village cricket ground.

Open all day all wk **Bar Meals** Av main course £9 food served all day **Restaurant** Fixed menu price fr £14 Av 3 course à la carte fr £21 food served all day ⊕ FREE HOUSE ◀ Red Top, Harvey's ♂ Westons Stowford Press. ♟ 12 **Facilities** ❧ Children welcome Children's menu Children's portions Garden Beer festival Parking Wi-fi

PICK OF THE PUBS

The Coastguard

ST MARGARET'S BAY   Map 7 TR34

CT15 6DY ☎ **01304 853176**
e-mail: bookings@thecoastguard.co.uk
web: www.thecoastguard.co.uk
dir: *A258 between Dover & Deal follow St Margaret's at Cliffe signs. 2m, through village towards sea*

Sitting on the suntrap terrace here, the hazy smudge on the horizon is likely to be the French coast, shimmering beyond the silently passing ferries and freighters. Crane your neck upwards and the view of Blighty's fine countryside is cut off by – well – Blighty's most famous natural feature; the White Cliffs of Dover thrust upwards behind this convivial waterside inn. The popular Heritage Coast footpath passes the door, whilst the watersport fans beach their kayaks here to indulge in a half of Gadds' The Ramsgate No 5 bitter or a sip of Rough Old Wife cider; Fyne Ales from western Scotland are also on handpump here, reflecting owner Nigel Wyndmus's roots. The food from Nigel's wife Sam and her team is renowned for its wonderful flavours, and all freshly made on the premises from local produce as far as possible. Many dishes have a story behind them: they might be based on an old Roman recipe, a reworked classic dish, or perhaps an

original creation in response to something particularly outstanding that becomes available. The menus change twice daily, depending on the weather and what's available. Bar bites and starters feature local pork and cider pie; rabbit and mushroom parfait with truffle oil and Melba toast; or a smoked haddock, spinach and cheddar omelette, enough for nibblers. Those with heartier appetites may progress to hot devilled crab topped with mature cheddar, smoked haddock roasted with a Shetland mussel and saffron cider cream, or gratin of Kentish broccoli with cider, mushrooms and leeks. Calorific desserts abound, or tackle the pub's award-winning Waterloo cheeseboard.

Open all day all wk 11-11 (Sun 11-10.30) ⊕ FREE HOUSE ◄ Gadds' The Ramsgate No 5, Fyne, Adnams ♂ Kent, Rough Old Wife, Hogan's.
Facilities Children welcome Children's portions Garden Beer festival Parking Wi-fi

Save on hotels. Book at **theAA.com/hotel**

KENT 311 ENGLAND

ST MARGARET'S BAY
Map 7 TR34

The Coastguard

PICK OF THE PUBS

See Pick of the Pubs on opposite page

SANDWICH
Map 7 TR35

George & Dragon Inn

Fisher St CT13 9EJ ☎ 01304 613106
e-mail: enquiries@georgeanddragon-sandwich.co.uk
web: www.georgeanddragon-sandwich.co.uk
dir: *Between Dover & Canterbury*

Built in 1446, ale was first sold here in 1549, but was only licensed under the name of George & Dragon in 1615. This town centre pub oozes charm and character, with its wood floors and open fires, and makes a welcome pitstop when exploring historic Sandwich on foot. Run by two brothers, you can refuel with a pint of well-kept Shepherd Neame Master Brew or a guest ale. The lunch board includes dishes like grilled pork with root vegetable mash, or chicken and mushroom pie. On the monthly-changing evening menu, expect rump of lamb on curried chickpeas, or butternut squash tart with sage parmesan crumble. Head outside to the picturesque suntrap courtyard in summer. Booking for meals may be required.

Open 11-3 6-11 (Sat 11-11 Sun 12-4) Closed: Sun eve **Bar Meals** L served all wk 12-2 D served Mon-Sat 6-9 **Restaurant** L served all wk 12-2 D served Mon-Sat 6-9 ⊕ ENTERPRISE INNS ◀ Shepherd Neame Master Brew, Guest ales ♂ Aspall. ♥ 9 **Facilities** ❤ Garden Wi-fi

See advert on page 309

SELLING
Map 7 TR05

The Rose and Crown

Perry Wood ME13 9RY ☎ 01227 752214
e-mail: info@roseandcrownperrywood.co.uk
dir: *From A28 right at Badgers Hill, left at end. 1st left signed Perry Wood. Pub at top*

Goldings hops are draped around this rambling, low-beamed 16th-century inn, with exposed brickwork, inglenooks, horse brasses, corn dollies and a bar offering Harvey's Sussex, Adnams Southwold real ales and Biddenden cider. Descend to the restaurant, where the ghost of Hammond Smith, murdered after a boozy day in 1889, may join you, but don't let his presence detract from the pleasure of home-cooked Kent fish pie; lamb shank; chicken and carrot casserole; or brie, bacon and walnut jacket potato. The flower-festooned garden is made for summer eating and drinking. Check for beer festival dates.

Open all wk 12-3 6.30-11 Closed: 25-26 Dec eve, 1 Jan eve, Mon eve **Bar Meals** L served all wk 12-2 D served Tue-Sat 6.30-9 **Restaurant** L served all wk 12-2 D served Tue-Sat 6.30-9 ⊕ FREE HOUSE ◀ Adnams Southwold Bitter, Harvey's Sussex Best Bitter, Guest ale ♂ Westons Stowford Press, Biddenden. **Facilities** ❤ Children welcome Children's menu Children's portions Play area Garden Beer festival Parking 🚐 (notice required)

SHIPBOURNE
Map 6 TQ55

The Chaser Inn

PICK OF THE PUBS

Stumble Hill TN11 9PE ☎ 01732 810360
e-mail: enquiries@thechaser.co.uk
dir: *N of Tonbridge take A227. Pub on left on main road*

The award-winning Chaser Inn takes its name from the pub's long association with the nearby Fairlawne racing stable, where the late Peter Cazalet trained horses for the Queen Mother and other leading owners. Once a haunt for stars such as Richard Burton and Elizabeth Taylor, it is now an informal, relaxed village inn, next to the church and overlooking the common, with log fires, a lovely beer garden and a covered courtyard that comes into its own in the winter months. Well-kept real ales, such as Old Speckled Hen, and plenty of wines by the glass are complemented by an extensive menu of sandwiches, light bites and main courses such as Irish lamb stew with root vegetables, pearl barley and Savoy cabbage; pan-roasted breast of chicken with bacon and mushroom risotto; and grilled High Field Farm sirloin of beef with grilled flat mushrooms, vine tomatoes, peppercorn sauce and chips.

Open all day all wk ⊕ WHITING AND HAMMOND ◀ Greene King IPA & Abbot Ale, Morland Old Speckled Hen, Guest ales. **Facilities** Children welcome Children's portions Garden Parking Wi-fi

SMARDEN
Map 7 TQ84

The Chequers Inn

PICK OF THE PUBS

The Street TN27 8QA ☎ 01233 770217
e-mail: spaldings@thechequerssmarden.com
dir: *Through Leeds village, left to Sutton Valence/ Headcorn then left for Smarden. Pub in village centre*

The former weavers' village of Smarden has around 200 buildings of architectural and historical interest, one of which is the clapboarded 14th-century Chequers Inn. Its beautiful landscaped garden features a large carp pond and an attractive south-facing courtyard. Ales brewed by Harvey's and Adnams are served in the low-beamed bars, and a beer festival is planned. Seasonal ingredients are sourced locally for the menus of traditional and modern food. Typical of the restaurant choices are starters of mussels and squid in a spicy sauce with garlic bread; and main courses like pan-fried chicken stuffed with goat's cheese and wrapped in bacon. The bar menu, carte and children's menu are all served on Sundays too, when traditional beef, lamb and pork roasts are joined by gammon and turkey. Time your visit for a Thursday evening if the weekly steak deal for two, including a carafe of wine, appeals.

Open all day all wk **Bar Meals** L served all wk 12-3 D served all wk 6-9 **Restaurant** L served all wk 12-3 D served all wk 6-9 ⊕ FREE HOUSE ◀ Harvey's, Adnams, Hancock's. **Facilities** Children welcome Children's menu Children's portions Garden Beer festival Parking Wi-fi 🚐

SPELDHURST
Map 6 TQ54

George & Dragon

PICK OF THE PUBS

Speldhurst Hill TN3 0NN ☎ 01892 863125
e-mail: julian@speldhurst.com
dir: *Telephone for directions*

Inside this award-winning, timber-clad village hostelry, built around 1500, possibly earlier, is a modern gastro-pub, and a very successful one too. The bar serves Larkins bitter, made about three miles away, Westerham Brewery's specially produced George's Marvellous Medicine, and local organic fruit juices. The seasonal menu promises organic, free-range and GM-free produce whenever possible, with just about everything drawn from within a 30-mile radius. British pub classics include Ashdown Forest venison stew with herb dumpling; and Speldhurst pork sausages, mash and onion gravy. A starter of a tin bucket of shell-on prawns, lemon and saffron aïoli could be followed by Turners Hill pheasant breast in bacon with confit leg and dauphinoise potato; chargrilled chicken salad with pine nuts and chorizo; or pan-fried fillets of wild sea bass with sautéed potatoes, poached fennel, roasted tomatoes and clams. Alphabetically, wines are from the Barossa Valley in Australia to Valdobbiadene in Italy. Booking for meals may be required.

continued

SPELDHURST *continued*

Open all day all wk **Bar Meals** L served all wk 12-2.30 D served Mon-Sat 7-9.45 **Restaurant** L served Sat 12-3, Sun 12-4 D served Fri 7-10, Sat 6.30-10 ⊕ FREE HOUSE ◀ Harvey's Sussex Best Bitter, Westerham George's Marvellous Medicine, Larkins Ŏ Westons Stowford Press. ₹ 11 **Facilities** Children welcome Children's portions Family room Garden Parking Wi-fi ⊞

STONE IN OXNEY
Map 7 TQ92

The Crown Inn

TN30 7JN ☎ **01233 758302**
e-mail: enquiries@thecrowninnstoneinoxney.co.uk
dir: *From Tenterden take B2082 towards Rye. Through Wittersham, in approx 0.75m left towards Stone in Oxney. Inn in 1.5m at bottom of hill*

In a hamlet on the Isle of Oxney, this 300-year-old, tile-hung pub with a contemporary interior is close to the old cliff-line above Romney Marsh, once the seabed. In the bar, Larkins' and Shepherd Neame's Kent-brewed ales and a big inglenook; in the wood-floored dining room menus vary according to the day of the week: on Thursdays and Fridays the Bistro menu offers home-made lasagne; leek and potato-topped fish pie; and feta, leek and parmesan 'pielets'. Wood-fired pizzas are prepared on Fridays and Saturdays. A west-facing patio overlooks the countryside. Booking for meals may be required.

Open 12-3 6-11 (Sun 12-5) Closed: Jan, Sun eve & Mon **Bar Meals** L served Tue-Sat 12-2, Sun 12.30-2.30 D served Tue-Sat 6.30-9 ⊕ FREE HOUSE ◀ Larkins Traditional, Shepherd Neame Spitfire. **Facilities** ❖ Children welcome Children's portions Garden Parking Wi-fi ⊞ (notice required)

STOWTING
Map 7 TR14

The Tiger Inn **NEW**

TN25 6BA ☎ **01303 862130**
e-mail: info@tigerinn.co.uk

Lost down winding lanes in a scattered North Downs hamlet, the 250-year-old Tiger Inn oozes traditional character and rural charm. The front bar is delightfully rustic and unpretentious, with stripped oak floors, two warming wood-burning stoves, old cushioned pews, and scrubbed old pine tables. Mingle with the locals at the bar with a pint of Master Brew, then order a hearty meal from the inviting chalkboard menu – Romney Marsh rack of lamb with redcurrant jus, whole Dover sole, chicken, ham and leek pie with shortcrust pastry. In summer dine alfresco on the suntrap front terrace. There are super local walks.

Open all day Closed: Tue **Bar Meals** L served Mon, Wed-Sun 12-9 D served Mon, Wed-Sun 12-9 Av main course £14 food served all day **Restaurant** L served Mon, Wed-Sun 12-9 D served Mon, Wed-Sun 12-9 food served all day ⊕ FREE HOUSE ◀ Shepherd Neame Master Brew, Harvey's, Old Dairy, Gadds', Hop Fuzz Ŏ Biddenden. ₹ 10 **Facilities** ❖ Children welcome Children's menu Children's portions Garden Parking Wi-fi ⊞

TENTERDEN
Map 7 TQ83

White Lion Inn

57 High St TN30 6BD ☎ **01580 765077**
e-mail: whitelion.tenterden@marstons.co.uk
dir: *On A28 (Ashford to Hastings road)*

This 16th-century coaching inn stands on a broad tree-lined street in 'the Jewel of the Weald'. Renovated and rejuvenated, the pub combines its many original features with a contemporary look and feel. Reasonably priced fresh food ranges from starters of roasted Portobello mushrooms, or shredded duck in crisp filo pastry, to mains such as harissa lamb kebabs or chicken Caesar salad. Look out for special offers on pub classics served all day. Reliable Marston's ales are the mainstay in the bar. Booking for meals may be required.

Open all wk 10am-11pm (wknds 10am-mdnt) ⊕ MARSTON'S ◀ Pedigree, Jennings Cumberland Ale. **Facilities** Children welcome Children's menu Children's portions Garden Parking Wi-fi

TONBRIDGE

See Penshurst

TUDELEY
Map 6 TQ64

The Poacher **NEW**

Hartlake Rd TN11 0PH ☎ **01732 358934**
e-mail: enquiries@thepoachertudeley.co.uk
dir: *A21 S onto A26 E, at rdbt turn right. After 2m turn sharp left into Hartlake Rd, 0.5m on right*

Cross Oak Inns lavished money on this unassuming rural pub a few years back and the result is impressive. Expect acres of wood floor, modern brown banquette seating, contemporary artwork on the walls, and a long, slate-fronted bar counter dispensing Doom Bar and local Tonbridge ales. Chunky low tables, a few plush stools and ultra-trendy striped chairs, and floor-to-ceiling wine chillers enhance the great 'bar' atmosphere. In keeping, food is bang up to date, so expect sharing platters, cinnamon braised pork belly; venison and root vegetable stew; steaks and burgers; and good puddings like pear and almond tart with ginger anglaise. Tudeley church is worth a visit to see the famous Chagall windows.

Open all wk 12-3.30 5.30-11 (Sun 12-10.30) Closed: 25 Dec **Bar Meals** L served all wk 12-2.30 D served all wk 6-9.30 Av main course £11 **Restaurant** L served all wk 12-2.30 D served all wk 6-9.30 Av 3 course à la carte fr £25 ⊕ FREE HOUSE/CROSS OAK INNS ◀ Sharp's Doom Bar, Shepherd Neame Spitfire, Tonbridge Ŏ Westons Stowford Press. ₹ 10 **Facilities** Children welcome Children's menu Children's portions Garden Parking ⊞ (notice required)

TUNBRIDGE WELLS (ROYAL)
Map 6 TQ53

The Beacon ★★★★ INN

PICK OF THE PUBS

See Pick of the Pubs on opposite page

The Crown Inn

The Green, Groombridge TN3 9QH ☎ **01892 864742**
e-mail: crowngroombridge@hotmail.co.uk
dir: *Take A264 W of Tunbridge Wells, then B2110 S*

Dating back to 1585, in the 18th century this charming free house was the infamous headquarters for a gang of smugglers. They hid their casks of tea in the passages between the cellar and Groombridge Place, which was later home to Sir Arthur Conan Doyle, who made The Crown his local. Today, its low beams and an inglenook fireplace are the setting for some great food and drink. Favourites include home-made pies, battered haddock, Cumberland sausage and mash, breaded scampi, and daily specials based on fresh local produce. Eat alfresco during the summer months. Booking for meals may be required.

Open all wk 11-3 6-11 (Sat 11-11 Sun 12-10.30 summer; Sun 12-5 winter) **Bar Meals** L served Mon-Fri 12-2.30, Sat-Sun 12-3 D served Mon-Thu 6.30-9, Fri-Sat 6.30-9.30 Av main course £10.50 **Restaurant** L served Mon-Fri 12-2.30, Sat-Sun 12-3 D served Mon-Thu 6.30-9, Fri-Sat 6.30-9.30 Av 3 course à la carte fr £22 ⊕ FREE HOUSE ◀ Harvey's Sussex Best Bitter, Royal Tunbridge Wells Royal Ŏ Westons Stowford Press. **Facilities** ❖ Children welcome Children's menu Children's portions Play area Garden Parking

The Hare on Langton Green

PICK OF THE PUBS

Langton Rd, Langton Green TN3 0JA ☎ **01892 862419**
e-mail: hare@brunningandprice.co.uk
dir: *From Tunbridge Wells follow A264 towards East Grinstead. The Hare is on the x-rds at Langton Green*

Situated on the edge of rolling Kent countryside, this site has been home to an inn since the 18th century. The current Hare's predecessor was extensively damaged in a fire in 1900, and the present Victorian-Tudor edifice was completed a year later in what is now a well-to-do suburb of Tunbridge Wells. The extensive menu changes daily. Starters might include sweet chilli chicken samosa with tzatziki and sesame noodle salad; followed by mains of sea bass with clams in a potato, leek, pea and saffron broth; or wild mushroom and lentil pie with sweet potato mash. There is also a choice of light bites and sandwiches. In addition to a choice of real ales and ciders, there's an impressive range of malt whiskies and wines. A woman holding a child is said to haunt the main staircase and cellar, though nobody has been able to identify the period she comes from.

Open all day all wk 12-11 (Fri-Sat 12-12 Sun 12-10.30) ⊕ BRUNNING & PRICE ◀ Greene King IPA, Ruddles Best & Abbot Ale, Morland Original, Hardys & Hansons Olde Trip Ŏ Westons Old Rosie & Wyld Wood Organic, Aspall. **Facilities** Children welcome Children's menu Children's portions Garden Parking

Save on hotels. Book at **theAA.com/hotel**

KENT 313 | ENGLAND

PICK OF THE PUBS

The Beacon ★★★★INN

TUNBRIDGE WELLS (ROYAL)   Map 6 TQ53

Tea Garden Ln TN3 9JH
☎ **01892 524252**
e-mail: info@the-beacon.co.uk
web: www.the-beacon.co.uk
dir: *From Tunbridge Wells take A264 towards East Grinstead. Pub 1m on left*

As the address suggests, there were tea gardens here in an area called Happy Valley. They were created about 1820, but the late Victorians presumably lost interest, because in 1895 Sir Walter Harris was able to buy the land and build a house, Rusthall Beacon, here. After a wartime spell as a hostel for Jewish refugees, in 1950 it became a hotel. Standing in nearly 17 acres, the building is jam-packed with impressive architectural features – moulded plaster ceilings and stained-glass windows in particular. The bar offers a trinity of real ales – Harvey's Best, Larkins Traditional and Timothy Taylor Landlord, as well as Stowford Press draught cider and Westons Organic bottled pear cider. Take a pint out to the terrace and enjoy the terrific views. Food is served in the bar, the restaurant, or in one of three private dining rooms, where the menus take full advantage of local produce, not least the fruit, vegetables and herbs from The Beacon's own kitchen garden. Start perhaps with roasted fennel and orange salad with balsamic dressing; or Shetland mussels with creamy cider sauce and Rusbridge bread from nearby Southborough. For a main course, select from a list

containing braised blade of beef with dauphinoise potatoes, caramelised onion, glazed French beans and red wine jus; home-cooked gammon with free-range egg and hand-cut chips; and seafood and saffron tagliatelle with Noilly Prat and dill sauce. There are plenty of others to choose from, as well as the daily specials board. A good wine list offers plenty of choice by the glass. The area offers a lot of things to do, making an overnight stay in one of the individually themed, impeccably furnished and decorated bedrooms something to consider.

Open all day all wk 11-11 (Sun 12-10.30) **Bar Meals** L served Mon-Thu 12-2.30, Fri-Sun 12-9.30 D served Mon-Thu 6.30-9.30, Fri-Sun 12-9.30 Av main course £12 **Restaurant** L served Mon-

Thu 12-2.30, Fri-Sun 12-9.30 D served Mon-Thu 6.30-9.30, Fri-Sun 12-9.30 Av 3 course à la carte fr £20 ⊕ FREE HOUSE ◀ Harvey's Sussex Best Bitter, Timothy Taylor Landlord, Larkins Traditional ♻ Westons Stowford Press & Westons Wyld Wood Organic Pear. ♟ 12 **Facilities** Children welcome Children's menu Children's portions Play area Garden Parking Wi-fi 🚌 (notice required) **Rooms 3**

WESTERHAM   Map 6 TQ45

The Fox & Hounds

Toys Hill TN16 1QG ☎ 01732 750328
e-mail: hickmott1@hotmail.com
dir: *Telephone for directions*

Chartwell, where Sir Winston Churchill lived, is not far from this late 18th-century alehouse surrounded by National Trust land high on Kent's Greensand Ridge. All food served in the bar and traditionally styled restaurant is made on the premises from locally sourced produce. A starter might be an individual baked camembert with confit garlic and onion marmalade, followed by fillet of fresh beer-battered fish; slow-cooked ox cheek; or roasted red pepper and basil risotto. Lunchtime filled rolls are available Tuesdays to Saturdays and there are hog roasts in summer. Booking for meals may be required.

Open all day 10am-11pm Closed: 25 Dec, Mon eve **Bar Meals** L served Mon-Sat 12-2, Sun 12-3 D served Tue-Sat 6-9 Av main course £10.50 **Restaurant** L served Mon-Sat 12-2, Sun 12-3 D served Tue-Sat 6-9 Fixed menu price fr £9 Av 3 course à la carte fr £20 ⊕ GREENE KING ◀ IPA, Abbot Ale & Ruddles County, Morland. ♟ 10 **Facilities** ❄ Children welcome Children's menu Garden Parking 🚌 (notice required)

Grasshopper on the Green

The Green TN16 1AS ☎ 01959 562926
e-mail: info@grasshopperonthegreen.com
dir: *M25 junct 5, A21 towards Sevenoaks, then A25 to Westerham. Or M25 junct 6, A22 towards East Grinstead, A25 to Westerham*

As its name suggests this beamed 700-year-old inn overlooks Westerham's pretty green and takes its name from the heraldic crest of the local 16th-century merchant and financier Thomas Gresham, founder of the Royal Exchange. Worth calling by for a pint of Westerham's Bull Dog and a plate of food by the log fire or in the peaceful summer garden. Look to chalkboard for daily dishes like beef stew with mash, home-made fishcakes with chilli dip, and liver and bacon with red wine jus. Winston Churchill's home Chartwell (now a National Trust property) is close by.

Open all day all wk **Bar Meals** L served all wk 12-9 D served all wk 12-9 Av main course £10 food served all day **Restaurant** L served all wk 12-9 D served all wk 12-9 food served all day ⊕ FREE HOUSE ◀ Grasshopper Ale, Adnams Broadside, Harvey's Sussex Best Bitter, Courage Best Bitter, Westerham British Bulldog BB. ♟ 12 **Facilities** ❄ Children welcome Children's menu Children's portions Play area Garden Parking Wi-fi 🚌 (notice required)

WEST MALLING   Map 6 TQ65

The Farmhouse

PICK OF THE PUBS

97 The High St ME19 6NA ☎ 01732 843257
e-mail: enquiries@thefarmhouse.biz
dir: *M20 junct 4, S on A228. Right to West Malling. Pub in village centre*

The Farmhouse is a handsome Elizabethan property in the heart of the beautiful old market town of West Malling. There's a friendly atmosphere in this modern gastro-pub's stylish bar and two dining areas. Outside is a pretty walled garden with an area of decking overlooking 15th-century stone barns. Local seasonal ingredients are used to produce a range of menus with a strong French influence. Expect starters such as seared wood pigeon breast with butternut squash purée; tiger prawns with garlic, coconut, lime and coriander; or baked camembert; and mains like oven-roasted whole partridge with brussel sprouts gratin, game chips and juniper berry jus; confit pork belly with bubble-and-squeak; or spicy winter root vegetable tagine. There are stone-baked pizzas and toasted paninis alongside the blackboard menu, which changes regularly.

Open all day all wk 11-11 **Bar Meals** L served Mon-Thu 12-3, Fri-Sat 12-9.45, Sun 12-9.30 D served Mon-Thu 6-9.45, Fri-Sat 12-9.45, Sun 12-9.30 Av main course £12 **Restaurant** L served Mon-Thu 12-3, Fri-Sat 12-7.45, Sun 12-9.30 D served Mon-Thu 6-9.30, Fri-Sat 12-9.45, Sun 12-9.30 Av 3 course à la carte fr £24 ⊕ ENTERPRISE INNS ◀ Harvey's, Guinness ♂ Biddenden, Aspall. ♟ 20 **Facilities** Children welcome Children's portions Garden Parking Wi-fi

WHITSTABLE   Map 7 TR16

The Sportsman @@

PICK OF THE PUBS

Faversham Rd, Seasalter CT5 4BP ☎ 01227 273370
e-mail: contact@thesportsmanseasalter.co.uk
dir: *3.5m W of Whitstable, on coast road between Whitstable & Faversham*

Reached via a winding lane across open marshland from Whitstable, and tucked beneath the sea wall, The Sportsman has a rustic and welcoming interior, with wooden floors and stripped pine furniture. There has been an inn on this site since 1642, but the surrounding area was entered in the Domesday Book as belonging to the kitchens of Canterbury Cathedral. A plaque on the wall commemorates the part played by the pub in a little known World War II episode, the Battle of Graveney Marshes: in 1940 a German Junkers 88 crashlanded near the pub, where a platoon of London Irish Rifles was billeted. After surrendering, the Germans were taken to the pub for a pint to await the POW authorities. Today's range of Shepherd Neame ales would certainly have gone down well in 1940. The pub is renowned for its food and the high standard of cooking is recognised with two AA Rosettes. Fish and seafood feature strongly - maybe poached rock oysters with pickled cucumber and Avruga caviar, followed by seared thornback ray with brown butter, cockles and sherry vinegar. Alternatives might include pork terrine followed by chicken with bread sauce and roasting juices. Booking for meals may be required.

Open all wk 12-3 6-11 Closed: 25-26 Dec, 1 Jan **Bar Meals** Av main course £18 **Restaurant** L served Tue-Sun 12-2 D served Tue-Sat 7-9 Av 3 course à la carte fr £33 ⊕ SHEPHERD NEAME ◀ Late Red, Master Brew, Original Porter, Early Bird, Goldings Ale, Whitstable Bay ♂ Thatchers Gold. ♟ 9 **Facilities** Children welcome Children's portions Family room Garden Parking

WROTHAM   Map 6 TQ65

The Bull ★★★★ INN @

Bull Ln TN15 7RF ☎ 01732 789800
e-mail: info@thebullhotel.com
web: www.thebullhotel.com
dir: *M20 junct 2, A20 (signed Paddock Wood, Gravesend & Tonbridge). At rdbt 3rd exit onto A20 (signed Wrotham, Tonbridge, Borough Green, M20 & M25). At rdbt take 4th exit into Bull Ln (signed Wrotham)*

In a quiet country location, this attractive three-storey building can be traced to 1385; it was first licensed under

Henry VII in 1495. More recently, World War II pilots relaxed here; stamps on the restaurant ceiling mark downed German planes, and dozens of pictures of Spitfires decorate the place. Ales from the award-winning Dark Star micro-brewery are supported by a 70-bottle wine list. Food follows classic lines, but as much as possible is sourced from local growers and suppliers: Hartley Bottom lamb and prune pie, and Woods Farm egg and cheese omelette are just two examples. Why not stay over in one of the refurbished bedrooms and try the circular walk from the pub? Booking for meals may be required.

The Bull

Open all day all wk **Bar Meals** L served Mon-Sat 12-2.30 D served Mon-Sat 6-9 **Restaurant** L served Mon-Sat 12-2.30, Sun 12-8 D served Mon-Sat 6-9 ⊕ FREE HOUSE ◀ Dark Star Partridge Best Bitter, Hophead ♂ Westons Stowford Press. ♀ 8 **Facilities** Children welcome Children's portions Garden Parking Wi-fi ⚌ **Rooms** 11

WYE   Map 7 TR04

The New Flying Horse

Upper Bridge St TN25 5AN ☎ 01233 812297
e-mail: newflyhorse@shepherd-neame.co.uk
dir: *Telephone for directions*

With a 400-year-old history, this village inn charms with its low ceilings, black beams, open brickwork and large open fireplace. In winter snuggle up by the fire, savour a pint of Late Red and select a couple of classics from the menu, such as sea bass with fennel and red pepper risotto; and roast pheasant with fondant potato and parsnip crisps. Very much the village local it has a rare bat and trap game, and a stunning World War II 'Soldier's Dream of Blighty' garden which won an award at the 2005 Chelsea Flower Show. Booking for meals may be required.

Open all day all wk **Bar Meals** L served all wk 12-2 D served all wk 6-9 Av main course £10 **Restaurant** L served all wk 12-2 D served all wk 6-9 ⊕ SHEPHERD NEAME ◀ Master Brew, Spitfire & Late Red, Guest ales. ♀ 12 **Facilities** Children welcome Children's menu Children's portions Play area Garden Parking ⚌

LANCASHIRE

ALTHAM   Map 18 SD73

The Walton Arms

Burnley Rd BB5 5UL ☎ 01282 774444
e-mail: walton-arms@btconnect.com
dir: *Just off M65 junct 8. On A678 between Accrington & Padiham*

A long-established way-station on an ancient highway linking Yorkshire and Lancashire, this sturdy, stone-built dining pub oozes history. Pilgrims to Whalley Abbey called at an inn here when Henry VII was king. Beams and brasses, rustic furniture and slabbed stone floors welcome today's pilgrims intent on sampling the comprehensive menu, either as a bar meal or in the atmospheric dining room. Typical choices include a pot of button mushrooms with creamed blue cheese sauce followed by hake fillet with a soft herb crust, new potatoes and seasonal vegetables or the inn's 'famous' shoulder of local lamb with roasted vegetables.

Open all wk Mon-Sat 12-2.30 5.30-11 (Sun 12-10.30) **Bar Meals** L served Mon-Sat 12-2, Sun 12-8.30 D served Mon-Sat 6-9, Sun 12-8.30 **Restaurant** L served Mon-Sat 12-2, Sun 12-8.30 D served Mon-Sat 6-9, Sun 12-8.30 ⊕ J W LEES ◀ Bitter. ♀ 16 **Facilities** Children welcome Children's menu Children's portions Parking Wi-fi ⚌ (notice required)

BASHALL EAVES   Map 18 SD64

The Red Pump Inn
PICK OF THE PUBS

Clitheroe Rd BB7 3DA ☎ 01254 826227
e-mail: info@theredpumpinn.co.uk
dir: *3m from Clitheroe, NW, follow 'Whitewell, Trough of Bowland & Bashall Eaves' signs*

There's some doubt about exactly when this old pub was built, although 1756 would be a reasonable guess since that's the date carved on a door lintel. It used to be a coaching inn and the horses would quench their thirst from the old red pump now in the bar. Real ale drinkers can quench theirs from a line-up including Tirril, Black Sheep and Moorhouse's. Of the restaurant side of things, owners Jonathan and Martina Myerscough say: "We love good honest, tasty food, prepared fresh from local-as-possible ingredients and presented well with thought, but without too much fuss". Either they, or their chefs, might change the menus on a whim, as well as seasonally, to offer typical mains of rich Lancashire ox-cheek pie; rabbit loin casserole with rabbit haggis, carrot mash and twice-fried chips; and linguine salsa verde. Look on the specials board for fish. Children have their own menu. Booking for meals may be required.

Open 12-3 6-11 (Sun 12-9) Closed: 2wks early Jan, Mon (ex BH) ⊕ FREE HOUSE ◀ Black Sheep, Moorhouse's, Tirril. **Facilities** Children welcome Children's menu Children's portions Garden Parking Wi-fi

BILSBORROW   Map 18 SD53

Owd Nell's Tavern

Guy's Thatched Hamlet, Canal Side PR3 0RS
☎ 01995 640010
e-mail: info@guysthatchedhamlet.com
dir: *M6 junct 32 N on A6. In approx 5m follow brown tourist signs to Guy's Thatched Hamlet*

This country-style tavern is full of old-world charm, with beams and flagstones aplenty. Run by the same family for over 30 years, it forms part of Guy's Thatched Hamlet, a cluster of eating and drinking venues beside the Lancaster Canal. Expect excellent ales, such as Owd Nell's Canalside Bitter or Pendle Witches Brew, and an authentic country pub ambience enhanced by flagged floors, fireplaces and low ceilings. All-day fare is typified by home-made soups, 'whale size' fish and chips, steak-and-kidney pie, and specials like beef goulash. Children's menus are available. There is a cider festival in the summer, and several other events to look out for.

Open all day all wk 7am-2am Closed: 25 Dec **Bar Meals** L served all wk 12-9 D served all wk 12-9 Av main course £9 food served all day **Restaurant** L served all wk 12-9 D served all wk 12-9 Av 3 course à la carte fr £17 food served all day ⊕ FREE HOUSE ◀ Moorhouse's Premier Bitter & Pendle Witches Brew, Owd Nell's Canalside Bitter, Bowland, Copper Dragon, Black Sheep, Thwaites, Hart ♂ Thatchers Heritage & Cheddar Valley. ♀ 20 **Facilities** ♣ Children welcome Children's menu Children's portions Family room Garden Beer festival Parking Wi-fi ⚌ (notice required)

BLACKBURN   Map 18 SD62

Clog and Billycock ◉
PICK OF THE PUBS

See Pick of the Pubs on page 316
See advert on page 317

The Millstone at Mellor ★★ HL ◉◉
PICK OF THE PUBS

See Pick of the Pubs on page 318
See advert on page 319

PICK OF THE PUBS

Clog and Billycock

Billinge End Rd, Pleasington BB2 6QB
☎ **01254 201163**
e-mail: enquiries@theclogandbillycock.com
web: www.theclogandbillycock.com
dir: *M6 junct 29 to M65 junct 3, follow Pleasington signs*

From the same stable as The Three Fishes at Whalley (see entry) and The Highwayman at Burrow (see entry), the team at Ribble Valley Inns have taken a good and popular dining inn and made it better still. In a village at the fringe of Blackburn, its hillside setting is in pleasantly wooded, countryside with the historic Hoghton Tower close by. Walks from the door lead to Witton Country Park, Pleasington Old Hall and there are riverside rambles through the striking gorge of the River Darwen. Originally the Bay Horse Inn, a century ago a new landlord took the reins; his favoured attire was a billycock hat and Lancashire clogs, his personality did the rest and the 'new' name stuck! It's a Thwaites' house, with their popular Lancaster Bomber the pick of the beers, whilst the wine list stretches to over 35 bins. Marry this to the well crafted menu created by award-winning chef Nigel Haworth and you've the start of a long friendship with this mid-Victorian inn, which is an engaging mix of contemporary and traditional styles, with a surprisingly airy interior, modern art and photos of local food heroes. It's

Lancashire produce that Nigel concentrates on; commence with treacle baked saddleback pork ribs or Greave's black pudding on an English muffin with poached egg. Ideal bedfellows for mains that promise heather-reared Lonk lamb Lancashire hotpot with pickled red cabbage, Goosnargh duck pie, toad in the hole or fish pie. The fish and chips includes mouth-watering chips cooked in dripping. Non-meat options are weighty with Lancashire's artisan cheese producers and the bounteous vegetables of the region. For afters, try Tomlinson's rhubarb jelly and custard, pineapple upside-down cake or chocolate and orange pudding.

Open all wk 12-11 (Sun 12-10.30) Closed: 25 Dec **Bar Meals** L served Mon-

Sat 12-2, Sun & BH 12-8 (afternoon bites Mon-Sat 2-6) D served Mon-Thu 5.30-8.30, Fri-Sat 5.30-9, Sun & BH 12-8 Av main course £12.50 **Restaurant** L served Mon-Sat 12-2, Sun & BH 12-8 D served Mon-Thu 5.30-8.30, Fri-Sat 5.30-9, Sun & BH 12-8 Av 3 course à la carte fr £24 ⊕ RIBBLE VALLEY INNS
◧ Thwaites Nutty Black, Wainwright, Original, Lancaster Bomber.
Facilities Children welcome Children's menu Children's portions Garden Parking

Save on hotels. Book at **theAA.com/hotel**

LANCASHIRE 317 ENGLAND

THE CLOG AND BILLYCOCK

Billinge End Road, Pleasington, Blackburn,
Lancashire BB2 6QB
Tel: 01254201163
Website: www.theclogandbillycock.com
Email: enquiries@theclogandbillycock.com

This is the third Ribble Valley Inn to open following the staggering success of *The Three Fishes* at Mitton, and *The Highwayman* at Nether Burrow. Like its stable mates, *The Clog and Billycock* is steeped in all the history you might expect of a rural treasure. Step inside and the atmosphere is immediately warm and welcoming. A popular Thwaites' house, where locals enjoy an impressive line up of ales, along with a wine list chosen to complement the menu. Nigel Haworth works closely with local producers and the menu reflects this, enjoy Ascroft's Deep Fried Cauliflower Fritters, Curried Mayonnaise followed by Goosnargh Cornfed Chicken, Mustard, Cayenne Pepper, Hint of Tabasco, Real Chips Cooked in Dripping and for afters, Jam Roly Poly & Real Custard.

PICK OF THE PUBS

The Millstone at Mellor ★★ HL 🌹🌹

BLACKBURN　　Map 18 SD62

Church Ln, Mellor BB2 7JR
☎ **01254 813333**
e-mail: relax@millstonehotel.co.uk
web: www.millstonehotel.co.uk
dir: *M6 junct 31, A59 towards Clitheroe, past British Aerospace. Right at rdbt signed Blackburn/Mellor. Next rdbt 2nd left. Hotel at top of hill on right*

An attractively presented old coaching inn owned by Blackburn brewery, Thwaites. Mellor is in the Ribble Valley, designated an Area of Outstanding Natural Beauty, whose place names often found their way into JRR Tolkien's 'Middle Earth'. Getting to know this beautiful area better is a good enough reason to visit or stay at The Millstone, especially for those who enjoy chef-patron Anson Bolton's classic and inventive food, which has been earning him two AA Rosettes year after year. Choose from a daytime or a dinner menu, whether you eat in the very English oak-panelled Miller's restaurant or in the bar. The former has the sandwiches, baps and wraps, while both offer a good choice of light dishes and starters, deli boards, grills and classics. Additionally at dinner is a seasonal selection, such as autumn's monkfish and prawn thermidor, and roast guinea fowl breast. Among the classics are beer-battered haddock; breast of chicken in chilli and pimento

marinade; slow-roasted shank of Pendle lamb; and woodland mushroom risotto. The menu suggests that women might prefer a six-ounce sirloin, which implies that the ten-ounce steaks are for men. Gluten-free choices are available. Desserts are represented by apple charlotte with clotted cream and warm custard sauce; and chocolate and coffee mousse affogato and amaretti crumb, perhaps with a glass of Chilean Sauvignon Blanc late harvest dessert wine. A dozen or so wines are available by the glass in each of three sizes. Among the guest rooms is one with a four-poster, and they all offer a good view of the village and its church, while the residents' lounge has the tranquil Remembrance Park in its sights.

Open all day all wk **Bar Meals** L served Mon-Sat 12-9.30, Sun 12-9 Av main course £13.50 food served all day 🍺 THWAITES INNS OF CHARACTER 🍺 Lancaster Bomber, Original, Wainwright Ŏ Kingstone Press. ▿ 10 **Facilities** Children's menu Children's portions Parking Wi-fi **Rooms** 23

BLACKO　　　　　　　　　Map 18 SD84

Moorcock Inn

Gisburn Rd BB9 6NG ☎ 01282 614186
e-mail: jamesseemann@live.co.uk
dir: *M65 junct 13, take A682 inn halfway between Blacko & Gisburn*

Beyond the folly of Blacko Tower, high on the road towards Gisburn on the Upper Admergill area, lies this family-run, 18th-century inn with traditional log fires and splendid views towards the Pendle Way. With Thwaites Wainwright and Kingstone Press cider served in the bar, home-prepared dishes are a speciality. There's a wide choice on the menu and specials board including salads and sandwiches, and vegetarian and children's meals. Main dishes are hearty and might include lasagne, various steaks, pork in orange and cider, and grilled trout. There's a folk/acoustic music night on the first Wednesday of each month, a traditional Lancashire menu on Thursday evenings, Steak Night every Friday, and a carvery on Sunday.

Open 12-2 6-9 (Sat 12-9 Sun 12-6) Closed: Mon eve **Bar Meals** L served Mon-Fri 12-2, Sat 12-9, Sun 12-6 D served Tue-Fri 6-9, Sat 12-9, Sun 12-6 Av main course £8.95 **Restaurant** L served Mon-Fri 12-2, Sat 12-9, Sun 12-6 D served Tue-Fri 6-9, Sat 12-9, Sun 12-6 ⊕ FREE HOUSE ◀ Thwaites Wainwright, Lancaster Bomber ♂ Kingstone Press. **Facilities** ✿ Children welcome Children's menu Children's portions Parking 🚌

BURROW　　　　　　　　Map 18 SD67

The Highwayman ◉

PICK OF THE PUBS

See Pick of the Pubs on page 320
See advert on page 321

CARNFORTH　　　　　　Map 18 SD47

The Longlands Inn and Restaurant

Tewitfield LA6 1JH ☎ 01524 781256
e-mail: info@longlandshotel.co.uk
dir: *Telephone for directions*

With its nooks and crannies, old beams and uneven floors, this family-run dog-friendly inn stands next to Tewitfield locks on the Lancaster Canal. The bar, with Tirril ales on tap, rocks to live bands on Monday evenings while hungry music lovers consume plates of pizza and pasta. Otherwise look to the restaurant for good country cooking, with meats from the Silverdale butcher, Morecambe Bay shrimps, and Lancaster Smokehouse products on the appetising menu. Children too are well catered for, with proper home-cooked dishes and activity bags to keep them busy. Booking for meals may be required.

Open all day all wk 11-11 **Bar Meals** L served Mon-Fri 12-2.30, Sat 12-4, Sun 12-9 D served Mon-Sat 6-9.30, Sun 12-9 **Restaurant** L served Mon-Fri 12-2.30, Sat 12-4, Sun 12-9 D served Mon-Sat 6-9.30, Sun 12-9 ⊕ FREE HOUSE ◀ Tirril Old Faithful, Black Sheep. ♚ 9 **Facilities** ✿ Children welcome Children's menu Garden Parking Wi-fi 🚌 (notice required)

CHIPPING　　　　　　　Map 18 SD64

Dog & Partridge

Hesketh Ln PR3 2TH ☎ 01995 61201
dir: *M6 junct 31A, follow Longridge signs. At Longridge left at 1st rbdt, straight on at next 3 rdbts. At Alston Arms turn right. 3m, pub on right*

Dating back to 1515, this pleasantly modernised rural pub in the Ribble Valley enjoys delightful views of the surrounding fells. The barn has been transformed into a welcoming dining area, where home-made food on the comprehensive bar snack menu is backed by a specials board featuring fresh fish and game dishes. A typical menu shows a starter of deep-fried garlic mushrooms; then mains of braised pork chops with home-made apple sauce and stuffing or home-made steak-and-kidney pie. Booking for meals may be required.

Open 11.45-3 6.45-11 (Sat 11.45-3 6-11 Sun 11.45-10.30) Closed: Mon **Bar Meals** L served Tue-Sat 12-1.45 **Restaurant** L served Tue-Sat 12-1.30, Sun 12-3 D served Tue-Sat 7-9, Sun 3-8.30 ⊕ FREE HOUSE ◀ Black Sheep, Tetley's, Guest ales. ♚ 8 **Facilities** Children welcome Children's menu Children's portions Parking 🚌

PICK OF THE PUBS

The Highwayman ❀

BURROW   Map 18 SD67

LA6 2RJ ☎ 01524 273338
e-mail: enquiries@highwaymaninn.co.uk
web: www.highwaymaninn.co.uk
dir: *M6 junct 36, A65 to Kirkby Lonsdale.*
A683 S. Burrow approx 2m

As with all good legends, it is sometimes difficult to separate fact from fiction. Here is no exception. That it started life in the 18th century as a coaching inn is not in doubt, although whether it was ever the haunt of Lancashire's notorious highwaymen is a little less certain. We're on solid ground though in saying that it's a Ribble Valley Inn, one of Nigel Haworth's thriving group of dining pubs. What you can expect here are craggy stone floors, warm solid wood furniture, log fires in winter and walled gardens in which to enjoy outdoor drinking and dining. Thwaites of Blackburn supply their Lancaster Bomber, Wainwright and Original cask ales, Aston Manor sends its draught cider, and the extensive list of fine wines is chosen by Craig Bancroft of Northcote, Nigel's award-winning restaurant in Langho. In fact, it's Nigel who inspires the menus for what some might call a gastro-pub, but which all here prefer to regard as a 21st-century version of 'the local'. The head chef and his team not only know the traditional specialities of the area but also how to give them that little contemporary nudge. Start with warm Morecambe Bay shrimps; baked Herefordshire snails; or creamed field mushrooms on toast. To follow, maybe Lancashire Lonk lamb hotpot; Cornvale duck pie; or breast of devilled Goosnargh corn-fed chicken, and then a typical dessert of lemon meringue pie; elderflower syllabub and jelly with Grasmere gingerbread; or the local cheeseboard. There are seasonal alternative menus, a very good children's menu and a gluten-free one too. The beautifully landscaped terraced gardens offer comfortable seating and outdoor heating, and the flowers and shrubs have been carefully chosen to help attract the region's butterflies and birds.

Open all day 12-11 (Sun 12-10.30)
Closed: 25 Dec, Mon **Bar Meals** L served Tue-Sat 12-2, Sun (& BH) 12-8

(afternoon bites Tue-Sat 2-6) D served Tue-Thu 6-9, Fri-Sat 5.30-9, Sun (& BH) 12-8 Av main course £12.75 food served all day **Restaurant** Av 3 course à la carte fr £24 ▥ RIBBLE VALLEY INNS ◧ Thwaites Original, Lancaster Bomber, Wainwright ♂ Kingstone Press, Aston Manor. **Facilities** Children welcome Children's menu Children's portions Garden Parking

Save on hotels. Book at **theAA.com/hotel**

LANCASHIRE 321 ENGLAND

THE HIGHWAYMAN

Burrow, Kirkby Lonsdale LA6 2RJ
Tel: 01524 273 338
Website: www.highwaymaninn.co.uk
Email: enquiries@highwaymaninn.co.uk

The Highwayman, an 18th century coaching inn, is the sister pub to *The Three Fishes* at Mitton, part of Nigel Haworth's Ribble Valley Inns establishments. Enjoy a smart civilised setting of stone floors, handsome wooden furniture and crackling log fires. In the summer relax in a wonderful terraced walled garden. Dishes inspired by local producers from, Mackenzie's Smoked Mackerel Pate; Lancashire Smokehouse Beech & Juniper Smoked Salmon, Seawater Prawns, Morecambe Bay Shrimps, Pickled Cucumber, Sour Cream Caper Dressing to Sandham's Mature Lancashire & Curd Cheese, Sour Cream Jacket, Tomato & Red Onion Salad. The Highwayman is the 21st century version of 'the local', with the addition of regional food of outstanding quality and imagination, a great line up of beers and wines to add even more to the perfect experience. For walkers, cyclists or those who simply like to take a gentle drive along meandering country lanes; this is a magnificent corner of Britain to explore.

CLITHEROE · Map 18 SD74

The Assheton Arms

PICK OF THE PUBS

See Pick of the Pubs on opposite page
See advert below

COLNE · Map 18 SD83

The Alma Inn ★★★★ INN NEW

Emmott Ln, Laneshawbridge BB8 7EG ☎ 01282 857830
e-mail: reception@thealmainn.com
dir: *M65, A6068 towards Keighley. At Laneshawbridge left into Emmott Ln. 0.5m, pub on left*

Stone floors, original beams and real fires have all been preserved in the restoration of this inn, which dates from 1725. Deep in Pendle's magnificent countryside, it offers a relaxed and welcoming setting for drinking or dining. The menu is built around local produce including steak (served with a choice of sauces) and Pendle Forest lamb shank, maybe braised in port with spring onion champ, garlic green beans and a mint and redcurrant sauce. Other options include sandwiches and filled crusty ciabattas. Finish with home-churned ice cream. Booking for meals may be required.

Open all day all wk **Bar Meals** L served all wk 12-9 D served all wk 12-9 food served all day **Restaurant** L served all wk 12-9 D served all wk 12-9 food served all day ⊕ FREE HOUSE ◀ John Smith's, Tetley's, Guest ales ♂ Rekorderlig. ₹ 10 **Facilities** ✿ Children welcome Children's menu Children's portions Garden Parking Wi-fi 🚐 **Rooms** 10

ELSWICK · Map 18 SD43

The Ship at Elswick

High St PR4 3ZB ☎ 01995 672777
e-mail: mail@theshipatelswick.co.uk
dir: *M55 junct 3, A585 signed Fleetwood. Right onto Thistleton Rd (B5269)*

In a quiet village on the Fylde and handy both for Blackpool and the quieter resorts of Cleveleys and Fleetwood, this former farmhouse is now a reliable village local and dining inn. From Fleetwood come some of the fish inhabiting the very traditional menu here; beef and Guinness pie is another favourite or start with a plate of Bury black pudding with poached egg hollandaise, chorizo and rocket. The owners are proud to use Lancashire produce in most of their dishes, although the standard beer is Yorkshire's Black Sheep Best Bitter!

Open all day all wk **Bar Meals** Av main course £10.95 food served all day **Restaurant** food served all day ⊕ PUNCH TAVERNS ◀ Jennings Cumberland Ale, Black Sheep, Guest ales. ₹ 8 **Facilities** Children welcome Children's menu Children's portions Play area Garden Parking Wi-fi 🚐

FENCE · Map 18 SD83

Fence Gate Inn

Wheatley Lane Rd BB12 9EE ☎ 01282 618101
e-mail: info@fencegate.co.uk
dir: *From M65 junct 13 towards Fence, 1.5m, pub set back on right opposite T-junct for Burnley*

Next to the village church at the edge of beautiful open countryside, this imposing building, dating back 300 years, was a private house until 1982 when today's comfortable inn was created. High quality furnishings, a brasserie and dining suites reveal its function as a foodie destination, but drinkers aren't forgotten, with a characterful wood-panelled bar and grand log fire where Lancashire-brewed beers are the order of the day. The Lancashire theme continues with the food; Bowland beef features strongly, home-made local pork sausages a speciality and Red Rose cheeses a fine final flourish to a meal.

Open all day all wk noon-close ⊕ FREE HOUSE ◀ Courage Directors, Caledonian Deuchars IPA, Theakston, Moorhouse's, Bowland, Guest ales ♂ Westons Stowford Press. **Facilities** Children welcome Children's menu Children's portions Garden Parking Wi-fi

---

The Assheton Arms

Downham, Clitheroe, Lancashire BB7 4BJ • Tel: 01200 441227
Website: www.asshetonarms.com
Email: info@asshetonarms.com

The 18th century *Assheton Arms* at Downham, with spectacular views of Pendle Hill reopened April 2012 after extensive refurbishment.

Alongside the historic pub which is still dog friendly, there are now two floors of dining area in the previously disused half of the building. *The Assheton Arms* now merges traditional surroundings with modern food, and an emphasis on great quality of food, beer, service and surroundings. You'll find a wide selection of quality fish dishes as well as classic favourites such as Pendle Hill steak and Gazegill Organics Lamb. In addition to the pub and restaurant we are able to offer private dining and host speciality evenings which we publicise in our news section and through twitter and facebook.

Save on hotels. Book at **theAA.com/hotel**

LANCASHIRE 323 ENGLAND

PICK OF THE PUBS

The Assheton Arms

CLITHEROE Map 18 SD74

Downham BB7 4BJ ☎ 01200 441227
e-mail: info@asshetonarms.com
web: www.asshetonarms.com
dir: *A59 to Chatburn, then follow*
Downham signs

One of the North West's most historic inns, The Assheton Arms was originally a farmhouse brewing beer just for the workers. It became the George and Dragon in 1872, then in 1950 was renamed in honour of the contribution Ralph Assheton, Lord Clitheroe, made to the war effort during World War II. In December 2011 the inn was taken over by the family-owned and operated Seafood Pub Company. They have now made some sweeping changes, including the renovation of a disused two-level dining area, which is now in use again. At the bar you'll find real ales from Thwaites, Black Sheep and Hawkshead as well as cider from Kingstone Press. Executive chef Antony Shirley has devised a fish and seafood menu full of interest, with typical choices including whole grilled plaice, roast halibut, king scallops and oysters. Besides the regular menu there are daily specials such as hake fillet with wild mushrooms and Jerusalem artichoke purée; roast cod with devilled black peas and mashed potato; and whole Morecambe Bay plaice with brown shrimp, caper butter and parsley potatoes. Calves' liver with bubble-and-squeak, scrumpy-battered onion rings

and smoked bacon; or venison sausages with crushed potatoes, lentils and smoked bacon gravy are attractive options for meat-lovers. Desserts run along the lines of syrup pudding with 'proper' custard; and milk chocolate pot with raspberry compôte and crushed amaretti biscuits. Local sourcing is a priority here, with Pendle Hill rib-eye steaks, organic lamb and pork from Gazegill Organics, and poultry and game from Johnson and Swarbrick all adding to the quality of the experience. If you're particularly keen on the seafood side of things, take note that the inn hosts a seafood festival in September. Booking for meals may be required.

Open all day all wk 12-10.30 (Fri-Sat 12-12) **Bar Meals** L served Mon-Sat 12-3, Sun 12-8 D served Mon-Thu

6-8.30 Fri-Sat 6-9 Av main course £12.50 **Restaurant** L served Mon-Sat 12-3, Sun 12-8 D served Mon-Thu 6-8.30 Fri-Sat 6-9 ⊕ FREE HOUSE ◼ Thwaites, Wainwright, Black Sheep, Hawkshead Ö Kingstone Press. **Facilities** Children welcome Children's menu Children's portions ❧ Garden Parking Wi-fi 🚐 (notice required)

FENISCOWLES
Map 18 SD62

Oyster & Otter NEW

631 Livesey Branch Rd BB2 5DQ ☎ 01254 203200
e-mail: info@oysterandotter.co.uk
web: www.oysterandotter.co.uk
dir: *M65 junct 3, right at lights right at mini rdbt into Livesey Branch Rd*

This seafood-driven gastro-pub opened in spring 2011 after an extensive refurbishment by a family of successful Fleetwood fish merchants. The relaxed and New England feel adds a contemporary edge to the pub, which is complemented by its seafront-style decking and wooden clapboard and stone exterior. Not surprisingly, fish and seafood dominates the menus which might include Morecambe Bay plaice or local sea bass. Non-fish eaters are well catered for with meat sourced from local producers. Leave room for warm Chorley cakes with Lancashire cheese or parkin pudding with treacle cream. There is a seafood festival in September. Booking for meals may be required.

Open all day all wk **Restaurant** L served Mon-Sat 12-3, Sun 12-9 D served Mon-Thu 5-9, Fri-Sat 5-10, Sun 12-9 Fixed menu price fr £14.95 Av 3 course à la carte fr £19 ⊕ THWAITES ◖ Wainwright, Lancaster Bomber, Original ♂ Kingstone Press. ♥ 9 **Facilities** Children welcome Children's menu Children's portions Garden Parking Wi-fi 🚐 (notice required)

See advert below

FORTON
Map 18 SD45

The Bay Horse Inn
PICK OF THE PUBS

LA2 0HR ☎ 01524 791204
e-mail: yvonne@bayhorseinn.com
dir: *M6 junct 33 take A6 towards Garstang, turn left for pub, approx 1m from M6*

Tucked down a country lane on the edge of the Forest of Bowland, the Wilkinson family has been at the helm of this charming 18th-century pub since 1992. They have continued to develop and improve the pub and its extended gardens, which lead to open fields where pheasants and deer can often be spotted. Mismatched furniture and a handsome stone fireplace with roaring winter log fires characterise the inn, which offers real cask beers, as well as an extensive wine list. Award-winning chef Craig Wilkinson specialises in simple, fresh and imaginative dishes. A fixed-price lunch carte offers two or three courses such as duck liver pâté with fig purée; fish pie glazed with Lancashire cheese; and lemon posset, gin-soaked berries and shortbread. A dinner selection could comprise cocktail of crab, smoked salmon and avocado purée, followed by slow-cooked Goosnargh duckling, potato purée, cherries and duck gravy. Booking for meals may be required.

Open 12-3 6-12 Closed: Mon (ex BH L) **Bar Meals** L served Tue-Sat 12-1.45, Sun 12-3 D served Tue-Sat 6-9 Av main course £14.45 **Restaurant** L served Tue-Sat 12-1.45, Sun 12-3 D served Tue-Sat 6-9 Fixed menu price fr £17.50 Av 3 course à la carte fr £22.50 ⊕ FREE HOUSE ◖ Moorhouse's Pendle Witches Brew, Black Sheep, Guest ale. ♥ 11 **Facilities** ❀ Children welcome Children's portions Garden Parking Wi-fi

---

Map 18 SD74

GRINDLETON

Duke of York NEW

Brow Top BB7 4QR ☎ 01200 441266
e-mail: info@dukeofyorkgrindleton.com
dir: *From A59 N of Clitheroe left to Chatburn. In Chatburn right into Ribble Ln. Over river, right at T-junct. Pub at brow of hill on left*

In the heart of the Ribble Valley, this creeper-clad pub dates from 1863 and remains the centre of village life. Low ceilings, flagstones and log fires provide plenty of character, as do the various nooks and crannies. Huddle around the bar for pints of Black Sheep with the locals, or head to the restaurant where modern dishes showcase the best local produce – potted shrimps on toast might be followed by roasted breast of Goosnargh chicken with celeriac and pearl barley risotto. A lovely garden is perfect for alfresco dining.

Open 12-3 6-11 (Sun 12-3 5-11) Closed: 25 Dec, Mon (ex BH) **Bar Meals** L served Tue-Sat 12-2, Sun 12-2.30 D served Tue-Sat 6-9, Sun 5-7.30 Av main course £11 **Restaurant** L served Tue-Sat 12-2, Sun 12-2.30 D served Tue-Sat 6-9, Sun 5-7.30 Fixed menu price fr £12.99 Av 3 course à la carte fr £29 ⊕ PUNCH TAVERNS ◼ Black Sheep Best Bitter, Thwaites Original. ♟ 20 **Facilities** ❖ Children welcome Children's menu Children's portions Garden Parking Wi-fi ▰ (notice required)

HESKIN GREEN
Map 15 SD51

Farmers Arms

85 Wood Ln PR7 5NP ☎ 01257 451276
e-mail: andy@farmersarms.co.uk
dir: *On B5250 between M6 & Eccleston*

This fine 17th-century pub used to be called the Pleasant Retreat, but in 1902 the name was changed. Never mind, because this long, creeper-covered building is still pleasant, very pleasant actually, and its flagstoned Vault

Bar is still a retreat. Malcolm and Ann Rothwell have been here for a quarter of a century, and now son Andrew and his wife Sue are slowly taking over the helm. The menu may include minted lamb cutlets or baked haddock gratin, while the main menu features Cumberland sausage, lasagna verdi, grills and steaks, and a selection of salads, jacket potatoes and sandwiches. Hand-pulled real ales include Silver Tally, named after the token that miners would exchange for a lamp.

Open all day all wk **Bar Meals** food served all day **Restaurant** food served all day ⊕ ENTERPRISE INNS ◼ Timothy Taylor Landlord, Marston's Pedigree, Prospect Silver Tally, Black Sheep, Tetley's. **Facilities** ❖ Children welcome Children's menu Children's portions Play area Garden Parking Wi-fi

HEST BANK
Map 18 SD46

Hest Bank Hotel

2 Hest Bank Ln LA2 6DN ☎ 01524 824339
e-mail: chef.glenn@btinternet.com
dir: *From Lancaster take A6 N, after 2m left to Hest Bank*

Comedian Eric Morecambe used to drink at this canalside former coaching inn, first licensed in 1554. Awash with history and 'many happy ghosts', it now offers cask ales and a wide selection of meals all day, with local suppliers playing an important role in maintaining food quality. The good value menu may range from a large pot of Bantry Bay mussels to the pub's own lamb hotpot made to a traditional recipe. The pub is family-friendly so perhaps while keeping an eye on the children you can enjoy a pint of Thwaites Wainwright or Black Sheep Best Bitter in the terraced garden.

Open all day all wk 11.30-11.30 (Sun 11.30-10.30) **Bar Meals** L served Mon-Sat 12-9, Sun 12-8 D served Mon-Sat 12-9, Sun 12-8 food served all day ⊕ PUNCH TAVERNS ◼ Thwaites Wainwright Blonde, Black Sheep Best Bitter, Guest ales. **Facilities** Children welcome Children's menu Children's portions Play area Garden Parking ▰ (notice required)

LANCASTER
Map 18 SD46

The Borough NEW

3 Dalton Square LA1 1PP ☎ 01524 64170
e-mail: vicki@theboroughlancaster.co.uk
dir: *Telephone for directions*

Following major refurbishment, Martin Harmer pushed open the doors to this smart town house pub in 2006 and hasn't looked back. Wooden floors, chunky tables, chesterfield sofas, warm green hues and masses of light from a huge bay window create a friendly, relaxed vibe for enjoying cracking Lancashire ales and a quality food offering. Using top-notch ingredients from local suppliers, including meat and eggs from surrounding farms, the seasonal menu may take in Morcambe Bay shrimps, 45-day aged rump steak with fat chips and peppercorn sauce, and sticky toffee pudding. There's a great value 'school dinners' menu.

Open all wk 12-11 (Fri noon-12.30am Sat 9am-12.20am) Closed: 25 Dec **Bar Meals** L served Sun-Thu 12-9, Fri-Sat 12-9.30 D served Sun-Thu 12-9, Fri-Sat 12-9.30 **Restaurant** L served Sun-Thu 12-9, Fri-Sat 12-9.30 D served Sun-Thu 12-9, Fri-Sat 12-9.30 Fixed menu price fr £20 ⊕ FREE HOUSE ◼ Borough IPA, Lancaster Amber, Young's Bitter, Wells Eagle IPA, Bowland Hen Harrier. ♟ 11 **Facilities** Children welcome Children's menu Garden Wi-fi ▰ (notice required)

Penny Street Bridge ★★★ TH

PICK OF THE PUBS

See Pick of the Pubs on page 326
See advert below

PICK OF THE PUBS

Penny Street Bridge ★★★ TH

LANCASTER   Map 18 SD46

Penny St LA1 1XT ☎ 01524 599900
e-mail: relax@pennystreetbridge.co.uk
web: www.pennystreetbridge.co.uk
dir: *In city centre*

Right in the centre of the city, the listed Penny Street Bridge was once a Corporation Toll House. Demolished in 1901, it was then rebuilt as two separate pubs, which Thwaites Brewery joined together again in 2007 to create a smart town-house hotel, bar and brasserie. Its wonderfully high ceilings make it feel light and modern, although retained period features can be seen everywhere, from the listed staircase to the servant bell hooks, and from the stained-glass windows to the rather special wardrobe in one of the bedrooms that the owners can't, and wouldn't ever want to, move. The atmosphere is quirkily elegant, with wooden floors in the brasserie, mismatched tables and tub chairs in the traditional bar and grill, and a stylish, contemporary feel in the refurbished bedrooms. Chef Andrew Nixon and his team prepare all food on the premises. Served all day, their seasonal menus make the most of the excellent Lancashire produce available locally, from corned beef hash with poached free-range egg; or onion soup with Lancashire cheese croûton for a starter, to main courses such as sea bass with brown shrimp risotto; wild boar sausage with baked apple, caramelised onion, mash and gravy; and baked spinach and ricotta cannelloni. Steaks aged for 28 days are seared on the charcoal grill and served with thick-cut chips and a Caesar side salad. Stone-baked pizzas made with fresh dough come with all the popular toppings, like pepperoni, spicy chicken and sweet bell pepper, and Parma ham, mushroom and olives. For pudding, try the rice pudding with Lyth Valley damson preserve, or Lancashire curd tart. Opposite the pub is Penny Street Bridge itself, under which runs the Lancaster Canal on its 42-mile journey from Tewitfield to Kendal.

Open all day all wk 9am–mdnt **Bar Meals** food served all day **Restaurant** food served all day ⊕ THWAITES INNS OF CHARACTER ◀ Wainwright, Lancaster Bomber, Original ♂ Kingstone Press. ♟ 9 **Facilities** Children welcome Children's menu Children's portions Parking Wi-fi **Rooms** 28

Save on hotels. Book at theAA.com/hotel

LANCASHIRE 327 **ENGLAND**

LANCASTER *continued*

The Stork Inn

Conder Green LA2 0AN ☎ 01524 751234
e-mail: tracy@thestorkinn.co.uk
dir: *M6 junct 33 take A6 N. Left at Galgate & next left to Conder Green*

The Stork is a white-painted coaching inn spread along the banks of the Conder estuary, with a colourful 300-year-history that includes several name changes. The quaint sea port of Glasson Dock is a short walk along the Lancashire Coastal Way, and the Lake District is easily accessible. In the bar you will find local ales such as Lancaster Black and Blonde. Seasonal specialities join home-cooked English and South African food like pan-fried chicken breast topped with Lancashire cheese and bacon; Boerewors - lightly spiced pure beef farmer's sausage, served with sweet potato mash and a balsamic, red onion and tomato relish; and minted pea risotto.

Open all day all wk 10am-11pm (Sat-Sun 8.30am-11pm) **Bar Meals** L served all wk 12-9 (Sat-Sun 8.30am-9pm) D served all wk 12-9 (Sat-Sun 8.30am-9pm) food served all day **Restaurant** food served all day ⊕ ENTERPRISE INNS ◀ Timothy Taylor Landlord, Lancaster Blonde & Lancaster Black, Marston's Pedigree, Black Sheep. ♟10 **Facilities** ❧ Children welcome Children's menu Children's portions Play area Garden Parking Wi-fi ▥

The Sun Hotel and Bar

PICK OF THE PUBS

LA1 1ET ☎ 01524 66006
e-mail: info@thesunhotelandbar.co.uk
dir: *6m from M6 junct 33*

First licensed as 'Stoop Hall' in 1680, The Sun was formerly Lancaster's premier coaching inn. Generals from the occupying Jacobean Army lodged at The Sun in 1745, and the artist JMW Turner stayed here whilst making sketches of Heysham in 1812. Now famous for its hospitality and wide selection of cask ales and wines, its lovely old bar is frequented throughout the day; first arrivals are the hotel guests and business breakfasters, then shoppers and people checking their e-mails over coffee. At lunchtime it's busy with customers keen to tuck into the locally sourced good food on the main and daily-changing specials menus. And in the evening there are the real ale enthusiasts, draught and bottled lager connoisseurs and wine lovers. The experienced kitchen brigade prepares home-cooked food, including the popular cheese, cold meat and pâté boards. There is a patio for alfresco dining in warmer weather and an annual beer festival in the summer.

Open all day all wk from 7.30am until late **Bar Meals** food served all day **Restaurant** food served all day ⊕ FREE HOUSE ◀ Lancaster Amber & Blonde, Thwaites Lancaster Bomber, Timmermans Strawberry ♂ Kingstone Press. ♟23 **Facilities** Children welcome Children's menu Children's portions Garden Beer festival ▥

The White Cross **NEW**

Quarry Rd LA1 4XT ☎ 01524 33999
e-mail: twcpub@yahoo.co.uk
dir: *S on one-way system, turn left after Town Hall. Over canal bridge on right*

Set in a 130-year-old former cotton mill warehouse on the edge of the Lancaster Canal, The White Cross is a short stroll from the city centre. A regularly changing selection of up to 14 cask ales includes beers from Copper Dragon, Timothy Taylor and Theakston breweries, but food is an equal draw at this popular waterfront venue. Home-made pork pie; lamb, mint and rosemary burger; lasagne al forno; and deli boards to share are typical menu choices.

Open all day all wk **Bar Meals** Av main course £7 food served all day **Restaurant** food served all day ⊕ ENTERPRISE INNS ◀ Copper Dragon Golden Pippin, Timothy Taylor Landlord, Theakston Old Peculier ♂ Westons Stowford Press & Old Rosie, Ribble Valley Gold. ♟13 **Facilities** Children welcome Children's menu Children's portions Garden Beer festival Parking Wi-fi ▥ (notice required)

LITTLE ECCLESTON   **Map 18 SD44**

The Cartford Inn

PICK OF THE PUBS

See Pick of the Pubs on page 328

NEWTON-IN-BOWLAND   **Map 18 SD65**

Parkers Arms

PICK OF THE PUBS

BB7 3DY ☎ 01200 446236
e-mail: enquiries@parkersarms.co.uk
web: www.parkersarms.co.uk
dir: *From Clitheroe take B6478 through Waddington to Newton-in-Bowland*

In a beautiful hamlet amidst the rolling hills of the Trough of Bowland, this Georgian dining inn is just yards from the River Hodder and enjoys panoramic views over Waddington Fell. It celebrates its rural location by serving the best of Lancashire produce. This includes ales from

the local breweries, meats raised on nearby moorland, vegetables from Ribble Valley farms and fresh fish from nearby Fleetwood. French chef-patron Stosie Madi even forages for ingredients herself. The simple, but elegant, modern dishes on the daily-changing, seasonal menu include Goosnargh corn-fed chicken and leek pie; slow-braised shin of Bowland beef in ale with creamed mash; and fillet of sea bass with pea gnocchi and a lemon reduction. For pudding could be 'Wet Nelly', a classic north-west dessert originally created for Lord Nelson in Liverpool and reworked by co-owner Kathy Smith.

Open all wk 12-3 6-12 (Sat-Sun 12-12) (open all day in summer) **Bar Meals** L served Mon-Fri 12-3, Sat-Sun all day D served Mon-Fri 6-9, Sat-Sun all day Av main course £10-£11 **Restaurant** L served Mon-Fri 12-3, Sat-Sun all day D served Mon-Fri 6-9, Sat-Sun all day Fixed menu price fr £10 Av 3 course à la carte fr £20 ⊕ FREE HOUSE/ENTERPRISE INNS ◀ Bowland Hen Harrier & Sawley Tempted, Lancaster Amber, Copper Dragon ♂ Westons Stowford Press. ♟9 **Facilities** ❧ Children welcome Children's menu Children's portions Garden Parking Wi-fi ▥

PARBOLD   **Map 15 SD41**

The Eagle & Child

PICK OF THE PUBS

Maltkiln Ln, Bispham Green L40 3SG ☎ 01257 462297
web: www.ainscoughs.co.uk
dir: *3m from M6 junct 27. Take A5209 to Parbold. Right onto B5246. 2.5m, Bispham Green on right*

The pub's unusual name derives from a local legend that Lord Derby's illegitimate son was discovered in an eagle's nest; a more prosaic local title is the Bird and Bastard. An award-winning dining pub in a pretty and peaceful location, its outside seating is positioned to enjoy bowling on the green during the summer months. The bar maintains its traditional atmosphere by offering a choice of real ciders and regularly-changing guest ales from a

continued

PICK OF THE PUBS

The Cartford Inn

LITTLE ECCLESTON Map 18 SD44

PR3 0YP ☎ 01995 670166
e-mail: info@thecartfordinn.co.uk
web: www.thecartfordinn.co.uk
dir: *Off A586*

Set in an idyllic location adjoining a toll bridge across the tidal Rive Wyre, this award-winning 17th-century coaching inn enjoys extensive views over the countryside towards the Trough of Bowland and Beacon Fell. Owners Julie and Patrick Beaume have created a pleasing mix of traditional and gastro décor: the stylish and contemporary interior is an appealing blend of striking colours, natural wood and polished floors, whilst the smart open fireplace and an eclectic selection of furniture adds a comfortable and relaxed feel to the bar lounge. Thanks to a new extension, The Cartford now also includes the impressive River Lounge restaurant and an attractive dining terrace, where you can enjoy an imaginative range of dishes based on quality ingredients from local suppliers. Lunchtime sandwiches like cold poached salmon or Cumbrian cured ham and chutney come on Pebby's fresh bread and are served with organic crisps, whilst wooden platters are the showcase for local antipasti, Fleetwood seafood, and organic crudités. Cartford favourites include Pilling Marsh lamb hotpot; and the ever-popular fish with

chunky chips and marrowfat peas. Other main course options range from a parmesan Swiss roll with ricotta, goat's cheese, crème fraîche and sundried tomato; to chargrilled tuna loin with paella, roast peppers, chorizo and rocket salad. Passionfruit tart with raspberry sorbet; and brioche and apricot jam pudding with custard are just two of the choices for dessert. The Cartford Inn makes an ideal spot from which to explore the surrounding area; Lancaster, the Royal Lytham Golf Club, and Blackpool with its Winter Gardens and Grand Theatre are all within easy reach. Accommodation is available.

Open all day Closed: 25 Dec, Mon L
Bar Meals L served Tue-Sat 12-2, Sun 12-8.30 D served Mon-Thu 5.30-9,

Fri-Sat 5.30-10 **Restaurant** L served Tue-Sat 12-2, Sun 12-8.30 D served Mon-Thu 5.30-9, Fri-Sat 5.30-10 ⊕ FREE HOUSE ◀ Moorhouse's Pride of Pendle, Hawkshead Lakeland Gold, Bowland Hen Harrier, Theakston Old Peculier Ö Westons. **Facilities** Children welcome Children's menu Children's portions Garden Parking Wi-fi

PARBOLD *continued*

dozen nearby micro-breweries; the annual early May Bank Holiday beer festival attracts up to 2,000 people to a huge marquee in the pub grounds. Menus for both bar and restaurant hinge on locally sourced and organic produce where possible. Typical of starters are sticky lamb stirfry with sweet chilli noodles, and queen scallops baked in the shell with a creamy garlic and herb sauce. Follow up with a simple grilled steak with green peppercorn and brandy sauce or braised chicken with a risotto of pearl barley, wild mushrooms and thyme. Booking for meals may be required.

Open all wk 12-3 5.30-11 (Fri-Sun 12-11) **Bar Meals** L served all wk 12-2 D served Sun-Thu 5.30-8.30, Fri-Sat 5.30-9 **Restaurant** L served all wk 12-2 D served Sun-Thu 5.30-8.30, Fri-Sat 5.30-9 ⊕ FREE HOUSE ◀ Moorhouse's Black Cat, Thwaites Original, Southport Golden Sands, Guest ales ♺ Kingstone Press. **Facilities** ✿ Children welcome Children's menu Children's portions Family room Garden Beer festival Parking ▄ (notice required)

PENDLETON   Map 18 SD73

The Swan with Two Necks NEW

BB7 1PT ☎ 01200 423112
e-mail: swanwith2necks@yahoo.co.uk
dir: *Exit A59 between Whalley & Chatburn follow Pendleton signs, 0.5m to pub*

Hidden away in the pretty village of Pendleton, The Swan with Two Necks is a charming, traditional village inn dating back to 1722. Pendleton nestles under Pendle Hill, which is famous for its witches, and that's not the only curious piece of history attached to this place; the inn's name refers to the tradition of marking the necks of swans belonging to the Worshipful Company of Vintners with two 'nicks' to distinguish them from swans belonging to the king or queen. Of course you won't find swan on the menu here, but this pub is renowned for its ales, so be sure to try the likes of Phoenix Wobbly Bob or Copper Dragon Golden Pippin.

Open 12-3 6-11 (Sun 12-10.30) Closed: 25 Dec, Mon L, Tue **Bar Meals** L served Wed-Sat 12-1.45, Sun 12-6.30 D served Wed-Sat 6-8.30 ⊕ FREE HOUSE ◀ Phoenix Wobbly Bob, Copper Dragon Golden Pippin, Prospect Nutty Slack, Marble ♺ Westons Traditional & Country Perry. ☗ 14 **Facilities** Children welcome Children's menu Children's portions Garden Parking ▄ (notice required)

SAWLEY   Map 18 SD74

The Spread Eagle
PICK OF THE PUBS

BB7 4NH ☎ 01200 441202
e-mail: spread.eagle@zen.co.uk
dir: *Just off A159 between Clitheroe & Skipton, 4m N of Clitheroe*

Beautifully refurbished in 2009, this handsome old stone inn stands on a quiet lane in the glorious Ribble Valley, flanked on one side by the impressive ruins of Sawley Abbey, and on other by the River Ribble. Inside, choose between the elegant, light-filled dining room with its lush river views through picture windows, or the charming 17th-century bar, where you'll find traditional stone-flagged floors, old oak furniture and roaring fires alongside trendy wallpaper, painted settles strewn with bright cushions, colourful upholstered chairs, eclectic objets d'art, and cool Farrow & Ball hues. The result is a cosy and relaxing setting for savouring a pint of Timothy Taylor Landlord and some decent modern pub food. Served throughout the inn and changing daily, the menu may include scallops and black pudding with saffron and orange dressing; a classic steak-and-kidney pudding; rib-eye steak with garlic butter and hand-cut chips; and warm chocolate brownie with maple ice cream. Don your boots and walk it all off in the Bowland hills.

Open all day all wk 11-11 (Sun 12-10.30) **Bar Meals** L served Mon-Sat 12-2, Sun 12-7.30 D served Mon-Sat 6-9.30, Sun 12-7.30 **Restaurant** L served Mon-Sat 12-2, Sun 12-7.30 D served Mon-Sat 6-9.30, Sun 12-7.30 ⊕ INDIVIDUAL INNS ◀ Thwaites Wainwright, Timothy Taylor Landlord, Moorhouse's ♺ Kingstone Press. ☗ 16 **Facilities** ✿ Children welcome Children's menu Children's portions Garden Parking ▄

TOCKHOLES   Map 15 SD62

The Royal Arms
PICK OF THE PUBS

Tockholes Rd BB3 0PA ☎ 01254 705373
dir: *M65 junct 4 follow Blackburn signs. Right at lights, 1st left. Up hill left at 3B's Brewery into Tockholes Rd. Pub in 3m on left*

The Royal Arms is an appealing, four-square old stone pub in a tiny fold of mill-workers' cottages beside a winding back road high in the West Pennine Moors; walks from the door drop into the deer-haunted Roddlesworth Woods around a picturesque string of reservoirs, or climb to the imposing Jubilee Tower on nearby Darwen Hill. There's an engaging hotchpotch of furnishings in the characterful, flag-floored, beamed little rooms with log fires together with fascinating old photos of the local villages in their mill-town heyday. The bar is rich with pickings from Lancashire micro-breweries. Take a glass

of Glen Top out to tables on the lawn; listen to curlews call on the reedy moors and study the appealing, regularly changing menu of home-cooked goodies, including cheeky leeky pie (chicken, leek and onion) and some great spicy dishes. Sunday roasts or a fulfilling steak and pepper pie take the chill off a bracing winter walk. The annual beer festival takes place in September.

Open all day Closed: Mon **Bar Meals** L served Tue-Fri 12-2, Sat 12-3, Sun 12-6 D served Wed-Sat 6-8.45, Sun 12-6 ◀ Rossendale Glen Top Bitter, Three B's, Guest ales. **Facilities** ✿ Children welcome Children's menu Children's portions Garden Beer festival Parking ▄

TUNSTALL   Map 18 SD67

The Lunesdale Arms
PICK OF THE PUBS

LA6 2QN ☎ 015242 74203
e-mail: info@thelunesdale.co.uk
dir: *M6 junct 36. A65 Kirkby Lonsdale. A638 Lancaster. Pub 2m on right*

Emma Gillibrand's bright, cheery and welcoming pub is set in a small rural village in the beautiful Lune Valley. Well established, with quite a reputation for its food, wines and fine regional beers (Black Sheep and Dent), it draws diners from far and wide for changing chalkboard menus that showcase locally sourced produce, including bread baked on the premises, meat from local farms and organically grown vegetables and salads. Both lunch and evening menus change on a daily basis according to the seasonality of ingredients and new ideas. Country terrine with medlar jelly; slow-roasted shoulder of lamb; butternut squash, sage and Lancashire blue cheese risotto; steak, Guinness and mushroom pie; and Yorkshire rhubarb pannacotta with poached rhubarb show the style. In winter, cosy up by the wood-burning stove in the light and airy bar, with its bare boards, stripped dining tables, comfortable sofas, and local artwork. Booking for meals may be required.

Open 11-3 6-12 (Sat Sun & BH 11-4 6-1am) Closed: 25-26 Dec, Mon (ex BH) **Bar Meals** L served Tue-Fri 12-2, Sat-Sun 12-2.30 D served Tue-Sun 6-9 **Restaurant** L served Tue-Fri 12-2, Sat-Sun 12-2.30 D served Tue-Sun 6-9 ⊕ FREE HOUSE ◀ Dent Aviator, Black Sheep, Brysons, Guinness ♺ Westons Stowford Press. **Facilities** ✿ Children welcome Children's portions Family room Garden Parking ▄

WHALLEY   Map 18 SD73

The Three Fishes ◉
PICK OF THE PUBS

See Pick of the Pubs on page 330
See advert on page 331

PICK OF THE PUBS

The Three Fishes ❀

WHALLEY　　　Map 18 SD73

Mitton Rd, Mitton BB7 9PQ
☎ **01254 826888**
e-mail: enquiries@thethreefishes.com
web: www.thethreefishes.com
dir: *M6 junct 31, A59 to Clitheroe. Follow Whalley signs, B6246, 2m*

For more than four centuries travellers in the short stretch of road between the Ribble bridge at Mitton and the 16th-century bridge over its tributary, the Hodder, have been stopping here for a swift half. With Pendle Hill forming one horizon, Longridge Fell another, this is the landscape that inspired parts of JRR Tolkien's *Lord of the Rings* trilogy. By the log fire in the contemporary, rambling interior try a 'beer bat', a wooden paddle holding three glasses, each a third of a pint, for sampling real ales from brewery partner Thwaites of Blackburn and the monthly guest. The menus are inspired by Nigel Haworth, chef-patron of Northcote, his renowned restaurant in nearby Langho, which like this pub is an associate company of Ribble Valley Inns. With an AA Rosette for inventiveness and presentation, the restaurant relies extensively on trusted regional suppliers whose portraits adorn the walls. Try Bury black pudding or game terrine with Gott's streaky bacon as a starter, followed by a main course of fish pie, Lancashire hotpot, a chargrill or an English tossed salad. Afternoon bites served from 2pm include

platter of the day, ploughman's and sandwiches. A six-variety Lancashire cheeseboard served with butter, home-made bread, biscuits, celery and chutney should go down well with caseophiles (that is, cheese-lovers). Southerners might raise an eyebrow at the Three Fishes' assertion that the Sunday roast was invented and perfected in the north of England, but it's probably best not to rise to the bait and simply enjoy dining on rib-eye of local beef; corn-fed chicken; Gloucester Old Spot pork loin; or organic shoulder of lamb. Those wishing to stay are recommended to consider Northcote, only ten minutes away.

Open all day all wk Closed: 25 Dec **Bar Meals** L served Mon-Sat 12-2, Sun 12-8 (afternoon bites Mon-Sat 2-5.30)

D served Mon-Thu 5.30-8.30, Fri-Sat 5.30-9, Sun 12-8 Av main course £10.50 food served all day **Restaurant** food served all day ⊕ RIBBLE VALLEY INNS ◀ Bowland Hen Harrier, Moorhouse's Black Cat, Thwaites ♻ Rekorderlig. ♟9 **Facilities** Children welcome Children's menu Children's portions Garden Parking

THE THREE FISHES

Mitton Road, Mitton, Nr Whalley, Lancashire BB7 9PQ
Tel: 01254 826888 • Fax: 01254 826026
Website: www.thethreefishes.com
Email: enquiries@thethreefishes.com

The Three Fishes is situated in the tiny picturesque hamlet of Mitton, in the rural haven of The Ribble Valley. A relaxing environment, with sprawling sun-terraces in the summer and crackling log fires in the winter. As the flagship and first born pub to Ribble Valley Inns, it has become a legend in these parts. A line up of the best cask ales, ciders and guest beers, plus a wine list which received the AA Notable Wine List award 2012. The food inspired by Nigel Haworth offers a delicious tribute to traditional specialities, and British classics using the produce of our local food heroes. Enjoy a nibble of North Sea Cod Cheeks in Scrumpy Batter, Sea Salt, Bramley Apple Aioli or Nigel's Free Range Rare Breed Chipolatas, Cumberland, Spicy Pork & Black Pudding, Mustard Mayonnaise. In the winter indulge in the classic Lancashire hotpot with heather reared Lonk lamb, King Edward Potatoes, Pickled Red Cabbage. The menu offers a large selection for vegetarians and a gluten free menu is available.

The Dressers Arms

Briers Brow PR6 8HD ☎ 01254 830041
e-mail: info@dressersarms.co.uk
dir: M61 junct 8, A674 to Blackburn. Follow sign for pub on right

Until the 1960s, this was the smallest pub in Lancashire. The long, low, creeper-festooned old gristone building is crammed with local photos, collectables and artefacts spread through a clutch of separate drinking areas; partly flagged floors are warmed by roaring fires in winter. Its appeal is enhanced by the choice of ales and a reliable raft of home-made pub grub: perhaps a hot sandwich of pan-fried chicken and bacon with melted cheese will hit the spot; otherwise look to the specials for a trio of lamb cutlets with port and rosemary sauce.

Open all day all wk **Bar Meals** food served all day **Restaurant** food served all day ⊕ FREE HOUSE ◀ The Dressers Arms Dressers Bitter, Black Sheep ♂ Westons. ☂ 20 **Facilities** ✿ Children welcome Children's menu Children's portions Family room Garden Parking Wi-fi ▭

The Inn at Whitewell ★★★★★ INN ◉

PICK OF THE PUBS

Forest of Bowland BB7 3AT ☎ 01200 448222
e-mail: reception@innatwhitewell.com
dir: From B6243 follow Whitewell signs

Little, if any, of the wild beauty of the Forest of Bowland can have changed since the 1300s, when this stone inn was built as a small manor house. It stands high on the banks of the River Hodder, where the owner Charles Bowman says he trusts it will remain (an example of his self-confessed "often misplaced sense of humour"). The somewhat eccentric interior is packed with random furnishings, antiques and pictures, a Bowman family passion. The kitchen produces consistently delicious food for the bar at lunch and supper, typically grilled Norfolk kipper, and cheese and onion pie, and also for the dining room in the evening, when you might choose smoked Goosnargh chicken salad; roast rack of lamb with cumin, tomatoes, garlic and Anna potatoes; and home-made ice cream. The whole complex embraces 23 individually decorated bedrooms, a wine merchant, an art gallery and a shop selling home-made goodies. Booking for meals may be required.

Open all day all wk 10am-1am **Bar Meals** L served all wk 12-2 D served all wk 7.30-9.30 Av main course £25 **Restaurant** D served all wk 7.30-9.30 Av 3 course à la carte fr £32 ⊕ FREE HOUSE ◀ Timothy Taylor Landlord, Bowland, Copper Dragon, Moorhouse's, Hawkshead ♂ Dunkertons Premium Organic. ☂ 16 **Facilities** Children welcome Children's portions Garden Parking Wi-fi ▭ (notice required) **Rooms** 23

The Queen's Head ★★★★ RR ◉

PICK OF THE PUBS

See Pick of the Pubs on opposite page

The White Horse

PICK OF THE PUBS

White Horse Ln LE4 4EF ☎ 0116 267 1038
e-mail: info@thewhitehorsebirstall.co.uk
dir: M1 junct 21A, A46 towards Newark 5.5m. Exit A46 at Loughborough

Overlooking Watermead Country Park, The White Horse (formerly The Mulberry Tree) is a former canal-worker's beerhouse whose tranquil garden was once a coal wharf serving the village of Birstall. Rebuilt in the 1920s, the pub has matured over the years into today's restful retreat, which delivers the very best expected of a village inn: reliable beers, good company and a sought-after range of dishes. Boaters and ramblers alike can look forward to vintage cheddar and leek frittata with salad leaves and balsamic glaze followed by classic pub main courses such as a hand-made burger with chips, relish and onion rings; gammon with egg and chips; or beef lasagne with dressed salad and garlic bread. Or just follow the locals' lead and tuck in to the renowned pie of the week with all the trimmings. For dessert, maybe home-made banoffee pie with toffee sauce.

Open all wk winter 12-3 5.30-11 (Sun 12-10.30); summer all day everyday **Bar Meals** L served Mon-Sat 12-2.30, Sun 12-4 D served Mon-Sat 6-9 Av main course £10 **Restaurant** L served Mon-Sat 12-2.30, Sun 12-4 D served Mon-Sat 6-9 ⊕ TRUST INNS ◀ Timothy Taylor Landlord, Jennings Cumberland Ale, Guest ale. **Facilities** ✿ Children welcome Children's menu Children's portions Play area Garden Parking ▭ (notice required)

The Three Horseshoes

Main St DE73 8AN ☎ 01332 695129
e-mail: ian@thehorseshoes.com
dir: 5m from M1 junct 23a. Pub in village centre

Originally a farrier's, the buildings here are around 250 years old; the pub has been here for at least a century, while the main kitchen, a farm shop and a chocolate workshop now occupy the smithy's and stables in the courtyard. Inside, numerous original features and old beams are supplemented by antique furniture, and sea-grass matting completes the warm and welcoming atmosphere. Typical dishes are tomato and vodka soup; salmon and sweet potato curry; roast vegetable casserole; fillet of beef with pepper sauce; and duck breast with cabbage and bacon. Try some of the hand-made chocolates for dessert. Booking for meals may be required.

Open 10.30-2.30 5.30-11 (Sun 12-3) Closed: 25-26 & 31 Dec-1 Jan, Sun eve **Bar Meals** L served Mon-Sat 12-2 D served Mon-Sat 5.30-9.15 Av main course £8.95 **Restaurant** L served Mon-Sat 12-2, Sun 12-3 D served Mon-Sat 6.30-9.15 Av 3 course à la carte fr £31 ⊕ FREE HOUSE ◀ Marston's Pedigree. **Facilities** ✿ Children welcome Children's portions Garden Parking

Joiners Arms

Church Walk LE17 5QH ☎ 0116 247 8258
e-mail: stephen@thejoinersarms.co.uk
dir: 4m from Lutterworth

More restaurant than village pub, with restored natural oak beams, tiled floor, pleasant décor, and lots of brassware and candles. Menus change constantly, and quality ingredients are sourced – beef from Scotland, Cornish lamb, Portland crab. From an impressive menu, dishes might include king scallops, Clonakilty black pudding and garlic mash; melon in elderflower and ginger jelly; medallions of Scottish beef fillet with Diane sauce; butternut squash and blue cheese risotto; liquorish pannacotta with blackcurrant sorbet; or mango and passionfruit Pavlova. Every Tuesday there's a three-course fixed menu 'Auberge Supper'. Booking for meals may be required.

Open 12-2 6.30-11 Closed: Mon ⊕ FREE HOUSE ◀ Greene King IPA, John Smith's, Guinness. **Facilities** Parking

Tollemache Arms

48 Main St NG33 5SA ☎ 01476 860477
e-mail: info@tollemache-arms.co.uk
dir: 4m off the A1, between Colsterworth and Melton Mowbray on the B676

Situated in the beautiful village of Buckminster, this striking, 18th-century building on the Tollemache Estate is now a thriving pub. Those looking to enjoy a drink are welcomed by the big oak bar which serves local Grainstore ales, while diners can get comfy in the stylish, oak-floored dining room and library and enjoy the good modern British food. Using local seasonal produce, daily menus may feature butternut, chilli and feta soup; pan-fried sea bass with blood orange and fennel salad; and cherry clafoutis with ice cream: Thursday evening is pie night. A community focused pub where dogs and children are welcome. Booking for meals may be required.

Open Tue-Sat 12-3 5-11 (Sun 12-5) Closed: 27-29 Dec, 2-9 Jan, Sun eve, Mon **Bar Meals** L served Tue-Sat 12-2, Sun 12-3 D served Tue-Sat 6.30-9 Av main course £10.50 **Restaurant** L served Tue-Sat 12-2, Sun 12-3 D served Tue-Sat 6.30-9 ⊕ FREE HOUSE ◀ The Grainstore Ten Fifty, Phipps NBC Red Star, John Smith's, Guinness, Guest ales, Local ales. ☂ 10 **Facilities** ✿ Children welcome Children's menu Children's portions Garden Parking Wi-fi ▭

PICK OF THE PUBS

The Queen's Head ★★★★RR ❀

BELTON   Map 11 SK42

2 Long St LE12 9TP ☎ 01530 222359
e-mail: enquiries@thequeenshead.org
web: www.thequeenshead.org
dir: *On B5324 between Coalville &
Loughborough*

A contemporary boutique-style pub/
restaurant with rooms in the centre of
the picturesque village of Belton. Its
transformation belies the fact that The
Queen's Head has been trading as the
village pub since the early 1800s. All-
round appeal starts with a clean and
uncluttered exterior, suggesting that its
owners might also have a fair idea of
what constitutes good interior design.
And so they have. Settle into a leather
sofa in the contemporary bar and
choose your refreshment. A real ale is
always on tap, changing every few days;
such is the focus on customer
satisfaction here that a favourite tipple
may be installed if it can be sourced. An
AA Rosette indicates that eating here is
no humdrum experience. The head chef
uses only fresh produce, locally sourced
if possible; for example, the pub has
exclusive access to Dexter beef raised
on a Leicestershire small holding. Yet
dishes are competitively priced and
include pub classics. Pie and mash is
actually two pies with different fillings,
cooked fresh to order and served with
Savoy cabbage and red wine jus. Other
favourites are shepherd's pie, and

home-made beer-battered fish with
hand-cut chips. Light lunches range
from sandwiches to starter-size portions
of salmon and prawn fishcake; or seared
scallops with pea textures and
pancetta. For a more extravagant outlay
you can enjoy a roast rump of local lamb
with root vegetables and a gruyère
cheese gratin; or slow-cooked belly of
pork with fresh king prawns, mustard
seed mash and Madeira jus. In addition
to roasts, Sunday lunch menus address
the needs of fish lovers and vegetarians,
and finish with desserts such as apple,
pear and cinnamon crumble with crème
anglaise. If staying overnight, you'll find
individually designed and styled
bedrooms. This is definitely a 'special
occasion' type of place, and is

occasionally closed to accommodate a
private booking. So telephone ahead to
clear the way for a memorable treat.

Open all day all wk Closed: 25-26 Dec
⊕ FREE HOUSE ◼ Marston's Pedigree,
Queen's Special. **Facilities** Children
welcome Children's portions Play area
Garden Parking Wi-fi **Rooms** 6

COLEORTON · Map 11 SK41

George Inn

Loughborough Rd LE67 8HF ☎ 01530 834639
e-mail: janice@jwilkinson781.orangehome.co.uk
dir: *Just off A42 junct 13 on A512*

Weary travellers should take note of this 300-year-old family-run free house as it makes a convenient refreshment stop close to the A42 and M1. Secluded away in rolling countryside the George has a traditional bar and homely lounge, with leather sofa and chairs fronting a wood-burning stove, providing a relaxing and comfortable setting for sampling some honest pub food. Dishes range from lunchtime panini sandwiches (stilton, bacon and mushroom) and lasagne and garlic bread to Thai green chicken curry and rib-eye steak with all the trimmings. Booking for meals may be required.

Open 12.30-3 5.30-11 (Fri-Sat 12-11 Sun 12-4) Closed: Sun eve, Mon **Bar Meals** L served Tue-Sat 12-2.30, Sun 12-3 D served Tue-Thu 6-9, Fri-Sat 6-9.30 Av main course £10 **Restaurant** L served Tue-Sat 12-2.30, Sun 12-3 D served Tue-Thu 6-9, Fri-Sat 6-9.30 Av 3 course à la carte fr £20 ⊕ FREE HOUSE ◀ Marston's Pedigree, Guest ales Ò Thatchers Gold. ♈ 12 **Facilities** Children welcome Children's portions Play area Garden Parking Wi-fi

EVINGTON · Map 11 SK60

The Cedars

Main St LE5 6DN ☎ 0116 273 0482
e-mail: pippa@king-henrys-taverns.co.uk
dir: *From Leicester take A6 towards Market Harborough. Left at lights, onto B667 to Evington. Pub in village centre*

At The Cedars you can choose to eat in the bar restaurant with its panoramic windows overlooking the fountain and pond, or just enjoy a drink in the lounge bar with its leather sofas and relaxed atmosphere. King Henry's Taverns, the owners, offer something for everyone on their menu of freshly prepared dishes – for small and large appetites alike. Choose from steaks, fish and rump burgers, as well as traditional favourites such as steak-and-ale pie, and international dishes like Mexican fajitas. The gardens are a great place for alfresco dining. For dessert, the chocolate lumpy bumpy pie is certainly a treat for chocoholics.

Open all day all wk 11.30-11 **Bar Meals** L served all wk 12-10 D served all wk 12-10 food served all day **Restaurant** L served all wk 12-10 D served all wk 12-10 food served all day ⊕ FREE HOUSE/KING HENRY'S TAVERNS ◀ Greene King IPA, Marston's Pedigree, Guinness. **Facilities** Children welcome Children's menu Children's portions Garden Parking ▄▄▄

GRIMSTON · Map 11 SK62

The Black Horse

3 Main St LE14 3BZ ☎ 01664 812358
e-mail: amanda.wayne@sky.com
dir: *Telephone for directions*

Amanda Sharpe's traditional 16th-century coaching inn overlooks the village green, and beyond that to the Vale of Belvoir, inspiration for the Belvoir Star Mild sold in the bar alongside real ales from Adnams, St Austell and Marston's. Traditional main courses include pan-fried trio of lamb; sizzling Cajun chicken; lamb cutlets; and lasagne, as well as a daily specials board listing fresh fish and some less familiar dishes. The outdoor eating area is popular.

Open all wk 12-3 6-11 (Sun 12-6) ⊕ FREE HOUSE ◀ Marston's Pedigree, St Austell Tribute, Belvoir Star Mild, Adnams, Guest ales Ò Thatchers Gold. **Facilities** Children welcome Children's portions Garden

KNOSSINGTON · Map 11 SK80

The Fox & Hounds

6 Somerby Rd LE15 8LY ☎ 01664 452129
dir: *4m from Oakham in Knossington*

High quality food and helpful, friendly service are the hallmarks of this 500-year-old pub, which recently reopened after a major refurb. Set in the village of Knossington close to Rutland Water, the building retains lots of traditional features, and the large rear garden and sitting area are ideal for alfresco summer dining. A typical lunch menu might include grilled lamb rump with ratatouille and tapenade; vegetable tart with stilton; or salmon with roasted aubergine, red pepper and coriander salsa. Booking for meals may be required.

Open 12-2.30 6.30-11 (Fri 12-3 5-11 Sun eve in summer) Closed: Mon, Tue L & Sun eve **Bar Meals** L served Wed-Sun 12-2 D served Tue-Sat 6.30-9.30 Av main course £13 **Restaurant** L served Wed-Sun 12-2 D served Tue-Sat 6.30-9.30 ⊕ ENTERPRISE INNS ◀ Wells Bombardier, Fuller's London Pride. **Facilities** ✿ Children's portions Garden Parking Wi-fi ▄▄▄ (notice required)

LEICESTER · Map 11 SK50

The Almanack

15 Bathhouse Ln, Highcross LE1 4SA ☎ 0116 216 0705
e-mail: hello@thealmanack-leicester.co.uk
dir: *In Highcross shopping centre (car parks nearby)*

A modern British gastro-pub with dramatic floor-to-ceiling windows and a vintage-inspired interior, The Almanack sits in the heart of Leicester's trendy Highcross restaurant quarter. Take a seat on one of the retro chairs or slide into a booth for a pint of Purity Gold and order from an extensive menu that includes deli boards, sandwiches and main dishes of sausages and mash; creamy fish stew with butterbeans and chorizo;

and Cotswold lamb canon with dauphinoise potatoes, spring vegetables and lamb jus.

Open all day all wk 10am-mdnt Closed: 25 Dec **Bar Meals** Av main course £14.50 food served all day **Restaurant** food served all day ⊕ FREE HOUSE/PEACH PUBS ◀ Purity Gold, Pure UBU. ♈ 10 **Facilities** ✿ Children welcome Children's menu Children's portions Wi-fi ▄▄▄

LONG WHATTON · Map 11 SK42

The Falcon Inn ★★★ INN

64 Main St LE12 5DG ☎ 01509 842416
e-mail: enquiries@thefalconinnlongwhatton.com
dir: *Telephone for directions*

Lebanese-born proprietor Jad Otaki brings a taste of the Middle East to this traditional country inn; the Mezzeh is akin to a tasting menu of some half dozen starters and four main courses. But The Falcon is at heart an English pub, decked out with award-winning flower displays and hosting real ale drinkers on the beautiful heated rear terrace. If spice is not your thing, you can plump for familiar bar meals such as goujons of lemon sole; or chicken breast in a cream and peppercorn sauce. Accommodation is available. Booking for meals may be required.

Open all day all wk **Bar Meals** L served Mon-Sat 12-2, Sun 12-4 D served Mon-Sat 6.30-9 **Restaurant** L served Mon-Sat 12-2, Sun 12-4 D served Mon-Sat 6.30-9 ⊕ EVERARDS ◀ Tiger & Original, Guest ale. **Facilities** Children welcome Family room Garden Parking Wi-fi ▄▄▄ **Rooms** 11

The Royal Oak ★★★★ INN ◉

PICK OF THE PUBS

26 The Green LE12 5DB ☎ 01509 843694
e-mail: enquiries@theroyaloaklongwhatton.co.uk
dir: *M1 junct 24, A6 to Kegworth. Right into Whatton Road (becomes Kegworth Ln) to Long Whatton. From Loughborough, A6 towards Kegworth. Left onto B5324, right into Hathern Rd leading to The Green*

Reopened in 2010 after a full refurbishment, The Royal Oak is now an award-winning gastro-pub, offering high quality, locally sourced food. In the smart bar, popular brews from Timothy Taylor and Blue Monkey Brewery stand shoulder-to-shoulder with regular guests and a carefully selected wine list with nine by the glass. In the equally stylish restaurant diners can expect some tough decisions: will it be rack of lamb cutlets marinated in chilli and honey, with a Moroccan spiced vegetable tagine, fruit and nut bulgar wheat and home-made coriander dough balls; slow-cooked fillet of beef topped with chicken liver parfait and served with shallot and wild mushroom Tatin, parsnip purée and red wine jus; or vegetarian suet pudding of roast squash and rosemary with a mixed bean, tomato and baby onion casserole? An annual April beer festival offers 30 real ales and 10 ciders. The impeccably furnished guest bedrooms are in a separate building. Booking for meals may be required.

Open all day all wk **Bar Meals** L served Mon-Sat 12-2.30, Sun 12-4 D served Mon-Sat 5.30-9.30 Av main course £8 **Restaurant** L served Mon-Sat 12-2.30, Sun 12-4 D served Mon-Sat 5.30-9.30 Fixed menu price fr £27 Av 3 course à la carte fr £22 ⦿ FREE HOUSE ◖ St Austell Tribute, Bass, Timothy Taylor Landlord, Blue Monkey, Guest ales ♡ Westons Old Rosie, Thatchers. ♟ 9 **Facilities** Children welcome Children's portions Garden Beer festival Parking Wi-fi **Rooms** 7

LOUGHBOROUGH   Map 11 SK51

The Swan in the Rushes

21 The Rushes LE11 5BE ☎ 01509 217014
e-mail: swanintherushes@castlerockbrewery.co.uk
dir: *On A6 (Derby road). Pub in front of Sainsbury's, 1m from railway station.*

A 1930s tile-fronted real ale pub, The Swan in the Rushes was acquired by the Castle Rock chain in 1986, making it the oldest in the group. There's a first-floor drinking terrace, a function room and bar that seats 80, and a family/dining area. This pub has a friendly atmosphere and always offers ten ales, including seven guests, a selection of real ciders and fruit wines. Expect traditional pub grub, music nights, a folk club and a skittle alley. Beer festivals are held at the end of May and in mid-November.

Open all day all wk 11-11 (Fri-Sat 11am-mdnt Sun 12-11) **Bar Meals** L served all wk 12-3 D served Mon-Fri 5-9.30, Sat 12-9.30 ⦿ FREE HOUSE/CASTLE ROCK ◖ Harvest Pale, Sheriff's Tipple & Elsie Mo, Adnams Southwold Bitter, 7 Guests ales ♡ Westons Stowford Press & Country Perry. ♟ 12 **Facilities** ♣ Children welcome Children's portions Family room Beer festival Parking Wi-fi 🚐

LUTTERWORTH   Map 11 SP58

Man at Arms

The Green, Bitteswell LE17 4SB ☎ 01455 552540
e-mail: pippa@king-henrys-taverns.co.uk
dir: *From Lutterworth take Lutterworth Rd towards Ullesthorpe. Turn left at small white cottage. Pub on left after college on village green*

This pub was named after a bequest by the Dowse Charity to the nearby village of Bitteswell in return for providing a 'man at arms' for times of war. It was the first pub bought by the King Henry's Taverns group. Now, 27 years later, it shares a common menu with its sister pubs. Along with traditional favourites such as steak-and-ale pie, sizeable options include a whole roast chicken; 'brontosaurus' lamb shank (a half leg); and the Titanic challenge – a rump steak weighing some three pounds.

Open all day all wk 11.30-11 **Bar Meals** food served all day **Restaurant** food served all day ⦿ FREE HOUSE/KING HENRY'S TAVERNS ◖ Greene King IPA, Wells Bombardier, Guinness, Bass. ♟ 16 **Facilities** Children welcome Children's menu Children's portions Garden Parking 🚐

MOUNTSORREL   Map 11 SK51

The Swan Inn ★★★★ INN

10 Loughborough Rd LE12 7AT ☎ 0116 230 2340
e-mail: swan@jvf.co.uk
dir: *On A6 between Leicester & Loughborough*

Originally built as two terraced cottages in 1688, this Grade II listed free house stands on the banks of the River Soar and has a secluded riverside garden, ideal for summer sipping and dining. Exposed beams, flagstone floors and roaring winter log fires characterise the cosy bar and dining areas. Fine wines and cask-conditioned beers from Theakston and Greene King accompany a varied, weekly-changing menu of British and European classics, as well as light lunches and snacks: salmon fillet with slow-cooked leeks in filo pastry, and duck breast with Savoy cabbage and pancetta are indicative of the standard. Luxury accommodation is available.

Open all wk 12-2.30 5.30-11 (Sat 12-11 Sun 12-3 7-10.30) **Bar Meals** L served all wk 12-2 D served Mon-Sat 6.30-9.30 Av main course £12 **Restaurant** L served all wk 12-2 D served Mon-Sat 6.30-9.30 Fixed menu price fr £10.90 Av 3 course à la carte fr £22 ⦿ FREE HOUSE ◖ Black Sheep Best Bitter, Theakston XB & Old Peculier, Greene King Ruddles County & Abbot Ale. **Facilities** ♣ Garden Parking **Rooms** 1

MOWSLEY   Map 11 SP68

The Staff of Life

PICK OF THE PUBS

Main St LE17 6NT ☎ 0116 240 2359
dir: *M1 junct 20, A4304 to Market Harborough. Left in Husbands Bosworth onto A5199. In 3m turn right to pub*

Were they to return, the residents of this well-proportioned Edwardian house would surely be amazed by the transformation of their home into such an appealing community local. The bar even has some traditional features – high-backed settles and flagstone floor, for example – along with a large woodburning stove. Look up to see not only a fine wood-panelled ceiling but also, not quite where you'd expect it, the wine cellar. Many wines are served by the glass, and ales from the likes of Fuller's are on tap. In the dining area, which overlooks the garden, carefully prepared dishes combine British and international influences: Parma ham and gorgonzola on a rocket and olive salad could be followed by a shortcrust pastry game pie stuffed with goose, rabbit, pigeon and pheasant. Desserts are prepared to order by Linda O'Neill, a former member of the Irish Panel of Chefs. A small patio area lies to the front with additional outside seating in the rear garden.

Open Mon-Sat 6-close (Sat 12-3 6-close Sun 12-10.30) Closed: Mon-Fri L **Bar Meals** L served Sat 12-2.15, Sun 12-3 D served Tue-Sat 6-9.15 Av main course £14 **Restaurant** L served Sat 12-2.15, Sun 12-3 D served Tue-Sat 6-9.15 Fixed menu price fr £14.95 ⦿ FREE HOUSE ◖ Sharp's Doom Bar, Fuller's London Pride, Timothy Taylor. ♟ 19 **Facilities** Children welcome Children's portions Garden Parking 🚐 (notice required)

NETHER BROUGHTON   Map 11 SK62

The Red House

23 Main St LE14 3HB ☎ 01664 822429
e-mail: bernie@mulberrypubco.com
dir: *M1 junct 21A, A46. Right onto A606. Or take A606 from Nottingham*

The Red House is a fine mixture of a 300-year-old village pub (with log fires in winter) and light, contemporary design. The lounge bar opens into an airy restaurant, and a conservatory area overlooks the outdoor bar, terrace and courtyard grill. Immaculate gardens include a small play area and a permanent marquee for weddings, parties and corporate functions. Dishes range from a selection of sandwiches or hot dishes like Guinness and beef sausages with mash and stout gravy in the bar, to roast rump of English lamb, pea mash and confit carrots in the restaurant. An ideal spot for walking, fishing and bird-watching. Booking for meals may be required.

Open all wk 7-3 5-11 (Fri-Sun all day) ⦿ FREE HOUSE/ MULBERRY PUB (UK) PLC ◖ Greene King IPA, Belvoir, Guinness ♡ Jacques. **Facilities** Children welcome Children's menu Children's portions Play area Garden Parking Wi-fi

OADBY   Map 11 SK60

Cow and Plough

PICK OF THE PUBS

Gartree Rd, Stoughton Farm LE2 2FB ☎ 0116 272 0852
e-mail: cowandplough@googlemail.com
dir: *3m Leicester Station A6 to Oadby. Turn off to Spire Hospital, pub 0.5m beyond*

Former Victorian farm buildings house this much-loved pub which dates back to 1989, when licensee Barry Lount approached the owners of Stoughton Grange Farm, who were in the process of opening the farm to the public. The farm park attraction has since closed, but the Cow and Plough continues to thrive, hosting functions and events including quarterly beer and cider festivals. The pub also brews its own award-winning Steamin' Billy beers, named in honour of the owners' Jack Russell terrier. The interior is decorated with historic inn signs and brewing memorabilia, providing a fascinating setting in which to enjoy food from the regularly changing menus. Typical choices include moules marinière with crusty bread followed by roasted rabbit hotpot with sweet cider sauce. A separate list of 'traditional dishes' offers the likes of sausages, mash and gravy or steak and Steamin' Billy ale pie. Puddings continue in a traditional vein with the likes of Bakewell tart or apple and cinnamon crumble. Booking for meals may be required.

Open all day all wk **Bar Meals** L served all wk 12-2.30 D served all wk 6-9 Av main course £10.95 **Restaurant** L served all wk 12-2.30 D served all wk 6-9 Fixed menu price fr £13.95 Av 3 course à la carte fr £22.95 ⦿ FREE HOUSE ◖ Steamin' Billy Bitter & Skydiver, Fuller's London Pride, Batemans Dark Mild, Abbeydale. ♟ 10 **Facilities** ♣ Children welcome Children's menu Children's portions Family room Garden Beer festival Parking Wi-fi 🚐

SILEBY
Map 11 SK61

The White Swan

Swan St LE12 7NW ☎ 01509 814832
e-mail: tamiller56@googlemail.com
dir: *From Leicester A6 towards Loughborough, turn right for Sileby; or take A46 towards Newark-on-Trent, turn left for Sileby*

Behind the unassuming exterior of this 1930s building, you'll find a free house of some character, with a book-lined restaurant and a homely bar with an open fire. A wide selection of home-made rolls, baguettes and snacks is on offer; menus change weekly, and there are blackboard specials, too. For main course, try the salmon and prawn pancake; roast cod with chorizo, tomatoes and garlic butter; pork fillet with wholegrain mustard, white wine and cream; or rump steak with all the trimmings. Save some room for desserts such as hot chocolate fudge cake.

Open Tue-Sat & Sun L Closed: 1-7 Jan, Sat L, Sun eve & Mon **Bar Meals** L served Tue-Sun 12-1.30 (ex Sat) D served Tue-Sat 7-8.30 **Restaurant** L served Sun 12-1.30 D served Tue-Sat 7-8.30 ⊕ FREE HOUSE ◀ Marston's Pedigree, Fuller's London Pride, Ansell's. ☂ 8 **Facilities** Children welcome Children's menu Children's portions Garden Parking Wi-fi

SOMERBY
Map 11 SK71

Stilton Cheese Inn

High St LE14 2QB ☎ 01664 454394
web: www.stiltoncheeseinn.co.uk
dir: *From A606 between Melton Mowbray & Oakham follow signs to Pickwell & Somerby. Enter village, 1st right to centre, pub on left*

Built from mellow local sandstone, this attractive 17th-century inn stands in the centre of the village surrounded by beautiful countryside; nearby is Melton Mowbray, famous for its pork pies and stilton cheese – hence the pub's name. It enjoys a good reputation for its food, and for its great selections of real ales, wines and malt whiskies. A typical meal might include stilton and onion soup followed by home-made lasagne or other pub classics such as deep fried scampi or macaroni cheese.

Open all wk 12-3 6-11 (Sun 12-3 7-11) **Bar Meals** L served all wk 12-2 D served Mon-Sat 6-9, Sun 7-9 Av main course £9 **Restaurant** L served all wk 12-2 D served Mon-Sat 6-9, Sun 7-9 Av 3 course à la carte fr £18 ⊕ FREE HOUSE ◀ The Grainstore Ten Fifty, Brewster's Hophead, Belvoir Star, Oakham Ales JHB,

Newby Wyke Kingston Topaz Ⓒ Westons Old Rosie & Bounds. ☂ 15 **Facilities** Children welcome Children's menu Children's portions Family room Garden Parking 🚌 (notice required)

STATHERN
Map 11 SK73

Red Lion Inn
PICK OF THE PUBS

Red Lion St LE14 4HS ☎ 01949 860868
e-mail: info@theredlioninn.co.uk
dir: *From A1 (Grantham), A607 towards Melton, turn right in Waltham, right at next x-rds then left to Stathern*

Whatever the season, the Red Lion Inn has plenty to offer: logs crackling in the stove, daily-changing specials boards, superb value lunch offers, cookery demonstrations, and wine evenings – all this and regional ales too. Located in the beautiful Vale of Belvoir, details like the stone-floored bar, the elegant dining room and the comfortable lounge (complete with plenty of reading material) make this establishment stand out. Menus change seasonally in accordance with locally supplied produce, and offer a mix of classic pub food and innovative country cooking. Typical of chef Sean Hope's dishes are braised pork fritters with apple and black pudding; fillet of salmon with beetroot, spätzle and a horseradish velouté; honey roast confit duck leg with beetroot champ mash and Madeira sauce; and vegetable curry with coriander rice and pistachio naan bread. Desserts too reflect a serious attention to detail: rhubarb and ginger pannacotta with rhubarb sorbet, and coffee pudding, toffee sauce and Amaretto ice cream are two examples. Booking for meals may be required.

Open 12-3 6-11 (Fri-Sat 12-11 Sun 12-7) Closed: Sun eve & Mon **Bar Meals** L served Tue-Sat 12-2, Sun 12-3 D served Tue-Thu 6-9, Fri 5.30-9.30, Sat 7-9.30 Av main course £10.50 **Restaurant** L served Tue-Sat 12-2, Sun 12-3 D served Tue-Thu 6-9, Fri 5.30-9.30, Sat 7-9.30 Fixed menu price fr £14.50 Av 3 course à la carte fr £29 ⊕ RUTLAND INN COMPANY LTD ◀ The Grainstore Red Lion Ale, Brewster's Marquis, Fuller's London Pride Ⓒ Aspall, Sheppy's. ☂ 8 **Facilities** Children welcome Children's menu Children's portions Garden Parking

SWITHLAND
Map 11 SK51

The Griffin Inn

174 Main St LE12 8TJ ☎ 01509 890535
e-mail: thegriffininn@swithland.info
dir: *From A46 into Anstey. Right at rdbt to Cropston. Right at x-rds, 1st left, 0.5m to Swithland. Follow brown signs for inn*

Parts of this welcoming, traditional, family-run country inn date back to the 15th century. There are three cosy bar areas serving a range of real ales, two dining rooms, a skittle alley and large patio. Menus and a wide range of specials offer unfussy, good-value food including smoked seafood terrine; chicken ballotine wrapped in Parma ham and filled with pesto, sundried tomatoes and mozzarella; and mushroom, spinach and cherry tomato frittata. The area is popular with walkers heading for Swithland

Woods, Beacon Hill and the Old John folly. There's also a steam railway nearby. Booking for meals may be required.

Open all day all wk **Bar Meals** L served Mon-Thu 12-2, Fri-Sun 12-9 D served Mon-Thu 6-9, Fri-Sun 12-9 Av main course £10-£15 **Restaurant** L served Mon-Thu 12-2, Fri-Sun 12-9 D served Mon-Thu 6-9, Fri-Sun 12-9 Av 3 course à la carte fr £20 ⊕ EVERARDS ◀ Adnams Southwold Bitter, 2 Guest ales. ☂ 9 **Facilities** Children welcome Children's portions Garden Parking Wi-fi 🚌

THORPE LANGTON
Map 11 SP79

The Bakers Arms

Main St LE16 7TS ☎ 01858 545201
dir: *Take A6 S from Leicester then left signed 'The Langtons', at rail bridge continue to x-rds. Straight on to Thorpe Langton. Pub on left*

Low beams, rug-strewn quarry-tiled floors, large pine tables and open fires create an intimate setting in this thatched pub set in an equally pretty village. It has an excellent local following, and the modern pub food is one of the key attractions, with the menu changing from week to week. Expect dishes like a warm tartlet of goat's cheese with sultanas, red onion marmalade and balsamic reduction; pork fillet wrapped in pancetta with a grain mustard sauce; and sticky toffee pudding with vanilla ice cream. The area is popular with walkers, riders and mountain bikers. Booking for meals may be required.

Open 6.30-11 (Sat 12-2.30 6.30-11 Sun 12-2.30) Closed: 1-7 Jan, Sun eve, Mon **Bar Meals** Av main course £15 **Restaurant** L served Sat-Sun 12-2.30 D served Tue-Sat 6.30-9.15 Av 3 course à la carte fr £27 ⊕ FREE HOUSE ◀ Langton Bakers Dozen Bitter. ☂ 9 **Facilities** Garden Parking Wi-fi

WELHAM
Map 11 SP79

The Old Red Lion

Main St LE16 7UJ ☎ 01858 565253
e-mail: pippa@king-henrys-taverns.co.uk
dir: *NE of Market Harborough take B664 to Weston by Welland. Left to Welham*

An old country pub belonging to the King Henry's Taverns group. Once a coaching inn, the small area opposite the main bar was originally the archway where coaches would swing in to offload their weary passengers. In winter the leather chesterfields around the log fires create a cosy feel, while in summer the surrounding footpaths and bridleways offer delightful walks. The menu of freshly prepared dishes has choices for both small and large appetites; two children's menus span ages 2 to 11. Typical dishes are wholetail golden scampi; calves' liver and bacon; Indian curries; and vegetable lasagne.

Open all day all wk 11.30-11 ⊕ FREE HOUSE/KING HENRY'S TAVERNS ◀ Greene King IPA, Marston's Pedigree, Guinness. ☂ 15 **Facilities** Children welcome Children's menu Children's portions Parking 🚌

WOODHOUSE EAVES — Map 11 SK51

The Wheatsheaf Inn ★★★★ INN

Brand Hill LE12 8SS ☎ 01509 890320
e-mail: richard@wheatsheafinn.net
dir: *M1 junct 22, follow Quorn signs*

In the heart of the Charnwood Forest, this privately-owned pub has been in the Dimblebee family for several generations and started life as an alehouse for local quarrymen at the turn of the 19th century. With a good selection of real ales, food includes seasonal daily specials and tempting dishes such as stilton and Guinness pâté; creamy fish pie; half a spit-roasted chicken; salmon and tuna fishcakes. Modern en suite bedrooms are available in the adjacent cottage annexe. Booking for meals may be required.

Open all wk **Closed:** Sun eve in winter **Bar Meals** L served Mon-Fri 12-2, Sat 12-2.30, Sun 12-3.30 D served Mon-Sat 6.30-9.15 **Restaurant** L served Mon-Fri 12-2, Sat 12-2.30, Sun 12-3.30 D served Mon-Sat 6.30-9.15 ⊕ FREE HOUSE ◀ Greene King Abbot Ale, Timothy Taylor Landlord, Adnams Broadside, Tetley's Smoothflow, Marston's Pedigree, Guest ale. ♟ 16 **Facilities** ❖ Children welcome Children's portions Garden Parking Wi-fi **Rooms** 2

LINCOLNSHIRE

ALLINGTON — Map 11 SK84

The Welby Arms ★★★★ INN

The Green NG32 2EA ☎ 01400 281361
web: www.thewelbyarmsallington.com
dir: *From Grantham take either A1 N, or A52 W. Allington 1.5m*

This is a lovely example of a traditional village inn, where the local Morris team dance, the resplendent creeper changes with the seasons and travellers through this rural part of south Lincolnshire can find a comfy bed for the night. Up to six real ales slake the thirst, whilst appetites are sated by a well-balanced menu, plus specials that may reveal a starter choice of pan-fried scallops, chorizo sausage and chilli sauce, leading to a wild mushroom Stroganoff with rice and vegetables, or braised lamb shank with redcurrant and mint sauce. Booking for meals may be required.

Open all wk 12-3 6-11 (Sun 12-10.30) **Bar Meals** L served Mon-Sat 12-2, Sun 12-8.30 D served Mon-Sat 6-9 **Restaurant** L served Mon-Sun 12-2, Sun 12-8.30 D served Mon-Sat 6-9 ⊕ ENTERPRISE INNS ◀ John Smith's, Bass, Timothy Taylor Landlord, Jennings Cumberland Ale, Badger Tanglefoot, Adnams Broadside, Courage Directors, Black Sheep Ö Westons Stowford Press. ♟ 22 **Facilities** Children welcome Children's menu Children's portions Garden Parking 🚃 **Rooms** 3

See advert below

ASWARBY — Map 12 TF03

The Tally Ho Inn

NG34 8SA ☎ 01529 455170
e-mail: info@thetallyhoinn.com
*dir: 3m S of Sleaford on A15 towards Bourne/
Peterborough*

Built as a farm around 1750, this handsome,
award-winning inn was until 1945 the home of the
manager of the Aswarby Estate. In fact, like the
surrounding parkland, it's still part of it. The old English
garden, complete with fruit trees, overlooks the estate
and grazing sheep. Among sturdy pillars, beams and
exposed stonework, dine on freshly prepared modern
British dishes created by chef-proprietor John Blenkiron.
Choices are Aberdeen Angus steak; pea, fava bean and
parmesan risotto; and honey-roast Gressingham duck
breast. On the August Bank Holiday, the pub holds a
family fun day with real ales, hog roast and live music.

Open 12-2.30 6-11 (Sun 12-3) Closed: Sun eve **Bar
Meals** L served Mon-Sat 12-2, Sun 12-2.30 D served
Mon-Thu 6-9, Fri-Sat 6-9.30 Av main course £9.50
Restaurant L served Mon-Sat 12-2, Sun 12-2.30 D served
Mon-Thu 6-9, Fri-Sat 6-9.30 Av 3 course à la carte fr
£22.50 ⊕ FREE HOUSE ◀ Timothy Taylor Landlord,
Greene King Abbot Ale, Guest ales ♻ Westons Wyld Wood
Organic. **Facilities** Children welcome Children's menu
Children's portions Play area Family room Garden Beer
festival Parking Wi-fi 🚌

BARNOLDBY LE BECK — Map 17 TA20

The Ship Inn

Main Rd DN37 0BG ☎ 01472 822308
e-mail: the_ship_inn@btinternet.com
*dir: M180 junct 5, A18 past Humberside Airport. At
Laceby Junction rdbt (A18 & A46) straight over follow
Skegness/Boston signs. Approx 2m turn left signed
Waltham & Barnoldby le Beck*

Set in a picturesque village on the edge of the
Lincolnshire Wolds, this 300-year-old inn has always
attracted an interesting mix of customers, from Grimsby's
seafarers to aviators from the county's World War II
airstrips. The bar is filled with maritime bric-à-brac and
serves a grand choice of ales, and there's a beautiful
garden outside. The Ship is perhaps best known for its
menu of fresh seafood: Grimsby smoked haddock with
poached egg makes a great starter, follow with pan-fried
skate wing and caper butter. Booking for meals may be
required.

Open 12-3 6-11 (Fri-Sat 12-3 6-12 Sun 12-5) Closed:
25 Dec, Sun eve **Bar Meals** L served Mon-Sat 12-2, Sun
12-5 D served Mon-Sat 6-9 **Restaurant** L served Mon-Sat
12-2, Sun 12-5 D served Mon-Sat 6-9 ⊕ FREE HOUSE/
INNOVATIVE SIGHT LTD ◀ Black Sheep Best Bitter, Tom
Wood's, Guinness. ♥ 9 **Facilities** Children welcome
Children's portions Garden Parking Wi-fi 🚌 (notice
required)

BELCHFORD — Map 17 TF27

The Blue Bell Inn

1 Main Rd LN9 6LQ ☎ 01507 533602
e-mail: bluebellbelchford@gmail.com
web: www.bluebellbelchford.co.uk
dir: Off A153 between Horncastle & Louth

In the heart of the Lincolnshire Wolds and located on the
Viking Way, this family-run traditional country free house
attracts locals and walkers alike. Rest your weary feet in
sumptuous armchairs with a pint of well-kept real ale
such as Black Sheep or Timothy Taylor Landlord and a
wide selection of wines. At lunchtime, choose between
tempting mackerel baps and corned beef hash cake,
whilst evening meals range from fresh Grimsby haddock
with chips and mushy peas, to beef, ale and mushroom
pie, or pork belly on sticky red cabbage.

Open all wk 11.30-2.30 6.30-11 Closed: 2nd & 3rd wk
Jan **Bar Meals** L served all wk 12-2 D served all wk
6.30-9 **Restaurant** L served all wk 12-2 D served all wk
6.30-9 ⊕ FREE HOUSE ◀ Timothy Taylor Landlord, Black
Sheep, Guest ale. **Facilities** Children welcome Children's
menu Children's portions Garden Parking

BOURNE — Map 12 TF02

The Wishing Well Inn

Main St, Dyke PE10 0AF ☎ 01778 422970
e-mail: wishingwell@hotmail.com
dir: Take A15 towards Sleaford. Inn in next village

This Lincolnshire village free house started life in 1879
as a one-room pub called the Crown. Several extensions
have since been sympathetically executed with recycled
stone and timbers; the well that gives the pub its name,
previously in the garden, is now a feature of the smaller
dining room. Loyal customers return again and again to
enjoy a comprehensive menu of traditional favourites in
the warm and welcoming atmosphere. Outside, an
attractive beer garden backs onto the children's play
area, and there is a beer festival over the August Bank
Holiday weekend.

Open all wk 11-3 5-11 (Fri-Sat 11am-mdnt Sun &
summer all wk 11-11) **Bar Meals** L served Mon-Thu
12-2.30, Fri-Sun 12-9 D served Mon-Thu 5.30-9, Fri-Sun
12-9 ⊕ FREE HOUSE ◀ Greene King Abbot Ale, Shepherd
Neame Spitfire, 3 Guest ales. **Facilities** Children welcome
Children's menu Children's portions Play area Garden
Beer festival Parking Wi-fi 🚌 (notice required)

CONINGSBY — Map 17 TF25

The Lea Gate Inn

Leagate Rd LN4 4RS ☎ 01526 342370
e-mail: theleagateinn@hotmail.com
web: www.the-leagate-inn.co.uk
dir: Off B1192 just outside Coningsby

The oldest licensed premises in the county, dating from
1542, this was the last of the Fen Guide Houses that
provided shelter before the treacherous marshes were
drained. The oak-beamed pub has a priest's hole and a
very old inglenook fireplace among its features. The same
family have been running the pub for over 25 years. Both
the bar and restaurant serve food and offer seasonal
menus with lots of local produce (including game in
season) and great fish choices, such as freshwater trout
and lobster.

Open all wk 11.30-3 6-11 (Sun 12-10.30) **Bar Meals** L
served Mon-Sat 11.45-2 Sun 12-9 D served Mon-Sat 6-9
Restaurant L served Mon-Sat 11.45-2, Sun 12-9 D served
Mon-Sat 6-9 ⊕ FREE HOUSE ◀ Wells Bombardier, Black
Sheep, Guest ales. **Facilities** 🐾 Children welcome
Children's menu Play area Garden Parking 🚌

DRY DODDINGTON — Map 11 SK84

Wheatsheaf Inn

NG23 5HU ☎ 01400 281458
e-mail: wheatsheafdrydoddington@hotmail.co.uk
web: www.wheatsheaf-pub.co.uk
*dir: From A1 between Newark-on-Trent & Grantham. Turn
into Doddington Ln for Dry Doddington*

The church, with its leaning tower, faces this
pantile-roofed inn across the village green. No one's sure
of the inn's age, but they can date the pre-Jurassic era
stones used to build it as 200 million years old! Abbot,
Batemans XB and Timothy Taylor Landlord are the regular
real ales, with Lincolnshire easily the biggest contributor

Save on hotels. Book at **theAA.com/hotel**

LINCOLNSHIRE 339 **ENGLAND**

of produce on the menus. Enjoy a starter of pea, mint and crème fraîche risotto, followed by slow-braised shoulder of lamb; fish of the day; or honey-roasted pepper and goat's cheese tart, in the bar, restaurant or sheltered garden.

Open 12-2.30 5-11 (Sat-Sun 12-close) Closed: Mon **Bar Meals** L served Tue-Sun 12-2 D served Tue-Sun 6-9 **Restaurant** L served Tue-Sat 12-2, Sun 12-4 D served Tue-Thu 6-9, Fri-Sat 6-9.30, Sun 5-7 ⊕ FREE HOUSE ◀ Timothy Taylor Landlord, Greene King Abbot Ale, Batemans XB Ò Hogan's. ♉ 12 **Facilities** ☻ Children welcome Children's menu Children's portions Garden Parking Wi-fi ▄▄ (notice required)

FROGNALL
Map 12 TF11

The Goat

155 Spalding Rd PE6 8SA ☎ 01778 347629
e-mail: debbiestokes@thegoatfrognall.com
web: www.thegoatfrognall.com
dir: *A1 to Peterborough, A15 to Market Deeping, old A16 to Spalding, pub approx 1.5m from A15 & A16 junct*

With five different guest ales every week, beer and cider is taken seriously here and you might want to time a visit for the June beer festival. Families are equally welcome at this friendly country free house, which has an open fire, a large conservatory with its own courtyard and a child-friendly garden. The extensive menu has broad appeal and main courses include lamb and mint pie; beef in red wine; mushroom and pepper curry; and home-cooked ham salad. Booking for meals may be required.

Open all wk Mon-Fri 11.30-3 6-11.30 (Sat 11.30-11.30 Sun 12-11) Closed: 25 Dec, 1 Jan **Bar Meals** L served Mon-Fri 12-2, Sat 12-9.30, Sun 12-9 D served Mon-Fri 6.30-9.30, Sat 12-9.30, Sun 12-9 **Restaurant** L served Mon-Fri 12-2, Sat 12-9.30, Sun 12-9 D served Mon-Fri 6.30-9.30, Sat 12-9.30, Sun 12-9 ⊕ FREE HOUSE ◀ Guest ales from Elgood's, Batemans, Abbeydale, Nethergate, Hopshackle Ò Westons Old Rosie, Moonshine, Thatchers Cheddar Valley. **Facilities** Children welcome Children's menu Children's portions Play area Family room Garden Beer festival Parking ▄▄ (notice required)

GOSBERTON
Map 12 TF23

The Black Horse

**66 Siltside, Gosberton Risegate PE11 4ET
☎ 01775 840995**
e-mail: cr8ionz@theblackhorserestaurant.net
dir: *From Spalding take A16 towards Boston. Left onto A152. At Gosberton take B1397 to Gosberton Risegate. Pub set back from road*

Tucked away in a village amidst the Fens outside Spalding, this lovely creeper-clad local is a showcase for Lincolnshire's wealth of food producers. Huddle up to the woodburning stove or catch the summer rays in the beer garden, sipping Black Sheep or Hobgoblin. The menu changes fortnightly and has Italian and Asian influences. Tuck into chicken satay skewers served on toasted naan; beef parmigiana topped with mushrooms and mozzarella; diced tandoori lamb shoulder; and steaks cooked at the table on a slab of volcanic rock. Finish with white chocolate and raspberry terrine. Booking for meals may be required.

Open Tue-Sat 6pm-late (Sun 12-3 6-9 Fri-Sun summer 12-late) Closed: Mon **Bar Meals** L served Fri-Sun 12-4 (summer) D served Tue-Sun 6-10 (summer) **Restaurant** L served Fri-Sun 12-3 D served Tue-Sun 6-10.30 Av 3 course à la carte fr £13.95 ⊕ FREE HOUSE ◀ Black Sheep Best Bitter, Wychwood Hobgoblin Ò Thatchers Gold. ♉ 9 **Facilities** ☻ Children welcome Children's menu Children's portions Garden Parking ▄▄ (notice required)

HOUGH-ON-THE-HILL
Map 11 SK94

The Brownlow Arms ★★★★★ INN ◉

High Rd NG32 2AZ ☎ 01400 250234
e-mail: armsinn@yahoo.co.uk
dir: *Take A607 (Grantham to Sleaford road). Hough-on-the-Hill signed from Barkston*

At the heart of a pretty village, this well-groomed 17th-century stone inn is named after former owner Lord Brownlow and it still has the look of a welcoming country house. In the convivial bar, enjoy a pint of real ale as you make your menu choices. The modern dishes include a starter of pan-fried grey mullet with curried chickpeas and sweet potato, which might be followed by steamed venison, shallot and port pudding. Leave room for the plum and stem ginger crumble. The landscaped terrace encourages alfresco dining. Accommodation is available. Booking for meals may be required.

Open Tue-Sat 6pm-11pm, Sun L Closed: 25-27 Dec, 31 Dec-1 Jan, Mon, Sun eve **Restaurant** L served Sun 12-2.30 D served Tue-Sat 6.30-9.30 Fixed menu price fr £21.95 Av 3 course à la carte fr £30 ⊕ FREE HOUSE ◀ Timothy Taylor Landlord, Marston's Pedigree. ♉ 10 **Facilities** Garden Parking Wi-fi **Rooms** 5

INGHAM
Map 17 SK98

Inn on the Green

34 The Green LN1 2XT ☎ 01522 730354
dir: *From Lincoln take A15 signed Scunthorpe. Left into Ingham Ln signed Ingham, Cammeringham. Right onto B1398 (Middle St), left to Ingham*

Its name neatly summarises the position of this charming Grade II listed country pub/restaurant, proud holder of many awards. In addition to the choice of real ales, seasonal dishes using local produce are served throughout the pub's three bars – cosy entrance bar with sofas, front bar with roaring log fire, and another one upstairs; restaurant seating is at the rear on the ground and first floors. Staples include chicken liver pâté with home-made red onion marmalade. Daily-changing specials range from potted local rabbit with poached rhubarb and cider jelly to seared Atlantic halibut. Super desserts, all home-made, and a range of vegetarian options complete the picture. Booking for meals may be required.

Open 11.30-3 6-11 (Fri 11.30-3 5-11 Sat 11.30-11 Sun 12-10.30) (Sat 11.30-3 6-11 in winter) Closed: Mon **Bar Meals** L served Wed-Sat 12-2, Sun 12-4.45 D served Tue-Sat 6-9 **Restaurant** L served Wed-Sat 12-2, Sun 12-4.45 D served Tue-Sat 6-9 ⊕ FREE HOUSE ◀ Batemans XB, Black Sheep, Adnams Ò Westons Stowford Press. ♉ 9 **Facilities** Children welcome Children's portions Garden Parking ▄▄ (notice required)

KIRKBY LA THORPE
Map 12 TF04

Queens Head

Church Ln NG34 9NU ☎ 01529 305743 & 307194
e-mail: clrjcc@aol.com
web: www.thequeensheadinn.com
dir: *Just off A17 (dual carriageway). Pub signed from A17*

Heavy beams, open log fires, antique furnishings and original watercolours - this award-winning destination dining pub ticks all the boxes when it comes to original features and traditional character. The French-trained chef-proprietor prepares everything on site, from breads to desserts, and local ingredients get star billing on the menu. A platter of Lincolnshire stuffed chine with mixed pickles and chutney might make way for slowly steamed suet steak-and-kidney pudding. Wash it down with local cask ales or wines from a well-considered list. Booking for meals may be required.

continued

KIRKBY LA THORPE *continued*

Open all wk 12-3 6-11 (Sun 12-11) **Bar Meals** L served Mon-Sat 12-2.30, Sun 12-8.30 D served Mon-Fri 6-9.30, Sat 6-10, Sun 12-8.30 Av main course £9.95 **Restaurant** L served Mon-Sat 12-2.30, Sun 12-8.30 D served Mon-Fri 6-9.30, Sat 6-10, Sun 12-8.30 Fixed menu price fr £12.95 Av 3 course à la carte fr £20 ⊕ FREE HOUSE ◀ Batemans XB, Guest ales. ♥ 9 **Facilities** Children welcome Children's menu Children's portions Garden Parking Wi-fi ▦ (notice required)

KIRTON IN LINDSEY · Map 17 SK99

The George

20 High St DN21 4LX ☎ 01652 640600
e-mail: enquiry@thegeorgekirton.co.uk
dir: *From A15 take B1205, turn right onto B1400*

Lincoln and the Wolds are within easy reach of this extensively restored yet traditional pub run by Glen and Neil McCartney. The 18th-century former coaching inn serves locally brewed Batemans ales and seasonally changing menus. Customers can dine in the comfortable bar area or in the informal restaurant. Favourite starters such as prawn cocktail, and bar meals such as lasagne with salad and hand-cut chips, are topped by regularly changing specials such as chicken schnitzel with a brandy and mushroom sauce; and game and blackcurrant pie.

Open all wk 5-11 (Sun 12-2.30) ⊕ FREE HOUSE ◀ Batemans XB. **Facilities** Children welcome Children's menu Children's portions Play area Garden ▦

LINCOLN · Map 17 SK97

Pyewipe Inn

Fossebank, Saxilby Rd LN1 2BG ☎ 01522 528708
e-mail: enquiries@pyewipe.co.uk
dir: *From Lincoln on A57 past Lincoln/A46 Bypass, pub signed in 0.5m*

There's a great view of nearby Lincoln Cathedral from the grounds of this waterside inn, which takes its name from the local dialect for lapwing. Set in four wooded acres beside the Roman-built Fossedyke Navigation, it serves real ales and home-made, locally sourced food. Expect dishes such as partridge and black pudding stack with a red wine sauce; pork belly with a cider and grain mustard sauce and mash; or loin of cod poached in Thai broth with noodles and stir-fried vegetables. There is a beer garden and riverside patio where you can enjoy your meal and a cold beer. Booking for meals may be required.

Open all day all wk 11-11 **Bar Meals** L served all wk 12-9.30 D served all wk 12-9.30 food served all day **Restaurant** L served all wk 12-9.30 D served all wk 12-9.30 food served all day ⊕ FREE HOUSE ◀ Guest ales. **Facilities** Children welcome Children's portions Garden Parking Wi-fi ▦

The Victoria

6 Union Rd LN1 3BJ ☎ 01522 541000
e-mail: jonathanjpc@aol.com
dir: *From city outskirts follow signs for Cathedral Quarter. Pub 2 mins' walk from all major up-hill car parks. Adjacent to the West Gate of Lincoln Castle*

Situated right next to the Westgate entrance of the castle and within a stone's throw of Lincoln Cathedral, a long-standing drinkers' pub with a range of real ales, including six changing guest beers, ciders and perries. As well as the fantastic views of the castle, the pub also offers great meals made from home-prepared food including hot baguettes and filled bacon rolls, Saturday breakfasts and Sunday lunches. House specials include sausage and mash, various pies, chilli con carne and home-made lasagne. Facilities include a large beer garden with children's play area. There are Halloween and winter beer festivals.

Open all day all wk 11am-mdnt (Fri-Sat 11am-1am Sun 12-12) **Bar Meals** L served all wk 12-2.30 Av main course £5.95 ⊕ BATEMANS ◀ XB, Timothy Taylor Landlord, Castle Rock Harvest Pale, Guest ales ♉ Westons. **Facilities** ✿ Children welcome Children's portions Play area Garden Beer festival Wi-fi ▦ (notice required)

Wig & Mitre

PICK OF THE PUBS

32 Steep Hill LN2 1LU ☎ 01522 535190
e-mail: email@wigandmitre.com
dir: *At top of Steep Hill, adjacent to cathedral & Lincoln Castle car parks*

Between the castle and the cathedral in the upper part of the medieval city, the Wig & Mitre is a mix of architectural styles from the 14th century onwards. Owned and operated by the same family since 1977, it's a music-free zone: instead you'll find a reading room and, since it's not tied to a brewery, real ales from Batemans, Black Sheep and Wells & Young's. Food includes full and small English breakfasts served until noon, all-day hot and cold sandwiches, ploughman's and light meals. Turning to the main menu, you might start with tomato and oxtail soup with potato dumplings; then salt hake with clams, creamed garlic, white beans, lardons and samphire; or chicken breast wrapped in pancetta with sage roast potatoes, purple sprouting broccoli and smoked tomato and herb sauce. Under 'puds' the menu lists sticky toffee pudding, and baked rice pudding with bitter chocolate praline. Booking for meals may be required.

Open all day all wk 8.30am-mdnt **Bar Meals** L served all wk 8.30am-10pm D served all wk 8.30am-10pm food served all day **Restaurant** L served all wk 8.30am-10pm D served all wk 8.30am-10pm Fixed menu price fr £12.95 Av 3 course à la carte fr £19.50 food served all day ⊕ FREE HOUSE ◀ Batemans XB, Young's London Gold, Black Sheep. ♥ 24 **Facilities** ✿ Children welcome Children's menu Children's portions

LITTLE BYTHAM · Map 11 TF01

The Willoughby Arms

Station Rd NG33 4RA ☎ 01780 410276
e-mail: info@willoughbyarms.co.uk
dir: *B6121 (Stamford to Bourne road), at junct follow signs to Careby/Little Bytham, inn 5m on right*

This beamed, traditional stone country inn started life as the booking office and waiting room for Lord Willoughby's private railway line. These days it has a fresher look whilst retaining its traditional charms. Expect a good selection of real ales - including several from local micro-breweries - with great, home-cooked food available every lunchtime and evening. Dishes range from sirloin steak topped with a Diane sauce to chargrilled tuna steak with lemon butter. As well as a cosy bar with open fire, and a light and airy sun lounge, there is also a large beer garden with stunning views to enjoy on warmer days.

Open all day all wk 12-11 **Bar Meals** L served Mon-Sat 12-2, Sun 12-4 D served all wk 6-9 ⊕ FREE HOUSE ◀ Ufford White Hart, Batemans XB, Abbeydale Absolution ♉ Bristol Port, Broadoak Kingston Black. ♥ 10 **Facilities** Children welcome Children's menu Children's portions Garden Beer festival Parking Wi-fi ▦ (notice required)

MARKET RASEN · Map 17 TF18

The Black Horse Inn

Magna Mile LN8 6AJ ☎ 01507 313645
e-mail: info@blackhorseludford.co.uk
dir: *In village on A631, between Louth & Market Rasen*

Expect beers from Lincolnshire micro-breweries at this village inn in the heart of the Lincolnshire Wolds. Recent refurbishment has introduced slate floors and uncovered terrazzo tiles, but hasn't compromised the character of the place. Comfy contemporary furnishings and open fires blend easily with displays recalling 101 Squadron, based at nearby Ludford Magna airfield in World War II. The pub was also once part of an estate owned by George Tennyson MP, grandfather of Alfred, Lord Tennyson. Food is a key part of the offering here. Diners can enjoy an eclectic menu of home-made, locally sourced meals: perhaps wild boar salami salad, or braised pork cheek to start; followed by sea cod with curly cale colcannon; macaroni with chestnut mushrooms and Colston Basset stilton; or shank of lamb with mash and roast parsnips. Try a baked ginger parkin or some steamed treacle sponge pudding for afters.

Open 12-2 6-10 (Sun 12-3) Closed: 2wks Jan, Sun eve, Mon **Bar Meals** L served Tue-Sat 12-2, Sun 12-3 D served Tue-Sat 6-10 **Restaurant** L served Tue-Sat 12-2, Sun 12-3 D served Tue-Sat 6-10 Fixed menu price fr £10 ⊕ FREE HOUSE ◀ Tom Wood's Best Bitter, Great Newsome Pricky Back Otchan, Poachers Monkey Hanger ♉ Skidbrooke. **Facilities** Children welcome Children's portions Garden Parking

Save on hotels. Book at theAA.com/hotel

LINCOLNSHIRE 341 ENGLAND

PARTNEY
Map 17 TF46

Red Lion Inn

PE23 4PG ☎ 01790 752271
e-mail: enquiries@redlioninnpartney.co.uk
dir: On A16 from Boston, or A158 from Horncastle

Warmed by wood burners, this welcoming village inn at the foot of the Lincolnshire Wolds is popular with walkers and cyclists who take refreshment here between visits to the nearby nature reserves and sandy beaches. Two real ales are always on tap, with ciders, lagers, and a good choice of wines too. The pub also has an excellent reputation for home-cooked food: maybe sugar-baked gammon and peaches, pheasant, venison and rabbit pie, or beef in beer with a garlic crust.

Open all wk 12-2 6-11 (Sun 12-2 6-10.30) **Bar Meals** L served all wk 12-2 D served all wk 6-9 **Restaurant** L served all wk 12-2 D served all wk 6-9 ⊕ FREE HOUSE ◀ Black Sheep, Guinness, Tetley's, Guest ales ♻ Westons 1st Quality. **Facilities** Children welcome Children's portions Parking Wi-fi 🚌 (notice required)

RAITHBY
Map 17 TF36

Red Lion Inn

PE23 4DS ☎ 01790 753727
dir: A158 from Horncastle, through Hagworthingham, right at top of hill signed Raithby

This traditional beamed village pub, parts of which date back 300 years, is situated on the edge of the Lincolnshire Wolds, a great place for walking and cycling. Inside is a wealth of character with log fires providing a warm welcome in winter. Dine in one of the four bars or on the comfort of the restaurant. A varied menu of home-made dishes is prepared using fresh local produce - sea bass with stir-fried vegetables; roast guinea fowl with tomato, garlic and bacon; and medallions of beef with peppercorn sauce. Meals can be taken in the garden in the warmer months.

Open 12-2 6-11 (Mon 7-11) Closed: Mon L **Bar Meals** L served Tue-Sun 12-2 D served Tue-Sat 7-8.30 **Restaurant** L served Tue-Sun 12-2 D served Tue-Sun 7-8.30 ⊕ FREE HOUSE ◀ Thwaites, Batemans. **Facilities** Children welcome Children's menu Children's portions Garden Parking 🚌 (notice required)

SKEGNESS
Map 17 TF56

Best Western Vine Hotel ★★★ HL

Vine Rd, Seacroft PE25 3DB ☎ 01754 763018 & 610611
e-mail: info@thevinehotel.com
dir: In Seacroft area of Skegness. S of town centre

Said to be the second oldest building in Skegness, the Vine has remained largely unchanged since 1770. Set amid two acres of beautiful gardens, the ivy-covered hotel was bought by the brewer Harry Bateman in 1927. This charming hostelry offers comfortable accommodation and a fine selection of Batemans ales. Typical food choices include pasta dishes such as spinach and mushroom tortellini or lasagne, a selection from the grill, and main courses including ham, egg and chips, and chicken pot pie. Booking for meals may be required.

Open all day all wk **Bar Meals** L served Mon-Fri 12-2 D served all wk 6-9 **Restaurant** L served Sun 12-2 D served all wk 6-9 ◀ Batemans XB, XXXB & Valiant, Black Sheep, Dixon's. ♀ 8 **Facilities** Children welcome Children's menu Children's portions Garden Parking 🚌 Rooms 25

SOUTH RAUCEBY
Map 11 TF04

The Bustard Inn & Restaurant ⊛

PICK OF THE PUBS

44 Main St NG34 8QG ☎ 01529 488250
e-mail: info@thebustardinn.co.uk
dir: A15 from Lincoln. Right onto B1429 for Cranwell, 1st left after village, straight across A17

Great bustard won't have been on the menu for some time, since legend has it that the last indigenous specimen was shot nearby in 1845 by the local lord of the manor; the pub's name recalls this deed. Situated above Lincoln Edge, the pub dates from 1860 and is an imposing Grade II listed building, at the heart of the pretty stone-built estate village. In the beer garden and courtyard, locals indulge in the house beer Cheeky Bustard, brewed by a local micro. Renovated in 2006, the light and airy interior is divided between the bar and an elegant restaurant, with dressed stone walls, beamed ceiling and tapestry chairs. Chef Phil Lowe's one AA-Rosette cuisine draws on local produce where possible. The bar menu features venison pie, moules marinière, Mediterranean sharing platter, and corned beef hash. Meanwhile the daily à la carte menu might offer pan-fried halibut with roast lobster, herb mash and lemon butter sauce; or tomato and mozzarella tart with mixed leaves and pesto. There is live jazz most Wednesday nights and special food nights.

Open 12-3 5.30-11 (Sun 12-3.30) Closed: 1 Jan, Sun eve, Mon **Bar Meals** L served Tue-Sat 12-2.30, Sun 12-3 D served Tue-Sat 6-9.30 Av main course £11.50 **Restaurant** L served Tue-Sat 12-2.30, Sun 12-3 D served Tue-Sat 6-9.30 Fixed menu price fr £13.20 Av 3 course à la carte fr £24.50 ⊕ FREE HOUSE ◀ Riverside Cheeky Bustard, Batemans XXXB, Guinness, Guest ale ♻ Aspall. ♀ 13 **Facilities** Children welcome Children's portions Garden Parking Wi-fi 🚌 (notice required)

SOUTH WITHAM
Map 11 SK91

Blue Cow Inn & Brewery

High St NG33 5QB ☎ 01572 768432
e-mail: enquiries@bluecowinn.co.uk
dir: Between Stamford & Grantham on A1

Named 'blue' after erstwhile owner the Duke of Buckminster's political allegiance to the Whigs, this partly medieval building has been a pub for over 400 years. Low beams, pillars, flagstone floors and dressed-stone walls characterise its ancient interior, with crackling log fires to take the edge off the fenland breezes; any remaining chill may be generated by the pub's ghosts – a lady and a dog. Licensee Simon Crathorn brews two of his own award-winning ales, ideally consumed on the colourful beer garden patio. Snacks, salads and sandwiches are offered, as well as mains like all-day breakfast, barbecue chicken, beer-battered haddock, and vegetable lasagne.

Open all day all wk 11-11 **Bar Meals** Av main course £8 food served all day **Restaurant** food served all day ⊕ FREE HOUSE ◀ Blue Cow Best Bitter. ♀ 10 **Facilities** ✿ Children welcome Children's menu Children's portions Family room Garden Parking Wi-fi 🚌 (notice required)

STAMFORD
Map 11 TF00

The George of Stamford ★★★★ HL ⊛

PICK OF THE PUBS

71 St Martins PE9 2LB ☎ 01780 750750
e-mail: reservations@georgehotelofstamford.com
web: www.georgehotelofstamford.com
dir: From Peterborough take A1 N. Onto B1081 for Stamford, down hill to lights. Hotel on left

Lord Burghley, Elizabeth I's Lord High Treasurer, erected the main block of this famous hotel in 1597. Outside, over the old Great North Road, is the gallows sign that warned highwaymen to stay away; under the Cocktail Bar is a medieval crypt; and there's a walled Monastery Garden, which pilgrims walked in, but monks never did. The London Room and York Bar were where passengers waited while one of the 'twenty up' and 'twenty down' daily stagecoaches changed horses. Today's visitors, few of whose arrivals involve a horse, can have soup, a sandwich or snack in the bar or lounge, or a light meal in the Garden Room or cobbled courtyard, while in the magnificent oak-panelled restaurant, traditional

continued

STAMFORD *continued*

steak-and-kidney pudding; aromatic steamed fillet of Atlantic cod; and poached eggs Benedict. Additionally, there are shellfish, seafood, pastas and cold buffets. Well-equipped bedrooms display the artistic skills of Julia Vannocci. Booking for meals may be required.

Open all day all wk 11-11 (Sun 12-11) **Bar Meals** L served all wk 12-2.30 Av main course £7.95 **Restaurant** L served all wk 12-2.30 (Garden Room all wk 12-11) D served all wk 7-10.30 Fixed menu price fr £23.50 Av 3 course à la carte fr £43.20 food served all day ⊕ FREE HOUSE ◀ Adnams Broadside, The Grainstore, Bass ○ Aspall. ♥ 21 **Facilities** Children welcome Children's portions Garden Parking Wi-fi **Rooms** 47

The Tobie Norris

PICK OF THE PUBS

12 Saint Pauls St PE9 2BE ☎ 01780 753800
e-mail: info@tobienorris.com
dir: *From A1 to Stamford on A6121, which becomes West St, then East St. After right bend turn right into Saint Pauls St*

After an award-winning restoration and remodelling, this medieval hall house dating from 1280 opened as a three-storey, seven-roomed pub in 2006. Tobie, or Tobias, Norris was a bell founder who lived in the property in the 16th century. As a free house it offers handpumps with badges declaring Adnams Southwold, Ufford Ales' White Hart and Rupert's War Dog, two micro-brewery guests, and real ciders. The kitchen specialises in stone-baked pizzas, cooked in imported Italian ovens, for which you can create your own toppings. There's also a full selection of seasonal specials, some Italian-inspired, such as antipasto carne and penne pomodoro, as well as wasabi chicken and crushed plum potatoes; belly pork and chickpea cassoulet; and sea bass Niçoise. The Italian influence appears again on the desserts list, with affogato, and sweetened calzone of the day. Right outside is a large enclosed patio.

Open all day all wk **Bar Meals** L served all wk 12-2.30 D served Mon-Sat 6-9 Av main course £11.95 ⊕ FREE HOUSE ◀ Ufford White Hart & Rupert's War Dog, Adnams Southwold Bitter, Guest ales ○ Hogan's, Westons Wyld Wood Organic Vintage. ♥ 18 **Facilities** ❀ Garden Wi-fi

SURFLEET SEAS END Map 12 TF22

The Ship Inn

154 Reservoir Rd PE11 4DH ☎ 01775 680547
e-mail: shipsurfleet@hotmail.com
dir: *Off A16 (Spalding to Boston). Follow tourist signs towards Surfleet Reservoir then The Ship Inn signs*

This successor to an earlier pub stands by two rivers, the Welland and the Glen, as well as Vernatti's Drain, named after the engineer who drained these fenlands in the mid-1600s. The bar is panelled in hand-crafted oak, while upstairs the restaurant overlooks the flat surrounding land, which is only just above sea level. Local ingredients in daily specials are served seven days a week, making up dishes such as chicken Napoleon cooked in a creamy wild mushroom, garlic and Cognac sauce. Fishing and golf parties are welcome.

Open all wk 11-3 5-12 (Sat-Sun 11am-mdnt) **Bar Meals** L served 12-2 D served 5-9 Av main course £10 **Restaurant** L served 12-2 D served 5-9 Fixed menu price fr £17.95 Av 3 course à la carte fr £25 ◀ Oakham, Elgood's, Local ales. **Facilities** ❀ Children welcome Children's menu Children's portions Parking Wi-fi 🚐

SUSWORTH Map 17 SE80

The Jenny Wren Inn

East Ferry Rd DN17 3AS ☎ 01724 784000
e-mail: info@jennywreninn.co.uk
dir: *Telephone for directions*

A beamed and wood-panelled former farmhouse with buckets of character. No better place then for the sampling of special cocktails and nibbles now served every evening; ale lovers can stick to the ever-reliable Theakston. The pub has won accolades for its food, especially for dishes involving line-caught fresh fish. Otherwise the Italian head chef and his team create both traditional pub favourites and authentic pasta, to be enjoyed in the ground-floor lounge with open fire; the upstairs function room overlooking the River Trent is popular for larger parties. Booking for meals may be required.

Open all wk 12-3 5.45-10.30 (Fri-Sun 11.30-10.30) **Bar Meals** L served Mon-Thu 12-2, Fri-Sun 12-9 D served Mon-Thu 5.45-9, Fri-Sun 12-9 Av main course £8.95 **Restaurant** L served Mon-Thu 12-2, Fri-Sun 12-9 D served Mon-Thu 5.45-9, Fri-Sun 12-9 Fixed menu price fr £9.95 Av 3 course à la carte fr £25 ⊕ FREE HOUSE ◀ Morland Old Speckled Hen, Theakston. **Facilities** Children welcome Children's menu Children's portions Family room Garden Parking Wi-fi 🚐

THEDDLETHORPE ALL SAINTS Map 17 TF48

Kings Head Inn **NEW**

Mill Rd LN12 1PB ☎ 01507 339798
e-mail: lordandladyhutton@hotmail.co.uk
dir: *From A1031 between Mablethorpe & Theddlethorpe, turn left into Mill Rd. Pub on right*

Two miles from the beach and close to a nature reserve, this thatched 16th-century inn is a sight for sore eyes. Inside are charming bars with traditional furnishings and very low ceilings. All food is locally sourced and vegetables are home grown. Fish is a speciality in the summer; game in the winter. Dishes range from Thai-style fishcakes with home-made sweet chilli sauce through to traditional favourites such as steak-and-ale pie or grilled steak with all the trimmings. There is a beer festival in July.

Open 12-3 6-11 (Sat 12-11 Sun 12-10.20 Summer; Sun 12-5 Winter) Closed: Mon (winter) **Bar Meals** L served Sun-Fri 12-2.30, Sat all day D served Sun-Fri 6-9, Sat all day **Restaurant** L served Sun-Fri 12-2.30, Sat all day D served Sun-Fri 6-9, Sat all day ⊕ FREE HOUSE ◀ Batemans XB, Black Sheep ○ Thatchers Gold, Skidbrooke. **Facilities** ❀ Children welcome Children's portions Family room Garden Beer festival Parking Wi-fi 🚐 (notice required)

TIMBERLAND Map 17 TF15

The Penny Farthing Inn

4 Station Rd LN4 3SA ☎ 01526 378359
dir: *From Sleaford take A153, left onto B1189. At junct with B1191 follow signs for Timberland*

Located in a charming village just outside Lincoln, The Penny Farthing has been refurbished in a traditional style. It's a popular and friendly pub and is worth noting if you're looking for somewhere comfortable and informal after exploring Lincoln and its cathedral. From the seasonal dinner menu, try twice-baked cheese soufflé with a spinach and grain mustard velouté followed by oven-roasted belly pork with fennel and bacon in cider jus. Finish with baked chocolate tart and ice cream. Booking for meals may be required.

Open all day Closed: Mon ⊕ FREE HOUSE ◀ Shepherd Neame Spitfire, John Smith's, Timothy Taylor Landlord, Wells Bombardier. **Facilities** Children welcome Children's portions Garden Parking Wi-fi

WOODHALL SPA   Map 17 TF16

Village Limits Country Pub, Restaurant & Motel

Stixwould Rd LN10 6UJ ☎ 01526 353312
e-mail: info@villagelimits.co.uk
dir: *At rdbt on main street follow Petwood Hotel signs. Motel 500yds past Petwood Hotel*

The pub and restaurant are situated in the original part of the building, so expect bare beams and old-world charm. Typical meals, championing the fresh ingredients of many local Lincolnshire suppliers, include creamy garlic and stilton mushrooms; or battered brie wedges; followed by chargrilled chicken with a mushroom and pepper sauce; or beer-battered haddock. Finish with Dennetts ice cream or a home-made pudding. There's a good choice of real ales to wash it all down, including Dixon's Major Bitter and Batemans XB. Booking for meals may be required.

Open 11.30-3 6.30-11 Closed: 26 Dec-2 Jan, Mon L **Bar Meals** L served Tue-Sun 11.30-2 D served all wk 6.30-9 Av main course £11 **Restaurant** L served Tue-Sun 11.30-2 D served all wk 6.30-9 ⊕ FREE HOUSE ◀ Batemans XB, Tom Wood's Best Bitter, Dixon's Major Bitter ☼ Thatchers. ♇ 8 **Facilities** Children welcome Children's menu Children's portions Garden Parking Wi-fi 🚐

WOOLSTHORPE   Map 11 SK83

The Chequers Inn
PICK OF THE PUBS

Main St NG32 1LU ☎ 01476 870701
e-mail: justinnabar@yahoo.co.uk
dir: *Approx 7m from Grantham. 3m from A607. Follow heritage signs to Belvoir Castle*

The modern rubs along with the traditional just fine in this 17th-century coaching inn next to the village cricket pitch, and from whose mature garden you can see Belvoir Castle. Interior delights are the five real fires, a bar that does a good line in real ales, namely Woodforde's Wherry and Batemans, and the Bakehouse Restaurant, where the oven from village bakery days remains in situ. Expect sophisticated pub food - monkfish pie with gruyère and herb crust, or pan-fried duck breast with sweet potato cake, sauté spinach and cherry jus. There are pub classics too, like beer-battered haddock and hand-cut chips, and gammon steak with fried organic egg. If the words '7th Heaven' appear against your chosen dish on the menu, it is one of seven served between six and seven o'clock every day of the week for £7.

Open all wk 12-3 5.30-11 (Sat-Sun all day) Closed: 25 Dec eve & 26 Dec eve, 1 Jan eve ⊕ FREE HOUSE ◀ Woodforde's Wherry, Batemans ☼ Aspall, Westons Old Rosie. **Facilities** Children welcome Children's menu Children's portions Family room Garden Parking

LONDON

E1

Town of Ramsgate   PLAN 2 G3

62 Wapping High St E1W 2NP ☎ 020 7481 8000
e-mail: peter@townoframsgate.co.uk
dir: *0.3m from Wapping tube station & Tower of London*

Close to The City, this Grade II listed building dates back 500 years and is steeped in history. Press gangs used to work the area, imprisoning men overnight in the cellar, and Judge Jeffreys was caught here while trying to flee the country. The pub retains much of its original character with bric-à-brac and old prints. The owners serve a range of real ales and more than a dozen wines by the glass. Enjoy dishes such as cottage pie in the bar or on the terrace overlooking the River Thames.

Open all day all wk 12-12 (Sun 12-11) **Bar Meals** L served all wk 12-4 D served all wk 5-9 Av main course £9.50 food served all day ⊕ FREE HOUSE ◀ Fuller's London Pride, Adnams, Young's ☼ Aspall. ♇ 13 **Facilities** ♣ Children welcome Garden Wi-fi 🚐 (notice required)

E8

The Cat & Mutton   PLAN 2 G4

76 Broadway Market, Hackney E8 4QJ
☎ 020 7254 5599
e-mail: andy@catandmutton.co.uk
dir: *Telephone for directions*

Formerly known as the 'Cattle & Shoulder of Mutton' the pub was used by workers on their way to London's livestock markets in the 17th century. Today, the revamped building has been reinvented as one of East London's busiest food pubs. At scrubbed tables in trendy, gentrified surroundings, order steak tartare with Melba toast; pan-fried sea trout Niçoise; or pot-roast spring chicken with baby vegetables. There are well-kept real ales and several wines are offered by the glass. Booking for meals may be required.

Open all day all wk 12-11 (Fri-Sat noon-1am) Closed: 25-26 Dec ⊕ SEAMLESS LTD ◀ Adnams Southwold Bitter, Shepherd Neame Spitfire, Caledonian Deuchars IPA ☼ Westons, Addlestones. **Facilities** Children welcome Children's portions Wi-fi

E9

The Empress   PLAN 2 G4
PICK OF THE PUBS

130 Lauriston Rd, Victoria Park E9 7LH
☎ 020 8533 5123
e-mail: info@theempressofindia.com
dir: *From Mile End Station turn right onto Grove Rd, leads onto Lauriston Rd*

New owners have taken over this classic East End pub, which has in its time been a nightclub, a print works and,

more recently, a floristry training school. The bar serves classic cocktails, beer from the East London Brewing Company and fine wines from around the globe, with 19 served by the glass. Classic British food, served from the open kitchen, offers options throughout the day, including weekend brunch (from 10am), lunch, dinner and all-day bar snacks. Rare breed meats and free-range eggs come from Ginger Pig in Yorkshire, charcuterie from Bindisa, and organic bread from E5 Bakehouse. In the evening, expect bone marrow, snails and parsley to be followed by beef cheek and turnips, steak and chips with caper and shallot dressing, or cod with curried cauliflower and lime dressing. The weekend brunch menu takes in eggs Benedict, pancakes with maple syrup and bananas, and a plate of Serrano ham; don't miss the Sunday roasts – served until 9pm.

Open all day all wk Closed: 25 Dec **Bar Meals** Av main course £13 food served all day **Restaurant** L served Mon-Fri 12-3, Sat 12.30-4, Sun 12.30-9 D served Mon-Sat 6-10, Sun 12.30-9 Av 3 course à la carte fr £23 ⊕ FREE HOUSE ◀ East London Foundation Bitter. ♇ 19 **Facilities** ♣ Children welcome Children's menu Children's portions Wi-fi 🚐

E14

The Grapes   PLAN 2 G3
PICK OF THE PUBS

76 Narrow St, Limehouse E14 8BP ☎ 020 7987 4396
e-mail: info@thegrapes.co.uk
dir: *Telephone for directions*

In *Our Mutual Friend*, Charles Dickens immortalised this old Thames-side pub, now in new hands, as the Six Jolly Fellowship Porters. While he might recognise the wood-panelled, Victorian long bar and The Dickens Snug, where as a child he reputedly danced on a table, much of surrounding Limehouse has changed beyond recognition. So too has the Isle of Dogs, as looking east from the small terrace over the river at the back to the skyscrapers of Canary Wharf proves. Cask-conditioned ales in the bar include Adnams, Marston's Pedigree, Timothy Taylor Landlord and guests, while in the tiny upstairs dining room the fresh seafood includes pan-seared scallops, chorizo and smoked chilli; grilled or crispy battered haddock fillet; and whole roasted sea bass. If you'd prefer steak and chips, or shepherd's pie, they're on the menu too. Salads, sandwiches and bar meals are always available, and there are traditional roasts on Sundays. Booking for meals may be required.

Open all day all wk 12-11 (Mon-Wed 12-3 5.30-11) Closed: 25-26 Dec, 1 Jan **Bar Meals** L served Mon-Sat 12-2.30, Sun 12-3.30 D served Mon-Sat 6.30-9.30 **Restaurant** L served Mon-Fri 12-2.30 D served Mon-Sat 6.30-9.30 ⊕ SPIRIT LEASED ◀ Marston's Pedigree, Timothy Taylor Landlord, Adnams, Guest ales ☼ Aspall. **Facilities** ♣

E14 *continued*

The Gun ⊛ PLAN 2 G3

27 Coldharbour, Docklands E14 9NS ☎ 020 7515 5222
e-mail: info@thegundocklands.com
dir: From South Quay DLR, east along Marsh Wall to mini rdbt. Turn left, over bridge then 1st right

The Gun stands on the banks of the Thames in an area once home to the dockside iron foundries which produced guns for the Royal Navy. The pub takes its name from the cannon fired to celebrate the opening of the West India docks in 1802; it was also, allegedly, where Nelson and Lady Hamilton sometimes met on their secret assignations. Destroyed by fire several years ago, the Grade II listed building reopened in 2004 following painstaking restoration work. It offers adjoining main bar and restaurant, two private dining rooms, two snugs, and a stunning riverside terrace overlooking the Millennium Dome. Right next door is the pub's latest addition – A Grelha serves traditional southern Portuguese food straight from the barbecue. Back in The Gun, you can snack on oysters from Borough Market, lunch on a plate of devilled whitebait from the pub menu, or choose a restaurant main course such as roast breast of Yorkshire guinea fowl. There is a strong wine list featuring over 100 bins. Booking for meals may be required.

Open all wk 11am-mdnt (Sun 11-11) Closed: 25-26 Dec ⊕ ETM GROUP ◀ Fuller's London Pride, Adnams, Guinness ♻ Aspall. **Facilities** Children welcome Children's portions Garden Wi-fi

The Bleeding Heart Tavern ⊛ PLAN 1 E4

19 Greville St EC1N 8SQ ☎ 020 7242 8238
e-mail: bookings@bleedingheart.co.uk
dir: Close to Farringdon tube station, at corner of Greville St & Bleeding Heart Yard

Standing just off London's famous Leather Lane, and dating from 1746, when Holborn had a boozer for every five houses and inns boasted that their customers could be 'drunk for a penny and dead drunk for twopence'. It traded until 1946, was a grill for 52 years, and reopened as The Tavern Bar in 1998. Today this Tavern offers traditional real ales and a light lunchtime menu if you're pressed for time. Downstairs, the warm and comforting dining room features an open rotisserie and grill serving free-range organic British meat, game and poultry alongside an extensive wine list. Typical menu choices might start with mackerel and whisky pâté as a prelude to braised beef in Adnams ale with dumplings, or spit-roast suckling pig with sage apple and onion stuffing and crushed garlic potatoes. Desserts include steamed chocolate pudding, treacle tart and a jam roly-poly. Booking for meals may be required.

Open all day 7am-11pm Closed: BHs, 10 days at Xmas, Sat-Sun ⊕ FREE HOUSE ◀ Adnams Southwold Bitter, Broadside, Fisherman, May Day ♻ Aspall.

The Coach & Horses PLAN 1 E5

26-28 Ray St, Clerkenwell EC1R 3DJ ☎ 020 7278 8990
e-mail: info@thecoachandhorses.com
dir: From Farringdon tube station right onto Cowcross St. At Farringdon Rd turn right, after 500yds left onto Ray St. Pub at bottom of hill

Located on the site of Hockley-in-the-Hole bear-baiting pit, this restored wood-panelled Victorian pub was built to serve the myriad artisans, many of them Italian, who once populated this characterful area. What is now the public bar used to be a sweet shop, people lived in the beer cellars, and there was a secret passage to the long-buried River Fleet, still running beneath the pub and audible from the cellar and a drain outside the front entrance. Unsurprisingly there are a few ghosts, including an old man and a black cat. The reasonably priced dishes on the modern European menu kick off with bar snacks such as pickled eggs, Welsh rarebit, and blinchiki – a Russian crêpe with beef, cheese and onion. Enjoy them with a pint of Fuller's or a glass of wine from the great list. Over the road is the original Clerk's Well from which this district takes its name.

Open all wk 12-11 (Sat 6-11 Sun 12.30-5) Closed: 24 Dec-1st Mon in Jan, BH **Bar Meals** L served Mon-Fri 12-3, Sun 1-4 D served Mon-Sat 6-10 Av main course £10-£11 **Restaurant** L served Mon-Fri 12-3, Sun 1-4 D served Mon-Sat 6-10 Av 3 course à la carte fr £20 ⊕ FREE HOUSE/PUNCH TAVERNS ◀ Timothy Taylor Landlord, Adnams Southwold Bitter, Fuller's London Pride ♻ Burrow Hill. ₱ 17 **Facilities** ❤ Children welcome Children's portions Garden Wi-fi ⊞ (notice required)

The Eagle PLAN 1 E5

159 Farringdon Rd EC1R 3AL ☎ 020 7837 1353
dir: Angel/Farringdon tube station. Pub at north end of Farringdon Rd

Now into its second decade, The Eagle blazed a trail in the early 1990s and paved the way for what we now except as stylish gastro-pubs. Despite considerable competition, The Eagle is still going strong and remains one of trendy Clerkenwell's top establishments. The lofty interior has barely changed since it opened and includes a wooden-floored bar and dining area, a mishmash of vintage furniture, and an open-to-view kitchen that produces a creatively modern, twice-daily changing menu which revels in bold, rustic flavours. Typical of the range are salt cod soup with paprika, peppers, garlic, bread and egg; Venetian-style calves' liver on toast with sweet onion, red wine vinegar and parsley; and rare grilled onglet with horseradish cream, roast potatoes and rocket. The tapas selection includes grilled asparagus with pecorino and desserts are limited to Portuguese-style custard tarts and good espresso coffee.

Open all day 12-11 (Sun 12-5) Closed: BH L (1wk Xmas), Sun eve **Bar Meals** L served Mon-Fri 12-3, Sat-Sun 12-3.30 D served Mon-Sat 6.30-10.30 Av main course £10 **Restaurant** L served Mon-Fri 12-3, Sat-Sun 12-3.30

D served Mon-Sat 6.30-10.30 ⊕ FREE HOUSE ◀ Wells Eagle IPA & Bombardier ♻ Westons, Addlestones. ₱ 15 **Facilities** ❤ Children welcome Children's portions

The Jerusalem Tavern PLAN 1 E4

55 Britton St, Clerkenwell EC1M 5NA ☎ 020 7490 4281
e-mail: thejerusalemtavern@gmail.com
dir: 100mtrs NE of Farringdon tube station; 300mtrs N of Smithfield

Owned by Suffolk's St Peter's Brewery, this historic tavern has close links to Samuel Johnson, Oliver Goldsmith, David Garrick and the young Handel, who used to drink here on his visits to London. Named after the Priory of St John of Jerusalem, founded in 1140, the pub can be traced back to the 14th century, having occupied several sites in the area including part of St John's Gate. The current premises date from 1720 although the shop frontage dates from about 1810, when it was a workshop for Clerkenwell's various watch and clock craftsmen. Its dimly lit Dickensian bar, with bare boards, rustic wooden tables, old tiles, candles, open fires and cosy corners, is the perfect film set - which is what it has been on many occasions. A classic pub in every sense, it offers the full range of cask and bottled beers from St Peter's Brewery, as well as a range of simple pub fare.

Open all day 11-11 Closed: 25 Dec-1 Jan, Sat-Sun **Bar Meals** L served Mon-Fri 12-3 Av main course £8 **Restaurant** Fixed menu price fr £6.90 ⊕ ST PETER'S BREWERY ◀ St Peter's (full range) ♻ Aspall. **Facilities** ❤ Wi-fi

The Peasant PLAN 1 E5

240 Saint John St EC1V 4PH ☎ 020 7336 7726
e-mail: eat@thepeasant.co.uk
dir: Exit Angel & Farringdon Rd tube station. Pub on corner of Saint John St & Percival St

A gastro-pub movement pioneer, this beautifully restored, Grade II listed former gin palace still looks very Victorian, with its mahogany horseshoe bar, mosaic floor and period chandeliers in the circus-memorabilia-filled restaurant. Real ales include Truman's Runner, a bitter that revives the name of one of that long-defunct brewery's favourites; there are good real ciders too, lots of bottled beers, including some Belgian Trappist varieties, and decent wines. Two menus: a carte for upstairs, and lighter meals in the bar, where, amid the cult-band posters and old speedway billboards, you can order fish, chips and pea purée, or roast chicken breast with stem broccoli and red wine jus. A typical dinner begins with warm salad of crispy squid, prawns, chorizo, semi-dried tomatoes and chilli oil, and follows with roast rump of lamb with potato and cumin pakora, celeriac purée, green beans and coriander jus. Beer festivals are in April and November.

Open all day all wk Closed: 24 Dec-2 Jan **Bar Meals** L served all wk 12-11 D served all wk 12-11 Av main course £12 food served all day **Restaurant** D served Tue-Sat

6-11 Av 3 course à la carte fr £30 ⊕ FREE HOUSE
◄■ Wells Bombardier, Crouch Vale Brewers Gold, Truman's
Runner, Guest ales ♂ Thatchers Pear & Katy, Aspall, The
Orchard Pig. ♥ 15 **Facilities** Children welcome Children's
portions Garden Beer festival ▬ (notice required)

Ye Olde Mitre   PLAN 1 E4

1 Ely Court, Ely Place, By 8 Hatton Garden EC1N 6SJ
☎ **020 7405 4751**
e-mail: yeoldemitre@fullers.co.uk
dir: *From Chancery Lane tube station exit 3 walk downhill
to Holborn Circus, left into Hatton Garden. Pub in alley
between 8 & 9 Hatton Garden.*

Built in 1546 in the shadow of the palace of the Bishops
of Ely, this quirky historic corner pub is in Ely Court, off
Hatton Garden. Choose from at least five real ales in the
magnificent wood-panelled rooms, with a range of bar
snacks or 'English tapas' that includes toasted
sandwiches, pork pies, Scotch eggs, sausage rolls, olives
and picked eggs. Beer festivals are held in May, August
and December, but the pub is closed at weekends and
Bank Holidays.

Open all day Closed: 25 Dec, 1 Jan, BHs, Sat-Sun (ex 1st
wknd Aug) **Bar Meals** L served Mon-Fri 11.30-9.30
D served Mon-Fri 11.30-9.30 food served all day
⊕ FULLER'S ◄■ London Pride, Geoge Gale & Co Seafarers,
Caledonian Deuchars IPA, Adnams Broadside, Guest ales
♂ Biddenden Bushels. ♥ 8 **Facilities** Garden Beer festival
Wi-fi

EC2

Old Dr Butler's Head   PLAN 1 F4

Mason's Av, Coleman St, Moorgate EC2V 5BT
☎ **020 7606 3504**
e-mail: olddoctorbutlers@shepherdneame.co.uk
dir: *Telephone for directions*

The sign says Dr, the fascia says Doctor. Butler was King
James I's Court Physician with a line in dodgy cures,
including plunging plague victims into cold water. He
also sold 'medicinal ale' through his alehouses, this
Shepherd Neame pub, rebuilt after the Great Fire of 1666,
being the sole survivor. Sandwiches are served in the
gas-lit bar, while the upstairs Chop House restaurant
offers lunchtime favourites such as steak and kidney suet
pudding, and an extensive wine list. Like many City of
London pubs, Dr Butler's closes at weekends. Booking for
meals may be required.

Open all day Closed: Sat-Sun **Bar Meals** L served Mon-Fri
12-3 D served Mon-Fri 6-9 Av main course £11
Restaurant L served Mon-Fri 12-3 Av 3 course à la carte
fr £25 ⊕ SHEPHERD NEAME ◄■ Spitfire, Bishops Finger,
Master Brew, Kent's Best. ♥ 12 **Facilities** Wi-fi ▬

EC4

The Black Friar   PLAN 1 E3

174 Queen Victoria St EC4V 4EG ☎ **020 7236 5474**
dir: *Opposite Blackfriars tube station*

Space permitting, so much could be written about this
1875 pub and its later art nouveau interior celebrating
the fanciful antics of the medieval Dominican monks,
who once lived here, known as the Blackfriars. Real ales
range from Adnams to Timothy Taylor, via Fuller's,
Sharp's and St Austell, with solid sustenance of
sandwiches and pies; Cumberland sausage and mash;
salmon and broccoli fishcakes; and roasted vegetable
risotto. On a triangular site by Blackfriars tube station,
it's popular with City suits.

Open all day all wk Mon-Sat 10am-11pm (Sun 12-10.30)
Closed: 25 Dec **Bar Meals** L served all wk 10-5 D served
all wk 5-10 ⊕ MITCHELLS & BUTLERS ◄■ Fuller's London
Pride, St Austell Tribute, Sharp's Doom Bar, Adnams,
Timothy Taylor ♂ Westons Wyld Wood Organic, Aspall.
♥ 14 **Facilities** Children welcome Garden

The Old Bank of England   PLAN 1 E4

194 Fleet St EC4A 2LT ☎ **020 7430 2255**
e-mail: oldbankofengland@fullers.co.uk
dir: *Pub by Courts of Justice*

This magnificent building previously housed the Law
Courts' branch of the Bank of England. Set between the
site of Sweeney Todd's barbershop and his mistress's pie
shop, it stands above the original bank vaults and the
tunnels in which Todd butchered his unfortunate victims.
Aptly, there's an extensive range of speciality pies
including game, brandy and redcurrant, and lamb and
red pepper, but other treats include roasted lemon and
thyme chicken breast on a pearl barley broth, and
caramelised onion and olive puff pastry tart.

Open all day Closed: BHs, Sat-Sun ⊕ FULLER'S ◄■ London
Pride, Chiswick Bitter, Discovery, ESB, Seasonal ales.
Facilities Garden Wi-fi

The White Swan ◉   PLAN 1 E4
PICK OF THE PUBS

108 Fetter Ln, Holborn EC4A 1ES ☎ **020 7242 9696**
e-mail: info@thewhiteswanlondon.com
dir: *Nearest tube: Chancery Lane. From station towards
St Paul's Cathedral. At HSBC bank left into Fetter Ln.
Pub on right*

Transformed from the old Mucky Duck pub, this is now a
handsome, traditional City watering hole. Downstairs is
the wood-panelled bar which serves a cosmopolitan
selection of beers and lagers, and plenty of wines by the

glass. Its fresh cream-coloured walls embrace
leather-covered bar stools and mixed wooden tables,
chairs and banquettes; beneath your feet the reclaimed
timber floorboards complete the sumptuous atmosphere.
Upstairs on the mezzanine is a beautifully restored dining
room with mirrored ceiling and linen-clad tables. Cooking
is modern British in style: a baby leek vinaigrette with
grated egg and anchovy dressing is a sample starter.
Fish fresh from Billingsgate each morning appears in
main courses such as roast fillet of Atlantic halibut with
leeks, mussels and crème fraîche. An alternative is rump
of Scottish Blackface mutton with hedgehog mushrooms
and fondant potatoes. To finish, the passionfruit
cheesecake, apple and blackberry crumble, and
home-made ice creams are all excellent. Booking for
meals may be required.

Open 11am-mdnt (Fri 11-1am) Closed: 25-26 Dec, 1 Jan,
Sat-Sun & BHs ⊕ ETM GROUP ◄■ Fuller's London Pride,
Adnams, Guinness ♂ Addlestones. **Facilities** Children
welcome Children's portions Wi-fi

N1

The Albion   PLAN 2 F4

10 Thornhill Rd, Islington N1 1HW ☎ **020 7607 7450**
e-mail: info@the-albion.co.uk
dir: *From Angel tube station, cross road into Liverpool
Rd past Sainsbury's, continue to Richmond Ave. Left. At
junct with Thornhill Rd turn right. Pub on right*

In the heart of Islington, just off Upper Street in the
Barnsbury conservation area, stands this Georgian gem
of a pub. The spacious walled garden and
wisteria-covered pergola draw the summer crowds –
perfect for relaxed alfresco drinking and tucking into
some cracking modern pub food prepared from top-notch
British produce. The brasserie-style menu centres around
the charcoal grill – whole mackerel, 28-day aged
Galloway rib-eye steak – alongside chicken, leek and
mushroom pie; smoked haddock fishcake with
hollandaise; and treacle sponge with crème anglaise. Log
fires warm the classic dark wood panels and tastefully
furnished interior in winter. Booking for meals may be
required.

Open all day all wk **Bar Meals** L served Mon-Fri 12-3, Sat
12-4, Sun 12-9 D served Mon-Sat 6-10, Sun 12-9
Restaurant L served Mon-Fri 12-3, Sat 12-4, Sun 12-9
D served Mon-Sat 6-10, Sun 12-9 Av 3 course à la carte
fr £30 ⊕ PUNCH TAVERNS ◄■ Ringwood Best Bitter,
Caledonian Deuchars IPA ♂ Addlestones. ♥ 12
Facilities ☺ Children welcome Children's menu
Children's portions Garden Wi-fi ▬ (notice required)

N1 continued

The Barnsbury PLAN 2 F4

209-211 Liverpool Rd, Islington N1 1LX
☎ 020 7607 5519
e-mail: thebarnsburypub@hotmail.com
dir: Telephone for directions

The Barnsbury, a 'free house and dining room' in the heart of Islington, is a welcome addition to the London scene. It's a gastro-pub where both the food and the prices are well conceived – and its walled garden makes it a secluded and sought-after summer oasis for alfresco relaxation. At least six guest ales are backed by an in-depth wine list. The food is cooked from daily supplies of fresh ingredients which have been bought direct from the market. Starter dishes range from smoked chicken and mango salad to a charcuterie board. Tempting mains might include pea and stilton risotto; and seared tuna with roasted tomato and basil fusilli.

Open all day all wk 12-11 (Sun 12-10.30) Closed: 25-26 Dec, 1 Jan ⊕ FREE HOUSE ◀ Guest ales.
Facilities Children welcome Garden

The Charles Lamb PLAN 2 F4

16 Elia St, Islington N1 8DE ☎ 020 7837 5040
e-mail: food@thecharleslambpub.com
dir: From Angel station turn left, at junct of City Rd turn left. Pass Duncan Terrace Gdns, left into Colebrooke Row. 1st right

Named after a local writer who lived in Islington in the 1830s, this cracking neighbourhood pub thrives thanks to the hard work and dedication of Camille and MJ Hobby-Limon, who took over the former Prince Albert in 2005. Locals beat a path to the door for micro-brewery ales and the hearty, home-cooked comfort food listed on the daily chalkboard menu. With inspiration from the Mediterranean, dishes may include Basque fish stew, wild mushroom and pearl barley risotto, and a rustic cassoulet. The pub hosts an annual Bastille Day event complete with petanque competition.

Open all wk Mon & Tue fr 4 Wed-Sun fr noon Closed: 23 Dec-1 Jan **Bar Meals** L served Wed-Fri 12-3, Sat 12-4, Sun 12-6 D served Mon-Sat 6-9.30, Sun 7-9 ⊕ FREE HOUSE ◀ Dark Star Hophead, Triple fff Alton's Pride, Guest ales Ö Thatchers. ♔ 9 **Facilities** Children welcome Beer festival Wi-fi

The Compton Arms PLAN 2 F4

4 Compton Av, Off Canonbury Rd N1 2XD
☎ 020 7359 6883
e-mail: andard07@btinternet.com
dir: Telephone for directions

George Orwell was once a customer at this peaceful pub, 'a country pub in the city', on Islington's backstreets. The late 17th-century building has a rural feel, and is frequented by a mix of locals, actors and musicians. One local described it as 'an island in a sea of gastro-pubs'. Expect real ales from the handpump, and good value steaks, mixed grills, big breakfasts and Sunday roasts.

The bar is busy when Arsenal are at home. Change of hands.

Open all day all wk Closed: 25 Dec pm ⊕ GREENE KING ◀ IPA & Abbot Ale, Guest ale. **Facilities** Garden

The Crown PLAN 2 F4

116 Cloudesley Rd, Islington N1 0EB ☎ 020 7837 7107
e-mail: crown.islington@fullers.co.uk
dir: From Angel tube station take Liverpool Rd, 6th left into Cloudesley Sq. Pub on opposite side of Square

A lovely Grade II listed Georgian building in the Barnsbury village conservation area of Islington, this pub boasts one of only two remaining barrel bars in London. It has a shaded outdoor area for good weather and a roaring log fire for winter. The pub specialises in quality gastro-pub food, along with Fuller's beers. The regularly changing menu focuses on fresh seasonal ingredients, offering hearty traditional English favourites and Sunday roasts. Bread is also freshly baked on the premises.

Open all day all wk Closed: 25 Dec ⊕ FULLER'S ◀ London Pride, Organic Honeydew, ESB, London Porter Ö Aspall. **Facilities** Children welcome Children's portions Garden Wi-fi

The Drapers Arms ⊛ PLAN 2 F4

PICK OF THE PUBS

44 Barnsbury St N1 1ER ☎ 020 7619 0348
e-mail: nick@thedrapersarms.com
dir: Turn right from Highbury & Islington station, 10 mins along Upper St. Barnsbury St on right opposite Shell service station

Built by the Drapers' Company in the 1830s, Nick Gibson's handsome Islington pub serves its local real ale and cider drinkers well, with Harvey's Sussex, Sambrook's Wandle (named after a South London river), Truman's Runner, plus Aspall and Westons Organic cider. Thought clearly goes into the menus too, as testified by pleasingly different, hearty starters like Cullen skink; haggis fritters with gribiche sauce; and potted beef with pickled red cabbage. The kitchen approaches mains in the same way, with kedgeree; grilled quail with braised red cabbage and prunes; and lentils with roast squash, chanterelles and chive crème fraîche; while a typical dessert might be burnt fennel and orange custard. The downstairs open-plan bar is illuminated by large picture windows, its unfussy interior furnished with a mix of squashy sofas and solid wooden tables. For a quieter pint, try the peaceful garden (yes, even in London). Look out for the August beer festival.

Open all day all wk ⊕ FREE HOUSE ◀ Harvey's Sussex, Sambrook's Wandle, Truman's Runner Ö Aspall, Westons Stowford Press & Wyld Wood Organic. **Facilities** Children welcome Children's menu Children's portions Garden Beer festival Wi-fi

The Duke of Cambridge PLAN 2 F4

PICK OF THE PUBS

30 Saint Peter's St N1 8JT ☎ 020 7359 3066
e-mail: duke@dukeorganic.co.uk
dir: Telephone for directions

Geetie Singh's obsession with achieving the lowest possible carbon footprint possible at her remarkable Islington gastro-pub, the first certified organic pub in Britain, has reached new heights. Everything possible is re-used or recycled and even the electricity is wind and solar generated. Sustainable, ethically-produced ingredients are approved by the Soil Association and Marine Conservation Society, and items such as bread, ice cream and pickles are all made on site. Beers from local micro-breweries, real ciders such as Luscombe, and organic wines go hand-in-hand with a mouthwatering seasonal menu that may change twice daily, with 80 per cent of ingredients sourced from the Home Counties. A spring choice could be mussels in tomato, chorizo and ale sauce, followed by Dover sole with Savoy cabbage, pancetta and sautéed potatoes. The winter menu may offer beetroot and cumin seed soup with crème fraîche, followed by rabbit and red wine stew with bubble-and-squeak. To finish, there could be rhubarb fool with coconut macaroon. Booking for meals may be required.

Open all day all wk Closed: 24-26 & 31 Dec, 1 Jan **Bar Meals** L served Mon-Fri 12.30-3, Sat-Sun 12.30-3.30 D served Mon-Sat 6.30-10.30, Sun 6.30-10 **Restaurant** L served Mon-Fri 12.30-3, Sat-Sun 12.30-3.30 D served Mon-Sat 6.30-10.30, Sun 6.30-10 ⊕ FREE HOUSE ◀ Pitfield SB Bitter, East Kent Goldings, Shoreditch Stout & Eco Warrior, St Peter's Best Bitter Ö Westons, Dunkertons, Luscombe. ♔ 12 **Facilities** ♣ Children welcome Children's portions 🚌

The House PLAN 2 F4

63-69 Canonbury Rd N1 2DG ☎ 020 7704 7410
e-mail: info@inthehouse.biz
dir: Telephone for directions

Situated in Islington's prestigious Canonbury district but moments away from the hustle and bustle of Upper Street, this successful gastro-pub has featured in a celebrity cookbook and garnered plenty of praise since it opened its doors a few years ago. Expect a thoroughly modern, seasonal British menu at lunch and dinner. Typical dishes include red onion tarte Tatin with melted goat's cheese and rocket; slow-roast pork belly with wholegrain mustard mash, curly kale, black pudding, apple sauce and cider jus; and rhubarb crumble with crème anglaise for dessert.

Open Mon-Fri 4-12 (Sat-Sun 10am-2am) Closed: Mon-Fri L (ex BH) **Restaurant** L served Sat-Sun 10-4 D served Mon-Fri 6-10.30, Sat-Sun 6-10 ⊕ PUNCH TAVERNS ◀ Sharp's Doom Bar, Guinness Ö Aspall. ♔ 8 **Facilities** ♣ Children welcome Children's menu Children's portions Garden Wi-fi 🚌

N6

The Flask　　　　　　PLAN 2 E5

PICK OF THE PUBS

77 Highgate West Hill N6 6BU ☎ 020 8348 7346
e-mail: theflaskhighgate@london-gastros.co.uk
dir: *Nearest tube: Archway/Highgate*

High on Highgate Hill, this north London institution may now be a gastro-pub with a big reputation but its name was made long ago when Dick Turpin frequented it. Dating from 1663 and made famous by Byron, Keats, Hogarth and Betjeman, this Grade II listed pub has become a London landmark. It retains much of its character and cosy atmosphere and a maze of small rooms is served by two bars, one of which houses the original sash windows. Fuller's, Butcombe and guest real ales are on offer alongside two dozen bottled ales and ciders, and some sensibly priced wines. Starters include grilled pigeon breast, radish and golden beetroot, while typical mains are roast poussin, sautéed courgettes and leeks; and whole lemon sole, fennel, lemon and caper butter. For dessert, try quince and almond tart or pear and golden raisin crumble. The large front garden is especially popular in the summer. Booking for meals may be required.

Open all day all wk 12-11 (Sun 12-10.30) Closed: 25 Dec **Bar Meals** L served Mon-Fri 12-3, Sat-Sun 12-4 D served Mon-Sat 6-10, Sun 6-9 ⊕ FULLER'S ◀ London Pride, ESB & Discovery, Butcombe Bitter, Guest ales Ö Aspall. ♥ 13 **Facilities** Children welcome Garden Wi-fi ⊞

N19

The Landseer　　　　　　PLAN 2 F5

37 Landseer Rd N19 4JU ☎ 020 7263 4658
e-mail: thelandseer@hotmail.com
dir: *Nearest tube stations: Archway & Tufnell Park*

Leather sofas, chunky farmhouse-style tables and much indoor greenery characterise this airy gastro-pub. This is an ideal spot to relax with the weekend papers, or while away an evening with one of the pub's extensive library of board games. Snack from the bar, brunch or tapas menu, indulge in chargrilled meat or fish steaks, or claim a classic sea bass with braised fennel; Sunday roasts are a major draw here. In warmer weather, enjoy a meal or a drink on the spacious patio. Booking for meals may be required.

Open all day all wk 12-12 (Sun-Tue 12-11) Closed: 25 Dec, 1 Jan ⊕ FREE HOUSE ◀ Staropramen, Guest ales Ö Brothers Pear, Aspall. **Facilities** Children welcome Children's portions Play area Wi-fi

NW1

The Chapel　　　　　　PLAN 1 B4

48 Chapel St NW1 5DP ☎ 020 7402 9220
e-mail: thechapel@btconnect.com
dir: *By A40 Marylebone Rd & Old Marylebone Rd junct. Off Edgware Rd by tube station*

An award-winning, child-friendly gastro-pub, The Chapel has a bright, open-plan interior of stripped floors and pine furniture, and one of central London's largest enclosed pub gardens. Owners Alison McGrath and Lakis Hondrogiannis take delivery of fresh produce daily for separate antipasti, canapé, lunch and dinner menus, the last two of which list Spanish pork, olive and pepper stew; beef and ginger stirfry with egg noodles and sweet chilli sauce; salmon and salt cod fishcake; and leek lasagne, tomato coulis and baby red chard salad. Many wines are by the glass.

Open all day all wk Closed: 25-26 Dec, 1 Jan, Etr **Restaurant** L served Mon-Sat 12-2.30, Sun 12.30-3 D served all wk 7-10 ⊕ FREE HOUSE/GREENE KING ◀ IPA, Morland Old Golden Hen Ö Aspall. ♥ 15 **Facilities** ✿ Children welcome Children's menu Children's portions Garden ⊞ (notice required)

The Engineer　　　　　　PLAN 2 E4

PICK OF THE PUBS

65 Gloucester Av, Primrose Hill NW1 8JH
☎ 020 7483 1890
e-mail: enquiries@theengineerprimrosehill.co.uk
dir: *Telephone for directions*

Built by Isambard Kingdom Brunel in 1841, this unassuming street corner pub stands tucked away in a residential part of Primrose Hill close to Camden Market. It attracts a discerning dining crowd who relish its imaginative and well-prepared food and friendly, laid-back atmosphere. Refurbished following a change of ownership, it has a spacious bar area, wood floors, sturdy wooden tables with candles, simple décor and cosy upstairs private dining rooms. A walled, paved and heated garden to the rear is popular in fine weather. In addition to cosmopolitan beers, the drinks list includes hand-crafted teas, freshly ground coffees, interesting wines, and a variety of whiskies. Regularly changing menus feature an eclectic mix of inspired home-made dishes using organic and free-range products. A typical Sunday lunch menu may feature rabbit terrine with piccalilli to start, followed by roast duck with plums and braised red cabbage, or lamb shoulder with confit garlic and mint sauce. Leave room for bitter chocolate pudding with malt ice cream. Booking for meals may be required.

Open all day all wk 9am-11pm (Sun & BH 9am-10.30pm) **Bar Meals** L served Mon-Fri 12-3, Sat-Sun 12.30-4 D served Mon-Sat 6.30-11, Sun & BH 6.30-10.30 Av main course £15 **Restaurant** L served Mon-Fri 12-3, Sat-Sun 12.30-4 D served Mon-Sat 6.30-11, Sun & BH 6.30-10.30 Fixed menu price fr £25 Av 3 course à la carte fr £32 ⊕ MITCHELLS & BUTLERS ◀ Adnams Gunhill, Timothy Taylor Landlord, Redemption Ö Pips. ♥ 19 **Facilities** ✿ Children welcome Children's menu Children's portions Family room Garden Beer festival Wi-fi ⊞

The Globe　　　　　　PLAN 1 B4

43-47 Marylebone Rd NW1 5JY ☎ 020 7935 6368
e-mail: globe.1018@thespiritgroup.com
dir: *At corner of Marylebone Rd & Baker St, opposite Baker St tube station*

Many famous and infamous characters have been patrons here including Charles Dickens. Built in 1735, the same year as the neighbouring Nash terraces, the pub retains much of its period charm, including William, the ghost of a former landlord. The first omnibus service from Holborn stopped here and the Metropolitan line was constructed under the road a few feet from the tavern. A good choice of real ales is offered alongside freshly cooked British pub food, such as bangers and mash, chicken tikka masala, Wiltshire cured ham, egg and chips, and steak-and-ale pie.

Open all day all wk 10am-11pm (Fri-Sat 10am-11.30pm Sun 10am-10.30pm) (Closed some eves after Wembley football matches) Closed: 25 Dec **Bar Meals** L served Mon-Sat 10-10, Sun 12-9.30 D served Mon-Sat 10-10, Sun 12-9.30 Av main course £9 food served all day **Restaurant** food served all day ⊕ PUNCH TAVERNS ◀ Greene King Abbot Ale, Wells Bombardier, Young's, Morland Old Speckled Hen, Guest ales. ♥ 13 **Facilities** Children welcome Children's menu Children's portions Wi-fi ⊞ (notice required)

The Lansdowne　　　　　　PLAN 2 E4

PICK OF THE PUBS

90 Gloucester Av, Primrose Hill NW1 8HX
☎ 020 7483 0409
e-mail: info@thelansdownepub.co.uk
dir: *Turn right from Chalk Farm tube station into Adelaide Rd, 1st left into Bridge Approach (on foot). Into Gloucester Av, 500yds. Pub on corner*

In 1992 The Lansdowne was one of the earliest dining pubs in Primrose Hill. The pub was stripped of its fruit machines, TVs and jukebox and replaced with solid wood furniture and back-to-basics décor; today, it blends a light, spacious bar and outdoor seating area with a slightly more formal upper dining room. All that apart, however, its success depends on the quality of its cooking. All food is freshly prepared on the premises, using organic or free-range ingredients wherever possible, and portions are invariably generous. The seasonal menu offers spiced red lentil soup with Greek yogurt; home-cured bresaola with rocket, capers and parmesan; pan-fried sardines on toast with watercress; confit pork belly with prunes, potatoes and lardons; poached sea trout with crushed herb potatoes; polenta with roast pumpkin, buffalo mozzarella and walnut.

Open all day all wk 12-11 (Sat 10am-11pm Sun 10am-10.30pm) ⊕ FREE HOUSE ◀ Wells Bombardier, Truman's Ö Aspall. **Facilities** Children welcome

NW1 *continued*

The Prince Albert PLAN 2 F4

163 Royal College St NW1 0SG ☎ 020 7485 0270
e-mail: info@princealbertcamden.com
dir: *From Camden tube station follow Camden Rd. Right onto Royal College St, 200mtrs on right*

Picnic tables furnish the small paved courtyard, while The Prince Albert's wooden floors and bentwood furniture make a welcoming interior for customers and their four-legged friends. Real ales there are, but you may fancy a refreshing San Miguel for a change, and wine drinkers have plenty of choice. Bar snacks range from home-roasted nuts to crispy salt and pepper chicken wings, which also feature on the great-value set menu; these can be followed by Old English pork sausages or beer-battered haddock. Two or three times a year the pub holds a three-day real ale festival. Booking for meals may be required.

Open all day all wk 12-11 (Sun 12.30-10.30) **Bar Meals** L served Mon-Sat 12-3, Sun 12-5 D served Mon-Sat 6-10 **Restaurant** L served Mon-Sat 12-3, Sun 12-5 D served Mon-Sat 6-10 ⊕ FREE HOUSE ◀ Adnams Broadside, Kirin Ichiban, Black Sheep Ŏ Westons Stowford Press. ▼ 20 **Facilities** ❖ Children welcome Children's menu Children's portions Garden Beer festival Wi-fi

The Queens PLAN 2 E4

49 Regents Park Rd, Primrose Hill NW1 8XD
☎ 020 7586 0408
e-mail: queens@youngs.co.uk
dir: *Nearest tube: Chalk Farm*

There's a traditional British menu at this cosy Victorian pub overlooking Primrose Hill. Located in one of London's most affluent and personality-studded areas, The Queens is steeped in celebrity history and is mentioned in many stars' autobiographies. The bar menu offers a range of sandwiches, supported by hot dishes like sausages, mash and onion gravy, and cod and chips in ale batter. Grab a seat on the terraced seating outdoors in good weather. An annual beer festival coincides with British Food Fortnight. Booking for meals may be required.

Open all day all wk 11-11 (Sun 12-10.30) ⊕ YOUNG'S ◀ Bitter & Special, Wells Bombardier, Guest ales. **Facilities** Children welcome Children's portions Beer festival Wi-fi

NW3

The Holly Bush PLAN 2 E4

Holly Mount, Hampstead NW3 6SG ☎ 020 7435 2892
e-mail: hollybush@fullers.co.uk
dir: *Nearest tube: Hampstead. Exit tube station onto Holly Hill, 1st right*

The Holly Bush was once the stables belonging to the home of English portraitist George Romney and became a pub after his death in 1802. The original panelled walls remain, and there are chandeliers in the restaurant. The building has been investigated by 'ghost busters', but

more tangible 21st-century media celebrities are easier to spot. Depending on your appetite, the menu offers pies; chicken with black pudding; and fillet of pork wrapped in prosciutto. There has been a change of hands.

Open all day all wk 12-11 (Sun 12-10.30) ⊕ FULLER'S ◀ London Pride & ESB, Harvey's Sussex Best Bitter, Butcombe Ŏ Aspall. **Facilities** Children welcome Children's portions Beer festival Wi-fi

NW5

The Bull and Last NEW PLAN 2 E5

168 Highgate Rd NW5 1QS ☎ 020 7267 3641
e-mail: info@thebullandlast.co.uk
dir: *From Kentish Town tube station N along Highgate Rd, 10min walk*

A historic free house in a Grade II listed building, a stone's throw from Hampstead Heath. Accolades have been won for its friendly front of house team and Sunday lunches. Children and dogs are welcome too, so this really is a relaxing place to sample a pint of Young's or one of 17 wines sold by the glass. Wondering whether to eat? A glance at the menu will make up your mind – who can resist mouthwatering starters like orecchiette (ear-shaped pasta) with chicken livers, or fish soup with rouille and gruyère croquettes? Move on to roast Cornish cod with oxtail ragout if you're determined to push the boat out. Booking for meals may be required.

Open all day all wk 12-11 (Fri-Sat 12-12 Sun 12-10.30) Closed: 24-25 Dec **Bar Meals** L served Mon-Fri 12-3, Sat-Sun 12.30-3.30 D served Mon-Sat 6.30-10, Sun 7.30-9 Av main course £17 **Restaurant** L served Sat-Sun 12.30-3.30 D served Tue-Sat 7-10, Sun 6.30-9 Fixed menu price fr £35 Av 3 course à la carte fr £23 ⊕ FREE HOUSE/ETIVE PUBS LTD ◀ Hook Norton Hooky Bitter, Sharp's Doom Bar, Ringwood Best Bitter, Young's London Porter Ŏ Addlestones. ▼ 17 **Facilities** ❖ Children welcome Children's menu Children's portions Wi-fi

Dartmouth Arms PLAN 2 E5

35 York Rise NW5 1SP ☎ 020 7485 3267
e-mail: dartmoutharms@faucetinn.com
dir: *5 min walk from Hampstead Heath, 2 mins from Tufnell Park tube station*

This welcoming local close to Hampstead Heath is open for breakfast from 10am at weekends and will happily serve you a Virgin Mary (a Bloody Mary without the vodka) along with your bacon buttie. Quiz nights every Tuesday are perhaps a better time to sample ales by Adnams, Westerham and Young's, and there's a good choice of real ciders too. Sustenance comes in the form of hearty, upmarket pub food: parsnip and apple soup; Bridge farm organic bangers with celeriac mash, roasting gravy and freshly battered onion rings; and apple crumble with crème anglaise are typical offerings.

Open all day all wk 11-11 (Fri 11am-mdnt Sat 10am-mdnt Sun 10am-10.30pm) **Bar Meals** L served Mon-Fri 12-10, Sat-Sun 10-10 D served Mon-Fri 12-10, Sat-Sun 10-10 Av main course £10 food served all day **Restaurant** L served Mon-Fri 12-10, Sat-Sun 10-10

D served Mon-Fri 12-10, Sat-Sun 10-10 Fixed menu price fr £8.50 Av 3 course à la carte fr £20 food served all day ⊕ FREE HOUSE ◀ Westerham Finchcocks Original, Adnams, Young's Ŏ Kingstone Press, Briska. ▼ 10 **Facilities** Children welcome Children's menu Children's portions Wi-fi ⟺ (notice required)

The Junction Tavern PLAN 2 E4

PICK OF THE PUBS

101 Fortess Rd NW5 1AG ☎ 020 7485 9400
dir: *Between Kentish Town & Tufnell Park tube stations*

A stalwart of London's gastro-pub scene, this friendly local stands halfway between Kentish Town and Tufnell Park tube stations. Handy for the green spaces of Hampstead Heath and Parliament Hill, as well as the shops and markets in Camden, the pub specialises in real ales, with pumps on the bar including Sambrook's Wandle and Twickenham Fine Ales. The seasonal menus change daily from brunch to dinner. Daytime options include scrambled eggs, chorizo and toast or steamed mussels, leeks, bacon and cider cream. In the evening, you could try smoked chicken, baby gem and apple, mustard dressing, followed by roast lamb chump, Jersey Royals, broad bean purée and mint dressing. Finish with lemon tart and English strawberries or mixed berry Pavlova. Regular beer festivals in the conservatory and large heated garden can offer a range of up to 50 beers served straight from the cask. Booking for meals may be required.

Open all wk 5pm-11pm (Fri 12-11 Sat 11.30-11 Sun 12-10.30) Closed: 24-26 Dec, 1 Jan, Mon-Thu L **Bar Meals** L served Fri 12-3, Sat-Sun 12-4 D served Mon-Sat 6.30-10.30, Sun 6.30-9.30 Av main course £15.50 **Restaurant** L served Fri 12-3, Sat-Sun 12-4 D served Mon-Sat 6.30-10.30, Sun 6.30-9.30 Av 3 course à la carte fr £28.50 ⊕ ENTERPRISE INNS ◀ Sambrook's Wandle, Twickenham, Guest ales Ŏ Westons Wyld Wood Organic. ▼ 16 **Facilities** ❖ Garden Beer festival Wi-fi ⟺

The Lord Palmerston PLAN 2 E5

33 Dartmouth Park Hill NW5 1HU ☎ 020 7485 1578
e-mail: lordpalmerston@geronimo-inns.co.uk
dir: *From Tufnell Park Station turn right. Up Dartmouth Park Hill. Pub on right, on corner of Chetwynd Rd*

The Lord Palmerston is a stylish London pub in the Dartmouth Park conservation area. It has two open fires in winter, plus a large front terrace and rear garden for dining in summer. Food is taken seriously, with dishes ranging from chicken liver parfait with plum chutney and toast, and venison and apple sausages with braised red cabbage and curly kale, to steamed Cornish mussels in garlic and white wine cream. Saturday brunch is served from noon until 4pm, when the venison and apple sausages, or confit duck leg dishes may prove too tempting. As well as a beer festival in February, the pub holds weekly quiz nights and film screenings. Booking for meals may be required.

Open all day all wk 12-11 (Sun 12-10.30) **Bar Meals** L served Mon-Fri 12-3, Sat 12-4, Sun 12-5 D served

Save on hotels. Book at **theAA.com/hotel**

LONDON 349 ENGLAND

Mon-Sat 6.30-10, Sun 6-8.30 Av main course £15 food served all day **Restaurant** L served Mon-Fri 12-3, Sat 12-4 D served Mon-Sat 6.30-10, Sun 6-9 Av 3 course à la carte fr £25 ⊕ GERONIMO INNS LTD ◀ Adnams Southwold Bitter, Sharp's Doom Bar, Twickenham Naked Ladies, Purity Pure UBU, Redemption ♂ Aspall. ♚ 24 **Facilities** ♣ Children welcome Garden Beer festival

NW6

The Salusbury Pub and Dining Room
PLAN 2 D4

50-52 Salusbury Rd NW6 6NN ☎ 020 7328 3286
e-mail: thesalusburypub@btconnect.com
dir: *100mtrs left from Queens Park tube & train station*

In the hub of the Queen's Park community, this gastro-pub has a lively and vibrant atmosphere, offering draft beers and a London restaurant-style menu without the associated prices. The award-winning wine list boasts more than 100 wines, including mature offerings from the cellar. The owners stick to their successful formula of fantastic Italian food, great wines and consistent service. Example dishes are beef carpaccio with rocket and parmesan; lobster tagliatelle; whole sea bream in a salt crust; confit pheasant with cauliflower purée and crispy parsnips; and wild mushroom risotto.

Open all day 12-11 (Thu-Sat 12-12 Sun 12-10.30) Closed: 25-26 Dec, Mon L (ex BHs) **Bar Meals** L served Tue-Fri 12-3, Sat-Sun 12.30-3.30 D served all wk 7-10.15 Av main course £14 **Restaurant** L served Tue-Fri 12-3, Sat-Sun 12.30-3.30 D served all wk 7-10.15 Av 3 course à la carte fr £25 ⊕ FREE HOUSE ◀ Morland Old Speckled Hen, Adnams ♂ Aspall. ♚ 15 **Facilities** ♣ Children welcome Children's portions Family room Wi-fi ▦ (notice required)

NW8

The New Inn
PLAN 2 E4

2 Allitsen Rd, St John's Wood NW8 6LA
☎ **020 7722 0726**
e-mail: thenewinn@gmail.com
dir: *Off A41 by St John's Wood tube station onto Acacia Rd, last right, to end on corner*

This convivial Regency inn is well-placed for nearby Regent's Park, Lord's (hence the background cricketing theme) and bustling Camden Lock and Market. Voluminous flower baskets and troughs break the lines of this traditional street-corner local, where pavement tables are a popular retreat for locals supping Abbot Ale and diners indulging in the sharing boards, pasta dish of the day or a lunchtime sandwich. Live music at weekends. There has been a change of hands.

Open all day all wk ⊕ GREENE KING ◀ Abbot Ale, IPA. **Facilities** Children welcome Children's portions Wi-fi

The Salt House
PLAN 2 E4

PICK OF THE PUBS

63 Abbey Rd, St John's Wood NW8 0AE
☎ **020 7328 6626**
e-mail: info@thesalthouse.co.uk
dir: *Turn right outside St John's Wood tube. Left onto Marlborough Place, right onto Abbey Rd, pub on left*

Describing itself as a mere scuttle from The Beatles' famous Abbey Road zebra crossing, this 18th-century inn promises a two-fold commitment to good food: to source excellent ingredients and to home cook them. With the exception of the odd bottle of ketchup, everything – including bread, buns and pasta – is made on site. Meats are accredited by the Rare Breed Survival Trust, and most fish served has been caught in Looe. Representative starters are Thai-style fishcake with lemon aïoli, and pork pâté with apple jelly and toast. Main courses include comfort dishes such as beer-battered fish and chips with pea purée, and pork and leek sausages with mustard mash. Warm pear and almond tart with Chantilly cream is a nice finish, or look to the cheeseboard for three varieties served with grapes, crackers and home-made chutney. A function room can be hired for larger parties, while outside heaters allow for alfresco dining even when the weather is inclement.

Open all day all wk 12-11 (Sat 12-12) ⊕ GREENE KING ◀ Abbot Ale, Guinness ♂ Aspall. **Facilities** Children welcome Family room

NW10

William IV Bar & Restaurant
PLAN 2 D4

786 Harrow Rd NW10 5JX ☎ 020 8969 5944
e-mail: info@williamivlondon.com
dir: *Nearest tube: Kensal Green*

Character is everywhere in this large, rambling gastro-pub, happily co-existing with cosmopolitan Kensal Green's cafés, delis and antique shops. Music plays in the bar, but you can always chill out in the sofa area. Classic and modern European food is represented by duck breast with pickled cabbage, bok choy and anise jus; baked cod, chorizo and potato cake, green beans and sweet wine dressing; and courgette parcel stuffed with wild rice, and saffron cream sauce.

Open all day all wk 12-11 (Fri-Sun noon-1am) ⊕ FREE HOUSE ◀ Fuller's London Pride, Morland Old Speckled Hen, Guest ales ♂ Aspall. **Facilities** Children welcome Children's menu Children's portions Garden Beer festival Wi-fi

SE1

The Anchor & Hope ◉◉
PLAN 1 E3

PICK OF THE PUBS

36 The Cut SE1 8LP ☎ 020 7928 9898
e-mail: anchorandhope@btconnect.com
dir: *Nearest tube: Southwark & Waterloo*

This gastro-pub has many accolades to its name, but is at heart a down-to-earth and lively place with a large bar. Children, parents, and dogs are all welcome; in fine weather, its pavement tables are much sought after. Refreshment choices range from Bombardier to continental lagers, while the wine list is notable for its straightforward pricing approach; many half bottles are half the cost of full ones – a factor much appreciated by the pub's faithful diners. A heavy curtain separates the bar from the dining area and open kitchen. The menu is a no-nonsense list of refreshingly unembroidered dishes, and may change twice daily according to demand. Expect robust, gutsy dishes along the lines of warm snail and bacon salad; Middlewhite faggots and chips; warm pickled herring with potato and sour cream; or cassoulet for two. Desserts are no less inspiring: pear and almond tart; and lemon pot with cassis and shortbread are two examples.

Open all day Closed: BH, Xmas, New Year, 2wks Aug, Sun eve, Mon L **Bar Meals** L served Tue-Sat 12-2.30, Sun 2pm fixed time D served Mon-Sat 6-10.30 Av main course £14 **Restaurant** Av 3 course à la carte fr £20 ⊕ CHARLES WELLS ◀ Bombardier & Eagle IPA, Young's, Erdinger, Kirin ♂ Luscombe. ♚ 18 **Facilities** ♣ Children welcome ▦ (notice required)

The Bridge House Bar & Dining Rooms
PLAN 1 G3

218 Tower Bridge Rd SE1 2UP ☎ 020 7407 5818
e-mail: the-bridgehouse@tiscali.co.uk
dir: *5 min walk from London Bridge/Tower Hill tube stations*

There are great views of the Thames, the Gherkin and the ever-changing City skyline from this, the nearest pub to Tower Bridge. It comprises a bar, dining room and café, plus facilities for private functions. A range of Adnams and guest ales are accompanied by meals produced from ingredients bought at the local markets. Typical dishes include traditional shepherd's pie with cheesy mash; grilled sea bass with spinach; and confit lamb chump with Swiss chard and oyster mushrooms.

Open all day all wk Closed: 25-26 Dec **Bar Meals** L served all wk 12-4.30 D served all wk 5.30-10.30 Av main course £10 **Restaurant** L served all wk 12-4.30 D served all wk 5.30-10.30 Fixed menu price fr £12 Av 3 course à la carte fr £16.50 ⊕ ADNAMS ◀ Southwold Bitter, Broadside & Explorer, Guest ale. ♚ 32 **Facilities** Children welcome Children's menu Children's portions Family room Wi-fi ▦

SE1 continued

The Fire Station   PLAN 1 E3

PICK OF THE PUBS

150 Waterloo Rd SE1 8SB ☎ 020 7620 2226
e-mail: info@thefirestationwaterloo.com
dir: *Turn right at exit 2 of Waterloo Station*

Close to Waterloo, and handy for the Old Vic Theatre and Imperial War Museum, this remarkable conversion of an early-Edwardian fire station has kept many of its former trappings intact. The bar offers plenty of beers - draught and bottles - as well as cocktails and wines. The rear dining room faces the open kitchen; there are breakfast, set lunch, Sunday, restaurant and pre-theatre menus to take your pick from, as well as bar snacks and light bites. Dishes are home-made, traditional British and European, for example maple marinated duck breast; bouillabaisse; and chicken, walnut and tarragon ballotine. Mouthwatering desserts include chocolate brownie cheesecake, glazed strawberry tart, and warm pear upside-down cake. The handy location means it can get very busy, but the friendly staff cover the ground with impressive speed. There has been a change of hands in early 2012.

Open all day all wk 9am-mdnt (Sun 11-11) Closed: 25-26 Dec, 1 Jan ⊕ MARSTON'S ◀ EPA, Fuller's London Pride, Ringwood. **Facilities** Children welcome Children's portions Wi-fi

The Garrison   PLAN 1 G2

PICK OF THE PUBS

99-101 Bermondsey St SE1 3XB ☎ 020 7089 9355
e-mail: info@thegarrison.co.uk
dir: *From London Bridge tube station, E towards Tower Bridge 200mtrs, right onto Bermondsey St. Pub in 100mtrs*

Transformed a while ago from a typical 'Sarf London' boozer, this busy, friendly neighbourhood gastro-pub may still look rather ordinary from the outside, but the cleverly restyled interior, with its delightful hotch-potch of decorative themes, has a French brasserie flavour. Antique odds and ends, including mismatched chairs and tables, add to the quirky charm. The place bounces with life from breakfast through to dinner and beyond, when the downstairs room doubles as a mini-cinema. Breakfast could be a croissant, porridge or a full cooked English; for lunch, maybe potted shrimp, then pumpkin, courgette and chickpea tagine; in the evening, try smoked ham hock and parsley terrine followed by pan-roasted venison pavé with courgette and potato rösti, caramelised onions and peppercorn sauce. On the side are dauphinoise potatoes, hand-cut chips, and various salads. Drinks include real ales from Adnams, Breton cider and a good few wines by the glass. Booking for meals may be required.

Open all day all wk 8am-11pm (Fri 8am-mdnt Sat 9am-mdnt Sun 9am-10.30pm) Closed: 25-26 Dec ⊕ FREE HOUSE ◀ Spaten-Franziskaner-Bräu Franziskaner Hefe-Weisse, Adnams, Staropramen ♂ Thatchers Pear. **Facilities** Wi-fi

The George Inn   PLAN 1 F3

77 Borough High St SE1 1NH ☎ 020 7407 2056
e-mail: 7781@greeneking.co.uk
dir: *From London Bridge tube station, take Borough High St exit, left. Pub 200yds on left*

The coming of the nearby railway meant demolition of part of what is now London's sole surviving example of a 17th-century, galleried coaching inn, but what's left is impressive. National Trust-owned, it still features some very old woodwork, like the simple wall seats. The house George Inn Ale is brewed by Adnams, while others are Greene King. The fairly-priced pub grub includes sandwiches, salads and dishes such as grilled smoked haddock with spinach and poached egg; 10-oz rump steak; Gloucester Old Spot sausages and mash; and mushroom, thyme and roasted garlic pappardelle.

Open all day all wk 11-11 (Sun 12-10.30) Closed: 25-26 Dec **Bar Meals** L served Mon-Sat 11-10, Sun 12-10 D served Mon-Sat 11-10, Sun 12-10 food served all day **Restaurant** L served Mon-Sat 11-10, Sun 12-10 D served Mon-Sat 11-10, Sun 12-10 food served all day ⊕ GREENE KING ◀ Royal London, Abbot Ale & IPA, Morland Old Speckled Hen, Adnams George Inn Ale, Guest ale ♂ Aspall. **Facilities** Children welcome Garden Wi-fi ▭

The Market Porter   PLAN 1 F3

9 Stoney St, Borough Market, London Bridge SE1 9AA ☎ 020 7407 2495
dir: *Close to London Bridge Station*

With as apt a name as you could wish for, this Borough Market pub is blessed with a really good atmosphere, especially on Thursdays, Fridays and Saturdays, when the retail market operates. The exceptional choice of real ales includes the resident Harvey's, others changing up to nine times a day and some international sidekicks. Apart from sandwiches and bar snacks are dishes such as Cumberland sausage with mash and red onion marmalade; slow-braised belly of Middle English pork with thyme; and tuna Niçoise salad. On weekdays the pub opens its doors at 6am. Booking for meals may be required.

Open all day all wk **Bar Meals** L served Sun-Fri 12-3 **Restaurant** L served Mon-Fri 12-3, Sat-Sun 12-5 ⊕ FREE HOUSE ◀ Harvey's Sussex Best Bitter, wide selection of international ales. ♇ 10 **Facilities** ▭

SE10

The Cutty Sark Tavern   PLAN 2 G3

4-6 Ballast Quay, Greenwich SE10 9PD ☎ 020 8858 3146
dir: *Nearest tube: Greenwich. From Cutty Sark ship follow river towards Millennium Dome (10 min walk)*

There's been a tavern on Ballast Quay for hundreds of years. The current building dates back to the early 1800s when it was called the Union Tavern. It was renamed when the world famous tea-clipper was dry-docked upriver in 1954. Inside there are low beams, creaking floorboards, dark panelling and, from the large bow window in the upstairs bar, commanding views of the Thames, Canary Wharf and the Millennium Dome. Well-kept beers, wines by the glass and a wide selection of malts are all available, along with a choice of light bites, salads, classics like poacher's chicken, steak-and-ale pie and Hawaiian burger, as well as vegetarian and fish dishes, and a children's menu. Busy at weekends, especially on fine days.

Open all day all wk ⊕ FREE HOUSE ◀ Fuller's London Pride, George Gale & Co Seafarers, Butcombe. **Facilities** Children welcome Children's menu Children's portions Garden

Greenwich Union Pub   PLAN 2 G3

PICK OF THE PUBS

56 Royal Hill SE10 8RT ☎ 020 8692 6258
e-mail: theunion@meantimebrewing.com
dir: *From Greenwich DLR & main station exit by main ticket hall, turn left, 2nd right into Royal Hill. Pub 100yds on right*

In the heart of Greenwich's bustling Royal Hill, this welcoming pub is a beer-drinker's idea of heaven. Comfortable leather sofas and flagstone floors help to keep the original character of this refurbished pub intact. Interesting beers from the award-winning Meantime Brewing Co, lagers and even freshly squeezed orange juice, along with a beer garden, make this a popular spot. The food is an eclectic range of traditional and modern dishes drawn from around the world. Everything is freshly prepared and sourced locally where possible; for example the fish comes straight from Billingsgate Market. The menu might include home-made pork and apple burger with chips and apple sauce, or pan-fried hake supreme with squid and black ink risotto. Try tempting bar snacks such as fish fingers with tartare sauce or a British cheeseboard. Round things off with bread pudding and chocolate ice cream.

Open all day all wk 12-11 (Sun 12-10.30) ⊕ FREE HOUSE ◀ Meantime Helles, Wheat & London Pale Ale, Kohler ♂ Aspall, Thatchers. **Facilities** Children welcome Garden

Save on hotels. Book at **theAA.com/hotel**

LONDON 351 **ENGLAND**

North Pole Bar & Restaurant   PLAN 2 G3

PICK OF THE PUBS

131 Greenwich High Rd, Greenwich SE10 8JA
☎ **020 8853 3020**
e-mail: info@northpolegreenwich.com
dir: *Right from Greenwich rail station, pass Novotel. Pub on right*

Dating from 1849, the name originated with the Victorian obsession for polar exploration, and North Pole Road adjoins the pub. Recently refurbished to a high standard, the pub now also boasts seating for 100 people in the beer garden; plans are afoot to develop a boutique hotel behind the pub. It's a stylish venue, offering a complete night out under one roof. Refreshments range from international beers such as Staropramen and Peroni to cocktails, while award-winning cooking continues to attract both visitors and loyal locals. A fishy start to the Piano restaurant's seasonally changing menus may be smoked mackerel with new potatoes; smoked sea trout salad; or grilled king scallops. In spring expect to find saddle of Welsh lamb stuffed with spinach and wild garlic, while summer promises Barbary duck breast on caramelised onion and buttered pear. Desserts range from cranberry cheesecake to dark chocolate and blackberry pie. Booking for meals may be required.

Open all day all wk noon-2am **Bar Meals** L served all wk 12-10 D served all wk 12-10 Av main price £8 food served all day **Restaurant** L served Sat-Sun 12-5 D served all wk 6-10.30 Fixed menu price fr £15 Av 3 course à la carte fr £19.95 ⊞ FREE HOUSE ◼ Guinness, Staropramen ♂ Aspall. ☗ 9 **Facilities** ❖ Children welcome Children's menu Children's portions Garden Wi-fi ▨ (notice required)

SE21

The Crown & Greyhound   PLAN 2 F2

73 Dulwich Village SE21 7BJ ☎ **020 8299 4976**
e-mail: enquiry@thecrownandgreyhound.co.uk
dir: *Nearest train: North Dulwich*

With a history reaching back to the 18th century, The Crown & Greyhound (nicknamed The Dog) counts Charles Dickens and John Ruskin amongst its celebrated patrons. In the olden days, the pub was split in two - The Crown served the gentry while The Greyhound housed the labourers. Modern day customers will find three bars and a restaurant in the heart of peaceful Dulwich Village. The ever-changing menu might feature Shropshire roast chicken with herb butter and fries, and sticky toffee pudding for dessert. There are daily salads, pasta and fish dishes, too.

Open all day all wk 11-11 (Thu-Sat 11am-mdnt Sun 11-10.30) **Bar Meals** L served Mon-Sat 12-10, Sun 12-9 D served Mon-Sat 12-10, Sun 12-9 Av main course £10.50 food served all day **Restaurant** L served Mon-Sat 12-10, Sun 12-9 D served Mon-Sat 12-10, Sun 12-9 food served all day ⊞ MITCHELLS & BUTLERS ◼ Harvey's Sussex Best Bitter, Sharp's Doom Bar, Guest ales ♂ Aspall. ☗ 20 **Facilities** ❖ Children welcome Children's menu Children's portions Garden ▨ (notice required)

SE22

Franklins ⊛   PLAN 2 F2

PICK OF THE PUBS

157 Lordship Ln, Dulwich SE22 8HX ☎ **020 8299 9598**
e-mail: info@franklinsrestaurant.com
dir: *0.5m S from East Dulwich station along Dog Kennel Hill & Lordship Ln*

This neighbourhood pub has a solid reputation for its food and also happens to serve a good selection of real ales, ciders and lagers. Internal surfaces are stripped back and exposed, and the furnishings are smart, although the bar retains a more traditional appearance. Meats are rare breeds from farms in southern England and include Gloucester Old Spot pigs, Red Poll cattle and Oxford Down lambs; fish and shellfish are sourced from sustainable British stocks; game is from Yorkshire and the Scottish Highlands; vegetables are Kent grown; and the water, for those who avoid London tap, is bottled in the 'Garden of England'. Start with ox heart, chicory, capers and seed mustard then move on to spring chicken with leeks, tarragon and cream. For dessert, maybe chocolate pannacotta and oranges – although you may prefer Welsh rarebit, Scotch woodcock or local cheeses.

Open all day all wk 11-11 Closed: 25-26 & 31 Dec, 1 Jan **Bar Meals** Av main course £15 food served all day **Restaurant** Fixed menu price fr £16.95 Av 3 course à la carte fr £25 food served all day ⊞ FREE HOUSE ◼ Shepherd Neame Original Porter, Harvey's, Meantime, Guinness ♂ Aspall, Biddenden. ☗ 13 **Facilities** ❖ Children welcome Children's portions Wi-fi

---

The Palmerston ⊛   PLAN 2 F2

91 Lordship Ln, East Dulwich SE22 8EP
☎ **020 8693 1629**
e-mail: info@thepalmerston.net
dir: *2m from Clapham, 0.5m from Dulwich Village, 10min walk from East Dulwich station*

A striking gastro-pub, heavy on the wood panelling, with much stripped floorboard and some great floor tiling. Occasional installations of photographic exhibitions add to the flair of this corner-plot destination dining pub in leafy Dulwich. Chef Jamie Younger's one AA Rosette results from his modern British menu with a Mediterranean twist; witness the mussel, bacon, dill and saffron chowder, offsetting roast rump of Dedham Vale lamb. Affable locals pop in for some flavoursome beers, too, from the likes of Sharp's and Harvey's. Booking for meals may be required.

Open all day all wk ⊞ ENTERPRISE INNS ◼ Sharp's Doom Bar, Harvey's ♂ Westons Stowford Press.
Facilities Children welcome Children's portions

SE23

The Dartmouth Arms   PLAN 2 G2

7 Dartmouth Rd, Forest Hill SE23 3HN
☎ **020 8488 3117**
e-mail: mail@thedartmoutharms.com
dir: *800mtrs from Horniman Museum on South Circular Rd*

The long-vanished Croydon Canal once ran behind this transformed old pub, and you can still see the towpath railings at the bottom of the car park. Smart bars serve snacks, traditional real ales, continental lagers, cocktails, coffees and teas, while the restaurant might offer devilled ox kidneys with black pudding or smoked haddock tart for starters, and mains might be pork belly with cannellini beans or scallops with cauliflower purée and crispy pancetta.

Open all wk Closed: 25-26 Dec, 1 Jan ⊞ ENTERPRISE INNS ◼ Fuller's London Pride, Timothy Taylor Landlord, Adnams Broadside. **Facilities** Children welcome Garden Parking Wi-fi

SW1

The Buckingham Arms   PLAN 1 D2

62 Petty France SW1H 9EU ☎ **020 7222 3386**
e-mail: buckinghamarms@youngs.co.uk
dir: *Nearest tube: St James's Park*

This elegant Young's pub was known as the Black Horse until 1903 and retains much of its old charm including etched mirrors and period light fittings in the bar. Close to Buckingham Palace, it is popular with pretty much everyone: tourists, business people, politicians, media types, real ale fans... Expect a good range of simple pub food, including sharing platters, sandwiches and hearty favourites such as sausages and mash, steak-and-ale pie and West Country beef burgers.

Open all day 11-11 (Sat 12-6 Sun 12-6 summer) Closed: 25-26 Dec, Sun (winter) **Bar Meals** L served all wk 12-3 D served Mon-Fri 3-8, Sat-Sun 3-5 Av main course £7.95 ⊞ YOUNG'S ◼ Bitter, Wells Bombardier, Sambrook's Wandel. ☗ 15 **Facilities** ❖ Children welcome Wi-fi

continued

SW1 continued

Nags Head PLAN 1 B2

PICK OF THE PUBS

53 Kinnerton St SW1X 8ED ☎ 020 7235 1135
dir: *Telephone for directions*

This pub was built in the early 19th century to cater for the footmen and stable hands who looked after the horses in these Belgravia mews. With its Dickensian frontage and an interior like a well-stocked bric-à-brac shop, the award-winning Nags Head stubbornly resists any contemporary touches. It's a mobile phone-free zone, too. Compact and bijou, it's located in a quiet mews near Harrods, its front and back bars connected by a narrow stairway and boasting wooden floors, panelled walls, and low ceilings. The walls are covered with photos, drawings, mirrors, helmets, model aeroplanes; there are even penny-slot machines. The atmosphere is best described as 'entertaining' if you're in the right frame of mind. The waist-high bar is another oddity, but the full Adnams range is served, along with a good value menu that includes salads, sandwiches, a daily roast and pie, and traditional pub favourites like chilli con carne and ploughman's.

Open all day all wk 11-11 **Bar Meals** L served all wk 11-9.30 Av main course £7.50 food served all day **Restaurant** food served all day ⊕ FREE HOUSE ◀ Adnams Southwold Bitter, Broadside, Fisherman, Regatta Ö Aspall. **Facilities** ❖ Children welcome

The Orange Public House & Hotel PLAN 1 C1

37 Pimlico Rd SW1W 8NE ☎ 020 7881 9844
e-mail: reservations@theorange.co.uk
dir: *Nearest tube stations: Victoria & Sloane Street*

Recognised for its approach to sustainability, The Orange comprises a number of light and airy adjoining rooms, which have a rustic Tuscan feel with their muted colours and potted orange trees on stripped wooden boards. Well-heeled locals quaff Adnams ales and Italian wines while selecting from menus of modern European dishes. Wood-fired pizzas and oven roasts lead the way, but the carte is full of good things: Carlingford rock oysters; spiced potted Kilravock Farm pork; steamed Norfolk mussels; and Dover sole to list but a few. Booking for meals may be required.

Open all day all wk 8am-11.30pm (Sun 8am-10.30pm) **Bar Meals** L served all wk 12-6 D served all wk 6-10 Av main course £17.50 food served all day **Restaurant** L served all wk 12-3 D served all wk 6-10 Av 3 course à la carte fr £30 ⊕ FREE HOUSE ◀ Adnams, Meantime Wheat & Pale Ale Ö Aspall. ♟ 15 **Facilities** Children welcome Children's menu Children's portions Wi-fi

The Thomas Cubitt NEW PLAN 1 C2

44 Elizabeth St SW1W 9PA ☎ 020 7730 6060
e-mail: reservations@thethomascubitt.co.uk
dir: *Nearest stations: Victoria & Sloane Square*

Belgravia's most exclusive pub honours London's legendary master builder and draws a discerning local crowd for fine wine and some of the best gastro-pub food in town. Expect a country-house feel throughout, with warm Farrow & Ball colours, high ceilings, oak floors, and floor-to-ceiling windows in buzzy downstairs bar. Here, opt for Adnams ale and tuck into oysters with shallot dressing, potted smoked salmon, braised lamb shank with red wine jus, and port poached pear with white chocolate sauce. The smart upstairs restaurant has a separate menu and it's essential to book for the memorable Sunday roasts. Booking for meals may be required.

Open all day all wk 12-11 (Sun 12-10.30) Closed: Xmas **Bar Meals** L served all wk all day D served all wk all day Av main course £14 food served all day **Restaurant** L served all wk 12-3.30 D served all wk 6-9.30 Fixed menu price fr £17.50 Av 3 course à la carte fr £37 ⊕ FREE HOUSE ◀ Caledonian Deuchars IPA, Adnams Ö Aspall. ♟ **Facilities** Children welcome Children's menu Children's portions ▭ (notice required)

The Wilton Arms PLAN 1 B2

71 Kinnerton St SW1X 8ED ☎ 020 7235 4854
e-mail: wilton@shepherd-neame.co.uk
dir: *Between Hyde Park Corner & Knightsbridge tube stations*

In summer The Wilton Arms is distinguished by fabulous flower-filled baskets and window boxes. Known locally as The Village Pub, this early 19th-century hostelry's other name is a reference to the 1st Earl of Wilton. High settles and bookcases create cosy, individual seating areas in the air-conditioned interior, and a conservatory covers the old garden. Shepherd Neame ales, including Spitfire, accompany traditional pub fare: ploughman's, toasted sandwiches, burgers, fish and chips, chicken Kiev, and roast beef.

Open all day all wk Closed: 25-26 Dec, BHs **Bar Meals** L served Mon-Fri 12-4, Sat 12-3 D served Mon-Fri 5.30-9 Av main course £7.50 ⊕ SHEPHERD NEAME ◀ Spitfire & Bishops Finger, Oranjeboom. **Facilities** Children welcome Children's portions ▭

SW3

The Admiral Codrington PLAN 1 B2

17 Mossop St SW3 2LY ☎ 020 7581 0005
e-mail: admiral.codrington@333holdingsltd.com
dir: *Nearest tube stations: South Kensington & Sloane Square. Telephone for detailed directions*

To habitués of this smart South Ken gastro-pub, it's The Cod, which explains the whimsical item on the menu – Admiral's cod, served with tomato, mushroom and herb crust. It's one of many modern British options that also include slow-cooked shoulder of lamb, root vegetables and rosemary, and three-cheese macaroni with crispy bacon. The restaurant's glass roof retracts to give 'alfresco' dining, and the heated beer garden has an all-weather awning. Snacks are available in the bar.

Open all day all wk 11.30am-mdnt (Fri-Sat 11.30am-1am Sun 12-10.30) ⊕ FREE HOUSE ◀ Shepherd Neame Spitfire, Black Sheep, Guinness. **Facilities** Children welcome Children's menu Garden Wi-fi

The Builders Arms PLAN 1 B1

PICK OF THE PUBS

13 Britten St SW3 3TY ☎ 020 7349 9040
e-mail: thebuildersarms@geronimo-inns.co.uk
dir: *From Sloane Square tube station down King's Rd. Right into Chelsea Manor St, at end right into Britten St, pub on right*

Tucked away in the back streets of Chelsea, just off trendy Kings Road, this stylish three-storey Georgian pub was built by the same crew that constructed St Luke's church over the way. Inside, leather sofas dot the spacious informal bar area, where your can enjoy a pint of Bombardier. A brief, daily-changing menu offers a wide range of modern English food with a twist, but if further ideas are needed, consult the specials board and dine in the restaurant. Starters on the main menu might include fresh Portland crab and apple salad on toast; or prawn and avocado tian with Marie Rose sauce. Typical main courses are pan-fried bream fillet with warm Niçoise salad and soft poached egg; marmalade glazed duck leg, Savoy cabbage and potato cake, rhubarb purée. There are more than 30 bins, plus many wines by the glass. When the sun shines the outdoor terrace is highly popular.

Open all wk Mon-Wed 11-11 Thu-Sat 11am-mdnt (Sun 12-10.30) **Restaurant** L served Mon-Fri 12-3, Sat 12-4, Sun 12-6 D served Mon-Wed 7-10, Thu-Sat 7-11, Sun 7-9 ⊕ GERONIMO INNS ◀ Wells Bombardier, Sharp's Doom Bar Ö Aspall. ♟ 16 **Facilities** ❖ Children welcome ▭

Save on hotels. Book at **theAA.com/hotel**

LONDON 353 **ENGLAND**

Coopers Arms
PLAN 1 B1

PICK OF THE PUBS

87 Flood St, Chelsea SW3 5TB ☎ 020 7376 3120
e-mail: coopersarms@youngs.co.uk
dir: *From Sloane Square tube station, straight onto King's Rd. Approx 1m W, opposite Waitrose, turn left. Pub half way down Flood St*

This is an upmarket, backstreet Chelsea pub close to the King's Road and the river. Celebrities and the notorious rub shoulders with the aristocracy and the local road sweeper in the bright, vibrant atmosphere, while the stuffed brown bear, Canadian moose and boar bring a character of their own to the bar. Food is served here and in the quiet upstairs dining room, with a focus on fish and steak. The menu also offers chilli con carne, home-made burgers, award-winning sausages, and roasts on Sundays. The interesting platters are great to share: a selection of mini pies; vegetarian meze; charcuterie and crusty bread; and whole baked camembert. Good staff-customer repartee makes for an entertaining atmosphere, and there are quiz and live music nights. There was a change of hands at the end of 2011.

Open all day all wk 12-11 (Sun 12-10.30) ⊕ YOUNG'S ◖ Special & Bitter, Wells Bombardier, Guinness. **Facilities** Children welcome Children's portions Garden

The Cross Keys
PLAN 2 E3

1 Lawrence St, Chelsea SW3 5NB ☎ 020 7349 9111
e-mail: info@thexkeys.co.uk
dir: *From Sloane Square walk down King's Rd, left onto Old Church St, then left onto Justice Walk, then right*

Established in 1765, this Chelsea pub counted JMW Turner, Whistler, DG Rossetti and Dylan Thomas among its customers. More recently it has been co-owned by the sculptor Rudy Weller, who created the *Horses of Helios* and the *Three Graces*, prominently displayed in Piccadilly Circus. While at the Cross Keys, Rudy created 'a magical kingdom' throughout its four rooms, which comprise the bar, conservatory restaurant, gallery and a room at the top. The modern European menu tempts with foie gras terrine; red snapper; and corn-fed Provençal chicken. The bar menu includes chicken Caesar salad and roast beef ciabatta. Booking for meals may be required.

Open all day all wk Closed: 25 Dec, 1-2 Jan **Bar Meals** L served Mon-Fri 12-3, Sat-Sun 12-10.30 D served Mon-Fri 6-10, Sat-Sun 12-10.30 **Restaurant** L served Wed-Sun 12-3 D served Mon-Sat 6-10.30 ⊕ FREE HOUSE ◖ Everards Tiger, Sharp's Doom Bar, Guinness, Guest ales. ♟ 15 **Facilities** ❖ Children welcome Children's portions Wi-fi ▱ (notice required)

The Pig's Ear
PLAN 1 A1

35 Old Church St SW3 5BS ☎ 020 7352 2908
e-mail: thepigsear@hotmail.co.uk
dir: *Telephone for directions*

Now in fresh hands, this award-winning gastro-pub off the King's Road specialises in real ales such as Pigs Ear and Sambrook's, as well as daily changing guests; you can also have Breton cider and Czech, Belgian and German bottled lagers. There's a traditional, timeless feel to the bar and the oak-panelled dining room on the first floor, where the British/French brasserie menu might offer a pork sharing board; Mediterranean fish soup; hand-chopped Scottish fillet steak tartare; line-caught whole sea bass en papillote; and risotto with seasonal wild mushrooms. Booking for meals may be required.

Open all day all wk **Bar Meals** L served Mon-Fri 12-3, Sat 12-4, Sun 12-9 D served Mon-Sat 6-10, Sun 12-9 Av main course £18 **Restaurant** L served Mon-Fri 12-3, Sat 12-4, Sun 12-9 D served Mon-Sat 6-10, Sun 12-9 Av 3 course à la carte fr £45 ⊕ FREE HOUSE ◖ Uley Pigs Ear, Sambrook's, Duchess IPA, Guinness, Guest ales. ♟ 10 **Facilities** ❖ Children welcome Children's portions Wi-fi

SW4

The Windmill on the Common
PLAN 2 E2

Clapham Common South Side SW4 9DE ☎ 020 8673 4578
e-mail: francesca@rochecom.com
dir: *5m from London, just off South Circular 205 at junct with A24 at Clapham*

Crackling open fires in winter and soft leather sofas make this pub a popular place for friends to meet. The original part of the building was known as Holly Lodge and at one time was the property of the founder of Young's Brewery. The Windmill today offers a varied menu with something for all tastes and appetites: 'Young's own famous pies' including steak-and-ale or chicken, leek and ham; fresh fish, grilled or in Young's beer-batter; sausage of the day; and poached pear with cinnamon pannacotta are typical.

Open all day all wk 11am-mdnt (Sun 12-10) ⊕ YOUNG'S ◖ Young's ♂ Rekorderlig, Kopparberg. **Facilities** Children welcome Garden Parking Wi-fi

SW6

The Atlas
PLAN 2 E3

PICK OF THE PUBS

16 Seagrave Rd, Fulham SW6 1RX ☎ 020 7385 9129
e-mail: theatlas@btconnect.com
dir: *2 mins walk from West Brompton tube station*

Just around the corner from West Brompton tube, The Atlas is one of only a handful of London pubs to have a walled garden. Located in a trendy part of town where a great many pubs have been reinvented to become diners or restaurants, here is a traditional, relaxed local that remains true to its cause with a spacious bar area split into eating and drinking sections. Typical menus might feature starters such as roast wood pigeon breast with Jerusalem artichoke gratin, mushroom and leek soup, or Caesar salad. Tempting mains demonstrate some European influences in dishes such as slow-roast tomato and saffron risotto, salmon and dill fishcakes, 'Fabada asturiana' (Spanish pork stew with chorizo, tomato, white beans and paprika) or grilled monkfish with rosemary. There's a wide-ranging wine list.

Open all day all wk Closed: 24-31 Dec **Bar Meals** L served Mon-Fri 12-2.30, Sat 12-4, Sun 12-10 D served Mon-Sat 6-10, Sun 12-10 Av main course £12-£15 ⊕ FREE HOUSE ◖ Fuller's London Pride, Caledonian Deuchars IPA, Timothy Taylor Landlord, Guest ale. ♟ 15 **Facilities** Children welcome Children's portions Garden Wi-fi ▱ (notice required)

The Jam Tree
PLAN 2 E3

541 King's Rd SW6 2EB ☎ 020 3397 3739
e-mail: info@thejamtree.com
dir: *Nearest stations: Imperial Wharf & Fulham Broadway*

Number two in The Jam Tree gastro-pub family, and now with a new owner, this Chelsea sibling echoes the quirkiness of the Kensington original (see entry). Antique mirrors, personalised artworks, old chesterfields and mismatched furniture give the interior a decidedly individual look. The modern British menu with colonial undertones offers curries; thali, an Indian tasting platter; chicken or vegetable Madras; and beef rang dang. Other possibilities are slow-roasted duck leg; and seared scallops with Malay potato cake. A long cocktail list, barbecue, plasma screen and resident DJs are additional reasons for visiting.

Open all day all wk **Bar Meals** L served Mon-Fri 12-3, Sat-Sun 11-5 D served Mon-Fri 6-10, Sat 5-10, Sun 5-9 Av main course £14 **Restaurant** L served Mon-Fri 12-3, Sat-Sun 11-5 D served Mon-Fri 6-10, Sat 5-10, Sun 5-9 Av 3 course à la carte fr £27.50 ⊕ FREE HOUSE ◖ Timothy Taylor Landlord ♂ Symonds. ♟ 9 **Facilities** ❖ Children welcome Children's menu Children's portions Garden Wi-fi

SW6 continued

The Sands End Pub NEW PLAN 2 E3

135-137 Stephendale Rd, Fulham SW6 2PR
☎ **020 7731 7823**
e-mail: thesandsend@hotmail.com
dir: *From Wandsworth Bridge Rd (A217) into Stephendale
Rd. Pub 300yds at junct with Broughton Rd*

The Sands End is a neighbourhood gem much loved by
fashionable Fulham foodies, as it has the feel and food
quality of a contemporary country pub. Expect to find
scrubbed farmhouse tables on rustic wooden floors,
locals quaffing pints of Doom Bar, chalkboard menus
listing terrific bar snacks and a food philosophy built
around the 'Field to Fork' mantra. Chef Chris Slaughter's
British seasonal cooking makes use of foraged and farm
sourced produce, including vegetables from the pub's
allotment, resulting in hearty and honest dishes like lamb
shank and swede pie; roe deer, winter chanterelles and
red cabbage; and raspberry and custard tart. A beer and
food festival is held in the summer.

Open all day all wk Closed: 25 Dec **Bar Meals** L served all
wk 12-3, snacks all day, brunch fr 10am wknds D served
all wk 6-10.30 Av main course £12.50 **Restaurant** L
served all wk 12-3 D served all wk 6-10.30 Fixed menu
price fr £13.50 Av 3 course à la carte fr £22.50 ⊕ PUNCH
TAVERNS ◗ St Austell Tribute, Sharp's Doom Bar, Black
Sheep Ŏ Aspall. ₹ 16 **Facilities** ❤ Children welcome
Children's portions Garden Beer festival Wi-fi

The White Horse PLAN 2 E3

PICK OF THE PUBS

1-3 Parson's Green, Fulham SW6 4UL ☎ **020 7736 2115**
e-mail: info@whitehorsesw6.com
dir: *140mtrs from Parson's Green tube*

The former late 18th-century coaching inn and Victorian
gin palace is a substantial sandstone pub with a
triangular walled front terrace overlooking Parson's
Green. These days it's a destination for lovers of
traditional British pub food and interesting real ales and
wines, with a restaurant in the former coach house, an
upstairs bar, and a luxurious private dining area. The
interior is a pleasing blend of polished mahogany and
wooden and flagstone floors, open fires and contemporary
lighting. From the modern pub menu start with pheasant
galantine with pumpkin and beetroot jus, follow with Red
Poll beef fillet with girolles, dauphinoise potatoes and
plum jus, or the classic beer-battered haddock with
hand-cut chips, and finish with winter fruit crumble and
custard. Every dish comes with a recommended beer to
drink, such partnering forming part of the pub's Beer
Academy Courses. Dubbed the 'Sloaney Pony', it's good
for Sunday brunch, summer barbeques and four beer
festivals a year.

Open all day all wk **Bar Meals** L served all wk 12-10.30
D served all wk 12-10.30 food served all day
Restaurant food served all day ⊕ MITCHELLS & BUTLERS
◗ Adnams Broadside, Harvey's Sussex Best Bitter,
Oakham JHB Ŏ Aspall. ₹ 20 **Facilities** ❤ Children
welcome Children's portions Garden Beer festival Wi-fi

SW7

The Anglesea Arms PLAN 1 A1

15 Selwood Ter, South Kensington SW7 3QG
☎ **020 7373 7960**
e-mail: enquiries@angleseaarms.com
dir: *Telephone for directions*

Feeling like a country pub in the middle of South
Kensington, the interior has barely changed since 1827,
though the dining area has been tastefully updated with
panelled walls and leather-clad chairs, plus there's
outside seating. Lunch and dinner menus place an
emphasis on quality ingredients, fresh preparation and
cosmopolitan flavours. Sunday lunches are popular, so
booking is advisable. From the menu expect perhaps
goat's cheese, spinach and fig tart; crispy fried baby
squid with risotto nero; wild boar and apple sausages
with mash, braised red cabbage and shallot gravy;
pan-fried skate wing with hand-cut chips, watercress
and aïoli; followed by rum pannacotta with rhubarb
compôte. Booking for meals may be required.

Open all day all wk Closed: 25-26 Dec ⊕ FREE HOUSE/
CAPITAL PUB COMPANY ◗ Fuller's London Pride, Adnams
Southwold Bitter & Broadside, Sambrook's Wandle,
Sharp's Doom Bar Ŏ Symonds. **Facilities** Children
welcome Children's portions Garden Wi-fi

SW8

The Masons Arms PLAN 2 E3

169 Battersea Park Rd SW8 4BT ☎ **020 7622 2007**
e-mail: masons.arms@london-gastros.co.uk
dir: *Opposite Battersea Park BR Station*

This Fuller's gastro-pub breaks the mould, with live jazz,
blues or folk at weekends adding a new dimension to the
indoor-outdoor choice of where to eat and sup. Worn
wooden floors, friendly, professional staff and a
welcoming atmosphere, all equally suited for a quiet
romantic dinner or a family outing. The food is British
with Italian and Asian influences and is freshly prepared
in an open kitchen, a touch of theatre whilst awaiting
perhaps squid stuffed with feta and chilli. The menu
changes on a daily basis.

Open all day all wk 12-11 (Fri 12-12 Sun 12-10.30)
Closed: 25 Dec ⊕ FULLER'S ◗ London Pride & Organic
Honeydew, Staropramen. **Facilities** Garden Wi-fi

SW10

The Hollywood Arms PLAN 1 A1

PICK OF THE PUBS

45 Hollywood Rd SW10 9HX ☎ **020 7349 7840**
e-mail: hollywoodarms@youngs.co.uk
dir: *1 min from Chelsea & Westminster Hospital, 200mtrs
down Hollywood Rd on right towards Fulham Rd*

In the heart of Chelsea, this listed building dates back to
the mid-17th century when it was the home of landowner
Henry Middleton, who owned land in England, Barbados
and America. The interior of this hidden treasure has
been elegantly refurbished, its original charm
complemented by rich natural woods, pastel shades and
modern fabrics. The large upstairs lounge has elegant
mouldings around the ceiling and large open fires, whilst
the ground floor pub and restaurant retains much of its
traditional atmosphere. Here the chefs lovingly create
menus from scratch using high-quality ingredients. Small
plates will produce diver-caught scallop gratin or potted
Wiltshire rabbit on sourdough, while main courses offer
game pie; Gressingham duck breast with rösti and spiced
red cabbage; or whole baked sea bass with fennel, orange
and caper salad. Classic puddings include treacle tart
and apple crumble with custard.

Open all day all wk 12-11.30 (Thu-Sat 12-12 Sun
12-10.30) **Bar Meals** L served Mon-Fri 12-3, Sat-Sun
12-10 D served Mon-Fri 5-10, Sat-Sun 12-10 Av main
course £14 **Restaurant** L served Mon-Fri 12-3, Sat-Sun
12-10 D served Mon-Fri 5-10, Sat-Sun 12-10 Av 3 course
à la carte fr £35 ⊕ YOUNG'S ◗ Bitter, Wells Bombardier,
Guinness, Guest ales Ŏ Aspall. ₹ 12 **Facilities** ❤
Children's portions Wi-fi ▭ (notice required)

Save on hotels. Book at **theAA.com/hotel**

LONDON 355 ENGLAND

PICK OF THE PUBS

The Idle Hour

SW13   **PLAN 2 D2**

62 Railway Side, Barnes SW13 0PQ
☎ **020 8878 5555**
e-mail: theidlehour@aol.com
web: www.theidlehour.co.uk
dir: *From Mortlake High St (A3003) into White Hart Ln. 5th left into Railway Side (at rail crossing). Pub just past school*

Stephen Thorp bought his mid 19th-century, Barnes-backwater free house on his birthday in 2001, since when it has become quite a landmark in this well-heeled Thames-side suburb. Being a little tricky to find doesn't fox the locals, nor apparently does it deter the custom of 'names' from music, film and TV. Although Stephen designed it with a nod to tradition, that is, lots of candles and fresh flowers everywhere and a real fire in the winter, it's still modern and stylish. A bit quirky too – for proof, check any of the wrong-time-telling clocks. A secluded garden doubles as a suntrap during the day and a romantic, candlelit spot for evening dining. What confirms its pub status is that there are always at least ten draught beers, including Adnams, many more in bottles, a 'mind-boggling' array of spirits, and a carefully selected, almost entirely organic, wine list, many by the glass. The small, frequently changing menu makes use of mainly organic ingredients for starters of seared scallops with pork belly and pea purée; grilled haloumi with chickpea and coriander salsa; and beef fillet carpaccio with horseradish cream. Aberdeen Angus steak and Harvey's Sussex ale pie kicks off a list of possible mains, followed by free-range, corn-fed spatchcock roast poussin with mash and sprouting broccoli; and wild mushroom, tarragon and pea risotto with parmesan and rocket. Among the desserts, you can expect lavender crème brûlée, and chocolate mousse with shortbread. Boards of artisan cheeses come with crackers, grapes, figs and home-made chutney. Begin Sunday lunch with a Bloody Mary made with freshly grated horseradish, and follow with a whole chicken or leg of lamb (for two) served in a roasting pan surrounded by goose fat-roasted potatoes, steamed broccoli, honey-roasted carrots and 'spectacular gravy that takes a week to make'.

Open all wk 12-12 (Fri-Sat noon-1am)
Closed: 25 Dec **Bar Meals** L served Mon-Fri 12-3, Sat-Sun 12.30-10 D served Mon-Fri 6-10, Sat-Sun 12.30-10 **Restaurant** L served Mon-Fri 12-3, Sat-Sun 12.30-10 D served Mon-Fri 6-10, Sat-Sun 12.30-10 ⊞ FREE HOUSE
🍺 Adnams, Guest ales ♻ Addlestones
🍷 15 **Facilities** Children welcome 🐾 Garden Wi-fi

SW10 continued

Lots Road Pub and Dining Room
PLAN 2 E3

PICK OF THE PUBS

114 Lots Rd, Chelsea SW10 0RJ ☎ 020 7352 6645
e-mail: lotsroad@foodandfuel.co.uk
dir: 5-10 mins walk from Fulham Broadway Station

Located just off the bustling King's Road, opposite the entrance to Chelsea Harbour, the Lots Road is a real star of the gastro-pub scene, appealing to well-heeled locals for the relaxing vibe and a daily menu that lists imaginative, modern pub food. Expect a smart, comfortable, well-designed space, which segues smoothly between jaunty bar area and the more secluded dining room. Slate grey and cream walls and wooden tables create a light, pared-down feel, and attentive staff are set on making you feel comfortable. There are real ales, an excellent wine list, and cocktails both quirky and classic. Food takes in a mix of seasonal pub classics and more innovative dishes, perhaps pumpkin and ginger soup; or steamed Isle of Lewis mussels, white wine, garlic and shallots; followed by lamb shoulder shepherd's pie and curly kale; or root vegetable and butter bean lasagne and French beans; then a pudding of sticky toffee pudding with honey pot ice cream; or chocolate mousse tart and orange syrup. Don't miss Saturday brunch and the Sunday family roasts.

Open all day all wk 11-11 (Sun 12-10.30) ⊕ FOOD AND FUEL ◀ Sharp's Doom Bar, Wells Bombardier & Eagle IPA, Guinness. **Facilities** Children welcome Children's menu Children's portions Wi-fi

---

SW11

The Bolingbroke Pub & Dining Room
PLAN 2 E2

172-174 Northcote Rd SW11 6RE ☎ 020 7228 4040
e-mail: info@thebolingbroke.com
dir: Nearest stations: Clapham South; Clapham Junction

Named after the first Viscount Bolingbroke, who managed to be both brilliant politician and reckless rake, this refined dining pub stands in a road known colloquially as 'Nappy Valley', due to its popularity with well-heeled young families. While it caters admirably for children, adults can enjoy the modern British menus offering pan-roasted hake; rabbit stuffed with spinach and hazelnut; and sunflower, mint, pea and shallot ravioli, alongside a bar menu with tempura-battered mackerel and chips; and traditional ploughman's. Weekend brunch includes boiled egg and soldiers for babies. On handpump is Timothy Taylor. Booking for meals may be required.

Open all day all wk Closed: 25-28 Dec, 1 Jan **Bar Meals** L served Mon-Fri 12-3.30, Sat 10-4, Sun 12-9 D served Mon-Sat 6-10.30, Sun 12-9 Av main course £12.50 **Restaurant** L served Mon-Fri 12-3.30, Sat 10-4, Sun 12-9 D served Mon-Sat 6-10.30, Sun 12-9 Av 3 course à la carte fr £21.50 ⊕ FREE HOUSE ◀ Timothy Taylor Landlord

---

Ö Aspall, Westons Wyld Wood Organic. ♀ 13 **Facilities** ♣ Children welcome Children's menu Children's portions Wi-fi ➡ (notice required)

The Fox & Hounds
PLAN 2 E2

PICK OF THE PUBS

66 Latchmere Rd, Battersea SW11 2JU
☎ 020 7924 5483
e-mail: foxandhoundsbattersea@btopenworld.com
dir: From Clapham Junction exit onto High St turn left, through lights into Lavender Hill. After post office, left at lights. Pub 200yds on left

This is one of those archetypal Victorian corner pubs that London still has in abundance but from the moment you step through the door you'll feel like one of the locals. Its style is simple: with bare wooden floors, an assortment of furniture, walled garden, extensive patio planting and a covered and heated seating area. Regulars head here for the good selection of real ales and an international wine list; the menu suggests the 'Wine of the Moment' with tasting notes, and Ales of the Week. Fresh ingredients are delivered daily from the London markets, enabling the Mediterranean-style menu and specials to change accordingly; all prepared in the open-to-view kitchen. So, you might start with saffron potato soup or squid and chorizo with prawns. Follow with roast spatchcock chicken with Parma ham; spinach and roast garlic risotto; rib-eye steak, roast potatoes and salsa verde; or pan-roasted salmon. A traditional British lunch is served on Sundays.

Open 12-3 5-11 (Mon 5-11 Fri-Sat 12-11 Sun 12-10.30) Closed: 24 Dec-1 Jan, Mon L **Bar Meals** L served Fri 12.30-3, Sat 12.30-4, Sun 12.30-10 D served all wk 6-10 Av main course £14 ⊕ FREE HOUSE ◀ Caledonian Deuchars IPA, Harvey's Sussex Best Bitter, Fuller's London Pride, St Austell Tribute. ♀ 14 **Facilities** Children welcome Children's portions Garden Wi-fi ➡ (notice required)

SW13

The Bull's Head
PLAN 2 D3

373 Lonsdale Rd, Barnes SW13 9PY ☎ 020 8876 5241
e-mail: jazz@thebullshead.com
dir: Telephone for directions

The Thames-side setting of this imposing 17th-century pub would be a draw in itself, but what really pulls the crowds in are the top-class jazz and blue groups that have made the pub internationally famous over 50 years. Countless famous musicians have wet their whistles with the fine cask-conditioned ales from Wells and Young's — and so can you in the bustling bar. Traditional bar lunches include salt beef sandwiches; sausages, mash and onion gravy; and plum and apple crumble, while authentic Thai food is available throughout the pub in the evening.

Open all day all wk 12-12 Closed: 25 Dec **Bar Meals** L served all wk 12-6 **Restaurant** D served all wk 6-10.30 ⊕ YOUNG'S ◀ Special, Bitter, Ramrod & Winter Warmer, Wells Bombardier, Guinness. ♀ 21 **Facilities** Children welcome Children's portions Family room Garden Wi-fi

---

The Idle Hour
PLAN 2 D2

PICK OF THE PUBS

See Pick of the Pubs on page 355

SW14

The Victoria
PLAN 2 C2

10 West Temple Sheen, East Sheen SW14 7RT
☎ 020 8876 4238
e-mail: bookings@thevictoria.net
dir: Nearest tube station: Mortlake

Close to Richmond Park, The Victoria is a warm and friendly pub with a large conservatory and a fabulous garden with a safe children's play area. With TV chef Paul Merrett and restaurateur Greg Bellamy at the helm, you can expect top award-winning food. Menus encompass casual bites like salt beef salad or potted fresh and smoked salmon rillette, as well as main courses such as cumin-roasted rump of lamb with roasted sweet potato, smoked aubergine and merguez sausage. Saturday brunch and Sunday lunch are particularly popular with families.

Open all day all wk **Bar Meals** L served Mon-Thu 12-10, Fri 12-10.30 D served Mon-Thu 12-10, Fri 12-10.30, Sat 6-10.30 food served all day **Restaurant** L served Mon-Fri 12-2.30, Sat-Sun 12-4 D served Mon-Thu 6-10, Fri-Sat 6-10.30, Sun 4.45-8 ⊕ ENTERPRISE INNS ◀ Fuller's London Pride, Timothy Taylor Landlord, Guest ale Ö Westons Wyld Wood Organic. ♀ 28 **Facilities** Children welcome Children's menu Children's portions Play area Garden Parking Wi-fi

---

SW15

The Spencer
PLAN 2 D2

PICK OF THE PUBS

237 Lower Richmond Rd, Putney SW15 1HJ
☎ 020 8788 0640
e-mail: info@thespencerpub.com
dir: Corner of Putney Common & Lower Richmond Rd, opposite Old Putney Hospital

The green and leafy expanse of Putney Common is the view from tables outside this long-established pub, out in the 'burbs and just a short stroll from the Thames Embankment; their beer garden is part of the Common. A light, bright and airy interior belies the rather traditional look of the place; revamped a few years ago, the emphasis is on good dining in a crisp, chic environment where locals are still welcomed to sup at the bar, with Sharp's Doom Bar or Fuller's London Pride the pick of the beers. Meals, in the bar or restaurant area, are a modern take on traditional favourites, such as a starter of Welsh rarebit with fresh beef tomato and pan-fried smoked bacon; or shredded duck, poached pear and walnut salad with stilton dressing. Mains take on a seasonal look to reflect the desire to use only the freshest ingredients; look for a linguine of fresh crab, parsley, cherry tomatoes, garlic and chilli; grilled Mediterranean sea bass with Jerusalem artichoke purée and wilted spinach; or honey-roast belly of pork, glazed apple and Puy lentils. Sunday roasts and rotisserie free-range chickens are a favourite with families. Booking for meals may be required.

Open all day all wk 10am-mdnt Closed: 25 Dec ⊕ FREE HOUSE ◀ Fuller's London Pride, Sharp's Doom Bar, Guinness Õ Aspall Draught & Peronelle's Blush, Westons Wyld Wood Organic. **Facilities** Children welcome Children's menu Children's portions Play area Garden Wi-fi

---

The Telegraph   PLAN 2 D2

Telegraph Rd, Putney Heath SW15 3TU
☎ **020 8788 2011**
e-mail: info@thetelegraphputney.co.uk
dir: *Nearest tube: East Putney. Nearest rail station: Putney High St*

This pub was close to an Admiralty telegraph station between London and Portsmouth, and has been involved in the sale of beer since before 1856. Although it's only five minutes from the hustle and bustle of Putney High Street, The Telegraph feels more like a country pub. Certainly the focus on well-kept real ales cannot be faulted, with Naked Ladies from Twickenham Fine Ales well worth a try. The menu, with its pub fare and contemporary European dishes, includes grazing boards and chicken, chorizo and haloumi skewers to start, and mains of braised lamb shank, roast duck breast, steaks and burgers. Booking for meals may be required.

Open all day all wk **Bar Meals** L served all wk all day D served Mon-Thu until 9.30, Fri-Sat until 10, Sun until 9 food served all day **Restaurant** L served all wk all day D served Mon-Thu until 9.30, Fri-Sat until 10, Sun until 9 food served all day ◀ Sharp's Doom Bar, Twickenham Naked Ladies, Brakspear Bitter, Adnams Broadside. **Facilities** Children welcome Children's menu Children's portions Garden Parking ▱

SW18

The Alma Tavern   PLAN 2 E2
PICK OF THE PUBS

499 Old York Rd, Wandsworth SW18 1TF
☎ **020 8870 2537**
e-mail: alma@youngs.co.uk
dir: *Opposite Wandsworth Town rail station*

Vivid green tiles covering part of the curving frontage of this street-corner inn can't fail to catch the eye, as do the belvedere tower and the imposing balustrading of this impressive Young's establishment. Not far from the Thames or the greenery of Wandsworth Common, step inside to a well renovated Victorian town pub, complete with decorative plaster frieze, a superb island bar, mosaics and feature mahogany staircase; the latter leads to the Bramford Room, which is licensed for weddings. The roomy bar has an interesting mix of highly polished wood and distressed tables, with lots of perching posts

for those days when Twickenham hosts international matches; off this is a more peaceful dining room where an enthusiastic mix of traditional pub grub and gastro-pub dishes attract diners from a wide area. A twice-baked cheddar soufflé or seared scallops with pea-mint purée set out the stall, followed by pan-fried fillet of line-caught mackerel, bacon and beetroot relish; Gressingham duck breast with Puy lentils and garlic mash; or an Alma burger with Somerset brie, bacon and French fries giving a flavour of the mains. Beers from Young's stable, plus guests from local micro-breweries and a good list of bins, provide ample accompaniment.

Open all day all wk ⊕ YOUNG'S ◀ Sambrook's Wandle Õ Addlestones. **Facilities** Children welcome Children's portions Beer festival Wi-fi

---

The Earl Spencer   PLAN 2 E2
PICK OF THE PUBS

260-262 Merton Rd, Southfields SW18 5JL
☎ **020 8870 9244**
e-mail: theearlspencer@hotmail.com
dir: *Exit Southfields tube station, down Replingham Rd, left at junct with Merton Rd, to junct with Kimber Rd*

A rare mix of community and gastro-pub only ten minutes from the Wimbledon Tennis Centre. Edwardian pubby grandeur, log fires and polished wood furnishings offer a relaxed, informal atmosphere, whilst a good selection of wines and real ales draws in a dedicated bunch of regulars. It's child-friendly too, something of a rarity in establishments where food is taken seriously. The emphasis is on fresh cooking (even the bread is home baked) with an international cast of chefs; the menu changes daily and reflects seasonal produce. Kick in with poached salted ox tongue, lentils and green sauce or Normandy oysters, shallot vinegar and lemon before progressing to neck end of pork, root vegetable mash, buttered kale, cider and mustard; or whole lemon sole accompanied by ratte potatoes, braised leeks, chives and vermouth. Round off with Bramley apple and blackberry crumble or prune and Armagnac iced parfait. Events are catered for in a large, self-contained function suite, or simply unwind with a beer on the front patio. As we went to press, we learnt of a change of hands.

Open all wk 11-11 (Fri-Sat 11am-mdnt Sun 12-10.30) Closed: 25 Dec ⊕ ENTERPRISE INNS ◀ Fuller's London Pride, Sharp's Doom Bar, Hook Norton, Guinness Õ Aspall. **Facilities** Children welcome Garden Wi-fi

---

The Roundhouse   PLAN 2 E2

2 Northside, Wandsworth Common SW18 2SS
☎ **020 7326 8580**
e-mail: roundhouse@sabretoothvintners.com
dir: *Telephone for directions*

Sambrook's Brewery in Battersea furnishes this pub with its Wandle and Junction ales, the former named after a nearby river and the latter for the famous station at Clapham. The young brewery's crafted ales fit well with The Roundhouse, which underwent a renaissance in name, décor and management a few years ago. The ambience is of a friendly local, with a round black walnut bar, open kitchen, eclectic art on the walls, daily-changing menus and those lip-smacking Sambrook's ales. The concise menu takes in a charcuterie board; home-made soup; lamb burger; beer-battered hake; and mushroom, spinach and ricotta cannelloni.

Open all wk Mon-Thu 4-11 Fri 3-12 Sat 12-12 Sun 12-10.30 **Bar Meals** L served Sat 12-4, Sun 12-4.30 D served Mon-Sat 6-10, Sun 6.30-9 Av main course £12 **Restaurant** L served Sat 12-4, Sun 12-4.30 D served Mon-Sat 6-10, Sun 6.30-9 ⊕ FREE HOUSE ◀ Sambrook's Wandle, Junction Õ Hogan's. ♀ 15 **Facilities** ❖ Children welcome Children's portions Garden Wi-fi ▱

The Ship Inn   PLAN 2 E2
PICK OF THE PUBS

41 Jew's Row SW18 1TB ☎ **020 8870 9667**
e-mail: drinks@theship.co.uk
dir: *Wandsworth Town BR station nearby. On S side of Wandsworth Bridge*

By its own admission, this late 18th-century Thames-side pub upriver from Wandsworth Bridge can't claim to be in one of London's most appealing locations, but it's fought hard to stay noticed and is really worth tracking down. Enter via the delightful, two-level, rose-covered terrace and you'll find a vibrant conservatory bar with bare floorboards, central wood-burning stove, motley collection of old wooden tables and chairs, and an open-plan kitchen that prepares jolly good pub food prepared from high quality produce. On days when the barbecue is fired up, grab a pint of Young's or Sambrook's Wandle and enjoy chargrilled sirloin steak, braised shallots, hand-cut chips and watercress; seared guinea fowl, truffled mash, wilted greens and mushroom jus; or parsnip, tomato and goat's cheese gratin, Jerusalem artichoke and spinach fricassée. Tuesdays are given over to lively acoustic Irish music, and other bands play on Thursdays and Sundays; quiz night is Wednesday.

Open all day all wk Sun-Wed 11-11 (Thu-Sat 11am-mdnt) **Bar Meals** L served all wk 12-6 D served all wk 6-10 Av main course £13 food served all day **Restaurant** L served Mon-Sat 12-4, Sun 12-5 D served Mon-Sat 6-10, Sun 7-10 ◀ Wells Bombardier, Sambrook's Wandle, Young's & Seasonal ales Õ Addlestones. ♀ 15 **Facilities** Children welcome Children's menu Children's portions Garden Wi-fi

W1

Duke of Wellington NEW   PLAN 1 B4

94a Crawford St W1H 2HQ ☎ 020 7723 2790
e-mail: theduke@hotmail.co.uk
dir: 5 mins' walk from Baker Street Station

It's worth alighting the tube at Baker Street for the five-minute stroll down charming Crawford Street to locate this delightfully unpretentious little gastro-pub. At rustic tables in the single bar – all bare boards, ornate ceiling and modern artwork – tuck into some robust modern British food that makes sound use of locally sourced produce. Start with dressed crab on toast, follow with shellfish and bacon chowder, or slow-roasted lamb shoulder with lemon ratte potatoes, and finish with a satisfying sticky toffee pudding with banana ice cream. Don't miss the Sunday roast lunches.

Open all day all wk Closed: 25 Dec-2 Jan **Bar Meals** L served all wk 12-4 D served all wk 6.30-10 Av main course £15 **Restaurant** L served all wk 12-4 D served all wk 7-10 Fixed menu price fr £14.95 Av 3 course à la carte fr £27 ⊕ PUNCH TAVERNS ◀ Sharp's Doom Bar, Fuller's London Pride, Black Sheep. ♟ **Facilities** ✿ Children welcome Children's portions Wi-fi ▱ (notice required)

French House   PLAN 1 D4

49 Dean St, Soho W1D 5BG ☎ 020 7437 2477
dir: Nearest tube stations: Piccadilly Circus, Tottenham Court Road, Covent Garden. Pub at Shaftesbury Avenue end of Dean St

This legendary Soho watering hole was patronised by General de Gaulle during the Second World War, and later by Dylan Thomas, Francis Bacon, Dan Farson and many other louche Soho habitués. Run by Lesley Lewis for over 20 years, the small, intimate and very atmospheric bar only serves half pints of Budvar, Leffe and Guinness. The upstairs restaurant Polpetto closed in summer 2012 and became a second bar, offering more informal drinking space; this area is also used as an art gallery. Only lunchtime bar food is served. Booking for meals may be required.

Open all day all wk 12-11 (Sun 12-10.30) Closed: 25 Dec **Bar Meals** L served Mon-Fri 12-4 ⊕ FREE HOUSE ◀ Budweiser Budvar, Kronenbourg, Leffe, Meteor, Guinness. ♟ 22 **Facilities** Wi-fi

The Grazing Goat   PLAN 1 B4

6 New Quebec St W1H 7RQ ☎ 020 7724 7243
e-mail: reservations@thegrazinggoat.co.uk
dir: Behind Marble Arch tube station, off Seymour St

Just minutes away from Oxford Street and Marble Arch, this classy, six-storey pub and hotel is full of period features including open fireplaces, oak floors and solid oak bars. The name is not mere whimsy; goats did once graze around here because the first Lady Portman was allergic to cow's milk. Expect modern British, seasonal cooking – maybe chilli salt squid with lime dressing followed by steak-and-ale pie with battered neeps, with coffee brûlée for dessert. Floor-to-ceiling glass doors are

opened in warmer weather for alfresco dining. Booking for meals may be required.

Open all day all wk 8am-11.30pm (Sun 8am-10.30pm) Closed: Xmas & New Year **Bar Meals** Av main course £15 food served all day **Restaurant** L served all wk 12-3 D served all wk 6-10 ⊕ FREE HOUSE ◀ Sharp's Doom Bar, Caledonian Deuchars IPA ♖ Aspall. ♟ 20 **Facilities** Children welcome Children's portions Wi-fi ▱ (notice required)

The Portman NEW   PLAN 1 B4

51 Upper Berkeley St W1H 7QW ☎ 020 7723 8996
e-mail: manager@theportmanmarylebone.com
dir: From Marble Arch along Great Cumberland Place, 3rd left into Upper Berkeley St

Tucked between the hustle of Oxford Street and the elegant shops of Marylebone, prisoners once stopped here for a final drink on their way to the gallows at Tyburn Cross. These days, this friendly central London pub is the perfect place for weary shoppers to refuel on Rebellion Brewery ales and seasonal British classics served all day, 365 days a year. Seared Barbary duck breast with thyme rösti and cherry sauce or the pie of the day are popular choices, as are the steaks and Angus beef burgers.

Open all day all wk **Bar Meals** Av main course £12.50 food served all wk **Restaurant** L served all wk 12-3 D served all wk 6-10 Av 3 course à la carte fr £26 ⊕ FREE HOUSE ◀ Rebellion, Guest ale ♖ Aspall. ♟ 12 **Facilities** Children welcome Children's portions Wi-fi

W2

The Cow   PLAN 2 E4

89 Westbourne Park Rd W2 5QH ☎ 020 7221 5400
e-mail: office@thecowlondon.co.uk
dir: Telephone for directions

Popular with the Notting Hill glitterati, this atmospheric Irish gastro-pub has a bustling downstairs bar and a tranquil first-floor dining room. 'Eat heartily and give the house a good name' is the sound philosophy here, and the stars of the show are oysters and Guinness. Daily specials include seafood plates and platters; bowls of whelks and winkles; and 'Cow classics' such as Londoner sausages with mash and gravy; hand-made taglioni with crab, tomato and chilli; or fish stew with rouille and croûtons. Booking for meals may be required.

Open all day all wk Closed: 25 Dec ⊕ FREE HOUSE ◀ Fuller's London Pride, Courage Directors, De Koninck, Guinness.

The Prince Bonaparte   PLAN 2 E4

80 Chepstow Rd W2 5BE ☎ 020 7313 9491
e-mail: princebonaparte@realpubs.co.uk
dir: Nearest tube: Notting Hill Gate or Westbourne Park

The building, originally a gin house built in 1850, is noted for its airy and open-plan interior. It became a first-generation gastro-pub in the early 1990s, featuring a large half-moon bar fronted by high tables; lofty ceiling

spaces, a skylight and theatre-style kitchen characterise the dining room. Guest ales and many bottled beers witness its credentials as a drinker's pub, confirmed by the beer festival held here in the third week of March. High-quality produce likely to feature on the excellent menu may include Dover sole, lamb from Devon and New Forest venison. Booking for meals may be required.

Open all day all wk 12-11 (Sun 12-10.30) **Bar Meals** L served Mon-Fri 12-3.30, Sat-Sun all day D served Mon-Fri 6-10.30 Av main course £14.50 **Restaurant** L served Mon-Fri 12-3.30, Sat-Sun all day D served Mon-Fri 6-10.30 Fixed menu price fr £9.50 Av 3 course à la carte fr £23.50 ⊕ FREE HOUSE/REAL PUBS ◀ Sharp's Doom Bar, 2 Guest ales ♖ Aspall. ♟ 13 **Facilities** Children welcome Children's portions Beer festival Wi-fi ▱ (notice required)

The Westbourne   PLAN 2 E4

101 Westbourne Park Villas W2 5ED ☎ 020 7221 1332
dir: On corner of Westbourne Park Rd & Westbourne Park Villas

Bare floorboards and a long green and zinc bar characterise this classic Notting Hill gastro-pub, much favoured by its bohemian and celebrity clientele. The popular terrace is a suntrap in summer and heated in winter, attracting many locals and visitors to enjoy good food and drinks in a unique atmosphere. Daily-changing imaginative dishes are listed on a large blackboard above the bar, using fresh ingredients from leading independent suppliers. Dishes might include Gloucester Old Spot pork loin chop with chorizo and black cabbage.

Open Tue-Sat 12-11 (Sun 12-10.30 Mon 5-11) Closed: 24 Dec-2 Jan, Mon L ⊕ FREE HOUSE ◀ Caledonian Deuchars IPA, Staropramen, Leffe, Hoegaarden, Flowers. **Facilities** Children welcome Children's portions Garden Wi-fi

W4   Map 6 TQ27

Sam's Brasserie & Bar ⊛   PLAN 2 D3

11 Barley Mow Passage, Chiswick W4 4PH
☎ 020 8987 0555
e-mail: info@samsbrasserie.co.uk
dir: Behind Chiswick High Rd, next to green, off Heathfield Terrace

Once the Sanderson wallpaper factory, this large converted red-brick warehouse is a very unique space. Open all day from breakfast onwards, Sam's Brasserie covers all bases with its food and drink offering. Enjoy a pint of London Pride and rock oysters in the bar or tuck in to main menu choices such as grilled pork chop with black pudding mash, winter greens and cider jus in the buzzy brasserie. Don't miss the Sunday roasts. Booking for meals may be required.

Open all day all wk Closed: 25-26 Dec ⊕ FREE HOUSE ◀ Fuller's London Pride. **Facilities** Children welcome Children's menu Children's portions Wi-fi

The Swan
PLAN 2 D3

PICK OF THE PUBS

1 Evershed Walk, 119 Acton Ln, Chiswick W4 5HH
☎ **020 8994 8262**
e-mail: theswanpub@btconnect.com
dir: *Pub on right at end of Evershed Walk*

A friendly gastro-pub, The Swan is the perfect spot for all seasons with its welcoming wood-panelled interior and a large lawned garden and patio for summertime refreshments. Good food is at the heart of the operation, and you can sit and eat wherever you like. The menu of modern, mostly Mediterranean cooking has a particular Italian influence, and vegetarians are not forgotten. Start perhaps with fried beef dumplings with sweet chilli relish; a vegetarian option could be baked goat's cheese bruschetta with Sicilian aubergine relish and pesto. Next comes the main course: roast poussin with lemon and thyme and sweet potato hash; or pheasant and wild mushroom risotto. If you still have an appetite, then finish off with pear and almond tart, or home-made ice cream. Real ale recommendations are shown on the menu.

Open all wk 5-11.30 (Sat 12-11.30 Sun 12-11) Closed: 24-31 Dec **Bar Meals** L served Sat 12.30-3, Sun 12.30-10 D served Sun-Thu 6-10, Fri-Sat 6-10.30 Av main course £12-£15 ⊕ FREE HOUSE ◼ Fuller's London Pride, Harvey's Sussex Best Bitter, St Austell Tribute, Otter Bitter, Guinness Ò Westons Wyld Wood Organic. ♟ 12 **Facilities** Children welcome Children's portions Garden

W5

The Wheatsheaf
PLAN 2 C4

41 Haven Ln, Ealing W5 2HZ ☎ **020 8997 5240**
e-mail: wheatsheaf@fullers.co.uk
dir: *1m from A40 junct with North Circular*

Just a few minutes from Ealing Broadway, this large Victorian pub has a rustic appearance inside. It's an ideal place to enjoy a big-screen sporting event and a drink among wooden floors, panelled walls, beams from an old barn, and real fires in winter. There are Fuller's beers and traditional pub grub that includes Cumberland sausages and mash; home-made fish pie; platters to share; Fuller's beer-battered cod and hand-cut chips; and spaghetti carbonara.

Open all day all wk 12-11 (Sun 12-10.30) ⊕ FULLER'S ◼ London Pride, Discovery, Chiswick Bitter, Seasonal ales Ò Aspall Draught. **Facilities** Children welcome Children's portions Garden Wi-fi

W6

Anglesea Arms @
PLAN 2 D3

PICK OF THE PUBS

35 Wingate Rd W6 0UR ☎ **020 8749 1291**
dir: *Telephone for directions*

Intimate and cosy, it's whispered that the Great Train Robbery was hatched here back in the 1960s. This traditional corner pub is close to Ravenscourt Park tube station. Today, real fires and a relaxed atmosphere are the attraction, together with a terrace where drinks and food can be served. Behind the Georgian façade, well-kept ales are dispensed from breweries as far apart as Suffolk and Cornwall, and the place positively buzzes with people eagerly seeking out the unashamedly gastro-pub food with one AA Rosette. Unusual dishes from the open kitchen shine out, including starters such as smoked eel. Mains may feature grilled partridge or sautéed rabbit with choucroute, carrots and mustard. Ricotta doughnuts with cinnamon and butterscotch sauce could be a pudding option, as could cheeses from Neal's Yard Dairy. There's a seriously impressive wine cellar here too, with 20 available by the glass. Nigella Lawson's early 'Domestic Goddess' cookery shows were filmed in the pub dining room.

Open all day all wk 11-11 (Sun 12-10.30) Closed: 25-27 Dec **Bar Meals** L served all wk 12.30-7 D served Mon-Sat 7-10.30, Sun 6.30-9.30 Av main course £16.50 **Restaurant** L served Mon-Fri 12.30-2.45, Sat 12.30-3, Sun 12.30-3.30 D served Mon-Sat 7-10.30, Sun 6.30-9.30 Av 3 course à la carte fr £30 ⊕ ENTERPRISE INNS ◼ Ringwood Fortyniner, St Austell Tribute, Sharp's Cornish Coaster, Otter Ale & Bitter, Woodforde's Wherry Ò Westons Wyld Wood Organic. ♟ 20 **Facilities** Children welcome Children's portions Garden

The Dartmouth Castle
PLAN 2 D3

PICK OF THE PUBS

26 Glenthorne Rd, Hammersmith W6 0LS
☎ **020 8748 3614**
e-mail: dartmouth.castle@btconnect.com
dir: *Nearest tube station: Hammersmith. 100yds from Hammersmith Broadway*

While it's very much a place to relax over a pint or two, the food is proving a great attraction at this corner pub. The monthly-changing menu ranges from imaginative sandwiches (mozzarella and slow-roast tomatoes with pesto; or marinated rump steak with onions, chilli and red wine) to gutsy Mediterranean fare that includes a wide range of canapé platters as well as main dishes like Spanish pork stew with chorizo, or fish stew with langoustines and tiger prawns. Vegetarians aren't forgotten either, with choices like linguine alla genovese or slow-roast tomato and saffron risotto. Typical desserts are apple and rhubarb crumble and home-made ice creams. The range of beers includes at least two real ales on tap at any one time, and there's a well-chosen international wine list with 15 available by the glass.

There's also a beer garden for the summer months and a function room.

Open all day 12-11 (Sat 5-11 Sun 12-10.30) Closed: Etr, 23 Dec-2 Jan, Sat L **Bar Meals** L served Mon-Fri 12-2.30, Sun 12-9.30 D served Mon-Fri 6-10, Sat 6-10, Sun 12-9.30 Av main course £12 **Restaurant** Fixed menu price fr £19.50 ⊕ FREE HOUSE ◼ Sharp's Doom Bar, Sambrook's Wandle, Otter Bitter, Guest ales Ò Aspall. ♟ 15 **Facilities** Garden Wi-fi

The Stonemasons Arms
PLAN 2 D3

54 Cambridge Grove W6 0LA ☎ **020 8748 1397**
e-mail: stonemasonsarms@london-gastros.co.uk
dir: *Hammersmith tube. Walk down King St, 2nd right up Cambridge Grove, pub at end*

Fascinating menu options make this imposing corner pub, just a short hop from Hammersmith tube station, well worth finding; the charcuterie plate or vegetarian meze plate to share, and O'Hagan's American smokey sausages with buttered vegetables, mash and onion gravy all tantalise the tastebuds, enhancing the popularity of the pub with local residents and business people alike. During warmer months a decking area can be used for alfresco dining, and there's a secluded, intimate restaurant area. The pub carries an ever-changing display of works by a local artist, and there are weekly quiz nights.

Open all day all wk 11-11 (Sun 12-10.30) ⊕ FULLER'S ◼ London Pride & Organic Honey Dew, Guinness Ò Symonds Founders Reserve. **Facilities** Children welcome Children's portions Garden Wi-fi

W8

The Mall Tavern @@ **NEW**
PLAN 2 E3

71-73 Palace Gardens Ter, Notting Hill W8 4RU
☎ **020 7729 3374**
e-mail: info@themalltavern.com
dir: *Nearest tube station: Notting Hill*

A Victorian pub built in 1856 midway between Notting Hill and Kensington, The Mall was, and remains, a true locals' tavern – albeit a rather stylish, upmarket one. With two AA Rosettes, expect a hearty modern take on pub food – maybe venison pork pie with pickled vegetables followed by chicken with white wine, beech mushrooms, baby onions and salsify, with champagne rhubarb trifle for dessert. Besides regular beers such as Sharp's Doom Bar and By the Horns Stiff Upper Lip, there's an impressive list of wines, with many available by the glass.

Open all day all wk Closed: 1wk Xmas **Bar Meals** L served 12-10 D served 12-10 Av main course £15 food served all day **Restaurant** L served 12-10 D served 12-10 food served all day ⊕ ENTERPRISE INNS ◼ Sharp's Doom Bar, By The Horns Stiff Upper Lip. ♟ **Facilities** Children welcome Children's portions Garden Wi-fi 🚌 (notice required)

W8 continued

The Scarsdale
PLAN 2 E3

23A Edwardes Square, Kensington W8 6HE
☎ 020 7937 1811
e-mail: scarsdale@fullers.co.uk
dir: *Exit Kensington High Street Station, turn left, 10 mins along High St. Edwardes Sq next left after Odeon Cinema*

The Scarsdale is a 19th-century free-standing building with colourful hanging baskets and window boxes spilling into the small terraced patio, in a leafy road just off Kensington High Street. The Frenchman who developed the site was supposedly one of Bonaparte's secret agents. A planned refurbishment worried the regulars, but the essence of the place has hardly been interfered with at all. The kitchen was updated though, allowing the introduction of a broader menu of brasserie-style dishes. Examples are mussels with lime and ginger, and chargrilled chicken sandwich on ciabatta with red peppers, spinach and mayonnaise. Booking for meals may be required.

Open all day all wk 12-11 (Sun 12-10.30) Closed: 25-26 Dec **Bar Meals** Av main course £9 food served all day **Restaurant** L served all wk 12-3 D served all wk 6-10 Fixed menu price fr £14 Av 3 course à la carte fr £25 ⊕ FULLER'S ◀ London Pride & Bengal Lancer, George Gale & Co Seafarers, Butcombe. ♟ 20 **Facilities** ♣ Garden Wi-fi

The Windsor Castle
PLAN 2 E3

114 Campden Hill Rd W8 7AR ☎ 020 7243 8797
dir: *From Notting Hill Gate, take south exit towards Holland Park, left onto Campden Hill Rd*

A surprisingly rural-looking pub in well-heeled Campden Hill, it dates from 1845 and takes its name from the royal abode 18 miles away, once visible from upstairs. Largely unmodernised for at least 100 years, its rambling, oak-panelled interior is warmed by two gas fires, and the large garden has its own bar. Very much a drinker's pub, it serves Sambrook's Wandle and Adnams Broadside real ales and several real ciders, but there's good food too, including Norfolk pork loin chop; beer-battered haddock and skin-on chips; and chestnut and wild mushroom risotto.

Open all day all wk 12-11 (Sun 12-10.30) **Bar Meals** food served all day **Restaurant** food served all day ⊕ MITCHELLS & BUTLERS ◀ Timothy Taylor Landlord, Adnams Broadside, Sambrook's Wandle ♂ Westons Old Rosie, Addlestones, Aspall. ♟ 12 **Facilities** ♣ Children welcome Children's menu Children's portions Garden

W9

The Waterway
PLAN 2 E4

54 Formosa St W9 2JU ☎ 020 7266 3557
e-mail: info@thewaterway.co.uk
dir: *From Warwick Avenue tube, up Warwick Av, turn left at Formosa St, pub is No. 54*

With its lovely canalside position in Maida Vale, The Waterway offers great alfresco opportunities with is outdoor terrace, where popular barbecues are held in summer. In colder weather, the bar is a great place to relax with its sumptuous sofas and open fires. There is a good choice of drinks, including champagne by the glass. The restaurant menu offers modern European food – chargrilled squid with sweet chilli sauce and mixed leaves; spiced pork belly, black pudding mash and Bramley apple sauce; roast monkfish, spring greens, Parma ham and barley risotto.

Open all day all wk 12-11 (Sat 10.30am-11pm Sun 11-10.30) **Bar Meals** L served all day D served all day Av main course £12 food served all day **Restaurant** L served Mon-Fri 12-3.30, Sat-Sun 12-4 D served Mon-Sat 6.30-10.30, Sun 6.30-10 Fixed menu price fr £16 Av 3 course à la carte fr £25 ⊕ ENTERPRISE INNS ◀ Sharp's Doom Bar, Fuller's London Pride, Skinner's Cornish Knocker ♂ Aspall. ♟ 16 **Facilities** Children welcome Children's menu Children's portions Garden Wi-fi ⛟

W11

Portobello Gold
PLAN 2 E3

95-97 Portobello Rd, Notting Hill W11 2QB
☎ 020 7460 4900
e-mail: reservations@portobellogold.com
dir: *From Notting Hill Gate tube station, follow signs to Portobello Market*

In the heart of famous Portobello Road Market, this quirky Notting Hill pub/wine bar/brasserie has been under the same ownership since 1985, and offers an interesting range of British ales and European beers, great wines and cocktails. Former US President Bill Clinton reportedly dropped into Portobello Gold with an entire motorcade, stayed an hour and left without paying! Menus always list game and seafood, including oysters. Dishes such as pasta, tortillas, burgers, bangers and steaks are all prepared from scratch on the premises. With the landlord's wife, Linda Bell, an established wine writer, 18 wines by the glass should be no surprise. Booking for meals may be required.

Open all day all wk **Bar Meals** L served all day D served all day Av main course £13 food served all day **Restaurant** L served all day D served all day food served all day ⊕ ENTERPRISE INNS ◀ Fuller's London Pride, Harvey's Sussex, Meantime, Leffe, Freedom, Guinness ♂ Thatchers Gold, Katy & Spartan. ♟ 18 **Facilities** Children welcome Children's portions Wi-fi ⛟ (notice required)

W14

The Albion NEW
PLAN 2 D3

121 Hammersmith Rd, West Kensington W14 0QL
☎ 020 7603 2826
e-mail: chris@downthealbion.com
dir: *Near Kensington Olympia & Barons Court tube stations*

Weary from wandering around Olympia and in need of refreshment? Then head across the road to The Albion, a fine old pub that takes its name from HMS *Albion* and has the look and feel of an old ship. Famous for its Easter Music and Real Ale Festival, it is also locally renowned for its stone-baked pizzas – try the chorizo and olive, the Moroccan lamb or the jerk chicken. Wash down with a pint of Deuchers IPA or Thwaites Wainwright.

Open all day all wk **Bar Meals** L served all wk 11-3 D served all wk 5-10 Av main course £8.50 ⊕ HEINEKEN ◀ Caledonian Deuchars IPA, Harvey's Albion Ale, Thwaites Wainwright ♂ Symonds. **Facilities** Garden Beer festival Wi-fi ⛟ (notice required)

The Cumberland Arms
PLAN 2 D3

PICK OF THE PUBS

29 North End Rd, Hammersmith W14 8SZ
☎ 020 7371 6806
e-mail: thecumberlandarmspub@btconnect.com
dir: *From Kensington Olympia, exit station, turn left at Hammersmith Rd right, at T-junct (North End Rd) left, 100yds, pub on left*

Eye-catching with its bold gold lettering and attractive blue-painted façade, gloriously festooned with flowers in summer, this gastro-pub is worth noting if visiting Olympia. Bag a pavement bench and table on sunny days or head indoors, where mellow furniture and stripped floorboards characterise its interior. Friendly staff, an affordable first-rate wine list and well-kept ales (Doom Bar, London Pride, Exmoor Gold) are the draw for those seeking after-work refreshment, but it is also a great place for plates of unpretentious Mediterranean-style food offered from a monthly-changing menu. Hearty dishes range through pork terrine with fruit chutney; a sharing plate of antipasti; home-made chicken, spinach and ricotta ravioli; lamb steak with braised barley and tomato and cavalo nero; and rib-eye steak with roast potatoes, rocket and salsa verde. Desserts and cheese revert to a more French/English style – lemon tart with mascarpone, and apple and blackberry crumble.

Open all day all wk 12-11 (Sun 12-10.30 Thu-Fri 12-12) Closed: 24 Dec-1 Jan **Bar Meals** Av main course £12-£15 **Restaurant** L served Mon-Sat 12-3, Sun 12.30-9.30 D served all wk 6-10 ⊕ FREE HOUSE/THE PURPLE TIGER ◀ Fuller's London Pride, Exmoor Gold, Sharp's Doom Bar, Staropramen. ♟ 16 **Facilities** Children welcome Children's portions Garden Wi-fi ⛟ (notice required)

Save on hotels. Book at theAA.com/hotel

LONDON 361 ENGLAND

The Havelock Tavern
PLAN 2 D3

57 Masbro Rd, Brook Green W14 0LS ☎ 020 7603 5374
e-mail: enquiries@thehavelocktavern.co.uk
dir: *Nearest tube stations: Shepherd's Bush & Kensington Olympia*

One of the most celebrated London gastro-pubs, The Havelock has maintained the correct balance between 'gastro' and 'pub' for more than 15 years. There has been a change of hands at this popular Brook Green local but it's very much business as usual, with plenty on offer for locals who want a pint of Sambrook's Wandle, or food-lovers choosing from a menu that changes twice a day and which might include beef and black bean chilli, or grilled Toulouse sausages with borlotti beans, bacon, tomato and greens.

Open all day all wk 11-11 (Sun 12-10.30) Closed: 25-26 Dec **Bar Meals** L served Mon-Sat 12-2.30, Sun 12.30-3 D served Mon-Sat 7-10, Sun 7.30-9.30 Av main course £13 **Restaurant** Av 3 course à la carte fr £25 ⊕ FREE HOUSE ◖ Sharp's Doom Bar, Sambrook's Wandle ᚖ Westons Stowford Press. ᛞ 28 **Facilities** ❀ Children welcome Children's portions Garden Beer festival Wi-fi

The Jam Tree
PLAN 2 D3

58 Milson Rd W14 0LB ☎ 020 7371 3999
e-mail: info@thejamtree.com
dir: *Nearest tube stations: Shepherd's Bush & Kensington Olympia*

You'll find this hugely individual pub tucked away behind Kensington Olympia. The bar is furnished with an eclectic mix of chairs, tables and artworks, and pavement tables add to its cosmopolitan appeal. Come for the good range of beers and spirits or delve into the interesting wine list that has been designed around menus that aim to set the pub apart from the usual gastro fare. From the all-day menu perhaps choose hot potted smoked haddock followed by roast duck leg with garlic mash and red wine jus, and peanut butter and strawberry jam cheesecake. Excellent Saturday brunch and Sunday lunch menus.

Open all day all wk **Bar Meals** L served Mon-Sat 12-3, Sun 12-8 D served Mon-Sat 6-10, Sun 12-8 **Restaurant** L served Mon-Sat 12-3, Sun 12-8 D served Mon-Sat 6-10, Sun 12-8 ⊕ FREE HOUSE ◖ Morland Old Speckled Hen, Greene King St Edmunds ᚖ Aspall. ᛞ **Facilities** Children welcome Children's menu Children's portions Wi-fi 🚌

WC1

The Bountiful Cow
PLAN 1 E4
PICK OF THE PUBS

51 Eagle St, Holborn WC1R 4AP ☎ 020 7404 0200
e-mail: manager@roxybeaujolais.com
web: www.thebountifulcow.co.uk
dir: *230mtrs NE from Holborn tube station, via Procter St. Walk through 2 arches into Eagle St. Pub between High Holborn & Red Lion Square*

With a pub cookbook to her name, and as a presenter on the BBC's *Full on Food* programme, Roxy Beaujolais needs little introduction. The proprietor of the ancient Seven Stars in WC2 (see entry), she found another pub in Holborn and turned it into The Bountiful Cow, 'a public house devoted to beef'. Two floor levels are bedecked with pictures of cows, bullfights, cowgirls, diagrams of meat cuts and posters of cow-themed films; jazzy but discreet music adds to an atmosphere halfway between funky bistro and stylish saloon. Ales are from Adnams and Dark Star, and the short wine list includes half a dozen gutsy reds. Menus are based on beef sourced at Smithfield Market and aged in-house. Starters such as garlic fried prawns and desserts like crème brûlée can top and tail the main event; a two-person steak board presents four half steaks on an engraved oak platter which can be bought (minus the steaks) as a memento. Booking for meals may be required.

Open all day 11-11 (Sat 12-11) Closed: 25-26 Dec, 1 Jan, Sun **Bar Meals** L served Mon-Sat 12-9.30 D served Mon-Sat 12-9.30 **Restaurant** L served Mon-Sat 12-3 D served Mon-Sat 5-10.30 ⊕ FREE HOUSE ◖ Adnams Southwold Bitter, Dark Star Hophead ᚖ Aspall. ᛞ **Facilities** Children welcome Wi-fi 🚌 (notice required)

The Lamb
PLAN 1 D5
PICK OF THE PUBS

94 Lamb's Conduit St WC1N 3LZ ☎ 020 7405 0713
e-mail: lambwc1@youngs.co.uk
dir: *Russell Square, turn right, 1st right, 1st left, 1st right*

This building was first recorded in 1729, was 'heavily improved' between 1836 and 1876, and frequented by Charles Dickens when he lived nearby in Doughty Street (now housing the Dickens Museum). This really is a gem of a place, with its distinctive green-tiled façade, very rare glass snob screens, dark polished wood, and original sepia photographs of music hall stars who performed at the nearby Holborn Empire. The absence of television,

piped music and fruit machines allows conversation to flow, although there is a working polyphon. Home-cooked bar food includes a vegetarian corner (vegetable curry, or burger); a fish choice including traditional fish and chips; steaks from the griddle; plus pies and baked dishes from the stove. Favourites are steak-and-ale pie (called the Celebration 1729 pie); sausage and mash; liver and bacon; and fried egg and chips. For something lighter, try a ploughman's or a vegetable samosa with mango chutney.

Open all day all wk 12-11 (Thu-Sat 12-12 Sun 12-10.30) ⊕ YOUNG'S ◖ Young's (full range). **Facilities** Children welcome Garden

Norfolk Arms
PLAN 1 D5

28 Leigh St WC1H 9EP ☎ 020 7388 3937
e-mail: info@norfolkarms.co.uk
dir: *Nearest tube stations: Russell Square, Kings Cross & Euston*

Located on a busy street corner in Bloomsbury, within five minutes' walk of St Pancras International, the Norfolk Arms is a London gastro-pub. Behind its Victorian frontage, the main bar and dining area are at ground level, with private dining on the first floor. The extensive and eclectic bar menu features British, European and Middle Eastern tapas: typical choices are stuffed vine leaves, Scotch egg, Valencian carrots and Serrano ham. The main menu includes oxtail stew and spicy Italian sausages. A great choice of beers and ten wines by the glass complete the picture.

Open all day all wk Closed: 25-26, 31 Dec & 1 Jan **Bar Meals** food served all day **Restaurant** food served all day ⊕ SCOTTISH & NEWCASTLE ◖ Theakston XB, Greene King IPA. ᛞ 10 **Facilities** Children welcome Children's portions Wi-fi

WC2

The George
PLAN 1 E4

213 Strand WC2R 1AP ☎ 020 7353 9638
e-mail: enquiries@georgeinthestrand.com
dir: *Opposite Royal Courts of Justice*

Facing the Royal Courts of Justice, The George was built as a coffee house in 1723, although the black-and-white façade is late Victorian. Once regulars included Horace Walpole and Samuel Johnson, today mingle with judges, barristers and court reporters over a pint of Sharp's Doom Bar, a lunchtime salad, an open sandwich or hot wrap. For something more substantial, try chargrilled rib-eye steak; smoked poached haddock with bubble-and-squeak; traditional Irish lamb stew with dumplings; or the roast carvery. There's a real ale and cider festival every March. Booking for meals may be required.

Open all day all wk Closed: 25-26 Dec ⊕ FREE HOUSE ◖ Sharp's Doom Bar, Hogs Back TEA, Sambrook's Wandle, Black Sheep, Purity Pure UBU, Adnams Southwold Bitter ᚖ Aspall. **Facilities** Children welcome Beer festival Wi-fi

WC2 *continued*

The Seven Stars PLAN 1 E4

PICK OF THE PUBS

53 Carey St WC2A 2JB ☎ 020 7242 8521
e-mail: roxy@roxybeaujolais.com
dir: *From Temple N via The Strand & Bell Yard to Carey St. From Holborn SE via Lincoln's Inn Fields & Searle St to Carey St*

The Seven Stars may never have seen better days in its four centuries of existence. Since Roxy Beaujolais took over this ancient Grade II listed pub behind the Royal Courts of Justice 12 years ago, delicate and undisruptive primping has produced nothing but accolades. Improvements have been managed with such tact by Roxy's architect husband that some think even his modern dumbwaiter is ancient. Strengthened by its ambience, The Seven Stars has bloomed into the ideal pub – the food is simple but well executed, the ales are kept perfectly, the wines are few but very good, and the staff are welcoming and efficient. Roxy cooks herself most of the time. The day's dishes, listed on the blackboard, change according to what's best in the market and what tickles Roxy's fancy. Recent examples are tuna kedgeree biryani; and hot smoked German sausages with sautéed potatoes.

Open all day all wk 11-11 (Sat 12-11 Sun 12-10.30) Closed: 25-26 Dec, 1 Jan **Bar Meals** L served Mon-Fri 12-9.30, Sat-Sun 1-9.30 D served Mon-Fri 12-9.30, Sat-Sun 1-9.30 **Restaurant** L served Mon-Fri 12-9.30, Sat-Sun 1-9.30 D served Mon-Fri 12-9.30, Sat-Sun 1-9.30 ⊕ FREE HOUSE ◀ Adnams Southwold Bitter & Broadside, Dark Star Hophead, Sambrook's Wandle ☼ Aspall, Weston Wyld Wood Organic Pear. **Facilities** Wi-fi

The Sherlock Holmes PLAN 1 D3

10 Northumberland St WC2N 5DB ☎ 020 7930 2644
e-mail: 7967@greeneking.co.uk
dir: *From Charing Cross tube station exit onto Villiers St. Through 'The Arches' (runs underneath Charing Cross station) straight across Craven St into Craven Passage to Northumberland St*

Painted black with etched glass windows and colourful hanging baskets, this traditional corner pub is chock-full of Holmes memorabilia, including photographs of Conan Doyle, mounted pages from manuscripts, and artefacts and pieces recording the adventures of the Master Detective. There's even a replica of Holmes' and Watson's sitting room and study. This split-level establishment has a bar on the ground floor and on the first floor an intimate covered roof garden and the restaurant. There's Sherlock Holmes Ale to drink, hot and cold bar food plus an à la carte menu offering such treats as grilled tuna steak salad, roast beef, cottage pie, and lamb shank. Finish with a seasonal fruit crumble. Booking for meals may be required.

Open all day all wk Closed: 25-26 Dec **Bar Meals** food served all day **Restaurant** food served all day ⊕ GREENE KING ◀ Sherlock Holmes Ale & Abbot Ale, Morland Old Speckled Hen ☼ Aspall. ♚ 14 **Facilities** Children welcome Garden Wi-fi ▦

GREATER LONDON

CARSHALTON Map 6 TQ26

The Sun

4 North St SM5 2HU ☎ 020 8773 4549
e-mail: thesuncarshalton@googlemail.com
dir: *Off A232 (Croydon Rd) between Croydon & Sutton*

Very much a family-friendly pub, The Sun is a popular stop after visiting Carshalton Ponds. Beer festivals with hog roasts and live music are held every June and November; at other times there are always five ales on the go, including Timothy Taylor Landlord. Menus of rustic comfort food with European influences use the freshest, seasonal, free-range and organic produce: gnocchi with roasted red pepper sauce; pork, apricot and pistachio terrine; half roast chicken with lemon and thyme. There is also a separate children's menu. The chefs move to the garden for summer barbecues, when the family bar, children's chalkboard wall and sandpit come into their own. Booking for meals may be required.

Open all day Closed: Mon until 5pm **Bar Meals** L served Tue-Sat 12-3, Sun 12-7 D served Mon 6-9, Tue-Sat 6-9.30 Av main course £15 ⊕ FREE HOUSE ◀ Timothy Taylor Landlord, Rudgate Ruby Mild ☼ Westons, Addlestones. ♚ 14 **Facilities** ♣ Children welcome Children's menu Children's portions Play area Family room Garden Beer festival Wi-fi ▦

CHELSFIELD Map 6 TQ46

The Five Bells

PICK OF THE PUBS

BR6 7RE ☎ 01689 821044
dir: *From M25 junct 4 take A224 towards Orpington. In approx 1m turn right into Church Rd. Pub on left*

Conveniently located just inside the M25 near junction 4, this family-run Grade II listed pub is situated in a protected conservation village, with many lovely walks in the area. Dating from 1668, The Five Bells takes its name from the magnificent bells at the St Martin of the Tours church just up the road. There are two bars: one is a dog-friendly front bar boasting an original inglenook fireplace; the other is larger and houses the restaurant area. This in turn leads to the patio and extensive garden, which comes complete with a swing and play area for the children. In the kitchen, chef Chris Miller's seasonal menu complements the real ales and wines on offer: garlic mushrooms, home-cured salmon, fish and chips, and honey-and-mustard glazed ham with egg and chips are some examples. Home-made pizzas can be served at any time during pub opening hours, and beer festivals take place at Easter and in October along with regular music, quizzes and other events.

Open all day all wk **Bar Meals** L served all wk 12-3 D served Thu-Sat 6.30-9 Av main course £11.25 **Restaurant** L served all wk 12-3 D served Thu-Sat 6.30-9 Av 3 course à la carte fr £18 ⊕ ENTERPRISE INNS ◀ Courage Best, Sharp's Doom Bar, Guinness. ♚ 13 **Facilities** ♣ Children welcome Children's menu Children's portions Play area Garden Beer festival Parking Wi-fi ▦ (notice required)

HAM

Hand & Flower PLAN 2 C2

24 Upper Ham Rd TW10 5LA ☎ 020 8332 2022
e-mail: info@handandflower.com
dir: *On A307*

Originally the old toll house on the turnpike opposite Ham Common, the revamped Hand & Flower stands a short stroll from Richmond Park. Follow a good summer walk with lunch in the stunning, award-winning garden, replete with pond, private dining area and secluded tables away from the bustling patio. On inclement days head indoors to the modern and spacious dining area for all-day food, the daily menu ranging from home-made burgers and sandwiches to dressed crab; Caesar salad; and sea bass with samphire, chilli and lime braised fennel, and vegetable and potato broth. Accompany with a pint of Pride or one of the many wines by the glass.

Open all day all wk ⊕ TOP TAVERNS LTD ◀ Fuller's London Pride, Harvey's. **Facilities** Children welcome Children's menu Children's portions Garden Wi-fi

MERSEYSIDE

BARNSTON   Map 15 SJ28

Fox and Hounds

Barnston Rd CH61 1BW ☎ 0151 648 7685
e-mail: ralphleech@hotmail.com
web: www.the-fox-hounds.co.uk
dir: *M53 junct 4 take A5137 to Heswall. Right to Barnston on B5138. Pub on A551*

The pub, located in a conservation area and built on the site of an alehouse and barn, became a centenarian in 2011; its Edwardian character has been preserved in the pitch pine woodwork and leaded windows. The Snug is adorned with period fixtures and fittings, an open fire and collections of 1920s/1930s memorabilia. A good selection of real ales is served alongside lunchtime salads, paninis, platters and traditional mains, while the specials board concentrates on beef and steak pie; lamb shank; lasagne; Somerset chicken; and battered fish and chips. The beautifully kept beer garden is a riot of colour in summer. Booking for meals may be required.

Open all day all wk 11-11 (Sun 12-10.30) **Bar Meals** L served Mon-Sat 12-2, Sun 12-2.30 D served Tue-Fri fr 5.30 Av main course £8.95 ⊕ FREE HOUSE ◀ Theakston Best Bitter & Old Peculier, Brimstage Trapper's Hat, Webster's, Guest ales. ☏ 12 **Facilities** Children welcome Children's portions Family room Garden Parking Wi-fi ➡ (notice required)

BROMBOROUGH   Map 15 SJ38

Dibbinsdale Inn ★★★★ INN

Dibbinsdale Rd CH63 0HJ ☎ 0151 334 9818
e-mail: info@thedibbinsdale.co.uk
dir: *M53 junct 5, A41 towards Birkenhead. In 2m left towards Bromborough rail station. Through 2 sets of lights. 2nd right into Dibbinsdale Rd. Inn 600yds on left*

When this urban-fringe pub was purchased by Thwaites a few years ago, the brewery gave it the contemporary makeover you see today, both inside and out, and it now offers comfortable accommodation too. No prizes for guessing whose cask ales are sold, backed by guests and Kingstone Press cider. Sourcing ingredients from carefully chosen suppliers, the kitchen creates an ever-changing menu of traditional favourites: baked field mushrooms topped with Cheshire cheese is a typical starter, while grills; a daily roast with seasonal vegetables; and beer-battered haddock with thick-cut chips and mushy peas feature among the main courses. Change of hands.

Open all day all wk ⊕ THWAITES ◀ Wainwright Ò Kingstone Press. **Facilities** Children welcome Children's menu Children's portions Parking Wi-fi **Rooms** 11

GREASBY   Map 15 SJ28

Irby Mill

Mill Ln CH49 3NT ☎ 0151 604 0194
e-mail: info@irbymill.co.uk
dir: *M53 junct 3, onto A552 signed Upton & Heswall. At lights onto A551 signed Upton & Greasby. At lights left into Arrowe Brook Rd. At rdbt 3rd exit into Mill Ln*

An eye-catching, solid, sandstone-block built old miller's cottage (the windmill was demolished in 1898, pub opened in 1980) just a short jog from the airy heights of Thurstaston Common at the heart of The Wirral Peninsula. One of the area's best choices of real ales meets an exceptional, very pubby menu strong on Wirral produce – steaks are from locally grazed Aberdeen Angus, sausages from an award-winning local butcher. Popular with ramblers and Sunday diners, there's a suntrap grassy garden for summer; log fire, low beams and York-stone floor for the winter.

Open all day all wk **Bar Meals** L served Mon-Sat 12-9, Sun 12-6 D served Mon-Sat 12-9 Av main course £8.95 **Restaurant** L served Mon-Sat 12-9, Sun 12-6 D served Mon-Sat 12-9 ⊕ SCOTTISH & NEWCASTLE ◀ Wells Bombardier, Greene King Abbot Ale, Jennings Cumberland Ale, Black Sheep, 4 Guest ales. ☏ 12 **Facilities** ☘ Children welcome Children's menu Children's portions Garden Parking Wi-fi ➡

HIGHTOWN   Map 15 SD30

The Pheasant Inn

20 Moss Ln L38 3RA ☎ 0151 929 2106
dir: *From A565 take B5193, follow signs to Hightown*

This former alehouse is just minutes from Crosby Beach, where sculptor Antony Gormley's 100 cast-iron figures gaze out to sea. Surrounded by fields and nearby golf courses, the pub retains an original brick in the restaurant wall dated 1719, when the pub was called the Ten Billets Inn. In the bar these days you'll find Thwaites Wainwright alongside Aspall ciders. The menu is changed twice a year so expect seasonal dishes like slow-roasted lamb shoulder with winter vegetables and truffle mashed potatoes, or grilled sea bass on a bed of roasted fennel, broad beans and peas. There are also grill nights, the legendary Sunday platter and Friday fish suppers to enjoy.

Open all day all wk 12-11 (Sun 12-10.30) **Bar Meals** food served all day **Restaurant** food served all day ⊕ MITCHELLS & BUTLERS ◀ Thwaites Wainwright Ò Aspall Draught & Organic. ☏ 30 **Facilities** Children welcome Children's menu Garden Parking

NORFOLK

BAWBURGH   Map 13 TG10

Kings Head

PICK OF THE PUBS

See Pick of the Pubs on page 364

BINHAM   Map 13 TF93

Chequers Inn

Front St NR21 0AL ☎ 01328 830297
e-mail: steve@binhamchequers.co.uk
dir: *On B1388 between Wells-next-the-Sea & Walsingham*

Just a few miles from the north Norfolk coast, the Chequers is home to the Front Street Brewery, but even though they brew their own beer they still have guest ales together with an extensive range of foreign bottled beers such as Küppers Kölsch and Chimay Red Label, and a connoisseur's selection of rare and vintage beers. The pub has been owned by a village charity since the 1640s, and was originally a trade hall. Many stones from the nearby Binham Priory were used in its construction. The daily-changing menu might include mixed bean and Mediterranean vegetable chilli or deep-fried catfish fillet. Contact the pub for its beer festival dates.

Open all wk 11.30-2.30 6-11 (Fri-Sat 11.30-2.30 6-11.30 Sun 12-3 7-11) **Bar Meals** L served Mon-Sat 12-2, Sun 12-2.30 D served Mon-Sat 6-9, Sun 7-9 ⊕ FREE HOUSE ◀ Front Street Binham Cheer, Callums Ale & Unity Strong, Seasonal specials. **Facilities** Children welcome Children's menu Children's portions Garden Beer festival Parking Wi-fi ➡

PICK OF THE PUBS

Kings Head

BAWBURGH   Map 13 TG10

Harts Ln NR9 3LS ☎ 01603 744977
e-mail: anton@kingshead-bawburgh.co.uk
web: www.kingshead-bawburgh.co.uk
dir: *From A47 W of Norwich take B1108 W*

Standing opposite the village green and just yards from the River Yare, this 17th-century free house has bags of traditional charm. There are solid oak beams, bulging walls, wooden floors and comfy leather seating, making it the perfect place to relax after a day exploring the delights of nearby Norwich. After running the Kings Head for 28 years, Anton and Pam Wimmer pride themselves on projecting a warm welcome to locals and visitors alike. The pub is named after King Edward VII who, says Anton, "invested the Edwardian era with a reputation for delicious if somewhat upholstered pleasures. We aim to continue this philosophy". Behind the bar you'll find East Anglian ales and ciders, including Woodforde's Wherry, Adnams Broadside and Aspall's Blush. Head chef Dan Savage and second chef Leigh Taylor create monthly menus and daily-changing specials that are firmly rooted in the local markets – and they can make many of the dishes dairy- or gluten-free on request. Menus might include starters of chickpea and chorizo stew with toasted garlic flatbread; and

a Norfolk seafood platter of prawns, smoked salmon, smoked mackerel, whitebait and pickled cockles. Further down the menu you'll find main courses such as slow-braised shin of beef and horseradish suet pudding with seasonal vegetables; pan-seared salmon with poached rhubarb, ginger velouté, green bean and potato salad; and roast butternut squash with potato gnocchi, blue cheese cream sauce and dressed leaves. Leave room for desserts like warm banana cake with caramel sauce; and chocolate and almond torte with clotted cream and almond brittle. Booking for meals may be required.

Open all day all wk Closed: 25-27 Dec eve, 1 Jan eve **Bar Meals** L served Mon-Sat 12-2, Sun 12-4, Summer Sun 12-3

D served Mon-Sat 5.30-9, Summer Sun 6-9 **Restaurant** L served Mon-Sat 12-2, Sun 12-4, Summer Sun 12-3 D served Mon-Sat 5.30-9, Summer Sun 6-9 ⊕ FREE HOUSE ◖ Adnams Southwold Bitter & Broadside, Woodforde's Wherry, Wadworth, Guest ale ♂ Aspall & Perronelle's Blush. ♟ 11
Facilities Children welcome Children's menu Children's portions Garden Parking Wi-fi 🚐

BLAKENEY   Map 13 TG04

The Blakeney White Horse
PICK OF THE PUBS

4 High St NR25 7AL ☎ **01263 740574**
e-mail: hello@blakeneywhitehorse.co.uk
dir: *From A148 (Cromer to King's Lynn road) onto A149 signed to Blakeney*

This former 17th-century coaching inn is tucked away in a cluster of narrow streets lined with fishermen's cottages winding down to Blakeney's small tidal harbour. All around are fabulous views over creeks, Glaven Valley estuary and vast marshes of sea lavender, samphire and mussel beds. New leaseholders Francis and Sarah Guildea have set about a tasteful refurbishment, using a palette of neutral colours throughout the entrance lobby, elegant semi-private dining area, and main bar where Adnams ales are still a welcome sight. If wine is your preference, 14 from the list can be served by the glass. On the menu, expect the likes of warm salt cod brandade; the pub's renowned chicken and clam cataplana – a Portuguese dish served with home-baked corn bread; and baked vanilla cheesecake. If not so hungry, a simple but delicious carte of light lunches includes bagels and baguettes served with a handful of fries. Booking for meals may be required.

Open all day all wk 10.30am–11pm Closed: 25 Dec **Bar Meals** L served all wk 12–2.15 D served Sun-Thu 6–9, Fri-Sat 6–9.30 Av main course £14.50 **Restaurant** Av 3 course à la carte fr £25 ⊕ ADNAMS ◄ Southwold Bitter, Broadside, Sole Star Ŏ Aspall. ♟ 14 **Facilities** ♣ Children welcome Children's menu Children's portions Family room Garden Parking Wi-fi

The Kings Arms

Westgate St NR25 7NQ ☎ **01263 740341**
e-mail: kingsarmsnorfolk@btconnect.com
dir: *From Holt or Fakenham take A148, then B1156 for 6m to Blakeney*

Tucked away in this popular fishing village close to the north Norfolk coastal path, this thriving free house is the perfect refreshment stop following an invigorating walk, time spent birdwatching, or a ferry trip to the nearby seal colony. An excellent selection of real ales, including Norfolk-brewed Woodforde's Wherry is backed by menus featuring locally caught fish and seasonal seafood – cod, prawn and bacon chowder; mussels in garlic cream sauce – together with braised pheasant with bacon jus; steak and Adnams ale suet pudding; and home-made lasagne.

Open all day all wk Closed: 25 Dec eve **Bar Meals** food served all day ⊕ FREE HOUSE ◄ Morland Old Speckled Hen, Woodforde's Wherry, Marston's Pedigree, Adnams Southwold Bitter. ♟ 10 **Facilities** ♣ Children welcome Children's menu Children's portions Play area Family room Garden Parking Wi-fi ▭

BLICKLING   Map 13 TG12

The Buckinghamshire Arms
PICK OF THE PUBS

Blickling Rd NR11 6NF ☎ **01263 732133**
e-mail: bucksarms@tiscali.co.uk
dir: *A410 from Cromer exit at Aylsham onto B1354, follow Blickling Hall signs*

A stunning late 17th-century coaching inn, 'The Bucks' stands by the gates of the National Trust's Blickling Hall. The lounge bar and restaurant, with their solid furniture and wood-burning stoves, have plenty of appeal. The Victorian cellar houses real ales from Norfolk's Wolf Brewery and Adnams in Suffolk. Meals can be taken in either the lounge bar or restaurant, with menus offering fresh local food served in both traditional and modern styles. Dishes from the dinner menu include starters of Mr Kew's Gunton venison sausage with braised Puy lentils; or gratin of smoked haddock and leek with brioche and gruyère crust. Robust main courses might take in slow-roasted Old Spot pork belly with curly kale and sweet potato dauphinoise; or confit duck with thyme roasted red onion, celeriac mash and rich Madeira sauce. Vegetarians may select the creamy gnocchi with butternut squash, baby spinach and toasted pine nuts. This beautiful inn is said to be haunted by Anne Boleyn's ghost, who wanders in the adjacent courtyard and charming garden. Booking for meals may be required.

Open all day 11–11 summer (1–3 6–11 winter) Closed: 25 Dec, Sun eve ⊕ FREE HOUSE ◄ Adnams Southwold Bitter & Regatta, Woodforde's Wherry & Nelson's Revenge, Wolf Coyote Ŏ Aspall, Norfolk. **Facilities** Children welcome Children's portions Garden Parking Wi-fi

BRANCASTER   Map 13 TF74

The Ship Hotel
PICK OF THE PUBS

Main Rd PE31 8AP ☎ **01485 210333**
e-mail: thebar@shiphotelnorfolk.co.uk
dir: *On A149 in village centre*

TV chef and hotelier Chris Coubrough snapped up the faded and forlorn Ship Hotel, set in a prime coastal location opposite the access road to Brancaster beach, in 2009 to enhance his portfolio of chic inns along the north Norfolk coast. He embarked on a stunning refurbishment of the property, pushing open the doors in May 2010 and business has been brisk ever since. Coast path walkers, beach bums and families flock by to rest and refuel on some cracking modern pub food prepared from fresh produce sourced from local farmers and fisherman. Be tempted by a 'Ship Classic', perhaps braised gammon with new potatoes and parsley sauce; or tuck into sea bass with shellfish and tomato linguine; slow-cooked duck hash with fried duck egg and wild mushroom jus; or confit duck leg and balsamic jus. Wash it down with a pint of Adnams and relax in the gorgeous bar and dining rooms, where you can expect rug-strewn wood floors, wood-burning stoves, contemporary Farrow & Ball hues, shelves full of books, quirky antiques, scrubbed wooden

tables and a distinct nautical feel. Booking for meals may be required.

Open all day all wk ⊕ FREE HOUSE/FLYING KIWI INNS ◄ Jo C's Norfolk Kiwi, Adnams Southwold Bitter Ŏ Aspall. **Facilities** Children welcome Children's menu Children's portions Garden Parking Wi-fi

BRANCASTER STAITHE   Map 13 TF74

The Jolly Sailors

PE31 8BJ ☎ **01485 210314**
e-mail: info@jollysailorsbrancaster.co.uk
dir: *On A149 coast road midway between Hunstanton & Wells-next-the-Sea*

Very much a hub of village life, The Jolly Sailors was restored to its former glory while retaining all of its unique charm and character. It's the brewery tap for the Brancaster micro-brewery, and also serves great pub food like whitebait with bread and butter; mussels caught 'just over there'; pan-fried pigeon breast with mash, red cabbage and gravy; and home-made hot or cold Scotch egg. A new addition is the 'Jolly' ice cream beach hut in the garden. There are quiz, themed and local live music nights, and an ale and music festival in June.

Open all wk Mon-Thu 12-3 6-11 Fri 12-3 5-11 (Mon-Fri all day spring & summer) Sat 12-11 Sun 12-10.30 **Bar Meals** L served (winter) Mon-Fri 12-2 (all day spring & summer), Sat-Sun 12-9 D served (winter) Mon-Fri 6-9 (all day spring & summer), Sat-Sun 12-9 Av main course £9.20 **Restaurant** Av 3 course à la carte fr £19.70 ⊕ FREE HOUSE ◄ Brancaster Oyster Catcher & Best, Woodforde's Wherry, Adnams, Guest ales Ŏ Westons Stowford Press. ♟ 10 **Facilities** ♣ Children welcome Children's menu Children's portions Play area Garden Beer festival Parking Wi-fi ▭ (notice required)

The White Horse ★★★ HL ⑩⑩
PICK OF THE PUBS

PE31 8BY ☎ **01485 210262**
e-mail: reception@whitehorsebrancaster.co.uk
dir: *A149 (coast road), midway between Hunstanton & Wells-next-the-Sea*

One of the best views in this part of Norfolk – straight over glorious tidal marshes to Scolt Head Island – can be savoured from the airy conservatory restaurant, summer sun deck and elegant bedrooms at this stylish inn on the Norfolk coastal path. Reflecting the view, colours are muted and natural, and beach-found objects are complemented by contemporary artworks. Scrubbed pine tables and high-backed settles in the bar create a welcoming atmosphere, while alfresco dining in the sunken front garden is a popular warm-weather option, accompanied by Brancaster Best bitter. The extensive, daily-changing conservatory restaurant menu (two AA Rosettes) champions the freshest local seafood, including seasonal fish and shellfish gathered at the foot of the garden. Typically, follow tempura Brancaster oysters, with mullet with a bean, chorizo and tomato ragout, or cod, smoked haddock and chive beignet with wholegrain

continued

BRANCASTER STAITHE *continued*

mustard cream. Meaty options may include Norfolk game and ale stew. There are also good bar meals, breakfasts and puddings – try the pistachio and olive oil cake. Booking for meals may be required.

Open all day all wk 11-11 (Sun 11-10.30) (open from 9am for breakfast) **Bar Meals** L served all wk 11-9 D served all wk 11-9 Av main course £14.50 food served all day **Restaurant** L served all wk 12-2 D served all wk 6.30-9 Av 3 course à la carte fr £28 ⊕ FREE HOUSE ◀ Adnams Southwold Bitter, Woodforde's Wherry, Brancaster Best & Oyster Catcher, Guest ales ♂ Aspall, Whin Hill. ♛ 16 **Facilities** ✿ Children welcome Children's menu Children's portions Garden Parking Wi-fi **Rooms** 15

BRISLEY   Map 13 TF92

The Brisley Bell Inn & Restaurant ★★★ INN

The Green NR20 5DW ☎ 01362 668686
e-mail: info@brisleybell-inn.co.uk
dir: *On B1145, between Fakenham & East Dereham*

The patio of this attractive 16th-century warm brick-built pub overlooks the largest piece of common land in Norfolk, the tranquil Brisley Common, which amounts to some 200 acres. Inside you'll find a small bar serving reliable ales including their own Taverner's Tipple, with old beams, a large brick fireplace and exposed brick walls. There's a separate dining room, and a wide-ranging menu that takes in bar snacks, fresh locally-sourced produce, and popular Sunday roasts. If you would like to stay over to explore the area, then there are comfortable bedrooms available. Look out for the beer festival. Booking for meals may be required.

Open all day all wk **Bar Meals** L served all wk 12-2.30 D served Sun-Thu 6-8, Fri-Sat 6-9 Av main course £5.95 **Restaurant** L served all wk 12-2.30 D served Sun-Thu

6-8, Fri-Sat 6-9 Fixed menu price fr £10.45 Av 3 course à la carte fr £17.95 ⊕ FREE HOUSE ◀ Taverner's Tipple, Greene King IPA, Hardys & Hansons Olde Trip, Woodforde's ♂ Aspall. **Facilities** Children welcome Children's menu Children's portions Garden Beer festival Parking Wi-fi 🚌 **Rooms** 3

BURNHAM MARKET   Map 13 TF84

The Hoste Arms ★★★ HL ⊛⊛

PICK OF THE PUBS

See Pick of the Pubs on opposite page
See advert below

BURNHAM THORPE   Map 13 TF84

The Lord Nelson

PICK OF THE PUBS

Walsingham Rd PE31 8HN ☎ 01328 738241
e-mail: enquiries@nelsonslocal.co.uk
web: www.nelsonslocal.co.uk
dir: *B1355 (Burnham Market to Fakenham road), pub 9m from Fakenham & 1.75m from Burnham Market. Pub near church opposite playing fields*

This pub started life in 1637 as The Plough and was renamed The Lord Nelson in 1798, to honour Horatio

Nelson who was born in the village. Located opposite the delightful village cricket ground and bowling green, it has an atmospheric interior that has changed little over the past 370 years; you can even sit on Nelson's high-backed settle. Drinks are served from the taproom, with real ales drawn straight from the cask. In the cosy bar you can also partake in unique rum-based tipples such as Nelson's Blood. The kitchen aims to cook dishes with balance between flavours, so that the quality of the ingredients shines. A typical meal is farmhouse pâté with toast and red onion marmalade followed by pan-fried salmon in a green herb crust with beurre blanc and duchess potatoes, with apple pie and vanilla ice cream for dessert. Children will enjoy the huge garden. From May to September, weekend walking tours of Nelson's village are available. Booking for meals may be required.

Open all wk 12-3 6-11 (Jul-Aug 12-11) **Bar Meals** L served all wk 12-2.30 D served all wk 6-9 **Restaurant** L served all wk 12-2.30 D served all wk 6-9 ⊕ GREENE KING ◀ Abbot Ale & IPA, Woodforde's Wherry. ♛ 14 **Facilities** ✿ Children welcome Children's menu Play area Garden Parking Wi-fi 🚌

Save on hotels. Book at **theAA.com/hotel**

NORFOLK 367 ENGLAND

PICK OF THE PUBS

The Hoste Arms ★★★ HL ❀❀

The Green PE31 8HD ☎ 01328 738777
e-mail: reception@hostearms.co.uk
web: www.hostearms.co.uk
dir: *Signed from B1155, 5m W of Wells-next-the-Sea*

It's a fascinating thought that one of Norfolk's most praised destination dining inns should once have been local boy Horatio Nelson's Saturday morning local. A magnificent combination of top-notch two-AA Rosette food and distinctive accommodation, this cream-painted, pantiled old village manor house couldn't want for a better location, being in an Area of Outstanding Natural Beauty, with the Peddars Way, Norfolk Coast Path, marshlands, endless beaches and tremendous wildlife, all virtually on the doorstep. A hotel since 1651, it has also been a courthouse, livestock market and even a brothel, but now, with bedrooms spread across six properties in and around Burnham Market, a cosy bar, three main restaurants, lounge, conservatory and pretty walled garden behind the terrace restaurant, it's a hotel like never before. The all-East Anglian real ale line-up includes, appropriately, Nelson's Revenge from Woodforde, while the 150-bin list features some of the world's finest wines. Examples of items on the lunch and dinner menus are starters of Brancaster oysters; the 'Norfolk coastline assiette' for two; and home-smoked pigeon breasts with pearl barley and portabello mushroom

risotto. Typical main courses are salmon, tiger prawn and peanut curry with jasmine rice, crushed peanuts and sliced chilli; loin of Holkham venison with sweet braised red cabbage, parsnip purée, buttered curly kale and redcurrant jus; and steamed steak and kidney suet pudding with honey-glazed parsnips, Chantenay carrots and wilted baby spinach. A vegetarian might home in on risotto of roasted butternut squash with sautéed wild mushrooms, shaved parmesan, pumpkin seeds and truffle oil. Traditional roast beef is available Sunday lunchtimes. A selection of Norfolk cheeses is offered as a dessert, as too are apple and vanilla tarte Tatin with Calvados ice cream, and Hoste trio, a partnership of iced yoghurt parfait, dark chocolate fondant and sticky toffee. Booking for meals may be required.

Open all day all wk **Bar Meals** L served all wk 12-2 D served all wk 6-9 Av main course £12.75 **Restaurant** L served all wk 12-2 D served all wk 6-9 Av 3 course à la carte fr £27.75 🛢 FREE HOUSE ◖ Adnams Broadside, Woodforde's Wherry & Nelson's Revenge. 🍷 16 **Facilities** Children's menu Children's portions 🐾 Garden Parking Wi-fi **Rooms** 34

BURSTON
Map 13 TM18

The Crown

Mill Rd IP22 5TW ☎ **01379 741257**
e-mail: enquiries@burstoncrown.com
dir: *NE of Diss*

Steve and Bev Kembery have transformed their 16th-century pub by the green into a cracking community pub, drawing locals in for top-notch ale and food, organising the village fête, hosting three beer festivals a year, and offering a weekly busker's night and regular theme nights. As well as a decent pint of Adnams, you can tuck into roast beef ciabatta with Dijon mayonnaise or sausages and mash in the bar, or look to the carte for salt and pepper squid, honey roast duck breast, and chicken supreme with tarragon and cream sauce. Well worth finding. Booking for meals may be required.

Open all day all wk **Bar Meals** L served Mon-Sat 12-2, Sun 12-4 D served Mon-Sat 6.30-9 Av main course £10 **Restaurant** L served Mon-Sat 12-2, Sun 12-4 D served Mon-Sat 6.30-9 Av 3 course à la carte fr £21 ⊕ FREE HOUSE ◀ Adnams Southwold Bitter & Old Ale, Elmtree Burston's Cuckoo, Greene King Abbot Ale, Elgood's ♂ Aspall, Burnards Norfolk Cider. **Facilities** Children welcome Children's menu Children's portions Garden Beer festival Parking Wi-fi ▭

CLEY NEXT THE SEA
Map 13 TG04

The George Hotel

PICK OF THE PUBS

See Pick of the Pubs on opposite page

COLTISHALL
Map 13 TG21

Kings Head

26 Wroxham Rd NR12 7EA ☎ **01603 737426**
e-mail: contact@kingsheadcoltishall.co.uk
dir: *A47 (Norwich ring road) onto B1150 to North Walsham at Coltishall. Right at petrol station, follow to right past church. Pub on right by car park*

Standing on the banks of the River Bure, this 17th-century free house is right in the heart of the Norfolk Broads. Hire cruisers are available at nearby Wroxham, and fishing boats can be hired at the pub. If you prefer to stay on dry land you'll find a warm welcome at the bar, with a range of real ales that includes Adnams Bitter, Directors and Marston's Pedigree. There's an inviting menu, too, served in both the bar and the restaurant. Booking for meals may be required.

Open all wk 11-3 6-12 Closed: 26 Dec ⊕ FREE HOUSE ◀ Adnams Southwold Bitter, Courage Directors, Marston's Pedigree, Fuller's London Pride. **Facilities** Children welcome Children's menu Children's portions Parking

CROMER
Map 13 TG24

The Red Lion Food and Rooms ★★★★ INN

Brook St NR27 9HD ☎ **01263 514964**
e-mail: info@redlion-cromer.co.uk
dir: *From A149 in Cromer right into Church St, leads to Garden St. Right into Jetty St, left into Tucker St. Pub on corner of Brook St*

Built on the late 1800s, The Red Lion stands in the heart of Cromer, overlooking the pier and award-winning beach. It was headquarters of the area's coastal defences during World War II, and tunnels reputedly connected it to other strategic buildings in town. Now refurbished it retains many original features. Beer options are an ale drinker's dream – try a pint of Green Jack Brewery Lurcher. Short but high quality menus proffer the likes of smoked haddock, crayfish and mussel chowder; and rump steak with peppercorn sauce and all the trimmings. There are light, comfortable rooms, many with sea views. Booking for meals may be required.

Open all day all wk **Bar Meals** L served all wk 12-2.30 D served all wk 6-9.30 **Restaurant** L served all wk 12-2.30 D served all wk 6-9.30 ⊕ FREE HOUSE ◀ Bees Wobble, Green Jack Lurcher Stout, Woodforde's Nelson's Revenge, Humpty Dumpty Railway Sleeper, Adnams Broadside. ₹ 9 **Facilities** ❖ Children welcome Children's menu Children's portions Beer festival Parking Wi-fi ▭ **Rooms** 15

EAST RUDHAM
Map 13 TF82

The Crown Inn

PICK OF THE PUBS

The Green PE31 8RD ☎ **01485 528530**
e-mail: reception@crowninnnorfolk.co.uk
dir: *On A148, 6m from Fakenham on King's Lynn road*

Standing at the head of the village green on the A148, the award-winning Crown at East Rudham is part of TV chef Chris Coubrough's thriving Flying Kiwi mini-empire of pubs along the Norfolk coast. It draws the crowds for its charming, spruced-up interior, which successfully blends traditional period features (low beams, rug-strewn wooden floor, open log fires) with contemporary comforts - cool Farrow & Ball colours, high-backed leather chairs at scrubbed tables, shelves of books, fresh flowers and chunky church candles. Equally bang up-to-date is the food, with the menu changing every two weeks and listing good modern British dishes prepared from fresh Norfolk produce. Tuck into salmon and brown shrimp rillettes with toast and caper berries; then follow with roast chump of lamb with roast Mediterranean vegetables, crispy polenta and black olive jus; leaving room for raspberry brûlée tart. Expect decent lunchtime sandwiches and proper kids' food.

Open all day all wk ⊕ FREE HOUSE/FLYING KIWI INNS ◀ Adnams Southwold Bitter & Broadside, Flying Kiwi Homebrew ♂ Aspall. **Facilities** Children welcome Children's menu Children's portions Parking Wi-fi

EAST RUSTON
Map 13 TG32

The Butchers Arms

Oak Ln NR12 9JG ☎ **01692 650237**
e-mail: info@thebutchersarms.biz
dir: *From A149 SE of North Walsham follow signs for Briggate, Honing & East Ruston. Oak Ln off School Rd*

In the heart of the Broads, this quintessential beamed pub started life as three terraced cottages in the early 1800s. Today it's a timeless village pub, without jukebox or pool table; you'll just find 'Mavis', a 1954 Comma fire engine, parked outside. Landlady Julie Oatham has been here for over 20 years, and ensures a welcoming atmosphere. Real ales from local breweries are served alongside traditional favourites of liver, bacon and tomato casserole or steak, ale and mushroom pie. There is a beer garden and vine-covered patio for summer dining.

Open 12-2.30 6.30-11 Closed: Mon (Jan-Mar) **Bar Meals** L served all wk 12-2 D served all wk 7-8.30 Av main course £8.75 **Restaurant** L served all wk 12-2 D served all wk 7-8.30 Fixed menu price fr £5 Av 3 course à la carte fr £11 ⊕ FREE HOUSE ◀ Morland Old Speckled Hen, Greene King IPA, Adnams, Woodforde's. **Facilities** ❖ Children welcome Children's menu Children's portions Garden Beer festival Parking ▭ (notice required) **Notes** ⊛

EATON
Map 13 TG20

The Red Lion

50 Eaton St NR4 7LD ☎ **01603 454787**
e-mail: admin@redlion-eaton.co.uk
dir: *Off A11, 2m S of Norwich city centre*

This heavily beamed 17th-century coaching inn has bags of character, thanks to its Dutch gable ends, panelled walls and inglenook fireplaces. The covered terrace enables customers to enjoy one of the real ales or sample a glass from the wine list outside during the summer months. The extensive menus offer everything from Hungarian beef goulash soup to pan-fried or deep-fried skate wing with capers, or Norfolk rabbit, bacon and leek puff pastry pie. There's a light meals and snack menu too. Booking for meals may be required.

Open all day all wk ◀ Adnams Southwold Bitter, Woodforde's Wherry, Fuller's London Pride. **Facilities** Children welcome Children's menu Children's portions Garden Parking Wi-fi

Save on hotels. Book at **theAA.com/hotel**

NORFOLK 369 ENGLAND

PICK OF THE PUBS

The George Hotel

CLEY NEXT THE SEA Map 13 TG04

High St NR25 7RN ☎ 01263 740652
e-mail: info@thegeorgehotelatcley.co.uk
web: www.thegeorgehotelatcley.co.uk
dir: *On A149 through Cley next the Sea,*
approx 4m from Holt

The salt marshes of the north Norfolk
coast are a paradise for birdwatchers,
which is good news for The George,
whose beer garden backs on to them,
and the village's famous mill and
Blakeney Harbour are just a mile away.
Indeed, this old hotel on historic Cley's
winding High Street, with its Georgian
and Flemish-style architecture, has
been an ornithological focal point for
many years. Ask to see its 'bird bible', a
record of sightings kept by visiting
observers. The welcoming bar is home to
several real ales, including Yetman's
from just along the coast at Holt. You
can snack in the lounge bar or dine in
the light, painting-filled restaurant. The
daily-changing menu offers only the
best of local fresh ingredients, and fish
and seafood is a real strength, of
course, not least that which has broken
its journey from sea to the kitchen in
Cley Smokehouse a few doors away, and
whose output can be sampled in a
smokehouse platter of smoked salmon,
mackerel and crevettes. At lunchtime

the menu offers starters of curried
potted prawns; and leek and potato
soup, and main meals, such as lamb
and mint pie, as well as sandwiches,
including ham and Dijon mustard; and
salmon and cream cheese, for example.
Dinner, depending on the season, might
bring an eight-ounce rib-eye steak with
slow-roasted tomato, French fries and
crispy onion rings; pan-fried pork chop
with chorizo, chickpea and pepper
casserole; and spinach, apple and
goat's cheese parcel with sautéed
potatoes and mixed leaf salad. Desserts
include star anise pannacotta with
rhubarb and ginger sorbet, and Black
Forest mess. Promotions include Pie and
a Pint, and Curry and a Pint evenings.

Open all day all wk 10.30am-11.30pm
Meals L served Mon-Sat 12-2.15, Sun
12.30-2.30 D served Mon-Sat 6.30-9,
Sun 6.30-8.30 Av main course £11.95
Fixed menu price fr £19.95 Av 3 course
à la carte fr £24.95 ⊕ FREE HOUSE
◀ Adnams Broadside, Woodforde's
Wherry, Yetman's, Guest ales ♂ Aspall.
♥ 8 **Facilities** Children welcome
Children's menu ✿ Garden Parking Wi-fi
🚌 (notice required)

ERPINGHAM — Map 13 TG13

The Saracen's Head

PICK OF THE PUBS

Wolterton NR11 7LZ ☎ 01263 768909
e-mail: info@saracenshead-norfolk.co.uk
dir: *From A140, 2.5m N of Aylsham, left, through
Erpingham. Pass Spread Eagle on left. Through
Calthorpe, 0.5m, pub on right*

The privately owned Saracen's Head is deep among the
fields down country lanes – and you do find yourself
wondering why there's a pub in such a lonely spot. The
answer is that it was once a coach house, built in Tuscan
farmhouse style in 1806 for neighbouring Wolterton Hall.
Its arty, parlour-room atmosphere is the legacy of the
former owner, who has now been succeeded by Tim and
Janie Elwes. You may eat in one of the bars, where Suffolk
and Norfolk real ales are on handpump, or in the
restaurant, where a sample three-course meal might
comprise grilled haloumi on lavender (a local crop) croûte
with sun-blushed tomatoes; roast Norfolk pheasant with
Calvados and cream; or baked Cromer crab with apple
and sherry; and poached pears in spicy red wine. For a
really quiet dinner or meal, sit out in the sheltered
courtyard garden. Booking for meals may be required.

Open 11.30-3 6-11 (Sun 12-3 7-10.30) **Closed:** 25-29
Dec, Mon (ex BH), Tue L (Oct-May) ⊕ FREE HOUSE
◀ Adnams Southwold Bitter, Woodforde's Wherry, Guest
ales. **Facilities** Children welcome Children's menu
Children's portions Garden Parking

FAKENHAM — Map 13 TF92

The Wensum Lodge Hotel

Bridge St NR21 9AY ☎ 01328 862100
e-mail: enquiries@wensumlodge.fsnet.co.uk
dir: *In town centre*

Idyllically located by the River Wensum just three
minutes' walk from Fakenham, this lovely pub has a
stream flowing through its garden and offers guests free
fishing on the river. The building dates from around 1700,
and was originally the grain store for the adjoining mill.
Fine ales are complemented by home-cooked food
prepared from locally supplied ingredients, with
baguettes, jacket potatoes and an all-day breakfast on
the light bite menu, and a carte menu for heartier fare.
An ideal base for cycling, bird-watching, fishing and
horse-racing.

Open all wk ⊕ FREE HOUSE ◀ Greene King Abbot Ale &
IPA, Old Mill Traditional Bitter. **Facilities** Children
welcome Garden Parking

GREAT RYBURGH — Map 13 TF92

The Blue Boar Inn

NR21 0DX ☎ 01328 829212
e-mail: blueboarinn@ryburgh.co.uk
dir: *Off A1067 4m S of Fakenham*

This former coaching inn, which dates back to 1685, has
been lovingly restored, retaining period features like the
inglenook fireplace and tiled floors. The inn stands
opposite the round towered Saxon church of St Andrew
with the River Wensum flowing nearby. Nowadays the inn
serves a good range of real ales alongside home-cooked,
locally sourced food. Typical choices include Norfolk beef
and ale pie; Brancaster mussels with cider and cream;
and marmalade bread-and-butter pudding.

Open 11.30-2.30 6.30-11.30 **Closed:** Tue **Bar Meals** L
served Sun-Mon, Wed-Fri 11.30-2 D served Wed-Mon 6-9
Av main course £9.95 **Restaurant** L served Sun-Mon,
Wed-Fri 11.30-2 D served Wed-Mon 6-9 ⊕ FREE HOUSE
◀ Adnams Southwold Bitter, Winter's Golden & Revenge,
Guinness, Staropramen, Yetman's Ⴢ Addlestones,
Westons Stowford Press, Aspall. ☻ 8 **Facilities** Children
welcome Children's menu Children's portions Play area
Family room Garden Parking Wi-fi ⛟

HEVINGHAM — Map 13 TG12

Marsham Arms Coaching Inn

Holt Rd NR10 5NP ☎ 01603 754268
e-mail: info@marshamarms.co.uk
dir: *On B1149 N of Norwich airport, 2m through Horsford
towards Holt*

The name of this country inn comes from Victorian
philanthropist and landowner Robert Marsham, who built
the Marsham Arms as a roadside hostel for poor farm
labourers. Some original features remain, including the
wooden beams and large open fireplace. Real ales are
served straight from the barrel. The seasonal menu uses
fresh local produce, and there are always vegetarian and
gluten-free options. Main courses might include whole
oven-roasted partridge, creamed bacon and cabbage
with Lyonnaise potatoes, Cajun-spiced salmon fillet, and
haunch of venison with a wild mushroom and red wine
sauce. There is a spacious garden with a paved patio.
Look out for events such as the monthly jazz evenings.
The inn holds a Green Tourism award.

Open all day all wk **Bar Meals** L served Mon-Fri 12-2.30,
Sat-Sun all day D served Mon-Fri 6-9, Sat-Sun all day
Restaurant L served Mon-Fri 12-2.30, Sat-Sun all day
D served Mon-Fri 6-9.30, Sat-Sun all day ⊕ FREE HOUSE
◀ Adnams Southwold Bitter & Broadside, Woodforde's
Wherry, Mauldons, Worthington's Ⴢ Aspall. ☻
Facilities ✿ Children welcome Children's menu
Children's portions Garden Parking Wi-fi ⛟ (notice
required)

HEYDON — Map 13 TG12

Earle Arms

The Street NR11 6AD ☎ 01263 587376
e-mail: theearlearms@gmail.com
dir: *Signed between Cawston & Corpusty on B1149 (Holt
to Norwich road)*

Horse-racing memorabilia adorn the walls of this
16th-century free house, courtesy of the horse-racing
mad landlord. Situated on the green in a pretty, privately
owned village, it is thought that Oliver Cromwell once
stayed here, and Heydon itself is often used as a film
location, so stars of stage and screen have enjoyed a
good choice of dishes complemented by daily specials.
One of the two rooms offers service through a hatch to
the tables in the attractive back garden. There is a beer
festival held on St George's Day. Booking for meals may
be required.

Open 12-3 6-11 **Closed:** Mon **Bar Meals** L served Tue-Sun
12-2 D served Tue-Sun 6-8.30 Av main course £10
Restaurant L served Tue-Sun 12-2 D served Tue-Sat
6-8.30 ⊕ FREE HOUSE ◀ Woodforde's Wherry, Adnams,
Guest ales. ☻ 16 **Facilities** Children welcome Children's
menu Children's portions Garden Beer festival Parking
Wi-fi ⛟

HINGHAM — Map 13 TG00

The White Hart Hotel

3 Market Place NR9 4AF ☎ 01953 850214
e-mail: whitehart@flyingkiwiinns.co.uk
dir: *In market square on B1108*

In picturesque Hingham's Georgian market place, this
long-established coaching inn reopened in 2011 after
extensive refurbishment. Elements of the old inn remain
in the beams and open fireplaces; however this is
unashamedly a gastro-pub drawing on the larder of East
Anglia, twinned with contemporary design ideals,
resulting in a memorable mix of retro rustic and exotic
touches. The Norfolk Kiwi beer here is brewed by Jo, the
wife of owner/TV chef Chris Coubrough. The modern
British cuisine is suitably inspiring; salt and cracked
black pepper squid with home-made chilli jam; and
marinated rump of lamb with tabouleh salad,
home-made houmous and baba ghanoush take the eye.

Open all day all wk **Bar Meals** L served all wk 12-2.30
D served all wk 6.30-9.30 Av main course £15.95
Restaurant L served all wk 12-2.30 D served all wk
6.30-9.30 Fixed menu price fr £15.95 Av 3 course à la
carte fr £28 ⊕ FREE HOUSE ◀ Adnams Southwold Bitter,
Jo C's Norfolk Kiwi, Guest ale Ⴢ Aspall. **Facilities** ✿
Children welcome Children's menu Children's portions
Garden Parking Wi-fi ⛟

Save on hotels. Book at **theAA.com/hotel**

NORFOLK 371 **ENGLAND**

HOLKHAM	Map 13 TF84

Victoria at Holkham ★★ SHL ◉◉

PICK OF THE PUBS

Park Rd NR23 1RG ☎ 01328 711008
e-mail: victoria@holkham.co.uk
dir: *On A149, 3m W of Wells-next-the-Sea*

The Victoria stands at the gates of landlord Lord Coke's Palladian ancestral home, Holkham Hall, just minutes from the golden sands of Holkham Beach. Its opulent, colonial-style interior is full of furniture and accessories from Rajahstan and other exotic places. Outside is a courtyard where summer barbecues are popular. Tom Coke would argue that the Victoria's main attraction is what he calls 'some of the most consistently good food in north Norfolk'. Key words here are fresh, local and seasonal, whether it be shellfish, fish or samphire from the north Norfolk coast; beef from farms on the Holkham Estate; organic chickens from a tenant farmer; venison from the herd of fallow deer or, in the winter, wild game from family shoots. Perhaps choices might be pumpkin and truffle risotto; slow-braised beef with pomme purée; or Holkham venison with braised red cabbage; and chilled vanilla rice pudding with stewed English plums. Booking for meals may be required.

Open all day all wk 11-11 ⊕ HOLKHAM ESTATE ◀ Adnams Southwold Bitter ◔ Aspall. **Facilities** Children welcome Children's menu Children's portions Play area Garden Parking Wi-fi **Rooms** 10

HOLT	Map 13 TG03

The Pigs

PICK OF THE PUBS

Norwich Rd, Edgefield NR24 2RL ☎ 01263 587634
e-mail: info@thepigs.org.uk
web: www.thepigs.org.uk
dir: *On B1149*

This 17th-century country inn was taken over by the three ambitious co-owners seven years ago and they have transformed the place into a thriving local pub where community spirit and culinary endeavour combine in a celebration of all things Norfolk. The lovely tranquil setting at the fringe of the village allows for a peaceful garden, whilst locals barter their fresh fruit and vegetables over the bar for a pint or two, practise darts or bar billiards and quaff Old Spot bitter – what else. An incredibly versatile menu emerges from the kitchen, utilising neglected cuts of meat and produce from the pub's adjoining allotment. Crispy pig's ears with tartare sauce, followed by the slow-cooked belly of pork should fit the bill. If pork-based treats aren't your thing, then slow-cooked duck leg with orange, pickled red cabbage, watercress and chips may tempt. A children's cookery school is particularly popular. Booking for meals may be required.

Open all wk Mon-Sat 11-2.30 6-11 (Sun & BH 12-9) **Bar Meals** L served Mon-Sat 12-2.30, Sun & BH 12-9 D served Mon-Sat 6-9 **Restaurant** L served Mon-Sat 12-2.30, Sun & BH 12-9 D served Mon-Sat 6-9 ⊕ FREE HOUSE ◀ Woodforde's Wherry, Greene King Abbot Ale, Wolf Old Spot, Adnams Broadside & Southwold Bitter. ♈ 17 **Facilities** Children welcome Children's menu Children's portions Play area Family room Garden Parking ▥ (notice required)

HORSTEAD	Map 13 TG21

Recruiting Sergeant

Norwich Rd NR12 7EE ☎ 01603 737077
dir: *On B1150 between Norwich & North Walsham*

Matthew and Nicola Colchester have developed an enviable local reputation for food at this award-winning colour-washed brick and flint free house. Fresh local produce is the foundation of their ever-changing menu, which might include Binham Blue salad with pickled pears; toasted steak sandwich, red onion marmalade and chips; chargrilled Cajun spiced swordfish and king prawn brochettes on Caesar salad; and a giant bowl of Brancaster mussels. Booking for meals may be required.

Open all day all wk 11-11 (Sun 12-10.30) ⊕ FREE HOUSE ◀ Greene King Abbot Ale, Adnams, Woodforde's, Courage ◔ Aspall. **Facilities** Children welcome Children's menu Children's portions Garden Parking

HUNSTANTON	Map 12 TF64

The Ancient Mariner Inn ★★★★ HL
NEW

Golf Course Rd, Old Hunstanton PE36 6JJ
☎ 01485 536390
e-mail: conference@lestrangearms.co.uk
dir: *Off A149 1m N of Hunstanton. Left at sharp right bend by pitch & putt course*

Adjoining Le Strange Arms Hotel in Old Hunstanton, whose grounds sweep down to a glorious beach, this traditional and very popular pub enjoys unrivalled sea views - best enjoyed at sunset when the sun sinks into The Wash. Close to RSPB reserves and Sandringham House, it makes a popular stop, the draw being the award-winning, Cask Marque ales. There is a seafaring atmosphere, and a classic pub menu is offered. Accommodation is available. Booking for meals may be required.

Open all day all wk **Bar Meals** L served all wk 12-9 D served all wk 12-9 Av main course £9 food served all day **Restaurant** L served all wk 12-9 D served all wk 12-9 food served all day ⊕ FREE HOUSE ◀ Adnams, Theakston, Wychwood, Shepherd Neame. ♈ 10

Facilities ⚘ Children welcome Children's menu Children's portions Play area Family room Garden Beer festival Parking Wi-fi ▥ (notice required) **Rooms** 43

The King William IV Country Inn & Restaurant

Heacham Rd, Sedgeford PE36 5LU ☎ 01485 571765
e-mail: info@thekingwilliamsedgeford.co.uk
web: www.thekingwilliamsedgeford.co.uk
dir: *A149 to Hunstanton, right at Norfolk Lavender in Heacham onto B1454, signed Docking. 2m to Sedgeford*

An inn for 175 years, this extensively refurbished and extended free house is tucked away in the village of Sedgeford and conveniently close to the north Norfolk coastline. Made cosy by winter log fires, it has four dining areas, plus a covered alfresco terrace for warmer months. At the height of the season, you'll find five real ales on tap, and extensive menus to please everyone: expect the likes of sautéed lamb's kidneys with pasta shells and cream sauce; poached salmon fillet with hollandaise; and French apricot tartlet. Booking for meals may be required.

Open all day 11-11 (Sun 12-10.30) Closed: Mon L (ex BH) **Bar Meals** L served Tue-Sat 12-2, Sun 12-2.30 D served all wk 6.30-9 **Restaurant** L served Tue-Sat 12-2, Sun 12-2.30 D served all wk 6.30-9 ⊕ FREE HOUSE ◀ Woodforde's Wherry, Adnams Southwold Bitter, Greene King Abbot Ale, Morland Old Speckled Hen, Guest ale. ♈ 9 **Facilities** ⚘ Children welcome Children's menu Children's portions Family room Garden Parking Wi-fi

HUNWORTH   Map 13 TG03

The Hunny Bell

PICK OF THE PUBS

The Green NR24 2AA ☎ 01263 712300
e-mail: hunnybell@animalinns.co.uk
dir: *From Holt take B1110. 1st right to Hunworth*

Set next to the green in pretty Hunworth in the peaceful
Glaven Valley, just two miles south of Holt, this
18th-century gem of a pub provides a quiet haven away
from the bustling beaches and villages on the coast.
In-the-know foodies retreat from the salt marshes to the
cosy snug and the rustic-chic beamed main bar, which
successfully blend historic charm with a contemporary
feel. From this blend you get real coffee, pints of Wherry
and some imaginative pub food. Kick off with pressed
Norfolk reared ham hock and green peppercorn terrine;
follow with braised Stody Estate pheasant coq au vin with
bubble-and-squeak, braised red cabbage and button
mushrooms; and finish with the assiette of chocolate
desserts. Walkers will find excellent lunchtime
sandwiches. Outside, there's a terrace overlooking the
green, as well as a charming old-world English garden. A
beer festival is held in late August. As we went to press, a
change of hands was taking place.

Open all wk 12-3 6-11 **Bar Meals** L served all wk 12-2.30
D served all wk 6-9 **Restaurant** L served all wk 12-2.30
D served all wk 6-9 ⊕ FREE HOUSE/ANIMAL INNS
◀ Woodforde's Wherry, Adnams, Greene King, Elgood's,
Oakham Ŏ Aspall. ♈ 10 **Facilities** Children welcome
Children's menu Children's portions Garden Beer festival
Parking Wi-fi ⊝ (notice required)

INGHAM   Map 13 TG32

The Ingham Swan

PICK OF THE PUBS

Swan Corner, Sea Palling Rd NR12 9AB
☎ 01692 581099
e-mail: info@theinghamswan.co.uk
dir: *From A149 through Stalham to Ingham*

Flanked by the ruins of Ingham Priory and overlooking
glorious countryside, the thatched and beautifully
preserved 14th-century Swan stands in a picture-book
village close to the Norfolk coast. A sympathetic
refurbishment has retained the building's heritage and
blended it with contemporary décor. Chef-patron Daniel
Smith used to work at Le Gavroche and Morston Hall, and
he sticks to his Norfolk roots with a menu packed with
local produce. Starters of chicken liver parfait with Wherry
chutney and celeriac remoulade, or scallops with
pancetta and cauliflower velouté might precede whole
lemon sole with Brancaster mussel broth, or roast duck
with rich orange jus. Round things off with vanilla
pannacotta served with blood orange sorbet, or rum and
raisin parfait with warm date cake, chocolate mousse
and hazelnut caramel. Local ales such as Woodforde's
Wherry are complemented by an interesting international
wine list that boasts a number of notable bottles from
France. Booking for meals may be required.

Open 11-3 6-11 Closed: 25-26 Dec, 2wks Jan, Mon **Bar
Meals** Av main course £17 **Restaurant** L served Tue-Sun
(all wk Apr-Oct) D served Tue-Sat (all wk Apr-Oct) Fixed
menu price fr £16.95 Av 3 course à la carte fr £27.50
⊕ WOODFORDE'S ◀ Wherry, Nelson's Revenge, Nog,
Sundew, Admiral's Reserve Ŏ Aspall. ♈ 10
Facilities Children welcome Children's portions Garden
Parking ⊝

ITTERINGHAM   Map 13 TG13

Walpole Arms

NR11 7AR ☎ 01263 587258
e-mail: info@thewalpolearms.co.uk
dir: *From Aylsham towards Blickling. After Blickling Hall
take 1st right to Itteringham*

Tucked away down narrow lanes on the edge of sleepy
Itteringham, close to Blickling Hall (National Trust), this
renowned rural dining venue has been bought by a local
farming family. Reopened in May 2012 following
extensive refurbishment, the oak-beamed bar offers local
Woodforde and Adnams ales on tap, while menus
champion top-notch meats and produce from the family
farm and local artisan producers. Typical dishes may
include ham hock terrine with piccalilli; confit duck leg
with braised chicory, Puy lentils and crispy bacon; and
baked rhubarb and custard cheesecake.

Open all wk 12-3 6-11 (Sat 12-11 Sun 12-5) ⊕ FREE
HOUSE ◀ Adnams Broadside & Southwold Bitter,
Woodforde's Wherry, Guest ales Ŏ Aspall. ♈ **Facilities** ✿
Children welcome Children's menu Play area Garden
Parking

KING'S LYNN   Map 12 TF62

The Stuart House Hotel, Bar &
Restaurant ★★★ HL

35 Goodwins Rd PE30 5QX ☎ 01553 772169
e-mail: reception@stuarthousehotel.co.uk
web: www.stuarthousehotel.co.uk
dir: *Follow signs to town centre, pass under Southgate
Arch, immediate right, in 100yds turn right*

A short walk from King's Lynn's historic town centre
stands this popular hotel and bar, set in attractive
grounds, including a patio and garden for summer
alfresco eating and drinking. Tip-top East Anglian ales
and traditional dishes are served in the bar, and there is
a separate restaurant offering a carte menu and daily
specials. A typical meal may start with brie and
mushroom tart, with pork belly on apple mash with cider

sauce, or sweet chilli beef with noodles for main course. A
programme of events includes regular live music, murder
mystery dinners and an annual beer festival.

Open all wk 5-11 **Bar Meals** D served all wk 6-9.30
Restaurant D served all wk 7-9.30 ⊕ FREE HOUSE
◀ Oakham JHB, Timothy Taylor Landlord, Adnams,
Woodforde's, Greene King. **Facilities** Children's portions
Play area Garden Beer festival Parking Wi-fi ⊝
Rooms 18

LARLING   Map 13 TL98

Angel Inn

PICK OF THE PUBS

NR16 2QU ☎ 01953 717963
e-mail: info@angel-larling.co.uk
dir: *5m from Attleborough, 8m from Thetford. 1m from
station*

On the edge of Breckland and Thetford Forest Park, this
17th-century former coaching inn has been run for more
than 80 years by three generations of the Stammers
family. There's a good, local feel to the heavily-beamed
public bar, with jukebox, dartboard and fruit machine,
while the oak-panelled lounge bar has dining tables with
cushioned wheel-back chairs, an oak settle, a wood
burner and a huge collection of water jugs. Five guest
ales, including a mild, are served, as well as more than a
hundred whiskies. Menus make good use of local
ingredients, with lighter snacks including freshly made
sandwiches, jacket potatoes, ploughman's, burgers and
salads. Typically among the mains are smoked haddock
mornay; Thai green chicken curry; stilton and mushroom
bake; and a pasta dish of salmon and prawn fusilli. Each
August the Angel hosts Norfolk's largest outdoor beer
festival, with over 100 real ales and ciders. Booking for
meals may be required.

Open all day all wk 10am-mdnt **Bar Meals** L served
Sun-Thu 12-9.30, Fri-Sat 12-10 D served Sun-Thu
12-9.30, Fri-Sat 12-10 Av main course £9.95 food served
all day **Restaurant** L served Sun-Thu 12-9.30, Fri-Sat
12-10 D served Sun-Thu 12-9.30, Fri-Sat 12-10 food
served all day ⊕ FREE HOUSE ◀ Adnams Southwold
Bitter, Caledonian Deuchars IPA, Timothy Taylor Landlord,
Mauldons, Hop Back Ŏ Aspall. ♈ 10 **Facilities** Children
welcome Children's menu Children's portions Play area
Garden Beer festival Parking Wi-fi ⊝

LETHERINGSETT   Map 13 TG03

The Kings Head

PICK OF THE PUBS

Holt Rd NR25 7AR ☎ 01263 712691
e-mail: thebar@kingsheadnorfolk.co.uk
dir: *On A148, 1m from Holt. Pub on corner*

Chris Coubrough's thriving Norfolk-based Flying Kiwi Inns
snapped up this rather grand, manor-like building on the
edge of upmarket Holt in 2009 and revamped it in
impressive style. Expect an elegant, rustic-chic feel
throughout the rambling dining areas that radiate from

Save on hotels. Book at **theAA.com/hotel**

NORFOLK 373 ENGLAND

the central bar, with rugs on terracotta tiles, squashy sofas and leather chairs fronting blazing winter log fires, feature bookcases, warm heritage hues, and an eclectic mix of old dining tables. The atmosphere is informal, the beer is East Anglian-brewed – try a pint of Adnams – and the food modern British and prepared from top-notch ingredients supplied by the pub's own herd of Dexter cows, local farmers, fisherman and artisan producers. This translates to ham hock, pistachio and mustard terrine with piccalilli; Norfolk duck cassoulet; sea bass with shellfish bouillabaisse, saffron potatoes and garlic rouille; and vanilla pannacotta with rhubarb. This award-winning gastro-pub has superb alfresco areas including an excellent children's garden and a gravelled front terrace with posh benches and brollies. Booking for meals may be required.

Open all day all wk ⊕ FREE HOUSE/FLYING KIWI INNS ◀ Adnams Southwold Bitter, Jo C's Norfolk Kiwi ♂ Aspall. **Facilities** Children welcome Children's menu Children's portions Play area Garden Parking Wi-fi

LITTLE FRANSHAM
Map 13 TF91

The Canary and Linnet

Main Rd NR19 2JW ☎ 01362 687027
dir: *On A47 between Dereham & Swaffham*

The sign outside this attractive, former blacksmith's cottage once showed footballers in Norwich City (Canaries) and King's Lynn (Linnets) strips, but now features two birds in a cage. Inside, the low ceilings, exposed beams and an inglenook fireplace enhance the pub's credentials as a traditional English country pub. Food offered throughout the bar, conservatory restaurant and garden includes leek, mushroom and parmesan crumble; steak-and-ale pie; and slow-roasted pork belly. Leave room for bread-and-butter pudding or sherry trifle. Booking for meals may be required.

Open all wk 12-3 6-11 (Sun 12-3 6.30-10.30) **Bar Meals** L served all wk 12-2 D served all wk 6-9 **Restaurant** L served all wk 12-2 D served all wk 6-9 ⊕ FREE HOUSE ◀ Greene King IPA, Adnams Southwold Bitter, Wolf ♂ Aspall. **Facilities** Children welcome Children's menu Garden Parking ▭

MARSHAM
Map 13 TG12

The Plough Inn
PICK OF THE PUBS

See Pick of the Pubs on page 374

MUNDFORD
Map 13 TL89

Crown Hotel

Crown Rd IP26 5HQ ☎ 01842 878233
e-mail: info@the-crown-hotel.co.uk
web: www.the-crown-hotel.co.uk
dir: *A11 to Barton Mills junct, then A1065 to Brandon & onto Mundford*

Originally a hunting lodge, this historic hillside inn on the edge of Thetford Forest dates back to 1652. Traditional, home-cooked food is served in the bars and two restaurants; perhaps pan-fried supreme of salmon with warm cherry tomato and basil salad or Jimmy Butler's slow-roasted pork belly with apple brandy sauce, baked apple and dauphinoise potatoes. In addition to the real ales and wines, there is a choice of over 50 malt whiskies. Being on a hill, the garden is on the first floor. Booking for meals may be required.

Open all day all wk 10.30-12 **Bar Meals** L served all wk 12-3 D served all wk 6.30-10 **Restaurant** L served all wk 12-3 D served all wk 6.30-10 ⊕ FREE HOUSE ◀ Courage Directors, Greene King Ruddles County, Hardys & Hansons Olde Trip, Woodforde's Wherry, Guest ales. **Facilities** ❀ Children welcome Children's portions Garden Parking Wi-fi ▭

NEWTON
Map 13 TF81

The George & Dragon

Swaffham Rd PE32 2BX ☎ 01760 755046
e-mail: info@newtongeorge.co.uk
dir: *3m N of Swaffham on A1065*

Found just north of the market town of Swaffham and a stone's throw from Castle Acre Priory, The George & Dragon has been refreshing weary travellers since 1740. These days, visitors can make use of the Wi-fi connection as they enjoy the pub's own Newton Bitter in the beamed bar or in the three acres of garden. The menu changes monthly and might include five spice pork belly or 'sausage of the month' with mash and red onion gravy.

Open 11-3 6-11 Closed: Sun eve & Mon L **Bar Meals** L served Tue-Sun 12-2 D served Mon-Sat 6-9 Av main course £10 **Restaurant** L served Tue-Sun 12-2 D served Mon-Sat 6-9 Av 3 course à la carte fr £16 ⊕ FREE HOUSE ◀ Newton Bitter, Guest ales ♂ Aspall. ♀ 13 **Facilities** ❀ Children welcome Children's menu Children's portions Play area Garden Parking Wi-fi

NORWICH
Map 13 TG20

Adam & Eve

Bishopsgate NR3 1RZ ☎ 01603 667423
e-mail: theadamandeve@hotmail.com
dir: *Behind the Anglican Cathedral, next to the Law Courts*

Norwich's oldest pub, the Adam & Eve has been serving ale since 1249, when it was the lodging house for craftsmen building the Anglican cathedral next door. The pub's name may refer to the arms of the medieval Fruitier's Company and its connection with the building from 1720. These days it remains a traditional pub undisturbed by TV or games machines, and counts a few ghosts among its regulars. Decked with award-winning flowers in summer, it offers real ales and plenty of traditional, home-made food with the likes of lasagne; chilli con carne; chicken and ham pie; salmon goujons with mango and lime dip; and ploughman's and jacket potatoes.

Open all day all wk 11-11 (Sun 12-10.30) Closed: 25-26 Dec, 1 Jan **Bar Meals** L served Mon-Sat 12-7, Sun 12-5 ⊕ ENTERPRISE INNS ◀ Adnams Southwold Bitter, Theakston Old Peculier, Wolf Straw Dog, Humpty Dumpty ♂ Aspall. ♀ 11 **Facilities** Parking Wi-fi ▭

The Mad Moose Arms
PICK OF THE PUBS

2 Warwick St NR2 3LB ☎ 01603 627687
e-mail: madmoose@animalinns.co.uk
dir: *1m from A11*

Popular with the locals, this friendly neighbourhood gastro-pub offer the best of both worlds, with a stylish ground-floor bar and a sophisticated upstairs dining room. Regulars know they can expect Norfolk real ales – Woodforde's Wherry and Wolf Straw Dog – and a bar menu offering a variety of interesting sandwiches, light meals and salads; and main dishes such as duck hash; smoked haddock gratin and toad-in-the-hole. On the first floor is the elegant 1Up restaurant with chandeliers, sea green drapes, and a feature wall depicting a fairytale forest. Confident and ambitious cooking is typified by a starter of seared scallops and chorizo, cauliflower beignets, quince purée, chorizo and lime oil. This might be followed by roast Norfolk venison loin, pomme sarladaise and baby onions, curly kale and mushroom jus. Among the desserts consider iced hazelnut parfait. There is a stylish outdoor patio for alfresco dining and beer festivals in May and October. As we went to press, a change of hands was taking place. Booking for meals may be required.

Open all day all wk 12-12 Closed: 25 Dec ⊕ FREE HOUSE/ ANIMAL INNS ◀ Woodforde's Wherry, Wolf Straw Dog, Oakham ♂ Aspall. **Facilities** Children welcome Children's menu Children's portions Garden Beer festival

PICK OF THE PUBS

The Plough Inn

MARSHAM Map 13 TG12

Norwich Rd NR10 5PS
☎ **01263 735000**
e-mail: enq@ploughinnmarsham.co.uk
web: www.ploughinnmarsham.co.uk
dir: *On A140, 10m N of Norwich, 1m S of Aylsham*

Roger and Val Stock, proprietors at this 18th-century countryside inn near the north Norfolk coast, take pride in their neatly presented hostelry. And rightly so – Marco Pierre White stayed here while filming locally, as did the *Relocation, Relocation* team. But you don't have to be a media luvvie to come here for a relaxing pint. Whether you're touring the Broads or on your way to Norwich Airport six miles away, the welcome will be warm, and experienced staff will ensure you enjoy your visit. New improvements include the garden area and car park, redecoration inside, and comfortable seats in the bar. Greene King IPA and Adnams are the ales on offer, together with lagers and a good range of wines. The restaurant uses local and seasonal produce if possible; the menus of modern British favourites are prepared in-house, and wheat- and gluten-free meals are a speciality. The range of lunchtime sandwiches, jacket potatoes

and omelettes offer fillings to suit every palate. Popular starters are creamy garlic mushrooms; deep-fried brie; and tiger prawns in home-made batter. Main courses range from lemon and herb chicken, to sweet potato and goat's cheese ravioli. The chef's signature dishes are slow-roasted belly of pork with crunchy crackling; and cheddar and chive soufflé. Children are well catered for – all their favourites are served, from garlic bread to chicken nuggets or fish fingers; they love puddings such as Harry Potter's cauldron of worms – vanilla ice cream with jelly worms and strawberry sauce.

Open all wk 12-2.30 6-11 (all day summer) **Bar Meals** L served all wk 12-2.30 D served all wk 6-9 ⬜ FREE HOUSE ◗ Greene King IPA, Adnams, John Smith's ⬤ Aspall. ♟ 10
Facilities Children welcome Children's menu Children's portions Garden Parking Wi-fi 🚐

Save on hotels. Book at **theAA.com/hotel**

NORFOLK 375 ENGLAND

NORWICH continued

Ribs of Beef

24 Wensum St NR3 1HY ☎ 01603 619517
e-mail: roger@cawdron.co.uk
dir: From Tombland (in front of cathedral) turn left at Maids Head Hotel. Pub 200yds on right on bridge

Roger and Anthea Cawdron have owned this historic riverside free house for over 25 years, and the welcoming atmosphere remains popular with holidaymakers cruising the Broads. The pub is famous for its range of cask ales, excellent wines and traditional English food using locally sourced produce. Breakfast baps start at 11am, whilst hearty choices like ham, eggs and chips; and lamb shank, mash and peas rub shoulders with sandwiches, burgers and jacket potatoes on the varied main menu. Sit outside on the terrace during the warmer months.

Open all day all wk 11-11 (Fri-Sat 11am-1am) **Bar Meals** L served Mon-Fri 12-2.30, Sat-Sun 12-5 Av main course £7.50 ⊕ FREE HOUSE ◀ Woodforde's Wherry, Adnams Southwold Bitter, Elgood's Black Dog, Oakham JHB, Fuller's London Pride ♂ Kingfisher Norfolk Cider. ♀ 9 **Facilities** Children welcome Children's menu Children's portions Family room Wi-fi ▭ (notice required)

RINGSTEAD   Map 12 TF74

The Gin Trap Inn ★★★★ INN ◉

PICK OF THE PUBS

6 High St PE36 5JU ☎ 01485 525264
e-mail: thegintrap@hotmail.co.uk
dir: A149 from King's Lynn towards Hunstanton. In 15m turn right at Heacham for Ringstead

The Peddars Way recreational path passes the door of this attractive pub in a pretty village just a couple of miles from the north Norfolk coast and its string of little ports, nature and bird reserves. Dating from 1667 and sympathetically upgraded over the years, it's a comfy base from which to explore this engaging countryside. The rustic bar has a relaxed and friendly atmosphere, exposed brickwork and beams, blazing log-burning stove for warmth throughout the winter, plus an intimate dining room and modern conservatory. There's also a pretty garden for summer alfresco drinking and dining. Walkers pop in for drinks (East Anglian real ales) and a meal to fortify them on their way. They pride themselves on the provenance of the produce that goes into the meals, much of which is extremely locally sourced. Carpaccio of beef with horseradish, celeriac remoulade and micro herbs to start, followed by grilled hake with home-made egg noodles, razor fish chowder and lemon oil are fine examples from the inspired, one AA-Rosette gastro-pub menu here. Stay over in one of the three bedrooms.

Open all day all wk 11.30-11 (11.30-2.30 6-11 in winter) ⊕ FREE HOUSE ◀ Adnams Southwold Bitter, Woodforde's Wherry, Guest ales ♂ Aspall. **Facilities** Children welcome Children's menu Children's portions Garden Parking Wi-fi **Rooms** 3

SALTHOUSE   Map 13 TG04

The Dun Cow

Coast Rd NR25 7XA ☎ 01263 740467
e-mail: salthouseduncow@gmail.com
dir: On A149 (coast road). 3m E of Blakeney, 6m W of Sheringham

In a quiet coastal village within an Area of Outstanding Natural Beauty, this traditional brick and flint pub probably originated as a cattle barn built around 1650. Today it overlooks some of Britain's finest salt marshes, so expect to share it, particularly the front garden, with birdwatchers and walkers. A tasteful refurbishment in 2012 reflects the surrounding farmlands and seascapes. Local suppliers provide high quality produce for select menus prepared from scratch, especially fresh shellfish and game from local shoots. Samphire, asparagus and soft fruit are all sourced within five miles.

Open all day all wk **Bar Meals** Av main course £10 food served all day **Restaurant** food served all day ⊕ PUNCH TAVERNS ◀ Woodforde's Wherry, Adnams, Guest ales ♂ Aspall. ♀ 19 **Facilities** ♣ Children welcome Children's menu Children's portions Garden Parking Wi-fi ▭ (notice required)

SNETTISHAM   Map 12 TF63

The Rose & Crown ★★ HL ◉

PICK OF THE PUBS

Old Church Rd PE31 7LX ☎ 01485 541382
e-mail: info@roseandcrownsnettisham.co.uk
dir: 10m N from King's Lynn on A149 signed Hunstanton. Inn in centre of Snettisham between market square & church

Anthony and Jeannette's splendid 14th-century inn was originally built to house the craftsmen who built the beautiful church up the road and is everything you'd expect from a Norfolk village inn. Beyond the rose-festooned façade lie twisting passages and hidden corners, leading to three charming bars, replete with heavy oak beams, uneven red-tiled floors, inglenook fireplaces, tip-top Adnams ale on tap, and an informal atmosphere. The menu makes good use of locally supplied produce – beef comes from cattle that grazed the nearby salt marshes; fishermen still in their waders deliver Brancaster mussels and Thornham oysters; and strawberries and asparagus are grown locally. Start with wood pigeon and wild mushroom mini pie, follow with a baked salmon fillet served with lemon and parsley risotto and roast balsamic potatoes, or roasted Mediterranean vegetable and pine nut linguine, leaving room for orange syllabub with zabaglione ice cream and Italian meringue. Stylish bedrooms offer excellent accommodation and the pretty walled garden was once the village bowling green. Booking for meals may be required.

Open all day all wk **Bar Meals** L served Mon-Fri 12-2, Sat-Sun 12-2.30 D served Sun-Thu 6-9, Fri-Sat 6-9.30 Av main course £12.25 **Restaurant** L served Mon-Fri 12-2, Sat-Sun 12-2.30 D served Sun-Thu 6-9, Fri-Sat 6-9.30 Av 3 course à la carte fr £25 ⊕ FREE HOUSE

◀ Adnams Southwold Bitter & Broadside, Bass, Fuller's London Pride, Greene King IPA. ♀ 12 **Facilities** ♣ Children welcome Children's menu Children's portions Play area Family room Garden Parking Wi-fi **Rooms** 16

STIFFKEY   Map 13 TF94

The Stiffkey Red Lion NEW

44 Wells Rd NR23 1AJ ☎ 01328 830552
e-mail: redlion@stiffkey.com
dir: On A149, 4m E of Wells-next-the-Sea; 4m W of Blakeney

The Red Lion started life in the 17th century as an inn before switching back and forth between house, pub and even a doctor's surgery. Located on the north Norfolk coast, this comfortable inn is now a popular bolt-hole for walkers and birdwatchers stepping off the nearby saltmarshes. Grab an old pew by one of the four log fires and warm up over a glass of Nelson's Revenge and locally sourced seasonal dishes such as Cromer crab salad, Norfolk game pie or Blakeney whitebait.

Open all day all wk **Bar Meals** L served Mon-Sat 12-2.30, Sun 12-9 D served Mon-Sat 6-9, Sun 12-9 Av main course £12 **Restaurant** L served Mon-Sat 12-2.30, Sun 12-9 D served Mon-Sat 6-9, Sun 12-9 ⊕ FREE HOUSE ◀ The Stiffkey Red Lion Stewkey Brew, Woodforde's Wherry & Nelson's Revenge. ♀ 12 **Facilities** ♣ Children welcome Children's menu Children's portions Garden Parking Wi-fi

---

STOKE HOLY CROSS   Map 13 TG20

The Wildebeest Arms

PICK OF THE PUBS

82-86 Norwich Rd NR14 8QJ ☎ 01508 492497
e-mail: wildebeest@animalinns.co.uk
dir: From A47 take A140, left to Dunston. At T-junct turn left, Wildebeest Arms on right

This charming village local is the perfect retreat from the hustle and bustle of nearby Norwich. Tastefully modernised with a modern rustic-chic look, expect thick, chunky wooden tables, wooden floors and oak beams, vases of fresh lilies, potted plants, crackling log fires and yellow rag-washed walls. What is striking is the quirky collection of African tribal art, which adds a touch of exoticism. Although the emphasis has been placed firmly on delivering great food, all are welcome to pop in for a pint of Adnams and a decent glass of wine (some are available by the glass). The kitchen takes a modern approach - underpinned by a classical French theme. Kick off with warm pigeon and Parma ham salad and move on to grilled smoked haddock with garlic creamed potato and buttered spinach. Leave room for pistachio cake and pistachio parfait with boozy cherries. As we went to press, a change of hands was taking place. Booking for meals may be required.

Open all wk Closed: 25-26 Dec ⊕ FREE HOUSE ◀ Adnams ♂ Aspall. **Facilities** Children welcome Children's portions Garden Parking

PICK OF THE PUBS

Chequers Inn

THOMPSON Map 13 TL99

Griston Rd IP24 1PX ☎ 01953 483360
e-mail: richard@thompsonchequers.co.uk
web: www.thompsonchequers.co.uk
dir: *Exit A1075 between Watton & Thetford*

Well off the beaten track, this splendid, long and low, thatched 17th-century inn is worth finding – a mile off the A1075 Watton to Thetford road along a tiny lane on the edge of the village – for its peaceful location and unspoilt charm. It takes its name from the chequered cloth used for counting money, wages and rents in medieval times. Manorial courts, held here from at least 1724, dealt with rents, letting of land, and petty crime. Beneath the steep-raked thatch of this ancient alehouse, once a row of several cottages, lies a series of low-ceilinged interconnecting rooms served by a long bar. Wonky wall timbers, low doorways, open log fires, a rustic mix of old furniture and old farming implements characterise the atmospheric interior. Eat in the bar for pub favourites such as steak-and-kidney pudding, deep-fried cod and chips, and home-made vegetable curry. In the evenings, choose from pork medallions with stilton and red onion, stuffed chicken breast with smoked salmon, sirloin steak with horseradish, brandy and mushroom sauce, or look to

the chalkboard for the day's fresh fish dishes, perhaps whole sea bream, and game in season. Round things off with home-made desserts like treacle and almond tart, or opt for a selection of English and continental cheeses served with grapes, celery and biscuits. The inn is an ideal base for exploring the heart of Norfolk and the Peddars Way National Trail. Alternatively, the eight-mile Great Eastern Pingo Trail follows a succession of shallow depressions in the ground that were formed during the last Ice Age. Dogs are welcome in the large rear garden, which offers picnic tables and children's play equipment, as well as extensive views over the surrounding countryside. Booking for meals may be required.

Open all wk 11.30-3 6.30-11 **Bar Meals** L served all wk 12-2 D served all wk 6.30-9 **Restaurant** L served all wk 12-2 D served all wk 6.30-9 ⊕ FREE HOUSE ◀ Fuller's London Pride, Adnams Southwold Bitter, Wolf Ale, Greene King IPA, Woodforde's Wherry. ♚ 8
Facilities Children welcome Children's menu Children's portions ❖ Play area Garden Parking Wi-fi 🚌 (notice required)

Save on hotels. Book at **theAA.com/hotel**

NORFOLK 377 ENGLAND

STOW BARDOLPH — Map 12 TF60

The Hare Arms

PICK OF THE PUBS

PE34 3HT ☎ 01366 382229
e-mail: trishmc@harearms222.wanadoo.co.uk
dir: *From King's Lynn take A10 to Downham Market. After 9m village signed on left*

No music drowns the conversation in the L-shaped bar and adjoining conservatory of this attractive ivy-clad pub, run for 36 years by Trish and David McManus. Full of fascinating bygones they have collected along the way, it's named after the Hare family, who have lived at Stow Hall since 1553. A large bar food menu is always available, supplemented by daily specials of, say, peppered swordfish steak with cream and brandy sauce; and chicken breast wrapped in oak-smoked bacon, coated in stilton sauce. The restaurant menu ranges from hot goat's cheese tart to Cajun-spiced red snapper, by way of monkfish and tiger prawn casserole; grilled local rump steak; and chicken-style Quorn and leek shortcrust pie. A choice of salads includes crayfish tails with smoked salmon, prawns and lemon crème fraîche; and Roquefort with pear, bacon and mustard and sherry dressing. Expect to see peacocks in the garden. Booking for meals may be required.

Open all wk 11-2.30 6-11 (Sun 12-10.30) Closed: 25-26 Dec **Bar Meals** L served Mon-Sat 12-2, Sun 12-10 D served Mon-Sat 6.30-10, Sun 12-10 Av main course £10 **Restaurant** D served Mon-Sat 7-9 Fixed menu price fr £17 Av 3 course à la carte fr £32 ⊕ GREENE KING ◀ Abbot Ale & IPA, Morland Old Speckled Hen, Guest ales ⍟ Aspall. ▾ 9 **Facilities** Children welcome Children's menu Children's portions Family room Garden Parking Wi-fi

SWANTON MORLEY — Map 13 TG01

Darbys Freehouse

1&2 Elsing Rd NR20 4NY ☎ 01362 637647
e-mail: louisedarby@hotmail.com
dir: *From A47 (Norwich to King's Lynn) take B1147 to Dereham*

A large country house, divided first into cottages in the late 19th century, then in 1988 converted into a pub. The old beams and inglenooks are still there, of course, while the spacious bar is furnished with stripped pine tables and benches, and stools are made from tractor seats. Mostly locally supplied, traditional pub food includes home-made curries; scampi and chips; chicken mozzarella melt; and vegetarian and children's selections. Guest ales join Norfolk and Suffolk regulars. Booking for meals may be required.

Open all wk Mon-Thu 11.30-3 6-11 (Fri-Sat 11.30-11 Sun 12-10.30). Food served all day Sat-Sun ◀ Woodforde's Wherry, Adnams Broadside & Southwold Bitter, 2 Guest ales. **Facilities** Children welcome Children's menu Children's portions Play area Family room Garden Parking

THOMPSON — Map 13 TL99

Chequers Inn

PICK OF THE PUBS

See Pick of the Pubs on page 376

THORNHAM — Map 12 TF74

Marco Pierre White The Lifeboat Inn

PICK OF THE PUBS

Ship Ln PE36 6LT ☎ 01485 512236
e-mail: reception@lifeboatinn.co.uk
dir: *A149 from Hunstanton for approx 6m. 1st left after Thornham sign*

A recent addition to the Marco Pierre White group, this rambling, 16th-century smugglers' inn, situated on the edge of a vast expanse of salt marsh, is a short stroll from sweeping beaches, renowned bird reserves, and bracing coastal path walks. The ramble of old rooms retain their original character, boasting low-beamed ceilings, rug-strewn tiled floors, low doors, half-panelled walls, five log-burning fires, and a rustic array of furniture, from carved oak tables to antique settles and pews. Antique oil lamps suspended from the ceiling and a wealth of nautical bric-à-brac enhance the charm, while the adjoining conservatory is renowned for its ancient vine and there's an adjacent walled patio garden. Food ranges from sausage and caramelised onion sandwiches, and starters like potted duck and salt and pepper calamari with lemon mayonnaise, to traditional fish and chips, braised lamb shank with roasted root vegetables and red wine jus, and grilled plaice with potted shrimps and lemon butter. It's perfectly placed for visiting Sandringham and Nelson's birthplace at Burnham Thorpe. Booking for meals may be required.

Open all day all wk **Bar Meals** food served all day **Restaurant** D served all wk 7-9.30 ⊕ FREE HOUSE ◀ Greene King Abbot Ale & IPA, Woodforde's Wherry, Adnams, Guest ales. ▾ 10 **Facilities** Children welcome Children's menu Children's portions Play area Garden Parking Wi-fi

---

The Orange Tree

PICK OF THE PUBS

See Pick of the Pubs on page 378

TITCHWELL — Map 13 TF74

Titchwell Manor Hotel ★★★ HL ⑳⑳

PICK OF THE PUBS

PE31 8BB ☎ 01485 210221
e-mail: margaret@titchwellmanor.com
dir: *A149 between Brancaster & Thornham*

On Norfolk's striking north coast, this former Victorian farmhouse looks out over Titchwell Marsh RSPB Reserve.

During 25 years here Margaret and Ian Snaith have tastefully modernised it, while their son Eric and his team are responsible for the two AA-Rosette cuisine in the elegant, candlelit Conservatory overlooking the walled garden. More informal are the Eating Rooms and bar, although in summer many head for the sea-view terrace. Indicative starters include Joselito Gran Reserva ham with melon and olive oil; and diver-caught scallops with oxtail lentils and smoked red wine; and main courses of Brancaster shellfish; fish, chips and mushy peas; grilled sirloin and rib-eye steaks; and roast celeriac pie with Binham Blue cheese. A noteworthy special is fillet of turbot, salt and vinegar mash, parsley, brown butter and charred onions. Accommodation is in the main period house, contemporary style rooms around the herb garden and the detached Potting Shed. Booking for meals may be required.

Open all day all wk **Bar Meals** L served all wk 12-2.30 D served all wk 6-9.30 **Restaurant** L served all wk 12-2.30 D served all wk 6-9.30 ⊕ FREE HOUSE/FLYING KIWI INNS ◀ Greene King IPA, Abbot Ale. ▾ 8 **Facilities** ☘ Children welcome Children's menu Children's portions Garden Parking Wi-fi ▭ (notice required) **Rooms** 26

WARHAM ALL SAINTS — Map 13 TF94

Three Horseshoes

PICK OF THE PUBS

NR23 1NL ☎ 01328 710547
dir: *From Wells A149 to Cromer, then right onto B1105 to Warham*

This gem of a pub first opened its doors in 1725. Its rambling old rooms, including a gas-lit main bar, are stone floored with scrubbed wooden tables. A grandfather clock ticks away in one corner, and a curious green and red dial in the ceiling turns out to be a rare example of Norfolk Twister, an ancient pub game. Vintage posters, clay pipes, photographs and memorabilia adorn the walls, while down a step are old one-arm bandits. Woodforde's Sundew and Nelson's Revenge are served from the cask through a hole in the bar wall. Home-made soups, pies and puddings dominate the menu, so start with creamy mushroom or vegetable soup; follow with macaroni cheese bake for a light lunch, or chicken and rabbit pie if more hungry. Date and banana sponge or Marsh mud pie are served with custard or cream. A no-chips policy applies, incidentally. Outside is a beer garden and covered courtyard.

Open all wk 12-2.30 6-11 **Bar Meals** L served all wk 12-1.45 D served all wk 6-8 Av main course £7.80-£9.40 ⊕ FREE HOUSE ◀ Woodforde's Wherry, Sundew, Nelson's Revenge ⍟ Whin Hill. **Facilities** ☘ Children welcome Children's portions Family room Garden Parking ▭ (notice required)

PICK OF THE PUBS

The Orange Tree

THORNHAM   Map 12 TF74

High St PE36 6LY ☎ **01485 512213**
e-mail: email@theorangetreethornham.co.uk
web: www.theorangetreethornham.co.uk
dir: *Telephone for directions*

Formerly a smugglers' haunt, this 400-year-old whitewashed inn has evolved into a stylish and contemporary country pub. Now run by Mark and Joanna Goode, it stands opposite Thornham church in the centre of the village and makes a useful stop for walkers on the ancient Peddars Way. Develop an appetite with a stroll to the local staithe, where working fishing boats still come and go through the creeks of Brancaster Bay, before returning for meal and a pint of East Anglian-brewed ale. Award-winning chef Philip Milner makes the most of freshly landed local seafood, with innovative dishes like garlic roasted halibut with sauté cod cheeks, saffron potatoes, baby fennel and langoustine broth. But it's not just the seafood that justifies his claim that the restaurant is the jewel in The Orange Tree's crown; the pub has a long established relationship with local suppliers, and most of the meat is sourced from the Sandringham Estate. The humble lunchtime sandwich gets celebrity treatment with options such as chargrilled rump steak with onions, mushrooms, fried duck egg and triple mustard mayo – which, like others on the list, can be served on ciabatta or multi-seed bloomer. Some dishes, including the organic salmon, chilli and freshwater crayfish fishcakes, are available as either a starter or main course, whilst others – like pan-roasted Norfolk pheasant with roast parsnips, wild damson sponge, black quinoa risotto and pomegranate molasses – are definitely aimed at larger appetites. But leave space to sample the appetising selection of desserts; winter fruit tart with clementine purée and cinnamon ice cream is a typical choice.

Open all day all wk **Bar Meals** L served all wk 12-3 D served all wk 6-9.30 Av main course £11.50 **Restaurant** L served all wk 12-3 D served all wk 6-9.30 Av 3 course à la carte fr £33 ⊞ PUNCH TAVERNS ◀ Woodforde's Wherry, Adnams Southwold Bitter, Crouch Vale Brewers Gold ♂ Aspall. ♟ 21 **Facilities** Children welcome Children's menu Children's portions Play area Garden Parking Wi-fi 🚐

WELLS-NEXT-THE-SEA   Map 13 TF94

The Crown Hotel
PICK OF THE PUBS

The Buttlands NR23 1EX ☎ 01328 710209
e-mail: reception@crownhotelnorfolk.co.uk
dir: *10m from Fakenham on B1105*

Overlooking the tree-lined green known as The Buttlands, the striking contemporary décor of this 17th-century former coaching inn blends effortlessly with its old-world charm. Beneath the bar's ancient beams, East Anglian ales and Aspall real cider are on tap. Whether you eat in the bar, more formally in the restaurant, in the cheerful Orangery, or outside with its great views, the ever-changing main menu features traditional favourites, the best of modern British cuisine, and international-influenced dishes. Perhaps pan-fried sea bass with ham hock, sweetcorn, chickpea and chilli broth; spiced chickpea burgers with pitta bread and tomato salsa; roast cod fillet on celery and apple mash with a shallot and thyme sauce. Try also one of the local seafood specials, or one of the colourful salads. Desserts might include chestnut parfait with balsamic roasted fig or warm bread-and-butter pudding. A good few wines are available by the glass and there are a few half-bottles. There are good choices on the children's menu. Booking for meals may be required.

Open all day all wk **Bar Meals** L served all wk 12-2.30 D served all wk 6.30-9.30 Av main course £15 **Restaurant** L served all wk 12-2.30 D served all wk 6.30-9.30 Av 3 course à la carte fr £15.95 ⊕ FREE HOUSE/FLYING KIWI INNS ◀ Adnams Southwold Bitter, Jo C's Norfolk Kiwi, Guest ale ♂ Aspall. ♟ 14 **Facilities** Children welcome Children's menu Children's portions Garden Parking Wi-fi ▭

The Globe Inn

The Buttlands NR23 1EU ☎ 01328 710206
e-mail: globe@holkham.co.uk
dir: *in village centre*

The Globe is a short stroll from the town's bustling quay and overlooks the leafy village green. It has a warm, welcoming bar and comfortable restaurant, with a sunny courtyard for alfresco drinking and dining. The menus take full advantage of the abundance of local produce from both land and sea – such as tender asparagus in early summer and game from the Holkham Estate in winter. Smoked mackerel pâté, horseradish crème fraîche and toast makes a delicious starter. To finish, share the Norfolk cheese selection with celery, quince jelly and biscuits. Booking for meals may be required.

Open all day all wk **Bar Meals** L served all wk 12-2.30 D served all wk 6.30-9 Av main course £14 **Restaurant** L served all wk 12-2.30 D served all wk 6.30-9 ⊕ ADNAMS ◀ Adnams ♂ Aspall. ♟ 10 **Facilities** ♣ Children welcome Children's menu Children's portions Garden Wi-fi ▭ (notice required)

WEST BECKHAM   Map 13 TG13

The Wheatsheaf

Manor Farm, Church Rd NR25 6NX ☎ 01263 822110
e-mail: manager@thewheatsheafwestbeckham.co.uk
dir: *2m inland from Sheringham on A148, turn opp Sheringham Park*

Situated in a quiet village just two miles from Sheringham and formerly known as the 'old manor farmhouse', this charming building was converted to a pub over 20 years ago and retains many original features. Sample one of the real ales from Woodforde's and relax in bar, one of the restaurants or the large garden. All food is made on the premises using fresh local produce. From the bar menu, dishes might include prime beef lasagne or beer-battered haddock, while typical choices from the restaurant menu are roasted pepper and cashew Stroganoff; and slow-roasted belly pork with bubble-and-squeak.

Open 11.30-3 6.30-11.30 Closed: Mon ⊕ FREE HOUSE ◀ Woodforde's Wherry, Greene King IPA, Guest ales ♂ Aspall. **Facilities** Children welcome Children's menu Children's portions Play area Garden Parking

WESTON LONGVILLE   Map 13 TG11

The Parson Woodforde ★★★★ INN ◉

Church St NR9 5JU ☎ 01603 881675
e-mail: manager@theparsonwoodforde.com
dir: *From Norwich take A1067 (Fakenham road). After Morton turn left in Marl Hill Rd to Weston Longville*

Just a 20-minute drive from Norwich, in the village of Weston Longville, this pub started life as the Five Ringers back in 1845. Now a free house with a great selection of real ales and a restaurant, it reopened a couple of years ago after an extensive refurbishment. A range of local cask ales are on offer alongside a menu that showcases Norfolk produce in dishes such as a duo of braised lamb and shank with a fruit terrine and horseradish mash with thyme. A beer festival is held in September. Accommodation is available. Booking for meals may be required.

Open all day all wk Closed: 25 Dec (drinks only 12-2.30), Mon (Jan-Feb) **Bar Meals** food served all day **Restaurant** L served Mon-Fri 12-2.30, Sat all day, Sun 12-9 D served Sat 12-9.30, Sun 12-9 ⊕ FREE HOUSE ◀ Grain Best Bitter, Wolf Straw Dog, Adnams Southwold Bitter, Winter's ♂ Aspall. ♟ 12 **Facilities** Children welcome Children's menu Children's portions Garden Beer festival Parking Wi-fi ▭ (notice required) **Rooms** 4

WINTERTON-ON-SEA   Map 13 TG41

Fishermans Return

The Lane NR29 4BN ☎ 01493 393305
e-mail: enquiries@fishermansreturn.com
web: www.fishermansreturn.com
dir: *8m N of Great Yarmouth on B1159*

This dog-friendly, 350-year-old brick and flint free house stands close to long beaches and National Trust land, making it the ideal spot to finish a walk. Guest ales support Woodforde's Norfolk Nog and Wherry behind the bar, whilst the menus range from popular favourites like omelettes and filled jacket potatoes to sirloin steak and three bean chilli. Look out for fish and seafood specials on the daily-changing blackboard, where freshly caught mackerel or sea bass may be on offer. The pub hosts a beer festival on August Bank Holiday.

Open all wk 11-2.30 5.30-11 (Sat-Sun 11-11) **Bar Meals** L served all wk 12-2.30 D served all wk 6-9 **Restaurant** L served all wk 12-2.30 D served all wk 6-9 ⊕ FREE HOUSE ◀ Woodforde's Wherry & Norfolk Nog, Guest ales ♂ Westons Stowford Press & Old Rosie Scrumpy, Local ciders. ♟ 9 **Facilities** ♣ Children welcome Children's menu Children's portions Play area Family room Garden Beer festival Parking Wi-fi ▭

continued

WIVETON — Map 13 TG04

Wiveton Bell ◉

PICK OF THE PUBS

Blakeney Rd NR25 7TL ☎ 01263 740101
e-mail: enquiries@wivetonbell.co.uk
dir: *1m from Blakeney. Wiveton Rd off A149*

Sleepy Wiveton stands just a mile inland from the glorious coastal salt marshes and the stylishly spruced-up Bell overlooks the peaceful village green and church. Expect a chic interior, with earthy heritage-coloured walls, stripped beams, chunky tables and oak-planked floors. Further character is provided by the bold, contemporary oil paintings by local artists that line the walls of the cosy bar and conservatory dining room, where Yetman's ale (brewed up the road), Aspall cider and a carefully selected wine list hold sway. In winter, head for the tables close to the inglenook fireplace, mingle with the locals and peruse the seasonal menu, which is bolstered by adventurous specials that champion local fish and game. Begin with game terrine with fig and pear chutney and follow with Melton Park venison casserole with braised red cabbage, or Cley Smokehouse haddock with mustard sauce. Don't miss the excellent Sunday roasts – booking essential. Booking for meals may be required.

Open all day all wk Closed: 25 Dec **Bar Meals** L served all wk 12-2.15 D served all wk 6-9 **Restaurant** L served all wk 12-2.15 D served all wk 6-9.15 ⊕ FREE HOUSE ◀ Woodforde's Wherry, Adnams Broadside, Yetman's Ö Aspall. ▼ 17 **Facilities** Children's menu Garden Parking Wi-fi

WOODBASTWICK — Map 13 TG31

The Fur & Feather Inn

Slad Ln NR13 6HQ ☎ 01603 720003
dir: *From A1151 (Norwich to Wroxham road), follow brown signs for Woodforde's Brewery. Pub next to Brewery*

An idyllic thatched country pub ideal for beer lovers. Eight real ales from Woodforde's Brewery next door are served straight from the cask, with no jukebox, TV or pool table to disturb the peace. The pub was originally two farm cottages, and now boasts three cosy bar areas and a smart restaurant. Here you can enjoy traditional home-made English fare: Norfolk venison and stilton pie; pan-fried skate wing; and lamb and mint burger are some examples. An interesting vegetarian selection and a 'think local' 30-mile menu complete the picture.

Open all day all wk **Bar Meals** Av main course £11 food served all day **Restaurant** Av 3 course à la carte fr £22 food served all day ◀ Woodforde's Wherry, Sundew, Norfolk Nog, Nelson's Revenge, Admiral's Reserve, Once Bittern, Headcracker, Mardler's Mild. ▼ 12 **Facilities** Children welcome Children's menu Garden Parking Wi-fi ▭ (notice required)

NORTHAMPTONSHIRE

ASHBY ST LEDGERS — Map 11 SP56

The Olde Coach House Inn

CV23 8UN ☎ 01788 890349
e-mail: info@oldecoachhouse.co.uk
dir: *M1 junct 18 follow A361/Daventry signs. Village on left*

This handsome creeper-clad stone inn has been carefully modernised and is furnished with all manner of chairs, squashy leather sofas, pale wooden tables, large mirrors, hunting scenes, an original old stove, and fresh flowers. There are several different eating and drinking areas, at least three real ales, a good choice of wines, friendly staff, and plenty of seating outside. Dining here is popular too and food ranges from stone-fired home-made pizzas, to game pie with herb shortcrust pastry and vegetarian chestnut and wild mushroom cottage pie. Booking for meals may be required.

Open all wk Mon-Thu 12-3 5.30-11 (Fri-Sun all day) **Bar Meals** L served Mon-Sat 12-2.30, Sun 12-8 D served Mon-Sat 6-9.30, Sun 12-8 Av main course £10 **Restaurant** L served Mon-Sat 12-2.30, Sun 12-8 D served Mon-Sat 6-9.30, Sun 12-8 Fixed menu price fr £6 Av 3 course à la carte fr £21 ⊕ CHARLES WELLS ◀ Bombardier, Everards Tiger, Hook Norton Old Hooky, Young's. ▼ 12 **Facilities** Children welcome Children's menu Children's portions Play area Garden Parking ▭ (notice required)

ASHTON — Map 11 SP74

The Old Crown

1 Stoke Rd NN7 2JN ☎ 01604 862268
e-mail: bex@theoldcrownashton.co.uk
dir: *M1 junct 15. 1m from A508 from Roade*

A well-appointed homely village local in the small rural community of Ashton. A pub for over 300 years, its pretty, sheltered gardens are a popular choice for summer dining, or settle in to the beamed bar room and look forward to choosing from the well thought out, balanced menus while sipping a pint of well-kept ale. Perhaps start with deep-fried squid with aïoli, followed by ginger and soy marinated chicken breast with sticky coconut rice; or trio of lamb (cutlet, mini shepherd's pie and slow cooked shoulder); then spiced pecan and chocolate tart. There are regular events held throughout the year.

Open 12-3 6-11 (Sat 12-11.30 Sun 12-10.30) Closed: Mon ⊕ CHARLES WELLS ◀ Eagle IPA, Courage Directors, Young's. **Facilities** Children welcome Children's portions Garden Parking Wi-fi

AYNHO — Map 11 SP53

The Great Western Arms

Station Rd OX17 3BP ☎ 01869 338288
e-mail: info@great-westernarms.co.uk
dir: *From Aynho take B4031 (Station Road) W towards Deddington. Turn right to pub*

Apparently Sat Navs don't always pinpoint this pretty village inn between the Oxford Canal and the former Great Western Railway line. Once found, though, you'll appreciate its double-sided fireplace (popular in winter), lovely courtyard (ditto summer), and Hook Norton ales and an extensive wine selection (ditto all year). Menus are full of good things from chef-patron René Klein's kitchen, like his Thai Massaman vegetable curry; Cajun salmon fillet; breast of pheasant with pheasant and venison pasty; and toasted beef sandwich with horseradish. October's first weekend is beer festival time.

Open all day all wk Closed: 25 Dec **Bar Meals** L served all wk 12-3 D served all wk 6-9 **Restaurant** L served all wk 12-3 D served all wk 6-9 ⊕ HOOK NORTON ◀ Hooky Bitter, Ali's Ale, Twelve Days Ö Westons Perry, Old Rosie & Stowford Press. ▼ 10 **Facilities** ❀ Children welcome Children's menu Children's portions Garden Beer festival Parking Wi-fi ▭ (notice required)

BULWICK — Map 11 SP99

The Queen's Head

PICK OF THE PUBS

Main St NN17 3DY ☎ 01780 450272
e-mail: queenshead-bulwick@tiscali.co.uk
dir: *Just off A43, between Corby & Stamford*

A 17th-century stone-built free house overlooking the village church, parts of The Queen's Head date back to 1400. Recently refurbished, the pub is a warren of small rooms with exposed wooden beams, four open fireplaces and flagstone floors. Relax by the fire or on the patio with a pint of real ale from the local Oakham or Rockingham breweries. Local shoots supply seasonal game such as teal, woodcock and partridge, and other ingredients often include village-grown fruit and vegetables brought in by customers and friends. Lunchtime brings a good selection of sandwich and snacks, and main dishes that have helped the pub to attract a string of awards. The evening menu might feature local pork sausages with mash and white onion and grainy mustard sauce. The menu is backed by a comprehensive wine list. The Queen's Head also has a outdoor oven for outside dining. Booking for meals may be required.

Open 12-11 Closed: Mon ⊕ FREE HOUSE ◀ Elland, Rockingham, Newby Wyke, Thornbridge, Oakham. **Facilities** Children welcome Children's portions Garden Parking

Save on hotels. Book at **theAA.com/hotel**

NORTHAMPTONSHIRE 381 ENGLAND

CHACOMBE — Map 11 SP44

George and Dragon
PICK OF THE PUBS

Silver St OX17 2JR ☎ 01295 711500
e-mail: georgeanddragonchacombe@googlemail.com
dir: *M40 junct 11, A361 (Daventry road). Chacombe 1st right*

Within easy reach of the Cotswolds and Silverstone racing circuit, this honey-stoned, 17th-century pub is tucked away beside the church in the pretty village of Chacombe. Situated in a Conservation Area, the pub retains a traditional, welcoming atmosphere: the three comfortable bars have an abundance of low beams, simple wooden chairs and settles, roaring log fires, and warm terracotta décor. The sun terrace is a good spot for sampling the cask ales in summer. The lunchtime menu offers sandwiches and baguettes with salad and tortilla chips or hand-cut chips; small bites such as soups, salads and fishcakes; and bigger bites like chilli con carne, beefburger and ratatouille vegetable lasagne; as well as a daily specials board. In the evening, the menu lists starters like Brixworth pâté with warm toast and red onion and port marmalade, followed by sirloin steak served with vine cherry tomatoes, mushroom, onion rings and hand-cut chips, or smoked haddock fillet on a bed of sautéed spinach served with creamy leek sauce. Booking for meals may be required.

Open all day all wk 12-11 ⊕ EVERARDS ◀ Tiger & Beacon, Guest ales. **Facilities** Children welcome Children's menu Children's portions Garden Parking Wi-fi

CRICK — Map 11 SP57

The Red Lion Inn

52 Main Rd NN6 7TX ☎ 01788 822342
dir: *From M1 junct 18, 0.75m E on A428, follows signs for Crick from new rdbt*

Exposed beams, low ceilings and open fires rack up the rustic charm in this thatched 17th-century coaching inn, which is easily accessible from the M1. The Marks family, landlords here for the last 32 years, give their customers exactly what they want - a friendly atmosphere, real ales - including a weekly guest ale - and traditional food. The daily home-made steak pie is a lunchtime favourite, while fillet and sirloin steaks are a speciality in the evening. Fish eaters will find trout, lemon sole and seafood platter. Children are welcome at lunch, but only those over 12 are permitted in the evening.

Open all wk 11-2.30 6.15-11 (Sun 12-3 7-11) **Bar Meals** L served all wk 12-2 D served Mon-Sat 6.30-9 Av main course £4.80-£5.75 **Restaurant** Fixed menu price fr £8 ⊕ FREE HOUSE ◀ Wells Bombardier, Morland Old Speckled Hen, Caledonian Deuchars IPA, Guest ale. **Facilities** ♣ Children welcome Children's menu Children's portions Garden Parking

EAST HADDON — Map 11 SP66

The Red Lion
PICK OF THE PUBS

Main St NN6 8BU ☎ 01604 770223
e-mail: nick@redlioneasthaddon.co.uk
dir: *Just off A428*

Since taking over in 2010, former Gary Rhodes chef Adam Gray and his partner Nick Bonner have put The Red Lion firmly on the map as a top destination gastro-pub. Such is the pub's reputation for culinary excellence that it even runs its own cookery school. Expect a high standard of food at this award-winning village pub, whether in snacks such as free-range pork Scotch egg, or potted mackerel with rhubarb and toasted spelt bread to begin; main dishes like braised red wine beef with carrots and creamy mash or poached organic salmon with red cabbage and wild mushrooms; and puddings along the lines of banana fool with toffee sauce. Accompany your meal with one of 14 wines served by the glass or a pint of Wells Bombardier. The landscaped gardens offer good views over rolling countryside.

Open all day all wk **Bar Meals** L served all wk 12-2.30 D served all wk 6-10 Av main course £12.50 **Restaurant** L served all wk 12-2.30 D served all wk 6-10 Av 3 course à la carte fr £26 ⊕ CHARLES WELLS ◀ Bombardier & Eagle IPA, Young's London Gold. ♥ 14 **Facilities** Children welcome Children's portions Garden Parking Wi-fi

EYDON — Map 11 SP54

Royal Oak @ Eydon NEW

6 Lime Av NN11 3PG ☎ 01327 263167
e-mail: info@theroyaloakateydon.co.uk
dir: *Telephone for directions*

John Crossan's mellow stone pub dates back 300 years and stands in the heart of pretty Eydon. Innovative modern pub food draws discerning diners from far and wide but it's still very much hub of the village, welcoming walkers, dogs and local drinkers into the bar and dining areas. Come for pints of Hooky by the inglenook or for daily menus that champion local seasonal produce, including vegetables from the village allotments. Tuck into braised beef with roasted root vegetables or pan-fried sea bass with surf clam and crayfish velouté, followed by dark chocolate fondant, or opt for a cracking home-made burger from the short bar menu.

Open 12-2.30 6-11 (Mon 6-11 Sat-Sun all day) Closed: Mon L **Bar Meals** L served Tue-Sun 12-2.30 D served Tue-Sat 7-9, Sun 6.30-8.30 Av main course £8-£12 **Restaurant** L served Tue-Sun 12-2.30 D served Tue-Sat 7-9, Sun 6.30-8.30 Fixed menu price fr £10 Av 3 course à la carte fr £22 ⊕ FREE HOUSE ◀ Fuller's London Pride, Timothy Taylor Landlord, Hook Norton Hooky Bitter ♂ Westons Stowford Press. ♥ 16 **Facilities** ♣ Children welcome Children's menu Children's portions Garden Beer festival Parking Wi-fi (notice required)

FARTHINGHOE — Map 11 SP53

The Fox

Baker St NN13 5PH ☎ 01295 713965
e-mail: enquiries@foxatfarthinghoe.co.uk
dir: *Follow A422, midway between Banbury & Brackley. On Baker Street directly off A422.*

This Charles Wells pub brings its customers fresh, locally sourced food with friendly service and a relaxing village atmosphere. In practice this translates as a varied menu offering pub favourites such as Brackley Butchers sausages and mash; tempting lunchtime sandwiches; charcuterie, seafood and vegetarian deli boards; and vegetarian options such as roasted vegetable coulibiac. There is even a take-out menu. Ladies' Night on Wednesdays means three courses and a glass of wine for £15. Tuesday evening is curry night, Thursdays and Fridays have extra seafood dishes while a roast is offered every Sunday lunch. Beers include Erdinger, Bombardier and guest ales. Booking for meals may be required.

Open all wk 12-3 6-11 (Fri-Sun 12-11) **Bar Meals** L served all wk 12-2.30 D served all wk 6-9.30 Av main course £12 **Restaurant** L served all wk 12-2.30 D served all wk 6-9.30 Fixed menu price fr £15 Av 3 course à la carte fr £25 ⊕ CHARLES WELLS ◀ Bombardier, Young's, Erdinger, Guest ale. ♥ 12 **Facilities** Children welcome Children's portions Garden Parking Wi-fi (notice required)

FARTHINGSTONE — Map 11 SP65

The Kings Arms
PICK OF THE PUBS

Main St NN12 8EZ ☎ 01327 361604
e-mail: paul@kingsarms.fsbusiness.co.uk
dir: *M1 junct 16, A45 towards Daventry. At Weedon take A5 towards Towcester. Right signed Farthingstone*

Tucked away in perfect walking country, this 300-year-old stone free house is close to the National Trust's Elizabethan mansion at Canon's Ashby. Paul and Denise Egerton grow their own salads and herbs in the pub's quirky garden, which is full of interesting recycled items, decorative trees and shrubs, and secluded corners. The terrace is the place to enjoy alfresco drinking on warmer days with red kites and buzzards overhead; in winter, real fires warm the stone-flagged interior. The Kings Arms is mainly a drinkers' pub, with up to five real ales and Westons Old Rosie cider on tap. But lunches served in the bar at weekends feature quality fine foods such as fish from Loch Fyne, Scottish venison and British cheeses. Expect dishes such as salmon and parsley fishcakes or chicken, feta and red pepper salad. Find out about summer barbecues or winter casserole evenings. Booking for meals may be required.

Open 7-11.30 (Fri 6.30-12 Sat-Sun 12-3.30 7-11.30) Closed: Mon **Bar Meals** L served Sat-Sun 12-2.30 D served last Fri in month ⊕ FREE HOUSE ◀ Young's Bitter, Vale VPA, St Austell Trelawny, Silverstone Pitstop, Adnams ♂ Westons Old Rosie. **Facilities** ♣ Children welcome Children's portions Family room Garden Parking

FOTHERINGHAY — Map 12 TL09

The Falcon Inn ⊛

PICK OF THE PUBS

PE8 5HZ ☎ 01832 226254
e-mail: info@thefalcon-inn.co.uk
dir: *N of A605 between Peterborough & Oundle*

First the history: it was in this sleepy village that Richard III was born in 1452, and 115 years later Mary, Queen of Scots was beheaded. The attractive 18th-century, stone-built pub stands in gardens redesigned by award-winning landscape architect Bunny Guinness. It's a real local, the Tap Bar regularly used by the village darts team, their throwing arms lubricated by pints of Fool's Nook ale and Aspall cider. The menus in both the bar and charming conservatory restaurant rely extensively on locally sourced ingredients. In the winter, offerings from the restaurant are Portland crab; crayfish and saffron tart; and ham hock terrine to start. Mains might be rack of lamb with dauphinoise potato, baby vegetables and red wine jus. The bar menu has sandwiches and a selection of starters and mains, such as sautéed king prawns, and shin of beef. For dessert, there's lemon meringue pie or chocolate nemesis.

Open all day 12-11 Closed: Sun eve Jan-Mar **Bar Meals** L served Mon-Sat 12-2.15, Sun 12-3 D served Mon-Sat 6.15-9.15, Sun 6.15-8.30 Av main course £9.50 **Restaurant** L served Mon-Sat 12-2.15, Sun 12-3 D served Mon-Sat 6.15-9.15, Sun 6.15-8.30 Av 3 course à la carte fr £22.50 ⊕ FREE HOUSE ◀ Greene King IPA, Digfield Fool's Nook, Fuller's London Pride, Guest ales ♦ Aspall. ⬛ 14 **Facilities** ❖ Children welcome Children's menu Children's portions Garden Beer festival Parking Wi-fi ▭ (notice required)

GRAFTON REGIS — Map 11 SP74

The White Hart

Northampton Rd NN12 7SR ☎ 01908 542123
e-mail: alan@pubgraftonregis.co.uk
dir: *M1 junct 15 onto A508 between Northampton & Milton Keynes*

This thatched, stone-built property dating from the 16th century is the focal point for a friendly village with around 100 residents. In 1464 Edward IV married Elizabeth Woodville in this historic place. The pub has been owned by the same family for 15 years and Alan, now the owner, is also chef. Menus change frequently according to available produce. Typical choices include braised British lamb's liver, local pheasant pie, spicy bean and vegetable casserole, or pork and cider apple casserole. Well-kept ales and 14 wines by the glass complete the picture. There's also a recent addition to the garden in the shape of a gazebo/band stand. Booking for meals may be required.

Open 12-2.30 6-11 Closed: Mon **Bar Meals** L served Tue-Sun 12-2 D served Tue-Sun 6-9.30 **Restaurant** D served Tue-Sun 6.30-9 ◀ Greene King, Abbot Ale, IPA. ⬛ 14 **Facilities** Children's portions Garden Parking

GREAT OXENDON — Map 11 SP78

The George Inn

PICK OF THE PUBS

LE16 8NA ☎ 01858 465205
e-mail: info@thegeorgegreatoxendon.co.uk
dir: *A508 towards Market Harborough*

There's been a pub on the site here at the fringe of the little village of Great Oxendon for at least 500 years; reports of ghostly apparitions add to the chatter at the welcoming bar, where beers from Timothy Taylor and Adnams are supplemented by regular guest ales. The inn has been lovingly restored and refurbished over the years, retaining much character, with beams, open log fires and comfy furnishings setting the scene for an indulgence in the excellent cuisine prepared by chef-patron David Dudley. Choose the airy conservatory overlooking the gardens and start with a light bite such as salmon, sweet potato and red pepper cake, or gruyère fritters with cranberry sauce. Mains are a good mix of solid inn fare; braised beef with horseradish mash and red wine jus, or escalope of salmon on crushed potatoes with a tarragon velouté. Vegetarian options offer up ricotta and spinach tortellini.

Open 12-3 5.30-11 (Sun 12-3) Closed: 25 Dec, Sun eve ⊕ FREE HOUSE ◀ Adnams Southwold Bitter, Timothy Taylor Landlord, Guest ales. **Facilities** Children welcome Children's portions Garden Parking

HARRINGWORTH — Map 11 SP99

The White Swan

Seaton Rd NN17 3AF ☎ 01572 747543
e-mail: adam@whiteswanharringworth.co.uk
dir: *From A47 between Uppingham & Duddington take B672 signed Coldacott & Seaton. Under Harringworth Viaduct to T-junct. Left signed Harringworth. Under viaduct again. Pub in village centre on left*

A handsome, ironstone-built old coaching inn set in the verdant Welland Valley, close to where it is crossed by England's longest railway viaduct, all 82 arches of it. The 16th-century village centre inn is well respected for a wide variety of dishes created from produce of the area; wood pigeon, home-smoked trout or roast breast of guinea fowl may feature, rounded off by calorific pudding treats. Local beers and ciders are championed here, with the Welland Valley Beer Festival hosted each year.

Open 12-2.30 6.30-11 Closed: Sun eve & Mon L ◀ Adnams Southwold Bitter, Shepherd Neame Spitfire, Digfield Ales Barnwell Bitter ♦ Welland Vineyard Roundhead. **Facilities** Children welcome Children's menu Children's portions Beer festival Parking

KILSBY — Map 11 SP57

The George

Watling St CV23 8YE ☎ 01788 822229
dir: *M1 junct 18, follow A361/ Daventry signs. Pub at rdbt junct of A361 & A5*

This village pub, with its warm welcome and great local atmosphere, has a traditional public bar and a high-ceilinged wood-panelled lounge which opens into a smarter but relaxed area with solidly comfortable furnishings. The full menu might include Arbroath smokie fishcakes, chicken and bacon Caesar salad and up to 16oz steaks. Adnams, Fuller's, Old Speckled Hen and a guest real ale are well-kept on handpumps. Mondays are Pie and Pint Nights, Wednesdays are Steak and Wine, while Thursdays are devoted to burgers. There's a beer festival every St George's Day weekend. Booking for meals may be required.

Open all wk 11.30-3 5.30-11.30 (Sun 12-5 6-11) ⊕ PUNCH TAVERNS ◀ Fuller's London Pride, Morland Old Speckled Hen, Adnams Southwold Bitter. **Facilities** Children welcome Children's menu Children's portions Garden Beer festival Parking Wi-fi

NASSINGTON — Map 12 TL09

The Queens Head Inn ★★★★ INN ⊛

54 Station Rd PE8 6QB ☎ 01780 784006
e-mail: info@queensheadnassington.co.uk
dir: *Exit A1 at Wansford, follow Yarwell & Nassington signs. Through Yarwell. Pub on left in Nassington*

The beheading of Mary, Queen of Scots at nearby Fotheringhay Castle in 1587 adds a certain piquancy to the name of this stone-built inn, now in new hands. Proud of its AA Rosette, it offers favourites old and new, including treacle-braised ox-cheek; Gressingham duck breast; salted Atlantic cod; and pie or suet pudding of the week. Local farm steaks receive the Josper charcoal grill treatment, while vegetarians might like the sun-blushed tomato with French goat's cheese tart. Dine outdoors in warmer weather. Stay in one of the nine en suite bedrooms.

Open all day all wk **Bar Meals** L served all wk 12-2 D served all wk 5.30-9.30 Av main course £12 **Restaurant** L served all wk 12-2.30 D served Mon-Sat 5.30-9.30 Av 3 course à la carte fr £23 ⊕ FREE HOUSE ◀ Greene King IPA, Oakham JHB. ⬛ 8 **Facilities** ❖ Children welcome Children's menu Children's portions Garden Parking Wi-fi ▭ (notice required) **Rooms** 9

NORTHAMPTON — Map 11 SP76

Althorp Coaching Inn

Main St, Great Brington NN7 4JA ☎ 01604 770651
e-mail: althorpcoachinginn@btconnect.com
dir: *From A428 pass main gates of Althorp House, left before rail bridge. Great Brington 1m*

The listed, 16th-century stone and thatched Althorp Coaching Inn is on the Althorp Estate, the Spencer

Save on hotels. Book at theAA.com/hotel

NORTHAMPTONSHIRE 383 ENGLAND

ancestral home. A brick and cobbled courtyard is surrounded by stable rooms, and the enclosed flower garden is a wonderfully peaceful spot in which to sample one of the real ales. With exposed beams and original décor throughout, you really are transported back to the past. The cellar restaurant specialises in traditional English cooking based on locally sourced ingredients. Look out for dishes such as smoked mackerel pâté; slow-braised Rockingham Estate venison with chestnut mushrooms in a red wine sauce; and fillet of sea bass on a bed of garlic-roasted fennel.

Open all day all wk 11-11 **Bar Meals** L served all wk 12-3 D served Sun-Thu 6.30-9.30, Fri-Sat 6.30-10 **Restaurant** L served all wk 12-3 D served Sun-Thu 6.30-9.30, Fri-Sat 6.30-10 ⊕ FREE HOUSE ◀ Greene King IPA & Abbot Ale, Fuller's London Pride, Cottage Puffing Billy, Tunnell Sweet Parish Ale, 5 Guest ales ♻ Farmhouse, Thatchers Heritage. ♟ 10 **Facilities** Children welcome Children's menu Children's portions Garden Beer festival Parking Wi-fi ▦ (notice required)

OUNDLE   Map 11 TL08

The Chequered Skipper

Ashton PE8 5LD ☎ **01832 273494**
e-mail: enquiries@chequeredskipper.co.uk
dir: A605 towards Dundle, at rdbt follow signs to Ashton. 1m turn left into Ashton, pub in village

The pub sign depicts a butterfly in honour of Dame Miriam Rothschild, a renowned entomologist who lived at the banking family's country house here. The little thatched village was built for the estate workers in the 1880s; huddled by the huge green the ironstone buildings are the epitome of rural England – the World Conker Championships are held here. The pub plays its part well, with timeless oak floor and beams, and a collection of butterfly display cases diverting attention from a bar stocking locally brewed beers (two beer festivals a year). The menu mixes speciality pizzas, traditional English and European dishes - smoked pigeon; pork and blueberry terrine; and linguine with marinated artichokes and feta cheese may appear.

Open all wk 11.30-3 6-11 (Sat 11.30-11 Sun 11.45-11) ⊕ FREE HOUSE ◀ Rockingham Ale, Brewster's Hophead, Oakham. **Facilities** Children welcome Children's portions Garden Beer festival Parking Wi-fi

SIBBERTOFT   Map 11 SP68

The Red Lion

PICK OF THE PUBS

43 Welland Rise LE16 9UD ☎ **01858 880011**
e-mail: andrew@redlionwinepub.co.uk
web: www.redlionwinepub.co.uk
dir: From Market Harborough take A4304, through Lubenham, left through Marston Trussell to Sibbertoft

Since taking over this friendly 300-year-old free house in 2004, Andrew and Sarah Banks have created an appealing blend of contemporary and classic décor, with

oak beams, leather upholstery and a smartly turned-out dining room. In fine weather, meals are served in the quiet garden – a favourite with local walkers and cyclists – and there's also a children's play area. Wine is the owners' special passion; over 200 bins appear on the ever-growing wine list, and 20 labels are served by the glass. After tasting, all the wines can be bought at take-home prices, avoiding the guesswork of supermarket purchases. Booking is required to sample the monthly-changing menu, which is served throughout the pub. For dinner, oven baked camembert, celery and crusty bread might herald hake fillet with prawn and caper butter and creamy mash, before rounding off with apple and sultana strudel. Booking for meals may be required.

Open 12-2 6.30-11 Closed: Mon L & Tue L, Sun eve **Bar Meals** L served Wed-Sun 12-2 D served Mon-Sat 6.30-9.30 Av main course £10 **Restaurant** L served Wed-Sun 12-2 D served Mon-Sat 6.30-9.30 Fixed menu price fr £12 Av 3 course à la carte fr £19 ⊕ FREE HOUSE ◀ Timothy Taylor Landlord, Black Sheep, Adnams ♻ Samuel Smith's Organic, Aspall. ♟ 20 **Facilities** Children welcome Children's menu Children's portions Play area Garden Parking Wi-fi ▦

STOKE BRUERNE   Map 11 SP74

The Boat Inn

NN12 7SB ☎ **01604 862428**
e-mail: info@boatinn.co.uk
web: www.boatinn.co.uk
dir: In village centre, just off A508 or A5

On the banks of the Grand Union Canal, just across the lock from the National Waterways Museum, this busy free house has been run by the Woodward family since 1877. The all-day bar menu proffers hot baguettes, light bites, burgers, and main courses such as full rack of ribs, fisherman's platter, and nut roast. For a more formal experience overlooking the peaceful waters, the Woodwards Restaurant offers à la carte and set menus, including beetroot and goat's cheese salad; butternut squash jalousie; and pork belly with apple and sage gravy. Booking for meals may be required.

Open all day all wk 9.30am-11pm (Sun 9.30am-10.30pm) **Bar Meals** L served all wk 9.30-9.30 D served all wk 9.30-9.30 Av main course £8.75 food served all day **Restaurant** L served Tue-Sun 12-2 D served all wk 7-9 Fixed menu price fr £14.95 Av 3 course à la carte fr £25 ⊕ FREE HOUSE ◀ Banks's Bitter, Marston's Pedigree, Frog Island Best Bitter, Marston's Old Empire, Wychwood Hobgoblin, Jennings Cumberland Ale ♻ Thatchers Traditional. ♟ 10 **Facilities** ✿ Children

welcome Children's menu Children's portions Garden Parking ▦

TITCHMARSH   Map 11 TL07

The Wheatsheaf at Titchmarsh

1 North St NN14 3DH ☎ **01832 732203**
e-mail: enquiries@thewheatsheafattitchmarsh.co.uk
dir: From A14 junct 13 take A605 towards Oundle, right to Titchmarsh. Or from A14 junct 14 follow signs for Titchmarsh

After Darren and Amy Harding took over this stone-built village pub in 2010, they made sure its delightful character remained unthreatened by refurbishment. Greene King real ales are backed by others from Fuller's, Butcombe and regularly changing guests, and sandwiches are made on demand. Among the light snacks are chicken and button mushroom casserole, and venison sausages with mash, while for a typical main meal consider sun-blushed tomato chicken breast in pancetta; confit duck leg; oven-roasted haddock glazed with Welsh rarebit; or chestnut and oyster mushroom tart. There are chargrills too. Booking for meals may be required.

Open all wk 12-3 6-11 (Sat-Sun 12-10) **Bar Meals** L served Mon-Thu 12-2, Fri-Sat 12-2.30, Sun 12-5 D served Mon-Sat 6-9.30 Av main course £7 **Restaurant** L served Mon-Thu 12-2, Fri-Sat 12-2.30, Sun 12-5 D served Mon-Sat 6-9.30 Fixed menu price fr £12 Av 3 course à la carte fr £27 ⊕ FREE HOUSE ◀ Greene King IPA, Sharp's Doom Bar, Fuller's London Pride, Butcombe, Guest ales ♻ Westons Stowford Press. ♟ 11 **Facilities** Children welcome Children's portions Garden Parking Wi-fi ▦ (notice required)

TOWCESTER   Map 11 SP64

The Saracens Head

219 Watling St NN12 8BX ☎ **01327 350414**
e-mail: saracenshead.towcester@greeneking.co.uk
dir: From M1 junct 15A, A43 towards Oxford. Take A5 signed Towcester

This imposing building dates back over 400 years, and is featured in Charles Dickens' first novel, The Pickwick Papers. The same home comforts that Dickens enjoyed when visiting Towcester have been updated to modern standards, and discerning customers will find excellent service in the restored pub. Main menu choices include guinea fowl stuffed with pancetta; baked salmon fillet with a tomato, pepper and white wine Provençale sauce; and Mediterranean vegetable lasagne with a dressed salad. Booking for meals may be required.

Open all day all wk ⊕ GREENE KING/OLD ENGLISH INNS ◀ Abbot Ale & IPA, Guest ale. **Facilities** Children welcome Children's menu Children's portions Garden Parking Wi-fi

PICK OF THE PUBS

The Crown

WESTON — Map 11 SP54

Helmdon Rd NN12 8PX
☎ **01295 760310**
e-mail: info@thecrownweston.co.uk
web: www.thecrownweston.co.uk
dir: *Accessed from A43 or B4525*

This 16th-century inn has been serving ale since the reign of Elizabeth I, the first recorded owner being All Souls College, Oxford. The pub is probably best known as the place where Lord Lucan was allegedly spotted enjoying a pint the day after the brutal murder of his children's nanny in 1974 and he was never seen again. The latest in a long line of proprietors is Robert Grover, who took over The Crown ten years ago. He has ensured that his pub continues to feature prominently in the life of the local community by hosting regular special events such as curry evenings. The pub is well known for the provision of excellent beers, a short but elegant range of dishes based on high quality ingredients, welcoming staff and its family-friendly atmosphere. Real ales are a strength, at least four in number, and wines are reasonably priced, from the gluggable house wines to sophisticated gems from top producers. New chef Veronica Drysdale flies the flag for local produce and her seasonal menus include at least four daily pies, including venison and Guinness; and

chicken, leek and ham in a creamy sauce. From the pub classics section of the menu, typical choices include lamb curry with rice and mango chutney; beer battered haddock with minted peas, chips and tartare sauce; and duck confit with purple sprouting broccoli, dauphinoise potatoes and a rich jus. Round off with marmalade sponge pudding and vanilla ice cream; chocolate and nut brownie; or rhubarb crème brûlée. Traditional roasts on Sundays are popular all year round and the meat comes from a local farm shop. Nearby attractions to the pub include Sulgrave Manor, the ancestral home of George Washington, and Silverstone racing circuit.

Open all wk 6-11.30 (Fri-Sat 12-3.30 6-11.30 Sun 12-3.30 7-11) Closed: 25 Dec **Bar Meals** L served Fri-Sun 12-2.30 D served Wed-Sat 6-9.30 Av main course £10 ⊕ FREE HOUSE ◀ Greene King IPA, Hook Norton Best, Timothy Taylor Landlord, St Austell Tribute, Black Sheep ♂ Westons Stowford Press. **Facilities** Children welcome Children's portions Family room ☆ Garden Parking Wi-fi 🚌 (notice required)

The King's Head

PICK OF THE PUBS

Church St PE8 5ST ☎ 01832 720024
e-mail: aletha@wadenhoekingshead.co.uk
dir: *From A605, 3m from Wadenhoe rdbt. 2m from Oundle*

Set in the unspoilt village of Wadenhoe, alongside the picturesque River Nene, this stone-built, partially thatched inn has been serving travellers since the 17th century. In the summer, grab a seat in extensive riverside gardens in the shade of the ancient willow trees and watch the colourful narrow boats over a pint of King's Head Bitter; August also brings a beer festival. In winter, head for the comfortable bar with its quarry-tiled and bare-boarded floors, heavy oak-beamed ceilings, pine furniture and open log fires. The pub offers the most modern facilities but has lost none of its old world charm. The lunchtime menu offers sandwiches, pies and light bites such as home-made burger topped with cheddar cheese and chips or a ploughman's. In the evening you can feast like a king on warm pork and black pudding terrine with apple sauce, or roast chicken, tarragon and shallot pot pie, minted new potatoes and purple sprouting broccoli.

Open all day all wk 11-11 (Sun 12-10 winter 11-2.30 5.30-11 Sun 12-6) Closed: Sun eve in winter **Bar Meals** L served all wk 12-2.30 D served all wk 6-9 Av main course £10.95 **Restaurant** L served all wk 12-2.30 D served all wk 6-9 ⊕ FREE HOUSE ◀ King's Head Bitter, Digfield Barnwell Bitter, Hogs Back BSA Ŏ Kingstone Press. ☻ 15 **Facilities** Children welcome Children's portions Garden Beer festival Parking ▨

The Crown

PICK OF THE PUBS

See Pick of the Pubs on opposite page

The Wollaston Inn

PICK OF THE PUBS

87 London Rd NN29 7QS ☎ 01933 666473
e-mail: info@wollaston-inn.co.uk
dir: *From Wellingborough, onto A509 towards Wollaston. After 2m, over rdbt, then immediately left. Inn at top of hill*

In the late Sixties and early Seventies when this was the Nags Head, the resident Sunday night DJ here was the late John Peel; its star-studded musical history includes appearances by U2, Rod Stewart and Thin Lizzie. Then, in 2003, it was reinvented as a restaurant within a pub. Renamed and restored, the 350-year-old building's interior provides a commendable backdrop to soft Italian leather sofas, casual tables and chairs, and ambient lighting. Today its association with live music is set for a revival, with the function room hosting up and coming bands on Saturday nights. Beer lovers have a great choice, with Marston's and guests among others, and Peroni on draught is a new addition. 'Great food at great prices' is The Wollaston's dining promise. The line-up starts with traditional pub lunch favourites (home-made steakburger; ham, double egg and chips); in the evening go for a chef's special such a Thai-style red curry, or minted lamb cutlets.

Open all day all wk **Bar Meals** Av main course £10-£15 food served all day **Restaurant** food served all day ⊕ FREE HOUSE ◀ Marston's Burton Bitter, Guinness, Guest ales. ☻ 16 **Facilities** ♣ Children welcome Children's menu Children's portions Garden Parking Wi-fi ▨ (notice required)

NORTHUMBERLAND

The Masons Arms

Stamford, Nr Rennington NE66 3RX ☎ 01665 577275
e-mail: bookings@masonsarms.net
web: www.masonsarms.net
dir: *NE of Alnwick on B1340, 0.5m past Rennington*

A tastefully modernised 200-year-old coaching inn, known by the local community as Stamford Cott. It is a useful staging post for visitors to Hadrian's Wall, Lindisfarne and the large number of nearby golf courses. There is a great range of beers to enjoy, including Farne Island and Secret Kingdom. The substantial home-cooked food is available in the bar and the restaurant, and is made using the best of local produce. Typical examples include lemon sole with prawns and parsley sauce, or Northumbrian game casserole.

Open all wk 12-2 6.30-11 (Sun 12-2 6.30-10.30) **Bar Meals** L served all wk 12-2 D served all wk 6.30-9 ⊕ FREE HOUSE ◀ John Smith's, Theakston Best Bitter, Hadrian Border Secret Kingdom, Gladiator & Farne Island. **Facilities** Children welcome Children's menu Children's portions Family room Garden Parking ▨

The Barrasford Arms **NEW**

NE48 4AA ☎ 01434 681237
e-mail: contact@barrasfordarms.co.uk
dir: *From A69 at Hexham take A6079 signed Acomb & Chollerford. In Chollerford by church turn left signed Barrasford*

Chef Tony Binks's destination food pub stands close to Hadrian's Wall deep in the glorious Northumbrian countryside. Despite the emphasis on food, it retains a traditional pub atmosphere, with local Wylam and Hadrian Border ales on tap in the time-honoured bar, which fills with locals and passing walkers and cyclists. Most beat a path to the door for Tony's short, imaginative menus, which bristle with local farm beef and lamb and seasonal game. Typically, tuck into ham hock terrine; grey mullet with pepper, chorizo, saffron and tomato broth; and vanilla and mascarpone rice pudding. His set lunches are great value. Booking for meals may be required.

Open 12-3 6-11 (Sat-Sun all day) Closed: 1st wk Jan, Mon L **Restaurant** L served Tue-Sun 12-2 D served Mon-Sat 6.30-9 Fixed menu price fr £11.50 Av 3 course à la carte fr £25 ⊕ FREE HOUSE ◀ Wylam Gold Tankard, Hadrian Border Gladiator. **Facilities** Garden Parking ▨ (notice required)

Blue Bell Hotel

Market Place NE70 7NE ☎ 01668 213543
e-mail: enquiries@bluebellhotel.com
dir: *Off A1, 15m N of Alnwick, 15m S of Berwick-upon-Tweed*

Halfway between Alnwick and Berwick on the old London to Edinburgh road, this independently run, creeper-covered 17th-century coaching inn stands in the heart of the village in fine gardens, beyond which, through the trees, rises Belford church tower. Local meats, game, fish and cheeses are employed to good effect in the Garden Restaurant, Tavern Bar and Bistro, whose menus present the tastes of Northumbria and beyond. The perfect spot to unwind after a day of walking, cycling, watersports or golf. Booking for meals may be required.

Open all day all wk 11am-mdnt ⊕ FREE HOUSE ◀ Tetley's Smoothflow, Calders, Black Sheep, Guinness. **Facilities** Children welcome Children's menu Children's portions Play area Garden Parking Wi-fi

CARTERWAY HEADS
Map 19 NZ05

The Manor House Inn

PICK OF THE PUBS

DH8 9LX ☎ **01207 255268**
e-mail: barrie.wray@schiedel.co.uk
dir: *A69 W from Newcastle, left onto A68 then S for 8m.
Inn on right*

Just 30 minutes from both Newcastle and Durham, this small family-run pub is an ideal base for exploring the region. Occupying an elevated position on the A68, overlooking open moorland and the stunning Derwent Valley, the pub was built around 1760. The stone-walled bar, with log fires, low-beamed ceiling and massive timber support, serves five real ales all year, among which are Theakston Best and Workie Ticket from the Mordue brewery in North Shields. The bar and lounge are good for a snack, while the restaurant is divided into two dining areas, the larger of which welcomes families with children. Most produce is local, and includes game birds from the fields around the pub, rabbit that is hawk-caught on the moors, and venison from local herds. A sample menu includes fish pie, sirloin steak, Cumberland sausage and mash, and vegetable pancake.

Open all day all wk 11-11 (Sun 12-10.30) **Bar Meals** Av main course £10.95 food served all day **Restaurant** food served all day ⊕ ENTERPRISE INNS ◀ Theakston Best Bitter, Mordue Workie Ticket, Greene King Ruddles County, Courage Directors, Morland Old Speckled Hen Ö Westons Old Rosie. ☗ 8 **Facilities** ❖ Children welcome Children's menu Children's portions Garden Parking Wi-fi ▭ (notice required)

CORBRIDGE
Map 21 NY96

The Angel of Corbridge

Main St NE45 5LA ☎ **01434 632119**
e-mail: info@theangelofcorbridge.com
dir: *0.5m off A69, signed Corbridge*

A coaching inn since 1726, this refurbished free house offers a stylish split-level bar, afternoon tea on squashy sofas in the comfortable wood panelled lounge, as well as a handsome new restaurant with a beamed and vaulted ceiling. The menu features classic dishes such as chargrilled sirloin steak with green peppercorn sauce and hand-cut chips, alongside more innovative meals like steamed fresh mussels in Bloody Mary sauce. Finish, perhaps, with lemon and lime cheesecake and elderflower sorbet.

Open all day all wk **Bar Meals** D served all wk except Sun Av main course £11 food served all day **Restaurant** D served all wk except Sun Av 3 course à la carte fr £21 food served all day ⊕ FREE HOUSE ◀ Timothy Taylor Landlord, Local ales. ☗ **Facilities** Children welcome Children's menu Children's portions Garden Parking Wi-fi ▭ (notice required)

CRASTER
Map 21 NU21

The Jolly Fisherman NEW

Haven Hill NE66 3TR ☎ **01665 576461**
e-mail: dkwhitehead@hotmail.com
dir: *Exit A1 at Denwick*

Choosing a splendid harbourside location, a fisherman called Chas Archbold opened this pub in 1847, when Craster was a thriving fishing village. Only a few boats, usually East Coast cobles, now go out, mostly for the herring that are smoked to become Craster's famous kippers. Lunchtime and evening house specialities are home-made crab soup with whisky and cream, crab sandwiches, and kipper pâté; toasties, pizza and burger and chips are also available. Mordue Brewery's Workie Ticket bitter is at the bar. A pub refurb was planned for 2012.

Open all day all wk **Bar Meals** food served all day **Restaurant** food served all day ⊕ PUNCH TAVERNS ◀ Mordue Workie Ticket, Black Sheep. ☗ 12 **Facilities** ❖ Children welcome Children's menu Children's portions Garden Parking Wi-fi ▭ (notice required)

ETAL
Map 21 NT93

Black Bull

TD12 4TL ☎ **01890 820200**
dir: *Off A697, left at junct for 1m then left into Etal*

The Black Bull stands by the ruins of Etal Castle, not far from the River Till, with the grand walking country of the Cheviots on the doorstep. The only thatched pub in Northumberland, it serves traditional pub food such as deep-fried fish with home-made chips and mushy peas; chilli con carne; and a selection of home-made suet crust pastry pies: try chicken, leek and stilton; or steak and black pudding. In the summer months the Heatherslaw Light Railway runs a steam engine to the village every half hour.

Open 12-3 6-11 (summer 11-11) Closed: Tue (winter) ⊕ PUBMASTER ◀ Caledonian Deuchars IPA, John Smith's Smooth. **Facilities** Children welcome Children's menu Garden Parking ▭

FALSTONE
Map 21 NY78

The Pheasant Inn ★★★★ INN

PICK OF THE PUBS

See Pick of the Pubs on opposite page

HALTWHISTLE
Map 21 NY76

Milecastle Inn

Military Rd, Cawfields NE49 9NN ☎ **01434 321372**
e-mail: clarehind@aol.com
dir: *From A69 into Haltwhistle. Pub approx 2m at junct with B6318*

A traditional pub decorated with horse brasses and local pictures, the Milecastle occupies a wonderfully remote

and peaceful location high on the moorland edge. One horizon is serrated by the line of Hadrian's Wall and there are easy walks up the lane past Roman camps to reach Milecastle 42 beside the Wall at Cawfield Crags. Tasty beers from Newcastle's Big Lamp Brewery are ample reward for a breezy stroll, accompanied perhaps by game pâté with toast; chicken curry with rice and chips; or a choice of pies. A roaring winter fire takes the chill, or you could sit outside and enjoy the curlew-haunted countryside.

Open all day all wk 12-11 (12-3 6-10 Nov-Mar) **Bar Meals** L served all wk 12-2.30 winter, 12-8.45 summer D served all wk 6-8.30 winter, 12-8.45 summer Av main course £10 **Restaurant** L served all wk 12-2.30 winter, 12-8.45 summer D served all wk 6-8.30 winter, 12-8.45 summer ⊕ FREE HOUSE ◀ Big Lamp Prince Bishop, Sunny Daze. **Facilities** Children welcome Children's menu Children's portions Garden Parking Wi-fi ▭ (notice required)

HAYDON BRIDGE
Map 21 NY86

The General Havelock Inn

Ratcliffe Rd NE47 6ER ☎ **01434 684376**
e-mail: info@generalhavelock.co.uk
dir: *On A69, 7m W of Hexham*

Built in around 1766, this riverside free house is named after a 19th-century British Army officer. The pub, with its restaurant in a converted stone barn overlooking the River Tyne, is a favourite with local showbusiness personalities. In summer, the patio area is covered by a marquee. The real ales are all sourced from a 15-mile radius: Mordue Workie Ticket, Geltsdale Cold Fell are but two. Owner/chef Gary Thompson makes everything by hand, including the bread and ice cream. Local ingredients are the foundation of his signature dishes, which include Cullen skink, duck with sugar snap pea salad, and bread-and-butter pudding. Look out for themed nights. Booking for meals may be required.

Open 12-2.30 7-12 Closed: Mon **Bar Meals** L served Tue-Sun 12-2 D served Tue-Sun 7-9 Av main course £12 **Restaurant** L served Tue-Sun 12-2 D served Tue-Sun 7-9 Fixed menu price fr £16 Av 3 course à la carte fr £25 ⊕ FREE HOUSE ◀ High House Farm Nel's Best, Geltsdale Cold Fell, Big Lamp Bitter, Mordue Workie Ticket, Cumberland Corby Blonde, Allendale. ☗ 15 **Facilities** ❖ Children welcome Children's portions Family room Garden Wi-fi ▭ (notice required)

HEDLEY ON THE HILL
Map 19 NZ05

The Feathers Inn

PICK OF THE PUBS

See Pick of the Pubs on page 388

Save on hotels. Book at theAA.com/hotel

NORTHUMBERLAND 387 ENGLAND

PICK OF THE PUBS

The Pheasant Inn ★★★★INN

FALSTONE Map 21 NY78

Stannersburn NE48 1DD
☎ **01434 240382**
e-mail: stay@thepheasantinn.com
web: www.thepheasantinn.com
dir: *A69, B6079, B6320, follow signs for Kielder Water*

Byroads thread this particularly pretty part of the Northumberland National Park, meandering between verdant valleys, high moors and tranquil woodlands at the edge of the Cheviot Hills. Here too are England's largest man-made forest and biggest reservoir, Kielder Water. Ideally sited to take full advantage is the ivy-clad Pheasant Inn, secluded at the forest's edge beside a lane heading towards the cycle tracks, sculpture trail, observatory, endless walks and superb wildlife watching (lots of red squirrels here) that set Kielder apart. Long before forest or lake existed, farmers visited a beerhouse at Stannersburn; from such beginnings as long ago as 1624 has developed today's archetypical old country inn; effortlessly welcoming, endlessly satisfying and with eight individually styled bedrooms to tempt travellers to tarry awhile. Photos of yesteryear's locals and trades festoon the exposed stone walls that support blackened beams; light from winter log fires flickers across antique artefacts and furniture whilst summer guests use a stream-side garden of utter tranquillity. There's also a tasteful,

terracotta-hued dining room where the daily-changing menu makes the most of Northumberland's generous larder, creatively cooked by Irene and Robin Kershaw. Caramelised red onion and goat's cheese tartlet, or farmhouse pâté with toast starters set the scene for confit of duck breast with a port and raspberry glaze, or roast sirloin of beef with Yorkshire pudding. A good range of fish fresh from North Shields fish quay add to the choice, including perhaps fresh dressed crab with new potatoes and salad. Excellent beers from Wylam Brewery satisfy guests eager to get their fill of Northumberland's bounty. Booking for meals may be required.

Open 12-3 6.30-11 Closed: 25-27 Dec, Mon-Tue (Nov-Mar) **Bar Meals** L served

Mon-Sat 12-2.30 D served all wk 7–9 Av main course £9.50 **Restaurant** L served Mon-Sat 12-2.30 D served Mon-Sat 6.30-8.30 Av 3 course à la carte fr £24.95 ⊕ FREE HOUSE ◄ Timothy Taylor Landlord, Wylam Gold Tankard, Rocket, Red Kite, Red Shot & Angel. **Facilities** Children welcome Children's menu Children's portions Play area Family room Garden Parking Wi-fi **Rooms** 8

PICK OF THE PUBS

The Feathers Inn

HEDLEY ON THE HILL   Map 19 NZ05

NE43 7SW ☎ 01661 843607
e-mail: info@thefeathers.net
web: www.thefeathers.net
dir: *Telephone for directions*

This small stone-built free house is well patronised locally, but strangers are frequently charmed by the friendly and relaxed atmosphere created here by owners Rhian Cradock and Helen Greer. It's also worth the detour for its tip-top Northumbrian micro-brewery ales, some cracking pub food and the splendid views across the Cheviot Hills. Old oak beams, stone walls decorated with local photographs, coal fires and rustic settles set the informal scene, and there's a good selection of traditional pub games like shove ha'penny and bar skittles. Rhian's impressive daily menu makes sound use of the freshest local ingredients – including game from local shoots, rare-breed local cattle and Longhorn beef – to create great British classics as well as regional dishes from the north east. You could start with potted local hare and middlewhite pork with toast and pickled walnuts, or Rhian's home-made black pudding with a village egg and devilled gravy. Typical main courses range from a hearty Angus steak-and-kidney pie with creamy mash and buttered carrots to grilled North Sea plaice with heritage potatoes, spinach, white wine and samphire velouté. Leave room for desserts like sticky date pudding

with butterscotch sauce and local cream, or dark chocolate tart with marmalade ice cream. Relax and sup one of the cask ales, perhaps Wylam Red Kite or Mordue Workie Ticket, beside a real open fire and dip into one of the many cookery books that spill out all over the place. The Feathers is the perfect location to enjoy a relaxing lunch with beautiful Northumbrian views, or meet with friends for an intimate dinner. Families are welcome, and a small side room can be booked in advance if required. The annual beer and food festival takes place over Easter and includes a barrel race, egg jarping, barbecue and a farmers' market. Booking for meals may be required.

Open all wk 12-11 (Mon 6-11 Sun 12-10.30) Closed: No food served 1st

2wks Jan **Bar Meals** L served Tue-Sat 12-2, Sun 12-2.30 D served Tue-Sat 6-8.30 Av main course £12 ⊕ FREE HOUSE ◧ Mordue Workie Ticket, Fuller's London Pride, Northumberland Pit Pony, Orkney Red MacGregor, Hadrian Border Gladiator, Wylam Red Kite, The Consett Ale Works Red Dust ♂ Westons 1st Quality & Old Rosie. ♀
Facilities Children welcome Children's portions Beer festival Parking Wi-fi

Save on hotels. Book at **theAA.com/hotel**

NORTHUMBERLAND 389 ENGLAND

HEXHAM   Map 21 NY96

Battlesteads Hotel & Restaurant
PICK OF THE PUBS

See Pick of the Pubs on page 390

Dipton Mill Inn
PICK OF THE PUBS

Dipton Mill Rd NE46 1YA ☎ 01434 606577
e-mail: ghb@hexhamshire.co.uk
dir: *2m S of Hexham on HGV route to Blanchland, B6306, Dipton Mill Rd*

A former farmhouse, with the millstream running right through the gardens, the pub was rebuilt some 400 years ago. It is surrounded by farmland and woods with footpaths for pleasant country walks, and Hadrian's Wall and other Roman sites are close by. The Dipton Mill is home to Hexhamshire Brewery ales, which include Devil's Water and Old Humbug. All dishes are freshly prepared from local produce where possible. Start with home-made soup, such as spiced parsnip served with a warm roll, followed by hearty dishes like mince and dumplings; lamb leg steak in wine and mustard sauce; or tomato, bean and vegetable casserole. Traditional desserts include creamy lemon tart; chocolate rum and truffle torte; and bread-and-butter pudding. Good cheese selection. Salads, sandwiches and ploughman's are also always available.

Open 12-2.30 6-11 (Sun 12-3) Closed: 25 Dec, Sun eve **Bar Meals** L served all wk 12-2 D served Mon-Sat 6.30-8 Av main course £7.50 ⊕ FREE HOUSE ◀ Hexhamshire Shire Bitter, Old Humbug, Devil's Water, Devil's Elbow, Whapweasel, Blackhall English Stout Ŏ Westons Old Rosie. ♈ 17 **Facilities** Children welcome Children's portions Garden ⊞ (notice required) **Notes** ⊛

Miners Arms Inn

Main St, Acomb NE46 4PW ☎ 01434 603909
e-mail: info@theminersacomb.com
dir: *17m W of Newcastle on A69. 2m W of Hexham*

A family-run village pub dating from 1746, The Miners occupies a peaceful spot near Hadrian's Wall. Three top local real ales are always available, with guest deliveries from further afield every weekend. Mainly locally sourced dishes, including vegetable or beef chilli; Cumberland sausage casserole; and wholetail scampi typify the traditional pub food. Visitors can enjoy the open hearth fire, the suntrap of a beer garden, or sitting out front absorbing village life. Beer festivals are held occasionally. Booking for meals may be required.

Open all wk 5-12 (Sat 2.30-12 Sun 12-12) ⊕ FREE HOUSE ◀ Wylam Bitter, Pilsner Urquell, Yates Best Bitter Ŏ Perry's Farm Pressed. **Facilities** ♚ Children welcome Garden Beer festival **Notes** ⊛

Rat Inn
PICK OF THE PUBS

NE46 4LN ☎ 01434 602814
e-mail: info@theratinn.com
dir: *2m from Hexham, Bridge End (A69) rdbt, take 4th exit signed Oakwood. Inn 500yds on right*

This former drovers' inn catered to farmers from the Borders stopping off on their way to the market in Hexham, which is only a mile away. Just how the Rat came by its name is shrouded in mystery. On sunny days soak up the spectacular views of the Tyne Valley from its glorious hillside garden. On cooler days retreat into the classic bar, where you'll find crackling log fires, a flagstone floor, old pews and benches and an impressive oak bar dispensing six local micro-brewery ales. Peruse the papers over a pint, then order a plate of food from an interesting daily menu that bristles with locally sourced ingredients – a blackboard in the bar details the farms where the day's meats have come from. In addition, herbs are grown in the pub garden and the cheeseboard features only Northumbrian cheeses. Typically, tuck into rack of lamb; confit duck leg; or pan haggerty, a potato and cheese layered dish - a Northumbrian favourite. Leave room for sticky toffee pudding. Booking for meals may be required.

Open all day all wk **Bar Meals** L served Tue-Sat 12-2, Sun 12-3 D served Tue-Sat 6-9 Av main course £12 **Restaurant** L served Tue-Sat 12-2, Sun 12-3 D served Tue-Sat 6-9 Av 3 course à la carte fr £20 ⊕ FREE HOUSE ◀ 6 Guest ales. ♈ **Facilities** Children welcome Children's portions Garden Parking Wi-fi

LONGFRAMLINGTON   Map 21 NU10

The Anglers Arms
PICK OF THE PUBS

Weldon Bridge NE65 8AX ☎ 01665 570271 & 570655
e-mail: johnyoung@anglersarms.fsnet.co.uk
dir: *Take A697 N of Morpeth signed Wooler & Coldstream. 7m, left to Weldon Bridge*

Commanding the picturesque Weldon Bridge over the River Coquet since the 1760s, this part-battlemented, former coaching inn on the road to Scotland is full of knick-knacks and curios, pictures and fishing memorabilia. Timothy Taylor Landlord and Theakston Best Bitter are among the real ales to accompany bar meals like Chinese duck salad or traditional cod and chips. An old Pullman railway carriage provides a different dining experience, with silver service as standard, and dishes such as tournedos Flodden, which is prime fillet stuffed with Applewood cheese wrapped in bacon and coated in garlic sauce; grilled fillet of salmon with new potatoes, baby corn, green beans, rocket and chilli sauce; and stir-fried vegetable sizzler. The carefully tended half-acre of garden is perfect for alfresco dining and includes a children's play park. You can fish on the pub's own mile of River Coquet. Booking for meals may be required.

Open all day all wk 11-11 (Sun 12-10.30) **Bar Meals** L served all wk 12-9.30 D served all wk 12-9.30 Av main

course £10 food served all day **Restaurant** L served all wk 12-9.30 D served all wk 12-9.30 Fixed menu price fr £15 Av 3 course à la carte fr £25 food served all day ⊕ FREE HOUSE ◀ Timothy Taylor Landlord, Morland Old Speckled Hen, Greene King Abbot Ale, Theakston Best Bitter. **Facilities** ♚ Children welcome Children's portions Play area Family room Garden Parking ⊞ (notice required)

LONGHORSLEY   Map 21 NZ19

Linden Tree ★★★★ HL ⊛⊛

Linden Hall NE65 8XF ☎ 01670 500033
e-mail: lindenhall@macdonald-hotels.co.uk
dir: *Off A1 on A697, 1m N of Longhorsley*

Golf shoes are certainly welcome at this friendly pub set within the grounds of Linden Hall, the impressive Georgian mansion that is now a popular golf and country club with 50 bedrooms. A sunny patio makes for a relaxed setting in summer and the brasserie-style menu might include a classic prawn cocktail; 21-day aged Scottish beefburger; grilled fillet of Scottish salmon with watercress sauce or steak-and-ale pie. Round off a long day with a nightcap in the golfers' lounge.

Open all wk Mon-Sat 11-11 (Sun 11-10.30) ⊕ FREE HOUSE ◀ Greene King IPA, Worthington's, Guinness. **Facilities** Children welcome Children's menu Children's portions Play area Garden Parking ⊞ (notice required) **Rooms** 50

LOW NEWTON BY THE SEA   Map 21 NU22

The Ship Inn

The Square NE66 3EL ☎ 01665 576262
e-mail: forsythchristine@hotmail.com
dir: *NE from A1 at Alnwick towards Seahouses*

Newton Haven beach is bang opposite this pretty inn on the green in a still delightfully unspoilt, 18th-century fishing village. The pub is self-sufficient in real ale because it brews its own next door. Barrels of Sea Coal, Dolly Day Dream, Ship Hop Ale and Sandcastles at Dawn are then rolled a mere 10ft to the cellar, from where they are pumped to the small curved bar. Here you can expect plenty of locally caught fresh and smoked fish, free-range meats, interesting vegetarian food, and old-fashioned puddings such as crumbles. Booking for meals may be required.

Open all wk seasonal variations, please telephone for details **Bar Meals** L served all wk 12-2.30 D served all wk 7-8 (some seasonal variations, please telephone for details) ⊕ FREE HOUSE ◀ The Ship Inn Sea Coal, Dolly Day Dream, Sea Wheat, Ship Hop Ale, Sandcastles at Dawn. **Facilities** ♚ Children welcome Garden **Notes** ⊛

PICK OF THE PUBS

Battlesteads Hotel & Restaurant

HEXHAM   Map 21 NY96

Wark NE48 3LS ☎ 01434 230209
e-mail: info@battlesteads.com
web: www.battlesteads.com
dir: *10m N of Hexham on B6320 (Kielder road)*

Outstanding green credentials, including a carbon-neutral heating system, account for some of the awards picked up by Richard and Dee Slade's hotel, restaurant and pub. Standing just a few miles north of Hadrian's Wall and close to Kielder Forest and Border Riever country, it was converted from an 18th-century farmhouse and is utterly charming – from the flower tubs and hanging baskets to Gilroy the cat, who long ago adopted the place as his home. Renowned for superb food, there are three dining options: a relaxed bar area, where Durham Magus and other regional real ales are on tap; the conservatory, with views of the secret walled garden; and the main restaurant where dark wood furnishings, low lighting and old British Railways travel posters create a more formal setting. Chef Eddie Shilton sources all the food from the two-acre gardens and polytunnels, or from no more than 25 miles away from the village. His style, primarily modern British with a smattering of international choices, leads to seasonal game, Cumbrian beef,

Northumbrian lamb, and fish and seafood from North Shields. Look out too for Louisiana chicken with a red onion, bacon and prawn cream sauce; confit of duck leg; and butternut squash risotto. Dee's desserts include award-winning whisky and marmalade bread-and-butter pudding; fruit Pavlova; and local cheeses that might be hard to find further south. Guests are encouraged to log the wildlife they see around the hotel, and someone who knows their birds has noted a leucistic, or albino, oystercatcher among the buzzards, ospreys and red kites. Richard is always pleased to conduct a tour of the hotel's green installations. There's usually a beer festival in summer. Booking for meals may be required.

Open all day all wk **Bar Meals** L served all wk 12-3 D served all wk 6.30-9.30 **Restaurant** L served all wk 12-3 D served all wk 6.30-9.30 ⊕ FREE HOUSE ◼ Durham Magus, Black Sheep Best Bitter, High House Farm Nel's Best, Guest ales ♂ Thatchers Gold. ☙ 13 **Facilities** Children welcome Children's portions ❖ Garden Beer festival Parking Wi-fi 🚌 (notice required)

Save on hotels. Book at **theAA.com/hotel**

NORTHUMBERLAND 391 **ENGLAND**

MILFIELD
Map 21 NT93

The Red Lion Inn

Main Rd NE71 6JD ☎ 01668 216224
e-mail: redlioninn@fsmail.net
web: www.redlionmilfield.co.uk
dir: *On A697, 9m S of Coldstream (6m N of Wooler)*

Three hundred years ago this stone building was a sheep drovers' pub. Later it became a stagecoach inn, then during World War II it was popular with fighter pilots based nearby. Situated on the edge of Northumberland National Park, it is within easy reach of fishing on both the Till and Tweed, walking routes in the Cheviot Hills, and the battle site of Flodden Field (AD1513). Locally sourced ingredients feature in dishes such as honey roast pork belly with bubble-and-squeak; home-made steak-and-ale pie; spinach and butternut squash curry; and poached salmon fillet wrapped in smoked bacon. There's also a choice of excellent guest beers to wash it all down with. Booking for meals may be required.

Open all wk 11-2 5-11 (Sat 11-11 Sun 11-10.30) Apr-Nov **Bar Meals** L served Mon-Fri 11-2, Sat-Sun 11-9 D served Mon-Fri 5-9, Sat-Sun 11-9 ⊕ FREE HOUSE ◀ Caledonian Deuchars IPA, Black Sheep, Guinness, Guest ales ♂ Thatchers Gold. **Facilities** Children welcome Children's menu Children's portions Garden Parking Wi-fi ⛟

NETHERTON
Map 21 NT90

The Star Inn

NE65 7HD ☎ 01669 630238
dir: *7m from Rothbury*

Little has changed at this timeless gem since the Wilson-Morton family took over in 1917. Lost in superb remote countryside north of Rothbury, The Star retains many period features and the bar is like stepping into someone's living room, comfortable and quiet, with no intrusive fruit machines or piped music. Don't expect any food, just cask ales (Camerons Strongarm) in the peak of condition, served from a hatch in the entrance hall. A real find.

Open Tue-Wed & Sun 7.30pm-10.30pm Fri-Sat 7.30pm-11pm Closed: Mon, Thu ⊕ FREE HOUSE ◀ Camerons Strongarm, Guest ales. **Facilities** Parking ⛟ (notice required) **Notes** ⊜

NEWTON
Map 21 NZ06

Duke of Wellington Inn **NEW**

NE43 7UL ☎ 01661 844446
e-mail: info@thedukeofwellingtoninn.co.uk
dir: *From Corbridge A69 towards Newcastle. 3m to village*

Just off the A69 near Corbridge, this early 19th-century pub overlooks the Tyne Valley and is a handy base for exploring the National Park and Hadrian's Wall. Now refurbished, the original oak and stone has been complemented by modern furniture and fabrics to create a comfortable pub with rooms offering local ales and enjoyable dishes such as English asparagus risotto; and pan-seared scallops with spiced chorizo and black pudding. There is a cycle and golf club store and boot room for visitors looking for a more active stay.

Open all day all wk **Bar Meals** Av main course £9.95 food served all day **Restaurant** Fixed menu price fr £14.95 Av 3 course à la carte fr £22 food served all day ⊕ FREE HOUSE ◀ Hadrian Border Tyneside Blond, Timothy Taylor Landlord. ♚ 11 **Facilities** ❀ Children welcome Children's menu Children's portions Garden Parking Wi-fi ⛟ (notice required)

NEWTON-ON-THE-MOOR
Map 21 NU10

The Cook and Barker Inn ★★★★ INN
PICK OF THE PUBS

NE65 9JY ☎ 01665 575234
e-mail: info@cookandbarkerinn.co.uk
dir: *0.5m from A1 S of Alnwick*

For a traditional Northumbrian country inn with smartly furnished en suite bedrooms, look no further, for that is what The Cook and Barker is. Enjoying outstanding views of the Northumberland coast and the Cheviot Hills, Phil Farmer's long-established family business goes way beyond providing 'pub grub with rooms', thanks to his deployment of expert front-of-house and skilled kitchen teams. As he also runs Hope House Farm eight miles away, he has no trouble sourcing the organic beef, lamb and pork that feature on the wide-ranging bar and lounge menus. Typically, these offer steamed fresh mussels in white wine, garlic and cream sauce; roast wood-pigeon with crispy bacon, creamed cabbage and honey and whisky sauce; while an example of seafood might be pan-roasted sea bass with a risotto of petit pois, spinach and parmesan cheese. The three-course dinner menu may well include slow-cooked and seared roe deer fillet with celeriac purée. Booking for meals may be required.

Open all day all wk 12-11 **Bar Meals** Av main course £8.95 **Restaurant** L served all wk 12-2 D served all wk 7-9 Fixed menu price fr £29 ⊕ FREE HOUSE ◀ Timothy Taylor Landlord, Black Sheep, Bass. **Facilities** Children welcome Children's portions Garden Parking Wi-fi ⛟ (notice required) **Rooms** 18

SEAHOUSES
Map 21 NU23

The Bamburgh Castle Inn ★★★ INN

NE68 7SQ ☎ 01665 720283
e-mail: enquiries@bamburghcastleinn.co.uk
dir: *A1 onto B1341 to Bamburgh, B1340 to Seahouses, follow signs to harbour*

With its prime location on the quayside giving wraparound sea views as far as the Farne Islands, this is surely one of the best positioned pub anywhere along Northumberland's stunning coast. Dating back to the 18th century, the inn has been transformed in recent years with superb bar and dining areas and seating outside. A beer festival is held in the garden every year, children and dogs are welcomed, and pub dishes of locally sourced food represent excellent value. Typical of these are venison and chilli pâté; home-made fishcakes; and Moroccan lamb steak.

Open all day all wk **Bar Meals** Av main course £9.95 food served all day **Restaurant** Fixed menu price fr £8.95 food served all day ⊕ FREE HOUSE ◀ Hadrian Border Farne Island. ♚ 11 **Facilities** ❀ Children welcome Children's menu Children's portions Family room Garden Beer festival Parking Wi-fi ⛟ (notice required) **Rooms** 29

The Olde Ship Inn ★★★★ INN
PICK OF THE PUBS

9 Main St NE68 7RD ☎ 01665 720200
e-mail: theoldeship@seahouses.co.uk
dir: *Lower end of main street above harbour*

Set above the bustling old harbour of Seahouses, this stone-built free house reflects the fishing heritage of this tiny port. Built as a farm around 1745, it has been in the present owners' family for 100 years. These days it is a residential inn with a long-established reputation for good food and drink in relaxing surroundings. Lit by stained-glass windows, the main saloon bar is full of character, with its wooden floor made from pine ships' decking. It offers whiskies as well as a selection of real ales, such as Old Speckled Hen and Farne Island. The inn's corridors and boat gallery are an Aladdin's cave of antique nautical artefacts, ranging from a figurehead to all manner of ship's brasses and dials. Bar foods include locally caught seafood and home-made soups. In the evenings, starters like duck and orange pâté are followed by chicken and mushroom casserole; crab salad; and rib-eye steak. The bedrooms have en suite bathrooms and are tastefully decorated; some have views of the Farne Islands. Booking for meals may be required.

Open all day all wk 11-11 (Sun 12-11) **Bar Meals** L served all wk 12-2.30 D served all wk 7-8.30 (no D late Nov-late Jan) Av main course £8 **Restaurant** L served Sun 12-2 D served all wk 7-8.30 (no D late Nov-late Jan) Fixed menu price fr £10 ⊕ FREE HOUSE ◀ Greene King Ruddles, Courage Directors, Hadrian Border Farne Island, Morland Old Speckled Hen, High House Farm Nel's Best, Black Sheep, Theakston. ♚ 10 **Facilities** Children welcome Children's portions Family room Garden Parking Wi-fi **Rooms** 18

SLAGGYFORD · Map 18 NY65

The Kirkstyle Inn

CA8 7PB ☎ 01434 381559
dir: *Just off A689, 6m N of Alston*

With enviable views of the South Tyne River and in an Area of Outstanding Natural Beauty, The Kirkstyle Inn takes its name from the stile into the adjacent churchyard of St Jude's. A real log fire heats the pub in winter, but there's a warm welcome here all the year round. Among the beers are real ales from local breweries including Yates Bitter and in summer a special Kirkstyle Ale is available. Expect lunchtime snacks and specials, including local sausages served with local honey mustard and either eggs and hand-cut chips, or mash and gravy. Friday and Saturday nights are Steak Night, and there's plenty of options for those with special dietary requirements. This dog-friendly pub is handy for both the Pennine Way and the South Tyne Trail.

Open all wk 12-3 6-11 Closed: Mon in winter **Bar Meals** L served all wk 12-2 D served Mon-Sat 6-8.30 **Restaurant** L served all wk 12-2 D served Mon-Sat 6-8.30 ⊕ FREE HOUSE ◀ Kirkstyle Ale, Yates Best Bitter, Guinness. **Facilities** ❤ Children welcome Children's portions Garden Parking 🚗 (notice required)

WARDEN · Map 21 NY96

The Boatside Inn

NE46 4SQ ☎ 01434 602233
e-mail: sales@theboatsideinn.com
web: www.theboatsideinn.com
dir: *Off A69 W of Hexham, follow signs to Warden Newborough & Fourstones*

The name of this stone-built country free house harks back to the days when a rowing boat ferried people across the river before the bridge was built. Standing beneath Warden Hill at the confluence of the North and South Tyne rivers, The Boatside welcomes children, walkers and cyclists; the inn also has fishing rights on the river. Local produce is used for main courses such as steamed haddock fillet; Bill Bell of Haltwhistle pork sausage with gravy and mash; Quorn and vegetable casserole; and steak and red wine casserole with leek suet pudding.

Open all day all wk 11-11 (Sun 11-10.30) **Bar Meals** L served Mon-Sat 11-9, Sun 12-8 D served Mon-Sat 11-9, Sun 12-8 Av main course £9.75 food served all day **Restaurant** L served Mon-Sat 12-2.30, Sun 12-8 D served Mon-Sat 6-9, Sun 12-8 ⊕ FREE HOUSE ◀ Black Sheep, John Smith's, Mordue, Wylam. **Facilities** Children

welcome Children's menu Children's portions Garden Parking Wi-fi 🚗 (notice required)

WARENFORD · Map 21 NU12

The White Swan ◉

NE70 7HY ☎ 01668 213453
e-mail: dianecuthbert@yahoo.com
dir: *100yds E of A1, 10m N of Alnwick*

This 200-year-old coaching inn stands near the original toll bridge over the Waren Burn. Formerly on the Great North Road, the building is now just a stone's throw from the A1. Inside, you'll find thick stone walls and an open fire for colder days; in summer, there's a small sheltered seating area, with further seats in the adjacent field. The Dukes of Northumberland once owned the pub, and its windows and plasterwork still bear the family crests. Visitors and locals alike enjoy the atmosphere and Northumbrian dishes: try Seahouses kippers with creamy horseradish sauce; venison pudding with suet crust and fresh vegetables; or roast pork hock with wine and herbs. Vegetarians are well catered for, with interesting dishes like beetroot and potato gratin; artichoke and leek pancakes; and celeriac pan haggerty with fresh tomato sauce.

Open all day all wk 12-12 ⊕ FREE HOUSE ◀ Black Sheep, John Smith's, Guest ales. **Facilities** Children welcome Children's menu Children's portions Garden Parking

NOTTINGHAMSHIRE

BEESTON · Map 11 SK53

Victoria Hotel

Dovecote Ln NG9 1JG ☎ 0115 925 4049
e-mail: victoriabeeston@btconnect.com
dir: *M1 junct 25, A52 E. Turn right at Nurseryman PH, right opp Rockaway Hotel into Barton St 1st left, next to railway station*

The Victoria dates from 1899 when it was built next to Beeston Railway Station, and the large, heated patio garden is still handy for a touch of train-spotting. It offers an excellent range of traditional ales, continental beers and lagers, traditional ciders, a good choice of wines by the glass and single malt whiskies. Specials might include fresh seafood risotto; steak, kidney and ale pie; Thai vegetable curry; and grilled wild sea bass with Niçoise vegetables. Half of the menu is vegetarian. Check out the dates of the four annual beer festivals – end of January, Easter, last two weeks in July, and October. Booking for meals may be required.

Open all day all wk 10.30am-11pm (Sun 12-11) Closed: 26 Dec **Bar Meals** L served Sun-Tue 12-8.45, Wed-Sat 12-9.30 D served Sun-Tue 12-8.45, Wed-Sat 12-9.30 Av main course £9 food served all day **Restaurant** L served Sun-Tue 12-8.45, Wed-Sat 12-9.30 food served all day ⊕ FREE HOUSE ◀ Batemans XB, Castle Rock Harvest Pale & Hemlock Bitter, Everards Tiger, Holden's Black Country Bitter, Blue Monkey, 6 Guest ales Ò Thatchers Traditional, Broadoak, Biddenden Bushels. ♛ 25 **Facilities** ❤ Garden Beer festival Parking

BLIDWORTH · Map 16 SK55

Fox & Hounds

Blidworth Bottoms NG21 0NW ☎ 01623 792383
e-mail: info@foxandhounds-pub.com
dir: *Right off B6020 between Ravenshead & Blidworth*

At the beginning of 2012 the pub closed briefly for an overhaul of its interior. A fusion of blues, creams, reds and new furniture and fabrics revitalises the pub without damaging the traditional country-style character stemming from its early 19th-century origins. For nearly 100 years the locals have performed a 'Plough Play' in the pub every January, recalling the days when Blidworth Bottoms was a larger community with shops and a post office. The Greene King ales are reliable as ever, and the refreshed menu still delivers well-priced dishes of popular home-made favourites, such as beef casserole and herb dumplings or cottage pie.

Open all day all wk 11.30-11.30 (Fri-Sat 11.30am-mdnt) **Bar Meals** L served all wk 11.30-9 D served all wk 11.30-9 food served all day **Restaurant** food served all day ⊕ GREENE KING ◀ Morland Old Speckled Hen, Hardys & Hansons Best Bitter & Olde Trip, Seasonal guest ales. ♛ 9 **Facilities** ❤ Children welcome Children's menu Children's portions Play area Garden Parking 🚗

CAUNTON · Map 17 SK76

Caunton Beck

NG23 6AB ☎ 01636 636793
e-mail: email@cauntonbeck.com
dir: *6m NW of Newark on A616 to Sheffield*

This beautifully restored village pub-restaurant grew from a 16th-century cottage; its colourful rose arbour reflects the work of late 19th-century horticulturalist Samuel Reynolds Hole, the local vicar and later Dean of Rochester. Batemans GHA, Marston's Pedigree and Black Sheep real ales complement a worthy international wine list, a good few of which are by the glass. Like its sister establishment the Wig & Mitre in Lincoln (see entry), meals begin with breakfast, light snacks and nibbles, and carry on throughout the day and evening. A typical main meal, available from late morning, would be roast shallot, thyme and Y-Fenni cheese tart; soft herb-encrusted brill fillet with chorizo picante and coriander risotto; and spiced clementine crème brûlée with cinnamon ice cream. Daily specials are on the blackboard, while the children's menu offers cheese on toast; roast breast of chicken; and, for that rarity, the truly health-conscious youngster, fresh raw vegetables. Booking for meals may be required.

Open all day all wk 8am-mdnt **Bar Meals** L served all wk 8am-10pm D served all wk 8am-10pm Av main course £10.50-£14.50 food served all day **Restaurant** L served all wk 8am-10pm D served all wk 8am-10pm Fixed menu price fr £12.95 Av 3 course à la carte fr £20.70 food served all day ⊕ FREE HOUSE ◀ Batemans GHA, Marston's Pedigree, Black Sheep, Guinness Ò Thatchers. ♛ 24 **Facilities** ❤ Children welcome Children's menu Children's portions Garden Parking

Save on hotels. Book at **theAA.com/hotel**

NOTTINGHAMSHIRE 393 ENGLAND

PICK OF THE PUBS

The Martin's Arms

COLSTON BASSETT   Map 11 SK73

School Ln NG12 3FD ☎ 01949 81361
e-mail: martins_arms@hotmail.co.uk
web: www.themartinsarms.co.uk
dir: *Exit A46 between Leicester &*
Newark

At the heart of village life since the 18th century, this old pub takes its name from Henry Martin, MP for Kinsale in County Cork, who was the local squire in the early 1800s. Situated at the corner of a leafy cul-de-sac by an old market cross owned by the National Trust, it's surrounded by ancient trees in the estate parkland to which it belonged until 1990, when the present owners, Jack Inguanta and Strafford Bryan, bought it, undertaking to maintain its character and atmosphere. This they have clearly managed to do, since much of the interior will take you straight back in time, especially the Jacobean fireplaces and the period furnishings. The bar has an impressive range of real ales, with Castle Rock Harvest Pale waving the flag for the county, while another local 'brew' is elderflower pressé from Belvoir Fruit Farms. Seasonal menus include dishes featuring village-made stilton cheese, which under EU law can only be produced in Nottinghamshire and the adjacent counties of Derbyshire and Leicestershire. Bread, preserves, sauces, terrines, soups, pasta and much, much more are all made on site. Classic pub dishes include ploughman's with Colston Bassett stilton

or Cornish Yarg pork pie; and fish and chips with minted crushed peas, tartare sauce and lemon salad; while mains from a winter carte include braised blade of beef, with bourguignon flavours and salt-baked celeriac; creamed turbot chowder and Avruga caviar; and Somerset brie risotto cake and roasted onion purée, confit garlic, wild mushrooms and poached egg. Among the desserts are bitter chocolate fondant and pistachio mousse; and baked rice pudding with plum jam and gingerbread. Prices for a good number of the fine wines begin at below £20. The one-acre garden incorporates a croquet lawn. Booking for meals may be required.

Open all wk 12-3.30 6-11 (Sun 12-5)
Closed: 25-26 Dec & 1 Jan eve **Bar**

Meals L served Mon-Sat 12-2, Sun 12-5
D served Mon-Sat 7-9.30
Restaurant L served all wk 12-2 D
served Mon-Sat 7-9.30 ⊞ FREE HOUSE
◖ Marston's Pedigree, Bass, Greene King Abbot Ale, Timothy Taylor Landlord, Black Sheep Best Bitter, Castle Rock Harvest Pale, Shepherd Neame Spitfire.
♟ **Facilities** Children welcome Children's portions Family room Garden Parking 🚐 (notice required)

CAYTHORPE — Map 11 SK64

Black Horse Inn

NG14 7ED ☎ 0115 966 3520
dir: 12m from Nottingham off A612 towards Southwell

Expect good old-fashioned hospitality in this small, beamed country pub, which has been run by the same family for three generations. It has its own brewery, producing Caythorpe Dover Beck Bitter (named after the stream that runs past the pub), a coal fire in the bar, and delicious home-cooked food prepared from seasonal ingredients. Fresh fish dishes such as mussels or fried fillet of cod with parsley sauce are a speciality. Other choices might include melon and continental ham followed by sausages with creamed potato and home-made gravy. Good local walks. Booking for meals may be required.

Open 12-2.30 5.30-11 (Sun 12-5 8-10.30) Closed: Mon (ex BH) & every 3rd Tue L **Bar Meals** L served Tue-Sat 12-1.45 D served Tue-Sat 6.30-8.30 Av main course £9 **Restaurant** L served Tue-Sat 12-1.45 D served Tue-Fri 6-8.30 ⊕ FREE HOUSE ◖ Greene King Abbot Ale, Caythorpe Dover Beck Bitter, Batemans XB, Adnams, Black Sheep Ö Westons Stowford Press. ♟ 8 **Facilities** Garden Parking Wi-fi **Notes** ⊜

COLSTON BASSETT — Map 11 SK73

The Martin's Arms

PICK OF THE PUBS

See Pick of the Pubs on page 393

EDWINSTOWE — Map 16 SK66

Forest Lodge ★★★★ INN

4 Church St NG21 9QA ☎ 01623 824443
e-mail: reception@forestlodgehotel.co.uk
web: www.forestlodgehotel.co.uk
dir: A614 towards Edwinstowe, turn onto B6034. Inn opposite church

This award-winning 18th-century coaching inn stands on the edge of Sherwood Forest opposite the church where Robin Hood reputedly married Maid Marian. Sympathetically restored by the Thompson family over the past decade, it includes stylish accommodation and a comfortable restaurant and bar. Five cask ales are always on tap in two beamed bars warmed by open fires. An impressive baronial-style dining hall is an ideal setting for wholesome fare such as balsamic-glazed red onion

and goat's cheese tart, or faggots of Derbyshire pork with mash and rich onion gravy. Booking for meals may be required.

Open all wk 11.30-3 5.30-11 (Fri 11.30-3 5-11 Sun 12-3 6-10.30) Closed: 1 Jan **Bar Meals** L served all wk 12-2.30 D served all wk 6-9.30 **Restaurant** L served all wk 12-2.30 D served all wk 6-9.30 ⊕ FREE HOUSE ◖ Wells Bombardier & Eagle IPA, Kelham Island Pale Rider & Easy Rider, Acorn Pale Ale. **Facilities** Children welcome Children's menu Children's portions Garden Parking Wi-fi ⛟ (notice required) **Rooms** 13

ELKESLEY — Map 17 SK67

Robin Hood Inn

High St DN22 8AJ ☎ 01777 838259
e-mail: a1robinhood@aol.com
dir: 5m SE of Worksop off A1 towards Newark-on-Trent

Parts of this unassuming village inn date back to the 14th century. Ceilings and floors are deep red, while the green walls are adorned with pictures of food. Real food is served in both the bar and restaurant, and includes a fixed price menu, carte and daily specials board. Typical dishes include soups; grilled Lincolnshire pork sausages with cheddar mash and onion gravy; poached fillet of smoked haddock and steamed spinach; the Robin Hood mixed grill; and prime steak hamburger and chips. For dessert enjoy raspberry jam sponge and custard or chocolate and roasted almond ice cream sundae. Kids eat free with each adult main course purchased.

Open 11.30-2.30 6-11 Closed: Sun eve & Mon **Bar Meals** L served Tue-Sun 12-2 D served Tue-Sat 6-8.30 Av main course £8-£10 **Restaurant** L served Tue-Sun 12-2 D served Tue-Sat 6-8.30 Fixed menu price fr £10.95 Av 3 course à la carte fr £14 ⊕ ENTERPRISE INNS ◖ John Smith's Extra Smooth, Black Sheep Best Bitter, Guest ale. **Facilities** ♣ Children welcome Children's menu Children's portions Play area Garden Parking ⛟

FARNDON — Map 17 SK75

The Farndon Boathouse ⊜

PICK OF THE PUBS

Riverside NG24 3SX ☎ 01636 676578
e-mail: info@farndonboathouse.co.uk
dir: From Newark-on-Trent take A46 to Farndon x-rds, turn right, continue to river. Boathouse on riverside

Clad in wood, with chunky exposed roof trusses, stone floors, warehouse-style lighting, and an abundance of glass, this modern bar and eatery, in the style of an old boathouse, sits wonderfully well on the banks of the River Trent. Just how well you'll realise if you approach from the river in your canoe, or watch a sunset through the extensively glazed frontage of the bar and restaurant. With the award of an AA Rosette, the food philosophy champions local sourcing and home preparation, with home-smoked meats, fish, spices and cheeses, for example, and herbs and leaves grown in the kitchen garden. Exciting dishes include smoked haddock on a kedgeree style risotto; Thai fish bowl; seared duck breast

on a frittata of potato and Iberico Belota chorizo; and chargrilled Scotch steaks. Cask-conditioned real ales change frequently, and live music is played every Sunday evening.

Open all day all wk 10am-11pm ⊕ FREE HOUSE ◖ Greene King IPA, Guest ales Ö Aspall. **Facilities** Children welcome Children's menu Children's portions Garden Parking Wi-fi

HARBY — Map 17 SK87

Bottle & Glass

High St NG23 7EB ☎ 01522 703438
e-mail: email@bottleandglassharby.com
dir: S of A57 (Lincoln to Markham Moor road)

Harby's claim to fame is that Edward I's wife Eleanor reputedly died here in 1290. Compact and convivial, this old free house with flagged floors and heavy beams offers great food, beginning with full English breakfast and with sandwiches and light meals available all day. Seasonal main dishes include Lincolnshire beef with Madagascan green peppercorn sauce; line-caught cod, chorizo and gruyère pizza; and roasted red onion and golden beetroot frittata. The terrace is inevitably popular on sunny days. Booking for meals may be required.

Open all day all wk 10am-11pm **Bar Meals** L served Mon-Fri & Sun 10-9.30, Sat 10-10 D served Mon-Fri & Sun 10-9.30, Sat 10-10 Av main course £10-£30 food served all day **Restaurant** L served Mon-Fri & Sun 10-9.30, Sat 10-10 D served Mon-Fri & Sun 10-9.30, Sat 10-10 Fixed menu price fr £12.95 Av 3 course à la carte fr £21.25 food served all day ⊕ FREE HOUSE ◖ Young's Bitter & London Gold, Black Sheep, Guinness Ö Thatchers Gold. ♟ 24 **Facilities** ♣ Children welcome Children's menu Children's portions Garden Parking

KIMBERLEY — Map 11 SK44

The Nelson & Railway Inn

12 Station Rd NG16 2NR ☎ 0115 938 2177
dir: 1m N of M1 junct 26

Originally 17th-century with Victorian additions, this popular village pub has been run by the same family for over 40 years. Next door is the Hardys & Hansons Brewery that supplies many of the beers, but the two nearby railway stations that once made it a railway inn are now sadly derelict. Interesting brewery prints and railway signs decorate the beamed bar and lounge. A hearty menu of pub favourites includes ploughman's and hot rolls, as well as grills and pub classics like lasagne, fish and chips and home-made cottage pie.

Open all day all wk 11am-mdnt **Bar Meals** L served Mon-Fri 12-2.30, Sat 12-9, Sun 12-6 D served Mon-Fri 5.30-9, Sat 12-9 **Restaurant** L served Mon-Fri 12-2.30, Sat 12-9, Sun 12-6 D served Mon-Fri 5.30-9, Sat 12-9 ⊕ GREENE KING ◖ Hardys & Hansons Best Bitter, Cool & Dark Mild, Guest ales. **Facilities** Children welcome Children's menu Children's portions Family room Garden Parking Wi-fi ⛟

PICK OF THE PUBS

The Full Moon Inn

MORTON   Map 17 SK75

Main St NG25 OUT ☎ 01636 830251
e-mail: info@thefullmoonmorton.co.uk
web: www.thefullmoonmorton.co.uk
dir: *Newark A617 to Mansfield. Past
Kelham, turn left to Rolleston & follow
signs to Morton*

When William and Rebecca White
arrived at this once dark and dated pub,
they transformed it into the
contemporary, comfortable and friendly
Trent Valley free house that you see
today. The couple exposed the old
beams and brickwork from the original
18th-century cottages, brought in
reclaimed panelling and furniture, and
secured the pub's year-round appeal
with a charming summer garden and
two log fires for those chilly winter days.
Five hand-pulls prove that William takes
his real ales seriously, whilst Rebecca's
forte is cooking. Her kitchen produces
farm-fresh food, mostly locally sourced,
with specials supporting the regular
lunchtime and evening menus. There's
plenty on offer, beginning at 10.30 every
morning with a full breakfast menu that
also includes vegetarian options. The
lunchtime selection includes omelettes
or filled baguettes, both served with
salad, as well as a choice of starters
and hot dishes like smoked cheese tart
with sun-blushed tomatoes, chutney
and parmesan pastry; and home-made

burger with smoked bacon, stilton and
red onion marmalade in a ciabatta bun
with skinny chips and salad. The
evening brings a more extensive modern
British menu: a typical selection might
begin with duck liver pâté, home-made
bread and chutney; followed by halibut
wrapped in pancetta, with scallop,
lemon and dill sauce, creamy mash and
pak choi. Finish, perhaps, with iced
brandy, apricot and currant parfait with
chocolate sauce. During the week,
additional choices are available at
lunchtime and on Monday-Thursday
evenings from the special fixed price
3-2-1 menu, and there's a children's
menu, too. Booking for meals may be
required.

Open all wk fr 10.30am **Bar Meals** L
served all wk 12-2.30 D served all wk
5.30-9 **Restaurant** L served all wk
12-2.30 D served all wk 5.30-9 ⊕ FREE
HOUSE ◅ Wells Bombardier, Caythorpe
Dover Beck Bitter, Abbeydale Moonshine,
Guest ales. ♟ 8 **Facilities** Children
welcome Children's menu Children's
portions Play area Family room Garden
Parking Wi-fi 🚌

LAXTON Map 17 SK76

The Dovecote Inn

Cross Hill NG22 0SX ☎ 01777 871586
e-mail: dovecote_inn@btconnect.com
dir: *Exit A1 at Tuxford through Egmanton to Laxton*

Like most of the village of Laxton, this family-run, 18th-century pub is Crown Estate property belonging to the Royal Family. Outside is a delightful beer garden with views of the church, while the interior has a bar as well as three cosy wining and dining rooms. The seasonal, home-cooked dishes could include oak smoked salmon with celeriac remoulade, cocktail sauce and brown bread and butter to start; and Lincolnshire sausages and mash with braised onion gravy to follow. The village still practises the medieval strip field farming method – there is a visitor centre in the pub car park. A beer festival is held on the last weekend in August. Booking for meals may be required.

Open all wk 11.30-3 5-11 (Sun 12-10.30) **Bar Meals** Av main course £10.50 **Restaurant** L served Mon-Sat 12-2, Sun 12.30-6 D served Mon-Sat 5-9 ⊕ FREE HOUSE ◀ Timothy Taylor Landlord, Batemans XB, Castle Rock Harvest Pale, Sharp's Doom Bar. ♀ 9 **Facilities** Children welcome Children's menu Children's portions Garden Beer festival Parking Wi-fi ➡ (notice required)

MORTON Map 17 SK75

The Full Moon Inn

PICK OF THE PUBS

See Pick of the Pubs on page 395

NEWARK-ON-TRENT Map 17 SK75

The Prince Rupert NEW

46 Stodman St NG24 1AW ☎ 01636 918121
e-mail: info@theprincerupert.co.uk
dir: *5mins walk from Castle on entry road to Market Sq*

Lovingly and sympathetically restored and refurbished to its former 15th-century glory by Michael Thurlby in 2010, The Prince Rupert oozes character and charm and is one of Newark's most historic pubs. Expect old beams, wood floors, crackling log fires and cosy corners in the series of small downstairs rooms; make sure you explore upstairs, as the ancient architectural features are stunning. To drink, there's Ufford Ales and Westons Vintage cider on tap, while menus take in pub classics and excellent stone-baked pizzas. There are regular live music events and the pub holds a beer festival every Bank Holiday.

Open all day all wk 11am-mdnt (Fri-Sat 11am-1am Sun 12-12) Closed: 25 Dec **Bar Meals** L served all wk 12-2.30 D served all wk 6-9 Av main course £5.95-£14.50 ⊕ FREE HOUSE ◀ Ufford Ales Rupert's War Dog, Thornbridge Wild Swan & Jaipur, Blue Monkey Ŏ Westons Wyld Wood Organic Vintage. ♀ 16 **Facilities** Children welcome Garden Beer festival Wi-fi ➡

NOTTINGHAM Map 11 SK53

Fellows Morton & Clayton

54 Canal St NG1 7EH ☎ 0115 950 6795
e-mail: office@fellowsmortonandclayton.co.uk
dir: *Telephone for directions*

Named after a major Victorian canal transportation company, FMC sits in the heart of the impressive Castle Wharf complex, with a cobbled courtyard overlooking the Nottingham Canal. The pub was converted from a warehouse over 30 years ago and these days is a regular 'Nottingham in Bloom' award winner. Inside, the giant plasma screen shows all the big sporting events while you tuck into home-cooked pub grub made from local ingredients, ranging from a toasted haloumi sandwich, mushroom burger, and sharing plates to chicken penne pasta and daily specials. Dine in the bar or the charming Gallery Restaurant.

Open all day all wk **Bar Meals** L served all wk 10-3 D served Thu-Sun 3-9 Av main course £7.50 food served all day ⊕ ENTERPRISE INNS ◀ Timothy Taylor Landlord, Fuller's London Pride, Nottingham EPA, St Austell Trelawny. **Facilities** Children's portions Garden Parking Wi-fi ➡

Ye Olde Trip to Jerusalem

PICK OF THE PUBS

1 Brewhouse Yard, Castle Rd NG1 6AD
☎ 0115 947 3171
e-mail: 4925@greeneking.co.uk
dir: *In town centre*

Castle Rock, upon which stands Nottingham Castle, is riddled by caves and passageways cut into the sandstone. The builders of this unusual pub made the most of this, incorporating some of the caves into the design of the inn, one of Britain's oldest, founded in AD1189. The name recalls that soldiers, clergy and penitents gathered here before embarking on the Crusade to the Holy Land – doubtless they drank to their quest at the castle's beerhouse before their trip to Jerusalem. Centuries of service and piecemeal renovations over the years give the Trip instant appeal, from the magpie collection of furnishings in the warren of rooms to the unique Rock Lounge (look for the Ring the Bull game), spooky alcoves (several ghosts here) and quirks such as the cursed galleon and the fertility chair. Beers from the Nottingham Brewery feature strongly, accompanying a reliable menu of old favourites (sausage and mash, steak-and-ale pie) and innovative new bites (cauliflower and cheddar cheese tart). There is a beer festival two or three times a year.

Open all day all wk 11-11 (Fri-Sat 11am-mdnt) ⊕ GREENE KING ◀ IPA & Abbot Ale, Morland Old Speckled Hen, Hardys & Hansons Olde Trip, Nottingham guest ales Ŏ Aspall. **Facilities** Children welcome Garden Beer festival

THURGARTON Map 17 SK64

The Red Lion

Southwell Rd NG14 7GP ☎ 01636 830351
dir: *On A612 between Nottingham & Southwell*

In the 16th century monks from nearby Thurgarton Priory would fall out of this alehouse and weave their way home. In 1936, as press cuttings in the porch record, the landlady was murdered in her bedroom, and her niece was found wounded in a horse trough. How tame by comparison life is today in this warren of oak-beamed rooms and welcoming open fires, and in the tree-shaded terraced garden. Pub food is represented by Cajun chicken; chargrilled gammon steak; Whitby scampi; and Mediterranean vegetable lasagne. Light meals include salads. Change of Hands.

Open all wk 11.30-2.30 6.30-11 (Sat-Sun & BH 11.30-11) **Bar Meals** L served all wk 12-2 D served Sun-Fri 6.30-9, Sat 6.30-9.30 **Restaurant** L served all wk 12-2 D served Sun-Fri 6.30-9, Sat 6.30-9.30 ⊕ FREE HOUSE ◀ Black Sheep, Guest ales. **Facilities** Children welcome Children's menu Children's portions Garden Parking Wi-fi ➡

TUXFORD Map 17 SK77

The Mussel & Crab

Sibthorpe Hill NG22 0PJ ☎ 01777 870491
e-mail: musselandcrab1@hotmail.com
web: www.musselandcrab.com
dir: *From Ollerton/Tuxford junct of A1& A57. N on B1164 to Sibthorpe Hill. Pub 800yds on right*

Landlocked Nottinghamshire may not offer sea views but Bruce and Allison Elliott-Bateman have turned this quirky pub into a renowned seafood restaurant since taking over in the late 1990s. Beautifully fresh fish and seafood dominate the menu, with food served in a multitude of rooms decked out in inimitable style. The piazza room is styled as an Italian courtyard and the beamed restaurant is big on rustic charm. Countless blackboards offer ever-changing dishes such as prawn linguine and lemon sole on the bone as well as non-fishy dishes like rump of lamb. Booking for meals may be required.

Open all wk 11-3 6-11 **Bar Meals** L served Mon-Sat 11-2.30, Sun 11-3 D served Mon-Sat 6-10, Sun 6-9 **Restaurant** L served Mon-Sat 11-2.30, Sun 11-3 D served Mon-Sat 6-10, Sun 6-9 ⊕ FREE HOUSE ◀ Tetley's Smoothflow & Cask, Guinness. ♀ 16 **Facilities** Children welcome Children's menu Family room Garden Parking

Save on hotels. Book at **theAA.com/hotel**

OXFORDSHIRE 397 ENGLAND

OXFORDSHIRE

ADDERBURY
Map 11 SP43

Red Lion ★★★ INN

The Green OX17 3LU ☎ 01295 810269
e-mail: 6496@greeneking.co.uk
dir: *Off M40, 3m from Banbury*

A fine stone-built coaching inn overlooking the village green. Dating back to English Civil War times, it was once owned by the Royalists who, a tad sycophantically, called it The King's Arms. A list of landlords since 1690 is displayed inside, where age-blackened 'duck or grouse' beams, oak panelling and great big fireplaces set the scene for daily newspapers, real ales and good wines. Classic dishes include British beef and Ruddles ale pie; slow-cooked lamb shank; chicken tikka masala; and grilled sea bass fillets. Accommodation is provided in 12 individually designed rooms. Booking for meals may be required.

Open all day all wk 7am-11pm (Sat 8am-11.30pm Sun 8am-11pm) **Bar Meals** Av main course £10 food served all day **Restaurant** food served all day ⊕ GREENE KING ◖ Abbot Ale, Morland Old Speckled Hen, Guest ales. ☗ 11 **Facilities** Children welcome Children's menu Children's portions Garden Parking Wi-fi ▭ (notice required) **Rooms** 12

ARDINGTON
Map 5 SU48

The Boar's Head ★★★★ INN ◉◉

PICK OF THE PUBS

See Pick of the Pubs on page 398

BAMPTON
Map 5 SP30

The Romany

Bridge St OX18 2HA ☎ 01993 850237
e-mail: theromanyinnbampton@yahoo.co.uk
dir: *Telephone for directions*

This 18th-century building of Cotswold stone was a shop until a couple of decades ago. Now a pretty inn, The Romany counts a beamed bar, log fires and intimate dining room among its many charms. The choice of food ranges from bar snacks and bar meals to a full carte, with home-made specials like lasagne, chicken Romany, or chilli and chips. There is also a good range of vegetarian choices. The garden might be just the spot to enjoy a pint of Hooky Bitter or London Pride. Regional singers provide live entertainment a couple of times a month.

Open all day all wk 12-12 **Bar Meals** L served Fri-Sat 12-9, Sun 12-3 D served Tue-Thu 4-9, Fri-Sat 12-9 Av main course £8.50 **Restaurant** L served Fri-Sat 12-9, Sun 12-3 D served Tue-Thu 4-9, Fri-Sat 12-9 Fixed menu price fr £7.50 Av 3 course à la carte fr £13.50 ⊕ PUNCH TAVERNS ◖ Hook Norton Hooky Bitter, Fuller's London Pride, Guest ales. **Facilities** Children welcome Children's menu Children's portions Play area Garden Wi-fi ▭

The Wykham Arms

Temple Mill Road, Sibford Gower, Banbury, Oxfordshire OX15 5RX

Tel: 01295 788808 / 788807

The Wykham Arms is a thoroughly modern freehouse set in a 16th century thatched inn where you are welcome to sit and enjoy a pint of well kept real cask ales or choose a glass of fine wine from the well regarded wine list. The food offering ranges from great value bar meals to a modern à la carte menu with the focus on local products and suppliers. The Sunday lunch menu proves very popular with families. Lovely patio area to sit and soak up the atmosphere of this Cotswold village.

Opening times:
Closed all day Monday.
Tues–Sat 12pm–3pm;
6pm–9.30pm for lunch and dinner.
Sunday lunch only 12pm–3pm.

Email: info@wykhamarms.co.uk
Web: www.wykhamarms.co.uk

PICK OF THE PUBS

The Boar's Head ★★★★INN ❀❀

ARDINGTON Map 5 SU48

Church St OX12 8QA ☎ 01235 833254
e-mail: info@boarsheadardington.co.uk
web: www.boarsheadardington.co.uk
dir: *Exit A417 E of Wantage, pub adjacent to church*

Ardington and its twin community, Lockinge, lie within the estate laid out in the 19th century by Lord Wantage, who would no doubt be delighted that it remains very much as he left it. The half-timbered Boar's Head has been serving the local community for over 150 years, today as pub, first-class restaurant and provider of three attractive en suite guest rooms, converted from the original barns and outbuildings. Its scrubbed pine tables, candles, fresh flowers and blazing log fires create just the atmosphere that so many pub-goers love. Local breweries, including Best Mates (in Ardington itself), Butts and West Berkshire, are given a good share of the bar action. Everything, from bread to ice cream, and from pasta to pastries, is made on the premises. In the two AA-Rosette restaurant, the regularly changing menu is well known for its fish specialities, featuring whatever is sent up daily from Cornish ports. A typical meal might begin with scallop tempura with chilli jam or artichoke velouté; to be followed by roast Newlyn cod with red wine vinaigrette and wild garlic; roast squab pigeon with black pudding and port wine sauce; or roast rack of spring lamb with herb crust and garlic confit. Finish with a praline soufflé and iced nougat, or toffee banana croustade with vanilla ice cream. A seven-course tasting menu is available. Ardington is surrounded by footpaths and cycle routes winding through nearby villages and running up to the ancient Ridgeway. Golfers will find several excellent courses nearby, while fly-fishers can obtain a day-pass for the area's well-stocked trout lakes.

Open all wk 🍺 FREE HOUSE ◼ West Berkshire Dr Hexter's, Butts Barbus barbus, Best Mates Ardington Ale ♉ Westons Stowford Press.
Facilities Children welcome Children's portions Garden Parking Wi-fi **Rooms** 3

Save on hotels. Book at **theAA.com/hotel**

OXFORDSHIRE 399 **ENGLAND**

BANBURY   Map 11 SP44

The Wykham Arms

Temple Mill Rd, Sibford Gower OX15 5RX
☎ **01295 788808**
e-mail: info@wykhamarms.co.uk
web: www.wykhamarms.co.uk
dir: *Between Banbury & Shipston-on-Stour off B4035.
15m S of Stratford-upon-Avon*

In the 14th century William of Wykeham was Bishop of Winchester, Chancellor of England and founder of Oxford colleges. He also built much of Windsor Castle, from which town, coincidentally, arrived proprietors and classically trained chefs Damian and Debbie Bradley in 2005 to run this Cotswold-stone free house. They offer well-kept real ales (Wye Valley HPA and Purity Pure UBU among them), good wines and impressive food, typically corn-fed chicken breast in smoked bacon with ragout; pavé of Shetland salmon with red wine risotto; and confit of Warwickshire pork belly with bubble-and-squeak.

Open 12-3 6-11 Closed: Mon **Bar Meals** L served Tue-Sun 12-2.30 D served Tue-Sat 6-9.30 Av main course £10 **Restaurant** L served Tue-Sun 12-2.30 D served Tue-Sat

6-9.30 Fixed menu price fr £20 Av 3 course à la carte fr £27 ⊕ FREE HOUSE ◀ St Austell Tribute, Wye Valley HPA, Purity Pure UBU, Guinness. ♚ 20 **Facilities** Children welcome Children's portions Family room Garden Parking Wi-fi

See advert on page 397

Ye Olde Reindeer Inn

47 Parsons St OX16 5NA ☎ **01295 264031**
e-mail: info@wearealsoknownas.co.uk
dir: *1m from M40 junct 11, in town centre just off market square*

The oldest pub in Banbury, the Reindeer dates back to 1570. During the Civil War, Oliver Cromwell met his men here in the magnificent Globe Room, which still has its original wood panelling. A great range of cask ales is kept (usually five at any one time) and a large selection of malt whiskies. Mulled wines are another house speciality. Menu favourites are bubble-and-squeak with honey roast ham, baked beans and fried egg; Yorkshire pudding filled with sausage, onion and gravy; and home-made beef and Hooky ale pie.

Open all day all wk 11am-11.30pm (Fri-Sun 12-12) **Bar Meals** L served Mon-Sat 11-4, Sun 12-3 D served Mon-Sat 6-10 **Restaurant** L served Mon-Sat 11-4, Sun 12-3 D served Mon-Sat 6-10 ⊕ HOOK NORTON ◀ Hooky Bitter, Old Hooky, Hooky Dark, Hooky Gold, First Light ♻ Westons 1st Quality, Stowford Press. **Facilities** ❧ Children welcome Children's menu Children's portions Family room Garden Parking ▦

BARNARD GATE   Map 5 SP41

The Boot Inn

PICK OF THE PUBS

OX29 6XE ☎ **01865 881231**
e-mail: info@theboot-inn.com
dir: *Off A40 between Witney & Eynsham*

The Boot is set in beautiful countryside on the edge of the Cotswolds, near the ancient village of Eynsham, just a few miles west of Oxford. Renowned for its celebrity boot collection - the Bee Gees, George Best and Jeremy Irons to name a few – exposed beams, stone-flagged floors and two fabulous open fires set the scene at the inn, which has a pleasant garden for summer use, a welcoming bar and secluded dining areas. Beers from well-known and reliable brewers are on tap, and the wine list would satisfy the most cosmopolitan of oenophiles. The lunch menu offers salads, doorstop sandwiches and a selection from the chargrill: burgers, sausages and steaks. Dinner options are along the lines of baked white onion and truffle tart; lightly smoked breast of chicken; and chocolate fondant with vanilla ice cream to finish.

Open all wk 12-3 6-11 (Sun all day) **Bar Meals** L served Mon-Sat 12-2.30, Sun 12-9 D served Mon-Sat 7-9.30, Sun 12-9 **Restaurant** L served Mon-Sat 12-2.30, Sun 12-9 D served Mon-Sat 7-9.30, Sun 12-9 ⊕ CHARLES WELLS ◀ Young's, Guest ales. ♚ 10 **Facilities** Children welcome Children's portions Garden Parking Wi-fi

BECKLEY   Map 5 SP51

The Abingdon Arms

High St OX3 9UU ☎ 01865 351311
e-mail: bookings@abingdonarms.co.uk
web: www.abingdonarms.co.uk
dir: *M40 junct 8, follow signs at Headington rdbt for Beckley, then brown tourist signs*

Evelyn Waugh, author of *Brideshead Revisited*, once enjoyed the warm hospitality of the Abingdon Arms and the pub is just as welcoming today. Set in a pretty village to the north of Oxford, the pub has been smartly updated but still retains a cosy and traditional atmosphere. Good food and beers from Brakspear have also helped put it on the map. A range of light meals is available at lunchtime, while dinner could feature rump of lamb wrapped in pancetta or king prawn and clam linguine. There are opportunities for many pleasant walks in the area.

Open all wk 12-3 6-11 (Sat-Sun all day) **Bar Meals** L served Mon-Fri 12-2.30, Sat 12-9.30, Sun all day D served Mon-Fri 6-9.30, Sat 12-9.30, Sun all day Av main course £11.95 **Restaurant** L served Mon-Fri 12-2.30, Sat 12-9.30, Sun all day D served Mon-Fri 6-9.30, Sat 12-9.30, Sun all day ⊕ BRAKSPEAR ◀ Bitter,

Special, Oxford Gold & Guest ale, Wychwood Hobgoblin, Marston's Pedigree Ö Symonds. **Facilities** ✿ Children welcome Children's portions Play area Garden Parking Wi-fi ⊜ (notice required)

See advert on page 399

BLACK BOURTON   Map 5 SP20

The Vines

PICK OF THE PUBS

See Pick of the Pubs on opposite page

BLOXHAM   Map 11 SP43

The Elephant & Castle

OX15 4LZ ☎ 0845 873 7358
e-mail: bloxhamelephant1@btconnect.com
dir: *M40 junct 11, pub just off A361, in village centre. 3m from Banbury*

The arch of this 15th-century Cotswold-stone coaching inn used to straddle the former Banbury to Chipping Norton turnpike. At night the gates of the pub were closed, and no traffic could get over the toll bridge. Locals play Aunt Sally or shove-ha'penny in the big wood-floored bar, whilst the lounge boasts a bar-billiards table and a large inglenook fireplace. The menu offers toasties and baguettes, and favourites like scampi, crispy cod and vegetarian shepherd's pie. The bar serves seasonal and guest ales as well as Westons ciders. The beer festival in May is part of the Bloxfest Music Festival.

Open all wk 10-3 6-12 (Fri 10-3 5-2am Sat 10am-2am Sun 10am-mdnt) **Bar Meals** L served Mon-Sat 12-2 Av main course £6 **Restaurant** L served Mon-Sat 12-2 ⊕ HOOK NORTON ◀ Hooky Bitter & Seasonal ales, Guest ales Ö Westons. **Facilities** ✿ Children welcome Children's menu Children's portions Family room Garden Beer festival Parking Wi-fi ⊜

BRIGHTWELL BALDWIN   Map 5 SU69

The Lord Nelson Inn

PICK OF THE PUBS

See Pick of the Pubs on page 402

BRIGHTWELL-CUM-SOTWELL   Map 5 SU59

The Red Lion

The Street OX10 0RT ☎ 01491 837373
e-mail: enquiries@redlion.biz
dir: *From A4130 (Didcot to Wallingford road) follow Brightwell-cum-Sotwell signs. Pub in village centre*

A picture-postcard thatched and timbered 16th-century village pub that's not only pretty but also a cracking community local, playing host to charity quiz nights, French and painting classes, various cuisine nights, live jazz, and an annual festival. Hearty, traditional pub food is freshly prepared from local produce. Look to the chalkboard for the famous short-crust pastry pies of the day, or the main menu for things like lasagne, pork tenderloin with black pudding and caramelised apple, or vegetable tagine. Don't miss the Sunday roast lunches. The pub holds a beer festival (with live music) for two days every summer. Behind the bar, beers come from the likes of West Berkshire, Loddon and Appleford breweries, while a choice of wine comes from the very local Brightwell Vineyard.

Open all wk 12-3 6-11 **Bar Meals** L served all wk 12-2 D served Tue-Sat 6.30-9 Av main course £7-£9 **Restaurant** L served all wk 12-2 D served Tue-Sat 6.30-9 Av 3 course à la carte fr £16 ⊕ FREE HOUSE ◀ West Berkshire Good Old Boy, Loddon Hoppit, Appleford Brightwell Gold Ö Westons Stowford Press, Tutts Clump. **Facilities** ✿ Children welcome Children's menu Children's portions Garden Beer festival Parking

BROUGHTON   Map 11 SP43

Saye and Sele Arms

Main Rd OX15 5ED ☎ 01295 263348
e-mail: mail@sayeandselearms.co.uk
dir: *3m from Banbury Cross*

Three miles from Banbury Cross and close to Broughton Castle, this attractive 16th-century inn has become a destination for foodies since Danny and Liz McGeehan took over eight years ago. Although food is the driving force here, beer is not overlooked and Adnams and Sharp's are joined by regular guests. Chef-proprietor Danny 's appealing menu includes a pie of the day and specials of confit duck with apple mash; coffee and walnut roulade is one of the popular desserts. In summer, bag a table in the well-stocked garden. Booking for meals may be required.

Open 11.30-2.30 7-11 (Sat 11.30-3 7-11 Sun 12-5) Closed: 25 Dec, Sun eve **Bar Meals** L served Mon-Sat 12-2 D served Mon-Sat 7-9.30 **Restaurant** L served Mon-Sat 12-2, Sun 12-3 D served Mon-Sat 7-9.30 ⊕ FREE HOUSE ◀ Adnams Southwold Bitter, Sharp's Doom Bar, 2 Guest ales Ö Westons Stowford Press, Thatchers Dry. ♟ 8 **Facilities** Children welcome Children's portions Garden Parking ⊜

PICK OF THE PUBS

The Vines

BLACK BOURTON   Map 5 SP20

Burford Rd OX18 2PF ☎ **01993 843559**
e-mail: info@vineshotel.com
web: www.vinesblackbourton.co.uk
dir: *A40 at Witney onto A4095 to Faringdon, 1st right after Bampton to Black Bourton*

Ahdy and Karen Gerges bought The Vines, already a highly regarded restaurant and bar, in 2002. Four years later they added 18 guest rooms, most in a separate wing overlooking the village church. Built of Cotswold stone, as virtually everywhere is round here, it has been an inn since only the 1940s, when it apparently helped relieve pressure on the village local caused by the influx of American servicemen based around here. But beyond the Cotswold-stone façade, nowhere else has an interior like it. The striking murals and reliefs in the restaurant and bar are the legacy of John Clegg, who created it for a BBC television programme. Take it all in over a pint of Old Hooky in the spacious and comfortably furnished lounge, or make for the patio, where you can stop playing art critic and play a challenging game of Aunt Sally. The menus list an imaginative choice of internationally influenced modern British dishes, all freshly prepared using locally sourced produce. Typical examples from the starters listed on the

carte include Roquefort cheesecake with quince dressing; and smoked salmon soufflé and celeriac remoulade. Then among the mains could be rack of lamb on sweet potato and swede purée with rich Madeira jus and parsnip crisps; smoked haddock, cream cheese and caper risotto, with fresh dill, rocket and a soft poached egg; and hand-made Glamorgan sausages on a bed of creamy Savoy cabbage with parsley mashed potatoes. For dessert, try profiteroles with chocolate sauce; Eton Mess; and warm apple cake and custard. There's always a Sunday roast and a good selection of Old and New World wines.

Open all wk **Bar Meals** L served Tue-Sun 12-2 D served Mon-Sat 6-9, Sun 7-9 Av main course £12.50 **Restaurant** L served Sat-Sun 12-2 D served Mon-Sat 6-9 Av 3 course à la carte fr £30 🛢 FREE HOUSE 🍺 Hook Norton Old Hooky, Tetley's Smoothflow.
Facilities Children welcome Children's menu Children's portions Garden Parking Wi-fi 🚌

PICK OF THE PUBS

The Lord Nelson Inn

BRIGHTWELL BALDWIN   Map 5 SU69

OX49 5NP ☎ 01491 612497
e-mail: ladyhamilton1@hotmail.co.uk
web: www.lordnelson-inn.co.uk
dir: *Off B4009 between Watlington & Benson*

Originally constructed as a thatched cottage, later additions to this 300-year-old stone-built inn include 18th-century gables and a quaint verandah facing the village church. In Nelson's day the pub was simply known as the Admiral Nelson; but when, in 1797, the great man was elevated to the peerage, the pub's name was elevated too. For more than a century after that, villagers slaked their thirst here until, in 1905, the inn was closed following complaints about over-indulgent estate workers. That could have been the end of the story – but, a generation later, the building was bought by a couple who just liked the look of it. They gave it a complete makeover, and The Lord Nelson finally reopened on Trafalgar Day, 1971. Now full of fresh flowers, candlelight and a splendid inglenook fireplace, it's just the place to relax after a country walk or a day at the office. And, during the summer, the pretty terraced garden with its weeping willow is popular for alfresco eating and drinking. All the food is freshly cooked, using local produce where possible. The house menu begins with a complimentary basket of bread and olives. Starters might include warm crispy shredded duck salad; or mixed leaf salad with bacon, mushrooms and onion topped with melted English goat's cheese. For light main course options, try a wild mushroom risotto or roast vegetable tart. Other main courses include English fillet of pork wrapped in Parma ham with a mustard sauce; and veal escalope with lemon and sage butter. Look out for red kites while you're in the area; the RSPB reintroduced them onto the nearby Chiltern escarpment in the early 1990s.

Open all wk 12-3 6-11 (Sun 12-10.30) (summer 11-3 6-11) Closed: 25 Dec **Bar Meals** L served Mon-Sat 12-3, Sun

12-3.30 D served Mon-Sat 6-10, Sun 7-9.30 **Restaurant** L served Mon-Sat 12-2.30, Sun 12-3.30 D served Mon-Sat 6-10, Sun 7-9.30 ⊕ FREE HOUSE ◀ Rebellion IPA, Adnams, Brakspear, Black Sheep ♂ Westons Stowford Press. ♟ 20 **Facilities** Children welcome Children's portions Garden Parking Wi-fi ▭ (notice required)

Save on hotels. Book at **theAA.com/hotel**

OXFORDSHIRE 403 **ENGLAND**

BURCOT | Map 5 SU59

The Chequers

OX14 3DP ☎ 01865 407771
e-mail: enquiries@thechequers-burcot.co.uk
dir: *On A415 (Dorchester to Abingdon road) between Clifton Hampden & Dorchester*

Taken over by chef Steven Sanderson in 2006, this is an impressive thatched, 400-year-old timber-framed pub, once a staging post for boats on the Thames, or the Isis, to give it its local name. On winter days the fire-warmed sofas are the favoured spots, especially for toasting marshmallows, although on warm days the enclosed beer garden wins hands down. The home-prepared food is serious but far from pretentious - try Old Spot crispy pork belly, Plymouth brill with wild mushrooms and truffles, Steve's shepherd's pie, or fish and chips with chips cooked in beef dripping. The kitchen garden provides many of the vegetables, and other ingredients are sourced with a real attention to quality, seasonality and ecology. A decent wine list is complemented by a cocktail menu. Booking for meals may be required.

Open all day all wk 12-11 (Sun 12-4) **Bar Meals** L served all wk 12-3 D served Mon-Sat 6.30-9.30 Av main course £12-£20 **Restaurant** L served all wk 12-3 D served Mon-Sat 6.30-9.30 Fixed menu price fr £14.95 Av 3 course à la carte fr £25 ⊕ FREE HOUSE ◀ St Austell Tribute, Young's, Guest ales ♂ Aspall. ♟ 20 **Facilities** Children welcome Children's menu Children's portions Garden Parking Wi-fi 🚌 (notice required)

BURFORD | Map 5 SP21

The Highway Inn NEW

117 High St OX18 4RG ☎ 01993 823661
e-mail: info@thehighwayinn.co.uk
dir: *From A40 onto A361*

Scott and Tally Nelson's renovated inn dates back to 1480 and enjoys the best views of Burford's high street from its top of the town position. Take in the bustling scene from pavement tables or retreat to the peace and quiet of the medieval rear courtyard. Character and charm abound inside, from the low beams, open fires and nooks and crannies in the bar and dining areas to the unique cellar dining room, which is popular with parties and weddings. Monthly menus brim with local produce, from Kelmscott pork belly with tarragon gravy to the Highway Shoot's pheasant served with pink peppercorn sauce.

Open all day all wk 12-11 Closed: 25-26 Dec, 1st 2wks Jan **Bar Meals** L served Mon-Sat 12-2.30, Sun 12-3 D served Sun-Thu 6-9, Fri-Sat 6-9.30 Av main course £10-£15 **Restaurant** Av 3 course à la carte fr £20 ⊕ FREE HOUSE ◀ Hook Norton Hooky Bitter, Wye Valley Butty Bach, Butcombe ♂ Westons Stowford Press, Cotswold. ♟ 15 **Facilities** ♣ Children welcome Children's menu Children's portions Family room Garden Beer festival Wi-fi 🚌 (notice required)

The Inn for All Seasons ★★★ RR

PICK OF THE PUBS

See Pick of the Pubs on page 404

The Lamb Inn ★★★ SHL ◉◉

PICK OF THE PUBS

Sheep St OX18 4LR ☎ 01993 823155
e-mail: info@lambinn-burford.co.uk
dir: *M40 junct 8, follow A40 & Burford signs, 1st turn, down hill into Sheep St*

Tucked down a quiet side street in this most attractive Cotswolds town, it's difficult to exaggerate the mellow charm of the 15th-century Lamb Inn. The flagstone floor, log fire, cosy armchairs, fine wines and traditional real ales like Cotswold Way provide a welcoming atmosphere in the bar. Throughout, the inn combines old-world charm with stylish interiors. The two-AA Rosette restaurant looks out to a gorgeous walled cottage garden through mullioned windows. Chef Sean Ducie presents contemporary English cooking based entirely on local produce. Lunch in the bar may take in a fish deli board to share, haddock rarebit, open sandwiches and main dishes such as sundried tomato and olive frittata, and chump of lamb. Cooking moves up a gear at dinner, the dining room menu offering salmon tartare with horseradish mayonnaise, roast pork with sage stuffing, and lemon tart. Comfortable bedrooms are the icing on the cake.

Open all day all wk **Bar Meals** L served all wk 12-2.30 D served all wk 6.30-9.30 **Restaurant** L served all wk 12-2.30 D served all wk 7-9.30 ⊕ FREE HOUSE ◀ Hook Norton Hooky Bitter, Wickwar Cotswold Way. ♟ 16 **Facilities** ♣ Children welcome Children's menu Children's portions Garden Parking Wi-fi **Rooms** 17

CASSINGTON | Map 5 SP41

The Chequers Inn

6 The Green OX29 4DG ☎ 01865 882620
dir: *From Oxford take A40 towards Witney. Right to Cassington*

Turn off the busy A40, and you'll find this imposing Cotswold-stone inn next to the church at the end of the village road. The interior is cosy yet stylish, with polished flagstone floors, winter log fires and wooden furniture adorned with pretty candles. Freshly prepared meals include starters of goat's cheese and caramelised plum crostini, or parsnip and sweet potato soup; followed by main courses of Thai chicken curry; honey and cider ham; and rib-eye steak with peppercorn sauce. There is a beautiful orangery, perfect for private parties and functions.

Open all day all wk **Bar Meals** L served Mon-Fri 12-2.30, Sat-Sun 12-3 D served all wk 6.30-9.30 Av main course £10.95 **Restaurant** L served Mon-Fri 12-2.30, Sat-Sun 12-3 D served all wk 6.30-9.30 Av 3 course à la carte fr £19.95 ⊕ YOUNG'S ◀ Wells Bombardier ♂ Westons Stowford Press. ♟ 10 **Facilities** Children welcome

---

Children's menu Children's portions Garden Parking Wi-fi 🚌 (notice required)

CAULCOTT | Map 11 SP52

Horse & Groom

Lower Heyford Rd OX25 4ND ☎ 01869 343257
web: www.horseandgroomcaulcott.co.uk
dir: *From Bicester take B3040 signed Witney. Through Middleton Stoney. Approx 2.3m to Caulcott*

A perfect mix of character and quality, this picture-perfect thatched village tavern has a great taproom, all wavy beams, settles, inglenook, and a bar well supplied with real ales and ciders. An elegant marriage is made with the weekly-changing top-drawer menu, eaten in the snug or the cosy little dining room. The French chef-patron has his finger firmly on the pulse of the freshest, locally sourced produce for his modern English dishes. The ploughman's makes a delicious light lunch, or choose between a dozen varieties of sausage. A beer festival is held in July. Booking for meals may be required.

Open all wk 12-3 6-11 **Bar Meals** L served Tue-Sun D served Tue-Sat **Restaurant** L served Tue-Sun D served Tue-Sat ⊕ FREE HOUSE ◀ Hook Norton Hooky Bitter, Sharp's Doom Bar, Vale Gravitas, St Austell Proper Job, White Horse Bitter ♂ Westons Old Rosie & Stowford Press, Moles Black Rat. **Facilities** Children's portions Garden Beer festival Parking Wi-fi 🚌

See advert on page 405

PICK OF THE PUBS

The Inn for All Seasons ★★★RR

BURFORD Map 5 SP21

The Barringtons OX18 4TN
☎ **01451 844324**
e-mail: sharp@innforallseasons.com
web: www.innforallseasons.com
dir: *3m W of Burford on A40*

Starting life as two quarry cottages, this 16th-century coaching inn once witnessed the dispatch of Cotswold stone for buildings such as Blenheim Palace and St Paul's Cathedral. Ale was probably dispensed here from the beginning, so the transition to an inn was simply a natural progression. The New Inn, as it was then, was one of three coaching inns owned by the Barrington Park Estate and remained estate-owned until the 1950s. In 1964 it was sold to Jeremy Taylor, who choreographed horses for films such as *Lawrence of Arabia* and *A Man for All Seasons*, hence the change of name. The Sharp family took over in the mid-1980s and have been here ever since. Within its solid Cotswold stone walls lies a treasure trove of ancient oak beams, leather chairs and interesting memorabilia, giving it that authentic country pub feel. The well-stocked bar offers Wadworth ales from Devizes and guest beers such as Sharp's Doom Bar, as well as an extensive wine list. Matthew Sharp selects seasonal local produce for his British-continental cuisine, including game from the Barrington Park Estate and local Gloucester pork and ham. The inn also

offers one of the best fresh fish boards in the area. Typical menu choices might begin with sautéed mixed forest mushrooms with Oxford Blue, Chardonnay and tarragon cream with toasted granary croûte; before moving on to pan-roasted Gloucester Old Spot loin steak with garlic and thyme confit potato, green beans and smoked bacon. Round off, perhaps, with poached peach tartlet with passionfruit, raspberries and custard. Meals are served in the bar area, as well as in the more formal restaurant and the lovely beer garden. There are ten comfortable en suite bedrooms, and dogs are welcome. Booking for meals may be required.

Open all day all wk 11-2.30 6-11 (Fri-Sat 11-11) **Bar Meals** L served all wk

12-2.30 D served all wk 6.30-9.30 Av main course £13.50 **Restaurant** L served all wk 12-2.30
D served all wk 6.30-9.30 Fixed menu price fr £10 Av 3 course à la carte fr £24.50 ⊕ FREE HOUSE ◀ Wadworth 6X & Horizon, Sharp's Doom Bar Ŏ Sharp's Orchard. ☘ 16 **Facilities** ✿ Children welcome Children's menu Children's portions Play area Garden Parking Wi-fi 🚐 **Rooms** 10

Save on hotels. Book at **theAA.com/hotel**

OXFORDSHIRE 405 **ENGLAND**

CHALGROVE
Map 5 SU69

The Red Lion Inn

PICK OF THE PUBS

The High St OX44 7SS ☎ 01865 890625
dir: *B480 from Oxford ring road, through Stadhampton,
left then right at mini rdbt. At Chalgrove Airfield right
into village*

Other than the occasional quack of inquisitive ducks, the
medieval village of Chalgrove may be tranquil these days
but that wasn't the case in 1643 when Prince Rupert
clashed with John Hampden's Parliamentarian forces
during the First Civil War. The stream-side beer garden of
this old inn overlooks the compact green at the heart of
the village, where thatched cottages slumber not far from
the church which is, unusually, owner of the pub. In the
bar, select from the great range of draught beers
complementing the appealing menu created from the
best local ingredients by chef-patron Raymond Sexton. The
choice may include salad of Serrano ham, buffalo
mozzarella and sun-blushed tomatoes, an appetiser for
sautéed lamb's liver and bacon with creamy mash and
red onion gravy, or breast of Gressingham duck with
rhubarb and ginger sauce. Finish with iced lemon
meringue parfait courtesy of Suzanne Sexton, an
accomplished pastry chef.

Open all wk 11.30-3 6-12 (Sat 11.30-3 6-1am Sun all
day) Closed: 25 Dec **Bar Meals** L served Mon-Sat 12-2,
Sun 12-3 D served Mon-Sat 6-9 **Restaurant** L served
Mon-Sat 12-2, Sun 12-3 D served Mon-Sat 6-9 ⊕ FREE
HOUSE ◀ Fuller's London Pride, Butcombe, Guest ale
Ò Aspall, Westons Stowford Press. **Facilities** ❖ Children
welcome Children's menu Children's portions Play area
Garden Wi-fi 🚌 (notice required)

CHARLBURY
Map 11 SP31

The Bull Inn

PICK OF THE PUBS

Sheep St OX7 3RR ☎ 01608 810689
e-mail: info@bullinn-charlbury.com
dir: *M40 junct 8, A40, A44 follow Woodstock/Blenheim
Palace signs. Through Woodstock take B4437 to
Charlbury, pub at x-rds in town*

A short hop from Woodstock, Blenheim Palace and the
attractions of the Cotswolds, this attractive stone-fronted
16th-century free house presides over Charlbury's main
street. Log fires burning in the inglenook fireplaces and
the beamed interior add to the charming period
character, as does the wooden-floored bar that offers a
range of Cotswold ales by Goffs. A tastefully furnished
lounge and dining room add to the relaxing space, while

outside the vine-covered terrace is a lovely backdrop for a
drink or meal in summer. Sandwiches served at
lunchtime from Tuesday to Saturday may suffice, but the
main menu may prove tempting with a starter of Thai
fishcake, Asian slaw and sweet chilli dressing and main
courses like pan-fried Barbary duck breast, Puy lentils,
candied red cabbage and bacon lardoons or chicken
casserole with chervil dumplings, baby onions and curly
kale. Leave room for the jam roly-poly and home-made
custard or selection of local cheeses. Booking for meals
may be required.

Open 12-2.30 6-11 Closed: 25-26 Dec, Sun eve & Mon
Bar Meals L served Tue-Fri 12-2, Sat-Sun 12-2.30
D served Tue-Sat 6.30-9 Av main course £13
Restaurant L served Tue-Fri 12-2, Sat-Sun 12-2.30
D served Tue-Sat 6.30-9 Av 3 course à la carte fr £19.50
⊕ FREE HOUSE ◀ Goffs, Loddon Ò Thatchers Gold. ♇ 10
Facilities Children welcome Children's portions Garden
Parking

CHECKENDON
Map 5 SU68

The Highwayman ◉

PICK OF THE PUBS

Exlade St RG8 0UA ☎ 01491 682020
dir: *On A4074 (Reading to Wallingford road)*

Tucked away in a secluded hamlet, overlooking open fields on the edge of the wooded Chiltern Hills, this rambling, beautifully refurbished 17th-century inn makes the perfect destination following a glorious walk through the surrounding beech woods. Traditional low beams, wooden floors and open fireplaces blend effortlessly with the smart, contemporary décor, providing a comfortable atmosphere in which to savour a pint of London Pride and interesting seasonal menus that offer good modern pub food prepared from locally-sourced produce. Typically, order cod and crab fishcakes with garlic mayonnaise or gravad lax and smoked salmon with lemon capers to start, then continue with duck breast with confit duck croquettes and glazed parsnips, or roast beef and Yorkshire pudding. A peaceful rear garden and suntrap terrace make for laid-back summer drinking.

Open 12-3 6-11 (Sun 12-10) Closed: Mon **Bar Meals** L served Tue-Sat 12-2, Sun 12-3 D served Tue-Sat 6-9 Av main course £10-£15 **Restaurant** L served Tue-Sat 12-2, Sun 12-3 D served Tue-Sat 6-9 Fixed menu price fr £11 ⊕ FREE HOUSE ◀ Fuller's London Pride, Loddon Ferryman's Gold, Butlers, Guest ale. **Facilities** ☻ Children welcome Children's portions Garden Parking Wi-fi ━ (notice required)

CHINNOR
Map 5 SP70

The Sir Charles Napier ◉◉

PICK OF THE PUBS

Spriggs Alley OX39 4BX ☎ 01494 483011
web: www.sircharlesnapier.co.uk
dir: *M40 junct 6, B4009 to Chinnor. Right at rdbt to Spriggs Alley*

High amidst the beech woods of the Chiltern Hills in an Area of Outstanding Natural Beauty, elegant red kites soar over this sublime flint-and-brick dining inn, which is also just ten minutes from the M40. Making the most of this secluded locale, seasonal forays to the hedgerows and woods (customers can join in) produce herbs, fungi and berries used in the inventive menus, whilst the plump local game finds its way into some of the extraordinary two AA-Rosette winning dishes here. Diners distribute themselves amidst a most eclectically furnished suite of rooms that showcase Michael Cooper's memorable sculptures and have comfy sofas set near warming winter log fires. Crispy confit pork shoulder with pumpkin purée gives a flavour of things to come; butter poached cod with farfalle, mussels and sea vegetables, or local beef fillet with tarragon chips and mushroom fricassée for example, accompanied by a choice from over 200 wines. Digestive time may be spent appreciating the superb grounds, where more sculptures are displayed. Booking for meals may be required.

Open 12-4 6-12 (Sun 12-6) Closed: 25-26 Dec, Mon, Sun eve **Bar Meals** L served Tue-Fri 12-2.30 D served Tue-Fri 6.30-9 Av main course £13.50 **Restaurant** L served Tue-Sat 12-2.30, Sun 12-3.30 D served Tue-Sat 6.30-10 Fixed menu price fr £15.50 Av 3 course à la carte fr £37.50 ⊕ FREE HOUSE ◀ Wadworth 6X, Henry's Original IPA. ☻ 12 **Facilities** Children welcome Children's menu Children's portions Garden Parking Wi-fi ━

CHIPPING NORTON
Map 10 SP32

The Chequers

Goddards Ln OX7 5NP ☎ 01608 644717
e-mail: info@chequers-pub.com
dir: *In town centre, next to theatre*

This traditional English pub stands next to Chipping Norton's popular theatre, making it ideal for pre-show drinks and suppers. The name dates back to 1750, but it's thought that an alehouse has stood on this site since the 16th century. Besides the cosy bar, there's a conservatory restaurant serving locally sourced home-made dishes such as cauliflower, spinach and potato curry; a daily shortcrust pie; and rich venison stew.

Open all day all wk 11-11 (Fri-Sat 11am-mdnt Sun 11-10.30) Closed: 25 Dec ⊕ FULLER'S ◀ Chiswick Bitter, London Pride & ESB, George Gale & Co HSB. **Facilities** Children welcome Children's menu Children's portions Wi-fi

CHISELHAMPTON
Map 5 SU59

Coach & Horses Inn ★★★ INN

PICK OF THE PUBS

Watlington Rd OX44 7UX ☎ 01865 890255
e-mail: enquiries@coachhorsesinn.co.uk
dir: *From Oxford on B480 towards Watlington, 5m*

This delightful 16th-century inn is set in peaceful countryside six miles south-east of Oxford. Inside you'll find roaring log fires, original exposed beams, an old bread oven and furniture styles that enhance the character of the building. A wide range of imaginative food is served, including a daily specials fish board; grills, poultry and game are also perennial favourites.

There are nine chalet-style en suite bedrooms available, all with lovely rural views. Booking for meals may be required.

Open all day all wk 11-11 (Sun 12-3.30 7-10.30) **Bar Meals** L served all wk 12-2 **Restaurant** L served all wk 12-2 D served Mon-Sat 7-9.30 ⊕ FREE HOUSE ◀ Hook Norton Hooky Bitter & Old Hooky, Goffs, Loddon, Guest ales. ☻ 10 **Facilities** Children welcome Children's menu Children's portions Garden Parking Wi-fi **Rooms** 9

CHRISTMAS COMMON
Map 5 SU79

The Fox and Hounds

OX49 5HL ☎ 01491 612599
e-mail: hello@thetopfox.co.uk
web: www.foxandhoundschristmascommon.co.uk
dir: *M40 junct 5, 2.5m to Christmas Common, on road towards Henley*

Standing high on the Chilterns escarpment, this pretty dining pub dates from around 1645. Known by locals as the 'Top Fox' (because there's a Fat one in nearby Watlington), its barn-style restaurant seats about 50 people, the bar another 25. Typical dinner mains are Brakspear ale-battered haddock, chunky chips and crushed peas; wild boar sausages in red wine and mushroom sauce; and aubergine parmigiana. Daily specials might include eggs Benedict. Although there's a suntrap garden, new landlords Sharon and Simon Edwards aren't bothered by dogs, muddy boots or children indoors.

Open all day all wk 12-11 (Sun 12-10.30) Closed: 25-26 Dec eve, 1 Jan eve **Bar Meals** L served Mon-Fri 12-2.30, Sat 12-3, Sun 12-4 D served Mon-Thu 7-9, Fri-Sat 7-9.30 **Restaurant** L served Mon-Fri 12-2.30, Sat 12-3, Sun 12-4 D served Mon-Thu 7-9, Fri-Sat 7-9.30 ⊕ BRAKSPEAR ◀ Bitter, Seasonal ales ♂ Addlestones. ☻ 11 **Facilities** ☻ Children welcome Children's menu Children's portions Garden Parking ━ (notice required)

PICK OF THE PUBS

Bear & Ragged Staff

CUMNOR   Map 5 SP40

28 Appleton Rd OX2 9QH
☎ **01865 862329**
e-mail: enquiries@bearandraggedstaff.com
web: www.bearandraggedstaff.com
dir: *A420 from Oxford, right onto B4017 signed Cumnor*

In typically tranquil Oxfordshire countryside, this 16th-century, stone-built dining pub has a rich history, not least having served as a billet for troops during the English Civil War. While the soldiers were here, Richard Cromwell, son of Oliver and Lord Protector of England, allegedly chiselled away the Royal Crest that once adorned the lintel above one of the doors in the bar, and Sir Walter Scott mentions this very Bear & Ragged Staff in his novel, *Kenilworth*. The chefs here take full advantage of the fresh, seasonal game available from local estates and shoots, since the surrounding woods and farmland teem with pheasant, partridge, deer, muntjac, rabbit, duck and pigeon. From the microwave-free kitchen (in other words, everything is cooked with fresh ingredients) come hearty, country-style casseroles, stews, steaks, bangers and mash and other pub classics. Install yourself in one of the traditional bar rooms, all dressed stone and warmed by log fires, relax on the stone-flagged patio, or settle in the comfortable

restaurant and ask for the eminently manageable menu. Start with meze, charcuterie, crispy duck leg pancakes or home-made soup; then choose vegetable tagine; pork and wild boar faggots; chargrilled venison steak; market fish of the day; or butternut squash, brown cap mushrooms and spinach risotto. Pizzas from an authentic oven are another option. If, to follow, upside-down apple pudding with Calvados crème anglaise, or creamy rice pudding with red plum compôte fail to tick the right box, call for the cheeseboard, full of British classics with crackers, celery, chutney and grapes. The Bear has a climbing frame for children and dogs are welcome in the bar area.

Open all day all wk **Bar meals** Av main course £14 food served all day **Restaurant** Fixed menu price fr £5.95 Av 3 course à la carte fr £25 food served all day ⊕ GREENE KING ◀ Guinness, Guest ales Õ Aspall, Hogan's. ♀ 14 **Facilities** ✿ Children welcome Children's menu Children's portions Play area Garden Parking Wi-fi 🚌 (notice required)

CHURCH ENSTONE   Map 11 SP32

The Crown Inn

PICK OF THE PUBS

Mill Ln OX7 4NN ☎ 01608 677262
dir: *Off A44, 15m N of Oxford*

Award-winning chef Tony Warburton runs this stone-built 17th-century free house on the eastern edge of the Cotswolds with his wife Caroline. During the summer season you can while away the long evenings eating or drinking in the quiet and secluded rear garden, which is sheltered from the wind but enjoys the best of the late sunshine. Inside you'll find a traditional rustic bar with an open fire, a spacious slate floored conservatory, and a richly decorated beamed dining room. All meals are prepared on the premises using fresh produce, including fish and shellfish, and pork, beef and game from the local farms and estates. Starters may include cream of mushroom and basil soup or duck and smoked pheasant terrine. Main course choices range from steak and Hooky pie to braised rabbit with Dijon mustard and roast potatoes, or poached smoked haddock and cheddar mash. A home-made dessert such as ginger sponge and custard will round things off nicely.

Open all wk 12-3 6-11 (Sun 12-4) Closed: 26 Dec, 1 Jan **Bar Meals** L served all wk 12-2 D served Mon-Sat 7-9 **Restaurant** L served all wk 12-2 D served Mon-Sat 7-9 ⊕ FREE HOUSE ◀ Hook Norton Hooky Bitter, Timothy Taylor Landlord, Wychwood Hobgoblin Ŏ Cotswold. ♥ 8 **Facilities** Children welcome Children's portions Garden Parking

CLIFTON   Map 11 SP43

Duke of Cumberland's Head

OX15 OPE ☎ 01869 338534
e-mail: info@thecliftonduke.com
dir: *A4260 from Banbury, then B4031 from Deddington. 7m from Banbury*

Believed to be Elizabethan, this thatched stone pub commemorates Prince Rupert of the Rhine, who fought alongside his uncle, Charles I, at the nearby Battle of Edge Hill in 1642. Many old features survive, including the inglenook fireplace and low exposed beams. Three real ales are always on tap, as is Addlestones cider; the newly opened whisky bar needs no explanation. Largely traditional pub favourites, sourced from local farmers, gamekeepers and suppliers, include pie of the day; slow-cooked pork belly; seafood linguine; and roasted butternut squash and sage risotto.

Open all wk 11-3 6-11 Closed: 25 Dec **Bar Meals** L served Mon-Sat 12-2.30, Sun 12-3 D served Mon-Thu 6.30-9, Fri-Sat 6.30-9.30 Av main course £13 **Restaurant** L served Mon-Sat 12-2.30, Sun 12-3 D served Mon-Thu 6.30-9, Fri-Sat 6.30-9.30 Av 3 course à la carte fr £21 ⊕ FREE HOUSE ◀ Hook Norton, Tring, Oxfordshire, Vale Ŏ Addlestones. ♥ 11 **Facilities** ♣ Children welcome Children's menu Children's portions Garden Parking Wi-fi

CRAY'S POND   Map 5 SU68

The White Lion

Goring Rd, Goring Heath RG8 7SH ☎ 01491 680471
e-mail: enquiries@thewhitelioncrayspond.com
dir: *From M4 junct 11 follow signs to Pangbourne, through toll on bridge to Whitchurch. N for 3m into Cray's Pond*

There has been a change of hands at this 250-year-old local, which is beautifully positioned high in the Chilterns Area of Outstanding Natural Beauty. An extensive makeover mixes traditional and contemporary and open fires take away the winter chill in this pub, which is popular with ramblers. Good, solid pub meals like toad-in-the-hole with mash; locally cured ham, egg and chips; and beer-battered haddock, chips and peas also warm the cockles, with meals taken in the conservatory restaurant or in the secluded garden when the weather allows.

Open all day all wk (No food Sun eve) **Bar Meals** Av main course £8.95 food served all day **Restaurant** food served all day ⊕ GREENE KING ◀ IPA, Morland Old Speckled Hen. ♥ **Facilities** ♣ Children welcome Children's menu Children's portions Play area Garden Parking Wi-fi ➡

CUMNOR   Map 5 SP40

Bear & Ragged Staff

PICK OF THE PUBS

See Pick of the Pubs on page 407

The Vine Inn

11 Abingdon Rd OX2 9QN ☎ 01865 862567
dir: *A420 from Oxford, right onto B4017*

A vine does indeed clamber over the whitewashed frontage of this 18th-century village pub. In 1560, nearby Cumnor Place was the scene of the suspicious death of the wife of Lord Robert Dudley, favourite of Elizabeth I; the house was pulled down in 1810. There's a selection of rotating real ales in the carpeted bar, and a typical seasonal menu includes hunter chicken with chips, peas and grilled tomato; sausage and mash with onion gravy; and classic Greek salad, with blackboard specials extending the choice. Children love the huge garden. Booking for meals may be required.

Open all wk (Sat-Sun all day) **Bar Meals** L served Mon-Fri 12-2, Sat 12-3, Sun 12-4 **Restaurant** L served Mon-Fri 12-2, Sat 12-3, Sun 12-4 D served Mon-Sat 6-9.15 ⊕ PUNCH TAVERNS ◀ Guest ales. **Facilities** Children welcome Children's menu Children's portions Play area Garden Parking ➡ (notice required)

DEDDINGTON   Map 11 SP43

Deddington Arms ★★★ HL ⊛

PICK OF THE PUBS

Horsefair OX15 OSH ☎ 01869 338364
e-mail: deddarms@oxfordshire-hotels.co.uk
dir: *M40 junct 11 to Banbury. Follow signs for hospital, then towards Adderbury & Deddington, on A4260*

Overlooking Deddington's pretty market square, this striking 16th-century former coaching inn, with a new landlord, boasts a wealth of timbering, flagstone floors, numerous nooks and crannies, crackling winter log fires and sought-after window seats in the beamed bar. Here you can savour a pint of Black Sheep or Adnams ale while perusing the great value set lunch menu or the imaginative carte. Eat in the bar or head for the elegant dining room and kick off a one AA-Rosette meal with smoked salmon and dill roulade with watercress pesto, followed by braised lamb shank with creamed potatoes and minted peas, or a freshly made pizza (goat's cheese, red onion and rocket), and stem ginger crème brûlée. From the market lunch menu perhaps choose smoked ham and stilton salad, and rabbit casserole with new potatoes. Accommodation includes 27 en suite bedrooms with cottage suites and four-poster luxury.

Open all day all wk 11am-mdnt (Sun 11-11) **Bar Meals** L served all wk 12-2.30 D served all wk 6.30-9.30 **Restaurant** L served all wk 12-2.30 D served all wk 6.30-9.30 ⊕ FREE HOUSE ◀ Black Sheep, Adnams, 2 Guest ales Ŏ Westons Stowford Press. ♥ 8 **Facilities** Children welcome Children's menu Children's portions Parking Wi-fi ➡ (notice required) **Rooms** 27

DORCHESTER (ON THAMES)   Map 5 SU59

The George ★★ HL

PICK OF THE PUBS

See Pick of the Pubs on opposite page

PICK OF THE PUBS

The George ★★ HL

DORCHESTER (ON THAMES)   Map 5 SU59

25 High St OX10 7HH ☎ 01865 340404
e-mail: georgedorchester@relaxinnz.co.uk
web: www.thegeorgedorchester.co.uk
dir: *From M40 junct 7, A329 S to A4074 at Shillingford. Follow Dorchester signs. From M4 junct 13, A34 to Abingdon then A415 E to Dorchester*

The multi-gabled, 15th-century George stands in the old town's picturesque high street, opposite the 12th-century Dorchester Abbey. Believed to be one of the country's oldest coaching inns, it has been a welcome haven for many an aristocrat, including Sarah Churchill, the first Duchess of Marlborough, while much later the non-aristocratic author D H Lawrence favoured it with his presence, perhaps while he was living in Hermitage, near Newbury. Oak beams and inglenook fireplaces characterise the interior, while the elevated restaurant offers a secret garden with a waterfall. The Potboys Bar, apparently named after the Abbey bell-ringers who used to gather in here, is a traditional taproom and therefore unquestionably the right place to enjoy a pint from one of the six breweries that make up The George's roll of honour – Brakspear, Butcombe, Fuller's, Sharp's, Skinner's and Wadworth – while tucking into pasta carbonara with garlic bread; bangers and mash with gravy; or an 8oz rump steak with fat chips from the bar menu. Food is all locally sourced: the Abbey gardens, for example, supply all the herbs used in the kitchen, customers contribute the occasional home-grown vegetables, and local shoots provide pheasants. In Carriages Restaurant the

menu offers confit of crisp belly pork with Puy lentils, local Toulouse sausages and crushed new potatoes; coq au vin with roasted garlic croutons and celeriac mash; fresh and smoked fish pie with potato and cheddar cheese glaze; and butternut squash risotto with red onion, fresh herbs, white truffle oil and parmesan shavings. Expect white chocolate and marmalade bread-and-butter pudding with Disaronno custard, and Eton Mess on the dessert list. There are four-poster feature rooms for that special occasion, family rooms and pretty doubles and singles, all well equipped, some with views of either the extensive gardens or the Abbey. Check for beer festival dates. Booking for meals may be required.

Open all day all wk 7am-mdnt **Bar Meals** L served all wk 12-3 D served all wk 6-9 Av main course £10

Restaurant L served all wk 12-3 D served all wk 6-9 Fixed menu price fr £20 Av 3 course à la carte fr £25 ⊕ CHAPMANS GROUP ◀ Wadworth 6X, Skinner's Betty Stogs, Fuller's London Pride, Sharp's Doom Bar, Butcombe, Brakspear ♂ Westons Stowford Press. **Facilities** Children welcome Children's menu Children's portions Garden Beer festival Parking Wi-fi 🚌 **Rooms** 17

DORCHESTER (ON THAMES) *continued*

The White Hart ★★★ HL

High St OX10 7HN ☎ 01865 340074
e-mail: whitehart@oxfordshire-hotels.co.uk
dir: *A4074 (Oxford to Reading), 5m from M40 junct 7/*
A329 to Wallingford

If this picture-perfect hotel looks familiar, that could be because it has played a starring role in the TV series *Midsomer Murders*. Set seven miles from Oxford in heart of historic Dorchester on Thames, it has welcomed travellers for around 400 years, and the bars attract locals, residents and diners alike. There is a great choice of real beers available. Log fires and candlelight create an intimate atmosphere for the enjoyment of innovative dishes prepared from fresh ingredients. A good-value fixed-price lunch is available Monday to Saturday, with a choice of three starters, mains and desserts. The carte menu doubles your choice and includes imaginative dishes such as pumpkin risotto or Thai-style fishcakes, followed by roasted loin of pork with braised red cabbage, caramelised apple and sweet potato crisps; fish and chips in beer-batter with crushed minted peas and hand-cut chips; or grilled peppered rump steak.

Open all day all wk 11am-mdnt (Sun 11-11) **Bar Meals** L served all wk 12-2.30 D served all wk 6.30-9.30 **Restaurant** L served all wk 12-2.30 D served all wk 6.30-9.30 ⊕ FREE HOUSE ◼ Adnams, Black Sheep ♻ Westons Stowford Press. 🍷 12 **Facilities** Children welcome Children's portions Garden Parking 🚌 **Rooms** 28

The Lamb at Buckland

Lamb Ln, Buckland SN7 8QN ☎ 01367 870484
e-mail: thelambatbuckland@googlemail.com
dir: *Just off A420, 3m E of Faringdon*

You can find The Lamb tucked away in the beautiful village of Buckland in the Vale of the White Horse and just 15 minutes' drive from Oxford. Built of Cotswold stone and dating from the 17th century, the pub is run by husband and wife Richard and Shelley Terry, and Christopher Green. All three are trained chefs, but you'll find Shelley running front of house while the two men work in the kitchen. The trio are united in their objective: to offer good food in a pub atmosphere, with relaxed and friendly service. To this end local producers of both ales and food are called upon to stock the bar and larder, and many of the vegetables are grown in the kitchen garden next to the suntrap patio. Typical dishes plucked from the menu might be pan-fried whole tiger prawns with chilli and ginger, followed by roasted whole partridge with buttered spinach and mushroom sauce. Booking for meals may be required.

Open all wk 11.30-3 6-11 Closed: Sun eve, Mon **Bar Meals** L served Tue-Sat 12-2, Sun 12-3 D served Tue-Sat 7-9 Av main course £12.95 **Restaurant** L served Tue-Sat

12-2, Sun 12-3 D served Tue-Sat 7-9 Av 3 course à la carte fr £24 ⊕ FREE HOUSE ◼ Brakspear Bitter, Ramsbury Gold, West Berkshire Good Old Boy, Loose Cannon Abingdon Bridge. 🍷 12 **Facilities** ♣ Children welcome Children's portions Garden Parking Wi-fi

The Trout at Tadpole Bridge ★★★★ INN ◉

Buckland Marsh SN7 8RF ☎ 01367 870382
e-mail: info@troutinn.co.uk
dir: *A420 onto A417 to Faringdon, take A4095 signed*
Bampton, pub approx 2m

On its long journey to the sea the Thames flows through peaceful spots like Tadpole Bridge, an isolated community limited to Gareth and Helen Pugh's 17th-century inn and one other house. River cruisers moor just downstream and their crews must be delighted to find The Trout so close. While taking food seriously, the Pughs shun the 'gastro-pub' label as it suggests drinkers aren't welcome, whereas locals pop in every night for a pint or two of Ramsbury, Loose Cannon or Wayland Smithy, or a Cotswold cider. Typical main dishes are breast of guinea fowl with haggis beignets and sweetbreads and Madeira ragout; Kelmscott pork belly, cheek and fillet with black pudding, bubble-and-squeak and cider sauce; and fillet of turbot with roasted cherry tomatoes, saffron and leek broth. The children's menu fails to mention chicken nuggets, but does offer penne pasta carbonara. There are six luxurious bedrooms. Booking for meals may be required.

Open all wk 11.30-3 6-11 (Sat-Sun all day) Closed: 25-26 Dec **Bar Meals** L served all wk 12-2 D served all wk 7-9 Av main course £14.95 **Restaurant** L served all wk 12-2 D served all wk 7-9 Fixed menu price fr £12.95 Av 3 course à la carte fr £25 ⊕ FREE HOUSE ◼ Ramsbury Bitter, Young's Bitter, White Horse Wayland Smithy, Loose Cannon Abingdon Bridge ♻ Westons Stowford Press, Cotswold. 🍷 12 **Facilities** ♣ Children welcome Children's menu Children's portions Garden Parking Wi-fi **Rooms** 6

The Woodman Inn

SN7 7NX ☎ 01367 820643
e-mail: enquiries@thewoodmaninn.net
dir: *M4 junct 15, A419 towards Swindon. Right onto A420*
signed Oxford/Shrivenham. Straight on at next 2 rdbts. At
x-rds left onto B4508 to Fernham

An annual beer festival at this picturesque 17th-century pub in a hamlet in the Vale of the White Horse confirms its real ale credentials. At other times gems from the local White Horse Brewery and Bath Ales are among the taps. Log fires burn through the winter, while friendly staff provide excellent table service on the terrace in summer. The restaurant, a medieval banqueting hall with minstrels' gallery, makes a great setting for carefully prepared pub dishes such as smoked chicken Caesar salad with crispy bacon; and half a roast duck coated in ginger and orange marmalade.

Open all day all wk **Bar Meals** L served Mon-Fri 12-2, Sat-Sun 12-2.30 D served all wk 6.30-9.30 Av main course £13.95 **Restaurant** L served Mon-Fri 12-2, Sat-Sun 12-2.30 D served all wk 6.30-9.30 Fixed menu price fr £13.95 Av 3 course à la carte fr £13.95 ⊕ FREE HOUSE ◼ Timothy Taylor Landlord, Wadworth 6X, Wychwood Hobgoblin, Oakham, Bath, White Horse ♻ Aspall, Thatchers Cheddar Valley. **Facilities** ♣ Children welcome Children's menu Children's portions Family room Garden Beer festival Parking Wi-fi 🚌

The Butchers Arms

OX27 8EB ☎ 01869 277363
e-mail: tg53@sky.com
dir: *4m from Bicester on A4421 towards Buckingham*

Lark Rise to Candleford author Flora Jane Thompson was born at Juniper Hill, a couple of miles from this pretty, creeper-covered pub. Her house there became Lark Rise, and Buckingham and Banbury metamorphosed into Candleford. Handpumps dispense Old Hooky, Doom Bar and Tring Brewery's bizarrely named Side Pocket for a Toad, while the menu offers a good traditional selection, including pie of the day; lemon sole; home-made curry; and beef or mushroom Stroganoff. You can watch the cricket from the patio and in mid-June there's a beer festival.

Open all day all wk **Bar Meals** L served all wk 12-2.30 D served all wk 6.30-9 **Restaurant** L served Mon-Sat 12-2.30, Sun 12-3.30 D served all wk 6.30-9 ⊕ PUNCH TAVERNS ◼ Hook Norton Old Hooky, Sharp's Doom Bar, Tring Side Pocket for a Toad ♻ Thatchers Katy, Westons Stowford Press. **Facilities** ♣ Children welcome Children's menu Children's portions Beer festival Parking Wi-fi 🚌 (notice required)

The Carpenters Arms

Fulbrook Hill OX18 4BH ☎ 01993 823275
e-mail: bridgett.howard@ntlworld.com
dir: *From rdbt on A40 at Burford take A361 signed*
Chipping Norton. Pub on right 150mtrs from mini rdbt
just after bridge

Expect oodles of charm and character from this 17th-century stone pub; the warren of cosy, beautifully decorated and furnished rooms draws a cosmopolitan crowd, many of whom stop to enjoy the modern British cooking. Choices range from bar snacks such as game pie with mash and carrots to more ambitious dishes such as goat's cheese tian with tomato, basil and olives followed by rack of lamb with sautéed potatoes, asparagus, lemon and rosemary. Change of hands. Booking for meals may be required.

Open Wed-Fri 12-2.30 Tue-Thu 6-9 Fri-Sat 12-3 6-9.30 Sun 12-3 Closed: Sun eve, Mon, Tue L (winter) **Bar Meals** L served Wed-Fri 12-2.30, Sat-Sun 12-3 D served Tue-Thu 6-9, Fri-Sat 6-9.30 **Restaurant** L served Wed-Fri 12-2.30, Sat-Sun 12-3 D served Tue-Thu 6-9, Fri-Sat 6-9.30 ⊕ GREENE KING ◼ IPA & Abbot Ale, Morland Old Speckled Hen ♻ Aspall. 🍷 10 **Facilities** ♣ Children welcome Children's portions Garden Parking Wi-fi

Save on hotels. Book at theAA.com/hotel

OXFORDSHIRE 411 ENGLAND

PICK OF THE PUBS

The White Hart ❀❀

FYFIELD   Map 5 SU49

Main Rd OX13 5LW ☎ 01865 390585
e-mail: info@whitehart-fyfield.com
web: www.whitehart-fyfield.com
dir: *7m S of Oxford, just off A420*
(Oxford to Swindon road)

Mark and Kay Chandler's 500-year-old former chantry house (abolished in 1548) is steeped in history and has been a pub since 1580 when St John's College in Oxford, large local landowners, leased it to tenants but reserved the right to 'occupy it if driven from Oxford in pestilence' – so far this has not been invoked! At some point the large hall was divided into two floors, but in 1963 this was removed, thereby restoring the main hall's original proportions and exposing the 15th-century arch-braced roof to view. There's still a splendid 30ft-high minstrels' gallery overlooking the restaurant and the interior features original oak beams, flagstone floors, and huge stone-flanked windows. Study the wonderful history and architecture over a pint of Hooky or Doom Bar, or one of the 14 wines served by the glass in the characterful bar – arrive early to bag the table beside roaring log fire in winter. Awarded two AA Rosettes for their food, chef Mark is steadfast in his pursuit of fresh, seasonal food from trusted local suppliers and their own kitchen garden, which provides a regular supply of fruit, vegetables and herbs. Mark's cooking reveals a high level of technical skill and his menus change daily, perhaps

featuring goat's cheese and lemon ravioli with pink peppercorns and basil, or crab toastie with dippy egg and brown shrimp butter among the short choice of starters. To follow, try rack of Cotswold lamb with lamb faggot, dauphinoise, peas and minted hollandaise, or grilled trout fillet, local crayfish bisque, smoked eel and horseradish croquette, local wild garlic and wild mushrooms. Make room for apple and Calvados mousse with cobnut praline. The lunchtime set menu is great value. Other attractions include the occasional Bank Holiday beer festivals, and takeaway fish and chips on Thursdays. Booking for meals may be required.

Open 12-3 5.30-11 (Sat 12-11 Sun 12-10.30) Closed: Mon (ex BH) **Bar Meals** L served Tue-Sat 12-2.30, Sun 12-3

D served Tue-Sat 7-9.30 Av main course £15.70 **Restaurant** L served Tue-Sat 12-2.30, Sun 12-3 D served Tue-Sat 7-9.30 Fixed menu price fr £16 Av 3 course à la carte fr £26 ⊕ FREE HOUSE ◖ Hook Norton Hooky Bitter, Sharp's Doom Bar, Loddon Hullabaloo, Guest ales ♂ Thatchers Cheddar Valley. ♟ 14 **Facilities** Children welcome Children's menu Children's portions Play area Garden Beer festival Parking Wi-fi 🚐

FYFIELD — Map 5 SU49

The White Hart ◉◉

PICK OF THE PUBS

See Pick of the Pubs on page 411

GORING — Map 5 SU68

Miller of Mansfield

PICK OF THE PUBS

See Pick of the Pubs on opposite page

GREAT TEW — Map 11 SP42

The Falkland Arms

PICK OF THE PUBS

OX7 4DB ☎ 01608 683653
e-mail: falklandarms@wadworth.co.uk
dir: *Off A361, 1.25m, signed Great Tew*

This 500-year-old inn takes its name from Lucius Carey, 2nd Viscount Falkland, who inherited the manor of Great Tew in 1629. Nestling at the end of a charming row of Cotswold-stone cottages, The Falkland Arms is a classic: flagstone floors, high-backed settles and an inglenook fireplace characterise the intimate bar, where a huge collection of beer and cider mugs and jugs hangs from the ceiling. Home-made specials such as cottage pie; pork, apple and mushroom pie; and mozzarella and mushroom risotto cakes supplement the lunchtime menu of filled baguettes and ploughman's; these can be enjoyed in the bar or the pub garden. In the evening, booking is essential for dinner in the small dining room. Expect pork fillet wrapped in bacon, creamy leek and mushroom tagliatelle, or pork and cashew stirfry. Being a genuine English pub, clay pipes and snuff are always on sale. Booking for meals may be required.

Open all day all wk 11.30-11 (Sun 12-10.30) **Bar Meals** L served all wk 12-2.30 D served all wk 6.30-9 Av main course £10-£11 **Restaurant** L served all wk 12-2.30 D served all wk 6.30-9 Av 3 course à la carte fr £25 ⊕ WADWORTH ◀ 6X, Henry's Original IPA & Horizon, Guest ales ◯ Westons Traditional & Perry. ♦ 18 **Facilities** ✿ Children welcome Children's portions Garden Beer festival Wi-fi ☷ (notice required)

HAMPTON POYLE — Map 11 SP51

The Bell

PICK OF THE PUBS

OX5 2QD ☎ 01865 376242
e-mail: contactus@thebelloxford.co.uk
dir: *From N: exit A34 signed Kidlington, over bridge. At mini rdbt turn right, left to Hampton Poyle (before slip road to rejoin A34). From Kidlington: at Oxford rd rdbt (junct of A4260 & A4165), take Bicester Rd (Sainsbury's on left & towards A34). Left to Hampton Poyle*

This welcoming dining inn nestles close to the Cherwell to the north of Oxford. The addition of a contemporary restaurant has done nothing to harm the historic heart of the old village pub, where limestone flagged floors, oak beams and comfortable leather armchairs still greet the bar regulars. Well behaved dogs are welcome here too, or out on the delightful south-facing terrace which has seating for 60. An eye-catching feature is a wood-burning oven where some dishes from the open kitchen are prepared, including legendary rustic pizzas. These, along with burgers and salads, can be served in the bar at any time. If a memorable meal is what you have in mind, head for the restaurant where you could start with coarse terrine of pork, goose, pheasant and pigeon; continue with fresh grilled tuna on watercress salad; and finish with a creamy rice pudding with warm vanilla poached pear. Grilled fish and great steaks are also recommended. Booking for meals may be required.

Open all day all wk 7am-11pm **Bar Meals** L served Mon-Sat 12-2.30, Sun 12-3 D served all wk 6-10 **Restaurant** L served Mon-Fri 12-2.30, Sat-Sun all day D served Mon-Fri 6-9.30, Sat-Sun 6-10 ⊕ FREE HOUSE ◀ Fuller's London Pride, Hook Norton Old Hooky, Wadworth ◯ Westons Stowford Press. ♦ 9 **Facilities** ✿ Children welcome Children's portions Family room Garden Parking Wi-fi ☷ (notice required)

HENLEY-ON-THAMES — Map 5 SU78

The Cherry Tree Inn

PICK OF THE PUBS

Stoke Row RG9 5QA ☎ 01491 680430
e-mail: info@thecherrytreeinn.com
dir: *B481 towards Reading & Sonning Common 2m, follow Stoke Row sign*

After a recent change of hands, this 400-year-old listed building was reopened in April 2012. Originally three flint cottages, The Cherry Tree has been comprehensively re-fitted, mixing the original flagstone floors, beamed ceilings and fireplaces with contemporary décor. The bar offers Brakspear real ales and around 30 different wines, including some served by the glass. Choices on the bar menu include lightly spiced whitebait with tartare sauce; slow-cooked pork belly with roast English asparagus and cider potato fondant; and crème brûlée with banana salsa. The restaurant menu might begin with glazed ham hock, bubble-and-squeak cake with champagne mustard; continue with roasted monkfish, sautéed spring greens and a cockle and chorizo broth; and finish with chocolate soup, toasted marshmallow and drunken cherry. Outside, the large south-facing garden is perfect for alfresco summer dining.

Open all wk 11-3 5-11 (Fri-Sat 11-11 Sun 12-10) Closed: 1 Jan **Bar Meals** L served Mon-Fri 12-3, Sat 12-4, Sun 12-10 D served Mon-Sat 7-10 **Restaurant** L served Mon-Fri 12-3, Sat 12-4, Sun 12-10 D served Mon-Sat 7-10 ⊕ BRAKSPEAR ◀ Bitter, Oxford Gold, Seasonal ales ◯ Symonds. ♦ 12 **Facilities** ✿ Children welcome Children's menu Garden Parking

The Five Horseshoes

PICK OF THE PUBS

Maidensgrove RG9 6EX ☎ 01491 641282
e-mail: admin@thefivehorseshoes.co.uk
dir: *From Henley-on-Thames take A4130, 1m, take B480 signed Stonor. In Stonor left, through woods, over common, pub on left*

There's every chance of seeing red kites wheeling around above this 16th-century, brick and flint pub overlooking the Chiltern Hills. Its two snug bar areas are characterised by beams, wrought iron, brasswork, open fires, traditional pub games and Brakspear's real ales on the handpumps. To dine in the large conservatory restaurant is to enjoy an approach to traditional English dishes that often involves tweaking them to intensify the flavours, thus a menu typically begins with Cornish oysters and Bloody Mary sorbet; and whole baked camembert stuffed with almonds and rosemary. Of appeal to follow might be a main course of roast haunch of muntjac venison; herb-crusted fillet of wild sea bass; goat's cheese and ratatouille ravioli; or even a Chateaubriand for two. Pub classics include beer-battered haddock and chips and doorstep sandwiches. Dogs are welcome in the bar and two large beer gardens, the location for summer weekend barbecues and Bank Holiday hog roasts. Booking for meals may be required.

Open all wk 12-3.30 6-11 (Sat 12-11 Sun 12-6) **Bar Meals** L served Mon-Fri 12-2.30, Sat 12-3, Sun 12-4 D served Mon-Sat 6.30-9.30 **Restaurant** L served Mon-Fri 12-2.30, Sat 12-3, Sun 12-4 D served Mon-Sat 6.30-9.30 ⊕ BRAKSPEAR ◀ Ordinary, Oxford Gold. **Facilities** ✿ Children welcome Children's portions Garden Parking ☷

The Little Angel

Remenham Ln RG9 2LS ☎ 01491 411008
e-mail: enquiries@thelittleangel.co.uk
dir: *From Henley-on-Thames take A4130 (White Hill) towards Maidenhead. Pub on left*

Especially on Fridays and Saturdays this rather engaging, whitewashed pub just over Henley's famous bridge from the town gets pretty packed – and for good reasons, including the really chic interior, with warming colours and an open fire (oh, and the odd black lab); the well compiled wine list; the real ales that come from Brakspear; and the exceptional modern menu. Try fish stew of conger eel, plaice, mussels and clams in rich tomato sauce; or pan-fried confit duck hash. Sundays are "unbelievably busy" but don't worry, lunch is served all day. Booking for meals may be required.

Open all day all wk 11-11 (Fri-Sat 11am-mdnt Sun 12-10) **Bar Meals** L served Mon-Fri 12-3, Sat-Sun all day D served Mon-Fri 7-10, Sat-Sun all day Av main course £11.25 **Restaurant** L served Mon-Fri 12-3, Sat-Sun all day D served Mon-Fri 7-10, Sat-Sun all day Fixed menu price fr £15 Av 3 course à la carte fr £23 ⊕ BRAKSPEAR ◀ Brakspear, Oxford Gold & Seasonal ales, Guinness. ♦ 11 **Facilities** ✿ Children welcome Children's portions Garden Parking Wi-fi ☷

Save on hotels. Book at **theAA.com/hotel**

OXFORDSHIRE 413 **ENGLAND**

PICK OF THE PUBS

Miller of Mansfield

GORING   Map 5 SU68

High St RG8 9AW ☎ 01491 872829
e-mail: reservations@millerofmansfield.com
web: www.millerofmansfield.com
dir: *From Pangbourne A329 to Streatley.*
Right on B4009, 0.5m to Goring

The beautiful red-brick Georgian coaching inn in this attractive Thames-side village has been stylishly renovated by Paul Suter, who has lavished money on the place. In an Area of Outstanding Natural Beauty, it makes the perfect bolt-hole for exploring the Thames Path (just along the road) and the Chiltern Hills. Despite having smart rooms and being highly rated as a restaurant with rooms, the Miller of Mansfield remains a focal point for the village. The cracking bar, replete with shiny wooden floors, fat candles on scrubbed tables and blazing log fires, welcomes local and visiting real ale drinkers, and wine lovers too; indeed, refreshments extend to triple-certified origin coffees and organic teas. The kitchen focuses on freshness of ingredients, so expect seasonality in its take on modern British cooking. Suppliers are carefully sourced, and just about everything that can be is home made. In the Philippe Starck-influenced dining room, each dish brims with flavour: lobster ravioli, lobster bisque, basil purée and olive tapenade foam;

poached monkfish, asparagus, wild mushroom risotto and courgette flowers; pistachio pork belly, braised cheek, parsnip purée, apple and pickled walnut chutney and Berkshire honey jus are just a selection. Yet you can order grilled lemongrass sardines, chorizo Scotch egg, a steak and red onion sandwich, or a pub classic like steak-and-kidney pudding with roasted root vegetables from the all-day menu in the bar, perhaps with a pint of Rebellion IPA or West Berkshire Brewery's Good Old Boy — ample demonstration of the lack of ostentation within this welcoming hostelry. Booking for meals may be required.

Open all day all wk 8am-11pm **Bar Meals** L served all wk 12-10 D served all wk 12-10 food served all day **Restaurant** L & D served all wk all day ⊕ FREE HOUSE ◖ West Berkshire Good Old Boy, Rebellion IPA.
Facilities Children welcome Children's menu Children's portions ✿ Garden Parking Wi-fi 🚌

HENLY-ON-THAMES *continued*

The Three Tuns

5 The Market Place RG9 2AA ☎ 01491 410138
e-mail: info@threetunshenley.co.uk
dir: *In town centre. Parking nearby*

Mark and Sandra Duggan have taken over this Brakspear pub, which, although not too obvious from the street, is one of the oldest in town. The cosy, matchboarded front bar has bare and carpeted floors, scrubbed tables, an open fire, and a miscellany of artefacts, posters and prints. From the adjacent intimate dining room, a passageway leads to the suntrap terrace garden. Freshly sourced local produce (the butcher's only next door!) underpins menus both traditional and modern: hand-made pies; fish and chips; home-cured salmon with beetroot; and mushroom risotto, for example.

Open all day 11.30-11 (Sat 11am-mdnt Sun 11-6) Closed: 25 Dec, Mon **Bar Meals** L served Tue-Fri 12-3, Sat-Sun 12-4 D served Tue-Sat 6-9.45 Av main course £14 **Restaurant** L served Tue-Fri 12-3, Sat-Sun 12-4 D served Tue-Sat 6-9.45 Fixed menu price fr £10 Av 3 course à la carte fr £20 ⊕ BRAKSPEAR ◀ Special, Oxford Gold ♂ Westons Wyld Wood. ☂ 12 **Facilities** ✿ Children welcome Children's portions Garden

WhiteHartNettlebed
PICK OF THE PUBS

High St, Nettlebed RG9 5DD ☎ 01491 641245
e-mail: whitehart@tmdining.co.uk
dir: *On A4130 between Henley-on-Thames & Wallingford*

Royalist and parliamentary soldiers made a habit of lodging in local taverns during the English Civil War; this 15th-century inn reputedly billeted troops loyal to the King. During the 17th and 18th centuries the area was plagued by highwaymen, including the notorious Isaac Darkin, who was eventually caught, tried and hung at Oxford Gaol. These days the beautifully restored property is favoured by a stylish crowd who appreciate the chic bar and restaurant. Heading the beer list is locally-brewed Brakspear, backed by popular internationals and a small selection of cosmopolitan bottles. A typical three-course meal selection could comprise sweet potato and gruyère tartlet with rocket; spinach, feta and cumin spanakopita with baba ganoush; and lemon and thyme pannacotta with red wine poached pear. Booking for meals may be required.

Open all day all wk 7am-11pm (Sun 8am-10pm) ⊕ BRAKSPEAR ◀ Brakspear, Guinness ♂ Symonds. **Facilities** Children welcome Children's menu Children's portions Play area Family room Garden Parking

---

Rising Sun

Witheridge Hill RG9 5PF ☎ 01491 640856
e-mail: info@risingsunwitheridgehill.co.uk
dir: *From Henley-on-Thames take A4130 towards Wallingford. Take B481, turn right to Highmoor*

Adjacent to the green in a small Chilterns hamlet, the path to this 17th-century pub passes through the garden. Its idyllic setting is matched by an interior rich in low beamed ceilings, wood-boarded floors, and richly coloured walls. Chalkboards list guest ales, wines and forthcoming events, while a tapas menu proffers a dozen appetisers ranging from pan-fried chorizo through battered calamari rings to houmous with toasted pitta. The thoughtfully decorated restaurant is divided into three sections, making for cosy tables – a great place to sample the game casserole with celeriac purée and stilton dumplings.

Open all wk Mon-Fri 12-3 5-11 (Sat 12-11 Sun 12-7) **Bar Meals** L served Mon-Fri 12-2, Sat-Sun 12-3 D served Mon-Sat 6.30-9 Av main course £14 **Restaurant** L served Mon-Fri 12-2, Sat-Sun 12-3 D served Mon-Sat 6.30-9 Av 3 course à la carte fr £26 ⊕ BRAKSPEAR ◀ Ordinary, Oxford Gold ♂ Westons Wyld Wood Organic. ☂ 10 **Facilities** ✿ Children welcome Children's menu Children's portions Family room Garden Parking Wi-fi ▭ (notice required)

The Plough Inn

GL7 3HG ☎ 01367 253543
e-mail: josie.plough@hotmail.co.uk
dir: *From M4 junct 15 onto A419 towards Cirencester then right onto A361 to Lechlade. A417 towards Faringdon, follow signs to Kelmscott*

Dating from 1631, this attractive Cotswold-stone inn stands on the Thames Path midway between Radcot and Lechlade, making it a haven for walkers and boaters. It's also just a short walk from Kelmscott Manor, once home to William Morris. Exposed stone walls and flagstone floors set the scene for real ales and an extensive, hearty menu. Dishes range from medallions of pork tenderloin to falafel burger with Mediterranean couscous. The pub holds a beer festival (please contact for dates).

Open all day all wk 11.30-11 (Sun 11-11) **Bar Meals** L served all wk 12-3 D served all wk 7-10 **Restaurant** L served all wk 12-3 D served all wk 7-10 ⊕ FREE HOUSE ◀ Wye Valley, Hook Norton, Box Steam, Guest ales ♂ Symonds Scrumpy Jack. **Facilities** Children welcome Children's menu Children's portions Garden Beer festival Wi-fi ▭

The Kingham Plough ★ ★ ★ ★ INN ◉◉
PICK OF THE PUBS

The Green OX7 6YD ☎ 01608 658327
e-mail: book@thekinghamplough.co.uk
dir: *B4450 from Chipping Norton to Churchill. 2nd right to Kingham, left at T-junct. Pub on right*

Situated on the village green in a beautiful Cotswold village, this quintessential inn has a relaxing bar where you can enjoy one of the real ales and daily-changing bar snacks like scotched quail eggs or venison sausage rolls. In the restaurant chef-proprietor Emily Watkins, who worked under Heston Blumenthal at The Fat Duck, changes the short menu daily to accommodate the deliveries from local farms, smallholdings and game estates. Expect two AA-Rosette dishes like game terrine with a red onion and star anise chutney served with brioche; venison loin with rosehip jelly and a salsify and celeriac gratin; pollock with crispy whitebait in a devilled butter sauce with baked mash potato and wilted spinach; plum lardy cake with clotted cream ice cream; and an exemplary local cheeseboard. Look out for events such as the annual farmers' market, cider festival, quiz nights and food tasting evenings. There are elegantly furnished bedrooms, all newly refurbished.

Open all day all wk Closed: 25 Dec **Bar Meals** L served Mon-Sat 12-9, Sun 12-8 D served Mon-Sat 12-9, Sun 12-8 food served all day **Restaurant** L served Mon-Sat 12-2, Sun 12-3 D served Mon-Thu 7-8.30, Fri-Sat 6.30-9 ⊕ FREE HOUSE ◀ Wye Valley HPA, Purity Mad Goose, Cotswold Wheat Beer, Hook Norton ♂ Westons Stowford Press. **Facilities** ✿ Children welcome Children's menu Children's portions Garden Parking Wi-fi **Rooms** 7

The Bell at Langford

GL7 3LF ☎ 01367 860249
dir: *From Swindon take A361 towards Lechlade & Burford. Through Lechlade, at rdbt right onto B4477 signed Carterton. Turn right for Langford*

Jacqui and Paul Wynne's busy little dining pub in a charming village has polished flagstones, an inglenook fireplace and simple, low-key furnishings. People like it this way, which is why they enjoy eating here. Paul is the chef and Jacqui runs front of house, and is passionate about the beers and wines. There's a lot to choose from: crab and leek tart glazed with gruyère in a white wine cream sauce; roasted fillet of pork with bubble-and-squeak and spinach in a Madeira and oyster mushroom sauce; and Chettinad chicken (tomatoes, coconut cream, spices, curry leaves and chilles) with rice, naan bread and poppadoms. Fish specials include seared scallops with chorizo and a rocket and parmesan salad.

Open 12-3 7-11 (Fri 12-3 7-12 Sat 12-3 7-11.30) Closed: Sun eve & Mon **Bar Meals** L served Tue-Sun 12-1.45 D served Tue-Sat 7-9 **Restaurant** L served Tue-Sun 12-1.45 D served Tue-Sat 7-9 ⊕ FREE HOUSE ◀ Sharp's Doom Bar, St Austell Tribute, Hook Norton ♂ Westons

Save on hotels. Book at **theAA.com/hotel**

OXFORDSHIRE 415 ENGLAND

Stowford Press. ₹ 12 **Facilities** ✿ Children welcome Children's menu Children's portions Play area Garden Parking 🚐

LOWER SHIPLAKE — Map 5 SU77

The Baskerville ★★★★ INN

PICK OF THE PUBS

See Pick of the Pubs on page 416

LOWER WOLVERCOTE — Map 5 SP40

The Trout Inn

PICK OF THE PUBS

195 Godstow Rd OX2 8PN ☎ 01865 510930
dir: *From A40 at Wolvercote rdbt (N of Oxford) follow signs for Wolvercote, through village to pub*

This utterly captivating waterside inn is threaded into the structure of one of Oxford's oldest buildings. A favourite with undergraduates, its renown was assured when Morse and Lewis sat on the terrace below the weir, supping local beers in several episodes of the iconic television detective series filmed here. It was already ancient when Lewis Carroll, and later CS Lewis took inspiration here; centuries before them it was a hospice for Godstow Nunnery, on the opposite bank of the Thames. With leaded windows, great oak beams, flagged floors and fireplaces glowing in winter, it is arguably Oxford's most atmospheric inn, enhanced by modern comforts. The comprehensive, top-notch menu has a distinct Mediterranen lineage, with starters of minted bulgar wheat, meze or garlic gambas setting the scene for a wide range of freshly made pastas and pizzas, backed up by reliable modern British fare like lemon and garlic spit-roasted chicken; or roast rump of lamb.

Open all day all wk 9am-close **Bar Meals** L served all wk 12-10 D served all wk 12-10 food served all day **Restaurant** L served all wk 12-10 D served all wk 12-10 food served all day ⊕ FREE HOUSE ◀ Brakspear Oxford Gold & Bitter, Adnams Lighthouse, Sharp's Doom Bar, Guest ales Ö Aspall. ₹ 21 **Facilities** Children welcome Garden Parking 🚐

MIDDLETON STONEY — Map 11 SP52

Best Western Jersey Arms Hotel ★★ HL

OX25 4AD ☎ 01869 343234
e-mail: jerseyarms@bestwestern.co.uk
dir: *3m from junct 9/10 of M4. 3m from A34 on B430*

Until 1951, when a family called Ansell bought it, this 13th-century country inn belonged to the Jersey Estate. In 1985 the Ansells sold it to Donald and Helen Livingston, making them only its third owners since 1243. Food can be taken in the Bar & Grill where the British menu is supplemented by daily specials. Start with salmon and coriander fishcake, then try slow-roasted shoulder of Oxfordshire pork with sage and onion sauce; chargrilled chicken, with onion, tomato and tarragon sauce; or

---

savoury pancake stuffed with spinach and cream cheese. Booking for meals may be required.

Open all day all wk **Bar Meals** L served all wk 12-2 D served all wk 6.30-9 Av main course £12.50 **Restaurant** L served all wk 12-2 D served all wk 6.30-9 Av 3 course à la carte fr £25 ⊕ FREE HOUSE ◀ Flowers. ₹ 9 **Facilities** Children welcome Children's menu Garden Parking Wi-fi **Rooms** 20

MURCOTT — Map 11 SP51

The Nut Tree Inn ◉ ◉

PICK OF THE PUBS

Main St OX5 2RE ☎ 01865 331253
dir: *M40 junct 9, A34 towards Oxford. Left onto B4027 signed Islip. At Red Lion turn left. Right signed Murcott, Fencott & Charlton-on-Otmoor. Pub on right in village*

The Nut Tree is a thatched, 15th-century free house overlooking the pond in Murcott, one of the 'Seven Towns' of Otmoor, an area of semi-wetland, part of which is an RSPB nature reserve. With oak beams, wood-burners, unusual carvings and an impressive portfolio of real ales on tap, it serves great modern British food, whenever possible free range, wild or organic. Salmon is home-smoked, breads and ice creams home-made, succulent meat comes from the pub's own rare-breed pigs, and fruit and vegetables are from its and neighbours' gardens. A typical selection in the two AA-Rosette restaurant might be parfait of chicken livers, followed by roast breast of Gressingham duck, or fillet of Cornish cod, then warm chocolate fondant with cardamom ice cream. A seven-course tasting menu wends its way through fillet of Cornish mackerel, slow-roasted belly of pork and boiled egg and soldiers. The 14-page wine list includes some impressive Bordeaux and Burgundies. Booking for meals may be required.

Open all day Closed: Sun eve & Mon **Bar Meals** L served Tue-Sat 12-2.30, Sun 12-3 D served Tue-Sat 7-9 Av main course £10 **Restaurant** L served Tue-Sat 12-2.30, Sun 12-3 D served Tue-Sat 7-9 Fixed menu price fr £18 Av 3 course à la carte fr £37.50 ⊕ FREE HOUSE ◀ Vale Best Bitter, Hadda's Winter Solstice & Wychert, Fuller's London Pride, Brains The Rev. James, Wickwar BOB, Shepherd Neame Spitfire. ₹ 16 **Facilities** Children welcome Children's portions Garden Parking 🚐

NORTH HINKSEY VILLAGE — Map 5 SP40

The Fishes

OX2 0NA ☎ 01865 249796
e-mail: fishes@peachpubs.com
dir: *From A34 S'bound (dual carriageway) left at junct after Botley Interchange, signed North Hinksey & Oxford Rugby Club. From A34 N'bound exit at Botley Interchange & return to A34 S'bound, then follow as above*

This attractive, tile-hung Victorian pub is a short walk from the centre of Oxford yet sits in three acres of wooded grounds running down to a stream – an ideal place for a picnic ordered at the bar or one of their regular

---

barbecues. Real ales can be enjoyed in the cosy snug, but you may well be tempted by the modern British food ranging from deli boards to full meals such as potted crab with smoked paprika mayonnaise, and watercress and radish salad, followed by Cornish lamb on the bone with shallot and parsley mash, sprouting broccoli and mint jus. Opt for vanilla pannacotta for dessert.

Open all day all wk Closed: 25 Dec **Bar Meals** Av main course £14 food served all day **Restaurant** Av 3 course à la carte fr £22 food served all day ⊕ PEACH PUBS ◀ Greene King IPA, Morland Old Speckled Hen, Guest ales Ö Aspall. ₹ 13 **Facilities** ✿ Children welcome Children's portions Play area Garden Parking Wi-fi 🚐 (notice required)

OXFORD — Map 5 SP50

The Anchor

PICK OF THE PUBS

2 Hayfield Rd, Walton Manor OX2 6TT ☎ 01865 510282
dir: *A34 (Oxford ring road N), exit Peartree rdbt, 1.5m down the Woodstock road, then right at Polstead Rd, follow road to end, pub on right*

Records show a pub on this site since 1752, but the current Anchor was built in 1933 by Hall's Brewery. Many of its original art deco features have been left untouched, including the large central bar. Very much a community pub, it's a base for coffee mornings, the book club, and charity fund-raising efforts. It's off the beaten track – but, for all that, remains firmly on the map for its well-kept Wadworth ales and small but carefully chosen wine list. The relaxed and comfortable surroundings extend to log fires and daily newspapers. Lunchtime bar snacks embrace merguez sausages with honey and yogurt dip, or scrambled eggs with smoked salmon. A typical lunch dish would be spiced smoked haddock fishcakes. The short but sweet dinner carte selection tempts with steamed Fowey mussels; grilled lamb steaks with salsa verde; and caramelised lemon tart with crème fraîche. There's a garden for alfresco dining, and major sporting events are shown in the Oak Bar. Booking for meals may be required.

Open all day all wk 12-11 Closed: 25-26 Dec **Bar Meals** L served Mon-Sat 12-2.30, Sun 12-3 D served Mon-Sat 6-9.30, Sun 6.30-8.30 **Restaurant** L served Mon-Sat 12-2.30, Sun 12-3 D served Mon-Sat 6-9.30, Sun 6.30-8.30 ⊕ WADWORTH ◀ 6X, Henry's Original IPA & Bishop's Tipple, Guest ale Ö Westons Stowford Press. **Facilities** Children welcome Children's menu Children's portions Garden Parking Wi-fi

PICK OF THE PUBS

The Baskerville ★★★★INN

LOWER SHIPLAKE Map 5 SU77

Station Rd RG9 3NY ☎ 0118 940 3332
e-mail: enquiries@thebaskerville.com
web: www.thebaskerville.com
dir: *Just off A4155, 1.5m from Henley towards Reading, follow signs at War Memorial junct*

On the popular Thames Path, close to Shiplake Station and just a few minutes from historic Henley-on-Thames, this brick-built pub may have a rather plain façade but inside is a modern-rustic pub of real quality. Walkers remove their muddy boots at the door before heading to the bar that's adorned with sporting memorabilia, and where pints of Loddon Hoppit, brewed two miles away, are served with welcoming smiles. Variety and choice for the customer is a top priority here, as witnessed by well-balanced menus covering breakfast, lunch, evening, Sunday lunch and children's choices. Whether it's the bar snacks blackboard menu or the à la carte, the objective is to serve really good food at a reasonable price in a relaxed and unpretentious atmosphere. Modern British describes the kitchen's approach, with continental and eastern influences. All produce is delivered daily, and all dishes, including the bread, are prepared on the premises; organic, sustainably sourced ingredients travel as few miles as possible, and a special fish menu runs throughout the summer months. Lunchtime open sandwiches include Baskerville smoked ham and mature cheddar with home-made chutney, or home-cured organic Shetland salmon and chunky tartare sauce.

Alternatively you could savour pan-fried English ox liver and smoked bacon with colcannon potatoes and a rich rosemary and onion gravy. A typical evening choice might start with smoked haddock, spring onion and saffron tart with celeriac remoulade and lemon vinaigrette dressed leaves, followed by oven-roast rump of Chiltern lamb and black pudding with parsnip and potato rösti, minted pea purée, buttered Savoy and redcurrant jus. The wine list extends to 50 bins, and owner Allan Hannah betrays his origins with his range of 40 malt whiskies. The pub also boasts an attractive garden, where summer Sunday barbecues are a common fixture, plus comfortable accommodation. Booking for meals may be required.

Open all day all wk 11-11 (Sun 12-10.30) Closed: 25 Dec, 1 Jan **Bar Meals** L served Mon-Sat 12-6, Sun

12-3.30 D served Mon-Thu 6-9.30, Fri-Sat 6-10 Av main course £16 food served all day **Restaurant** L served Mon-Sat 12-6, Sun 12-3.30 D served Mon-Thu 6-9.30, Fri-Sat 6-10 Fixed menu price fr £16.50 Av 3 course à la carte fr £28 food served all day ◙ Fuller's London Pride, Loddon Hoppit, Timothy Taylor Landlord Ö Thatchers. ♟ 12 **Facilities** Children welcome Children's menu Children's portions Play area ♣ Garden Parking Wi-fi **Rooms** 4

Save on hotels. Book at **theAA.com/hotel**

OXFORDSHIRE 417 **ENGLAND**

OXFORD *continued*

The Magdalen Arms NEW

243 Iffley Rd OX4 1SJ ☎ 01865 243159
e-mail: info@magdalenarms.co.uk
dir: *On the corner of Iffley Rd & Magdalen Rd*

A short walk from Oxford city centre, this bustling food pub is run by the same team behind Waterloo's hugely influential Anchor & Hope gastro-boozer (see entry). There is a similar boho feel to the place with its dark red walls and vintage furniture and the nose-to-tail menu will be familiar to anybody who knows the pub's London sibling. Expect the likes of spiced parsnip soup; pork schnitzel with purple sprouting broccoli and anchovy dressing; and steamed ginger pudding with custard. Real ales are complemented by a vibrant modern wine list. Booking for meals may be required.

Open 11-11 (Tue 5-11) Closed: 1st 2wks Aug, Mon **Bar Meals** L served Wed-Sat 12-2.30, Sun 12-3 D served Tue-Sat 6-10, Sun 6-9.30 Av main course £13 **Restaurant** L served Wed-Sat 12-2.30, Sun 12-3 D served Tue-Sat 6-10, Sun 6-9.30 Av 3 course à la carte fr £20 ⊕ SCOTTISH & NEWCASTLE ◀ Caledonian Deuchars IPA, Ringwood Fortyniner, Theakston Best Bitter ♂ Symonds. ♀ 16 **Facilities** ✿ Children welcome Garden Beer festival

The Oxford Retreat

1-2 Hythe Bridge St OX1 2EW ☎ 01865 250309
e-mail: info@theoxfordretreat.com
dir: *In city centre. 200mtrs from rail station towards centre*

Smack beside the River Isis, the decked, tree-shaded waterside garden at this imposing gabled pub is the place to be seen and is best enjoyed after a day exploring the city of dreaming spires. Arrive early and relax sipping cocktails or a pint of London Pride, then order from the eclectic pub menu, including locally potted pork with spicy chutney; a ham hock sharing plate served with home-made breads; a pepperoni pizza; or sirloin steak with dauphinoise potatoes and red wine jus. In winter retreat inside and cosy up around the log fire.

Open all wk 4-close (Fri & Sun noon-close Sat noon-3am) Closed: 25-26 Dec & 1 Jan **Bar Meals** L served Fri-Sat 12-10, Sun 12-8 D served Mon-Thu 4-10, Fri-Sat 12-10, Sun 12-8 **Restaurant** L served Fri-Sat 12-10, Sun 12-8 D served Mon-Thu 4-10, Fri-Sat 12-10, Sun 12-8 ⊕ FREE HOUSE ◀ Fuller's London Pride, Guinness, Staropramen ♂ Westons Wyld Wood Organic. ♀ 10 **Facilities** Children welcome Children's portions Garden Wi-fi 🚌 (notice required)

Turf Tavern

4 Bath Place, off Holywell St OX1 3SU ☎ 01865 243235
e-mail: 8004@greeneking.co.uk
dir: *Telephone for directions*

A jewel of a pub, and consequently one of Oxford's most popular, although it's not easy to find, as it is approached through hidden alleyways, which, if anything, adds to its allure. Previously called the Spotted Cow, it became the

Turf in 1842, probably in deference to its gambling clientele; it has also had brushes with literature, film and politics. The Turf Tavern is certainly one of Oxford's oldest pubs, with some 13th-century foundations and a 17th-century low-beamed front bar. Three beer gardens help ease overcrowding, but the 11 real ales and reasonably priced pub grub keep the students, locals and visitors flowing in.

Open all day all wk Mon-Sat 11-11 (Sun 12-10.30) Closed: 25 Dec **Bar Meals** food served all day ⊕ GREENE KING ◀ Guest ales ♂ Westons Old Rosie. **Facilities** ✿ Children welcome Garden Wi-fi 🚌

PISHILL — Map 5 SU78

The Crown Inn

PICK OF THE PUBS

See Pick of the Pubs on page 418

RAMSDEN — Map 11 SP31

The Royal Oak

PICK OF THE PUBS

See Pick of the Pubs on page 419

ROTHERFIELD PEPPARD — Map 5 SU78

The Unicorn NEW

Colmore Ln, Kingwood RG9 5LX ☎ 01491 628674
e-mail: enquiries@unicornkingwood.co.uk
dir: *Exit A4074 (Reading to Wallingford), follow Sonning Common & Peppard signs. Left in Peppard Common signed Stoke Row. Right into Colmore Ln at Unicorn sign*

A village local set in the Chilterns, The Unicorn is five miles from Henley-on-Thames and Reading. Petitioning villagers recently saved the pub from closure and change of use. Now, with children and dogs welcome, expect to have to fight your way in on a Friday or Saturday evening, or during the beer festival, such is The Unicorn's reputation as a friendly drinking pub. It's also becoming known as a food destination, serving light lunches such as ploughman's or classic Welsh rarebit with salad and fries; and dinner highlights such as crab and sweetcorn risotto followed by luxury fish pie. Booking for meals may be required.

Open all wk 11-3 5.30-11 (Fri-Sat 11am-mdnt Sun 12-10) **Bar Meals** L served Mon-Fri 12-3, Sat-Sun all day D served Mon-Fri 7-10, Sat-Sun all day Av main course £11.50 **Restaurant** L served Mon-Fri 12-3, Sat-Sun all day D served Mon-Fri 7-10, Sat-Sun all day ⊕ BRAKSPEAR ◀ Bitter & Oxford Gold, Marston's Pedigree, Hook Norton ♂ Westons Wyld Wood Organic, Symonds. **Facilities** ✿ Children welcome Children's portions Garden Beer festival Parking Wi-fi 🚌 (notice required)

SHILTON — Map 5 SP20

Rose & Crown

OX18 4AB ☎ 01993 842280
dir: *From A40 at Burford take A361 towards Lechlade on Thames. Right, follow Shilton signs on left. Or from A40 E of Burford take B4020 towards Carterton*

A traditional Cotswold-stone inn dating back to the 17th century, two miles south of Burford. Each of the two rooms has original beams and a log fire, helping to meld seamlessly its twin functions of friendly village local and destination food pub. Two mainstay real ales are augmented by a regularly changing guest and Westons Wyld Wood Vintage cider. Chef-landlord Martin Coldicott and head chef Jamie Webber are both classically trained (The Connaught and The Ivy respectively), so expect way above average dishes featuring locally sourced produce – roast venison or steak, ale and mushroom pie. You can eat and drink in the garden on warmer days.

Open all wk 11.30-3 6-11 (Fri-Sun & BH 11.30-11) **Bar Meals** L served Mon-Fri 12-2, Sat-Sun & BH 12-2.45 D served all wk 7-9 Av main course £12 **Restaurant** L served Mon-Fri 12-2, Sat-Sun & BH 12-2.45 D served all wk 7-9 Av 3 course à la carte fr £20 ⊕ FREE HOUSE ◀ Hook Norton Old Hooky, Young's Bitter ♂ Westons Wyld Wood Organic Vintage. ♀ 10 **Facilities** ✿ Children welcome Garden Parking

SHIPTON-UNDER-WYCHWOOD — Map 10 SP21

The Shaven Crown Hotel

High St OX7 6BA ☎ 01993 830330
e-mail: relax@theshavencrown.co.uk
dir: *On A361, halfway between Burford & Chipping Norton opposite village green & church*

This 14th-century coaching inn was built by the monks of Bruern Abbey as a hospice for the poor. Following the Dissolution of the Monasteries, Elizabeth I used it as a hunting lodge before giving it to the village in 1580, when it became the Crown Inn. Thus it stayed until 1930, when a brewery with a sense of humour changed the name as homage to the familiar monastic tonsure. Its interior is full of original architectural features, like the Great Hall. Light meals and real ales are served in the bar, while the restaurant offers Cotswold ham, beef, lamb and venison pie; beer-battered fish and chips; and winter vegetable and bean hotpot.

Open all wk 11-3 5-11 (Sat-Sun 11-11) **Bar Meals** L served Mon-Fri 12-2, Sat 12-9.30, Sun 12-9 D served Mon-Fri 6-9.30, Sat 12-9.30, Sun 12-9 Av main course £13 **Restaurant** L served Mon-Fri 12-2, Sat 12-9.30, Sun 12-9 D served Mon-Fri 6-9.30, Sat 12-9.30, Sun 12-9 ⊕ FREE HOUSE ◀ Hook Norton, Wye Valley, Goffs, Cottage ♂ Westons Stowford Press. ♀ 10 **Facilities** ✿ Children welcome Children's menu Children's portions Garden Parking Wi-fi 🚌 (notice required)

PICK OF THE PUBS

The Crown Inn

PISHILL   Map 5 SU78

RG9 6HH ☎ 01491 638364
e-mail: enquiries@thecrowninnpishill.co.uk
web: www.thecrowninnpishill.co.uk
dir: *A4130 from Henley-on-Thames,*
right onto B480 to Pishill

A pretty 15th-century brick and flint
former coaching inn, The Crown has
enjoyed a colourful history. It began life
in medieval times, serving ale to
members of the thriving monastic
community, then in later years, served
as a refuge for Catholic priests
escaping Henry VIII's draconian rule. It
contains possibly the largest priest hole
in the country, complete with a sad story
about one Father Dominique, who met
his end there and whose ghost is
occasionally seen in the pub. Moving
forward to the swinging 60s, the
thatched barn housed a nightclub
hosting the likes of George Harrison and
Dusty Springfield. Nowadays, the barn is
licensed for civil ceremonies as well as
serving as a function room. In the pub
itself, the bar is supplied by mostly local
breweries, including Rebellion, and the
menu changes frequently, including
sandwiches and ploughman's at lunch-

times, and features local produce
cooked fresh to order. Lunch and dinner
are served every day and can be enjoyed
inside the pub with its three log fires or
in the picturesque garden overlooking
the valley, depending on the season. The
name of the village is often a subject of
conversation, some say it was to do with
wagon horses relieving themselves once
they had got to the top of the hill or
maybe simply because peas used to be
ground around here! Self-contained
cottage accommodation is available.

Open all wk 12-3 6-11 (Sun 12-10)
Closed: 25-26 Dec **Bar Meals** L served
all wk 12-2.30 D served all wk
6.30-9.30 **Restaurant** L served all wk
12-2.30 D served all wk 6.30-9.30
⊕ FREE HOUSE ◖ Brakspear, West
Berkshire, Loddon, Rebellion.
Facilities Children welcome Children's
portions ❧ Garden Parking 🚌 (notice
required)

PICK OF THE PUBS

The Royal Oak

RAMSDEN　　　　　Map 11 SP31

High St OX7 3AU ☎ 01993 868213
e-mail: jo@royaloakramsden.com
web: www.royaloakramsden.com
dir: *B4022 from Witney towards Charlbury, right before Hailey, through Poffley End*

Built of Cotswold stone and facing Ramsden's fine parish church, this former 17th-century coaching inn is a popular refuelling stop for walkers exploring nearby Wychwood Forest and visitors touring the pretty villages and visiting Blenheim Palace. Whether you are walking or not, the cosy inn oozes traditional charm and character, with its old beams, warm fires and stone walls, and long-serving landlords John and Jo Oldham provide a very warm welcome. A free house, it dispenses beers sourced from local breweries, such as Hook Norton Hooky Bitter and Old Hooky, alongside Adnams Broadside and Young's Special. Somerset's Original Cider Company supplies the bar with Pheasant Plucker cider, alongside Westons Old Rosie from Herefordshire. With a strong kitchen team, the main menu, built on the very best of fresh local and seasonal ingredients, regularly features a pie of the week topped with puff pastry or the popular suet pudding; there are other pub favourites such as confit duck with Puy lentils and garlic potatoes; half shoulder of lamb with rosemary and garlic jus; and a bowl of chilli with rice and tortillas. Aberdeen Angus beef is available in the form of sirloin and rump steaks, cooked to your liking on the chargrill. Among the daily specials you may find a hearty and traditional fish and vegetable stew; scallops with asparagus and smoked bacon; and roast local partridge with game chips and a port and redcurrant glaze. For a lighter bite try the devilled lambs' kidneys or the Kelmscott bacon salad. Every Thursday evening there is a special offer of steak, with a glass of wine and dessert included. Carefully selected by the owner, the wine list has over 200 wines, specialising in those from Bordeaux and Languedoc, with 30 of them served by the glass.

Open all wk 11.30-3 6.30-11 (Sun 11.30-3 7-10.30) Closed: 25 Dec **Bar Meals** L served all wk 12-2 D served Mon-Sat 7-9.45, Sun 7-9 **Restaurant** L served all wk 12-2 D served Mon-Sat 7-9.45, Sun 7-9 🛢 FREE HOUSE ◀ Hook Norton Old Hooky & Hooky Bitter, Adnams Broadside, Young's Special, Wye Valley ♻ Westons Old Rosie, Pheasant Plucker. 🍷 30 **Facilities** Children's portions 🐾 Garden Parking

SHUTFORD
Map 11 SP34

The George & Dragon

PICK OF THE PUBS

See Pick of the Pubs on opposite page

SOUTH STOKE
Map 5 SU58

The Perch and Pike ★★★ INN

RG8 0JS ☎ 01491 872415
e-mail: info@perchandpike.co.uk
dir: *On Ridgeway Hiking Trail. 1.5m N of Goring & 4m S of Wallingford on B4009*

There is a genuinely warm welcome at this 17th-century village pub, just a two-minute walk from the River Thames. The adjoining barn conversion houses the 42-seater restaurant, where food ranges from a selection of salads, baguettes and ploughman's to the likes of traditional pub meals of scampi and chips or the home-made pie to the more exotic South African dish of Bobotie (lightly spiced beef mince with dried apricots and raisins with rice). Four comfortable bedrooms are available. Booking for meals may be required.

Open all wk 11.30-3 5.30-11 (Sat-Sun 11.30-11) **Bar Meals** L served Mon-Sat 12-2.30 D served Mon-Sat 7-9.30 **Restaurant** L served Sun 12-2.30 D served Mon-Sat 7-9.30 ⊕ BRAKSPEAR ◀ Brakspear, Guest ale. ₹ 10 **Facilities** ✿ Children welcome Children's portions Garden Parking Wi-fi **Rooms** 4

STEEPLE ASTON
Map 11 SP42

The Red Lion

South Side OX25 4RY ☎ 01869 340225
e-mail: redlionsa@aol.com
dir: *0.5m off A4260 (Oxford Rd). Follow brown tourist signs for pub*

Close to Blenheim Palace and Banbury Cross, this unspoilt 18th-century pub is a popular place for thirsty walkers to enjoy a pint of local Hook Norton beer. Situated high in the beautiful north Oxfordshire village of Steeple Aston, it has a majestic view of the Cherwell Valley from its pretty floral suntrap terrace. The conservatory-style oak dining room offers dishes ranging from a range of thin-crust pizzas to traditional favourites such as chicken liver pâté with rustic chutney, followed by chicken and mushroom shortcrust pie with mashed potatoes and greens. Booking for meals may be required.

Open all wk 12-3 5.30-11 (Sat 12-11 Sun 12-5) (Jun-Oct all day) Closed: Sun eve from 5pm **Bar Meals** L served all wk 12-2.30 D served Mon-Sat 6-9 **Restaurant** L served all wk 12-2.30 D served Mon-Sat 6-9 ⊕ HOOK NORTON ◀ Hooky Bitter, Double Stout, Seasonal ales Ŏ Westons Stowford Press. **Facilities** ✿ Children welcome Children's portions Garden Parking Wi-fi ➡ (notice required)

STOKE ROW
Map 5 SU68

Crooked Billet

PICK OF THE PUBS

RG9 5PU ☎ 01491 681048
dir: *From Henley towards Oxford on A4130. Left at Nettlebed for Stoke Row*

Built in 1642, the Crooked Billet was once the hideout of notorious highwayman Dick Turpin. Tucked away down a single track lane in deepest Oxfordshire, this charmingly rustic pub is now a popular hideaway for the well-heeled and the well known. Many of its finest features are unchanged, including the low beams, tiled floors and open fires that are so integral to its character. Local produce and organic fare are the mainstays of the kitchen, to the extent that the chef-proprietor will even exchange a lunch or dinner for the locals' excess vegetables. Menu offerings include starters like onion tart, chilli mussels or wild mushroom and mozzarella risotto cakes. To follow, there's a good range of fish mains, including John Dory with wild mushrooms and cauliflower purée, lemon sole with seared scallops, or roast brill with cider steamed mussels. Other alternatives include venison with haggis and roast figs; or ricotta, spinach and red pepper filo parcel. The pub hosts music nights, wine tastings and other events. Booking for meals may be required.

Open all wk 12-3 7-12 (Sat-Sun 12-12) Closed: 25 Dec **Bar Meals** L served Mon-Fri 12-2.30, Sat 12-10.30, Sun 12-10 D served Mon-Fri 7-10, Sat 12-10.30, Sun 12-10 **Restaurant** L served Mon-Fri 12-2.30, Sat 12-10.30, Sun 12-10 D served Mon-Fri 7-10, Sat 12-10.30, Sun 12-10 Fixed menu price fr £15 Av 3 course à la carte fr £30 ⊕ BRAKSPEAR ◀ Bitter. ₹ 10 **Facilities** Children welcome Children's portions Garden Parking

SWERFORD
Map 11 SP33

The Mason's Arms

Banbury Rd OX7 4AP ☎ 01608 683212
e-mail: admin@masons-arms.com
dir: *Between Banbury & Chipping Norton on A361*

A 300-year-old, stone-built former Masonic lodge, this pub in the Cotswolds has retained its traditional, informal feel. Owners Jude Kelly and Vicky Robertson took over in summer 2010. The modern British cooking concentrates on local produce where possible. You might begin with wild mussels steamed in cider, or pickled fillet of black bream with pickled samphire and orange oil, followed perhaps by roasted loin of rabbit wrapped in Parma ham with roast new potatoes. They also offer pub classics - dishes like home-baked ham, duck egg and chips; or faggots with mash, Hooky gravy and peas. Booking for meals may be required.

Open all wk 10-3 6-11 (Sun 12-dusk) Closed: 27-28 Dec **Bar Meals** L served Mon-Sat 12-2.30, Sun 12-dusk D served Mon-Sat 7-9, Sun 12-dusk **Restaurant** L served Mon-Sat 12-2.30, Sun 12-dusk D served Mon-Sat 7-9, Sun 12-dusk ⊕ FREE HOUSE ◀ Wychwood Hobgoblin, Brakspear. ₹ 20 **Facilities** ✿ Children welcome Children's menu Garden Parking Wi-fi ➡

SWINBROOK
Map 5 SP21

The Swan Inn ★★★★ INN ⊚⊚

PICK OF THE PUBS

OX18 4DY ☎ 01993 823339
e-mail: info@theswanswinbrook.co.uk
dir: *A40 towards Cheltenham, left towards Swinbrook, pub 1m before Burford*

Hidden in the Windrush Valley you will find the idyllic village of Swinbrook where time stands still. Owners Archie and Nicola Orr-Ewing took on the lease of this dreamy, wisteria-clad stone pub from the Dowager Duchess of Devonshire, the last surviving Mitford sister, in 2007. The Swan is the perfect English country pub – it stands by the River Windrush near the village cricket pitch, overlooking unspoilt Cotswold countryside. It gets even better inside: the two cottage-style front rooms, replete with worn flagstones, crackling log fires, low beams and country furnishings, lead through to a cracking bar and classy conservatory extension. First-class pub food ranges from simple bar snacks to more substantial main courses of guinea fowl, apricot and chickpea tagine; and Cornish hake with a casserole of butter beans, tomato and chorizo. You won't want to leave, so book one of the stunning en suite rooms in the restored barn. Booking for meals may be required.

Open all wk (Closed afternoons Nov-15 Mar) Closed: 25 Dec **Bar Meals** L served Mon-Fri 12-2, Sat-Sun 12-2.30 D served Mon-Thu 7-9, Fri-Sat 7-9.30 **Restaurant** L served Mon-Fri 12-2, Sat-Sun 12-2.30 D served Mon-Thu 7-9, Fri-Sat 7-9.30 ⊕ FREE HOUSE ◀ Hook Norton, Guest ales Ŏ Addlestones, Westons Wyld Wood Organic & Stowford Press, Cotswold. ₹ 9 **Facilities** Children welcome Children's menu Children's portions Garden Parking Wi-fi **Rooms** 6

Save on hotels. Book at **theAA.com/hotel**

OXFORDSHIRE 421 ENGLAND

PICK OF THE PUBS

The George & Dragon

SHUTFORD   Map 11 SP34

Church Ln OX15 6PG ☎ 01295 780320
web: www.thegeorgeanddragon.com
dir: *A422 from Banbury. 4m, turn left at sign for Shutford, follow directly to pub*

This attractive Cotswold-stone country pub is built into the side of a hill, with the village church directly above. Dating back to the 13th century, the pub is conveniently located at the start of the popular Shutford Walk and is a favourite rest stop for ramblers who congregate in the beer garden overlooking the picturesque village. Legend has it that several ghosts haunt the pub, and that a secret tunnel links it to the manor house. The bar (where in winter the locals play dominoes by the roaring fire) is probably unique in that it is actually 12 feet underground. That's surely something to think about while ordering one of the five real ales, or a refreshing glass of wine. Everything on the seasonal menus, except for the locally baked bread, is made from scratch; villagers bring in game and vegetables from their allotments. In the restaurant, look to the specials list to find pan-roasted cod fillet, or local game casserole with sweet potato purée. The à la carte menu will tempt with pan-fried naturally smoked haddock; Hooky venison haunch steak with braised red cabbage and fondant potato, or roasted vegetable Wellington with tomato cream and roast baby potatoes. To finish, caramelised lemon tart with blackcurrant sorbet, or

steamed treacle pudding with custard cannot be resisted. If you just want a bar snack before heading off round the ancient tracks of the Shutford Walk, try a mature cheddar ploughman's with apple and celery salad, or warm steak and onion sandwich with chips and salad. Alternatively, forget the walk and time your visit for a Sunday – you'll be choosing from the likes of roast striploin of Oxfordshire beef with roast potatoes and Yorkshire pudding, followed by apple and blackberry crumble with custard.

Open all wk 6-11 (Fri 12-2.30 6-11 Sat-Sun & BH all day) **Bar Meals** L served Fri-Sun 12-2.30 D served Mon-Sat 6-9 Av main course £10 **Restaurant** L served Fri-Sun 12-2.30 D served Mon-Sat 6-9 Fixed menu price fr £10

Av 3 course à la carte fr £20 ⊕ FREE HOUSE ◀ Hook Norton Hooky Bitter, Fuller's London Pride, Theakston Old Peculier, Marston's Pedigree, Wells Bombardier. ♚ 8 **Facilities** Children welcome Children's menu Children's portions Garden Beer festival 🚌 (notice required)

SYDENHAM
Map 5 SP70

The Crown Inn
PICK OF THE PUBS

Sydenham Rd OX39 4NB ☎ 01844 351634
dir: *M40 junct 6, B4009 towards Chinnor. Left onto A40. At Postcombe right to Sydenham*

In a small village below the scarp slopes of the Chilterns, this pretty 16th-century inn shows how careful refurbishment can successfully incorporate both traditional and modern styles. Old photographs, for example, hang contentedly alongside contemporary paintings. The menu is short – barely a dozen items are featured – but expect good things of those that are, such as main courses of slow-roasted Moroccan spiced lamb shank pie with baked potato mash; seafood and chorizo risotto; and pan-fried pork escalope with avocado, mature cheddar and cream. Desserts include chocolate fondant and apple and almond tart. In the bar, a pint of Brakspear would go well with a ploughman's, omelette, baguette or pizza. Treasure hunts starting and finishing at The Crown take you through some of the prettiest villages in this part of Oxfordshire, while the pub also holds quizzes and live music.

Open 12-3 5.30-11 (Sat 12-11 Sun 12-3) Closed: Sun eve, Mon **Bar Meals** L served Tue-Sat 12-2.30 D served Tue-Sat 7-9.30 **Restaurant** L served Tue-Sun 12-2.30 D served Tue-Sat 7-9.30 ⊕ FREE HOUSE/THE SYDENHAM PUB CO ◀ Fuller's London Pride, Brakspear, Guinness, Guest ale ⭘ Westons Stowford Press, Thatchers Gold. **Facilities** ✿ Children welcome Children's portions Garden ⛟

TETSWORTH
Map 5 SP60

The Old Red Lion

40 High St OX9 7AS ☎ 01844 281274
e-mail: info@theoldredliontetsworth.co.uk
dir: *Oxford Service area, turn right onto A40. At T-junct turn left then right onto A40 signed Stokenchurch, via Milton Common to Tetsworth*

Watch winter football and summer cricket on the village green directly outside this stylish pink-washed pub. (The green also has a large enclosed children's play area.) In the relaxing bar area real ales change seasonally. Food can be enjoyed in Nemards restaurant behind the bar, or in the quieter Library room for private dining, which is popular for family meals. There is a Sunday carvery with three meats to choose from plus regular events, from a mini Easter festival to cheese and wine evenings and quiz nights. Head outside to the patio area on warmer days and watch red kites being fed.

Open all wk 11-2.30 5-11 (Sat 12-11 Sun 12-7) **Bar Meals** L served all wk 12-2.30 D served all wk 5-9 Av main course £9 **Restaurant** L served all wk 12-2.30 D served all wk 5-9 ⊕ FREE HOUSE ◀ Green King IPA, Ruddles Best. **Facilities** Children welcome Children's menu Children's portions Garden Beer festival Parking Wi-fi ⛟

THAME
Map 5 SP70

The James Figg
PICK OF THE PUBS

21 Cornmarket OX9 2BL ☎ 01844 260166
e-mail: thejamesfigg@peachpubs.com
dir: *In town centre*

This pub's name celebrates one of the town's most famous sons – England's first undisputed champion boxer who lived in the pub 300 years ago before moving to London to run a school teaching the gentry the noble art of self-defence. An attractive 18th-century pub close to Thame's market place, it has a traditional look with dark wood floors, Ercol Windsor chairs, a double-sided open fire and a curving bar dispensing three real ales including the locally brewed Vale Best Bitter. A tempting list of snacks offers Scotch eggs, pork pies and breaded camembert, while other light options include sandwiches and toasties. If you're seeking something more substantial, look to favourites such as classic prawn cocktail followed by Newitt's sausages and mash with onion gravy or roast of the day with all the trimmings. For pudding, maybe apple crumble. Beyond The Stables function room, you'll find the pub's secret garden.

Open all day all wk 11am-mdnt Closed: 25 Dec **Bar Meals** L served all wk 12-2.30 D served all wk 6-9.30 Av main course £9 ⊕ FREE HOUSE/PEACH PUBS ◀ Vale Best Bitter, Purity Mad Goose ⭘ Addlestones, Aspall. ⬤ 10 **Facilities** ✿ Children welcome Children's portions Garden Parking Wi-fi

The Thatch

29-30 Lower High St OX9 2AA ☎ 01844 214340
e-mail: thatch@peachpubs.com
dir: *In town centre*

A striking thatched, black and white half-timbered pub, The Thatch was originally a row of 16th-century cottages. It remains a cosy warren of rooms with inglenook fireplaces and antique furniture. If you make it past the bar without being tempted by coffee, cakes or a pint of Doom Bar, you'll find yourself in the restaurant overlooking the sunny courtyard garden. The kitchen focuses on the best seasonal ingredients – ham hock ballotine with mustard pickle might be followed by leg of lamb with salsa verde, broad beans and new potatoes. Booking for meals may be required.

Open all day all wk Closed: 25 Dec **Bar Meals** L served all wk 12-10 D served all wk 12-10 food served all day **Restaurant** L served all wk 12-2.45 D served all wk 6-10 ⊕ PEACH PUBS ◀ Vale Wychert, Sharp's Doom Bar ⭘ Aspall. ⬤ 12 **Facilities** ✿ Children welcome Children's portions Garden Beer festival Parking Wi-fi ⛟ (notice required)

TOOT BALDON
Map 5 SP50

The Mole Inn ◉◉
PICK OF THE PUBS

OX44 9NG ☎ 01865 340001
e-mail: info@themoleinn.com
dir: *5m SE from Oxford city centre off B480*

Discerning customers travel to this amusingly named village to relax with pints of Hook Norton in the 300-year-old, Grade II listed Mole Inn. They come to enjoy the exciting, two AA-Rosette-awarded culinary output of award-winning chef/host Gary Witchalls and the front-of-house professionalism of his wife, Jenny, amid leather sofas, stripped beams, solid white walls and terracotta floors. Together with Moodley's micro-brewery, they have developed 'The Mole's Pleasure', a real ale which is particularly suited to their dry-aged steaks from Aberdeenshire. Pick from rib-eye, rump, sirloin or fillet steaks and then choose your sauce. Other main courses could include grilled mixed fish with lime aïoli, a rocket and cherry tomato salad and skinny fries; and wild mushroom and cherry tomato linguine with a parmesan cream. Mango and passionfruit Pavlova; treacle tart with ice cream; and a British cheeseboard are among the desserts. Booking for meals may be required.

Open all day all wk 12-12 (Sun 12-11) Closed: 25 Dec **Bar Meals** Av main course £15 **Restaurant** L served Mon-Sat 12-2.30, Sun 12-4 D served Mon-Sat 7-9.30, Sun 6-9 Av 3 course à la carte fr £28 ⊕ FREE HOUSE ◀ The Mole's Pleasure, Fuller's London Pride, Shepherd Neame Spitfire, Hook Norton, Guinness. ⬤ 11 **Facilities** Children welcome Children's menu Children's portions Garden Parking

WALLINGFORD
Map 5 SU68

The Partridge ◉◉

32 Saint Mary St OX10 0ET ☎ 01491 825005
e-mail: contact@partridge-inn.com
dir: *From M40 junct 6, B4009, follow Wallingford signs through Watlington to Benson. A4074 to rdbt. Right through Crowmarsh Gifford to Wallingford*

Leather chairs, wood fires and lovely mirrors form the background to a menu of modern British and French rustic dishes at this Wallingford venue. Owner and chef José Cau has created a foodie's haven with two AA-Rosettes where the à la carte menu might feature foie gras ballotine; partridge wrapped in smoked pancetta; or rump of lamb. The daily Market Menu offers as less expensive alternative and could include chestnut mushroom lasagne or Cornish skate wings. Good ales, a formidable wine list and a pleasant garden complete the picture. Booking for meals may be required.

Open all wk 12-3 5-11 **Bar Meals** L served all wk 12-2.30 D served all wk 6-9.30 Av main course £12 **Restaurant** L served all wk 12-2.30 D served all wk 6-9.30 Fixed menu price fr £10 Av 3 course à la carte fr £35 ⊕ GREENE KING ◀ Abbot Ale, Morland Old Speckled Hen. ⬤ 12 **Facilities** Children welcome Children's menu Children's portions Garden Wi-fi ⛟ (notice required)

WEST HANNEY   Map 5 SU49

Plough Inn

Church St OX12 0LN ☎ 01235 868674
e-mail: info@ploughwesthanney.co.uk
dir: *From Wantage take A338 towards Oxford. Inn in 1m*

A pub for 'only' 180 years, the thatched building dates back to around 1525 when it was built as a workers' cottage on an estate. Trevor and Ann Cooper have created a friendly village inn, with log fires, roast chestnuts, mulled wine and their own damson gin. Sharp's Doom Bar is the house beer. From the kitchen comes home-cooked, seasonal dishes such as Turkey stirfry and deep-fried whitebait, as well as daily specials and snacks. Dining outside in the pretty walled garden is an option in summer, and beer festivals take place on May and August Bank Holidays. Booking for meals may be required.

Open all wk 12-3 6-12 (Sat-Sun all day) **Bar Meals** L served all wk 12-3 D served all wk 6-9 **Restaurant** L served all wk 12-2 D served all wk 6-9 ⊕ FREE HOUSE ◀ West Berkshire, Loddon, Vale, Wychwood, Sharp's Doom Bar ♂ Westons, Thatchers Gold. ♟ 10 **Facilities** ☺ Children welcome Children's menu Children's portions Play area Garden Beer festival Parking Wi-fi ▭

WESTON-ON-THE-GREEN   Map 11 SP51

The Ben Jonson

OX25 3RA ☎ 01869 351153
e-mail: dine@thebenjonsonpub.co.uk
dir: *M40 junct 9, A34 towards Oxford. 1st exit onto B430. At rdbt right into village. Pub on left*

Dating from 1742, the pub was named after the English Renaissance dramatist, poet and actor, who would stop at the pub on his way to visit William Shakespeare in Stratford. The pub has a separate bar and dining area, as well as a secluded terrace garden. The food is sourced as locally as possible and all real ales are from Oxfordshire, as are a number of wines. Simple, seasonal dishes on the daily changing menu might include baguettes, ploughman's, Oxfordshire cheeses, starters of smoked trout salad, and ham hock terrine, and mains of wild venison pie, and Charolais rib-eye steak. Booking for meals may be required.

Open all day all wk 12-11 **Bar Meals** L served all wk 12-9 D served all wk 12-9 food served all day **Restaurant** L served all wk 12-9 D served all wk 12-9 food served all day ⊕ FREE HOUSE ◀ Brakspear, Wychwood Hobgoblin, Hook Norton Old Hooky, White Horse. ♟ 14 **Facilities** Children welcome Children's menu Children's portions Garden Parking Wi-fi

WHEATLEY   Map 5 SP50

Bat & Ball Inn

28 High St, Cuddesdon OX44 9HJ ☎ 01865 874379
e-mail: info@batball.co.uk
dir: *Through Wheatley towards Garsington, turn left signed Cuddesdon*

No surprise that the bar here is packed to the gunnels with cricketing memorabilia, but the charm of this former coaching inn extends to beamed ceilings, flagstone floors and solid wood furniture warmed by an open log fire. The house ale 'LBW' is flanked by interesting and well-kept guests. A comprehensive seasonal menu, supplemented by daily specials, is likely to include the Bat burger, home made from steak and with a choice of toppings; and slow-braised shoulder of lamb. Look out for clay pigeon shoots, pig roasts, steak nights and sausage and mash evenings. The pub is in an ideal spot for walkers. Booking for meals may be required.

Open all day all wk ⊕ MARSTON'S ◀ Pedigree, LBW Bitter, Guinness ♂ Thatchers Gold. **Facilities** Children welcome Children's menu Children's portions Garden Parking Wi-fi

WITNEY   Map 5 SP31

The Fleece ★★★ INN

11 Church Green OX28 4AZ ☎ 01993 892270
e-mail: fleece@peachpubs.com
dir: *In town centre*

Overlooking the village's beautiful church green in the heart of picturesque Witney, this fine Georgian building was once the home of Clinch's brewery. Nowadays, it serves food and drink all day, from porridge and golden syrup or eggs Benedict at breakfast to dinner, with well-kept ales attracting locals and visitors alike. The appealing modern British menu might include pumpkin, blue cheese and red onion tart; free-range duck breast with butternut squash purée; or roast cod with garlic creamed peas and leeks. Excellent deli boards are also available, as well as the option of spacious accommodation if you want to stay over. Booking for meals may be required.

Open all day all wk **Bar Meals** L served all wk 12-6.30 D served all wk 6.30-10 food served all day **Restaurant** L served all wk 12-2.30 D served all wk 6.30-10 food served all day ⊕ PEACH PUBS ◀ Greene King IPA, Morland Old Speckled Hen, Guest ale ♂ Aspall. ♟ **Facilities** ☺ Children welcome Children's portions Parking Wi-fi **Rooms** 10

The Three Horseshoes

78 Corn St OX28 6BS ☎ 01993 703086
e-mail: thehorseshoeswitney@hotmail.co.uk
dir: *From Oxford on A40 towards Cheltenham take 2nd turn to Witney. At rdbt take 5th exit to Witney. Over flyover, through lights. At next rdbt take 5th exit into Corn St. Pub on left*

Built of Cotswold stone, the historic Grade II listed building sits on Witney's original main street. A traditional family-run pub, it has a charming and stylish interior with stone walls, low ceilings, wood and flagstone floors, and blazing log fires in winter. An impressive selection of ales includes Ringwood Fortyniner and Wychwood Hobgoblin; there's an annual beer festival on August Bank Holiday. Dishes range from simple sandwiches and a grill menu through to dishes such as Cornish crab cake with vanilla and lime mayonnaise, followed by Gressingham duck breast with fondant potato.

Open all day all wk 11am-12.30am ⊕ ADMIRAL TAVERNS ◀ Ringwood Fortyniner, Wychwood Hobgoblin, Brakspear Bitter, Hook Norton, White Horse ♂ Thatchers Green Goblin, Westons Stowford Press. **Facilities** Children welcome Children's portions Garden Beer festival Wi-fi

WOODSTOCK   Map 11 SP41

The Kings Arms ★★★ HL ⊛

PICK OF THE PUBS

See Pick of the Pubs on page 424

WOOLSTONE   Map 5 SU28

The White Horse

SN7 7QL ☎ 01367 820726
e-mail: info@whitehorsewoolstone.co.uk
dir: *Off A420 at Watchfield onto B4508 towards Longcot signed Woolstone*

The black-and-white-timbered, thatched, Elizabethan village pub is the perfect rest and refuelling stop following an invigorating Ridgeway walk across White Horse Hill. Upholstered stools line the traditional bar, where a fireplace conceals two priest holes, visible to those who don't mind getting their knees dirty. Accompany a pint of Arkell's ale with an open black pudding and bacon sandwich, or a lunchtime plate of ham, duck egg and chips, or sausages, mash and gravy. Evening extras may include roast skate wing and beef fillet with triple-cooked chips and roast tomato sauce. Booking for meals may be required.

Open all day all wk 11-11 **Bar Meals** L served Mon-Sat 12-2.30, Sun 12-3 D served Mon-Sat 6-9 Av main course £13.95 **Restaurant** L served all wk 12-2.30 D served all wk 6-9 Fixed menu price fr £21.95 Av 3 course à la carte fr £26.95 ⊕ ARKELL'S ◀ Moonlight & Wiltshire Gold, Guinness ♂ Westons Stowford Press. **Facilities** ☺ Children welcome Children's portions Garden Parking Wi-fi ▭

PICK OF THE PUBS

The Kings Arms ★★★HL 🏵

WOODSTOCK　　　　　**Map 11 SP41**

19 Market St OX20 1SU
☎ **01993 813636**
e-mail: stay@kingshotelwoodstock.co.uk
web: www.kingshotelwoodstock.co.uk
dir: *In town centre, on corner of Market St & A44*

An imposing Georgian building in the middle of the town, yet this pub is less than five minutes' walk to Blenheim Palace, home of the Dukes of Marlborough and birthplace of Winston Churchill. The comfortable bar areas have stripped wooden floors, a log-burning stove and marble-topped counters, where a guest real ale accompanies regulars Brakspear Bitter and Oxford Gold. A bar meal could be as simple as cream of spiced parsnip soup with chives, or at the more serious end of the menu, honey and mustard baked Kelmscott Farm ham with free-range eggs and chips. Sandwiches too, of course, and cream tea is available all day. For rather more stylish surroundings, go to the Atrium Restaurant, where the AA has awarded a Rosette for the modern and classic English cuisine. The lunch menu differs from dinner, so depending what time of day you visit, you might begin with natural smoked haddock and watercress kedgeree with poached egg; or pressed rabbit and ham hock terrine with spiced rhubarb compôte. These menus are concise, but they still offer a good choice of main dishes, including cod and crayfish fishcakes with buttered curly kale and tomato butter sauce; free-range peppered chicken breast, pear and fig salad with toasted hazelnuts; braised shank of lamb with rosemary mash, port sauce and braised leeks; and organic brie, spinach and red onion Wellington with rich mushroom sauce and roast carrots. And there are enough desserts to keep anyone happy: ginger brûlée with mulled plums and buttered shortbread; autumn fruit crumble with vanilla custard; and a range of natural ice creams and sorbets. Accommodation consists of 15 en suite bedrooms, with uncluttered décor, cool colours, crisp linen and a flat-screen TV. Booking for meals may be required.

Open all day all wk **Bar Meals** L served Mon-Fri 12-2.30, Sat 12-3, Sun all day D served Mon-Sat 6.30-9, Sun all day Av main course £10 **Restaurant** L served Mon-Fri 12-2.30, Sat 12-3, Sun all day D served Mon-Sat 6.30-9, Sun all day Av 3 course à la carte fr £35 ⊞ FREE HOUSE 🛢 Brakspear Bitter & Oxford Gold, Guest ales ♂ Thatchers Green Goblin. ♛ 15 **Facilities** Children welcome Children's portions Wi-fi 🚌 **Rooms** 15

WYTHAM   Map 5 SP40

White Hart

OX2 8QA ☎ 01865 244372
e-mail: whitehartwytham@btconnect.com
dir: *Just off A34 NW of Oxford*

In a sleepy hamlet west of Oxford, this Cotswold-stone pub was featured in the *Inspector Morse* TV series. The pub is more 'smart gastro-pub' than traditional village local, the bold interior blending flagged floors and big stone fireplaces with a contemporary style. You can pop in for a pint but this is predominantly a place to eat, and boasts an extensive wine list. In summer, dine alfresco on the Mediterranean-style terrace.

Open all wk 12-4 6-11 (Sat-Sun 12-11) ⊕ WADWORTH ◄ Henry's IPA & 6X, Guest ales ♂ Westons Stowford Press. **Facilities** Children welcome Children's menu Garden Parking Wi-fi

RUTLAND

BARROWDEN   Map 11 SK90

Exeter Arms

PICK OF THE PUBS

LE15 8EQ ☎ 01572 747247
e-mail: enquiries@exeterarmsrutland.co.uk
dir: *From A47 turn at landmark windmill, village 0.75m S. 6m E of Uppingham & 17m W of Peterborough*

Situated in the heart of pretty Barrowden, overlooking the village green, duck pond and open countryside, this 17th-century building is a cracking country pub and boasts a vast garden with a pétanque court for lazy summer days. The attractive stone building has seen many roles in its long life, including a smithy, a dairy and a postal collection point. Landlord Martin Allsopp brews ales such as Beech, Bevin, Hop Gear and Attitude Two in the on-site micro-brewery, and also offers a range of ten wines by the glass. Expect a nice traditional feel to the spacious bar and an informal atmosphere for enjoying some good pub food. At lunchtime, tuck into hot beef and horseradish mayonnaise sandwiches, or heartier appetites will find steak-and-ale pie with hand-cut chips, and smoked haddock with spring onion mash and a pea and herb cream sauce. A typical dinner could begin with chicken liver pâté, followed by roast pork belly with apple compôte.

Open 12-2.30 6-11 Closed: Sun eve, Mon L **Bar Meals** L served Tue-Sat 12-2 Av main course £10 **Restaurant** L served Sun 12-2 D served Tue-Sat 6.30-9 ⊕ FREE HOUSE ◄ Exeter Arms Beech, Bevin, Owngear, Hop Gear, Attitude Two, Pilot, Blackadder. ☂ 10 **Facilities** ✿ Garden Parking 🚌 (notice required)

BRAUNSTON   Map 11 SK80

The Blue Ball **NEW**

6 Cedar St LE15 8QS ☎ 01572 722135
e-mail: dominicway@hotmail.com
dir: *From Oakham N on B640. Left onto Cold Overton Rd, 2nd left onto West Rd, onto Braunston Rd (becomes Oakham Rd). In village 2nd left into Cedar St. Pub on left opposite church*

'The warmest welcome at the oldest inn in Rutland county' is the proud claim at the 17th-century thatched Blue Ball. Refurbishment to a high standard has left original features untouched and its traditional appeal intact. Landlord Dominic Way certainly looks after his Marston's ales, as locals in the beamed and cosy bar will testify. The pub is also a destination restaurant – even the bread is home-baked – and a Young Diners menu confirms the pub's family-friendly credentials. Expect modern British cuisine like roast rack of Launde Farm lamb, and duo of pork with sweet potato fondants. Booking for meals may be required.

Open all wk 12-3 6-11 (Sat-Sun all day) Closed: 25 Dec **Bar Meals** L served all wk 12-2 D served all wk 6.30-9 Av main course £10 **Restaurant** L served all wk 12-2 D served all wk 6.30-9 Av 3 course à la carte fr £30 ⊕ MARSTON'S ◄ EPA & Burton Bitter, Jennings Cumberland Ale. ☂ 10 **Facilities** Children welcome Children's menu Children's portions Garden Wi-fi

CLIPSHAM   Map 11 SK91

The Olive Branch ★★★★ INN ⊛⊛

PICK OF THE PUBS

Main St LE15 7SH ☎ 01780 410355
e-mail: info@theolivebranchpub.com
dir: *2m off A1 at B664 junct, N of Stamford*

In the pretty village of Clipsam, The Olive Branch was originally three farm labourers' cottages, knocked together to make a pub in 1890. Inside, the interior has an eclectic mix of antique and pine furniture, bookshelves, and log fires and roasted chestnuts in winter. The bar serves a good selection of bottled beers, and local ales including The Grainstore Ten Fifty. From chef and co-owner Sean Hope's two AA-Rosette kitchen come classics pan-fried fillet of pollock with rösti potato and cauliflower cheese; and Lincolnshire sausages with English mustard mash and red cabbage. There are also set lunch and dinner menus, which might start with roast pumpkin bread or moules marinière, continue with venison and chestnut suet pudding with root vegetable purée and buttered kale, and finish with dark chocolate and hazelnut Pavlova. Outside is an attractive front garden and terrace where home-made lemonade is served in summer. Elegant accommodation is available. Booking for meals may be required.

Open all wk 12-3.30 6-11 (Sat 12-11 Sun 12-10.30) Closed: 25 Dec eve **Bar Meals** L served Mon-Fri 12-2, Sat 12-2 & 2.30-5.30, Sun 12-3 D served Mon-Sat 7-9.30, Sun 7-9 **Restaurant** L served Mon-Sat 12-2, Sun 12-3 D served Mon-Sat 7-9.30, Sun 7-9 ⊕ FREE HOUSE/ RUTLAND INN COMPANY LTD ◄ The Grainstore Ten Fifty & Olive Oil, Fenland, Brewster's VPA ♂ Sheppy's Dabinett Apple, Oakwood Special & Cider with Honey. ☂ 13 **Facilities** ✿ Children welcome Children's menu Children's portions Garden Parking Wi-fi **Rooms** 6

EMPINGHAM   Map 11 SK90

The White Horse Inn ★★★ INN

Main St LE15 8PS ☎ 01780 460221
e-mail: info@whitehorserutland.co.uk
web: www.whitehorserutland.co.uk
dir: *From A1 take A606 signed Oakham & Rutland Water. From Oakham take A606 to Stamford*

This stone-built former 17th-century courthouse has lost none of its period charm. The open fire, beamed bar, great selection of real ales and friendly staff makes it an ideal place to relax after a walk or cycle ride around Rutland Water. The comprehensive menus kick off with baguettes and sandwiches, and progress through pub classics, starters and salads to main courses. These are home-made using quality ingredients, locally produced if possible, in the likes of slow-roast belly pork with a cider sauce; supreme of salmon with a herb crust; and venison haunch steak. Accommodation is available.

Open all day all wk Closed: 25 Dec **Bar Meals** L served all wk 12-9 D served all wk 12-9 Av main course £10 food served all day **Restaurant** L served all wk 12-9 D served all wk 12-9 Av 3 course à la carte fr £20 food served all day ⊕ ENTERPRISE INNS ◄ John Smith's, Adnams Southwold Bitter, Sharp's Doom Bar, Timothy Taylor Landlord, Black Sheep Best Bitter. ☂ 14 **Facilities** Children welcome Children's menu Children's portions Garden Parking 🚌 **Rooms** 13

EXTON
Map 11 SK91

Fox & Hounds
PICK OF THE PUBS

19, The Green LE15 8AP ☎ 01572 812403
e-mail: sandra@foxandhoundsrutland.co.uk
dir: *Take A606 from Oakham towards Stamford, at Barnsdale turn left, after 1.5m turn right towards Exton. Pub in village centre*

Traditional English and Italian food is the hallmark of this imposing 17th-century free house, which stands opposite the green amid the charming stone and thatched cottages in the village centre. There's a delightful walled garden, making this former coaching inn a perfect spot for a sunny day. The pub has a reputation for good food and hospitality, and is an ideal stopping-off point for walkers and cyclists exploring nearby Rutland Water and the surrounding area. Its menu is the work of Italian chef-proprietor Valter Floris and his team, and in the evenings there's an impressive list of authentic, thin-crust pizzas. In addition, the main menu features coq au vin with bacon, chestnut mushrooms, Savoy cabbage and new potatoes; roasted pumpkin and goat's cheese filo tartlets; and calves' liver with mash and onion gravy. Good beers include Grainstore Rutland Bitter. Booking for meals may be required.

Open 11-3 6-11 Closed: Mon (ex BH) ⊕ FREE HOUSE ◀ Greene King IPA, The Grainstore Ten Fifty & Rutland Bitter ♂ St Helier Pear, Aspall. **Facilities** Children welcome Children's menu Children's portions Family room Garden Parking Wi-fi

GREAT CASTERTON
Map 11 TF00

The Plough Inn **NEW**

Main St PE9 4AA ☎ 01780 762178
dir: *From A1, NW of Stamford, follow Great Casterton signs onto B1081*

The landlords of this 17th-century pub on the old Great North Road have worked hard to turn it into a popular dining destination. There are low beams in the restaurant, and a large beer garden where you can also dine. Locally sourced, freshly prepared lasagne, burgers and sausages and mash appear on the bar menu, while the carte offers slow-roasted belly of pork with haggis mash; pan-seared Rutland Water trout; red snapper with mussel and chorizo linguine; loin of venison; and penne pasta with baby spinach, asparagus and rich gorgonzola sauce.

Open 12-3 6-close Closed: 25 Dec, Sun eve & Mon **Bar Meals** L served Tue-Sat 12-2.30, Sun 12-3 D served Tue-Sat 6-9.30 Av main course £8.95-£12.95 **Restaurant** L served Tue-Sat 12-2.30, Sun 12-3 D served Tue-Sat 6-9.30 Fixed menu price fr £10 Av 3 course à la carte fr £19.75 ⊕ PUNCH TAVERNS ◀ Wychwood Hobgoblin, Bass. **Facilities** ✿ Children welcome Children's menu Children's portions Play area Garden Parking ⚍ (notice required)

GREETHAM
Map 11 SK91

The Wheatsheaf **NEW**

1 Stretton Rd LE15 7NP ☎ 01572 812325
e-mail: enquiries@wheatsheaf-greetham.co.uk
dir: *From A1 follow signs for Oakham onto B668 to Greetham, pub on left*

Lovingly run by husband and wife team Carol and Scott Craddock, this 18th-century village pub is a homely refuge with an emphasis on home-cooked food. Carol has notched up more than 20 years working in some renowned kitchens (including Bibendum under Simon Hopkinson) and her experience is put to good use here. A typical meal might include baked razor clams with chilli, lime and smoked paprika butter followed by rare roast venison with mash, Savoy cabbage, treacle cured bacon, red wine sauce and horseradish cream. For dessert, maybe flourless chocolate and almond cake with yogurt ice cream. Booking for meals may be required.

Open 12-3 6-close (Sat-Sun all day & Fri in Summer) Closed: Mon (ex BH) **Bar Meals** L served Tue-Fri 12-2, Sat 12-2.30, Sun 12-3 D served Tue-Sat 6.30-9 **Restaurant** L served Tue-Fri 12-2, Sat 12-2.30, Sun 12-3 D served Tue-Sat 6.30-9 Fixed menu price fr £12 Av 3 course à la carte fr £15 ⊕ PUNCH TAVERNS ◀ Greene King IPA, Oldershaw Newton's Drop, Brewsters Decadence. ♀ 11 **Facilities** ✿ Children welcome Children's menu Children's portions Garden Parking Wi-fi ⚍ (notice required)

LYDDINGTON
Map 11 SP89

The Marquess of Exeter ★★★★ INN

52 Main St LE15 9LT ☎ 01572 822477
e-mail: info@marquessexeter.co.uk
dir: *A1(N) exit towards Leicester/A4. At rdbt onto A47 towards Leicester. At Uppingham rdbt onto A6003/Ayston Rd. Through Uppingham to Stoke Rd. Left into Lyddington, left onto Main St. Pub on left*

Renowned local chef Brian Baker's old village inn fits perfectly into Lyddington's long, yellow-brown ironstone streetscape. Tasteful contemporary design works well together with traditional pub essentials, to wit, beams, flagstone floors and winter fires. Modern British menus offer Brian's signature sharing dish of grilled rib of Derbyshire beef; roasted fillet of cod with wild mushroom risotto; and caramelised onion, field mushroom and goat's cheese tart. Add a shady garden and the mix is complete for an enjoyable overnight stay, especially now that guest rooms have been given the luxury treatment. Booking for meals may be required.

Open all day all wk **Bar Meals** L served Mon-Sat 12-2.30, Sun 12-3 D served Mon-Sat 6.30-9.30, Sun 6-9 Av main course £14.25 **Restaurant** L served Mon-Sat 12-2.30, Sun 12-3 D served Mon-Sat 6.30-9.30, Sun 6-9 Fixed menu price fr £12 Av 3 course à la carte fr £22.85 ⊕ MARSTON'S ◀ Pedigree, Brakspear ♂ Thatchers. ♀ 14 **Facilities** Children welcome Children's menu Children's portions Garden Parking Wi-fi ⚍ (notice required) **Rooms** 17

Old White Hart ★★★★ INN

51 Main St LE15 9LR ☎ 01572 821703
e-mail: mail@oldwhitehart.co.uk
dir: *From A6003 between Uppingham & Corby take B672. Pub on main street opp village green*

Honey-coloured sandstone cottages surround this similarly constructed, 17th-century free house opposite the village green. Beamed ceilings, stone walls and open fires make for a comfortable interior, although on warm days customers tend to take their pint of Great Oakley bitter (this and more at the summer beer festival), or Aspall cider out into the well-stocked gardens. Dishes served in the restaurants include traditional roast rack of lamb; White Hart pork and sage sausages; rare-breed pork loin; daily fresh fish; and vegetarian choices. Accommodation is in converted cottages alongside the pub. Booking for meals may be required.

Open all wk 12-3 6.30-11 (Sun 12-3 7-10.30) Closed: 25 Dec, 26 Dec eve **Bar Meals** L served Mon-Sat 12-2, Sun 12-2.30 D served all wk 6.30-9 Av main course £12.95 **Restaurant** L served Mon-Sat 12-2, Sun 12-2.30 D served all wk 6.30-9 Fixed menu price fr £10.95 Av 3 course à la carte fr £20.70 ⊕ FREE HOUSE ◀ Greene King IPA, Timothy Taylor Landlord & Golden Best, The Grainstore, Great Oakley ♂ Aspall. ♀ 10 **Facilities** Children welcome Children's portions Play area Garden Beer festival Parking Wi-fi ⚍ **Rooms** 11

MANTON
Map 11 SK80

The Horse and Jockey **NEW**

2 St Marys Rd LE15 8SU ☎ 01572 737335
e-mail: enquiries@horseandjockeyrutland.co.uk
dir: *Exit A6003 between Oakham & Uppingham signed Rutland Water South Shore. 1st left in Manton into St Marys Rd*

A privately owned, award-winning free house only half a mile from Rutland Water's southern shore, this stone-built pub is handsomely proportioned. At the heart of the refurbished interior, a low-beamed, stone-floored bar offers local Grainstore real ales, Jollydale Cyder and a wide choice of wines. Wholesome home-cooked meals include freshly made baguettes; creamy garlic mushrooms, and black pudding fritters as starters; and mains of rump, sirloin and gammon steaks; beer-battered haddock and chips; and vegetarian tartlet. Check for specials, too. Booking for meals may be required.

Open all day all wk **Bar Meals** L served Mon-Fri 12-3 (Apr-Sep) 12-2.30 (Oct-Mar), Sat-Sun 12-9 D served Mon-Fri 6-9, Sat-Sun 12-9 Av main course £9.95 **Restaurant** L served Mon-Fri 12-3 (Apr-Sep) 12-2.30 (Oct-Mar), Sat-Sun 12-9 D served Mon-Fri 6-9, Sat-Sun 12-9 ⊕ FREE HOUSE ◀ The Grainstore Cooking, Morland Old Speckled Hen ♂ Jollydale. ♀ 12 **Facilities** ✿ Children welcome Children's portions Garden Parking Wi-fi ⚍ (notice required)

Save on hotels. Book at **theAA.com/hotel**

RUTLAND 427 ENGLAND

PICK OF THE PUBS

Kings Arms ★★★★INN ◉◉

WING — Map 11 SK80

Top St LE15 8SE ☎ **01572 737634**
e-mail: info@thekingsarms-wing.co.uk
web: www.thekingsarms-wing.co.uk
dir: *1m off B6003 between Uppingham & Oakham*

Dating from 1649, this attractive, stone-built free house has been run by the Goss family since 2004. Husband and wife team James and Ali look after the kitchen and front-of-house, while parents David and Gisa Goss are always ready lend a hand. The bar, the oldest part of the building, has flagstone floors, low-beamed ceilings, nooks, crannies and two open fires, and offers a wide selection of traditional cask ales, including Grainstore Cooking bitter from Oakham, and Sheppy's and Jollydale real ciders. Lunchtime bar meals are supplemented in the two AA-Rosette restaurant by an à la carte menu and daily specials. The menu has artisanal overtones, which isn't at all surprising given the close links the Gosses have forged with local farmers, millers, smallholders, hunters and fishermen. This cooking style is well represented by such dishes as bouillabaisse, which is made with tempura oysters, Dover sole, mussels, cod cheeks and crab; osso buco Milanese; and grey-legged partridge or woodcock, with rösti, roots, pancetta chips and Madeira jus. And then from the on-site smokehouse come eel, trout, meats, black pudding and other products that owe much to James's experience of Swiss air-drying techniques, and Danish fish-curing and smoking. These are presented in various ways, a good example being

smoked Stamford cider-and-mustard-roast ham. On the 'classics' part of the menu might be Rutland shepherd's pie; beer-battered fish of the day; and quail's egg and pancetta salad. Served at lunchtime only are freshly baked cobs with home-made beef dripping chips, filled with roast Hambleton beef, Colston Basset stilton, pork loin with apple compôte, BLT, or you can have one filled with salad. Ice creams and sorbets are homemade, preferably using seasonal windfall fruits and flowers. Eight spacious en suite letting rooms with their own private entrance are set away from the pub; guests may even leave motorised campers and light boats in the large car park. Booking for meals may be required.

Open Tue-Sun 12-3 6.30-11 (seasonal times) Closed: Sun eve, Mon, Tue L (Oct-Mar), Sun eve, Mon L (Apr-Sep)

Bar Meals L served Tue-Sun 12-2.30 D served Tue-Sat 6.30-8.30 **Restaurant** L served Tue-Sun 12-2.30 D served Mon-Sat 6.30-8.30 ⊕ FREE HOUSE ◼ Shepherd Neame Spitfire, The Grainstore Cooking, Marston's Pedigree ♉ Sheppy's, Jollydale, Stamford. ♟ 33 **Facilities** Children welcome Children's menu Children's portions ✤ Garden Parking Wi-fi ☞ (notice required) **Rooms 8**

OAKHAM
Map 11 SK80

Barnsdale Lodge Hotel ★★★ HL 🏵

The Avenue, Rutland Water, North Shore LE15 8AH
☎ **01572 724678**
e-mail: enquiries@barnsdalelodge.co.uk
dir: *A1 onto A606. Hotel 5m on right, 2m E of Oakham*

This former farmhouse has been in the proprietor's family since 1760 and is part of the adjoining Exton Estate. It overlooks Rutland Water in the heart of this picturesque little county. There's a cosy bar with comfortable chairs and a courtyard with outdoor seating. The bistro-style one AA-Rosette menu draws on local produce and offers dishes such as tiger prawns with Caesar salad followed by seared spring lamb rump with chorizo, new potatoes and pea and mint jus. Accommodation comprises 44 stylish en suite rooms.

Open all day all wk ⊕ FREE HOUSE ◀ The Grainstore Rutland Bitter, Tetley's, Guinness. **Facilities** Children welcome Children's menu Children's portions Play area Garden Parking Wi-fi **Rooms** 44

The Finch's Arms

Oakham Rd, Hambleton LE15 8TL ☎ **01572 756575**
e-mail: info@finchsarms.co.uk
dir: *From Oakham take A606 signed Stamford. Turn right signed Upper Hambleton. Pub on left*

Beamed ceilings, cask ales and a small bustling bar characterise this traditional 17th-century free house, with magnificent views overlooking Rutland Water. Log fires warm the snug seating areas in winter, whilst in summer months there's an appealing outside terrace. Typical dishes in the Garden Room restaurant might include roast chicken with pea, smoked bacon and parmesan risotto; or baked Cornish cod with buttered cabbage and hazelnut crust.

Open all day all wk ⊕ FREE HOUSE/PROPER PUB COMPANY ◀ Timothy Taylor Landlord, Black Sheep. **Facilities** Children welcome Children's portions Garden Parking Wi-fi

The Grainstore Brewery

Station Approach LE15 6RE ☎ **01572 770065**
e-mail: enquiries@grainstorebrewery.com
web: www.grainstorebrewery.com
dir: *Next to Oakham rail station*

Founded in 1995, Davis's Brewing Company is housed in the three-storey Victorian grain store next to Oakham

railway station. Finest quality hops and ingredients are used to make the beers that can be sampled in the pub's taproom. Food is wholesome and straightforward, with the ales playing an important part in recipes for steamed fresh mussels; cheddar and ale soup; Quenby Hall stilton and Rutland Panther pâté; and beef and Panther stew. A full diary of events includes live music and the annual August Bank Holiday beer festival.

Open all day all wk Sun-Thu 11-11 (Fri-Sat 11-12) **Bar Meals** L served all wk 11-3 ⊕ FREE HOUSE ◀ The Grainstore Rutland Panther, Triple B, Ten Fifty, Silly Billy, Rutland Beast, Nip, Seasonal beers Ŏ Sheppy's. **Facilities** Children welcome Children's portions Garden Beer festival Parking Wi-fi

SOUTH LUFFENHAM
Map 11 SK90

The Coach House Inn

3 Stamford Rd LE15 8NT ☎ **01780 720166**
e-mail: thecoachhouse123@aol.com
dir: *On A6121, off A47 between Morcroft & Stamford*

Horses were once stabled here while weary travellers enjoyed a drink in what is now a private house next door. This elegantly appointed, attractive stone inn offers a comfortable 40-cover dining room and a cosy bar serving Adnams, Morland and Timothy Taylor Landlord. A short, appealing menu in the Ostler's Restaurant might feature chicken liver pâté with orange and cranberry chutney; and lamb shank with garlic mash, root vegetables and redcurrant jus. In the bar tuck into roast cod with hand-cut chips and pea purée; or beef and ale casserole. Booking for meals may be required.

Open 12-2 5-11 (Sat all day) Closed: 25 Dec, 1 Jan, Sun eve, Mon L **Bar Meals** L served Tue-Sat 12-2 D served Mon-Sat 6.30-9 Av main course £9.50 **Restaurant** L served Tue-Sun 12-2 D served Mon-Sat 6.30-9 Av 3 course à la carte fr £25 ⊕ FREE HOUSE ◀ Timothy Taylor Landlord, Morland Old Speckled Hen, Adnams, Guinness Ŏ Aspall. **Facilities** Children welcome Children's portions Garden Parking Wi-fi (notice required)

STRETTON
Map 11 SK91

The Jackson Stops Country Inn
PICK OF THE PUBS

Rookery Rd LE15 7RA ☎ **01780 410237**
dir: *From A1 follow Stretton signs*

The long, low, stone-built partly thatched building dates from 1721, and has plenty of appeal: stone fireplaces with log fires, exposed stone, quarry-tiled floors, scrubbed wood tables and five intimate dining rooms. In the timeless and beamed snug bar, the choice of real ales lifts the heart, boding well for the excellent value to be had from the dishes on the seasonally changing menu, all freshly prepared and cooked by the kitchen staff. Children can choose from their own menu or take smaller portions from the adult choice. And, if you were wondering about the pub's name: there can be few pubs in the country that have acquired their name by virtue of a 'For Sale' sign. One was planted outside the pub for so long

during a previous change of ownership that the locals dispensed with the old name in favour of the name of the estate agent on the board. Booking for meals may be required.

Open 12-3.30 6-11 (Sun 12-5) Closed: Sun eve, Mon **Bar Meals** L served Tue-Sat 12-5, Sun 12-5 D served Tue-Sat 6.30-9.30 **Restaurant** L served Tue-Sat 12-3, Sun 12-5 D served Tue-Sat 6.30-9.30 ⊕ FREE HOUSE ◀ Oakham JHB, Guest ales. **Facilities** ✿ Children welcome Children's menu Children's portions Garden Beer festival Parking

WHITWELL
Map 11 SK90

The Noel @ Whitwell NEW

Main Rd LE15 8BW ☎ **01780 460347**
e-mail: info@thenoel.co.uk
dir: *Between Oakham & Stamford on A606 N shore of Rutland Water*

The part-thatched village inn stands just a 15-minute stroll from the north shore of Rutland Water, so worth noting if you are walking or pedalling the lakeside trail and in need of refreshment. The friendly, spruced-up bar and dining room have stylish modern feel and feature flagstone floors, heritage colours and a warming winter log fires. Expect to find local Grainstore ales on tap and a wide-ranging menu listing pasta and salad dishes alongside shoulder of lamb with red wine gravy; beef bourguignon; and Cajun salmon with chilli dressing.

Open 12-3 6-close Closed: Mon **Bar Meals** L served Tue-Sat 12-2, Sun 12-3 D served Tue-Sat 6.30-9 Av main course £9-£11 **Restaurant** L served Tue-Sat 12-2, Sun 12-3 D served Tue-Sat 6.30-9 Fixed menu price fr £13.95 Av 3 course à la carte fr £18 ⊕ ENTERPRISE INNS ◀ Greene King Ruddles County, The Grainstore Cooking Ŏ Westons Stowford Press. ▼ 10 **Facilities** ✿ Children welcome Children's menu Children's portions Garden Parking Wi-fi (notice required)

WING
Map 11 SK80

Kings Arms ★★★★ INN 🏵🏵
PICK OF THE PUBS

See Pick of the Pubs on page 427

Save on hotels. Book at **theAA.com/hotel**

SHROPSHIRE 429 **ENGLAND**

SHROPSHIRE

ADMASTON — Map 10 SJ61

The Pheasant Inn at Admaston

TF5 0AD ☎ 01952 251989
e-mail: info@thepheasantadmaston.co.uk
web: www.thepheasantadmaston.co.uk
dir: *M54 junct 6 follow A5223 towards Whitchurch then follow B5063 towards Shawbirch & Admaston. Pub is on left of main rd*

This lovely old country pub dates from the 19th century and is renowned for its well-kept beers and food. Its stylish interior décor and real fire add character to the dining areas, whilst the large enclosed garden is ideal for families. Using the best of local produce, expect pan-fried chorizo and chilli squid to start, followed by roasted pepper stuffed with spiced couscous or trio of Wenlock Edge Farm sausages. Sticky toffee roulade and Bailey's cheesecake are just two options for dessert. There is also a good menu for children under ten. Booking for meals may be required.

Open all day all wk 11-11 (Thu 11am-11.30pm Fri-Sat 11am-mdnt) **Bar Meals** L served Mon-Fri 12-2, Sat 12-9.15, Sun 12-7 **Restaurant** L served Mon-Fri 12-2, Sat 12-9.15, Sun 12-7 ⊕ ENTERPRISE INNS ◀ Salopian Shropshire Gold, Greene King IPA, Guinness. ₹ 10 **Facilities** Children welcome Children's menu Children's portions Play area Garden Parking ☞

BASCHURCH — Map 15 SJ42

The New Inn

Church Rd SY4 2EF ☎ 01939 260335
e-mail: eat@thenewinnbaschurch.co.uk
dir: *8m from Shrewsbury, 8m from Oswestry*

Near the medieval church, this stylishly modernised old whitewashed village pub is a focal point for all things Welsh Marches, with beers from nearby Oswestry's Stonehouse brewery amongst five ales stocked, meats from the village's Moor Farm or Shrewsbury's renowned market, and cheeses from a Cheshire supplier. Chef-patron Marcus and his team transform these into tempting fare such as ham hock fritters with mustard mayonnaise; free range chicken breast with chorizo mash, sweetcorn purée, spinach and chicken jus; and caramelised lemon tart with Chantilly cream. Booking for meals may be required.

Open Tue-Fri 11-3 6-11 (Sat 11-11 Sun 12-11) Closed: 26 Dec, 1 Jan, Mon **Bar Meals** L served Tue-Sat 12-2, Sun 12-6 D served Tue-Sat 6-9 **Restaurant** L served Tue-Sat 12-2, Sun 12-6 D served Tue-Sat 6-9 ⊕ FREE HOUSE ◀ Banks's Bitter, Stonehouse Station Bitter, Hobsons Best Bitter, Guest ales Ò Thatchers Gold.
Facilities Children welcome Children's menu Children's portions Garden Beer festival Parking Wi-fi

BISHOP'S CASTLE — Map 15 SO38

The Three Tuns Inn

PICK OF THE PUBS

Salop St SY9 5BW ☎ 01588 638797
e-mail: timce@talk21.com
dir: *From Ludlow take A49 through Craven Arms, then left onto A489 to Lydham, then A488 to Bishop's Castle, inn at top of the town.*

Since 2003 this mid 17th-century pub and the identically named brewery have been separate businesses, although they work very closely together, which explains the array of Three Tuns real ales in the bar, including 1642, the golden bitter that commemorates the date of the inn's first brewing licence. The public, snug and lounge bars are free from piped music and games machines, although there's occasional live jazz, rock, classical music and Morris dancing in the garden or function room. A beer festival over the second weekend of July involves all the town's pubs. In the classy, oak-framed, glass-walled dining room the menu offers mixed game, port and black pudding pie; smoked paprika escalope of pork with prosciutto; and grilled supreme of salmon. For vegetarians, bean and lentil burger with melting mozzarella and wild mushroom risotto with parmesan are possibilities. Dogs are welcome in the bar, restaurant and garden. Booking for meals may be required.

Open all day all wk **Bar Meals** L served all wk 12-3 D served Mon-Sat 7-9 Av main course £10 **Restaurant** L served all wk 12-3 D served Mon-Sat 7-9 ⊕ SCOTTISH & NEWCASTLE ◀ Three Tuns XXX, Solstice, Old Scrooge, Cleric's Cure, 1642. ₹ 12 **Facilities** ✿ Children welcome Children's menu Children's portions Garden Beer festival

BRIDGNORTH — Map 10 SO79

Halfway House Inn ★★★ INN

Cleobury Rd, Eardington WV16 5LS ☎ 01746 762670
e-mail: info@halfwayhouseinn.co.uk
dir: *M54 junct 4, A442 to Bridgnorth. Or M5 junct 4, A491 towards Stourbridge. A458 to Bridgnorth. Follow tourist signs on B4363*

Originally called the Old Red Lion, this 17th-century coaching inn was renamed in 1823 after a young Princess Victoria paid a visit en route between Shrewsbury and Worcester. An original Elizabethan mural has been preserved behind glass for all to enjoy, and the pub is renowned for a good selection of real ales, 40 malts, and around 100 wines. Home-cooked dishes range from light lunchtime bites to pork loin steak with peppercorn sauce; and rainbow trout with lemon and rosemary butter. Accommodation is available.

Open 5-11.30 (Fri-Sat 11am-11.30pm Sun 11-6) Closed: Sun eve (ex BH) **Bar Meals** L served Fri-Sun 12-2 D served Mon-Sat 6-9 Av main course £8.95 **Restaurant** L served Sat-Sun 12-3 D served Mon-Sat 6-9 Fixed menu price fr £20 Av 3 course à la carte fr £22 ⊕ FREE HOUSE ◀ Holden's Golden Glow, Wood's Shropshire Lad, Guinness Ò Westons Stowford Press. ₹ 10 **Facilities** ✿ Children welcome Children's menu Children's portions Play area Garden Parking Wi-fi ☞ (notice required) **Rooms** 10

BURLTON — Map 15 SJ42

The Burlton Inn ★★★★ INN

PICK OF THE PUBS

SY4 5TB ☎ 01939 270284
e-mail: enquiries@burltoninn.com
dir: *10m N of Shrewsbury on A528 towards Ellesmere*

A classy, contemporary interpretation of an 18th-century inn, this pretty old building stands on the road between Shrewsbury and Ellesmere. Inside there's a fresh looking dining area, a soft-furnished space for relaxation, and a traditional bar - the perfect place to enjoy a pint of Robinsons Unicorn and other seasonal bitters. Behind the main building are en suite guest rooms and the terrace, ideal for alfresco summer dining. The menu offers nibbles such as artisan bread with balsamic and oil or Belgian fries with garlic mayonnaise, followed perhaps by a starter of poached sea bream with red Thai sauce and coconut salad; and a main course of duo of Gressingham duck with winter vegetables, Puy lentils and braising juices. For dessert, try walnut chocolate brownie with caramelised bananas, chocolate sauce and ice cream. A separate children's menu offers the likes of pasta with home-made tomato sauce; and haddock goujons with chips. Booking for meals may be required.

Open all wk 12-3 6-11 (Sun 12-5) Closed: 25 Dec **Bar Meals** L served Mon-Sat 12-2, Sun 12-3 D served Mon-Sat 6-9 Av main course £9.50 **Restaurant** L served Mon-Sat 12-2, Sun 12-3 D served Mon-Sat 6-9 ⊕ FREDERIC ROBINSON ◀ Build a Rocket Boys! & Unicorn, Hartleys Cumbria Way Ò Westons Stowford Press. ₹ 9 **Facilities** Children welcome Children's menu Children's portions Garden Parking Wi-fi **Rooms** 6

CARDINGTON — Map 10 SO59

The Royal Oak

SY6 7JZ ☎ 01694 771266
e-mail: inntoxicated@gmail.com
dir: *Turn right off A49 N of Church Stretton; 2m off B4371 (Church Stretton-Much Wenlock road)*

Said to be the oldest continuously licensed pub in Shropshire, this free house in a conservation village can trace its roots to the 15th century. The rambling low-beamed bar with vast inglenook (complete with cauldron, black kettle and pewter jugs) and comfortable beamed dining room are refreshingly undisturbed by music, TV or games machines. Choose from the excellent cask ales and ponder your choice of sustenance: good-value home-made fare includes 'fidget pie', a Shropshire recipe of gammon, apples, cider and puff pastry. Or try the vegetable tagine, grilled trout with almonds, or pork loin with black pudding.

Open 12-2.30 (Sun 12-3.30) Tue-Wed 6.30-11 (Thu-Sat 6.30-12 Sun 7-12) Closed: Mon (incl BH Mon) **Bar Meals** L served Tue-Sat 12-2, Sun 12-2.30 D served Tue-Sat 6.30-9, Sun 7-9 **Restaurant** L served Tue-Sat 12-2, Sun 12-2.30 D served Tue-Sat 6.30-9, Sun 7-9 ⊕ FREE HOUSE ◀ Hobsons Best Bitter, Three Tuns XXX, Wye Valley Butty Bach, Marston's Pedigree, Salopian Hop Twister. **Facilities** ✿ Children welcome Children's menu Garden Parking Wi-fi 🚌 (notice required)

CHURCH STRETTON — Map 15 SO49

The Bucks Head ★★★★ INN

42 High St SY6 6BX ☎ 01694 722898
e-mail: lnutting@btinternet.com
dir: *12m from Shrewsbury & Ludlow*

Only a five-minute walk from the hills and open countryside, The Bucks Head is a charming old building, parts of which may have been built as a hunting lodge for the Marquis of Bath. A tunnel is rumoured to run from the cellar under the beer garden. At the heart of the local community, the inn is known for its well-kept Banks's, Marston's and guest ales; its steaks and specials board; and welcoming accommodation. So bring your boots, ramble along the Long Mynd, and return to plaice fillet in breadcrumbs; gammon with fried egg or pineapple; or cream cheese and broccoli bake.

Open all day all wk **Bar Meals** L served all wk 12-2.30 D served all wk 6-9 **Restaurant** L served all wk 12-2.30 D served all wk 6-9 ⊕ MARSTON'S ◀ Pedigree, Banks's Original & Bitter, 2 Guest ales. **Facilities** Children welcome Children's menu Children's portions Garden Wi-fi 🚌 (notice required) **Rooms** 4

CLAVERLEY — Map 10 SO79

The Woodman

Danford Ln WV5 7DG ☎ 01746 710553
dir: *On B4176 (Bridgnorth to Dudley road)*

Village farms, butcher and baker supply much of the produce used in the well-respected dishes here at this sibling-run, three-storey Victorian inn. Outside a picturesque settlement deep in the east Shropshire countryside, the beer, too, comes from just down the lane in Enville, whilst the notable wine list spreads its wings worldwide to source some bins unique in England to The Woodman. The contemporary interior is a comfy mix of village local and bistro, where breast of Shropshire pheasant with chestnuts and smoked bacon, sautéed scallops, or the very popular honeycomb ice cream show the quality of the fare here. Alfresco dining is a popular summer option, indulging in grand rural views to the ridge of Abbot's Castle Hill. Booking for meals may be required.

Open all day Closed: Sun eve ⊕ PUNCH TAVERNS ◀ Black Sheep, Enville Ale. **Facilities** Children welcome Children's portions Garden Parking Wi-fi

CLEOBURY MORTIMER — Map 10 SO67

The Crown Inn

PICK OF THE PUBS

Hopton Wafers DY14 0NB ☎ 01299 270372
dir: *On A4117 8m E of Ludlow, 2m W of Cleobury Mortimer*

This 16th-century creeper-clad inn is in an ideal spot for walking in the lush countryside surrounding the small village of Hopton Wafers. The inn retains much of its original character and has an enviable reputation for good food made with ingredients sourced from regional producers. Eat in one of three eating areas: in the Shropshire Restaurant overlooking the countryside; in Poachers, with exposed beams, stonework and large inglenook fireplace; and in the Rent Room, which offers daily menus, light bites and specials - and more of those rural views. In Poachers, a typical meal might be pan-seared scallops and asparagus on a salad of radish and red onion with a lemon dressing; followed by fillet of beef on beetroot risotto with a port reduction. The wine list has been selected by a local merchant and includes a wide range of fine ports, Armagnacs and Cognacs. The Crown is in an ideal spot for walking in the lush surrounding countryside.

Open all day all wk **Bar Meals** L served all wk 12-2.30 D served all wk 6-9 **Restaurant** L served Mon-Fri 12.30-2, Sat 12-2.30, Sun 12-8 D served Mon-Fri 6-9, Sat 6-9.30, Sun 12-8 ⊕ FREE HOUSE ◀ Hobsons Best Bitter, Guest ales. ♒ 25 **Facilities** Children welcome Children's menu Children's portions Play area Garden Parking 🚌

CLUN — Map 9 SO38

The White Horse Inn

The Square SY7 8JA ☎ 01588 640305
e-mail: pub@whi-clun.co.uk
web: www.whi-clun.co.uk
dir: *On A488 in village centre*

Gloriously unspoilt and unpretentious, a great survival of a village inn oozing character, beams, wizened wood and slab floors upon which may be spilled beers brewed in their own micro-brewery, together with others selected from Shropshire's many craft breweries. Heart-warming pub grub, derived from very local suppliers awaits visitors drawn to AE Housman's 'Quietest place under the sun'. An A4 sheet lists the provenance of pretty much everything on the menu, and none of it has come very far. Regular events take place here, including the Clun Valley beer festival each October.

Open all day all wk **Bar Meals** L served Mon-Sat 12-2, Sun 12.30-2.30 D served all wk 6.30-8.30 Av main course £8.95 **Restaurant** L served Mon-Sat 12-2, Sun 12.30-2.30 D served all wk 6.30-8.30 ⊕ FREE HOUSE ◀ The White Horse Inn Clun Pale Ale, Wye Valley Butty Bach, Hobsons Best Bitter, Salopian Shropshire Gold Ö Westons 1st Quality & Perry, Robinsons Flagon. **Facilities** ✿ Children welcome Children's portions Garden Beer festival Wi-fi 🚌 (notice required)

Save on hotels. Book at **theAA.com/hotel**

SHROPSHIRE 431 | **ENGLAND**

COCKSHUTT   Map 15 SJ42

The Leaking Tap

Shrewsbury Rd SY12 0JQ ☎ 01939 270636
e-mail: lesley@theleakingtap.org
dir: *On A528 (Shrewsbury to Ellesmere road)*

Saved from closure in 2009 and now privately owned, this traditional old coaching inn is in the heart of beautiful Shropshire countryside on the road from Shrewsbury to Ellesmere. The Leaking Tap has a unique atmosphere and charm and features oak beams and log fires, along with a selection of ales and food cooked from local produce. Regularly changing lunchtime or evening menus are available and might include chicken breast wrapped in bacon in a brandy and stilton sauce, or leek and parsnip cheese bake.

Open all wk 12-2 5.30-11.30 ⊕ FREE HOUSE
◄ Worthington's, Guest ales. **Facilities** Children welcome Children's menu Children's portions Parking

---

CRAVEN ARMS   Map 9 SO48

The Sun Inn

Corfton SY7 9DF ☎ 01584 861239
e-mail: normanspride@btconnect.com
dir: *On B4368, 7m N of Ludlow*

First licensed in 1613, this historic pub has been run by the Pearce family since 1984. Landlord Norman Pearce brews the Corvedale ales in what was the pub's old chicken and lumber shed, using local borehole water; Mahorall cider, from just down the road, is another drinks option. Teresa Pearce uses local produce in a delicious array of traditional dishes — faggots and mushy peas, ocean pie, beef in ale. There are plenty of vegetarian and some vegan options. The pub holds a beer festival in May and is close to the ramblers' paradise of Clee Hill and Long Mynd.

Open all wk 12-2.30 6-11 (Sun 12-3 7-11) **Bar Meals** L served Mon-Sat 12-2, Sun 12-2.45 D served Mon-Sat 6-9, Sun 7-9 Av main course £9 **Restaurant** L served Mon-Sat 12-2, Sun 12-2.45 D served Mon-Sat 6-9, Sun 7-9 ⊕ FREE HOUSE ◄ Corvedale Norman's Pride, Dark & Delicious, Katie's Pride, Farmer Rays Ò Mahorall Farm. ❦ 8 **Facilities** ❧ Children welcome Children's menu Children's portions Play area Garden Beer festival Parking Wi-fi ▭ (notice required)

CRESSAGE   Map 10 SJ50

The Riverside Inn

Cound SY5 6AF ☎ 01952 510900
dir: *On A458 7m from Shrewsbury, 1m from Cressage*

This inn sits in three acres of gardens alongside the River Severn, offering customers delightful river views both outdoors and from a modern conservatory. Originally a vicarage for St Peter's church in the village, the building also housed a girls' school and a railway halt before becoming a pub in 1878. The pub is popular with anglers. The monthly-changing menu might open with melon and ginger cocktail or a smoked salmon roulade, followed perhaps by cod mornay or Burgundy chicken. Comforting desserts include home-made toffee cheesecake. Their own brew, Riverside Inn Bitter, is available in the cosy bar.

Open all wk Sat-Sun all day May-Sep **Bar Meals** L served all wk 12-2.30 D served all wk 6.30-9.30 Av main course £10 **Restaurant** L served all wk 12-2.30 D served all wk 6.30-9.30 ⊕ FREE HOUSE ◄ Riverside Inn Bitter, Guest ales. ❦ **Facilities** ❧ Garden Parking Wi-fi

---

HODNET   Map 15 SJ62

The Bear at Hodnet

TF9 3NH ☎ 01630 685214
e-mail: reception@bearathodnet.co.uk
dir: *At junct of A53 & A442 turn right at rdbt. Inn in village centre*

With its old beams and fireplaces, and secret passages leading to the parish church, this 16th-century coaching inn is steeped in history. Standing opposite Hodnet Hall Gardens, the pub has a bar that is full of character with plenty of real ales such as Shropshire Gold. Famous for medieval banquets in the refurbished hall, food in the bar includes rare-breed meats (Black Mountain Farm Dexter beefburger) and pub classics like beer-battered haddock and hand-cut chips; and coq au vin with fondant potato. Round off with a treacle, lemon and walnut tart.

Open 11-11 Closed: Sun eve **Bar Meals** L served Mon-Sat 12-2.30 D served Mon-Sat 6-9.30 **Restaurant** L served all wk 12-2.30 D served Mon-Sat 6-9.30 ⊕ FREE HOUSE ◄ Salopian Shropshire Gold, Guinness, Guest ales Ò Westons Stowford Press. **Facilities** Children welcome Children's portions Garden Parking Wi-fi ▭ (notice required)

IRONBRIDGE   Map 10 SJ60

The Malthouse

The Wharfage TF8 7NH ☎ 01952 433712
e-mail: mcdonald740@msn.com
dir: *Telephone for directions*

In the Severn Gorge, within a mile of the famous Iron Bridge, the 18th-century Malthouse is known for its Friday and Saturday night live music. But for a different way to spend the evening try the restaurant, where candlelit tables and an extensive menu feature home-made steak and Guinness pie; king prawn linguine; braised shoulder of Shropshire lamb; and mushroom, pepper and spinach Stroganoff. There's pubbier grub too, such as thick pork sausages with black pudding mash. Brakspear, Wood's and Titanic make up the real ale portfolio.

Open all day all wk **Bar Meals** L served all wk 11-10 D served all wk 11-10 food served all day **Restaurant** L served all wk 11-10 D served all wk 11-10 food served all day ⊕ FREE HOUSE ◄ Wychwood Hobgoblin, Wood's Shropshire Lad, Brakspear, Titanic Ò Thatchers Gold & Pear. ❦ 10 **Facilities** Children welcome Children's menu Children's portions Garden Parking Wi-fi ▭

LEEBOTWOOD   Map 15 SO49

Pound Inn

SY6 6ND ☎ 01694 751477
e-mail: info@thepound.org.uk
dir: *On A49, 9m S of Shrewsbury*

An eye-catching pub in a memorable location; this thatched, 15th century drovers' inn lies at the foot of the jagged, whaleback hills of mid-Shropshire, with The Lawley thrusting steeply up beyond the garden. Recently refurbished in a contemporary airy style, a happy mix of traditional village pub (it's the oldest building in the village) and smart dining destination draws in ramblers to sup Salopian Brewery beers and to try a taste of grilled ox tongue and cauliflower cheese fritter to start, followed by Shropshire sausages with cheddar mash or roast venison with butternut squash.

Open all wk 12-2.30 6-10.30 ◄ Wye Valley Butty Bach, Salopian Shropshire Gold Ò Westons Stowford Press. **Facilities** Children welcome Children's portions Garden Parking

---

LITTLE STRETTON   Map 15 SO49

The Ragleth Inn

Ludlow Rd SY6 6RB ☎ 01694 722711
e-mail: wendyjd65@hotmail.com
dir: *From Shrewsbury take A49 towards Leominster. At lights in Church Stretton turn right. 3rd left into High St. Continue to Little Stretton. Inn on right*

Midway between Shrewsbury and Ludlow, this 17th-century country inn lies in beautiful countryside at the foot of the Long Mynd hills. The pretty, traditional exterior includes a large beer garden with plenty of wooden benches and a children's play area, matched within by two bars and a restaurant with oak beams, antiques and inglenook fireplaces. A good range of ales accompanies classic pub dishes, baked potatoes and baguettes on the bar menu; chef's specials; and the restaurant menu. Typical options are lasagne, grilled steak, fish and chips, vegetable curry, and lamb cutlets. All diets can be catered for. The pub holds a beer festival during the first weekend of July.

Open all wk **Bar Meals** L served Mon-Sat 12-2.15, Sun all day D served Mon-Sat 6.30-9, Sun all day Av main course £10.50 **Restaurant** L served Mon-Sat 12-2.15, Sun all day D served Mon-Sat 6.30-9, Sun all day Fixed menu price fr £8 Av 3 course à la carte fr £20 ⊕ FREE HOUSE ◄ Greene King Abbot Reserve, Wye Valley Butty Bach, Hobsons, Three Tuns Ò Westons Stowford Press. **Facilities** ❧ Children welcome Children's menu Children's portions Play area Garden Beer festival Parking Wi-fi ▭ (notice required)

LLANFAIR WATERDINE — Map 9 SO27

The Waterdine

PICK OF THE PUBS

LD7 1TU ☎ 01547 528214
e-mail: info@waterdine.com
dir: *4.5m W of Knighton off B4355, turn right opposite Lloyney Inn, 0.5m into village, last on left opp church*

The Waterdine is a low-slung, whitewashed former drovers' inn dating from the late 16th century, with original timber floors and leaded windows. The old parish church stands opposite, and the River Teme flows along the bottom of the pretty garden from which there are beautiful views. The family of Lord Hunt, of Everest Expedition fame, lived in the village, and some of the planning reputedly took place in the lounge bar. Today it serves an excellent range of real ales, ciders and wines; wood-burning stoves create a cosy atmosphere in winter. There are two dining rooms: the Garden Room looks out over the river, and the taproom has a massive oak mantle which displays burn marks from long-extinguished candles. Concise menus are based on home-grown, locally supplied produce in dishes such as Cornish mackerel fillet on Lebanese spices; organic Welsh mountain lamb loin with boulangère potatoes; and pancakes in orange and Grand Marnier syrup. Booking for meals may be required.

Open 12-3 7-11 Closed: 1wk winter, 1wk spring, Sun eve & Mon (ex BH), Tue-Wed L **Bar Meals** L served Thu-Sun 12.15-1.30 **Restaurant** L served Thu-Sun 12.15-1.30 D served Tue-Sat 7-8.30 Fixed menu price fr £22.50 ⊕ FREE HOUSE ◀ Wood's Shropshire Legends, Parish Bitter, Shropshire Lad ♂ Brook Farm. **Facilities** Children welcome Children's portions Garden Parking

LUDLOW — Map 10 SO57

The Church Inn ★★★★ INN

Buttercross SY8 1AW ☎ 01584 872174
web: www.thechurchinn.com
dir: *In town centre, behind Buttercross*

The inn stands on one of the oldest sites in Ludlow town centre, dating back some seven centuries, and through the ages has been occupied by a blacksmith, saddler, apothecary and barber-surgeon. These days it enjoys a reputation for providing a good range of up to ten real ales in the cosy bar areas alongside the fine products of the Ludlow Pie Company. Up to 30 different pies are available at any one time. There are ten comfortable en suite bedrooms with smart modern bathrooms.

Open all day all wk Bar Meals L served Mon-Fri 12-2.30, Sat-Sun 12-3 D served Mon-Sat 6.30-9, Sun 6.30-8.30 ⊕ FREE HOUSE ◀ Hobsons Town Crier & Hobsons Mild, Weetwood, Wye Valley Bitter, Ludlow Gold & Boiling Well, Guest ales ♂ Stowford, Aspall, Robinsons. **Facilities** Children welcome ⛟ **Rooms** 10

The Clive Bar & Restaurant with Rooms ★★★★★ RR ⊛⊛

PICK OF THE PUBS

Bromfield SY8 2JR ☎ 01584 856565
e-mail: info@theclive.co.uk
web: www.theclive.co.uk
dir: *2m N of Ludlow on A49, between Hereford & Shrewsbury*

This classy bar and restaurant with rooms is situated on the Earl of Plymouth's estate. Built as a farmhouse in the 18th century, it was home to Robert Clive, who laid the foundation of British rule in India. It was converted into a public house in the late 1900s to cater to the workers on the estate. Inside the handsome Georgian building, traditional and contemporary looks blend well. The bar is bright and modern; here local real ales and ciders are dispensed, along with light snacks. Relax on the sofas by an enormous fireplace in the 18th-century lounge with its beams and brick and stone walls - Clive's original coat of arms is on one wall. A more contemporary upper area leads to a sheltered non-smoking courtyard with tables and parasols for the warmer months. Expect high-quality cuisine built around the best of local and seasonal produce: a starter of rillette of duck, truffle butter, herb salad, spiced gingerbread and hazelnut dressing says it all. Accommodation is available in the tastefully converted period outbuildings. Booking for meals may be required.

Open all day all wk Closed: 25-26 Dec **Bar Meals** L served Mon-Fri 12-3, Sat-Sun 12-6.30 D served Mon-Sat 6.30-10, Sun 6.30-9.30 Av main course £10.95 **Restaurant** L served all wk 12-3 D served Mon-Sat 6.30-10, Sun 6.30-9.30 Av 3 course à la carte fr £30 ⊕ FREE HOUSE ◀ Hobsons Best Bitter, Ludlow Gold ♂ Dunkertons, Mahorall Farm, Thatchers Old Rascal. ♟ 9 **Facilities** Children welcome Children's portions Garden Parking ⛟ (notice required) **Rooms** 15

MADELEY — Map 10 SJ60

All Nations Inn

20 Coalport Rd TF7 5DP ☎ 01952 585747
dir: *On Coalport Rd, overlooking Blists Hill Museum*

Opened as a brewhouse in 1831, this friendly and largely unspoilt free house has a relaxed and friendly atmosphere. And a brewhouse it remains, with a real fire and outside seating overlooking Blists Hill open-air museum. You'll search in vain for a jukebox, pool table or fruit machine, although Six Nations rugby matches are shown on a TV propped up on barrels. There's no restaurant either, but quality pork pies and rolls are always available.

Open all day all wk 12-12 ⊕ FREE HOUSE ◀ Shires Dabley Ale, Dabley Gold & Coalport Dodger Mild, Guest ales ♂ Westons. **Facilities** Children welcome Garden Parking **Notes** ⊛

The New Inn

Blists Hill Victorian Town, Legges Way TF7 5DU ☎ 01952 601018
e-mail: sales@jenkinsonscaterers.co.uk
dir: *Between Telford & Broseley*

Here's something different - a Victorian pub that was moved brick by brick from the Black Country and re-erected at the Ironbridge Gorge Open Air Museum. The building remains basically as it was in 1890, and customers can buy traditionally brewed beer at five-pence farthing per pint - roughly £2.10 in today's terms - using pre-decimal currency bought from the bank. The mainly traditional menu includes home-made soup; steak-and-kidney pudding; and ham and leek pie. Tea and coffee are served from 10 to 2.30, and afternoon tea from 2.30 to 3.30.

Open all wk 10-4 winter, 10-5 summer Closed: 25 Dec, 1 Jan **Restaurant** L served all wk 12-2.30 ⊕ IRONBRIDGE GORGE MUSEUMS ◀ Banks's Bitter & Original, Marston's Pedigree. **Facilities** Children welcome Garden Parking ⛟

MARTON — Map 15 SJ20

The Lowfield Inn

SY21 8JX ☎ 01743 891313
e-mail: lowfieldinn@tiscali.co.uk
dir: *From Shrewsbury take B4386 towards Montgomery. Through Westbury & Brockton. Pub on right in 13m just before Marton*

In the village of Marton on the Shropshire/Powys border, this pub was built on the site of the 'old' Lowfield Inn. The views of the countryside from the large garden are stunning. Inside, the atmosphere is relaxed and informal, with comfy sofas and local artworks on the walls. While locally brewed real ales and ciders quench the thirst, the kitchen produces modern British dishes with international influences. Ingredients are sourced from the surrounding countryside whenever possible. You could try the bubble-and-squeak potato cakes to start, followed by

Thai chicken curry, or pork and leek sausages. The inn hosts an annual charity garden party.

Open all day all wk **Bar Meals** L served all wk 12-9.30 D served all wk 12-9.30 Av main course £11 food served all day **Restaurant** L served all wk 12-9.30 D served all wk 12-9.30 Fixed menu price fr £13.25 Av 3 course à la carte fr £19.75 food served all day ⊕ FREE HOUSE ◀ Three Tuns XXX & 1642, Monty's Moonrise & Mojo, Wood's Shropshire Lad, Salopian Shropshire Gold ♂ Inch's Stonehouse, Westons Old Rosie, Gwynt y Ddraig Dog Dancer. ₹ 18 **Facilities** ❖ Children welcome Children's menu Children's portions Garden Parking Wi-fi ▥

The Sun Inn

SY21 8JP ☎ **01938 561211**
e-mail: suninnmarton@googlemail.com
dir: On B4386 (Shrewsbury to Montgomery road), in centre of Marton opp village shop

Tucked away in a small hamlet in stunning Shropshire countryside, The Sun Inn is a classic stone-built free house dating back to the early 1800s. Run by the Gartell family, it's very much a convivial local, with darts, dominoes, regular quiz nights and local Hobsons ale on tap, as well as a respected dining venue offering a modern Mediterranean-inspired menu in the contemporary restaurant. Typically, follow king prawns in coconut and chilli sauce, with roast partridge and pear in ginger wine, and iced lemon parfait. Booking for meals may be required.

Open 12-3 7-12 Closed: Sun eve, Mon, Tue L **Bar Meals** L served Wed-Sat 12-2.30 D served Tue-Fri from 7pm **Restaurant** L served Wed-Sun 12-2.30 D served Tue-Sat from 7pm ⊕ FREE HOUSE ◀ Hobsons Best Bitter, Guest ales. ₹ 8 **Facilities** Children welcome Children's portions Garden Parking ▥ (notice required)

MUCH WENLOCK   Map 10 SO69

The George & Dragon

2 High St TF13 6AA ☎ **01952 727312**
e-mail: thegeorge.dragon@btinternet.com
dir: On A458 halfway between Shrewsbury & Bridgnorth, on right of the High Street

A traditional black-and-white 17th-century inn at the heart of Much Wenlock, The George & Dragon oozes history, charm and character and has many a spooky tale attached. Sited next to the market square, Guildhall and ruined priory, the inn welcomes everyone, from locals to celebrities - John Cleese, Tony Robinson, Jennifer Jones and George Cole are among those who have popped in for refreshment. Run by locals Bev and James, it offers five traditional cask ales and home-cooked food such as Welsh rarebit, home-made pie of the day, or pan-fried Gressingham duck breast with black cherry sauce. The town is well known for its Wenlock Olympic Games, which have taken place every July since 1850, and were a big inspiration to the modern Olympic movement.

Open all day all wk 11-11 (Fri-Sat 11am-mdnt) **Bar Meals** L served all wk 12-2.30 D served Mon-Tue, Thu-Sat

6-9 **Restaurant** L served all wk 12-2.30 D served Mon-Tue, Thu-Sat 6-9 ⊕ PUNCH TAVERNS ◀ Greene King Abbot Ale, Wadworth 6X, St Austell Tribute, Guest ales ♂ Westons Wyld Wood Organic. **Facilities** ❖ Children welcome Children's menu Children's portions Beer festival Wi-fi ▥

The Talbot Inn

High St TF13 6AA ☎ **01952 727077**
e-mail: the_talbot_inn@hotmail.com
dir: M54 junct 4, follow Ironbridge Gorge Museum signs, then Much Wenlock signs. Much Wenlock on A458, 11m from Shrewsbury, 9m from Bridgnorth

Built in 1361, originally as an Abbott's House, The Talbot has also been an almshouse and a coaching inn. Through an archway you can see its delightful old courtyard, while inside are the oak beams and log fires so indicative of great age. Most of the food is freshly prepared from local produce for extensive, regularly changing menus featuring sandwiches, salads, jacket potatoes, steaks, fish and large filled Yorkshire puds. Bread-and-butter pudding is a fixture.

Open all day all wk 11am-2am **Bar Meals** L served all wk 12-2.30 D served Mon-Sat 6-9, Sun 6-8.30 Av main course £8.95 **Restaurant** L served all wk 12-2.30 D served Mon-Sat 6-9, Sun 6-8.30 Fixed menu price fr £4.95 Av 3 course à la carte fr £12.95 ⊕ FREE HOUSE ◀ Bass, Guest ales. ₹ 11 **Facilities** Children welcome Children's portions Garden Parking ▥ (notice required)

Wenlock Edge Inn

PICK OF THE PUBS

Hilltop, Wenlock Edge TF13 6DJ ☎ **01746 785678**
e-mail: info@wenlockedgeinn.co.uk
dir: 4.5m from Much Wenlock on B4371

From the patio of this old pub high up on the dramatic wooded escarpment of Wenlock Edge there are superb views west to Caer Caradoc and the Long Mynd. Originally a row of 17th-century quarrymen's cottages, it is an almost obligatory stopping point for walkers and horse riders, as well as farmers, business people and other locals. Its cosy interior contains a small country-style dining room and several bars, one with a wood-burning stove. Here, you'll find Enville, Hobsons and Three Tuns real ales, Thatchers Gold cider and a good few wines by the glass. Local and regional produce is used for regular British pub dishes of slow-roasted belly of pork with apple mash; beer-battered pollock, chips and minted peas; and caramelised onion and camembert soufflé tart. There is also a daily fish board and special fish nights with lobster and beer-battered scallops typically on the menu.

Open all day all wk 11-11 **Bar Meals** L served all wk 12-3 D served all wk 6-9 **Restaurant** L served all wk 12-3 D served all wk 6-9 ⊕ FREE HOUSE ◀ Hobsons Best Bitter & Town Crier, Three Tuns, Enville Ale ♂ Thatchers Gold. ₹ 8 **Facilities** ❖ Children welcome Children's portions Garden Parking ▥

MUNSLOW   Map 10 SO58

The Crown Country Inn ★★★★ INN ◉◉

PICK OF THE PUBS

See Pick of the Pubs on page 434

NORTON   Map 10 SJ70

The Hundred House ★★★★ INN ◉◉

PICK OF THE PUBS

Bridgnorth Rd TF11 9EE ☎ **01952 580240**
e-mail: reservations@hundredhouse.co.uk
dir: On A442, 6m N of Bridgnorth, 5m S of Telford centre

Surrounded by rolling Severn Valley countryside and just a ten-minute drive from Ironbridge Gorge and its many museums, this historic 14th-century pub has been run as a popular inn by the Phillips family for the past 25 years. Downstairs is an amazing interconnecting warren of lavishly decorated bars and dining rooms with old quarry-tiled floors, exposed brickwork, beamed ceilings and Jacobean oak panelling. Younger son Stuart Phillips continues to head kitchen operations, producing a mix of innovative new dishes and pub favourites with two AA Rosettes. The à la carte might offer griddled scallops with risotto cake, stir-fried vegetables, carrot and ginger oil, or rich Provençale fish soup, which might be followed by roast breast of free-range chicken stuffed with tarragon mousse served with tomato and wild mushroom sauce, or roast chump of Shropshire lamb with leek, parsnip and lamb cake with sautéed kidney and rosemary jus. Cookery classes are also available.

Open all day all wk Closed: 25 Dec eve **Bar Meals** L served all wk 12-2.30 D served all wk 6-9.30 Av main course £13.95 **Restaurant** L served Mon-Sat 12-2.30, Sun 12-9 D served Mon-Sat 6-9.30, Sun 12-9 Av 3 course à la carte fr £24.85 ⊕ FREE HOUSE ◀ Marston's Oyster Stout, Ironbridge Steam & Gold, Three Tuns ♂ Rosie's. ₹ 10 **Facilities** ❖ Children welcome Children's menu Children's portions Family room Garden Parking Wi-fi ▥ (notice required) **Rooms** 9

PICK OF THE PUBS

The Crown Country Inn ★★★★INN ❀❀

SY7 9ET ☎ 01584 841205
e-mail: info@crowncountryinn.co.uk
web: www.crowncountryinn.co.uk
dir: *On B4368 between Craven Arms &*
Much Wenlock

The Grade II-listed Crown has stood in its lovely setting below the limestone escarpment of Wenlock Edge since Tudor times. An impressive three-storey building, it served for a while as a Hundred House, a type of court, where the infamous 'Hanging' Judge Jeffreys sometimes presided over proceedings. Could it be that the black-swathed Charlotte, whose ghost is sometimes seen in the pub, once appeared before him? The main bar retains its sturdy oak beams, flagstone floors and prominent inglenook fireplace, while free house status means Mahorall Farm ciders and a good range of ales, including bitters from Ludlow and Holden's breweries, are available. Owners Richard and Jane Arnold are well known for their strong commitment to good food, Richard being not only head chef but Shropshire's only Master Chef of Great Britain, a title he has cherished for many years. Meals based on top-quality local produce from trusted sources are served in the main bar, the Bay dining area, and the Corvedale restaurant, the former court room. These may include starters of smooth parfait of chicken livers with home-made chutneys and toasted Tuscan bread; and crisp-crumbed, naturally smoked haddock fishcake, leeks, smoked Tanatside cheese with sweet chilli and

tomato jam. Typical main courses would be griddled rib-eye steak with garlic button mushrooms, grilled tomatoes and spiced potato wedges; confit of Gressingham duck leg with fricassée of butter beans, roasted vegetables and chorizo, and warmed apple chutney; and wild mushroom and barley risotto, goat's cheese and red wine syrup. Sundays here are deservedly popular, when a typical lunch might start with split pea and pancetta soup; continue with fried red gurnard with tomato and crab risotto; and finish with lemon and mandarin crème brûlée and lemon shortbread. Three large bedrooms are located in a converted Georgian stable block. Booking for meals may be required.

Open Tue-Sat 12-3.30 6.45-11 (Sun 12-3.30) Closed: Xmas, Sun eve, Mon

Bar Meals L served Tue-Sun 12-2 D served Tue-Sat 6.45-8.45 Av main course £16 **Restaurant** L served Tue-Sun 12-2 D served Tue-Sat 6.45-8.45 Fixed menu price fr £20 Av 3 course à la carte fr £28.75 ⊕ FREE HOUSE
◧ Holden's Black Country Bitter & Golden Glow, Ludlow Gold & Black Knight ♂ Mahorall Farm. **Facilities** Children welcome Children's portions Play area Garden Parking 🚌 **Rooms** 3

OSWESTRY	Map 15 SJ22

The Bradford Arms ★★★★ INN

Llanymynech SY22 6EJ ☎ 01691 830582
e-mail: robinbarsteward@tesco.net
dir: *5.5m S of Oswestry on A483 in Llanymynech*

Once part of the Earl of Bradford's estate, between Oswestry and Welshpool, this 17th-century coaching inn is ideally situated for golfing, fishing and walking. It has also won awards as a community pub serving first-class real ales. Eating in the spotless, quietly elegant bar, dining rooms and conservatory is a rewarding experience, with every taste catered for. For lunch try oven-roast chicken supreme, giant filled Yorkshire pudding, or steak-and-kidney pudding; while a typical dinner menu features stilton chicken, beef Stroganoff, fisherman's pie, and leek, mushroom and onion pancake. Comfortable accommodation is available.

Open all wk 11.30-3 5.30-12 **Bar Meals** L served all wk 11.30-2 Av main course £7.95 **Restaurant** L served all wk 11.30-2 D served all wk 5.30-9 Fixed menu price fr £8.95 Av 3 course à la carte fr £17.95 ⊕ FREE HOUSE ◀ Black Sheep Best Bitter, Tetley's Smoothflow, Guinness, 2 Guest ales. **Facilities** ❀ Children welcome Children's menu Children's portions Garden Parking Wi-fi ▭ (notice required) **Rooms** 5

PAVE LANE	Map 10 SJ71

The Fox

TF10 9LQ ☎ 01952 815940
e-mail: fox@brunningandprice.co.uk
dir: *1m S of Newport, just off A41*

One of the Brunning & Price pub family, The Fox is a grand Edwardian building with spacious rooms and little nooks wrapped around a busy central bar, where plenty of Shropshire real ales demand attention. The menu offers sandwiches and light meals (beef stirfry, crab linguine), as well as smoked haddock and salmon fishcakes with tomato salad; pan-fried lamb rump served with Greek salad; and venison, black pudding and apple pie with mash, vegetables and gravy. Choose from ice cream, cheese or traditional puddings like Bakewell tart and steamed chocolate sponge. Enjoy the gently rolling countryside and wooded hills from the south-facing terrace.

Open all day all wk 12-11 (Sun 12-10.30) **Bar Meals** food served all day **Restaurant** food served all day ⊕ FREE HOUSE/BRUNNING & PRICE ◀ Timothy Taylor Landlord, Wood's Shropshire Lad, Thwaites Original, Titanic Mild, Holden's Golden Glow. ♟ **Facilities** Children welcome Children's portions Garden Parking

SHIFNAL	Map 10 SJ70

Odfellows Wine Bar

Market Place TF11 9AU ☎ 01952 461517
e-mail: reservations@odley.co.uk
web: www.odleyinns.co.uk
dir: *M54 junct 4, 3rd exit at rdbt, at next rdbt take 3rd exit, past petrol station, round bend under rail bridge. Bar on left*

No, it's not a mistake. The 'od' spelling stems from Odley Inns, who own this quirky, town centre café bar and restaurant. Hobsons, Joule's, Salopian, Slater's and Titanic breweries supply the real ales, Addlestones and Thatchers the ciders. Ethically and locally sourced food is served in an elevated dining area and attractive conservatory, the seasonal menus offering nasi goreng with king prawns and chicken; filo-wrapped pheasant breast; gammon steak with pineapple salsa; and ciabatta-based veggie supreme, not forgetting the beef Odburger. Live music on Sundays and a May beer festival.

Open all day all wk 12-12 Closed: 25-26 Dec, 1 Jan **Bar Meals** L served all wk 12-2.30 Av main course £10 **Restaurant** L served all wk 12-2.30 D served all wk 6-10 Fixed menu price fr £10 Av 3 course à la carte fr £18 ⊕ FREE HOUSE ◀ Salopian, Slater's, Hobsons, Joule's, Titanic Ở Thatchers, Addlestones. ♟ 11 **Facilities** Children welcome Children's menu Children's portions Garden Beer festival Parking Wi-fi

SHREWSBURY	Map 15 SJ41

The Armoury

Victoria Quay, Victoria Av SY1 1HH ☎ 01743 340525
e-mail: armoury@brunningandprice.co.uk
dir: *Telephone for directions*

On the opposite bank of the river from Shrewsbury's Theatre Severn, this converted armoury building makes an impressive, large-scale pub with its vast warehouse windows. Inside, huge bookcases dominate the bar and restaurant area, where the comprehensive menu is accompanied by a great range of real ales such as Wood's Shropshire Lad, local cider and a well-considered wine list. Typical dishes are braised shoulder of lamb with minted new potatoes, vegetables and gravy; and pan-fried fillet of sea bass with noodles, pak choi, sweet and sour sauce and basmati rice.

Open all day all wk Closed: 25 Dec drinks only **Bar Meals** food served all day **Restaurant** food served all day ⊕ FREE HOUSE/BRUNNING & PRICE ◀ Roosters YPA, Salopian Shropshire Gold, Caledonian Deuchars IPA, Wood's Shropshire Lad, Three Tuns Castle Steamer Ở Westons Stowford Press, Ludlow Vineyard. ♟ **Facilities** Children welcome Children's portions

The Mytton & Mermaid
Hotel ★★★ HL ◉◉

PICK OF THE PUBS

Atcham SY5 6QG ☎ 01743 761220
e-mail: reception@myttonandmermaid.co.uk
dir: *From M54 junct 7 signed Shrewsbury, at 2nd rdbt take 1st left signed Ironbridge/Atcham. In 1.5m hotel on right after bridge*

Reputedly linked by a secret tunnel to nearby St Eata's church and situated opposite Attingham Park (National Trust), this Grade II listed property dates from 1735 and enjoys spectacular views over the River Severn. Tastefully decorated throughout, the interior recalls the atmosphere of its coaching days. There's a relaxed gastro-pub feel about the place, especially the bar, which features a wood floor, scrubbed tables, comfy sofas and an open log fire. Here you can quaff a pint of local Shropshire Lad and tuck into some appetising dishes like venison cottage pie and smoked duck Caesar salad. Top-notch Shropshire ingredients drive the seasonal, modern British menu in the restaurant with its two AA Rosettes. Starters such as ravioli of lobster herald main course options that might encompass chicken breast with sage and onion risotto, or pan-fried sea bass steak. Leave space for dessert; passion fruit iced parfait is a typical choice.

Open all day all wk 7am-11pm Closed: 25 Dec **Bar Meals** Av main course £13.95 food served all day **Restaurant** L served Mon-Sat 12-2.30, Sun 12-9 D served Mon-Sat 7-10, Sun 12-9 Av 3 course à la carte fr £30 ⊕ FREE HOUSE ◀ Wood's Shropshire Lad, Salopian Shropshire Gold, Hobsons Best Bitter, Wye Valley. ♟ 12 **Facilities** Children welcome Children's menu Garden Parking Wi-fi ▭ (notice required) **Rooms** 18

SHREWSBURY *continued*

The Plume of Feathers

Harley SY5 6LP ☎ 01952 727360
e-mail: feathersatharley@aol.com
dir: *Telephone for directions*

Nestling under Wenlock Edge, this beamed 16th-century country inn has stunning views across the valley, particularly from the garden. Look for the Charles I oak bedhead, full-size cider press and inglenook fireplace. Food reflects the four seasons, and there are early-bird specials and light bites. The main menu might feature sticky barbecued ribs to start, Moroccan-style potato cakes with grilled goat's cheese on a chunky tomato sauce or grilled sea bass fillets on courgette ribbons in a coriander butter to follow. Real ales from local breweries feature strongly, along with an extensive wine list served by the glass. It's a popular spot for anyone fond of outdoor pursuits.

Open all wk 12-2.30 5-11 (Fri-Sun all day) **Bar Meals** L served all wk 12-2.30 D served all wk 5.30-9.30 Av main course £8.95 **Restaurant** L served Mon-Fri 12-2.30, Sat-Sun all day D served all wk 6-9 Fixed menu price fr £10 Av 3 course à la carte fr £20 ⊕ FREE HOUSE ◀ Courage Directors, Enville Ale, Guinness, Guest ales. ♥ **Facilities** ❄ Children welcome Children's menu Children's portions Play area Garden Parking Wi-fi ➡

STOTTESDON
Map 10 SO68

Fighting Cocks

1 High St DY14 8TZ ☎ 01746 718270
e-mail: sandrafc_5@hotmail.com
dir: *11m from Bridgnorth off B4376*

According to a framed newspaper cutting on the pub wall, 'Nipper Cook' drank 30 pints of cider each night at this unassuming 18th-century rural free house. Today, this lively local hosts regular music nights, as well as an apple day each October and an annual beer festival in November. Expect home-made pâtés, curries, pies and puddings on the menu. The owners' neighbouring shop supplies local meats, home-made pies, sausages, and produce from the gardens. Booking for meals may be required.

Open all wk 6pm-mdnt (Fri 5pm-1am Sat 12-12 Sun 12-10.30) **Bar Meals** L served Sat-Sun 12-2.30 Av main course £10 **Restaurant** L served Sat-Sun 12-2.30 D served Mon-Sat 7-9 ⊕ FREE HOUSE ◀ Hobsons Best Bitter, Town Crier & Mild, Wye Valley HPA & Bitter, Ludlow Gold Ö Westons Stowford Press, Robinsons Flagon. **Facilities** Children welcome Children's menu Garden Beer festival Parking Wi-fi

WELLINGTON
Map 10 SJ61

The Old Orleton Inn

Holyhead Rd TF1 2HA ☎ 01952 255011
e-mail: aapub@theoldorleton.com
dir: *From M54 junct 7 take B5061 (Holyhead Rd), 400yds on left on corner of Haygate Rd & Holyhead Rd*

The old and new blend effortlessly throughout this refurbished 17th-century former coaching inn. Overlooking the famous Wrekin Hill, it is popular with walkers exploring the Shropshire countryside. Expect a relaxed and informal atmosphere, local Hobsons ales on tap and modern British food, with lunch in the brasserie taking in soup, sandwiches, salad platters and ham, egg and chips. Evening extras include Shropshire lamb, seared sea bass, and rib-eye steak with stilton sauce. Booking for meals may be required.

Open 12-3 5-11 Closed: 1st 2wks Jan, Sun eve ⊕ FREE HOUSE ◀ Hobsons Best Bitter, Town Crier Ö Westons Stowford Press. **Facilities** Garden Parking Wi-fi

WENTNOR
Map 15 SO39

The Crown Inn

SY9 5EE ☎ 01588 650613
dir: *From Shrewsbury A49 to Church Stretton, follow signs over Long Mynd to Asterton, right to Wentnor*

Deep amid the Shropshire Hills, this inviting 16th-century timbered inn was taken over by new owners in early 2012. It is popular with walkers who warm themselves at wood-burning stoves in winter and on the outside decking in the summer; here you can sup Three Tuns bitter and gaze at the Long Mynd's lofty ridge. The pub's homely atmosphere, enhanced by beams and horse brasses, makes eating and drinking here a pleasure. Meals are served in the bar or separate restaurant; expect pub classics like garlic mushrooms and chicken balti with rice, chips and naan bread.

Open all day all wk **Bar Meals** L served all wk 12-9.30 D served all wk 12-9.30 Av main course £8.50 food served all day **Restaurant** L served all wk 12-9.30 D served all wk 12-9.30 food served all day ⊕ FREE HOUSE ◀ Brains The Rev. James, Hobsons Old Henry, Three Tuns Ö Westons Scrumpy. ♥ 8 **Facilities** Children welcome Children's menu Children's portions Play area Garden Parking Wi-fi ➡

WHITCHURCH
Map 15 SJ54

Willeymoor Lock Tavern

Tarporley Rd SY13 4HF ☎ 01948 663274
dir: *2m N of Whitchurch on A49 (Warrington to Tarporley road)*

You can watch narrow boats negotiating the lock from this much-extended former lock-keeper's cottage on the attractive and busy Llangollen Canal. In the bar, Shropshire Gold represents the county, teapots hang from low beams and there are open log fires. Competitively priced food includes grills, beef and onion pie, salad platters and ham, egg and chips. The children's play area and large beer garden make this an ideal warm weather location, and it's a popular refreshment spot for walkers exploring the nearby Sandstone Trail and the Bishop Bennett Way.

Open all wk 12-2.30 6-11 (Sun 12-2.30 6-10.30) Closed: 25 Dec **Bar Meals** L served all wk 12-2 D served all wk 6-9 **Restaurant** L served all wk 12-2 D served all wk 6-9 ⊕ FREE HOUSE ◀ Weetwood Eastgate Ale, Timothy Taylor Landlord, Greene King IPA, Morland Old Speckled Hen, Salopian Shropshire Gold, Stonehouse. ♥ 9 **Facilities** Children welcome Children's menu Play area Garden Parking

SOMERSET

APPLEY
Map 3 ST02

The Globe Inn

TA21 0HJ ☎ 01823 672327
e-mail: globeinnappley@btconnect.com
dir: *From M5 junct 26 take A38 towards Exeter. Village signed in 5m*

Hidden in a maze of lanes on the Somerset-Devon border, this Grade II listed inn dates back 500 years and is known for its large collection of Corgi and Dinky cars, *Titanic* memorabilia, old advertising posters and enamel signs. The smart beer gardens have lovely views over rolling hills. Local seasonal produce is used in 'good honest food' made from scratch on the premises; maybe mushroom Stroganoff followed by venison pie or a selection from the grill, with pear and ginger pudding for dessert. A beer festival is held the first weekend in September. Booking for meals may be required.

Open Tue-Sun 12-3 6.30-11 Closed: 25-26 Dec, Mon (ex BH) Sun eve Nov-Apr **Bar Meals** L served Tue-Sun 12-2 D served Tue-Sun 7-9.30 Av main course £12 **Restaurant** L served Tue-Sun 12-2 D served Tue-Sun 7-9.30 Av 3 course à la carte fr £23 ⊕ FREE HOUSE ◀ Appley's Ale, Sharp's Doom Bar, St Austell Tribute, Cotleigh Harrier, Otter Ale, O'Hanlon's Yellow Hammer, Exmoor Ö Thatchers Gold, Healey's Cornish Rattler. ♥ 8 **Facilities** Children welcome Children's menu Children's portions Play area Garden Beer festival Parking ➡

ASHCOTT — Map 4 ST43

Ring O'Bells

High St TA7 9PZ ☎ 01458 210232
e-mail: info@ringobells.com
dir: *M5 junct 23 follow A39 & Glastonbury signs. In Ashcott turn left, at post office follow church & village hall signs*

An independent free house successfully run by the same family for 25 years. Parts of the building date from 1750, so the traditional village pub interior has beams, split-level bars, an old fireplace and a collection of bells and horse brasses. The pub is close to the Somerset Levels, RSPB reserve at Ham Wall and National Nature Reserve at Shapwick Heath. Local ales and ciders are a speciality, while all food is made on the premises. Expect good-value dishes and daily specials such as deep-fried stilton-stuffed mushrooms, or spicy crab cakes with sweet chilli dip, to start; followed by pork tenderloin in Somerset cider and apple sauce; chicken chasseur; or braised liver and onions. Treat yourself to an ice cream sundae for dessert.

Open all wk 12-3 7-11 (Sun 7-10.30) Closed: 25 Dec **Bar Meals** L served all wk 12-2 D served all wk 7-10 Av main course £10 **Restaurant** L served all wk 12-2 D served all wk 7-10 Av 3 course à la carte fr £18 ⊕ FREE HOUSE ◀ Guest ales Ŏ Wilkins Farmhouse, The Orchard Pig. ♥ 8 **Facilities** ✤ Children welcome Children's menu Children's portions Play area Garden Parking Wi-fi ᔎ (notice required)

ASHILL — Map 4 ST31

Square & Compass ★★★★ INN

Windmill Hill TA19 9NX ☎ 01823 480467
e-mail: squareandcompass@tiscali.co.uk
dir: *Exit A358 at Stewley Cross service station onto Wood Rd. 1m to pub in Windmill Hill*

Beautifully located overlooking the Blackdown Hills in the heart of rural Somerset, this traditional family-owned country pub has been a labour of love for owners Chris and Janet Slow for over 15 years. A warm and friendly atmosphere pervades the bar with its hand-made settles and tables. Exmoor ales head the refreshments list, while reasonably priced and freshly made pub dishes are prepared in the state-of-the-art kitchen. Chef's specials may tempt with fillets of sea bass, lamb noisettes, or pork tenderloin. The barn next door hosts weddings and regular live music, while eight bedrooms built in 2010 offer four-star accommodation.

Open 12-3 6.30-late (Sun 7-late) Closed: 25-26 Dec, Tue-Thu L **Bar Meals** L served Fri-Mon 12-2 D served all wk 7-9.30 **Restaurant** L served Fri-Mon 12-2 D served all wk 7-9.30 ⊕ FREE HOUSE ◀ St Austell Tribute & Trelawny, Exmoor. **Facilities** ✤ Children welcome Children's menu Children's portions Garden Parking Wi-fi **Rooms** 8

AXBRIDGE — Map 4 ST45

Lamb Inn

The Square BS26 2AP ☎ 01934 732253
dir: *10m from Wells & Weston-Super-Mare on A370*

Parts of this rambling 15th-century inn were once the guildhall, but it was licensed in 1830 when the new town hall was built. Standing across the medieval square from King John's Hunting Lodge, the pub's comfortable bars have log fires and offer Butcombe ales; there's also a skittle alley and large terraced garden. Snacks and pub favourites support home-made dishes like Thai red vegetable curry, chicken parmigiana, beef and Butcombe pie, and Mexican spicy chicken. Booking for meals may be required.

Open all wk 11-3 6-11 (Thu-Sat 11am-11.30pm Sun 12-10.30) **Bar Meals** L served all wk 12-2.30 D served Mon-Sat 6-9 ⊕ BUTCOMBE ◀ Bitter & Gold, Guest ales Ŏ Thatchers, Ashton Press. **Facilities** Children's menu Children's portions Garden Wi-fi ᔎ (notice required)

BABCARY — Map 4 ST52

Red Lion

TA11 7ED ☎ 01458 223230
e-mail: redlionbabcary@btinternet.com
dir: *Please telephone for directions*

This multi-gabled stone free house has been beautifully appointed, with rich colour-washed walls, heavy beams and simple wooden furniture. The bar has a great selection of real ales, and you can dine there, in the restaurant or garden. The daily menus feature pub favourites as well as dishes such as artichoke, leek and smoked cheese crêpes; confit belly of pork with a bubble-and-squeak potato cake and black pudding; and chicken, leek and ham pie. All bread is baked on the premises and local suppliers are used whenever possible.

Open all wk **Bar Meals** L served all wk 12-2.30 D served Mon-Sat 7-9.30 **Restaurant** L served all wk 12-2.30 D served Mon-Sat 7-9.30 ⊕ FREE HOUSE ◀ Teignworthy, O'Hanlon's, Otter, Bath Ŏ Westons Stowford Press. ♥ 12 **Facilities** Children welcome Play area Garden Parking Wi-fi ᔎ

BACKWELL — Map 4 ST46

The New Inn

86 West Town Rd BS48 3BE ☎ 01275 462199
e-mail: info@newinn-backwell.co.uk
dir: *From Bristol A370 towards Weston-Super-Mare. Pub on right just after Backwell in West Town. Or from M5 junct 21, A370 towards Bristol*

This 18th-century country pub has a relaxed and welcoming atmosphere inside, and a rear garden perfect for summertime Sunday evening barbecues. A good selection of draught beers and ciders is sold at the bar, while attentive staff look after diners tucking in to French- and English-inspired dishes that range from the traditional to the contemporary: potato and roasted garlic

soup, for example, could be followed by pan-roasted Gressingham duck breast with celeriac purée. Dogs are allowed in the bar and garden, and there is plenty of parking. Change of hands.

Open all day all wk 12-12 Closed: 25 Dec **Bar Meals** food served all day **Restaurant** L served Mon-Sat 12-2.30, Sun 12-3.30 D served Mon-Thu 6-9.30, Fri-Sat 6.30-10 ⊕ ENTERPRISE INNS ◀ Sharp's Doom Bar, Timothy Taylor Landlord, Butcombe Brunel IPA Ŏ Weston Stowford Press & Wyld Wood Organic. ♥ 15 **Facilities** ✤ Children welcome Children's portions Garden Parking ᔎ

BATH — Map 4 ST76

The Chequers

50 Rivers St BA1 2QA ☎ 01225 360017
e-mail: info@thechequersbath.com
dir: *In city centre, near the Royal Crescent*

There has been a pub on this site since 1776 when the main customers were tired sedan-chair men carrying aristocrats to nearby lodging houses. A short walk from Bath's most famous landmarks, this smart food pub is now run by the team behind the nearby Marlborough Tavern (see entry). The bar offers a range of pub classics and sandwiches, whilst the refined upstairs restaurant is the place to enjoy à la carte choices like roasted Cornish cod, wilted Savoy cabbage and cassoulet of haricot beans and chorizo.

Open all day all wk Closed: 25 Dec **Bar Meals** L served Mon-Sat 12-2.30, Sun 12-6 D served Mon-Sat 6-9.30, Sun 12-6 Av main course £16.50 **Restaurant** Fixed menu price fr £10 Av 3 course à la carte fr £22 ⊕ ENTERPRISE INNS ◀ Butcombe Bitter, Bath Gem Ŏ Westons Wyld Wood Organic, Addlestones. ♥ 19 **Facilities** ✤ Children welcome Children's portions Wi-fi ᔎ (notice required)

The Garricks Head NEW

7-8 St John's Place BA1 1ET ☎ 01225 318368
e-mail: info@garricksheadpub.com
dir: *Adjacent to Theatre Royal. Follow Theatre Royal brown tourist signs*

One of the oldest Georgian buildings in Bath, this is the former home of Beau Nash, the bon viveur who put Bath on the map as a resort. Now surrounded by the Theatre Royal, much of its customers are theatregoers. The menu is as locally sourced as possible; typical dishes include Cornish crab and apple salad with celeriac remoulade and brown crab dressing followed by braised Somerset beef shin and horseradish suet pudding with buttered greens, roasted carrots and shallot sauce. For dessert maybe rich chocolate tart with white chocolate sauce and vanilla ice cream. Booking for meals may be required.

Open all day all wk Closed: 25-25 Dec **Bar Meals** L served Mon-Sat 12-3, Sun 12-4 D served Mon-Sat 5.30-10, Sun 5.30-9 Av main course £13.95 **Restaurant** L served Mon-Sat 12-3, Sun 12-4 D served Mon-Sat 5.30-10, Sun 5.30-9 Fixed menu price fr £15.95 Av 3 course à la carte fr £27.95 ⊕ FREE HOUSE ◀ Otter Bitter, Palmers. ♥ 20 **Facilities** ✤ Children welcome Children's portions Garden Wi-fi

BATH *continued*

The Hop Pole

PICK OF THE PUBS

7 Albion Buildings, Upper Bristol Rd BA1 3AR
☎ **01225 446327**
e-mail: hoppole@bathales.co.uk
dir: *On A4 from city centre towards Bristol. Pub opposite Royal Victoria Park*

Since the last edition of the guide appeared, Phil Cotton has taken over this delightful pub just off the River Avon towpath, opposite Royal Victoria Park. Described as both a country pub in the heart of a city, and as a 'secret oasis', it has a stripped-down, stylish interior and a lovingly restored, spacious beer garden, which Phil has refreshed with a grapevine canopy. Bath Ales, now elevated from micro-brewery to regional brewery status, supplies many beers from its stable – here you'll find Barnsey (formerly Barnstormer), Festivity, Gem, SPA and Wild Hare. All food is home cooked, from the bar snacks to the main meals such as River Fowey mussels with cider and saffron sauce; honey and clove ham hock, piccalilli and cauliflower cheese; grilled cod with chorizo and haricot cassoulet; and grilled vegetable tart with rocket, parmesan shavings and potato salad. Children are served smaller portions from the main menu.

Open all day all wk 12-11 (Fri-Sat 12-12) **Bar Meals** L served Mon-Fri 12-3, Sat 12-9.30, Sun 12-4 D served Mon-Fri 6-9, Sat 12-9.30 Av main course £10 **Restaurant** L served Mon-Fri 12-3, Sat 12-9.30, Sun 12-4 D served Mon-Fri 6-9, Sat 12-9.30 Fixed menu price fr £10 Av 3 course à la carte fr £20 ⊕ BATH ALES ◀ Gem, SPA, Barnsey, Festivity, Wild Hare Ŏ Bath Ciders Bounders. ₸ 14 **Facilities** ☺ Children welcome Children's menu Children's portions Garden Wi-fi ⛲ (notice required)

King William

PICK OF THE PUBS

See Pick of the Pubs on opposite page

The Marlborough Tavern ◉◉

PICK OF THE PUBS

35 Marlborough Buildings BA1 2LY ☎ **01225 423731**
e-mail: info@marlborough-tavern.com
dir: *200mtrs from W end of Royal Crescent*

This admirable pub just around the corner from the famous Royal Crescent has been providing food and drink since the 18th century, when it was a favoured pull-up for foot-weary sedan-chair carriers. Today's clientele are more likely to be exhausted from a morning or afternoon spent traipsing round Bath's shops and boutiques, now eager for refreshment in the contemporary, retro and classic-style bars or courtyard garden. Butcombe, Landlord and Totty Pot dark porter occupy the handpumps, and the number of wines sold by the glass now exceeds 20. The classy menu delivers gutsy, full-flavoured dishes prepared from local seasonal and organic produce, among which a typical starter is potted game with red onion compôte and toast; to follow, whole South Coast plaice with caper brown butter, fried pink fir potatoes and wilted cavolo nero; or pork, tomato, chorizo and bean casserole. For vegetarians, chestnut, mushroom and pearl barley risotto, perhaps. Booking for meals may be required.

Open all day all wk 12-11 (Fri-Sat noon-12.30am) Closed: 25 Dec Bar Meals Av main course £15 **Restaurant** L served Mon-Sat 12-2.30, Sun 12.30-4 D served Mon-Thu 6-9.30, Sat 6-9 Fixed menu price fr £12 Av 3 course à la carte fr £28 ⊕ FREE HOUSE ◀ Butcombe Bitter, Timothy Taylor Landlord, Cheddar Totty Pot Ŏ Addlestones. ₸ 23 **Facilities** ☺ Children welcome Children's portions Garden Wi-fi ⛲ (notice required)

The Star Inn

23 Vineyards BA1 5NA ☎ **01225 425072**
e-mail: landlord@star-inn-bath.co.uk
dir: *On A4, 300mtrs from centre of Bath*

Set amid glorious Georgian architecture and first licensed in 1760, the impressive Star Inn is one of Bath's oldest pubs and is of outstanding historical interest, with a rare and totally unspoiled interior. Original features in the four drinking areas include 19th-century Gaskell and Chambers bar fittings, a barrel lift from the cellar, and even complimentary pinches of snuff found in tins in the smaller bar! Long famous for its pints of Bass served from the jug, these days Abbey Ales from Bath's only brewery are also popular. Fresh filled rolls are available and free snacks on Sundays. A beer festival is held twice a year.

Open all wk 12-2.30 5.30-12 (Fri 12-2.30 5.30-1am Sat noon-1am Sun 12-12) ⊕ PUNCH TAVERNS ◀ Abbey Bellringer, Bath Star, Twelfth Night & White Friar, Bass Ŏ Abbey Ales Hells Bells. **Facilities** ☺ Children welcome Beer festival Wi-fi ⛲

BAWDRIP
Map 4 ST33

The Knowle Inn

TA7 8PN ☎ **01278 683330**
e-mail: peter@matthews3.wanadoo.co.uk
dir: *M5 junct 23 or A39 from Bridgwater towards Glastonbury*

This 16th-century pub, just a mile from the M5, nestles beneath the Polden Hills on the edge of the Somerset levels and between the Quantock and Mendip Hills. A true community pub, with live music, skittles and darts, it also specialises in fresh seafood, with sea bass and John Dory often among the catch delivered from Plymouth. A full range of sandwiches and light meals is backed by pub favourites such as gammon steak with egg or pineapple, steak-and-ale pie, and chicken with barbecue sauce and cheese. A Mediterranean-style garden, complete with fish pond, is ideal for summer alfresco meals.

Open all day all wk **Bar Meals** L served all wk 11-3 D served all wk 6-9 **Restaurant** L served all wk 11-3 D served all wk 6-9 ⊕ ENTERPRISE INNS ◀ Otter, Guest ales Ŏ Thatchers, Natch. **Facilities** ☺ Children welcome Children's menu Children's portions Garden Parking ⛲ (notice required)

BECKINGTON
Map 4 ST85

Woolpack Inn ★★★★ INN

BA11 6SP ☎ **01373 831244**
e-mail: 6534@greeneking.co.uk
dir: *Just off A36 near junct with A361*

Standing in the middle of the village, this charming, stone-built coaching inn dates back to the 1500s. Inside there's an attractive, flagstone floor in the bar and outside at the back, a delightful terraced garden. The lunch menu offers soup and sandwich platters, and larger dishes such as home-made sausages and mash; fresh herb and tomato omelette; steak-and-ale pie; and beer-battered cod and chips. Some of these are also listed on the evening bar menu. Eleven en suite bedrooms, including one four-poster room and one family room, are available. Booking for meals may be required.

Open all day all wk 11-11 (Sun 11-10) ⊕ OLD ENGLISH INNS & HOTELS ◀ Greene King IPA & Abbot Ale, Guest ale Ŏ Moles Black Rat. **Facilities** Children welcome Children's menu Children's portions Garden Parking Wi-fi **Rooms** 11

BISHOPSWOOD
Map 4 ST21

Candlelight Inn NEW

TA20 3RS ☎ **01460 234476**
e-mail: info@candlelight-inn.co.uk
dir: *From A303 SW of Newtown, right a x-rds signed Bishopswood & Churchinford. Pub on right in village*

Persevere down tiny lanes off the A303 to locate Debbie and Tom's 17th-century pub deep in the Blackdown Hills. Having been closed for a year, the experienced couple have breathed new life into the rustic rural local. Expect exposed flint walls, wooden floors, crackling log fires and a warm and friendly atmosphere in the bar, where locals gather for tip-top pints of Exmoor or Otter drawn straight from the cask. Food will not disappoint; follow mussel and parsley risotto with stuffed pork loin with mustard mash and cider sauce, leaving room for crème Catalan. Look out for occasional beer festivals. Booking for meals may be required.

Open 12-3 6-11 (Sun all day) Closed: 25-27 Dec, Mon **Bar Meals** L served Tue-Fri 12-2, Sat-Sun 12-2.30 D served Tue-Thu & Sun 7-9, Fri-Sat 7-9.30 Av main course £14 **Restaurant** L served Tue-Fri 12-2, Sat-Sun 12-2.30 D served Tue-Thu & Sun 7-9, Fri-Sat 7-9.30 Fixed menu price fr £16 Av 3 course à la carte fr £25 ⊕ FREE HOUSE ◀ Otter Bitter, Bass, Exmoor, Branscombe Ŏ Thatchers, Sheppy's, Tricky. ₸ 9 **Facilities** ☺ Children welcome Children's portions Garden Beer festival Parking Wi-fi ⛲ (notice required)

Save on hotels. Book at **theAA.com/hotel**

SOMERSET 439 ENGLAND

PICK OF THE PUBS

King William

BATH   Map 4 ST76

36 Thomas St BA1 5NN
☎ **01225 428096**
e-mail: info@kingwilliampub.com
web: www.kingwilliampub.com
dir: *At junct of Thomas St & A4 (London Rd), on left from Bath towards London. 15 mins walk from Bath Spa main line station*

You could walk past this unassuming free house and scarcely give it a second look. Yet that would be a mistake, for within the plain Bath stone building lies an appealing city pub that exudes the charm and character that other places can only yearn for. It's a happy mix of destination dining inn and locals' pub, effortlessly catering for both these markets, with a cosy snug and traditional bar beneath the memorable upstairs dining room. Real ale buffs will generally find a regular Palmers ale, supplemented by guest beers from local micro-breweries such as Stonehenge Ales, Yeovil Ales and the Milk Street Brewery. There's no food on Monday or Tuesday lunchtimes, but on other days the bar menu offers lighter dishes such as slow-roast beef skirt, horseradish cream and dripping toast; fresh Cornish mussels steamed in Somerset cider with triple-cooked chips; and a grazing board of Bertinet bread, marinated olives, beetroot pesto, Fussels rapeseed oil and

English balsamic. Serious diners will seek out the daily-changing restaurant menu, packed with inspiring dishes from locally-produced seasonal ingredients. Starters like home-smoked salmon with roast beetroot pesto, organic leaves and crème fraîche; or roast artichoke with mixed herb and Lord of the Hundreds ewes' cheese shavings, might herald a main course of local lamb rump, fondant potato, English asparagus, shallot purée and rosemary sauce; or pan-roast hake with shellfish and vegetable broth, potato and herb dumplings. Lemon posset with cinnamon ice cream and shortbread completes an evening of easy eating, with a good wine list for a bracing accompaniment. Booking for meals may be required.

Open 12-3 5-close (Sat-Sun 12-close) Closed: 25 Dec, Mon-Tue L **Bar Meals** L served Wed-Sun 12-3 D served Mon-Sat 6-10, Sun 6-9 **Restaurant** L served Sun 12-3 D served Wed-Sat 6-10 ⊕ FREE HOUSE ◀ Stonehenge Danish Dynamite, Palmers Dorset Gold, Milk Street Funky Monkey, Yeovil ♂ Pheasant Plucker, Westons Wyld Wood Organic, The Orchard Pig. ♟ 14 **Facilities** Children welcome Children's portions Wi-fi

BLUE ANCHOR   Map 3 ST04

The Smugglers

TA24 6JS ☎ 01984 640385
e-mail: info@take2chefs.co.uk
web: www.take2chefs.co.uk
dir: *Off A3191, midway between Minehead & Watchet*

'Fresh food, cooked well' is the simple philosophy at this friendly 300-year-old inn. It stands just yards from Blue Anchor Bay on one side, with a backdrop of the Exmoor Hills on the other. Head to the Cellar Bar for refreshment, and to order food. Starters and light bites include sardines and local mussels, while the stoves and grill proffer steaks, Lashford's award-winning sausages, and weekly specials such as lamb rump marinated in cider and honey. In fine weather families can eat in the large walled garden where children enjoy the bouncy castle.

Open 12-3 6-11 (Sat-Sun 12-11) Closed: Sun eve, Mon-Tue (Nov-Feb only) **Bar Meals** L served all wk 12-2.15 D served all wk 6-9 **Restaurant** L served all wk 12-2.15 D served all wk 6-9 ⊕ FREE HOUSE ◀ Otter Smuggled Otter & Ale, John Smith's ♂ Westons Traditional. ♟ 8 **Facilities** ♣ Children welcome Children's menu Children's portions Play area Garden Parking Wi-fi ▄▄ (notice required)

BRADFORD-ON-TONE   Map 4 ST12

White Horse Inn

Regent St TA4 1HF ☎ 01823 461239
e-mail: glenwhitehorse@googlemail.com
dir: *N of A38 between Taunton & Wellington*

Opposite the church in the heart of a delightful thatched village, this stone-built inn dates back over 300 years. Very much a community pub, it has a bar area, restaurant, outdoor skittle lane or boules pitch, garden and patio. Real ales brewed in the south west include varied guests, while home-cooked food favours tried-and-tested popular dishes: a pint of shell-on Atlantic prawns; sausages and mash with vegetables and onion gravy; and slow-roasted ham with egg and chips. There's a curry night on Wednesdays.

Open all day all wk **Bar Meals** L served all wk 12-2 D served all wk 6-9 **Restaurant** L served all wk 12-2 D served all wk 6-9 ⊕ ENTERPRISE INNS ◀ Sharp's Doom Bar, Exmoor Ale, Otter Ale ♂ Thatchers Gold. **Facilities** ♣ Children welcome Children's menu Children's portions Garden Parking Wi-fi ▄▄ (notice required)

CATCOTT   Map 4 ST33

The Crown Inn

1 The Nydon TA7 9HQ ☎ 01278 722288
e-mail: catcottcrownin@aol.com
dir: *M5 junct 23, A39 towards Glastonbury. Turn left to Catcott*

Perhaps 400 years old, this low-beamed, flagstoned pub in the Somerset levels originated as a beer house serving local peat-cutters. The winter log fire takes the chill off Bristol Channel winds; in summer the half-acre beer garden is great for families and sun worshippers. Food is plentiful, imaginative and home-made, with highlights including well-matured local steaks, fresh fish, and local game when in season. A good range of cask ales and ciders from regional suppliers completes the picture.

Open 12-2.30 6-late Closed: Mon L **Bar Meals** L served Tue-Sun 12-2 (booking advisable Sun) D served all wk 6-9 **Restaurant** L served Tue-Sun 12-2 (booking advisable Sun) D served Sun-Thu 6-9, Fri-Sat 6-9.30 (booking advisable Fri-Sat) ⊕ FREE HOUSE ◀ Sharp's Doom Bar, Butcombe ♂ Ashton Press. ♟ 10 **Facilities** Children welcome Children's menu Children's portions Play area Garden Parking ▄▄

CHEW MAGNA   Map 4 ST56

The Bear and Swan

PICK OF THE PUBS

South Pde BS40 8SL ☎ 01275 331100
e-mail: bearandswan@fullers.co.uk
dir: *A37 from Bristol. Turn right signed Chew Magna onto B3130. Or from A38 turn left on B3130*

The Victorians clearly didn't like the frontage of this early 18th-century pub, so they gave it one of their own. Inside, the oak-beamed rooms with scrubbed wooden floors and diverse collection of reclaimed tables, chairs and assorted artefacts all contribute to its warm and friendly atmosphere. It's owned by Fuller's, so expect London Pride, but you'll also find Butcombe Bitter, local real ciders and a list of well selected wines. The restaurant offers daily one-, two- and three-course menus with good choices of fish, game, seafood, meats and vegetarian dishes. You might care to start with wasabi tuna and tiger prawn satay with pepper salad; before moving on to aubergine rarebit with tomato, caper and pesto risotto; or baked cod with pancetta crust, fennel and rocket linguine and sweet roasted garlic velouté. The August Bank Holiday weekend cider festival also features a barbecue and live music. Booking for meals may be required.

Open all day Closed: 25 Dec, Sun eve **Bar Meals** L served Mon-Sat 12-2.30, Sun 12-3 D served Mon-Sat 6.30-9.30 Av main course £10.25 **Restaurant** L served Mon-Sat 12-2.30, Sun 12-3 D served Mon-Sat 6.30-9.30 Av 3 course à la carte fr £23 ⊕ FULLER'S ◀ London Pride, Butcombe Bitter ♂ Ashton Press, Aspall, Symonds. ♟ 12 **Facilities** ♣ Children welcome Children's portions Garden Parking Wi-fi ▄▄ (notice required)

The Pony and Trap ◉

Knowle Hill, Newton BS40 8TQ ☎ 01275 332627
e-mail: josh@theponyandtrap.co.uk
dir: *Take A37 S from Bristol. After Pensfold turn right at rdbt onto A368 towards Weston-Super-Mare. In 1.5m right signed Chew Magna & Winford. Pub 1m on right*

A 200-year-old country cottage pub/restaurant with fantastic views across the Chew Valley, Josh Eggleton's award-winning Pony and Trap still feels like a rural local despite the acclaim it has achieved with its food. Committed to sourcing all ingredients as locally as possible, everything on the menu is made on the premises, right down to the bread and butter. Try Valley Smokehouse smoked salmon terrine with piccalilli; ox liver with truffle mash and smoked bacon; or the home-made burger. Fine wines, local real ales and ciders complete the picture. Booking for meals may be required.

Open 11.30-3 6.30-12 (Sun all day) Closed: Mon (ex BH & Dec) **Bar Meals** L served Tue-Sat 12-2.30, Sun 12-3.30 D served Tue-Sun 7-9.30 Av main course £15 **Restaurant** L served Tue-Sat 12-2.30, Sun 12-3.30 D served Tue-Sun 7-9.30 Av 3 course à la carte fr £28 ⊕ FREE HOUSE ◀ Butcombe Bitter, Sharp's Doom Bar, Guest ale ♂ Ashton Press, The Orchard Pig. ♟ 12 **Facilities** Children welcome Children's portions Garden Parking Wi-fi

CHISELBOROUGH   Map 4 ST41

The Cat Head Inn

Cat St TA14 6TT ☎ 01935 881231
e-mail: info@thecatheadinn.co.uk
dir: *Leave A303 onto A356 towards Crewkerne, take 3rd left turn (at 1.4m) signposted Chiselborough, then after 0.2m turn left*

Once a farmhouse, and probably creeper-clad back then too, The Cat Head's flagstoned, open fire-warmed interior is furnished with light wooden tables and chairs, and high-backed settles. Changing hands in 2011, Otter and Butcombe are now the resident real ales in the picturesque bar, along with beer from the Moor Brewery, which is only 15 minutes from the pub. The bar menu lists sandwiches, ploughman's, light bites, and a handful of pub classics. The evening menu offers pan-fried monkfish tail wrapped in Parma ham; trio of local sausages; and artichoke and leek risotto. Outside are attractive gardens and play area. Booking for meals may be required.

Open all wk 12-2.30 6-11 Closed: Mon in winter ⊕ ENTERPRISE INNS ◀ Butcombe, Otter, Moor ♂ Thatchers Cheddar Valley, Symonds. **Facilities** Children welcome Children's menu Children's portions Play area Family room Garden Wi-fi

PICK OF THE PUBS

The Hunters Rest ★★★★INN

CLUTTON　　　　　　　　**Map 4 ST65**

King Ln, Clutton Hill BS39 5QL
☎ **01761 452303**
e-mail: info@huntersrest.co.uk
web: www.huntersrest.co.uk
dir: *On A37 follow signs for Wells through Pensford, at large rdbt left towards Bath, 100mtrs right into country lane, pub 1m up hill*

The Earl of Warwick made a canny decision when he chose this particular spot around 1750 to build his hunting lodge, because he would have been able to see clear over the Cam Valley to the Mendip Hills, and across the Chew Valley towards Bristol. And you still can. When the estate was sold in 1872, the building became a tavern serving the growing number of coal miners working in the area, but all the mines closed long ago and the place has been transformed into a popular and attractive inn, with five individually decorated bedrooms, including two four-poster suites. Paul Thomas has been running the place for 25 years (he told the AA he's 'getting old'), during which time he has established a great reputation for good home-made food, real ales – typically Butcombe, Bath Gem and Otter – and a well-stocked wine cellar, with a fair number by the glass. The menu includes Norwegian prawn cocktail; warm chicken and bacon salad; and giant pastries called oggies, which might come with a variety of fillings, such

as beef steak and stilton, mixed smoked fish, and cauliflower cheese. Other hot dishes include Somerset faggots with onion gravy; lamb's liver and bacon; chicken madras; chilli burritos; and from the specials blackboard a selection of daily-delivered, Brixham-landed sea bass and other fish; rosy veal with confit shallots; noisettes of lamb with rosemary gravy; and griddled English asparagus and wild mushroom risotto. There's also a children's menu offering battered haddock, beefburger and chicken nuggets, and a dozen popular desserts such as tarte au citron, and maple and walnut cheesecake. In summer you can sit out in the landscaped grounds.

Open all day all wk **Bar Meals** L served all wk 12-9.45 D served all wk 12-9.45

Av main course £10 food served all day **Restaurant** L served all wk 12-9.45 D served all wk 12-9.45 Av 3 course à la carte fr £22.50 food served all day ⊕ FREE HOUSE ◀ Bath Gem, Otter Ale, Butcombe Ö Broadoak, Thatchers. ♟ 10 **Facilities** Children welcome Children's menu Children's portions Play area Family room 🐾 Garden Parking Wi-fi 🚌 (notice required) **Rooms** 5

CHURCHILL Map 4 ST45

The Crown Inn

The Batch BS25 5PP ☎ **01934 852995**
dir: *From Bristol take A38 S. Right at Churchill lights, left in 200mtrs, up hill to pub*

It's hard to believe that this gem of a pub could once have been a stop on what was then the Bristol to Exeter coach road. Ten real ales are served straight from the cask in the two flagstone-floored bars, where open fires blaze on cold days. Freshly prepared bar lunches, including sandwiches, filled jacket potatoes, sausages and mash and pork casserole, are made from the best local ingredients. In fact the beef comes straight from the pub's own fields. Enjoy a meal in the beautiful gardens.

Open all day all wk 11-11 (Fri 11am-mdnt) **Bar Meals** L served all wk 12-2.30 Av main course £6.40 ⊕ FREE HOUSE ◀ Palmers IPA, Bass, RCH PG Steam & Hewish IPA, Bath Gem, St Austell Tribute, Butcombe ♂ Thatchers, Ashton Press, Healey's Cornish Rattler, Bath Ciders Bounders. **Facilities** Children welcome Children's portions Garden Parking ▭ **Notes** ⊛

CLAPTON-IN-GORDANO Map 4 ST47

The Black Horse
PICK OF THE PUBS

Clevedon Ln BS20 7RH ☎ **01275 842105**
e-mail: theblackhorse@talktalkbusiness.net
dir: *M5 junct 19, 3m to village. 2m from Portishead, 10m from Bristol*

The bars on one of the windows of this attractive, whitewashed inn near Bristol are a reminder that the Black Horse's Snug Bar was once the village lock-up. Built in the 14th century, the traditional bar of this pub features low beams, flagstone floors, wooden settles and old guns above the big open fireplace. Real ales served straight from the barrel include local Butcombe Best and Wadworth 6X, whilst cider fans will rejoice at the sight of Thatchers Heritage. The small kitchen in this listed building limits its output to traditional pub food served lunchtimes only (Monday to Saturday). The repertoire includes hot and cold filled baguettes and rolls; home-made soup of the day; pies and seasonal specials. The large rear garden includes a children's play area, and there's a separate family room.

Open all day all wk **Bar Meals** L served Mon-Sat 12-2 ⊕ ENTERPRISE INNS ◀ Courage Best Bitter, Wadworth 6X, Shepherd Neame Spitfire, Butcombe Bitter, Exmoor Gold, Otter Bitter ♂ Thatchers & Heritage. ♟ 8 **Facilities** Children welcome Play area Family room Garden Parking

CLUTTON Map 4 ST65

The Hunters Rest ★★★★ INN
PICK OF THE PUBS

See Pick of the Pubs on page 441

COMBE HAY Map 4 ST75

The Wheatsheaf
PICK OF THE PUBS

See Pick of the Pubs on opposite page

COMPTON DANDO Map 4 ST66

The Compton Inn

Court Hill BS39 4JZ ☎ **01761 490321**
e-mail: paul@huntersrest.co.uk
dir: *From A368 between Chelwood & Marksbury follow Hunstrete & Compton Dando signs*

A former farmhouse, the Grade II listed Compton Inn has only been a pub since World War II, but it has been sympathetically restored. Located in the picturesque Compton Dando, with its imposing church and hump-backed bridge crossing the River Chew, it is only a few miles from the bustling city of Bristol. It's an ideal bolt-hole to enjoy local ale and cider, and well-cooked dishes like moussaka with Greek salad in a lemon dressing; and noisettes of lamb in a rosemary gravy with sauté potatoes and vegetables. Sweets include Eton Mess and Baileys crème brûlée.

Open all day all wk **Bar Meals** L served Mon-Sat 12-2.15, Sun 12-6 D served Mon-Sat 6.15-9.15 Av main course £11.50 **Restaurant** L served Mon-Sat 12-2.15, Sun 12-6 D served Mon-Sat 6.15-9.15 Av 3 course à la carte fr £22.50 ⊕ PUNCH TAVERNS ◀ Bath Ales Gem, Sharp's Doom Bar, Butcombe ♂ Thatchers Traditional. ♟ 10 **Facilities** ❀ Children welcome Children's menu Children's portions Garden Parking Wi-fi ▭ (notice required)

The White Hart

Wrington Road, Congresbury BS49 5AR • Tel: 01934 833303
Website: www.whitehartcongresbury.co.uk
Email: whitehart.waspcatering@gmail.com

The White Hart with its old wooden beams, open fires and quirky pub characteristics is a hidden gem tucked away between Congresbury and Wrington. Phil and Cathy Sullivan with business partner Adam Williams took over the pub in early october 2011 and have already built up a regular client base. Between them they have over 40 years' experience in catering and have a firm belief in using good quality locally sourced ingredients. There is a warm and welcoming atmosphere, with staff that are attentive and who take pride in what they do. Serving freshly prepared food, the menu is seasonal and is enhanced by the daily specials produced by Chef Phil Sullivan and his team. Examples of the menu include Ham Hock Terrine with Triple Plat Toast and Cider and Apple Chutney, Pan Roasted Duck Breast, with Parsnip Mash and an Orange and Thyme Sauce and Belgian Dark Chocolate and Baileys Mousse Torte with Cotswold Double Cream. With Specials such as Oven Roasted Seabass with Creamed Leeks and Saute Potatoes or Beef and Tanglefoot Pie with Handcut Chips and Garden Peas there is plenty of choice. With a large private beer garden and car park for 50 cars the White Hart is the place to be.

Save on hotels. Book at **theAA.com/hotel**

SOMERSET 443 ENGLAND

PICK OF THE PUBS

The Wheatsheaf

COMBE HAY   Map 4 ST75

BA2 7EG ☎ 01225 833504

e-mail: info@wheatsheafcombehay.com
web: www.wheatsheafcombehay.co.uk
dir: *From Bath take A369 (Exeter road) to Odd Down, left at park & ride & immediately right towards Combe Hay. 2m to thatched cottage, turn left*

A long, whitewashed free house with a pantiled roof, standing on a peaceful hillside near the route of the former Somerset Coal Canal, which closed well over a century ago. The pub was built in 1576 as a farmhouse, but not until the 18th century did it begin its life as an alehouse, and today its old persona rubs shoulders companionably with the new, country-chic interior. The building is decorated with flowers in summer, when the gorgeous south-facing garden makes an ideal spot for outdoor drinking and dining. In the stylishly decorated, rambling bar with its massive wooden tables, sporting prints and open fires, the resident real ale is Butcombe Bitter, with back-up from guests, and the ciders are Cheddar Valley and Ashton Press. The wines are mostly from France, and Bordeaux in particular (sorry, no New World, says proprietor and wine specialist, Ian Barton), although there is one from the vineyard directly above the pub's kitchen garden. The garden is home to free-range chickens, ducks and bees, blissfully unaware of the importance of their various contributions to the daily

menus prepared by head chef, Eddy Rains. Eddy, a Gordon Ramsay protégé, is wholly committed to the use of the freshest seasonal ingredients to create his impressive and memorable dishes, from his ploughman's to his seven-course Taste of the West Country menu. Lunch or dinner might begin with roast parsnip soup with port glaze; or Weymouth lobster ravioli and fennel céviche, and be followed by 21-day aged Hereford sirloin, hand-cut chips, with either fried duck egg or Barkham Blue cheese butter; loin of Exmoor venison, wild mushroom faggot, beetroot and smoked cherry juice; or fish special, depending on that day's landing. For dessert, options include milk chocolate semi-fredo and Jaffa cakes; and warm treacle tart with malted milk ice cream.

Open 10.30-3 6-11 (Sun 11-5.30) Closed: 25-26 Dec & 1st wk Jan, Sun eve, Mon (ex BH) **Bar Meals** L served Tue-Sat 12-2.30 D served Tue-Sat 6.30-9.30 **Restaurant** L served Tue-Sun 12-2 D served Tue-Sat 6.30-9.30 ⊕ FREE HOUSE ◀ Butcombe Bitter, Bath ♂ Thatchers & Cheddar Valley, Ashton Press. ♟ 13 **Facilities** Children welcome ❧ Garden Parking Wi-fi

CONGRESBURY — Map 4 ST46

The White Hart NEW

Wrington Rd BS49 5AR ☎ 01934 833303
e-mail: whitehart.waspcatering@gmail.com
web: www.whitehartcongresbury.co.uk
dir: *From Congresbury on A370 towards Bristol, right into Wrington Rd. Pub in 0.75m*

Combined quaint village pub and dining venue hidden down a long lane off the A370, The White Hart is now owned by Hall & Woodhouse. A conventional line in sandwiches and bar meals is supplemented by some more enterprising home-cooked food: lamb shank with rosemary and red wine gravy; pork loin on mustard mash with sage and cider jus; and sea bass with lemon and chive sauce. An increasing attraction is Sunday lunch, best enjoyed by the fire in the beamed snug bar, or in the airy conservatory, which looks across the garden towards the Mendips Hills. Find out about the summer beer festival.

Open all wk 12-3 6-11 (Sat 12-11 Sun 12-10.30) Closed: 25-26 Dec **Bar Meals** L served Mon-Fri 12-3, Sat all day, Sun 12-6.30 D served Mon-Fri 6-9.30, Sat all day Av main course £7.50 **Restaurant** L served Mon-Fri 12-3, Sat all day, Sun 12-6.30 D served Mon-Fri 6-9.30, Sat all day Av 3 course à la carte fr £17.50 ⊕ HALL & WOODHOUSE ◀ Badger Tanglefoot ♻ Westons Stowford Press. ♟ 11
Facilities ✿ Children welcome Children's menu Children's portions Garden Parking 🚌 (notice required)

See advert on page 442

CORTON DENHAM — Map 4 ST62

The Queens Arms ★★★★ INN ◉

PICK OF THE PUBS

See Pick of the Pubs on opposite page

CRANMORE — Map 4 ST64

Strode Arms

BA4 4QJ ☎ 01749 880450
dir: *S of A361, 3.5m E of Shepton Mallet, 7.5m W of Frome*

Just up the road from the East Somerset Railway, this rambling old coaching inn boasts a splendid front terrace overlooking the village duck pond. Spacious bar areas are neatly laid out with comfortable country furnishings and warmed by winter log fires; the perfect setting to enjoy a pint of Bishop's Tipple or Strong in the Arm. Expect dishes such as smoked salmon and smoked haddock cheesy pot or Thai fishcakes to start; and mains like roasted guinea fowl breast on a bed of chestnut and bacon purée or pan-fried plaice fillet topped with melted lemon and chervil butter. There's also a bar menu with pies, and other wholesome stuff.

Open all wk 11.30-3 6-11 **Bar Meals** L served all wk 12-2 D served Mon-Sat 6-9 Av main course £9.65 **Restaurant** L served all wk 12-2 D served Mon-Sat 6-9 Fixed menu price fr £11.75 ⊕ WADWORTH ◀ Henry's Original IPA, 6X, Bishop's Tipple, Strong in the Arm ♻ Westons Traditional.
Facilities ✿ Children welcome Children's menu Children's portions Family room Garden Parking Wi-fi

CREWKERNE — Map 4 ST40

The George Inn ★★★ INN

Market Square TA18 7LP ☎ 01460 73650
e-mail: georgecrewkerne@btconnect.com
web: www.thegeorgehotelcrewkerne.co.uk
dir: *Telephone for directions*

Situated in the heart of Crewkerne, The George has been welcoming travellers since 1541, though the present

hamstone building dates from 1832, and the current landlord has held sway since 1994. Kingstone Press ciders sit alongside four real ales in the bar, while the kitchen produces an array of popular dishes for bar snacks and more substantial meals from the daily specials board. Vegetarian and vegan meals are always available. Thirteen comfortable en suite bedrooms are traditionally styled and include four-poster rooms.

Open all day all wk **Bar Meals** L served all wk 12-2 D served all wk 7-9 Av main course £5.95 **Restaurant** L served all wk 12-2 D served all wk 7-9 Fixed menu price fr £8.25 Av 3 course à la carte fr £16 ⊕ FREE HOUSE ◀ St Austell Tribute, Dartmoor Legend, Boddingtons ♻ Thatchers Gold, Kingstone Press. ♟ 8
Facilities Children welcome Children's menu Children's portions Wi-fi 🚌 **Rooms** 13

The Manor Arms

North Perrott TA18 7SG ☎ 01460 72901
dir: *From A30 (Yeovil/Honiton) take A3066 towards Bridport. North Perrott 1.5m*

On the Dorset/Somerset border, this 16th-century Grade II listed pub and its neighbouring hamstone cottages overlook the village green. According to the new landlord, The Manor Arms has "a long history of happy times." The inn has been lovingly restored and an inglenook fireplace, flagstone floors and oak beams are among the charming features inside. Dogs and children are welcome, there's a good beer garden for warmer days and there are plenty of rambling opportunities on the doorstep. To accompany ales like Exmoor, and Ashton Press cider, expect wholesome traditional food such as diced venison and veg with a red wine sauce served in a Yorkshire pudding; roast partridge with pears and blue cheese sauce; and lamb cutlets on chive mash with redcurrant jus.

Open all wk 12-11 **Bar Meals** L served all wk 12-2.30 D served all wk 6.30-9 **Restaurant** L served all wk 12-2.30 D served all wk 6.30-9 ⊕ FREE HOUSE ◀ Sharp's Doom Bar, Exmoor, Butcombe ♻ Ashton Press.
Facilities ✿ Children welcome Children's menu Children's portions Garden Parking Wi-fi

Save on hotels. Book at **theAA.com/hotel**

SOMERSET 445 **ENGLAND**

PICK OF THE PUBS

The Queens Arms ★★★★INN ✿

CORTON DENHAM   Map 4 ST62

DT9 4LR ☎ **01963 220317**
e-mail: relax@thequeensarms.com
web: www.thequeensarms.com
dir: *A303 follow signs for Sutton Montis, South Cadbury & Corton Denham. Through South Cadbury, 0.25m, left, up hill signed Corton Denham. Left at hill top to village, approx 1m. Pub on right*

You will find this late 18th-century, stone-built former cider house in a web of lanes meandering through stunning countryside on the Somerset/Dorset border. Footpaths work their way up on to grassy downs and alongside gurgling trout streams; it's the ideal place to chill out after a good ramble. Beneath the old beams in the engagingly furnished bar and separate dining room are old scrubbed tables beside grand, open fireplaces, gentlemen's leather chairs tucked into quiet corners of the gently colourwashed walls, and barrel seats and sofas dotting wood and flagstoned floors. Outside, a sheltered terrace against creeper-clad walls and sunny garden tick all the boxes needed for outdoor eating and drinking. Owners Gordon and Jeanette Reid stand by a commitment to provide over 30 bottled world beers, draught ales from Pitney micro-brewery Moor's to the Czech Republic's Pilsner Urquell, and The Orchard Pig and other local farm ciders, scrumpy and apple juices. They champion low food miles and animal welfare; pork is from their own pigs, and their free-range chickens and ducks provide the poultry and eggs. There's a great wine list, too. Food is simple, high quality and seasonal; earthy dishes such as a starter of broccoli and Cashell Blue soup, or smoked haddock and clam chowder with home-made dill bread set the scene for mains that might include roasted Gilcombe Farm lamb rump, cauliflower pancake, root vegetables and lamb and cranberry jus; duo of Cornish sea bass and Scottish salmon, gratin potato, fine beans, wasabi beurre blanc and pickled ginger; baked local game pie; and spiced aubergine and haloumi pithiviers, coriander couscous, harissa and carrot purée. A beer festival was held for the first time in February 2012 – watch out for another. The spacious guest rooms are all en suite and look out over the rolling countryside. Booking for meals may be required.

Open all day all wk **Bar Meals** L served all wk 12-3 D served Mon-Sat 6-10, Sun 6-9.30 Av main course £10
Restaurant L served all wk 12-3

D served Mon-Sat 6-10, Sun 6-9.30 Av 3 course à la carte fr £27.50 ⊕ FREE HOUSE ◀ Moor Revival & Northern Star, Guest ales ○ Thatchers Gold, Hecks, Wilkins Farmhouse, Burrow Hill, The Orchard Pig. ♀ 23 **Facilities** Children welcome Children's menu Children's portions ❖ Garden Beer festival Parking Wi-fi **Rooms** 8

CROSCOMBE
Map 4 ST54

The Bull Terrier ★★★ INN

Long St BA5 3QJ ☎ 01749 343658
e-mail: barry.vidler@bullterrierpub.co.uk
dir: *Halfway between Wells & Shepton Mallet on A371*

Originally called The Rose and Crown, this unspoiled village free house was first licensed in 1612 and is one of Somerset's oldest pubs. The pub changed its name to The Bull Terrier in 1976 but the building itself dates from the late 15th century, the fireplace and ceiling in the inglenook bar being added in the 16th century. One menu is offered throughout, including steak-and-kidney pie, and trout and almonds. In summer, enjoy the pretty walled garden. For those wanting to stay overnight, there are two bedrooms.

Open all wk 12-2.45 7-late **Bar Meals** L served all wk 12-2 D served all wk 7-9 Av main course £8.50 **Restaurant** L served all wk 12-2 D served all wk 7-9 ⊕ FREE HOUSE ◀ Courage Directors, Marston's Pedigree, Morland Old Speckled Hen, Greene King Ruddles County, Cheddar Ŏ Thatchers Cheddar Valley, Thatchers Gold. ♥ 8 **Facilities** ❤ Children welcome Children's menu Children's portions Family room Garden Parking ☞ **Rooms** 2

The George Inn

Long St BA5 3QH ☎ 01749 342306 & 345189
e-mail: pg@thegeorgeinn.co.uk
dir: *On A371 midway between Shepton Mallet & Wells*

It is 12 years since the Graham family bought this 17th-century village pub and the renovations are ongoing. Enjoy local ales such as Moor Revival in the softly lit bar with its large inglenook fireplace and family grandfather clock. There are real ciders too, including The Orchard Pig, and diners can enjoy locally sourced quality food, with daily specials such as game pie and pan-fried rump of lamb complementing old favourites. The garden terrace incorporates an all-weather patio and children's area.

Open all wk 12-2.30 6-11 **Bar Meals** L served all wk 12-2 D served all wk 6-9 Av main course £9 **Restaurant** L served all wk 12-2 D served all wk 6-9 ⊕ FREE HOUSE ◀ Butcombe Bitter, Moor Revival, Blindmans Ŏ Thatchers Cheddar Valley, The Orchard Pig, Westons Stowford Press. ♥ 9 **Facilities** ❤ Children welcome Children's menu Children's portions Play area Family room Garden Beer festival Parking Wi-fi

---

DINNINGTON
Map 4 ST41

Dinnington Docks

TA17 8SX ☎ 01460 52397
e-mail: hilary@dinningtondocks.co.uk
dir: *S of A303 between South Petherton & Ilminster*

Formerly known as the Rose & Crown, this traditional village pub on the old Fosse Way has been licensed for over 250 years and has no loud music, pool tables or fruit machines to drown out the conversation. Inside you will find pictures, signs and memorabilia of its rail and maritime past. Good-quality cask ales and farmhouse cider are served, and freshly prepared food including the likes of crab cakes, faggots, snapper, steak, and lamb shank for two. There's a quiz night every Sunday, and pub is located in an ideal place for cycling and walking.

Open all wk 11.30-3 6-12 (Sat-Sun all day) **Bar Meals** L served all wk 12-2 D served all wk 7-9 **Restaurant** L served all wk 12-2 D served all wk 7-9 ⊕ FREE HOUSE ◀ Butcombe Bitter, Guest ales Ŏ Burrow Hill, Westons Stowford Press, Thatchers Gold. **Facilities** Children welcome Children's menu Children's portions Play area Family room Garden Parking ☞

DITCHEAT
Map 4 ST63

The Manor House Inn

PICK OF THE PUBS

BA4 6RB ☎ 01749 860276
e-mail: landlord@manorhouseinn.co.uk
dir: *From Shepton Mallet take A371 towards Castle Cary, in 3m turn right to Ditcheat*

In the pretty village of Ditcheat, between Shepton Mallet and Castle Cary, this handsome red-brick, 17th-century free house belonged to the lord of the manor about 150 years ago when it was known as the White Hart. Convenient for the Royal Bath and West Showground and the East Somerset Steam Railway, it is also boasts views of the Mendips. Flagstone floors and warming log fires in winter add to the charm of the friendly bar, which serves local Butcombe Bitter and regular guest ales, Thatchers cider and up to nine wines by the glass. The seasonal menu may offer starters such as home-baked ratatouille with rich provençale sauce; and scallops in shells with lemon and lime dressing; followed by main courses of braised brisket of beef with creamy horseradish mash and rich Guinness sauce; or guinea fowl breast with spinach, fondant potato and Marsala sauce. Booking for meals may be required.

Open all day all wk Mon-Sat (Sun 12-9) **Bar Meals** L served Mon-Sat 12-2.30, Sun 12-5 D served Mon-Thu 6.30-9, Fri-Sat 6.30-9.30 Av main course £10 **Restaurant** L served Mon-Sat 12-2.30, Sun 12-5 D served Mon-Thu 6.30-9, Fri-Sat 6.30-9.30 Av 3 course à la carte fr £20 ⊕ FREE HOUSE ◀ Butcombe Bitter, Guest ales Ŏ Ashton Press, Thatchers & Thatchers Pear. ♥ 9 **Facilities** Children welcome Children's portions Garden Parking Wi-fi ☞ (notice required)

DULVERTON
Map 3 SS92

Woods Bar and Restaurant ◉

4 Bank Square TA22 9BU ☎ 01398 324007
e-mail: woodsdulverton@hotmail.com
dir: *From Tiverton take A396 N. At Machine Cross take B3222 to Dulverton. Establishment adjacent to church*

In the rural town of Dulverton on the edge of Exmoor, this is a bar and restaurant where food and drink are taken seriously, but without detriment to its friendly atmosphere. It's run by owners with a passion for wine – every bottle on the comprehensive list can be opened for a single glass. The cosy bar crackles with conversation while dishes of modern British cooking with a French accent leave the kitchen. Typical of these one AA-Rosette dishes are roast loin of Somerset pork with black pudding; and whole grilled plaice with turnip fondants. Booking for meals may be required.

Open all wk 11-3 6-11.30 (Sun 12-3 7-11) **Bar Meals** L served all wk 12-2 D served all wk 6-9.30 **Restaurant** L served all wk 12-2 D served all wk 7-9.30 ⊕ FREE HOUSE ◀ St Austell Tribute, HSD, Dartmoor Ŏ Thatchers, Healey's Cornish Rattler. **Facilities** Children welcome Children's menu Children's portions Garden

---

DUNSTER
Map 3 SS94

The Luttrell Arms

PICK OF THE PUBS

High St TA24 6SG ☎ 01643 821555
e-mail: info@luttrellarms.fsnet.co.uk
dir: *From A39 (Bridgwater to Minehead), left onto A396 to Dunster (2m from Minehead)*

Built in the 15th century this beguiling hotel was used as a guest house by the Abbots of Cleeve. Oozing history and charm, the building also served as a headquarters for Cromwell during his siege of Dunster Castle. Its open fires and oak beams make the bar a welcoming place in winter, while the garden in summer offers delightful views of the surrounding medieval village and Exmoor National Park. Pick up a pint of the guest ale or Thatchers Cheddar Valley cider and ponder your choice from the menu, which can be eaten in the bar, in the more formal restaurant, or outside. Flavoursome lunchtime sandwiches and baguettes include warm salt beef with dill pickles. Main courses range from a full rack of pork ribs in a smokey barbecue sauce served with coleslaw and chips to a deep-fried wedge of Somerset brie with a sweet chilli dip and mixed salad. Booking for meals may be required.

Open all wk 8am-11pm **Bar Meals** L served all wk 11.30-3, all day summer D served all wk 7-10 **Restaurant** L served Sun 12-3 D served all wk 7-10 ⊕ FREE HOUSE ◀ Exmoor Fox, Sharp's Doom Bar, Skinner's, Guest ale Ŏ Thatchers Cheddar Valley. **Facilities** Children welcome Children's menu Children's portions Family room Garden ☞

EAST COKER — Map 4 ST51

The Helyar Arms ★★★ INN

PICK OF THE PUBS

Moor Ln BA22 9JR ☎ 01935 862332
e-mail: info@helyar-arms.co.uk
dir: *3m from Yeovil. Take A57 or A30, follow East Coker signs*

In one of Somerset's most picturesque villages, parts of this lovely old pub date back to the mid-15th century. Named after Archdeacon Helyar, a chaplain to Queen Elizabeth I, the pub retains much of its original character with log fires in the charming old-world bar, where Butcombe and Exmoor ales are backed by Thatchers and Taunton Original ciders. The kitchen makes full use of local produce, including Somerset game and fish from the south Devon coast. There's plenty of choice, from sandwiches and lighter-bite starters such as pea and mint blini with Scottish smoked salmon and lime crème fraîche, followed by confit Creedy Carver duck leg with bubble-and-squeak and Madeira jus. Succulent local steaks can be cut to order and grilled, plus their steak sandwich has won awards. All puddings are home made and might include glazed lemon and lime tart. Comfortable accommodation is available.

Open all wk 11-3 6-11 Closed: 25 Dec eve **Bar Meals** L served all wk 12-2.30 D served all wk 6.30-9.30 **Restaurant** L served all wk 12-2.30 D served all wk 6.30-9.30 ⊕ PUNCH TAVERNS ◀ Butcombe Bitter, Sharp's Doom Bar, Exmoor Ŏ Thatchers Gold, Taunton Original. **Facilities** ❖ Children welcome Children's portions Family room Garden Parking Wi-fi ➡ (notice required) **Rooms** 6

EXFORD — Map 3 SS83

The Crown Hotel ★★★ HL ◉

PICK OF THE PUBS

TA24 7PP ☎ 01643 831554
e-mail: info@crownhotelexmoor.co.uk
dir: *From M5 junct 25 follow Taunton signs. Take A358 then B3224 via Wheddon Cross to Exford*

A family-run 17th-century purpose-built coaching inn on Exmoor; today's incarnation, a comfy mix of elegance and tradition, recalls the days of stalwart service. Right at the heart of the National Park, The Crown has three acres of its own grounds and a tributary of the infant River Exe flowing through its woodland. Not surprisingly it's popular with outdoor pursuit enthusiasts, but the cosy bar is very much the social heart of the village; many of the patrons enjoy the Exmoor Ales from Wiveliscombe just down the road. The AA-Rosette menu promises a meal of a higher order, especially with Exmoor's profuse organic produce on the doorstep and the kitchen's close attention to sustainable sources. The bar menu could tempt with steamed Cornish mussels, or seared Brixham scallops. Restaurant main courses could include slow-roasted belly of Somerset pork; or a trio of Heal Farm hand-made sausages. Round off with The Crown's 'infamous' sticky toffee pudding.

Open all day all wk 12-11 **Bar Meals** L served all wk 12-2.30 D served all wk 5.30-9.30 Av main course £14 **Restaurant** D served all wk 7-9 Fixed menu price fr £30 ⊕ FREE HOUSE ◀ Exmoor Ale & Gold, Guest ales Ŏ Thatchers Gold, Healey's Cornish Rattler. ₹ 10 **Facilities** ❖ Children welcome Children's portions Garden Parking Wi-fi ➡ **Rooms** 16

FAULKLAND — Map 4 ST75

Tuckers Grave

BA3 5XF ☎ 01373 834230
dir: *From Bath take A36 towards Warminster. Turn right on A366, through Norton St Philip towards Faulkland. In Radstock, left at x-rds, pub on left*

Tapped Butcombe ale and Cheddar Valley cider draw local aficionados to this unspoilt rural gem, which was threatened with permanent closure in 2011. Somerset's smallest pub has a tiny atmospheric bar with old settles but no counter, or music, television or jukebox either. Lunchtime sandwiches are available, and a large lawn with flower borders makes an attractive outdoor seating area, with the countryside adjacent. The 'grave' in the pub's name is the unmarked one of Edward Tucker, who hung himself here in 1747.

Open 11.30-3 6-11 (Sun 12-3 7-10.30) Closed: 25 Dec, Mon L ⊕ FREE HOUSE ◀ Fuller's London Pride, Butcombe Bitter Ŏ Thatchers Cheddar Valley. **Facilities** Children welcome Family room Garden Parking **Notes** ☺

FRESHFORD — Map 4 ST76

The Inn at Freshford

The Hill BA2 7WG ☎ 01225 722250
e-mail: landlord@theinnatfreshford.co.uk
dir: *1m from A36 between Beckington & Limpley Stoke*

Popular with walkers and their dogs, this family-run 15th-century inn in the Limpley Stoke valley is ideally placed for strolling along the nearby Kennet and Avon Canal. Extensive gardens host a beer festival in August, while at other times the delights of Wiltshire's Box Steam Brewery take their turn in the bar. Here wooden floors, original beams and log fires add tremendous charm. The varied and contemporary menu changes weekly, but choices might include devilled kidneys on toast with fried egg; pan-fried medallions of venison; and puddings such as pear and cranberry frangipane tart.

Open all wk Mar-Dec all day; Jan-Feb Mon-Thu 10.30-3 6-11 Fri-Sat all day Sun 10.30-6 **Bar Meals** L served Mon-Sat 12-2.30, Sun 12-5 D served Mon-Sat 6.30-9 Av main course £12.50 **Restaurant** Av 3 course à la carte fr £22 ⊕ FREE HOUSE ◀ Box Steam, Guest ale. ₹ 12 **Facilities** ❖ Children welcome Children's menu Children's portions Garden Beer festival Parking Wi-fi ➡ (notice required)

HASELBURY PLUCKNETT — Map 4 ST41

The White Horse at Haselbury

PICK OF THE PUBS

North St TA18 7RJ ☎ 01460 78873
e-mail: haselbury@btconnect.com
dir: *Just off A30 between Crewkerne & Yeovil on B3066*

This pub in the peaceful village of Haselbury Plucknett started life as a rope works and flax store, later becoming a cider house. Its interior feels fresh and warm, but retains the original character of exposed stone and open fires. Patrick and Jan Howard have run the hostelry for over ten years, with the explicit promise to provide the best food, service and value for money possible. This is confirmed by the early-bird set menu served early evening from Tuesday to Friday, when salmon filo tart could be followed by Somerset pork steak, and rounded off with banoffee cheesecake. The eclectic carte menu might include pork, chicken and apricot terrine; sweet and sour vegetable stirfry; Barnsley lamb chop with a mint-infused gravy; plus an excellent selection of fish specials. Enjoy your meal with a glass of Otter Ale, Burrow Hill cider or one of the ten wines by the glass.

Open 12-2.30 6.30-11 Closed: Sun eve, Mon **Bar Meals** L served Tue-Sun 12-2 D served Tue-Sat 6.30-9.30 **Restaurant** L served Tue-Sun 12-2 D served Tue-Sat 6.30-9.30 ⊕ FREE HOUSE ◀ Palmers Best Bitter, Otter Ale Ŏ Thatchers, Burrow Hill. ₹ 10 **Facilities** Children welcome Children's menu Children's portions Garden Parking

HINTON BLEWETT — Map 4 ST55

Ring O'Bells

BS39 5AN ☎ 01761 452239
e-mail: ringobells@butcombe.com
dir: *11m S of Bristol on A37 towards Wells. Turn right from either Clutton or Temple Cloud to Hinton Blewett*

On the edge of the Mendips, this 200-year-old inn describes itself as the 'archetypal village green pub' and offers good views of the Chew Valley. An all-year-round cosy atmosphere is boosted by a log fire in winter, and a wide choice of well-kept real ales. An extra dining area/function room was added a few years ago. There's always something going on, whether it's a tour of the brewery, pig racing night or fishing competitions. Good-value dishes include beer-battered haddock fillet with chips; pie of the day with mashed potato; or Ashton cider-braised pork belly and pork cheek on a black pudding mash. Baguettes, sandwiches, jacket potatoes and ploughman's are also available. Booking for meals may be required.

Open all wk Mon-Thu 12-3 5-11 (Fri-Sun all day) ⊕ BUTCOMBE ◀ Bitter & Gold, Fuller's London Pride, Guest ales Ŏ Ashton Press & Still. **Facilities** Children welcome Children's menu Children's portions Garden Parking Wi-fi

HINTON ST GEORGE · Map 4 ST41

The Lord Poulett Arms

PICK OF THE PUBS

See Pick of the Pubs on opposite page

HOLCOMBE · Map 4 ST64

The Holcombe Inn ★★★★★ INN ◉◉

Stratton Rd BA3 5EB ☎ 01761 232478
e-mail: bookings@holcombeinn.co.uk
web: www.holcombeinn.co.uk
dir: *On A367 to Stratton-on-the-Fosse, take concealed left turn opposite Downside Abbey signed Holcombe, take next right, pub 1.5m on left*

From the lovely gardens of this Grade II listed, 17th-century country inn you can see Downside Abbey and beyond. Full of log-fired, flagstone-floored charm, assisted by tucked-away corners with sofas, this is where Adam Dwyer's top-notch, local produce-inspired menu offers Goan monkfish curry; pan-roasted faggots; slow-roasted beef short rib; and aubergine and ricotta cannelloni. Otter and Bath ales, and Thatchers and The Orchard Pig real ciders are on tap, plenty of wines are by the glass, and some 'top shelf' whiskies are from defunct distilleries. Luxury accommodation incorporates limestone bathrooms with rain showers.

Open all wk 12-3 6-11 (Fri-Sun all day) **Bar Meals** L served all wk 12-2.30 D served all wk 6.30-9.30 **Restaurant** L served all wk 12-2.30 D served all wk 6.30-9.30 ⊕ FREE HOUSE ◐ Otter Ale, Bath Gem Ď Thatchers, The Orchard Pig. ♀ 17 **Facilities** Children welcome Children's menu Children's portions Garden Parking Wi-fi ▣ **Rooms** 7

HOLTON · Map 4 ST62

The Old Inn **NEW**

BA9 8AR ☎ 01963 32002
e-mail: carolyn@theoldinnrestaurant.co.uk
dir: *Telephone for directions*

A 400-year-old coaching inn just outside Wincanton, restored yet with its character preserved, and now winning awards for its food cooked over charcoal. Settle in front of the log fire with a pint of Butcombe or Thatchers cider, while choosing from the short menu of quality dishes. The pub's own farm just two miles up the road supplies much of the produce, particularly pork, beef and eggs; any unclaimed game from the day's shoot is prepared and delivered here too. Fresh fish is also a feature – look for Devon crab with fried duck egg; Brixham mussels; and whole lemon sole. Booking for meals may be required.

Open 12-3 6-11 (Sat 12-11 Sun 12-6) Closed: Sun eve **Bar Meals** L served Mon-Sat 12-2, Sun 12-4 D served Mon-Sat 6-9 **Restaurant** L served Mon-Sat 12-2, Sun 12-4 D served Mon-Sat 6-9.30 ⊕ FREE HOUSE ◐ Wadworth Boundary, Butcombe, Cheddar Ď Thatchers, Addlestones. **Facilities** Parking Wi-fi

HUISH EPISCOPI · Map 4 ST42

Rose & Crown

TA10 9QT ☎ 01458 250494
dir: *M5 junct 25, A358 towards Ilminster. Left onto A378. Huish Episcopi in 14m (1m from Langport). Pub near church in village*

Locked in a glorious time-warp, this 17th-century thatched inn, affectionately known as Eli's, (named after the current landlord's grandfather) has been in the Pittard family for over 140 years. Don't expect to find a bar counter, there's just a flagstoned taproom where customers congregate among the ale and farmhouse cider casks. In a side room are a sit-up-and-beg piano, time-honoured pub games, old photos and fairly basic furniture. Home-made food includes popular steak-and-ale pie, sandwiches, jacket potatoes or pork cobbler. Monthly folk-singing evenings are fun.

Open all wk 11.30-3 5.30-11 (Fri-Sat 11.30-11.30 Sun 12-10.30) **Bar Meals** L served all wk 12-2 D served Mon-Sat 5.30-7.30 Av main course £7 ⊕ FREE HOUSE ◐ Teignworthy Reel Ale, Glastonbury Mystery Tor, Hop Back Summer Lightning, Butcombe Bitter, Branscombe Vale Summa That Ď Burrow Hill. **Facilities** ♣ Children welcome Play area Family room Garden Parking ▣ (notice required) **Notes** ◉

ILCHESTER · Map 4 ST52

Ilchester Arms

The Square BA22 8LN ☎ 01935 840220
e-mail: mail@ilchesterarms.com
dir: *From A303 take A37 signed Ilchester/Yeovil, left at 2nd Ilchester sign. Hotel 100yds on right*

An elegant Georgian-fronted house with lots of character, this establishment was first licensed in 1686; attractive features include open fires and a lovely walled garden. Between 1962 and 1985 it was owned by the man who developed Ilchester cheese, and its association with good food continues: chef-proprietor Brendan McGee takes pride in producing modern British dishes such as breast of chicken filled with wild mushroom mousse; pan-fried medallions of pork tenderloin on a bed of baked sweet potato purée; and wild and forest mushroom casserole.

Open all day all wk 7am-11pm Closed: 26 Dec **Bar Meals** L served Mon-Sat 12-2.30 D served Mon-Sat 7-9 Av main course £10 **Restaurant** L served all wk 12-2.30 D served Mon-Sat 7-9 Fixed menu price fr £12.95 Av 3 course à la carte fr £22.95 ⊕ FREE HOUSE ◐ Flowers IPA, Butcombe, Bass, Local ales Ď Thatchers Gold & Pear. ♀ 14 **Facilities** Children welcome Children's menu Children's portions Play area Family room Garden Beer festival Parking Wi-fi ▣

ILMINSTER · Map 4 ST31

New Inn ★★★★ INN

Dowlish Wake TA19 0NZ ☎ 01460 52413
dir: *From Ilminster follow Kingstone & Perry's Cider Museum signs, in Dowlish Wake follow pub signs*

Deep in rural Somerset, this 350-year-old stone-built pub is tucked away in the village of Dowlish Wake, close to Perry's thatched Cider Mill and Museum. Inside are two bars with wood-burning stoves and a restaurant, where menus of home-cooked food capitalise on the quality and freshness of local produce. You could opt for a signature dish such as stilton chicken topped with a generous helping of smoked bacon; or stick to pub favourites such as West Country crab cakes with chips, salad and garlic mayonnaise. There are four guest rooms situated in the pleasant garden.

Open all wk 11.30-3 6-11 ⊕ FREE HOUSE ◐ Butcombe Bitter, Otter Ale & Bitter Ď Thatchers Gold. **Facilities** Children welcome Children's menu Children's portions Garden Parking Wi-fi **Rooms** 4

PICK OF THE PUBS

The Lord Poulett Arms

HINTON ST GEORGE　　Map 4 ST41

High St TA17 8SE ☎ 01460 73149
e-mail: reservations@lordpoulettarms.com
web: www.lordpoulettarms.com
dir: *2m N of Crewkerne, 1.5m S of A303*

There's a hint of France in the secluded garden of this handsome stone village inn; the click of boules drifts across tumbled spreads of lavender, whilst a wisteria-shrouded pergola is tucked in next to an old fives wall. Within, sheltered by a thatched roof, all is firmly English, with a marvellous magpie-mix of polished antique furniture sprinkled liberally across timeworn boarded floors, polished old flagstones and a vast fireplace where demi-trees burn for winter warmth, pumping out the heat into tastefully decorated rooms. The feel is unstuffy and relaxed, and glowing evening candles create a classy comfortable look. The inner sanctum bar is popular with locals and dispenses cracking pints of Branscombe Vale Brewery ales and West Country ciders straight from the cask. With such a classic interior you wouldn't expect a modern twist on food, yet the kitchen delivers an eclectic menu that bristles with imagination and local raw ingredients. Everything is handled with aplomb, from salt beef brisket on home-made rye bread with pickle, mustard and triple-cooked chips, to the spicy West Bay crab linguine on the appealing daily-changing lunchtime menu. In the

evening, perhaps start with roasted pumpkin soup with pumpkin seed pesto, then follow with chargrilled venison loin with confit walnuts, braised red cabbage, celeriac purée and port jus, or sea bass with smoked haddock and bacon hash and lemon butter sauce. Puddings include quince and walnut rice pudding, toffee apple crème brûlée with spiced shortbread, and a fine selection of West Country cheeses served with home-made chutney. There's a decent wine list, too, a summer weekend beer festival, and the set Sunday lunch menu is great value (two-course £16; three-course £19). Booking for meals may be required.

Open all day all wk 12-11 Closed: 26 Dec, 1 Jan **Bar Meals** L served all wk

12-2.30, bar menu 3-6.30 D served all wk 7-9.15 Av main course £13 **Restaurant** L served all wk 12-2.30, bar menu 3-6.30 D served all wk 7-9.15 Av 3 course à la carte fr £25 ⊕ FREE HOUSE ◀ Hop Back, Branscombe Vale, Otter, Dorset Ö Thatchers Gold, Burrow Hill. ♟ 14 **Facilities** Children welcome Children's portions Garden Beer festival Parking Wi-fi

---

KILVE	Map 3 ST14

The Hood Arms ★★★★ INN

TA5 1EA ☎ 01278 741210
e-mail: info@thehoodarms.com
web: www.thehoodarms.com
dir: *From M5 junct 23/24 follow A39 to Kilve. Village between Bridgwater & Minehead*

The Quantock Hills rise up behind this family-run 17th-century coaching inn, just an ammonite's throw from Kilve's fossil-rich beach. Real ales to enjoy in the beamed bar or in the garden include regulars from Otter and Palmers, guests Jurassic and Harbour Master, and local ciders, any of which will happily accompany a warm foccacia roll, jacket potato or something from the main menu, such as pheasant breasts in streaky bacon; osso buco; sea bass fillets with crayfish and dill risotto; or mixed squash with pequillo peppers. Specials are chalked up daily. There are 12 stylish guest rooms, some with four-poster beds. Booking for meals may be required.

Open all day all wk **Bar Meals** L served Mon-Sat 12-2, Sun 12-3 D served Mon-Sat 6-9, Sun 6-8 Av main course £12 **Restaurant** L served Mon-Sat 12-2, Sun 12-3 D served Mon-Sat 6-9, Sun 6-8 Av 3 course à la carte fr £25 ⊕ FREE HOUSE ◀ Otter Head, Palmers Copper Ale, Fuller's London Pride, Guinness, Guest ales ♂ Thatchers Gold. ₹ 12 **Facilities** ✿ Children welcome Children's portions Play area Family room Garden Parking Wi-fi **Rooms** 12

KINGSDON	Map 4 ST52

Kingsdon Inn

TA11 7LG ☎ 01935 840543
e-mail: enquiries@kingsdoninn.co.uk
dir: *A303 onto A372, right onto B3151, right into village, right at post office*

The three charmingly decorated, saggy-beamed rooms in this pretty thatched pub have a relaxed and friendly feel. Formerly a cider house, it is furnished with stripped pine tables and cushioned farmhouse chairs, and there are enough open fires to keep everywhere well warmed. Menus make excellent use of seasonal, local and often organic produce - a typical meal might include wild rabbit terrine with roast pistachio and orange followed by marinated haunch of venison with braised shallot, dauphinoise potato, roast sprouts, chestnut and port. Change of hands. Booking for meals may be required.

Open all wk 12-3 6-11 (Sun 12-3 7-10.30) **Bar Meals** L served all wk 12-2 D served all wk 6.30-9 Av main course £12 **Restaurant** Av 3 course à la carte fr £21 ⊕ FREE HOUSE/GAME BIRD INNS ◀ Sharp's Doom Bar, Butcombe, Otter ♂ Burrow Hill. ₹ 10 **Facilities** ✿ Children welcome Children's menu Children's portions Garden Parking Wi-fi ▦ (notice required)

LANGLEY MARSH	Map 3 ST02

The Three Horseshoes

TA4 2UL ☎ 01984 623763
e-mail: mark_jules96@hotmail.com
dir: *M5 junct 25 take B3227 to Wiveliscombe. Turn right up hill at lights. From square, turn right, follow Langley Marsh signs, pub in 1m*

Surrounded by beautiful countryside, this handsome 17th-century red sandstone pub has had only four landlords during the last century. It remains a free house, with traditional opening hours, a good choice of ales straight from the barrel and a warm, friendly welcome. The landlord's wife prepares home-cooked meals, incorporating local ingredients and vegetables from the pub garden. Popular with locals, walkers and cyclists, there's an enclosed garden with outdoor seating to enjoy in warmer weather.

Open 7pm-11pm (Sat 12-2.30 7-11 Sun 12-2.30) Closed: Sun eve, Mon, Tue-Fri L **Bar Meals** L served Sat-Sun 12-1.45 D served Tue-Sat 7-9 Av main course £9.95 ⊕ FREE HOUSE ◀ Otter Ale, Exmoor Ale, Cotleigh 25, St Austell Tribute ♂ Sheppy's. **Facilities** Children welcome Garden Parking

---

LANGPORT	Map 4 ST42

The Old Pound Inn

Aller TA10 0RA ☎ 01458 250469
e-mail: oldpoundinn@btconnect.com
dir: *2.5m N of Langport on A372. 8m SE of Bridgwater on A372*

With parts dating from 1571 and 1756, this cider house was originally known as the White Lion. It was renamed in 1980 to commemorate the fact that its garden was once the village pound. Plenty of historic character has been retained with oak beams and open fires. Locally it has a reputation as a friendly pub selling a range of real ales, whiskies, and good home-cooked food: Somerset beef features in burgers and prime steaks, while vegetarians will enjoy the Mediterranean vegetable tart. There is also a skittle alley.

Open all wk 11.30-2.30 5-11 (Sat 11.30-mdnt Sun 12-10) ⊕ FREE HOUSE ◀ St Austell Tribute, Sharp's, Cotleigh, Branscombe, Glastonbury, Teignworthy, Butcombe ♂ Thatchers Gold. **Facilities** Children welcome Children's menu Children's portions Garden Parking Wi-fi

---

LONG SUTTON	Map 4 ST42

The Devonshire Arms ★★★★ INN ◉

PICK OF THE PUBS

TA10 9LP ☎ 01458 241271
e-mail: mail@thedevonshirearms.com
dir: *Exit A303 at Podimore rdbt onto A372. Continue for 4m, left onto B3165*

Once a hunting lodge, this fine-looking, stone-built pub stands on a pretty village green. Beyond its imposing portico showing the Devonshire family crest, unexpectedly contemporary styling complements the large open fire and other original features. In the bar the handpump badges denote Bath SPA, Cheddar Potholer and two real ales from the Moor brewery at Pitney, and Burrow Hill and Olde Harry's farmhouse ciders. Based to a great extent on locally sourced produce, the daily-changing menu invites you to try smoked salmon platter with confit beetroot and lime; or organic sausages with mustard mash and grilled red onion for lunch; and duo of Dorset crab; Quantock duck confit; or beef chuck cooked in ruby port in the evening. You may also drink and dine in the courtyard, large walled garden or overlooking the green at the front. The en suite bedrooms have been designed in a fresh modern style. Booking for meals may be required.

Open all wk 12-3 6-11 Closed: 25-26 Dec, 1 Jan **Bar Meals** L served all wk 12-2.30 D served all wk 7-9.30 Av main course £12.95 **Restaurant** D served all wk 7-9.30 Av 3 course à la carte fr £27.50 ⊕ FREE HOUSE ◀ Bath SPA, Cheddar Potholer, Moor Revival & Merlin's Magic ♂ Burrow Hill, Olde Harry's. ₹ 10 **Facilities** Children welcome Children's menu Play area Garden Parking Wi-fi **Rooms** 9

Save on hotels. Book at **theAA.com/hotel**

SOMERSET 451 ENGLAND

LOWER LANGFORD Map 4 ST46

The Langford Inn ★★★★ INN

BS40 5BL ☎ **01934 863059**
e-mail: langfordinn@aol.com
web: www.langfordinn.com
dir: M5 junct 21, A370 towards Bristol. At Congresbury turn right onto B3133 to Lower Langford. Village on A38

Owned by Cardiff brewery Brains, this award-winning Mendip pub and restaurant also offers accommodation in converted 17th-century barns. Brains beers are joined by local Butcombe ales in the bar, which is adorned with local memorabilia. The daily-changing menu proffers traditional dishes such as cod and chips; fish pie; or lasagne, but sizzling stir-fried beef and oyster sauce or red Thai curry offer something different. There's a good choice of 24 wines by the glass to accompany your meal.

Open all day all wk **Bar Meals** L served 12-9 food served all day **Restaurant** L served 12-9 D served Fri-Sat 12-9.30 food served all day ⊕ BRAINS ◀ SA, Butcombe, Guinness Ö Thatchers Gold & Katy. ♈ 24
Facilities Children welcome Children's menu Children's portions Garden Parking Wi-fi ▥ **Rooms** 7

LOWER VOBSTER Map 4 ST74

Vobster Inn ★★★★ INN ◉◉

PICK OF THE PUBS

BA3 5RJ ☎ **01373 812920**
e-mail: info@vobsterinn.co.uk
dir: 4m W of Frome

Set in four acres of glorious countryside in the pretty hamlet of Lower Vobster, it is believed the inn originated in the 16th-century and was used by King James II and his army of Royalists prior to the battle of Sedgemoor in 1685. Raf and Peta Davila have been making their mark here ever since they arrived, a process that includes being awarded two AA Rosettes. The tapas menu offers roast Catalan tomato bread, Spanish meatballs, and grilled garlic mushrooms. For lunch, choose a filled baguette, omelette, ploughman's, or a steak. On the main menu you'll find rib-eye of beef with egg, fries and onion rings; pea, courgette and parmesan risotto; and roast

chicken breast with Catalan tomato sauce. All desserts are home-made, with choices like iced banana and praline parfait, and sticky toffee pudding. Special events like paella night and pudding night are popular. Three individually furnished bedrooms are available. Booking for meals may be required.

Open 12-3 6.30-11 Closed: Sun eve & Mon (ex BH L) **Bar Meals** L served Tue-Sun 12-2 D served Tue-Sat 6.30-9 Av main course £12 **Restaurant** L served Tue-Sun 12-2 D served Tue-Sat 6.30-9 Av 3 course à la carte fr £22.50 ⊕ FREE HOUSE ◀ Butcombe Blond, Bitter Ö Ashton Press, The Orchard Pig. ♈ 10 **Facilities** Children welcome Children's menu Children's portions Family room Garden Parking Wi-fi ▥ (notice required) **Rooms** 3

LUXBOROUGH Map 3 SS93

The Royal Oak Inn **NEW**

TA23 0SH ☎ **01984 640319**
e-mail: info@theroyaloakinnluxborough.co.uk
dir: B3228 follow signs to Luxborough

Nestling by a stream at the bottom of a steep-sided valley, deep in Exmoor's Brendon Hills, the thatched Royal Oak is a truly rural 14th-century inn. Locals, walkers and visitors mingle in the unspoilt main bar, all flagstoned or cobbled floors, low beams, old kitchen tables and uncontrived charm. Pints of Exmoor Gold are delivered through the hatchway, best enjoyed by the roaring fire in winter, or on the suntrap patio when the sun shines. Good country food is served in the bar and adjoining cosy dining rooms, with a typical autumn menu offering venison casserole, braised lamb shanks, and smoked haddock and chive risotto. Superb local walks. Booking for meals may be required.

Open all wk 12-2.30 6-11 (wknds & summer holidays all day) Closed: 25 Dec **Bar Meals** L served all wk 12-2 Av main course £7.95 **Restaurant** L served all wk 12-2 D served all wk 7-9 Av 3 course à la carte fr £30 ⊕ FREE HOUSE ◀ Exmoor Ale & Gold, St Austell Tribute Ö Thatchers Cheddar Valley. ♈ 15 **Facilities** ❖ Children welcome Children's menu Garden Parking ▥ (notice required)

MARTOCK Map 4 ST41

The Nag's Head Inn

East St TA12 6NF ☎ **01935 823432**
dir: Telephone for directions

This 16th-century former cider house is set in a lovely hamstone street in a picturesque south Somerset village. The large rear garden is partly walled and has pretty borders and trees. Ales, wines and home-cooked food are served in both the public and lounge/diner bars, where crib, dominoes, darts and pool are available. The pub also has a separate skittle alley. There's a poker evening on Thursday and Sunday evening is quiz night.

Open all wk 12-3 6-11 (Fri-Sun 12-12) **Bar Meals** L served all wk 12-2 D served Mon-Tue 6-8, Wed-Sat 6-9 Av main course £8.50 **Restaurant** L served all wk 12-2 D served Mon-Tue 6-8, Wed-Sat 6-9 Av 3 course à la

carte fr £18 ◀ Yeovil Ruby, Local guest ales Ö Thatchers Gold, Westons Stowford Press. **Facilities** Children welcome Children's menu Children's portions Family room Garden Parking

MILVERTON Map 3 ST12

The Globe ★★★ INN ◉

PICK OF THE PUBS

See Pick of the Pubs on page 452

MONTACUTE Map 4 ST41

The Kings Arms Inn

49 Bishopston TA15 6UU ☎ **01935 822255**
e-mail: info@thekingsarmsinn.co.uk
dir: From A303 onto A3088 at rdbt signed Montacute. Hotel in village centre

The hamstone-built, refurbished Kings Arms has stood in this picturesque village, at the foot of Mons Acutus (thus, supposedly, Montacute) since 1632. Along with cask ales and fine wines, you can eat in the fire-warmed bar or lounge, in the large beer garden, or in the restaurant. Starters include deep-fried whitebait, or duck and orange pâté, with main courses of chicken supreme with bacon, mushroom and shallot cream sauce; or battered cod and chips. A bar favourite is the succulent salt beef sandwich. There are plenty of events to watch out for. As we went to press, we learnt of a change of hands. Booking for meals may be required.

Open all wk 7.30am-11pm ⊕ GREENE KING ◀ Ruddles Best & IPA, Morland Old Speckled Hen Ö Aspall, Thatchers. **Facilities** Children welcome Garden Parking Wi-fi

---

The Phelips Arms

The Borough TA15 6XB ☎ **01935 822557**
e-mail: phelipsarmsmontacute@talktalk.net
dir: From Cartgate rdbt on A303 follow signs for Montacute

Overlooking the village square and close to the National Trust's historic Montacute House, this 17th-century listed hamstone building offers warm hospitality and wonderful home-cooked food. You'll find well-kept Palmers beers and Thatchers cider behind the bar, whilst meals are freshly prepared using the best local and West Country produce. The menu features dishes such as pan-fried sea bass with cashew, spinach and rocket pesto; and stuffed belly pork with pear and apple jus. The beautiful walled garden is an ideal place to relax on a summer's day. Booking for meals may be required.

Open all wk 12-2.30 6-11 Closed: 25 Dec **Bar Meals** L served all wk 12-2 D served all wk 6.30-9 Av main course £5-£12 **Restaurant** L served all wk 12-2 D served all wk 6.30-9 ⊕ PALMERS ◀ Best Bitter, 200, Copper Ale Ö Thatchers Gold. ♈ 10 **Facilities** ❖ Children welcome Children's menu Children's portions Garden Parking Wi-fi ▥

PICK OF THE PUBS

The Globe ★★★INN ❀

MILVERTON Map 3 ST12

Fore St TA4 1JX ☎ **01823 400534**
e-mail: info@theglobemilverton.co.uk
web: www.theglobemilverton.co.uk
dir: *On B3187*

The Globe is a free house that is clearly very much part of the village and local community, thanks to husband and wife team, Mark and Adele Tarry. They've been presiding over this old coaching inn for over six years, its clean-lined, contemporary interior sitting comfortably within the Grade II listed structure. Local artists display their paintings on the walls of the restaurant and bar area, whilst a wood-burning stove and a sun terrace provide for all seasons. One of Mark's passions is local ales; Exmoor and Otter are the regulars, while guest ales come from other Somerset brewers. Sheppy's local cider and English wines are also available. An extensive menu ranges from traditional steak-and-kidney pie and home-made burgers at lunchtime, to the main menu with slow-roasted Gloucester Old Spot belly pork, and a wide selection of fish specials, among them sea trout, scallops and River Fowey mussels. Everything is home made, including the bread. For a quick and easy lunch option there are baguettes and ciabattas with fillings like Parma ham, brie and rocket; and roasted vegetables with feta cheese. The kitchen uses West Country produce extensively in the production of sea bass fillets with chorizo pesto and rocket; chargrilled rib-eye steak with brandy and green peppercorn sauce and home-made fat chips; roasted Barbary duck breast with celeriac purée and spiced orange sauce; and wild mushroom and gruyère cheese tart with red onion jam. Home-made (with a little help from Mark's mum) desserts include classic crème brûlée; mascarpone and Amaretto tiramisù; and lemon tart with raspberry cream. There is a carefully thought-out children's menu too. Stay over in one of the comfortable bedrooms because Milverton is a good base from which to explore the Quantock Hills and Exmoor. Booking for meals may be required.

Open 12-3 6-11 (Fri-Sat 12-3 6-11.30)
Closed: Sun eve, Mon L 🛢 FREE HOUSE
🍺 Exmoor Ale, Butcombe Bitter, Otter Bitter, Guest ales 🍏 Sheppy's.
Facilities Children welcome Children's menu Parking Wi-fi **Rooms** 3

Save on hotels. Book at theAA.com/hotel

SOMERSET 453 ENGLAND

NORTH CURRY — Map 4 ST32

The Bird in Hand

1 Queen Square TA3 6LT ☎ 01823 490248
dir: *M5 junct 25, A358 towards Ilminster, left onto A378 towards Langport. Left to North Curry*

Cheerful staff provide a warm welcome to this friendly 300-year-old village inn, which boasts large inglenook fireplaces, flagstone floors, exposed beams and studwork. The place is very atmospheric at night by candlelight, and the daily-changing blackboard menus feature local produce, including game casserole, curries and bubble-and-squeak with sausage, bacon, eggs and mushrooms. The à la carte menu always has three or four fresh fish dishes, steaks and home-made desserts. Booking for meals may be required.

Open all wk 12-3 6-11 **Bar Meals** L served Mon-Sat 12-2, Sun 12-3 D served Sun-Thu 6.45-9, Fri-Sat 7-9.30 **Restaurant** L served Mon-Sat 12-2, Sun 12-3 D served Sun-Thu 6.45-9, Fri-Sat 7-9.30 ⊕ FREE HOUSE ◀ Otter Bitter & Ale, Exmoor Gold, Cotleigh Barn Owl, Butcombe Gold, Teignworthy Old Moggie, Hop Back Ö Parsons Choice, Ashton Press. ▾ 9 **Facilities** ❖ Children welcome Children's portions Parking Wi-fi

NORTON ST PHILIP — Map 4 ST75

George Inn

PICK OF THE PUBS

See Pick of the Pubs on page 454

NUNNEY — Map 4 ST74

The George at Nunney

Church St BA11 4LW ☎ 01373 836458
e-mail: info@thegeorgeatnunney.co.uk
dir: *0.5m N off A361, Frome/Shepton Mallet*

Set in a classic English village complete with moated castle ruins, this rambling inn has established itself as the hub of the village's lively community. Taken over by the Hedges family in spring 2012, it serves a choice of real ales, ciders and imported beers in the comfortable beamed bar. Lunch and dinner menus change every few weeks and the specials change weekly. A typical selection could comprise goat's cheese fritters, followed by paprika-infused chicken breast, bacon crisps and garlic and ginger cousous, and a banoffee tower to finish. Booking for meals may be required.

Open all wk 12-3 6-11 (Sun 7-10.30) ⊕ FREE HOUSE ◀ Wadworth 6X, Wychwood Hobgoblin Ö Westons Stowford Press. **Facilities** Garden Parking Wi-fi

OAKHILL — Map 4 ST64

The Oakhill Inn ★★★★ INN ◉

PICK OF THE PUBS

See Pick of the Pubs on page 455

OVER STRATTON — Map 4 ST41

The Royal Oak

TA13 5LQ ☎ 01460 240906
e-mail: info@the-royal-oak.net
dir: *Exit A303 at Hayes End rdbt (South Petherton). 1st left after Esso garage signed Over Stratton*

With X-shaped tie-bar ends securing its aged hamstone walls, thatched roof, blackened beams, flagstones, log fires, old church pews and settles, this 17th-century former farmhouse certainly looks like a textbook example of an English country pub. The real ales are from Hall & Woodhouse in Blandford. With different prices for small or normal appetites, home-cooked dishes on the menu range from Moroccan spiced vegetable curry, via pan-fried fillets of sea bass, to chargrilled sirloin steak. Added attractions are the beer garden, children's play area and barbecue. Booking for meals may be required.

Open Tue-Sun Closed: Mon **Bar Meals** L served Tue-Sun 12-2 D served Tue-Sun 6-9 **Restaurant** L served Tue-Sun 12-2 D served Tue-Sun 6-9 ⊕ HALL & WOODHOUSE ◀ Badger Dorset Best, Tanglefoot, K&B Sussex. **Facilities** ❖ Children welcome Children's menu Children's portions Play area Family room Garden Parking

PITNEY — Map 4 ST42

The Halfway House

TA10 9AB ☎ 01458 252513
dir: *On B3153, 2m from Langport & Somerton*

This pub is largely dedicated to the promotion of real ale, with a beer festival in March, and always six to ten ales available in tip-top condition, including Moor Northern Star and Teignworthy. This delightfully old fashioned rural pub has three homely rooms boasting open fires, books and games, but no music or electronic games. Home-cooked rustic food made using local ingredients (except Sundays when it is too busy with drinkers) include soups, local sausages, sandwiches and a good selection of curries and casseroles.

Open all wk 11.30-3 5.30-11 (Fri-Sat 11.30-3 5.30-12 Sun all day) **Bar Meals** L served Mon-Sat 12-2.30, Sun 2-5 D served Mon-Sat 7-9.30 Av main course £7.95 ⊕ FREE HOUSE ◀ Butcombe Bitter, Otter Ale, Hop Back Summer Lightning, Moor Northern Star, Teignworthy Ö Kingstone Black, Burrow Hill, Wilkins Farmhouse. ▾ 8 **Facilities** ❖ Children welcome Children's portions Play area Garden Beer festival Parking Wi-fi

PORLOCK — Map 3 SS84

The Bottom Ship

Porlock Weir TA24 8PB ☎ 01643 863288
e-mail: enquiries@shipinnporlockweir.co.uk
dir: *Telephone for directions*

Enjoy superb views across the Bristol Channel to south Wales from the suntrap terrace at this thatched waterside pub, best enjoyed following a coast path stroll. Exmoor ales are the mainstay in the beamed bar, with a couple of

real ciders (Cheddar Valley and Pear and Apple Rattlers) also on tap. Home-made food using fresh local produce includes most pub favourites, from deep-fried whitebait to steak-and-ale pie. Children have their own menu and dogs are welcome. Don't miss the music and ale festival in early July.

Open all day all wk **Bar Meals** L served all wk 12-3 D served all wk 5.30-8.30 ⊕ FREE HOUSE ◀ Exmoor Ale & Stag, Otter Bright, St Austell Proper Job Ö Healey's Pear & Cornish Rattler, Thatchers Cheddar Valley. **Facilities** ❖ Children welcome Children's menu Children's portions Garden Beer festival Parking ▭

The Ship Inn

High St TA24 8QD ☎ 01643 862507
e-mail: enquiries@shipinnporlock.co.uk
dir: *A358 to Williton, then A39 to Porlock. 6m from Minehead*

Reputedly one of the oldest inns on Exmoor, this 13th-century free house stands at the foot of Porlock's notorious hill, where Exmoor tumbles into the sea. In the past it's attracted the sinister attentions of Nelson's press gang, but now its thatched roof and traditional interior provide a more welcoming atmosphere. Regularly changing menus include an appealing selection of hot and cold baguettes, and hot dishes from sausage and mash to guinea fowl breast with crispy bacon and red wine jus. There's also a beer garden and children's play area. Booking for meals may be required.

Open all day all wk **Bar Meals** L served all wk 12-2.30 D served all wk 6-9 **Restaurant** L served all wk 12-2.30 D served all wk 6-9 ⊕ FREE HOUSE ◀ St Austell Tribute & Proper Job, Exmoor Ale, Cotleigh Tawny Owl, Otter Ö Thatchers & Cheddar Valley. **Facilities** ❖ Children welcome Children's menu Children's portions Play area Garden Parking Wi-fi ▭

RODE — Map 4 ST85

The Mill at Rode

BA11 6AG ☎ 01373 831100
e-mail: info@themillatrode.co.uk
dir: *6m S of Bath*

A converted grist mill on the banks of the beautiful River Frome, this magnificent multi-storeyed Georgian building sits in its own landscaped grounds in the rural hinterland south of Bath. The dining-terrace overhangs the rushing waters, a great location in which to indulge in local beers or select from the West Country-based menu; maybe terrine of local game with apple chutney and warm toast, followed by fillets of Cornish plaice stuffed with mushrooms and spinach and topped with a vintage cheddar sauce. A children's playroom offers grown-ups the chance of escape and a peaceful chinwag. Booking for meals may be required.

Open all day all wk 12-11 Closed: 25 Dec ⊕ FREE HOUSE ◀ Butcombe Bitter, Marston's Pedigree, Guinness, Guest ales Ö Black Rat, Ashton Press. **Facilities** Children welcome Children's menu Children's portions Play area Family room Garden Parking Wi-fi

PICK OF THE PUBS

George Inn

NORTON ST PHILIP Map 4 ST75

High St BA2 7LH ☎ 01373 834224
e-mail: georgeinn@wadworth.co.uk
web: www.georgeinnsp.co.uk
dir: *A36 from Bath to Warminster, 6m,*
right onto A366 to Radstock, village 1m

Nearly eight centuries old, this is a truly remarkable building. Grade I listed and with an international reputation, it was built, so historians believe, in 1223 as temporary accommodation for Carthusian monks while they constructed Hinton Priory two miles away. In 1397, the Prior granted it a licence to sell ale, making it one of the country's oldest continuously licensed inns. Originally only one storey, the large upper floor was added to provide extra accommodation and storage space as Norton developed into a thriving wool trade centre. When Wadworth, the Devizes brewery, carried out a major restoration, it uncovered medieval wall paintings, which are now preserved, as are other interesting features like the stone-tiled roof, massive doorway, turreted staircase, cobbled courtyard and open-air gallery leading to the bedrooms. At one time, a five-foot high tunnel led from the George to the Priory and although now blocked, a few years back someone managed to trace it all the way with a divining rod. There are two menus, the carte and Monmouth's, the former typically offering roasted monkfish wrapped in Parma ham with piccalilli; chicken filled with roasted pepper, spinach and feta on a bed of roasted

aubergine; and maybe Serbian gibanica, a flaky pastry ensemble of apple, feta, cider and grapes. Monmouth's is easier on the wallet, with most dishes around the £10 mark, including masala-style chicken curry with pilau rice; beer-battered fish and chips with mint and pea purée; and steak, mushroom and Wadworth 6X ale pie, with shortcrust pastry. For a lighter option, a selection of ciabattas is served until 6pm. Among the wines are a white and a red from a'Beckett's Vineyard, near Devizes. Outside, you can eat in the ancient and atmospheric courtyard and from the beer garden watch cricket on the Mead. Change of hands. Booking for meals may be required.

Open all day all wk 11.30-11 (Sun 12-10.30) **Bar Meals** L served Mon-Thu

11.30-9, Fri-Sat 11.30-9.30, Sun 12-9 food served all day **Restaurant** L served Mon-Thu 11.30-9, Fri-Sat 11.30-9.30, Sun 12-9 food served all day ⊕ WADWORTH ◀ 6X, Henry's Original IPA, Bishop's Tipple Ö Westons Stowford Press, Thatchers Gold. ☐
Facilities Children welcome Children's menu Children's portions Play area ❖ Garden Parking Wi-fi 🚌

PICK OF THE PUBS

The Oakhill Inn ★★★★INN ❀

OAKHILL Map 4 ST64

Fosse Rd BA3 5HU ☎ 01749 840442
e-mail: info@theoakhillinn.com
web: www.theoakhillinn.com
dir: *On A367 between Stratton-on-the-Fosse & Shepton Mallet*

One of the deep duck-egg blue walls in this spacious, attractively decorated and furnished inn features an eye-catching display of over 20 clocks. Assorted rugs cover the floors, and bar stools covered with the same blue material line the bar, where homage is paid to the village's former brewing tradition by at least three rotating real ales from local micro-breweries, including the new Devilfish in nearby Hemington. Alongside these are long-term incumbents from Palmers and Butcombe, various draught lagers and three draught local farmhouse ciders, including Lilley's Pheasant Plucker. Head chef Neil Creese – a man who insists that his menus must conform to free-range and organic principles – has won national recognition for his cooking; his mantra "local food tastes better" means that he sources dairy products and free-range eggs from a farm less than three miles away, that from the car park you can see the herd supplying his organic beef, and that free-range chicken and guinea fowl need only make a short journey from Bradford-on-Avon. Of necessity, the daily deliveries of fish and seafood come from further away in

Cornwall. So settle back with a seasonal menu and go for a three-course lunch or dinner of deep-fried tiger prawns with salad; roast duck breast, pink fir apple potatoes, greens and Seville orange sauce; or fillets of plaice with new potatoes and leek and mussel sauce; and hot chocolate pot and cream. The bar menu offers a good choice of steaks, as well as beefburger with tomato and pear relish, chips and salad; Montgomery cheddar ploughman's; and chargrilled chicken and mayonnaise sandwich. If the weather is fine wander into the landscaped garden to have a look at the village church and the gently undulating Mendip Hills. The inn keeps a collection of Ordnance Survey maps for walking and cycling enthusiasts. Booking for meals may be required.

Open all wk Mon-Fri 12-3 5-11 (Sat-Sun 12-12) **Bar Meals** L served all wk 12-3 D served all wk 6-9 **Restaurant** L served all wk 12-3 D served all wk 6-9 🍴 FREE HOUSE ◀ Butcombe Bitter, Devilfish Devil Best, Palmers ♨ The Orchard Pig, Pheasant Plucker. ☿ **Facilities** Children welcome Children's menu Children's portions ✿ Garden Parking Wi-fi 🚌 (notice required) **Rooms** 5

RUDGE   Map 4 ST85

The Full Moon at Rudge ★★★ INN

BA11 2QF ☎ **01373 830936**
e-mail: info@thefullmoon.co.uk
dir: *From A36 (Bath to Warminster road) follow Rudge signs*

Just seven miles from Longleat, this venerable 16th-century old cider house is located at the crossing of two old drove roads and enjoys great views of Westbury White Horse. Sympathetically updated, the pub retains its stone-floored rooms furnished with scrubbed tables. The modern menus change to reflect the seasons, with Barnsley lamb chop with rosemary jus or Somerset sirloin steak being examples of the fare. There is a large garden with play area, and 17 comfortable bedrooms for those wishing to stay longer.

Open all day all wk 11.30-11 (Sun 12-10.30)
◀ Butcombe Bitter, Fuller's London Pride, Guest ale ♖ Thatchers Cheddar Valley, Rich's Farmhouse.
Facilities Children welcome Children's menu Play area Garden Parking Wi-fi **Rooms** 17

SHEPTON BEAUCHAMP   Map 4 ST41

Duke of York

North St TA19 0LW ☎ **01460 240314**
e-mail: sheptonduke@tiscali.co.uk
dir: *M5 junct 25 Taunton or A303*

In March 2012 husband and wife team Paul and Hayley Rowlands, along with Purdy the 'famous' pub dog, celebrated their tenth anniversary at the helm of this 17th-century free house. The bar stocks good West Country ales and local ciders, and the restaurant's short menu pleases locals and tourists alike. Chargrilled steaks are a staple – two evenings a week are devoted to them. Lighter options are pie of the day or burgers, all home-made. Gardens, a skittle alley, and a beer festival in September round off the attractions of this homely pub. Booking for meals may be required.

Open all day 12-12 (Mon 5.30-11) Closed: Mon L **Bar Meals** L served Tue-Sun 12-2 D served Tue-Sat 6.45-9 Av main course £9.50 **Restaurant** L served Sun 12-2.30 D served Tue-Sat 6.45-9 ⊕ FREE HOUSE ◀ Teignworthy Reel Ale, Otter Ale ♖ Thatchers Gold. ♟ 9
Facilities Children welcome Children's menu Children's portions Family room Garden Beer festival Parking Wi-fi 🚐

SHEPTON MALLET   Map 4 ST64

The Three Horseshoes Inn ★★★★ INN

PICK OF THE PUBS

Batcombe BA4 6HE ☎ **01749 850359**
e-mail: info@thethreehorseshoesinn.com
dir: *Take A359 from Frome to Bruton. Batcombe signed on right. Pub by church*

This honey-coloured stone inn enjoys a peaceful position squirrelled away in the very rural Batcombe Vale, and the lovely rear garden overlooks the old parish church. The long and low-ceilinged main bar has exposed stripped beams, a huge stone inglenook with log fire, and is warmly and tastefully decorated, with pale blue walls hung with old paintings, creating a homely atmosphere. From gleaming handpumps on the bar come foaming pints of locally brewed Cheddar Potholer. Menus draw on the wealth of fresh seasonal produce available locally, with lunches taking in cumin spiced lamb salad with new potatoes and fine beans, or Somerset ham and local eggs with chips. Choice at dinner extends to pan-fried bream with fennel and creamed leeks, or a more classic rib-eye steak and chips. Desserts include boozy orange parfait or a board of local cheeses. There are three stylishly decorated letting bedrooms available. Booking for meals may be required.

Open all wk Mon-Fri 11-3 6-11 (Sat 11-11 Sun 12-10.30) ⊕ FREE HOUSE ◀ Butcombe Bitter, Moor Revival, Cheddar Potholer ♖ The Orchard Pig, Ashton Press.
Facilities Children welcome Children's menu Children's portions Garden Parking Wi-fi **Rooms** 3

The Waggon and Horses

PICK OF THE PUBS

Frome Rd, Doulting Beacon BA4 4LA ☎ **01749 880302**
e-mail: waggon.horses09@googlemail.com
dir: *1.5m N of Shepton Mallet at x-roads with Old Wells-Frome road, 1m off A37*

A pretty, whitewashed building with leaded windows, this friendly family-run, 18th-century coaching inn sits high in the Mendips with views over Glastonbury. There is a large enclosed garden where drinks and meals can be enjoyed outside in fine weather. A varying range of local real beers and ciders are served alongside traditional home-cooked dishes. You could begin with chicken liver pâté and toast or crab cakes with home-made dill sauce; followed by mushroom and spinach lasagne with chips and garlic bread; chicken breast in a tarragon sauce; or steak-and-ale pie. Baguettes, jacket potatoes, ploughman's and other light bites are available at

lunchtime. Children are most welcome, and the building is accessible for wheelchairs. Other facilities include the skittle alley and a function room, plus there are bike nights and Italian chefs' nights.

Open all wk Mon-Sat 12-2.30 6-11 (Sun 12-3 6-10) **Bar Meals** L served Mon-Sat 12-2.30, Sun 12-3 D served Mon-Sat 6-9, Sun 6-8 **Restaurant** L served Mon-Sat 12-2.30, Sun 12-3 D served Mon-Sat 6-9, Sun 6-8 ⊕ FREE HOUSE ◀ Wadworth 6X, Butcombe ♖ Wilkins Farmhouse, Ashton Press. **Facilities** Children welcome Children's menu Children's portions Garden Parking 🚐

SHEPTON MONTAGUE   Map 4 ST63

The Montague Inn

PICK OF THE PUBS

BA9 8JW ☎ **01749 813213**
e-mail: themontagueinn@aol.com
dir: *From Wincanton & Castle Cary turn right off A371*

Nestling in rolling unspoilt Somerset countryside on the edge of sleepy Shepton Montague, this award-winning 18th-century stone-built village inn is hidden down winding country lanes close to Castle Cary. Tastefully decorated throughout, with the homely bar featuring old dark pine and an open log fire, and a cosy, yellow-painted dining room, the focus and draw of this rural dining pub is the careful sourcing of local foods from artisan producers and the kitchen's imaginative seasonal menus. Expect to find cask ales from Bath Ales, salads, fruit and vegetables from local farms, and free-range eggs from Blackacre Farm. This translates to lunchtime dishes like duck liver parfait and orange jelly; smoked haddock soufflé; and devilled chicken livers on toast. Evening specials might include rump of lamb with roasted garlic and parsley mash, ending with strawberry parfait and berry compôte. The attractive rear terrace with rural views is perfect for summer sipping. Families are most welcome. Booking for meals may be required.

Open 12-3 6-11.30 Closed: Sun eve ⊕ FREE HOUSE ◀ Wadworth 6X, Camerons Strongarm, Bath, Guest ales ♖ Thatchers Gold, Addlestones, Local Cider.
Facilities Children welcome Children's portions Family room Garden Parking Wi-fi

STANTON WICK   Map 4 ST66

The Carpenters Arms

PICK OF THE PUBS

See Pick of the Pubs on opposite page

PICK OF THE PUBS

The Carpenters Arms

STANTON WICK　　　　　Map 4 ST66

BS39 4BX ☎ 01761 490202
e-mail: carpenters@buccaneer.co.uk
web: www.the-carpenters-arms.co.uk
dir: *From A37 at Chelwood rdbt take A368 signed Bishop Sutton. Right to Stanton Wick*

Overlooking the Chew Valley, this charming stone-built free house is well placed, especially if you want to visit Bath, Bristol or the delightful cathedral city of Wells. Actually, it's well placed whatever your plans, even if you just want a quick lunchtime pint of Butcombe Bitter, Sharp's Doom Bar or Otter Ale. Converted from a row of miners' cottages, the inn has become a popular retreat over the years for anyone appreciating good food and fine wines. Outside you'll find an attractively landscaped patio, while behind the flower-bedecked façade low beams, old pews and squashy sofas offer a relaxed welcome in the rustic bar. Logs stacked neatly from floor to ceiling frame the large fireplace and add to the appeal of the chatty, music-free atmosphere. The extensive menus are changed regularly to make the best of local and seasonal produce. From the many possibilities are chilli con carne with rice; pan-roasted fillet of sea bass with crushed new potatoes, spinach, and crayfish and chive cream sauce; steak, mushroom and red wine in cheese suet pastry with mash and peas; Thai chicken curry with coriander rice; and linguine with sun-blushed tomato, garlic, roasted red pepper, and rocket and pesto dressing. And then there are the specials: pan-fried pork belly with creamed potato, braised cabbage and grain mustard sauce; and pan-fried duck breast with crisp vegetable stirfry, noodles and plum and apple sauce. Not to mention the delicious home-made desserts would be unforgiveable, especially the glazed pannetone bread-and-butter pudding, and the treacle tart with lemon curd ice cream. Baguettes filled with brie and red onion marmalade; smoked salmon and citrus mayonnaise; or honey-roast ham, rocket and tomato chutney are snack options. The extensive wine list combines New and Old World favourites. Booking for meals may be required.

Open all day all wk 11-11 (Sun 12-10.30) Closed: 25-26 Dec **Bar Meals** L served Mon-Sat 12-2.30, Sun 12-9 D served Mon-Thu 6-9.30, Fri-Sat 6-10, Sun 12-9 **Restaurant** L served Mon-Sat 12-2.30, Sun 12-9 D served Mon-Thu 6-9.30, Fri-Sat 6-10, Sun 12-9 ⊕ FREE HOUSE ◀ Butcombe Bitter, Sharp's Doom Bar, Otter Ale. ☘ 10 **Facilities** Children welcome Children's menu Children's portions Garden Parking 🚌

STOGUMBER · Map 3 ST03

The White Horse

High St TA4 3TA ☎ 01984 656277

e-mail: info@whitehorsestogumber.co.uk
dir: *From Taunton take A358 to Minehead. In 8m left to Stogumber, 2m into village centre. Right at T-junct & right again. Pub opp church*

Under different ownership since July 2011, this traditional free house on the edge of the Quantock Hills is ideally situated for walkers and visitors to the nearby West Somerset Steam Railway. Formerly the village's Market Hall and Reading Room, the dining room is now the place to study a menu of home-cooked dishes such as Caribbean pork with apple, mango and ginger; steak-and-kidney pudding; or local gammon steak, egg and chips. Enjoy local ales such as Otter Bitter in the courtyard garden.

Open all day all wk **Bar Meals** L served all wk 12-2 D served all wk 7-9 Av main course £8.50 **Restaurant** L served all wk 12-2 D served all wk 7-9 Av 3 course à la carte fr £18.50 ⊞ FREE HOUSE ◀ St Austell Proper Job, Otter Bitter, Local ale, Guest ales Ò Thatchers Cheddar Valley, Healey's Cornish Rattler. **Facilities** ✿ Children welcome Children's menu Family room Garden Parking ⊞ (notice required)

STOKE ST GREGORY · Map 4 ST32

Rose & Crown

Woodhill TA3 6EW ☎ 01823 490296

e-mail: info@browningpubs.com
dir: *M5 junct 25, A358 towards Langport, left at Thornfalcon, left again, follow signs to Stoke St Gregory*

Stephen and Richard Browning run this Somerset Levels pub, having taken over from their parents, who came here in 1979. The brothers are also the chefs, responsible for its well-deserved reputation for good food, while partners Sally and Leonie look after front of house. Classic pub dishes appear alongside the more innovative crispy pressed Somerset pork belly with spiced apple and gravy; sizzling tandoori chicken with onions and sweet bell peppers; and creamy vegetable Stroganoff with basmati rice. West County real ales aplenty and farmhouse ciders in the bar. Booking for meals may be required.

Open all wk 11-3 6-11 **Bar Meals** L served all wk 12-2 D served all wk 7-9 Av main course £7.95 **Restaurant** L served all wk 12-2 D served all wk 7-9 Fixed menu price fr £10.95 Av 3 course à la carte fr £22.95 ⊞ FREE HOUSE ◀ Exmoor Ale, Fox & Stag, Otter Ale, Butcombe, Wickwar, Guest ales Ò Thatchers Gold, Local cider. **Facilities** ✿ Children welcome Children's menu Children's portions Garden Parking Wi-fi ⊞ (notice required)

STREET · Map 4 ST43

The Two Brewers ★★★★ INN

38 Leigh Rd BA16 0HB ☎ 01458 442421

e-mail: richard@thetwobrewers.co.uk
dir: *In town centre*

'A country pub in a town', this stone inn successfully achieves a balance between town local and country pub. Behind the bar, which serves cask-conditioned ales like Courage Best bitter, is a collection of unusual pump-clips. Both alley skittles and boules in the enclosed garden are taken seriously. Guests staying over in the converted stable accommodation may plan visits to nearby Glastonbury Tor over a meal of freshly home-cooked goodies, such as the crispy vegetable platter; salmon goujons; succulent rump steak; or cheese and bacon toastie. Children's portions are available.

Open all wk Mon-Sat 11-3 6-11 (Sun 11.30-3 6-10.30) Closed: 25-26 Dec **Bar Meals** L served all wk 12-2 D served all wk 6-9 Av main course £7 **Restaurant** L served all wk 12-2 D served all wk 6-9 Av 3 course à la carte fr £14 ⊞ FREE HOUSE ◀ St Austell Tribute, Courage Best, 2 Guest ales Ò Westons Stowford Press. **Facilities** Children welcome Children's menu Children's portions Garden Parking Wi-fi **Rooms** 3

TAUNTON · Map 4 ST22

The Hatch Inn

Village Rd, Hatch Beauchamp TA3 6SG ☎ 01823 480245

e-mail: lizrx8@hotmail.co.uk
dir: *M5 junct 25, S on A358 for 3m. Left to Hatch Beauchamp, pub in 1m*

Surrounded by splendid Somerset countryside, this family-run pub dates back to the mid-1800s and has its share of ghostly occupants. The inn prides itself on its friendly atmosphere and the quality of its wines and beers – there are always four real ales available, rotating regularly via local brewers. Wholesome home-made food is served, prepared from local produce, with a good choice of snacks and meals served in the both the bar and restaurant. There's a roast on Sunday, and a children's menu is also offered.

Open all day all wk 12-3 5-11 (Thu 12-3 5-12 Fri-Sat 12-12 Sun 12-10.30) **Bar Meals** L served all wk 12-3 D served all wk 6-9 Av main course £8.95 **Restaurant** L served all wk 12-3 D served all wk 6-9 ⊞ FREE HOUSE ◀ Local guest ales Ò Lilley's Pigs Swill & Crazy Goat. ☶ 10 **Facilities** ✿ Children welcome Children's menu Children's portions Parking Wi-fi ⊞ (notice required)

TINTINHULL · Map 4 ST41

The Crown and Victoria Inn ★★★★ INN ⊛

14 Farm St BA22 8PZ ☎ 01935 823341

e-mail: info@thecrownandvictoria.co.uk
dir: *Next to the National Trust gardens at Tintinhull House*

This 300-year-old inn occupies an enviable rural setting amidst sweeping willow trees. Now a friendly family-orientated pub with a peaceful beer garden, Mark Hilyard and Isabel Thomas have worked wonders since taking it over in 2006. Along with award-winning beers and a good selection of wines, the locally sourced food, much of it organic and free-range, has built up a following of its own and has been awarded an AA Rosette. Typical dishes on the extensive menu might include Yeovil Marsh free-range chicken, ham and leek pie with mustard sauce, Savoy cabbage and mash; butternut squash and parsnip risotto with sage and truffle oil and parmesan crackling; chargrilled rib-eye steak with grilled beef tomato, portobello mushroom, onion rings and Dorset red watercress with triple-cooked chips. Finish with lemon posset and Garibaldi biscuits, or hot chocolate fondant with hazelnut ice cream and sesame wafer. The five spacious, well-equipped bedrooms complete the package. Booking for meals may be required.

Open all wk 10-4 5.30-late ⊞ FREE HOUSE ◀ Sharp's Doom Bar, Butcombe, Cheddar, Cotleigh, Yeovil Ò Ashton Press. **Facilities** Children welcome Children's menu Children's portions Garden Beer festival Parking Wi-fi **Rooms** 5

TRISCOMBE · Map 4 ST13

The Blue Ball

TA4 3HE ☎ 01984 618242

e-mail: enq@blueballinn.info
dir: *From Taunton take A358 past Bishops Lydeard towards Minehead*

Anyone who hasn't been to the 18th-century Blue Ball since 2001 might be a little confused since, although it's still down the same narrow lane in the Quantock Hills, it isn't quite where it was. Until then ale was pumped from a cellar in the old stables across the road. Today, said stables are the pub, looking south to the Brendon Hills and serving Cotleigh Tawny, Exmoor Gold and Stag, and Otter Head real ales, and Thatchers and Mad Apple ciders. Lunch might be a hot or cold sandwich; Severn and Wye smoked salmon and crayfish cocktail: or devilled rabbit kidneys and mushrooms. The frequently changing dinner menu might offer monkfish and langoustine Goan curry; Creedy Carver duck plate; or oven-dried tomato tart with melting goat's cheese and purple basil jam. On the first Saturday in September is Triscombefest, the beer festival. Booking for meals may be required.

Open 12-3 6-11 (Fri-Sat 12-11 Sun 12-8.30) Closed: 25 Dec, 26 Dec eve, 1 Jan eve, Mon, Sun eve (winter only)

Save on hotels. Book at **theAA.com/hotel**

SOMERSET 459 **ENGLAND**

Restaurant L served Tue-Sat 12-2, Sun 12-3 D served Tue-Sat 7-9, Sun (summer only) 7-8.30 Fixed menu price fr £19.95 Av 3 course à la carte fr £28 ⊞ FREE HOUSE ◀ Cotleigh Tawny Owl, Exmoor Gold & Stag, St Austell Tribute, Otter Head ♂ Thatchers, Mad Apple. **Facilities** ✿ Children welcome Children's portions Garden Beer festival Parking Wi-fi ▦ (notice required)

WATERROW
Map 3 ST02

The Rock Inn ★★★★ INN

PICK OF THE PUBS

See Pick of the Pubs on page 460

WELLS
Map 4 ST54

The City Arms

69 High St BA5 2AG ☎ 01749 673916
e-mail: cityofwellspubcoltd@hotmail.com
dir: *On corner of Queen St & Lower High St*

This building was once the city gaol (Judge Jeffreys passed sentence here) and original features include barred windows, a solitary cell, chains and locks. The pub offers traditional standards of quality and service, and a choice of seven real ales, draught ciders and menus of fresh local produce. The bar menu might offer grilled sardine fillets with a sweet chilli, coriander and garlic dressing; whole baked camembert; and chicken liver and apricot brandy pâté. The specials board changes weekly and there are also special events, such as carvery demonstrations. Booking for meals may be required.

Open all wk 9am-11pm (Fri-Sat 9am-mdnt Sun 10am-11pm) **Bar Meals** L served all wk 12-9.30 D served all wk 12-9.30 Av main course £7.95 food served all day **Restaurant** L served all wk 12-3 D served all wk 6-10.30 (May-Sep Fri-Sun 7-10) Av 3 course à la carte fr £16.95 ⊞ FREE HOUSE ◀ Cheddar Potholer, Butts Barbus barbus, Glastonbury Hedge Monkey & Golden Chalice, Sharp's ♂ Ashton Press, Aspall, Addlestones, Symonds. ♀ 10 **Facilities** Children welcome Children's menu Children's portions Family room Garden ▦

The Crown at Wells ★★★★ INN

Market Place BA5 2RP ☎ 01749 673457
e-mail: eat@crownatwells.co.uk
dir: *On entering Wells follow signs for Hotels & Deliveries, in Market Place*

The exterior of this 15th-century coaching inn located in the Market Place of England's smallest city will be familiar to movie buffs as it featured in the hit film *Hot Fuzz*. A stone's throw from the city's magnificent cathedral and moated Bishop's Palace, the pub is full of character with three original fireplaces, and is comfortably furnished. Bar menu choices include home-made fish pie; local River Axe mussels in white wine, tomato and chilli sauce, and breaded baked Somerset brie with cranberry sauce. There are 15 charming bedrooms available. Booking for meals may be required.

Open all day all wk Closed: 25 Dec **Bar Meals** L served Sun-Tue & Thu-Fri 12-2, Wed & Sat 12-9 D served all wk 6-9 Av main course £7.25 **Restaurant** L served Mon-Sat 12-2, Sun 12-2.30 D served all wk 6-9.30 Fixed menu price fr £10.95 Av 3 course à la carte fr £19.20 ⊞ FREE HOUSE ◀ Sharp's Doom Bar, Glastonbury Holy Thorn, Butcombe ♂ Ashton Press. **Facilities** Children welcome Children's menu Children's portions Garden Parking Wi-fi ▦ (notice required) **Rooms** 15

The Fountain Inn & Boxer's Restaurant

PICK OF THE PUBS

1 Saint Thomas St BA5 2UU ☎ 01749 672317
e-mail: eat@fountaininn.co.uk
dir: *In city centre, at A371 & B3139 junct. Follow signs for The Horringtons. Inn on junct of Tor St & Saint Thomas St*

Run by the Lawrence family for the past 30 years, this attractive 18th-century pub was originally built to accommodate men working on nearby Wells Cathedral. Yellow-painted with blue shutters and pretty window boxes, the interior is just as enticing with its large open fire in winter, interesting bric-à-brac, unobtrusive music and board games. The upstairs Boxer's restaurant is run by head chef Julie Pearce, who uses the finest local produce to create an impressive selection of quality home-cooked food for both the restaurant and the bar below. Among the favourites are beef, mushroom and ale pie topped with puff pastry; honey-glazed duck breast with orange and honey jus; and roasted local lamb with fresh mint and red wine jus. Round things off with warm Bakewell tart and local clotted cream or scoops of Lovington's ice cream. Parking is available opposite.

Open all wk Mon-Sat 12-2.30 6-11 (Sun 12-2.30 7-11) Closed: 25-26 Dec **Bar Meals** L served all wk 12-2 D served Mon-Sat 6-9, Sun 7-9 **Restaurant** L served all wk 12-2 D served Mon-Sat 6-9, Sun 7-9 ⊞ PUNCH TAVERNS ◀ Butcombe Bitter, Sharp's Doom Bar. ♀ 23 **Facilities** Children welcome Children's menu Children's portions Parking ▦

WEST BAGBOROUGH
Map 4 ST13

The Rising Sun Inn

TA4 3EF ☎ 01823 432575
e-mail: jon@risingsuninn.info
dir: *Telephone for directions*

This traditional, 16th-century village pub serving West Country ales lies in the picturesque Quantock Hills. After a fire the inn was rebuilt around the cob walls and magnificent door; the décor is both bold and smart. A good choice of food, using produce from local suppliers, includes main courses such as corned beef hash topped with a fried egg; fillet of salmon with a cheddar crust; and warm chicken and bacon salad. Among the many options for dessert are jam roly-poly and chocolate brownies. A gallery restaurant above the bar is ideal for private functions.

Open all wk 10.30-3 6-11 **Bar Meals** L served all wk 12-2 D served all wk 6.30-9.30 Av main course £17 **Restaurant** L served all wk 12-2 D served all wk

6.30-9.30 Av 3 course à la carte fr £30 ⊞ FREE HOUSE ◀ Exmoor Ale, St Austell Proper Job, Butcombe. ♀ **Facilities** Children welcome Children's portions

WEST CAMEL
Map 4 ST52

The Walnut Tree

PICK OF THE PUBS

Fore St BA22 7QW ☎ 01935 851292
e-mail: info@thewalnuttreehotel.com
dir: *Off A303 between Sparkford & Yeovilton Air Base*

The A303 to the West Country can be a tedious drive, so it's worth making a half-mile detour to this smartly modernised and extended family-run village inn between Sparkford and Ilchester. The eponymous tree provides the terrace with welcoming dappled shade on warm sunny days, while in the black-beamed, part-oak, part-flagstone-floored bar, burgundy leather furniture sets the scene. Otter real ales and Thatchers Gold cider can accompany lunchtime smoked haddock, prawn and pasta bake; Thai red chicken curry and basmati rice; or ham and mushroom omelette, chips and salad. The evening menu, served in the Rosewood restaurant, changes seasonally to offer starters such as Cornish mussels in white wine cream, onion and garlic sauce; and baked figs with goat's cheese and Parma ham; followed perhaps by a main course of fillet of beef Rossini with pâté and rich Madeira sauce; or smoked haddock fillet with cheese and chive sauce. Booking for meals may be required.

Open 11-3 5.30-11 Closed: 25-26 Dec, 1 Jan, Sun eve, Mon L, Tue L **Bar Meals** L served Wed-Sun 12-2 D served Mon-Sat 6-9 Av main course £11 **Restaurant** L served Wed-Sun 12-2 D served Mon-Sat 6-9 Av 3 course à la carte fr £27 ⊞ FREE HOUSE ◀ Otter Ale, Bitter ♂ Thatchers Gold. ♀ 9 **Facilities** Children welcome Children's portions Garden Parking Wi-fi

WEST HUNTSPILL
Map 4 ST34

Crossways Inn ★★★★ INN

PICK OF THE PUBS

See Pick of the Pubs on page 461

PICK OF THE PUBS

The Rock Inn ★★★★INN

WATERROW   Map 3 ST02

TA4 2AX ☎ **01984 623293**
e-mail: lnp@rockinn.co.uk
web: www.rockinn.co.uk
dir: *From Taunton take B3227. Waterrow*
approx 14m W. Or from M5 junct 27,
A361 towards Tiverton, then A396 N,
right to Bampton, then B3227 to
Waterrow

In a lovely green valley beside the River Tone stands this 400-year-old, half-timbered former smithy and coaching inn, part of which is carved out of solid rock, as you can see in the bar. Here, local farmers stand on the well-worn floors or sit at the scrubbed tables in front of a big log fire drinking peak condition local beers with appropriate West Country-sounding names like Cotleigh Tawny, Exmoor Gold and Otter Ale, and Sheppy's Taunton-made cider. You can eat in the dog-friendly bar (the dartboard doesn't interfere with the tables), or mount a few steps to the small, bistro-style restaurant where chunky tables are topped with church candles, and food is locally sourced, freshly prepared and cooked to order. Both eating areas share the same ever-changing menu, written up on blackboards and featuring the best cuts of West Country meat (Aberdeen Angus beef comes from landlords Matt Harvey and Joanna Oldman's own farm), fish is delivered daily from Brixham, and

shoots on Exmoor provide the game. Lunch may include French onion soup or crayfish cocktail, followed by locally made sausages and mash, or perhaps lasagne and salad. Dinner options might include chargrilled ten-ounce Devon Red rib-eye steak with home-made chips; roasted Barbary duck breast with sautéed potato, and honey and soy reduction; grilled fillets of Brixham cod with crushed new potatoes, langoustines, prawns and mussels; and spinach, ricotta and pine nut pancake with leaf salad. And finally, for pudding try baked lemon cheesecake, or pannacotta and gin-soaked plums. There is also a private dining room for up to 14 people. Stop off for a night or two in one of the cosy bedrooms.

Open all wk **Bar Meals** L served all wk 12-2.30 D served all wk 6.30-9.30 Av main course £11.50 **Restaurant** L served all wk 12-2.30 D served all wk 6.30-9.30 Av 3 course à la carte fr £25 ⊕ FREE HOUSE ◄ Cotleigh Tawny Owl & Barn Owl, Exmoor Gold & Antler, Otter Ale Ŏ Sheppy's. ♀ 9 **Facilities** Children welcome Children's menu Children's portions ❤ Parking Wi-fi ▭ **Rooms** 8

PICK OF THE PUBS

Crossways Inn ★★★★ INN

WEST HUNTSPILL   Map 4 ST34

Withy Rd TA9 3RA ☎ 01278 783756
e-mail: info@crosswaysinn.com
web: www.crosswaysinn.com
dir: *M5 juncts 22 or 23 on A38*

A family-run 17th century, tile-hung coaching inn ideally positioned for visitors to the Somerset Levels or walkers looking for a cosy respite from the rigours of the Mendip Hills. The Crossways Inn has benefited from major renovation work in recent years, including the revamped skittle alley and new state-of-the-art kitchen. Warmed by two open log fireplaces, the cosy, wavy-beamed interior has an array of fine old photos of the area. Draw close to the bar to inspect the ever-rotating selection of excellent beers, often from micro-breweries in Somerset, such as Moor and RCH. The beer choice increases significantly during the pub's popular August Bank Holiday beer festival. Cider drinkers are spoiled for choice, too, with Thatchers on tap and Rich's Cider created at a local farm just a couple of miles away. The classic food here also tends to be very locally sourced, like Somerset rump and sirloin steaks, which come with home-made peppercorn, stilton or white wine and mushroom sauce. Cottage pie, sausages and mash, curry of the day, and scampi and chips are all popular options, but you will need to check the specials board for the daily pie. The pasta

section of the menu offers lasagne, spaghetti bolognese and, for vegetarians, roasted vegetable and four-cheese bake. Lighter meals include sandwiches, baguettes, ploughman's and jacket potatoes. Interesting desserts are toffee and Dime Bar crunch pie, and Alabama chocolate fudge cake, while the under-10s can have ice creams topped with sprinkles or a flake, as long as they have eaten all their chicken nuggets, macaroni cheese or whatever they ordered from their own main menu. In summer, the large enclosed beer garden and children's play area comes into its own, as does the heated gazebo.

Open all day all wk Closed: 25 Dec
Bar Meals food served all day

Restaurant food served all day
⊕ FREE HOUSE ◪ Exmoor Stag, Cotleigh Snowy, Sharp's Doom Bar, Otter Ale, RCH Double Header, Moor, Butcombe ♻ Thatchers Gold, Dry & Heritage, Rich's. ♚ 16
Facilities Children welcome Children's menu Children's portions Play area Family room ♣ Garden Beer festival Parking Wi-fi 🚌 (notice required)
Rooms 7

WEST MONKTON — Map 4 ST22

The Monkton Inn

PICK OF THE PUBS

Blundells Ln TA2 8NP ☎ 01823 412414

dir: *M5 junct 25 to Taunton, right at Creech Castle for 1m, left into West Monkton, right at Procters Farm, 0.5m on left*

A little bit tucked away on the edge of the village, this convivial pub has been run since autumn 2011 by Peter Mustoe. Once inside you'll undoubtedly be struck by the polished floorboards, stone walls, log fire, leather sofas, smart dining furniture, in fact, by the whole set-up. At the bar you'll be able to order Butcombe, Exmoor and Sharp's real ales, as well as your food, but meals are served only in the restaurant or on the patio. Lunch could be Cape Malay chicken and apricot curry, or the more prosaic steak, egg and chips, while the dinner menu offers pan-fried fillet of plaice in white wine cream sauce; grilled tiger prawns with rice, lemon butter and piri-piri sauce; Somerset lamb cutlets with redcurrant and mint jus; and fresh tagliatelle, tomato and basil. On Sundays expect roasts, fish and chips, a curry and chargrills. Booking for meals may be required.

Open all wk 12-3 6-11 **Bar Meals** L served all wk 12-2 D served all wk 6-9 **Restaurant** L served all wk 12-2 D served all wk 6-9 ⊕ ENTERPRISE INNS ◀ Butcombe Bitter, Sharp's Doom Bar, Exmoor Ale & Gold, Morland Old Speckled Hen ◐ Thatchers Gold. **Facilities** ❖ Children welcome Children's menu Children's portions Play area Garden Parking

WHEDDON CROSS — Map 3 SS93

The Rest and Be Thankful Inn ★★★★ INN

TA24 7DR ☎ 01643 841222
e-mail: stay@restandbethankful.co.uk
web: www.restandbethankful.co.uk
dir: *5m S of Dunster*

Almost 1,000 feet up in Exmoor National Park's highest village, this early 19th-century coaching inn blends old-world charm with friendly hospitality. Today's travellers are welcomed with log fires warming the bar in winter; traditional entertainments of skittle alley and pool table are at the disposal of the energetic. Menus of carefully prepared pub favourites may include deep-fried brie wedges; Exmoor sausages in red onion gravy; a 'taste of the West' cheeseboard; and Somerset farmhouse ice

creams. The popular Sunday carvery represents excellent value. A beer festival is planned, details to be confirmed. Booking for meals may be required.

Open all wk 10-3 6-close **Bar Meals** L served all wk 12-2 D served all wk 6.30-9 **Restaurant** L served all wk 12-2 D served all wk 6.30-9 ⊕ FREE HOUSE ◀ Exmoor Ale, St Austell Proper Job & Tribute, Sharp's Own, Guinness ◐ Thatchers Gold, Healey's Cornish Rattler. ♚ 9 **Facilities** Children welcome Children's menu Children's portions Garden Beer festival Parking Wi-fi ▭ **Rooms** 8

WINSFORD — Map 3 SS93

Royal Oak Inn

TA24 7JE ☎ 01643 851455
e-mail: enquiries@royaloakexmoor.co.uk
dir: *Off A396 (Minehead to Tiverton road)*

Previously a farmhouse and dairy, the Royal Oak is a breathtaking, thatched ancient inn in one of Exmoor's prettiest villages, huddled beneath the rising moors beside the River Exe. Inside its all big fires, comfy chairs, restrained paraphernalia and restful décor, all the better to enjoy the twin treats of good honest Exmoor beers and rich local produce on the seasonal bar and restaurant menus, including slow-braised lamb shank with pan-fried gnocchi and red wine jus; butternut squash risotto cake; and deep-fried scampi in stout batter and chips. Booking for meals may be required.

Open all wk 11-3 6-11 ⊕ ENTERPRISE INNS ◀ Exmoor Ale, Stag, Gold ◐ Thatchers. **Facilities** Children welcome Children's menu Children's portions Garden Parking Wi-fi

WIVELISCOMBE — Map 3 ST02

White Hart ★★★★ INN

PICK OF THE PUBS

West St TA4 2JP ☎ 01984 623344
e-mail: reservations@whitehartwiveliscombe.co.uk
dir: *M5 junct 26. Pub in town centre*

Located at the foot of the Brendon Hills and nearby Quantocks, this former coaching inn dates back some 350 years and offers an attractive gateway to Exmoor. Completely transformed after a major renovation, it offers high standards and modern comforts, whilst still retaining its traditional appeal. Wiveliscombe has been described as Somerset's capital of brewing and, with its rich history dating back over 200 years, it is now home to both the Cotleigh and Exmoor breweries. Both companies' products are regularly on offer in the vibrant, friendly bar. Head chef Dave Gaughan's reputation for high-quality, freshly cooked food using locally sourced produce is apparent in his pub classics, such as steak and Tawny ale pie; and Beech Hayes Farm sausages with apple mash and onion gravy. Other favourites include River Exe mussels cooked in white wine and cream, and West Country duck breast served on confit garlic mash with an orange and rosemary sauce. The 16 en suite bedrooms have blend of original and contemporary features. Booking for meals may be required.

Open all day all wk 10.30am-11pm (Fri-Sat 9am-mdnt) ⊕ FREE HOUSE ◀ Exmoor, Cotleigh, Guest ales. **Facilities** Children welcome Children's menu Children's portions Garden Parking Wi-fi **Rooms** 16

WOOKEY — Map 4 ST54

The Burcott Inn

Wells Rd BA5 1NJ ☎ 01749 673874
e-mail: ian@burcottinn.co.uk
dir: *2m from Wells on B3139*

The Mendip Hills rise up to the north of this 300-year-old stone pub on the edge of a charming village. Its age is confirmed by the low-beamed ceilings, flagstone floors and log fires, while another notable feature is its copper-topped bar with five real ales and Addlestones cider on hand-pull. Here, you can have a snack or a daily special, while in the restaurant typical dishes include pan-fried steaks; grilled gammon; oven-baked Moroccan-spiced cod; salad options; and mushroom and tomato fusilli. There are also specials board choices.

Open 11.30-2.30 6-11 (Sun 12-3) Closed: 25-26 Dec, 1 Jan, Sun eve **Bar Meals** L served all wk 12-2 D served Tue-Sat 6.30-9 Av main course £9.50 **Restaurant** L served all wk 12-2 D served Tue-Sat 6.30-9 Av 3 course à la carte fr £20 ⊕ FREE HOUSE ◀ Teignworthy Old Moggie, RCH Pitchfork, Hop Back Summer Lightning, Cheddar Potholer, Butts Barbus barbus ◐ Addlestones. **Facilities** Children welcome Children's menu Children's portions Family room Garden Parking ▭ (notice required)

WOOKEY HOLE — Map 4 ST54

Wookey Hole Inn ◉ NEW

High St BA5 1BP ☎ 01749 676677
e-mail: mail@wookeyholeinn.com
dir: *Opposite Wookey Hole caves*

Opposite the famous caves, this family-run hotel, restaurant and bar is outwardly traditional, although the interior looks and feels very laid-back. Somerset and continental draught and bottled beers include Glastonbury's Love Monkey, Quantock's specially brewed Wook Ale, and fruity Belgian Früli; local Wilkins tempts cider-heads. There are plenty of lunchtime snacks and other dishes, and in the evening Mediterranean haloumi kebabs with couscous; fillet of West Country beef with roast tomato and portabella mushrooms; and pan-fried cod with olive oil mash. Mussels, duck legs, pork belly and pheasant are all possible specials. Booking for meals may be required.

Open all wk Closed: 25-26 Dec, Sun eve **Bar Meals** L served all wk 12-2.30 D served Mon-Sat 7-9.30 Av main course £5.95-£15.95 **Restaurant** L served all wk 12-2.30 D served Mon-Sat 7-9.30 Fixed menu price fr £14 Av 3 course à la carte fr £13.95 ⊕ FREE HOUSE ◀ Quantock Wook Ale, Glastonbury Love Monkey, Cheddar, Yeovil, Cottage ◐ Wilkins Farmhouse. **Facilities** ❖ Children welcome Children's menu Children's portions Garden Parking Wi-fi ▭ (notice required)

YARLINGTON　　　Map 4 ST62

The Stags Head Inn

Pound Ln BA9 8DG ☎ 01963 440393
e-mail: mrandall1960@tiscali.co.uk
dir: *Exit A303 at Wincanton onto A37 signed Castle Cary. In 3m turn left signed Yarlington, take 2nd right into village. Pub opposite church*

Halfway between Wincanton and Castle Cary lies this completely unspoilt country inn with flagstones and real fires, its authentic atmosphere undisturbed by electronic intrusions. The annual fair in the village of Yarlington is reputedly the one referred to by Thomas Hardy in *The Mayor of Casterbridge* – although wives and children are no longer sold to visiting sailors as far as anyone knows. Real ales include Greene King and guests, backed by Thatchers and Aspall ciders; food revolves around home-cooked favourites served in the restaurant, the snug bar, or alfresco in fine weather. Booking for meals may be required.

Open Mon-Sun L Closed: 25 Dec, Sun (eve) ⊕ FREE HOUSE ◀ Greene King IPA, Bass, Guest ales Ö Thatchers Gold, Aspall. **Facilities** Children welcome Children's menu Garden Parking Wi-fi

YEOVIL　　　Map 4 ST51

The Half Moon Inn ★★★ INN

Main St, Mudford BA21 5TF ☎ 01935 850289
e-mail: enquiries@thehalfmoon.co.uk
dir: *A303 at Sparkford onto A359 to Yeovil, 3.5m on left*

The exposed beams and flagstone floors retain the character of this painstakingly restored 17th-century village pub just north of Yeovil. Local East Street Cream ale is one of the beers on tap and there are ten wines by the glass to accompany the extensive menu of home-cooked food, which includes pub classics and main meals such as pork Stroganoff, venison casserole, and a mixed grill of sea bass, salmon and haddock. The large cobbled courtyard is ideal for alfresco dining and spacious, well-equipped bedrooms are also available.

Open all day all wk Closed: 25-26 Dec **Bar Meals** L served all wk 12-6 D served all wk 12-9.30 food served all day **Restaurant** L served all wk 12-9.30 D served all wk 6-9.30 food served all day ⊕ FREE HOUSE ◀ RCH Pitchfork, East Street Cream Ö Westons Old Rosie & Perry. ♀ 10 **Facilities** Children welcome Children's menu Children's portions Garden Parking Wi-fi **Rooms** 14

The Masons Arms ★★★★ INN

PICK OF THE PUBS

41 Lower Odcombe BA22 8TX ☎ 01935 862591
e-mail: paula@masonsarmsodcombe.co.uk
dir: *A3088 to Yeovil, right to Montacute, through village, 3rd right after petrol station to Lower Odcombe*

Believed to be the oldest building in the village, this 16th-century inn has a thatched roof and four thatched 'eyebrows' above its upper windows. Originally a traditional cider house comprising three cottages, it had a small parlour where thirsty masons from the local quarry were served. These days, the bar serves pints from the pub's own micro-brewery. Proprietors Drew and Paula have built strong green credentials, recycling anything and everything, and growing many of their own vegetables and fruit. The wine list reflects this commitment, with organic, vegetarian, biodynamic and fairly traded choices. Drew also runs the kitchen, producing freshly prepared dishes for seasonal and daily-changing menus. 'Pub grub' might include fishcakes; beef and Odcombe ale casserole; corned beef hash and egg; and Thai yellow vegetable and fruit curry. The comfortable en suite letting rooms are set back from the road and overlook the garden. Booking for meals may be required.

Open all wk 12-3 6-12 **Bar Meals** L served all wk 12-2 D served all wk 6.30-9.30 Av main course £10 **Restaurant** L served all wk 12-2 D served all wk 6.30-9.30 Fixed menu price fr £13.50 Av 3 course à la carte fr £22.50 ⊕ FREE HOUSE ◀ Odcombe No 1, Spring, Roly Poly, Winters Tail, Half Jack Ö Thatchers Gold & Heritage. ♀ 8 **Facilities** ❖ Children welcome Children's menu Children's portions Garden Parking Wi-fi **Rooms** 6

STAFFORDSHIRE

ALSTONEFIELD　　　Map 16 SK15

The George

PICK OF THE PUBS

DE6 2FX ☎ 01335 310205
e-mail: emily@thegeorgeatalstonefield.com
dir: *7m N of Ashbourne, signed Alstonefield to left off A515*

The nearby valley is much favoured by ramblers, many of whom seek well-earned refreshment at this friendly 18th-century coaching inn. Run by three generations of the same family, the current landlady warmly welcomes all-comers, as long as muddy boots are left at the door. The appeal of this fine pub, other than the wonderful location and welcome, includes a splendid range of real ales and wines by the glass, and excellent home-cooked food; fresh flowers, and candlelight in the evenings are elegant finishing touches. The pub's pesticide-free garden supplies home-grown vegetables, salad leaves and herbs in season, and other ingredients are sourced as locally as possible. A light lunch could comprise creamed wild mushrooms and leeks with toasted sourdough; a more filling option could be the trio of Tissington sausages with black pudding mash. Leave space for the Yorkshire rhubarb and frangipane tart, or apple and nutmeg crumble served with traditional custard. Booking for meals may be required.

Open all wk Mon-Fri 11.30-3 6-11 (Sat 11.30-11 Sun 12-9.30) Closed: 25 Dec ⊕ MARSTON'S ◀ Burton Bitter & Pedigree, Jennings Cumberland Ale, Brakspear Oxford Gold, Guest ale Ö Thatchers. **Facilities** Children welcome Children's portions Garden Parking

The Watts Russell Arms

PICK OF THE PUBS

See Pick of the Pubs on page 464

ALTON　　　Map 10 SK04

Bulls Head Inn

High St ST10 4AQ ☎ 01538 702307
e-mail: janet@thebullsheadalton.co.uk
dir: *M6 junct 14, A518 to Uttoxeter. Follow Alton Towers signs. Onto B5030 to Rocester, then B5032 to Alton. Pub in village centre*

This family-run 17th-century coaching inn is situated less than a mile from Alton Towers theme park. Oak beams and an inglenook fireplace set the scene for the old-world bar, and the country-style dining room with its pine furniture and slate floor. Serving a selection of real ales from three handpumps, the main courses on the menu might include baked chicken supreme with wild mushroom and white wine sauce; home-made cottage pie; and curry or pie of the day; plus succulent steaks. Booking for meals may be required.

Open all wk 11-11 ⊕ FREE HOUSE ◀ Bass, Greene King Abbot Ale & Ruddles County, Fuller's London Pride, Sharp's Doom Bar, Wells Bombardier, Hancock's Ö Kopparberg. **Facilities** Children welcome Children's menu Children's portions Garden Parking

ANSLOW　　　Map 10 SK22

The Burnt Gate at Anslow

Hopley Rd DE13 9PY ☎ 01283 563664
e-mail: info@burntgate.co.uk
dir: *From Burton take B5017 towards Abbots Bromley. At top of Henhurst Hill turn right Inn on Hopley Rd, 2m from town centre*

There's a country-house feel to this hanging-basket bedecked village inn, set in pleasant countryside near Tutbury. Named after a tollhouse that was burned to the ground centuries ago, light oak beams and colour-washed walls brighten the interior, where patrons can look forward to locally brewed real ale and a generous menu crafted largely from Staffordshire-sourced materials; chicken breast stuffed with fresh spinach and mushrooms in Madeira sauce hits the spot. Vegans, vegetarians and coeliacs will be particularly pleased with the choices available here.

Open all day all wk Closed: 31 Dec ⊕ FREE HOUSE ◀ Marston's Pedigree, Guest ales. **Facilities** Children's menu Parking Wi-fi

PICK OF THE PUBS

The Watts Russell Arms

ALSTONEFIELD Map 16 SK15

Hopedale DE6 2GD ☎ 01335 310126
e-mail: contact@wattsrussell.co.uk
web: www.wattsrussell.co.uk
dir: *Take A515 N towards Buxton. In 6.5m left to Alstonefield & Mildale. Cross River Dove, take left fork to Mildale. 1.5m to pub*

A charming 18th-century stone-built inn in the beautiful Peak District National Park, within walking distance of the Dove and Manifold Valleys. Originally a farmstead, it later became a beer house called the New Inn, which was renamed in 1851 after the wife of wealthy industrialist Jesse Watts-Russell, whose father built the neo-Gothic Ilam Hall down the road, the surviving part of which is now a youth hostel. Husband and wife team Bruce and Chris Elliott run the pub, whose cosy interior makes everyone feel pleased to be here, and even dogs are welcome in the terraced gardens and courtyard. At the bar, made from old oak barrels, Chris serves well-kept real ales from ever-changing local breweries, Thornbridge in Bakewell, for example; hand-crafted lagers from the Freedom Brewery in Abbots Bromley; single malts from a 15-strong selection; and eight wines by the glass. In the kitchen, Bruce prepares everything from scratch, using mostly locally supplied produce and ingredients, and with prior notice most dietary requirements can be catered for. Chris and Bruce insist that

theirs is not a 'gastro-pub', and that it's not a problem if you want a starter or a pudding on its own. At lunchtime there are tempting sandwiches, tortilla wraps, soups, hand-made pizzas and hot plates such as vegetable curry and lasagne bolognese, while typical in the evening would be pan-fried fillet of Scottish salmon; slow-cooked belly of pork; and lobby, a Staffordshire country beef casserole. Among the vegetarian dishes, of which there are usually at least three, might be 'vegetable whim', the ingredients donated by a villager. On Friday evenings 'tapas with a twist' are served, while Sunday lunches include prime topside of beef served pink, and chicken roasted with garlic and herbs. Booking for meals may be required.

Open Mon 12-2.30 Tue-Fri 12-10 (Sat 12-11 Sun 12-8) Closed: Mon eve **Bar Meals** L served Mon 12-2, Tue-Sat 12-4, Sun 12-7 D served Tue-Sat 7-9 ⊕ FREE HOUSE ◼ Guest ales. ♟ 8 **Facilities** Children welcome Children's portions ♣ Garden Parking

Save on hotels. Book at **theAA.com/hotel**

STAFFORDSHIRE 465 ENGLAND

BARTON-UNDER-NEEDWOOD   Map 10 SK11

The Waterfront

Barton Marina DE13 8DZ ☎ 01283 711500
e-mail: waterfront@bartonmarina.co.uk
web: www.bartonmarina.co.uk
dir: *Off A38, 1st left signed Barton-under-Needwood*

Part of a purpose-built marina complex, this modern pub opened in 2007, making use of reclaimed materials to resemble an old canalside warehouse. Overlooking busy moorings, it offers beers specially brewed for the pub, a fair few classic cocktails, and an extensive menu of snacks, oven-fired pizzas, and old favourites of chicken balti and rice; breaded scampi and chips; and mushroom and red pepper risotto. Daily specials offer additional choice. A walk along the Trent & Mersey towpath leads to the nearby National Memorial Arboretum, the UK's Centre of Remembrance. Booking for meals may be required.

Open all day all wk **Bar Meals** L served 10-6 D served 6-9.30 Av main course £11 food served all day **Restaurant** L served Mon-Sat 12-3, Sun 12-8 D served Mon-Sat 6-9.30 Fixed menu price fr £15 Av 3 course à la carte fr £22 ⊕ FREE HOUSE ◀ Waterfront Barton Pale & Marina Bitter, St Austell Tribute, Marston's Pedigree Ö Thatchers. ₹ 20 **Facilities** Children welcome Children's menu Children's portions Garden Parking Wi-fi 🚐 (notice required)

See advert below

BURTON UPON TRENT   Map 10 SK22

Burton Bridge Inn

24 Bridge St DE14 1SY ☎ 01283 536596
dir: *Telephone for directions*

The oldest pub in the historic brewing town of Burton, this former coaching inn has its own brewery at the back in an old stable block. The old-fashioned interior has oak panelling, feature fireplaces, and a distinct lack of electronic entertainment. A full range of Burton Bridge ales is available on tap, as well as the locally produced Freedom Four lager. The menu offers straightforward dishes, sandwiches and jacket potatoes, and the pub hosts beer festivals twice a year. A skittle alley is also available for hire.

Open all wk 11.30-2.30 5-11 (Sun 12-3 7-10.30) **Bar Meals** L served Mon-Sat 12-2 ⊕ BURTON BRIDGE BREWERY ◀ Gold Medal Ale, Festival Ale, Golden Delicious, Bridge Bitter. ₹ 15 **Facilities** ❀ Garden Beer festival Wi-fi

CAULDON · Map 16 SK04

Yew Tree Inn

ST10 3EJ ☎ 01538 308348
dir: Between A52 & A523. 4.5m from Alton Towers

Alan East's 300-year-old pub is home to his amazing collection of antiques and curiosities, including a 3,000-year-old Grecian urn, several penny-farthings, polyphons, a pair of Queen Victoria's stockings, a crank handle telephone and a pub lantern. No wonder he's been nicknamed the Moorland Magpie. A snacks-only menu offers locally made, hand-raised pork pies, sandwiches, baps, quiches and desserts, all ready to be accompanied by a pint of Bass, Burton Bridge or Rudgate Ruby Mild.

Open all wk 10.30-2.30 6-12 (Sun 12-3 7-12) **Bar Meals** L served 10.30-2.30, Sun 12-3 ⊕ FREE HOUSE ◀ Burton Bridge, Bass, Rudgate Ruby Mild. **Facilities** Children welcome Family room Parking 🚗 **Notes** ☺

CHEADLE · Map 10 SK04

The Queens At Freehay

Counslow Rd, Freehay ST10 1RF ☎ 01538 722383
e-mail: mail@queensatfreehay.co.uk
dir: 4m from Alton Towers, 2m from Cheadle

Tucked away in a quiet village, and surrounded by mature trees and well-tended gardens, this 18th-century, family-run pub and restaurant has a refreshing, modern interior. With a good reputation for food, its main menu is supplemented by chef's specials on the fresh fish and meat boards. Expect Moroccan lamb tagine; home-made beef and Merlot pie; roasted shoulder of Staffordshire lamb; and leek, goat's cheese and oatcake gratin. Iconic draught Burton and the more local Alton Abbey are among the beers on handpump in the bar. Booking for meals may be required.

Open all wk 12-3 6-11 (Sun 12-4 6.30-11) Closed: 25-26, 31 Dec-1 Jan **Bar Meals** L served Mon-Sat 12-2, Sun 12-2.30 D served Mon-Sat 6-9.30, Sun 6.30-9.30 Av main course £10.95 **Restaurant** L served Mon-Sat 12-2, Sun 12-2.30 D served Mon-Sat 6-9.30, Sun 6.30-9.30 Fixed menu price fr £11.95 Av 3 course à la carte fr £19.95 ⊕ FREE HOUSE ◀ Burton Ale, Peakstones Rock Alton Abbey, Wells Bombardier, Guinness. ☻ **Facilities** Children welcome Children's portions Garden Parking Wi-fi

COLTON · Map 10 SK02

The Yorkshireman

PICK OF THE PUBS

See Pick of the Pubs on opposite page

ECCLESHALL · Map 15 SJ82

The George

Castle St ST21 6DF ☎ 01785 850300
e-mail: vicki@slatersales.co.uk
dir: From M6 junct 14 take A5013 to Eccleshall (6m)

In 2011, long-term owners, the Slaters, bid their managers farewell and now run the pub themselves once more. Effectively, it's the taphouse for the family micro-brewery, whose Top Totty bitter was withdrawn as a guest ale from a House of Commons bar in February 2012, because its pump badge upset the shadow equalities minister. Available in both the open-fired bar and restaurant are snacks and light meals; grilled steaks; pork medallions in whisky and mushroom sauce; battered coley and hand-cut chips; and roast beetroot and asparagus risotto. A beer festival is held over Easter.

Open all day all wk 11am-1.30am (Fri-Sat 11am-2.30am Sun 12-12) **Bar Meals** L served Mon-Fri 12-3, Sat 12-9, Sun 12-6 D served Mon-Fri 6-9, Sat 12-9 **Restaurant** L served Mon-Fri 12-3, Sat 12-9, Sun 12-6 D served Mon-Fri 6-9, Sat 12-9 ⊕ SLATER'S ALES ◀ Slater's Ales. ☻ 10 **Facilities** ✿ Children welcome Children's menu Children's portions Beer festival Parking Wi-fi 🚗

HOAR CROSS · Map 10 SK12

The Meynell Ingram Arms **NEW**

Abbots Bromley Rd DE13 8RB ☎ 01283 575202
e-mail: info@themeynell.co.uk
dir: B5017 from Burton upon Trent towards Abbots Bromley. At Needham rdbt straight on. At x-rds with A515, left towards Lichfield. 0.5m, right on entering Newchurch. Right, follow pub signs

The Meynell is an elegant pub set in rolling Staffordshire countryside and draws foodies and walkers from nearby Burton upon Trent for its relaxing atmosphere, the peaceful garden and enjoyable pub food. It is also a good place to start and finish a country walk, and the function room and marquee make it a popular wedding venue. Varied menus offer sandwiches and grazing boards, alongside pub classics (Meynell burger with hand-cut chips), and dishes like oxtail casserole and lamb fillet with thyme jus. Wash down with a pint of Pedigree or one of 16 wines served by the glass.

Open all day all wk **Bar Meals** L served Mon-Fri 12-2, Sat 12-2.30, Sun 12-7 D served Mon-Sat 6.30-9, Sun 12-7 Av main course £10.95 **Restaurant** L served Mon-Fri 12-2, Sat 12-2.30, Sun 12-7 D served Mon-Sat 6.30-9, Sun 12-7 Fixed menu price fr £10 Av 3 course à la carte fr £18.95 ⊕ FREE HOUSE ◀ Marston's Pedigree, Burton Bridge, Guest ale. ☻ 16 **Facilities** ✿ Children welcome Children's portions Garden Parking Wi-fi 🚗 (notice required)

LEEK · Map 16 SJ95

Three Horseshoes Inn ★★★ HL ⑳⑳

Buxton Rd, Blackshaw Moor ST13 8TW ☎ 01538 300296
e-mail: enquiries@3shoesinn.co.uk
dir: On A53, 3m N of Leek

A family-run inn and country hotel in the Peak District National Park, the Three Horseshoes offers breathtaking views of the moorlands, Tittesworth reservoir and rock formations from the attractive gardens. Inside this creeper-covered inn are ancient beams, gleaming brass, rustic furniture and wood fires in the winter, with a good selection of real ales. Using the best Staffordshire produce, visitors can choose from three dining options: locally-reared roast meat in the bar carvery, the relaxed atmosphere of the brasserie offering modern British and Thai dishes with two AA Rosettes, or Kirks Restaurant. Delicious afternoon teas are also available. Booking for meals may be required.

Open all day all wk ⊕ FREE HOUSE ◀ Theakston XB, Courage Directors, Morland Old Speckled Hen, John Smith's. **Facilities** Children welcome Children's menu Children's portions Play area Garden Parking **Rooms** 26

NORBURY JUNCTION · Map 15 SJ72

The Junction Inn

ST20 0PN ☎ 01785 284288
e-mail: junctioninn1@hotmail.co.uk
dir: From M6 junct 14 take A5013 for Eccleshall, left at Great Bridgeford onto B5405 towards Woodseaves, left onto A519 towards Newport, left for Norbury Junction

Situated on a beautiful stretch of waterway where the Shropshire Union Canal meets the disused Newport arm, the inn's large beer garden has a ringside view of everything happening on the canal. Famous for its Junction steak pie, the pub also serves other home-made dishes such as pork faggots and beef lasagne. There's a Sunday carvery with local meat and barbecues in the garden in summer. There are cosy open fires in winter and plenty of real ales include a choice of guest ales.

Open all wk 11-3 6-11 (Fri 11-11 Sat 11am-mdnt Sun 12-10.30 open all day in summer) Closed: 3-6pm in winter ⊕ FREE HOUSE ◀ Banks's Mild & Bitter, Sambrook's Junction, Guest ales. **Facilities** Children welcome Children's menu Children's portions Play area Family room Garden Parking

Save on hotels. Book at **theAA.com/hotel**

STAFFORDSHIRE 467 ENGLAND

PICK OF THE PUBS

The Yorkshireman

COLTON   Map 10 SK02

Colton Rd WS15 3HB ☎ 01889 583977
e-mail: theyorkshireman@wine-dine.co.uk
web: www.wine-dine.co.uk
dir: *From A51 rdbt in Rugeley follow rail*
station signs, under rail bridge, to pub

The heritage of this edge-of-town pub opposite Rugeley's Trent Valley railway station is lost in the mists of time, or possibly lost in steam billowing from express engines, as it may have been established as a tavern to serve the new railway in the 19th century. It's seen a lot of life since those days, including a boisterous period as a local known as 'Wilf and Rosa's Tavern' and as a meeting place for farmers and soldiers when the sawdust and straw on the floor was doubtless put to good use. It's rather more sedate these days, emerging from a complete refurbishment just a few years ago as a panelled, wood-floored dining pub specialising in dishes using the best of Staffordshire produce and offering beers from a local micro-brewery including, unusually, a lager. Bought at nearby auctions, the eclectic furnishings are part of the charm, and the faux Stubbs paintings attract much comment. Just as much part of the furnishings is the pub's greyhound, Dahl. The menu is updated regularly, as season and supply allow, but a good range covering all the

bases is assured. Taken from a sample menu, starters may encompass duo of chicken liver and cranberry pâté with duck liver; stout and black pudding pâté; or potted smoked trout served with Melba toast and cucumber relish. The treats continue with mains such as trio of Johnson's of Yoxall sausages with creamy mash and onion gravy; or grilled fillet of seabass with beurre blanc sauce, crushed lemon and parsley new potatoes. Staffordshire-reared steaks are a speciality, as are dishes featuring rare-breed Gloucester Old Spot pork. There's a special Sunday menu, and the pub's name comes from a scion of the White Rose county who was once landlord here! Booking for meals may be required.

Open all wk 12-2.30 5.30-10 (Sat 12-11 Sun 12-6) **Bar Meals** L served Mon-Sat 12-2.30, Sun 12-6 D served Mon-Sat 6-9 **Restaurant** L served Mon-Sat 12-2.30, Sun 12-6 Bistro menu Mon-Sat 12-2 D served Mon-Sat 6-9 ⊕ FREE HOUSE ◼ Blythe ♻ Westons Stowford Press. ♀ 10 **Facilities** Children welcome Children's portions ✤ Garden Parking Wi-fi 🚌

ONNELEY — Map 15 SJ74

The Wheatsheaf Inn ★★★★ INN

Bar Hill Rd CW3 9QF ☎ 01782 751581
e-mail: pub@wheatsheafpub.co.uk
web: www.wheatsheafpub.co.uk
dir: *On A525 between Madeley & Woore*

This attractive whitewashed pub started life as a coaching inn in 1769 and although it has been modernised in recent years, the old beams and fires are still in place, making for a cosy setting to enjoy real ales or a meal in the restaurant. Meat from the local farm appears on the menu, which includes caramelised chicken livers with wilted spinach and garlic bread; rack of lamb with dauphinoise potatoes and redcurrant jus; and steak-and-ale pie. The pub adjoins a golf course so don't forget to pack your clubs and maybe stay over in the guest rooms situated in converted stables.

Open all day all wk **Bar Meals** L served Mon-Sat 12-9 D served Mon-Sat 12-9 food served all day **Restaurant** L served Mon-Sat 12-9 D served Mon-Sat 12-9 food served all day ⊕ FREE HOUSE ◀ Wells Bombardier, Timothy Taylor Landlord, Guest ales. **Facilities** ✿ Children welcome Children's menu Children's portions Play area Family room Garden Parking Wi-fi **Rooms** 10

STAFFORD — Map 10 SJ92

The Holly Bush Inn

PICK OF THE PUBS

See Pick of the Pubs on opposite page

STOURTON — Map 10 SO88

The Fox Inn

Bridgnorth Rd DY7 5BL ☎ 01384 872614 & 872123
e-mail: foxinnstourton@gmail.com
dir: *5m from Stourbridge town centre. On A458 (Stourbridge to Bridgnorth road)*

A late 18th-century inn set in unspoilt countryside on an estate once owned by Lady Jane Grey, The Fox is steeped in history and retains many original features. In the 40 years Stefan Caron has been running it, he has built its reputation for quality and value for money. Typical evening meal choices could include warm bacon, potato and black pudding salad, followed by half a lobster with garlic butter, garlic mayonnaise and fries. A large garden with weeping willow, gazebo and attractive patio area

completes the picture. Booking for meals may be required.

Open all wk 10.30-3 5-11 (Sat-Sun 10.30am-11pm) **Bar Meals** L served Mon-Sat 12-2.30 D served Tue-Sat 7-9.30 **Restaurant** L served Tue-Sat 12-2.30, Sun 12.30-5 D served Tue-Sat 7-9.30 ⊕ FREE HOUSE ◀ Bathams, Wye Valley HPA, Guinness ⓩ Robinsons, Thatchers. **Facilities** Children welcome Children's menu Children's portions Garden Parking 🚌

SUMMERHILL — Map 10 SK00

Oddfellows in the Boat

The Boat, Walsall Rd WS14 0BU ☎ 01543 361692
e-mail: info@oddfellowsintheboat.com
dir: *A461 (Lichfield towards Walsall). At rdbt junct with A5 (Muckley Corner) continue on A461. In 600mtrs establishment is visible. Continue 500mtrs, U-turn on dual carriageway back to establishment*

On the main road between Walsall and Lichfield, the Boat once served bargees on the now-disused Curly Wyrley Canal to the rear. Although the pub does hold its own beer festival, real ale lovers can enjoy what amounts to a rolling beer festival all year thanks to an ever-changing choice from local micro-breweries. Locally sourced dishes are prepared in an open kitchen and chalked up daily, with popular options including slow-roast shoulder of lamb with buttered greens and red wine jus, and cod fillet with prawns and brown shrimp.

Open all wk 11-3 6-11 (Sun 12-11) Closed: 25 Dec **Bar Meals** L served Mon-Sat 12-2.15, Sun 12-8.15 D served Mon-Sat 6-9.30, Sun 12-8.15 Av main course £11 **Restaurant** L served Mon-Sat 12-2.15, Sun 12-8.15 D served Mon-Sat 6-9.30, Sun 12-8.15 Fixed menu price fr £8.95 Av 3 course à la carte fr £20 ⊕ FREE HOUSE ◀ 3 Guest ales. ☘ 13 **Facilities** Children welcome Garden Beer festival Parking Wi-fi

TAMWORTH — Map 10 SK20

The Globe Inn ★★★ INN

Lower Gungate B79 7AT ☎ 01827 60455
e-mail: info@theglobetamworth.com
dir: *Telephone for directions*

A popular meeting place in the 19th century, The Globe was rebuilt in 1901 and completely refurbished nearly 100 years later. The restored exterior shows off its original appearance, while interior decoration has followed design styles of the era – the elegant carved bar and fireplaces reinforce its period character; air conditioning in public areas and satellite television are two concessions to 21st-century living. Beers from large breweries, menus of pub grub, a function room, and en suite accommodation complete the picture.

Open all day all wk 11-11 (Thu-Sat 11am-mdnt Sun 11-4 7-11) Closed: 25 Dec, 1 Jan **Bar Meals** L served all wk 11-2 D served Mon-Sat 6-9 Av main course £7.50 **Restaurant** L served all wk 11-2 D served Mon-Sat 6-9 Fixed menu price fr £16 ⊕ FREE HOUSE ◀ Bass, Worthington's. **Facilities** Children welcome Children's

menu Children's portions Parking Wi-fi 🚌 (notice required) **Rooms** 18

TUTBURY — Map 10 SK22

Ye Olde Dog & Partridge Inn

High St DE13 9LS ☎ 01283 813030
dir: *From A38 in Burton upon Trent take A511 signed Uttoxter at Derby Turn rdbt. Tutbury approx 4.5m*

The oldest building on a quaint and traditional High Street close to Tutbury Castle, this medieval half-timbered pub dates back to the 15th century. The heavily beamed interior shelters nooks and alcoves where you can tuck into a menu that covers the whole gamut, from classics such as steak-and-ale pie, steak burgers and organic Shetland salmon wrapped in pancetta with cheese mash and green beans, all washed down with real ales and a good list of wines.

Open all day all wk **Bar Meals** L served all wk 12-10 Av main course £8 food served all day **Restaurant** L served all wk 12-10 Fixed menu price fr £9.99 food served all day ⊕ SPIRIT PUB COMPANY ◀ Marston's Pedigree, Courage, 3 Guest ales. ☘ 12 **Facilities** Children welcome Children's menu Children's portions Garden Parking Wi-fi 🚌

WETTON — Map 16 SK15

Ye Olde Royal Oak

DE6 2AF ☎ 01335 310287
e-mail: royaloakwetton@live.co.uk
dir: *A515 towards Buxton, left in 4m to Manifold Valley-Alstonfield, follow signs to Wetton*

In the Manifold Valley, this white-painted, stone-built inn dates back to at least 1760. Attractions such as Thors Cave, Wetton Mill and the stepping-stones at Dovedale are within walking distance, so ramblers, campers and cyclists are always calling in for a pint or two of Wincle brewery's Sir Philip, or Belvoir's Gordon Bennett, which are now on tap after a change of hands. Of course, they're normally hungry too, and order home-cooked sirloin steak with onion rings and mushrooms; Greek-style lamb with mixed rice; or roasted vegetable and Wensleydale cheese bake. The pub has a moorland garden.

Open 12-2 7-closing Closed: Mon-Tue in winter **Bar Meals** L served Wed-Sun 12-2 D served Wed-Sun 7-9 Av main course £8.15 ⊕ FREE HOUSE ◀ Whim Hartington Bitter, Morland Old Speckled Hen, Belvoir Gordon Bennett, Wincle Sir Philip. **Facilities** ✿ Children welcome Children's menu Family room Garden Parking 🚌 (notice required)

PICK OF THE PUBS

The Holly Bush Inn

STAFFORD   Map 10 SJ92

Salt ST18 0BX ☎ 01889 508234
e-mail: geoff@hollybushinn.co.uk
web: www.hollybushinn.co.uk
dir: *Telephone for directions*

This thatched inn is situated in the village of Salt, probably a settlement originating from the Saxon period due to its sheltered position and proximity to the River Trent. It's believed to be only the second pub in the country to receive, back in Charles II's reign, a licence to sell alcohol, although the building itself possibly dates from as long ago as 1190; and when landlord Geoff Holland's son Joseph became a joint licensee at the age of 18 years and 6 days, he was the youngest person ever to be granted a licence. The pub's comfortably old-fashioned interior contains all the essential ingredients: heavy carved beams, open fires, attractive prints and cosy alcoves. In the kitchen there's a strong commitment to limiting food miles by supporting local producers, and to ensuring that animals supplying meat have lived stress-free lives. The main menu features traditional dishes such as steak-and-kidney pudding; battered cod with mushy peas; and mixed grill; but also included are the still-traditional-but-less-well-known, such as braised venison with chestnuts; and slow-cooked lamb and barley stew. The specials board changes every session, but will usually include Staffordshire oatcakes stuffed with bacon and cheese; hand-made pork, leek and stilton sausages with fried eggs and chips; and a roast meat, perhaps topside of beef; or ham with sweet Madeira gravy. The evening specials board may offer home-smoked fillet of Blythe Field trout with creamy horseradish sauce; warm pan-fried duck and pear salad; Scottish mussels steamed with cider and cream; rabbit casserole with dumplings; or slow-cooked mutton with caper sauce. Cheeses are all hand-made to old English recipes, while seasonal puddings include the unquestionably traditional bread-and-butter pudding, and apple crumble with cinnamon and nutmeg dusting. During the warmer months hand-made pizzas are cooked in

a wood-fired brick oven; in addition to the usual favourites, try the surf and turf, or seafood special.

Open all day all wk 12-11 (Sun 12-10.30) **Bar Meals** L served Mon-Sat 12-9.30, Sun 12-9 Av main course £11.50 food served all day ⏣ FREE HOUSE 🍺 Marston's Pedigree, Adnams, Guest ales. ♟ 12 **Facilities** Garden Beer festival Parking Wi-fi

PICK OF THE PUBS

The Crown Inn

WRINEHILL Map 15 SJ74

Den Ln CW3 9BT ☎ 01270 820472
e-mail: info@thecrownatwrinehill.co.uk
web: www.thecrownatwrinehill.co.uk
dir: *Village on A531, 1m S of Betley.*
6m S of Crewe; 6m N of
Newcastle-under-Lyme

Charles and Sue Davenhill have owned this 19th-century, former coaching inn for more than 35 years, which Charles reckons makes him Staffordshire's longest-serving licensee. Joint proprietor with him is son-in-law Mark Condliffe, whose wife Anna is also part of the business. With an open-plan layout the pub nevertheless retains its oak beams and famously large inglenook fireplace, always a welcome feature. The bar does a good line in well-kept real ales, with always a choice of six, two each from Jennings and Marston's, one from Salopian Ales and a regularly changing micro-brewery guest; ten wines are offered by the glass. Food is a major reason for the success of The Crown, not just for its consistent quality but for the generosity of how much appears on the plate. Regularly changing menus are jam-packed with choice: at one end are modestly priced light meals, such as minced beef or roasted vegetable lasagne al forno; and breaded plaice fillets with chips, peas and home-made tartare sauce. At the other are head chef Steve's trademark piri-piri chicken; smoked haddock and salmon fishcakes

flavoured with spring onion and chives; and local pork and leek sausages with four-ounce fillet steak, bacon, egg, tomato, mushrooms, chips and petit pois. Vegetarians themselves, Sue and Anna recognise that choice should extend beyond mushroom Stroganoff, so always offer such alternatives as cheshire cheese and thyme sausages with wholegrain mustard mash and caramelised onion gravy; and veggie burritos filled with courgettes, baby corn and mixed peppers in tomato sauce. From the puddings menu, try home-made spotted dick with lashings of custard; or Belgian chocolate bombe with a swirl of cream. On the children's menu children will find home-roasted ham with free-range egg, and farfalle pasta with tomato sauce and cheese.

Open 12-3 6-11 (Sun 12-4 6-10.30)
Closed: 25-26 Dec, Mon L **Bar Meals** L
served Tue-Fri 12-2, Sat-Sun 12-3
D served Sun-Thu 6-9, Fri 6-9.30, Sat
6-10 ⊕ FREE HOUSE ◀ Marston's
Pedigree & Burton Bitter, Jennings
Cumberland Ale & Sneck Lifter,
Salopian, Guest ales. ♥ 10
Facilities Children welcome Children's
menu Children's portions Garden
Parking 🚌 (notice required)

WOODSEAVES · Map 15 SJ72

The Plough Inn

Newport Rd ST20 0NP ☎ 01785 284210
dir: *From Stafford take A5013 towards Eccleshall. Turn left onto B4505. Woodseaves at junct with A519. 5m from Eccleshall on A519 towards Newport*

This mid-18th century inn, which was built for workers constructing the nearby canal, has returned to its roots as a traditional country pub. The restored large inglenook fireplace gives a warm, welcoming feel, there's a good selection of real ales, and home-cooked, traditional pub dishes are served. Expect beef lasagne with salad; home-made pie; or plaice, chips and peas. Pie night and steak night are held once a month, and an Italian gourmet night is held every three months.

Open all wk 12-3 5-11 (Mon 5-11 Fri-Sat 12-12 Sun 12-10 BH all day) ⊕ FREE HOUSE ◀ Banks's Bitter & Mild, Marston's Pedigree, Jennings Cumberland Ale ♻ Thatchers Gold. **Facilities** Children welcome Children's menu Children's portions Family room Garden Parking Wi-fi

WRINEHILL · Map 15 SJ74

The Crown Inn
PICK OF THE PUBS

See Pick of the Pubs on opposite page

The Hand & Trumpet

Main Rd CW3 9BJ ☎ 01270 820048
e-mail: hand.and.trumpet@brunningandprice.co.uk
dir: *M6 junct 16, A351, follow Keele signs, 7m, pub on right in village*

A deck to the rear of this relaxed country pub overlooks sizeable grounds, which include a large pond. The pub has a comfortable interior with original floors, old furniture, open fires and rugs. Six cask ales including guests and over 70 malt whiskies are offered, along with a locally sourced menu. Typical dishes are potted Mrs Kirkham's Lancashire cheese with chicory, grape and walnut salad; venison, pigeon and duck meatloaf with bubble-and-squeak. There is a beer festival in the last week of January.

Open all day all wk 11.30-11 (Sun 11.30-10.30) **Bar Meals** L served all wk 12-10 D served all wk 12-10 Av main course £11.25 food served all day **Restaurant** L served all wk 12-10 D served all wk 12-10 ⊕ BRUNNING & PRICE ◀ Caledonian Deuchars IPA, Hawkshead Lakeland Gold, Guest ales ♻ Aspall. ♀ 12 **Facilities** ❖ Children welcome Children's portions Garden Beer festival Parking

SUFFOLK

ALDRINGHAM · Map 13 TM46

The Parrot and Punchbowl Inn & Restaurant

Aldringham Ln IP16 4PY ☎ 01728 830221
dir: *On B1122, 1m from Leiston, 3m from Aldeburgh, on x-rds to Thorpeness*

If you thought bizarre pub names were a late 20th-century fad, think again. Originally called The Case is Altered, this old smugglers' inn became The Parrot and Punchbowl in 1604. With contraband hooch no longer available (not here, anyway), normal commercial principles now apply and money needs to change hands for drinks, including glasses of wine and pints of Adnams or Woodforde's Wherry. The good-value menu offers shortcrust steak-and-ale pie; scampi and chips; and ham, egg and chips. Daily specials and vegetarian meals also have very reasonable price tags. Booking for meals may be required.

Open 12-2.30 6-11 (Sun 12-2) Closed: Mon Jan-Mar **Bar Meals** L served all wk 12-2 D served Mon-Sat 6.30-9 Av main course £10 **Restaurant** L served all wk 12-2 D served Mon-Sat 6.30-9 ⊕ ENTERPRISE INNS ◀ Woodforde's Wherry, Adnams, Guest ale ♻ Aspall. **Facilities** ❖ Children welcome Children's portions Play area Family room Garden Parking Wi-fi ▭

BRANDESTON · Map 13 TM26

The Queens Head ◉
PICK OF THE PUBS

See Pick of the Pubs on page 472

BURY ST EDMUNDS · Map 13 TL86

The Linden Tree

7 Out Northgate IP33 1JQ ☎ 01284 754600
e-mail: lindentree@live.com
dir: *Opposite railway station*

Built to serve the railway station, this is a large, friendly Victorian pub, with stripped pine bar, dining area, conservatory and charming garden. Along with real ales and regular guests, the family-orientated menu ranges from stilton and leek tart or chicken and pesto pasta to stout-braised beef and wild mushroom casserole, pie of the week and grilled Suffolk gammon. Leave room for one of the desserts like banoffee cream slice or pecan and maple waffles. Booking for meals may be required.

Open all wk 12-11 (Fri-Sat 11-11 Sun 12-10) Closed: 25 Dec ⊕ GREENE KING ◀ IPA, Morland Old Speckled Hen, Guest ale ♻ Aspall. **Facilities** Children welcome Children's menu Children's portions Play area Garden

The Nutshell

17 The Traverse IP33 1BJ ☎ 01284 764867
dir: *Telephone for directions*

Measuring just 15ft by 7ft, this unique pub has been confirmed as Britain's smallest by *Guinness World Records*; and somehow more than 100 people and a dog managed to fit inside in the 1980s. It has certainly become a tourist attraction and there's lots to talk about while you enjoy a drink – a mummified cat and the bar ceiling, which is covered with paper money. There have been regular sightings of ghosts around the building, including a nun and a monk who apparently weren't praying! No food is available, though the pub jokes about its dining area for parties of two or fewer.

Open all day all wk ⊕ GREENE KING ◀ IPA & Abbot Ale, Guest ales. **Facilities** ▭ Notes ◉

The Old Cannon Brewery ★★★ INN
PICK OF THE PUBS

See Pick of the Pubs on page 473

The Three Kings ★★★★ INN

Hengrave Rd, Fornham All Saints IP28 6LA ☎ 01284 766979
e-mail: thethreekings@keme.co.uk
dir: *Bury St Edmunds (2m), A14 junct 42 (1m)*

It is perhaps fitting, albeit tenuously, that brewer's Greene King should own this 18th-century coaching inn, named after three Saxon kings reputedly buried locally. Family run, it has all the necessary elements – wood-panelled bars, restaurant, conservatory and courtyard. Bar food is mainly baguettes, sandwiches, ploughman's, salads and burgers, while the more ambitious evening carte offers rabbit, wild mushroom and bacon stew; fresh fish of the day; pan-roasted chicken breast; and winter vegetable hotpot. Daily specials add a further choice of meat and fish dishes. Comfortable accommodation is available in converted outbuildings. Booking for meals may be required.

Open all day all wk 12-12 **Bar Meals** L served Mon-Fri 12-2, Sat-Sun 12-2.30 D served Mon 6-8, Tue-Sat 5.30-9 **Restaurant** L served Sun 12-2.30 ⊕ GREENE KING ◀ IPA & Abbot Ale, Guest ales. ♀ 14 **Facilities** Children welcome Children's menu Children's portions Garden Parking ▭ (notice required) **Rooms** 9

PICK OF THE PUBS

The Queens Head ❀

BRANDESTON   Map 13 TM26

The Street IP13 7AD ☎ 01728 685307
e-mail: thequeensheadinn@btconnect.com
web: www.queenshead-brandeston.com
dir: *From A14 take A1120 to Earl Soham, then S to Brandeston*

This smart Adnams pub, created from four cottages and first opened in 1811, stands slightly off the beaten track in a sleepy village deep in peaceful Suffolk countryside. A detour is well worthwhile to sample one of the cracking Southwold ales, or a meal prepared to AA-Rosette standard. Now under the guiding hand of landlord Oliver Coote, the family- and dog-friendly hostelry has a well-furnished summer garden, and a camping area at the rear for those wanting to explore Suffolk on foot or bicycle. Inside, a warm and richly coloured décor complements the traditional homely features of wood panelling, quarry-tiled floors and open log fires. Family-based events are organised throughout the year, including barbecues in the garden and a beer festival in June to coincide with the village fête. Sunday lunches are always popular, usually offering a choice of roasts, a fish dish and a vegetarian option, topped and tailed by tempting starters and puddings. The modern British menu, described as 'pub food with a twist', is based on local produce where possible, and bristles with interest. How often do you come across a starter of roast pig's head with sauce gribiche, yolk and crispy ear? Or Peking duck consommé, roulade and tortellini? Main courses, accompanied by seasonal vegetables, may include braised feather blade of beef with mashed potato; roast Felixstowe hake with boulangère potatoes and pak choi; and venison shepherd's pie with wilted greens. To round off sweetly, a chocolate tart with rhubarb sorbet, or sour cherry Arctic roll both hit the spot. Alternatively the savoury selection of Suffolk cheeses is served with frozen grapes. Booking for meals may be required.

Open 12-3 5-12 (Sun 12-5) Closed: Sun eve, Mon **Bar Meals** L served Tue-Sat 12-2, Sun 12-3 D served Tue-Sat 6-9 **Restaurant** L served Tue-Sat 12-2, Sun 12-3 D served Tue-Sat 6-9 ⊞ ADNAMS ◀ Broadside, Southwold Bitter, Seasonal ales ♂ Aspall. **Facilities** ❤ Children welcome Children's menu Children's portions Garden Beer festival Parking Wi-fi 🚐

Save on hotels. Book at **theAA.com/hotel**

SUFFOLK 473 **ENGLAND**

PICK OF THE PUBS

The Old Cannon Brewery ★★★ INN

BURY ST EDMUNDS Map 13 TL86

86 Cannon St IP33 1JR
☎ **01284 768769**
e-mail: info@oldcannonbrewery.co.uk
web: www.oldcannonbrewery.co.uk
dir: *From A14 junct 43 follow signs to Bury St Edmunds town centre, at 1st rdbt 1st left into Northgate St, then 1st into Cadney Ln, left at end into Cannon St, pub 100yds on left*

Two giant stainless steel brewing vessels dominate the bar of the only independent brewpub in Bury St Edmunds – you'll find this revitalised Victorian pub tucked away down Bury's back streets, so follow the directions carefully. The brewery vessels are not just for show, they are used to brew the ales dispensed from the gleaming row of handpumps on the bar. The brewer uses East Anglian-grown and malted barley; choice hops and ale aficionados have at least three to choose between at the bar, including Old Cannon Best, Gunner's Daughter and Hornblower, which are augmented by a seasonal beer, or brew for a special occasion such as St Edmund's Head, an annual brew to celebrate St Edmund's Day on 20 November. In keeping with having a brewery inside the bar-cum-dining room, the décor is light and airy, with some walls painted in a rich, earthy colour, plus you can expect wooden floors and rustic scrubbed tables. In true brasserie style, the Brewery Kitchen serves 'cannon fodder', freshly prepared from great local produce. Some starters and light bites can be upped in size, such as salads and Thai currys. Of the main courses, duck leg with braised red cabbage and plum sauce; and roast salmon with creamy cabbage, bacon and cockles are typical choices. Beef comes from a Suffolk herd of Red Polls and local estate game appears on the seasonal specials board, while puddings may include steamed sponge, cheesecake and crème brûlée. Overnight guests are catered for in the converted Brewery Rooms, just across the courtyard from the bar.

Open all day all wk 12-11 (Sun 12-10.30) **Bar Meals** L served all wk 12-9 D served all wk 12-9 Av main

course £11 food served all day **Restaurant** L served all wk 12-9 D served all wk 12-9 food served all day 🍺 FREE HOUSE ◀ The Old Cannon Best Bitter, Gunner's Daughter, Hornblower, Blonde Bombshell & Seasonal ales, Adnams Southwold Bitter, Guest ales ♂ Aspall. 🍷 12 **Facilities** Garden Beer festival Parking Wi-fi **Rooms** 7

CAVENDISH — Map 13 TL84

Bull Inn

High St CO10 8AX ☎ 01787 280245
e-mail: knaffton@aol.com
dir: *A134 (Bury St Edmunds to Long Melford), then right at green, pub 3m on right*

A fine double-fronted, probably Victorian façade masks the splendid 15th-century beamed interior of this pub in one of Suffolk's prettiest villages. The atmosphere's good, the beers are from Adnams and a guest brewery, and the food's jolly decent too, with a menu listing perhaps rustic steak, mushroom and Irish ale pie; beer-battered fish and chips; smoked salmon and crayfish tagliatelle; and Mediterranean vegetable lasagne. Sunday roast may be selected from joints of beef, pork, lamb, chicken and turkey. Dogs are welcome downstairs in the public bar and in the patio garden.

Open all wk 11-3 6.30-11 **Bar Meals** L served all wk 12-3 D served all wk 6.30-9 **Restaurant** L served all wk 12-3 D served all wk 6.30-9 ⊕ ADNAMS ◀ Southwold Bitter & Broadside, Guest ales Õ Aspall. **Facilities** ❄ Children welcome Children's menu Children's portions Garden Parking ▭ (notice required)

CHILLESFORD — Map 13 TM35

The Froize Inn ◉

The Street IP12 3PU ☎ 01394 450282
e-mail: dine@froize.co.uk
dir: *On B1084 between Woodbridge (8m) & Orford (3m)*

Built on the site of Chillesford Friary and originally a pair of gamekeeper's cottages, this distinctive red-brick free house dates from 1490 and stands on today's popular Suffolk Coastal Path. Chef-owner David Grimwood may operate The Froize as more of a restaurant than a pub, but the atmosphere is informal and there's always a decent pint of Adnams on tap. Daily menus champion East Anglian growers and suppliers, and excellent one-Rosette dishes are served buffet-style on a groaning hot table; in winter perhaps baked Orford cod with crayfish risotto; or breast of guinea fowl with butternut squash and redcurrants. Booking for meals may be required.

Open Tue-Sun Closed: Mon **Restaurant** L served Tue-Sun 12-3 D served Thu-Sat from 7pm ⊕ FREE HOUSE ◀ Adnams Õ Aspall. ♟ 12 **Facilities** Children welcome Children's portions Garden Parking Wi-fi ▭ (notice required)

CRATFIELD — Map 13 TM37

The Cratfield Poacher

Bell Green IP19 0BL ☎ 01986 798206
e-mail: cratfieldpoacher@yahoo.co.uk
dir: *From Halesworth take B1117 towards Eye. At Laxfield turn right, follow Cratfield signs (3m). Or, from Diss, take A143 towards Bungay. Right at Harleston onto B1123 towards Halesworth. Through Metfield, 1m, turn right & follow Cratfield signs (2m)*

A pub for the past 350 years, this handsome longhouse in deepest rural Suffolk is off the beaten track but well worth the detour. Boasting some impressive exterior plasterwork pargeting, it is just as charming inside, with low beams and tiled floors. There's always eight draught beers available at weekends, often from the Adnams and Oakham breweries, plus local Aspall cider. Home-cooked food, especially smoked mackerel salad and shepherd's pie, with daily-changing specials completing the pleasing picture at this proper village local, which is the hub of the community.

Open 12-2.30 6-12 (Sat-Sun all day) Closed: Mon, Tue L **Bar Meals** L served Wed-Fri 12-2.30 (Sat-Sun all day) D served Tue-Fri 6-9 (Sat-Sun all day) Av main course £8.95 **Restaurant** L served Wed-Fri 12-2.30 (Sat-Sun all day) D served Tue-Fri 6-9 (Sat-Sun all day) Fixed menu price fr £8.50 Av 3 course à la carte fr £13.95 ⊕ FREE HOUSE ◀ Crouch Vale Brewers Gold, Oakham JHB, Earl Soham Victoria Bitter & Gannet Mild, Adnams Õ Aspall. **Facilities** ❄ Children welcome Children's menu Children's portions Garden Parking ▭ (notice required)

DENNINGTON — Map 13 TM26

Dennington Queen

The Square IP13 8AB ☎ 01728 638241
e-mail: denningtonqueen@yahoo.co.uk
dir: *From Ipswich A14 to exit for Lowestoft (A12), then B1116 to Framlingham then follow signs to Dennington*

A 16th-century inn with bags of old-world charm including open fires, a coffin hatch, a bricked-up tunnel to the neighbouring church and a ghost. Locally brewed Aspall cider accompanies real ales from Adnams, Black Sheep, Timothy Taylor, St Austell and, from Woodbridge, Earl Soham. Suggestions from the modern British menu include Thai fishcakes with sweet chilli jam; calves' liver with champ mash, Bramfield bacon and red onion jus; and wild mushroom and smoked cheddar risotto. A typical daily special is spinach and pea linguine with salsa verde. Booking for meals may be required.

Open all wk 12-3 6-close **Bar Meals** L served all wk 12-2 D served all wk 6.30-9 **Restaurant** L served all wk 12-2 D served all wk 6.30-9 ⊕ FREE HOUSE ◀ St Austell Tribute, Earl Soham Victoria Bitter, Timothy Taylor Landlord, Adnams, Black Sheep Õ Aspall. **Facilities** Children welcome Children's menu Children's portions Garden Parking ▭ (notice required)

DUNWICH — Map 13 TM47

The Ship at Dunwich ★★ SHL ◉

PICK OF THE PUBS

See Pick of the Pubs on opposite page

EARL SOHAM — Map 13 TM26

Victoria

The Street IP13 7RL ☎ 01728 685758
dir: *From A14 at Stowmarket take A1120 towards Yoxford*

This friendly, down-to-earth free house is a showcase for Earl Soham beers, which for many years were produced from a micro-brewery behind the pub. Some ten years ago the brewery moved to the Old Forge building a few yards away, where production still continues. Inside this traditional pub, simple furnishings, bare floorboards and an open fire set the scene for traditional home-cooked pub fare, including ploughman's, jacket potatoes and macaroni cheese. Heartier meals include a variety of casseroles and curries, followed by home-made desserts. A specials board and vegetarian dishes add to the choices.

Open all wk 11.30-3 6-11 **Bar Meals** L served all wk 12-2 D served all wk 7-10 Av main course £9.50 ⊕ FREE HOUSE/EARL SOHAM BREWERY ◀ Earl Soham Victoria Bitter, Albert Ale, Brandeston Gold, Sir Roger's Porter Õ Aspall. **Facilities** Children welcome Children's portions Garden Parking ▭ (notice required)

ELVEDEN — Map 13 TL88

Elveden Inn ♨ NEW

Brandon Rd IP24 3TP ☎ 01842 890876
e-mail: info@elvedeninn.com
dir: *From Mildenhall on A11 towards Thetford. Left onto B1106, pub on left*

The Elveden Estate have lavished money on their village inn, pushing open the doors of the revamped pub in November 2011 to reveal a relaxed and contemporary bar and dining rooms, and four luxury guest rooms. Expect a family-friendly atmosphere, blazing log fires in winter, East Anglian ales on tap, and a modern pub menu that brims with produce sourced from the estate farm and surrounding countryside. From classics like steak-and-ale pie and the Elveden burger, the choice also takes in ham hock and rabbit terrine, game hotpot, and lemon tart with spiced berry compôte. Don't miss the mid-June beer festival.

Open all day all wk **Bar Meals** L served all wk 12-9 D served all wk 12-9 Av main course £11.95 food served all day **Restaurant** L served all wk 12-9 D served all wk 12-9 Av 3 course à la carte fr £22.95 food served all day ⊕ FREE HOUSE ◀ Purity Mad Goose, Adnams Broadside, Southwold & East Green Õ Aspall & Perronelle's Blush. ♟ 9 **Facilities** ❄ Children welcome Children's menu Children's portions Garden Beer festival Parking Wi-fi ▭ (notice required) **Rooms** 4

Save on hotels. Book at **theAA.com/hotel**

SUFFOLK 475 ENGLAND

PICK OF THE PUBS

The Ship at Dunwich ★★ SHL ✿

DUNWICH — Map 13 TM47

Saint James St IP17 3DT
☎ **01728 648219**
e-mail: info@shipatdunwich.co.uk
web: www.shipatdunwich.co.uk
dir: *N on A12 from Ipswich through Yoxford, right signed Dunwich*

Two minutes' stroll from the beach, The Ship at Dunwich is a well-loved old smugglers' inn overlooking the salt marshes and sea, and is popular with walkers and birdwatchers visiting the nearby RSPB Minsmere reserve. Dunwich was at one time a medieval port of some size and importance, but then the original village was virtually destroyed by a terrible storm in 1326. Further storms and erosion followed and now the place is little more than a hamlet beside a shingle beach. The Ship keeps Dunwich on the map with hearty meals and ales from Adnams, Earl Soham and Green Jack – to name just a few. Its delightful unspoilt public bar offers nautical bric-à-brac, a wood-burning stove in a huge fireplace, flagged floors and simple wooden furnishings. Sympathetically spruced up in recent years, with the addition of clean, comfortable and contemporary-style bedrooms, it is locally renowned for its fish and chips, which include a choice of cod, whiting, plaice or hake. Other dishes plough a traditional

furrow. You could start with a home-made Scotch egg of Blythburgh pork, black pudding and free-range egg served with home-made piccalilli and salad, or potted prawns with granary toast and butter, followed perhaps by pie of the day with mashed potatoes and vegetables, or slow-cooked pork belly with sautéed potatoes, black pudding, seasonal vegetables and a lightly spiced gravy. Desserts continue in a similar vein – maybe classic Bakewell tart or apple and cinnamon baked cheesecake. Look for the ancient fig tree in the garden, and take note of the inn's two annual beer festivals, one towards the end of March and the other at the end of September. Booking for meals may be required.

Open all day all wk **Bar Meals** L served all wk 12-3 D served all wk 6-9 Av main course £12.50 **Restaurant** L served all wk 12-3 D served all wk 6-9 ⊕ FREE HOUSE ◀ Adnams Southwold Bitter, Humpty Dumpty, Brandon Rusty Bucket, Earl Soham, Green Jack ☼ Aspall. ♀ 9 **Facilities** Children welcome Children's menu Children's portions Family room ❀ Garden Beer festival Parking Wi-fi **Rooms** 15

EYE
Map 13 TM17

The White Horse Inn ★★★★ INN

Stoke Ash IP23 7ET ☎ 01379 678222
e-mail: mail@whitehorse-suffolk.co.uk
dir: On A140 between Ipswich & Norwich

Midway between Norwich and Ipswich, this 17th-century coaching inn is set amid lovely Suffolk countryside. The heavily timbered interior accommodates an inglenook fireplace, two bars and a restaurant. An extensive menu is supplemented by lunchtime snacks, grills and daily specials from the blackboard. Try salmon pâté or smoked duck salad to start. Main courses include red pepper and goat's cheese lasagne; honey and mustard chicken; venison casserole; chicken madras; and baked salmon with a sage and parmesan crust. There are 11 spacious motel bedrooms in the grounds, as well as a patio and secluded grassy area.

Open all day all wk 7am-11pm (Sat 8am-11pm Sun 8am-10.30pm) **Bar Meals** food served all day **Restaurant** food served all day ⊕ FREE HOUSE ◀ Greene King Abbot Ale, Adnams Ò Aspall. **Facilities** Children welcome Children's menu Children's portions Garden Parking Wi-fi ➡ **Rooms** 11

FRAMLINGHAM
Map 13 TM26

The Station Hotel

Station Rd IP13 9EE ☎ 01728 723455
e-mail: framstation@btinternet.com
dir: Bypass Ipswich towards Lowestoft on A12. Approx 6m left onto B1116 towards Framlingham

Built as part of the local railway in the 19th century, The Station Hotel has been a pub since the 1950s, outliving the railway which closed in 1962. You will find scrubbed tables and an eclectic mix of furniture. During the last decade it has established a fine reputation for its gutsy and earthy food listed on the ever-changing blackboard menu. A typical lunch could be the Station cheeseburger; dinner might include pigeon breast with bubble-and-squeak and smoked bacon; or roast loin of venison with a red wine and mushroom risotto. Try beers such as Victoria Bitter and Albert Ale, supplied by the Earl Soham Brewery. There is a beer festival in mid-July. Booking for meals may be required.

Open all wk 12-2.30 5-11 (Sun 12-3 7-10.30) **Bar Meals** L served all wk 12-2 D served Sun-Thu 6.30-9, Fri-Sat 6.30-9.30 ⊕ FREE HOUSE ◀ Earl Soham Victoria Bitter, Albert Ale & Gannet Mild, Veltins, Crouch Vale, Guinness Ò Aspall. **Facilities** ✿ Children welcome Children's portions Family room Garden Beer festival Parking ➡

FRAMSDEN
Map 13 TM15

The Dobermann Inn

The Street IP14 6HG ☎ 01473 890461
dir: S off A1120 (Stowmarket to Yoxford road) 10m from Ipswich on B1077 towards Debenham

Previously called The Greyhound, this pretty country pub was renamed by its current proprietor, a prominent breeder and judge of Dobermanns. The thatched roofing, gnarled beams, open fire and assorted furniture reflect its 16th-century origins. With a selection of Adnams ales on offer and Mauldons Dickens bitter, food ranges from sandwiches, hearty ploughman's and salads to main courses featuring plenty of fish and vegetarian choices. Reliable favourites include chilli con carne, spicy nut loaf, Dover sole, and steak and mushroom pie.

Open 12-3 7-11 Closed: 25-26 Dec, Sun eve, Mon **Bar Meals** L served Tue-Sun 12-2 D served Tue-Sat 7-9 Av main course £10.75 ⊕ FREE HOUSE ◀ Adnams Southwold Bitter, Old Ale & Broadside, Mauldons Dickens Ò Aspall. **Facilities** Garden Parking ➡ (notice required) **Notes** ☺

GREAT BRICETT
Map 13 TM05

The Veggie Red Lion

PICK OF THE PUBS

Green Street Green IP7 7DD ☎ 01473 657799
e-mail: janwise@fsmail.net
dir: 4.5m from Needham Market on B1078

In an inspired move a few years ago, Jan Wise re-invented the old 17th-century village pub at Great Bricett as a ground-breaking vegetarian and vegan destination dining inn. Set in large peaceful grounds amidst pockets of woodland, the pub was reinvigorated and became instantly popular. It continues to serve a tasty drop of Greene King IPA and Old Speckled Hen. Jan's unfailing commitment to developing exquisite dishes has won accolades – you'll find no hint of anything that once grazed, swam or pecked; special diets are usually no problem either. Settle down in the rustic beamed and colour-washed interior to experience the delightful difficulty of deciding just what treats to try. Start with parsnip and pecan bruschetta drizzled with white truffle oil. Next could come an African sweet potato stew, with roasted red peppers, fine beans and baby corn. Lashings of custard could accompany a closing crumble of Bramley apple and cinnamon. Weekend booking is strongly recommended.

Open 12-3 6-11 Closed: Sun eve & Mon **Bar Meals** L served Tue-Sun 12-2 D served Tue-Sat 6-9 ⊕ GREENE KING ◀ IPA, Morland Old Speckled Hen Ò Aspall. **Facilities** Children welcome Children's menu Children's portions Play area Garden Parking Wi-fi

HALESWORTH
Map 13 TM37

The Queen's Head

PICK OF THE PUBS

The Street, Bramfield IP19 9HT ☎ 01986 784214
e-mail: qhbfield@aol.com
dir: 2m from A12 on A144 towards Halesworth

A lovely Grade II listed building in the centre of Bramfield on the edge of the Suffolk Heritage Coast near historic Southwold. The enclosed garden, ideal for children, is overlooked by the thatched village church which has an unusual separate round bell tower. The pub's interior welcomes with scrubbed pine tables, exposed beams, a vaulted ceiling in the bar and enormous fireplaces. In the same capable hands for over 15 years, the pub's landlord enthusiastically supports the 'local and organic' movement – reflected by a menu which proudly names the farms and suppliers from which the carefully chosen ingredients are sourced. There is nonetheless a definite cosmopolitan twist in dishes such as Moat Farm smoked duck breast with marinated beetroot, walnut and grilled goat's cheese salad; and Blythburgh pork chop with braised Puy lentils with an apple and cider sauce. Amanda's home-made puddings and ice creams are tempting, as is the platter of three local cheeses with celery – Shipcord, Suffolk Blue and Norfolk White Lady.

Open all wk 10.30-2.30 6.30-11 (Sun 12-3 7-10.30) Closed: 25 Dec **Bar Meals** L served all wk 12-2 D served Mon-Fri 6.30-9.15, Sat 6.30-10, Sun 7-9 Av main course £12.95 ⊕ ADNAMS ◀ Southwold Bitter, Broadside Ò Aspall. ♟ 8 **Facilities** ✿ Children welcome Children's menu Children's portions Family room Garden Parking Wi-fi ➡ (notice required)

HITCHAM
Map 13 TL95

The White Horse Inn

The Street IP7 7NQ ☎ 01449 740981
e-mail: lewis@thewhitehorse.wanadoo.co.uk
dir: 13m from Ipswich & Bury St Edmunds, 7m Stowmarket, 7m Hadleigh

The 400-year-old inn was originally a staging post between London and Norwich and once had a blacksmith's forge attached to the pub. Today, this rural village local is the perfect setting for quaffing Suffolk real ales – Rattlesden Best - playing traditional pub games and enjoying regular live entertainment. Freshly prepared meals take in bar meals like roast beef and horseradish sandwiches, and steak-and-ale pie; and baked sea bass and beef bourguignon on the evening menu. In summer, the beer garden is open for barbecues. Booking for meals may be required.

Open all wk 12-3 6-11 **Bar Meals** L served all wk 12-2.30 D served all wk 6-9 **Restaurant** L served all wk 12-2.30 D served all wk 6-9 ⊕ FREE HOUSE ◀ Adnams Southwold Bitter & Fisherman, Rattlesden Best, Cox and Holbrook Stowmarket Porter Ò Aspall. ♟ **Facilities** ✿ Children welcome Children's menu Children's portions Garden Parking Wi-fi ➡ (notice required)

Save on hotels. Book at **theAA.com/hotel**

SUFFOLK 477 ENGLAND

HOLBROOK
Map 13 TM13

The Compasses

Ipswich Rd IP9 2QR ☎ 01473 328332
e-mail: compasses.holbrook@virgin.net
dir: *From A137 S of Ipswich, take B1080 to Holbrook, pub on left. From Ipswich take B1456 to Shotley. At Freston Water Tower right onto B1080 to Holbrook. Pub 2m right*

Standing on the spectacular Shotley peninsula bordered by the rivers Orwell and Stour, this traditional 17th-century country pub offers a simple, good-value menu. Choices range from filled jacket potatoes and lunchtime baguettes to hot pub favourites like liver and bacon casserole or Hungarian goulash. Fish dishes include an unusual seafood lasagne, whilst Thai green butternut and pineapple curry is amongst the vegetarian options. A monthly quiz night and pensioners' weekday lunches complete The Compasses' honest offerings. Booking for meals may be required.

Open 11.30-2.30 6-11 (Sun 12-3 6-10.30) Closed: 26 Dec-1 Jan, Tue eve **Bar Meals** L served all wk 12-2.15 D served Wed-Mon 6-9.15 Av main course £9 **Restaurant** L served all wk 12-2.15 D served Wed-Mon 6-9.15 ⊕ PUNCH TAVERNS ◀ Adnams Southwold Bitter, Sharp's Doom Bar ♂ Aspall. ♟ 12 **Facilities** Children welcome Children's menu Children's portions Play area Garden Parking Wi-fi ☛ (notice required)

HONEY TYE
Map 13 TL93

The Lion

CO6 4NX ☎ 01206 263434
e-mail: enquiries@lionhoneytye.co.uk
dir: *On A134 midway between Colchester & Sudbury*

A traditional country dining pub, located in an Area of Outstanding Natural Beauty, The Lion has a walled beer garden for outside eating and drinking. The spacious restaurant is decorated in a modern, comfortable style and the bar has low-beamed ceilings and an open log fire. The bar menu offers a good choice of sandwiches, jackets and pub classics, while the main menu includes smoked salmon and apple rösti stack; tiger prawn spaghetti; roasted pepper filled with basil and vegetable couscous; and lamb meatballs in a tomato and mint cream sauce.

Open all wk 11.30-3 6-11 (Sun 12-10) ◀ Adnams. **Facilities** Children welcome Children's menu Children's portions Garden Parking

HOXNE
Map 13 TM17

The Swan

Low St IP21 5AS ☎ 01379 668275
e-mail: info@hoxneswan.co.uk
dir: *Telephone for directions*

This 15th-century Grade II listed lodge, reputedly built for the Bishop of Norwich, has large gardens running down to the River Dove, with a vast willow tree. Inside, the restaurant and front bar boast a 10ft inglenook fireplace, ornate beamed ceilings and old planked floors. Food includes starters like pan-fried pigeon breast with celeriac and apple gratin; or smoked mackerel fishcakes; followed by silverside and oxtail braise with horseradish mash, millefeuille of pork, apricot and almonds; or aubergine, chickpea and sweet potato tagine. Booking for meals may be required.

Open all wk ⊕ ENTERPRISE INNS ◀ Adnams Southwold Bitter, Woodforde's Wherry, Guest ales ♂ Aspall. **Facilities** Children welcome Children's portions Garden Parking

INGHAM
Map 13 TL87

The Cadogan ★★★★ INN ◉

The Street IP31 1NG ☎ 01284 728443
e-mail: info@thecadogan.co.uk
dir: *A14 junct 42, 1st exit onto B1106. At rdbt take 1st exit (A134). 3m to Ingham. Pub on left*

Just four miles from the centre of Bury St Edmunds, The Cadogan is a friendly and inviting pub with seven en suite bedrooms for those who want to stay longer. The emphasis on the food is seasonality and local produce; lunchtime sandwiches and light bites are complemented by dinner options such as spiced chickpea and parmesan bake; or slow-roasted duck leg with pork and white bean stew. Open all day, there is a large garden, with a children's play area, perfect for alfresco dining.

Open all day all wk Closed: 25 Dec-1 Jan **Bar Meals** L served all wk 12-2.30 D served all wk 6-9.30 Av main course £12 **Restaurant** L served all wk 12-2.30 D served all wk 6-9.30 Av 3 course à la carte fr £21 ⊕ GREENE KING ◀ IPA, Abbot Ale ♂ Aspall. ♟ 14 **Facilities** Children welcome Children's menu Children's portions Play area Garden Parking Wi-fi ☛ (notice required) **Rooms** 7

IPSWICH
Map 13 TM14

The Fat Cat

288 Spring Rd IP4 5NL ☎ 01473 726524
e-mail: fatcatipswich@btconnect.com
dir: *rom A12 take A1214 towards town centre, becomes A1071 (Woodbridge Road East). At mini rdbt 2nd left into Spring Rd*

Good beer and conversation are the two main ingredients in this no-frills free house. The Fat Cat is a mecca for beer aficionados, with a friendly atmosphere in two homely bars and a raft of real ales served in tip-top condition from the taproom behind the bar. The head-scratching choice – up to 22 every day – come from Dark Star, Elgood's, Green Jack and a host of local micro-breweries. Soak up the beer with simple bar snacks like beef and Guinness pasties, sausage rolls, pork pies and baguettes.

Open all day all wk **Bar Meals** food served all day ⊕ FREE HOUSE ◀ Adnams Old Ale, Dark Star Hophead, Elgood's Black Dog, Green Jack Gone Fishing, Guest ales ♂ Aspall. ♟ 8 **Facilities** Garden ☛ (notice required) **Notes** ◉

LAXFIELD
Map 13 TM27

The Kings Head (The Low House)

PICK OF THE PUBS

Gorams Mill Ln IP13 8DW ☎ 01986 798395
e-mail: lowhouse@keme.co.uk
dir: *On B1117*

This unspoilt thatched 16th-century alehouse is a rare Suffolk gem that oozes charm and character. Locals know it as The Low House because it lies in a dip below the churchyard. Tip-top Adnams ales are served straight from the cask in the original taproom – this is one of the few pubs in Britain which has no bar. Order a pint of Broadside and retire to an ancient fireplace with a horseshoe of high-backed settles with an oak table in the middle. Traditional lunchtime fare includes sandwiches and baguettes, perhaps a BLT or roast beef and horseradish. Home-cooked dishes range from classics like sausages with mash and onion gravy to slow-roasted Dingley Dell pork and lamb shank cooked in Guinness. Beer festivals in May and September are unforgettable occasions thanks to the beautiful situation of the pub overlooking the river; its grounds, now with rose gardens and an arbour, were formerly the village bowling green.

Open all wk 12-3 6-close (all day Apr-Sep) **Bar Meals** L served all wk 12-2 D served Mon-Sat 7-9 Av main course £8.50 **Restaurant** L served all wk 12-2 D served Mon-Sat 7-9 Fixed menu price fr £10 Av 3 course à la carte fr £19.50 ⊕ ADNAMS ◀ Southwold Bitter, Broadside & Seasonal ales, Guest ales ♂ Aspall. ♟ 11 **Facilities** ❖ Children welcome Children's portions Play area Family room Garden Beer festival Parking Wi-fi ☛ (notice required)

LEVINGTON — Map 13 TM23

The Ship Inn

PICK OF THE PUBS

Church Ln IP10 0LQ ☎ 01473 659573
e-mail: theshipinnlevington@hotmail.co.uk
dir: *Off A14 towards Felixstowe. Nr Levington Marina*

The timbers of this 13th-century thatched inn overlooking the River Orwell are impregnated with the salt of the sea, and ghosts of bygone smugglers still occupy the many nooks and crannies. The Ship Inn stands within sight of the Suffolk marshes, where the hulks of beached sailing vessels were broken up for their precious beams. Indeed, families are welcome to enjoy the estuary views outside on the attractive front seats or on the rear patio. The interior walls and surfaces, however, are so full of maritime lamps, compasses and keepsakes that it's deemed an unsafe environment for children. There are two log-burning stoves in wintertime to keep things cosy. The service is informal, friendly and attentive. The sophisticated menu changes daily and focuses on executing a select number of dishes well. Starters may include pan-fried sardines with tomato and coriander salsa, and might be followed by a main course confit of duck leg with red wine-braised cabbage and sweet potato fries.

Open all wk 11.30-3 6-11 (Sat 11.30-11 Sun 12-10.30) ⊕ ADNAMS ◀ Southwold Bitter & Broadside, Guest ale ♂ Aspall. **Facilities** Children welcome Garden Parking Wi-fi

LIDGATE — Map 12 TL75

The Star Inn

PICK OF THE PUBS

The Street CB8 9PP ☎ 01638 500275
dir: *From Newmarket clocktower in High St follow signs towards Clare on B1063. Lidgate 7m*

Now under new ownership, this quintessentially English pub dates back to the 14th-century. An important meeting place for local residents, the pub is popular with Newmarket trainers on race days, and with dealers and agents from all over the world during bloodstock sales. Originally two cottages, the two traditionally furnished bars still fit the old-world bill with heavy oak beams, log fires, pine tables and antique furniture, but the dishes on the menu are a mix of Spanish and British. On the Spanish side are starters like whole baby squid with garlic and chilli or fish soup, which might be followed by bean and chorizo stew. British tastes are also catered for, with dishes such as warm chicken liver salad; venison steaks in port; and pigs' cheeks. There's an extensive wine list, too, with a number of well-priced Riojas jostling for position alongside the real ales on tap. Booking for meals may be required.

Open 12-3 6-12 Closed: 25-26 Dec, 1 Jan, Mon ⊕ GREENE KING ◀ IPA, Ruddles County, Abbot Ale ♂ Aspall. **Facilities** Children welcome Children's portions Garden Parking

LINDSEY TYE — Map 13 TL94

The Lindsey Rose

IP7 6PP ☎ 01449 741424
e-mail: thelindseyrose@hotmail.co.uk
dir: *From A12 between Ipswich & Sudbury take A1141 signed Lavenham. Ignore 1st sign for Lindsey, follow 2nd sign and pub sign*

Set in the beautiful Suffolk countryside between Ipswich and Sudbury, The Lindsey Rose has been the village local for over 500 years. Local ales are stocked in the bar and also take centre stage at the pub's annual beer festival. The region's produce is also celebrated on the menu, which might include their famous Red Poll beefburger venison; beer-battered haddock and chips; and sticky toffee pudding. Children are very welcome here and get their own menu and activity area outside. Booking for meals may be required.

Open all wk 11-3 5.30-11 (Sun all day) **Bar Meals** L served Mon-Sat 12-2.30, Sun 12-3 D served Mon-Sat 6.30-9.30, Sun 7-9 Av main course £15 **Restaurant** L served Mon-Sat 12-2.30, Sun 12-3 D served Mon-Sat 6.30-9.30, Sun 7-9 Av 3 course à la carte fr £27 ⊕ FREE HOUSE ◀ Adnams Southwold Bitter, Mauldons ♂ Aspall. **Facilities** ✿ Children welcome Children's menu Children's portions Play area Garden Beer festival Parking Wi-fi (notice required)

MELTON — Map 13 TM25

Wilford Bridge

Wilford Bridge Rd IP12 2PA ☎ 01394 386141
e-mail: wilfordbridge@debeninns.com
web: www.debeninns.co.uk/wilfordbridge
dir: *From A12 towards coast, follow signs to Bawdsey & Orford, cross rail lines, next pub on left*

On the other side of the River Deben from the pub - over Wilford Bridge, in fact - is Sutton Hoo (National Trust), where the famous seventh-century ship-burial was found in 1939. Mike and Anne Lomas have been running this free house for the last 20 years, he specialising in classic English dishes, especially featuring seafood, such as haddock, salmon and prawn pie; Shingle Street cod fillet; and plenty of shellfish, while from the chargrill come lamb and veal cutlets, steaks, and tournedos Rossini. In the bar, Adnams is joined by guest ales.

Open all day all wk **Bar Meals** L served all wk 11-9.30 D served all wk 11-9.30 food served all day **Restaurant** D served all wk 11-9.30 food served all day ⊕ FREE HOUSE

◀ Adnams Southwold Bitter & Broadside, John Smith's, Guest ales ♂ Aspall. 💲 9 **Facilities** Children welcome Children's menu Garden Parking

MILDENHALL — Map 12 TL77

The Olde Bull Inn ★★★ HL ◉

PICK OF THE PUBS

See Pick of the Pubs on opposite page

MONKS ELEIGH — Map 13 TL94

The Swan Inn ◉◉

PICK OF THE PUBS

The Street IP7 7AU ☎ 01449 741391
e-mail: carol@monkseleigh.com
dir: *On B1115 between Sudbury & Hadleigh*

Just across from the village green, the thatched Swan Inn blends easily with Monks Eleigh's colour-washed cottages, pretty gardens and imposing church. Wealth came from the wool trade and the original inn may have been the manorial court before affluent wool merchants first dined out here. Vestiges of the original 14th-century building remain, including the old smoke hole, wattle-and-daub panels and some fine beams supporting the thatched roof. Woodcock, teal and courgette flowers may feature on the menu here; a season for everything, and everything in its season is a guiding principal followed by chef-proprietor Nigel Ramsbottom, who honed his considerable skills at The Walnut Tree, Abergavenny, explaining the Italian influence to some dishes. Settle in with pork rillete with green tomato chutney before taking time over braised lamb knuckle with Puy lentil sauce, or monkfish wrapped in Parma ham and sage leaves, served on vegetable paella. Hot caramelised fig tart with vanilla ice cream is a fitting final flourish.

Open 12-2 7-11 Closed: 25-26 Dec, 2wks in summer, Sun eve & Mon **Bar Meals** L served Tue-Sun 12-2 D served Tue-Sat 7-9 Av main course £25 **Restaurant** L served Tue-Sun 12-2 D served Tue-Sat 7-9 Fixed menu price fr £15.75 Av 3 course à la carte fr £25 ⊕ FREE HOUSE ◀ Greene King IPA, Adnams Southwold Bitter & Broadside ♂ Aspall, Thatchers Katy, Savanna. 💲 **Facilities** Children welcome Children's portions Garden Parking

Save on hotels. Book at **theAA.com/hotel**

SUFFOLK 479 **ENGLAND**

PICK OF THE PUBS

The Olde Bull Inn ★★★ HL ✿

MILDENHALL   Map 12 TL77

The Street, Barton Mills IP28 6AA
☎ **01638 711001**
e-mail: bookings@bullinn-bartonmills.com
web: www.bullinn-bartonmills.com
dir: *Exit A11 between Newmarket &*
Mildenhall, signed Barton Mills

Travelling the A11 and in need of a
welcome pitstop en route to the Norfolk
coast? Then pull off just before Barton
Mills roundabout to locate this 16th-
century coaching inn. With its fine gables
and dormer windows and impressive
coaching courtyard, the rambling
building certainly has the look and feel of
a traditional roadside inn. However, step
inside the spruced-up bar, restaurant
and rooms and expect to be wowed by
Cheryl, Wayne and Sonia's contemporary
makeover, which successfully blends
original oak beams, big fireplaces and
wooden floors with funky fabrics,
designer wallpapers and bold colours –
best experienced in the quirky and very
individual boutique-style bedrooms. The
hands-on family have breathed new life
into this once faded old inn and the hub
of the building (and village) is the
refurbished bar, all muted Farrow & Ball
hues, scrubbed pine tables and cosy
seats by a blazing winter fire. Relax and
peruse the bar and restaurant menus
with a tip-top pint of East Anglian ale,
perhaps a local Humpty Dumpty brew.
Menus evolve with the seasons and every
effort is made to reduce 'food miles' and

source food from local farms and
producers. In the bar, tuck into pub
classics like Newmarket sausages with
mash and caramelised red onion gravy;
fresh Lowestoft cod in beer batter with
hand-cut chips; or Blythburgh ham, eggs
and chips. Eat alfresco on sunny days in
the delightful courtyard. Cooking moves
up a gear in the AA-Rosette Oak Room
Restaurant, where a meal may kick off
with marinated king prawn risotto with
coriander and sweet chilli sauce,
followed by rump of Denham Estate lamb
with gratin potato and red wine and
thyme jus, or Red Poll beef fillet with
creamy pepper sauce and smoked garlic
mash. To finish, try Matt's sticky toffee
pudding with rock salt caramel and
vanilla pod ice cream.

Open all day all wk 8am-11pm **Bar
Meals** L served all wk 12-9 (bkfst 8-12)
D served all wk 12-9 Av main course
£10 food served all day **Restaurant** L
served Sun 12-3 D served all wk 6-9
⌂ FREE HOUSE ◄ Adnams Broadside,
Greene King IPA, Brandon Rusty Bucket,
Humpty Dumpty, Wolf ♂ Aspall. ♀ 11
Facilities Children welcome Children's
menu Children's portions Garden
Parking Wi-fi ☛ (notice required)
Rooms 14

NAYLAND
Map 13 TL93

Anchor Inn

PICK OF THE PUBS

26 Court St CO6 4JL ☎ 01206 262313
e-mail: info@anchornayland.co.uk
dir: *Follow A134 Colchester to Sudbury for 3.5m through Gt Horkesley, bottom of hill turn right to Nayland, Horkesley Road. Pub on right after bridge*

The Anchor Inn Heritage Farm delivers a wealth of fresh produce to this 15th-century pub's kitchen, and the menu reflects this close relationship. The farm, which welcomes visitors, is run on traditional lines, with working Suffolk Punch horses helping to produce good old-fashioned food in the time-honoured way. Starters include a smoked platter fish, meat and cheeses from their own smokehouse; wild boar goulash with steamed dumpling bread served with home-baked rolls; and country pâté with quince and apple chutney. Classic mains include home-made traditional pork sausages; mussels in white wine cream sauce; and broccoli and stilton tartlet; as well as a choice of roasts on Sunday. Ales from Greene King and Adnams are drawn, and wines include an award-winner from their own vineyard just three miles away. Set on the banks of the River Stour, the Anchor is reputedly the last remaining place from which press-gangs recruited their 'volunteers'. Bought by Exclusive Inns in spring 2012 – expect big changes to the interior and food offering. Booking for meals may be required.

Open all wk Tue-Sun all day (Mon 11-3 5-11) **Bar Meals** L served Mon-Fri 12-2, Sat 12-2.30, Sun 12-4 D served Mon-Fri 6.30-9, Sat 6.30-9.30 Av main course £9.95 **Restaurant** L served Mon-Fri 12-2, Sat 12-2.30, Sun 12-4 D served Mon-Fri 6.30-9, Sat 6.30-9.30 ⊕ FREE HOUSE/EXCLUSIVE INNS ◀ Greene King IPA, Adnams, Local ales Ŏ Aspall, Carter's. **Facilities** Children welcome Children's menu Children's portions Garden Beer festival Parking ▱

ORFORD
Map 13 TM45

Jolly Sailor Inn

Quay St IP12 2NU ☎ 01394 450243
dir: *On B1084 E of Woodbridge, Orford signed from A12 approx 10m*

This timber-framed 16th-century quayside inn draws yachtsmen and landlubbers alike for a pint of Adnams while they ponder the charms of this reputed smugglers' haunt. Fishermen still use the sheltered anchorage protected by Orford Ness's shingle bank, and birdwatchers gather here to see the unique habitat and breeding grounds of Havergate Island. Views over the marshes, saltings and castle from the pub's extensive garden are more reasons to tarry, and perhaps order a light bite of Suffolk game and pork terrine; or a plate of Suffolk ham with bubble-and-squeak and free-range fried egg. Change of hands.

Open all wk 11-3 6-12 (Sat & summer all wk 11-11 Sun 12-11) **Bar Meals** L served Mon-Fri 12-3, Sat-Sun 11-9.30 D served Mon-Fri 6-9.30, Sat-Sun 11-9.30 **Restaurant** L served Mon-Fri 12-3, Sat-Sun 11-9.30 D served Mon-Fri 6-9.30, Sat-Sun 11-9.30 ⊕ ADNAMS ◀ Southwold Bitter, Broadside, Explorer Ŏ Aspall. ♑ 14 **Facilities** ♥ Children welcome Children's menu Children's portions Play area Family room Garden Parking Wi-fi ▱

REDE
Map 13 TL85

The Plough

IP29 4BE ☎ 01284 789208
dir: *On A143 between Bury St Edmunds & Haverhill*

Gracing the front lawn of this part-thatched, 16th-century pub is an old plough, its weather-beaten ironwork brushed by a weeping willow. On long-standing landlord Brian Desborough's ever-changing blackboard menu look for diced Highland beef in cream with wholegrain mustard and whisky sauce; minted local venison in chilli sauce with potato and cheese topping; and sea bass fillets in cream with bacon, butterbean and sweetcorn sauce. The bar serves Fuller's, Adnams, Ringwood and Sharp's ales and ten wines by the glass. At 128 metres above sea level, Rede is Suffolk's highest point.

Open all wk 11-3 6-12 (Sun 12-3) **Bar Meals** L served all wk 12-2 D served Mon-Sat 6-9 Av main course £12.50 **Restaurant** L served all wk 12-2 D served Mon-Sat 6-9 ⊕ ADMIRAL TAVERNS ◀ Fuller's London Pride, Ringwood Best Bitter, Sharp's Cornish Coaster, Adnams Ŏ Aspall. ♑ 10 **Facilities** Children welcome Children's portions Garden Parking Wi-fi ▱ (notice required)

SIBTON
Map 13 TM36

Sibton White Horse Inn ★★★★ INN ⦿

PICK OF THE PUBS

See Pick of the Pubs on opposite page

SNAPE
Map 13 TM35

The Crown Inn

PICK OF THE PUBS

Bridge Rd IP17 1SL ☎ 01728 688324
e-mail: snapecrown@tiscali.co.uk
dir: *A12 from Ipswich towards Lowestoft, right onto A1094 towards Aldeburgh. In Snape right at x-rds by church, pub at bottom of hill*

First-time visitors to this 15th-century former smugglers' inn are often astonished by the adjoining smallholding where a veritable menagerie of livestock is lovingly reared by Teresa and Garry Cook. It pays not to become too attached however, as these are destined for the table at this marvellously atmospheric pub (no gaming machines or background music here), with abundant old beams, log fire, brick floors and, around the large inglenook, a very fine double Suffolk settle. Fish from Orford fishermen and locally raised beef feature in the strong British menus, with daily specials adding to the tally. The menus are forever changing but dishes such as crab spring roll with chilli crème fraîche; pork terrine with piccalilli (both home made of course); Orford smoked fish platter with lemon mayonnaise; and chicken breast with beansprouts, shiitake mushrooms and lemongrass broth might appear, all helped along with Adnams beers or a choice of wines by the glass. There is a spacious garden for summer dining.

Being close to Snape Maltings Concert Hall, pre- and post-concert dining is available. Booking for meals may be required.

Open all wk ⊕ ADNAMS ◀ Southwold Bitter, Broadside, Seasonal ales Ŏ Aspall. **Facilities** Children welcome Children's portions Garden Parking

The Golden Key

PICK OF THE PUBS

Priory Ln IP17 1SQ ☎ 01728 688510
dir: *Telephone for directions*

Tucked away in the village, this delightful and tasteful 15th-century, cottage-style pub stands close to Snape Maltings Concert Hall and galleries, and oozes traditional charm. Inside, the time-honoured main bar has quarry-tiled floor, scrubbed pine tables, cosy nooks and alcoves, and some fine old curved settles fronting one of two roaring winter log fires. Mingle with the locals quaffing tip-top pints of Adnams ales, brewed up the road in Southwold, or head through to the pine-furnished dining room to sample dishes from the menu, which draws strongly on ultra-local produce. Fish is delivered daily from nearby Aldeburgh beach; organic vegetables come from the parson's garden; game from a nearby shoot and lamb from a neighbouring farm. Typically, this translates to bone marrow salad, rabbit pie, and fish and chips. The wine list stretches to 43 bins; on good days enjoy a glass outside beside the boules pitch. The pub also holds a beer festival. Booking for meals may be required.

Open all wk 12-3 6-11 (Sun all day) **Bar Meals** L served all wk 12-3 D served all wk 6-9 **Restaurant** L served all wk 12-3 D served all wk 6-9 ⊕ ADNAMS ◀ Southwold Bitter, Broadside, Explorer, Old Ale, Oyster Stout Ŏ Aspall. ♑ 15 **Facilities** ♥ Children welcome Children's portions Garden Beer festival Parking Wi-fi ▱

Save on hotels. Book at **theAA.com/hotel**

SUFFOLK 481 ENGLAND

PICK OF THE PUBS

Sibton White Horse Inn ★★★★INN

SIBTON   Map 13 TM36

Halesworth Rd IP17 2JJ
☎ 01728 660337
e-mail: info@sibtonwhitehorseinn.co.uk
web: www.sibtonwhitehorseinn.co.uk
dir: *A12 at Yoxford onto A1120, 3m to Peasenhall. Right opposite butchers, inn 600mtrs*

Off the beaten track, but just five minutes from the A12 at Yoxford in the heart of the Suffolk countryside, this rustic 16th-century free house retains much of its Tudor charm and incorporates stone floors, exposed brickwork and ships' timbers believed to have come from Woodbridge shipyard. A genuine free house, the bar is the place to enjoy pints of Green Jack Trawlerboys or Woodforde's Once Bittern, with a choice of dining areas to sample the award-winning food. Owners Neil and Gill Mason are committed to producing high-quality food from fresh local ingredients – and, to prove it, they grow many of their vegetables in the raised beds behind the pub. In the buzzy restaurant, you can order old favourites like tiger prawn cocktail with roasted pepper and baby gem lettuce; or Adnams beer-battered haddock with hand-cut chips, pea purée and tartare sauce. For those diners in search of something a little more special, wild duck and pheasant terrine with honey and hoi sin glaze, salad leaves and sweet chilli dressing; or salad of smoked ham hock with broad bean,

tomato and gherkin, honey and mustard dressing might be followed by Blythburgh pork fillet wrapped in streaky bacon, sautéed potato, mange tout, chestnut purée, spinach and basil pesto; or poached Scottish salmon fillet with sautéed new potato, wilted chard, orange fennel and tomato and red onion salsa. Finish, perhaps, with apple and forest fruit crumble with apple ice cream or vanilla pannacotta with strawberry soup. A secluded courtyard has a Mediterranean feel when the sun comes out. Time a visit for one of the pub's August beer festivals. Well-behaved children are welcome. Booking for meals may be required.

Open all wk 12-2.30 6.30-11 (Sun 6-11 in winter; Sun 12-3.30 6-11 in summer) Closed: 26-27 Dec **Bar Meals** L served

Mon-Sat 12-2, Sun 12-2.30 D served Mon-Sat 7-9, Sun 7-8.30 **Restaurant** L served Mon-Sat 12-2, Sun 12-2.30 D served Mon-Sat 7-9, Sun 7-8.30 Av 3 course à la carte fr £26 ⊕ FREE HOUSE ◀ Adnams Southwold Bitter, Woodforde's Once Bittern, Green Jack Trawlerboys Best Bitter ♂ Aspall. ♛ 9 **Facilities** Children welcome Children's portions ♨ Garden Beer festival Parking Wi-fi **Rooms** 6

SNAPE continued

Plough & Sail

Snape Maltings IP17 1SR ☎ 01728 688413
dir: *Snape Maltings on B1069 S of Snape. Signed from A12*

A pink, pantiled old inn at the heart of the renowned Snape Maltings complex, handy for the cultural and shopping opportunities here and close to splendid coastal walks. The interior is a comfy mix of dining and avant-garde destination pub; local ales and a good bin of wines accompany a solid menu, featuring an Orford smoked fish platter or slow-roast belly of pork with Suffolk cider apple chutney, plus a wide range of starters, nibbles and sandwiches. As we went to press, we learnt of a change of hands.

Open all day all wk ⊕ FREE HOUSE ◀ Adnams Broadside, Southwold Bitter & Explorer, Woodforde's Wherry ♂ Aspall. **Facilities** Children welcome Children's menu Children's portions Garden Parking Wi-fi

---

SOUTHWOLD Map 13 TM57

The Crown Hotel ★★ HL ⊛

PICK OF THE PUBS

The High St IP18 6DP ☎ 01502 722275
e-mail: crown.hotel@adnams.co.uk
dir: *A12 onto A1095 to Southwold. Into town centre, pub on left*

Centrally located in the seaside town of Southwold, The Crown dates back to the 18th century, when it was a coaching inn. Now the flagship hotel for Adnams Brewery, it offers a range of excellent ales on tap, as well as local Aspall cider. The high standard of cooking is recognised with an AA Rosette, and the whole place buzzes with lively informality. The seaside location brings impressive seafood options such as pan-fried sea bass fillet with mussels; cauliflower risotto and saffron velouté; or fillet of cod with buttered spinach and shellfish chowder. Other options might include hay-braised belly of local pork, black pudding purée, Savoy cabbage, apple and prune compôte; or pheasant breast with parsnip purée, sprouts, Chantenay carrots and sloe gin jus. Excellent puddings include blood orange cheesecake with pistachio ice cream. The Crown's 14 refurbished bedrooms are reached through twisting corridors and staircases.

Open all wk 8am-11pm (Sun 8am-10.30pm) **Bar Meals** L served Sun-Fri 12-2, Sat 12-2.30 D served Sun-Fri 6-9, Sat 6-9.30 (5.30-9.30 summer) **Restaurant** L served Sun-Fri 12-2, Sat 12-2.30 D served Sun-Fri 6-9, Sat 6-9.30 (5.30-9.30 summer) ⊕ ADNAMS ◀ Adnams ♂ Aspall. ♀ 20 **Facilities** Children welcome Children's menu Children's portions Garden Parking Wi-fi **Rooms** 14

The Randolph

PICK OF THE PUBS

41 Wangford Rd, Reydon IP18 6PZ ☎ 01502 723603
e-mail: reception@therandolph.co.uk
dir: *A1095 from A12 at Blythburgh 4m, Southwold 9m from Darsham train station*

Named after Sir Winston Churchill's father, this award-winning establishment is just a 15-minute walk from the centre of picturesque Southwold and an ideal base for exploring the Suffolk Heritage Coast. Built by the town's Adnams Brewery, this grand, late-Victorian hotel boasts a light and airy lounge bar with contemporary furnishings including high-backed chairs and comfortable sofas. Adnams beers such as Broadside are sold today, alongside real cider from another Suffolk maker, Aspall. Sandwiches and lighter meals are served in the bar, whereas in the large dining area the cooking style is modern British. Locally sourced ingredients produce starters and light meals such as Basque squid stew or tea-smoked pigeon breast, watercress and fig salad, and main courses ranging from dressed crab salad with buttered new potatoes and lemon and herb mayonnaise to chicken, ham and pea risotto. To one side of the building lies a large garden.

Open all day all wk **Bar Meals** L served all wk 12-2 D served all wk 6.30-9 Av main course £12-£16 **Restaurant** L served all wk 12-2 D served all wk 6.30-9 ⊕ ADNAMS ◀ Southwold Bitter, Broadside, Explorer, Old Ale ♂ Aspall. **Facilities** Children welcome Children's menu Children's portions Garden Parking Wi-fi 🚌

STANSFIELD Map 13 TL75

The Compasses Stansfield **NEW**

High St CO10 8LN ☎ 01284 789486
e-mail: ron@compasses.uk.com
dir: *From Bury St Edmunds take A143 towards Haverhill. Left signed Denston. Bear right into Stansfield, pub on right*

With its outer walls painted yellow you'll easily spot The Compasses, a village-centre pub run by Ron and Jaqcue van Straalen. With a prestigious restaurant career in Holland behind him, Ron likes to serve Dutch mussels, but other culinary ideas for his regularly changing menus come from this side of the North Sea, such as starters of locally smoked goose breast; and sautéed creamy garlic mushrooms. Main courses are Adnams ale pie; slow-cooked lamb shank; pheasant breast; liver and bacon; halibut fillet; and vegetarian specials. There's live music on Wednesdays.

Open 12-2 5-11 (Sat-Sun all day) Closed: 3wks Jan, Mon, Tue **Bar Meals** L served Wed-Sat 12-2, Sun 12-3 D served Wed-Sun 6-9 **Restaurant** L served Wed-Sat 12-2, Sun 12-3 D served Wed-Sun 6-9 ⊕ FREE HOUSE ◀ Woodforde's, Adnams, Earl Soham, Nethergate. **Facilities** ♣ Children welcome Children's menu Children's portions Garden Parking Wi-fi 🚌 (notice required)

STANTON Map 13 TL97

The Rose & Crown

Bury Rd IP31 2BZ ☎ 01359 250236
e-mail: roseandcrownstanton@btconnect.com
dir: *On A143 from Bury St Edmunds towards Diss*

Set in three acres of landscaped grounds, this 16th-century former coaching inn offers a varied snack menu, daily specials and a Sunday carvery. Settle on one of the comfy sofas in the split-level bar for a pint of Southwold-brewed Adnams, before tucking into tiger prawn, salmon and crayfish spaghetti; hand-carved ham with eggs and chips; or a warm goat's cheese salad with mango coulis and croûtons. A Tuesday quiz is amongst the regular weekday evening events, and children can enjoy a bouncy castle on summer weekends.

Open all day all wk **Bar Meals** L served Mon-Thu 12-3, Fri-Sat 12-9.30, Sun 12-8.30 D served Mon-Thu 5-9, Fri-Sat 12-9.30, Sun 12-8.30 **Restaurant** L served Mon-Thu 12-3, Fri-Sat 12-9.30, Sun 12-8.30 D served Mon-Thu 5-9, Fri-Sat 12-9.30, Sun 12-8.30 ◀ Greene King IPA, St Austell Tribute, Timothy Taylor Landlord, Adnams, Guinness ♂ Aspall. ♀ 12 **Facilities** ♣ Children welcome Children's menu Children's portions Play area Garden Beer festival Parking Wi-fi 🚌

STOKE-BY-NAYLAND Map 13 TL93

The Angel Inn

PICK OF THE PUBS

CO6 4SA ☎ 01206 263245
e-mail: info@angelinnsuffolk.co.uk
dir: *From Colchester take A134 towards Sudbury, 5m to Nayland. Or from A12 between juncts 30 & 31 take B1068, then B1087 to Nayland*

Set in Constable country, this Grade II listed 16th-century coaching inn is under new ownership and has undergone a full refurbishment. It may offer the most modern of facilities but it has retained plenty of its original features and charm with beamed bars, log fires and cosy snug areas. The relaxed, contemporary feel extends to the air-conditioned conservatory, patio and sun terrace. With its high ceiling and 52-ft deep well, The Well Room is certainly a focal point, and booking for lunch or dinner is recommended. Dining in the bar is on a first-come, first-served basis but the same menu is served throughout. Main courses offer a range of meat, seafood and vegetarian options, typically including pan-fried hake fillet with beetroot fritter, braised chicory and orange beurre blanc, or smoked bacon and cheddar chicken Kiev with tomato salsa and potato wedges. There is an extensive wine list.

Open all day all wk 11-11 (Sun 11-10.30) **Bar Meals** L served Mon-Fri 12-3.30, Sat 12-9.30, Sun 12-9 D served Mon-Fri 6-9.30, Sat 12-9.30, Sun 12-9 **Restaurant** L served Mon-Fri 12-3.30, Sat 12-9.30, Sun 12-9 D served Mon-Fri 6-9.45, Sat 12-9.30, Sun 12-9 ⊕ FREE HOUSE/ EXCLUSIVE INNS ◀ Adnams Southwold Bitter, Greene

---

Save on hotels. Book at **theAA.com/hotel**

SUFFOLK 483 ENGLAND

King, Nethergate, 2 Guest ales ♻ Aspall. ♟ 12
Facilities ✿ Children welcome Children's menu
Children's portions Family room Garden Parking Wi-fi
🚐 (notice required)

The Crown ★★★ SHL ◉◉

PICK OF THE PUBS

CO6 4SE ☎ 01206 262001
e-mail: info@crowninn.net
dir: *Exit A12 signed Stratford St Mary/Dedham. Through
Stratford St Mary 0.5m, left, follow signs to Higham. At
village green turn left, left again 2m, pub on right*

In the heart of Constable country and within easy reach of
the timeless villages of Lavenham, Kersey and Long
Melford, this 16th-century free house sits above the Stour
and Box river valleys on the Suffolk and Essex border.
Stylishly updated to create a contemporary bar and
informal dining areas, the pub also has 11 luxury en suite
bedrooms. Local produce underpins the modern British
menu, with dishes freshly prepared to order. Lunch brings
full meals and lighter options, or look to the chalkboard
for the daily East Coast fish selection. An evening meal
might begin with pheasant, rabbit and venison terrine
with red onion marmalade, followed by confit duck and
new potato hash with watercress and fried egg. Blood
orange tart with citrus yogurt makes for a refreshing end
to the meal. Every dish is given a wine match, and a
decent selection of ales complements the superb wine
list.

Open all day all wk 7.30am-11pm (Sun 8am-10.30pm)
Closed: 25-26 Dec **Bar Meals** L served Mon-Sat 12-2.30,
Sun 12-9 D served Mon-Thu 6-9.30, Fri-Sat 6-10, Sun
12-9 Av main course £14 **Restaurant** L served Mon-Sat
12-2.30, Sun 12-9 D served Mon-Thu 6-9.30, Fri-Sat
6-10, Sun 12-9 Av 3 course à la carte fr £25 ⊕ FREE
HOUSE ◀ Adnams Southwold Bitter, Crouch Vale Brewers
Gold, Woodforde's Wherry, Guest ales ♻ Aspall. ♟ 32
Facilities Children welcome Children's menu Children's
portions Garden Parking Wi-fi **Rooms** 11

STOWMARKET — Map 13 TM05

The Buxhall Crown

PICK OF THE PUBS

Mill Rd, Buxhall IP14 3DW ☎ 01449 736521
e-mail: thebuxhallcrown@hotmail.co.uk
dir: *3m from Stowmarket and A14*

A 17th-century building, The Buxhall Crown has a classic
old bar with intimate corners and an open fire, and a
second bar with a lighter, more modern feel. The owners
and staff pride themselves on the friendly family feel of
the pub, and the high quality of the food they serve.
Dishes are prepared from locally sourced produce, and
breads, biscuits, ice creams and sorbets are all freshly
made on the premises. Anything from bar snacks to a full
four-course meal is catered for, and the menu changes
regularly to suit the weather and the availability of
ingredients. To start, spiced parsnip soup with apple
crème fraîche, and pressed ham hock terrine with

redcurrants, Russet apple salad and piccalilli; followed
by Suffolk chicken breast, chanterelle mushroom mousse,
fondant potatoes and smoked bacon velouté; St Edmunds
beer-battered haddock fillet, triple cooked chips and
minted crushed peas; and woodland mushroom and
vegetable nage risotto all appeared on a winter menu.

Open 12-3 7-11 (Sat 12-3 6.30-11) Closed: 25 & 26 Dec,
Sun eve ⊕ GREENE KING ◀ IPA, Hardys & Hansons Olde
Trip, Morland Old Speckled Hen, Guest Ale ♻ Aspall.
Facilities Children welcome Children's menu Children's
portions Garden Parking Wi-fi

STRADBROKE — Map 13 TM27

The Ivy House

Wilby Rd IP21 5JN ☎ 01379 384634
e-mail: stensethhome@aol.com
dir: *Telephone for directions*

Just around the corner from Stradbroke's main street, this
Grade II listed thatched pub offers real ales and wine
from Adnams wine cellar. The weekly-changing menu in
the well-appointed restaurant makes good use of local
and seasonal produce, and in warmer weather you can sit
outside at the front or in the garden. Typical dishes
include skate wing with caper butter, new potatoes and
samphire; and roast loin of local venison with braised red
cabbage, celeriac and mash. Leave room for lemon and
amaretti cake or Pavlova with summer berries. Booking
for meals may be required.

Open all wk 12-3 6-11 **Restaurant** L served all wk 12-2
D served all wk 6.30-9 ⊕ FREE HOUSE ◀ Adnams,
Woodforde's, Buffy's ♻ Aspall. ♟ 12 **Facilities** ✿ Garden
Parking

SWILLAND — Map 13 TM15

Moon & Mushroom Inn

High Rd IP6 9LR ☎ 01473 785320
e-mail: themoonandmushroom@live.co.uk
dir: *Take B1077 (Westerfield road) from Ipswich. Approx
6m right to Swilland*

This award-winning 400-year-old free house promises to
serve 'home-cooked food at its very best', but that
statement makes no mention of the lip-smacking array of
East Anglian real ales served here straight from the
barrel. The pub was reputedly a staging post for the
despatch of convicts to Australia, and the records at
Ipswich Assizes do indeed show that a previous landlord
was deported for stealing two ducks and pig. A point to
ponder as you tuck into your ham, eggs and chips…
Booking for meals may be required.

Open Tue-Sat (Sun L & Mon L) Closed: Sun eve & Mon eve
Bar Meals L served Mon-Sat 12-2, Sun 12-2.30 D served
Tue-Sat 6.30-9 Av main course £10 **Restaurant** L served
Mon-Sat 12-2, Sun 12-2.30 D served Tue-Sat 6.30-9
⊕ FREE HOUSE ◀ Nethergate Suffolk County,
Woodforde's Wherry & Admiral's Reserve, Wolf Ale &
Golden Jackal ♻ Aspall. **Facilities** ✿ Children welcome
Children's portions Garden Parking

THORPENESS — Map 13 TM45

The Dolphin Inn

Peace Place IP16 4NA ☎ 01728 454994
e-mail: dolphininn@hotmail.co.uk
dir: *A12 onto A1094 & follow Thorpeness signs*

Just a short stroll from miles of unspoilt Suffolk coastline,
you'll find this friendly pub. In 1910, local landowner
Stuart Ogilvie started building a seaside holiday village
in Aldringham-cum-Thorpe; Ogilvie renamed his creation
Thorpeness. The original pub predated all this, but
unfortunately it burnt down. This 1995 rebuild stocks real
ales from independent local breweries, and serves locally
sourced produce such as grilled cod, garden peas and
chunky chips; and Procters Old English sausages,
creamed mash and roast onion gravy. Very much a
community pub, the kitchen also supplies preserves, pies
and pastries to the attached village store. Booking for
meals may be required.

Open 11-3 6-11 (Sat all day Sun 11-5) Closed: Sun eve &
Mon in winter **Bar Meals** L served all wk 12-2.30 D served
all wk 6.30-9.30 Av main course £12 **Restaurant** L served
all wk 12-2.30 D served all wk 6.30-9.30 Fixed menu
price fr £14.95 Av 3 course à la carte fr £23 ⊕ FREE
HOUSE ◀ Adnams Southwold Bitter & Broadside,
Brandon Rusty Bucket, Mauldons Midsummer Gold,
Woodforde's Wherry ♻ Aspall. ♟ 18 **Facilities** ✿ Children
welcome Children's menu Children's portions Garden
Parking Wi-fi 🚐

TUDDENHAM — Map 13 TM14

The Fountain

The Street IP6 9BT ☎ 01473 785377
e-mail: fountainpub@btconnect.com
dir: *From Ipswich take B1077 (Westerfield Rd) signed
Debenham. At Westerfield turn right for Tuddenham*

Only three miles north of Ipswich in the lovely village of
Tuddenham St Martin, this 16th-century country pub
combines old fashioned pub hospitality with an informal
bistro-style restaurant. The menu changes frequently and
there is an emphasis on local produce in dishes such as
haddock and smoked cheddar rarebit with tomato and
onion salad; braised pork belly with potato, pancetta and
Savoy cabbage broth; and baked lemon tart with
blackcurrant and cassis sorbet. Wash it all down with
pints of Adnams ale or Aspall cider. Booking for meals
may be required.

Open all wk 12-3 6-11 **Bar Meals** L served all wk 12-2
D served Mon-Fri 6-9, Sat 6-9.30 Av main course £12
Restaurant L served Mon-Sat 12-2, Sun 12-7 D served
Mon-Fri 6-9, Sat 6-9.30 Fixed menu price fr £13.25 Av 3
course à la carte fr £22 ⊕ FREE HOUSE ◀ Adnams
♻ Aspall. ♟ 9 **Facilities** Children welcome Children's
menu Children's portions Garden Parking

PICK OF THE PUBS

The Westleton Crown ★★★HL ❀❀

WESTLETON　　　Map 13 TM46

The Street IP17 3AD ☎ **01728 648777**
e-mail: info@westletoncrown.co.uk
web: www.westletoncrown.co.uk
dir: *A12 N, turn right for Westleton just after Yoxford. Hotel opposite on entering Westleton*

Standing opposite the parish church in a peaceful village close to the RSPB's Minsmere, this traditional coaching inn dates back to the 12th century and provides a comfortable base for exploring Suffolk's glorious Heritage Coast. The pub retains plenty of character and rustic charm, complemented by all the comforts of contemporary living. On winter days you'll find three crackling log fires, local real ales including Brandon Rusty Bucket and Adnams Southwold Bitter, as well as a good list of wines (with 11 available by the glass). There's also an extensive menu that includes innovative daily specials and classic dishes with a twist, all freshly prepared from the best local produce available. You can eat in the cosy bar, in the elegant dining room, or in the refurbished garden room. Sandwiches are made with a choice of The Crown's own breads, and served with sea-salted crisps and a dressed salad. More substantial appetites might choose from starters like a terrine of Blythburgh pork belly and garlic sausage with sauce gribiche; or Orford

smoked haddock risotto finished with crème fraîche and a baby caper salad. Follow up with main course choices such as pan-fried fillet of halibut with thyme creamed potato, curly kale, oxtail tortellini and chive beurre blanc; or suet pudding filled with slow-cooked Suffolk chicken, mushroom and tarragon, sautéed spinach, creamed potato and chicken jus. Save some space for accomplished desserts like rich chocolate Charlotte with caramelised chestnuts and yogurt sauce; or fig tarte Tatin with whisky and honey ice cream. Retire to one of the 34 comfortably refurbished and individually styled bedrooms, complete with flat-screen TV. Outside, the large terraced gardens are floodlit in the evening.

Open all day all wk 7am-11pm (Sun 7.30am-10.30pm) **Bar Meals** L served all wk 12-2.30 D served all wk 6.30-9.30 **Restaurant** L served all wk 12-2.30 D served all wk 6.30-9.30 ⊞ FREE HOUSE ◀ Adnams Southwold Bitter, Brandon Rusty Bucket Ö Aspall Harry Sparrow. ♀ 11 **Facilities** Children welcome Children's menu Children's portions ❖ Garden Parking Wi-fi 🚌 (notice required) **Rooms** 34

PICK OF THE PUBS

The White Horse ✿

WHEPSTEAD　　　　　　　Map 13 TL85

Rede Rd IP29 4SS ☎ 01284 735760
web: www.whitehorsewhepstead.co.uk
dir: *From Bury St Edmunds take A143 towards Haverhill. Left onto B1066 to Whepstead. In Whepstead right into Church Hill, leads into Rede Rd*

In the village of Whepstead, surrounded by rural public footpaths, The White Horse was built as a farmhouse in the early 17th century and extended during the Victorian era. The country pub was on the verge of extinction in 2009 when Gary and Di Kingshott recognised its potential and succeeded in buying it. The new owners closed it for a few months while it was being refurbished, and reopened it to the great delight of the locals and tremendously loyal staff. The bright, spacious interior makes it a great space for the display and sale of artworks by local painters. The large, copper-topped bar, open fire and comfortable wooden chairs make you feel instantly at home, while nostalgic touches like the Tuck Shop - which sells ice cream, sweets and chocolate - appeal to adults and children alike. As well as reliable Suffolk ales and real cider behind the bar, the AA Rosette-awarded menus change on a daily basis. Gary oversees the kitchen, and his passion for great, uncomplicated food is evident in every dish. Seasonal ingredients are locally sourced where

possible and always fresh. Starters could include the likes of smoked pigeon breast with balsamic beetroot; bruschetta of melting goat's cheese with honey and walnuts; and crayfish tails in a tomato mayonnaise. Main course options might be Marrakesh lamb cooked with dates, cinnamon, sultanas and couscous; steamed fillet of plaice filled with pea purée and white wine sauce; and honey, lemon and thyme roast chicken breast. Sticky Brazil nut tart, chocolate and cherry knickerbocker glory, and lemon bread-and-butter pudding are dessert choices. Di runs the front of house and her years of experience ensure quick and friendly service. Skye, the dog, can be found snoozing in a corner when he is not gently greeting customers.

Open 11.30-3 7-11 Closed: 25-26 Dec, Sun eve **Bar Meals** L served all wk 12-2 D served Mon-Sat 7-9.30 Av main course £10.95 **Restaurant** L served all wk 12-2 D served Mon-Sat 7-9.30 Fixed menu price fr £12.95 Av 3 course à la carte fr £25 ⊕ FREE HOUSE ◀ Adnams Southwold Bitter & Broadside, Guest Ale Ŏ Aspall. ♀ 10 **Facilities** Children welcome Children's portions Garden Parking 🚐

WALBERSWICK — Map 13 TM47

The Anchor ◉◉

PICK OF THE PUBS

Main St IP18 6UA ☎ 01502 722112
e-mail: info@anchoratwalberswick.com
dir: *A12 onto B1387, follow Walberswick signs*

Close to the seashore in trendy Walberswick, this striking
Arts and Crafts building is a sight for sore eyes. Diners
here are in for an education as well as a gastronomic
treat as each meal is twinned with a recommended beer
or award-winning wine. Game terrine with roast pears
and chutney is paired with Flying Dog IPA or Pouilly Loche
en Chantonne 2007 for instance, whilst smoked haddock
fishcake with creamy leeks and hand-cut chips could
come with Schneider Weisse or Forrest Estate Sauvignon
Blanc 2009. Good conversation, food and drink is the
mission statement of licensees Mark and Sophie Dorber;
Mark oversees the drinks side of the business whilst
Sophie continually invents culinary treats; she cut her
chef-teeth catering for cast and crew of the *Star Wars*
films, so expect some very unusual dishes! Chinese water
deer, slip soles and snipe may feature on her
award-winning menu. The rule-of-thumb here is to use
only the freshest, most local produce available, so the
salt marsh lamb or rabbit may have matured as
near-neighbours on the coastal strip outside the village,
stretching away from the sheltered terrace and wildflower
meadow beside the pub. A mid-August beer festival is
something to look forward to. Booking for meals may be
required.

Open all day all wk **Bar Meals** food served all day
Restaurant L served all wk 12-3 D served all wk 6-9
⊕ ADNAMS ◀ Southwold Bitter, Broadside & Seasonal
ales, Meantime Helles & Pale Ale, Bitburger, Guest ales
Ö Aspall. ☎ 22 **Facilities** Children welcome Children's
menu Children's portions Family room Garden Beer
festival Parking Wi-fi

WESTLETON — Map 13 TM46

The Westleton Crown ★★★ HL ◉◉

PICK OF THE PUBS

See Pick of the Pubs on page 484

WHEPSTEAD — Map 13 TL85

The White Horse ◉

PICK OF THE PUBS

See Pick of the Pubs on page 485

SURREY

ABINGER — Map 6 TQ14

The Stephan Langton

PICK OF THE PUBS

See Pick of the Pubs on opposite page

The Volunteer

Water Ln, Sutton RH5 6PR ☎ 01306 730985
e-mail: volunteer247@btinternet
dir: *Between Guildford & Dorking, 1m S of A25*

Enjoying a delightful rural setting with views over the
River Mole, this popular village pub was originally farm
cottages and first licensed about 1870. Under the
ownership of Hall & Woodhouse, it remains an ideal
watering hole for walkers who want to relax over a pint in
the attractive three-tier pub garden, or in the bustling
bar with its two fireplaces. Typical dishes include red
Thai curry; chicken and asparagus pie; and the renowned
Volunteer fish pie. Sandwiches, baguettes, melts, toasted
sandwiches and jacket potatoes are all available too.

Open all day all wk 11.30-11 (Sat 11-11 Sun 12-11) **Bar
Meals** L served all wk 12-11 **Restaurant** L served all wk
12-2.30 D served all wk 6.30-9.30 ⊕ HALL & WOODHOUSE
◀ Badger Tanglefoot, K&B Sussex, Guest ales Ö Westons
Stowford Press. ☎ 9 **Facilities** ☙ Children welcome
Children's menu Children's portions Garden Parking Wi-fi
🚐 (notice required)

ALBURY — Map 6 TQ04

The Drummond at Albury ★★★ INN

The Street GU5 9AG ☎ 01483 202039
e-mail: drummondarms@aol.com
dir: *6m from Guildford*

This eye-catching village inn, reopened and renamed in
2010 by the Duke of Northumberland whose family have
historic links to the pub, stands beside the River
Tillingbourne in the hearty of the Surrey Hills. Expect a
comforting mix of great local real ales from the Hogs
Back brewery, and the best of modern and traditional
British cooking – whole baked camembert to share,
braised lamb shank with red wine gravy, and hot
chocolate fondant. Individually appointed letting rooms
make the pub a good base from which to explore the
North Downs.

Open all day all wk 11-11 (Fri-Sat 11am-mdnt Sun
12-10.30) **Bar Meals** L served Mon-Fri 12-3, Sat 12-6,
Sun 12-8 D served Mon-Sat 6-9.30, Sun 12-8
Restaurant L served Mon-Fri 12-3, Sat 12-6, Sun 12-8
D served Mon-Sat 6-9.30, Sun 12-8 ⊕ FREE HOUSE
◀ Courage Best Bitter, Fuller's London Pride, Hogs Back
TEA, Adnams. ☎ 10 **Facilities** ☙ Children welcome
Children's portions Garden Parking Wi-fi **Rooms** 9

William IV

Little London GU5 9DG ☎ 01483 202685
web: www.williamivalbury.com
dir: *Just off A25 between Guildford & Dorking. Near Shere*

Deep in the Surrey Hills yet only a stone's throw from
Guildford, this 16th-century free house provides 'proper
pub food' made from mostly local produce. Sometimes
it's the free-range pork raised by landlord Giles written on
the blackboards, but more usually it's liver and bacon,
beer-battered cod and chips, or pan-fried Cajun chicken,
all served in the bar and dining room. Young's and two
Surrey breweries supply the real ales. It is great walking
and riding country, and the attractive garden is ideal for
post-ramble relaxation. Booking for meals may be
required.

Open all wk 11-3 5.30-11 (Sat 11-11 Sun 12-11) **Bar
Meals** L served all wk 12-2 D served Mon-Sat 7-9 ⊕ FREE
HOUSE ◀ Young's, Hogs Back, Surrey Hills Ö Westons
Stowford Press & Bounds. **Facilities** ☙ Children welcome
Children's portions Garden Parking 🚐 (notice required)

BETCHWORTH — Map 6 TQ25

The Red Lion

Old Rd, Buckland RH3 7DS ☎ 01737 843336
e-mail: info@redlionbetchworth.co.uk
dir: *Telephone for directions*

The family-run Red Lion dates back to 1795 and is set in
18 acres next to a cricket ground. It is home to a wisteria
thought to be 250 years old, and enjoys lovely rolling
countryside views, all just 15 minutes from Gatwick
Airport. Starters from a sample menu include smoked
haddock fishcakes, soup with crusty bread, or free-range
chicken liver parfait with granary toast and pear chutney.
Follow on with fisherman's pie, full rack of marinated
ribs, fish and chips, or short-crust pastry pie of the week.
There are two unusual function areas: a fully
air-conditioned cellar, and an outdoor area covered with
a cedar shingle roof. The area is ideal for walkers.

Open all day all wk 11am-11.30pm (Fri-Sat 11am-mdnt)
Bar Meals L served Sun-Fri 12-2.30, Sat 12-4
Restaurant L served Mon-Fri 12-2.30, Sat-Sun 12-4
D served Mon-Thu 6.30-9, Fri-Sat 6.30-9.30, Sun 6.30-8
⊕ PUNCH TAVERNS ◀ Adnams Southwold Bitter, Sharp's
Doom Bar, Hogs Back TEA, Fuller's London Pride
Ö Addlestones, Westons Stowford Press. ☎ 9 **Facilities** ☙
Children welcome Children's menu Children's portions
Garden Parking Wi-fi 🚐 (notice required)

PICK OF THE PUBS

The Stephan Langton

ABINGER   Map 6 TQ14

Friday St RH5 6JR
☎ **01306 730775** & **737129**
e-mail: info@stephanlangtonpub.co.uk
web: www.stephanlangtonpub.com
dir: *Exit A25 between Dorking &
Guildford at Hollow Ln. 1.5m, left into
Friday St*

Undulating mixed woodland surrounds
this secluded hamlet at the base of
Leith Hill, which is nothing more than a
tranquil hammer pond and a handful of
stone and timber cottages. This is prime
Surrey walking country and a popular
pitstop is The Stephan Langton, a 1930s
building named after the first
archbishop of Canterbury, who was
supposedly born in Friday Street. He
helped draw up the Magna Carta and a
copy of the document is pinned to a wall
in the rustic, bare-boarded bar. Equally
unpretentious is the adjoining dining
room, with its cream-washed walls,
simple wooden tables and chairs, and
open fires. Having conquered Leith Hill,
the highest summit in south-east
England, relax on the suntrap patio and
savour a thirst-quenching pint of locally
brewed Hogs Back TEA or Surrey Hills
Shere Drop. Peruse the short, inviting
menu that hits the spot with lunchtime
sandwiches and starters like smoked
chicken and leek risotto, and local
smoked trout with potato scones, mixed

leaves and walnut pesto dressing.
Typical hearty main dishes take in
grilled cod with Tuscan bean broth; beef
slow-braised in beer with root
vegetables, bashed neeps and tatties;
seared venison with roasted beetroot,
local watercress and crème de cassis
jus; and thyme and sage roasted rack of
lamb with sweet potato gratin, cavalo
nero and red wine jus. Changing daily
specials make the most of local
produce, much of it sourced from the
surrounding Wooton Estate. Mathew
Granger and Marissa Waters took over
the pub in November 2009 and are
gradually upgrading the place and
developing the food side of the
operation. Booking for meals may be
required.

Open 11.30-3 5.30-11 (Sat 11-11 Sun
12-9) Closed: Mon **Bar & Restaurant** L
Tue-Sat 12-2.30, Sun 12-4 D Tue-Sat
6.30-9.30 Av main course £13 Fixed
menu price fr £12 Av 3 course à la carte
fr £25 Booking advised ⊕ FREE HOUSE
◀ Ringwood Best Bitter, Hogs Back
TEA, Surrey Hills Shere Drop
Ŏ Thatchers. **Facilities** Children
welcome Children's portions ❧ Garden
Parking 🚌 (notice required)

BRAMLEY
Map 6 TQ04

Jolly Farmer Inn

High St GU5 0HB ☎ 01483 893355
e-mail: enquiries@jollyfarmer.co.uk
dir: *From Guildford take A281 (Horsham road). Bramley 3.5m S of Guildford*

Originally a coaching inn steeped in character and history, this friendly 16th-century family-run traditional free house has a passion for beer. Besides the impressive range of Belgian bottled beers, you'll always find up to eight constantly-changing cask real ales on the counter. The pub offers a high standard of food all freshly cooked, with daily specials board featuring Scottish sirloin and vegetable stirfry; home-made lasagne; Caesar salad and a full rack of barbecue pork ribs with chips and salad.

Open all day all wk 11-11 **Bar Meals** L served all wk 12-2.30 D served all wk 6-9.30 Av main course £10 **Restaurant** L served all wk 12-2.30 D served all wk 6-9.30 Av 3 course à la carte fr £22 ⊕ FREE HOUSE ◀ 8 Guest ales ♂ Westons Stowford Press, Aspall. ♟ 16 **Facilities** ❖ Children welcome Children's menu Garden Parking Wi-fi ▭ (notice required)

BUCKLAND
Map 6 TQ25

The Jolly Farmers Deli Pub & Restaurant

Reigate Rd RH3 7BG ☎ 01737 221355
e-mail: info@thejollyfarmersreigate.co.uk
dir: *On A25 approx 2m from Reigate & 4m from Dorking*

A unique free house beside the A25 between Reigate and Dorking. It may look like a traditional pub but step inside and you'll find a cracking deli/farmshop that showcases local foods and artisan producers smack next to the comfortable, wood-floored bar and restaurant. What's more, it is open all day, serving breakfast (at weekends), lunch, cream teas and dinner, or you can just pop in for some deli produce. Typical dishes include warm salad of pork belly, chorizo and new potatoes; lamb and wild mushroom suet pudding; calves' liver with herb and garlic butter; and sticky toffee pudding. Local ales, farmers' markets and beer festivals are added attractions.

Open all day all wk ⊕ FREE HOUSE ◀ Dark Star Hophead, WJ King Horsham Best. **Facilities** Children welcome Children's menu Children's portions Garden Beer festival Parking Wi-fi

CHIDDINGFOLD
Map 6 SU93

The Crown Inn ★★★★★ INN

The Green GU8 4TX ☎ 01428 682255
e-mail: enquiries@thecrownchiddingfold.com
dir: *On A283 between Milford & Petworth*

Set by the village green and dating back over 700 years, this historic and beautifully appointed inn oozes charm and character, featuring ancient panelling, open fires, distinctive carvings, huge beams, and eight comfortable

bedrooms. Food ranges from decent snacks like roast beef, horseradish and watercress sandwiches to Crown favourites like steak-and-kidney pudding, and imaginative dishes, perhaps roast duck on braised Savoy cabbage with smoked bacon and mash. Puddings include apple and rhubarb crumble. Booking for meals may be required.

Open all day all wk **Bar Meals** L served Mon-Sat 12-2.30, Sun 12-3 D served Mon-Sat 6.30-10, Sun 6.30-9.30 Av main course £12.50 **Restaurant** L served Mon-Sat 12-2.30, Sun 12-3 D served Mon-Sat 6.30-10, Sun 6.30-9.30 Fixed menu price fr £19.50 Av 3 course à la carte fr £22.50 ⊕ FREE HOUSE/FGH INNS ◀ Crown Bitter, Fuller's London Pride, Tiple fff Moondance, Hop Back Summer Lightning. **Facilities** Children welcome Children's menu Children's portions Garden Wi-fi ▭ **Rooms** 8

The Swan Inn ★★★★ INN ◉ NEW

PICK OF THE PUBS

Petworth Rd GU8 4TY ☎ 01428 684688
e-mail: info@theswaninnchiddingfold.com
dir: *From A3 follow Milford/Petworth/A283 signs. At rdbt 1st exit onto A238. Slight right onto Guildford & Godalming bypass. Right into Portsmouth Rd, left (continue on A283), to Chiddingfold*

Nestling among the Surrey Hills in the village of Chiddingfold between Guildford and Petworth, The Swan is typical of the coaching inns that used to serve customers travelling to or from the South Coast. Rebuilt in the 1880s and refurbished to a high standard in 2010, The Swan today combines village pub with fine dining and luxurious boutique-style accommodation. Among the ales are those brewed by the Surrey Hills Brewery, and more than a dozen wines from the cosmopolitan list are served by the glass. The menu also has international appeal, with tasty produce such as Scottish salmon, Parma ham and foie gras appearing among the best of local ingredients. A typical choice could be an appetiser of confit chicken and pork rillettes with sauce gribiche; a main course of pan-seared lamb's liver with celeriac mash; and dessert of apricot and frangipane tart with vanilla ice cream. The inn holds an annual beer festival in September. Booking for meals may be required.

Open all day all wk 11-11 (Sun 12-10.30) **Bar Meals** L served all wk 12-3 D served Mon-Sat 6.30-10, Sun 6.30-9 Av main course £12.50 **Restaurant** L served all wk 12-3 D served Mon-Sat 6.30-10, Sun 6.30-9 Av 3 course à la carte fr £22 ⊕ FREE HOUSE ◀ Adnams Southwold Bitter, Surrey Hills Shere Drop ♂ Hogan's, Aspall. ♟ 16 **Facilities** ❖ Children welcome Children's menu Children's portions Garden Beer festival Parking Wi-fi **Rooms** 10

CHURT
Map 5 SU83

Pride of the Valley

PICK OF THE PUBS

Tilford Rd GU10 2LH ☎ 01428 605799
e-mail: reservations@prideofthevalleyhotel.com
dir: *4m from Farnham on outskirts of Churt. 3m from Haslemere*

Named after a local beauty spot, this coaching inn was built in 1867 and is set in some of Surrey's most picturesque countryside. It was once a watering hole for Prime Minister David Lloyd George, who retired locally in the 1920s. Now a comfortable country house hotel, the building is distinguished by some fine art nouveau touches and wonderful wood panelling. The owner is an enthusiastic supporter of the local Hogs Back Brewery and maintains a first-class wine list, all of which complements the regularly refreshed menus reflecting seasonal, locally sourced produce. A typical day may find lamb tagine or trio of sausages on the bar meu; and wild boar and apple burger, accompanied by white pudding sausage roll, fried quail's egg, apple purée and parsnip crisps on the restaurant menu. Finish with milk chocolate mousse or orange and date sticky pudding. The large garden to the rear has picnic tables. Booking for meals may be required.

Open all day all wk **Bar Meals** L served Mon-Sat 12-2.30, Sun 12-3 D served all wk 6.30-9.30 Av main course £10 **Restaurant** L served Thu-Sat 12-2.30, Sun 12-3 D served Thu-Sat 6.30-9.30 Av 3 course à la carte fr £25 ⊕ FREE HOUSE ◀ Hogs Back TEA, Sharp's Doom Bar. **Facilities** ❖ Children welcome Children's menu Children's portions Garden Parking Wi-fi ▭ (notice required)

COBHAM
Map 6 TQ16

The Cricketers

Downside KT11 3NX ☎ 01932 862105
e-mail: info@thecricketersdownside.co.uk
dir: *M25 junct 10, A3 towards London. 1st exit signed Cobham. Straight over 1st rdbt, right at 2nd. In 1m right opposite Waitrose into Downside Bridge Rd*

Under new ownership in 2011, parts of this pub, with its oak beams and log fires, date back to 1540. The inn's charming rural setting makes it popular with walkers, and the pretty River Mole is close by. Chef-patron Max offers an all-day speciality pasta menu, as well as sharing boards and mains like bangers and mash; pie of the day; steamed rainbow trout; and a choice of burgers. Sandwiches and flatbreads are also served at lunchtime. The beer garden overlooks Downside Common and the village green.

Open all day all wk ◀ Morland Old Speckled Hen, Fuller's London Pride. **Facilities** Children welcome Children's menu Children's portions Play area Garden Parking

Save on hotels. Book at **theAA.com/hotel**

SURREY 489 **ENGLAND**

COLDHARBOUR
Map 6 TQ14

The Plough Inn
PICK OF THE PUBS

Coldharbour Ln RH5 6HD ☎ **01306 711793**
e-mail: theploughinn@btinternet.com
dir: *M25 junct 9, A24 to Dorking. A25 towards Guildford. Coldharbour signed from one-way system*

Known to date from 1641, the Abrehart family's old coaching inn gets much of its footfall from walkers and cyclists scaling nearby 965-ft Leith Hill, the highest point in south-eastern England. Earlier visitors were smugglers en route from the South Coast to London, which may be why the resident ghost is a sailor. Another high point is the landlord's own micro-brewery, producing Tallywhacker porter, Crooked Furrow bitter and the lighter Beautiful South, as well as Biddenden cider. The Abrehart's 23-year residency has produced a family-friendly place with big fires, a pretty garden and an evening steakhouse with a malt whisky bar serving 21-day, dry-aged local award-winning Aberdeen Angus steaks and other chargrills. On the menus expect lamb, mint and coriander sausages and mash with Merlot gravy; cod, haddock, prawn and salmon pie; and Mediterranean vegetable and goat's cheese tart. Home-made puddings include spotted dick and a daily crumble. Booking for meals may be required.

Open all day all wk 11.30am-mdnt Closed: 25 Dec **Bar Meals** L served Mon-Fri 12-2.30, Sat-Sun 12-3 D served Mon 7-9.30 Av main course £10 **Restaurant** D served Tue-Sun 7-10 ⊕ FREE HOUSE ◀ Leith Hill Crooked Furrow, Tallywhacker & The Beautiful South, Shepherd Neame Spitfire ᚖ Biddenden. **Facilities** Children welcome Children's menu Children's portions Garden Parking Wi-fi ➡ (notice required)

COMPTON
Map 6 SU94

The Withies Inn

Withies Ln GU3 1JA ☎ **01483 421158**
dir: *Telephone for directions*

Set amid unspoiled country on Compton Common just below the Hog's Back, this low-beamed 16th-century pub has been carefully modernised to incorporate a small restaurant. There is also a splendid garden where meals and drinks can be served under the pergola. Snacks available in the bar range from sandwiches and jackets to home-made quiche or soup of the day. In the restaurant dishes include seafood crêpe mornay; home-made Withies pâté; half a roast duckling with orange or peach sauce; whole local trout; and individual beef Wellington.

Open 11-3 6-11 (Fri 11-11) Closed: Sun eve **Bar Meals** L served all wk 12-2.30 D served Mon-Sat 7-10 **Restaurant** L served all wk 12-2.30 D served Mon-Sat 7-10 ⊕ FREE HOUSE ◀ Hogs Back TEA, Greene King IPA, Adnams ᚖ Aspall. **Facilities** Children welcome Garden Parking Wi-fi

CRANLEIGH
Map 6 TQ03

The Richard Onslow

113-117 High St GU6 8AU ☎ **01483 274922**
e-mail: therichardonslow@peachpubs.com
dir: *From A281 between Guildford & Horsham take B2130 to Cranleigh, pub in village centre*

A grand old tile-hung pub, the former Onslow Arms reopened in 2009 after a major refurbishment. Inside, it has retained its character, and its original brick inglenook, whilst benefiting from contemporary décor and a new dining room. Enjoy pints of local Surrey Hills ale and tuck into all-day menus offering tempting sandwiches, deli boards, daily roasts, salads and three-course meals such as moules marinière, followed by sausages, mash and gravy, with tiramisù for dessert.

Open all day all wk Closed: 25 Dec **Bar Meals** Av main course £14 food served all day **Restaurant** Av 3 course à la carte fr £22 food served all day ⊕ PEACH PUBS ◀ Surrey Hills Shere Drop, Adnams Lighthouse, Purity Pure UBU, Sharp's Doom Bar ᚖ Aspall, Addlestones. ♈ 13 **Facilities** ☙ Children welcome Children's portions Garden Parking Wi-fi ➡ (notice required)

DUNSFOLD
Map 6 TQ03

The Sun Inn

The Common GU8 4LE ☎ **01483 200242**
e-mail: suninn@dunsfold.net
dir: *A281 through Shalford & Bramley, take B2130 to Godalming. Dunsfold on left after 2m*

Opposite the cricket green and village pond in a chocolate-box village, this traditional 17th-century inn delivers a warm welcome, blazing fires and an array of real ales from the likes of Adnams and Harvey's. The award-winning, home-made healthy eating dishes use produce from the inn's own vegetable garden. Typical choices include crab and avocado salad or deep fried breaded brie to start, followed perhaps by chilli con carne with basmati rice, sour cream and garlic bread, or a hand-made Puy lentil and root vegetable burger. Enjoy the quiz every Sunday evening.

Open all day all wk **Bar Meals** L served all wk 12-2.30 D served Mon-Sat 7-9.15, Sun 7-8.30 Av main course £8.95 **Restaurant** L served all wk 12-2.30 D served Mon-Sat 7-9.15, Sun 7-8.30 ⊕ PUNCH TAVERNS ◀ Sharp's Doom Bar, George Gale & Co HSB, Harvey's Sussex, Adnams, Guinness ᚖ Westons Old Rosie. ♈ 10 **Facilities** ☙ Children welcome Children's menu Children's portions Garden Parking Wi-fi ➡ (notice required)

EASHING
Map 6 SU94

The Stag on the River NEW

Lower Eashing GU7 2QG ☎ **01483 421568**
e-mail: bookings@stagontherivereashing.co.uk
dir: *From A3 S'bound exit signed Eashing, 200yds over river bridge. Pub on right*

The river is the Wey, and this comfortable, well-appointed village inn on its banks takes full advantage, with a large beer garden and separate patio. Fixtures on handpump in the bar are Hogs Back TEA (Traditional English Ale) and Surrey Hills Shere Drop, named after a nearby village; others rotate. A seasonal menu might begin with fresh crab bruschetta in lime and chilli mayonnaise, or a charcuterie sharing board. Main courses include smoked haddock and prawn pie in spinach, bacon and mascarpone sauce; and supreme of chicken with dauphinoise potatoes.

Open all wk all day (ex Mon-Thu 3-5) Closed: 25 Dec **Bar Meals** L served Mon-Sat 12-3, Sun 12-8.30 D served Mon-Sat 6-9, Sun 12-8.30 Av main course £10-£15 **Restaurant** L served Mon-Sat 12-3, Sun 12-8.30 D served Mon-Sat 6-9, Sun 12-8.30 Fixed menu price fr £10 Av 3 course à la carte fr £10 ⊕ FREE HOUSE ◀ Hogs Back TEA, Surrey Hills Shere Drop, Guest ales. ♈ 12 **Facilities** ☙ Children welcome Children's menu Children's portions Garden Parking Wi-fi

EAST CLANDON
Map 6 TQ05

The Queens Head

The Street GU4 7RY ☎ **01483 222332**
e-mail: mark.williams@redmistleisure.co.uk
dir: *4m E of Guildford on A246. Signed*

This bustling brick-built village pub close to the North Downs Way is a haven for ramblers and locals seeking the best local produce. Beer is courtesy of the nearby Surrey Hills Brewery, while the food majors on locally sourced seasonal produce including meat from a 100-acre working farm. A hearty plate of braised lamb shank with parsley mash, braised cabbage and rosemary jus will revive after a long winter walk, or share a fish board, including crayfish, Devon crab and smoked mackerel, in the tree-shaded garden. Booking for meals may be required.

Open all wk 12-3 6-11 (Sat 12-11 Sun 12-9) **Bar Meals** L served Mon-Fri 12-2.30, Sat 12-9.30, Sun 12-8 D served Mon-Thu 6-9, Fri 6-9.30, Sat 12-9.30, Sun 12-8 Av main course £12 **Restaurant** L served Mon-Fri 12-2.30, Sat 12-9.30, Sun 12-8 D served Mon-Thu 6-9, Fri 6-9.30, Sat 12-9.30, Sun 12-8 Av 3 course à la carte fr £24 ⊕ FREE HOUSE ◀ Surrey Hills Shere Drop, Hogs Back TEA, Brakspear Oxford Gold, Shepherd Neame Spitfire, Sharp's Doom Bar. ♈ 13 **Facilities** ☙ Children welcome Children's menu Children's portions Garden Parking Wi-fi ➡

EFFINGHAM — Map 6 TQ15

The Plough

Orestan Ln KT24 5SW ☎ **01372 458121**
dir: *Between Guildford & Leatherhead on A246*

Off the beaten track near Polesden Lacey, an opulent National Trust country house, this pub's history is unclear, but it probably dates from the mid-1870s, judging by the beamed and matchboarded interior. Monthly-changing, freshly prepared contemporary and traditional British blackboard favourites include bacon and avocado salad; bangers and mash; chestnut-stuffed guinea fowl; and pan-fried sea bream with red wine, chorizo and pea risotto. Sunday roasts come with huge Yorkshire puds. Surrey Hills ramblers are often to be found in the garden and terrace, and shooting parties may turn up.

Open all wk 11.30-3 5.30-11 (Sun 12-3 7-10.30) Closed: 25-26 Dec & 31 Dec eve **Bar Meals** L served all wk 12-2.30 D served Mon-Sat 7-10, Sun 7-9 **Restaurant** L served all wk 12-2.30 D served Mon-Sat 7-10, Sun 7-9 ⊕ YOUNG'S ◀ Special & Winter Warmer, Wells Bombardier, Courage Directors, St Austell Tribute. **Facilities** Children welcome Children's menu Children's portions Garden Parking

ELSTEAD — Map 6 SU94

The Golden Fleece

Farnham Rd GU8 6DB ☎ **01252 702349**
e-mail: sheilapride@aol.com
dir: *From A3 at Milford follow Elstead signs on B3001. Pub past village green on left*

Situated in the tranquil village of Elstead, surrounded by beautiful countryside, this family-run pub offers a warm and traditional welcome with real log fire and hand-pulled ales. What sets it apart, however, is the extensive and authentic Thai menu that runs alongside more traditional pub classics. The pub also offers a Thai takeaway service during opening hours, and an enclosed beer garden is ideal for families with children.

Open all wk 11.30-3.30 5.30-11.30 (Fri-Sun all day) ⊕ ENTERPRISE INNS ◀ Otter Ale, Surrey Hills Shere Drop, Adnams Broadside, Ringwood Fortyniner ᵹ Thatchers. **Facilities** Children welcome Children's menu Children's portions Family room Garden Parking Wi-fi

The Woolpack

The Green, Milford Rd GU8 6HD ☎ **01252 703106**
e-mail: info@woolpackelstead.co.uk
dir: *A3 S, take Milford exit, follow signs for Elstead on B3001*

A traditional country pub, originally a wool exchange dating back to the 17th century. Weaving shuttles and other remnants of the wool industry make appealing features, as do the open log fires, low beams, high-backed settles, window seats and spindle-backed chairs. Select cask-conditioned ales are rotated, backed by a good choice of ciders. On the menu, starters such as pan-fried chicken livers are followed by home-made suet steak-and-kidney pudding; chunky minted lamb casserole; and desserts like all-spiced apple crumble with custard. The surrounding common land attracts ramblers galore, especially at lunchtime. As we went to press we learnt that the new owners were refurbishing the pub.

Open all day all wk Mon-Fri 10am-late (Sat-Sun 12-late) **Bar Meals** L served all wk 12-3 D served all wk 6-9 Av main course £6 food served all day **Restaurant** L served Mon-Sat 12-3, Sun 12-8 D served all wk 6-9 Fixed menu price fr £10 Av 3 course à la carte fr £20 food served all day ⊕ PUNCH TAVERNS ◀ Greene King Abbot Ale, Ringwood Fortyniner, Hogs Back TEA, Otter Ale, Sharp's Doom Bar, Brakspear, Young's ᵹ Westons Stowford Press, Addlestones, Aspall. ♟ 10 **Facilities** ❧ Children welcome Children's menu Children's portions Play area Garden Parking Wi-fi ▭ (notice required)

ENGLEFIELD GREEN — Map 6 SU97

The Fox and Hounds **NEW**

Bishopsgate Rd TW20 0XU ☎ **01784 433098**
e-mail: info@thefoxandhoundsrestaurant.com
dir: *With village green on left, left into Bishopsgate Rd*

Slap bang next to the Bishopsgate entrance to Windsor Great Park in the village of Englefield Green, The Fox and Hounds dates back to 1780. Under ambitious new ownership and reopened after an extensive four-month refurbishment, you can now enjoy a drink in the stylish bar or enjoy a slap-up meal in the light and elegant conservatory restaurant. A starter of Scottish mussels in Thai coconut broth might be followed by coq au vin or cheese and onion pie with purple sprouting broccoli.

Open all day all wk 8am-11pm **Bar Meals** L served all wk 12-9 D served all wk 12-9 Av main course £9 **Restaurant** L served all wk 12-3 D served Mon-Sat 6.30-9.30, Sun 6-9 Av 3 course à la carte fr £25.85 ⊕ FREE HOUSE/ENTERPRISE INNS ◀ Windsor & Eton Knight of the Garter, Sharp's Doom Bar, Brakspear ᵹ Addlestones. ♟ 22 **Facilities** ❧ Children welcome Children's menu Children's portions Garden Parking Wi-fi

FARNHAM — Map 5 SU84

The Bat & Ball Freehouse

PICK OF THE PUBS

See Pick of the Pubs on opposite page
See advert on page 492

The Spotted Cow at Lower Bourne

Bourne Grove, Lower Bourne GU10 3QT
☎ **01252 726541**
e-mail: thespottedcow@btinternet.com
web: www.thespottedcowpub.com
dir: *From Farnham Station left onto Approach Rd. Left onto A287 continue onto Vicarage Hill, left onto Bourne Grove.*

The Spotted Cow is set in four acres of secluded, woodland-shaded grounds and two gardens, one of which is enclosed and especially suitable for young children. Indulge in some of the great TEA beer from nearby Hogs Back Brewery and consider the ever-changing menu of tried-and-tested favourites, all made fresh on the premises. Sandwiches, jackets and ploughman's are on the bar lunch menu, while Thai green chicken curry, slow-roasted belly of pork, and 'ultimate' veggie burger all have a place on the main menu. Keep an eye out for specials like chorizo, cherry tomato and spiced chicken skewers.

Open all wk 12-3 5.30-11 (Sat 12-11 Sun 12-10.30) **Bar Meals** L served Mon-Sat 12-2.30 D served Mon-Sat 6-9.15 Av main course £10 **Restaurant** L served Mon-Sat 12-2.30, Sun 12-7 D served Mon-Sat 6-9.15 Av 3 course à la carte fr £25 ⊕ FREE HOUSE ◀ Timothy Taylor Landlord, Hogs Back TEA, Otter ᵹ Addlestones. **Facilities** ❧ Children welcome Children's portions Play area Garden Parking Wi-fi

Save on hotels. Book at **theAA.com/hotel**

SURREY 491   ENGLAND

PICK OF THE PUBS

The Bat & Ball Freehouse

FARNHAM   Map 5 SU84

15 Bat & Ball Ln, Boundstone GU10 4SA
☎ **01252 792108**
e-mail: info@thebatandball.co.uk
web: www.thebatandball.co.uk
dir: *From A31 (Farnham bypass) onto A325 signed Birdworld. Left at Bengal Lounge. At T-junct right, immediately left into Sandrock Hill Rd. 0.25m left into Upper Bourne Ln. Follow signs.*

Tucked down a lane in a wooded valley south of Farnham, this 150-year-old inn is not that easy to find, but well worth hunting out. Hops for the local breweries in Farnham and Alton were grown in the valley, and originally the hop-pickers were paid in the building that eventually became the pub. An enterprising tenant grasped the business opportunity that presented itself, and began to provide the pickers with ale, relieving them of some of their hard-earned cash! Very much a community pub, the interior features terracotta floors, oak beams, a roaring fire and plenty of cricketing memorabilia. The lovely garden has a terrace with vine-topped pergola and a children's play fort. Expect six regularly changing cask-conditioned ales, perhaps including brews from local Bowman, Ballards, Arundel and Weltons micro-breweries, a good range of wines (eight by the glass) and home-cooked food. Enjoy a sharing platter laden with dips, prosciutto ham, olives, sun-dried tomatoes and mixed breads; or a light

meal or starter of home-made Scotch egg served with piccalilli, smoked mackerel, lemon and horseradish paté; or a mixed cheese ploughman's with pickles and warm crusty bread. The extensive choice of main courses takes in chicken and ham pie; lamb shank braised in red wine, tomato, garlic and thyme; chorizo and pork belly stew; lambs' liver, onion and bacon with mash and onion gravy; and Moroccan vegetable tagine on couscous with mint yoghurt dip. There's live music on the last Sunday of the month, and don't miss the popular Beer, Cider and Music Festival on the second weekend in June. Booking for meals may be required.

Open all day all wk 11-11 (Sun 12-10.30) **Bar Meals** L served Mon-Sat

12-2.15, Sun 12-3 D served Mon-Sat 7-9.30, Sun 6-8.30 Av main course £10.95 **Restaurant** ⊕ FREE HOUSE
◀ Hogs Back TEA, Triple fff, Bowman, Ballards, Andwell, Arundel, Weltons.
Ŏ Westons Stowford Press ☙ 8
Facilities Children welcome Children's menu Children's portions Play area Family room ☙ Garden Beer festival Parking Wi-fi

The Bat and Ball Freehouse

Bat and Ball Lane, Boundstone, Farnham, Surrey GU10 4SA
www.thebatandball.co.uk

Tel: 01252 792108
E-mail: info@thebatandball.co.uk

The Bat and Ball Freehouse nestles in the bottom of the Bourne valley in Boundstone near Farnham. Over 150 years old, the Pub has a relaxed, rural feel, surrounded by woodland and wildlife, and is the focal point of 5 footpaths which connect to local villages. Customers can eat or drink throughout the Pub, patio area and the large south-facing garden (which backs onto the Bourne stream and has a popular children's play structure). All the food is cooked in-house and this is very much a pub that serves restaurant quality food and not a restaurant that sells beer! The bar area has both a traditional and modern style to it to provide for our differing customer tastes, both young and old, and we have a tempting selection of 6 well-kept Cask Ales.

Save on hotels. Book at **theAA.com/hotel**

SURREY 493 ENGLAND

The Bell

Bell Ln KT22 9ND ☎ 01372 372624
e-mail: bellfetcham@youngs.co.uk
dir: *From A245 in Leatherhead take Waterway Rd
(B2122). At rdbt 2nd exit into Guildford Rd (B2122). At
mini rdbt right into Cobham Rd. Straight on at next 2
mini rdbts. Left into School Ln, left into Bell Ln*

The striking 1930s building in the pretty Mole Valley is
one of Young's Brewery's 'flagship' dining pubs. Expect a
smart terrace for alfresco drinking and dining, a light
and airy wood-panelled restaurant, and a comfortable
bar, replete with leather sofas and chairs. Using quality,
seasonal produce, including vegetables from Secretts
Farm and pork from Dingley Dell Farms, everything on the
menus is cooked from scratch. The traditional British
cuisine is a cut above the norm, with the likes roast
Gressingham duck leg, and pan-fried sea bream on the
main menu. Classic bar food, Sunday roasts (booking
essential) and an autumn beer festival complete the
picture.

Open all day all wk **Bar Meals** Av main course £10 food
served all day **Restaurant** Av 3 course à la carte fr £25
food served all day ⊕ YOUNG'S ◀ Special, Wells
Bombardier, Guest ale ◐ Aspall. ♟ 22 **Facilities** Children
welcome Children's portions Garden Beer festival Parking
Wi-fi 🚌 (notice required)

The Parrot Inn

PICK OF THE PUBS

RH5 5RZ ☎ 01306 621339
e-mail: drinks@theparrot.co.uk
dir: *B2126 from A29 at Ockley, signed Forest Green*

With its oak beams and huge fire, this attractive
17th-century building is in many ways the archetypal
English inn, right down to its location opposite the village
green and cricket pitch. But in addition to the expected
features, it has its own butchery, bakery, charcuterie and
farm shop called The Butcher's Hall and Country Grocer.
The owners have a farm just a few miles away where they
raise Shorthorn cattle, Middle White pigs, Dorset sheep
and Black Rock hens. The pub makes its own sausages,
preserves and chutneys, and much of the menu uses
these home-grown or home-made products. Dishes blend
modern, traditional and European: pork and pheasant
terrine; mushroom, chestnut and lentil filo parcel; and
slow-cooked pork belly with spiced chorizo and bean
stew. Not to be forgotten is a good range of real ales,
which can be enjoyed in the bar or one of the gardens or
on the terrace. Booking for meals may be required.

Open all day all wk Closed: 25 Dec **Bar Meals** L served
Mon-Sat 12-3, Sun 12-5 D served Mon-Sat 6-10 Av main
course £9-£13 **Restaurant** L served Mon-Sat 12-3, Sun
12-5 D served Mon-Sat 6-10 Av 3 course à la carte fr £25
⊕ FREE HOUSE ◀ Ringwood Best Bitter & Old Thumper,

Timothy Taylor Landlord, Dorking DB Number One,
Young's. ♟ 14 **Facilities** ❖ Children's portions Garden
Parking Wi-fi

The Boatman

Millbrook GU1 3XJ ☎ 01483 568024
e-mail: contact@boatman-guildford.co.uk
web: www.boatman-guildford.co.uk
dir: *From Guildford take A281 towards Shalford. Pub
on right*

Just half a mile from Guildford, this tranquil pub is set on
the banks of the River Wey, with views across the river to
parkland. Extensive terraced seating leads down to the
river where you can enjoy a pint of Hogs Back or one of
the 14 wines by the glass, or there's a covered garden
area if the weather is being unkind. Food served
throughout the day centres on pub favourites: pork and
apple sausage mash; home-made pie of the day;
slow-roasted lamb shoulder with mash and mint gravy.

Open all wk 12-11 (Sun 12-10.30) **Bar Meals** L served
Mon-Sat 12-9.30, Sun 12-7 D served Mon-Sat 12-9.30,
Sun 12-7 **Restaurant** L served Mon-Sat 12-9.30, Sun
12-7 D served Mon-Sat 12-9.30, Sun 12-7 ⊕ FREE HOUSE
◀ Otter Bitter, Hogs Back TEA. ♟ 14 **Facilities** Children
welcome Children's menu Garden Parking Wi-fi

The Keystone

3 Portsmouth Rd GU2 4BL ☎ 01483 575089
e-mail: drink@thekeystone.co.uk
web: www.thekeystone.co.uk
dir: *From Guildford rail station turn right. Cross 2nd
pedestrian crossing, follow road downhill. past Savills
Estate Agents. Pub 200yds on left*

Just off the bottom of Guildford's bustling High Street,
this easy-going and unpretentious pub features squashy
leather sofas, pub art and a secluded outdoor terrace.
Live music and an annual July cider festival are amongst
the things to look out for. Along with real ales and cider,
expect fairly priced, modern pub food including salads,
steaks and award-winning pies. Main course options
range from sweet potato, chickpea and red pepper curry
to lime and coriander chicken breast with wild rice.

Open all day all wk 12-11 (Fri-Sat 12-12 Sun 12-5)
Closed: 25-26 Dec, 1 Jan **Bar Meals** L served all wk 12-3
D served Mon-Sat 6-9 ⊕ PUNCH TAVERNS ◀ Wadworth
6X, Tiple fff Alton's Pride, Guest ales ◐ Westons Wyld
Wood Organic, Addlestones. ♟ 10 **Facilities** Children
welcome Children's menu Children's portions Garden
Beer festival

The White Horse

The Street GU8 4JA ☎ 01483 208258
e-mail: pub@whitehorsehascombe.co.uk
dir: *From Godalming take B2130. Pub on left 0.5m after
Hascombe*

Surrounded by prime walking country, this 16th-century
pub's flower-filled garden is a summer stunner. Other
selling points include its traditional interior, impressive
tally of real ales and ciders, popular family room and
ample outdoor seating; then there's the high standard of
food, with meats coming from organic pedigree breeds. A
meal might take in chicken liver and brandy pâté, with
chutney and toast; chargrilled salmon fillet with spinach,
new potatoes and beurre blanc; or Angus beef keema
masala, steamed rice and red onion salad; and lemon tart.

Open all day all wk **Bar Meals** food served all day
Restaurant food served all day ⊕ PUNCH TAVERNS ◀ St
Austell Tribute, Triple fff Alton's Pride, Sharp's Doom Bar,
Adnams Southwold Bitter, Hogs Back TEA, Harvey's,
Guest ales ◐ Thatchers Green Goblin, Kopparberg Pear,
Westons Old Rosie & Wyld Wood Organic. ♟ 11
Facilities ❖ Children welcome Children's menu
Children's portions Play area Family room Garden Parking
Wi-fi 🚌 (notice required)

HASLEMERE
Map 6 SU93

The Wheatsheaf Inn ★★★ INN

Grayswood Rd, Grayswood GU27 2DE ☎ **01428 644440**
e-mail: thewheatsheaf@aol.com
dir: *Exit A3 at Milford, A286 to Haslemere. Grayswood approx 7.5m N*

This friendly, award-winning village inn nestles in the tranquil Surrey Hills. The Edwardian building has a stunning display of hanging baskets and an airy conservatory; the magnificent viewpoint at Black Down, beloved of Alfred, Lord Tennyson, is nearby. You may be tempted by this to book a B&B stay, or perhaps just to enjoy a meal once you've seen the inviting menus of classics and specials – Scottish smoked salmon; ale-battered fillet of hake; rib-eye or fillet steak; and beef lasagne; followed by chocolate and almond torte. You could, of course, just relax with a pint of Sharp's Doom Bar beer or Aspall cider in the peaceful garden. Booking for meals may be required.

Open all wk 11-3 6-11 (Sun 12-3 7-10.30) **Bar Meals** L served all wk 12-2 D served all wk 7-9.45 Av main course £11.95 **Restaurant** L served all wk 12-2 D served all wk 7-9.45 Fixed menu price fr £11.95 Av 3 course à la carte fr £22 ⊕ FREE HOUSE ◀ Fuller's London Pride, Sharp's Doom Bar, Greene King Abbot Ale, Langham Hip Hop ♻ Aspall. **Facilities** ♣ Children welcome Children's menu Children's portions Garden Parking Wi-fi **Rooms** 7

LEIGH
Map 6 TQ24

The Plough

Church Rd RH2 8NJ ☎ **01306 611348**
e-mail: sarah@theploughleigh.wanadoo.co.uk
dir: *Telephone for directions*

On the village green opposite the church, this white-painted, featherboarded country pub has been run by Sarah Bloomfield and family for 21 years. The lounge, restaurant and bar have all now been refurbished. The lounge's low beams date from the late 15th century, while the bar, where you can play traditional pub games and enjoy mulled wine during the winter, is positively new by comparison, being only 112 years old. The kitchen offers home-cooked food such as creamy garlic mushrooms, oven-roast hake fillet, Greek salad, burgers and pub favourites. It's a popular destination for walkers.

Open all wk 11-11 (Sun 12-11) **Bar Meals** Av main course £10.95 food served all day **Restaurant** food served all day ⊕ HALL & WOODHOUSE ◀ Badger Dorset Best, Tanglefoot, K&B Sussex. ♥ 11 **Facilities** ♣ Children welcome Children's menu Children's portions Garden Parking Wi-fi 🚐

The Seven Stars

PICK OF THE PUBS

See Pick of the Pubs on opposite page
See advert below

LINGFIELD
Map 6 TQ34

Hare and Hounds

PICK OF THE PUBS

See Pick of the Pubs on page 496

LONG DITTON
Map 6 TQ16

The Ditton

64 Ditton Hill Rd KT6 5JD ☎ **020 8339 0785**
e-mail: goodfood@theditton.co.uk
dir: *Telephone for directions*

The pub part opened first, in 2008, followed a year later by adjoining Long's Brasserie. A 1930s building, it looks as though it was once two semi-detached houses but, whatever its origin, it has become a community local, with beers from Sharp's and Young's, and pub favourites of chilli con carne; chicken and chorizo linguine; beef bourguignon; and vegetable strudel. The Brasserie's style is slow-roasted belly of pork on cauliflower and parmesan purée; and veal T-bone steak with beetroot rösti. Summer barbecues are held in the large beer garden. Booking for meals may be required.

Open all day all wk 12-11 **Bar Meals** L served all wk 12-9 D served all wk 12-9 Av main course £9.95 food served all day **Restaurant** L served Wed-Sun 12-9 D served Wed-Sat 12-9 Av 3 course à la carte fr £24.95 ⊕ ENTERPRISE INNS ◀ Sharp's Doom Bar, Greene King IPA, Young's. ♥ 10 **Facilities** Children welcome Children's menu Children's portions Play area Garden Parking Wi-fi 🚐 (notice required)

THE SEVEN STARS

Bunce Common Road, Dawes Green, Leigh, Reigate, Surrey RH2 8NP   Tel: 01306 611254   www.thesevenstarsleigh.co.uk

Located in the Southern reaches of the Mole Valley between the old Market Towns of Reigate and Dorking can be found *The Seven Stars*, a truly traditional inn dating back to early 1600. The Seven Stars GRADE II listed building can be found in a tiny hamlet called Dawes Green.

Children are very welcome during the warmer months when food is served outside but unfortunately cannot be accommodated inside – the Premises Licence allows only young adults over the age of fourteen to dine with their parents.

The Seven Stars concentrates on serving quality beer and food, which is freshly prepared by a team of chefs and home smoked meat and fish can often be found on the Specials Board.

Save on hotels. Book at **theAA.com/hotel**

SURREY 495 ENGLAND

PICK OF THE PUBS

The Seven Stars

LEIGH Map 6 TQ24

**Bunce Common Rd, Dawes Green
RH2 8NP ☎ 01306 611254**
e-mail: davepellen@aol.com
web: www.thesevenstarsleigh.co.uk
dir: *S of A25 (Dorking to Reigate road)*

An early 17th-century, tile-hung tavern tucked away in the rural southern reaches of the Mole Valley. Its generous measure of charm and character is enhanced by the absence of games machines, TV screens and piped music; some might also appreciate the licence that prohibits under-14s from dining. The older bar is centred on an inglenook fireplace at one end and a log-burning stove at the other. On a wall a carefully preserved inscription quotes one William Eades in 1637: "Gentleman, you are welcome to sit down for your ease, pay what you call for and drink what you please". Today this could mean Young's and Fuller's London Pride real ales and a cider. Dogs are allowed, as long as they "keep their owners under control". The restaurant has its own bar, which is always available to use when open. The food served is of high quality and is prepared by a team of three chefs using local produce whenever possible. Among the starters and light meals you might find spicy chorizo and crayfish tail salad; pâté with toasted bloomer; and field mushroom topped with spinach and Welsh rarebit. Examples of main dishes include pan-scorched calves' liver and bacon with Dijon mustard mash; marinated pork chop with sweet potato chips, cabbage, and honey and sherry jus; and grilled monkfish and curried mussel sauce with mash and spinach. From the specials selection come home-smoked ribs, and fillet of John Dory with creamy prawn, coconut and coriander risotto, while if you want something more traditional, try curry and rice with poppadoms, or porcini ravioli in a mushroom, leek, pea and parmesan sauce. At the front is a garden for those with a drink, at the side a patio and garden for diners, and there's plenty of parking space. Booking for meals may be required.

Open all wk 12-3 5.30-11 (Sun 12-8)
Closed: 25-26 Dec, 1 Jan **Bar Meals** L served Mon-Sat 12-3, Sun 12-4
D served Mon-Thu 6-9, Fri-Sat 6.30-9.30 **Restaurant** L served Mon-Sat 12-3, Sun 12-4 D served Mon-Thu 6-9, Fri-Sat 6.30-9.30 ⊕ PUNCH TAVERNS ◀ Morland Old Speckled Hen, Fuller's London Pride, Young's. ☻ 12
Facilities ❖ Garden Parking

PICK OF THE PUBS

Hare and Hounds

LINGFIELD Map 6 TQ34

Common Rd RH7 6BZ ☎ 01342 832351
e-mail: info@hareandhoundspublichouse.co.uk
web: www.hareandhoundspublichouse.co.uk
dir: From A22 follow Lingfield Racecourse signs into Common Rd

Not far from Lingfield Park racecourse, this pale-blue-washed, 18th-century country pub has adopted the fashionable shabby-chic look for its interior, all mismatched furniture, shelves full of old books, a stone rabbit sitting on what looks like an old packing case... but it's a style that works. The pub has made a good name for its modern and classic food, no doubt partly attributable to the fact that chef and owner Eric Payet incorporates into the menus tastes and flavours from his Indian Ocean island childhood home of Réunion. Further inspiration comes from Eric and his wife Tracy's many years of working in restaurants throughout France and the UK. Using local produce where possible, a meal may start with chilled squid and chorizo spring roll, crème fraîche and chickpeas; or smooth sweetcorn soup, ricotta gnocchi and black truffle dressing. This might be followed by braised blade of beef, confit turnip, boulangère potato and red wine sauce; roast stone bass, courgette beignet, smooth mussel sauce and tapenade; or hand-rolled tagliatelle, soft poached egg, black truffle and aged

parmesan. Among the possible ways to finish are iced tutti frutti with warm madeleine and passionfruit; or lemon curd and raspberry 'Fabergé' egg. Blackboards list light lunches, pub classics and specials, respective examples being croque monsieur, or indeed, croque madame; roast Toulouse sausages with caramelised onion and mash potato; and braised shoulder of lamb pie with Moroccan spice, crushed swede and pastry. On a sunny day, the split-level decked garden is a good spot for a pint of Harvey's Sussex bitter, Woodforde's Wherry, or a glass of wine selected by Nick Hillman's merchant vintners' company in the village.

Open all day Closed: 1-5 Jan, Sun eve
Bar Meals L served Mon-Sat 12-2.30,

Sun 12-3 D served Mon-Sat 7-9.30
Restaurant L served Mon-Sat 12-2.30, Sun 12-3 D served Mon-Sat 7-9.30
🍺 PUNCH TAVERNS ◀ Woodforde's Wherry, Harvey's Sussex, Guinness 🍏 Westons Stowford Press.
Facilities Children welcome Children's portions Garden Parking

Save on hotels. Book at **theAA.com/hotel**

SURREY 497 **ENGLAND**

MICKLEHAM Map 6 TQ15

King William IV

Byttom Hill RH5 6EL ☎ 01372 372590
dir: *From M25 junct 9, A24 signed to Dorking, pub just before Mickleham*

The King Billy, built in 1790 for local estate workers, has a panelled snug and larger back bar with an open fire, cast-iron tables and grandfather clock. The terraced garden is ideal for summer socialising and offers panoramic views of the Mole Valley, where earlier you might have been walking. Hogs Back TEA and Shere Drop are in the bar, with food such as tournedos Rossini; Thai-spiced free-range chicken; and Scottish fillet steak.

Open all wk 11.30-3 6-11 (Sun 12-10.30) ⊕ FREE HOUSE
◀ Hogs Back TEA, Surrey Hills Shere Drop ♂ Westons Stowford Press. **Facilities** Children welcome Children's portions Garden Parking

The Running Horses

Old London Rd RH5 6DU ☎ 01372 372279
e-mail: info@therunninghorses.co.uk
web: www.therunninghorses.co.uk
dir: *1.5m from M25 junct 9. Off A24 between Leatherhead & Dorking*

Near the foot of Box Hill amid lovely National Trust countryside, The Running Horses has been welcoming travellers for more than 400 years and has a history of sheltering highwaymen. The interior still resonates with the past, right down to its bare beams and real fires. Food ranges from lunchtime chunky sandwiches and ploughman's platters to inventive dishes such as Welsh rarebit crostinis with chargrilled peppers and ratatouille dressing, followed by ham hock and leek pie topped with a split pea purée. There's also a good selection from the grill. Booking for meals may be required.

Open all day all wk 12-11 (Sun 12-10.30) **Bar Meals** L served Mon-Fri 12-2.30, Sat-Sun 12-3 D served Mon-Sat 7-9.30, Sun 6.30-9 **Restaurant** L served Mon-Fri 12-2.30, Sat-Sun 12-3 D served Mon-Sat 7-9.30, Sun 6.30-9 ⊕ FREE HOUSE ◀ Fuller's London Pride & Chiswick Bitter, George Gale & Co HSB, Young's Bitter ♂ Aspall. ⬩ 9 **Facilities** ❤ Children welcome Children's portions Garden Wi-fi ▭ (notice required)

NEWDIGATE Map 6 TQ14

The Surrey Oaks

Parkgate Rd RH5 5DZ ☎ 01306 631200
e-mail: ken@surreyoaks.co.uk
dir: *From A24 follow signs to Newdigate, at T-junct turn left, pub 1m on left*

Dating back to 1570, this pretty oak-beamed pub stands beside a quiet lane about a mile outside the village of Newdigate. There are two rambling bars, one with an inglenook fireplace and a great range of real ales on tap, including Surrey Hills Ranmore Ale, as well as a restaurant area, patio and beer garden with boules pitch. From the specials board order squid pan fried in garlic butter, followed by lamb's liver, bacon and mash, or whole plaice with parsley butter. Beer festivals are held at Whitsun and August Bank Holiday.

Open all wk 11.30-2.30 5.30-11 (Sat 11.30-3 6-11 Sun 12-10) **Bar Meals** L served Mon-Sat 12-2, Sun 12-2.30 D served Tue-Sat 6.30-9.30 Av main course £10 **Restaurant** L served Mon-Sat 12-2, Sun 12-2.30 D served Tue-Sat 6.30-9.30 Av 3 course à la carte fr £18 ⊕ ADMIRAL TAVERNS ◀ Harvey's Sussex Best, Surrey Hills Ranmore Ale, Guest ales ♂ Moles Black Rat, Westons Country Perry. **Facilities** ❤ Children welcome Children's menu Children's portions Play area Garden Beer festival Parking Wi-fi ▭ (notice required)

NUTFIELD Map 6 TQ35

The Inn on the Pond NEW

Nutfield Marsh Rd RH1 4EU ☎ 01737 643000
e-mail: enquiries@theinnonthepondnutfield.co.uk
dir: *From A25 E from Redhill, turn left after Nutfield village & down Church Hill. 1m on left*

Part of the select Cross Oak Inns group, the beautifully appointed Inn on the Pond lives up to its name – it stands next to a duck pond, and the village cricket pitch and overlooks Nutfield Marsh Nature Reserve (monthly wildlife walks). Time your arrival for sunset and you can savour a pint of Hogs Back TEA on the front terrace and watch the sun sink into the Surrey Hills. Inside, there are log fires, a contemporary décor and modern pub menus listing herb-crusted lamb with thyme jus, and salmon and dill fishcakes.

Open all wk 12-3 5.30-11 (all day Sat-Sun in summer) Closed: 25 Dec **Bar Meals** L served Mon-Sat 12-2.30, Sun 12-9.30 summer only D served all wk 6-9.30 Av main course £11 **Restaurant** L served all wk 12-2.30 D served all wk 6-9.30 Av 3 course à la carte fr £25 ⊕ FREE HOUSE/CROSS OAK INNS ◀ Hogs Back TEA, Sharp's Doom Bar, Pilgrim Progress, Tonbridge Blonde Ambition ♂ Westons Stowford Press. ⬩ 10 **Facilities** ❤ Children welcome Children's menu Children's portions Garden Parking ▭ (notice required)

OCKHAM Map 6 TQ05

The Black Swan

Old Ln KT11 1NG ☎ 01932 862364
e-mail: enquiries@blackswanockham.com
dir: *M25 junct 10, A3 towards Guildford. Approx 2m turn left to Ockham*

Pubs with this name tend to get called the Mucky Duck, but after Geronimo Inns bought this one locals became more respectful. Inside are rough sawn timbers, wooden rafters, unusual antique furnishings, great beers and wine, and good food at affordable prices. Using the best of local produce, dishes include Dexter rump or sirloin steak with hand-cut chips, field mushroom and peppercorn sauce; prawn and salmon penne pasta with white wine sauce; and aubergine and vegetable stack with tomato sauce. The pub holds a quiz night every Tuesday.

Open all day all wk ⊕ FREE HOUSE/GERONIMO INNS ◀ Surrey Hills Shere Drop, Sharp's Doom Bar, Hogs Back TEA, Bitburger, Guinness ♂ Aspall. **Facilities** Children welcome Children's menu Children's portions Garden Parking Wi-fi

OCKLEY   Map 6 TQ14

Bryce's at The Old School House ◉

PICK OF THE PUBS

RH5 5TH ☎ **01306 627430**
e-mail: fish@bryces.co.uk
web: www.bryces.co.uk
dir: *8m S of Dorking on A29*

Having notched up some 20 years under owner Bill Bryce, this Grade II listed former boarding school dates back to 1750. The current custodian is passionate about fresh fish and offers a huge range, despite the land-locked location in rural Surrey. These days, it's more of a restaurant than a pub, although there is a bar with its own menu and a range of real ales including Horsham Bitter. The dishes on the restaurant menu are nearly all fish, with a few specials for non-piscivores. Options to start include New England clam chowder; potted brown shrimps on granary toast and queenie scallops with wilted spinach and hollandaise. Main courses include pan-fried wing of South Coast skate with caperberry and lime brown butter; or roast cod fillet with parmesan crust on creamed courgettes. Look to the blackboard for the home-made desserts. You can also order takeaway fish and chips at the bar.

Open 12-3 6-11 Closed: 25-26 Dec, 1 Jan, Sun pm Nov, Jan-Feb **Bar Meals** L served all wk 12-2.30 D served all wk 6-9.30 Av main course £12.95 **Restaurant** L served all wk 12-2.30 D served all wk 7-9.30 Fixed menu price fr £12.50 Av 3 course à la carte fr £34 ⊕ FREE HOUSE ◀ Fuller's London Pride, Weltons Horsham Bitter, John Smith's Extra Smooth. ♀ 15 **Facilities** ♣ Children welcome Children's portions Parking ➡ (notice required)

The Kings Arms Inn

Stane St RH5 5TS ☎ **01306 711224**
e-mail: enquiries@thekingsarmsockley.co.uk
dir: *From M25 junct 9 take A24 through Dorking towards Horsham, A29 to Ockley*

Welcoming log fires, a priest hole, a friendly ghost and an award-winning garden are just a few charms of this oak-beamed 16th-century inn. In the picturesque village of Ockley and overlooked by the tower of Leith Hill, it's an ideal setting in which to enjoy a pint and wholesome food after climbing the hill. Choices prepared by chef Alex Rustani include sandwiches, a Greek meze sharing plate, pie of the day; and more adventurous dishes such as chicken liver parfait followed by confit of duck with château potatoes, spiced braised red cabbage, Morello cherries and orange sauce.

Open all wk 12-3 6-11 **Bar Meals** L served all wk 12-3 D served all wk 6.30-9.30 Av main course £12 **Restaurant** L served all wk 12-3 D served all wk 6.30-9.30 Fixed menu price fr £12.50 Av 3 course à la carte fr £25 ⊕ FREE HOUSE/CROSS OAK INNS ◀ WJ King Horsham Best, Sharp's Doom Bar, Hogs Back TEA ♨ Westons Stowford Press. ♀ 10 **Facilities** Children welcome Children's menu Children's portions Garden Parking Wi-fi ➡ (notice required)

RIPLEY   Map 6 TQ05

The Talbot Inn ★★★★ INN ◉

PICK OF THE PUBS

High St GU23 6BB ☎ **01483 225188**
e-mail: info.thetalbot@bespokehotels.com
dir: *Telephone for directions*

One of England's finest 15th-century coaching inns, The Talbot is said to have provided the stage for Lord Nelson and Lady Hamilton's love affair in 1798. Although the inn has been refurbished, it has retained its impressive historic features, and the cosy beamed bar boasts open fires and real ales. In contrast, the chic dining room has a copper ceiling and modern glass conservatory extension. One AA-Rosette food blends pub classics like fish and chips or local sausages and mash with more innovative dishes like venison loin with chestnut purée and spiced pears, or brill paupiettes with creamed leeks and shellfish sauce. Finish with hot apple and rhubarb crumble and crème anglaise. The 39 stylish bedrooms are smart and contemporary, ranging from beamed rooms in the inn to new-build rooms overlooking the garden. The pub is conveniently positioned just 20 minutes from Heathrow and Gatwick International airports. Booking for meals may be required.

Open all day all wk 12-11 (Sun 12-10) ⊕ BESPOKE HOTELS ◀ Surrey Hills Shere Drop, Greene King Abbot Ale & IPA ♨ Westons Stowford Press. **Facilities** Children welcome Children's menu Children's portions Garden Parking Wi-fi **Rooms** 39

SOUTH GODSTONE   Map 6 TQ34

Fox & Hounds

Tilburstow Hill Rd RH9 8LY ☎ **01342 893474**
dir: *4m from M25 junct 6*

Seventeenth-century pirate and smuggler John Trenchman is said to haunt this building, which dates in part to 1368 and has been a pub since 1601. A large inglenook in the restaurant and a real fire in the lower bar add to the old-world charm. Food-wise there's plenty to choose from, including a starter of crispy deep-fried brie with a cranberry coulis; and mains ranging from chilli con carne to rump steak and Normandy chicken (in a cream sauce of cider, bacon and leeks). Other imaginative choices include specials such as a venison, red wine and chocolate pie. The large garden offers rural views and home-grown vegetables; marquees are erected in summer for alfresco dining.

Open all day all wk **Bar Meals** L served all wk 12-9 D served all wk 12-9 food served all day **Restaurant** L served all wk 12-9 D served all wk 12-9 food served all day ⊕ GREENE KING ◀ Abbot Ale & IPA, Guest ales. ♀ 12 **Facilities** Children welcome Children's menu Children's portions Garden Parking ➡ (notice required)

TILFORD   Map 5 SU84

The Duke of Cambridge **NEW**

Tilford Rd GU10 2DD ☎ **01252 792236**
e-mail: amy.corstin@redmistleisure.co.uk
dir: *From Guildford on A31 towards Farnham follow Tongham, Seale, Runfield signs. Right at end, follow Eashing signs. Left at end, 1st right (signed Tilford St). Over bridge, 1st left, 0.5m*

Not one but two annual beer festivals are among the many attractions of this attractive pub in the Surrey countryside outside Farnham. In May fundraising for a local charity is the excuse for a celebration of beers and music; another festival in October brings a marriage of ales and traditional food. Expect a friendly welcome then, children and dogs included, with garden and terrace beckoning in summer and open fire with hearty food for the winter evenings. Typical of the menu are slow-cooked Tilford beef; fresh crab linguine; and pea and gorgonzola risotto. Booking for meals may be required.

Open all wk 11-3 5-11 (Sat 11-11 Sun 12-10.30) Closed: 25 Dec & 31 Dec eve **Restaurant** L served Mon-Fri 12-2.30, Sat 12-3.30, Sun 12-8.30 D served Mon-Fri 6-9, Fri-Sat 6-9.30, Sun 12-8.30 Av 3 course à la carte fr £20 ⊕ FREE HOUSE/RED MIST LEISURE LTD ◀ Hogs Back TEA, Ringwood Fortyniner, Surrey Hills Shere Drop ♨ Thatchers Gold. ♀ 15 **Facilities** ♣ Children welcome Children's menu Children's portions Play area Garden Beer festival Parking Wi-fi

Save on hotels. Book at **theAA.com/hotel**

SURREY – SUSSEX, EAST 499 | **ENGLAND**

WEST END | Map 6 SU96

The Inn @ West End

PICK OF THE PUBS

42 Guildford Rd GU24 9PW ☎ 01276 858652
e-mail: greatfood@the-inn.co.uk
dir: *On A322 towards Guildford. 3m from M3 junct 3, just beyond Gordon Boys rdbt*

Gerry and Ann Price have created an establishment that out-manoeuvres many a competitor with weekly fish nights, monthly quizzes and special events linked to their expanding wine business. But this doesn't preclude anyone from simply enjoying a pint of Exmoor or Fuller's London Pride with the newspaper in the bar; on a fine evening the clematis-hung terrace overlooking the garden and boules pitch is a blissful spot. The modern interior is open plan with wooden floors, yellow walls, tasteful checks, crisp linen-clothed tables and an open fire. The kitchen team continues to make great use of the pub's fruit and vegetable garden in the creation of seasonal dishes. Organic Saddleback pork pâté with apple and walnut salad could precede a casserole of slowly cooked game with juniper, herbs and red wine. Home-made desserts such as rice pudding with caramelised apples round things off nicely. Booking for meals may be required.

Open all wk 11-3 5-11 (Sat 11-11 Sun 12-10.30) **Bar Meals** L served all wk 12-2.30 D served all wk 6-9.30 Av main course £16.95 **Restaurant** L served all wk 12-2.30 D served all wk 6-9.30 Fixed menu price fr £13.75 Av 3 course à la carte fr £27.95 ⊕ ENTERPRISE INNS ◖ Timothy Taylor Landlord, Fuller's London Pride, Exmoor. ♟ 15 **Facilities** ✿ Children's portions Garden Parking Wi-fi

WEST HORSLEY | Map 6 TQ05

The King William IV

PICK OF THE PUBS

83 The Street KT24 6BG ☎ 01483 282318
e-mail: info@kingwilliam4th.com
dir: *On The Street off A246 (Leatherhead to Guildford)*

Named in honour of the monarch who relaxed England's brewing laws, this popular gastro-pub is situated in a leafy Surrey village. The business was started by a miller, Edmund Collins, who knocked two cottages together to create an alehouse. Many of the original Georgian features have been preserved, but there is also an airy conservatory restaurant and a large garden and terrace to the rear, with colourful tubs and floral baskets. It's popular with walkers, as it is close to the Royal Horticultural Society's Wisley Gardens and many other places of interest. Local beers include Shere Drop and

Courage Directors, plus a guest ale of the month, and a dozen wines are offered by the glass. The well-priced menu ranges from burgers and fish pie to platters, oven-baked salmon fillet and rump steak. Leave room for banoffee pie, chocolate fudge cake or crème brûlée to finish.

Open all day all wk 11.30am-mdnt (Sun 12-10.30) **Bar Meals** L served all wk 12-3 D served Mon-Fri 6-9, Sat all day Av main course £9.50 **Restaurant** L served all wk 12-3 D served Mon-Fri 6-9, Sat all day Fixed menu price fr £7.95 Av 3 course à la carte fr £18 ⊕ ENTERPRISE INNS ◖ Surrey Hills Shere Drop, Courage Best & Directors, Sharp's Doom Bar, Greene King Ruddles, Guest ales. ♟ 12 **Facilities** ✿ Children welcome Children's menu Children's portions Family room Garden Parking Wi-fi 🚐

WINDLESHAM | Map 6 SU96

The Half Moon **NEW**

Church Rd GU20 6BN ☎ 01276 473329
e-mail: c@sturt.tv
dir: *M3 junct 3, A322 follow Windlesham signs into New Rd; right at T-junct into Church Rd, pub on right*

Owned by the Sturt family for over a century, this slate-floored, low-beamed, 17th-century free house offers the traditional country pub experience. Big hitter Fuller's shares real ale bar space with Hogs Back and Sharp's, and Old Rosie scrumpy. There's plenty of choice at lunchtime, while dinner options include calves' liver, bacon, bubble-and-squeak; grilled sea bass, spicy tomato and king prawn sauce; ricotta, spinach and wild mushroom cannelloni; and local game in season. There's a children's play area in the beer garden. Events include a beer festival. Booking for meals may be required.

Open 11-3 5-11 Closed: Sun after 7pm **Bar Meals** L served all wk 12-2.15 D served Mon-Sat 6-9.15 Av main course £12 **Restaurant** L served all wk 12-2.15 D served Mon-Sat 6-9.15 Fixed menu price fr £15 Av 3 course à la carte fr £25 ⊕ FREE HOUSE ◖ Sharp's, Theakston, Fuller's, Timothy Taylor, Hogs Back ⚈ Lilley's Bee Sting Pear, Westons Old Rosie. ♟ 10 **Facilities** ✿ Children welcome Children's menu Children's portions Play area Garden Beer festival Parking Wi-fi 🚐 (notice required)

SUSSEX, EAST

ALCISTON | Map 6 TQ50

Rose Cottage Inn

PICK OF THE PUBS

BN26 6UW ☎ 01323 870377
e-mail: ian@alciston.freeserve.co.uk
dir: *Off A27 between Eastbourne & Lewes*

Expect a warm welcome at this traditional Sussex village pub, complete with roses round the door. At the foot of the South Downs, ramblers will find it a good base for long walks in unspoilt countryside, especially along the old traffic-free coach road to the south. The inn has been in the same family for over 50 years, and is well known for its good, home-cooked food, including organic vegetables and the best local meats, poultry and game. From the wide selection of fish, try fillet of lemon sole stuffed with smoked salmon pâté with white wine, cream and prawn sauce. You might opt for Kashmiri-style chicken curry or whole baked camembert from the daily specials. Classic pub dishes, salads and light bites are also available. When in season, fresh mussels are delivered from Scotland every Friday. The inn sells a number of items from local suppliers for customers to buy, including honey, eggs and game. Booking for meals may be required.

Open all wk 11.30-3 6.30-11 Closed: 25-26 Dec **Bar Meals** L served all wk 12-2 D served all wk 7-9.30 Av main course £11 **Restaurant** L served all wk 12-2 D served all wk 7-9.30 Av 3 course à la carte fr £21 ⊕ FREE HOUSE ◖ Harvey's Sussex Best Bitter, Dark Star ⚈ Biddenden. ♟ 8 **Facilities** Garden Parking Wi-fi

ALFRISTON | Map 6 TQ50

George Inn

High St BN26 5SY ☎ 01323 870319
e-mail: info@thegeorge-alfriston.com
dir: *Telephone for directions*

First licensed to sell beer as far back as 1397, this splendid Grade II listed flint and half-timbered inn is set in a picturesque South Downs' village. The heavy oak beams and ancient inglenook fireplace add plenty of character to the bar, whilst the kitchen serves delights such as rustic boards to share; steamed Thai-style mussels; crayfish, crab and avocado terrine; Mediterranean fish stew; and pork tenderloin with button mushrooms and Marsala wine sauce. A network of smugglers' tunnels leads from the pub's cellars. Booking for meals may be required.

Open all day all wk Closed: 25-26 Dec **Bar Meals** L served Sun-Thu 12-9, Fri-Sat 12-10 D served Sun-Thu 12-9, Fri-Sat 12-10 Av main course £12 food served all day **Restaurant** L served Sun-Thu 12-9, Fri-Sat 12-10 D served Sun-Thu 12-9, Fri-Sat 12-10 Av 3 course à la carte fr £20 food served all day ⊕ GREENE KING ◖ IPA & Abbot Ale, 2 Guest ales ⚈ Aspall. **Facilities** ✿ Children welcome Children's menu Children's portions Garden Wi-fi 🚐

ASHBURNHAM PLACE   Map 6 TQ61

Ash Tree Inn

Brownbread St TN33 9NX ☎ 01424 892104
dir: *From Eastbourne take A271 at Boreham Bridge towards Battle. Next left, follow pub signs*

Tucked down the delightfully named Brownbread Street deep in the Sussex countryside, the 400-year-old Ash Tree has been revamped and now boasts a warm and bright interior, replete with stripped wooden floors, new tables and chairs, and a spanking new bar. It still retains its original character, with four fireplaces (two of them inglenooks), exposed beams and a friendly local atmosphere. Expect to find Harvey's ale on tap and traditional home-cooked food, the menu offering steak-and-kidney pudding, sausages and mash, beer-battered haddock, and a roast on Sundays. Booking for meals may be required.

Open 12-4 7-11 (Sat-Sun 11.30am-mdnt) Closed: Mon pm (Sun pm winter) **Bar Meals** L served Tue-Sun 12-3 D served Tue-Sat 7-9 Av main course £8.95 **Restaurant** L served Tue-Sun 12-3 D served Tue-Sat 7-9 Av 3 course à la carte fr £19 ⊕ FREE HOUSE ◀ Harvey's Sussex Best Bitter, Guest ales Ď Westons Stowford Press. **Facilities** ♣ Children welcome Children's portions Garden Parking ▭ (notice required)

BERWICK   Map 6 TQ50

The Cricketers Arms
PICK OF THE PUBS

BN26 6SP ☎ 01323 870469
e-mail: pbthecricketers@aol.com
dir: *Off A27 between Polegate & Lewes, follow signs for Berwick Church*

A Grade II listed flintstone pub in beautiful cottage gardens close to many popular walks, not least the South Downs Way running along the crest of the chalk scarp between here and the sea. In the 16th century it was two farmworkers' cottages, then an alehouse for 200 years, until around 50 years ago Harveys of Lewes, Sussex's oldest brewery, bought it and turned it into a 'proper' pub. Three beamed, music-free rooms with stone floors and open fires are simply furnished with old pine furniture. A short menu of home-made food includes crispy whitebait, and houmous and pitta bread starters. Steak-and-ale pie is an ever-popular main course, as are cod in beer-batter, and pork and herb sausages with free-range egg and chunky chips. Nearby is Charleston Farmhouse, the country rendezvous of the Bloomsbury Group of writers, painters and intellectuals, and venue for an annual literary festival. Booking for meals may be required.

Open all wk Mon-Fri 11-3 6-11 Sat 11-11 Sun 12-9 (May-Sep Mon-Sat 11-11 Sun 12-10.30) Closed: 25 Dec **Bar Meals** L served Oct-Apr Mon-Fri 12-2.15, Sat-Sun 12-9, May-Sep all wk 12-9 D served Oct-Apr Mon-Fri 6.15-9, Sat-Sun 12-9, May-Sep all wk 12-9 Av main course £9.50 **Restaurant** L served Oct-Apr Mon-Fri 12-2.15, Sat-Sun 12-9, May-Sep all wk 12-9 D served

Oct-Apr Mon-Fri 6.15-9, Sat-Sun 12-9, May-Sep all wk 12-9 ⊕ HARVEYS OF LEWES ◀ Sussex Best Bitter, Armada Ale Ď Thatchers. ₹ 12 **Facilities** ♣ Children welcome Children's portions Family room Garden Parking ▭ (notice required)

BLACKBOYS   Map 6 TQ52

The Blackboys Inn

Lewes Rd TN22 5LG ☎ 01825 890283
e-mail: info@theblackboys.co.uk
dir: *From A22 at Uckfield take B2102 towards Cross in Hand. Or from A267 at Esso service station in Cross in Hand take B2102 towards Uckfield. Village in 1.5m at junct of B2102 & B2192*

Set in the heart of East Sussex, this 14th-century, and part-weatherboarded, pub was once a favourite with local charcoal-burners, or blackboys, whose soot-caked skin can just about be imagined. Today's well-scrubbed visitors enjoy beers from Harvey's in one of two bars, and in the restaurant, vegetables from the garden, game from local shoots, and fish from Rye and Hastings. Pan-fried halibut with prawn, crab and brandy cream sauce, and fillet steak, mushrooms and onions are typical. Outside are rambling grounds and an orchard. There is also a function room available for hire. Quiz nights and live music every month. Recent change of hands.

Open all day all wk 12-12 **Bar Meals** L served Mon-Fri 12-3, Sat 12-10, Sun 12-9 D served Sun-Mon 6-9, Tue-Sat 6-10 **Restaurant** L served Mon-Fri 12-3, Sat 12-10, Sun 12-9 D served Sun-Mon 6-9, Tue-Sat 6-10 ⊕ HARVEYS OF LEWES ◀ Sussex Best Bitter, Sussex Hadlow Bitter, Sussex Old Ale, Seasonal ales. ₹ 15 **Facilities** ♣ Children welcome Children's menu Children's portions Garden Beer festival Parking Wi-fi ▭

BRIGHTON & HOVE   Map 6 TQ30

The Basketmakers Arms

12 Gloucester Rd BN1 4AD ☎ 01273 689006
e-mail: bluedowd@hotmail.co.uk
dir: *From Brighton station main entrance 1st left (Gloucester Rd). Pub on right at bottom of hill*

A Victorian backstreet local tucked away in the North Laine area of the city and run with passion and pride by Peter Dowd for 25 years. Expect to find a mind-boggling choice of drinks, including eight changing real ales, around 100 malt whiskies and large selections of vodka, gin, and bourbon. Food on the pub menu is all cooked in-house and prepared from locally sourced produce. Fish is bought daily straight from the local fishermen and dishes include beer-battered fish and chips, mussels in white wine, shallots and garlic, and roast beef sandwiches.

Open all day all wk 11-11 (Fri-Sat 11am-mdnt Sun 12-11) **Bar Meals** L served Mon-Fri 12-8.30, Sat 12-7, Sun 12-6 D served Mon-Fri 12-8.30, Sat 12-7, Sun 12-6 food served all day ⊕ FULLER'S ◀ London Pride, ESB, Discovery & Bengal Lancer, George Gale & Co HSB & Seafarers, Guest ales. **Facilities** ♣ Children welcome

The Greys
PICK OF THE PUBS

105 Southover St BN2 9UA ☎ 01273 680734
e-mail: chris@greyspub.com
dir: *0.5m from St Peter's Church in Hanover area of Brighton*

Climb the Old Steine towards Kemp Town to find this eye-catching turquoise-painted pub. It's a gem, described by the landlord as a 'shoebox', and delights in its role as a thriving community pub in the bohemian area of Hanover in central Brighton. A compact backstreet local, stripped-wood and flagstone floors, and timber-panelled walls give the sense of a country pub in the town, and with the wood-burning stove glowing in the fireplace, there is no finer place to relax with a pint of Harvey's bitter or a Breton cider. There is a great selection of Belgian beers, too, and annual Sussex and Belgian beer festival on August Bank Holiday weekend. An eclectic, ever-changing menu is based on local, seasonal produce, so expect anything from warm tomato tart with home-made pesto to duck breast on mustard mash with cider jus, and top-notch Sunday roasts, perhaps rib of beef with creamed horseradish. The Greys is also known for its live country/folk/bluegrass music on Monday nights, featuring many leading artistes. Booking for meals may be required.

Open all wk 4-11 (Sat noon-12.30am Sun 12-11) **Bar Meals** L served Sun 12-4.30 D served Tue-Thu & Sat 6-9 Av main course £12 **Restaurant** L served Sun 12-4.30 D served Tue-Thu & Sat 6-9 Av 3 course à la carte fr £22 ⊕ ENTERPRISE INNS ◀ Timothy Taylor Landlord, Harvey's Sussex Best Bitter Ď Westons Stowford Press, Wyld Wood Organic. **Facilities** Beer festival Parking Wi-fi

The Market Inn ★★★ INN

1 Market St BN1 1HH ☎ 01273 329483
e-mail: marketinn@reallondonpubs.com
dir: *In The Lanes area, 50mtrs from junct of North St & East St*

Set in the historic Lanes area, this fine traditional English pub is located a short walk from the Brighton Pavilion, seafront and pier. A traditional English menu is served all day along with local and regional ales, and a good range of wines; a wide-screen television shows all the major sporting events. Food is made on the premises from locally sourced produce. To stay over and enjoy this famous seaside city, two attractively decorated en suite rooms are available, with a separate guest entrance.

Open all wk 11-11 (Fri-Sat 11am-mdnt Sun 12-10.30) ◀ Wells Bombardier, Shepherd Neame Spitfire, Harvey's. **Facilities** Children welcome Children's menu Children's portions Wi-fi **Rooms** 2

PICK OF THE PUBS

The Merrie Harriers

COWBEECH   Map 6 TQ61

BN27 4JQ ☎ **01323 833108**

e-mail: ben@sussexcountrytaverns.co.uk
web: www.merrieharriers.co.uk
dir: *Exit A271, between Hailsham & Herstmonceux*

Owned by Ben and Nicky West and a brother-in-law, Gary Neate, this attractive, white-painted clapboard village inn is very much the hub of the community. Built in 1624, its external good looks are matched inside by the wealth of oak beams, and a huge inglenook fireplace that takes centre stage in the bar area. Look out for the female ghost who apparently wanders around and likes looking out of the kitchen window. Outside, the terrace overlooks its own acre of the Weald where the pub grows fruit and vegetables, and the tug-of-war team practises. Studying the modern British, daily-changing menu should ideally take place over one of the ten wines by the glass or a pint of Harvey's, Timothy Taylor or WJ King real ale. Ben's commitment to cooking with locally grown ingredients is evident wherever you look: for example, the fish (Dover sole, sea bass, crab, lobster and scallops) are caught in The Channel off Eastbourne and are always in demand, especially on seafood nights. Then there's the beef, the organic lamb and the pork, all Sussex reared and bred, while the game – roebuck deer,

pheasant, teal, wood pigeon and hare – is all bought from or traded with local gamekeepers. Ben uses traditional, but often forgotten, cuts of meat, such as crispy pig's cheeks and 21-day aged onglet steak. They also provide classic pub dishes such as liver and bacon, fish pie and ploughman's. The Merrie Harriers is also renowned for its Sunday lunch with a choice of roasts, served with real gravy and horseradish from the garden. There is a private dining room available for parties and wedding breakfasts. The garden can be used for larger events which include wedding receptions, private parties, hog roasts and barbecues, in a marquee or in the open air. Their beer and music festival is held every August Bank Holiday, and entrance is free.

Open all wk Mon-Thu 11.30-3 6-12 (Fri-Sun all day) **Bar Meals** L served all wk 12-2.30 D served all wk 6.30-9 **Restaurant** L served all wk 12-2.30 D served all wk 6.30-9 ⊞ FREE HOUSE ◀ Harvey's, Timothy Taylor, WJ King ♂ Westons Stowford Press. ♀ 10 **Facilities** Children welcome Children's menu Children's portions Play area ✿ Garden Beer festival Parking Wi-fi 🚌

BRIGHTON & HOVE *continued*

Preston Park Tavern

88 Havelock Rd BN1 6GF ☎ 01273 542271
e-mail: info@prestonparktavern.co.uk
web: www.prestonparktavern.co.uk
dir: *From N towards Brighton on A23, at Mill Rd rdbt take 2nd exit, continue on A23 (follow Brighton, then Town Centre signs). Left (one-way) onto Stanford Ave (A23), left into Havelock Rd*

Preston Park Tavern is a must-visit family-friendly food pub. Tucked away in the residential backstreets of Brighton, this light and airy gastro-pub with its open kitchen offers lunchtime sandwiches and main courses of smoked haddock fishcakes and burgers. The evening menu moves up a gear with Redlands Farm rib-eye steak; roasted fillet of cod in a Puy lentil and chestnut mushroom broth; and butternut squash and Sussex kale risotto. Sunday lunches are worth booking for and children have their own menus. Booking for meals may be required.

Open all day all wk Closed: 25 Dec & 1 Jan **Bar Meals** L served Mon-Fri 12-2.30, Sat 12-4, Sun 12-6 D served Mon-Sat 6-9.45 **Restaurant** L served Mon-Fri 12-2.30, Sat 12-4, Sun 12-6 D served Mon-Sat 6-9.45 ⊕ FREE HOUSE ◀ Harvey's Sussex Best Bitter, Timothy Taylor Landlord. ♚ 22 **Facilities** ❀ Children welcome Children's menu Children's portions Garden Wi-fi

CHAILEY   Map 6 TQ31

The Five Bells Restaurant and Bar

East Grinstead Rd BN8 4DA ☎ 01825 722259
e-mail: the5bells@hotmail.com
dir: *5m N of Lewes on A275*

This 500-year-old pub retains many original features, including a large inglenook fireplace. It is run now by the Fisher family, who have created a homely, relaxed atmosphere in the snug with its log fires and in the restaurant. All the dishes are made on the premises. The pub hosts live music evenings. In summer, the large bar terrace and secluded restaurant garden come into their own, and barbecues are held there. Car and motorcycle clubs are welcomed and it is a venue for car events, plus it's handy for Sheffield Park, the Bluebell Railway, Plumpton racecourse and walks around Chailey.

Open all wk 12-3 6-12 (Sat-Sun all day) ⊕ ENTERPRISE INNS ◀ Harvey's Sussex Best, Sharp's Doom Bar ♻ Aspall. **Facilities** Children welcome Children's portions Garden Parking Wi-fi

CHIDDINGLY   Map 6 TQ51

The Six Bells

BN8 6HE ☎ 01825 872227
dir: *E of A22 between Hailsham & Uckfield. Turn opp Golden Cross PH*

Inglenook fireplaces and plenty of bric-à-brac are to be found at this large free house, which is where various veteran car and motorbike enthusiasts meet on club nights. The jury in the famous Onion Pie Murder trial sat and deliberated in the bar before finding the defendant guilty. Exceptionally good-value bar food includes green lip mussels with salad and French bread; cauliflower and broccoli bake; rack of ribs; chicken curry; and spicy ravioli with salad. Enjoy the fortnightly popular folk and blues evenings.

Open all wk 10-3 6-11 (Fri-Sun all day) ⊕ FREE HOUSE ◀ Courage Directors, Harvey's Sussex Best Bitter. **Facilities** Children welcome Family room Garden Parking

COOKSBRIDGE   Map 6 TQ41

Marco Pierre White The Rainbow Inn

PICK OF THE PUBS

Resting Oak Hill BN8 4SS ☎ 01273 400334
e-mail: enquires@rainbowsussex.co.uk
dir: *3m outside Lewes on A275 towards Haywards Heath*

The long history of warm hospitality and superior refreshment continues at this 18th-century flint-built pub. Now associated with Marco Pierre White, The Rainbow's characterful interior attracts both locals and travellers alike. The rustic bar and three sumptuously decorated dining areas are united by their décor – parquet floors and deep brown carpets, gleaming mahogany furniture, filigree-covered tables and wood-framed pictures. It helps, of course, that Harvey's ales are always available, backed by a regularly-changing guest, and that the extensive wine carte includes a fine selection from Burgundy and Bordeaux. Fixed-priced lunch and evening menus represent excellent value. A typical à la carte choice could open with Maxim's quails' eggs; continue with speciality fish of the day, or grilled calves' liver with bacon; and finish with Mr White's rice pudding with prunes d'Agen à l'Armagnac. A suntrap enclosed rear terrace and grassy beer garden with views to the South Downs complete the picture.

Open all day all wk 12-11 **Bar Meals** L served all wk 12-3 D served all wk 6.30-10 **Restaurant** L served all wk 12-3 D served all wk 6.30-10 ⊕ FREE HOUSE/STERLING PUB COMPANY ◀ Harvey's Sussex Best Bitter, Dark Star, Guinness, Guest ale ♻ Westons Stowford Press. ♚ 10 **Facilities** Children welcome Children's menu Children's portions Garden Parking Wi-fi 🚐

COWBEECH   Map 6 TQ61

The Merrie Harriers

PICK OF THE PUBS

See Pick of the Pubs on page 501

DANEHILL   Map 6 TQ42

The Coach and Horses

PICK OF THE PUBS

See Pick of the Pubs on opposite page

DITCHLING   Map 6 TQ31

The Bull ★★★★ INN

PICK OF THE PUBS

See Pick of the Pubs on page 504

EAST CHILTINGTON   Map 6 TQ31

The Jolly Sportsman ◉

Chapel Ln BN7 3BA ☎ 01273 890400
e-mail: info@thejollysportsman.com
dir: *From Lewes take A275, left at Offham onto B2166 towards Plumpton, take Novington Ln, after approx 1m left into Chapel Ln*

Bruce Wass's isolated dining pub enjoys a lovely garden setting on a peaceful dead-end lane looking out to the South Downs. The bar retains some of the character of a Victorian alehouse, with Dark Star Hophead on tap, while the dining room strikes a cool, modern-rustic pose. Well-sourced food with one AA Rosette shines on daily-changing menus, served throughout the pub, from smoked garlic soup with pancetta and thyme dumplings to roast pork fillet and braised cheek with quince aïoli and grain mustard mash. Fixed-price and children's menus are also available. Well worth finding. Booking for meals may be required.

Open all wk (Sat & Summer all day) Closed: 25 Dec **Bar Meals** L served Mon-Sat 12-2.30, Sun 12.15-3.30 D served Sun-Thu 6.30-9.30, Fri-Sat 6.30-10 Av main course £15.75 **Restaurant** L served Mon-Sat 12.15-2.30, Sun 12.15-3.30 D served Mon-Thu 7-9.30, Fri-Sat 7-10, Sun 7-9 Fixed menu price fr £13.50 Av 3 course à la carte fr £29 ⊕ FREE HOUSE ◀ Dark Star Hophead, Harvey's Sussex Best Bitter ♻ Thatchers. ♚ 14 **Facilities** ❀ Children welcome Children's menu Children's portions Play area Garden Parking Wi-fi

Save on hotels. Book at **theAA.com/hotel**

SUSSEX, EAST 503 ENGLAND

PICK OF THE PUBS

The Coach and Horses

DANEHILL Map 6 TQ42

RH17 7JF ☎ 01825 740369
e-mail: coachandhorses@danehill.biz
web: www.coachandhorses.danehill.biz
dir: *From East Grinstead, S through Forest Row on A22 to junct with A275 (Lewes road), right on A275, 2m to Danehill, left onto School Lane, 0.5m, pub on left*

For a long, long time after 1847, when it opened, The Coach served its immediate community on the edge of Ashdown Forest as a simple alehouse with stabling. Today the community it serves is much larger, and what it offers goes way beyond beer, since it is now an award-winning country pub and restaurant. Inside, vaulted ceilings, panelling and stone and wood flooring add to the charm. The bars are busy, not only with locals, but with those from further afield who know its appeal, or who chance upon it, perhaps with the help of the AA *Pub Guide*. An enormous maple tree dominates the sunny, child-free terrace at the rear, while from the peaceful front garden, where children can play, you can see the South Downs. Drinkers enjoy real ales from Harveys of Lewes and weekly-changing guests, local Danehill Black Pig Farmhouse Cider, or some eight wines by the glass. A light-lunch menu is available in the day and a selection of pub classics is prepared for both lunch and dinner. Local sourcing is the guiding principle wherever possible, with fish from Seaford Bay, lamb from Danehill itself,

and veal, beef, game, vegetables, wild mushrooms and eggs from surrounding villages. Typically, lunch might be pheasant and prune rillette with toasted soda bread; Sussex sirloin steak, cherry vine tomatoes, portabello mushroom and hand-cut chips; and warmed poached pear with filo biscuits and glazed marzipan. Also typically, dinner might begin with salmon fishcake and cucumber velouté; continue with Moroccan spiced chickpea fritters; and finish with sticky toffee pudding with vanilla ice cream. Those who like their pub classics are looked after with local pork and herb sausages, mash and red onion gravy; and beer-battered fish and chips.

Open all wk 11.30-3 6-11 (Sat-Sun 12-11) Closed: 26 Dec **Bar Meals** L served Mon-Fri 12-2.30, Sun 12-3

D served Mon-Fri 7-9, Sat 7-9.30 Av main course £13 **Restaurant** L served Mon-Fri 12-2, Sun 12-3 D served Mon-Thu 7-9, Fri-Sat 7-9.30 Av 3 course à la carte fr £26 ⊕ FREE HOUSE ◄ Sharp's Doom Bar, WJ King, Harvey's, Hammerpot, Guest ales ♉ Westons Stowford Press, Black Rat, Black Pig. ♟ 8 **Facilities** Children welcome Children's menu Children's portions Play area ♣ Garden Parking Wi-fi

PICK OF THE PUBS

The Bull ★★★★INN

DITCHLING Map 6 TQ31

2 High St BN6 8TA ☎ 01273 843147
e-mail: info@thebullditchling.com
web: www.thebullditchling.com
dir: *From Brighton on A27 take A23, follow Pyecombe/Hassocks signs, then Ditchling signs, 3m*

This venerable 450-year-old inn started life as monks' lodgings. Today's cosy retreat is a far cry from those spartan days – The Bull's memorable interior pushes all the right buttons with open fires, wavy beams, leather sofas, cosy corners, candlelight, bare floorboards, scrubbed tables and a locals' bar brimming with good Sussex beers. Dominic and Vanessa Worral have toiled tirelessly to create the archetypal English village inn with a refreshing contemporary edge. The monks' draughty rooms have been replaced with individually designed guest accommodation, very popular with visitors to the South Downs National Park within which The Bull stands. The rounded tops of the hills rise steeply beyond the village to the commanding Ditchling Beacon; a self-guided walk from the pub will take you there, and the South Downs Way National Trail also crosses the Beacon. Views from the sheltered terrace and garden stretch towards the grassy ridges which protect pretty Ditchling from the sea breezes at Brighton, just 15 minutes away by car. Sussex farms and estates provide the chefs with a panoply of delights with which to create their refreshingly modern gourmet British dishes. Typical 'small plate' starters could include Thai beef noodle salad with mirin dressing; and pan-seared scallops with roasted pancetta, sautéed kale and celeriac purée. Luxurious main courses take the form of ballotine of rabbit stuffed with prunes, smoked bacon and Puy lentil soup; or sea trout en papillote, with clams, fennel and sorrel. Vegetarian options are no less flavoursome: one example is sesame and sumac-seared aubergine, parmesan doughnuts, vodka cherry tomatoes and skordalia. Desserts include spiced apple and pistachio clafoutis, and home-made ice creams. Wine-lovers will delight in a generous list, including more than 20 served by the glass.

Open all day all wk 11-11 (Sat 8.30am-11pm Sun 8.30am-10.30pm) **Bar Meals** L served Mon-Fri 12-2.30, Sat 12-9.30, Sun 12-9 (Sat-Sun bkfst 8.30-10.30am) D served Mon-Sat 6-9.30, Sun 12-9 ⊕ FREE HOUSE ◁ Harvey's Sussex Best Bitter, Timothy Taylor Landlord, Hop Back Summer Lightning, Dark Star ♂ Westons Traditional. ♟ 21
Facilities Children welcome Children's menu Children's portions Play area Garden Parking Wi-fi **Rooms** 4

Map 6 TV59

The Tiger Inn

PICK OF THE PUBS

The Green BN20 0DA ☎ 01323 423209
e-mail: tiger@beachyhead.org.uk
dir: From A259 between Eastbourne & Seaford. Pub 0.5m

If you fancy a stroll around Beachy Head followed by a pint at The Tiger, chances are you will not be alone. Even in midwinter, such are the charms of this estate-owned pub that its popularity still ensures the bar is bustling. It sits beside a village green lined with picture-postcard cottages and enjoys wonderful downland views. The interior is quintessentially English too, with log fires, beams, stone floors and ancient settles. Its own micro-brewery supplies award-winning ales such as Legless Rambler. Good-value and high-quality home-cooked dishes stream out of the kitchen, and include the likes of slow-roasted pork belly with thyme buttered carrots and bubble-and-squeak; sirloin steak with chips; and braised lamb shoulder with sautéed potatoes, fennel and spring onion.

Open all day all wk **Bar Meals** L served all wk 12-3 D served all wk 6-9 Av main course £8.50 **Restaurant** L served all wk 12-3 D served all wk 6-9 Av 3 course à la carte fr £20 ⊕ FREE HOUSE/BEACHY HEAD BREWERY ◀ Legless Rambler & Original Ale, Harvey's ♂ Westons Stowford Press. ♟ 10 **Facilities** ✿ Children welcome Children's portions Garden Beer festival Parking Wi-fi

Map 6 TQ42

The Griffin Inn

PICK OF THE PUBS

TN22 3SS ☎ 01825 722890
e-mail: info@thegriffininn.co.uk
dir: M23 junct 10 to East Grinstead, then A22, then A275. Village signed on left, 15m from M23

Don't be surprised if you hear a steam whistle drifting across The Griffin's huge landscaped gardens, for this imposing Grade II listed inn is little more than a mile from the heritage Bluebell Railway at Sheffield Park. There are views to Ashdown Forest and the Sussex Downs from the gardens, whilst the 16th-century interior simply oozes charm from its beams, panelling, settles and log fires. The bar boasts handpumps dispensing the best of local ales, and there's a generous wine list, too. Walkers and cyclists arriving to join destination diners will revel in the terrific menu, created from the freshest of local produce. Current popular dishes include starters like pan-roasted smoked paprika and lemon chicken breast; braised wild boar sausages, champ mash and sweet chicory; or pan-fried skate wing with new potatoes and cockle vinaigrette. Booking for meals may be required.

Open all day all wk 12-11 Closed: 25 Dec **Bar Meals** L served Mon-Fri 12-2.30, Sat-Sun 12-3 D served all wk 7-9.30 Av main course £13.50 **Restaurant** L served Mon-Fri 12-2.30, Sat-Sun 12-3 D served Mon-Sat 7-9.30 Fixed menu price fr £30 Av 3 course à la carte fr £30

⊕ FREE HOUSE ◀ Harvey's Sussex Best Bitter, WJ King, Hepworth & Co ♂ Westons Stowford Press. ♟ 16 **Facilities** ✿ Children welcome Children's menu Children's portions Play area Garden Parking Wi-fi

Map 6 TQ51

The Gun

PICK OF THE PUBS

TN21 0JU ☎ 01825 872361
e-mail: enquiries@thegunhouse.co.uk
dir: 5m S of Heathfield, 1m off A267 towards Gun Hill. 4m off A22 between Uckfield & Hailsham

This charming 15th-century pub is tucked away in the heart of the Sussex countryside and was once the main courthouse serving the neighbouring towns and villages. Its wooden floors and beams, and lots of hideaway places provide the perfect setting for quiet eating and drinking. A separate panelled dining room with a stunning fireplace is ideal for private parties. The first-class food is seasonal and sourced from local suppliers. Two deli boards can be shared by a gathering of friends - the Asian board has Thai crab cake, tandoori chicken skewers, marinated king prawns, raita, sweet chilli sauce, poppadoms and pickled ginger salad. Main courses might include pumpkin ravioli with wild mushroom, chestnut and sage sauce, and rocket and parmesan salad; and venison pie with braised red cabbage and root vegetable mash. On sunny days, dine alfresco in the large garden or on the terrace, and enjoy the views across the countryside. The Old Coach House behind The Gun has been transformed into a farmers' market selling organic foods, fish and meats.

Open all wk 11.30-3 5.30-11 (Sun 11.30-10.30) **Bar Meals** L served Mon-Sat 12-3, Sun 12-9.30 D served Mon-Sat 6-9.45, Sun 12-9.30 Av main course £12 **Restaurant** L served Mon-Sat 12-3, Sun 12-9.30 D served Mon-Sat 6-9.45, Sun 12-9.30 Av 3 course à la carte fr £24 ⊕ FREE HOUSE ◀ Sharp's Doom Bar, Harvey's, Guinness ♂ Biddenden, Aspall. ♟ 14 **Facilities** ✿ Children welcome Children's menu Children's portions Play area Garden Parking Wi-fi

Map 6 TQ43

Anchor Inn

Church St TN7 4AG ☎ 01892 770424
e-mail: info@anchorhartfield.com
dir: On B2110

This friendly, family-orientated free house in the heart of 'Winnie the Pooh' country has been taken over by the previous owner's son. It was built in 1465 and has been a pub since the late 19th century. Locals meet in the front bar with its stone floors and heavy wooden beams, whilst an inglenook fireplace and library area give the back bar a more intimate feel. There's a hot and cold snack menu, with grills, fish and vegetarian options to satisfy heartier appetites. The front verandah and large garden are a bonus on warm sunny days. Booking for meals may be required.

Open all day all wk **Bar Meals** L served Mon-Fri 12-3, Sat 12-10, Sun 12-9 D served Mon-Thu 6-9, Fri 6-10, Sat 12-10, Sun 12-9 Av main course £9.95 **Restaurant** L served Mon-Fri 12-3, Sat 12-10, Sun 12-9 D served Mon-Thu 6-9, Fri 6-10, Sat 12-10, Sun 12-9 Fixed menu price fr £13.95 Av 3 course à la carte fr £16.95 ⊕ FREE HOUSE ◀ Harvey's Sussex Best Bitter, Moorhouse's Black Cat, Larkins ♂ Westons Stowford Press. **Facilities** ✿ Children welcome Children's menu Children's portions Garden Parking Wi-fi 🚍 (notice required)

The Hatch Inn

PICK OF THE PUBS

See Pick of the Pubs on page 506

Map 6 TQ52

Star Inn **NEW**

Church St, Old Heathfield TN21 9AH ☎ 01435 863570
dir: Behind Old Heathfield church

Built as an inn for the stonemasons who constructed the 14th-century church, this creeper-clad stone building has a stunning summer garden that affords impressive views across the High Weald; a view once painted by Turner. Equally appealing is the atmospheric, low-beamed main bar with its rustic furnishings and huge inglenook fireplace – all very cosy and welcoming in winter. Note the unusual barrel-vaulted ceiling in the upstairs dining room and the chalkboard menu that lists fresh fish and seafood direct from the day boats in Hastings.

Open all day all wk **Bar Meals** L served Mon-Sat 12-2.30, Sun 12-3 D served all wk 7-9.30 Av main course £12.95 **Restaurant** L served Mon-Sat 12-2.30, Sun 12-3 D served all wk 7-9.30 Av 3 course à la carte fr £23 ⊕ FREE HOUSE ◀ Fuller's London Pride, Shepherd Neame Master Brew, Harvey's ♂ Thatchers. ♟ 10 **Facilities** ✿ Children welcome Children's portions Garden Parking Wi-fi 🚍 (notice required)

PICK OF THE PUBS

The Hatch Inn

HARTFIELD   Map 6 TQ43

Coleman's Hatch TN7 4EJ
☎ **01342 822363**
e-mail: nickad@mac.com
web: www.hatchinn.co.uk
dir: *A22 at Forest Row rdbt, 3m to Coleman's Hatch, right by church*

If AA Milne could populate Ashdown Forest with a bear called Winnie the Pooh, a tiger called Tigger and a kangaroo called Kanga, why shouldn't llamas and reindeer live here? Well, they do, on a farm in nearby Wych Cross, not far from this eye-catching old inn at the site of one of the medieval gates into what was then dense woodland with valuable iron and timber reserves. Built around 1430, the part-weatherboarded building may have been cottages for iron workers, although it has been a pub for nearly 300 years, it was no doubt much appreciated by the dry-throated charcoal burners who used to work in these parts, and even passing smugglers. Classic beams and open fires draw an appreciative crowd to sample beers from Fuller's, Larkins and Harvey's, and the food, a fusion of classic and modern, for which during the past 16 years proprietor Nicholas Drillsma and partner Sandy Barton have built an enviable reputation. Their daily-changing menus are complemented by an extensive wine list, including ten by the glass. With plenty of local suppliers to draw on, fresh seasonal produce features in just about everything, with starters of home-made carrot and coriander soup; and potato

gnocchi in creamy stilton and spring onion sauce. Lunchtime mains include tagine of lamb with coriander and jasmine rice; and deep-fried Whitby Bay scampi tails with fries. A reservation is needed for evening dining, when choices include slow-braised belly of pork, purple sprouting broccoli and apple jus; breast of chicken, chorizo and wild mushroom risotto; and goat's cheese, artichoke heart and sun-blushed tomato tarte Tatin. Finish with home-made marshmallow, chocolate fondue and fruits, or orange upside-down sponge and custard. The Ashdown Forest beer festival is held here in June, when the views across the Forest from the two large gardens are especially fine. Booking for meals may be required.

Open all wk 11.30-3 5.30-11 (Sat-Sun all day) Closed: 25 Dec drinks only **Bar**

Meals L served all wk 12-2.15 D served Mon-Thu 7-9.15, Fri-Sat 7-9.30 **Restaurant** L served all wk 12-2.15 D served Mon-Thu 7-9.15, Fri-Sat 7-9.30 ⊕ FREE HOUSE ◀ Harvey's & Sussex Old Ale, Fuller's London Pride, Sharp's Doom Bar, Larkins ♂ Westons Stowford Press. ♟ 10 **Facilities** Children welcome Children's portions Play area ♣ Garden Beer festival

Save on hotels. Book at **theAA.com/hotel**

SUSSEX, EAST 507 ENGLAND

ICKLESHAM   Map 7 TQ81

The Queen's Head

Parsonage Ln TN36 4BL ☎ **01424 814552**

dir: *Between Hastings & Rye on A259. Pub in village on x-rds near church*

Praised by the national press, this award-winning 17th-century tile-hung pub enjoys a magnificent view across the Brede Valley to Rye. The traditional atmosphere has been preserved, with vaulted ceilings, large inglenook fireplaces, church pews, antique farm implements, and a bar from the old Midland Bank in Eastbourne. Customers are kept happy with at least six real ales, an annual beer festival on the first weekend in October, and menus ranging from salads, sandwiches, jackets and ploughman's to specials, fresh fish and pub classics like lamb and mint pie; beef lasagne; all-day breakfast; and pork chops.

Open all wk 11-11 (Sun 11-10.30) Closed: 25 & 26 Dec (eve) **Bar Meals** L served Mon-Fri 12-2.30, Sat-Sun 12-9.30 D served Mon-Fri 6-9.30, Sat-Sun 12-9.30 Av main course £7.95-£9.50 ⊕ FREE HOUSE ◀ Rother Valley Level Best, Greene King Abbot Ale, Harvey's Sussex Best Bitter, Ringwood Fortyniner, Dark Star ♂ Biddenden, Westons Old Rosie. ♈ 12 **Facilities** ❧ Children welcome Children's menu Children's portions Play area Garden Beer festival Parking Wi-fi 🚐 (notice required)

MAYFIELD   Map 6 TQ52

The Middle House

PICK OF THE PUBS

See Pick of the Pubs on page 508

MILTON STREET   Map 6 TQ50

The Sussex Ox

BN26 5RL ☎ **01323 870840**

e-mail: mail@thesussexox.co.uk
dir: *Off A27 between Wilmington & Drusillas. Follow brown signs to pub*

Drink deeply of old Sussex here, with the wonderful, matchboarded old bar rooms, wood and sealed-brick floors oozing character and a lawned beer garden looking out to the Long Man of Wilmington. Dine in the bar, the Garden Room, or the more formal Dining Room; the daily-changing menu relies on the best local ingredients. To start, perhaps pickled Eastbourne herrings or pressed ham hock and caper terrine. Follow with braised Sussex rabbit or pumpkin pie topped with cheesy puff pastry. Bar snacks such as root vegetable crisps and peppers stuffed with feta are also available, washed down with the pub's own Oxhead bitter from Dark Star Brewery. Booking for meals may be required.

Open all wk 11.30-3 6-11 Closed: 25-26 Dec **Bar Meals** L served all wk 12-2 D served all wk 6-9 Av main course £10 **Restaurant** L served all wk 12-2 D served all wk 6-9 ⊕ FREE HOUSE ◀ Harvey's Sussex Best Bitter, Dark Star Oxhead & Golden Gate, Crouch Vale Brewers Gold

---

♂ Westons Perry. ♈ 17 **Facilities** ❧ Children welcome Children's portions Family room Garden Parking Wi-fi

---

OFFHAM   Map 6 TQ41

The Blacksmiths Arms ★★★★ INN

London Rd BN7 3QD ☎ **01273 472971**
e-mail: blacksmithsarms@shineadsl.co.uk
web: www.theblacksmithsarms-offham.co.uk
dir: *2m N of Lewes on A275*

A hostelry since the mid-18th century, this free house in the South Downs National Park is just two miles from the lovely old town of Lewes. So that makes two reasons to visit, or even stay in the charming, high-quality accommodation. A third reason is Bernard and Sylvia Booker's flavoursome cooking using the best sustainably sourced local produce for lemon sole Walewska; steak-and-kidney pie; and spinach and ricotta cannelloni. And a fourth is Harvey's real ales in a bar with a log fire in the inglenook. Booking for meals may be required.

Open 12-3 6.30-10.30 Closed: Sun eve, Mon winter, Mon L summer **Bar Meals** L served Tue-Sun 12-2 Av main course £12 **Restaurant** L served Tue-Sun 12-2 D served Tue-Sat 6.30-9 Fixed menu price fr £11.95 Av 3 course à la carte fr £24 ⊕ FREE HOUSE ◀ Harvey's, Bitburger. ♈ 10 **Facilities** Children welcome Children's portions Garden Parking Wi-fi **Rooms** 4

PLUMPTON   Map 6 TQ31

Half Moon **NEW**

Ditchling Rd BN7 3AF ☎ **01273 890253**
e-mail: info@halfmoonplumpton.com

At the foot of the South Downs National Park and just ten minutes from Lewes, this lovely 200-year-old former coach house is all you could hope for when it comes to quintessential English inn. Enjoy foaming pints of local Harvey's ales by the fire in the stone-walled bar. Alternatively, settle down in the well-appointed, antique-filled dining room for comforting dishes such as fish soup; venison carpaccio; hand-carved ham, free-range eggs and chips; or pan-fried chicken breast with chorizo sausage and spinach risotto. Booking for meals may be required.

Open all day Closed: Sun eve **Bar Meals** L served all wk 12-6 D served Mon-Sat 6-9 food served all day **Restaurant** L served all wk 12-3 D served Mon-Sat 6-9 ⊕ FREE HOUSE ◀ Harvey's, WJ King, Hammerpot ♂ Westons, Severn. ♈ 10 **Facilities** ❧ Garden Parking Wi-fi 🚐

RINGMER   Map 6 TQ41

The Cock

Uckfield Rd BN8 5RX ☎ **01273 812040**
e-mail: matt@cockpub.co.uk
web: www.cockpub.co.uk
dir: *Just off A26 approx 2m N of Lewes just outside Ringmer*

This 16th-century inn takes its name from a bygone era when a cock horse was a spare horse used by coachmen to pull heavy loads – immortalised in the nursery rhyme 'Ride a Cock Horse to Banbury Cross'. Once a mustering point during the Civil War, the interior of the main bar is pretty much unaltered since Cromwell's time, including oak beams, flagstone floors and a blazing fire in the inglenook. Harvey's and Dark Star ales accompany the extensive menu of favourites, among which dishes of local venison burger and home-made chicken curry may be found. Booking for meals may be required.

Open all wk 11-3 6-11.30 (Sun 11-11) Closed: 26 Dec **Bar Meals** L served Mon-Fri 12-2, Sat 12-2.30 D served Mon-Sat 6-9.30, Sun 12-9.30 **Restaurant** L served Mon-Fri 12-2, Sat 12-2.30 D served Mon-Sat 6-9.30, Sun 12-9.30 ⊕ FREE HOUSE ◀ Harvey's Sussex Best Bitter & Old Ale, Fuller's London Pride, Dark Star Hophead, Hogs Back, Hammerpot Guest ales ♂ Westons 1st Quality. ♈ 10 **Facilities** ❧ Children welcome Children's menu Children's portions Play area Garden Parking 🚐 (notice required)

See advert on page 509

PICK OF THE PUBS

The Middle House

MAYFIELD   Map 6 TQ52

High St TN20 6AB ☎ **01435 872146**
e-mail: kirsty@middle-house.com
web: www.middlehousemayfield.co.uk
dir: E of A267, S of Tunbridge Wells

Once described as 'one of the finest examples of a timber-framed building in Sussex', this Grade I listed, 16th-century village inn dominates Mayfield's High Street. It has been here since 1575, when it was built for Sir Thomas Gresham, Elizabeth I's Keeper of the Privy Purse and founder of the London Stock Exchange. The entrance hall features a large ornately carved wooden fireplace by master carver Grinling Gibbons, wattle-and-daub infill, a splendid oak-panelled restaurant and secret priest holes. A private residence until the 1920s, it is now a family-run business. Real ale drinkers do well here, with a handsome choice, including Harvey's Sussex Best Bitter from Lewes and Fuller's London Pride. As in all good kitchens, the meats, poultry, game and vegetables come from local farms and producers, and here guarantee a bar menu comprising over 40 dishes, including classics of home-cooked smoked gammon with two free-range fried eggs; deep-fried wholetail scampi with chunky chips; home-made sausages of the day; fresh salads, vegetarian options and a children's healthy-eating menu. For something a little less traditional, try pot-roast shank of local lamb tagine, or roast boneless quail filled with mixed forest mushrooms. It isn't just the building

that has been described in superlative terms – the private chapel in the restaurant is regarded as 'one of the most magnificent in England'. The carte offers whole large grilled Cornish sardines with garlic butter; fanned marinated duck breast with chorizo and sun-blushed tomato risotto; and corn fritter and harissa-roasted vegetable stack with toasted feta cheese. And of the desserts, special mention is warranted for pine nut and maple pannacotta with roasted blueberries, pistachio ice cream and lavender honeycomb; and hot coconut and Malibu soufflé. Head outside to the lovely terraced gardens for views of the rolling countryside. Booking for meals may be required.

Open all day all wk **Bar Meals** L served Mon-Fri 12-2, Sat 12-2.30 D served

Mon-Sat 6.30-9.30, Sun all day **Restaurant** L served Tue-Sun 12-2 D served Tue-Sat 6.30-9 ⊞ FREE HOUSE ◀ Harvey's Sussex Best Bitter, Greene King Abbot Ale, Black Sheep Best Bitter, Theakston Best Bitter, Adnams Southwold Bitter, Sharp's Doom Bar, Fuller's London Pride ♂ Thatchers Gold. ♟ 9 **Facilities** Children welcome Children's menu Children's portions Play area Garden Parking Wi-fi

RUSHLAKE GREEN   Map 6 TQ61

Horse & Groom

PICK OF THE PUBS

TN21 9QE ☎ 01435 830320
e-mail: chappellhatpeg@aol.com
dir: *Telephone for directions*

An appealing pub-restaurant at the edge of the enormous green that gives the village its name. Residents have supped here for over 230 years and the pub retains much rustic character, with heavy beams, hearth, lots of brass and copper, and a cosy Gun Room restaurant complete with antique firearms. Outside a huge garden offers a grand prospect over the pretty East Sussex countryside, a much sought-after spot for summertime refreshment. Drinkers delight in Harvey's ales all year round, whilst diners are rewarded by a fulfilling menu of home-cooked fare, including blackboard specials. Typical choices include starters of deep-fried whitebait dusted with cayenne pepper; and glazed goat's cheese and caramelised onion tartlet. Main courses may feature a fresh fillet of Hastings cod in chef's beer-batter with thick-cut chips, mushy peas and home-produced tartare sauce; or a marinated duck breast, oven-roasted and served on a bed of stir-fried vegetables. Booking for meals may be required.

Open all wk 11.30-3 6-11 (Sun all day) ⊕ SHEPHERD NEAME ◀ Master Brew, Spitfire, Kent's Best, Late Red & Bishops Finger, Harvey's Sussex Best Bitter ♂ Thatchers Gold. **Facilities** Children welcome Children's portions Garden Parking Wi-fi

RYE   Map 7 TQ92

The George Tap ★★★★ HL ◉

98 High St TN31 7JT ☎ 01797 222114
e-mail: stay@thegeorgeinrye.com
dir: *M20 junct 10, A2070 to Brenzett, A259 to Rye*

Dating back to 1575, this town-centre inn offers a fascinating mix of old and new, with an exquisite original Georgian ballroom and plenty of antique and contemporary furnishings and locally produced art. In the bar, the draw is beers from Dark Star and Harvey's breweries and a tasty, light bar menu. Diners taking the one AA-Rosette meals can enjoy fruits of the sea from local boats, perhaps grilled Rye Bay lobster with garlic, chilli and parsley; or tackle a spiced Romney Marsh lamb burger. Booking for meals may be required.

Open all day all wk **Bar Meals** L served all wk 12-6 D served all wk 6-10 food served all day **Restaurant** L served all wk 12-3 D served all wk 6-10 ⊕ FREE HOUSE ◀ White Chilly Willy, Dark Star American Pale Ale, Harvey's Sussex Best Bitter ♂ Biddenden Bushell. ₹ 15 **Facilities** Children welcome Children's menu Children's portions Garden Wi-fi ▭ **Rooms** 34

The Globe Inn

10 Military Rd TN31 7NX ☎ 01797 227918
e-mail: info@theglobe-inn.com
dir: *M20 junct 10 onto A2070, A259 & A268*

A traditional weather-boarded inn built in 1839, this friendly free house is located just outside the ancient town walls of Rye. With no distractions such as TV screens or jukeboxes, this is a pub where conversation flows over pints of British Bulldog or one of the ten wines served by the glass. In the smartly appointed restaurant, enjoy dishes such as crisp pork belly, sherry and Calvados jus; local sausages with Dijon and honey mash; treacle tart with toffee ice cream. In summer, the garden offers excellent alfresco potential. Booking for meals may be required.

Open 12-3.30 6-11 (BHs all day) Closed: Mon, Sun eve **Bar Meals** L served Tue-Sun 12-3 D served Tue-Sat 6-9 Av main course £14 **Restaurant** L served Tue-Sun 12-3 D served Tue-Sat 6-9 Fixed menu price fr £8.95 Av 3 course à la carte fr £23.95 ⊕ FREE HOUSE ◀ Westerham British Bulldog BB & Audit Ale, Harvey's ♂ Westons Stowford Press. ₹ 10 **Facilities** ✿ Children welcome Children's portions Garden Parking Wi-fi ▭ (notice required)

The Cock Inn

Uckfield Road, Ringmer, Lewes, East Sussex   BN8 5RX
Tel: 01273 812040   Website: www.cockpub.co.uk

This is a 16th century family run dining pub where the landlords still find time to personally greet both new and returning customers. Walk into the pub and you are met by a huge blackboard that seems to list every pub dish that has ever existed! Should that not be enough choice then this is supplemented by a daily Specials Board – we try to offer something for all tastes, appetites and budgets and also cater for Coeliacs and Vegans.

There is a well stocked bar that features Harveys' Best Bitter, plus 2 other locally sourced seasonal beers.

The garden has plenty of space to enjoy fine weather with patio areas, grass and views to the South Downs; and if you are lucky spectacular sunsets on clear evenings. The pub welcomes dogs in the garden and bar area with dog chews and water bowls.

RYE continued

Mermaid Inn ★★★ HL ⊕

PICK OF THE PUBS

Mermaid St TN31 7EY ☎ 01797 223065
e-mail: info@mermaidinn.com
dir: *A259, follow signs to town centre, into Mermaid St*

In 1156 Rye became one of Edward the Confessor's confederation of Cinque Ports; the same year, someone built the cellars of this ancient inn. Opening on to a cobbled street, the main building is only (relatively speaking) 600 years old, with ships' timbers for beams and huge open fireplaces carved from French stone ballast dredged from Rye harbour. The infamous Hawkhurst Gang of smugglers used to meet in the Giant's Fireplace bar, audaciously displaying their loaded pistols to deter interference by magistrates; in the chimney breast there's a priest's hole. British and French-style food is served in both the bar and linenfold-panelled, AA-Rosette restaurant, and under sunshades on the patio. Roasted quail and baked salmon might be on the lunch menu, while dinner choices can include local pheasant breast with venison liver; pan-fried halibut; and sweet potato cakes. The Elizabethan Chamber is one of eight delightfully furnished bedrooms with a four-poster. Booking for meals may be required.

Open all wk 12-11 **Bar Meals** L served all wk 12-2.30 D served all wk 6-9 **Restaurant** L served all wk 12-2.30 D served all wk 7-9.30 ⊕ FREE HOUSE ◀ Morland Old Speckled Hen, Fuller's London Pride, Harvey's ○ Kingstone Press. ♚ 15 **Facilities** Children welcome Children's menu Children's portions Garden Parking Wi-fi ▬ (notice required) **Rooms** 31

The Ypres Castle Inn

PICK OF THE PUBS

See Pick of the Pubs on opposite page
See advert on page 512

Salehurst Halt

PICK OF THE PUBS

Church Ln TN32 5PH ☎ 01580 880620
dir: *0.5m from A21 (Tunbridge Wells to Hastings road). Exit at Robertsbridge rdbt to Salehurst*

Built in the 1860s, when it was known as the Old Eight Bells. Legend puts the name change down to a church organist who commuted to the village from Bodiam, necessitating a new halt on the Robertsbridge to Tenterden line. Despite use by many a hop-picker thereafter, the steam railway eventually closed. Today the hop crop is sold to Harvey's in Lewes, and returned as one of the ales sold by the pub – its traditional cellar is much prized for maintaining ale in top condition. The hop-growing farm also supplies the pub's meats, including Buster's burgers; note that evening meals are only served from Wednesday to Saturday. The landscaped

garden has a wonderful terrace with beautiful views over the Rother Valley; here a wood-fired pizza oven runs almost continually during the summer, with orders taken at the garden counter. Before leaving, have a stroll around this picturesque hamlet and the 12th-century church. Booking for meals may be required.

Open Tue-Wed 12-3 6-11 (Thu-Sun 12-11) Closed: Mon **Bar Meals** L served Tue-Sun 12-2.30 D served Wed-Sat 7-9 Av main course £7-£17 ⊕ FREE HOUSE ◀ Harvey's Sussex Best Bitter, Dark Star, Old Dairy, Guest ales ○ Biddenden Bushels, East Stour. **Facilities** Children welcome Children's portions Garden

The Peacock Inn

PICK OF THE PUBS

TN22 3XA ☎ 01825 762463
e-mail: enquiries@peacock-inn.co.uk
dir: *Just off A272 (Haywards Heath to Uckfield road) & A26 (Uckfield to Lewes road)*

Today it may be renowned for its food and the resident ghost of Mrs Fuller, but The Peacock Inn dates from 1567 and was mentioned in Samuel Pepys' diary. This traditional inn is full of old-world charm, both inside and out. The large rear patio garden is a delightful spot in summer. Woodcote Bitter and a guest ale keeps beer-lovers happy, and there are eight wines by the glass. For the hungry there are starters such as baked figs stuffed with brie, Parma ham and red pepper syrup; sweet chilli chicken salad with avocado and crispy bacon; followed by seared sea bass fillet, creamed fennel and leek, sauté potatoes and port reduction; or roast lamb rump with mint crust, creamy mash, red cabbage and lamb jus. For the non-meat eaters there's chestnut mushroom risotto, truffle oil and parmesan shavings.

Open all wk 11-3 6-11 Closed: 25-26 Dec **Bar Meals** L served Mon-Sat 12-3, Sun 12-6 D served Mon-Sat 6-9.30, Sun 12-6 **Restaurant** L served Mon-Sat 12-3, Sun 12-6 D served Mon-Sat 6-9.30, Sun 12-6 ⊕ FREE HOUSE ◀ Harvey's Sussex Best Bitter, Hammerpot Woodcote Bitter, Guest ale. ♚ 8 **Facilities** ♣ Children welcome Children's menu Children's portions Garden Parking

The Bull

Dunster Mill Ln TN5 7HH ☎ 01580 200586
e-mail: enquiries@thebullinn.co.uk
dir: *From M25 exit at Sevenoaks toward Hastings, right at x-rds onto B2087, right onto B2099 through Ticehurst, right for Three Legged Cross*

The Bull started life as a 14th-century Wealden Hall House, reputedly one of the oldest dwelling places in the country, and is set in a hamlet close to Bewl Water. The interior features oak beams, inglenook fireplaces, quarry-tiled floors, and a mass of small intimate areas in the bar. The extensive gardens are popular with families who enjoy the duck pond, petanque pitch, aviary and children's play area. Menus offer pub favourites ranging

from freshly baked baguettes and bar snacks to hearty dishes full of comfort, such as bangers and mash and treacle tart.

Open all day all wk 12-12 Closed: 25-26 Dec eve **Bar Meals** L served Mon-Fri 12-2.30, Sat 12-3, Sun 12-8 D served Mon-Sat 6.30-9, Sun 6.30-8 Av main course £8.50 **Restaurant** L served Mon-Fri 12-2.30, Sat 12-3, Sun 12-8 D served Mon-Sat 6.30-9, Sun 6.30-8 Av 3 course à la carte fr £15 ⊕ FREE HOUSE ◀ Harvey's Sussex Best Bitter & Armada Ale, Timothy Taylor Landlord, Guest ales ○ Westons Stowford Press. **Facilities** ♣ Children welcome Children's menu Children's portions Play area Garden Parking Wi-fi ▬ (notice required)

The Best Beech Inn

PICK OF THE PUBS

Best Beech Hill TN5 6JH ☎ 01892 782046
e-mail: info@thebestbeech.co.uk
dir: *7m from Tunbridge Wells. On A246 at lights turn left onto London Rd (A26), left at mini rdbt onto A267, left then right onto B2100. At Mark Cross signed Wadhurst, 3m on right*

The Best Beech Inn is in the perfect country-pub setting - in an Area of Outstanding Natural Beauty near the Kent and Sussex border. Once a coaching house dating back to 1680, the pub has been sympathetically refurbished to preserve the essentially Victorian character of its heyday, with comfy chairs, exposed brickwork and open fireplaces. The atmosphere is relaxed and welcoming while the décor combines both old and new. The seasonal menus offer the freshest, most dynamic ingredients sourced from local suppliers. Starters might include chicken liver parfait, followed by main courses such as leek, mushroom and almond loaf, or game pie. Enjoy apple pie with rhubarb compôte or local Sussex cheeses for pudding. Sandwiches and children's choices are also available. The award-winning ales and great selection of wines can be enjoyed by the fire in winter or out on the terrace in summer. Booking for meals may be required.

Open all wk 12-3 6-11 (Mon 6-11 Sat 9am-11pm Sun 12-6) Closed: Sun eve & Mon L **Bar Meals** L served Tue-Fri 12-2.30, Sat all day, Sun 12-3.30 D served Tue-Fri 6-9.30, Sat all day Av main course £10.50 **Restaurant** L served Tue-Fri 12-2.30, Sat all day, Sun 12-3.30 D served Tue-Fri 6-9.30, Sat all day Av 3 course à la carte fr £19.50 ⊕ SHEPHERD NEAME ◀ Master Brew, Spitfire ○ Thatchers Gold. ♚ 9 **Facilities** Children welcome Children's menu Children's portions Parking Wi-fi ▬ (notice required)

Save on hotels. Book at **theAA.com/hotel**

SUSSEX, EAST 511 ENGLAND

PICK OF THE PUBS

The Ypres Castle Inn

RYE Map 7 TQ92

Gun Garden TN31 7HH
☎ **01797 223248**
e-mail: info@yprescastleinn.co.uk
web: www.yprescastleinn.co.uk
dir: *Behind church & adjacent to Ypres Tower*

The ancient town of Rye's best-kept secret, the pretty Ypres Castle Inn, known as 'The Wipers' by the locals, sits beneath the ramparts of the Ypres Castle Tower, thought to have been built in 1249 as part of the town's defences. The white weather-boarded free-house has been providing hospitality since 1640. It is reached by 16th-century steps designed to make sword-fighting even more treacherous for invading hordes and was once the haunt of local wool smugglers — known as 'Owlers' because of their bird-like signals to each other. These days, the welcoming and sophisticated interior creates a relaxed, friendly atmosphere and offers a reading room stocked with an eclectic literary mix, together with daily newspapers, children's games and free Wi-fi. The pretty bar, featuring the original timber frame of the building, serves local Harvey's Sussex Best Bitter, best enjoyed sitting next to the roaring log fire or relaxing at one of the large oak tables. From the garden there are magnificent views of Romney Marsh and the River Rother, whose working fishing fleet provides most of the seafood offered on the menu, including the famous Rye Bay

Scallop. Other local produce on the menu includes Winchelsea Pork, Romney Marsh Lamb and home-cooked Biddenden cider-soaked ham. Lunchtime brings daily home-made soups as well as freshly baked baguettes, seafood salads and beer-battered cod and chips. Don't miss the home-made pickles, especially the piccalilli. There are morning and afternoon teas and coffees and home-made cakes, baked fresh every morning. Booking for dinner is advisable in summer and always for the traditional Sunday roasts. Live music by local artistes from a varied programme on Friday nights, Sundays and in the garden in summer. Dogs are welcome — ask for a free dog treat; there's even a dog menu with recommendations by Spud, the pub's terrier. Booking for meals may be required.

Open all day all wk **Bar Meals** L all wk 12-3 D Mon-Sat 6-9 **Restaurant** L all wk 12-3 D Sat-Thu 6-9, Fri 6-8 ⊕ FREE HOUSE ◗ Harvey's Sussex Best Bitter, Timothy Taylor Landlord, Larkins Best Bitter, Guest ales ♂ Biddenden Bushell. ⬚ 12 **Facilities** Children welcome Children's menu Children's portions Garden ⚘ Wi-fi

WILMINGTON   Map 6 TQ50

The Giants Rest

The Street BN26 5SQ ☎ 01323 870207
e-mail: abecjane@aol.com
dir: *2m from Polegate on A27 towards Brighton*

With the famous chalk figure of the Long Man of Wilmington standing guard further up the lane, this family-owned Victorian free house can properly claim to be one of the most Druid-friendly pubs in Sussex. The rustic wooden-floored bar is decorated with Beryl Cook prints. Take a seat at a pine table, each with its own wooden puzzle, and order some home-prepared food: wild garlic king prawns; shepherd's pie topped with cumin mashed potato; Sussex Downs rabbit and bacon pie; slow-roast belly of pork; warm haloumi salad; and hake fishcakes. Booking for meals may be required.

Open all wk 11-3 6-11 (Sat-Sun all day) **Bar Meals** L served Mon-Fri 11.30-2, Sat-Sun all day D served Mon-Fri 6.30-9, Sat-Sun all day Av main course £10.50 **Restaurant** L served Mon-Fri 11.30-2, Sat-Sun all day D served Mon-Fri 6.30-9, Sat-Sun all day ⊕ FREE HOUSE ◀ Harvey's Sussex Best Bitter, Timothy Taylor Landlord, Hop Back Summer Lightning Ŏ Westons Stowford Press. **Facilities** ❤ Children welcome Children's portions Garden Parking 🚐

WINCHELSEA   Map 7 TQ91

The New Inn

German St TN36 4EN ☎ 01797 226252
e-mail: thenewinnwinchelsea@sky.com
dir: *Telephone for directions*

It may not be a thriving seaport any more but Winchelsea boasts one of the finest collections of heritage medieval buildings in Britain and the historic 18th-century New Inn welcomes visitors and locals alike. Known today for its comfort, hospitality and excellent cuisine, it offers a light bite menu (moules marinière, local sausages and mash) or a dining menu that features the likes of Rye Bay seafood linguine, rack of Sussex lamb and hot Thai red chicken curry. The lovely walled garden is a delight on a sunny day.

Open all day all wk ◀ Morland Original & Old Speckled Hen, Greene King IPA & Abbot Ale Ŏ Westons Stowford Press. **Facilities** Children welcome Children's menu Children's portions Family room Garden Parking Wi-fi

WITHYHAM   Map 6 TQ43

The Dorset Arms

PICK OF THE PUBS

TN7 4BD ☎ 01892 770278
e-mail: pete@dorset-arms.co.uk
dir: *4m W of Tunbridge Wells on B2110 between Groombridge & Hartfield*

The picture-postcard perfection of this centuries-old building is a jigsaw of ages and styles - slender chimney stacks, sharp gables, gleaming white weatherboarding and careworn tiles. Licensed some 200 years ago when it took the name of the local landowning family, once Earls of Dorset, the interior doesn't disappoint, with a comfy, period mix of flagstoned and oak-boarded floors, vast open fireplace, undulating beams, and magpie furniture. It remains at heart a true village local, with darts, good Sussex ales from Harvey's and a vibrant community atmosphere. The produce of the kitchen is also a major draw, with an extensive, daily-changing specials board complementing the respectable carte menu. Starters range from avocado, mozzarella and tomato salad to devilled whitebait. The main event might include Thai green chicken curry; linguine marinara; and whole grilled lemon sole. All desserts are home-made. Tables on the green outside allow summertime alfresco dining.

Open all wk 11.30-3 6-11 (Sat-Sun all day) ⊕ HARVEYS OF LEWES ◀ Sussex Best Bitter, Seasonal ales. **Facilities** Garden Parking Wi-fi

SUSSEX, WEST

AMBERLEY   Map 6 TQ01

The Bridge Inn

Houghton Bridge BN18 9LR ☎ 01798 831619
e-mail: bridgeamberley@btinternet.com
web: www.bridgeinnamberley.com
dir: *5m N of Arundel on B2139. Next to Amberley main line station*

Ramblers hiking the South Downs Way throng the riverside garden in summer at this traditional 17th-century free house beside the River Arun at the mid-point of the long-distance trail. Inside, the candlelit bar and log fires draw folk in on cold winter evenings for Westons ciders and tip-top real ales like Sharp's Cornish Coaster and local Kings Old Ale. Food will satisfy the heartiest of walking appetites, with the menu listing steak-and-kidney-suet-pudding; rack of barbecued pork ribs; and a ham ploughman's lunch served with coleslaw, potato salad and a baguette.

Open all day all wk 11-11 (Sun 12-10.30) **Bar Meals** L served Mon-Fri 12-2.30, Sat-Sun 12-4 D served Mon-Sat 6-9, Sun 5.30-8 Av main course £10 **Restaurant** L served Mon-Fri 12-2.30, Sat-Sun 12-4 D served Mon-Sat 6-9, Sun 5.30-8 ⊕ FREE HOUSE ◀ Skinner's Betty Stogs, Sharp's Cornish Coaster, WJ King Kings Old Ale & Brighton Blonde, Harvey's Sussex Ŏ Westons Stowford Press & Old Rosie. **Facilities** ❤ Children welcome Children's menu Children's portions Garden Parking 🚐 (notice required)

ASHURST   Map 6 TQ11

The Fountain Inn

PICK OF THE PUBS

See Pick of the Pubs on page 514

BALCOMBE   Map 6 TQ33

The Cowdray

RH17 6QD ☎ 01444 811280
e-mail: alexandandy@hotmail.co.uk
dir: *From M23 junct 10a take the B2036 towards Balcombe*

This once run-down village boozer has been transformed into a plushly upholstered dining pub. Inside you'll find wood floors, a fresh, crisp décor, and a pub menu that's a cut above average. Alex and Andy Owen, who previously worked for Gordon Ramsay, specialise in sourcing ingredients within Sussex if possible. Notable exceptions are the Scottish Angus and Longhorn beef cuts which appear on the separate rare-breeds steak menu. Other dishes might include pigeon with raisin purée, onion marmalade and mixed leaves; roasted lamb chump with honey-glazed root vegetables and dauphinoise potatoes; and tarte Tatin for pudding. Booking for meals may be required.

Open all day all wk Closed: 25 Dec eve **Bar Meals** L served Mon-Sat 12-3, Sun 12-4 D served Mon-Thu 5.30-9.30, Fri-Sat 6-10 Av main course £13.95 food served all day **Restaurant** L served Mon-Sat 12-3, Sun 12-4 D served Sun-Thu 5.30-9.30, Fri-Sat 6-10 Fixed menu price fr £15.95 Av 3 course à la carte fr £25 ⊕ GREENE KING ◀ IPA, Morland Original, Guinness. ♀ 11 **Facilities** ❤ Children welcome Children's menu Children's portions Play area Family room Garden Parking Wi-fi 🚐 (notice required)

PICK OF THE PUBS

The Fountain Inn

ASHURST   Map 6 TQ11

BN44 3AP ☎ 01403 710219
e-mail: manager@fountainashurst.co.uk
web: www.fountainashurst.co.uk
dir: *On B2135 N of Steyning*

Set in the picturesque village of Ashurst, this 16th-century listed building is a fine example of a traditional English pub, complete with wonky floorboards, inglenook fireplaces and the smell of home cooking. The South Downs are visible from the pretty gardens (there's a great duck pond, too) while inside, a huge brick chimney stack vents the capacious inglenook. Other charming features include flagstone floors, traditional beams, rustic furnishings and a skittle alley. The pub has seen an impressive series of famous admirers: Sir Laurence Olivier was a regular, and Sir Paul McCartney loved the place so much he filmed part of the video for 'Wonderful Christmas Time' here in 1979. Hilaire Belloc set part of his book *The Four Men*, published in 1902, in the pub. Local beers from Harvey's and other regional breweries accompany the tasty, freshly cooked pub food that attracts walkers, cyclists, locals and those from further afield. At lunchtime there are light bites such as a Sussex ham and cheese ploughman's or warm chicken and bacon salad with honey and mustard dressing, or at lunch or dinner you could opt for the full three courses; maybe pan-seared scallops

with crispy pancetta, spinach and cauliflower purée followed by pan-fried duck breast with wilted spinach, wild mushrooms and new potatoes, with sticky toffee pudding and clotted cream for dessert. If you're seeking a classic, look to the list of 'favourites', which includes sausage and mash with onion gravy; local fish and chips with crushed peas and tartare sauce; and the Fountain burger with streaky bacon, Swiss cheese and chips. Look out for events including live music and comedy. Booking for meals may be required.

Open all day all wk 11-11 (Sun 11-10.30) **Bar Meals** L served Mon-Sat 12-2.30, Sun 12-3 D served Mon-Sat 6-9.30, Sun 6-9 Av main course £12 **Restaurant** L served Mon-Sat 12-2.30,

Sun 12-3 D served Mon-Sat 6-9.30, Sun 6-9 ⊕ ENTERPRISE INNS ◀ Harvey's Sussex, Sharp's Doom Bar, Fuller's, Seasonal ales, Guest ales ♉ Weston Stowford Press. ♟ 23 **Facilities** Children welcome Children's menu Children's portions ♣ Garden Beer festival Parking 🚌

BOSHAM   Map 5 SU80

The Anchor Bleu

High St PO18 8LS ☎ **01243 573956**
dir: *From A27 SW of Chichester take A259. Follow Fishbourne signs, then Bosham signs*

If you park your car opposite The Anchor Bleu, check the tide times as this 17th century harbourside inn as it floods during most high tides. Flagstone floors, low beams, an open log fire and two terraces, one overlooking Chichester Harbour, add to the charm of this popular pitstop for walkers and cyclists. Five real ales are on offer, and local seafood is showcased on the menu. Eat on the terraces, or inside in either the restaurant or bar area and choose dishes that are based on locally sourced, seasonal ingredients. Reservations for the evening are recommended but there are no bookings taken for lunch. Booking for meals may be required.

Open all wk all day (12-3 5.30-11 Oct-Apr) **Bar Meals** L served all wk 12-3 D served all wk 6.30-9.30 Av main course £7.95 **Restaurant** L served all wk 12-3 D served all wk 6.30-9.30 ⊕ ENTERPRISE INNS ◀ Sharp's Cornish Coaster & Doom Bar, Ringwood Fortyniner, Otter Ale, Hop Back Summer Lightning, Bath Gem ♂ Westons Stowford Press. ♀ 10 **Facilities** Children welcome Children's menu Children's portions Garden ⛟ (notice required)

BURGESS HILL   Map 6 TQ31

The Oak Barn

Cuckfield Rd RH15 8RE ☎ **01444 258222**
e-mail: enquiries@oakbarnrestaurant.co.uk
web: www.oakbarnrestaurant.co.uk
dir: *Telephone for directions*

As its name suggests, this popular pub-restaurant occupies a 250-year-old barn that has been lovingly restored using salvaged timbers from wooden ships. Brimming with charm and atmosphere, the interior is rich in oak flooring, authentic wagon wheel chandeliers, and fine stained glass. Lofty raftered ceilings, a galleried restaurant, and leather chairs fronting a huge fireplace are an idyllic setting for supping a pint of Harvey's and tucking into home-smoked mackerel fishcakes, followed by braised shoulder of lamb with a honey and herb crust and dauphinoise potatoes. Outside is an enclosed courtyard and patios, with water features. Booking for meals may be required.

Open all day all wk 10am-11pm (Sun 11-11) **Bar Meals** L served all wk 12-2.30 D served all wk 6-9.30 **Restaurant** L served all wk 12-2.30 D served all wk 6-9.30 ⊕ FREE HOUSE ◀ Harvey's, Guinness. ♀ 8 **Facilities** Children welcome Children's portions Garden Parking Wi-fi

See advert below

BURPHAM
Map 6 TQ00

George & Dragon ®

PICK OF THE PUBS

BN18 9RR ☎ **01903 883131**
e-mail: sara.cheney@btinternet.com
dir: *Off A27 1m E of Arundel, signed Burpham, 2.5m pub on left*

Tucked away down a long 'no through road', Burpham looks across the Arun Valley to the mighty Arundel Castle. There are excellent riverside and downland walks on the doorstep of this 300-year-old free house, and walkers are welcome in the bar. Step inside and you'll find beamed ceilings and modern prints on the walls, with worn stone flags on the floor. The original rooms have been opened out to form a large space that catches the late sunshine, but there are still a couple of alcoves with tables for an intimate drink. You'll also discover a small bar hidden around a corner. This is very much a dining pub, attracting visitors from far and wide. The à la carte menu and specials board offer a good choice of dishes between them: for starters you could try pan-seared scallops or Thai-marinated tiger prawns with noodles. Main courses might include chicken and wild mushroom pie, or seafood risotto. There are tables outside, ideal for whiling away an afternoon or evening in summer, listening to the cricket being played on the green. Booking for meals may be required.

Open all wk 12-3 6-11 ⊕ FREE HOUSE ◀ Arundel, Guest ales ♂ Aspall. **Facilities** Children welcome Children's menu Garden Parking

BURY
Map 6 TQ01

The Squire & Horse

Bury Common RH20 1NS ☎ **01798 831343**
e-mail: squireandhorse@btconnect.com
dir: *On A29, 4m S of Pulborough, 4m N of Arundel*

The original 16th-century building was extended several years ago, with old wooden beams and country fireplaces throughout. All the food is freshly cooked to order and sourced locally wherever possible. With the head chef originating from Australia there are innovative gastro-pub style dishes on offer here. These could include springbok Wellington with confit potato, or pork escalopes layered with ratatouille and three cheeses. You can also dine outside in the stylish seating area. There is a members' dining club to join with discounts throughout the year.

Open all wk 11-3 6-11 ⊕ FREE HOUSE ◀ Greene King IPA, Harvey's Sussex, Guest ales. **Facilities** Children welcome Children's menu Garden Parking

CHARLTON
Map 6 SU81

The Fox Goes Free ★★★★ INN

PICK OF THE PUBS

See Pick of the Pubs on opposite page

CHICHESTER
Map 5 SU80

The Bull's Head ★★★★ INN

99 Fishbourne Road West PO19 3JP ☎ **01243 839895**
e-mail: julie@bullsheadfishbourne.net
dir: *A27 onto A259, 0.5m on left*

Proud holder of a Fuller's Master Cellarman certificate, The Bull's Head serves five real ales all in tip-top condition. This traditional roadside pub with large open fire has been a hostelry since some time in the 17th century, and before that it was a farm house. Its position just outside Chichester is perfect for visiting Fishbourne Roman Palace and Bosham harbour. Live jazz is played every month, special events are hosted throughout the year, and four en suite bedrooms in a converted stables offer contemporary comforts. Home-cooked food is based on locally sourced ingredients. Booking for meals may be required.

Open all wk 11-3 5.30-11 (Sat-Sun all day) **Bar Meals** L served Mon-Fri 12-2, Sat 12-9.30, Sun 12-3 D served Mon-Fri 6-9, Sat 12-9.30, Sun 6-8.30 Av main course £9.50 **Restaurant** L served Mon-Fri 12-2, Sat 12-9.30, Sun 12-3 D served Mon-Fri 6-9, Sat 12-9, Sun 6-8.30 Av 3 course à la carte fr £16.95 ⊕ FULLER'S ◀ London Pride, Geoge Gale & Co Seafarers ♂ Aspall. ♥ 10 **Facilities** ❄ Children welcome Children's portions Parking Wi-fi ▭ (notice required) **Rooms** 4

The Earl of March ®®

PICK OF THE PUBS

Lavant Rd, Lavant PO18 0BQ ☎ **01243 533993**
e-mail: info@theearlofmarch.com
dir: *On A286, 1m N of Chichester*

Named after the local landowning dynasty, The Earl nestles at the foot of the South Downs National Park and is an inspirational place to stay awhile. William Blake wrote the words to 'Jerusalem' whilst sitting in the east-facing bay window here in 1803; today's visitors can enjoy much the same views that prompted his outpourings. With two AA Rosettes, the sublime choice of dishes are prepared from the bounty of local estates and the nearby Channel. Velouté of Jerusalem artichokes with morels and truffle oil whets the appetite, then fully sated with roast butternut squash risotto cake, glazed chestnuts and sage butter sauce, and white chocolate ice cream for dessert. Such top-notch dishes are crafted by Giles Thompson, former Executive Chef at London's Ritz Hotel and now proprietor of this delightful 18th-century coaching inn, rescued in 2005 from five years of closure and refurbished in 'country plush' style. Booking for meals may be required.

Open all day all wk **Bar Meals** L served all wk 12-2.30 winter, 12-9 summer D served all wk 12-9 summer Av main course £17.50 **Restaurant** L served all wk 12-2.30 winter, Sun 12-3 summer D served Mon-Sat 5.30-9.30, Sun 6-9 Fixed menu price fr £18.50 Av 3 course à la carte fr £30 ⊕ ENTERPRISE INNS ◀ Hop Back Summer Lightning, Fuller's London Pride, Harvey's ♂ Westons Stowford Press. ♥ 31 **Facilities** ❄ Children welcome Children's menu Children's portions Garden Parking Wi-fi

Royal Oak Inn ★★★★★ INN ®

PICK OF THE PUBS

Pook Ln, East Lavant PO18 0AX ☎ **01243 527434**
e-mail: info@royaloakeastlavant.co.uk
dir: *2m N of Chichester. Exit A286 to East Lavant centre*

Set within the South Downs National Park and just up the hill from Goodwood racecourse, the Royal Oak is also perfectly situated for nearby Chichester. Two centuries old, the creeper-clad Georgian inn is at the heart of the historic village and is now a smart dining pub blessed with luxury accommodation. The brick-lined restaurant and beamed bar achieve a crisp, rustic brand of chic: details include open fires, fresh flowers, candles, and wine attractively displayed in alcoves set into the walls; Horsham Best and Gospel Green champagne cider are among the thirst-quenchers on offer. The seasonal menu is an easy mix of English classics and modern Mediterranean dishes, and much of the produce is grown by villagers in return for pints. Pace yourself with a starter of game and pistachio terrine with hedgerow jelly prior to smoked haddock Florentine with spinach, cheese sauce and poached hen's egg, or beef Bourguignon. Booking for meals may be required.

Open all day all wk 7am-11.30pm **Bar Meals** L served Mon-Sat 12-2.30 Av main course £13 **Restaurant** L served all wk 12-2.30 Fixed menu price fr £16.95 Av 3 course à la carte fr £26.70 ⊕ FREE HOUSE ◀ Skinner's Betty Stogs, Sharp's Doom Bar, Arundel Sussex Gold, WJ King Horsham Best, McMullen Country Bitter ♂ Gospel Green Champagne & Cidermakers, Thatchers. ♥ 20 **Facilities** Children welcome Children's portions Garden Parking Wi-fi **Rooms** 8

COMPTON
Map 5 SU71

Coach & Horses

The Square PO18 9HA ☎ **023 9263 1228**
dir: *On B2146 S of Petersfield, to Emsworth, in centre of Compton*

A 17th-century coaching inn and Victorian bar are comfortably combined here to make a charming village pub. Set in a pretty Downland village, it's a popular spot for walkers and cyclists. In the same hands for over a quarter of a century, the front bar features two open fires and a bar billiards table, while the restaurant is in the oldest part of the pub, with many exposed beams. Beers from independent breweries, like Dark Star Hophead and Ballards Best, are available. Expect proper cooking such as steak-and-kidney pudding, slow-roasted belly pork, and pheasant braised in red wine. Booking for meals may be required.

Open all wk 11.30-3 6-11 **Bar Meals** L served all wk 12-2 D served all wk 7-9 **Restaurant** L served all wk 12-2 D served all wk 7-9 ⊕ FREE HOUSE ◀ Ballards Best Bitter, Dark Star Hophead, Hammerpot Bottle Wreck Porter ♂ Thatchers, Appledram. **Facilities** ❄ Children welcome Children's portions ▭

PICK OF THE PUBS

The Fox Goes Free ★★★★ INN

CHARLTON Map 6 SU81

PO18 0HU ☎ **01243 811461**
e-mail: enquiries@thefoxgoesfree.com
web: www.thefoxgoesfree.com
dir: *A286, 6m from Chichester towards Midhurst*

Standing in unspoiled countryside at the foot of the South Downs, this lovely old brick and flint free house was a favoured hunting lodge of William III. With its three huge fireplaces, old pews and brick floors, the 15th-century building simply exudes charm and character. The pub, which hosted the first Women's Institute meeting in 1915, lies close to the rambling Weald and Downland Open Air Museum, where over 45 historic buildings from around southern England have been reconstructed to form a unique collection. Goodwood Estate is also close by, and The Fox attracts many customers during the racing season and the annual Festival of Speed. Comfortable accommodation is available here if you would like to stay over. Away from the high life, you can watch the world go by from the solid timber benches and tables to the front, or relax under the apples trees in the lawned rear garden. Lest all this sounds rather extravagant, you'll find that The Fox is a friendly and welcoming drinkers' pub with a good selection of real ales that includes the eponymous Fox Goes Free bitter. Everything from the chips to the ice cream is home-made and, whether you're looking for a quick bar snack or something more substantial, the daily-changing menus offer something for every taste. Bar meals

include home-made sausages and mash with onion marmalade and vegetables; and beer-battered cod and chips with mushy peas and home-made tartare sauce; as well as a selection of ciabattas. À la carte choices may start with home-baked bread and marinated olives, or whole baked camembert, confit garlic and toasted fingers. Continue with meat and fish main courses such as twice-cooked pork belly with home-made black pudding and mash, or roasted fillet of salmon with chorizo creamed spinach. Salads can be prepared for both small and large appetites, and there are some appealing vegetarian options, too. Booking for meals may be required.

Open all day all wk 11-11 (Sun 12-11) Closed: 25 Dec eve **Bar Meals** L served Mon-Fri 12-2.30, Sat-Sun 12-10 D

served Mon-Fri 6.30-10, Sat-Sun 12-10 Av main course £11.50-£16.50 **Restaurant** L served all wk 12-2.30 D served all wk 6.30-10 Av 3 course à la carte fr £28 ⊕ FREE HOUSE ◗ The Fox Goes Free, Ballards Best Bitter, Otter. **Facilities** Children welcome Children's menu Children's portions ✿ Garden Parking Wi-fi 🚌 **Rooms** 5

CUCKFIELD Map 6 TQ32

The Talbot NEW

High St RH17 5JX ☎ 01444 455898
e-mail: info@thetalbotcuckfield.co.uk
dir: *B2036 into village centre*

At the heart of the historic village of Cuckfield, The Talbot was fully refurbished in 2010 by the current owners. The result is a contemporary pub and restaurant that prides itself on making the most of the local larder, whether it's Dark Star or Harvey's ales or seasonal dishes such as seared Newhaven scallops with parsnip purée and black pudding, or roasted field mushroom with home-smoked blue cheese. Such is the pub's commitment to local food, there is a monthly producers' market in the courtyard.

Open all day all wk **Bar Meals** L served all wk 12-2.30 D served Mon-Sat 6-9.30, Sun 12-5 Av main course £13.70 **Restaurant** L served all wk 12-2.30 D served Mon-Sat 6-9.30 FREE HOUSE Harvey's Sussex Best Bitter, Dark Star, Guest ales. 17 **Facilities** Children welcome Children's menu Children's portions Garden Wi-fi (notice required)

DIAL POST Map 6 TQ11

The Crown Inn

Worthing Rd RH13 8NH ☎ 01403 710902
e-mail: crowninndialpost@aol.com
dir: *8m S of Horsham, off A24*

A family-owned free house overlooking the village green, The Crown offers a relaxed pub atmosphere for those who just want a pint of Harvey's, but food is a key part of what's on offer here. Local sourcing doesn't get much better than lamb and pork from the family farm, and everything is made on the premises, from celeriac and truffle oil soup to the Sussex smokie – natural-smoked haddock with cream and Sussex Charmer cheese on a bed of spinach topped with prawns. Finish with sticky toffee pudding with home-made ice cream. Booking for meals may be required.

Open all wk Mon-Sat 11-3 6-11 (Sun 12-4) **Bar Meals** L served all wk 12-2.15 D served Mon-Sat 6-9.15 Av main course £15 **Restaurant** L served all wk 12-2.15 D served Mon-Sat 6-9.15 Fixed menu price fr £10 FREE HOUSE Harvey's Sussex Best Bitter, Devil's Dyke Porter, Kissingate Best Thatchers Gold, JB. 12 **Facilities** Children welcome Children's portions Garden Parking Wi-fi (notice required)

DUNCTON Map 6 SU91

The Cricketers

GU28 0LB ☎ 01798 342473
e-mail: info@thecricketersduncton.co.uk
dir: *On A285, 3m from Petworth, 8m from Chichester*

Dating to the 16th century, this attractive white-painted pub with inglenook fireplace sits in beautiful gardens behind Goodwood in the lovely South Downs. The inn, little changed over the years, is named to commemorate its one-time owner John Wisden, the first-class cricketer and creator of the famous sporting almanac. Well-kept real ales include Arundel Sussex Gold, while the blackboard menu offers traditional favourites, home-cooked from locally sourced ingredients. Look for the likes of slow-braised pork belly; a trio of venison sausages; or a steak cut to order and cooked to your liking. Children are welcome, with a menu for younger tastes.

Open all day all wk **Bar Meals** L served Mon-Fri 12-2.30, Sat-Sun 12-6 D served Mon-Fri 6-9, Sat-Sun 12-9 **Restaurant** L served Mon-Fri 12-2.30, Sat-Sun 12-6 D served Mon-Fri 6-9, Sat-Sun 12-9 FREE HOUSE Skinner's Betty Stogs, WJ King Horsham Best, Arundel Sussex Gold, Guest ale Thatchers & Heritage. **Facilities** Children welcome Children's menu Children's portions Play area Garden Parking

EAST ASHLING Map 5 SU80

Horse and Groom ★★★★ INN

PO18 9AX ☎ 01243 575339
e-mail: info@thehorseandgroomchichester.co.uk
web: www.thehorseandgroomchichester.co.uk
dir: *3m from Chichester on B1278 between Chichester & Rowland's Castle. 2m off A27 at Fishbourne*

This 400-year-old village inn with rooms has long been popular with visitors exploring Bosham Harbour and the South Downs National Park to the north. The inn retains much of its heritage; timber frames, oak beams and flagstoned floors offer a comfy retreat in which to try traditional ales such as Hophead. In the restaurant, enjoy the extensive menu of mains and specials; half a duck with balsamic and honey glaze; and cheese-topped smoked haddock with spinach take the eye here. On a summer day, head to the suntrap beer garden. Booking for meals may be required.

Open 12-3 6-11 (Sun 12-6) Closed: Sun eve **Bar Meals** L served Mon-Sat 12-2.15, Sun 12-2.30 D served Mon-Sat 6.30-9.15 **Restaurant** L served Mon-Sat 12-2.15, Sun 12-2.30 D served Mon-Sat 6.30-9.15 FREE HOUSE Hop Back Summer Lightning, Dark Star Hophead, Sharp's Doom Bar, Harvey's, Young's Westons Stowford Press, Addlestones. **Facilities** Children welcome Children's menu Children's portions Garden Parking Wi-fi **Rooms** 11

EAST DEAN Map 6 SU91

The Star & Garter

PICK OF THE PUBS

PO18 0JG ☎ 01243 811318
e-mail: thestarandgarter@hotmail.com
dir: *On A286 between Chichester & Midhurst. Exit A286 at Singleton. Village in 2m*

Built as a pub from traditional Sussex flint in about 1740, The Star & Garter stands close to the village pond in the pretty downland village of East Dean and was taken over by a new owner in 2011. The interior has been opened out to give a light and airy atmosphere with original brickwork, antique panelling, scrubbed tables and a wood-burning stove. In the bar, two locally brewed real ales are served from the barrel alongside two ciders and a range of wines by the glass. Locally renowned for an excellent selection of fish and shellfish, the menu also includes fine meat and vegetarian dishes, plus sharing platters. Typical choices include roasted guinea fowl with creamy Shropshire blue sauce; couscous-crusted goat's cheese with red onion salad; and pan-seared scallops with crispy pancetta and salad. A sunny sheltered patio, an original well and attractive lawned gardens complete the picture. Goodwood racecourse and motor racing venues are just a short hop in the car. Booking for meals may be required.

Open all wk 11-3 6-11 (Fri 5.30-11 Sat-Sun all day) **Bar Meals** L served Mon-Fri 12-2.30, Sat-Sun all day D served Mon-Fri 6.30-11, Sat-Sun all day **Restaurant** L served Mon-Fri 12-2.30, Sat-Sun all day D served Mon-Fri 6.30-10, Sat-Sun all day FREE HOUSE Arundel Castle, Sussex Gold Westons 1st Quality, Aspall. 11 **Facilities** Children welcome Children's menu Children's portions Garden Parking Wi-fi

Save on hotels. Book at **theAA.com/hotel**

SUSSEX, WEST 519 ENGLAND

PICK OF THE PUBS

The Foresters Arms

GRAFFHAM   Map 6 SU91

The Street GU28 0QA ☎ 01798 867202
e-mail: info@forestersgraffham.co.uk
web: www.forestersgraffham.co.uk
dir: *From Midhurst S on A285, left to Heyshott straight on to Graffham; From Petworth S on A286, turn right to Graffham, left fork into village centre*

New life has been breathed into this 17th-century inn hidden away in a tranquil cul-de-sac village at the foot of the South Downs. It's worth seeking out as it's ideally placed for post-walking and biking refreshments, and it's handy for Goodwood racing, polo at Cowdray Park and antique hunting in Petworth and Arundel. In the bar you'll find old beams, exposed stone walls and a large smoke-blackened fireplace, as well as a real ale choice likely to embrace tip-top ales from local Harvey's, Langham and Dark Star breweries, or there are 15 wines served by the glass. The pub offers an imaginative short menu that trawls the Mediterranean for inspiration and reflects the seasons. They make sound use of quality Sussex produce and dishes are freshly prepared – no corners are cut in the pub's objective to offer the best in quality and value. For a starter or light lunch choose watercress and basil soup, served with Farretti's Italian bakery ciabatta; a salad of Sussex Ash goat's cheese and confit beetroot with baby leaves and a chilli and herb dressing; or warm ciabatta roll

filled with rare beef, horseradish crème fraîche and baby leaves. Having cycled or tramped miles across the Downs, tuck into a hearty chicken, tarragon and saffron pie; a plate of spaghetti with seared tiger prawns; chorizo, baby red chard and prawn bisque; roast rump of lamb with crushed celeriac and rosemary jus; or try the wild sea bass with smoked shrimp velouté. Leave room for blueberry and apple crumble with warm crème anglaise, or orange and brandy brioche butter pudding, then walk it all off with a downland stroll. Don't miss the monthly Saturday live jazz evenings. Booking for meals may be required.

Open all wk 12-3 6-late (all day Sat-Sun in Jul-Aug) **Bar Meals** L served all

wk 12-2.30 D served Mon-Sat 6-9.15, Sun 6-8 Av main course £6.50-£14 **Restaurant** L served all wk 12-2.30 D served Mon-Sat 6-9.15, Sun 6-8 Fixed menu price fr £11 Av 3 course à la carte fr £24.50 🛢 FREE HOUSE ◼ Harvey's Sussex Best Bitter, Dark Star Hophead, Langham seasonal ale Ŏ Thatchers Gold. ♟ 15 **Facilities** Children welcome Children's menu Children's portions 🐾 Garden Parking Wi-fi

ELSTED   Map 5 SU81

The Three Horseshoes

PICK OF THE PUBS

GU29 0JY ☎ 01730 825746

dir: *A272 from Midhurst towards Petersfield, after 2m left to Harting & Elsted, after 3m pub on left*

Tucked below the steep scarp slope of the South Downs National Park in the peaceful village of Elsted, this 16th-century former drovers' alehouse is one of those quintessential English country pubs that Sussex specialises in, full of rustic charm. Expect unspoilt cottage-style bars, worn stone-flagged floors, low beams, latch doors, a vast inglenook, and a mix of antique furnishings. On fine days the extensive rear garden, with roaming chickens and stunning southerly views, is hugely popular. Tip-top real ales, including Bowman and Flower Pots from across the Hampshire border, are drawn from the cask, and a daily-changing blackboard menu offers classic country cooking. Game such as pheasant is abundant in season; alternatively fish of the day comes with dauphinoise potatoes.

Open all wk ⊕ FREE HOUSE ◀ Ballards Best Bitter, Fuller's London Pride, Timothy Taylor Landlord, Hop Back Summer Lightning, Bowman Wallops Wood, Flower Pots. **Facilities** Garden Parking

FERNHURST   Map 6 SU82

The Red Lion

The Green GU27 3HY ☎ 01428 643112

dir: *Just off A286 midway between Haslemere & Midhurst*

Renowned for its warm welcome and friendly atmosphere, this attractive 16th-century inn with oak beams and open fires is set in its own lovely gardens on the village green. The good choice of beers includes Fuller's ESB, Chiswick and London Pride along with seasonal guest ales. Freshly cooked, mostly traditional English food is offered from the menus, featuring the likes of smoked haddock fishcakes; steak, kidney and ale pudding; cold poached salmon and prawn salad with new potatoes; and chilli con carne. Sandwiches, jackets and salads are available on the snack menu. Look out for the specials, too. Booking for meals may be required.

Open all day all wk 11.30-11 (Sun 11.30-10.30) **Bar Meals** L served all wk 12-3 D served all wk 6-9.30 **Restaurant** L served all wk 12-3 D served all wk 6-9.30 ⊕ FULLER'S ◀ ESB, Chiswick Bitter & London Pride, Guest ale ♻ Aspall. ♟ 8 **Facilities** ✿ Children welcome Children's menu Children's portions Garden Parking ⛟

GRAFFHAM   Map 6 SU91

The Foresters Arms

PICK OF THE PUBS

See Pick of the Pubs on page 519

HALNAKER   Map 6 SU90

The Anglesey Arms at Halnaker

PICK OF THE PUBS

See Pick of the Pubs on opposite page

HENLEY   Map 6 SU82

Duke of Cumberland Arms

GU27 3HQ ☎ 01428 652280

e-mail: info@thedukeofcumberland.com
dir: *Between Haslemere & Midhurst, just off A286 south of Fernhurst*

Many fine words have been written about this beautiful, 15th-century pub perched on a wooded hillside in the South Downs National Park. Inside are flagstones, brick floors, scrubbed tables, and ales served straight from the barrels Harvey's and Langham breweries deliver them in. The first-rate menus impress at lunchtime with Sussex venison ragout, and pan-seared scallop salad, and again in the evening with confit free-range pork belly with apple and Calvados glaze, and whole roasted Sussex partridge with black pudding mash. Check the date of the summer Dukefest beer festival. Booking for meals may be required.

Open all day all wk **Bar Meals** L served all wk 12-2 D served Tue-Sat 7-9 Av main course £12.95 **Restaurant** L served all wk 12-2 D served Tue-Sat 7-9 Av 3 course à la carte fr £30 ⊕ FREE HOUSE ◀ Harvey's Sussex, Langham Best Bitter & Hip Hop ♻ Westons Stowford Press. ♟ **Facilities** ✿ Children welcome Children's portions Garden Beer festival Parking Wi-fi

HEYSHOTT   Map 6 SU81

Unicorn Inn

PICK OF THE PUBS

GU29 0DL ☎ 01730 813486

e-mail: unicorninnheyshott@hotmail.co.uk
dir: *Telephone for directions*

Jenni Halpin's 18th-century free house stands in a sleepy Sussex village and enjoys stunning views of the South Downs from its beautiful, south-facing rear garden, the perfect spot to relax on sunny day with a pint of Horsham Best or Sussex Gold. Being within the South Downs National Park, it's a fair bet that you'll share the pub with walkers and cyclists (and, of course, some locals) seeking out the home-cooked food listed on seasonal menus that make sound use of locally sourced produce. The bar, with beams and a large log fire, is particularly atmospheric, while the subtly lit, cream-painted restaurant is where you can sample fresh fish from Selsey – try wild sea bass fillet with white wine and chive sauce – or dishes likes slow-roasted lamb shank with mash and a redcurrant and rosemary sauce, or confit duck leg with elderberry and balsamic sauce. Good sandwiches (roast beef and horseradish) and popular Sunday lunches complete the pleasing picture. Booking for meals may be required.

Open 11.30-3 6-11 (Sun 12-4) Closed: 2wks Jan, Sun eve & Mon **Bar Meals** L served Tue-Sat 12-2, Sun 12-2.30 D served Tue-Sat 7-9 **Restaurant** L served Tue-Sat 12-2, Sun 12-2.30 D served Tue-Sat 7-9 ⊕ FREE HOUSE ◀ WJ King Horsham Best, Arundel Sussex Gold ♻ Westons Stowford Press. **Facilities** ✿ Children welcome Children's menu Children's portions Garden Parking ⛟ (notice required)

HORSHAM   Map 6 TQ13

The Black Jug

31 North St RH12 1RJ ☎ 01403 253526

e-mail: black.jug@brunningandprice.co.uk
dir: *Telephone for directions*

'When our week's work is over, to the Jug we repair'. So begins some mid-Victorian doggerel about this busy town-centre pub, a replacement for the 19th-century original which burnt down in the 1930s. Inside, classic wood panelling and flooring, old furniture and bookcases; outside, a conservatory-cum-courtyard. All-day meals (from noon) are freshly prepared using local ingredients wherever possible, typically crab linguine with ginger, red chilli and coriander; sweet potato and coconut curry with jasmine rice; smoked duck breast with pecan, avocado and mango salad; and smoked haddock and salmon fishcakes. Booking for meals may be required.

Open all day all wk **Bar Meals** L served Mon-Sat 12-10, Sun 12-9.30 D served Mon-Sat 12-10, Sun 12-9.30 Av main course £11.95 food served all day **Restaurant** L served Mon-Sat 12-10, Sun 12-9.30 D served Mon-Sat 12-10, Sun 12-9.30 food served all day ⊕ BRUNNING & PRICE ◀ Harvey's Sussex, Caledonian Deuchars IPA, Theakston Old Peculier ♻ Westons Wyld Wood Vintage Cider, Gwynt y Ddraig Black Dragon. ♟ 15 **Facilities** ✿ Children welcome Children's portions Garden

KINGSFOLD   Map 6 TQ13

The Dog and Duck

Dorking Rd RH12 3SA ☎ 01306 627295

e-mail: info@thedoganduck.fsnet.co.uk
dir: *On A24, 3m N of Horsham*

The Dog and Duck is a 16th-century family-run and family-friendly country pub. There's plenty of children's play equipment in the huge garden, and three very large fields encourage dogs and energetic owners to stretch their legs. In the summer a native American camp is set up, complete with tepees and camp fire. The rest of the year sees the diary chock-full of celebratory and fundraising events.

Open all wk 12-3 6-11 (Fri 12-3 6-12 Sat 12-12 Sun 12-10) **Bar Meals** L served all wk 12-2.30 (3pm Sun) D served Mon-Sat 6-9 Av main course £7.95-£12.95 **Restaurant** L served all wk 12-2.30 (3pm Sun) D served Mon-Sat 6-9 ⊕ HALL & WOODHOUSE ◀ Badger K&B Sussex, Dorset Best, Seasonal ales ♻ Westons Stowford Press. **Facilities** ✿ Children welcome Children's menu Children's portions Play area Garden Beer festival Parking ⛟ (notice required)

PICK OF THE PUBS

The Anglesey Arms at Halnaker

HALNAKER   Map 6 SU90

PO18 0NQ ☎ 01243 773474
e-mail: info@angleseyarms.co.uk
web: www.angleseyarms.co.uk
dir: *From centre of Chichester 4m E on A285 (Petworth road)*

Jools and George Jackson's charming, old-fashioned Georgian country pub stands in two acres of landscaped grounds on the Goodwood Estate, famous for its horse racing, the Festival of Speed and the Goodwood Revival. The village name, in which the 'l' is silent, comes from the Old English for 'half an acre'; many centuries earlier the Romans pushed Stane Street, their road from Chichester to London, through here. Head first to the wood-floored bar to enjoy hand-pulled Young's Bitter, Bowman Swift One or Black Sheep Best Bitter, or one of the unusual wines from small vineyards. Hand-cut sandwiches; local sausages; smoked salmon and poached egg toasted muffin; and Thai fishcakes are available along with a full lunchtime menu. The kitchen team makes skilful use of meats from traceable and organically raised animals, as well as locally caught fish from sustainable stocks. The Anglesey has built a special reputation for its Sussex steaks, hung for at least 21 days. For dinner, try a starter of home-made Selsey crab pâté, or salad of sun-blushed tomatoes, olives, artichokes,

brie and croûtons, then follow with calves' liver and bacon with mash and onion gravy; confit of duck with bubble-and-squeak and plum sauce; or pumpkin and potato pudding on roast squash with garlic sauce, dressed salad and parmesan crisps. At both lunch and dinner, blackboards list daily local meat and fish dishes. On Sundays the menu breaks the traditional roast mould by also offering, for example, fresh Cornish sardines with spiced tomato, black olive and new potato salad; steak-and-ale pie; and white onion and Tallegio cheese tart. Within a mile of the pub is a now-famous archaeological site, where in 1993 the 500,000 year-old shin-bone of Boxgrove Man was found. Booking for meals may be required.

Open all wk 11-3 5.30-11 (Fri-Sun 11-11) **Bar Meals** L served Mon-Sat 12-2.30, Sun 12-3 D served Mon-Sat 6.30-9.30 **Restaurant** L served Mon-Sat 12-2.30, Sun 12-3 D served Mon-Sat 6.30-9.30 ⊕ PUNCH TAVERNS ◀ Young's Bitter, Bowman Swift One, Black Sheep Best Bitter ♂ Westons Stowford Press. ♟ 12 **Facilities** Children welcome Children's portions ♣ Garden Parking Wi-fi 🚐

KINGSFOLD *continued*

The Owl at Kingsfold

Dorking Rd RH12 3SA ☎ 01306 628499
e-mail: info@theowl-kingsfold.co.uk
web: www.theowl-kingsfold.co.uk
dir: *On A24, 4m N of Horsham*

Nigel and Jean White gave The Owl a stylish makeover after they took over the pub in 2010. However, it remains a traditional country free house, with wooden beams, flagstone floors and log burners. It occupies a prominent roadside site in the village, with plenty of parking and a garden with views to the Surrey Hills; composer Ralph Vaughan Williams reputedly arranged the 'Kingsfold Hymn' here. There are three real ales to choose from, while the dinner menu includes roasted pepper and tomato bruschetta drizzled with pesto to start; and home-made beef, Guinness and stilton pie; and Cajun-spiced chicken breast as mains.

Open all day all wk **Bar Meals** food served all day **Restaurant** food served all day ⊕ FREE HOUSE ◀ Otter Ale, Hogs Back TEA, St Austell Tribute Ö Westons. ▼ 12 **Facilities** Children welcome Children's menu Children's portions Garden Parking Wi-fi

KIRDFORD Map 6 TQ02

The Half Moon Inn
PICK OF THE PUBS

RH14 0LT ☎ 01403 820223
dir: *Off A272 between Billingshurst & Petworth. At Wisborough Green follow Kirdford signs*

Set directly opposite the church in this quiet, unspoilt Sussex village near the River Arun, this picturesque, red-tiled 16th-century village inn is covered in climbing roses. A bit off the beaten track, the pub is made up of cottages that were once craftsmen's workshops. Although drinkers are welcome, the Half Moon is mainly a dining pub. The interior consists of an attractive bar with adjoining wooden-floored restaurant area. The furniture and paintings charmingly reflect the oak beams, tiled floors, open fireplaces and log fires in winter. The chef serves honest wholesome food, locally sourced from healthy well-reared stock. The à la carte, daily set menus and lunchtime snacks reflect the best of the season's ingredients. At dinner, the atmosphere changes, with candlelight, linen tablecloths and polished glassware. Private dining is available. Well-tended gardens at the front and rear are an added draw in the summer. There

are also a number of walks and cycle routes in the area if you want to work up an appetite.

Open 11-3 6-11 Closed: Sun eve, Mon eve ◀ Ballards, Local ale. **Facilities** Children welcome Children's portions Garden Parking

LAMBS GREEN Map 6 TQ23

The Lamb Inn

RH12 4RG ☎ 01293 871336 & 871933
e-mail: lambinnrusper@yahoo.co.uk
dir: *6m from Horsham between Rusper & Faygate. 5m from Crawley*

Follow an invigorating rural ramble with a pint of local Kings Old Ale or Langham LSD in the homely beamed bar of this traditional country pub. It remains a rustic and unspoilt local, thanks to landlords Ben and Chris, who maintain the unchanging atmosphere, so expect a crackling fire in the inglenook, and a conservatory dining room. Menus feature as much locally sourced produce as possible and dishes may take in Springs Sussex salmon with home-made mayonnaise; braised lamb shoulder with tarragon, white wine and slow-roasted tomatoes; and whole grilled sea bass. The annual August beer festival draws a loyal crowd.

Open all wk Mon-Thu 11.30-3 5.30-11 (Fri-Sat 11.30-11 Sun 12-10.30) Closed: 25-26 Dec **Bar Meals** L served Mon-Thu 12-2, Fri-Sat 12-9.30, Sun 12-9 D served Mon-Thu 6.30-9.30, Fri-Sat 12-9.30, Sun 12-9 Av main course £12 **Restaurant** L served Mon-Thu 12-2, Fri-Sat 12-9.30, Sun 12-9 D served Mon-Thu 6.30-9.30, Fri-Sat 12-9.30, Sun 12-9 Fixed menu price fr £9 Av 3 course à la carte fr £23 ⊕ FREE HOUSE ◀ WJ King Kings Old Ale, Weltons Old Cocky, Langham LSD, Dark Star Hophead & Partridge Best Bitter Ö Westons Stowford Press, Biddenden, Rekorderlig. ▼ 12 **Facilities** Children welcome Children's menu Children's portions Garden Beer festival Parking Wi-fi ▥ (notice required)

LODSWORTH Map 6 SU92

The Halfway Bridge Inn
PICK OF THE PUBS

See Pick of the Pubs on opposite page

The Hollist Arms
PICK OF THE PUBS

The Street GU28 9BZ ☎ 01798 861310
e-mail: info@thehollistarms.com
dir: *0.5m between Midhurst & Petworth, 1m N of A272, adjacent to Country Park*

A family-friendly, 15th-century public house outside which, on the lawn, stands a grand old tree ringed by a bench. The pub overlooks the green in a picturesque village that is now within the South Downs National Park, created in 2011. Inglenook fireplaces, low beams and a blissful absence of games machines imbue it with traditional pub charm and character, but what differentiates it from others is the impression that the owners, Sally and Serge, have transplanted a bistro from rural France. A window table in the atmospheric dining room is rather popular, but alternatives are in the snug and several small rooms. Seasonal menus of home-cooked French and English food may feature bouillabaisse; falafel, guacamole and piperade salad; and venison steak with root vegetable gratin and juniper jus. Real ales come from Otter, Timothy Taylor and Lodsworth-brewed Langham. Well-behaved dogs usually find a tasty bone to gnaw on. Booking for meals may be required.

Open all day all wk 11-11 **Bar Meals** L served all wk 12-2.30 D served all wk 6-9 **Restaurant** L served all wk 12-2.30 D served all wk 6-9 ⊕ FREE HOUSE ◀ Timothy Taylor Landlord, Otter Ale, Langham Ö Westons Stowford Press. ▼ 9 **Facilities** ♣ Children welcome Children's menu Children's portions Garden Parking Wi-fi ▥ (notice required)

LURGASHALL Map 6 SU92

The Noah's Ark

The Green GU28 9ET ☎ 01428 707346
e-mail: amy@noahsarkinn.co.uk
dir: *B2131 from Haslemere follow signs to Petworth/ Lurgashall. A3 from London towards Portsmouth. At Milford take A283 signed Petworth. Follow signs to Lurgashall*

In a picturesque village beneath Blackdown Hill, this attractive 16th-century inn overlooks the cricket green. The interior is full of warmth thanks to the charm of old beams, a large inglenook fireplace, and the enthusiasm of its owners. Ales include a regularly changing guest, and the traditional British food with a contemporary twist uses seasonal ingredients carefully sourced from the best local suppliers: brie filo parcel with Cumberland sauce with chicory and walnut salad may precede main courses such as smoked haddock gratin and rib-eye steak. Booking for meals may be required.

Open all day all wk 11-11 (Sun 11-10 summer Sun 11-7 winter) **Bar Meals** L served all wk 12-2.30 D served all wk 7-9.30 Av main course £12 **Restaurant** L served all wk 12-2.30 D served all wk 7-9.30 Av 3 course à la carte fr £25 ⊕ GREENE KING ◀ IPA & Abbot Ale, Guest ale Ö Westons Stowford Press. **Facilities** ♣ Children welcome Children's portions Family room Garden Parking Wi-fi ▥ (notice required)

PICK OF THE PUBS

The Halfway Bridge Inn

LODSWORTH   Map 6 SU92

Halfway Bridge GU28 9BP
☎ **01798 861281**
e-mail: enquiries@halfwaybridge.co.uk
web: www.halfwaybridge.co.uk
dir: *Between Petworth & Midhurst, next to Cowdray Estate & Golf Club on A272*

The A272, on which this red-brick, 17th-century coaching inn stands, halfway between Petworth and Midhurst, is a delightful road, but it can be slow. So instead of fuming behind that tractor with its laden trailer, pull in to The Halfway's large car park, beyond which you will discover a delightful mix of traditional pub and contemporary dining inn, where beams, log fires and polished wood floors characterise the tastefully furnished rooms, with Paul and Sue Carter's modern touches adding a more contemporary note. In the bar, order a pint of Moondance from Alton's Triple fff brewery, pull up one of the comfortable oak chairs and study one of the regularly changing menus and daily specials featuring traditional and modern British dishes, all largely made with ingredients from trusted local suppliers. Start with naturally smoked haddock rarebit, sweet and sour plum tomato and watercress salad; or potted duck leg with roasted hazelnut bread, and carrot and orange remoulade. Options to follow could include fillet of sea trout with slow-cooked lentils, cauliflower purée, glazed chicory and

crispy leeks; chargrilled venison haunch with celeriac and wholegrain mustard gratin, red cabbage and parsnip crisps; and pumpkin, squash and coconut curry with spiced basmati rice and cucumber raita. Blackberry Bakewell tart with apple and nutmeg crunch fool; and rhubarb and ginger syllabub with roasted pecan biscotti are among the desserts. There's a peaceful patio and garden. The land on which the pub stands is part of the Cowdray Estate, which is centred around Easebourne, near Midhurst. That's where you'll find Cowdray Park, famous as the home of British polo.

Open all wk 11-11 (Sun 12-10.30) Closed: 25 Dec **Bar Meals** L served all wk 12-2.30 D served all wk 6.30-9.15

Av main course £8.95 **Restaurant** L served all wk 12-2.30 D served all wk 6.30-9.15 ⊕ FREE HOUSE ◧ Sharp's Doom Bar, Otter Amber, Triple fff Moondance ♺ Westons Stowford Press. ⬤ 12 **Facilities** Children welcome Children's menu Children's portions Garden Parking Wi-fi

MAPLEHURST
Map 6 TQ12

The White Horse

Park Ln RH13 6LL ☎ 01403 891208
dir: 5m SE of Horsham, between A281 & A272

This award-winning rural free house has been under the same ownership for 30 years and lies deep in the Sussex countryside. It offers a welcome haven free from music and fruit machines. Hearty home-cooked pub food and an enticing selection of five real ales are served over what is reputed to be the widest bar counter in Sussex. Sip a pint of Harvey's Sussex Best Bitter or King's Red River whilst admiring the rolling countryside from the large, quiet, south-facing garden. Village-brewed cider is a speciality.

Open all wk 12-2.30 6-11 (Sun 12-3 7-11) **Bar Meals** L served all wk 12-2 D served Mon-Sat 6-9, Sun 7-9 ⊕ FREE HOUSE ◀ Harvey's Sussex Best Bitter, Weltons Pridenjoy, Dark Star Espresso, King's Red River Ŏ JB, Local cider. ♀ 11 **Facilities** Children welcome Children's menu Children's portions Play area Family room Garden Parking ▭ **Notes** ⊛

MIDHURST
Map 6 SU82

The Angel Hotel

North St GU29 9DN ☎ 01730 812421
e-mail: info@theangelmidhurst.co.uk
dir: Telephone for directions

The true Tudor origins of this historic former coaching inn are hidden behind an imposing and well-proportioned late-Georgian façade. Its frontage overlooks the town's main street, while at the rear attractive gardens give way to meadowland and the ruins of Cowdray Castle. A reliable pint of Fuller's could be followed by dinner in the new Bentley's Grill, where a range of the finest Argentinean steaks can be cut to suit appetites large and small. Other choices include sautéed Bignor Park pheasant with wild mushroom risotto. A sympathetic refurbishment retained and enhanced original features.

Open all day all wk ⊕ FREE HOUSE ◀ George Gale & Co HSB, Fuller's London Pride, Guinness Ŏ Aspall. **Facilities** Children welcome Children's menu Children's portions Garden Parking Wi-fi

NUTHURST
Map 6 TQ12

Black Horse Inn
PICK OF THE PUBS

Nuthurst St RH13 6LH ☎ 01403 891272
e-mail: enquiries@theblackhorseinn.com
dir: 4m S of Horsham, off A281, A24 & A272

The Black Horse's 18th-century features – stone-flagged floors, exposed wattle-and-daub walls, inglenook fire – have been combined with touches of contemporary style to create a truly relaxing dining pub. The lovely old building, half masked by impressive window boxes in summer, was originally part of a row of workers' cottages on the Sedgwick Park estate; it was first recorded as an inn in 1817. Today the award-winning hostelry's real ales and ciders are backed by a concise but complete menu of dishes from the kitchen. Lunch sees a range of open sandwiches competing with classic hot plates and specials. In the evening expect more complex fare such as forest mushroom lasagne, or loin of pork with dauphinoise potatoes. Home-made puddings follow simple but classic lines such as lemon meringue pie. On sunny days you can sit out on the terraces at the front and rear, or take drinks across the stone bridge over a stream into the delightful back garden. Booking for meals may be required.

Open all wk 12-3 6-11 (Sat 12-11 Sun 12-9 BH all day) ⊕ FREE HOUSE/MR SMITHS PUBS ◀ Dark Star Hophead, Harvey's Sussex, WJ King, Hepworth & Co, Guest ales Ŏ Westons Stowford Press. **Facilities** Children welcome Children's menu Children's portions Garden Parking

OVING
Map 6 SU90

The Gribble Inn

PO20 2BP ☎ 01243 786893
dir: From A27 take A259. After 1m left at rdbt, 1st right to Oving, 1st left in village

This charming 16th-century inn is a peaceful spot to quietly sup any of the eight real ales from its on-site micro-brewery plus a choice of five or six seasonal extras; takeaway polypins are also sold. Named after local schoolmistress Rose Gribble, it has large open fireplaces, wood burners, low beams and no background music. Enjoy traditional pub food with a twist: rabbit and Stowford Press cider with mustard mash; West Sussex rump of lamb with rosemary roasted potatoes and red wine jus; or savoury baked four-cheese cheesecake with roasted tomatoes and kale. The inn hosts summer and winter beer festivals, and there is also a skittle alley, enjoyed by parties and works' social functions. Booking for meals may be required.

Open all wk 11-3 5.30-11 (Fri-Sun 11-11) ⊕ HALL & WOODHOUSE ◀ Badger First Gold, Gribble Ale, Reg's Tipple, Pig's Ear, Fuzzy Duck, Plucking Pheasant, Mocha Mole & Sussex Quad Hopper, Flints Full Glory Ŏ Westons Stowford Press. **Facilities** Children welcome Children's menu Children's portions Family room Garden Beer festival Parking

PETWORTH
Map 6 SU92

The Angel Inn ★★★★ INN NEW

Angel St GU28 0BG ☎ 01798 344445 & 342153
e-mail: enquiries@angelinnpetworth.co.uk
web: www.angelinnpetworth.co.uk
dir: From Petworth centre take A283, E towards Fittleworth, Pub on left

Just a stroll away from the town centre, the newly refurbished Angel dates from medieval times and bowed walls, exposed beams, head-cracking doorways, big fireplaces and sloping floors all testify to its antiquity. The jumble of centuries is particularly apparent in the comfortable bedrooms. Cosy up by one of crackling log fires with a pint of local Arundel ale and choose from the extensive menu. Follow crab and ginger risotto with beef Stroganoff, or spit-roasted lamb (cooked over the fire), and finish with rhubarb crumble. The walled patio garden is a delight in sunny days. Booking for meals may be required.

Open all day all wk 10.30am-11pm (Sun 11.30-10.30) **Bar Meals** L served all wk 12-2.30 D served Mon-Sat 6.30-9.30, Sun 6-9 Av main course £11 ⊕ FREE HOUSE ◀ Arundel, Langham, Guest ales Ŏ Aspall, Addlestones. ♀ 25 **Facilities** ✿ Children welcome Children's menu Children's portions Garden Parking Wi-fi **Rooms** 6

See advert on opposite page

Save on hotels. Book at **theAA.com/hotel**

SUSSEX, WEST 525 ENGLAND

The Grove Inn

PICK OF THE PUBS

Grove Ln GU28 0HY ☎ 01798 343659
e-mail: steveandvaleria@tiscali.co.uk
dir: *Outskirts of village, just off A283*

A 17th-century free house a stone's throw south of historic Petworth. It nestles in beautiful gardens with 360-degree views of the South Downs; a patio area with a shady pergola is ideal for alfresco drinks. The pub's idyllic situation and generous outdoor spaces make it an ideal venue for the beer festival held here every summer. Inside is a bar with oak-beamed ceilings and large fireplace, while the conservatory restaurant is the place to sample a seasonal menu. The pub is hosted by a husband and wife partnership: Valeria looks after front of house, warmly welcoming locals and visitors alike, while husband Stephen runs the kitchen operation. His simple objective is to serve quality dishes at prices that do not detract from their enjoyment. Typical starters include spicy devilled kidneys; main courses embrace confit duck legs with black cherry and honey sauce; and what better for dessert than apple crumble with vanilla ice cream?

Open Tue-Sat 12-3 6-11 (Sun 12-3) Closed: Sun eve & Mon (ex BH) **Bar Meals** L served Tue-Sun 12-2.30 D served Tue-Sat 6-9.15 Av main course £12.50 **Restaurant** L served Tue-Sun 12-2.30 D served Tue-Sat 6-9.15 Fixed menu price fr £19.95 Av 3 course à la carte fr £24 ⊕ FREE HOUSE ◀ Skinner's Betty Stogs, Sharp's Doom Bar, Langham Halfway to Heaven, Young's. **Facilities** Children welcome Children's portions Garden Beer festival Parking Wi-fi 🚐 (notice required)

POYNINGS   Map 6 TQ21

Royal Oak

PICK OF THE PUBS

See Pick of the Pubs on page 526

ROWHOOK   Map 6 TQ13

The Chequers Inn ◉

PICK OF THE PUBS

RH12 3PY ☎ 01403 790480
e-mail: thechequersrowhook@googlemail.com
dir: *Off A29 NW of Horsham*

Expect to find a classic interior of flagstone floor, low beams, blazing fire in the inglenook and all the trimmings at this striking, 400-year-old higgledy-piggledy country pub. Operated by accomplished chef Tim Neal, member of the prestigious Master Chefs of Great Britain and holder of an AA Rosette, it offers Harvey's Sussex on tap and a very impressive wine list to partner an extensive bar menu (sausages with mash and onion gravy; Sussex cheese ploughman's), which may also be eaten in the inn's restaurant. Tim delights in using only the best local produce, taking this to the extreme by going native and sourcing seasonal wild mushrooms and even truffles from the generous woodlands near the hamlet of Rowhook. From the restaurant menu (also served in the bar), order scallops on curried cauliflower purée and coriander oil, then follow with lamb chump with dauphinoise and thyme jus, leaving room for rich chocolate tart with raspberry sorbet, or a plate of British cheeses. Booking for meals may be required.

Open 11.30-3.30 6-11.30 (Sun 12-3.30) Closed: 25 Dec, Sun & BH eve **Bar Meals** L served all wk 12-2 D served Mon-Fri 7-9 Av main course £5.50-£16.75 **Restaurant** L served all wk 12-2 D served Mon-Sat 7-9 Av 3 course à la carte fr £27.50 ⊕ FREE HOUSE ◀ Harvey's Sussex, Guest ale ♂ Thatchers Gold. ♟ 30 **Facilities** Children's portions Garden Parking

---

SHIPLEY   Map 6 TQ12

The Countryman Inn

PICK OF THE PUBS

See Pick of the Pubs on page 527

George & Dragon

Dragons Green RH13 8GE ☎ 01403 741320
e-mail: marlenegrace@googlemail.com
dir: *Signed from A272 between Coolham & A24*

Set amid beautiful Sussex countryside, this 17th-century cottage is a haven of peace and quiet, especially on balmy summer evenings when the garden is a welcome retreat. Its interior is all head-banging beams and inglenook fireplaces, with an excellent choice of real ales at the bar. Food-wise, expect pub classics such as sausage, mash and onion gravy; seared salmon fillet with new potatoes; and pesto chicken and bacon salad. Shipley is famous for its smock mill. A change of hands was underway as we went to press. Booking for meals may be required.

Open all wk 12-3 6-11 (Sat-Sun all day) ⊕ FREE HOUSE ◀ Badger Dorset Best, Fursty Ferret & Pickled Partridge, Harvey's Sussex Best Bitter, Guest ale ♂ Westons Stowford Press. **Facilities** Children welcome Children's portions Play area Family room Garden Parking Wi-fi

---

~ *The Angel Inn* ~

Angel Street, Petworth GU28 0BG • Tel: 01798 344445
Website: www.angelinnpetworth.co.uk • Email: enquiries@angelinnpetworth.co.uk

The Angel Inn is a pub with good food and comfortable rooms. The inn, which has mediaeval origins, was re-opened in June 2011 after an extensive refurbishment programme. We pride ourselves on being a pub first and foremost, with three real ales on tap (currently Arundel, Langham and a Guest) and a cooled stillage for serving three guest beers straight off the barrel. Malt whiskies and over sixty wines also feature. The pub has a central oval bar and three working fires, one of which is used to spit roast joints of meat. Food is predominantly English influenced and sourced locally where possible, Classic dishes feature strongly and are reasonably priced. Outside the sheltered garden enjoys sandstone paving, stone and brick walls and is a delightful place to relax with a drink or a meal. The bedrooms and the ensuites are of a high standard and have also been refurbished.

PICK OF THE PUBS

Royal Oak

POYNINGS Map 6 TQ21

The Street BN45 7AQ ☎ 01273 857389
e-mail: ropoynings@aol.com
web: www.royaloakpoynings.biz
dir: *From A23 onto A281 signed Henfield & Poynings*

Licensed since the 1880s, this award-winning pub has been steered by Paul Day and Lewis Robinson since 1996. Occupying a lovely spot in a pretty village below the South Downs and surrounded by glorious downland walks, the pub has plenty to offer all year round. In summer, the wonderful garden boasts excellent barbecue facilities, serene rural views, and all-day food. The rest of the year, the eye-catching window blinds and cream-painted exterior draw customers into a building with solid oak floors, where old beams hung with hop bines blend effortlessly with contemporary décor and sumptuous sofas. In the bar, Sussex-brewed Harvey's Sussex Best Bitter sits alongside Westons cider and perry, and an accessible wine list includes New and Old World wines with up to 14 available by the glass. The menu changes seasonally and is driven by local produce. The broad range of meals suits most appetites. A charcuterie sharing platter comes laden with a selection of cured meats, salamis, shaved parmesan, olives and warm ciabatta; or you can opt for a smoked salmon, cucumber and mascarpone ciabatta sandwich platter. Moving up the scale, good old fashioned pub favourites like free-range boiled gammon with bubble-and-squeak and fried egg; or home-made beefburger with Sussex cheddar, smoked bacon, fries and roasted red pepper chutney rub shoulders with more ambitious dishes. For starters, try the creamed leek and smoked cheddar tart; or Selsey crab rarebit with soft poached egg. Main course options might include free-range Sussex chicken and oyster mushroom pie; or oak-smoked haddock with creamed potatoes, wilted spinach, poached egg and parmesan cream. Some puddings (including cherry and almond frangipane tart) are served with hand-made ice cream from local dairy herd. Summer barbecue menus and

winter themed menus prove popular. Booking for meals may be required.

Open all day all wk 11-11 (Sun 12-10.30) **Bar Meals** L served all wk 12-9.30 D served all wk 12-9.30 **Restaurant** L served all wk 12-9.30 D served all wk 12-9.30 ⊕ FREE HOUSE ◀ Harvey's Sussex Best Bitter ♻ Westons & Herefordshire Country Perry. ♇ 14 **Facilities** Children welcome Children's menu Children's portions Play area Garden Parking Wi-fi 🚌 (notice required)

Save on hotels. Book at theAA.com/hotel

SUSSEX, WEST 527 ENGLAND

PICK OF THE PUBS

The Countryman Inn

SHIPLEY　　　Map 6 TQ12

Countryman Ln RH13 8PZ
☎ **01403 741383**
e-mail: countrymaninn@btinternet.com
web: www.countrymanshipley.co.uk
dir: *A272 at Coolham into Smithers Hill Ln. 1m, left at T-junct*

Alan Vaughan and his family have run this traditional rural free house since 1986. Surrounding it are 3,500 acres of farmland owned by the Knepp Castle Estate, now gradually returning to a more natural state since the introduction of fallow deer, free-roaming Tamworth pigs, Exmoor ponies and Longhorn cattle. Wild birds have also been encouraged to return, attracted by newly planted wild grasses. In the open log fire-warmed bar, you'll find cask-conditioned Harvey's, Fuller's London Pride and Dark Star ales, and more than 30 wines from around the world. Local game, free-range meats from local farms and vegetables from the pub's own garden make their appearance on the menu, alongside fish from the two nearest Sussex ports of Shoreham and Newhaven. Pub-grub lovers will find what they're looking for in bangers 'n' mash; ham, egg and chips; and scampi and chips, for example, as well as sandwiches and baguettes, salads and platters. Typical starters on the main menu include potted ham hock with rustic bread and piccalilli, and breaded brie with redcurrant dip; and to follow, mains of bacon and onion roly-poly with smoked bacon, roasted vegetables, mash and parsley sauce; plaice and Serrano ham paupiettes with parmesan and chilli fettuccine, tomato and onion salad; and red pepper and chickpea dhansak with jasmine rice, naan bread and chutney. Please note that very young children are not permitted in the restaurant, but if the weather's good enough they are welcome to eat in the garden. Here, a new feature is the open-air kitchen serving ploughman's lunches with home-baked bread and other snacks, grills and shellfish. In the pub's own farm shop you can buy a wide range of food, including free-range eggs, home-made preserves, pickles and relishes.

Open all wk 10-4 6-11 **Bar Meals** L served all wk 11.30-3.30 D served all wk 6-10 Av main course £11 **Restaurant** L served all wk 11.30-3.30 D served all wk 6-10 Av 3 course à la carte fr £21 ⊕ FREE HOUSE ◼ Fuller's London Pride, Harvey's, Dark Star ⚬ Thatchers Gold. ♟ 18 **Facilities** Garden Parking Wi-fi

SINGLETON
Map 5 SU81

The Partridge Inn

PO18 0EY ☎ 01243 811251
e-mail: info@thepartridgeinn.co.uk
dir: Telephone for directions

Set within the picturesque Goodwood Estate in the South Downs village of Singleton, this pub dates back to the 16th century when it was part of a huge hunting park owned by the Fitzalan Earls of Arundel. Today, it is popular with walkers enjoying the rolling Sussex countryside and visitors to Goodwood for motor and horse-racing. Now run by Giles Thompson, former executive head chef of The Ritz London, you can expect a friendly welcome and great food, from tempting sandwiches, salads and light bites to main courses of corn-fed breast of chicken with pancetta, mash and rosemary jus; and pan-fried sea bream fillet with wilted spinach, creamed leeks and mash. Booking for meals may be required.

Open all wk (Sat-Sun all day) **Bar Meals** L served Mon-Fri 12-2, Sat-Sun 12-3 D served Mon-Thu 6-9, Fri-Sat 6-9.30 Av main course £15 **Restaurant** L served Mon-Fri 12-2, Sat-Sun 12-3 D served Mon-Thu 6-9, Fri-Sat 6-9.30 Av 3 course à la carte fr £25 ⊕ ENTERPRISE INNS ◀ Fuller's London Pride, Harvey's Sussex, Hop Back Summer Lightning Ò Westons Stowford Press. ♀ 15 **Facilities** ♣ Children welcome Children's menu Children's portions Garden Parking Wi-fi

SLINDON
Map 6 SU90

The Spur

BN18 0NE ☎ 01243 814216
e-mail: thespurslindon@btinternet.com
dir: Off A27 on A29 outside Slindon

Set just outside the village of Slindon on top of the rolling South Downs, this 17th-century pub is a an ideal stopping-off point on a day out in the country. It has been praised for its friendly atmosphere and for generous portions of food. Outside are large pub gardens and a courtyard, inside is an open-plan bar and restaurant, warmed by crackling log fires. Daily-changing bar meals are on the blackboard, and may include lamb cutlets, steak-and-kidney pie, and fresh fish and shellfish. The restaurant menu changes every few months, and a typical selection of dishes from this includes seafood risotto, half shoulder of Southdown lamb, and goat's cheese and roasted pepper savoury cheesecake. A skittle alley and function room are also available. Booking for meals may be required.

Open all wk 11.30-3 6-11 (Sun 12-3 7-10.30) **Bar Meals** L served all wk 12-2 D served Sun-Tue 7-9, Wed-Sat 7-9.30 **Restaurant** L served all wk 12-2 D served Sun-Tue 7-9, Wed-Sat 7-9.30 ⊕ FREE HOUSE ◀ Sharp's Doom Bar, Courage Directors Ò Thatchers Gold. ♀ 10 **Facilities** Children welcome Children's menu Children's portions Garden Parking

STEDHAM
Map 5 SU82

Hamilton Arms/Nava Thai Restaurant

Hamilton Arms School Ln GU29 0NZ ☎ 01730 812555
e-mail: hamiltonarms@hotmail.com
web: www.thehamiltonarms.co.uk
dir: Off A272 between Midhurst & Petersfield

In this whitewashed free house opposite the village common, smiling Thai staff serve authentic Thai food and beers. Or, if you prefer, you can have English bar snacks and beers, including the Hamilton's own draught Armless. The extensive menu lists Thai soups, salads and curries, and beef, pork, chicken, duck, fish and seafood dishes. For £10 on Sundays, eat as much as you want from the Thai or English-roast buffets. Takeaways are available too. The pub is home to the Mudita Trust, which helps abused and underprivileged children in Thailand. Booking for meals may be required.

Open all day Closed: Mon (ex BH) **Bar Meals** L served Tue-Sun 12-2.30 D served Tue-Sun 6-10 Av main course £9.50 **Restaurant** L served Tue-Sun 12-2.30 D served Tue-Sun 6-10 Fixed menu price fr £24.50 Av 3 course à la carte fr £25 ⊕ FREE HOUSE ◀ Fuller's London Pride, Triple fff Alton's Pride, Hamilton Armless Ò Westons Vintage & Stowford Press. ♀ 8 **Facilities** ♣ Children welcome Children's menu Children's portions Play area Garden Parking Wi-fi

SUTTON
Map 6 SU91

The White Horse Inn

PICK OF THE PUBS

The Street RH20 1PS ☎ 01798 869221
e-mail: mail@whitehorse-sutton.co.uk
dir: From Petworth follow signs for Roman villa then to Sutton village

In a sleepy village tucked beneath the South Downs amid a maze of the narrow lanes, this 250-year-old pub has been transformed into a stylish modern country inn. Being so handy for polo at Cowdray Park and racing at Goodwood, it makes a great watering hole at the end of a hard day's entertainment. Handpumps in the smart wooden-floored bar dispense the likes of local Harvey's and Adnams ales, while menus make good use of seasonal produce from local suppliers to create some imaginative and good-value dishes. Perhaps start with mussels grilled with garlic and herb butter, then follow

with confit duck with dauphinoise, green beans and red wine jus, and round off with sticky toffee pudding with butterscotch sauce and vanilla ice cream. Lighter options include Sussex cheddar and pickle sandwiches; ham, egg and chips; and smoked chicken, avocado, chorizo and tomato salad. Super terrace and garden for summer alfresco meals. Booking for meals may be required.

Open all wk 11-3 6-11 **Bar Meals** L served all wk 11.30-2.30 D served all wk 6.30-9.30 **Restaurant** L served all wk 11.30-2.30 D served all wk 6.30-9.30 ⊕ ENTERPRISE INNS ◀ Sharp's Doom Bar, Fuller's London Pride, Harvey's, Adnams Ò Westons Stowford Press. **Facilities** Children welcome Children's portions Garden Parking Wi-fi

TILLINGTON
Map 6 SU92

The Horseguards Inn ★★★★ INN ⊛

PICK OF THE PUBS

GU28 9AF ☎ 01798 342332
e-mail: info@thehorseguardsinn.co.uk
dir: From Petworth towards Midhurst on A272. In 1m turn right signed Tillington. Inn 300mtrs up hill opposite church

Standing somewhat higher than the lane passing by, this charming 300-year-old inn took its name in the 1840s when the Household Cavalry would refresh themselves here while their horses grazed in Petworth Park nearby. Opposite is the parish church, with an unusual Scots Crown tower. Inside the pub is a series of tastefully refurbished rooms with sagging beams, original pine panelling, open fires (you can roast chestnuts on one), antique and pine furnishings, fresh flowers and candles. The small daily-changing menu reflects what has been sourced from local suppliers, dug from the pub's vegetable patch, and foraged from Sussex hedgerows and seashores. Chalkboards declare where the day's meats have come from. Order warm salad of smoked sprats with sausage, beetroot, chicory and horseradish cream; organic rose veal fillet with wild mushrooms; or South Coast mackerel with sautéed potatoes. Three bright bedrooms provide the answer for an overnight stay. Booking for meals may be required.

Open all day all wk **Bar Meals** L served Mon-Fri 12-2.30, Sat 12-3, Sun 12-3.30 D served all wk 6.30-9 **Restaurant** L served Mon-Fri 12-2.30, Sat 12-3, Sun 12-3.30 D served all wk 6.30-9 ⊕ ENTERPRISE INNS ◀ Harvey's Sussex Best Bitter, Skinner's Betty Stogs, Staropramen, Guinness Ò Westons Stowford Press. ♀ 16 **Facilities** ♣ Children welcome Children's menu Children's portions Garden Wi-fi (notice required) Rooms 3

PICK OF THE PUBS

The Cat Inn

WEST HOATHLY Map 6 TQ33

North Ln RH19 4PP ☎ 01342 810369
e-mail: thecatinn@googlemail.com
web: www.catinn.co.uk
dir: *From East Grinstead centre take
A22 towards Forest Row. Into left lane,
into B2110 (Beeching Way) signed
Turners Hill. Left into Vowels Ln signed
Kingscote & West Hoathly. Left into
Selsfield Rd, forward into Chapel Row,
right into North Ln*

The 16th-century Cat Inn commands a
prime spot opposite the church in
picturesque West Hoathly, a hilltop village
on the edge of the Ashdown Forest.
Landlord Andrew Russell swapped grand
Gravetye Manor for this thriving free house
in 2009, then placed local chef Max
Leonard in the kitchen and hasn't looked
back since. Step inside the characterful
old bar to find an enormous fireplace, oak
beams, fine wooden panelling and floors,
and a buzzy atmosphere. Beyond are the
light and airy garden room, and the
suntrap terrace for summer alfresco
dining at smart teak tables. Max draws on
fresh, seasonal produce, including local
South Downs lamb, Rye Bay fish and
seafood, estate game and locally foraged
ingredients. This translates to starters of
game terrine with Indian military chutney;
crispy cod fishcake with minted pea purée;
and soft black pudding and roast pork
belly served on crushed celeriac and
caramelised apple. For mains, choose sea
bass with brown shrimp and caper butter;
the traditional Harvey's beer-battered fish
and chips; or steak, mushroom and ale pie
with mash and vegetables; or go for the
steaming bowl of mussels in a pancetta
and leek cream, and served with warm
dipping bread and chips. Pace yourself as
you will need room for Max's Valrhona
chocolate salted caramel tart with
Chantilly cream, or his quince, apple and
raspberry crumble. Wash down with a
cracking pint of local Dark Star ale or
delve into the excellent list of wines; ten
offered by the glass. There are super local
walks and make time to visit the
fascinating Priests House in the village.
Booking for meals may be required.

Open all day 12-11.30 Closed: Sun eve
Bar Meals L served Mon-Thu 12-2, Fri-

Sun 12-2.30 D served Mon-Thu 6-9,
Fri-Sat 6-9.30 Av main course £13
Restaurant L served Mon-Thu 12-2,
Fri-Sun 12-2.30 D served Mon-Thu 6-9,
Fri-Sat 6-9.30 Av 3 course à la carte fr
£25 ⊕ FREE HOUSE ◖ Harvey's Sussex
Best Bitter, Moorhouse's Black Cat,
Larkins, Dark Star ♻ Westons Stowford
Press. ♟ 10 **Facilities** Children welcome
Children's portions ❖ Garden Parking
Wi-fi

TROTTON — Map 5 SU82

The Keepers Arms ◉

PICK OF THE PUBS

GU31 5ER ☎ **01730 813724**
e-mail: ss@keepersarms.co.uk
dir: *5m from Petersfield on A272, pub on right just after narrow bridge*

Low ceilings, wooden floorboards and an open log fire greet you as you enter this charming 17th-century free house perched above the A272, one of England's most delightful cross-country roads. The arrival in April 2011 of new owner Salvinia McGrath is not expected to change the line-up of Dark Star, Ringwood, Ballards and Otter real ales in the convivial bar, or the wide range of wines and spirits. Oak dining tables and comfortable upholstered chairs furnish the restaurant, whose look was inspired by a Scottish hunting lodge, thus the rich tartan fabrics. Real effort is made to source locally for menus and blackboards likely to offer sun-blushed tomato risotto with goat's cheese and pesto; pan-fried fillet of turbot with Thai crab tartlet; and roasted belly and braised shoulder of pork, celeriac dauphinoise and carrot and coriander purée. There are views of the South Downs from both the restaurant and terrace.

Open all wk 12-3.30 6-11 **Bar Meals** L served all wk 12-2 D served all wk 7-9.30 **Restaurant** L served all wk 12-2 D served all wk 7-9.30 ⊕ FREE HOUSE ◀ Dark Star Hophead, Ringwood Best Bitter & Fortyniner, Ballards Best Bitter, Otter Ale Ö Thatchers Gold. ♥ 8 **Facilities** ✿ Children welcome Children's portions Garden Parking

WALDERTON — Map 5 SU71

The Barley Mow

PO18 9ED ☎ **023 9263 1321**
e-mail: info@thebarleymowpub.co.uk
dir: *B2146 from Chichester towards Petersfield. Turn right signed Walderton, pub 100yds on left*

Popular with walkers, cyclists and horse-riders out exploring the Kingley Vale nature reserve, this ivy-clad 18th-century pub was used by the local Home Guard as its HQ in World War II; it's famous locally for its skittle alley. The secluded, stream-bordered garden is a real suntrap, perfect for a pint of Doom Bar; in winter months the log fires crackle. The menu covers the usual favourites such as lightly fried breaded whitebait; chef's mixed grill; sausage and mash; and curry of the day. Look out for jazz suppers every third Tuesday of the month (booking advised).

Open all wk 11-3 6-11 (Sun 12-10.30) **Bar Meals** L served Mon-Sat 12-2.30, Sun all day D served all wk 6-9.30 Av main course £9.95 **Restaurant** L served all wk 12-2.30 D served all wk 6-9.30 ⊕ FREE HOUSE · ◀ Ringwood Old Thumper & Fortyniner, Fuller's London Pride, Harvey's Sussex Best Bitter, Sharp's Doom Bar, Adnams, Otter Ö Westons Stowford Press, Thatchers. ♥ 10 **Facilities** ✿ Children welcome Children's menu Children's portions Garden Parking ▭

WARNINGLID — Map 6 TQ22

The Half Moon

The Street RH17 5TR ☎ **01444 461227**
e-mail: info@thehalfmoonwarninglid.co.uk
dir: *1m from Warninglid/Cuckfield junct of A23 & 6m from Haywards Heath*

This picture-perfect Grade II listed building dates from the 18th century and has been sympathetically extended to preserve its traditional feel. Look out for the glass-topped well as you come in. Enjoy a pint of Harvey's or a real cider while perusing the menu, which offers specials and pub classics. Try oriental crispy pork balls with satay sauce and star anise drizzle; gnocchi in a wild mushroom and tarragon mustard cream; butternut squash falafel burger served with hand-cut chips; and chicken rogan josh served with onion bhaji, basmati rice, mango chutney and a poppadom. The pub garden is home to a 250-year-old cider press. Booking for meals may be required.

Open all wk 11.30-2.30 5.30-11 (Sat 11.30-11 Sun 11.30-10.30) **Bar Meals** L served Mon-Sat 12-2, Sun 12-3 D served Mon-Sat 6-9.30 Av main course £13 **Restaurant** L served Mon-Sat 12-2, Sun 12-3 D served Mon-Sat 6-9.30 ⊕ FREE HOUSE ◀ Harvey's Sussex & Old Ale, Dark Star Ö Symonds, Westons. ♥ 12 **Facilities** ✿ Children welcome Children's menu Children's portions Family room Garden Parking Wi-fi ▭ (notice required)

WEST CHILTINGTON — Map 6 TQ01

The Queens Head

The Hollow RH20 2JN ☎ **01798 812244**
e-mail: enquiries@thequeensheadsussex.co.uk
dir: *Telephone for directions*

The new, three-generation family running this mostly 17th-century, textbook country pub serves a good selection of local and more distantly brewed real ales in their beamed, low-ceilinged, open-fired bars. It's named after Anne of Cleves, to whom Henry VIII gave nearby Nyetimber (now a vineyard) on divorcing her. Locally sourced seasonal meals include pork belly with black pudding; supreme of chicken; sea bass; Cumberland sausages and mash; and confit garlic soufflé with ratatouille. Stone-baked and deep-pan pizzas are available at lunchtime and in the evening. Sandwiches at lunchtime too.

Open all day all wk 12-11 (Mon 6-11 ex BH 12-11 Sun 12-10.30) **Bar Meals** L served Tue-Sat 12-2.30, Sun & BH 12-4 D served Mon-Sat 6-9.30 **Restaurant** L served Tue-Sat 12-2.30, Sun & BH 12-4 D served Mon-Sat 6-9.30 ⊕ ENTERPRISE INNS ◀ Harvey's Sussex Best Bitter, Fuller's London Pride, Ballards Best Bitter, Sharp's Doom Bar, Arundel Sussex Gold. **Facilities** ✿ Children welcome Children's menu Children's portions Garden Parking Wi-fi ▭ (notice required)

WEST HOATHLY — Map 6 TQ33

The Cat Inn

PICK OF THE PUBS

See Pick of the Pubs on page 529

WINEHAM — Map 6 TQ22

The Royal Oak

BN5 9AY ☎ **01444 881252**
e-mail: theroyaloakwineham@sky.com
dir: *Wineham between A272 (Cowfold to Bolney) & B2116 (Hurst to Henfield)*

Tucked away on a quiet country lane between the A272 and B2116 near Henfield, this part-tiled, black-and-white timbered cottage is a classic alehouse, a true rural survivor that has been serving the locals for 300 years. Dating from the 14th century, it has head-cracking low beams, a huge inglenook with warming winter fire, brick and stone-flagged floors, rustic furnishings and time-honoured pub games. Harvey's and Dark Star ales are drawn straight from the drum and home-cooked pub food ranges from ploughman's boards to hearty Sussex beef, stout and mushroom pie with new potatoes and baby carrots. Extensive gardens for summer alfresco drinking. Booking for meals may be required.

Open all wk 11-3 5.30-close (Sat 11-3 6-close Sun 11-3 7-close) **Bar Meals** L served all wk 12-2.30 D served all wk 7-9.30 Av main course £10-£14 **Restaurant** L served all wk 12-2.30 D served all wk 7-9.30 Av 3 course à la carte fr £20 ⊕ FREE HOUSE ◀ Harvey's Sussex Best Bitter, Dark Star Hophead Ö Thatchers Gold, Westons Old Rosie. ♥ 20 **Facilities** ✿ Children welcome Children's portions Garden Beer festival Parking Wi-fi ▭

WISBOROUGH GREEN — Map 6 TQ02

Cricketers Arms

Loxwood Rd RH14 0DG ☎ **01403 700369**
e-mail: craig@cricketersarms.com
dir: *On A272 between Billingshurst & Petworth. In centre of Wisborough Green turn at junct next to village green, pub 100yds on right*

A traditional village pub dating from the 16th century with oak beams, wooden floors and open fires. Fans of extreme sports should be aware that the Cricketers is the home of the British Lawn Mower Racing Association. Alongside real ales there are many wines by the glass in the bar, with a menu ranging from snacks to three course meals and Sunday roasts, with plenty of specials. Typical dishes include steak pie, sea bass in a prawn and oyster sauce, game dishes in season, and 'mega' salads. There are live music and quiz nights, as well as an annual hog roast.

Open all day all wk ⊕ ENTERPRISE INNS ◀ Harvey's Sussex, Fuller's London Pride, Bowman Swift One. **Facilities** ✿ Children welcome Children's menu Children's portions Garden Parking Wi-fi

Save on hotels. Book at **theAA.com/hotel**

TYNE & WEAR – WARWICKSHIRE 531 | ENGLAND

TYNE & WEAR

NEWCASTLE UPON TYNE | Map 21 NZ26

Shiremoor House Farm

Middle Engine Ln, New York NE29 8DZ
☎ **0191 257 6302**
dir: *Telephone for directions*

Brilliantly converted from old farm buildings and in the same hands for 24 years, this popular north Tyneside pub in the village of New York is a perfect place for a swift pint of Jarrow Rivet Catcher or Mordue Workie Ticket. Particularly appealing is the glazed former granary where a wide range of traditional, home-cooked pub food is served. Choices from the daily-changing blackboard menu could include steak, ale and mushroom casserole, or fillet of salmon with prawn and dill sauce. Look out for kebab nights on Tuesdays and fish nights on Wednesdays.

Open all day all wk **Closed:** 25 Dec eve **Bar Meals** L served all wk 11-10 D served all wk 11-10 Av main course £9.95 food served all day ⊕ FREE HOUSE ◀ Timothy Taylor Landlord, Mordue Workie Ticket, Theakston Best Bitter, John Smith's, Jarrow Rivet Catcher Ō Batemans Rosie Nosey. ♟ 12 **Facilities** Children welcome Children's menu Children's portions Family room Garden Parking 🚌

TYNEMOUTH | Map 21 NZ36

Copperfields ★★★ HL

Grand Hotel, Grand Pde NE30 4ER ☎ **0191 293 6666**
e-mail: info30@grandhotel-uk.com
dir: *On NE coast, 10m from Newcastle upon Tyne*

Copperfields bar is at the rear of the imposing Grand Hotel away from the hustle and bustle, where Stan Laurel and Oliver Hardy always stayed when they played Newcastle's Theatre Royal. Worth a visit for the great views up and down the coast, as well as an extensive bar menu that includes butternut squash and sage risotto, chicken tagine, lamb stew, beer-battered haddock and ciabatta steak sandwich. A blackboard lists daily specials.

Open all day all wk ⊕ FREE HOUSE ◀ Caledonian Deuchars IPA, Black Sheep. **Facilities** Children welcome Children's menu Garden Parking Wi-fi **Rooms** 45

WARWICKSHIRE

ALCESTER | Map 10 SP05

The Holly Bush

PICK OF THE PUBS

37 Henley St B49 5QX ☎ **01789 762482**
e-mail: thehollybushpub@btconnect.com
dir: *M40 junct 15 for Warwick/Stratford, take A46 to Stratford. From Stratford take A46 to Redditch, follow Alcester signs*

The 17th-century Holly Bush has been transformed from a one-bar boozer into a cracking town-centre pub run with passion and panache – and there's an award-winning garden too. Two bars serve eight regional brews and a local cider, supped cheerfully in five characterful rooms along with plates of contemporary and traditional food from the kitchen: asparagus, Parma ham and parmesan tartlet; and crispy confit of duck with crushed new potatoes give a flavour of the treats in store. Specials continue the focus on flavoursome ingredients in such dishes as smoked haddock and Applewood cheese fishcake with rocket and Chardonnay cream sauce; and pan-fried red snapper with coriander rice. Accompanying wines from a well-priced selection are easily chosen thanks to the succinct guidance on the list. Come here to enjoy not just the food and drink but also the exceptional friendly service. Watch out for regular live music nights, as well as beer festivals in June and October.

Open all day all wk 12-12 (Fri-Sat noon-1am) ⊕ FREE HOUSE ◀ Sharp's Doom Bar, Purity Gold & Mad Goose, Uley Bitter, Black Sheep Ō Hogan's, Local cider. **Facilities** Children welcome Children's menu Children's portions Garden Beer festival Parking

ALDERMINSTER | Map 10 SP24

The Bell

PICK OF THE PUBS

See Pick of the Pubs on page 532

ALVESTON | Map 10 SP25

The Baraset Barn

PICK OF THE PUBS

1 Pimlico Ln CV37 7RJ ☎ **01789 295510**
e-mail: barasetbarn@lovelypubs.co.uk
dir: *Telephone for directions*

Barn is what it's called, because barn is what it was. Not any more, though. True, the original flagstones reflect its 200-year existence, but it is now a light and modern gastro-pub with a dramatic interior styled in granite, pewter and oak. Stone steps lead from the bar to the main dining area with brick walls and high oak beams, while the open mezzanine level offers a good view of the glass-fronted kitchen. The luxurious lounge is furnished with comfortable sofas for whiling away the morning with a coffee and the papers. The menu successfully blends classic British with Mediterranean ideas, such as sharing plates of tapas; starters of vodka- and beetroot-cured salmon, capers, sieved egg and horseradish crème fraîche; and spiced pumpkin and cauliflower fritters. Follow with Purity real ale-battered fish, chips, minted pea purée and sauce gribiche; or calves' liver and onions. The continental-style patio garden is made for outdoor dining. Booking for meals may be required.

Open all day 12-12 **Closed:** 25 Dec & 1 Jan, Sun eve, Mon (Jan-Feb) **Bar Meals** L served all wk 12-2.30 D served Mon-Sat 6.30-9.30 Av main course £14 **Restaurant** L served Mon-Sat 12-2.30, Sun 12-3.30 D served Mon-Sat 6.30-9.30 Fixed menu price fr £13 Av 3 course à la carte fr £30 ⊕ FREE HOUSE ◀ Purity Pure UBU. **Facilities** ❀ Children welcome Children's portions Garden Parking Wi-fi 🚌

ARDENS GRAFTON | Map 10 SP15

The Golden Cross

PICK OF THE PUBS

Wixford Rd B50 4LG ☎ **01789 772420**
e-mail: info@thegoldencross.net
dir: *Telephone for directions*

If you like faggots then this 18th-century country inn is the place to come, because an old recipe that went walkabout has recently been rediscovered, much to the delight of locals. With other traditional favourites they appear on the single menu served throughout, listing starters and light bites such as potted shrimps, and chargrilled chicken Caesar salad, with main courses of grilled sea bass; rump and rib-eye steaks; and spinach pancakes. Blackboards announce the ever-changing specials. If you eat in the pastel-toned dining room take a good look at the attractive plasterwork on the ceiling, or if you prefer to stay in the rug-strewn, flagstone-floored bar, the hefty beams are worth more than a cursory glance. The real ales here come from Wells, Purity Brewing or a guest. The garden is large and safe, and the covered patio is heated. Song and steak night is on Thursday.

Open all wk **Bar Meals** L served all wk 12-2.30 D served all wk 5-9 Av main course £10 **Restaurant** L served all wk 12-2.30 D served all wk 5-9 Av 3 course à la carte fr £20 ⊕ CHARLES WELLS ◀ Bombardier, Purity, Guest ales Ō Thatchers Heritage. **Facilities** Children welcome Children's menu Children's portions Garden Parking Wi-fi 🚌 (notice required)

PICK OF THE PUBS

The Bell

ALDERMINSTER Map 10 SP24

CV37 8NY ☎ 01789 450414
e-mail: info@thebellald.co.uk
web: www.thebellald.co.uk
dir: *On A3400, 3.5m S of Stratford-upon-Avon*

Set in the heart of a picturesque village between Stratford-upon-Avon and Shipston on Stour, this striking Georgian coaching inn has been beautifully upgraded and refurbished by the Alscot Estate. The result is a refreshing mix of contemporary comforts and rustic charm, with the historic core of beamed ceilings, blazing log fires and flagged floors combining well with bold colours and stylish fabrics and the modern dining courtyard. This is located beside a grassy garden and the riverside meadow that ripples down to the River Stour is perfect for enjoying summer picnics. The restaurant oozes charm and is cunningly designed into quirky zones, each with its own distinct atmosphere, and a place for all occasions with a buzzing atmosphere. Time to enjoy a pint of Hook Norton or the inn's locally-brewed Alscot Ale and nibble on a self-selected grazing platter, perhaps laden with hams, olives, mozzarella, pesto, balsamic shallots, vine tomatoes and garlic focaccia, before considering the indulgent daily-changing menu. Typically, begin with Alscot game terrine wrapped in Parma ham and served with

plum chutney, then follow with braised brisket of beef with horseradish mash and red wine jus, or monkfish wrapped in smoked salmon with seafood risotto. Round off with warm dark chocolate and fudge tart with strawberry ice cream, or a plate of local cheeses with home-made chutney. In the bar, sandwiches (rump steak with red onion marmalade and cheddar cheese) are served with hand-cut chips and salad, or you can try a Bell classic, perhaps the beef and thyme burger, or bangers and mash. Much of the produce is local, with vegetables and herbs harvested from Alscot's historic kitchen garden, and game and venison is reared on the estate. Booking for meals may be required.

Open all wk 9.30-3 6-11 (Fri-Sat 9.30am-11pm Sun 9.30-5) **Bar Meals** L served Mon-Fri 12-2, Sat 12-2.30, Sun 12-3 D served Mon-Thu 7-9, Fri-Sat 6-9 **Restaurant** L served Mon-Fri 12-2, Sat 12-2.30, Sun 12-3 D served Mon-Thu 7-9, Fri-Sat 6-9 ⊞ FREE HOUSE ◄ Hook Norton, Alscot Ale Ŏ Hogan's. ♀ 14 **Facilities** Children welcome Children's menu Garden Parking Wi-fi 🚌

ASTON CANTLOW   Map 10 SP16

The King's Head NEW

21 Bearley Rd B95 6HY ☎ 01789 488242
e-mail: info@thekh.co.uk
dir: *Exit A3400 between Stratford-upon-Avon &
Henley-in-Arden. Follow Aston Cantlow signs*

Flanked by a huge spreading chestnut tree and oozing
historic charm, this impressive black-and-white timbered
Tudor building has been sensitively refurbished in modern
style. Tastefully rustic inside, with lime-washed low
beams, huge polished flagstones, painted brick walls, old
scrubbed pine tables and crackling log fires, it draws
diners for innovative pub food. Tuck into the famous duck
supper; a classic beef and Guinness pie; cod with crab
and chilli noodles; or the Greek meze sharing board.
There's a smart rear terrace and a cider bar serving up to
seven traditional ciders.

Open all wk 12-3 6-11 (Sat 12-11 Sun 12-8.30) Closed:
25 Dec **Bar Meals** L served all wk 12-2.30 D served all wk
6.30-9.30 Av main course £14 **Restaurant** L served all wk
12-2.30 D served all wk 6.30-9.30 Fixed menu price fr
£12 Av 3 course à la carte fr £25 ⊕ ENTERPRISE INNS
◀ Purity Gold & Pure UBU, Greene King Abbot Ale, M&B
Brew XI ♨ Hogan's, Westons, Thatchers. ▮ 11
Facilities ♣ Children welcome Children's menu
Children's portions Garden Parking Wi-fi 🚌 (notice
required)

BARFORD   Map 10 SP26

The Granville @ Barford

PICK OF THE PUBS

52 Wellesbourne Rd CV35 8DS ☎ 01926 624236
e-mail: info@granvillebarford.co.uk
dir: *1m from M40 junct 15. Take A429 signed Stow.
Located at furthest end of Barford village*

Situated in the heart of Shakespeare country, this
impressive brick building dates back to Georgian times.
The comfortable dining pub benefits from stylish décor
and warm, friendly service, which has made it a firm
favourite with locals and visitors alike. Relax on the
leather sofas in the lounge with a drink - a pint of Purity
Gold perhaps, or choose from the accessible wine list. The
Granville's ever-changing seasonal menus offer varied,
interesting choices and good value. At lunch, the offering
ranges from doorstep sandwiches and wraps to starters
like linguine in a lightly spiced crab broth with spring
onion, lime and coriander. An evening meal might begin
with salmon and haddock fishcakes, wilted spinach,
lemon and butter sauce, followed by North African spiced
lamb patties, winter fruit saffron couscous, mint and
cucumber yogurt. Enjoy alfresco dining in the spacious
patio garden. There is a calendar of events to entertain
customers.

Open all wk 12-3 5.30-11 (Fri-Sat 12-11.30 Sun 12-11)
⊕ ENTERPRISE INNS ◀ Hook Norton Hooky Bitter, Purity
Gold & Pure UBU. **Facilities** Children welcome Children's
portions Play area Garden Parking Wi-fi

EDGEHILL   Map 11 SP34

The Castle Inn

OX15 6DJ ☎ 01295 670255
e-mail: castleinnedgehill@gmail.com
dir: *M40 junct 11 then A422 towards
Stratford-upon-Avon. 6m to Upton House, next right, 1.5m
to Edgehill*

A man called Sanderson Miller built this curious,
castellated property on top of Edgehill in 1742, right
where Charles I had raised his standard before engaging
with the Parliamentarians in the first major clash of the
English Civil War. In 1922, 100 years after it became an
alehouse, Hook Norton acquired it and the two bars still
serve that brewery's own and guest ales today. Plentiful,
traditional food includes pork, stilton and mushroom
bake; seafood platter; steak, mushroom and Hooky ale pie
(aka Boozy Bullock); and veggie pie of the day.

Open all day all wk 11.30am-close **Bar Meals** L served
Mon-Sat 12-2.30, Sun 12-8 D served Mon-Sat 6.30-9,
Sun 12-8 Av main course £8.50 ⊕ HOOK NORTON
◀ Hooky Bitter, Old Hooky, Hooky Dark & Hooky Gold,
Guest ales ♨ Westons Old Rosie. **Facilities** ♣ Children
welcome Children's menu Children's portions Garden
Beer festival Parking 🚌 (notice required)

ETTINGTON   Map 10 SP24

The Chequers Inn

PICK OF THE PUBS

91 Banbury Rd CV37 7SR ☎ 01789 740387
e-mail: hello@the-chequers-ettington.co.uk
dir: *Take A422 from Stratford-upon-Avon towards
Banbury. Ettington in 5m, after junction with A429*

Whilst its origins are uncertain, this welcoming pub near
Stratford-upon-Avon may have been named after the
ancient Chequers tree that once stood in front of the
building. With its tasteful French undertones, beautiful
tapestries and sumptuous armchairs, this comfortably
appointed country dining inn radiates a homely feel.
Today, you can choose between the relaxed setting of the
bar, the well-appointed restaurant, and the large garden
overlooking the chef's vegetable patch. Cooking is
modern European with a nod to traditional English
favourites, and there's a very popular monthly fish night.
Lunchtime brings sandwiches and light meals like pie of
the day, whilst main menu selections might start with
spiced game kofta kebab. Main course options include
braised lamb shoulder, ratatouille and herb crust with
herb mash and rosemary jus, or pan-fried sea bass with
chorizo mash. A good selection of real ales and ciders,
plus an approachable wine list complete the package.
Booking for meals may be required.

Open 12-3 5-11 (Sat 12-11 Sun 12-6) Closed: Sun eve,
Mon **Bar Meals** L served Tue-Sat 12-2.30, Sun 12.30-3.30
D served Tue-Sat 6.30-9.30 **Restaurant** L served Tue-Sat
12-2.30, Sun 12.30-3.30 D served Tue-Sat 6.30-9.30
⊕ INDEPENDENT ◀ Greene King IPA, Fuller's London
Pride, St Austell Tribute ♨ Thatchers Gold. ▮ 8
Facilities ♣ Children welcome Children's menu
Children's portions Garden Parking 🚌 (notice required)

The Houndshill

Banbury Rd CV37 7NS ☎ 01789 740267
e-mail: info@thehoundshill.co.uk
web: www.thehoundshill.co.uk
dir: *On A422 SE of Stratford-upon-Avon*

Family-run for over 30 years, this inn is set in 12 acres of
garden and woodland in the beautiful Warwickshire
countryside, and a perfect base for exploring popular
tourist attractions such as Oxford, Blenheim, Stratford
and the Cotswolds. The pleasant tree-lined garden is
especially popular with families. Typical dishes include
grilled sirloin steak with fries, tomatoes, mushrooms and
peas; chilli con carne; home-made chicken curry; baked
lasagne; or The Houndshill platter – smoked salmon,
avocado, prawns, melon and cold poached salmon.

Open all wk 12-3 6-11 Closed: 24 Dec-1 Jan **Bar Meals** L
served all wk 12-2 D served all wk 7-9.30 **Restaurant** L
served all wk 12-2 D served all wk 7-9.30 ⊕ FREE HOUSE
◀ Purity Gold & Pure UBU. **Facilities** Children welcome
Children's menu Children's portions Play area Garden
Parking Wi-fi 🚌

FARNBOROUGH   Map 11 SP44

The Inn at Farnborough

PICK OF THE PUBS

OX17 1DZ ☎ 01295 690615
e-mail: enquiries@theinnfarnborough.co.uk
dir: *M40 junct 11 towards Banbury. Right at 3rd rdbt onto
A423 signed Southam. 4m & onto A423. Left onto single
track road signed Farnborough. Approx 1m turn right into
village, pub on right*

Built of locally quarried, honey-coloured Hornton stone,
this Grade II listed, 16th-century property used to be the
Butcher's Arms, having once belonged to the butcher on
the now National Trust-owned Farnborough Park Estate.
Tasteful restoration has ensured the retention of a fine
inglenook fireplace and other original features. The bar
serves Hook Norton real ales, locally made Hogan's cider,
and plenty of wines served by the glass. The concise
menu lists British pub classic dishes, and others with a
Mediterranean influence, but quality ingredients and high
culinary skills ensure impressive results whatever your
choice. Starters include baby spinach and Oxford Blue
risotto with poached egg; and among the mains are
chargrilled Aberdeenshire rib-eye steak; grilled fillet of
sea bass; Ditchford Mill Farm bangers and mash; and
roasted butternut squash. Local game is a speciality.
Trained baristas serve 'proper' coffee – have a pot in the

continued

FARNBOROUGH *continued*

terraced garden or covered decking area. Booking for meals may be required.

Open all wk 10-3 6-11 (Sat-Sun all day) Closed: 25 Dec **Bar Meals** L served all wk 12-3 D served all wk 6-10 Av main course £10 **Restaurant** L served all wk 12-3 D served Mon-Fri 6-10, wknd 10am-mdnt Fixed menu price fr £14.95 Av 3 course à la carte fr £27 ⊕ FREE HOUSE ◄ Hook Norton Hooky Bitter Ŏ Hogan's, Local ciders. ☗ 14 **Facilities** ✿ Children welcome Children's menu Children's portions Play area Garden Parking Wi-fi ⛟ (notice required)

GAYDON   Map 11 SP35

The Malt Shovel

Church Rd CV35 0ET ☎ 01926 641221
e-mail: malt.shovel@btconnect.com
dir: *M40 junct 12 follow B4451 to Gaydon*

Although historical detail proves elusive, no one disputes that the pub Richard and Debi Morisot run so successfully dates from the 16th century. In the dining room, where the pub's original entrance door has been incorporated as a feature, options include wild boar and apple sausages braised in Calvados; gammon, egg and chips; smoked haddock Welsh rarebit; and four-cheese ravioli. Snacks include chunky granary sandwiches, baguettes and hot paninis. Hook Norton, Fuller's and Timothy Taylor are normally among the real ales. Well-behaved children and dogs are welcome. Booking for meals may be required.

Open all wk 11-3 5-11 (Fri-Sat 11-11 Sun 12-10.30) **Bar Meals** L served all wk 12-2 D served all wk 6.30-9 Av main course £10 **Restaurant** L served all wk 12-2 D served all wk 6.30-9 ⊕ ENTERPRISE INNS ◄ Fuller's London Pride, Timothy Taylor Landlord, Everards Tiger, Wadworth 6X, Hook Norton. ☗ 10 **Facilities** ✿ Children welcome Children's portions Parking ⛟ (notice required)

GREAT WOLFORD   Map 10 SP23

The Fox & Hounds Inn
PICK OF THE PUBS

CV36 5NQ ☎ 01608 674220
e-mail: enquiries@thefoxandhoundsinn.com
dir: *Off A44 NE of Moreton-in-Marsh*

This family-run village inn is nestled in the heart of Warwickshire on the edge of the Cotswolds, and is as unspoilt as the wonderful countryside around it. The quintessential English inn ambience - settles, log fires and beams festooned with hops – is an ideal place to sup pints of Hook Norton or Purity ales. The busy kitchen uses local produce such as Dexter beef and seasonal game from local shoots. Herbs and vegetables come from the productive kitchen garden, and mushrooms are wild; only fresh fish comes from further afield, with deliveries from Scotland and Cornwall. Even the bread is baked using fresh yeast and organic flour milled in the Cotswolds. A typical selection from the modern British menu could

include baked Kitebrook egg with chard, crispy capers and sourdough soldiers; oxtail risotto with horseradish, tarragon, carrots and crispy parmesan; slow-roast belly pork, home-made black pudding, roast Cox's pippins, cider and juices. There is a daily-changing menu on the blackboard.

Open 12-2.30 6-11.30 (Sun 12-10.30) Closed: 1st 2wks Jan, Mon ⊕ FREE HOUSE ◄ Hook Norton Hooky Bitter, Purity, Guest ales Ŏ Westons Stowford Press. **Facilities** Children welcome Children's portions Garden Parking

---

HENLEY-IN-ARDEN   Map 10 SP16

The Bluebell ◉◉

93 High St B95 5AT ☎ 01564 793049
e-mail: info@bluebellhenley.co.uk
dir: *Opposite police station on A3400 in town centre*

On the picturesque High Street in Henley-in-Arden, this 500-year-old former coaching inn has been boldly updated by Leigh and Duncan Taylor. Be wowed by the swanky interior design, which combines original beams, worn flagstones and open fireplaces with bold colours and an eclectic mix of furnishings and fabrics. The bar and dining room ooze style and atmosphere and both throng with drinkers and diners, with seasonal menus brimming with local or home-grown produce. Typically, tuck into pork and chicken liver pâté, followed by beer-braised ox cheek with bone marrow fritter. Booking for meals may be required.

Open all day Closed: Mon **Bar Meals** L served Tue-Sat 12-2.30, Sun 12-3.30 D served Tue-Sat 6-9.30 Av main course £16 **Restaurant** L served Tue-Sat 12-2.30, Sun 12-3.30 D served Tue-Sat 6-9.30 Fixed menu price fr £15 Av 3 course à la carte fr £29 ⊕ FREE HOUSE ◄ Purity Pure UBU & Mad Goose, Church End What The Fox's Hat, Hook Norton Hooky Bitter Ŏ Hogan's. ☗ 16 **Facilities** ✿ Children welcome Children's portions Garden Parking Wi-fi

---

HUNNINGHAM   Map 11 SP36

The Red Lion, Hunningham
PICK OF THE PUBS

Main St CV33 9DY ☎ 01926 632715
e-mail: sam@redlionhunningham.co.uk
dir: *From Leamington Spa take B4453, through Cubbington to Weston under Wetherby. Follow Hunningham signs (turn sharp right as road bends left towards Princethorpe)*

Located beside a 14th-century bridge, this quirky country pub's beer garden leads down to the River Leam and offers lovely countryside views. Set in the heart of rural Warwickshire, this friendly pub's real fires and original features are enhanced by contemporary touches such as framed vintage comic book covers. A series of dining areas stretches out from the entrance and the tables and chairs are an eclectic mix of styles that seem to fit perfectly with the building. Peruse the appealing, well-executed menu then hop up to the bar (where you'll

find delicious pork pies sitting there as an additional temptation) to place your order. Locally sourced produce drives the generous dishes - a winter menu included Buttercross black pudding, bacon, smoked cheese and walnut salad; and field mushroom with blue cheese rarebit as starters, followed by the ever-popular fishcakes, in this case salmon and crayfish with spinach, butter sauce and poached Offchurch egg; and Warwickshire steak burger with bacon, cheese, coleslaw and hand-cut chips. On August Bank Holiday park your car (and tent if you like) in one of two fields for the annual outdoor film and beer festival; look out for the other events that take place.

Open all day all wk **Bar Meals** L served all wk 12-9.30 D served all wk 12-9.30 Av main course £10.95 food served all day **Restaurant** L served all wk 12-9.30 D served all wk 12-9.30 Av 3 course à la carte fr £22 food served all day ⊕ GREENE KING ◄ IPA & Abbot Ale, Hook Norton Old Hooky, BrewDog Alpha Dog, Guest ales. ☗ 28 **Facilities** ✿ Children welcome Children's portions Garden Beer festival Parking Wi-fi

---

ILMINGTON   Map 10 SP24

The Howard Arms
PICK OF THE PUBS

See Pick of the Pubs on opposite page

KENILWORTH   Map 10 SP27

The Almanack

Abbey End North CV8 1QJ ☎ 01926 353637
e-mail: hello@thealmanack-kenilworth.co.uk
dir: *Exit A46 at Kenilworth & brown Castle sign, towards town centre. Turn left onto Abbey Hill (B4104) signed Balsall Common. At rdbt into Abbey End. Opposite Holiday Inn*

This award-winning modern British gastro-pub was inspired by the 1960s Kinks' hit 'Autumn Almanac'. Stylish and contemporary, it is furnished with retro Danish teak furniture, original album covers and a huge island bar separating the lounge from the eatery and open kitchen. The pub is open all day for breakfast, coffee and cake, lunch and dinner; menu choices include deli boards, a daily roast, a selection from the chargrill, and full meals such as cheese fondue with crudités and country bread, followed by creamy fish stew with clams, butterbeans and chorizo, with crème brûlée for dessert. There's a special kids' menu, too.

Open all day all wk Closed: 25 Dec **Bar Meals** Av main course £14 food served all day **Restaurant** Av 3 course à la carte fr £22 food served all day ⊕ FREE HOUSE/PEACH PUBS ◄ Purity Pure UBU & Gold, Sharp's Doom Bar Ŏ Addlestones, Aspall. ☗ 13 **Facilities** ✿ Children welcome Children's menu Children's portions Wi-fi ⛟ (notice required)

Save on hotels. Book at **theAA.com/hotel**

WARWICKSHIRE 535 ENGLAND

PICK OF THE PUBS

The Howard Arms

ILMINGTON Map 10 SP24

Lower Green CV36 4LT
☎ **01608 682226**
e-mail: info@howardarms.com
web: www.howardarms.com
dir: *Exit A429 or A3400, 9m from Stratford-upon-Avon*

Set in the beautiful Cotswold Hills, The Howard Arms is the start and finish to a number of fabulous local walks and is popular with ramblers. A detailed guide of walks can be bought at the bar for a small donation, with all the monies going to the church funds. A stunning 400-year-old Cotswold-stone inn on the picturesque village green of Ilmington, it is at the centre of village life. The flagstoned bar and open-plan dining room create a civilised look without sacrificing period charm, and it is all imbued with an informal atmosphere and a log fire that burns for most of the year. The breadth of choice among handpumps and bottles in the bar indicates a well-considered approach to meeting the demands of locals and visitors alike. Award-winning ales feature with famous local names to the area such as Purity, Hook Norton and Wye Valley, while wine drinkers can choose from a carefully selected list of over 30 wines by the glass. Equally serious are the inn's efforts to source excellent seasonal ingredients and always strive to use local suppliers. Why not begin with a tian of crab with pickled cucumber and horseradish cream, or poached pear, toasted brioche, blue cheese mousse and candied walnuts? Then move on to a main course of three way lamb (breast, cutlet and kidney), sweet potato rösti, sticky carrots and red wine jus, or pig's cheeks with bubble-and-squeak, fried egg and black pudding perhaps. Alternatively go more traditional and try lemon-battered fish and chips with pea purée and hand-cut chips, or lamb hotpot with spiced red cabbage. A dessert might be caramelised baby pineapple, Garibaldi biscuit with rum and raisin ice cream, or Jamaican gingerbread, gingerbread men and vanilla ice cream. Accommodation is available. Booking for meals may be required.

Open all day all wk **Bar & Restaurant** L served Mon-Fri 12-2.30, Sat-Sun 12-4 D served Mon-Sat 6.30-9.30, Sun 6.30-9 🛢 FREE HOUSE ◾ Warwickshire Lady Godiva, Wye Valley Bitter, Hook Norton Old Hooky, Purity. ☍ 30
Facilities Children welcome Children's portions Garden Parking Wi-fi 🚌 (notice required)

LAPWORTH — Map 10 SP17

The Boot Inn

PICK OF THE PUBS

Old Warwick Rd B94 6JU ☎ 01564 782464
e-mail: bootinn@hotmail.com
dir: *Telephone for directions*

Beside the Grand Union Canal in the unspoilt village of Lapworth, this lively and convivial 16th-century former coaching inn is reputedly haunted by a former waitress from the 19th century. Apart from its smart interior with its soft modern furnishings complementing the old-world feel, the attractive garden is a great place to relax or dine on warm days, while a canopy and patio heaters make it a comfortable place to sit even on cooler evenings. Being a free house, there is a good choice of real ales to enjoy – Fuller's London Pride or Purity Pure UBU maybe. But the main draw is the modern brasserie-style food. Choose a filled wrap, pitta or sandwich for lunch. For dinner, a starter of devilled kidneys on toast; or freshly made soup perhaps followed by a main of spit-roasted piri-piri chicken; confit of duck, fondant potato, wilted spinach and tomato compôte; and Thai vegetable curry. Children and 'well-natured' dogs are welcome, while the friendly staff can cater for any dietary requirements. The annual fireworks display attracts a huge crowd.

Open all day all wk 11-11 (Thu-Sat 11am-mdnt Sun 11-10.30) **Bar Meals** L served all wk 12-2.30 D served Mon-Fri 7-9.30, Sat 6.30-9.30, Sun 7-9 Av main course £11.95 **Restaurant** L served all wk 12-2.30 D served Mon-Fri 7-9.30, Sat 6.30-9.30, Sun 7-9 Fixed menu price fr £13.50 Av 3 course à la carte fr £30 ⊕ FREE HOUSE ◀ Fuller's London Pride, Purity Pure UBU, St Austell Tribute ⭘ Thatchers Gold. ♟ 9 **Facilities** ✿ Children welcome Children's menu Children's portions Garden Parking ⛟ (notice required)

LEAMINGTON SPA (ROYAL) — Map 10 SP36

The Moorings at Myton NEW

Myton Rd CV31 3NY ☎ 01926 425043
e-mail: info@themoorings.co.uk
web: www.themoorings.co.uk
dir: *M40 junct 14 or 13 follow A452 towards Leamington Spa. At 4th rdbt after crossing canal, The Moorings on left*

Raymond Blanc protégés Charles Harris and Nigel Brown have transformed this canalside gastro-pub after a stylish £250k refurbishment. A relaxed, maritime New

England-style makeover has enhanced the building's architectural features and made full use of its unique waterside location. A wide range of ales is on offer but wine buffs will be drawn to the excellent list. Trusted local suppliers are the cornerstone of an Anglo-French menu that includes soufflés, sharing plates, salads and steaks alongside main courses such as roasted salmon fishcake with pea sauce and poached egg.

Open all day all wk **Bar Meals** L served all wk 12-2.30 D served all wk 6-9.30 Av main course £12 **Restaurant** L served all wk 12-2.30 D served all wk 6-9.30 Av 3 course à la carte fr £22 ⊕ CHARLES WELLS ◀ Bombardier, Young's London Gold, Courage Directors, Warwickshire Darling Buds. ♟ 13 **Facilities** ✿ Children welcome Children's menu Children's portions Family room Garden Parking Wi-fi ⛟ (notice required)

See advert on opposite page

LONG COMPTON — Map 10 SP23

The Red Lion ★★★★ INN ⊛

PICK OF THE PUBS

Main St CV36 5JS ☎ 01608 684221
e-mail: info@redlion-longcompton.co.uk
web: www.redlion-longcompton.co.uk
dir: *On A3400 between Shipston on Stour & Chipping Norton*

Originally built as a coaching inn in 1748, The Red Lion makes a good base from which to explore the Cotswolds and the fascinating towns of Stratford-upon-Avon and Warwick. Although still very much the village local, it appeals equally to those seeking a decent meal or stay, with oak beams, wood-burning stoves and open fires in the stone-flagged bar and the cosy, well-decorated dining areas. The menu and blackboards cater for all tastes, beginning with interesting sandwiches like hot steak, tomato and horseradish on ciabatta, or battered cod and chips served on the 'Red Lion Times'. Serious diners might start with pork and chicken liver terrine, before moving on to rib-eye steak with Café de Paris butter, followed by rhubarb and ginger crumble tart with crème anglaise. Children have their own menu. Five elegant en suite bedrooms feature such modern luxuries as Egyptian cotton bed linen, fluffy towels and flat-screen televisions.

Open all wk Mon-Thu 10-2.30 6-11 (Fri-Sun all day) ⊕ FREE HOUSE ◀ Hook Norton Hooky Bitter, Adnams, Timothy Taylor. **Facilities** Children welcome Children's menu Children's portions Play area Garden Parking Wi-fi **Rooms** 5

LONG ITCHINGTON — Map 11 SP46

The Duck on the Pond

The Green CV47 9QJ ☎ 01926 815876
dir: *On A423 in village centre, 1m N of Southam*

Children will be delighted to discover that the name of this attractive village inn does indeed indicate the presence of a pond complete with drakes and mallards. Winter fires light an intriguing interior, crammed with fascinating bric-à-brac, while the menu offers a selection of pub favourites including battered fish, gammon and steaks, as well as vegetarian choices like aubergine and walnut bake or spinach and ricotta cannelloni. There is a lovely outdoor area for alfresco dining and a beer festival on the first May Bank Holiday.

Open all day all wk ⊕ CHARLES WELLS ◀ Bombardier & Eagle IPA, Young's Bitter, Guinness. **Facilities** Children welcome Children's menu Children's portions Beer festival Parking

MONKS KIRBY — Map 11 SP48

The Bell Inn

Bell Ln CV23 0QY ☎ 01788 832352
e-mail: belindagb@aol.com
dir: *Village off B4455 (Fosse Way)*

This quaint, timbered inn was once the gatehouse of a Benedictine priory and then a brewhouse cottage. The pine bar top came from a tree grown in Leire churchyard nearby. The Spanish owners describe their pub as "a corner of Spain in the heart of England". Mediterranean and traditional cuisine play an important role on the truly extensive menu. Enjoy a glass of Ruddles while taking time to make your choices. Chateaubriand; salmon à la béchamel; lobster mornay; and mushroom Stroganoff all make a showing.

Open Tue-Sun Closed: 26 Dec, 1 Jan, Mon ⊕ FREE HOUSE ◀ Greene King IPA, Ruddles. **Facilities** Children welcome Garden Parking ⛟

OFFCHURCH   Map 11 SP36

The Stag at Offchurch

Welsh Rd CV33 9AQ ☎ 01926 425801
e-mail: info@thestagatoffchurch.com
web: www.thestagatoffchurch.com
dir: *From Leamington Spa take A425 towards Southam. At Radford Semele turn left onto Offchurch Ln to Offchurch*

A 16th-century thatched pub in the centre of the picturesque village of Offchurch, The Stag is a former coaching inn that has been refurbished but retained its character. Walkers and locals mingle in the bar with its oak floor and open fires, while diners can choose between two comfortable restaurant areas. The imaginative menu offers plenty of choice and meat from local farms – start with black fig, crispy prosciutto, toasted walnut and Roquefort, then continue with slow-roast pork collar with sage and apple crust, or pan-fried sea bass with confit, garlic crushed potatoes, spinach, pea and shellfish sauce. A selection of locally-butchered steaks are also available, along with sharing plates and various things on toast. Booking for meals may be required.

Open all day all wk **Bar Meals** L served all wk 12-2.30 D served all wk 6-9.30 Av main course £13 **Restaurant** L served all wk 12-2.30 D served all wk 6-9.30 Av 3 course à la carte fr £22 ⊕ FREE HOUSE ◄ Warwickshire, Purity ♂ Hogan's Dry. ♀ 13 **Facilities** ♣ Children welcome Children's menu Children's portions Garden Parking Wi-fi

See advert on page 537

OXHILL   Map 10 SP34

The Peacock

Main St CV35 0QU ☎ 01295 688060
e-mail: info@thepeacockoxhill.co.uk
dir: *From Stratford-upon-Avon take A422 towards Banbury. Turn right to Oxhill*

Successfully combining traditional old-world charm with a contemporary feel, this 16th-century stone-built pub can be found by meandering down leafy lanes between Stratford and Banbury to locate Oxhill. The kitchen focuses on sourcing local meats and vegetables from local farms, and the seasonal menus and chalkboard specials have found favour with local diners. Typical choices may include seared scallops on black pudding with chilli oil; fillet of beef Wellington with red wine and mushroom sauce; and pan-fried chicken breast with brie, peppercorn, brandy and cream sauce. Booking for meals may be required.

Open all day all wk 12-11 **Bar Meals** L served Mon-Sat 12-2, Sun 12-8 D served Mon-Sat 6-9, Sun 12-8 **Restaurant** L served Mon-Sat 12-2, Sun 12-8 D served Mon-Sat 6-9, Sun 12-8 ◄ Timothy Taylor Golden Best, Wye Valley HPA & Butty Bach, Guest ales ♂ Thatchers Pear & Gold, Healey's Cornish Rattler. ♀ 12 **Facilities** Children welcome Children's menu Children's portions Garden Parking Wi-fi 🚐

PRESTON BAGOT   Map 10 SP16

The Crabmill

B95 5EE ☎ 01926 843342
e-mail: thecrabmill@lovelypubs.co.uk
dir: *M42 junct 8, A3400 towards Stratford-upon-Avon. Take A4189 Henley-in-Arden lights. Left, pub 1.5m on left*

The name is a reminder that crab apple cider was once made at this 15th-century hostelry, which is set in beautiful rural surroundings. Restored to create an upmarket venue, the pub has a comfortable, light, open feel. Even the menu is fresh and exciting, with a lunchtime hoi sin duck wrap or ploughman's, to evening dishes such as grilled sea bream fillet with smoked haddock, potato and clam chowder; and pork tenderloin wrapped in Parma ham, black pudding, sage potato cake and mustard cream.

Open all day 11-11 Closed: Sun eve **Bar Meals** L served Mon-Thu 12-2.30, Fri-Sat 12-5 D served Mon-Sat 6.30-9.30 Av main course £14 **Restaurant** L served Mon-Sat 12-2.30 D served Mon-Sat 6.30-9.30 Fixed menu price fr £13.10 Av 3 course à la carte fr £25 ⊕ FREE HOUSE ◄ Greene King Abbot Ale, Purity Gold, St Austell Tribute. ♀ 9 **Facilities** ♣ Children welcome Children's menu Children's portions Garden Parking Wi-fi

PRIORS MARSTON   Map 11 SP45

The Hollybush Inn

PICK OF THE PUBS

Hollybush Ln CV47 7RW ☎ 01327 260934
e-mail: enquiries@hollybushatpriorsmarston.co.uk
dir: *From Southam A425, off bypass, 1st right, 6m to Priors Marston. Left after war memorial, next left, 150yds left again*

Originally a farmhouse, The Hollybush only became a fully licensed pub in 1947. Set in the beautiful village of Priors Marston in the heart of Warwickshire, it's a warm hub of village social activity with a very relaxed atmosphere and real fires; people can eat and/or drink wherever they choose. The menus range from open sandwiches and sharing boards to a comprehensive main menu selection - perhaps a starter of peppered carpaccio of beef with a wild rocket and parmesan salad and fresh lemon juice; followed by pan-fried red mullet fillets with a rustic Italian ratatouille and sautéed potatoes. For those in search of pub classics, beer-battered haddock and chips; and ham, egg and chips are also on offer. Desserts could include profiteroles or sticky toffee pudding. Smaller portions can be ordered for most of the grown-up dishes.

Look out for live music and other events during the year. Booking for meals may be required.

Open all wk 12-3 5.30-11 (Sat-Sun 12-11) **Bar Meals** L served all wk 12-2.30 D served Mon-Sat 6.30-9.30 **Restaurant** L served Mon-Sat 12-2.30, Sun 12-4 D served Mon-Sat 6-9.30, Sun 12-4 ⊕ PUNCH TAVERNS ◄ Morland Old Speckled Hen, Hook Norton, Fuller's ♂ Westons Stowford Press. ♀ 12 **Facilities** Children welcome Children's portions Garden Parking Wi-fi 🚐

RATLEY   Map 11 SP34

The Rose and Crown

OX15 6DS ☎ 01295 678148
e-mail: k.marples@btinternet.com
dir: *Follow Edgehill signs, 7m N of Banbury (13m SE of Stratford-upon-Avon) on A422*

First, a grisly tale: following the Battle of Edge Hill in 1642, a Roundhead was discovered hiding in the chimney of this 12th-century pub and promptly beheaded. His ghost now reputedly haunts the building, but don't let that spoil your enjoyment of the peaceful village location, the fine ales and the home-made pub meals, perhaps cottage pie; ham, eggs and chips; haddock and spring onion fishcakes; vegetarian options; as well as one of the Sunday roasts. Booking for meals may be required.

Open all wk 12-2.30 6-11 **Bar Meals** L served Mon-Sun 12-2.30 D served Mon-Sat 6.30-9 ◄ Wells Bombardier & Eagle IPA, Morland Old Speckled Hen, Guest ale. **Facilities** Children welcome Children's portions Family room Garden Parking

RED HILL   Map 10 SP15

The Stag at Redhill

PICK OF THE PUBS

Alcester Rd B49 6NQ ☎ 01789 764634
e-mail: info@thestagatredhill.co.uk
dir: *On A46 between Stratford-upon-Avon & Alcester*

If Stratford-upon-Avon gets too busy, take the Alcester road for this 16th-century, Greene King-owned country inn. It was originally Stratford's courthouse and jail, and you can still see one of the old cell doors preserved inside. Food service begins with breakfast and runs through to dinner, every day of the year. The Sunday carvery always includes two joints of beef, one cooked rare. Wednesday is pie-and-a-pint night, Friday is grill night accompanied by a piano player, and there's usually a good-value fixed-price lunch menu during the week. Typical mains include meat, fish and vegetable sharing platters; Indonesian pork curry; beer-battered haddock and chips; and oven-roasted field mushrooms. There's also a separate tapas menu, and frequently changing specials. If you plan to arrive by helicopter, the hotel will advise you not to overfly the rare breeds farm next door as they "don't want the lambs having kittens!"

Open all day all wk 7am-11pm **Bar Meals** L served all wk 12-5 D served all wk 5-9 food served all day **Restaurant** L

Save on hotels. Book at **theAA.com/hotel**

WARWICKSHIRE 539 ENGLAND

served all wk 12-5 D served all wk 5-9 food served all day ⊕ GREENE KING ◀ IPA, Abbot Ale & Ruddles, Morland Old Speckled Hen & Original ⌀ Westons Stowford Press. ♈ 9 **Facilities** Children welcome Children's menu Children's portions Garden Parking Wi-fi ▭ (notice required)

RUGBY
Map 11 SP57

Golden Lion ★★★ HL

PICK OF THE PUBS

Easenhall CV23 0JA ☎ 01788 832265
e-mail: reception@goldenlionhotel.org
dir: *From Rugby take A426, take 1st exit Newbold road B4112. Through Newbold. At Harborough Parva follow brown sign, turn left, pub in 1m*

Set in idyllic Warwickshire countryside, this charming free house has its bar and restaurant in the original 16th-century building, which retains many original features, including log fires, low beams and wattle-and-daub walls. Run by the Austin family since 1931, you'll find real ales such as Young's Bitter and Wells Bombardier in the bar, as well as excellent food and service, with a wide choice of sandwiches, baguettes and ploughman's; a traditional Sunday lunch carvery and speciality nights - the French bistro or the taste of Asia evening perhaps. The restaurant menu may feature seared scallops, black pudding and bacon salad; mussels braised in cream and cider; or garlic and stilton mushrooms on toasted ciabatta to start; followed by lamb and apricot pie; braised lamb shank with creamy mash and redcurrant jus; or a red Thai chicken curry. The adjoining contemporary hotel has 20 well-equipped bedrooms.

Open all day all wk 11-11 (Sun 12-11) **Bar Meals** L served Mon-Sat 12-2, Sun 12-2.30 D served Mon-Sat 4.30-9.30, Sun 3-8.45 **Restaurant** L served Mon-Sat 12-2, Sun 12-2.30 D served Mon-Sat 4.30-9.30, Sun 3-8.45 ⊕ FREE HOUSE ◀ Courage Directors, Purity Pure UBU, Wells Bombardier, Young's Bitter ⌀ Westons Stowford Press, Brothers. ♈ 10 **Facilities** Children welcome Children's menu Children's portions Garden Parking Wi-fi ▭ (notice required) **Rooms** 20

Old Smithy

1 Green Ln, Church Lawford CV23 9EF ☎ 02476 542333
e-mail: pippa@king-henrys-taverns.co.uk
dir: *From Rugby take A428 (Lawford Rd) towards Coventry. Turn right to Church Lawford*

One of King Henry's Taverns, a prettier building is hard to imagine; the garden and patio are much sought-after in summer. The interior is inviting too, with huge logs fires adding warmth and atmosphere in winter, a modern conservatory-style dining room, and spacious bar where Marston's Pedigree is one of the choices. The menu of generous dishes will delight the hungry, but can cater for smaller appetites too, with paninis and jacket potatoes. International flavours include Mexican fillet fajitas; and pollo los marinos (chicken breast in a mushroom and white wine sauce) for a taste of Spain.

Open all day all wk 11.30-11 **Bar Meals** food served all day **Restaurant** food served all day ⊕ FREE HOUSE/KING HENRY'S TAVERNS ◀ Marston's Pedigree, Guinness. ♈ 16 **Facilities** Children welcome Children's menu Children's portions Garden Parking ▭

SALFORD PRIORS
Map 10 SP05

The Bell at Salford Priors

Evesham Rd WR11 8UU ☎ 01789 772112
e-mail: info@thebellatsalfordpriors.com
web: www.thebellatsalfordpriors.com
dir: *From A46 (Bidford Island) towards Salford Priors. Through village. Pub on left*

Close to Stratford-upon-Avon, the Cotswolds and within easy reach of the NEC at Birmingham, this country pub draws diners for its rural location and the daily menu that champions local seasonal produce. Expect a warm welcome, glowing fires and three real ales on tap, including Sharp's Doom Bar. Typically, follow black pudding and bacon spring rolls with Ragley blade of beef cooked in red wine and mushroom sauce, and hot chocolate pudding. Game lovers will not resist partridge breast with pear purée followed by venison Wellington with red wine sauce. Booking for meals may be required.

Open all day all wk **Bar Meals** Av main course £12 food served all day **Restaurant** L served Mon-Fri 12-3, Sat-Sun all day D served Mon-Fri fr 6, Sat-Sun all day Fixed menu price fr £8 ⊕ ENTERPRISE INNS ◀ Wye Valley HPA, Sharp's Doom Bar, Wickwar BOB ⌀ Westons Old Rosie. ♈ 10 **Facilities** 🐾 Children welcome Children's menu Children's portions Garden Parking Wi-fi

SHIPSTON ON STOUR
Map 10 SP24

White Bear Hotel

High St CV36 4AJ ☎ 01608 661558
e-mail: info@whitebearshipston.co.uk
dir: *From M40 junct 15, follow signs to Stratford-upon-Avon, then take A3400 to Shipston on Stour*

Situated in the market town square and providing the hub of the local community, the refurbished bars of this Georgian hotel have a comfortable, timeless appeal, with open fires and wooden settles. You'll find a range of real ales and keg beers, with several wines available by the glass. Food-wise, expect simple offerings such as filled jacket potatoes, fresh salads or pie of the day. Visit in the afternoon and you can enjoy a scone with clotted cream and jam.

Open all day all wk ⊕ PUNCH TAVERNS ◀ Fuller's London Pride, Caledonian Deuchars IPA, Hook Norton Hooky Bitter, St Austell Tribute, Adnams, Black Sheep, 3 Guest ales ⌀ Westons Old Rosie. **Facilities** Children welcome Children's menu Children's portions Garden Beer festival Parking Wi-fi

SHREWLEY
Map 10 SP26

The Durham Ox Restaurant and Country Pub

PICK OF THE PUBS

Shrewley Common CV35 7AY ☎ 01926 842283
e-mail: enquiries@thedurhamox.com
dir: *M40 junct 15 onto A46 towards Coventry. 1st exit signed Warwick, turn left onto A4177. After Hatton Country World, pub signed 1.5m*

An award-winning pub/restaurant in a peaceful village just four miles from Warwick and Leamington. Warm and inviting, its old beams, roaring fire and traditional hospitality combine with a city chic that give it a competitive edge. Success is in no small measure due to the restaurant, where impressive, seasonally changing classic and contemporary dishes are prepared. A meal might consist of beef carpaccio; leg of lamb, boulangère potatoes, tomato confit, fine beans and red wine jus; and vanilla pannacotta with toffee sauce. Bar food includes snacks and sandwiches for lunch, and hearty pub classics and snacks in the evening, such as breaded mushrooms, sausage and mash, and pizza. Children are offered spaghetti bolognese or fish and chips from their own menu. Extensive gardens incorporate a safe children's play area.

Open all wk 11-11 (Sun 12-10) ⊕ GREENE KING ◀ Ruddles County & IPA, Guest ales ⌀ Westons Stowford Press. **Facilities** Children welcome Children's menu Play area Garden Parking

STRATFORD-UPON-AVON   Map 10 SP25

The Fox & Goose Inn

PICK OF THE PUBS

Armscote CV37 8DD ☎ 01608 682635
e-mail: mail@foxandgoosecountryinn.co.uk
dir: *1m off A3400, between Shipston on Stour & Stratford-upon-Avon*

Converted from cottages and a blacksmith's forge, this ivy-clad inn stands in an off-the-beaten track village in rolling countryside close to Stratford-upon-Avon. An ideal base for exploring the Cotswolds, the stylish pub/restaurant has rustic-chic interior comprising a cosy locals' bar with squishy velvet cushions on benches and pews, and a smart dining room with open log fire and an eclectic mix of furnishings on flagstone floors. Expect to find local Hooky or London Pride on tap, or coincide your visit with the champagne happy hour in the early evening from Monday to Saturday and enjoy a glass (or bottle) of fizz. For more solid sustenance, look to the country-style menu: guinea fowl and pheasant terrine with apricot marmalade could be followed by grilled mullet with braised fennel and dill butter; or rib-eye steak with chunky chips and red onion butter. There's alfresco decking for dining under the vines, and lovely countryside views. Booking for meals may be required.

Open all day all wk **Bar Meals** Av main course £12.95 food served all day **Restaurant** Fixed menu price fr £12.95 Av 3 course à la carte fr £18.50 food served all day ⊕ FREE HOUSE ◀ Wadworth 6X, Hook Norton Hooky Bitter, Fuller's London Pride, Purity Pure UBU, Local guest ales ♂ Thatchers Gold. ♀ 10 **Facilities** ♣ Children welcome Children's menu Children's portions Garden Parking Wi-fi ▄▄ (notice required)

The One Elm

PICK OF THE PUBS

1 Guild St CV37 6QZ ☎ 01789 404919
e-mail: theoneelm@peachpubs.com
dir: *In town centre*

A stroll from the river and theatre, The One Elm is in a prime location in the town centre and mirrors the chic, contemporary look and style of menus to be found at other Peach Pubs, the innovative small pub group founded by Lee Cash and Hamish Stoddart. Opening at 9.30am for coffee and breakfast, there's an informal, almost continental feel about the place, especially in the stylish front lounge area with its wood floor, bright painted walls, leather sofas and low tables displaying the day's newspapers. Beyond the central, open-to-view kitchen is the more formal dining area, while the upstairs seating area has an even grander feel. From deli boards offering tapas-style starters or nibbles of charcuterie, cheese, and rustic breads, the menu is an eclectic list of modern pub food. Enjoy starter or main course size moules marinière or begin with chicken liver pâté with apple chutney, then follow with pan-fried cod with creamy chorizo, butter beans and leeks, and finally dark

chocolate tart. The secluded terrace induces a feeling of being abroad. Booking for meals may be required.

Open all day all wk 9.30am-11pm (Thu 9.30am-mdnt Fri-Sat 9.30am-1am Sun 9.30am-10.30pm) Closed: 25 Dec **Bar Meals** L served all wk 12-6 D served all wk 6-10 food served all day **Restaurant** L served all wk 12-2.30 D served all wk 6-10 ⊕ FREE HOUSE/PEACH PUBS ◀ Purity Pure UBU & Gold, Black Sheep ♂ Addlestones. ♀ 8 **Facilities** ♣ Children welcome Children's menu Children's portions Garden Parking Wi-fi ▄▄

STRETTON ON FOSSE   Map 10 SP23

The Plough Inn

GL56 9QX ☎ 01608 661053
e-mail: saravol@aol.com
dir: *From Moreton-in-Marsh, 4m on A429 N. From Stratford-upon-Avon, 10m on A429 S*

A classic award-winning village pub built from mellow Cotswold stone, The Plough has the requisite exposed beams and real fire. Four real ales are usually on tap, ciders include Black Rat, and there's a good range of wines too. It's a family-run affair, with French chef and co-owner Jean-Pierre in charge of the kitchen; so expect traditional French dishes on the specials board. With a spit-roast in the inglenook fireplace in winter and spring, entertainment on Sunday evenings ranges from quizzes to folk music.

Open 11.30-2.30 6-11.30 (Sun 12-3) Closed: 25 Dec eve, Sun eve & Mon L (ex BH) **Bar Meals** L served Tue-Sun 12-2 D served Tue-Sat 7-9 ⊕ FREE HOUSE ◀ Ansell's Mild, Shepherd Neame Spitfire, Hook Norton, Purity, Local ales ♂ Thatchers Katy & Traditional, Black Rat. ♀ 9 **Facilities** Children welcome Children's portions Play area Garden Parking Wi-fi ▄▄ (notice required)

TEMPLE GRAFTON   Map 10 SP15

The Blue Boar Inn ★★★ INN

B49 6NR ☎ 01789 750010
e-mail: info@theblueboar.co.uk
dir: *From A46 (Stratford to Alcester) turn left to Temple Grafton. Pub at 1st x-rds*

An alehouse from the outset, the oldest part of this village inn dates from the early 1600s. Water from the glass-covered well in the bar area was once used for brewing, but nowadays it's a home for goldfish. Warmth in the bar and restaurant comes from four open fires, while in the summer there is a patio garden with views of the Cotswold Hills. Regularly changing menus include steak from local Freeman's Farm; penne provençale; and grilled pork, apple and black pudding stack. Wash it down with one of their ales: Jennings, Banks's Original, Marston's Pedigree or Wychwood Hobgoblin. Accommodation is available in the form of 14 attractive bedrooms.

Open all day all wk **Bar Meals** L served all wk 12-3 D served all wk 6-10 **Restaurant** L served Mon-Fri 12-3, Sat 12-10, Sun 12-9 D served Mon-Fri 6-10, Sat 12-10,

Sun 12-9 ⊕ MARSTON'S ◀ Pedigree, Wychwood Hobgoblin, Banks's Original, Jennings ♂ Thatchers Gold. ♀ **Facilities** ♣ Children welcome Children's menu Children's portions Garden Parking Wi-fi ▄▄ (notice required) **Rooms** 14

WARWICK   Map 10 SP26

The Rose & Crown

PICK OF THE PUBS

30 Market Place CV34 4SH ☎ 01926 411117
e-mail: roseandcrown@peachpubs.com
dir: *M40 junct 15 follow signs to Warwick. Pass castle car park entrance up hill to West Gate, left into Bowling Green St, 1st right, then turn right into Market Square*

Lee Cash and Hamish Stoddart created the innovative Peach Pub Company over a decade ago and The Rose & Crown – their flagship venture - continues to thrive. A vibrant and stylish gastro-pub in the heart of Warwick, it has a laid-back vibe and a contemporary look that sits comfortably with period features and homely touches such as leather sofas and coffee tables with the day's newspapers. The pub opens early for breakfast (free toast), and offers a modern pub menu that's served all day. Deli boards offer small tapas-style portions of cheeses, charcuterie and fish, and the seasonal menu also offers a wide selection of dishes to suit the occasion and time of day. There are breakfast sarnies, small or large plates of risotto, filled herb pancakes and salads, then main dishes like organic salmon fishcake with watercress and gremolata; and bangers and mash. Puddings may include crème brûlée, or ginger and orange sponge with custard. A beer festival is usually held during May.

Open all day all wk Closed: 25 Dec **Bar Meals** Av main course £14 food served all day **Restaurant** Av 3 course à la carte fr £22 food served all day ⊕ FREE HOUSE/PEACH PUBS ◀ Purity Pure UBU & Gold, Sharp's Doom Bar ♂ Addlestones, Aspall. ♀ 13 **Facilities** ♣ Children welcome Children's portions Beer festival Wi-fi ▄▄ (notice required)

WELFORD-ON-AVON   Map 10 SP15

The Bell Inn

PICK OF THE PUBS

Binton Rd CV37 8EB ☎ 01789 750353
e-mail: info@thebellwelford.co.uk
dir: *Please telephone for directions*

Reputedly one of the oldest pubs in the Warwickshire Cotswolds, The Bell dates from the early 16th century. Handy for Stratford, legend has it that William Shakespeare contracted fatal pneumonia after stumbling home from here in the pouring rain. Although it is now a contemporary restaurant, the historic bar with its limestone-flagged floors, beams, oak furniture and open fires still serves at least five real ales. Owners Colin and Teresa Ombler have always aimed to proffer a warm welcome and a simple pint, with dishes of quality food and outstanding service when desired. These are certainly

Save on hotels. Book at **theAA.com/hotel**

WARWICKSHIRE 541 ENGLAND

hard to resist, the menu proudly listing all the local suppliers of fresh and seasonal produce. Starters and light meals include crayfish, prawn and seasonal melon cocktail with Marie Rose sauce; and deep-fried brie with ginger and apricot compôte; specials range from roasted whole sea bass on lemon and herb potatoes with basil dressing to steak and onion pie with a shortcrust pastry lid. There are sharing deli plates and hot sandwich of the week too. Booking for meals may be required.

Open all wk 11.30-3 6-11 (Sat 11.30-11 Sun 12-10.30) **Bar Meals** L served Mon-Fri 11.30-2.30, Sat 11.30-3, Sun all day D served Mon-Thu 6-9.30, Fri-Sat 6-10, Sun all day Av main course £13.95 **Restaurant** L served Mon-Sat 11.30-2.30, Sun all day D served Mon-Thu 6-9.30, Fri-Sat 6-10, Sun all day Fixed menu price fr £12.95 Av 3 course à la carte fr £25.95 ⊕ ENTERPRISE INNS ◀ Wells Bombardier, Hobsons Best Bitter, Flowers Best Bitter & IPA, Purity Gold & Pure UBU, Hook Norton. ⚑ 16 **Facilities** Children welcome Children's menu Children's portions Garden Parking Wi-fi 🚐 (notice required)

WITHYBROOK　　　　　　Map 11 SP48

The Pheasant

Main St CV7 9LT ☎ **01455 220480**
e-mail: thepheasant01@hotmail.com
web: www.thepheasanteatinghouse.com
dir: *7m NE of Coventry, on B4112*

A warm welcome awaits you at this 17th-century inn, idyllically situated beside the brook where withies were once cut for fencing, hence the village's name, Withybrook. The Pheasant is a popular free house, cosy and full of character with an inglenook fireplace, farm implements and horse-racing photographs on display. The chalkboard displays daily and seasonal specials, complementing a wealth of food choices from the extensive main menu. Specials include fresh fish (ranging from cod to lemon sole), local game, pasta and home-made pies. Options from the main menu are half

roast duck, tuna steak, plaice goujons, lamb shank and lasagne. Vegetarian dishes are also available. Outside, the benches on the patio area overlooking the Withy Brook can accommodate 100 people – perfect for a leisurely lunch or a thirst-quenching pint of real ale after a walk in the beautiful surrounding countryside. Booking for meals may be required.

Open all wk 11-3 6-11.30 (Sun & BH 11-11) Closed: 25-26 Dec **Bar Meals** Av main course £11.75 **Restaurant** L served Mon-Sat 12-2, Sun 12-8.30/9 D served Mon-Sat 6-10, Sun 12-8.30/9 ⊕ FREE HOUSE ◀ Courage Directors, Theakston Best Bitter, John Smith's Extra Smooth, Young's Bitter. ⚑ 16 **Facilities** Children welcome Children's menu Children's portions Garden Parking Wi-fi 🚐

See advert below

WOOTTON WAWEN — Map 10 SP16

The Bulls Head

PICK OF THE PUBS

Stratford Rd B95 6BD ☎ 01564 792511
e-mail: info@thebullsheadwoottonwawen.co.uk
dir: *On B3400, 4m N of Stratford-upon-Avon, 1m S of Henley-in-Arden*

A smart, black-and-white timber-framed pub, just one of the notable old buildings in Wootton Wawen. It's only a mile or so from the picturesque village of Henley-in-Arden and ideally placed for touring and exploring Warwickshire and the Cotswolds. Originally two separate cottages, it displays a stone with the date 1317, and the bar and snug areas feature rug-strewn flagstone floors, low, gnarled oak beams, old church pews, and leather sofas fronting log fires. Ale drinkers will find Marston's Pedigree, Banks's Original and Wychwood Hobgoblin ales on tap in the bar, while the food offering here takes in ham, egg and chips; classic fish and chips; and the hearty Bull's Head club sandwich filled with bacon, chicken, lettuce, tomato and egg mayonnaise. The same tone and style are maintained in the magnificent 'great hall' restaurant, with its vaulted ceiling and yet more exposed beams. Here you can tuck into braised lamb shank with caramelised onion gravy, or roast salmon with watercress sauce, followed by sticky toffee pudding.

Open all day all wk ⊕ BILLESLEY PUB COMPANY ◀ Marston's Pedigree, Banks's Bitter & Original, Wychwood Hobgoblin, Guest ales. **Facilities** Children welcome Children's portions Garden Parking Wi-fi

WEST MIDLANDS

BARSTON — Map 10 SP27

The Malt Shovel at Barston ◉◉

PICK OF THE PUBS

See Pick of the Pubs on opposite page
See advert below

BIRMINGHAM — Map 10 SP08

The Old Joint Stock

4 Temple Row West B2 5NY ☎ 0121 200 1892
e-mail: oldjointstock@fullers.co.uk
dir: *Opposite main entrance to St Philip's Cathedral, just off Colmore Row*

A former bank, this impressively colonnaded building was originally a library, designed by the same architect as part of St Philip's Cathedral opposite. The high-Victorian Gothic interior incorporates an immense domed ceiling, stately-home fittings and towering mahogany island bar. Speciality pies take up a chunk of the menu, which also features liver and onions; bangers and mash; and bacon and smoked cheddar steakburger. Fuller's, the owner, has developed the second floor as an 80-seat theatre for productions from Shakespeare to fashion shows. A beer festival is held twice yearly.

Open all wk all day (Sun 12-5) **Bar Meals** L served all wk 12-5 D served Mon-Sat 5-10 Av main course £9.50 food served all day **Restaurant** L served all wk 12-5 D served Mon-Sat 5-10 food served all day ⊕ FULLER'S ◀ London Pride, ESB, Discovery. ♟ 16 **Facilities** Children welcome Family room Garden Beer festival Wi-fi ▭

Penny Blacks

132-134 Wharfside St, The Mailbox B1 1RQ
☎ 0121 632 1460
e-mail: info@penny-blacks.com
dir: *In Mailbox district in city centre. Nearest station: Birmingham New Street*

Part of the regenerated Mailbox area of Birmingham, a short walk from the National Indoor Arena and Symphony Hall, this large canalside bar has a traditional pub feel with a warm and welcoming atmosphere. With five to seven real ales on tap and a vast range of wines, it has become a popular meeting place for locals and tourists alike. The bar menu is a mix of pub classics and modern British dishes, from bar bites, sharing plates, pies or speciality sausages with a choice of mash, to steaks, fish and chips and vegetarian options. There is also a restaurant, a wine bar, sporting events on TV, and a DJ on Thursday, Friday and Saturday night.

Open all day all wk Closed: 25-26 Dec, 1 Jan ⊕ FREE HOUSE/CROPTHORNE INNS ◀ Wyre Piddle, Hook Norton, St Austell, Church End, Cottage, Wentworth, Slater's. **Facilities** Children welcome Children's menu Children's portions Garden Wi-fi

THE MALT SHOVEL AT BARSTON

A delightful village pub a short hop from Birmingham, set in the Solihull countryside. The Malt Shovel is a bustling, award-winning free house with modern soft furnishings and interesting artifacts. Natural wood and pastel colours characterise the interiors of this converted early 20th-century mill building. The bar is charming and relaxed with winter log fires, and a beautiful garden for summer alfresco dining. The restaurant is housed in an adjacent stylishly converted barn.

Food is cooked to order with imaginative, modern British dishes making the best of fresh seasonal ingredients. The seafood menu includes seared Scottish scallops on pea purée, Colnakilty black pudding, crisp bacon; mildly spiced king prawns, passion fruit and chilli sauce, cracker salad; or the well known salmon fishcake on spinach, fresh farm poached egg, tarragon hollandaise. Followed by grilled plaice, roast sweet potato, crab and black Tuscan olive oil dressing; Cornish wild turbot with shelled mussels, crayfish, samphire and saffron broth; or lamb slow roasted in Thai spices with coconut milk, pickled ginger, spring onion & rice.

Temptingly ended by raspberry Eton mess; strawberry trio – wild strawberry torte, jelly and ice cream; or pear, rum and raison brioche bread and butter pudding!

Barston Lane, Barston, Solihull, B92 0JP
Tel/fax: 01675 443 223 • Mobile: 07968 784 985
www.themaltshovelatbarston.com

Save on hotels. Book at **theAA.com/hotel**

WEST MIDLANDS 543 **ENGLAND**

PICK OF THE PUBS

The Malt Shovel at Barston 🌸🌸

BARSTON Map 10 SP27

Barston Ln B92 0JP ☎ 01675 443223
web: www.themaltshovelatbarston.com
dir: *M42 junct 5, A4141 towards Knowle.*
Left into Jacobean Ln, right at T-junct
(Hampton Ln). Left into Barston Ln,
0.5m

Sitting comfortably in the countryside and safely outside Birmingham's motorway box, the award-winning Malt Shovel is an airy, well-designed free house with modern soft furnishings and interesting artefacts. Natural wood and pastel colours characterise the interiors of this stylishly converted early 20th-century mill building, and flowers decorate the unclothed tables in the tiled dining area. The bar is cosy and relaxed with winter log fires, there's an attractive garden for alfresco summer dining, and the restaurant is located in the adjacent converted barn. Head chef Max Murphy is proud of the pub's two AA Rosettes, and meals are freshly prepared and stylishly presented. The extensive choice of modern British dishes makes the best of fresh seasonal ingredients, and the daily fish specials board is popular with lovers of seafood. A quick canter through the imaginative menu finds starters like breaded brie with pear and apricot chutney; charred red pepper tartlet with Serrano ham, mozzarella and pine nuts; and seared peppered tuna with celeriac, horseradish and enoki mushrooms. Main course dishes are just as appetising: try baked cod on beetroot and potato gratin with English asparagus and Lincolnshire smoked bacon; venison with green beans, creamed mash and quince jus; or gnocchi with Shiraz roasted tomatoes, basil, olives and rocket. The dessert menu doesn't disappoint, with flavours as varied as raspberry and hibiscus flower cheesecake with pannacotta ice cream; pear, rum and raisin brioche and butter pudding with vanilla bean custard; and dark chocolate meringue pie with pecan honeycomb. Finally, a board of English and European cheeses with grapes, celery, apple and sultana chutney and crispbread will fill any remaining corners. Booking for meals may be required.

Open all day all wk **Bar Meals** L served Mon-Sat 12-2.30, Sun 12-4 D served Mon-Sat 6-9.30 Av main course £13.95 **Restaurant** L served Sun 12-4 D served Mon-Sat 7-9.30 Av 3 course à la carte fr £28.95 ⊕ FREE HOUSE ◀ St Austell Tribute, M&B Brew XI, Timothy Taylor Landlord. ♛ 10 **Facilities** Garden Parking

CHADWICK END   Map 10 SP27

The Orange Tree

PICK OF THE PUBS

Warwick Rd B93 0BN ☎ **01564 785364**
e-mail: theorangetree@lovelypubs.co.uk
dir: 3m from Knowle towards Warwick

A destination dining pub that ticks all the right boxes, The Orange Tree is one of a small and select chain of comfy, chic pubs in the West Midlands owned by Paul Salisbury and Paul Hales. Chunky wooden furniture, airy interiors dappled with prints on thick walls supporting old beams all meld easily with a labyrinth of more traditional rustic, pubby corners with leather sofas in quiet alcoves, log fires, antique-style mirrors and colour-washed walls creating an inviting ambience. The dining experience is summed up as 'simple but up-to-the-minute' and encapsulates a good range such as sharing plates, pizzas and pastas from the stone-fired ovens together with modern European and global dishes. Tempura soft-shelled crab with calamari, Asian slaw and mirin dressing is a typical starter, possibly followed by lamb pavé with butternut ratatouille, spring onion sauce and apple and mint jelly. Summer diners can indulge in a feast on the sunny patio or amidst landscaped gardens in the tranquil countryside. Booking for meals may be required.

Open all day all wk 11-11 Closed: 25 Dec **Bar Meals** L served Mon-Sat 12-2.30, Sun 12-7 D served Mon-Sat 6-9.30 **Restaurant** L served Mon-Sat 12-2.30, Sun 12-7 D served Mon-Sat 6-9.30 ⊕ FREE HOUSE ◀ Fuller's London Pride, Purity Pure UBU. ☕ 10 **Facilities** ❤ Children welcome Children's portions Play area Garden Parking Wi-fi ▭ (notice required)

HAMPTON IN ARDEN   Map 10 SP28

The White Lion Inn

PICK OF THE PUBS

10 High St B92 0AA ☎ **01675 442833**
e-mail: info@thewhitelioninn.com
dir: Opposite church

Originally a farmhouse, this 17th-century timber-framed pub has been licensed since at least 1836. Landlord Chris Roach and partner FanFan draw on their considerable experience from managing (and, of course, visiting) many restaurants, bistros and gastro-pubs in England and France. The bright and modern interior is wood floored, decorated with fresh flowers and furnished with wicker chairs. The simple bistro-style, seasonal menu nods fairly vigorously across the English Channel, with items like black pudding St Malo; blanquette de veau (veal ragout) with rice; and coq au vin. Non-Gallic finds are likely to include Scottish sirloin and fillet steaks; calves' liver, bacon and onions; fish and other daily specials; and mushroom, cherry tomato and pepper

risotto. There are also sandwiches (toasted if preferred) and jacket potatoes. The traditional Sunday lunches are a must. The bar offers a good selection of real ales and ciders, including Brew XI, Mad Goose, Tribute and Doom Bar.

Open all day all wk noon-12.30am (Sun 12-10.30) **Bar Meals** L served all wk 12-2.30 D served all wk 6.30-9.30 **Restaurant** L served all wk 12-2.30 D served all wk 6.30-9.30 ⊕ PUNCH TAVERNS ◀ M&B Brew XI, Purity Mad Goose, St Austell Tribute, Sharp's Doom Bar, Hobsons ♂ Westons Stowford Press, Aspall. **Facilities** ❤ Children welcome Children's menu Children's portions Garden Parking Wi-fi ▭ (notice required)

OLDBURY   Map 10 SO98

Waggon & Horses

PICK OF THE PUBS

17a Church St B69 3AD ☎ **0121 552 5467**
e-mail: andrew.gale.17a@hotmail.com
dir: Telephone for directions

Tucked away in the remnants of the old town centre, the Waggon & Horses is a Grade II listed Victorian pub. It's popular with shoppers and office workers who come to see the ornate tiled walls, the lovely copper-panelled ceiling, the fine Holts Brewery etched windows, and the huge tie collection in the splendid back bar. The side room has big old tables and high-backed settles, where you can also enjoy freshly prepared hot and cold pub food and bar snacks at lunch and in the evening. Ale drinkers can sup contentedly as the choice is good, including Brains, Holden's Golden Glow, Salopian Shropshire Gold and guest ales.

Open all wk Closed: Sun eve in winter **Bar Meals** L served Mon-Sat 12-2.30 D served Tue-Fri 5.30-7.30 ⊕ BRAINS ◀ Brains, Salopian Shropshire Gold & Oracle, Holden's Golden Glow, Guest ale. **Facilities** Children welcome Children's portions Family room Parking ▭

SEDGLEY   Map 10 SO99

Beacon Hotel & Sarah Hughes Brewery

PICK OF THE PUBS

129 Bilston St DY3 1JE ☎ **01902 883380**
dir: Telephone for directions

Home of the Sarah Hughes Brewery and the famous Dark Ruby Mild, the Beacon Hotel is a restored Victorian tap house that has barely changed in 150 years. Proprietor John Hughes reopened the adjoining Sarah Hughes Brewery in 1987, 66 years after his grandmother became the licensee. The rare snob-screened island bar serves a simple taproom, with its old wall benches and a fine blackened range; a super cosy snug replete with a green-tiled marble fireplace, dark woodwork, velvet curtains and huge old tables; and a large smoke-room with an adjoining, plant-festooned conservatory. On a

tour of the brewery you can see the original grist case and rare open-topped copper that add to the Victorian charm and give unique character to the brews. Flagship beers are Sarah Hughes Dark Ruby, Surprise and Amber, with seasonal bitter and two guest beers from small micro-breweries also available. Food in the pub is limited to filled cob rolls but there is a designated children's room and play area, as well as a large garden.

Open all wk 12-2.30 5.30-11 (Fri 12-3 Sat-12-3 6-11 Sun 12-3 7-10.30) **Bar Meals** food served all day ⊕ FREE HOUSE ◀ Sarah Hughes Dark Ruby, Sedgley Surprise & Amber, Guest ales. **Facilities** Children welcome Play area Family room Garden Parking ▭ **Notes** ⊛

WEST BROMWICH   Map 10 SP09

The Vine

Roebuck St B70 6RD ☎ **0121 553 2866**
e-mail: bharat@thevine.co.uk
dir: 0.5m from M5 junct 1.2m from town centre

Well-known, family-run business renowned for its excellent curries and cheap drinks. Since 1978 the typically Victorian alehouse has provided the setting for Suresh 'Suki' Patel's eclectic menu. Choose from a comprehensive range of Indian dishes (lamb rajastani, goat curry, chicken methi), a barbecue menu and Thursday spit-roast, offered alongside traditional pub fare like sandwiches, jacket potatoes and toasties. The Vine boasts the Midlands' only indoor tandoori barbeque, plus it is a stone's throw from The Hawthorns, West Bromwich Albion's football ground.

Open all wk (Fri-Sun all day) **Bar Meals** L served Mon-Fri 11.30-2.30, Sat-Sun 12-10.30 D served Mon-Fri 5-10.30, Sat-Sun 12-10.30 **Restaurant** L served Mon-Fri 11.30-2.30, Sat-Sun 12-10.30 D served Mon-Fri 5-10.30, Sat-Sun 12-10.30 Av 3 course à la carte fr £12 ⊕ FREE HOUSE ◀ Bathams, Holden's, Wye Valley, Burton Bridge. **Facilities** Children welcome Garden ▭ (notice required)

Save on hotels. Book at **theAA.com/hotel**

WIGHT, ISLE OF 545 ENGLAND

WIGHT, ISLE OF

ARRETON
Map 5 SZ58

The White Lion

Main Rd PO30 3AA ☎ 01983 528479
e-mail: chrisandkatieiow@hotmail.co.uk
web: www.white-lion-arreton.com
dir: *B3056 (Newport to Sandown road)*

Fast approaching its 300th birthday, this former coaching inn sits in the old part of the village in an outstandingly beautiful conservation area. Expect a warm welcome amid oak beams, polished brass and open fires. An outside seating area enjoys views of the Arreton scenery. Well-kept ales and pub grub are served all day, ranging from traditional treats such as whitebait through to Mexican fajitas and Indonesian nasi goreng. Ask about the small window in the corner of the bar and the Arreton ghost walk.

Open all day all wk **Bar Meals** L served all wk 12-9 D served all wk 12-9 food served all day **Restaurant** L served all wk 12-9 D served all wk 12-9 food served all day ⊕ ENTERPRISE INNS ◀ Sharp's Doom Bar, Timothy Taylor Landlord Ō Westons Stowford Press, Thatchers Pear. **Facilities** ❖ Children welcome Children's menu Children's portions Family room Garden Parking ▥

BEMBRIDGE
Map 5 SZ68

The Crab & Lobster Inn ★★★★ INN

32 Forelands Field Rd PO35 5TR ☎ 01983 872244
e-mail: info@crabandlobsterinn.co.uk
dir: *From Bembridge village, 1st left after Boots onto Forelands Rd to Windmill Hotel. Left onto Lane End Rd, 2nd right onto Egerton Rd, left onto Howgate Rd & immediately right onto Forelands Field Rd*

Adorned with summer flower baskets and troughs, this Victorian spirit merchant's inn sports a fine beamed interior, whilst the stunning coastal location beside Bembridge Ledge means the raised deck and patio is the

place to sup Wight-brewed Goddards Fuggle-Dee-Dum bitter, idly watching yachts and fishing boats. Locally caught seafood is one of the pub's great attractions, with dishes such whole lobster, chilli penne with prawns, battered calamari, and home-made crab cakes. There are meat and vegetarian dishes too, and sandwiches at lunchtime. Some of the light and airy bedrooms have memorable sea views. Booking for meals may be required.

Open all day all wk 11-11 (Sun 11-10.30) **Bar Meals** L served all wk 12-2.30 (summer Sat-Sun & BH 2.30-5.30 limited menu) D served Sun-Thu 6-9, Fri-Sat 6-9.30 Av main course £7-£8 **Restaurant** L served all wk 12-2.30 (summer Sat-Sun & BH 2.30-5.30 limited menu) D served Sun-Thu 6-9, Fri-Sat 6-9.30 ⊕ ENTERPRISE INNS ◀ Sharp's Doom Bar, Goddards Fuggle-Dee-Dum, Greene King IPA, John Smith's Ō Westons Stowford Press. ♟ 12 **Facilities** ❖ Children welcome Children's menu Children's portions Garden Parking Wi-fi **Rooms** 5

The Windmill Inn ★★★★ INN

1 Steyne Rd PO35 5UH ☎ 01983 872875
e-mail: enquiries@windmill-inn.com
dir: *From Sandown take B3395 (Sandown Rd). Straight on at rdbt into Steyne Rd in Bembridge. Inn on right*

Located in the peaceful village of Bembridge, this family-friendly pub with 14 bedrooms offers a wide range of local ales and wines to complement the extensive menus. Not surprisingly, fresh local fish drives the main menu and the daily-changing choice might include Bembridge crab or lobster. There is also a range of pub classics, steaks, burgers, light bites and lunchtime sandwiches. An all-day Sunday carvery is especially popular with families and there is a good children's menu.

Open all day all wk **Bar Meals** L served all wk 11.30-2 D served all wk 5-9 Av main course £6-£15 **Restaurant** L served all wk 12-2 D served all wk 5-9 Av 3 course à la carte fr £14 ⊕ FREE HOUSE ◀ Ringwood Best Bitter, Goddards Fuggle-Dee-Dum & Special Bitter, Greene King IPA, Sharp's Doom Bar Ō Westons Stowford Press. ♟ 12 **Facilities** ❖ Children welcome Children's menu Children's portions Garden Parking Wi-fi ▥ **Rooms** 14

BONCHURCH
Map 5 SZ57

The Bonchurch Inn

Bonchurch Shute PO38 1NU ☎ 01983 852611
e-mail: gillian@bonchurch-inn.co.uk
dir: *Off A3055 in Bonchurch*

Tucked away in a secluded Dickensian-style courtyard, this small family-run free house inn is in a quiet, off the road location. In fact, little has changed here since this former coaching inn and stables was granted its first licence in the 1840s. Food is available lunchtime and evenings in the bar; choices range from sandwiches and salads to plenty of fresh fish and chicken dishes and juicy steaks. Italian specialities are a prominent feature; try the minestrone soup, crab linguine or spinach cannelloni. Desserts also have an Italian bias – perhaps

zabaglione, cassata or tiramisù. Booking for meals may be required.

Open all wk 11-3 6.30-11 Closed: 25 Dec **Bar Meals** L served all wk 12-2 D served all wk 6.30-9 Av main course £14.95 **Restaurant** D served all wk 7-8.45 ⊕ FREE HOUSE ◀ Courage Directors, Best Bitter. **Facilities** ❖ Children welcome Children's menu Children's portions Family room Garden Parking Wi-fi

COWES
Map 5 SZ49

Duke of York Inn ★★★ INN

Mill Hill Rd PO31 7BT ☎ 01983 295171
e-mail: bookings@dukeofyorkcowes.co.uk
dir: *In town centre*

Situated close to the centre of Cowes and the marina, this former coaching inn has been run by the same family for over 40 years. Fittingly, a nautical theme runs throughout this friendly and informal pub, where everyone is welcome, even soggy, wet yachtsmen. Quality home-cooked food is available in the bar and restaurant and includes daily specials, fresh seafood, snacks, roast lunches on Sunday, and pub staples such as lamb cutlets, chicken goujons and cheeseburger. Real ales include Goddards Fuggle-Dee-Dum with real ciders too. Comfortable, individually decorated bedrooms are available. Booking for meals may be required.

Open all day all wk **Bar Meals** L served all wk 12-2.30 D served all wk 6-10 **Restaurant** L served all wk 12-2.30 D served all wk 6-10 ⊕ ENTERPRISE INNS ◀ Goddards Fuggle-Dee-Dum, Sharp's Doom Bar, Ringwood Best Bitter Ō Westons 1st Quality & Old Rosie. **Facilities** ❖ Children welcome Children's menu Children's portions Parking Wi-fi ▥ **Rooms** 13

The Fountain Inn ★★★ INN

High St PO31 7AW ☎ 01983 292397
e-mail: 6447@greeneking.co.uk
dir: *Adjacent to Red Jet passenger ferry in town centre*

On the quay, just yards from the Southampton ferry, with a deck overlooking the harbour, which makes it ideal for boat-watching. American president Thomas Jefferson stayed here in 1789, following a state visit to England. Enjoy a pint of Goddards, the island's only brewery, and something from the extensive menu, such as a steak, lasagne, grilled sea bass, chicken tikka masala, or a chef's special. Nice as Pie is every Tuesday, Get Spicy every Wednesday, and Go for a Sizzler on Thursday. Some of the en suite bedrooms have sea views.

Open all day all wk **Bar Meals** L served all wk 12-9 D served all wk 12-9 food served all day **Restaurant** L served all wk 12-9 D served all wk 12-9 food served all day ⊕ GREENE KING ◀ IPA, Goddards. ♟ **Facilities** ❖ Children welcome Children's menu Children's portions Wi-fi **Rooms** 20

FRESHWATER   Map 5 SZ38

The Red Lion

PICK OF THE PUBS

Church Place PO40 9BP ☎ 01983 754925
dir: *In Old Freshwater follow signs for All Saints Church*

Situated in the centre of the village, there's been a pub on this site since the 11th century, although today's climber-clad red-brick building is more recent. Only a short walk from Yarmouth harbour, it's a popular drinking spot for visiting yachtsmen, as well as walkers and golfers. The garden is well furnished with hardwood chairs and tables, and a canvas dome comes into its own for alfresco dining. The bar is comfortable with settles and chairs around scrubbed pine tables, the log fire burns throughout the winter, and peace and quiet is preferred to music. Much of the produce used in Lorna Mence's filling meals comes from the island; most of the herbs and some of the vegetables are grown in the pub's garden. The light lunch menu includes pub favourites, as well as sandwiches and salads. Old favourites are beef madras, shepherd's pie, and gammon steak, while main course specials include kedgeree, whole grilled plaice, pan-fried scallops wrapped in bacon, and mushroom Stroganoff. Round off the meal with sticky toffee pudding or sherry trifle. Booking for meals may be required.

Open all wk 11.30-3 5.30-11 (Sun 12-3 7-10.30) **Bar Meals** L served all wk 12-2 D served Mon-Sat 6.30-9, Sun 7-9 Av main course £11.50 **Restaurant** L served all wk 12-2 D served Mon-Sat 6.30-9, Sun 7-9 Av 3 course à la carte fr £15 ⊕ ENTERPRISE INNS ◀ Goddards Special Bitter & Fuggle-Dee-Dum, Sharp's Doom Bar ☼ Thatchers. **Facilities** ❉ Garden Parking

GODSHILL   Map 5 SZ58

The Taverners

PICK OF THE PUBS

High St PO38 3HZ ☎ 01983 840707
dir: *Please telephone for directions*

The Taverners has filled many roles in its history, including a tea room reputedly graced by a visit from Queen Victoria. Today's pub is run by islanders Roger Serjent and Lisa Choi, who are committed to producing a high-quality menu while keeping their food and drink miles as low as possible. To this end they grow their own vegetables and source as much as they can from the island; meat, poultry, eggs and dairy produce all come from within a couple of miles' radius, whilst seafood arrives from nearby Ventnor and Bembridge. They even advertise for home-grown fruit and vegetables, so local growers drop by to sell their fresh produce. Traditional choices from the menu could be beef and ale pie; or dry-cured ham with eggs and hand-cut chips. The specials board has a selection of dishes made from seasonal produce, and is only written once the deliveries have arrived. An in-pub shop sells home-made food items from the kitchen, fine wines, and island products. In the garden is a toddlers' play area. Booking for meals may be required.

Open all day all wk Closed: 1st 3wks Jan **Bar Meals** L served all wk 12-3 D served Sun-Thu 6-9, Fri-Sat 6-9.30 Av main course £11 **Restaurant** L served all wk 12-3 D served Sun-Thu 6-9, Fri-Sat 6-9.30 Av 3 course à la carte fr £22 ⊕ PUNCH TAVERNS ◀ Taverners Own, Sharp's Doom Bar, Brains The Rev. James, Black Sheep, Butcombe ☼ Westons Stowford Press, Godshill. ♉ 10 **Facilities** ❉ Children welcome Children's menu Children's portions Play area Garden Parking ☷ (notice required)

HULVERSTONE   Map 5 SZ38

The Sun Inn at Hulverstone

Main Rd PO30 4EH ☎ 01983 741124
e-mail: lesleyblanchard@btconnect.com
dir: *Between Mottistone & Brook on B3399*

Once a haunt for smugglers, this 600-year-old pub and restaurant in beautiful countryside has a huge beer garden and an outstanding sea view. Before Mark and Lesley Blanchard bought it in 2009, it nearly became a private house, a move forestalled by local opposition and strong council backing. The menu relies on island-raised lamb, Aberdeen Angus beef, free-range rare breed pigs and locally caught fish for home-made burgers, chillis and curries; beer-battered fish of the day; and hand-cut ham with local free-range eggs. Wight brewery Goddards supplies the beers. Booking for meals may be required.

Open all day all wk **Bar Meals** L served all wk 12-9 D served all wk 12-9 food served all day **Restaurant** L served all wk 12-9 D served all wk 12-9 food served all day ⊕ ENTERPRISE INNS ◀ Ringwood Fortyniner, Goddards Fuggle-Dee-Dum, Adnams Southwold Bitter, Otter Ale ☼ Weston Stowford Press. **Facilities** ❉ Children welcome Children's portions Garden Parking Wi-fi ☷ (notice required)

NINGWOOD   Map 5 SZ38

Horse & Groom

Main Rd PO30 4NW ☎ 01983 760672
e-mail: info@horse-and-groom.com
dir: *On A3054 (Yarmouth to Newport road)*

This large family-friendly pub is a landmark on the Newport road, just a couple of miles west of Yarmouth. There's a nice garden with a large children's play area, and four-footed family members are also welcome on the stone and wood floored indoor areas. Food is served daily from noon until 9pm, and the offering ranges from baguettes and light bites to pub favourites like beef and local ale pie, battered fish and chips, and locally made sausages with mash and onion gravy, plus a specials board offering seasonal specialities. There is a real ale festival each September. Booking for meals may be required.

Open all day all wk **Bar Meals** L served all wk 12-9 D served all wk 12-9 Av main course £9 food served all day **Restaurant** L served all wk 12-9 D served all wk 12-9 food served all day ⊕ ENTERPRISE INNS ◀ Ringwood, Goddards. ♉ 15 **Facilities** ❉ Children welcome Children's

menu Children's portions Play area Garden Beer festival Parking Wi-fi ☷ (notice required)

NITON   Map 5 SZ57

Buddle Inn

St Catherines Rd PO38 2NE ☎ 01983 730243
e-mail: sayhi@buddleinn.co.uk
dir: *Take A3055 from Ventnor. In Niton take 1st left signed 'to the lighthouse'*

Flanked by the English Channel on one side and the coastal path on the other, this 16th-century, former cliff-top farmhouse is one of the island's oldest hostelries. Popular with hikers and ramblers (and their muddy boots), the interior has the full traditional complement - stone flags, oak beams and a large open fire, plus great real ales on tap. Expect hearty home-made food such as home-made pâté with red onion compôte followed by home-made steak-and-ale pie with a choice of potatoes and gravy. Two beer festivals a year.

Open all day all wk 11-11 (Fri-Sat 11am-mdnt Sun 12-10.30) **Bar Meals** L served all wk 12-9 D served all wk 12-9 Av main course £10 food served all day **Restaurant** L served all wk 12-9 D served all wk 12-9 food served all day ⊕ ENTERPRISE INNS ◀ Buddle Best, Fuller's London Pride, Adnams ☼ Thatchers Gold. ♉ 8 **Facilities** Children welcome Children's menu Children's portions Family room Garden Beer festival Parking Wi-fi ☷ (notice required)

NORTHWOOD   Map 5 SZ49

Travellers Joy

85 Pallance Rd PO31 8LS ☎ 01983 298024
e-mail: tjoy@globalnet.co.uk
dir: *Telephone for directions*

Ruth, Derek and Andy run this 300-year-old alehouse, just a little way inland from Cowes. They keep eight real ales on handpump all year round, including St Austell Tribute, Island Ales Wight Gold and Timothy Taylor Landlord. Don't expect dishes described on the menu as 'drizzled' or 'pan-roasted' here because the food is home cooked and uncomplicated but with all the trimmings — ham, egg and chips; chicken burger; breaded plaice; vegetarian pasta. Sandwiches, baguettes and jacked potatoes are lighter options. Children's portions are available. Outside is a pétanque terrain and pets' corner.

Open all wk 12-2.30 5-11 (Fri-Sun 12-11.30) **Bar Meals** L served all wk 12-2 D served all wk 6.30-9.30 Av main course £7.70 ⊕ FREE HOUSE ◀ Island Wight Gold, Courage Directors, Caledonian Deuchars IPA, St Austell Tribute, Timothy Taylor Landlord. **Facilities** ❉ Children welcome Children's menu Children's portions Family room Garden Parking ☷ (notice required)

PICK OF THE PUBS

The Seaview Hotel & Restaurant ★★★HL

SEAVIEW　　　　　　　　　Map 5 SZ69

High St PO34 5EX ☎ 01983 612711
e-mail: reception@seaviewhotel.co.uk
web: www.seaviewhotel.co.uk
dir: *B3330 from Ryde, left signed*
Puckpool, along seafront, hotel on left

The Pump Bar is the hidden gem of the Seaview Hotel. Warm and welcoming, it is perfect for ladies who lunch, old friends spinning yarns or families chilling out. The hotel's quiet location just a short stroll from the seafront means that from selected vantage points, particularly The Terrace, there are fantastic views of the Solent. The Pump Bar's décor reflects the seaside location with a quirky selection of lobster pots, oars, masts and other nautical memorabilia. At the bar you'll find Isle of Wight ales and a wide range of spirits and liqueurs, plus 'healthier options'. There's also an extensive menu featuring ingredients from the hotel's own farm. Expect a pleasing mix of traditional and innovative dishes, including locally caught fresh fish and seafood specials – maybe a crab ramekin with ciabatta croûtons followed by roasted sea bass with braised fennel, saffron potatoes and bouillabaisse sauce. Other choices could include local beef tartare with beef tea and dill pickle ahead of a main course of slow-cooked ox cheek and tongue with fondant potato and creamed celeriac. There's also a selection of 'Seaview classics' including breaded wholetail scampi with chips and salad; and venison sausages with creamed potato and onion. A decent selection of meat-free options might include chicory and pear salad with pear purée, pickled girolles and white wine jelly; and roasted vegetable risotto with tomato confit and parmesan. Classic desserts like sticky toffee pudding with caramel and pecan nut sauce and vanilla ice cream or vanilla pannacotta with spiced pineapple purée and froth round things off nicely. Booking for meals may be required.

Open all wk 11-3 6-11 **Bar Meals** L served all wk 12-2.30 D served all wk 6.30-9.30 **Restaurant** L served all wk 12-2.30 D served all wk 6.30-9.30 ⊕ FREE HOUSE ◗◼ Ventnor Golden Bitter, Goddards, Guest ale ⵗ Westons Stowford Press. **Facilities** Children welcome Children's portions **Rooms** 28

PICK OF THE PUBS

The New Inn

SHALFLEET   Map 5 SZ48

Main Rd PO30 4NS ☎ 01983 531314
e-mail: info@thenew-inn.co.uk
web: www.thenew-inn.co.uk
dir: *6m from Newport to Yarmouth on A3054*

Set on the National Trust-owned Newtown River estuary, this charming whitewashed pub is an absolute mecca for yachties. One of the island's best-known dining pubs, its name reflects how it rose phoenix-like from the charred remains of an older inn, which burnt down in 1743; original inglenook fireplaces, flagstone floors and low-beamed ceilings give it bags of character. The waterside location sets the tone for the menu; the pub has a reputation for excellent seafood dishes, with lobster and cracked local crab usually available. Daily specials are chalked on blackboards around the place. Further fish options may include seafood royale (a gargantuan fish and shellfish platter); the New Inn fish pie; and grilled fillets of sole with roasted leek and truffle oil. Meat lovers could try black pudding with bacon and stilton salad followed by slow-roasted belly pork with caramelised onion and red sage. Vegetarians can enjoy the likes of goat's cheese tartlet with tomato and thyme chutney; and gnocchi with roasted butternut squash, garlic,

rosemary, fresh parmesan and local cream. International influences are evident in dishes such as spiced swordfish steak with pak choi and roasted rice, or lamb steak with Moroccan-style bean salad. There's also a list of dishes for 'smaller appetites', including local sausage with chips and peas; hand-sliced ham with egg and chips; and beer-battered fish and chips – but if it's a light lunch you're seeking, be sure to consider the best-selling crab baguettes. At the bar you'll find Goddards Fuggle-Dee-Dum and Greene King among others, and over 60 worldwide wines comprise one of the island's most extensive selections. Booking for meals may be required.

Open all day all wk **Bar Meals** L served all wk 12-2.30 D served all wk 6-9.30 Av main course £12 **Restaurant** L served all wk 12-2.30 D served all wk 6-9.30 ⊕ ENTERPRISE INNS ◀ Bass, Goddards Fuggle-Dee-Dum, Greene King IPA, Marston's Pedigree ♂ Westons Stowford Press. ☙ 11 **Facilities** Children welcome Children's portions ❧ Garden Parking Wi-fi

Save on hotels. Book at **theAA.com/hotel**

WIGHT, ISLE OF – WILTSHIRE 549 **ENGLAND**

| ROOKLEY | Map 5 SZ58 |

The Chequers

Niton Rd PO38 3NZ ☎ 01983 840314
e-mail: richard@chequersinn-iow.co.uk
dir: *Telephone for directions*

Surrounded by farms in the centre of the island, this family-friendly country free house with log fires and a large garden has a reputation for good food at reasonable prices. Choose from jackets, sandwiches, cold platters, light bites, grilled meats, the carvery or the main menu. Favourites are steak, mushroom and ale pie; Bembridge crab and clam tagliatelle verdi; or pan-seared tuna steak. There are also plenty of choices for children, who get their own menu. There's a wide range of ice creams for dessert. Check out the date for the next beer festival.

Open all day all wk **Bar Meals** food served all day **Restaurant** food served all day ⊕ FREE HOUSE ◀ Ringwood Best Bitter & Fortyniner, Guest ales Ö Thatchers. ℗ **Facilities** ♣ Children welcome Children's menu Children's portions Play area Family room Garden Beer festival Parking Wi-fi

| SEAVIEW | Map 5 SZ69 |

The Boathouse ★★★★ INN

Springvale Rd PO34 5AW ☎ 01983 810616
e-mail: info@theboathouseiow.co.uk
dir: *From Ryde take A3055. Left onto A3330, left into Puckpool Hill. Pub 0.25m on right*

The Boathouse is in a lovely Edwardian building, painted blue to reflect its spectacular setting on a promenade overlooking the Solent. There are four stylish rooms available, should you want to take further advantage of the views. Well-kept ales and an extensive wine selection complement exciting specials boards that make the most of freshly landed local fish. Other choices include lunchtime baguettes and pub favourites such as ham, eggs and chips; and locally made sausages on chef's special mash. Booking for meals may be required.

Open all day all wk 9-11 **Bar Meals** L served all week 12-2.30 D served all week 6-9.30 Av main course £12 **Restaurant** L served all wk 12-2.30 D served all wk 6-9.30 Fixed menu price fr £17.50 ⊕ PUNCH TAVERNS ◀ Ringwood Best Bitter, Sharp's Doom Bar, Bass, Greene King IPA Ö Westons Stowford Press. ℗ 11 **Facilities** Children welcome Children's portions Garden Parking Wi-fi **Rooms** 4

The Seaview Hotel & Restaurant ★★★ HL ◉

PICK OF THE PUBS

See Pick of the Pubs on page 547

| SHALFLEET | Map 5 SZ48 |

The New Inn

PICK OF THE PUBS

See Pick of the Pubs on opposite page

| SHORWELL | Map 5 SZ48 |

The Crown Inn

PICK OF THE PUBS

Walkers Ln PO30 3JZ ☎ 01983 740293
e-mail: enquiries@crowninnshorwell.co.uk
web: www.crowninnshorwell.co.uk
dir: *Left at top of Carisbrooke High Street. Shorwell approx 6m*

A traditional country pub in a pretty village, parts of The Crown date from the 17th century, although its varying floor levels suggest many subsequent alterations. Log fires and antique furniture abound and if you're lucky you might glimpse the friendly female ghost who seems to disapprove of customers playing cards. Outside are a children's play area and a beautiful stream, whose trout grow fat exclusively for the herons it seems. Six real ales include Sharp's Doom Bar and Adnams Broadside. Good use is made of locally sourced lamb, beef, game and fish on bi-annually revised menus that offer pub staples like fisherman's pie, curry and home-made beef lasagne, while further study reveals a good range of starters (maybe the chef's home-made pâté of the day or traditional prawn cocktail), a selection from the grill, hot and cold sharing platters, pizzas and a vegetarian selection offering the likes of vegetable curry and vegetable kebabs. Booking for meals may be required.

Open all day all wk **Bar Meals** L served all wk 12-9.30 D served all wk 12-9.30 food served all day **Restaurant** L served all wk 12-9.30 D served all wk 12-9.30 food served all day ⊕ ENTERPRISE INNS ◀ Ringwood Fortyniner & Best Bitter, Sharp's Doom Bar, Adnams Broadside, Goddards Ö Westons Stowford Press. ℗ 12 **Facilities** Children welcome Children's menu Children's portions Play area Garden Parking Wi-fi 🚍 (notice required)

| WHIPPINGHAM | Map 5 SZ59 |

The Folly

Folly Ln PO32 6NB ☎ 01983 297171
dir: *Telephone for directions*

The Folly stands beside the River Medina and you can, if you wish, travel here from Cowes on the pub's own waterbus. In the bar are timbers from the hull of an old barge, and even the restaurant tables are named after boats. The menus offer a wide choice of sandwiches and wraps, jacket potatoes, gourmet burgers, and classics like beef and ale pie; breaded wholetail Scottish scampi; pan-seared Barbary duck; and spinach and ricotta cannelloni. There is a large beer garden and patio, and a sheltered area.

Open all day all wk ⊕ GREENE KING ◀ IPA, Morland Old Speckled Hen, Goddards Special Bitter Ö Aspall. **Facilities** Children welcome Children's menu Children's portions Garden Parking

| WILTSHIRE | |
| ALDBOURNE | Map 5 SU27 |

The Blue Boar

20 The Green SN8 2EN ☎ 01672 540237
e-mail: blueboar.green@btconnect.com
dir: *From Salisbury take B4192 to Aldbourne. Or M4 junct 14 take A338 to Hungerford, B4192 to Aldbourne & follow brown signs*

A traditional, 16th-century pub with two open fires, The Blue Boar serves Wadworth and regularly-changing guest ales from a perfect location on the village green. Eating outside is a joy, with views of beautiful houses, the church and a Celtic cross. Typical home-prepared food includes baked camembert; ratatouille pancake; and steak-and-kidney pie. The bar menu has sandwiches, filled jackets and pub classics. Beer festivals are held in April and October. Enthusiasts periodically relive the days of the American 'Screaming Eagles', who were billeted in Aldbourne from 1941 to 1945 and used the pub as the officers' mess. Booking for meals may be required.

Open all wk 11.30-3 5.30-11 (Fri-Sun 11.30-11) **Bar Meals** L served all wk 12-2 D served all wk 6.30-9.30 **Restaurant** L served Mon-Fri 12-2, Sat-Sun 12-2.30 D served all wk 6.30-9.30 ⊕ WADWORTH ◀ 6X & Henry's Original IPA, Guest ales Ö Westons Stowford Press. **Facilities** Children welcome Children's portions Garden Beer festival Wi-fi 🚍

PICK OF THE PUBS

Red Lion Inn

AXFORD Map 5 SU27

SN8 2HA ☎ 01672 520271
e-mail: info@redlionaxford.com
web: www.redlionaxford.com
dir: *M4 junct 15, A246 Marlborough centre. Follow Ramsbury signs. Inn 3m*

For over 400 years, this eye-catching old inn has welcomed travellers on lanes threading along the Kennet Valley just outside the stirring Georgian town of Marlborough. From the flower-bedecked terrace (perfect for alfresco summer dining), divine views percolate to the river and this most peaceful stretch of countryside. It's located in the North Wessex Downs Area of Outstanding Natural Beauty and close to the popular walks in the remarkable, ancient Savernake Forest; ample opportunity to work up an appetite to sate at one of Wiltshire's finest dining inns. Tables and chairs cunningly constructed from half-barrels and squashy, all-too comfortable sofas dot the timeworn parquet flooring of the convivial bar, all beams and boards focussed on a huge inglenook fireplace. Elsewhere, brick and flint feature walls are the backdrop for the well-appointed lounges and Garden Restaurant, offering a choice of dining areas. Settle in with a vintage from the extensive wine list or a glass of own-label Axford Ale from the nearby Ramsbury micro-brewery and consider a menu which is strong on seasonal game and fish dishes with a contemporary

European flavour. In the restaurant, start with twice-baked goat's cheese soufflé with beetroot or perhaps tempura of king prawns in beer batter and chilli dip. Mains that make the most of Wiltshire's larder include braised rabbit with prunes and Madeira, flash-fried calves' liver with caramelised onions and bacon, or slowly braised lamb shank with a rosemary jus. Vegetarian options include home-made caramelised onion and fig tart with smoked cheddar and tomato. Completing the calorie top-up is a daily-changing dessert choice. The bar menu offers steak and Ramsbury ale pie, fish pie and Red Lion Aberdeen Angus burger with French fries, plus a variety of Caesar salads.

Open 12-3 6-11 ⊕ FREE HOUSE
🛢 Ramsbury Axford Ale & Gold, Guest ales ♉ Westons Stowford Press.
Facilities Children welcome Children's portions Garden Parking

Save on hotels. Book at **theAA.com/hotel**

WILTSHIRE 551 ENGLAND

PICK OF THE PUBS

The Kings Arms U

BRADFORD-ON-AVON   Map 4 ST86

Monkton Farleigh BA15 2QH
☎ 01225 858705
e-mail: enquiries@kingsarms-bath.co.uk
web: www.kingsarms-bath.co.uk
dir: *Exit A363 (Bath to Bradford-on-Avon road), follow brown tourist signs to pub*

The origins of this stone-built village inn go back to the 1100s, when a Cluniac Priory was established here; later medieval times are evident in the wonderful mullioned windows, stone doorways and vast inglenook fireplace, allegedly the largest in the county. In the 1880s quarrying for Bath stone began to the north-west of the village, and it was probably then that the building first became an alehouse. Widely known for being haunted, one story involves a ghostly monk who enjoys practical jokes and another features a woman wailing pitifully on the anniversary of her death, caused by her runaway coach crashing into the wall of the pub. A key hanging behind the bar was unearthed recently, but nobody knows what lock it fits, which could be something to ponder while choosing between Butcombe Bitter, St Austell Tribute, a guest ale or an Addlestones or Aspall real cider. The seasonal menus here are locally sourced, with fish and seafood delivered by Kingfisher from Brixham Market in time for lunch, perhaps tempura red

mullet with sweet fennel tart and aubergine caviar as a starter, or popcorn confit chicken with apple and pink fir potato salad, mustard and pea shoots, followed by rosemary- and thyme-crusted lamb cannon, fondant potato and parsnip and vanilla purée; baked hake fillet and yellow lentil, saffron, tarragon and chorizo broth; or beer-battered haloumi, tomato fondue, tartare salad and hand-cut chips. For dessert, try quince pannacotta, oat and raisin biscuit and apple purée; or salted chocolate truffle, hazelnut sablé and Guinness ice cream. The wine list categorises by style, with a fair number by the glass and half bottle. Booking for meals may be required.

Open all wk 12-3 6-11 (Sat-Sun 12-11.30)

Bar Meals L served Mon-Fri 12-3, Sat 12-10, Sun 12-7.30 D served Mon-Fri 6-10, Sat 12-10, Sun 12-7.30 Av main course £10-£12.95 **Restaurant** L served Mon-Fri 12-3, Sat 12-10, Sun 12-7.30 D served Mon-Fri 6-10, Sat 12-10, Sun 12-7.30 Av 3 course à la carte fr £35
⊕ PUNCH TAVERNS ◼ Butcombe Bitter, St Austell Tribute, Guest ale ♂ Addlestones, Aspall. ♟ 17 **Facilities** Children welcome Children's menu ✿ Garden Parking Wi-fi ▭ (notice required) **Rooms** 4

ALDBOURNE *continued*

The Crown Inn

The Square SN8 2DU ☎ 01672 540214
e-mail: bookings@thecrownaldbourne.co.uk
dir: *M4 junct 15, N on A419, signed to Aldbourne*

In the heart of historic Aldbourne in the Marlborough Downs, The Crown overlooks the village square and duck pond. This well-groomed 18th-century inn has a cosy, traditional beamed bar and a comfortable, wooden-floored dining room. A change of hands has ensured The Crown is still very much the village inn and with local Ramsbury Gold on tap, it offers a good selection of home-cooked dishes, from soup and sandwiches to Sunday roasts and a popular tapas menu. The courtyard is a pleasant spot for alfresco summer sipping. Beer festivals are held in May and August.

Open all day all wk 12-12 **Bar Meals** Av main course £8.50 food served all day **Restaurant** Av 3 course à la carte fr £25 food served all day ⊕ ENTERPRISE INNS ◀ Shepherds Neame Spitfire, Ramsbury Gold, Sharp's Doom Bar, Guest ales ♂ Westons Stowford Press, Aspall. ₹ 16 **Facilities** ❤ Children welcome Children's menu Children's portions Play area Garden Beer festival Parking Wi-fi ▭

| AXFORD | Map 5 SU27 |

Red Lion Inn

PICK OF THE PUBS

See Pick of the Pubs on page 550

| BERWICK ST JOHN | Map 4 ST92 |

The Talbot Inn

The Cross SP7 0HA ☎ 01747 828222
dir: *From Shaftesbury take A30 towards Salisbury. Right to Berwick St John. Pub 1.5m*

A typical old English country pub nestling in the beautiful Chalke Valley; the building dates from the 17th century and has the beams, low ceilings and huge inglenook fireplace so typical of its kind. It used to be three cottages, one of them the village shop, before becoming an alehouse in 1835. Real ales plus good home-cooked food shown on the menus and specials board are on offer; try the crispy whitebait, or deep fried brie with redcurrant jelly to start; followed by a Thai or Indian curry; beef or lamb stew with dumplings; or sausages, mash and onion gravy; and for dessert there's nothing better than the sticky toffee pudding and cream. Booking for meals may be required.

Open 12-2.30 6.30-11 (Sun 12-4) Closed: Sun eve & Mon **Bar Meals** L served Tue-Sun 12-2 D served Tue-Sat 6.30-9 Av main course £10.50 ⊕ FREE HOUSE ◀ Ringwood Best Bitter & Fortyniner, Wadworth 6X ♂ Westons Stowford Press. **Facilities** ❤ Children welcome Children's portions Garden Parking

| BISHOPSTONE | Map 5 SU28 |

The Royal Oak **NEW**

Cues Ln SN6 8PH ☎ 01793 790481
e-mail: royaloak@helenbrowningorganics.co.uk
dir: *M4 junct 15, A419 towards Swindon. At rdbt right into Pack Hill signed Wanborough. In Bishopstone left into Cues Ln. Pub on right*

Rescued from closure in 2006 by local organic farmer Helen Browning, the delightfully simple Royal Oak stands tucked away in a glorious village below the Wiltshire Downs. Rustic, relaxed and very friendly, you can expect a cracking community atmosphere, Arkell's ales, roaring logs fires, and interesting, daily-changing menus featuring allotment-grown vegetables and farm-reared meat. For supper, try the pork and partridge terrine with celeriac remoulade, follow with roast gurnard on saffron potatoes with a fennel, curry and mussel broth, and finish with sticky toffee pudding. Book one of the farm safari tours followed by lunch at the pub.

Open all wk 12-3 6-11 (Sat 12-12 Sun 12-10) **Bar Meals** L served all wk 12-3 D served all wk 6-9.30 Av main course £14 **Restaurant** Av 3 course à la carte fr £27 ⊕ ARKELL'S ◀ Moonlight & 3B, Donnington SBA ♂ Westons Old Rosie, Wyld Wood Organic & Perry. **Facilities** ❤ Children welcome Children's menu Children's portions Play area Garden Parking Wi-fi ▭ (notice required)

| BOX | Map 4 ST86 |

The Northey ★★★★★ INN

Bath Rd SN13 8AE ☎ 01225 742333
e-mail: thenorthey@ohhcompany.co.uk
dir: *4m from Bath on A4 towards Chippenham. Between M4 juncts 17 & 18*

This former station hotel was built by Brunel for his workers, who were building a box tunnel when stone was sent up north by train to build houses. These days this stylishly transformed inn with three en suite bedrooms is a favourite in the area for eating and drinking. The interior makes good use of wood and flagstone flooring, high-backed oak chairs, leather loungers and handcrafted tables around the bar, where inviting sandwiches, ciabattas and Italian platters hold sway. The main menu ranges from calves' liver and bacon; rack of spring lamb; pan-fried gnocchi; to the pub's speciality fish dishes and great steaks.

Open all day all wk Closed: 25-26 Dec **Bar Meals** L served all wk 11-6 food served all day **Restaurant** L served all wk 11-6 D served all wk 6-10 food served all day ⊕ WADWORTH ◀ 6X, Warburtons ♂ Westons Stowford Press, Thatchers Gold. ₹ 14 **Facilities** Children welcome Children's menu Children's portions Garden Parking Wi-fi ▭ **Rooms** 3

The Quarrymans Arms

Box Hill SN13 8HN ☎ 01225 743569
e-mail: pub@quarrymans-arms.co.uk
dir: *Telephone for directions*

A display of quarrying memorabilia bears witness to the years Brunel's navvies spent driving the Great Western Railway through Box Tunnel (spot the bar's replica fireplace) deep beneath this 300-year-old pub. The resultant honeycomb of Bath stone workings attract potholers and cavers, who slake their thirsts on local ales and ciders, and replace lost calories with spaghetti carbonara, pork dijonnaise, tuna Niçoise, or something from the comprehensive vegetarian selection. 'Mini ale weeks' are held throughout the year. Superb views of the Box Valley can be enjoyed; from outside you can see Solsbury Hill. Booking for meals may be required.

Open all day all wk 11am-11.30pm **Bar Meals** L served all wk 11-3 D served all wk fr 6 Av main course £10 **Restaurant** L served all wk fr 11 D served all wk fr 6 Av 3 course à la carte fr £16 ⊕ FREE HOUSE ◀ Butcombe Bitter, Wadworth 6X, Moles Best, Local guest ales ♂ Westons Stowford Press, Black Rat. ₹ 13 **Facilities** ❤ Children welcome Children's menu Children's portions Family room Garden Beer festival Parking Wi-fi ▭ (notice required)

| BRADFORD-ON-AVON | Map 4 ST86 |

The Dandy Lion

35 Market St BA15 1LL ☎ 01225 863433
e-mail: Dandylion35@aol.com
dir: *Telephone for directions*

In the centre of the lovely market town of Bradford-on-Avon, this 18th-century inn was once a boot and shoe shop and a grocery. It is now a popular bar and restaurant offering well-kept Wadworth ales and continental lagers, together with a mix of traditional English and rustic European food. The bar menu offers hot filled flatbreads, light bites and 'things on toast', whilst the choice in the upstairs restaurant menu might include chicken Kiev; steak, mushroom and ale pie; and home-baked Wiltshire ham, free-range eggs and triple cooked chips. Booking for meals may be required.

Open all wk 11-3 6-11 (Fri-Sat 11-11 Sun 11.30-10.30) Closed: 25 Dec **Bar Meals** L served all wk 12-2.30 D served all wk 6-9.30 **Restaurant** D served Fri-Sat 7-9.30 ⊕ WADWORTH ◀ 6X, Henry's Original IPA, Seasonal ales ♂ Westons Stowford Press & Wyld Wood Organic. ₹ 21 **Facilities** ❤ Children welcome Children's portions

The Kings Arms ▯

PICK OF THE PUBS

See Pick of the Pubs on page 551

Save on hotels. Book at **theAA.com/hotel**

WILTSHIRE 553 | ENGLAND

PICK OF THE PUBS

The Tollgate Inn ★★★★INN ❀❀

BRADFORD-ON-AVON Map 4 ST86

Holt BA14 6PX ☎ 01225 782326
e-mail: alison@tollgateholt.co.uk
web: www.tollgateholt.co.uk
dir: *M4 junct 18, A46 towards Bath,
then A363 to Bradford-on-Avon, then
B3107 towards Melksham, pub on right*

Standing just off the village green, this
stone-built, part 16th-century
amalgamation of weaving shed and
chapel was a village local when Alex
Venables and Alison Ward-Baptiste
bought it over 12 years ago. They have
transformed it, so much so that it is
now an exemplary country inn offering
top-notch, two-AA Rosette cuisine and
elegant accommodation. Its extensive
grounds include a garden and a
paddock with ever-munching sheep and
goats. The richly furnished, oak-floored
main bar area has a wood-burning
stove and comfy sofas, and serves real
ales from, among others, small local
breweries like Glastonbury and Moles,
and Ashton Press and Lilley's Bee Sting
real ciders. There are two dining rooms,
one upstairs in the original chapel, once
used by the weavers working below.
Here the menu changes daily, always
with an emphasis on local produce
whose provenance is open for
inspection, including hand-reared beef
from the lush pastures of Broughton
Gifford, lamb from Limpley Stoke, pork
from Woolley Farm, game from local
shoots, and vegetables from the fertile
soils around Bromham. Fresh fish is
delivered daily from Brixham in Devon.

Top chef Alex cooks in a modern English
style but with Mediterranean influences
to produce starters of bresaola of home-
cured beef with truffle dressing; and
game terrine. His main courses include
pan-fried chicken breast stuffed with
olives and goat's cheese on tomato
ragout; Cornish fish and mussel hotpot
in creamy saffron sauce; and roasted
vegetable and brie Wellington with
wilted curly kale infused with chilli and
garlic. 'Seasons' deli and farm shop in
the barn alongside sells Alex's recipes
and ingredients for his classic dishes.
Guest rooms are individually styled with
antiques, open fires and oak beams;
from two you can see the Westbury
White Horse, and from the other two,
the village.

Open 11.30-3 5.30-11 (Sun 11.30-3)
Closed: Sun eve **Bar Meals** L served all

wk 12-2 D served Mon-Sat 7-9 Av main
course £14.50 **Restaurant** L served all
wk 12-2 D served Mon-Sat 7-9 Fixed
menu price fr £17.95 Av 3 course à la
carte fr £28 ⊕ FREE HOUSE ◼ Moles
Best, Sharp's Own & Doom Bar,
Glastonbury Mystery Tor, St Austell
♂ Thatchers Traditional, Ashton Press,
Lilley's Bee Sting Pear. ☙ 10
Facilities Children welcome Children's
portions Garden Parking Wi-fi **Rooms** 4

BRADFORD-ON-AVON *continued*

The Tollgate Inn ★★★★ INN ⊚⊚

PICK OF THE PUBS

See Pick of the Pubs on page 553

BRINKWORTH · Map 4 SU08

The Three Crowns

PICK OF THE PUBS

See Pick of the Pubs on opposite page

BROAD CHALKE · Map 5 SU02

The Queens Head Inn

1 North St SP5 5EN ☎ 01722 780344
e-mail: ryan.prince@btinternet.com
dir: *A354 from Salisbury towards Blandford Forum, at Coombe Bissett right towards Bishopstone, pub in 4m*

Located halfway along the Chalke Valley and just eight miles from Salisbury, this former cottage has been the hub of the village for 150 years. Low beams and an open fire add to the cosy ambience in the bar, where well-kept Badger ales are the main attraction. Fresh, locally sourced produce is used to create a traditional and seasonal range of dishes such as pan-fried whole trout glazed with lemon and parsley butter or steak-and-ale pie. Head out to the courtyard in warmer weather. Booking for meals may be required.

Open all wk 11-3 6-11 (Fri 11-3 6-12 Sat 11-11.30 Sun 12-8) **Bar Meals** L served all wk 12-2.30 D served Mon-Sat 7-9.30 **Restaurant** L served all wk 12-2.30 D served Mon-Sat 7-9.30 ⊕ HALL & WOODHOUSE ◀ Badger Dorset Best, Tanglefoot, Hopping Hare, Pickled Partridge, Lemony Cricket, Fursty Ferret, Furkin Fox ♂ Westons Stowford Press. **Facilities** Children welcome Children's menu Children's portions Family room Garden Beer festival Parking Wi-fi ▥ (notice required)

BROUGHTON GIFFORD · Map 4 ST86

The Fox

The Street SN12 8PN ☎ 01225 782949
e-mail: alexgeneen@gmail.com
dir: *From Melksham take B3107 towards Holt. Turn right to Broughton Gifford. Pub in village centre*

Expect lovely ales from Bath, Otter, Butcombe and Fuller's at this village pub, augmented in the summer months when it hosts a beer festival. Food standards are high too. The owners raise their own chickens, ducks and pigs, tend an extensive vegetable and herb garden, and barter with villagers for wildfowl and other produce. From these raw ingredients come highly seasonal dishes and the pub's own bacon, ham, charcuterie and sausages. Typical of the menu are oxtail and leek terrine with sourdough toast; and home-reared pork chop with braised red cabbage.

Open all day all wk **Bar Meals** L served all wk 12-2.30 D served all wk 6.30-9.30 Av main course £15 **Restaurant** L served all wk 12-2.30 D served all wk 6.30-9.30 Fixed menu price fr £14.95 ⊕ FREE HOUSE ◀ Bath Gem, Otter Bitter, Butcombe Bitter, Fuller's London Pride. ♚ 18 **Facilities** Children welcome Children's menu Children's portions Garden Beer festival Parking Wi-fi

---

BURCOMBE · Map 5 SU03

The Ship Inn

Burcombe Ln SP2 0EJ ☎ 01722 743182
e-mail: theshipburcombe@mail.com
web: www.theshipburcombe.co.uk
dir: *In Burcombe, off A30, 1m from Wilton & 5m W of Salisbury*

A 17th-century village pub with low ceilings, oak beams and a large open fire. In summer the riverside garden is where you'd enjoy a leisurely meal in the company of the resident ducks. Seasonal menu examples include braised lamb shank with creamy garlic and rosemary mash, and Savoy cabbage; pan-seared lamb's liver with crispy bacon, mash and green beans; chicken casserole with mushrooms, shallots, herbed fries and bacon and red wine; and mixed seafood risotto. In the bar Wadworth 6X, Ringwood Best and Butcombe hold the fort on hand-pull.

Open all wk 11-3 6-11 **Bar Meals** L served all wk 12-2.30 D served all wk 6-9 Av main course £13 **Restaurant** L served all wk 12-2.30 D served all wk 6-9 Av 3 course à la carte fr £23 ⊕ ENTERPRISE INNS ◀ Wadworth 6X, Ringwood Best Bitter, Butcombe. ♚ 9 **Facilities** ♨ Children welcome Children's menu Children's portions Garden Parking Wi-fi ▥

BURTON · Map 4 ST87

The Old House at Home ★★★★★ INN

SN14 7LT ☎ 01454 218227
e-mail: office@ohhcompany.co.uk
dir: *On B4039 NW of Chippenham*

This ivy-clad, stone built free house dates from the early 19th century and is one of three run by the Warburton family; dad David has been here for years and still happily pulls pints of Maiden Voyage, Wadworth 6X and Thatchers Gold in the low-beamed bar. The finest seasonal ingredients are used to create impressive menu favourites like spiced salmon and crab cakes; guinea fowl with apricot stuffing; moules marinière; and vegetable pie. The beautifully landscaped gardens feature a waterfall. Six high quality bedrooms are available in a stylish annexe.

Open all day all wk **Bar Meals** L served all wk 12-9.30 food served all day **Restaurant** L served all wk 12-9.30 food served all day ⊕ FREE HOUSE ◀ Ales of Scilly Maiden Voyage, Wadworth 6X, Guest ales ♂ Thatchers Gold & Traditional. ♚ 12 **Facilities** ♨ Children welcome Children's menu Children's portions Garden Parking Wi-fi ▥ (notice required) **Rooms** 6

COLLINGBOURNE DUCIS · Map 5 SU25

The Shears Inn

The Cadley Rd SN8 3ED ☎ 01264 850304
e-mail: info@theshears.co.uk
dir: *Just off A338 between Marlborough & Salisbury*

Dating from the 18th century, this traditional family-run country inn was once a shearing shed for market-bound sheep. The original part of the building is thatched, while inside you'll find wooden and slate floors, low-beamed ceilings and a large inglenook dominating the restaurant. Typical choices from the tasty modern British menu may include beer-battered haggis and black pudding; honey and watercress sausages and mash; and lemon posset with raspberry shortbread. The enclosed sunny garden is an ideal venue for the annual beer festival held in early June. Booking for meals may be required.

Open 11-3 6-11 (Sat 11-11 summer, Sun fr 12) Closed: Sun eve **Bar Meals** L served Mon-Sat 12-2, Sun 12-3.30 D served Mon-Sat 6-9.30 Av main course £9-£12 **Restaurant** L served Mon-Sat 12-2, Sun 12-3.30 D served Mon-Fri 7-9.15, Sat 7-9.30 Av 3 course à la carte fr £27.50 ⊕ BRAKSPEAR ◀ Bitter, Wychwood Hobgoblin, Guest ales ♂ Westons Wyld Wood Organic. ♚ 12 **Facilities** ♨ Children welcome Children's portions Garden Beer festival Parking Wi-fi ▥

Save on hotels. Book at **theAA.com/hotel**

WILTSHIRE 555 ENGLAND

PICK OF THE PUBS

The Three Crowns

BRINKWORTH　　　　　Map 4 SU08

SN15 5AF ☎ 01666 510366
e-mail: allyson@threecrowns.co.uk
web: www.threecrowns.co.uk
dir: *From Swindon take A3102 to Royal Wootton Bassett, take B4042, 5m to Brinkworth*

Lots of greenery inside and out here, with the conservatory restaurant festooned with potted plants and the little village green fronting this traditional old inn. The village sits in rich farming countryside on a low ridge above the River Avon; glimpses of Daunstey Vale catch the eye from the pub's secluded beer garden and tree-shaded patio, where heaters bring additional comfort as the evenings draw in. It's a thriving community pub, hosting locals and their dogs, the local hunt when it meets, and families set on celebrating a special occasion. Amiable staff greet you in the beamed, fire-warmed old bar, where ales include one brewed by proprietors Anthony and Allyson Windle's sister establishment, the Weighbridge Brewhouse in Swindon. Wine is another of Anthony's specialities; great pride has gone into selecting the carte of over 80 bottles, all tasted and approved by the owner. The menu has long been recognised for its ambition and variety. The lunch list includes the classic ploughman's, but hot dishes of venison faggots, traditional bangers and mash, and home-made curries are difficult to resist. In the evening, choices will warm the hearts of the adventurous and the hungry: strips of crocodile are marinaded in the pub's blend of Thai spices, then steam-fried with lime and fresh ginger; wild boar is cooked on the griddle and served with a shallot and sun-dried apricot sauce. For those with more conventional tastes, home-made pies include steak and kidney, veal and mushroom, and minted lamb. For fish lovers, a fillet of North Atlantic cod is gently poached in Italian vermouth with fresh basil, leeks and diced tomatoes. Generously calorific puddings round off a meal to remember. Booking for meals may be required.

Open all day all wk 10am-mdnt Closed: 25-26 Dec **Bar Meals** L served Mon-Sat

12-2, Sun 12-9 D served Mon-Sat 6-9.30, Sun 12-9 **Restaurant** L served Mon-Sat 12-2, Sun 12-9 D served Mon-Sat 6-9.30, Sun 12-9 ⊕ ENTERPRISE INNS ◀ Greene King IPA, Timothy Taylor Landlord, Weighbridge Ŏ Westons Stowford Press. ♀ 27 **Facilities** Children welcome Children's menu Children's portions Play area ❤ Garden Parking Wi-fi

CORTON — Map 4 ST94

The Dove Inn ★★★ INN ⊛

PICK OF THE PUBS

See Pick of the Pubs on opposite page

CRICKLADE — Map 5 SU09

The Red Lion Inn NEW

74 High St SN6 6DD ☎ 01793 750776
e-mail: info@theredlioninncricklade.co.uk
web: www.theredlioninncricklade.co.uk
dir: *M4 junct 15, A419 towards Cirencester. Left onto B4040 into Cricklade. Right at T-junct (mini-rdbt) into High St. Inn on right*

Situated just off the Thames Path as it passes through historic Cricklade, this early-17th-century pub's many historic features are instrumental in creating a classic atmosphere. A micro-brewery in the garden will soon augment the bar line-up of ten real ales and ciders. Home-prepared restaurant food is noteworthy for using locally foraged and wild ingredients, rare-breed meats and sustainable fish. Try Gloucester Old Spot pork chop, or pan-fried grey mullet, and look out for a revival of forgotten cuts of meat. It's the first weekend in June for the beer festival.

Open all day all wk **Bar Meals** L served Mon-Sat 12-2.30, Sun 12-3 D served Mon-Thu 6.30-9 Av main course £9.50 **Restaurant** L served Mon-Sat 12-2.30, Sun 12-3 D served Tue-Thu 6.30-9, Fri-Sat 6.30-9.30 Av 3 course à la carte fr £20 ⊕ FREE HOUSE ◀ Butcombe Bitter, Moles Best, Wadworth 6X ♂ Westons Old Rosie, Mates Ravens Roost. ☘ 9 **Facilities** ✿ Children welcome Children's menu Children's portions Garden Beer festival Wi-fi ▄▄▄ (notice required)

CRUDWELL — Map 4 ST99

The Potting Shed NEW

The Street SN16 9EW ☎ 01666 577833
e-mail: bookings@thepottingshedpub.com
dir: *On A429 between Malmesbury & Cirencester*

Light pastel shades and beams scrubbed down to their natural hue characterise the appealing interior of this Cotswold dining pub. With dogs and children welcome, The Potting Shed aims to provide a warm and welcoming atmosphere for all-comers. A typical three-course choice from the menu could start with confit duck and roasted plum boudin; continue with beer-battered pollock with triple-cooked chips; and round off with chocolate and banana loaf. Food and drink can be served outside; two acres of grounds allow plenty of space for lawns, fruit trees and vegetable plots which supply fresh produce for the kitchen.

Open all day all wk **Bar Meals** L served Mon-Sat 12-2.30, Sun 12-3 D served Mon-Sat 7-9.30, Sun 7-9 **Restaurant** L served Mon-Sat 12-2.30, Sun 12-3 D served Mon-Sat 7-9.30, Sun 7-9 ⊕ ENTERPRISE INNS ◀ Butcombe Bitter ♂ Westons Stowford Press. **Facilities** ✿ Children welcome Children's portions Garden Parking Wi-fi ▄▄▄ (notice required)

DEVIZES — Map 4 SU06

The Bear Hotel ★★★ HL ⊛⊛

The Market Place SN10 1HS ☎ 01380 722444
e-mail: info@thebearhotel.net
dir: *In town centre, follow Market Place signs*

Slap bang in the heart of Devizes, close to the Wadworth Brewery that owns it, this characterful coaching inn dates from around 1559. Notable former guests include Judge Jeffreys, George III and Harold Macmillan, all of whom would have enjoyed the abundance of old beams and log fires. With two AA Rosettes a meal here might include pork and duck rillette followed by whole grilled plaice with fine beans, new potatoes, parsley and caper butter. Music fans should check out the weekly jazz sessions. On sunny days, grab a seat in the courtyard. Accommodation is available.

Open all day all wk 9.30am-11pm **Bar Meals** L served all wk 11.30-2.30 D served all wk 7-9.30 Av main course £8-£10 **Restaurant** L served Sun 12-2.30 D served Mon-Sat 7-9.45 Av 3 course à la carte fr £28 ⊕ WADWORTH ◀ 6X, Henry's Original IPA, Old Timer, Malt & Hops, Boundary, Horizon, Seasonal ales. ☘ 15 **Facilities** ✿ Children welcome Children's menu Children's portions Garden Parking Wi-fi ▄▄▄ **Rooms** 25

The Raven Inn

Poulshot Rd SN10 1RW ☎ 01380 828271
e-mail: theraveninnpoulshot@yahoo.co.uk
dir: *A361 from Devizes towards Trowbridge, left at Poulshot sign*

Worth noting if walking the Kennet and Avon Canal towpath or visiting the famous Caen Hill flight of locks, as this refurbished half-timbered 18th-century pub is just a short walk away. Divert for tip-top Wadworth ales and the weekly-changing menu, which offers a mixture of modern pub classics and more imaginative dishes. Expect to find the Raven burger, ham, egg and chips, and steak-and-kidney pie alongside rabbit braised in cider and grilled sole with lemon and parsley butter. Leave room for warm chocolate brownie with chocolate sauce. The pub is dog friendly.

Open 11.30-2.30 6-11 (Sun 12-3 6-10) Closed: Mon (Oct-Etr) **Bar Meals** L served all wk 12-2 D served all wk 6.30-9 Av main course £12 **Restaurant** L served all wk 12-2 D served all wk 6.30-9 ⊕ WADWORTH ◀ 6X, Henry's Original IPA, Horizon, Old Timer ♂ Thatchers Gold. ☘ 12 **Facilities** ✿ Children welcome Children's menu Children's portions Garden Beer festival Parking Wi-fi ▄▄▄ (notice required)

DONHEAD ST ANDREW — Map 4 ST92

The Forester

PICK OF THE PUBS

Lower St SP7 9EE ☎ 01747 828038
e-mail: possums1@btinternet.com
dir: *4.5m from Shaftesbury off A30 towards Salisbury*

Close to Wardour Castle in the pretty little village of Donhead St Andrew, this lovely old pub is an ideal place to put your feet up after one of the long local walks. Traditional in style, it has warm stone walls, a thatched roof, original beams and an inglenook fireplace. An extension provides a restaurant plus a restaurant/meeting room, with double doors opening on to the lower patio area. The restaurant has a good reputation for freshly cooked meals and specialises in Cornish seafood – there is a separate seafood menu available during the week. These quality ingredients are treated with a mix of traditional and cosmopolitan flavours to create dishes such as pan-fried Cornish plaice fillet, crab-crushed potatoes, purple kale, and shellfish butter; and Donhead Estate venison suet pudding, roasted root vegetables and braised red cabbage. To finish, maybe try lavender pannacotta with honeycomb or order the award-winning cheeseboard. Booking for meals may be required.

Open 12-2 6.30-11 Closed: 25-26 Dec, Sun eve **Bar Meals** L served all wk 12-2 D served Mon-Sat 7-9 Av main course £10-£12 **Restaurant** L served all wk 12-2 D served Mon-Sat 7-9 Fixed menu price fr £15.50 Av 3 course à la carte fr £25.50 ⊕ FREE HOUSE ◀ Butcombe, Otter ♂ Westons Wyld Wood Organic. ☘ 15 **Facilities** Children welcome Children's menu Children's portions Garden Parking Wi-fi

Save on hotels. Book at **theAA.com/hotel**

WILTSHIRE 557 ENGLAND

PICK OF THE PUBS

The Dove Inn ★★★ INN ✿

CORTON   Map 4 ST94

BA12 0SZ ☎ 01985 850109
e-mail: info@thedove.co.uk
web: www.thedove.co.uk
dir: *5m SE of Warminster. Exit A36 to Corton*

Squirreled away in the delightful Wylye Valley in the heart of Wiltshire, this bustling 19th-century pub guarantees a warm welcome for locals and visitors alike. A striking central fireplace is a feature of the bar with a wood-burning stove and flagstone and oak floors, and the spacious garden is the perfect spot for barbecues or a drink on long summer days. The appealing menu is based firmly on West Country produce, with many ingredients coming from within just a few miles of the kitchen. Popular lunchtime bar snacks and ciabattas give way to a full evening carte featuring well-made and hearty pub classics. Typical starters include steamed Shetland Isle mussels, chorizo and Stowford Press cider sauce or an Italian-style salad of Parma ham, sweet peaches, shaved parmesan, wild rocket and basil dressing. These might be followed by whole grilled Cornish lemon sole, new potatoes, anchovy, caper and parsley butter, or local rabbit, pancetta, wild mushroom and cider pie with shortcrust pastry. Hot chocolate fondant pot with vanilla ice cream, and apple and blackberry crumble with vanilla mascarpone are crowd-pleasing desserts. Seven en suite bedrooms arranged around a courtyard make The Dove an ideal touring base - Bath, Longleat, Salisbury and Stonehenge are all close by. And for those visitors who haven't got time to stay for lunch or dinner, beer-battered fish and chips and the famous Dove burger and chips are available to take away, wrapped traditionally in newspaper. Children are welcome and get to choose from their own two-course menu.

Open all wk 12-3 6-11.30 ⊕ FREE HOUSE ◾ Fuller's London Pride, Sharp's Doom Bar, Hop Back GFB ♂ Westons Stowford Press. **Facilities** Children welcome Children's menu Children's portions Garden Parking Wi-fi **Rooms** 7

EAST CHISENBURY   Map 5 SU15

Red Lion

SN9 6AQ ☎ 01980 671124
e-mail: enquiries@redlionfreehouse.com
dir: *From A303 take A345 N. Exit at Enford. Left at T-junct towards East Chisenbury. Pub 1m on right*

On the edge of Salisbury Plain and with fishing rights on the River Avon, the Red Lion attracts country sports enthusiasts, not to mention locals who cannot resist the pub's guest ales and excellent food. Run by three chefs, including a pastry specialist, everything from butter to lime cordial is made on the premises using prime seasonal ingredients. A three-course treat could start with spiced parsnip soup; continue with roast rump of Ashdale beef; and finish with Bramley apple crumble. Go for the May Bank Holiday beer festival and see what's cooking. Booking for meals may be required.

Open all day all wk **Bar Meals** L served Mon-Sat 12-2, Sun 12-3 D served all wk 6.30-9 Av main course £18 **Restaurant** L served Mon-Sat 12-2, Sun 12-3 D served all wk 6.30-9 Fixed menu price fr £18 Av 3 course à la carte fr £32 ⊕ FREE HOUSE ◀ Guest ales ♂ Westons Stowford Press Wyld Wood Organic, Aspall. ♟ 10 **Facilities** ♣ Children welcome Children's portions Garden Beer festival Parking Wi-fi

EAST KNOYLE   Map 4 ST83

The Fox and Hounds

PICK OF THE PUBS

See Pick of the Pubs on opposite page

EBBESBOURNE WAKE   Map 4 ST92

The Horseshoe

PICK OF THE PUBS

Handley St SP5 5JF ☎ 01722 780474
dir: *Telephone for directions*

Dating from the 17th century, the family-run Horseshoe is a genuine old English pub in the pretty village of Ebbesbourne Wake. The original building has not changed much, except for a conservatory extension to accommodate more diners, and there's a lovely flower-filled garden. Beyond the climbing roses are two rooms adorned with simple furniture, old farming implements and country bygones, linked to a central servery where well-kept cask-conditioned ales are dispensed straight from their barrels – Bowman Swift One, Otter Bitter and Palmers Copper – plus real ciders, too. Good-value traditional bar food is offered from a varied menu. Freshly prepared from local produce, dishes include local faggots in onion gravy; ham, egg and chips; lamb hotpot; and lunchtime sandwiches. The home-made pies are a firm favourite – venison and mushroom; chicken, ham and mushroom; steak and kidney; and game. Ice creams are provided by Buttercup Ice Cream in Wardour. Booking for meals may be required.

Open all wk 12-3 6.30-11 (Sun 12-4) Closed: 26 Dec, Sun eve & Mon L **Bar Meals** L served Tue-Sat 12-2 D served Tue-Sat 7-9 **Restaurant** L served Sun 12-2.30 D served Tue-Sat 7-9 ⊕ FREE HOUSE ◀ Otter Bitter, Bowman Swift One & Nutz, Palmers Copper Ale, Sixpenny 6D Best ♂ Hecks Farmhouse Cider, Thatchers Gold.
Facilities Children welcome Children's portions Play area Garden Parking

FONTHILL GIFFORD   Map 4 ST93

The Beckford Arms

PICK OF THE PUBS

See Pick of the Pubs on page 560

FROXFIELD   Map 5 SU26

The Pelican Inn

Bath Rd SN8 3JY ☎ 01488 682479
e-mail: enquiries@pelicaninn.co.uk
web: www.pelicaninn.co.uk
dir: *On A4 midway between Marlborough & Hungerford*

Tom and Jen Sunley took over this 17th-century roadside pub in early 2012 and are working hard to restore its fortunes, sprucing up the rambling bar and dining areas in contemporary style. Just 300 yards from the Kennet and Avon Canal, it is a popular refuelling stop for walkers, cyclists and the boating fraternity, as well as weary A4 travellers – the pub is midway between Marlborough and Hungerford. Expect Otter Bitter and local guest ales on tap, a raft of wines by the glass, and freshly prepared food, the menu offering traditional pub favourites alongside chef Tom's chalkboard fish specials, and a choice of roasts on Sundays.

Open all day all wk 11.30-11 (Sun 12-10) **Bar Meals** L served Mon-Sat 12-2.30, Sun 12-7 D served Mon-Fri 6-9, Sat 6-9.30, Sun 12-7 **Restaurant** L served Mon-Sat 12-2.30, Sun 12-7 D served Mon-Fri 6-9, Sat 6-9.30, Sun 12-7 ⊕ FREE HOUSE ◀ Otter Bitter, Guest ales ♂ Westons Old Rosie. ♟ 11 **Facilities** ♣ Children welcome Children's menu Children's portions Garden Parking Wi-fi 🚐 (notice required)

GREAT CHEVERELL   Map 4 ST95

The Bell Inn

PICK OF THE PUBS

High St SN10 5TH ☎ 01380 813277
e-mail: gary06weston@aol.com
dir: *From Salisbury take A360 towards Devizes, through West Lavington, 1st left after black & yellow striped bridge onto B3098. Right to Great Cheverell*

Mentioned in the Domesday Book, this property became a drovers' inn in the 18th century. The Grade II listed building has achieved more recent fame featuring on the television programme Location, Location, Location. Sharp's Doom Bar and Wadworth 6X are among the ales on offer in the bar with its welcoming log fire. Home-cooked West Country food is served in the elegantly styled, oak-beamed restaurant. The imaginative and varied menu makes use of top-quality ingredients which you'll find in starters such as creamy garlic and mushroom tart; smoked trout pâté; and prawn and Brixham crab cocktail. Main courses extend to beef Stroganoff; sea bass fillets served with chilli and soy noodles; and hunters' chicken. Pub classics like home-made steak-and-ale pie, and venison casserole also have a place on the menu. The sunny, secluded garden is set in tranquil surroundings with lots of wooden benches and a patio area, enjoyed by families and locals long into the evening.

Open all wk ⊕ FREE HOUSE ◀ Wadworth 6X, IPA, Sharp's Doom Bar, Guest ale ♂ Westons Stowford Press.
Facilities Children welcome Children's menu Children's portions Garden Parking Wi-fi

HANNINGTON   Map 5 SU19

The Jolly Tar

Queens Rd SN6 7RP ☎ 01793 762245
e-mail: jolly.tar@sky.com
dir: *M4 junct 15, A419 towards Cirencester. At Bunsdon/Highworth sign follow B4109. Towards Highworth, left at Freke Arms, follow Hannington & Jolly Tar pub signs*

Although far from the sea, there's a nautical reason for this former farmhouse's name – a retired sea captain married into the Freke family, who once owned it. Old timbers and locally brewed Arkell's ales are served in its two bars, making this pretty inn an appealing destination. All food is freshly prepared and from the daily menu choose home hock terrine, then follow with steak-and-ale pie with chunky chips or pork belly with garlic and chilli crushed potatoes and cider gravy. The conservatory restaurant overlooks the sun terrace and spacious garden, replete with a children's play area. Booking for meals may be required.

Open 12-3 6-11 (Sun 12-3 7-11) Closed: Mon L (ex BHs) **Restaurant** L served Tue-Sun 12-2 D served Mon-Sat 6.30-9, Sun 7-9 ⊕ ARKELL'S ◀ 3B, Noel Ale, Kingsdown. ♟ 9 **Facilities** Children welcome Children's menu Play area Garden Parking Wi-fi

Save on hotels. Book at **theAA.com/hotel**

WILTSHIRE 559 ENGLAND

PICK OF THE PUBS

The Fox and Hounds

EAST KNOYLE   Map 4 ST83

The Green SP3 6BN ☎ 01747 830573
e-mail: fox.hounds@virgin.net
web: www.foxandhounds-eastknoyle.co.
uk
dir: *From A303 follow Blandford/East
Knoyle signs onto A350, follow brown
pub signs*

This partly thatched and half-timbered,
rustic 15th-century inn makes the most
of its stunning Blackmore Vale location.
There are exceptional views from the
patio beer garden and nearby East
Knoyle village green across these
Wiltshire and Dorset boundary-lands,
where Sir Christopher Wren was born
and the family of Jane Seymour (Henry
VIII's third wife) were based. Hidden in a
timeless village on a greensand ridge,
the engaging exterior is well matched by
the atmospheric interior, with lots of
flagstone flooring, wood-burning fires
and restful stripped wood furniture.
Locals eager to partake of Thatchers
Cheddar Valley cider or Hop Back Crop
Circle rub shoulders with diners keen to
make the acquaintance of the eclectic
menu. Blackboard menus increase the
choice, dependant entirely on the
availability of the freshest local fare.
Starters might include deep-fried
rosemary and garlic-crusted brie
wedges with cranberry jelly or tempura-
battered king prawns with sweet chilli
dip. When it comes to main courses,

good, wholesome pub grub like fish pie;
chicken pie with chips and vegetables
and home-made sausages, mash and
gravy share the board with lamb shank
braised in red wine; slow-roasted belly
pork with an apple and cider sauce;
duck breast with damson sauce and
spring onion mash; or Thai green curry
with lemongrass-scented jasmine rice.
Stone-baked pizzas from a clay oven
and a comprehensive children's menu
add to the fray, whilst desserts include
fresh Dorset apple cake with golden
syrup and cream or chocolate and
raspberry tart with mascarpone cream.
There is also a gluten-free chocolate
fondant and ice cream.

Open all wk 11.30-3 5.30-11 **Bar
Meals** L served all wk 12-2.30 D served

all wk 6-9 Av main course £10.50
Restaurant L served all wk 12-2.30
D served all wk 6-9 Av 3 course à la
carte fr £25 ⊞ FREE HOUSE ◄ Hop Back
Crop Circle & Summer Lightning,
Wickwar BOB, Adnams Broadside,
Palmers Dorset Gold, St Austell Tribute,
Butcombe ♂ Thatchers Cheddar Valley.
♀ 15 **Facilities** Children welcome
Children's menu ❧ Garden Parking Wi-fi
🚌 (notice required)

PICK OF THE PUBS

The Beckford Arms

FONTHILL GIFFORD   Map 4 ST93

SP3 6PX ☎ 01747 870385
e-mail: info@beckfordarms.com
web: www.beckfordarms.com
dir: *From A303 (E of Wincanton) follow Fonthill Bishop sign. At T-junct in village right, 1st left signed Fonthill Gifford & Tisbury. Through Fonthill Estate arch to pub*

One way of approaching this Georgian country coaching inn is through an impressive arch on the edge of Lord Margadale's 10,000-acre Fonthill Estate. Dan Brod and Charlie Luxton reopened the inn in 2011 after refurbishing it in the wake of a terrible fire the previous year, but it all looks pretty good now. The herringbone-patterned, parquet-floored bar serves local real ales, including Dorset Piddle's Jimmy Riddle, Keystone's Beckford Phoenix (in memory of the fire) and several real ciders. One of the wines by the glass is Fonthill Glebe, a locally produced white, the house summer cocktail is the Beckford Bellini and Fonthill Forest is its counterpart in winter. That's when the huge open fire in the bar is used to spit-roast a suckling pig. The restaurant's glass wall opens on to the terrace and the pretty garden where hammocks hang between the trees, you can play pétanque, children can run around and there's even a bath for hosing down a muddy dog. Deciding what temptations to eat from the daily-changing menu could prove tricky. Will you start with

Exmoor venison terrine with pistachios, green peppercorns and apricot chutney; or Jerusalem artichoke salad, Laverstoke mozzarella (from Jody Scheckter's organic buffalo herd), beans and roasted garlic vinaigrette? Then there are the mains: gnocchi with Dorset mushrooms, butternut squash purée, sage, pumpkin seeds and parmesan; seared fillet of salmon with crushed new potatoes, horseradish and parsley butter; or braised shoulder of lamb with mash, roasted carrots, cannellini beans and rosemary. Among the bar meals are salad Niçoise with smoked mackerel; and Creedy Carver duck with Pythouse greens (from a kitchen garden near Tisbury), dauphinoise potatoes and green peppercorn jus. Afternoon tea is served on the terrace and on comfy sofas by an open fire in the sitting room.

Open all day all wk **Bar Meals** L served all wk 12-2.30 D served all wk 6-9.30 Av main course £12.50 **Restaurant** L served Mon-Sat 12-2.30, Sun 12-3 D served all wk 6-9.30 ⊕ FREE HOUSE ◄ Keystone Beckford Phoenix, Dorset Piddle Jimmy Riddle, Butcombe, Erdinger ♂ Ashton Press, Westons Wyld Wood Organic, Sheppy's. ♥ 12 **Facilities** Children welcome Children's menu Children's portions Play area 🐾 Garden Parking Wi-fi

Save on hotels. Book at **theAA.com/hotel**

WILTSHIRE 561 **ENGLAND**

HEYTESBURY   Map 4 ST94

The Angel Coaching Inn
PICK OF THE PUBS

See Pick of the Pubs on page 562

HINDON   Map 4 ST93

Angel Inn
PICK OF THE PUBS

High St SP3 6DJ ☎ 01747 820696
e-mail: info@angel-inn-at-hindon.co.uk
dir: *1.5m from A303, on B3089 towards Salisbury*

In the heart of rural Wiltshire, minutes from the ancient mounds and henges of Salisbury Plain, this beautifully restored 18th-century coaching inn offers many original features, wooden floors, beams and a huge stone fireplace. An elegant gastro-pub where rustic charm meets urbane sophistication, outside is an attractive paved courtyard and garden furniture, where food can be served in fine weather. The interior is characterised by natural wood flooring, beams, large stone fireplace and comfortable leather seating. Behind the bar are Brakspear and Timothy Taylor ales. Pine country-style tables and chairs, together with the day's newspapers, lend a friendly and relaxed atmosphere. An eclectic mix of traditional and modern dishes characterise the brasserie-style menu, based on quality seasonal ingredients. A typical starter is warm pigeon, lentil and bacon salad. The main courses could be slow-cooked blade of beef with oxtail faggot and horseradish mash; and roasted pork fillet, barley risotto, caramelised turnips and apple compôte. Desserts are on the blackboard, as are the day's set menu and specials. Booking for meals may be required.

Open all day all wk 11-11 (Sun 12-4) ⊕ FREE HOUSE ◀ Timothy Taylor Landlord, Sharp's, Brakspear ♂ Thatchers Gold. **Facilities** Children welcome Children's portions Garden Parking Wi-fi

The Lamb at Hindon ★★★★ INN ⊛
PICK OF THE PUBS

High St SP3 6DP ☎ 01747 820573
e-mail: info@lambathindon.co.uk
dir: *From A303 follow Hindon signs. At Fonthill Bishop right onto B3089 to Hindon. Pub on left*

The Lamb began trading as a public house in this charming Wiltshire village as early as the 12th century. Today's wisteria smothered Georgian building continues this selfless service and weary A303 travellers should note that it opens from 7.30am for breakfast and coffee – it beats stopping at the services. The interior of the stone-built inn is divided into several cosy areas and oozes olde-worlde charm, with sturdy period furnishings, flagstone floors, and terracotta walls hung with old prints and paintings; the splendid old stone fireplace with crackling log fire adds the finishing touch to the warm, homely atmosphere. Where better to enjoy a pint of

Young's Bitter or Wiltshire's largest selection of malt whiskies? From the bar menu, tuck into classic Red Poll burgers or roast beef and horseradish sandwiches. The main menu, recognised with an AA Rosette, brings its own pleasures: trout pâté with beetroot coulis, followed by sea bream with caper and herb butter, and baked vanilla cheesecake with fruit compôte. The accommodation here includes four-poster bedrooms. Booking for meals may be required.

Open all day all wk 7.30am-11pm **Bar Meals** L served all wk 12-2.30 D served all wk 6.30-9.30 Av main course £14 **Restaurant** L served all wk 12-2.30 D served all wk 6.30-9.30 Av 3 course à la carte fr £25 ⊕ BOISDALE ◀ Young's Bitter, St Austell Tribute, Butcombe ♂ Westons Stowford Press. ♥10 **Facilities** ♣ Children welcome Children's menu Children's portions Garden Parking Wi-fi **Rooms** 19

HORNINGSHAM   Map 4 ST84

The Bath Arms at Longleat ★★★★ INN ⊛⊛
PICK OF THE PUBS

BA12 7LY ☎ 01985 844308
e-mail: enquiries@batharms.co.uk
dir: *Off B3092 S of Frome*

Built in the 17th century, The Bath Arms occupies a prime position at one of the entrances to Longleat Estate and the famous Safari Park. The building became a public house with rooms in 1732 called the New Inn; it was later renamed the Weymouth Arms, and became the Marquess of Bath Arms in 1850. An ivy-clad stone inn, it has been comfortably refurbished and features two fine beamed bars – one traditional with settles, old wooden tables and an open fire, and a bar for dining. The Wessex Brewery furnishes the public bar with its much-cherished Horningsham Pride ale, while most food is sourced within 50 miles of the pub. Simple menus focus on quality produce, with minimal use of international influences and an emphasis on traditional preserving methods – smoking, curing, potting and pickling. The lunchtime menu has traditional favourites such as traditional fish and chips, chicken Caesar salad and rib-eye steak, but these belie the kitchen team's culinary expertise which has won two AA Rosettes - revealed in dinner dishes such as pan-fried fillet of sea bass, brown shrimps and white bean cassoulet; and roasted guinea fowl with fondant potato, mushrooms and bacon. Stylish accommodation is available. Booking for meals may be required.

Open all day all wk **Bar Meals** L served all wk 12-2.30 D served all wk 7-9 Av main course £10 **Restaurant** L served all wk 12-2.30 D served all wk 7-9 Fixed menu price fr £18.50 Av 3 course à la carte fr £29.50 ⊕ HILLBROOKE HOTELS ◀ Wessex Horningsham Pride & Horningsham PIG, Guest ales ♂ Westons Stowford Press. ♥9 **Facilities** ♣ Children welcome Children's menu Children's portions Garden Beer festival Parking Wi-fi ☛ (notice required) **Rooms** 15

LACOCK   Map 4 ST96

The George Inn

4 West St SN15 2LH ☎ 01249 730263
e-mail: thegeorge01@btconnect.com
dir: *M4 junct 17 take A350, S, between Chippenham and Melksham*

Steeped in history and much used as a film and television location, the beautiful National Trust village of Lacock includes this atmospheric inn. The George dates from 1361 and boasts a medieval fireplace, a low-beamed ceiling, mullioned windows, flagstone floors, plenty of copper and brass, and an old tread wheel by which a dog would drive the spit. Locals and visitors discuss the merits of the ale selection at the bar, while menus proffer a selection of steaks and flavoursome pies, with fish options among the summertime specials; finish with home-made bread-and-butter pudding.

Open all wk 9-2.30 5-11 (Fri-Sat 9am-11pm Sun 9am-10.30pm) Closed: 25 Dec **Bar Meals** L served all wk 12-2 D served all wk 6-9 **Restaurant** L served all wk 12-2 D served all wk 6-9 ⊕ WADWORTH ◀ 6X, Henry's Original IPA, JCB, Henry's Smooth ♂ Westons Stowford Press. ♥9 **Facilities** Children welcome Children's menu Children's portions Play area Garden Parking ☛

Red Lion Inn

1 High St SN15 2LQ ☎ 01249 730456
e-mail: redlionlacock@wadworth.co.uk
dir: *Just off A350 between Chippenham & Melksham. Follow Lacock signs*

A historic 18th-century inn at the heart of the National Trust village of Lacock, whose famous abbey has featured in many films. The pub's Georgian interior with large open fireplace and flagstone floors creates an atmosphere conducive to the enjoyment of Wadworth ales and a wondrous choice of real ciders – many of which can be tasted during the pub's annual cider festival. Home-cooked food follows traditional lines, from sharing boards of meats, fish or cheeses to main plates of wild boar and apple sausages; free-range chicken breast with a stilton and bacon cream; or a Red Lion beefburger topped with red onion marmalade and goat's cheese.

Open all day all wk 8am-11pm (Sat 9am-11pm Sun 9am-10.30pm) ⊕ WADWORTH ◀ 6X, Henry's Original IPA, Horizon, Swordfish ♂ Westons Stowford Press, Thatchers Gold. **Facilities** Children welcome Children's menu Children's portions Garden Beer festival Parking Wi-fi

PICK OF THE PUBS

The Angel Coaching Inn

HEYTESBURY   Map 4 ST94

High St BA12 0ED ☎ 01985 840330
e-mail: admin@angelheytesbury.co.uk
web: www.angelheytesbury.co.uk
dir: *A303 onto A36 towards Bath, 8m, Heytesbury on left*

A sympathetically refurbished 17th-century coaching inn tucked away in a sleepy, upmarket village, close to the tranquil River Wylye and Warminster. The inn is also well placed for exploring Bath, Salisbury and the nearby Longleat Estate. It successfully retains the traditional charm and character of a coaching inn, although these days it is more of a dining destination, yet the atmosphere is relaxed and informal. Either reserve a table in the convivial main beamed bar, surrounded by old scrubbed pine tables, fine prints and a roaring log fire in the inglenook, or relax into a deep sofa with a drink in the lounge before dining in the lighter, more modern and formal restaurant; summer alfresco meals can be enjoyed in the secluded courtyard garden. Menus change daily and typically offer a sharing board starter of baked camembert fondue with bread sticks and red onion jam; or perhaps devilled lambs' kidneys on toasted sourdough toast; or a warming winter vegetable soup topped with crispy sage and served with spelt bread. For a main

course, opt for traditional ale-battered haddock with chunky chips, crushed peas and tartare sauce; or a classic steak-and-kidney pie. More inventive choices take in cider-braised pork belly with mash, Savoy cabbage and apple sauce; and roast duck with chestnuts and smoked bacon. Simpler lunchtime meals include chicken sandwich with pesto mayonnaise and eggs Benedict. For pudding, try the baked white chocolate cheesecake with clementine ice cream. Wash it all down with a pint of Morland or a glass of house wine from the extensive list, then walk it all off with a wonderful stroll through the stunning river valley and surrounding downland.

Open all day all wk **Bar Meals** L served all wk 12-2.30 D served all wk 6.30-9.30 **Restaurant** L served all wk 12-2.30 D served all wk 6.30-9.30 ⊕ GREENE KING ◖ IPA, Morland, Wadworth 6X ♂ Westons Stowford Press. ♟ 8 **Facilities** Children welcome Children's portions ✿ Garden Parking Wi-fi 🚐

Save on hotels. Book at **theAA.com/hotel**

WILTSHIRE 563 ENGLAND

LIMPLEY STOKE — Map 4 ST76

The Hop Pole Inn

Woods Hill, Lower Limpley Stoke BA2 7FS
☎ **01225 723134**
dir: *Telephone for directions*

Set in the beautiful Avon Valley, The Hop Pole dates from 1580 and takes its name from the hop plant that still grows outside the pub. Eagle-eyed film fans may recognise it as the hostelry in the 1993 film *The Remains of the Day*. A hearty menu includes Thai vegetable curry, home-made pies, fresh local trout, and steaks. Food can be enjoyed with one of the many ales, or one of the wines served by the glass.

Open all wk 11-2.30 6-11 (Sun 12-3 7-10.30) Closed: 25 Dec **Bar Meals** L served Mon-Sat 12-2, Sun 12-2.15 D served Mon-Thu 6-9, Fri-Sat 6-9.30, Sun 7-9 Av main course £9.25 **Restaurant** L served Mon-Sat 12-2, Sun 12-2.15 D served Mon-Thu 6-9, Fri-Sat 6-9.30, Sun 7-9 ⊕ FREE HOUSE ◀ Sharp's Doom Bar, Bath Gem, Guest ales ♂ Westons Stowford Press. ♥ 11 **Facilities** Children welcome Children's menu Children's portions Family room Garden Parking Wi-fi

LOWER CHICKSGROVE — Map 4 ST92

Compasses Inn ★★★★ INN ⊛

PICK OF THE PUBS

SP3 6NB ☎ **01722 714318**
e-mail: thecompasses@aol.com
dir: *On A30 (1.5m W of Fovant) take 3rd right to Lower Chicksgrove. In 1.5m turn left into Lagpond Ln, pub 1m on left*

Amid rolling Wiltshire countryside in a tiny hamlet, you're bound to be charmed by this picture-perfect 14th-century thatched inn. An old cobbled path leads to the low latched door that opens into a delightful bar with worn flagstones and old beams. Snuggle up to the large inglenook fireplace or relax in the intimate booth seating, perfect on a winter's evening. You can be certain to find three or four real ales on tap, and the wine list is comprehensive. Be sure to try the food: the kitchen team has won an AA Rosette for their freshly made seasonal dishes; these are written on a blackboard because they change so frequently. Examples of starters are pork, liver and pistachio terrine, or spiced crab cake. Main dishes may feature Wiltshire pheasant leg shepherd's pie and roasted pheasant breast, or pan-fried sea tout, roasted beetroot and new potatoes. Five bedrooms are available, providing an ideal base for exploring the beautiful surrounding countryside.

Open 12-3 6-11 (Sun 12-3 7-10.30) Closed: 25-26 Dec, Mon L Jan-Mar **Bar Meals** L served all wk 12-2 D served all wk 6.30-9 Av main course £15 **Restaurant** Av 3 course à la carte fr £21 ⊕ FREE HOUSE ◀ Keystone Large One, Stonehenge Spire Ale, Plain Inntrigue, Butcombe ♂ Thatchers Gold, Ashton Still. ♥ 8 **Facilities** ♣ Children welcome Children's menu Children's portions Garden Parking Wi-fi ⇌ **Rooms** 5

MALMESBURY — Map 4 ST98

The Horse & Groom Inn

PICK OF THE PUBS

The Street, Charlton SN16 9DL ☎ **01666 823904**
e-mail: info.horseandgroominn@bespokehotels.com
dir: *M4 junct 17 follow signs to Cirencester on A429. Through Corston & Malmesbury. Straight on at Priory rdbt, at next rdbt take 3rd exit to Cricklade, then to Charlton*

Fronted by a tree-sheltered lawn and surrounded by its own paddock, this 16th-century, Cotswold-stone coaching inn has all the charm and character you'd expect from original stone flags, open fires, solid oak tables and rug-strewn wooden floors. In the Charlton Bar, Wadworth 6X house beer is joined by guest ales, while outside, there's plenty of space, including a lovely walled garden and separate play area. In the kitchen, almost all the ingredients come from within 40 miles of the pub. Beef, for example, comes from Jesse Smith's, a local family butcher. Their rib-eye steaks are hung for 28 days and are delivered on the bone when required; pork belly and bacon comes from nearby Bromham; free-range chickens from a farm in Stroud; and lamb from the Cotswolds. Sausage and mash, and home-made pies are among the traditional dishes, while the modern British are represented by lamb rump with garlic mash and broad beans, or pheasant with fondant potato, cabbage and bacon.

Open all wk 9am-11pm (Sun 11-10.30) ⊕ FREE HOUSE ◀ Wadworth 6X, Guest ales ♂ Westons Stowford Press. **Facilities** Children welcome Children's menu Children's portions Play area Garden Parking Wi-fi

The Smoking Dog

62 The High St SN16 9AT ☎ **01666 825823**
e-mail: smokindog@sabrain.com
dir: *5m N of M4 junct 17*

This compact town centre pub was built of stone in the 17th century and known as The Greyhound until 1986. Log fires and wooden floors enhance its warm and cosy interior, and the pub is one of the few in Malmesbury to boast a secure family garden at the rear. The menu mixes pub favourites like pie and mash with more imaginative fare such as wild mushroom risotto with blue cheese topping, and a renowned beer and sausage festival is held over the Spring Bank Holiday weekend. Booking for meals may be required.

Open all day all wk 12-11 (Fri-Sat 12-12 Sun 12-10.30) **Bar Meals** L served Mon-Fri 12-2.30, Sat-Sun 12-3 D served Mon-Sat 6.30-9.30, Sun 6.30-8.30 **Restaurant** L served Mon-Fri 12-2.30, Sat-Sun 12-3 D served Mon-Sat 6.30-9.30, Sun 6.30-8.30 ⊕ BRAINS ◀ The Rev. James, Butcombe Bitter, 3 Guest ales. **Facilities** ♣ Children welcome Children's menu Children's portions Garden Beer festival Wi-fi

The Vine Tree

PICK OF THE PUBS

Foxley Rd, Norton SN16 0JP ☎ **01666 837654**
e-mail: tiggi@thevinetree.co.uk
dir: *M4 junct 17, A429 towards Malmesbury. Turn left for village*

The Vine Tree used to be a mill, and workers apparently passed beverages out through front windows to passing carriages - an early drive-through it would seem. These days, it is well worth seeking out for its interesting modern pub food and memorable outdoor summer dining. In the central bar a large open fireplace burns wood all winter, and there's a wealth of old beams, flagstone and oak floors. Ramblers and cyclists exploring Wiltshire's charms are frequent visitors, and the inn is situated on the official county cycle route. Cooking is modern British in style, with menus changing daily in response to local produce availability. Dishes include salads, light bites and vegetarian options, local game and well-sourced fish and meats. Perhaps start with skewer of Moroccan chargrilled boned quail with minted couscous and tzatziki; followed by pan-fried wild sea bass from Looe, rustic ratatouille and cannellini beans. There are also great real ales and a terrific stock of wines, with many by the glass. In addition to the suntrap terrace, there's a two-acre garden with two boules pitches.

Open all wk 12-3 6-12 (Sun 12-4 6-11) ⊕ FREE HOUSE ◀ St Austell Tinners Ale & Tribute, Uley Bitter, Stonehenge Pigswill, Guest ales ♂ Westons Stowford Press. **Facilities** Children welcome Children's menu Children's portions Play area Garden Parking Wi-fi

MARDEN — Map 5 SU05

The Millstream **NEW**

SN10 3RH ☎ **01380 848490**
e-mail: enquiries@themillstreammarden.co.uk
web: www.themillstreammarden.co.uk
dir: *6m E of Devizes, N of A342*

An attractive village pub near Devizes, set in the heart of the Pewsey Vale. The large garden is a wonderfully peaceful spot for an alfresco drink or meal. Inside, the three fireplaces make for a cosy and romantic atmosphere in which to sip a regional cider and refuel with a bar snack: a ham, mustard and cheddar ciabatta melt perhaps, or a breakfast bap. A more fulfilling meal could comprise a leek and gruyère tartlet; a Stokes Marsh Farm 28-day aged rib-eye steak; and a Burcombe mess to finish.

continued

MARDEN *continued*

Open all wk 11-3 6-11 Closed: 25 Dec **Bar Meals** L served all wk 12-2.30 D served all wk 6-9 Av main course £13 **Restaurant** L served all wk 12-2.30 D served all wk 6-9 Av 3 course à la carte fr £23 ⊕ WADWORTH ◀ 6X, IPA, Horizon ♻ Thatchers Gold. ♚ 10 **Facilities** ❀ Children welcome Children's menu Children's portions Garden Parking ⛟ (notice required)

MARLBOROUGH — Map 5 SU16

The Lamb Inn ★★★ INN

The Parade SN8 1NE ☎ **01672 512668**
e-mail: thelambinnmarlboro@fsmail.net
dir: *E along High St (A4) turn right into The Parade, pub 50yds on left*

Overlooking Marlborough's impressively wide main street, this coaching inn dates from 1673. It's a dog-friendly and welcoming hostelry today, but the dining room, converted from the stable, is reputed to be haunted since a woman was killed when pushed down the stairs. Landlady and chef Jackie Scott uses prime local ingredients including Wiltshire beef, pork from farms close by, game in season, and herbs and berries from the hedgerows. Expect the likes of pigeon and wild mushroom pâté; and a home-made cassoulet of smoked ham, garlic sausage, lamb and duck. Booking for meals may be required.

Open all day all wk **Bar Meals** L served all wk 12-2.30 D served Mon-Thu 6.30-9 Av main course £11 ⊕ WADWORTH ◀ 6X, Guest ales. ♚ 10 **Facilities** ❀ Children welcome Children's portions Garden Wi-fi **Rooms** 6

MINETY — Map 5 SU09

Vale of the White Horse Inn

PICK OF THE PUBS

SN16 9QY ☎ **01666 860175**
dir: *On B4040 (3m W of Cricklade, 6m E of Malmesbury)*

An eye-catching and beautifully restored inn overlooking a large pond. Built in the early 1800s, the building's true history is something of a mystery, but it was registered by its current name in the 1881 census. It closed in 1999, but was rescued and reopened in 2002. Today, sitting under a parasol on the large raised terrace, it's hard to think of a better spot. The village bar is popular with the local community, drawn by a good selection of real ales and events such as skittles evenings, live music and quizzes. Upstairs, lunch and dinner are served in the stone-walled restaurant with its polished tables and bentwood chairs. The ethos is to serve good home-cooked food at sensible prices. The bar menu has a range of baguettes; nachos topped with cheese, guacamole, salsa and jalapeños; and specials that change with the day of the week. Most pub favourites will be found on the main menu, ranging from prawn and crayfish cocktail to deep-fried scampi and chips; grills include a half-pound burger.

Open all wk 11.45-2.45 4.45-11 (Thu-Sat 11.45-11 Sun 11.45-10.30) ⊕ FREE HOUSE ◀ Three Castles Vale Ale & Saxon Archer, Hancock's, Braydon ♻ Westons Stowford Press. **Facilities** Children welcome Children's menu Children's portions Family room Garden Parking Wi-fi

NEWTON TONY — Map 5 SU24

The Malet Arms

PICK OF THE PUBS

SP4 0HF ☎ **01980 629279**
e-mail: info@maletarms.com
dir: *8m N of Salisbury on A338, 2m from A303*

Off the beaten track, in a quiet village on the River Bourne, this 17th-century inn was originally built as a dwelling house. Much later it became The Three Horseshoes, named after a nearby smithy. An earlier Malet Arms, owned by lord of the manor Sir Henry Malet, closed in the 1890s and its name was transferred. It's not just the village that's quiet: the pub is too, as fruit machines and piped music are banned. There is a good range of real ales and whiskies, and all the food on the ever-changing blackboard menu is home cooked. Game is plentiful in season, often courtesy of the landlord who shoots pheasant and deer. In fine weather you can sit outside in the garden, where there is a children's play area. Look out for the beer festival in July. Booking for meals may be required.

Open all wk 11-3 6-11 (Sun 12-3 6-10.30) Closed: 25-26 Dec, 1 Jan ⊕ FREE HOUSE ◀ Ramsbury, Stonehenge, Triple fff, Palmers, Andwell ♻ Westons Old Rosie & Stowford Press, Ashton Press. **Facilities** Children welcome Children's menu Play area Garden Beer festival Parking

NUNTON — Map 5 SU12

The Radnor Arms

SP5 4HS ☎ **01722 329722**
dir: *From Salisbury ring road take A338 to Ringwood. Nunton signed on right*

Not far from Salisbury this is a popular pub in the centre of Nunton dating from around 1750. In 1855 it was owned by the local multi-talented brewer/baker/grocer, and bought by Lord Radnor in 1919. It has recently been refurbished and became a free house in early 2012. Bar snacks are supplemented by an extensive fish choice and daily specials, which might include braised lamb shank, wild mushroom risotto, turbot with spinach or Scotch rib-eye fillet, all freshly prepared. There is a summer garden with rural views to enjoy, and the pub hosts an annual pumpkin competition in October.

Open all wk 11-3.30 6-11.30 **Bar Meals** L served all wk 12-2 D served all wk 6-9 Av main course £8.95 **Restaurant** L served all wk 12-2 D served all wk 6-9 Av 3 course à la carte fr £25 ⊕ FREE HOUSE ◀ Hook Norton Old Hooky, Sharp's Doom Bar, Downton Quadhop, Otter ♻ Westons Stowford Press. **Facilities** ❀ Children welcome Children's portions Play area Family room Garden Parking Wi-fi ⛟

OAKSEY — Map 4 ST99

The Wheatsheaf at Oaksey ◉◉

PICK OF THE PUBS

Wheatsheaf Ln SN16 9TB ☎ **01666 577348**
e-mail: info@thewheatsheafatoaksey.co.uk
dir: *Off A419, 6m S of Cirencester, through waterparks, follow signs for Oaksey*

The origins of this mellow Cotswold-stone inn go back over 700 years. The sophisticated dining pub with old-world charm has two AA Rosettes. The huge old fireplace, beams, parquet floor and comfortably lived-in bar furniture are instantly welcoming, whilst in the restaurant area, Elizabethan England is replaced by inspiring, contemporary décor, light wood and striking prints. Handy for the Cotswold Water Park and Roman Cirencester, explorers chancing on The Wheatsheaf are rewarded with innovative dishes created by chef-patron Tony Robson-Burrell and his Ritz London-trained son Jack. From simple bar snacks to 32-day hung beef, all appetites can be sated. Enjoy a starter of Indian-spiced mackerel and then stretch to mains of Italian vegetable tart or beef and mushroom suet pudding, aiding the digestion with a good list of bins. Alternatively, choose from nine gourmet burgers. The pub has a dedicated band of locals who revel in the choice of beers from Butcombe Bitter to Sharp's Doom Bar.

Open Tue-Fri 12-2 6-11 (Sat 12-11 Sun 12-6) Closed: Sun eve, Mon **Bar Meals** L served Tue-Sun 12-2 D served Tue-Sat 6.30-9 Av main course £10 **Restaurant** L served Tue-Sun 12-2 D served Tue-Sat 6.30-9 Av 3 course à la carte fr £30 ⊕ FREE HOUSE ◀ Sharp's Doom Bar, Butcombe Bitter, Timothy Taylor Landlord. ♚ 14 **Facilities** ❀ Children welcome Children's menu Children's portions Garden Parking Wi-fi ⛟ (notice required)

OGBOURNE ST ANDREW   Map 5 SU17

Silks on the Downs

Main Rd SN8 1RZ ☎ 01672 841229
e-mail: silks@silksonthedowns.co.uk
web: www.silksonthedowns.co.uk
dir: *M4 junct 15, A346 towards Marlborough. Approx 6m to Ogbourne St Andrew. Pub on A346*

Tucked away in rolling downland, a mile north of the bustling market town of Marlborough, the name of this award-winning village pub reflects the racing heritage of the Berkshire Downs. Framed silks of leading racehorse owners and jockeys adorn the walls and the pub offers local Ramsbury ales, fine wines and an informal dining experience. There are filled freshly baked organic baguettes at lunchtime or classics like haddock in beer-batter, with carpaccio of venison and guinea fowl with wild mushroom risotto among the evening additions. Booking for meals may be required.

Open 12-3 6.30-11 Closed: 25 & 26 Dec, Sun eve **Bar Meals** L served all wk 12-3 Av main course £14 **Restaurant** L served all wk 12-3 D served Mon-Sat 7-9.30 ⊕ FREE HOUSE ◀ Ramsbury Gold, Wadworth 6X & Henry's Original IPA Ŏ Aspall. ▼ 11 **Facilities** Children welcome Children's menu Children's portions Garden Parking Wi-fi

PEWSEY   Map 5 SU16

The Seven Stars

Bottlesford SN9 6LW ☎ 01672 851325
e-mail: info@thesevenstars.co.uk
dir: *Off A345*

In the heart of the Vale of Pewsey between Salisbury Plain and the Marlborough Downs, this 16th-century free house is a 15-minute drive from the stone circles of Avebury and five minutes from two of Wiltshire's famous white horses. A handsome thatched building with seven acres of garden, the bar maintains its original character with low beams and oak paneling. Expect local Wadworth 6X and Ramsbury Gold on tap and a menu of no-frills modern classics: perhaps roast butternut squash risotto followed by the pie of the day.

Open 12-3 6-11 Closed: Mon & Tue L ⊕ FREE HOUSE ◀ Wadworth 6X, Ramsbury Gold, Timothy Taylor Landlord, Guest Ales Ŏ Westons Stowford Press, Lilley's Apples & Pears. **Facilities** Children welcome Children's menu Children's portions Garden Parking Wi-fi

PITTON   Map 5 SU23

The Silver Plough

PICK OF THE PUBS

White Hill SP5 1DU ☎ 01722 712266
e-mail: info@silverplough-pitton.co.uk
dir: *From Salisbury take A30 towards Andover, Pitton signed. Approx 3m*

After a change of management in July 2011, The Silver Plough has had a gentle spruce up but retains much of its charm with wood-burning stoves, heavy-beamed rooms and eclectic furnishings. From the lawns of this characterful country pub, the views across the thatched cottages and tree-feathered ridge tops mark the adjacent Salisbury Downs. It all makes for a lovely spot to enjoy a glass of Badger First Gold ale or tuck into generous plates of locally-sourced seasonal food from the menu, which is supplemented with daily changing specials. Starters of mussels with smoked mackerel marinière or grilled goat's cheese and honey salad might be followed by gammon steak and root vegetable mash with parsley sauce; steak-and-ale herb crust pie with mash or cod loin, samphire, pan-fried scallops with hollandaise sauce. There is also a private dining room and traditional skittle alley.

Open all wk 12-3 6-11 (Sun all day) **Bar Meals** L served all wk 12-2 D served all wk 6-9 Av main course £10 **Restaurant** L served Mon-Sat 12-2, Sun all day D served Mon-Sat 6-9, Sun all day Fixed menu price fr £12.50 Av 3 course à la carte fr £22 ⊕ HALL & WOODHOUSE ◀ Badger Tanglefoot, First Gold & K&B Sussex, Guest ale Ŏ Westons Stowford Press. ▼ 15 **Facilities** ✿ Children welcome Children's menu Children's portions Family room Garden Parking Wi-fi 🚐 (notice required)

RAMSBURY   Map 5 SU27

The Bell at Ramsbury NEW

The Square SN8 2PE ☎ 01672 520230
e-mail: thebell@thebellramsbury.com
dir: *M4 junct 14, A338 to Hungerford. B4192 towards Swindon. Left to Ramsbury*

This 17th-century coaching inn occupies a lovely position at the centre of the village in the Kennet Valley on the Wiltshire/Berkshire border. Enjoy light bites in the cosy bar area with its wood-burners and comfortable sofas. Alternatively, book a table in the restaurant and order from an à la carte that might include loin of local venison; roasted saddle of rabbit; or home-made pie of the day. The Bell even has its own micro-brewery, which supplies the bar with the exclusive Ramsbury Gold and Bitter. Booking for meals may be required.

Open all wk 12-3 6-11 (Sun 12-10) **Bar Meals** L served Mon-Sat 12-2.30 D served Mon-Sat 6-9, Sun 6-8 Av main course £10 **Restaurant** L served all wk 12-2.30 D served Mon-Sat 6-9 Fixed menu price fr £20 Av 3 course à la carte fr £30 ⊕ FREE HOUSE ◀ Ramsbury Bitter, Gold Ŏ Thatchers Gold, Lilley's Apples & Pears. ▼ 12 **Facilities** ✿ Children welcome Children's menu Children's portions Garden Parking Wi-fi

ROWDE   Map 4 ST96

The George & Dragon ★★★★ RR ⊛⊛

PICK OF THE PUBS

High St SN10 2PN ☎ 01380 723053
e-mail: thegandd@tiscali.co.uk
dir: *1m from Devizes, take A342 towards Chippenham*

In 1917 the writer Edward Hutton said that Rowde had a 'curious inn', although whether, since there were then four inns in the village, he meant this 16th-century coaching inn isn't known. Not curious, but certainly interesting, is that the Tudor Rose of Elizabeth I is carved on the old beams in the cosy interior, with large open fireplaces, wooden floors, antique rugs and candlelit tables. The two-AA Rosette restaurant specialises in fresh fish and seafood, while other temptations include baked fresh fig with goat's cheese and prosciutto; paillard of beef fillet with anchovy butter; and roast rack of lamb with mint pea purée and red wine jus. Narrowboaters from the nearby Kennet & Avon Canal enjoy coming here for a pint of Bath Ales Gem and Ringwood Fortyniner, especially after they've just navigated their way through the 29 locks of the Caen Flight. Quality accommodation is provided in individually designed bedrooms. Booking for meals may be required.

Open 12-3 6.30-10 (Sat 12-4 6.30-10 Sun 12-4) Closed: Sun eve **Bar Meals** L served Mon-Fri 12-3, Sat-Sun 12-4 D served Mon-Sat 6.30-10 Av main course £13.50 **Restaurant** L served Mon-Fri 12-3, Sat-Sun 12-4 D served Mon-Sat 6.30-10 Fixed menu price fr £16.50 Av 3 course à la carte fr £24.50 ⊕ FREE HOUSE ◀ Butcombe Bitter, Sharp's Doom Bar, Bath Gem, Fuller's ESB & London Pride, Ringwood Fortyniner Ŏ Ashton Press. ▼ 10 **Facilities** Children welcome Children's menu Children's portions Garden Parking Wi-fi 🚐 **Rooms** 3

SALISBURY — Map 5 SU12

The Cloisters

83 Catherine St SP1 2DH ☎ 01722 338102
e-mail: thecloisters83@gmail.com
dir: *In city centre, near cathedral*

The Cloisters is a mid 18th-century pub with Victorian windows that look into a beamed interior warmed by a pair of open fires. The choice of ales includes Hop Back's Summer Lightning and a weekly changing guest ale. The Cloisters has a reputation in the city for good honest food, thanks to a well-qualified chef. The menu comprises popular pub plates, from toasted sandwiches at lunchtime to all-day grills, salads, and dishes such as asparagus and spring onion tart; pork and apple sausages with mash; and chicken with bacon and brie. Booking is advised for the Sunday carvery.

Open all day all wk 11-10 (Thu-Sat 11am-12.30am Sun 12-10) **Bar Meals** L served Mon-Fri 11-3, Sat 11-9, Sun 12-9 D served Mon-Fri 6-9, Sat 11-9, Sun 12-9 Av main course £7-£8 **Restaurant** L served Mon-Fri 11-3, Sat 11-9, Sun 12-9 D served Mon-Fri 6-9, Sat 11-9, Sun 12-9 ⊕ ENTERPRISE INNS ◀ Sharp's Doom Bar, Hop Back Summer Lightning, Guest ales. ☕ **Facilities** Children welcome Children's menu Children's portions ▭

Old Mill ★★★ INN

Town Path SP2 8EU ☎ 01722 327517
e-mail: theoldmill@simonandsteve.com
dir: *From A338 onto A3094, take 3rd right*

Just ten minutes from Salisbury Cathedral, this pub is split between two buildings: the flagstone bar, originally a Georgian yarn factory, and the restaurant, which is in a 15th-century former paper mill, England's first. You can see the mill races through a glass panel. Menus typically offer mixed game suet pudding, chargrilled rump steak, fish specials, and linguine pomodoro. The large beer garden straddles the River Nadder just before it joins the Avon. Beer festivals are held in October and May. En suite guest rooms with original beams look across the water meadows.

Open all day all wk **Bar Meals** L served all wk 12-9 Av main course £11 food served all day **Restaurant** L served all wk 12-2.30 D served all wk 7-8.45 Av 3 course à la carte fr £20 ⊕ GREENE KING ◀ IPA & Abbot Ale, Morland Old Speckled Hen ☕ Aspall. ☕ 10 **Facilities** ☕ Children welcome Children's menu Children's portions Garden Beer festival Parking Wi-fi ▭ **Rooms** 11

The Wig and Quill

1 New St SP1 2PH ☎ 01722 335665
e-mail: enquiries@wigandquill.co.uk
dir: *On approach to Salisbury follow brown Old George Mall Car Park signs. Pub opposite car park*

New Street is very close to the cathedral, whose superlative spire soars skywards just behind this traditional city pub, which saw a change of hands in early 2012. In the roomy, beamed bar with its open fires, flagstone and wooden floored, enjoy a pint of 6X or a

guest cider. From the menu choose between trio of local sausages and mash; warm chicken and bacon salad; and scampi and chips. Try apple pie or hot chocolate fudge cake for dessert. Lying behind the pub is a sheltered courtyard garden for the summer months.

Open all wk 11-4 5-2.30am (Sat-Sun all day) ⊕ WADWORTH ◀ 6X, Bishop's Tipple, Henry's Original IPA & Horizon, Guest ales ☕ Westons Stowford Press, Guest ciders. **Facilities** Children welcome Children's menu Children's portions Garden

SEEND — Map 4 ST96

Bell Inn

Bell Hill SN12 6SA ☎ 01380 828338
e-mail: fgfdevizes@aol.com
dir: *On A361 between Devizes & Semington*

Oliver Cromwell and his troops reputedly enjoyed breakfast at this inn, quite possibly on 18 September 1645 when he was advancing from Trowbridge to attack Devizes Castle. Its other claim to fame is that John Wesley opened the chapel next door and preached against the 'evils' of drink outside the pub. The restaurant of this barn conversion has lovely valley views and offers a tempting menu of home-cooked fare using locally sourced organic meats and produce. A selection could include pan-fried fillet of venison with redcurrant and wine sauce, and sweet potato and chickpea tagine with couscous.

Open all wk 12-2.30 5.30-11.30 **Bar Meals** L served all wk 12-2.30 D served all wk 5.30-10 **Restaurant** L served all wk 12-2.30 D served all wk 5.30-10 ⊕ WADWORTH ◀ 6X, Henry's Original IPA, Bishop's Tipple ☕ Westons Stowford Press. **Facilities** ☕ Children welcome Children's menu Children's portions Play area Garden Parking ▭

SEMINGTON — Map 4 ST86

The Lamb on the Strand

99 The Strand BA14 6LL ☎ 01380 870263
e-mail: info@thelambonthestrand.co.uk
dir: *1.5m E on A361 from junct with A350*

This popular dining pub began life as an 18th-century farmhouse, later developing into a beer and cider house. Today, customers can choose from real ales like Sharp's and Box Steam, as well as 15 wines served by the glass. Food is freshly prepared from locally sourced ingredients, with an appetising choice of hot dishes, salads and doorstep sandwiches at lunchtime. The evening carte is more extensive; Lacock pork chop with creamed potatoes, courgette ribbons and mushroom Diane sauce is typical of the modern British fare. Booking for meals may be required.

Open 12-3 6-11 Closed: Sun eve 1st Sun Nov-1st Sun Mar **Bar Meals** L served all wk 12-3 D served Mon-Sat 6-9.30 **Restaurant** L served all wk 12-3 D served Mon-Sat 6-9.30 ⊕ FREE HOUSE ◀ Bath Gem, Box Steam, Sharp's, Guinness ☕ Bath Ciders Bounders, Westons Stowford Press. ☕ 15 **Facilities** ☕ Children welcome Children's

menu Children's portions Play area Family room Garden Beer festival Parking Wi-fi ▭ (notice required)

The Somerset Arms ★★★★ INN

High St BA14 6JR ☎ 01380 870067
dir: *A361 from Devizes towards Trowbridge, right at 2nd rdbt into Semington*

A slate-roofed, whitewashed, 17th-century coaching inn 500 yards from Semington Locks on the Kennet & Avon Canal, and the short aqueducts carrying it over a brook and the village by-pass. Very much a community pub, its bar and lounge feature exposed beams, tiled floors, log fires, leather sofas and warmly coloured walls. Ales from within a 50-mile radius include Summerset from Yeovil and Danish Dynamite which, despite its name, comes from the Stonehenge Brewery. Real ale lovers might also note the pub's May and August Bank Holiday beer festivals. Stylish interior design extends to the contemporary dining room, with light-wood furniture and jazzy wall coverings, and upstairs to the boutique-style bedrooms. With the comprehensive wine list to hand, consult the seasonal menu for dishes such as wild mushroom suet pudding with stilton mash and Calvados jus; stuffed pork tenderloin in home-cured pancetta; and pan-fried cod with saffron clam chowder sauce. Booking for meals may be required.

Open all day all wk **Bar Meals** L served Tue-Sun 12-3 D served Tue-Sat 6.30-9 Av main course £10 **Restaurant** L served Tue-Sun 12-3 D served Tue-Thu 6.30-9, Fri-Sat 6.30-9.30 Av 3 course à la carte fr £20 ⊕ FREE HOUSE ◀ Bath Gem, Hop Back Summer Lightning, Box Steam Golden Bolt, Stonehenge Danish Dynamite, Yeovil Summerset ☕ Broadoak Perry, Thatchers Cheddar Valley, Broadoak Old Bristolian, Moonraker. ☕ 16 **Facilities** ☕ Children welcome Children's menu Children's portions Family room Garden Beer festival Parking Wi-fi **Rooms** 3

SHERSTON — Map 4 ST88

The Rattlebone Inn

Church St SN16 0LR ☎ 01666 840871
e-mail: eat@therattlebone.co.uk
dir: *M4 junct 17, A429 to Malmesbury. 2m after passing petrol station at Stanton St Quentin, turn left signed Sherston*

The Rattlebone is named after the legendary Saxon warrior John Rattlebone, who is said to haunt this lovely 16th-century Cotswolds pub, which boasts roaring winter fires and bags of character. A lively drinkers' pub, it offers real ales, organic cider and many wines by the glass. Its menus, created by head chef Roger Payne, are best described as 'country bistro' and proffer such delights as breast of pheasant with black pudding and wild mushroom and chestnut tagliatelle. Outside are three boules pistes, two gardens and a beautiful skittle alley. It's also the home of Mangold Hurling, a slightly insane West Country sport.

Save on hotels. Book at **theAA.com/hotel**

WILTSHIRE 567 ENGLAND

Open all wk 12-3 5-11 (Fri 12-3 5-12 Sat 12-12 Sun 12-11) **Bar Meals** L served Mon-Sat 12-2.30, Sun 12-3 D served Mon-Sat 6-9.30 Av main course £9 **Restaurant** L served Mon-Sat 12-2.30, Sun 12-3 D served Mon-Sat 6-9.30 Fixed menu price fr £12.50 Av 3 course à la carte fr £20 ⊕ YOUNG'S ◀ Bitter, Wells Bombardier, St Austell Tribute ♻ Westons Stowford Press & Wyld Wood Organic, Thatchers Gold. ♟ 14 **Facilities** ♣ Children welcome Children's portions Garden Wi-fi ▰ (notice required)

STOURTON   Map 4 ST73

Spread Eagle Inn ★★★★ INN

PICK OF THE PUBS

BA12 6QE ☎ 01747 840587
e-mail: enquiries@spreadeagleinn.com
dir: N of A303 off B3092

This charming 19th-century inn is in an enviable position right at the heart of the 2,650-acre Stourhead Estate, one of the country's most loved National Trust properties. Before or after a walk through the magnificent gardens and landscapes, there is plenty on offer here, including real ales brewed in a nearby village and traditional countryside cooking using produce from local specialists in and around North Dorset, West Wiltshire and South Somerset. Even the simple ploughman's is prepared with local bread with a Dorset Blue cheese or Keene's mature cheddar served with home-made chutney. In the restaurant, expect oven-baked Cornish sea bass fillets on a bed of parmesan mash; free-range tarragon-stuffed chicken suprême with Parmentier potatoes; and chef's crème brûlée to finish. The interior is smartly traditional, and in the bedrooms, antiques sit side by side with modern comforts.

Open all day all wk 9.30am-11pm ⊕ FREE HOUSE ◀ Wessex Kilmington Best, Butcombe, Guest ales ♻ Ashton Press. **Facilities** Children welcome Garden Parking **Rooms** 5

TOLLARD ROYAL   Map 4 ST91

King John Inn

PICK OF THE PUBS

SP5 5PS ☎ 01725 516207
e-mail: info@kingjohninn.co.uk
dir: On B3081 (7m E of Shaftesbury)

This attractive Victorian pub stands in idyllic Tollard Royal, deep in unspoilt downland on the Wiltshire/Dorset border. Rescued and revamped with style and flair by Alex and Gretchen Boon, its airy, open-plan bar and dining areas are stylishly uncluttered and have an upmarket feel, featuring rugs on terracotta tiles, old pine tables, snug alcoves, warming winter log fires, and a sold oak bar. Peruse the daily papers, sup a pint of Butcombe Bitter or delve in Alex's impressive list of wines by the glass, then tuck into some hearty, modern British food from the delicious daily menu that brims with local produce. Perhaps start with moules marinière followed by sika venison haunch with beetroot pearl barley and greens, then finish with lemon posset and stewed berries.

There's a super summer terrace for alfresco meals and don't miss Alex's wine shop across the car park. Booking for meals may be required.

Open all wk 12-3 6-11 **Bar Meals** L served Mon-Fri 12-2.30, Sat-Sun 12-3 D served all wk 7-9.30 **Restaurant** L served Mon-Fri 12-2.30, Sat-Sun 12-3 D served all wk 7-9.30 ⊕ FREE HOUSE ◀ Butcombe Bitter, Wadworth 6X, Guest ales ♻ Ashton Press. ♟ 16 **Facilities** ♣ Children's portions Garden Parking Wi-fi

UPPER CHUTE   Map 5 SU25

The Cross Keys Inn

SP11 9ER ☎ 01264 730295
e-mail: crosskeysinn@upperchute.com
dir: From Andover take A342 towards Ludgershall signed Devizes. Turn right for Upper Chute

This early 18th-century building has been an alehouse for most of its existence. Set on top of a hill in some beautiful countryside, it's no surprise that there are stunning views. Serving freshly prepared meals and plenty of locally brewed ales, The Cross Keys is family and pet-friendly, and provides a relaxed and welcoming atmosphere. As well as a regularly changing menu of classics such as seafood pie, fish and chips, and baked smoked haddock, there's a famous pie menu, which offers the likes of chicken, ham and leek; rabbit and venison; chicken and mushroom; and minted lamb and spring onion. Booking for meals may be required.

Open all wk 11-2.30 6-11 (Mon 6-11 Sun 12-3) Closed: Mon L, Sun eve **Bar Meals** L served Tue-Fri 12-2, Sat-Sun 12-2.30 D served Mon-Sat 6-9 Av main course £9.99 **Restaurant** L served Tue-Fri 12-2, Sat-Sun 12-2.30 D served Mon-Sat 6-9 ⊕ FREE HOUSE ◀ Fuller's London Pride, Hop Back GFB ♻ Westons Stowford Press. ♟ 9 **Facilities** ♣ Children welcome Children's menu Children's portions Play area Garden Beer festival Parking Wi-fi ▰ (notice required)

UPPER WOODFORD   Map 5 SU13

The Bridge Inn

SP4 6NU ☎ 01722 782323
e-mail: enquiries@thebridgewoodford.co.uk
web: www.thebridgewoodford.co.uk
dir: From Salisbury take A360. Turn right for Middle Woodford & Upper Woodford. (Village between A360 & A345 5m N of Salisbury)

On a quiet lane running along the west side of the broad Wiltshire Avon, this charming pub has a large, grassy

garden running down to the wide sweep of the river. Seasonal starter choices might include gravad lax with warm potato cake, dill and mustard crème fraîche; and leek and gruyère tartlet. Appearing among the half-dozen winter menu mains were open ravioli with roasted vegetables and cheese sauce; home-made fishcakes with mushrooms, shallots, herbed fries and bacon and red wine; and rib-eye steak with chips and sautéed mange-tout.

Open all wk 11-3 6-11 **Bar Meals** L served all wk 12-2.30 D served all wk 6-9 Av main course £13 **Restaurant** L served all wk 12-2.30 D served all wk 6-9 Av 3 course à la carte fr £23 ⊕ ENTERPRISE INNS ◀ Hop Back Summer Lightning, Wadworth 6X, Ringwood Best Bitter. ♟ 10 **Facilities** ♣ Children welcome Children's menu Children's portions Garden Parking Wi-fi ▰ (notice required)

UPTON LOVELL   Map 4 ST94

Prince Leopold Inn

BA12 0JP ☎ 01985 850460
e-mail: princeleopold@live.co.uk
dir: From Warminster take A36 after 4.5m turn left into Upton Lovell

Enjoying an idyllic setting beside the River Wylye, this archetypal country inn was built in 1887 and named after Queen Victoria's popular youngest son. The panelled bar serves three ales, perhaps to be enjoyed in the Victorian snug, complete with a log fire but updated with the creature comforts of sofas and the day's papers. Lunchtime classics include devilled lamb's kidneys on toast, while roast haunch of wild boar with juniper sauce may feature at dinner. The pub overlooks water meadows and the garden is a particular draw in summer.

Open all wk 11-3 6-11 **Bar Meals** L served all wk 12-2.30 D served all wk 6.30-9.30 Av main course £9 **Restaurant** L served all wk 12-2.30 D served all wk 6.30-9.30 Fixed menu price fr £15 Av 3 course à la carte fr £20 ⊕ FREE HOUSE ◀ Wadworth 6X, Butcombe, Guest ales ♻ Ashton Press. ♟ 30 **Facilities** Children welcome Children's menu Children's portions Garden Beer festival Parking Wi-fi

WARMINSTER Map 4 ST84

The Angel Inn
PICK OF THE PUBS

Upton Scudamore BA12 0AG ☎ 01985 213225
e-mail: mail@theangelinn.co.uk
dir: *From Warminster take A350 towards Westbury or A36 towards Bath*

With Longleat Safari & Adventure Park five miles away, this restored 16th-century coaching inn is also very well placed for Bath and Salisbury (although they lie in opposite directions). Access is via a walled garden and terrace where meals and drinks can be served, while inside, open fires and natural wood flooring help to create a welcoming feel, with Wadworth, Butcombe and guest ales adding their own important contribution. Lunchtime choices and specials might include parmentiere of beef and black pudding, sweet potato mash and wholegrain mustard-roasted butternut squash; or marinated shoulder of lamb tagine, jewelled fruit couscous and roasted Mediterranean vegetables. The modern British style continues at dinner with a pigeon breast starter, which comes with smoked cheese and apple tarte Tatin, hazelnut, Madeira and citrus dressing, followed perhaps by fillet of sea trout with fennel, citrus fruit and ginger concassé, broad beans, black sesame seeds, udon noodles and oyster sauce. Booking for meals may be required.

Open all wk 11-3 6-11 Bar Meals L served all wk 12-2 D served all wk 6-9 Av main course £15 Restaurant L served all wk 12-3 D served all wk 6-9.30 Fixed menu price fr £15 Av 3 course à la carte fr £25 ⊕ FREE HOUSE ◀ Wadworth 6X, Butcombe, John Smith's Extra Smooth, Guest ales. ♀ 10 Facilities Children welcome Children's menu Children's portions Garden Parking Wi-fi

The Bath Arms

Clay St, Crockerton BA12 8AJ ☎ 01985 212262
e-mail: batharms@aol.com
dir: *From Warminster on A36 take A350 towards Shaftesbury then left to Crockerton, follow signs for Shearwater*

Set on the Longleat Estate close to the Shearwater Lake, this whitewashed country pub attracts locals, walkers and tourists. The garden has been landscaped to provide a pleasant spot for outdoor drinking and dining, and the Garden Suite, with views across the lawn, provides additional seating on busy weekends. Expect stylish food such as sticky beef with braised red cabbage; grilled salmon with fennel and rocket salad; and chicken breast with parsnip mash, beans and lentils. Baguettes are also available.

Open all day all wk 11-3 6-11 (Sat-Sun 11-11) Bar Meals L served all wk 12-2 D served all wk 6.30-9 Restaurant L served all wk 12-2 D served all wk 6.30-9 ⊕ FREE HOUSE ◀ Wessex Crockerton Classic & Potters Ale, Guest ales. Facilities ♣ Children welcome Children's portions Play area Garden Parking Wi-fi ⌨ (notice required)

The George Inn ★★★★ INN

Longbridge Deverell BA12 7DG ☎ 01985 840396
e-mail: info@the-georgeinn.co.uk
dir: *Telephone for directions*

A 17th-century coaching inn overlooking the grassy banks of the River Wylye, The George is a very popular spot on fine days. Food served in the traditional, oak-beamed Smithy Bar and in the two restaurants reflects the seasons, so beef stew and dumplings, for example, is a typical winter dish. Other possibilities include chicken Madras and pan-seared salmon; there's also a dedicated steak menu and Sunday carvery. One of the real ales – Deverill's Advocate – is brewed in the village and is always in demand at the pub's August beer festival. En suite accommodation is available.

Open all day all wk 11-11 (Sun 12-10.30) Closed: 25 Dec fr 3, 26 Dec (1 Jan open 11-3) Bar Meals L served Mon-Thu 12-2.30, Fri-Sat 12-9.30, Sun 12-9 D served Mon-Thu 6-9.30, Fri-Sat 12-9.30, Sun 12-9 Av main course £9.50 Restaurant L served Mon-Thu 12-2.30, Fri-Sat 12-9.30, Sun 12-9 D served Mon-Thu 6-9.30, Fri-Sat 12-9.30, Sun 12-9 ⊕ POWDER TRAIN ◀ Wadworth 6X, Wessex Deverill's Advocate, John Smith's ♙ Thatchers Cheddar Valley. ♀ 11 Facilities Children welcome Children's menu Children's portions Play area Garden Beer festival Parking Wi-fi ⌨ (notice required) Rooms 12

WHITLEY Map 4 ST86

Marco Pierre White The Pear Tree Inn ⓤ
PICK OF THE PUBS

Top Ln SN12 8QX ☎ 01225 709131
e-mail: info@wheelerspeartree.com
dir: *A365 from Melksham towards Bath, at Shaw right onto B3353 to Whitley, 1st left*

This wisteria-clad stone pub epitomises the best of modern interior design, from the beautifully crafted furniture to the positioning of the stone ginger beer jars. Even so, farmhouse character remains, from the flagstone floors to the grand open fires and eclectic collection of agricultural artefacts. Like other inns belonging to Mr White, it offers The Governor ale, named after the

celebrity chef's family greyhound, and a carefully selected worldwide wine list. Dine in the bar, restaurant or peaceful gardens on British and European dishes chosen from a menu that differentiates itself by offering not starters, but hors d'oeuvres, such as Maxim's quail eggs; petit chou farci à l'ancienne (stuffed cabbage); and Wheeler's (of St James's) pea and ham soup. The quality continues with wing of skate with winkles and jus à la Parisienne; Mr Lamb's shepherd's pie; and caramelised honey-roast pork belly with Marco Polo glaze. Accommodation is available.

Open all day all wk bkfst-11pm Bar Meals L served all wk 12-2.30 D served all wk 6.30-9.30 Restaurant L served all wk 12-2.30 D served all wk 6.30-9.30 ◀ JW Lees The Governor, Wadworth 6X, Sharp's Doom Bar, Fuller's London Pride ♙ Thatchers Gold. ♀ Facilities Children welcome Children's menu Garden Parking Wi-fi Rooms 6

WOOTTON RIVERS Map 5 SU16

Royal Oak
PICK OF THE PUBS

SN8 4NQ ☎ 01672 810322
e-mail: royaloak35@hotmail.com
dir: *3m S from Marlborough*

This much expanded 16th-century thatched and timbered pub is perfectly situated for Stonehenge, Bath and Winchester and for exploring the ancient oaks of Savernake Forest. Only 100 yards from the Kennet and Avon Canal and the Mid-Wilts Way, it has an interior as charming as the setting, with low, oak-beamed ceilings, exposed brickwork and wide open fireplaces. In the bar you'll find Wadworth 6X and guest ales, including local Ramsbury Bitter. The menus cover all manner of pubby favourites, including cottage pie with vegetables; local game pie with claret and juniper; surf 'n' turf; and a cheeseburger with home-made relish, salad and chips. Other options include a starter of pigeon terrine with fig compôte, followed perhaps by lamb cutlets with leek fondue. There's also a decent selection of international favourites ranging from pork goulash to Thai chicken curry with rice. To finish, maybe sherry trifle or apple crumble with fresh cream.

Open all wk 10-3 6-11 (Sat-Sun all day) Bar Meals L served Mon-Sat 12-2.30, Sun 12-8.30 D served Mon-Sat 6-9.30, Sun 12-8.30 Restaurant L served Mon-Sat 12-2.30, Sun 12-8.30 D served Mon-Sat 6-9.30, Sun 12-8.30 ⊕ FREE HOUSE ◀ Wadworth 6X, Local guest ales ♙ Westons Stowford Press. ♀ 9 Facilities ♣ Children welcome Children's menu Children's portions Family room Garden Parking Wi-fi ⌨ (notice required)

Save on hotels. Book at **theAA.com/hotel**

WORCESTERSHIRE 569 ENGLAND

WORCESTERSHIRE

BECKFORD — Map 10 SO93

The Beckford ★★★★ INN

Cheltenham Rd GL20 7AN ☎ 01386 881532
e-mail: enquiries@thebeckford.com
web: www.thebeckford.com
dir: On A46 (Evesham to Cheltenham road) 5m from M5 junct 9

Midway between Tewkesbury and Evesham, this rambling Georgian country inn has the Cotswolds beckoning just to the east and shapely Bredon Hill rising immediately to the north. Painstakingly upgraded and refurbished over recent years, the result is an enticing mix of contemporary comforts and traditional fixtures throughout the public areas and the comfortable bedrooms. A typical meal might include pan-seared scallops with spicy chorizo on a bed of leaves with a sweet balsamic reduction; chargrilled duck breast with home-made tipsy Oxford marmalade sauce laced with whisky and served with new potatoes; and creamy chocolate pannacotta with fruits of the forest compôte. Look out for an October beer festival.

Open all day all wk **Bar Meals** Av main course £12.95 food served all day **Restaurant** Av 3 course à la carte fr £20 food served all day ⊕ FREE HOUSE ◀ Fuller's London Pride, Courage Best Bitter, Wye Valley, Wickwar, Prescott ☼ Westons Stowford Press. ⚑ 14 **Facilities** ☙ Children welcome Children's menu Children's portions Garden Beer festival Parking Wi-fi ▄▄ (notice required) **Rooms** 13

BEWDLEY — Map 10 SO77

Little Pack Horse

31 High St DY12 2DH ☎ 01299 403762
e-mail: enquires@littlepackhorse.co.uk
dir: From Kidderminster follow ring road & Safari Park signs. Then follow Bewdley signs over bridge, turn left, then right, right at top of Lax Ln. Pub in 20mtrs

The sign of the Pack Horse indicates that this historic timber-framed inn was a carrier's pub and a clearing house for goods in transit. The beams are low, the bar is made of elm and there are log fires. Expect a good selection of real ales, including Worcestershire Way from Bewdley, and real ciders. The menu relies on locally sourced, seasonal produce for chargrilled steaks; wholetail scampi; Lancashire cheese and thyme sausages; and its ten 'famous' pies, including, especially for Dandy fans, the Herefordshire beef Desperate Dan cow pie. Booking for meals may be required.

Open all wk 12-2.30 6-11.30 (Sat-Sun 12-12) **Bar Meals** L served Mon-Fri 12-2.15, Sat-Sun 12-4 D served Mon-Thu 6-9, Fri 6-9.30, Sat-Sun 5.30-9.30 Av main course £8.25-£15 **Restaurant** L served Mon-Fri 12-2.15, Sat-Sun 12-4 D served Mon-Thu 6-9, Fri 6-9.30, Sat-Sun 5.30-9.30 ⊕ PUNCH TAVERNS ◀ St Austell Tribute, Bewdley Worcestershire Way, Everards Tiger ☼ Thatchers Katy, Westons Stowford Press & Wyld Wood Organic. ⚑ 10 **Facilities** ☙ Children welcome Children's menu Children's portions Family room Garden Wi-fi ▄▄ **Notes** ⊕

The Mug House Inn & Angry Chef Restaurant ★★★★ INN ◉

PICK OF THE PUBS

12 Severnside North DY12 2EE ☎ 01299 402543
e-mail: drew@mughousebewdley.co.uk
dir: A456 from Kidderminster to Bewdley. Pub in town on river

This inn's unusual name dates back to the 17th century when 'mug house' was a popular term for an alehouse. It sits beside the River Severn in picturesque Bewdley, and has plenty of outdoor riverside seating for warmer days. You'll find at least two guest ales at the bar, alongside regulars such as Hereford Pale Ale (HPA) and Westons Traditional scrumpy. There is an annual beer festival on May Day Bank Holiday weekend, when the rear garden comes into its own. It's a wonderful suntrap, there are regular barbecues, and a glass-covered patio with heaters can be used if rain or chilly winds threaten. Food follows pub favourite lines, but quality is not sacrificed and prices are reasonable: chunky crusty bread 'sarnies' and jacket potatoes are available at lunchtime, while AA Rosette-standard options from the short restaurant carte might include chicken and pork pâté with melba toast followed by roasted rump of lamb with ratatouille, roasted shallots, potato rösti and a thyme scented jus. Accommodation is comfortable and thoughtfully furnished. Booking for meals may be required.

Open all day all wk 12-11 **Bar Meals** L served Mon-Sat 12-2.30, Sun 12-5 **Restaurant** L served Mon-Sat 12-2.30, Sun 12-5 D served Mon-Sat 6.30-9 ⊕ PUNCH TAVERNS ◀ Timothy Taylor Landlord, Wye Valley HPA, 2 Guest ales ☼ Westons Traditional. ⚑ 10 **Facilities** ☙ Garden Beer festival Wi-fi **Rooms** 7

Woodcolliers Arms ★★★ INN

76 Welch Gate DY12 2AU ☎ 01299 400589
e-mail: roger@woodcolliers.co.uk
dir: 3m from Kidderminster. 2 mins walk from No 2 bus stop

If you've never tried atbivnaya, you can at this 17th-century, family-run free house built into a hillside just across the river from the Severn Valley steam railway. Battered pork steak, it's one of the several dishes Russian chef Boris Rumba serves alongside largely locally sourced more traditional pub favourites, such as beef Stroganoff (although this too is Russian style), salmon fillet, and cauliflower cheese. There's always a weekly-changing roll-call of local real ales on offer, and Herefordshire ciders. Comfortable accommodation includes the Secret Room, once blocked off and 'lost' for years. Booking for meals may be required.

Open all wk 5pm-12.30am (Sat 12.30-12.30 Sun 12.30-11) **Bar Meals** L served Sat-Sun 12.30-3 D served all wk 6-9 Av main course £10 **Restaurant** L served Sat-Sun 12.30-3 D served all wk 6-9 Av 3 course à la carte fr £16 ⊕ FREE HOUSE/OLIVERS INNS LTD ◀ Ludlow Gold, Three Tuns 1642, Kinver Edge ☼ Thatchers Gold, Westons Old Rosie. ⚑ 14 **Facilities** ☙ Children welcome Garden Parking Wi-fi ▄▄ (notice required) **Rooms** 5

BRANSFORD — Map 10 SO75

The Bear & Ragged Staff

Station Rd WR6 5JH ☎ 01886 833399
e-mail: mail@bear.uk.com
dir: 3m from Worcester or Malvern, clearly signed from A4103 or A449

Built in 1861 as an estate rent office and stables, this lovely old free house still has its original stable doors. Just minutes from both Malvern and Worcester, the pub is also handy for the Malvern Hills and fishing on the River Teme. These days it has a reputation for good beers and food. A meal might take in pressed duck and chicken terrine with lemon and thyme followed by braised blade of beef in coriander and pomegranate with kale and braising liquor. Blackboard specials include traditional fish and chips.

Open 11.30-2 6-11 Closed: 25 Dec eve, 1 Jan eve, Sun eve **Bar Meals** L served all wk 12-2 D served Mon-Sat 6.30-9 Av main course £15 **Restaurant** L served all wk 12-2 D served Mon-Sat 6.30-9.30 Av 3 course à la carte fr £27 ⊕ FREE HOUSE ◀ Hobsons Twisted Spire, Sharp's Doom Bar ☼ Westons Stowford Press. ⚑ 10 **Facilities** ☙ Children welcome Children's menu Children's portions Garden Parking Wi-fi ▄▄ (notice required)

The Fleece Inn

PICK OF THE PUBS

The Cross WR11 7JE ☎ 01386 831173
e-mail: nigel@thefleeceinn.co.uk
dir: *From Evesham follow signs for B4035 towards Chipping Campden. Through Badsey into Bretforton. Right at village hall, past church, pub in open parking area*

Originally built in the time of Chaucer, The Fleece Inn remained in the ownership of a single family until the last of the descendents, Lola Taplin, passed away in front of the fire in the snug in 1977. A quintessential English pub, now owned by the National Trust, the beautiful timbered building was originally a longhouse. The pub was nearly lost in a tragic fire in 2004; a massive renovation followed, when its features and integrity were restored. Real ale devotees will admire one of England's oldest pewter collections as they order a pint of Pigs Ear; and cider lovers can try the home-brewed Ark cider. Families will enjoy the summer sunshine in the apple orchard while children use the play area. Typical dishes on the menu are beef madras, steak-and-kidney pie, game casserole, and beer-battered cod. An apple and ale festival is held in October, during which over 40 ales and ciders can be sampled.

Open all wk 11-11 (Sep-May Mon-Tue 11-3 6-11 Wed-Sun 11-11) **Bar Meals** L served Mon-Sat 12-2.30, Sun 12-4 D served Mon-Sat 6.30-9, Sun 6.30-8.30 Av main course £9-£11 **Restaurant** Fixed menu price fr £7.95 ⊕ FREE HOUSE ◀ Uley Pigs Ear, Hook Norton Hooky Bitter Ŏ Thatchers Heritage, The Ark. ♟ 12 **Facilities** Children welcome Children's menu Children's portions Play area Garden Beer festival Wi-fi ▭ (notice required)

Crown & Trumpet NEW

Church St WR12 7AE ☎ 01386 853202
e-mail: info@cotswoldholidays.co.uk
dir: *From High St follow Snowshill sign. Pub 600yds on left*

Close to church and village green in this famous, picture-postcard village on the edge of the Cotswolds, the Crown & Trumpet is a traditional, 17th-century mellow stone inn. Step inside the classic beamed bar and quaff a pint of local Stanway bitter or a glass of mulled wine by the blazing fire in winter. In summer, head outside to make the most of the peaceful patio garden. In keeping, the menu features classic pub food, so expect ploughman's lunches, sausages and mash, steak-and-kidney pie, lasagne and garlic bread, and home-made rhubarb crumble and custard.

Open all wk 11-3 5-11 (Fri-Sat 11am-mdnt Sun 12-11) **Bar Meals** L served Mon-Fri 12-2.30, Sat-Sun 12-5 D served Mon-Fri 6-9.30, Sat-Sun 5-9.30 Av main course £7.95 **Restaurant** L served Mon-Fri 12-2.30, Sat-Sun 12-5 D served Mon-Fri 6-9.30, Sat-Sun 5-9.30 ⊕ ENTERPRISE INNS ◀ Stroud Tom Long, Cotswold

Spring Codrington Codger, Stanway Ŏ Gwatkin. ♟ 9 **Facilities** ❄ Children welcome Children's menu Children's portions Garden Beer festival Parking Wi-fi ▭ (notice required)

The Bell & Cross

PICK OF THE PUBS

Holy Cross DY9 9QL ☎ 01562 730319
dir: *Telephone for directions*

Dating from the early 19th century, this award-winning pub has been refurbished in recent years but retains its original character. Head for the bar for traditional hand-pulled beers and an inviting log fire in winter, or the covered and heated patio for comfortable alfresco dining on cooler nights. The Bell & Cross is run by Roger Narbett, the chef to the England football team (as is The Chequers, Droitwich; see entry), so you can be sure that the food here hits the spot. Expect modern British food in a traditional setting; light options include a range of sandwiches and deli platters, as well as 'pub snacks' (maybe a pork pie or a Scotch egg) and light bites such as nachos with chive sour cream and sweet chilli or fishcakes with white wine, prawn and chive sauce. Main courses range from traditional fish and chips through to yellow Thai curry with chicken, carrot, coriander, jasmine rice and crackers. For pudding, maybe New York lemon curd cheesecake with honeycomb crisp or warm Bakewell tart with toasted almonds and raspberry mascarpone. Booking for meals may be required.

Open all wk 12-3 6-11 (Sun 12-10.30) Closed: 25 Dec, 26 Dec eve, 31 Dec & 1 Jan eve **Bar Meals** L served all wk 12-2 D served Mon-Sat 6.30-9.15 Av main course £13.50 **Restaurant** L served Mon-Sat 12-2, Sun 12-7 D served Mon-Sat 6.30-9.15, Sun 12-7 Fixed menu price fr £13.95 Av 3 course à la carte fr £19.75 ⊕ ENTERPRISE INNS ◀ Marston's Pedigree & Burton Bitter, Timothy Taylor Landlord, Guest ales. ♟ 15 **Facilities** ❄ Children welcome Children's menu Children's portions Garden Parking ▭ (notice required)

The Chequers

PICK OF THE PUBS

Kidderminster Rd, Cutnall Green WR9 0PJ
☎ 01299 851292
dir: *Telephone for directions*

Roger Narbett, chef to the England football team, runs this traditionally charming pub with his wife Joanne - and it's not just the memorabilia on the bar wall that's in the premier league. The pub has retained its traditional features (open fire, church panel bar, richly coloured furnishings) following a makeover and offers a goodly range of real ales including Hook Norton and Greene King at the bar. Next to the bar is the modern country-style Garden Room with warmly painted walls, a plush sofa and hanging tankards. The menus here cover all bases, with choices ranging from deli platters and light bites

(garlic cheesy ciabatta; chicken yuk sung with crispy noodles, baby gem leaves and soy dip) to pub classic main courses such as bangers of the day with mash, cabbage and onion gravy or a burger with melted cheese, fries and sweet chilli mayo. Desserts also play to the crowd, offering the likes of warm sticky toffee pudding with caramel sauce and toffee ripple ice cream; and Cornish fudge cheesecake with butterscotch sauce, pralines and cream. Booking for meals may be required.

Open all wk 12-3 6-11 (Sun 12-4 6-10.30) Closed: 25 Dec, 1 Jan eve **Bar Meals** L served Mon-Sat 12-2, Sun 12-2.30 D served all wk 6.30-9.15 **Restaurant** L served Mon-Sat 12-2, Sun 12-2.30 D served all wk 6.30-9.15 ⊕ FREE HOUSE ◀ Enville Ale, Greene King Ruddles, Wye Valley HPA, Timothy Taylor, Hook Norton. ♟ 15 **Facilities** ❄ Children welcome Children's menu Children's portions Family room Garden Parking ▭

The Honey Bee

Doverdale Ln, Doverdale WR9 0QB ☎ 01299 851620
e-mail: honey@king-henrys-taverns.co.uk
dir: *From Droitwich take A442 towards Kidderminster. Left into Dovedale Lane to Dovedale*

This spacious, modern and friendly pub has a garden and a play area for children. There are plenty of areas, inside or out, to enjoy a drink or the freshly prepared dishes which will satisfy small and large appetites alike. Choose from steaks, fish and seafood, rumpburgers, traditional favourites, and international and vegetarian dishes. The pub is set in four and half acres with two fishing lakes that are stocked with carp.

Open all day all wk 11.30-11 ⊕ FREE HOUSE/KING HENRY'S TAVERNS ◀ Greene King IPA, Marston's Pedigree, Guinness. **Facilities** Children welcome Children's menu Children's portions Play area Garden Parking

The Old Cock Inn

Friar St WR9 8EQ ☎ 01905 770754
e-mail: pub@oldcockinn.co.uk
dir: *M5 junct 5, A449 in Droitwich town centre opposite theatre*

Three stained-glass windows, rescued from a church destroyed during the Civil War, are a feature of this charming pub, first licensed during the reign of Queen Anne. The stone carving with a frog emerging from its mouth above the front entrance is believed to portray Judge Jeffreys, who is said to have held one of his assizes here. A varied menu, including snacks, platters and more substantial dishes – salmon with a sweet chilli coating; pasta with roasted vegetables and pesto; lamb chop trio; and bacon, egg and chips - is supplemented by the daily specials. Booking for meals may be required.

Open 12-3 6-11 (Sun-Mon 12-6 Sat all day) Closed: Sun eve & Mon eve **Bar Meals** L served Tue-Sat 12-2.30 D served Tue-Sat 6-9 Av main course £7-£8 ⊕ MARSTON'S ◀ EPA, Guest ales Ŏ Thatchers Heritage. **Facilities** ❄ Children welcome Children's portions Garden Wi-fi ▭ (notice required)

PICK OF THE PUBS

The Boot Inn ★★★★ INN

FLYFORD FLAVELL | Map 10 SO95

Radford Rd WR7 4BS ☎ 01386 462658
e-mail: enquiries@thebootinn.com
web: www.thebootinn.com
dir: *A422 from Worcester towards Stratford. Turn right to village*

Parts of this family-run, award-winning, traditional coaching inn can be traced back to the 13th century, and for evidence you need only to look at the heavy beams and slanting doorways. Keep an eye out too for the friendly ghost, age uncertain. The large bar area is comfortable, the pool table and TV having been banished to a separate room, while regulars like Old Speckled Hen, London Pride and Black Sheep, and an extensive wine list complement the varied and imaginative menus which change every six weeks. You can eat from the lunchtime sandwich and bar snack menu, from the extensive specials board, or from the full à la carte, but no matter which you choose, or indeed where — including the conservatory — only the best and freshest, mostly county-sourced, produce is used. A sample menu therefore may include starters of Portobello mushroom stuffed with crispy bacon and goat's cheese, and mango and crayfish salad; followed by something from the griddle, such as

English steaks hung for 21 days; sea bass fillets with sizzled ginger, chilli, spring onion and hoi sin; pork rib-eye steak with walnut crust and cider apple sauce; roasted lamb shank with redcurrant and rosemary gravy; or chive savoury pancakes filled with roasted vegetables and melted brie. Sundays are devoted to roasts — beef, pork and turkey are served, along with the specials menu. Gardens and a shaded patio area are especially suited to summer dining. The comfortable en suite bedrooms in the converted coach house are furnished in antique pine and equipped with practical goodies.

Open all day all wk **Bar Meals** L served all wk 12-2 D served all wk 6.30-10 **Restaurant** L served all wk 12-2 D served all wk 6.30-10 🍺 PUNCH TAVERNS 🛢 Morland Old Speckled Hen, Fuller's London Pride, Black Sheep Ö Westons Stowford Press. 🍷 8 **Facilities** Children welcome Children's menu Children's portions Garden Parking Wi-fi 🚌 (notice required) **Rooms** 5

FAR FOREST
Map 10 SO77

The Plough Inn NEW

Cleobury Rd DY14 9TE ☎ 01299 266237
e-mail: info@nostalgiainns.co.uk
dir: On A417

The location in beautiful rolling countryside, the excellent range of locally brewed real ales, and one of the best carvery dining operations for miles draw local foodies to this family-owned, former 18th-century coaching inn. It's also popular with walkers and cyclists, so arrive early to get the pick of the four roasted joints, perhaps leg of lamb, Far Forest venison, local pork and Scottish beef, all served with a choice of 12 vegetables. Alternatively, try ale-battered cod followed by Baileys profiteroles. The gorgeous summer garden comes with its own bar.

Open all wk 12-3 6-11 (Fri-Sat 12-11 Sun 12-10) **Bar Meals** L served Mon-Fri 12-2, Sat 12-9, Sun 12-6 D served Mon-Fri 6-9, Sat 12-9 **Restaurant** L served Mon-Fri 12-2, Sat 12-9, Sun 12-6 D served Mon-Fri 6-9, Sat 12-9 Fixed menu price fr £5.95 Av 3 course à la carte fr £11.95 ⊕ FREE HOUSE ◀ Wood's Shropshire Lad, Greene King Abbot Ale ♻ Aspall, Westons Stowford Press. **Facilities** Children welcome Children's menu Children's portions Garden Parking Wi-fi 🚌 (notice required)

FLADBURY
Map 10 SO94

Chequers Inn

Chequers Ln WR10 2PZ ☎ 01386 860276
e-mail: 123_lee@live.co.uk
dir: Off A44 between Evesham & Pershore

Tucked away in a pretty village with views of the glorious Bredon Hills, this 14th-century inn has bags of rustic charm including plenty of beams and an open fire. Local produce from the Vale of Evesham provides the basis for home-cooked dishes such as crispy whitebait salad; pan-fried calves' liver with wholegrain mustard mash; and chocolate and caramel salted torte with caramel sauce. There is also a traditional Sunday carvery. The pretty walled garden enjoys outstanding views - a great setting for drinking or dining - and the nearby River Avon is ideal for walking.

Open 12-3 6-11 Closed: Sun eve **Bar Meals** L served Mon-Sat 12-2 D served Mon-Sat 6-9 Av main course £10 **Restaurant** L served all wk 12-2 D served Mon-Sat 6-9 ⊕ ENTERPRISE INNS ◀ Sharp's Doom Bar, Black Sheep ♻ Westons Stowford Press, Aspall. **Facilities** ❤ Children welcome Children's menu Children's portions Play area Garden Parking 🚌 (notice required)

FLYFORD FLAVELL
Map 10 SO95

The Boot Inn ★★★★ INN

PICK OF THE PUBS

See Pick of the Pubs on page 571

GUARLFORD
Map 10 SO84

Plough and Harrow

Rhydd Rd WR13 6NY ☎ 01684 310453
e-mail: info@theploughandharrow.co.uk
dir: From Great Malvern take B4211 (Guarlford Rd). Through Guarlford, pub on left

Formerly a dray house and stable, this is a charming country pub with views of the Malvern Hills from its back garden. Customers can choose from a selection of beers and wines including Wadworth IPA while enjoying home-made meals served in comfortable surroundings, with winter fires and alfresco summer dining. Seasonal produce from the pub's own kitchen garden drives menu options that graduate from lunchtime light bites and salads to evening choices like roast corn-fed chicken with creamed cabbage and pancetta, and pear bread-and-butter pudding with star anise ice cream.

Open 11-3 6-11.30 Closed: 25 Dec, 1 Jan, 1wk spring, 1wk autumn, Sun eve & Mon **Bar Meals** L served Tue-Sun 12-2 D served Tue-Sat 6.30-9 Av main course £12.95 **Restaurant** L served Tue-Sun 12-2 D served Tue-Sat 6.30-9 Fixed menu price fr £13.95 Av 3 course à la carte fr £29.95 ⊕ WADWORTH ◀ Henry's Original IPA, 6X. **Facilities** ❤ Children welcome Children's portions Garden Parking Wi-fi 🚌 (notice required)

KEMPSEY
Map 10 SO84

Walter de Cantelupe Inn ★★★ INN

PICK OF THE PUBS

Main Rd WR5 3NA ☎ 01905 820572
dir: 4m S of Worcester city centre on A38. Pub in village centre

Situated in the village of Kempsey, just four miles from Worcester city centre, this privately owned and run free house commemorates a 13th-century Bishop of Worcester, who was strongly against his parishioners' habit of brewing and selling ales as a way to raise church funds. With its whitewashed walls bedecked with flowers, parts of the pub date from the 17th century. Outside, a walled and paved garden has been fragrantly planted with clematis, roses and honeysuckle, and its south-facing position can be a real suntrap. The menu is written up each day on a blackboard, with choices to appeal to both traditionalists and those seeking something more contemporary. You could begin with Worcestershire rare titbit and follow with Malvern Victorian sausages and mash, or the pie of the day. Three or four cask ales are usually on offer, including Timothy Taylor Landlord. The pub also has accommodation. Booking for meals may be required.

Open 12-2.30 6-11 (Sun 12-3 6-10.30) Closed: 25-26 Dec, 1 Jan, Mon (ex BH) ⊕ FREE HOUSE ◀ Timothy Taylor Landlord, Cannon Royall Kings Shilling, Mayfields Copper Fox ♻ Westons Stowford Press. **Facilities** Children welcome Children's portions Garden Parking Wi-fi **Rooms** 3

KNIGHTWICK
Map 10 SO75

The Talbot

PICK OF THE PUBS

WR6 5PH ☎ 01886 821235
e-mail: info@the-talbot.co.uk
web: www.the-talbot.co.uk
dir: A44 (Leominster road) through Worcester, 8m W right onto B4197 at River Teme bridge

The Talbot is a traditional coaching inn, which has stood by the ford across the sleepy River Teme for over 500 years, surrounded by hop yards and meadows. The inn is also home to the Teme Valley Brewery, which uses locally grown hops in a range of curiously named cask-conditioned ales called This, That, T'Other and Wot. Nearly everything on the menus is made in-house, including bread, preserves, black pudding and raised pies. Salads, herbs and vegetables are grown in the large organic kitchen garden, and wild foods are gathered from the fields and hedgerows; everything else comes from a local source, with the exception of fish, which comes from Cornwall and Wales. The pub hosts a produce market on the second Sunday of the month and a beer festival is held the second weekend in October. The bar menu offers ploughman's, filled rolls and hot dishes, whilst in the restaurant, starters might include smoked haddock rarebit, followed by duo of pork served on roasted root vegetables. Leave space for white chocolate cheesecake.

Open all day all wk 7.30am-11.30pm **Bar Meals** L served all wk 12-9 D served all wk 12-9 food served all day **Restaurant** L served all wk 12-6.30 D served all wk 6.30-9 food served all day ⊕ FREE HOUSE ◀ Teme Valley This, That, T'Other & Wot, Hobsons Best Bitter ♻ Kingstone Press, Robinsons. ♟ 12 **Facilities** ❤ Children welcome Children's portions Garden Beer festival Parking Wi-fi 🚌

LOWER BROADHEATH　　　Map 10 SO85

The Dewdrop Inn

Bell Ln WR2 6RR ☎ 01905 640012
e-mail: enquiries@thedewdrop-inn.co.uk
dir: *From Worcester take A443 towards Kidderminster. Left onto B4202 towards Martley. Left into Bell Ln on entering Lower Broadheath. Pub 400yds on right.*

In the leafy village of Lower Broadheath near the city of Worcester, this painstakingly refurbished country inn sits on the Elgar Route just a few minutes' walk from the birthplace of Sir Edward Elgar. The menu is packed with classic dishes such as outdoor reared pork belly with a mustard and honey dressing followed by home-braised lamb shank with Lyonnaise potatoes, fine green beans and a red wine jus. Booking for meals may be required.

Open all day all wk **Bar Meals** L served all wk 12-2.30 D served all wk 5.30-9 Av main course £8.95 **Restaurant** L served all wk 12-2.30 D served all wk 5.30-9 Fixed menu price fr £12 Av 3 course à la carte fr £22 ⊕ FREE HOUSE ◖ Bewdley Worcestershire Way, Wye Valley Ò Robinsons. **Facilities** Children welcome Children's menu Children's portions Play area Garden Parking Wi-fi ▄▄ (notice required)

MALVERN　　　Map 10 SO74

The Inn at Welland

Drake St, Welland WR13 6LN ☎ 01684 592317
e-mail: info@theinnatwelland.co.uk
dir: *M50 junct 1, A38 follow signs for Upton upon Severn. Left onto A4104, through Upton upon Severn, 2.5m. Pub on right*

This newly refurbished 17th-century country inn, formerly known as the Anchor, is ideally located between Upton on Severn and Malvern. With spectacular views of the Malvern Hills and close to the Three Counties Showground, there is a stylish alfresco terrace for the warmer months, and a wood-burner and open fire for the winter. Food centres around seasonal local produce, with daily classic rotisserie specialities, accompanied by Wye Valley ale plus guests. Typical dishes might include oak-smoked salmon with potato pancake, followed by slow-roasted pork belly with garlic and honey glaze.

Open Tue-Sat 9.30am-11pm (Sun 9.30-6) Closed: Mon **Bar Meals** L served Tue-Sun 12-2.30 D served Tue-Sat 6.30-9.30 Av main course £11.50 **Restaurant** L served Tue-Sun 12-2.30 D served Tue-Sat 6.30-9.30 ⊕ FREE HOUSE ◖ Otter Bitter, Wye Valley, Malvern Hills, Guest ales Ò Westons Stowford Press. ♟ 10 **Facilities** Children welcome Children's menu Children's portions Garden Parking ▄▄ (notice required)

Nags Head

19-21 Bank St WR14 2JG ☎ 01684 574373
e-mail: enquiries@nagsheadmalvern.co.uk
dir: *Off A449 in Malvern*

From the garden the looming presence of North Hill, northernmost top of the stunning Malvern Hills takes the

eye, if only momentarily, away from the panoply of delights that mark out this enterprising free house. Up to 14 micro-brewery marvels (including the pub's own St George's) adorn the bar, with an interior dotted with snugs, log fires and a magpie's nest of artefacts. The annual beer festival on St George's Day offers more than 40 real ales, and with a marvellous menu (try the Moroccan lamb or steamed sea bass) to enjoy, the hills can wait!

Open all day all wk **Bar Meals** L served all wk 12-2 Av main course £7.50 **Restaurant** D served all wk 6.30-8.30 ⊕ FREE HOUSE ◖ St George's Friar Tuck, Tennent's Charger, Holden's Dragon's Blood, Bathams Ò Thatchers Heritage, Westons 1st Quality. **Facilities** ✿ Children welcome Children's portions Garden Beer festival Parking ▄▄

The Wyche Inn ★★★★ INN

74 Wyche Rd WR14 4EQ ☎ 01684 575396
e-mail: thewycheinn@googlemail.com
dir: *1.5m S of Malvern. On B4218 towards Malvern & Colwall. Off A449 (Worcester to Ross/Ledbury road)*

Start or end a walk in the Malvern Hills in this traditional, dog-friendly country inn, probably the highest in Worcestershire. Indeed, the views from various nearby high points are quite something; from Malvern Beacon, for instance, you can see seven counties. Beers come from Hobsons and Wye Valley, while home-cooked dishes include pie of the day, chicken curry and battered cod. Themed food nights feature sirloin steak (Tuesday/Saturday) and mixed grill (Wednesday), and roast lunches are served on Sundays. Well-behaved pets are welcome in the six rooms.

Open all day all wk **Bar Meals** L served Mon-Fri 12-2.30, Sat 12-8.30, Sun 12-6 (winter Sat 12-2.30, Sun 12-3.30) D served Mon-Fri 6-8.30, Sat 12-8.30 (winter Sat 5-8.30) **Restaurant** L served Mon-Fri 12-2.30, Sat 12-8.30, Sun 12-6 (winter Sat 12-2.30, Sun 12-3.30) D served Mon-Fri 6-8.30, Sat 12-8.30 (winter Sat 5-8.30) ⊕ FREE HOUSE ◖ Hobsons Best Bitter, Wye Valley HPA. ♟ 9 **Facilities** Children welcome Children's menu Children's portions Garden Parking Wi-fi **Rooms** 6

MARTLEY　　　Map 10 SO76

Admiral Rodney Inn ★★★★ INN

Berrow Green, WR6 6PL ☎ 01886 821375
e-mail: rodney@admiral.fslife.co.uk
dir: *M5 junct 7, A44 signed Leominster. Approx 7m at Knightwick right onto B4197. Inn 2m on left at Berrow Green*

An early 17th-century farmhouse, now with two bars serving Wye Valley Bitter and HPA as regular ales, three local guests, Robinsons Tenbury cider and, in summer, draught perry. Traditional pub food includes lunchtime sandwiches, baguettes and rump steak, fried egg and mushrooms. Mains in the evening might extend to faggots with mash; Cajun chicken quesadilla; and roasted Mediterranean vegetable pancake. Fish are a speciality on their own weekly changing menu. The large,

separate dining room opens at weekends. Well-behaved dogs are welcome in the pub and in the en suite bedrooms.

Open all wk 12-3 5-11 (Mon 5-11 Sat 12-11 Sun 12-10.30) **Bar Meals** L served Tue-Sat 12.15-2.15, Sun 12.30-4 D served Tue-Sat 6.30-9 **Restaurant** L served Tue-Sat 12.15-2.15, Sun 12.30-4 D served Tue-Sat 6.30-9 ⊕ FREE HOUSE ◖ Wye Valley Bitter, HPA, Local guest ales (Black Pear, Malvern Hills, Kinver, Hobsons, Birds) Ò Westons Stowford Press, Robinsons Cask. **Facilities** ✿ Children welcome Children's menu Garden Parking Wi-fi ▄▄ (notice required) **Rooms** 3

PERSHORE　　　Map 10 SO94

The Defford Arms

Upton Rd, Defford WR8 9BD ☎ 01386 750378
dir: *From Pershore take A4104 towards Upton upon Severn. Pub on left in village*

Rescued from dereliction by Neil and Sue Overton in 2007, The Defford stands testament to their efforts: they have eschewed music, gambling machines and TV in favour of old fashioned values. It's in a great location too, so days out at Croome Park, the Three Counties Showground at Malvern, Cheltenham racecourse or Pershore plum festival could all include a welcome break here. Expect traditional home-made food such as chicken liver pâté and red onion jam; cottage pie; and cinnamon bread-and-butter pudding.

Open all wk Mon 5.30-9 Tue 12-2.30 5.30-9.30 Wed 12-2.30 5.30-10 Thu 12-2.30 5.30-10.30 Fri 12-2.30 5.30-11 Sat 12-11.30 Sun 12-4 **Bar Meals** L served Tue-Sun D served all wk until 9 Av main course £8.95 **Restaurant** L served Tue-Sun D served all wk until 9 ⊕ FREE HOUSE ◖ Guest ales Ò Westons Stowford Press. **Facilities** ✿ Children welcome Children's menu Children's portions Garden Parking ▄▄ (notice required)

POWICK　　　Map 10 SO85

The Halfway House Inn

Bastonford WR2 4SL ☎ 01905 831098
dir: *From M5 junct 7 take A4440 then A449*

Standing halfway between Worcester and Malvern on the main road, this aptly named Georgian free house boasts winter log fires and a mature shady garden at the side. Steaks and seafood are a speciality, but the menu also features a good choice of fresh, locally sourced hot dishes such as pork medallions and black pudding on mashed potatoes with creamy, coarse-grain mustard. The extensive lunchtime menu offers salads, sandwiches and jacket potatoes, as well as hot dishes and a range of ploughman's.

Open 12-3 6-11 Closed: Mon-Tue **Bar Meals** L served Wed-Sun 12-2 D served Wed-Sun 6-9 **Restaurant** L served Wed-Sun 12-2 D served Wed-Sun 6-9 ⊕ FREE HOUSE ◖ Greene King Abbot Ale, Fuller's London Pride, St George's, Timothy Taylor Ò Westons Stowford Press. **Facilities** Children welcome Children's menu Children's portions Garden Parking Wi-fi ▄▄

UPTON SNODSBURY — Map 10 SO95

Bants ★★★★ INN

Worcester Rd WR7 4NN ☎ 01905 381282
e-mail: info@bants.co.uk
dir: *Exit M5 junct 6, follow Evesham signs. At 2nd rdbt left onto A422 towards Stratford. Bants 2m on left*

This 16th-century free house takes its name from the Bant family who have run the pub since 1985. A former coaching inn serving traditional ales, it has real fires in winter warming an eclectic mix of old beams and contemporary furnishings. Traditional dishes with a modern twist are served in three lounge bars and the dedicated conservatory restaurant. The food has a high comfort factor: typical choices include poached fillet of salmon on saffron and dill risotto; and calves' liver pan-fried in Marsala wine. There are nine en suite rooms.

Open all day all wk **Bar Meals** food served all day **Restaurant** food served all day ⊕ FREE HOUSE ◀ Local ales ♻ Local ciders. ▼ 12 **Facilities** ♣ Children welcome Children's menu Children's portions Garden Parking Wi-fi ▥ (notice required) **Rooms** 9

YORKSHIRE, EAST RIDING OF

BARMBY ON THE MARSH — Map 17 SE62

The King's Head

High St DN14 7HT ☎ 01757 630705
e-mail: rainderpubcoltd@tiscali.co.uk
dir: *M62 junct 37 follow A614/Bridlington/York/Howden signs. Left at A63. At rdbt 1st exit onto A614/Booth Ferry Rd towards Goole. At rdbt 4th exit on B1228/Booth Ferry Rd. Left, through Asselby to Barmby on the Marsh*

In the 17th century this pub served a ferry that crossed the Rivers Ouse and Derwent. The family-run village pub was painstakingly refurbished some four years ago, producing a place for all tastes; from the beamed bar through a bright, modern lounge to the cosy, intimate restaurant. Several members of the family are trained chefs and make the most of Yorkshire's burgeoning larder; braised beef with clementines and ginger wine served with herb cobbler and mash is just one of the tempting mains here. Their innovative Yorkshire tapas menu features haddock goujons, confit lamb croquettes, and baked mussels. There are great open sandwiches and a take-away deli menu (including ice creams), too. Booking for meals may be required.

Open Wed-Thu 12-2 5-11 (Mon-Tue 5-11 Fri 12-2 5-12 Sat 12-12 Sun 12-11) Closed: Mon L, Tue L **Bar Meals** L served Wed-Fri 12-2, Sat-Sun all day D served Tue-Thu 5-8.30, Fri 5-9, Sat-Sun all day **Restaurant** L served Sat-Sun all day D served Tue-Thu 5-8.30, Fri 5-9, Sat-Sun all day ⊕ FREE HOUSE ◀ Black Sheep Best Bitter, 3 Guest ales. **Facilities** Children welcome Children's menu Children's portions Garden Parking ▥ (notice required)

BEVERLEY — Map 17 TA03

The Ferguson Fawsitt Arms & Country Lodge

East End, Walkington HU17 8RX ☎ 01482 882665
e-mail: admin@fergusonfawsitt.com
web: www.fergusonfawsitt.co.uk
dir: *M62 junct 38 onto B1230, left on A1034, right onto B1230, on left in centre of Walkington*

Step back in time here, where little has changed since Victorian villagers first enjoyed hospitality in the 1860s; until the 1950s part of the inn was the village smithy. Open fires, dark-wood panelling, carved settles, beams and some decent tiling to the floor welcomes those set on sampling a pint of Copper Dragon Golden Pippin, or diners intent on a good Sunday roast, steak pie from the carvery or a poached fish duo of salmon wrapped with pangasius fish. Booking for meals may be required.

Open all day all wk 11-11 (Sun 12-11) Closed: 25 Dec **Bar Meals** L served Sun-Thu 12-9, Fri-Sat 12-9.30 D served Sun-Thu 12-9, Fri-Sat 12-9.30 food served all day **Restaurant** L served Sun-Thu 12-9, Fri-Sat 12-9.30 D served Sun-Thu 12-9, Fri-Sat 12-9.30 ⊕ FREE HOUSE ◀ Greene King Abbot Ale, Morland Old Speckled Hen, Copper Dragon Golden Pippin. ▼ 10 **Facilities** Children welcome Children's menu Children's portions Parking Wi-fi ▥

Green Dragon NEW

51 Saturday Market HU17 8AA ☎ 01482 889801
dir: *Telephone for directions*

This historic Tudor-fronted inn has a sleek, stylish interior with polished wood floors, modern bar furniture and heritage colours on the walls. It is reputedly haunted by the ghost of a young Danish soldier who was executed after killing a comrade in a duel in 1689. Expect handpicked real ales from all over the UK and hearty, modern pub food such as chicken wings with piri-piri sauce; smoked haddock fishcakes with baby potatoes,

mixed seasonal salad and tartare sauce; and Cumberland sausages and mash.

Open all day all wk Closed: 25 Dec **Bar Meals** L served all wk 11-10 D served all wk 11-10 Av main course £7 food served all day **Restaurant** L served all wk 11-10 D served all wk 11-10 food served all day ⊕ NICHOLSONS ◀ Leeds Pale, Thornbridge Pica Pica ♻ Westons Old Rosie, Aspall. ▼ 18 **Facilities** Children welcome Children's menu Children's portions Garden ▥

DRIFFIELD — Map 17 TA05

Best Western The Bell ★★★ HL

46 Market Place YO25 6AN ☎ 01377 256661
e-mail: bell@bestwestern.co.uk
dir: *Enter town from A164, right at lights. Car park 50yds on left behind black railings*

In the centre of Driffield, this listed 18th-century coaching inn is now a hotel furnished with antiques and fine art. The Oak Bar flies the flag for local breweries and the ever-changing selection might showcase beers from Hambleton and Tom Wood's. Add to the equation the jaw-dropping choice of 300 malt whiskies and an overnight stay in one of the 16 bedrooms might be the order of the day. In the oak-panelled dining room, rump of lamb with spring onion mash and mint gravy is a typical main course. Booking for meals may be required.

Open all day all wk Closed: 25 Dec, 1 Jan **Bar Meals** L served Mon-Sat 12-1.30 D served all wk 5-8.30 Av main course £7 **Restaurant** L served Sun 12-1.30 D served Mon-Sat 6.30-8.30 Av 3 course à la carte fr £18.50 ⊕ FREE HOUSE ◀ Wold Top Falling Stone & Mars Magic, Hambleton Stallion & Stud, Tom Wood's Shepherds Delight. ▼ 10 **Facilities** Children welcome Children's portions Parking Wi-fi ▥ (notice required) **Rooms** 16

FLAMBOROUGH — Map 17 TA27

The Seabirds Inn

Tower St YO15 1PD ☎ 01262 850242
dir: *On B1255 E of Bridlington, 6m from train station*

Head westwards from famous Flamborough Head and its lighthouse, and you'll swiftly arrive at this 200-year-old village pub. Good eating is the emphasis here, with a daily-changing specials board. Fresh fish dishes include grilled lemon sole, salmon hollandaise, and a platter laden with seafood. Carnivores are not forgotten, the menu offers a good range of steaks, gammon with egg or pineapple or both; and lamb steak with red wine and rosemary sauce. There are headland walks and a golf course close by. Booking for meals may be required.

Open 12-3 6-11 Closed: Mon (winter) **Bar Meals** L served all wk 12-2 D served Sun-Fri 6-8.30, Sat 6-9.30 Av main course £6.95 **Restaurant** L served all wk 12-2 D served Sun-Fri 6-8.30, Sat 6-9.30 Fixed menu price fr £6.95 Av 3 course à la carte fr £27.95 ⊕ FREE HOUSE ◼ John Smith's, Tetley's Smoothflow, Guest ales. ♥ 9 **Facilities** Children's menu Children's portions Garden Parking ▥

HUGGATE   Map 19 SE85

The Wolds Inn ★★★ INN

YO42 1YH ☎ 01377 288217
e-mail: huggate@woldsinn.freeserve.co.uk
dir: S off A166 between York & Driffield

Sixteenth century in origin, this family-run hostelry is, at 525 feet above sea level, the highest in the Yorkshire Wolds. Copper pans and gleaming brassware fill the wood-panelled interior, where the open fires still burn good old-fashioned coal. The restaurant is widely known for serving large portions of, among other things, locally sourced Barnsley chops; crispy fresh farm duckling; fillet of plaice; chicken breast stuffed with spinach; and Wolds Topper, "the mixed grill to remember". The overnight accommodation is particularly popular with those exploring the countryside and coast. Booking for meals may be required.

Open 12-2 6-11 (Sun 12-10.30) Closed: Mon (ex BH) **Bar Meals** L served Tue-Sun 12-2 D served Tue-Sun 6-9 Av main course £7 **Restaurant** L served Tue-Sat 12-2, Sun 12-4.30 D served Tue-Sat 6-9, Sun 4.30-9 Av 3 course à la carte fr £22 ⊕ FREE HOUSE ◼ Timothy Taylor Landlord & Golden Best, John Smith's ♂ Kingstone Press. **Facilities** Children welcome Children's menu Children's portions Garden Parking ▥ (notice required) **Rooms** 3

KILHAM   Map 17 TA06

The Old Star Inn

Church St YO25 4RG ☎ 01262 420619
e-mail: oldstarkilham@hotmail.com
dir: Between Driffield & Bridlington on A164. 6m from Driffield. 9m from Bridlington

Standing opposite the village church, this pantiled, multi-roomed old village pub with open fires is handy for the Wolds, the spectacular Flamborough Head and the old fishing port of Filey. Home-cooked food is sourced from local suppliers, with particular attention to reducing the travelling time of ingredients. Special diets are catered for, and children have half price portions. The licensee is a dedicated supporter of Yorkshire beers, with regulars such as Daleside and Copper Dragon complemented by a popular annual beer and cider festival each September. Booking for meals may be required.

Open all wk 5pm-11pm (Mon 6pm-11pm Fri (Summer only) 12-2 4-12 Sat 12-12 Sun 12-10.30) ⊕ ENTERPRISE INNS ◼ John Smith's, Black Sheep, Theakston, Copper Dragon, Timothy Taylor, Daleside. **Facilities** Children welcome Children's portions Garden Beer festival Parking Wi-fi

LOW CATTON   Map 17 SE75

The Gold Cup Inn

YO41 1EA ☎ 01759 371354
dir: 1m S of A166 or 1m N of A1079, E of York

Solid tables and pews - reputedly made from a single oak tree - feature in the restaurant of this 300-year-old, family-run free house. There's a large beer garden, for just enjoying a pint of Black Bull perhaps, plus an adjoining paddock that runs down to the River Derwent. On the bar menu expect to find breaded brie wedges, spicy Cajun chicken, and poached salmon salad. The à la carte menu features sea bass fillets with pesto dressing; vegetable Stroganoff with saffron rice; and roast rack of lamb with a rosemary and mint glaze. Booking for meals may be required.

Open 12-2.30 6-11 (Sat-Sun 12-11) Closed: Mon L **Bar Meals** L served Tue-Fri 12-2.30, Sat-Sun 12-6 D served all wk 6-9 **Restaurant** L served Sun 12-8.30 D served all wk 6-9 ⊕ FREE HOUSE ◼ Theakston Black Bull. ♥ 13 **Facilities** ✿ Children welcome Children's menu Children's portions Play area Garden Parking ▥

LUND   Map 17 SE94

The Wellington Inn

19 The Green YO25 9TE ☎ 01377 217294
e-mail: tellmemore@thewellingtoninn.co.uk
dir: On B1248 NE of Beverley

Nicely situated opposite the picture-postcard village green in a stunning rural location, this country pub is popular with locals and visitors alike, whether for a pint of real ale, a glass of wine, or a plate of decent food. Inside is a unique blend of old and new where you can choose from the traditional pub menu or from the carte in the more formal restaurant. Expect mouthwatering dishes like Godminster cheddar and cumin seed twice-baked soufflé; pea and honey-roast ham hock risotto; pan-fried lamb's liver and sautéed lamb's kidney with potato and bacon hotpot; or grilled Cornish mackerel fillets on paella risotto. Booking for meals may be required.

Open 12-3 6.30-11 Closed: Mon L ⊕ FREE HOUSE ◼ Timothy Taylor Landlord, Black Sheep Best Bitter, John Smith's, Copper Dragon, Regular guest ale. **Facilities** Children welcome Children's menu Children's portions Garden Parking Wi-fi

SANCTON   Map 17 SE83

The Star NEW

King St YO43 4QP ☎ 01430 827269
e-mail: benandlindsey@thestaratsancton.co.uk
dir: 2m SE of Market Weighton on A1034

Built as a farmhouse and converted into a pub in 1710, the sandstone Star stands in a pretty Yorkshire Wolds village and thrives as a traditional local serving top-notch pub food. Owner-chef Ben Cox and his partner Lindsey spruced up and extended the pub a couple of years ago, adding a stylish dining area, so expect stone floors, log-burning stoves and a modern feel. Ben is passionate about using local produce and his impressive dishes range from old favourites like steak-and-ale pie to turbot with roast salsify, cauliflower purée and cod cheek fritter. There's an excellent vegetarian menu and the set lunch menu is a steal. Booking for meals may be required.

Open 12-3 6-11 (Sun all day) Closed: Mon **Bar Meals** L served Tue-Sat 12-2, Sun 12-3 D served Tue-Sat 6-9.30, Sun 6-8 Av main course £12 **Restaurant** L served Tue-Sat 12-2, Sun 12-3 D served Tue-Sat 6-9.30, Sun 6-8 Fixed menu price fr £15 Av 3 course à la carte fr £30 ⊕ FREE HOUSE ◼ Black Sheep, Copper Dragon, Wold Top, Great Newsome ♂ Moorlands Farm. ♥ 21 **Facilities** Children welcome Children's menu Children's portions Play area Garden Parking

SOUTH CAVE   Map 17 SE93

The Fox and Coney Inn

52 Market Place HU15 2AT ☎ 01430 424044
e-mail: info@foxandconey.co.uk
dir: 4m E of M62 on A63. 4m N of Brough mainline railway

In the heart of South Cave, this former coaching inn dating from 1739 is probably the oldest building in the village; it was just called the Fox until William Goodlad added the Coney (rabbit) in 1788. It's a handy dog-friendly watering hole for walkers on the nearby Wolds Way, with two original fireplaces burning on wintry days, beams, and popular lunchtime sandwiches. In the restaurant, where a daily menu and seasonal specials are served, tables are set with crisp white tablecloths and napkins. Food is sourced locally, especially meats, which are all free range.

Open all day all wk 11.30-11 **Bar Meals** L served Mon-Sat 12-3, Sun 12-8 D served Mon-Sat 4.30-9, Sun 12-8 **Restaurant** L served Mon-Sat 12-3, Sun 12-8 D served Mon-Sat 4.30-9, Sun 12-8 ◼ Timothy Taylor Landlord, John Smith's, Theakston Cool Cask, Caledonian Deuchars IPA, Guest ales. ♥ 10 **Facilities** ✿ Children welcome Children's menu Children's portions Family room Garden Parking Wi-fi ▥

SOUTH DALTON · Map 17 SE94

The Pipe & Glass Inn ◉◉

PICK OF THE PUBS

West End HU17 7PN ☎ 01430 810246
e-mail: email@pipeandglass.co.uk
dir: *Just off B1248 (Beverley to Malton road). 7m from Beverley*

Part 15th-century, part 17th, the inn occupies the site of the original gatehouse to Dalton Hall, family seat of Lord Hotham. James and Kate Mackenzie's transformation of their inn has helped to earn it two AA Rosettes, but it still feels like the village local, with Copper Dragon, Cropton, Wold Top and other locally brewed ales, and Old Rosie cider in the bar. The restaurant is more contemporary in style and the conservatory looks out over the garden. James sources top-notch local and seasonal produce for modern British menus, which at lunchtime may feature fillet of English beef with roast shallots; and beetroot and Yellison Farm (in the Yorkshire Dales) goat's cheese tart. Evening possibilities include slow-cooked crispy lamb with mutton and kidney faggot; and a special of turbot fillet with monkfish cheek fritter and braised oxtail and horseradish sauce. The new Hotham Room has its own kitchen for private dining. Booking for meals may be required.

Open all day 12-11 (Sun 12-10.30) Closed: 2wks Jan, Mon (ex BH) **Bar Meals** L served Tue-Sat 12-2, Sun 12-4 D served Tue-Sat 6.30-9.30 **Restaurant** L served Tue-Sat 12-2, Sun 12-4 D served Tue-Sat 6.30-9.30 ⊕ FREE HOUSE ◀ Wold Top, Copper Dragon, Black Sheep, Cropton, John Smith's, York ♂ Westons Old Rosie. ♟ 15 **Facilities** Children welcome Children's menu Children's portions Garden Parking Wi-fi

SUTTON UPON DERWENT · Map 17 SE74

St Vincent Arms

Main St YO41 4BN ☎ 01904 608349
e-mail: enquiries@stvincentarms.co.uk
dir: *From A64 follow signs for A1079. Turn right, follow signs for Elvington on B1228. Through Elvington to Sutton upon Derwent*

The pub is named after John Jervis, who was mentor to Admiral Lord Nelson and who became the first Earl of St Vincent in the 18th century. This is a warm family-run pub with an old fashioned welcoming atmosphere, minus music or gaming machines but with the addition of great food and an excellent selection of beers and wines. Lunches follow popular lines with salads, home-made lasagne, or large haddock with chips and mushy peas. Specials, served both at lunch and in the evening, may include gratin of queenie scallops; pan-fried Dover sole; or Toulouse sausages on parsley mash.

Open all wk 11.30-3 6-11 (Sun 12-3 6.30-10.30) **Bar Meals** L served all wk 12-2 D served all wk 6.30-9.30 **Restaurant** L served all wk 12-2 D served all wk 6.30-9.30 ⊕ FREE HOUSE ◀ Timothy Taylor Landlord, Fuller's ESB & London Pride, York Yorkshire Terrier, Wells Bombardier, Old Mill Traditional Bitter. ♟ 16 **Facilities** Children welcome Garden Parking

YORKSHIRE, NORTH

AKEBAR · Map 19 SE19

The Friar's Head

Akebar Park DL8 5LY ☎ 01677 450201 & 450591
e-mail: info@akebarpark.com
dir: *From A1 at Leeming Bar onto A684, 7m towards Leyburn. Entrance at Akebar Park*

A typical stone-built Dales pub at the entrance to Akebar Holiday Park, overlooking beautiful countryside and grounds where you can play bowls, croquet and pétanque. Inside you'll find exposed beams and stonework and a good fire in winter, with hand-pulled Yorkshire ales from the bar. The lush plants and vines of the Cloister conservatory dining room give it a tropical appearance; in the evening it's candlelit. Typical dishes include crisp-roasted half-duckling; medallions of pork; deep-fried king prawn tails; and linguine with mushrooms, leeks and sun-blushed tomatoes. Booking for meals may be required.

Open all wk 10-3 6-11.30 (Fri-Sun 10am-11.30pm Jul-Sep) Closed: 25 Dec, 26 Dec eve **Bar Meals** L served all wk 12-2.30 D served all wk 6-9.30 **Restaurant** L served all wk 12-2.30 D served all wk 6-9.30 ⊕ FREE HOUSE ◀ John Smith's, Theakston Best Bitter, Black Sheep Best Bitter, Timothy Taylor Landlord. ♟ 12 **Facilities** Children welcome Children's portions Garden Parking

ALDWARK · Map 19 SE46

The Aldwark Arms ◉◉

YO61 1UB ☎ 01347 838324
e-mail: enquiries@aldwarkarms.co.uk
dir: *From York ring road take A19 N. Left into Warehill Ln signed Tollerton & Helperby. Through Tollerton, follow Aldwark signs*

Nestled in the Vale of York and extensively renovated a few years ago, this handsome pub has risen phoenix-like under its new guise as a dining inn dedicated to supporting farms and estates in the Hambleton area of Yorkshire. Sofas, open fires, wooden floors and a large garden terrace all draw locals to indulge in a pint of Timothy Taylor, while diners travel considerable distances to sample chef-patron Chris Hill's exceptional, two AA-Rosette restaurant menu – think mains of slow-cooked oxtail with honeyed root vegetables; and medallions of monkfish with a herb crust, Parma ham, scallops and shrimps. The cosy bar serves lighter meals like rump steak sandwich and French onion soup. Booking for meals may be required.

Open all day Closed: Mon **Bar Meals** L served Tue-Fri 12-2, Sat-Sun all day D served Tue-Fri 5-9, Sat-Sun all day Av main course £7.95 **Restaurant** L served Tue-Fri 12-2, Sat-Sun all day D served Tue-Fri 5-9, Sat-Sun all day Fixed menu price fr £20 Av 3 course à la carte fr £25 ⊕ FREE HOUSE ◀ Timothy Taylor. ♟ 12 **Facilities** Children welcome Children's menu Children's portions Play area Garden Parking 🚌 (notice required)

APPLETON-LE-MOORS · Map 19 SE78

The Moors Inn

YO62 6TF ☎ 01751 417435
e-mail: enquiries@moorsinn.co.uk
dir: *On A170 between Pickering & Kirbymoorside*

Whether you're interested in walking or sightseeing by car, this 18th-century Grade II listed inn is a good choice for its location and good home-cooked food. Taken over by the Frank family in 2012, the pub is set in a small moors village with lovely scenery in every direction; in summer you can sit in the large garden and enjoy the splendid views. Dishes include pork medallions in a cider cream sauce; twice baked four cheese soufflé; and orange marmalade bread-and-butter pudding. Many of the vegetables are grown by the landlord. In addition to hand-pumped local ales, there is a selection of malt whiskies and a good choice of wines by the glass. Booking for meals may be required.

Open all day all wk ⊕ FREE HOUSE ◀ Theakston Black Bull Bitter, Timothy Taylor Landlord, Black Sheep ♂ Westons Stowford Press. **Facilities** Children welcome Children's menu Children's portions Garden Parking Wi-fi

APPLETREEWICK · Map 19 SE06

The Craven Arms

BD23 6DA ☎ 01756 720270
e-mail: info@craven-cruckbarn.co.uk
dir: *2m E of Burnsall off B6160*

Enjoy spectacular views of the River Wharfe and Simon's Seat from this 16th-century Dales pub, which was originally a farm and later used as a weaving shed and courthouse. The village stocks are still outside. The building retains its original beams, flagstone floors, gas lighting and magnificent fireplace. Traditional real ales are served and there's a beer festival every October. The menu, on a blackboard on the wall, offers a choice of around 12 mains that change daily, using locally-sourced food. A heather-thatched cruck barn to the rear serves as restaurant and function room.

Open all day all wk ⊕ FREE HOUSE ◀ Dark Horse Cruck Barn Bitter & Hetton Pale Ale, Saltaire Raspberry Blonde, Moorhouse's Blond Witch & Black Witch ♂ Kingstone Press. **Facilities** Children welcome Children's menu Children's portions Play area Garden Beer festival Parking Wi-fi

ASENBY · Map 19 SE37

Crab & Lobster ★★★★★ RR ◉◉

PICK OF THE PUBS

Dishforth Rd YO7 3QL ☎ 01845 577286
e-mail: reservations@crabandlobster.co.uk
dir: *From A1(M) take A168 towards Thirsk, follow signs for Asenby*

This unique 17th-century thatched pub with its friendly bar is set amid seven acres of garden, lake and streams in the heart of the North Yorkshire countryside. Inside and

Save on hotels. Book at theAA.com/hotel

YORKSHIRE, NORTH 577 ENGLAND

out it is festooned with everything from old advertising signs to fishing nets, an Aladdin's cave of antiques and artefacts from around the world. Equally famous for its innovative two AA-Rosette cuisine and special gourmet extravaganzas, the menus show influences from France and Italy. Starters leave no doubt you are in seafood heaven: the pub's famous fish club sandwich; steamed Shetland mussels with thyme, shallots, garlic and wine; and grilled queenies scallop are just a few of the offerings. The theme continues into main courses with the likes of fish pie, tandoori marinated monkfish and grilled halibut with crushed peas, creamy leek, sweetcorn and scallop chowder and buttery mash. For those who prefer meat, the range of locally-sourced ingredients will not disappoint: a tagine of local pork with aubergine purée and harissa sauce is just one example. Desserts such as baked orange and cranberry cheesecake with honey ice cream and Grand Marnier crème Anglaise are equally appealing. Accommodation is available.

Open all day all wk **Bar Meals** L served all wk 12-2.30 D served Sun-Fri 7-9, Sat 6.30-9.30 Av main course £12.50 **Restaurant** Fixed menu price fr £18.95 Av 3 course à la carte fr £35 ⊕ FREE HOUSE ◀ Copper Dragon Golden Pippin, John Smith's, Hambleton, Guinness. **Facilities** Children welcome Children's portions Garden Parking Wi-fi **Rooms** 14

AUSTWICK
Map 18 SD76

The Game Cock Inn

The Green LA2 8BB ☎ 015242 51226
e-mail: eric.coupey@hotmail.co.uk
dir: Follow the A65 from Skipton or Kendal, then follow signs for Austwick

A traditional, award-winning Thwaites pub in a village below Oxenber Hill, capped with a magnificent limestone pavement. In the bar, winter log fires; outside a large garden with children's play area. Wherever possible, Eric Coupey, who runs the pub with his wife Maree, chooses local firms to supply fresh produce for his imaginative menus of English, French and Mediterranean dishes. The Gallic influence continues with Breton night on Tuesdays and French on Wednesdays; locally sourced steaks are Thursdays, and on Fridays you can take away fish, chips and mushy peas. Booking for meals may be required.

Open Tue-Fri 11.30-3 5-close (Sat-Sun all day) Closed: Mon **Bar Meals** L served Tue-Fri 11.30-2, Sat-Sun 11.30-9 D served Tue-Fri 5-9, Sat-Sun 11.30-9 **Restaurant** L served Tue-Fri 11.30-2, Sat-Sun 11.30-9 D served Tue-Fri 5-9, Sat-Sun 11.30-9 ⊕ THWAITES ◀ Original, Lancaster Bomber, Wainwright & Nutty Black, Guest ales ♻ Kingstone Press. **Facilities** Children welcome Children's menu Children's portions Play area Garden Parking Wi-fi 🚌 (notice required)

AYSGARTH
Map 19 SE08

The George & Dragon Inn

PICK OF THE PUBS

DL8 3AD ☎ 01969 663358
e-mail: info@georgeanddragonaysgarth.co.uk
web: www.georgeanddragonaysgarth.co.uk
dir: On A684 midway between Leyburn & Hawes. Pub in village centre

The George & Dragon Inn is a 17th-century Grade II listed building in a superb location in the Yorkshire Dales National Park, near the beautiful Aysgarth Falls. The area is perfect for walking, touring and visiting local attractions, including Forbidden Corner, the Wensleydale Railway, and the cheese factory. The owners are proud to continue a centuries-long tradition of Yorkshire hospitality at the inn, with customers keeping cosy in winter by the fireside, and in summer enjoying their drinks and meals out on the furnished flower-filled patio. Well-kept real ales are served, and the inn has a great reputation for its traditional food, including steak pie and fish and chips. In the early evening a fixed-price menu meets the needs of ravenous walkers, while a broader à la carte choice comes into force after 7pm. Choices could be home-made chicken liver pâté with apple chutney; Wensleydale pork sausages and mash; or braised pork belly, mash, choucroute and cider reduction.

Open all wk 12-close **Bar Meals** L served all wk 12-2 D served all wk 6-8.30, May-Sep 5.30-9 ⊕ FREE HOUSE ◀ Black Sheep Best Bitter, John Smith's Cask, Yorkshire Dales, Guest ales ♻ Thatchers Gold. ⚑ 16 **Facilities** Children welcome Garden Parking 🚌

BEDALE
Map 19 SE28

The Castle Arms Inn ★★★★ INN

Meadow Ln, Snape DL8 2TB ☎ 01677 470270
e-mail: castlearms@aol.com
dir: From A1 (M) at Leeming Bar take A684 to Bedale. A x-rds in town centre take B6268 to Masham. Approx 2m, turn left to Thorp Perrow Arboretum. In 0.5m left for Snape

A family-run 14th-century pub with bed and breakfast accommodation in the sleepy village of Snape, this inn is a good starting point for walking and cycling, and visiting local stately homes, castles and film locations. The homely interior has exposed beams and horse brasses and a real fire in the bar, home to Marston's, Brakspear and Jennings real ales. A meal in the restaurant selected from the ever-changing menu might feature sautéed

queen scallops and gruyère cheese, followed by grilled gammon steak, free-range eggs and hand-cut chips, and finish with warm Belgian chocolate fondant.

Open all wk 12-3 6-12 **Bar Meals** L served all wk 12-2 D served all wk 7-9 (ex Sun winter) **Restaurant** L served all wk 12-2 D served all wk 7-9 (ex Sun winter) ⊕ MARSTON'S ◀ Pedigree, Jennings Bitter, Brakspear Bitter. **Facilities** Children welcome Children's menu Children's portions Garden Parking **Rooms** 9

BOROUGHBRIDGE
Map 19 SE36

The Black Bull Inn

PICK OF THE PUBS

See Pick of the Pubs on page 578

Crown Inn Roecliffe ★★★★★ RR ◉

PICK OF THE PUBS

Roecliffe YO51 9LY ☎ 01423 322300
e-mail: info@crowninnroecliffe.co.uk
dir: A1(M) junct 48, follow Boroughbridge signs. At rdbt to Roecliffe

Karl and Amanda Mainey have worked wonders since taking over this handsome 16th-century former coaching inn in 2007. Just minutes from the A1(M) (junction 48) and smack beside pretty Roecliffe's neatly trimmed green, the striking green-painted pub has been restored to its former glory, with stone-flagged floors, old oak beams and crackling log fires featuring prominently in the civilised and smartly furnished bar and dining rooms. Local produce is name-checked – farm meats, game shoots, Whitby fish and crab, and kippers, salmon and haddock are smoked in-house – and put to fine use on a clearly focused modern British menu, backed up by daily chalkboard specials. Everything is home-made, from Southfield Farm pressed duck terrine, sweet clementine and home-made grilled crumpet for a starter, to fish pie with a grilled Wensleydale crust, or Gloucester Old Spot belly pork with Bramley apple and sage mash for main course. Delicious puddings may include pannetone bread-and-butter pudding, or try a plate of hand-made Yorkshire cheeses. The four elegant bedrooms, each with sleigh beds, authentic antiques and free-standing baths, are the icing on the cake.

Open all wk 12-3.30 5-12 (Sun 12-7) **Bar Meals** L served Mon-Sat 12-2.30, Sun 12-7 D served Mon-Sat 6-9.30, Sun 12-7 Av main course £15 **Restaurant** L served Mon-Sat 12-2.30, Sun 12-7 D served Mon-Sat 6-9.30, Sun 12-7 Fixed menu price fr £16.95 Av 3 course à la carte fr £27 ⊕ FREE HOUSE ◀ Timothy Taylor Landlord, Ilkley Gold & Mary Jane, Theakston, Black Sheep. ⚑ 30 **Facilities** Children welcome Children's menu Children's portions Garden Parking Wi-fi 🚌 (notice required) **Rooms** 4

PICK OF THE PUBS

The Black Bull Inn

BOROUGHBRIDGE   Map 19 SE36

6 St James Square YO51 9AR
☎ **01423 322413**
web: www.blackbullboroughbridge.co.uk
dir: *A1(M) junct 48, B6265 E for 1m*

Using a false name, highwayman Dick Turpin stayed at this ancient inn which stands in a quiet corner of the market square and was one of the main stopping points for travellers on the long road between London and the North. Today you have to turn off the A1(M), but it's well worth it to discover an inn built in 1258 that retains its ancient beams, low ceilings and roaring open fires, not to mention one that also gives houseroom to the supposed ghosts of a monk, a blacksmith, a cavalier and a small boy. Tony Burgess is the landlord and the man responsible for high standards that exclude anything electronic which makes a noise. The hot and cold sandwich selection in the bar is wide, while in the dining room expect a good choice of traditional pub food on menus offering lamb shank on creamy mash in port and honey gravy; salmon steak on fried noodles with spicy oriental sauce; Barnsley chop and other grills; and Sizzlers, such as Mexican spiced vegetables in a hot sweet salsa sauce; and pan-fried duck breast topped with peppers, mushrooms, bamboo shoots and sweet and sour sauce. Frequently changing blackboard specials widen the choice to include halibut steak with smoked salmon and fresh prawns in white wine sauce; and wild button mushroom ragout with fresh salad. Possible followers are apple pie and custard; citrus lemon tart; or mixed ice creams, brandy snaps and fruit purées. In the bar, real ale drinkers will find favourites from Timothy Taylor, Cottage Brewery and Theakston, while the wine list shows all the signs of careful compilation. Booking for meals may be required.

Open all day all wk 11-11 (Fri-Sat 11am-mdnt Sun 12-11) ⊕ FREE HOUSE ◀ John Smith's, Timothy Taylor Best Bitter, Wells Bombardier, Theakston, Cottage, Guest ale. **Facilities** Children welcome Children's menu Children's portions Parking

PICK OF THE PUBS

Malt Shovel Inn

BREARTON   Map 19 SE36

HG3 3BX ☎ 01423 862929

e-mail: bleikers@themaltshovelbrearton.co.uk
web: www.themaltshovelbrearton.co.uk
dir: *A61 (Ripon to Harrogate) onto B6165 towards Knaresborough. Left, follow Brearton signs. 1m, right to village*

Swiss-born Jürg Bleiker bought this lovely 16th-century country pub in 2006, having previously set up and run Bleiker's Smokehouse, now in the hands of his two daughters and their husbands. Parts of the original structure catch the eye in the busy interior, where log fires will draw you into the jigsaw of spaces and corners, with their reclaimed church panelling. Big leather chairs and pianos dot stone-flagged floors of the bar, curiously named The Monkey; more intimate settings in the Red Room and the elegant Green Room all meld together, while the fern-draped conservatory serves as a striking contrast. With Jürg as head chef, front of house is run by his wife Jane and son D'Arcy and his wife Anna, both of whom are internationally renowned operatic soloists (check for dates of opera-with-dinner evenings). Wine lovers will appreciate the well-balanced list, while beer drinkers can enjoy Black Sheep Best, Timothy Taylor Landlord or a guest; the cider is Aspall. The brasserie-style menu is strong on fish dishes: goujons of East Coast monkfish in lager beer batter, and stir-fried tiger prawns and sweet chilli sauce, for example. Jürg has established a smokery here too, from which emanates his signature Kiln Platter, which features all of his home-smoked products. Other dishes include Wiener schnitzel with capers, anchovy and lemon; roast whole local partridge; rustic cassoulet with home-made Toulouse sausages from the pub's own pigs; freshly made fishcakes with garlic mayonnaise, salad and chunky chips; and Swiss rösti potato with gruyère cheese and salad. Accompanying organic vegetables are sourced from the pub's own smallholding. Jürg personally selects and intelligently describes his wines on a list stating that all house wines are served by the 500ml carafe, as well as by the glass. Jazz is played on most Sunday lunchtimes. Booking for meals may be required.

Open 12-3 5.30-11 (Sun 12-4) Closed: 25 Dec, Sun eve, Mon & Tue **Bar Meals** L served Wed-Sat 12-2, Sun 12-4 D served Wed-Sat 6-9 Av main course £14.95 **Restaurant** L served Wed-Sat 12-2, Sun 12-4 D served Wed-Sat 6-9 Fixed menu price fr £12.95 Av 3 course à la carte fr £26.40 ⊕ FREE HOUSE ◀ Black Sheep Best Bitter, Timothy Taylor Landlord, Guest ale ♂ Aspall. ☗ 21 **Facilities** Children welcome Children's portions Garden Parking

BREARTON Map 19 SE36

Malt Shovel Inn

PICK OF THE PUBS

See Pick of the Pubs on page 579
See advert below

BROMPTON-BY-SAWDON Map 17 SE98

The Cayley Arms

YO13 9DA ☎ 01723 859372
e-mail: joannabou@hotmail.co.uk
dir: *On A170 in Brompton-by-Sawdon between Pickering & Scarborough*

Named after pioneering aviator Sir George Cayley, this pub stands in the heart of picturesque Brompton-by-Sawdon. Its cosy log fire and friendly atmosphere have been the centre of village life for over a century. All food is sourced locally and specials include crab, lobster and mussels. Chunky lunchtime sandwiches with home-made crisps and hot baguettes are supplemented by hot dishes such as warm chicken and bacon salad or fisherman's pie. Outside is an award-winning garden and decking area where you can enjoy a pint of Black Sheep or Hobgoblin.

Open 12-3 5-close (Mon 6-close) Closed: Mon L **Bar Meals** L served Tue-Sun 12-2 D served Mon-Sat 6-9 Av main course £8 **Restaurant** L served Tue-Sat 12-2 D served Mon-Sat 6-9 ⊕ PUNCH TAVERNS ◀ Tetley's Cask, Wychwood Hobgoblin, Black Sheep. ♟ 10 **Facilities** Children welcome Children's menu Children's portions Play area Garden Parking Wi-fi 🚐

BROUGHTON Map 18 SD95

The Bull ⊚

PICK OF THE PUBS

See Pick of the Pubs on opposite page
See advert on page 582

BURNSALL Map 19 SE06

The Devonshire Fell ★★★★ RR ⊚⊚

PICK OF THE PUBS

BD23 6BT ☎ 01756 729000
e-mail: manager@devonshirefell.co.uk
dir: *On B6160, 6m from Bolton Abbey rdbt, A59 junct*

Perched on a hillside overlooking the river and with unparalleled views of the Yorkshire Dales, this former Victorian club for gentlemen mill-owners stands on the edge of the Duke of Devonshire's estate. Given the lineage and the stunning setting, one would expect polished antiques and a classic country-house feel, but the décor is bright and lively, with vibrant colours, polished floorboards, and bold, contemporary works of art throughout the relaxing, open-plan lounge bar and conservatory restaurant, and the quirky, hugely individual boutique-style bedrooms. Equally bang up-to-date are the modern, Mediterranean-inspired dishes, which have been awarded two AA Rosettes and may take in sea bass fillet with Morecambe Bay brown shrimp and shellfish foam; honey-roasted duck breast, champ potatoes, baby turnips and blackberry sauce; and dark chocolate marquise with basil ice cream in the restaurant. Simpler dishes like eggs Benedict, sausage and mash; and steak and chips are served in the bar, alongside local Copper Dragon ales.

Open all day all wk **Bar Meals** Av main course £16.25 food served all day **Restaurant** food served all day ⊕ FREE HOUSE/DEVONSHIRE HOTELS & RESTAURANTS ◀ Copper Dragon Scotts 1816 & Golden Pippin, Truman's. ♟ 10 **Facilities** Children welcome Children's menu Children's portions Garden Parking Wi-fi **Rooms** 12

The Red Lion ★★ HL

PICK OF THE PUBS

By the Bridge BD23 6BU ☎ 01756 720204
e-mail: info@redlion.co.uk
dir: *From Skipton take A59 E, take B6160 towards Bolton Abbey, Burnsall 7m*

This 16th-century ferryman's inn overlooks the River Wharfe as it gently curves under a magnificent five-arch bridge. Large gardens and terraces make it an ideal spot for sunny days. The Grayshon family have sympathetically upgraded the interior, retaining its beamed ceilings and creaky sloping floors. The original 'one-up, one-down' structure, now the oak-panelled and floored main bar, is the focal point of the hotel. Bar food includes lunchtime sandwiches and light meals such as ham hock terrine with shallot compôte; and shepherd's pie or pork belly with a spring vegetable and smoked bacon jardinière in the evening. The main menu ups the ante with the likes of Thai-style fish fritters, followed by oxtail and potato pie. If you are staying over in one of the bedrooms look out for the horse trough – it was easier to build the steps around it.

Open all day all wk 8am-11.30pm ⊕ FREE HOUSE ◀ Timothy Taylor Golden Best, Theakston Best Bitter, Copper Dragon. **Facilities** Children welcome Play area Family room Garden Parking **Rooms** 25

The Malt Shovel

Main Street, Brearton,
North Yorkshire HG3 3BX
Tel: 01423 862929

Website: www.themaltshovelbrearton.co.uk
Email: bleikers@themaltshovelbrearton.co.uk

The Malt Shovel has been offering hospitality and refreshment to locals and visitors for over four hundred years.

At the heart of the tiny North Yorkshire village of Brearton, just four miles from Harrogate and Knaresborough, *The Malt Shovel* has become a gastronomic destination in its own right. But it remains, above all, a local, family-run country Inn, offering excellent food, friendly service and the warmest of welcomes.

PICK OF THE PUBS

The Bull ✤

BROUGHTON   Map 18 SD95

BD23 3AE ☎ 01756 792065
e-mail: enquiries@thebullatbroughton.com
web: www.thebullatbroughton.com
dir: *3m from Skipton on A59, on right*

Tucked away off a busy main road, The Bull belongs to another, less frantic era; the unhurried, relaxed atmosphere of this Ribble Valley Inns dining pub eases you seamlessly into this lost world. The setting helps, of course; The Bull is part of the historic Broughton Estate, 3,000 acres of prime Yorkshire turf owned by the Tempest family for 900 years. The stunning mansion is close by and the pedigree shorthorn cattle, after which the pub is named, graze pastures skirting the Aire Valley. A dining pub it may be, but The Bull welcomes beer drinkers with plenty of choice: try Dark Horse Hetton, a golden ale made with a blend of four different hops which give a spicy flavour with mild bitterness. Award-winning chefs make the most of the largesse offered by carefully selected producers across Yorkshire and Lancashire; provenance and traceability are key to the ingredients used in the extensive modern English menus here. By welcoming children with their own menu scaled down from the adult version, The Bull hopes to widen kiddies' understanding of fine and fresh local food; there are fun sheets and competitions for them too. How better to start than with Gloucester Old Spot

crispy pork croquette, crackling and Tomlinson's rhubarb chutney? Main courses and grills feature the famous beef — perhaps in the form of a burger in an English muffin, served with real chips cooked in dripping, battered onion rings and tomato relish. Alternatively you'll find a North Sea fish pie stuffed with good things and topped with Wensleydale mash, and welfare-friendly English veal kidneys, jacket mash, streaky bacon, English onions and mushroom sauce. You can round off with traditional pancakes and choose your filling — hazelnut and chocolate is very popular.

Open all day 12-11 (Sun 12-10.30) Closed: 25 Dec, Mon **Bar Meals** L served Tue-Sat 12-2, afternoon bites Tue-Sat 2-5.30, Sun 12-8 D served Tue-Thu

5.30-8.30, Fri-Sat 5.30-9, Sun 12-8 Av main course £10.50 food served all day **Restaurant** food served all day ⊕ RIBBLE VALLEY INNS ◖ Dark Horse Hetton Pale Ale, Moorhouse's Pride of Pendle, Copper Dragon Scotts 1816. **Facilities** Children welcome Children's menu Garden Parking

THE BULL AT BROUGHTON

Broughton, Skipton, North Yorkshire BD23 3AE
Tel: 01756 792065
Website: www.thebullatbroughton.com
Email: enquiries@thebullatbroughton.com

The historic pub – now the fourth Ribble Valley Inn – is part of the beautiful 3,000 acre Broughton Hall Estate and only four miles from Skipton Town Centre. Nigel Haworth works with Yorkshire's amazing farmers, growers and fine food suppliers to develop dishes full of tradition and provenance, but with a deliciously contemporary twist. It is the same formula which has brought countless top awards to the first three Ribble Valley Inns. This is a real treat for the taste buds, enjoy a starter of Gloucester Old Spot Crispy Pork Croquette, Crackling, Tomlinson's Rhubarb Chutney followed by Toad in the Hole, Nigel's Free Range Rare Breed Sausages, Maris Piper Mash, English Onion Gravy and indulge in our Classic Baked Alaska for dessert. Enjoy alfresco dining on craggy terraces in the summers and blazing log fires in the winter.

Save on hotels. Book at theAA.com/hotel

YORKSHIRE, NORTH 583 ENGLAND

PICK OF THE PUBS

Ye Old Sun Inn

COLTON Map 16 SE54

Main St LS24 8EP ☎ 01904 744261
e-mail: info@yeoldsuninn.co.uk
web: www.yeoldsuninn.co.uk
dir: *3-4m from York, off A64*

Young Ashley and Kelly McCarthy took over this 17th-century country pub in 2004 and have worked hard in transforming its fortunes from a run-down local to a thriving inn. They have added a new bar area and extended the dining area, allowing them more space to increase the excellent themed events and cookery demonstrations and classes that have proved so popular in recent years. The former deli to the rear of the pub has made way for Ashley's new state-of-the-art kitchen, with the deli now placed in the dining room, where diners can buy freshly baked bread, home-made jams and chutneys, fresh fish, and daily essentials. A marquee in the garden overlooks rolling countryside and is used for large functions, which includes a summer beer festival and regular farmers' markets. Ashley takes pride in sourcing food and ale from small local producers and suppliers, including salads from his own polytunnel, and his menus are innovative and exciting. Lunches include light bites such as sandwiches, salads and wraps, plus there's an excellent Sunday lunch menu featuring locally sourced roasted meats, chef's specials and a dinner menu. Expect

Yorkshire-style main courses such as braised beef cheeks with horseradish mash and casseroled vegetables; steak and Black Sheep Bitter pie with shortcrust pastry; or rack of Yorkshire lamb with bubble-and-squeak and red wine jus. Precede with roasted tomato and pesto soup and finish with upside-down plum sponge with home-made plum sorbet, or tuck into Ashley's tasting platter of desserts. All dishes come with a wine recommendation, or look to the handpumps: Rudgate Battle Axe or Timothy Taylor Landlord are among the choice of seven real ales. Booking for meals may be required.

Open all wk 12-2.30 6-11 (Sun 12-10.30) **Bar Meals** L served Mon-Sat 12-2, Sun 12-7 D served Mon-Sat

6-9.30 Av main course £14
Restaurant L served Mon-Sat 12-2, Sun 12-7 D served Mon-Sat 6-9.30 ⊕ FREE HOUSE ◼ Timothy Taylor Landlord & Golden Best, Rudgate Battle Axe, Black Sheep, Ossett, Moorhouse's, Guest ale Ŏ Aspall. ♇ 18 **Facilities** Children welcome Children's menu Children's portions Garden Beer festival Parking Wi-fi 🚌

CALDWELL
Map 19 NZ11

Brownlow Arms

DL11 7QH ☎ 01325 718471
e-mail: brownlowarms@mail.com
dir: *From A1 at Scotch Corner take A66 towards Bowes. Right onto B6274 to Caldwell. Or from A1 junct 56 take B6275 N. 1st left through Mesonby to junct with B6274. Right to Caldwell*

Set in delightful rolling countryside between Barnard Castle and Darlington, this updated stone inn in the tiny village of Caldwell is a great place to seek out. With ten wines by the glass, plenty more bins and reliable Yorkshire real ales, time passes easily here. A blend of traditional and modern rooms is the setting for unpicking a phenomenally comprehensive menu. How do you like your chicken, for example? Cajun? Satay? Stuffed with spinach and blue cheese? Kiev? In a red Thai curry? Filleted with tarragon and lime? The choice is yours at the Brownlow. Booking for meals may be required.

Open all wk 5.30pm-10.30pm (Sat-Sun 12-11) **Bar Meals** L served Sat-Sun all day fr 12 D served Mon-Fri 5.30-9 **Restaurant** L served Sat-Sun all day fr 12 D served Mon-Fri 5.30-9, Sat-Sun 5-9.30 ⊕ FREE HOUSE ◀ Timothy Taylor Landlord, Black Sheep, John Smith's, Guinness. ♀ 10 **Facilities** Children welcome Children's menu Children's portions Garden Parking Wi-fi

CARTHORPE
Map 19 SE38

The Fox & Hounds

PICK OF THE PUBS

DL8 2LG ☎ 01845 567433
dir: *Off A1, signed on both N'bound & S'bound carriageways*

In the sleepy village of Carthorpe, the cosy Fox and Hounds has been a country inn for over 200 years. The restaurant was once the village smithy, and the old anvil and other tools of the trade are still on display. A family-run pub with a warm welcome, Helen Taylor (whose parents bought the pub some 20 years ago) and her husband Vincent take pride in the quality of their refreshments and food, and have won many awards to prove it. Beers include Black Sheep brewed nearby at Masham, while the wine choice is plentiful and global in scope. The pub's excellent reputation for food is built on named suppliers and daily fresh fish deliveries; a typical dinner choice could begin with whole dressed crab, continue with roast rack of lamb served on a blackcurrant croûton with roast gravy, and finish with spiced dark and white chocolate brownie with vanilla ice cream. There are separate vegetarian and cheese menus.

Open Tue-Sun 12-3 7-11 Closed: 25 Dec & 1st 2wks Jan, Mon **Bar Meals** L served Tue-Sun 12-2 D served Tue-Sun 7-9.30 **Restaurant** L served Tue-Sun 12-2 D served Tue-Sun 7-9.30 ⊕ FREE HOUSE ◀ Black Sheep Best Bitter, Worthington's, Guest ale Ŏ Thatchers Gold. **Facilities** Children welcome Children's portions Parking

CHAPEL LE DALE
Map 18 SD77

The Old Hill Inn

LA6 3AR ☎ 015242 41256
dir: *From Ingleton take B6255 4m, on right*

Originally built as a farm, part of this inn dates back to 1615 and once served passing drovers. You'll find beautiful views of the Dales and many walks on the doorstep, and some of Yorkshire's most famous ales behind the bar. The inn is run by a family of four chefs, one of whom is renowned for his spectacular sugar sculptures (some of which are on display). Lunchtime snacks embrace sandwiches, hot or cold ham and home-made sausages. Larger plates may include beef casserole; mushroom stuffed with ratatouille and chickpeas; and penne all'arrabbiata (pasta in a spicy tomato sauce). Booking for meals may be required.

Open Tue-Sun Closed: 24-25 Dec, Mon (ex BH) **Bar Meals** L served Tue-Sat 12-2.30, Sun 12-3 D served Tue-Fri & Sun 6.30-8.45, Sat 6-8.45 **Restaurant** L served Tue-Sat 12-2.30, Sun 12-3 D served Tue-Fri & Sun 6.30-8.45, Sat 6-8.45 ⊕ FREE HOUSE ◀ Black Sheep Best Bitter, Theakston Best Bitter, Dent Aviator, Guest beer Ŏ Thatchers Gold, Aspall. **Facilities** ♣ Children welcome Children's menu Children's portions Garden Parking ➡ (notice required)

COLTON
Map 16 SE54

Ye Old Sun Inn

PICK OF THE PUBS

See Pick of the Pubs on page 583

CRATHORNE
Map 19 NZ40

The Crathorne Arms NEW

PICK OF THE PUBS

See Pick of the Pubs on opposite page

CRAY
Map 18 SD97

The White Lion Inn

PICK OF THE PUBS

BD23 5JB ☎ 01756 760262
e-mail: admin@whitelioncray.com
dir: *B6265 from Skipton to Grassington, then B6160 towards Aysgarth. Or from Leyburn take A684 towards Hawes. At Aysgarth take B6160 towards Grassington. Cray in 10m*

The celebrated fell-walker Wainwright once described this former drovers' hostelry as a 'tiny oasis', a claim that's just as accurate today. Nestling beneath Buckden Pike, The White Lion is Wharfedale's highest inn and boasts some spectacular scenery. All the qualities of a traditional Yorkshire inn have been maintained here, from warm hospitality to oak beams, log fire and flagstone floors. A good choice of hand-pulled real ales is offered and 20-plus malt whiskies. You can eat and drink in the bar or dining room, though the sight of the cascading Cray Gill, which runs past the inn, is sure to entice children out to the garden. In the bar, lunchtime options include filled baguettes, ploughman's, and plate-sized Yorkshire puddings with a choice of fillings. Also available is a variety of substantial dishes such as roast belly pork stuffed with black pudding; and horseshoe gammon with eggs or pineapple.

Open all day all wk 10am-11pm **Bar Meals** L served all wk 12-2 D served all wk 6-8 Av main course £8.95 ⊕ FREE HOUSE ◀ Timothy Taylor Best, Copper Dragon, Golden Pippin & Best Bitter, John Smith's Cask Ŏ Westons Stowford Press. **Facilities** Children welcome Children's menu Children's portions Garden Parking Wi-fi ➡ (notice required)

CRAYKE
Map 19 SE57

The Durham Ox

PICK OF THE PUBS

See Pick of the Pubs on page 586

CROPTON
Map 19 SE78

The New Inn

YO18 8HH ☎ 01751 417330
e-mail: info@croptonbrewery.com
dir: *Telephone for directions*

On the edge of the North York Moors National Park, this family-run free house is fortunate to have the award-winning Cropton micro-brewery at the bottom of the garden. Popular with locals and visitors alike, the pub is a draw to ale lovers and there is an annual beer festival in November. Meals are served in the restored village bar and in the elegant Victorian restaurant: choices could include Yorkshire coast fishcakes or crisp belly pork with dauphinoise potatoes; an extensive range from the grill; plus lunchtime sandwiches and ciabatta rolls.

Open all day all wk 11-11 (Sun 11-10.30) **Bar Meals** L served all wk 12-2 D served all wk 6-9 Av main course £9.75 **Restaurant** D served all wk 6-9 ⊕ FREE HOUSE ◀ Cropton Two Pints, Yorkshire Warrior, Blackout, Monkmans Slaughter, Yorkshire Moors Bitter & Honey Gold Ŏ Mr Whitehead's. **Facilities** ♣ Children welcome Children's menu Children's portions Play area Family room Garden Beer festival Parking Wi-fi ➡ (notice required)

Save on hotels. Book at **theAA.com/hotel**

YORKSHIRE, NORTH 585 ENGLAND

PICK OF THE PUBS

The Crathorne Arms NEW

CRATHORNE   Map 19 NZ40

TS15 0BA ☎ 01642 701931
e-mail: info@crathorne-arms.co.uk
web: www.crathorne-arms.co.uk
dir: *From Yarm onto A67. At rdbt,
straight on, pass Kirklevington. Over
flyover (A19), 1st right to Crathorne,
pass Crathorne Hall, 200yds on right*

This country pub and restaurant, which
belongs to Lord Crathorne, the current
Lord-Lieutenant of North Yorkshire, is
more than the average hosterly. It has
been trading as a pub since the early
1900s and is full of historical features,
from original beams to old photographs
on the walls. In the bar you'll find
glowing fires and an impressive line-up
of real ales including Black Sheep, Bass
and a weekly guest which can be enjoyed
in 'old school' dimpled pint glasses.
Proprietor Tom Sturman heads up the
kitchen team of very skilled chefs, who
create freshly prepared dishes from local
and seasonal ingredients whenever
possible. You'll often see the Crathorne
Estate gamekeeper enjoying a pint
having dropped off the day's shoot. So
naturally, in season, game features
strongly on the menu – as in a starter of
pigeon breast with apple purée, black
pudding mousse, crispy ham and
beignets of confit pigeon and black
pudding, or a main course of pheasant
breast with crispy leg, pickled cabbage
and shallot, game sausage, juniper
hollandaise and game jus. If game isn't
your thing, you could try seared queen
scallops and pressed pork belly with

spiced pumpkin purée, devilled sauce
and toasted pumpkin seeds; or salad of
beetroot three ways with marinated
Yellison goat's cheese, followed by
smoked paprika dusted monkfish,
chorizo mash, fine beans, baby spinach
and mussel beurre blanc; or pan-fried
chicken breast, truffle sautéed potatoes,
pancetta and pea fricassée. Typical
desserts include banana cake, vanilla
syrup, pecan and almond brittle, banana
smoothie and caramelised banana; and
sticky toffee pudding with toffee sauce
and pistachio ice cream. The Crathorne
Arms hosts a number of events
throughout the year including the annual
Hurworth Hunt and shooting party
breakfasts and dinners. Booking for
meals may be required.

Open Mon 5-11, Tue-Thu 12-3 5-11, Fri
12-3 5-12 **Bar Meals** L served Tue-Sat

12-2.30, Sun 12-5 D served Mon-Sat
5.30-9.30 Av main course £13.95
Restaurant L served Tue-Sat 12-2.30,
Sun 12-5 D served Mon-Sat 5.30-9.30
Fixed menu price fr £10.95 Av 3 course
à la carte fr £20.95 ⊕ FREE HOUSE
◀ Bass, Black Sheep, Guest ales
♻ Gaymers. **Facilities** Children welcome
Children's menu Children's portions
Parking Wi-fi 🚌 (notice required)

PICK OF THE PUBS

The Durham Ox

Westway YO61 4TE ☎ 01347 821506
e-mail: enquiries@thedurhamox.com
web: www.thedurhamox.com
dir: *From A19 through Easingwold to Crayke. From market place left up hill, pub on right*

Whether you march in, arrive by helicopter or take a break on a ramble, the finest of Yorkshire welcomes awaits you at this hilltop pub. The pretty pantiled free house is set in the beautiful Howardian Hills, an Area of Outstanding Natural Beauty just a 20-minute drive from York, whilst Herriot country and the sublime Castle Howard are nearby. A former AA Pub of The Year, The Durham Ox is named after an eponymous ox that was born in 1796 and grew to massive proportions. A print hanging in the bottom bar is dedicated to the Ox's first owner, the Rt Hon Lord Somerville. Another claim to fame is that the Grand Old Duke of York is said to have marched his men up and down the hill outside the inn. With its flagstone floors, exposed beams, oak panelling and roaring winter fires in the main bar, The Durham Ox ticks all the right boxes. The White Rose county provides real ales and the produce for many of the award-winning meals produced in the kitchen, with fish and game being especially well regarded.

Sandwiches and pub classics like fish and chips with mushy peas and chunky chips provide everyday fare, whilst more discerning palates will also find plenty of choice. Start your meal, maybe, with Mrs Bell's twice-baked blue cheese soufflé with cauliflower purée and walnut dressing, before moving on to rump of Dales spring lamb, dauphinoise potatoes, spring cabbage, rosemary and redcurrant reduction. Desserts are no less appealing, with strawberry Eton Mess a typical choice. Booking for meals may be required.

Open all wk all day 12-11.30 (Sun 12-10.30) Closed: 25 Dec **Bar Meals** L served Mon-Sat 12-2.30, Sun 12-3 D served Mon-Sat 5.30-9.30, Sun

5.30-8.30 Av main course £15.95 **Restaurant** L served Mon-Sat 12-2.30, Sun 12-3 D served Mon-Sat 5.30-9.30, Sun 5.30-8.30 Av 3 course à la carte fr £28 ⊕ FREE HOUSE ◀ Timothy Taylor Landlord, Black Sheep Best Bitter. ♟ 10 **Facilities** Children welcome Children's menu Children's portions Garden Parking Wi-fi

Save on hotels. Book at theAA.com/hotel

YORKSHIRE, NORTH 587 ENGLAND

The Blue Lion

PICK OF THE PUBS

DL8 4SN ☎ 01969 624273
e-mail: enquiries@thebluelion.co.uk
web: www.thebluelion.co.uk
dir: *From Ripon take A6108 towards Leyburn*

This smart 18th-century coaching inn, tucked away in an unspoilt estate village close to Jervaulx Abbey, once frequented by drovers and travellers journeying through Wensleydale, has become one of North Yorkshire's finest inns run by Paul and Helen Klein. An extensive but sympathetic refurbishment has created rural chic interiors with stacks of atmosphere and charm. The classic bar with its open fire and flagstone floor is a beer drinker's haven, where the best of North Yorkshire's breweries present a pleasant dilemma for the real ale lover. A blackboard displays imaginative but unpretentious bar meals, while diners in the candlelit restaurant can expect culinary treats incorporating a variety of Yorkshire ingredients, notably seasonal game. A memorable meal may comprise pan-fried king scallops with apple, smoked bacon and black pudding salad; or butternut squash and cep risotto with parmesan and truffle oil; followed by whole roast partridge, buttered cabbage and bread sauce, or slow-braised beef shin, confit garlic mash potato, pancetta and spinach; and warm hazelnut cake, hazelnut mousse and filo crisps to finish.

Open all day all wk 11-11 Closed: 25 Dec **Bar Meals** L served all wk 12-2.15 D served all wk 7-9.30 Av main course £18.95 **Restaurant** L served all wk 12-2.15 D served all wk 7-9.30 Av 3 course à la carte fr £27.50 ⊕ FREE HOUSE ◀ Black Sheep Best Bitter & Riggwelter, Theakston Best Bitter, Worthington's Ŏ Thatchers Gold. ♀ 12 **Facilities** ♣ Children welcome Children's portions Garden Parking Wi-fi

The Cover Bridge Inn

DL8 4SQ ☎ 01969 623250
e-mail: enquiries@thecoverbridgeinn.co.uk
dir: *On A6108 between Middleham & East Witton*

A cunning door-latch befuddles many a first-time visitor to this magnificent little pub, snuggling beside the River Cover at one end of a venerable arched bridge. The pub's oldest part was probably built around 1670, to cater for the increasing trade on the drovers' route from Coverdale.

The ancient interior rewards with wrinkled beams, a vast hearth and open fires, settles and fulfilling fodder, including grand home-made pies and a huge ham and eggs. Settle in the riverside garden with your choice from eight ales on tap and watch the river drift gently by.

Open all day all wk **Bar Meals** L served all wk 12-2 D served all wk 6-9 Av main course £9 ⊕ FREE HOUSE ◀ Guest ales Ŏ Westons Old Rosie, Gwynt y Ddraig Happy Daze. **Facilities** ♣ Children welcome Children's menu Children's portions Play area Garden Parking 🚌 (notice required)

The Wheatsheaf Inn

PICK OF THE PUBS

YO21 1TZ ☎ 01947 895271
e-mail: info@wheatsheafegton.com
dir: *Off A169 NW of Grosmont*

This modest old pub is very popular with fishermen, as the River Esk runs along at the foot of the hill, and is a big draw for fly-fishers in particular. The pub sits back from the wide main road and it would be easy to drive past it, but that would be a mistake as the welcoming main bar is cosy and traditional, with low beams, dark green walls and comfy settles. The menu offers sandwiches, soup and hot foccacia rolls at lunchtime, as well as a range of light lunches, including wholetail Whitby scampi. In the evening, the supper menu might include a starter of lambs' kidneys with bacon, Madeira and redcurrant gravy and main courses such as chicken and smoked bacon puff pastry pie. There's a locals' bar too, but it only holds about a dozen people, so get there early.

Open 11.30-3 5.30-11.30 (Sat 11.30-11.30 Sun 11.30-11) Closed: Mon **Bar Meals** L served Tue-Sun 12-2 D served Tue-Sat 6-9 ⊕ FREE HOUSE ◀ Black Sheep Best Bitter & Golden Sheep, John Smith's, Timothy Taylor Landlord, Guest ales Ŏ Thatchers Gold. **Facilities** Children welcome Garden Parking

Horseshoe Hotel

YO21 1XE ☎ 01947 895245
e-mail: horseshoehotel@yahoo.co.uk
dir: *From Whitby take A171 towards Middlesborough. Village signed in 5m*

The Horseshoe Hotel is an 18th-century country house set in beautiful grounds by the River Esk, handy for visiting Whitby, Robin Hood's Bay, the North Yorkshire Moors Railway and TV's *Heartbeat* country. Inside the welcoming bar are oak settles and tables, local artists' paintings, and plates around the picture rails. Along with some great beers, such as Durham Brewery ale, local ingredients are used to create the varied menu. Change of hands.

Open all wk 11.30-3 6.30-11 (Sat 11.30-11 Sun 12-10.30) **Bar Meals** L served all wk 12-2 D served all wk 6-9 **Restaurant** L served all wk 12-2 D served all wk 6-9 ⊕ FREE HOUSE ◀ John Smith's Cask, Durham, Black Sheep, Theakston, Guest ales. **Facilities** Children welcome Children's menu Children's portions Family room Garden Parking 🚌 (notice required)

The Postgate NEW

YO21 1UX ☎ 01947 895241
dir: *Telephone for directions*

Set in the Esk Valley within a stone's throw of the river, The Postgate is a typical North York Moors country inn; it played the part of the Black Dog in TV's *Heartbeat* programme. Being on the coast-to-coast trail, and becoming known as a food destination, the pub is popular with walkers who chat amiably with locals in the bar over their pints of Black Sheep. A myriad of food choices written on blackboards change with seasonal availability. Fresh fish and seafood are strengths, while hearty dishes of local lamb and mature beef are served with your choice of vegetables, potatoes or salads.

Open all wk 12-3 5.30-12 **Bar Meals** L served all wk 12-2.30 D served all wk 6-9 Av main course £7.95 **Restaurant** L served all wk 12-2.30 D served all wk 6-9 Fixed menu price fr £10.95 Av 3 course à la carte fr £20 ⊕ PUNCH TAVERNS ◀ Timothy Taylor Landlord, Black Sheep Bitter. **Facilities** ♣ Children welcome Children's menu Children's portions Garden Parking Wi-fi 🚌 (notice required)

Black Horse Hotel

32 Church St BD24 0BE ☎ 01729 822506
e-mail: theblackhorse-giggle@tiscali.co.uk
dir: *Telephone for directions*

Set next to the church and behind the market cross in the 17th-century main street, this traditional free house is as charming as Giggleswick itself. Down in the warm and friendly bar you'll find a range of hand-pulled ales, with local guest beer sometimes available. The menu of freshly prepared pub favourites ranges from hot sandwiches, home-made pizzas or giant filled Yorkshire puddings, to main course dishes like traditional lamb hotpot or horseshoe of local gammon. Booking for meals may be required.

Open 12-2.30 5.30-11 (Sat-Sun 12-11) Closed: Mon **Bar Meals** L served Tue-Sun 12-1.45 D served Tue-Sun 7-8.45 Av main course £8 **Restaurant** L served Sun 12-1.45 D served Tue-Sun 7-8.45 ⊕ FREE HOUSE ◀ Timothy Taylor Landlord & Golden Best, John Smith's. **Facilities** Children welcome Children's menu Children's portions Garden Parking Wi-fi

GOATHLAND — Map 19 NZ80

Birch Hall Inn

Beck Hole YO22 5LE ☎ 01947 896245
e-mail: glenys@birchhallinn.fsnet.co.uk
dir: *9m from Whitby on A169*

Beck Hole is a tiny hamlet of nine cottages and a pub hidden in the steep Murk Esk valley close to the North York Moors steam railway. This delightful little free house has just two tiny rooms separated by a sweet shop. The main bar offers well-kept local ales to sup beside an open fire in winter, including the pub's house ale, Beckwatter. In warm weather, food and drink can be enjoyed in the large garden, which has peaceful views of the local walks. The local quoits team play on the village green on summer evenings. The pub has been under the same ownership for over 25 years and the simple menu features the local butcher's pies, old-fashioned flatcakes filled with ham, cheese, corned beef or farmhouse pâté, and home-made scones and buttered beer cake.

Open 11-3 7.30-11 (11-11 summer) Closed: Mon eve & Tue in winter **Bar Meals** L served food served all day in summer ⊕ FREE HOUSE ◁ Birch Hall Inn Beckwatter, Black Sheep Best Bitter, Durham Black Velvet, York Guzzler. **Facilities** ❤ Children welcome Family room Garden **Notes** ⊜

GRASSINGTON — Map 19 SE06

Grassington House ★★★★★ RR ⊛⊛ NEW

5 The Square BD23 5AQ ☎ 01756 752406
e-mail: bookings@grassingtonhousehotel.co.uk
dir: *A59 into Grassington, in town square opposite post office*

Overlooking Grassington's cobbled square and surrounded by the limestone hills of Wharfedale, John and Sue Rudden's elegant pub/restaurant with rooms was built as a private house in 1760, its Georgian architecture still very much an important feature. Fresh local produce, including the Ruddens' own hand-reared, rare-breed pork, joins internationally sourced speciality ingredients for a menu offering celeriac and apple soup; grilled whiting fillet with smoked haddock risotto; pan-roast chicken breast with black pudding; and taster slates of tapas-style dishes. Thwaites and Dark Horse's Hetton Pale Ale from Skipton are in the bar.

Open all day all wk **Bar Meals** L served Mon-Fri 12-2.30, Sat 12-4, Sun 12-8 D served Mon-Sat 6-9.30, Sun 12-8 Av main course £15 **Restaurant** L served all wk 12-2.30 D served Mon-Sat 6-9.30, Sun 6-8 Fixed menu price fr £16.50 Av 3 course à la carte fr £28 ⊕ FREE HOUSE ◁ Dark Horse Hetton Pale Ale, Thwaites Original & Wainwright. ☂ 14 **Facilities** Children welcome Children's menu Children's portions Garden Parking Wi-fi ▭ (notice required) **Rooms** 9

GREAT AYTON — Map 19 NZ51

The Royal Oak ★★★ INN

123 High St TS9 6BW ☎ 01642 722361
e-mail: info@royaloak-hotel.co.uk
dir: *Telephone for directions*

Opposite the green in the village where explorer Captain James Cook went to school, this 18th-century inn has been run by the Monaghan family since 1978. Original features, including beamed ceilings and open fires in the public bar and restaurant, are very much part of its charm and character. An extensive range of food is available all day: from an evening menu come crispy beer-battered cod fillet; shortcrust pie of the day; Chinese-style chicken curry; and vegetable and Yorkshire pudding platter. Stay over in one of the five comfortable bedrooms.

Open all day all wk Closed: 25 Dec **Bar Meals** L served all wk 12-6 D served all wk 6-9.30 Av main course £6 food served all day **Restaurant** L served all wk 12-2 D served all wk 6-9.30 Fixed menu price fr £11.25 ⊕ SCOTTISH & NEWCASTLE ◁ John Smith's Smooth, Courage Directors, Theakston. ☂ 10 **Facilities** ❤ Children welcome Children's menu Children's portions Garden Wi-fi ▭ (notice required) **Rooms** 5

GREAT HABTON — Map 19 SE77

The Grapes Inn NEW

YO17 6TU ☎ 01653 669166
e-mail: info@thegrapes-inn.co.uk
dir: *From Malton take B1257 towards Helmsley. In Amotherby right into Amotherby Ln. After Newsham Bridge right into Habton Ln & follow pubs signs. 0.75m to pub*

Adam and Katie Myers have breathed new life into this once unloved village local, which stands in picturesque Great Habton within easy reach of the North York Moors. Regulars quaffing pints of Ringwood Best fill the cosy bar, replete with roaring winter log fire, while the refurbished dining areas are the domain of local foodies, who come for Adam's imaginative cooking. Fresh local produce is used to create seared scallops on crab risotto with crisp Parma ham, beef fillet on truffle mash with wild mushroom ragout, and bar meals like chicken and leek pie. Leave room for gingerbread sponge. Booking for meals may be required.

Open Tue-Fri 6pm-close (Sat 12-2 6-close Sun open all day) Closed: fr 2 Jan for 2wks, Mon **Bar Meals** L served Sat-Sun 12-2 D served Tue-Sat 6.30-8.30, Sun 7-8.30 Av main course £9-£20 **Restaurant** L served Sat-Sun 12-2 D served Tue-Sat 6.30-8.30, Sun 7-8.30 ⊕ MARSTON'S ◁ Ringwood Best Bitter ♻ Thatchers Gold. **Facilities** Children welcome Children's menu Children's portions Parking

GREEN HAMMERTON — Map 19 SE45

The Bay Horse Inn

York Rd YO26 8BN ☎ 01423 330338
e-mail: enquiry@bayhorsegreenhammerton.co.uk
dir: *A1 junct 47 follow signs for A59 towards York. After 3m, turn left into village, on right opposite post office*

This traditional inn is part of the original settlement of Green Hammerton, positioned on the old Roman road from York to Aldborough. The pub has served travellers and villagers for over 200 years; many original features remain in the beamed, fire-warmed interior. Reliable Yorkshire cask beers accompany home-made meals strong on local produce; excellent matured steaks, gammon and chicken breasts are always available. Daily-changing dishes include haunch of venison steak with pear, cranberry and port sauce; and pork fillet with cider and apple sauce. Outside is a garden and patio area.

Open all wk 11.30-2.30 5.30-12 (Sat 11.30am-mdnt Sun 11.30-8) **Bar Meals** L served all wk 12-2.30 D served Mon-Fri 6-9, Sat 12-9 Av main course £9.95 **Restaurant** L served all wk 12-2.30 D served Mon-Fri 6-9, Sat 12-9, Sun 12-7.30 ⊕ GREENE KING ◁ IPA, Timothy Taylor, Black Sheep, Guest ale. **Facilities** ❤ Children welcome Children's portions Garden Parking Wi-fi ▭ (notice required)

GRINTON — Map 19 SE09

The Bridge Inn

PICK OF THE PUBS

See Pick of the Pubs on opposite page

HARDRAW — Map 18 SD89

The Green Dragon Inn NEW

DL8 3LZ ☎ 01969 667392
e-mail: info@greendragonhardraw.com
dir: *From Hawes take A684. Towards Sedbergh. Right to Hardraw, approx 1.5m*

Step back in time when you enter this North Yorkshire hostelry whose history, reputedly stretching back to the 13th century, is as colourful as JMW Turner's depiction of Hardraw Force, sketched when he stayed here. Whilst revelling in its past, proprietor D. Mark Thompson is not resting on his laurels. The pub hosts the annual Hardraw Scar Brass Band festival, three beer festivals, and regular live folk music. Visitors on a budget will relish the choice of real ales and a short selection of unpretentious pub meals. If you're in the area, don't miss this one.

Open all day all wk **Bar Meals** Av main course £9.95 food served all day **Restaurant** Fixed menu price fr £9.95 Av 3 course à la carte fr £18 food served all day ◁ Timothy Taylor Landlord, Theakston Best Bitter & Old Peculier, Wensleydale, Yorkshire Dales ♻ Olivers, Gwatkins, Dunkertons, Ralph's. **Facilities** Children welcome Children's menu Children's portions Family room Garden Beer festival Parking Wi-fi ▭ (notice required)

PICK OF THE PUBS

The Bridge Inn

GRINTON   Map 19 SE09

DL11 6HH ☎ **01748 884224**
e-mail: atkinbridge@btinternet.com
web: www.bridgeinngrinton.co.uk
dir: *Exit A1 at Scotch Corner onto
A6108, through Richmond. Left onto
B6270 towards Grinton & Reeth*

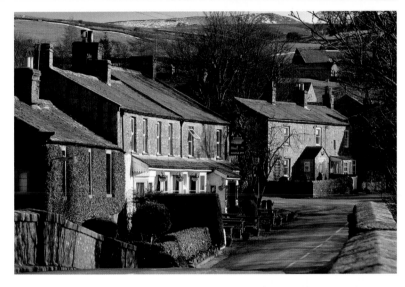

The Bridge is a happy mix of village pub
and dining inn, with locals enjoying the
bustling games room and beamed old
bar whilst a more tranquil restaurant
area caters for those after a more
intimate meal experience. Two of the
Yorkshire Dales' wildest and prettiest
dales meet here in Grinton;
Arkengarthdale and Swaledale collide in
a symphony of fells, moors, waterfalls
and cataracts, at the heart of which
Grinton has stood for nearly 1,000 years.
The inn is just a tad younger; a 13th-
century riverside building close to one of
Yorkshire's finest old churches, known
as the Cathedral of the Dales. Lanes
and tracks slope down from the heights,
bringing ramblers and riders to
appreciate the good range of northern
beers that Andrew Atkin matches with
his fine foods; York Brewery's Yorkshire
Terrier being a case in point. Resident
chef John Scott is in charge of the food,
his menu inspired by carefully chosen
seasonal local game, meats, fish and
other produce, including herbs plucked

from the garden. Expect traditional
English dishes with a modern twist,
enhanced by daily-changing specials.
Starters range from a black pudding
Scotch egg to lamb koftas with mini
spiced poppadums and a roasted garlic
dip. Mains reflect a similar scope,
running from homely steak-and-ale pie,
or cod in real ale and dill batter with
chips to Asian duck leg on noodles with
a black pudding spring roll and a sweet
chilli and plum sauce. Finish with Liz's
ginger pudding; Amaretto cheesecake;
summer pudding; or a selection of
Swaledale cheeses with savoury biscuits
and chutney. For entertainment there is
musicians' night every Thursday.

Open all day all wk **Bar Meals** Av main
course £10 food served all day
Restaurant food served all day
⊕ JENNINGS ◼ Cumberland Ale &
Cocker Hoop, Caledonian Deuchars IPA,
York Yorkshire Terrier, Adnams.
Facilities Children welcome Children's
menu Children's portions ✸ Garden
Parking Wi-fi ▭

HAROME
Map 19 SE68

The Star Inn ⊛⊛

PICK OF THE PUBS

YO62 5JE ☎ 01439 770397

e-mail: reservations@thestarinnatharome.co.uk
dir: *From Helmsley take A170 towards Kirkbymoorside 0.5m. Turn right for Harome*

This 14th-century thatched gem on the fringe of the North Yorkshire Moors National Park has long been one of the jewels in England's gastro-pub crown, but the pubby bar is worth the journey alone. Locals and visitors can glory in Black Sheep or Hambleton Ales from the nearby village of that name, eagerly awaiting the call to dine on Andrew Pern's daily-changing seasonal menu crafted largely from hyper-local produce. Treat yourself to risotto of York ham, flat leaf parsley and grain mustard with garlic-roast Hereford snails and cheddar 'crackling' before moving on to roast rack of Ryedale lamb with a 'hotpot' pie, smoked garlic mash, braised salsify, pearl barley and rosemary juices. Finish with caramelised vanilla rice pudding and Ampleforth apple brandy prunes. Eagle-eyed visitors to the bar might spot the trademark carved mouse which decorates the classic oak furniture created by 'Mouseman' Thompson's works in nearby Kilburn. Booking for meals may be required.

Open all wk 11.30-3 6.30-11 (Mon 6.30-11 Sun 12-11) Closed: 1 Jan, Mon L **Bar Meals** L served Tue-Sat 11.30-2, Sun 12-6 D served Mon-Sat 6.30-9.30 **Restaurant** L served Tue-Sat 11.30-2, Sun 12-6 D served Mon-Sat 6.30-9.30 ⊕ FREE HOUSE ◀ Theakston Best Bitter, Black Sheep, Copper Dragon, Hambleton, Cropton ○ Westons Stowford Press, Ampleforth Abbey. ♀ 24 **Facilities** Children welcome Children's menu Children's portions Garden Parking 🚌 (notice required)

HAWES
Map 18 SD88

The Moorcock Inn

Garsdale Head LA10 5PU ☎ 01969 667488

e-mail: admin@moorcockinn.com
dir: *On A684 5m from Hawes, 10m from Sedbergh at junct for Kirkby Stephen (10m). Garsdale Station 1m*

At the tip of Wensleydale, this 18th-century inn stands alone in open countryside, although it is only three-quarters of a mile from Garsdale Station. Inside is a traditional blend of original stonework and bright colours, comfortable sofas, wooden chairs and an open fire in winter. Savour a glass of local real ale or one of the 50 malt whiskies, and enjoy the spectacular views from the garden. Home-cooked lunches include jackets, sandwiches and pub classics. For dinner, a starter of chicken liver pâté might be followed with game and chestnut stew; bangers and mash; or cherry tomato and red onion tart.

Open all day all wk 12-12 **Bar Meals** L served all wk 12-3 Av main course £9 **Restaurant** D served all wk 6.30-9 Fixed menu price fr £8 ⊕ FREE HOUSE ◀ Black Sheep, Copper Dragon, Theakston, Guest ales ○ Thatchers. ♀ 8 **Facilities** ❀ Children welcome Children's menu

Children's portions Family room Garden Parking Wi-fi 🚌 (notice required)

HAWNBY
Map 19 SE58

The Inn at Hawnby ★★★★ INN ⊛

PICK OF THE PUBS

YO62 5QS ☎ 01439 798202

e-mail: info@innathawnby.co.uk
web: www.innathawnby.co.uk
dir: *Off B1257 between Stokesley & Helmsley*

At the top of a hill in the village of Hawnby, this charming 19th-century former drovers' inn with rooms is set in the heart of the North Yorkshire Moors, and offers panoramic views of the surrounding countryside. With hands-on and welcoming proprietors, Kathryn and David Young, the award-winning, one AA-Rosette cuisine majors on local produce. Dishes such as seared scallops, cauliflower jelly, black pudding and Yorkshire apple; rump of lamb, salt-baked turnips, lardons, potatoes and Cumberland sauce; and smoked haddock risotto with chopped hen's eggs can be enjoyed with a pint of light and quaffable Hawnby Hops ale brewed especially for the pub. Puddings include pistachio cake with blackberry sorbet; and chocolate nemesis with vanilla ice cream. For designated drivers, there's even free water from the inn's own spring. If you would like to stay over, there are nine comfortable rooms.

Open all wk 10-3 6-11 (Fri-Sun all day) Closed: 25 Dec **Bar Meals** L served all wk 12-2 D served all wk 7-9 Av main course £12.95 **Restaurant** L served all wk 12-2 D served all wk 7-9 Av 3 course à la carte fr £25 ⊕ FREE HOUSE ◀ Timothy Taylor Landlord, Black Sheep, Hawnby Hops ○ Westons Stowford Press. ♀ 8 **Facilities** Children welcome Children's menu Children's portions Garden Parking Wi-fi 🚌 (notice required) **Rooms** 9

HIGH GRANTLEY
Map 19 SE26

The Grantley Arms NEW

HG4 3PJ ☎ 01765 620227

e-mail: vsails2@aol.com
dir: *From Ripon on B6265 towards Pateley Bridge (pass Fountains Abbey) take 2nd right signed Grantley. 0.5m pub on left*

You'll find this 17th-century inn in the picturesque village of High Grantley on the edge of the Yorkshire Dales National Park three miles from Fountains Abbey and five miles from the market town of Ripon. Valerie Sails and Eric Broadwith have been at the helm here since 2001

and they pride themselves on their friendly welcome, locally brewed ales and home-cooked food. Typical dishes include pan-fried scallops with apple and black pudding velouté; locally farmed fillet of beef with oxtail, foie gras and Puy lentils; and fruit crumble with crème anglaise.

Open 12-2 5.30-11 Closed: Mon (Nov-Mar) **Bar Meals** L served all wk 12-2 D served all wk 5.30-9 **Restaurant** L served all wk 12-2 D served all wk 5.30-9 ⊕ FREE HOUSE ◀ Theakston, Hambleton, Daleside, Great Newsome, Black Sheep ○ Thatchers Gold. ♀ 10 **Facilities** Children welcome Children's menu Children's portions Parking 🚌 (notice required)

HOVINGHAM
Map 19 SE67

The Malt Shovel

Main St YO62 4LF ☎ 01653 628264

e-mail: info@themaltshovelhovingham.com
dir: *18m NE of York, 5m from Castle Howard*

Tucked away in the Duchess of Kent's home village, the stone-built 18th-century Malt Shovel offers a friendly atmosphere with well-kept ales and food prepared from quality local ingredients. There are two dining rooms where you can enjoy starters of whitebait with lime and chili mayonnaise, chicken liver pâté with chutney, or black pudding and apple fritters, followed by swordfish with tomato and anchovy sauce, mustard chicken, or chickpea curry. There is also a large beer garden at the rear of the pub where you can sit and enjoy a pint or two in lovely surroundings. Booking for meals may be required.

Open all wk Winter 11.30-2 6-11 (Sun & Summer 11.30-2.30 5.30-11) **Bar Meals** L served Mon-Sat 11.30-2 (winter) 11.30-2.30 (summer), Sun 12-2.30 D served Mon-Sat 6-9 (winter) 5.30-9 (summer), Sun 5.30-8 **Restaurant** L served Mon-Sat 11.30-2 (winter) 11.30-2.30 (summer), Sun 12-2.30 D served Mon-Sat 6-9 (winter) 5.30-9 (summer), Sun 5.30-8 ⊕ PUNCH TAVERNS ◀ Copper Dragon Golden Pippin, Theakston Best Bitter, Black Sheep, Guest ale. **Facilities** Children welcome Children's menu Children's portions Garden Parking 🚌 (notice required)

The Worsley Arms Hotel

PICK OF THE PUBS

Main St YO62 4LA ☎ 01653 628234

e-mail: enquiries@worsleyarms.co.uk
dir: *On B1257 between Malton & Helmsley*

The Worsley Arms has been welcoming guests to the village of Hovingham since 1841, when Sir William Worsley built a spa house and a hotel. The spa failed, but the hotel survived and, together with the separate pub, forms part of the Worsley family's historic Hovingham Hall Estate, birthplace of the Duchess of Kent, and currently home to her nephew. You can eat in the restaurant or the Cricketer's Bar (the local team has played on the village green for over 150 years). Hambleton beers from nearby Thirsk are on tap, and food choices in the pub include home-made chicken liver parfait flavoured with port and Armagnac; steak, ale and button mushroom pie with puff pastry lid; classic Caesar salad and a range of ciabatta sandwiches. A short drive from Pickering and Thirsk, the pub is a magnificent base for exploring North Yorkshire. Booking for meals may be required.

Open all day all wk 11-11 ⊕ FREE HOUSE ◀ Tetley's, Hambleton. **Facilities** Children welcome Garden Parking

HUBBERHOLME　　　　Map 18 SD97

The George Inn

BD23 5JE ☎ 01756 760223
dir: *From Skipton take B6265 to Threshfield. B6160 to Buckden. Follow signs for Hubberholme*

To check if the bar is open, look for a lighted candle in the window. Another old tradition is the annual land-letting auction on the first Monday night of the year, when local farmers bid for 16 acres of land owned by the church. Stunningly located beside the River Wharfe in the Yorkshire Dales National Park, this pub has flagstone floors, stone walls, mullioned windows, an open fire and an inviting summer terrace. With beers from Black Sheep and Yorkshire Dales breweries, evening menus include Wensleydale pork escalope, and Thai-style fishcakes. There's a reduced lunch menu with the addition of baguettes. Booking for meals may be required.

Open 12-3 6-11 Closed: 1st 2wks Dec, Mon **Bar Meals** L served Tue-Sun 12-2 D served Tue-Sun 6.30-8 Av main course £10 ⊕ FREE HOUSE ◀ Black Sheep, Yorkshire Dales ♂ Thatchers Gold. **Facilities** Children welcome Children's menu Garden Parking

KETTLEWELL　　　　Map 18 SD97

The Kings Head

The Green BD23 5RD ☎ 01756 760242
e-mail: info@kingsheadkettlewell.co.uk
dir: *Take B6160 to Kettlewell from either A684, or A59 at Bolton Bridge*

A traditional pub with an inglenook fireplace and fabulous views, The Kings Head is a great base from which to explore the breathtaking scenery of the Yorkshire Dales – and the village of Kettlewell is as quaint and pretty as its name suggests. Expect to find local cask ales and an appealing menu of home-cooked favourites such as a warm Wensleydale flan to start, followed by steak-and-ale pie, with a warm chocolate fudge brownie for dessert. The pub welcomes children and dogs.

Open all day all wk **Bar Meals** L served all wk 12-2.30 D served all wk 5-8.30 Av main course £12 **Restaurant** Av 3 course à la carte fr £19.95 ⊕ FREE HOUSE ◀ Black Sheep Bitter, Tetley's, Kings Head ♂ Thatchers Gold. **Facilities** ♣ Children welcome Children's menu Children's portions Parking Wi-fi ▆

KILBURN　　　　Map 19 SE57

The Forresters Arms Inn

The Square YO61 4AH ☎ 01347 868386
e-mail: admin@forrestersarms.com
dir: *From Thirsk take A170, after 3m turn right signed Kilburn. At Kilburn Rd junct, turn right, Inn on left in village square*

A sturdy stone-built former coaching inn still catering for travellers passing close by the famous White Horse of Kilburn on the North York Moors. Next door is the famous Robert Thompson workshop; fine examples of his early work, with the distinctive mouse symbol on every piece, can be seen in both bars. Visiting coachmen would undoubtedly have enjoyed the log fires, cask ales and good food as much as today's visitors. Dishes include starters like prawn Marie Rose with brown bread or pheasant and ham terrine served with apple and walnut chutney, and continue with steak-and-ale pie, haddock fillet in Hambleton ale batter, or slow-roasted belly pork with mash and braised red cabbage. There's also a specials board and a selection of lunchtime snacks.

Open all day all wk 9am-11pm **Bar Meals** L served Mon-Fri 12-3, off season 12-2.30, Sat-Sun all day D served all wk 6-9, off season 6-8 **Restaurant** L served Mon-Fri 12-3, off season 12-2.30, Sat-Sun all day D served all wk 6-9, off season 6-8 ⊕ ENTERPRISE INNS ◀ John Smith's Cask, Hambleton Best Bitter, Guest ales ♂ Symonds Founder Reserve. **Facilities** ♣ Children welcome Children's menu Children's portions Garden Beer festival Parking Wi-fi ▆

KIRBY HILL　　　　Map 19 NZ10

The Shoulder of Mutton Inn

DL11 7JH ☎ 01748 822772
e-mail: info@shoulderofmutton.net
dir: *From A1 Scotch Corner junct take A66. Approx 6m follow signs for Kirby Hill on left*

Enjoying an elevated village position, this ivy-clad 18th-century inn enjoys stunning views over Holmedale from its garden and sheltered patio. Open log fires warm the traditional interior, where you can sup local Daleside ales, while the stone-walled restaurant, replete with original beams and white linen, is the place to tuck into daily-changing home-cooked dishes. Follow local black pudding, blue cheese and apple salad, with roast duck on bubble-and-squeak with Madeira sauce; or pork loin with a cream tarragon and mushroom sauce. Good hearty bar snacks are also served. Look out for the beer festival. Booking for meals may be required.

Open all wk 6-11 (Sat-Sun 12-3 6-11) **Bar Meals** L served Sat-Sun 12-2 D served Wed-Sun 6.30-9 Av main course £8.50-£15 **Restaurant** L served Sun 12-2 D served Wed-Sun 6.30-9 Av 3 course à la carte fr £22.50 ⊕ FREE HOUSE ◀ Daleside, Guest ales ♂ Thatchers. **Facilities** Children welcome Garden Beer festival Parking

KIRKBY FLEETHAM　　　　Map 19 SE29

The Black Horse Inn ★★★★★ RR ◉◉

Lumley Ln DL7 0SH ☎ 01609 749010
e-mail: gm@blackhorsekirkbyfleetham.com
dir: *Village signed from A1 between Catterick & Leeming Bar*

Legend has it that Dick Turpin eloped with his lady from this village pub in the Swale valley, just off the vast village green; the inn was named after the outlaw's steed in celebration. The pub garden adjoins fields, and the interior, including the seven characterful bedrooms, has been stylishly remodelled to create a pleasing mix of tradition and comfort. No surprise then that locals and visitors are encouraged to tarry a while, to sup a grand Yorkshire pint and enjoy accomplished two AA-Rosette food that covers all the bases. Look for signature starters such as chef's black pudding with parsnip mash, and main courses like baked monkfish and Parma ham.

Open all day all wk **Bar Meals** L served Mon-Sat 12-2.30, Sun 12-7 D served Mon-Sat 5-9.30, Sun 12-7 Av main course £10 **Restaurant** L served Mon-Sat 12-2.30, Sun 12-7 D served Mon-Sat 5-9.30, Sun 12-7 Av 3 course à la carte fr £21 ⊕ FREE HOUSE ◀ Black Sheep, Copper Dragon, Timothy Taylor Landlord. ♟ 10 **Facilities** Children welcome Children's menu Children's portions Garden Parking Wi-fi **Rooms** 7

KIRKBYMOORSIDE　　　　Map 19 SE68

George & Dragon Hotel
PICK OF THE PUBS

17 Market Place YO62 6AA ☎ 01751 433334
e-mail: reception@georgeanddragon.net
dir: *Just off A170 between Scarborough & Thirsk. In town centre*

The G&D, as it is affectionately known, is a family-owned, town-centre coaching inn. Its undoubted charm is due to many things – the log fire in the bar, the sheltered courtyard and fountain, the collection of cricketing, golf and rugby paraphernalia. Order a pint of Copper Dragon, Daleside or one of the other real ales and grab a seat in one of the nooks and crannies. Then, in the adjoining bistro and restaurant, tuck into a lunchtime Cajun salmon fillet, or curry of the day. Or, if an evening meal in wooden-floored Knight's Restaurant suits you better, begin with crispy fried Somerset brie, then enjoy Yorkshire venison steak with baby boar sausage, mash and crispy leeks, creamed cabbage and redcurrant sauce; or roast fillet of sea bass, crab and spring onion mash and lemon and prawn butter sauce. The traditional Sunday carvery is hugely popular.

Open all day all wk 10.30am-11pm **Bar Meals** L served all wk 12-2 D served all wk 6-9 Av main course £8 **Restaurant** L served all wk 12-2 D served all wk 6-9 Av 3 course à la carte fr £20 ⊕ FREE HOUSE ◀ Greene King Abbot Ale, Copper Dragon, Daleside, Black Sheep, Guest ales. ♟ 12 **Facilities** Children welcome Children's menu Children's portions Garden Parking Wi-fi ▆

KIRKHAM — Map 19 SE76

Stone Trough Inn

PICK OF THE PUBS

Kirkham Abbey YO60 7JS ☎ 01653 618713
e-mail: timstonetroughinn@live.co.uk
dir: *1.5m off A64, between York & Malton*

Set amongst the Howardian Hills in a stunning location overlooking Kirkham Priory and the River Derwent, this free house has a great reputation for fine food and a great selection of real ales. Stone Trough Cottage was converted to an inn during the early 1980s, and took its name from the base of a 12th-century cross erected by a French knight to commemorate a son killed in a riding accident. The cross has long since disappeared, but its hollowed-out base now stands at the entrance to the car park. A real fire, bare beams and wooden settles make for a pleasingly traditional interior. Food-wise, the menu includes salmon fillet on champ mashed potato with a saffron, leek and prawn sauce; potato, chickpea and spinach curry with tomato, fresh ginger and yogurt; and chicken fillet in bacon with saffron rice and lightly curried coconut cream.

Open all day all wk 11-11 (Sun 12-11) ⊕ FREE HOUSE ◀ Tetley's Cask, Timothy Taylor Landlord, Black Sheep Best Bitter, York, Cropton, Wold Top, Guest ales. **Facilities** Children welcome Children's menu Children's portions Garden Parking

KNARESBOROUGH — Map 19 SE35

The General Tarleton Inn ★★★★★ RR ⑥⑥

PICK OF THE PUBS

See Pick of the Pubs on opposite page

LANGTHWAITE — Map 19 NZ00

The Red Lion Inn

DL11 6RE ☎ 01748 884218
e-mail: rlionlangthwaite@aol.com
web: www.redlionlangthwaite.co.uk
dir: *Through Reeth into Arkengarthdale, 18m from A1*

The Red Lion is a traditional country pub owned by the same family for 47 years. It hosts two darts teams in winter, a quoits team in summer, and bar snacks are served all year round. There are some wonderful walks in this part of the Dales and relevant books and maps are on sale in the bar. In the tiny snug there are photographs relating to the various films and TV programmes filmed at this unusually photogenic pub (including *All Creatures Great and Small*, *A Woman of Substance* and *Hold the Dream*). Ice cream, chocolates and sweets are available as well.

Open all wk 11-3 7-11 **Bar Meals** L served all wk 11-3 ⊕ FREE HOUSE ◀ Black Sheep Best Bitter & Riggwelter, Worthington's Creamflow, Guinness Ŏ Thatchers Gold. ₹ 9 **Facilities** Family room Garden Parking

LASTINGHAM — Map 19 SE79

Blacksmiths Arms

YO62 6TN ☎ 01751 417247
e-mail: pete.hils@blacksmithslastingham.co.uk
dir: *7m from Pickering & 4m from Kirkbymoorside. A170 (Pickering to Kirbymoorside road), follow Lastingham & Appleton-le-Moors signs*

Opposite St Mary's Church (renowned for its Saxon crypt) in the National Park area, this stone-built free house retains its original 17th-century low-beamed ceilings and open range fireplace. Outside there's a cottage garden and decked seating area. Home-cooked dishes prepared from locally supplied ingredients are served in the smartly decorated dining areas, and include home-made steak-and-ale pie; Whitby wholetail scampi with home-made tartare sauce; and jumbo crispy cod with chips and mushy peas. There is a takeaway service too. Enjoy the food with a pint of Theakston Best Bitter or one of the guest ales. Booking for meals may be required.

Open all day all wk **Bar Meals** L served all wk 12-5 D served all wk 6.30-8.45 Av main course £10 **Restaurant** L served all wk 12-5 D served Mon-Sat 6.30-8.45 ⊕ FREE HOUSE ◀ Theakston Best Bitter, 2 Guest ales. **Facilities** Children welcome Children's menu Children's portions Family room Garden Wi-fi ➡

LEVISHAM — Map 19 SE89

Horseshoe Inn ★★★★ INN

Main St YO18 7NL ☎ 01751 460240
e-mail: info@horseshoelevisham.co.uk
dir: *A169, 5m from Pickering. 4m, pass Fox & Rabbit Inn on right. In 0.5m left to Lockton. Follow steep winding road to village*

This welcoming country inn sits at the head of a tranquil village on the edge of the North York Moors National Park. It makes an ideal base for walking, cycling and touring the moors – don't miss a trip on the nearby steam railway. Charles and Toby Wood have created an inviting atmosphere in the beamed bar, with its polished plank floor and roaring log fire, offering tip-top ales and hearty country cooking - maybe Whitby haddock with chips and mushy peas, wild mushroom risotto with parmesan, duck breast on sweet potato mash, or venison suet pudding with sloe gin gravy. There are nine comfortable bedrooms available. Booking for meals may be required.

Open all day all wk **Bar Meals** L served all wk 12-2 D served all wk 6-8.30 Av main course £10 **Restaurant** L served all wk 12-2 D served all wk 6-8.30 Av 3 course à la carte fr £20 ⊕ FREE HOUSE ◀ Black Sheep Best Bitter, Cropton Yorkshire Moors, Two Pints, Yorkshire Warrior & Endeavour Ŏ Thatchers Gold. ₹ 12 **Facilities** ♣ Children welcome Children's menu Children's portions Garden Parking Wi-fi **Rooms** 9

LEYBURN — Map 19 SE19

The Queens Head ★★★★ INN

Westmoor Ln, Finghall DL8 1QZ ☎ 01677 450259
e-mail: enquiries@queensfinghall.co.uk
dir: *From Bedale follow A684 W towards Leyburn, just after pub & caravan park turn left signed to Finghall. Follow road, on left*

The dining room at this 18th-century village inn overlooks Wild Wood – believed to be one of the inspirations for Kenneth Grahame to write *The Wind in the Willows*. Set on a hillside terrace above Wensleydale, this is a place where drinkers can quaff a pint of Black Sheep by the fire and diners can order from a menu ranging from sandwiches and pub favourites to contemporary dishes like smoked haddock and leek fishcake or roast lamb rump, braised lamb rissole, creamed spinach and mint. Spacious accommodation is located in the adjacent annexe.

Open all wk 12-3 6-close Closed: 26 Dec & 1 Jan **Bar Meals** L served all wk 12-2 D served all wk 6-9 **Restaurant** L served all wk 12-2 D served all wk 6-9 ⊕ FREE HOUSE ◀ Black Sheep Best Bitter, Theakston Best Bitter. ₹ 10 **Facilities** Children welcome Children's menu Children's portions Garden Parking ➡ (notice required) **Rooms** 3

PICK OF THE PUBS

The General Tarleton Inn ★★★★★ RR

KNARESBOROUGH Map 19 SE35

Boroughbridge Rd, Ferrensby HG5 0PZ
☎ **01423 340284**
e-mail: gti@generaltarleton.co.uk
web: www.generaltarleton.co.uk
dir: *A1(M) junct 48 at Boroughbridge,
take A6055 to Knaresborough. Inn 4m
on right*

General Banastre Tarleton gained a bit of a
reputation during the American War of
Independence, and it was probably a British
soldier who'd fought alongside him who later
asked his permission to rename this 18th-
century coaching inn in his honour. Standing
in pleasant surroundings just north of
Knaresborough, it's handy for the Yorkshire
Dales. The much renovated interior still
retains its old beams and original log fires,
while the sofas encourage guests to settle
down with one of the seasonal menus that
have helped chef-proprietor John Topham
and his capable team earn two AA Rosettes.
That John supports the use of Yorkshire
produce is immediately apparent when you
read that East Coast fish is delivered daily,
local vegetables arrive the day they've been
picked, and the game comes from nearby
shoots. His 'Food with Yorkshire Roots' may
be eaten in the Bar Brasserie, in the fine-
dining restaurant, or in the terrace garden
and courtyard. If you start with Little
Moneybags, you'll experience the inn's widely
renowned signature starter of crisp pastry
seafood parcels in lobster sauce. Other
tempting openers include warm shredded
duck salad with chorizo, lardons, croûtons
and salad leaves, and chicken liver parfait
with toasted brioche, quince purée and
pickled walnuts. Among the mains look out
for a rabbit extravaganza of roast loin, best
end and herb-stuffed leg in bacon, with
mini-rabbit pie, celeriac purée, girolles,
broad beans and truffle jus. Also appearing
might be seafood thermidor – salmon,
haddock, cod, monkfish and prawns in a
brandy, mustard and cheese sauce; and
ricotta and basil cannelloni. Accompanying
wines can be selected from a list of 150,
many from smaller producers. The bedrooms
are individually decorated and have
everything you'd expect, including Auntie
Bertha's daily baked biscuits, made to an
old Topham family recipe. Booking for meals
may be required.

Open all wk 12-3 5.30-11 **Bar Meals** L
served all wk 12-2 D served all wk
5.30-9.15 Av main course £16
Restaurant L served Sun 12-1.45
D served Mon-Sat 6-9.15 Av 3 course à
la carte fr £27.65 ⊕ FREE HOUSE
◧ Black Sheep Best Bitter, Timothy
Taylor Landlord Ŏ Aspall. ⬤ 11
Facilities Children welcome Children's
menu Children's portions Garden
Parking Wi-fi **Rooms** 13

LEYBURN *continued*

Sandpiper Inn

PICK OF THE PUBS

Market Place DL8 5AT ☎ **01969 622206**
e-mail: hsandpiper99@aol.com
dir: *A1 onto A684 to Leyburn*

This 17th-century, ivy-clad inn occupies the oldest building in Leyburn, but has only been a pub for some 30 years. Handy for Wensleydale and many other Yorkshire attractions, it has a bar and snug where you can enjoy a pint of Copper Dragon or take your pick from 100 single malts. Chef-proprietor Jonathan Harrison has established an excellent reputation for preparing modern British food using the finest ingredients. Head for the dining room to peruse the list of exciting and varied traditional and international dishes such as pork and pheasant sausage with creamed wild garlic followed by breast of Nidderdale chicken with black bacon, roasted vegetables and potato dauphinoise. Lunch brings sandwiches and light meals such as omelette Arnold Bennett or sausages and mash with gravy. For desert, maybe apple and plum crumble with custard. Booking for meals may be required.

Open 11.30-3 6.30-11 (Sun 12-2.30 6.30-10.30) Closed: Mon & occasionally Tue **Bar Meals** L served Tue-Sun 12-2.30 **Restaurant** L served Tue-Sun 12-2.30 D served Tue-Thu & Sun 6.30-9, Fri-Sat 6.30-9.30 ⊕ FREE HOUSE ◀ Black Sheep Best Bitter, Daleside, Copper Dragon, Archers, Yorkshire Dales ♻ Thatchers Gold. ♟ 10 **Facilities** Children welcome Children's menu Family room Garden Wi-fi

---

LITTON   Map 18 SD97

Queens Arms

BD23 5QJ ☎ **01756 770208**
e-mail: queens.litton@gmail.com
dir: *N of Skipton*

Dating from the 18th century, this drovers' inn is full of original features including flagstones and beams. The open fire offers a warm winter welcome to outdoor enthusiasts, fresh from enjoying the Yorkshire Dales countryside. Cask-conditioned ales from the on-site micro-brewery accompany home-cooked dishes like local lamb chops, beer-battered haddock or chef's veggie tart. There are stunning views from the bars and garden. Booking for meals may be required.

Open 12-3 6.30-11.30 (Sun 7-11) Closed: Mon ⊕ FREE HOUSE ◀ Litton Ale, Tetley's Cask, Guest ales ♻ Westons Stowford Press. **Facilities** Children welcome Children's portions Family room Garden Parking

---

LONG PRESTON   Map 18 SD85

Maypole Inn

Maypole Green BD23 4PH ☎ **01729 840219**
e-mail: robert@maypole.co.uk
dir: *On A65 between Settle & Skipton*

It was 1695 when Ambrose Wigglesworth first threw open the doors of this inn in on the edge of what is now the Yorkshire Dales National Park. The village maypole stands on the green outside and seating provides great views of Long Preston Moor. The pub's commitment to real ale and cider has earned it top honours, while its traditional home cooking ensures eminently satisfying food. The beamed dining room and cosy bar with open fire are welcoming, so relax and sup a pint of Bowland while your Hellifield sausages with mash and onion gravy are being prepared.

Open all day all wk **Bar Meals** L served Sun-Thu 12-9, Fri-Sat 12-9.30 Av main course £9.50 food served all day

---

Restaurant L served Mon-Fri 12-2.30, Sat-Sun all day D served Mon-Fri 6-9, Sat-Sun all day ⊕ ENTERPRISE INNS ◀ Timothy Taylor Landlord, Moorhouse's Premier Bitter, Jennings, Cumberland, Copper Dragon, Bowland ♻ Westons Wyld Organic Vintage, Gwynt y Ddraig Black Dragon, Sandford Orchards Devon Scrumpy, Saxon Ruby Tuesday. ♟ 11 **Facilities** ♣ Children welcome Children's menu Children's portions Garden Parking Wi-fi 🚌 (notice required)

LOW ROW   Map 18 SD99

The Punch Bowl Inn ★★★★ INN

DL11 6PF ☎ **01748 886233**
e-mail: info@pbinn.co.uk
web: www.pbinn.co.uk
dir: *A1 from Scotch Corner take A6108 to Richmond. Through Richmond then right onto B6270 to Low Row*

Located in Swaledale with Wainwright's Coast to Coast Walk on the doorstep, this Grade II listed, refurbished pub dates back to the 17th century. During a refurbishment a couple of years ago, the bar and bar stools were hand-crafted by Robert 'The Mouseman' Thompson's Craftsmen Ltd (see if you can spot the mice around the bar). Typical food choices include cream of cauliflower and cheddar soup; herb-crusted salmon fillet with prawns and Bercy sauce; and poached pear in spiced red wine and crème fraiche. Local cask-conditioned ales also feature. If you would like to stay over for the Swaledale festivals, there are stylish bedrooms available, all with spectacular views. Booking for meals may be required.

Open all day all wk 11am-mdnt Closed: 25 Dec **Bar Meals** L served all wk 12-2 D served all wk 6-9 Av main course £13.75 **Restaurant** L served all wk 12-2 D served all wk 6-9 Av 3 course à la carte fr £24.50 ⊕ FREE HOUSE ◖ Theakston Best Bitter, Black Sheep Best Bitter & Riggwelter, Timothy Taylor Landlord Ö Thatchers Gold. ♟ 13 **Facilities** Children welcome Children's menu Children's portions Parking Wi-fi ▨ (notice required) **Rooms** 11

MALHAM　　　　　　Map 18 SD96

The Lister Arms ★★★★ INN

PICK OF THE PUBS

See Pick of the Pubs on page 596
See advert on opposite page

MASHAM　　　　　　Map 19 SE28

The Black Sheep Brewery

Wellgarth HG4 4EN ☎ 01765 680101 & 680100
e-mail: sue.dempsey@blacksheep.co.uk
web: www.blacksheepbrewery.co.uk
dir: *Off A6108, 9m from Ripon & 7m from Bedale*

Set up by Paul Theakston, a member of Masham's famous brewery family, in the former Wellgarth Maltings in 1992, the complex includes an excellent visitor centre and a popular bar-cum-bistro. Take a fascinating tour of the brewery, then take in the wonderful views over the River Ure and surrounding countryside as you sup tip-top pints of Riggwelter and Golden Sheep. Tuck into a good plate of food, perhaps braised beef, fish pie, pan-fried lamb's liver with black pudding, mash and rich onion gravy, or a roast beef sandwich. Booking for meals may be required.

Open all wk 10.30-4.30 (Thu-Sat 10.30am-late) **Restaurant** L served Mon-Sat 12-2.30, Sun 12-3 D served Thu-Sat 6.30-9 ⊕ BLACK SHEEP BREWERY ◖ Best Bitter, Riggwelter, Ale, Golden Sheep. **Facilities** Children welcome Children's menu Children's portions Garden Parking Wi-fi ▨

The White Bear NEW

Wellgarth HG4 4EN ☎ 01765 689319
e-mail: sue@whitebearmasham.co.uk
dir: *Signed from A1 between Bedale & Ripon*

Theakston Brewery's flagship inn stands just a short stroll from the legendary brewhouse and market square in this bustling market town and provides the perfect base for exploring the Yorkshire Dales. Handsome and refurbished with style in recent years, there's a snug taproom for quaffing pints of Old Peculier by the glowing fire, oak-floored lounges with deep sofas and chairs for perusing the daily papers, and an elegant dining room. Menus take in lamb shank with ratatouille, hot roast beef baguette, and specials like game pie and smoked haddock and pea risotto. Expect 30 cask ales at the late June beer festival.

Open all day all wk **Bar Meals** food served all day **Restaurant** food served all day ⊕ FREE HOUSE/ THEAKSTON ◖ Best Bitter, Black Bull Bitter, Lightfoot & Old Peculier, Caledonian Deuchars IPA. **Facilities** ❀ Children welcome Children's menu Children's portions Garden Beer festival Parking Wi-fi ▨ (notice required)

MIDDLEHAM　　　　　Map 19 SE18

Black Swan Hotel

Market Place DL8 4NP ☎ 01969 622221
e-mail: theblackswanmiddleham@yahoo.com
dir: *Telephone for directions*

Backing onto Middleham Castle, home of Richard III, this historic 17th-century pub stands in the village square and is at the heart of Yorkshire's racing country. Horses can be seen passing outside every morning on their way to the gallops. In the beamed bar quaff Black Sheep ales and tuck into a hearty bar meal, perhaps steak and Guinness pie or a bowl of mussels cooked in white wine. More adventurous dishes are offer in the restaurant, from tuna marinated in ginger, chilli, garlic and soy to rabbit stew and grilled ostrich with red wine and redcurrant sauce. Change of hands. Booking for meals may be required.

Open all day all wk **Bar Meals** L served all wk 12-3 D served all wk 5-9 Av main course £8.50 **Restaurant** D served all wk 5-9 Fixed menu price fr £10.50 Av 3 course à la carte fr £17 ⊕ ENTERPRISE INNS ◖ John Smith's, Theakston Best Bitter & Old Peculier, Black Sheep. ♟ 10 **Facilities** ❀ Children welcome Children's menu Children's portions Garden Wi-fi ▨

The White Swan

Market Place DL8 4PE ☎ 01969 622093
e-mail: enquiries@whiteswanhotel.co.uk
dir: *From A1, take A684 towards Leyburn then A6108 to Ripon, 1.5m to Middleham*

Paul Klein's Tudor coaching inn stands in the cobbled market square in the shadow if Middleham's ruined castle and, like the village, is steeped in the history of the turf, with several top horseracing stables located in the area. Expect to find oak beams, flagstones and roaring log fires in the atmospheric bar, where you can quaff tip-top Black Sheep ales and enjoy modern British pub food. Using quality Yorkshire produce the menu takes in baked egg Florentine, braised leg of lamb with mash and a rich jus, and glazed lemon tart with raspberry sauce. Booking for meals may be required.

Open all day all wk 10.30am-11pm (mdnt at wknds) **Bar Meals** Av main course £12.50 food served all day **Restaurant** L served all wk 8am-9.30pm (bkfst fr 8am) D served all wk 8am-9.30pm (bkfst fr 8am) Fixed menu price fr £14.95 Av 3 course à la carte fr £26.95 food served all day ⊕ FREE HOUSE ◖ Black Sheep Best Bitter, John Smith's, Theakston Ö Thatchers Gold. ♟ 9 **Facilities** Children welcome Children's portions Family room Parking Wi-fi ▨

MIDDLESMOOR　　　　Map 19 SE07

Crown Hotel

HG3 5ST ☎ 01423 755204
dir: *Telephone for directions*

There are great views towards Gouthwaite Reservoir from this breezy 900-ft high hilltop village with its cobbled streets. This family-run traditional free house dates back to the 17th century and is in an ideal spot for anyone following the popular Nidderdale Way. Visitors can enjoy a good pint of local beer and food by the cosy, roaring log fire, or in the sunny pub garden. A large selection of malt whiskies is also on offer.

Open Tue-Sun Closed: all day Mon, Tue-Thu L (winter) **Bar Meals** L served Tue-Sun 12-2 D served Tue-Sun 7-8.30 ⊕ FREE HOUSE ◖ Black Sheep Best Bitter, Wensleydale Bitter, Guinness. **Facilities** ❀ Children welcome Garden Parking **Notes** ◉

MUKER　　　　　　　Map 18 SD99

The Farmers Arms

DL11 6QG ☎ 01748 886297
e-mail: enquiries@farmersarmsmuker.co.uk
dir: *From Richmond take A6108 towards Leyburn, turn right onto B6270*

Located at the head of beautiful Swaledale, the pub is understandably popular with walkers and in summer the south facing patio is a relaxing place to enjoy a pint of Black Sheep. The menu includes lunchtime filled Yorkshire puddings and light bites such as toasted sandwiches or home-made soup, and full evening meals along the lines of prawn cocktail followed by home-made beef casserole with a choice of potatoes and vegetables. Finish with home-made fruit crumble. There is a separate children's menu.

Open all day all wk **Bar Meals** L served all wk 12-2.30 D served all wk 6-8.30 ⊕ FREE HOUSE ◖ Theakston Best Bitter & Old Peculier, John Smith's, Black Sheep, Guest ales Ö Thatchers Gold. ♟ 9 **Facilities** ❀ Children welcome Children's menu Children's portions Garden Parking

PICK OF THE PUBS

The Lister Arms ★★★★INN

MALHAM   Map 18 SD96

BD23 4DB ☎ 01729 830330
e-mail: relax@listerarms.co.uk
web: www.listerarms.co.uk
dir: *In town centre*

Thomas Lister of Gisburne Park, who was created the first Lord Ribblesdale in 1797, gave his name to this beautiful old stone coaching inn. Grade I listed, the house itself is now an independent private hospital. Being right on the village green makes it a good place to stop for morning coffee, a pint of one of the guest ales, or Thwaites Wainwright bitter, named after Blackburn-born Alfred Wainwright, famous for his Lakeland Fells guides. History is visible wherever you look: outside, there's a traditional mounting block for horse riders, and a beautiful tiled entrance way; inside, the renovated ground floor is divided into little nooks, with original beams, wood floors and fireplaces. Food from chef-patron Terry Quinn's kitchen is seasonal, local and always freshly prepared, with daily 'Lister Loves' dishes displayed on a board hanging above the fireplace in the bar. For lunch try one of the Home Comforts, such as a hot chargrilled steak sandwich; beefsteak, mushroom and Thwaites Nutty Black ale pie with creamy mash, peas and a jug of gravy; or rigatoni pasta with spinach, broad beans and

parmesan. Dinner might begin with tempura tiger prawns with spicy chilli sauce and fresh lime; continue with poached fillet of fresh Scottish salmon with parsley new potatoes, wilted greens and hollandaise sauce; and finish with Yorkshire Dales ice cream, or lemon meringue pie. Children can choose from their own menu, tuck into complimentary fresh fruit, top up their soft drinks free and receive a goodie box. Well-behaved dogs, muddy boots and cycles are also happily tolerated. Wake up to a full Yorkshire breakfast following a night in one of the en suite guest rooms, from some of which you can see the distant rock amphitheatre of Malham Cove.

Open all day all wk ⊕ THWAITES INNS OF CHARACTER ◖ Wainwright, Original ♉ Kingstone Press. **Facilities** ❧ Children welcome Children's menu Children's portions Garden Parking Wi-fi **Rooms** 9

PICK OF THE PUBS

The Black Swan at Oldstead ★★★★★ RR ❀❀❀

OLDSTEAD   Map 19 SE57

Main St YO61 4BL ☎ 01347 868387
e-mail: enquiries@blackswanoldstead.co.uk
web: www.blackswanoldstead.co.uk
dir: *A1 junct 49, A168, A19S, after 3m left to Coxwold then Byland Abbey. In 2m left for Oldstead, pub 1m on left*

Dating back to the 16th century and set in a sleepy hamlet below the North York Moors, The Black Swan is owned and run by the Banks family, who have farmed in the village for generations. In the bar you'll find a stone-flagged floor, an open log fire, original wooden window seats, soft cushions, and fittings by Robert 'Mousey' Thompson who, in the 1930s, was a prolific maker of traditional handcrafted English oak furniture. Expect tip-top real ales, cracking wines by the glass, malt whiskies and vintage port, while the first-class food on offer changes with the seasons, being sourced mainly from local farms. So there are pub classics, such as sausages and mash, and smoked salmon with tartare sauce sandwiches, for example. The cooking style moves upmarket in the comfortable restaurant (with three AA Rosettes to its credit), where Persian rugs line an oak floor, the furniture is antique, and candles in old brass holders create light soft enough to be romantic, but bright enough to read the innovative modern country menu by. Start perhaps with free-range chicken and leek terrine with Madeira and trompette mushrooms; or Japanese-style tuna with wasabi, ginger, radish and coriander; move on to venison saddle and venison pithiviers with braised red cabbage, parsnips and juniper juice; and finish with hazelnut parfait, chocolate, and mango and cinder toffee, accompanied by a glass of red Muscatel. The bedrooms have solid oak floors and are furnished with quality antiques, classy soft fabrics, and paintings. Bathrooms are fitted with an iron roll-top bath and a walk-in wet room shower, which sounds like just the place to head for after one of the pleasant walks radiating from the front of the building (route details are available at the bar). Booking for meals may be required.

Open 12-3 6-11 Closed: 1wk Jan, Mon L, Tue L, Wed L **Bar Meals** L served Thu-Sun 12-2 D served all wk 6-9 Av main course £14 **Restaurant** L served Thu-Sun 12-2 D served all wk 6-9 Fixed menu price fr £20 Av 3 course à la carte fr £45 ⊕ FREE HOUSE ◀ Black Sheep, Copper Dragon. ♟ 19 **Facilities** Children welcome Children's menu Children's portions Garden Parking Wi-fi **Rooms** 4

NEWTON ON OUSE — Map 19 SE55

The Dawnay Arms NEW

YO30 2BR ☎ 01347 848345
e-mail: dine@thedawnay.co.uk
dir: *From A19 follow Newton on Ouse signs*

The Dawnay Arms sits on the banks of the River Ouse, in the middle of a picture-perfect village. Its origins are Georgian, and its large rear garden runs down to moorings for those arriving by boat. The refurbished interior, all chunky beams and tables, hosts a great array of cask ales including Treboom, a relatively recent addition to York's renowned micro-breweries; the well-chosen wine list also deserves mention. Food, British in style, comprises hearty dishes of locally sourced ingredients, with game and seafood the specialities: pheasant and wild mushroom pasty; and roast chunk of Whitby cod with a crab crust and tagliatelle.

Open 12-3 6-11 (Sat-Sun all day) Closed: 1st wk Jan, Mon **Bar Meals** L served Tue-Sat 12-2.30, Sun 12-6 D served Tue-Sat 6-9.30, Sun 12-6 Av main course £15.95 **Restaurant** L served Tue-Sat 12-2.30, Sun 12-6 D served Tue-Sat 6-9.30, Sun 12-6 Fixed menu price fr £11.95 Av 3 course à la carte fr £23 ⊕ FREE HOUSE ◀ Timothy Taylor Golden Best, Treboom Drum Beat, Black Sheep Best Bitter & Golden Sheep. ☗ 12 **Facilities** ❀ Children welcome Children's menu Children's portions Garden Parking Wi-fi ▭ (notice required)

NUNNINGTON — Map 19 SE67

The Royal Oak Inn

Church St YO62 5US ☎ 01439 748271
dir: *Village centre, close to Nunnington Hall*

This Grade II listed, 18th-century solid stone country inn welcomes with an open-plan bar furnished with scrubbed pine and decorated with farming memorabilia, open fires in winter and fresh flowers in summer. The sign on the front door says it all: 'Real ale, real food, real people'. True to this promise, head chef Ed Woodhill uses the best local produce to create innovative interpretations of traditional dishes. Typical choices include ham hock croquette with home-made piccalilli; gorgonzola and pear chutney tart and pheasant en croûte.

Open 12-2.30 6.30-11 (Sun 12-3 6.30-11 summer 12-3 winter) Closed: Mon (ex BH 12-2) **Bar Meals** L served Tue-Sun 12-2 (booking required Sun) D served Tue-Sun 6.30-9 (summer), Tue-Sat fr 6.30 (winter) Av main course £12 **Restaurant** L served Tue-Sat 12-2, Sun12-3 (booking required Sun) D served Tue-Sun 6.30-9 (summer),

Tue-Sat fr 6.30 (winter) ⊕ FREE HOUSE ◀ Black Sheep, Wold Top, John Smith's. ☗ 10 **Facilities** ❀ Children welcome Children's menu Children's portions Garden Parking

OLDSTEAD — Map 19 SE57

The Black Swan at Oldstead ★★★★★ RR ⑩⑩⑩

PICK OF THE PUBS

See Pick of the Pubs on page 597

OSMOTHERLEY — Map 19 SE49

The Golden Lion

PICK OF THE PUBS

6 West End DL6 3AA ☎ 01609 883526
e-mail: goldenlionosmotherley@yahoo.co.uk
dir: *Telephone for directions*

The Golden Lion is a cosy sandstone building of some 250 years standing. The atmosphere is warm and welcoming, with open fires and wooden flooring on one side of the downstairs area. Furnishings are simple with a wooden bar, bench seating and tables, whitewashed walls, mirrors and fresh flowers. The extensive menu ranges through basic pub grub to more refined dishes. The starters are divided between fish, soups, vegetarian, pastas and risottos, meat and salads, and might include smoked salmon; buffalo mozzarella with tomato and basil; spicy pork ribs; and avocado and king prawn salad. Mains are along the lines of grilled sea bass with new potatoes and peas; coq au vin; calves' liver with fried onions and mash; home-made beefburger with Mexican salsa; and spicy chilladas with fresh tomato sauce. There are also interesting specials like pork Stroganoff and rice, or lamb and feta lasagne. Sherry trifle, and bread-and-butter pudding with cream, are popular desserts.

Open 12-3 6-11 Closed: 25 Dec, Mon L, Tue L ⊕ FREE HOUSE ◀ Timothy Taylor Landlord, York Guzzler, Yorkshire Dales ♻ Herefordshire. **Facilities** Children welcome Children's menu Garden

PATELEY BRIDGE — Map 19 SE16

The Sportsmans Arms Hotel

PICK OF THE PUBS

Wath-in-Nidderdale HG3 5PP ☎ 01423 711306
e-mail: sportsmansarms@btconnect.com
dir: *A59/B6451, hotel 2m N of Pateley Bridge*

Wath is a conservation village, picturesque and unspoilt, set in beautiful Nidderdale, one of the loveliest of the Yorkshire Dales. Ray and June Carter have been running their 17th-century restaurant, reached by a packhorse bridge across the Nidd, for over 30 years, although son Jamie and daughter Sarah have leading roles too these days. Enter the hallway and find open log fires, comfortable chairs, a warm and welcoming bar and a

calm, softly lit restaurant, dominated at one end by a Victorian sideboard and substantial wine rack. As much of the food as possible is locally sourced: fish arrives daily from Whitby and other East Coast harbours. Always a good choice are the Nidderdale lamb, pork, beef, fresh trout and especially game (season permitting) from the Moors. The wine list offers a wide selection of styles and prices to complement any dish. The Sportsmans Arms stands on the 53-mile, circular Nidderdale Way, hard by the dam over the River Nidd (some fishing rights belong to the hotel) that creates Gouthwaite Reservoir.

Open all wk 12-2.30 6.30-11 Closed: 25 Dec ⊕ FREE HOUSE ◀ Black Sheep, Worthington's, Timothy Taylor ♻ Thatchers Gold. **Facilities** Children's portions Garden Parking Wi-fi

PICKERING — Map 19 SE78

Fox & Hounds Country Inn ★★ HL ⑩

PICK OF THE PUBS

Sinnington YO62 6SQ ☎ 01751 431577
e-mail: fox.houndsinn@btconnect.com
dir: *3m W of town, off A170 between Pickering & Helmsley*

Proprietors Andrew and Catherine Stephens and their friendly, efficient staff ensure a warm welcome at this handsome 18th-century coaching inn with its oak-beamed ceilings, old wood panelling and open fires. Situated in Sinnington, on a quiet road between Pickering and Kirkbymoorside, a gentle walk from the pub passes the village green to the pretty riverside where ducks swim in the shallows and an ancient packhorse bridge leads to more footpaths through the woods. You can enjoy a pint of Copper Dragon Best Bitter, or perhaps try one of the unusual whiskies, such as Ledaig and The Balvenie. The menu is full of locally farmed produce; a lighter menu, served during lunch and early supper, accompanies the main à la carte. Expect the likes of crab cakes with a red pepper pesto; chargrilled minute steak with a pepper sauce and fries; beer-battered haddock and chips; and lamb hotpot. The inn has ten well-equipped en suite bedrooms. Booking for meals may be required.

Open all wk 12-2 5.30-11 (Sat 12-2 6-11 Sun 12-2.30 6-10.30) Closed: 25-26 Dec **Bar Meals** L served all wk 12-2 D served Mon-Fri 5.30-9, Sat-Sun 6-9 Av main course £13.25 **Restaurant** L served all wk 12-2 D served all wk 6.30-9 Av 3 course à la carte fr £20.95 ⊕ FREE HOUSE ◀ Copper Dragon Best Bitter, Wold Top Falling Stone ♻ Thatchers Gold. ☗ 9 **Facilities** Children welcome Children's menu Children's portions Garden Parking ▭ **Rooms** 10

The Fox & Rabbit Inn

Whitby Rd, Lockton YO18 7NQ ☎ 01751 460213
e-mail: info@foxandrabbit.co.uk
dir: *From Pickering take A169 towards Whitby. Lockton in 5m*

Charles and Toby Wood's attractive 18th-century pub stands virtually alone on the Pickering to Whitby road. Dalby Forest is to the east, the North York Moors to the north-west, which together attract outdoor leisure enthusiasts in droves to the area, so all-day food and drink is greatly appreciated. Usually available are deep-fried Whitby haddock; slow-braised lamb shank; wild mushroom risotto; and specials such as beef curry with basmati rice. With anything on the menu, of course, a pint of local Cropton or Black Sheep real ale goes down a treat.

Open all day all wk **Bar Meals** Av main course £12 ⊕ FREE HOUSE ◀ Black Sheep Best Bitter, John Smith's Extra Smooth, Marston's Oyster Stout, Cropton, Guest ales ☼ Thatchers Gold. ♟ 13 **Facilities** ❖ Children welcome Children's menu Children's portions Garden Parking ▭ (notice required)

The White Swan Inn ★★★ HL ☺

PICK OF THE PUBS

Market Place YO18 7AA ☎ 01751 472288
e-mail: welcome@white-swan.co.uk
dir: *From N: A19 or A1 to Thirsk, A170 to Pickering, left at lights, 1st right onto Market Place. Pub on left. From S: A1 or A1(M) to A64 to Malton rdbt, A169 to Pickering*

The award-winning White Swan is the inn every market town wishes it had. Two miles from the North Yorkshire Moors National Park in the middle of *Heartbeat* Country, this stylish inn offers great food and comfortable accommodation, with the city of York only half an hour away. Close links with top London butcher The Ginger Pig, whose farm is seven miles from the pub, means that rare-breed meat gets star billing on a seasonal menu that has wowed critics and visitors. Tempting dishes include the likes of Black Sheep battered Whitby haddock with chips and mushy peas, Jerusalem artichoke and spinach risotto, or Ginger Pig sausage and mash, which may follow potted pork and black pudding, quail's egg and onion chutney, or spiced mussel stew. Make room for comforting puddings: spiced Ampleforth apple and bramble crumble and custard; glazed lemon tart, prune and treacle ice cream. Fine ales and carefully chosen wines complete the picture. Booking for meals may be required.

Open all day all wk **Bar Meals** L served all wk 12-2 D served all wk 6.45-9 **Restaurant** L served all wk 12-2 D served all wk 6.45-9 ⊕ FREE HOUSE ◀ Black Sheep, World Top, Copper Dragon ☼ Westons Old Rosie. ♟ 13 **Facilities** ❖ Children welcome Children's menu Children's portions Garden Parking Wi-fi ▭ (notice required) **Rooms** 21

| PICKHILL | Map 19 SE38 |

Nags Head Country Inn ★★★★ INN ☺☺

PICK OF THE PUBS

YO7 4JG ☎ 01845 567391
e-mail: enquiries@nagsheadpickhill.co.uk
dir: *From the South, junct 50 (A61). From the North, junct 51 (A684). Join A6055*

For nearly 40 years the Boynton family have been welcoming visitors to their extended, former 17th-century coaching inn set in a peaceful village just off the A1 north of Thirsk. Synonymous with Yorkshire hospitality at its best, notably among weary travellers and the local racing fraternity, the inn comprises a beamed lounge and a traditional taproom bar with flagged and tiled floors, beams adorned with ties and a magpie selection of tables and chairs tucked around open fires. A terrific menu is the icing on the cake here; a small but perfectly formed taproom menu offers sandwiches and simple meals such as steak and chips with all the trimmings or Thai chicken, vegetable and noodle stirfry. In the lounge or elegant restaurant, order mushroom and roasted garlic risotto to start, followed perhaps by corn-fed chicken with a small wing Kiev, buttered cabbage, potato dumplings and pearl barley broth. Tempting, calorific puddings seal the deal, perhaps forced Yorkshire rhubarb pithivier with frangipane and ewe's milk ice cream. If all this leaves you feeling too full to move, consider staying in one of the inn's comfortably furnished bedrooms. Booking for meals may be required.

Open all wk 11-11 (Sun 11-10.30) Closed: 25 Dec **Bar Meals** L served Mon-Sat 12-2, Sun 12-8 D served Mon-Sat 6-9.30, Sun 12-8 Av main course £13 **Restaurant** L served Mon-Sat 12-2, Sun 12-5 D served Mon-Sat 6-9.30, Sun 5-8 Av 3 course à la carte fr £18 ⊕ FREE HOUSE ◀ Black Sheep Best Bitter, Theakston Old Peculier, Best Bitter & Black Bull, York Guzzler ☼ Thatchers Gold. ♟ 8 **Facilities** Children welcome Children's menu Children's portions Garden Parking Wi-fi ▭ (notice required) **Rooms** 13

| PICTON | Map 19 NZ40 |

The Station Hotel

TS15 0AE ☎ 01642 700067
e-mail: info@thestationhotelpicton.co.uk
dir: *1.5m from A19*

A short hop from the A19 and ten minutes from Yarm, this traditional pub welcomes families and the fact the beer garden is located next to the village play area makes it ideal for those with young children. Inside, relax in front of the open fire with a pint of Tetley's or head for the dining area for a range of home-cooked dishes that make good use of produce from local farmers and butchers. Everything is home-made, from Wensleydale chicken with brandy, walnut and cranberry cream sauce to hand-cut chips. Booking for meals may be required.

Open all wk 5-11.30 (Sat 12-2.30 5-11.30 Sun 12-7) **Bar Meals** L served Sat 12-2.30, Sun 12-7 D served all wk 5-9

Av main course £16 **Restaurant** L served Sat 12-2.30 D served all wk 5-9 Fixed menu price fr £22 ⊕ FREE HOUSE ◀ Tetley's Cask & Smoothflow, Black Sheep, Guinness, Guest ales. ♟ 14 **Facilities** Children welcome Children's menu Children's portions Play area Garden Parking Wi-fi ▭ (notice required)

| REETH | Map 19 SE09 |

Charles Bathurst Inn ★★★★ INN

PICK OF THE PUBS

Arkengarthdale DL11 6EN ☎ 01748 884567
e-mail: info@cbinn.co.uk
web: www.cbinn.co.uk
dir: *From A1 exit at Scotch Corner onto A6108, through Richmond, left onto B6270 to Reeth. At Buck Hotel right signed Langthwaite, pass church on right, inn 0.5m on right*

Television fans will recognise the spectacularly rugged Dales scenery around this 18th-century inn, as it appeared in the series *All Creatures Great and Small*. This remote country inn takes its name from the son of Oliver Cromwell's physician who built it for his workers. In winter, it caters for serious ramblers tackling The Pennine Way and the Coast to Coast route, and it offers a welcome escape from the rigours of the moors. English classics meet modern European dishes on a menu written up on the mirror hanging above the stone fireplace. Choose from a selection of real ales including Black Sheep and enjoy white onion and blue cheese tartlet with spiced tomato chutney, followed by Gressingham duck breast, confit fennel, potato rösti and orange sauce. A decent bin of wines includes 12 by the glass. The 19 bedrooms with fabulous Dales views may tempt others to extend their visit. Booking for meals may be required.

Open all day all wk 11am-mdnt Closed: 25 Dec **Bar Meals** L served all wk 12-2 D served all wk 6-9 Av main course £13.95 **Restaurant** L served all wk 12-2 D served all wk 6-9 Av 3 course à la carte fr £24.50 ⊕ FREE HOUSE ◀ Black Sheep Best Bitter & Riggwelter, Rudgate Jorvik Blonde, Theakston. ♟ 12 **Facilities** Children welcome Children's menu Children's portions Play area Garden Parking Wi-fi ▭ (notice required) **Rooms** 19

RIPON — Map 19 SE37

The George at Wath ★★★★ INN ◉

Main St, Wath HG4 5EN ☎ 01765 641324
e-mail: richard@thegeorgeatwath.co.uk
dir: *From A1 (dual carriageway) N'bound turn left signed Melmerby & Wath. From A 1 S'bound exit at slip road signed A61. At T-junct right (signed Ripon). Approx 0.5m turn right for Melmerby & Wath*

The George at Wath, a brick-built double-fronted free house dating from the 18th century, is just three miles from the cathedral city of Ripon. This traditional Yorkshire pub retains its flagstone floors, log-burning fires and cosy atmosphere, while the contemporary dining room proffers seasonal and locally sourced ingredients for its mix of classic and bistro-style dishes: salt cod fritters could be followed by glazed gammon with chips cooked in dripping; finish with a chocolate tart, or rhubarb and custard. The George is child and dog friendly, and hosts Bank Holiday beer festivals.

Open 12-3 5-11 (Sat-Sun all day) Closed: Mon & Tue L **Bar Meals** L served Wed-Sun 12-3 D served Mon-Sat fr 5.30 Av main course £15 **Restaurant** L served Wed-Sun 12-3 D served Mon-Sat 5.30-9 Fixed menu price fr £10 Av 3 course à la carte fr £26 ⊕ FREE HOUSE ◀ Theakston, Rudgate. ▾ 14 **Facilities** ❤ Children welcome Children's menu Children's portions Garden Beer festival Parking Wi-fi ▭ (notice required) **Rooms** 5

The Royal Oak ★★★★ INN ◉

36 Kirkgate HG4 1PB ☎ 01765 602284
e-mail: info@royaloakripon.co.uk
dir: *In town centre*

Built as a coaching inn, this refurbished city centre venue now has a clean, modern and open feel, with wooden floorboards in the bright, spacious bar and comfortable leather settees in the one AA-Rosette restaurant. Owned by Timothy Taylor brewery you can obviously expect excellent ales. Lunchtime brings 'knife and fork' sandwiches with hand-cut chips, and there's also a good range of pub classics like pie and mash. Other mains include line caught bass with peanut and lime risotto, prawns and Thai red curry sauce. Regular food and wine tasting events and modern accommodation complete the package.

Open all day all wk ⊕ TIMOTHY TAYLOR & CO LTD ◀ Landlord, Best Bitter, Golden Best, Ram Tam. **Facilities** Children welcome Children's menu Children's portions Garden Parking Wi-fi **Rooms** 6

ROBIN HOOD'S BAY — Map 19 NZ90

Laurel Inn

New Rd YO22 4SE ☎ 01947 880400
dir: *Telephone for directions*

Given its location it's hardly surprising that this was once the haunt of smugglers who used a network of underground tunnels and secret passages to bring the booty ashore. Nowadays it's the haunt of holidaymakers and walkers, and the setting for this small, traditional pub which retains lots of character features, including beams and an open fire. The bar is decorated with old photographs, and an international collection of lager bottles. This popular free house serves Theakston Old Peculier and Best Bitter and Adnams.

Open all wk ⊕ FREE HOUSE ◀ Theakston Best Bitter & Old Peculier, Adnams. **Facilities** ❤ Children welcome Family room Wi-fi **Notes** ◉

SAWDON — Map 17 SE98

The Anvil Inn
PICK OF THE PUBS

Main St YO13 9DY ☎ 01723 859896
e-mail: info@theanvilinnsawdon.co.uk
dir: *1.5m N of Brompton-by-Sawdon, on A170 8m E of Pickering & 6m W of Scarborough*

The bar was once the blacksmith's forge, which is why it's crammed with artefacts, including the furnace, bellows, tools and, of course, an anvil. It has been a pub since only the mid-1980s, when it became a welcome new amenity for locals, walkers and mountain bikers in this sleepy village on the edge of the North Riding Forest Park. Weekly changing beers tend to come from local micro-breweries, so you may encounter Daleside's Old Leg Over (but be careful how you ask for it!). Another big draw is chef-patron Mark Wilson's modern European cooking, typically pan-roast breast and slow-roast leg of guinea fowl with Morcilla black pudding, chorizo and sherry jus; grilled fillet of plaice with sautéed queen scallops, parisienne potatoes and chilli, lime and coconut cream; and twice-baked roast shallot soufflé with Kashmir Gold saffron and Ryedale cheese. Ask the waitress for details of the trio of English puddings. Booking for meals may be required.

Open 12-2.30 6-11 Closed: 26 Dec, 1 Jan & varying annual holiday, Mon-Tue **Bar Meals** L served Wed-Sat 12-2, Sun 12-2.30 D served Wed-Sat 6.30-9, Sun 6-8 Av main course £14 **Restaurant** L served Wed-Sat 12-2, Sun 12-2.30 D served Wed-Sat 6.30-9, Sun 6-8 Av 3 course à la carte fr £22.50 ⊕ FREE HOUSE ◀ Daleside Old Leg Over, Wold Top Angler's Reward, Leeds Midnight Bell ♂ Westons Stowford Press. ▾ 11 **Facilities** ❤ Children welcome Children's portions Garden Parking

SAWLEY — Map 19 SE26

The Sawley Arms

HG4 3EQ ☎ 01765 620642
e-mail: info@sawleyarms.co.uk
dir: *A1(M) junct 47, A59 to Knaresborough, B6165 to Ripley, A61 towards Ripon, left for Sawley. Or from Ripon B6265 towards Pateley Bridge, left to Sawley. Pub 1m from Fountains Abbey*

After 42 years in the same family, this delightful 200-year-old free house has now passed to the next generation, Robin and Nicky Jaques. Just a mile from Fountains Abbey and surrounded by stunning gardens, it was a frequent haunt of the late author and vet James Herriot. The varied modern British menu lists dishes that range from roast Nidderdale lamb rump with bubble-and-squeak mash and red wine and rosemary gravy; to butternut squash, spinach and Yorkshire fettle pie with smoked tomato sauce. Booking for meals may be required.

Open 11.30-3 6-11 Closed: Mon eve in winter **Bar Meals** L served all wk 12-2.30 D served all wk 6.30-9.30 Av main course £10.95 **Restaurant** L served all wk 12-2.30 D served all wk 6.30-9.30 Av 3 course à la carte fr £18.95 ⊕ FREE HOUSE ◀ Theakston Best Bitter, John Smith's. ▾ 12 **Facilities** Children welcome Children's portions Garden Parking ▭ (notice required)

SCAWTON — Map 19 SE58

The Hare Inn ◉
PICK OF THE PUBS

YO7 2HG ☎ 01845 597769
e-mail: info@thehareinn.co.uk
dir: *Telephone for directions*

Built in the 13th century and allegedly used as a brewhouse by the monks who built Rievaulx Abbey, The Hare also boasts a friendly ghost! Later, in the 17th century, ale was brewed here for local iron workers. Inside, you'll find low-beamed ceilings and flagstone floors, a wood-burning stove offering a warm welcome in the bar, and an old-fashioned kitchen range in the dining area. Eating here promises food of AA Rosette standard, with the kitchen ringing the changes according to availability of locally sourced ingredients. The full à la carte menu is complemented by light lunch and early bird options, offering quality dining at value prices. A representative choice might start with roast goat's cheese in filo pastry with pine nuts and basil dressing; continuing with pan-fried breast of guinea fowl with tarragon mousse and wild mushrooms; and finishing with passionfruit crème brûlée. Booking for meals may be required.

Open Tue-Sat 12-2 6-9.30 (Sun 12-4) Closed: Mon, Sun eve (ex BHs) ⊕ FREE HOUSE ◀ Timothy Taylor Landlord, Black Sheep, Guest ales ♂ Thatchers. **Facilities** Children welcome Children's portions Garden Parking

SETTLE　　　　　　　　　Map 18 SD86

The Lion at Settle ★★★★ INN

Duke St BD24 9DU ☎ 01729 822203
e-mail: relax@thelionsettle.co.uk
web: www.thelionsettle.co.uk
dir: *Telephone for directions*

This traditional Dales coaching inn is situated in the heart of Settle's 17th-century market place. Owner Thwaites Brewery completely refurbished the inn early in 2011, sprucing up the bedrooms and revamping the cosy bars and the spacious restaurant, which ooze history and atmosphere with original inglenook fireplaces, wooden floors and a grand staircase lined with pictures that trace back through the town's history. It's now a comfortable base for exploring the Dales and meets the needs of travellers experiencing the spectacular Settle to Carlisle railway line. In addition, expect decent cask ales and a classic pub menu offering freshly prepared pub favourites with a strong Yorkshire influence and sound use of local, seasonal produce. Typically, tuck into warm Blue Pig black pudding; bacon and potato salad; haddock in beer-batter; or beef and ale suet pudding. Desserts could include toffee apple crumble.

Open all day all wk 11-11 (Fri-Sat 11am-11.30pm Sun 12-10.30) **Bar Meals** L served Mon-Sat 12-9, Sun 12-8 D served Mon-Sat 12-9, Sun 12-8 food served all day **Restaurant** L served Mon-Sat 12-9, Sun 12-8 D served Mon-Sat 12-9, Sun 12-8 food served all day ⊕ THWAITES INNS OF CHARACTER ◖ Original, Lancaster Bomber & Wainwright, Guest ales ⚬ Kingstone Press. ♟ 9 **Facilities** ✿ Children welcome Children's menu Children's portions Garden Parking 🚌 **Rooms** 14

See advert below

SKIPTON　　　　　　　　Map 18 SD95

Devonshire Arms

Grassington Rd, Cracoe BD23 6LA ☎ 01756 730237
e-mail: info@devonshirecracoe.co.uk
dir: *Telephone for directions*

The original setting for the Rhylstone Ladies WI calendar, this convivial, lovingly renovated 17th-century inn is conveniently located for the Three Peaks and has excellent views of Rhylstone Fell. In the hands of experienced licensees Barbara and Nathan Hutchinson you will find character, quality and service here. A wide range of cask ales plus an extensive wine list will wash down a menu that runs from spiced whitebait with lime and paprika mayonnaise to pan-seared Yorkshire lamb rump with dauphinoise potatoes and apricot and mint gravy.

Open all day all wk **Bar Meals** L served all wk 8.30-8.30 D served all wk 8.30-8.30 food served all day **Restaurant** L served all wk 8.30-8.30 D served all wk 8.30-8.30 food served all day ⊕ MARSTON'S ◖ EPA & Burton Bitter, Jennings Bitter. ♟ 11 **Facilities** ✿ Children welcome Children's menu Children's portions Play area Garden Parking Wi-fi 🚌 (notice required)

SNAINTON — Map 17 SE98

The Coachman Inn ★★★★ RR ◉

Pickering Road West YO13 9PL ☎ **01723 859231**
e-mail: info@coachmaninn.co.uk
web: www.coachmaninn.co.uk
dir: *5m from Pickering, off A170 onto B1258, 9m from Scarborough off A170 onto B1258*

Built in 1776, this Grade II listed Georgian coaching inn is superbly located to make the most of coast and countryside. The Coachman offers award-winning food and holds the coveted AA Rosette for culinary excellence. Food is served in the romantic candlelit Carriages Restaurant, rustic Coachman Bar or outside in the gardens and bistro courtyard. Typical dishes include penne pasta with roasted vegetables in tomato and basil sauce with mozzarella; and Yorkshire venison haunch with celeriac, spinach and elderflower jus. Traditional beers are available and a wide selection of wines by the glass. Six individually designed bedrooms are available. Booking for meals may be required.

Open all wk 12-12 **Bar Meals** L served all wk 12-9 D served all wk 12-9 Av main course £11.50 **Restaurant** L served Mon-Sat 12-9, Sun 12-3 D served Mon-Sat 12-9, Sun 4-9 Fixed menu price fr £25 Av 3 course à la carte fr £20 ⊕ FREE HOUSE ◀ John Smith's, Wold Top, Guinness. ☗ 15 **Facilities** Children welcome Children's menu Children's portions Garden Parking Wi-fi **Rooms** 6

STARBOTTON — Map 18 SD97

Fox & Hounds Inn

BD23 5HY ☎ **01756 760269 & 760367**
e-mail: starbottonfox@aol.com
dir: *Telephone for directions*

Built as a private house some 400 years ago, this pub has been serving this picturesque limestone Yorkshire Dales village since the 1840s. Make for the bar, with its large stone fireplace, oak beams and flagged floor to enjoy a pint of Black Sheep or Timothy Taylor Landlord, or one of the wide selection of malts. Head to the dining room for home-cooked pork medallions in brandy and mustard sauce; Thai cod and prawn fishcakes; or broccoli and stilton quiche. The area is renowned for its spectacular walks.

Open 12-3 6-11 (Sun 12-3.30 5.30-10.30) Closed: 1-22 Jan, Mon ⊕ FREE HOUSE ◀ Timothy Taylor Landlord, Black Sheep, Moorhouse's, Guest ales ᵹ Thatchers Gold. **Facilities** Children welcome Garden Parking

SUTTON-ON-THE-FOREST — Map 19 SE56

The Blackwell Ox Inn ★★★★ INN ◉

PICK OF THE PUBS

Huby Rd YO61 1DT ☎ **01347 810328**
e-mail: enquiries@blackwelloxinn.co.uk
dir: *A1237 onto B1363 to Sutton-on-the-Forest. Left at T-junct, 50yds on right*

Built around 1823 as a private house, the inn's name celebrates a shorthorn Teeswater Ox that stood 6ft high at the crop and weighed 1,033 kilos. When the beast was slaughtered in 1779 its meat fetched £110, about £7,000 today. Blending period charm with modern elegance, the pub offers a well-stocked bar with attractively priced Black Sheep Bitter, Timothy Taylor Landlord and Copper Dragon on the pumps. Lunchtime snacks and some restaurant menu items can be eaten in the bar too, or out on the terrace. The simple cooking style owes much to a North Yorkshire-focused sourcing policy for lunchtime hot and cold sandwiches, alongside mussels, chips and aïoli; sausage and mash; and croque madame with chips and salad. Among restaurant main courses look for pan-roasted cod loin; rib-eye steak; and feta cheese and roast vegetable tart. Only seven miles from York, the inn offers comfortable, individually designed bedrooms.

Open all wk 12-3 5.30-11 (Sun 12-10.30) Closed: 25 Dec, 1 Jan **Bar Meals** L served all wk 12-2 D served all wk 6-9.30 **Restaurant** L served all wk 12-2 D served all wk 6-9.30 ⊕ FREE HOUSE ◀ Timothy Taylor Landlord, Black Sheep Best Bitter, Copper Dragon, Guinness. ☗ 14 **Facilities** Children welcome Children's menu Children's portions Garden Parking Wi-fi ⌖ (notice required) **Rooms** 7

THORNTON LE DALE — Map 19 SE88

The New Inn

Maltongate YO18 7LF ☎ **01751 474226**
e-mail: enquire@the-new-inn.com
dir: *A64 N from York towards Scarborough. At Malton take A169 to Pickering. At Pickering rdbt right onto A170, 2m, pub on right*

Standing at the heart of a picturesque village complete with stocks and a market cross, this family-run Georgian coaching house dates back to 1720. The old-world charm of the location is echoed inside the bar and restaurant, with real log fires and exposed beams. Enjoy well-kept Theakston Black Bull and guest ales, bitters, lagers and wines and tuck into beef and ale casserole; breast of duckling with sweet orange sauce; and chicken wrapped in Parma ham and topped with mozzarella.

Open all wk 12-2.30 5-11 (summer all day) **Bar Meals** L served Mon-Sat 12-2, Sun 12-2.30 (winter Tue-Sat) D served Mon-Sat 6-8.30, Sun 6.30-8.30 (winter Mon-Sat) **Restaurant** L served Mon-Sat 12-2, Sun 12-2.30 (winter Tue-Sat) D served Mon-Sat 6-8.30, Sun 6.30-8.30 (winter Mon-Sat) ⊕ SCOTTISH & NEWCASTLE ◀ Theakston Black Bull, Guest ales. **Facilities** Children welcome Children's menu Children's portions Garden Parking Wi-fi ⌖

THORNTON WATLASS — Map 19 SE28

The Buck Inn ★★★ INN

PICK OF THE PUBS

See Pick of the Pubs on opposite page

WASS — Map 19 SE57

Wombwell Arms

PICK OF THE PUBS

YO61 4BE ☎ **01347 868280**
e-mail: info@wombwellarms.co.uk
dir: *From A1 take A168 to A19 junct. Take York exit, then left after 2.5m, left at Coxwold to Ampleforth. Wass 2m*

Sitting in the shadow of the Hambleton Hills, Ian and Eunice Walker's whitewashed village inn dates from 1620, when it was built as a granary using stones from the ruins of nearby Byland Abbey. There are two oak-beamed, flagstone-floored bars, one with a huge inglenook fireplace, the other with a wood-burning stove, and the atmosphere is relaxed and informal. Locals, walkers and cyclists quaff pints of Timothy Taylor Landlord. High quality, modern British meals with a South African twist are prepared from local produce as far as possible. Tuck into decent sandwiches for lunch and choose one of the Wombwell classics for dinner, perhaps the Masham pork and apple sausages with mash and gravy. Or try the South African Bobotie – a mild and fruity mince curry dish served with rice. Leave room for the pistachio brownie with pistachio ice cream, or a plate of local cheeses. Booking for meals may be required.

Open 12-3 6-11 (Sat 12-11 Sun 12-4 6-10.30) Closed: Sun eve & Mon Nov-Mar **Bar Meals** L served Mon-Thu 12-2, Fri-Sat 12-2.30, Sun 12-3 D served Mon-Thu 6.30-9, Fri-Sat 6.30-9.30, Sun 6.30-8.30 Av main course £12 **Restaurant** L served Mon-Thu 12-2, Fri-Sat 12-2.30, Sun 12-3 D served Mon-Thu 6.30-9, Fri-Sat 6.30-9.30, Sun 6.30-8.30 Av 3 course à la carte fr £20 ⊕ FREE HOUSE ◀ Timothy Taylor Landlord, Theakston Best Bitter, Caledonian Deuchars IPA ᵹ Galtres Gold. ☗ 11 **Facilities** Children welcome Children's menu Children's portions Garden Parking Wi-fi ⌖ (notice required)

Save on hotels. Book at **theAA.com/hotel**

YORKSHIRE, NORTH 603 ENGLAND

PICK OF THE PUBS

The Buck Inn ★★★ INN

THORNTON WATLASS   Map 19 SE28

HG4 4AH ☎ 01677 422461
e-mail: innwatlass1@btconnect.com
web: www.buckwatlass.co.uk
dir: *From A1 at Leeming Bar take A684
to Bedale, B6268 towards Masham.
Village in 2m*

A traditional, well-run friendly institution
that has been in the experienced hands
of Michael and Margaret Fox for over 20
years, who have no trouble in
maintaining its welcoming and relaxed
atmosphere. The inn doesn't just
overlook the village green and cricket
pitch; players score four runs for hitting
the pub wall, and six if the ball goes over
the roof! Very much the quintessential
village scene in beautiful Thornton
Watlass, Bedale is where Wensleydale,
gateway to the Yorkshire Dales National
Park, begins, and this glorious area is
where much of the TV programme
Heartbeat was filmed. There are three
separate dining areas – the bar for
informality, the restaurant for dining by
candlelight, and for busy days the large
function room. The menu ranges from
traditional, freshly prepared pub fare to
exciting modern cuisine backed by daily
changing blackboard specials. Typical
bar favourites are Masham rarebit
(Wensleydale cheese with local ale
topped with bacon and served with pear
chutney); steak-and-ale pie; oven-baked
lasagne; lamb cutlets with rosemary and
redcurrant sauce; and beer-battered fish

and chips. Hearty and wholesome daily
specials may take in seared scallops
with frizzy salad and five spice sauce;
prawn and crab tian; or smoked duck
salad. Main courses include grilled
smoked haddock with buttery mash,
saffron cream and crisp onion rings;
salmon fillet with buttered noodles and
tomato and garlic sauce; venison
sausages with Lyonnaise potatoes and
rosemary gravy; or pan-fried duck breast
with stir-fried vegetables and hoi sin
sauce. Beer drinkers have a choice of
five real ales, including Masham-brewed
Black Sheep, while whisky drinkers have
a selection of some 40 different malts to
try, ideal when relaxing by the coal fire.
There's live jazz music most Sunday
lunchtimes. Cottage-style bedrooms
provide a comfortable night's sleep.

Open all wk 11am-mdnt Closed: 25 Dec
eve ⊕ FREE HOUSE ◖ Black Sheep Best
Bitter, 4 Guest ales ♂ Thatchers Gold.
Facilities Children welcome Children's
menu Children's portions Play area
Family room Garden Parking **Rooms** 7

WEST BURTON · Map 19 SE08

Fox & Hounds

DL8 4JY ☎ 01969 663111
e-mail: the_fox_hounds@unicombox.co.uk
dir: *A468 between Hawes & Leyburn, 0.5m E of Aysgarth*

In a beautiful Dales setting, this is a traditional pub overlooking the large village green, which has swings and football goals, and its own hidden waterfalls. Parents can happily sit at the front and enjoy a drink while keeping an eye on their children. A proper local, the pub hosts men's and women's darts teams and a dominoes team. In summer customers play quoits out on the green. Real ales, some from the Black Sheep Brewery down the road, and home-made food prepared from fresh ingredients is served. In addition to the pizzas cooked in the pizza oven, dishes include chicken curry, steak-and-kidney pie, lasagne, steaks and other pub favourites. Booking for meals may be required.

Open all day all wk ⊕ FREE HOUSE ◀ Theakston Best Bitter, Black Sheep, John Smith's, Copper Dragon. **Facilities** Children welcome Children's menu Children's portions Parking

WEST TANFIELD · Map 19 SE27

The Bruce Arms

PICK OF THE PUBS

Main St HG4 5JJ ☎ 01677 470325
e-mail: halc123@yahoo.co.uk
dir: *On A6108 between Ripon & Masham*

Set in the pretty riverside village of West Tanfield, this 18th-century stone-built pub is a great base for exploring the Yorkshire Dales. The pub's bistro-style interior exudes charm with traditional exposed beams, log fires and candles on the tables. Expect a good wine list, real ales from the local Black Sheep Brewery, and heartfelt cooking from owner Hugh Carruthers using the best of local produce. Choices include home-cured ham, egg and chips, and contemporary British and European cuisine. There is a lovely alfresco dining area for summer. It's a handy base for visiting the races at both Ripon and Thirsk, and famous sights such as Fountains Abbey.

Open 12-2.30 6-9.30 (Sun 12-3.30) Closed: Mon ⊕ FREE HOUSE ◀ Black Sheep Best Bitter, Guest ales Ö Aspall. **Facilities** Children welcome Garden Parking

WEST WITTON · Map 19 SE08

The Wensleydale
Heifer ★★★★ RR ⊚⊚

PICK OF THE PUBS

Main St DL8 4LS ☎ 01969 622322
dir: *A1 to Leeming Bar junct, A684 towards Bedale for approx 10m to Leyburn, then towards Hawes, 3.5m to West Witton*

Located between Leyburn and Hawes in the heart of the Yorkshire Dales National Park, this refurbished

17th-century coaching inn offers guests all the modern comforts of a stylish boutique restaurant with rooms but retains many of its original features. As well as an inviting lounge with roaring log fires and real ales, the pub offers two different dining experiences. The fish bar is less formal with seagrass flooring, wooden tables and rattan chairs, whilst the light and airy seafood restaurant has a much more contemporary and casually formal atmosphere. In the kitchen, fresh fish and seafood and locally sourced meats are handled with simplicity. Whitby lobster bisque or baked king scallops gruyère might be followed by smoked haddock and garden pea risotto or salmon and scallop Rockefeller. Leave room for desserts of cappuccino and chocolate pannacotta, or classic crème brûlée with butter shortbread. Little Heifers get their own well-considered menu.

Open all day all wk **Bar Meals** L served all wk 12.30-2.30 D served all wk 6-9.30 Av main course £12 **Restaurant** L served all wk 12.30-2.30 D served all wk 6-9.30 Fixed menu price fr £19.95 Av 3 course à la carte fr £32 ⊕ FREE HOUSE ◀ Heifer Gold, Black Sheep Ö Aspall. ⬥ **Facilities** ✿ Children welcome Children's menu Children's portions Garden Parking Wi-fi ⬛ Rooms 13

WHITBY · Map 19 NZ81

The Magpie Café

14 Pier Rd YO21 3PU ☎ 01947 602058
e-mail: ian@magpiecafe.co.uk
dir: *Telephone for directions*

More a licensed restaurant than a pub, the award-winning Magpie has been the home of North Yorkshire's best-ever fish and chips since the late 1930s. You could pop in for a pint of Cropton, but the excellent views of the harbour from the dining room, together with the prospect of fresh seafood, could prove too much of a temptation. Up to ten fish dishes are served daily, perhaps including Whitby Cullen skink; and Scarborough woof (a type of catfish) with chips.

Open all day all wk Closed: 1-21 Jan ⊕ FREE HOUSE ◀ Cropton Scoresby Stout, Tetley's Bitter. **Facilities** Children welcome Children's menu Children's portions

WIGGLESWORTH · Map 18 SD85

The Plough Inn

BD23 4RJ ☎ 01729 840243
e-mail: info@theploughatwigglesworth.co.uk
dir: *From A65 between Skipton & Long Preston take B6478 to Wigglesworth*

Dating back to 1720, the bar of this traditional country free house features oak beams and an open fire. There are fine views of the surrounding hills from the conservatory restaurant, where the pub's precarious position on the Yorkshire/Lancashire border is reflected in a culinary 'War of the Roses'. Yorkshire pudding with beef casserole challenges Lancashire hotpot and pickled red cabbage - the latest score is published beside the daily blackboard specials!

Open Wed-Sun Closed: Mon-Tue ⊕ FREE HOUSE ◀ Guest ales. **Facilities** Children welcome Children's portions Parking

YORK · Map 16 SE65

Blue Bell

PICK OF THE PUBS

53 Fossgate YO1 9TF ☎ 01904 654904
e-mail: robsonhardie@aol.com
dir: *In city centre*

Its slimline frontage is easy to miss, but don't walk past this charming pub – the smallest in York – which has been serving customers in the ancient heart of the city for 200 years. In 1903 it was given a typical Edwardian makeover, and since then almost nothing has changed – so the Grade II listed interior still includes varnished wall and ceiling panelling, cast-iron tiled fireplaces, and charming old settles. The layout is original too, with the taproom at the front and the snug down a long corridor at the rear, both with servery hatches. The only slight drawback is that the pub's size leaves no room for a kitchen, so don't expect anything more complicated than lunchtime sandwiches. However, there's a good selection of real ales: no fewer than seven are usually on tap, including rotating guests. The pub has won awards for its efforts in fund-raising.

Open all day all wk **Bar Meals** L served Mon-Sat 12-2.30 ⊕ PUNCH TAVERNS ◀ Timothy Taylor Landlord Ö Westons Traditional. **Facilities** ✿ Wi-fi Notes ⊛

Lamb & Lion Inn ★★★★ INN ⊚

2-4 High Petergate YO1 7EH ☎ 01904 612078
e-mail: gm@lambandlionyork.com
dir: *From York Station, turn left. Stay in left lane, over Lendal Bridge. At lights left (Theatre Royal on right). At next lights pub on right under Bootham Bar (medieval gate)*

Right in the historical centre of York, this rambling Georgian inn has unrivalled views of nearby York Minster from its elevated beer garden. Conjoined to the medieval Bootham Bar gateway, it is furnished and styled in keeping with its grand heritage. A warren of snugs and corridors radiate from a bar offering a challenging array of beers, including Golden Mane, brewed for the inn. Equally enticing is the menu, offering comforting classics ranging from croque monsieur or cheese omelette to hay-baked chicken breast and sage mash. Finish with British cheeses or ginger burnt cream with rhubarb compôte.

Open all day all wk **Bar Meals** Av main course £12.95 food served all day **Restaurant** food served all day ⊕ FREE HOUSE ◀ Great Heck Golden Mane, Black Sheep Best Bitter, Copper Dragon Golden Pippin. ⬥ 10 **Facilities** ✿ Children welcome Children's menu Children's portions Garden Wi-fi **Rooms** 12

Lysander Arms

Manor Ln, Shipton Rd YO30 5TZ ☎ 01904 640845
e-mail: christine@lysanderarms.co.uk
dir: *Telephone for directions*

This pub stands on a former RAF airfield where No. 4 Squadron's Westland Lysander aircraft were based early in World War II. Still relatively modern, which accounts for the contemporary feel of the interior, it has a long, fully air-conditioned bar with up-to-date furnishings, brick-built fireplace and large-screen TV. Brasserie restaurant meals range from 'light bites' such as Yorkshire Blue cheese and chive rarebit with pickled red cabbage to hearty meals such as steak, mushroom and ale pie or slow-cooked belly pork with crispy crackling, black pudding, creamed potatoes and roasted apple. Booking for meals may be required.

Open all day all wk **Bar Meals** L served Tue-Sun 12-2 D served Tue-Sat 5-9 Av main course £9 **Restaurant** L served Tue-Sun 12-2 D served Tue-Sat 5-9 ⊕ FREE HOUSE ◀ John Smith's Extra Smooth, York Guzzler, Wychwood Hobgoblin, Copper Dragon, Black Sheep, Theakston ♂ Kopparberg. ♚ 8 **Facilities** ❀ Children welcome Children's menu Children's portions Play area Garden Parking Wi-fi

YORKSHIRE, SOUTH

BRADFIELD   Map 16 SK29

The Strines Inn

Bradfield Dale S6 6JE ☎ 0114 285 1247
e-mail: thestrinesinn@yahoo.co.uk
dir: *N off A57 between Sheffield & Manchester*

Strines is an old English word meaning 'the meeting of waters', and this popular free house overlooks Strines Reservoir. Although it was built as a manor house in the 13th century, most of the present building is 16th century and it has been an inn since 1771. Traditional home-made fare ranges from sandwiches and salads, to 'giant' Yorkshire puddings with a choice of fillings and a pie of the day. There is an enclosed play area and a separate area for peacocks, geese and chickens, which roam freely.

Open all wk 10.30-3 5.30-11 (Sat-Sun 10.30am-11pm; all day Apr-Oct) Closed: 25 Dec **Bar Meals** L served Mon-Fri 12-2.30, Sat-Sun 12-9 (summer all wk 12-9) D served Mon-Fri 5.30-9, Sat-Sun 12-9 (summer all wk 12-9) Av main course £8.95 ⊕ FREE HOUSE ◀ Marston's Pedigree, Jennings Cocker Hoop, Bradfield Farmers Bitter, Wychwood Hobgoblin. ♚ 10 **Facilities** ❀ Children welcome Children's menu Children's portions Play area Garden Parking 🚌

CADEBY   Map 16 SE50

Cadeby Inn
PICK OF THE PUBS

Main St DN5 7SW ☎ 01709 864009
e-mail: info@cadebyinn.co.uk
dir: *In the centre of village*

The date on the gable is 1751, but records of a pub on the site in this peaceful Yorkshire village go a lot further back. Standing behind a tree-shaded beer garden at the edge of the village, this Georgian gem fuses the welcome of a village local with the quiet sophistication of a destination dining pub. Beers from Yorkshire breweries take the eye at the bar (a changing beer from the local Wentworth micro is a favourite), whilst the extensive regular menu, with mains such as chilli fried chicken with spiced noodles and garlic naan bread; crispy belly pork, mustard mash and sticky red cabbage; or slow roasted lamb shank with red wine, rosemary, garlic and shallots. Mini toffee nests with Netherthorpe Dairy fresh cream; or double chocolate fudge brownie with vanilla ice cream could complete the feast.

Open all wk 12-11 ⊕ FREE HOUSE ◀ John Smith's Cask, Black Sheep Best Bitter, Guest ales. **Facilities** Children welcome Children's menu Children's portions Garden Parking Wi-fi

DONCASTER   Map 16 SE50

Waterfront Inn

Canal Ln, West Stockwith DN10 4ET ☎ 01427 891223
e-mail: keithescreet@gmail.com
dir: *From Gainsborough take either A159 N, then minor road to village. Or A631 towards Bawtry/Rotherham, right onto A161, then onto minor road*

This 19th-century pub is located at the end of the Chesterfield Canal and overlooks the picturesque marina at West Stockwith. Walkers and visitors to this lovely spot beat a path here, lured by the promise of real ales and good-value food. The restaurant has views on all sides of the marina and large beer garden. The pub welcomes families and offers a children's menu and a play area.

Open 12-2.30 6-11 (Sat 12-11 Sun 12-9) Closed: Mon (ex BH) **Bar Meals** L served Tue-Sun 12-2.30 D served Tue-Sun 6.30-9 **Restaurant** L served Tue-Sun 12-2.30 D served Tue-Sun 6.30-9 ⊕ ENTERPRISE INNS ◀ John Smith's Cask, Morland Old Speckled Hen, Greene King ♂ Westons Stowford Press. **Facilities** Children welcome Children's menu Children's portions Play area Garden Parking 🚌

PENISTONE   Map 16 SE20

Cubley Hall
PICK OF THE PUBS

Mortimer Rd, Cubley S36 9DF ☎ 01226 766086
e-mail: info@cubleyhall.co.uk
dir: *M1 junct 37, A628 towards Manchester, or M1 junct 35a, A616. Hall just S of Penistone*

Built as a farm in the 1700s, Cubley Hall was a gentleman's residence in Queen Victoria's reign and later became a children's home before being transformed into pub in 1982. In 1990 the massive, oak-beamed bar was converted into the restaurant and furnished with old pine tables, chairs and church pews, and the building was extended to incorporate the hotel, which was designed to harmonise with the original mosaic floors, ornate plaster ceilings, oak panelling and stained glass. On the edge of the Peak District National Park, the hall is reputedly haunted by Florence Lockley, who married there in 1904 and is affectionately known as Flo. Food-wise, take your pick from light bites, chalkboard specials and an extensive main menu listing pub classics and home-made pizzas. Typically, choose from a Crawshaw beefburger with all the trimmings; fish and chips; pork and leek sausages; mash and onion gravy; and chicken and mushroom carbonara. Booking for meals may be required.

Open all day all wk **Bar Meals** L served all wk 12-9.30 D served Mon-Sat 12-9.30, Sun 12-9 food served all day **Restaurant** L served Sun 2 sittings 12-3.30 & 3-5.30 ⊕ FREE HOUSE ◀ Tetley's Bitter, Black Sheep Best Bitter. **Facilities** Children welcome Children's menu Children's portions Play area Family room Garden Parking Wi-fi 🚌 (notice required)

The Fountain Inn Hotel

Wellthorne Ln, Ingbirchworth S36 7GJ ☎ 01226 763125
e-mail: wineaboutwine@hotmail.co.uk
dir: *M1 junct 37, A628 to Manchester then A629 to Huddersfield*

Attractively located by Ingbirchworth Reservoir in the foothills of the southern Pennines, parts of this former coaching inn date from the 17th century. The interior is cosy and stylish, the locals' bar has real log fires and traditional games. Under new owners, the food focus is still on quality with value for money: expect the likes of steak pie, Whitby scampi, and toffee and ginger roulade. In the summer, enjoy the garden with its large decking and seating area, or time your visits for the May and August beer festivals.

Open all day all wk **Bar Meals** L served all wk 12-9 D served all wk 12-9 Av main course £10 food served all day **Restaurant** L served all wk 12-9 D served all wk 12-9 Fixed menu price fr £7.95 Av 3 course à la carte fr £16.95 food served all day ⊕ INTREPID LEISURE ◀ John Smith's Extra Smooth, Timothy Taylor Landlord, Jennings Sneck Lifter, Copper Dragon, Black Sheep. ♚ 8 **Facilities** ❀ Children welcome Children's menu Children's portions Play area Family room Garden Beer festival Parking Wi-fi 🚌 (notice required)

SHEFFIELD Map 16 SK38

The Fat Cat

PICK OF THE PUBS

23 Alma St S3 8SA ☎ 0114 249 4801
e-mail: info@thefatcat.co.uk
dir: *Telephone for directions*

Built in 1832, it was known as The Alma Hotel for many years, then in 1981 it was the first Sheffield pub to introduce guest beers. The policy continues, with constantly changing, mainly micro-brewery, guests from across the country, two handpumped ciders, unusual bottled beers, Belgian pure fruit juices and British country wines. The pub's own Kelham Island Brewery accounts for at least four of the 11 traditional draught real ales. The smart interior is very much that of a traditional, welcoming back-street pub, with real fires making it feel very cosy, while outside is an attractive walled garden with Victorian-style lanterns and bench seating. Except on Sunday evenings, typical home-cooked food from a simple weekly menu is broccoli cheddar pasta; Mexican mince and nachos; and savoury bean casserole. Events include the Monday quiz and curry night, and £1.30 a pint evening beer offers.

Open all wk 12-11 (Fri-Sat 12-12) Closed: 25 Dec **Bar Meals** L served Mon-Fri & Sun 12-3, Sat 12-8 D served Mon-Fri 6-8, Sat 12-8 ⊕ FREE HOUSE ◀ Timothy Taylor Landlord, Kelham Island Best Bitter & Pale Rider, Guest ales ♻ Westons Stowford Press, Guest ciders. **Facilities** Children welcome Children's portions Family room Garden Parking Wi-fi 🚐

Kelham Island Tavern

PICK OF THE PUBS

62 Russell St S3 8RW ☎ 0114 272 2482
e-mail: kelhamislandtav@aol.com
dir: *Just off A61 (inner ring road). Follow brown tourist signs for Kelham Island*

This 1830s backstreet pub was built to quench the thirst of steelmakers who lived and worked nearby. The semi-derelict pub was rescued in 2001 by Lewis Gonda and Trevor Wraith, who transformed it into an award-winning 'small gem'. The pub is in a conservation and popular walking area, with old buildings converted into stylish apartments, and The Kelham Island Museum round the corner in Alma Street telling the story of the city's industrial heritage. The real ale list is formidable: residents Barnsley Bitter, Brewers Gold and Farmers Blonde are joined by ten ever-changing guests, as well as Westons Old Rosie cider, and a midsummer beer festival is held every year at the end of June. Constantly updated blackboards typically offer beef bourguignon; steak-and-ale pie; broccoli and cheese pie; and soups, pâtés and various bar snacks. Great in the summer, the pub has won awards for its beer garden and floral displays.

Open all day all wk 12-12 **Bar Meals** L served Mon-Sat 12-3 Av main course £6 ⊕ FREE HOUSE ◀ Barnsley Bitter, Crouch Vale Brewers Gold, Bradfield Farmers

Blonde, 10 Guest ales ♻ Westons Old Rosie. **Facilities** ♣ Children welcome Children's portions Family room Garden Beer festival Parking 🚐

The Sheffield Tap NEW

Platform 1B, Sheffield Station, Sheaf St S1 2BP
☎ 0114 273 7558
dir: *Access from Sheaf St & from Platform 1B. NB limited access from Platform 1B on Fri & Sat*

For more than 30 years disused, derelict and vandalised, the former Edwardian refreshment room and dining rooms of Sheffield Midland Railway Station are now an award-winning Grade II listed free house. Painstakingly restored to its former glory by the current custodians, with help from the Railway Heritage Trust, The Sheffield Tap is now a beer mecca offering ten real ales, one real cider, 12 keg products and more than 200 bottled beers from around the world. Food is limited to bagged bar snacks, and children are welcome until 8pm every day.

Open all day all wk Closed: 25-26 Dec, 1 Jan ⊕ FREE HOUSE ◀ Thornbridge ♻ Thistly Cross. **Facilities** ♣ Children welcome Garden Wi-fi 🚐 (notice required)

TOTLEY Map 16 SK37

The Cricket Inn

PICK OF THE PUBS

Penny Ln, Totley Bents S17 3AZ ☎ 0114 236 5256
e-mail: info@brewkitchen.co.uk
dir: *Follow A621 from Sheffield 8m. Turn right onto Hillfoot Rd, 1st left onto Penny Ln*

Partly owned by Bakewell's Thornbridge Brewery, this former farmhouse once sold beer to navvies building the nearby Totley Tunnel on the Sheffield to Manchester railway. Now a popular seafood- and game-led gastro-pub, it attracts Peak District walkers, whilst dogs and children are made to feel very welcome. Not surprisingly for a pub owned by a brewery, the beer selection is impressive, with four Thornbridge ales on tap as well as a small selection of bottled Belgian beers. Snacks include local black pudding with sticky onion jam; and Huntsman pie with home-made piccalilli. Alternatively, go for roast scallops with risotto of smashed garden peas and squid ink; classic fish pie with buttered greens; lamb shank and lamb mince shepherd's pie; or grilled cod with Niçoise salad. Desserts might include warm treacle tart with clotted cream, or baked 'New York-style' lemon cheesecake with lemon sorbet and griottine cherries.

Open all day all wk 11-11 **Bar Meals** L served Mon-Fri 12-2.30, Sat-Sun all day D served Mon-Fri 5-8.30, Sat-Sun all day Av main course £12 **Restaurant** L served Mon-Fri 12-2.30, Sat-Sun all day D served Mon-Fri 5-8.30, Sat-Sun all day Fixed menu price fr £25 Av 3 course à la carte fr £20 ⊕ BREWKITCHEN LTD ◀ Thornbridge Wild Swan, Lord Marples, Jaipur. 🍷 10 **Facilities** ♣ Children welcome Children's menu Children's portions Garden Parking 🚐

YORKSHIRE, WEST

ADDINGHAM Map 19 SE04

The Fleece

PICK OF THE PUBS

154 Main St LS29 0LY ☎ 01943 830491
e-mail: info@fleeceinnaddingham.co.uk
dir: *Between Ilkley & Skipton*

After establishing a string of successful gastro-pubs, Craig Minto has returned to this 17th-century coaching inn, once owned by his father. Located where several well-tramped footpaths meet, it's popular with walkers, food and drink being served on the front terrace and in the stone-flagged interior with its enormous fireplace, wooden settles and bar offering real ales like Copper Dragon and Ilkley. Much of the produce is local and organic, with beef and lamb coming from a nearby farm, surplus vegetables from allotment holders, and game straight from the shoot. The daily chalkboard and rolling menus offer pan-roasted chicken supreme stuffed with mushroom duxelle, buttered kale and red wine jus; sirloin of Yorkshire beef, caramelised onion and Blacksticks Blue cheese; sea bass fillets, tenderstem broccoli and brown shrimp and dill risotto; and ricotta, basil and roast pumpkin cannelloni. An on-site deli sells 'proper Yorkshire' produce, including ready meals from The Fleece's kitchen. Booking for meals may be required.

Open all day all wk 12-11 (Sun 12-10.30) **Bar Meals** L served Mon-Sat 12-2.15, Sun 12-8 D served Mon-Sat 5-9, Sun 12-8 Av main course £12 **Restaurant** L served Mon-Sat 12-2.15, Sun 12-8 D served Mon-Sat 5-9, Sun 12-8 Fixed menu price fr £12.95 ⊕ PUNCH TAVERNS ◀ Timothy Taylor Landlord, Black Sheep, Copper Dragon, Ilkley ♻ Westons Stowford Press. 🍷 30 **Facilities** ♣ Children welcome Children's menu Children's portions Play area Garden Parking Wi-fi 🚐 (notice required)

BRADFORD Map 19 SE13

New Beehive Inn

171 Westgate BD1 3AA ☎ 01274 721784
e-mail: newbeehiveinn+21@btinternet.com
dir: *A606 into Bradford, A6161 200yds B6144, left after lights, pub on left*

Dating from 1901 and centrally situated with many tourist attractions nearby, this classic Edwardian inn retains its period Arts and Crafts atmosphere with five separate bars and gas lighting. It is on the national inventory list of historic pubs. Outside, with a complete change of mood, you can relax in the Mediterranean-style courtyard. The pub offers a good range of unusual real ales, such as Salamander Mudpuppy and Abbeydale Moonshine, and a selection of over 100 malt whiskies, served alongside some simple bar snacks. Music fans should attend the cellar bar, which is open at weekends and features regular live bands.

Open all day all wk ⊕ FREE HOUSE ◀ Kelham Island Best Bitter, Abbeydale Moonshine, Salamander Mudpuppy, Ilkley Mary Jane, Saltaire Cascade Pale Ale ♻ Westons Old Rosie. **Facilities** Children welcome Family room Garden Parking Wi-fi 🚐

PICK OF THE PUBS

Shibden Mill Inn ★★★★ INN 🏵🏵

HALIFAX Map 19 SE02

Shibden Mill Fold HX3 7UL
☎ 01422 365840
e-mail: enquiries@shibdenmillinn.com
web: www.shibdenmillinn.com
dir: *From A58 into Kell Ln. 0.5m, left into Blake Hill*

The Shibden Valley used to be an important wool production area, the waters of Red Beck powering this 17th-century, former spinning mill until the industry collapsed in the late 1800s. Now it's a charming inn, with open fires, oak beams, small windows and heavy tiles, happily enjoying a more civilised existence below overhanging trees in a wooded glen that makes Halifax just down the road seem a thousand miles away. The beer garden is extremely popular, not least with beer fans who come here to sample a real ale called Shibden Mill, brewed specially for the inn, Black Sheep or one of the three guest ales. With two AA Rosettes, the restaurant attracts those who enjoy food prepared from trusted local growers and suppliers, and a seasonal menu offering newly conceived dishes and old favourites. Two starters to consider might be assiette of pork (pulled and potted belly, crispy cheek and miniature pork pie) with black pudding bread, and beetroot and orange coleslaw; and potato and spinach soup with poached quail's egg and nettle pesto. Turn over the page for possibilities such as pan-fried, garlic-studded Cornish mackerel with wild mushrooms, scallop mousse tortellini, potato rösti and oyster velouté sauce; pan-roasted Barnsley chop with basil and mint pesto, sun-blushed tomato purée, black peas and devils on horseback; and curried cauliflower risotto with smoked cheese fritters and rocket. Among the old favourites mentioned earlier are corned beef hash; steamed steak and ale suet pudding; and beer-battered Scottish haddock. A gourmet menu proposes Yorkshire artisan cheeses served with home-made chutney, oat biscuits, celery and Eccles cakes, ideally accompanied by a glass of vintage port. Stay overnight in one of the individually designed luxury bedrooms, with a full Yorkshire breakfast to look forward to next morning.

Open all wk 12-2.30 5.30-11 (Sat-Sun 12-11) Closed: 25-26 Dec eve & 1 Jan eve **Bar Meals** L served Mon-Sat 12-2, Sun all day D served Mon-Sat 6-9.30 **Restaurant** L served Sun 12-7.30 D served Fri-Sat 6-9.30 FREE HOUSE John Smith's, Black Sheep, Shibden Mill, 3 Guest ales. 🍷 12 **Facilities** Children welcome Children's menu Children's portions Garden Parking Wi-fi **Rooms** 11

CLIFTON   Map 16 SE12

The Black Horse Inn ⊛

HD6 4HJ ☎ 01484 713862
e-mail: mail@blackhorseclifton.co.uk
dir: 1m from Brighouse town centre. 0.5m from M62 junct 25

Past guests at this pretty 17th-century inn tucked away in a quiet village above the Calder Valley included Roy Orbison, who spent his second honeymoon here, and Shirley Bassey. There's plenty to sing praises about here, with the finest Yorkshire fare gaining one AA Rosette; look forward to accompanying a pint of own-label Black Horse Brew (from Sowerby Bridge) with a starter of smoked haddock kedgeree with coconut foam, leading to a terrine of Pateley Bridge pork with black pudding crumble. *Last of the Summer Wine* was filmed here; with over 100 bins to choose from, it's a minor miracle that they're not still here.

Open all day all wk 12-12 ⊕ FREE HOUSE ◖ Black Horse Brew, Timothy Taylor Landlord. **Facilities** Children welcome Children's menu Children's portions Garden Parking Wi-fi

EMLEY   Map 16 SE21

The White Horse

2 Chapel Ln HD8 9SP ☎ 01924 849823
dir: M1 junct 38, A637 towards Huddersfield. At rdbt left onto A636, then right to Emley

On the old coaching route to Huddersfield and Halifax, this 18th-century pub's bar is warmed by a working Yorkshire range; the restaurant has a fire too. Of the eight cask ales, five are permanent, three are ever-rotating guests, featuring micro-breweries and their own Ossett Brewery ales. A simple menu offers the likes of seafood salad, black pudding and poached egg crostini, steak-and-ale pie, mixed grill, chilli, and sausage and mash with onion gravy. The pub is something of a community hub, and is popular with walkers and cyclists and locals, of course. Booking for meals may be required.

Open all wk 12-11 (Mon 4-11 Fri-Sat 12-11.30 Sun 12-10.30) **Bar Meals** L served Tue-Sat 12-2 D served Tue-Fri 5-8, Sat 5-9 Av main course £6.50 **Restaurant** L served Sun 12-5 D served Tue-Fri 5-8, Sat 5-9 ⊕ FREE HOUSE ◖ Ossett Excelsior, Emley Cross & Pale Gold, Bob's White Lion, Copper Dragon, Guest ales ♂ Westons Old Rosie. ♀ 9 **Facilities** Children welcome Children's portions Family room Garden Parking 🚌

HALIFAX   Map 19 SE02

The Rock Inn Hotel

Holywell Green HX4 9BS ☎ 01422 379721
e-mail: enquiries@therockhotel.co.uk
dir: From M62 junct 24 follow Blackley signs, left at x-rds, approx 0.5m on left

Set in the scenic rural valley of Holywell Green between Halifax and Huddersfield, this pretty 17th-century wayside inn is now a thriving hotel and conference venue and ideally located for Leeds and Manchester. All-day dining in the brasserie-style conservatory is a thoroughly international affair; kick off with sautéed chicken livers with tandoori spices or deep-fried belly pork croquettes and move on to Thai green chicken curry or beef lasagne al forno. The bar serves a choice of beers and around ten wines by the glass. Booking for meals may be required.

Open all day all wk 12-11 **Bar Meals** L served Mon-Sat 12-2, Sun 12-5.30 D served Mon-Sat 5.30-9 Av main course £8 **Restaurant** L served Mon-Sat 12-2 D served Mon-Sat 5.30-9 Fixed menu price fr £6.95 Av 3 course à la carte fr £15.95 ⊕ ENTERPRISE INNS ◖ Timothy Taylor Landlord, John Smith's. ♀ 9 **Facilities** Children welcome Children's menu Children's portions Garden Parking Wi-fi 🚌 (notice required)

Shibden Mill Inn ★★★★ INN ⊛⊛

PICK OF THE PUBS

See Pick of the Pubs on page 607

The Three Pigeons

1 Sun Fold, South Pde HX1 2LX ☎ 01422 347001
e-mail: threepigeons@ossett-brewery.co.uk
dir: From A629 (Skircoat Rd) in Halifax turn into Hunger Hill. Left into Union St, right into Heath View St, left into South Parade, right into Sun Fold

When Ossett Brewery took over this great little real ale pub they restored its period features to their former glory. The interior is divided into four small rooms or snugs, and each has its own character and charm. There is an amazing art deco painted ceiling in the central bar which has gained the pub its Grade II listed status. Good ales are the draw here, with Three Pigeons ale and three other beers always available. Expect live jamming sessions every Sunday night.

Open all wk 4-11 (Fri-Sat 12-12 Sun 12-11) ⊕ OSSETT BREWERY ◖ Three Pigeons, Pale Gold, Silver King, Excelsior, Yorkshire Blonde & Big Red, Guest ales ♂ Westons Traditional, Perry & Old Rosie. **Facilities** 🐾 Beer festival 🚌 (notice required) **Notes** ⊛

HARTSHEAD   Map 16 SE12

The Gray Ox

15 Hartshead Ln WF15 8AL ☎ 01274 872845
e-mail: grayox@hotmail.co.uk
dir: M62 junct 25, A644 signed Dewsbury. Take A62, then branch left signed Hartshead & Moor Top B6119. Left again to Hartshead

Originally a farmhouse dating back to 1709, The Gray Ox enjoys a commanding position overlooking Brighouse, Huddersfield and the surrounding countryside. Jennings ales and a dozen wines are sold by the glass at the bar. Booking for the award-winning restaurant is advisable; regional and fresh produce drives the menu – suppliers are named on a 'local heroes' board. Can anyone resist Westmoor outdoor-reared slow-cooked belly pork with langoustine Scotch egg, asparagus spears, parisienne potatoes and pea sauce? Alternatively time your visit for a Sunday roast of local beef, with a log fire and the day's papers. Booking for meals may be required.

Open all wk 12-3.30 6-12 (Sun 12-10.30) **Bar Meals** L served Mon-Sat 12-2, Sun 12-7 D served Mon-Fri 6-9, Sat 6-9.30, Sun 12-7 **Restaurant** L served Mon-Sat 12-2, Sun 12-7 D served Mon-Fri 6-9, Sat 6-9.30, Sun 12-7 ⊕ MARSTON'S ◖ Jennings Cumberland Ale, Cocker Hoop, Sneck Lifter. ♀ 12 **Facilities** Children welcome Children's portions Garden Parking Wi-fi 🚌

HAWORTH   Map 19 SE03

The Old White Lion Hotel

Main St BD22 8DU ☎ 01535 642313
e-mail: enquiries@oldwhitelionhotel.com
dir: A629 onto B6142, 0.5m past Haworth Station

Set in the famous Brontë village of Haworth, this traditional family-run 300-year-old coaching inn looks down onto the famous cobbled Main Street. In the charming bar the ceiling beams are supported by timber posts, and locals appreciatively quaff their pints of guest ale. Food is taken seriously and 'dispensed with hospitality and good measure'. Bar snacks include burgers, salads and jackets, while a meal in the award-winning Gimmerton Restaurant might start with garlic mushrooms; continue with rolled loin and noisette of Wharfedale lamb; and complete with one of chef's home-made desserts. Booking for meals may be required.

Open all day all wk 11-11 (Sun 12-10.30) **Bar Meals** L served Mon-Fri 12-2.30, Sat-Sun all day D served Mon-Fri 6-9.30, Sat-Sun all day Av main course £8.95 **Restaurant** L served Sun 12-2.30 D served all wk 7-9.30 Fixed menu price fr £17.50 Av 3 course à la carte fr £22.50 ⊕ FREE HOUSE ◖ Tetley's Bitter, John Smith's, Local guest ales. ♀ 9 **Facilities** Children welcome Children's menu Children's portions Parking Wi-fi 🚌

HEPWORTH Map 16 SE10

The Butchers Arms NEW

PICK OF THE PUBS

38 Towngate HD9 1TE ☎ 01484 682361
e-mail: info@thebutchersarmshepworth.co.uk
dir: *A616 into Hepworth. Butchers Arms in village centre*

When Yorkshire chef Tim Bilton took over this Hepworth pub in 2008, it was a failing business with an uncertain future. Four years on and it is one of the region's most popular gastro-pubs with a clutch of awards. Whether it's the Black Sheep ale served in the bustling bar or the excellent food, the emphasis here is very much on 'local'. A strict sourcing policy means that the majority of ingredients are from within a 75-mile radius, including some produce grown by villagers in their own gardens and allotments. In the bar, enjoy classics such as Whitby kippers or the pie of the day, but things move up a gear in the restaurant, where a starter of seared king scallops with Yorkshire black pudding and apple purée might be followed by Round Green Farm venison loin with a venison cottage pie, roast beets, butternut squash and Pontefract cake jus. Booking for meals may be required.

Open all day all wk **Bar Meals** L served Mon-Fri 12-2, Sat-Sun all day D served Mon-Fri 5-9, Sat-Sun all day **Restaurant** L served Mon-Fri 12-2, Sat-Sun all day D served Mon-Fri 5-9, Sat-Sun all day Fixed menu price fr £12 Av 3 course à la carte fr £35 ⊕ ENTERPRISE INNS ◀ Black Sheep, Copper Dragon. ♀ 16 **Facilities** Children welcome Children's portions Garden Parking

HOLMFIRTH Map 16 SE10

Farmers Arms NEW

2-4 Liphill Bank Rd HD9 2LR ☎ 01484 683713
e-mail: farmersarms2@gmail.com
dir: *From Holmfirth take A635 (Greenfield Rd) on right signed Manchester. Left at Compo's Café. 2nd right into Liphill Bank Rd*

The picturesque Holme Valley is typical *Last of the Summer Wine* country. Seek out the Farmers Arms – a small village pub run with pride by Sam Page and Danielle Montgomery whose rewardingly expansive ideas include a beer festival. Seven cask ales embrace local guests from the likes of Ossett Brewery and Castle Rock. The menu appeals too, with fresh dishes prepared from scratch including bread, pasta and corned beef; salads and herbs are picked from the garden. Settle by the log fire while awaiting the likes of VIP mushrooms on toast, or ox stew and dumplings.

Open Tue-Thu 12-3 5-12 (Fri-Sun 12-12 Mon 5-12) Closed: Mon L **Bar Meals** L served Tue-Thu 12-2, Fri-Sat 12-3, Sun 12-8 D served Tue-Thu 6-9.30, Sat 5-9.30, Sun 12-8 Av main course £9 ⊕ PUNCH TAVERNS ◀ Timothy Taylor Landlord, Copper Dragon Golden Pippin, Greene King IPA, Guest ales Ŏ Thatchers Gold, Westons Wyld Wood Organic. ♀ 13 **Facilities** ✿ Children welcome Children's portions Garden Beer festival Parking Wi-fi ▦ (notice required)

ILKLEY Map 19 SE14

Ilkley Moor Vaults NEW

Stockeld Rd LS29 9HD ☎ 01943 607012
e-mail: info@ilkleymoorvaults.co.uk
dir: *From Ilkley on A65 towards Skipton. Pub on right*

Known locally as The Taps, this pub was once attached to the Victorian Ilkley Moor Hotel, which burnt down in the early 1970s. Located at the start of the Dales Way and near the 'old bridge' that crosses the River Wharfe, it is now a stylish establishment with a welcome emphasis on food; sample dishes include Mediterranean fish soup with rouille, gruyère and croûtons; Hungarian chicken paprikash, and sticky toffee pudding and ice cream for dessert. There's an impressive children's menu too.

Open 12-3 5-11 (Sat-Sun all day) Closed: Mon (ex BH) **Bar Meals** L served Tue-Sat 12-2.30, Sun 12-7 D served Tue-Sat 6-9, Sun 12-7 Av main course £11.50 **Restaurant** L served Tue-Sat 12-2.30, Sun 12-7 D served Tue-Sat 6-9, Sun 12-7 Fixed menu price fr £16.95 Av 3 course à la carte fr £21 ⊕ SCOTTISH & NEWCASTLE ◀ Timothy Taylor Landlord, Theakston Best Bitter, Caledonian Deuchars IPA. ♀ 9 **Facilities** ✿ Children welcome Children's menu Children's portions Garden Parking ▦ (notice required)

KIRKBURTON Map 16 SE11

The Woodman Inn ★★★★ INN

Thunderbridge HD8 0PX ☎ 01484 605778
e-mail: thewoodman@connectfree.co.uk
dir: *Approx 5m S of Huddersfield, just off A629*

The family that owns this lovely old stone-built inn has been in the licensed trade since 1817. Set in the wooded hamlet of Thunderbridge, the pub offers one menu throughout so customers can eat in the downstairs bar with a pint of Timothy Taylor Landlord or the more formal upstairs restaurant with one of 13 wines offered by the glass. Dishes include daily fish (smoked haddock topped with smoked bacon and rarebit crust), and the likes of steak-and-ale pie. Accommodation is provided in adjacent converted weavers' cottages.

Open all day all wk 12-11 (Fri-Sat 12-12 Sun 12-10.30) **Bar Meals** Av main course £10 food served all day **Restaurant** Av 3 course à la carte fr £25 food served all day ⊕ FREE HOUSE ◀ Timothy Taylor Landlord, Black Sheep, Guest ales Ŏ Aspall. ♀ 13 **Facilities** ✿ Children welcome Children's menu Children's portions Garden Parking Wi-fi ▦ (notice required) **Rooms** 12

LEEDS Map 19 SE23

The Cross Keys

PICK OF THE PUBS

107 Water Ln LS11 5WD ☎ 0113 243 3711
e-mail: info@the-crosskeys.com
dir: *0.5m from Leeds Station: right onto Neville St, right onto Water Ln. Pass Globe Rd, pub on left*

James Watt, famed inventor of the steam engine, reputedly hired a room here to spy on his competitor Matthew Murray; to learn Murray's trade secrets Watt simply bought drinks for foundry workers relaxing here after work. Incredibly, this historic landmark from the peak of Leeds' industrial history was closed in the 1980s; when the current owners discovered it, it was a tyre storage depot for a local garage. Today, the pub proudly combines a city centre restaurant with a country pub atmosphere, serving hand-pulled pints from local micro-breweries, and food recreated from long lost recipes for traditional British dishes. Well-trained staff will happily talk you through the menus, which use the best of seasonal produce in starters such as haggis, neeps and tatties, and Shetland mussels with celery, bacon and ale cream sauce, and main courses of pan-fried calves' liver with smoked mashed potato, bacon and onion sauce; and Yorkshire venison puff pastry pie. For dessert, maybe Blackberry Eton Mess or spiced apple and pear crumble with custard.

Open all wk 12-11 (Fri-Sat 12-12 Sun 12-10.30) **Bar Meals** L served Mon-Sat 12-3, Sun 12-5 D served Mon-Sat 6-10 **Restaurant** L served Mon-Sat 12-3, Sun 12-5 D served Mon-Sat 6-10 ⊕ FREE HOUSE ◀ Kirkstall, Magic Rock, Thornbridge Ŏ Westons Wyld Wood Organic & Organic Pear, Aspall. ♀ 13 **Facilities** Children welcome Children's menu Children's portions Garden Wi-fi ▦

North Bar NEW

24 New Briggate LS1 6NU ☎ 0113 242 4540
e-mail: info@northbar.com
dir: *From rail station towards Corn Exchange, left into Briggate (main shopping area). At x-rds with The Headrow straight on into New Briggate. Bar 100mtrs on right*

This pioneering beer bar in the heart of Leeds is heaven for beer aficionados and in 2012 it celebrates 15 years of serving up to 150 beers from around the globe as any one time. Since 1997 it has served over 1,000 draught beers and over 100,000 bottled beers, yet pride of place on the vast bar are handpumped beers from local micro-breweries, notably Roosters ales. It's a trendy European-style bar, full of characters and great conversation, as well as a venue for music and local art exhibitions. Don't miss the regular beer festivals.

Open all day all wk 11am-2am Closed: 25 Dec **Bar Meals** Av main course £5 food served all day ⊕ FREE HOUSE ◀ Kirkstall, Roosters, Thornbridge, Marble, Buxton Ŏ Black Rat, Oliver's. **Facilities** ✿ Children welcome Beer festival Parking Wi-fi

LINTHWAITE　　　　　Map 16 SE11

The Sair Inn

Lane Top HD7 5SG ☎ 01484 842370
dir: *From Huddersfield take A62 (Oldham road) for 3.5m. Left just before lights at bus stop (in centre of road) into Hoyle Ing & follow sign*

You won't be able to eat here, but this old hilltop alehouse has enough character in its four small rooms to make up for that. Three are heated by hot Yorkshire ranges in winter. Landlord Ron Crabtree has brewed his own beers for over 25 years and they are much sought after by real ale aficionados. Imported German and Czech lagers are available, too. In summer the outside drinking area catches the afternoon sun and commands views across the Colne Valley.

Open all wk 5-11 (Sat 12-11 Sun 12-10.30) ⊕ FREE HOUSE ◀ Linfit Bitter, Special Bitter, Gold Medal, Autumn Gold, Old Eli ♂ Westons 1st Quality. **Facilities** ❖ Children welcome ▥ (notice required) **Notes** ◉

LINTON　　　　　Map 16 SE34

The Windmill Inn

Main St LS22 4HT ☎ 01937 582209
web: www.thewindmillinnwetherby.co.uk
dir: *From A1 exit at Tadcaster/Otley junct, follow Otley signs. In Collingham follow Linton signs*

The small beamed rooms in this pleasant village pub, once the home of the long-disappeared miller, have been stripped back to bare stone, presumably the original 14th-century walls. A coaching inn since the 18th century, polished antique settles, log fires, oak beams and copper-topped cast-iron tables set the scene in which to enjoy good food in the bar or Pear Tree restaurant. Dishes on offer include Moroccan spiced lamb shank, piri-piri chicken and home-made pie of the day. A beer festival is held in July.

Open all wk 11-3 5.30-11 (Fri-Sat 11-11 Sun 12-10.30) Closed: 1 Jan **Bar Meals** L served Mon-Fri 12-2, Sat 12-2.30, Sun 12-5.45 Av main course £9.95 **Restaurant** L served Mon-Fri 12-2, Sat 12-2.30, Sun 12-5.45 D served Mon-Tue 5.30-8.30, Wed-Sat 5.30-9 ⊕ HEINEKEN ◀ Theakston Best Bitter, Greene King Ruddles County, John Smith's, Daleside. ₹ 12 **Facilities** ❖ Children welcome Children's portions Garden Beer festival Parking ▥ (notice required)

MARSDEN　　　　　Map 16 SE01

The Olive Branch ★★★★ RR ◉

Manchester Rd HD7 6LU ☎ 01484 844487
e-mail: eat@olivebranch.uk.com
dir: *On A62 between Marsden & Slaithwaite, 6m from Huddersfield*

Enter this traditional 19th-century inn on a former packhorse route above the River Colne and the Huddersfield Canal and you'll find yourself in a rambling series of rooms, fire-warmed in winter. The restaurant's highly regarded brasserie-style food is exemplified by starters of carpaccio of Hartshead beef fillet; and shellfish thermidor, while typical main dishes include braised Welsh lamb shank; hake fillet and crab stirfry; and wild mushroom and thyme risotto. Enjoy a pint of Greenfield's Dobcross Bitter from Saddleworth on the sun deck. Three designer bedrooms are available. Booking for meals may be required.

Open all wk Mon-Sat 6.30pm-11pm (Sun 12.30-10.30) Closed: 1st 2wks Jan **Bar Meals** L served Sun 1-8.30 **Restaurant** L served Sun 1-8.30 D served Mon-Sat 6.30-9.30, Sun 1-8 ⊕ FREE HOUSE ◀ Greenfield Dobcross Bitter, Ale. ₹ 12 **Facilities** Children welcome Children's menu Children's portions Garden Parking Wi-fi **Rooms** 3

The Riverhead Brewery Tap & Dining Room

PICK OF THE PUBS

2 Peel St HD7 6BR ☎ 01484 841270 & 844324
e-mail: riverhead@ossett-brewery.co.uk
dir: *In town centre*

The lively River Colne cascades through the centre of this engaging little mill town, beside which stands a modest, stone-built Victorian former co-op building. Re-emerging in 1995 as a micro-brewery and thriving pub, its beers, named after reservoirs nestling in the enfolding high South Pennine moors, are a major draw on the popular Trans-Pennine Rail Ale Trail. Now owned by Ossett Brewery, the beers are still brewed in the brewery just off the bar; it's an immensely popular spot for ramblers, rail-alers and locals, a genuine melting pot. Enjoy a pint of March Haigh in the bare-boarded, wood-rich bar, dappled with great local photos, or pop upstairs to the dining room for some classic lunchtime pub grub, enhanced in the evenings by tip-top modern dishes such as starter of black pudding and chestnut spring roll with slowly roasted belly pork, preceding medallion of turkey with spatchcock quail and a herb, leek and smoked cheese polenta, crispy skin and port sauce.

Open all day all wk ⊕ OSSETT BREWERY ◀ Riverhead March Haigh, Butterley Bitter, Redbrook, Black Moss Stout. **Facilities** Children welcome Children's portions

OSSETT　　　　　Map 16 SE22

Ossett Brewery Tap

2 The Green WF5 8JS ☎ 01924 272215
e-mail: ossetttap@ossett-brewery.co.uk
dir: *M1 junct 40, A638 signed Wakefield. At lights right into Queens Dr, right into Station Rd (B6128), left into Southdale Rd, right into The Green*

Taking on the mantle from the original brewery pub in the adjacent Calder Valley; the Tap fires on all cylinders with a great range of Ossett's award-winning beers (plus guests) always available over the ornately-moulded wooden bar of this locals' pub with a heart of gold. Updating has spruced up the traditional interior, with real fires warming flagstone-floored and oak-boarded rooms liberally spread with Britannia tables, and upholstered wall-benches threaded amongst tastefully decorated stone and colour-washed rooms.

Open all wk 3-12 (Fri-Sat noon-1am, Sun 12-12) ⊕ OSSETT BREWERY ◀ Pale Gold, Silver King, Excelsior & Yorkshire Blonde, Fuller's London Pride. **Facilities** Garden Parking **Notes** ◉

PICK OF THE PUBS

Ring O'Bells Country Pub & Restaurant

THORNTON   Map 19 SE03

212 Hilltop Rd BD13 3QL
☎ **01274 832296**
e-mail: enquiries@theringobells.com
web: www.theringobells.com
dir: *From M62 take A58 for 5m, right onto A644. 4.5m follow Denholme signs, into Well Head Rd into Hilltop Rd*

Thornton is the village where the Brontë Sisters, whose father was the rector, were born, christened and lived. Originally, the Ring O' Bells, high above the village, was a Wesleyan chapel overlooking the dramatic Yorkshire Pennines where, on a clear day, the views stretch for over 40 miles. Ann and Clive Preston have successfully run the pub for 20 years, and their cuisine, service and professionalism have been recognised with accolades from both the trade and visitors. Recent refurbishment of the bar and dining area has done nothing to dilute its traditional, historical feel, enhanced by prints of the village in the 1920s on the walls, although contemporary art is displayed in the restaurant. The air-conditioned Brontë Restaurant, once mill workers' cottages, now has a conservatory running its whole length with stunning valley views. Local farmers and suppliers of meat, fish, game and veg know that everything will be carefully prepared and cooked by a team of award-winning chefs, whose à la carte menu and daily specials board offer

traditional British dishes with European influences. Expect starters such as Scottish salmon and crab fishcakes, Thai sweet chilli marinated haddock, or lamb and spinach meatballs. Main courses may include roasted topside of beef with Yorkshire pudding; pea and mint risotto; grilled fillet of mackerel; or braised boneless shoulder of Yorkshire lamb; and a choice of award-winning pies. There's also a daily vegetarian dish on the blackboard. Among the desserts, all made to order, are warm apple pie and toffee sauce; brandy snap basket with ice cream berry sundae; and glazed lemon tart. Booking for meals may be required.

Open all wk 11.30-4 5.30-11.30 (Sat-Sun 11.30-4 6.15-11.30) Closed: 25 Dec **Bar**

Meals L served all wk 12-2 D served Mon-Fri 5.30-9.30, Sat-Sun 6.15-9.30 Av main course £10.95 **Restaurant** L served all wk 12-2 D served all wk 5.30-9.30, Sat-Sun 6.15-9.30 Fixed menu price fr £8.95 Av 3 course à la carte fr £22.95 ⊞ FREE HOUSE ◄ John Smith's, Courage Directors, Black Sheep, Copper Dragon, Otter. ♟ 12 **Facilities** Children welcome Children's menu Children's portions Parking Wi-fi 🚐 (notice required)

Old Bridge Inn

Priest Ln HX6 4DF ☎ 01422 822595
web: www.theoldbridgeinn.co.uk
dir: 5m from Halifax in village centre by church, over a pack horse bridge

This ancient inn has changed very little over the last 700 years. Approached by an old packhorse bridge in a Pennine conservation village, the whitewashed, award-winning pub has three traditional bars, with antique furniture and open fires. In addition to Timothy Taylor ales, they always offer two guest beers from independent brewers. Tranquil landscaped seating outside overlooks the River Ryburn. Expect good old-fashioned dishes like Hinchliffes championship pork pie and mushy peas, lamb and mint sausages with crushed new potatoes, or sea bass fillet with samphire, new potatoes and crab sauce. Booking for meals may be required.

Open all wk 12-3 5.30-11 (Fri-Sat 12-11.30 Sun 12-10.30) **Bar Meals** L served all wk 12-2 D served Mon-Sat 6.30-9.30 ⊕ FREE HOUSE ◀ Timothy Taylor Landlord, Golden Best & Best Bitter, Guest ales. ♟ 12 **Facilities** Children's portions Garden Parking Wi-fi

The Three Acres Inn

PICK OF THE PUBS

HD8 8LR ☎ 01484 602606
e-mail: info@3acres.com
dir: From Huddersfield take A629 then B6116, turn left for village

This old drovers' inn is an ideal stopping off place for travellers heading north to the Yorkshire Dales. Brian Orme and Neil Truelove have built a reputation for good quality food and a welcoming atmosphere. The inn's spacious interior is lavishly traditional with exposed beams and large fireplaces. On summer evenings, sit out on the deck with a pint of Black Sheep (to remind you of the drovers), or a glass of wine and soak up the fabulous views. The food served in both bar and restaurant

successfully fuses traditional English with international influences. A starter of warm salad of crispy roast duck might be followed by honey and mustard roast gammon or spiced aubergine and tomato cottage pie. Finish with lemon tart, chocolate mousse or orange pannacotta. A generous range of light meals and sandwiches with interesting fillings makes a great lunchtime choice. Booking for meals may be required.

Open all wk 12-3 6-11 **Closed:** 25-26 Dec eve, 1 Jan eve **Bar Meals** L served all wk 12-2 D served all wk 6.30-9.30 Av main course £17.95 **Restaurant** L served all wk 12-2 D served all wk 6.30-9.30 Fixed menu price fr £39.95 Av 3 course à la carte fr £35 ⊕ FREE HOUSE ◀ Timothy Taylor Landlord & Golden Best, Black Sheep, Copper Dragon, Leeds Pale. ♟ 19 **Facilities** Children welcome Children's portions Garden Parking Wi-fi

The Alma Inn & Fresco Italian Restaurant

Cotton Stones HX6 4NS ☎ 01422 823334
e-mail: info@almainn.com
dir: Exit A58 at Triangle between Sowerby Bridge & Ripponden. Follow signs for Cotton Stones

An old stone inn set in a dramatically beautiful location at Cotton Stones with stunning views of the Ryburn Valley. Outside seating can accommodate 200 customers, while the interior features stone-flagged floors and real fires. The cosy bar serves several ales including a guest, and a vast selection of Belgian bottled beers, each with its individual glass; a beer festival in late September is the high-point of hop-based celebrations. The appeal of the Fresco Italian Restaurant revolves around the wood-burning pizza oven on display in the restaurant, the only one in the Calderdale area.

Open all day all wk 12-10.30 **Bar Meals** L served Mon-Thu 12-10, Fri-Sat 12-10.30, Sun 12-9 D served Mon-Thu 12-10, Fri-Sat 12-10.30, Sun 12-9 Av main course £9.95 food served all day **Restaurant** L served Mon-Thu 12-10, Fri-Sat 12-10.30, Sun 12-9 D served Mon-Thu 12-10, Fri-Sat 12-10.30, Sun 12-9 food served all day ⊕ FREE HOUSE ◀ Timothy Taylor Landlord & Golden Best, Tetley's Bitter, Guest ales. ♟ **Facilities** ☙ Children welcome Children's portions Garden Beer festival Parking Wi-fi 🚌 (notice required)

Ring O'Bells Country Pub & Restaurant

PICK OF THE PUBS

See Pick of the Pubs on page 611

See Pick of the Pubs on page 611

Pack Horse Inn

HX7 7AT ☎ 01422 842803
dir: Off A646 & A6033

The Pack Horse is a converted Laithe farmhouse dating from the early 1600s. Its beautiful location is just 300 yards from the Pennine Way, which makes it popular with walkers, mountain bikers, and horse riders hacking the Mary Towneley Loop. Subdued lighting, cosy log fires and historical pictures characterise the interior. Equally attractive are the home-cooked meals, a good range of real ales and a fabulous choice of 130 single malt whiskies. Note that from October to Easter the pub is only open in the evening.

Open summer 12-3 7-11 **Closed:** Mon & Tue-Fri L (Oct-Etr) **Bar Meals** L served Tue-Sun summer only D served Tue-Sun Av main course £9.95 ⊕ FREE HOUSE ◀ Theakston XB, Black Sheep Best Bitter, Copper Dragon Golden Pippin, Thwaites Lancaster Bomber. ♟ 12 **Facilities** ☙ Children welcome Parking

Fleur du Jardin

PICK OF THE PUBS

Kings Mills GY5 7JT ☎ 01481 257996
e-mail: info@fleurdujardin.com
dir: 2.5m from town centre

Guernsey's finest sandy beaches are but a short stroll from this friendly hotel, bar and restaurant, named after one of the island's most famous breeds of cow. Dating from the 15th century, it has been restyled with a modern shabby-chic appeal, but historical features such as granite walls, wood beams and fireplaces remain untouched. The low bar might require some to stoop, but that needn't hamper the enjoyment of a pint of Sunbeam, brewed by Channel Island brewery, Liberation. Kitchen watchwords are seasonality and freshness - it isn't unusual to see a local fisherman delivering a 10lb sea bass. Expect steaks, lasagne and burgers; confit of salmon teriyaki; pot-roast barbecue pork; Thai chicken curry; and, of course, seafood. Sunday lunch could be roast sirloin of beef; chicken and leek pasta bake; or steamed haddock mornay. Desserts along traditional lines include warm chocolate fudge cake with Guernsey cream. Booking for meals may be required.

Open all day all wk ⊕ FREE HOUSE ◀ Liberation Guernsey Sunbeam, Fuller's London Pride, Guest ales ♺ Roquette. **Facilities** Children welcome Children's menu Children's portions Garden Parking Wi-fi

Save on hotels. Book at theAA.com/hotel

CHANNEL ISLANDS 613 ENGLAND

ST PETER PORT — Map 24

The Admiral de Saumarez ★★★ HL

Duke of Normandie Hotel, Lefebvre St GY1 2JP
☎ **01481 721431**
e-mail: enquiries@dukeofnormandie.com
dir: *From harbour rdbt St Julians Av, 3rd left into Anns Place, continue to right, up hill, then left into Lefebvre St, archway entrance on right*

Part of the Duke of Normandie Hotel, this thoughtfully restored bar attracts a happy mix of Guernsey locals and hotel residents. It is full of architectural salvage, including old timbers (now painted with well-known amusing sayings) and maritime memorabilia. Details of the great naval victories of the Admiral himself are engraved on the tables. You can be served your refreshments out in the suntrap beer garden in warmer weather. The lunch and dinner menus proffer traditional pub favourites: local hand-picked crab cakes with red pepper dressing make a great starter; continue with deep-fried goujons of local plaice with straw fries. Booking for meals may be required.

Open all day all wk 11am-11.30pm **Bar Meals** L served all wk 12-2 D served all wk 6-9 Av main course £8 **Restaurant** L served all wk 12-2 D served all wk 6-9 Fixed menu price fr £12.50 ⊕ FREE HOUSE ◀ Randall's of Guernsey Patois, Morland Old Speckled Hen ♂ Rocquette. **Facilities** Children welcome Children's menu Children's portions Garden Parking ➡ **Rooms** 37

The Ship & Crown, Crow's Nest Brasserie NEW

The Quay GY1 2NB ☎ **01481 728994**
e-mail: ship_crown@hotmail.com
dir: *Opposite Crown Pier*

Occupying a historic building on the waterfront at St Peter Port, this busy Guernsey town pub and stylish brasserie boasts magnificent views across the Victoria Marina to the neighbouring Channel Islands. Run by the same family for more than 30 years, the pub offers a wide range of beers and ciders, but it is equally well known for its extensive menus and all-day bar meals. The freshly picked local crab sandwiches and range of salads are especially popular, as are the traditional fish pie and the lamb cutlets.

Open all day all wk **Bar Meals** L served all wk 11-9 D served all wk 11-9 Av main course £7 food served all day **Restaurant** L served all wk 12-3 D served all wk 6-10 Fixed menu price fr £10.50 Av 3 course à la carte fr £24.95 ⊕ FREE HOUSE ◀ Fuller's London Pride, Wells Bombardier, Sharp's Doom Bar, Wychwood Hobgoblin, Liberation ♂ Addlestones. ₹ 8 **Facilities** Children welcome Children's menu Children's portions Parking Wi-fi ➡

JERSEY

GOREY — Map 24

Castle Green

La Route de la Cote JE3 6DR ☎ **01534 840218**
e-mail: enquiries@jerseypottery.com
dir: *Opposite main entrance of Gorey Castle*

Arrive early for a seat on the sunny terrace outside this stylish pub as the views are breathtaking — it overlooks Gorey Harbour and Grouville Bay, with dramatic Mont Orgueil looming above the harbour. Jersey produce, especially fresh fish and seafood, features on the seasonally evolving menu. Choices range from fish soup through mixed fish grill with Mediterranean salsa to sea bass with salsa verde. For meat eaters there are home-made beefburgers and pork belly with mustard sauce. Round it off with a comforting dessert such as plum and almond tart.

Open 11.30-3 6-11 (all day in summer) Closed: Sun eve & Mon L **Bar Meals** L served Tue-Sun 12-2.30 D served Mon-Sat 6-9 Av main course £11.50-£12.95 **Restaurant** L served Tue-Sun 12-2.30 D served Mon-Sat 6-9 Av 3 course à la carte fr £22 ◀ Courage Directors, John Smith's Extra Smooth, Theakston, Bass. ₹ 8 **Facilities** Children welcome Children's menu Children's portions Garden Wi-fi ➡

ST AUBIN — Map 24

Old Court House Inn

St Aubin's Harbour JE3 8AB ☎ **01534 746433**
e-mail: info@oldcourthousejersey.com
dir: *From Jersey Airport, right at exit, left at lights, 0.5m to St Aubin*

This historic hotel and pub overlooks the harbour and has a popular alfresco eating trade and a long history dating back to 1450. The original courthouse at the rear of the property was first restored in 1611, while beneath the front part are enormous cellars where privateers stored their plunder. Three bars offer food, and there are two restaurants with terrific harbour views, plus there's an attractive courtyard. There's lots of locally caught fish on the menus of course, plus confit duck leg with thyme jus and lamb shank with red wine jus. Real ales include some from the Liberation Brewery.

Open all day all wk Closed: 25 Dec, Mon Jan-Feb **Bar Meals** L served all wk 12.30-2.30 D served Mon-Sat 7.30-10 **Restaurant** L served all wk 12.30-2.30 D served all wk 7.30-10 ⊕ FREE HOUSE ◀ Courage Directors, Theakston, John Smith's, Liberation. **Facilities** Children welcome Children's menu Children's portions Beer festival Wi-fi ➡ (notice required)

ST BRELADE — Map 24

The Portelet Inn NEW

La Route de Noirmont JE3 8AJ ☎ **01534 741899**
e-mail: portelet@randalls.je
dir: *Telephone for directions*

Transformed from a 17th-century farmhouse into a pub in 1948, The Portelet is a popular, family-friendly pub situated a short walk from the coast in St Brelade. While adults relax in the bar, children can let off steam in Pirate Pete's excellent indoor or outdoor play areas, and the Carvery restaurant is ideal for family dining. Kids have their own menu, while parents can tuck into classic pub food, the wide-ranging menu taking in beer-battered fish and chips; lamb shank with champ and thyme sauce; and sticky toffee pudding. Booking for meals may be required.

Open all day Closed: Mon (Jan-Mar) **Bar Meals** L served Mon-Thu 12-8.30, Fri-Sat 12-9, Sun & PH 12-8 D served Mon-Thu 12-8.30, Fri-Sat 12-9, Sun & PH 12-8 Av main course £10.50 food served all day **Restaurant** L served Mon-Thu 12-8.30, Fri-Sat 12-9, Sun & PH 12-8 D served Mon-Thu 12-8.30, Fri-Sat 12-9, Sun & PH 12-8 Fixed menu price fr £15 Av 3 course à la carte fr £21.50 food served all day ⊕ RANDALLS ◀ Wells Bombardier. **Facilities** Children welcome Children's menu Children's portions Play area Family room Garden Parking Wi-fi ➡ (notice required)

ST MARTIN — Map 24

Royal Hotel

La Grande Route de Faldouet JE3 6UG ☎ **01534 856289**
e-mail: johnbarker@jerseymail.co.uk
dir: *2m from Five Oaks rdbt towards St Martin. Pub on right next to St Martin's Church*

A friendly local in the heart of St Martin, this former coaching inn prides itself on offering quality food and drink. Landlord John Barker has been welcoming guests for almost 25 years. A roaring log fire in the spacious lounge warm winter visitors, and there's a sunny beer garden to enjoy during the summer months. On the menu are traditional home-made favourites such as baby rack of ribs, chicken curry, and braised lamb shank. The pub also makes its own pizzas with a variety of toppings. Burgers, filled jacket potatoes, grills and children's choices are on offer, too.

Open all day all wk **Bar Meals** L served all wk 12-2.15 D served Mon-Sat 6-8.30 **Restaurant** L served all wk 12-2.15 D served Mon-Sat 6-8.30 ⊕ RANDALLS ◀ Ringwood Best Bitter, John Smith's Smooth, Theakston Cool Cask, Guinness, Bass ♂ Westons Stowford Press. ₹ 9 **Facilities** Children welcome Children's menu Children's portions Play area Garden Parking Wi-fi ➡ (notice required)

ST MARY — Map 24

St Mary's Country Inn NEW

La Rue des Buttes JE3 3DS ☎ 01534 482897
e-mail: stmarys@liberationpubco.com
dir: *Telephone for directions*

Jersey's Liberation Brewery owns this appealing country inn with smart, contemporary interior. The menu offers imaginative food at reasonable prices, including roasts and grills; espetadas (Portuguese chargrilled skewered meats and fish); murgh makhani (butter chicken curry); duck cassoulet; ale-battered cod with chunky chips; and stir-fried bok choy. There are just three prices on the wine list, but choice extends to half-litre carafes and plenty by the glass. In the bar you'll find continental lagers, island-brewed Mary Ann and flagship cask-conditioned Liberation Ale. There's a delightful seating area outside. Booking for meals may be required.

Open all day all wk **Bar Meals** L served all wk 12-2.30 D served all wk 6-9 Av main course **£9 Restaurant** L served all wk 12-2.30 D served all wk 6-9 ⊕ LIBERATION GROUP ◀ Liberation Ale, Mary Ann Special. ♥ 19 **Facilities** ❖ Children welcome Children's menu Children's portions Garden Parking Wi-fi ➡ (notice required)

ISLE OF MAN

PEEL — Map 24 SC28

The Creek Inn

Station Place IM5 1AT ☎ 01624 842216
e-mail: thecreekinn@manx.net
dir: *On quayside opposite House of Manannan Museum*

On the quayside, overlooked by Peel Hill, the family-run Creek Inn is a real ale drinkers' paradise, with locally brewed Okells ales, up to five changing guests, and a beer festival in March. Bands play every weekend, and nightly during the TT and Manx Grand Prix, when the pub becomes the town's focal point. There's a huge selection of dishes on the menu, from local fish, steaks and burgers, to vegetarian options and salads, alongside sandwiches, hot baguettes and toasties.

Open all day all wk **Bar Meals** L served all wk 11-9.30 D served all wk 11-9.30 food served all day **Restaurant** L served all wk 11-9.30 D served all wk 11-9.30 food served all day ⊕ FREE HOUSE ◀ Okells Bitter & Seasonal ales, Bushy's, 4 Guest ales ♂ Thatchers Green Goblin, St Helier, Manx Apple. ♥ 12 **Facilities** Children welcome Children's menu Children's portions Garden Beer festival Parking Wi-fi ➡

PORT ERIN — Map 24 SC26

Falcon's Nest Hotel ★★ HL

The Promenade, Station Rd IM9 6AF ☎ 01624 834077
e-mail: falconsnest@enterprise.net
dir: *Follow coast road, S from airport or ferry. Hotel on seafront, immediately after steam railway station*

Once owned by local locksmith William Milner, this magnificent pub-hotel overlooks a beautiful sheltered harbour and beach. Head for the saloon bar, 'Ophidian's Lair', for the pool table, jukebox and live sports via satellite; alternatively the residents' lounge, also open to the public, serves the same local ales from Okells and Bushy's, among others, and over 70 whiskies. The former ballroom has been restored and turned into a Victorian-style dining room, where local seafood dishes include crab, prawns, sea bass, marlin, lobster and local scallops known as 'queenies'; the carvery here is also very popular.

Open all day all wk **Bar Meals** L served all wk 12-9 Av main course **£8.95** food served all day **Restaurant** L served all wk 12-2 D served all wk 6-9 Fixed menu price fr £16 Av 3 course à la carte fr £22 ⊕ FREE HOUSE ◀ John Smith's, Okells, Bushy's, Guinness, Manx guest ale, Guest ales. **Facilities** Children welcome Children's menu Children's portions Family room Beer festival Parking Wi-fi ➡ **Rooms** 39

Save on hotels. Book at **theAA.com/hotel**

ISLE OF MAN 615 **ENGLAND**

Scotland

Ben Macdui viewed from Glen Lui near Braemar in the Cairngorms National Park

ABERDEEN, CITY OF

ABERDEEN   Map 23 NJ90

Old Blackfriars

52 Castle St AB11 5BB ☎ 01224 581922
e-mail: oldblackfriars.aberdeen@belhavenpubs.net
dir: *From train station turn right along Guild St then left into Market St, at end turn right onto Union St. Pub on right at end of road*

Situated in Aberdeen's historic Castlegate, this traditional split-level city centre pub stands on the site of property owned by Blackfriars Dominican monks, hence the name. Inside you'll find stunning stained glass, plus well-kept real ales (nine handpumps) and a large selection of malt whiskies. The pub is also renowned for excellent food and an unobtrusive atmosphere (no background music and no television). The wide-ranging menu has all the pub favourites and more – chicken Balmoral, chicken tikka makhani, sweet potato curry, and baked lasagne. There is a weekly quiz and live music every Thursday.

Open all day all wk 11am-mdnt (Fri-Sat 11am-1am Sun 11-11) Closed: 25 Dec, 1 Jan ⊕ BELHAVEN ◀ Caledonian Deuchars IPA, Inveralmond Ossian, Greene King Ruddles County, Guest ales. **Facilities** Children welcome Children's menu Family room Wi-fi

ABERDEENSHIRE

BALMEDIE   Map 23 NJ91

The Cock & Bull Bar & Restaurant ◉

Ellon Rd, Blairton AB23 8XY ☎ 01358 743249
e-mail: info@thecockandbull.co.uk
dir: *11m N of city centre, on left of A90 between Balmedie junct & Foveran*

A cast-iron range warms the bar in this whitewashed, stone-built coaching inn, standing quite alone in open farmland north of Aberdeen. Conversation is easily stimulated by local artist Irene Morrison's paintings and assorted hanging artefacts. Affordably priced food in the AA-Rosette restaurant uses Marine Stewardship Council-approved white fish and Peterhead-landed shellfish, and beef and pork from the region's stock farms. A seasonal menu might list venison and haggis burger; haddock, mushy peas and rustic chips; and pumpkin gnocchi.

Open all day all wk 10am-11.30pm (Sun 12-7.30) Closed: 26-27 Dec, 2-3 Jan **Bar Meals** L served Mon-Sat 10-8.45, Sun 12-7.30 D served Mon-Sat 10-8.45, Sun 12-7.30 food served all day **Restaurant** L served Mon-Sat 10-8.45, Sun 12-7.30 D served Mon-Sat 10-8.45, Sun 12-7.30 food served all day ⊕ FREE HOUSE ◀ Caledonian 80/-, Guinness. **Facilities** Children welcome Children's menu Play area Garden Parking Wi-fi 🚐

MARYCULTER   Map 23 NO89

Old Mill Inn

South Deeside Rd AB12 5FX ☎ 01224 733212
e-mail: info@oldmillinn.co.uk
dir: *5m W of Aberdeen on B9077*

This delightful family-run 200-year-old country inn stands on the edge of the River Dee, five miles from Aberdeen city centre. A former mill house, the 18th-century granite building has been tastefully modernised to include a restaurant where the finest Scottish ingredients feature on the menu: start with marinated herring salad or black pudding parcel, then continue with pan-roasted lamb cutlets, roast vegetable and pesto tagliatelle, or grilled salmon fillet on sweet potato mash. Food and drink can be enjoyed in the garden in warmer months.

Open all day all wk **Bar Meals** L served all wk 12-2 D served all wk 5.30-9 **Restaurant** L served all wk 12-2 D served all wk 5.30-9 ⊕ FREE HOUSE ◀ Caledonian Deuchars IPA, Timothy Taylor Landlord, Fuller's London Pride. **Facilities** Children welcome Children's menu Children's portions Garden Parking 🚐

NETHERLEY   Map 23 NO89

The Lairhillock Inn

PICK OF THE PUBS

AB39 3QS ☎ 01569 730001
e-mail: info@lairhillock.co.uk
dir: *From Aberdeen take A90. Right towards Durris on B9077 then left onto B979 to Netherley*

Formerly a farmhouse and then a coaching inn, the 17th-century Lairhillock stands alone surrounded by fields. There's a rustic feel inside, especially in the fine old bar with its exposed stone, panelling, settles and log fires. Menus change every three months to keep up with the best seasonal Scottish produce, while the daily specials prove that the kitchen never lets any interesting ingredient slip by. Thus, langoustines from Gourdon, Shetland mussels, Orkney scallops, Highlands wild boar and venison, and salmon from the Dee all make a showing, while Aberdeen Angus steaks are always a cert. Lairies gambas are king prawns cooked in lime, chilli, sweet pepper and coconut sauce; fish, chicken and duck are peat-smoked on the premises. Although the chip output is kept to a minimum, you can, for example, have them with smoked bacon and caramelised onion burger. The more formal Crynoch Restaurant offers roast cannon of lamb; and spring vegetable tagliatelle. Booking for meals may be required.

Open all day all wk Closed: 25-26 Dec, 1-2 Jan **Bar Meals** L served all wk 12-2 D served all wk 6-9.30 **Restaurant** L served Sun 12-2 D served Tue-Sat 7-9.30 ⊕ FREE HOUSE ◀ Timothy Taylor Landlord, Caledonian Deuchars IPA, Guest ales. **Facilities** 🐾 Children welcome Children's menu Children's portions Garden Parking 🚐 (notice required)

OLDMELDRUM   Map 23 NJ82

The Redgarth

Kirk Brae AB51 0DJ ☎ 01651 872353
e-mail: redgarth1@aol.com
dir: *From A947 (Oldmeldrum bypass) follow signs to Golf Club/Pleasure Park. Establishment E of bypass*

Built as a house in 1928 and situated in a small village, this friendly family-run inn has an attractive garden that offers magnificent views of Bennachie and the surrounding countryside. Cask-conditioned ales, such as Highland Scapa and Inveralmond Thrappledouser, and interesting wines are served along with dishes prepared on the premises using fresh local produce. A typical selection might include Moroccan lamb casserole with minted couscous, or duo of fillet beef and venison with leek mash. Booking for meals may be required.

Open all wk 11-3 5-11 (Fri-Sat 11-3 5-11.45) Closed: 25-26 Dec, 1-3 Jan **Bar Meals** L served all wk 12-2 D served Sun-Thu 5-9, Fri-Sat 5-9.30 **Restaurant** L served all wk 12-2 D served Sun-Thu 5-9, Fri-Sat 5-9.30 ⊕ FREE HOUSE ◀ Inveralmond Thrappledouser, Timothy Taylor Landlord, Highland Scapa Special & Orkney Best, Kelburn Pivo Estivo. **Facilities** Children welcome Children's menu Children's portions Garden Parking Wi-fi 🚐

ARGYLL & BUTE

ARDUAINE   Map 20 NM71

Loch Melfort Hotel ★★★ HL ◉◉

PICK OF THE PUBS

PA34 4XG ☎ 01852 200233
e-mail: reception@lochmelfort.co.uk
dir: *On A816, midway between Oban & Lochgilphead*

Perfect for garden enthusiasts, sailors or simply those looking for tranquility, the Chartroom II is part of the Loch Melfort Hotel, previously the Campbell family home. The hotel is located on the path to the NTS Arduaine Gardens with spectacular views over Asknish Bay towards Jura and beyond. The relaxed atmosphere of this modern bar and bistro with two AA Rosettes is the place to enjoy all-day drinks and home baking, as well as light lunches and suppers. It has the finest views on the West Coast and serves home-made Scottish fare including plenty of locally landed seafood, such as fantastic langoustines, scallops, crabs, lobsters and mussels; Highland beefburgers, and steak-and-ale pies. You can sit outside and enjoy a drink in warmer weather watching magical sunsets or sit around the cosy fire in winter and watch the waves crashing against the rocks. The Chartroom II is family friendly and serves children's meals or smaller portions from the main menu, plus there is a playground. There are also four free moorings from April to October. Booking for meals may be required.

Open all wk 11-10 ⊕ FREE HOUSE ◀ Caledonian 80/-, Belhaven, Fyne. **Facilities** Children welcome Children's menu Children's portions Play area Garden Parking **Rooms** 25

Save on hotels. Book at **theAA.com/hotel**

ARGYLL & BUTE 619 SCOTLAND

PICK OF THE PUBS

Tigh an Truish Inn

CLACHAN-SEIL Map 20 NM71

PA34 4QZ ☎ 01852 300242
web: www.tighantruish.co.uk
dir: *12m S of Oban take A816. Onto
B844 towards Atlantic Bridge*

The Brunner family's fiercely traditional 18th-century inn – right by the single-span 'Bridge over the Atlantic' at the top of Seil Sound – is not signposted from the B816, so make sure you find the turning on to the B844 (towards Easdale and on to the Isle of Luing). The inn's name has quite a tale attached, as roughly translated, Tigh an Truish is Gaelic for 'House of Trousers'. After the Battle of Culloden in 1746, the wearing of kilts was outlawed and anyone caught wearing one faced execution. Many Seil islanders defied this ruling and it was at this historic, white-painted inn that they swapped their kilts for trousers before travelling to the mainland. These days people pause here for single malts, regularly changing ales from local brewers, including Atlas and Fyne ales, and a menu that brims with seafood: salmon and mussels from Argyll producers, and lobster and prawns caught by local fishermen working the Firth of Lorne. This translates to smoked mackerel pâté with oatcakes; a steaming bowl of moules marinière; delicious

langoustines served with garlic mayonnaise; and daily fresh fish dishes on the chalkboard menu. Fish-free options include macaroni cheese; home-made steak-and-ale pie; and sirloin steak with chive and ginger butter. The bar is delightfully unchanged and simple, while for families, a separate lounge off the main bar is furnished with children's books – another indication of the pub's genuinely warm welcome. Popular with tourists and members of the yachting fraternity, the inn's waterfront beer garden is much in demand on summer days, when the tides can be watched as they swirl around the famous bridge.

Open all wk 11-11 (Mon-Fri 11-2.30 5-11 Oct-Mar) Closed: 25 Dec & 1 Jan **Bar Meals** L served all wk 12-2 D served all wk 6-8.30 (Apr-Oct) ⊕ FREE HOUSE ◄ Local guest ales. **Facilities** Children welcome Children's menu Children's portions Family room ❀ Garden Parking 🚌 (notice required)

CAIRNDOW — Map 20 NN11

Cairndow Stagecoach Inn ★★★ INN

PA26 8BN ☎ **01499 600286**
e-mail: enq@cairndowinn.com
dir: *N of Glasgow take A82, left on A83 at Arrochar. Through Rest and be Thankful to Cairndow. Follow signs for inn*

On the upper reaches of Loch Fyne, this old coaching inn offers plenty of fine views of mountains, magnificent woodlands and rivers. Sample one of many malt whiskies in the friendly bar by the roaring fire, or idle away the time in the loch-side garden watching the oyster-catchers while sipping the local Fyne Ales. The menu in the candlelit Stables Restaurant offers pan-fried scallops with chilli garlic butter; chicken stuffed with haggis with creamy peppercorn sauce; salmon from the loch; and home-made meatballs, tomato and herb sauce with linguine. Meals are also served all day in the bar and lounges. Accommodation is available if you would like to stay over and explore the area. On your way to the pub you should look out for Britain's tallest tree! Booking for meals may be required.

Open all day all wk **Bar Meals** L served all wk 12-6 D served all wk 6-9 Av main course £7 food served all day **Restaurant** L served all wk 12-6 D served all wk 6-9 Av 3 course à la carte fr £25 food served all day ⊕ FREE HOUSE ◀ Fyne Hurricane Jack, Avalanche, Piper's Gold, Maverick, Jarl. **Facilities** ❄ Children welcome Children's menu Children's portions Family room Garden Parking Wi-fi ▭ (notice required) **Rooms** 18

CLACHAN-SEIL — Map 20 NM71

Tigh an Truish Inn
PICK OF THE PUBS

See Pick of the Pubs on page 619

CONNEL — Map 20 NM93

The Oyster Inn
PICK OF THE PUBS

PA37 1PJ ☎ **01631 710666**
e-mail: stay@oysterinn.co.uk
dir: *Telephone for directions*

A comfortable informal inn, The Oyster overlooks the tidal whirlpools and white water of the Falls of Lora, with glorious views to Mull. It was built in the 18th century to serve ferry passengers, but the ferry has long since been superseded by the modern road bridge. Ferryman's Bar in the pub next door was, and still is, known as the Glue Pot. Years ago canny locals knew they could be 'stuck' here between ferries and evade Oban's Sunday licensing laws; additionally, a blacksmith's shop behind the pub melted down horses' hooves for glue — the pots hang from the bar ceiling. Food is served from midday in the bar and from 6pm in the restaurant. Locally sourced quality ingredients go into the short but succulent menu of real food: half a dozen West Coast oysters or a trio of seafood

is a great way to start. Catch of the day could follow, or a rack of Highland lamb.

Open all day all wk 12-12 **Bar Meals** L served all wk 12-6 D served all wk 6-9.30 Av main course £10 food served all day **Restaurant** D served all wk 6-9.30 Av 3 course à la carte fr £25 ⊕ FREE HOUSE ◀ Guinness, John Smith's. **Facilities** ❄ Children welcome Children's menu Children's portions Family room Garden Parking Wi-fi

CRINAN — Map 20 NR79

Crinan Hotel
PICK OF THE PUBS

PA31 8SR ☎ **01546 830261**
e-mail: reservations@crinanhotel.com
dir: *From M8, at end of bridge take A82, at Tarbert left onto A83. At Inveraray follow Campbeltown signs to Lochgilphead, follow signs for A816 to Oban. 2m, left to Crinan on B841*

At the north end of the Crinan Canal which connects Loch Fyne to the Atlantic Ocean, the Crinan is a romantic retreat enjoying fabulous views across the Sound of Jura. It's a long-standing place of welcome at the heart of community life in this tiny fishing village. The hotel dates back some 200 years and has been run by owners Nick and Frances Ryan for around 40 of them. Eat in the Crinan Seafood Bar or the Westward Restaurant. The cuisine is firmly based on the freshest of seafood – it's landed daily just 50 metres from the hotel. Starters could include brochettes of Loch Fyne scallops with organic salad leaves and balsamic reduction. For a main course perhaps choose grilled fillet of monkfish with caper lemon butter, or roast rack of Argyll Hill lamb. Boat trips can be arranged to the islands, and there is a classic boats regatta in the summer. Look for the 'secret garden' just behind the hotel. Booking for meals may be required.

Open all day all wk 11-11 Closed: 25 Dec ◀ Fyne, Worthington's, Tennent's Velvet, Guinness. **Facilities** Children welcome Children's menu Children's portions Garden Parking Wi-fi

DUNOON — Map 20 NS17

Coylet Inn

Loch Eck PA23 8SG ☎ **01369 840426**
e-mail: info@coyletinn.co.uk
dir: *N of Dunoon on A815*

Here on Loch Eck's shores you wouldn't want a television or games machines to disturb your drink or meal. Well, they won't, at least not in this charming, beautifully appointed 17th-century coaching inn, where you can relax with a glass of wine or a pint of Piper's Gold or Highlander in peace by a log fire. Fully traceability lies behind menus offering haggis, neeps and tatties; beer-battered West Coast haddock; Scottish rib-eye steak; and home-made courgette and herb bites. Ice Age glaciers created the perfect surroundings for walking, cycling and fishing.

Open all day Closed: 3-26 Jan, Mon & Tue (Oct-Mar) **Bar Meals** L served all wk 12-2.30 D served all wk 6-8.30

Restaurant L served all wk 12-2.30 D served all wk 6-8.30 ⊕ FREE HOUSE ◀ Fyne Highlander & Piper's Gold, Guest ales. **Facilities** ❄ Children welcome Children's menu Children's portions Garden Parking

INVERARAY — Map 20 NN00

George Hotel **NEW**

Main Street East PA32 8TT ☎ **01499 302111**
e-mail: info@thegeorgehotel.co.uk
dir: *On A83*

In the centre of a historic conservation town, the George was built in 1776 and has been in the ownership of the Clark family since 1860. Although there have been sensitive additions over the years, nothing detracts from the original flagstone floors and four roaring log fires. More than 100 whiskies and a range of Fyne ales are complemented by an extensive bar menu that includes traditional haggis, neeps and tatties. The award-winning restaurant showcases local produce; try the baked Loch Duart salmon fillet with smoked mussel and pistachio risotto. The George holds beer and music festivals on the May and August Bank Holidays.

Open all day all wk 11am-1am Closed: 25 Dec **Bar Meals** Av main course £8-£14 food served all day **Restaurant** food served all day ⊕ FREE HOUSE ◀ Fyne. ☘ 9 **Facilities** ❄ Children welcome Children's menu Children's portions Garden Beer festival Parking Wi-fi ▭ (notice required)

KILFINAN — Map 20 NR97

Kilfinan Hotel Bar

PA21 2EP ☎ **01700 821201**
e-mail: info@kilfinan.com
dir: *8m N of Tighnabruaich on B8000*

On the eastern shore of Loch Fyne, set amid spectacular Highland scenery on a working estate, this hotel has been welcoming travellers since the 1760s. The bars are cosy with log fires in winter, and offer a fine selection of malts. There are two intimate dining rooms, with the Lamont room for larger parties. Menus change daily and offer the best of local produce: Loch Fyne langoustines grilled in garlic and butter; pan-seared Loch Fyne scallops with crispy bacon and sage; or Isle of Bute venison steak. Enjoy the views from the garden on warmer days. Booking for meals may be required.

Open all wk Closed: winter ⊕ FREE HOUSE ◀ McEwan's 80/-, Fyne. **Facilities** Children welcome Children's menu Children's portions Family room Garden Parking

LOCHGILPHEAD	Map 20 NR88

Cairnbaan Hotel ★★★ HL ◉

PICK OF THE PUBS

Cairnbaan PA31 8SJ ☎ 01546 603668
e-mail: info@cairnbaan.com
dir: *2m N, take A816 from Lochgilphead, hotel off B841*

Built in 1801 to coincide with the opening of the Crinan Canal, which it overlooks, this historic hotel has been run by Darren and Christine Dobson for the past decade. Lighter meals are served from the bistro-style menu in the relaxed atmosphere of the bar, conservatory lounge, or alfresco. For a more formal occasion dine in the serene, AA-Rosetted restaurant, where the carte specialises in the use of fresh local produce, notably seafood and game. Look for starters of Tarbet landed langoustine with bread, salad and mayonnaise. Mains might include Sound of Jura scallops wrapped in pancetta with garlic butter and new potatoes. Round off, perhaps, with sticky toffee pudding with vanilla ice cream. From nearby Oban there are sailings to the islands of Mull, Coll and Tiree. Inveraray Castle is also well worth a visit, as is Dunadd Fort where the ancient kings of Scotland were crowned.

Open all wk 8am-11pm Closed: 25 Dec ⊕ FREE HOUSE ◖ Local ales. **Facilities** Children welcome Children's menu Children's portions Garden Parking Wi-fi **Rooms** 12

LUSS	Map 20 NS39

The Inn at Inverbeg ★★★★ INN

PICK OF THE PUBS

G83 8PD ☎ 01436 860678
e-mail: inverbeg.reception@loch-lomond.co.uk
dir: *12m N of Balloch*

Today a good road skirts Loch Lomond's western shore, but it wouldn't have been so good in 1814, when this wayside inn opened its doors. Now completely remodelled, it incorporates Mr C's Fish & Whisky Restaurant and Bar, which specialises in the obvious. Starting with the fish, expect haddock and cod, West Coast oysters, langoustines, squid, steamed mussels, tempura tiger prawns and Thai fish curry. Try Cullen skink, a thick fish soup. But it offers meat dishes too, including chargrilled Buccleuch steak burger; Cajun chicken; and black pudding and haggis fritters. Mr C's other commodity is, of course, malt whiskies, more than 200 of them. If you prefer a real ale, there's Deuchars IPA, Highlander and Houston's Killellan. Live folk music is played nightly throughout the summer. Individually styled rooms are split between the inn and a sumptuous beach house right on Loch Lomond's bonnie, bonnie banks.

Open all day all wk 11-11 (Fri-Sat 11am-mdnt) **Bar Meals** L served all wk 12-9 D served all wk 12-9 food served all day **Restaurant** L served all wk 12-9 D served all wk 12-9 food served all day ⊕ FREE HOUSE ◖ Houston Killellan, Fyne Highlander, Caledonian Deuchars IPA. ♟ 30 **Facilities** Children welcome Children's menu Children's portions Parking Wi-fi ⛟ (notice required) **Rooms** 20

PORT APPIN	Map 20 NM94

The Pierhouse Hotel & Seafood Restaurant ★★★ SHL ◉

PICK OF THE PUBS

PA38 4DE ☎ 01631 730302
e-mail: reservations@pierhousehotel.co.uk
dir: *A828 from Ballachulish to Oban. In Appin right at Port Appin & Lismore ferry sign. After 2.5m left after post office, hotel at end of road by pier*

With breathtaking views to the islands of Lismore and Mull, it would be hard to imagine a more spectacular setting for this family-run hotel and renowned seafood restaurant with one AA Rosette. Once home to the piermaster, the distinctive building now houses a popular bar, pool room, terrace and dining area, and offers a selection of menus featuring the finest seasonal Scottish seafood, meat, game and vegetables. Lunches in the Ferry bar range from freshly-filled ciabattas and baked potatoes to burgers, pastas and fish dishes. Meanwhile a typical three-course restaurant meal might start with velvet crab bisque, seafood medley and lemon oil; before progressing to roast loin of Kingairloch venison with truffle mashed potato, creamy Savoy cabbage and venison jus. The tempting desserts include Pierhouse sorbets and chocolate fondant with clotted cream. Twelve individually designed bedrooms include two with four-poster beds and superb loch views, and a couple of family rooms. Booking for meals may be required.

Open all wk 11-11 Closed: 25-26 Dec ⊕ FREE HOUSE ◖ Calders 80/-, Belhaven Best, Guinness. **Facilities** Children welcome Children's portions Family room Garden Parking **Rooms** 12

STRACHUR	Map 20 NN00

Creggans Inn ★★★ HL ◉◉

PICK OF THE PUBS

PA27 8BX ☎ 01369 860279
e-mail: info@creggans-inn.co.uk
dir: *A82 from Glasgow, at Tarbet take A83 towards Cairndow, left onto A815 to Strachur*

Standing on the shores of Loch Fyne and a coaching inn since the days of Mary, Queen of Scots, this small, informal and very comfortable inn enjoys glorious vistas across the Mull of Kintyre to the Western Isles. A good range of Scottish ales, including Atlas Latitude and Harviestoun Bitter & Twisted, and some fine malt whiskies are all served at the bar. Regional produce plays a key role in the seasonal menus: the famed Loch Fyne oysters of course, but also salmon and scallops from the same waters, perhaps a potted hot smoked salmon and horseradish pâté as a starter. Robust main courses may feature roast lamb with port and basil jus in the dining room, or chicken with pearl barley, cabbage and bacon broth, or steak and local ale pie in the bar. Toasted almond pannacotta with roast peaches and orange caramel makes a fulfilling conclusion. There's a formal terraced garden and patio for alfresco summer enjoyment

– both make the most of the view. Booking for meals may be required.

Open all day all wk 11am-mdnt **Bar Meals** L served all wk 12-2.30 D served all wk 6-8.30 **Restaurant** D served all wk 7-8.30 ◖ Fyne Highlander, Atlas Latitude, Caledonian Deuchars IPA, Harviestoun Bitter & Twisted. **Facilities** Children welcome Children's menu Children's portions Garden Parking Wi-fi **Rooms** 14

TAYVALLICH	Map 20 NR78

Tayvallich Inn

PA31 8PL ☎ 01546 870282
dir: *From Lochgilphead take A816 then B841/B8025*

Established for over 30 years, the inn stands in a picturesque fishing village overlooking the natural harbour of Tayvallich Bay at the head of Loch Sween. There are unrivalled views, particularly from the outside area of decking, where food and a great selection of real ales can be enjoyed. Not surprisingly given the location, fresh seafood features strongly – the catch is landed from the boats right outside the front door! Lobster, crab and langoustine are available in the summer, while typical dishes in winter might be fragrant Thai mussels, pan-seared king scallops served with sweet chilli and ginger sauce; and smoked haddock chowder. Booking for meals may be required.

Open all wk all day in summer (closed 3-6 Mon-Fri in winter) Closed: 25-26 Dec, Mon (Nov-Mar) **Bar Meals** L served all wk 12-2.30 D served all wk 6-9 Av main course £9.95 **Restaurant** L served all wk 12-2.30 D served all wk 6-9 Av 3 course à la carte fr £22.95 ⊕ FREE HOUSE ◖ Belhaven Best, Fyne Maverick, Avalanche & Piper's Gold, Guinness. ♟ 8 **Facilities** Children welcome Children's menu Children's portions Garden Parking ⛟ (notice required)

CLACKMANNANSHIRE	

DOLLAR	Map 21 NS99

Castle Campbell Hotel

11 Bridge St FK14 7DE ☎ 01259 742519
e-mail: bookings@castle-campbell.co.uk
dir: *A91 (Stirling to St Andrews road). In Dollar centre by bridge overlooking clock tower*

Handy for Dollar Glen's spectacular gorges, this 19th-century coaching inn offers a real taste of Scotland. Built in 1821, pictures on the walls date back to that period. Recognised as a Whisky Ambassador, the hotel has over 50 malts; local ale is always on tap and the wine list runs to several pages. Prime Scottish produce features on the menus, with options ranging from filled ciabattas, salads and pastas in the bar to pan-fried mullet fillets with spring onion mash and ratatouille in the restaurant. Booking for meals may be required.

Open all wk ⊕ FREE HOUSE ◖ Harviestoun Bitter & Twisted, McEwan's 70/-, Caledonian Deuchars IPA (guest). **Facilities** Children welcome Children's menu Children's portions Parking

DUMFRIES & GALLOWAY

BARGRENNAN | Map 20 NX37

House O'Hill Hotel NEW

DG8 6RN ☎ 01671 840243
e-mail: enquiries@houseohill.co.uk
dir: *From Newton Stewart take A714 towards Girvan, 8m. Hotel signed*

This free house in the Galloway Forest Park is around 250 years old and was originally a crofters' cottage. Saved from closure in 2010 by the current owners, it is now a comfortable hotel offering a range of Scottish real ales and more than 20 single malts. Two log fires make the bar a perfect place to put your feet up after a walk in the forest and take advantage of a menu driven by local produce; home-made haggis and black pudding patties might be followed by local game casserole. There are beer festivals in March and September. Booking for meals may be required.

Open all day all wk **Closed:** 3-25 Jan **Bar Meals** L served all wk 12-2.45 D served all wk 6-8.45 Av main course £10 **Restaurant** L served all wk 12-2.45 D served all wk 6-8.45 Fixed menu price fr £15 Av 3 course à la carte fr £18 ⊕ FREE HOUSE ◄ Sulwath, Stewart's, Ayr, Fyne ♻ Aspall. **Facilities** ❤ Children welcome Children's menu Family room Garden Beer festival Parking Wi-fi 🚐

ISLE OF WHITHORN | Map 20 NX43

The Steam Packet Inn

PICK OF THE PUBS

Harbour Row DG8 8LL ☎ 01988 500334
e-mail: steampacketinn@btconnect.com
dir: *From Newton Stewart take A714, then A746 to Whithorn, then Isle of Whithorn*

This lively quayside pub stands in a picturesque village at the tip of the Machars peninsula. Personally run by the Scoular family for over 20 years, it is the perfect place to escape from the pressures of modern living. Sit in one of the comfortable bars, undisturbed by television, fruit machines or piped music, and enjoy one of the real ales, a malt whisky from the great selection, or a glass of wine. Glance out of the picture windows and watch the fishermen at work, then look to the menu for a chance to sample the fruits of their labours. Extensive seafood choices - perhaps a kettle of mussels cooked in a cream and white wine sauce; isle-landed monkfish tail; or fillet of bream - are supported by the likes of haggis-stuffed mushroom; and braised Galloway lamb shank.

Open all wk 11-11 (Sun 12-11) **Closed:** 25 Dec, winter Tue-Thu 2.30-6 ⊕ FREE HOUSE ◄ Timothy Taylor Landlord, Guest ales. **Facilities** Children welcome Children's menu Children's portions Garden Parking

KIRKCUDBRIGHT | Map 20 NX65

Selkirk Arms Hotel

Old High St DG6 4JG ☎ 01557 330402
e-mail: reception@selkirkarmshotel.co.uk
dir: *M74 & M6 to A75, halfway between Dumfries & Stranraer on A75*

Robert Burns reputedly wrote the 'Selkirk Grace' at this privately owned hotel on one of his Galloway tours. The hotel's Selkirk Grace ale was produced in conjunction with Sulwath Brewers to celebrate the fact. The public rooms include two bars, and a great choice of dishes is offered in The Bistro or more intimate Artistas Restaurant, including local specialities like seared Kirkcudbright king scallops on a leek compôte with air-dried ham followed by Galloway beef, black pudding and caramelised onion pie. Finish with Ecclefechan tart with whisky ice cream. Booking for meals may be required.

Open all day all wk **Bar Meals** L served all wk 12-2 D served all wk 6-9 Av main course £10.95 **Restaurant** L served Sun 12-2 D served all wk 7-9 Av 3 course à la carte fr £29 ⊕ FREE HOUSE ◄ Timothy Taylor Landlord, Sulwath Selkirk Grace, Dark Horse Hetton Pale Ale, Caledonian Deuchars IPA. 🍷 8 **Facilities** Children welcome Children's menu Children's portions Garden Parking Wi-fi 🚐

MOFFAT | Map 21 NT00

Annandale Arms ★★★ HL ⊚

High St DG10 9HF ☎ 01683 220013
e-mail: margaret@annandalearmshotel.co.uk
dir: *A74(M) junct 15. Take A701, Moffat 1m*

A major Moffat landmark for over 250 years, it used to be a matter of pride that this hostelry could change a coach and four in less than a minute, in which time the driver would down a pint of ale; today, Broughton's Merlin deserves much more time and appreciation. The award-winning food, a mix of traditional Scottish and international dishes, is also worth pondering over: choose between locally made haggis with neeps and tatties, poacher's game pie, Annandale salmon fishcakes, steak and stout pie, and roast marinated chump of lamb set on honey and cumin roast carrots and parsnips with a lamb jus. Besides the à la carte menu, there are daily specials and a selection of choices from the chargrill. Booking for meals may be required.

Open all day all wk **Bar Meals** L served all wk 12-2 D served all wk 5-9 Av main course £8.95 **Restaurant** L served all wk 12-2 D served all wk 6-9 Fixed menu price fr £18.50 Av 3 course à la carte fr £30 ⊕ FREE HOUSE ◄ Broughton Merlin ♻ Westons Stowford Press. **Facilities** ❤ Children welcome Children's menu Children's portions Garden Parking Wi-fi 🚐 (notice required) **Rooms** 16

NEW GALLOWAY | Map 20 NX67

Cross Keys Hotel

High St DG7 3RN ☎ 01644 420494
e-mail: enquiries@thecrosskeys-newgalloway.co.uk
dir: *At N end of Loch Ken, 10m from Castle Douglas on A712*

This 17th-century former coaching inn sits in a stunning location at the top of Loch Ken and on the edge of Galloway Forest Park, a superb area for walking, fishing, birdwatching, golf, watersports, painting and photography. Part of the hotel was once the police station and in the beamed period bar the food is served in restored, stone-walled cells. The à la carte restaurant offers hearty food with a Scottish accent, such as home-made Galloway steak pie, fish in cider batter, and minted shoulder of lamb. Real ales are a speciality, and there's a good choice of malts in the whisky bar.

Open 6-11.30 **Closed:** Sun & Mon eve winter ⊕ FREE HOUSE ◄ Houston, Sulwath, Guest ales ♻ Westons Stowford Press. **Facilities** Children's menu Garden Wi-fi

NEWTON STEWART | Map 20 NX46

Creebridge House Hotel

PICK OF THE PUBS

Minnigaff DG8 6NP ☎ 01671 402121
e-mail: info@creebridge.co.uk
dir: *From A75 into Newton Stewart, turn right over river bridge, hotel 200yds on left*

A listed building dating from 1760, this family-run, country house hotel stands in three acres of tranquil gardens and woodland at the foot of Kirroughtree Forest. Taking its name from the River Cree, the hotel used to be the Earl of Galloway's shooting lodge and the grounds part of his estate. The bar and brasserie offer malt whiskies and real ales, including Deuchars. For lunch or candlelit dinner in the restaurant, the well-filled menu offers plenty of dishes with Scottish credentials, such as grilled locally made haggis with melted cheddar and rich whisky cream sauce; pan-fried haunch of Highland venison; Galloway wholetail scampi; and West Coast prawn and salmon penne pasta. Home-made desserts include pear and almond tart with custard, and lemon posset with shortbread. If you're an outdoor sort, this is the place to be as there is fishing, golf, cycling, horse riding walking and deer stalking.

Open all wk 12-2 6-11.30 (Fri-Sat 12-2 6-1am) **Closed:** 1st 3wks Jan ⊕ FREE HOUSE ◄ Caledonian Deuchars IPA, Guinness, Guest ales. **Facilities** Children welcome Garden Parking

The Galloway Arms Hotel

54-58 Victoria St DG8 6DB ☎ 01671 402653
e-mail: info@gallowayarmshotel.com
web: www.gallowayarmshotel.com
dir: *In town centre, opposite clock*

Founded 260 years ago by 6th Earl of Galloway, the hotel acted as the focus for developing the 'planted' market town of Newton Stewart, first established in the 1650s. On the banks of the River Cree, the town is well sited to explore Galloway Forest or the Machars of Whithorn, working up an appetite for traditional Scottish dishes such as chicken, leek and Highland crowdie or the prosaically-named Bonnie Prince Charlie's Balls (deep-fried haggis in Drambuie-based sauce), accompanied by a dram from the most extensive selection of malts in Galloway.

Open all day all wk 11am-mdnt **Bar Meals** L served all wk 12-2 D served all wk 6-9 **Restaurant** D served all wk

6-9 ⊕ FREE HOUSE ◀ Belhaven Best & 70/- Shilling, Caledonian Deuchars IPA, Guinness. ♟ 11 **Facilities** ❄ Children welcome Children's menu Children's portions Garden Parking 🚐

See advert below

SANDHEAD	Map 20 NX04

Tigh Na Mara Hotel

Main St DG9 9JF ☎ 01776 830210
e-mail: tighnamara@btconnect.com
dir: *A75 from Dumfries towards Stranraer. Left onto B7084 to Sandhead. Hotel in village centre*

Tigh na Mara means 'house by the sea', which seems appropriate for this family-run village hotel is set in the tranquil seaside village of Sandhead and boasts breathtaking views of the Sands of Luce. An extensive menu of dishes created from top-quality local ingredients might include local seafood pancakes with white wine sauce; loin of Border lamb with Lyonnaise potatoes; or poached salmon and king prawns with Chablis cream. Relax with a glass of Belhaven Best in the garden, comfortable lounge or beside the fire in the public bar. Booking for meals may be required.

Open all day all wk **Bar Meals** L served all wk 12-2.30 D served all wk 6-9 Av main course £8-£22 **Restaurant** L served all wk 12-2.30 D served all wk 6-9 Fixed menu price fr £10.95 Av 3 course à la carte fr £15.95 ⊕ BELHAVEN ◀ Best, Morland Old Speckled Hen. **Facilities** Children welcome Children's menu Children's portions Family room Garden Parking Wi-fi

The Royal Arch Bar

285 Brook St DD5 2DS ☎ 01382 779741
dir: *3m from Dundee. 0.5 min from Broughty Ferry rail station*

Commemorating the vanished Masonic Arch, an unearthed lump of which is now on display, this charismatic local has been successively The Royal Arch Tavern, Hotel, Arms and now Bar. Behind its tile-hung exterior is a traditional public bar featuring a carved-wood gantry from a demolished pub, and a homely art deco lounge (note the furniture legs and stained glass), converted from an old cottage. McEwan's 80/- and Belhaven Best beers are backed by guests. In addition to snacks, meals include beef olives; breaded haddock; chicken tikka masala; and filled omelettes. Booking for meals may be required.

Open all day all wk **Bar Meals** L served Mon-Fri 12-2.15, Sat-Sun 12-5 D served all wk 5-7.30 Av main course £5-£8 **Restaurant** L served Mon-Fri 12-2.15, Sat-Sun 12-5 D served all wk 5-7.30 Fixed menu price fr £9.50 Av 3 course à la carte fr £10 ⊕ FREE HOUSE ◀ McEwan's 80/-, Belhaven Best, Caledonian Deuchars IPA, Angus Mashie Niblick Cask. ♟ 30 **Facilities** Children welcome Children's portions Family room Garden Beer festival Wi-fi 🚐

DUNDEE — Map 21 NO43

Speedwell Bar

165-167 Perth Rd DD2 1AS ☎ 01382 667783
*dir: From A92 (Tay Bridge), A991 signed Perth/A85/
Coupar Angus/A923. At Riverside rdbt 3rd exit (A991). At
lights left into Nethergate signed Parking/South Tay St.
Forward into Perth Rd. Pass university. Bar on right*

This fine example of an unspoiled Edwardian art deco bar
is worth visiting for its interior alone; all the fitments in
the bar and sitting rooms are beautifully crafted
mahogany – gantry, drink shelves, dado panelling and
fireplace. Internal doors are all glazed with etched glass.
The same family owned it for 90 years, until the present
landlord's father bought it in 1995. As well as the
cask-conditioned ales, 157 whiskies and imported bottles
are offered. A kitchen would be good, but since the pub is
listed this is impossible. Visitors are encouraged to bring
their own snacks from nearby bakeries. This community
pub is home to several clubs and has live Scottish music
from time to time on a Tuesday.

Open all day all wk 11am-mdnt ⊕ FREE HOUSE
◀ Caledonian Deuchars IPA, Harviestoun Bitter &
Twisted, Williams Bros Seven Giraffes ♡ Addlestones.
♟ 18 **Facilities** ✿ Beer festival Wi-fi ⌷ Notes ⊠

EAST AYRSHIRE

DALRYMPLE — Map 20 NS31

The Kirkton Inn

1 Main St KA6 6DF ☎ 01292 560241
e-mail: kirkton@cqm.co.uk
dir: 6m SE from centre of Ayr just off A77

In the heart of the village of Dalrymple, this inn was built
in 1879 as a coaching inn and has been providing
sustenance to travellers ever since; the welcoming
atmosphere makes it easy to feel at home. It's a stoutly
traditional setting, with open fires and polished brasses.
Eat traditional and wholesome dishes in the Coach Room
in the oldest part of the building, and perhaps choose
chicken and leek pie, or Kirkton burger, followed by hot
chocolate fudge cake. Lighter options are soup and
sandwiches. Dining is also available in another room
which overlooks the River Doon.

Open all day all wk **Bar Meals** L served all wk 12-2.30
D served all wk 5-8 **Restaurant** L served all wk 12-2.30
D served all wk 5-9 ⊕ SCOTTISH & NEWCASTLE ◀ John
Smith's, Guinness. **Facilities** Children welcome Children's
menu Children's portions Play area Family room Garden
Parking Wi-fi ⌷

GATEHEAD — Map 20 NS33

The Cochrane Inn

45 Main Rd KA2 0AP ☎ 01563 570122
*dir: From Glasgow A77 to Kilmarnock, then A759 to
Gatehead*

There's a friendly, bustling atmosphere inside this
traditional ivy-covered village centre pub, which sits just
a short drive from the Ayrshire coast. The interior has
natural stone walls adorned with gleaming brasses and
log fires in winter. The menus combine British and
international flavours in hearty, wholesome food. This
might translate as salt and pepper squid with jalapeño
salsa or smoked duck breast with apple salad, walnuts
and orange dressing; then haggis, neeps and tatties;
chicken stuffed with cream cheese, chorizo and garlic; or
steak and sausage pie. As we went to press, a change of
hands had just taken place.

Open all wk 12-2.30 5.30 onwards (Sun 12-9) ⊕ FREE
HOUSE ◀ John Smith's. **Facilities** Children welcome
Children's menu Children's portions Garden Parking Wi-fi

SORN — Map 20 NS52

The Sorn Inn ★★★★ RR @@

PICK OF THE PUBS

35 Main St KA5 6HU ☎ 01290 551305
e-mail: craig@sorninn.com
dir: A70 from S; or A76 from N onto B743 to Sorn

Dating back to the 18th century when it was a coaching
inn on the old Edinburgh to Kilmarnock route, The Sorn
Inn is now a smart gastro-pub with comfortably
refurbished rooms. Along with award-winning real ales
from Renfrewshire's Houston Brewery, 12 wines are
served by the glass. Chef-patron Craig Grant and his
team have won accolades for their cuisine too, including
two AA Rosettes. Menus in both the Chop House and
Restaurant offer a fusion of fine dining and
brasserie-style food using the best of imported and
seasonal ingredients. A sharing board of Italian
appetisers strikes all the right notes with focaccia, pasta
salad, salamis, pickled vegetables, pesto and rosemary
polenta. Otherwise look out for Gressingham duck and
orange rissoles. Pastas and steaks from the grill are
augmented by the likes of Mum's steak pie; and pan-fried
skate cheeks. If you have the appetite you could round off
with a selection of Scottish cheeses. Alternatively try the
whisky cream and butterscotch foam with peanut brittle.
Accommodation is available. Booking for meals may be
required.

Open 12-2.30 6-10 (Fri 12-2.30 6-12 Sat 12-12 Sun
12-10) Closed: 2wks Jan, Mon **Bar Meals** L served Tue-Fri
12-2.30, Sat 12-9, Sun 12-8 D served Tue-Fri 6-9, Sat
12-9, Sun 12-8 Av main course £14 **Restaurant** L served
Tue-Fri 12-2.30, Sat 12-9, Sun 12-8 D served Tue-Fri 6-9,
Sat 12-9, Sun 12-8 Fixed menu price fr £13.95 Av 3
course à la carte fr £27 ⊕ FREE HOUSE ◀ John Smith's,
Houston Texas, Guinness. ♟ 12 **Facilities** ✿ Children
welcome Children's menu Children's portions Parking
Wi-fi ⌷ (notice required) **Rooms** 4

EAST LOTHIAN

GULLANE — Map 21 NT48

The Old Clubhouse NEW

East Links Rd EH31 2AF ☎ 01620 842008
*dir: A198 into Gullane, 3rd right on to East Links Rd, pass
church, on left*

Established in 1890 as the home of Gullane Golf Club,
this building had a chequered past after the golfers
moved on to larger premises, including stints as a disco
and as tea rooms. In 1989 the Campanile family took the
reins and it hasn't looked back. Roaring winter fires and
walls crammed with golfing memorabilia make a good
first impression, and the menu delivers a lengthy list of
pub classics including regional specialities such as
Cullen skink or Hornings haggis with Stornoway black
pudding. For dessert, maybe home-made ice cream.
Booking for meals may be required.

Open all day all wk Closed: 25 Dec & 1 Jan **Bar Meals** L
served all wk 12-9.30 D served all wk 12-9.30 Av main
course £11 food served all day **Restaurant** L served all wk
12-9.30 D served all wk 12-9.30 food served all day
⊕ FREE HOUSE ◀ Timothy Taylor Landlord, Caledonian
Deuchars IPA ♡ Thistly Cross. ♟ 9 **Facilities** ✿ Children
welcome Children's menu Children's portions Garden
Wi-fi ⌷ (notice required)

LONGNIDDRY — Map 21 NT47

The Longniddry Inn

Main St EH32 0NF ☎ 01875 852401
e-mail: info@longniddryinn.com
dir: On A198 (Main St), near rail station

Now that the old public bar has been turned into The
Stables restaurant, this combination of a former
blacksmith's forge and four cottages on Longniddry's
Main Street is proving more inviting than ever. Already
held in high esteem locally for friendly service and good
food, it offers an extensive menu featuring Stornoway
black pudding and poached egg; haggis, neeps and
tatties; chef's stirfry; macaroni cheese; and chicken and
combo sizzlers from the grill. In warmer weather take your
pint of Belhaven Best, glass of wine or freshly ground
coffee outside. Booking for meals may be required.

Open all day all wk **Bar Meals** L served Mon-Sat 12-2.30
D served Mon-Sat 5-8.30 **Restaurant** L served Sun 1-7.30
⊕ PUNCH TAVERNS ◀ Belhaven Best. **Facilities** Children
welcome Children's menu Children's portions Garden
Parking Wi-fi ⌷

Save on hotels. Book at **theAA**.com/hotel

EDINBURGH, CITY OF 625 SCOTLAND

EDINBURGH, CITY OF

EDINBURGH
Map 21 NT27

Bennets Bar

8 Leven St EH3 9LG ☎ 0131 229 5143
e-mail: bennetsbar@hotmail.co.uk
dir: *Next to Kings Theatre. Please phone for more detailed directions*

Bennets is a listed property dating from 1839 with hand-painted tiles and murals on the walls, original stained-glass windows, intricate wood carving on bar fitments and brass beer taps. It's a friendly pub, popular with performers from the adjacent Kings Theatre. The traditional bar has some contemporary twists and serves real ales, over 120 malt whiskies and a decent selection of wines. The home-made food, at a reasonable price, ranges from toasties, burgers and salads to stovies (potato and meat stew), steak pie, and Scottish fare. There's also a daily roast and traditional puddings. Coffee and tea are served all day.

Open all day all wk 11am-1am Closed: 25 Dec ⊕ IONA PUB ◀ Caledonian Deuchars IPA & 80/-, Guinness. **Facilities** Children welcome Children's menu Children's portions Family room Wi-fi

Bert's Bar NEW

29-31 William St EH3 7NG ☎ 0131 225 5748
e-mail: bertsbar@maclay.co.uk

Although it has changed names a few times, Bert's has been a popular Edinburgh watering hole since the 1930s. Popular with rugby fans, it retains many of its original features although the food and drink offering is thoroughly modern. Enjoy a well-kept pint of Deuchars or Thistly Cross cider or order from a broad menu that offers plenty of choice. Start, perhaps, with local smoked salmon and move on to beef steak pie; Cajun chicken; curry of the day or the more traditional haggis, neeps and tatties.

Open all day all wk Closed: 25 Dec **Bar Meals** L served all wk 12-8 D served all wk 12-8 Av main course £6.95 food served all day ⊕ MACLAY ◀ Caledonian Deuchars IPA, Harviestoun Bitter & Twisted, Timothy Taylor Landlord, Orkney Dark Island ⚫ Thistly Cross. **Facilities** ☘ Wi-fi

The Bow Bar

80 The West Bow EH1 2HH ☎ 0131 226 7667
dir: *Telephone for directions*

If there is one free house that reflects the history and traditions of Edinburgh's Old Town, it is The Bow Bar. With some 220 malt whiskies, eight real ales poured from traditional tall founts and 30 bottled beers, the focus may be on liquid refreshment but the range of snacks includes haggis, cheese and chilli pies and bridies (meat pastries). Tables from old train carriages and a church gantry add to the unique feel of a bar where the sound of conversation makes up for the lack of gaming machines and music. Twice a year in January and July, the pub holds ten-day long beer festivals.

Open all day all wk Closed: 25-26 Dec, 1-2 Jan **Bar Meals** L served Mon-Sat 12-3, Sun 12.30-3 ⊕ FREE HOUSE ◀ Caledonian Deuchars IPA, Stewart Edinburgh No 3 & Pentland IPA, Harviestoun Bitter & Twisted, Atlas Latitude, Fyne Avalanche & Jarl, Cairngorm Black Gold, Tempest, Thornbridge ⚫ Westons Stowford Press, Pipsqueak. **Facilities** ☘ Beer festival Wi-fi

The Café Royal ◉

PICK OF THE PUBS

19 West Register St EH2 2AA ☎ 0131 556 1884
e-mail: info@caferoyal.org.uk
dir: *Off Princes St, in city centre*

Little has changed at The Café Royal since it moved across the road from its original site in 1863. Designed by local architect Robert Paterson, it is a glorious example of Victorian and Baroque, with an interior seemingly frozen in time. Elegant stained glass and fine late Victorian plasterwork dominate the building, as do irreplaceable Doulton ceramic murals in the bar and restaurant. The whole building and its interior were listed in 1970 so future generations can enjoy the unique building which still sticks to its early 19th-century roots by serving local ales, wine, coffee and fresh oysters in the bar and restaurant. Scottish produce dominates the menu, from starters of Cullen skink with Arbroath smokie or game pie with redcurrant and ginger chutney to main courses of Scottish beef and ale pie or haggis and whisky cream pie with chips. Booking for meals may be required.

Open all day all wk **Bar Meals** Av main course £9 food served all day **Restaurant** L served all wk 12-2.30 D served all wk 5-9.30 Av 3 course à la carte fr £25 ⊕ SPIRIT PUB COMPANY ◀ Caledonian Deuchars IPA, Kelburn Ca'Canny & Goldihops, Harviestoun Bitter & Twisted. ☐ 10 **Facilities** Children welcome Children's portions Wi-fi ⊞

Doric Tavern

PICK OF THE PUBS

15-16 Market St EH1 1DE ☎ 0131 225 1084
e-mail: info@the-doric.com
dir: *In city centre opp Waverly Station & Edinburgh Dungeons*

Housed in a 17th-century building, the Doric claims to be Edinburgh's oldest food-serving hostelry; certainly records show a pub on this site since 1823. Its name is taken from an old language once spoken in north-east Scotland, mainly Aberdeenshire. Conveniently located for Waverley Station, the pub is just a short walk from Princes Street and Edinburgh Castle. Public rooms include a refurbished ground-floor bar, and a wine bar and bistro upstairs. In these pleasantly informal surroundings, a wide choice of fresh, locally sourced food is prepared by the chefs on site. While supping a pint of Edinburgh Gold, you can nibble on marinated olives or haggis spring rolls. Mains from the grill include a Border beef rib-eye, while chef's specials may include a home-made game pie with chargrilled asparagus. Seafood is delivered fresh each morning: haddock is deep-fried in the pub's own beer-batter and served with hand-cut chips and home-made tartare sauce.

Open all day all wk 11.30am-mdnt (Thu-Sat 11.30am-1am) Closed: 25-26 Dec **Bar Meals** Av main course £12.50 food served all day **Restaurant** Fixed menu price fr £15 Av 3 course à la carte fr £25 food served all day ⊕ FREE HOUSE ◀ Caledonian Deuchars IPA, Stewart's 80/- & Edinburgh Gold, Guinness. **Facilities** Children welcome Children's menu Children's portions Family room ⊞

The Guildford Arms NEW

1-5 West Register St EH2 2AA ☎ 0131 556 4312
e-mail: manager@guildfordarms.com
dir: *Opposite Balmoral Hotel at E end of Princes St*

A magnificent Jacobean-style ceiling and other late-Victorian design features get customers talking in this wonderful free house and galleried restaurant. Renowned for seafood, beef and a devotion to beers, the pub has seven Scottish and two English real ales, European draught lagers, brewery showcase weekends, and two ten-day beer festivals. Unsurprisingly, it becomes an Edinburgh Fringe venue. Menus offer lunchtime haggis, neeps and tatties; and East Coast breaded haddock; evenings include duck breast in cranberry and rosemary gravy; fillet steak medallions in mushrooms and Blue Monday stilton; and chargrilled Aberdeen Angus steaks. Booking for meals may be required.

Open all day all wk Closed: 25-26 Dec, 1 Jan **Bar Meals** L served all wk 12-3, snacks 3-9 Av main course £13 food served all day **Restaurant** L served all wk 12-3 D served Sun-Thu 5.30-9.30, Fri-Sat 5-10 Av 3 course à la carte fr £18.50 ⊕ FREE HOUSE ◀ Harviesoun Bitter & Twisted, Fyne Jarl, Orkney Dark Island, Caledonian Deuchars IPA, rotating Stewart, Highland ⚫ Thistly Cross, Westons 1st Quality. ☐ 13 **Facilities** Children's portions Beer festival

EDINBURGH *continued*

Halfway House NEW

24 Fleshmarket Close EH1 1BX ☎ **0131 225 7101**
e-mail: stevewhiting@straitmail.co.uk
dir: *From Royal Mile (close to x-rds with North & South bridges) into Cockburn St. Into Fleshmarket Cl, or take flight of steps off Cockburn St on right*

Edinburgh's smallest pub is an iconic institution hidden down an Old Town 'close' or flight of steps linking the city's Old and New towns. The cosy interior is adorned with railway memorabilia and throngs with beer aficionados supping interesting ales from Scottish micro-breweries, perhaps Pentland IPA and Cairngorm Trade Winds. Mop up the ale with some traditional Scottish bar food made from fresh produce: Cullen skink, haggis, neeps and tatties; or black boar sausages with mash and mustard gravy. If beer is not your thing, then sample the 40 or so whiskies behind the bar. Look out for regular beer festivals.

Open all day all wk **Bar Meals** Av main course £6.50 food served all day ⊕ FREE HOUSE ◀ Stewart Pentland IPA, Harviestoun Bitter & Twisted, Cairngorm Trade Winds, Houston Peter's Well ♂ Westons Stowford Press. **Facilities** ❧ Children welcome Beer festival Wi-fi **Notes** ⊛

The Shore Bar & Restaurant

3 Shore, Leith EH6 6QW ☎ **0131 553 5080**
e-mail: info@theshore.biz
dir: *Telephone for directions*

The Shore occupies a historic 17th-century building and overlooks the Water of Leith in the heart of Leith Docks. It has a dedicated following for its bustling, informal atmosphere and high standards in a kitchen that specialises in fresh Scottish seafood. Food is served all day, the choice ranging from snacks like calamari with chilli sauce and bar classics like steak-and-kidney pie, to

such daily specials as scallops with beetroot and orange butter and grey mullet with crab and chervil risotto. Leave room for treacle tart with clotted cream ice cream. Booking for meals may be required.

Open all wk noon-1am (Sun 12.30pm-1am) Closed: 25-26 Dec, 1 Jan **Bar Meals** L served all wk 12-6 D served all wk 6-10.30 food served all day **Restaurant** L served all wk 12-6 D served all wk 6-10.30 food served all day ⊕ FREE HOUSE ◀ Belhaven 80/-, Caledonian Deuchars IPA, Guinness. ♀ 14 **Facilities** Children welcome Children's portions Wi-fi ⛛

Whiski Bar & Restaurant NEW

119 High St EH1 1SG ☎ **0131 556 3095**
e-mail: info@whiskibar.co.uk
web: www.whiskibar.co.uk
dir: *Midway along The Royal Mile*

Strolling down Edinburgh's high street (The Royal Mile) and in need of sustenance and a 'wee' dram, then seek out this award-winning bar at number 119. Choose from over 300 malt whiskies (why not try a 'Whisky Flight' tasting tour) and tuck into some traditional Scottish food. Served all day, the menu makes good use of Buccleuch beef and daily deliveries of seafood from local fishermen. Typically, try smoked salmon and haddock fishcakes; venison steak with redcurrant jus; then cranachan for pudding. Come for the traditional Scottish music in the evening – this bar is famous for its fiddle music.

Open all day all wk **Bar Meals** L served Mon-Thu 10-10, Fri-Sun 10-10.30 D served Mon-Thu 10-10, Fri-Sun 10-10.30 Av main course £10 food served all day **Restaurant** L served Mon-Thu 10-10, Fri-Sun 10-10.30 D served Mon-Thu 10-10, Fri-Sun 10-10.30 Av 3 course à la carte fr £24 food served all day ⊕ FREE HOUSE ◀ Innis & Gunn ♂ Thistly Cross. ♀ 9 **Facilities** Children welcome Children's menu Children's portions ⛛ (notice required)

See advert below

| RATHO | Map 21 NT17 |

The Bridge Inn

PICK OF THE PUBS

27 Baird Rd EH28 8RA ☎ **0131 333 1320**
e-mail: info@bridgeinn.com
dir: *From Newbridge at B7030 junct, follow signs for Ratho and Edinburgh Canal Centre*

This canal-side inn makes the most of its idyllic waterside location, catering for boaters, cyclists and ramblers using the tree-lined Union Canal. The inn even has two floating restaurants on renovated barges, which travel the popular waterway most weekends. The waterside beer garden is a popular summertime venue, where a grand selection of beers from Scotland's burgeoning micro-brewery sector is the order of the day. Inside, the bistro offers a menu created from local

---

Save on hotels. Book at **theAA.com/hotel**

EDINBURGH, CITY OF – FIFE 627 SCOTLAND

produce: maybe saddleback pork belly with haggis bonbons and orange and vinegar emulsion followed by a duo of Sutherland venison with baby pear, red wine, mash, greens and chocolate chilli oil, and then cooked and set Scottish cream with toasted pine nut praline and berry compôte for dessert. Lunch includes lighter options such as Cullen skink followed by home-made pie of the week. Booking for meals may be required.

Open all day all wk 11-11 (Fri-Sat 11am-mdnt) Closed: 25-26 Dec, 2 Jan **Bar Meals** L served Mon-Fri 12-3, Sat 12-9, Sun 12.30-8.30 D served Mon-Fri 5.30-9, Sat 12-9, Sun 12.30-8.30 **Restaurant** L served Mon-Fri 12-3, Sat 12-9, Sun 12.30-8.30 D served Mon-Fri 5.30-9, Sat 12-9, Sun 12.30-8.30 ⊕ FREE HOUSE ◀ Caledonian Deuchars IPA, Belhaven, Guest ales ♂ Aspall. ♟ 21
Facilities Children welcome Children's menu Children's portions Garden Beer festival Parking Wi-fi ▭

FIFE

BURNTISLAND   Map 21 NT28

Burntisland Sands Hotel

Lochies Rd KY3 9JX ☎ 01592 872230
e-mail: mail@burntislandsands.co.uk
dir: *Towards Kirkcaldy, Burntisland on A921. Hotel on right before Kinghorn*

Once a highly regarded girls' boarding school, this small, family-run hotel stands just 50 yards from an award-winning sandy beach. Visitors can expect reasonably priced breakfasts, snacks, lunches and evening meals, including internationally themed evenings. Typical dishes include seared tuna steak with lemon butter, crispy shredded beef in a choice of oriental sauces, mixed grill deluxe, mushroom Stroganoff, brie and redcurrant tart, and broccoli and cauliflower mornay. Relax and enjoy a drink in the bar and lounge area or in the courtyard. Booking for meals may be required.

Open all day all wk **Bar Meals** L served Mon-Fri 12-2.30, Sat-Sun all day D served Mon-Fri 5-8.30 Av main course £8 **Restaurant** L served Mon-Fri 12-2.30, Sat-Sun all day D served Mon-Fri 5-8.30 Av 3 course à la carte fr £20 ⊕ FREE HOUSE ◀ Caledonian Deuchars IPA, John Smith's, Tennent's, Courage, Guinness, Guest ales.
Facilities Children welcome Children's menu Children's portions Play area Garden Parking Wi-fi ▭ (notice required)

EARLSFERRY   Map 21 NO40

The Golf Tavern NEW

5 Links Rd KY9 1AW ☎ 01333 330610
e-mail: richard@ship-elie.com
dir: *From Lundin Links take A915, then A917 towards Elie. Turn right signed Earlsferry, through golf course to T-junct. Right into one-way system, Tavern on right near 4th tee*

Close to the fourth tee on the Elie Golf Course, the '19th' – as locals know it – has become the hub of Earlsferry since Richard and Jill Philip took over four years ago. Although sport is the focus here, whether it's golf, pool or live rugby on the TV, it offers something for everybody. Enjoy a pint of Deuchars IPA and order from the traditional menu that includes chicken curry, rib-eye steak and chips, or quiche of the day. During July and August, freshly prepared sandwiches are served at lunchtimes.

Open all day all wk Closed: 25 Dec **Bar Meals** L served Mon-Sat 12-2.30, Sun 12.30-3 D served Sun-Thu 6-9, Fri-Sat 6-9.30 Av main course £8-£10 **Restaurant** L served Mon-Sat 12-2.30, Sun 12.30-3 D served Sun-Thu 6-9, Fri-Sat 6-9.30 Fixed menu price fr £7.95 ⊕ FREE HOUSE ◀ Caledonian Deuchars IPA. **Facilities** ❖ Children welcome Children's menu Children's portions Wi-fi

ELIE   Map 21 NO40

The Ship Inn

The Toft KY9 1DT ☎ 01333 330246
e-mail: info@ship-elie.com
dir: *Follow A915 & A917 to Elie. From High Street follow signs to Watersport Centre & The Toft*

The enthusiastic Philip family (who also run The Golf Tavern, Earlsferry; see entry) has run this lively free house for over 20 years. A pub since 1838, it sits right on the waterfront at Elie Bay. The cricket team plays regular fixtures on the beach, live music is regularly staged, and a full programme of charity and celebratory events runs throughout the year, including a barbecue on New Year's Day. The best of local produce features on the concise menu that offers the likes of deep-fried haddock in beer-batter, and steak and Guinness pie.

Open all day all wk Closed: 25 Dec **Bar Meals** L served Mon-Sat 12-2.30, Sun 12.30-3 D served Mon-Thu 6-9, Fri-Sat 6-9.30 **Restaurant** L served Mon-Sat 12-2.30, Sun 12.30-3 D served Mon-Thu 6-9, Fri-Sat 6-9.30 ⊕ FREE HOUSE ◀ Caledonian Deuchars IPA & 80/-, Belhaven Best, Younger's Tartan Special. **Facilities** ❖ Children welcome Children's menu Children's portions Play area Family room Garden ▭

KINCARDINE   Map 21 NS98

The Unicorn

15 Excise St FK10 4LN ☎ 01259 739129
e-mail: info@theunicorn.co.uk
dir: *Exit M9 junct 7 towards Kincardine Bridge. Cross bridge, bear left. 1st left, then sharp left at rdbt*

This 17th-century pub-restaurant in the historic River Forth port of Kincardine used to be a coaching inn. Pub quizzers might care to know (if you don't already) that Sir James Dewar, inventor of the vacuum flask, was born here in 1842. Brasserie meals include Scottish rib-eye steak; Moroccan spiced lamb; duo of smoked salmon and prawns; and roasted haloumi and rosemary vegetable stack. Enjoy a pint of Bitter & Twisted, Old Engine Oil or Schiehallion with a ham and brie panini by the open fire in the comfortable lounge bar. Booking for meals may be required.

Open 9-4 5.30-12 (Sun 12-7) Closed: 3rd wk Jul, Mon **Bar Meals** L served incl bkfst Tue-Sat 9-12 **Restaurant** L served Tue-Sat 12-4, Sun 12-3.45 D served Tue-Thu 5.30-9.30, Fri-Sat 6-9.30 ⊕ FREE HOUSE ◀ Harviestoun Bitter & Twisted, Schiehallion, Old Engine Oil.
Facilities Children welcome Children's menu Children's portions Garden Parking Wi-fi ▭

ST ANDREWS   Map 21 NO51

The Inn at Lathones ★★★★ INN ⊛⊛

PICK OF THE PUBS

Largoward KY9 1JE ☎ 01334 840494
e-mail: lathones@innatlathones.com
dir: *5m from St Andrews on A915*

Although many people associate St Andrews purely with golf, this 400-year-old coaching inn with rooms is the exception to the rule as it doubles up as an award-winning live music venue. Lindisfarne and Curtis Stigers are among the many luminaries who perform here, and the walls display one of the best collections of music memorabilia in the country. Ancient meets modern here and guests can relax in deep sofas and enjoy excellent ales from Orkney Brewery around log-burners. For the past 14 years the chefs here have been awarded two AA Rosettes; their innovative cooking of well-sourced local ingredients can be judged from starters that include game spiced terrine, or leek and Dunsyre Blue tart with mixed leaves and hazelnut dressing. Mains come up trumps, too, with roasted sea bass with mussels and prawns, lemon and fennel sauce, or slow-roasted belly of pork with sautéed wild mushrooms and pak choi. Smart, contemporary accommodation is available.

Open all day all wk Closed: 2wks Jan ⊕ FREE HOUSE ◀ Orkney Dark Island, Atlas Three Sisters, Belhaven Best.
Facilities Children welcome Garden Parking **Rooms** 21

ST ANDREWS *continued*

The Jigger Inn

PICK OF THE PUBS

The Old Course Hotel KY16 9SP ☎ **01334 474371**
e-mail: reservations@oldcoursehotel.co.uk
dir: *M90 junct 8, A91 to St Andrews*

Steeped in history, The Jigger was a stationmaster's lodge in the 1800s on a railway line that disappeared many years ago. Located in the grounds of The Old Course Hotel, its close proximity to the world-famous St Andrews golf course means that it is home to some impressive golfing memorabilia. Don't be surprised if you are sharing the bar with a caddy or a golfing legend fresh from a game. Crackling open-hearth fires, traditional Scottish pub hospitality and plenty of golfing gossip are the backdrop for a selection of Scottish beers, including St Andrews and Jigger Ale. All-day availability is one advantage of a short, simple menu that lists soups, inviting sandwiches and quenelles of haggis, neeps and tatties as starters, and continues with Jigger burger with Mull cheddar, Ayrshire bacon and fries; shepherd's pie with roasted root vegetables; pork and honey sausages on colcannon mash; and desserts such as apple and pear crumble. Booking for meals may be required.

Open all day all wk 11-11 (Sun 12-11) ⊕ FREE HOUSE
◀ The Jigger Inn Jigger Ale, St Andrews, Guinness.
Facilities Children welcome Garden Parking

GLASGOW, CITY OF

GLASGOW　　　　　　　　Map 20 NS56

Bon Accord

153 North St G3 7DA ☎ **0141 248 4427**
e-mail: paul.bonaccord@ntlbusiness.com
dir: *M8 junct 19 merge onto A804 (North Street) signed Charing Cross*

Tourists from all over the world come to the 'Bon', Paul McDonagh and son Thomas's multi-award-winning alehouse and malt whisky bar. The reason? To sample some of the annual tally of a thousand-plus different beers, over 40 ciders (maybe at one of the four beer and cider festivals), or 240-strong malts collection (a far cry from the original five on offer). To line the stomach are all-day breakfasts, baguettes, giant Yorkshire puddings, chilli con carne, fish and chips, grilled steaks, chicken salads, macaroni cheese and vegetarian Glamorgan sausage.

Open all day all wk **Bar Meals** L served all wk 12-8 D served all wk 12-8 Av main course £5.95 food served all day **Restaurant** Fixed menu price fr £4.95 food served all day ⊕ FREE HOUSE ◀ Over 1,000 real ales per year ⊙ Over 40 ciders per year. ♟ 11 **Facilities** Children welcome Garden Beer festival Wi-fi 🚌

Rab Ha's

83 Hutchieson St G1 1SH ☎ **0141 572 0400**
e-mail: management@rabhas.com
dir: *Telephone for directions*

In the heart of Glasgow's revitalised Merchant City, Rab Ha's takes its name from Robert Hall, a local 19th-century character known as 'The Glasgow Glutton'. This hotel, restaurant and bar blend Victorian character with contemporary Scottish décor. Pre-theatre and set menus show extensive use of carefully sourced Scottish produce in starters like poached egg on grilled Stornoway black pudding, and pan-seared Oban scallops, followed by roast saddle of Rannoch Moor venison. Change of hands.

Open all day all wk 12-12 (Sun 12.30-12) ⊕ FREE HOUSE
◀ Tennent's. **Facilities** Children welcome Children's portions

Stravaigin ◉◉

PICK OF THE PUBS

26-30 Gibson St G12 8NX ☎ **0141 334 2665**
e-mail: stravaigin@btinternet.com
dir: *Telephone for directions*

Located in a busy street close to the university, this popular café-bar has picked up several awards for its food (including two AA Rosettes) and design. The modern split-level basement restaurant draws the crowds with its contemporary décor, stone and leather-covered walls, modern art and quirky antiques. The award-winning bar offers an extensive wine list and real ales like Fyne Ales Chip 71 and Belhaven Best. Expect innovative and exciting fusion food cooked from top-notch Scottish ingredients. The wide range of eclectic dishes may include sticky Korean pork cheek with a brown rice cake and kimchi (spicy pickled cabbage); Mexican meatball, black bean and tortilla soup; Pentland pheasant Kiev with poppy seed and horseradish rösti and pickled cabbage; haggis, neeps and tatties (veggie version available); and pistachio and olive oil cake, pistachio sabayon, date pastilla and coffee mascarpone for dessert (wines are recommended with each dessert).

Open all day all wk Closed: 25 Dec, 1 Jan **Bar Meals** L served all wk 11-5 D served all wk 5-11 Av main course £13.95 food served all day **Restaurant** L served Sat-Sun 12-11 D served all wk 5-11 ⊕ FREE HOUSE ◀ Caledonian Deuchars IPA, Belhaven Best, Fyne Chip 71 ⊙ Westons Wyld Wood Organic Classic. ♟ 22 **Facilities** ✿ Children welcome Children's menu Children's portions Wi-fi

Ubiquitous Chip ◉◉

PICK OF THE PUBS

12 Ashton Ln G12 8SJ ☎ **0141 334 5007**
e-mail: mail@ubiquitouschip.co.uk
dir: *In West End of Glasgow, off Byres Rd. Beside Hillhead subway station*

Down a cobbled mews in the West End, this Glasgow stalwart has been one of the city's most celebrated eateries since 1971. The main dining area opens into a green and leafy, vine-covered courtyard, while upstairs is the brasserie-style, two-AA Rosette restaurant. There are three drinking areas: the traditional Big Pub, serving real ales, nearly 30 wines by the glass and more than 150 malt whiskies; the Wee Bar, which lives up to its name by being possibly the 'wee-est' bar in Scotland; and the Corner Bar, which serves cocktails across a granite slab reclaimed from a mortuary. The kitchen showcases the very best of Scotland's produce on the menu in the shape of pan-fried guinea fowl breast, confit leg, sultana and Brazil nut farce and wine reduction; roast halibut, parsnip rösti, Jerusalem artichoke, parsnip crisps, watercress and spinach sauce; clementine and lemon parfait, lemon sorbet and lime sherbet. Booking for meals may be required.

Open all day all wk 11am-1am (Sun 12.30pm-1am) Closed: 25 Dec, 1 Jan **Bar Meals** L served Mon-Sat 11-5, Sun 12.30-5 D served all wk 5-11 Av main course £14 food served all day **Restaurant** L served Mon-Sat 12-2.30, Sun 12.30-3.30 D served all wk 5-11 Fixed menu price fr £19.95 ⊕ FREE HOUSE ◀ Caledonian Deuchars IPA, Fyne Chip 71 ⊙ Addlestones. ♟ 29 **Facilities** Children welcome Children's menu Children's portions Wi-fi 🚌 (notice required)

West Brewery **NEW**

AA PUB OF THE YEAR FOR SCOTLAND 2012-2013

PICK OF THE PUBS

Templeton Building, Glasgow Green G40 1AW
☎ **0141 550 0135**
e-mail: info@westbeer.com

This buzzy brewery pub/restaurant occupies the old Winding House of the former Templeton Carpet Factory, one of Glasgow's most unique Victorian buildings, modelled on the Doge's Palace in Venice. West is the only brewery in the UK to produce all of its beers according to the German Purity Law, which means they are free from artificial additives, colourings and preservatives. Look down into the brewhouse from the beer hall and watch the brewers making the lagers and wheat beers, including St Mungo, Dunkel, Munich and Hefeweizen, with equipment imported from Germany. Brewery tours are conducted on selected days of the week. The all-day menu offers German dishes like Wiener schnitzel, spätzle (Bavarian noodles with caramelised onions and melted cheese) and Nuremberg sausages served with sauerkraut. Grills, burgers and British pub grub also feature. For dessert is the adults-only Hefeweizen ice cream, made by hand and infused with their award-winning wheat beer. Brunch is available at weekends. Look out for the Oktoberfest beer festival. Booking for meals may be required.

Open all day all wk Closed: 25-26 Dec, 1-2 Jan **Bar Meals** L served all wk 12-5 D served all wk 5-9 Av main course £10.95 **Restaurant** L served all wk 12-5 D served all wk 5-9 Fixed menu price fr £14.95 Av 3 course à la carte fr £23 ⌖ FREE HOUSE ◀ West Munich Red ○ Aspall. **Facilities** Children welcome Children's menu Children's portions Garden Beer festival Parking ▦ (notice required)

HIGHLAND

ACHILTIBUIE   Map 22 NC00

Summer Isles Hotel & Bar ◉◉
PICK OF THE PUBS

IV26 2YG ☎ 01854 622282
e-mail: info@summerisleshotel.com
dir: *Take A835 N from Ullapool for 10m, Achiltibuie signed on left, 15m to village. Hotel 1m on left*

A wild and largely untouched landscape, where the weather can change in days from Arctic to Aegean, provides the backdrop for this highly praised hotel. Fabulous is the only word for the views out to Badentarbat Bay and the Summer Isles. The informal all-day bar serves fresh ground coffee, snacks, lunch, afternoon tea and evening meals, but note that restaurant food is not served between November and March. Where once crofters gathered to drink, today's guests are mostly locals (some of whom may well be crofters) from the scattering of houses along this remote road, plus tourists, of course. Those old farmers are remembered in Crofters' Pale, one of the bar's three An Teallach Ale Company's brews. Nearly everything you eat is home produced, locally caught or at least Scottish – scallops, lobster, langoustines, crab, halibut, turbot, salmon, venison, quail, Shetland lamb.

Open all wk 12-11 Closed: 31 Oct-3 Apr **Bar Meals** L served all wk 12-2.30, soup & snacks till 5 D served all wk 5-8.30 Av main course £18 food served all day **Restaurant** L served Apr-Oct all wk 12.30-2.30 D served Apr-Oct all wk till 8 ⌖ FREE HOUSE ◀ An Teallach Crofters' Pale Ale, Beinn Deorg. ⚑ **Facilities** Children welcome Children's menu Children's portions Garden Parking Wi-fi ▦ (notice required)

AVIEMORE   Map 23 NH81

The Old Bridge Inn

Dalfaber Rd PH22 1PU ☎ 01479 811137
e-mail: sayhello@oldbridgeinn.co.uk
dir: *Exit A9 to Aviemore, 1st right to Ski Rd, then 1st left again 200mtrs*

Overlooking the River Spey, this friendly pub is in an area popular for outdoor pursuits. Drink in the attractive riverside garden or in the relaxing bars warmed by a roaring log fire. Here malt whiskies naturally have their place, but not to the exclusion of excellent real ales. In winter try a warming seasonal cocktail while perusing the après-ski menu in the comfortable restaurant. After an active day, a Dalfour brown trout starter could easily be followed by roast Gressingham duck with spring onion mash and spring greens. There is a varied music programme with regular funk/soul/disco nights. Booking for meals may be required.

Open all day all wk 11am-mdnt (Fri-Sat 11am-1am Sun 12.30-12) ⌖ FREE HOUSE ◀ Caledonian Deuchars IPA, Cairngorm Trade Winds & Black Gold, Atlas Nimbus, Harviestoun Schiehallion ○ Thistly Cross. **Facilities** Children welcome Children's portions Garden Parking Wi-fi

CARRBRIDGE   Map 23 NH92

The Cairn

PH23 3AS ☎ 01479 841212
e-mail: info@cairnhotel.co.uk
dir: *In village centre*

In the Highland village of Carrbridge, this family-run dog-friendly inn makes a perfect base for exploring the Cairngorms, the Moray coast and the Malt Whisky Trail. In the homely tartan-carpeted bar, you'll find blazing winter log fires and cracking local Cairngorm ales on handpump. Gastro-pub-style food using Highland produce represents excellent value for money. Toasted sandwiches can be served whenever you arrive. Hearty bar meals are both tasty and filling: tempura chicken, for example, or haggis-filled tartlets glazed with goat's cheese. Otherwise try a succulent pork loin with caramelised apple. There are regular live music events.

Open all day all wk 11am-mdnt (Fri-Sat 11am-1am) **Bar Meals** L served all wk 12-2.30 D served all wk 6-8.30 Av main course £9 **Restaurant** Av 3 course à la carte fr £18 ⌖ FREE HOUSE ◀ Cairngorm, Black Isle, Guest ales. ⚑ 9 **Facilities** ❖ Children welcome Children's menu Children's portions Garden Parking Wi-fi

CAWDOR   Map 23 NH85

Cawdor Tavern
PICK OF THE PUBS

See Pick of the Pubs on page 630

FORTROSE   Map 23 NH75

The Anderson
PICK OF THE PUBS

Union St IV10 8TD ☎ 01381 620236
e-mail: info@theanderson.co.uk
dir: *From Inverness take A9 N signed Wick. Right onto B9161 signed Munlochy, Cromarty A832. At T-junct right onto A832 to Fortrose*

On the beautiful Black Isle to the north of Inverness, this striking black-and-white painted pub enjoys a tranquil seaside setting; a short walk from its door passes the gaunt, ruined cathedral before happening on the picturesque harbour at Fortrose, with sweeping views across the Moray Firth. Nearby Chanonry Point lighthouse is renowned as one of the best places from which to watch the dolphins of the Firth. But why leave an inn famed for its classic range of finest Scottish micro-brewery beers, vast array of Belgian beers and 230 single malts selected by American proprietor Jim Anderson? The 'global cuisine' created with freshest Scottish produce is equally comprehensive. Aberdeen beef, West Coast seafood and Highland game are amongst dishes on the daily-changing menu: seafood chowder or fried ravioli are typical starters, followed perhaps by Stornoway guinea fowl stuffed with Munro's white pudding and served with a creamy leek and cider sauce. You could finish with apple rhubarb crumble tartlet with vanilla ice cream. Booking for meals may be required.

Open all wk 4pm-11pm Closed: mid Nov-mid Dec **Bar Meals** D served all wk 6-9.30 **Restaurant** D served all wk 6-9.30 Av 3 course à la carte fr £20 ⌖ FREE HOUSE ◀ Rotating ales ○ Addlestones, Moorlands Farm. ⚑ 13 **Facilities** ❖ Children welcome Children's menu Garden Beer festival Parking Wi-fi

PICK OF THE PUBS

Cawdor Tavern

CAWDOR Map 23 NH85

The Lane IV12 5XP ☎ 01667 404777
e-mail: enquiries@cawdortavern.co.uk
web: www.cawdortavern.co.uk
dir: *A96 onto B9006, follow Cawdor Castle signs. Tavern in village centre*

The Tavern is tucked away in the heart of Cawdor's pretty conservation village, just off the Inverness to Nairn road; near by is the castle where Macbeth held court. Pretty wooded countryside slides away from the pub, offering umpteen opportunities for rambles, games of golf, and challenging cycle routes. Exercise over, repair to this homely hostelry to enjoy the welcoming mix of fine Scottish food and island micro-brewery ales that makes the pub a destination in its own right. Norman and Christine Sinclair are approaching their 20th anniversary at the helm, and still it goes from strength to strength. A new venture and excellent value is a Sunday high tea starting at 4.30pm, when freshly cooked main courses are followed by a selection of home baking with teas and coffees. There's an almost baronial feel to the bars, created from the Cawdor Estate's joinery workshop in the 1960s. The lounge bar's wonderful panelling came from Cawdor Castle's dining room as a gift from a former laird; log fires and stoves add winter warmth, as does the impressive choice of Orkney Brewery beers and Highland and Island malts. A highly accomplished menu balances meat, fish, game and vegetarian options, prepared in

a modern Scottish style with first class Scottish produce. Settle in the delightful restaurant beneath wrought iron Jacobean chandeliers and contemplate starting with a trio of Scottish puddings – black pudding, prize haggis and white pudding layered together and served with home-made chutney. Next may come a venison burger from the grill, topped with smoked bacon, tomato relish and melting mozzarella. Classic sweets include sticky toffee pudding, and chocolate brownie with warm chocolate sauce. Alfresco drinking and dining is possible on the colourful patio area at the front of the Tavern during the warm summer months. Booking for meals may be required.

Open all wk 11-3 5-11 (Sat 11am-mdnt Sun 12.30-11) all day in summer Closed: 25 Dec, 1 Jan **Bar Meals** L

served Mon-Sat 12-2, Sun 12.30-3 D served all wk 5.30-9 **Restaurant** L served Mon-Sat 12-2, Sun 12.30-3 D served all wk 5.30-9 🛢 FREE HOUSE 🍺 Orkney Red MacGregor, Raven Ale, Clootie Dumpling & Dark Island, Atlas Latitude Highland Pilsner, Three Sisters, Nimbus & Wayfarer Ŏ Thatchers Gold. ☐ 9 **Facilities** Children welcome Children's menu Children's portions 🐾 Garden Parking 🚌

Save on hotels. Book at theAA.com/hotel

HIGHLAND 631 SCOTLAND

FORT WILLIAM — Map 22 NN17

Moorings Hotel ★★★ HL ◉

Banavie PH33 7LY ☎ 01397 772797
e-mail: reservations@moorings-fortwilliam.co.uk
dir: *From A82 in Fort William follow signs for Mallaig, then left onto A830 for 1m. Cross canal bridge then 1st right signed Banavie*

Smack beside the historic Caledonian Canal and Neptune's Staircase, the famous flight of eight locks, the Moorings is a modern hotel and pub that enjoys panoramic views on clear days towards Ben Nevis. The view is best savoured from the Upper Deck lounge bar and the bedrooms. Food, served in the nautically themed Mariners cellar bar, the lounge and the fine-dining Jacobean Restaurant features local fish and seafood. Dishes in the bar and lounge include steak-and-ale pie, Irish stew with colcannon, pork steak with mash and peppercorn sauce, and lemon tart. There is access to the canal towpath from the gardens. Booking for meals may be required.

Open all day all wk Closed: 24-26 Dec **Bar Meals** L served all wk 12-9.30 D served all wk 12-9.30 Av main course £10.95 food served all day **Restaurant** D served all wk 7-9.30 Av 3 course à la carte fr £24 ⊕ FREE HOUSE ◀ Tetley's Bitter, Caledonian Deuchars IPA, Guinness. **Facilities** Children welcome Children's menu Garden Parking Wi-fi ⛵ (notice required) **Rooms** 27

GAIRLOCH — Map 22 NG87

The Old Inn

PICK OF THE PUBS

IV21 2BD ☎ 01445 712006
e-mail: info@theoldinn.net
dir: *Just off A832, near harbour at south end of village*

Gairloch's oldest hostelry enjoys a wonderful setting at the foot of the Flowerdale Valley with views of the Outer Hebrides. Built in 1750, it was once a changing post for horses but now attracts herds of outdoor enthusiasts, especially walkers. Owner Alastair Pearson opened the pub's very own on-site micro-brewery in 2010, so expect the pints of The Slattadale, The Flowerdale, Blind Piper and The Erradale to be in tip-top condition at the bar. It's not just the beer that's home-made: the pub has its own smokery producing smoked meats, fish and cheese, and bread is baked in-house. Local fish and game feature strongly on menus that run from simple grills and hearty home-made pies to pizza and pasta dishes. Picnic tables on the large grassy area by the stream make an attractive spot for eating and enjoying the views. Dogs are welcomed with bowls, baskets and rugs to help them feel at home. Booking for meals may be required.

Open all day all wk 11am-mdnt (Sun 12-12) **Bar Meals** L served all wk 12-2.30, summer 12-4.30 D served all wk 5-9.30 Av main course £9.75 **Restaurant** D served all wk

6-9.30 Av 3 course à la carte fr £27.50 ⊕ FREE HOUSE ◀ The Old Inn The Erradale, The Flowerdale, The Slattadale, Three Sisters & Blind Piper, Adnams Southwold Bitter, An Teallach Crofters' Pale Ale, Cairngorm Trade Winds. **Facilities** ☘ Children welcome Children's menu Children's portions Garden Parking Wi-fi ⛵ (notice required)

GLENCOE — Map 22 NN15

Clachaig Inn NEW

PH49 4HX ☎ 01855 811252
e-mail: frontdesk@clachaig.com
dir: *Glencoe village signed from A82. Inn 3m S of village*

Set in the heart of Glencoe against a backdrop of spectacular mountains, this award-winning Highland inn has provided hospitality for over 300 years. In the traditional bar, expect anything up to 15 local real ales and a breathtaking selection of over 200 malt whiskies, which can be enjoyed with traditional local dishes such as Clachaig venison casserole; Crofter's salmon; or haggis, neeps and tatties. As well as occasional beer and whisky tastings, the pub also holds beer festivals throughout the year including February and October.

Open all day all wk Closed: 24-26 Dec **Bar Meals** L served all wk 12-9 D served all wk 12-9 Av main course £10 food served all day ⊕ FREE HOUSE ◀ Local ales (up to 15 at one time) ⓞ Westons. **Facilities** ☘ Children welcome Children's menu Children's portions Play area Family room Garden Beer festival Parking Wi-fi ⛵

GLENUIG — Map 22 NM67

Glenuig Inn NEW

PH38 4NG ☎ 01687 470219
e-mail: bookings@glenuig.com
dir: *From Fort William on A830 towards Mallaig. Left onto A861, 8m to Glenuig Bay*

Dating back to around 1746 and Bonnie Prince Charlie's time, the Glenuig Inn is now an award-winning 'green' pub and popular base for sea-kayakers drawn to the stunning beaches in the Sound of Arisaig. The emphasis here is 'as local as we can get it' and this philosophy applies to the bar, where only local real ale is served, and the kitchen. A typical menu might include local prawn tails cooked in garlic butter, followed by pheasant and wild mushroom pie; roasted smoked duck breast; or mackerel fishcakes.

Open all day all wk **Bar Meals** Av main course £10 food served all day **Restaurant** Fixed menu price fr £10 Av 3 course à la carte fr £20 food served all day ⊕ FREE HOUSE ◀ Cairngorm Trade Winds, Black Gold, Stag ⓞ Thistly Cross. ⬤ 9 **Facilities** ☘ Children welcome Children's menu Children's portions Play area Family room Garden Parking Wi-fi

INVERGARRY — Map 22 NH30

The Invergarry Inn

PH35 4HJ ☎ 01809 501206
e-mail: info@invergarryhotel.co.uk
dir: *At junct of A82 & A87*

A real Highland atmosphere pervades this refurbished roadside inn set in glorious mountain scenery between Fort William and Fort Augustus. Spruced-up bars make it a great base from which to explore Loch Ness, Glencoe and the West Coast. Relax by the crackling log fire with a wee dram or a pint of Garry Ale, then tuck into a good meal. Perhaps try Lochaber haggis, bashit neeps and tatties to start; followed by sea bream en papiette or a succulent 10oz rib-eye Scottish beefsteak and hand-cut chips. There are excellent walks from the front door.

Open all day all wk Closed: Dec-Jan ⊕ FREE HOUSE ◀ The Invergarry Inn Garry Ale, Timothy Taylor, Guinness. **Facilities** Children welcome Children's menu Children's portions Family room Garden Parking

INVERIE — Map 22 NG70

The Old Forge

PH41 4PL ☎ 01687 462267
e-mail: info@theoldforge.co.uk
dir: *From Fort William take A830 (Road to the Isles) towards Mallaig. Take ferry from Mallaig to Inverie (boat details on website)*

Britain's most remote mainland pub is – ironically - only accessible by boat (unless you're in the mood for an 18-hour hike). It stands literally between heaven and hell; Loch Nevis is Gaelic for heaven and Loch Hourn is Gaelic for hell. It's popular with everyone from locals to hill walkers, and is renowned for its impromptu ceilidhs. It is also the ideal place to sample local fish and seafood and there's no better way than choosing the seafood platter of rope mussels, langoustines, oak-smoked salmon and smoked trout. Other dishes might include smoked venison salad with home-made red onion marmalade; home-made haggis lasagne; and crème brûlée for dessert. There are 12 boat moorings and a daily ferry from Mallaig.

Open all day all wk **Bar Meals** L served all wk 12-3 D served all wk 6-9.30 Av main course £10-£15 **Restaurant** L served all wk 12-3 D served all wk 6-9.30 ⊕ FREE HOUSE ◀ Guinness, Guest ales. **Facilities** ☘ Children welcome Children's menu Children's portions Play area Family room Garden Parking Wi-fi ⛵

Kylesku Hotel

PICK OF THE PUBS

IV27 4HW ☎ **01971 502231**
e-mail: info@kyleskuhotel.co.uk
dir: *A835, then A837 & A894 into Kylesku. Hotel at end of road at Old Ferry Pier*

The hotel sits at the centre of the North West Highlands Global Geopark – 2,000 square kilometres of lochs, mountains and wild coast – and close to Britain's highest waterfall. Bypassed by the new bridge over Loch Glencoul in 1984, the former 17th-century coaching inn enjoys a glorious situation down by the old ferry slipway. Here today's fishing boats land the creel-caught seafood that forms the backbone of the daily chalkboard menu. Views from the bar and restaurant are truly memorable – you may catch sight of seals, dolphins, otters, eagles and terns. So settle down with an An Teallach or Skye real ale, and ponder your choice of the morning's catch. You could start with mussels, rope-grown in the loch outside, or go straight for the langoustines, served either hot with garlic butter, or cold with garlic mayonnaise. If meat is preferred local butchers and crofters supply wild venison, duck, chicken and Scottish rib-eye steaks. Booking for meals may be required.

Open all day all wk Closed: Nov-Feb **Bar Meals** L served all wk 12-6 D served all wk 6-9 Av main course £13 food served all day **Restaurant** D served all wk 7-9 ⊕ FREE

HOUSE ◧ An Teallach, Isle of Skye. 🏆 10 **Facilities** ✿ Children welcome Children's menu Children's portions Garden Wi-fi

Loch Leven Hotel

Old Ferry Rd PH33 6SA ☎ **01855 821236**
e-mail: reception@lochlevenhotel.co.uk
web: www.lochlevenhotel.co.uk
dir: *Off A82, N of Ballachulish Bridge*

The slipway into Loch Leven at the foot of the garden recalls the origins of this 17th-century inn as one staging

point on the old ferry linking the Road to The Isles. This extraordinary location, near the foot of Glencoe and with horizons peppered by Munro peaks rising above azure sea lochs, is also gifted with superb seafood from the local depths. Indulge in scampi, haddock, or chunky lamb Celtic casserole. Sip beers from Cairngorm Brewery or a wee dram from a choice of over 75 malts, making the best of the sun terrace which must have one of Scotland's most idyllic views.

Open all day all wk 11-11 (Thu-Sat 11am-mdnt Sun 12.30-11) **Bar Meals** L served all wk 12-3 D served all wk 6-9 **Restaurant** L served all wk 12-3 D served all wk 6-9 ⊕ FREE HOUSE ◧ Cairngorm, Atlas, River Leven. **Facilities** ✿ Children welcome Children's menu Children's portions Play area Family room Garden Parking Wi-fi 🚌

See advert below

PICK OF THE PUBS

Plockton Inn & Seafood Restaurant

PLOCKTON   Map 22 NG83

Innes St IV52 8TW ☎ 01599 544222
e-mail: info@plocktoninn.co.uk
web: www.plocktoninn.co.uk
dir: *A87 towards Kyle of Lochalsh. At Balmacara follow Plockton signs, 7m*

Mary Gollan and her brother Kenny's great-grandfather built this attractive stone free house just 100 metres from the harbour as a manse. They were born and bred in the village and since buying this enviably well located establishment in 1997, have run it with Kenny's partner, Susan Trowbridge, the three of them sharing the honours for making it an out-and-out award winner. The ladies double up in the role of chef, while Kenny manages the bar, where you'll find Plockton Crags and Plockton Bay real ales from the village brewery. An easygoing atmosphere is apparent throughout, with winter fires in both bars, and a selection of over 50 malt whiskies. A meal in the reasonably formal Dining Room or the more relaxed Lounge Bar is a must, with a wealth of freshly caught local fish and shellfish, West Highland beef, lamb, game and home-made vegetarian dishes on the set menu, plus daily specials. Martin, the barman, catches the Plockton prawns (called langoustines here) in Loch Carron, then Kenny takes them and other seafood off to his smokehouse. Starters include a vegetable or fish-based soup; chicken liver pâté and toast; haggis or vegetarian haggis clapshot with neeps, tatties and home-

pickled beetroot; and grilled goat's cheese. Among the main dishes could be those langoustines of Martin's, served hot with garlic or cold with Marie Rose sauce; skate wing with black butter, lemon and capers; smoked haddock and salmon fishcakes; grilled chicken marinated in chilli, lemon, saffron and mint; pork goulash and rice; and lentil and hazelnut roast. Desserts include sticky toffee pudding; cranachan ice cream; and Scottish cheeses served with Orkney oatcakes. The public bar is alive on Tuesdays and Thursdays with music from local musicians, who are often joined by talented youngsters from the National Centre of Excellence in Traditional Music in the village. Booking for meals may be required.

Open all day all wk **Bar Meals** L served all wk 12-2.30 D served all wk 6-9 Av main course £11 **Restaurant** D served all wk 6-9 Av 3 course à la carte fr £20 🛢 FREE HOUSE ◀ Greene King Abbot Ale, Fuller's London Pride, Young's Special, Plockton Crags Ale & Bay. **Facilities** Children welcome Children's menu Children's portions Play area 🐾 Garden Parking Wi-fi 🚌 (notice required)

PICK OF THE PUBS

Shieldaig Bar & Coastal Kitchen ★ SHL ❀❀

SHIELDAIG   Map 22 NG85

IV54 8XN ☎ **01520 755251**

e-mail: tighaneilean@keme.co.uk
web: www.shieldaigbarandcoastalkitchen.co.uk
dir: *Exit A896, in village centre*

The Ordnance Survey doesn't mark much on the map here — just a clutch of houses, a couple of jetties, a memorial and a hotel. The hotel is the award-winning Tigh an Eilean Hotel, of which the Shieldaig Bar & Coastal Kitchen is part. The location is where the magnificent Torridon Mountains meet the Western Seas; offshore is Shieldaig Island, owned by the National Trust for Scotland, while Upper Loch Torridon is just round the corner, and the road to remote Applecross curves round the bay from the inn. Be prepared to be left almost speechless by the abundance of wildlife visible from this extraordinary waterside setting — otters and seals, white-tailed sea eagles, oyster catchers, pine martens... An Teallach Brewery supplies the traditional bar, where live music and ceilidhs add a weekend buzz to this tiny village, and watching one of the spectacular sunsets will add a thrill to your stay. Only someone with no knowledge of local geography would be surprised that the sea provides much of what appears on the menu, especially the shellfish landed daily by fishermen who employ environmentally responsible creel-fishing and hand-diving techniques. Ways of sampling this local bounty include seafood stew and fisherman's pie, while other sustainable fish, including pollock and sea bream, will likely as not feature as blackboard daily specials. Among the meat dishes are venison bangers and mash, steak tartare and home-made beefburgers, while from the wood-fired oven come hand-made pizzas, with toppings from 'sea, hill or garden'. Outside by the loch is a courtyard with benches and tables. Most of the bedrooms have fabulous views westward out to sea, while the rest look up the hill towards Bein Shieldaig. None has a TV — they're deemed unnecessary in such a peaceful place, although there are some downstairs. Booking for meals may be required.

Open all day all wk **Bar Meals** L served all wk 12-2.30 D served all wk 6-9 **Restaurant** L served all wk 12-2.30 D served all wk 6-9 🍺 FREE HOUSE 🍺 An Teallach. 🍷 8 **Facilities** Children welcome Children's menu Children's portions Garden Parking Wi-fi 🚌 (notice required) **Rooms** 11

Save on hotels. Book at **theAA.com/hotel**

HIGHLAND 635 SCOTLAND

PLOCKTON	Map 22 NG83

The Plockton Hotel ★★★ SHL

PICK OF THE PUBS

Harbour St IV52 8TN ☎ 01599 544274
e-mail: info@plocktonhotel.co.uk
web: www.plocktonhotel.co.uk
dir: *A87 towards Kyle of Lochalsh. At Balmacara follow Plockton signs, 7m*

The Pearson family has run this award-winning harbourside hotel for the past 22 years, and the business has grown to include 15 en suite bedrooms. Dating from 1827, the original black fronted building is thought to have been a ships' chandlery before it was converted to serve as the village inn. Set with the mountains on one side and the deep blue waters of Loch Carron on the other, the hotel specialises in seafood – including freshly landed fish and locally caught langoustines – supplemented by Highland steaks and locally reared beef.

Lunchtime features light bites, warm bloomers and toasted paninis, as well as hot main dishes ranging from haggis, neeps and tatties to Highland venison casserole. Evening choices might include roasted pepper and goat's cheese salad; pan-fried herring in oatmeal; or flamed peppered whisky steak. A fine range of malts is available to round off that perfect Highland day. Booking for meals may be required.

Open all day all wk 11am-mdnt (Sun 12.30-11) Closed: 25 Dec, 1 Jan **Bar Meals** L served Mon-Sat 12-2.15, Sun 12.30-2.15 D served all wk 6-10 **Restaurant** L served Mon-Sat 12-2.15, Sun 12.30-2.15 D served all wk 6-9 ⊕ FREE HOUSE ◀ Plockton Bay & Crags Ale, Houston. **Facilities** Children welcome Children's menu Children's portions Family room Garden Wi-fi **Rooms** 15

Plockton Inn & Seafood Restaurant

PICK OF THE PUBS

See Pick of the Pubs on page 633

SHIELDAIG	Map 22 NG85

Shieldaig Bar & Coastal Kitchen ★ SHL ◎◎

PICK OF THE PUBS

See Pick of the Pubs on opposite page

TORRIDON	Map 22 NG95

The Torridon Inn ★★★★ INN

PICK OF THE PUBS

IV22 2EY ☎ 01445 791242
e-mail: inn@thetorridon.com
dir: *From Inverness take A9 N, then follow signs to Ullapool. Take A835 then A832. In Kinlochewe take A896 to Annat. Pub 200yds on right after village*

A fine hostelry idyllically set in 58 acres of parkland overlooking Loch Torridon and surrounded by lofty mountains. The inn was created by converting the estate stable block, buttery and farm buildings, yet the atmosphere is an informal mix of modern convenience and cosy comfort. Its success ensues from its continued promotion of local real ales, as witnessed by a beer festival held in late September, and menus that source as many ingredients as possible from the surrounding area. During the day you can tuck into hearty soups, sandwiches and bar meals, while in the evening you can linger over a delicious choice on menus likely to feature platters of local seafood; Balmoral chicken breast with local haggis; and a Torridon whisky crème brûlée, served with home-made shortbread and raspberry compôte. Last but not the least of its attractions is an ever-growing range of malt whiskies.

continued

PICK OF THE PUBS

The Sun Inn ★★★★INN ❀

DALKEITH   Map 21 NT36

Lothian Bridge EH22 4TR
☎ **0131 663 2456**
e-mail: thesuninn@live.co.uk
web: www.thesuninnedinburgh.co.uk
dir: *On A7 towards Galashiels, opposite Newbattle Viaduct*

This family-run former coaching inn stands in wooded grounds close to the banks of the River Esk. Appointed in contemporary style, the owners have blended the original fireplace, oak beams and exposed stone walls with a new wooden floor and feature wallpapers to realise their vision of a thoroughly modern gastro-pub. The friendly and obliging staff make this a great place to eat, drink and relax, helped along with winter log fires and a bright summer patio. Local cask ales have pride of place behind the bar, which also offers an extensive wine list. Food in the more formal restaurant is modern British, masterminded by owner and head chef Ian Minto and his son Craig. Locally sourced Scottish ingredients form the backbone of the menus, with lunchtime offerings that might include Eyemouth fish pie topped with mash and melting gruyère cheese; skirt of Borders beef with herb dumplings, Savoy cabbage and chive mash; or stuffed Portobello mushroom with rarebit topping, dauphinoise potato, chive cream and house salad. At

dinner, chicken liver pâté, tomato chutney and olive oil ciabatta toasts; or ham hock potato cake with wilted spinach, poached hen's egg and hollandaise sauce could precede a main course of sea bass fillets with tenderstem broccoli, brown shrimp and dill risotto and white wine cream; whilst meat eaters might opt for John Gilmour's rib-eye steak with roast vine tomato, field mushroom and proper chips. Modestly priced puddings include a classic crème brûlée with butter shortbread; and white wine poached pears with chocolate sauce and vanilla ice cream. Five individually styled en suite bedrooms complete the picture of this comfortable inn. Booking for meals may be required.

Open all day all wk Closed: 26 Dec, 1 Jan **Bar Meals** L served Mon-Sat 12-2, Sun 12-7 D served Mon-Sat 6-9, Sun 12-7 **Restaurant** L served Mon-Sat 12-2, Sun 12-7 D served Mon-Sat 6-9, Sun 12-7 🍺 FREE HOUSE ◀ Caledonian Deuchars IPA, Belhaven Best, Timothy Taylor. ♟ 10 **Facilities** Children welcome Children's portions Garden Parking Wi-fi **Rooms** 5

TORRIDON *continued*

Open all day all wk **Closed:** Jan **Bar Meals** L served all wk 12-2 D served all wk 6-9 Av main course £12 **Restaurant** L served all wk 12-2 D served all wk 6-9 Av 3 course à la carte fr £20 ⊕ FREE HOUSE ◀ Isle of Skye Red Cuillin, Torridon Ale, Cairngorm Trade Winds, An Teallach & Crofters Pale Ale, Cromarty Happy Chappy. **Facilities** Children welcome Children's menu Children's portions Play area Garden Beer festival Parking Wi-fi 🚌 **Rooms** 12

MIDLOTHIAN

DALKEITH   Map 21 NT36

The Sun Inn ★★★★ INN ⊛

PICK OF THE PUBS

*See Pick of the Pubs on opposite page
See advert on page 635*

PENICUIK   Map 21 NT25

The Howgate Restaurant

Howgate EH26 8PY ☎ 01968 670000
e-mail: peter@howgate.com
dir: *10m N of Peebles. 3m E of Penicuik on A6094 between Leadburn junct & Howgate*

This beautifully converted farm building was formerly the home of Howgate cheeses. Its fire-warmed bar offers bistro-style meals, while the candlelit restaurant serves a full carte. Executive and head chefs, Steven Worth and Sean Blake, respectively, use the finest Scottish produce, especially beef and lamb, which are cooked in the charcoal grill; other options might include Cullen skink; steamed Shetland mussels; smoked haddock and wild mushroom risotto; and penne pasta in an asparagus and cream sauce. There are fine beers to enjoy and an impressively produced wine list roams the globe. Booking for meals may be required.

Open all wk **Closed:** 25-26 Dec, 1 Jan **Bar Meals** L served all wk 12-2 D served all wk 6-9.30 Av main course £9.95 **Restaurant** L served all wk 12-2 D served all wk 6-9.30 Av 3 course à la carte fr £20 ⊕ FREE HOUSE ◀ Belhaven Best, Hoegaarden. ♟ 14 **Facilities** Children welcome Children's portions Garden Parking Wi-fi 🚌 (notice required)

ROSLIN   Map 21 NT26

The Original Rosslyn Inn ★★★★ INN

2-4 Main St EH25 9LE ☎ 0131 440 2384
e-mail: enquiries@theoriginalhotel.co.uk
dir: *Off city bypass at Straiton for A703 (inn near Rosslyn Chapel)*

Just eight miles from central Edinburgh, this family-run village inn has been in the Harris family for 38 years. A short walk from the famous Rosslyn Chapel, Robert Burns, the famous Scottish poet, once stayed here and wrote a small poem about his visit. Catch up with the locals in the village bar, or relax by the fire in the lounge whilst choosing from the menu. Soups, jackets and paninis are supplemented by main course options like haggis with tatties and neeps; breaded haddock and chips; and vegetarian harvester pie. Alternatively, the Grail Restaurant offers more comprehensive dining options. There are well-equipped bedrooms, four with four-posters.

Open all day all wk ⊕ FREE HOUSE ◀ Belhaven Best. **Facilities** Children welcome Children's menu Children's portions Garden Parking Wi-fi **Rooms** 6

MORAY

FOCHABERS   Map 23 NJ35

Gordon Arms Hotel

80 High St IV32 7DH ☎ 01343 820508
e-mail: enquiries@gordonarms.co.uk
dir: *A96 approx halfway between Aberdeen & Inverness, 9m from Elgin*

This 200-year-old former coaching inn, close to the River Spey and within easy reach of Speyside's whisky distilleries, is understandably popular with salmon fishers, golfers and walkers. Its public rooms have been carefully refurbished, and the hotel makes an ideal base from which to explore this scenic corner of Scotland. The cuisine makes full use of local produce: venison, lamb and game from the uplands, fish and seafood from the Moray coast, beef from Aberdeenshire and salmon from the Spey - barely a stone's throw from the kitchen!

Open all day all wk 11-11 (Thu 11am-mdnt Fri-Sat 11am-12.30am) ⊕ FREE HOUSE ◀ Caledonian Deuchars IPA, John Smith's Extra Smooth, Guest ales. **Facilities** Children welcome Parking

NORTH LANARKSHIRE

CUMBERNAULD   Map 21 NS77

Castlecary House Hotel

Castlecary Rd G68 0HD ☎ 01324 840233
e-mail: enquiries@castlecaryhotel.com
dir: *A80 onto B816 between Glasgow & Stirling. 7m from Falkirk, 9m from Stirling*

Run by the same family for years, this friendly hotel is located close to the historic Antonine Wall and the Forth and Clyde Canal. Meals in the lounge bars plough a traditional furrow with options such as mince and tatties, steak pie, and beer-battered haddock. Home-made puddings include meringue banoffee nest and steamed chocolate pudding. More formal fare is available in Camerons Restaurant. There is an excellent selection of real ales on offer, including Arran Blonde and Houston Peter's Well. A beer festival is held once or twice a year – contact the hotel for details of the dates. Booking for meals may be required.

Open all day all wk **Closed:** 1 Jan **Bar Meals** L served 12-9 D served 12-9 Av main course £8 food served all day **Restaurant** L served Sun 12.30-3 D served Mon-Sat 6-9.30 Fixed menu price fr £10.95 ⊕ FREE HOUSE ◀ Arran Blonde, Harviestoun Bitter & Twisted, Inveralmond Ossian's Ale, Houston Peter's Well, Caledonian Deuchars IPA. ♟ 8 **Facilities** Children welcome Children's menu Children's portions Garden Beer festival Parking Wi-fi 🚌

PERTH & KINROSS

GLENFARG   Map 21 NO11

The Famous Bein Inn ★★★ INN ⊛

PH2 9PY ☎ 01577 83021
e-mail: enquiries@beininn.com
dir: *From S: M90 junct 8, A91 towards Cupar. Left onto B996 to Bein Inn. From N: M90 junct 9, A912 towards Gateside*

Standing by the river in the glorious wooded Glen of Farg, this former drovers' inn is just minutes from the M90. While enjoying a refreshing pint of Inveralmond ale by the log fire or out on the sundeck, choose from the list of locally sourced and freshly prepared food served all day from midday. Awarded one AA Rosette, the Balvaird Restaurant is the place to taste rib-eye steak with peppercorn sauce, while plates in the bistro range from chicken liver parfait to coq au vin, pork belly with apple and cinnamon purée, and sticky toffee pudding with toffee sauce. Accommodation is available.

Open all day all wk **Closed:** 25-26 Dec **Bar Meals** Av main course £9.25-£10.95 food served all day **Restaurant** food served all day ⊕ FREE HOUSE ◀ Belhaven Best, Inveralmond, Guinness, Tennent's. **Facilities** Children welcome Children's menu Children's portions Garden Parking Wi-fi 🚌 **Rooms** 11

PICK OF THE PUBS

The Killiecrankie Hotel ★★★ SHL ❀❀

KILLIECRANKIE Map 23 NN96

PH16 5LG ☎ 01796 473220
e-mail: enquiries@killiecrankiehotel.co.uk
web: www.killiecrankiehotel.co.uk
dir: *Take B8079 N from Pitlochry. Hotel in 3m after NT Visitor Centre*

This white-painted Victorian manse gleams amidst woodland at the Pass of Killiecrankie, the gateway to the Highlands. This magnificent gorge, famed for the battle in 1689 when the Jacobites routed the forces of King William III, is a stronghold for red squirrels and a renowned birdwatching area. The hotel's logo shows Royalist soldier Donald McBean leaping the gorge to escape pursuing Highlanders. There are countless walks into the hills, including majestic Ben Vrackie rising directly behind the hotel, riverside walks and the nearby lochs in the Tummel Valley, with a garland of shapely mountains. Less active guests explore the area's distilleries, including that at Edradour, outside nearby Pitlochry, which is Scotland's smallest. Standing in a four-acre estate, the hotel retains much of the character of old combined with modern comforts. The cosy, wood-panelled bar is a popular haunt, while the snug sitting room (with a grand fire for winter days) opens on to a small patio and a fine herbaceous border. Arm yourself with a beer from the likes of Orkney or Belhaven and relax beside the tranquil rose garden, studying an uplifting menu that makes the most of Scotland's diverse produce and which has gained head chef Mark Easton two AA Rosettes. Creative starters range from terrine of scallop and twice-baked goat's cheese brûlée to fulfilling home-made soups; the ever-evolving mains selection could see pan-fried fillet of Highland venison and breast of woodpigeon; or pan-seared fillet of Ayrshire pork in black peppercorn and herb crust with Lochaber smoked cheese sauce. Each main is matched on the menu with a specific wine suggestion from the hotel's notable list of quality bins. Finish with a traditional cranachan – toasted oatmeal and Drambuie cream with raspberries and shortbread. Lighter lunchtime meals may be taken in the conservatory.

Open all day all wk Closed: Jan & Feb
🍺 FREE HOUSE ◀ Orkney Red MacGregor, Caledonian Deuchars IPA, Belhaven Best ♉ Kopparberg.
Facilities Children welcome Children's menu Garden Parking **Rooms** 10

KILLIECRANKIE — Map 23 NN96

Killiecrankie House
Hotel ★★★ SHL ◉◉

PICK OF THE PUBS

See Pick of the Pubs on opposite page

MEIKLEOUR — Map 21 NO13

Meikleour Hotel

PH2 6EB ☎ 01250 883206
e-mail: visitus@meikleourhotel.co.uk
dir: *From A93 (between Perth & Blairgowrie) take A984 into village centre*

The famous Beech Hedge of Meikleour, planted in 1745, is the world's tallest and longest hedge. There's abundant foliage too at this creeper-clad, gabled coaching inn, where real ale drinkers in the flagstone-floored, fishing- and shooting-themed bar can enjoy Lure of Meikleour from the Inveralmond Brewery in Perth, as well as a beer festival on the last Sunday in May. Top-quality chefs prepare imaginative bistro food entirely in-house, from Toulouse sausage and pulled-pork cassoulet to beer-battered Scottish haddock, chips and peas. On Tuesdays pre-booked guests can gamble against the house to see who pays for dinner (but not drinks). Booking for meals may be required.

Open all wk 11-3 6-11 Closed: 25-30 Dec **Bar Meals** L served all wk 12.15-2.30 D served all wk 6.30-9 Av main course £10.50 **Restaurant** L served all wk 12.15-2.30 D served all wk 6.30-9 Av 3 course à la carte fr £20 ⊕ FREE HOUSE ◀ Inveralmond Lure of Meikleour Ö Westons Wyld Wood Organic Vintage. **Facilities** ✿ Children welcome Children's menu Children's portions Garden Beer festival Parking Wi-fi

PITLOCHRY — Map 23 NN95

Moulin Hotel

PICK OF THE PUBS

11-13 Kirkmichael Rd, Moulin PH16 5EH
☎ 01796 472196
e-mail: enquiries@moulinhotel.co.uk
dir: *From A924 at Pitlochry take A923. Moulin 0.75m*

At the foot of Ben Vrackie on an old drovers' road, this great all-round inn was built in 1695 and is a popular base for walking and touring. Locals are drawn to the bar for the excellent home-brewed beers, with Ale of Atholl, Braveheart, Moulin Light, and Old Remedial served on handpump. The interior boasts beautiful stone walls and lots of cosy niches, with blazing log fires in winter; while the courtyard garden is lovely in summer. Menus offer the opportunity to try something local such as Scotsman's Bunnet (batter pudding filled with a Highland meat and vegetable stew); Skye mussels; deep-fried haggis; and sporran of plenty (minute steak stuffed with haggis). You might then round off your meal with bread and Lockerbie butter pudding, or sticky whisky fudge cake. A specials board broadens the choice further. Over 20 wines by the glass and more than 30 malt whiskies are available. Booking for meals may be required.

Open all day all wk 11-11 (Fri-Sat 11am-11.45pm Sun 12-11) **Bar Meals** L served all wk 12-9.30 D served all wk 12-9.30 Av main course £10 food served all day **Restaurant** D served all wk 6-9 Fixed menu price fr £23 Av 3 course à la carte fr £27 ⊕ FREE HOUSE ◀ Moulin Braveheart, Old Remedial, Ale of Atholl & Moulin Light, Belhaven Best. ☝ 25 **Facilities** Children welcome Children's menu Children's portions Garden Parking Wi-fi ⇔ (notice required)

RENFREWSHIRE

HOUSTON — Map 20 NS46

Fox & Hounds

South St PA6 7EN ☎ 01505 612448 & 612991
e-mail: jonathon.wengel@btconnect.com
web: www.foxandhoundshouston.co.uk
dir: *A737, W from Glasgow. Take Johnstone Bridge off Weir exit, follow signs for Houston. Pub in village centre*

This welcoming old coaching inn is very much at the heart of the attractive village of Houston, and pulls in the plaudits for the beers which flow from its micro-brewery; beer festivals in May and August add spice. The homely menu centres around classics such as home-made fish pie; slow-braised shoulder of lamb with red wine and rosemary jus; and fresh Scottish scampi tails in ale batter. A list of around 150 whiskies, including some rare ones, is the icing on the cake here.

Open all day all wk 11am-mdnt (Fri-Sat 11am-1am Sun fr 12.30) **Bar Meals** L served all wk 12-5 D served Mon-Sat 5-10, Sun 5-9 Av main course £8 food served all day **Restaurant** L served all wk 12-5 D served Mon-Sat 5-10, Sun 5-9 Fixed menu price fr £10.95 Av 3 course à la carte fr £18 food served all day ⊕ FREE HOUSE ◀ Houston Killellan, Warlock Stout, Texas, Jock Frost, Peter's Well Ö Addlestones. ☝ 10 **Facilities** ✿ Children welcome Children's menu Children's portions Garden Beer festival Parking Wi-fi ⇔ (notice required)

SCOTTISH BORDERS

ALLANTON — Map 21 NT85

Allanton Inn

TD11 3JZ ☎ 01890 818260
e-mail: info@allantoninn.co.uk
dir: *From A1 at Berwick take A6105 for Chirnside (5m). At Chirnside Inn take Coldstream Rd for 1m to Allanton*

This family-run 18th-century coaching inn is a perfect base to explore the Borders, and it has built up a formidable reputation for its local ales and excellent food. A large beer garden with fruit trees overlooking open countryside is an ideal spot to sup a pint of Bitter & Twisted or tuck into locally-sourced dishes such as beer-battered whiting and chunky chips, or pork cutlet in a red wine jus. Barbecues are held in the summer. Booking for meals may be required.

Open all day all wk 12-11 Closed: 2wks Feb (dates vary) **Bar Meals** L served all wk 12-3 D served all wk 6-9 Av main course £14 **Restaurant** L served all wk 12-3 D served all wk 6-9 Av 3 course à la carte fr £23 ⊕ FREE HOUSE ◀ Inveralmond Ossian, Scottish Borders Game Bird, Harviestoun Bitter & Twisted, Fyne Piper's Gold. ☝ 10 **Facilities** Children welcome Children's menu Children's portions Garden Wi-fi

ETTRICK — Map 21 NT21

Tushielaw Inn

TD7 5HT ☎ 01750 62205
e-mail: robin@tushielaw-inn.co.uk
dir: *At junct of B709 & B711(W of Hawick)*

This 18th-century former toll house and drovers' halt on the banks of Ettrick Water makes a good base for touring the Borders, trout fishing (salmon fishing can be arranged), wildlife and birdwatching, and those tackling the Southern Upland Way. An extensive menu is always available with daily-changing specials. Fresh produce is used according to season, with local lamb and Aberdeen Angus beef regular specialities. Local haggis smothered in melted Lockerbie cheddar and steak-and-ale pie are popular choices.

Open all wk ⊕ FREE HOUSE ◀ Belhaven Best, Guinness, Tennent's. **Facilities** Children welcome Parking ⇔

GALASHIELS
Map 21 NT43

Kingsknowes Hotel ★★★ HL

1 Selkirk Rd TD1 3HY ☎ 01896 758375
e-mail: enquiries@kingsknowes.co.uk
dir: *Off A7 at Galashiels/Selkirk rdbt*

In over three acres of grounds on the banks of the Tweed, this splendid baronial mansion was built in 1869 for a textile magnate. There are lovely views of the Eildon Hills and Abbotsford House, Sir Walter Scott's ancestral home. Meals are served in two restaurants and the Courtyard Bar, where fresh local or regional produce is used as much as possible. The impressive glass conservatory is the ideal place to enjoy a drink. Accommodation is available.

Open all day all wk Mon-Wed 12-11 (Thu-Sat noon-1am Sun 12-11) ⊕ FREE HOUSE ◀ McEwan's 70/-, John Smith's. **Facilities** Children welcome Children's menu Play area Garden Parking **Rooms** 12

INNERLEITHEN
Map 21 NT33

Traquair Arms Hotel

Traquair Rd EH44 6PD ☎ 01896 830229
e-mail: info@traquairarmshotel.co.uk
dir: *From A72 (Peebles to Galashiels road) take B709 for St Mary's Loch & Traquair*

Amidst the heather-covered hills of the Scottish Borders stands this imposing pub/hotel with tranquil beer garden. Expect to share it with muddy mountain bikers – downhill and cross-country trails are right on the doorstep. It's one of only two places where you can drink Traquair Bear Ale, brewed a stone's throw away at Traquair House. An unusual combination of Scottish and Italian food is prepared by the resident Italian chef. Sample dishes include local Borders lamb; tiger prawns with spaghetti, cherry tomatoes and flat leaf parsley; and a dessert of summer pudding with crème Chantilly. Booking for meals may be required.

Open all day all wk Closed: 25 Dec **Bar Meals** L served Mon-Fri 12-2.30, Sat-Sun all day D served Mon-Fri 5-9, Sat-Sun all day Av main course £10 **Restaurant** L served Mon-Fri 12-2.30, Sat-Sun all day D served Mon-Fri 5-9, Sat-Sun all day ⊕ FREE HOUSE ◀ Caledonian Deuchars IPA, Timothy Taylor Landlord, Traquair Bear Ale. **Facilities** Children welcome Children's menu Children's portions Garden Parking Wi-fi 🚌

KELSO
Map 21 NT73

The Cobbles Inn ⊛

PICK OF THE PUBS

See Pick of the Pubs on opposite page

KIRK YETHOLM
Map 21 NT82

The Border Hotel

The Green TD5 8PQ ☎ 01573 420237
e-mail: borderhotel@aol.com
dir: *From A698 in Kelso take B6352 for 7m to Kirk Yetholm*

Marking the end of the 268-mile-long Pennine Way walk, this 18th-century former coaching inn is a welcoming and most hospitable place to revive after any journey, be it on foot or by car. Cracking pints of Pennine Way Bitter will slake parched throats and the traditional British menu, which features local game and farm meats, will satisfy healthy appetites. Follow chicken liver parfait with red onion jam with venison suet pudding or pork belly with cider and apple gravy, leaving room for a hearty pudding. Refurbished in 2012, the stone-flagged bar has a blazing winter log fire, and the conservatory dining room looks over the patio and beer garden. Booking for meals may be required.

Open all day all wk Closed: 25 Dec **Bar Meals** L served all wk 12-2 D served all wk 6-8.45 Av main course £9.95 **Restaurant** L served all wk 12-2 D served all wk 6-8.45 ⊕ FREE HOUSE ◀ Broughton Pennine Way Bitter, Scottish Borders Game Bird, Orkney Raven Ale Ò Westons Old Rosie. ♀ 10 **Facilities** ♣ Children welcome Children's menu Children's portions Play area Garden Parking Wi-fi 🚌 (notice required)

LAUDER
Map 21 NT54

The Black Bull ★★★★ INN ⊛

PICK OF THE PUBS

Market Place TD2 6SR ☎ 01578 722208
e-mail: enquiries@blackbull-lauder.com
dir: *In centre of Lauder on A68*

In the heart of the Scottish Borders, on the edge of the Lammermuir Hills, this whitewashed, three-storey coaching inn dates from 1750. After a day of walking in the hills, visiting Thirlestane Castle, playing golf or checking out the Princes Street bargains in nearby Edinburgh, enjoy a gastro-pub-style lunch in the relaxed Harness Room bar or the more formal lounge bar. A light lunch menu of snacks and sandwiches is served from midday, while a typical supper might lead you to begin with Cullen skink or terrine of pheasant, hare and mallard. Follow with Border beef, Guinness and mushroom pie, or something from the grill might appeal. To finish, there is brioche bread-and-butter pudding; or a selection of Scottish cheeses - Cooleeney, Gubbeens and Dunsyre Blue - with oatcakes. The inn has eight superb en suite rooms. Booking for meals may be required.

Open all day all wk ⊕ BLACKBULL HOTEL (LAUDER) LTD ◀ Timothy Taylor Landlord, Caledonian Deuchars IPA, Morland Old Speckled Hen, Marston's Pedigree, Tetley's, Guinness. **Facilities** Children welcome Children's menu Children's portions Parking Wi-fi **Rooms** 8

LEITHOLM
Map 21 NT74

The Plough Hotel

Main St TD12 4JN ☎ 01890 840252
e-mail: theplough@leitholm.wanadoo.co.uk
dir: *5m N of Coldstream on A697. Take B6461, Leitholm in 1m*

Set in a small village in rich farming country south of the Lammermuir Hills, this compact old coaching inn specialises in Aberdeen Angus steaks. The beef is sourced by the local butcher from the foremost livestock market in the Borders and well aged before preparation. The wide-ranging menu also features chicken and haggis stack in Drambuie sauce; hand-pulled beers draw in the locals, whilst the beer garden is a tranquil retreat.

Open all wk Mon-Tue 4-12 Wed-Thu & Sun 12-12 Fri-Sat noon-1am ⊕ FREE HOUSE ◀ Guinness, Guest ale. **Facilities** Children welcome Garden Parking

MELROSE
Map 21 NT53

Burts Hotel ★★★ HL ⊛⊛

PICK OF THE PUBS

Market Square TD6 9PL ☎ 01896 822285
e-mail: enquiries@burtshotel.co.uk
dir: *A6091, 2m from A68 3m S of Earlston*

In Melrose's picturesque market square stands this 18th-century hotel, owned by the Henderson family for some 40 years. Since it's a listed building, restoration and extensions have necessarily been sympathetic, yet all the refinements of a modern first-class hotel are evident. After a day out, perhaps visiting Sir Walter Scott's Abbotsford home, settle down with one of the 90 malts, or a pint of Caledonian 80/-. Lying in the shadow of the Eildon Hills, the town is surrounded by the rich countryside and waters which provide much of the produce used in the kitchen. The Bistro Bar's extensive lunch and supper menu lists steamed West Coast mussels; and braised shank of Borders lamb, while the restaurant, holder of two AA Rosettes since 1995, offers, among much more, tasting of pig, namely belly, fillet, and cheek tortellini with apples and anise jus. En suite rooms are equipped to a high standard. Booking for meals may be required.

Open all wk 12-2.30 5-11 **Bar Meals** L served all wk 12-2 D served all wk 6-9.30 Av main course £12 **Restaurant** L served Sat-Sun D served all wk 7-9 Av 3 course à la carte fr £26 ⊕ FREE HOUSE ◀ Caledonian Deuchars IPA & 80/-, Timothy Taylor Landlord, Fuller's London Pride. ♀ 10 **Facilities** ♣ Children welcome Children's portions Garden Parking Wi-fi **Rooms** 20

PICK OF THE PUBS

The Cobbles Inn ✿

KELSO   Map 21 NT73

7 Bowmont St TD5 7JH
☎ **01573 223548**
e-mail: info@thecobblesinn.co.uk
web: www.thecobblesinn.co.uk
dir: *In town centre*

There's an abundance of character and atmosphere in this attractively modernised 19th-century coaching inn, which sits on the cobbled town square in the heart of picturesque Kelso. Sit by the roaring log fire in winter and enjoy single malts, continental beers or the pub's own ales from their local Tempest Brewing Co (they have a craft brewery in town). The well-established restaurant has an AA Rosette for the quality of its food. Expect a frequently changing menu dominated by local fish and shellfish, Border lamb, beef and pork or game in season. Influences come from far and wide, with traditional British food, modern European classics and Pacific Rim dishes all rubbing shoulders on menus that offer everything from light bites to full three course meals. For lunch you could try a hand-made beefburger with mature cheddar or Belhaven smoked trout salad with spicy tomato and pepper relish and new potatoes. Alternatively there are bagel sandwiches and nibbles including olives and crispy potato skins with sweet chilli and chive cream dips. Bar meals range from classics such as beer-battered

fillet of haddock and chips or grilled sirloin through to spicy options such as a stirfry with vermicelli rice noodles or a spiced lentil burger. An excellent value set-price dining menu offers evening dishes such as house-smoked roe deer with quince and apple jelly and savoury chestnut shortbread, followed by pan-fried fillet of sea bass with fondant potatoes, roast Jerusalem artichokes, crispy pancetta and morel sauce, along with an ever-changing selection of home-made desserts from the blackboard. The inn is a popular choice for small wedding receptions, business meetings and private functions thanks to its upstairs dining and function room, where a bespoke menu is available. Live music session every Friday night.

Open all day 11.30-11 Closed: 25-26 Dec, Mon Nov-Mar **Bar Meals** L served Tue-Sun 12-2 D served Tue-Sat 6-9, Sun 6-8 Av main course £9.95 **Restaurant** L served Tue-Sun 12-2 D served Tue-Sat 6-9, Sun 6-8 Fixed menu price fr £16.95 Av 3 course à la carte fr £20 ⊕ FREE HOUSE ◀ Tempest ♂ Thistly Cross. **Facilities** Children welcome Children's menu Children's portions Parking Wi-fi 🚌 (notice required)

PICK OF THE PUBS

The Wheatsheaf at Swinton

SWINTON   Map 21 NT84

Main St TD11 3JJ ☎ 01890 860257
e-mail: reception@wheatsheaf-swinton.co.uk
web: www.wheatsheaf-swinton.co.uk
dir: *From Edinburgh A697 onto B6461.*
From East Lothian A1 onto B6461

Husband and wife team Chris and Jan Winson have built up an impressive reputation for their dining destination in this attractive village. Whether you choose to eat in the Sun Room or the Dining Room, the latter overlooking the village green, the menus feature home-made food using locally sourced produce, including daily delivered fresh seafood from Eyemouth 12 miles away, and beef from livestock raised on the surrounding Borders pastures. Also likely to appear, according to the season, are wild salmon, venison, partridge, pheasant, woodcock and duck. The bar and garden menu is likely to offer a club sandwich, steak and ale pie, beefburger and lamb's liver with onion, mash and crispy bacon. One way to start a meal in the restaurant might be with pan-seared woodland pigeon breast, Stornoway black pudding purée, crispy apple and light game jus; another could be home-made Thai crab cake with sweet chilli sauce. Head chef John Forrestier, who comes from Nancy in France, specialises in fish, so a main course definitely worth considering is his baked Dover sole with scallop mousse, clams, beurre blanc and pickled cockle salad. Alternatives might include roast

Scottish venison with celeriac purée, seared poached pears, rösti potato and light beetroot and chocolate sauce; or pan-seared goat's cheese gnocchi and morel mushroom fricassée, buttered kale and truffle oil. Typical specials include langoustines as a starter, and mains of beer-battered haddock; pan-fried medallions of monkfish; and wild halibut. Other regular meat dishes include oven-roast pork fillet, and slow-braised Borders beef blade. Finally, a couple of the desserts: glazed pomegranate tart and lemon sorbet; and baked Malteser cheesecake with passionfruit coulis. The bar stocks Deuchars IPA, Belhaven Best, and draught Peroni. Here too is a whisky map and tasting notes to study before choosing your single malt. Booking for meals may be required.

Open 4-11 (Sat 12-12 Sun 12-11)
Closed: 23-24 & 26 Dec, 2-3 Jan, Mon-Fri L **Bar Meals** L served Sat-Sun 12-2 D served Mon-Sat 6-9, Sun 6-8.30 **Restaurant** L served Sat-Sun 12-2 D served Mon-Sat 6-9, Sun 6-8.30 ⊕ FREE HOUSE ◖ Caledonian Deuchars IPA, Belhaven Best, Guinness. ♀ 12
Facilities Children welcome Garden Parking 🚌

NEWCASTLETON   Map 21 NY48

Liddesdale ★★★★ INN NEW

17 Douglas Square TD9 0QD ☎ 01387 375255
dir: *In centre of Newcastleton*

Fully refurbished by new owners in 2008, this inn sits in Douglas Square at the heart of Newcastleton (sometimes referred to as Copshaw Holm), a 17th-century village planned by the third Duke of Buccleugh. An ideal base for exploring the unspoiled countryside in this area, the inn has a bar stocked with over 20 malt whiskies and a different cask-conditioned ale every week in the summer. A typical meal might include jalapeño peppers stuffed with cream cheese; haggis and pork sausages with horseradish mash and onion gravy; and sticky toffee pudding with vanilla ice cream.

Open all day all wk **Bar Meals** L served all wk 12-2 D served all wk 5-9 **Restaurant** L served Sat-Sun 12-2 D served all wk 5-9 ⊕ FREE HOUSE ◀ Samuel Smith's ◓ Samuel Smith's Organic. **Facilities** Children welcome Children's menu Children's portions Garden Beer festival Wi-fi ▭ (notice required) **Rooms** 6

ST BOSWELLS   Map 21 NT53

Buccleuch Arms Hotel

PICK OF THE PUBS

The Green TD6 0EW ☎ 01835 822243
e-mail: info@buccleucharms.com
dir: *On A68, 10m N of Jedburgh. Hotel on village green*

Dating from the 16th century, this smart and friendly country-house hotel, which celebrated its 175th anniversary in 2011, was originally an inn for the fox-hunting aristocracy. Set beside the village cricket pitch, it's an attractive brick and stone building with an immaculate garden. Inside, a large and comfortable lounge is warmed by a log fire in winter, while the spacious enclosed garden comes into its own during the warmer months. The bar serves one real ale at a time, but turnover is high so locals keep coming back to find out what's on offer - the Stewart Brewery, Broughton Ales, and the Hadrian Border Brewery are just three of the regular suppliers. Menus change seasonally, but the specials may well change twice daily to reflect the availability of ingredients from the Scottish Borders countryside. Typical dishes include pressed ham hock with caramelised onions and parsley; fillet of Eyemouth haddock in crispy beer-batter with chips, garden peas and home-made tartare sauce; and slow-cooked lamb casserole with pearl barley and red cabbage. Booking for meals may be required.

Open all day all wk 7am-11pm Closed: 25 Dec ⊕ FREE HOUSE ◀ McEwan's 70/-, Stewart, Atlas, Orkney, Northumberland, Broughton, Hadrian Border, Guest ales. **Facilities** Children welcome Children's menu Children's portions Play area Garden Parking

SWINTON   Map 21 NT84

The Wheatsheaf at Swinton

PICK OF THE PUBS

See Pick of the Pubs on opposite page

TIBBIE SHIELS INN   Map 21 NT22

Tibbie Shiels Inn

PICK OF THE PUBS

St Mary's Loch TD7 5LH ☎ 01750 42231
dir: *From Moffat take A708. Inn 14m on right*

The inn itself is a lovely whitewashed cottage with later additions and stands between St Mary's Loch and the Loch of the Lowes in the glorious Yarrow Valley. Isabella 'Tibbie' Shiels was the first licensee in 1826 and her famously unforgettable name lives on still. Well-known visitors during her time included Walter Scott, Thomas Carlyle and Robert Louis Stevenson. She is rumoured to still keep watch over the bar, where the selection of over 50 malt whiskies helps sustain long periods of ghost watching. The majority of the ingredients on the traditional pub menu are local, including the famous hill-farmed lamb, game and even herbs grown in the garden. Sandwiches, salads, ploughman's and paninis are all on offer, while the straightforward carte may tempt with Arbroath smokies with tartare sauce followed by home-made venison burger with chips, salad and red pepper relish, steak-and-ale pie, or sirloin steak with pepper sauce and all the trimmings. There are plenty of evening events throughout the year.

Open all day all wk 8am-mdnt **Bar Meals** L served all wk 12-3.30 D served all wk 5.30-9 **Restaurant** L served all wk 12-3.30 D served all wk 5.30-9 ⊕ FREE HOUSE ◀ Belhaven 80/-, Broughton Greenmantle Ale, Tibbie Shiels Ale & The Reiver ◓ Westons Stowford Press. **Facilities** ✿ Children welcome Children's menu Children's portions Play area Garden Parking Wi-fi ▭

SOUTH AYRSHIRE

SYMINGTON   Map 20 NS33

Wheatsheaf Inn

Main St KA1 5QB ☎ 01563 830307
dir: *In Symington, off A77 between Ayr & Kilmarnock*

Log fires burn in every room of this charming 17th-century free house, which has been run by Martin and Marnie Thompson for over 25 years. The former coaching inn stands close to the Royal Troon Golf Course, and the interior is decorated with the work of local artists. The varied menu offers plenty of choice, with dishes like fillet of sole with shrimps in lemon and dill cream sauce contrasting with more homely favourites such as gammon steak with pineapple or fried egg. Desserts include pear and ginger crumble.

Open all day all wk 11-11 (Fri-Sat 11am-mdnt) Closed: 25 Dec, 1 Jan **Bar Meals** L served all wk all day D served all wk all day Av main course £10 food served all day

Restaurant L served all wk 12-2 D served all wk 5-9 Fixed menu price fr £9.95 Av 3 course à la carte fr £20 ⊕ FREE HOUSE ◀ Belhaven Best, Morland Old Speckled Hen, Guinness. **Facilities** Children welcome Children's menu Children's portions Garden Parking ▭ (notice required)

STIRLING

CALLANDER   Map 20 NN60

The Lade Inn

Kilmahog FK17 8HD ☎ 01877 330152
e-mail: info@theladeinn.com
dir: *From Stirling take A84 to Callander. 1m N of Callander, left at Kilmahog Woollen Mills onto A821 towards Aberfoyle. Pub immediately on left*

A stone's throw from the River Teith in the heart of the Trossachs National Park, the stone-built Lade Inn is part of the surrounding Leny Estate, built as a tearoom in 1935. First licensed in the 1960s, the inn is noted for real ales brewed by the Trossachs Craft Brewery at the side of the pub, and for its week-long beer festival in late August/early September. Dog- and family-friendly, the inn's home-cooked menu offers many smaller portions and/or allergen-free dishes; it's served in both restaurant and bar. There is live folk music on Friday and Saturday evenings. Booking for meals may be required.

Open all day all wk **Bar Meals** L served Mon-Sat 12-9, Sun 12.30-9 D served Mon-Sat 12-9, Sun 12.30-9 Av main course £9.50 **Restaurant** L served Mon-Sat 12-9, Sun 12.30-9 D served Mon-Sat 12-9, Sun 12.30-9 Fixed menu price fr £14.50 Av 3 course à la carte fr £20 ⊕ FREE HOUSE ◀ Trossachs Waylade, LadeBack & LadeOut, Belhaven Best, Tennent's ◓ Thistly Cross. ☂ 9 **Facilities** ✿ Children welcome Children's menu Children's portions Play area Family room Garden Beer festival Parking Wi-fi ▭ (notice required)

DRYMEN   Map 20 NS48

The Clachan Inn

2 Main St G63 0BG ☎ 01360 660824
e-mail: info@clachaninndrymen.co.uk
dir: *Telephone for directions*

Established in 1734, The Clachan is believed to be the oldest licensed pub in Scotland; this quaint white-painted cottage on the West Highland Way was once owned by Rob Roy's sister. Family-run for the past 30 years the bar stocks frequently changing guest ales while a warming log fire keeps things cosy. More comfort comes with the food – choose from pub favourites such as deep-fried potato skins with dips; jumbo sausage with baked beans and chips; and home-made toffee sponge pudding.

Open all day all wk Closed: 25 Dec & 1 Jan **Bar Meals** L served Mon-Sat 12-3.45 D served Mon-Sat 6-9.45 Av main course £8-£9 **Restaurant** L served Mon-Sat 12-3.45 D served Mon-Sat 6-9.45 ⊕ FREE HOUSE ◀ Harviestoun Bitter & Twisted, Cairngorm Trade Winds, Guinness. ☂ 9 **Facilities** ✿ Children welcome Children's menu Children's portions Wi-fi ▭ (notice required)

Cross Keys Hotel

Main St FK8 3DN ☎ 01786 870293
e-mail: info@kippencrosskeys.co.uk
dir: *10m W of Stirling, 20m from Loch Lomond off A811*

The 300-year-old Cross Keys stands on Kippen's Main Street and offers seasonally changing menus and a good pint of Harviestoun Bitter & Twisted. The pub's welcoming interior, warmed by three log fires, is perfect for resting your feet after a walk in nearby Burnside Wood, or you can sit in the garden when the weather permits. The menu takes in beetroot, feta and walnut risotto; seafood linguine with roasted lemons; chicken with chorizo, spinach and bean broth, and a good range of pub classics, perhaps rib-eye steak, horseradish and caramelised onion sandwich or haddock and chips. Dogs are welcome in the top bar.

Open all wk 12-3 5-11 (Fri 12-3 5-1am Sat noon-1am Sun 12-12) Closed: 1 Jan **Bar Meals** L served Mon-Fri 12-3, Sat 12-9, Sun 12-8 D served Mon-Fri 5-9, Sat 12-9, Sun 12-8 Av main course £8-£19 **Restaurant** L served Mon-Fri 12-3, Sat 12-9, Sun 12-8 D served Mon-Fri 5-9, Sat 12-9, Sun 12-8 ⊕ FREE HOUSE ◀ Belhaven Best, Harviestoun Bitter & Twisted, Guinness, Guest ales ♻ Addlestones. ♣ 10 **Facilities** Children welcome Children's menu Children's portions Play area Family room Garden Parking Wi-fi 🚌

The Inn at Kippen

PICK OF THE PUBS

Fore Rd FK8 3DT ☎ 01786 870500
e-mail: info@theinnatkippen.co.uk
dir: *From Stirling take A811 to Loch Lomond. 1st left at Kippen station rdbt, 1st right onto Fore Rd. Inn on left*

Located in a picturesque village at the foot of the Campsie Hills, this traditional whitewashed free house enjoys views across the Forth valley to the Highlands. The stylish bar is a relaxing place to sample the extensive range of cask ales and wines, as well as a superb selection of spirits that reflects the proprietor's long career in the Scotch whisky business. Two separate areas offer a choice of casual or more formal dining from a menu driven by seasonal, locally sourced ingredients. Traditional and contemporary dishes reveal British, European and Oriental influences. Start, perhaps, with a twice-baked parmesan soufflé before moving on to steak pie with seasonal vegetables; Thai seafood broth with sea bass, mussels and king prawns; or butternut squash, sage and parmesan risotto. Tempting desserts include treacle and stem ginger pudding with coconut ice cream. There's a pretty garden area for summer dining, and a heated smoking deck. Booking for meals may be required.

Open all day all wk ⊕ FREE HOUSE ◀ George Killian's Irish Red. **Facilities** Children welcome Children's menu Children's portions Garden Parking Wi-fi

Champany Inn - The Chop and Ale House ◉◉

PICK OF THE PUBS

See Pick of the Pubs on opposite page

The Four Marys

65/67 High St EH49 7ED ☎ 01506 842171
dir: *M9 junct 3 or 4 take A803 to Linlithgow. Pub in town centre*

Named after one of the four ladies-in-waiting of Mary, Queen of Scots, who was born in nearby Linlithgow Palace, this town house dates from 1500. It was 481 years old when it was licensed for the first time, having served as a chemist, newsagent and printing works beforehand. It now thrives as one of Scotland's top real ale pubs, serving predominantly Scottish brews and hosting popular beer festivals in May and October. A no-nonsense menu presents sandwiches; hand-pressed burgers; lighter dishes such as British ham hock salad; and mains like Balmoral chicken.

Open all day all wk **Bar Meals** L served all wk 12-5 D served all wk 5-9 Av main course £8 food served all day **Restaurant** L served all wk 12-5 D served all wk 5-9 food served all day ⊕ BELHAVEN/GREENE KING ◀ Belhaven 80/- & Four Marys, Morland Old Speckled Hen, Caledonian Deuchars IPA, Stewart Edinburgh Gold. ♥ 9 **Facilities** Children welcome Children's menu Children's portions Garden Beer festival 🚌

Coll Hotel

PICK OF THE PUBS

PA78 6SZ ☎ 01879 230334
e-mail: info@collhotel.com
dir: *Ferry from Oban. Hotel at head of Arinagour Bay, 1m from Pier (collections by arrangement)*

Being the only inn on the Isle of Coll, it's no surprise that the bar of this award-winning hotel is the hub of the island community. Come here to meet the locals, soak in the atmosphere, and enjoy stunning views over the sea to Jura and Mull. The most popular drinks are pints of Fyne ale and malt whiskies from the list, but there is a good wine selection too. In the summer months the fabulous

garden acts as an extension to the bar or the Gannet restaurant; watch the yachts coming and going while enjoying a glass of Pimm's. Fresh produce is landed and delivered from around the island every day and features on the specials board. Famed for its seafood, you'll find it in dishes such as seared scallops in garlic and lemon butter, and a platter of Coll langoustines that can be served hot or cold, with seasonal salad or fried potatoes. Among the non-fish options, try the chicken topped with haggis in a whisky sauce. Booking for meals may be required.

Open all day all wk ⊕ FREE HOUSE ◀ Fyne Piper's Gold, Guinness. **Facilities** Children welcome Children's menu Children's portions Play area Family room Garden Parking Wi-fi

The Port Charlotte Hotel

Main St PA48 7TU ☎ 01496 850360
e-mail: info@portcharlottehotel.co.uk
dir: *From Port Askaig take A846 towards Bowmore. Right onto A847, through Blackrock. Take unclassified road to Port Charlotte*

This sympathetically restored Victorian hotel is perfectly positioned on the west shore of Loch Indaal in an attractive conservation village. With their warming fires, the lounge and public bar are convivial gathering points, and lovers of Scottish art will enjoy the work on display. Islay ales and whiskies make a great way to warm up before enjoying a menu packed with local produce – perhaps beef and ale pie or seafood landed by the Islay fishing fleet. A large conservatory opens out into the garden and directly onto the beach.

Open all day all wk Closed: 24-26 Dec **Bar Meals** L served all wk 12-2 D served all wk 6-9 Av main course £11.95 **Restaurant** D served all wk 6-9 Av 3 course à la carte fr £32 ⊕ FREE HOUSE ◀ Islay. ♥ 9 **Facilities** Children welcome Children's menu Children's portions Play area Family room Garden Parking Wi-fi 🚌

PICK OF THE PUBS

Champany Inn - The Chop and Ale House

LINLITHGOW   Map 21 NS97

Champany EH49 7LU ☎ 01506 834532
e-mail: reception@champany.com
web: www.champany.com
dir: *2m NE of Linlithgow on corner of A904 & A803*

Within striking distance of Edinburgh is this famous inn, a cluster of buildings, some dating back to the 16th century, which houses The Chop and Ale House, as well as the restaurant, which was once a millhouse. Of the two splendid restaurants, the more informal and homely is The Chop and Ale House, a converted farmer's bothy which was once the public bar of an former inn here. With a pint of Belhaven in hand, or a glass of the Champany's own-label South African wine, settle in your chosen spot with the bistro-style menu. Beef is the big thing here – Aberdeen Angus of course – whether it be steaks or the same steak minced and formed in half-pound burgers. Starters include chicken tikka; smoked salmon roulade; lightly grilled home-smoked chorizo sausage with pickled red cabbage; and beetroot and goat's cheese salad, while main course alternatives to steak are home-made boerewors or vegetarian sausages; deep-fried haddock in home-made batter; and chicken Caesar salad. If you can manage a dessert, cranachan is on the carte, as is home-made carrot cake with ice cream; and hot malted waffles with maple syrup. Its worth taking time to check out the new Champany Cellars wine shop; on display are wines from around the world, and especially worthy of note are those shipped directly from a number of South African wineries. Devotees of the single malt surely won't walk past the section of Highlands and Islands whiskies. If you're staying over then there's lots of interesting places to explore outside Edinburgh – Hopetoun House and Bo'ness and Kinneil Steam Railway, and just across the Firth of Forth via the famous bridge is the beautiful county of Fife. Booking for meals may be required.

Open all wk 12-2 6.30-10 (Fri-Sun 12-10) Closed: 25-26 Dec, 1 Jan **Bar Meals** L served all wk 12-2 D served all wk 6.30-10 **Restaurant** L served all wk 12.30-2 D served all wk 6.30-10 ⊕ FREE HOUSE ◀ Belhaven. **Facilities** Children welcome Children's portions Garden Parking

MULL, ISLE OF

DERVAIG — Map 22 NM45

The Bellachroy Hotel **NEW**

PA75 6QW ☎ 01688 400314
e-mail: info@thebellachroy.co.uk
dir: *Take ferry from Oban to Craignure. A849 towards Tobermory. Left at T-junct onto B8073 to Dervaig*

Built in 1608, the historic drovers' inn is Mull's oldest inn and enjoys a stunning location overlooking Loch Cuin in the pretty village of Dervaig. The draw, other than the character bar and the alfresco dining terrace, are the tip-top Fyne ales – try a pint of Highlander – the mind-boggling range of Island malt whiskies, and the fresh local produce on the daily menus. Expect Iona mutton, Dervaig pork, Mull venison and cheeses, and delicious langoustines, lobster, scallops and oysters, all landed at local harbours. Booking for meals may be required.

Open all day all wk **Bar Meals** L served all wk 12-2.30 D served all wk 6-8.30 Av main course £10 **Restaurant** L served all wk 12-2.30 D served all wk 6-8.30 Av 3 course à la carte fr £22 ⊕ FREE HOUSE ◀ Fyne Avalanche, Highlander. **Facilities** ❀ Children welcome Children's menu Children's portions Garden Parking Wi-fi

ORKNEY

ST MARY'S — Map 24 HY40

The Commodore **NEW**

Holm KW17 2RU ☎ 01856 781788
dir: *On A961 (Kirkwall to St Margarets Hope road)*

Just outside St Mary's village in Holm and only a ten-minute drive from Kirkwall, this family-friendly pub and restaurant enjoys stunning views over the Scapa Flow, the Churchill Barriers and the Italian Chapel. A number of local ales such as Orkney Best are showcased in the bar and this sourcing policy extends to the menu in the light and airy restaurant. Bar meals of steak pie or chicken Kiev are complemented by Westray salmon in pastry, or Egilsay pork chops glazed with whisky, mustard and brandy from the main menu. Booking for meals may be required.

Open all wk all day May-Oct (6pm-late Nov-Apr) Closed: 26 Dec & 1-2 Jan **Bar Meals** L served all wk 12-2 (May-Oct) D served all wk 6-9 Av main course £10 **Restaurant** L served all wk 12-2 (May-Oct) D served all wk 6-9 Fixed menu price fr £15 Av 3 course à la carte fr £30 ⊕ FREE HOUSE ◀ Highland Orkney Blast, Scapa & Best, Orkney Raven Ale & Red MacGregor ♂ Kopparberg. ▾ **Facilities** ❀ Children welcome Children's menu Children's portions Garden Parking Wi-fi 🚐

STROMNESS — Map 24 HY20

Ferry Inn **NEW**

John St KW16 3AD ☎ 01856 850280
e-mail: info@ferryinn.com
dir: *Opposite ferry terminal*

With its prominent harbour-front location, the Ferry Inn has long enjoyed a reputation for local ales. The pub has now installed racking for a further ten local ales on top of the five handpulls on the bar and although the beers change regularly you may be lucky to find Red MacGregor or Skull Splitter. If beer isn't your thing, there are plenty of wines and malt whiskies to choose from, as well as an appealing menu that can include haggis and clap shot with whisky sauce or an Orkney seafood platter.

Open all day all wk 9am-mdnt (Thu-Sat 9am-1am Sun 9.30am-mdnt) Closed: 25 Dec & 1 Jan **Bar Meals** Av main course £8 food served all day **Restaurant** Av 3 course à la carte fr £18 food served all day ⊕ FREE HOUSE ◀ Highland Scapa Special & Orkney IPA, Orkney Dark Island & Skull Splitter. **Facilities** Children welcome Children's menu Children's portions Parking Wi-fi 🚐

SKYE, ISLE OF

ARDVASAR — Map 22 NG60

Ardvasar Hotel ★★★ SHL

IV45 8RS ☎ 01471 844223
e-mail: richard@ardvasar-hotel.demon.co.uk
web: www.ardvasarhotel.com
dir: *From ferry terminal, 50yds & turn left*

Beside the road towards the southern tip of Skye, sit out front to drink in the extraordinary views to the rocky foreshore, Sound of Sleat and the mountains of the Knoydart Peninsula, a ferry ride away via Mallaig. Once you've sipped your Skye-brewed beer or local malt, retire to the comfy lounge bar or dining room to indulge in some of Skye's most renowned seafood meals; the local boats may land salmon, crab, lobster or scallops. Estate venison and Aberdeen Angus beef extend the choice. Residents in the individually designed rooms can look to a fine Scottish breakfast to set another day in paradise going.

Open all day all wk 11am-mdnt (Sun 12-11) **Bar Meals** L served all wk 12-2.30 D served all wk 5.30-9 ⊕ FREE HOUSE ◀ Isle of Skye Red Cuillin. **Facilities** Children welcome Children's menu Children's portions Garden Parking **Rooms** 10

CARBOST — Map 22 NG33

The Old Inn and Waterfront Bunkhouse

PICK OF THE PUBS

IV47 8SR ☎ 01478 640205
e-mail: enquiries@theoldinnskye.co.uk
web: www.theoldinnskye.co.uk
dir: *From Skye Bridge follow A87 N. Take A863, then B8009 to inn*

The Old Inn and Waterfront Bunkhouse, on the shores of Loch Harport near the Talisker distillery, is a charming, 200-year-old island cottage very popular among the walking and climbing fraternity. Arrive early for a table on the waterside patio and savour the breathtaking views of the Cuillin Hills with a pint of Hebridean ale in hand. Inside, open fires welcome winter visitors, and live Highland music is a regular feature most weekends. The menu includes daily home-cooked specials with numerous fresh fish dishes such as local prawns and oysters, and mackerel from the loch. A typical choice could start with crispy confit duck leg salad or hot smoked salmon with Achmore crème fraîche; continue with a chargrilled Highland sirloin steak or Thai green vegetable curry; and finish with home-made rice pudding with dried apricots, raisins and toasted almonds.

Open all day all wk 11am-mdnt **Bar Meals** L served all wk 12-9.30 D served all wk food served all day **Restaurant** D served all wk food served all day ⊕ FREE HOUSE ◀ Isle of Skye Red Cuillin & Black Cuillin, Cuillin Skye Ale & Pinnacle Ale, Hebridean. **Facilities** Children welcome Children's portions Family room Garden Parking Wi-fi 🚐

Save on hotels. Book at **theAA.com/hotel**

SCOTTISH ISLANDS 647 SCOTLAND

ISLEORNSAY — Map 22 NG71

Hotel Eilean Iarmain ★★★ SHL ◉◉

PICK OF THE PUBS

IV43 8QR ☎ 01471 833332
e-mail: hotel@eilean-iarmain.co.uk
dir: A851, A852 right to Isleornsay harbour front

This award-winning Hebridean hotel with its own pier overlooks the Isle of Ornsay harbour and Sleat Sound. The old-fashioned character of the hotel remains intact, and décor is mainly cotton and linen chintzes with traditional furniture. More a small private hotel than a pub, the bar and restaurant ensure that the standards of food and drinks served here are exacting. The head chef declares: 'We never accept second best, it shines through in the standard of food served in our restaurant'. Here you can try dishes like Eilean Iarmain Estate venison casserole, pan-seared sirloin steak, or grilled fillet of cod with hollandaise sauce. If you call in at lunchtime, a range of baked potatoes, sandwiches and toasties is also available. Half portions are served for children. Booking for meals may be required.

Open all day all wk 11am-11.30pm (Thu 11am-mdnt Fri 11am-1am Sat 11am-12.30am) ⊕ FREE HOUSE ◖ McEwan's 80/-, Isle of Skye, Guinness.
Facilities Children welcome Children's portions Garden Parking **Rooms** 16

STEIN — Map 22 NG25

Stein Inn

Macleod's Ter IV55 8GA ☎ 01470 592362
e-mail: angus.teresa@steininn.co.uk
dir: A87 from Portree. In 5m take A850 for 15m. Right onto B886, 3m to T-junct. Turn left

The location of Skye's oldest inn is sublime, for about 20 paces from the front door, across some grass with pub tables, are the waters of Loch Bay. The island's abundant fresh fish and shellfish are fully exploited by the kitchen, as are its sheep, wild deer and Highland cattle. Choices include West Coast mussels meunière; venison pie; and steak braised in local ale. At lunchtime try a haggis toastie, smoked salmon platter, or fresh crab sandwich. The bar stocks 125 malts and Reeling Deck beer from the Isle of Skye brewery.

Open all day all wk 11am-mdnt Closed: 25 Dec, 1 Jan **Bar Meals** L served all wk 12-4 D served all wk 6-9.30 Av main course £9 **Restaurant** D served all wk 6-9.30 Av 3 course à la carte fr £19 ⊕ FREE HOUSE ◖ Isle of Skye Red Cuillin & Reeling Deck, Cairngorm Trade Winds, Caledonian Deuchars IPA, Orkney Dark Island. ♟ 9
Facilities ❧ Children welcome Children's menu Children's portions Play area Family room Garden Parking Wi-fi 🚌

SOUTH UIST

LOCHBOISDALE — Map 22 NF71

The Polochar Inn

Polochar HS8 5TT ☎ 01878 700215
e-mail: polocharinn@aol.com
dir: W from Lochboisdale, take B888. Hotel at end of road

Standing virtually alone overlooking the Sound of Eriskay and a prehistoric standing stone, this white-painted inn is the former change-house, where travellers waited for the ferry to Barra. Owned by sisters Morag MacKinnon and Margaret Campbell, it serves Hebridean real ales and specialises in local seafood and meats, as well as pasta dishes, all made with fresh, seasonal ingredients and served in a dining room with outstanding views of the sea. From the beer garden watch dolphins playing and the brilliant sunsets. On summer Saturday nights live music fills the bar.

Open all day all wk 11-11 (Fri-Sat 11am-1am Sun 12.30pm-1am) **Bar Meals** L served Mon-Sat 12.30-8.30, Sun 1-8.30 (winter all wk 12-2.30) D served Mon-Sat 12.30-8.30, Sun 1-8.30 (winter all wk 5-8.30) food served all day ⊕ FREE HOUSE ◖ Hebridean, Guest ales.
Facilities Children welcome Children's menu Children's portions Family room Garden Parking Wi-fi 🚌 (notice required)

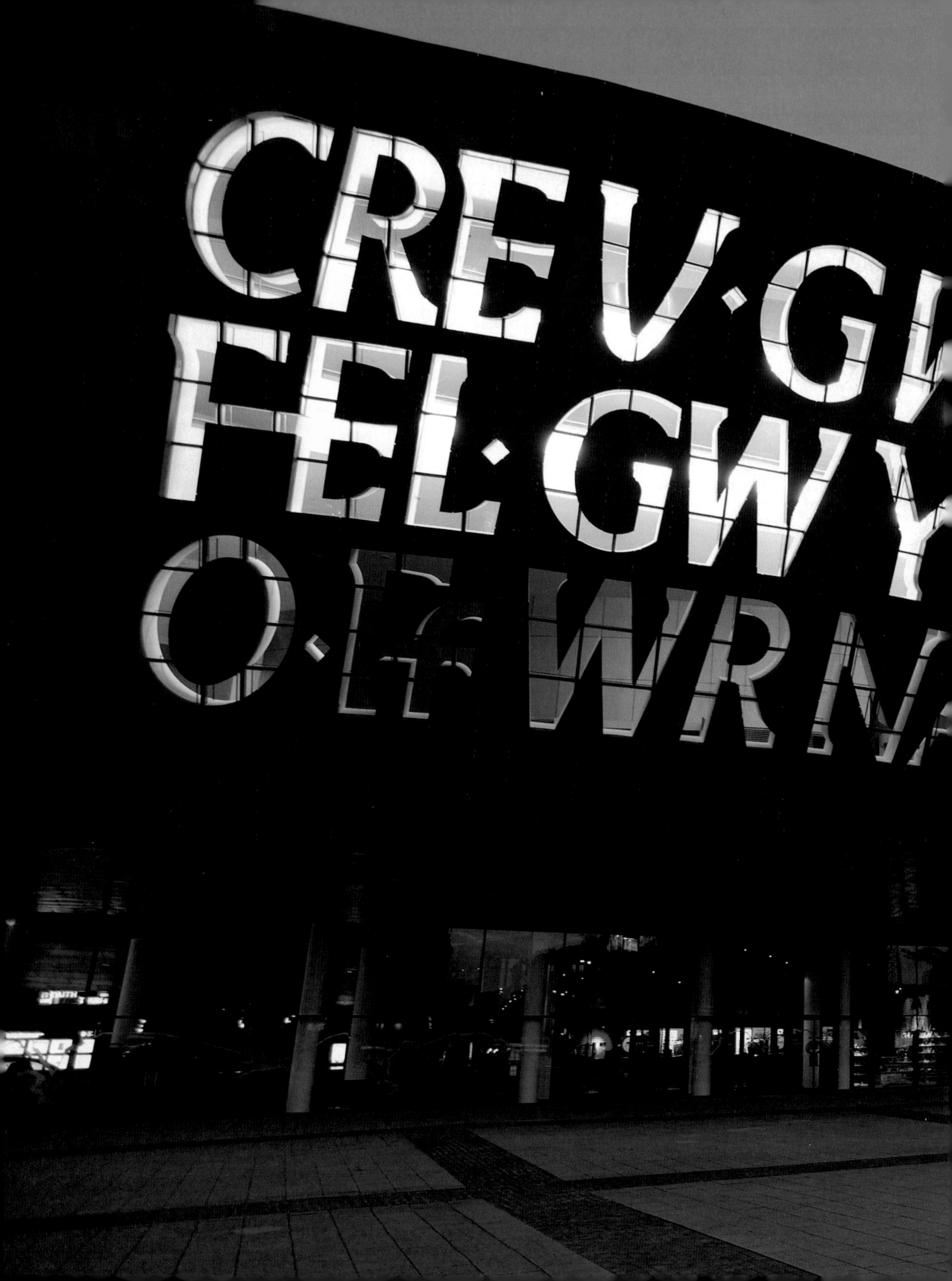

Wales

Millennium Centre, Cardiff

PICK OF THE PUBS

Ye Olde Bulls Head Inn ★★★★★ INN

BEAUMARIS Map 14 SH67

Castle St LL58 8AP ☎ 01248 810329
e-mail: info@bullsheadinn.co.uk
web: www.bullsheadinn.co.uk
dir: *From Britannia Road Bridge follow A545. Inn in town centre*

A stone's throw from the gates of Beaumaris' medieval castle, this 15th-century pub started life as a staging post and inn on the route to Ireland. The Bull was commandeered by Cromwell's General Mytton whose forces laid siege to the Royalist-held castle during the English Civil War in 1645. The town became a fashionable tourist destination after Princess Victoria visited in 1832 and today's imposing establishment retains much of the character of Georgian and Victorian times, underscored by tasteful contemporary additions. The light and airy Brasserie has been moulded from the former stables; the Welsh slate floor, oak tables and open fire a relaxing location at any time. The bar itself transports drinkers back to Dickensian times (the man himself stayed here), with settles, antique furnishings and artefacts, including the town's old ducking stool and remarkable old weaponry; Bass and Hancock's are supplemented by regularly changing guest ales. The Bull's happy location in the midst of a rich larder of seafood and Welsh livestock farms means that the menus here are exceptional; this potential has been realised and recognised by the award of two AA Rosettes. The popular Brasserie offers a children's menu and portions and a good range of modern global dishes; mussels cooked with white wine, garlic, parsley and cream; chickpea, almond and coriander falafels with Moroccan spiced couscous, but it is the intimate Loft Restaurant where the boat is pushed out. Start with Penmon Bay lobster and poached guinea fowl risotto with tarragon velouté, leading to fillet of Welsh beef, salt beef and potato hash, carrots and swede, girolle mushroom and mustard jus. The exceptional accommodation here comes with a full Welsh breakfast, ample repast before exploring the treasure trove that is Ynys Môn, the Isle of Anglesey. Booking for meals may be required.

Open all day all wk **Closed:** 25 Dec **Bar Meals** L served Mon-Sat 12-2, Sun 12-3 Av main course £5-£6.50 **Restaurant** L served Mon-Sat 12-2, Sun 12-3 D served Brasserie all wk 6-9; Loft Restaurant Tue-Thu 7-9.30, Fri-Sat 6.30-9 Av 3 course à la carte fr £12.50 ⊕ FREE HOUSE ◼ Bass, Hancock's, Guest ales. ♀ 20 **Facilities** Children welcome Children's menu Children's portions Parking Wi-fi **Rooms** 26

ANGLESEY, ISLE OF

BEAUMARIS Map 14 SH67

Ye Olde Bulls Head

Inn ★★★★★ INN ◉◉

PICK OF THE PUBS

See Pick of the Pubs on page 650

RED WHARF BAY Map 14 SH58

The Ship Inn

PICK OF THE PUBS

LL75 8RJ ☎ 01248 852568
dir: *Telephone for directions*

Wading birds flock here to feed on the extensive sands of Red Wharf Bay, making The Ship's waterside beer garden a birdwatcher's paradise on warm days. In the Kennealy family's hands for around 40 years, the pub faces east on the lee side of a hill, sheltered from prevailing winds and catching the morning and afternoon sun perfectly. Before the age of steam, sailing ships landed cargoes here from all over the world; now the boats bring fresh Conwy Bay fish and seafood to the kitchens of this traditional free house. Real ales are carefully tended and a single menu applies to both bars and restaurant. Typical starters include a charred bundle of asparagus with a balsamic and honey dressing; and frittata of locally reared duck egg with curried mayonnaise and seasonal salad. Move on to bangers and mash with onion gravy or a minted lamb burger with sour cream, chips and a Greek-style side salad. Other options include lunchtime sandwiches and wraps and a separate children's menu. Booking for meals may be required.

Open all day all wk **Bar Meals** L served all wk 12-2.30 D served all wk 6-9 **Restaurant** D served Sat-Sun ⊕ FREE HOUSE ◀ Conwy Rampart, Adnams, Guest ales Ö Westons Wyld Wood Organic. **Facilities** Children welcome Children's menu Play area Family room Garden Parking Wi-fi

BRIDGEND

KENFIG Map 9 SS88

Prince of Wales Inn

CF33 4PR ☎ 01656 740356
e-mail: prince-of-wales@btconnect.com
dir: *M4 junct 37 into North Cornelly. Left at x-rds, follow signs for Kenfig & Porthcawl. Pub 600yds on right*

Thought to be one of the most haunted pubs in Wales, this 16th-century stone-built free house was formerly the seat of local government for the lost city of Kenfig. Just as remarkably, it is also the only pub in Britain to have held a Sunday school continuously from 1857 to 2000. Welsh brunch, and beef and traditional Welsh ale pie are amongst the local dishes on the menu, and the daily blackboard specials are also worth attention. Ring for details of the pub's occasional beer festivals.

Open all day all wk **Bar Meals** L served all wk 12-2.30 D served all wk 6-8.30 Av main course £8.50-£9 **Restaurant** L served all wk 12-2.30 D served all wk 6-8.30 ⊕ FREE HOUSE ◀ Bass, Sharp's Doom Bar, Worthington's, Guest ales Ö Tomos Watkin Taffy Apples. **Facilities** ❤ Children welcome Children's menu Children's portions Garden Beer festival Parking Wi-fi 🚌 (notice required)

CARDIFF

CREIGIAU Map 9 ST08

Caesars Arms

PICK OF THE PUBS

See Pick of the Pubs on page 653

GWAELOD-Y-GARTH Map 9 ST18

Gwaelod-y-Garth Inn

Main Rd CF15 9HH ☎ 029 2081 0408 & 07855 313247
e-mail: gwaelo-dinn@btconnect.com
web: www.gwaelodinn.co.uk
dir: *From M4 junct 32, N on A470, left at next exit, at rdbt turn right 0.5m. Right into village*

This stone-built hillside cottage hugs lanes criss-crossing the thickly wooded flank of Garth Hill, high above Taffs Well. Across the vale is the fairytale Victorian sham castle of Castell Coch – one diversion amongst many in this pretty corner of the Taff Valley just north of Cardiff. Guest ales from as far afield as Essex and Derbyshire rub shoulders with local brews at the bar, along with a farm cider from Pontypridd. A pleasing selection of home-cooked pub food produces dishes of roast Glamorgan turkey, and rack of lamb with herb crust. Booking for meals may be required.

Open all day all wk 11am-mdnt (Sun 12-11) **Bar Meals** L served Mon-Thu 12-2, Fri-Sat 11-9, Sun 12-3 D served Mon-Sat 6.30-9 **Restaurant** L served Mon-Thu 12-2, Fri-Sat 11-9, Sun 12-3 D served Mon-Sat 6.30-9 ⊕ FREE HOUSE ◀ Wye Valley HPA, Swansea Three Cliffs Gold, RCH Pitchfork, Vale of Glamorgan, Crouch Vale Brewers Gold, Thornbridge Jaipur, Gower Ö Local cider. **Facilities** ❤ Children welcome Children's menu Children's portions Garden Parking 🚌

See advert on page 652

CARMARTHENSHIRE

ABERGORLECH Map 8 SN53

The Black Lion

SA32 7SN ☎ 01558 685271
e-mail: georgerashbrook@hotmail.com
dir: *A40 E from Carmarthen, then B4310 signed Brechfa & Abergorlech*

A drive through the pretty Cothi Valley brings you to this attractive, 16th-century village pub run by George and Louise Rashbrook. Louise does all the cooking and George wisely gives her a generous credit on the pub's website for doing so. You can eat from an extensive menu in the flagstoned bar, while the evening menu in the more modern, candlelit dining room offers beef, almond, mint and lemon casserole; mustard-stuffed chicken in bacon; scampi and chips; and mushroom, brie and cranberry Wellington. The award-winning beer garden overlooks a Roman bridge. Booking for meals may be required.

Open 12-3 7-11 (Sat-Sun & BH all day) Closed: Mon (ex BH) **Bar Meals** L served Tue-Sun 12-2.30 D served Tue-Sun 7-9 Av main course £7.95 **Restaurant** D served Tue-Sun 7-9 ⊕ FREE HOUSE ◀ Rhymney Ö Westons Stowford Press. **Facilities** ❤ Children welcome Children's menu Children's portions Garden Parking Wi-fi 🚌 (notice required)

LLANDDAROG Map 8 SN51

Butchers Arms NEW

SA32 8NS ☎ 01267 275330
e-mail: b5dmj@aol.com
dir: *From A48 between Carmarthen & Cross Hands follow Llanddarog/B4310 signs. Pub by church in village*

Well into a third decade at this pretty old pub, self-taught butcher and accomplished chef David James continues to run his kitchen with unbridled enthusiasm. Hidden up a side road off the A48 beside the church, it's worth dropping in following a visit to the National Botanic Garden (two miles). Arrive early and with an appetite, then marvel at the Toby jug collection before ordering a pint of Double Dragon to accompany some hearty pub food – lamb shank with mint and cider sauce; hot shellfish platter; and chicken curry. The mixed grill is for the serious meat-eater.

Open 12-3 6-11 Closed: 24-26 Dec, Sun & Mon **Bar Meals** L served Tue-Sat 12-2.30 D served Tue-Sat 6-9.30 Av main course £8.95-£16.95 **Restaurant** L served Tue-Sat 12-2.30 D served Tue-Sat 6-9.30 Av 3 course à la carte fr £20 ⊕ FREE HOUSE ◀ Felinfoel Cambrian Bitter, Double Dragon, Celtic Pride. ♆ 10 **Facilities** Children welcome Children's menu Garden Wi-fi 🚌 (notice required)

Gwaelod y Garth Inn

It's just a short ride out of the city, but here, above the valley, in the shelter of the Garth, the pace of life is slower. The welcome at the Gwaelod y Garth Inn is a genuine one, so we're a much favoured watering-hole for walkers, cyclists, hang-gliders, and our colourful locals, too.

The village and the pub have exceptional views of the Taff Vale and the Bristol Channel beyond, and our terrace is a marvellous place just to meet and watch the world go by. Inside, in the cosy bar and in the pool-room, you'll find plenty of choice of drinks, including good real ales, tasty bar-food, friendly company and, when it's cold outside, open fires. Upstairs, Chef ensures that our comfortable award-winning restaurant serves a fine extensive menu with wines to match, and on Sundays there is always a traditional roast.

The pub has recently been given a Highly Commended Award from CAMRA. B&B is also available (awaiting rating - see website for up to date information). The rest is up to you.

Licenced restaurant

CAMRA Commended bar

Open fires

Main Rd, Gwaelod y Garth, Cardiff, CF15 9HH

Tel: 029 20810408   **Email:** gwaelo-dinn@btconnect.com   **Website:** www.gwaelodinn.co.uk

Save on hotels. Book at **theAA.com/hotel**

CARDIFF 653 WALES

PICK OF THE PUBS

Caesars Arms

CREIGIAU Map 9 ST08

Cardiff Rd CF15 9NN ☎ 029 2089 0486
e-mail: info@caesarsarms.co.uk
web: www.caesarsarms.co.uk
dir: M4 junct 34, A4119 towards
Llantrisant/Rhondda. Approx 0.5m right
at lights signed Groesfaen. Through
Groesfaen, past Dynevor Arms pub. Next
left, signed Creigiau. 1m, left at T-junct,
pass Creigiau Golf Course. Pub 1m on
left

An upmarket country dining pub and
farm shop tucked away down winding
lanes just ten miles from Cardiff. The
whitewashed building is older than it
looks, and inside you'll find an
appealing bar and dining area, and fine
views over extensive gardens and
surrounding countryside from the
heated patio and terrace. There's so
much more here than the excellent ales
from Llanelli's Felinfoel Brewery and the
award-winning wine list, which extends
to more than 100 bottles. The pub has
its own beehives and makes its own
honey; the vegetables, herbs and salads
from its own gardens are used in the
kitchen, and there's an in-house
smokery, giving a truly local flavour. The
excellent farm shop is well stocked with
free-range eggs, rare-breed pork
products, honey from their hives, Welsh
cheeses, home-baked bread and chef's
ready prepared meals to take away. The
inn prides itself on the vast selection of
fresh fish, seafood, meat and game
displayed on shaven ice. Fresh seafood
is an undoubted strength, with
deliveries taken twice daily. Start with
Pembrokeshire dressed crab, tiger
prawns cooked in garlic, or scallops
with leek and bacon, then follow with
hake, salmon, John Dory, Dover sole
or lobster in season. For a real
showstopper, order sea bass baked
in rock salt – it will be theatrically
cracked open and filleted at your table.
Carnivores can choose from mountain
lamb, plus Carmarthenshire Welsh beef,
venison from the Brecon Beacons, and
free-range chickens from the Wye Valley.
Bajan fishcakes, or cherry-smoked duck
breast with organic beetroot give an
indication of the flavours that await in
this much favoured hostelry. There is
private parking for over 100 cars.

Open 12-2.30 6-10 (Sun 12-4) Closed:
25-26 Dec, 1 Jan, Sun eve **Bar Meals** L
served Mon-Sat 12-2.30 **Restaurant** L
served Mon-Sat 12-2.30, Sun 12-4 D
served Mon-Sat 6-10 Fixed menu price
fr £8.95 Av 3 course à la carte fr £25.95
⊕ FREE HOUSE ◆■ Felinfoel Double
Dragon, Brains Smooth, Guinness
Ö Gwynt y Ddraig Orchard Gold.
Facilities Children welcome Children's
portions Garden Parking 🚌

PICK OF THE PUBS

White Hart Thatched Inn & Brewery

LLANDDAROG   Map 8 SN51

SA32 8NT ☎ 01267 275395
e-mail: bestpubinwales@aol.com
web: www.thebestpubinwales.co.uk
dir: *A48, 6m E of Carmarthen towards
Swansea, onto B4310 signed
Llanddarog*

Built in 1371, this lovely old free house
has been run by the Coles family since
1994. It is thought to have started life
as a hostel for the stonemasons who
built the nearby village church – but the
White Hart has proved more durable, for
the church burnt down in 1850 and was
replaced by the present building a few
years later. Throughout its long history
the pub continued to cater for the
working population, and home-brewed
ale was an essential ingredient of the
cakes baked here for drovers attending
the famous Llanddarog fair. Nowadays
the bar is crammed with antiques,
including the heavily carved oak settles
beside the open log fire. The theme
continues in the converted barn that
forms the dining room, where a Towy
River coracle is amongst dozens of
artefacts decorating the high rafters.
Ales are brewed on-site using top-
quality malted barley, whole hop cones
and water from the 300-foot deep well;
Cwrw Blasus (meaning tasty ale) is
always available, along with a selection
of other cask-conditioned ales. Food at
the White Hart gets the same careful

attention – the business is now a
member of Prince Charles' exclusive
Welsh lamb club, and also serves
pedigree Welsh Black beef alongside its
own eggs and home-produced pork. The
varied menu offers bar snacks, steaks,
poultry and fish, whilst typical
blackboard specials might include
traditional Welsh cawl; belly pork with
vegetables; sea bass fillets in lemon
butter; hunter's chicken; and salmon in
sweet chilli. In summer, the flower-filled
patio garden is perfect for alfresco
dining. Children will enjoy the play area
and seeing the pigs, chickens, ducks
and turkeys on the small home farm.

Open 12-3.30 6-11 (Sun 12-3.30
7-10.30) Closed: Jan, Wed **Bar Meals** L

served Thu-Tue 11.30-3 D served Mon-
Tue & Thu-Sat 6.30-11, Sun 7-10
Restaurant L served Thu-Tue 11.30-3
D Mon-Tue & Thu-Sat 6.30-11, Sun 7-10
🛢 FREE HOUSE ◀ Coles Cwrw Blasus,
Roasted Barley Stout, Cwrw Llanddarog,
Bramling Cross & Swn y Dail Ö Seidr,
Carmarthen Gold. **Facilities** Children
welcome Children's menu Children's
portions Play area Garden Parking
🚌 (notice required)

Save on hotels. Book at **theAA.com/hotel**

CARMARTHENSHIRE 655 WALES

LLANDDAROG *continued*

White Hart Thatched Inn & Brewery
PICK OF THE PUBS

See Pick of the Pubs on opposite page

LLANDEILO   Map 8 SN62

The Angel Hotel

Rhosmaen St SA19 6EN ☎ 01558 822765
e-mail: capelbach@hotmail.com
dir: *In town centre next to post office*

In the heart of bustling Llandeilo, The Angel is handy for anyone browsing its boutiques or enjoying a walk in the stunning countryside that surrounds this small, historic town. Locals rest easy in the café-bar with its choice of real ales and lively events calendar; diners favour the thriving Y Capel Bach (The Little Chapel) bistro, where dishes could include chorizo, sautéed potato and balsamic salad followed by slow-roasted rabbit in a rich herb and garlic gravy, with baked banana cheesecake for dessert. The upstairs function room features memorable Sistine Chapel-like frescoes, whilst a secluded walled garden offers the ultimate escape. Booking for meals may be required.

Open 11.30-3 6-11 Closed: Sun **Bar Meals** L served Mon-Sat 11.30-2.30 D served Mon-Sat 6-9 Av main course £6.50 **Restaurant** L served Mon-Sat 11.30-2.30 D served Mon-Sat 6-9 Fixed menu price fr £13.50 Av 3 course à la carte fr £18 ⊕ FREE HOUSE ◀ Evan Evans, Tetley's. ♈ 10 **Facilities** ✿ Children welcome Children's menu Children's portions Garden Wi-fi ▭ (notice required)

LLANDOVERY   Map 9 SN73

The Kings Head NEW

1 Market Square SA20 0AB ☎ 01550 720393
e-mail: info@kingsheadcoachinginn.co.uk
dir: *M4 junct 49, A483 through Ammanford, Llandeilo onto A40 to Llandovery. Pub in town centre opposite market clock tower*

A family-run, former coaching inn on the edge of the Brecon Beacons National Park, with exposed beams and a wood-burning fire. Mondays to Fridays there's a £5 lunch deal – choose from pub classics like steak-and-ale pie, and faggots and mash, while on the regular menu are pan-fried cockles with Penclawdd laverbread; Welsh rump and rib-eye steaks; marinated chicken breast; venison steak with port and juniper sauce; fresh gnocchi arrabiata; and pan-seared salmon fillet. Evan Evans and guest real ales, with pool and darts.

Open all day all wk 10am-mdnt Closed: 25 Dec **Bar Meals** L served all wk 12-2.30 D served all wk 6-9.30 Av main course £7-£12 **Restaurant** L served all wk 12-2.30 D served all wk 6-9.30 ⊕ FREE HOUSE ◀ Evan Evans, Guest ales. **Facilities** ✿ Children welcome Children's menu Children's portions Parking Wi-fi ▭ (notice required)

LLANGADOG   Map 9 SN72

The Red Lion NEW

Church St SA19 9AA ☎ 01550 777357
e-mail: info@redlioncoachinginn.co.uk
dir: *A40 from Llandeilo towards Llandovery. Right at rdbt into Llangadog. 1m, pub on left*

A traditional coaching inn with a history reaching back to Cromwell's time, The Red Lion has been lovingly refurbished with an eye for its traditional features. Set in the beautiful Towy Valley, it's popular with locals and visitors alike. The menu caters for all comers with dishes ranging from taster-sized 'Welsh tid bits' (Glamorgan sausages; Welsh rarebit) to classy numbers such as Towy Valley lamb shank pot roasted in rosemary, port and red wine and served with chive potato mash and caramelised shallots. To finish, maybe hot chocolate and orange fondant.

Open all day all wk **Bar Meals** L served all wk 12-3 D served all wk 6-9.30 Av main course £11.50 **Restaurant** L served all wk 12-3 D served all wk 6-9.30 Fixed menu price fr £10 ⊕ FREE HOUSE ◀ Evan Evans Cwrw, Sharp's Doom Bar. **Facilities** ✿ Children welcome Children's menu Children's portions Parking Wi-fi ▭

LLANLLWNI   Map 8 SN43

Belle @ Llanllwni

SA40 9SQ ☎ 01570 480495
e-mail: mail@bellevueinn.co.uk
dir: *Midway between Carmarthen & Lampeter on A485*

Surrounded by countryside and with stunning views, this cosy and welcoming roadside inn sits on the A485 between Carmarthen and Lampeter. Head this way on a sunny day and dine alfresco. There are two rotating ales here to enjoy along with local bottled Welsh ciders. In the dining room, smoked mackerel and crayfish salad with lemon dressed leaves and roasted tomatoes may be followed by braised lamb shank with whisky and orange gravy on mash, finished with a sweet like winter berry bavarois with pomegranate water ice. Expect excellent ingredients including free-range local meats.

Open 12-3 5.30-11 Closed: Mon (ex BHs) **Bar Meals** L served Wed-Sat 12-3 D served Tue-Sun 6-9.30 Av main course £11 **Restaurant** L served Sun 12-3 D served Tue-Sun 6-9.30 Fixed menu price fr £9.95 Av 3 course à la carte fr £25 ⊕ FREE HOUSE ◀ Guinness, Guest ales ♻ Westons Stowford Press, Gwynt y Ddraig. **Facilities** Children welcome Children's menu Children's portions Parking ▭ (notice required)

NANTGAREDIG   Map 8 SN42

Y Polyn ◉◉
PICK OF THE PUBS

SA32 7LH ☎ 01267 290000
e-mail: ypolyn@hotmail.com
dir: *From A48 follow signs to National Botanic Garden of Wales. Then follow brown signs to Y Polyn*

With a trout fishery nearby, bracing walks in the Towy Valley just down the hill and the inspiring National Botanic Garden of Wales a mile or so up the road, this former tollhouse outside the attractive county town of Carmarthen is an established destination pub for lovers of Welsh food. West Wales is rapidly becoming one of the hotspots for organic and homespun cuisine, and the bounty of the local area is to the forefront in the tempting dishes that come from the modest kitchen here. Treats include roast rack of Machynlleth salt marsh lamb with onion, garlic and thyme purée; and potato, leek, courgette and goat's cheese pie. Warm plum and frangipane tart or baked sultana and nutmeg cheesecake served with a pear compôte seal the deal. All this has gained the inn two AA Rosettes for its accomplished country-pub cooking. The excellent beers come from Pontypridd. Booking for meals may be required.

Open all wk 12-4 7-11 Closed: Mon, Sun eve **Bar Meals** Av main course £14.50 **Restaurant** L served Tue-Sun 12-2 D served Tue-Sat 7-9 Fixed menu price fr £12.50 ⊕ FREE HOUSE ◀ Otley 01, 03 Boss. ♈ 12 **Facilities** Children welcome Children's portions Garden Parking Wi-fi

CEREDIGION

ABERAERON — Map 8 SN46

The Harbourmaster

PICK OF THE PUBS

Pen Cei SA46 0BT ☎ 01545 570755
e-mail: info@harbour-master.com
dir: *From A487. In Aberaeron follow Tourist Information Centre signs. Pub next door*

The harbourmaster's old house has been the focal point of Aberaeron's Georgian quayside since 1811. Its mauve walls harmonise perfectly with those of its pastel-coloured quayside neighbours, no two painted the same shade. The former grain store next door is now a relaxing bar overlooking the harbour – the perfect spot for a pint of Glaslyn, HM Best, a Welsh real cider or one of the 18 wines sold by the glass. The carefully chosen shades of the interior bring out the best in the original features, especially the listed spiral staircase and the Welsh slate. The kitchen's dishes feature carefully sourced produce, typically the bar menu's prawn and Cardigan Bay crab cocktail; and leek and Hafod cheese tartlet with beetroot salad. A three-course evening meal might be smoked haddock and cockle soup; shepherd's pie made with pan-roasted Welsh lamb cutlets and shoulder; and baked Alaska with raspberry sauce. Booking for meals may be required.

Open all day all wk 10am-11.30pm Closed: 25 Dec **Bar Meals** L served all wk 12-2.30 D served all wk 6-9 Av main course £14 **Restaurant** L served all wk 12-2.30 D served all wk 6.30-9 Av 3 course à la carte fr £30 ⊕ FREE HOUSE ◄ Purple Moose Glaslyn Ale, HM Best Bitter Ŏ Gwynt y Ddraig Black Dragon & Orchard Gold. ☂ 18 **Facilities** Children welcome Children's menu Children's portions Parking Wi-fi

LLWYNDAFYDD — Map 8 SN35

The Crown Inn & Restaurant

SA44 6BU ☎ 01545 560396
e-mail: thecrowninnandrestaurant@hotmail.co.uk
dir: *Off A487 NE of Cardigan*

Dating from 1799, this traditional Welsh longhouse has original beams, open fireplaces and a pretty restaurant. There's a carvery every Sunday and a varied menu with a good selection of dishes, including cranberry, mushroom and brie Wellington served with potato gratin, sautéed mushrooms and fine green beans; and trio of braised mixed sausages served on a bed of garlic mashed potato in a giant Yorkshire pudding with gravy and peas. Blackboard specials, a children's menu, light snacks and bar food are also available. Outside is a delightful, award-winning garden, while an easy walk down the lane leads to a cove with caves and National Trust cliffs.

Open all day all wk **Bar Meals** L served all wk 12-3 D served all wk 6-9 **Restaurant** L served all wk 12-3 D served all wk 6-9 ⊕ FREE HOUSE ◄ Flowers IPA,

Morland Old Speckled Hen, Cottage, Guest ales. ☂ 12 **Facilities** ❤ Children welcome Children's menu Children's portions Play area Family room Garden Parking ⇌ (notice required)

CONWY

BETWS-Y-COED — Map 14 SH75

Ty Gwyn Inn ★★★ INN

PICK OF THE PUBS

LL24 0SG ☎ 01690 710383 & 710787
e-mail: mratcl1050@aol.com
dir: *At junct of A5 & A470, 100yds S of Waterloo Bridge*

The Ratcliffe family has owned and run this former coaching inn for the past 28 years, and now Martin (the chef for all that time) and his wife Nicola are in charge. Located on the old London to Holyhead road, it was welcoming travellers long before Thomas Telford built his impressive cast iron Waterloo Bridge over the River Conwy opposite in 1815. Much of the original 17th-century character is evident inside. Real ales come from as near as Conwy's Great Orme brewery, as well as from much further afield. Martin's cooking relies heavily on quality local produce including home-grown veg. Typical starters range from slow-braised lamb's heart with rosemary and Burgundy gravy with horseradish mash; to confit of crispy aromatic duck with spicy Thai salad, sweet chilli, soy and sesame. Main courses have more of a European feel, with typical choices including lobster thermidor and pot-roasted chicken with Beaujolais, mushroom and fresh rosemary jus. Some of Nicola's own-designed en suite rooms have four-posters. Booking for meals may be required.

Open all wk 12-2 6.30-11 Closed: 1wk Jan **Bar Meals** L served all wk 12-2 D served all wk 6.30-9 Av main course £8.95-£21 **Restaurant** L served all wk 12-2 D served all wk 6.30-9 Fixed menu price fr £14.95 ⊕ FREE HOUSE ◄ Adnams Broadside, Brains The Rev. James, Morland Old Speckled Hen, Great Orme. **Facilities** Children welcome Children's menu Children's portions Parking Wi-fi ⇌ **Rooms** 13

BETWS-YN-RHOS — Map 14 SH97

The Wheatsheaf Inn

LL22 8AW ☎ 01492 680218
e-mail: wheatsheafinn@hotmail.co.uk
dir: *A55 to Abergele, take A548 to Llanrwst from High Street. 2m turn right B5381, 1m to Betws-yn-Rhos*

Although the building dates back to the 1200s, The Wheatsheaf was licensed as a coaching inn in the 17th-century, serving the mail route between Conwy and Chester. The pub oozes old-world character with oak beams and stone pillars. Bar snacks are served in addition to the restaurant menu, which makes good use of local produce. A starter of mussels in garlic and white wine might be followed by Welsh Black steak-and-ale pie. Booking for meals may be required.

Open Tue-Wed 6-10 Thu 6-11 Fri 5-11 Sat 12-11 Sun 12-10 Closed: Mon **Bar Meals** L served Sat 12-2 D served Tue-Sun 6-9 **Restaurant** L served Sat 12-2, Sun 12-8 D served Tue-Sat 6-9, Sun 12-8 ⊕ ENTERPRISE INNS ◄ Morland Old Speckled Hen, Caledonian Deuchars IPA, Sharp's Doom Bar, Black Sheep, Guinness Ŏ Kopparberg. **Facilities** ❤ Children welcome Children's menu Children's portions Family room Garden Parking ⇌ (notice required)

CAPEL CURIG — Map 14 SH75

Bryn Tyrch Inn **NEW**

LL24 0EL ☎ 01690 720223
e-mail: info@bryntyrchinn.co.uk
dir: *On A5, 6m from Betws-y-Coed*

Occupying an idyllic position in the heart of the Snowdonia National Park with breathtaking views of Snowdon and Moel Siabod, this remote hotel and bar is an ideal base for exploring the stunning mountains of the region. Welsh produce dominates the menu, which can be enjoyed in the informal bar or the terrace restaurant. Beef stew with leek dumplings; Welsh lamb burger and chips; and pan-fried salmon and smoked haddock chowder are typical choices. Look out for hog roasts in the garden during the summer. Booking for meals may be required.

Open all wk (L only wknds & hols) Closed: mid Dec-27 Dec, 3-21 Jan **Bar Meals** L served wknds & hols 12-3 D served all wk 6-9 Av main course £12.95 **Restaurant** L served wknds & hols 12-3 D served all wk 6-9 Av 3 course à la carte fr £30 ⊕ FREE HOUSE ◄ Purple Moose Dark Side of the Moose, Snowdonia. **Facilities** Children welcome Children's menu Children's portions Garden Parking Wi-fi

Cobdens Hotel ★★ SHL

LL24 0EE ☎ 01690 720243
e-mail: info@cobdens.co.uk
dir: *On A5, 5m W of Betws-y-Coed*

This 250-year-old inn sits at the foot of Moel Siabod in a beautiful mountain village deep in Snowdonia, with Snowdon itself a couple of miles down the valley. No surprise then that it's a haven for outdoor pursuit enthusiasts of all descriptions, taking refreshment, rebuilding their strength or enjoying live music in the famous Mountain Bar built into the rock face. Typical dishes include pear and endive salad with gorgonzola and walnuts; halibut steak Provençale with fine salad and new potatoes; and hearty meat options such as Welsh rib-eye steak with peppercorn sauce.

Open all day all wk 12-11 (Sun 12-10.30) Closed: 6-20 Jan **Bar Meals** L served all wk 12-2 D served all wk 6-9 Av main course £7.95 **Restaurant** L served all wk 12-2 D served all wk 6-9 Fixed menu price fr £12.95 Av 3 course à la carte fr £22.50 ⊕ FREE HOUSE ◄ Conwy Rampart, Cobdens Ale, Honey Fayre, Telford Porter, Guest ales Ŏ Rosie's Perfect Pear & Wicked Wasp. **Facilities** ❤ Children welcome Children's menu Children's portions Garden Parking Wi-fi ⇌ **Rooms** 17

Save on hotels. Book at **theAA.com/hotel**

CONWY 657 WALES

COLWYN BAY   Map 14 SH87

Pen-y-Bryn

PICK OF THE PUBS

Pen-y-Bryn Rd LL29 6DD ☎ 01492 533360
e-mail: pen.y.bryn@brunningandprice.co.uk
dir: *1m from A55. Follow signs to Welsh Mountain Zoo. Establishment at top of hill*

Looks can be deceiving. This unprepossessing 1970s building may look like a medical centre but step inside to find a handsomely refurbished interior, where you'll find a friendly and chatty atmosphere with local ales and cracking pub food served throughout the day. The interior has character in spades, with oak floors, open fires, rugs, bookcases and old furniture, whilst the stunning rear garden and terrace enjoy panoramic views over the sea and the Great Orme headland. The modern British menu offers a great choice of sandwiches and lighter meals, perhaps Welsh rarebit on thick toast with chutney, or you might opt for mussels cooked in white wine, garlic and cream. Main course options range from chargrilled chicken on tagliatelle with a spiced saffron butter sauce, to braised shoulder of lamb on crushed new potatoes with rosemary gravy. Chocolate brownie with chocolate sauce and ice cream, or lemon tart with fruit compôte will round things off nicely.

Open all day all wk **Bar Meals** L served Mon-Sat 12-9.30, Sun 12-9 D served Mon-Sat 12-9.30, Sun 12-9 Av main course £10.95 food served all day **Restaurant** L served Mon-Sat 12-9.30, Sun 12-9 D served Mon-Sat 12-9.30, Sun 12-9 food served all day ⊕ BRUNNING & PRICE ◀ Original, Purple Moose Snowdonia Ale, Great Orme Ö Aspall. ♚ 14 **Facilities** Children welcome Children's menu Children's portions Garden Beer festival Parking

CONWY   Map 14 SH77

The Groes Inn ★★★★★ INN ⬤

PICK OF THE PUBS

See Pick of the Pubs on page 658

DOLWYDDELAN   Map 14 SH75

Elen's Castle Hotel

LL25 0EJ ☎ 01690 750207
e-mail: stay@hotelinsnowdonia.co.uk
dir: *5m S of Betws-y-Coed, follow A470*

Elen's Castle was once owned by the Earl of Ancaster, who sold it to his gamekeeper. The latter opened it as a coaching inn around 1880, specialising in hunting parties. Now a family-run free house, it boasts an old-world bar with a wood-burning stove and an intimate restaurant with breathtaking views of the mountains and Lledr River. Sample dishes include chicken Cymru, a succulent chicken breast served in a leek, mushroom, cream and Caerphilly cheese sauce with seasonal vegetables; and Welsh Black beefburger served with chunky chips. Water from the on-site Roman well is said to have healing properties.

Open vary by season Closed: 1st 2wks Jan, wk days in quiet winter periods **Bar Meals** D served 6.30-9 Av main course £9 **Restaurant** D served 6.30-9 ⊕ FREE HOUSE ◀ Shepherd Neame Spitfire, Wychwood Hobgoblin, Brains, Worthington's, Black Sheep Ö Westons Stowford Press. **Facilities** Children welcome Children's menu Children's portions Play area Family room Garden Parking Wi-fi 🚌 (notice required)

LLANDUDNO JUNCTION   Map 14 SH77

The Queens Head

PICK OF THE PUBS

See Pick of the Pubs on page 659
See advert below

THE QUEEN'S HEAD

Glanwydden, Conwy, North Wales LL31 9JP • Tel: 01492 546570 • Fax: 01492 546487
Website: www.queensheadglanwydden.co.uk • Email: enquiries@queensheadglanwydden.co.uk

The village of Glanwydden is just five minutes' drive from the Victorian seaside resort of Llandudno. In the other direction lies Snowdonia National Park, making this 18th-century pub and restaurant well placed for both.

One of the finest and best-known inns in Wales, which attracts food lovers from far and wide, the old wheelwright's cottage has gone up in the world. Low beams, polished tables, walls strewn with maps and a roaring log fire in the bar. Professional chefs who have a passion for local produce prepare an impressive range of delicious dishes that in the summer might include fresh Conwy crab and Great Orme lobster. Friendly, smartly turned-out staff serves starters of crispy duck leg or Conwy fish soup, and mains of salmon and coriander fishcakes or Welsh rump steak, desserts might include bara brith bread and butter pudding. An impressive selection of wines and beers are available, and can be taken out on the pretty terrace on a hot summer's day.

Robert and Sally Cureton have been here for 29 years, nurturing a country local and their efforts paid off when they were awarded AA's Pub of the Year for Wales 2009–2010.

PICK OF THE PUBS

The Groes Inn ★★★★★ INN ✿

Ty'n-y-Groes LL32 8TN
☎ **01492 650545**
e-mail: reception@groesinn.com
web: www.groesinn.com
dir: *Exit A55 to Conwy, left at mini rdbt by Conwy Castle onto B5106, 2.5m inn on right*

As the first licensed house in Wales, this charming creeper-clad inn has been welcoming customers since 1573. It nestles between the easternmost summits of the Carneddau mountain range and the rich riverside pastures of the verdant Conwy Valley - Snowdonia at its most benign, with extraordinary views from the flowery gardens one good reason to linger; another is the range luxuriously appointed yet ultra traditional bedroom suites. Rambling rooms, beamed ceilings, careworn settles, military hats (there's a connection to the Duke of Wellington here), historic cooking utensils, a stag's head over an open fire – this inn has plenty to point out and even snigger over (namely, the saucy Victorian postcards) – but don't expect a jukebox, gaming machines or pool table. The walled town of Conwy is just two miles away and the front of the inn has magnificent views of the River Conwy and the hills behind, which rise towards Snowdonia. In spring and summer the flower-bedecked frontage and secluded gardens beckon; on colder days, take advantage of the real fire, which lends a warm glow to the cosy interior. Naturally there's a distinctly Welsh tilt to the menu, awarded one AA Rosette, with lamb and game from nearby estates and an infinitely varied selection of fruits of the sea brought in through Conwy's quay or Anglesey's boats; try the seafood pie, fishcakes or the smoked fish platter. Other options could include Welsh rarebit or garlic stilton mushrooms to start, followed by winter root vegetable stew with cheddar dumplings; chicken curry; or cottage pie with cheddar mash. For pudding, try rice pudding with fresh cream and strawberry jam or orange syllabub with lemon shortbread. Be sure to taste the beers, which mostly come from the Great Orme micro-brewery.

Open all wk 12-3 6-11 **Bar Meals** L served all wk 12-2 D served all wk 6.30-9 Av main course £12 **Restaurant** L served all wk 12-2 D served all wk 6.30-9 Fixed menu price fr £18 ⊕ FREE HOUSE ◀ Burton Ale, Great Orme Welsh Black, Orme & Groes Ale, Tetley's ♂ Westons Stowford Press. ♟ 14 **Facilities** Children's menu Children's portions Family room Garden Parking Wi-fi ▭ (notice required) **Rooms 14**

Save on hotels. Book at **theAA.com/hotel**

CONWY 659 | WALES

PICK OF THE PUBS

The Queens Head

LLANDUDNO JUNCTION   Map 14 SH77

Glanwydden LL31 9JP
☎ **01492 546570**
e-mail: enquiries@
queensheadglanwydden.co.uk
web: www.queensheadglanwydden.
co.uk
dir: *A55 onto A470 towards Llandudno.
At 3rd rdbt right towards Penrhyn Bay,
2nd right into Glanwydden, pub on left*

A former AA Pub of the Year for Wales,
this charming country pub is located in
a pretty rural village just a five-minute
drive from the Victorian seaside town of
Llandudno. Once the storehouse of the
Llangwestennin Parish, this early 18th-
century pub is perfectly situated for
country walks, cycling, or a day on the
beach. The Queens Head continues to
attract discerning customers with its
warm welcome, effortless charm and
excellent service. The stylish terrace is
great for summer evenings, whilst on
colder nights the relaxed atmosphere in
the bar is perfect for a pre-dinner drink
by the log fire; real ales include Great
Orme brews, and the lip-smacking wine
list with description notes on the back
of the menu has plenty of choice. The
dedicated kitchen makes excellent use
of local produce in varied menus that
might include a starter of Conwy fish
soup finished with brandy and tomato;
award-winning smoked breast of
Barbary duck with tomato and red onion

chutney; or deep-fried Welsh brie with
home-made cranberry and orange
chutney. Local fish and seafood is the
cornerstone of the menu and typical
examples are home-made salmon and
coriander fishcakes; seared Anglesey
king scallops with pea purée, pancetta
and rocket or baked fillet of cod topped
with Welsh rarebit served with creamy
leeks, roasted vine tomatoes and chunky
chips. Meat-lovers and vegetarians are
certainly not overlooked, with the likes
of home-made steak, mushroom and ale
pie; grilled pork and leek sausages and
chargrilled haloumi with roasted
pepper, vine tomatoes, asparagus and
dauphinoise potatoes. Booking for
meals may be required.

Open all wk 11.30-3 6-10.30 (Sat-Sun
11.30-10.30) **Bar Meals** L served Mon-
Fri 12-2, Sat-Sun 12-9 D served Mon-Fri
6-9, Sat-Sun 12-9 **Restaurant** L served
Mon-Fri 12-2, Sat-Sun 12-9 D served
Mon-Fri 6-9, Sat-Sun 12-9 ⊕ FREE
HOUSE ◀ Great Orme. ♀ 10
Facilities Children's portions Garden
Parking 🚌

LLANELIAN-YN-RHÔS	Map 14 SH87

The White Lion Inn

LL29 8YA ☎ **01492 515807**
e-mail: info@whitelioninn.co.uk
dir: *A55 junct 22, left signed Old Colwyn, A547. At rdbt 2nd exit onto B5383 signed Betwys-yn-Rhos. In 1m turn right into Llanelian Rd, follow to village. Pub on right*

At the crossroads of the hamlet of Llanelian, a place with plenty of history around St Elian's Well, you'll find this traditional family-run inn. It still retains its original slate floor and oak-beamed ceiling, and there is an old salt cellar by the inglenook fireplace. The Cole family have restored and preserved many aspects of traditional village life revolving around the pub, including reinstating the snug next to the bar. The food is traditional, home cooked, and wherever possible locally sourced, including of course shoulder of Welsh lamb. Other dishes on the comprehensive main menu and specials board include wholetail scampi with chips, and shortcrust steak-and-kidney pie. Booking for meals may be required.

Open Tue-Fri 11.30-3 6-11 (Sat 11.30-4 6-11.30 Sun 12-10.30) Closed: Mon (ex BHs) **Bar Meals** L served Tue-Sat 12-2, Sun 12-9 D served Tue-Sat 6-9, Sun 12-9 Av main course £9.95 **Restaurant** L served Tue-Sat 12-2, Sun 12-9 D served Tue-Sat 6-9, Sun 12-9 ⊕ FREE HOUSE ◀ Marston's Pedigree, Mansfield Smooth Creamy Ale & Dark Mild, Guest ale. ♥ 11 **Facilities** Children welcome Children's menu Children's portions Garden Parking Wi-fi ▥ (notice required)

LLANNEFYDD	Map 14 SH97

The Hawk & Buckle Inn

LL16 5ED ☎ **01745 540249**
e-mail: enquiries@hawkandbuckleinn.com
dir: *Telephone for directions*

From high in the north Wales hills, this lovingly restored 17th-century coaching inn enjoys spectacular views across the local countryside to Blackpool Tower and beyond. The real ale selection includes The Rev. James and Conwy Celebration, and fresh local produce is used wherever possible to create dishes such as chicken, wild mushroom and broccoli pasta bake; or the 8oz Hawk burger topped with Welsh cheese and smoked bacon. Substantial afternoon teas feature sandwiches, Bara Brith, home-made Welsh cakes and scones with jam and cream. Booking for meals may be required.

Open all wk Mon-Tue & Thu-Fri 6-11 Wed 12-3 Sat 6-12 Sun 12-6 (summer Mon-Tue & Thu-Fri 6-11 Wed 12-3 Sat 12-12 Sun 12-10.30) **Bar Meals** L served Wed 12-3, Sat 6-9, Sun 12-6 (winter), Wed 12-3, Sat-Sun 12-9 (summer) D served Mon-Sat 6-9 (Sat-Sun summer 12-9) **Restaurant** L served Wed 12-3, Sat 6-9, Sun 12-6 (winter), Wed 12-3, Sat-Sun 12-9 (summer) D served Mon-Sat 6-9 (Sat-Sun summer 12-9) ⊕ FREE HOUSE ◀ Brains The Rev. James, Purple Moose Glaslyn Ale, Conwy Celebration Ale. **Facilities** Parking Wi-fi

TREFRIW	Map 14 SH76

The Old Ship NEW

High St LL27 0JH ☎ **01492 640013**
e-mail: rhian.barlow@btopenworld.com
dir: *From A470 between Tal-y-Bont & Betws-y-Coed follow Trefriw signs*

Situated in a peaceful village in the wooded eastern edge of the Snowdonia National Park, this traditional inn is the perfect refuelling stop following a tramp in the hills. Warm up by the log fire with a refreshing pint of Purple Moose Glaslyn Ale and peruse the daily chalkboard menu. Using locally sourced ingredients, freshly prepared dishes take in steaming bowl of Conwy mussels cooked in garlic, white wine and cream, followed by Spanish-style hake casserole, oxtail braised in ale with mash and vegetables, and sticky toffee pudding for dessert.

Open 12-3 6-11 (Sat-Sun 12-11) Closed: Mon (ex BHs) **Bar Meals** L served Tue-Sat 12-2.30, Sun 12-9 D served Tue-Sat 6-9, Sun 12-9 Av main course £8.95 ⊕ FREE HOUSE ◀ Banks's Bitter, Purple Moose Glaslyn Ale, Bragdyr Nant Cwrw Coryn, Great Orme. ♥ **Facilities** Children welcome Children's menu Children's portions Garden Parking

DENBIGHSHIRE	

LLANELIDAN	Map 15 SJ15

The Leyland Arms NEW

LL15 2PT ☎ **01824 750822**
e-mail: info@leylandarms.co.uk
dir: *Midway between Ruthin & Gwyddelwern on A494, turn left to Llanelidan. Pub next to church*

Overlooking the cricket pitch and adjacent to St Elidan church in sleepy Llanelidan, deep in the Clwydian Hill, The Leyland Arms is the heart and soul of the village. A true community pub, it's the home of the cricket team and the annual nativity play is held in the stables at the back of the pub. In summer enjoy the views from the terraced garden and hunker down by the fire in winter with a pint Thwaites Original. Food is prepared from locally sourced ingredients and the daily menu may include salmon, crab, lime and ginger fishcake salad; beef and ale pie; and apple and pear crumble with custard.

Open 12-3 6-11 Closed: Mon **Bar Meals** L served Tue-Sun 12-3 D served Tue-Sat 6-9 Av main course £7-£10 **Restaurant** L served Tue-Sun 12-2.30 D served Tue-Sun 6-9 Fixed menu price fr £10 ⊕ FREE HOUSE ◀ Thwaites Original & Triple C, Guest ale ♻ Kingstone Press. ♥ 12 **Facilities** Children welcome Children's portions Garden Parking Wi-fi ▥ (notice required)

RHEWL	Map 15 SJ16

The Drovers Arms, Rhewl

Denbigh Rd LL15 2UD ☎ **01824 703163**
dir: *1.3m from Ruthin on A525*

A small countryside village pub whose name recalls a past written up and illustrated on storyboards displayed inside. Main courses are divided on the menu into poultry, traditional meat, fish, grills and vegetarian; examples from each section are chicken in tarragon sauce; Welsh lamb's liver and onions; Vale of Clwyd sirloin steak; home-made fish pie; and mushroom Stroganoff. Ales are from J W Lees, including Coronation Street, and can be enjoyed in the garden in summer.

Open all wk 12-3 5.30-11 (Sat 12-3 5.30-12 Sun 12-11 Jun-Sep all day) Closed: Tue L ⊕ J W LEES ◀ Bitter, Coronation Street. **Facilities** Children welcome Children's menu Children's portions Play area Family room Garden Parking Wi-fi

ST ASAPH	Map 15 SJ07

The Plough Inn

The Roe LL17 0LU ☎ **01745 585080**
e-mail: ploughsa@gmail.com
dir: *Exit A55 at Rhyl/St Asaph signs, left at rdbt, pub 200yds on left*

In Simon Rodenhurst's ten years at this 18th-century coaching inn, his first-floor open kitchen has prepared more than half a million meals. The bar is traditional, with open fires, rustic furniture and real ales from North Wales; the restaurant, though modern, retains a vaulted ceiling from its days as a ballroom. Dine here on poached chicken with goat's cheese and chorizo; honey-glazed pork chop with bubble-and-squeak; fish of the day; or leek and cheese croquettes, and help Simon towards his millionth meal. There's live music on Friday nights. Booking for meals may be required.

Open all day all wk **Bar Meals** L served 12-9 D served 12-9 Av main course £10 food served all day **Restaurant** L served 12-9 D served 7-11 Fixed menu price fr £12.95 Av 3 course à la carte fr £17.70 ⊕ FREE HOUSE ◀ Conwy, Great Orme, Plassey. ♥ 10 **Facilities** Children welcome Children's menu Children's portions Garden Parking Wi-fi ▥

Save on hotels. Book at **theAA.com/hotel**

FLINTSHIRE – GWYNEDD 661 | WALES

FLINTSHIRE

BABELL — Map 15 SJ17

Black Lion Inn

CH8 8PZ ☎ 01352 720239
e-mail: theblacklioninn@btinternet.com
dir: *A55 junct 31 to Caerwys. Left at x-roads signed Babell. In 3m turn right*

From its stunning rural location, this 13th-century free house commands breathtaking views across the surrounding Area of Outstanding Natural Beauty. The former coaching inn has a chilling history of ghost stories – nowadays, offset by the warmth of the welcome, the comfy sofas and a cosy open fire. Locally brewed cask ales complement the appealing modern British menu, featuring dishes like Welsh lamb shank with minted potato crush. Wednesday is traditional pie night, and the pub takes part in the annual Ale Trail around ten local pubs in late April.

Open all day Closed: Mon, Tue **Bar Meals** L served Wed-Sun 12-9 D served Wed-Sun 12-9 Av main course £10.95 food served all day **Restaurant** L served Wed-Sun 12-9 D served Wed-Sun 12-9 Av 3 course à la carte fr £23.95 food served all day ⊕ FREE HOUSE ◀ Purple Moose Myrica Gale, Black Lion Bitter, Great Orme Celtica. ♟ 8 **Facilities** Children welcome Children's menu Children's portions Play area Garden Beer festival Parking ▭ (notice required)

CILCAIN — Map 15 SJ16

White Horse Inn

CH7 5NN ☎ 01352 740142
e-mail: christine.jeory@btopenworld.com
dir: *From Mold take A541 towards Denbigh. After approx 6m turn left*

This 400-year-old pub is the last survivor of five originally to be found in this lovely hillside village, probably because it was the centre of the local gold-mining industry in the 19th century. Today, the White Horse is popular with walkers, cyclists and horse-riders. Food here is home made by the landlord's wife using the best quality local ingredients, and is accompanied by a good range of real ales. A typical meal might start with garlic and ginger breaded prawns with curry mayonnaise, followed by home-made steak-and-kidney pie or, for a vegetarian option, three-bean smokey chilli served with basmati rice.

Open all wk 12-3 6.30-11 (Sat 12-11 Sun 12-10.30) **Bar Meals** L served Mon-Sat 12-2.15, Sun 12-3 D served all wk 7-9 Av main course £8 ⊕ FREE HOUSE ◀ Marston's Pedigree, Banks's Bitter, Timothy Taylor Landlord, Bass, Archers Gold, Fuller's London Pride. ♟ 9 **Facilities** ✿ Garden Parking

MOLD — Map 15 SJ26

Glasfryn

PICK OF THE PUBS

Raikes Ln, Sychdyn CH7 6LR ☎ 01352 750500
e-mail: glasfryn@brunningandprice.co.uk
dir: *From Mold follow signs to Theatr Clwyd, 1m from town centre*

On a hilltop overlooking Mold, Glasfryn was built as a judge's residence in about 1900; the market town's popular theatre is just over the road. Rescued by the present owners at the end of the last century, it's been transformed into a busy pub attracting everybody from holidaymakers to farmers and business people. Locals wouldn't miss its two beer festivals: the first, in March, celebrates Welsh food and drink; in October it's the turn of British Pie Week together with Champion Beers of Britain. The pub's 12 real ale pumps are the tip of the refreshment iceberg – the wine and malt whisky lists are comprehensive too. Why not have a bite to eat in the bright open interior with polished furniture, or out in the attractively landscaped garden? A mature cheddar rarebit with green salad, perhaps, or a dish of home-smoked duck with red chard, will make your visit memorable. Booking for meals may be required.

Open all day all wk **Bar Meals** L served Mon-Sat 12-9.30, Sun 12-9 D served Mon-Sat 12-9.30, Sun 12-9 food served all day **Restaurant** L served Mon-Sat 12-9.30, Sun 12-9 D served Mon-Sat 12-9.30, Sun 12-9 food served all day ⊕ BRUNNING & PRICE ◀ Purple Moose Snowdonia Ale, Flowers Original. ♟ 16 **Facilities** ✿ Children welcome Children's portions Garden Beer festival Parking ▭ (notice required)

NORTHOP — Map 15 SJ26

Stables Bar Restaurant

CH7 6AB ☎ 01352 840577
e-mail: info@soughtonhall.co.uk
dir: *From A55, take A119 through Northop*

This unusual free house dates from the 18th century and was created from Soughton Hall's stable block, and original features like the cobbled floors and roof timbers remain intact; the magnificent main house was built as a bishop's palace. The selection of real ales includes Stables Bitter, or diners can browse the wine shop for a bottle to accompany their meal. The Classic menu offers ciabatta sandwiches, platters to share and hearty main courses, while the seasonal à la carte dinner menu features perhaps chicken, chorizo and polenta croquette on red onion relish with crispy pancetta. Enjoy the gardens in summer. Booking for meals may be required.

Open all day all wk **Bar Meals** L served all wk 12-9.30 D served all wk 12-9.30 Av main course £11.95 food served all day **Restaurant** L served Sun 12-4 D served all wk 7-9.30 Fixed menu price fr £14.95 Av 3 course à la carte fr £28.95 ⊕ FREE HOUSE ◀ Coach House Honeypot Best Bitter & Dick Turpin Premium Bitter, Plassey Bitter, Stables Bitter. **Facilities** Children welcome Children's menu Children's portions Family room Garden Parking Wi-fi ▭

GWYNEDD

ABERDYFI — Map 14 SN69

Penhelig Arms Hotel & Restaurant

PICK OF THE PUBS

Terrace Rd LL35 0LT ☎ 01654 767215
e-mail: info@penheligarms.com
web: www.penheligarms.com
dir: *On A493, W of Machynlleth*

This popular waterside inn is perfectly situated for visitors to Cader Idris, the Snowdonia National Park and several historic castles in the area. The Penhelig Arms has been serving travellers and locals since 1870 and offers spectacular views over the tidal Dyfi Estuary. Music and TV-free, the wood-panelled and log-fire-warmed Fisherman's Bar is a cosy bolt-hole to enjoy Brains real ales and bar meals such as creamed cockles and bacon on toast. The award-winning waterfront restaurant offers a more brasserie-style experience and menus showcase the abundant local seafood and Welsh beef and lamb. A typical menu might include crab cakes with aïoli and lime; baked loin of cod with wilted spinach, butternut squash and sweet potato dauphinoise, Puy lentils and lemon oil; or braised beef brisket with carrot and swede mash, braised red cabbage and gravy. Leave room for the Baileys cheesecake. The short wine list is attractively priced. Booking for meals may be required.

Open all day all wk Closed: 25 Dec **Bar Meals** L served all wk 12-2 (Jun-Sep 12-9) D served all wk 6-9 Av main course £9.95 **Restaurant** L served all wk 12-2 D served all wk 7-9 Av 3 course à la carte fr £23 ⊕ BRAINS ◀ Bitter & The Rev. James, Guest ale Ŏ Westons Stowford Press, Thatchers Katy. ♟ 20 **Facilities** ✿ Children welcome Children's menu Children's portions Garden Parking Wi-fi ▭ (notice required)

BEDDGELERT   Map 14 SH54

Tanronnen Inn ★★★★ INN

LL55 4YB ☎ 01766 890347
e-mail: guestservice@tanronnen.co.uk
dir: *In village centre opposite river bridge*

Originally part of the Beddgelert Estate, this stone-built building was the stables for the passing coach trade in 1809; after conversion to a cottage, it opened as a beer house in 1830. By the end of the 19th century, it had two letting bedrooms and was serving meals for visitors. Badly damaged by flooding in 1906, the shop at the back was incorporated to provide more accommodation. Today's inn has two attractive small bars serving Robinsons ales, a large lounge with open fire, a dining room open to non-residents in which to enjoy home-cooked meals, and attractive accommodation.

Open all day all wk ⊕ FREDERIC ROBINSON ◀ Unicorn, Dizzy Blonde. **Facilities** Children welcome Children's menu Children's portions Parking **Rooms** 7

BLAENAU FFESTINIOG   Map 14 SH74

The Miners Arms

Llechwedd Slate Caverns LL41 3NB ☎ 01766 830306
e-mail: bookings@llechwedd.co.uk
dir: *From Llandudno take A470 S. Through Betwys-y-Coed, 16m to Blaenau Ffestiniog*

Housed in two former miners' cottages on the site of Llechwedd Slate Caverns, this welcoming pub is a great place to finish an underground tour, where you can glimpse the life of a Victorian slate quarryman. Slate floors, open fires and staff in Victorian costume emphasise the heritage theme and this extends to the menu which includes tasty home-made soup, sandwiches, a 'traditional miner's lunch' and lobsgows, a local speciality stew that reputedly dates back to Blaenau Ffestiniog's trading links with Hamburg. Welsh treats such as bara brith (a moist fruit bread) and Welsh cakes are also available.

Open all wk 10-5.45 Closed: Oct-Etr **Bar Meals** L served all wk 11-4 ⊕ FREE HOUSE ◀ Purple Moose. **Facilities** Children welcome Children's portions Play area Family room Garden Parking 🚌

CAERNARFON   Map 14 SH46

Black Boy Inn ★★★★ INN

Northgate St LL55 1RW ☎ 01286 673604
e-mail: office@black-boy-inn.com
web: www.black-boy-inn.com
dir: *A55 junct 9 onto A487, follow signs for Caernarfon. Within town walls between castle & Victoria Dock*

Character oozes from the very fabric of this ancient inn, one of the oldest in Wales (built 1522) and standing within the town walls in the shadow of the unforgettable Caernarfon Castle. Outside all gables and flower displays; within are restful real-fire warmed, low-ceilinged rooms sewn amidst beams and struts rescued from old ships. Meat and other products are generally local, and dishes from a recent menu include hand-battered cod, dressed crab meat, fiery dragon chicken curry, stokers lamb cobbler and baked whole aubergine filled with honey-roasted vegetables. The well-proportioned bedrooms are an ideal base from which to explore the Lleyn Peninsula or catch the newly reopened Welsh Highland Railway.

Open all day all wk **Bar Meals** L served 12-9 D served 12-9 Av main course £6 food served all day **Restaurant** L served 12-9 D served 12-9 food served all day ⊕ FREE HOUSE ◀ Purple Moose Snowdonia Ale, Brains The Rev. James, Hancock's. **Facilities** Children welcome Children's menu Children's portions Play area Garden Parking Wi-fi 🚌 **Rooms** 15

LLANBEDR   Map 14 SH52

Victoria Inn ★★★★ INN

LL45 2LD ☎ 01341 241213
e-mail: junevicinn@aol.com
dir: *On A496 between Barmouth and Harlech*

Fascinating features for pub connoisseurs are the circular wooden settle, ancient stove, grandfather clock and flagged floors in the atmospheric bar of the Victoria. Home-made food is served in the lounge bar and restaurant, complemented by a range of Robinsons traditional ales. A children's play area has been incorporated into the well-kept garden, with a playhouse, slides and swings. Situated beside the River Artro, the Rhinog mountain range and the famous Roman Steps are right on the doorstep. If you would like to explore the area, there are five spacious and thoughtfully furnished bedrooms.

Open all day all wk 11-11 (Sun 12-10.30) **Bar Meals** L served Mon-Fri 12-3, Sat-Sun 12-9 D served Mon-Fri 5-9, Sat-Sun 12-9 ⊕ FREDERIC ROBINSON ◀ Unicorn, Guest ales Ö Westons Stowford Press. ♀10 **Facilities** Children welcome Children's menu Children's portions Play area Garden Parking 🚌 (notice required) **Rooms** 5

PENNAL   Map 14 SH60

Glan yr Afon/Riverside NEW

Riverside Hotel SY20 9DW ☎ 01654 791285
e-mail: info@riversidehotel-pennal.co.uk
dir: *3m from Machynlleth on A493 towards Aberdovey. Pub on left*

Since taking over this riverside free house, set beside the River Sychan in sleepy Pennal village, Glyn and Corina Davies have spruced up and transformed the interior adding slate floors, modern light oak furnishings and bold funky fabrics. There's a wood-burning stove pumping out heat in winter, Dark Side of the Moose ale on tap, and a good range of modern pub food on the menu. Relax and opt for a starter fishcake with chilli and lime mayonnaise, then a hearty fish stew or Welsh Black sirloin steak with creamy peppercorn sauce, before tucking into a chocolate and pear tart. Booking for meals may be required.

Open all wk 12-3 6-11 Closed: 25-26 Dec, 2wks Jan **Bar Meals** L served all wk 12-2 D served all wk 6-9 Av main course £12.95 **Restaurant** L served all wk 12-2 D served all wk 6-9 Av 3 course à la carte fr £24.50 ⊕ FREE HOUSE ◀ Sharp's Doom Bar, Purple Moose Dark Side of the Moose & Snowdonia Ale, Salopian Golden Thread, Stonehouse Ö Westons Stowford Press. ♀12 **Facilities** 🌸 Children welcome Children's menu Children's portions Garden Parking Wi-fi 🚌 (notice required)

TUDWEILIOG
Map 14 SH23

Lion Hotel

LL53 8ND ☎ **01758 770244**
e-mail: martlee.lion@gmail.com
dir: *A487 from Caernarfon onto A499 towards Pwllheli. Right onto B4417 to Nefyn, onto Edern then onto Tudweiliog*

Run by the Lee family for the past 40 years, the Lion stands in an Lleyn Peninsula Area of Outstanding Natural Beauty three miles from Nefyn Golf Club and a ten-minute walk from the beach. The bar features an extensive list of whiskies alongside ales from the Purple Moose brewery. A typical menu might offer peeled prawns in garlic butter; steak-and-kidney pie; spare ribs in barbecue sauce; and spinach and ricotta cannelloni. The large garden and children's play area makes the pub especially popular with cyclists, walkers and families.

Open all wk 11-3 6-11 (summer all day) **Bar Meals** L served all wk 12-2 D served all wk 6-9 Av main course £9.50 ⊕ FREE HOUSE ◖ Cwrw Llyn Brenin Enlli, Big Bog, Purple Moose, Guinness. **Facilities** Children welcome Children's menu Children's portions Play area Family room Garden Parking Wi-fi 🚐 (notice required)

WAUNFAWR
Map 14 SH55

Snowdonia Parc Brewpub & Campsite

LL55 4AQ ☎ **01286 650409 & 650218**
e-mail: info@snowdonia-park.co.uk
dir: *Telephone for directions*

In the heart of Snowdonia, a short drive from Mount Snowdon, this popular walkers' pub is located at Waunfawr Station on the Welsh Highland Railway. There are steam trains on site (the building was originally the stationmaster's house), plus a micro-brewery and campsite. Home-cooked food ranges from chicken, leek and ham pie to vegetable curry and roast Welsh beef with all the trimmings. Naturally the pub serves its own Welsh Highland Bitter along with other ales. The Welsh Highland Railway Rail Ale Festival is held in mid-May.

Open all day all wk 11-11 (Fri-Sat 11am-11.30pm) **Bar Meals** food served all day **Restaurant** food served all day ⊕ FREE HOUSE ◖ Snowdonia Welsh Highland Bitter, Summer Ale, Carmen Sutra & Gwyrfai. **Facilities** Children welcome Children's menu Play area Family room Garden Beer festival Parking Wi-fi 🚐 (notice required)

ABERGAVENNY
Map 9 SO21

Clytha Arms

PICK OF THE PUBS

See Pick of the Pubs on page 664

LLANGYBI
Map 9 ST39

The White Hart Village Inn ◉◉

PICK OF THE PUBS

See Pick of the Pubs on page 665

LLANTRISANT
Map 9 ST39

The Greyhound Inn

PICK OF THE PUBS

NP15 1LE ☎ **01291 672505 & 673447**
e-mail: enquiry@greyhound-inn.com
web: www.greyhound-inn.com
dir: *M4 junct 24, A449 towards Monmouth, exit at 1st junct signed Usk. 2nd left for Llantrisant. Or from Monmouth A40, A449 exit for Usk. In Usk left into Twyn Sq follow Llantrisant signs. 2.5m under A449 bridge. Inn on right*

Established as a country inn in 1845, The Greyhound Inn was originally a 17th-century Welsh longhouse and part of a 400-acre farm. In the same family's hands for the past three decades, the pub has two acres of award-winning beautiful gardens, a four-acre paddock and an array of restored outbuildings. The lounges are served by one bar with a range of real ales including a monthly guest, and ciders such as Wales' own Gwynt y Ddraig. Owner Nick Davies heads the kitchen team; enjoy the fruits of their labours in one of the four eating areas, one of which is a candlelit dining room. Dishes range from old favourites such as steak-and-kidney pie or home-cooked ham with peas and chips to freshly grilled local trout with garden peas and chipped potatoes, or Brazil nut and spinach roast with a fresh salad and coconut korma sauce. There's also a selection from the grill. Booking for meals may be required.

Open all day 11-11 Closed: 25 & 31 Dec, 1 Jan, Sun eve **Bar Meals** L served all wk 12-2.15 D served Mon-Sat 6-10 Av main course £9.50 **Restaurant** L served all wk 12-2.15 D served Mon-Sat 6-10 Av 3 course à la carte fr £22.50 ⊕ FREE HOUSE ◖ Flowers Original & Bass, Greene King Abbot Ale, Guest ale Ŏ Gwynt y Ddraig, Kingstone Press. ♟ 10 **Facilities** ♥ Children welcome Children's menu Family room Garden Parking Wi-fi 🚐

LLANVAIR DISCOED
Map 9 ST49

The Woodlands Tavern Country Pub & Dining

PICK OF THE PUBS

NP16 6LX ☎ **01633 400313**
e-mail: info@thewoodlandstavern.co.uk
dir: *5m from Caldicot & Magor*

The Woodlands Tavern is a friendly, family-run village free house at the foot of Gray Hill, close to the Roman fortress town of Caerwent and walking trails through Wentwood Forest. A patio ensures that food and drink can be served outside in fine weather. As well as being popular with walkers, cyclists and fishermen who quench their thirsts with pints of Felinfoel, Bevan's Bitter and regularly changing guest ales, The Woodlands draws diners from far and wide for its modern British menu and daily chalkboard specials. Typically, you can tuck into a platter of smoked salmon and Portland crab, and follow that with a duo of lamb – slow-braised shoulder and loin chop. Fish specials appear on the blackboard: perhaps pan-fried tiger prawns with garlic, lemon and sweet chilli sauce. The popular Sunday three-course lunch will probably feature roast sirloin of beef with Yorkshire pudding. Apple pie with creamy custard is an irresistible pud with which to finish. Booking for meals may be required.

Open 12-3 6-12 (Sun 12-4) Closed: 1 Jan, Sun eve, Mon **Bar Meals** L served Tue-Fri 12-2, Sat 12-2.30, Sun 12-4 D served Tue-Fri 6-9, Sat 6-9.30 **Restaurant** L served Tue-Fri 12-2, Sat 12-2.30, Sun 12-4 D served Tue-Fri 6-9, Sat 6-9.30 ⊕ FREE HOUSE ◖ Rhymney Bevan's Bitter, Felinfoel, Guest ales. ♟ 10 **Facilities** ♥ Children welcome Children's menu Children's portions Parking Wi-fi 🚐 (notice required)

PICK OF THE PUBS

Clytha Arms

ABERGAVENNY Map 9 SO21

Clytha NP7 9BW ☎ 01873 840206
e-mail: theclythaarms@btinternet.com
web: www.clytha-arms.com
dir: *From A449/A40 junction (E of Abergavenny) follow 'Old Road Abergavenny/Clytha' signs*

Tucked away off the old Abergavenny to Raglan road, this eye-catching converted dower house stands on the edge of parkland dotted with small woods and the occasional folly. There are enchanting views from the large garden across the lush Vale of Gwent towards Blorenge Mountain and the shapely Skirrid Hill, whilst the Usk Valley Walk follows the nearby river. The main bar is full of character, with old pews, tables and rustic furnishings, as well as posters and a wood-burning stove. The pub is renowned for its range of real ales, with Wye Valley Bitter and over 300 guest ales every year supporting some great artisan ciders and perrys. Drinkers who feel the need for a little more choice can enjoy the Clytha's annual Welsh Cider Festival, or the Welsh Beer, Cheese and Music festival, held over the late May and August Bank Holiday weekends respectively. Grazers can have a simple tapas from Andrew Canning's widely fêted gastro-pub menu, or tuck into a full restaurant meal accompanied by a choice of over 100 wines, including a

white from the nearby Monnow Valley vineyard. Starters like grilled oysters with laverbread and Caerphilly; or charcuterie with celeriac salad might herald a main course of stuffed ham with cider sauce and sauté potatoes; Caerphilly and walnut stuffed aubergine with basil risotto; or wild boar and duck cassoulet. Mango brûlée with coconut ice cream is a typical choice for dessert. Local attractions include Raglan Castle, as well as golf, fishing and countryside walks.

Open 12-3 6-12 (Fri-Sun 12-12) Closed: 25 Dec, Mon L **Bar Meals** L served Tue-Sun 12.30-2.30 D served Mon-Sat 7-9.30 Av main course £14.50 **Restaurant** L served Tue-Sun

12.30-2.30 D served Mon-Sat 7-9.30 Fixed menu price fr £21.50 Av 3 course à la carte fr £27.50 ⊕ FREE HOUSE
🛢 Banks's Mild, Rhymney Bitter, Wye Valley Bitter, 4 Guest ales (300+ per year) ⚑ Gwynt y Ddraig Black Dragon, Ragan Perry, Clytha Perry. ⚲ 12
Facilities Children welcome Children's menu Children's portions Play area Garden Beer festival Parking Wi-fi 🚌

Save on hotels. Book at **theAA.com/hotel**

MONMOUTHSHIRE 665 WALES

PICK OF THE PUBS

The White Hart Village Inn ❀❀

LLANGYBI   Map 9 ST39

NP15 1NP ☎ 01633 450258

e-mail: enquiries@thewhitehartvillageinn.com
web: www.thewhitehartvillageinn.com
dir: *M4 junct 25 onto B4596 (Caerleon road) through Caerleon High St, straight over rdbt into Usk Rd, continue to Llangybi*

Situated in the beautiful Usk Valley, in the pretty village of Llangybi, a warm welcome awaits at this picturesque, lovely historic inn where no less than 11 fireplaces can be found. Henry VIII became owner-by-default upon receiving it in the dowry of Jane Seymour, whilst arch-republican Oliver Cromwell based himself here during local Civil War campaigns. Add a priest hole, a wealth of exposed beams, precious Tudor plasterwork and a mention in TS Eliot's poem *Usk,* and you've a destination to savour. Chef-patron Michael Bates, formerly at Celtic Manor, is at the helm, offering village drinkers reliable beers from the likes of Ringwood Best, as well as a variety of ciders. It's the two AA-Rosette menu that keeps visitors returning time and again, though. Using fresh local produce, and combining exciting ingredients and complementary flavours, head chef Adam Whittle prepares and presents dishes with the utmost care and attention to detail. Lunchtime menus suggest chestnut and

truffle risotto followed by pan-fried bream with cabbage, bacon, shallot and potato, whilst the broader dinner menu may include curried parsnip soup, or chicken liver parfait with apple and plum; followed by Cwrw Braf battered cod and chips, or celeriac and potato royale with parsnip and leek, finishing with rice pudding and passionfruit, or orange and olive oil cake with milk chocolate mousse. In summer, head outside to the extensive seating area.

Open all day 12-11 (Sun 12-10) Closed: Mon **Bar Meals** Av main course £15.75 food served all day **Restaurant** L served Tue-Sat 12-3, Sun 12-4 D served Tue-Sat 6-10 Fixed menu price fr £18.95 Av 3 course à la carte fr £24 ⊕ FREE

HOUSE 🍺 Ringwood Best Bitter, Wye Valley Butty Bach ⚘ Tomos Watkin Taffy Apple, Thatchers Gold, Ty Gwyn. ♟ 15 **Facilities** Children welcome Children's menu Children's portions Garden Parking Wi-fi

PANTYGELLI   Map 9 SO31

PANTYGELLI   Map 9 SO31

The Crown

Old Hereford Rd NP7 7HR ☎ 01873 853314
e-mail: crown@pantygelli.com
web: www.thecrownatpantygelli.com
dir: Telephone for directions

Dating from the 16th century, this charming family-run free house in the Black Mountains has fine views of Skirrid, in Welsh Ysgyrid Fawr, known also as Holy Mountain. Walkers and cyclists love it, but it's a genuine community pub too, serving Bass, Rhymney Bitter, Wye Valley and guest real ales and Gwatkin cider, all ideal before or with Welsh Black rib-eye steak; salmon supreme; or something spicy from far away. Specials are typified by duck breast, courgettes and roasted onion; and baked avocado with blue cheese, fennel and French beans.

Open 12-2.30 6-11 (Sat 12-3 6-11 Sun 12-3 6-10.30) Closed: Mon L **Bar Meals** L served Tue-Sun 12-2 D served Tue-Sat 7-9 **Restaurant** L served Tue-Sun 12-2 D served Tue-Sat 7-9 ⊕ FREE HOUSE ◀ Rhymney Bitter, Wye Valley HPA, Bass, Guest ales Ꝺ Westons Stowford Press, Gwatkin Yarlington Mill. **Facilities** ✿ Children welcome Children's portions Garden Parking Wi-fi

PENALLT   Map 4 SO51

The Boat Inn

Lone Ln NP25 4AJ ☎ 01600 712615
dir: From Monmouth take A466. In Redbrook, pub car park signed. Access by foot across rail bridge over River Wye

Dating back over 360 years, this riverside pub has served as a hostelry for quarry, mill, paper and tin mine workers, and even had a landlord operating a ferry across the Wye at shift times. The unspoilt slate floor is testament to the age of the place. The excellent selection of real ales complements the menu well, with choices ranging from various ploughman's to lamb stifado or the charmingly named pan haggerty. Ideal for walkers taking the Offa's Dyke or Wye Valley walks.

Open all wk 12-11 (Sun 12-10.30) ⊕ FREE HOUSE ◀ Wye Valley, Guest ales Ꝺ Westons Stowford Press. **Facilities** Children welcome Garden Parking

The Inn at Penallt ★★★★ INN ◉

PICK OF THE PUBS

NP25 4SE ☎ 01600 772765
e-mail: enquiries@theinnatpenallt.co.uk
dir: From Monmouth take B4293 to Trellech. Up hill, in approx 2m left signed Penallt. In village at x-roads, turn left. Inn approx 0.3m on right

Built as a farmhouse in the 17th century, Bush Farm started serving cider, ale and perry in the early 1800s before becoming the Bush Inn in the 1890s. Spruced up and renamed by Jackie and Andrew Murphy a few years ago, the pub maintains its time-honoured reputation for serving quality local ales and ciders from breweries within 30 miles, alongside AA-Rosette standard food made from sustainable produce. Tuck into seared scallops, pea purée, roasted garlic and smoked Welsh bacon; or home-made faggots and creamed mashed potato with onion gravy and crushed peas. Finish with lemon-scented treacle tart with ginger ice cream. Dog-friendly accommodation is available. Booking for meals may be required.

Open Tue-Thu 6-11 Fri-Sun 12-11 winter (Tue-Fri 12-3 6-11 Sat-Sun 12-11 summer) Closed: 1st 2wks Jan, Mon **Bar Meals** L served Fri-Sun 12-2.30 D served Tue-Sat 6-9 Av main course £14 **Restaurant** L served Fri-Sun 12-2.30 D served Tue-Sat 6-9 Fixed menu price fr £13.95 Av 3 course à la carte fr £25 ⊕ FREE HOUSE ◀ Wye Valley Butty Bach, Kingstone Classic Bitter, Newmans Wolvers Ale Ꝺ Ty Gwyn, Gwynt y Ddraig Black Dragon. ♀ **Facilities** ✿ Children welcome Children's menu Children's portions Play area Garden Parking Wi-fi ▭ **Rooms** 4

RAGLAN   Map 9 SO40

The Beaufort Arms Coaching Inn & Brasserie ★★★ HL ◉

PICK OF THE PUBS

High St NP15 2DY ☎ 01291 690412
e-mail: enquiries@beaufortraglan.co.uk
dir: 0.5m from junct of A40 & A449 Abergavenny/ Monmouth, midway between M50 & M4

This grandly proportioned former coaching inn has always had strong links with nearby Raglan Castle; during the Civil War Roundhead soldiers frequented the bar during the siege of 1646. Nowadays, the place is equally popular when re-enactments are held at the castle, so it's not unusual to see men in full medieval armour tucking into a full Welsh breakfast in the brasserie. The inn has been beautifully appointed with many delightful design features, while holding strong to its traditional roots. A handsome display of fishing trophies dominates the country bar, where locals and visitors gather and chat over pints of The Rev. James. The inn offers well-kept real ales, ciders, and Belgian and German beers. Food is served in the lounge, with its carved bar, deep leather settees, and large stone fireplace ('lifted', some say, from

the castle), as well as in the private dining room and brasserie. Enjoy skilfully presented modern dishes like crispy Thai fishcakes with fresh chilli jam and mixed leaves; roasted pork belly with a boudin fritter, garlic crushed potatoes and honey star anise jus; and chocolate fondant. The weekly-changing specials board includes fresh fish from Devon. Booking for meals may be required.

Open all day all wk Closed: 25 Dec **Bar Meals** L served Mon-Thu 12-3, Fri-Sat 12-5 D served all wk 6-9.30 Av main course £12.95 **Restaurant** L served Mon-Thu 12-3, Fri-Sat 12-5, Sun 12-4 D served Mon-Sat 6-9.30, Sun 6-8.30 Fixed menu price fr £12.95 Av 3 course à la carte fr £30 ⊕ FREE HOUSE ◀ Fuller's London Pride, Brains The Rev. James, Morland Old Speckled Hen, Wye Valley Butty Bach Ꝺ Westons Stowford Press, Thatchers Gold. ♀ 16 **Facilities** Children welcome Children's menu Children's portions Garden Parking Wi-fi ▭ (notice required) **Rooms** 15

RHYD-Y-MEIRCH   Map 9 SO30

Goose and Cuckoo Inn

Upper Llanover NP7 9ER ☎ 01873 880277
e-mail: gooseandcuckoo@lineone.net
dir: From Abergavenny take A4042 towards Pontypool. Turn left after Llanover, follow signs for inn

This friendly, whitewashed pub in the Brecon Beacons National Park is popular with walkers. It has a garden with views of the Malvern Hills and a traditional interior with flagstoned bar area and a wood-burning stove. So, the perfect setting for a pint of well-kept Rhymney Bitter or one of the 85 single malt whiskies. All the food is home-made by landlady Carol Dollery; typical dishes include bean soup with a home-made roll; beef casserole; and cheese and rocket quiche. The pub hosts two beer festivals – in May and August.

Open Tue-Thu 11.30-3 7-11 (Fri-Sun all day) Closed: Mon (ex BH) **Bar Meals** L served Tue-Sun 11.30-3 D served Tue-Sun 7-9 Av main course £8 ⊕ FREE HOUSE ◀ Rhymney Bitter, Newmans Red Stag Ꝺ Kingstone Press. **Facilities** ✿ Children welcome Children's portions Family room Garden Beer festival Parking **Notes** ◉

SHIRENEWTON   Map 9 ST49

The Carpenters Arms

Usk Rd NP16 6BU ☎ 01291 641231
dir: M48 junct 2, A48 to Chepstow then A4661, B4235. Village 3m on left

A 400-year-old traditional country pub in a wooded location in the valley of the Mounton Brook between the rivers Wye and Usk. Formerly a smithy and carpenter's shop, today's four bars have flagstone floors, open fires, church pew seating and lots of old chamber pots. Home-made food is typified by rainbow trout with sage and bacon butter; chef's steak pie; Welsh faggots, mash and mushy peas; lasagne with hand-cut chips; and, for vegetarians, a special vegetable shepherd's pie with goat's cheese mash. Traditional Sunday roasts are popular.

Save on hotels. Book at **theAA.com/hotel**

MONMOUTHSHIRE 667 WALES

Open all wk 12-3 5.30-12 (Sat all day Sun 12-4.30) ⊕ PUNCH TAVERNS ◀ Fuller's London Pride, Shepherd Neame Spitfire, Bath Gem ♂ Thatchers Traditional. **Facilities** Children welcome Children's menu Children's portions Family room Parking Wi-fi

SKENFRITH   Map 9 SO42

The Bell at Skenfrith ★★★★★ RR ◉◉

PICK OF THE PUBS

NP7 8UH ☎ 01600 750235
e-mail: enquiries@skenfrith.co.uk
dir: *M4 junct 24 onto A449. Exit onto A40, through tunnel & lights. At rdbt take 1st exit, right at lights onto A466 towards Hereford road. Left onto B4521 towards Abergavenny, 3m on left*

Occupying a beautiful rural spot on the banks of the River Monnow, this award-winning, 17th-century coaching inn has splendid views of Skenfrith Castle. Character oozes from the fully restored oak bar, flagstone floors, comfortable sofas and old settles, while 11 individually decorated and well-equipped bedrooms, some with four-posters, provide high quality accommodation. On draught are Wye Valley Bitter and Hereford Pale Ale, Kingstone Classic Bitter, as well as Ty Gwyn local cider. The two AA-Rosette restaurant uses produce from its fully certified organic kitchen garden in its regularly changing menus and daily specials board. For lunch, you could choose hake en papillote with new potatoes, vegetables and caviar cream. For a thoroughly satisfying three-course dinner, perhaps smoked salmon ravioli with crème fraîche, cucumber textures and capers; seared rare bavette of Brecon beef with oxtail beignet with mash potato; and dark chocolate and chestnut fondant with malted milk ice cream. The award-winning wine list offers a well-chosen world selection. Booking for meals may be required.

Open all day Closed: last wk Jan & 1st wk Feb, Tue Nov-Mar **Bar Meals** L served all wk 12-2.30 D served Mon-Sat 7-9.30, Sun 7-9 Av main course £17 **Restaurant** L served all wk 12-2.30 D served Mon-Sat 7-9.30, Sun 7-9 Fixed menu price fr £26 Av 3 course à la carte fr £33 ⊕ FREE HOUSE ◀ Wye Valley Bitter & HPA, Kingstone Classic Bitter ♂ Westons Stowford Press, Ty Gwyn, Local cider. ☂ 13 **Facilities** Children welcome Children's menu Garden Parking Wi-fi **Rooms** 11

TINTERN PARVA   Map 4 SO50

Fountain Inn

Trellech Grange NP16 6QW ☎ 01291 689303
e-mail: fountaininntintern@btconnect.com
dir: *From M48 junct 2 follow Chepstow then A466/Tintern signs. In Tintern turn by George Hotel for Raglan. Bear right, inn at top of hill, 2m from A466*

A fine old inn dating from 1611 in lovely countryside, with a garden overlooking the Wye Valley. New owners offer several curries, including chicken Kashmiri, and fruit and vegetable Jalfrezi; and Welsh Black beef, Welsh lamb and roasted ham, all with fresh vegetables, roast potatoes, Yorkshire pudding and beer gravy. They also have a fresh

fish menu with whole griddled flounder; sizzling crevettes; and beer-battered cod and chips. Their passion for real ales and ciders is evident both in the great bar line-up, and at the Easter and September beer festivals.

Open all day all wk **Bar Meals** L served Tue-Sun 12-2.30 D served all wk 6-9 Av main course £6.95 **Restaurant** L served Tue-Sun 12-2.30 D served all wk 6-9 Fixed menu price fr £6.95 ⊕ FREE HOUSE ◀ Wychwood Hobgoblin, Brains The Rev. James, Kingstone Classic Bitter, Whittingtons Cats Whiskers, Butcombe, Mayfields, Rhymney, Hook Norton, Hereford, Ring O'Bells, Bass ♂ Thatchers Gold, Broadoak. ☂ 9 **Facilities** 🐾 Children welcome Children's menu Children's portions Family room Garden Beer festival Parking Wi-fi 🚌 (notice required)

TREDUNNOCK   Map 9 ST39

Newbridge on Usk ★★★★ RR ◉◉

PICK OF THE PUBS

NP15 1LY ☎ 01633 451000
e-mail: newbridgeonusk@celtic-manor.com
dir: *M4 junct 24 follow Newport signs. Right at Toby Carvery, B4236 to Caerleon. Right over bridge, through Caerleon to mini rdbt. Straight ahead onto Llangibby/Usk road*

Set above a bend in the river in the verdant Vale of Usk, this smart residential (six en suite rooms) gastro-pub is the latest incarnation of a hostelry that has served passers-by for 200 years. With medieval Usk and Roman Caerleon on the doorstep and myriad sporting opportunities locally (including golf at the Ryder Cup venue Celtic Manor, owners of the inn), the pub offers a relaxing end to a busy day. Cosy, rustic, old-world fittings meld seamlessly with contemporary comforts; on summer evenings the riverside garden is a winning place to sup a glass of The Rev. James and contemplate the sunset illuminating Wentwood and the beautiful Monmouthshire hills. Welsh produce is used creatively to create dishes worthy of two AA Rosettes, with tasters like free-range saddleback ham hock cured in Welsh cider; and mains such as sewin (sea trout) with Lyonnaise potatoes, samphire, Penclawdd cockles and pastis beurre blanc; Preseli Blue Mountain Welsh lamb rump with wild garlic crust; or perhaps warm salad of quinoa and soft herbs.

Open all wk 11am-mdnt **Bar Meals** L served all wk 12-2.30 D served all wk 7-10 **Restaurant** L served all wk 12-2.30 D served all wk 7-10 ⊕ FREE HOUSE ◀ Brains The Rev. James & Smooth, Guest ale ♂ Tomos Watkin Taffy Apples. ☂ 12 **Facilities** Children welcome Children's menu Children's portions Garden Parking Wi-fi 🚌 **Rooms** 6

TRELLECH   Map 4 SO50

The Lion Inn

PICK OF THE PUBS

NP25 4PA ☎ 01600 860322
e-mail: debs@globalnet.co.uk
dir: *From A40 S of Monmouth take B4293, follow Trellech signs. From M8 junct 2, straight across rdbt, 2nd left at 2nd rdbt, B4293 to Trellech*

When a naval captain, presumably retired, built this former brewhouse and inn in 1580, he used ships' timbers for the main structural beams to remind himself of the sea. Now in the same hands for 17 years, its many awards reflect everything it offers, from the real fires to the wholesome food, real ales and local ciders. The extensive menu embraces bar snacks, basket meals, ideas for small appetites and numerous specials – one blackboard each for steaks and sauces, Thai curries, fish and the rest. Regularly featured are trio of sausages; chicken in tarragon; beef in black bean sauce; pan-fried kangaroo steak; South African game grill; Russian-style monkfish; swordfish steak; and mushroom Stroganoff. Children and those with smaller appetites have plenty of favourites to choose from. The pub garden features a stream and an aviary, and the suntrap courtyard has beautiful views. Check dates for summer and winter beer festivals. Booking for meals may be required.

Open 12-3 6-11 (Mon 12-3 7-11 Thu 12-3 6-12 Fri-Sat 12-12 Sun 12-4.30) Closed: Sun eve ⊕ FREE HOUSE ◀ Wye Valley Butty Bach, Sharp's Cornish Coaster, Rhymney Bitter, Butcombe Gold, Bath. **Facilities** Children welcome Children's portions Garden Beer festival Parking

USK   Map 9 SO30

The Nags Head Inn

Twyn Square NP15 1BH ☎ 01291 672820
e-mail: keynags@tiscali.co.uk
dir: *On A472*

Owned by the Key family for over 40 years, this 15th-century coaching inn overlooks the square just a short stroll from the River Usk, and boasts magnificent hanging flower baskets. A good range of beers is available in the traditional bar, which is furnished with polished tables and chairs, and decorated with collections of horse brasses, farming tools and lanterns hanging from exposed oak beams. Game in season figures strongly among the speciality dishes, including whole stuffed partridge, pheasant in port, home-made rabbit pie and brace of quails.

Open all wk 10.30-2.30 5-11 Closed: 25 Dec **Bar Meals** L served all wk 11.45-1.45 D served all wk 5.30-9.30 **Restaurant** L served all wk 11.45-1.45 D served all wk 5.30-9.30 ⊕ FREE HOUSE ◀ Brains Bitter, Buckley's Bitter, The Rev. James & Bread of Heaven, Sharp's Doom Bar ♂ Westons Stowford Press. ☂ 9 **Facilities** Children welcome Children's portions Garden Parking 🚌

USK *continued*

Raglan Arms ®

PICK OF THE PUBS

Llandenny NP15 1DL ☎ 01291 690800
e-mail: raglanarms@gmail.com
dir: *From Monmouth take A449 to Raglan, left in village. From M4 take A449 exit. Signposted to Llandenny on right*

This mid 19th-century stone-built pub enjoys a pretty village location. Its simple interior reflects traditional values, including a firm emphasis on locally sourced food, which is so good it holds an AA Rosette. Dine at rustic tables around the bar, where you'll find Wye Valley Bitter and Butty Bach, or in the conservatory. In summer, head for the decked area outside and soak up the sun while you eat. Some dishes, such as Thai fishcakes with plum and mirin dipping sauces, imam bayildli with crème fraîche or home-made bratwurst with white wine onion sauce and mashed potato, reflect an enthusiasm for international flavours, while others (maybe trio of Welsh lamb with dauphinoise potatoes or gratin of smoked haddock fillet with leeks, Cornish crab and mashed potatoes) take their cues from classical French and traditional British cuisine. Egg custard with blackcurrant sorbet is a typical dessert but take note that a Raglan hallmark is its excellent selection of Welsh and English cheeses. Look out for the special events with tasting menus. Booking for meals may be required.

Open Tue-Sat 12-2.30 6.30-9.30 (Sun 12-3) Closed: 25-27 Dec, Sun eve & Mon **Bar Meals** L served Tue-Sat 12-2.30, Sun 12-3 D served Tue-Sat 6.30-9.30 Av main course £15 **Restaurant** L served Tue-Sat 12-2.30, Sun 12-3 D served Tue-Sat 6.30-9.30 Av 3 course à la carte fr £28 ⊕ FREE HOUSE ◄ Wye Valley Bitter & Butty Bach, Guinness Ö Thatchers Gold. ♀ 12 **Facilities** Children welcome Children's portions Garden Parking

NEWPORT

CAERLEON | Map 9 ST39

The Bell at Caerleon **NEW**

Bulmore Rd NP18 1QQ ☎ 01633 420613
e-mail: thebellinn@hotmail.co.uk

This 17th-century coaching inn has stood in ancient Caerleon on the banks of the River Usk for more than 400 years. Situated close to an ancient Roman burial ground (also believed by some to be the location of King Arthur's Camelot), the pub has won several awards for its food and drink, particularly its range of local cider and perry. The pub holds annual real ale and cider festivals with barbecues and free entertainment. Local produce drives the menu, which might include Carmarthen Bay mussels steamed in smoked bacon, shallot and local cider, or pan-roasted pheasant with rosemary, thyme and wholegrain mustard mash.

Open all day all wk **Bar Meals** L served Mon-Sat 12-2.30, Sun 12-4 D served all wk 6-9.30 Av main course £8-£15 **Restaurant** L served Mon-Sat 12-2.30, Sun 12-4 D served all wk 6-9.30 Fixed menu price fr £9.95 Av 3 course à la carte fr £26 ⊕ ENTERPRISE INNS ◄ Sharp's Doom Bar,

Felinfoel Double Dragon, Bath Gem, 3 Rotating ales Ö Gwynt y Ddraig Black Dragon & Happy Daze, Hallets Real. ♀ 10 **Facilities** ♣ Children welcome Children's portions Garden Beer festival Parking Wi-fi ⛟ (notice required)

PEMBROKESHIRE

ABERCYCH | Map 8 SN24

Nags Head Inn

SA37 0HJ ☎ 01239 841200
dir: *On B4332 (Carmarthen to Newcastle Emlyn road)*

Situated at the entrance to the enchanted valley in the famous Welsh folk tales of *Mabinogion*, this famous old inn is the first building you see over the county boundary when crossing into Pembrokeshire from the Teifi Falls at Cenarth. In one of the outbuildings the old forge still remains where the blacksmith crafted the first horse-drawn ploughs for export to America. Old Emrys ale is brewed on the premises ready for consuming in the beamed bars and riverside gardens. The fine fare includes home-made cawl with cheese and crusty bread; steak, Guinness and mushroom pie; and Cardigan Island crab salad.

Open Tue-Sun Closed: Mon **Bar Meals** L served Tue-Sun 12-2 D served Tue-Sun 6-9 Av main course £9 **Restaurant** L served Tue-Sun 12-2 D served Tue-Sun 6-9 Fixed menu price fr £11.95 ⊕ FREE HOUSE ◄ Old Emrys. **Facilities** Children welcome Play area Garden Parking ⛟

AMROTH | Map 8 SN10

The New Inn

SA67 8NW ☎ 01834 812368
e-mail: paulluger@hotmail.com
dir: *A48 to Carmarthen, A40 to St Clears, A477 to Llanteg then left, follow road to sea front, turn left. 0.25m on left*

This is a 16th-century inn was originally a farmhouse. Belonging to Amroth Castle Estate it has been family run for some 37 years. It has old world charm with beamed ceilings, a Flemish chimney, a flagstone floor and an inglenook fireplace. It is close to the beach with views towards Saundersfoot and Tenby from the dining room upstairs. Locally caught fish and shellfish are specialities along with Welsh beef; home-made dishes include soup, pies and curries. Enjoy food or drink outside on the large lawn complete with picnic benches.

Open all day all wk Mar-Oct 11-11 (Oct-Mar eve & wknds only) **Bar Meals** Av main course £8.50 food served all day **Restaurant** food served all day ⊕ FREE HOUSE ◄ Sharp's Doom Bar, Hancock's, Guinness, Guest ales. **Facilities** ♣ Children welcome Children's menu Children's portions Family room Garden Parking ⛟

CAREW | Map 8 SN00

Carew Inn

SA70 8SL ☎ 01646 651267
e-mail: mandy@carewinn.co.uk
dir: *From A477 take A4075. Inn 400yds opp castle & Celtic cross*

A traditional stone-built country inn situated opposite the Carew Celtic cross and Norman castle. Enjoy the one-mile circular walk around the castle and millpond. A good range of bar meals includes Welsh Black steak-and-kidney pie; chilli con carne; Thai red chicken curry; and seafood pancakes. Fruit crumble and old favourite jam roly-poly feature among the puddings. There's a children's play area in the garden, which also hosts regular barbecues in the summer.

Open all day all wk 11am-mdnt (Sun 12-12) Closed: 25 Dec ⊕ FREE HOUSE ◄ Worthington's, Brains The Rev. James, Guest ales. **Facilities** Children welcome Children's menu Children's portions Play area Garden Parking

LETTERSTON | Map 8 SM92

The Harp Inn

31 Haverfordwest Rd SA62 5UA ☎ 01348 840061
e-mail: info@theharpatletterston.co.uk
dir: *On A40, 10m from Haverfordwest, 4m from Fishguard ferry.*

Formerly a working farm and home to a weekly market, this 15th-century free house remained largely unchanged for 500 years. Owned by the Sandall family since 1982, the building has now been fully renovated so that diners in the stylish conservatory restaurant can enjoy local favourites like Welsh fillet steak; venison Roquefort; and whole sea bass. Alternatively, the bar lunch menu offers classic pub meals including crispy battered cod and chips. Enjoy lunch with your children in the fenced garden.

Open all day all wk **Bar Meals** food served all day **Restaurant** food served all day ⊕ FREE HOUSE ◄ Tetley's, Greene King Abbot Ale Ö Thatchers Gold. **Facilities** Children welcome Children's menu Children's portions Play area Garden Parking Wi-fi ⛟

Save on hotels. Book at **theAA.com/hotel**

PEMBROKESHIRE 669 WALES

| **LITTLE HAVEN** | Map 8 SM81 |

St Brides Inn

St Brides Rd SA62 3UN ☎ 01437 781266
e-mail: kgardham@btinternet.com
dir: *From Haverfordwest take B4341 signed Broad Haven. Through Broad Haven to Little Haven*

In the seaside village of Little Haven in the Pembrokeshire National Park, this attractive inn is an ideal stop for walkers on the nearby coastal path. It has the added attraction of an indoor ancient well, as well as a pretty floral beer garden. Food-wise expect the likes of spiced salmon and prawn fishcakes with a sweet chilli dip; cod in home-made beer-batter with chips and mushy peas; and home-made pies with a choice of vegetables. Children get to choose from their own menu. Look out for themed evenings throughout the year.

Open all wk 11.30-3 5.30-11.30 (all day summer) **Bar Meals** L served all wk 12-2.30 D served all wk 6-9 **Restaurant** L served all wk 12-2.30 D served all wk 6-9 ⊕ MARSTON'S ◀ Pedigree, Banks's Bitter. **Facilities** ✿ Children welcome Children's menu Children's portions Garden ▬ (notice required)

The Swan Inn

PICK OF THE PUBS

Point Rd SA62 3UL ☎ 01437 781880
e-mail: enquiries@theswanlittlehaven.co.uk
dir: *B4341 from Haverfordwest. In Broad Haven follow seafront/Little Haven signs 0.75m*

Arrive early to bag a window table and savour one of the best views in Pembrokeshire from this 200-year-old pub perched above a rocky cove overlooking St Brides Bay. Paul and Tracy Morris's award-winning free house buzzes with chatter and contented diners, dispensing well-kept real ales and a decent choice of wines in the comfortably rustic bar, furnished with old settles, polished oak tables and leather armchairs beside the fireplace. There's also an intimate dining room, with an elegant contemporary-style restaurant upstairs; cooking is modern British, with a commitment to seasonal and local produce. Choose from open sandwiches and pub favourites like pie of the day and peas, or treat yourself to the full works. A typical meal might start with crayfish mousseline with wild mushroom and tarragon cream sauce; followed by duck leg confit with port and juniper sauce; and finishing with lemon tart with Chantilly cream and fruit coulis. Booking for meals may be required.

Open all day all wk 11am-mdnt Closed: 3 Jan-18 Feb, Sun out of season **Bar Meals** L served all wk 12-2 D served all wk 6-9 **Restaurant** L served all wk 12-2 D served all wk 6-9 ⊕ FREE HOUSE ◀ Morland Old Speckled Hen, Penlon Cottage, Brains The Rev. James, Worthington's, Guinness. **Facilities** Children welcome Children's menu Children's portions Garden Wi-fi ▬ (notice required)

| **NEWPORT** | Map 8 SN03 |

Salutation Inn

Felindre Farchog, Crymych SA41 3UY ☎ 01239 820564
e-mail: johndenley@aol.com
web: www.salutationcountryhotel.co.uk
dir: *On A487 between Cardigan & Fishguard*

This tastefully modernised, 16th-century coaching inn stands on the River Nevern in the Pembrokeshire Coast National Park. Owners since 2000 are John Denley, a veteran of 20 years in restaurants in North Africa and the Middle East, and his wife Gwawr, born two miles away on the slopes of Carningli Mountain. There is an emphasis on fresh locally sourced produce for the menu, which lists deep-fried butterfly prawns in coconut with chilli jam; chicken breast paprika with tagliatelle; and vegetable lasagne. Felinfoel, Brains and a local guest are on tap. Booking for meals may be required.

Open all day Closed: Tue in winter **Bar Meals** L served all wk 12.30-2.30 D served all wk 6.30-9 **Restaurant** L served Sun 12.30-2.30 D served Sat-Sun 7-9 ⊕ FREE HOUSE ◀ Felinfoel, Brains, Local guest ales ♂ Thatchers Gold. **Facilities** ✿ Children welcome Children's menu Children's portions Garden Parking Wi-fi ▬ (notice required)

| **PORTHGAIN** | Map 8 SM83 |

The Sloop Inn

SA62 5BN ☎ 01348 831449
e-mail: matthew@sloop-inn.freeserve.co.uk
dir: *Take A487 NE from St Davids for 6m. Left at Croesgoch for 2m to Porthgain*

Possibly the most famous pub on the north Pembrokeshire coast, The Sloop Inn is located in beautiful quarrying village of Porthgain and is especially welcome on a cold winter's day. The walls and ceilings are packed with pictures and memorabilia from nearby shipwrecks. The harbour is less than 100 yards from the door and there is a village green to the front and a large south-facing patio. With ales like Felinfoel and Greene King IPA on the pump, a varied menu includes breakfasts, snacks, pub favourites, steaks and home-caught fish. Booking for meals may be required.

Open all day all wk 9.30am-11pm (winter 11.30-11) Closed: 25 Dec **Bar Meals** L served all wk 12-2.30 D served all wk 6-9.30 **Restaurant** L served all wk 12-2.30 D served all wk 6-9.30 ⊕ FREE HOUSE/B G BETTERSPOONS Ltd ◀ Cropton Yorkshire Warrior, Hancock's HB, Felinfoel, Greene King IPA Guest ale. **Facilities** Children welcome Children's menu Garden Parking Wi-fi ▬

| **ROSEBUSH** | Map 8 SN02 |

Tafarn Sinc

Preseli SA66 7QT ☎ 01437 532214
e-mail: briandavies2@btconnect.com
dir: *Telephone for directions*

Built to serve the railway that no longer exists, this large red corrugated-iron free house stands testament to its rapid construction in 1876. This idiosyncratic establishment refuses to be modernised and boasts wood-burning stoves, a sawdust floor, and a charming garden. Set high in the Preseli Hills amid stunning scenery, it is popular with walkers, who can refuel on traditional favourites like local lamb burgers; prime Welsh sirloin steak; home-cooked ham; and Glamorgan sausages with chutney.

Open all day 12-11 Closed: Mon (ex BH & summer) **Bar Meals** L served Tue-Sat 12-2 D served Tue-Sat 6-9 **Restaurant** L served Tue-Sat 12-2 D served Tue-Sat 6-9 ⊕ FREE HOUSE ◀ Worthington's, Tafarn Sinc, Guest ale. **Facilities** Children welcome Children's menu Garden Parking ▬ (notice required)

| **ST DOGMAELS** | Map 8 SN14 |

Webley Waterfront Inn & Hotel

Poppit Sands SA43 3LN ☎ 01239 612085
e-mail: enquiries@webleyhotel.co.uk
dir: *A484 from Carmarthen to Cardigan, then to St Dogmaels, right in village centre to Poppit Sands on B4546*

This long-established family business is spectacularly situated at the start of the Pembrokeshire Coast National Park. The inn offers outstanding views across the River Teifi and Poppit Sands to Cardigan Bay. The bar serves Gwynt y Ddraig Welsh cider together with a selection of ales. Not surprisingly, local seafood and fish dominate the menu: seared rainbow trout with toasted almonds, and sea bass with Puy lentils and salsa verde. The specials board might feature Cardigan Bay lobster and crab. Other dishes include chilli con carne and curry of the day. Booking for meals may be required.

Open all day all wk **Bar Meals** L served all wk 12-2.30 D served all wk 6-8.30 Av main course £12 **Restaurant** D served all wk 6-9 Av 3 course à la carte fr £25.30 ⊕ FREE HOUSE ◀ Brains Buckley's Bitter & The Rev. James, Worthington's, Guest ales ♂ Gwynt y Ddraig. ♥ 8 **Facilities** ✿ Children welcome Children's menu Children's portions Family room Garden Parking Wi-fi ▬

PICK OF THE PUBS

The Stackpole Inn

STACKPOLE   Map 8 SR99

SA71 5DF ☎ 01646 672324
e-mail: info@stackpoleinn.co.uk
web: www.stackpoleinn.co.uk
dir: *From Pembroke take B4319, follow Stackpole signs, approx 4m*

This traditional inn is a walker's delight, set in pristine gardens at the heart of the National Trust's Stackpole Estate and close to the spectacular Pembrokeshire coastal path. There's a rare George V postbox in the mellow stone wall outside, a survival from the time when one of the two original stone cottages was a post office. Nowadays the pub offers facilities for walkers, cyclists, fishermen and climbers, as well as those who simply prefer to relax and do nothing. Once inside, you'll find a slate bar, ceiling beams made from ash trees grown on the estate, and a wood-burning stove set within the stone fireplace. The pub's free house status means that there's always a guest beer from around the UK to accompany three Welsh ales, a couple of real ciders and a varied wine list. Local produce from the surrounding countryside and fish from the coast play a major part in the home-cooked menu. A lighter lunch menu offers freshly baked Couronne loaves with an appetising selection of fillings

that includes Welsh brie with locally cured bacon, and tuna with tarragon mayonnaise. Three-course appetites might begin with creamy Welsh blue cheese on bitter leaf salad with pickled walnuts and poached grapes, or smoked salmon on potato blini with herb crème fraîche. Main course options range from seared Welsh lamb with Moroccan couscous and tomato jus with seasonal vegetables; to wild sea bass fillet with fennel and saffron risotto. Round things off with caramelised lemon tart and passionfruit sorbet, or creamy rice pudding with cinnamon and apple. Booking for meals may be required.

Open all wk 12-3 6-11 Closed: Sun eve (winter) ⊕ FREE HOUSE ◀ Brains The Rev. James, Felinfoel Double Dragon, Guest ale ♻ Westons Stowford Press & Old Rosie. **Facilities** Children welcome Children's menu Children's portions Garden Parking Wi-fi

Save on hotels. Book at **theAA.com/hotel**

PEMBROKESHIRE – POWYS 671 WALES

SOLVA   Map 8 SM82

The Cambrian Inn

Main St SA62 6UU ☎ 01437 721210
e-mail: thecambrianinn@btconnect.com
dir: *13m from Haverfordwest on A487 towards St Davids*

This Grade II listed inn is something of an institution in this pretty fishing village, and attracts local and returning visitors alike. Full of charm and character, a major refurbishment was completed a few years ago. A sample bar menu offers local Welsh lamb cutlets, gammon steak or Welsh sirloin steak, while the carte dinner menu offers lots of fresh fish dishes. Local and Welsh real ales are served and can be enjoyed in the outside seating area in warmer weather. Recent change of hands.

Open all day all wk ⊕ FREE HOUSE ◀ Tomos Watkin OSB & Cwrw Braf, Wye Valley Butty Bach, Guest ales.
Facilities Children welcome Children's menu Children's portions Garden Parking

STACKPOLE   Map 8 SR99

The Stackpole Inn

PICK OF THE PUBS

See Pick of the Pubs on opposite page

WOLF'S CASTLE   Map 8 SM92

The Wolfe Inn

SA62 5LS ☎ 01437 741662
dir: *On A40 between Haverfordwest & Fishguard. 7m from both towns*

The Wolfe is an oak-beamed, stone-built property in a lovely village setting. The building has three-foot walls, and despite being decorated in neutral tones it still has an olde-worlde feel. The bar-brasserie and restaurant comprise four interconnecting but distinctly different rooms: the Victorian Parlour, Hunters' Lodge, Brasserie and a conservatory. There is a bar menu (perhaps Texan barbecue chicken or Chinese crispy beef) and full à la carte - roast duck with fresh orange Cointreau and ginger sauce, or a mixed grill. Desserts could be lemon lush pie or strawberry trifle. Booking for meals may be required.

Open all wk (all day in summer) **Bar Meals** L served all wk 12-2.30 D served all wk 6-9 **Restaurant** D served all wk 7-9 ⊕ BRAINS ◀ Worthington's, Guest ale.
Facilities Children welcome Children's menu Children's portions Garden Parking Wi-fi ▬ (notice required)

POWYS

BERRIEW   Map 15 SJ10

The Lion Hotel

SY21 8PQ ☎ 01686 640452
e-mail: trudi.jones@btconnect.com
dir: *5m from Welshpool on A483, right to Berriew. In village centre next to church*

Behind the black-and-white timbered exterior of this 17th-century family-run coaching inn lie bars and dining areas where yet more old timbers testify to its age. Menus, based on local produce, include a starter of ballotine of mackerel, potato and chive salad, coriander and lemon mayo; then mains might be loin of Welsh lamb with boulangère potatoes, or dill gnocchi with white wine cream sauce. Yogurt pannacotta with candied orange or a selection of Welsh farmhouse cheese finish things off nicely. There is a separate bar area where you can enjoy a pint of real ale from the selection on tap including Banks's Bitter, Pedigree and Old Empire. Booking for meals may be required.

Open all wk 12-3 5-11 (Fri-Sat 12-11 Sun 12-3 6-10.30) ⊕ MARSTON'S ◀ Pedigree & Old Empire, Banks's Bitter, Guest ales. **Facilities** Children welcome Children's portions Parking Wi-fi

BRECON   Map 9 SO02

The Felin Fach Griffin ★★★★ INN ◉◉

PICK OF THE PUBS

Felin Fach LD3 0UB ☎ 01874 620111
e-mail: enquiries@felinfachgriffin.co.uk
dir: *4.5m N of Brecon on A470 (Brecon to Hay-on-Wye road)*

With no Wi-fi signal at all, The Felin Fach Griffin is perfect for those who really do want to get away from it all. Charles and Edmund Inkin's mantra of 'the simple things, done well' is typified by this inn with rooms, whether it's the well-considered drinks list, the quality cooking or the en suite bedrooms. In the bar, sink into leather sofas in front of the open fire with a glass of local ale. Food is served in bare-floored rooms where original features, including an Aga, are teamed with tasteful modern touches. The Griffin draws much of its ingredients from the Brecons, while the garden keeps up a steady flow of organic produce. The lunchtime menu includes minute steak sandwich with fried egg and triple cooked chips, whilst the freshest seafood could feature Cornish pollock with sautéed new potatoes, spinach and clam broth. Sixteen wines are offered by the glass. Booking for meals may be required.

Open all day all wk 11.30-11 (Sun 11-10.30) Closed: 24-25 Dec, 4 days early Jan **Bar Meals** L served all wk 12-2.30 D served Sun-Thu 6-9, Fri-Sat 6-9.30 **Restaurant** L served all wk 12-2.30 D served Sun-Thu 6-9, Fri-Sat 6-9.30 ⊕ FREE HOUSE ◀ Breconshire, Montgomery, Tomos Watkin, Otley, The Waen ♂ Westons Stowford Press, Ty Gwyn, Pips. ♟ 16 **Facilities** Children welcome Children's menu Children's portions Garden Parking **Rooms** 7

The Usk Inn ★★★★ INN

PICK OF THE PUBS

See Pick of the Pubs on page 672

The White Swan Inn

PICK OF THE PUBS

Llanfrynach LD3 7BZ ☎ 01874 665276
e-mail: lee.havard@hotmail.co.uk
dir: *A40, 3m E of Brecon onto B4558 follow Llanfrynach signs*

Originally a coaching inn in the 17th century, The White Swan is set opposite the ancient church of St Brynach and enjoys an impressive backdrop of the Brecon Beacons. An atmospheric gastro-pub featuring stone walls, exposed oak beams, stone-flagged floor and log fires, it offers a warm and cosy welcome, whether you eat in the spacious Flagstone Restaurant or the more informal bar, which also offers a lighter snack menu and Brains beers on handpump. The inventive menus change monthly and all dishes are freshly prepared using locally sourced produce. Lunch might be home-made faggots with mushy peas and creamy mash followed by Baileys cream cheesecake. Typical evening dishes include herb crusted best end and confit shoulder of Welsh lamb with leek mash and lamb jus. Puddings might include glazed apple tart with crème anglaise and vanilla ice cream. There's also a selection from the grill.

Open Wed-Sun 11.30-3 6.30-11.30 Closed: 25-26 Dec, 1st 2wks Jan, Mon & Tue (ex summer, Dec & BH) **Bar Meals** L served Wed-Sat 12-2, Sun 12-2.30 D served Wed-Sun 7-9 Av main course £12.95 **Restaurant** L served Wed-Sat 12-2, Sun 12-2.30 D served Wed-Sun 7-9 Fixed menu price fr £15 Av 3 course à la carte fr £28 ⊕ FREE HOUSE ◀ Hancock's HB, Brains SA, Smooth & The Rev. James, Guinness. ♟ 8 **Facilities** Children welcome Children's menu Children's portions Garden Parking Wi-fi ▬ (notice required)

PICK OF THE PUBS

The Usk Inn ★★★★INN

BRECON Map 9 SO02

Talybont-on-Usk LD3 7JE
☎ 01874 676251
e-mail: stay@uskinn.co.uk
web: www.uskinn.co.uk
dir: *6m E of Brecon, just off A40 towards Abergavenny & Crickhowell*

The village of Talybont-on-Usk lies on the picturesque Abergavenny to Brecon road. The inn opened in the 1840s, just as the Brecon to Merthyr railway line was being built alongside it. In 1878 the locomotive *Hercules* failed to stop at the station opposite and crashed into Station Road, seriously disrupting conversation and beer consumption at the bar. The pub still enjoys its enviable position about 300 metres from the village centre, attracting locals and visitors to the Brecon Beacons National Park in equal number. Another source of custom is the Brecon to Monmouthshire canal that passes through the village – sometimes at roof level. Over the years The Usk has been transformed from an ordinary pub into a country inn with restaurant and rooms. Refurbishments have been sympathetic, preserving its traditional ambience. Ten bedrooms are cheerfully bright, decorated in refreshing colours. Expect a choice of guest ales at the bar, along with ciders and popular wines. The Usk's reputation for good cooking and good value is based on the kitchen's selection of carefully sourced ingredients, served in a blend of traditional and modern dishes. So the menu lists a prawn cocktail alongside a warm scallop and black pudding salad with coarse mustard dressing. The set menu appeals with tomato and mozzarella bake, followed by fillet of salmon with a saffron and herb sauce. Light bites at lunchtime include a grilled baguette with real Caerphilly cheese, lettuce and tomato; or a more substantial beef and Guinness pie with mash. Look to the specials list for a fulfilling dinner, which could kick off with tortellini with prosciutto and a tomato and basil sauce. Next, a roasted breast of pheasant stuffed with cranberry and roasted vegetables and wrapped in streaky bacon. Pudding could take the form of a banoffee Pavlova – a meringue nest with fudge ice cream and chopped banana.

Open all day all wk 11am-11.30pm (Sun 11-10.30) Closed: 25-26 Dec eve **Bar Meals** L served all wk 12-2.30 Av main course £12.95 **Restaurant** L served Sun 12-2.30 D served all wk 6.30-9.30 Fixed menu price fr £14.95 Av 3 course à la carte fr £20.95 FREE HOUSE Guinness, Guest ales Thatchers, Robinsons. 11 **Facilities** Children welcome Children's portions Garden Parking (notice required) **Rooms** 10

Save on hotels. Book at **theAA.com/hotel**

POWYS 673 WALES

COEDWAY
Map 15 SJ31

The Old Hand and Diamond Inn

SY5 9AR ☎ **01743 884379**
e-mail: moz123@aol.com
web: www.oldhandanddiamond.co.uk
dir: *9m from Shrewsbury*

Just 15 minutes' drive from the medieval market town of Shrewsbury, this 17th-century inn is conveniently positioned on the Powys/Shropshire border. The pub retains much of its original character, with exposed beams and inglenook fireplace. This is the place to enjoy a pint of local Shropshire Lad ale, whilst choosing from an extensive menu that uses the best from local suppliers. Dishes might include grilled lamb chops with Shrewsbury sauce or home-made burger topped with bacon and cheese. The beer garden has plenty of seating and a children's play area.

Open all day all wk 11am-1am **Bar Meals** L served Mon-Thu 12-2.30, Fri-Sun 12-9.30 D served Mon-Thu 6-9.30, Fri-Sun 12-9.30 **Restaurant** L served Mon-Thu 12-2.30, Fri-Sun 12-9.30 D served Mon-Thu 6-9.30, Fri-Sun 12-9.30 ⊕ FREE HOUSE ◀ Worthington's, Wood's Shropshire Lad, Guest ales. **Facilities** ✿ Children welcome Children's portions Play area Garden Parking ▨

CRICKHOWELL
Map 9 SO21

The Bear Hotel ★★★ HL ®

PICK OF THE PUBS

See Pick of the Pubs on page 674

Nantyffin Cider Mill Inn

PICK OF THE PUBS

Brecon Rd NP8 1SG ☎ **01873 810775**
e-mail: info@cidermill.co.uk
dir: *At junct of A40 & A479, 1.5m W of Crickhowell*

Tucked above the River Usk, views from the inn's garden sweep across to wooded hills beneath Llangattock Mountain and the distant Brecon Beacons, whilst behind rise the shapely summits of the secluded Black Mountains. For centuries, drovers driving cattle, sheep or geese to market stopped here to sample the home-made cider. Pressing ceased in the 1960s, although excellent local cider still flies the flag at this colour-washed old cider mill where the original press, still fully usable, can be seen in the Mill Room Restaurant. Dressed stone walls, precarious beams and vast fireplace fit the scene to a T, whilst the stunning restaurant is a destination dining favourite. Welsh produce is to the fore, with cobbler of local lamb or chargrilled dry-aged rib-eye steak hitting the spot; the specials board updates the daily catch available from local rivers and harbours, perhaps hake, leek and pancetta thermidor. Splendid beers from breweries in the Welsh Valleys, and a good bin of wines seal the deal. Booking for meals may be required.

Open 12-3 6-11 Closed: Mon (ex BH), Sun eve Oct-Mar ⊕ FREE HOUSE ◀ Brains The Rev. James, Rhymney Bitter, Felinfoel Best Bitter ♂ Thatchers Gold & Green Goblin, Kingstone Press. **Facilities** Children welcome Children's portions Garden Parking

GLADESTRY
Map 9 SO25

The Royal Oak Inn

HR5 3NR ☎ **01544 370669 & 370342**
e-mail: brianhall@btinternet.com
dir: *4m W of Kington, 10m from Hay-on-Wye on B4594*

This 400-year-old inn once welcomed drovers taking store cattle from Wales to England. The huge inglenook fireplace, heavily beamed ceilings and a flagstone floor set the scene for the home-made fare served in the lounge bar/dining area, including bar snacks, soups, jacket potatoes, sandwiches and salads. A roast is served every Sunday. Offa's Dyke footpath is nearby, and there's an exhilarating four-mile walk from Kington along Hergest Ridge with its breathtaking views. Booking for meals may be required.

Open all day all wk Etr-Aug (Oct-Mar reduced hrs) Closed: Thu eve in winter ⊕ FREE HOUSE ◀ Brains The Rev. James, Wye Valley Butty Bach, Worthington's, Guest ales ♂ Westons Stowford Press. **Facilities** Children welcome Children's portions Garden Parking **Notes** ☺

GLANGRWYNEY
Map 9 SO21

The Bell NEW

NP8 1EH ☎ **01873 811115**
e-mail: enquiries@thebellcountrypub.co.uk
dir: *On A40 halfway between Abergavenny & Crickhowell*

Just outside Abergavenny in the tiny village of Glangrwyney, this lovely country pub is located within the Brecon Beacons National Park and is the perfect pitstop for walkers or those in search of a comfortable refuel. A constantly changing selection of local ales and ciders is complemented by a menu that makes the most of abundant local produce. Try the venison shepherd's pie; steak-and-ale pie; or the board of award-winning Welsh cheeses. Real ale fans should time a visit for the Easter or August Bank Holiday beer festivals. Booking for meals may be required.

Open all day 12-11.30 Closed: Mon (ex holiday periods) **Bar Meals** L served Tue-Sun 12-3 D served Tue-Sun 6-9 Av main course £11 **Restaurant** L served Tue-Sun 12-3 D served Tue-Sun 6-9 Fixed menu price fr £10 Av 3 course à la carte fr £24 ⊕ BRAINS ◀ 4 Guest ales ♂ Westons, Gwynt y Ddraig Orchard Gold. ♥ 9 **Facilities** Children welcome Children's menu Children's portions Garden Beer festival Parking Wi-fi ▨ (notice required)

GLASBURY
Map 9 SO31

The Harp Inn NEW

HR3 5NR ☎ **01497 847373**
e-mail: info@theharpinn.co.uk
web: www.theharpinn.co.uk
dir: *In village centre on B4350, approx 3.5m from Hay-on-Wye*

A pub since the 16th century, this comfortable inn overlooks the River Wye and is just three miles from Hay-on-Wye itself. In the bar, grab a table by the log fire and enjoy a pint of one of several local real ales on offer or one of the ten wines available by the glass. The tempting menu offers delicious classics of home-made steak and Wye Valley stout pie, and Welsh lamb hotpot. Regular music events include monthly folk and Irish sessions and occasional jazz nights.

Open 12-3 6-12 Closed: Mon **Bar Meals** L served Tue-Sun 12-2 D served Tue-Sun 6.30-9 **Restaurant** L served Tue-Sun 12-2 D served Tue-Sun 6.30-9 ⊕ FREE HOUSE ◀ Wye Valley Dorothy Goodbody's Country Ale, Butty Bach ♂ Westons Stowford Press. ♥ 10 **Facilities** ✿ Children welcome Children's menu Children's portions Garden Parking Wi-fi ▨ (notice required)

PICK OF THE PUBS

The Bear Hotel ★★★ HL ❀

Brecon Rd NP8 1BW ☎ 01873 810408
e-mail: bearhotel@aol.com
web: www.bearhotel.co.uk
dir: *On A40 between Abergavenny & Brecon*

Dating back to 1432, this wonderful old coaching inn has been at the heart of life in the market town of Crickhowell for nearly 600 years. It retains oodles of the character derived from successive generations, with a superb old bar brimming with antique furnishings on the rug-strewn floor, sheltered cobbled courtyard and memorable hanging baskets. With the lovely Usk Valley walk, nearby canal and the tops of the Black Mountains and Brecon Beacons looming large, visitors wanting peace, tranquility and adventure seek out the comfortably appointed bedrooms, whilst the cuisine has gained an AA Rosette for the skilled chef and kitchen team. Taken in the bar or in two restaurant areas, the fare is strongly influenced by availability of local produce for which the area is widely renowned. A meal here might kick off with crab and sweetcorn chowder; Welsh rarebit on toasted bloomer; or chicken liver and Cognac parfait with red onion marmalade. Welsh Black beef features in several dishes (try the home-made cottage pie or one of the steaks, grilled to your liking and served with a

range of classic sauces), or sample slow-roasted belly pork with colcannon, black pudding and cider cream or home-made Welsh lamb burger with sweet tomato, rosemary and garlic chutney and chips. Vegetarians are well catered for and may be tempted by cauliflower and potato cake with green vegetables, tomato coulis and creamy cheese sauce. Round things off with bread-and-butter pudding, one of the many comforting desserts on offer. Booking for meals may be required.

Open all wk 11-3 6-11 Closed: 25 Dec **Bar Meals** L served all wk 12-2 D served Mon-Sat 6-10, Sun 7-9.30 Av main course £10 **Restaurant** L served Sun

12-2 D served Mon-Sat 6-10 Av 3 course à la carte fr £34 ⊕ FREE HOUSE ◀ Bass, Greene King Ruddles Best, Brains The Rev. James, John Smith's. ♟ 10 **Facilities** Children welcome Children's menu Children's portions Family room ✿ Garden Parking Wi-fi 🚌 **Rooms** 34

Save on hotels. Book at theAA.com/hotel

POWYS 675 WALES

HAY-ON-WYE
Map 9 SO24

The Old Black Lion ★★★★ INN ◉
PICK OF THE PUBS

HR3 5AD ☎ 01497 820841
e-mail: info@oldblacklion.co.uk
dir: *In town centre*

Parts of this charming whitewashed inn date from the 1300s, although structurally most of it is 17th century. It is situated close to what was known as the Lion Gate, one of the original entrances to the old walled town of Hay-on-Wye. The oak-timbered bar is furnished with scrubbed pine tables, comfy armchairs and a log-burning stove – perfect for savouring a pint of Old Black Lion Ale. The inn has a long-standing reputation for its food – witness the AA Rosette – and the pretty dining room overlooking the garden terrace is where to enjoy bar favourites of baked loin of cod with fennel, leeks and cheese sauce. In the restaurant the menu typically offers supreme of guinea fowl with spinach, sun-blushed tomatoes and Madeira sauce; and herb-crusted rack of local lamb with sweet potatoes and rosemary and port jus. Guest rooms are available. Hay, of course, has bookshops at every turn, and it is also home to a renowned annual literary festival. Only children over eight are welcome.

Open all day all wk 8am-11pm Closed: 24-26 Dec **Bar Meals** L served Mon-Fri 12-2, Sat-Sun 12-2.30 D served Sun-Thu 6.30-9, Fri-Sat 6.30-9.30 **Restaurant** L served Mon-Fri 12-2, Sat-Sun 12-2.30 D served Sun-Thu 6.30-9, Fri-Sat 6.30-9.30 ⊕ FREE HOUSE ◖ Old Black Lion Ale, Sharp's Doom Bar ♂ Westons Stowford Press. ⬥ 8 **Facilities** Garden Parking Wi-fi **Rooms** 10

The Three Tuns NEW

4 Broad St HR3 5DB ☎ 01497 821855
e-mail: info@three-tuns.com
dir: *In town centre*

Despite a devastating fire a few years ago, this 16th-century, possibly older, pub has attracted an eclectic roll-call of famous, even infamous, visitors, from Jools Holland to the Great Train Robbers. In the bar is an old settle, reclaimed from the fire and restored for that welcome pint of Wye Valley Bitter or Butty Bach, and a plate of cured Talgarth ham with rosemary sweet potatoes, a pizza or a ciabatta. A wider choice at dinner includes slow-cooked pork roulade; traditional Welsh faggots; pan-fried sea bass; and winter vegetable ratatouille moussaka. Booking for meals may be required.

Open 11-3 6-11 Closed: 25 Dec, Mon & Tue (winter) **Bar Meals** L served all wk 12-2 D served all wk 6-9 Av main course £13 **Restaurant** L served all wk 12-2 D served all wk 6-9 ⊕ FREE HOUSE ◖ Wye Valley Bitter, Butty Bach ♂ Westons Old Rosie. **Facilities** Children welcome Children's portions Garden Wi-fi ▬

LLANDRINDOD WELLS
Map 9 SO06

The Bell Country Inn

Llanyre LD1 6DY ☎ 01597 823959
e-mail: info@bellcountryinn.co.uk
dir: *1.5m NW of Llandrindod Wells on A4081*

Sitting high in the hills above Llandrindod Wells, this smartly refurbished former drovers' inn is now a pleasing mix of old and new. Two bars and a restaurant serve a range of beers and seasonally changing menus. Local ingredients are used with meat coming from neighbouring farms and woodland. A meal might include seared scallops on cauliflower purée and black pudding, followed by breast of Gressingham duck with honey-glazed onions, minted pea purée, château potato and a Madeira sauce. Finish with home-made lemon tart. Booking for meals may be required.

Open 12-3 6-11.30 Closed: Sun eve ⊕ FREE HOUSE ◖ Guinness, Guest ales. **Facilities** Children welcome Children's menu Children's portions Garden Parking Wi-fi

The Laughing Dog

Howey LD1 5PT ☎ 01597 822406
dir: *From A483 between Builth Wells & Llandrindod Wells follow Howey signs. Pub in village centre*

The original part of this traditional country pub dates back to the 17th century when it was used as a stop for drovers. The pub comprises a public bar, snug, games room, restaurant and an attractive, dog-friendly beer garden. Wye Valley and Rhymney Bevan's bitters are the resident real ales. Locally sourced, home-made British food with some Asian-influenced dishes is the order of the day: slow-roasted pork belly with cider gravy, apple jelly and crackling; vegetable dansak; and breast of corn-fed chicken in a red wine and mushroom sauce. Desserts to look out for are baked vanilla cheesecake with orange syrup; and white chocolate and Penderyn whisky tart. Booking for meals may be required.

Open all wk 6-11 (Fri 5.30-11 Sat-Sun all day) **Bar Meals** L served Sun 12-2 D served Fri-Sat 6.30-9 Av main course £10.95 **Restaurant** L served Sun 12-2 D served Fri-Sat 6.30-9 Av 3 course à la carte fr £21 ⊕ FREE HOUSE ◖ Wye Valley Bitter, Newmans Wolvers Ale, The Celt Experience Celt-Bronze Ale, Felinfoel Double Dragon, Rhymney Bevan's Bitter. **Facilities** ✿ Children welcome Children's portions Garden ▬ (notice required)

LLANFYLLIN
Map 15 SJ11

Cain Valley Hotel

High St SY22 5AQ ☎ 01691 648366
e-mail: info@cainvalleyhotel.co.uk
dir: *From Shrewsbury & Oswestry follow signs for Lake Vyrnwy & onto A490 to Llanfyllin. Hotel on right*

Formerly The Wynnstay Arms, this town centre inn has been Llanfyllin's principal hostelry since the 17th century. Its imposing staircase, oak-panelled lounge bar and heavily beamed restaurant with exposed hand-made bricks all date from that time, while the brick front and Tuscan porch were built around 1800. A full bar menu is available at lunchtime and in the evening typically offers Welsh lamb, port, plum and ginger casserole; and home-made steak-and-ale pie. Lovers of mild ale will find Ansell's in the bar. Booking for meals may be required.

Open all day all wk 11.30am-mdnt (Sun 12-11pm) Closed: 25 Dec **Bar Meals** L served all wk 12-2 D served all wk 7-9 Av main course £8.50 **Restaurant** D served all wk 7-9 Av 3 course à la carte fr £19 ⊕ FREE HOUSE ◖ Worthington's, Ansell's Mild, Guinness ♂ Thatchers Gold. **Facilities** Children welcome Children's menu Children's portions Parking Wi-fi ▬ (notice required)

LLANGYNIDR
Map 9 SO11

The Coach & Horses

Cwmcrawnon Rd NP8 1LS ☎ 01874 730245
e-mail: info@coachandhorses.org
dir: *Take A40 from Abergavenny towards Brecon. At Crickhowell left onto B4558 to Llangynidr (NB narrow river bridge), or from Beaufort take B4560 through Brynmawr to Llangynidr*

Just two minutes' walk from the nearby canal moorings and surrounded by the Brecon Beacons, this early 18th-century free house is also a popular meeting place for car club members - the car park can accommodate over 70 vehicles. Changing real ales are sourced from a 40-mile radius, and include the inn's own Llangynidr Canal Water ale. The talented chefs prepare the likes of deep-fried brie followed by home-made venison faggots with horseradish mash and a red wine sauce, finishing with chilled banana terrine. The beer garden has lovely views over the countryside, and there are beer festivals in May and July. Booking for meals may be required.

Open all day all wk 12-12 Closed: Mon in winter **Bar Meals** L served all wk 12-2 D served all wk 6-9 Av main course £9.95 **Restaurant** L served Mon-Sat 12-2, Sun 12-3 D served Sun 6-9 ⊕ FREE HOUSE ◖ Llangynidr Canal Water, Guest ales ♂ Westons Stowford Press, Gwynt y Ddraig. **Facilities** ✿ Children welcome Children's menu Children's portions Garden Beer festival Parking Wi-fi ▬ (notice required)

PICK OF THE PUBS

The Dragon ★★★★ INN 🌹

MONTGOMERY　　　　Map 15 SO29

SY15 6PA ☎ 01686 668359
e-mail: reception@dragonhotel.com
web: www.dragonhotel.com
dir: *A483 towards Welshpool, right onto
B4386 then B4385. Behind town hall*

Set in the stunning Welsh Marches, this
black-and-white timber-framed
coaching inn dates back to the 1600s.
It is full of historical features, including
the enclosed patio which has been
created from the former coach entrance,
and the masonry in the bar, lounge and
most bedrooms, which was allegedly
removed from Montgomery Castle after
its destruction by Oliver Cromwell.
Husband and wife team Mark and Sue
Michaels oversee the bar and kitchen
respectively. Ales from the Montgomery
Brewery, wines from the Penarth
Vineyard and local Old Monty cider are
among the refreshments on offer.
Awarded an AA Rosette for its fine food
for over ten years, this inn offers an
excellent range of light snacks and full
meals. Snack-wise, you can choose from
a huge range of fillings, served in a
sandwich, a baguette or a jacket potato.
Ploughman's lunches and jumbo Welsh
rarebits are also on offer. If you prefer a
lengthy meal, kick off with nibbles such
as marinated artichoke hearts and
mushrooms or a selection of pickles,
then move on to chicken liver pâté with

beetroot salad and toast or Thai-spiced
fishcakes with sweet chilli dip. Typical
main courses range from spaghetti with
salmon and prawns through to a hearty
chicken pot pie with seasonal
vegetables. There's also a good choice
of vegetarian options (Welsh goat's
cheese and sun-dried tomato salad;
stirfry of fresh vegetables with teriyaki
sauce) and a please-all children's
menu, which includes pint-sized
portions of many of the adult's main
courses and simple meals such as
sausages and chips. Twenty en suite
rooms make the Dragon an ideal base
for touring, walking Offa's Dyke, and
fishing on the Severn. Booking for meals
may be required.

Open all wk 12-11 **Bar Meals** L served
all wk 12-2 D served all wk 7-9 Av main
course £9 **Restaurant** L served all wk
12-2 D served all wk 7-9 Fixed menu
price fr £26.50 Av 3 course à la carte fr
£30 ⊕ FREE HOUSE ◼ Wood's Special
Bitter, Bass, Montgomery Ö Old Monty.
Facilities Children welcome Children's
menu Children's portions Parking Wi-fi
🚌 (notice required) **Rooms** 20

Save on hotels. Book at **theAA.com/hotel**

POWYS 677 WALES

| MACHYNLLETH | Map 14 SH70 |

Wynnstay Hotel

PICK OF THE PUBS

SY20 8AE ☎ 01654 702941

e-mail: info@wynnstay-hotel.com

dir: *At junct A487 & A489. 5m from A470*

'Mach', as the locals call it, is a vibrant market town where, in the late 18th century, Sir Watcyn Williams-Wynne built his pied-à-terre. Now the Wynnstay, Herbert Arms and Unicorn Hotel (to give it its full title), it's run by Gareth Johns, a Master Chef of Great Britain, and his brother Paul. For their attractive, award-winning restaurant Gareth sources whatever ingredients he can within 50 miles, as Welsh place names on the menu testify. So were you to choose a three-course meal based on the appeal of where it comes from, you could start with Rhydlewis smoked fresh salmon rillettes; continue with Mathafarn pheasant breast with Puy lentils and smoked bacon; and round off with Llaeth-Y-Llan pannacotta with winter fruit compôte and mango coulis. Alternatively just drop in for a Welsh-brewed real ale in the bar where no piped music is played, although you might hear the occasional impromptu rendition by a visiting choir. Booking for meals may be required.

Open all wk 12-2.30 6-11 Closed: 1wk over New Year **Bar Meals** Av main course £13 **Restaurant** L served all wk 12-2 D served all wk 6.30-9 Av 3 course à la carte fr £19 ⊕ FREE HOUSE ◀ Greene King IPA, The Celt Experience Celt-Golden Ale, Monty's Moonrise, Evan Evans Warrior, Guinness. ☕ 10 **Facilities** ☆ Children welcome Children's portions Parking 🚌 (notice required)

| MONTGOMERY | Map 15 SO29 |

The Dragon ★★★★ INN ◉

PICK OF THE PUBS

See Pick of the Pubs on opposite page

| NEW RADNOR | Map 9 SO26 |

Red Lion Inn

PICK OF THE PUBS

Llanfihangel-nant-Melan LD8 2TN ☎ 01544 350220

e-mail: theredlioninn@yahoo.co.uk

dir: *A483 to Crossgates then right onto A44, 6m to pub. 3m W of New Radnor on A44*

Here in the wild landscape of mid-Wales is an ancient drover's inn that still provides water, though nowadays it's for hosing down muddy bikes, rather than for livestock to drink. There's a beamed lounge bar and a locals' bar offering guest real ales, two small restaurants and a suntrap garden. Traditional and modern cookery is based on fresh, local produce, some of the most popular dishes being Welsh Black sirloin steaks, Welsh lamb and organic salmon. Other main courses include game terrine with Cognac and grape preserve; and leek, wild mushroom and chestnut gâteau. Add imaginative

vegetarian dishes and traditional Sunday roasts. Round off with Welsh cheeses and home-made walnut bread. Welsh cream teas are served during the afternoon. Next door is St Michael's church, one of four so named encircling the burial place of the last Welsh dragon. According to legend, should anything happen to them the dragon will rise again.

Open 12-11.30 (Sun 12-7.30) Closed: Tue ⊕ FREE HOUSE ◀ Guest ales ♂ Westons Stowford Press. **Facilities** Children welcome Family room Garden Parking

| OLD RADNOR | Map 9 SO25 |

The Harp

PICK OF THE PUBS

LD8 2RH ☎ 01544 350655

e-mail: mail@harpinnradnor.co.uk

dir: *Old Radnor signed from A44 between Kington & New Radnor*

The Harp is a stone-built Welsh longhouse, believed to date from the 15th century. Views of the Radnor Valley are spectacular. Open the simple wooden door and you step into a cosy lounge and bars with oak beams, log fires, semi-circular wooden settles and slate floors; books, board games and hop bines complete the warmly traditional appeal. Real ales from Shropshire are rotated, and an annual June beer festival is hugely popular. The food focus is on fresh and seasonal produce, and local sources are identified on the pleasingly straightforward menu. Artisan bread with rapeseed oil and balsamic dip tides you over while your choices are being prepared. Black Mountains Smokery kipper, served warm with crushed new potato and chive salad, makes a tasty starter. Welsh lamb and beef will probably feature in the main course, or grilled sea bass fillets for fish lovers. Finish with a selection of Welsh cheeses; or rhubarb with custard, fresh cream and ginger crumb. Booking for meals may be required.

Open Tue-Fri 6-11 (Sat-Sun 12-3 6-11) Closed: Mon **Bar Meals** L served Sat-Sun 12-2.30 D served Tue-Sun 6-9 Av main course £14 **Restaurant** L served Sat-Sun 12-2.30 D served Tue-Sun 6-9 Av 3 course à la carte fr £20 ⊕ FREE HOUSE ◀ Three Tuns, Wye Valley, Hobsons, Ludlow, Salopian ♂ Kingston Rosy, Dunkertons, Westons Stowford Press. **Facilities** ☆ Children welcome Children's portions Garden Beer festival Parking Wi-fi

| TALGARTH | Map 9 SO13 |

Castle Inn

Pengenffordd LD3 0EP ☎ 01874 711353

e-mail: info@thecastleinn.co.uk

dir: *4m S of Talgarth on A479*

This welcoming inn enjoys a spectacular location in the heart of the Black Mountains, in the Brecon Beacons National Park. It is named after the Iron Age hill fort that tops the hill behind it – Castell Dinas. Numerous walks and mountain bike routes begin and end at its door, making it popular with outdoor enthusiasts. With a good selection of real local ales, substantial pub food includes steaks, beef, lamb, venison swordfish and tuna cooked on hot rocks; chicken and leek pie; and vegetable chilli. Look out for the Black Mountains' Beast – a large black cat that has been seen by several customers!

Open Wed-Fri 6-11 (Sat-Sun 12-11) Closed: Mon-Tue ⊕ FREE HOUSE ◀ Wye Valley Butty Bach, Rhymney Bitter & Hobby Horse, Brains The Rev. James, Evan Evans, Guest ales ♂ Westons Stowford Press & Vintage, Thatchers Gold. **Facilities** Children welcome Children's portions Garden Parking Wi-fi

| TALYBONT-ON-USK | Map 9 SO12 |

Star Inn

LD3 7YX ☎ 01874 676635

e-mail: anna@starinntalybont.co.uk

dir: *6m off A40 from Brecon towards Crickhowell*

Standing where the River Caerfanell runs under the Brecon and Monmouth Canal, the Star Inn is ideally placed for walkers, cyclists and boaters. This unmodernised 250-year-old inn is known, indeed revered, for its constantly changing beer selection of around 500 different ales a year. The hearty bar food is typically Welsh lamb shank with a rosemary and redcurrant jus; beef lasagne; and veggie Glamorgan sausages with a sweet red pepper sauce. There are regular pie and fish nights, and beer festivals in June and October.

Open all wk 11.30-3 5-11 (summer Mon-Fri 11.30-11 Sat-Sun 11-11) **Bar Meals** L served Mon-Fri 12-2, Sat-Sun 12-2.30 D served all wk 6-9 **Restaurant** L served Mon-Fri 12-2, Sat-Sun 12-2.30 D served all wk 6-9 ⊕ PUNCH TAVERNS ◀ Hancock's HB, Wadworth 6X, Guest ales ♂ Gwynt y Ddraig. **Facilities** ☆ Children welcome Children's menu Children's portions Garden Beer festival Wi-fi

| TRECASTLE | Map 9 SN82 |

The Castle Coaching Inn

PICK OF THE PUBS

See Pick of the Pubs on page 678

PICK OF THE PUBS

The Castle Coaching Inn

TRECASTLE   Map 9 SN82

LD3 8UH ☎ **01874 636354**
e-mail: reservations@castle-coaching-inn.co.uk
web: www.castle-coaching-inn.co.uk
dir: *On A40, W of Brecon*

Privately owned and run by the Porter family, this Georgian coaching inn sits on the old London to Carmarthen route in the northern part of the Brecon Beacons National Park. It makes an ideal base for the pursuit of outdoor activities or, for the less energetic, the simple appreciation of mountain views, lakes, waterfalls and wildlife. Restoration of the inn has been careful and considered over the years – there are lovely old fireplaces and a remarkable bow-fronted window looking out from the bar, where an open log fire burns throughout the winter. The focus on customer satisfaction makes this a relaxing hostelry, even at weekends when it becomes especially lively. Two real ales on tap change weekly, ensuring a pint in tip-top condition; wines and a good selection of Scottish and Irish whiskies are also served. While settling back to enjoy your drink and the pub's great atmosphere, take a look at the menu and specials board. Some guests prefer to stay in the bar to eat; the menu is the same both here and in the restaurant, although additional bar food includes fresh sandwiches, ploughman's, hot filled baguettes and

jackets. Starters range from home-made soup of the day with crusty bread, to duck and orange pâté; deep-fried camembert; and a salmon, cod and prawn fishcake served with home-made tartare sauce. Main courses typically include Welsh sirloin steak cooked to your liking with mushrooms, cherry tomatoes and onion rings; supreme of chicken stuffed with stilton, wrapped in bacon, with a white wine and cream sauce; and slow-roasted belly pork with cider apple and Calvados sauce. Desserts press all the right buttons with the likes of Belgian triple chocolate praline torte with vanilla ice cream; and lemon posset with shortbread. Outside, the peaceful terrace and garden beckon on sunny days.

Open all wk Sat-Sun 12-3, Mon-Sat 6-11, Sun 7-11 **Bar Meals** L served Sat-Sun 12-2 D served Mon-Sat 6.30-9, Sun 7-9 **Restaurant** L served Sat-Sun 12-2 D served Mon-Sat 6.30-9, Sun 7-9
⊕ FREE HOUSE ◖ Guest ales.
Facilities Children welcome Children's menu Children's portions ❧ Garden Parking Wi-fi

RHONDDA CYNON TAFF

PONTYPRIDD — Map 9 ST08

Bunch of Grapes

Ynysangharad Rd CF37 4DA ☎ 01443 402934
e-mail: info@bunchofgrapes.org.uk
dir: *From A470 onto A4054 (Pentrebach Rd/Merthyr Rd) into Ynysangharad Rd*

The Bunch of Grapes backs on to one of the last remnants of the Glamorganshire Canal, built in 1792. Now tastefully and sympathetically refurbished, the Bunch prides itself on quality, locally sourced foods and "back-slappingly friendly service". The pub has its own micro-brewery, so Otley ales are among the refreshments on offer at the bar. Head for the separate dining room to choose from the list of modern British dishes which uses sustainably farmed ingredients: deep-fried pollock fillet with hand-cut chips; grilled wood pigeon breast with celeriac purée and pomegranate salsa; or braised lamb shank are some examples. If you enjoy the signature dessert of sticky toffee pudding, you can buy the butterscotch sauce from the pub's deli. Booking for meals may be required.

Open all day all wk **Bar Meals** Av main course £8 food served all day **Restaurant** L served all wk 12-2.30 D served all wk 6.30-9.30 Av 3 course à la carte fr £24 ⊕ FREE HOUSE ◀ Otley O1, Guest ales ♂ Gwynt y Ddraig, Blaengawney. **Facilities** ✿ Children welcome Children's menu Children's portions Garden Beer festival Parking

SWANSEA

LLANGENNITH — Map 8 SS49

Kings Head ★★★★ INN

SA3 1HX ☎ 01792 386212
e-mail: info@kingsheadgower.co.uk
dir: *M4 junct 47, follow signs for Gower A483, 2nd exit at rdbt, right at lights onto B495 towards Old Walls, left at fork to Llangennith, pub on right*

A lane to Rhossili Bay starts just along from this 17th-century village inn, which still displays plenty of old beams, exposed stonework and a large open fire. The bar serves a weekly rotating schedule of real ales from the Gower Brewery, which pub landlord Chris Stevens co-founded in 2011. Well regarded home-made food using local produce includes Vietnamese, Goan and Thai curries; pizzas; creamy chicken and leek pie; salt marsh lamb steak; and fillet of sea bass. Comfortable, pet-friendly accommodation is available. A beer festival is held during the last weekend of November.

Open all day all wk 9am-11pm (Sun 9am-10.30pm) **Bar Meals** L served all wk 9am-9.30pm D served all wk 9am-9.30pm food served all day **Restaurant** L served all wk 9am-9.30pm D served all wk 9am-9.30pm food served all day ⊕ FREE HOUSE ◀ Gower, Guinness. **Facilities** ✿ Children welcome Children's menu Children's portions Garden Beer festival Parking ⛟ **Rooms** 27

REYNOLDSTON — Map 8 SS48

King Arthur Hotel

Higher Green SA3 1AD ☎ 01792 390775
e-mail: info@kingarthurhotel.co.uk
dir: *Just N of A4118 SW of Swansea*

Sheep graze on the village green opposite this charming inn set in a pretty village at the heart of the beautiful Gower Peninsula. Inside you'll find real log fires, bare wood floors and walls decorated with nautical memorabilia. Eat in the restaurant, main bar or family room, where choices range from pub favourites such as fillet of cod in a lager batter with home-made tartare sauce or a chicken fillet Kiev through to healthy salads (maybe Greek, ham or chicken Caesar). Enjoy the food with a choice of well-kept local ales, or one of 11 wines served by the glass. Booking for meals may be required.

Open all day all wk Closed: 25 Dec **Bar Meals** food served all day **Restaurant** L served all wk 12-2.30 D served Sun-Thu 6-9, Fri-Sat 6-9.30 ⊕ FREE HOUSE ◀ Felinfoel Double Dragon, Tomos Watkin OSB, Cottage King Arthur, Worthington's, Bass. ♈ 11 **Facilities** Children welcome Children's menu Children's portions Family room Garden Parking ⛟

VALE OF GLAMORGAN

COWBRIDGE — Map 9 SS97

The Cross Inn

Church Rd, Llanblethian CF71 7JF ☎ 01446 772995
e-mail: enquiry@crossinncowbridge.co.uk
web: www.crossinncowbridge.co.uk
dir: *Leave Cowbridge on B4270 towards Llantwit Major, pub 0.5m on right*

First licensed as a coaching inn in 1671, the picturesque Cross is tucked away on the fringes of Cowbridge in a peaceful corner of the Vale of Glamorgan, just a few miles from the splendid Heritage Coast. Fresh produce is sourced as locally as possible, with fish, meat and poultry delivered on a daily basis for dishes and specials such as home-made Glamorgan sausages; pie of the day; and slow-braised lamb shank. With lovely hanging flower baskets, the inn has won 'in bloom' awards. Look out for the mini beer and cider festivals in April and September.

Open all day all wk 10am-11pm **Bar Meals** L served Mon-Fri 12-2.30, Sat 12-9, Sun 12-3.30 D served Mon-Fri 5.30-9, Sat 12-9, Sun 5-8 Av main course £7.95 **Restaurant** L served Mon-Fri 12-2.30, Sat 12-9, Sun 12-3.30 D served Mon-Fri 5.30-9, Sat 12-9, Sun 5-8 Av 3 course à la carte fr £18.95 ⊕ FREE HOUSE ◀ Hancock's HB, Wye Valley Butty Bach, Evan Evans Crwr, Shepherd Neame Bishops Finger, Thornbridge Jaipur ♂ Westons & Stowford Press, Thatchers Gold. **Facilities** ✿ Children welcome Children's menu Children's portions Garden Beer festival Parking Wi-fi ⛟

Victoria Inn

Sigingstone CF71 7LP ☎ 01446 773943
e-mail: oleary445@aol.com
dir: *Off B4270 in Sigingstone*

In the heart of the Vale of Glamorgan, this much-loved, family-owned village inn, whose beamed interior is absolutely stuffed with photographs, prints and antiques has a reputation for good quality, home-prepared food. The daily breakfast, lunchtime and evening menus are extensive, with dishes such as pan-fried chicken breast, lamb chops, lasagne, salmon and prawn salad, fish pancake, and a juicy steak. Daily specials, including beautifully fresh fish, are chalked up on the blackboard. Thursday is curry night. The cosy snug is the perfect place to relax and enjoy a pint.

Open all wk 9.30-3 5.30-11.30 **Bar Meals** L served all wk 11.45-2.30 D served all wk 5.30-9 Av main course £8.95 **Restaurant** L served all wk 11.45-2.30 D served all wk 5.30-9 Fixed menu price fr £9.95 ⊕ FREE HOUSE ◀ Hancocks HB, Worthington's Creamflow, Sharp's Doom Bar, Brains SA Smooth. **Facilities** Children welcome Children's menu Garden Parking Wi-fi ⛟ (notice required)

EAST ABERTHAW — Map 9 ST06

Blue Anchor Inn

PICK OF THE PUBS

CF62 3DD ☎ 01446 750329
e-mail: blueanchor@gmail.com
dir: *From Barry take A4226, then B4265 towards Llantwit Major. Follow signs, turn left for East Aberthaw. 3m W of Cardiff Airport*

The grandfather of the present owners, Jeremy and Andrew Coleman, acquired this pretty, stone-built and heavily thatched inn in 1941, when he bought it from a large local estate. The inn has been trading almost continuously since 1380, the only break being in 2004 when a serious fire destroyed the top half of the building, forcing its closure for restoration. The interior remains warmly traditional; a warren of small rooms with low, beamed ceilings and open fires, including a large inglenook. A selection of well-kept real ales, including Wye Valley plus guests, is always on tap. An enticing range of food is offered in both the bar and the upstairs restaurant. Choose pub classics like gammon steak with egg and chips or more upmarket offerings such as pan-fried red mullet with broad beans and sorrel sauce followed by roasted local venison with roasted beetroot and red onion purée. A good choice is offered for Sunday lunch. Booking for meals may be required.

Open all day all wk 11-11 (25 Dec 12-2) **Bar Meals** L served Mon-Sat 12-2 D served Mon-Sat 6-9 Av main course £9 **Restaurant** L served Sun 12.30-2.30 D served Mon-Sat 7-9.30 Fixed menu price fr £10.50 Av 3 course à la carte fr £21 ⊕ FREE HOUSE ◀ Theakston Old Peculier, Wadworth 6X, Wye Valley HPA, Brains Bitter. **Facilities** 🐾 Children welcome Garden Parking 🚭

MONKNASH — Map 9 SS97

The Plough & Harrow

CF71 7QQ ☎ 01656 890209
e-mail: info@theploughmonknash.com
dir: *M4 junct 35 take dual carriageway to Bridgend. At rdbt follow St Brides sign, then brown tourist signs. Pub 3m NW of Llantwit Major*

Set in peaceful countryside on the edge of a small village with views across the fields to the Bristol Channel, this area is great for walkers attracted to the coastline. Dating back to 1383, the low, slate-roofed building was originally built as the chapter house of a monastery, although it has been a pub for 500 years. Expect an atmospheric interior, open fires, real ciders, up to eight guest ales on tap, and home-cooked food. Booking for meals may be required.

Open all day all wk **Bar Meals** L served Mon-Fri 12-2.30, Sat-Sun 12-5 D served all wk 6-8.30 **Restaurant** L served Mon-Fri 12-2.30, Sat-Sun 12-5 D served Mon-Sat 6-9 ⊕ FREE HOUSE ◀ Otley O1, Shepherd Neame Spitfire, Wye Valley HPA, Sharp's Atlantic IPA, Bass, Guest ales Ö Gwynt y Ddraig Happy Daze, Fiery Fox & Black Dragon. **Facilities** Children welcome Children's menu Children's portions Garden Beer festival Parking 🚭

WREXHAM

BURTON GREEN — Map 15 SJ35

The Golden Grove **NEW**

LLyndir Ln LL12 0AS ☎ 01244 571006
e-mail: enquiries@golden-grove.com
dir: *Exit B5445 (Old Chester to Wrexham road) into Llyndir Ln. Over level crossing. 1.5m to pub*

Having won recognition locally for its hospitality, The Golden Grove sets high standards as a family-run business. You'll find the pub in a beautiful rural setting, its venerable black-and-white timber framing betraying its 13th-century origins. A cosy bar, even cosier snug and spacious restaurant each have a real fire, while the summer months see much demand for the tranquil garden and comfortably furnished terrace. Marston's ales are backed by weekly guests, while menus include pub classics (fish and chips, steak-and-ale pie) and more complex dishes such as duck and sweet potato hotpot. Booking for meals may be required.

Open all day Closed: Mon **Bar Meals** L served Tue-Sat 12-9.30, Sun 12-9 D served Tue-Sat 12-9.30, Sun 12-9 Av main course £10 food served all day **Restaurant** L served Tue-Sat 12-9.30, Sun 12-9 D served Tue-Sat 12-9.30, Sun 12-9 Fixed menu price fr £10 Av 3 course à la carte fr £20 food served all day ⊕ MARSTON'S ◀ Burton Bitter, Brakspear Oxford Gold, Guest ale. ♥ 11 **Facilities** 🐾 Children welcome Children's portions Garden Parking Wi-fi 🚭 (notice required)

ERBISTOCK — Map 15 SJ34

Cross Foxes

Overton Bridge LL13 0DR ☎ 01978 780380
e-mail: cross.foxes@brunningandprice.co.uk
dir: *From Wrexham take A525 S. At Marchwiel take A528 signed Ellesmere to Erbistock*

Smack beside the River Dee close to the Shropshire border, this spruced-up 18th-century former coaching inn offers great river views from its raised terrace and through picture-windows in the one of the light and airy dining rooms. In typical Brunning & Price style, the interior is smart and comfortable, the choice of ales wines and spirits is impressive, and the all-day food operation is not only good value but a cut above the norm. Take potted salmon and crab, lamb shank with bubble-and-squeak and rosemary sauce, and sticky toffee pudding.

Open all day all wk Closed: 25 Dec ⊕ BRUNNING & PRICE ◀ Ringwood Best Bitter, Mansfield Riding Bitter, Brakspear Ö Westons. **Facilities** Children welcome Children's portions Play area Garden Parking

GRESFORD — Map 15 SJ35

Pant-yr-Ochain

PICK OF THE PUBS

Old Wrexham Rd LL12 8TY ☎ 01978 853525
e-mail: pant.yr.ochain@brunningandprice.co.uk
dir: *From Chester take exit for Nantwich. Holt off A483. Take 2nd left, also signed Nantwich Holt. Turn left at 'The Flash' sign. Pub 500yds on right*

A sweeping drive lined by majestic trees leads to this decoratively gabled manor house overlooking a lake and award-winning gardens. Although there has been a building on this site since the 13th-century, today's structure originally dates from the 1530s, as you can see from the Tudor wattle-and-daub walls and timber in the snug. The interior also has an inglenook fireplace and a host of nooks and crannies. The bar dispenses well-kept real ales such as Purple Moose, with Taffy Apples cider in support. Wine lovers too will not be disappointed by having to choose between over two dozen options. A daily-changing menu may offer a starter of chargrilled aubergine and tomato rolls with pomegranate and chilli yogurt; a light bite such as seafood risotto with parmesan shavings and dill dressing; and main courses such as Moroccan chicken, couscous, fig and pistachio salad with coriander dressing; or beef goulash with mash and sour cream. Eton Mess or vanilla cheesecake with cherry compôte could be dessert options.

Open all wk 12-11.30 (Sun 12-11) Closed: 25 Dec **Bar Meals** Av main course £11.95 food served all day **Restaurant** food served all day ⊕ FREE HOUSE/BRUNNING & PRICE ◀ Flowers Original, Weetwood Cheshire Cat, Brunning & Price Original Bitter, Purple Moose Ö Tomas Watkin Taffy Apples, Westons Stowford Press, Aspall. ♥ 22 **Facilities** 🐾 Children welcome Children's menu Children's portions Play area Garden Parking

HANMER — Map 15 SJ43

The Hanmer Arms ★★★★ INN

SY13 3DE ☎ 01948 830532
e-mail: info@hanmerarms.co.uk
dir: *Between Wrexham & Whitchurch on A539, off A525*

Locals fill the beamed and wooden-floored bars of this traditional free house, set beside the parish church in a peaceful, rural location on the Welsh border. The daily set dinner for two includes a glass of house wine, whilst the menu options include starters such as chicken liver pâté with toasted brioche and house chutney, followed by roast lamb rump with boulangère potatoes, or fresh fillet of salmon with a champagne herb sauce. Comfortable en suite rooms make the Hanmer Arms a good touring base.

Open all day all wk ⊕ FREE HOUSE ◀ Timothy Taylor Landlord, Adnams, Stonehouse Ö Westons Stowford Press. **Facilities** Children welcome Children's menu Children's portions Garden Parking Wi-fi **Rooms** 11

Save on hotels. Book at **theAA.com/hotel**

WREXHAM 681 WALES

PICK OF THE PUBS

The Hand at Llanarmon ★★★★ INN

LLANARMON DYFFRYN CEIRIOG Map 15 SJ13

LL20 7LD ☎ **01691 600666**
e-mail: reception@thehandhotel.co.uk
web: www.thehandhotel.com
dir: *Exit A5 at Chirk follow B4500 for 11m. Through Ceiriog Valley to Llanarmon D C. Pub straight ahead*

Make the journey up the remote Ceiriog Valley in the shadow of the Berwyn Mountains, and you'll find this classic country inn with its unique dining room and 13 comfortable en suite bedrooms. Still very much at the heart of the local community, the 16th-century free house was once a natural stopping place for drovers and their flocks on the old drovers' road from London to Anglesey. The Hand continued to operate as a working farm until the mid-20th century, and only became a fully-fledged inn in the late 1950s. Not surprising, then, that original oak beams, burnished brass and large fireplaces set the scene in the bar, where travellers and locals mingle in a buzz of friendly conversation over a pint of Weetwood Cheshire Cat or Brains The Rev. James. In recent years chef Grant Mulholland has established a strong reputation for no-nonsense dishes, cooked from scratch with flair and imagination; the same menu is served in the bar, the restaurant and on the sunny patio garden. The pub menu includes traditional favourites such as Hand shepherd's pie with parmesan mash and buttered cabbage, or Weetwood-

battered haddock with home-made chips, tartare sauce and peas. Restaurant diners can expect starters like Welsh organic smoked salmon and lemon mayonnaise with brown bread and butter; or goat's cheese brûlée with basil jam and toasted organic bread. Main course options might include pan-fried Welsh black sirloin steak with glazed Perl Lâs cheese and parsley butter; or crab bhajis with smoked haddock risotto and roasted cherry tomatoes. Home-made pudding choices feature Bramley apple money bag with vanilla ice cream; and spiced, roasted pineapple with pistachio cream. Booking for meals may be required.

Open all day all wk 11-11 (Sun 12-10.30) **Bar Meals** L served Mon-Sat 12-2.20, Sun 12.30-2.45 D served all wk

6.30-8.45 Av main course £12.25 **Restaurant** L served Mon-Sat 12-2.20, Sun 12.30-2.45 D served all wk 6.30-8.45 Av 3 course à la carte fr £26.50 ⊕ FREE HOUSE ◼ Weetwood Cheshire Cat, Brains The Rev. James, Monty's Sunshine ♻ Westons Stowford Press. **Facilities** Children welcome Children's portions ❖ Garden Parking 🚌 (notice required) **Rooms** 13

LLANARMON DYFFRYN CEIRIOG   Map 15 SJ13

The Hand at Llanarmon ★★★★ INN ◉

PICK OF THE PUBS

See Pick of the Pubs on page 681

West Arms ★★★★ INN ◉

PICK OF THE PUBS

LL20 7LD ☎ **01691 600665**
e-mail: info@thewestarms.co.uk
dir: *Off A483/A5 at Chirk, take B4500 to Ceiriog Valley*

The early 20th-century Prime Minister David Lloyd George described the Ceiriog Valley as 'a little piece of heaven on earth'. Way off the beaten track in this secret valley is the West Arms, built as a hostelry for drovers and now a magnet for ramblers. Its 16th-century labyrinthine rooms are full of character, with inglenook fireplaces, slate-flagged floors and wizened oak beams. A great selection of real ales includes Cambrian Gold, while

celebrity chef Grant Williams continues to prepare dishes to AA Rosette standard. These are based on the Ceiriog Valley's abundant ingredients and home-grown produce from the vast garden. You may need to look no further than the bar menu, if the bacon, turkey and mayonnaise baguette will suffice. Alternatively go for the appetite-satisfying hot plate of venison fillet wrapped in pastry with a wild mushroom duxelle in a Burgundy sauce. Your enjoyment will only be compounded by the warm welcome, friendly service and stunning views. Booking for meals may be required.

Open all day all wk **Bar Meals** L served Mon-Fri 12-2.30, Sat-Sun 12-9 D served Mon-Fri 6.30-9, Sat-Sun 12-9 Av main course £15.95 **Restaurant** L served Sun 12-2.30 D served all wk 7-9 Fixed menu price fr £27.95 Av 3 course à la carte fr £32.95 ⊕ FREE HOUSE ◀ Stonehouse Cambrian Gold & Station Bitter, Three Tuns XXX, Guinness, Guest ales ♂ Gwynt y Ddraig Black Dragon, Westons Stowford Press. **Facilities** ❧ Children welcome Children's menu Children's portions Garden Parking Wi-fi ▭ **Rooms** 15

MARFORD   Map 15 SJ35

MARFORD   Map 15 SJ35

Trevor Arms Hotel

LL12 8TA ☎ **01244 570436**
e-mail: thetrevorarmshotel@live.co.uk
dir: *Off A483 onto B5102 then right onto B5445 into Marford*

The early 19th-century coaching inn takes its name from Lord Trevor of Trevallin, who was killed in a duel; public executions, both by beheading and hanging, took place in the village. Grisly history notwithstanding, today's Trevor Arms is a charming hostelry, offering a selection of real ales and a varied menu of home-cooked dishes. Starters may include chicken liver pâté or prawn cocktail; then a main course of a mixed grill; beer-battered fish; or crispy Chinese glazed pork belly. Lite bites could be a duck wrap or salmon fishcakes. Booking for meals may be required.

Open all day all wk ◀ John Smith's, Guinness, Guest ales. **Facilities** Children welcome Children's menu Children's portions Garden Parking

Save on hotels. Book at **theAA.com/hotel**

WREXHAM 683 WALES

How to Find a Pub in the Atlas Section

Pubs are located in the gazetteer under the name of the nearest town or village. If a pub is in a small village or rural area, it may appear under a town within five miles of its actual location. The black dots and town names shown in the atlas refer to the gazetteer location in the guide. Please use the directions in the pub entry to find the pub on foot or by car. If directions are not given, or are not clear, please telephone the pub for details.

Key to County Map

The county map shown here will help you identify the counties within each country. You can look up each county in the guide using the county names at the top of each page. Towns featured in the guide use the atlas pages and index following this map.

England

1 Bedfordshire
2 Berkshire
3 Bristol
4 Buckinghamshire
5 Cambridgeshire
6 Greater Manchester
7 Herefordshire
8 Hertfordshire
9 Leicestershire
10 Northamptonshire
11 Nottinghamshire
12 Rutland
13 Staffordshire
14 Warwickshire
15 West Midlands
16 Worcestershire

Scotland

17 City of Glasgow
18 Clackmannanshire
19 East Ayrshire
20 East Dunbartonshire
21 East Renfrewshire
22 Perth & Kinross
23 Renfrewshire
24 South Lanarkshire
25 West Dunbartonshire

Wales

26 Blaenau Gwent
27 Bridgent
28 Caerphilly
29 Denbighshire
30 Flintshire
31 Merthyr Tydfil
32 Monmouthshire
33 Neath Port Talbot
34 Newport
35 Rhondda Cynon Taff
36 Torfaen
37 Vale of Glamorgan
38 Wrexham

Orkney Islands

Shetland Islands

Na h-Eileanan
an Iar

Highland

Moray

SCOTLAND

Aberdeenshire

City of
Aberdeen

Angus

Perth &
Kinross

City of
Dundee

Argyll
& Bute

Stirling

Fife

East
Lothian

North
Ayrshire

19

24

Scottish
Borders

South
Ayrshire

Dumfries &
Galloway

Northumberland

Argyll
& Bute

Stirling

18

22

Fife

Inverclyde

25

20

Falkirk

23

17

North
Lanarkshire

West
Lothian

City of
Edinburgh

North
Ayrshire

21

Midlothian

19

South Lanarkshire

Scottish
Borders

Tyne & Wear

Cumbria

Durham

Isle
of Man

North
Yorkshire

East Riding
of Yorkshire

Lancashire

West
Yorkshire

Isle of
Anglesey

Merseyside

6

South
Yorkshire

Lincolnshire

Conwy

30

Cheshire

Derbyshire

29

38

11

Gwynedd

13

Norfolk

Shropshire

9

12

WALES

15

5

Ceredigion

Powys

16

14

10

Suffolk

Pembrokeshire

7

1

Carmarthenshire

Gloucestershire

8

Essex

Swansea

3

Oxfordshire

Greater
London

4

2

31

26

32

Wiltshire

Surrey

Kent

33

36

35

28

34

Somerset

Hampshire

West
Sussex

East
Sussex

27

Cardiff

37

Devon

Dorset

Isle of
Wight

Cornwall

Isles of
Scilly

Guernsey

Jersey

ENGLAND

0   20   40   60   80   100 miles

0   20 40 60 80 100 120 140 160 kilometres

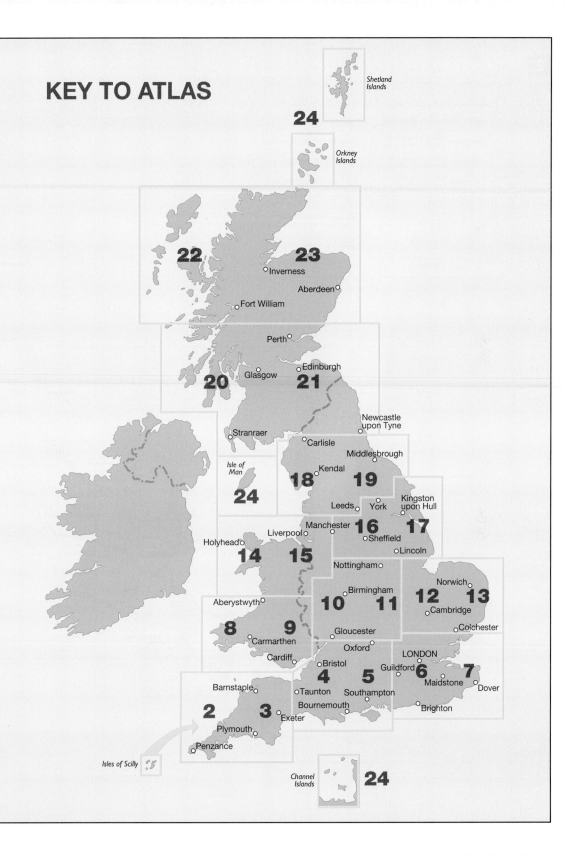

KEY TO ATLAS

Shetland Islands

24

Orkney Islands

22

23

○ Inverness

Aberdeen ○

○ Fort William

Perth ○

○ Edinburgh

20

Glasgow ○

21

○ Stranraer

Newcastle upon Tyne ○

○ Carlisle

Middlesbrough ○

Isle of Man

18

Kendal ○

19

24

Leeds ○

York ○

Kingston upon Hull ○

Holyhead ○

Liverpool ○

Manchester ○

16

Sheffield ○

17

14

15

Lincoln ○

Nottingham ○

Aberystwyth ○

Birmingham ○

Norwich ○

12

13

10

11

Cambridge ○

8

9

Gloucester ○

Colchester ○

Carmarthen ○

Oxford ○

LONDON

Cardiff ○

Bristol ○

Guildford ○

6

7

Barnstaple ○

4

5

Southampton ○

Maidstone ○

Dover ○

Taunton ○

Bournemouth ○

Brighton ○

2

3

Exeter ○

Plymouth ○

Isles of Scilly

Penzance ○

Channel Islands

24

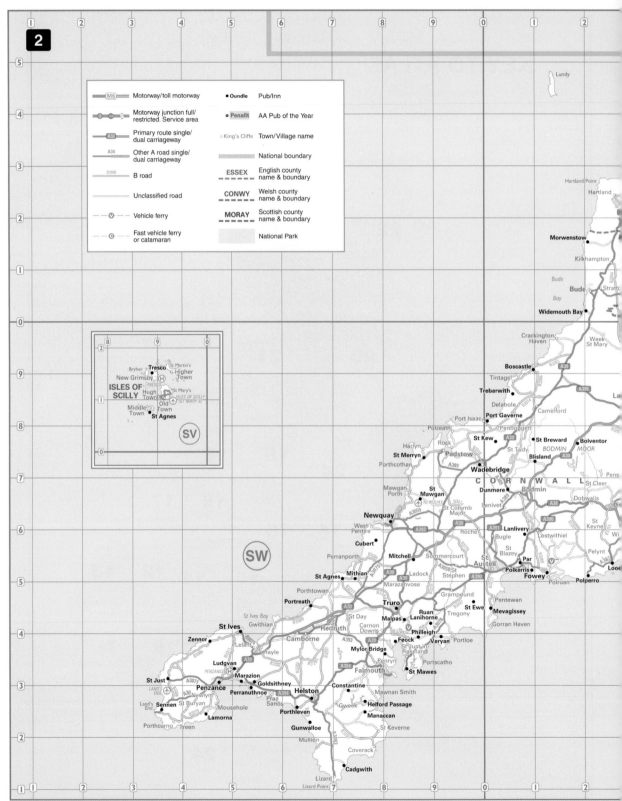

Motorway/toll motorway

Motorway junction full/ restricted. Service area

Primary route single/ dual carriageway

Other A road single/ dual carriageway

B road

Unclassified road

Vehicle ferry

Fast vehicle ferry or catamaran

●Oundle Pub/Inn

●Penallt AA Pub of the Year

○King's Cliffe Town/Village name

National boundary

ESSEX English county name & boundary

CONWY Welsh county name & boundary

MORAY Scottish county name & boundary

National Park

Lundy

ISLES OF SCILLY

Bryher Tresco St Martin's
New Grimsby Higher Town
Hugh Town St Mary's
Old Town ISLES OF SCILLY (ST MARY'S)
Middle Town St Agnes

SV

Hartland Point
Hartland

Morwenstow

Kilkhampton

Bude
Bude
Stratton
Bay
Widemouth Bay

Crackington Haven
Week St Mary

Boscastle

Tintagel
Trebarwith
Delabole Camelford
Port Isaac Port Gaverne
Polzeath
Harlyn Rock St Kew St Tudy St Breward Bolventor
St Merryn Padstow BODMIN MOOR
Porthcothan Blisland
Wadebridge
A389

CORNWALL
St Cleer
Mawgan Porth St Mawgan Dunmere Bodmin
Lanivet Dobwalls
Newquay St Columb Major St Keyne
West Pentire Roche Lanlivery Lostwithiel
Cubert Bugle St Blazey Pelynt
Perranporth Summercourt Par
Mitchell St Austell Polkerris Looe
St Agnes Ladock St Stephen Fowey Polperro
Mithian Marazanvose Polruan
Porthtowan Grampound Pentewan
Portreath St Ewe Mevagissey
St Day Truro Tregony Gorran Haven
Redruth Malpas Ruan Lanihorne
Carnon Dowris Veryan
Gwithian Camborne Feock Portloe
St Ives Lelant Philleigh Portscatho
Zennor St Just-in-Roseland
Hayle Mylor Bridge St Mawes
Ludgvan Penryn
Marazion Falmouth
St Just Penzance Goldsithney Constantine
Newlyn Perranuthnoe Mawnan Smith
Land's End Sennen St Buryan Helston Helford Passage
Mousehole Praa Sands Gweek Manaccan
Lamorna Porthleven St Keverne
Porthcurno Treen Gunwalloe
Mullion
Coverack
Cadgwith
Lizard
Lizard Point

SW

For continuation pages refer to numbered arrows

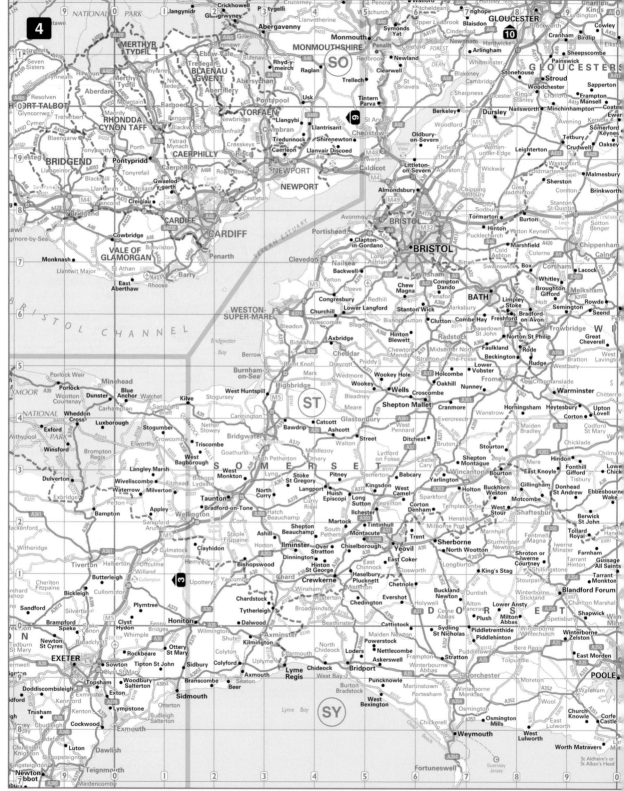

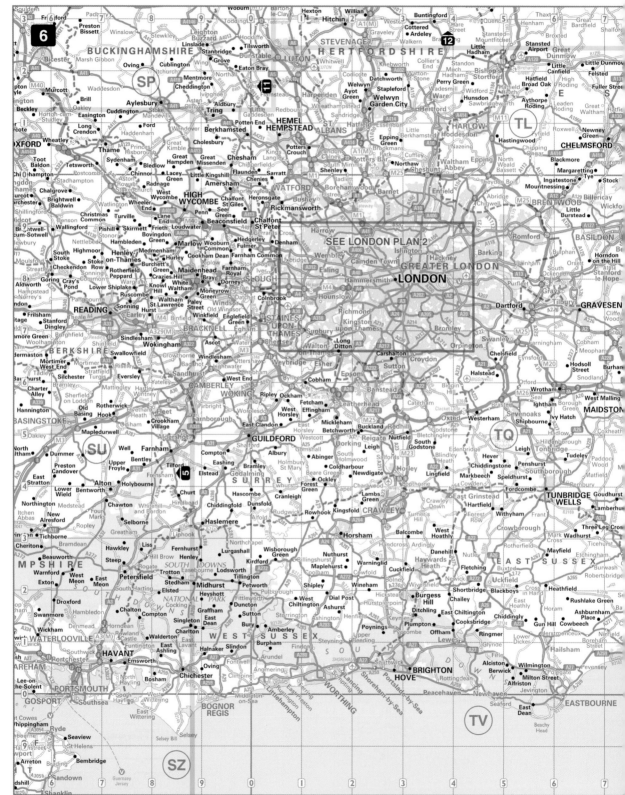

For continuation pages refer to numbered arrows

For continuation pages refer to numbered arrows

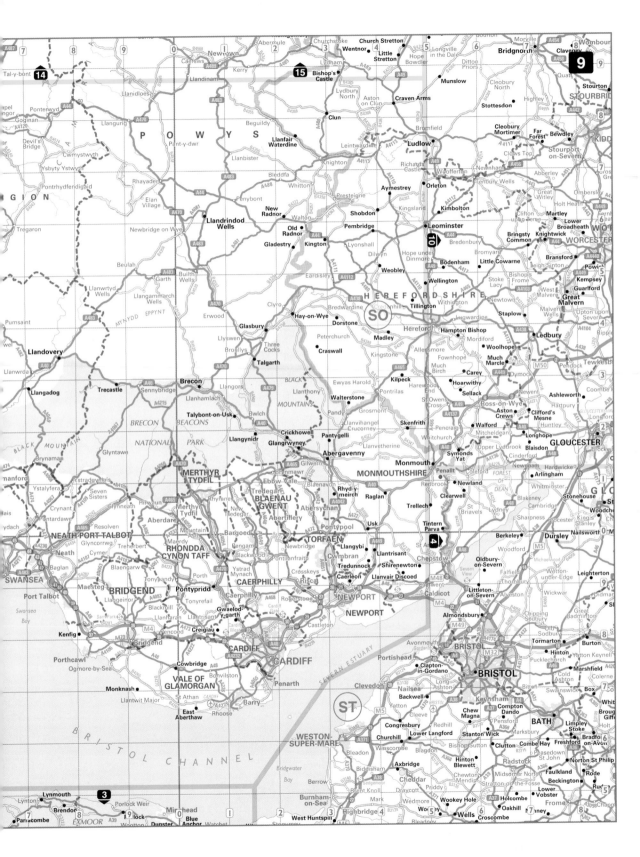

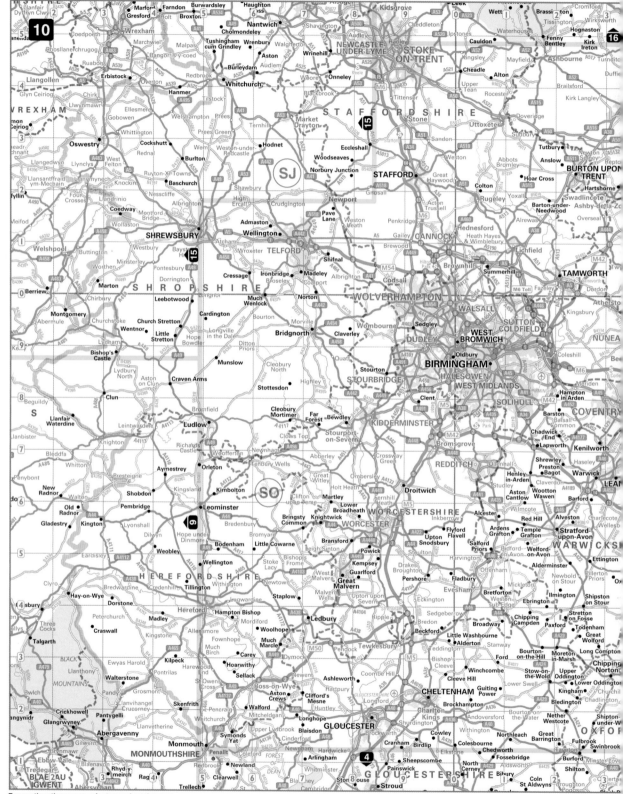

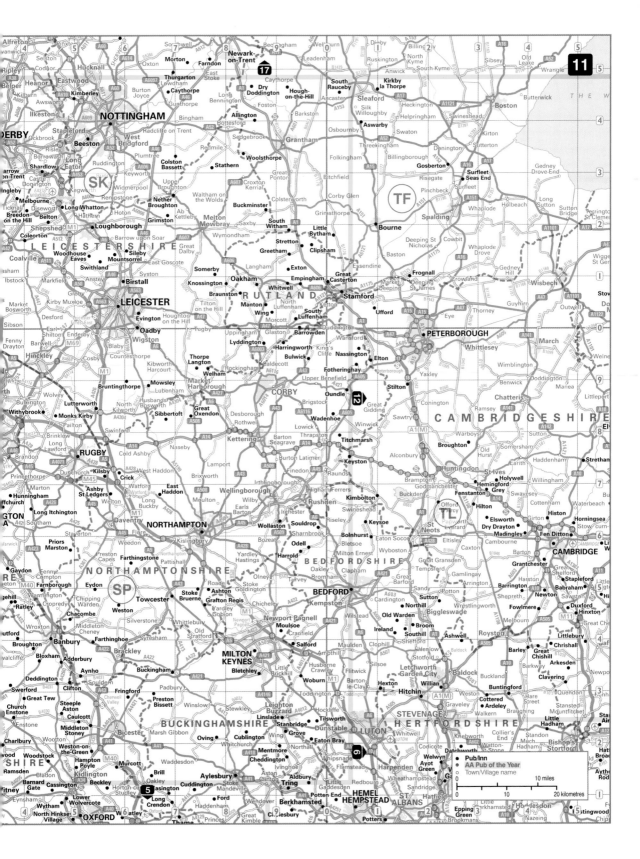

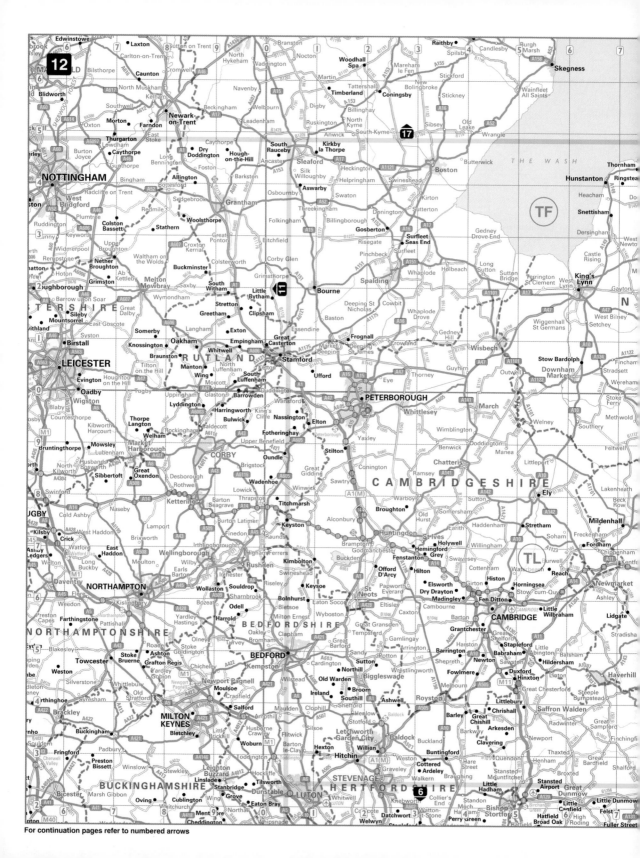

13

Pub/Inn
AA Pub of the Year
Town/Village name

0   10 miles
0   10   20 kilometres

7

ISLE OF
ANGLESEY

Cemaes
Amlwch
Llanerchymedd
Holyhead
Llanfachraeth
Benllech
Red
Wharf Bay
Llangoed
Pentraeth
Trearddur Bay
Holy
Island
Llangefni
Rhosneigr
Menai
Bridge
Bangor
Llanfair
P.G.
Y Felinheli
Aberffraw
Newborough
Llanllechid
Bethesda
Caernarfon
Llanrug
Bontnewydd
Waunfawr
Llanwnda
Llanberis
Llandwrog
Llanwnda
Caernarfon
Bay
Penygroes
Rhyd Ddu
Clynnog-fawr

Llandudno
Rhôs-
on-Sea
Colwyn Bay
Aberg
Deganwy
Llandudno Junction
Conwy
Llanddulas
Penmaenmawr
Llanelian-
yn-Rhôs
Beaumaris
Llanfairfechan
Llansantffraid
Glan Conwy
Betws-
yn-Rhos
Llannefy
Tal-y-Cafn
Llanfair
Talhaiarn
Llansanna
Tal-y-Bont
Llangernyw
Bylchau
Trefriw
Llanrwst
CONWY
Capel Curig
Betws-y-Coed
Dolwyddelan
Penmachno
Pentrefoelas
Cerrigydrudion
SNOWDONIA
Beddgelert
Blaenau Ffestiniog
Prenteg
Penmachno
Y Mae
Tremadog
Maentwrog
Ffestiniog
Morfa Nefyn
Nefyn
Llanystumdwy
Porthmadog
Penrhyndeudraeth
NATIONAL
Handde
Bodfuan
Tudweiliog
Criccieth
Borth-y-Gest
Talsarnau
Trawsfynydd
Bala
Pwllheli
Harlech
GWYNEDD
Sarn
Llanbedrog
Llanuwchllyn
PARK
Y Rhiw
Abersoch
Llanbedr
Ganllwyd
Aberdaron
Dyffryn Ardudwy
Bardsey
Island
Tal-y-bont
Llanw
Barmouth
Dolgellau
Dinas-Mawddwy
Fairbourne
Mallwyd
Llangad
Llwyngwril
Corris
Cemmaes
Road
Llanbrynmair
Tywyn
Bryncrug
Pennal
Machynlleth
Carno
SN
Aberdyfi
Borth
Tal-y-bont
CARDIGAN BAY
Llandre
Llanidloes
Aberystwyth
Bangor
Capel
Ponterwyd
Llanidloe

Pub/Inn
AA Pub of the Year
○ Town/Village name

0   10 miles
0   10   20 kilometres

For continuation pages refer to numbered arrows

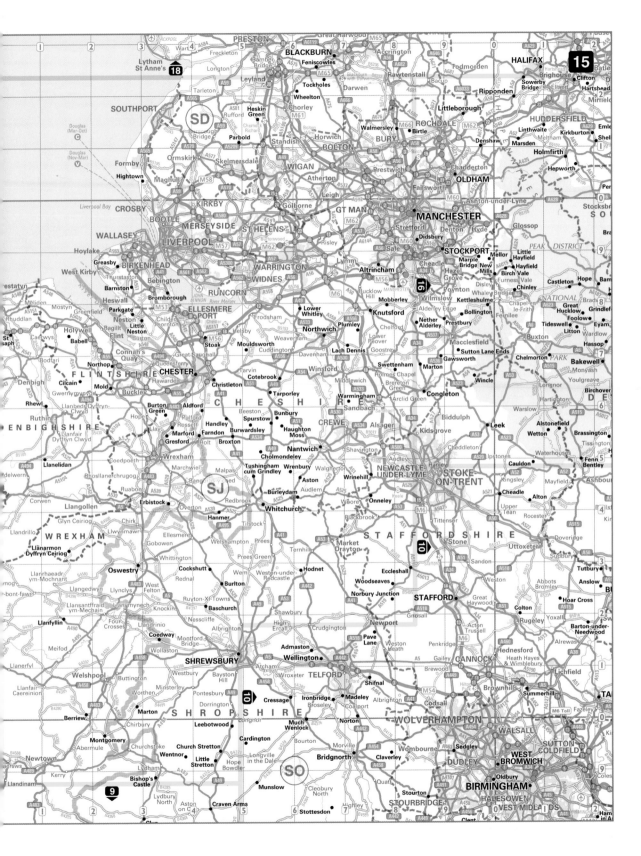

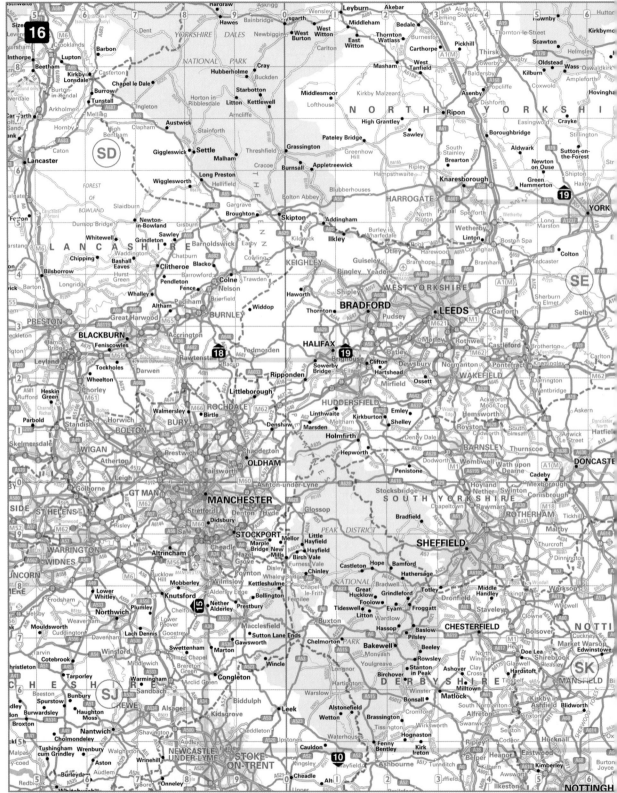

For continuation pages refer to numbered arrows

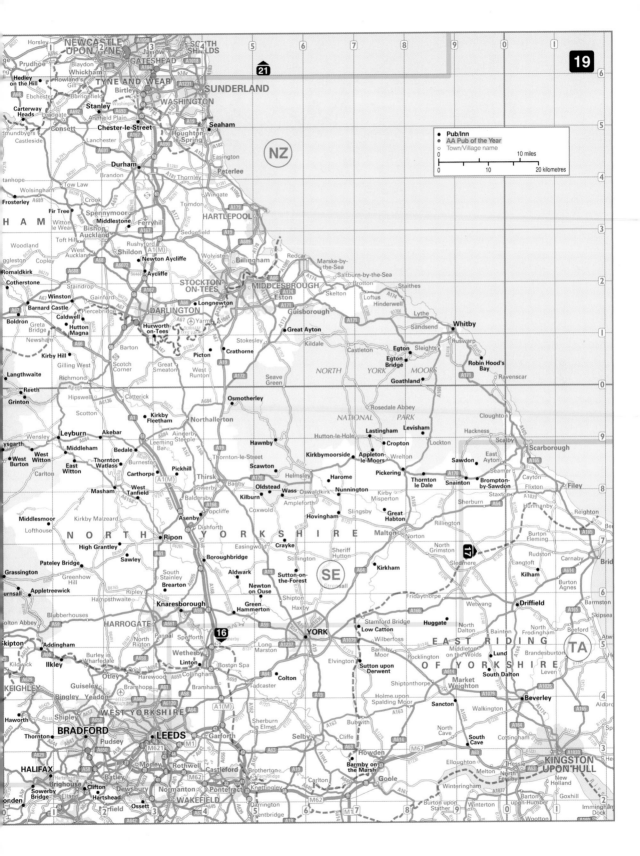

C EDIN	City of Edinburgh
C GLAS	City of Glasgow
CLACKS	Clackmannanshire
C DUND	City of Dundee
E DUNS	East Dunbartonshire
E RENS	East Renfrewshire
INVER	Inverclyde
MDLOTH	Midlothian
N LANS	North Lanarkshire
RENS	Renfrewshire
W DUNS	West Dunbartonshire
W LOTH	West Lothian

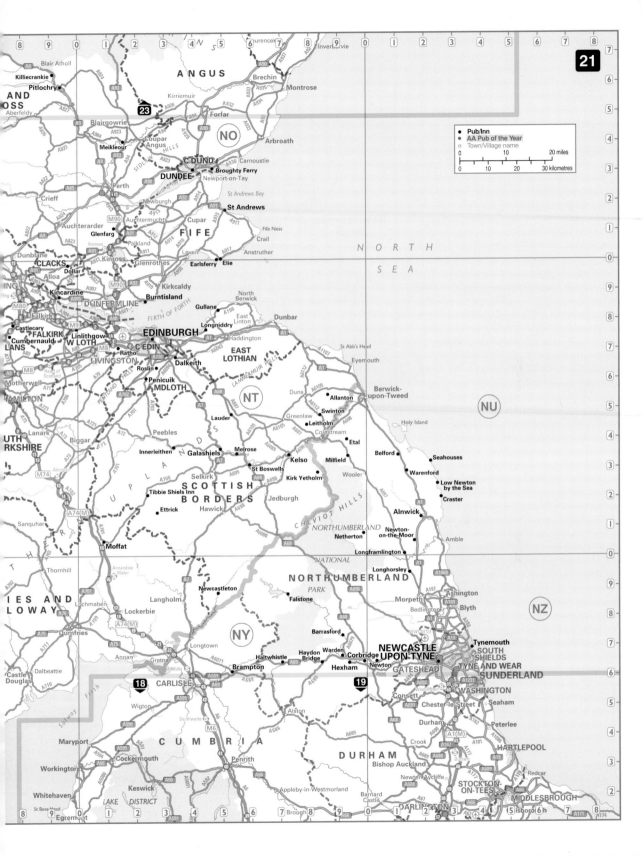

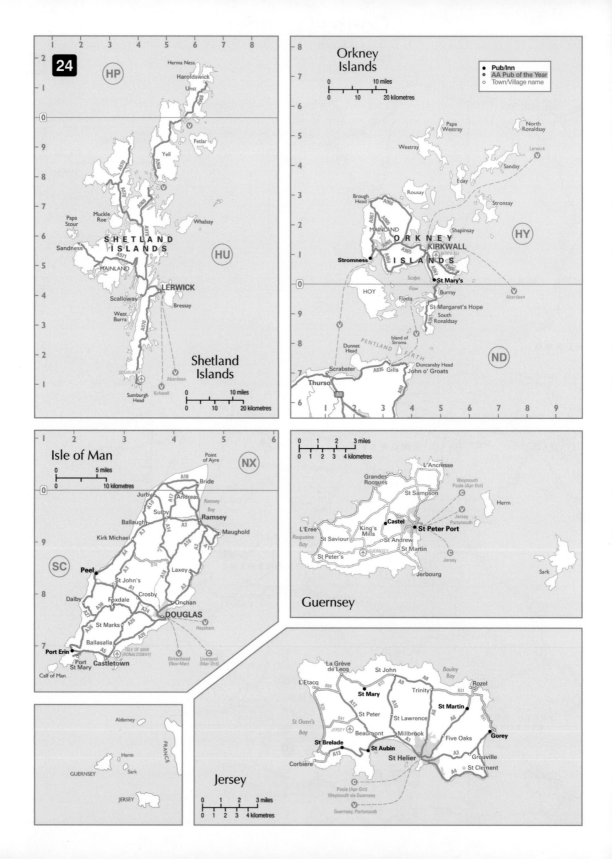

Central London

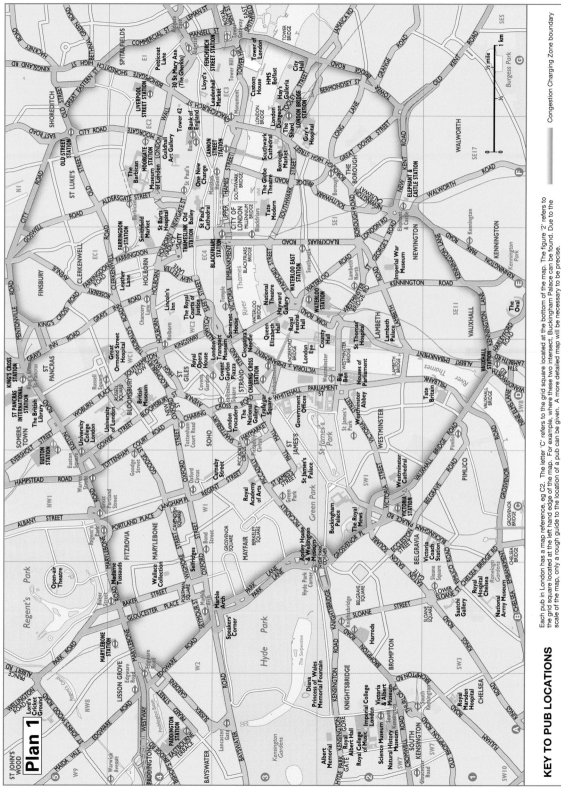

KEY TO PUB LOCATIONS

Each pub in London has a map reference, eg C2. The letter 'C' refers to the grid square located at the bottom of the map. The figure '2' refers to the grid square located at the left hand edge of the map. For example, where these two intersect, Buckingham Palace can be found. Due to the scale of the map, only a rough guide to the location of a pub can be given. A more detailed map will be necessary to be precise.

Congestion Charging Zone boundary

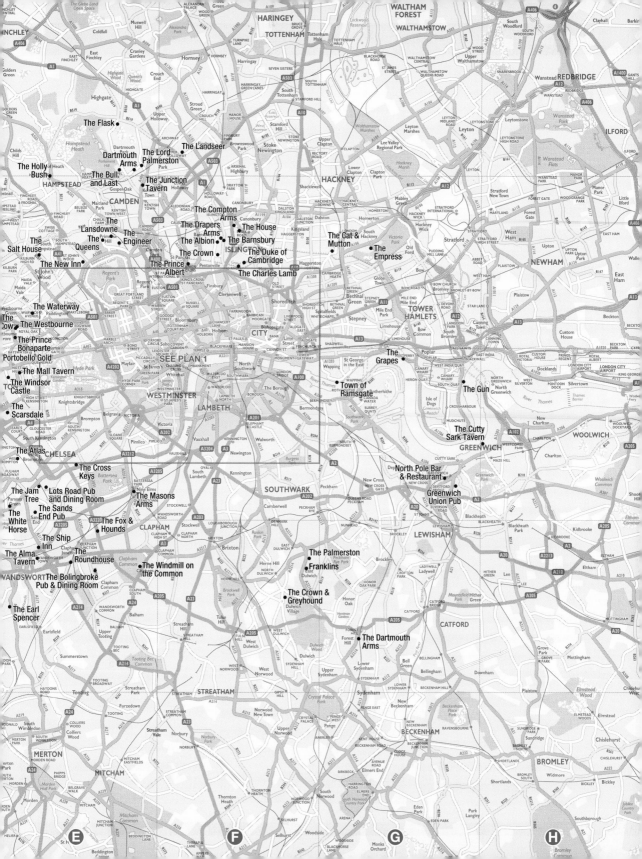

Index

Red entries are Pick of the Pubs

Acknowledgments

The Automobile Association would like to thank the following photographers, companies and picture libraries for their assistance in the preparation of this book.

Abbreviations for the picture credits are as follows – (t) top; (b) bottom; (c) centre; (l) left; (r) right; (AA) AA World Travel Library.

1b AA/Michael Moody; 2l AA/Caroline Jones; 3tl Chefshots - Eric Futran/StockFood; 5br AA/David Clapp; 6bl AA/James Tims; 7r Hemis/Alamy; 8b Courtesy of The Black Swan; 9tr Courtesy of The West Brewery; 9br Courtesy of The Inn at Penallt; 10b Roy Shakespeare/LOOP IMAGES; 11b AA/Clive Sawyer; 12 Matteo Carassale/SIME; 14t Courtesy of The Star Inn at Ringwood; 15t Courtesy of The Seafood Pub Company; 15b Courtesy of The Albion Taverna, Faversham; 17tl Courtesy of The Wheatsheaf Oaksey; 17tr Courtesy of Pavel Szylobryt/Oyster & Otter; 18br Courtesy of Brook House Inn; 19t Courtesy of The Old Hall Inn; 23tl Courtesy of The Three Tuns Inn; 26-27 AA/Tom Mackie; 614b AA/Wyn Voysey; 615 Colin Palmer Photography/Alamy; 616-617 AA/Mark Hamblin; 647b AA/AA; 648-649 AA/Rebecca Duke; 682b AA/Mark Bauer; 683 AA/Stephen Lewis; 686 Morris, Steven/StockFood

Photographs in the gazetteer are provided by the establishments.

Every effort has been made to trace the copyright holders, and we apologise in advance for any unintentional omissions or errors. We would be pleased to apply any corrections in a following edition of this publication.

Readers' Report Form

Please send this form to:–
Editor, The Pub Guide,
Lifestyle Guides,
AA Media,
Fanum House,
Basingstoke RG21 4EA

e-mail: lifestyleguides@theAA.com

Please use this form to tell us about any pub or inn you have visited, whether it is in the guide or not currently listed. We are interested in the quality of food, the selection of beers and the overall ambience of the establishment.

Feedback from readers helps us to keep our guide accurate and up to date. However, if you have a complaint to make during a visit, we do recommend that you discuss the matter with the pub management there and then, so that they have a chance to put things right before your visit is spoilt.

Please note that the AA does not undertake to arbitrate between you and the pub management, or to obtain compensation or engage in protracted correspondence.

Date

Your name (BLOCK CAPITALS)

Your address (BLOCK CAPITALS)

Post code

E-mail address

Name of pub

Location

Comments

(please attach a separate sheet if necessary)

Please tick here ☐ if you DO NOT wish to receive details of AA offers or products

PTO

Readers' Report Form *continued*

Have you bought this guide before? ☐ YES ☐ NO

Do you regularly use any other pub, accommodation or food guides? ☐ YES ☐ NO
If YES, which ones?

What do you find most useful about The AA Pub Guide?

Do you read the editorial features in the guide? ☐ YES ☐ NO

Do you use the location atlas? ☐ YES ☐ NO

Is there any other information you would like to see added to this guide?

What are your main reasons for visiting pubs (tick all that apply)
Food ☐   Business ☐   Accommodation ☐
Beer ☐   Celebrations ☐   Entertainment ☐
Atmosphere ☐   Leisure ☐
Other

How often do you visit a pub for a meal?
more than once a week ☐
once a week ☐
once a fortnight ☐
once a month ☐
once in six months ☐